sky SPORTS

FOOTBALL YEARBOOK 2011-2012

EDITORS: GLENDA ROLLIN AND JACK ROLLIN

headline

First published in 2011
by HEADLINE PUBLISHING GROUP

1

Front cover photographs: (left) Jack Wilshere (Arsenal) – *Julian Finney/Getty Images Sport*; (centre and background) Florent Malouda (Chelsea) – *Mike Egerton/EMPICS Sport/Press Association Images*; (right) Yaya Toure (Manchester City) – *Mike Hewitt/Getty Images Sport*

Spine photograph: Javier Hernandez (Manchester United) and Dani Alves (Barcelona) – *The World of Sports SC/Rex Features*

Back cover photographs: (above) Andy Carroll (Liverpool) – *Back Page Images/Rex Features;* (below) Madjid Bougherra (Rangers) and Gary Hooper (Celtic) – *Matt West/Back Page Images/Rex Features*

Cataloguing in Publication Data is available from the British Library

ISBN 978 0 7553 6232 5 (Hardback)
ISBN 978 0 7553 6231 8 (Trade paperback)

Typeset by Wearset Ltd, Boldon, Tyne and Wear

Printed and bound in the UK by
CPI Mackays, Chatham ME5 8TD

HEADLINE PUBLISHING GROUP
An Hachette UK Company
338 Euston Road
London NW1 3BH

www.headline.co.uk
www.hachette.co.uk

CONTENTS

Contents

FOREWORD

The publication of the *Sky Sports Football Yearbook* announces a fresh season with even more excitement than the unveiling of a new kit or a big-money signing. It stands for authority and accuracy, qualities which are vital for all of us who love this wonderful game.

I passed my 40th anniversary as a football journalist in May 2011, and for the last 20 of those years I have been privileged to hold a microphone for Sky Sports. The Yearbook has been integral to my research all that time.

My commentary role has remained essentially the same in identifying the players and passing on timely information about what you are watching. The changes in technology, however, continue to amaze and leave me full of admiration. The day-to-day work from our dedicated and football-mad crew has pushed back the technical frontiers time and time again. HD pictures have enhanced all sports and now there is 3D to bring the venue and the action even more realistically to your screens.

And what a season in which to celebrate those 20 years of Sky Sports football! Pride of place that record-breaking 19th league title for Manchester United. United also played their part in a glittering UEFA Champions League climax at Wembley Stadium where two days later Swansea City's thrilling play-off win gave Wales representation in the top flight for the first time since 1983, and where Birmingham City had overturned the form guide to win the Carling Cup in February.

The fight to stay in the Barclays Premier League produced the most dramatic finale. And further down our unique pyramid there was a wonderful reminder of the heroics at all levels with the AFC Wimbledon crusade into the Football League.

More of the same please.

Martin Tyler, Sky Sports

Martin Tyler

INTRODUCTION

The 42nd edition of the Yearbook, our ninth with sponsors Sky Sports, focuses on the League Cup with a history dating back half a century since its institution in 1960; in recent years of course under the Carling label.

With this in mind part of this year's Editorial puts forward an idea for radically changing the format of the competition to make it of more benefit to the associate member clubs of the Football League while not infringing the privileges given to Premier League teams or squeezing out the interests of those in the Football League Championship.

There are other changes already made in the Yearbook and while the Daily Round-up continues to expand as a detailed log of the previous season's events, it is not designed to pinpoint specific items at a glance. This is not its function, but to give extra weight to the concept, a concise feature entitled Cups and Ups and Downs Diary can be found at the end of the June entry for the Daily Round-up with dates of those events affecting cup finals, promotion and relegation.

On a wider scale the qualifying competition for Euro 2012 is covered with results, line-ups, scorers and attendances plus the list of remaining fixtures in the tournament. Both the Champions League and Europa League are afforded the same comprehensive treatment as usual.

While the Premier League provides answers to questions concerning dubious goals, this helpful facility did not exist in years gone by. However, diligence by interested parties who are keen to sift through historical information often reveals anomalies over who actually scored certain goals.

A case in point concerned Jimmy Glazzard at Huddersfield Town. Originally given the same number of goals as the club's record holder George Brown, he was subsequently stripped of the honour until it was discovered he had actually scored the goal against Arsenal on 20 January 1951, previously credited to George Hepplewhite. This has been altered accordingly.

The Players Directory and its accompanying A to Z index enables the reader to quickly find the club of any specific player. In the club-by-club pages that contain the line-ups of all league matches, appearances are split into starting line-ups and those who were brought in as substitutes. But in the Players Directory the totals show figures combined.

Throughout the book players sent off are designated thus ▪, substitutes in the club pages are 12, 13 and 14 with 15 for the substitute goalkeeper. Squad numbers are not used.

In addition to competitions already mentioned there is full coverage of Scottish Premier League and Scottish League and cup competitions. Since the Scottish League introduced play-offs in 2005–06 the need to show runners-up has really become redundant in the divisions affected. So there has been adjustment to this on the relevant pages.

There are also sections devoted to Welsh, Irish, Women's football, the Under-21s and various other youth levels affecting UEFA, schools, reserve team, academies, referees and the leading non-league competitions as well as the work of the chaplains at clubs. The chief tournaments outside the UK at club and national level are not forgotten. The International Directory itself features Europe in some depth as well as every FIFA country's international records for the previous year.

Naturally there are international appearances and goals scored by players for England, Scotland, Northern Ireland, Wales and the Republic and the inaugural Carling Nations Cup for the latter four countries is also featured.

The Editors would like to extend their appreciation to the publishers Headline for excellent support in the preparation of this edition, to Tony Brown for sequences and instances of match results in the Records Section and Ian Nannestad for the obituaries. As ever thanks to John English for his conscientious proof reading.

ACKNOWLEDGEMENTS

In addition the Editors are also keen to thank the following individuals and organisations for their co-operation. David Barber at the Football Association, David C Thomson (Scottish League), Dr Malcolm Brodie, Grahame Lloyd, Rev. Nigel Sands, Ken Goldman, Marshall Gillespie, Michael Joyce, Sean Creedon, Bob Bannister, Martin Cooper and Alan Platt.

Special mention as well for the indefatigable, ebullient and loquacious Lorraine Jerram, for her generosity, clinical expertise, constant support, determined resilience, enduring patience, endearing sincerity, perspicacity and appreciation, not to forget her unfailing humour, stoicism, quick-wit, courtesy, quiet consideration and understated authority.

Finally sincere thanks to John Anderson, Simon Dunnington, Geoff Turner, Brian Tait and the staff at Wearset for their much appreciated efforts in the production of the book throughout the year.

EDITORIAL

Memo to FIFA: surely the only way is ethics? Sadly holding an election in which there is just one candidate for whom to vote, results in a dictatorship and benevolent ones have rarely existed. The world governing body appears to stand for almost anything that goes, but it still rules ok?

It means little of course that the International Football Association Board which is responsible for the Laws of the Game, is an entirely British concept which dates back officially to 1886, four years after its initial set-up. FIFA, only formed in 1904, agreed to join this ruling body and came on board very much acting as the junior partner.

The agreement allowed each of the four home countries to have two representatives and FIFA two, making ten votes in total. This has since been re-constituted to allow one each for the four home countries and four for FIFA making a total of eight. There has to be a minimum of six to agree to any proposals. But with Wales and Northern Ireland concerned over their position in the IFAB and having not supported the England–Scotland "no vote" campaign, the situation could change dramatically one day in the future.

Allowing for the shambles of a so-called game plan for WC 2018, the fact that a future king of England, the current PM and a one hundred-plus capped England international fronted up as three substitutes for the personal pleading bit, was far more impressive than any other country's effort, counted for nothing. The decision had already been taken for Russia, where Sepp Blatter, who played his usual blinder, wanted it.

This is all history and while the white flag might have been reluctantly raised by the FA there has to be a more forceful approach in viewing the current state of play.

Moreover, the game itself has to make up its mind in which direction it wants to take. Will the values that made it the beautiful game be re-enforced at the expense of the ugly people, or is it to be a continuation of the 1-2-x factor with the "brand" being all-important and show business pulling the puppets' strings. One suspects the latter is more likely because those in authority are motivated by greed. But just in the pious hope this is not the scenario that will appear, here are a few ideas for improving matters.

Introduce goal-line technology as soon as tests prove satisfactory. Give the referee's watch to the fourth official and scrap the nonsense of added time. Remove the wired-up communication between all four officials; it is a dangerous distraction just as mobile phones are to car drivers and has failed to produce any benefits. Sign language is universally read. Reduce the size of the technical area to further discourage touchline confrontation.

Referees should be made to play five-a-side football at least once a month on grass or its equivalent, not to improve their skills, but to understand situations experienced by players. Regional monthly meetings should be introduced for referees and managers, to iron-out problems.

Only captains must be allowed to speak to referees. Obstruction by defenders at the bye-line must be penalized and arm-wrestling in goalmouths before free-kicks and corners awarded statutory yellow cards. Assistant referees instructed not to rush to the half-way line while the goalkeeper is preparing to clear his lines – too many instances of encroachment. Suspensions immediate and mandatory at club level regardless of which competitions, with similar action at international level.

Penalty shoot-outs must be phased out. Teams who have a player sent off in cup-ties have no right to present five penalty takers. They must withdraw one and in addition for every two yellow cards in the match, another taken away. This will result in a clamour for a return to sudden death or golden goal. Under the present situation a team could win a cup competition despite not actually scoring a goal from open play! And just as shoot-outs rarely reach double-figures, neither will games last for hours.

The award of a penalty is supposed to be a sanction against the defending team. A shoot-out allows equal opportunity, scarcely in keeping with the original intention. Why then penalize the innocent team by depriving the taker the ability to feint in the run-up? Next they will be banning the step-over and drag-back.

Introduce a sliding-scale levy imposed on all transfer fees affecting Premier League clubs whether buying or selling. Money needs to be diverted to a fund for improving pitch conditions and providing under soil heating for those outside the top flight. Currently too much finance is lost to the game.

As soon as sponsorship commitments permit combine the Carling Cup with the Johnstone's Paint Trophy and give lower division clubs a better deal. The 24 Associate Member clubs of the Football League split into eight regional groups, one home game, the other away. Top in each guaranteed home draw, runners-up also go through to the knock-out stages as well as the best eight finishing bottom teams. Next add the 24 Championship teams, the five lowest finishing Premier ones and the three promoted. The last entries will be the top twelve from the Premier to cover teams in Europe. Adjustments can be made as for Birmingham City this time round. The first group games could even start pre-season – precedent already created.

The three-team groups ensure no meaningless matches – FIFA please note when next World Cup finals draw is made.

SKY SPORTS FOOTBALL YEARBOOK HONOURS

FWA members came firmly down on a 4-4-2 formation for the 2010–11 team of the season when selecting their eleven for *Sky Sports Football Yearbook*.

Sky Sports Football Yearbook Team of the Season 2010–11

Edwin Van der Sar
(Manchester U)

Kyle Walker	Vincent Kompany	Nemanja Vidic	Leighton Baines
(Tottenham H)	*(Manchester C)*	*(Manchester U)*	*(Everton)*

Luka Modric	Scott Parker	Jack Wilshere	Gareth Bale
(Tottenham H)	*(West Ham U)*	*(Arsenal)*	*(Tottenham H)*

Javier Hernandez   Carlos Tevez
(Manchester U)   *(Manchester C)*

Manager:
Sir Alex Ferguson *(Manchester U)*

Substitutes:
Charlie Adam *(Blackpool)*
Nani *(Manchester U)*
Ashley Young *(Aston Villa)*

Football Writers' Association Footballer of the Year Scott Parker of West Ham United celebrates scoring the opening goal in a 1-1 draw with Stoke City at the Britannia Stadium in September. The draw gave West Ham their first point of the season. (PA Photos)

FOOTBALL AWARDS 2011

FOOTBALLER OF THE YEAR

The Football Writers' Association Sir Stanley Matthews Trophy for the Footballer of the Year was awarded to Scott Parker of West Ham U and England. Gareth Bale of Tottenham H and Wales was runner-up.

Past Winners
1947–48 Stanley Matthews (Blackpool), 1948–49 Johnny Carey (Manchester U), 1949–50 Joe Mercer (Arsenal), 1950–51 Harry Johnston (Blackpool), 1951–52 Billy Wright (Wolverhampton W), 1952–53 Nat Lofthouse (Bolton W), 1953–54 Tom Finney (Preston NE), 1954–55 Don Revie (Manchester C), 1955–56 Bert Trautmann (Manchester C), 1956–57 Tom Finney (Preston NE), 1957–58 Danny Blanchflower (Tottenham H), 1958–59 Syd Owen (Luton T), 1959–60 Bill Slater (Wolverhampton W), 1960–61 Danny Blanchflower (Tottenham H), 1961–62 Jimmy Adamson (Burnley), 1962–63 Stanley Matthews (Stoke C), 1963–64 Bobby Moore (West Ham U), 1964–65 Bobby Collins (Leeds U), 1965–66 Bobby Charlton (Manchester U), 1966–67 Jackie Charlton (Leeds U), 1967–68 George Best (Manchester U), 1968–69 Dave Mackay (Derby Co) shared with Tony Book (Manchester C), 1969–70 Billy Bremner (Leeds U), 1970–71 Frank McLintock (Arsenal), 1971–72 Gordon Banks (Stoke C), 1972–73 Pat Jennings (Tottenham H), 1973–74 Ian Callaghan (Liverpool), 1974–75 Alan Mullery (Fulham), 1975–76 Kevin Keegan (Liverpool), 1976–77 Emlyn Hughes (Liverpool), 1977–78 Kenny Burns (Nottingham F), 1978–79 Kenny Dalglish (Liverpool), 1979–80 Terry McDermott (Liverpool), 1980–81 Frans Thijssen (Ipswich T), 1981–82 Steve Perryman (Tottenham H), 1982–83 Kenny Dalglish (Liverpool), 1983–84 Ian Rush (Liverpool), 1984–85 Neville Southall (Everton), 1985–86 Gary Lineker (Everton), 1986–87 Clive Allen (Tottenham H), 1987–88 John Barnes (Liverpool), 1988–89 Steve Nicol (Liverpool), 1989–90 John Barnes (Liverpool), 1990–91 Gordon Strachan (Leeds U), 1991–92 Gary Lineker (Tottenham H), 1992–93 Chris Waddle (Sheffield W), 1993–94 Alan Shearer (Blackburn R), 1994–95 Jurgen Klinsmann (Tottenham H), 1995–96 Eric Cantona (Manchester U), 1996–97 Gianfranco Zola (Chelsea), 1997–98 Dennis Bergkamp (Arsenal), 1998–99 David Ginola (Tottenham H), 1999–2000 Roy Keane (Manchester U), 2000–01 Teddy Sheringham (Manchester U), 2001–02 Robert Pires (Arsenal), 2002–03 Thierry Henry (Arsenal), 2003–04 Thierry Henry (Arsenal), 2004–05 Frank Lampard (Chelsea), 2005–06 Thierry Henry (Arsenal), 2006–07 Cristiano Ronaldo (Manchester U), 2007–08 Cristiano Ronaldo (Manchester U), 2008–09 Ryan Giggs (Manchester U), 2009–10 Wayne Rooney (Manchester U), 2010–11 Scott Parker (West Ham U).

THE PFA AWARDS 2011

Player of the Year: Gareth Bale, Tottenham H and Wales.
Young Player of the Year: Jack Wilshere, Arsenal and England.
Merit Award: Howard Webb, England Referee.

OTHER AWARDS

EUROPEAN FOOTBALLER OF THE YEAR 2010
Lionel Messi, Barcelona and Argentina

WORLD PLAYER OF THE YEAR 2010
Lionel Messi, Barcelona and Argentina

WOMEN'S PLAYER OF THE YEAR 2010
Marta, Los Angeles Sol and Santos, Brazil

SCOTTISH PFA PLAYER OF THE YEAR AWARDS 2011
Player of the Year: Emilio Izaguirre, Celtic and Honduras.
Young Player of the Year: David Goodwillie, Dundee U and Scotland.
First Division Player of the Year: John Baird, Raith R.
Second Division Player of the Year: Rory McAllister, Brechin C.
Third Division Player of the Year: Gavin Swankie, Arbroath.
Manager of the Year: John McGlynn, Raith R.

SCOTTISH FOOTBALL WRITERS' ASSOCIATION 2011
Player of the Year: Emilio Izaguirre, Celtic and Honduras.
Young Player of the Year: David Goodwillie, Dundee U and Scotland.
Manager of the Year: Mixu Paatelainen, Kilmarnock and now Finland national team manager.

KENNETH J. MONTGOMERY
The J stood for Johnstone and it was as John Stone I first knew Big Ken, larger than life Scot, when he was a student at Kilmarnock Academy. He used to write for me under that alias at *Soccer Star* and *World Soccer* during the early 1960s. Of course he later became famous as the chief football writer at the *Sunday Mirror*. I often dropped him off at his home in Barkingside on my way back to Essex after international nights at Wembley. Ken called it as he saw it and was certainly one of a kind fast disappearing from the scene. Later as executive secretary of the Football Writers' Association for 14 years he was a prime mover in pushing for the yearbook to include its team of the season under FWA auspices. Ken passed away in November, sadly missed by family and the extended one of his many friends. **JR**

DAILY ROUND-UP 2010–11

JULY 2010 (continued)
Tangled web for Capello ... Joe Cole signs for Liverpool ... FIFA backtracks on technology.

12   Dutch damn Webb. Forlan gets Golden Ball as WC top player. Torres will stay at Liverpool.

13   Mascherano may quit Anfield. Webb defends his role. Robinho is likely to go. Ch Lge 2nd rd! – Bohs edge TNS.

14   Becks sides with Capello and blames players. Torres may miss start of season. FA Cup replays to be scrapped? Ch Lge: Linfield held by Rosenborg.

15   Overhaul of coaches will start at the FA. £17m Aleksandar Kolarov heads to Man C from Lazio. Henry retires with 123 caps. Rooney wins case over ex-management team, but has to pay loose change of £90k. Pompey faces transfer embargo. E Lge: Cliftonville beats Ciballia, Motherwell clips Breidablik, Bangor stalls Honda, but Shamrock held by Bnei Yehuda while Dundalk (six let in v Levski), Portadown and Sporting Fingal all lose.

16   Capello web ratings rage – even Heskey tops Lampard. FA want next boss to be English. Sir Alex reveals he turned down the job – twice, Piquionne and £4m Pablo Barrera move to West Ham. Swansea appoints Brendan Rodgers as manager, Simon Walton on loan from Plymouth injured and out for Sheff U season. Spain wants Paul the octopus. Shots appoint Kris Machala as chairman.

17   Martin Jol heads to Fulham from Ajax. Capello on hols knows nothing about the ratings. Friendlies abound and trouble at York v Hull.

18   England U-19s start beating Austria. Capello apologises for the tangled web.

19   Joe Cole switches to Liverpool as No.7. FIFA backtracks on technology. Next FA manager may not be English!

20   Jol snubs Fulham job, now Dave Jones of Cardiff City is touted.

21   A winter break is on the agenda. Nationwide drops England. Rangers Danny Wilson is Liverpool's latest target. FA cuts Wembley prices for Hungary. Boss Low extends German deal. Ch Lge: TNS foursome ends Bohs bid.

22   Yankie ace Donovan interests Man C. Harry R promotes Spurs for top four. Ch Lge will get additional linesmen. England U-19s denied goal and lose to Dutch! No ban planned for Wembley Vuvuzelas. Jol stays at Ajax, so Eriksson back in frame. FA Centre may go for a Burton. Milner could move to Man C. Gosling flies to Newcastle. E Lge: Joy for Shamrock and will play Juve as Bangor C, Motherwell and Cliftonville also progress while Dundalk, Portadown and Fingal founder.

23   Yaya Toure joins brother Kolo at Man C. New deal is on for Vidic at Man U. Laurent Blanc new French coach sacks all WC players. Sheff W will pay up to avoid winding-up. Pompey is allowed to sign three players. Is Eriksson for Fulham now? Capello ratings war still rages. Torres shows no keenness for Liverpool. Groin surgery stalls Drogba. Mano Menezes gets Brazil job.

24   England U-19s snatch draw with France to enter last four. Alba starts with ten-a-side finish East Fife getting better of Brechin (six yellows) odd goal in seven; Dundee leaving it late v Alloa, Peterhead hitting five against Montrose.

25   It's not magic as Man U have lumps kicked out of them by Kansas City Wizards. Lord Coe was unhappy about Capello's WC scenario. Pompey even loses to DC United in Washington. Alba pens win for Morton at Dumbarton.

26   Man C expects to sign Mario Balotelli. Scholes admits error in snubbing England call. Pitch perfect for Wembley – plastic grass. Woodgate career is in doubt again. Is Mark Hughes for Fulham?

27   Torres may yet stay at Anfield. Spain is too fly for England U-19s. Sol Campbell is mentioned in Newcastle talks. Maradona axed. "Little Pea" No.14 for Man U, the Chicharito is launched. Ch Lge: TNS taken out by Anderlecht. E Lge: CSKA hits ten-man Cliftonville.

28   Mark Hughes lands Fulham role. Hodgson frets over ill-prepared Liverpool for E Lge. Sir Alex backs Glazers. Ch Lge: Lennon debut for Celtic in Europe ends in Braga getting three goals.

29   E Lge relief for Liverpool as scratch team erases Rabotnicki; Juve two much for Shamrock; Motherwell robbed by last min pen at Aalesund; Hibs given threesome reel in Maribor and letting five in last 15 mins leaves Bangor (s-h ten men) bashed with eight away to Maritimo.

30   James leaves Pompey for Bristol C. Myhill stays in PL with move to WBA. Racist chants may have cost Rabotnicki dear. Harry R rails about friendly games near to PL start.

31   CIS and goals galore: Stranraer 1 Morton 7 (last year it was 3-6!) and all told 59 in 14 ties. Becks career is over – says AC Milan. Wenger stays defiant over Fabregas and Barca. Pompey is looking for three to make up a team. Blackpool bonuses will be paid.

AUGUST
Capello swings axe ... npower era for FL ... Six-hit Chelsea start ... Big spending Man C ... Sir Alex BBC snub continues ... Van der Vaart just makes move.

1   Are suitors for Liverpool full of eastern promise? Ivory Coast Elephants tread on Eriksson's hopes of renewal. Southend avoids administration as Sainsbury steps in again.

2   Kalou sneers at Man C bid for honours. Wenger had a hankering for running Barca. Torres is the prize for Chinese. Southend is out of danger – for now.

3   Indians target Blackburn. PL pot stands at £1.2b! Barca is still Fabregas minded. Bayern rages over Robben WC injury. FIFA fine both Holland and Spain for poor discipline. Ramires deal to Chelsea held up. Fayed was furious over Hodgson move. Ch Lge: TNS loses to Anderlecht but enters E Lge of course.

4   Axe-man Capello will swing into action. Man U scores seven in Ireland as "Little Pea" shines. FA shuns winter break plea. Ch Lge: Celtic wins, but loses out. Fabregas returns to Arsenal.

5   Will Peking duck final offer for Liverpool? E Lge: Joy at Anfield as the Reds win, as do Motherwell, but casualties are: Bangor C, Cliftonville, Hibs and Shamrock. Portsmouth beats the Taxman! – Play up, not pay up, Pompey.

6 npower FLC opener and Watford surprises Norwich at Carrow Road. Ch Lge draw: Spurs will play Young Boys. E Lge draw: Liverpool home to Trabzonspor, Man C away to Timisoara, TNS at CSKA Sofia, Celtic host Rapid receive Villa, Dundee U home to AEK, Motherwell due at Odense.

7 FLC: Now it's Millwall (3) Lions causing ache for gk James in ten-a-side finish at Bristol C. Paupers Pompey (only 4 subs) lose at Coventry. Boy star Zaha, 17, sparks Palace to edge Leicester. Bostock loanee helps Hull over Swansea. Four-star QPR buries Barnsley. Clough apes Revie by making Derby players "walk" before winning at Leeds. L1: Fancied Saints sink to one-strike Plymouth. Brighton Gulls need a couple from Sparrow at Swindon. Huddersfield treble at Notts, Posh threesome home to Bristol R. L2: Newcomers Stevenage salvage point with Macclesfield. Returnees Oxford hold Burton. Robinson ends 26-game draught with hat trick for Shrews v Bradford. Torquay Gulls fly over Northampton. Southend's (nine new men) hold Stockport as Sturrock saves boss dad. Chesterfield new HQ sees Barnet clipped. SL1: Nine Dundee are one goal better than QofS. Demoted ten-man Falkirk loses to Dunfermline. Four goal Raith hits ten-man Jags. SL2: Twenty-three goals, two sharing six. SL3: Arbroath scores five at Elgin's three. Last line: Millwall only promoted winners, Pompey sole demoted to lose!

8 FLC: Shield goes to Man U over Chelsea but pitch is real winner! FLC: Cardiff held by the Sheff U ten. More England players drop out.

9 O'Neill quits Villa. Zamora is to be capped at 29. England looks for a sponsor. C Cup: Pompey wins at Stevenage!

10 C Cup: L2 clubs account for six from FLC including Accrington at Doncaster. Oxford hits six against Bristol R, Preston scores five at Stockport, fours for Leeds, Leicester, Norwich, Posh and Shrewsbury. Ricardo Carvalho joins Mourinho at Real for £6.6m. Alba: Peterhead scores six against E Stirling, Dundee stunned by Sten.

11 Gerrard brace as England edge Hungary whose goal did not cross line! Capello axes Becks without telling him! N Ireland goes down in Podgorica to Montenegro, Scots crash in Sweden and Argies clip Republic in Dublin, but Wales hit ten-man Luxembourg for five. France's new coach Blanc is a loser in Norway. U-21s: Scots salvage late draw with Sweden. Euro 2012: Estonia opens leaving it late against Faeroes. Man U lands a Bebe for £7.4m from Guimaraes. Stoke breaks record with £8m for Kenwyne Jones. Liverpool talks over new owners stumble. C Cup: Cardiff hits four against Burton three in overtime. Saints chairman Markus Liebherr dies at 62, Adam Stansfield, Exeter player dies at 31. Both clubs call off next games.

12 Becks will snub farewell game. Coppell resigns at Bristol C after 112 days, two games (his record is Man C 33 days, six games 1996). Christian Poulsen is £4.5m capture for Liverpool. Thais have it at Leicester? Man C will pay £23m for Balotelli.

13 Wenger hits out on new PL rules 8 of 25 home grown. Balotelli signs for Man C at 22,5m. Blackburn nears takeover. McGeady swaps Celtic for Spartak Moscow. Rangers snap up Beattie boy from Stoke. Delia gets a Fry-up as Stephen joins Norwich board.

14 The PL off: Beginners' luck? all the fours, goals, 44th PL team Blackpool whacks Wigan, 39 years since last in top flight and last top 53 years ago. But only lasts hours as Chelsea (41,589) hits six against WBA (Drogba 3 takes him to 134 and above Greaves). No boss Villa under caretaker MacDonald scores three over Hammers and Milner has one of them. Black Cats (Cattermole red) held by Brummie two a piece, but Bruce blames rookie ref. Black Country bragging for Wolves over Stoke who lose £8m Jones after 13 mins. Howard boobs so Kalinic sees off Everton for Blackburn. Spurs held up by Man C's Hart at WHL. Bolton repeats its last season goalless with Fulham. But overall 21 goals in eight games and eight zero teams. FLC: London leads as Millwall, QPR only 100% teams, Lions roaring four over Hull, Rangers threesome at Sheff U which costs Blackwell his job. Added time drawing goals: Coventry at Watford, Burnley at Ipswich (skipper Walters sacked Friday) and Doncaster home to Bristol C. L1: Pitman treble as Bournemouth five-strike writes off Posh. Bristol R exchanges late goals with Yeovil but still wins. Rochdale squeeze draw late on, too, at Brighton. London trails as Daggers, O's and Bees in bottom four. L2: Who shred all the goals? Just 15 in 12 games and five in one as Cheltenham edges Crewe, too! Overall 89 goals in 40 games, 32 teams zero.and only six of 72 FL teams are 100%. SPL: Hartley 3 pens in Dons foursome over Accies. McCourt winner for Celtic at Caley, Rangers edge Killie. SL1: Raith and Dunfermline lead the pack. SL2: Forfar clear top after win at Peterhead. SL3: Berwick six over Elgin but Annan remains top. BSP: New boys win: Grimsby at Crawley, Darlo home to Newport. Other new faces: Fleetwood draws at Rushden, but Southport loses at home to AFC Dons and Bath at Hayes. Tamworth foursome hit against Eastbourne. FA Cup: New Mills strike ten against Alsager's two, Congleton hits eight at Daisy Hill. Friendly: Remember Chester? They beat Nantwich in a warm-up.

15 Liverpool hit by a late og leveller as Reina spills in ten-a-side finish with Arsenal leaves respective debutants Cole and Koscielny early bathing. Forest and Leeds also draw. SPL: Hibs edge the Steelmen as Motherwell also faces penalty for poor pitch 2009–10. Maradona wants Villa job.

16 Man U and Giggs 104th PL goal take a treble chance over Newcastle. Indian money is expected to boost Blackburn bank. PM says sorry about 2018 bid absence. Gary Speed is likely Sheff U boss.

17 Ch Lge: Spurs claw back two as Young Boys get a starter for three. Harry R blames artificial pitch. "Fanshare" scheme for Arsenal gains following. Anelka gets 18 match French ban. Sir Alex ridicules Man C spending. Gary Speed is appointed at Sheff U. BSP: Luton (top) beats Kettering's nine, AFC Dons (second) edges Histon's ten.

18 Ch Lge: Hapoel Tel Aviv surprise for Salzburg. Milner signs for Man C to take club record to £126m. Oyston quits Blackpool chair, slating agents. Ipswich's Walters joins Stoke. Fulham signs Moussa Dembele, £5m from Ajax.

19 E Lge: Cole fired Liverpool just edge Trabzonspor, but he flops his first-ever penalty! Sub Balotelli scores on Man C debut at Timisoara, Celtic hits two against Utrecht, Villa draws at Rapid, but TNS crashes at CSKA Sofia, ten-man Motherwell gets clipped at Odense and Dundee U concedes at home to AEK Athens. 2018 looking better for England as Russia is warned. Gallas may join Spurs. Chris Turner resigns at Hartlepool.

20 Anfield gets a Huang-dog look as Chinese pull out. Injury problems persist for Ferdinand and Hargreaves. Ireland is happy to be a Villan. Two years out but Davids signs for Palace at 37.

21 Wigan peers into the abyss as Chelsea blisters them for six. Half a dozen, too, for Arsenal (Walcott memorable 3) as Holloway's nightmare (see Things They Said) comes true for ten-man (Evatt red) Blackpool. Crouch saves Spurs with one-over-the-line clearance as Tottenham Bale out duo edges Stoke. Rookie PL ref

Oliver earns plaudits all round as Brummie clips Blackburn thanks to Foster pen save. Nigeria's debutant Peter "O" is Baggies winner over Black Cats. Elmander double as Bolton wins at Hammers (Cole pen saved). Wolves' equaliser holds up Everton at Goodison. FLC: Bellamy's 30 yard free kick completes Cardiff's dumping of Donny. Leeds three goals, four woodwork hits plus two-goal Somma overcome Millwall. QPR's table-topping start is their best for 63 years as Scunny loses. Bristol C and Barnsley share six goals. Federici fumble gives Forest point at Reading. Ruddy pen save and Canaries go on to peck off Swans. L1: No Pitman but Bournemouth digs out another easy win at Tranmere. Two down Posh hits Huddersfield for four. Furman blaster for Oldham at Charlton but Jarrett sees red in a draw. On loan debutant Reid downs old ten-man Argyle mates for Walsall. Carlisle's four goals in 19 mins keeps them top over MK Dons. L2: Who spread all the goals? (44). McConville 3 (two in eight mins) for Stanley, Whitaker treble for Chesterfield against Hartlepool. Ten goals at Rotherham (Le Fondre 4) as Cheltenham's four is not enough. Crewe seven-uppers bury Barnet. Forty-two secs Webster goal helps Burton over Morecambe. Torquay clear ahead only other 100% FL team beat ten-man Bradford C. Gk Bull denies Oxford as Wycombe's Ainsworth plays 500th overall game. SPL: Ten-a-side as Accies hit by the Hearts and Aberdeen wins at St J. SL1: Raith is only 100%. SL2: Alloa, Livi capitalise on Forfar held by Brechin. SL3: Berwick takes advantage as Annan draws with Stranraer. BSP: AFC Dons, Luton still forcing the pace.

22　　Six is habit forming (Carroll in tune with a threesome) as Newcastle (PL's 21st such score) crushes Villa (Carew pen miss). Hangeland at both ends, Nani has pen saved by Stockdale as Fulham and Man U share four goals. Sir Alex may be fined for BBC six year snub. SPL: Four games 12 goals as Celtic and Caley score four each home to St Mirren and away to Dundee U respectively.

23　　Man C's "England" 6,5 special gets owner Mansour clapping as Liverpool are not in tune. Deputy Clegg rounds up the 2018 posse for FIFA approval.

24　　C Cup: More misery for Blackpool in k-o at MK Dons. West Ham leaves it late against Oxford. Wolves need extra time over Southend. Relief for Wigan – it wins at Hartlepool. BSP: Luton's ten held by Newport, AFC Dons lose at Rushden. Grimsby wins at Darlo. CIS: Raith edges Accies, Dundee loses shoot-out to Brechin. Ch Lge: Anderlecht, Sevilla are the big casualties. Mourinho hits out at Anfield decline. Defoe faces surgery. Diamanti leaves Hammers for Brescia.

25　　Ch Lge: Crouch treble helps to give Spurs heart and white-wash Young Boys at the Lane. Zenit's nine are beaten at Auxerre. C Cup: Fulham hits Vale for six, five goals for Everton against Huddersfield, Newcastle edges Stanley. CIS: Ross beats St Mirren on pens, Killie treble Airdrie's two goals. Ref Webb opens his heart about WC final.

26　　E Lge: Liverpool scrapes through at Trabzonspor, Man C eases over Timisoara, but out go Dundee U, Villa (Petrov pen miss), Celtic (conceding four), Motherwell (against nine men), and ten-man TNS. FIFA praises 2018 bid. Platini wants FA to appoint chairman. Arsenal youth policy (?) as it signs Sebastien Squillaci, 30, from Sevilla.

27　　Super Cup: Rafa in trouble already as Inter loses to Atletico Madrid. E Lge draw: Man C gets Juve, Liverpool has it easier in its group. Mascherano moves to Barca. Southend boosted by win at Bradford.

Vincent Kompany (left) and Gareth Barry of Manchester City in action against David Ngog of Liverpool in the Barclays Premier League match at The City of Manchester Stadium. City ran out emphatic 3-0 winners with the opener from Gareth Barry and two second half goals from Carlos Tevez. (Action Images/Jason Cairnduff)

28 Lamps flops from the spot (Simonsen save), Drogba shows him how as Chelsea takes two off Stoke. Rooney overall drought pain ends in 1115th min with pen as Man U is the first to hoist 1500 pt in PL and adds to Hammers worst start for 33 years and first to hoist 1500th pt in PL. Wigan lives! Rodallega ten mins from time wins it at Spurs erasing memory of that 9-1. Walcott stars again as Arsenal edges Blackburn. Late Etuhu foils Blackpool victory over Fulham. Wolves held by Carroll-starring Newcastle but still go fourth in game of dozen yellows. FLC: Rangers 92nd and 96th goals salvage a point at Derby. Pompey's decline continues at home to Cardiff. Debut loanee Calve carves Sheff U the points over Preston. Leicester unhappy over denied leveller against Reading. Forest makes it ten games no win. Donny is grateful for Woods 65 sec goal on way to beating Hull. Millwall get og starter for three against Coventry. £1m record buy Sinclair aids Swans to say bye-bye Burnley. L1: Saints flourish a foursome at Bristol R. Posh old boys punish Plymouth. Bournemouth, Notts share joy of six. Orient achieves first win over Exeter. Five-goal Sheff W stuns Hartlepool away. L2: Who shred all the goals (2): only 23 scored in 11. Torquay concedes after 998 mins to stay clear over Vale. Shrews stuff ex-boss Simpson with four at Stockport. Vet Warne is Millers winner at Hereford. SPL: Killie down the Dons. Hamilton surprises Caley Rangers top edging St J. SL1: Raith sole 100% edges Morton. Dundee loses gk to red but smacks Bairns. SL2: Livi maintains two-point lead against Forfar. SL3: Berwick clear at top as Annan draws at Montrose. BSP: Luton slumps at Tamworth, AFC Dons take two point lead with win at Eastbourne. FA Cup: Six teams hit six, Clevedon and Met Police (hullo hullo) both away. C Cup draw: Spurs get Arsenal. Capello does a Becks u-turn.

29 Tevez miss of the week so Man C pays the penalty with an added time Bent spot kick after Richards tango. Two drawn to Brummie and without sent off goalie Bolton bounces back for a point. Volley boy Torres lives! First goal for the Spaniard beats ten-man finishing WBA. One goal is enough, too, for Villa against Everton. SPL: Motherwell concedes pen and match to Celtic who go top. Poor start for JM at Real in scoreless affair at Mallorca. FA Cup: Lincoln M Rail shunt Glapwell for six.

30 Robinho may be on the way to AC Milan. Pardew axed at Soton. Capello faces injury crisis. Portugal boss Queiroz expects six month ban. Rafa goalless, too, as Inter held at Bologna!. New BSP leaders as Mansfield hits four at Altrincham while Luton held by Hayes and AFC Dons by Newport. Crawley's nine edge Forest's nine.

31 Van der Vaart jumps under the transfer window in time to get his Spurs in £8m deal. JPT: Shock for managerless Saints, dumped by Swindon. FA Cup: Wednesfield six hitters over Castle Vale.

SEPTEMBER
Rooney grabbed by the tabloids ... Houllier back at Villa ... Extra time may go ... PL League of Nations ... Wenger's tackling issue ... Becks heads 2018 bid.

1 Rio gets a run out for Man U stiffs. UEFA trumpets ban on vuvuzelas.

2 FIFA herald Rooney as "outstanding in WC 2010." Houllier is latest to be touted for Villa after Eriksson and Bradley (USA).

3 Friday is Euro 2012 night: Three Lions Defoe treble in England foursome over Bulgaria; Double Irish joy Northern (ending seven no goal run) and Republic via Slovenia and Armenia respectively; Wales downed in Montenegro and Collins injured. Wasteful Scots held in Lithuania. It's Tor-Tor Torres in Spanish four-play, blankety-Blanc for French losers in Paris to Belarus! Portugal forced to share eight with Cyprus. U-21s Sturridge on target for England in Portugal, N Ireland hits four against San Marino, Scots draw in Belarus, but Republic edged in Switzerland.

4 L1: Ten finishing MK Dons edge pen-claiming Hartlepool. Vincelot double as Daggers win E London derby with Orient. Wasteful Austin costs Swindon in goalless at Carlisle. Exeter added time pen nails Charlton. Notts four play floors Yeovil. First win for Tranmere against Posh. L2: Nine goals at Bury, 7 in 27 mins, as Gills just clipped by the odd goal. First win in 20 for Stockport at Macc. Barnet recovers from 66 sec Cheltenham goal for three points. Vale of tears for homers at Bradford. Wilting Southend still ends Torquay run. Hullo, hullo, Constable on triple beat for Oxford v Morecambe. BSP: AFC Dons regain lead at Kettering as Mansfield lose at home to Tamworth. Four no win Luton loses at Grimsby. Alba q-f: Ross, Partick and QoS are through. Vase: St Helens, Tividale behind the eight ball strikes. Fall out from Paki cricket lands Croydon Ath in chaos. Welsh U-21s win in Hungary.

5 L1 leaders Sheff W stung by Brentford. Alba: Peterhead completes four for semis. Toshack prepared to quit Wales if results show no improvement. WC ref Webb officiates at Rotherham Sunday League game!

6 Rooney in wake of sex allegations prepares to play away in Switzerland, Levein cools over goal glut predictions against Liechtenstein as do the Republic facing Andorra. Houllier heads towards Villa. Blackburn touting tycoon may be skint.

7 Euro 2012: Roo scores as England beats ten-man Swiss. Scots manage a winner – in the 97th min! Republic nets three against Andorra. Goals galore: six for Germany, Sweden plus five for Italy. France even succeeds in winning. Portugal is a loser in Norway. Baros misses pen as Czechs blanked by Lithuania. Spain crashes in friendly to Argies. U-21s: England defeats Lithuania to enter play-offs, Republic loses in Turkey, Wales in Italy and N Ireland in Germany, but Scots edge Austria to top its group.

8 Capello will retire in 2012. England manager candidates: Roy H, Stuart P, Harry R, Sam A, Steve B. Gerrard likely to keep armband. Balotelli, Rodwell, Kuyt injury scares. Houllier is new Villa boss. Ilkeston Town wound up. Chester attracts 2743 to six goals.

9 Arsenal has 76 players! Walcott and Defoe are latest injury victims. Ref Webb is about to come back. FIFA is likely to scrap extra time. Banned Queiroz is sacked by Portugal. Toshack stands down for Wales.

10 RBS is to mastermind Liverpool sale. 700 up for Sir Alex tomorrow in terms of PL, as one of seven everpresent teams will line-up this weekend.

11 Sir Alex rues sparing Roo at Everton as sloppy Man U concedes two in added time to share joy of six. Chelsea concedes a goal but hit three at West Ham as Green gaffes again. Arsenal foursome flattens Trotters ten men as Song Bellong tunes in with 1000th Pl goal of Wenger era. Blackpool getting the PL hang of it, wins at Newcastle. Dembele doubles up over Wolves but Zamora broken leg misery for Fulham. Moneybags Man C gets little change out of Blackburn in Rovers 900th PL pt after Hart fumble. Spurs have to settle for WBA draw (17 different countries represented) as ref Webb returns to PL and Modric is injured. Sub Gyan debut goal earns ten-man Sunderland (Cattermole off again) pt at Wigan. FLC: Millwall is unhappy over Forest leveller. Loanee Olofinjana helps to stuff own masters Hull for Cardiff. Burnley recovers from two-goal deficit

to beat Preston with three in six mins in odd goal in seven win. Scunny hit by Bristol C as boss Adkins wants away to Soton. L1: Elliot pen save then Anyinsah wins it for Charlton against Notts. Sheff W back from admin-brink loses to Carlisle on U's first success at Hillsborough. Posh five-star response to Oldham's initial two. L2: Three down Burton looks to Harrad treble for a pt at Rotherham. Unbeaten Torquay held by Crewe. Gills first win over Shrewsbury, Northampton, too, beating Southend. Shot shy Hereford blanked by Oxford. SPL: Rangers leave it late for Miller goal at Hamilton, Celtic get three against Hearts. SL1: Raith drops first two points at Ross. SL2: Four goal Alloa, Templeman treble for Forfar. SL3: Gribben grabs hat trick for Berwick and Stranraer traps Spiders in ten-a-side. BSP: AFC Dons, Crawley, Mansfield, Tamworth, Fleetwood, Luton and Darlo – all seven winners at the top. FA Cup: Oxhey Jets shot down by eight-goal Hornchurch Flack (threesome). Yetton trebles in Truro eight, too. Super sub Burnell hits foursome for Wealdstone. JM gets first Real win (Ricardo Carvalho!) as Barca loses to Hercules.

12　Torres quiet again as Reina helps Liverpool to a pt at Birmingham. Modric is ok. Nigel Adkins gets Soton job. England Ladies hit two against Swiss in WC first leg p-o.

13　Stoke edge Villa to give boss Pulis something on day his mother died. Hammers fine "fat boy" McCarthy. Ajax's Evander Sno, suffers heart attack at 23.

14　Ch Lge: Man U with Rooney, but odd other choices, held goalless by Rangers and Valencia ankle k-o for term. Spurs two up in 18 mins have to settle for a Werder draw. Inter also level away to Twente. Messi day for Barca, two goals, one missed pen and two woodwork hits, in five v Panathinaikos. Valencia takes four off Bursa. Benfica has two-goal lead over Hapoel TA. Ten-man Schalke loses at Lyon. Late goal gives FC Copenhagen lead over Rubin. FLC goal glut: 39. Barnsley five-star shakes Leeds, Palace foursome (loanee Vaughan treble) over poor Pompey. Boss-less Scunny cracks four at Sheff U. First win for Forest at PNE. Kink dinks late for Boro over Burnley. Coppinger is treble shooter for Donny against Norwich.

15　Ch Lge: Arsenal inspired by Fabregas hits Braga for six, Chelsea nets four at Zilina. JM is happy with a couple for Real against Ajax. Ibrahimovic double for AC Milan beats Auxerre. Spartak Moscow shakes Marseille. Shakhtar edges Partizan. Bayern late show defeats Roma. Cluj surprises Basle. Adkins debut sees Soton lose to MK Dons. Skint FA? – National Football Centre might really go for a Burton. Hammers give Grant religious weekend leave. Houllier hopes to have McAllister as No.2. England rises to sixth in rankings!

16　E Lge: Liverpool minus Torres hits four against Steaua, Man C takes two goal lead at Salzburg. Lech surprise Juve with a draw. Aris edges Atletico Madrid. England Ladies shrug off dismissal to beat Swiss and reach WC finals. Shearer says he was offered Toon job, then heard nothing.

17　FLC: Wenger under fire from some PL bosses over tackling issue. Big Sam wants to reign in Spain. Vet gk Sullivan holds firm as Donny goes goalless with Leeds. L2: Stanley another fine win over Imps. BSP: Shock for AFC Dons at Luton (7283).

18　Wenger strop as Bent levels for Sunderland 15 secs over four mins overtime denies ten-man Arsenal (Song off, 50th red under AW). Spurs three in last 13 mins upsets Wolves lead at WHL. Ben Arfa 25 yd strike for Newcastle puts misery into Merseyside for Everton. Fulham draws at hard ball Blackburn. Houllier's watching brief reveals his Villa problems in pt apiece with Bolton. Baggies bring Midland bragging rights over Brummie. West Ham first pt at Stoke but odds already 14-5 against its survival! FLC: QPR continues best start since 1947 at Leicester. Watford earns joy of six at Millwall in best away for 112 years. Robson 24 secs opener for Boro is fastest at Riverside and helps to down Reading. Coventry achieves first win at Bristol C for 47 years. Preston's worst start for nearly 90 years as NE loses to Norwich. Kid Wickham inspires Ipswich over Cardiff. L1: Hughes hat trick for Bristol R depresses Daggers. Having a laugh? Not really as Walsall fun day ends with Swindon winning. Ten-man Plymouth adds to Sheff W slide. No goal Soton held by Colchester. Huddersfield shrugs off two goal Yeovil lead and doubles it to go top as Posh is held at Exeter. L2: Bauza debut pen for Hereforfd, Bartlett saves one so Bury has to settle for a draw. Top three: Shrewsbury, Port Vale and Chesterfield seal and all win. BSP: New leaders as Tubbs double aids Crawley. SPL: Rangers hit Dundee U for four. SL1: Dunfermline leads as Raith held at Dundee. SL2: Roberts three pens – then sent off for Ayr! SL3: Stranraer holds ten-man Berwick. Vase: South Shields strike eight at Ryton. Gornal, Shoreham both score seven in wins. JM's Real edges home at Real Sociedad.

19　Buoyant Berbatov's three is one better than Gerrard's pair as Man U clips Liverpool. Tevez is the main man for Man C at Wigan. Chelsea adds another four with reply from Blackpool. SPL: Killie early strike is not enough to stop Celtic. Bobby Smith, ex-Chelsea, Spurs and England striker dies at 77.

20　Becks is spearheading 2018 WC bid. Hicks move to cement his association with Liverpool does not set.

21　C Cup: Arsenal finishes in overtime with foursome at WHL to Spurs chagrin. Everton racked with woe as the Brentford Bees sting in a shoot-out thanks to reserve gk Lee. Pussy-footing Black Cats under the Hammers. Wolves need extra time to end ten-man Notts resistance. Sinclair hat trickster preens for Swans at Posh. Fulham's interest extinguished at Stoke. Pompey falls to Leicester. Now Ipswich takes out Millwall at the New Den. Lancs derby goes Burnley way against Bolton. Birmingham's four in four mins punishes MK Dons. L1: Brighton moves second at Plymouth. BSP: Mansfield five-star hits York. CIS: Rangers hit seven against Fifers, St J treble shooters over Q o S, Motherwell double at Brechin, Falkirk edges Hearts odd goal in seven. Spain: JM sees Real threesome over Espanyol.

22　C Cup: Cobblers, Liverpool as Northampton wins Anfield shoot-out. Seven goals again at Stamford Bridge, but Newcastle get four of them against Chelsea. Man U five hit (Owen two) at Scunny. Red faced Blue Moon slips away as Baggies brace beats Man C. Houllier off to a Young double for Villa against Blackburn. Added time win for Wigan over Preston. CIS: Celtic hits Caley for six, Dundee U needs extra time to oust Ross, Killie beats the Hi-Bees. Dons edge Raith.

23　Rooney feels the heat under media lights. Capello to award four day break to players. BSP: AFC Dons edge Crawley to regain top place.

24　Mancini tips Chelsea ahead of clash. Hodgson is unhappy over Sir Alex on Torres. Pompey six hitters hound ten Leicester Foxes. Brentford goes west at the Orient.

25　Crisis club Chelsea? Man C skipper Tevez wins Battle of the Blues against them. Almunia saves WBA pen then flaps Baggies to victory at Arsenal. Gerrard straightens Liverpool out for a point again after Bent double for Sunderland, but both Hodgson and Bruce castigate ref Atwell. Hammers off the foot (Green "stiffs" media) as Spurs continue their London blip. Ten-man Birmingham finish goalless with Wigan, same score line for ten-man Birmingham and Wigan. Lancs clash of the "Blacks", sees "Burn" win at "Pool." FLC: QPR strides on over Donny. Watford 17 secs start and take out Boro. Ten-man Reading late blast sees off

Barnsley. Reliable Alexander misses first spot kick in 19 as Burnley is held by Bristol C. Preston ride luck at Coventry to win. Hull end away win drought after 31 games at Norwich. Cardiff clip ten-man Millwall. Leeds secure first win over Sheff U for 17 years. Derby hits five against ten-man Palace. L1: Brighton Seagulls peck off Oldham to soar to first place. Posh win local derby with MK Dons. Adkins snaps first win for Soton at financial-worried Sheff W ending 510 mins of no goals. Colchester is only unbeaten side in the division after beating Tranmere. L2: Port Vale extends lead at the head after victory over Accrington. Barnet, Shots both throw two-goal leads for a point apiece at Morecambe and Stockport respectively. Loanee Holroyd gives Stevenage first away win at Liincoln. Macc stops Torquay on the coast. BSP: Mansfield foursome over Eastbourne keeps them top. Luton loses at Gateshead. Fleetwood splash out in third place after Bath. SPL: Celtic win Green battle with Hibs. Referee gives two yellow to St J's Anderson but he stays on at Dundee U! SL1: Winners Dunfermline, Raith both move away from pack. SL2: Livi held by East Fife, so Brechin goes closer beating Dumbarton. SL3: Berwick held at East Stirling, so Stranraer is level after four-play finishes Arbroath. FA Cup: Sam Higgins four goals in Chelmsford seven; AFC Telford five goals (best gate 1447) v Stourbridge. Real held goalless at Levante! Inter loses at Roma.

26   Man U has to settle for a draw at Bolton and Roo is substituted. Magpies Perch at the wrong end as Stoke wins at St James Park. Villa with re-born Heskey delights Houllier in victory at Wolves. SPL: Pear shaped for Dons late on against Rangers, down to ten men and edged out. BSP: Crawley wins at Rushden to resume at the top. AFC Dons slip up at Harriers. Winter, the St J ref. thinks of quitting.

27   Arsenal, Chelsea plan changes for Ch Lge games. Rooney is out with ankle injury. BSP: ex-FL neighbours York, Darlo in goalless draw.

28   Ch Lge: Fabianski glows in the dark as Arsenal shrugs off blackout to win convincingly at ten-man Partizan. Chelsea is back to winning and clean sheet against Marseille. Bayern comes back to edge Basle. Roma clips Cluj. Spartak eases against Zilina. AC Milan makes a point at Ajax. JM gets his one at Auxerre for Real. Donetsk takes three at Braga. FLC: Ten goals at Leeds as PNE come back from the dead to score five in a row and win (Parkin treble). Rangers held by Millwall, but crowd trouble mars it all. Norwich odd goal in seven win against Leicester (Fryatt two, then red card). Swans sting the Hornets at Watford. Palace manages a draw at Cardiff. Ten-a-side draw between Reading and Ipswich. L1: Brighton, Bournemouth, Carlisle (four at Hartlepool) and Rochdale leading foursome all win, but Posh loses ten-a-side with Notts. Tranmere makes ground at Bristol R. Another ten each side affair sees Plymouth successful at Swindon. L2: Crucial win for Port Vale over Shrewsbury. Holroyd hat trick as Stevenage shows four-play at Hereford. Bury hits four at Morecambe, Wycombe similarly at home against Barnet. Entertaining Shots? Only goal at Torquay but just 13 in their nine matches! BSP: Fleetwood flows to the top at Barrow. Newport goes second beating Forest.

29   Ch Lge: V der Vaart misses pen, scores then sent off as Ruskie shows him how with two spot on in Spurs four-play against Twente. "Chicharito" takes out Valencia for Man U. Even Rangers win against Bursa. Eto'o is treble shooter for Inter over Werder. Lyon wins away to Hapoel. Schalke is two much for Benfica. Copenhagen double hits at Panathinaikos. Barca draws away to Rubin. BSP: Crawley is back on top after beating Tamworth and Tubbs hit another two. AFC Dons move to second place after beating Cambridge. Lincoln parts company with boss Sutton.

30   E Lge: Man C held by Juve and post loss of £121m. Liverpool scoreless in Utrecht draw but still lead Group K. Hotel idea may rescue Burton Centre. Spurs new ground close by is given the nod. Dundee on the brink, owing money to HMRC and no wages paid to players.

OCTOBER

Eriksson at Leicester ... Man U record turnover and loss ... Henry is Liverpool new owner ... Dundee in crisis ... Rooney wants away ... Goals and cards soar.

1   Leicester axes Paulo Sousa, Eriksson is in line. Keith Gillespie is bankrupt. Sky Sports Victory Shield: Scots beat Irish.

2   Man U held at Sunderland where unlucky boss Bruce has not beaten his old boss Sir Alex in 13 attempts. Everton gains first win at Birmingham who fail to beat 103 year home record and – shock, horror – go above Liverpool, first time in 26 years! V der V doubles up again for Spurs to edge Villa. Baggies draw with Bolton. Stoke climbs to 7th with one goal against Blackburn. Fulham pt still leaves Hammers at the bottom. Henry red after horror tackle as Wigan beats ten-tame Wolves. FLC: Leicester parades boss to be Sven before defeating Scunny. Millwall's 125th anniversary but Burnley gets a draw. Bellamy back and scores for Cardiff winners at Hull. Injury hit Palace loses to leaders QPR. Ten man Leeds beaten at Ipswich. L1: Brighton draws at Tranmere but stays top as Posh close gap at Carlisle. Lambert two pens swipe off Bournemouth. Bristol R 94th min winner stuns Huddersfield. Brentford swaps bottom spot with Walsall after edging Charlton while the Saddlers lose at home to Yeovil. Daggers come back after 44 secs Swindon goal to climb to 20th. L2: Two games 21 goals, 10 just 20! Stanley put the Gills in first mess scoring seven to their four. Three goals deficit but Chesterfield fights back to share ten with Crewe! Port Vale loses at Oxford after levelling in added time! Cheltenham achieves first win away at the Shots. Rotherham remains third after draw at Bury. SPL: Hearts in trouble after missiles in defeat by Rangers. Celtic comes back from behind at Accies. SL1: Dunfermline, Raith are losers as gap closes. SL2: Livi suffers first defeat so Brechin goes top after beating Peterhead. SL3: Albion new leaders after edging E Stirling. S Cup: Five goal Deveronvale sends Works loco. BSP: Crawley resumes at the head as AFC Dons can only draw with Forest Green. Trophy: Six goals ahead AFC Sudbury concedes Merstham four-play! Vase: St Neots eleven goals after Felixstowe loses keeper (Stefan Moore debut foursome). Saltash scores nine. Welsh: Bang on Bangor makes it eight wins edging TNS.

3   Drogba makes it 13 goals in 13 games for Chelsea against Arsenal. Liverpool lament limps on as Blackpool wins at Anfield. Ben Arfa suffers serious leg injury from De Jong tackle as Man C makes hard work of beating Newcastle. Six-hit RM crushes La Coruna as Barca only draws with Mallorca. Inter held by Juve, so Lazio winners over Brescia goes top.

4   Capello's youth policy kicks in with Kevin Davies, 33, in squad. FIFA bans Nigeria until government stops interfering. Is Hodgson out of his depth at Liverpool? De Jong axed by Dutch national team. Hereford sacks Davey and No 2 Fensome. Hughes parts company with Hibs.

5   Red Sox boss bids for Liverpool as G and H battle back. McClaren could be favourite for England job post-Capello? RM and Tevez are at loggerheads? Newcastle wants De Jong chastised. JPT: Half of away teams win, Crewe top with four goals – and both Maccs!

6   JPT: Sheff W need pens to oust Chesterfield, Rotherham a spot kick to beat Burton. Steve Parkin is appointed coach at Scunthorpe.

7   Fulham skipper Murphy lays into managers who acquiesce over bad tackles. Battle of Liverpool will go on. Man U is to establish first £100m operating profit. Man C is to target Ch Lge place. Will Ferdinand be axed? Healy back for N Ireland, Scots drop Miller, caretaker Flynn is upbeat for Wales as Matthaus leads the Bulgarians. Trapattoni aims to keep Republic on right track.

8   Euro: Montenegro (who?) beats Swiss to top England's group. Wales already looking out of it as Bulgaria does enough. Scots wall fails to prevent Czechs winning. Republic fight back not enough after Russians treble. N Ireland holds Italy scoreless. Elsewhere, Hungary nets six against San Marino, Slovenia five against Faeroes. Three wins now for Germany, Holland and Norway. U-21s: England edges Romania in first leg p-o. Man U has record turnover, record loss £83.6m! Liverpool might face a deduction of points!

9   L1: Brighton boss Poyet smarts at late Bournemouth pen that smacks leveller. Posh missing pen loses at Hartlepool, so Carlisle goes second beating Notts. London woe: Daggers, Orient and Bees in bottom four. L2: Port Vale held by Hereford ten. Chesterfield added time winner against Southend. Nine man Stanley turned over at Bury. Crewe in six goals share (22 goals in a week) but miss pen v Torquay. Ten Shots win at Oxford. Lincoln ends 464 mins goalless. Ainsworth's 100th career goal as Wycombe wins at Burton. BSP: Crawley held at Barrow so AFC Dons cut lead. SL3: Stranraer draws at Montrose to go third. Alba s-f: Q of S wins at Peterhead. Welsh: Bangor nine out of nine. FA Cup: best gate: 1835 as Halifax beats Harrogate. Euro: France, Croatia both win to top groups. Rooney wants winter break and McClaren turns down any return to England job.

10 Capello gives Rio back the armband, Crouch is in for injured Bent. Scots are retreating again (plus U-21s lose out to Iceland). N Ireland watches over Faeroes. Wales are hoping for a Bale in. Alba s-f: Ross needs pens to oust Jags.

11 LMA defend attitudes to tackling problem. Brazil beats Ukraine at Derby (where else!). Swindon edges Bristol R. Icy k-o for Scots at U-21 level. Liverpool heads for the High Court as NESV aims takeover vice G and H. Montenegro will be without star striker Vucinic. Lim from Asia enters Liverpool bidding.

12 Euro: Denied pen but that's all folks as Montenegro gets a scoreless draw. Scots give Spain a fright and restore some faith in defeat. Bale, yes, but Wales, no, in Switzerland. Keane pen miss so Republic draws in Slovakia. N Ireland held in Faeroes. Serb fans riot to end game in Italy after seven minutes. U-21s: England gets the draw it needs in Romania. JM rates Sir Alex! Sunderland's Ferdinand has court date.

13 Now it is High Court drama as G and H file injunction over Liverpool. And it's "Anklegate" as Rooney says he is not injured. Benayoun is out for six months. Blatter makes positive noises re-2018. Accrington withdraws from the JPT over fielding still suspended Ray Putterill; Tranmere is reinstated. Eddie Baily inside-forward during Spurs push and run success in 1950–51, dies at 85.

14 Battle for Anfield continues in Texas! Shearer wants England job. Becks snubs call up for friendly. Big Sam lays into Murphy, backed by the LMA. Torres fit for derby. Hargreaves is on brink of coming back. Dundee may fold. Pompey stays in administration. Steve Tilson is the new Lincoln boss. Big Mal (Malcolm) Allison, flamboyant manager, dies at 83.

15 Henry and the Red Sox beat G and H after Texas stand off to take over Liverpool. USA quits battle for WC 2018. More bosses line up to criticise Murphy. Mancini bans booze, not sex. Sky Sports Victory Shield: Wales shocks England with foursome. Dundee announces severe cuts and appoints new manager in Barry Smith.

16 Man U chucks two-goal lead, Roo (leaving?) is 71st min sub, V der S spills one so WBA pt makes it six no loss. Wenger red-faced on 800th game as Wilshere sees red as Brummies fail at Arsenal (no win there since 1957). Chelsea held scoreless at Villa who have best record against them at home. Ref Dean changes his mind over off-side Huddlestone goal, so Fulham loses unbeaten record to Spurs. N'Zogbia 107 secs double for Wigan against old Newcastle mates but Toon gets 94th min leveller. Sub Klasnic 181 seconds of one yellow card, one goal, another yellow in Bolton's first home win against Stoke. Noble pens a pt at Wolves but Hammers have gone 22 away without a win now. FLC: Millwall wins at ten-man Palace. Leeds gives pain for ex-boss Strachan at Boro. Sheff U and Burnley share six goals. Swans boss McDermott joy at old Reading base. Derby's Savage pen on 600th outing as ten-man PNE loses. Pompey wins again and may be out of administration soon. Coventry achieves first win at Ipswich since 1994. Hoolahan pen miss but Norwich draws at QPR (best gate 18,059 for six years). Gray's 100th career goal as Barnsley beats Forest. Whittingham back on the goal standard as Cardiff recovers two-goal deficit to beat lowly Bristol C. L1: Bubbling Brighton sounds a foursome bell at Charlton (six year worst at home). Brentford first away win comes at Tranmere. Og gives Posh odd goal in nine win over Swindon. Hold up at Huddersfield for injured lino, but Town beats Soton anyway. L2: Davies double does it for Chesterfield at Wycombe. Struggling Hereford claws back three goals to win at ten-man Northampton. Port Vale fails to beat stoic Gills who have gone club record 33 away without a win. A 92nd min winner stuns ten-man Accrington for Rotherham. Macc retrieves two-goals to stun Oxford. Bury just edges Torquay with odd goal in seven. SPL: Rangers again come back to beat Motherwell. SL1: Dunfermline, Raith back to winning ways. Dire straits Dundee gets a draw at Stirling. SL2: Brechin, Livi back to win bonuses. Ayr, Airdrie finish with nine and both lose. SL3: Stranraer One show, goal, first minute and first place at E Stirling. BSP: Newport shakes Crawley, so AFC Dons are top again. Trophy: Ross Hannah seven goals of Matlock 10. FC United best gate (1035). Wales: Bangor ten out of ten now. Barca wins at home, Real Madrid away are both successful. Two FIFA officials accused of taking bribes for votes.

17 New owner Henry sees second from bottom Liverpool flop at Everton. Sexy Man C edges Blackpool to go second top. Celtic matches Rangers for eighth win at Dundee U.

18 Ten-man Blackburn manages a draw with Sunderland. No more bucks for Rooney, so it looks final. Strachan walks away from Boro. Calderwood leaves Toon No.2 for Hibs No.1 – and Carroll must move in with the Nolans. Red Socks boss wants Becks to pull their strings up.

19 Ch Lge: Arsenal gives it five against Shakhtar, Chelsea a couple over Spartak in Moscow. Another clean sheet for Real as AC Milan loses. Braga puts Partizan at the bottom. Ajax ten see off Auxerre nine. Marseille edges it against Zilina. Bayern needs two ogs to clip Cluj. Basle surprises Roma. FLC: Kenny pen stop saves QPR pt at Swansea but Cardiff closes the gap at Coventry – just one of seven away winners. First travel

success for Palace at Norwich. Watford goes third after home win against Ipswich. BSP: Luton six hitters cut down Forest GR. Sir Alex outlines Rooney departure.

20   Ch Lge: Inter foursome so Bale's treble not enough for Spurs. Man U goes for the minimum against Bursa while crisis meeting is called at Old Trafford. Edu for both sides as Rangers draw with Valencia. Twente and Werder share the points. Benfica's ten suffer in Lyon. Schalke ease against Hapoel TA. Barca twosome takes out FC Copenhagen. Panathinaikos and Rubin draw and seem out of it. Hawk-Eye might still come in from the cold. It's looking good for 2018 as England rivals face investigation.

21   E Lge: Adebayor threesome finishes off Lech for Man C. Liverpool manages a draw in cauldron of Napoli. Suitors lined up for Rooney as agent seen as key figure while anti-Rooney protests begin inside and out.

22   Rooney stays with better deal! It's either a farce or a neatly staged conspiracy. QPR scrapes a late draw at Bristol C to ensure club record unbeaten run. Pompey faces demand for payment from ex-owner.

23   Chelsea eight home PL games without conceding in 781 minutes carry on winning as Wolves get off nine shots on target. Landlord and lodger get Newcastle goals to hit 250th in the PL with win at West Ham. OG King Dunne (8th) gives Sunderland the points against Villa. V der V rushes to the rescue for Spurs held by Everton. WBA goes fourth, club's highest since 1981, edging Fulham. McCarthy injury for Wigan as Bolton manages a draw there. Diamond switching Brummies sound a warning to Blackpool. FLC: Loanee Emnes starts Swans on victory trail against Leicester. Parkin 100th, 101st career goals as PNE clips Palace by odd goal in seven. Reading raids Burnley with foursome. Forest makes it three losses in a row for Ipswich. L1: Brighton ten unbeaten forges ahead against Yeovil. Tranmere four-play does it at Walsall. Charlton leaves it late to get its odd goal in seven win at Carlisle. L2: Four up Chesterfield hold on to beat battling Shrews. Wycombe lucky pen stuns Rotherham in another best of seven goals win. Flying Crewe makes it eleven without defeat to beat the Shots. SPL: Skacel treble for Hearts finishes St M. SL1: Raith edges Ross to move ahead as cash-strapped Dundee hits back to draw with Dunfermline. SL2: Wins for Brechin, Livi. S Cup: Stranraer club record nine demolishes St Cuthberts. Bo'Ness catches the QP Spiders. Buckie scores seven at Wigtown, Beith eight against Glasgow Univ. FA Cup: Hythe reaches first round first time in 99 years. Darlo hits six at Mossley. Harrow shakes Eastbourne with Troy Hewitt treble. Havant is on the rise again. Morgan-Smith hat trick for Luton overwhelms St Albans. Ronaldo foursome in Real's six hits; Messi adds couple for Barca.

24   85 mins minus Boyata is a red too much for Man C as Arsenal stays second. Hernandez double cheers Man U at Stoke. Torres lives! He hits winner against Blackburn for Liverpool. SPL: Rangers beat Celtic at Parkhead to forge in front. FA Cup: FC U of Man tips up Barrow boys.

25   FIFA on the back foot over bribery claims, Platini treads water against technology. Cardiff four-play surprises slipping Leeds.

26   C Cup: "Little pea" pops winner again for Man U to edge Wolves. Birmingham needs pens to swipe the Brentford Bees. Ipswich staves off Northampton lead. WBA foursome ends Leicester hopes. Swans 4500 fans get nothing for trip to Wigan. CIS: Dons and Motherwell make the semis. No big bucks for Hodgson at Liverpool. Blackburn will receive only a paltry sum for Indian poultry takeaway. Tevez is homesick. Tony Mowbray is new Middlesbrough boss. FA Cup replays: Tamworth wins at Grimsby. Bang goes understrength Bangor – as TNS hits nine in Welsh LC.

27   C Cup: Newcastle backs boss Hughton, but the Toon hit by awesome Arsenal four-play. Villa's ten men struggle to beat Burnley. Hammers go the extra time to beat Stoke. CIS: Celtic, Rangers in last four – surprise? Ince seems likely Notts manager. Russia steps up anti-England 2018 bid.

28   Russia says sorry, Ince is confirmed at Notts Co. New No.2 at Newcastle may be difficult to find and Steve Clarke turns down offer.

29   Grant is under pressure at West Ham despite earlier win. Mancini warns boozers. FIFA snubs England stars (?) for Golden Ball nominations. Italy gets statutory Euro win for abandoned Serbia game. Bangor back to winning as Bala loses. Sky Sports Victory Shield: Wales holds Scots. BSP: Southport, Kiddy get a draw in ten-a-side.

30   Farce as Man U's hands on Nani gets free shot in 2004 reprise error against Spurs by ref Clattenburg. Blackburn makes Chelsea fight for late win, but misses easy chance. Hammers push Arsenal even further before losing. Brittle bottlers Man C (Tevez at home) edged out by Wolves. Everton improvement continues over Stoke but Pulis rages over disallowed goal. Deputy striker Dempsey doubles up for Fulham against Wigan. FLC: Palace's Burley boys suffer bug and bitten by the Swans. Fifth draw in six for QPR in Burnley draw (Alexander back to pen success). Cardiff takes pole position against Norwich. Boro slumps to 23rd in Bristol C defeat. Pompey's best gate of season (19,719) sees Forest pruned. Fifth win in six for Coventry at Sheff U. Japanese Abe does it for Leicester as PNE loses. Reading gets best of seven goals against Donny. Derby's foursome over Watford lifts them to seventh. Howson has hat trick in another four-play episode for Leeds at Scunny. L1: Brace by Brighton's birthday boy Barnes as Posh loses at home. Huddersfield needs just one to beat bottom club Walsall. Colchester also takes advantage by winning at Bournemouth. Four star winners: Brentford at Exeter, Tranmere at home to MK Dons and Oldham hosting nine man Plymouth. Saints move up with win at Notts. Parkinson's 100th in charge of Charlton is rewarded against Sheff W. Yeovil chuck two goal lead to share six with Swindon. L2: Ten men Bradford hit Oxford's nine for five. Chesterfield held at Stevenage, Port Vale clips Crewe and Bury wins at nine-man Shots who also have boss Dillon red carded after two goals are disallowed. Hereford five star showing at Stockport as old boy Purdie returns on loan. SPL: Rangers lose 100% in draw with Caley, but Celtic closes gap at St J. SL1: Raith, Dunfermline are winners, Dundee shares six at Falkirk; SL2: Ayr at Peterhead and Dumbarton home to E Fife get four. SL3: Stranraer leaves it late to defeat Elgin. S Cup: Annan hits five in Preston replay. BSP: Crawley foursome hits Mansfield, Goal machine Luton celebrates 125th birthday with 7003 and three points. AFC Dons slip up to Darlo. Trophy: Dennis Egan three for Chasetown and Matt Cooper for Paulton who lose to Super-mariners. FC U of M/c has 1259 gate. Goal note: PL 12 in 6; FL 122 in 36. Card note: 26: PL (0), FL (15), SPL (1), Sl (7), SC (1) BSP (2). Spain: Barca, Real are winners (Ronaldo 38 goals in 38 games now).

31   Liverpool rides out the storm at Bolton and Maxi wins it. Nolan treble strike for Toon as ten-man Sunderland sinks on the Tyne. Midland derby ends goalless between Villa and Birmingham. SPL: Killie improves its position at Hearts.

NOVEMBER

Aberdeen record defeat ... Rangers, Celtic both losers ... France beats England ... Messi hits ton mark ... Rooney back in fold ... Mourinho card scam trumped.

1   Baggies nine men just edged out at Blackpool. Harry R defies FA over comments about refs. Dundee suffers severe 25 pt penalty. Wilshere signs for five more years at Arsenal. Quinn says sorry to Sunderland fans.

2   Ch Lge: Another bracing Spurs show from Bale belts Inter. Man U threesome away to Bursa. Rangers treble loss in Valencia. Twente sees off ten-man Werder. Four up Benfica is nearly caught by the Lyon. Hapoel first point in goalless with Schalke. Barca gets a draw at FC Copenhagen. Rubin and Panathinaikos share no goals. L1: Two waterlogged abandoned. Brighton stays on crest over Exeter. Huddersfield Yorkshire success at Sheff W. Orient chucks two goals to lose at Colchester. Foursome floors Daggers at Soton. L2: Floodlights fail at Cheltenham. Chesterfield hits Stanley five times. Shaker for Bury as Bradford wins.

3   Ch Lge: Chelsea qualifies with fourth victory as Spartak concedes four. Bayern achieves the same double-four trick away to Cluj. Arsenal clipped by old boy Eduardo for Shakhtar. Roma wins at ten-finishing Basle. Marseille delights in seventh heaven of Zilina. Real snatches last gasp leveller to qualify at AC Milan. Auxerre edges Ajax and Clattenburg gets hands right! Braga adds to Partizan misery. Liverpool appoints Damien Comolli as D of F.

4   E Lge: Super sub Gerrard rescues Liverpool with treble against Napoli. Blue Moon pig of a defeat to leaders Lech as lack lustre Man C loses three on the trot. David Gold hits out at Birmingham C owners. FC U of Man prepares for FA Cup shock. N Ireland – England Victory Shield waterlogged off.

5   FA Cup: FC U of Man's Mike Norton (a tiler) puts the lid on Rochdale with dodgy late winner. Rooney sent to USA for recuperation. BBC may screen unfavourable WC 2018 story quickly to limit damage. Brummies ban Gold. Ancelotti hails Gerrard.

6   PL: 5 pts separate 4th to 16th! Man U double Park (92nd minute winner) leaves Wolves clamped – but Hargreaves lasts 4 mins 40 secs after 777 day-absence. Four-play Bolton ties up Bale, rides out ten-starting foreign Spurs comeback. Gyan (Sunderland's only other scorer) brace puts skids under four in a row losing ten-man Stoke. Cahill's 50th PL goal (28th header) aids Everton draw at twice-leading Blackpool (Eardley birthday scorer). Grant rages at no pen as two up Hammers draw at Birmingham. Blackburn stops the rot edging Wigan (but Martinez raps ref). FLC: Rangers back to winning ways over ten-man Reading. Derby goes fourth above Coventry beaten by Leeds, by defeating Pompey. Boro wins at last to swap bottom spot with Palace. FA Cup: Three shocks: Dover wins at ten-man Gills to hit old boss Hessenthaler (7475) as losers players up for sale; Crewe tanned at Tamworth; Darlo ends seven year wait beating Bristol R. Replays earned: home: Corby edging Luton; Cambridge on Huddersfield Clark's 100th i/c; tiring Dartford outplaying Port Vale; Fleetwood holding ten-man Walsall; ten-man Hartlepool by Vauxhall. Away: Woking at Brighton; York at Rotherham. Best gate: Soton (10,400) but had to wait for two late goals v Shrews. Swindon foursome strikes at ten-man Plymouth. Moneybags Crawley hits five at Guiseley. McQuoid treble in Bournemouth's five against Tranmere three; Colchester four to Bradford's treble. New first rounders: Hythe let in five at Hereford, Tipton six at Carlisle (Madine 4), but Super for Marine debut against Eastwood. 18 Non-leaguers in the draw! SPL: Nine goals, ten-man Celtic inflict record nine goal defeat on Aberdeen (Stokes, Hooper trebles). SL1: Raith, Dunfermline beaten, Dundee edges Partick, nine man Stirling loses five at Cowden. SL2: Livi beats Dumbarton to lead by a point as Brechin held at Sten. Campbells are going – I and R off for Forfar in Peterhead draw! SL3: Leaders Stranraer recover from goal down to beat nine-finishing QP.

7   Another red card for Arsenal as Carroll calls the tune for Toon at the Emirates. Tor-Tor-Torres double strike stuns Chelsea for Liverpool. Balotelli brace and red card as Man C shakes off run of defeats at WBA. FA Cup: Sheff W late five-goal show beats Southport; Burton edges Oxford. SPL; Hearts win the Edinburgh derby as Hibs are 11th!

8   Praises sung for Carroll towards England place. Mancunians gear up for derby day.

9   Spurs under par again finish all square with Sunderland but Harry R unhappy with ref Webb over Cattermole challenge on Modric. Ref Clattenburg misses a handball so Stoke edges Birmingham. FLC: Pens and cards in QPR draw at Pompey. Palace clips Watford in best of five goals. Boro even win away at Scunny. Derby keeps the fourth at Ipswich. JPT: Northern semi places for Carlisle, Huddersfield, Tranmere; South: Brentford, Bristol R (doubling Wycombe three!), Charlton Ath and Exeter. BSP: AFC Dons win at Altrincham and go top. SPL: Dons lose again to Caley. Loosemores: TNS and Llanelli for final.

10   Derby-day and a goalless dead heat at Eastlands. Early and late Chamakh seals it for Arsenal at Wolves. Liverpool's Spanish FT index shows shares even at Wigan. Goal man Essien settles West London derby for Chelsea but gets a card against Fulham. Holloway rings the changes for Blackpool at Villa, loses and threatens to quit if fined for weak team. Beckford lives to save Everton's ten in Bolton draw. Big Sam beams as Blackburn wins at Newcastle. West Ham in another draw with WBA. FLC: Cardiff draws at Reading, but Bristol C take a liberty at Swansea to win. JPT: Sheff W completes the Northern last four. SPL: Shock! Horror! Both Rangers, home to Hibs and Celtic at Hearts lose and don't score. Dundee U loses to St Mirren and gate is lower than Dundee's last Saturday!

11   Barton banned for punch in Rovers game. Butch Wilkins axed by Chelsea. WC 2018 prospects improve? BSP: Luton loses at Wrexham.

12   Fergie junior misery goes on as Hull wins (first in nine) at PNE. Lampard return delayed again. Rooney is back. Wolves want Blackpool fined.

13   Villa lets slip two-goal lead so Man U grabs a pt. Goalless again at Eastlands with Man C and Birmingham. Odd goal in five win for Bolton and fifth place at Wolves. Century outing and Bale bracing for injury-hit Spurs four-play over Blackburn. Another no goals affair involves Newcastle and Fulham. Stoke puts a brake on Liverpool revival. Moses leads Wigan out of bottom three against WBA. Nil-all, too, as Hammers are held by change-back Blackpool. FLC: Capello call-up boy Bothroyd celebrates with twosome as Cardiff wins at Scunny. Forest and Rangers in unison with no goals and ref complaints! Howard's way for Leicester downs Derby. Reading recovers two-goal deficit to share six with Norwich. Becchio treble as Leeds see off Bristol C. Ipswich slips up at home again to Barnsley. Palace wins again, Coventry its victim! L1: Another McQuoid hat trick for Bournemouth deflates Walsall. Brighton's ten crash at Hartlepool. Charlton's five strikes at Posh, takes them to second. D & R staggers Yeovil. L2: Chesterfield home record goes for a Burton. Port Vale held goalless at Northampton. Crewe sees off the Gills ten men. Shrews nab a point at Stevenage. SPL: Injury-hit Rangers back to winning over desperate Dons. Hearts capture third spot at St J as Hibs edge Motherwell.

Liverpool captain Steven Gerrard scores the second goal of his hat-trick for Liverpool from the penalty spot during the UEFA Europa League Group K match at Anfield against Napoli. The Reds eventually ran out 3-1 winners after Napoli had taken the lead on 28 minutes through Ezequiel Lavezzi. (Action Images/Carl Recine)

SL1: Dundee wins again at Ross as Dunfermline draws with Raith. SL2: Livi winning at Airdrie, has three pt lead after Brechin an Forfar draw. SL3: Stranraer clings to top on goal difference after fight back draw with Annan. Albion plays catch up at QP. BSP: AFC Dons wheeled out at Barrow. Crawley held at Darlo. Vase: Tunbridge Wells digs eight against Holyport.

14 Crisis club Chelsea as Sunderland hits three at the Bridge. Arsenal sneaks second at Everton. FLC: Swans stop Boro sprint. SPL: Late goal for Celtic at St M.

15 Glazers will pay off Man U debt. Henry is behind Hodgson at Anfield.

16 Carroll will start for England against new-look France. PM wants BBC to drop anti-FIFA show – for now. Red Knights still hovering at Old Trafford. Ageing Pires is to sign for Villa. Defoe is on road to recovery. Scots beat Faeroes by three. U 21s: England finish with ten men as Germany score twice. FA Cup replays: Woking push Brighton to a shoot-out, Stevenage pens help avoid possible AFC Dons problem by beating MK Dons. Sheff W may be heading for administration.

17 Frogs leap over sad-looking England as Gerrard injury riles Liverpool. Chamakh on the mark as Morocco holds N Ireland. Republic is beaten by Norway. U-21s: Scots beat N Ireland, Wales clip Austria. FA Cup replays: York surprises Rotherham. Euro: Finns hit eight against San Marino. Friendly: Messi enough for Argies against Brazil.

18 Fall-out continues after England display. FA Cup replay: AFC Dons are so late winners at Ebbsfleet – almost Friday!

19 Bridge structure undermined at Chelsea? Terry has better fitness news. Rooney awaits fans response. Blatter gets his chopper out. Tennis could end 2018 chance. Blackburn is taken over by chicken outfit. Hughes is anxious to down Man C at Fulham. Sky Sports Victory Shield: Irish beat Welsh. Bury wins at Burton.

20 Two down Spurs beat Gunners – sweet seventeen years and Alan Sugar days since a Spurs win at Arsenal. One shot Brummies and Foster foil Chelsea. Wigan's nine men fall to Man U and sub Rooney. Bolton goes fourth after five hit on Newcastle. Liverpool sews up sad West Ham (Grant job safe!) in first half. Varney volley damages Wolves as Blackpool has HRH the boy William watching. Stoke add to Baggies bother (five games one pt). FLC: QPR back top – PNE stays bottom. Cardiff loses at home again to Forest. Sixth straight home win for ten-man Derby over Scunny. Bristol C adds to Leicester concern. Five goals, three pens and two reds as Sheff U edges Palace. L1: Super sub Tehoue double earns pt for O's against Bournemouth. Saints foursome on 125th birthday pounds Posh. Brighton caught by Bristol R leveller. Sheff W celebrates court delay with four-play over MK Dons. Another Jackson double lefts Charlton to second clipping Yeovil. Swindon 38 secs opener and share six with Rochdale. L2: Shot-shy Shots cave in to Chesterfield. Port Vale edges out Wycombe. First away win in 35 for Gills at Oxford. First win in six for four-goal Barnet against Northampton. SPL: Miller treble (two pens) snips Killie. Dundee U hits late equaliser at Celtic. S Cup: Beith, Threave seconds away form wins at Airdrie, Sten. BSP: Seven up Crawley sinks Alty. Luton hits five over Histon. York foursome rattles Rushden. Barca's eight at Almeria, Hat trick Messi now 101 goals in 154 games. Ronaldo strikes threesome for Real. Rafa's Inter lose at Chievo – fifth no win.

21 Blue moon ascends in four-play at Fulham to snatch fourth. Rovers climb over Villa. Scots refs will strike! BSP: AFC Dons hold off Kettering revival to go top.

22 Sunderland shares four with Everton. Scots seek oversees refs. Panorama castigated by FIFA's Warner.

23 Ch Lge: Wenger furious over fifth official failure to spot pen at Braga exposes poor Arsenal defending. Shakhtar top-up win at Partizan to lead group. Chelsea makes hard work of Zilina. JM takes advantage of ludicrous card rules to get two sent off as nine-man Real strolls on at Ajax. Two down Roma surprises

Bayern. Basle winners over Cluj will need to beat Germans now. Marseille secures second spot away to Spartak. AC Milan does enough to qualify at Auxerre. Hammers No.2 is axed. L1: Brighton in goalless share at Soton. Charlton held by Bristol R. Bournemouth, Sheff W and Huddersfield make ground with wins. L2: Oxford bounces back at Chesterfield, to Vale's five at ten-man Stockport put them top. Bury another five-star team wins at Lincoln. Cameron to do his PM bit for 2018 bid.

24   Ch Lge: Modric inspired Spurs go marching on to k-o stage via threesome over Werder. Rooney late pen – equals Charlton's 22 Euro goals – seals Man U in at Rangers, too. Inter qualifies edging Twente. Schalke takes three off Lyon but both move on. Hapoel T-A beats Benfica but neither will benefit. Valencia six-hit leaves Bursa without a point. Barca treble leaves Panathinaikos at the foot. Rubin clips FC Copenhagen and both are in the running. Harry R rates Gallas in Moore class, but Spurs fans veto Stratford switch. Arsenal players say sorry for Braga. UEFA investigates JM card episode. Suarez (Ajax) gets seven games for "biting."

25   Foreign refs rescue is on for Scots, but only for SPL and cup. Spurs new ground at home gets approval.

26   Old boy Pires faces Gunners with Villa. SOS game for West Ham looms. Everton seeks Becks. Some foreign refs decline. FA Cup: Crawley holds Swindon.

27   Sevens all round: Man U goals (go top) as Blackburn with those injured, Berbatov's first of five in 72 secs, last 70th. Still shaky Gunners four-play holds off Villa. Etherington equaliser at Soke spoils it for Man C on RM's birthday. Bolton forced to scramble for wonder Mark Davies leveller against Blackpool. Injury-hit Wolves super subs snatch it against Sunderland. Baggies bounce staggers Everton with foursome. Draw leaders Fulham (nine) held by Birmingham. Parker leads Hammers revival over Wigan who misses another pen. FLC: QPR beats Cardiff who boos Jones riles over ref Friend being foe! Burnley surprises Derby. Barmy pen fluff but Hull gets a draw at Boro. Ten-man PNE held goalless by Millwall. FA Cup: 2 ties off. Dover dumps Dillon's Shots. Ten-man FC U of Man earns draw at Brighton as Sam Ashton saves added time pen. Tamworth frightens Carlisle for a while. Super-marines makes Colchester battle. Six-up Huddersfield gives Macc the knife. SPL: Caley grabs draw at Celtic. SL and cup succumb to frost and no refs! BSP: 3 off. Newport consolidates fourth over Hayes.

28   Early Carroll denies Chelsea singing the Blues in second place. Skrtel at both ends but Spurs edge it 92nd minute over Liverpool. Goal note: 41 w/e PL, all score (a record). Weather hits Scots games.

29   PM Dave heads for crucial FIFA vote after Panorama damage. Sheff Wed safe as Mandaric stumps up takeover. Leicester wins East-Midland derby against Forest. FA Cup: Orient draws at Droylsden. JM's bad week at the office as Barca slam five against Real.

30   HRH the boy Wills and Becks join exodus for Zurich D-Day. Carragher is out for three months. JM gets one-match UEFA ban and fine; two players also suspended.

DECEMBER
England loses to Russia in 2018 bid ... Hughton axed at Newcastle ... Weather disrupts fixtures ... Ref Webb favours technology.

1   No show for Putin leaves England camp happy. E Lge: Man C eases over Salzburg to head group. C Cup: Birmingham clips Villa but rioting fans mar it all. Ipswich cheers at last as Albion are bagged. Trapattoni takes Irish pay cut. Terry and Essien back for Chelsea.

2   Ruskies get it! England manages two votes (one of their own) as fury erupts. Qatar is 2022 host! Did Putin know ahead? E Lge: Liverpool draw at Steaua – despite Reina boob – is enough to keep them top.

3   Gloves off for toys-out-of-pram FA in FIFA battle. Man C's Balotelli and Boateng in a scrap. Weather is likely to curtail programme.

4   Arsenal hip-hops to top edging Fulham as Man U's game at Blackpool falls to no-under soil heating and likely fine! Tevez wins it for ten-man Man C against Bolton but then throws wobbly against boss RM when subbed. Crisis club Chelsea now held by Everton. Spurs poor travel outside M25 means a draw at Birmingham. Blackburn keep Wolves penned in relegation bay as Big Sam applauds Russia and Qatar venues! Wigan and Stoke share four goals. FLC: 5 off. Cardiff needs 93rd min leveller to thwart PNE. Norwich wins at Derby, but Ipswich slips at home to Swansea. Leicester just fails at Watford. Millwall leaves it to Morison against Scunny. King spot on for Coventry aids Boro misery. Leeds owe it to Becchio brace against Palace. L1: 11 off. Swindon edges Sheff W. L2: 10 off. Oxford's fight back ends Barnet. Northampton moves up after taking out Stockport. BSP: all off. Wipe out for SPL and SL except for artificial Alloa's draw with Peterhead as ref Smith wears tights and long sleeve vest! Welsh: Bangor breaks British record with 14th consecutive League win from start with eight against Pt Talbot (Jamie Reed 5). Vase: one survivor only! Barca by train and coach 300 miles to win at Osasuna. Ronaldo double for Real at Valencia.

5   Sunderland in seventh place as Hammers succumb. Baggies hit poor Newcastle and Toon boss Hughton is unhappy. Mayor Johnson is to ban FIFA officials from the Dorchester!

6   Sacked Hughton is even sadder. Jol who quits Ajax is mentioned. Liverpool makes Houllier return for Villa a wretched one despite crowd cheering him. Ex-FA chairman Triesman joins the anti-FIFA brigade.

7   Ch Lge: Man U holds Valencia as they both qualify 1st and 2nd respectively and Sir Alex tinkers for the 150th consecutive time! Rangers (for the EL) draw in Bursa. Spurs share six at Twente to finish top (gk Boschker, 40, air shot og) while another tinker-man Benitez sees already qualified Inter crashes at Werder. Schalke wins away to Benfica, Lyon also qualified draws with Hapoel TA. Much-changed Barca still beats Rubin, FC Copenhagen makes second place beating Panathinaikos. FA Cup: ten goals, four red cards as Orient comes from two down to hit Droylsden for eight in nine-a-side! Moneybags Crawley beats Swindon in extra time. BSP: Hayes progress at Eastbourne expense. FIFA's Warner blames British press. MPs are to investigate English football.

8   Ch Lge: Arsenal finally slips in gear against Partizan, but qualify second behind Shakhtar, winners over Braga. Chelsea loses at Marseille (one win in six now) yet both teams progress. Spartak Moscow wins to keep Zilina bottom. Real Madrid shrugs off recent drama to hit Auxerre for four. AC Milan joined them despite loss to Ajax. Roma draw at Cluj is enough as Basle loses to group winners Bayern. FA Cup: FC U of M/c dream ends as Brighton strikes four. WCC: p-o: Wanda (UAE) beat Hekan (New Guinea)! Blatter dubs England as bad losers. Alan Pardew is appointed Newcastle manager.

9   FA Cup: Charlton takes out plucky Luton. Capello says England is improving.

10   QPR loses unbeaten record as Watford eases to Loftus Road win. Swans held by Millwall. L1: Posh edges Rochdale to move couple of places. WCC: q-f: Englebert beats Pachuca! Chilean miners will watch Man U.

£125m deal from Qatar (!) Foundation breaks Barca no-shirt policy. England will meet Denmark in a friendly match.

11 Man C rise level with leaders Arsenal, pushing Hammers into more mire – but suspended Tevez wants away. Pardew off to a flier for Toon as Liverpool is beaten, but Barton might be in trouble. Blackpool surprises Stoke at the Britannia. Villa with Heskey scoring edges out Albion again – 31 years since Baggies lge win there. Fulham equals PL draw record with 10th against Sunderland. Everton is off target – especially Saha – in another goalless with Wigan. FLC: (1 off). Sharp's 100th career goal but Leicester hits Donny for five. First win for Pompey at Norwich (ten-men) for 23 years. Burnley two goals ahead loses to Leeds. Cardiff slump goes on at Boro. Ipswich suffers ninth loss in 11. Tykes edge Blades (Speed off to Wales?). L1: 1 off. Sheff W six-hit whacks Bristol R. Brighton beaten at Huddersfield. Bees sting Saints. L2: 1 off. Wycombe end Bury's away run. Crewe shares six with Stockport. Gills win away again at Macc. Shots fluff pen and lose at Rotherham. Port Vale loses at Morecambe. Barnet welcomes win over Stanley. SPL: 3 off. Rangers held at Caley. Craig Brown new Aberdeen boss sees team lose to Hearts. SL1: 2 off. Dunf edges Q of S. Dundee wins again at Morton. SL2: 3 off. East Fife six-hit over Sten's ten. Brechin gets five at Peterhead. SL£: 3 off. Leaders Stranraer fights back for Berwick point. Wales: Bangor (just) keeps on winning at Aberystwyth. Trophy: 5 off, 1 aban. Holders Barrow wheeled out by Guiseley. Dartford holds Crawley, Chasetown – Kettering, Hayes loses at Ebbsfleet. Eastwood earns Rushden draw. Boston wins at York.

12 Gomes fluffs then foils Drogba as Spurs hold Chelsea. Wolves get first clean sheet beating Brummies. Bolton ten edges Blackburn. Walsall is off FLC bottom at Charlton. Barca hits another five, Real wins too with threesome.

13 Park keeps unbeaten Man U top against Arsenal but Rooney wayward spot kick and Wenger blames pitch. Blackburn sacks Allardyce in transfer dispute. Barking Blatter is in Qatar gay joke controversy. New Liverpool owners seek title in five years. Gary Speed appointed as Wales manager.

14 FA Cup: Hartlepool, Notts Co both win ties. JPT: Huddersfield completes last four with Brentford and Exeter C. SPL: Hearts beat Motherwell ten. SL1: Dundee eases over Cowden, Dunfermline and Ross are both held. Wales: Bangor run ends in added time leveller with Airbus..

15 E Lge: Liverpool held goalless by Utrecht but in knock-out stage with Villarreal, PAOK, Dynamo Kiev, BATE Borisov, CSKA Moscow, Sparta, PSG, Sevilla, Napoli, Porto and Besiktas. Alleged betting scam surfaces over Motherwell's Jennings red card. Spurs cleared for Olympic ground but all-English team for 2012 may face legal action. CWC: Inter reaches final. Paul Trollope axed by Bristol R.

16 E Lge: Man C gets draw at Juve and heads group. Holders Atletico Madrid held at Leverkusen and go out. Qualifers: Man C, Lech, Leverkusen, Aris, Sp Lisbon, Lille, Zenit, Anderlecht, Stuttgart, Young Boys, PSV, Metalist. SPL wage bill is £109m – PL big four are £109m plus each!

17 Ch Lge draw: Arsenal gets Barca! Man U start away to Marseille, Spurs at AC Milan and Chelsea at FC Copenhagen. E Lge: Away first legs for Liverpool at Sparta, Man C at Aris Salonika. Dundee pts deduction is confirmed. Death announced of Ralph Coates, Spurs and England at 64

18 Off – Arsenal (snow), Birmingham (frost), Liverpool (safety) and Wigan (snow). Welbeck clips the Trotters for Black Cats and Gordon wonder-saves from Knight. Sam-less Blackburn held by the Hammers. FLC: Off: 2 snow, 2 for safety. Snow joke for Sven as Ipswich ends six defeats to blizzard Leicester; even ref Atwell halts for pitch to be marked again. Gradel doubts shoots Leeds second as QPR loses another game. Reading's Long makes it four reverses on the spin for Rams. Holt stops ten-man Coventry for Norwich. Loanee Tudgay debut for Forest against Palace. Caretaker Carver cuts Swans down to size for Blades. L1: Off – 8 frozen, 3 for safety. Exeter five star stuffs the Owls from Sheff W. L2: all off – 9 frozen, 3 for safety. BSP: All off save for Fleetwood being held by Newport, while blizzard ends Luton v York. SPL: 4 off, but Caley holds Hearts and Killie edges ten man Hibs. SL: one survivor for each division. Deducted Dundee wins once more on the goal standard against Stirling, Airdrie surprises Alloa late on and Elgin levels at QP. Vase: all off. Another five goals for Barca (37 in 8) hit Espanyol.

19 Blackpool, Chelsea and WBA: all off for safety reasons. Tevez will play on. Real win – just – but get nine yellow cards (one red) in ten-a-side finish with Sevilla. Inter wins the CWC but Benitez might be chopped.

20 Tevez back and Man C out-shoots Everton five to one, but Howard bars way, so Toffees three points in ten-a-side.

21 Celtic drops two more points as Killie gets a draw. Death announced of Enzo Bearzot, 83, Italy's 1982 World Cup-winning coach.

22 David Bernstein, ex-Man C chairman, wins FA job to chagrin of David Dein. Eight-game misery for Wolfsburg spells problems for boss McClaren. Eight for Real in cup win – Ronaldo and Benzema trebles. Wages bar to Hammers getting Keane. Another Kean – Steve is confirmed at Blackburn helm for season. Benitez bows out at Inter. WC ref Webb is in favour of technology.

23 Aston Villa keen to keep Ashley Young. Arsenal and FA may fall out over Wilshere.but Wenger eyes Becks.

24 Weather likely to hit Boxing Day programme severely. Sir Alex intends to go on and on.

25 Reina is chased by Sir Alex. Liverpool wants Dzeko (Wolfsburg). Woodgate may be loaned by Spurs. No snoods at Everton. Battle of the basement is on for Fulham and West Ham.

26 Two off.(Blackpool frost, Everton burst pipes). Only two goals as Man U cruises with Berbatov double over Sunderland in 29th PL/Ch Lge unbeaten. Man C blistering start – 73 secs, 4 mins – is finally enough at Newcastle (RM's anniversary). V der V brace for Spurs at Villa, but Defoe is 8th red this term. Hammers give Fulham goal start and win at the Cottage. Baggies fritter chances and lose at Bolton. Wigan win at Wolves is bad news for Molineux. Stoke gets first win at Blackburn since 1965–66. FLC: 5 off (inc. Ipswich with no snow!). Rangers savage the Swans (no win there) in foursome effort. Leeds squanders two goal lead in draw at Leicester. Bellamy inspired Cardiff second again after beating Coventry. Another Long double for Reading in four-play over Bristol C. Super sub Bullard wins it for Hull at faltering Sheff U. First away win for Burnley at Barnsley. Pompey denies Millwall two more points. L1: 11 off. McSweeney strikes for Hartlepool at Huddersfield. L2: 11 off. Strevens late denies Hereford a point at Wycombe. SPL: 2 off. Celtic at home Rangers, Aberdeen (off bottom) and St Mirren all win away. SL: all off except Partick drawing with Raith and Livi getting a point at Alloa. BSP: all off.

27 Arsenal convinces against Chelsea. Fulham boss is under fire. Plymouth chairman and CEO both resign.

28 Sir Alex in a strop as "hands" denies Man U win at Birmingham. Balotelli treble (2 pens) aids four-play for Man C against Villa. Tottenham beats Newcastle but another red card (Kaboul). Blackpool upsets Black Cats

in the Stadium of Light. FLC: QPR extends lead to seven points at Coventry. Cardiff floored by Watford's four-play. Swansea just edges Barnsley. Leeds has to share points with Pompey after O'Brien double og. Norwich fight back topples Sheff U. Burnley lose at home to Scunny, Preston similarly to Boro. L1: 7 off. Saints foursome finishes Huddersfield. L2: 8 off. Improving Gills stun Port Vale. BSP: AFC Dons keep top over Eastbourne, Newport moves second and Mansfield gets five at Cambridge.

29   Now Liverpool loses to Wolves at Anfield! Chelsea scrapes a win over Bolton. Arsenal denied win at ten-man Wigan by a late og. FLC: Five-goal Forest piles on agony for Derby. L1: Brighton's ten held by Charlton. SPL: Ten-man Celtic edge no-shot Motherwell to go top as Rangers game at St J is called off. SL1: Dunfermline improves top berth with five against Cowden. Managers axed: Darren Ferguson (Preston), Brian Laws (Burnley).

30   Managers-go-round: Micky Adams in at Sheff U; Stuart McCall at Motherwell, Davie Irons at Stenhousemuir. Roy Hodgson faces angry Liverpool fans comments. Caretakers: Stuart Gray (Burnley), David Unsworth (PNE), Geoff Horsfield and Mark Grew (jointly at Port Vale). Peter Ridsdale joins Plymouth as consultant. McLean moves, Posh to Hull £1m. Is Ljungberg for Celtic?

31   Hodgson is on borrowed time despite sorry to fans. Becks loan to Spurs?

JANUARY 2011
Hodgson out – Dalglish in at Anfield … Crawley giant-killing … More managerial casualties … Lofthouse, Lion of Vienna, dies … Olympic stadium row … Torres to Chelsea for £50m.

1   Roo scores (first open play for 277 days 1418 mins) Sir Alex soars in admiration as Man U snips the pen-missing Baggies. Tevez spot-failure, too, as tenth clean sheet but edgy Man C clips Blackpool. 93rd min offside goal by Cole saves Hodgson job as Bolton is beaten ninth in a row by Liverpool. Arsenal impressive threesome at Birmingham whose Bowyer likely receive post for stamping. Another Sunderland clean sheet and three goals scored against Blackburn. Fourth unbeaten Hammers leap to 15th as Wolves cower at Upton Park. Stoke leaves Everton with just one win in ten – at Man C! Fulham tied up by Bale at WHL. FLC: QPR end with ten men and defeat at Norwich. Cardiff is well beaten at Bristol C. Added time leveller 90 mins 32 secs by Becchio saves Leeds against Boro. Watford four-play floors Pompey. Puncheon treble for Millwall ends Burley reign at Palace. Swans fly to second beating Reading. Forest just preserves 31 unbeaten at home in Barnsley draw. New boss Adams sees Sheff U seen off at no-shots Burnley. Forgotten Porter wheels Derby in at PNE. Donny downs Scunny. Cunningham breaks leg as Leicester wins at Hull. L1: Five out of five as Hartlepool beats Oldham. Murray is hat trick man for five-star Brighton against O's. Do Prado helps Saints into second place in foursome over Exeter. Charlton shares six at Colchester. L2: No-bss Vale (gk red) hit for five at Rotherham. Lester threesome for Chesterfield hits Stockport. Wycombe goes third at Cheltenham. Stimson sacked at Barnet after Shots win. Gills hit play-off bracket against Stevenage. SPL: Hearts edge Hibs in derby thanks to Kyle. BSP: Four of top five win: AFC Dons, Crawley, Luton and Fleetwood but Grimsby gets seven (Bore 3) against Mansfield.

2   Six-goal thrilling at the Bridge, but Chelsea drops another two crucial points to battling Villa. Ameobi goal is enough for Toon at Wigan. SPL: Samaras double for Celtic at Ibrox puts them four points ahead of two-in-hand Rangers. SL: Programme hit by weather: 9 off. Raith beats Dunfermline, Dundee stay second beating Ross. Falkirk doubles Stirling two goals. Alloa wins at Sten, Ayr at home over Dumbarton. Nine-man Montrose ships five to Abroath. Wales: Bangor loses first time in 18 at Prestatyn. Spain: Xavi 549th Barca outing equals club record.

3   Just seven from the last 18 points as QPR is held by Bristol C. Norwich og Boro a point at the Riverside. Swans concede at Leicester. Seven losses in nine for Ipswich as Forest win there. Sheff U needs a 96th min leveller against Donny in the local. Iversen is a hit for Palace on debut against PNE. Another new man Fryatt helps Hull overcome Pompey at Fratton. Floodlight failure does not stop Watford at Scunny. L1: Brighton leaves it late at Exeter. Saints cruise at Daggers. Bournemouth takes care of Brentford. Huddersfield edges the Yorks derby with Sheff W. Posh four-play keeps Walsall at the foot. Swindon surprises Charlton at The Valley. L2L Chesterfield has to fight back at Accrington for a point. Rotherham stays in contention at Macc. Wycombe stop Gills revival. Ten-man Vale back to winning ways as Burton loses. Hereford climbs off the bottom at sad Shots. BSP: Crawley cuts AFC Dons lead at FGR and have two games in hand. Grimsby hits five at Histon. Southport is another five-goal winner against Gateshead. SPL: Killie takes the points at St M. Peter Taylor may become Toon No.2. Becks chases loan deal. Blackburn aims for Ronaldinho.

4   Nani scores, Chicarito scores and shines in Roo role and still under-par Man U beat Stoke. Late strike Brummies get first away win since March at Blackpool. FLC: Bellamy back and scorer as Cardiff go second edging Leeds. Fulham flies high with threesome hitting WBA. Axe wielded as Parkinson (Charlton), Simpson (Stockport) and Hutchings (Walsall) join bosses dole qugets five at Annan. BSP: Luton third after win at Hayes. SPL favours two 10-club divisions though fans want one of 16 or 18!

5   Off days: Frustrated Arsenal draws with Man C in ten-a-side finish, Sunderland win at Villa in similar shortage – then off from Chelsea gives og winner to Wolves, even Gerrard misses a pen as Liverpool crashes at Blackburn and Spurs are clipped at Everton, but Hammers nailed five times at Newcastle (Best trio) as Toon sign Ben Arfa. Bolton and stoic Wigan share the points. Aldershot list Morgan for "death wish to booing fans." Bangor bubble bursts again at Llanelli.

6   Villa gets a Bridge loan from Man C. PNE appoints Phil Brown as manager. Roy Keane will be on his way from Ipswich with Paul Jewell likely replacement. Blatter appears much safer as chief rival fails to get votes. Jim Gannon appointed at Port Vale.

7   Becks is to be loan star for Spurs. Edin Dzeko £27m, Wolfsburg to Man C. Sidwell moves to Fulham from Villa.

8   FA Cup: Morning departure for Hodgson at Anfield, Dalglish i/c. N-E hotbed of soccer, your're having a laugh: ten-man Newcastle seen off at Stevenage, Sunderland at home to Notts, Boro at Harrad double strike Burton. Leeds and Schmichael earn replay with nine-change Arsenal in pen-a-piece (Walcott admits dive, then gets legit one). Nine-change Blackpool loses at Soton. No-change Fulham hits Posh for six (Kamara 3). Dover dream fades at Huddersfield. Orient's ex-Canaries loanee Smith smites Norwich. Ten Baggies are beaten at Reading – as last season. Everton gets five at Scunny. Doncaster holds ten-man Wolves. QPR (at Blackburn) continue cup misery – no win in ten years but lose Mackie with broken leg as Warnock rages over E-H Diouf reaction. Brighton deals Pompey – seven yellow, one red card – a seeing-off. Cardiff earns draw at

QPR's Leon Clarke arrives just ahead of Norwich City's Korey Smith during the npower Championship match at Carrow Road on New Year's Day. An early goal from Russell Martin saw Norwich move up to third in the table.
(PA Photos)

Stoke. York pushes Bolton before defeat. Four goals for Birmingham, Burnley, Swansea, Watford – even Hereford in second round replay at Lincoln! 93 goals scored in 27 ties. L1: Bournemouth takes advantage of cup ties to move second beating Plymouth. L2: Chesterfield pen Shrimpers in at Southend. Gills whack five at Stockport. First away win for Barnet at Bradford. Wycombe succumbs at Crewe. BSP: AFC Dons held goalless at Darlo, Luton similarly at Bath. Alty is off bottom winning at Rushden. S Cup: Maguire h-t in Aberdeen six goals over E Fife. Peterhead holds St M. Ross earns draw at Dundee U. Hamilton first home win of season against ten-man finishing Alloa (gk sent off but sub striker Gormley saves pen!). Caley leaves it late against Elgin. Montrose earns replay against Dunfermline, Ayr at Hibs. Welsh: Bangor back banging in six. Vase: Whitley Bay seven over AFC Liverpool (Paul Chow h-t).

9   FA Cup: Kenny boy start at Liverpool ends with Giggs pen for Man U and Gerrard sent off. Seven-up Chelsea wrecks no-boss Ipswich. Hart fumble gives Leicester replay in four-share with Man C. Defoe double makes it eight goals in eight for Spurs against old boys Charlton. S Cup: 2 off. Celtic wins at Berwick but tenman Dundee concedes four to Motherwell. Celtic players get bullets in post. Ronaldo gets three for Real. Henry will train with Arsenal.

10 FA Cup: Mega-bucks Crawley edge Derby. S Cup: Rangers ease over Killie. Liverpool adds Steve Clarke as first-team coach. Maradona claims English offer. Chopper out again as Gary Johnson (Posh), Dillon (Shots) go. Bristol R appoints Dave Penney and Paul Jewell moves in at Ipswich. Messi is FIFA world player of the year, Mourinho coach of the year. Villa Res score ten against ten-man Arsenal. Richard Butcher (Macclesfield) dies at 29.

11 C Cup: Foster fumbles Hammers to edge lead Brummie. Vermaelen hit by injury blow. Dzeko gets No.10 at Man C. Becks is no nearer Spurs loan. LMA claims 1023 managers have changed clubs since Sir Alex took over in 1986. S Cup: Brechin surprises QoS, St J trumps Hearts. L1: Plymouth two ahead at Huddersfield loses and have two sent off. Six-hitting Saints shock Oldham. Dougie Freedman is new Palace boss, Dean Holdsworth at Aldershot and Darren Ferguson back at Peterborough. Fleetwood gets five at Mansfield in BSP. Newport has two sent off late at Tamworth.

12 C Cup: Jewell watches as gem of a performance by Ipswich ousts Arsenal. Blackpool completes rare League double over Liverpool! McCourt is third N Ireland Celtic player to get a bullet. Milliband D is latest Sunderland board signing. Bellamy charged with assault. SPL: Celtic ten-men, lucky late pen win at Hamilton (nine men). S Cup: Sten gets five at Threave. FIFA may stretch Qatar WC wider!

13 Fabregas moan at long-ball Ipswich. RM says scrapping is good for Man C players. Chris Powell is likely Charlton choice.

14 L1: Brentford saves point against Exeter; Colchester edges Bournemouth set to lose boss Eddie Howe to Burnley. Robbie Keane £6m move from Spurs to Birmingham is on. Dundee loses appeal against pts deduction. UEFA investigates 47 alleged match-fixing European games.

15 Four T-type scorers drive Man C top against battling Wolves. Arsenal may have sounded last post for West Ham boss as Walcott scores on 100th PL outing. Peter O double for Baggies edges Blackpool. Andy Johnson is back on goal standard for Fulham at Wigan. Chelsea takes out Blackburn but lacks old style (Cech 102nd clean sheet). Etherington pen is Stoke's 100th PL goal as Bolton gk flops. FLC: QPR is goalless making a pt at Burnley. Swansea crystallizes second place beating Palace as last gasp Norwich denies Cardiff win. Leeds

four-play hits Scunny. Watford piles pressure as Rams recede. Boro gets four at Bristol C. Barnsley's nine lose at Hull. Forest 32 home run is saved by late strikes. L1: Chesterfield, Wycombe make ground but Rotherham lose to Southend. Crewe edges Port Vale in derby game. Bury held by the Shots, but Gills keep winning. First home win notched for Hereford. SPL: Celtic, Rangers both win. SL1: Ten-man Dundee (now bottom) draws at Dunfermline. SL2: Ayr pt ahead after win at Alloa. SL3: Stranraer clips QP to stay in front. BSP: Crawley takes advantage edging Kettering. Trophy: AFC Dons, Altrincham, Grimsby and Wrexham ousted by lower teams; Shaw h-t in Gateshead six. Welsh: Bangor leaves it late at Newtown. Leyton is no more. Nat Lofthouse, Lion of Vienna, dies at 85.

16 Four draws: Kenny D delight at Liverpool holding Everton! No-show fans (22,287) see Friedel's 250th consecutive record PL game for Villa at Birmingham. Gyan "fluke" robs Newcastle at Sunderland. Man U back in pole position as Spurs fail to break them.

17 Bent likely to go for £24m from Sunderland to Villa. Suarez eyes move to Liverpool from Ajax. Pienaar goes to Spurs for £3m. Robbie Keane deal collapses. O'Neill not interested in Hammers so Grant may get reprieve. PL and taxman are in talks over income loopholes. Qatar spent big bucks for WC. JPT: Exeter holds Brentford in South final f/l.

18 FA Cup: Man C doubles Leicester double but defence concerns. Wolves corner Donny five times. Stoke surprises Cardiff. L1: Plymouth shakes MK Dons. JPT: Carlisle takes four off Huddersfield in North final f/l. BSP: Crawley consolidates at Bath as AFC Dons are held at Fleetwood. Luton hits five against ten-man York. S Cup: Ayr k-o's Hibs. McGowan three as St M scores six at Peterhead. SPL: Rangers just beat Caley to go two pts behind Celtic with two in hand. Trophy: Alfreton whack three in extra time at Cambridge.

19 FA Cup: Arsenal takes Leeds more seriously and wins. S Cup: Buckie's ten (red card for slapping team mate!) push East Stirling till late. Spurs fans are unhappy about Games stadium move. Cantona is Cosmos saviour. Barca 28 no loss ends in cup away to Betis.

20 Row grows over Olympic stadium future. Kean is safe till 2013. Dier, just 17, goes to Everton from Sporting. Wheater £2.3m Boro to Bolton move. Carew nears Stoke. Wolves nab Hammill from Barnsley. JM and Real may be on collision course.

21 Scouting Harry R is mugged in Madrid and Forlan wants too many euros. Greaves and Pele join list pushing for Spurs at Olympic. Southend snatches Bury draw.

22 Berbatov third PL h-t (best since V Nist 8 yrs ago) in Man U (27 PL unbeaten) five hits on Birmingham. Villa winner Bent 3rd debut goal in five moves totalling £53m moves floors flaky Man C. Arsenal's Van Persie h-t and balloons pen against ten-finishing Wigan. Tor-tor-Torres helps Kenny's Liverpool to knock off Wolves. 91st min Lennon foils Newcastle for Spurs leveller. No Bent, just Richardson duo for Sunderland angles Blackpool. Hammers' Piquionne scores, gets two yellows then Fellaini 91st equaliser for Everton. Dempsey brace flushes out ten-man Stoke. FLC: Cardiff ends Watford seven wins in a row. Norwich completes double over Sheff U. Swans get a pt at Barnsley. Lights fail but Somma time earns Leeds one, too, at Pompey. Ex-Ram Earnshaw earns Forest first win in 17 years at Derby (33,010). Leicester moves to tenth beating Millwall. L1: Bournemouth's Feeney baffles Brighton in top-two clash. Huddersfield held by Colchester loses Rhodes injured. Three goals in seven s/h mins lead to Posh's four-play over Hartlepool. Orient second half foursome grounds Owls. Saints go down at Tranmere. L2: 2 off. Gk Bull keeps Chairboys standing against ten-man Rotherham. Change for Crewe: shunted by Shots. Six- unbeaten Chesterfield draws at Shrewsbury. Port Vale's ten fall to Cheltenham. Lincoln (Grimes 3) get odd goal in seven win at Stockport. SPL: Hearts deal Rangers a blow. SL1: 3 off. Raith two pts clear after drawing Morton. Dundee wins again! SL2: 3 off. Ayr moves pt nearer Livi in Peterhead draw. SL3: Stranraer suffers first away defeat at Elgin but stays top. Vase: Chow time keeps Herne at bay for Whitley. Leiston hits six at nine-finishing Guildford. BSP: Crawley held at Grimsby, Luton held by ten-man Gateshead, AFC Dons hit five over Southport.

23 Rovers are in seventh PL haven (six up since Sam) after beating Baggies in "UN game" (see Landmarks) but Di Matteo unhappy over ref Clattenburg pen miss. Rangers extend lead to five points. Sky's Gray and Keys apologise over Saturday's sexist remarks re-assistant ref Sian Massey. Coe is against Spurs Olympic bid.

24 Chelsea lives despite premature obit as Trotters are pig-sick over four-play. Orient in running for Olympic stadium. Suspended Gray and Keys may be sacked. Liverpool and Ajax stay in odds over Suarez.

25 Man U gives Blackpool two-goals and still wins. Villa wins again at Wigan. C Cup: Arsenal wears down Ipswich to reach final. FLC: Forest moves to fifth edging Bristol C. L1: Brighton beats ten-man Colchester. Sheff W held by nine-man Yeovil. L2: Chesterfield stops Gills home run. Crewe ten still edge Bradford. Hereford (home), Lincoln (away) keep winning. BSP: Crawley advances more as AFC Dons are held at Bath. S Cup: Morton gets five at ten-man Airdrie and it's the old One (two) for Stranraer getting odd goal in seven better than Sten. SL3: East Stirling five bests Arbroath's three. Sky axes Gray. Bernstein confirmed as FA Chairman.

26 C Cup: Brummies from behind as ace strike Bowyer fires comeback against old Hammers mates to reach first Wembley final since 1956, but crowd trouble again. Liverpool give Kenny first home win with bizarre og from Fulham. Adebayor goes to RM on loan. Keys follows Gray route.

27 Blackpool fined £25.000 for fielding weak team. Liverpool turns down £35m Chelsea bid for Torres. FA will demand player release for internationals. Lucky Buckie – E Stirling out of S Cup (ineligible player).

28 Torres wants away as Suarez prepares to move in. Spurs offer £25m for Carroll. Holloway is staying. Grant "safe" at Hammers. Millwall takes out Barnsley. Posh goes down at Colchester. Shrews lose at Bury. AFC Dons win at Gateshead. Lucky Buckie – East Stirling out of S Cup: ineligible player. JM thinks of another Real plan.

29 FA Cup: Saints alive and frighten Man U until old nut Owen and new pea Hernandez settle it. Tubbs pots it away for moneybags Crawley at Torquay, as sixth post-war n-l side in fifth round. Brighton is grateful for gk error at Watford. Coventry squanders two-goal lead as Birmingham comes back yet again to win. Burnley Eagles is two-fly for Burton. Orient surprises the Swans in Wales. Hereford pays for lead as four-play sees Sheff W through. Unconvincing, but Chelsea earns draw at Everton. Born-again Villa marches on over Blackburn. Reading just about puts Stevenage in its place. Low-key Lancs affair as Wigan gets replay at Bolton. FLC: No goals but Norwich pt at Palace and similarly for QPR at Hull – second and first respectively. L1: Walsall off the bottom with six-pack – best for 25 years beating Bristol R. Bournemouth edges Argyle in Plymouth. L2: Chesterfield scrapes draw with Bradford. Rotherham foursome takes out County. Lincoln keeps on winning trail, Vale losing again. CIS: Celtic four shakes the Dons. SPL: Hamilton still at the foot despite

gaining Killie draw. SL1: Raith at home, Dunfermline away are both beaten. SL2: Three goals not enough for East Fife at Livi and Sten at Ayr. SL3: Three at home insufficient for Stranraer toppled by Arbroath. BSP: Wrexham progresses at Mansfield, Fleetwood, Kiddy also win.

30   FA Cup: Murphy twice pens in ex-Spurs mates in Fulham foursome. Arsenal needs pen and og to edge out Huddersfield, but Nasri injured. Obinna hat trick man soars over Forest. Stoke owes win to Sorensen pen save at Wolves. CIS: Rangers just clip Motherwell to meet Celtic in final. Chelsea make final offer of £45m for Torres. Crawley gets plum draw at Old Trafford.

31   Transfer records tumble as Torres goes to Chelsea for £50m, who also grab Luiz from Benfica at £25m, Carroll to Liverpool for £35m who also get Suarez (Ajax) at £23m. Record £135m spent on the day. Chelsea announces loss of £71m. Southgate gets a job at the FA.

FEBRUARY

PL goals galore ... Rooney "volley" good – then bad ... Spurs scale heights in Milan ... Arsenal in classic with Barcelona ... Raul's Euro record ... Birmingham stun Gunners in Carling Cup.

1   Even Rooney gets on the score sheet twice as Man U defeat Villa and equal their 29 League unbeaten record. Chelsea manage four doubling Sunderland's effort with new boys, too. Arsenal have to come from behind to beat Everton. Baggies share four goals with Wigan. FLC: Rangers happy with Pompey gk error as starter for them. Swans add to Bristol C grief. Forest climbs above Cardiff – held by Reading – by winning at Coventry. Leeds draw at Hull. Bottom three Sheff U, Scunthorpe and Preston beaten again. L1: Brighton goalless draw at Orient but Bournemouth has better of Swindon as does Huddersfield against Carlisle. Saints leave it late to win at Exeter. Posh's five outdo the three-timer Owls. Oldham four-play is too much for Hartlepool. L2: Cheltenham only manages a point at Stockport, but Wycombe edges Cheltenham. Vale on win place again to shake Rotherham. Northampton hits Crewe for six, Bury gets four at Macc. Shots-Barnet fogged off at h-t. BSP: AFC Dons ship four at York, while Darlo lets in the same at Luton. SPL: Celtic beats Aberdeen – again.

2   Suarez scrapes a goal on his debut as Liverpool defeats Stoke. Man C slack again in draw at Birmingham. Crouch as usual is Spurs winner against Blackburn. Fulham edges no-Carroll Newcastle. Obinna again the main man for Hammers at Blackpool and loan-star Keane gets one,too. Zubar boob puts Wolves on the back foot at Bolton. L1: Bristol R loses again as MK Dons move to sixth. SPL: Rangers need just one goal against Hearts. Killie's ten win at Motherwell. Gary Neville retires after 602 Man U games. Fabregas admits to being upset on Tuesday.

3   Pub land – lady threatens Saturday TV blackout. FA warns politicians over FIFA watch. Alan Irvine loses his Sheff W job. Neil Young, Man C FA Cup finalist dies at 66. West Ham seeks compensation for injured Ashton after FA settles with player. Crawley held at Kettering.

4   QPR moves further ahead at Reading. 84 percent of Chelsea money goes on wages. Benitez jibe at "give-away" Torres saying he was worth £70m. Wenger hits out at spending spree. FIFA will ban snoods. PL predicts £100m player. Gary Megson is appointed Sheff W manager. Oldham may become homeless.

5   41 PL goals (7 pens) in 8 games! Arsenal four in 26 mins, gets one sent off, then Newcastle fights back to draw. Wolves (!) end Man U's 29-unbeaten League run as Doyle hits PL's 700th of the term. Saha four strikes (robbed by ref of fifth) as Everton's five betters Blackpool treble. Birthday boy (27) Tevez f/h hat trick baffles Baggies for Man C. Spurs need 92nd Kranjcar to edge Bolton as V der V scores one pen, misses another. Huth 93rd min winner of two as Stoke clips Sunderland. Wigan relieved with best of seven goals over Blackburn. Og ace Pantsil helps Villa make a point with Fulham. FLC: 51 secs for Forest to go second and secure Watford. Burnley pushes Norwich down a place. Leicester celebrates Sven's 63rd with four-play against Barnsley. Leeds has one enough to beat Coventry. Ipswich continues improvement at Sheff U expense. Palace clips Boro in basement battle. Hull five-star (Fryatt 3) rattles Scunny. L1: Posh and Saints share eight goals and four pens! Huddersfield foursome stuns Exeter. Fourth win for Walsall at Carlisle, four for Brighton, too, at Bristol R. Orient holds Bournemouth. Nine MK Dons hold Sheff W. L2: Bull rescues Wycombe with pen save in Port Vale draw. Lass Massey ok on the line as Shots get pt at Chesterfield. Lincoln makes it five on the trot at Hereford. Rotherham scuppers Crewe. S Cup: Buckie neither disgraced by Brechin, nor Stranraer by Motherwell. Five hits for Caley over Morton. Hamilton is taken out by Dundee U. St Mirren just wins at Ayr. SL1: Raith increases lead, Dundee wins at QoS. SL2: Dumbarton off the bottom at Alloa. SL3: Arbroath clear leaders after trio against Albion. BSP: Dons leave it late against Fleetwood. Trophy: Only three BSP definitely through – Darlo, Gateshead, Luton. History made for Chasetown. Barca La Liga record 16th straight win (Messi 3) v At Madrid, beating Real's 1960–61 run.

6   Liverpool steal Torres thunder as he lasts just 66 mins for beaten Chelsea. Birmingham dumps West Ham bottom again. FLC: Cardiff gets Welsh pecking order, up to third, Swans down to fifth. S Cup: Rangers and Celtic in ten-a-side draw. Og agony for Dunfermline in dying seconds at Aberdeen. Di Matteo sacked at WBA.

7   Ashley Cole is national team player of year. McClaren sacked by Wolfsburg. Carling Nations Cup raises hope for Republic. JPT: Brentford makes it to the final edging Exeter.

8   CN Cup: Dublin delight as threesome Republic beats Wales on Speed first i/c game. England U-21s undone by Mee red and Man U's Macheda pen for Italy. U-19s: England loses to Germany – of course. L1: Orient moves into top half beating Swindon. L2: Shrewsbury gets five to stop Lincoln run (Ainsworth f/h to go). Gills beat Rotherham, Bury progresses, too, against Stevenage. England give captain's armband to Lampard, Wilshere to play in midfield against Denmark. Gray and Keys get TalkSport jobs. Triesman spills gen over FA and PL to MPs. Dundee is back from the brink.

9   Denmark trip is a winner for England. CN Cup: Scots destroy Irish. U-21s: Wales beat Irish, too, Cyprus holds the Republic. S Cup: St J's complete the last eight against Thistle. France beats England U-19s. West Ham gets Olympic approval. PL has seven clubs among top 20's rich-list.

10   Court is likely to be next venue for Hammers/Spurs. Hodgson is the favourite for Albion. Former Test cricketer and amateur footballer Trevor Bailey, dies in flat fire at 87.

11   Manchester derby match might be City's last chance at title. Lass Massey is back on PL line. Hammers want retractable seats at Olympic site. Burton takes care of Chesterfield.

12   Man U (give it to them now?) rescued by Rooney acrobatic bicycle-kick volley in 144th derby with Man C. Two-goal Van Persie is VIP for Walcott-inspired Arsenal against Wolves. Spurs become 6th PL team to post

1000 points in come back at Sunderland. WBA spills three goal lead as Hammers react to Parker pep-talk and level with two-goal Ba boy. Wigan stops the KD band wagon at Liverpool in drawn affair. Last gasp Zigic wins it for Birmingham over Stoke. Shot-shy Blackburn ends goalless with Newcastle. Ten-man Villa gets a draw at Blackpool. FLC: Cardiff struggles to edge Scunthorpe. Leeds spoil James 850th game in win at Bristol C. Norwich does it again 94th min winner over Reading's ten-men. Boro's three goals are not enough to stop Swans four-play. Seventeen places climbed Leicester celebrates Sven's 63rd birthday at ragged Rams. L1: Brighton foursome too much for Hartlepool. Bournemouth stops Walsall mini-revival. Oldham frustrates Huddersfield. Saints leave it to Lambert's 50thgoal (14th this term) to beat Carlisle' ten men. Addicks glad of og to clip Posh. Orient four-play heaps more concern on Bristol R. L2: Shrews close on leaders edging Stevenage. Wycombe surprised by Bradford as are Rotherham at Oxford. Stockport ends poor run defeating Bury. SPL: £4m Jelavic treble as Rangers hit six against Motherwell. SL1: Dundee leaves it late but beats leaders Raith in 14th unbeaten game! SL2: Livi keeps ahead at Ayr. SL3: Stranraer slips to third held by Peterhead as Arbroath draws and Albion wins. BSP: Unstoppable Crawley, two down, beats ten-finishing Wrexham. Luton fails at home to Fleetwood. Vase: Holders Whitley hit five against Dunstable.

13   Everton on a bad day loses at Bolton. Ten-man Forest holds QPR at Loftus Road. Celtic stays in pole position at Dundee U. McStay loses Ross Co job after nine weeks.

14   Cech pen stop from Dempsey (Murphy had been subbed) saves Chelseaa (Torres subbed, too) at Fulham. Raheem Sterling, 16, gets five of nine for Liverpool Youth v Southend.

15   Ch Lge: It's Crouch as Spurs climb Milan heights but Gattuso plumbs the depths in attack on Jordan. Evergreen Raul strikes in Schalke draw at Valencia with 69th Euro goal beating Muller record. E Lge: Aris and Man C in soulless, goalless. PL: Newcastle menace Birmingham. FLC: Cardiff held by late Burnley leveller. Ipswich hits six at Doncaster (Wickham 3)! L1: 2 off. Sheff W ten-man lose at Tranmere. Walsall wins cellar battle with Daggers. Orient edges MK Dons. L2: Cobblers and Shrimps share six goals. Southend upsets Wycombe. Chesterfield held at Bury. BSP: 1 off. Crawley settles for point at Wrexham. SPL: Motherwell beats ten-man Aberdeen. SL1: 2 off. Dunfermline held by Falkirk. SL2: 1 off. Dumbarton wins again at E Fife. Livi progress, too. SL3: Arbroath, Stranraer win away. Losers Berwick at Clyde are now five without a win. Chairman Clarke warns FL clubs of debt black hole. Sunderland reports loss of nearly £28m.

16   Ch Lge: Emirates classic as Arsenal come back just nips Barca. Shakhtar edges Roma. FA up: One enough for Bolton at Wigan. FLC: Forest run ends at Scunthorpe.

17   E Lge: Liverpool stalemate away to Sparta and Rangers held at Ibrox by Sporting. Row erupts over Wembley final prices.

18:   Added time aids Leicester beat Bristol C. Port Vale back winning as Bradford C loses. BSP: Luton drops two points at Newport. Crawley is ready for big day at Old Trafford. Bernstein heads FA reform.

19   FA Cup: Shoot-out suffering Chelsea ends three year unbeaten cup run with Everton's Howard saving Baines blushes by stopping Anelka and Cole firing over. Cultured pass-masters Crawley almost force a draw at Man U as Brodie hits bar. Sheff W keels over at Birmingham (less than 15,000) three times and Brighton does likewise at Stoke. FLC: QPR held in the 11-no-win-Preston basement. Earnshaw does in old mates as Forest snatch second place beating Cardiff in 35th unbeaten homer. Swansea adds to injury-ravaged Doncaster's worries. Norwich held at Leeds in a classic. Bottle-throwers at Millwall as Boro win there first in 28 years. Ambrose rasper for Palace downs no-win-in-ten-Sheff U. L1: 1 off. Huddersfield earns draw at Bournemouth. Posh goes fourth against Tranmere. MK Dons are sixth after win at Hartlepool as Charlton loses to Exeter. Off bottom Bristol R edge Oldham. Ten-no-win Swindon is beaten by Carlisle. L2: I off. Chesterfield is winning again at Lincoln. Wycombe loses three in a week latest to Stanley. SPL: Aberdeen hits five against Killie. Kello pen savour for ten-man Hearts against Dundee U. SL1: 2 off. Raith wins well at Cowden. Weatherston 3 for Q of S. Ten-man Dundee 15th unbeaten wins in Stirling. SL2: 1 off. Livi 11 pts clear as Brechin held at E Fife. SL3: 1 off. Stranraer is within a pt of Arbroath by beating E Stirling. BSP: Shaw 19 seconds opener and treble as Gateshead gets seven at Wrexham. AFC Dons hit five at Tamworth. Real serve up JM's 148th unbeaten home game in nine years (only one loss in 166 for Porto v Benfica).

20   FA Cup: Late man Tehoue earns O's trip to LA sneaking draw with Arsenal. Bolton needs just one at Fulham. Man C ties in five against Notts. PL: Loanee Vela just keeps Wolves away from winning at WBA. SPL: Celtic damages Rangers again, with eight points lead but two games more.

21   FA Cup: Injury-plagued Hitzlsperger sparks Hammer five-star show to erase Burnley. Four match ban shock for Gattuso. Man U Anderson out with injury. Redknapp is realistic over top four. Ten-point penalty issued for Plymouth. Cup cash will help Orient stadium case.

22   Ch Lge: Anelka double aids Chelsea in Copenhagen. Real has to settle for draw in Lyon. PL: Squander bugs post-Euro Spurs in reverse at Blackpool. FLC: Cardiff, now third, puts breaks on Leicester. Swans at Coventry, QPR home to Ipswich also keep second and first positions respectively. Sheff U concedes two-goal lead and lose with ten men at Scunthorpe. Forest retains home record but PNE makes a point. Leeds are sharing again: six goals with Barnsley. Donny snatches a pt with og at Norwich. L1: Brighton takes it out on poor Plymouth. Draw team: Owls are goalless at Bournemouth, Saints, too, at Hartlepool and Posh shares two with Colchester. L2: Wycombe wins Burton for four. Chesterfield needs just a goal at Bradford. Crewe and Port Vale continue to slip up. BSP: AFC Dons taken out by Wrexham so Crawley are three points behind with five games in hand. Gateshead carries on scoring. SPL: Aberdeen edges Hamilton.

23   Ch Lge: Man U scoreless draw in Marseille. Last gasp Gomez wins it for Bayern at Inter. E Lge: Porto loses at home to Sevilla but goes through. PL: Arsenal beats Stoke but Fabregas (hamstring) and Walcott (ankle) are injured. SPL: Crucial win for St M at Motherwell. SL3: Arbroath, Stranraer (One 3!) retain positions.

24   E Lge: Better late than not at all for Liverpool against Sparta. Dzeko double for Man C winners. Rangers snatch it at the death on away goals at Sporting. Draw: Liverpool home to Braga, Man C at Dynamo Kiev while Rangers meet PSV. Peter Taylor is to leave Bradford. Platini warns Serbs over behaviour.

25   Sir Alex claims Arsenal are the only rivals. Glazers will not sell Man U. Bruce is to stay at Sunderland until 2014. Port Vale management reported in chaos. KD receives praise from owner Henry. Notts edge penmissing Charlton.

26   V der S (125th clean sheet) shines but four-timer Man U overcomes Wigan (12th win in 12: 37-4 goals) though "el bow" Rooney lucky to stay on. Loanee Sturridge four in four outings as Bolton holds ten-man Toon. Brace man Beckford 100th career goal hoists Everton to underscore Sunderland boss Bruce's poor record there. Villa whacks four past Blackburn. The Wolves are running – foursome against ten-man and

Adam-less Blackpool – for a 31 year top flight best. FLC: Warnock celebrates QPR year downing Boro. Swans spot of upping Leeds watched by 19,309. Cardiff wants to keep Arsenal loanees Ramsey and E-T longer after win at Hull. Six-absent Forest gets a pt at Millwall. Palace 30-sec opener ends in six goal share with Reading. Even Derby wins at 19-no-win Sheff U. Fourth win in a row for Pompey at Ipswich. Norwich aided by Crofts double-strike at Barnsley. Coventry puts brake on Leicester. Preston loses derby with Burnley. L1: Ten-man MK Dons stop Brighton – 4 hours 48 mins since conceding now. Saints four-timer breaks Swindon hoodoo. Posh benefit for boss Fergie's old man training camp with five goals at Oldham. Plymouth ends run of six loses. Ten-man Orient recovers to level at Huddersfield. Bournemouth gets late winner at Dagenham. L2: Hurst does in old Chesterfield mates for Morecambe. Gills get a pt at Shrewsbury. Wee Bennett inspires Bury against Crewe. Rotherham recovers to beat Burton. Stockport's nine clipped at Bradford. Northampton equals club six successive draw at Southend. Vale shrugs off boss chaos to beat The Shots. Cole save inspires Barnet over Lincoln. Ten-man Wycombe ko's nine from Macc in brawl finish. SPL: Hearts loses chance for second place in goalless at Aberdeen. Accies still chasing home win in Dundee U draw. SL1: Raith, Dunfermline and Falkirk all win. Dundee draws. SL2: Livi 11 pts ahead as Brechin loses at Ayr. SL3: top three all beaten. BSP: Crawley leaves it late to beat Barrow. AFC Dons score four, but Wrexham loses at Kiddy. Trophy: BSP rules ok – Luton, Gateshead and Darlo in semis. W Cup: Connah's Quay, TNS and Bangor (21st consecutive win in it) earn semi places. Barca equals La Liga away record of 19 unbeaten, but Real held at La Coruna.

27   C Cup Final: Arsenal defensive errors hand Birmingham trophy. PL: Hammers deal blow to Liverpool and Man C held by Fulham to end their title hopes. SPL: Chance for Rangers as Celtic loses to Motherwell. W S's men are five points behind with two games in hand.

28   Rooney will escape censure and Ashley Cole's shooting accident will be ignored. Vela is good for Baggies in Stoke draw. Port Vale bosses seek guidance! Villa announces £37m loss. Saha unhurt in crash.

MARCH
Giggs overtakes Sir Bobby . . . FA gunning for Blatter? . . . Balotelli goes to grass . . . Brits outed in Europa . . . New Villa record (Spanish) . . . Ghana holds England.

1   PL: Nine years since win at the Bridge, Man U hoist on their own . . . as Luiz luckily stays on to help Chelsea turn the tables, to Sir Alex fury as Reds have Vidic sent off late, while Giggs equals Bobby Charlton's 606 League games. FA Cup: Reading takes out Everton at Goodison. FLC: Even Donny wins at Derby. Forest is fortunate to get a late leveller at Boro. Pompey five wins no goals conceded beat Scunny. L1: Notts nine hold on for pt at Brentford. Saints lose at Walsall. Brighton goes back to winning at Yeovil. L2: Bury get three at Shrewsbury, Chesterfield foursome finishes Wycombe. Rotherham held at Torquay. SPL: Hibs inflict more misery on Accies. BSP: AFC Dons drop crucial pt at Hayes. Gash gets four in Rushden's five. Luton edges FGR. SL2: Livi now 13 pts ahead as Brechin is held. SL3: Stranraer back on top beating Clyde. Van Persie will miss three weeks. Nicky Forster gets Brentford post to season's end. PFA has to pay Argyle wages.

2   FA Cup: Bendtner hat trick as Arsenal takes five off Orient. Man C takes advantage of Villa selection. Sir Alex is likely to be fined for his ref outburst on Atkinson. S Cup: Celtic beats eight Rangers (one off before the whistle, another after it) in disgraceful encounter. Bosses chopped: Wilson at Swindon, Sampson at Northampton. Kelly Smith scores in her 100th England game as Italy is beaten.

3   Toure K fails drug test. Sir Alex will respond. Investigation starts over Auld Firm clash. Paul Hart moves in at Swindon. Ronaldo treble in Real's seven spree but gets injured. Police are to look at Cole shooting affair. Goal line technology on the FIFA agenda again.

4   Clattenburg was on point of quitting over Rooney. Houllier says he is sorry to Villa fans. Gary Johnson becomes new Northampton manager. Plymouth goes into administration. Mourinho escapes stabbing! Scots women beat England. FIFA outlaws snoods!

5   Wenger speechless over ref Taylor for no pen and goal ruled out in goalless with Sunderland (last seven previous with Black Cats raised only eight goals). Gk lapse for Wigan spoon feeds Silva for Man C winner. Young pen miss costs Villa at Bolton. Everton shrugs off cup loss to win at Newcastle – first in nine free. Three goals again for Hammers as loanee Ba helps down Stoke who wanted him in January. Baggies banish Brummies in midland derby. Clattenburg stays in the controversial news as Fulham clips Blackburn. FLC: Birthday boy Miller sees QPR home against Leicester for eight pt lead as Swans are beached at Scunthorpe and Cardiff Bluebirds grounded by Ipswich. Norwich's Hoolahan puff-pen gaffe allows Preston a point. Forest's 18 month home record is ended by Hull. Leeds again on goal trail with five against Donny's two (67-57 ratio this season). Cup form Reading similarly defeats Boro. Bristol C revival continues in four-play at failing Coventry. Pomey sixth in a row – Sheff U 13 no win. L1: Brighton hits 94th min winner to get advantage over Carlisle in seven goals affair. Unbeaten in ten, Bournemouth takes out Oldham. Skint Plymouth revels in foursome at Sheff W. MK Dons keep winning and inflict Rochdale's first reverse in a dozen. L2: Chesterfield stays 11 pts clear after win at Cheltenham. Bury's Lowe scores for club record eighth successive time as Hereford slumps. Wycombe held by the Shots. Donaldson treble-shooter stars for Crewe against Burton. SPL: Celtic adds to Accies plight. Hearts slip up to ten-man Killie. SL1: Raith edges ahead as Dunfermline loses to Morton. Dundee adds another point. SL2: Livi, Brechin, five-goal Ayr all win. SL3: Arbroath regains top as Stranraer loses at home to Albion. BSP: Crawley takes advantage of nine-man Histon. AFC Dons beat by Grimsby's ten-men, Luton draws with Kiddy. W Lge: Bangor loses home record now. Llanelli reaches cup semi. Vase: Chow double for Whitley Bay who join, Coalville, Kings Lynn and Poole clinch semi-final places.

6   Sir Alex is silent Knight as six yard-master Kuyt treble opens up the race beating Man U, though Carragher lucky to escape red – but Giggs beats Sir Bobby's record. Wolves share the joy of six with Spurs. SPL: Rangers need one to beat St M.

7   Chelsea back in the race? Blackpool disputes a pen but are well beaten. FA alleged to be gunning for Blatter. Bristol R sack Penney and put skipper Campbell in charge. Canada (!) beat England women. Dorchester p/m sent off for tackling pitch invader at Havant!

8   Ch Lge: Messi and Co put Arsenal on the Barca rack after Fabregas suicidal back-heel as Wenger blames ref for Persie "joke" second yellow when scores level. Shakhtar takes care of Roma's ten men. FLC: Rangers ten come a cropper at Millwall, Cardiff falters at Palace and Swansea is held by Watford. Norwich inflict another defeat on Leicester, Leeds push Preston further into trouble and Sheff U wins at last – beating Forest.

Burnley handily placed with games in hand and Reading both look dangerous now. Boro add to Derby woe before smallest Riverside gate (13,712). L1: Only one of top eight fails to win – Bournemouth losing at Exeter. Orient with games in hand is the fancied outsiders now after win at Walsall. Bristol R wins at Tranmere! L2: Chesterfield, Bury and Wycombe keep their automatic spots, Shrewsbury and Port Vale share four goals but Rotherham loses at Bradford. Shots edge Torquay to end blank spell. Defeated Stockport and Barnet are looking more isolated at the bottom. SL1: Dundee – quite naturally – wins at Cowden. SL2: Livi romping away as Brechin is beaten again at Forfar. SL3: Arbroath goes four pts ahead winning at Albion as Ten-man Stranraer loses at Annan. Trophy: Mansfield replay winners over Chasetown make it an all-BSP semi-final. Chris Armstrong (Reading), 29, retires with MS.

9   Ch Lge: Nervy night for Spurs at the Lane but AC Milan hits the exit. Schalke accounts for Valencia to give under the cosh boss Magath a breather. Wenger and Nasri charged for remarks to referee in Barcelona. PL: Birmingham manages a pt at Everton.

10   E Lge: Fragile Man C shafted by Shevchenko and co in Kiev as Balotelli suffers grass allergy! Liverpool penned in at Braga. Rangers reserve gk gains goalless draw at PSV. Spartak surprises Ajax, Villarreal edges Leverkusen and Porto beats CSKA away. Benfica takes narrow lead over PSG but Twente hits Zenit for three. Wenger hits back at dictators at UEFA. FIFA to probe six officials over two games all with pens! Flavio Paixao defies snood ban for Accies. QPR faces Faurlin fixture investigation.

11   Sir Alex hits out on Carragher tackle. Gerrard is out with injury again. TNS nears Bangor in four-play over Prestatyn.

12   FA Cup: 13 days of whine and losses for Wenger and Arsenal as Man U (record 27th semi now) change system with Silva boys R and F shining. Bolton's lucky charm Lee (eighth goal in eight overall wins) hits 90th min winner to edge Birmingham odd goal in five. FLC: Bottle-throwers mar ten-pt leaders QPR clipping ten-man Palace. Swansea gives Derby a rare win. No goal games: Leeds against Ipswich, Forest meeting Donny and Pompey with Boro. Hull beats 62 year old club record with 14th away unbeaten at losing Coventry. Watford beats nine-man Sheff U and Graham's 23rd goal is best since Luther Blissett 26 years before. Leicester wins at Scunny but Burnley comes unstuck to Millwall. L1: Brighton, Huddersfield retain automatic places, six-goal Posh even miss two pens to overcome ten-man Carlisle but hoist 100th goal of season. Saints leap frog Bournemouth to fifth place in the coastal derby and Barnard strikes his 20th for them. Baldock trebles it for MK Dons at Colchester. M'Poku shoots late 35 yard Orient winner over Oldham. Brentford achieves first win at Charlton in 85 years. L2: Chesterfield suffers at Crewe. Bury and Rotherham settles for no goals, but Wycombe loses at home to ten-man Stevenage. Shrews dumped by own player Robinson in five goal defeat at Torquay. Barnet shows relief for win at Hereford. S Cup: Brechin earns replay with St J. Aberdeen just thwarts St M in another draw. SL: five off (snow!). Thistle wins at Raith, Fifers at Falkirk and Dundee 20th undefeated recovers to edge QoS. Second Div: Ayr makes ground against Alloa. Third Div: Arbroath, Albion and Annan are winners, Stranraer held at Queen's Park. Wales: Bangor drops two pts at Llanelli. Trophy: Darlo gives advantage over Gateshead. BSP: Crawley three pts ahead – five games in hand as AFC Dons slip up to Kiddy. RM beats Hercules in JM's 150th unbeaten home game. John Rooney signs for New York Red Bulls.

13   FA Cup: Grant unhappy about ref as Hammers are edged out by Stoke. Man C makes it to a tie with Man U after just about beating Reading. FLC: Cardiff drops two points at home to Barnsley. SPL: Rangers grateful for og in Killie clipping. S Cup: Motherwell earns draw at Dundee U. Caley – Celtic waterlogged off. Trophy: Advantage Mansfield against Luton in first leg semi. Two off on each side in Liverpool – Man U Youth Cup!

14   Capello will hand Terry the armband – not Rio. Norwich late again winning games take out Bristol C. Arsenal may recruit Lehmann, 41, out of retirement! Coventry – ten in ten years – chops another boss Boothroyd.

15   Ch Lge: Little Pea shoots uncertain Man U through against Marseille. Inter's late show foils Bayern. FLC: PNE treble hits Scunny as in Watford's threesome at Ipswich. L1: Four-play Posh, Huddersfield and Orient keep on winning ways. L2: Torquay surprises Bury at Gigg Lane. BSP: Luton is no-scorer in Cambridge draw, but Crawley strikes another five. Weather hits SL programme again, but Raith wins in Div 1 and Albion hits six, Annan first in away successes in Div 3. Rio injury concerns.

16   Ch Lge: Chelsea scoreless with Danes but qualifies. Real treble takes out Lyon. SPL: Hearts hit again at Dundee U. S Cup: Ledley double for Celtic at Caley. Aberdeen edges St M. Five-game ban for Sir Alex. Rooney will stay at Old Trafford – again.

17   E Lge: Brits out! Balotelli misses two chances then sent off as Man C's one is not enough to stop Dynamo Kiev. Braga prevents Liverpool from scoring at Anfield. Rangers slip to PSV. Zenit twosome is insufficient against Twente. Villarreal does enough to beat Leverkusen as does Porto against CSKA Moscow. Benfica draw puts PSG out. Spartak completes whitewash of Ajax. UEFA bans Wenger, Nasri and Joe Jordan for one match. Scunthorpe dismisses Ian Baraclough. Blatter is to face Mohammed bin Hammam for FIFA job.

18   Two games but nine goals – Chesterfield fiver hits Rotherham, Shrimpers foursome downs Hereford. BSP: Crawley sees off AFC Dons for good? Ch Lge draw: Chelsea v Man U; Real M v Spurs; Schalke v Inter and Shakhtar v Barca. Baggies bag man Matthews celebrates 50 years there.

19   Super sub Berbatov 88th min wins it for ten-man Man U over Bolton. Almunia gambles and loses – Peter O pounces as Arsenal drops two pts at WBA. Spurs held up by Green as Defoe stalls on 99 goals against Hammers at goalless WHL. Fulham – no win at Everton 62 years – edged out by Everton again. Four-play Stoke four too many for Toon. Hoillett 93rd min rescue for Blackburn as Blackpool's Adam pen (ref Webb gaffe!) hits PL's 800th season goal. Wolves win at Villa puts more pressure on Houllier. Wigan clips Birmingham with 92nd min winner for Figueroa on his 110th outing. FLC: QPR's 21st clean sheet aids narrow win over Donny. Norwich held at Hull. Cardiff has to share six goals at ten-man finishing Millwall as City fan escapes fall from stand. Swans are grateful for loanee Borini double cutting Forest down. Game and Manset for Reading sub at Barnsley. PNE wins again to inflict Coventry's seventh no win. On loan Riise lifts Sheff U against Leeds! Pompey shakes limping Leicester. Clough sees derby draw at Palace on his 45th birthday. L1: One enough for Brighton at Oldham. Only a pt for Huddersfield as Swindon digs in and Bournemouth loses at Carlisle as Saints beat Sheff W stay fourth. Loanee gk Logan saves pen for winners Bristol R at Notts. Ex-O's Alexander does in old boys for Brentford with 150th career goal. Cureton's 200th League goal but Exeter loses to Yeovil. L2: Bury fails against Cheltenham. Wycombe has lucky leveller at Shrewsbury. Macc shares six with Torquay. 93rd min Shots finish ten-man Stockport. Barnet also loses to Morecambe. Gills get a draw at Burton. SPL: Hearts, Dundee U, Killie all win as Accies still seek home win in St J draw. SL1: Hardie 3 for

Dunfermline over Stirling's ten men but Raith held at Morton. Dundee recovers to level at Falkirk. SL2: Livi foursome strike at Forfar. Ayr clear second place at Peterhead. SL3: Swankie treble as Arbroath hits five at E Stir. Albion is held, Stranraer loses. BSP: Play off prospects improves for Fleetwood beating Wrexham. Trophy: Nine-man Luton held by Mansfield go out but Darlo draw with Gateshead enough for final place, too. Welsh: TNS edges Bangor to close gap to three pts with game in hand!

20   Blues rise over fragile Man C with Chelsea's Brazilians scoring. Ten-man Sunderland is beaten by Liverpool but Bruce riles over ref Friend change to pen award. Benfica's 18th League and Cup win is sequence record in Portugal.

21   Capello lists untried Jarvis and may use Carroll with Rooney. FA hands over some TV rights to UEFA. Gordon Taylor reminds his members about order of priorities. Man U Evans J says sorry to Holden for tackle. Bin Hammam may seek Platini deal. Rest cure works for Tevez. Posh hit buffers at MK Dons.

22   Captain Terry will stand up to any fan abuse. Parker could take Lampard role. Miss Wales to aid Dragon cause. Ex-FA CEO Watmore joins their critics. Platini flexes his FIFA muscle wants, but world body worries over match-fixing. L1: Brighton snatches win over Notts. Orient just save game with pen against Daggers. L2: Port Vale just scrapes a pt against Hereford. Goal note: Eleven FL games, 17 goals! S Cup: St J edges Brechin in replay. SL1: Trialist Hyde saves Dundee against Fifers in 22nd unbeaten. Raith also held by Ross. SL3: Ten-man Arbroath draws at Clyde. BSP: Crawley pushes further ahead at Eastbourne but Luton wins at Rushden.

23   Has Man U green and gold revolt ended? Sir Alex defends his ref Atkinson tirade. SL2: Ayr blown out by Forfar.

24   Bale out will aid England's cause. U-21s: England foursome in Denmark, Scots clipped in Belgium. Ex-Man C Etuhu jailed for brawl. Finns have a dozen players involved in match-fixing. Merseyside stiffs game 2336 for Liver-Ever two-two.

25   Euro 2012: N Ireland edged out in Serbia. Dutch treat Hungary to four goal pasting – V d V, Kuyt and V Persie among scorers. David Villa breaks Raul's Spanish record with 46th goal as Czechs are beaten. Belgium surprises Austria. U-21: Republic loses two late goals in Portugal. L1: Posh away, MK Dons at home both draw. Schlupp double boosts Brentford against Carlisle. L2: Rotherham impales Lincoln Imps six times, Thomas-Moore hat trick. Piazon, 17, will join Chelsea from Sao Paulo – one day. U-17: England edges N Ireland.

26   Euro 2012: Wail of the Welsh dragon, game over 14 mins as England wins in Cardiff, but Rooney book and ban. Bulgaria (Villa's Petrov's 100th) held by Swiss. Republic edges Macedonia Keane's 46th goal, but Doyle injured. Five out of five as Germans four-play (Klose, Muller 2 each) hits Azers. Crucial Dzeko goal aids Bosnia. Russians stalemate in Armenia. L1: Brighton seventh win in a row, Dicker one pen, misses, too (team's seventh such). Charlton shares pts at Bournemouth. Colchester's five-strike floors Exeter's nine men. MacDonald treble as Yeovil shakes ten-man Orient at home. L2: Wycombe three in ten mins effective at Morecambe. Bury's ten earns pt at PV. Sub Bradshaw at the double for Shrews at Bradford. Bottom two late fight backs: Stockport clips Southend, Barnet holds leaders Chesterfield. Stevenage goes fourth with four at Macc. SL1: Bairns put Raith to bed. Fifers held by the Jags. Trialist Hyde hits two for Dundee as Cowden hold them. SL2: McKenna treble for six-hit Brechin over Sons, but Ayr slips up. Livi keeps on going at E Fife. SL3: Two in a minute helps Stranraer at ten-man Arbroath, Albion held as well but Annan goes second at QP! BSP: Crawley settles for another nil-nil away at Gateshead. Dons win, Luton loses but only 23 goals in 11 matches! Vase: Coalville digs out three against Kings Lynn, W Bay sinks Poole.

27   Neymar stars as Brazil new look beats Scots at Emirates. Huddersfield 18th unbeaten tangles Notts. Another brace for McDonald sees Gills home at Cheltenham. Burton's nine rowed out at Oxford.

28   Mourinho claims to have been offered England job. Capello needs just 100 English words. Burnham is latest to blast FA. Barry will lead all-change England. U-21: England frozen out by Iceland!

29   Gyan snatches draw for Ghana at Wembley after Carroll opener for England. Uruguay holds off Republic come back. Euro 2012: N Ireland makes a pt against Slovenia. Five out of five for treble-hitting Spain away win in Lithuania. Dutch fiver, too, as Hungary hits three. U21: Wales takes up win in Andorra. L1: Brighton adds to run at Daggers. Owls now stung by Bees. L2: Shrews upset Rotherham, but PV manages to beat Lincoln. SL1: Dunfermline regains lead at Ross. SL2: Livi makes Blue Toon pay five times for lead. SL3: Annan surprised by Clyde, Stranraer shares six at Berwick. Capello contract row returns. Grassroots are suffering from ref abuse. Lehmann gets game with Arsenal stiffs. German threw banana at Neymar. Birmingham fined for pitch invasion. Man U will spend in summer.

30   Capello on offensive – can match Germans. Is Sir Alex having a laugh? – warns players about ref decisions. Spurs go on Olympic attack. Court stops Spanish strike. Takeover of Rangers nears. S Cup: Motherwell outs holders Dundee U. Burton edges Macc.

31   Kraut General Manager Bierhoff ridicules England boasts. Spurs flex Olympic legal muscles. Brazil WC 2014 plans hit snags. Hammers Grant complains about refs costing pts. U17: England beats Spain!

APRIL

Rooney century and ban ... Real effect for Spurs ... Man C OK Ya (Ya) ... Torres scores! ... Dundee escapes drop ... Barca boys see off JM.

1   Sir Alex wades in on PL's respect campaign proposals. Bosnia suspended by FIFA and UEFA over ethnic divisions. Posh has to share six with fight-back Bournemouth. Bangor loses to Prestatyn.

2   Rooney treble (now 101 PL goals), Rooney trouble over foul-mouth TV rant as foursome Man U twice fails to be penned in (club PL record) at West Ham, but Vidic lucky to stay on. Blank Gunners lack fire against ten-finishing Blackburn. Sub Torres unable to lift Chelsea to win at Stoke. Spurs held goalless at Wigan. Brunt spot on too, as Baggies on Hodgson revenge day beat Liverpool first time since 1981. Everton shares four goals with visiting Villa. Birmingham, sparked by vet Phillips, 37, oldest PL outfield player and scorer, leaps to 15th beating Bolton. Newcastle rises to ninth with four-play defeating Wolves. FLC: Double h-t as Holt and sub Jackson (3 in 15 mins) for Norwich as Scunny give new boss "Knill" response. Swans clipped out at off bottom Preston, so Cardiff snatches third place hitting Derby for four. Leeds – another Gradel brace – foursome costs ten-man Forest p-o slot. Long lengthens Reading push over Pompey. L1: Brighton has to take draw at Rochdale. Tenth away win for Huddersfield at Tranmere. Saints give Dons two goals start and win. First home win in four months for Sheff W as Colchester lose. Bristol R list welcome win

at Yeovil. L2: Chesterfield racing to the wire as PV succumbs. Wycombe gives Stockport sinking feeling. Kabba, dappa does it four times for Barnet at Burton! Crewe hits Cheltenham (worst since 1969) for eight (Donaldson, Grant h-t each). Macc punished for lead against four-play Shrews. Stevenage, Torquay both win but Gills held. SPL: Rangers fail to take advantage of Celtic waterlogged at Caley by losing to Dundee U. SL1: Dundee's 23 game run ends away to Raith, but only in the 91st min when down to ten men. Dunfermline stays top at Cowdenbeath. SL2: Livi held by Brechin. SL3: Annan, Albion (beating Arbroath) and Stranraer make progress. BSP: Crawley winners over Darlo need two more wins. Fleetwood moves fifth beating Tamworth. Wrexham lose to Hayes, Dons beat Barrow but Luton has to share six at Kiddy. Irish Lge Cup: Lisburn Distillery beats Portadown in final. Vase: Coalville, Whitley win again for final places. Mourinho home record goes after nine years on 150 unbeaten as Gijon wins.

3 Five-alive Man C renews Ch Lge bid as Sunderland wilts. Fulham force Blackpool nearer drop zone. JPT final: Brentford's ten finishing edged by Carlisle. SPL: Hibs held by ten Hearts. Paul Ince leaves Notts post.

4 QPR goes nine pts clear with treble over Sheff U. Man U will fight any Rooney ban. FL TV income is to fall.

5 Ch Lge: Shame is the Spur as Crouch gets two early yellows making it all white on the night for a foursome "Real." Inter is unable to curb Schalke's five star outing. FLC: Reading maintains winning attitude. L1: Bristol R moves out of danger beating Bournemouth. Saints at home, Posh away are additional winners. Even Sheff W gets four! L2: Wycombe held at Hereford, Stanley moves into play-offs beating ten-man Southend. BSP: Crawley pt at York leaves them needing five. SPL: Rangers go one pt in front of Celtic with game more by win at S J. SL2: Brechin loses to Airdrie so Livi look to promotion.

6 Ch Lge: Advantage Man U as Rooney side-foots the only goal as Chelsea denied an obvious penalty. Barca rattles Shakhtar with five goal salvo. SPL: Celtic returns to head as Hibs are beaten. Hereford have three points deducted, Torquay one for ineligible players in same game. Baseball star LeBron gets small slice of Anfield set up. Barnsley is first to go for "Solar" energy.

7 Sir Alex unhappy about Rooney two-game ban, but Police chief talks of "locking up." Rangers will fight any charge of sectarian chants. E Lge: Four timers Benfica hit PSV, Shevy off as Kiev is held by Braga, Porto five-star hits Spartak as does Villarreal's nap hand over Twente.

8 Sir Alex turns on ref Mason for Rooney situ. Wycombe suspends assistant Kuhl over alleged exchange with a player. Gerrard is out for season. Wenger will content himself with second.

9 Man U opens 10 pt lead, has superior goal difference and coasting as Fulham (only PL no red cards) is beaten – yet Sir Alex still unhappy! Sub Torres fails goal sink again but Chelsea edges Wigan. Crouch buries double yellow nightmare with bracing show for Stoke-clipping Spurs. Everton demolishes Wolves first half. Bolton puts more relegation pressure on Hammers – eighth such in a row. Free-fall Sunderland one pt in 24 as Baggies edge it. Blackburn and Birmingham finish level. FLC: 49 goals! Knill turns to kill as sunny Scunny four-play floors QPR. Sub Koumas rescues Cardiff victory at Doncaster. Fly Swans too strong for flapping Canaries. Forest dumped goal win for six-in-a-row Reading in game of seven goals three pens. Sheff U is beaten again by Boro. Leicester foursome revives promotion hope over Burnley, so PNE off foot in draw at Pompey. 3D programme and new dimension as Millwall beats Leeds. Boy Carson duo sparks Ipswich. L1: Brighton finishes with ten but still defeats Sheff W in 11th home win in a row. Saints with close to 4000 travelling fans see Orient go west. Huddersfield and Posh settle for level pegging. MK Dons go fifth defeating Carlisle because Tranmere shakes Bournemouth. Daggers leap-frog hits Notts. Vet Stewart, 38, ends his career for Exeter with win at first club Bristol R. Swindon wins – first in 19 – at Brentford. L2: Chesterfield loses at Hereford! Wycombe held at Oxford. Bury doubles Northampton's brace. Shots best shoots Shrews. Docked Torquay lands another win at Bradford. Stevenage held at Stockport, but Barnet wins again beating Crewe as Burton falls at Morecambe. Gills continue four-fold at Lincoln. BSP: Crawley clinches title. Sixes for Fleetwood and Luton while Dons win to ensure p-o berth but Wrexham held. Histon relegated at Gateshead. SPL; Celtic just defeats St M and moves five pts ahead of game-in-hand Rangers. Motherwell pt at Hearts as Caley misses out. SL1: Raith draws with Cowden. SL2: Livi promoted as Brechin loses to E Fife. SL3: Arbroath eases at Clyde, Albion and Annan scoreless but Stranraer beats E Stirling. Welsh Cup: Semi wins for Bangor, Llanelli over Connah's Q and TNS. Irish Cup: Semi wins for Linfield, Crusaders against Glentoran and Portadown.

10 Arsenal's win at Blackpool leaves them seven points adrift of Man U with game in hand. Villa needs just one goal to beat Newcastle. SPL: Rangers require only one for two at Hamilton. SL1: Stirling draws at Dundee but is relegated. Alba: Ross wins final over Q of S. Youth Cup semi: Chelsea takes slender lead over Man U in first leg.

11 Carroll on song with two for Liverpool as sad Man C lose injured Tevez and three goals. Kroenke takes control of Arsenal as seven others cash their chips. Allen quits Barnet for Notts after three games! Fair play entry beckons for Fulham in Europe?

12 Ch Lge: Ten-man Chelsea no match for Giggs pass-mastering Man U on another torrid Torres night. Messi (his 48th season goal) cleans up Shakhtar for Barca to reach final, too. FLC: 47 secs enough to Taarabt and QPR at Barnsley. Blades blunted yet again by Cardiff. Norwich shares foursome at Watford. Swans held by Hull. Reading ends Scunny revival. Leeds even loses at Derby. Forest puts last nine in the locker to beat Burnley. Millwall, Leicester and Preston all involved in draws. L1: Brighton wins promotion with five games in hand with best of seven win against Daggers. Saints lose it at Rochdale. L2: Bury's nine beat Burton's ten. BSP: Luton draws at ten-finishing Crawley. SPL: Celtic goes five pts ahead of one-in-hand Rangers again at St J. SL2: Ayr eases at Brechin.

13 Ch Lge: Gomes gaffe and Spurs exit to Real Madrid. Schalke finishes off Inter and awaits Man U in semi. Pressure mounts on Ancelotti at Chelsea. Arsenal will increase ticket prices. Death announced of Arsenal director Fiszman. Rotherham appoints Andy Scott as boss. Women's Super League starts: two games, two goals.

14 FA Cup hikes ticket for final. Orient steps up opposition to Olympic for Hammers. E Lge: Iberia rules ok? Benfica, Braga and Porto from Portugal, Villarreal from Spain make last four. Women's Super: two games, ten goals!,

15 FLC: Holt stops his ex-Forest mates with 20th Lge goal as Canaries go second in pecking order. L2: No outing for Bradford as Southend hits four. Utd the favourites as City await semi-final with trepidation. Is Ancelotti on borrowed time at the Bridge?

16 FA Cup: Man C Toure de force, okay, Ya (Ya) as Roo-less (and no Giggs) Man U loses Scholes to a card and the semi-tie. PL: Chelsea unloads the Baggies – sub Torres goal disallowed. Seven unbeaten Everton home run goes on at Rovers expense. 91st minute Villa puts Hammers in a pickle. Wigan inflicts 12th defeat of last 16 for Blackpool by the seaside. Birmingham punishes Sunderland for another loss – eight of last nine games and one pt from 27. FLC: Cardiff snatches second place as Pompey's ten go under. Eight in a row Reading hits Leicester ambitions. Swansea edged out at Burnley for whom Alexander reaches a great 1000 games. Division's top scorers Leeds and Watford share four goals. Even PNE adds to Sheff U misery. Scunny wins crucially at Palace. Boro – Tykes affair is drawn and has a brawl. L1: Top six all winners. Brighton becomes champions at Walsall. Saints one only from pressure against Bristol R. Huddersfield, Bournemouth and MK Dons are away day successes, Posh at home to Plymouth though gk Lewis saves pen and victory. L2: Chesterfield mathematically almost there as Macc is beaten. Bury strolls on to add concern for Barnet, as does Shrewsbury to Stockport. Wycombe held by Northampton. Torquay goes goalless with Vale. Ten undefeated Shots hold Stevenage. Sixteen unbeaten Gills make a pt with Morecambe. S Cup: Motherwell takes out St J in semi. SPL: Rangers just clip St M. SL1: Fifers score six in ten-a-side with Q of S. Raith wins at Stirling. Dundee adds another win at Morton. SL2: Forfar closes on Ayr held at Livi. SL3: Arbroath held, Annan loses, Albion wins away, Stranraer loses. BSP: Four more for Crawley, AFC Dons, too, but Luton held goalless. Wrexham, Fleetwood both win. Eastbourne relegated. Welsh: Bangor crash as Llanelli strikes five. Real's ten men hold Barca as Messi (49th goal) gets visitors goal from pen – his first time against a JM team.

17 FA Cup: Stoke high five demolishes Bolton to reach first final. PL: Added time farce as Arsenal hit 98th min pen, Liverpool spot on leveller 102 mins! S Cup: Celtic foursome against Dons ten men. SPL: Accies win at Hibs.

18 QPR finds Derby determined in draw. FA will send bill to Man U for Wembley heated "wall" game.

19 Pen appeals both sides but no goals at Toon-Man U leaves latter seven ahead of game in hand Arsenal. Burnley win over Boro puts them in range of play-offs. Notts out of danger zone at Tranmere. Another pt achieved for Burton at Bradford. BSP: Luton beaten at York, but p-o place safe. SPL: Dundee U finish with eight men, Rangers four goals (two pens). SL1: Winners Falkirk keeps hoping. Ross leaders hit by Q of S floodlight failure. SL2: Livi clips ten-man Ayr. SL3: Clyde swaps bottom self with E Stirling! Ref Atkinson (NB Sir Alex) gets FA Cup final. Fabregas has pop at his boss. Spurs want fixture change.

20 Spurs fights back to level with Arsenal sharing six, but pt favours neither, so Chelsea moves second beating Birmingham. Youth Cup: Man U takes out Chelsea to reach final. Celtic's "Anglos" foursome scorers going pt behind Rangers with game in hand, but manager Lennon receives parcel bomb. Ronaldo goal so Real Madrid edges Spanish Cup final against Barca. Carlton Cole fined £20,000 for tweeting. Blatter mounts new FIFA bid.

21 Ill Houllier will miss rest of season. Burton centre job is for Sheepshanks. Man U fans seek price cut. Wenger expects cash for players. Norwich whacks five at Ipswich but crowd trouble mars it. U-18: Scots clip England.

22 Sir Alex writes off Arsenal to upgrade Chelsea. Man C may sell Tevez. Al Ahli sacks O'Leary. FLC: Forest takes advantage of Leicester error. McCarthy saves Reading a pt at Leeds. L1: Orient dents Posh, but Huddersfield shines at MK Dons. L2: Chesterfield promoted without playing as Wycombe is held at Torquay. Stevenage sinks at Southend, Bury needs just one against Lincoln. BSP: Yet another foursome for Crawley;

Jack Wilshere of Arsenal skips past Tottenham Hotspur's Tom Huddlestone in the local derby at White Hart Lane. True to form the match was a pulsating affair ending 3-3 after Arsenal had led 3-1. (Action Images/Carl Recine)

AFC Dons recover to beat Mansfield. Kiddy sinks Fleetwood to boost p-o chance. Welsh: TNS goes under to Neath.

23 Lunchtime "Little Pea" digests Everton as Man U equals club record winning 13 home PL games in a row. Torres scores! Goal drought of 734 mins ends as Chelsea sends West Ham to the bottom. Defoe's PL goal century hoisted, but Spurs still drop two pts to WBA. Maxi treble as five-hit Liverpool punishes Birmingham. Leaky Wigan lets in four at Sunderland as Bruce celebrates 500th boss game. PL record for Blackpool – 17th scoring and conceding in same home game as Newcastle takes a pt. Friedel makes it 262 games on the trot as Villa holds Stoke. The "W" formation completed as Fulham draws at Wolves leaving the Molineux boys, Wigan and West Ham as last three. FLC: Two up Cardiff surrenders pt to QPR. Swansea is held at Pompey. Four-play for both Burnley and Millwall enhances prospects. Sheff U wins! – Bristol C edged at Bramall Lane. L1: Saints late show pulls curtain down on Brighton's – FL's last home record. Bournemouth held at Yeovil. Notts pile more grief on Swindon. L2: Shrewsbury's local derby win at Hereford pushes them into automatic slot. Accrington consolidates play-off hopes beating Bradford. Barnet shakes Gills four times, Stockport wins at Vale but Burton ends Shots run. SPL: Dundee U firms up fourth placing beating Killie. SL1: Dunfermline goes four pts ahead beating Raith. Dundee is safe at last – winning at Ross. Cowden's nine draws with QoS ten. SL2: Forfar beats ten-man Brechin to move within three pts of them in play-off berth. Peterhead relegated by E Fife. SL3: Arbroath confirms promotion beating Montrose, but Albion loses to in-form QP and Stranraer and Annan draw. Bangor closes gap on TNS winning at Pt Talbot. BSP: Wrexham wins at Gateshead but faces play-off axe over tax bill. JM rests nine Real players but doubles Valencia's three; Midget Messi scores 50th – first La Liga player as high.

24 Arsenal challenge ends as Cohen scores Bolton winner with 40 secs to spare. SPL: McGregor saves Samaras pen as still favourites Celtic draws at Rangers.

25 Sub Dzeko's goal helps Man C go fourth as Blackburn loses at home. FLC: Nerves affect QPR in another draw with Hull. Jackson at the treble edges Derby for Norwich. Whittingham goal for Cardiff sends Preston down. Swansea progresses against Ipswich as Reading slips up to give Sheff U a lift to 22nd. Forest continues in play-off zone at Bristol C. Marquis at the double as Millwall adds to Scunny worries. Donny draws locally at Barnsley, but Palace's Danns beats Leeds before late red card. L1: Brighton settles for pt at Colchester. Saints beat Hartlepool's ten-men. Huddersfield clips Daggers, but Posh is held by Yeovil and MK Dons manage to lose at Plymouth which relegates Swindon beaten at Sheff W. Bournemouth beats Bristol R in ten-a-side finish. L2: Bury wins promotion at Chesterfield. Wycombe climbs back to third beating Crewe as Shrewsbury is held by in-form Accrington. Struggles draw: Stockport with Northampton, Barnet with Oxford. Bradford eases concern with late winner over Shots. BSP: Another clean sheet for Crawley at Newport. AFC Dons are held, but Luton, Wrexham and p-o landing Fleetwood all win as Kiddy loses at Rushden.

26 Ch Lge: Even Schalke's Neuer is unable to stop Man U booking likely Wembley place. War of words erupts between Mourinho and Guardiola ahead of other semi. PL: Wolves stay trapped in danger zone as Stoke hits three. Police investigate another suspect package for Lennon. Parliament virtually writes off the FA!

27 Ch Lge: Pepe red-carded, non-playing Barca sub, too, JM banished to terrace, then Messi destroys Real (second goal 8 sec run beating four men over 43 yards). Rooney anguishes over his ex-wanting to leave OT. PL: Fulham piles on latest Bolton problems. Scottish Youth final: Celtic beats Rangers (of course). Groom-to-be HRH the boy Wills plays football with mates in Battersea Park!

Rangers' Nikica Jelavic and Celtic's Daniel Majstorovic battle for the ball during the Clydesdale Bank Scottish Premier League match at Ibrox Stadium. (PA Photos)

28 E Lge: Falcao foursome in five-star Porto win over Villarreal makes for Portuguese final as Benfica edges Braga in first leg semis. Mourinho heads for trouble with UEFA and Barca. Arsenal fans want ticket price block. Rangers fined for sectarian songs. Coventry appoints Andy Thorn as manager. Swindon axes Paul Hart and his assistant. Becks, Brooking and Madejski are Royal wedding guests.

29 QPR is facing penalty points over third-party player ownership. Torquay draws with Chesterfield and has 5002 gate. FIFA stats show Chicarito was the fastest at WC. JM faces opposition from Ronaldo now. Carragher on brink of 665th Liverpool outing.

30 No Hawk-Eye, just one lino getting the bird for giving Chelsea a goal, the other for not spotting off-side as Spurs suffer crucially in (Terry's 500th). Al Habsi saves Arteta pen, Baines gets one against Latics old boys as Everton draws with Wigan. Leaky Bolton even loses at Blackburn. Blackpool's first goalless draw all season at home v Stoke. Peter O is Africa's king of PL scorers as ten-men sand-Baggies do for Villa. Fulham puts Sunderland back on the rack. FLC: QPR celebrates title at Watford – for now? Swans put an end to Millwall hopes. Reading makes a pt at Coventry. In-form Forest (third win in 8 days) relegates Scunthorpe for a fiver. Leeds just about keeps hoping for p-o berth after edging Burnley. Sheff U demoted after draw with Barnsley. L1: Saints storm on at Brentford, but unbeaten in 24 Huddersfield stays in their wake to beach Brighton. Posh held at Rochdale, MK Dons clip Notts and Bournemouth gets a pt at Hartlepool (gk Flinders head 'pools leveller) as the three remain in right zone. Orient misses out, well beaten by Tranmere. Walsall continues to tread water after beating Charlton leaving winning Daggers, drawing Bristol R and losing Plymouth in the deep. L2: Stunning win for Wycombe at Bury keeps Shrewsbury only hoping after win at Cheltenham. Accrington (Ryan 3) play-off assured but Barnet menaced. Crewe confirms Stockport relegation. Nine-man Stevenage loses at Northampton (first win in 19), but Gills slip up at home again to Macc. Seven up Vale inflicts Morecame's worst lge defeat with Richards J and Dodds 3 each). Hereford rescue in Bradford draw, but Lincoln stays worried after loss at Oxford. SPL: Rangers pile on five goals at Motherwell. SL1: Dunfermline achieves promotion at Morton as Raith loses at QofS. Dundee wins again (7746 is better than three SPL gates). SL2: Ayr, Forfar in p-o mode but Brechin chased by E Fife now. SL3: Stranraer losers at Albion, overtaken in fourth by QP as Spiders win at Clyde. BSP: Southport losers at Kettering are relegated with Altrincham beaten by already doomed Eastbourne. FGR and their vanquishers Tamworth survive. Newport scores seven as Gateshead have gk sent off. Welsh: Bangor (1707) edges TNS for the title! Dortmund is Bundesliga champion, Real and Barca both lose in Spain.

MAY

Man U's 19th title ... Birmingham, Blackpool & West Ham go down ... QPR, Norwich and Swansea for PL ... Classy Barca beats Man U ... Celtic's Lennon suffers hatred ... FIFA in chaos.

1 Ramsey gives Chelsea a life-line as Arsenal beats Man U, both teams denied penalties. Man C adds to West Ham misery, Wolves unable to beat ten-man Birmingham but Liverpool threesome against Newcastle puts them fifth. SPL: Celtic (pt behind Rangers and game in hand) hits Dundee U for four and hoists century of goals overall in season.

2 Cardiff's afternoon crash to Boro helps Norwich winners at Pompey to promotion. Soton virtually assured of automatic spot as they relegate Argyle. Ten-a-side finish sees Accies win at St M. Real and Barca still sniping at each other. WPL Cup: TNS needs extra time to get best of seven over Llanelli.

3 Ch Lge: Barca clinches final place despite Real's equaliser in second leg, but the visitors rage over disallowed goal. England U-17s draw with France. Ken Bates buys Leeds. QC is to defend QPR. Arsenal will raise ticket prices; fans unhappy. FIFA set down rules for goal-line technology trial.

4 Ch Lge: Man U coasts to Wembley with foursome against Schalke. SPL: Caley shocks Celtic, now Rangers lead by a point.

5 E Lge: All-Portuguese final as Braga wins on away goals against Benfica and Porto on aggregate after losing to Villarreal. BSP p-o: Luton takes commanding lead at Wrexham. *The Daily Telegraph* exposes world-wide match-fixing. Black Market flourishes in Ch Lge final ticket racket. No-goal Chelsea lino is rested. Race row escalates in France over national team coach Blanc. Sugar's pill may not be swallowed by PL.

6 Sir Alex is confident ahead of Chelsea game. England U-17s lose to Danes. Thompson and Platini lead UEFA backing of Blatter. Mourinho receives five-match ban. The end for Tampere linked to match-fixer's company and exits Finnish football with several RoPs players, too. MPs will study gambling effect on the game. AFC Dons take BSP p-o lead at Fleetwood.

7 Adam's ail – misses one pen, scores another (in 66 secs) and escapes card for Bale tackle as Spurs scrape dramatic draw with Blackpool. Man C flops again at Everton. Sunderland ends (just) away day drought (447 mins) at Bolton. Newcastle puts pressure on ten-man Birmingham but McLeish goes ref unhappy. Wigan gets draw at Villa where Heskey charge might be changed. Hammers usual first half horror, then a pt before Keane miss against Blackburn. FLC: £875,000 fine for QPR but no pts deduction, just defeat by Leeds who fails to make p-o as four in a row Forest achieves it at ten-man Palace. Foursome Swans lick ten-man Sheff U, Reading edges Derby but Cardiff only salvages a pt late at Burnley. L1: Wonder goal from "Oxo" is the right brew for uplifting Saints against relegation surviving Walsall because Daggers downed by Posh's nap hand (87 in total), demoted but Bristol R losers at Colchester. Huddersfield shares eight goals with Brentford. L2: Wycombe clinches automatic place against Southend. Pts deducted Torquay suffers first reverse in 12 at Rotherham but goal difference better for p-o than beaten Gills at Chesterfield. Grazie says Grazioli to fleeting, three-game Mad Dog Allen after McLeod pen beats Port Vale and Shots send Lincoln into BSP. Stevenage six-share with Bury and Accrington level with Burton await play-offs. Crewe gets five (87 in all their games!) at Bradford (Donaldson reaches 28 goals). SPL: Another four for Rangers beats Hearts. Accies first home win over ten-man Hibs brings hope as St M loses at Caley. SL2: E Fife held so Brechin makes play-offs. SL3: Stranraer beats Clyde but misses out as QP snatches fourth place against Montrose. Trophy: Senior service for Darlo put Stags at final bay in extra time. Irish Cup: Linfield beats Crusaders.

8 Thirty-six seconds and almost there Man U put the skids under Chelsea, winning easier than the odd goal in three suggests. Wolves grab bragging rights over Baggies to move out of danger. Arsenal disappoints once more at Stoke. SPL: Celtic beats Killie but is a pt behind Rangers. AC Milan end five-year Inter title reign. Vase: Chow cooks up another brace for Whitley to bury Coalville. Welsh Cup: Llanelli four-play disposes of Bangor.

Chelsea's Didier Drogba (right) and Manchester United's Ryan Giggs battle for the ball in the Premier League match at Old Trafford. (PA Photos)

9   FA's WC bid team accused of underhand scheming; Blatter hits out. Maxi treble (32 sec start) as Liverpool whacks five at Fulham. UEFA U-17: England beats Serbia to reach last four. Morecambe parts with boss McIlroy.

10   Crouch og lifts Man C into Ch Lge as Spurs slip up. Rangers beat Dundee U to stay ahead. Hamilton loses a player, penalty and SPL status at St J. BSP: Luton reaches final edging Wrexham. Triesman alleges widespread corruption over FIFA bribes, but dismisses FA wrongdoing.

11   Neil Lennon attacked by spectator as Celtic wins at Hearts in ten-a-side game. SL p-os: Brechin held by Cowden; Ayr takes lead at Forfar; Annan edges Alloa and Albion draws at QP. BSP: AFC Dons hit Fleetwood for six and reach final. Barca held by Levante but win title. Foster quits England team. Poles worry over security ahead of 2012 Euro.

12   Three more years King Kenny walks on – Mersey water. Late afternoon ko for 2012 FA Cup final. FA will investigate Triesman claims. FLC p-o: ten-man Swansea keeps Forest still. U-17s: England beaten by Arsenal's Dutchman Ebecilio. Barnsley sacks boss Robins.

13   Sir Alex in trouble in praising ref Webb! Managers appointed: FLC p-o: No goals for either Reading or Cardiff. Adams is back at Vale; Lawrie Sanchez at Barnet and Jim Bentley as player-boss at Morecambe. Tevez can leave Man C if he so desires. Ancelotti admits error over Torres signing.

14   Manchester does rule ok? United lunchtime landmark English record 19th championship (12th PL), Giggs PL record 573rd game) in Rooney pen draw at Blackburn; City teatime pot of the FA Cup, first such for 35 years, edging Stoke courtesy of Toure K. Blackpool's Campbell hits 1000th PL season goal as Bolton just on wrong end of seven-goal thriller. Wolves leap to 16th as leaky Sunderland crashes at home again. Everton manager Moyes (350th PL game – 4th in list) riles over red card as Baggies climb to 10th. Play-offs: L1: Huddersfield draws at Bournemouth; L2: Torquay takes two-goal lead over Shrews. SL play-offs: 1: Ayr held by Forfar but move on as Brechin demotes Cowden. 2: Albion end QP run; Alloa relegated by Annan.

15   West Ham goes from Ba, Ba two-goal lead to bye, bye PL as N'Zogbia double strike for Wigan relegates them and boss Grant is then sacked. Spurs ruin Dalglish day at Liverpool. Fulham shoves Birmingham nearer danger zone at St Andrews. Arsenal booed despite all-out assault, peppering as brace man Bent leads Villa out of trouble. Chelsea held at the Bridge by Toon. Five in peril: Blackburn, Wolves, Birmingham, Blackpool and Wigan. L1 p-o: MK Dons clips Posh but remain unhappy over penalty. SPL: Celtic hits four against Motherwell, but Rangers third title in a row after five-star finish at Killie (three in first seven mins and Lafferty treble).

16   Swans leave Forest flapping in FLC p-o. Hammer fans accused of starting riot at West Ham party after Ba (humbug!) allegedly refuses to sign autograph. Blackburn boss Kean is on drink driving charge; one Rovers player faces illegal payment allegation. Fulham is likely to receive fair-play Europa League place. Sir Alex ignores latest FA charge. Maradona lands Dubai club deal. Chelsea stiffs beat Blackburn in North-South play-off. Cowdenbeath chairman receives suspect packet.

17   Blue Moon continues rising, third spot now as Stoke suffers treble loss to Man C. FLC p-o: Reading shakes Cardiff with threesome. Ferguson and Ancelotti both charged for respectively praising and criticising the same ref! Ba accuses fan of racial abuse. England Women beat Swedes. FA Youth Cup: Man U held at Sheff U in first leg final.

18   E Lge: JM II (Villas-Boras) carries on Porto record just beating defensive Braga. L1 p-o: Bournemouth loses a player in extra time and the shoot-out to Huddersfield after six share. SL: 1: Brechin holds Ayr. 2: Albion's Love treble hits Annan.

19   L1 p-o: Posh overturns MK Dons lead. FA protests with no vote for either Blatter or Bin Hammam.
20   L2 p-o: Another fine mess for Stanley as Stevenage finishes off nine-men. Torquay holds Shrews to reach
     final, too. Ancelotti remains unconcerned over future. Sir Alex acknowledges criticism if they lose to Black-
     pool. Paolo Di Canio is the Swindon boss.
21   S Cup final: Celtic eases to sink 'Well. AFC Dons need shoot-out to gain FL status against Luton. Women's
     Final: Arsenal beats Bristol Academy. Ronaldo breaks La Liga record with 39th and 40th goals. .
22   Blackpool even leads Man U but loses, Birmingham draws level at Spurs before the same fate, but there's no
     PL room for this B & B as both are relegated. Wolves fight back three down, still get edged by Blackburn but
     survive as does Wigan winners at Stoke. The-man Everton beats second-placed Chelsea who then sacks
     manager Ancelotti! Fulham gets its first red card in draw with Arsenal. Newcastle chucks three goal lead as
     treble-shooter Tchoyi levels for WBA. Bolton's ten-men lose to Man C. Villa just clip Liverpool, but Sunder-
     land threesome strikes already doomed Hammers. Thirty-two goals on the day takes total to PL record 1063
     for season. SL: Ayr wins promotion to Div 1 beating Brechin, Albion edges Annan to reach Div 2. Man U
     axes injury-hit Hargreaves. BBC Panorama will expose FIFA. Porto wins the Portuguese Cup, Schalke the
     German one.
23   Man U boys win the FA Youth Cup for record 10th time. Volcanic ash threatens Ch Lge final. Hiddink may
     return to Chelsea. Wilshere is to have a rest. McLeish is safe at Birmingham. Balotelli misses the Man C
     parade. England bid team to be investigated.
24   Twitter and Parliament having exposed alleged affair involving Giggs, he plays in Neville testimonial (Man U
     lose to Juvé) watched by 42,000. O'Neill reaches Villa settlement. Green is back for England. Blatter turns
     down British political inquiry. C Nations Cup: Keane double as Republic easily beats Northern Ireland.
25   FIFA in crisis: Chuck Blazer throws a curve ball accusing Warner and Bin Hammam of bribery! Kolo Toure
     might be banned for nine months. C Nations Cup: Scots fight back floors Wales.
26   Wembley presents best pitch: grass and plastic fibres for Ch Lge finale. Blatter denies alleged frame-up.
     Fulham granted E Lge via fair-play. Kolo Toure gets six months ban backdated to March.
27   FIFA Ethics committee will probe allegations. Ch Lge fever rises but Sir Alex remains confident. Wales beats
     N Ireland in C Nations.
28   Ch Lge final: Messi scores his first goal on English soil but Man U bites the dust as Barca sweeps to majestic
     victory with Sir Alex's tactics and selection again queried. Bin Hammam quits FIFA race as accusations con-
     tinue to fly. Platini is against goal-line technology. Stevenage beats Torquay to gain p-o lift to League One.
29   FIFA clears Blatter, but Warner and Bin Hammam under threat. Fergie jnr joy as three goals in 12 mins by
     Posh ends Huddersfield 27-game unbeaten run, rising Peterborough to Championship. C Nations Cup:
     Keane's 49th goal gives Republic the cup beating Scots. Big Sam aims for West Ham? Monaco relegated.
30   Swansea makes PL stage in fine encounter with Reading. Cardiff sacks Jones. Blatter takes offensive. Buckle
     leaves Torquay for Bristol R.
31   HRH Wills joins anti-FIFA election cry. Sponsors are angry. Warner fights back. Now Blazer goes! Scholes
     retires to join coaching staff – 675 games, 150 goals (102 PL 18th centurion), 66 caps, 14 goals. Houllier is to
     be retired on medical grounds. Kolo Toure plans appeal. Ruskies will take over Pompey. N Ireland U-21s
     held in Faeroes. England U-19s beat Montenegro.

Manchester United manager Sir Alex Ferguson celebrates with the Premier League trophy. (PA Photos)

JUNE
Blatter re-elected unopposed . . . More FIFA revelations . . . Fulham plays in June.

1   Dictator Blatter wins vote 171 to 17 as FA fails to get even Wales and N Ireland onside. Allardyce for West Ham, Richie Barker at Bury. Match-fixing: arrests made in Italy.

2   Hughes walks out on Fulham. FIFA declares war on England. England U-19s beat Swiss.

3   Euro 2012: Gomez double as Germany stays 100 percent in Austria; France held in Belarus; Lichtenstein surprises Lithuania. Friedel, 40, joins Spurs. FIFA will investigate international match-fixing.

4   Tired England held by Swiss who take two-goal lead, but Montenegro drops two points to Bulgaria. Republic goes top in group away to Macedonia; Portugal avenges Norway defeat.

5   England U-21s beat Norway, U-19s draw with Spain. PL clubs seeking managers widen range.

6   Blatter will sign Placido Domingo and Henry Kissinger for new committee! FA signals white flag with FIFA. Year off Ancelotti rules out come back. Hiddink is linked with Chelsea again and Abramovich said to be after Modric, Neymar and Sanchez. £3.5m Graham may join Swansea in record move. Rooney sports new hairline.

7   Martin Jol returns as Fulham manager. Henderson is to switch from Sunderland to Liverpool £20m. "Weak" Republic beats Italy in Liege!

8   All change for the Paul Jones – Rovers to Man U £16m? PM Dave has swipe at FIFA.

9   Villa seeks Martinez. Peter Withe may replace Bryan Robson – in Thai post. Is Exodus likely from Arsenal? Five fail drug test in Mexico squad. Surinam says bungs prevalent in Caribbean.

10 Loyal Martinez snubs Villa. Uwe Rosler gets Brentford job. FL will adopt UEFA fair play system. Jones deal held up for Man U. Bebe is loaned to Besiktas.

11 Liverpool puts late bid for Man U-bound Jones. Rushden axed from Blue Square Premier. Southport is reprieved. Killie expects to promote Kenny Shiels to boss.

12 McLeish quits Birmingham, Davies is sacked by Forest. McLeish is the favourite for Villa and McClaren awaits call to the woods. Steve Eyre gets Rochdale post. UEFA praises FL stance. U21s snatch draw with Spain.

13 Brummies want money for McLeish. McClaren sweeps in at Forest. Becks seeks GB 2012 place. Arsenal blame gas prices for ticket increase. Martin Ling gets Torquay job. Jones will go to Man U.

14 Shearer is in Cardiff frame. Gullit sacked by Terek Grozny.

15 U21s goalless with Ukraine must now beat Czechs. Chelsea chases Modric. Shearer says no to Cardiff. Udinese's Sanchez is chased by a PL pack.

16 By Eck – even Sir Alex backs McLeish at Villa! Hiddink and Villas-Boas head Chelsea list.

17 Modric wants for Chelsea. Baldini aims for dual role: England/Roma. England U-17s win first FIFA Under-17 WC game against Rwanda.

18 Tug-of-war erupts over Modric. Malky Mackay is given Cardiff position. England U21s on the brink.

19 U21s lead then are bounced out by the Czechs.

20 Jack Warner jumps ship at FIFA. Villas-Boas moves nearer Chelsea.

21 Boss jobs: Villas-Boras at Chelsea (£13.3m transfer!), Sean Dyche at Watford and Chris Hughton at Birmingham. GB plan hits Celtic no interest. O'Hara moves to Wolves for £5m.

22 Young moves to Man U for around £17m. Carroll returns to early training for Liverpool.

23 Arsenal snubs Fabregas bid from Barca. High Court rejects Spurs/Orient Olympic stadium challenge. Worthington breaks Celtic GB boycott. England U17s held by Canada whose gk scores with a punt.

24 Liverpool goes for Adam and Downing. Brazil plans for WC are in tatters. Ipswich want Swansea banned from transfers.

25 Stu Pearce and Hope Powell will run boys and girls GB 2012 teams. Hammers may have to flog Parker. U17s beat Uruguay to qualify for second WC round.

26 Spain wins the Euro U21 final beating Switzerland; Belarus edges ten-Czechs for third place.

27 De Gea moves towards Old Trafford. England women are held by WC by Mexicans.

28 Neymar is destined for either Chelsea or Real Madrid. Mexico suspends eight misbehaving players. Ch Lge begins!

29 Lee leaves Liverpool post. FIFA ref goes missing. England now ranked fourth in world! Di Matteo is No. 2 at the Bridge now.

30 E Lge starts and Fulham beats NSI. Birmingham is ok despite owner's court charge. Sunderland makes it three signings: Wickham, Ji and Gardner. U17s beat Argies on pens.

CUPS AND UPS AND DOWNS DIARY

FEBRUARY
27 Carling Cup final: Birmingham City 2 Arsenal 1.

MARCH
20 CIS Insurance Cup final: Rangers 2 Celtic 1.

APRIL
 3 Johnstone's Paint Trophy: Carlisle United 1 Brentford 0.
 9 Livingston promoted to Scottish League Div 1.
    Crawley Town promoted to League Two as Blue Square Premier champions.
    Histon relegated from Blue Square Premier.
10 Stirling Albion relegated to Scottish League Div 2.
    Alba Challenge Cup final: Ross County 2 Queen of the South 0.
12 Brighton & Hove Albion promoted to Football League Championship.
16 Brighton & Hove Albion League One champions.
    Eastbourne Borough relegated from Blue Square Premier.
22 Chesterfield promoted to League One.
23 Arbroath promoted to Scottish League Div 2.
    Peterhead relegated to Scottish League Div 3.
25 Preston North End relegated to League One.
    Swindon Town relegated to League Two.
    Bury promoted to League One.
30 Queens Park Rangers Football League Champions.
    Sheffield United and Scunthorpe United relegated to League One.
    Stockport County relegated to Blue Square Premier.
    Dunfermline Athletic promoted to Scottish Premier League.
    Altrincham and Southport relegated from Blue Square Premier.
    Bangor City Welsh Premier League champions.

MAY
 2 Norwich City promoted to Premier League.
    Plymouth Argyle relegated to League Two.
 7 Southampton promoted to Championship.
    Wycombe Wanderers promoted to League One.
    Chesterfield become League Two champions.
    Dagenham & Redbridge relegated to League Two.
    Bristol Rovers relegated to League Two.
    Lincoln City relegated to Blue Square Premier.
    FA Trophy final: Darlington 1 Mansfield Town 0.
    Irish Cup final: Linfield 2 Crusaders 1.
 8 FA Vase final: Whitley Bay 3 Coalville Town 2.
    Welsh Cup final: Llanelli 4 Bangor City 1.
10 Hamilton Academical relegated to Scottish League Div 1.
14 Manchester United Premier League champions.
    FA Cup final: Manchester City 1 Stoke City 0.
    Cowdenbeath relegated to Scottish League Div 2.
    Alloa Athletic relegated to Scottish League Div 3.
15 West Ham United relegated to Football League Championship.
18 Europa League final: Porto 1 Braga 0.
21 Active Nation Scottish Cup final: Celtic 3 Motherwell 0.
    Blue Square Premier Play-off final: AFC Wimbledon 0 Luton Town 0
    (AFC Wimbledon win 4-3 on penalties and promoted to League Two).
    Women's FA Cup final: Arsenal 2 Bristol Academy 0.
22 Birmingham City and Blackpool relegated to Football League Championship.
    Ayr United promoted to Scottish League Div 1.
    Albion Rovers promoted to Scottish League Div 2.
28 Champions League final: Barcelona 3 Manchester United 1.
    League Two play-off final: Stevenage 1 Torquay United 0.
    (Stevenage promoted to League Two).
29 League One play-off final: Peterborough United 3 Huddersfield Town 0.
    (Peterborough United promoted to Championship).
30 Championship play-off final: Swansea City 4 Reading 2.
    (Swansea City promoted to Premier League).

ENGLISH LEAGUE TABLES 2010–11

(P) *Promoted into division at end of 2009–10 season.*   (R) *Relegated into division at end of 2009–10 season.*

BARCLAYS PREMIER LEAGUE 2010–11

		Total					Home					Away						
		P	W	D	L	F	A	W	D	L	F	A	W	D	L	F	A	GD	Pts
1	Manchester U	38	23	11	4	78	37	18	1	0	49	12	5	10	4	29	25	41	80
2	Chelsea	38	21	8	9	69	33	14	3	2	39	13	7	5	7	30	20	36	71
3	Manchester C	38	21	8	9	60	33	13	4	2	34	12	8	4	7	26	21	27	71
4	Arsenal	38	19	11	8	72	43	11	4	4	33	15	8	7	4	39	28	29	68
5	Tottenham H	38	16	14	8	55	46	9	9	1	30	19	7	5	7	25	27	9	62
6	Liverpool	38	17	7	14	59	44	12	4	3	37	14	5	3	11	22	30	15	58
7	Everton	38	13	15	10	51	45	9	7	3	31	23	4	8	7	20	22	6	54
8	Fulham	38	11	16	11	49	43	8	7	4	30	23	3	9	7	19	20	6	49
9	Aston Villa	38	12	12	14	48	59	8	7	4	26	19	4	5	10	22	40	–11	48
10	Sunderland	38	12	11	15	45	56	7	5	7	25	27	5	6	8	20	29	–11	47
11	WBA (P)	38	12	11	15	56	71	8	6	5	30	30	4	5	10	26	41	–15	47
12	Newcastle U (P)	38	11	13	14	56	57	6	8	5	41	27	5	5	9	15	30	–1	46
13	Stoke C	38	13	7	18	46	48	10	4	5	31	18	3	3	13	15	30	–2	46
14	Bolton W	38	12	10	16	52	56	10	5	4	34	24	2	5	12	18	32	–4	46
15	Blackburn R	38	11	10	17	46	59	7	7	5	22	16	4	3	12	24	43	–13	43
16	Wigan Ath	38	9	15	14	40	61	5	8	6	22	34	4	7	8	18	27	–21	42
17	Wolverhampton W	38	11	7	20	46	66	8	4	7	30	30	3	3	13	16	36	–20	40
18	Birmingham C	38	8	15	15	37	58	6	8	5	19	22	2	7	10	18	36	–21	39
19	Blackpool (P)	38	10	9	19	55	78	5	5	9	30	37	5	4	10	25	41	–23	39
20	West Ham U	38	7	12	19	43	70	5	5	9	24	31	2	7	10	19	39	–27	33

NPOWER CHAMPIONSHIP 2010–11

		Total					Home					Away						
		P	W	D	L	F	A	W	D	L	F	A	W	D	L	F	A	GD	Pts
1	QPR	46	24	16	6	71	32	14	7	2	43	15	10	9	4	28	17	39	88
2	Norwich C (P)	46	23	15	8	83	58	13	6	4	47	30	10	9	4	36	28	25	84
3	Swansea C¶	46	24	8	14	69	42	15	5	3	41	11	9	3	11	28	31	27	80
4	Cardiff C	46	23	11	12	76	54	12	7	4	41	25	11	4	8	35	29	22	80
5	Reading	46	20	17	9	77	51	12	7	4	43	25	8	10	5	34	26	26	77
6	Nottingham F	46	20	15	11	69	50	13	8	2	43	22	7	7	9	26	28	19	75
7	Leeds U (P)	46	19	15	12	81	70	11	8	4	47	34	8	7	8	34	36	11	72
8	Burnley (R)	46	18	14	14	65	61	12	6	5	40	30	6	8	9	25	31	4	68
9	Millwall (P)	46	18	13	15	62	48	12	6	5	39	22	6	7	10	23	26	14	67
10	Leicester C	46	19	10	17	76	71	13	6	4	48	27	6	4	13	28	44	5	67
11	Hull C (R)	46	16	17	13	52	51	7	8	8	21	19	9	9	5	31	32	1	65
12	Middlesbrough	46	17	11	18	68	68	10	7	6	37	32	7	4	12	31	36	0	62
13	Ipswich T	46	18	8	20	62	68	10	3	10	33	37	8	5	10	29	31	–6	62
14	Watford	46	16	13	17	77	71	9	7	7	39	32	7	6	10	38	39	6	61
15	Bristol C	46	17	9	20	62	65	10	4	9	30	29	7	5	11	32	36	–3	60
16	Portsmouth (R)	46	15	13	18	53	60	8	9	6	31	26	7	4	12	22	34	–7	58
17	Barnsley	46	14	14	18	55	66	11	6	6	32	23	3	8	12	23	43	–11	56
18	Coventry C	46	14	13	19	54	58	9	5	9	27	26	5	8	10	27	32	–4	55
19	Derby Co	46	13	10	23	58	71	8	4	11	35	32	5	6	12	23	39	–13	49
20	Crystal Palace	46	12	12	22	44	69	11	6	6	28	24	1	6	16	16	45	–25	48
21	Doncaster R	46	11	15	20	55	81	9	7	7	26	31	4	6	13	29	50	–26	48
22	Preston NE	46	10	12	24	54	79	7	4	12	27	36	3	8	12	27	43	–25	42
23	Sheffield U	46	11	9	26	44	79	7	5	11	27	36	4	4	15	17	43	–35	42
24	Scunthorpe U	46	12	6	28	43	87	5	5	13	21	40	7	1	15	22	47	–44	42

¶*Swansea C promoted via play-offs.*

NPOWER LEAGUE 1 2010–11

		P	W	D	L	F	A	W	D	L	F	A	W	D	L	F	A	GD	Pts
				Total						Home					Away				
1	Brighton & HA	46	28	11	7	85	40	17	4	2	54	22	11	7	5	31	18	45	95
2	Southampton	46	28	8	10	86	38	16	4	3	44	13	12	4	7	42	25	48	92
3	Huddersfield T	46	25	12	9	77	48	12	8	3	38	21	13	4	6	39	27	29	87
4	Peterborough U¶ (R)	46	23	10	13	106	75	15	5	3	69	40	8	5	10	37	35	31	79
5	Milton Keynes D	46	23	8	15	67	60	14	5	4	35	23	9	3	11	32	37	7	77
6	Bournemouth (P)	46	19	14	13	75	54	13	5	5	47	24	6	9	8	28	30	21	71
7	Leyton Orient	46	19	13	14	71	62	12	6	5	37	25	7	7	9	34	37	9	70
8	Exeter C	46	20	10	16	66	73	12	5	6	40	31	8	5	10	26	42	-7	70
9	Rochdale (P)	46	18	14	14	63	55	9	8	6	36	30	9	6	8	27	25	8	68
10	Colchester U	46	16	14	16	57	63	12	7	4	38	30	4	7	12	19	33	-6	62
11	Brentford	46	17	10	19	55	62	9	5	9	24	28	8	5	10	31	34	-7	61
12	Carlisle U	46	16	11	19	60	62	9	7	7	34	26	7	4	12	26	36	-2	59
13	Charlton Ath	46	15	14	17	62	66	10	6	7	29	29	5	8	10	33	37	-4	59
14	Yeovil T	46	16	11	19	56	66	8	6	9	27	30	8	5	10	29	36	-10	59
15	Sheffield W (R)	46	16	10	20	67	67	10	5	8	38	29	6	5	12	29	38	0	58
16	Hartlepool U	46	15	12	19	47	65	9	6	8	32	32	6	6	11	15	33	-18	57
17	Oldham Ath	46	13	17	16	53	60	7	9	7	29	31	6	8	9	24	29	-7	56
17	Tranmere R	46	15	11	20	53	60	9	4	10	28	27	6	7	10	25	33	-7	56
19	Notts Co (P)	46	14	8	24	46	60	9	3	11	24	25	5	5	13	22	35	-14	50
20	Walsall	46	12	12	22	56	75	9	3	11	33	36	3	9	11	23	39	-19	48
21	Dagenham and R (P)	46	12	11	23	52	70	8	6	9	28	27	4	5	14	24	43	-18	47
22	Bristol R	46	11	12	23	48	82	6	7	10	24	35	5	5	13	24	47	-34	45
23	Plymouth Arg (R)	46	15	7	24	51	74	9	4	10	27	33	6	3	14	24	41	-23	42
24	Swindon T	46	9	14	23	50	72	5	9	9	20	27	4	5	14	30	45	-22	41

Plymouth Arg deducted 10 points. ¶Peterborough U promoted via play-offs.

NPOWER LEAGUE 2 2010–11

		P	W	D	L	F	A	W	D	L	F	A	W	D	L	F	A	GD	Pts
				Total						Home					Away				
1	Chesterfield	46	24	14	8	85	51	16	3	4	59	31	8	11	4	26	20	34	86
2	Bury	46	23	12	11	82	50	11	6	6	35	23	12	6	5	47	27	32	81
3	Wycombe W (R)	46	22	14	10	69	50	12	6	5	38	25	10	8	5	31	25	19	80
4	Shrewsbury T	46	22	13	11	72	49	11	9	3	36	18	11	4	8	36	31	23	79
5	Accrington S	46	18	19	9	73	55	15	5	3	53	24	3	14	6	20	31	18	73
6	Stevenage¶ (P)	46	18	15	13	62	45	9	11	3	37	24	9	4	10	25	21	17	69
7	Torquay U	46	17	18	11	74	53	10	8	5	36	22	7	10	6	38	31	21	68
8	Gillingham (R)	46	17	17	12	67	57	10	7	6	29	24	7	10	6	38	33	10	68
9	Rotherham U	46	17	15	14	75	60	10	8	5	41	26	7	7	9	34	34	15	66
10	Crewe Alex	46	18	11	17	87	65	13	6	4	49	18	5	5	13	38	47	22	65
11	Port Vale	46	17	14	15	54	49	11	7	5	32	22	6	7	10	22	27	5	65
12	Oxford U (P)	46	17	12	17	58	60	11	4	8	32	25	6	8	9	26	35	-2	63
13	Southend U (R)	46	16	13	17	62	56	10	7	6	37	28	6	6	11	25	28	6	61
14	Aldershot T	46	14	19	13	54	54	8	8	7	26	26	6	11	6	28	28	0	61
15	Macclesfield T	46	14	13	19	59	73	6	7	10	25	36	8	6	9	34	37	-14	55
16	Northampton T	46	11	19	16	63	71	8	9	6	40	33	3	10	10	23	38	-8	52
17	Cheltenham T	46	13	13	20	56	77	6	6	11	24	32	7	7	9	32	45	-21	52
18	Bradford C	46	15	7	24	43	68	10	3	10	27	30	5	4	14	16	38	-25	52
19	Burton Alb	46	12	15	19	56	70	9	8	6	36	31	3	7	13	20	39	-14	51
20	Morecambe	46	13	12	21	54	73	6	8	9	26	31	7	4	12	28	42	-19	51
21	Hereford U	46	12	17	17	50	66	4	11	8	23	30	8	6	9	27	36	-16	50
22	Barnet	46	12	12	22	58	77	8	5	10	30	35	4	7	12	28	42	-19	48
23	Lincoln C	46	13	8	25	45	81	7	4	12	18	41	6	4	13	27	40	-36	47
24	Stockport Co (R)	46	9	14	23	48	96	4	12	7	31	51	5	2	16	17	45	-48	41

Torquay U deducted 1 point. Hereford U deducted 3 points. ¶Stevenage promoted via play-offs.

FOOTBALL LEAGUE PLAY-OFFS 2010–11

CHAMPIONSHIP FIRST LEG

Thursday, 12 May 2011
Nottingham F (0) 0
Swansea C (0) 0   27,881
Nottingham F: Camp; Gunter, Moloney, McKenna (McCleary), Morgan, Chambers, Anderson, McGugan, Earnshaw (Tyson), Boyd (Tudgay), Cohen.
Swansea C: De Vries; Rangel, Taylor■, Britton, Tate, Williams, Dyer, Allen (Gower), Borini (Moore), Dobbie (Monk), Sinclair.

Friday, 13 May 2011
Reading (0) 0
Cardiff C (0) 0   21,485
Reading: Federici; Griffin, Harte, Karacan, Mills, Khizanishvili, McAnuff, Leigertwood, Long, Hunt (Howard), Robson-Kanu (Manset).
Cardiff C: Bywater; Quinn (Naylor), Blake, Olofinjana, McNaughton, Keinan, Whittingham, Emmanuel-Thomas (Koumas), Bothroyd, Bellamy (Chopra), Burke.

CHAMPIONSHIP SECOND LEG

Monday, 16 May 2011
Swansea C (2) 3 *(Britton 28, Dobbie 33, Pratley 90)*
Nottingham F (0) 1 *(Earnshaw 80)*   19,816
Swansea C: De Vries; Rangel, Tate, Britton, Monk, Williams, Dyer, Allen (Moore), Borini, Dobbie (Pratley), Sinclair (Serran).
Nottingham F: Camp; Gunter, Moloney, Moussi, Morgan, Chambers, McGoldrick (Earnshaw), McGugan, Tyson (Majewski), Tudgay (Boyd), Cohen.

Tuesday, 17 May 2011
Cardiff C (0) 0
Reading (2) 3 *(Long 28, 45 (pen), McAnuff 84)*   24,081
Cardiff C: Bywater; McNaughton, Samuel (Matthews), Olofinjana, Blake, Keinan, Whittingham, Emmanuel-Thomas (Koumas), Bothroyd, Chopra (Parkin), Burke.
Reading: Federici; Griffin, Harte, Karacan (Tabb), Mills, Khizanishvili, Cummings, Leigertwood, Long (Church), Hunt, McAnuff.

CHAMPIONSHIP FINAL (at Wembley)

Monday, 30 May 2011
Reading (0) 2 *(Allen 49 (og), Mills 57)*
Swansea C (3) 4 *(Sinclair 21 (pen), 22, 80 (pen), Dobbie 40)*   86,581
Reading: Federici; Griffin (Robson-Kanu), Harte, Karacan, Mills, Khizanishvili, Kebe, Leigertwood, Long, Hunt (Church), McAnuff.
Swansea C: De Vries; Rangel, Tate, Britton (Gower), Monk, Williams, Dyer, Allen (Moore), Borini, Dobbie (Pratley), Sinclair.
Unused substitute Tabb sent off at half-time.
Referee: P. Dowd (Staffordshire).

LEAGUE ONE FIRST LEG

Saturday, 14 May 2011
Bournemouth (0) 1 *(McDermott 60)*
Huddersfield T (1) 1 *(Kilbane 22)*   9043
Bournemouth: Jalal; Wiggins, Smith, Hollands, Pearce, Cooper, McDermott (Pugh), Robinson, Ings (Williamson), Lovell (Fletcher), Feeney.
Huddersfield T: Bennett; Peltier (Hunt), Naysmith, Gudjonsson, Clarke P, Kay, Arfield, Kilbane, Afobe (Novak), Ward (Cadamarteri), Roberts.

Sunday, 15 May 2011
Milton Keynes D (0) 3 *(Powell 47, Baldock S 50, Balanta 56)*
Peterborough U (1) 2 *(Mackail-Smith 8, McCann 81 (pen))*   12,662
Milton Keynes D: Martin; Doumbe, Lewington, Clayton, MacKenzie, O'Hanlon, Gleeson■, Balanta (Ibehre), Baldock S, Powell (Marsh-Brown), Chadwick.
Peterborough U: Lewis (Jones); Little, Lee■, McCann, Zakuani (Langmead), Bennett, Mendez-Laing (Ball), Rowe, Mackail-Smith, Tomlin, Boyd.

Huddersfield Town's Lee Peltier (right) rolls past Peterborough United's George Boyd in the npower Football League One Play-Off Final at Old Trafford. Three late goals gave Posh a comfortable 3-0 victory and a quick return to the Championship. (PA Photos)

Darius Charles (right) of Stevenage tracked by Chris Robertson of Torquay United in the npower Football League Two Play-Off Final at Old Trafford. John Mousinho scored the winner to make it successive promotions for Stevenage.
(Action Images/Paul Burrows)

LEAGUE ONE SECOND LEG

Wednesday, 18 May 2011

Huddersfield T (2) 3 *(Peltier 26, Ward 45, Kay 105)*
Bournemouth (1) 3 *(Lovell 44 (pen), 63, Ings 104)* 16,444
Huddersfield T: Bennett; Hunt, Naysmith, Kay, Clarke P, Kilbane, Peltier (McCombe), Ward, Rhodes (Novak), Afobe (Lee), Roberts.
Bournemouth: Jalal; Wiggins, Smith, Hollands, Pearce■, Cooper, McDermott (Pugh), Robinson, Ings (Baudry), Lovell (Symes), Feeney.
aet; Huddersfield T won 4-2 on penalties.

Thursday, 19 May 2011

Peterborough U (1) 2 *(McCann 11, Mackail-Smith 54)*
Milton Keynes D (0) 0 11,920
Peterborough U: Jones; Little, Basey, McCann (Whelpdale), Zakuani, Bennett, Wesolowski, Rowe, Mackail-Smith, Boyd.
Milton Keynes D: Martin; Doumbe, Lewington, Clayton, MacKenzie, O'Hanlon (Guy), Gleeson, Powell (Marsh-Brown), Baldock S, Balanta, Chadwick (Ibehre).

LEAGUE ONE FINAL (at Old Trafford)

Sunday, 29 May 2011

Huddersfield T (0) 0
Peterborough U (0) 3 *(Rowe 78, Mackail-Smith 80, McCann 85)* 48,410
Huddersfield T: Bennett; Hunt, Naysmith, Kilbane, Clarke P, Kay, Peltier, Arfield (Lee), Afobe (Rhodes), Ward (Cadamarteri), Roberts.
Peterborough U: Jones; Little, Basey (Lee), McCann, Zakuani, Bennett, Wesolowski, Rowe (Whelpdale), Mackail-Smith, Tomlin (Ball), Boyd.
Referee: S. Tanner (Somerset).

LEAGUE TWO FIRST LEG

Saturday, 14 May 2011

Torquay U (2) 2 *(Zebroski 29, O'Kane 45)*
Shrewsbury T (0) 0 4130
Torquay U: Bevan; Mansell, Nicholson, Robertson, Branston, Lathrope, Tomlin (Stevens), O'Kane, Kee (Oastler), Robinson, Zebroski.
Shrewsbury T: Smith; Grandison, Sadler, Wroe, Sharps (Canavan), Cansdell-Sherriff, Wright, Davis, Harrold, Collins (Bradshaw), Taylor J (Ainsworth).

Sunday, 15 May 2011

Stevenage (2) 2 *(Long 24, Byrom 45)*
Accrington S (0) 0 4424
Stevenage: Day; Henry, Laird, Roberts, Ashton, Bostwick, Wilson, Long (Beardsley), Reid (Harrison), Charles (Murphy), Byrom.
Accrington S: Cisak; Winnard, Jacobson, Hessey, Edwards, Procter, Ryan, Craney (Putterill), Gornell, McConville, Joyce.

LEAGUE TWO SECOND LEG

Friday, 20 May 2011

Accrington S (0) 0
Stevenage (0) 1 *(Beardsley 90)* 4185
Accrington S: Cisak; Winnard, Jacobson■, Hessey, Edwards, Procter, Ryan, Craney (Turner), Gornell, McConville■, Joyce.
Stevenage: Day; Henry, Laird, Roberts, Bostwick, Wilson (Winn), Murphy, Byrom, Charles (Beardsley), Reid (Harrison), Long.

Shrewsbury T (0) 0
Torquay U (0) 0 8452
Shrewsbury T: Smith; Grandison (Collins), Sadler, Wroe, Sharps, Cansdell-Sherriff, Wright, Davis (Leslie), Harrold, Ainsworth (Bradshaw), Taylor J.
Torquay U: Bevan; Mansell, Nicholson, Robertson, Branston, Lathrope, Kee (Oastler), O'Kane, Tomlin (Macklin), Robinson (Rowe-Turner), Zebroski.

LEAGUE TWO FINAL (at Old Trafford)

Saturday, 28 May 2011

Stevenage (1) 1 *(Mousinho 41)*
Torquay U (0) 0 11,484
Stevenage: Day; Henry, Laird, Mousinho, Roberts, Bostwick, Wilson, Byrom (Murphy), Charles (Beardsley), Reid (Harrison), Long.
Torquay U: Bevan; Mansell, Nicholson (Rowe-Turner), Robertson, Branston, Lathrope (Oastler), Robinson (Stevens), O'Kane, Kee, Tomlin, Zebroski.
Referee: D. Deadman (Cambridgeshire).

LEADING GOALSCORERS 2010–11

	League	Carling Cup	FA Cup	Other	Total
BARCLAYS PREMIERSHIP					
Only goals scored in the same division are included.					
Carlos Tevez *(Manchester C)*	20	0	3	0	23
Dimitar Berbatov *(Manchester U)*	20	0	0	1	21
Robin Van Persie *(Arsenal)*	18	1	1	2	22
Darren Bent *(Aston Villa)*	17	2	1	0	20
(*Includes 8 League goals, 2 Carling Cup goals and 1 FA Cup goal for Sunderland*).					
Peter Odemwingie *(WBA)*	15	0	0	0	15
Javier Hernandez *(Manchester U)*	13	1	1	5	20
Dirk Kuyt *(Liverpool)*	13	0	0	2	15
Rafael Van der Vaart *(Tottenham H)*	13	0	0	2	15
Florent Malouda *(Chelsea)*	13	0	0	1	14
Dudley Campbell *(Blackpool)*	13	0	0	0	13
Andy Carroll *(Liverpool)*	13	0	0	0	13
(*Includes 11 League goals for Newcastle U*).					
Charlie Adam *(Blackpool)*	12	1	0	0	13
Clint Dempsey *(Fulham)*	12	1	0	0	13
Kevin Nolan *(Newcastle U)*	12	0	0	0	12
NPOWER CHAMPIONSHIP					
Danny Graham *(Watford)*	23	2	1	0	26
Shane Long *(Reading)*	21	0	2	2	25
Grant Holt *(Norwich C)*	21	2	0	0	23
Scott Sinclair *(Swansea C)*	19	4	1	3	27
Luciano Becchio *(Leeds U)*	19	1	0	0	20
Adel Taarabt *(QPR)*	19	0	0	0	19
Jay Bothroyd *(Cardiff C)*	18	2	0	0	20
Max Gradel *(Leeds U)*	18	0	0	0	18
Steve Morison *(Millwall)*	15	2	0	0	17
Andy King *(Leicester C)*	15	0	1	0	16
Billy Sharp *(Doncaster R)*	15	0	1	0	16
Jay Rodriguez *(Burnley)*	14	0	1	0	15
NPOWER LEAGUE 1					
Craig Mackail-Smith *(Peterborough U)*	27	3	2	3	35
Glenn Murray *(Brighton & HA)*	22	0	0	0	22
Bradley Wright Phillips *(Charlton Ath)*	22	0	0	0	22
(*Includes 13 league goals for Plymouth Arg*)					
Richard Lambert *(Southampton)*	21	0	0	0	21
Ashley Barnes *(Brighton & HA)*	18	0	2	0	20
Gary Jones *(Rochdale)*	17	2	0	0	19
Will Hoskins *(Bristol R)*	17	0	1	2	20
Jamie Cureton *(Exeter C)*	17	0	0	3	20
Jordan Rhodes *(Huddersfield T)*	16	1	1	4	22
George Boyd *(Peterborough U)*	15	2	0	0	17
Dean Bowditch *(Yeovil T)*	15	0	0	0	15
Lee Barnard *(Southampton)*	14	0	1	0	15
NPOWER LEAGUE 2					
Clayton Donaldson *(Crewe Alex)*	28	0	0	1	29
Ryan Lowe *(Bury)*	27	0	1	0	28
Cody McDonald *(Gillingham on loan from Norwich C).*	25	0	0	0	25
Craig Davies *(Chesterfield)*	23	0	1	1	25
Adam Le Fondre *(Rotherham U)*	23	0	0	1	24
Barry Corr *(Southend U)*	18	1	2	0	21
Wesley Thomas *(Cheltenham T)*	18	0	1	0	19
Shaun Miller *(Crewe Alex)*	18	0	0	0	18
Jack Lester *(Chesterfield)*	17	0	0	0	17
Marc Richards *(Port Vale)*	16	0	2	2	20
Shaun Harrad *(Northampton T)*	16	1	2	0	19
(*Includes 10 league goals, 1 Carling Cup and 2 FA Cup for Burton Alb*)					
James Constable *(Oxford U)*	15	2	0	0	17
Ashley Grimes *(Lincoln C on loan from Millwall).*	15	0	2	0	17
Jake Robinson *(Shrewbury T)*	15	1	0	0	16
(*Includes 7 league goals on loan to Torquay U*)					
Danny Whitaker *(Chesterfield)*	15	0	0	0	15

Other matches consist of European games, J Paint Trophy, Community Shield and Football League play-offs. Players listed in order of League goals total.

REVIEW OF THE SEASON

Quantity not quality seems to have been the general appraisal of the 2010–11 season that witnessed Manchester United becoming the most successful championship-winning team in the history of English football when they won their 19th title, twelve of which had been achieved in the Premier League. Yet surely this quantification smacks of unfair criticism.

Overall more goals were scored in the Premier League than previously with 1063 registered from 380 matches for an average of 2.80. United was unsure of its triumph until the penultimate encounter when a draw at Blackburn Rovers secured the prize and the relegation battle went to the wire when five clubs were striving to avoid the remaining two places in the drop zone on that fateful Sunday in May.

Against this there were twenty-five goalless games, while drawn affairs in general accounted for almost a third of the entire 380, as many as 111 to be exact. Are three points no longer an incentive? Yet among the four top divisions another record was set with 46 matches finishing 3-0.

Yet one of the constant problems is the unrealistic expectancy that grips those teams aiming for more than survival in the top echelon. The so-called big four became the famous five as Manchester City and Tottenham Hotspur edged into the quartet to push Liverpool down to sixth.

One might imagine second place for Chelsea was good enough but it did not save manager Carlo Ancelotti's job. Even despite Manchester City's best season in League and Cup – victory at Wembley in the FA Cup – for more than 30 years, there were those who said they should have done even better. Arsenal were even considered to have had a poor season finishing third. Tottenham probably felt fifth place was one lower than they had hoped and expected.

Everton in seventh place faced the usual Merseyside anguish of finishing below neighbours Liverpool. Not so draw specialists Fulham in eighth place and content enough it seems. Moreover with just one dismissal in the final match, their disciplinary record enabled them to reach Europe producing the fair play card. And so down the list there were varying degrees of both disappointment and satisfaction. Not that this applied at the top.

The achievement of Manchester United was based on fortress Old Trafford, the only English team from the top four divisions to have an unbeaten home record. Just West Bromwich Albion escaped with a point, amazingly also scoring twice. Away, United did not register the same level of success, drawing ten times which was more than any other Premier side.

Sir Alex Ferguson again masterminded the show. As tinker-man general he swung the changes constantly to the extent that at one stage it was stated he had switched the starting line-up 150 times in a row. Eagle-eyed anoraks would spot consecutive league games with no changes, but there was a cup-tie in between. At times Sir Alex made mistakes in selection, but fewer than anyone else and he had a stronger squad from which to choose. He called upon 29 different players in the Premier League alone. None was ever present. Javier "Chicarito" Hernandez was the discovery of the season. Disappointment was losing in the Champions League final.

As to the overall facts only 16 players appeared in every match and only two outfield players the Merseyside pairing of Leighton Baines at Everton and Martin Skrtel of Liverpool stayed on continually throughout the 3,420 minutes.

Twenty-four unbeaten Premier matches until losing at Wolverhampton in February, United stumbled in March with successive defeats at Chelsea and Liverpool but only their drawing habit kept interest alive for challengers.

Manchester United's Wayne Rooney scores the equaliser after Blackburn Rovers' Brett Emerton had opened the scoring in the Barclays Premier League at Ewood Park on the penultimate weekend of the season. The point confirmed United's record-breaking 19th overall championship and the club's 12th in Premier League terms alone.
(Action Images/Lee Smith)

Chelsea after an impressive opening bid stalled around November and December. Recovery in March revived them, but they needed to win at Old Trafford in May where most others had failed. Fernando Torres proved to be a costly disappointment. Manchester City had their best season for decades of course. The defence was pretty solid throughout and claimed more clean sheets than anyone else in the top echelon. Carlos Tevez was the Blues' only consistent marksman, finishing level on 20 goals with Dimitar Berbatov across the city at Manchester United.

Fourth placed Arsenal scored 119 goals in all competitive matches and probably made as many chances again with their often delightful approach. But there was fragility there and only three times did they win a trio of Premier games in a row. Then there was the Carling Cup defeat to Birmingham City.

Amazingly Tottenham Hotspur mirrored their North London rivals' erratic statistic of no more than three consecutive wins three times! They won only three Premier matches from mid-February. Liverpool improved substantially when Kenny Dalglish returned as manager. But they suffered 14 defeats and in Europe a dozen games yielded only 12 goals. Everton had a much better last third of the season to stay in seventh place but goals were often difficult to find and the defence carried more than its fair share.

Mark Hughes surprisingly quit Fulham at the season's end. There was a managerial change at Aston Villa, too, but Gerard Houllier, who came back to take over from Martin O'Neill, retired on medical advice. Because the danger zone often involved half of the league, Aston Villa did finish ninth but owed it to four wins in the last eight.

Sunderland was put at risk after just one point accruing from a possible 27 until a mid-April mini-revival, while a change at the helm at West Bromwich Albion with Roy Hodgson coming from Liverpool restored the stability that had existed early in the season.

Newcastle United, concerned in a managerial switch, too, with Alan Pardew taking over, were as high as fifth early November after defeating Arsenal 1-0 at The Emirates. The team was also four down to the Gunners in the return before a second half recovery snatched a draw. Stoke City, who finished beaten FA Cup finalists, only slipped from eighth in the last two games and could consider it a fair season in their circumstances.

Bolton Wanderers slumped alarmingly from the top six in December and lost their last five in a row, while Blackburn Rovers, who were guided by Steve Kean in the last half of the season, found problems lasted until the final day when they held off a comeback by Wolves. Only once did they manage two wins in succession.

Wigan Athletic, bottom for several weeks to early April, won at Stoke on the last Sunday to escape. It was their eighth point out of 12. Wolverhampton Wanderers, survived despite demotion having appeared the likely outcome after accruing just nine points from the first 14 games.

Sadly for West Ham United the curtain had descended weeks before. Only two points were derived from the last possible 27. Incredibly the Hammers had inflicted Manchester United's worst defeat in the Carling Cup. Both Blackpool and Birmingham were involved in the see-saw finale. Blackpool even led at Old Trafford before defeat, City sucked in during the last six games fell, too, though had the Carling Cup and a Europa League place.

Despite Queens Park Rangers appearing to run away with the Football League Championship – an unbeaten 19-game start – they only finished four points ahead of Norwich City. The last tweet Canaries, renowned for crucial late goals, matched Rangers' away record. So much for the automatic places, the play-offs produced a different story.

Swansea City prevailed to accompany these two clubs after an uncertain opening month. Bursts of form from then on and finished with three straight wins. Nottingham Forest and Reading were then beaten in the play-offs. Cardiff City

Cesc Fabregas (right) of Arsenal holds off Paulo Ferreira of Chelsea in his team's 3-1 win at the Emirates Stadium in the Barclays Premier League. (Action Images/Tony O'Brien)

Tottenham Hotspur's Luka Modric dashes between Yaya Toure (left) and Micah Richards of Manchester City in the Barclays Premier League in May. In an ironic twist of fate, City's place in the Champions League was secured by Peter Crouch who put through his own goal at the same end as his winning effort which saw Spurs through to the Champions League last season. (Action Images/Paul Thomas)

headed the table briefly in mid-November yet ironically had their best spell of eight without a win to the end of April then drifted out of automatic placing. Reading beat them in the play-offs and had their best run from mid-February with 13 unbeaten. Forest kept in contact on the back of a lengthy home run and four straight wins at the death.

Once again Leeds United failed. Twelve undefeated was their best but significantly half were drawn. Burnley dropped from a promising position early March managing only three more wins. Millwall had good spells of nine and six without loss but only two successes in the last six. Leicester City's ambition was boosted until mid-February, thence just isolated wins.

Hull City – 17 draws as had Reading – never threatened beyond the fringe and nine without loss was their best. Middlesbrough with a disastrous first three months hauled themselves to mid-table. Ipswich Town's season was virtually decided by early December when just two wins came from 11 matches. Watford had six wins in a row at the turn of the year but were unable to top that sequence.

Bristol City extracted themselves from the bottom places in the second half of the season. Portsmouth, too, recovered from just two points from a possible 21 at the beginning despite only four points from the last eight games.

For Barnsley picking up wins here and there in the second half of the campaign kept them safe but Coventry City slumped with ten games without a win to early February. Derby County, too, fourth in November almost hit free-fall before snatching enough points.

Crystal Palace hovered dangerously close to the drop zone most of the season yet with only two wins from the last eight proved enough for safety. Doncaster Rovers mid-table in January grabbed only two more wins yet survived.

The relegated trio was Preston North End, Sheffield United and Scunthorpe United. Preston with three wins into April showed a too late glimmer after only six points from 14 games. Sheffield United fared even worse with four from the same number into March. Goals were a problem for Scunthorpe just ten in 18 games into April.

Brighton & Hove Albion, never headed from September, hit top gear in March dropping just two points from a possible 36 and had made it by mid-April. Southampton climbed steadily from a poor opening and lost only two of the last 21 to accompany them. Huddersfield Town missed out despite remaining undefeated throughout 2011 until losing in the play-off final to Peterborough United.

Prolifically scoring Posh stayed consistently in fourth place most of the season and only failed to find the net on four occasions. The other unlucky pairing in the play-offs were Milton Keynes Dons and Bournemouth. The Dons stronger in the last third of the season always appeared play-off material from then on and pushed Posh in the play-offs, too.

Bournemouth appeared primed for automatic promotion until early March, lost six matches and then slipped out to Huddersfield on penalties in the play-off. Leyton Orient deceivingly looked similar candidates with 14 unbeaten but Exeter City's best sequence of seven wins from eight was also too late.

One good run for Rochdale of 11 without loss to the end of February needed to be repeated but did not happen. Colchester United third in November drifted gradually away and one point from 21 into February settled mid-table for Brentford.

Fourth place during November was the pinnacle for Carlisle United but they did win the Johnstone's Paint Trophy at the expense of Brentford. Charlton Athletic appeared well fixed in second place in November, too, but 11 without a win to the end of March caused the damage.

At the half-way stage Yeovil Town seemed likely relegation material until a better finish improved matters. Sheffield Wednesday were able to arrest a slide that had yielded only four points from ten games and Hartlepool United's inconsistency in scoring often put them at risk in the bottom third of the table.

Oldham Athletic, also on 17 drawn affairs, suffered even more in attack. In the last 19 matches they scraped only ten goals yet scratched out 13 points! Tranmere Rovers unimpressive first half of the campaign needed four wins from the last seven games. But it was a close-run thing for Notts County who also suffered from a lack of goals. Nine successive defeats, too, required a remedy and two wins and two draws in the last five saved them.

Walsall, firmly cellar dwellers in January, did succeed with enough points here and there to avoid the fate of Dagenham & Redbridge, Bristol Rovers, Plymouth Argyle and Swindon Town.

Six without defeat was Dagenham's best but the dark clouds were never far off. Bristol Rovers slipped away after a better run of four without defeat into April and the deduction of points for Plymouth sealed their fate in February when in mid-table. Swindon looked doomed from mid-January and only two wins were derived from the last 22 fixtures.

League Two champions Chesterfield's position seemed likely from October. Runs of seven and ten without loss kept them buoyant. Bury had six successive wins from April after looking play-off material anyway. Joining these two clubs were Wycombe Wanderers in the automatic slot, staying undefeated in the last ten matches.

Shrewsbury Town missed out only by a point, one defeat in the last ten of a consistent season. But Torquay United beat them in the play-offs before they lost in turn to Stevenage. For Torquay 11 games undefeated secured its seventh place prior to the last match.

Stevenage beat Accrington Stanley in the play-off semi-final. Six wins in a row into April represented their best sequence at a crucial time. For Accrington it was scant reward for 13 games without defeat.

There was similar disappointment for Gillingham especially after 16 without loss, albeit with ten draws to mid-April. Rotherham United, second in January, only subsequently had a couple of wins in a row. Goals were plentiful at both ends in games involving Crewe Alexandra and the team was still in a play-off berth in February.

Neighbours Port Vale, second in early December, won only two games from early March while Oxford United's six wins out of seven to late January was their best. For Southend United the middle part of the season produced their most encouraging results and Aldershot Town steadied the ship from March.

Macclesfield Town survived a ten-game spell without a win mid-season and Northampton Town, as with Stanley and the Shots an amazing 19 draws, pulled themselves from danger after 15 matches lacking a win staying unbeaten in the last five. Even though Cheltenham Town were in a play-off situation in January only spasmodic wins kept them from danger.

Bradford City flirted with the drop zone and never registered more than two wins in succession, while the peril facing Burton Albion was a stack of games in hand needing ten games in a month to produce enough points. Morecambe remained in the last third, their worst period nine games lacking a victory.

Deduction of points menaced Hereford United at a crucial time but only one reverse came from the last eight games. However, the escape artists proved to be Barnet scarcely out of danger but clawing four wins from the last seven fixtures.

Dramatic falling Lincoln City slithered into the Conference having taken just two points from the last 11 games. They were joined by Stockport County never out of the last two places ironically after losing to Lincoln in January. Up from the Blue Square Premier: well heeled Crawley Town and a re-tread restoration of AFC Wimbledon.

Swansea City's Scott Sinclair (bottom) celebrates after scoring his team's second goal in the 4-2 win over Reading at Wembley in the npower Football League Championship Play-Off Final. (PA Photos)

THE FA CHARITY SHIELD WINNERS 1908–2010

1908	Manchester U v QPR	4-0 after 1-1 draw	1967	Manchester U v Tottenham H		3-3*
1909	Newcastle U v Northampton T	2-0	1968	Manchester C v WBA		6-1
1910	Brighton v Aston Villa	1-0	1969	Leeds U v Manchester C		2-1
1911	Manchester U v Swindon T	8-4	1970	Everton v Chelsea		2-1
1912	Blackburn R v QPR	2-1	1971	Leicester C v Liverpool		1-0
1913	Professionals v Amateurs	7-2	1972	Manchester C v Aston Villa		1-0
1920	WBA v Tottenham H	2-0	1973	Burnley v Manchester C		1-0
1921	Tottenham H v Burnley	2-0	1974	Liverpool† v Leeds U		1-1
1922	Huddersfield T v Liverpool	1-0	1975	Derby Co v West Ham U		2-0
1923	Professionals v Amateurs	2-0	1976	Liverpool v Southampton		1-0
1924	Professionals v Amateurs	3-1	1977	Liverpool v Manchester U		0-0*
1925	Amateurs v Professionals	6-1	1978	Nottingham F v Ipswich T		5-0
1926	Amateurs v Professionals	6-3	1979	Liverpool v Arsenal		3-1
1927	Cardiff C v Corinthians	2-1	1980	Liverpool v West Ham U		1-0
1928	Everton v Blackburn R	2-1	1981	Aston Villa v Tottenham H		2-2*
1929	Professionals v Amateurs	3-0	1982	Liverpool v Tottenham H		1-0
1930	Arsenal v Sheffield W	2-1	1983	Manchester U v Liverpool		2-0
1931	Arsenal v WBA	1-0	1984	Everton v Liverpool		1-0
1932	Everton v Newcastle U	5-3	1985	Everton v Manchester U		2-0
1933	Arsenal v Everton	3-0	1986	Everton v Liverpool		1-1*
1934	Arsenal v Manchester C	4-0	1987	Everton v Coventry C		1-0
1935	Sheffield W v Arsenal	1-0	1988	Liverpool v Wimbledon		2-1
1936	Sunderland v Arsenal	2-1	1989	Liverpool v Arsenal		1-0
1937	Manchester C v Sunderland	2-0	1990	Liverpool v Manchester U		1-1*
1938	Arsenal v Preston NE	2-1	1991	Arsenal v Tottenham H		0-0*
1948	Arsenal v Manchester U	4-3	1992	Leeds U v Liverpool		4-3
1949	Portsmouth v Wolverhampton W	1-1*	1993	Manchester U† v Arsenal		1-1
1950	World Cup Team v Canadian Touring Team	4-2	1994	Manchester U v Blackburn R		2-0
1951	Tottenham H v Newcastle U	2-1	1995	Everton v Blackburn R		1-0
1952	Manchester U v Newcastle U	4-2	1996	Manchester U v Newcastle U		4-0
1953	Arsenal v Blackpool	3-1	1997	Manchester U† v Chelsea		1-1
1954	Wolverhampton W v WBA	4-4*	1998	Arsenal v Manchester U		3-0
1955	Chelsea v Newcastle U	3-0	1999	Arsenal v Manchester U		2-1
1956	Manchester U v Manchester C	1-0	2000	Chelsea v Manchester U		2-0
1957	Manchester U v Aston Villa	4-0	2001	Liverpool v Manchester U		2-1
1958	Bolton W v Wolverhampton W	4-1	2002	Arsenal v Liverpool		1-0
1959	Wolverhampton W v Nottingham F	3-1	2003	Manchester U† v Arsenal		1-1
1960	Burnley v Wolverhampton W	2-2*	2004	Arsenal v Manchester U		3-1
1961	Tottenham H v FA XI	3-2	2005	Chelsea v Arsenal		2-1
1962	Tottenham H v Ipswich T	5-1	2006	Liverpool v Chelsea		2-1
1963	Everton v Manchester U	4-0	2007	Manchester U† v Chelsea		1-1
1964	Liverpool v West Ham U	2-2*	2008	Manchester U† v Portsmouth		0-0
1965	Manchester U v Liverpool	2-2*	2009	Chelsea† v Manchester U		2-2
1966	Liverpool v Everton	1-0	2010	Manchester U v Chelsea		3-1

Each club retained shield for six months.   † *Won on penalties.*

THE FA COMMUNITY SHIELD 2010

Chelsea (0) 1, Manchester U (1) 3

At Wembley Stadium, 8 August 2010, attendance 84,623

Chelsea: Hilario; Paulo Ferreira (Zhirkov 79), Cole (Bruma 79), Mikel (Drogba 60), Terry, Ivanovic, Essien, Lampard, Anelka (Sturridge 61), Kalou, Malouda (Benayoun 73).
Scorer: Kalou 83.

Manchester United: Van der Sar; O'Shea, Fabio (Smalling 71), Carrick (Giggs 79), Evans J, Vidic, Valencia, Scholes (Fletcher 79), Owen (Nani 46), Rooney (Berbatov 46), Park (Hernandez 46).
Scorers: Valencia 41, Hernandez 76, Berbatov 90.

Referee: A. Marriner (West Midlands).

ACCRINGTON STANLEY FL Championship 2

FOUNDATION

Accrington Football Club, founder members of the Football League in 1888, were not connected with Accrington Stanley. In fact both clubs ran concurrently between 1891 when Stanley were formed and 1895 when Accrington FC folded. Actually Stanley Villa was the original name, those responsible for forming the club living in Stanley Street and using the Stanley Arms as their meeting place. They became Accrington Stanley in 1893. In 1894–95 they joined the Accrington & District League, playing at Moorhead Park. Subsequently they played in the North-East Lancashire Combination and the Lancashire Combination before becoming founder members of the Third Division (North) in 1921, two years after moving to Peel Park. In 1962 they resigned from the Football League, were wound up, reformed 1963, disbanded in 1966 only to restart as Accrington Stanley (1968), returning to the Lancashire Combination in 1970.

The Fraser Eagle Stadium, Livingstone Road, Accrington, Lancashire BB5 5BX.

Telephone: (0871) 434 1968.

Ticket Office: (01254) 356 950/(01254) 336 954.

Fax: (01254) 356 951.

Website: www.accringtonstanley.co.uk

Email: info@accringtonstanley.co.uk

Ground Capacity: 5,057.

Record Attendance: 13,181 v Hull C, Division 3 (N), 28 September 1948 (at Peel Park). 4,368 v Colchester U, FA Cup 1st rd, 3 January 2004 (at Fraser Eagle Stadium – Crown Inn).

Pitch Measurements: 111yd × 72yd.

Chairman: Ilyas Khan.

President: Peter Marsden.

Managing Director: David O'Neill.

Secretary: Hannah Bailey.

Manager: John Coleman.

Assistant Manager: Jimmy Bell.

Physio: Joe Hinnigan.

Club Nickname: 'Reds'.

Colours: All red. *Change Colours:* All yellow.

Year Formed: 1891, reformed 1968.

HONOURS

Football League – Division 3 (N): *Runners-up* 1954–55, 1957–58.

Conference: *Champions* 2005–06.

FA Cup: 4th rd 1927, 1937, 1959, 2010.

Football League Cup: never past 2nd rd.

Northern Premier League: *Champions* 2002–03.

Northern League – Division 1: *Champions* 1999–2000.

North West Counties: *Runners-up* 1986–87.

Cheshire County League – Division 2: *Champions* 1980–81; *Runners-up* 1979–80.

Lancashire Combination: *Champions* 1973–74, 1977–78; *Runners-up* 1971–72, 1975–76.

Lancashire Combination Cup: *Winners* 1971–72, 1972–73, 1973–74, 1976–77.

Turned Professional: 1919.

Grounds: 1891, Moorhead Park; 1897, Bell's Ground; 1919, Peel Park; 1970, Crown Inn.

First Football League Game: 27 August 1921, Division 3 (N), v Rochdale (a) L 3-6 – Tattersall; Newton, Baines, Crawshaw, Popplewell, Burkinshaw, Oxley, Makin, Green (1), Hosker (2), Hartles.

sky SPORTS FACT FILE

For the first floodlight game at Peel Park on 15 February 1954, Accrington Stanley beat East Fife 4-1 in a friendly. Les Cocker scored twice, David Musgrave and Charlie Sneddon one each. Both Cocker and Sneddon had received benefits at the club in 1959.

Record League Victory: 8–0 v New Brighton, Division 3 (N), 17 March 1934 – Maidment; Armstrong (pen), Price, Dodds, Crawshaw, McCulloch, Wyper, Lennox (2), Cheetham (4), Leedham (1), Watson.

Record Cup Victory: 7–0 v Spennymoor U, FA Cup 2nd rd, 8 December 1938 – Tootill; Armstrong, Whittaker, Latham, Curran, Lee, Parry (2), Chadwick, Jepson (3), McLoughlin (2), Barclay.

Record Defeat: 9–1 v Lincoln C, Division 3 (N), 3 March 1951.

Most League Points (2 for a win): 61, Division 3 (N), 1954–55.

Most League Points (3 for a win): 73, FL 2, 2010–11.

Most League Goals: 96, Division 3 (N), 1954–55.

Highest League Scorer in Season: George Stewart, 35, Division 3 (N), 1955–56; George Hudson, 35, Division 4, 1960–61.

Most League Goals in Total Aggregate: George Stewart, 136, 1954–58.

Most League Goals in One Match: 5, Billy Harker v Gateshead, Division 3 (N), 16 November 1935; George Stewart v Gateshead, Division 3 (N), 27 November 1954.

Most Capped Player: Romuald Boco, 19 (42), Benin.

Most League Appearances: Jim Armstrong, 260, 1927–34.

Youngest League Player: Ian Gibson, 15 years 358 days, v Norwich C, 23 March 1959.

Record Transfer Fee Received: £250,000 (including sell-on from Blackpool 2001) for Brett Ormerod, March 1997.

Record Transfer Fee Paid: £85,000 to Swansea C for Ian Craney, January 2008.

Football League Record: 1921 Original Member of Division 3 (N); 1958–60 Division 3; 1960–62 Division 4; 2006– FL 2.

MANAGERS

William Cronshaw *c.*1894
John Haworth 1897–1910
Johnson Haworth *c.*1916
Sam Pilkingson 1919–24
   (*Tommy Booth p-m 1923–24*)
Ernie Blackburn 1924–32
Amos Wade 1932–35
John Hacking 1935–49
Jimmy Porter 1949–51
Walter Crook 1951–53
Walter Galbraith 1953–58
George Eastham snr 1958–59
Harold Bodle 1959–60
James Harrower 1960–61
Harold Mather 1962–63
Jimmy Hinksman 1963–64
Terry Neville 1964–65
Ian Bryson 1965
Danny Parker 1965–66
Gerry Keenan
Gary Pierce
Dave Thornley
Phil Staley
Eric Whalley
Stan Allen 1995–96
Tony Greenwood 1996–98
Billy Rodaway 1998
Wayne Harrison 1998–99
John Coleman May 1999–

LATEST SEQUENCES

Longest Sequence of League Wins: 7, 27.12.1954 – 5.2.1955.

Longest Sequence of League Defeats: 9, 8.3.1030 – 21.4.1930.

Longest Sequence of League Draws: 4, 10.9.1927 – 27.9.1927.

Longest Sequence of Unbeaten League Matches: 13, 15.3.2011 onwards.

Longest Sequence Without a League Win: 18, 17.9.1938 – 31.12.1938.

Successive Scoring Runs: 22 from 14.11.1936.

Successive Non-scoring Runs: 5 from 15.3.1930.

TEN YEAR LEAGUE RECORD

		P	W	D	L	F	A	Pts	Pos
2001-02	U Pr	44	21	9	14	89	64	72	6
2002-03	U Pr	44	30	10	4	97	44	100	1
2003-04	Conf	42	15	13	14	68	61	58	10
2004-05	Conf	42	18	11	13	72	58	65	10
2005-06	Conf	42	28	7	7	76	45	91	1
2006-07	FL 2	46	13	11	22	70	81	50	20
2007-08	FL 2	46	16	3	27	49	83	51	17
2008-09	FL 2	46	13	11	22	42	59	50	16
2009-10	FL 2	46	18	7	21	62	74	61	15
2010-11	FL 2	46	18	19	9	73	55	73	5

DID YOU KNOW ?

Goalkeeper Alf Tootill was turned down by Accrington Stanley, returned to his local club Ramsbottom United. Stanley thought again, signed him in 1927 and subsequently launched him on a long career with Wolverhampton Wanderers, Fulham and Crystal Palace.

ACCRINGTON STANLEY 2010–11 LEAGUE RECORD

Match No.	Date	Venue	Opponents	Result	H/T Score	Lg Pos.	Goalscorers	Attendance
1	Aug 7	H	Aldershot T	D	0-0	0-0	—	1624
2	14	A	Northampton T	D	0-0	0-0	14	4042
3	21	H	Macclesfield T	W	3-0	2-0	6	McConville 3 [29, 38, 72]	1371
4	28	A	Oxford U	D	0-0	0-0	7		6428
5	Sept 4	H	Wycombe W	D	1-1	0-0	8	Boulding [90]	1610
6	11	A	Torquay U	D	0-0	0-0	10		2598
7	17	H	Lincoln C	W	3-0	2-0	—	McConville [16], Gornell 2 [19, 60]	1844
8	25	A	Port Vale	L	0-2	0-1	7		5777
9	28	A	Stockport Co	D	2-2	1-0	—	Procter [40], Gornell [76]	3584
10	Oct 2	H	Gillingham	W	7-4	3-2	6	McConville [13], Parkinson [34], Barnett [43], Edwards 2 (2 pens) [58, 62], Gornell [73], Ryan [90]	1933
11	9	A	Bury	L	0-3	0-2	9		4164
12	16	H	Rotherham U	L	2-3	1-1	12	Parkinson [9], Ryan [49]	2256
13	23	A	Hereford U	D	1-1	1-0	14	Ryan [25]	2434
14	30	H	Cheltenham T	L	2-4	0-2	17	Gornell [51], Edwards (pen) [88]	1427
15	Nov 2	A	Chesterfield	L	2-5	1-3	—	Edwards (pen) [17], Gornell [60]	6034
16	13	A	Southend U	D	1-1	1-0	17	Ryan [26]	4748
17	20	H	Stevenage	W	1-0	0-0	13	McConville [67]	1370
18	23	A	Bradford C	D	1-1	1-0	—	Edwards (pen) [21]	10,392
19	Dec 11	A	Barnet	L	0-2	0-2	18		2250
20	Jan 1	A	Morecambe	W	2-1	1-1	18	Edwards (pen) [17], Ryan [82]	2702
21	3	A	Chesterfield	D	2-2	2-0	18	McConville [10], Gornell [24]	2041
22	8	H	Bury	W	1-0	0-0	13	Jacobson [77]	2481
23	15	A	Cheltenham T	W	2-1	1-0	12	Gornell [39], Richardson [89]	2736
24	18	H	Shrewsbury T	L	1-3	0-0	—	Gornell [47]	1362
25	Feb 1	H	Morecambe	D	1-1	1-0	15	Edwards (pen) [73]	1675
26	5	A	Stevenage	D	2-2	0-1	16	Gornell [88], Procter [90]	2265
27	15	A	Rotherham U	L	0-2	0-0	—		2529
28	19	A	Wycombe W	W	2-1	1-0	17	Jacobson [43], Edwards [82]	3747
29	22	H	Crewe Alex	W	3-2	1-1	—	Barnett [12], Craney [47], McConville [75]	1356
30	26	H	Torquay U	W	1-0	0-0	13	Craney [78]	1543
31	Mar 5	A	Lincoln C	D	0-0	0-0	14		2868
32	8	H	Stockport Co	W	3-0	3-0	—	Hessey [28], Edwards 2 (2 pens) [35, 42]	1831
33	12	A	Gillingham	L	1-3	1-2	13	McConville [14]	5299
34	15	H	Burton Alb	W	3-1	1-0	—	Edwards [24], Craney [48], Procter [67]	1445
35	19	H	Port Vale	W	3-0	1-0	11	McConville [43], Craney [86], Procter [90]	2413
36	22	A	Crewe Alex	D	0-0	0-0	—		3701
37	26	A	Aldershot T	D	1-1	1-0	—	Boulding [17]	2555
38	30	H	Hereford U	W	4-0	3-0	—	Gornell 2 [16, 56], Ryan [43], McConville [45]	1632
39	Apr 2	H	Northampton T	W	3-1	3-0	8	Craney 2 [16, 27], McConville [35]	1876
40	5	H	Southend U	W	3-1	1-0	—	Craney [10], Gornell [80], Edwards (pen) [84]	2222
41	8	A	Macclesfield T	D	2-2	0-1	—	Procter [73], Edwards (pen) [79]	1674
42	16	A	Oxford U	D	0-0	0-0	8		2066
43	23	H	Bradford C	W	3-0	3-0	5	Joyce [9], Procter [16], McConville [45]	2815
44	25	A	Shrewsbury T	D	0-0	0-0	5		7038
45	30	H	Barnet	W	3-1	1-1	5	Ryan 3 [4, 56, 66]	2764
46	May 7	A	Burton Alb	D	1-1	0-0	5	Winnard [84]	3491

Final League Position: 5

GOALSCORERS

League (73): Edwards 13 (11 pens), Gornell 13, McConville 13, Ryan 9, Craney 7, Procter 6, Barnett 2, Boulding 2, Jacobson 2, Parkinson 2, Hessey 1, Joyce 1, Richardson 1, Winnard 1.
Carling Cup (4): Hessey 1, Lindfield 1, Putterill 1, Turner 1.
FA Cup (3): Putterill 2, Ryan 1.
J Paint Trophy (1): Putterill 1.
Play-Offs (0).

Dunbavin I 25	Bateson J 12	Winnard D 45	Hessey S 40 + 1	Edwards P 44	Procter A 42 + 1	Ryan J 45 + 1	Barnett C 31 + 9	McConville S 37 + 6	Boulding R 6 + 9	Putterill R 11 + 13	Parkinson A 10 + 8	Turner C — + 13	Lindfield C 2 + 14	Joyce L 24 + 3	Owens A — + 3	Gornell T 40	Richardson L 3 + 8	Murphy P 5 + 8	Long K 11 + 4	Smyth T 3 + 1	Cisak A 21	Craney I 22	Jacobson J 26	Burton A 1	Match No.
1	2	3	4	5	6	7	8	9^1	10^2	11	12	13													1
1	2	3	4	5	6	7	8^3	9^2		11^1	12	13		10	14										2
1	2	3	4^3	5	6	7	8^2	9	10^1	11	12	13	14												3
1	2	3	4	5	6	7	8	9^2		11^1	12	13				10									4
1	2^1	3	4	5	6	7	8	9	13	11^2	12					10									5
1	2	3	4	5	6	7	8	9		11						10									6
1	2	3	4	5	6	7^2	8^3	9^1		11	12					10	13	14							7
1	2	3	4	5	6	7^2	8	9		11^1	12	13				10									8
1	2	3	4	5	6	7	8	9^1		11^2	12		14			10^3	13								9
1	2	3	4	5	6	7	8	9^1		11^2	12	13				10^3	14								10
1	2^1	3	4	5	6^4	7	8	9^1		11^2	12	13				10									11
1		3	4	2		7	8^3	9^1	10^2	14	11		13	6				5	12						12
		3	4	5		7^2	8	12		11	13			6		9	10^1			2	1				13
	2		4	5		7	8^2	9		11	12	13		6		10				3	1				14
	2	3		5	6	7	8^2	9			12		13			10		11^1	4		1				15
1		3	4		6	7	12	9^2		11						8^1	13	10		2^4	5				16
1		3	4	2	6	7		9^2		11^1	12					8	13	10			5				17
1		3	4	2	6	7^2	8^3	9^1		11	12			13		10	14				5				18
1		3	4	2	6	7	8^2			13	12			9				5				10	11^1		19
1	2			5	6	7^2	8	9			12					10	13		4			11^1	3		20
1	2			5	6	7	8	9^1			12					10			4			11	3		21
1	2			5	6	7	8	9		11^1						10	12		4				3		22
1	2	12		5	6	7	8	9^2	14	11^2						10	13		4^1				3		23
1			4	5^1	6	7	8	9^1	14	11^2	12					10	13	2					3		24
1	2		4	5	6	7	8	9^2		11^1	12					10	3						3		25
1	2		4	5	6	11^1	8			13	12		14			9	7^2					10	3^3		26
1	3		4	5	6	7	8^1	12		13				11		9						10^2	2		27
	2	4	5	6	7	7^1	8	12		11	9	13									1	10^2	3		28
	2	4	5	6	7	8^2	12			11	9	13									1	10^1	3		29
	2	4	5	6	7^3	8^1	12		13	11	9	14									1	10^2	3		30
	2	4	5	6	7^2	8^1	12		13	11	9										1	10	3		31
	2	4	5	6	7^1		10^3		13	14	12	11	9								1	8^2	3		32
	2	4	5	6	7^1		9			12	11	10									1	8	3		33
	2	4	5	6	7		9^1	14		13	11^{12}	10	12								1	8^3	3		34
	2	4	5	6	7	12	9^1			11	10										1	8^2	3		35
	2	4	5	6	7	13	9	12		11	10^1										1	8^2	3		36
	2	4	5	6	7	10	9^1			12	11										1	8	3		37
	2	4	5	6^2	7	12	10			11	9	13	14								1	8	3^3		38
	2	4^1	5	6	7^2	13	10			11	9	12									1	8	3		39
	2	4	5	6	7^3	12	10	14		11^2	9	13									1	8^1	3		40
	2	4	5	6	7	10^1				11	9	12									1	8	3		41
	2	4	5	6	7	13	10^1	12		11	9										1	8	3^2		42
	2	4	5	6	7^3	12	10^2	14		13	11	9									1	8^1	3		43
	2	4	5	6	7^2	13	10^1	14		12	11	9^3									1	8^2	3		44
	2	4^1	5	6	7^2	8	10			11	9	13	12								1		3		45
1	2			13	12	8^2		9^3	11		14	10						3	4	5^1	6			7	46

FA Cup

First Round	Oldham Ath	(h)	3-2
Second Round	Port Vale	(a)	0-1

Carling Cup

First Round	Doncaster	(a)	2-1
Second Round	Newcastle U	(h)	2-3

J Paint Trophy

First Round	Tranmere R	(a)	1-1

Play-Offs

Semi-Final	Stevenage	(a)	0-2
		(h)	0-1

AFC WIMBLEDON   FL Championship 2

FOUNDATION

While the history of AFC Wimbledon is straightforward since it was a new club formed in 2002, there were in effect two clubs operating for two years with Wimbledon connections. The other club was MK Dons, of course. In August 2001, the Football League had rejected the existing Wimbledon's application to move to Milton Keynes. In May 2002, they rejected local sites and were given permission to move by an independent commission set up by the Football League. AFC Wimbledon was founded in the summer of 2002 and held its first trials on Wimbledon Common. In subsequent years, there was considerable debate over the rightful home of the trophies obtained by the former Wimbledon football club. In October 2006, an agreement was reached between Milton Keynes Dons FC, its Supporters Association, the Wimbledon Independent Supporters Association and the Football Supporters Federation to transfer such trophies and honours to the London Borough of Merton.

The Cherry Red Records Fans' Stadium, Kingsmeadow, Jack Goodchild Way, 422a Kingston Road, Kingston-upon-Thames, Surrey KT1 3PB.

Telephone: (0208) 547 3528.

Fax: (0808) 2800 816.

Website: www.afcwimbledon.co.uk

Email: info@afcwimbledon.co.uk

Ground Capacity: 5,194 (1,265 seated).

Record Attendance: 4,722 v St Albans C, Blue Square Premier, 25 April 2009.

Chairman: Erik Samuelson.

Secretary: David Charles.

Manager: Terry Brown.

Assistant Manager: Stuart Cash.

Coach: Simon Bassey.

Physio: Mike Rayner.

Club Nickname: "The Dons".

Colours: All blue with yellow trim.

Change Colours: All yellow with blue sleeves and blue trim.

MANAGERS

Terry Eames 2002–04
Nicky English *(Caretaker)* 2004
Dave Anderson 2004–07
Terry Brown 2007–

sky SPORTS FACT FILE

AFC Wimbledon held extensive trials for any interested players wishing to be considered for the new club in the summer of 2002 and played their first pre-season friendly against Sutton United, the match attracting an encouragingly large attendance of 4657.

Year Formed: 2002.

Turned Professional: 2002.

Record League Victory: 9-0 v Slough T, Isthmian Premier League 31 March 2007.

Record Defeat: 5-0 v York C, Blue Square Premier, 7 April 2010.

Most League Points (3 for a win): 130, Combined Counties League 2003-04.

Most League Goals: 180, Combined Counties League, 2003-04.

Highest League Scorer in Season: Kevin Cooper, 53, 2003-04.

Most League Goals in Total Aggregate: Kevin Cooper, 107, 2002-04.

Most Appearances: Anthony Howard, 189, 2004-08.

LATEST SEQUENCES

Inherited records from Wimbledon

Longest Sequence of League wins: 7, 9.4.1983 – 7.5.1983.

Longest Sequence of League Defeats: 11, 10.1.2004 – 27.3.2004.

Longest Sequence of League Draws: 4, 3.3.1984 – 17.3.1984.

Longest Sequence of Unbeaten League Matches: 22, 15.1.1983 – 14.5.1983.

Longest Sequence Without a League Win: 14, 23.2.1980 – 15.4.1980.

Successive Scoring Runs: 23 from 18.2.1984 – 22.9.1984.

Successive Non-scoring Runs: 7 from 7.2.2004 – 24.3.2004.

HONOURS

Blue Square Conference: *Runners-up* 2010–11.

Blue Square South: *Champions* 2008–09.

Isthmian League – Premier Division: *Play-off Winners* 2007–08. **Division 1:** *Champions* 2004–05.

Combined Counties League: *Champions* 2003–04.

Combined Counties League: *Challenge Cup Winners* 2004.

Surrey Senior Cup: *Winners* 2005; *Runners-up* 2006.

Supporters Direct Cup: *Winners* 2003, 2006, 2010; *Runners-up* 2005, 2007.

Phil Ledger Memorial Cup: *Winners* 2011.

Inherited records from Wimbledon
FA Premier League: best season: 6th, 1993–94.

Football League: Division 3 – *Runners-up* 1983–84; **Division 4 –** *Champions* 1982–83.

FA Cup: *Winners* 1988.

Football League Cup: *Semi-final* 1996–97, 1998–99.

League Group Cup: *Runners-up* 1982.

Amateur Cup: *Winners* 1963; *Runners-up* 1935, 1947.

European Competitions
Intertoto Cup: 1995.

TEN YEAR LEAGUE RECORD

		P	W	D	L	F	A	Pts	Pos
2002-03	CC	46	36	3	7	125	46	111	3
2003-04	CC	46	42	4	0	180	32	130	1
2004-05	Isth DI	42	29	10	3	91	33	97	1
2005-06	Isth PR	42	22	11	9	67	36	77	4
2006-07	Isth PR	42	21	15	6	76	37	75	5
2007-08	Isth PR	42	22	9	11	81	47	75	3
2008-09	BSS	42	26	10	6	86	36	88	1
2009-10	BSP	44	18	10	16	61	47	64	8
2010-11	BSP	46	27	9	10	83	47	90	2

DID YOU KNOW ?

In a comparative short existence AFC Wimbledon has become extremely successful. Many records have been established. After 22 February 2003 and before defeat on 4 December 2004, they set a formidable UK record of remaining unbeaten in 78 league matches.

ALDERSHOT TOWN   FL Championship 2

FOUNDATION

It was through the initiative of Councillor Jack White, a local newsagent, who immediately captured the interest of the Town Clerk D. Llewellyn Griffiths, that Aldershot Town was formed in 1926. Having established a limited liability company under the chairmanship of Norman Clinton, an Aldershot resident and chairman of the Hampshire County FA, they rented the Recreation Ground from the Aldershot Borough Council. Admitted to the Southern League for 1927–28, they were elected to the Football League in 1932 but were removed from the competition in March 1992 and their record expunged. Re-formed almost immediately as Aldershot Town Football Club.

The EBB Stadium at the Recreation Ground, High Street, Aldershot GU11 1TW.

Telephone: 01252 320211.

Fax: 01252 324347.

Ticket Office: 01252 320211.

Website: www.theshots.co.uk

Ground capacity: 7,100.

Record Attendance: 19,138 v Carlisle U, FA Cup 4th rd (replay), 28 January 1970.

Pitch Measurements: 117yd × 74yd.

Chairman: Kris Machala.

Chief Executive: Peter Duffy.

Secretary: Bob Green.

Manager: Dean Holdsworth.

Assistant Manager: Matthew Bishop.

Physio: Nick Brink.

Colours: All red shirts with blue sleeves, red shorts with blue and white trim, red stockings with blue and white trim.

Change Colours: All black with red, blue and white trim.

Year Formed: 1926.

Turned Professional: 1927. *Ltd Co.:* 1927.

Previous Names: 1926, Aldershot Town; c.1937 Aldershot; 1992, Aldershot Town.

Club nickname: 'The Shots'.

Ground: 1927, Recreation Ground.

First Football League Game: 27 August 1932, Division 3 (S), v Southend U (h) L 1–2 – Robb; Wade, McDougall, Lawson, Spence, Middleton, Proud, White, Gamble, Douglas, Fishlock (1).

HONOURS

Football League: Best season: 8th, Division 3, 1973–74.

FA Cup: Best season: 5th rd, 1932–33, 5th rd replay, 1978–79.

Football League Cup: Best season: 3rd rd replay, 1984–85.

Blue Square Premier League: *Champions* 2007–08.

Conference: *Runners-up* 2003–04.

Southern League: *Champions* 1929–30; *Runners-up* 1930–31.

Football Combination Division 2: *Champions* 1930–31.

Isthmian League Division 3: *Champions* 1992–93.

Isthmian First Division Champions: 1997–98.

Isthmian League Premier Division: *Champions* 2002–03.

Hampshire Senior Cup: *Winners* 1928, 1999, 2000, 2002, 2003, 2007.

Setanta Shield: *Winners* 2008.

sky SPORTS FACT FILE

Pre-war Aldershot had the largest playing area in the Football League measuring 120 yards by 74. Currently the length has been trimmed to 117 yards. The pre-war Wembley pitch was 117 yards by 75. Oddly enough the Shots pared a yard off their width in recent times.

Record League Victory: 8–1 v Gateshead, Division 4, 13 September 1958 – Marshall; Henry, Jackson, Mundy, Price, Gough, Walters, Stepney (3), Lacey (3), Matthews (2), Tyrer.

Record Cup Victory: 7–0 v Chelmsford, FA Cup, 1st rd, 28 November 1931 – Robb; Twine, McDougall (1), Norman Wilson, Gardiner, Middleton (1), Blackbourne, Stevenson (1), Thom (3), Hopkins (1), Edgar. 7–0 v Newport (IW), FA Cup, 2nd rd, 8 December 1945 – Reynolds; Horton, Sheppard, Ray, White, Summerbee, Sinclair, Hold (1), Brooks (5), Fitzgerald, Hobbs (1). *N.B.* 11–1 v Kingstonian, FA Cup, 4th qual rd, 16 November 1929 – Mobbs; Thomas, McDougall, Norman Wilson, Gardiner, Middleton (2), Young (1), Common (1), Horton (2), Hopkins (3), Edgar (2).

Record Defeat: – 1–10 v Southend U, Leyland Daf Cup, Pr rd, 6 November 1990.

Most League Points: (2 for a win): 57, Division 4, 1978–79.

Most League Points (3 for a win): 75, Division 4, 1983–84.

Most League Goals: 83, Division 4, 1963–64.

Highest League Scorer in Season: John Dungworth, 26, Division 4, 1978–79.

Most League Goals in Total Aggregate: Jack Howarth, 171, 1965–71 and 1972–77.

Most League Goals in One Match: 5, Charlie Mortimore v Leyton Orient, Division 3 (S), 25 February 1950.

Most Capped Player: Anthony Straker, 5, Grenada.

Most League Appearances: Murray Brodie, 461, 1970–83.

Youngest League Player: Clive Jackman, 16 years 135 days v Leyton Orient, 16 April 1953.

Record Transfer Fee Received: Reported £200,000 from Swansea C for Scott Donnelly, July 2010.

Record Transfer Fee Paid: £54,000 to Portsmouth for Colin Garwood, February 1980.

Football League Record: 1932 Elected to Division 3 (S); 1958–73 Division 4; 1973–76 Division 3; 1976–87 Division 4; 1987–89 Division 3; 1989–92 Division 4; 1992–93 Isthmian League Division 3; 1993–94 Isthmian League Division 2; 1994–98 Isthmian League Division 1; 1998–2003 Isthmian League Premier Division; 2003–08 Conference; 2008– FL 2.

MANAGERS

Angus Seed 1927–37
Bill McCracken 1937–49
Gordon Clark 1950–55
Harry Evans 1955–59
Dave Smith 1959–71
  (GM from 1967)
Tommy McAnearney 1967–68
Jimmy Melia 1968–72
Tommy McAnearney 1972–81
Len Walker 1981–84
Ron Harris (GM) 1984–85
Len Walker 1985–91
Brian Talbot 1991
Ian McDonald 1991–92
Steve Wignall 1992–95
Steve Wigley 1995–97
George Borg 1997–2002
Terry Brown 2002–07
Gary Waddock 2007–09
Kevin Dillon 2009–11
Dean Holdsworth January 2011–

LATEST SEQUENCES

Longest Sequence of League Wins: 5, 16.9.1961 – 2.10.61.

Longest Sequence of League Defeats: 9, 20.11.1965 – 5.2.1966.

Longest Sequence of League Draws: 6, 6.10.1962 – 27.10.1962.

Longest Sequence of Unbeaten League Matches: 13, 30.9.1978 – 26.12.1978.

Longest Sequence Without a League Win: 17, 10.10.1936 – 30.1.1937.

Successive Scoring Runs: 29 from 1.4.1961.

Successive Non-scoring Runs: 6 from 22.3.1988.

TEN YEAR LEAGUE RECORD

		P	W	D	L	F	A	Pts	Pos
2001-02	Isth PR	42	22	7	13	76	51	73	3
2002-03	Isth PR	46	33	6	7	81	36	105	1
2003-04	Conf	42	20	10	12	80	67	70	5
2004-05	Conf	42	21	10	11	68	52	73	4
2005-06	Conf	42	16	6	20	61	74	54	13
2006-07	Conf	46	18	11	17	64	62	65	9
2007-08	B Sq Pr	46	31	8	7	82	48	101	1
2008-09	FL 2	46	14	12	20	59	80	54	15
2009-10	FL 2	46	20	12	14	69	56	72	6
2010-11	FL 2	46	14	19	13	54	54	61	14

DID YOU KNOW ?

Although Aldershot finished only tenth in 1938–39 it was their best pre-war season in Division Three (South). On 12 September a goalless draw at Bristol Rovers put them second on goal average and twice they were top on 17 September and again on 1 October.

ALDERSHOT TOWN 2010–11 LEAGUE RECORD

Match No.	Date	Venue	Opponents	Result	H/T Score	Lg Pos.	Goalscorers	Attendance
1	Aug 7	A	Accrington S	D	0-0	0-0	—	1624
2	14	H	Southend U	W	1-0	0-0	8	Morgan [81]	3011
3	21	A	Shrewsbury T	D	1-1	1-1	9	Charles [31]	5353
4	28	H	Stevenage	D	1-1	0-0	9	Spencer [63]	2525
5	Sept 4	H	Northampton T	D	1-1	0-1	10	Harding [90]	2739
6	11	A	Port Vale	L	0-1	0-1	13		5360
7	18	H	Wycombe W	D	0-0	0-0	14		3722
8	25	A	Stockport Co	D	2-2	2-0	18	Straker [27], Morgan [38]	4231
9	28	A	Torquay U	W	1-0	0-0	—	Morgan [86]	2167
10	Oct 2	H	Cheltenham T	L	0-2	0-1	15		2509
11	9	A	Oxford U	W	1-0	0-0	10	Morgan [58]	7808
12	16	H	Morecambe	W	2-1	2-0	7	Spencer [27], Morgan [36]	2308
13	23	A	Crewe Alex	L	1-3	0-2	9	Straker [52]	4164
14	30	H	Bury	L	1-3	1-1	11	Little [11]	2526
15	Nov 2	A	Hereford U	D	2-2	1-2	—	McGlashan [20], Small [87]	2126
16	13	A	Macclesfield T	L	0-2	0-1	14		1519
17	20	H	Chesterfield	L	0-2	0-0	16		2479
18	23	A	Burton Alb	W	2-1	2-1	—	Small 2 [16, 26]	1904
19	Dec 11	A	Rotherham U	L	0-1	0-1	17		2754
20	Jan 1	A	Barnet	W	2-1	2-0	16	Harding [35], Small [41]	1902
21	3	H	Hereford U	L	1-2	0-1	19	Guttridge [90]	2767
22	8	H	Oxford U	L	1-2	0-1	20	Guttridge [76]	3129
23	15	A	Bury	D	1-1	1-0	19	Guttridge [9]	2537
24	18	H	Bradford C	W	1-0	1-0	—	Charles [23]	2160
25	22	H	Crewe Alex	W	3-2	1-2	12	Small [24], Vincenti [63], Guttridge [90]	2613
26	29	A	Gillingham	L	1-2	0-0	—	Rodman [90]	4810
27	Feb 5	A	Chesterfield	D	2-2	0-1	17	Sills 2 [61, 79]	5669
28	8	A	Morecambe	D	1-1	0-0	—	Rodman [74]	1703
29	12	H	Macclesfield T	D	0-0	0-0	16		2373
30	15	H	Lincoln C	D	2-2	1-0	—	Charles (pen) [18], Rodman [48]	1847
31	19	A	Northampton T	D	1-1	0-1	16	Vincenti [78]	5011
32	26	H	Port Vale	L	1-2	0-1	18	Vincenti [68]	2506
33	Mar 1	H	Gillingham	D	1-1	0-0	—	Hylton [77]	2038
34	5	A	Wycombe W	D	2-2	1-1	18	Guttridge [26], Halls [76]	4421
35	8	H	Torquay U	W	1-0	0-0	—	Guttridge [53]	1939
36	12	A	Cheltenham T	W	2-1	1-0	14	Charles [10], Vincenti [55]	2697
37	19	H	Stockport Co	W	1-0	0-0	14	Spencer [90]	2263
38	22	H	Barnet	W	1-0	0-0	—	Hylton [60]	2420
39	26	H	Accrington S	D	1-1	0-1	—	Jones [52]	2555
40	Apr 2	A	Southend U	D	0-0	0-0	13		5557
41	9	H	Shrewsbury T	W	3-0	2-0	12	Hylton 2 (1 pen) [24, 77 (p)], Herd [29]	2371
42	16	A	Stevenage	D	2-2	1-1	12	Rodman 2 [43, 48]	3031
43	23	A	Burton Alb	L	1-2	1-1	14	Spencer [26]	2308
44	25	A	Bradford C	L	1-2	1-1	14	Vincenti [43]	10,965
45	30	H	Rotherham U	D	2-2	2-1	14	Charles [5], Vincenti [11]	2107
46	May 7	A	Lincoln C	W	3-0	0-0	14	Hylton (pen) [57], Guttridge 2 [69, 86]	7932

Final League Position: 14

GOALSCORERS

League (54): Guttridge 8, Vincenti 6, Charles 5 (1 pen), Hylton 5 (2 pens), Morgan 5, Rodman 5, Small 5, Spencer 4, Harding 2, Sills 2, Straker 2, Halls 1, Herd 1, Jones 1, Little 1, McGlashan 1.
Carling Cup (0).
FA Cup (2): Small 2.
J Paint Trophy (2): Hylton 1, Spencer 1.

Young J 46	Herd B 43	Vincent J 22 + 1	Panther M 20 + 3	Jones D 42 + 1	Charles A 41	Guttridge L 36 + 5	Harding B 29 + 6	Morgan M 19	Little G 13 + 1	Straker A 35 + 3	Small W 18 + 11	Spencer D 9 + 9	Morris A 13 + 9	Hylton D 24 + 9	McGlashan J 23 + 15	Halls J 16 + 7	Jackson M 4 + 5	Randall J — + 1	Fortune C 3 + 4	Ngo Baheng W — + 3	Connolly R — + 5	Henderson L 1	Vincenti P 22 + 1	Sills T 8 + 11	Rodman A 9 + 5	Grand S 6	Mekki A 2 + 6	Jarrett A 2 + 2	Medley L — + 4	Bergqvist D — + 1	Match No.
1	2	3	4	5	6	7	8	9	10^1	11	12																				1
1	2	3	4	5	6	7^2	8^1	9	10^3	11	14	12	13																		2
1	2	3	4	5	6	7^1	8^2	9	10^3	11	14		13	12																	3
1	2	3	4	5	6	7^1	8	9	10^2	11^3	13	12		14																	4
1	2	3	4^2	5	6	10	8	9		11^1	7^3	12		14	13																5
1	2	3	4^3	5	6	7^1	8	9	10^2	11	14		13	12																	6
1	2	3	4		6		8	9		11			12	5	7^2	13	10^1															7
1	2	3	4^1	5	6	13	8	9^3	10	11			14		7^2	12															8
1	2	3		5	6	13	8^2	9		11			10^1	4	7		12														9
1		3	4^3	5	6	8		9		11	10^2	13	2	7^1	14		12														10
1	2	3^8	4	5	6	13	8	9^3	10^1	11			14	12	7^2																11
1	2			4	5	6	13	8^2	11	10^1	3	9^3	12	14	7																12
1	2	3	4^3	5	6	8	9	11		13	10^1	12	14	7^2																	13
1	2	3	5^8		6	4		9^8	10^3	11			12	13	7^3	8^2	14														14
1	2	3			6	4	8^2		10^3	11	12			5	13	7		9^1	14												15
1	2	3	4^1	5		10	8		12	11	9	6			7^2	13															16
1	2	3		5	4	12	11^3	10^1	8	9		6		14	7^2	13															17
1	2	3	4	5		8		10	7^1	11			9^2	13	12		6														18
1	2	3^8	4^1	5		10	7		11	8			9^2	6									12	13							19
1	2			4	13	6			11	8	10		3	9^2	5	12	7^1														20
1	2			4^1	5	6			11	8	10^3		3	9^2		12		7	13	14											21
1	2	14		5	6	4	8		11^3	3	9		12	7^2	13								10^1								22
1	2	3	12	5	6	4	8			11^1			9^3	14	13	7							10^2								23
1	2	3	12	5	6	4	8^3						9	14	11^2	7							10^1	13							24
1	2	3	12	5	6	4	8						14	9^2	11^3	7							10^1	13							25
1	2	3^3		5	6	4	8						14	9^1	11	7							10^2	13	12						26
1	2			4	5	6	8						13	12	11^2		14						10^1	9^3	7	3					27
1			4^1	5	6		8						11^2	2	7^3		13	14					10	9	12	3					28
1			4^1	5	6	12	8						9	2	7^3		13						10^2	11	3	14					29
1	2			5	6	4	8						9^3		11^1	14	12						10^2	13	7	3					30
1	2			5	6	4	8						9^1		11^2		14						10^3	12	7	3	13				31
1	2			5	6	4^3	8						9^2		11	12	14						10	13	3		7^1				32
1	2			5	6	4^2	12						3		11^3	7	8^1						13	10			9		14		33
1	2			5	6	4	12						3^1		11^3	7	8						10	9^2			14	13			34
1	2			5	6	4							3		11^3		8						14	10		9^2	12	7^1	13		35
1	2			5	6	4							3	14	7^3	12	8						10	9^2			11^1	13			36
1	2			5	6		8^3						3	14	11	7^1	4						10	9^2	13		12				37
1	2			5	6	4	14						3	12	9	13	8						10^3	7^2	11^1						38
1	2			5	6	4	14						3	13	9^2	11	12						8^3	10	7^1						39
1	2			5	6	4							3	14	9^2	11^1	7^3	8					10	13	12						40
1	2			5	6	4	13						3	14	9^1	11	7^3	8					10^2	12							41
1	2			5	6	4	12						3		9^2	10	7^1	8						13	11						42
1	2			5		4							3		9^1	11	12	8	6				10^2	13	7^3						43
1	2			5	6	4							3		9^3	7^2	8				13		10	14	11^1	12					44
1	2			5	6	4							10		11	7^2	8			3^1				9	12		13				45
1	2					6	4						3	9^1	5^3	11	7^2	8					12	10	13					14	46

FA Cup

First Round	Brentford	(a)	1-1	
		(h)	1-0	
Second Round	Dover Ath	(a)	0-2	

Carling Cup

First Round	Watford	(h)	0-3

J Paint Trophy

First Round	Oxford U	(h)	2-0
Second Round	Bristol R	(a)	0-1

ARSENAL

FA Premiership

FOUNDATION

Formed by workers at the Royal Arsenal, Woolwich in 1886, they began as Dial Square (name of one of the workshops), and included two former Nottingham Forest players, Fred Beardsley and Morris Bates. Beardsley wrote to his old club seeking help and they provided the new club with a full set of red jerseys and a ball. The club became known as the 'Woolwich Reds' although their official title soon after formation was Woolwich Arsenal.

Emirates Stadium, Highbury House, 75 Drayton Park, Islington, London N5 1BU.

Telephone: (0207) 619 5003.

Fax: (0207) 704 4001.

Ticket Office: (0207) 619 5000.

Website: www.arsenal.com

Email: contactafc@arsenal.com

Ground Capacity: 60,361.

Record Attendance: 73,295 v Sunderland, Div 1, 9 March 1935 (at Highbury). 73,707 v RC Lens, UEFA Champions League, 25 November 1998 (at Wembley). 60,162 v Manchester U, FA Premier League, 3 November 2007 (at Emirates).

Pitch Measurements: 105m × 68m.

Chairman: Peter Hill-Wood.

Acting Managing Director: Ken Friar OBE.

Secretary: David Miles.

Manager: Arsène Wenger.

Assistant Manager: Pat Rice.

Physio: Colin Lewin.

Colours: Red shirts with white trim, white shorts, white stockings with red tops.

Change Colours: Yellow shirts with black sleeves, black shorts, yellow stockings with black trim.

Year Formed: 1886.

Turned Professional: 1891.

Ltd Co: 1893.

Previous Names: 1886, Dial Square; 1886, Royal Arsenal; 1891, Woolwich Arsenal; 1914 Arsenal.

Club Nickname: 'Gunners'.

HONOURS

FA Premier League:
Champions 1997–98, 2001–02, 2003–04. *Runners-up* 1998–99, 1999–2000, 2000–01, 2002–03, 2004–05.

Football League – Division 1:
Champions 1930–31, 1932–33, 1933–34, 1934–35, 1937–38, 1947–48, 1952–53, 1970–71, 1988–89, 1990–91;
Runners-up 1925–26, 1931–32, 1972–73;
Division 2: *Runners-up* 1903–04.

FA Cup: *Winners* 1930, 1936, 1950, 1971, 1979, 1993, 1998, 2002, 2003, 2005; *Runners-up* 1927, 1932, 1952, 1972, 1978, 1980, 2001.

Double performed: 1970–71, 1997–98, 2001–02.

Football League Cup: *Winners* 1987, 1993; *Runners-up* 1968, 1969, 1988, 2007, 2011.

European Competitions
European Cup: 1971–72, 1991–92.
UEFA Champions League: 1998–99, 1999–2000, 2000–01, 2001–02, 2002–03, 2003–04, 2004–05, 2005–06 (*runners-up*), 2006–07, 2007–08 (*q-f*), 2008–09 (*s-f*), 2009–10, 2010–11.
Fairs Cup: 1963–64, 1969–70 (*winners*), 1970–71. **UEFA Cup:** 1978–79, 1981–82, 1982–83, 1996–97, 1997–98, 1999–2000 (*runners-up*).
European Cup-Winners' Cup: 1979–80 (*runners-up*), 1993–94 (*winners*), 1994–95 (*runners-up*). **Super Cup:** 1994 (*runners-up*).

sky SPORTS FACT FILE

Arsenal adopted their first crest in 1888. It was based on the coat of arms of the Borough of Woolwich with its long military history. It chiefly comprised three cannons which looked like columns. A replica can be seen on a stained glass window in the Woolwich Town Hall.

Grounds: 1886, Plumstead Common; 1887, Sportsman Ground; 1888, Manor Ground; 1890, Invicta Ground; 1893, Manor Ground; 1913, Highbury; 2006, Emirates Stadium.

First Football League Game: 2 September 1893, Division 2, v Newcastle U (h) D 2–2 – Williams; Powell, Jeffrey; Devine, Buist, Howat; Gemmell, Henderson, Shaw (1), Elliott (1), Booth.

Record League Victory: 12–0 v Loughborough T, Division 2, 12 March 1900 – Orr; McNichol, Jackson; Moir, Dick (2), Anderson (1); Hunt, Cottrell (2), Main (2), Gaudie (3), Tennant (2).

Record Cup Victory: 11–1 v Darwen, FA Cup 3rd rd, 9 January 1932 – Moss; Parker, Hapgood; Jones, Roberts, John; Hulme (2), Jack (3), Lambert (2), James, Bastin (4).

Record Defeat: 0–8 v Loughborough T, Division 2, 12 December 1896.

Most League Points (2 for a win): 66, Division 1, 1930–31.

Most League Points (3 for a win): 90, FA Premier League, 2003–04.

Most League Goals: 127, Division 1, 1930–31.

Highest League Scorer in Season: Ted Drake, 42, 1934–35.

Most League Goals in Total Aggregate: Thierry Henry, 174, 1999–2007.

Most League Goals in One Match: 7, Ted Drake v Aston Villa, Division 1, 14 December 1935.

Most Capped Player: Thierry Henry, 81 (123), France.

Most League Appearances: David O'Leary, 558, 1975–93.

Youngest League Player: Jack Wilshere, 16 years 256 days v Blackburn R, 13 September 2008.

Record Transfer Fee Received: £25,000,000 from Manchester C for Emmanuel Adebayor, July 2009.

Record Transfer Fee Paid: £15,000,000 to Zenit for Andrei Arshavin, February 2009.

Football League Record: 1893 Elected to Division 2; 1904–13 Division 1; 1913–19 Division 2; 1919–92 Division 1; 1992– FA Premier League.

MANAGERS

Sam Hollis 1894–97
Tom Mitchell 1897–98
George Elcoat 1898–99
Harry Bradshaw 1899–1904
Phil Kelso 1904–08
George Morrell 1908–15
Leslie Knighton 1919–25
Herbert Chapman 1925–34
George Allison 1934–47
Tom Whittaker 1947–56
Jack Crayston 1956–58
George Swindin 1958–62
Billy Wright 1962–66
Bertie Mee 1966–76
Terry Neill 1976–83
Don Howe 1984–86
George Graham 1986–95
Bruce Rioch 1995–96
Arsène Wenger September 1996–

LATEST SEQUENCES

Longest Sequence of League Wins: 14, 10.2.2002 – 18.8.2002.

Longest Sequence of League Defeats: 7, 12.2.1977 – 12.3.1977.

Longest Sequence of League Draws: 6, 4.3.1961 – 1.4.1961.

Longest Sequence of Unbeaten League Matches: 49, 7.5.2003 – 24.10.2004.

Longest Sequence Without a League Win: 23, 28.9.1912 – 1.3.1913.

Successive Scoring Runs: 55 from 19.5.2001.

Successive Non-scoring Runs: 6 from 25.2.1987.

TEN YEAR LEAGUE RECORD

		P	W	D	L	F	A	Pts	Pos
2001-02	PR Lge	38	26	9	3	79	36	87	1
2002-03	PR Lge	38	23	9	6	85	42	78	2
2003-04	PR Lge	38	26	12	0	73	26	90	1
2004-05	PR Lge	38	25	8	5	87	36	83	2
2005-06	PR Lge	38	20	7	11	68	31	67	4
2006-07	PR Lge	38	19	11	8	63	35	68	4
2007-08	PR Lge	38	24	11	3	74	31	83	3
2008-09	PR Lge	38	20	12	6	68	37	72	4
2009-10	PR Lge	38	23	6	9	83	41	75	3
2010-11	PR Lge	38	19	11	8	72	43	68	4

DID YOU KNOW ?

On 12 February 2011 Robin Van Persie scored the 300th and 301st goals scored by Arsenal at the Emirates in less than five years since they took up residence. Gilberto Silva had the first, Emmanuel Adebayor was responsible for the 100th and Theo Walcott notched the 200th.

ARSENAL 2010–11 LEAGUE RECORD

Match No.	Date	Venue	Opponents	Result	H/T Score	Lg Pos.	Goalscorers	Attendance
1	Aug 15	A	Liverpool	D	1-1	0-0	—	Reina (og) [90]	44,722
2	21	H	Blackpool	W	6-0	3-0	2	Walcott 3 [12, 39, 58], Arshavin (pen) [32], Diaby [49], Chamakh [83]	60,032
3	28	A	Blackburn R	W	2-1	1-1	2	Walcott [20], Arshavin [51]	25,059
4	Sept 11	H	Bolton W	W	4-1	1-1	2	Koscielny [24], Chamakh [58], Song Billong [78], Vela [83]	59,876
5	18	A	Sunderland	D	1-1	1-0	2	Fabregas [13]	38,950
6	25	H	WBA	L	2-3	0-0	3	Nasri 2 [75, 90]	60,025
7	Oct 3	A	Chelsea	L	0-2	0-1	4		41,828
8	16	H	Birmingham C	W	2-1	1-1	3	Nasri (pen) [41], Chamakh [47]	60,070
9	24	A	Manchester C	W	3-0	1-0	2	Nasri [20], Song Billong [66], Bendtner [88]	47,393
10	30	H	West Ham U	W	1-0	0-0	2	Song Billong [88]	60,086
11	Nov 7	H	Newcastle U	L	0-1	0-1	3		60,059
12	10	A	Wolverhampton W	W	2-0	1-0	—	Chamakh 2 [1, 90]	27,329
13	14	H	Everton	W	2-1	1-0	2	Sagna [36], Fabregas [48]	36,279
14	20	H	Tottenham H	L	2-3	2-0	3	Nasri [9], Chamakh [27]	60,102
15	27	A	Aston Villa	W	4-2	2-0	3	Arshavin [39], Nasri [45], Chamakh [56], Wilshere [90]	38,544
16	Dec 4	H	Fulham	W	2-1	1-1	1	Nasri 2 [14, 75]	60,049
17	13	A	Manchester U	L	0-1	0-1	—		75,227
18	27	H	Chelsea	W	3-1	1-0	—	Song Billong [4], Fabregas [51], Walcott [53]	60,112
19	29	A	Wigan Ath	D	2-2	2-1	—	Arshavin [39], Bendtner [44]	17,014
20	Jan 1	A	Birmingham C	W	3-0	1-0	3	Van Persie [13], Nasri [58], Johnson (og) [66]	24,341
21	5	H	Manchester C	D	0-0	0-0	3		60,085
22	15	A	West Ham U	W	3-0	2-0	3	Van Persie 2 (1 pen) [13, 77 (p)], Walcott [41]	32,682
23	22	H	Wigan Ath	W	3-0	1-0	2	Van Persie 3 [21, 58, 85]	59,552
24	Feb 1	H	Everton	W	2-1	0-1	—	Arshavin [70], Koscielny [75]	60,014
25	5	A	Newcastle U	D	4-4	4-0	2	Walcott [1], Djourou [3], Van Persie 2 [10, 26]	51,561
26	12	H	Wolverhampton W	W	2-0	1-0	2	Van Persie 2 [16, 56]	60,050
27	23	H	Stoke C	W	1-0	1-0	—	Squillaci [8]	60,041
28	Mar 5	A	Sunderland	D	0-0	0-0	2		60,081
29	19	A	WBA	D	2-2	0-1	2	Arshavin [70], Van Persie [78]	25,729
30	Apr 2	H	Blackburn R	D	0-0	0-0	2		60,087
31	10	A	Blackpool	W	3-1	2-0	2	Diaby [18], Eboue [21], Van Persie [76]	16,030
32	17	H	Liverpool	D	1-1	0-0	2	Van Persie (pen) [89]	60,029
33	20	A	Tottenham H	D	3-3	3-2	3	Walcott [5], Nasri [12], Van Persie [40]	36,138
34	24	A	Bolton W	L	1-2	0-1	3	Van Persie [48]	26,881
35	May 1	H	Manchester U	W	1-0	0-0	3	Ramsey [56]	60,107
36	8	A	Stoke C	L	1-3	0-2	3	Van Persie [81]	27,478
37	15	H	Aston Villa	L	1-2	0-2	3	Van Persie [89]	60,023
38	22	A	Fulham	D	2-2	1-1	4	Van Persie [29], Walcott [89]	25,674

Final League Position: 4

GOALSCORERS

League (72): Van Persie 18 (2 pens), Nasri 10 (1 pen), Walcott 9, Chamakh 7, Arshavin 6 (1 pen), Song Billong 4, Fabregas 3, Bendtner 2, Diaby 2, Koscielny 2, Djourou 1, Eboue 1, Ramsey 1, Sagna 1, Squillaci 1, Vela 1, Wilshere 1, own goals 2.
Carling Cup (14): Bendtner 3, Nasri 2 (2 pens), Walcott 2, Arshavin 1, Fabregas 1, Koscielny 1, Lansbury 1, Van Persie 1, own goals 2.
FA Cup (12): Bendtner 3 (1 pen), Fabregas 2 (2 pens), Chamakh 1, Clichy 1, Nasri 1, Rosicky 1, Sagna 1, Van Persie 1, own goal 1.
Champions League (21): Arshavin 3, Chamakh 3, Fabregas 3 (2 pens), Nasri 2, Van Persie 2 (1 pen), Vela 2, Walcott 2, Song Billong 1, Squillaci 1, Wilshere 1, own goal 1.

Almunia M 8	Sagna B 33	Clichy G 33	Diaby V 13 + 3	Vermaelen T 5	Koscielny L 30	Eboue E 8 + 5	Wilshere J 31 + 4	Chamakh M 18 + 11	Arshavin A 25 + 12	Nasri S 28 + 2	Walcott T 19 + 9	Rosicky T 8 + 13	Van Persie R 19 + 6	Song Billong A 30 + 1	Fabregas F 22 + 3	Vela C — + 4	Gibbs K 4 + 3	Squillaci S 20 + 2	Denilson 6 + 10	Fabianski L 14	Emmanuel-Thomas J — + 1	Djourou J 20 + 2	Bendtner N 3 + 14	Szczesny W 15	Ramsey A 5 + 2	Lehmann J 1	Match No.
1	2	3	4^{3}	5	$6^{\blacksquare}$	7^{1}	8^{2}	9	10	11	12	13	14														1
1	2	3	4^{1}	5			8	9	10^{2}		7^{3}	11	13		6	12	14										2
1	2	3	4	5	6			14	12	10^{3}	11	13	9^{1}		7	8^{2}											3
1			12^{2}		6	2	7^{1}	9^{3}	10		11			4	8	14		3	5	13							4
1	2	3			6		7	9	10^{2}	11	12			$4^{\blacksquare}$	8^{1}			5	13								5
1	2	3	4^{1}		6^{3}	7^{2}	13	9	10	11	12				8		14	5									6
	2	3	4^{1}		6		8^{2}	9	10^{3}	11	12		7		14			5		1	13						7
		3	4		6	2	$8^{\blacksquare}$	9^{2}	10^{1}	11	12		7					5	13	1							8
	2	3			6		9^{2}	10^{1}	11	14	12		7	4	8^{3}			5	13	1							9
	2	3			6		14	9^{3}	10^{2}	11	12		7	4^{1}	8			5	13	1							10
	2	3			$6^{\blacksquare}$		10^{3}	9^{2}	12	11^{3}	7	13		4	8			5	14	1							11
	2	3			6		7^{1}	9^{3}	10^{2}	11	13			4	8		14	5	12	1							12
	2	3			6	14	7^{1}	9^{3}	10^{2}	11	13			4	8			5	12	1							13
	2	3			6			9^{1}	10^{3}	11^{2}	7	13		4	8		14	5	12	1							14
	2	3			6		8	9	10^{2}	11^{1}	7^{3}			4			13	5	12	1			14				15
	2	3			6^{1}		8^{3}	9	10	11	7^{2}	14		4				5	13	1			12				16
	2	3			6		8^{2}	9	10^{3}	11	7^{1}	14		4	13			5	12	1							17
	2	3	12		6			9^{1}	10^{2}	11	7	13		4	8^{3}	14		5		1							18
		3			6	2	7^{1}	12^{3}	9	10^{2}	11	13		4	8	14		5		1							19
	2	3			6			9^{2}	13	11	7^{1}		10	4	8			5	12	1							20
	2	3			6		7^{2}	12		11	8^{1}		10	4	9			5	13	1							21
		3			6	2		9	13	11^{3}	7^{2}		10	4	8^{1}			5	14			12		1			22
	2	3			6		7	14	12	11		9	10	4	8^{2}			5	13					1			23
	2	3	12		6			9^{3}	13	11^{2}	7		10	4^{1}	8			5	14					1			24
	2	3	$4^{\blacksquare}$		6		14	9^{2}	13	11	7^{3}		10		8			5^{1}	12					1			25
	2	3			6			9^{2}	12	11^{3}	7		10^{1}	4	8			5	14			13		1			26
	2	3			6	14			12	11	7^{2}		10	4	8^{1}			5	13					1	9^{3}		27
	2	3			6		7^{2}	8	12	11		13	10	4^{1}	9			5						1			28
1	2	3			6		7	12	9	11			10	4^{1}				5	13				8^{2}				29
1	2	3			6		8	13	9^{1}	11^{3}	7^{2}		10	4				5	12				14				30
		3			6	2	7		9^{1}	11^{2}	12		10	4	8^{3}			5	13						14	1	31
		3	4^{3}		6	2		9^{1}	12	11	7^{2}	14	10		8			5	13					1			32
	2	3			6		7^{1}	12	13	11^{3}		9^{2}	10	4	8			5					14	1			33
	2	3			6			9^{3}	12	11	7^{2}	13	10	4^{1}	8			5					14	1			34
	2	3			6	14		9	12	11^{1}	7^{3}		10	4				5^{2}	13					1	8		35
	2				6			9	12	11^{2}	7	14	10	4^{3}			3	5	13					1	8^{1}		36
	2	3			6^{1}			9^{2}	12	11	7		10	4				5	13					1	8		37
	2		4^{3}		6	13	7	9	14	11	12		10					3^{2}	5					1	8^{1}		38

FA Cup

Third Round	Leeds U	(h)	1-1
		(a)	3-1
Fourth Round	Huddersfield T	(h)	2-1
Fifth Round	Leyton Orient	(a)	1-1
		(h)	5-0
Sixth Round	Manchester U	(a)	0-2

Champions League

Group H	Braga	(h)	6-0
	Partizan Belgrade	(a)	3-1
	Shakhtar Donetsk	(a)	1-2
		(h)	5-1
	Braga	(a)	0-2
	Partizan Belgrade	(h)	3-1
Knock-Out Round	Barcelona	(h)	2-1
		(a)	1-3

Carling Cup

Third Round	Tottenham H	(a)	4-1
Fourth Round	Newcastle U	(a)	4-0
Quarter-Final	Wigan Ath	(h)	2-0
Semi-Final	Ipswich T	(a)	0-1
		(h)	3-0
Final	Birmingham C		1-2

(at Wembley).

ASTON VILLA   FA Premiership

FOUNDATION

Cricketing enthusiasts of Villa Cross Wesleyan Chapel, Aston, Birmingham decided to form a football club during the winter of 1874–75. Football clubs were few and far between in the Birmingham area and in their first game against Aston Brook St Mary's Rugby team they played one half rugby and the other soccer. In 1876 they were joined by a Scottish soccer enthusiast George Ramsay who was immediately appointed captain and went on to lead Aston Villa from obscurity to one of the country's top clubs in a period of less than 10 years.

Villa Park, Birmingham B6 6HE.
Telephone: (0121) 327 2299.
Fax: (0121) 322 2107.
Ticket Office/Consumer Sales: (0800) 612 0970.
Website: www.avfc.co.uk
Email: postmaster@avfc.co.uk
Ground Capacity: 42,582.
Record Attendance: 76,588 v Derby Co, FA Cup 6th rd, 2 March 1946.
Pitch Measurements: 115yd × 75yd.
Chairman: Randolph Lerner.
Secretary: Sharon Barnhurst.
Manager: Alex McLeish.
First Team Coach: Gordon Cowans.
Physio: Alan Smith.
Colours: Claret body, blue sleeve shirts, white shorts, sky blue stockings.
Change Colours: White shirts with blue trim, blue shorts, white stockings.
Year Formed: 1874.
Turned Professional: 1885.
Ltd Co.: 1896.
Public Ltd Company: 1969.
Club Nickname: 'The Villans'.
Grounds: 1874, Wilson Road and Aston Park (also used Aston Lower Grounds for some matches); 1876, Wellington Road, Perry Barr; 1897, Villa Park.
First Football League Game: 8 September 1888, Football League, v Wolverhampton W (a) D 1–1 – Warner; Cox, Coulton; Yates, Harry Devey, Dawson; Albert Brown, Green (1), Allen, Garvey, Hodgetts.

HONOURS

FA Premier League:
Runners-up 1992–93.
Football League – Division 1:
Champions 1893–94, 1895–96, 1896–97, 1898–99, 1899–1900, 1909–10, 1980–81;
Runners-up 1888–89, 1902–03, 1907–08, 1910–11, 1912–13, 1913–14, 1930–31, 1932–33, 1989–90;
Division 2: *Champions* 1937–38, 1959–60; *Runners-up* 1974–75, 1987–88;
Division 3: *Champions* 1971–72.
FA Cup: *Winners* 1887, 1895, 1897, 1905, 1913, 1920, 1957;
Runners-up 1892, 1924, 2000.
Double Performed: 1896–97.
Football League Cup: *Winners* 1961, 1975, 1977, 1994, 1996;
Runners-up 1963, 1971, 2010.
European Competitions
European Cup: 1981–82 (*winners*), 1982–83. **UEFA Cup:** 1975–76, 1977–78, 1983–84, 1990–91, 1993–94, 1994–95, 1996–97, 1997–98, 1998–99, 2001–02, 2008–09.
Europa League: 2009–10, 2010–11.
World Club Championship: 1982.
Super Cup: 1982 (*winners*). **Intertoto Cup:** 2000, 2001 (*winners*), 2002, 2008 (*winners*).

sky SPORTS FACT FILE

On 29 August 1925, the first day of the change in the off-side law, home teams in the Football League scored 105 goals, 55 away (two 0-0 draws). Aston Villa produced the best performance beating Burnley 10-0 with Len Capewell scoring five times, Billy Walker a hat-trick.

Record League Victory: 12–2 v Accrington S, Division 1, 12 March 1892 – Warner; Evans, Cox; Harry Devey, Jimmy Cowan, Baird; Athersmith (1), Dickson (2), John Devey (4), Lewis Campbell (4), Hodgetts (1).

Record Cup Victory: 13–0 v Wednesbury Old Ath, FA Cup 1st rd, 30 October 1886 – Warner; Coulton, Simmonds; Yates, Robertson, Burton (2); Richard Davis (1), Albert Brown (3), Hunter (3), Loach (2), Hodgetts (2).

Record Defeat: 1–8 v Blackburn R, FA Cup 3rd rd, 16 February 1889.

Most League Points (2 for a win): 70, Division 3, 1971–72.

Most League Points (3 for a win): 78, Division 2, 1987–88.

Most League Goals: 128, Division 1, 1930–31.

Highest League Scorer in Season: 'Pongo' Waring, 49, Division 1, 1930–31.

Most League Goals in Total Aggregate: Harry Hampton, 215, 1904–15.

Most League Goals in One Match: 5, Harry Hampton v Sheffield W, Division 1, 5 October 1912; 5, Harold Halse v Derby Co, Division 1, 19 October 1912; 5, Len Capewell v Burnley, Division 1, 29 August 1925; 5, George Brown v Leicester C, Division 1, 2 January 1932; 5, Gerry Hitchens v Charlton Ath, Division 2, 18 November 1959.

Most Capped Player: Steve Staunton 64 (102), Republic of Ireland.

Most League Appearances: Charlie Aitken, 561, 1961–76.

Youngest League Player: Jimmy Brown, 15 years 349 days v Bolton W, 17 September 1969.

Record Transfer Fee Received: £24,000,000 from Manchester C for James Milner, August 2010.

Record Transfer Fee Paid: £19,000,000 to Sunderland for Darren Bent, January 2011.

Football League Record: 1888 Founder Member of the League; 1936–38 Division 2; 1938–59 Division 1; 1959–60 Division 2; 1960–67 Division 1; 1967–70 Division 2; 1970–72 Division 3; 1972–75 Division 2; 1975–87 Division 1; 1987–88 Division 2; 1988–92 Division 1; 1992– FA Premier League.

MANAGERS

George Ramsay 1884–1926
  (Secretary-Manager)
W. J. Smith 1926–34
  (Secretary-Manager)
Jimmy McMullan 1934–35
Jimmy Hogan 1936–44
Alex Massie 1945–50
George Martin 1950–53
Eric Houghton 1953–58
Joe Mercer 1958–64
Dick Taylor 1964–67
Tommy Cummings 1967–68
Tommy Docherty 1968–70
Vic Crowe 1970–74
Ron Saunders 1974–82
Tony Barton 1982–84
Graham Turner 1984–86
Billy McNeill 1986–87
Graham Taylor 1987–90
Dr Jozef Venglos 1990–91
Ron Atkinson 1991–94
Brian Little 1994–98
John Gregory 1998–2002
Graham Taylor OBE 2002–03
David O'Leary 2003–06
Martin O'Neill 2006–10
Gerard Houllier 2010–11
Alex McLeish June 2011–

LATEST SEQUENCES

Longest Sequence of League Wins: 9, 15.10.1910 – 10.12.1910.

Longest Sequence of League Defeats: 11, 23.3.1963 – 4.5.1963.

Longest Sequence of League Draws: 6, 12.9.1981 – 10.10.1981.

Longest Sequence of Unbeaten League Matches: 15, 12.3.1949 – 27.8.1949.

Longest Sequence Without a League Win: 12, 27.12.1986 – 25.3.1987.

Successive Scoring Runs: 35 from 10.11.1895.

Successive Non-scoring Runs: 5 from 29.2.1992.

TEN YEAR LEAGUE RECORD

		P	W	D	L	F	A	Pts	Pos
2001-02	PR Lge	38	12	14	12	46	47	50	8
2002-03	PR Lge	38	12	9	17	42	47	45	16
2003-04	PR Lge	38	15	11	12	48	44	56	6
2004-05	PR Lge	38	12	11	15	45	52	47	10
2005-06	PR Lge	38	10	12	16	42	55	42	16
2006-07	PR Lge	38	11	17	10	43	41	50	11
2007-08	PR Lge	38	16	12	10	71	51	60	6
2008-09	PR Lge	38	17	11	10	54	48	62	6
2009-10	PR Lge	38	17	13	8	52	39	64	6
2010-11	PR Lge	38	12	12	14	48	59	48	9

DID YOU KNOW ❓

Even in the 1930s when the legendary coach Jimmy Hogan was manager of Aston Villa, the club employed 18 scouts to scour the country for talent. They sent in their reports on a Monday morning and the manager then acted upon the information received.

ASTON VILLA 2010–11 LEAGUE RECORD

Match No.	Date	Venue	Opponents	Result	H/T Score	Lg Pos.	Goalscorers	Attendance
1	Aug 14	H	West Ham U	W 3-0	2-0	—	Downing [15], Petrov [40], Milner [66]	36,604
2	22	A	Newcastle U	L 0-6	0-3	11		43,546
3	29	H	Everton	W 1-0	1-0	4	Young, L [9]	34,725
4	Sept13	A	Stoke C	L 1-2	1-0	—	Downing [35]	25,899
5	18	H	Bolton W	D 1-1	1-1	8	Young, A [13]	34,655
6	26	A	Wolverhampton W	W 2-1	1-0	5	Downing [25], Heskey [88]	27,511
7	Oct 2	A	Tottenham H	L 1-2	1-1	8	Albrighton [16]	35,871
8	16	H	Chelsea	D 0-0	0-0	8		40,122
9	23	A	Sunderland	L 0-1	0-1	10		41,506
10	31	H	Birmingham C	D 0-0	0-0	13		40,688
11	Nov 6	A	Fulham	D 1-1	1-0	14	Albrighton [41]	23,654
12	10	H	Blackpool	W 3-2	1-1	—	Downing [28], Delfouneso [60], Collins, James M [89]	34,330
13	13	H	Manchester U	D 2-2	0-0	9	Young, A (pen) [72], Albrighton [76]	40,073
14	21	A	Blackburn R	L 0-2	0-1	13		21,848
15	27	H	Arsenal	L 2-4	0-2	15	Clark 2 [52, 70]	38,544
16	Dec 6	A	Liverpool	L 0-3	0-2	—		39,079
17	11	H	WBA	W 2-1	1-0	14	Downing [25], Heskey [80]	37,015
18	26	H	Tottenham H	L 1-2	0-1	15	Albrighton [82]	39,411
19	28	A	Manchester C	L 0-4	0-3	15		46,716
20	Jan 2	A	Chelsea	D 3-3	1-1	15	Young, A (pen) [41], Heskey [47], Clark [90]	41,222
21	5	H	Sunderland	L 0-1	0-0	18		32,627
22	16	A	Birmingham C	D 1-1	0-0	17	Collins, James M [73]	22,287
23	22	H	Manchester C	W 1-0	1-0	16	Bent [18]	37,315
24	25	A	Wigan Ath	W 2-1	0-0	—	Agbonlahor [49], Young, A (pen) [62]	16,442
25	Feb 1	A	Manchester U	L 1-3	0-2	—	Bent [58]	75,256
26	5	H	Fulham	D 2-2	1-0	14	Pantsil (og) [13], Walker [72]	35,899
27	12	A	Blackpool	D 1-1	1-1	15	Agbonlahor [10]	16,000
28	26	A	Blackburn R	W 4-1	0-0	12	Young, A 2 (1 pen) [49 (p), 82], Hanley (og) [62], Downing [64]	34,309
29	Mar 5	A	Bolton W	L 2-3	1-1	13	Bent [15], Albrighton [64]	22,533
30	19	H	Wolverhampton W	L 0-1	0-1	14		38,965
31	Apr 2	A	Everton	D 2-2	0-1	16	Bent 2 [47, 68]	37,619
32	10	H	Newcastle U	W 1-0	1-0	14	Collins, James M [24]	37,090
33	16	A	West Ham U	W 2-1	1-1	9	Bent [36], Agbonlahor [90]	34,672
34	23	H	Stoke C	D 1-1	1-1	11	Bent [43]	35,235
35	30	A	WBA	L 1-2	1-0	13	Meite (og) [4]	25,889
36	May 7	H	Wigan Ath	D 1-1	1-1	14	Young, A [17]	36,293
37	15	A	Arsenal	W 2-1	2-0	13	Bent 2 [11, 15]	60,023
38	22	H	Liverpool	W 1-0	1-0	9	Downing [33]	42,785

Final League Position: 9

GOALSCORERS

League (48): Bent 9, Downing 7, Young, A 7 (4 pens), Albrighton 5, Agbonlahor 3, Clark 3, Collins, James M 3, Heskey 3, Delfouneso 1, Milner 1, Petrov 1, Walker 1, Young, L 1, own goals 3.
Carling Cup (6): Heskey 2, Young, A 2, Agbonlahor 1, Downing 1.
FA Cup (6): Albrighton 1, Clark 1, Delfouneso 1, Petkov 1, Pires 1, Walker 1.
Europa League (3): Agbonlahor 1, Bannan 1, Heskey 1.

Friedel B 38	Young L 23	Warnock S 19	Clark C 16+3	Dunne R 32	Petrov S 23+4	Albrighton M 20+9	Milner J 1	Young A 34	Carew J 6+4	Downing S 38	Reo-Coker N 24+6	Weimann A —+1	Bannan B 7+5	Ireland S 6+4	Heskey E 11+8	Beye H 2+1	Collins James M 31+1	Agbonlahor G 17+9	Cuellar C 10+2	Sidwell S 1+3	Delfouneso N 2+9	Lichaj E 3+2	Hogg J 5	Herd C 1+5	Pires R 2+7	Delph F 4+3	Walker K 15	Bent D 16	Baker N 4	Makoun J 7	Bradley M —+3	Match No.
1	2	3	4	5	6	7³	8¹	9²	10	11	12	13	14																			1
1	2	3	4³	5	6	7¹		9	10²	11	13				8	12	14															2
1	2	3		5	6	7		9	10¹	11					8		4	12														3
1	2	3		5	6	7			10	11					8	12	4	9¹														4
1	2	3		5¹	6	7			10	13	11				8²		4	9	12													5
1	2	3			6²	7¹		9		11					8	10	4	12	5	13												6
1	2	3		5	6³	7²		9	12	11					8	14	13	10¹	4													7
1		3	12	5¹	6			9	10²	11					8		7³	2	4	14	13											8
1		3		5	6¹	13		9		11					8		7²	10	2	4	12											9
1	2	3	4	5				9	13	11	7²				12		10	6	8¹													10
1	2	3	12	5		7		9		11	4¹				8		13	6			10²											11
1	2	3	4	5		7²		9		11					8³	13	6	12	10¹		14											12
1	2	3		5		7²		9		11					8		6	10¹	12	13					4³	14						13
1	2	3	4	5				9		11					8		7¹	10²	13					6³	14	12						14
1	2	3	4	5				9	10²	11					8³	13	6	12	14	7¹												15
1	2	3	4¹	5		7²		9		11		14					6	10³	12	8	13											16
1		3				7³		9		11	12				8¹		10²	6	5				13	2	4²	14						17
1		3	13			7				11							10¹	6	9	5			12	2	4²	14	8³					18
1		3			6	7¹				11					8³		10²	4	9	5			12	2	14	13						19
1		3		5	6	12		7		11	8				10		4	9¹						2								20
1		3		5	6¹	12		7		11	8¹	13			10⁴		4	9						2								21
1		3		5	6	7		10²		11	8¹				13		4	9	12					2								22
1		3		5	6¹	7	8	11	12								4	9						2				10				23
1		5	12	13		8³		11		4	6				9²									2	14			10	3	7¹		24
1		3		5	6²	7¹		9		11³		14		12			4		13							8	2	10				25
1		3		5	6¹	12		7		11					13		4	9²								8	2	10				26
1		3		5				9		11	8				13		12		7³	4¹							2	10²	6⁴	14		27
1			6	5	13	7		9		11	4							14							8²	1	7	10¹	3¹			28
1		3	6	12		7²		9		11	4							13								8¹	2	10		5		29
1		3				7³		9		11					4²		14		5				3	13	12		2	10	6¹	8		30
1		3		5		7				11					8		12	6	9¹								2	10	4			31
1		3		5	8	7				11					12		6	9¹	13						14		2²	10	4¹			32
1		3		5	6	7				11					8		4	9¹	12								2	10				33
1		3		5	6	12		7		11³					8		9²		4	13							2	10				34
1		3	12	5¹	6³	7		7		11		14			8²		4	9	13								2	10				35
1		3		5	6	12		7		11					8		9¹		4								2	10				36
1		3		5	6¹			9		11					8		13		4							7²	2	10		12		37
1		3		5	6	12		9³		11					8²		4		13							7¹	2	10			14	38

FA Cup

Third Round	Sheffield U	(a)	3-1
Fourth Round	Blackburn R	(h)	3-1
Fifth Round	Manchester C	(a)	0-3

Europa League

Play-Off	Rapid Vienna	(a)	1-1
		(h)	2-3

Carling Cup

Third Round	Blackburn R	(h)	3-1
Fourth Round	Burnley	(h)	2-1
Quarter-Final	Birmingham C	(a)	1-2

BARNET   FL Championship 2

FOUNDATION

Barnet Football Club was formed in 1888 as an amateur organisation and they played at a ground in Queen's Road until they disbanded in 1901. A club known as Alston Works FC was then
formed and they played at Totteridge Lane until changing to
Barnet Alston FC in 1906. They moved to their present ground a
year later, combining with The Avenue to form Barnet and Alston
in 1912. The club progressed to senior amateur football by way of
the Athenian and Isthmian Leagues, turning professional in 1965.
It was as a Southern League and Conference club that they made
their name.

Underhill Stadium, Barnet Lane, Barnet, Herts
EN5 2DN.

Telephone: (020) 8441 6932.

Fax: (020) 8447 0655.

Ticket Office: 0208 449 6325.

Website: www.barnetfc.com

Email: info@barnetfc.com

Ground Capacity: 5,345.

Record Attendance: 11,026 v Wycombe Wanderers,
FA Amateur Cup 4th Round 1951–52.

Record Receipts: £31,202 v Portsmouth, FA Cup
3rd Round, 5 January 1991.

Pitch Measurements: 100m × 64m.

Chairman: Anthony Kleanthous.

Group Finance Director: Andrew Adie.

Manager: Lawrie Sanchez.

Assistant Manager: Giuliano Grazioli.

Physio: Mark Stein.

Colours: All black with amber trim.

Change Colours: White shirts with black trim, red shorts, red stockings.

Year Formed: 1888.

Turned Professional: 1965.

Previous Name: 1906, Barnet Alston FC; 1919, Barnet.

Club Nickname: The Bees.

Grounds: 1888, Queens Road; 1901, Totteridge Lane; 1907, Barnet Lane.

First Football League Game: 17 August 1991, Division 4, v Crewe Alex (h) L 4–7 – Phillips;
Blackford, Cooper (Murphy), Horton, Bodley (Stein), Johnson, Showler, Carter (2), Bull (2), Lowe,
Evans.

HONOURS

Football League – Division 2:
Best season: 24th, 1993–94.

FA Amateur Cup: *Winners* 1946.

FA Trophy: *Runners-up* 1972.

GM Vauxhall Conference:
Winners 1990–91.
Conference: *Winners* 2004–05.

FA Cup: 4th rd, 2007, 2008.

League Cup: Best season: 3rd rd,
2006.

sky SPORTS FACT FILE

When Barnet reached the FA Cup first round proper for
the first time in 1925–26 they produced an outstanding
performance in spite of losing 3-1 at Brentford, then in
Division Three (South). The referee was Stanley Rous,
later FA Secretary, Knighted and then FIFA President.

Record League Victory: 7–0 v Blackpool, Division 3, 11 November 2000 – Naisbitt; Stockley, Sawyers, Niven (Brown), Heald, Arber (1), Currie (3), Doolan, Richards (2) (McGleish), Cottee (1) (Riza), Toms.

Record Cup Victory: 6–1 v Newport Co, FA Cup 1st rd, 21 November 1970 – McClelland; Lye, Jenkins, Ward, Embery, King, Powell (1), Ferry, Adams (1), Gray, George (3), (1 og).

Record Defeat: 1–9 v Peterborough U, Division 3, 5 September 1998.

Most League Points (3 for a win): 79, Division 3, 1992–93.

Most League Goals: 81, Division 4, 1991–92.

Highest League Scorer in Season: Dougie Freedman, 24, Division 3, 1994–95.

Most League Goals in Total Aggregate: Sean Devine, 47, 1995–99.

Most League Goals in One Match: 4, Dougie Freedman v Rochdale, Division 3, 13 September 1994; 4, Lee Hodges v Rochdale, Division 3, 8 April 1996.

Most Capped Player: Ken Charlery, 4, St Lucia.

Most League Appearances: Lee Harrison, 270, 1996–2002, 2006–09.

Youngest League Player: Kieran Adams, 17 years 71 days v Mansfield T, 31 December 1994.

Record Transfer Fee Received: £800,000 from Crystal Palace for Dougie Freedman, September 1995.

Record Transfer Fee Paid: £130,000 to Peterborough U for Greg Heald, August 1997.

Football League Record: 1991 Promoted to Division 4 from GMVC; 1991–92 Division 4; 1992–93 Division 3; 1993–94 Division 2; 1994–2001 Division 3; 2001–05 Conference; 2005– FL 2.

MANAGERS

Lester Finch
George Wheeler
Dexter Adams
Tommy Coleman
Gerry Ward
Gordon Ferry
Brian Kelly
Bill Meadows 1976–79
Barry Fry 1979–85
Roger Thompson 1985
Don McAllister 1985–86
Barry Fry 1986–93
Edwin Stein 1993
Gary Phillips (*Player–Manager*) 1993–94
Ray Clemence 1994–96
Alan Mullery (*Director of Football*) 1996–97
Terry Bullivant 1997
John Still 1997–2000
Tony Cottee 2000–01
John Still 2001–02
Peter Shreeves 2002–03
Martin Allen 2003–04
Paul Fairclough 2004–08
Ian Hendon 2008–10
Mark Stimson 2010–11
Martin Allen 2011
Lawrie Sanchez May 2011–

LATEST SEQUENCES

Longest Sequence of League Wins: 6, 28.8.1993 – 25.9.1999.

Longest Sequence of League Defeats: 11, 8.5.1993 – 2.10.1993.

Longest Sequence of League Draws: 4, 22.1.1994 – 12.2.1994.

Longest Sequence of Unbeaten League Matches: 12, 5.12.1992 – 2.3.1993.

Longest Sequence Without a League Win: 14, 24.4.1993 – 10.10.1993.

Successive Scoring Runs: 12 from 19.3.1995.

Successive Non-scoring Runs: 5 from 12.2.2000.

TEN YEAR LEAGUE RECORD

		P	W	D	L	F	A	Pts	Pos
2001-02	Conf	42	19	10	13	64	48	67	5
2002-03	Conf	42	13	14	15	65	68	53	11
2003-04	Conf	42	19	14	9	60	48	71	4
2004-05	Conf	42	26	8	8	90	44	86	1
2005-06	FL 2	46	12	18	16	44	57	54	18
2006-07	FL 2	46	16	11	19	55	70	59	14
2007-08	FL 2	46	16	12	18	56	63	60	12
2008-09	FL 2	46	11	15	20	56	74	48	17
2009-10	FL 2	46	12	12	22	47	63	48	21
2010-11	FL 2	46	12	12	22	58	77	48	22

DID YOU KNOW ?

Centre-forward George Sparrow, a one-club Barnet player, became the club's first capped amateur international when he was selected to play for England against Wales at Plymouth on 21 March 1925. England won 2-1. He was in distinguished company including Edgar Kail.

BARNET 2010–11 LEAGUE RECORD

Match No.	Date	Venue	Opponents	Result	H/T Score	Lg Pos.	Goalscorers	Attendance
1	Aug 7	A	Chesterfield	L	1-2	0-1	—	Poole [70]	6431
2	14	H	Burton Alb	D	0-0	0-0	18		1655
3	21	A	Crewe Alex	L	0-7	0-2	24		3171
4	28	H	Bury	D	1-1	0-0	24	Marshall [75]	1563
5	Sept 4	H	Cheltenham T	W	3-1	1-1	17	Walsh 2 [12, 65], Marshall [80]	2082
6	11	A	Lincoln C	L	0-1	0-1	21		2884
7	18	H	Rotherham U	L	1-4	0-0	24	Byrne [81]	1731
8	25	A	Morecambe	D	2-2	0-0	23	Kabba [53], Southam (pen) [69]	2221
9	28	A	Wycombe W	L	2-4	0-3	—	Walsh [74], Kabba [86]	3518
10	Oct 2	H	Hereford U	W	2-0	1-0	21	Marshall [14], Townsend (og) [78]	1745
11	9	H	Bradford C	L	0-2	0-0	23		2435
12	16	A	Stockport Co	L	1-2	0-0	23	Byrne [46]	4177
13	23	H	Macclesfield T	W	1-0	1-0	22	Byrne [9]	1594
14	30	A	Shrewsbury T	L	1-2	0-2	24	Parkes [61]	5331
15	Nov 2	H	Stevenage	L	0-3	0-2	—		2722
16	13	A	Torquay U	D	1-1	1-1	24	Byrne [20]	2257
17	20	H	Northampton T	W	4-1	2-1	23	Kabba 2 (1 pen) [10 (p), 43], Basey [47], Holmes [90]	1918
18	23	H	Gillingham	L	1-2	1-0	—	Gallen [31]	2519
19	Dec 4	A	Oxford U	L	1-2	1-0	—	Marshall [35]	6004
20	11	H	Accrington S	W	2-0	2-0	23	McLeod 2 [12, 45]	2250
21	28	H	Stockport Co	L	1-3	0-0	—	McLeod [54]	2045
22	Jan 1	H	Aldershot T	L	1-2	0-2	23	McLeod [54]	1902
23	3	A	Stevenage	L	2-4	0-3	24	McLeod [73], Marshall [76]	3744
24	8	A	Bradford C	W	3-1	0-1	22	Kiernan (og) [61], Uddin [64], Holmes [67]	10,514
25	15	H	Shrewsbury T	D	1-1	0-1	22	Taylor [90]	2164
26	22	A	Macclesfield T	D	1-1	0-0	21	McLeod (pen) [55]	1655
27	25	A	Port Vale	D	0-0	0-0	—		4112
28	29	H	Southend U	L	0-2	0-1	—		2867
29	Feb 5	A	Northampton T	D	0-0	0-0	22		4573
30	12	H	Torquay U	L	0-3	0-1	24		2168
31	19	A	Cheltenham T	D	1-1	0-0	24	Devera [90]	2926
32	22	A	Southend U	L	1-2	0-2	—	Kabba [88]	5501
33	26	H	Lincoln C	W	4-2	3-0	22	Kabba 2 (1 pen) [6, 15 (p)], Hughes [38], McLeod [68]	2226
34	Mar 5	A	Rotherham U	D	0-0	0-0	23		3566
35	8	H	Wycombe W	L	0-1	0-1	—		1520
36	12	A	Hereford U	W	2-1	1-1	23	McLeod 2 [44, 78]	2517
37	19	H	Morecambe	L	1-2	1-2	23	Byrne [21]	2510
38	22	A	Aldershot T	L	0-1	0-0	—		2420
39	26	H	Chesterfield	D	2-2	0-1	—	Deering 2 [52, 90]	2012
40	Apr 2	A	Burton Alb	W	4-1	0-1	23	Kabba 4 (1 pen) [53, 64, 67 (p), 79]	2774
41	9	H	Crewe Alex	W	2-1	2-1	23	Leach [11], McLeod [26]	2212
42	16	A	Bury	L	0-2	0-2	23		3082
43	23	A	Gillingham	W	4-2	2-1	23	Byrne [13], McLeod 3 (1 pen) [45, 52, 70 (p)]	6170
44	25	H	Oxford U	D	2-2	1-1	23	Kamdjo [11], Hughes [60]	3425
45	30	A	Accrington S	L	1-3	1-1	23	Marshall [7]	2764
46	May 7	H	Port Vale	W	1-0	0-0	22	McLeod (pen) [48]	4478

Final League Position: 22

GOALSCORERS

League (58): McLeod 14 (3 pens), Kabba 11 (3 pens), Byrne 6, Marshall 6, Walsh 3, Deering 2, Holmes 2, Hughes 2, Basey 1, Devera 1, Gallen 1, Kamdjo 1, Leach 1, Parkes 1, Poole 1, Southam 1 (1 pen), Taylor 1, Uddin 1, own goals 2.
Carling Cup (0).
FA Cup (0).
J Paint Trophy (1): Marshall 1.

Cole J 31	Devera J 43	Leach D 14	Southam G 31+2	Parkes J 37+3	Uddin A 28+2	Jarvis R 12+10	Poole G 6+4	Kabba S 23	Marshall M 45+1	Byrne M 26+2	Holmes R 14+11	Dennehy D 4+1	Kelly D —+3	Hughes M 31+2	Walsh P 6+3	Kamdjo C 28+4	Taylor C 2+16	Cox S 5+5	Stimson C —+6	Basey G 11	Vilhete M 6+14	Francomb G 13	Gallen K 6+1	Dobson C —+1	McLeod J 25+4	Coulton T 1	O'Brien L 7+1	Fraser T 10+5	Dunleavy J 1+2	Pulis A 4	Deering S 14+2	Adjeman-Pamboe K —+1	Parsons M 7+1	Midson J 3+2	Walker S 7	Stirling J 5+1	Match No.
1	2	3	4	5²	6	7¹	8	9²	10	11	12	13	14																								1
1		2	4	3	5	7			10¹	11	9	6	8	12																							2
1		3	4	2	6	14	8²		9¹	11	10	5	13	7³	12																						3
1	2	3	4²		6	7	8¹		12	11	10	5		13	9																						4
1	2	3	4	12	6			9	7	11	8	5¹	13	10²																							5
1	2	3	4	5	6		12	9	10	11	8¹			7																							6
1	2	3¹	4	5	6		13	9	8	11	7²			10	12																						7
1	2²		4	5	6		8	9¹	10	11	7³			3	12	13	14																				8
1	2		4	5	6	14	8¹	9	10	11³	7²			12	3	13																					9
1	2	4¹	5		12		9	10³	11	13			7	3	8²	6	14																				10
1			5	12	7		10		11	8	9	3	4¹	6	2																						11
1	2	4²	5	6¹			10	11	13	8	3	12	9	7																							12
1	2	4	5	6	13		10	11		7	3		9²	8¹	12																						13
1	2	4³	5	6	12		9	11	14	8¹	3²		13	7	10																						14
1	2	4⁷	5		12		9	11	14	3¹			6	8	7	10³	13																				15
1	2		5	6			9	8²	11	13	4		3	12	7	10¹																					16
1	2	4	5	6			9	11	12²	14	8¹		13	3		7³	10																				17
1	2	8	6	5			9	11	13³		4²		3	14	7	10¹	12																				18
1	2	4	5	6	13		9	11	12	8²	3		7³	10¹	14																						19
1	2	4	6¹				9	11	8²	12	5	14	3	13	7	10³																					20
1	2	4					9	11	8¹	6	7	3	12	5	10																						21
1	2	4					10	11	7	12	6	3	8¹	5	9																						22
	2	4³	6	12	14		8	10	11	5¹	7²	3	13	9	1																						23
	2	4	3	5	7		8	10²	11	12	13	6¹	9	1																							24
	2	4	3	5	7	12	8	11¹	6	13	10²	9	1																								25
	2	4	3	5	7		10	11	6	9	1	8																									26
	2	4²	3	5	7		10	11³	6	14	13	12	9	1	8¹																						27
	2	4	3	5	7		10	11	6²	12	13	9	1	8	14																						28
1	2	4	3	5			9²	7	11	6	13	12	10	8¹																							29
1	2	12	3	5			9	7	13	6	14	10³	8²	4⁸	11¹																						30
1	2	4¹	3	5	13		9	7	11	6	12	8²	10																								31
1	2	4	3	5	14		9	7	11³	6¹	13	8²	12	10																							32
1	2		3	5	12		9	8	4		12	10¹	6	11²· 13																							33
1	2		12	3	5¹	14	9²	8	13	11	6	10	4³	7	3																						34
1	2	3		7⁸			8	11¹	4³	6	13	12	10	14	9²	5																					35
1	2	3					7	11³	8	6	14	12	13	10	4¹	9²	5																				36
1	2	3	7¹				8³	11²	4	6	13	12	14	10	9	5																					37
	2	3					7	11	4¹	6	14	10³	1	12	8²	9	5⁸	13																			38
	2	3	7²	9	11				6	4³	14	10	8¹	12	13	1	5																				39
	2	3					9	8	11	4²	6¹	14	10³	13	7	12	1	5																			40
	2	6	12				9	8	11		13⁶	10²	15	4	7¹	5	1⁸	3																			41
	2	3	8²	12			9	7	11		14	10³	1	4	13	5¹	6																				42
	2	6	3				7	11	4³	12	13	10²	14	8	9	1	5¹																				43
	2	5	8	3			7	11	12	4	6	9	10¹	1																							44
	2	5²	3				7	11	12	4	6	10	8¹	9	1	13																					45
	2	5	3				7	11²		4	6	12	10¹	8	9	1																					46

FA Cup
First Round   Charlton Ath   (h)   0-0
                                                    (a)   0-1

Carling Cup
First Round   Swansea C   (a)   0-3

J Paint Trophy
Second Round   Southend U   (h)   1-3

BARNSLEY   FL Championship

FOUNDATION

Many clubs owe their inception to the church and Barnsley
are among them, for they were formed in 1887 by the
Rev. T. T. Preedy, curate of Barnsley St Peter's and went
under that name until it was dropped in 1897 a year before
being admitted to the Second Division of the Football League.

Oakwell Stadium, Grove Street, Barnsley,
South Yorkshire S71 1ET.

Telephone: (01226) 211 211.

Fax: (01226) 211 444.

Ticket Office: (0871) 22 66 777.

Website: www.barnsleyfc.co.uk

Email: thereds@barnsleyfc.co.uk

Ground Capacity: 23,186.

Record Attendance: 40,255 v Stoke C, FA Cup 5th rd,
15 February 1936.

Pitch Measurements: 110yd × 73yd.

Owner: Patrick Cryne.

Director: Barry Taylor.

General Manager/Secretary: Albert Donald Rowing.

Manager: Keith Hill. *Assistant Manager:* David Flitcroft.

Physio: Chris Burton.

Colours: Red shirts with white trim, white shorts, red stockings.

Change Colours: Black shirts, mustard shorts, mustard stockings.

Year Formed: 1887.

Turned Professional: 1888.

Ltd Co.: 1899.

Previous Name: 1887, Barnsley St Peter's; 1897, Barnsley.

Club Nickname: 'The Tykes', 'Reds' or 'Colliers'.

Ground: 1887, Oakwell.

HONOURS

Football League – Division 1:
Runners-up 1996–97;
Division 3 (N): *Champions* 1933–34,
1938–39, 1954–55; *Runners-up* 1953–54;
Division 3: *Runners-up* 1980–81;
Division 4: *Runners-up* 1967–68.
FA Cup: *Winners* 1912;
Runners-up 1910.
Football League Cup: Best season:
5th rd, 1982.

First Football League Game: 1 September 1898, Division 2, v Lincoln C (a) L 0–1 – Fawcett;
McArtney, Nixon; King, Burleigh, Porteous; Davis, Lees, Murray, McCullough, McGee.

Record League Victory: 9–0 v Loughborough T, Division 2, 28 January 1899 – Greaves; McArtney,
Nixon; Porteous, Burleigh, Howard; Davis (4), Hepworth (1), Lees (1), McCullough (1), Jones (2).
9–0 v Accrington S, Division 3 (N), 3 February 1934 – Ellis; Cookson, Shotton; Harper, Henderson,
Whitworth; Spence (2), Smith (1), Blight (4), Andrews (1), Ashton (1).

Record Cup Victory: 6–0 v Blackpool, FA Cup 1st rd replay, 20 January 1910 – Mearns; Downs, Ness;
Glendinning, Boyle (1), Utley; Bartrop, Gadsby (1), Lillycrop (2), Tufnell (2), Forman. 6–0 v
Peterborough U, League Cup 1st rd 2nd leg, 15 September 1981 – Horn; Joyce, Chambers, Glavin (2),
Banks, McCarthy, Evans, Parker (2), Aylott (1), McHale, Barrowclough (1).

sky SPORTS FACT FILE

Ernie Hine, the overall record goal scorer for Barnsley,
made his debut in an FA Cup replay away to Norwich
City on 12 January 1922. Team skipper Brough Fletcher
told him to take the penalty awarded to the Tykes; Hine
equalised and Barnsley went on to win 2-1.

Record Defeat: 0–9 v Notts Co, Division 2, 19 November 1927.

Most League Points (2 for a win): 67, Division 3 (N), 1938–39.

Most League Points (3 for a win): 82, Division 1, 1999–2000.

Most League Goals: 118, Division 3 (N), 1933–34.

Highest League Scorer in Season: Cecil McCormack, 33, Division 2, 1950–51.

Most League Goals in Total Aggregate: Ernest Hine, 123, 1921–26 and 1934–38.

Most League Goals in One Match: 5, Frank Eaton v South Shields, Division 3 (N), 9 April 1927; 5, Peter Cunningham v Darlington, Division 3 (N), 4 February 1933; 5, Beau Asquith v Darlington, Division 3 (N), 12 November 1938; 5, Cecil McCormack v Luton T, Division 2, 9 September 1950.

Most Capped Player: Gerry Taggart, 35 (50), Northern Ireland.

Most League Appearances: Barry Murphy, 514, 1962–78.

Youngest League Player: Reuben Noble-Lazarus, 15 years 45 days v Ipswich T, 30 September 2008.

Record Transfer Fee Received: £4,500,000 from Blackburn R for Ashley Ward, December 1998.

Record Transfer Fee Paid: £1,500,000 to Partizan Belgrade for Georgi Hristov, July 1997.

Football League Record: 1898 Elected to Division 2; 1932–34 Division 3 (N); 1934–38 Division 2; 1938–39 Division 3 (N); 1946–53 Division 2; 1953–55 Division 3 (N); 1955–59 Division 2; 1959–65 Division 3; 1965–68 Division 4; 1968–72 Division 3; 1972–79 Division 4; 1979–81 Division 3; 1981–92 Division 2; 1992–97 Division 1; 1997–98 FA Premier League; 1998–2002 Division 1; 2002–04 Division 2; 2004–06 FL 1; 2006– FL C.

LATEST SEQUENCES

Longest Sequence of League Wins: 10, 5.3.1955 – 23.4.1955.

Longest Sequence of League Defeats: 9, 14.3.1953 – 25.4.1953.

Longest Sequence of League Draws: 7, 28.3.1911 – 22.4.1911.

Longest Sequence of Unbeaten League Matches: 21, 1.1.1934 – 5.5.1934.

Longest Sequence Without a League Win: 26, 13.12.1952 – 26.8.1953.

Successive Scoring Runs: 44 from 2.10.1926.

Successive Non-scoring Runs: 6 from 7.10.1899.

MANAGERS

Arthur Fairclough 1898–1901
 (*Secretary-Manager*)
John McCartney 1901–04
 (*Secretary-Manager*)
Arthur Fairclough 1904–12
John Hastie 1912–14
Percy Lewis 1914–19
Peter Sant 1919–26
John Commins 1926–29
Arthur Fairclough 1929–30
Brough Fletcher 1930–37
Angus Seed 1937–53
Tim Ward 1953–60
Johnny Steele 1960–71
 (*continued as General Manager*)
John McSeveney 1971–72
Johnny Steele (*General Manager*) 1972–73
Jim Iley 1973–78
Allan Clarke 1978–80
Norman Hunter 1980–84
Bobby Collins 1984–85
Allan Clarke 1985–89
Mel Machin 1989–93
Viv Anderson 1993–94
Danny Wilson 1994–98
John Hendrie 1998–99
Dave Bassett 1999–2000
Nigel Spackman 2001
Steve Parkin 2001–02
Glyn Hodges 2002–03
Gudjon Thordarson 2003–04
Paul Hart 2004–05
Andy Ritchie 2005–06
Simon Davey 2007–10
 (*caretaker from November 2006*)
Mark Robins 2009–11
Keith Hill June 2011–

TEN YEAR LEAGUE RECORD

		P	W	D	L	F	A	Pts	Pos
2001-02	Div 1	46	11	15	20	59	86	48	23
2002-03	Div 2	46	13	13	20	51	64	52	19
2003-04	Div 2	46	15	17	14	54	58	62	12
2004-05	FL 1	46	14	19	13	69	64	61	13
2005-06	FL 1	46	18	18	10	62	44	72	5
2006-07	FL C	46	15	5	26	53	85	50	20
2007-08	FL C	46	14	13	19	52	65	55	18
2008-09	FL C	46	13	13	20	45	58	52	20
2009-10	FL C	46	14	12	20	53	69	54	18
2010-11	FL C	46	14	14	18	55	66	56	17

DID YOU KNOW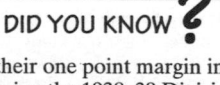

In their one point margin in winning the 1938–39 Division Three (North) championship, Barnsley had five forwards who reached double figures. Beau Asquith led with 28, followed by Johnny Steele on 17 goals, Danny McGarry with 12 and George Bullock and Johnny Lang on ten.

BARNSLEY 2010–11 LEAGUE RECORD

Match No.	Date		Venue	Opponents	Result		H/T Score	Lg Pos.	Goalscorers	Attendance
1	Aug	7	A	QPR	L	0-4	0-1	—		13,445
2		14	H	Crystal Palace	W	1-0	1-0	15	McCarthy (og) [35]	11,353
3		21	A	Bristol C	D	3-3	2-2	13	Gray 2 (1 pen) [4 (pl. 12], Hammill [51]	13,585
4		28	H	Middlesbrough	W	2-0	1-0	10	Shackell [28], Hammill [90]	11,767
5	Sept	11	A	Norwich C	L	1-2	1-0	11	McEveley [45]	24,624
6		14	H	Leeds U	W	5-2	1-1	—	O'Connor [42], O'Brien [49], Arismendi [66], Collins (og) [82], Hammill [83]	20,309
7		18	H	Derby Co	D	1-1	0-1	10	Hammill [48]	12,089
8		25	A	Reading	L	0-3	0-0	14		14,830
9		28	A	Scunthorpe U	D	0-0	0-0	—		5421
10	Oct	2	H	Cardiff C	L	1-2	0-1	15	Shackell [63]	11,211
11		16	H	Nottingham F	W	3-1	1-0	14	Doyle [4], Gray (pen) [56], Butterfield [87]	12,844
12		19	A	Burnley	L	0-3	0-0	—		14,428
13		23	A	Coventry C	L	0-3	0-1	17		14,573
14		30	H	Hull C	D	1-1	1-0	17	Hammill [24]	10,566
15	Nov	6	H	Leicester C	L	0-2	0-1	18		12,360
16		9	A	Preston NE	W	2-1	1-1	—	Hammill [44], O'Connor [89]	8994
17		13	A	Ipswich T	W	3-1	2-0	15	Lovre [21], Fulop (og) [27], O'Connor [50]	18,024
18		20	H	Portsmouth	W	1-0	1-0	12	Hammill [13]	10,908
19		27	H	Watford	D	0-0	0-0	12		10,653
20	Dec	11	H	Sheffield U	W	1-0	1-0	10	Colace [37]	12,976
21		26	H	Burnley	L	1-2	1-0	16	Hammill [25]	14,219
22		28	A	Swansea C	L	0-1	0-1	16		15,093
23	Jan	1	A	Nottingham F	D	2-2	1-0	18	Hill [17], Gray [50]	22,179
24		3	H	Coventry C	W	2-1	1-1	16	Doyle [4], Lovre [57]	11,118
25		15	A	Hull C	L	0-2	0-0	16		21,222
26		22	H	Swansea C	D	1-1	1-0	16	Hassell [14]	10,481
27		25	A	Doncaster R	W	2-0	0-0	—	Haynes 2 [54, 67]	10,740
28		28	A	Millwall	L	0-2	0-2	—		10,087
29	Feb	1	H	Preston NE	W	2-0	1-0	12	O'Connor [22], Haynes [90]	10,740
30		5	A	Leicester C	L	1-4	1-2	13	Mellis [45]	22,667
31		12	H	Ipswich T	D	1-1	0-0	13	Mellis [90]	10,904
32		19	A	Portsmouth	L	0-1	0-0	14		14,318
33		22	A	Leeds U	D	3-3	1-2	—	Shackell [2], Hill [48], Trippier [82]	26,289
34		26	H	Norwich C	L	0-2	0-2	15		12,461
35	Mar	5	A	Derby Co	D	0-0	0-0	16		26,251
36		8	H	Scunthorpe U	W	2-1	0-0	—	Harewood 2 [62, 83]	10,250
37		13	A	Cardiff C	D	2-2	1-1	15	Gray 2 [29, 89]	23,065
38		19	H	Reading	L	0-1	0-0	16		10,284
39	Apr	2	A	Crystal Palace	L	1-2	1-1	16	Harewood [43]	19,344
40		9	H	Bristol C	W	4-2	3-1	16	Gray (pen) [32], Haynes [40], Butterfield [45], McShane [56]	10,257
41		12	H	QPR	L	0-1	0-1	—		11,381
42		16	A	Middlesbrough	D	1-1	1-0	17	Harewood [22]	16,107
43		23	A	Watford	L	0-1	0-1	18		14,098
44		25	H	Doncaster R	D	2-2	0-0	18	Foster [69], Trippier [87]	12,418
45		30	A	Sheffield U	D	2-2	1-1	18	Haynes 2 [15, 84]	22,366
46	May	7	H	Millwall	W	1-0	0-0	17	Noble-Lazarus [60]	11,136

Final League Position: 17

GOALSCORERS

League (55): Hammill 8, Gray 7 (3 pens), Haynes 6, Harewood 4, O'Connor 4, Shackell 3, Butterfield 2, Doyle 2, Hill 2, Lovre 2, Mellis 2, Trippier 2, Arismendi 1, Colace 1, Foster 1, Hassell 1, McEveley 1, McShane 1, Noble-Lazarus 1, O'Brien 1, own goals 3.
Carling Cup (0).
FA Cup (0).

Steele L 46	Hassall B 34+3	McEveley J 15+2	Shackell J 44	Doyle N 35+8	Foster S 32+1	Devaney M 1+5	Colace R 24+2	Lovre G 19+2	Gray A 24+10	Hammill A 25	Hume I —+1	Newmann J —+5	Butterfield J 18+22	Arismendi D 24+7	Trippier K 37+2	O'Brien J 20+13	Dickinson L —+3	O'Connor G 19+3	Wood C 4+3	Potter L 2+2	Hill M 23	Hayes P 2+5	Bennett S —+4	Haynes D 20	Taylor A —+2	Nouble F 4	Mellis J 14+1	Noble-Lazarus R 1+6	McShane P 10	Harewood M 9+1	Clark J —+4	Rose D —+1	Match No.
1	2	3	4	5	6	7¹	8		9³	10	11²	12	13	14																			1
1	2	3	4	12	5	13	8³	9	10	11			14	6¹	7²																		2
1	2	3	4	12	5		8	9	10	11			13	6¹	7²																		3
1	2	3	4¹	13	5		8	9	10	11			14	6²	7³	12																	4
1	2	3	4	5¹	6			9²	10	11	12			8	7³	14	13																5
1	2	3¹	4	12	5				10	11			6	8	7			9															6
1	2	3	4	14	5			10²	11				6³	8	12	7¹	13	9															7
1	2	3¹	4	13	5	6³	14		11				8	7	9²	10	12																8
1	2¹		4	12	5				9	10²	11		6	8	7			13	3														9
1		3	4		5	8			12	11		13	6²	2	7			9	10¹														10
1	12	3	4	2	5		8	9²	10	11			13		7¹	6²		14															11
1	2²	3¹	4	6	5		8	9²	10	11			7	13		14	12																12
1			4	6	5			9³		11		14	7	8¹	2	12	13	10²		3													13
1	2		4	6	5		8¹		10	11	13	12		7²						3	9												14
1	2		4	12	5		8		13	11	14	6		7				10²	3³	9¹													15
1	3		4	6	5		7¹	9²	10²	11	14	12	2	8				13															16
1	3		4	6	5		7	9¹	11²		13		2	8	10						12												17
1	3		4	6	5		7	9	11				2	8	10																		18
1	3		4		5		7¹	9²	11		12	6	2	8	10						13												19
1	3		4	6	5		7	9¹	11				2	8	10						12												20
1	3		4	6	5		7²	9¹	10³	11		13	2	8							12	14											21
1	3		4	6¹	5		7	9	10²	11	14	12	2	8³							13												22
1	2		4	6	5		13	9²	10	11¹			8	7	12			3															23
1	2		4	6	5			9¹	12	11	13		8	7	10²			3															24
1	3		4⁸	8	5⁸		7¹	12	11		6	2			10			9															25
1	5			6			7	13	4	11	2	8¹	10²	3				9	12														26
1	2		4	6	5²		8	14	11	13	7¹	12	10³	3				9															27
1	5		4	6			7¹	11³	12	2	8	10²	3	13	8	14	9																28
1	5		4	6				13	8	2	12	10¹	3	7	9	11²																	29
1	5		4	6				12	13	8¹	2	10²	3	7	9	11³	14																30
1	2		4	6	5¹			13	8³	12	14	10²	3	7	9	11																	31
1	3		4	6				14	13	8	2	10¹	12	7	9²	11³	5																32
1	2²		4	6¹				14	13	8	7	12	10	3	9	11³	5																33
1	2¹		4²					9	14	6	8	7	13	10⁸	3	11	5	12															34
1		3	4	6		13			12	8	2	10³	14	7	11¹	5	9²																35
1		3	4	6		12			14	8	2	10¹	7²	11³	5	9																	36
1		3	4	6		12			14	8	2	13	11³	10¹	7²	5	9																37
1	5¹		4	6		12	7²	10³	13	8	2	11	3	14	9																		38
1	2¹		4	6		13	11	10³	8	12	14	3	7²	5	9																		39
1			4	5	8¹	10³	11	13	2²	3	7	12	14	6	9																		40
1	13		4	6		10³	11	2	3¹	7	8²	14	5	9	12																		41
1			4	6	12	10	11	14	2	13	3	7²	8¹	5⁸	9³																		42
1	13		4	6	5	10³	11	2	3	7	8²	12	9¹	14																			43
1	12		4	6	5	10	11	2	3	7³	8¹	9²	13	14																			44
1	2²		4	6	5	10	11	7	3	9	8¹	12	13																				45
1	2	13	4	6	5	10	11	7	14	3²	9³	8¹	12																				46

FA Cup
Third Round   West Ham U   (a)   0-2

Carling Cup
First Round   Rochdale   (h)   0-1

BIRMINGHAM CITY   FL Championship

FOUNDATION

In 1875, cricketing enthusiasts who were largely members of Trinity Church, Bordesley, determined to continue their sporting relationships throughout the year by forming a football club which they called Small Heath Alliance. For their earliest games played on waste land in Arthur Street, the team included three Edden brothers and two James brothers.

St Andrews Stadium, Birmingham B9 4RL.
Telephone: 0844 557 1875.
Fax: 0844 557 1975.
Ticket Office: (0844) 557 1875 (then option 2).
Website: www.bcfc.com
Email: reception@bcfc.com
Ground Capacity: 30,079.
Record Attendance: 66,844 v Everton, FA Cup 5th rd, 11 February 1939.
Pitch Measurements: 101m × 68m.
President: Carson Yeung.
Vice-president: Michael Wiseman.
Chairman: Vico Hui.
Vice-chairman: Peter Pannu.
Secretary: Julia Shelton.
Manager: Chris Hughton.
First-Team Coach: Andy Watson.
Head of Sports Science: Nick Davies.

HONOURS

Football League – FL C:
Runners-up 2006–07, 2008–09;
Division 2: *Champions* 1892–93, 1920–21, 1947–48, 1954–55, 1994–95;
Runners-up 1893–94, 1900–01, 1902–03, 1971–72, 1984–85;
Division 3: *Runners-up* 1991–92.
FA Cup: *Runners-up* 1931, 1956.
Football League Cup: *Winners* 1963, 2011; *Runners-up* 2001.
Leyland Daf Cup: *Winners* 1991.
Auto Windscreens Shield: *Winners* 1995.
European Competitions
European Fairs Cup: 1955–58, 1958–60 (*runners-up*), 1960–61 (*runners-up*), 1961–62.

Colours: Blue shirts with white trim, white shorts, blue stockings.
Change Colours: All black.
Year Formed: 1875.   *Turned Professional:* 1885.   *Ltd Co.:* 1888.
Previous Names: 1875, Small Heath Alliance; 1888, dropped 'Alliance'; 1905, Birmingham; 1945, Birmingham City.
Club Nickname: 'Blues'.
Grounds: 1875, waste ground near Arthur St; 1877, Muntz St, Small Heath; 1906, St Andrews.
First Football League game: 3 September 1892, Division 2, v Burslem Port Vale (h) W 5–1 – Charsley; Bayley, Speller; Ollis, Jenkyns, Devey; Hallam (1), Edwards (1), Short (1), Wheldon (2), Hands.
Record League Victory: 12–0 v Walsall T Swifts, Division 2, 17 December 1892 – Charsley; Bayley, Jones; Ollis, Jenkyns, Devey; Hallam (2), Walton (3), Mobley (3), Wheldon (2), Hands (2). 12–0 v Doncaster R, Division 2, 11 April 1903 – Dorrington; Goldie, Wassell; Beer, Dougherty (1), Howard; Athersmith, Leonard (4), McRoberts (1), Wilcox (4), Field (1), (1 og).
Record Cup Victory: 9–2 v Burton W, FA Cup 1st rd, 31 October 1885 – Hedges; Jones, Evetts (1); Fred James, Felton, Arthur James (1); Davenport (2), Stanley (4), Simms, Figures, Morris (1).

sky SPORTS FACT FILE

In the first three post-war seasons from 1946–47, Birmingham City established a fine home record losing just eight of 63 League fixtures and conceding only 102 goals in 126 games home and away. In 1947–48 they let in just 24 goals in winning promotion to Division One.

Record Defeat: 1–9 v Sheffield W, Division 1, 13 December 1930. 1–9 v Blackburn R, Division 1, 5 January 1895.

Most League Points (2 for a win): 59, Division 2, 1947–48.

Most League Points (3 for a win): 89, Division 2, 1994–95.

Most League Goals: 103, Division 2, 1893–94 (only 28 games).

Highest League Scorer in Season: Joe Bradford, 29, Division 1, 1927–28.

Most League Goals in Total Aggregate: Joe Bradford, 249, 1920–35.

Most League Goals in One Match: 5, Walter Abbott v Darwen, Division 2, 26 November, 1898; 5, John McMillan v Blackpool, Division 2, 2 March 1901; 5, James Windridge v Glossop, Division 2, 23 January 1915.

Most Capped Player: Maik Taylor, 50 (87), Northern Ireland.

Most League Appearances: Frank Womack, 491, 1908–28.

Youngest League Player: Trevor Francis, 16 years 7 months v Cardiff C, 5 September 1970.

Record Transfer Fee Received: £6,800,000 from Liverpool for Jermaine Pennant, July 2006.

Record Transfer Fee Paid: £8,500,000 to Santos Laguna for Christian Benitez, July 2009.

Football League Record: 1892 Elected to Division 2; 1894–96 Division 1; 1896–1901 Division 2; 1901–02 Division 1; 1902–03 Division 2; 1903–08 Division 1; 1908–21 Division 2; 1921–39 Division 1; 1946–48 Division 2; 1948–50 Division 1; 1950–55 Division 2; 1955–65 Division 1; 1965–72 Division 2; 1972–79 Division 1; 1979–80 Division 2; 1980–84 Division 1; 1984–85 Division 2; 1985–86 Division 1; 1986–89 Division 2; 1989–92 Division 3; 1992–94 Division 1; 1994–95 Division 2; 1995–2002 Division 1; 2002–06 FA Premier League; 2006–07 FL C; 2007–08 FA Premier League; 2008–09 FL C; 2009–11 FA Premier League; 2011– FL C.

LATEST SEQUENCES

Longest Sequence of League Wins: 13, 17.12.1892 – 16.9.1893.

Longest Sequence of League Defeats: 8, 28.9.1985 – 23.11.1985.

Longest Sequence of League Draws: 8, 18.9.1990 – 23.10.1990.

Longest Sequence of Unbeaten League Matches: 20, 3.9.1994 – 2.1.1995.

Longest Sequence Without a League Win: 17, 28.9.1985 – 18.1.1986.

Successive Scoring Runs: 24 from 24.9.1892.

Successive Non-scoring Runs: 6 from 1.10.1949.

MANAGERS

Alfred Jones 1892–1908
  (*Secretary-Manager*)
Alec Watson 1908–10
Bob McRoberts 1910–15
Frank Richards 1915–23
Billy Beer 1923–27
William Harvey 1927–28
Leslie Knighton 1928–33
George Liddell 1933–39
William Camkin and Ted Goodier
  were in charge during 1939–45
Harry Storer 1945–48
Bob Brocklebank 1949–54
Arthur Turner 1954–58
Pat Beasley 1959–60
Gil Merrick 1960–64
Joe Mallett 1964–65
Stan Cullis 1965–70
Fred Goodwin 1970–75
Willie Bell 1975–77
Sir Alf Ramsay 1977–78
Jim Smith 1978–82
Ron Saunders 1982–86
John Bond 1986–87
Garry Pendrey 1987–89
Dave Mackay 1989–91
Lou Macari 1991
Terry Cooper 1991–93
Barry Fry 1993–96
Trevor Francis 1996–2001
Steve Bruce 2001–07
Alex McLeish 2007–11
Chris Hughton June 2011–

TEN YEAR LEAGUE RECORD

		P	W	D	L	F	A	Pts	Pos
2001-02	Div 1	46	21	13	12	70	49	76	5
2002-03	PR Lge	38	13	9	16	41	49	48	13
2003-04	PR Lge	38	12	14	12	43	48	50	10
2004-05	PR Lge	38	11	12	15	40	46	45	12
2005-06	PR Lge	38	8	10	20	28	50	34	18
2006-07	FL C	46	26	8	12	67	42	86	2
2007-08	PR Lge	38	8	11	19	46	62	35	19
2008-09	FL C	46	23	14	9	54	37	83	2
2009-10	PR Lge	38	13	11	14	38	47	50	9
2010-11	PR Lge	38	8	15	15	37	58	39	18

DID YOU KNOW ?

Before entering the Football League, Birmingham (as Small Heath) also had a 12-0 win under the belts from the Football Alliance. On 8 March 1890 they hit Nottingham Forest with Will Devey getting six, George Short a hat-trick, Ted Devey with two goals and Jack Hallam another one.

BIRMINGHAM CITY 2010–11 LEAGUE RECORD

Match No.	Date	Venue	Opponents	Result		H/T Score	Lg Pos.	Goalscorers	Attendance
1	Aug 14	A	Sunderland	D	2-2	0-1	—	Dann [77], Ridgewell [88]	38,390
2	21	H	Blackburn R	W	2-1	0-0	5	Gardner 2 [57, 71]	21,394
3	29	A	Bolton W	D	2-2	1-0	6	Johnson [4], Gardner [50]	18,139
4	Sept 12	H	Liverpool	D	0-0	0-0	5		27,333
5	18	A	WBA	L	1-3	1-0	12	Jerome [15]	23,062
6	25	H	Wigan Ath	D	0-0	0-0	13		22,186
7	Oct 2	H	Everton	L	0-2	0-0	16		23,138
8	16	A	Arsenal	L	1-2	1-1	17	Zigic [33]	60,070
9	23	H	Blackpool	W	2-0	1-0	12	Ridgewell [36], Zigic [56]	26,850
10	31	A	Aston Villa	D	0-0	0-0	14		40,688
11	Nov 6	H	West Ham U	D	2-2	0-0	15	Jerome [64], Ridgewell [73]	26,474
12	9	A	Stoke C	L	2-3	0-1	—	Fahey [74], Jerome [76]	26,381
13	13	A	Manchester C	D	0-0	0-0	18		44,321
14	20	H	Chelsea	W	1-0	1-0	14	Bowyer [17]	24,357
15	27	A	Fulham	D	1-1	1-0	14	Larsson [20]	24,391
16	Dec 4	H	Tottenham H	D	1-1	0-1	14	Gardner [81]	25,770
17	12	A	Wolverhampton W	L	0-1	0-1	16		25,150
18	28	H	Manchester U	D	1-1	0-0	16	Bowyer [89]	28,242
19	Jan 1	H	Arsenal	L	0-3	0-1	19		24,341
20	4	A	Blackpool	W	2-1	1-0	15	Hleb [24], Dann [89]	14,550
21	16	H	Aston Villa	D	1-1	0-0	16	Johnson [49]	22,287
22	22	A	Manchester U	L	0-5	0-3	17		75,326
23	Feb 2	H	Manchester C	D	2-2	1-2	—	Zigic [23], Gardner (pen) [77]	24,379
24	6	A	West Ham U	W	1-0	0-0	16	Zigic [65]	32,927
25	12	H	Stoke C	W	1-0	0-0	14	Zigic [90]	23,660
26	15	H	Newcastle U	L	0-2	0-1	14	—	28,270
27	Mar 5	H	WBA	L	1-3	0-0	18	Beausejour [48]	27,013
28	9	A	Everton	D	1-1	1-1	—	Beausejour [17]	33,974
29	19	A	Wigan Ath	L	1-2	1-1	19	Ridgewell [6]	16,421
30	Apr 2	H	Bolton W	W	2-1	1-0	15	Phillips [4], Gardner [59]	26,142
31	9	A	Blackburn R	D	1-1	1-1	16	Bowyer [32]	28,426
32	16	H	Sunderland	W	2-0	1-0	14	Larsson [41], Gardner [66]	28,108
33	20	A	Chelsea	L	1-3	0-2	—	Larsson (pen) [76]	40,848
34	23	A	Liverpool	L	0-5	0-2	15		44,734
35	May 1	H	Wolverhampton W	D	1-1	1-1	15	Larsson [27]	26,072
36	7	A	Newcastle U	L	1-2	1-2	16	Bowyer [45]	47,409
37	15	H	Fulham	L	0-2	0-1	17		27,759
38	22	A	Tottenham H	L	1-2	0-0	18	Gardner [79]	36,119

Final League Position: 18

GOALSCORERS

League (37): Gardner 8 (1 pen), Zigic 5, Bowyer 4, Larsson 4 (1 pen), Ridgewell 4, Jerome 3, Beausejour 2, Dann 2, Johnson 2, Fahey 1, Hleb 1, Phillips 1.
Carling Cup (15): Zigic 3, Gardner 2, Bowyer 1, Derbyshire 1, Hleb 1, Johnson 1, Larsson 1 (pen), McFadden 1 (pen), Martins 1, Murphy 1, Phillips 1, Ridgewell 1.
FA Cup (12): Derbyshire 2, Jerome 2, Murphy 2, Phillips 2, Beausejour 1, Bentley 1, Martins 1, Parnaby 1.

Foster B 38	Carr S 38	Ridgewell L 36	Bowyer L 24+5	Dann S 20	Johnson R 38	Larsson S 31+4	Ferguson B 35	Jerome C 30+4	O'Connor G 2+1	Fahey K 19+5	McFadden J 3+1	Zigic N 13+12	Gardner C 25+4	Derbyshire M 4+9	Hleb A 13+6	Beausejour J 9+8	Phillips K 5+9	Murphy D 3+7	Bentley D 9+4	Mutch J 3	Jiranek M 10	Martins O 3+1	Davies C 2+4	Parnaby S 5	Doyle C — +1	Match No.
1	2^3	3	4	5	6	7	8	9	10^2	11^3	12	13	14													1
1	2	3	13	5	6	7	4	9		14	11^2	10^1	8^3	12												2
1	2	3	4	5	6	7^2	8	9			11^1	12	10													3
1	2	3	4	5	6	7	8	9		11^1		12	10													4
1	2	3	4^1	5	6	7	8	9^2				12	10	13	11^3	14										5
1	2	3	4^1	5	6	7	8	9^3				12	10^2		11^2	13	14									6
1	2	3	4	5	6	7	8	9^2		10^1		12	13	11												7
1	2	3	4^2	5	6	7	8			13	10^1	9		11		12										8
1	2	3	12	5	6	7	4	9^3	8^1	10		14	11^2		13											9
1	2	3		5	6	7	8	12		10		9	4		11^1											10
1	2	3	14	5	6	7	4	9^3		8^2		10	12		11^1	13										11
1	2	3		5	6	7	4	9		12		10	8		11^1											12
1	2	3	12	5	6	7	4	9		11		10^2	8^1	13												13
1	2	3	4	5	6	7	8	9		11		10^1		12												14
1	2	3	4	5	6	7	8	9		10^2		12	11^1	13												15
1	2	3	4^2	5	6	13	8	9		11^1		12	10		7^1	14										16
1	2		4^3	5	6	7	8	9		11^1		10^2	12		13	14	3									17
1	2	3	4	5	6	7^1	8	9^3		13		10	12		11^1	14										18
1	2	3	4^2	5	6	7	8	9^3		13		10	12		11^1	14										19
1	2	3		5	6	12	4	9		11^1		8	10^2	7^3	13	14										20
1	2	8	13	5		4		10		12		8	9^4	11^1					3	7						21
1	2	6		5	13	4	12	10^2		14	9	11^1							3	7^3	8					22
1	2	3	4^1		6		8	9^2		10	11		12	13			5		7							23
1	2	3	4		6	12	8	9^1		10	11						5		7							24
1	2	3		6	7	4	12			10	8					11	5	9^1								25
1	2	3		6	7^3	4	12			10	8		14	13	11		5^2	9^1								26
1	2	3^2	4		6		9	8		7^1	12	13	11				10	5								27
1	2	3	4		6	7		9^2		13			10		12	11^1	8	5								28
1	2	3			6	7	4	9		8			10^2		13	11^3	5^1	14	12							29
1	2^2	3	4^1		6	7	8	9^3		12		14	11		10	13			5							30
1	2	3	4		6^1	7	8	9				11			10				12	5						31
1	2	3	4		6	7^2	8	9^3		13		11	14	12	10^1				5							32
1	2	6		5	7	4	9^2			10		8	13	11^1		12			14	3^2						33
1^6	2	3	4	5	7		9	10		8^2		11^1	13	12		6							15			34
1	2	3	4		6	7	8	9		11^8		12	10^1			5										35
1	2	3^2	4		6	7	8	9		11^1		12	10			5										36
1	2		4^1		6	7	8					10	12	13	9	11	5^2		14	3^2						37
1	2	3			6	7^1	4	9		11		8	12	10		5										38

FA Cup

Third Round	Millwall	(a)	4-1
Fourth Round	Coventry C	(h)	3-2
Fifth Round	Sheffield W	(h)	3-0
Sixth Round	Bolton W	(h)	2-3

Carling Cup

Second Round	Rochdale	(h)	3-2
Third Round	Milton Keynes D	(h)	3-1
Fourth Round	Brentford	(h)	1-1
Sixth Round	Aston Villa	(h)	2-1
Semi-Final	West Ham U	(a)	1-2
		(h)	3-1
Final	Arsenal		2-1
(at Wembley).			

BLACKBURN ROVERS   FA Premiership

FOUNDATION

It was in 1875 that some Public School old boys called a meeting at which the Blackburn Rovers club was formed and the colours blue and white adopted. The leading light was John Lewis, later to become a founder of the Lancashire FA, a famous referee who was in charge of two FA Cup Finals, and a vice-president of both the FA and the Football League.

Ewood Park, Blackburn, Lancs BB2 4JF.

Telephone: 0871 702 1875.

Fax: (01254) 671 042.

Ticket Office: 0871 222 1444.

Website: www.rovers.co.uk

Email: enquiries@rovers.co.uk

Ground Capacity: 31,367.

Record Attendance: 62,522 v Bolton W, FA Cup 6th rd, 2 March 1929.

Pitch Measurements: 105m × 65.8m.

Deputy Chief Executive: Paul Hunt.

Company Secretary: Martin Goodman.

Football Secretary: Anthony Bloch.

Manager: Steve Kean.

Assistant Manager: John Jensen.

Physio: Dave Fevre.

Colours: Blue and white halved shirts, white shorts, blue stockings.

Change Colours: All red with black trim.

Year Formed: 1875. *Turned Professional:* 1880.

Ltd Co.: 1897.

Club Nickname: Rovers.

Grounds: 1875, all matches played away; 1876, Oozehead Ground; 1877, Pleasington Cricket Ground; 1878, Alexandra Meadows; 1881, Leamington Road; 1890, Ewood Park.

First Football League Game: 15 September 1888, Football League, v Accrington (h) D 5–5 – Arthur; Beverley, James Southworth; Douglas, Almond, Forrest; Beresford (1), Walton, John Southworth (1), Fecitt (1), Townley (2).

Record League Victory: 9–0 v Middlesbrough, Division 2, 6 November 1954 – Elvy; Suart, Eckersley; Clayton, Kelly, Bell; Mooney (3), Crossan (2), Briggs, Quigley (3), Langton (1).

HONOURS

FA Premier League:
Champions 1994–95;
Runners-up 1993–94.
Football League: Division 1:
Champions 1911–12, 1913–14;
Runners-up 2000–01;
Division 2: *Champions* 1938–39;
Runners-up 1957–58;
Division 3: *Champions* 1974–75;
Runners-up 1979–80.
FA Cup: *Winners* 1884, 1885, 1886, 1890, 1891, 1928; *Runners-up* 1882, 1960.
Football League Cup: *Winners* 2002.
Full Members' Cup: *Winners* 1987.
European Competitions
European Cup: 1995–96.
UEFA Cup: 1994–95, 1998–99, 2002–03, 2003–04, 2006–07, 2007–08.
Intertoto Cup: 2007.

sky SPORTS FACT FILE

On 23 January 2011 when Blackburn Rovers defeated West Bromwich Albion 2-0 at Ewood Park, players from twenty-two different nationalities were featured during the match. Nineteen different such representatives began the match, eleven of them on the visiting team.

Record Cup Victory: 11–0 v Rossendale, FA Cup 1st rd, 13 October 1884 – Arthur; Hopwood, McIntyre; Forrest, Blenkhorn, Lofthouse; Sowerbutts (2), Jimmy Brown (1), Fecitt (4), Barton (3), Birtwistle (1).

Record Defeat: 0–8 v Arsenal, Division 1, 25 February 1933.

Most League Points (2 for a win): 60, Division 3, 1974–75.

Most League Points (3 for a win): 91, Division 1, 2000–01.

Most League Goals: 114, Division 2, 1954–55.

Highest League Scorer in Season: Ted Harper, 43, Division 1, 1925–26.

Most League Goals in Total Aggregate: Simon Garner, 168, 1978–92.

Most League Goals in One Match: 7, Tommy Briggs v Bristol R, Division 2, 5 February 1955.

Most Capped Player: Henning Berg, 58 (100), Norway.

Most League Appearances: Derek Fazackerley, 596, 1970–86.

Youngest League Player: Harry Dennison, 16 years 155 days v Bristol C, 8 April 1911.

Record Transfer Fee Received: £18,000,000 from Manchester C for Roque Santa Cruz, June 2009.

Record Transfer Fee Paid: £7,500,000 to Manchester U for Andy Cole, December 2001.

Football League Record: 1888 Founder Member of the League; 1936–39 Division 2; 1946–48 Division 1; 1948–58 Division 2; 1958–66 Division 1; 1966–71 Division 2; 1971–75 Division 3; 1975–79 Division 2; 1979–80 Division 3; 1980–92 Division 2; 1992–99 FA Premier League; 1999–2001 Division 1; 2001– FA Premier League.

LATEST SEQUENCES

Longest Sequence of League Wins: 8, 1.3.1980 – 7.4.1980.

Longest Sequence of League Defeats: 7, 12.3.1966 – 16.4.1966.

Longest Sequence of League Draws: 5, 11.10.1975 – 1.11.1975.

Longest Sequence of Unbeaten League Matches: 23, 30.9.1987 – 27.3.1988.

Longest Sequence Without a League Win: 16, 11.11.1978 – 24.3.1979.

Successive Scoring Runs: 32 from 24.4.1954.

Successive Non-scoring Runs: 4 from 12.12.1908.

MANAGERS

Thomas Mitchell 1884–96
(Secretary-Manager)
J. Walmsley 1896–1903
((Secretary-Manager)
R. B. Middleton 1903–25
Jack Carr 1922–26
(Team Manager under Middleton to 1925)
Bob Crompton 1926–31
(Hon. Team Manager)
Arthur Barritt 1931–36
(had been Secretary from 1927)
Reg Taylor 1936–38
Bob Crompton 1938–41
Eddie Hapgood 1944–47
Will Scott 1947
Jack Bruton 1947–49
Jackie Bestall 1949–53
Johnny Carey 1953–58
Dally Duncan 1958–60
Jack Marshall 1960–67
Eddie Quigley 1967–70
Johnny Carey 1970–71
Ken Furphy 1971–73
Gordon Lee 1974–75
Jim Smith 1975–78
Jim Iley 1978
John Pickering 1978–79
Howard Kendall 1979–81
Bobby Saxton 1981–86
Don Mackay 1987–91
Kenny Dalglish 1991–95
Ray Harford 1995–96
Roy Hodgson 1997–98
Brian Kidd 1998–99
Graeme Souness 2000–04
Mark Hughes 2004–08
Paul Ince 2008
Sam Allardyce 2008–10
Steve Kean December 2010–

TEN YEAR LEAGUE RECORD			P	W	D	L	F	A	Pts	Pos
2001-02	PR Lge	38	12	10	16	55	51	46	10
2002-03	PR Lge	38	16	12	10	52	43	60	6
2003-04	PR Lge	38	12	8	18	51	59	44	15
2004-05	PR Lge	38	9	15	14	32	43	42	15
2005-06	PR Lge	38	19	6	13	51	42	63	6
2006-07	PR Lge	38	15	7	16	52	54	52	10
2007-08	PR Lge	38	15	13	10	50	48	58	7
2008-09	PR Lge	38	10	11	17	40	60	41	15
2009-10	PR Lge	38	13	11	14	41	55	50	10
2010-11	PR Lge	38	11	10	17	46	59	43	15

DID YOU KNOW ?

While Jimmy Brown's FA Cup scoring record with Blackburn Rovers in the 19th century is outstanding with 28 goals in 32 matches, Jack Southworth with 25 from the same number of games is amazing. On retiring he had another string to his bow, as a professional violinist.

BLACKBURN ROVERS 2010–11 LEAGUE RECORD

Match No.	Date	Venue	Opponents	Result	H/T Score	Lg Pos.	Goalscorers	Attendance
1	Aug 14	H	Everton	W 1-0	1-0	—	Kalinic [14]	25,869
2	21	A	Birmingham C	L 1-2	0-0	9	N'Zonzi [54]	21,394
3	28	H	Arsenal	L 1-2	1-1	15	Biram Diouf [27]	25,059
4	Sept 11	A	Manchester C	D 1-1	1-0	15	Kalinic [25]	44,246
5	18	H	Fulham	D 1-1	1-0	14	Samba [30]	23,759
6	25	A	Blackpool	W 2-1	1-0	9	Adam (og) [20], Emerton [90]	15,901
7	Oct 2	A	Stoke C	L 0-1	0-0	13		25,515
8	18	H	Sunderland	D 0-0	0-0	—		21,894
9	24	A	Liverpool	L 1-2	0-0	17	Carragher (og) [50]	43,328
10	30	H	Chelsea	L 1-2	1-1	18	Mwaruwari [21]	25,836
11	Nov 6	H	Wigan Ath	W 2-1	0-0	16	Pedersen [58], Roberts [67]	24,413
12	10	A	Newcastle U	W 2-1	1-0	—	Pedersen [3], Roberts [82]	41,053
13	13	A	Tottenham H	L 2-4	0-2	14	Nelsen [80], Givet [90]	35,700
14	21	H	Aston Villa	W 2-0	1-0	11	Pedersen 2 [45, 66]	21,848
15	27	A	Manchester U	L 1-7	0-3	13	Samba [83]	74,850
16	Dec 4	H	Wolverhampton W	W 3-0	2-0	10	Dunn [29], Emerton [43], Nelsen [55]	22,314
17	12	A	Bolton W	L 1-2	0-0	13	Biram Diouf [87]	24,471
18	18	H	West Ham U	D 1-1	0-0	—	Nelsen [51]	21,934
19	26	H	Stoke C	L 0-2	0-0	13		25,440
20	28	A	WBA	W 3-1	1-1	9	Kalinic 2 [3, 53], Biram Diouf [62]	24,440
21	Jan 1	A	Sunderland	L 0-3	0-2	12		36,242
22	5	H	Liverpool	W 3-1	2-0	9	Olsson [32], Mwaruwari 2 [38, 57]	24,522
23	15	A	Chelsea	L 0-2	0-0	11		40,846
24	23	H	WBA	W 2-0	1-0	7	Tamas (og) [41], Hoilett [47]	24,057
25	Feb 2	H	Tottenham H	L 0-1	0-1	—		23,253
26	5	A	Wigan Ath	L 3-4	1-1	11	Roberts [23], Samba [58], Dunn (pen) [81]	18,567
27	12	A	Newcastle U	D 0-0	0-0	11		26,781
28	26	A	Aston Villa	L 1-4	0-0	14	Kalinic [81]	34,309
29	Mar 5	A	Fulham	L 2-3	1-1	14	Hangeland (og) [45], Hoilett [65]	25,687
30	19	H	Blackpool	D 2-2	0-2	13	Samba [49], Hoilett [90]	27,209
31	Apr 2	A	Arsenal	D 0-0	0-0	14		60,087
32	9	H	Birmingham C	D 1-1	1-1	15	Hoilett [45]	28,426
33	16	A	Everton	L 0-2	0-0	16		35,857
34	25	H	Manchester C	L 0-1	0-0	—		23,529
35	30	H	Bolton W	W 1-0	1-0	16	Olsson [20]	28,985
36	May 7	A	West Ham U	D 1-1	1-0	15	Roberts [12]	33,789
37	14	A	Manchester U	D 1-1	1-0	15	Emerton [20]	29,867
38	22	A	Wolverhampton W	W 3-2	3-0	15	Roberts [22], Emerton [38], Hoilett [45]	29,009

Final League Position: 15

GOALSCORERS

League (46): Hoilett 5, Kalinic 5, Roberts 5, Emerton 4, Pedersen 4, Samba 4, Biram Diouf 3, Mwaruwari 3, Nelsen 3, Dunn 2 (1 pen), Olsson 2, Givet 1, N'Zonzi 1, own goals 4.
Carling Cup (4): Biram Diouf 3, Givet 1.
FA Cup (2): Hoilett 1, Kalinic 1.

Robinson P 36	Salgado M 36	Olsson M 25+4	Samba C 33	Jones P 24+2	Nelsen R 28	Givet G 29	Dunn D 17+10	Kalinic N 15+3	Diouf E 18+2	Pedersen M 27+8	N'Zonzi S 13+8	Biram Diouf M 17+9	Emerton B 24+6	Hoilett D 17+7	Grella V 4+1	Chimbonda P 3+3	Mwaruwari B 6+12	Andrews K 2+3	Roberts J 13+12	Goulon H 1+3	Linganzi A —+1	Morris J —+4	Hanley G 5+2	Bunn M 2+1	Lowe J —+1	Santa Cruz R 7+2	Jones J 15	Rochina R 1+3	Match No.
1	2	3	4	5	6	7	8^1	9	10	11	12	13																	1
1	2	8	4	5^1	6	3^2		9	10	11	7	13	12	14															2
1	2	13	4	6	5	3	12	9^2	10	11	14	7^3					8^1												3
1	2^2	12	4	6	5^1	3		9	10	11	14	7					8^3		13										4
1	2		4	6	5	3		9^2	10	11^1	14	7	12				8^3		13										5
1	2		4	6	5	3		9^3	10	11		7^2	12				8^1		14				13						6
1	2	12	4	6	5	3	10^1	11^3	8	9	7^2		14						13										7
1	2^2	3	4*	6	5	13	9^1	10	11	8	14	7					12^3												8
1	2	3	6	5	8^3	9^2	10	11	4^1	7	14	12					13												9
1	2	12	4	6	5	3^1	14	10^3	11	8	7						9^2		13										10
1	2		4	6	5	3	13	10^3	11	8^2	7	14					9^1		12										11
1	2		4	6	5	3	13	9^1	11	7	10^2	8					12												12
1	2^1		4	6	5	3	14	9^2	12	11^3	7	10	8				13												13
1	2		4	6	5	3^1	7	10	11^3	13	8^2	12					9		14										14
1	2		4	6	5	8	10^3					7^2	12	3			9		11^1				13					14	15
1	2		4	6	5	3	8^1	10^2	11	12	7		14				9^3		13										16
1	2^2	8^1	4	6	5	3	13	10^3	11	12	7	14					9												17
1	2	4^2	13^3		5	3	8	10	11	6	7	12					9^1		14										18
1	2	3		5	6		8^1	9		11	10	7	12										4						19
1^G	2^1	3		5	4		9^1	10^2	11	8	7	12	13										6	15					20
	3		5	2	4^3		10	11	8	7	9^1		12		14	13	6^1	1											21
	2	6^1	4		5	3	8^2	12	11	10	7		9^3		14	13	1												22
1	2	6	4		5	3	8^1	9^2	11	10	7^3		14						12	13									23
1	2^3	3	6		5	8	8^1	9^2	11	12	7	13	14				10	4											24
1	2	3	6		5		8^2	13	12	10^3	11		14	4			9									7^1			25
1	2	3	6		5	12		11	14	13	7^1	8	10^2				9									4^3			26
1	2	3	6		5	8^3	9	12	7	14	11^1	13														10^2	4		27
1	2	3	5*			12		11	14	7	10^2	4^1	13				6									9^3	R		28
1	2^3	11	5		3^1	12	7	10	14	8^2	9		6													4	13		29
1	2	3	6	12	5	13	14	8^2	11^3	7^1	10	13														9	4		30
1	2	3	6	4	5	13	$11*$	7	10	12																9^1	8^2		31
1	2	3	6	4	5^1	8	11	14	10^3	13	12															9^2	7		32
1	2	5	6	4	3^2	8	13	7	14	12																9^1	11	10^3	33
1	2	11	5	4	3^3	8^1	13	14	7	10^2	9															6	12		34
1	2^2	11	5	6	3	12	14	8	13	7	9^1	10^3															4		35
1		3	6	5		11	7	8^3	2	9^1	12	10^2	13													4	14		36
1	2	11	5^3	6	3	13	12	8	7	9^1	14	10															4^2		37
1	2	11	5	6	3	12	8	7	9^1	10																	4		38

FA Cup
Third Round	QPR	(h)	1-0
Fourth Round	Aston Villa	(a)	1-3

Carling Cup
Second Round	Norwich C	(h)	3-1
Third Round	Aston Villa	(a)	1-3

BLACKPOOL

FOUNDATION

Old boys of St John's School who had formed themselves into a football club decided to establish a club bearing the name of their town and Blackpool FC came into being at a meeting at the Stanley Arms Hotel in the summer of 1887. In their first season playing at Raikes Hall Gardens, the club won both the Lancashire Junior Cup and the Fylde Cup.

Bloomfield Road, Seasiders Way, Blackpool FY1 6JJ.
Telephone: (0871) 6221 953.
Fax: (01253) 405 011.
Ticket Office: (0871) 6221 953.
Website: www.blackpoolfc.co.uk
Email: info@blackpoolfc.co.uk
Ground Capacity: 9,491.
Record Attendance: 38,098 v Wolverhampton W, Division 1, 17 September 1955.
Pitch Measurements: 110yd × 74yd.
Chairman: Karl Oyston.
Secretary: Matt Williams.
Manager: Ian Holloway.
Assistant Manager: Steve Thompson.
Physio: Phil Horner.

HONOURS

Football League – Division 1:
Runners-up 1955–56;
Division 2: *Champions* 1929–30;
Runners-up 1936–37, 1969–70;
Division 4: *Runners-up* 1984–85.
FA Cup: *Winners* 1953;
Runners-up 1948, 1951.
Football League Cup: Semi-final 1962.
Anglo-Italian Cup: *Winners* 1971;
Runners-up 1972.
LDV Vans Trophy: *Winners* 2002, 2004.

Colours: Tangerine shirts with white trim, white shorts, tangerine stockings with white tops.
Change Colours: White shirts with tangerine trim, tangerine shorts, white stockings.
Year Formed: 1887.
Turned Professional: 1887.
Ltd Co.: 1896.
Previous Name: 'South Shore' combined with Blackpool in 1899, twelve years after the latter had been formed on the breaking up of the old 'Blackpool St John's' club.
Club Nickname: 'The Seasiders'.
Grounds: 1887, Raikes Hall Gardens; 1897, Athletic Grounds; 1899, Raikes Hall Gardens; 1899, Bloomfield Road.
First Football League game: 5 September 1896, Division 2, v Lincoln C (a) L 1–3 – Douglas; Parr, Bowman; Stuart, Stirzaker, Norris; Clarkin, Donnelly, Robert Parkinson, Mount (1), Jack Parkinson.
Record League Victory: 7–0 v Reading, Division 2, 10 November 1928 – Mercer; Gibson, Hamilton, Watson, Wilson, Grant, Ritchie, Oxberry (2), Hampson (5), Tufnell, Neal. 7–0 v Preston NE (away), Division 1, 1 May 1948 – Robinson; Shimwell, Crosland; Buchan, Hayward, Kelly; Hobson, Munro (1), McIntosh (5), McCall, Rickett (1). 7–0 v Sunderland, Division 1, 5 October 1957 – Farm; Armfield, Garrett, Kelly J, Gratrix, Kelly H, Matthews, Taylor (2), Charnley (2), Durie (2), Perry (1).

sky SPORTS FACT FILE

In 2010–11 Blackpool achieved their first League double over Liverpool since 1946–47. Then they won 3-2 at both Bloomfield Road and Anfield. Stan Mortensen scored three of their six goals that season. It was an outstanding performance because Liverpool were champions that term.

Record Cup Victory: 7–1 v Charlton Ath, League Cup 2nd rd, 25 September 1963 – Harvey; Armfield, Martin; Crawford, Gratrix, Cranston; Lea, Ball (1), Charnley (4), Durie (1), Oates (1).

Record Defeat: 1–10 v Small Heath, Division 2, 2 March 1901 and v Huddersfield T, Division 1, 13 December 1930.

Most League Points (2 for a win): 58, Division 2, 1929–30 and Division 2, 1967–68.

Most League Points (3 for a win): 86, Division 4, 1984–85.

Most League Goals: 98, Division 2, 1929–30.

Highest League Scorer in Season: Jimmy Hampson, 45, Division 2, 1929–30.

Most League Goals in Total Aggregate: Jimmy Hampson, 248, 1927–38.

Most League Goals in One Match: 5, Jimmy Hampson v Reading, Division 2, 10 November 1928; 5, Jimmy McIntosh v Preston NE, Division 1, 1 May 1948.

Most Capped Player: Jimmy Armfield, 43, England.

Most League Appearances: Jimmy Armfield, 568, 1952–71.

Youngest League Player: Matty Kay, 16 years 32 days v Scunthorpe U, 13 November 2005.

Record Transfer Fee Received: £1,750,000 from Southampton for Brett Ormerod, December 2001.

Record Transfer Fee Paid: £1,500,000 to Leicester C for D.J. Campbell, August 2010.

Football League Record: 1896 Elected to Division 2; 1899 Failed re-election; 1900 Re-elected; 1900–30 Division 2; 1930–33 Division 1; 1933–37 Division 2; 1937–67 Division 1; 1967–70 Division 2; 1970–71 Division 1; 1971–78 Division 2; 1978–81 Division 3; 1981–85 Division 4; 1985–90 Division 3; 1990–92 Division 4; 1992–2000 Division 2; 2000–01 Division 3; 2001–04 Division 2; 2004–07 FL 1; 2007–10 FL C; 2010–11 FA Premier League; 2011– FL C.

MANAGERS

Tom Barcroft 1903–33
(Secretary-Manager)
John Cox 1909–11
Bill Norman 1919–23
Maj. Frank Buckley 1923–27
Sid Beaumont 1927–28
Harry Evans 1928–33
(Hon. Team Manager)
Alex 'Sandy' Macfarlane 1933–35
Joe Smith 1935–58
Ronnie Suart 1958–67
Stan Mortensen 1967–69
Les Shannon 1969–70
Bob Stokoe 1970–72
Harry Potts 1972–76
Allan Brown 1976–78
Bob Stokoe 1978–79
Stan Ternent 1979–80
Alan Ball 1980–81
Allan Brown 1981–82
Sam Ellis 1982–89
Jimmy Mullen 1989–90
Graham Carr 1990
Bill Ayre 1990–94
Sam Allardyce 1994–96
Gary Megson 1996–97
Nigel Worthington 1997–99
Steve McMahon 2000–04
Colin Hendry 2004–05
Simon Grayson 2005–08
Ian Holloway May 2009–

LATEST SEQUENCES

Longest Sequence of League Wins: 9, 21.11.1936 – 1.1.1937.

Longest Sequence of League Defeats: 8, 26.11.1898 – 7.1.1899.

Longest Sequence of League Draws: 5, 4.12.1976 – 1.1.1977.

Longest Sequence of Unbeaten League Matches: 17, 6.4.1968 – 21.9.1968.

Longest Sequence Without a League Win: 19, 19.12.1970 – 24.4.1971.

Successive Scoring Runs: 33 from 23.2.1929.

Successive Non-scoring Runs: 5 from 12.4.1975.

TEN YEAR LEAGUE RECORD

		P	W	D	L	F	A	Pts	Pos
2001-02	Div 2	46	14	14	18	66	69	56	16
2002-03	Div 2	46	15	13	18	56	64	58	13
2003-04	Div 2	46	16	11	19	58	65	59	14
2004-05	FL 1	46	15	12	19	54	59	57	16
2005-06	FL 1	46	12	17	17	56	64	53	19
2006-07	FL 1	46	24	11	11	76	49	83	3
2007-08	FL C	46	12	18	16	59	64	54	19
2008-09	FL C	46	13	17	16	47	58	56	16
2009-10	FL C	46	19	13	14	74	58	70	6
2010-11	PR Lge	38	10	9	19	55	78	39	19

DID YOU KNOW ?

Blackpool reached the play-offs in successive seasons, losing to Torquay United in a shoot-out in 1990–91, before similarly defeating Scunthorpe United 4-3 on penalties the following term. Goalkeeper Steve McIlhargey made the crucial save to ensure victory.

BLACKPOOL 2010–11 LEAGUE RECORD

Match No.	Date	Venue	Opponents	Result	H/T Score	Lg Pos.	Goalscorers	Attendance
1	Aug 14	A	Wigan Ath	W 4-0	3-0	—	Taylor-Fletcher [16], Harewood 2 [38, 43], John-Baptiste [75]	16,152
2	21	A	Arsenal	L 0-6	0-3	10		60,032
3	28	H	Fulham	D 2-2	0-1	12	Pantsil (og) [71], Varney [76]	15,529
4	Sept 11	A	Newcastle U	W 2-0	1-0	4	Adam (pen) [45], Campbell [90]	49,597
5	19	A	Chelsea	L 0-4	0-4	9		41,761
6	25	H	Blackburn R	L 1-2	0-1	15	Phillips [85]	15,901
7	Oct 3	A	Liverpool	W 2-1	2-0	9	Adam (pen) [29], Varney [45]	43,156
8	17	H	Manchester C	L 2-3	0-0	10	Harewood [78], Taylor-Fletcher [90]	16,116
9	23	A	Birmingham C	L 0-2	0-1	14		26,850
10	Nov 1	H	WBA	W 2-1	1-0	—	Adam (pen) [12], Varney [62]	15,210
11	6	H	Everton	D 2-2	1-1	12	Eardley [10], Vaughan [48]	16,094
12	10	A	Aston Villa	L 2-3	1-1	—	Harewood [45], Campbell [87]	34,330
13	13	A	West Ham U	D 0-0	0-0	15		31,194
14	20	H	Wolverhampton W	W 2-1	2-0	12	Varney [3], Harewood [44]	15,922
15	27	A	Bolton W	D 2-2	1-0	11	Evatt [28], Varney [57]	25,851
16	Dec 11	H	Stoke C	W 1-0	0-0	10	Campbell [48]	26,879
17	28	A	Sunderland	W 2-0	0-0	8	Campbell 2 [50, 90]	42,892
18	Jan 1	A	Manchester C	L 0-1	0-1	11		47,296
19	4	H	Birmingham C	L 1-2	0-1	13	Campbell [68]	14,550
20	12	H	Liverpool	W 2-1	1-1	—	Taylor-Fletcher [12], Campbell [69]	16,089
21	15	A	WBA	L 2-3	1-1	10	Vaughan [11], Taylor-Fletcher [80]	25,316
22	22	H	Sunderland	L 1-2	0-2	12	Adam (pen) [86]	16,037
23	25	H	Manchester U	L 2-3	2-0	—	Cathcart [15], Campbell [43]	15,574
24	Feb 2	H	West Ham U	L 1-3	1-3	—	Adam [42]	15,095
25	5	A	Everton	L 3-5	1-1	15	John-Baptiste [37], Puncheon [62], Adam [64]	38,202
26	12	H	Aston Villa	D 1-1	1-1	16	Grandin [14]	16,000
27	22	H	Tottenham H	W 3-1	2-0	—	Adam (pen) [18], Campbell [44], Ormerod [80]	16,069
28	26	A	Wolverhampton W	L 0-4	0-1	15		29,086
29	Mar 7	H	Chelsea	L 1-3	0-1	—	Puncheon [86]	15,584
30	19	A	Blackburn R	D 2-2	2-0	15	Adam 2 (1 pen) [25 (p), 29]	27,209
31	Apr 3	A	Fulham	L 0-3	0-2	17		25,692
32	10	H	Arsenal	L 1-3	0-2	17	Taylor-Fletcher [52]	16,030
33	16	H	Wigan Ath	L 1-3	0-2	18	Campbell [83]	16,030
34	23	A	Newcastle U	D 1-1	1-1	17	Campbell [32]	16,003
35	30	H	Stoke C	D 0-0	0-0	17		16,003
36	May 7	A	Tottenham H	D 1-1	0-0	18	Adam (pen) [76]	35,585
37	14	H	Bolton W	W 4-3	3-2	18	Campbell 2 [9, 45], Puncheon [19], Adam [63]	15,979
38	22	A	Manchester U	L 2-4	1-1	19	Adam [40], Taylor-Fletcher [57]	75,400

Final League Position: 19

GOALSCORERS

League (55): Campbell 13, Adam 12 (7 pens), Taylor-Fletcher 6, Harewood 5, Varney 5, Puncheon 3, John-Baptiste 2, Vaughan 2, Cathcart 1, Eardley 1, Evatt 1, Grandin 1, Ormerod 1, Phillips 1, own goal 1.
Carling Cup (3): Adam 1 (pen), Ormerod 1, Sylvestre 1.
FA Cup (0).

Gilks M 18	John-Baptiste A 19+2	Crainey S 31	Adam C 34+1	Cathcart C 28+2	Evatt I 36+2	Taylor-Fletcher G 29+2	Grandin E 21+2	Harewood M 7+9	Ormerod B 6+13	Vaughan D 35	Sylvestre L 6+2	Basham C 1+1	Euell J 1+2	Keinan D 3+3	Demontagnac I —+1	Varney L 24+6	Eardley N 30+1	Campbell D 30+1	Southern K 11+10	Carney D 5+6	Phillips M 6+21	Kingson R 19+1	Edwards R 1+1	Rachubka P 1+1	Reid A 2+3	Beattie J 5+4	Puncheon J 6+5	Kornilenko S 3+3	Halstead M —+1	Match No.
1	2	3	4	5	6	7^3	8	9^2	10^1	11	12	13	14																	1
1	2	3	4	5	6^4	10^3	8	9^2	13	11	7^1		12	14																2
1	2	3	4	5	6^1	7	8		10	11						9	12													3
1		3	4		6		8^3	12	10^1	11			2			7^2	5	9	13	14										4
1	2	3	4		6	12	8^2	13	14	11			7			10^3	5^1	9												5
1		3	4	5	6	7	13	9^2	10^1	11						12	2^3	8	14											6
1		3	4	5^1	6	7	8^3			11				12		10	2^2	9	14	13										7
1		3	4	5	6	7	8^1	12		11						10	2^2	9		13										8
1		3	4	4^1	5	6	7	9^2	14	11						10^3	2	8	12	13										9
1		3	4	5^2	6	7	8			11				14		10^3	2^1	9	13	12										10
1		3	4	5	6	7^2	14	13		11						10^3	2	9	8^1	12										11
		12		13				9^3	10			7	2	8^1	6^2	14	4	3	11	1	5									12
1^6		3	4	5	6	7	8^1	13		11						10	2	9^2	12	15										13
		3^1	4	5	6	12		9^2		11	13					10	2	8	14	7^1		1								14
		3	4	5	6	7^1	8^3	12		11						10^2	2	9	13	14		1								15
		3	4	5	6	7	8^1			11						10	2	9	12			1								16
		3		5	6	7^3	8^1		11				4^2			10	2	9	14	13	12	1								17
		3	4	5	6	7^2		13		11			8^1			10^3	2	9	14	12		1								18
		3	4	5	6	7^2		12		11				13		10^3	2	9	14	8^1		1								19
	14	3	4	5	6	7^3	8^1	13		11						10^2	2	9	13		12	1								20
	14	3	4	5	6	7	8^1		13	11						10^3	2^2	9			12	1								21
		3^1	4	5	6	7	8^2	13	12	11						10	2	9	10	15										22
		3	4	5	6	7^2	8	13		11						10^1	2	9			12	1								23
	6		4	5^1	12	7		13		11						10^1	2	9	3			1				8^2	14			24
	5		4		6		8	14		11						2	9^2	12	3	13		1				10^3	7^1			25
	2		4	5	6	7^2	8^1			11						10^3		9	3	13		1			14	12				26
	3		4	5	6	7^1		13		11							2	9	12	14		1			10^2	8^3				27
	3			5	6	7^2		13		11						12	2	10^4	4	14		1				9^3	8^1			28
	5	3				8		12^1		11						2	4	8^2	13	10		1			10^1	9	7		15	29
	2	3	4^3	5	6	9	8^2			11						10^1			14	12		1				13	7			30
	2	3	4	5	6	7	8^1	9^2		11						12						1					10^3	14	13	31
	2	3	4	5	6	7										10^1		9	8^2	13		1					12	11^3	14	32
1		3	4	5	6	7^1	11^2			11						10^3	2	9	8		12						13	14		33
1	5	3	4		6				10^2	11						12	2	9	8							7^1	13			34
1	5	3	4		6				10^2	11						12	2	9	7							8^1		13		35
1	5	3	4	13	6	7^2				11							2^3	9	8								14	12	10^1	36
1	5	3	4^3	14	6	7^2				11		13					2	9	8								12		10^1	37
1	5	3	4		6	7^2	14			11		13					2	9	8^3		12								10^1	38

FA Cup
Third Round   Southampton   (a)   0-2   **Carling Cup**
Second Round   Milton Keynes D   (a)   3-4

BOLTON WANDERERS   FA Premiership

FOUNDATION

In 1874 boys of Christ Church Sunday School, Blackburn Street, led by their master Thomas Ogden, established a football club which went under the name of the school and whose president was Vicar of Christ Church. Membership was 6d (two and a half pence). When their president began to lay down too many rules about the use of church premises, the club broke away and formed Bolton Wanderers in 1877, holding their earliest meetings at the Gladstone Hotel.

The Reebok Stadium, Burnden Way, Lostock, Bolton BL6 6JW.

Telephone: (0844) 871 2932. *Fax:* (01204) 673 773.

Ticket Office: (0844) 871 2932.

Website: www.bwfc.co.uk

Email: reception@bwfc.co.uk

Ground Capacity: 28,101.

Record Attendance: 69,912 v Manchester C, FA Cup 5th rd, 18 February 1933 (at Burnden Park). 28,353 v Leicester C, FA Premier League, 23 December 2003 (at The Reebok Stadium).

Pitch Measurements: 105m × 68m.

Chairman: Phil A. Gartside.

Chief Executive: Allan Duckworth.

Vice-chairman: Brett Warburton.

Secretary: Simon Marland.

Manager: Owen Coyle.

Assistant Manager: Sandy Stewart.

Fitness Coach: Michael Rawson.

Colours: White shirts with blue body trim, blue shorts, white stockings.

Change Colours: Blue shirts with red trim, white shorts, blue stockings.

Year Formed: 1874. *Turned Professional:* 1880. *Ltd Co.:* 1895.

Previous Name: 1874, Christ Church FC; 1877, Bolton Wanderers.

Club Nickname: 'The Trotters'.

Grounds: Park Recreation Ground and Cockle's Field before moving to Pike's Lane ground 1881; 1895, Burnden Park; 1997, Reebok Stadium.

First Football League Game: 8 September 1888, Football League, v Derby Co (h) L 3–6 – Harrison; Robinson, Mitchell; Roberts, Weir, Bullough, Davenport (2), Milne, Coupar, Barbour, Brogan (1).

Record League Victory: 8–0 v Barnsley, Division 2, 6 October 1934 – Jones; Smith, Finney; Goslin, Atkinson, George Taylor; George T. Taylor (2), Eastham, Milsom (1), Westwood (4), Cook, (1 og).

HONOURS

Football League – Division 1: *Champions* 1996–97;
Division 2: *Champions* 1908–09, 1977–78; *Runners-up* 1899–1900, 1904–05, 1910–11, 1934–35, 1992–93;
Division 3: *Champions* 1972–73.
FA Cup: *Winners* 1923, 1926, 1929, 1958; *Runners-up* 1894, 1904, 1953.
Football League Cup: *Runners-up* 1995, 2004.
Freight Rover Trophy: *Runners-up* 1986.
Sherpa Van Trophy: *Winners* 1989.
European Competitions
UEFA Cup: 2005–06, 2007–08.

sky SPORTS FACT FILE

On 20 November 2010 Bolton Wanderers defeated Newcastle United 5-1 to move into fourth place in the Premier League table. The second goal of the match scored by Chung-Yong Lee was also the 500th registered by the Trotters in the competition since 1992–93.

Record Cup Victory: 13–0 v Sheffield U, FA Cup 2nd rd, 1 February 1890 – Parkinson; Robinson (1), Jones; Bullough, Davenport, Roberts; Rushton, Brogan (3), Cassidy (5), McNee, Weir (4).

Record Defeat: 1–9 v Preston NE, FA Cup 2nd rd, 10 December 1887.

Most League Points (2 for a win): 61, Division 3, 1972–73.

Most League Points (3 for a win): 98, Division 1, 1996–97.

Most League Goals: 100, Division 1, 1996–97.

Highest League Scorer in Season: Joe Smith, 38, Division 1, 1920–21.

Most League Goals in Total Aggregate: Nat Lofthouse, 255, 1946–61.

Most League Goals in One Match: 5, Tony Caldwell v Walsall, Division 3, 10 September 1983.

Most Capped Player: Mark Fish, 34 (62), South Africa.

Most League Appearances: Eddie Hopkinson, 519, 1956–70.

Youngest League Player: Ray Parry, 15 years 267 days v Wolverhampton W, 13 October 1951.

Record Transfer Fee Received: £15,000,000 from Chelsea for Nicolas Anelka, January 2008.

Record Transfer Fee Paid: £8,200,000 to Toulouse for Johan Elmander, July 2008.

Football League Record: 1888 Founder Member of the League; 1899–1900 Division 2; 1900–05 Division 1; 1903–05 Division 2; 1905–08 Division 1; 1908–09 Division 2; 1909–10 Division 1; 1910–11 Division 2; 1911–33 Division 1; 1933–35 Division 2; 1935–64 Division 1; 1964–71 Division 2; 1971–73 Division 3; 1973–78 Division 2; 1978–80 Division 1; 1980–83 Division 2; 1983–87 Division 3; 1987–88 Division 4; 1988–92 Division 3; 1992–93 Division 2; 1993–95 Division 1; 1995–96 FA Premier League; 1996–97 Division 1; 1997–98 FA Premier League; 1998–2001 Division 1; 2001– FA Premier League.

LATEST SEQUENCES

Longest Sequence of League Wins: 11, 5.11.1904 – 2.1.1905.

Longest Sequence of League Defeats: 11, 7.4.1902 – 18.10.1902.

Longest Sequence of League Draws: 6, 25.1.1913 – 8.3.1913.

Longest Sequence of Unbeaten League Matches: 23, 13.10.1990 – 9.3.1991.

Longest Sequence Without a League Win: 26, 7.4.1902 – 10.1.1903.

Successive Scoring Runs: 24 from 22.11.1996.

Successive Non-scoring Runs: 5 from 3.1.1898.

MANAGERS

Tom Rawthorne 1874–85
(Secretary)
J. J. Bentley 1885–86
(Secretary)
W. G. Struthers 1886–87
(Secretary)
Fitzroy Norris 1887
(Secretary)
J. J. Bentley 1887–95
(Secretary)
Harry Downs 1895–96
(Secretary)
Frank Brettell 1896–98
(Secretary)
John Somerville 1898–1910
Will Settle 1910–15
Tom Mather 1915–19
Charles Foweraker 1919–44
Walter Rowley 1944–50
Bill Ridding 1951–68
Nat Lofthouse 1968–70
Jimmy McIlroy 1970
Jimmy Meadows 1971
Nat Lofthouse 1971
(then Admin. Manager to 1972)
Jimmy Armfield 1971–74
Ian Greaves 1974–80
Stan Anderson 1980–81
George Mulhall 1981–82
John McGovern 1982–85
Charlie Wright 1985
Phil Neal 1985–92
Bruce Rioch 1992–95
Roy McFarland 1995–96
Colin Todd 1996–99
McFarland and Todd joint managers 1995–96
Sam Allardyce 1999–2007
Sammy Lee 2007
Gary Megson 2007–09
Owen Coyle January 2010–

TEN YEAR LEAGUE RECORD

		P	W	D	L	F	A	Pts	Pos
2001-02	PR Lge	38	9	13	16	44	62	40	16
2002-03	PR Lge	38	10	14	14	41	51	44	17
2003-04	PR Lge	38	14	11	13	48	56	53	8
2004-05	PR Lge	38	16	10	12	49	44	58	6
2005-06	PR Lge	38	15	11	12	49	41	56	8
2006-07	PR Lge	38	16	8	14	47	52	56	7
2007-08	PR Lge	38	9	10	19	36	54	37	16
2008-09	PR Lge	38	11	8	19	41	53	41	13
2009-10	PR Lge	38	10	9	19	42	67	39	14
2010-11	PR Lge	38	12	10	16	52	56	46	14

DID YOU KNOW

Centre-forward William Struthers signed by Bolton Wanderers from Rangers in 1881 played in 19 of the team's 24 FA Cup ties between then and 1887. He scored 18 goals in these matches including five against Bootle in a 6-1 victory on 4 November 1882.

BOLTON WANDERERS 2010–11 LEAGUE RECORD

Match No.	Date	Venue	Opponents	Result	H/T Score	Lg Pos.	Goalscorers	Attendance
1	Aug 14	H	Fulham	D	0-0	0-0	—	20,352
2	21	A	West Ham U	W	3-1	0-0	4	Upson (og) [48], Elmander 2 [68, 84]	32,533
3	29	H	Birmingham C	D	2-2	0-1	5	Davies, K (pen) [71], Blake [81]	18,139
4	Sept 11	A	Arsenal	L	1-4	1-1	12	Elmander [44]	59,876
5	18	A	Aston Villa	D	1-1	1-1	13	Davies, K [35]	34,655
6	26	H	Manchester U	D	2-2	1-1	12	Knight [6], Petrov [67]	23,926
7	Oct 2	A	WBA	D	1-1	0-0	12	Elmander [64]	22,846
8	16	H	Stoke C	W	2-1	1-0	7	Lee [22], Klasnic [90]	22,975
9	23	A	Wigan Ath	D	1-1	0-0	8	Elmander [66]	17,100
10	31	H	Liverpool	L	0-1	0-0	10		25,171
11	Nov 6	H	Tottenham H	W	4-2	1-0	6	Davies, K 2 (1 pen) [31, 76 (p)], Steinsson [56], Petrov [90]	20,255
12	10	A	Everton	D	1-1	0-0	—	Klasnic [79]	31,808
13	13	A	Wolverhampton W	W	3-2	1-0	5	Stearman (og) [1], Elmander [62], Holden [67]	27,508
14	20	H	Newcastle U	W	5-1	2-0	5	Davies, K 2 (2 pens) [18, 90], Lee [39], Elmander 2 [50, 72]	22,203
15	27	H	Blackpool	D	2-2	0-1	6	Petrov [76], Davies, M [89]	25,851
16	Dec 4	A	Manchester C	L	0-1	0-1	6		46,860
17	12	H	Blackburn R	W	2-1	0-0	6	Muamba [65], Holden [88]	24,471
18	18	A	Sunderland	L	0-1	0-1	—		35,101
19	26	H	WBA	W	2-0	1-0	6	Taylor [40], Elmander [86]	23,413
20	29	A	Chelsea	L	0-1	0-0	—		40,982
21	Jan 1	A	Liverpool	L	1-2	1-0	7	Davies, K [43]	35,400
22	5	H	Wigan Ath	D	1-1	0-0	7	Moreno [54]	18,852
23	15	A	Stoke C	L	0-2	0-1	7		26,809
24	24	H	Chelsea	L	0-4	0-2	—		22,837
25	Feb 2	H	Wolverhampton W	W	1-0	0-0	—	Sturridge [90]	18,944
26	5	A	Tottenham H	L	1-2	0-1	8	Sturridge [55]	36,197
27	13	H	Everton	W	2-0	1-0	8	Cahill [10], Sturridge [67]	22,986
28	26	A	Newcastle U	D	1-1	1-1	7	Sturridge [38]	48,062
29	Mar 5	A	Aston Villa	W	3-2	1-1	7	Cahill 2 [45, 75], Klasnic [86]	22,533
30	19	A	Manchester U	L	0-1	0-0	7		75,486
31	Apr 2	A	Birmingham C	L	1-2	0-1	8	Elmander [70]	26,142
32	9	H	West Ham U	W	3-0	2-0	8	Sturridge 2 [14, 51], Lee [20]	25,857
33	24	H	Arsenal	W	2-1	1-0	8	Sturridge [38], Cohen [90]	26,881
34	27	A	Fulham	L	0-3	0-1	—		23,222
35	30	A	Blackburn R	L	0-1	0-1	8		28,985
36	May 7	H	Sunderland	L	1-2	0-1	9	Klasnic [87]	22,597
37	14	A	Blackpool	L	3-4	2-3	10	Davies, K [6], Taylor [24], Sturridge [53]	15,979
38	22	H	Manchester C	L	0-2	0-1	14		26,285

Final League Position: 14

GOALSCORERS

League (52): Elmander 10, Davies, K 8 (4 pens), Sturridge 8, Klasnic 4, Cahill 3, Lee 3, Petrov 3, Holden 2, Taylor 2, Blake 1, Cohen 1, Davies, M 1, Knight 1, Moreno 1, Muamba 1, Steinsson 1, own goals 2.
Carling Cup (1): Klasnic 1.
FA Cup (7): Davies, K 2 (1 pen), Elmander 2, Klasnic 2, Lee 1.

Jaaskelainen J 35	Steinsson G 23	Robinson P 35	Muamba F 32+4	Knight Z 34	Cahill G 36	Lee C 25+6	Holden S 26	Elmander J 37	Davies K 38	Petrov M 18+10	Taylor M 22+14	Davies M 9+15	Klasnic I —+22	Blake R —+8	Bogdan A 3+1	O'Brien A 1+1	Ricketts S 14+3	Moreno R 4+13	Cohen T 3+5	Alonso M 4	Sturridge D 11+1	Wheater D 5+2	Gardner R 3+2	Match No.
1	2	3	4^1	5	6	7	8	9^3	10	11^2	12	13	14											1
1	2	3	4	5	6	7^1	8	9^3	10	11^3	12	13		14										2
1^1	2	3	4	5	6	7	8^2	9^1	10	11^6		13	12	15										3
	2	3	4	5	6^1	7^2	8	9^3	10	11^1		13		14	1	12								4
	2	3	4^2	5		7	8	9	10	11^3	14	13			1		6^1	12						5
1	2	4^1	5		7^3	8	9	10	11^2	14	12		13				6							6
1	2	3	4	5	6	7^1	8	9	10	11	12	13												7
1	2	3	4	5	6	7^3	8	9^2	10	11^1	12	14	13^8											8
1	2	3	4^3	5	6	7^1	8	9	10	11^2	12	14					13							9
1	2	3	4	5	6	7^1	8	9^1	10		11^3	13	14				12							10
1	2	3	4	5	6	7	8	9^3	10^2	12	11^1	13	14											11
1	2^1	3	4	5	6	7	8	9^3	10	11							12							12
1		3	4	5	6	7	8	9	10	13	11^2		12				2							13
1		3	4	5	6	7^3	8		9	10	12	11^1		13			2	14						14
1		3	4^3	5	6	7^1		9	10	12	11^2	8	14				2	13						15
1		3	4	5	6	7^3		9	10	11^1	12	8	13				2	14						16
1		3	12	5	6	7^1	8	9	10	11^2	13	4^8					2							17
1		3	4^3	5	6		8	9	10	11^1	7^2		12				2	13	14					18
1	2^1	3	4^2	5	6	7^3	8	9	10		11	13	14				12							19
1		3	4	5	6		8^3	9	10	13	11^2	14	12				2	7^1						20
1			4	5	6			9	10	13	11^0	8	12				2	7^1	3					21
1		3	4	5	6			9	10	12	11^2	8		13			2	7^1						22
1		3	4^1	5	6		8^3	9	10	12	11^2	7					2	13	14					23
1	2	3	4^2	5	6		8^6	9	10	7^1	11	12	14				13							24
1		3	14	5	6	7^1	4	9	10^3		11^2	8					2	13			12			25
1		3	14	5	6	12	4^3	9^1	10	13	11^2	8					2				7			26
1		3	14	5^1	6	13	4	7	10		11^2	8					2				9^3	12		27
1		3	4^1		6		8	7	10	11^2	13	12								2	9	5		28
1	2	3	4^1		5	13	8	7^3	10	11^2		12	14								9	6		29
1	2	3	4^3		5	12	8^2	7	10	11	13		14								9^1	6		30
1	2		4^3		5	12		7	10	11^2	14		13				8^1	3			9	6		31
1	2		4	6	5	7^1		8	10^3	11^2	12		14				13	3			9			32
1	2	3	4^1	6	5	8		7^3	10		11	12	14				13				9^2			33
1	2^1	3	4^2	6	5	7		9	10^3		11		14				8				12	13		34
	2		6	5	12			9^3	10	13	11^2		14		1		7^1	8			4	3		35
1	2	3	4^1	6	5	8^2		7	10		11^3		13				14				9	12		36
1	2	3	4^1	6	5	7		10^3	11			13					14	12			9	8^2		37
1	2	3		6	5	8^2		7^1	10		11^3		13				14	12			9^8	4		38

FA Cup

Third Round	York C	(h)	2-0
Fourth Round	Wigan Ath	(h)	0-0
		(a)	1-0
Fifth Round	Fulham	(a)	1-0
Sixth Round	Birmingham C	(a)	3-2
Semi-Final	Stoke C		0-5

(at Wembley).

Carling Cup

Second Round	Southampton	(a)	1-0
Third Round	Burnley	(a)	0-1

AFC BOURNEMOUTH   FL Championship 1

FOUNDATION

There was a Bournemouth FC as early as 1875, but the present club arose out of the remnants of the Boscombe St John's club (formed 1890). The meeting at which Boscombe FC came into being was held at a house in Gladstone Road in 1899. They began by playing in the Boscombe and District Junior League.

Dean Court, Kings Park, Bournemouth, Dorset BH7 7AF.

Telephone: (01202) 726 300.

Fax: (01202) 726 373.

Ticket Office: (01202) 726 338.

Website: www.afcb.co.uk

Email: enquiries@afcb.co.uk

Ground Capacity: 10,375 (with temporary stand, 9,776 without).

Record Attendance: 28,799 v Manchester U, FA Cup 6th rd, 2 March 1957.

Pitch Measurements: 105m × 78m.

Chairman: Eddie Mitchell.

Chief Executive: Neill Blake.

Secretary: Neil Vacher (Football Administrator).

Manager: Lee Bradbury.

Assistant Manager: Steve Fletcher.

Physio: Steve Hard.

Colours: Red shirts with thin black vertical stripes, black shorts, black stockings.

Change Colours: All black with red trim.

Year Formed: 1899.

Turned Professional: 1910.

Ltd Co.: 1914.

Previous Names: 1890, Boscombe St Johns; 1899, Boscombe FC; 1923, Bournemouth & Boscombe Ath FC; 1971, AFC Bournemouth.

Club Nickname: 'Cherries'.

Grounds: 1899, Castlemain Road, Pokesdown; 1910, Dean Court.

First Football League Game: 25 August 1923, Division 3 (S), v Swindon T (a) L 1–3 – Heron; Wingham, Lamb; Butt, Charles Smith, Voisey; Miller, Lister (1), Davey, Simpson, Robinson.

Record League Victory: 7–0 v Swindon T, Division 3 (S), 22 September 1956 – Godwin; Cunningham, Keetley; Clayton, Crosland, Rushworth; Siddall (1), Norris (2), Arnott (1), Newsham (2), Cutler (1). 10–0 win v Northampton T at start of 1939–40 expunged from the records on outbreak of war.

HONOURS

Football League:
Division 3: *Champions* 1986–87;
Division 3 (S): *Runners-up* 1947–48;
Division 4: *Runners-up* 1970–71.
FL 2: *Runners-up* 2009–10.
FA Cup: Best season: 6th rd, 1957.
Football League Cup: Best season: 4th rd, 1962, 1964.
Associate Members' Cup: *Winners* 1984.
Auto Windscreens Shield: *Runners-up* 1998.

sky SPORTS FACT FILE

In 2009–10 Brett Pitman scored 26 League goals for Bournemouth. It was the highest figure achieved in the competition by one of the club's players since 1971–72 when Ted MacDougall had scored 35 in Division Three, the season Bournemouth finished third.

Record Cup Victory: 11–0 v Margate, FA Cup 1st rd, 20 November 1971 – Davies; Machin (1), Kitchener, Benson, Jones, Powell, Cave (1), Boyer, MacDougall (9 incl. 1p), Miller, Scott (De Garis).

Record Defeat: 0–9 v Lincoln C, Division 3, 18 December 1982.

Most League Points (2 for a win): 62, Division 3, 1971–72.

Most League Points (3 for a win): 97, Division 3, 1986–87.

Most League Goals: 88, Division 3 (S), 1956–57.

Highest League Scorer in Season: Ted MacDougall, 42, 1970–71.

Most League Goals in Total Aggregate: Ron Eyre, 202, 1924–33.

Most League Goals in One Match: 4, Jack Russell v Clapton Orient, Division 3 (S), 7 January 1933; 4, Jack Russell v Bristol C, Division 3 (S), 28 January 1933; 4, Harry Mardon v Southend U, Division 3 (S), 1 January 1938; 4, Jack McDonald v Torquay U, Division 3 (S), 8 November 1947; 4, Ted MacDougall v Colchester U, 18 September 1970; 4, Brian Clark v Rotherham U, 10 October 1972; 4, Luther Blissett v Hull C, 29 November 1988; 4, James Hayter v Bury, Division 2, 21 October 2000.

Most Capped Player: Gerry Peyton, 7 (33), Republic of Ireland.

Most League Appearances: Steve Fletcher, 597, 1992–2007; 2008–.

Youngest League Player: Jimmy White, 15 years 321 days v Brentford, 30 April 1958.

Record Transfer Fee Received: £800,000 from Everton for Joe Parkinson, March 1994 and £800,000 from Ipswich T for Matt Holland, July 1997.

Record Transfer Fee Paid: £210,000 to Gillingham for Gavin Peacock, August 1989.

MANAGERS

Vincent Kitcher 1914–23
(Secretary-Manager)
Harry Kinghorn 1923–25
Leslie Knighton 1925–28
Frank Richards 1928–30
Billy Birrell 1930–35
Bob Crompton 1935–36
Charlie Bell 1936–39
Harry Kinghorn 1939–47
Harry Lowe 1947–50
Jack Bruton 1950–56
Fred Cox 1956–58
Don Welsh 1958–61
Bill McGarry 1961–63
Reg Flewin 1963–65
Fred Cox 1965–70
John Bond 1970–73
Trevor Hartley 1974–75
John Benson 1975–78
Alec Stock 1979–80
David Webb 1980–82
Don Megson 1983
Harry Redknapp 1983–92
Tony Pulis 1992–94
Mel Machin 1994–2000
Sean O'Driscoll 2000–06
Kevin Bond 2006–08
Jimmy Quinn 2008
Eddie Howe 2008–11
Lee Bradbury January 2011–

Football League Record: 1923 Elected to Division 3 (S) and remained a Third Division club for record number of years until 1970; 1970–71 Division 4; 1971–75 Division 3; 1975–82 Division 4; 1982–87 Division 3; 1987–90 Division 2; 1990–92 Division 3; 1992–2002 Division 2; 2002–03 Division 3; 2003–04 Division 2; 2004–08 FL 1; 2008–10 FL 2; 2010– FL 1.

LATEST SEQUENCES

Longest Sequence of League Wins: 7, 22.8.1970 – 23.9.1970.

Longest Sequence of League Defeats: 7, 13.8.1994 – 13.9.1994.

Longest Sequence of League Draws: 5, 25.4.2000 – 12.8.2000.

Longest Sequence of Unbeaten League Matches: 18, 6.3.1982 – 28.8.1982.

Longest Sequence Without a League Win: 14, 6.3.1974 – 27.4.1974.

Successive Scoring Runs: 31 from 28.10.2000.

Successive Non-scoring Runs: 6 from 1.2.1975.

TEN YEAR LEAGUE RECORD

		P	W	D	L	F	A	Pts	Pos
2001-02	Div 2	46	10	14	22	56	71	44	21
2002-03	Div 3	46	20	14	12	60	48	74	4
2003-04	Div 2	46	17	15	14	56	51	66	9
2004-05	FL 1	46	20	10	16	77	64	70	8
2005-06	FL 1	46	12	19	15	49	53	55	17
2006-07	FL 1	46	13	13	20	50	64	52	19
2007-08	FL 1	46	17	7	22	62	72	48*	21
2008-09	FL 2	46	17	12	17	59	51	46†	21
2009-10	FL 2	46	25	8	13	61	44	83	2
2010-11	FL 1	46	19	14	13	75	54	71	6

*10 pts deducted; †17 points deducted.

DID YOU KNOW ?

Bournemouth managed the remarkable feat of gaining promotion in 2009–10 with the same nineteen registered professional players as the club had when it was relegated the season before. All told they used just 25 in League games. Brett Pitman was the only ever present.

AFC BOURNEMOUTH 2010–11 LEAGUE RECORD

Match No.	Date	Venue	Opponents	Result	H/T Score	Lg Pos.	Goalscorers	Attendance
1	Aug 7	A	Charlton Ath	L 0-1	0-1	—		16,236
2	14	H	Peterborough U	W 5-1	2-0	8	Pugh [10], Robinson [20], Pitman 3 [50, 57, 65]	5949
3	21	A	Tranmere R	W 3-0	2-0	5	McQuoid [8], Symes (pen) [18], Pugh [61]	4847
4	28	H	Notts Co	D 3-3	3-1	5	McQuoid 2 [3, 25], Robinson [28]	6447
5	Sept 4	A	Huddersfield T	D 2-2	1-1	7	McQuoid [33], Pugh [79]	12,426
6	11	H	Dagenham & R	W 3-0	2-0	3	Pearce [38], McQuoid [42], Wiggins [55]	5501
7	18	A	Oldham Ath	L 1-2	1-0	7	Wiggins [45]	3912
8	25	H	Carlisle U	W 2-0	0-0	3	Garry [48], Symes (pen) [64]	6103
9	28	H	Exeter C	W 3-0	2-0	—	Symes 2 (1 pen) [2, 68 (p)], Pugh [29]	6823
10	Oct 2	A	Southampton	L 0-2	0-1	3		26,289
11	9	A	Brighton & HA	D 1-1	0-0	4	Pugh (pen) [90]	7348
12	16	H	Milton Keynes D	W 3-2	0-1	3	Hollands [55], Robinson [65], Pugh [71]	6715
13	23	A	Sheffield W	D 1-1	1-0	2	Garry [25]	17,868
14	30	H	Colchester U	L 1-2	0-1	4	Fletcher [87]	6575
15	Nov 2	A	Brentford	D 1-1	0-0	—	Hollands [64]	5278
16	13	H	Walsall	W 3-0	1-0	3	McQuoid 3 [29, 70, 87]	5601
17	20	A	Leyton Orient	D 2-2	1-0	4	Pugh 2 [2, 48]	4531
18	23	H	Yeovil T	W 2-0	2-0	—	Hollands [19], McQuoid [36]	6465
19	Dec 11	H	Hartlepool U	L 0-1	0-1	5		6129
20	28	A	Milton Keynes D	L 0-2	0-1	—		7638
21	Jan 1	A	Swindon T	W 2-1	1-1	4	Pugh [12], Pearce [80]	8874
22	3	H	Brentford	W 3-1	1-0	3	Feeney [11], Bartley [70], Fletcher [88]	6877
23	8	H	Plymouth Arg	W 3-0	2-0	—	Hollands [4], Feeney [38], Pugh (pen) [55]	7589
24	14	A	Colchester U	L 1-2	0-0	—	Fletcher [54]	3445
25	18	A	Rochdale	D 0-0	0-0	—		2312
26	22	H	Brighton & HA	W 1-0	0-0	2	Feeney [62]	9762
27	29	A	Plymouth Arg	W 2-1	1-0	—	Pugh [19], Fletcher [84]	8836
28	Feb 1	H	Swindon T	W 3-2	2-1	2	Feeney [8], Ings [27], Hollands [73]	7212
29	5	A	Leyton Orient	D 1-1	1-0	2	Symes [39]	6717
30	12	A	Walsall	W 1-0	0-0	2	Symes [52]	4103
31	19	H	Huddersfield T	D 1-1	0-0	2	Symes [74]	7923
32	22	H	Sheffield W	D 0-0	0-0	—		7268
33	26	A	Dagenham & R	W 2-1	0-0	2	Ings [56], Robinson [88]	2768
34	Mar 5	H	Oldham Ath	W 3-0	1-0	2	Hollands [20], Symes [47], Dalla Valle [80]	7075
35	8	A	Exeter C	L 0-2	0-1	—		4537
36	12	H	Southampton	L 1-3	1-1	5	Dalla Valle [6]	10,008
37	19	A	Carlisle U	L 0-1	0-1	5		4385
38	26	H	Charlton Ath	D 2-2	1-1	—	Pugh [30], Hollands [57]	7752
39	Apr 1	A	Peterborough U	D 3-3	1-3	—	Ings [35], Fletcher [71], Smith [90]	6670
40	5	A	Bristol R	L 0-1	0-1	—		6691
41	9	H	Tranmere R	L 1-2	0-1	6	Ings [90]	6004
42	16	A	Notts Co	W 2-0	0-0	6	Robinson [67], Ings [77]	6010
43	23	A	Yeovil T	D 2-2	0-0	—	Ings 2 (1 pen) [55 (p), 68]	6150
44	25	H	Bristol R	W 2-1	0-1	6	Baudry [84], Fletcher [88]	7869
45	30	A	Hartlepool U	D 2-2	2-0	6	Lovell [29], McDermott [38]	3159
46	May 7	H	Rochdale	L 1-2	1-1	6	Pearce [27]	9005

Final League Position: 6

GOALSCORERS

League (75): Pugh 12 (2 pens), McQuoid 9, Symes 8 (3 pens), Ings 7 (1 pen), Hollands 7, Fletcher 6, Robinson 5, Feeney 4, Pearce 3, Pitman 3, Dalla Valle 2, Garry 2, Wiggins 2, Bartley 1, Baudry 1, Lovell 1, McDermott 1, Smith 1.
Carling Cup (0).
FA Cup (6): McQuoid 3, Feeney 1, Fletcher 1, Pugh 1.
J Paint Trophy (0).
Play-Offs (4): Lovell 2 (1 pen), Ings 1, McDermott 1.

Jalal S 43	Purches S 6+3	Wiggins R 34+1	Cooper S 33+3	Pearce J 46	Bartley M 24+2	Pugh M 40+1	Robinson A 45	Pitman B 2	Arter H 7+11	Feeney L 44+2	Bradbury L 8+6	Symes M 16+6	Hollands D 31+11	McQuoid D 15+2	Cummings W 9+5	Stockley J —+4	Taylor L 2+9	Garry R 10	Fletcher S 7+31	Smith A 38	Bignall N 3+2	Stewart J 3+1	Partington J 2+3	Ings D 21+5	Williamson B —+4	Dalla Valle L 5+3	Molesley M —+2	Baudry M 1+2	McDermott D 6+3	Lovell S 5+2	Match No.
1	14	3	4	5	6^2	7	8	9	10^1	11		2^3	12	13																	1
1	2	3	4	5	6	7^3	8	9	13	11^2			10^1	12	14																2
1	2	3	4	5	6	7	8			11^2	12	10^3	13	9^1	14																3
1	2	3	4	5	6	7	8			11^1	14	10^3	12	9^2	13																4
1		3	2^2	5	4	7	8		13	11^3	10^1		12	9	14			6													5
1		3	4	5	10^2	7	8		13	11	2		12	9^1	14			6^3													6
1			4^2	5	10^3	7	8		14	11^1	2		12	9				6	13												7
1	2	4^1		5	10	7^2	8			11^3		12		9	14			6	13	3											8
1		3	4^3	5		7	8			11	2	10^2	14	9^1	12			6	13												9
1		3		5	4^2	7	8			11^1	12	10^3	13	9				6	14	2^8											10
1		3	4	5	10^2	7	8			11^3	2		14	9^1	12			6	13												11
1	2			5	10^1	7	8			11	4		9					6	12	3											12
1	2			5	10	7	8			11^1	4		9^2				13	6	12	3											13
1	2	4^2		5	10^1	7	8	14		11^3	13		6	9					12	3											14
1	2			5	6	7^1	8			11	10		4	9					12	3											15
1	2			5	14	7	8	13		11^3			4	9^2				6	12	3	10^1										16
1^6	2	4^1		5	12	7	8			11^2	13		6	9			10		3	15											17
	2			5	6		8		7	11^3	14	13	4	9^1					10^2	3	12	1									18
	2			5		7	8			11^2	13		14	4			12		10^3	3	9^1	1	6								19
1	2	13	6	5			8^2			11			4					10^3	12	3	14		9^1								20
1		2	4	5	6	7^3	8			11	13				9^1		10		3				12							21
1		2	4	5	6	7^2	8			11	9		12						13	3			10^1								22
1				5	6	7	8			11^2	12	13	4		2	14			10^1	3			9^3								23
1		2	14	5	6	7	8			11	10^1		4^3				13		12	3			9^2								24
1		2	6	5	7	10	8			11			12	4						3			9^1								25
1		2	4	5	6^1	7	8			11			10^2	12					13	3			9								26
1			4	5	6	7	8^2			11			10^1	13	2		14		12	3			9^3								27
1			6	5		7	8	13		11			10^1	4	2				12	3			9^2								28
1			6	5		7	8			11			10^1	4	2				12	3			9^2	13							29
1		13	6	5		7	8			11			10^3	4	2^2				14	3			9^1	12							30
1		2^2	6	5		7	8^3			11			10^1	4	13				12	3			14	9							31
1	2		6	5		7^3	8	14		11			10^1	4			13		12	3			9^2								32
1	14	2	6	5		7	8			11			10^2	4^3					13	3			9^1	12							33
1			6	5		7	8			11			10^2	4^3	2				13	3			9^1		12	14					34
1		2		5		7^3	8			11			10^1	4					13	3			12	14	9^2	6					35
1		2^1	6	5		7	8			11			4		12				13	3			14	9^1	10^3						36
1	2		6	5		7^2	8			11			4		13				12	3			9	10^1							37
	2	6	5			7^3	8			11^3			4		12			9^1	3	1			13	10^2			14				38
1	2	6	5			7^1	8	14		11			4^3						12	3			9^2					10	13		39
1	2		6	5		7	8			11			4						10	3^1			9^2	13			12				40
1			6	5		7^1	8			11			4		2				10	3^3			14	9^2			12	13			41
1	2^1		6	5			8	12		11			4						13	3			9^3			14	7	10^2		42
1			6	5	12				7	11			4		2				14	3			9^3	13			8^1	10^2		43
1			6	5				8^3	12	11			4^8		2				13	3			9			14	7^2	10^1		44
1	2		6	5			8		7^2	11									12	3			9^3	14		13	4	10^1		45
1	14	2	6	5		7	8			11			4						13	3^2			12					9^1	10^3	46

FA Cup

First Round	Tranmere R	(h)	5-3	
Second Round	Notts Co	(a)	1-3	

Carling Cup

First Round	Southampton	(a)	0-2

J Paint Trophy

First Round	Torquay U	(h)	0-0

Play-Offs

Semi-Final	Huddersfield T	(h)	1-1
		(a)	3-3

BRADFORD CITY   FL Championship 2

FOUNDATION

Bradford was a rugby stronghold around the turn of the century but after Manningham RFC held an archery contest to help them out of financial difficulties in 1903, they were persuaded to give up the handling code and turn to soccer. So they formed Bradford City and continued at Valley Parade. Recognising this as an opportunity of spreading the dribbling code in this part of Yorkshire, the Football League immediately accepted the new club's first application for membership of the Second Division.

Coral Window Stadium, Valley Parade, Bradford, West Yorkshire BD8 7DY.

Telephone: (01274) 773 355.

Fax: (01274) 773 356.

Ticket Office: (01274) 770 012.

Website: www.bradfordcityfc.co.uk

Email: bradfordcityfc@compuserve.com

Ground Capacity: 25,136.

Record Attendance: 39,146 v Burnley, FA Cup 4th rd, 11 March 1911.

Pitch Measurements: 113yd × 70yd.

Joint Chairmen: Julian Rhodes and Mark Lawn.

Director of Operations: David Baldwin.

Football Club Secretary: Kath Brown.

Manager: Peter Jackson.

Assistant Manager: Colin Cooper.

Physios: Chris Royston, Mark Cox.

Colours: Claret and amber striped shirts with claret sleeves, black shorts, black stockings.

Change Colours: All white with black trimmed sleeves.

Year Formed: 1903.

Turned Professional: 1903.

Ltd Co.: 1908.

Club Nickname: 'The Bantams'.

Ground: 1903, Valley Parade.

First Football League Game: 1 September 1903, Division 2, v Grimsby T (a) L 0–2 – Seymour; Wilson, Halliday; Robinson, Millar, Farnall; Guy, Beckram, Forrest, McMillan, Graham.

Record League Victory: 11–1 v Rotherham U, Division 3 (N), 25 August 1928 – Sherlaw; Russell, Watson; Burkinshaw (1), Summers, Bauld; Harvey (2), Edmunds (3), White (3), Cairns, Scriven (2).

Record Cup Victory: 11–3 v Walker Celtic, FA Cup 1st rd (replay), 1 December 1937 – Parker; Rookes, McDermott; Murphy, Mackie, Moore; Bagley (1), Whittingham (1), Deakin (4 incl. 1p), Cooke (1), Bartholomew (4).

HONOURS

Football League –
Division 1: *Runners-up* 1998–99;
Division 2: *Champions* 1907–08;
Division 3: *Champions* 1984–85;
Division 3 (N): *Champions* 1928–29;
Division 4: *Runners-up* 1981–82.

FA Cup: *Winners* 1911.

Football League Cup: Best season: 5th rd, 1965, 1989.

European Competitions:
Intertoto Cup: 2000.

sky SPORTS FACT FILE

In 1987–88 Bradford City had an impressive run in the Simod Cup – the sponsors of the Full Members Cup. They beat Aston Villa 5-0 away then at home defeated Newcastle United 2-1 and Southampton 1-0 before losing 2-1 after extra time away to Reading in round four.

Record Defeat: 1–9 v Colchester U, Division 4, 30 December 1961.

Most League Points (2 for a win): 63, Division 3 (N), 1928–29.

Most League Points (3 for a win): 94, Division 3, 1984–85.

Most League Goals: 128, Division 3 (N), 1928–29.

Highest League Scorer in Season: David Layne, 34, Division 4, 1961–62.

Most League Goals in Total Aggregate: Bobby Campbell, 121, 1981–84, 1984–86.

Most League Goals in One Match: 7, Albert Whitehurst v Tranmere R, Division 3 (N), 6 March 1929.

Most Capped Player: Jamie Lawrence, 19 (24), Jamaica.

Most League Appearances: Cec Podd, 502, 1970–84.

Youngest League Player: Robert Cullingford, 16 years 141 days v Mansfield T, 22 April 1970.

Record Transfer Fee Received: £2,000,000 from Newcastle U for Des Hamilton, March 1997 and £2,000,000 from Newcastle U for Andrew O'Brien, March 2001.

Record Transfer Fee Paid: £2,500,000 to Leeds U for David Hopkin, July 2000.

Football League Record: 1903 Elected to Division 2; 1908–22 Division 1; 1922–27 Division 2; 1927–29 Division 3 (N); 1929–37 Division 2; 1937–61 Division 3; 1961–69 Division 4; 1969–72 Division 3; 1972–77 Division 4; 1977–78 Division 3; 1978–82 Division 4; 1982–85 Division 3; 1985–90 Division 2; 1990–92 Division 3; 1992–96 Division 2; 1996–99 Division 1; 1999–2001 FA Premier League; 2001–04 Division 1; 2004–07 FL 1; 2007– FL 2.

LATEST SEQUENCES

Longest Sequence of League Wins: 10, 26.11.1983 – 3.2.1984.

Longest Sequence of League Defeats: 8, 21.1.1933 – 11.3.1933.

Longest Sequence of League Draws: 6, 30.1.1976 – 13.3.1976.

Longest Sequence of Unbeaten League Matches: 21, 11.1.1969 – 2.5.1969.

Longest Sequence Without a League Win: 16, 28.8.1948 – 20.11.1948.

Successive Scoring Runs: 30 from 26.12.1961.

Successive Non-scoring Runs: 7 from 18.4.1925.

MANAGERS

Robert Campbell 1903–05
Peter O'Rourke 1905–21
David Menzies 1921–26
Colin Veitch 1926–28
Peter O'Rourke 1928–30
Jack Peart 1930–35
Dick Ray 1935–37
Fred Westgarth 1938–43
Bob Sharp 1943–46
Jack Barker 1946–47
John Milburn 1947–48
David Steele 1948–52
Albert Harris 1952
Ivor Powell 1952–55
Peter Jackson 1955–61
Bob Brocklebank 1961–64
Bill Harris 1965–66
Willie Watson 1966–69
Grenville Hair 1967–68
Jimmy Wheeler 1968–71
Bryan Edwards 1971–75
Bobby Kennedy 1975–78
John Napier 1978
George Mulhall 1978–81
Roy McFarland 1981–82
Trevor Cherry 1982–87
Terry Dolan 1987–89
Terry Yorath 1989–90
John Docherty 1990–91
Frank Stapleton 1991–94
Lennie Lawrence 1994–95
Chris Kamara 1995–98
Paul Jewell 1998–2000
Chris Hutchings 2000
Jim Jefferies 2000–01
Nicky Law 2001–03
Bryan Robson 2003–04
Colin Todd 2004–07
Stuart McCall 2007–10
Peter Taylor 2010–11
Peter Jackson March 2011–

TEN YEAR LEAGUE RECORD

		P	W	D	L	F	A	Pts	Pos
2001-02	Div 1	46	15	10	21	69	76	55	15
2002-03	Div 1	46	14	10	22	51	73	52	19
2003-04	Div 1	46	10	6	30	38	69	36	23
2004-05	FL 1	46	17	14	15	64	62	65	11
2005-06	FL 1	46	14	19	13	51	49	61	11
2006-07	FL 1	46	11	14	21	47	65	47	22
2007-08	FL 2	46	17	11	18	63	61	62	10
2008-09	FL 2	46	18	13	15	66	55	67	9
2009-10	FL 2	46	16	14	16	59	62	62	14
2010-11	FL 2	46	15	7	24	43	68	52	18

DID YOU KNOW ?

In 1931–32 Bradford City won home and away in Division Two against Tottenham Hotspur. After an impressive 5-1 win at White Hart Lane on 5 December they completed the double 2-0 at Valley Parade on 16 April. It enabled City to edge Spurs out of seventh place.

BRADFORD CITY 2010–11 LEAGUE RECORD

Match No.	Date		Venue	Opponents	Result		H/T Score	Lg Pos.	Goalscorers	Attendance
1	Aug	7	A	Shrewsbury T	L	1-3	1-1	—	Adeyemi [24]	6993
2		14	H	Stevenage	W	1-0	1-0	11	Evans (pen) [32]	10,967
3		21	A	Torquay U	L	0-2	0-1	16		2941
4		27	H	Southend U	L	0-2	0-1	—		10,752
5	Sept	4	H	Port Vale	L	0-2	0-1	22		10,834
6		11	A	Stockport Co	D	1-1	0-0	22	Syers [56]	4277
7		18	H	Gillingham	W	1-0	0-0	19	Williams [90]	10,722
8		25	A	Northampton T	L	0-2	0-0	22		4646
9		28	A	Rotherham U	D	0-0	0-0	—		3872
10	Oct	2	H	Morecambe	L	0-1	0-1	23		10,640
11		9	A	Barnet	W	2-0	0-0	21	Osborne [65], Adeyemi [69]	2435
12		16	H	Cheltenham T	W	3-1	1-1	19	Syers [32], Hendrie [74], Hanson [87]	10,537
13		23	A	Burton Alb	L	0-3	0-1	20		3143
14		30	H	Oxford U	W	5-0	0-0	16	Daley 2 [48, 57], Hendrie (pen) [66], Syers [87], Moult [90]	11,376
15	Nov	2	A	Bury	W	1-0	1-0	—	Daley (pen) [30]	3521
16		13	A	Wycombe W	L	0-1	0-0	13		4077
17		20	H	Macclesfield T	L	0-1	0-1	14		10,779
18		23	H	Accrington S	D	1-1	0-1	—	Price [54]	10,392
19	Dec	11	H	Hereford U	W	1-0	1-0	14	Syers [8]	10,460
20		28	A	Cheltenham T	L	0-4	0-2	—		2666
21	Jan	1	A	Lincoln C	W	2-1	2-1	11	Hanson [2], Evans [42]	3225
22		3	H	Bury	W	1-0	1-0	10	Daley [45]	11,384
23		8	H	Barnet	L	1-3	1-0	11	Oliver [45]	10,514
24		15	A	Oxford U	L	1-2	1-0	14	Syers [9]	7068
25		18	A	Aldershot T	L	0-1	0-1	—		2160
26		25	A	Crewe Alex	L	1-2	1-2	—	Duff [39]	3665
27		29	A	Chesterfield	D	2-2	1-1	—	Syers [12], Hanson [53]	7556
28	Feb	1	H	Lincoln C	L	1-2	1-1	18	Hanson [4]	10,543
29		12	H	Wycombe W	W	1-0	0-0	17	Ellison [69]	10,897
30		18	A	Port Vale	L	1-2	0-0	—	Adeyemi [84]	4775
31		22	H	Chesterfield	L	0-1	0-1	—		10,782
32		26	H	Stockport Co	W	3-2	1-2	20	Williams 2 [14, 74], Evans [90]	15,332
33	Mar	5	A	Gillingham	L	0-2	0-1	20		5019
34		8	H	Rotherham U	W	2-1	1-1	—	Hunt [16], Adeyemi [90]	10,910
35		12	A	Morecambe	W	1-0	1-0	17	Hanson [33]	3521
36		19	H	Northampton T	D	1-1	1-0	17	Speight (pen) [8]	10,684
37		26	H	Shrewsbury T	L	1-2	0-0	—	Adeyemi [67]	10,735
38	Apr	2	A	Stevenage	L	1-2	0-1	20	Syers [72]	3079
39		5	A	Macclesfield T	W	1-0	1-0	—	Hanson [24]	1207
40		9	H	Torquay U	L	0-3	0-1	17		10,894
41		15	A	Southend U	L	0-4	0-2	—		5217
42		19	H	Burton Alb	D	1-1	0-1	—	Speight [74]	13,814
43		23	A	Accrington S	L	0-3	0-3	19		2815
44		25	H	Aldershot T	W	2-1	1-1	18	Daley [4], Syers [90]	10,965
45		30	A	Hereford U	D	1-1	0-0	16	Speight (pen) [81]	3219
46	May	7	H	Crewe Alex	L	1-5	1-4	18	Speight (pen) [23]	11,030

Final League Position: 18

GOALSCORERS

League (43): Syers 8, Hanson 6, Adeyemi 5, Daley 5 (1 pen), Speight 4 (3 pens), Evans 3 (1 pen), Williams 3, Hendrie 2 (1 pen), Duff 1, Ellison 1, Hunt 1, Moult 1, Oliver 1, Osborne 1, Price 1.
Carling Cup (3): Hanson 1, Speight 1, Syers 1.
FA Cup (3): Hanson 2, Syers 1.
J Paint Trophy (0).

McLaughlin J 25	Hunt L 24	Threlfall R 16+4	Bullock L 22+4	Williams S 26+2	Oliver L 41+1	Ramsden S 2	Adeyemi T 30+4	Evans G 28+8	Hanson J 31+5	Neilson S 1	Moult L 4+7	Doherty T 17+1	Speight J 13+15	O'Brien L 37+5	Duff S 14	Daley O 22+4	Rehman Z 5+3	Syers D 30+7	Osborne L 10+12	Hendrie L 8+4	Brown R 3	Gill O 4	Chilaka C —+4	Price J 6+4	Pidgeley L 21	Kiernan R 6+2	Eckersley R 12	Cullen M 1+3	Worthington J 16	Flynn M 16+3	Ellison K 6+1	Dobie S 8+5	Stephenson D —+1	Rowe D 1+1	Dean L —+1	Flett A —+1	Match No.
1	2	3	4³	5¹	6	7	8	9	10	11¹	12	13	14																								1
1	2		4		6		8	9	10		14	7²		3		5¹	11³	12	13																		2
1	2³	3⁴	4		6		8	9	10		11¹	7²		13	5		12	14																			3
1	2	14	4¹	5	6			9	10²	11³		8		12	3		7	13																			4
1	2	3			6		8¹	9				12		7	10	11²	5		4	13																	5
1	2	3²	4		6			9¹				12		8	10	11	5		7	13																	6
1	2	3³	4	5	6			14				9³		8	10²	11	7		13	12																	7
1	2¹		4	5	9							11²	8³	10	3	6		12	7	14	13																8
1			4	5	6		8	9				10¹	12	7	3	11²	2			13																	9
1			4	5	6¹		8	9				12	14	11	7²				10³	2	3	13															10
1				5	6³		8	14				10	12	4		7²	2	13	11	9¹	3																11
1		13	5									10³	14	8²	3		11¹	7	6	9	2	4	12														12
1			5									10	12	8	13	3		11¹	7	4	2	6	9²														13
			5	6			8		10⁴			14	4²	3		11	2	13	7³	9			12	1													14
		13	5	6	8			12				4²		3		11	2	7	10				9	1													15
			6		8	12		4⁴						3		11	2	7	13	10²			9	1	5												16
		4²	6		8¹	10								3		11	7	13	9		12	1	2	5													17
	14		6		8	13	10					4		3		12		7¹	11²		9³	1	2	5													18
	14		6		8		10					4		3		11²	7	12	9¹		13	1	2¹	5													19
			6		8¹	9	10					4		3		7	12		11	1	5	2															20
	3¹	4	5		8		10					11	8	12		7				1	2																21
	14	4	5¹	6	8	9	13					3		11³		7			10²	1	12	2															22
		4		6	8²	9	10					3		5¹	11	7			1	12	2	13															23
	3²	4		6	8	12	14					13	11	10²		7			1	5	2	9¹															24
1	3³	4¹		6	8	13	10					11	5	9²		7	12			2	14																25
1				6	4	9¹	10					13	3	5	12	7	8⁰			2		11²	14														26
1				6	8	9	10					3	5	12	7	4¹				2		11²	13														27
1				6	8	9	10					3	5	11²	4					2	13	7¹	12														28
	2			14	6	5	13	12	10¹			3				8³						1						7²	4	9	11						29
	2			5	6	8	9					12	3			7¹						1						4	11	10							30
	2	7³	5	6	8	9²	13					12	3			14						1						4	11	10¹							31
	2	14	4²	5	6³	8¹	12	10				13	3			7						1						9	11								32
	2			5	6	12	9	10				8	3						12	14		1						7¹	4	11²	13						33
	2			5	6	13	9¹	10				8	3			12	14					1						11²	4		7¹						34
1	2			5	6		9	10				8	3									1						11	4	12	7¹						35
1	2			5	6¹	13	9	10				8³	3			12						1						7⁴	4³	11	14						36
1	2			5		7	9					8¹	3			6	13					1						4	11²	12							37
1	6			5	13	8	9	10³				14	3			2	7²			12		1						4	11¹								38
1	2	3		5	6	8	9	10¹								7						1						11	4	12							39
1		2	10	5	6	8	9¹					12	3²			7						1						11	4	13							40
1		2	5		6	8¹	9¹					13	3			7	12					1						11	4	10²	14						41
	2	3		5	6		9	10				12	13	7²		8						1						11	4¹								42
	2	3	12	5¹	6			10²				9		11³		8				14		1						7	4	13							43
	2	3	5		6		12	10				9²		11		8			13			1						7	4¹								44
	2	3	5	13	6		9¹	10				8³	12	11²		4						1						7					14				45
1	2	3	5		6			10²				9	12	11¹		4						1						7				8	13				46

FA Cup
First Round   Colchester U   (a)   3-4

Carling Cup
First Round   Nottingham F   (h)   2-1
Second Round   Preston NE   (h)   1-2

J Paint Trophy
Second Round   Hartlepool U   (a)   0-1

BRENTFORD   FL Championship 1

FOUNDATION

Formed as a small amateur concern in 1889 they were very successful in local circles. They won the championship of the West London Alliance in 1893 and a year later the West Middlesex Junior Cup before carrying off the Senior Cup in 1895. After winning both the London Senior Amateur Cup and the Middlesex Senior Cup in 1898 they were admitted to the Second Division of the Southern League.

Griffin Park, Braemar Road, Brentford, Middlesex TW8 0NT.

Telephone: 0845 3456 442.

Fax: (0208) 568 9940.

Ticket Office: 0845 3456 442.

Website: www.brentfordfc.co.uk

E-mail: enquiries@brentfordfc.co.uk

Ground Capacity: 12,400.

Record Attendance: 38,678 v Leicester C, FA Cup 6th rd, 26 February 1949.

Pitch Measurements: 111yd × 74yd.

Chairman: Greg Dyke.

Executive Director: Alan Bird.

Secretary: Lisa Hall.

Manager: Uwe Rosler.

Assistant Manager: Peter Farrell.

Colours: White shirts with red sleeves and black trim underneath, four separated red vertical stripes on body, black shorts, black stockings.

Change Colours: Black shirts with gold trim, black shorts with gold trim, black stockings.

Year Formed: 1889.   *Turned Professional:* 1899.   *Ltd Co.:* 1901.

Club Nickname: 'The Bees'.

Grounds: 1889, Clifden Road; 1891, Benns Fields, Little Ealing; 1895, Shotters Field; 1898, Cross Road, S. Ealing; 1900, Boston Park; 1904, Griffin Park.

First Football League Game: 28 August 1920, Division 3, v Exeter C (a) L 0–3 – Young; Hodson, Rosier, Jimmy Elliott, Levitt, Amos, Smith, Thompson, Spreadbury, Morley, Henery.

Record League Victory: 9–0 v Wrexham, Division 3, 15 October 1963 – Cakebread; Coote, Jones; Slater, Scott, Higginson; Summers (1), Brooks (2), McAdams (2), Ward (2), Hales (1), (1 og).

Record Cup Victory: 7–0 v Windsor & Eton (away), FA Cup 1st rd, 20 November 1982 – Roche; Rowe, Harris (Booker), McNichol (1), Whitehead, Hurlock (2), Kamara, Joseph (1), Mahoney (3), Bowles, Roberts. *N.B.* 8–0 v Uxbridge: Frail, Jock Watson, Caie, Bellingham, Parsonage (1), Jay, Atherton, Leigh (1), Bell (2), Buchanan (2), Underwood (2), FA Cup, 3rd Qual rd, 31 October 1903.

HONOURS

Football League – Division 1: Best season: 5th, 1935–36;

Division 2: *Champions* 1934–35, 1994–95; **Division 3:** *Champions* 1991–92, 1998–99;

Division 3 (S): *Champions* 1932–33, *Runners-up* 1929–30, 1957–58;

Division 4: *Champions* 1962–63;

FL 2: *Champions* 2008–09.

FA Cup: Best season: 6th rd, 1938, 1946, 1949, 1989.

Football League Cup: Best season: 4th rd, 1983, 2011.

Freight Rover Trophy: *Runners-up* 1985.

LDV Vans Trophy: *Runners-up* 2001.

Johnstone's Paint Trophy: *Runners-up* 2011.

sky SPORTS FACT FILE

Inside-right Bert White was a prolific scorer for Brentford in Southern League and First World War matches. He played in England's international trial match for the South v North in 1919 and subsequently signed for Arsenal to launch a successful Football League career.

Record Defeat: 0–7 v Swansea T, Division 3 (S), 8 November 1924; v Walsall, Division 3 (S), 19 January 1957; v Peterborough U, 24 November 2007.

Most League Points (2 for a win): 62, Division 3 (S), 1932–33 and Division 4, 1962–63.

Most League Points (3 for a win): 85, Division 2, 1994–95, Division 3, 1998–99 and FL 2, 2008–09.

Most League Goals: 98, Division 4, 1962–63.

Highest League Scorer in Season: Jack Holliday, 38, Division 3 (S), 1932–33.

Most League Goals in Total Aggregate: Jim Towers, 153, 1954–61.

Most League Goals in One Match: 5, Jack Holliday v Luton T, Division 3 (S), 28 January 1933; 5, Billy Scott v Barnsley, Division 2, 15 December 1934; 5, Peter McKennan v Bury, Division 2, 18 February 1949.

Most Capped Player: John Buttigieg, 22 (98), Malta.

Most League Appearances: Ken Coote, 514, 1949–64.

Youngest League Player: Danis Salman, 15 years 248 days v Watford, 15 November 1975.

Record Transfer Fee Received: £2,500,000 from Wimbledon for Hermann Hreidarsson, October 1999.

Record Transfer Fee Paid: £750,000 to Crystal Palace for Hermann Hreidarsson, September 1998.

Football League Record: 1920 Original Member of Division 3; 1921–33 Division 3 (S); 1933–35 Division 2; 1935–47 Division 1; 1947–54 Division 2; 1954–62 Division 3 (S); 1962–63 Division 4; 1963–66 Division 3; 1966–72 Division 4; 1972–73 Division 3; 1973–78 Division 4; 1978–92 Division 3; 1992–93 Division 1; 1993–98 Division 2; 1998–99 Division 3; 1999–04 Division 2; 2004–07 FL 1; 2007–09 FL 2; 2009– FL 1.

LATEST SEQUENCES

Longest Sequence of League Wins: 9, 30.4.1932 – 24.9.1932.

Longest Sequence of League Defeats: 9, 20.10.1928 – 25.12.1928.

Longest Sequence of League Draws: 5, 16.3.1957 – 6.4.1957.

Longest Sequence of Unbeaten League Matches: 26, 20.2.1999 – 16.10.1999.

Longest Sequence Without a League Win: 18, 9.9.2006 – 26.12.2006.

Successive Scoring Runs: 26 from 4.3.1963.

Successive Non-scoring Runs: 7 from 7.3.2000.

MANAGERS

Will Lewis 1900–03
  (*Secretary-Manager*)
Dick Molyneux 1902–06
W. G. Brown 1906–08
Fred Halliday 1908–12, 1915–21, 1924–26
  (*only Secretary to 1922*)
Ephraim Rhodes 1912–15
Archie Mitchell 1921–24
Harry Curtis 1926–49
Jackie Gibbons 1949–52
Jimmy Bain 1952–53
Tommy Lawton 1953
Bill Dodgin Snr 1953–57
Malcolm Macdonald 1957–65
Tommy Cavanagh 1965–66
Billy Gray 1966–67
Jimmy Sirrel 1967–69
Frank Blunstone 1969–73
Mike Everitt 1973–75
John Docherty 1975–76
Bill Dodgin Jnr 1976–80
Fred Callaghan 1980–84
Frank McLintock 1984–87
Steve Perryman 1987–90
Phil Holder 1990–93
David Webb 1993–97
Eddie May 1997
Micky Adams 1997–98
Ron Noades 1998–2000
Ray Lewington 2000–01
Steve Coppell 2001–02
Wally Downes 2002–04
Martin Allen 2004–06
Leroy Rosenior 2006
Scott Fitzgerald 2006–07
Terry Butcher 2007
Andy Scott 2007–11
Nicky Forster 2011
Uwe Rosler June 2011–

TEN YEAR LEAGUE RECORD

		P	W	D	L	F	A	Pts	Pos
2001-02	Div 2	46	24	11	11	77	43	83	3
2002-03	Div 2	46	14	12	20	47	56	54	16
2003-04	Div 2	46	14	11	21	52	69	53	17
2004-05	FL 1	46	22	9	15	57	60	75	4
2005-06	FL 1	46	20	16	10	72	52	76	3
2006-07	FL 1	46	8	13	25	40	79	37	24
2007-08	FL 2	46	17	8	21	52	70	59	14
2008-09	FL 2	46	23	16	7	65	36	85	1
2009-10	FL 1	46	14	20	12	55	52	62	9
2010-11	FL 1	46	17	10	19	55	62	61	11

DID YOU KNOW ?

Brentford had immediate success entering a League competition, winning the West London Alliance unbeaten in 1892–93. Sadly because of a lack of funds the club was awarded neither a trophy nor medals for its outstanding first-time achievement.

BRENTFORD 2010–11 LEAGUE RECORD

Match No.	Date		Venue	Opponents	Result	H/T Score	Lg Pos.	Goalscorers	Attendance
1	Aug	7	A	Carlisle U	L 0-2	0-2	—		5913
2		14	H	Walsall	L 1-2	1-1	23	Alexander [44]	4544
3		21	A	Swindon T	D 1-1	1-1	22	MacDonald [8]	8132
4		28	H	Rochdale	L 1-3	1-1	24	Simpson [27]	4636
5	Sept	5	H	Sheffield W	W 1-0	1-0	22	MacDonald [41]	5396
6		11	A	Bristol R	D 0-0	0-0	19		5609
7		18	H	Hartlepool U	D 0-0	0-0	19		4710
8		24	A	Leyton Orient	L 0-1	0-1	—		4485
9		28	A	Brighton & HA	L 0-1	0-0	—		6740
10	Oct	2	H	Charlton Ath	W 2-1	2-0	23	Alexander [13], Diagouraga [31]	6342
11		9	H	Oldham Ath	L 1-3	1-1	24	Weston [4]	5339
12		16	A	Tranmere R	W 3-0	1-0	21	O'Connor 2 (1 pen) [7 (p), 67], Bean [81]	4929
13		23	H	Peterborough U	W 2-1	1-1	19	Woodman [39], Alexander [58]	6543
14		30	A	Exeter C	W 4-2	1-1	15	Legge [4], Alexander [62], Wood [64], MacDonald [72]	5510
15	Nov	2	H	Bournemouth	D 1-1	0-0	—	Grabban (pen) [66]	5278
16		13	H	Milton Keynes D	L 0-2	0-0	18		4789
17		20	A	Plymouth Arg	W 2-1	1-1	13	Bean [26], MacDonald [67]	6939
18		23	A	Colchester U	W 2-0	1-0	—	Alexander [26], MacDonald [90]	3172
19	Dec	11	A	Southampton	W 2-0	2-0	10	Alexander [13], MacDonald [28]	19,641
20	Jan	1	H	Dagenham & R	W 2-1	1-1	9	Simpson [10], Alexander [87]	5405
21		3	A	Bournemouth	L 1-3	0-1	10	Bradbury (og) [65]	6877
22		8	A	Yeovil T	L 0-2	0-1	—		3688
23		11	A	Peterborough U	L 1-2	0-1	—	Laird [74]	4667
24		14	A	Exeter C	D 1-1	0-1	—	Forster [90]	4767
25		22	A	Oldham Ath	L 1-2	0-1	16	Simpson [82]	3759
26		29	H	Yeovil T	L 1-2	1-1	—	MacDonald [39]	4753
27	Feb	1	A	Dagenham & R	L 1-4	0-1	18	MacDonald [90]	1907
28		5	H	Plymouth Arg	W 2-0	1-0	14	Weston 2 [35, 56]	5613
29		12	A	Milton Keynes D	D 1-1	0-0	15	Grabban [50]	8636
30		22	H	Tranmere R	W 2-1	1-0	—	MacDonald [2], Legge [90]	4192
31		26	H	Bristol R	W 1-0	1-0	14	Alexander (pen) [20]	5944
32	Mar	1	H	Notts Co	D 1-1	0-1	—	Osborne [74]	3795
33		5	A	Hartlepool U	L 0-3	0-1	14		2936
34		8	H	Brighton & HA	L 0-1	0-0	—		5694
35		12	A	Charlton Ath	W 1-0	0-0	14	Legge [89]	14,985
36		15	H	Huddersfield T	L 0-1	0-0	—		4402
37		19	H	Leyton Orient	W 2-1	2-0	11	Bean [6], Alexander [24]	6368
38		25	H	Carlisle U	W 2-1	0-0	—	Schlupp 2 [74, 83]	4365
39		29	A	Sheffield W	W 3-1	2-1	—	Spillane [3], Schlupp [18], Saunders [82]	14,797
40	Apr	9	H	Swindon T	L 0-1	0-0	11		4593
41		12	A	Walsall	L 2-3	1-1	—	Balkestein [30], Grabban [62]	3154
42		16	A	Rochdale	W 1-0	0-0	10	Simpson [79]	2963
43		22	H	Colchester U	D 1-1	0-1	—	Saunders [74]	4480
44		25	A	Notts Co	D 1-1	0-0	11	Schlupp [90]	6879
45		30	H	Southampton	L 0-3	0-2	10		7015
46	May	7	A	Huddersfield T	D 4-4	1-2	11	Schlupp 2 [45, 50], Grabban 2 [58, 68]	13,977

Final League Position: 11

GOALSCORERS

League (55): Alexander 9 (1 pen), MacDonald 9, Schlupp 6, Grabban 5 (1 pen), Simpson 4, Bean 3, Legge 3, Weston 3, O'Connor 2 (1 pen), Saunders 2, Balkestein 1, Diagouraga 1, Forster 1, Laird 1, Osborne 1, Spillane 1, Wood 1, Woodman 1, own goal 1.
Carling Cup (6): Simpson 2, Alexander 1, Bean 1, Wood 1, Woodman 1.
FA Cup (1): MacDonald 1.
J Paint Trophy (5): Alexander 2, Simpson 2, Saunders 1.

Moore S 9+1	Osborne K 41+1	Woodman C 40+1	Benn M 32+5	McCracken D 1+1	Balkestein P 17+3	Spillane M 18+6	O'Connor K 39+2	Alexander G 37+1	Forster N 6+12	Weston M 33+9	Simpson R 11+16	Legge L 27+3	MacDonald C 28+2	McCarthy A 3	Diagouraga T 32	Wood S 13+7	Adams N 3+4	Cort C —+3	Hamer B 10	Hunt D —+3	Saunders S 18+3	Hudson K —+2	Grabban L 13+9	Wright S 9+2	Lee R 22	Laird M 4	Tudur Jones O 4+2	Royce S 1+1	Bignall N 1+5	Neilson R 15	Byrne N 4+7	Reed A 8+3	Schlupp J 6+3	Carson T 1	Hacker L —+1	Reeves J —+1	Match No.
1	2	3	4	5^1	6	7^2	8	9	10^3	11	12	13	14																								1
	3	4			6		2	9	13	12	7	5	10^2	1	8	11^1																					2
5	3	4					2	9	13	11	7^1	6	10^2	1	8	12																					3
5	3	4^2					2	9^1		11	7	6	10	1	8	12	13																				4
5	3				6	2	4	9^2		11^3	7		10^1		8	14	12		1	13																	5
5	3				6	2	8	9		11			10			4	7		1																		6
5	3				6	2	8	9^2	13	11			10			4	7^1		1		12																7
5	3				6	2^1	8	9	14	11			10			4	7^1	13	1		12																8
2	3	4			6^1	7	5	9^2		10	11	12			8^3	14	13		1																		9
2	3	12				7	8	9		10^3	11	5				4	6^2		1	13	14																10
6	3	12				2^3	8	9	13	11		5	10			4^1	14		1		7^2																11
6	3	4				7	2	9^1		11		5	10		8				1		12																12
5	3	4				2	8	9		11		6	10^1		7				1		12																13
5	3	4	14			2^1	8	9^2		11	13	6^3	10		7				1		12																14
5	3	4					8	9^2	13	11		6	10		7^1						12		2		1												15
5	3	4			6^6		8	9	13	11^2	12		10		7^1									2	1												16
6	3	4	14			2	8^3	9^2	13			5	10		11^1					12	7				1												17
6	3	4					8	9^3	13	12^2	14	5	10		11^1					7				2	1												18
6	3	4^2					13	11	9	12	14	5	10^3							7				2	1												19
6	3		14				8	9	13	12^2	7^3	5	10		4	11^1								2	1												20
6	3	4^2				13	8	9		11^3	12	14	5		10						7^1			2	1												21
6	3	4^1	14			7		9^2	12	11	13	5^3	10											2	1	8											22
6	3	4	5		2	8	9^1	12	11			10												1	7												23
5	3	4^1	6			2^3	8	9	13	11^2	12		10								14	1	7														24
	3					2	9^2	10	11	13	5	12		7^1							6	1	4	8													25
5	3				6	2^3	4	9	13	11	7^6		10								12	1^8	8	15													26
5	3				6		4	9^2	14	12			10		13						7^1	2		8	1	11^3											27
5	3	13				2	9^3	11			6		10		8						7^1	12		1		4^2	14										28
5	3	4	12			2^1	9	11	13			6			8^9						7	10^2		1		14											29
5	3	4					9			11^2	12	6	10^1		8						7	13		1			2										30
5	3	4^1	13				12	9		11^3		6^2	10		8						7			1			2	14									31
5	3	4			6		9^2			11^1	12		10^3		8						7			1		14	2	13									32
5	3	4^1	6				9			11^3	10^2	13			8						7	14		1			2		12								33
5	3						9	13	12	6		10^1			8						7	14		1			2	4^3	11^2								34
5	3	13					9	12		6		4			7^1	10^3						1				14	2	11^2	8								35
5	3	14				2	9			11^2	6	4			10^1							1				13	7	8^3	12								36
15	5	4				2	9			11^2	6				7	13					10^1	1^6				3		8	12								37
1		3	4	6		13	9			11^3	5				8	14											2^2	12	7^1	10							38
	5	3	4	6	2	8^3				11^2	13					9							14	12		7		10^1	1							39
1		3	4^2	6		8	9^3	14		5					13						7	12					2	11	10^1								40
1	12	3	4	6						13	5^1	8			7	9											2	14	11^3	10^2							41
1	5	12	4	6		2^1		2		11	10				8	13					7^2	9					3										42
1	6	4^2				2^1	5			11^3	10				8	12					7	9					3	14	13								43
1	5^2	4				13	2			11	10				8	6					7	9^1					3		12								44
1	5	4			6					12					8	11					7^3	9					3	14	2^1	10^2	13						45
1	5	4				2^1				11^3					8^2	3					7	9					6	12	13	10						14	46

FA Cup

First Round	Aldershot T	(h)	1-1	
		(a)	0-1	

Carling Cup

First Round	Cheltenham T	(h)	2-1
Second Round	Hull C	(h)	2-1
Third Round	Everton	(h)	1-1
Fourth Round	Birmingham C	(a)	1-1

J Paint Trophy

First Round	Stevenage	(a)	1-0
Second Round	Leyton Orient	(a)	0-0
Southern Quarter-Final	Swindon T	(a)	1-1
Southern Semi-Final	Charlton Ath	(h)	0-0
Southern Final	Exeter C	(h)	1-1
		(a)	2-1
Final	Carlisle U		0-1
(at Wembley).			

BRIGHTON & HOVE ALBION   FL Championship

FOUNDATION

A professional club Brighton United was formed in November 1897 at the Imperial Hotel, Queen's Road, but folded in March 1900 after less than two seasons in the Southern League at the County Ground. An amateur team Brighton & Hove Rangers was then formed by some prominent United supporters and after one season at Withdean, decided to turn semi-professional and play at the County Ground. Rangers were accepted into the Southern League but then also folded June 1901. John Jackson the former United manager organised a meeting at the Seven Stars public house, Ship Street on 24 June 1901 at which a new third club Brighton & Hove United was formed. They took over Rangers' place in the Southern League and pitch at County Ground. The name was changed to Brighton & Hove Albion before a match was played because of objections by Hove FC.

American Express Community Stadium, Village Way, Falmer, Brighton BN1 9BL.
Telephone: (01273) 878 288.
Fax: (01273) 878 238.
Ticket Office: (0845) 496 1901 (128 Queen's Road).
Website: www.seagulls.co.uk
Email: seagulls@bhafc.co.uk
Ground Capacity: 22,374.
Record Attendance: 36,747 v Fulham, Division 2, 27 December 1958 (at Goldstone Ground). 8,691 v Leeds U, FL 1, 20 October 2007 (at Withdean).
Pitch Measurements: 110yd × 70yd.
Chairman: Tony Bloom.
Managing Director: Ken Brown.
Chief Executive: Martin Perry.
Secretary: Derek J. Allan.
Manager: Gus Poyet.

HONOURS

Football League – Division 1: Best season: 13th, 1981–82;
Division 2: *Champions* 2001–02; *Runners-up* 1978–79;
FL 1: *Champions* 2010–11.
Division 3 (S): *Champions* 1957–58; *Runners-up* 1953–54, 1955–56;
Division 3: *Champions* 2000–01; *Runners-up* 1971–72, 1976–77, 1987–88;
Division 4: *Champions* 1964–65.
FA Cup: *Runners-up* 1983.
Football League Cup: Best season: 5th rd, 1979.

Assistant Manager: Mauricio Taricco. *Physio:* Nathan Ring.
Colours: Blue and white striped shirts, white sleeves with blue trim, white shorts, white stockings.
Change Colours: Yellow and navy blue striped shirts with blue sleeves, navy blue shorts, navy blue stockings.
Year Formed: 1901. *Turned Professional:* 1901. *Ltd Co.:* 1904.
Grounds: 1901, County Ground; 1902, Goldstone Ground; 1997, groundshare at Gillingham FC; 1999, Withdean Stadium; 2011, American Express Community Stadium.
Club Nickname: 'The Seagulls'.
First Football League Game: 28 August 1920, Division 3, v Southend U (a) L 0–2 – Hayes; Woodhouse, Little; Hall, Comber, Bentley; Longstaff, Ritchie, Doran, Rodgerson, March.
Record League Victory: 9–1 v Newport Co, Division 3 (S), 18 April 1951 – Ball; Tennant (1p), Mansell (1p); Willard, McCoy, Wilson; Reed, McNichol (4), Garbutt, Bennett (2), Keene (1). 9–1 v

sky SPORTS FACT FILE

In 1950–51, centre-forward Cyril Thompson set a Brighton & Hove Albion record when he scored in eight successive League matches from 13 September to 28 October. Formerly with Southend United and Derby County, he had been a Second World War POW.

Southend U, Division 3, 27 November 1965 – Powney; Magill, Baxter; Leck, Gall, Turner; Gould (1), Collins (1), Livesey (2), Smith (3), Goodchild (2).

Record Cup Victory: 10–1 v Wisbech, FA Cup 1st rd, 13 November 1965 – Powney; Magill, Baxter; Collins (1), Gall, Turner; Gould, Smith (2), Livesey (3), Cassidy (2), Goodchild (1), (1 og).

Record Defeat: 0–9 v Middlesbrough, Division 2, 23 August 1958.

Most League Points (2 for a win): 65, Division 3 (S), 1955–56 and Division 3, 1971–72.

Most League Points (3 for a win): 95, FL 1, 2010–11.

Most League Goals: 112, Division 3 (S), 1955–56.

Highest League Scorer in Season: Peter Ward, 32, Division 3, 1976–77.

Most League Goals in Total Aggregate: Tommy Cook, 114, 1922–29.

Most League Goals in One Match: 5, Jack Doran v Northampton T, Division 3 (S), 5 November 1921; 5, Adrian Thorne v Watford, Division 3 (S), 30 April 1958.

Most Capped Player: Steve Penney, 17, Northern Ireland.

Most League Appearances: 'Tug' Wilson, 509, 1922–36.

Youngest League Player: Ian Chapman, 16 years 259 days v Birmingham C, 14 February 1987.

Record Transfer Fee Received: £1,500,000 from Tottenham H for Bobby Zamora, July 2003 and £1,500,000 from Celtic for Adam Virgo, July 2005.

Record Transfer Fee Paid: £1,000,000 to Watford for Will Buckley, June 2011.

Football League Record: 1920 Original Member of Division 3; 1921–58 Division 3 (S); 1958–62 Division 2; 1962–63 Division 3; 1963–65 Division 4; 1965–72 Division 3; 1972–73 Division 2; 1973–77 Division 3; 1977–79 Division 2; 1979–83 Division 1; 1983–87 Division 2; 1987–88 Division 3; 1988–96 Division 2; 1996–2001 Division 3; 2001–02 Division 2; 2002–03 Division 1; 2003–04 Division 2; 2004–06 FL C; 2006–11 FL 1; 2011– FL C.

MANAGERS

John Jackson 1901–05
Frank Scott-Walford 1905–08
John Robson 1908–14
Charles Webb 1919–47
Tommy Cook 1947
Don Welsh 1947–51
Billy Lane 1951–61
George Curtis 1961–63
Archie Macaulay 1963–68
Fred Goodwin 1968–70
Pat Saward 1970–73
Brian Clough 1973–74
Peter Taylor 1974–76
Alan Mullery 1976–81
Mike Bailey 1981–82
Jimmy Melia 1982–83
Chris Cattlin 1983–86
Alan Mullery 1986–87
Barry Lloyd 1987–93
Liam Brady 1993–95
Jimmy Case 1995–96
Steve Gritt 1996–98
Brian Horton 1998–99
Jeff Wood 1999
Micky Adams 1999–2001
Peter Taylor 2001–02
Martin Hinshelwood 2002
Steve Coppell 2002–03
Mark McGhee 2003–06
Dean Wilkins 2006–08
Micky Adams 2008–09
Russell Slade 2009
Gus Poyet November 2009–

LATEST SEQUENCES

Longest Sequence of League Wins: 9, 2.10.1926 – 20.11.1926.
Longest Sequence of League Defeats: 12, 17.8.2002 – 26.10.2002.
Longest Sequence of League Draws: 6, 16.2.1980 – 15.3.1980.
Longest Sequence of Unbeaten League Matches: 16, 8.10.1930 – 28.1.1931.
Longest Sequence Without a League Win: 15, 21.10.1972 – 27.1.1973
Successive Scoring Runs: 31 from 4.2.1956.
Successive Non-scoring Runs: 6 from 8.11.1924.

TEN YEAR LEAGUE RECORD

		P	W	D	L	F	A	Pts	Pos
2001-02	Div 2	46	25	15	6	66	42	90	1
2002-03	Div 1	46	11	12	23	49	67	45	23
2003-04	Div 2	46	22	11	13	64	43	77	4
2004-05	FL C	46	13	12	21	40	65	51	20
2005-06	FL C	46	7	17	22	39	71	38	24
2006-07	FL 1	46	14	11	21	49	58	53	18
2007-08	FL 1	46	19	12	15	58	50	69	7
2008-09	FL 1	46	13	13	20	55	70	52	16
2009-10	FL 1	46	15	14	17	56	60	59	13
2010-11	FL 1	46	28	11	7	85	40	95	1

DID YOU KNOW ?

In its long-running campaign to receive permission to move to a new ground, Brighton & Hove Albion supporters in February 2005 produced a CD single "Tom Hark (We want Falmer)" which immediately entered the UK chart at No. 17 and was then featured on Radio 1.

BRIGHTON & HOVE ALBION 2010–11 LEAGUE RECORD

Match No.	Date	Venue	Opponents	Result	H/T Score	Lg Pos.	Goalscorers	Attendance
1	Aug 7	A	Swindon T	W 2-1	1-0	—	Sparrow 2 [19, 75]	10,392
2	14	H	Rochdale	D 2-2	0-0	6	Murray [47], Bennett [67]	6602
3	21	A	Sheffield W	L 0-1	0-1	11		18,674
4	28	H	Walsall	W 2-1	0-0	7	Barnes [68], Painter [81]	6474
5	Sept 11	H	Milton Keynes D	W 2-0	0-0	7	LuaLua [48], Murray [75]	6683
6	18	A	Carlisle U	D 0-0	0-0	8		6039
7	21	A	Plymouth Arg	W 2-0	2-0	—	Elphick [22], Barnes [42]	7079
8	25	H	Oldham Ath	W 2-1	1-1	1	Barnes [44], Sandaza [90]	7148
9	28	H	Brentford	W 1-0	0-0	—	LuaLua [78]	6740
10	Oct 2	A	Tranmere R	D 1-1	1-0	1	Murray [35]	5421
11	9	H	Bournemouth	D 1-1	0-0	1	LuaLua [61]	7348
12	16	A	Charlton Ath	W 4-0	1-0	1	Calderon [26], Murray [62], LuaLua [81], Sparrow [90]	18,949
13	23	H	Yeovil T	W 2-0	1-0	1	Murray [43], Calderon [56]	7253
14	30	A	Peterborough U	W 3-0	2-0	1	Barnes 2 (1 pen) [16, 62 (pl)], Calderon [33]	10,116
15	Nov 2	H	Exeter C	W 3-0	2-0	—	El-Abd [7], Barnes 2 (1 pen) [30 (pl), 77]	7212
16	13	A	Hartlepool U	L 1-3	0-1	1	Dicker [57]	3073
17	20	H	Bristol R	D 2-2	0-1	1	Hughes (og) [62], Wood (pen) [73]	7407
18	23	A	Southampton	D 0-0	0-0	—		26,237
19	Dec 11	A	Huddersfield T	L 1-2	0-0	1	Murray [54]	14,398
20	29	H	Charlton Ath	D 1-1	1-1	—	Murray [36]	8374
21	Jan 1	H	Leyton Orient	W 5-0	2-0	1	Murray 3 [29, 50, 60], Jones (og) [31], Barnes [73]	7198
22	3	A	Exeter C	W 2-1	0-1	1	Murray [64], Barnes [90]	6352
23	15	H	Peterborough U	W 3-1	2-0	1	Wood 2 [25, 55], Bennett [27]	7233
24	22	A	Bournemouth	L 0-1	0-0	1		9762
25	25	H	Colchester U	W 2-0	1-0	—	Calderon [45], Noone [76]	6798
26	Feb 1	A	Leyton Orient	D 0-0	0-0	1		5872
27	5	A	Bristol R	W 4-2	1-1	1	Barnes [38], Bennett [52], Bolger (og) [73], Murray [79]	6683
28	12	H	Hartlepool U	W 4-1	2-0	1	Wood [12], Murray 2 [17, 56], Noone [53]	7296
29	22	H	Plymouth Arg	W 4-0	2-0	—	Murray 2 [28, 48], Wood [41], Sandaza [90]	7261
30	26	A	Milton Keynes D	L 0-1	0-1	1		9327
31	Mar 1	A	Yeovil T	W 1-0	1-0	—	Bennett [25]	3832
32	5	H	Carlisle U	W 4-3	1-1	1	Murray [23], Barnes 2 [53, 63], Bridcutt [90]	7466
33	8	A	Brentford	W 1-0	0-0	—	Osborne (og) [74]	5694
34	12	H	Tranmere R	W 2-0	0-0	1	Wood (pen) [63], Murray [71]	7461
35	19	A	Oldham Ath	W 1-0	0-0	1	Barnes [67]	3863
36	22	H	Notts Co	W 1-0	0-0	—	Calderon [63]	7264
37	26	H	Swindon T	W 2-1	1-1	—	Dicker (pen) [12], Murray [64]	7562
38	29	A	Dagenham & R	W 1-0	0-0	—	Murray [59]	3604
39	Apr 2	A	Rochdale	D 2-2	1-1	1	Wood (pen) [29], Dicker [51]	3959
40	9	H	Sheffield W	W 2-0	1-0	1	Wood (pen) [44], Bennett [74]	8107
41	12	H	Dagenham & R	W 4-3	2-1	—	Calderon [18], Murray [19], Bridcutt [56], Barnes [63]	7619
42	16	A	Walsall	W 3-1	1-1	1	Calderon [6], Murray [47], Bennett [90]	6015
43	23	H	Southampton	L 1-2	1-0	—	Barnes [45]	8169
44	25	A	Colchester U	D 1-1	0-1	1	Barnes [72]	5132
45	30	H	Huddersfield T	L 2-3	0-1	1	Barnes [47], Sparrow [69]	8416
46	May 7	A	Notts Co	D 1-1	1-1	1	Barnes [12]	10,347

Final League Position: 1

GOALSCORERS

League (85): **Murray 22, Barnes 18 (2 pens), Wood 8 (4 pens), Calderon 7, Bennett 6, LuaLua 4, Sparrow 4, Dicker 3 (1 pen), Bridcutt 2, Noone 2, Sandaza 2, El-Abd 1, Elphick 1, Painter 1, own goals 4.**
Carling Cup (0).
FA Cup (11): **Barnes 2 (1 pen), Bennett 2, Sandaza 2, Sparrow 2, Calderon 1, Taricco 1, Wood 1.**
J Paint Trophy (0).

Ankergren C 45	Calderon I 44	Painter M 46	Kishishev R 21+11	Elphick T 22+5	El-Abd A 36+1	Sparrow M 21+8	Navarro A 2+2	Barnes A 31+11	Smith J 3+5	Bennett E 45+1	Dicker G 38+8	Hart G —+3	Greer G 32	Murray G 38+4	Battipiedi A 3+5	Baz C —+7	Holroyd C —+3	LuaLua K 7+4	Bridcutt L 31+6	Sandaza F 3+12	Dunk L 2+3	Wood C 22+7	Taricco M 2+2	Noone C 10+13	Brezovan P 1+1	Kasim Y 1	Match No.
1	2	3	4¹	5	6	7	8	9	10²	11	12	13															1
1	2	3	4	5	12			9³	7¹	11²	8	13	6¹	10	14												2
1	2	3	4¹	5	6			9	7²	11	8			10	13	12											3
1	2	3	4	5	6			9	12	11²	8			10	7¹	13											4
1	2	3	4³	5	6	7¹		9	13	11	12			10					8²	14							5
1	2	3	4	5	6	7		13		11¹	8			10	12				9²								6
1	2	3		5	6	7¹		9		11	8			10²					12	4	13						7
1	2	3	12	5	6			9		11	8			10²					7	4¹	13						8
1	2	3	4³	5	6	7¹		9		11	12			13					8	14	10²						9
1	2	3	12	5		7²		9¹		11	8			10³					14	6	13	4					10
1	2	3	4¹	5	6			9		11	8			10	13				7²	12							11
1	2	3	4		6	7		9¹		11	8		5	10					12								12
1	2	3	4	12	6¹			9²		11	8		5	10	14				7³	13							13
1	2	3	4²		6			9		11	8		5	10¹	13	12			7								14
1	2	3	4		6			9		11¹	8³		5	10²	14	13			7	12							15
1	2	3	4²		6¹	13		9		11	8		5	10		14			12³	7⁸							16
1	2	3	4	14	6			9¹	13	11	8		5³	12	7²							10					17
1	2	3	4		6¹			9¹	13	11	8		5	14	7²							12	10				18
1	2	3	4³		6			13	14	11	8¹		5	10					7	12		9²					19
1	2⁸	3	13		6	7		12		11	8²		5	10					4			9¹					20
1		3	13		6	7		12		11	8		5	10³		14			4			9¹	2²				21
1		3	14		6	7		13		11	8¹		5	10					4			12	2³	9²			22
1	2	3	13		6	7²		14		11	12		5	10³					4			9		8¹			23
1	2	3	12		6	7¹		8		11	13		5	14					4³			9		10²			24
1	2	3	4²		6			12		11	8		5	10³					7	14		9¹		13			25
1	2	3			6	7¹		9		11	8		5	10²					4			13		12			26
1	2	3			6			7		11	8		5	10²					4	13		9¹		12			27
1	2	3			6			7²		11³	8		5	10	13			14	4			8¹		12			28
1	2	3			6	14		7²		11³	8		5	10					4	13		9¹		12			29
1	2²	3³			6	13		7¹		11	8		5	10					4	12		9	14				30
1	2	3	14		6	13		7¹		11³	8		5	10					4			9²		12			31
1	2	3	13		6			9³		11	8		5	10²					4	14		12		7¹			32
1	2	3²	4		6			7		9¹			11³	14					5	10		8		12	13		33
1	2	3	4²		6	7¹		14		11	8		5	10					12			9³		13			34
1	2	3	4¹		6	7		12³		11	13		5	10					8			9²		14			35
1	2	3		12	6¹	7				11²	8		5	10					4	14		9³		13			36
1	2	3	13	6		7¹				12	8		5	10					4	9³	14			11²			37
1	2	3	12	6				13		11¹	8²		5	10					4	9		14		7³			38
1	2	3	4²	6				13		11	8		5	10					7¹	14		9³		12			39
1	2	3	14	6	13			12		11³	8		5⁸	10					4			9¹		7²			40
1	2	3	14	5	6	13		12		11	8³			10					4			9¹		7²			41
1	2	3		5	6	7	14	9²		11³	8			10					4			13		12			42
1	2	3		5	6	7³		9²		11	8			10¹					4	14		12		13			43
1⁸	2	3		5			4	9		11	8									6	10			7		15	44
	2	3		6			12	9		11	8	13	5						4			10²		7¹	1		45
1	2	3		6¹		7²		10		11	13		5						4			12	9	14		8³	46

FA Cup

First Round	Woking	(h)	0-0
		(a)	2-2
Second Round	FC United of Manchester	(h)	1-1
		(a)	4-0
Third Round	Portsmouth	(h)	3-1
Fourth Round	Watford	(a)	1-0
Fifth Round	Stoke C	(a)	0-3

Carling Cup

First Round	Northampton T	(a)	0-2

J Paint Trophy

First Round	Leyton Orient	(h)	0-1

BRISTOL CITY   FL Championship

FOUNDATION

The name Bristol City came into being in 1897 when the Bristol South End club, formed three years earlier, decided to adopt professionalism and apply for admission to the Southern League after competing in the Western League. The historic meeting was held at The Albert Hall, Bedminster. Bristol City employed Sam Hollis from Woolwich Arsenal as manager and gave him £40 to buy players. In 1900 they merged with Bedminster, another leading Bristol club.

Ashton Gate Stadium, Bristol BS3 2EJ.

Telephone: (0871) 222 6666.

Fax: (0117) 9630 700.

Ticket Office: 0871 222 6666 (option 1).

Website: www.bcfc.co.uk

Email: enquiries@bcfc.co.uk

Ground Capacity: 21,804.

Record Attendance: 43,335 v Preston NE, FA Cup 5th rd, 16 February 1935.

Pitch Measurements: 115yd × 75yd.

Chairman: Colin Sexstone.

Vice-chairman: Keith Dawe.

Chief Executive: Guy Price.

Secretary: Michelle McDonald.

Manager: Keith Millen.

Assistant Manager: Steve Wigley.

Physio: Nick Dawes.

Colours: Red shirts with white trim, white shorts, red stockings.

Change Colours: White shirts with red trim, red shorts, white stockings.

Year Formed: 1894. *Turned Professional:* 1897.

Ltd Co.: 1897. Bristol City Football Club Ltd.

Previous Name: 1894, Bristol South End; 1897, Bristol City.

Club Nickname: 'Robins'.

Grounds: 1894, St John's Lane; 1904, Ashton Gate.

First Football League Game: 7 September 1901, Division 2, v Blackpool (a) W 2–0 – Moles; Tuft, Davies; Jones, McLean, Chambers; Bradbury, Connor, Boucher, O'Brien (2), Flynn.

Record League Victory: 9–0 v Aldershot, Division 3 (S), 28 December 1946 – Eddols; Morgan, Fox; Peacock, Roberts, Jones (1); Chilcott, Thomas, Clark (4 incl. 1p), Cyril Williams (1), Hargreaves (3).

HONOURS

Football League –
Division 1: *Runners-up* 1906–07;
Division 2: *Champions* 1905–06;
Runners-up 1975–76, 1997–98;
FL 1: *Runners-up* 2006–07;
Division 3 (S): *Champions* 1922–23, 1926–27, 1954–55;
Runners-up 1937–38;
Division 3: *Runners-up* 1964–65, 1989–90.

FA Cup: *Runners-up* 1909.

Football League Cup: Semi-final 1971, 1989.

Welsh Cup: *Winners* 1934.

Anglo-Scottish Cup: *Winners* 1978.

Freight Rover Trophy: *Winners* 1986; *Runners-up* 1987.

Auto Windscreens Shield: *Runners-up* 2000.

LDV Vans Trophy: *Winners* 2003.

sky SPORTS FACT FILE

On 1 May 1939 Bristol City achieved the unusual feat of winning two cup finals. At Thornbury the reserves beat a Berkeley and District XI 7-4 in the Berkeley Hunt Cup, while at Twerton Park the first eleven defeated Swindon Town 2-0 in the Bath Coronation Cup.

Record Cup Victory: 11–0 v Chichester C, FA Cup 1st rd, 5 November 1960 – Cook; Collinson, Thresher; Connor, Alan Williams, Etheridge; Tait (1), Bobby Williams (1), Atyeo (5), Adrian Williams (3), Derrick, (1 og).

Record Defeat: 0–9 v Coventry C, Division 3 (S), 28 April 1934.

Most League Points (2 for a win): 70, Division 3 (S), 1954–55.

Most League Points (3 for a win): 91, Division 3, 1989–90.

Most League Goals: 104, Division 3 (S), 1926–27.

Highest League Scorer in Season: Don Clark, 36, Division 3 (S), 1946–47.

Most League Goals in Total Aggregate: John Atyeo, 314, 1951–66.

Most League Goals in One Match: 6, Tommy 'Tot' Walsh v Gillingham, Division 3 (S), 15 January 1927.

Most Capped Player: Billy Wedlock, 26, England.

Most League Appearances: John Atyeo, 597, 1951–66.

Youngest League Player: Marvin Brown, 16 years 105 days v Bristol R, 17 October 1999.

Record Transfer Fee Received: £3,000,000 from Wolverhampton W for Ade Akinbiyi, September 1999.

Record Transfer Fee Paid: £2,250,000 to Crewe Alex for Nicky Maynard, August 2008.

Football League Record: 1901 Elected to Division 2; 1906–11 Division 1; 1911–22 Division 2; 1922–23 Division 3 (S); 1923–24 Division 2; 1924–27 Division 3 (S); 1927–32 Division 2; 1932–55 Division 3 (S); 1955–60 Division 2; 1960–65 Division 3; 1965–76 Division 2; 1976–80 Division 1; 1980–81 Division 2; 1981–82 Division 3; 1982–84 Division 4; 1984–90 Division 3; 1990–92 Division 2; 1992–95 Division 3; 1995–98 Division 2; 1998–99 Division 1; 1999–04 Division 2; 2004–07 FL 1; 2007– FL C.

MANAGERS

Sam Hollis 1897–99
Bob Campbell 1899–1901
Sam Hollis 1901–05
Harry Thickett 1905–10
Frank Bacon 1910–11
Sam Hollis 1911–13
George Hedley 1913–17
Jack Hamilton 1917–19
Joe Palmer 1919–21
Alex Raisbeck 1921–29
Joe Bradshaw 1929–32
Bob Hewison 1932–49
  (*under suspension 1938–39*)
Bob Wright 1949–50
Pat Beasley 1950–58
Peter Doherty 1958–60
Fred Ford 1960–67
Alan Dicks 1967–80
Bobby Houghton 1980–82
Roy Hodgson 1982
Terry Cooper 1982–88
  (*Director from 1983*)
Joe Jordan 1988–90
Jimmy Lumsden 1990–92
Denis Smith 1992–93
Russell Osman 1993–94
Joe Jordan 1994–97
John Ward 1997–98
Benny Lennartsson 1998–99
Tony Pulis 1999–2000
Tony Fawthrop 2000
Danny Wilson 2000–04
Brian Tinnion 2004–05
Gary Johnson 2005–10
Steve Coppell 2010
Keith Millen August 2010–

LATEST SEQUENCES

Longest Sequence of League Wins: 14, 9.9.1905 – 2.12.1905.

Longest Sequence of League Defeats: 7, 3.10.1970 – 7.11.1970.

Longest Sequence of League Draws: 4, 6.11.1999 – 27.11.1999.

Longest Sequence of Unbeaten League Matches: 24, 9.9.1905 – 10.2.1906.

Longest Sequence Without a League Win: 15, 29.4.1933 – 4.11.1933.

Successive Scoring Runs: 25 from 26.12.1905.

Successive Non-scoring Runs: 6 from 10.9.1910.

TEN YEAR LEAGUE RECORD

		P	W	D	L	F	A	Pts	Pos
2001-02	Div 2	46	21	10	15	68	53	73	7
2002-03	Div 2	46	24	11	11	79	48	83	3
2003-04	Div 2	46	23	13	10	58	37	82	3
2004-05	FL 1	46	18	16	12	74	57	70	7
2005-06	FL 1	46	18	11	17	66	62	65	9
2006-07	FL 1	46	25	10	11	63	39	85	2
2007-08	FL C	46	20	14	12	54	53	74	4
2008-09	FL C	46	15	16	15	54	54	61	10
2009-10	FL C	46	15	18	13	56	65	63	10
2010-11	FL C	46	17	9	20	62	65	60	15

DID YOU KNOW ?

Billy Jones was the first Bristol City player to win England international honours when he was capped against Ireland in 1901. He was also the first of their players to be awarded a benefit during his sixth season with the club. Initially a versatile forward, he became a wing-half.

BRISTOL CITY 2010–11 LEAGUE RECORD

Match No.	Date	Venue	Opponents	Result	H/T Score	Lg Pos.	Goalscorers	Attendance
1	Aug 7	H	Millwall	L	0-3	0-1	—	18,308
2	14	A	Doncaster R	D	1-1	0-0	22	Stewart 49	9291
3	21	H	Barnsley	D	3-3	2-2	21	Elliott 19, Adomah 21, Clarkson (pen) 62	13,585
4	28	A	Ipswich T	L	0-2	0-0	22		19,011
5	Sept 11	A	Scunthorpe U	W	2-0	1-0	16	Adomah 16, Clarkson 90	5185
6	14	H	Watford	L	0-2	0-1	—		13,998
7	18	H	Coventry C	L	1-2	1-2	21	Elliott 42	13,428
8	25	A	Burnley	D	0-0	0-0	21		14,540
9	28	A	Portsmouth	L	1-3	0-0	—	Stead 53	14,417
10	Oct 2	H	Norwich C	L	0-3	0-2	24		14,124
11	16	A	Cardiff C	L	2-3	2-1	24	Caulker 6, Stead 8	22,444
12	19	H	Reading	W	1-0	1-0	—	Haynes 28	13,519
13	22	H	QPR	D	1-1	1-0	—	Stead 16	14,552
14	30	A	Middlesbrough	W	2-1	1-1	22	Adomah 35, Elliott 49	19,039
15	Nov 6	H	Preston NE	D	1-1	0-1	22	Jones (og) 71	14,429
16	10	A	Swansea C	W	1-0	1-0	—	Stead 6	14,741
17	13	A	Leeds U	L	1-3	0-0	22	Stead 68	27,567
18	20	H	Leicester C	W	2-0	0-0	21	Pitman 57, Clarkson 90	14,517
19	27	H	Sheffield U	W	3-0	2-0	17	Pitman 2 (2 pens) 6, 34, McAllister 62	13,376
20	Dec 11	A	Derby Co	W	2-0	0-0	17	Pitman 2 48, 68	14,029
21	18	A	Hull C	L	0-2	0-1	19		20,299
22	26	A	Reading	L	1-4	1-2	19	Stead 15	19,293
23	28	H	Crystal Palace	D	1-1	0-1	19	Pitman (pen) 90	15,760
24	Jan 1	H	Cardiff C	W	3-0	2-0	17	Pitman 3, Johnson 39, Campbell-Ryce 55	15,683
25	3	A	QPR	D	2-2	0-0	17	Pitman 50, Caulker 90	15,618
26	15	H	Middlesbrough	L	0-4	0-1	19		13,699
27	22	A	Crystal Palace	D	0-0	0-0	17		14,128
28	25	A	Nottingham F	L	0-1	0-0	—		19,694
29	Feb 1	H	Swansea C	L	0-2	0-1	19		14,366
30	5	A	Preston NE	W	4-0	1-0	18	Keogh 5, Clarkson 2 56, 65, Pitman 85	11,784
31	12	H	Leeds U	L	0-2	0-1	19		18,000
32	18	A	Leicester C	L	1-2	0-1	—	Elliott 57	28,768
33	22	A	Watford	W	3-1	1-1	—	Maynard 32, Elliott 69, Pitman 90	12,125
34	26	H	Scunthorpe U	W	2-0	1-0	16	Clarkson 13, Maynard 49	14,423
35	Mar 5	A	Coventry C	W	4-1	3-0	15	Maynard 15, Nyatanga 24, Clarkson (pen) 44, Elliott 82	15,157
36	8	H	Portsmouth	W	2-1	1-0	—	Adomah 40, Halford (og) 66	13,886
37	14	A	Norwich C	L	1-3	0-1	—	Adomah 65	24,428
38	19	H	Burnley	W	2-0	1-0	14	Pitman 43, Maynard 70	14,360
39	Apr 2	H	Doncaster R	W	1-0	0-0	14	Maynard 76	13,726
40	9	A	Barnsley	L	2-4	1-3	15	Elliott 6, Maynard (pen) 83	10,257
41	12	A	Millwall	D	0-0	0-0	—		11,108
42	16	A	Ipswich T	L	0-1	0-0	15		14,159
43	23	A	Sheffield U	L	2-3	1-2	15	Simonsen (og) 10, Pitman (pen) 60	18,151
44	25	H	Nottingham F	L	2-3	0-2	16	Elliott 49, Stead 60	14,867
45	30	A	Derby Co	W	2-0	1-0	14	Stead 6, Skuse 66	25,745
46	May 7	H	Hull C	W	3-0	2-0	15	Stead 3, Pitman 14, Campbell-Ryce 56	15,112

Final League Position: 15

GOALSCORERS

League (62): Pitman 13 (4 pens), Stead 9, Elliott 8, Clarkson 7 (2 pens), Maynard 6 (1 pen), Adomah 5, Campbell-Ryce 2, Caulker 2, Haynes 1, Johnson 1, Keogh 1, McAllister 1, Nyatanga 1, Skuse 1, Stewart 1, own goals 3.
Carling Cup (2): McAllister 1, Sproule 1.
FA Cup (0).

James D 45	Hunt N 6+1	McAllister J 33+1	Fontaine L 30+1	Stewart D 18+3	Skuse C 25+5	Elliott M 46	Sproule I 4+7	Clarkson D 17+17	Adomah A 45+1	Campbell-Ryce J 21+10	Vokes S —+1	Jackson M —+4	Williams G —+3	Akinde J —+2	Johnson L 14+6	Cisse K 19+10	Pitman B 21+18	Stead J 24+3	Williams T —+1	Carey L 20+1	Rose D 13+4	Ribeiro C 8+1	Haynes D 10+3	Caulker S 29	Nyatanga L 18+2	Keogh A 4+5	Woolford M 10+5	Edwards J 1+1	Maynard N 11+2	Spence J 11	Gerken D 1	Wilson J 2	Reid B —+1	Match No.
1	2	3	4	5[4]	6	7	8[3]	9	10	11[1]	12[2]	13	14																					1
1	2	3	4	5	6	7	8[1]	10	9[2]	11		12	13																					2
1	2	3	4	5	6[1]	7	8	9[3]	10	11[2]		14	13	12																				3
1	2	3[1]	4	5		7	8			11					6	9	10	12																4
1	2	3	4	5[2]	6	7	12	14	11[1]						8	9[3]	10			13													5
1	2[1]	3	4	5	6	7	13	14	11						8[3]	9[2]	10				12												6
1		3	4		6	7[1]	12	9							13	14	10			5	11	2[3]	8[2]											7
1		3	4		6	7				11					12		10			5	8	2	9[1]											8
1	11[2]	2			6	7[1]		9							12		10			5	8	3	13	4										9
1	3[1]	2			6	7		9		11					12	13	10[2]			5	8			4										10
1		3	4		6[2]	7	12	14	11[1]							13	10			2	8			9[3]	5									11
1		3	4			7	14	8	11[2]						6	12	10			2	13			9[1]	5									12
1		3	4			7		8[1]							6	12	10			2	11			9	5									13
1		3	4			7		8[2]	14						6[1]	12	13	10		2	11			9[3]	5									14
1		3	4			7		8							6	12	10			2	11			9[1]	5									15
1		3[3]	4		14	7		8	11						6	12	13	10[1]		2				9[2]	5									16
1	13	3	4			7		8	11						6[3]	12	10			2[2]	14			9[1]	5									17
1		3	4		6	7	13	9[3]							8[1]	14	12	10[2]			11	2			5									18
1		3	4		6	7[2]	8	10[3]	14						12	13	9				11	2[1]			5									19
1		3		5	6	7	8[1]	9[2]	13						14	10	12				11	2			4									20
1		3		5	8	7	9[1]	8							13	10	12				11	2[2]			4									21
1	3[1]			5	6	7		8	14							9[2]	10			11[3]	2	13			4	12								22
1			2			7	13	8	11[1]						6	4	12	10[3]		14				9[2]	5	3								23
1			2			7	13	14	8[2]	11					6	4	9	10[3]							5	3	12							24
1			14	2		7	12	8[2]	11						6[3]	4	9	10[1]							5	3	13							25
1[*]	12		2			7	13	14	8	11[3]					6	4[1]	9	10[2]							5	3								26
1	2		4[2]		6	7	12	10[1]	8	11					13	9						3			5									27
1		3	4		6	7	12	10[1]	8	11[2]					13	9				2					5									28
1	12	3			6[1]	7	14	8	11[2]						4[3]	13	10			2					5									29
1		3			6	7		10	8[1]						4	12				2[2]					5	9	11	13						30
1		3			6	7		8	12						4	10				2[1]					5	9[2]	11		13					31
1		3[2]			6	7		10[1]	8	14					4					2					5	13	9[1]	11	12					32
1					6	7		10[1]	8						4	13				2					5	3	12	11	9[2]					33
1			12		6	7		10	8[2]						13	4				2					5[1]	3	14	11	9[3]					34
1			12		6	7		10[3]	8						4	14									5[1]	3	13	11	9[2]	2				35
1			5		6	7		10[1]	8						12	4									13	3	14	11[3]	9[2]	2				36
1					6	7		10[2]	8						12	4				13					5	3		11[1]	9	2				37
1					6	7	13	8	11						12	4[1]	10[2]								5	3	14		9[3]	2				38
1	3			5		7	13	8[3]	12	11					4[1]	9[2]									6		14		10	2				39
1	3[3]					7	13	8	12	11					6[2]	4	9[1]								5		14		10	2				40
1	3			5		7	14	8	4[1]						12	9[2]	13								6		11[3]		10	2				41
1	3			5	13	7[3]		8		11					4[2]	12	10[1]								6		14		9	2				42
1	3			5	12	7		8	13						4[3]	9	14								6		11[2]		10[*]	2				43
1	3					4	7	9[1]	8	11		13				12	10		5[2]						6					2				44
	3					4	7	13	8[2]	11		14				9[1]	10[3]								6		12				2	1	5	45
1	3[3]					4	7	14	8[1]	11[2]						9	10								5		12	2				6	13	46

FA Cup
Third Round   Sheffield W   (h)   0-3

Carling Cup
First Round   Southend U   (a)   2-3

BRISTOL ROVERS   FL Championship 2

FOUNDATION

Bristol Rovers were formed at a meeting in Stapleton Road, Eastville, in 1883. However, they first went under the name of the Black Arabs (wearing black shirts). Changing their name to Eastville Rovers in their second season, they won the Gloucestershire Senior Cup in 1888–89. Original members of the Bristol & District League in 1892, this eventually became the Western League and Eastville Rovers adopted professionalism in 1897.

The Memorial Stadium, Filton Avenue, Horfield, Bristol BS7 0BF.

Telephone: (0117) 909 6648.

Fax: (0117) 907 4312.

Ticket Office: (0117) 909 8848.

Website: www.bristolrovers.co.uk

Email: rodwesson@bristolrovers.co.uk; dave@bristolrovers.co.uk

Ground Capacity: 11,626.

Record Attendance: 38,472 v Preston NE, FA Cup 4th rd, 30 January 1960 (at Eastville). 9,464 v Liverpool, FA Cup 4th rd, 8 February 1992 (at Twerton Park). 12,011 v WBA, FA Cup 6th rd, 9 March 2008 (at Memorial Stadium).

Pitch Measurements: 110yd × 73yd 6in.

Chairman: Nick Higgs.

Secretary: Rod Wesson.

Manager: Paul Buckle.

Assistant Manager: Shaun North.

Physio: Phil Kite.

Colours: Blue and white quarters, white shorts, white stockings.

Change Colours: Black and gold quartered shirts, black shorts, gold stockings.

Year Formed: 1883. *Turned Professional:* 1897. *Ltd Co.:* 1896.

Previous Names: 1883, Black Arabs; 1884, Eastville Rovers; 1897, Bristol Eastville Rovers; 1898, Bristol Rovers. *Club Nickname:* 'Pirates'.

Grounds: 1883, Purdown; Three Acres, Ashley Hill; Rudgeway, Fishponds; 1897, Eastville; 1986, Twerton Park; 1996, The Memorial Stadium.

First Football League Game: 28 August 1920, Division 3, v Millwall (a) L 0–2 – Stansfield; Bethune, Panes; Boxley, Kenny, Steele; Chance, Bird, Sims, Bell, Palmer.

Record League Victory: 7–0 v Brighton & HA, Division 3 (S), 29 November 1952 – Hoyle; Bamford, Fox; Pitt, Warren, Sampson; McIlvenny, Roost (2), Lambden (1), Bradford (1), Petherbridge (2), (1 og). 7–0 v Swansea T, Division 2, 2 October 1954 – Radford; Bamford, Watkins; Pitt, Muir, Anderson; Petherbridge, Bradford (2), Meyer, Roost (1), Hooper (2), (2 og). 7–0 v Shrewsbury T, Division 3, 21 March 1964 – Hall; Hillard, Gwyn Jones; Oldfield, Stone (1), Mabbutt; Jarman (2), Brown (1), Biggs (1p), Hamilton, Bobby Jones (2).

HONOURS

Football League – Division 2: Best season: 4th, 1994–95; **Division 3 (S):** *Champions* 1952–53; **Division 3:** *Champions* 1989–90; *Runners-up* 1973–74.

FA Cup: Best season: 6th rd, 1951, 1958, 2008.

Football League Cup: Best season: 5th rd, 1971, 1972.

Leyland Daf: *Runners-up* 1990.

Johnstone's Paint Trophy: *Runners-up* 2007.

sky SPORTS FACT FILE

Bill Culley was the first Bristol Rovers player to score two hat-tricks in the Football League. His first trio came at home against Reading (4-2) on 2 April 1926, the second the following season on 15 April at Swindon Town (5-3). In both matches he scored once from the penalty spot.

Record Cup Victory: 6–0 v Merthyr Tydfil, FA Cup 1st rd, 14 November 1987 – Martyn; Alexander (Dryden), Tanner, Hibbitt, Twentyman, Vaughan Jones, Holloway, Meacham (1), White (2), Penrice (3) (Reece), Purnell.

Most League Points (2 for a win): 64, Division 3 (S), 1952–53.

Most League Points (3 for a win): 93, Division 3, 1989–90.

Most League Goals: 92, Division 3 (S), 1952–53.

Highest League Scorer in Season: Geoff Bradford, 33, Division 3 (S), 1952–53.

Most League Goals in Total Aggregate: Geoff Bradford, 242, 1949–64.

Most League Goals in One Match: 4, Sidney Leigh v Exeter C, Division 3 (S), 2 May 1921; 4, Jonah Wilcox v Bournemouth, Division 3 (S), 12 December 1925; 4, Bill Culley v QPR, Division 3 (S), 5 March 1927; 4, Frank Curran v Swindon T, Division 3 (S), 25 March 1939; 4, Vic Lambden v Aldershot, Division 3 (S), 29 March 1947; 4, George Petherbridge v Torquay U, Division 3 (S), 1 December 1951; 4, Vic Lambden v Colchester U, Division 3 (S), 14 May 1952; 4, Geoff Bradford v Rotherham U, Division 2, 14 March 1959; 4, Robin Stubbs v Gillingham, Division 2, 10 October 1970; 4, Alan Warboys v Brighton & HA, Division 3, 1 December 1973; 4, Jamie Cureton v Reading, Division 2, 16 January 1999.

Most Capped Player: Vitalijs Astafjevs, 31 (167), Latvia.

Most League Appearances: Stuart Taylor, 546, 1966–80.

Youngest League Player: Ronnie Dix, 15 years 173 days v Charlton Ath, 25 February 1928.

Record Transfer Fee Received: £2,100,000 from Fulham for Barry Hayles, November 1998 and £2,100,000 from WBA for Jason Roberts, July 2000.

Record Transfer Fee Paid: £375,000 to QPR for Andy Tillson, November 1992.

Football League Record: 1920 Original Member of Division 3; 1921–53 Division 3 (S); 1953–62 Division 2; 1962–74 Division 3; 1974–81 Division 2; 1981–90 Division 3; 1990–92 Division 2. 1992–93 Division 1; 1993–2001 Division 2; 2001–04 Division 3; 2004–07 FL 2; 2007–11 FL 1; 2011– FL 2.

MANAGERS

Alfred Homer 1899–1920
  (*continued as Secretary to 1928*)
Ben Hall 1920–21
Andy Wilson 1921–26
Joe Palmer 1926–29
Dave McLean 1929–30
Albert Prince-Cox 1930–36
Percy Smith 1936–37
Brough Fletcher 1938–49
Bert Tann 1950–68 (*continued as General Manager to 1972*)
Fred Ford 1968–69
Bill Dodgin Snr 1969–72
Don Megson 1972–77
Bobby Campbell 1978–79
Harold Jarman 1979–80
Terry Cooper 1980–81
Bobby Gould 1981–83
David Williams 1983–85
Bobby Gould 1985–87
Gerry Francis 1987–91
Martin Dobson 1991
Dennis Rofe 1992
Malcolm Allison 1992–93
John Ward 1993–96
Ian Holloway 1996–2001
Garry Thompson 2001
Gerry Francis 2001
Garry Thompson 2001–02
Ray Graydon 2002–04
Ian Atkins 2004–05
Paul Trollope 2005–10
Dave Penney 2011
Paul Buckle May 2011–

LATEST SEQUENCES

Longest Sequence of League Wins: 12, 18.10.1952 – 17.1.1953.

Longest Sequence of League Defeats: 8, 26.10.2002 – 21.12.2002.

Longest Sequence of League Draws: 5, 1.11.1975 – 22.11.1975.

Longest Sequence of Unbeaten League Matches: 32, 7.4.1973 – 27.1.1974.

Longest Sequence Without a League Win: 20, 5.4.1980 – 1.11.1980.

Successive Scoring Runs: 26 from 26.3.1927.

Successive Non-scoring Runs: 6 from 14.10.1922.

TEN YEAR LEAGUE RECORD

		P	W	D	L	F	A	Pts	Pos
2001-02	Div 3	46	11	12	23	40	60	45	23
2002-03	Div 3	46	12	15	19	50	57	51	20
2003-04	Div 3	46	14	13	19	50	61	55	15
2004-05	FL 2	46	13	21	12	60	57	60	12
2005-06	FL 2	46	17	9	20	59	67	60	12
2006-07	FL 2	46	20	12	14	49	42	72	6
2007-08	FL 1	46	12	17	17	45	53	53	16
2008-09	FL 1	46	17	12	17	79	61	63	11
2009-10	FL 1	46	19	5	22	59	70	62	11
2010-11	FL 1	46	11	12	23	48	82	45	22

DID YOU KNOW ❓

While Vic Lambden holds the record for the fastest Bristol Rovers goal in the FA Cup against Aldershot on 10 January 1951 after eight seconds, in Football League terms for the club Kenny Ronaldson registered after 28 seconds on 23 September 1967 against Southport.

BRISTOL ROVERS 2010–11 LEAGUE RECORD

Match No.	Date		Venue	Opponents	Result		H/T Score	Lg Pos.	Goalscorers	Atten-dance
1	Aug	7	A	Peterborough U	L	0-3	0-0	—		7113
2		14	H	Yeovil T	W	2-1	1-0	13	Osei-Kuffour [45], Anthony [90]	6438
3		21	A	Exeter C	D	2-2	1-1	13	Osei-Kuffour [45], Hoskins [54]	7401
4		28	H	Southampton	L	0-4	0-2	19		8226
5	Sept	4	A	Oldham Ath	D	1-1	1-1	17	Hoskins [8]	4039
6		11	H	Brentford	D	0-0	0-0	17		5609
7		18	A	Dagenham & R	W	3-0	2-0	15	Hughes 3 (1 pen) [27, 32, 87 (p)]	2287
8		25	H	Notts Co	W	2-1	1-0	13	Hoskins 2 [5, 56]	5962
9		28	H	Tranmere R	L	0-1	0-1	—		5589
10	Oct	2	A	Huddersfield T	W	1-0	0-0	9	Hoskins [90]	12,344
11		11	A	Swindon T	L	1-2	0-1	—	Hughes (pen) [90]	9065
12		16	H	Rochdale	W	2-1	1-0	9	Hughes (pen) [45], Lines [82]	5872
13		23	A	Hartlepool U	D	2-2	0-1	12	Osei-Kuffour [85], Anthony [90]	2792
14		30	H	Carlisle U	D	1-1	0-0	12	Lines [48]	6144
15	Nov	2	A	Plymouth Arg	L	1-3	0-0	—	Hoskins [67]	7413
16		13	H	Leyton Orient	L	0-3	0-2	15		5541
17		20	A	Brighton & HA	D	2-2	1-0	16	Anthony [24], Painter (og) [90]	7407
18		23	A	Charlton Ath	D	1-1	0-0	—	Brown [63]	13,468
19	Dec	11	A	Sheffield W	L	2-6	1-4	21	Hoskins 2 [7, 66]	19,242
20	Jan	1	A	Milton Keynes D	L	0-2	0-2	21		7185
21		4	A	Plymouth Arg	L	2-3	2-0	—	Hoskins 2 [8, 11]	5943
22		11	H	Walsall	D	2-2	0-1	—	Hoskins [53], Osei-Kuffour [54]	5369
23		15	A	Carlisle U	L	0-4	0-1	22		4229
24		18	A	Hartlepool U	D	0-0	0-0	—		5285
25		22	H	Swindon T	W	3-1	1-0	21	Hoskins [7], Osei-Kuffour [48], Hughes [74]	6972
26		29	A	Walsall	L	1-6	0-3	—	Hughes [49]	4023
27	Feb	2	H	Milton Keynes D	L	1-2	0-1	—	Hughes (pen) [83]	4829
28		5	H	Brighton & HA	L	2-4	1-1	23	Hoskins 2 [2, 86]	6683
29		8	A	Rochdale	L	1-3	0-0	—	Hoskins [79]	2372
30		12	A	Leyton Orient	L	1-4	0-2	24	Chorley (og) [52]	4913
31		19	H	Oldham Ath	W	1-0	0-0	23	Howe [73]	5379
32		26	A	Brentford	L	0-1	0-1	22		5944
33	Mar	1	H	Colchester U	L	0-1	0-1	—		5181
34		5	H	Dagenham & R	L	0-2	0-1	23		5716
35		8	A	Tranmere R	W	1-0	1-0	—	Lines [19]	4110
36		12	H	Huddersfield T	L	0-1	0-1	23		7380
37		19	A	Notts Co	W	1-0	0-0	22	Hoskins [62]	5691
38		25	H	Peterborough U	D	2-2	1-1	—	Osei-Kuffour [6], Hughes [57]	6589
39	Apr	2	A	Yeovil T	W	1-0	0-0	22	Williams [76]	6281
40		5	H	Bournemouth	W	1-0	1-0	—	Hughes (pen) [33]	6691
41		9	H	Exeter C	L	0-2	0-0	20		7500
42		16	A	Southampton	L	0-1	0-0	21		23,647
43		23	H	Charlton Ath	D	2-2	0-1	—	Brown [66], Williams [84]	6586
44		25	A	Bournemouth	L	1-2	1-0	22	Brown [4]	7869
45		30	H	Sheffield W	D	1-1	1-1	22	Hoskins (pen) [12]	8340
46	May	7	A	Colchester U	L	1-2	0-2	22	Richards [72]	4759

Final League Position: 22

GOALSCORERS

League (48): Hoskins 17 (1 pen), Hughes 10 (5 pens), Osei-Kuffour 6, Anthony 3, Brown 3, Lines 3, Williams 2, Howe 1, Richards 1, own goals 2.
Carling Cup (1): Lines 1.
FA Cup (1): Hoskins 1.
J Paint Trophy (9): Osei-Kuffour 3, Hoskins 2, Swallow 2, Hughes 1 (pen), Lines 1.

Andersen M 19	Anthony B 36 + 1	Sawyer G 37	Campbell S 37	Coles D 37	Tunnicliffe J 21 + 4	Blizzard D 3 + 2	Brown W 12 + 13	Hoskins W 41 + 2	Osei-Kuffour J 33 + 9	Hughes J 40 + 2	Lines C 41 + 1	Duffy D — + 3	Reece C 6 + 8	Green M 2	Regan C 19 + 2	Akinde J 9 + 5	Richards E 2 + 11	Swallow B 11 + 6	Pell H 7 + 3	Daniels L 9	McCracken D 5 + 5	Davies S 4 + 3	Howe R 8 + 4	Bolger C 4 + 2	Kalala J 10 + 1	Williams G 17 + 2	Logan C 16	Senda D 15	Ifil J 3	Lambe R 1 + 6	Harrison E — + 1	Powell L — + 1	Clough C 1 + 1	Clarke O — + 1	Match No.
1	2	3	4	5	6	7	8²	9	10	11¹	12	13																							1
1	2	3	4	5	6		8	9	10	11	7																								2
1	2	3	4	5	6		8²	9¹	10	11	7	12	13																						3
1	2	3	4	5	6		8¹	9	10	11	7	13	12²																						4
	6	3	4	5¹	13	7¹		9	10²	11	8			1	2	12																			5
1	5	3⁴	4				12	9¹	10	11	7				2	8																			6
1	3		4	5	6		12	9¹	10	11	7				2	8																			7
1	6	3	4	5³	14		12	9²	10	11	7				2	8¹	13																		8
1	6	3	4¹	5			12	9	10	11	7				2	8																			9
1	6	3	4	5	13		12	9	10	11	7				2²	8¹																			10
	6	3	4	5				9	10	11	7	12		1	2	8¹																			11
1	6	3	4	5			12	9	10²	11	7		8¹		2	13																			12
1	6	3	4	5			14	9³	10	11²	8		7¹		2	13	12																		13
1	6	3	4	5				9	10¹	11	8		7		2	12																			14
1	6	3	4¹	5			12	9	10	11	8		7²		2		13																		15
1	6	3	4³	5	12		8¹		10	11	7				2⁴	9²	13	14																	16
1	6	3	4	5			2²	12	10	11	7					9¹	13	8																	17
1	2		4	5	6		8	12	10	3	7					9¹	11																		18
1	2	3	4	5	6		7¹	9	10³	11²	8		14		12		13																		19
1	6	3	4	5				9	10	12	8		7¹		12		13	11²																	20
1	6	3	4				5¹	9	12	11	0		13		2		10	7²																	21
	3	4	5	6	13			9	12	11	8²				2		10¹	7		1															22
12	3³	4	5⁴	6	14	13		9	10²	11	8				2		7¹			1															23
5	3	8		6				9	10		7		12		2¹	13	11²			1	4														24
6	3	4						9	10	11	8				2		7			1	5														25
6	3	4				8		9	10²	11					7³		7¹			1	5	12	13	14											26
2	3³	4²						9	14	11					13					1	5¹	8	10	6	7	12									27
2			5					9	12	3	4				13					1	11	10¹	6	8²	7										28
2	3		5			13		9		11					12					1		8¹	10	6⁴	4	7²									29
2	3		5	6				9	13	11					12					1		8¹	10		4	7²									30
6	3		5					9		12	4						11¹					13	10		8	7²	1	2							31
	3		5					9²	12	11	4		13										10		8	7²	1	2¹	6						32
			5					9²	11	3	4				13							12	10¹		8	7	1	2	6						33
	3	4	5³					9²	13	11	8				14								10	12	2	7¹	1			6⁸					34
	3	4		6				9		11	8	10¹			13	12						5				7²	1	2							35
	3	4²	5	6				9	14	11	8	12			13		7¹									10³	1	2							36
	3	4	5	6				9²	12	11	8				13		7³						14		13	10¹	1	2							37
	3		4	5	6			9	10	11	8						7¹										1	2	12						38
	3		4³	5	6		14	9	10²	11	8						7¹					13				12	1	2							39
	3³		4²	5	6			9¹	10	11	8				13							14				7	1	2	12						40
	3²		5	6	13				10	11	4				12						8	14				7	1	2³		9¹					41
	3		4³	5	6				10²	11	8						7¹									9	1	2		12	13	14			42
	3		4	5²	6³		14	9	10	11¹	8											13				7	1	2		12					43
5	3		4¹				11³	9²	10		8										6⁸		14		12	7	1	2		13					44
6	3²		5¹				11	9	10		8				13								14		4	7²	1	2				12			45
6							7¹	9³			4				12	11	3²						8		10		1	2		14			5	13	46

FA Cup
First Round   Darlington   (a) 1-2

Carling Cup
First Round   Oxford U   (a) 1-6

J Paint Trophy
Second Round   Aldershot T   (h) 1-0
Southern Quarter-Final   Wycombe W   (a) 6-3
Southern Semi-Final   Exeter C   (h) 2-2

BURNLEY   FL Championship

FOUNDATION

On 18 May 1882 Burnley (Association) Football Club was still known as Burnley Rovers as members of that Rugby Club had decided on that date to play Association Football in the future. It was only a matter of days later that the members met again and decided to drop Rovers from the club's name.

Turf Moor, Harry Potts Way, Burnley, Lancashire BB10 4BX.

Telephone: 0871 221 1882.

Fax: (01282) 700 014.

Ticket Office: 0871 221 1914.

Website: www.burnleyfc.com

Email: info@burnleyfc.com

Ground Capacity: 22,610.

Record Attendance: 54,775 v Huddersfield T, FA Cup 3rd rd, 23 February 1924.

Pitch Measurements: 112yd × 70yd.

Chairman: Barry Kilby.

Joint Operational Directors: Brendon Flood, Clive Holt.

Manager: Eddie Howe.

Assistant Manager: Jason Tindall.

Football Secretary: Pauline Scott.

Head Physio: Alasdair Beattie.

Colours: Claret shirts with blue sleeves, white shorts, claret stockings.

Change Colours: White shirts, light blue shorts, light blue stockings.

Year Formed: 1882.

Turned Professional: 1883. *Ltd Co.:* 1897.

Previous Name: 1882, Burnley Rovers; 1882, Burnley.

Club Nickname: 'The Clarets'.

Grounds: 1882, Calder Vale; 1883, Turf Moor.

First Football League Game: 8 September 1888, Football League, v Preston NE (a) L 2–5 – Smith; Lang, Bury, Abrahams, Friel, Keenan, Brady, Tait, Poland (1), Gallocher (1), Yates.

Record League Victory: 9–0 v Darwen, Division 1, 9 January 1892 – Hillman; Walker, McFettridge, Lang, Matthews, Keenan, Nicol (3), Bowes, Espie (1), McLardie (3), Hill (2).

Record Cup Victory: 9–0 v Crystal Palace, FA Cup 2nd rd (replay), 10 February 1909 – Dawson; Barron, McLean; Cretney (2), Leake, Moffat; Morley, Ogden, Smith (3), Abbott (2), Smethams (1). 9–0 v New Brighton, FA Cup 4th rd, 26 January 1957 – Blacklaw; Angus, Winton; Seith, Adamson, Miller; Newlands (1), McIlroy (3), Lawson (3), Cheesebrough (1), Pilkington (1). 9–0 v Penrith, FA Cup 1st rd, 17 November 1984 – Hansbury; Miller, Hampton, Phelan, Overson (Kennedy), Hird (3 incl. 1p), Grewcock (1), Powell (2), Taylor (3), Biggins, Hutchison.

HONOURS

Football League – Division 1: *Champions* 1920–21, 1959–60; *Runners-up* 1919–20, 1961–62; **Division 2:** *Champions* 1897–98, 1972–73; *Runners-up* 1912–13, 1946–47, 1999–2000; **Division 3:** *Champions* 1981–82; **Division 4:** *Champions* 1991–92. Record 30 consecutive Division 1 games without defeat 1920–21.

FA Cup: *Winners* 1914; *Runners-up* 1947, 1962.

Football League Cup: Semi-final 1961, 1969, 1983, 2009.

Anglo–Scottish Cup: *Winners* 1979.

Sherpa Van Trophy: *Runners-up* 1988.

European Competitions European Cup: 1960–61. **European Fairs Cup:** 1966–67.

sky SPORTS FACT FILE

On 11 September 2010 Burnley were trailing 3-1 in the 70th minute at Turf Moor against Preston North End. The recovery began in the 84th minute with Chris Iwelumo, the first of three goals in six minutes, the completion of his hat-trick and the winning header from Jay Rodriguez.

Record Defeat: 0–10 v Aston Villa, Division 1, 29 August 1925 and v Sheffield U, Division 1, 19 January 1929.

Most League Points (2 for a win): 62, Division 2, 1972–73.

Most League Points (3 for a win): 88, Division 2, 1999–2000.

Most League Goals: 102, Division 1, 1960–61.

Highest League Scorer in Season: George Beel, 35, Division 1, 1927–28.

Most League Goals in Total Aggregate: George Beel, 179, 1923–32.

Most League Goals in One Match: 6, Louis Page v Birmingham C, Division 1, 10 April 1926.

Most Capped Player: Jimmy McIlroy, 51 (55), Northern Ireland.

Most League Appearances: Jerry Dawson, 522, 1907–28.

Youngest League Player: Tommy Lawton, 16 years 174 days v Doncaster R, 28 March 1936.

Record Transfer Fee Received: £6,500,000 from Wolverhampton W for Steven Fletcher, June 2010.

Record Transfer Fee Paid: £3,000,000 to Hibernian for Steven Fletcher, June 2009.

Football League Record: 1888 Original Member of the Football League; 1897–98 Division 2; 1898–1900 Division 1; 1900–13 Division 2; 1913–30 Division 1; 1930–47 Division 2; 1947–71 Division 1; 1971–73 Division 2; 1973–76 Division 1; 1976–80 Division 2; 1980–82 Division 3; 1982–83 Division 2; 1983–85 Division 3; 1985–92 Division 4; 1992–94 Division 2; 1994–95 Division 1; 1995–2000 Division 2; 2000–04 Division 1; 2004–09 FL C; 2009–10 FA Premier League; 2010– FL C.

LATEST SEQUENCES

Longest Sequence of League Wins: 10, 16.11.1912 – 18.1.1913.

Longest Sequence of League Defeats: 8, 2.1.1995 – 25.2.1995.

Longest Sequence of League Draws: 6, 21.2.1931 – 28.3.1931.

Longest Sequence of Unbeaten League Matches: 30, 6.9.1920 – 25.3.1921.

Longest Sequence Without a League Win: 24, 16.4.1979 – 17.11.1979.

Successive Scoring Runs: 27 from 13.2.1926.

Successive Non-scoring Runs: 6 from 9.8.1997.

MANAGERS

Harry Bradshaw 1894–99
 (*Secretary-Manager from 1897*)
Club Directors 1899–1900
J. Ernest Mangnall 1900–03
 (*Secretary-Manager*)
Spen Whittaker 1903–10
 (*Secretary-Manager*)
John Haworth 1910–24
 (*Secretary-Manager*)
Albert Pickles 1925–31
 (*Secretary-Manager*)
Tom Bromilow 1932–35
Selection Committee 1935–45
Cliff Britton 1945–48
Frank Hill 1948–54
Alan Brown 1954–57
Billy Dougall 1957–58
Harry Potts 1958–70
 (*General Manager to 1972*)
Jimmy Adamson 1970–76
Joe Brown 1976–77
Harry Potts 1977–79
Brian Miller 1979–83
John Bond 1983–84
John Benson 1984–85
Martin Buchan 1985
Tommy Cavanagh 1985–86
Brian Miller 1986–89
Frank Casper 1989–91
Jimmy Mullen 1991–96
Adrian Heath 1996–97
Chris Waddle 1997–98
Stan Ternent 1998–2004
Steve Cotterill 2004–07
Owen Coyle 2007–10
Brian Laws 2010
Eddie Howe January 2011–

TEN YEAR LEAGUE RECORD

		P	W	D	L	F	A	Pts	Pos
2001-02	Div 1	46	21	12	13	70	62	75	7
2002-03	Div 1	46	15	10	21	65	89	55	16
2003-04	Div 1	46	13	14	19	60	77	53	19
2004-05	FL C	46	15	15	16	38	39	60	13
2005-06	FL C	46	14	12	20	46	54	54	17
2006-07	FL C	46	15	12	19	52	49	57	15
2007-08	FL C	46	16	14	16	60	67	62	13
2008-09	FL C	46	21	13	12	72	60	76	5
2009-10	PR Lge	38	8	6	24	42	82	30	18
2010-11	FL C	46	18	14	14	65	61	68	8

DID YOU KNOW ?

Clarke Carlisle, the Burnley central defender and PFA chairman, made an appearance as a guest on the BBC's *Question Time* television programme on 20 January 2011. A former quiz winner as Britain's Brainiest Footballer in 2002, he won two *Countdown* rounds in 2010.

BURNLEY 2010–11 LEAGUE RECORD

Match No.	Date	Venue	Opponents	Result	H/T Score	Lg Pos.	Goalscorers	Attendance
1	Aug 7	H	Nottingham F	W 1-0	1-0	—	Iwelumo [45]	17,496
2	14	A	Ipswich T	D 1-1	0-0	8	Carlisle [90]	19,317
3	21	H	Leicester C	W 3-0	1-0	3	Wallace [45], Iwelumo [62], Alexander (pen) [74]	15,516
4	28	A	Swansea C	L 0-1	0-1	5		15,135
5	Sept 11	H	Preston NE	W 4-3	1-2	5	Iwelumo 3 [9, 84, 88], Rodriguez [90]	15,509
6	14	A	Middlesbrough	L 1-2	0-0	—	Bikey [66]	15,033
7	18	A	Crystal Palace	D 0-0	0-0	8		14,451
8	25	H	Bristol C	D 0-0	0-0	8		14,540
9	28	H	Hull C	W 4-0	2-0	—	Iwelumo 2 [14, 53], Eagles 2 (1 pen) [24, 50 (p)]	14,458
10	Oct 2	A	Millwall	D 1-1	1-1	6	Rodriguez [22]	12,330
11	16	A	Sheffield U	D 3-3	0-0	8	Marney [49], Eagles (pen) [54], Rodriguez [90]	22,936
12	19	H	Barnsley	W 3-0	0-0	—	Eagles 2 (1 pen) [50, 66 (p)], Iwelumo [82]	14,428
13	23	H	Reading	L 0-4	0-1	7		14,895
14	30	A	QPR	D 1-1	1-1	8	Alexander (pen) [45]	15,620
15	Nov 6	A	Norwich C	D 2-2	2-0	9	Paterson 2 [26, 33]	24,519
16	9	H	Doncaster R	D 1-1	0-1	—	Cork [63]	13,655
17	13	H	Watford	W 3-2	1-1	6	Iwelumo [25], Wallace [70], Alexander (pen) [77]	14,160
18	20	A	Coventry C	L 0-1	0-0	10		14,432
19	27	H	Derby Co	W 2-1	0-1	7	Mears [82], Cork [90]	13,790
20	Dec 11	H	Leeds U	L 2-3	0-2	9	Easton [29], Rodriguez [37]	20,453
21	26	A	Barnsley	W 2-1	0-1	8	Guidetti [49], Bikey [54]	14,219
22	28	H	Scunthorpe U	L 0-2	0-1	9		15,043
23	Jan 1	H	Sheffield U	W 4-2	3-1	8	Eagles [29], Iwelumo [44], Rodriguez [45], Thompson [85]	14,897
24	3	A	Reading	L 1-2	1-1	10	Wallace [28]	16,151
25	15	H	QPR	D 0-0	0-0	10		14,819
26	22	A	Scunthorpe U	D 0-0	0-0	11		4334
27	25	A	Portsmouth	W 2-1	2-1	—	Rodriguez [31], Marney [37]	13,345
28	Feb 1	A	Doncaster R	L 0-1	0-0	11		8893
29	5	H	Norwich C	W 2-1	1-0	10	Marney [33], Rodriguez [81]	14,859
30	12	A	Watford	W 3-1	1-1	8	Bennett (og) [8], Eagles [66], Iwelumo [75]	13,103
31	15	A	Cardiff C	D 1-1	0-1	—	Thompson [83]	21,307
32	26	A	Preston NE	W 2-1	1-1	8	Rodriguez [32], Cork [84]	17,136
33	Mar 5	H	Crystal Palace	W 1-0	1-0	7	Rodriguez [3]	14,848
34	8	A	Hull C	W 1-0	1-0	—	Delfouneso [5]	20,218
35	12	H	Millwall	L 0-3	0-0	7		14,589
36	15	H	Coventry C	D 2-2	1-0	—	Rodriguez 2 [18, 79]	13,802
37	19	A	Bristol C	L 0-2	0-1	8		14,360
38	Apr 2	A	Ipswich T	L 1-2	0-2	9	Rodriguez [68]	14,483
39	9	A	Leicester C	L 0-4	0-1	11		24,039
40	12	A	Nottingham F	L 0-2	0-0	—		19,411
41	16	H	Swansea C	W 2-1	0-0	11	Williams (og) [57], Eagles (pen) [77]	13,675
42	19	H	Middlesbrough	W 3-1	3-0	—	Rodriguez [22], Elliott [23], Duff [37]	14,366
43	23	A	Derby Co	W 4-2	1-2	8	Eagles 2 [15, 62], Elliott [65], McCann [74]	25,187
44	25	H	Portsmouth	D 1-1	0-0	8	Eagles [74]	14,927
45	30	A	Leeds U	L 0-1	0-1	9		31,186
46	May 7	H	Cardiff C	D 1-1	1-0	8	Rodriguez [13]	14,197

Final League Position: 8

GOALSCORERS

League (65): Rodriguez 14, Eagles 11 (4 pens), Iwelumo 11, Alexander 3 (3 pens), Cork 3, Marney 3, Wallace 3, Bikey 2, Elliott 2, Paterson 2, Thompson 2, Carlisle 1, Delfouneso 1, Duff 1, Easton 1, Guidetti 1, McCann 1, Mears 1, own goals 2.
Carling Cup (5): Carlisle 1, Eagles 1, Elliott 1, McDonald 1, Thompson 1 (pen).
FA Cup (8): Eagles 3, Alexander 1 (pen), Carlisle 1, Mears 1, Paterson 1, Rodriguez 1.

Jensen B 21	Mears T 44	Fox D 35	Duff M 27+1	Bikey A 27+1	Marney D 34+2	Elliott W 37+7	Alexander G 15+17	Iwelumo C 29+16	Paterson M 7+4	Wallace R 24+16	Carlisle C 33+2	Rodriguez J 37+5	Thompson S 2+27	Edgar D 3+4	Eagles C 37+6	Cork J 36+4	Cort L 3+1	Easton B 11+1	Grant L 25	Guidetti J 2+3	Austin C 2+2	Bartley M 3+2	Delfouneso N 7+4	Duffy S 1	McCann C 4	Match No.
1	2	3	4[1]	5	6	7	8	9[3]	10[2]	11	12	13	14													1
1		3		5	4	7	8	9[2]	10[1]	11	6		13	2[4]	12											2
1	2	3		5	6[1]	7	8	9[3]	10	11[2]	4		14		13	12										3
1	2[4]	3		5	4[3]	7	8[1]	9	10[2]	11	6	13			14	12										4
1		3		5	6[1]	7	8	9	10[2]	11	4		14	2[3]	13	12										5
1	2	3		5		7	8	9[1]		11	6	13	12		10[2]	4										6
1	2	3		5	6	7		9[2]		11[1]	4	12	13		10	8										7
1	2	3		5	12	7	8[1]	9[2]		14	6	10[3]	13		11	4										8
1	2	3		5	6	7[1]		9[3]	12	13	4	10[2]	14		11	8										9
1	2	3	12	5[2]	6[1]	7		9[3]				4[4]	10	14	11	8	13									10
1	2	3[1]		5	6	7		9[2]		14		10	13	12	11[3]	8	4									11
1	2			5	6[3]	7	14	9[2]	13	12		10			11[1]	8	4	3								12
1	2	3		5	6[1]	7		9[3]	14	12		10[2]	13		11	8	4[4]									13
	2	3	4		6	7	8	9[2]		12	5	10	13		11[1]				1							14
	2	3	4		6[2]	7	8	14	10[3]	12	5	9			11[1]		13		1							15
	2	3[2]	4		6	7	13	12	10[1]	14	5	9			11[3]	8			1							16
	2		4		14	7[1]	8	9[2]		13	5	10	12		11[3]	6		3	1							17
	2		4			7	8	9[2]		12	5	10	13		11	6[1]		3	1							18
	2			5	6[3]	7	14	9[1]		11	4	10[2]	12			8		3	1	13						19
	2			5	6	7		9[1]		11[2]	4	10	12			8		3	1	13						20
	2			5		7	8			11	4	10			12	6		3	1	9[1]						21
	2			5		7[1]	8	13		11[3]	4	10	14		12	6		3	1	9[2]						22
	2		4		6	7[2]	8	9[1]			5	10	12	13	11			3	1							23
	2		4		6[1]	7		14		11	5	12	9[2]		10	8		3[3]	1	13						24
	2	3	4		6	7	8[2]	9[1]			5	10	12	13	11	6			1							25
	2	3	4	12	6	7		13		11[2]	5[1]	10			9	8			1							26
	2	3	4		6	7	13	12			5	10	9[1]		11[2]	8			1							27
	2	3	4		6	7[1]		12	13	14	5	9[1]			11	8			1		10[2]					28
	2	7	4		6		12	14		13	5	3[2]	9		11[3]	8			1		10[1]					29
	2	3	4		6		13	9[1]		11	5	10	12		7[3]	8[2]			1		14					30
	2	3	4		6[2]		14	9[1]		11	5	10[2]	13		7	8			1		12					31
	2	3	4		6	12	14	9[1]		11[2]	5	10			7[3]	8			1		13					32
	2	3	4		6	12	13	9[1]		11[3]	5	10		14	7[2]	8			1							33
	2	3	4		6	12		13		11[1]	5	10			7[2]	8						9				34
	2	3	4		6[3]	13	14	12		11	5	10			7[1]	8						9[2]				35
	2	3	4		6[1]	12		14		11[2]	5	10			7	8[3]						13	9			36
	2	3		4		9[3]	14	13		11[2]	5	10			7	8[1]						6	12			37
	2			5	6	13	14	12		11[1]		10			7[2]			3	1				8[3]	9	4	38
1	2		4	5	6	7	14	9[2]			12		8[3]	13	11			3			10					39
1	2	3	4	5[3]	6	7[2]		13		12		14		10[1]	8						11[4]	9				40
1	2	3	4	5	6	7	13	12			10[3]		14	11[2]	8							9[1]				41
1	2	3	4	5[1]	6[3]	7	14	9		12		10			11[2]	8						13				42
1	2	3	4	5		7	13	9[1]		14		10	12		11[3]	6						8[2]				43
1	2	3	6	5[3]		7		9[2]		14		10	13		11	8						12		4[1]		44
1	2	3	4[2]	5		7		9[3]		13		10	14		11	6						12		8[1]		45
1	2	3		5[1]		7	14	13		11[2]		10		6	9[3]	8				12				4		46

FA Cup

Third Round	Port Vale	(h)	4-2
Fourth Round	Burton Alb	(h)	3-1
Fifth Round	West Ham U	(a)	1-5

Carling Cup

Second Round	Morecambe	(a)	3-1
Third Round	Bolton W	(h)	1-0
Fourth Round	Aston Villa	(a)	1-2

BURTON ALBION   FL Championship 2

FOUNDATION

Once upon a time there were three Football League clubs bearing the name Burton. Then there was none. In reality it had been two. Originally Burton Swifts and Burton Wanderers competed in it until 1901 when they amalgamated to form Burton United. This club disbanded in 1910. There was no senior club representing the town until 1924 when Burton Town, formerly known as Burton All Saints played in the Birmingham & District League, subsequently joining the Midland League in 1935–36. When the Second World War broke out the club fielded a team in a truncated version of the Birmingham & District League taking over from the club's reserves. But it was not revived in peacetime. So it was not until a further decade that a club bearing the name of Burton reappeared. Founded in 1950 Burton Albion made progress from the Birmingham & District League, too, then into the Southern League and because of its geographical situation later had spells in the Northern Premier League. In April 2009 Burton Albion restored the name of the town to the Football League competition as champions of the Blue Square Premier League.

Pirelli Stadium, Princess Way, Burton-on-Trent, Staffordshire DE13 0AR.

Telephone: (01283) 565 938.

Fax: (01283) 523 199.

Website: www.burtonalbionfc.co.uk

Email: bafc@burtonalbionfc.co.uk

Ground Capactiy: 6,350 (2,034 seated).

Record attendance: 5,806 v Weymouth, Southern League Cup final 2nd leg 1964 (at Eton Park). 6,192 v Oxford U, Blue Square Premier, 17 April 2009 (at Pirelli Stadium).

Pitch Measurements: 110yd × 72yd.

Chairman: Ben Robinson.

Football Secretary: Fleur Robinson.

Manager: Paul Peschisolido.

Assistant Manager: Gary Rowett.

Physio: Guy Johnson.

Colours: Yellow shirts with black insert, black shorts, black stockings.

Change Colours: White shirts with blue trim, blue shorts, blue stockings.

HONOURS

Conference: *Champions* 2008–09.
FA Cup: 4th rd 2011.
FA Trophy: *Runners-up* 1986–87.
Southern League – Premier Division: *Runners-up* 1999–2000, 2000–01; **Division 1 (N):** *Runners-up* 1971–72, 1973–74. **Shared Cup:** 2000. **Southern League Cup:** *Winners* 1964, 1997, 2000; *Runners-up* 1989.
Northern Premier League: *Champions* 2001–02.
Northern Premier League Shield: 1983. **Challenge Cup:** *Winners* 1983; *Runners-up* 1987.
President's Cup: *Runners-up* 1983, 1986.
Birmingham Senior Cup: *Winners* 1954, 1997; *Runners-up* 1970, 1971, 1987.
Staffordshire Senior Cup: *Winners* 1956; *Runners-up* 1977.
Midland Floodlit Cup: *Winners* 1976; *Runners-up* 1973.

sky SPORTS FACT FILE

On 11 September 2010 Burton Albion were trailing 3-0 away to Rotherham United at half-time. Shaun Harrad reduced the arrears in the first minute of the second half, converted a penalty on 63 minutes and completed his hat-trick in the 83rd minute to achieve a point.

Year Formed: 1950.

Club nickname: Brewers.

Grounds: 1950, Eton Park; 2005, Pirelli Stadium.

First Football League Game: 8 August 2009, FL 2, v Shrewsbury T (a) L 1–3 – Redmond; Edworthy, Boertien, Austin, Branston, McGrath, Maghoma, Penn, Phillips (Stride), Walker, Shroot (Pearson) (1).

Record League Victory: 6-1 v Aldershot T, FL 2, 12 December 2009 – Krysiak; James, Boertien, Stride, Webster, McGrath, Jackson, Penn, Kabba (2), Pearson (3) (Harrad) (1), Gilroy (Maghoma).

Record Cup Victory: 12–1 v Coalville T, Birmingham Senior Cup, 6 September 1954.

Record Defeat: 0–10 v Barnet, Southern League, 7 February 1970.

Most League Points (3 for a win): 62, FL 2, 2009–10.

Most League Goals: 71, FL 2, 2009–10.

Highest League Scorer in Season: Shaun Harrad, 21, 2009–10.

Most League Goals in Total Aggregate: Shaun Harrad, 31, 2009–11.

Most League Goals in One Match: 3, Greg Pearson v Aldershot T, FL 2, 12 December 2009; 3, Shaun Harrad v Rotherham U, FL 2, 11 September 2010.

Most Capped Player: Jacques Maghoma, 2, DR Congo.

Youngest League Player: Tom Parkes, 18 years 8 days v Torquay U, 23 January 2010.

Most League Appearances: John McGrath, 86, 2009–11.

Record Transfer Fee Received: £130,000 from Crewe Alex for John Brayford, September 2008.

Record Transfer Fee Paid: £20,000 to Kidderminster H for Russell Penn, July 2009.

Football League Record: Promoted from Blue Square Premier 2008–09; 2009– FL 2.

MANAGERS

Reg Weston
Sammy Crooks 1957
Eddie Shimwell 1958
Bill Townsend 1959–62
Peter Taylor 1962–65
Richie Norman
Reg Gutteridge
Harold Bodle 1974–76
Ian Storey-Moore 1978–81
Neil Warnock 1981–86
Brian Fidler 1986–88
Vic Halom 1988
Bobby Hope 1988
Chris Wright 1988–89
Ken Blair 1989–90
Frank Upton (*caretaker*) 1990
Steve Powell 1990–91
Brian Fidler 1991–92
Brian Kenning 1992–94
John Barton 1994–98
Nigel Clough 1998–2009
Roy McFarland 2009
Paul Peschisolido May 2009–

LATEST SEQUENCES

Longest Sequence of League Wins: 3, 4.10.2009 – 17.10.2009.

Longest Sequence of League Defeats: 2, 19.9.2009 – 26.9.2009.

Longest Sequence of League Draws: 2, 5.9.2009 – 12.9.2009.

Longest Sequence of Unbeaten League Matches: 6, 16.4.2011 onwards.

Longest Sequence Without a League Win: 7, 27.3.2010 – 24.4.2010.

Successive Scoring Runs: 13 from 5.12.2009.

Successive Non-scoring Runs: 2 from 19.9.2009.

TEN YEAR LEAGUE RECORD

		P	W	D	L	F	A	Pts	Pos
2001-02	UNI	44	31	11	2	106	30	104	1
2002-03	Conf	42	13	10	19	52	77	49	16
2003-04	Conf	42	15	7	20	57	59	51*	14
2004-05	Conf	42	13	11	18	50	66	50	16
2005-06	Conf	42	16	12	14	50	52	60	9
2006-07	Conf	46	22	9	15	52	47	75	6
2007-08	B Sq Pr	46	23	12	11	79	56	81	5
2008-09	B Sq Pr	46	27	7	12	81	52	88	1
2009-10	FL 2	46	17	11	18	71	71	62	13
2010-11	FL 2	46	12	15	19	56	70	51	19

*1 pt deducted.

DID YOU KNOW ?

Three times Burton Albion have reached a century of goals in a season. In 1953–54 in the Birmingham & District League the Brewers scored 120 in 46 matches. In the same competition they hit 100 in 38 during 1954–55. Then in the 1964–65 Southern League it was 121 from 46.

BURTON ALBION 2010–11 LEAGUE RECORD

Match No.	Date	Venue	Opponents	Result	H/T Score	Lg Pos.	Goalscorers	Attendance
1	Aug 7	H	Oxford U	D	0-0	0-0	—	4321
2	14	A	Barnet	D	0-0	0-0	15	1655
3	21	H	Morecambe	W	3-2	1-1	8	Webster 2 [1, 75], Pearson (pen) [81]	2072
4	28	A	Cheltenham T	L	1-2	1-0	11	Harrad [36]	3221
5	Sept 4	H	Hereford U	W	3-0	2-0	6	Walker [27], Harrad [31], Penn [47]	2556
6	11	A	Rotherham U	D	3-3	0-3	8	Harrad 3 (1 pen) [46, 62 (p), 83]	3516
7	18	H	Crewe Alex	D	1-1	1-0	7	Maghoma [44]	3093
8	25	A	Gillingham	L	0-1	0-0	10		4823
9	28	A	Lincoln C	D	0-0	0-0	—		2510
10	Oct 2	H	Stockport Co	W	2-1	0-1	10	Webster 2 [64, 66]	3107
11	9	H	Wycombe W	L	1-2	0-2	12	Harrad [50]	3042
12	16	A	Stevenage	L	1-2	0-1	15	Webster [48]	2550
13	23	H	Bradford C	W	3-0	1-0	12	Harrad (pen) [31], Collins [54], Penn [88]	3143
14	30	A	Macclesfield T	L	1-2	0-1	13	Collins [63]	1791
15	Nov 2	H	Port Vale	D	0-0	0-0	—		4027
16	13	A	Chesterfield	W	2-1	1-1	12	Collins [5], Harrad [84]	7864
17	19	H	Bury	L	1-3	1-1	—	Collins [29]	2738
18	23	H	Aldershot T	L	1-2	1-2	—	Harrad [45]	1904
19	Dec 11	H	Southend U	W	3-1	2-0	12	Maghoma [37], Prosser (og) [45], Webster [57]	2604
20	Jan 1	H	Shrewsbury T	D	0-0	0-0	15		3594
21	3	A	Port Vale	L	1-2	0-2	17	Harrad [60]	5681
22	Feb 1	A	Shrewsbury T	L	0-3	0-0	22		4343
23	11	H	Chesterfield	W	1-0	1-0	—	Webster [5]	4260
24	15	A	Torquay U	L	0-1	0-0	—		1602
25	19	A	Hereford U	D	0-0	0-0	22		2773
26	22	A	Wycombe W	L	1-4	0-3	—	Winnall [56]	3345
27	26	H	Rotherham U	L	2-4	2-1	23	Pearson [2], Webster [34]	3596
28	Mar 1	A	Northampton T	W	3-2	3-1	—	Corbett [22], McGrath [37], Dunn (og) [39]	3423
29	5	A	Crewe Alex	L	1-4	0-3	22	Winnall [83]	3882
30	8	H	Lincoln C	W	3-1	1-0	—	Winnall 2 (1 pen) [11, 75 (p)], Webster [48]	2051
31	12	A	Stockport Co	D	0-0	0-0	22		4278
32	15	A	Accrington S	L	1-3	0-1	—	Pearson [88]	1445
33	19	H	Gillingham	D	1-1	1-0	22	Winnall [26]	3230
34	22	H	Stevenage	L	0-2	0-1	—		1962
35	27	A	Oxford U	L	0-3	0-1	—		7127
36	30	H	Macclesfield T	W	3-2	1-1	—	Zola [43], Bolder [86], Winnall (pen) [89]	1974
37	Apr 2	H	Barnet	L	1-4	1-0	22	Winnall [11]	2774
38	5	H	Northampton T	D	1-1	1-1	—	Webster [43]	2536
39	9	A	Morecambe	L	1-2	0-1	22	Maghoma [78]	1877
40	12	A	Bury	L	0-1	0-0	—		2580
41	16	H	Cheltenham T	W	2-0	1-0	22	Pearson (pen) [31], Maghoma [79]	2444
42	19	A	Bradford C	D	1-1	1-0	—	McGrath [42]	13,814
43	23	A	Aldershot T	W	2-1	1-1	17	Webster [12], Zola [74]	2308
44	25	H	Torquay U	D	3-3	2-2	19	McGrath [26], Pearson [41], Zola [56]	3280
45	30	A	Southend U	D	1-1	1-1	19	Malone [28]	5730
46	May 7	H	Accrington S	D	1-1	0-0	19	Penn [46]	3491

Final League Position: 19

GOALSCORERS

League (56): Webster 11, Harrad 10 (2 pens), Winnall 7 (2 pens), Pearson 5 (2 pens), Collins 4, Maghoma 4, McGrath 3, Penn 3, Zola 3, Bolder 1, Corbett 1, Malone 1, Walker 1, own goals 2.
Carling Cup (1): Harrad 1.
FA Cup (7): Harrad 2, Webster 2, Collins 1, Maghoma 1, Zola 1.
J Paint Trophy (1): Walker 1.

Legzdins A 46	Corbett A 36 + 4	Boertien P 15 + 1	Stanton N 23	Moore D 32 + 2	McGrath J 38 + 3	Penn R 39 + 2	Bolder A 32 + 5	Harrad S 16 + 4	Pearson G 16 + 19	Webster A 38 + 4	Young L 9 + 10	Maghoma J 39 + 2	James T 25 + 2	Walker R 9 + 9	Phillips J 10 + 13	Ellison J — + 2	Austin R 20 + 4	Grocott K — + 2	Gilroy K — + 1	Collins J 9 + 1	Malone S 18 + 4	Hughes B 1	Zola C 14 + 4	Winnall S 12 + 7	Whaley S 1 + 2	Rodney N — + 3	Dyer J 4 + 1	Parkes T 4 + 1	Preen G — + 1	Match No.
1	2	3	4	5	6	7	8^2	9^1	10	11	12	13																		1
1		2	4	5	6^2	7	8	9	10^1	11	13		3	12																2
1	2	3^1	4	5	12	7	8^2	9^1	10	11	6				14	13														3
1	2		4	5	6	7	8^1	9		11		3^2	10		13	12														4
1	2	4^1	5	6	7		9^2	13	3	8	11	12	10^3		14															5
1	2			6	7		9	14	3^1	8^2	11	5	10^3	13			4	12												6
1	2			6	7		9	12	3	13	11	5	10^1	8^2			4													7
1	2		5	6	7		9	13	3	12	11	5	10^2	8^1			4													8
1	2		5	6	8	12	9^2	10	3		7		13	11^1			4													9
1	13	3	4	5^1	6		8^2	14	9		11		7^2		10			2	12											10
1	12	3	4	5^1	6		8^2		9		11		7		10	13	2													11
1	2	3^1	4			8	9	14	11	6^3	7		10^2		5	12				13										12
1	2		5	6	12	8	9^2			7^1	11		13	4			10	3												13
1	2		5	6^3	12	8	9	14		7^1	11^2		13	4			10	3												14
1	13		4	5^2	6	7	8	9	12	11			2		10^1	3														15
1		4^1	12	6	7^3	8	13		9	14	11^{12}	5		2			10	3												16
1		4		6^3	7^1	8	12		9	13	11^{12}	5		14			2	10	3											17
1	12		4	5	6		8	9	13	11	7			2^1			10^2	3												18
1	2		4	5	6	7	8	12		9^1	11^2		13				10	3												19
1	2		4	5	6	7^2	8		12			11					13				10	9^1								20
1	13		4	5	6	7	8	14	12^1	0^1	11			2			10^4	3^2												21
1			4	5	13	7^2	8		9	12		6^3	11			14	2				3			10^3						22
1	2	3	4^2	13	6	7^1	8		14	9		11	5											10^3	12					23
1	2	3	4		6	7	8^2		13	9^3		11	5	14										10	12					24
1	2	3	4		6	7^3	8		14	9^1	13	11^{12}	5								12			10^3						25
1	3		5	6		8		12	13	11		4		7^2			2							10^1	9					26
1	2	3	4		6	7^2	8		10	9		11^1	5	12											13					27
1	10	3	4	5	6	7	8		9		12	11^1					2													28
1	8^1	3	4		6^1	7	10^2		9			11	5	12			2							14	13					29
1	2	3		5	6	7^1	8			9^2		11	4											10	12	13				30
1	2	3^1		5		7	8		13	9		11^2	4		14						6			10^3		12				31
1	2				7	8			13	9^1		11^3	5				4				3			10	6^2	14	12			32
1	2		5	6	7^2	8		14	12	11		4	13	10^1							3			9^3						33
1	2		5	6	7	8		13	10	11^1		4			14						3^3		12	9^2						34
1	2		5^3		7	8		13	3	11^1	14		12								10^2		9^3		4	6^3				35
1	2					8		11^1	3		7	5	13				4				10^2		9		6		12			36
1	2	4		6		8		14	3	11		5^2					13				12		10	9^3		7^1				37
1	2		5	6	7			11		12			9^1								3		10	8			4			38
1	2		5	6^1	7	8		3	12	11		10^2									13		9				4			39
1	2		5	6^3	7			8^2	3	12	11	4	14	10^1							13		9^8							40
1	2		5^3	6	7	13		8	3	11	4	10^1	9^2								12				14					41
1	2		5	6	7	12		8	3	11^2	4	9									13		10^1							42
1	2		5	6	8			9	3	11	4	13	7^1								12		10^2							43
1	2		5	6	7			8^1	3	9	4	13									11^2		10	12						44
1	2		5	6	8	12		9^1	3	7^8	4										11		10^2	13						45
1	2		13	7	8			9^3	3		5	14									11		10^1	12		4^2	6			46

FA Cup

First Round	Oxford U	(h)	1-0	
Second Round	Chesterfield	(h)	3-1	
Third Round	Middlesbrough	(h)	2-1	
Fourth Round	Burnley	(a)	1-3	

Carling Cup

First Round	Cardiff C	(a)	1-4

J Paint Trophy

Second Round	Rotherham U	(h)	1-2

BURY

FL Championship 1

FOUNDATION

A meeting at the Waggon & Horses Hotel, attended largely by members of Bury Wesleyans and Bury Unitarians football clubs, decided to form a new Bury club. This was officially formed at a subsequent gathering at the Old White Horse Hotel, Fleet Street, Bury on 24 April 1885.

Gigg Lane, Bury, Lancs BL9 9HR.

Telephone: (08445) 790009.

Fax: (0161) 764 5521.

Ticket Office: (08445) 790009.

Website: www.buryfc.co.uk

Email: info@buryfc.co.uk

Ground Capacity: 11,669.

Record Attendance: 35,000 v Bolton W, FA Cup 3rd rd, 9 January 1960.

Pitch Measurements: 112yd × 72yd.

Secretary: Jill Neville.

HONOURS

Football League – Division 1: Best season: 4th, 1925–26; **Division 2:** *Champions* 1894–95, 1996–97; *Runners-up* 1923–24; **Division 3:** *Champions* 1960–61; *Runners-up* 1967–68; **FL 2:** *Runners-up* 2010–11. **FA Cup:** *Winners* 1900, 1903. **Football League Cup:** Semi-final 1963.

Directors: Mark Catlin, Brian Fenton, Jeremy Rothwell, Margaret Ladkin.

Manager: Richie Barker.

Assistant Manager: Peter Shirtliff.

Physio: Tom Walsh.

Colours: Black and blue halved shirts, white shorts, black stockings

Change Colours: Red and white striped shirts, black shorts, black stockings.

Year Formed: 1885.

Turned Professional: 1885.

Ltd Co.: 1897.

Club Nickname: 'Shakers'.

Ground: 1885, Gigg Lane.

First Football League Game: 1 September 1894, Division 2, v Manchester C (h) W 4–2 – Lowe; Gillespie, Davies; White, Clegg, Ross; Wylie, Barbour (2), Millar (1), Ostler (1), Plant.

Record League Victory: 8–0 v Tranmere R, Division 3, 10 January 1970 – Forrest; Tinney, Saile; Anderson, Turner, McDermott; Hince (1), Arrowsmith (1), Jones (4), Kerr (1), Grundy, (1 og).

Record Cup Victory: 12–1 v Stockton, FA Cup 1st rd (replay), 2 February 1897 – Montgomery; Darroch, Barbour; Hendry (1), Clegg, Ross (1); Wylie (3), Pangbourn, Millar (4), Henderson (2), Plant, (1 og).

Record Defeat: 0–10 v Blackburn R, FA Cup pr rd, 1 October 1887. 0–10 v West Ham U, Milk Cup 2nd rd 2nd leg, 25 October 1983.

sky SPORTS FACT FILE

In 1931–32 Bury signed Don "Dickie" Bird, an inside-forward from Cardiff C for whom he had made a scoring debut. He made just one first team appearance for the Shakers, a 2-1 FA Cup win over Swansea T on 9 January then went to Torquay, Derby, Sheffield U and Southend!

Most League Points (2 for a win): 68, Division 3, 1960–61.

Most League Points (3 for a win): 84, Division 4, 1984–85 and Division 2, 1996–97.

Most League Goals: 108, Division 3, 1960–61.

Highest League Scorer in Season: Craig Madden, 35, Division 4, 1981–82.

Most League Goals in Total Aggregate: Craig Madden, 129, 1978–86.

Most League Goals in One Match: 5, Eddie Quigley v Millwall, Division 2, 15 February 1947; 5, Ray Pointer v Rotherham U, Division 2, 2 October 1965.

Most Capped Player: Bill Gorman, 11 (13), Republic of Ireland and (4), Northern Ireland.

Most League Appearances: Norman Bullock, 506, 1920–35.

Youngest League Player: Brian Williams, 16 years 133 days v Stockport Co, 18 March 1972.

Record Transfer Fee Received: £1,100,000 from Ipswich T for David Johnson, November 1997.

Record Transfer Fee Paid: £200,000 to Ipswich T for Chris Swailes, November 1997 and £200,000 to Swindon T for Darren Bullock, February 1999.

Football League Record: 1894 Elected to Division 2; 1895–1912 Division 1; 1912–24 Division 2; 1924–29 Division 1; 1929–57 Division 2; 1957–61 Division 3; 1961–67 Division 2; 1967–68 Division 3; 1968–69 Division 2; 1969–71 Division 3; 1971–74 Division 4; 1974–80 Division 3; 1980–85 Division 4; 1985–96 Division 3; 1996–97 Division 2; 1997–99 Division 1; 1999–2002 Division 2; 2002–04 Division 3; 2004–11 FL 2; 2011– FL 1.

LATEST SEQUENCES

Longest Sequence of League Wins: 9, 26.9.1960 – 19.11.1960.

Longest Sequence of League Defeats: 8, 18.8.2001 – 25.9.2001.

Longest Sequence of League Draws: 6, 6.3.1999 – 3.4.1999.

Longest Sequence of Unbeaten League Matches: 18, 4.2.1961 – 29.4.1961.

Longest Sequence Without a League Win: 19, 1.4.1911 – 2.12.1911.

Successive Scoring Runs: 24 from 1.9.1894.

Successive Non-scoring Runs: 6 from 11.1.1969.

MANAGERS

T. Hargreaves 1887
  (*Secretary-Manager*)
H. S. Hamer 1887–1907
  (*Secretary-Manager*)
Archie Montgomery 1907–15
William Cameron 1919–23
James Hunter Thompson 1923–27
Percy Smith 1927–30
Arthur Paine 1930–34
Norman Bullock 1934–38
Charlie Dean 1938–44
Jim Porter 1944–45
Norman Bullock 1945–49
John McNeil 1950–53
Dave Russell 1953–61
Bob Stokoe 1961–65
Bert Head 1965–66
Les Shannon 1966–69
Jack Marshall 1969
Colin McDonald 1970
Les Hart 1970
Tommy McAnearney 1970–72
Alan Brown 1972–73
Bobby Smith 1973–77
Bob Stokoe 1977–78
David Hatton 1978–79
Dave Connor 1979–80
Jim Iley 1980–84
Martin Dobson 1984–89
Sam Ellis 1989–90
Mike Walsh 1990–95
Stan Ternent 1995–98
Neil Warnock 1998–99
Andy Preece 1999–2003
Graham Barrow 2003–05
Chris Casper 2005–08
Alan Knill 2008–11
Richie Barker April 2011–

TEN YEAR LEAGUE RECORD

		P	W	D	L	F	A	Pts	Pos
2001-02	Div 2	46	11	11	24	43	75	44	22
2002-03	Div 3	46	18	16	12	57	56	70	7
2003-04	Div 3	46	15	11	20	54	64	56	12
2004-05	FL 2	46	14	16	16	54	54	58	17
2005-06	FL 2	46	12	17	17	45	57	52*	19
2006-07	FL 2	46	13	11	22	46	61	50	21
2007-08	FL 2	46	16	11	19	58	61	59	13
2008-09	FL 2	46	21	15	10	63	43	78	4
2009-10	FL 2	46	19	12	15	54	59	69	9
2010-11	FL 2	46	23	12	11	82	50	81	2

*1 pt deducted.

DID YOU KNOW ?

On 26 September 1925, the First Division produced ten home wins and one draw. Of the 59 goals scored overall, the highest aggregate was Bury 7 Sheffield United 4. Norman Bullock scored three of the Bury goals.

BURY 2010–11 LEAGUE RECORD

Match No.	Date	Venue	Opponents	Result	H/T Score	Lg Pos.	Goalscorers	Attendance
1	Aug 7	H	Port Vale	L 0-1	0-0	—		4681
2	14	A	Oxford U	W 2-1	1-1	10	Lees [26], Lowe [79]	7552
3	21	H	Northampton T	D 1-1	0-1	11	Worrall [69]	2845
4	28	A	Barnet	D 1-1	0-0	12	Lowe [56]	1563
5	Sept 4	H	Gillingham	W 5-4	2-0	7	Bishop 2 [15, 50], Lowe 2 (1 pen) [34 (p), 73], Sodje [62]	2700
6	11	A	Crewe Alex	L 0-3	0-2	11		4030
7	18	H	Hereford U	D 1-1	0-0	11	Lowe [90]	2753
8	25	A	Cheltenham T	W 2-0	1-0	6	Lowe (pen) [11], Jones, M [85]	2758
9	28	A	Morecambe	W 4-1	2-1	—	Jones, M [3], Schumacher 2 [21, 89], Haworth [78]	2607
10	Oct 2	H	Rotherham U	D 1-1	1-0	5	Lowe [41]	3788
11	9	H	Accrington S	W 3-0	2-0	4	Lowe 2 [13, 45], Ajose [57]	4164
12	16	A	Torquay U	W 4-3	2-2	4	Lowe (pen) [27], Ajose [33], Schumacher [51], Jones, M [71]	2553
13	23	H	Southend U	W 1-0	1-0	3	Skarz [41]	3531
14	30	A	Aldershot T	W 3-1	1-1	3	Jones, M 2 [44, 66], Ajose [77]	2526
15	Nov 2	H	Bradford C	L 0-1	0-1	—		3521
16	13	H	Stockport Co	L 0-1	0-1	5		4244
17	19	A	Burton Alb	W 3-1	1-1	—	Jones, M [10], Ajose [53], Sodje [73]	2738
18	23	A	Lincoln C	W 5-0	3-0	—	Haworth [10], Ajose 2 [21, 71], Lowe 2 [23, 90]	3659
19	Dec 11	A	Wycombe W	L 0-1	0-0	3		3673
20	Jan 1	H	Macclesfield T	D 2-2	0-1	5	Lowe [83], John-Lewis [89]	2860
21	3	A	Bradford C	L 0-1	0-1	5		11,384
22	8	A	Accrington S	L 0-1	0-0	6		2481
23	15	H	Aldershot T	D 1-1	0-1	6	Schumacher [71]	2537
24	21	A	Southend U	D 1-1	1-0	—	Mozika [65]	5175
25	28	A	Shrewsbury T	W 1-0	1-0	—	Lowe [39]	2917
26	Feb 1	A	Macclesfield T	W 4-2	3-2	4	Jones, M [8], Lowe 2 [33, 86], Ajose [36]	1267
27	8	H	Stevenage	W 3-0	1-0	—	Bishop [8], Sodje [61], Lowe [70]	2080
28	12	A	Stockport Co	L 1-2	0-0	5	Lowe [88]	4903
29	15	H	Chesterfield	D 1-1	0-1	—	Lowe [46]	2517
30	19	A	Gillingham	D 1-1	0-1	5	Lowe [72]	5021
31	26	H	Crewe Alex	W 3-1	0-1	5	Bennett 2 [64, 68], Lowe [76]	3308
32	Mar 1	A	Shrewsbury T	W 3-0	1-0	—	Bishop [21], Lowe [53], Schumacher [80]	5298
33	5	A	Hereford U	W 3-0	1-0	2	Schumacher 2 [3, 51], Lowe [86]	2650
34	8	A	Morecambe	W 1-0	0-0	—	John-Lewis [85]	2480
35	12	A	Rotherham U	D 0-0	0-0	2		4620
36	15	H	Torquay U	L 1-2	1-0	—	Holroyd [4]	2757
37	19	H	Cheltenham T	L 2-3	1-2	2	Futcher [9], Haworth [68]	2870
38	26	H	Port Vale	D 0-0	0-0	—		5510
39	Apr 2	H	Oxford U	W 3-0	1-0	4	Ajose 2 [1, 70], Lowe [63]	3515
40	9	A	Northampton T	W 4-2	3-0	3	Lowe [24], Ajose 2 [28, 57], Mozika [42]	5077
41	12	H	Burton Alb	W 1-0	0-0	—	Lees [77]	2580
42	16	H	Barnet	W 2-0	2-0	2	Ajose [16], Jones, M [21]	3082
43	22	A	Lincoln C	W 1-0	0-0	—	Lees [56]	4248
44	25	A	Chesterfield	W 3-2	1-0	2	Lees [12], Worrall [55], Lowe [87]	9614
45	30	H	Wycombe W	L 1-3	1-1	2	Lowe (pen) [10]	6238
46	May 7	A	Stevenage	D 3-3	2-2	2	Schumacher 2 [16, 70], Ajose [31]	5016

Final League Position: 2

GOALSCORERS

League (82): Lowe 27 (4 pens), Ajose 13, Schumacher 9, Jones, M 8, Bishop 4, Lees 4, Haworth 3, Sodje 3, Bennett 2, John-Lewis 2, Mozika 2, Worrall 2, Futcher 1, Holroyd 1, Skarz 1.
Carling Cup (0).
FA Cup (3): Lees 1, Lowe 1, Sodje 1.
J Paint Trophy (0).

Belford C 39	Picken P 38	Skarz J 46	Lees T 45	Sodje E 40	Sweeney P 18+7	Worrall D 27+13	Schumacher S 42+1	Lowe R 46	Bishop A 14+5	Haworth A 20+20	Jones M 37+5	Bennett K 13+19	John-Lewis L 6+33	Futcher B 6+5	Carlton D —+3	Mozika D 32+1	Ajose N 22+6	Branagan R 1+1	Williams O 6	Gunning G 2	Holroyd C 3+1	Eckersley R 3	Harrop M —+3	Jones A —+1	McCarthy L —+1	Match No.
1	2	3	4	5	6	7^1	8	9^3	10	11^2	12	13	14													1
1	2	3	4	5	6	12	8	9^2	10^3	11	7^1	13	14													2
1	2	3	4	5^3	6	12	8	9	10^2	11	7^1	13	14													3
1	2	3	4	5	6	7^1	8	9^2	13	11^3	10	14		12												4
1	2^2	3	4	5	6	13	8	9	10^3	11^1	7			14	12											5
1	2	3	4	5	6	12	8	9	10^2	11^3	7^1			13	14											6
1	2^3	3	4	5	6	12		9	10^2	11^1	7	14		13	8											7
1	2	3	4	5		7^3	8	9^2	10^1	11	14	12				6	13									8
1	2^3	3	4	5		7^1	8	9^2	12	11	10	13				6	14									9
1	2	3	4	5		7^2	8	9	13	11^1	12	10^3				6	14									10
1	2	3	4	5		7^1	8	9	12	11^2	13					6	10									11
1	2	3	4	5		7^1	8	9	12	11^2	13	14				6	10^3									12
1^0	2	3	4	5		7	8	9	13	11^2		12				6	10^1	15								13
	2	3	4	5	13	7^1	8	9^3	12	11		14				6^2	10	1								14
	2	3	4	5		7^1	8	9		11		12				6	10	1								15
	2	3	4	5		12	8	9		11^1	7^3	14	13			6	10^2	1								16
	2	3	4	5	12	13	8^1	9^3		11^2	7		14			6	10	1								17
	2	3	4	5	12	13	8^1	9		11^2	7^3		14			6	10	1								18
		3	4	5	12		8	9		11^2	7^1		13			6	10	1	2							19
	2^1	3		5			8	9		11^2	7	12	13			6	10	1	4							20
1	2	3	4	5		8^2	9		11^1	7	13	12				6	10									21
1	2^3	3	4	5	14	8	9		11^2	7	13	12				6	10^1									22
1	2	3	4	5		8	9	13	7^1	11^2	10					6	12									23
1	2^3	3	4	5	7^1	8	9		12	13	11^2	10	14			6										24
1	2	3	4	5		8	9^1	12	11	7						6	10									25
1	2	3	4	5		12	8	9	13	11^1	7^3	14				6	10^2									26
1	2	3	4	5		12	8	9	10^3	11^2	7^1	13	14			6										27
1	2^2	3	4^1	5		13	8		10	11^3	7	14	12			6										28
1	2	3	4	5		13	8	9	10^1	11^2	7		12			6										29
1	2	3	4	5	13	7^1	8	9		12	11					10^2	6										30
1	2^2	3	4	5		7	8	9	14	12	11^1	13	10^3			6										31
1	2	3	4	5	14	7	8	9^2	10^1	13		11	12			6^3										32
1	2	3	4	5	14	7	8	9^1		13	11^2	12				6^3										33
1	2	3	4	5	6	7^2	8	9	10^3	12	13	11^1	14													34
1	2	3	4	5	6	7	8	9	10^2	12		11^1									13					35
1		3	4		7^1	8	9	13		12	11	14	5^3	6^2							10	2				36
1		3	4		7^1	8	9		12		11	14	5^2	6	13						10^3	2				37
1		3	4	5	6	8^0	9		7^1		11^3	13		12						10^2	2	14				38
1	2	3	4	5	6	7^1		9^3		13	11^2	12	14			8	10									39
1	2	3	4	5^3	6	7^1		9		11	12	13				8	10^2						14			40
1	2	3	4	5^3	8	7	12	9		11^2	13	14				6^8	10^3									41
1	2^1	3	4		6	7	8	9		13	11^2	12	14	5		10^3										42
1		3	4		6	2	8	9^3		12	11	7	13	5		10^2							14			43
1		3	4		6	2	8	9		12	11^1	7^2	13	5		10										44
1		3	4		6^3	2^2	8	9		12	7^1	11	13	5		10							14			45
1		3	4	5	6	2	8	9		12	7^1	11^3	13			10^2								14		46

FA Cup
First Round   Exeter C   (h)   2-0
Second Round   Peterborough U   (h)   1-2

Carling Cup
First Round   Sheffield W   (a)   0-1

J Paint Trophy
Second Round   Shrewsbury T   (h)   0-0
Northern Quarter-Final
       Tranmere R   (h)   0-1

CARDIFF CITY FL Championship

FOUNDATION

Credit for the establishment of a first class professional football club in such a rugby stronghold as Cardiff, is due to members of the Riverside club formed in 1899 out of a cricket club of that name. Cardiff became a city in 1905 and in 1908 the South Wales and Monmouthshire FA granted Riverside permission to call themselves Cardiff City. The club turned professional under that name in 1910.

Cardiff City Stadium, Leckwith Road, Cardiff CF11 8AZ.

Telephone: (0845) 365 1115. *Fax:* (0845) 365 1116.

Ticket Office: 0845 345 1400.

Website: www.cardiffcityfc.co.uk

Email: club@cardiffcityfc.co.uk

Ground Capacity: 26,828.

Record Attendance: 62,634, Wales v England, 17 October 1959 (at Ninian Park); 26,055 v Leicester C, FL C Play-Off semi-final 2nd leg 12 May 2010 (at Cardiff City Stadium).

Club Record Attendance: 57,893 v Arsenal, Division 1, 22 April 1953.

Pitch Measurements: 110yd × 75yd.

Chairman: Dato Chan Tien Ghee.

Chief Executive: Gethin Jenkins.

Secretary: Nick Alford.

Manager: Malky Mackay.

Physio: Sean Connelly BHSc MCSP, SRP.

Colours: Blue shirts with yellow trim, white shorts, white stockings.

Change Colours: Yellow shirts, blue shorts, blue stockings.

Year Formed: 1899. *Turned Professional:* 1910.

Ltd Co.: 1910.

HONOURS

Football League Division 1: *Runners-up* 1923–24;
Division 2: *Runners-up* 1920–21, 1951–52, 1959–60;
Division 3 (S): *Champions* 1946–47;
Division 3: *Champions* 1992–93. *Runners-up* 1975–76, 1982–83, 2000–01;
Division 4: *Runners-up* 1987–88.

FA Cup: *Winners* 1927 (only occasion the Cup has been won by a club outside England); *Runners-up* 1925, 2008.

Football League Cup: Semi-final 1966.

Welsh Cup: *Winners* 22 times (joint record).

Charity Shield: Winners 1927.

European Competitions
European Cup-Winners' Cup: 1964–65, 1965–66, 1967–68 (*s-f*), 1968–69, 1969–70, 1970–71, 1971–72, 1973–74, 1974–75, 1976–77, 1977–78, 1988–89, 1992–93, 1993–94.

Previous Names: 1899, Riverside; 1902, Riverside Albion; 1908, Cardiff City.

Club Nickname: 'Bluebirds'.

Grounds: Riverside, Sophia Gardens, Old Park and Fir Gardens. 1910, Ninian Park; 2009, Cardiff City Stadium.

First Football League Game: 28 August 1920, Division 2, v Stockport Co (a) W 5–2 – Kneeshaw; Brittan, Leyton; Keenor (1), Smith, Hardy; Grimshaw (1), Gill (2), Cashmore, West, Evans (1).

Record League Victory: 9–2 v Thames, Division 3 (S), 6 February 1932 – Farquharson; Eric Morris, Roberts; Galbraith, Harris, Ronan; Emmerson (1), Keating (1), Jones (1), McCambridge (1), Robbins (5).

sky SPORTS FACT FILE

In 1951–52, despite winning only two fixtures away from Ninian Park, Cardiff City won promotion back to the First Division as runners-up after 23 years out of it. They thwarted Birmingham City by just 0.14 of goal average on the last day of the season, beating Leeds United 3-1.

Record Cup Victory: 8–0 v Enfield, FA Cup 1st rd, 28 November 1931 – Farquharson; Smith, Roberts; Harris (1), Galbraith, Ronan; Emmerson (2), Keating (3); O'Neill (2), Robbins, McCambridge.

Record Defeat: 2–11 v Sheffield U, Division 1, 1 January 1926.

Most League Points (2 for a win): 66, Division 3 (S), 1946–47.

Most League Points (3 for a win): 86, Division 3, 1982–83.

Most League Goals: 95, Division 3, 2000–01.

Highest League Scorer in Season: Robert Earnshaw, 31, Division 2, 2002–03.

Most League Goals in Total Aggregate: Len Davies, 128, 1920–31.

Most League Goals in One Match: 5, Hugh Ferguson v Burnley, Division 1, 1 September 1928; 5, Walter Robbins v Thames, Division 3 (S), 6 February 1932; 5, William Henderson v Northampton T, Division 3 (S), 22 April 1933.

Most Capped Player: Alf Sherwood, 39 (41), Wales.

Most League Appearances: Phil Dwyer, 471, 1972–85.

Youngest League Player: Bob Adams, 15 years 355 days v Southend U, 18 February 1933.

Record Transfer Fee Received: £5,000,000 from Sunderland for Michael Chopra, August 2006; £5,000,000 from Arsenal for Aaron Ramsey, June 2008; £5,000,000 from Birmingham C for Roger Johnson, June 2009.

Record Transfer Fee Paid: £3,000,000 to Sunderland for Michael Chopra, July 2009.

Football League Record: 1920 Elected to Division 2; 1921–29 Division 1; 1929–31 Division 2; 1931–47 Division 3 (S); 1947–52 Division 2; 1952–57 Division 1; 1957–60 Division 2; 1960–62 Division 1; 1962–75 Division 2; 1975–76 Division 3; 1976–82 Division 2; 1982–83 Division 3; 1983–85 Division 2; 1985–86 Division 3; 1986–88 Division 4; 1988–90 Division 3; 1990–92 Division 4; 1992–93 Division 3; 1993–95 Division 2; 1995–99 Division 3; 1999–2000 Division 2; 2000–01 Division 3; 2001–03 Division 2; 2003–04 Division 1; 2004– FL C.

MANAGERS

Davy McDougall 1910–11
Fred Stewart 1911–33
Bartley Wilson 1933–34
B. Watts-Jones 1934–37
Bill Jennings 1937–39
Cyril Spiers 1939–46
Billy McCandless 1946–48
Cyril Spiers 1948–54
Trevor Morris 1954–58
Bill Jones 1958–62
George Swindin 1962–64
Jimmy Scoular 1964–73
Frank O'Farrell 1973–74
Jimmy Andrews 1974–78
Richie Morgan 1978–81
Graham Williams 1981–82
Len Ashurst 1982–84
Jimmy Goodfellow 1984
Alan Durban 1984–86
Frank Burrows 1986–89
Len Ashurst 1989–91
Eddie May 1991–94
Terry Yorath 1994–95
Eddie May 1995
Kenny Hibbitt (*Chief Coach*) 1995
Phil Neal 1996
Russell Osman 1996–97
Kenny Hibbitt 1997–98
Frank Burrows 1998–2000
Billy Ayre 2000
Bobby Gould 2000
Alan Cork 2000–02
Lennie Lawrence 2002–05
Dave Jones 2005–11
Malky Mackay June 2011–

LATEST SEQUENCES

Longest Sequence of League Wins: 9, 26.10.1946 – 28.12.1946.

Longest Sequence of League Defeats: 7, 4.11.1933 – 25.12.1933.

Longest Sequence of League Draws: 6, 29.11.1980 – 17.1.1981.

Longest Sequence of Unbeaten League Matches: 21, 21.9.1946 – 1.3.1947.

Longest Sequence Without a League Win: 15, 21.11.1936 – 6.3.1937.

Successive Scoring Runs: 23 from 24.10.1992.

Successive Non-scoring Runs: 8 from 20.12.1952.

TEN YEAR LEAGUE RECORD

		P	W	D	L	F	A	Pts	Pos
2001-02	Div 2	46	23	14	9	75	50	83	4
2002-03	Div 2	46	23	12	11	68	43	81	6
2003-04	Div 1	46	17	14	15	68	58	65	13
2004-05	FL C	46	13	15	18	48	51	54	16
2005-06	FL C	46	16	12	18	58	59	60	11
2006-07	FL C	46	17	13	16	57	53	64	13
2007-08	FL C	46	16	16	14	59	55	64	12
2008-09	FL C	46	19	17	10	65	53	74	7
2009-10	FL C	46	22	10	14	73	54	76	4
2010-11	FL C	46	23	11	12	76	54	80	4

DID YOU KNOW ?

In the 1967–68 European Cup-Winner's Cup, Cardiff City met Moscow Torpedo. At home on 6 March a goal by Barrie Jones gave Cardiff the lead. The return leg was played in Tashkent where Torpedo won 1-0. The decider in Augsburg saw Norman Dean win the tie.

CARDIFF CITY 2010–11 LEAGUE RECORD

Match No.	Date	Venue	Opponents	Result	H/T Score	Lg Pos.	Goalscorers	Attendance
1	Aug 8	H	Sheffield U	D	1-1	0-1	—	Bothroyd [62]	20,573
2	14	A	Derby Co	W	2-1	1-1	7	Chopra [15], Burke [78]	25,103
3	21	H	Doncaster R	W	4-0	1-0	2	Bothroyd 2 [36, 62], Burke [68], Bellamy [84]	24,027
4	28	A	Portsmouth	W	2-0	1-0	2	Mullins (og) [37], Bothroyd [49]	15,866
5	Sept 11	H	Hull C	W	2-0	1-0	2	Olofinjana [20], Rae [81]	24,083
6	14	A	Leicester C	L	1-2	1-0	—	Naylor [26]	20,510
7	18	A	Ipswich T	L	0-2	0-0	3		22,599
8	25	H	Millwall	W	2-1	1-1	2	Bothroyd [24], Keogh [89]	23,010
9	28	H	Crystal Palace	D	0-0	0-0	—		22,007
10	Oct 2	A	Barnsley	W	2-1	1-0	2	Bellamy [42], Olofinjana [67]	11,211
11	16	H	Bristol C	W	3-2	1-2	2	Bothroyd [12], Whittingham 2 [46, 78]	22,444
12	19	A	Coventry C	W	2-1	1-1	—	Whittingham (pen) [5], Bothroyd [87]	14,604
13	25	H	Leeds U	W	4-0	1-0	—	Bothroyd 2 [22, 56], Chopra [51], Naylor [60]	20,747
14	30	H	Norwich C	W	3-1	3-1	1	Bothroyd [9], Chopra [12], Whittingham (pen) [37]	24,634
15	Nov 7	H	Swansea C	L	0-1	0-0	2		26,049
16	10	A	Reading	D	1-1	0-1	—	Bothroyd [77]	17,960
17	13	A	Scunthorpe U	W	4-2	3-1	1	Bothroyd 2 [2, 34], Chopra [9], Olofinjana [79]	5333
18	20	H	Nottingham F	L	0-2	0-1	2		23,526
19	27	A	QPR	L	1-2	1-1	2	Bellamy [13]	17,316
20	Dec 4	H	Preston NE	D	1-1	0-1	—	Keogh [90]	21,151
21	11	A	Middlesbrough	L	0-1	0-1	2		14,250
22	26	H	Coventry C	W	2-0	1-0	2	Olofinjana [21], Bellamy [83]	24,595
23	28	A	Watford	L	1-4	1-1	2	Whittingham [16]	14,560
24	Jan 1	A	Bristol C	L	0-3	0-2	5		15,683
25	4	H	Leeds U	W	2-1	1-0	—	Bellamy [11], Chopra [79]	25,010
26	15	A	Norwich C	D	1-1	1-0	3	Parkin [7]	25,270
27	22	H	Watford	W	4-2	3-1	2	Bellamy [14], Chopra [17], Bothroyd [31], Gyepes [83]	23,702
28	Feb 1	H	Reading	D	2-2	0-1	5	Bothroyd [48], Bellamy [90]	21,405
29	6	A	Swansea C	W	1-0	0-0	3	Bellamy [85]	18,280
30	12	H	Scunthorpe U	W	1-0	0-0	2	Olofinjana [85]	21,604
31	15	H	Burnley	D	1-1	1-0	—	Chopra [45]	21,307
32	19	A	Nottingham F	L	1-2	0-1	4	Whittingham (pen) [64]	26,019
33	22	H	Leicester C	W	2-0	1-0	—	Chopra [21], Ramsey [52]	22,410
34	26	A	Hull C	W	2-0	0-0	3	Chopra [66], Emmanuel-Thomas [90]	21,441
35	Mar 5	H	Ipswich T	L	0-2	0-0	3		21,347
36	8	A	Crystal Palace	L	0-1	0-0	—		12,549
37	13	H	Barnsley	D	2-2	1-1	4	Whittingham [21], Keinan [83]	23,065
38	19	A	Millwall	D	3-3	0-0	4	Burke 2 [49, 80], Whittingham [73]	15,039
39	Apr 2	H	Derby Co	W	4-1	1-0	3	Bothroyd (pen) [7], Keinan [48], Quinn [56], Whittingham [68]	22,254
40	9	A	Doncaster R	W	3-1	1-0	3	Burke [15], Koumas 2 [89, 90]	9174
41	12	A	Sheffield U	W	2-0	1-0	—	Bellamy [21], Emmanuel-Thomas [71]	18,230
42	16	H	Portsmouth	W	3-0	2-0	2	Olofinjana [6], Bothroyd [45], Whittingham [73]	24,007
43	23	H	QPR	D	2-2	2-1	3	Bothroyd [6], Bellamy [35]	26,058
44	25	A	Preston NE	W	1-0	1-0	3	Whittingham [6]	12,818
45	May 2	H	Middlesbrough	L	0-3	0-3	—		25,183
46	7	A	Burnley	D	1-1	0-1	4	Bellamy [90]	14,197

Final League Position: 4

GOALSCORERS

League (76): Bothroyd 18 (1 pen), Bellamy 11, Whittingham 11 (3 pens), Chopra 9, Olofinjana 6, Burke 5, Emmanuel-Thomas 2, Keinan 2, Keogh 2, Koumas 2, Naylor 2, Gyepes 1, Parkin 1, Quinn 1, Rae 1, Ramsey 1, own goal 1.
Carling Cup (5): Bothroyd 2, McCormack 2, Chopra 1.
FA Cup (1): Chopra 1.
Play-Offs (0).

Marshall D 11	McNaughton K 44	Blake D 13+13	Rae G 2+5	Hudson M 39+1	Gyepes G 16+5	Whittingham P 45	Drinkwater D 7+2	Bothroyd J 37	Chopra M 25+7	Burke C 31+13	McCormack R —+2	Olofinjana S 38+1	Matthews A 2+6	Bellamy C 34+1	Naylor L 25+2	Koumas J 5+18	Keogh A 11+5	McPhail S 23+5	Wildig A —+2	Heaton T 27	Quinn P 22+1	Riggott C 2	Parkin J 2+9	Emmanuel-Thomas J 7+7	Ramsey A 6	Keinan D 18	Bywater S 8	Samuel J 6	Match No.
1	2	3	4[1]	5	6	7	8	9	10	11	12																		1
1	2[1]	3		5	6	7	8	9	10[2]	11	13	4	12																2
1	2[1]			5	6	7	8	9[3]		11	12	4	3	10[3]	14														3
1	2[1]			5	6	7	8	9[3]	10[2]	11	12	4	14	13	3														4
1	2		12	5	6	7	8	9	10[2]	11		4[1]		13	3														5
1	2		13	5	6	7	8[2]	9	10[1]	11	12	4			3														6
1	2[1]		12	5	6	7	8[2]	9[3]	10	11	13	4	14		3														7
	2	4[2]	13	5	6	7		9		11		3	12	10				8[1]		1									8
	2	3		5		7		9		11		4	12	10		6[1]		8		1									9
	2	4[4]		5	6	7		9		11				10	3			8		1									10
	2			5	6	7		9	10	11		4			3	12	13	8[1]		1									11
	2			5	6	7		9	10[1]	11		4		8[2]	3	12	13			1									12
	2			5	6	7		9	10[1]	11		4		8	3	12				1									13
	2			5	6	7		9	10[2]	11		4		8[1]	3	12	13			1									14
	2[2]		13	5	6	7	8[3]		10	11	12	4	14	9[1]	3					1									15
	2		13	5	6	7		9	10[2]	11		4			3	12		8[1]		1									16
	2		13	5	6[2]	7		9	10	11		4	14		3[3]	12		8		1									17
	2	3[2]	13	5	6	7	12	9	10[1]	11		4						8		1									18
	2		13	5	6	7	8[1]	9		11		4		10	3	12				1									19
1	2	3[2]	13	5	6	7	8[3]	9[1]		11		4	14	10		12													20
1	2			5	6	7	8[1]	9	12	11		4		10	3														21
1	2		12	5		7		9	10	11		4			3			8			6[1]								22
1	2		13	5	6		8[3]	9	10	11	12	4			3[1]														23
	2		12	5		7[2]		9[2]	10	11		4	13		3			8		1	6[1]								24
	2		12	5		7		9	10	11		4		8[2]	3		13			1	6[1]								25
	2		12	5		7		9	10	11		4			3			8[1]		1	6								26
	2		12	5		7[3]		9[2]	10	11		4	14		3[1]		13	8		1	6								27
	2		12	5		7		9[3]	10	11		4[1]	14		3		13	8		1	6								28
	2[1]		12	5		7[7]		9	10[3]	11		4	14		3		13	8		1	6								29
	2		12	5		7[1]		9	10[2]	11		4	14		3		13	8		1	6								30
	2		13	5		7		9	10[2]	11		4			3[1]	12		8		1	6								31
	2			5		7		9	10[2]	11		4			3	12	13	8		1	6								32
	2			5		7		9[2]	10[1]	11		4[3]	14		3	12	13	8		1	6								33
	2			5		7		9	10[2]	11		4			3	12	13	8		1	6								34
	2		13	5		7		9	10[3]	11		4	14		3[2]	12		8		1	6								35
	2			5		7		9	10[1]	11		4			3	12		8		1	6								36
	2			5		7		9[3]	10[1]	11		4	14		3	12	13	8		1	6								37
	2		13	5[2]		7		9[1]		11		4	14	10	3[3]	12		8		1	6								38
	2		12	5		7		9[2]		11		4	14	10[3]			13	8								6	1	3[1]	39
	2			5		7		9		11[2]		4		10		12	13	8								6	1	3[1]	40
	2		12	5		7		9		11		4		10	3[1]		13	8[2]								6	1		41
	2			5[3]		7		9[1]		11		4	14	10		12	13	8[2]								6	1	3	42
	2			5		7		9		11[1]		4		10[2]		12	13	8								6	1	3	43
	2[1]		12	5		7		9		11		4		10[2]			13	8								6	1	3	44
	2		13	5[3]		7		9		11		4	14	10		12		8[2]								6	1	3[1]	45
	2		12	5[1]		7		9		11[2]		4[3]	14	10	3		13	8								6	1		46

FA Cup
Third Round   Stoke C   (a) 1-1 / (h) 0-2

Carling Cup
First Round   Burton Alb   (h) 4-1
Second Round   Peterborough U   (a) 1-2

Play-Offs
Semi-Final   Reading   (a) 0-0 / (h) 0-3

CARLISLE UNITED   FL Championship 1

FOUNDATION

Carlisle United came into being when members of Shaddongate United voted to change its name on 17 May 1904. The new club was admitted to the Second Division of the Lancashire Combination in 1905–06, winning promotion the following season. Devonshire Park was officially opened on 2 September 1905, when St Helens Town were the visitors. Despite defeat in a disappointing 3-2 start, a respectable mid-table position was achieved.

Brunton Park, Warwick Road, Carlisle CA1 1LL.
Telephone: (01228) 526 237.
Fax: (01228) 554 141.
Ticket Office: (0844) 371 1921.
Website: www.carlisleunited.co.uk
Email: enquiries@carlisleunited.co.uk
Ground Capacity: 16,981.
Record Attendance: 27,500 v Birmingham C, FA Cup 3rd rd, 5 January 1957 and v Middlesbrough, FA Cup 5th rd, 7 February 1970.
Pitch Measurements: 114yd × 74yd.
Chairman: Andrew Jenkins.
Managing Director: John Nixon.
Secretary: Sarah McKnight.
Manager: Greg Abbott.
Assistant Manager: Graham Kavanagh.
Physio: Neil Dalton.
Colours: Blue shirts with white and red trim, white shorts, white stockings.
Change Colours: All red with blue trim on sleeves.
Year Formed: 1904.   *Ltd Co.:* 1904.
Previous Name: 1904, Shaddongate United; 1904, Carlisle United.
Club Nicknames: 'Cumbrians' or 'The Blues'.
Grounds: 1904, Milholme Bank; 1905, Devonshire Park; 1909, Brunton Park.

HONOURS

Football League – Division 1: 22nd, 1974–75;
Division 3: *Champions* 1964–65, 1994–95; *Runners-up* 1981–82;
Division 4: *Runners-up* 1963–64;
FL 2: *Champions* 2005–06.
FA Cup: 6th rd 1975.
Football League Cup: Semi-final 1970.
Auto Windscreens Shield: *Winners* 1997; *Runners-up* 1995.
LDV Vans Trophy: *Runners-up* 2003, 2006.
Johnstone's Paint Trophy: *Winners* 2011; *Runners-up* 2010.

First Football League Game: 25 August 1928, Division 3 (N), v Accrington S (a) W 3–2 – Prout; Coulthard, Cook; Harrison, Ross, Pigg; Agar (1), Hutchison, McConnell (1), Ward (1), Watson.
Record League Victory: 8–0 v Hartlepool U, Division 3 (N), 1 September 1928 – Prout; Smiles, Cook; Robinson (1) Ross, Pigg; Agar (1), Hutchison (1), McConnell (4), Ward (1), Watson. 8–0 v Scunthorpe U, Division 3 (N), 25 December 1952 – MacLaren; Hill, Scott; Stokoe, Twentyman, Waters; Harrison (1), Whitehouse (5), Ashman (2), Duffett, Bond.
Record Cup Victory: 6–0 v Shepshed Dynamo, FA Cup 1st rd, 16 November 1996 – Caig; Hopper, Archdeacon (pen), Walling, Robinson, Pounewatchy, Peacock (1), Conway (1) (Jansen), Smart (McAlindon (1)), Hayward, Aspinall (Thorpe), (2 og).

sky SPORTS FACT FILE

In the seven FA Cup matches in which Carlisle United scored over three seasons from 1956–57, Alf Ackerman was on target in each of them. His sequence of goals was 2 2 3 1 1 1 2. He also scored 61 Football League goals in 97 outings for them during the same period.

Record Defeat: 1–11 v Hull C, Division 3 (N), 14 January 1939.

Most League Points (2 for a win): 62, Division 3 (N), 1950–51.

Most League Points (3 for a win): 91, Division 3, 1994–95.

Most League Goals: 113, Division 4, 1963–64.

Highest League Scorer in Season: Jimmy McConnell, 42, Division 3 (N), 1928–29.

Most League Goals in Total Aggregate: Jimmy McConnell, 126, 1928–32.

Most League Goals in One Match: 5, Hugh Mills v Halifax T, Division 3 (N), 11 September 1937; 5, Jim Whitehouse v Scunthorpe U, Division 3 (N), 25 December 1952.

Most Capped Player: Eric Welsh, 4, Northern Ireland.

Most League Appearances: Allan Ross, 466, 1963–79.

Youngest League Player: John Slaven, 16 years 162 days v Scunthorpe U, 16 March 2002.

Record Transfer Fee Received: £1,500,000 from Crystal Palace for Matt Jansen, February 1998.

Record Transfer Fee Paid: £140,000 to Blackburn R for Joe Garner, August 2007.

Football League Record: 1928 Elected to Division 3 (N); 1958–62 Division 4; 1962–63 Division 3; 1963–64 Division 4; 1964–65 Division 3; 1965–74 Division 2; 1974–75 Division 1; 1975–77 Division 3; 1977–82 Division 3; 1982–86 Division 2; 1986–87 Division 3; 1987–92 Division 4; 1992–95 Division 3; 1995–96 Division 2; 1996–97 Division 3; 1997–98 Division 2; 1998–04 Division 3; 2004–05 Conference; 2005–06 FL 2; 2006– FL 1.

LATEST SEQUENCES

Longest Sequence of League Wins: 7, 18.2.06 – 8.4.06.

Longest Sequence of League Defeats: 12, 27.9.2003 – 13.12.2003.

Longest Sequence of League Draws: 6, 11.2.1978 – 11.3.1978.

Longest Sequence of Unbeaten League Matches: 19, 1.10.1994 – 11.2.1995.

Longest Sequence Without a League Win: 14, 19.1.1935 – 19.4.1935.

Successive Scoring Runs: 26 from 23.8.1947.

Successive Non-scoring Runs: 5 from 24.8.1968.

MANAGERS

Harry Kirkbride 1904–05 (*Secretary-Manager*)
McCumiskey 1905–06 (*Secretary-Manager*)
Jack Houston 1906–08 (*Secretary-Manager*)
Bert Stansfield 1908–10
Jack Houston 1910–12
Davie Graham 1912–13
George Bristow 1913–30
Billy Hampson 1930–33
Bill Clarke 1933–35
Robert Kelly 1935–36
Fred Westgarth 1936–38
David Taylor 1938–40
Howard Harkness 1940–45
Bill Clark 1945–46 (*Secretary-Manager*)
Ivor Broadis 1946–49
Bill Shankly 1949–51
Fred Emery 1951–58
Andy Beattie 1958–60
Ivor Powell 1960–63
Alan Ashman 1963–67
Tim Ward 1967–68
Bob Stokoe 1968–70
Ian MacFarlane 1970–72
Alan Ashman 1972–75
Dick Young 1975–76
Bobby Moncur 1976–80
Martin Harvey 1980
Bob Stokoe 1980–85
Bryan 'Pop' Robson 1985
Bob Stokoe 1985–86
Harry Gregg 1986–87
Cliff Middlemass 1987–91
Aidan McCaffery 1991–92
David McCreery 1992–93
Mick Wadsworth (*Director of Coaching*) 1993–96
Mervyn Day 1996–97
David Wilkes and John Halpin (*Directors of Coaching*), and **Michael Knighton** 1997–99
Nigel Pearson 1998–99
Keith Mincher 1999
Martin Wilkinson 1999–2000
Ian Atkins 2000–01
Roddy Collins 2001–02; 2002–03
Paul Simpson 2003–06
Neil McDonald 2006–07
John Ward 2007–08
Greg Abbott December 2008–

TEN YEAR LEAGUE RECORD

		P	W	D	L	F	A	Pts	Pos
2001-02	Div 3	46	12	16	18	49	56	52	17
2002-03	Div 3	46	13	10	23	52	78	49	22
2003-04	Div 3	46	12	9	25	46	69	45	23
2004-05	Conf	42	20	13	9	74	37	73	3
2005-06	FL 2	46	25	11	10	84	42	86	1
2006-07	FL 1	46	19	11	16	54	55	68	8
2007-08	FL 1	46	23	11	12	64	46	80	4
2008-09	FL 1	46	12	14	20	56	69	50	20
2009-10	FL 1	46	15	13	18	63	66	58	14
2010-11	FL 1	46	16	11	19	60	62	59	12

DID YOU KNOW ?

History was made for Carlisle United on 14 February 1955 when the club hosted a friendly match against Austrian club Columbia based in Vienna, the first overseas team to play at Brunton Park. Jimmy Whitehouse, Allan Ashman and Tommy Moran scored in a 3-2 United win.

CARLISLE UNITED 2010–11 LEAGUE RECORD

Match No.	Date		Venue	Opponents	Result		H/T Score	Lg Pos.	Goalscorers	Attendance
1	Aug	7	H	Brentford	W	2-0	2-0	—	Madine [22], Harte (pen) [45]	5913
2		14	A	Plymouth Arg	D	1-1	0-0	4	Harte [68]	7782
3		21	H	Milton Keynes D	W	4-1	2-0	1	Zoko [42], Berrett [45], Madine [55], Taiwo [61]	5205
4		27	A	Colchester U	D	1-1	0-1	—	Thirlwell [90]	4475
5	Sept	4	H	Swindon T	D	0-0	0-0	2		5689
6		11	H	Sheffield W	W	1-0	1-0	2	Curran [36]	20,282
7		18	H	Brighton & HA	D	0-0	0-0	3		6039
8		25	A	Bournemouth	L	0-2	0-0	7		6103
9		28	A	Hartlepool U	W	4-0	3-0	—	Michalik [8], Madine 3 [26, 36, 71]	3419
10	Oct	2	H	Peterborough U	L	0-1	0-1	4		5735
11		9	H	Notts Co	W	1-0	0-0	2	Madine [68]	5599
12		16	A	Exeter C	L	1-2	0-2	6	Robson [71]	5324
13		23	H	Charlton Ath	L	3-4	0-2	8	Grella [58], Curran [61], Madine [77]	5624
14		30	A	Bristol R	D	1-1	0-0	10	Grella [87]	6144
15	Nov	2	H	Tranmere R	W	2-0	1-0	—	Berrett [42], Murphy [49]	3744
16		13	H	Southampton	W	3-2	2-0	4	Marshall [21], Harding (og) [30], Chester [57]	6578
17		20	A	Walsall	L	1-2	1-1	8	Grella [26]	4256
18		23	H	Rochdale	D	1-1	1-0	—	Madine [20]	7412
19	Dec	11	A	Dagenham & R	L	0-2	0-0	11		4380
20	Jan	1	H	Huddersfield T	D	2-2	0-1	14	Zoko [71], Chester [82]	5904
21		3	A	Tranmere R	L	1-2	0-1	15	Berrett [78]	5128
22		15	H	Bristol R	W	4-0	1-0	14	Berrett 2 (2 pens) [44, 82], Curran [57], Cooper [73]	4229
23		22	A	Notts Co	W	1-0	0-0	11	Zoko [55]	6327
24		29	H	Oldham Ath	D	2-2	0-2	—	Zoko [75], Berrett (pen) [90]	5389
25	Feb	1	A	Huddersfield T	L	0-2	0-2	11		11,572
26		5	H	Walsall	L	1-3	0-1	13	Murphy [90]	4332
27		12	A	Southampton	L	0-1	0-1	16		25,076
28		15	A	Oldham Ath	W	1-0	0-0	—	Curran [80]	8564
29		19	A	Swindon T	W	1-0	1-0	12	Berrett [29]	7592
30		22	H	Exeter C	D	2-2	2-2	—	Curran [9], Zoko [45]	3962
31		26	H	Sheffield W	L	0-1	0-1	13		6834
32	Mar	1	A	Charlton Ath	W	3-1	1-1	—	Marshall [27], Curran [62], Loy [80]	12,797
33		5	A	Brighton & HA	L	3-4	1-1	12	Taiwo [3], Marshall [60], Arter [89]	7466
34		8	H	Hartlepool U	W	1-0	0-0	—	Zoko [67]	3898
35		12	A	Peterborough U	L	0-6	0-3	10		6467
36		15	H	Plymouth Arg	D	1-1	1-0	—	Berrett [34]	3354
37		19	A	Bournemouth	W	1-0	1-0	8	Murphy [26]	4385
38		25	A	Brentford	L	1-2	0-0	—	Michalik [88]	4365
39		29	A	Yeovil T	L	0-1	0-0	—		3331
40	Apr	9	A	Milton Keynes D	L	2-3	1-1	14	Noble [28], Berrett (pen) [69]	10,795
41		12	A	Leyton Orient	D	0-0	0-0	—		3228
42		16	H	Colchester U	W	4-1	3-0	12	Berrett [9], Curran 2 [26, 61], Noble [31]	4405
43		23	A	Rochdale	W	3-2	1-1	—	Holness (og) [25], Noble [60], Robson [65]	3762
44		25	H	Leyton Orient	L	0-1	0-1	10		4685
45		30	A	Dagenham & R	L	0-3	0-2	11		2693
46	May	7	H	Yeovil T	L	0-2	0-1	12		6473

Final League Position: 12

GOALSCORERS

League (60): Berrett 10 (4 pens), Curran 8, Madine 8, Zoko 6, Grella 3, Marshall 3, Murphy 3, Noble 3, Chester 2, Harte 2 (1 pen), Michalik 2, Robson 2, Taiwo 2, Arter 1, Cooper 1, Loy 1, Thirlwell 1, own goals 2.
Carling Cup (0).
FA Cup (9): Madine 5, Zoko 3, Chester 1.
J Paint Trophy (13): Murphy 4, Marshall 2, Michalik 2, Chester 1, Price 1, Taiwo 1, Zoko 1, own goal 1.

Collin A 46	Simek F 46	McDaid S 12	Thirlwell P 21+2	Chester J 18	Harte I 4	Taiwo T 44+2	Berrett J 46	Curran C 36+9	Zoko F 40+4	Madine G 21	Bridge-Wilkinson M —+3	Robson M 27+15	Murphy P 32+2	Kavanagh G —+1	Michalik L 32	Marshall B 27+6	Norwood O 4+2	Price J —+3	Grella M 7+3	Kane T —+1	Evans C 1	Livesey D 5+5	Cruise T 3	Hurst K —+2	Bowman R —+3	Cooper L 6	Noble L 18+3	Wells N —+3	Dudgeon J 1+1	Loy R 5+12	Madden P 1+12	Borrowdale G 1	McKenna B —+1	Arter H 2+3	Match No.
1	2	3	4	5	6	7	8	9	10^1	11	12																								1
1	2	3	4	5	6	7	8	9	10^1	11	12																								2
1	2	3	4	5	6	7	8^1	9	10^2	11	13	12																							3
1	2	3	4	5	6^2	7^3	8^1	9	10	11		12	13	14																					4
1	2	3	4	5		7^2	8	9	10^1	11		13			6	12																			5
1	2	3	4	5		11^2	8	9^1	10			12			6	13																			6
1	2	3		5	6^1	7	8^2	9^3	10			13			4	12	11	14																	7
1	2	3		5	6		8	9^3	10^2	11		13			4	12	7^1	14																	8
1	2	3		5	6^3	7	13	9	10	11^{12}		12			4^1	8	14																		9
1	2	3		5	6	7^3	12	9	10	11^{12}			4			8^1	13	14																	10
1	2	3		5	6	7	8	9	10	12			4			11^1																			11
1	2	3		5	6	7	9^2	11	10	13			4		8^1	12																			12
1	2			5^1	6	7		9	10^2	11			3	4		13		8	12																13
1	2				6	8	9^1		10				11	3	5	12		7	4^2		13														14
1	2				6	7	12	9^1	10				3	4	5	8		11																	15
1	2			5	6	7	13	9^2	10^1				12	3	4	8		11																	16
1	2			5	6	7	13	9^1	10				12		4	8		11						3^2											17
1	2			5	6	7	14	9^3	10				12		4^8	8		11^2						3^1	13										18
1	2	8		5	6^1	7		9^2	10				13		4	11		12						3											19
1	2	12		5	6	7	9^3	13	11				3		4	8^1		10^2							14										20
1	2		4			3^2	8	9^1	12	10			11^3	6	5	7		13							14										21
1	2		4^1				7	8	10	9^3				3	6	11^2									14		5	12	13						22
1	2						7	8	9	10				3	6	11											5	4							23
1	2	12					7^2	8	9	10			14	3^1	6	11											5	4^3	13						24
1	2		4				7^1	8^2	9^3	10			12		6	11											5	13	3	14					25
1	2						12	8	9	10			11^2	3	6	7^1						5^3					4			13	14				26
1	2						11	8	14	9^3			12	6	5	7											4^2	13		10^1		3^8			27
1	2						11	8	12	9			3	6	5	7											4			10^1					28
1	2						11	8	13	9^3			3	6	5^1	7			12								4			10^2	14				29
1	2						11	8	9	10			3	6		7^1						5					4			12					30
1	2						11	8	9^3	10^2			3	6		7						5					4^1			12	13		14		31
1	2						11	8	9				3	6		7						5					4			10					32
1	2						11	8	9^3	12			3	6		7						5					4^2			10^1	14			13	33
1	2						11	8	9	10^1			3	6		7									5		4^8			12					34
1	2						4	8	9	10^1			3	6		7^3									5^8		14			13	12		11^2		35
1	2		4				8^1	9	10				3	6	5	7																	12		36
1	2		4				11^1	8	9	10			3	6	5	7															12				37
1	2		4			7	8^2	9	13				11^3	3	5	10						14								12			6		38
1	2		4				11^2	8^3	9	10^1			3	6	5	7											13			14			12		39
1	2		4				11	8^1	9	10			3	6	5												7			12					40
1	2		4				11	8	9	10^1			3	6	5												7			12					41
1	2		4				11	8	9	10^1			3	6	5												7				12				42
1	2		4				11^2	8	9	10^1			3	6	5												7			13	12				43
1	2		4				11^1	8	9	10^3			3	6	5								13				7^2			14	12				44
1	2		4				11^1	8	9^3	10			3	6	5^2							13					7			14	12				45
1	2^1		4				12	8^2	9	10			3	6	5							13					7			14	11^3				46

FA Cup

First Round	Tipton T	(h)	6-0
Second Round	Tamworth	(h)	3-2
Third Round	Torquay U	(a)	0-1

Carling Cup

First Round	Huddersfield T	(a)	0-1

J Paint Trophy

Second Round	Port Vale	(h)	2-2
Northern Quarter-Final	Crewe Alex	(h)	3-1
Northern Semi-Final	Sheffield W	(h)	3-1
Northern Final	Huddersfield T	(h)	4-0
		(a)	0-3
Final	Brentford		1-0

(at Wembley).

CHARLTON ATHLETIC   FL Championship 1

FOUNDATION

The club was formed on 9 June 1905, by a group of 14- and 15-year-old youths living in streets by the Thames in the area which now borders the Thames Barrier. The club's progress through local leagues was so rapid that after the First World War they joined the Kent League where they spent a season before turning professional and joining the Southern League in 1920. A year later they were elected to the Football League's Division 3 (South).

The Valley, Floyd Road, Charlton, London SE7 8BL.

Telephone: (020) 8333 4000.

Fax: (020) 8333 4001.

Ticket Office: (0871) 226 1905.

Website: www.cafc.co.uk

Email: info@cafc.co.uk

Ground Capacity: 27,111.

Record Attendance: 75,031 v Aston Villa, FA Cup 5th rd, 12 February 1938 (at The Valley).

Pitch Measurements: 101.5m × 65.8m.

Chairman: Michael Slater.

Chief Executive: Stephen Kavanagh.

Football Secretary: Chris Parkes.

Manager: Chris Powell.

Assistant Manager: Alex Dyer.

Head Physio: Erol Umut.

HONOURS

Football League – Division 1: *Champions* 1999–2000; *Runners-up* 1936–37; **Division 2:** *Runners-up* 1935–36, 1985–86; **Division 3 (S):** *Champions* 1928–29, 1934–35. **FA Cup:** *Winners* 1947; *Runners-up* 1946. **Football League Cup:** Quarter-final 2007. **Full Members' Cup:** *Runners-up* 1987.

Colours: Red shirts with white trim, white shorts, white stockings with red tops.

Change Colours: Black and blue striped shirts, black shorts, blue stockings.

Year Formed: 1905.

Turned Professional: 1920.

Ltd Co.: 1919.

Club Nickname: 'Addicks'.

Grounds: 1906, Siemen's Meadow; 1907, Woolwich Common; 1909, Pound Park; 1913, Horn Lane; 1920, The Valley; 1923, Catford (The Mount); 1924, The Valley; 1985, Selhurst Park; 1991, Upton Park; 1992, The Valley.

First Football League Game: 27 August 1921, Division 3 (S), v Exeter C (h) W 1–0 – Hughes; Johnny Mitchell, Goodman; Dowling (1), Hampson, Dunn; Castle, Bailey, Halse, Green, Wilson.

Record League Victory: 8–1 v Middlesbrough, Division 1, 12 September 1953 – Bartram; Campbell, Ellis; Fenton, Ufton, Hammond; Hurst (2), O'Linn (2), Leary (1), Firmani (3), Kiernan.

sky SPORTS FACT FILE

Luke Varney, a £2,500,000 signing from Crewe Alexandra, opened his Charlton Athletic scoring account against Leicester City on 22 September 2007. He had previously scored for Crewe against City in just 27 seconds on 25 August 2005.

Record Cup Victory: 7–0 v Burton A, FA Cup 3rd rd, 7 January 1956 – Bartram; Campbell, Townsend; Hewie, Ufton, Hammond; Hurst (1), Gauld (1), Leary (3), White, Kiernan (2).

Record Defeat: 1–11 v Aston Villa, Division 2, 14 November 1959.

Most League Points (2 for a win): 61, Division 3 (S), 1934–35.

Most League Points (3 for a win): 91, Division 1, 1999–2000.

Most League Goals: 107, Division 2, 1957–58.

Highest League Scorer in Season: Ralph Allen, 32, Division 3 (S), 1934–35.

Most League Goals in Total Aggregate: Stuart Leary, 153, 1953–62.

Most League Goals in One Match: 5, Wilson Lennox v Exeter C, Division 3 (S), 2 February 1929; 5, Eddie Firmani v Aston Villa, Division 1, 5 February 1955; 5, John Summers v Huddersfield T, Division 2, 21 December 1957; 5, John Summers v Portsmouth, Division 2, 1 October 1960.

Most Capped Player: Jonatan Johansson, 42 (105), Finland.

Most League Appearances: Sam Bartram, 579, 1934–56.

Youngest League Player: Jonjo Shelvey, 16 years 59 days v Burnley, 26 April 2008.

Record Transfer Fee Received: £16,500,000 from Tottenham H for Darren Bent, May 2007

Record Transfer Fee Paid: £5,380,000 to Ipswich T for Darren Bent, June 2005.

Football League Record: 1921 Elected to Division 3 (S); 1929–33 Division 2, 1933–35 Division 3 (S); 1935–36 Division 2; 1936–57 Division 1; 1957–72 Division 2; 1972–75 Division 3; 1975–80 Division 2; 1980–81 Division 3; 1981–86 Division 2; 1986–90 Division 1; 1990–92 Division 2; 1992–98 Division 1; 1998–99 FA Premier League; 1999–2000 Division 1; 2000–07 FA Premier League; 2007–09 FL C; 2009– FL 1.

MANAGERS

Walter Rayner 1920–25
Alex Macfarlane 1925–27
Albert Lindon 1928
Alex Macfarlane 1928–32
Albert Lindon 1932–33
Jimmy Seed 1933–56
Jimmy Trotter 1956–61
Frank Hill 1961–65
Bob Stokoe 1965–67
Eddie Firmani 1967–70
Theo Foley 1970–74
Andy Nelson 1974–79
Mike Bailey 1979–81
Alan Mullery 1981–82
Ken Craggs 1982
Lennie Lawrence 1982–91
Steve Gritt/Alan Curbishley 1991–95
Alan Curbishley 1995–2006
Iain Dowie 2006
Les Reed 2006
Alan Pardew 2006–08
Phil Parkinson 2008–10
Chris Powell January 2011–

LATEST SEQUENCES

Longest Sequence of League Wins: 12, 26.12.1999 – 7.3.2000.

Longest Sequence of League Defeats: 10, 11.4.1990 – 15.9.1990.

Longest Sequence of League Draws: 6, 13.12.1992 – 16.1.1993.

Longest Sequence of Unbeaten League Matches: 15, 4.10.1980 – 20.12.1980.

Longest Sequence Without a League Win: 18, 18.8.2008 – 17.1.2009.

Successive Scoring Runs: 25 from 26.12.1935.

Successive Non-scoring Runs: 5 from 6.9.1922.

TEN YEAR LEAGUE RECORD

		P	W	D	L	F	A	Pts	Pos
2001-02	PR Lge	38	10	14	14	38	49	44	14
2002-03	PR Lge	38	14	7	17	45	56	49	12
2003-04	PR Lge	38	14	11	13	51	51	53	7
2004-05	PR Lge	38	12	10	16	42	58	46	11
2005-06	PR Lge	38	13	8	17	41	55	47	13
2006-07	PR Lge	38	8	10	20	34	60	34	19
2007-08	FL C	46	17	13	16	63	58	64	11
2008-09	FL C	46	8	15	23	52	74	39	24
2009-10	FL 1	46	23	15	8	71	48	84	4
2010-11	FL 1	46	15	14	17	62	66	59	13

DID YOU KNOW ?

One of the first overseas born players to turn out for Charlton Athletic in the 1920s was goalkeeper Charlie "Spider" Preedy, a bit of a show-boater who had been born in India. He made 140 League and Cup appearances, joined Arsenal and won an FA Cup medal in 1930.

CHARLTON ATHLETIC 2010–11 LEAGUE RECORD

Match No.	Date	Venue	Opponents	Result	H/T Score	Lg Pos.	Goalscorers	Attendance
1	Aug 7	H	Bournemouth	W 1-0	1-0	—	Sodje [22]	16,236
2	13	A	Leyton Orient	W 3-1	1-0	—	McCormack [28], Wagstaff [62], Solly [90]	5535
3	21	H	Oldham Ath	D 1-1	1-1	3	Wagstaff [24]	14,842
4	28	A	Huddersfield T	L 1-3	0-2	8	Fry [90]	13,858
5	Sept 4	A	Exeter C	L 0-1	0-0	11		5743
6	11	H	Notts Co	W 1-0	0-0	9	Anyinsah [85]	14,436
7	18	A	Tranmere R	D 1-1	1-0	10	Wagstaff [6]	4735
8	25	H	Dagenham & R	D 2-2	1-1	11	Llera [10], Jackson [89]	14,806
9	28	H	Milton Keynes D	W 1-0	0-0	—	Benson [86]	13,155
10	Oct 2	A	Brentford	L 1-2	0-2	8	Wagstaff [74]	6342
11	9	A	Plymouth Arg	D 2-2	1-1	10	Benson 2 [35, 90]	7738
12	16	H	Brighton & HA	L 0-4	0-1	14		18,949
13	23	A	Carlisle U	W 4-3	2-0	10	Jackson [23], Anyinsah [38], Benson 2 [47, 90]	5624
14	30	H	Sheffield W	W 3-0	1-0	6	Wagstaff [23]	17,365
15	Nov 2	A	Swindon T	W 3-0	1-0	—	Jackson [13], Anyinsah [51], Benson [74]	7939
16	13	A	Peterborough U	W 5-1	4-0	2	Jackson 2 (1 pen) [15 (p), 36], Racon [25], Martin 2 [38, 65]	7477
17	20	H	Yeovil T	W 3-2	2-1	2	Jackson 2 (1 pen) [11, 85 (p)], Racon [26]	15,184
18	23	H	Bristol R	D 1-1	0-0	—	Benson [77]	13,468
19	Dec 12	H	Walsall	L 0-1	0-0	4		14,938
20	29	A	Brighton & HA	D 1-1	1-1	—	Jackson (pen) [3]	8374
21	Jan 1	A	Colchester U	D 3-3	2-2	3	Jackson 2 (2 pens) [18, 40], Benson [76]	6112
22	3	H	Swindon T	L 2-4	1-1	5	Jackson [22], Abbott [87]	14,740
23	15	A	Sheffield W	D 2-2	2-0	7	Wagstaff [4], Jackson (pen) [6]	19,051
24	22	H	Plymouth Arg	W 2-0	0-0	7	Wagstaff [55], Eccleston [90]	16,607
25	Feb 1	H	Colchester U	W 1-0	0-0	7	Wright-Phillips [78]	13,830
26	5	A	Yeovil T	W 1-0	0-0	5	Wright-Phillips [63]	4651
27	12	H	Peterborough U	W 3-2	0-1	5	Jackson [57], Wright-Phillips [59], Abbott [80]	15,909
28	15	A	Hartlepool U	L 1-2	0-1	—	Eccleston [54]	2289
29	19	H	Exeter C	L 1-3	0-0	7	Wright-Phillips [86]	24,767
30	25	A	Notts Co	L 0-1	0-0	—		8141
31	Mar 1	H	Carlisle U	L 1-3	1-1	—	Wright-Phillips [10]	12,797
32	5	H	Tranmere R	D 1-1	0-1	7	Wright-Phillips [54]	14,015
33	8	A	Milton Keynes D	L 0-2	0-0	—		7026
34	12	H	Brentford	L 0-1	0-0	11		14,985
35	19	A	Dagenham & R	L 1-2	0-1	13	Nouble [90]	3505
36	22	H	Southampton	D 1-1	0-0	—	Wright-Phillips [86]	16,550
37	26	A	Bournemouth	D 2-2	1-1	—	Wagstaff [28], Wright-Phillips [81]	7752
38	29	A	Rochdale	L 0-2	0-1	—		2589
39	Apr 2	H	Leyton Orient	W 3-1	0-1	12	Benson [50], Wright-Phillips [73], Semedo [87]	15,875
40	5	A	Southampton	L 0-2	0-1	—		20,112
41	9	A	Oldham Ath	D 0-0	0-0	12		3562
42	16	H	Huddersfield T	L 0-1	0-0	13		15,879
43	23	A	Bristol R	D 2-2	1-0	—	Benson [8], Reid [46]	6586
44	25	H	Rochdale	W 3-1	1-0	13	Racon [31], Parrett [52], Eccleston [76]	13,253
45	30	A	Walsall	L 0-2	0-1	14		5088
46	May 7	H	Hartlepool U	D 0-0	0-0	13		15,804

Final League Position: 13

GOALSCORERS

League (62): Jackson 13 (6 pens), Benson 10, Wright-Phillips 9, Wagstaff 8, Anyinsah 3, Eccleston 3, Racon 3, Abbott 2, Martin 2, Fry 1, Llera 1, McCormack 1, Nouble 1, Parrett 1, Reid 1, Semedo 1, Sodje 1, Solly 1.
Carling Cup (3): Abbott 2, Martin 1.
FA Cup (6): Anyinsah 2, Jackson 1, Racon 1, Reid 1, Wagstaff 1.
J Paint Trophy (4): Racon 2, Abbott 1, Wagstaff 1.

Elliot R 35	Solly C 9+5	Jackson J 29+1	McCormack A 18+6	Doherty G 35+3	Dailly C 32	Wagstaff S 35+5	Semedo J 42	Abbott P 10+7	Sodje A 1+14	Reid K 13+19	Racon T 34+5	Martin L 14+6	Francis S 32+2	Llera M 14+1	Worner R 7+1	Fry M 20+5	Benson P 28+4	Anyinsah J 14+5	Fortune J 12+4	Eccleston N 8+13	Bessone F 13	Wright-Phillips B 20+1	Jenkinson C 7+1	Nouble F 4+5	Parrett D 9	Stewart M 6+3	Sullivan J 4	Harriott C 1+2	Match No.
1	2	3	4	5	6	7^2	8	9^1	10^3	11	12	13	14																1
1	14	3	4	5	6	7		9^2	13	11^1	8	10^3	2	12															2
1		3	4	5		7		9	12	11	8^1	10	2	6															3
	3^2	4	5	6		7^1	8	9	12	11		10	2		1	13													4
1	13	4	5		12		8	9^3	14	11^1	7^2		2	6		3	10												5
1	6	4^1	5				8	9^3	14	11	12	7	2			3	10^2	13											6
	3^2		5			7	8		12	13	4	11^3	2	6	1	14	10	9^1											7
	3		5			7^2	8		12	13^3	4	11	2	6	1	14	10	9^1											8
	11^2		5			7^1	8		12	13	4	10	2		1	3	9	6											9
1	11		5			7	8		12	14	13	4	10^2	2		3^1	9	6^3											10
1	3		5	6		7^1	8	9^2		11	4	12				10	13	2											11
1	3		5	6	14		8	9^2		11^3	4	7	12			10	13	2^1											12
1	11	13	5	6		7	8		12		4^2		2			3	10	9^1											13
1	11	13	5	6		7	8				4^2	12	2			3	10	9^1											14
1	11		5	6		7	8				4		2			3	10	9											15
1	11	13	5	6		7^2	8^3		14		4	12	2			3	10	9^1											16
1	11	14	5	6		8			12	7^2	4	9^3	2			3^1	10	13											17
1	11	12	5			7^3	8^1		14	13	4	10	2			3^2	9	6											18
1	11		5			7^3	8		14	13	4	12	2			3^1	10	9^2	6										19
1	11		5	6		7^3	8^2		14	13	4	12	2			3	10	9^1											20
1	11		5	6		7^1	8		12	13	4^2		2			3	10^8	9											21
1	3	7^2		6	12		8	13	14	11	4	9^1	2			10		5^3											22
1	11	10^3	5	6		7	8		12	13	4^2		2			3		9^1	14										23
1	11^{10}		5	6		7	8		14		12	4^2	2			3		9^4	13										24
1	11	4	5	6		7	8				2					13	12	9^1	14	3^2	10^3								25
1	11	4^1	5	6		7	8			12			2			3	14	9^2	13	10^3									26
1	11	8	5	6		9^1	7	12		14			2			13		4	3^2	10^3									27
1	11	4^2	5	6		8	9			13			2^1			3		7		10	12								28
1	11	4^1	5	6		14	8	9		13		12				3^2			7^3	10	2								29
1	11^1		5	6	12	8		13		4			2			9			7^2	10	3								30
1		5^1		6	7	8		11		4			2			13		12	9^2	10	3								31
1^8	11^2		5		7	8		13		4			2	6	15	9		12		10^1	3								32
	10^1		5		7	8		11^2		4			2	6	1	9^8		13		12	3								33
	13	11	5^1		7	8		14		4^3			6	1	3			12		10	2^2	9							34
	13	11^3	5		7^2	8		12					6	1	3^1			14		10	2	9	4						35
1	2		14	5	7^1	8		4					6			13		12	3	10		9^2	11^3						36
1	2		14	5	7	8		4					6			12		13	3^3	10		9^1	11^2						37
1	2			5	7^2	8^3		4					6			12	9^1		13	3	10		11	14					38
1	2			5	7	8		4					6			9^3			13	3	10^2	14	11^1	12					39
1	2			5	7	8		4					6			9^2		14	3	10^3	13	11^1	12					40
1	2		14	5	6^8	7	8	4^1					9			12		3	10^2	13	11^3	1							41
1	2			5		7	8		12	4^1			9	6		3			10			11	1						42
1	12			5		7^8		11^8		2			9^2	6		8	3			13	10^1		4						43
1	12			5				4		2			9^1	6		7	3^2	10		13	11^3	8	1	14					44
1				5				4^1		2			9	6		7	3	10		11	8		12						45
1	11			12		7^2	8		13				5	9		6	6^1	14	3	10			4	2^3					46

FA Cup

First Round	Barnet	(a)	0-0
		(h)	1-0
Second Round	Luton T	(h)	2-2
		(a)	3-1
Third Round	Tottenham H	(a)	0-3

Carling Cup

First Round	Shrewsbury T	(a)	3-4

J Paint Trophy

First Round	Dagenham & R	(h)	1-0
Second Round	Milton Keynes D	(a)	2-1
Southern Quarter-Final	Southend U	(a)	1-0
Southern Semi-Final	Brentford	(a)	0-0

CHELSEA   FA Premiership

FOUNDATION

Chelsea may never have existed but for the fact that Fulham rejected an offer to rent the Stamford Bridge ground from Mr H. A. Mears who had owned it since 1904. Fortunately he was determined to develop it as a football stadium rather than sell it to the Great Western Railway and got together with Frederick Parker, who persuaded Mears of the financial advantages of developing a major sporting venue. Chelsea FC was formed in 1905 and applications made to join both the Southern League and Football League. The latter competition was decided upon because of its comparatively meagre representation in the south of England.

Stamford Bridge, Fulham Road, London SW6 1HS.
Telephone: 0871 984 1955.
Fax: (020) 7381 4831.
Ticket Office: 0871 984 1905.
Website: www.chelseafc.com
Ground Capacity: 41,841.
Record Attendance: 82,905 v Arsenal, Division 1, 12 October 1935.
Pitch Measurements: 103m × 67m.
Chairman: Bruce Buck.
Director: Eugene Tenenbaum.
Chief Executive: Ron Gourlay.
Secretary: David Barnard.
Manager: Andre Villas-Boas.
Technical Director: Michael Emenalo.
Assistant First Team Coaches: Roberto Di Matteo, Steve Holland, Paul Clement.
Fitness Coaches: Glen Driscoll, Jose Mario Rocha.
Colours: Reflex blue shirt, reflex blue shorts, white stockings with blue trim.
Change Colours: Blue and black hooped shirts with yellow trim, black shorts with yellow trim, black stockings with yellow tops.
Year Formed: 1905.
Turned Professional: 1905.
Ltd Co.: 1905.
Club Nickname: 'The Blues'.
Ground: 1905, Stamford Bridge.
First Football League Game: 2 September 1905, Division 2, v Stockport Co (a) L 0–1 – Foulke; Mackie, McEwan; Key, Harris, Miller; Moran, Jack Robertson, Copeland, Windridge, Kirwan.

HONOURS

FA Premier League:
Champions 2004–05, 2005–06, 2009–10.
Runners-up 2003–04, 2006–07, 2007–08, 2010–11.

Football League – Division 1:
Champions 1954–55; **Division 2:**
Champions 1983–84, 1988–89;
Runners-up 1906–07, 1911–12, 1929–30, 1962–63, 1976–77.

FA Cup: Winners 1970, 1997, 2000, 2007, 2009, 2010. **Runners-up** 1915, 1967, 1994, 2002.

Football League Cup: Winners 1965, 1998, 2005, 2007; **Runners-up** 1972, 2008.

Full Members' Cup: Winners 1986.

Zenith Data Systems Cup:
Winners 1990.

European Competitions
Champions League: 1999–2000, 2003–04 (s-f), 2004–05 (s-f), 2005–06, 2006–07 (s-f), 2007–08 (runners-up), 2008–09 (s-f), 2009–10, 2010–11.
European Fairs Cup: 1958–60, 1965–66, 1968–69.
European Cup-Winners' Cup:
1970–71 (winners), 1971–72, 1994–95, 1997–98 (winners), 1998–99 (s-f).
UEFA Cup: 2000–01, 2001–02, 2002–03. **Super Cup:** 1998–99 (winners).

sky SPORTS FACT FILE

Frank Lampard captained England for the first time v Denmark on 9 February 2011 playing with ex-England skipper John Terry. On 18 August 2009 Terry plus national captains Ballack (Germany) and Shevchenko (Ukraine) played for Chelsea against Sunderland.

Record League Victory: 8-0 v Wigan Ath, FA Premier League, 9 May 2010 – Cech; Ivanovic (Belletti), Ashley Cole (1), Ballack (Matic), Terry, Alex, Kalou (1) (Joe Cole), Lampard (pen), Anelka (2), Drogba (3, 1 pen), Malouda.

Record Cup Victory: 13–0 v Jeunesse Hautcharage, ECWC, 1st rd 2nd leg, 29 September 1971 – Bonetti; Boyle, Harris (1), Hollins (1p), Webb (1), Hinton, Cooke, Baldwin (3), Osgood (5), Hudson (1), Houseman (1).

Record Defeat: 1–8 v Wolverhampton W, Division 1, 26 September 1953.

Most League Points (2 for a win): 57, Division 2, 1906–07.

Most League Points (3 for a win): 99, Division 2, 1988–89.

Most League Goals: 103, FA Premier League, 2009–10.

Highest League Scorer in Season: Jimmy Greaves, 41, 1960–61.

Most League Goals in Total Aggregate: Bobby Tambling, 164, 1958–70.

Most League Goals in One Match: 5, George Hilsdon v Glossop, Division 2, 1 September 1906; 5, Jimmy Greaves v Wolverhampton W, Division 1, 30 August 1958; 5, Jimmy Greaves v Preston NE, Division 1, 19 December 1959; 5, Jimmy Greaves v WBA, Division 1, 3 December 1960; 5, Bobby Tambling v Aston Villa, Division 1, 17 September 1966; 5, Gordon Durie v Walsall, Division 2, 4 February 1989.

Most Capped Player: Frank Lampard, 84 (86), England.

Most League Appearances: Ron Harris, 655, 1962–80.

Youngest League Player: Ian Hamilton, 16 years 138 days v Tottenham H, 18 March 1967.

Record Transfer Fee Received: £12,000,000 from Rangers for Tore Andre Flo, November 2000; £12,000,000 from Manchester C for Wayne Bridge, January 2009.

Record Transfer Fee Paid: £50,000,000 to Liverpool for Fernando Torres, January 2011.

Football League Record: 1905 Elected to Division 2; 1907–10 Division 1; 1910–12 Division 2; 1912–24 Division 1; 1924–30 Division 2; 1930–62 Division 1; 1962–63 Division 2; 1963–75 Division 1; 1975–77 Division 2; 1977–79 Division 1; 1979–84 Division 2; 1984–88 Division 1; 1988–89 Division 2; 1989–92 Division 1; 1992– FA Premier League.

MANAGERS

John Tait Robertson 1905–07
David Calderhead 1907–33
Leslie Knighton 1933–39
Billy Birrell 1939–52
Ted Drake 1952–61
Tommy Docherty 1961–67
Dave Sexton 1967–74
Ron Suart 1974–75
Eddie McCreadie 1975–77
Ken Shellito 1977–78
Danny Blanchflower 1978–79
Geoff Hurst 1979–81
John Neal 1981–85 (*Director to 1986*)
John Hollins 1985–88
Bobby Campbell 1988–91
Ian Porterfield 1991–93
David Webb 1993
Glenn Hoddle 1993–96
Ruud Gullit 1996–98
Gianluca Vialli 1998–2000
Claudio Ranieri 2000–04
Jose Mourinho 2004–07
Avram Grant 2007–08
Luiz Felipe Scolari 2008–09
Guus Hiddink 2009
Carlo Ancelotti 2009–2011
Andre Villas-Boas June 2011–

LATEST SEQUENCES

Longest Sequence of League Wins: 11, 25.4.2009 – 20.9.2009.

Longest Sequence of League Defeats: 7, 1.11.1952 – 20.12.1952.

Longest Sequence of League Draws: 6, 20.8.1969 – 13.9.1969.

Longest Sequence of Unbeaten League Matches: 40, 23.10.2004 – 29.10.2005.

Longest Sequence Without a League Win: 21, 3.11.1987 – 2.4.1988.

Successive Scoring Runs: 27 from 29.10.1988.

Successive Non-scoring Runs: 9 from 14.3.1981.

TEN YEAR LEAGUE RECORD

		P	W	D	L	F	A	Pts	Pos
2001-02	PR Lge	38	17	13	8	66	38	64	6
2002-03	PR Lge	38	19	10	9	68	38	67	4
2003-04	PR Lge	38	24	7	7	67	30	79	2
2004-05	PR Lge	38	29	8	1	72	15	95	1
2005-06	PR Lge	38	29	4	5	72	22	91	1
2006-07	PR Lge	38	24	11	3	64	24	83	2
2007-08	PR Lge	38	25	10	3	65	26	85	2
2008-09	PR Lge	38	25	8	5	68	24	83	3
2009-10	PR Lge	38	27	5	6	103	32	86	1
2010-11	PR Lge	38	21	8	9	69	33	71	2

DID YOU KNOW ?

On 9 January 2011 when Chelsea beat Ipswich Town 7-0 in the FA Cup third round, goalkeeper Petr Cech had kept his 151st clean sheet in 301 League and Cup appearances. The club's record holder is Peter Bonetti with 208 unbeaten matches from a career total of 729.

CHELSEA 2010–11 LEAGUE RECORD

Match No.	Date	Venue	Opponents	Result	H/T Score	Lg Pos.	Goalscorers	Attendance
1	Aug 14	H	WBA	W 6-0	2-0	—	Malouda 2 [6, 90], Drogba 3 [45, 55, 68], Lampard [63]	41,589
2	21	A	Wigan Ath	W 6-0	1-0	1	Malouda [34], Anelka 2 [48, 52], Kalou 2 [78, 89], Benayoun [90]	14,476
3	28	H	Stoke C	W 2-0	1-0	1	Malouda [32], Drogba (pen) [77]	40,931
4	Sept 11	A	West Ham U	W 3-1	2-0	1	Essien 2 [2, 83], Kalou [18]	33,014
5	19	H	Blackpool	W 4-0	4-0	1	Kalou [2], Malouda 2 [12, 41], Evatt (og) [30]	41,761
6	25	A	Manchester C ·	L 0-1	0-0	1		47,203
7	Oct 3	H	Arsenal	W 2-0	1-0	1	Drogba [39], Alex [85]	41,828
8	16	A	Aston Villa	D 0-0	0-0	1		40,122
9	23	H	Wolverhampton W	W 2-0	1-0	1	Malouda [23], Kalou [81]	41,752
10	30	A	Blackburn R	W 2-1	1-1	1	Anelka [39], Ivanovic [84]	25,836
11	Nov 7	A	Liverpool	L 0-2	0-2	1		44,238
12	10	H	Fulham	W 1-0	1-0	—	Essien [30]	41,593
13	14	H	Sunderland	L 0-3	0-1	1		41,072
14	20	A	Birmingham C	L 0-1	0-1	1		24,357
15	28	A	Newcastle U	D 1-1	1-1	2	Kalou [45]	46,469
16	Dec 4	H	Everton	D 1-1	1-0	3	Drogba (pen) [42]	41,642
17	12	A	Tottenham H	D 1-1	0-1	4	Drogba [70]	35,787
18	27	A	Arsenal	L 1-3	0-1	—	Ivanovic [57]	60,112
19	29	H	Bolton W	W 1-0	0-0	—	Malouda [61]	40,982
20	Jan 2	H	Aston Villa	D 3-3	1-1	5	Lampard (pen) [23], Drogba [84], Terry [89]	41,222
21	5	A	Wolverhampton W	L 0-1	0-1	5		26,432
22	15	H	Blackburn R	W 2-0	0-0	4	Ivanovic [57], Anelka [76]	40,846
23	24	A	Bolton W	W 4-0	2-0	—	Drogba [11], Malouda [41], Anelka [56], Ramires [74]	22,837
24	Feb 1	A	Sunderland	W 4-2	2-2	—	Lampard (pen) [15], Kalou [23], Terry [60], Anelka [90]	37,855
25	6	H	Liverpool	L 0-1	0-0	4		41,829
26	14	A	Fulham	D 0-0	0-0	—		25,685
27	Mar 1	H	Manchester U	W 2-1	0-0	—	Luiz [54], Lampard (pen) [80]	41,825
28	7	A	Blackpool	W 3-1	1-0	—	Terry [20], Lampard 2 (1 pen) [62 (p), 66]	15,584
29	20	H	Manchester C	W 2-0	0-0	3	Luiz [78], Ramires [90]	41,741
30	Apr 2	A	Stoke C	D 1-1	1-1	4	Drogba [33]	27,508
31	9	A	Wigan Ath	W 1-0	0-0	3	Malouda [67]	40,734
32	16	A	WBA	W 3-1	3-1	3	Drogba [22], Kalou [26], Lampard [45]	25,163
33	20	H	Birmingham C	W 3-1	2-0	—	Malouda 2 [3, 62], Kalou [26]	40,848
34	23	H	West Ham U	W 3-0	1-0	2	Lampard [44], Torres [84], Malouda [90]	41,656
35	30	H	Tottenham H	W 2-1	1-1	2	Lampard [45], Kalou [89]	41,681
36	May 8	A	Manchester U	L 1-2	0-2	2	Lampard [68]	75,445
37	15	H	Newcastle U	D 2-2	1-1	2	Ivanovic [2], Alex [83]	41,739
38	22	A	Everton	L 0-1	0-0	2		38,712

Final League Position: 2

GOALSCORERS

League (69): Malouda 13, Drogba 11 (2 pens), Kalou 10, Lampard 10 (4 pens), Anelka 6, Ivanovic 4, Essien 3, Terry 3, Alex 2, Luiz 2, Ramires 2, Benayoun 1, Torres 1, own goal 1.
Carling Cup (3): Anelka 2 (1 pen), Van Aanholt 1.
FA Cup (9): Lampard 3, Kalou 2, Sturridge 2, Anelka 1, own goal 1.
Champions League (17): Anelka 7 (1 pen), Drogba 2 (1 pen), Ivanovic 2, Sturridge 2, Essien 1, Malouda 1, Terry 1, Zhirkov 1.
Community Shield (1): Kalou 1.

Cech P 38	Paulo Ferreira 12 + 9	Cole A 38	Mikel J 28	Terry J 33	Alex 12 + 3	Essien M 32 + 1	Lampard F 23 + 1	Anelka N 27 + 5	Drogba D 30 + 6	Malouda F 33 + 5	Ivanovic B 32 + 2	Benayoun Y 1 + 6	Kalou S 16 + 15	Sturridge D — + 13	Ramires 22 + 7	Kakuta G 1 + 4	Bruma J 1 + 1	Zhirkov Y 6 + 6	McEachran J 1 + 8	Bosingwa J 13 + 7	Torres F 8 + 6	Luiz D 11 + 1	Bertrand R — + 1	Match No.
1	2^1	3	4	5	6	7	8^2	9	10^3	11	12	13	14											1
1	12	3	4	5	6	7^3	8	9	10	11^2	2^1	14	13											2
1	2	3	4	5	6	7^3	8^1	9^2	10	11		12	13	14										3
1	2	3	4	5^2	13	7		9^1	10	14	6		8^3		11	12								4
1	2	3	4^3		6^1	7		10	11	5	14	9		8^2		12	13							5
1		3	4^1	5	6	7		9	10^2	11	2		13	8^3		12	14							6
1	12	3	4^3	5	6	7		9	10	11	2^1		14	8^2		13								7
1	2^2	3	4	5		7		9		11	6		8^3	10^1		12	14	13						8
1	13	3	4	5		8		9	10	7^1	6		12		11^3	14	2^2							9
1	13	3	4	5	6	8		9^2	10	7^1	2		12		11									10
1		3	4	5	6		9	12	7	2^2		10^1	14	8		11^3	13							11
1	14	3	4	5		8^4		10	7^1	6		9^2	13	12	11	2^3								12
1	5	3	4				9	10	7^1	6		12		8^2	14		11^3	13	2					13
1	2^1	3	4		6		9	10	11	5		7	13	8^2			12							14
1		3	4^1		6		9	10	11	5		8	12	7			2							15
1	12	3	4^3	5		7		9^2	10	11	6		8	14	13		2^1							16
1	2	3	4^1	5		7	14	9	12	11^3	6		10^2	13	8									17
1	2^3	3	4^1	5		7	8		10	11^2	6		9		12	13		14						18
1	12	3		5		7	8	9^2	10	11	6		13		4			2^1						19
1	2^1	3		5		7	9^2	10	11			13	14	4^2	6		12							20
1		3		5		7	8	12^1	10	11^3	6		9^1	13	4^7	14		2						21
1		3		5		7^2	8	9^1	10	11^3	6		12	14	4			13	2					22
1		3	4^1	5		7		9	10	11	6		13		8^2			12	2					23
1	14	3	4^1	5		7	8	9	10	13	6		11^2		12			2^3						24
1		3	4^2	5		7	8	11	10	13	6		12					2^3		9^1	14			25
1		3		5		7	8	10^1	13	11	2		12		4					9^2	6			26
1		3		5		7	8	10^1	12	11^2	2		6			13		14	9	4^3				27
1		3		5		7	8		10^1	13			12		4^3			11^4	14	2	9	6		28
1		3		5		4	8	13	12	11^2	2		10^3		7			14			9^1	6		29
1		3		5		4	8	9^2	10	11	14		12		7^1					2^3	13	6		30
1	2^3	3	4^1		14		8	9^2	10	11	5	12		7						13	6			31
1		3	4	5		7	8^2		10^3	11	2^1	13	9							12	14	6		32
1	2	3^1	4	5		7	8	14	10	11^3			9^2							13	6	12		33
1		3	4	5		7^1	8	13	10^3	11	2	12	9^2							14	6			34
1		3	4	5		7^1	8	14	10	11^3	2		13		12					9^2	6			35
1		3	4^2	5	13	7	8		10	11	2		9^3		12					14	6^1			36
1		3		5	6	12	8	10	13	14	2	11^3		7^1					4^2		9			37
1	13	3	4^1	5	6^2	7^3	8	10		11	2		12						14		9			38

FA Cup

Third Round	Ipswich T	(h)	7-0
Fourth Round	Everton	(a)	1-1
		(h)	1-1

Champions League

Group F	Zilina	(a)	4-1
	Marseille	(h)	2-0
	Spartak Moscow	(a)	2-0
		(h)	4-1
	Zilina	(h)	2-1
	Marseille	(a)	0-1
Knock-Out Round	FC Copenhagen	(a)	2-0
		(h)	0-0
Quarter-Final	Manchester U	(h)	0-1
		(a)	1-2

Carling Cup

Third Round	Newcastle U	(h)	3-4

Community Shield

Manchester U		1-3
(at Wembley).		

CHELTENHAM TOWN   FL Championship 2

FOUNDATION

Although a scratch team representing Cheltenham played a match against Gloucester in 1884, the earliest recorded match for Cheltenham Town FC was a friendly against Dean Close School on 12 March 1892. The School won 4–3 and the match was played at Prestbury (half a mile from Whaddon Road). Cheltenham Town played Wednesday afternoon friendlies at a local cricket ground until entering the Mid Gloucester League. In those days the club played in deep red coloured shirts and were nicknamed 'the Rubies'. The club moved to Whaddon Lane for season 1901–02 and changed to red and white colours two years later.

The Abbey Business Stadium, Whaddon Road, Cheltenham, Gloucestershire GL52 5NA.

Telephone: (01242) 573 558.

Fax: (01242) 224 675.

Ticket Office: (01242) 573 558 (option 1).

Website: www.ctfc.com

Email: info@ctfc.com

Ground Capacity: 7,136.

Record Attendance: 10,389 v Blackpool, FA Cup 3rd rd, 13 January 1934 (at Cheltenham Athletic Ground). 8,326 v Reading, FA Cup 1st rd, 17 November 1956 (at Whaddon Road).

Pitch Measurements: 112yd × 72yd.

Chairman: Paul Baker.

Vice-chairman: Colin Farmer.

Secretary: Paul Godfrey.

Manager: Mark Yates.

Assistant Manager: Neil Howarth.

Physio: Ian Weston.

Colours: All red with white trim.

Change Colours: All black with red trim.

Year Formed: 1892.

Turned Professional: 1932.

Ltd Co.: 1937.

Club Nickname: 'The Robins'.

Grounds: Pre-1932, Agg-Gardner's Recreation Ground; Whaddon Lane; Carter's Lane; 1932, Whaddon Road.

HONOURS

Football League: Best Season Division 3 2001–02 (4th).

FA Cup: Best season: 5th rd 2002.

Football League Cup: never past 2nd rd.

Football Conference: *Champions* 1998–99, *Runners-up* 1997–98.

Trophy: *Winners* 1997–98.

Southern League: *Champions* 1984–85; **Southern League Cup:** *Winners* 1957–58, *runners-up* 1968–69, 1984–85; **Southern League Merit Cup:** *Winners* 1984–85; **Southern League Championship Shield:** *Winners* 1985.

Gloucestershire Senior Cup: *Winners* 1998–99; **Gloucestershire Northern Senior Professional Cup:** *Winners* 30 times; **Midland Floodlit Cup:** *Winners* 1985–86, 1986–87, 1987–88; **Mid Gloucester League:** *Champions* 1896–97; **Gloucester and District League:** *Champions* 1902–03, 1905–06; **Cheltenham League:** *Champions* 1910–11, 1913–14; **North Gloucestershire League:** *Champions* 1913–14; **Gloucestershire Northern Senior League:** *Champions* 1928–29, **1932–33;** **Gloucestershire Northern Senior Amateur Cup:** *Winners* 1929–30, 1930–31, 1932–33, 1933–34, 1934–35; **Leamington Hospital Cup:** *Winners* 1934–35.

sky SPORTS FACT FILE

Peter Hauser, a South African born wing-half and underground surveyor by profession, joined Cheltenham Town from Blackpool in 1962 while on the transfer list at £15,000. After a season he moved on, carving out a position for himself as Player-Manager of Chester.

Record League Victory: 11–0 v Bourneville Ath, Birmingham Combination, 29 April 1933 – Davis; Jones, Williams; Lang (1), Blackburn, Draper; Evans, Hazard (4), Haycox (4), Goodger (1), Hill (1).

Record Cup Victory: 12–0 v Chippenham R, FA Cup 3rd qual. rd, 2 November 1935 – Bowles; Whitehouse, Williams; Lang, Devonport (1), Partridge (2); Perkins, Hackett, Jones (4), Black (4), Griffiths (1).

Record Defeat: 0–7 v Crystal Palace, League Cup 2nd rd, 2 October 2002.
N.B. 1–10 v Merthyr T, Southern League, 8 March 1952.

Most League Points (2 for a win): 60, Southern League Division 1, 1963–64.

Most League Points (3 for a win): 78, Division 3, 2001–02.

Most League Goals: 66, Division 3, 2001–02.

Highest League Scorer in Season: Julian Alsop, 20, Division 3, 2001–02.

Most League Goals in Total Aggregate: Julian Alsop, 39, 2000–03; 2009–10.

Most League Goals in One Match: 3, Damien Spencer v Milton Keynes D, FL 1, 31 January 2009; 3, Michael Pook v Burton Alb, FL 2, 13 March 2010.

Most Capped Player: Grant McCann, 7 (33), Northern Ireland.

Most League Appearances: David Bird, 288, 2001–11.

Youngest League Player: Kyle Haynes, 17 years, 2 months, 26 days v Oldham Ath, FL 1, 24 March 2009.

Record Transfer Fee Received: £400,000 from Colchester U for Steve Gillespie, July 2008.

Record Transfer Fee Paid: £50,000 to West Ham U for Grant McCann, January 2003 and £50,000 to Stoke C for Brian Wilson, March 2004.

Football League Record: 1999 Promoted to Division 3; 2002 Division 2; 2003–04 Division 3; 2004–06 FL 2; 2006–09 FL 1; 2009– FL 2.

MANAGERS

George Blackburn 1932–34
George Carr 1934–37
Jimmy Brain 1937–48
Cyril Dean 1948–50
George Summerbee 1950–52
William Raeside 1952–53
Arch Anderson 1953–58
Ron Lewin 1958–60
Peter Donnelly 1960–61
Tommy Cavanagh 1961
Arch Anderson 1961–65
Harold Fletcher 1965–66
Bob Etheridge 1966–73
Willie Penman 1973–74
Dennis Allen 1974–79
Terry Paine 1979
Alan Grundy 1979–82
Alan Wood 1982–83
John Murphy 1983–88
Jim Barron 1988–90
John Murphy 1990
Dave Lewis 1990–91
Ally Robertson 1991–92
Lindsay Parsons 1992–95
Chris Robinson 1995–97
Steve Cotterill 1997–2002
Graham Allner 2002–03
Bobby Gould 2003
John Ward 2003–07
Keith Downing 2007–08
Martin Allen 2008–09
Mark Yates December 2009–

LATEST SEQUENCES

Longest Sequence of League Wins: 4, 29.4.2006 – 8.8.2006.
Longest Sequence of League Defeats: 7, 27.1.2009 – 28.2.2009
Longest Sequence of League Draws: 5, 5.4.2003 – 21.4.2003.
Longest Sequence of Unbeaten League Matches: 16, 1.12.2001 – 12.3.2002.
Longest Sequence Without a League Win: 14, 20.12.2008 – 7.3.2009
Successive Scoring Runs: 17 from 16.2.2008.
Successive Non-scoring Runs: 4 from 12.9.1999.

TEN YEAR LEAGUE RECORD

		P	W	D	L	F	A	Pts	Pos
2001-02	Div 3	46	21	15	10	66	49	78	4
2002-03	Div 2	46	10	18	18	53	68	48	21
2003-04	Div 3	46	14	14	18	57	71	56	14
2004-05	FL 2	46	16	12	18	51	54	60	14
2005-06	FL 2	46	19	15	12	65	53	72	5
2006-07	FL 1	46	15	9	22	49	61	54	17
2007-08	FL 1	46	13	12	21	42	64	51	19
2008-09	FL 1	46	9	12	25	51	91	39	23
2009-10	FL 2	46	10	18	18	54	71	48	22
2010-11	FL 2	46	13	13	20	56	77	52	17

DID YOU KNOW ?

In the post-war period, Cheltenham Town signed two players from Bristol City both also Gloucestershire County cricketers. Midfield player Bobby Etheridge came in 1964–65 while goalkeeper Ron Nicholls originally transferred to Bristol Rovers from Cheltenham in 1954.

CHELTENHAM TOWN 2010–11 LEAGUE RECORD

Match No.	Date	Venue	Opponents	Result		H/T Score	Lg Pos.	Goalscorers	Attendance
1	Aug 7	A	Gillingham	D	1-1	0-0	—	Thomas [53]	5655
2	14	H	Crewe Alex	W	3-2	2-1	4	Thomas 2 [22, 42], Goulding [62]	3537
3	21	A	Rotherham U	L	4-6	3-2	12	Goulding [4], Thomas [28], Jeffers [36], Lowe [90]	3072
4	28	H	Burton Alb	W	2-1	0-1	6	Thomas [80], Low [82]	3221
5	Sept 4	A	Barnet	L	1-3	1-1	12	Artus [2]	2082
6	11	H	Stevenage	W	1-0	0-0	6	Thomas [69]	2805
7	18	A	Chesterfield	L	0-3	0-1	8		5503
8	25	H	Bury	L	0-2	0-1	15		2758
9	28	H	Oxford U	D	1-1	1-0	—	Thomas [29]	4349
10	Oct 2	A	Aldershot T	W	2-0	1-0	12	Andrew [13], Goulding [62]	2509
11	9	H	Northampton T	W	1-0	0-0	7	Smikle [60]	3016
12	16	A	Bradford C	L	1-3	1-1	9	Low [7]	10,537
13	23	H	Port Vale	D	0-0	0-0	10		3167
14	30	A	Accrington S	W	4-2	2-0	7	Smikle [4], Goulding 2 [18, 74], Shroot [80]	1427
15	Nov 13	A	Hereford U	D	1-1	0-1	10	Goulding [65]	3264
16	20	H	Morecambe	D	1-1	1-0	10	Low [43]	2524
17	23	A	Macclesfield T	W	2-0	2-0	—	Low [8], Smikle [32]	1870
18	Dec 11	A	Shrewsbury T	D	1-1	1-0	8	Thomas [26]	4901
19	14	H	Southend U	L	0-2	0-2	—		2229
20	28	H	Bradford C	W	4-0	2-0	—	Goulding 2 [31, 67], Pack [35], Thomas [76]	2666
21	Jan 1	H	Wycombe W	L	1-2	1-1	8	Andrew [12]	3326
22	3	A	Southend U	W	2-1	2-0	7	Pack [4], Thomas [5]	4942
23	8	A	Northampton T	D	1-1	0-1	8	Thomas [48]	4031
24	15	H	Accrington S	L	1-2	0-1	10	Thomas [83]	2736
25	22	A	Port Vale	W	1-0	0-0	9	Goulding [55]	5163
26	25	H	Lincoln C	L	1-2	1-2	—	Artus [31]	2292
27	29	A	Oxford U	D	1-1	1-1	—	Thomas [25]	7738
28	Feb 1	H	Wycombe W	L	1-2	0-1	11	Thomas [56]	3409
29	5	A	Morecambe	D	1-1	0-0	11	Artus [69]	10,691
30	12	H	Hereford U	L	0-3	0-1	12		3643
31	19	H	Barnet	D	1-1	0-0	12	Thomas [61]	2926
32	22	A	Torquay U	D	2-2	0-1	—	Goulding [79], Thomas [90]	2977
33	26	A	Stevenage	L	0-4	0-2	14		2733
34	Mar 1	H	Stockport Co	W	2-1	1-1	—	Thomson [22], Thomas [67]	2191
35	5	H	Chesterfield	L	0-3	0-1	13		2870
36	12	H	Aldershot T	L	1-2	0-1	16	Pook [83]	2697
37	19	A	Bury	W	3-2	2-1	15	Gallinagh [3], Low 2 [7, 68]	2870
38	22	A	Torquay U	L	1-2	0-1	—	Andrew [89]	2186
39	27	H	Gillingham	L	1-2	1-0	—	Elliott [3]	3157
40	Apr 2	A	Crewe Alex	L	1-8	0-4	15	Thomas [50]	3682
41	9	H	Rotherham U	D	1-1	0-1	16	Gallinagh [62]	2413
42	16	A	Burton Alb	L	0-2	0-1	16		2444
43	23	H	Macclesfield T	L	0-1	0-1	18		2757
44	25	A	Lincoln C	W	2-0	0-0	17	Low [65], Andrew [88]	3007
45	30	H	Shrewsbury T	L	0-1	0-1	18		4288
46	May 7	A	Stockport Co	D	1-1	1-0	17	Smikle [23]	5027

Final League Position: 17

GOALSCORERS

League (56): Thomas 18, Goulding 10, Low 7, Andrew 4, Smikle 4, Artus 3, Gallinagh 2, Pack 2, Elliott 1, Jeffers 1, Lowe 1, Pook 1, Shroot 1, Thomson 1.
Carling Cup (1): Jeffers 1.
FA Cup (1): Thomas 1.
J Paint Trophy (0).

Brown S 46	Lowe K 36	Andrew D 43	Pook M 25+4	Elliott S 39+2	Riley M 26	Low J 28+2	Artus F 21+8	Thomas W 40+1	Goulding J 34+5	Smikle B 37+9	Bird D 27+12	Jeffers S 3+19	Melligan J 14+13	Shroot R 4+3	Pack M 32+6	Gallinagh A 20+4	Lewis T 8+14	Watkins M —+1	Eastham A 8+1	Walsh P —+4	Green M 10+9	Thomson J 3+2	Elito M 1+1	Haynes K 1	Match No.
1	2	3	4	5	6	7	8^3	9^1	10^2	11	12	13	14												1
1	2	3	4	5	6^1	7	8	9^1	10^3	11	12	13	14												2
1	6	3	4	5		7^3	8	9	10^1	11	2	12	14	13											3
1	2	3	4	5	6^1	7	8	9	10^3	11^2	12		14	13											4
1	6	3	4	5		7	8^1	9	10^3	11	2^2		14	13	12										5
1	2	3	4	5		7		9	14	12		10^1	11^2		8^1	13	6								6
1	2	3	4	5				9^2	12	7	13	10^1	11^3		8	6	14								7
1	2	3	4^1	5				9	10	7	13	12	11^3		8^2	6	14								8
1	2	3	4	5				9^2	10	11	8	12	7^1		6	13									9
1	2	3	4	5		7			10	11^2	8	13	9^1		6	12									10
1	2	3	4^1	5		7			10	11	8		9		6	12									11
1	2	3	4^1	5		7	12		10	11		13	8		6		9^2								12
1	2	3		5^3		7	8^1		10	11	14	13	9^2		4	6	12								13
1	2		6		7	10^1	11	3	12		8	9^2			4	5	13								14
1	2	3				7	13	12	10	11	4	8^1	9^2		6	5									15
1	2	3^3			6	7	8^1	9^2	10	11	12	14	13		4	5									16
1	2	3	13		6	7^2		9^1	10	11	4	12			8	5									17
1	2	3	13		6	7		9^2	10^1	11	4	12			8	5									18
1	2	3	14		6	7^1		9	10	11	4^2	13	12		8	5^3									19
1	2	3	4^1	5	6			9^2	10	11	12	13	7^3		8			14							20
1	2	3	4^1	5	6			9	10	11^2	12	13	7		8										21
1	2	3	4	5	6^1			9^3	10^2	11	14	13	7		8	12									22
1	2	3	4	5		12		9^3	10^2	11	14		7^1		8				6		13				23
1	2	3	4	5^3		12	13	9	10	11^2			7^1		8				6		14				24
1	2	3		5	11^1	7		9^2	10^3	12	4	13			8				6		14				25
1	2	3		5	11^1	7^2		9	10	13	4	12			8^3				6		14				26
1	2	3		5	6	7^1		9	10	11	4				8				12						27
1	2	3		5^2		7^1		9	10	11	4				8	13			6		12				28
1	2	3		5^1	6	7		9^1	10	11	4				8^2	13			12		14				29
1	2	3		5	6	7^2		9	10^3	11^1	4	13			8				12		14				30
1	2	3	14	5	6	12		9^3	13	11	4		7^2		8^1						10				31
1	2^1	3		5	6	7		9	10	11^2	4	12	13		8										32
1		3		5	6^1	13	7	9	10	14	2^2				8	12					11		4^3		33
1		3	4	5	2	14		9	10	12	13				8^2				6		11^3	7^1			34
1		3	4	5	2			9	10^2	13	14				8^3				6		11	7^1	12		35
1	2		4	5	3			9	12	11^2	8		7^3						6		13	14	10^1		36
1	2	3	8		6	7	11^1	9^2		12	4	13			5						10				37
1	2	3	8		6	7^3		11^1	9	12	14				4	5					10^2	13			38
1	2^1	3		5	6	7	8^3	9	10	13	12				4						11^2	14			39
1		3	4^2	5	6	7^3		9	10^1	11	2	13			8						14		12		40
1		3	13	5	6	12		9		11	4		7^1		8	2					10^2				41
1		3	12	5	6	7^2		9		11	4				8	2^4	13				10^1				42
1		3		5	6	7^2		9		11	4	13			8	2^1	12				10				43
1		3	10	5	6	2	14	9^3		11^2	4	13			8						7^1		12		44
1		3	4	5^1	6	7^3		9		11	2	14			8	12					10^2	13			45
1		3			6	7	8^2	9^3		11	13	14			4	5					10^1	12		2	46

FA Cup
First Round   Morecambe   (h)   1-0
Second Round   Southampton   (a)   0-3

Carling Cup
First Round   Brentford   (a)   1-2

J Paint Trophy
Second Round   Plymouth Arg   (h)   0-2

CHESTERFIELD FL Championship 1

FOUNDATION

Chesterfield are fourth only to Stoke, Notts County and Nottingham Forest in age for they can trace their existence as far back as 1866, although it is fair to say that they were somewhat casual in the first few years of their history playing only a few friendlies a year. However, their rules of 1871 are still in existence showing an annual membership of 2s (10p), but it was not until 1891 that they won a trophy (the Barnes Cup) and followed this a year later by winning the Sheffield Cup, Barnes Cup and the Derbyshire Junior Cup.

b2net stadium, 1866 Sheffield Road, Whittington Moor, Chesterfield S41 8NZ.
Telephone: (01246) 209 765.
Fax: (01246) 556 799.
Ticket Office: (01246) 209 765.
Website: www.chesterfield-fc.co.uk
Email: reception@chesterfield-fc.co.uk
Ground Capacity: 8,502.
Record Attendance: 30,968 v Newcastle U, Division 2, 7 April 1939 (at Saltergate).
Pitch Measurements: 111yd × 71yd.
Chairman: Barrie Hubbard.
Vice-chairman: David C. Jones.
Managing Director: Mike Warner.
Finance Director: Alan Walters.
Manager: John Sheridan.
Assistant Manager: Tommy Wright.
Physio: Jamie Hewitt.
Colours: Blue shirts with white trim, white shorts, white stockings.
Change Colours: Red shirts with white sleeves, red shorts, red stockings.
Year Formed: 1866.
Turned Professional: 1891.
Ltd Co: 1871.
Previous Name: 1867, Chesterfield Town; 1919, Chesterfield.
Club Nicknames: 'Blues' or 'Spireites'.
Grounds: 1867, Drill Field; 1871, Recreation Ground; 2010, b2net stadium.
First Football League Game: 2 September 1899, Division 2, v Sheffield W (a) L 1–5 – Hancock; Pilgrim, Fletcher; Ballantyne, Bell, Downie; Morley, Thacker, Gooing, Munday (1), Geary.
Record League Victory: 10–0 v Glossop NE, Division 2, 17 January 1903 – Clutterbuck; Thorpe, Lerper; Haig, Banner, Thacker; Tomlinson (2), Newton (1), Milward (3), Munday (2), Steel (2).
Record Cup Victory: 5–0 v Wath Ath (a), FA Cup 1st rd, 28 November 1925 – Birch; Saxby, Dennis; Wass, Abbott, Thompson; Fisher (1), Roseboom (1), Cookson (2), Whitfield (1), Hopkinson.

HONOURS

Football League – Division 2:
Best season: 4th, 1946–47;
Division 3 (N): *Champions* 1930–31, 1935–36; *Runners-up* 1933–34;
FL 2: *Champions* 2010–11;
Division 4: *Champions* 1969–70, 1984–85.
FA Cup: Semi-final 1997.
Football League Cup: Best season: 4th rd, 1965, 2007.
Anglo-Scottish Cup: *Winners* 1981.

sky SPORTS FACT FILE

On 2 October 2010 Chesterfield found itself losing 4-1 at home to Crewe Alexandra after just 26 minutes. With two minutes remaining the visitors were still leading 5-3, before the Spireites rallied to level the scores, Craig Clay equalising in the 92nd minute during added time.

Record Defeat: 0–10 v Gillingham, Division 3, 5 September 1987.

Most League Points (2 for a win): 64, Division 4, 1969–70.

Most League Points (3 for a win): 91, Division 4, 1984–85.

Most League Goals: 102, Division 3 (N), 1930–31.

Highest League Scorer in Season: Jimmy Cookson, 44, Division 3 (N), 1925–26.

Most League Goals in Total Aggregate: Ernie Moss, 161, 1969–76, 1979–81 and 1984–86.

Most League Goals in One Match: 4, Jimmy Cookson v Accrington S, Division 3 (N), 16 January 1926; 4, Jimmy Cookson v Ashington, Division 3 (N), 1 May 1926; 4, Jimmy Cookson v Wigan Borough, Division 3 (N), 4 September 1926; 4, Tommy Lyon v Southampton, Division 2, 3 December 1938.

Most Capped Player: Walter McMillen, 4 (7), Northern Ireland; Mark Williams, 4 (30), Northern Ireland.

Most League Appearances: Dave Blakey, 613, 1948–67.

Youngest League Player: Dennis Thompson, 16 years 160 days v Notts Co, 26 December 1950.

Record Transfer Fee Received: £750,000 from Southampton for Kevin Davies, May 1997.

Record Transfer Fee Paid: £250,000 to Watford for Jason Lee, August 1998.

Football League Record: 1899 Elected to Division 2; 1909 failed re-election; 1921–31 Division 3 (N); 1931–33 Division 2; 1933–36 Division 3 (N); 1936–51 Division 2; 1951–58 Division 3 (N); 1958–61 Division 3, 1961–70 Division 4; 1970–83 Division 3; 1983–85 Division 4; 1985–89 Division 3; 1989–92 Division 4; 1992–95 Division 3; 1995–2000 Division 2; 2000–01 Division 3; 2001–04 Division 2; 2004–07 FL 1; 2007–11 FL 2; 2011– FL 1.

LATEST SEQUENCES

Longest Sequence of League Wins: 10, 6.9.1933 – 4.11.1933.

Longest Sequence of League Defeats: 9, 22.10.1960 – 27.12.1960.

Longest Sequence of League Draws: 8, 26.11.2005 – 2.1.2006.

Longest Sequence of Unbeaten League Matches: 21, 26.12.1994 – 29.4.1995.

Longest Sequence Without a League Win: 18, 11.9.1999 – 3.1.2000.

Successive Scoring Runs: 46 from 25.12.1929.

Successive Non-scoring Runs: 7 from 23.9.1977.

MANAGERS

E. Russell Timmeus 1891–95 (*Secretary-Manager*)
Gilbert Gillies 1895–1901
E. F. Hind 1901–02
Jack Hoskin 1902–06
W. Furness 1906–07
George Swift 1907–10
G. H. Jones 1911–13
R. L. Weston 1913–17
T. Callaghan 1919
J. J. Caffrey 1920–22
Harry Hadley 1922
Harry Parkes 1922–27
Alec Campbell 1927
Ted Davison 1927–32
Bill Harvey 1932–38
Norman Bullock 1938–45
Bob Brocklebank 1945–48
Bobby Marshall 1948–52
Ted Davison 1952–58
Duggie Livingstone 1958–62
Tony McShane 1962–67
Jimmy McGuigan 1967–73
Joe Shaw 1973–76
Arthur Cox 1976–80
Frank Barlow 1980–83
John Duncan 1983–87
Kevin Randall 1987–88
Paul Hart 1988–91
Chris McMenemy 1991–93
John Duncan 1993–2000
Nicky Law 2000–01
Dave Rushbury 2002–03
Roy McFarland 2003–07
Lee Richardson 2007–09
John Sheridan June 2009–

TEN YEAR LEAGUE RECORD

		P	W	D	L	F	A	Pts	Pos
2001-02	Div 2	46	13	13	20	53	65	52	18
2002-03	Div 2	46	14	8	24	43	73	50	20
2003-04	Div 2	46	12	15	19	49	71	51	20
2004-05	FL 1	46	14	15	17	55	62	57	17
2005-06	FL 1	46	14	14	18	63	73	56	16
2006-07	FL 1	46	12	11	23	45	53	47	21
2007-08	FL 2	46	19	12	15	76	56	69	8
2008-09	FL 2	46	16	15	15	62	57	63	10
2009-10	FL 2	46	21	7	18	61	62	70	8
2010-11	FL 2	46	24	14	8	85	51	86	1

DID YOU KNOW ?

Centre-forward Tommy Swinscoe was discovered at 26 in wartime services football playing in representative matches in Italy. Previously with Shirebrook Supporters, he signed for Chesterfield and was joint top scorer in 1946–47 with 13 goals during the club's best season.

CHESTERFIELD 2010–11 LEAGUE RECORD

Match No.	Date	Venue	Opponents	Result	H/T Score	Lg Pos.	Goalscorers	Attendance
1	Aug 7	H	Barnet	W 2-1	1-0	—	Mattis [24], Lester [59]	6431
2	14	A	Port Vale	D 1-1	0-1	5	Mattis [79]	6444
3	21	H	Hereford U	W 4-0	2-0	2	Whitaker 3 (1 pen) [9 (p), 33, 60], Forde [63]	4970
4	28	A	Macclesfield T	D 1-1	0-0	4	Davies [68]	2176
5	Sept 4	H	Lincoln C	W 2-1	1-0	3	Mattis [36], Davies [62]	6429
6	11	A	Morecambe	D 1-1	0-1	4	Boden [83]	2323
7	18	H	Cheltenham T	W 3-0	1-0	3	Talbot [14], Davies 2 [48, 66]	5503
8	25	A	Rotherham U	L 0-1	0-0	4		5365
9	28	A	Northampton T	W 2-1	0-1	—	Morgan [71], Davies [75]	4025
10	Oct 2	H	Crewe Alex	D 5-5	1-4	2	Lester 2 [23, 74], Whitaker 2 (2 pens) [79, 89], Clay [90]	6047
11	9	H	Southend U	W 2-1	1-1	2	Whitaker (pen) [27], Boden [90]	6557
12	16	A	Wycombe W	W 2-1	1-0	1	Davies 2 [27, 73]	5211
13	23	H	Shrewsbury T	W 4-3	3-0	1	Talbot [29], Lester [42], Davies 2 [45, 62]	7777
14	30	A	Stevenage	D 0-0	0-0	1		3556
15	Nov 2	H	Accrington S	W 5-2	3-1	—	Davies 2 [8, 88], Whitaker 2 (1 pen) [41 (p), 56], Lester [42]	6034
16	13	A	Burton Alb	L 1-2	1-1	1	Niven [44]	7864
17	20	A	Aldershot T	W 2-0	0-0	1	Davies [61], Whitaker [63]	2479
18	23	H	Oxford U	L 1-2	1-0	—	Morris [14]	5929
19	Dec 11	H	Torquay U	W 1-0	1-0	1	Lester [28]	4801
20	Jan 1	H	Stockport Co	W 4-1	1-1	1	Lester 3 [13, 62, 67], Davies [90]	7542
21	3	A	Accrington S	D 2-2	0-2	1	Smalley [88], Boden [90]	2041
22	8	A	Southend U	W 3-2	2-0	1	Whitaker 2 (2 pens) [12, 62], Smalley [19]	5021
23	15	H	Stevenage	W 1-0	1-0	1	Talbot [42]	6219
24	22	A	Shrewsbury T	D 0-0	0-0	1		6483
25	25	A	Gillingham	W 2-0	1-0	—	Smalley 2 [13, 49]	4770
26	29	H	Bradford C	D 2-2	1-1	—	Whitaker [11], Bowery [90]	7556
27	Feb 1	A	Stockport Co	D 1-1	0-0	1	Smalley [74]	4092
28	5	H	Aldershot T	D 2-2	1-1	1	Smalley 2 [7, 84]	5669
29	11	A	Burton Alb	L 0-1	0-1	—		4260
30	15	A	Bury	D 1-1	1-0	—	Davies [20]	2517
31	19	A	Lincoln C	W 2-0	1-0	1	Davies [15], Holden [84]	4172
32	22	A	Bradford C	W 1-0	1-0	1	Smalley [16]	10,782
33	26	H	Morecambe	L 0-2	0-1	1		6441
34	Mar 1	H	Wycombe W	W 4-1	2-0	—	Smalley [27], Whitaker (pen) [36], Lester [46], Davies [88]	6392
35	5	A	Cheltenham T	W 3-0	1-0	1	Davies 2 [34, 87], Djilali [47]	2870
36	8	H	Northampton T	W 2-1	0-0	1	Davies [63], Lester [68]	5661
37	12	A	Crewe Alex	L 0-2	0-1	1		4503
38	18	H	Rotherham U	W 5-0	3-0	—	Holden [21], Davies [31], Lester 3 [45, 81, 83]	10,089
39	26	A	Barnet	D 2-2	1-0	—	Smalley [21], Davies [46]	2012
40	Apr 2	H	Port Vale	W 2-0	0-0	1	Lester [48], Smalley [71]	8606
41	9	A	Hereford U	L 0-3	0-1	1		2492
42	16	A	Macclesfield T	W 2-1	0-1	1	Davies [60], Whitaker [76]	8206
43	23	A	Oxford U	D 0-0	0-0	1		8195
44	25	H	Bury	L 2-3	0-1	1	Davies [50], Lester [63]	9614
45	29	A	Torquay U	D 0-0	0-0	—		5002
46	May 7	H	Gillingham	W 3-1	0-0	1	Whitaker [54], Lester [76], Smalley [82]	10,023

Final League Position: 1

GOALSCORERS

League (85): Davies 23, Lester 17, Whitaker 15 (8 pens), Smalley 12, Boden 3, Mattis 3, Talbot 3, Holden 2, Bowery 1, Clay 1, Djilali 1, Forde 1, Morgan 1, Morris 1, Niven 1.
Carling Cup (1): Mattis 1.
FA Cup (3): Boden 1, Bowery 1, Davies 1.
J Paint Trophy (4): Morgan 2, Bowery 1, Davies 1.

Lee T 46	Hunt J 18 + 2	Morris J 113 + 6	Mattis D 35 + 3	Breckin J 119 + 6	Forde S 31	Talbot D 44	Allott M 33 + 3	Davies C 41	Lester J 29 + 11	Whitaker D 43 + 3	Griffiths S 28 + 1	Bowery J 5 + 22	Niven D 24 + 11	Boden S 2 + 21	Morgan D 18 + 3	Clay C 1 + 2	Gray D 1 + 1	Lomax K 3 + 1	Smalley D 22 + 6	Robertson G 21	Page R — + 1	Vidal J 5 + 1	Holden D 17	Djilali K 7 + 3	Lowry J — + 3	Match No.
1	2	3¹	4	5	6	7	8	9⁸	10²	11	12	13														1
1	2		9	5	6	7	8		10²	11	3	12	4¹	13												2
1	2		4	5	6	7	8²		10¹	11	3	12	13	14	9³											3
1	2		4	5	6	7	8	9	10¹	11	3				12											4
1	2		5	14	6	7	8	9²	10¹	4	3	12	13		11³											5
1	2		4		5	7²	8	9		6	3	10¹	12	13	11											6
1	2		4		5	7¹	8³	9	10²	6	3		12	13	11	14										7
1	2		4		5	7	8¹	9	10²	6	3		12		11		13									8
1	2		4	5	6	7¹		9	12	11	3		8		10											9
1	2		4	5¹	6			9	10	7	3		8		11	12										10
1	2	12	5		4	6	7		9²	10³	8	3	14	4	13	11¹										11
1	2	3¹	4		6	7			9	12	11	5	10²	8	13											12
1		12	4		5	7	8¹	9³	10²	11	3	13	6	14		2										13
1	2		4		5	7	8	9	12	11	3	10¹	6													14
1	2¹		4		5	7	8	9	10³	11	3		6²	14					12	13						15
1	2		4		5	7	8	9²	10¹	11		13	6⁴		12				3							16
1	2	6¹	4		5	7	8	9³	10²	11		14		13					3	12						17
1	2	4²		6	7	8	9	10¹	11		13		12		3³			5	14							18
1			4	5	6	7	8		10²	11		9¹	2	13					12	3						19
1	13	12	4²	5	2	7		9	10³	8		14	6		11¹					3						20
1	12	11¹	4	5	2	7			10³	8		9²	6	14					13	3						21
1	2	11¹	4	5	8	7			10			13	12						9²	3						22
1			4	5	2	7	8	9¹	10	11		6							12	3						23
1			4	5	6	7	8	9¹	12	11		13							10⁷	3	2					24
1		6	4		5	7	8	9²	12	11		13							10¹	3	2					25
1			4	5	2¹	7	8	9	10²	11		14	6³						13	3	12					26
1	6¹	4	5		7	8	9			11	3	12	13						10²		2					27
1	12	4	5		7	8	9	10²	6	3	13								11		2					28
1		4¹	12	5	7	8	9²		11	3	13	6¹	14						10			2				29
1	4		12	5		7	9		8²		13	14							10⁸	3	6¹	2	11³			30
1	8			5	6¹	7		9	13	12		4	10²							3		2	11¹³	14		31
1	4			5		7		9	12	13		6	10¹						8	3		2	11²			32
1	6			5		7		9	10²	12		4³	13						8	3		2	11¹	14		33
1	13			7		9³	10¹		6	3		4	12	11²					8	5		2	14			34
1				7	13	9		6	3			4³	12	10²					8	5		2	11¹	14		35
1	14			7	8	9²	10³	6	3	13		4¹							11	5		2	12			36
1	3			7	12	9	13	6				4¹	14	10³					8	5		2	11²			37
1	14			7	8³	9¹	10²	6	3	12			11						4	5		2	13			38
1	12			7	8	9	13	6	3				10²						4	5		2	11¹			39
1	5¹	12		7	8	9	10²	6		14	13	11							4³	3		2				40
1	4	14		7	12	9	10²	6		3¹		13	11						8	5³		2				41
1	5			7	8	9	10¹	6	3			12	11						4			2				42
1	6	5		7	8	9²	14	11	3			12	4³	13	10¹				2							43
1	5			7	8	9	10	6	3²	13	12	11¹							4			2				44
1	12	6		5	7	8	9	13	11	3		10¹							4²			2				45
1	4²	13	5	7	8	9¹	10³	6	3			14	12						11			2				46

FA Cup
First Round   Harrow Bor   (a)   2-0
Second Round   Burton Alb   (a)   1-3

Carling Cup
First Round   Middlesbrough   (h)   1-2

J Paint Trophy
First Round   Walsall   (a)   2-1
Second Round   Sheffield W   (a)   2-2

COLCHESTER UNITED   FL Championship 1

FOUNDATION

Colchester United was formed in 1937 when a number of enthusiasts of the much older Colchester Town club decided to establish a professional concern as a limited liability company. The new club continued at Layer Road which had been the amateur club's home since 1909.

Weston Homes Community Stadium, United Way, Colchester, Essex CO4 5UP.

Telephone: (01206) 755 100.

Fax: (01206) 755 112.

Ticket Office: (0845) 437 9089.

Website: www.cu-fc.com

Email: caroline@colchesterunited.net

Ground Capacity: 10,000.

Record Attendance: 19,072 v Reading, FA Cup 1st rd, 27 November 1948 (at Layer Road). 10,064 v Norwich C, FL 1, 16 January 2010 (at Community Stadium).

Pitch Measurements: 106m × 68m.

Executive Chairman: Robbie Cowling.

Vice-chairman: Richard Cowling.

Football Secretary: Caroline Pugh.

Manager: John Ward.

Assistant Manager: Joe Dunne.

Physio: Tony Flynn.

Colours: Royal blue and white striped shirts with white sleeves, royal blue shorts, white stockings.

Change Colours: All black.

Year Formed: 1937.

Turned Professional: 1937.

Ltd Co.: 1937.

Club Nickname: 'The U's'.

Grounds: 1937, Layer Road; 2008, Weston Homes Community Stadium.

First Football League Game: 19 August 1950, Division 3 (S), v Gillingham (a) D 0–0 – Wright; Kettle, Allen; Bearryman, Stewart, Elder; Jones, Curry, Turner, McKim, Church.

Record League Victory: 9–1 v Bradford C, Division 4, 30 December 1961 – Ames; Millar, Fowler; Harris, Abrey, Ron Hunt; Foster, Bobby Hunt (4), King (4), Hill (1), Wright.

HONOURS

Football League – FL 1:
Runners-up 2005–06;
Division 4: *Runners-up* 1961–62.
FA Cup: Best season: 6th rd, 1971.
Football League Cup: Best season: 5th rd, 1975.
Auto Windscreens Shield: *Runners-up* 1997.
GM Vauxhall Conference: *Winners* 1991–92.
FA Trophy: *Winners* 1992.

sky SPORTS FACT FILE

Signed from West Ham United in 1948, winger Stan Foxall became a firm favourite at Layer Road. After two seasons Colchester United gained Football League status and since he had received injury compensation with the Hammers he was unable to play for the U's again.

Record Cup Victory: 9-1 v Leamington, FA Cup 1st rd, 5 November 2005 – Davison; Stockley (Garcia), Duguid, Brown (1), Chilvers, Watson (1), Halford (1), Izzet (Danns) (2), Iwelumo (1) (Williams), Cureton (2), Yeates (1).

Record Defeat: 0–8 v Leyton Orient, Division 4, 15 October 1988.

Most League Points (2 for a win): 60, Division 4, 1973–74.

Most League Points (3 for a win): 81, Division 4, 1982–83.

Most League Goals: 104, Division 4, 1961–62.

Highest League Scorer in Season: Bobby Hunt, 38, Division 4, 1961–62.

Most League Goals in Total Aggregate: Martyn King, 130, 1956–64.

Most League Goals in One Match: 4, Bobby Hunt v Bradford C, Division 4, 30 December 1961; 4, Martyn King v Bradford C, Division 4, 30 December 1961; 4, Bobby Hunt v Doncaster R, Division 4, 30 April 1962.

Most Capped Player: Bela Balogh, 2 (9), Hungary.

Most League Appearances: Micky Cook, 613, 1969–84.

Youngest League Player: Lindsay Smith, 16 years 218 days v Grimsby T, 24 April 1971.

Record Transfer Fee Received: £2,500,000 from Reading for Greg Halford, January 2007.

Record Transfer Fee Paid: £400,000 to Cheltenham T for Steve Gillespie, July 2008.

MANAGERS

Ted Fenton 1946–48
Jimmy Allen 1948–53
Jack Butler 1953–55
Benny Fenton 1955–63
Neil Franklin 1963–68
Dick Graham 1968–72
Jim Smith 1972–75
Bobby Roberts 1975–82
Allan Hunter 1982–83
Cyril Lea 1983–86
Mike Walker 1986–87
Roger Brown 1987–88
Jock Wallace 1989
Mick Mills 1990
Ian Atkins 1990–91
Roy McDonough 1991–94
George Burley 1994
Steve Wignall 1995–99
Mick Wadsworth 1999
Steve Whitton 1999–2003
Phil Parkinson 2003–06
Geraint Williams 2006–08
Paul Lambert 2008–09
Aidy Boothroyd 2009–10
John Ward May 2010–

Football League Record: 1950 Elected to Division 3 (S); 1958–61 Division 3; 1961–62 Division 4; 1962–65 Division 3; 1965–66 Division 4; 1966–68 Division 3; 1968–74 Division 4; 1974–76 Division 3; 1976–77 Division 4; 1977–81 Division 3; 1981–90 Division 4; 1990–92 GM Vauxhall Conference; 1992–98 Division 3; 1998–04 Division 2; 2004–06 FL 1; 2006–08 FL C; 2008– FL 1.

LATEST SEQUENCES

Longest Sequence of League Wins: 7, 29.11.1968 – 1.2.1969.

Longest Sequence of League Defeats: 8, 9.10.1954 – 4.12.1954.

Longest Sequence of League Draws: 6, 21.3.1977 – 11.4.1977.

Longest Sequence of Unbeaten League Matches: 20, 22.12.1956 – 19.4.1957.

Longest Sequence Without a League Win: 20, 2.3.1968 – 31.8.1968.

Successive Scoring Runs: 24 from 15.9.1962.

Successive Non-scoring Runs: 5 from 7.4.1981.

TEN YEAR LEAGUE RECORD

		P	W	D	L	F	A	Pts	Pos
2001-02	Div 2	46	15	12	19	65	76	57	15
2002-03	Div 2	46	14	16	16	52	56	58	12
2003-04	Div 2	46	17	13	16	52	56	64	11
2004-05	FL 1	46	14	17	15	60	50	59	15
2005-06	FL 1	46	22	13	11	58	40	79	2
2006-07	FL C	46	20	9	17	70	56	69	10
2007-08	FL C	46	7	17	22	62	86	38	24
2008-09	FL 1	46	18	9	19	58	58	63	12
2009-10	FL 1	46	20	12	14	64	52	72	8
2010-11	FL 1	46	16	14	16	57	63	62	10

DID YOU KNOW ?

In 1937–38 Colchester United sold Reg Smith to Wolverhampton Wanderers, Cliff Fairchild to Arsenal. As part of the deal a Challenge Match was arranged at Layer Road between the Wolves and the Gunners. A then record crowd of 17,000 watched Wolves win 1-0.

COLCHESTER UNITED 2010–11 LEAGUE RECORD

Match No.	Date	Venue	Opponents	Result	H/T Score	Lg Pos.	Goalscorers	Attendance
1	Aug 7	A	Exeter C	D 2-2	2-1	—	Wordsworth 2 [10, 11]	5927
2	14	H	Sheffield W	D 1-1	0-0	14	Bond [50]	6011
3	21	A	Rochdale	W 2-1	1-0	9	Bond [38], Henderson, I [84]	3016
4	27	H	Carlisle U	D 1-1	1-0	—	Mooney [29]	4475
5	Sept 4	A	Walsall	W 1-0	0-0	5	Bond [83]	3416
6	11	H	Plymouth Arg	D 1-1	1-0	8	Bond [22]	4201
7	18	A	Southampton	D 0-0	0-0	9		17,857
8	25	H	Tranmere R	W 3-1	3-0	5	Mooney [6], Wordsworth [16], Okuonghae [31]	3637
9	28	H	Dagenham & R	D 2-2	1-1	—	Vincent [43], Mooney [65]	4515
10	Oct 2	A	Milton Keynes D	D 1-1	1-0	6	Okuonghae [26]	11,280
11	9	H	Huddersfield T	L 0-3	0-2	11		4211
12	16	A	Oldham Ath	D 0-0	0-0	10		4136
13	23	H	Notts Co	W 2-1	0-1	6	Odejayi 2 [76, 83]	3811
14	30	A	Bournemouth	W 2-1	1-0	3	Williams, T [16], Henderson, I [80]	6575
15	Nov 2	H	Leyton Orient	W 3-2	2-2	—	Heath [22], Mooney (pen) [32], Wilson [80]	3899
16	13	A	Swindon T	L 1-2	1-1	6	Vincent [45]	7679
17	20	H	Hartlepool U	W 3-2	0-1	3	Bond [57], Odejayi [60], Henderson, I (pen) [90]	3640
18	23	H	Brentford	L 0-2	0-1	—		3172
19	Dec 11	H	Yeovil T	D 0-0	0-0	6		3748
20	Jan 1	H	Charlton Ath	D 3-3	2-2	10	Heath [16], Bond [24], Wordsworth [64]	6112
21	3	A	Leyton Orient	L 2-4	0-1	11	Wordsworth [69], Henderson, I [81]	4339
22	14	H	Bournemouth	W 2-1	0-0	—	Gillespie 2 [77, 84]	3445
23	22	A	Huddersfield T	D 0-0	0-0	10		12,689
24	25	A	Brighton & HA	L 0-2	0-1	—		6798
25	28	H	Peterborough U	W 2-1	1-1	—	Gillespie [37], Mooney [86]	4645
26	Feb 1	A	Charlton Ath	L 0-1	0-0	9		13,830
27	5	A	Hartlepool U	L 0-1	0-0	10		2646
28	12	H	Swindon T	W 2-1	1-0	10	Mooney (pen) [7], Gillespie [90]	3624
29	15	A	Notts Co	L 0-2	0-2	—		4041
30	19	H	Walsall	W 2-0	1-0	10	Perkins [18], Mooney (pen) [56]	3439
31	22	A	Peterborough U	D 1-1	1-1	—	Henderson, I [17]	5758
32	26	A	Plymouth Arg	L 1-2	1-1	10	Zubar (og) [41]	8982
33	Mar 1	A	Bristol R	W 1-0	1-0	—	Odejayi [22]	5181
34	5	H	Southampton	L 0-2	0-1	8		6523
35	8	A	Dagenham & R	L 0-1	0-1	—		2140
36	12	H	Milton Keynes D	L 1-3	1-0	12	Gillespie [29]	4103
37	19	A	Tranmere R	L 0-1	0-0	14		4292
38	22	A	Oldham Ath	W 1-0	0-0	—	Vincent [52]	2892
39	26	H	Exeter C	W 5-1	1-1	—	Gillespie 2 [31, 77], Mooney (pen) [73], Vincent [76], Bond [86]	3629
40	Apr 2	A	Sheffield W	L 1-2	0-1	11	Gillespie [90]	15,663
41	9	H	Rochdale	W 1-0	0-0	10	Henderson, I [87]	4052
42	16	A	Carlisle U	L 1-4	0-3	11	Gillespie [71]	4405
43	22	A	Brentford	D 1-1	1-0	—	Henderson, I [15]	4480
44	25	H	Brighton & HA	D 1-1	1-0	12	Henderson, I [16]	5132
45	30	A	Yeovil T	L 2-4	1-3	12	Vincent [43], Mooney [63]	3797
46	May 7	H	Bristol R	W 2-1	2-0	10	Henderson, I 2 [28, 30]	4759

Final League Position: 10

GOALSCORERS

League (57): Henderson, I 10 (1 pen), Gillespie 9, Mooney 9 (4 pens), Bond 7, Vincent 5, Wordsworth 5, Odejayi 4, Heath 2, Okuonghae 2, Perkins 1, Williams, T 1, Wilson 1, own goal 1.
Carling Cup (3): Mooney 2, Henderson, I 1.
FA Cup (5): Mooney 3 (1 pen), Bond 1, Wilson 1.
J Paint Trophy (0).

Cousins M 13+1	Wilson B 25+1	Tierney M 12+1	Perkins D 36	Okuonghae M 14	Reid P 17+1	Bond A 36+7	Izzet K 38+3	Odejayi K 18+26	Wordsworth A 26+9	Henderson I 24+12	Mooney D 37+2	Vincent A 28+9	Beevers L 12+7	Baldwin P 10+1	White J 15+7	James L 17+11	Henderson L —+8	Heath M 26+1	Williams T 7	Williams B 33	Hackney S —+1	Coker B 20	Gillespie S 11+7	Vilhjalmsson M —+3	Clarke N 18	O'Toole J 5+6	Smith T 6	Powell C 2	Sanderson J —+1	Match No.
1	2	3	4	5	6	7	8^3	9^1	10^2	11	12	13	14																	1
1	2	3	4	5	6	7	8	13	10	11^1	9^2	12																		2
1	2	3	4^1	5	6^2	7	8	14	10	11	9^3	12	13																	3
1	2	3	4^1	5		7	8	13	10^2	11	9^3	12		6	14															4
1	2	3	4	5		7	8	12	10	11^1	9^2			6	13															5
1	2^1	3	4	5		7	8	13	10		9^2	11		6	12															6
1		3^1	4	5	13	7	8	14	10	11	9^3				6^2	2	12													7
1		3	4	5	6	7^3	8	13	10	14	9^2	11^1				2	12													8
1		3^1	4	5^2	6	7^1	8	12	10	9	11					2	14	13												9
1			4	5	6	7	8	12	10^3	13	9^1	11^2				2	14	3												10
	2		4	5	6	7	8	13	10^1	9	11^2	12						3		1										11
	2		4	5	6	7^1	8	14	10^3	13	9	11^2	12					3		1										12
	2		4		6	7^2	8	12	10^1	13	9	11^3	14					3	5	1										13
	2	13	4		6	7	8^3	10	12	9^1	11^2	14						3	5	1										14
	2		4		6	7	8^1	9^2	14	10^3	11	12	13					3	5	1										15
	2	3	4^2	5	6	7	8^1	9	12	13	10	11^3	14							1										16
	2	3	4^2	5	6	7	12	9	10^1	8	11^3	13	14							1										17
	2	3	4		6	7	9^1	13	10^2	8	11				5	12				1										18
	2		4		6	8^3	9^2	10	7	12	11^1	5	14	13				3		1										19
			4		6	7	12	10	13	9^2	11^1	2			3	8			5	1										20
					6	7^2	12	10	8	9	11^1	2			3	4			5	1	13									21
		4				7	8^2	14	10	9^3	11^1	2		5	13		6			1			3	12						22
		4				7	8	12	10	9^3	11^1	2^2		5	13	14	6			1			3							23
		4				7	8^2	12	10	11^1	9^3	5^1	2			6				1			3	13	14					24
		4				7	8	12	13	9^3	2	14	11^1			3				1			5		10^2	6				25
15		4^1				7	8	13	12	9	2	11				5				1^6			3		10^2	6				26
1		4^1				7	8	13	12	9^2	14	2				11^3				5			3		10	6				27
1		4^3				7	8^1	12	10	9	11^2	2	5				6						3	13						28
1		4				7^1	12	10	11^2	8^9	9	3			2	13	6									14	5			29
		4				12	8^1	10^2	7	9^3	14	2	11			5			1		3		13	6						30
		4^1				14	8	10^3	12	7	9	13	2			11^1				5		1	3			6				31
		4^1				14	8^3	10	13	7	9^2	2	11				5			1		3		12		6				32
						7	8^2	9^1	11	10^3	14	2	4				5			1		3	12			6	13			33
						13	8^2	10^3	11^1	7	9^4	14	2			4	5			1		3	12			6				34
						7	8	9^3	10^2	11	13	2	4^1			5				1		3	12			6	14			35
14		4				12		9	11^2	7^1	13	3^3	2		8	5				1		10				6				36
	2	4				12		9	8^1	13	11^2	7^3				1		3		10			6	14	5					37
	2	4				7	8	12		14	9^1	11^2				5				1		3	10^3			6	13			38
	2	4				7	8^1		13	9	11^2	12			12				5	1		3	10			6				39
	2	4^1				7	8^9	13			9^2	11				12				5	1		3	10			6	14		40
	2					7	4	12		13	9^1	11^2	14							1		3	10^3			6	8	5		41
	2					7	4	11		10		12								1		3	9			6	8^1	5		42
	2						4^3	12	14	7	9	11^2			8		6			1			10^1		13			5	3	43
	2					12	4		13	10	9	11^2			8		6			1					7^1			5	3	44
	2						4	13		10^2	9	11	12		7					1		3				6	8	5^1		45
	2					7^2	13	10		9		11	6		3	4				5	1						8^1		12	46

FA Cup
First Round	Bradford C	(h)	4-3
Second Round	Swindon Supermarine	(h)	1-0
Third Round	Swansea C	(a)	0-4

Carling Cup
First Round	Hereford U	(a)	3-0
Second Round	Sunderland	(a)	0-2

J Paint Trophy
Second Round	Wycombe W	(h)	0-2

COVENTRY CITY · FL Championship

FOUNDATION

Workers at Singers' cycle factory formed a club in 1883. The first success of Singers' FC was to win the Birmingham Junior Cup in 1891 and this led in 1894 to their election to the Birmingham and District League. Four years later they changed their name to Coventry City and joined the Southern League in 1908 at which time they were playing in blue and white quarters.

The Ricoh Arena, Phoenix Way, Foleshill, Coventry CV6 6GE.

Telephone: (0844) 873 1883.

Fax: 0870 421 1988.

Ticket Office: (0844) 873 1883 (option 1).

Website: www.ccfc.co.uk

Email: info@ccfc.co.uk

Ground Capacity: 32,609.

Record Attendance: 51,455 v Wolverhampton W, Division 2, 29 April 1967 (at Highfield Road). 31,407 v Chelsea, FA Cup 6th rd, 7 March 2009 (at Ricoh Arena).

Pitch Measurements: 110yd × 75yd.

Chairman: Ken Dulieu.

Vice-chairman: John Clarke OBE.

Chief Executive: Paul Clouting.

Secretary: Pam Hindson.

Manager: Andy Thorn.

First Team Coach: Steve Harrison.

Physio: Michael McBride.

Colours: Sky blue shirts with grey horizontal stripes, white shorts, sky blue stockings.

Change Colours: Green shirts with black vertical stripes, black shorts and stockings.

Year Formed: 1883.   *Turned Professional:* 1893.   *Ltd Co.:* 1907.

Previous Name: 1883, Singers FC; 1898, Coventry City FC.

Club Nickname: 'Sky Blues'.

Grounds: 1883, Binley Road; 1887, Stoke Road; 1899, Highfield Road; 2005, Ricoh Arena.

First Football League Game: 30 August 1919, Division 2, v Tottenham H (h) L 0–5 – Lindon; Roberts, Chaplin, Allan, Hawley, Clarke, Sheldon, Mercer, Sambrooke, Lowes, Gibson.

Record League Victory: 9–0 v Bristol C, Division 3 (S), 28 April 1934 – Pearson; Brown, Bisby; Perry, Davidson, Frith; White (2), Lauderdale, Bourton (5), Jones (2), Lake.

Record Cup Victory: 8–0 v Rushden & D, League Cup 2nd rd, 2 October 2002 – Debec; Caldwell, Quinn, Betts (1p), Konjic (Shaw), Davenport, Pipe, Safri (Stanford), Mills (2) (Bothroyd (2)), McSheffery (3), Partridge.

Record Defeat: 2–10 v Norwich C, Division 3 (S), 15 March 1930.

HONOURS

Football League – Division 1: Best season: 6th, 1969–70;
Division 2: *Champions* 1966–67;
Division 3: *Champions* 1963–64;
Division 3 (S): *Champions* 1935–36;
Runners-up 1933–34;
Division 4: *Runners-up* 1958–59.
FA Cup: *Winners* 1987.
Football League Cup: Semi-final 1981, 1990.
European Competitions
European Fairs Cup: 1970–71.

sky SPORTS FACT FILE

On 8 November 1956 Coventry City hosted the Third Division South v its Northern colleagues. City manager Harry Warren was in charge of the South team, his coach George Raynor acted as trainer. The North was managed by ex-Coventry manager Harry Storer. South won 2-1.

Most League Points (2 for a win): 60, Division 4, 1958–59 and Division 3, 1963–64.

Most League Points (3 for a win): 66, Division 1, 2001–02.

Most League Goals: 108, Division 3 (S), 1931–32.

Highest League Scorer in Season: Clarrie Bourton, 49, Division 3 (S), 1931–32.

Most League Goals in Total Aggregate: Clarrie Bourton, 171, 1931–37.

Most League Goals in One Match: 5, Clarrie Bourton v Bournemouth, Division 3 (S), 17 October 1931; 5, Arthur Bacon v Gillingham, Division 3 (S), 30 December 1933.

Most Capped Player: Magnus Hedman, 44 (58), Sweden.

Most League Appearances: Steve Ogrizovic, 507, 1984–2000.

Youngest League Player: Ben Mackey, 16 years 167 days v Ipswich T, 12 April 2003.

Record Transfer Fee Received: £13,000,000 from Internazionale for Robbie Keane, July 2000.

Record Transfer Fee Paid: £6,500,000 to Wolverhampton W for Robbie Keane, August 1999; £6,500,000 to Norwich C for Craig Bellamy, August 2000.

Football League Record: 1919 Elected to Division 2; 1925–26 Division 3 (N); 1926–36 Division 3 (S); 1936–52 Division 2; 1952–58 Division 3 (S); 1958–59 Division 4; 1959–64 Division 3; 1964–67 Division 2; 1967–92 Division 1; 1992–2001 FA Premier League; 2001–04 Division 1; 2004– FL C.

LATEST SEQUENCES

Longest Sequence of League Wins: 6, 25.4.1964 – 5.9.1964.

Longest Sequence of League Defeats: 9, 30.8.1919 – 11.10.1919.

Longest Sequence of League Draws: 6, 1.11.2003 – 29.11.2003.

Longest Sequence of Unbeaten League Matches: 25, 26.11.1966 – 13.5.1967.

Longest Sequence Without a League Win: 19, 30.8.1919 – 20.12.1919.

Successive Scoring Runs: 25 from 10.9.1966.

Successive Non-scoring Runs: 11 from 11.10.1919.

MANAGERS

H. R. Buckle 1909–10
Robert Wallace 1910–13
   (*Secretary-Manager*)
Frank Scott-Walford 1913–15
William Clayton 1917–19
H. Pollitt 1919–20
Albert Evans 1920–24
Jimmy Kerr 1924–28
James McIntyre 1928–31
Harry Storer 1931–45
Dick Bayliss 1945–47
Billy Frith 1947–48
Harry Storer 1948–53
Jack Fairbrother 1953–54
Charlie Elliott 1954–55
Jesse Carver 1955–56
George Raynor 1956
Harry Warren 1956–57
Billy Frith 1957–61
Jimmy Hill 1961–67
Noel Cantwell 1967–72
Bob Dennison 1972
Joe Mercer 1972–75
Gordon Milne 1972–81
Dave Sexton 1981–83
Bobby Gould 1983–84
Don Mackay 1985–86
George Curtis 1986–87
   (*became Managing Director*)
John Sillett 1987–90
Terry Butcher 1990–92
Don Howe 1992
Bobby Gould 1992–93
   (*Bobby Gould and Don Howe
   joint managers June 1992*)
Phil Neal 1993–95
Ron Atkinson 1995–96
   (*became Director of Football*)
Gordon Strachan 1996–2001
Roland Nilsson 2001–02
Gary McAllister 2002–04
Eric Black 2004
Peter Reid 2004–05
Micky Adams 2005–07
Iain Dowie 2007–08
Chris Coleman 2008–10
Aidy Boothroyd 2010–11
Andy Thorn April 2011–

TEN YEAR LEAGUE RECORD

		P	W	D	L	F	A	Pts	Pos
2001-02	Div 1	46	20	6	20	59	53	66	11
2002-03	Div 1	46	12	14	20	46	62	50	20
2003-04	Div 1	46	17	14	15	67	54	65	12
2004-05	FL C	46	13	13	20	61	73	52	19
2005-06	FL C	46	16	15	15	62	65	63	8
2006-07	FL C	46	16	8	22	47	62	56	17
2007-08	FL C	46	14	11	21	52	64	53	21
2008-09	FL C	46	13	15	18	47	58	54	17
2009-10	FL C	46	13	15	18	47	64	54	19
2010-11	FL C	46	14	13	19	54	58	55	18

DID YOU KNOW ?

The youngest player to appear for Coventry City outside of the Football League competition was Johnson Clarke-Harris, aged 16 years 20 days when he came on as a substitute against Morecambe in the Carling Cup on 10 August 2010.

COVENTRY CITY 2010–11 LEAGUE RECORD

Match No.	Date	Venue	Opponents	Result	H/T Score	Lg Pos.	Goalscorers	Attendance
1	Aug 7	H	Portsmouth	W 2-0	1-0	—	Eastwood 2 [4, 70]	18,814
2	14	A	Watford	D 2-2	0-1	3	Bell [88], Jutkiewicz (pen) [90]	12,813
3	21	H	Derby Co	W 2-1	1-0	4	Jutkiewicz (pen) [33], Turner, B [80]	13,169
4	28	A	Millwall	L 1-3	0-1	8	Gunnarsson [60]	11,688
5	Sept 11	H	Leicester C	D 1-1	1-0	9	Platt [40]	20,060
6	14	A	Swansea C	L 1-2	0-1	—	Turner, B [56]	12,411
7	18	A	Bristol C	W 2-1	2-1	11	Platt [22], Turner, B [45]	13,428
8	25	H	Preston NE	L 1-2	0-2	13	Gunnarsson [61]	14,945
9	28	H	Doncaster R	W 2-1	1-1	—	Gunnarsson [2], McSheffrey [86]	12,292
10	Oct 2	A	Hull C	D 0-0	0-0	9		20,626
11	16	A	Ipswich T	W 2-1	1-0	7	Platt [19], Jutkiewicz (pen) [56]	19,100
12	19	H	Cardiff C	L 1-2	1-1	—	McSheffrey [44]	14,604
13	23	H	Barnsley	W 3-0	1-0	6	McSheffrey [9], Baker [86], Clarke [90]	14,573
14	30	A	Sheffield U	W 1-0	1-0	4	McSheffrey [23]	20,059
15	Nov 6	H	Leeds U	L 2-3	0-2	5	Jutkiewicz [52], Turner, B [64]	28,184
16	9	A	Nottingham F	L 1-2	1-1	—	Chambers (og) [35]	19,501
17	13	A	Crystal Palace	L 0-2	0-1	11		13,278
18	20	H	Burnley	W 1-0	0-0	9	Doyle, M [57]	14,432
19	27	A	Scunthorpe U	W 2-0	1-0	6	McSheffrey [31], Murphy (og) [73]	4397
20	Dec 4	H	Middlesbrough	W 1-0	0-0	—	King (pen) [78]	15,768
21	11	A	Reading	D 0-0	0-0	5		14,029
22	18	H	Norwich C	L 1-2	0-0	6	King [73]	15,230
23	26	A	Cardiff C	L 0-2	0-1	6		24,595
24	28	H	QPR	L 0-2	0-0	7		17,678
25	Jan 1	H	Ipswich T	D 1-1	0-1	9	Eastwood [48]	14,412
26	3	A	Barnsley	L 1-2	1-1	11	Eastwood [35]	11,118
27	15	H	Sheffield U	D 0-0	0-0	11		14,854
28	23	A	QPR	L 1-2	1-1	13	King [25]	13,185
29	Feb 1	H	Nottingham F	L 1-2	1-2	15	King [26]	14,631
30	5	A	Leeds U	L 0-1	0-0	16		27,033
31	12	H	Crystal Palace	W 2-1	1-0	14	Wood [34], King [79]	16,454
32	22	H	Swansea C	L 0-1	0-0	—		13,481
33	26	A	Leicester C	D 1-1	1-1	17	King [14]	25,356
34	Mar 5	H	Bristol C	L 1-4	0-3	19	Jutkiewicz [53]	15,157
35	8	A	Doncaster R	D 1-1	1-0	—	Eastwood [23]	7921
36	12	H	Hull C	L 0-1	0-1	19		14,370
37	15	A	Burnley	D 2-2	0-1	—	Jutkiewicz [61], McSheffrey [75]	13,802
38	19	H	Preston NE	L 1-2	0-1	20	Bell [71]	12,269
39	Apr 2	H	Watford	W 2-0	1-0	17	McSheffrey [27], Jutkiewicz [66]	16,519
40	9	A	Derby Co	D 2-2	2-2	18	Gunnarsson [16], King [39]	25,546
41	12	A	Portsmouth	W 3-0	1-0	—	King 2 (2 pens) [19, 70], McSheffrey [58]	13,132
42	16	H	Millwall	W 2-1	1-0	16	King 2 [7, 84]	16,354
43	22	H	Scunthorpe U	D 1-1	1-1	—	King [5]	16,705
44	25	A	Middlesbrough	L 1-2	1-1	17	Jutkiewicz [10]	15,817
45	30	H	Reading	D 0-0	0-0	17		22,436
46	May 7	A	Norwich C	D 2-2	0-0	18	Keogh [54], Jutkiewicz [64]	26,268

Final League Position: 18

GOALSCORERS
League (54): King 12 (3 pens), Jutkiewicz 9 (3 pens), McSheffrey 8, Eastwood 5, Gunnarsson 4, Turner, B 4, Platt 3, Bell 2, Baker 1, Clarke 1, Doyle, M 1, Keogh 1, Wood 1, own goals 2.
Carling Cup (0).
FA Cup (4): Baker 1, Eastwood 1, King 1, Wood 1.

Westwood K 41	Keogh R 46	Cranie M 32+4	Doyle M 15+3	Turner B 14	Cameron N 22+3	Bell D 20+2	Carsley L 25	Jutkiewicz L 34+8	Eastwood F 14+13	McSheffrey G 30+3	Platt C 22+12	Baker C 19+13	Turner I 2	Gunnarsson A 37+5	Quirke M 3+1	Clarke J 12+9	Clingan S 26+2	Wood R 35+5	McPake J 11+1	Ward D 4+1	McIndoe M —+6	King M 24+4	O'Donovan R —+2	O'Halloran S 10+1	Wilson C —+1	Hussey C 8+3	Ireland D —+1	Deegan G —+1	Match No.
1	2	3	4	5	6	7^2	8	9^1	10	11	12	13																	1
	2	3	4	5	6	7	8	9	10^1	11^2	12			1^6	13	15													2
1	2	3	4	5	6	7^2	8	9^1	10^3	11	12			14		13													3
	2	3			6	7^1	8		13	11	9	12^4		1		10^2		4	5^3	14									4
1	2	14	5			8	9^3		11^1	10				13	3	4	6		7^2	12									5
1	2	13	5			8	9		11	12				7	3^2	4	6					10^1						6
1	2	3	5			8	9	10	11					7		4	6											7
1	2	3	5		13	8	9^3		10	11^1				7^2		4	6	14				12						8
1	2	3	5			8	13	12	9					7		4	6		11^1			10^2						9
1	2	3	5			8	10		9	12				11		4	6		7^1									10
1	2	3	13	5		8	9		11^2	10	12			7^1		4	6											11
1	2	3	5			8	9^1	11	10					7		4	6		12									12
1	2	3	5			8	9^3		11^3	10	12			7^1	13	4	6				14							13
1	2	3	5			8	9^2		11^3	10	12			7^1	14	4	6		13									14
1	2	3^2	5			8	9		11	10^1	13			7		4	6		12									15
1	2	3	14		12	8	9		11^2	13				7		4^3	6	5^1				10						16
1	2	3^3	4			8	9	13	11			7^1		12		6	5					10^2	14					17
1	2		4	3		8	13		11^3	9	7^1			12	14	6	5					10^2						18
1	2		4	3		8	12	13	11^3	9				7^2	14	6	5					10^1						19
1	2		4	3		8	13	12	11^3	9				7^1	14	6	5					10^2						20
1	2		4	6		8			11	9				7^1	12	3	5					10						21
1	2	12	4		3^1	7^1		13	14	11	9^2		8^4			6	5^3				10							22
1	2		4	3		8	9	12	11^2	13					7^1	6	5					10						23
1	2		4	6	7^2	8		14	11	9						3^1	5^3					10	12	13				24
1	2	13	4	6	7^1	8	9	11^2		12						3	5					10^4						25
1	2	12	4		3	8			10	11	9			7		6	5^1											26
1	2	5	4					9^1	10	11	12	7		8			6								3			27
1	2	5	4^1					14	10^3	11^2	13	7		8		12	6				9					3			28
1	2	5				8^1		13	10^3	11^2	14	7		4	12		6				9					3			29
1		5	8					9	10^1	12	11	7		4	2		6									3			30
1	2		8			5		9	12		11^1	7		4			6					10					3			31
1	2		8			5	7	9		12		11^1		4			6					10					3			32
1	2	8^1				5	7	9	13			11^2		4		12	6					10	3^1						33
1^6	2					5	7	9	13			11^2		4			6					10^4	3^1	12	15				34
	2	3				5	7^1	9	10	11		12		8	1		4	6											35
1	2	3^3				5^2	7^1	9	10	11		12		8	14	4	6							13					36
1	5							9	10	11		7		8	2	4	6							3^1	12				37
1	5			14	12			9	10	11^2		7^1		8	2	4	6^3		13						3				38
1	5	6		12	7^3			13	10^2	11				8	2^1	4			14	9					3				39
1	2	5			6	7		9^2		11^1	13	12		8		4						10				3			40
1	2	5			6	7		9^1		11^2	12	13		8		4						10				3			41
1	6	5				7		9^2			13	11		8^1		2^3	4	14				12	10			3			42
1	5	6				7		9^2	13			11^1		8		2	4	14				12	10			3^3			43
1	5	6				7		9	13		10^2	11		8^1		2	4	12				14				3^1			44
	6	5^1				7		9^2			13	11		8	1	2	4	12				10				3			45
	6	5				7		9	14			11^1		8	1	3^2	4	13				10^3				2	12		46

FA Cup
Third Round   Crystal Palace   (h)   2-1
Fourth Round   Birmingham C   (a)   2-3

Carling Cup
First Round   Morecambe   (a)   0-2

CRAWLEY TOWN   FL Championship 2

FOUNDATION

Formed in 1896, Crawley Town initially entered the West Sussex League before switching to the mid-Sussex League in 1901, winning the Second Division in its second season. The club remained at such level until 1951 when it became members of the Sussex County League and five years later moved to the Metropolitan League while remaining as an amateur club. It was not until 1962 that the club turned semi-professional and a year later, joined the Southern League. Many honours came the club's way, but the most successful run was achieved in 2010–11 when they reached the fifith round of the FA Cup and played before a crowd of 74,778 spectators at Old Trafford against Manchester United. Crawley Town spent 48 years at the Town Mead ground before a new site was occupied at Broadfield in 1997, ideally suited to access from the neighbouring motorway. History was also made on 9 April when the team won promotion to the Football League after beating Tamworth 3-0 to stretch their unbeaten League record to 26 games. They finished the season with a Conference record points total of 105 and at the same time, established another milestone for the longest unbeaten run, having extended it to 30 matches by the end of the season.

Broadfield Stadium, Winfield Way, Crawley, Sussex RH11 9RX.

Telephone: (01293) 410 000.

Fax: (01293) 410 002.

Website: www.crawleytownfc.com

Email: info@crawleytownfc.com

Ground Capacity: 4,996 (1,150 seated).

Record Attendance: 4,522 v Weymouth, Doc Martens Premier League, 6 March 2004.

Pitch Measurements: 110yd × 72yd.

Chairman: Victor Marley.

Manager: Steve Evans.

Assistant Manager: Paul Raynor.

Coach: Craig Brewster.

Club Nickname: "Red Devils"

MANAGERS

Managers have included:
Tom Jarvie
John Hollins
Colin Pates
Francis Vines
Simon Wormull
David Woozley
Steve Evans May 2007–

sky SPORTS FACT FILE

Though comparative newcomers to the FA Cup, having not entered until 1959, Crawley Town reached the first round proper for the first time in 1970–71. In 1991–92 they made it to the third round and of course surpassed this by getting to the fifth round in 2010–11.

Colours: All red.

Change Colours: White shirts, purple shorts, purple stockings.

Year Formed: 1896.

Turned Professional: 1962.

Grounds: Town Mead to 1997; Broadfield Stadium 1997.

Record Conference Victory: 7-0 v Altrincham, 20 November 2010.

Most League Points (3 for a win): 105, Blue Square Premier, 2010–11.

Most League Goals: 93, Blue Square Premier, 2010–11.

Highest League and Cup Scorer in Season: Matt Tubbs, 40, Blue Square Premier, 2010–11.

Most League and Cup Appearances since 2007: Glenn Wilson, 164.

HONOURS

FA Cup: Best Season: 5th rd 2011.

Blue Square Premier: *Champions* 2010–11.

Southern League: *Champions* 2003–04.

Southern League Cup: *Winners* 2003, 2004.

Southern League Championship Trophy: *Winners* 2004, 2005.

Southern League Merit Cup: *Winners* 1971.

Sussex Professional Cup: *Winners* 1970.

Sussex Senior Cup: *Winners* 1990, 1991, 2003, 2005.

Sussex Intermediate Cup: *Winners* 1928.

Sussex Floodlit Cup: *Winners* 1991, 1992, 1993, 1999.

Southern Counties Floodlit League: *Champions* 1985–86.

Mid-Sussex Senior League: *Champions* 1902–03.

Montgomery Cup: *Winners* 1926.

Gilbert Rice Floodlit Cup: *Winners* 1980, 1984.

Roy Hayden Trophy: *Winners* 1991, 1992.

William Hill Senior Cup: *Winners* 1993.

Metropolitan League Challenge Cup: *Winners* 1959.

Highest Placed Amateur Award: 1961–62.

FA Ronnie Radford Award: 2011.

TEN YEAR LEAGUE RECORD

		P	W	D	L	F	A	Pts	Pos
2001-02	S PR	42	21	10	11	67	48	73	4
2002-03	S PR	42	17	13	12	64	51	64	7
2003-04	S PR	42	25	9	8	77	43	84	1
2004-05	Conf	42	16	9	17	50	50	57	12
2005-06	Conf	42	12	11	19	48	55	44	17
2006-07	Conf	46	17	12	17	52	52	53	18
2007-08	BSP	46	19	9	18	73	67	60	15
2008-09	BSP	46	19	14	13	77	55	70	9
2009-10	BSP	44	19	9	16	50	57	66	7
2010-11	BSP	46	31	12	3	93	50	105	1

DID YOU KNOW ?

In 2010–11 Crawley Town won the award for the best performance in the FA Cup when they reached the fifth round before losing to Manchester U 1-0 at Old Trafford. Their victims had been Newport Co, Guiseley, Swindon T, Derby Co and Torquay U.

CREWE ALEXANDRA   FL Championship 2

FOUNDATION

The first match played at Crewe was on 1 December 1877 against Basford, the leading North Staffordshire team of that time. During the club's history they have also played in a number of other leagues including the Football Alliance, Football Combination, Lancashire League, Manchester League, Central League and Lancashire Combination. Two former players, Aaron Scragg in 1899 and Jackie Pearson in 1911, had the distinction of refereeing FA Cup finals. Pearson was also capped for England against Ireland in 1892.

The Alexandra Stadium, Gresty Road, Crewe, Cheshire CW2 6EB.

Telephone: (01270) 213 014.

Fax: (01270) 216 320.

Ticket Office: (01270) 252 610.

Website: www.crewealex.net

Email: info@crewealex.net

Ground Capacity: 10,107.

Record Attendance: 20,000 v Tottenham H, FA Cup 4th rd, 30 January 1960.

Pitch Measurements: 112m × 74m.

Chairman: John Bowler.

Vice-chairman: David Rowlinson.

Finance Operations Manager: Andrew Blakemore.

Manager: Dario Gradi MBE.

Assistant Manager: Steve Davis.

Physio: Rob Sharp.

Colours: Red shirts with white trim, white shorts, red stockings.

Change Colours: White shirts with tangerine trim, tangerine shorts, tangerine stockings.

Year Formed: 1877.

Turned Professional: 1893.

Ltd Co.: 1892.

Club Nickname: 'Railwaymen'.

Ground: 1898, Gresty Road.

First Football League Game: 3 September 1892, Division 2, v Burton Swifts (a) L 1–7 – Hickton; Moore, Cope; Linnell, Johnson, Osborne; Bennett, Pearson (1), Bailey, Barnett, Roberts.

Record League Victory: 8–0 v Rotherham U, Division 3 (N), 1 October 1932 – Foster; Pringle, Dawson; Ward, Keenor (1), Turner (1); Gillespie, Swindells (1), McConnell (2), Deacon (2), Weale (1).

HONOURS

Football League – Division 2: *Runners-up* 2002–03.

FA Cup: Semi-final 1888.

Football League Cup: never past 3rd round.

Welsh Cup: *Winners* 1936, 1937.

sky SPORTS FACT FILE

In the eight days from 2 October to 9 October 2010, Crewe Alexandra were involved in a 5-5 League Two draw away to Chesterfield, a 4-2 away win in the Johnstone's Paint Trophy at Macclesfield and a 3-3 home League Two draw with Torquay and missed a penalty!

Record Cup Victory: 8–0 v Hartlepool U, Auto Windscreens Shield 1st rd, 17 October 1995 – Gayle; Collins (1), Booty, Westwood (Unsworth), Macauley (1), Whalley (1), Garvey (1), Murphy (1), Savage (1) (Rivers (1p)), Lennon, Edwards, (1 og). 8–0 v Doncaster R, LDV Vans Trophy 3rd rd, 10 November 2002 – Bankole; Wright, Walker, Foster, Tierney; Lunt (1), Brammer, Sorvel, Vaughan (1) (Bell); Ashton (3) (Miles), Jack (2) (Jones (1)).

Record Defeat: 2–13 v Tottenham H, FA Cup 4th rd replay, 3 February 1960.

Most League Points (2 for a win): 59, Division 4, 1962–63.

Most League Points (3 for a win): 86, Division 2, 2002–03.

Most League Goals: 95, Division 3 (N), 1931–32.

Highest League Scorer in Season: Terry Harkin, 35, Division 4, 1964–65.

Most League Goals in Total Aggregate: Bert Swindells, 126, 1928–37.

Most League Goals in One Match: 5, Tony Naylor v Colchester U, Division 3, 24 April 1993.

Most Capped Player: Clayton Ince, 38 (79), Trinidad & Tobago.

Most League Appearances: Tommy Lowry, 436, 1966–78.

Youngest League Player: Steve Walters, 16 years 119 days v Peterborough U, 6 May 1988.

Record Transfer Fee Received: £4,000,000 from Derby Co for Seth Johnson, May 1999 (including sell-on).

Record Transfer Fee Paid: £650,000 to Torquay U for Rodney Jack, June 1998.

Football League Record: 1892 Original Member of Division 2; 1896 Failed re-election; 1921 Re-entered Division (N); 1958–63 Division 4; 1963–64 Division 3; 1964–68 Division 4; 1968–69 Division 3; 1969–89 Division 4; 1989–91 Division 3; 1991–92 Division 4; 1992–94 Division 4; 1994–97 Division 3; 1997–2002 Division 1; 2002–03 Division 2; 2003–04 Division 1; 2004–06 FL C; 2006–09 FL 1; 2009– FL 2.

MANAGERS

W. C. McNeill 1892–94 *(Secretary-Manager)*
J. G. Hall 1895–96 *(Secretary-Manager)*
R. Roberts *(1st team Secretary-Manager)* 1897
J. B. Blomerley 1898–1911 *(Secretary-Manager, continued as Hon. Secretary to 1925)*
Tom Bailey *(Secretary only)* 1925–38
George Lillycrop *(Trainer)* 1938–44
Frank Hill 1944–48
Arthur Turner 1948–51
Harry Catterick 1951–53
Ralph Ward 1953–55
Maurice Lindley 1956–57
Willie Cook 1957–58
Harry Ware 1958–60
Jimmy McGuigan 1960–64
Ernie Tagg 1964–71 *(continued as Secretary to 1972)*
Dennis Viollet 1971
Jimmy Melia 1972–74
Ernie Tagg 1974
Harry Gregg 1975–78
Warwick Rimmer 1978–79
Tony Waddington 1979–81
Arfon Griffiths 1981–82
Peter Morris 1982–83
Dario Gradi 1983–2007
Steve Holland 2007–08
Gudjon Thordarson 2008–09
Dario Gradi October 2009–

LATEST SEQUENCES

Longest Sequence of League Wins: 7, 30.4.1994 – 3.9.1994.

Longest Sequence of League Defeats: 10, 16.4.1979 – 22.8.1979.

Longest Sequence of League Draws: 5, 31.8.1987 – 18.9.1987.

Longest Sequence of Unbeaten League Matches: 17, 25.3.1995 – 16.9.1995.

Longest Sequence Without a League Win: 30, 22.9.1956 – 6.4.1957.

Successive Scoring Runs: 26 from 7.4.1934.

Successive Non-scoring Runs: 9 from 6.11.1974.

TEN YEAR LEAGUE RECORD

		P	W	D	L	F	A	Pts	Pos
2001-02	Div 1	46	12	13	21	47	76	49	22
2002-03	Div 2	46	25	11	10	76	40	86	2
2003-04	Div 1	46	14	11	21	57	66	53	18
2004-05	FL C	46	12	14	20	66	86	50	21
2005-06	FL C	46	9	15	22	57	86	42	22
2006-07	FL 1	46	17	9	20	66	72	60	13
2007-08	FL 1	46	12	14	20	47	65	50	20
2008-09	FL 1	46	12	10	24	59	82	46	22
2009-10	FL 2	46	15	10	21	68	73	55	18
2010-11	FL 2	46	18	11	17	87	65	65	10

DID YOU KNOW ?

Ralph Williams was but briefly at Crewe Alexandra in 1931–32, yet crucially scored 16 goals in 13 League and Cup appearances and had another strike ruled out when Wigan Borough resigned from the competition. Crewe were one of eighteen different clubs for whom he played!

CREWE ALEXANDRA 2010–11 LEAGUE RECORD

Match No.	Date	Venue	Opponents	Result	H/T Score	Lg Pos.	Goalscorers	Attendance
1	Aug 7	H	Hereford U	L 0-1	0-1	—		4343
2	14	A	Cheltenham T	L 2-3	1-2	23	Ada [4], Zola [49]	3537
3	21	H	Barnet	W 7-0	2-0	14	Miller 2 [4, 77], Donaldson 2 [34, 59], Grant [47], Artell [57], Leitch-Smith [82]	3171
4	28	A	Lincoln C	D 1-1	1-1	13	Miller [23]	3024
5	Sept 4	A	Stevenage	D 1-1	0-1	15	Westwood, Ashley R [56]	3431
6	11	H	Bury	W 3-0	2-0	9	Miller [3], Artell [18], Murphy [71]	4030
7	18	A	Burton Alb	D 1-1	0-1	9	Murphy [63]	3093
8	25	H	Oxford U	D 1-1	1-0	8	Artell [38]	4584
9	28	H	Macclesfield T	D 1-1	0-0	—	Leitch-Smith [87]	3659
10	Oct 2	A	Chesterfield	D 5-5	4-1	14	Murphy [4], Bell [6], Moore [13], Miller [26], Donaldson [80]	6047
11	9	H	Torquay U	D 3-3	1-2	15	Donaldson [45], Westwood, Ashley R 2 (1 pen) [73, 78 (p)]	4445
12	16	A	Southend U	W 2-0	0-0	10	Donaldson [56], Miller [77]	5506
13	23	H	Aldershot T	W 3-1	2-0	7	Moore [43], Grant [44], Westwood, Ashley R [58]	4164
14	30	A	Port Vale	L 1-2	0-1	9	Donaldson (pen) [82]	8607
15	Nov 2	H	Shrewsbury T	L 1-2	0-1	—	Miller [49]	4594
16	13	A	Gillingham	W 3-1	2-0	9	Moore [36], Donaldson [45], Miller [77]	5292
17	20	H	Rotherham U	L 0-1	0-1	11		4301
18	27	A	Morecambe	W 2-1	2-0	—	Donaldson [4], Moore [45]	1793
19	Dec 11	A	Stockport Co	D 3-3	1-1	9	Donaldson 2 [45, 47], Shelley [64]	4036
20	Jan 1	H	Northampton T	W 2-0	1-0	9	Donaldson [43], Miller [59]	3835
21	3	A	Shrewsbury T	W 1-0	0-0	8	Miller [67]	6561
22	8	H	Wycombe W	W 3-0	0-0	5	Donaldson 2 [71, 72], Miller [86]	3727
23	11	A	Torquay U	L 1-2	0-2	—	Shelley [59]	1955
24	15	H	Port Vale	W 2-1	1-0	5	Miller [18], Dugdale [81]	7183
25	22	A	Aldershot T	L 2-3	2-1	6	Shelley [19], Donaldson [43]	2613
26	25	H	Bradford C	W 2-1	2-1	—	Donaldson [15], Moore [40]	3665
27	Feb 1	A	Northampton T	L 2-6	1-3	7	Leitch-Smith [5], Sarcevic [88]	4021
28	5	A	Rotherham U	L 1-3	0-1	8	Leitch-Smith [62]	3750
29	12	H	Gillingham	D 1-1	1-0	9	Sinclair (og) [26]	4012
30	19	H	Stevenage	L 0-1	0-0	11		3793
31	22	A	Accrington S	L 2-3	1-1	—	Moore [8], Artell [72]	1356
32	26	A	Bury	L 1-3	1-0	12	Miller [41]	3308
33	Mar 5	H	Burton Alb	W 4-1	3-0	11	Donaldson 3 (1 pen) [2, 27 (p), 90], Miller [7]	3882
34	8	A	Macclesfield T	L 0-1	0-1	—		1485
35	12	H	Chesterfield	W 2-0	1-0	10	Donaldson [36], Shelley [87]	4503
36	15	H	Southend U	W 1-0	0-0	—	Miller [65]	3319
37	19	A	Oxford U	L 1-2	0-1	12	Leitch-Smith [90]	6751
38	22	H	Accrington S	D 0-0	0-0	—		3701
39	27	A	Hereford U	L 0-1	0-1	—		2334
40	Apr 2	H	Cheltenham T	W 8-1	4-0	12	Donaldson 3 (1 pen) [4, 33, 67 (p)], Miller [11], Grant 3 (1 pen) [37, 73, 88 (p)], Westwood, Ashley R [58]	3682
41	9	A	Barnet	L 1-2	1-2	13	Donaldson (pen) [45]	2212
42	16	A	Lincoln C	D 1-1	0-0	13	Donaldson (pen) [77]	3731
43	22	H	Morecambe	W 2-1	0-0	—	Donaldson 2 [72, 90]	3614
44	25	H	Wycombe W	L 0-2	0-2	13		4615
45	30	H	Stockport Co	W 2-0	0-0	12	Goodall (og) [62], Donaldson [65]	4799
46	May 7	A	Bradford C	W 5-1	4-1	10	Miller 2 [12, 32], Donaldson [34], Shelley 2 [45, 67]	11,030

Final League Position: 10

GOALSCORERS

League (87): Donaldson 28 (5 pens), Miller 18, Moore 6, Shelley 6, Grant 5 (1 pen), Leitch-Smith 5, Westwood, Ashley R 5 (1 pen), Artell 4, Murphy 3, Ada 1, Bell 1, Dugdale 1, Sarcevic 1, Zola 1, own goals 2.
Carling Cup (1): own goal 1.
FA Cup (1): Westwood Ashley R 1.
J Paint Trophy (5): Artell 1, Bell 1 (pen), Donaldson 1, Grant 1, own goal 1.

Taylor R 44	Tootle M 36 + 3	Blanchett D 38 + 1	Murphy L 36 + 3	Artell D 40	Ada P 39 + 1	Westwood Ashley R 45 + 1	Bell L 45	Zola C 4 + 2	Miller S 38 + 4	Donaldson C 42 + 1	Grant J 16 + 9	Leitch-Smith A 5 + 11	Powell N — + 17	Moore B 28 + 10	Shelley D 17 + 8	Mitchel-King M 9 + 5	Dugdale A 15 + 5	Mellor K — + 1	Phillips S 2 + 1	Sarcevic A — + 6	Westwood Ashley M 7 + 1	Connerton J — + 1	Clayton M — + 2	Turton O — + 1	Hughes C — + 1	Davis H — + 1	Match No.
1	2	3	4	5	6	7	8	9^1	10^2	11	12	13															1
1	2	3	4	5	6	7	8	9	10	11^1			12														2
1	2	3	4^3	5	6	7	8		9	10^2	11^1	13		12	14												3
1		3	4^2	5	6	7	8	12	10	9	11^1			13		2											4
1		3	4	5	6	7	8	9^2	10^1	11			12	13		2											5
1	2^2	3	4	5	6	7	8	9^3	10^1	11		14	12		13												6
1	12	3	4	5	6	7	8		10^3	9	11^2		13	14		2^1											7
1	2	3	4	5	6	7	8	12	9	10	11^1																8
1	2	3	4^2	5	6	7	8	10	9^3	11^1	14	12	13														9
1	2	3	4	5	6	7	8	10	12	13	11^1			9^2													10
1	2	3	4	5	6	7	8	12	10^2	11^3	13	14	9^1														11
1	2	3^1	4	5	6	7	8	13	10^2	11		9^3		12	14												12
1	2	3^1	4	5	6	7	8	13	10^2	11^3		9		12	14												13
1	2		4	5	6	7	8	12	10	11^1		9				3^2	13										14
1	2	3^1	4	5	6	7	8	10^2	11	13		9		12													15
1	2		4	5	3	7	8	10^1	11	12		9				6											16
1	2^1	12	4	5	6	3	8	9	10		11					7											17
1	2	3	4	5		7	8	10^1	11^3	13	12	9^2				6	14										18
1	2	3	4	5	12	7		10	11		9	8				6^1											19
1	2	3	4	5	6	7	8	10^1	11	12				9													20
1	2	3	4	5	6	7	8	9	10^2	11^1		13		12													21
1	2	3	4	5	6	7^1	8^3	10^2	11	13	14	9		12													22
1	2	3	4^1	5	6	12	8	10	11	13	9	7^2															23
1	2	3	4	5^1	6	7	8	10^2	11	13	9			12													24
1^1	2	3	12		6	7	8	10^5	11	13	9^2	4^1			5		15										25
	2	3	4		6	7	8	10^1	11■	12	9				5				1								26
1	2	3	4	5	6	7	8	9^1		12	11^3	13		10^2							14						27
1	2		4^1	5	6	7	8		10	13	9	11^2			3						12						28
1	2		4	5	6	7	8		11		9	10			3												29
1	2		4^1	5	6	7	8	10		12	9	11			3												30
1	2	3	12	5	6	4	7	10	11		9	8^1															31
1	2	3		5	6	4	7	10	11^2	8^3	12	9^1		13							14						32
1		3	4	5	6	7	8	10^1	11	12	9^2	13				2											33
1		3	4^2	5	6	7	8	10	11	13	9^1			12		2											34
1		3	4	5^1	6	7^1	8	10	11		9			12		2							13				35
1		3	4	5	6	7^1	8	10	11	13	9^2			12		2											36
1	12	3^1	4	5	6	7	8	10	11	13	9^2					2											37
1		3	4^2	5	6	7	8	10	11	12	13	9^1				2											38
13		3	4	5	6^2	7	8	9^3	10	12	14	11^1							1	2							39
1	2	3		5		4	8	9^1	10	11	13	7^2								6	12						40
1	2	3	12	5^2		4	7^1	9	10	11	8	13								6							41
1	2	3		6	4		8	9	10	11^1	13	12				7^2				5							42
1	2	3		4	7			9^1	10	11	8^2	13			5	6							12				43
1	2	3		4	7			9^3	10	11^1	13	8^2			5					12	6		14				44
1	2		6	4^3	7			10	11		9	8^1		5^2		3				12				13	14		45
1	2		5	4			8	10	11		9	7^2		3		6				13						12	46

FA Cup

First Round   Tamworth   (a)   1-2

Carling Cup

First Round   Derby Co   (h)   1-0
Second Round   Ipswich T   (h)   0-1

J Paint Trophy

Second Round   Macclesfield T   (a)   4-2
Northern Quarter-Final
   Carlisle U   (a)   1-3

CRYSTAL PALACE   FL Championship

FOUNDATION

There was a Crystal Palace club as early as 1861 but the present organisation was born in 1905 after the formation of a club by the company that controlled the Crystal Palace (building), had been rejected by the FA who did not like the idea of the Cup Final hosts running their own club. A separate company had to be formed and they had their home on the old Cup Final ground until 1915.

Selhurst Park Stadium, Whitehorse Lane, London SE25 6PU.

Telephone: (020) 8768 6000.

Fax: (020) 8771 5311.

Ticket Office: 0871 200 0071.

Website: www.cpfc.co.uk

Email: info@cpfc.co.uk

Ground Capacity: 26,225.

Record Attendance: 51,482 v Burnley, Division 2, 11 May 1979 (at Selhurst Park).

Pitch Measurements: 110yd × 74yd.

Co-Chairmen: Steve Parish and Martin Long.

Chief Executive: Phil Alexander.

Manager: Dougie Freedman.

Assistant Manager: Lennie Lawrence.

Physio: Alex Manos.

Colours: Red and blue striped shirts, blue shorts, blue stockings.

HONOURS

**Football League –
Division 1:** *Champions* 1993–94;
Division 2: *Champions* 1978–79;
Runners-up 1968–69;
Division 3: *Runners-up* 1963–64;
Division 3 (S): *Champions* 1920–21;
Runners-up 1928–29, 1930–31, 1938–39;
Division 4: *Runners-up* 1960–61.
FA Cup: *Runners-up* 1990.
Football League Cup: Semi-final 1993, 1995, 2001.
**Zenith Data Systems Cup:
Winners** 1991.
**European Competition
Intertoto Cup:** 1998.

Change Colours: White shirt with one blue and one red diagonal stripe, white shorts, white stockings.

Year Formed: 1905.

Turned Professional: 1905.

Ltd Co.: 1905.

Club Nickname: 'The Eagles'.

Grounds: 1905, Crystal Palace; 1915, Herne Hill; 1918, The Nest; 1924, Selhurst Park.

First Football League Game: 28 August 1920, Division 3, v Merthyr T (a) L 1–2 – Alderson; Little, Rhodes; McCracken, Jones, Feebury; Bateman, Conner, Smith, Milligan (1), Whibley.

Record League Victory: 9–0 v Barrow, Division 4, 10 October 1959 – Rouse; Long, Noakes; Truett, Evans, McNichol; Gavin (1), Summersby (4 incl. 1p), Sexton, Byrne (2), Colfar (2).

Record Cup Victory: 8–0 v Southend U, Rumbelows League Cup 2nd rd (1st leg), 25 September 1990 – Martyn; Humphrey (Thompson (1)), Shaw, Pardew, Young, Thorn, McGoldrick, Thomas, Bright (3), Wright (3), Barber (Hodges (1)).

sky SPORTS FACT FILE

On 3 January 2011 Crystal Palace defeated Preston North End with a Steffen Iversen goal. He was making his debut for the club and returning to English football which he left in March 2004 when the ex-Tottenham Hotspur forward was playing for Wolverhampton Wanderers.

Record Defeat: 0–9 v Burnley, FA Cup 2nd rd replay, 10 February 1909. 0–9 v Liverpool, Division 1, 12 September 1990.

Most League Points (2 for a win): 64, Division 4, 1960–61.

Most League Points (3 for a win): 90, Division 1, 1993–94.

Most League Goals: 110, Division 4, 1960–61.

Highest League Scorer in Season: Peter Simpson, 46, Division 3 (S), 1930–31.

Most League Goals in Total Aggregate: Peter Simpson, 153, 1930–36.

Most League Goals in One Match: 6, Peter Simpson v Exeter C, Division 3 (S), 4 October 1930.

Most Capped Player: Aleksandrs Kolinko, 23 (86), Latvia.

Most League Appearances: Jim Cannon, 571, 1973–88.

Youngest League Player: John Bostock, 15 years 287 days v Watford, 29 October 2007.

Record Transfer Fee Received: £8,500,000 from Everton for Andy Johnson, May 2006.

Record Transfer Fee Paid: £2,750,000 to RC Strasbourg for Valerien Ismael, January 1998.

Football League Record: 1920 Original Members of Division 3; 1921–25 Division 2; 1925–58 Division 3 (S); 1958–61 Division 4; 1961–64 Division 3; 1964–69 Division 2; 1969–73 Division 1; 1973–74 Division 2; 1974–77 Division 3; 1977–79 Division 2; 1979–81 Division 1; 1981–89 Division 2; 1989–92 Division 1; 1992–93 FA Premier League; 1993–94 Division 1; 1994–95 FA Premier League; 1995–97 Division 1; 1997–98 FA Premier League; 1998–2004 Division 1; 2004–05 FA Premier League; 2005– FL C.

LATEST SEQUENCES

Longest Sequence of League Wins: 8, 9.2.1921 – 26.3.1921.

Longest Sequence of League Defeats: 8, 10.1.1998 – 14.3.1998.

Longest Sequence of League Draws: 5, 21.9.2002 – 19.10.2002.

Longest Sequence of Unbeaten League Matches: 18, 22.2.1969 – 13.8.1969.

Longest Sequence Without a League Win: 20, 3.3.1962 – 8.9.1962.

Successive Scoring Runs: 24 from 27.4.1929.

Successive Non-scoring Runs: 9 from 19.11.1994.

MANAGERS

John T. Robson 1905–07
Edmund Goodman 1907–25
(had been Secretary since 1905 and afterwards continued in this position to 1933)
Alex Maley 1925–27
Fred Mavin 1927–30
Jack Tresadern 1930–35
Tom Bromilow 1935–36
R. S. Moyes 1936
Tom Bromilow 1936–39
George Irwin 1939–47
Jack Butler 1947–49
Ronnie Rooke 1949–50
Charlie Slade and Fred Dawes *(Joint Managers)* 1950–51
Laurie Scott 1951–54
Cyril Spiers 1954–58
George Smith 1958–60
Arthur Rowe 1960–62
Dick Graham 1962–66
Bert Head 1966–72 *(continued as General Manager to 1973)*
Malcolm Allison 1973–76
Terry Venables 1976–80
Ernie Walley 1980
Malcolm Allison 1980–81
Dario Gradi 1981
Steve Kember 1981–82
Alan Mullery 1982–84
Steve Coppell 1984–93
Alan Smith 1993–95
Steve Coppell *(Technical Director)* 1995–96
Dave Bassett 1996–97
Steve Coppell 1997–98
Attilio Lombardo 1998
Terry Venables *(Head Coach)* 1998–99
Steve Coppell 1999–2000
Alan Smith 2000–01
Steve Bruce 2001
Trevor Francis 2001–03
Steve Kember 2003
Iain Dowie 2003–06
Peter Taylor 2006–07
Neil Warnock 2007–10
Paul Hart 2010
George Burley 2010–11
Dougie Freedman January 2011–

TEN YEAR LEAGUE RECORD

		P	W	D	L	F	A	Pts	Pos
2001-02	Div 1	46	20	6	20	70	62	66	10
2002-03	Div 1	46	14	17	15	59	52	59	14
2003-04	Div 1	46	21	10	15	72	61	73	6
2004-05	PR Lge	38	7	12	19	41	62	33	18
2005-06	FL C	46	21	12	13	67	48	75	6
2006-07	FL C	46	18	11	17	59	51	65	12
2007-08	FL C	46	18	17	11	58	42	71	5
2008-09	FL C	46	15	12	19	52	55	57	15
2009-10	FL C	46	14	17	15	50	53	49*	21
2010-11	FL C	46	12	12	22	44	69	48	20

* 10 pts deducted.

DID YOU KNOW ?

On 30 January 1926 Crystal Palace defeated Chelsea 2-1 in a fourth round FA Cup tie at Selhurst Park. The attendance that day of 41,000 was at the time a record crowd for the venue. Receipts from the match were nearly £2,545 and the gate remained a record for 40 years.

CRYSTAL PALACE 2010–11 LEAGUE RECORD

Match No.	Date	Venue	Opponents	Result	H/T Score	Lg Pos.	Goalscorers	Attendance
1	Aug 7	H	Leicester C	W 3-2	3-0	—	Zaha [19], Ambrose [26], Lee [41]	17,486
2	14	A	Barnsley	L 0-1	0-1	10		11,353
3	21	H	Ipswich T	L 1-2	0-0	15	Danns [90]	15,781
4	28	A	Scunthorpe U	L 0-3	0-2	20		5292
5	Sept 11	A	Reading	L 0-3	0-1	21		17,921
6	14	H	Portsmouth	W 4-1	1-1	—	Vaughan 3 [14, 55, 59], Danns (pen) [81]	14,219
7	18	H	Burnley	D 0-0	0-0	19		14,451
8	25	A	Derby Co	L 0-5	0-2	19		25,258
9	28	A	Cardiff C	D 0-0	0-0	—		22,007
10	Oct 2	H	QPR	L 1-2	0-0	23	Cadogan [89]	17,171
11	16	H	Millwall	L 0-1	0-0	23		16,693
12	19	A	Norwich C	W 2-1	0-1	—	Bennett [56], Gardner [63]	24,975
13	23	A	Preston NE	L 3-4	1-3	23	Garvan [20], Dorman [69], Vaughan (pen) [80]	10,116
14	30	H	Swansea C	L 0-3	0-1	24		16,223
15	Nov 6	A	Middlesbrough	L 1-2	1-0	24	Counago [29]	15,400
16	9	H	Watford	W 3-2	1-0	—	Ambrose [18], Garvan 2 [56, 59]	12,353
17	13	H	Coventry C	W 2-0	1-0	23	Ambrose 2 (1 pen) [33, 54 (p)]	13,278
18	20	A	Sheffield U	L 2-3	1-1	23	Danns (pen) [18], Vaughan [63]	20,240
19	27	H	Doncaster R	W 1-0	1-0	22	Counago [35]	12,470
20	Dec 4	A	Leeds U	L 1-2	1-0	—	Danns [44]	25,476
21	11	H	Hull C	D 0-0	0-0	22		13,341
22	18	A	Nottingham F	L 0-3	0-1	22		22,359
23	28	A	Bristol C	D 1-1	1-0	23	Danns [2]	15,760
24	Jan 1	A	Millwall	L 0-3	0-1	23		16,170
25	3	H	Preston NE	W 1-0	0-0	22	Iversen [58]	14,961
26	15	A	Swansea C	L 0-3	0-1	22		13,369
27	22	H	Bristol C	D 0-0	0-0	22		14,128
28	29	H	Norwich C	D 0-0	0-0	—		16,327
29	Feb 1	A	Watford	D 1-1	1-1	21	Vaughan [40]	12,664
30	5	H	Middlesbrough	W 1-0	1-0	21	Vaughan [36]	14,060
31	12	A	Coventry C	L 1-2	0-1	21	Iversen [90]	16,454
32	19	H	Sheffield U	W 1-0	0-0	21	Ambrose [69]	14,214
33	22	A	Portsmouth	L 0-1	0-0	—		15,641
34	26	H	Reading	D 3-3	2-1	21	Ambrose [1], Danns [25], Easter [68]	13,845
35	Mar 5	A	Burnley	L 0-1	0-1	21		14,848
36	8	H	Cardiff C	W 1-0	0-0	—	Dikgacoi [82]	12,549
37	12	A	QPR	L 1-2	1-1	21	Vaughan [40]	18,116
38	19	H	Derby Co	D 2-2	1-1	21	Moxey [21], Ambrose (pen) [88]	14,686
39	Apr 2	H	Barnsley	W 2-1	1-1	21	Danns [29], Vaughan (pen) [75]	19,344
40	9	A	Ipswich T	L 1-2	0-1	21	McCarthy [73]	24,378
41	12	A	Leicester C	D 1-1	1-0	—	Scannell [31]	22,303
42	16	H	Scunthorpe U	L 1-2	0-1	21	Scannell [70]	17,810
43	22	A	Doncaster R	D 0-0	0-0	—		14,312
44	25	H	Leeds U	W 1-0	1-0	20	Danns [2]	20,142
45	30	A	Hull C	D 1-1	0-1	20	Sekajja [88]	20,407
46	May 7	H	Nottingham F	L 0-3	0-1	20		18,443

Final League Position: 20

GOALSCORERS

League (44): Vaughan 9 (2 pens), Danns 8 (2 pens), Ambrose 7 (2 pens), Garvan 3, Counago 2, Iversen 2, Scannell 2, Bennett 1, Cadogan 1, Dikgacoi 1, Dorman 1, Easter 1, Gardner 1, Lee 1, McCarthy 1, Moxey 1, Sekajja 1, Zaha 1.
Carling Cup (2): Lee 1, own goal 1.
FA Cup (1): Danns 1.

Speroni J 45	Clyne N 46	Bennett J 10+3	Davis C 17+7	McCarthy P 43	Garvan O 26	Ambrose D 27+1	Cadogan K 7+9	Lee A 3	Zaha W 26+15	Dorman A 14+6	N'Diaye A 4+8	Andrew C 1+12	Djilali K 10+4	Wright D 27+1	Danns N 36+1	Barrett A 5+2	Obika J —+7	Marrow A 20+1	Davids E 6	Counago P 17+13	Gardner A 26+2	Vaughan J 28+2	O'Keefe S 1+3	Scannell S 5+14	Iversen S 11+6	Easter J 6+8	Parsons M 2	Moxey D 17	Dikgacoi K 13	Price L 1	Agustien K 6+2	Sekajja I —+1	Match No.
1	2		4	5	6	7	8^1		9^2	10^3	11	12	13	14																			1
1	2		4	5	6	7	8^1		9	10	11^2		13		3	12																	2
1	2	3	4●	5	6		8^1		9^3	10	11^2			7	12	13	14																3
1	2		4	5^1	6		8^2		13	14		9	11		12	7	3	10^3															4
1	2	3		5	6	13			10^1	14	11	8		7^2	12	4	9^3																5
1	2			5	6	8			10	12	11	7^2		3	13	4	9^1																6
1	2	13	4	5	6	8^1		12	10^2		14	11^3	7		3		9																7
1	2	12	4	5	6			10^2	14	13	11^1	7		3	8^3		9●																8
1	2	12	4^1	5	6	14		9	13	11^3	7^2		3	8	10																		9
1	2	3		5	6	12		9	11^3	14	7	4	8^2	10^1	13																		10
1	2	3	4●	5	6	8^1		9	7^2	12	13	11	10																				11
1	2	3		5	6	9	7	12	11	8^1	13	4	10^2																				12
1	2	3		5	6	13	9	8^2	14	11^1	7^3	12	4	10																			13
1	2			5	6^1	13	9	8	14	11^2	3	4	12	7^3	10																		14
1	2			5	6	7	12	13	14	3^3	8^2	4	11	10^1	9																		15
1	2	13		5	6	7^3	12	14	3	8	4^2	11	10^1	9																			16
1	2		4^1	5	6	7^3	9	14	3	8	11	13	12	10^2																			17
1	2		4	5^1	6●	9	7	3	8	11	13	10	12^2																				18
1	2		4		7^2	8	12	13	3	6	14	11^1	10	5	9●																		19
1	2		4		7	13	8^2	11^1	3	6	10	5	9	12																			20
1	2		4	5	6	9^2	11	3	7	13	10	8^1	12																				21
1	2		4	5	6	7^3	12	11^1	9	13	3	8	10^2	14																			22
1	2	11	4^1	5		7	13	9	3	6	12	14	8^3																				23
1	2			5	6	7^3	13	12	14	8	4	11^1	10^2	9																			24
1	2	3		5	6	12		9^3	11	13	14	8		4	7^1	10^2																	25
1	2			5	6	8	11^1	12	3	7				10^3	4	14	9^2	13															26
1	2			5		7^3	8	14	3	4	11	10^1	6	13	12	9^2																	27
1	2			5		7	12	3	4	11	6	9	10^1	8																			28
1	2	14		5		7^1	10^3	3	8	6	11	9^2	12	13	4																		29
1	2			5		7^1	10	3	11	13	4	9^3	12	14	8^2	6																	30
1	2			5	6	7^2	8	11	13	4	9^3	12	14	10^1	3																		31
1	2	13	5		7^2	8^1	11	4	14	6	9^3	10^1	14	13	3	10																	32
1	2			5		7	12	11	4^2	6	9^3	10^1	14	13	3	8																	33
1	2			5		8	14	11	4^3	6	10^1	13	9^2	12	3	7																	34
	2			5		7	3^2	4	13	6	9	12	10^2	14	11	8^1	1																35
1	2	13	5		7^2	11	4	12	6	9^3	14	10^1	3	8																			36
1	2	12	5●	7	14	11^3	4	6	9^2	10^1	13	3	8																					37
1	2	5		7	14	11^3	4	13	6	9^1	10^2	12	3	8																				38
1	2	5		7^1	12	4^2	6	9^3	13	10	14	3	8	11																			39
1	2	5		7^1 14	13	4	6	9^2	12	10	3	8	11^3																				40
1	2	5	7^1	9●	4	10^1	6	13	11^2 14	3	8	12																						41
1	2	5	7^3	12	4	14	6	9	13● 10	3	8^1	11^2																						42
1	2	5	7	13	9^2	4	10^1	6	12	3	8	11																						43
1	2	14	5	7	11	4●	6	12	10^3	9^1	3	8^2	13																					44
1	2	4	5	6^1	7	12	9^2 13	11	10^3	3	8	14																						45
1	2	12	5	7	14	11^3	4	10^1	6	13	9^2	3●	8																					46

FA Cup

Third Round	Coventry C	(a)	1-2

Carling Cup

First Round	Yeovil T	(a)	1-0
Second Round	Portsmouth	(a)	1-1

DAGENHAM & REDBRIDGE   FL Championship 2

FOUNDATION

The roots of Dagenham & Redbridge live firmly in the Essex side of the Greater London area. Though only formed in 1992 their complex origins date back to the 19th century involving Ilford (founded 1881) and Leytonstone (1886) who merged in 1979 to form Leytonstone-Ilford. They and Walthamstow Avenue (1900) joined together in 1988 to becom Redbridge Forest who in turn merged with Dagenham FC (1949) in 1992. Victoria Road has existed as a football ground since 1917. Initially used by Sterling Works, in the summer of 1955 Briggs Sports vacated the premises and Dagenham FC moved in and the pitch was enclosed.

The London Borough of Barking and Dagenham Stadium, Victoria Road, Dagenham, Essex RM10 7XL.

Telephone: (0208) 592 1549.

Fax: (020) 8593 7227.

Ticket Office: (020) 8592 1549 (extension 21).

Website: www.daggers.co.uk

Email: info@daggers.co.uk

Ground Capacity: 6,007.

Record Attendance: 4,791 v Shrewsbury T, FL 2, 2 May 2009.

Pitch Measurements: 100m × 64.5m.

Chairman: David J. Andrews.

Vice-chairman: David E. Ward.

Managing Director: Stephen R. Thompson.

Secretary: Terry Grover.

Manager: John L. Still.

Assistant Manager: Terry W. Harris.

Physio: John Gowens.

Colours: Red shirts with blue sleeves and red trim, blue shorts, blue stockings.

Change Colours: All yellow.

Year Formed: 1992.

Ground: 1992, Victoria Road.

Club Nickname: The Daggers.

First Football League Game: 11 August 2007, FL 2 v Stockport Co (a) L 0–1 – Roberts; Foster, Griffiths, Rainford, Uddin, Boardman, Saunders (Strevens), Southam, Benson (Moore), Nurse, Sloma (Huke).

MANAGERS

John Still 1992–94
Dave Cusack 1994–95
Graham Carr 1995–96
Ted Hardy 1996–99
Garry Hill 1999–2004
John Still April 2004–

sky SPORTS FACT FILE

Dagenham & Redbridge created a record in the play-offs for promotion to League One on 16 May 2010 when they defeated Morecambe 6-0 in the first leg of their tie. It was not the only first to come from the match as Josh Scott scored four of the goals, the highest at this stage.

Record League Victory: 6–0 v Chester C, FL 2, 9 August 2008 – Roberts; Okuonghae, Griffiths, Arber, Uddin, Taiwo, Saunders (2), Green (1) (Southam), Benson (1) (Nurse), Strevens (1p) (Nwokeji (1)), Gain.

Record Cup Victory: 6–1 v Stowmarket T, FA Cup 2nd qual rd, 28 September 1992; 6–1 v Wealdstone (a), FA Cup 3rd qual rd, 12 October 1992.

Record Defeat: 0–9 v Hereford U, Conference, 27 February 2004.

Most League Points (3 for a win): 72, FL 2, 2009–10.

Most League Goals: 77, FL 2, 2008–09.

Highest League Scorer in Season: Paul Benson, 28, Conference, 2006–07.

Most League Goals in Total Aggregate: 40, Paul Benson, 2007–.

Most League Goals in One Match: 4, Paul Benson v Shrewsbury T, FL 2, 18 August 2009.

Most Capped Player: Jon Nurse, 4, Barbados.

Most League Appearances: Tony Roberts, 175, 2007–.

Youngest League Player: Dominic Green, 18 years 93 days v Brentford, 2 October 2007.

Record Transfer Fee Received: £200,000 from Cardiff C for Solomon Taiwo, August 2009.

Record Transfer Fee Paid: £20,000 to Plymouth Arg for Damien McCrory, February 2010.

Football League Record: 2006–07 Promoted from Conference; 2007–10 FL 2; 2010–11 FL 1; 2011– FL 2.

LATEST SEQUENCES

Longest Sequence of League Wins: 5, 12.2.2008 – 1.3.2008.

Longest Sequence of League Defeats: 4, 27.10.2007 – 17.11.2007.

Longest Sequence of League Draws: 3, 21.9.2010 – 28.9.2010.

Longest Sequence of Unbeaten League Matches: 6, 6.12.2008 – 17.1.2009.

Longest Sequence Without a League Win: 9, 6.10.2007 – 4.12.2007.

Successive Scoring Runs: 16 from 12.4.2008.

Successive Non-scoring Runs: 3 from 12.1.2008.

HONOURS

FA Cup: Best season: 3rd rd, 2008.

Conference: *Champions* 2006–07. *Runners-up* 2001–02.

Isthmian League (Premier): *Champions* 1999–2000.

Essex Senior Cup: *Winners* 1997–98, 2000–01; *Runners-up* 2001–02.

AS DAGENHAM FC

FA Trophy: *Winners* 1979–80; *Runners-up* 1976–77.

Amateur Cup: *Runners-up* 1969–70, 1970–71.

AS ILFORD

FA Amateur Cup: *Winners* 1929, 1930. **Isthmian League:** *Champions* 1906–07, 1920–21, 1921–22.

AS LEYTONSTONE

FA Amateur Cup: *Winners* 1947, 1948, 1968.

Isthmian League: *Champions* 1918–19, 1937–38, 1938–39, 1946–47, 1947–48, 1949–50, 1950–51, 1951–52, 1965–66.

AS LEYTONSTONE/ILFORD

Isthmian League: *Champions* 1981–82, 1988–89.

AS WALTHAMSTOW AVENUE

FA Amateur Cup: *Winners* 1952, 1961. **Isthmian League:** *Champions* 1945–46, 1948–49, 1952–53, 1954–55. **Athenian League:** *Champions* 1929–30, 1932–33, 1933–34, 1937–38, 1938–39.

AS REDBRIDGE FOREST

Isthmian League: *Winners* 1990–91.

TEN YEAR LEAGUE RECORD

		P	W	D	L	F	A	Pts	Pos
2001-02	Conf	42	24	12	8	70	47	84	3
2002-03	Conf	42	21	9	12	71	59	72	5
2003-04	Conf	42	15	9	18	59	64	54	13
2004-05	Conf	42	19	8	15	68	60	65	11
2005-06	Conf	42	16	19	16	63	59	58	10
2006-07	Conf	46	28	11	7	93	48	95	1
2007-08	FL 2	46	13	10	23	49	70	49	20
2008-09	FL 2	46	19	11	16	77	53	68	8
2009-10	FL 2	46	20	12	14	69	58	72	7
2010-11	FL 1	46	12	11	23	52	70	47	21

DID YOU KNOW ?

In a fourth qualifying round of the FA Cup in October 2001, Tony Roberts made history by becoming the first goalkeeper in the history of the competition to score direct from open play in the 2-2 draw at Basingstoke Town. The Daggers won the replay 3-0.

DAGENHAM & REDBRIDGE 2010–11 LEAGUE RECORD

Match No.	Date	Venue	Opponents	Result	H/T Score	Lg Pos.	Goalscorers	Attendance
1	Aug 7	A	Sheffield W	L 0-2	0-2	—		23,081
2	21	A	Notts Co	L 0-1	0-0	24		5210
3	28	H	Tranmere R	D 2-2	0-0	23	Vincelot [52], Arber [71]	2256
4	Sept 4	H	Leyton Orient	W 2-0	1-0	19	Vincelot 2 [8, 50]	4195
5	11	A	Bournemouth	L 0-3	0-2	24		5501
6	18	H	Bristol R	L 0-3	0-2	24		2287
7	21	H	Exeter C	D 1-1	0-1	—	Vincelot [71]	2005
8	25	A	Charlton Ath	D 2-2	1-1	23	Green, Danny (pen) [45], Nurse [90]	14,806
9	28	A	Colchester U	D 2-2	1-1	—	Savage [15], Vincelot [72]	4515
10	Oct 2	H	Swindon T	W 2-1	0-1	20	Scannell [48], Savage [80]	2767
11	9	A	Milton Keynes D	L 0-2	0-0	21		7083
12	16	H	Walsall	D 1-1	1-0	23	Currie [26]	2666
13	23	A	Rochdale	L 2-3	0-2	24	Scannell [64], Arber [68]	2650
14	30	H	Hartlepool U	D 1-1	0-0	23	Hartley (og) [49]	2464
15	Nov 2	A	Southampton	L 0-4	0-2	—		20,161
16	13	A	Yeovil T	W 3-1	1-1	22	Antwi [18], Ogogo [81], Elito [87]	3586
17	20	H	Oldham Ath	L 0-1	0-0	22		2239
18	23	A	Plymouth Arg	L 1-2	1-0	—	Tomlin [9]	4960
19	Dec 11	A	Carlisle U	W 2-0	0-0	22	Elito [82], Green, Danny [89]	4380
20	Jan 1	A	Brentford	L 1-2	1-1	22	Vincelot [34]	5405
21	3	H	Southampton	L 1-3	0-0	23	Scott [84]	3585
22	8	H	Rochdale	L 0-1	0-0	—		1948
23	15	A	Hartlepool U	W 1-0	0-0	23	Tomlin [86]	2939
24	22	H	Milton Keynes D	L 0-1	0-0	23		4446
25	Feb 1	H	Brentford	W 4-1	1-0	23	Nurse 2 [19, 66], Osborne (og) [56], Vincelot [67]	1907
26	5	A	Oldham Ath	D 1-1	0-0	24	Vincelot [73]	4121
27	12	H	Yeovil T	W 2-1	1-1	22	Vincelot [30], Nurse [72]	2119
28	15	A	Walsall	L 0-1	0-0	—		3174
29	22	H	Huddersfield T	D 1-1	0-1	—	Green, Danny (pen) [59]	2336
30	26	H	Bournemouth	L 1-2	0-0	23	Nurse [48]	2768
31	Mar 5	A	Bristol R	W 2-0	1-0	21	Green, Danny [45], Vincelot [83]	5716
32	8	H	Colchester U	W 1-0	1-0	—	Savage [11]	2140
33	12	A	Swindon T	D 1-1	0-1	20	Nurse [83]	7864
34	19	H	Charlton Ath	W 2-1	1-0	20	Nurse [33], Green, Danny [55]	3505
35	22	A	Leyton Orient	D 1-1	1-0	—	Green, Danny [12]	4581
36	26	H	Sheffield W	D 1-1	0-1	—	Green, Danny (pen) [80]	3549
37	29	H	Brighton & HA	L 0-1	0-0	—		3604
38	Apr 2	A	Exeter C	L 1-2	0-0	20	Vincelot [76]	4598
39	5	H	Peterborough U	L 0-2	0-2	—		2063
40	9	H	Notts Co	W 3-1	3-0	19	Akinde [16], Green, Danny 2 (1 pen) [41, 45 (p)]	2608
41	12	A	Brighton & HA	L 3-4	1-2	—	Akinde [1], Nurse [48], Green, Danny (pen) [51]	7619
42	16	A	Tranmere R	L 0-2	0-2	19		4562
43	22	H	Plymouth Arg	L 0-1	0-0	—		3559
44	25	A	Huddersfield T	L 1-2	1-2	20	Vincelot [28]	14,072
45	30	H	Carlisle U	W 3-0	2-0	21	Nurse 2 [4, 29], Green, Danny [84]	2693
46	May 7	A	Peterborough U	L 0-5	0-1	21		7519

Final League Position: 21

GOALSCORERS

League (52): Vincelot 12, Green, Danny 11 (5 pens), Nurse 10, Savage 3, Akinde 2, Arber 2, Elito 2, Scannell 2, Tomlin 2, Antwi 1, Currie 1, Ogogo 1, Scott 1, own goals 2.
Carling Cup (1): McCrory 1.
FA Cup (3): Danny Green 2 (1 pen), Taiwo 1.
J Paint Trophy (0).

Roberts T 43	Ogogo A 33	McCrory D 22+1	Arber M 44	Doe S 38	Vincelot R 46	Green Danny 41	Lewis S 7+3	Benson P 3	Tomlin G 16+3	Gain P 35+2	Nurse J 24+14	Scott J 8+8	Scannell D 14+6	Currie D 12+10	Antwi W 9+2	Ifil P 13+1	Savage B 21+15	Gwillim G —+2	Bingham B 4+2	Taiwo S 16+2	Walsh P —+3	Lewington C 3	Pinney N —+1	Palsson V 2	Elito M 8+2	Ilesanmi F 24+1	Brown K 3	Morgan M 5+7	Lancaster C —+4	Lee O 4+1	Akinde J 8+1	Green Danny J —+3	Match No.
1	2	3	4	5	6	7^1	8	9	10^2	11^3	12	13	14																				1
1	2	3^1	4	5	6	7	8^1	9	11	13	10^2	12	14																				2
1	2	3	4	5	6	7	8	9	11		10																						3
1	2^1	3	4	5	6	7	13		9^3	8	14	10		11^2	12																		4
1		3	4	5	6	7^2	14		9^1	8	12	10	13	11^3		2																	5
1		3	4	5	6	7	8^1		9	11	12	10^2				2	13																6
1		3	4	5	6	7	8		9	11		10^2				2^1	13	12															7
1		3	4	5	6	7^3	8		9	11	12^2	13	14			2	10^1																8
1		3	4	5	6^1	7	8		9^2	11	13					2	10		12														9
1		3	4	5	6	7^3			9^1	8	12	14	11			2^2	10	13															10
1		3	4	5	6	7	12		9^1	8	13	11				2	10^2																11
1		3	4	5	6	7			8			12	9^1	11		2	10																12
1		3	4	5	6	7			9	8		12	11			2	10^1																13
1		3	4	5	6				9		14	10^2	11^3	7		2^1	13				8	12											14
		3	4	5^1	6	7			9^3		12	10	11^1			2					8	13	1	14									15
	2	3	4		6	7			13	9^2					5		10				8		1		11^1	12							16
	2		4		6	7			12	9^2		14			5		13				8		1		11^3	3	10^1						17
1	2		4		6	7			9^2	12					5		13				8	11				3	10^1						18
1	2		4		6	7						12			5		10^1				8				11	3	9						19
1	3		2		6	7									5		10	9	8						11	4							20
1	2			5	6	7			12	13		14			4		10^3	9^1	8^2						11	0							21
1	2		4	5	6	7			9^3	8		12		14			10^2								11^1	3		13					22
1	2		4	5	6	7			9	8		12													11^1	3		10					23
1	2		4	5	6	7			9	8		12													11^1	3		10					24
1	2		4	5	6				8	9^2		11^1	7				13								12	3		10					25
1	2		4	5	6				11	9		7					12		8^1	13						3		10^2					26
1	2		4	5^1	6				9			11	7				12		8	13						3		10^1					27
1	2		4	5	6	7^2			13	9		11^1					10		0							3		12					28
1	7	12^2	4	5	6	7			9			11					10^2		8							3^1		13					29
1	2	3	4		6	7			5	9		13	11^2				10^1		8									12					30
1	3^1	2	5	6		7			11	9		10^2			4		13		8						12								31
1	2		4	5	6	7			11	9							10^1		8							3		12					32
1	2		4	5	6	7			11	9			13				10^3	12^2	8^1							3		14					33
1	2		4	5	6	7			8	9		11^1					10		12							3							34
1	2		4	5	6	7			8	9		11^2				13	10^1									3^1		12					35
1	2	3	4	5	6	7			8	9		11^2	13				10^1													12			36
1	2	3	4	5	6	7			8	9		11^2	13				10^1													12			37
1	2	3	4	5	6				8	9							10^1														11	12	38
1	2	3	4	5	6	7^2			11	9		12	13																		8	10^1	39
1	2		4	5	6	7			8	9		11^1					13									3				12	10^2		40
1	2		4	5	6	7			11	9		12														3					8^1	10	41
1	2		4	5	6	7^3			11	9		13					12									3			14	8^2	10^1		42
1	2		4	5^1	6	7			8	9		11	12			14										3^3					10^2	13	43
1	2		4		6	7			11	9^2		14			5		13		8^1							3^3					10	12	44
1	2		4		6	7^4			8	9		5					12					11				3					10^1		45
1			4		6				11^3	9		7	5	2	12		8									3^2				14	10^1	13	46

FA Cup
First Round　　Leyton Orient　　(h)　1-1
　　　　　　　　　　　　　　　　　(a)　2-3

Carling Cup
First Round　　Milton Keynes D　　(a)　1-2

J Paint Trophy
First Round　　Charlton Ath　　(a)　0-1

DERBY COUNTY   FL Championship

FOUNDATION

Derby County was formed by members of the Derbyshire County Cricket Club in 1884, when football was booming in the area and the cricketers thought that a football club would help boost finances for the summer game. To begin with, they sported the cricket club's colours of amber, chocolate and pale blue, and went into the game at the top immediately entering the FA Cup.

Pride Park Stadium, Derby DE24 8XL.
Telephone: 0871 472 1884.
Fax: (01332) 667 519.
Ticket Office: 0871 472 1884.
Website: www.dcfc.co.uk
Email: derby.county@dcfc.co.uk
Ground Capacity: 33,597.
Record Attendance: 41,826 v Tottenham H, Division 1, 20 September 1969 (at Baseball Ground). 33,597 England v Mexico, 25 May 2001 (at Pride Park).
Pitch Measurements: 100.58m × 67.66m.
Chairman of GSC and Club Chairman: Andy Appleby.
Vice-chairman of GSC and Vice Club Chairman: Lionel Margolick.
President and Chief Executive: Tom Glick.
Secretary: Clare Morris.
Manager: Nigel Clough.
Coaches: Gary Crosby, Andy Garner, Martin Taylor, Johnny Metgod.
Physio: Neil Sullivan.

HONOURS

Football League – Division 1:
Champions 1971–72, 1974–75;
Runners-up 1895–96, 1929–30, 1935–36, 1995–96;
Division 2: *Champions* 1911–12, 1914–15, 1968–69, 1986–87;
Runners-up 1925–26;
Division 3 (N): *Champions* 1956–57;
Runners-up 1955–56.
FA Cup: *Winners* 1946;
Runners-up 1898, 1899, 1903.
Football League Cup: Semi-final 1968, 2009.
Texaco Cup: *Winners* 1972.
European Competitions
European Cup: 1972–73, 1975–76.
UEFA Cup: 1974–75, 1976–77.
Anglo-Italian Cup: *Runners-up* 1993.

Colours: White shirts with black trim, black shorts with white trim, white stockings with black trim.
Change Colours: Black shirts with white trim, grey shorts with black and white trim, black stockings with grey and white trim.
Year Formed: 1884. *Turned Professional:* 1884. *Ltd Co.:* 1896.
Club Nickname: 'The Rams'.
Grounds: 1884, Racecourse Ground; 1895, Baseball Ground; 1997, Pride Park.
First Football League Game: 8 September 1888, Football League, v Bolton W (a) W 6–3 – Marshall; Latham, Ferguson, Williamson; Monks, Walter Roulstone; Bakewell (2), Cooper (2), Higgins, Harry Plackett, Lol Plackett (2).
Record League Victory: 9–0 v Wolverhampton W, Division 1, 10 January 1891 – Bunyan; Archie Goodall, Roberts; Walker, Chalmers, Walter Roulstone (1); Bakewell, McLachlan, Johnny Goodall (1), Holmes (2), McMillan (5). 9–0 v Sheffield W, Division 1, 21 January 1899 – Fryer; Methven, Staley; Cox, Archie Goodall, May; Oakden (1), Bloomer (6), Boag, McDonald (1), Allen, (1 og).

sky SPORTS FACT FILE

In 1909–10, Derby County relied heavily on the scoring partnership of Jimmy Bauchop and Alf Bentley with 21 and 30 League goals respectively from a total of 72. The Rams finished fourth but the top four were separated by just one point. They took only two out of a possible last six.

Record Cup Victory: 12–0 v Finn Harps, UEFA Cup 1st rd 1st leg, 15 September 1976 – Moseley; Thomas, Nish, Rioch (1), McFarland, Todd (King), Macken, Gemmill, Hector (5), George (3), James (3).

Record Defeat: 2–11 v Everton, FA Cup 1st rd, 1889–90.

Most League Points (2 for a win): 63, Division 2, 1968–69 and Division 3 (N), 1955–56 and 1956–57.

Most League Points (3 for a win): 84, Division 3, 1985–86, Division 3, 1986–87 and FL C, 2006–07.

Most League Goals: 111, Division 3 (N), 1956–57.

Highest League Scorer in Season: Jack Bowers, 37, Division 1, 1930–31; Ray Straw, 37 Division 3 (N), 1956–57.

Most League Goals in Total Aggregate: Steve Bloomer, 292, 1892–1906 and 1910–14.

Most League Goals in One Match: 6, Steve Bloomer v Sheffield W, Division 1, 2 January 1899.

Most Capped Player: Deon Burton, 42 (59), Jamaica.

Most League Appearances: Kevin Hector, 486, 1966–78 and 1980–82.

Youngest League Player: Lee Holmes, 15 years 268 days v Grimsby T, 26 December 2002.

Record Transfer Fee Received: £7,000,000 rising to £9,000,000 for Seth Johnson from Leeds U, October 2001.

Record Transfer Fee Paid: £4,000,000 to Crewe Alex for Seth Johnson, May 1999 (including sell-on).

Football League Record: 1888 Founder Member of the Football League; 1907–12 Division 2; 1912–14 Division 1; 1914–15 Division 2; 1915–21 Division 1; 1921–26 Division 2; 1926–53 Division 1; 1953–55 Division 2; 1955–57 Division 3 (N); 1957–69 Division 2; 1969–80 Division 1; 1980–84 Division 2; 1984–86 Division 3; 1986–87 Division 2; 1987–91 Division 1; 1991–92 Division 2; 1992–96 Division 1; 1996–2002 FA Premier League; 2002–04 Division 1; 2004–07 FL C; 2007–08 FA Premier League; 2008– FL C.

MANAGERS

W. D. Clark 1896–1900
Harry Newbould 1900–06
Jimmy Methven 1906–22
Cecil Potter 1922–25
George Jobey 1925–41
Ted Magner 1944–46
Stuart McMillan 1946–53
Jack Barker 1953–55
Harry Storer 1955–62
Tim Ward 1962–67
Brian Clough 1967–73
Dave Mackay 1973–76
Colin Murphy 1977
Tommy Docherty 1977–79
Colin Addison 1979–82
Johnny Newman 1982
Peter Taylor 1982–84
Roy McFarland 1984
Arthur Cox 1984–93
Roy McFarland 1993–95
Jim Smith 1995–2001
Colin Todd 2001–02
John Gregory 2002–03
George Burley 2003–05
Phil Brown 2005–06
Billy Davies 2006–07
Paul Jewell 2007–08
Nigel Clough January 2009–

LATEST SEQUENCES

Longest Sequence of League Wins: 9, 15.3.1969 – 19.4.1969.

Longest Sequence of League Defeats: 8, 12.12.1987 – 10.2.1988.

Longest Sequence of League Draws: 6, 26.3.1927 – 18.4.1927.

Longest Sequence of Unbeaten League Matches: 22, 8.3.1969 – 20.9.1969.

Longest Sequence Without a League Win: 36, 22.9.2007 – 30.8.2008.

Successive Scoring Runs: 29 from 3.12.1960.

Successive Non-scoring Runs: 8 from 30.10.1920.

TEN YEAR LEAGUE RECORD

		P	W	D	L	F	A	Pts	Pos
2001-02	PR Lge	38	8	6	24	33	63	30	19
2002-03	Div 1	46	15	7	24	55	74	52	18
2003-04	Div 1	46	13	13	20	53	67	52	20
2004-05	FL C	46	22	10	14	71	60	76	4
2005-06	FL C	46	10	20	16	53	67	50	20
2006-07	FL C	46	25	9	12	62	46	84	3
2007-08	PR Lge	38	1	8	29	20	89	11	20
2008-09	FL C	46	14	12	20	55	67	54	18
2009-10	FL C	46	15	11	20	53	63	56	14
2010-11	FL C	46	13	10	23	58	71	49	19

DID YOU KNOW ?

Benjamin Ward Spilsbury scored the first Derby County goal against Blackburn Olympic on 27 September 1884. He became the club's first England international and the first to score hat-tricks in successive FA Cup ties in 1887, initially against Ecclesfield, then Owlerton.

DERBY COUNTY 2010–11 LEAGUE RECORD

Match No.	Date		Venue	Opponents	Result		H/T Score	Lg Pos.	Goalscorers	Attendance
1	Aug	7	A	Leeds U	W	2-1	2-1	—	Hulse [13], Commons (pen) [27]	26,761
2		14	H	Cardiff C	L	1-2	1-1	11	Cywka [25]	25,103
3		21	A	Coventry C	L	1-2	0-1	16	Moxey [52]	13,169
4		28	H	QPR	D	2-2	1-0	15	Commons [40], Bailey [59]	25,874
5	Sept	11	H	Sheffield U	L	0-1	0-1	18		25,749
6		14	A	Hull C	L	0-2	0-1	—		19,714
7		18	A	Barnsley	D	1-1	1-0	20	Leacock [14]	12,089
8		25	H	Crystal Palace	W	5-0	2-0	19	Bueno 2 [14, 62], Commons [41], Green [68], Kuqi [73]	25,258
9		28	H	Middlesbrough	W	3-1	1-1	—	Barker [45], Commons 2 [51, 60]	24,739
10	Oct	2	A	Swansea C	D	0-0	0-0	14		15,071
11		16	H	Preston NE	W	3-0	2-0	13	Moxey [21], Bueno [32], Savage (pen) [90]	26,117
12		19	A	Doncaster R	W	3-2	1-0	—	Moore [19], Commons 2 [59, 72]	9000
13		23	A	Millwall	L	0-2	0-1	12		12,024
14		30	H	Watford	W	4-1	2-0	7	Brayford [14], Cywka 2 [36, 81], Kuqi [65]	27,119
15	Nov	6	H	Portsmouth	W	2-0	1-0	4	Savage (pen) [23], Green [58]	29,086
16		9	A	Ipswich T	W	2-0	0-0	—	Commons 2 [58, 76]	17,572
17		13	A	Leicester C	L	0-2	0-1	4		25,930
18		20	H	Scunthorpe U	W	3-2	2-1	4	Cywka [3], Commons (pen) [37], Moore [59]	25,189
19		27	A	Burnley	L	1-2	1-0	4	Moore [19]	13,790
20	Dec	4	H	Norwich C	L	1-2	1-2	—	Commons [17]	26,134
21		11	A	Bristol C	L	.0-2	0-0	7		14,029
22		18	H	Reading	L	1-2	0-1	9	Commons [61]	24,514
23		29	A	Nottingham F	L	2-5	1-3	—	Moore [14], Commons [55]	29,490
24	Jan	1	A	Preston NE	W	2-1	0-0	12	Porter 2 [70, 84]	11,198
25		3	H	Millwall	D	0-0	0-0	13		24,239
26		15	A	Watford	L	0-3	0-3	14		12,917
27		22	H	Nottingham F	L	0-1	0-0	14		33,010
28	Feb	1	H	Ipswich T	L	1-2	1-1	16	Bueno [7]	23,159
29		5	A	Portsmouth	D	1-1	1-0	17	Davies, S [34]	14,555
30		12	H	Leicester C	L	0-2	0-2	17		26,142
31		19	A	Scunthorpe U	D	0-0	0-0	18		5696
32		22	H	Hull C	L	0-1	0-0	—		24,533
33		26	A	Sheffield U	W	1-0	1-0	18	Robinson [27]	21,084
34	Mar	1	H	Doncaster R	L	1-3	0-1	—	Davies, S [90]	24,239
35		5	H	Barnsley	D	0-0	0-0	18		26,251
36		8	A	Middlesbrough	L	1-2	1-0	—	Ward (pen) [32]	13,712
37		12	H	Swansea C	W	2-1	1-0	18	Williams (og) [7], Davies, S [54]	25,341
38		19	A	Crystal Palace	D	2-2	1-1	17	Pearson [7], Ward [63]	14,686
39	Apr	2	A	Cardiff C	L	1-4	0-1	19	Savage (pen) [90]	22,254
40		9	H	Coventry C	D	2-2	2-2	19	Davies, S [41], Savage (pen) [45]	25,546
41		12	H	Leeds U	W	2-1	0-0	—	Ward [61], Davies, B [63]	27,252
42		18	A	QPR	D	0-0	0-0	—		16,745
43		23	H	Burnley	L	2-4	2-1	19	Robinson [6], Ward [31]	25,187
44		25	A	Norwich C	L	2-3	0-1	19	Davies, S [54], Bueno [63]	26,078
45		30	H	Bristol C	L	0-2	0-1	19		25,745
46	May	7	A	Reading	L	1-2	1-1	19	Ward [32]	21,902

Final League Position: 19

GOALSCORERS

League (58): Commons 13 (2 pens), Bueno 5, Davies, S 5, Ward 5 (1 pen), Cywka 4, Moore 4, Savage 4 (4 pens), Green 2, Kuqi 2, Moxey 2, Porter 2, Robinson 2, Bailey 1, Barker 1, Brayford 1, Davies, B 1, Hulse 1, Leacock 1, Pearson 1, own goal 1.
Carling Cup (0).
FA Cup (1): Addison 1.

Bywater S 22	Brayford J 46	Roberts G 24+2	Bailey J 32+4	Anderson R 4+7	Leacock D 22+3	Green P 36	Savage R 37+3	Hulse R 1	Commons K 25+1	Cywka T 21+10	Barker S 42+1	Pringle B 3+12	Porter C 6+12	Varney L 1	Doyle C 5+9	Moxey D 20+2	Martin D —+2	Ball C 1+4	Bueno A 25+4	Kuqi S 8+4	Pearson S 21+9	O'Brien M —+2	Moore L 9+4	Noble R —+1	Fielding F 16	Addison M 10+11	Davies S 14+6	Davies B 10+3	Ayala D 16+1	Ward J 13	Robinson T 8+5	Severn J —+1	Buxton J —+1	Jones B 7	Hendrick J —+4	Atkins R 1	Match No.
1	2	3	4	5^1	6	7	8	9	10^3	11^2	12	13	14																								1
1	2	3	4		6	7	8^1		10^2	11^3	5	13	14						9	12																	2
1	2	3	4		6	7	8^2		10	12	5	13							9^1	11																	3
1	2	3	4		6	7	8		10^1	12	5								9^2	11^3		13	14														4
1	2	3^2	4		6	7^1	8^3		10	9	5								14	11		13	12														5
1	2		4		6	7	8		12	9^1	5	13							14	11^3	3^2		10														6
1	2		4		6	7				11^2	5	13						8	9^1	10^3	3	12	14														7
1	2		4		6^1	7	8^3			11	5	13				12			9	10^2	3	14															8
1	2		4		6^3	7	8			11^1	5	13				12			9^2	10	3	14															9
1	2		4		6	7	8			11^1	5	13				12			9^2	10^3	3	14															10
1	2		4	14	6	7	8			11^2	5	13				12			9^1	10^3	3																11
1	2		4	14	6	7	8			11^3	5	13				12			9^2	10^1	3																12
1	2		4	14	6	7^2	8^1		12	11	5	13							9^2	10	3^3																13
1	2		4	14	6	7^2	8		10	11^3	5	13				12			9^1		3																14
1	2		4		6	7	8			11^3	5	13				12			9	10^2	3	14															15
1	2		4		6^3	7	8			11^2	5	13				12			9	10^1	3	14															16
1	2		4		6	7	8^1		10		5^2	13				12			9	11^1	3	14															17
1	2	3			6	7	8			11^2	5	13				12	4		9^1			14	10^3														18
1	2		4		6	7	8				5	13				12			9^1	11^2	3	14	10^3														19
1	2	3	4		6	7	8^1		10	11	5					12			9																		20
1	2	3^1			6	7			10	11^3	5	13				12	4	8^2	9																		21
1	2				6^1	7			10	11	5	13				12	4^2	8^3	9		3	14															22
1	2		4		6	7			10	11^2	5	13				12		8^1	9		3																23
1	2	3	4^2			7	8		10^1		5								9^3				6			12	11			13	14						24
1	2		4			7	8^3		10		5				12				9		3		6^1			11^2	13			14							25
1	2	3	4^2		6		8		12		5								9	11^1			10^3				13	7		14							26
1	2				6		8^1		12		5		10^2				3^b	4	9	11								13	7								27
1	2	3	4				8^2				5	13	10^1						9	11						12		7	6								28
1	2	3	4^1				8		12		5	13							11			14	10^3					7	6	9^2							29
1	2	3	4				8		12		5	13	10^2						11^1			14						7	6^3	9							30
1	2	3	4				8		12		5	13							11									7	6	9^2	7	10^1					31
1^6	2	3^2					8				5	13					4		11							12			6	9^1	7	10	15				32
	2		4				8		12		5		10^2						11^1						1	3	13	7^2	6	9	14						33
	2		4				8				5	13							12	14	11				1	3^2	9	7^3	6	10^1							34
	2	3	4			7^2	8^1				5								11						1	12	13	9	6	10							35
	2	3	4				8^2		12		5								11						1	7	13	9	6	10^1							36
	2	3	4^1				8		12		5								11				7		1		13	9^3	6	10^2					14		37
	2	3	4	14			8				5								11^3				7^1		1		13	9^2	6	10	12						38
	2	3^2	4^1				8				5^3	13			12				11		9	14	7						6	10				1			39
	2		4^3		6^2		8				5	13									11^1	14	7			3			10	9	12			1			40
	2	3	4				8				5	13									11^1	14	7				9^3		6	10^2	12			1			41
	2	3	4				8		12		5	13									11		7^1				9^2		6	10				1			42
	2	3^3	4				8^2				5					3			12		11	14	7^1				9		6	10^8				1	13		43
	2	3^3	4	14			8^2				5								12		10	11	7^1						6	9				1	13		44
	2	3	4				8^3				5	13							12		11		7						6	9^2	10^1			1	14		45
	2		4^3		6		8				5	13			12				11^1		9		7^2			3				10				1	14		46

FA Cup
Third Round   Crawley T   (a)   1-2

Carling Cup
First Round   Crewe Alex   (a)   0-1

DONCASTER ROVERS   FL Championship

FOUNDATION

In 1879, Mr Albert Jenkins assembled a team to play a match against the Yorkshire Institution for the Deaf. The players remained together as Doncaster Rovers, joining the Midland Alliance in 1889 and the Midland Counties League in 1891.

Keepmoat Stadium, Stadium Way, Lakeside, Doncaster, South Yorkshire DN4 5JW.

Telephone: (01302) 764 664.

Fax: (01302) 363 525.

Ticket Office: (01302) 762 576.

Website: www.doncasterroversfc.co.uk

Email: info@doncasterroversfc.co.uk

Ground Capacity: 15,231.

Record Attendance: 37,149 v Hull C, Division 3 (N), 2 October 1948 (at Belle Vue). 15,001 v Leeds U, FL 1, 1 April 2008 (at Keepmoat Stadium).

Pitch Measurements: 100m × 70m.

Chairman: John Ryan.

Vice-chairman: Dick Watson.

Chief Executive/Secretary: David Morris.

Manager: Sean O'Driscoll.

Assistant Manager: Richard O'Kelly.

Physio: John Dickens.

Colours: Red and white hooped shirts, red sleeves with black trim, black shorts with red trim, black stockings with red tops.

Change Colours: Black shirts with red trim, red shorts, red stockings.

Year Formed: 1879. *Turned Professional:* 1885.

Ltd Co.: 1905 & 1920.

Club Nickname: 'Rovers'.

HONOURS

Football League: Best season 2007–08.
Division 3: *Champions* 2003–04;
Division 3 (N): *Champions* – 1934–35, 1946–47, 1949–50;
Runners-up 1937–38, 1938–39;
Division 4: *Champions* 1965–66, 1968–69; *Runners-up* 1983–84.

FA Cup: Best season 5th rd, 1952, 1954, 1955, 1956.

Football League Cup: Best season: 5th rd, 1976, 2006.

J Paint Trophy: *Winners* 2007.

Football Conference:
Champions 2002–03

Sheffield County Cup: *Winners* 1891, 1912, 1936, 1938, 1956, 1968, 1976, 1986.

Midland Counties League:
Champions 1897, 1899.

Conference Trophy: *Winners* 1999, 2000.

Sheffield & Hallamshire Senior Cup:
Winners 2001, 2002.

Grounds: 1880–1916, Intake Ground; 1920, Benetthorpe Ground; 1922, Low Pasture, Belle Vue; 2007, Keepmoat Stadium.

First Football League Game: 7 September 1901, Division 2, v Burslem Port Vale (h) D 3–3 – Eggett; Simpson, Layton; Longden, Jones, Wright, Langham, Murphy, Price, Goodson (2), Bailey (1).

Record League Victory: 10–0 v Darlington, Division 4, 25 January 1964: Potter; Raine, Meadows, Windross (1), White, Ripley (2), Robinson, Book (2), Hale (4), Jeffrey, Broadbent (1).

Record Cup Victory: 7–0 v Blyth Spartans, FA Cup 1st rd, 27 November 1937: Imrie; Shaw, Rodgers, McFarlane, Bycroft, Cyril Smith, Burton (1), Killourhy (4), Morgan (2), Malam, Dutton.

sky SPORTS FACT FILE

The first player to be awarded full international honours with Doncaster Rovers was Pat McConnell, an inside-forward signed from Bradford City in 1925. He was capped for Northern Ireland against Wales on 4 February 1928. He later played for Southport.

Record Defeat: 0–12 v Small Heath, Division 2, 11 April 1903.

Most League Points (2 for a win): 72, Division 3 (N), 1946–47.

Most League Points (3 for a win): 92, Division 3, 2003–04.

Most League Goals: 123, Division 3 (N), 1946–47.

Highest League Scorer in Season: Clarrie Jordan, 42, Division 3 (N), 1946–47.

Most League Goals in Total Aggregate: Tom Keetley, 180, 1923–29.

Most League Goals in One Match: 6, Tom Keetley v Ashington, Division 3 (N), 16 February 1929.

Most Capped Player: Len Graham, 14, Northern Ireland.

Most League Appearances: Fred Emery, 417, 1925–36.

Youngest League Player: Alick Jeffrey, 15 years 229 days v Fulham, 15 September 1954.

Record Transfer Fee Received: £2,000,000 from Reading for Matthew Mills, July 2009.

Record Transfer Fee Paid: £1,150,000 to Sheffield U for Billy Sharp, August 2010.

Football League Record: 1901 Elected to Division 2; 1903 Failed re-election; 1904 Re-elected; 1905 Failed re-election; 1923 Re-elected to Division 3 (N); 1935–37 Division 2; 1937–47 Division 3 (N); 1947–48 Division 2; 1948–50 Division 3 (N); 1950–58 Division 2; 1958–59 Division 3; 1959–66 Division 4; 1966–67 Division 3; 1967–69 Division 4; 1969–71 Division 3; 1971–81 Division 4; 1981–83 Division 3; 1983–84 Division 4; 1984–88 Division 3; 1988–92 Division 4; 1992–98 Division 3; 1998–2003 Conference; 2003–04 Division 3; 2004–08 FL 1; 2008– FL C.

LATEST SEQUENCES

Longest Sequence of League Wins: 10, 22.1.1947 – 4.4.1947.

Longest Sequence of League Defeats: 9, 14.1.1905 – 1.4.1905.

Longest Sequence of League Draws: 4, 29.10.1932 – 19.11.1932.

Longest Sequence of Unbeaten League Matches: 20, 26.12.1968 – 12.4.1969.

Longest Sequence Without a League Win: 20, 9.8.1997 – 29.11.1997.

Successive Scoring Runs: 27 from 10.11.1934.

Successive Non-scoring Runs: 7 from 27.9.1947.

MANAGERS

Arthur Porter 1920–21
Harry Tufnell 1921–22
Arthur Porter 1922–23
Dick Ray 1923–27
David Menzies 1928–36
Fred Emery 1936–40
Bill Marsden 1944–46
Jackie Bestall 1946–49
Peter Doherty 1949–58
Jack Hodgson and Sid Bycroft (*Joint Managers*) 1958
Jack Crayston 1958–59 (*continued as Secretary-Manager to 1961*)
Jackie Bestall (*TM*) 1959–60
Norman Curtis 1960–61
Danny Malloy 1961–62
Oscar Hold 1962–64
Bill Leivers 1964–66
Keith Kettleborough 1966–67
George Raynor 1967–68
Lawrie McMenemy 1968–71
Morris Setters 1971–74
Stan Anderson 1975–78
Billy Bremner 1978–85
Dave Cusack 1985–87
Dave Mackay 1987–89
Billy Bremner 1989–91
Steve Beaglehole 1991–93
Ian Atkins 1994
Sammy Chung 1994–96
Kerry Dixon (*Player-Manager*) 1996–97
Dave Cowling 1997
Mark Weaver 1997–98
Ian Snodin 1998–99
Steve Wignall 1999–2001
Dave Penney 2002–06
Sean O'Driscoll September 2006–

TEN YEAR LEAGUE RECORD

		P	W	D	L	F	A	Pts	Pos
2001-02	Conf.	42	18	13	11	68	46	67	4
2002-03	Conf.	42	22	12	8	73	47	78	3
2003-04	Div 3	46	27	11	8	79	37	92	1
2004-05	FL 1	46	16	18	12	65	60	66	10
2005-06	FL 1	46	20	9	17	55	51	69	8
2006-07	FL 1	46	16	15	15	52	47	63	11
2007-08	FL 1	46	23	11	12	65	41	80	3
2008-09	FL C	46	17	7	22	42	53	58	14
2009-10	FL C	46	15	15	16	59	58	60	12
2010-11	FL C	46	11	15	20	55	81	48	21

DID YOU KNOW ?

In 1938–39 when Doncaster Rovers finished runners-up in Division Three (North), six players reached double figures in goals: Mick Kilhouhry and Eddie Perry on 14, Fred Dell 12, Charlie Leyfield and Albert Malam with 11 each plus George Little on ten goals.

DONCASTER ROVERS 2010–11 LEAGUE RECORD

Match No.	Date		Venue	Opponents	Result		H/T Score	Lg Pos.	Goalscorers	Attendance
1	Aug	7	A	Preston NE	W	2-0	2-0	—	O'Connor [12], Hayter [18]	12,190
2		14	H	Bristol C	D	1-1	0-0	5	Sharp (pen) [90]	9291
3		21	A	Cardiff C	L	0-4	0-1	11		24,027
4		28	H	Hull C	W	3-1	2-1	9	Woods, M [2], Sharp (pen) [44], Coppinger [69]	11,149
5	Sept	11	A	Watford	D	2-2	1-0	10	Gillett [32], Friend [90]	15,101
6		14	H	Norwich C	W	3-1	1-0	—	Coppinger 3 [14, 50, 86]	9314
7		17	H	Leeds U	D	0-0	0-0	—		13,293
8		25	A	QPR	L	0-3	0-0	10		13,990
9		28	A	Coventry C	L	1-2	1-1	—	Sharp [43]	12,292
10	Oct	2	H	Nottingham F	D	1-1	1-1	13	Lockwood [33]	10,759
11		16	A	Scunthorpe U	W	3-1	1-1	12	Sharp 2 (1 pen) [31, 59 (p)], O'Connor [72]	7005
12		19	H	Derby Co	L	2-3	0-1	—	Shiels 2 [66, 68]	9000
13		23	H	Sheffield U	W	2-0	2-0	11	Coppinger [33], Sharp [42]	8985
14		30	A	Reading	L	3-4	2-1	15	Hayter [26], Martis [42], Shiels [50]	15,553
15	Nov	6	H	Millwall	W	2-1	0-1	12	Hayter [56], Healy [58]	10,356
16		9	A	Burnley	D	1-1	1-0	—	Hayter [13]	13,655
17		13	A	Portsmouth	W	3-2	2-0	7	Hayter [15], Coppinger [26], Healy [79]	14,828
18		20	H	Swansea C	D	1-1	1-0	7	Hayter [16]	13,614
19		27	A	Crystal Palace	L	0-1	0-1	10		12,470
20	Dec	11	A	Leicester C	L	1-5	1-1	16	Sharp [6]	27,549
21		17	H	Middlesbrough	W	2-1	1-1	—	Hayter [22], Stock [90]	9543
22	Jan	1	H	Scunthorpe U	W	3-0	3-0	13	Sharp [26], Hayter [38], Mills [45]	9447
23		3	A	Sheffield U	D	2-2	0-0	14	Sharp 2 (1 pen) [66, 74 (p)]	21,102
24		15	H	Reading	L	0-3	0-1	15		9496
25		22	A	Ipswich T	L	2-3	1-0	15	Sharp 2 [6, 61]	17,298
26		25	H	Barnsley	L	0-2	0-0	—		10,740
27	Feb	1	H	Burnley	W	1-0	0-0	14	Duff (og) [59]	8893
28		5	A	Millwall	L	0-1	0-0	15		11,427
29		12	H	Portsmouth	L	0-2	0-1	16		10,288
30		15	H	Ipswich T	L	0-6	0-3	—		8448
31		19	A	Swansea C	L	0-3	0-2	17		13,309
32		22	A	Norwich C	D	1-1	0-1	—	Drury (og) [83]	25,529
33		26	H	Watford	D	1-1	1-1	19	Euell [45]	8954
34	Mar	1	A	Derby Co	W	3-1	1-0	—	Sharp 2 [41, 48], Mills [71]	24,239
35		5	A	Leeds U	L	2-5	1-1	17	Sharp [45], Moussa [49]	27,027
36		8	H	Coventry C	D	1-1	0-1	—	Hayter [88]	7921
37		12	A	Nottingham F	D	0-0	0-0	17		25,442
38		19	H	QPR	L	0-1	0-0	19		11,747
39	Apr	2	A	Bristol C	L	0-1	0-0	20		13,726
40		9	H	Cardiff C	L	1-3	0-1	20	Coppinger [78]	9174
41		12	H	Preston NE	D	1-1	0-0	—	Stock [77]	9456
42		16	A	Hull C	L	1-3	1-2	20	Moussa [16]	21,395
43		22	H	Crystal Palace	D	0-0	0-0	—		14,312
44		25	A	Barnsley	D	2-2	0-0	21	Euell 2 [59, 73]	12,418
45		30	H	Leicester C	D	1-1	0-0	21	Brooker [50] -	11,757
46	May	7	A	Middlesbrough	L	0-3	0-1	21		19,978

Final League Position: 21

GOALSCORERS

League (55): Sharp 15 (4 pens), Hayter 9, Coppinger 7, Euell 3, Shiels 3, Healy 2, Mills 2, Moussa 2, O'Connor 2, Stock 2, Brooker 1, Friend 1, Gillett 1, Lockwood 1, Martis 1, Woods, M 1, own goals 2.
Carling Cup (1): Payne 1.
FA Cup (2): Hayter 1, Sharp 1.

Sullivan N 30+1	O'Connor J 34	Friend G 30+2	Martis S 24+2	Lockwood A 13+3	Stock B 31+6	Coppinger J 38+2	Woods M 13+2	Hayter J 28+4	Sharp B 22+2	Gillett S 21+1	Shiels D 15+18	Brooker S 1+12	Hird S 20+12	Mason R 5+10	Thomas W 17+4	Dumbuya M 17+6	Oster J 41	Wilson M 15+13	Fairhurst W —+2	Mills J 17+1	Webster B 1+6	Healy D 6+2	Souza D 3+5	Chambers J 6+1	Kilgallon M 7+5	Keegan P 9+1	Woods G 16	Burge R —+1	Moussa F 14	Euell J 7+5	Match No.
1	2	3	4	5	6	7^1	8	9^3	10^2	11■	12	13	14																		1
1	2	3	4^2	5	6^1	12	8		10	11	9		14		7^3	13															2
1	2	3^2		5	6	9	7		10	11^3	12	13			8^1	4	14														3
1	2	3	4	5^1	6^3	9	8		10	11	13		12		14		7^2														4
1	2	3	4	5^1	6^2	9	8		10	11	13		12		14		7^3														5
1	5	3	4		12	9	8		10^3	11^2	13				14	2	7^1	6													6
1	5	3	4		12	9		6	10	11^3	8^2				14	2	7^1	13													7
1	5	3	4			9		6	10	11^1	12			8		2	7														8
1	2	3	4^1	5	13	9	8		10	11^2				6	12		7^3	14													9
1	6	3	5	12		8	4	9	10	11^1					14	2^3	7^2	13													10
1	4	3^1	5	13		8	6	9	10	11^3				12		2	7^2	14													11
1			14	6	8	12	13	10	11^1	9				5		2	7^2			3^3	4										12
1	5	4^2	13	6	7	8^3	9	10^1	12	14				2	11					3											13
1	5	4		6	7	8	9	10^2	12					2	11^1					3	13										14
1	2	4		6	7^3	9		8^1	12		5	14	11	13	3		10^2														15
1	2	4		6^3	7	9		8^1	13	14	5	3	11	12			10^2														16
1	2	4		6	7	9		12	8^1	5	3	11^2	13	14			10^3														17
1	3			6	7	9			13	12	4	5	2	11^2	8		10^1														18
1	2	4		6	7	9	14	12	13	5^2	3	11^1	8^3	10																	19
1	2^1	4		6	7^3	9	10	13	3	5	11	14	8^2	12																	20
1		4^2	5	6	7^3	9	10	14	2	11	8				12	13		3^1													21
1	2	4^1	12	6^2	7	9^3	10	13	5■	11	8				3	14															22
1	2		5	7^2		9	10^3	8^1		11	4				3	13	14	$6^■$	12												23
1	2	17	5		7	13	9^3	10		14	4^2				11	8		3^1					6								24
1	2		5		7		9	10	8^1	14	12				11	4^3	13						3^2	6							25
1	2	13	5		7		9	10	8	14					11	4^1							3^2	6^3	12						26
	4	3			6^2	7		9^1	10	14	12	5			11^3			13		2					8		1				27
	2	3			6^1			10	13	$9^■$	5	4			11			12		7					8		1				28
	2	11			$0^■$	$9^■$		10	13	5^1	12				7		14			3	4				8		1				29
	2	11				9		10^2		5	12				7	4		6			$3^■$				8	1		13			30
1		3				7		6^2		5^1				11	10		2	13		14				12	8^3				4	9	31
1		3			6^1			12		4				5	11		7	2				13			8				9^2	10	32
		3			6			10		2				5	11		12	4							8	1		7^1	9	33
		3			6^1			10^2	14	9				2	5		11	12		4			13		8	1		7^3		34
		3			6^3	12		13	10	9^1				2	5		11	14		7					8^2	1		4		35
		3	4^2		6	11		9	10^1		13	12		5	8			2^3				14				1		7		36
		3	4^1		6	10		9	11		2^3	13		14	8^2		5	12								1		7		37
		3	4		6	10		9^2	7^3		2	12		14	11^1		5								1		8	13		38
		3	4		6^1	10		9^3	7		13	2		11	12		5								1		8^2	14		39
		3	4		6	10		9	7^3		2			11^2	14		5^1	12							1		8	13		40
2		3	4		6	10^2		9^3	7		13			12	11^1		5								1		8	14		41
2		3	4^3		6	10		9^2	7		13	14			11^1		5								1		8	12		42
		4	3	13	6			9^3	12		7	14		5	2^2		11								1		8^1	10		43
15	2	3				8		9	7		13	6		4^1	5		11	12							$1^■$			10^2		44
1	4	3		13		10		9	7^2		12	14		6^3	5		2	11							8			8^1		45
1		3		14				9	12		7^2	13		5	2^3		11	4							6			10^1	8	46

FA Cup
Third Round   Wolverhampton W   (h) 2-2
                                   (a) 0-5

Carling Cup
First Round   Accrington S   (h) 1-2

EVERTON

FA Premiership

FOUNDATION

St Domingo Church Sunday School formed a football club in 1878 which played at Stanley Park. Enthusiasm was so great that in November 1879 they decided to expand membership and changed the name to Everton playing in black shirts with a scarlet sash and nicknamed the 'Black Watch'. After wearing several other colours, royal blue was adopted in 1901.

Goodison Park, Goodison Road, Liverpool L4 4EL.

Telephone: (0871) 663 1878.

Fax: (0151) 286 9112.

Ticket Office: (0871) 663 1878.

Website: www.evertonfc.com

Email: everton@evertonfc.com

Ground Capacity: 40,158.

Record Attendance: 78,299 v Liverpool, Division 1, 18 September 1948.

Pitch Measurements: 100.48m × 68m.

Chairman: Bill Kenwright CBE.

Deputy Chairman: Jon Woods.

Chief Executive: Robert Elstone.

Secretary: David Harrison.

Manager: David Moyes.

Assistant Manager: Steve Round.

Fitness Coach: Dave Billows.

Colours: Blue shirts with white trim, white shorts, white stockings.

Change Colours: Pink shirts with blue trim, black shorts, black stockings.

Year Formed: 1878.

Turned Professional: 1885.

Ltd Co.: 1892.

Previous Name: 1878, St Domingo FC; 1879, Everton.

Club Nickname: 'The Toffees'.

Grounds: 1878, Stanley Park; 1882, Priory Road; 1884, Anfield Road; 1892, Goodison Park.

First Football League Game: 8 September 1888, Football League, v Accrington (h) W 2–1 – Smalley; Dick, Ross; Holt, Jones, Dobson; Fleming (2), Waugh, Lewis, Edgar Chadwick, Farmer.

HONOURS

Football League – Division 1:
Champions 1890–91, 1914–15, 1927–28, 1931–32, 1938–39, 1962–63, 1969–70, 1984–85, 1986–87;
Runners-up 1889–90, 1894–95, 1901–02, 1904–05, 1908–09, 1911–12, 1985–86;
Division 2: *Champions* 1930–31;
Runners-up 1953–54.
FA Cup: *Winners* 1906, 1933, 1966, 1984, 1995; *Runners-up* 1893, 1897, 1907, 1968, 1985, 1986, 1989, 2009.
Football League Cup:
Runners-up 1977, 1984.
League Super Cup: *Runners-up* 1986.
Simod Cup: *Runners-up* 1989.
Zenith Data Systems Cup:
Runners-up 1991.
European Competitions
European Cup: 1963–64, 1970–71.
European Cup-Winners' Cup:
1966–67, 1984–85 (*winners*), 1995–96.
European Fairs Cup: 1962–63, 1964–65, 1965–66.
Champions League: 2005–06.
UEFA Cup: 1975–76, 1978–79, 1979–80, 2005–06, 2007–08, 2008–09.
Europa League: 2009–10.

---

sky SPORTS FACT FILE

Ever the pioneers, Everton installed under soil heating at the club's training ground as far back as during the 1937–38 season, designed to offset the effects of frost and snow that have become commonplace in the higher echelons of the game in this country.

Record League Victory: 9–1 v Manchester C, Division 1, 3 September 1906 – Scott; Balmer, Crelley; Booth, Taylor (1), Abbott (1); Sharp, Bolton (1), Young (4), Settle (2), George Wilson. 9–1 v Plymouth Arg, Division 2, 27 December 1930 – Coggins; Williams, Cresswell; McPherson, Griffiths, Thomson; Critchley, Dunn, Dean (4), Johnson (1), Stein (4).

Record Cup Victory: 11–2 v Derby Co, FA Cup 1st rd, 18 January 1890 – Smalley; Hannah, Doyle (1); Kirkwood, Holt (1), Parry; Latta, Brady (3), Geary (3), Edgar Chadwick, Millward (3).

Record Defeat: 4–10 v Tottenham H, Division 1, 11 October 1958.

Most League Points (2 for a win): 66, Division 1, 1969–70.

Most League Points (3 for a win): 90, Division 1, 1984–85.

Most League Goals: 121, Division 2, 1930–31.

Highest League Scorer in Season: William Ralph 'Dixie' Dean, 60, Division 1, 1927–28 (All-time League record).

Most League Goals in Total Aggregate: William Ralph 'Dixie' Dean, 349, 1925–37.

Most League Goals in One Match: 6, Jack Southworth v WBA, Division 1, 30 December 1893.

Most Capped Player: Neville Southall, 92, Wales.

Most League Appearances: Neville Southall, 578, 1981–98.

Youngest League Player: James Vaughan, 16 years 271 days v Crystal Palace, 10 April 2005.

MANAGERS
W. E. Barclay 1888–89 *(Secretary-Manager)*
Dick Molyneux 1889–1901 *(Secretary-Manager)*
William C. Cuff 1901–18 *(Secretary-Manager)*
W. J. Sawyer 1918–19 *(Secretary-Manager)*
Thomas H. McIntosh 1919–35 *(Secretary-Manager)*
Theo Kelly 1936–48
Cliff Britton 1948–56
Ian Buchan 1956–58
Johnny Carey 1958–61
Harry Catterick 1961–73
Billy Bingham 1973–77
Gordon Lee 1977–81
Howard Kendall 1981–87
Colin Harvey 1987–90
Howard Kendall 1990–93
Mike Walker 1994
Joe Royle 1994–97
Howard Kendall 1997–98
Walter Smith 1998–2002
David Moyes March 2002–

Record Transfer Fee Received: £25,000,000 rising to £29,000,000 from Manchester U for Wayne Rooney, August 2004.

Record Transfer Fee Paid: £15,000,000 to Standard Liege for Marouane Fellaini, September 2008.

Football League Record: 1888 Founder Member of the Football League; 1930–31 Division 2; 1931–51 Division 1; 1951–54 Division 2; 1954–92 Division 1; 1992– FA Premier League.

LATEST SEQUENCES

Longest Sequence of League Wins: 12, 24.3.1894 – 13.10.1894.

Longest Sequence of League Defeats: 6, 26.12.1996 – 29.1.1997.

Longest Sequence of League Draws: 5, 4.5.1977 – 16.5.1977.

Longest Sequence of Unbeaten League Matches: 20, 29.4.1978 – 16.12.1978.

Longest Sequence Without a League Win: 14, 6.3.1937 – 4.9.1937.

Successive Scoring Runs: 40 from 15.3.1930.

Successive Non-scoring Runs: 6 from 3.3.1951.

TEN YEAR LEAGUE RECORD

			P	W	D	L	F	A	Pts	Pos
2001-02	PR Lge	38	11	10	17	45	57	43		15
2002-03	PR Lge	38	17	8	13	48	49	59		7
2003-04	PR Lge	38	9	12	17	45	57	39		17
2004-05	PR Lge	38	18	7	13	45	46	61		4
2005-06	PR Lge	38	14	8	16	34	49	50		11
2006-07	PR Lge	38	15	13	10	52	36	58		6
2007-08	PR Lge	38	19	8	11	55	33	65		5
2008-09	PR Lge	38	17	12	9	55	37	63		5
2009-10	PR Lge	38	16	13	9	60	49	61		8
2010-11	PR Lge	38	13	15	10	51	45	54		7

DID YOU KNOW ?

On 5 February 2011 Louis Saha scored four goals as Everton defeated Blackpool 5-3 at Goodison Park. It was the first time an Everton player had hit as many since Graeme Sharp scored all four at Southampton on 3 October 1987.

EVERTON 2010–11 LEAGUE RECORD

Match No.	Date	Venue	Opponents	Result	H/T Score	Lg Pos.	Goalscorers	Attendance
1	Aug 14	A	Blackburn R	L	0-1	0-1	—	25,869
2	21	H	Wolverhampton W	D	1-1	1-0	17	Cahill [43]	37,767
3	29	A	Aston Villa	L	0-1	0-1	18		34,725
4	Sept 11	H	Manchester U	D	3-3	1-1	18	Pienaar [39], Cahill [89], Arteta [90]	36,556
5	18	H	Newcastle U	L	0-1	0-1	19		38,019
6	25	A	Fulham	D	0-0	0-0	20		25,598
7	Oct 2	A	Birmingham C	W	2-0	0-0	17	Johnson (og) [54], Cahill [90]	23,138
8	17	H	Liverpool	W	2-0	1-0	11	Cahill [34], Arteta [50]	39,673
9	23	A	Tottenham H	D	1-1	1-1	11	Baines [17]	35,967
10	30	H	Stoke C	W	1-0	0-0	8	Yakubu [67]	35,513
11	Nov 6	A	Blackpool	D	2-2	1-1	11	Cahill [13], Coleman [50]	16,094
12	10	H	Bolton W	D	1-1	0-0	—	Beckford [90]	31,808
13	14	H	Arsenal	L	1-2	0-1	13	Cahill [89]	36,279
14	22	A	Sunderland	D	2-2	1-1	—	Cahill [6], Arteta [83]	37,331
15	27	H	WBA	L	1-4	1-2	16	Cahill [42]	35,237
16	Dec 4	A	Chelsea	D	1-1	0-1	15	Beckford [86]	41,642
17	11	H	Wigan Ath	D	0-0	0-0	15		32,853
18	20	A	Manchester C	W	2-1	2-0	—	Cahill [4], Baines [19]	45,028
19	28	A	West Ham U	D	1-1	1-1	11	Coleman [42]	33,422
20	Jan 1	A	Stoke C	L	0-2	0-1	13		27,418
21	5	H	Tottenham H	W	2-1	1-1	11	Saha [3], Coleman [75]	34,124
22	16	A	Liverpool	D	2-2	0-1	12	Distin [46], Beckford [52]	44,795
23	22	H	West Ham U	D	2-2	0-1	13	Bilyaletdinov [77], Fellaini [90]	34,179
24	Feb 1	A	Arsenal	L	1-2	1-0	—	Saha [24]	60,014
25	5	H	Blackpool	W	5-3	1-1	13	Saha 4 [20, 47, 76, 84], Beckford [80]	38,202
26	13	A	Bolton W	L	0-2	0-1	13		22,986
27	26	H	Sunderland	W	2-0	2-0	10	Beckford 2 [8, 39]	37,776
28	Mar 5	A	Newcastle U	W	2-1	2-1	10	Osman [31], Jagielka [36]	50,128
29	9	H	Birmingham C	D	1-1	1-1	—	Heitinga [35]	33,974
30	19	H	Fulham	W	2-1	1-0	8	Coleman [36], Saha [49]	33,239
31	Apr 2	H	Aston Villa	D	2-2	1-0	7	Osman [38], Baines (pen) [83]	37,619
32	9	A	Wolverhampton W	W	3-0	3-0	7	Beckford [21], Neville [39], Bilyaletdinov [45]	28,352
33	16	A	Blackburn R	W	2-0	0-0	7	Osman [54], Baines (pen) [75]	35,857
34	23	A	Manchester U	L	0-1	0-0	7		75,300
35	30	A	Wigan Ath	D	1-1	0-1	7	Baines (pen) [78]	17,051
36	May 7	H	Manchester C	W	2-1	0-1	7	Distin [65], Osman [72]	37,351
37	14	A	WBA	L	0-1	0-1	7		25,838
38	22	H	Chelsea	W	1-0	0-0	7	Beckford [74]	38,712

Final League Position: 7

GOALSCORERS

League (51): Cahill 9, Beckford 8, Saha 7, Baines 5 (3 pens), Coleman 4, Osman 4, Arteta 3, Bilyaletdinov 2, Distin 2, Fellaini 1, Heitinga 1, Jagielka 1, Neville 1, Pienaar 1, Yakubu 1, own goal 1.
Carling Cup (6): Beckford 1 (pen), Coleman 1, Fellaini 1, Osman 1, Rodwell 1, Saha 1.
FA Cup (7): Baines 2, Saha 2, Beckford 1, Coleman 1, Fellaini 1.

Howard T 38	Baines L 38	Jagielka P 31+2	Cahill T 22+5	Distin S 38	Neville P 31	Osman L 20+6	Pienaar S 18	Saha L 14+8	Fellaini M 19+1	Arteta M 29	Beckford J 14+18	Bilyaletdinov D 10+16	Rodwell J 14+10	Hibbert T 17+3	Heitinga J 23+4	Coleman S 25+9	Yakubu A 7+7	Anichebe V 8+8	Vaughan J —+1	Baxter J —+1	Gueye M 2+3	Vellios A —+3	Forshaw A —+1	Match No.
1	2	3	4	5	6	7^1	8	9^2	10^3	11	12	13	14											1
1	3	6	10	5		13	8	12	14	11	9^1	7^3			2	4^2								2
1	3	6	10	5		7	12	8	11	9^1			4^2	2^3	14	13								3
1	3	6		5		8	7	9		11			2^1	4^2	12	13								4
1	3	6		5		7	8		10	11	9^2	14	2^1	4^3	13	12								5
1	3	4	10^1	5	6	12	7	8		11	13					2^2	9							6
1	3	4	10	5	6	7		8		11	13				12	2^2	9^1							7
1	3	6	10	5	2	8^1			11^3	14	12		13	4^2	7	9								8
1	11	6	10	5	3		8	12		14	7		13	4^2	2^3	9^1								9
1	3	6	10	5	2		8	12		11		13		4	7^1	9^2								10
1	3	6	10	5	2		8^2	12		11	14	13		4^3	7	9^1								11
1	3	6	4	5	2^2		8	9^3	10^4	11	13	7^1			12	14								12
1	3	6	10	5	2^2		8	9		11^3	13		12	4^1	7	14								13
1	3	6	10	5	2		8	9^2		11	14		12	4^3	7^1	13								14
1	3	6		7	5		8	12		11^4	13		14		2	4^1		9^2	10^3					15
1	3	6	10	5	2		8^2	9^1		11	12	13		4	7									16
1	3	6	10	5	2	11^2	9^1	8		12				4	7	13								17
1	3	6^3	10	5	2	8^1	13		11		12		4	14	7^2	9^4								18
1	3		10	5	2	9^3	8	11^2		14	13		6^1	4	7	12								19
1	3	6	4	5	2^1	12	8	9^3	10	11^2	14				7	13								20
1	3			5		13	6^2	9^3	8	11	10^1	14		4	7	12								21
1	3			5		4^2	8	11	10^1	14	13	6		7	9^3	12								22
1	3			5	2^3	6	12	8	11	10^1	13	14		4	7	9^2								23
1	3	13		5	2^2	12	9	8	11	10^1			4	6	7^3	14								24
1	3	14	13	5	2	9^3	8	11	12	10^2	4^1	6			7									25
1	3	4		5	2	13	8	11	12	10^2	6	7^1			9^3	14								26
1	3	6	13	5	2	4	9^3	8^1	11	10^2	14				12	7								27
1	3	6		5	8^1	7^3	9		11	10^2	4		2		12	14	13							28
1	3	6		5	7		9		11^1	10^2	14	8	2		4^3	12	13							29
1	3	6	10^1	5	8	11	9^3		14	13			4^2	2	12	7								30
1	3	6	5^2	8	11		10	9		2	4	7^1									12	13		31
1	3	6	5	8	11	10^2	9^3		2	4									12	7^1	13	14		32
1	3	6	5	8	11	10^3	9	12	2	4^1	13										7^2	14		33
1	3	6	12	5	8	11	10^2	9^1	4	2	7^3	13									14			34
1	3	6	10^2	5	8	7	11^1	12	4	2	13	9^3									14			35
1	3	6	13	5	8	7	11	12	10^2	2^1	4	14	9^3											36
1	3	6	5	8^2	10	11	12	13^4	14	2	4	7^1	9^3											37
1	3	6	13	5	10	11^2	9^1	8	2	4	7^3	12												38

FA Cup

Third Round	Scunthorpe U	(a)	5-1
Fourth Round	Chelsea	(h)	1-1
		(a)	1-1
Fifth Round	Reading	(h)	0-1

Carling Cup

Second Round	Huddersfield T	(h)	5-1
Third Round	Brentford	(a)	1-1

EXETER CITY   FL Championship 1

FOUNDATION

Exeter City was formed in 1904 by the amalgamation of St Sidwell's United and Exeter United. The club first played in the East Devon League and then the Plymouth & District League. After an exhibition match between West Bromwich Albion and Woolwich Arsenal which was held to test interest as Exeter was then a rugby stronghold, it was decided to form Exeter City. At a meeting at the Red Lion Hotel in 1908, the club turned professional.

St James Park, Stadium Way, Exeter EX4 6PX.

Telephone: (01392) 411 243.

Fax: (01392) 413 959.

Website: www.exetercityfc.co.uk

Email: reception@exetercityfc.co.uk

Training Ground: (01395) 232784.

Ground Capacity: 8,830.

Record Attendance: 20,984 v Sunderland, FA Cup 6th rd (replay), 4 March 1931.

Record Receipts: £59,862.98 v Aston Villa, FA Cup 3rd rd, 8 January 1994.

Pitch Measurements: 114yd × 73yd.

Chairman: Edward Chorlton OBE.

Vice-chairman: Julian Tagg.

Club Secretary: Mike Radford.

Manager: Paul Tisdale.

First Team Coach: Rob Edwards.

Sports Medicine: Ian Andrews.

Colours: Red and white striped shirts, red sleeves, white shorts, white stockings.

Change Colours: All black with red trim.

Year Formed: 1904.

Turned Professional: 1908.

Ltd Co.: 1908.

Club Nickname: 'The Grecians'.

Ground: 1904, St James Park.

First Football League Game: 28 August 1920, Division 3, v Brentford (h) W 3–0 – Pym; Coleburne, Feebury (1p); Crawshaw, Carrick, Mitton; Appleton, Makin, Wright (1), Vowles (1), Dockray.

Record League Victory: 8–1 v Coventry C, Division 3 (S), 4 December 1926 – Bailey; Pollard, Charlton; Pullen, Pool, Garrett; Purcell (2), McDevitt, Blackmore (2), Dent (2), Compton (2). 8–1 v Aldershot, Division 3 (S), 4 May 1935 – Chesters; Gray, Miller; Risdon, Webb, Angus; Jack Scott (1), Wrightson (1), Poulter (3), McArthur (1), Dryden (1), (1 og).

HONOURS

Football League – Division 3:
Best season: 8th, 1979–80;
Division 3 (S): *Runners-up* 1932–33;
Division 4: *Champions* 1989–90;
Runners-up 1976–77;
FL 2: *Runners-up* 2008–09.

FA Cup: est season: 6th rd replay, 1931, 6th rd 1981.

Football League Cup: never beyond 4th rd.

Division 3 (S) Cup: *Winners* 1934.

sky SPORTS FACT FILE

Centre-forward Rod Williams tended not to dwell too long at one club in his 1930s career in the Football League. At Exeter City in 1936–37 he was top scorer with 29 League goals and added seven in a fine FA Cup to the fifth round including doubles in three successive games.

Record Cup Victory: 14–0 v Weymouth, FA Cup 1st qual rd, 3 October 1908 – Fletcher; Craig, Bulcock; Ambler, Chadwick, Wake; Parnell (1), Watson (1), McGuigan (4), Bell (6), Copestake (2).

Record Defeat: 0–9 v Notts Co, Division 3 (S), 16 October 1948. 0–9 v Northampton T, Division 3 (S), 12 April 1958.

Most League Points (2 for a win): 62, Division 4, 1976–77.

Most League Points (3 for a win): 89, Division 4, 1989–90.

Most League Goals: 88, Division 3 (S), 1932–33.

Highest League Scorer in Season: Fred Whitlow, 33, Division 3 (S), 1932–33.

Most League Goals in Total Aggregate: Tony Kellow, 129, 1976–78, 1980–83, 1985–88.

Most League Goals in One Match: 4, Harold 'Jazzo' Kirk v Portsmouth, Division 3 (S), 3 March 1923; 4, Fred Dent v Bristol R, Division 3 (S), 5 November 1927; 4, Fred Whitlow v Watford, Division 3 (S), 29 October 1932.

Most Capped Player: Dermot Curtis, 1 (17), Eire.

Most League Appearances: Arnold Mitchell, 495, 1952–66.

Youngest League Player: Cliff Bastin, 16 years 31 days v Coventry C, 14 April 1928.

Record Transfer Fee Received: £500,000 from Manchester C for Martin Phillips, November 1995.

Record Transfer Fee Paid: £65,000 to Blackpool for Tony Kellow, March 1980.

Football League Record: 1920 Elected to Division 3; 1921–58 Division 3 (S); 1958–64 Division 4; 1964–66 Division 3; 1966–77 Division 4; 1977–84 Division 3; 1984–90 Division 4; 1990–92 Division 3; 1992–94 Division 2; 1994–2003 Division 3; 2003–08 Conference; 2008–09 FL 2; 2009– FL 1.

MANAGERS

Arthur Chadwick 1910–22
Fred Mavin 1923–27
Dave Wilson 1928–29
Billy McDevitt 1929–35
Jack English 1935–39
George Roughton 1945–52
Norman Kirkman 1952–53
Norman Dodgin 1953–57
Bill Thompson 1957–58
Frank Broome 1958–60
Glen Wilson 1960–62
Cyril Spiers 1962–63
Jack Edwards 1963–65
Ellis Stuttard 1965–66
Jock Basford 1966–67
Frank Broome 1967–69
Johnny Newman 1969–76
Bobby Saxton 1977–79
Brian Godfrey 1979–83
Gerry Francis 1983–84
Jim Iley 1984–85
Colin Appleton 1985–87
Terry Cooper 1988–91
Alan Ball 1991–94
Terry Cooper 1994–95
Peter Fox 1995–2000
Noel Blake 2000–01
John Cornforth 2001–02
Neil McNab 2002–03
Gary Peters 2003
Eamonn Dolan 2003–04
Alex Inglethorpe 2004–06
Paul Tisdale June 2006–

LATEST SEQUENCES

Longest Sequence of League Wins: 7, 23.4.1977 – 20.8.1977.

Longest Sequence of League Defeats: 7, 14.1.1984 – 25.2.1984.

Longest Sequence of League Draws: 6, 13.9.1986 – 4.10.1986.

Longest Sequence of Unbeaten League Matches: 13, 23.8.1986 – 25.10.1986.

Longest Sequence Without a League Win: 18, 21.2.1995 – 19.8.1995.

Successive Scoring Runs: 22 from 15.9.1958.

Successive Non-scoring Runs: 6 from 24.11.1923.

TEN YEAR LEAGUE RECORD

		P	W	D	L	F	A	Pts	Pos
2001-02	Div 3	46	14	13	19	48	73	55	16
2002-03	Div 3	46	11	15	20	50	64	48	23
2003-04	Conf	42	19	12	11	71	51	69	6
2004-05	Conf	42	20	11	11	71	50	71	6
2005-06	Conf	42	18	9	15	65	48	63	7
2006-07	Conf	46	22	12	12	67	48	78	5
2007-08	B Sq Pr	46	22	17	7	83	58	83	4
2008-09	FL 2	46	22	13	11	65	50	79	2
2009-10	FL 1	46	11	18	17	48	60	51	18
2010-11	FL 1	46	20	10	16	66	73	70	8

DID YOU KNOW ?

The first player to reach double figures for goal scoring in the FA Cup for Exeter City once they entered the Football League was George Purcell with twelve from 22 games between 1926 and 1932. It was a fine effort as he played either on the right wing or at inside-right.

EXETER CITY 2010–11 LEAGUE RECORD

Match No.	Date	Venue	Opponents	Result	H/T Score	Lg Pos.	Goalscorers	Attendance
1	Aug 7	H	Colchester U	D	2-2	1-2	—	Harley (pen) [7], Logan [87]	5927
2	21	H	Bristol R	D	2-2	1-1	17	Nardiello [9], O'Flynn (pen) [75]	7401
3	28	A	Leyton Orient	L	0-3	0-1	21		4145
4	Sept 4	H	Charlton Ath	W	1-0	0-0	14	Harley (pen) [90]	5743
5	11	A	Hartlepool U	W	3-2	1-2	12	Harley [12], O'Flynn 2 [48, 57]	2641
6	18	H	Peterborough U	D	2-2	0-1	14	Nardiello [54], Cureton [71]	5146
7	21	A	Dagenham & R	D	1-1	1-0	—	Logan [5]	2005
8	25	A	Yeovil T	W	3-1	1-0	8	Logan 2 [23, 58], Harley [75]	5886
9	28	A	Bournemouth	L	0-3	0-2	—		6823
10	Oct 2	H	Rochdale	W	1-0	0-0	7	Cureton [49]	5363
11	9	A	Walsall	L	1-2	0-2	12	Harley [53]	3776
12	16	H	Carlisle U	W	2-1	2-0	7	Logan 2 [19, 22]	5324
13	23	A	Milton Keynes D	L	0-1	0-0	11		8002
14	30	H	Brentford	L	2-4	1-1	14	Cureton 2 [28, 78]	5510
15	Nov 2	A	Brighton & HA	L	0-3	0-2	—		7212
16	13	H	Notts Co	W	3-1	2-1	12	Cureton [18], Logan [32], Harley [66]	5302
17	20	A	Huddersfield T	W	1-0	1-0	12	Duffy [36]	13,108
18	23	A	Oldham Ath	D	3-3	0-3	—	Logan [77], Cureton [85], Nardiello [89]	3561
19	Dec 11	A	Plymouth Arg	L	0-2	0-1	13		14,347
20	18	H	Sheffield W	W	5-1	1-1	—	Cureton 2 [29, 72], Sercombe [58], Golbourne [61], O'Flynn [88]	5524
21	Jan 1	A	Southampton	L	0-4	0-1	13		22,465
22	3	H	Brighton & HA	L	1-2	1-0	14	Logan [8]	6352
23	8	H	Milton Keynes D	D	1-1	1-0	—	Cureton [8]	4544
24	14	A	Brentford	D	1-1	1-0	—	O'Flynn [2]	4767
25	22	H	Walsall	W	2-1	1-0	13	Duffy [4], Nardiello [77]	4853
26	29	A	Swindon T	D	0-0	0-0	—		8132
27	Feb 1	H	Southampton	L	1-2	1-0	13	Nardiello [39]	6370
28	5	H	Huddersfield T	L	1-4	0-0	15	Nardiello [90]	4786
29	12	A	Notts Co	W	2-0	0-0	12	Tully [54], Taylor [73]	6176
30	19	A	Charlton Ath	W	3-1	0-0	13	Sercombe [64], O'Flynn [77], Harley (pen) [84]	24,767
31	22	A	Carlisle U	D	2-2	2-2	—	Harley 2 [13, 27]	3962
32	26	H	Hartlepool U	L	1-2	0-2	15	Cureton [59]	4931
33	Mar 1	H	Tranmere R	D	1-1	0-1	—	Sercombe [65]	3456
34	5	A	Peterborough U	L	0-3	0-1	15		6174
35	8	H	Bournemouth	W	2-0	1-0	—	Cureton [16], Logan [59]	4537
36	12	A	Rochdale	W	1-0	1-0	9	Cureton [30]	2726
37	19	H	Yeovil T	L	2-3	2-1	12	Cureton 2 [25, 45]	5841
38	26	A	Colchester U	L	1-5	1-1	—	Nardiello [21]	3629
39	29	H	Swindon T	W	1-0	0-0	—	Harley (pen) [79]	4174
40	Apr 2	H	Dagenham & R	W	2-1	0-0	10	Taylor [81], Logan [87]	4598
41	9	A	Bristol R	W	2-0	0-0	9	Nardiello 2 [78, 90]	7500
42	16	A	Leyton Orient	W	2-1	1-1	9	Cureton 2 [4, 79]	5036
43	22	H	Oldham Ath	W	2-0	2-0	—	Golbourne [34], Cureton [42]	5458
44	25	A	Tranmere R	L	0-4	0-1	9		5017
45	30	H	Plymouth Arg	W	1-0	0-0	8	Dunne [46]	7869
46	May 7	A	Sheffield W	W	2-1	0-1	8	Nardiello [76], Archibald-Henville [89]	21,085

Final League Position: 8

GOALSCORERS

League (66): Cureton 17, Logan 11, Harley 10 (4 pens), Nardiello 10, O'Flynn 6 (1 pen), Sercombe 3, Duffy 2, Golbourne 2, Taylor 2, Archibald-Henville 1, Dunne 1, Tully 1.
Carling Cup (2): Harley 2.
FA Cup (0).
J Paint Trophy (12): Cureton 3, Harley 3, Nardiello 3 (1 pen), Duffy 1, O'Flynn 1, own goal 1.

Jones P 18	Duffy R 41 + 1	Golbourne S 42 + 2	Noble D 29 + 7	Jones B 27 + 2	Taylor M 26 + 2	Harley R 40 + 2	Sercombe L 38 + 4	O'Flynn J 22 + 9	Nardiello D 15 + 15	Tully S 42 + 1	Cureton J 34 + 7	Logan R 22 + 18	Thomson J 1 + 15	Edwards R 6 + 3	Dunne J 36 + 6	Cozic B 4 + 7	Archibald-Henville T 32 + 4	Stewart M 2 + 6	Krysiak A 10	Norwood J 1	Hamer B 18	Bennett S — + 1	Nichols T — + 1	Tisdale P — + 1	Match No.
1	2	3	4	5	6	7	8	9¹	10²	11³	12	13	14												1
1	2⁴	11	4²	5			8	9	10¹	3	12			6	7	13									2
1		11	4	5		7	3	9		2	10¹	12	14	6³	8²		13								3
1	2	11		5		8	4	9¹	10²	3	13	12		14	7	6³									4
1	2³	11		5		7	4	9²	10¹	3	13	12		14	8	6									5
1	2	11		5		8	4	9¹	10²	3	13	12			7	6									6
1	2	11³	13	5		7	4		12	3	10¹	9	14		8²	6									7
1	2	11	4²	5		7	12			3	10	9			13	8¹	6								8
1	2¹	11	12	5		7	4			3	10³	9	13		8²		6	14							9
1	2	11		5		7	4			3	10¹	9			8		6	12							10
1	2	11	4	5		7	14	12	13³	3	10²	9¹			8	6⁴									11
1	2	11	12	5		7	4	9		3		10		6¹	8										12
1	2	11	4³	5		7	8	9		3²		10	13	6¹	14		12								13
1	2	11	14	5		7³	8	9¹		3²	12	10	13		4	6									14
	12	4	3				8		14	2		13		5	11	7¹	6	9²	1		10²				15
	2	11				6	7	8		3	10	9²		4¹	12	5	13	1							16
	2	11				6	7	8	12	13	3	10²	9¹	4		5		1							17
	2¹	11	12			6	7	8		13	3	10	9	4²		5		1							18
	2	3	4	12	6¹	13	8	14	11³		10	9²		7		5		1							19
	2	11	4¹	5	6	7³	8	13		3	10	9²	14	12				1							20
1	2	11	4	5¹	6	7	8	14	12	3²	10³	9	13												21
1	2	11	4²	5	6¹	7	8	14		3	10³	9		13		12									22
1	2¹	11	4³	5	6	14	8	13		3	10	9²		7	12										23
1	3	13	4	2	6		8	9	10³	12	14		7²		11		5¹								24
3	11	4	5¹	6		8	13	12	2	10	9²			7							1				25
2³	11	4		6	7	5	9²	8	3	10¹	13	12			14						1				26
2		4	3	6	7²	8	9	10¹		13			11		5	12					1				27
2	11	12		4		14	10	3¹		9³	13	5		7²	6	8		1							28
7	11	8		6	7	12	0		3¹	10		4		5							1				29
2¹	11	4		6	8	12	9³		3	10	14		7²	13	5						1				30
	3	11³	4¹	6	7	8	9²	12	2	10		13	14	5							1				31
2³	11	4	5¹	6	7		9²	14	3	10	13	12	8								1				32
	3	4		6	7	11	9²	12	2	10	13		8¹	5							1				33
2	11	4²		6	7	8		9¹	3	10	12		13	5							1				34
3	11			6	7	8		2	10	9			4	5							1				35
12	3	4¹		6	11	8	13	2	10	9²			7	5							1				36
3²	11	12		6	7	8		14	2¹	10	9³		4	5	13						1				37
3	11⁴		12		7	8	6³	9¹	2¹	10²	14		4	13	5						1				38
3		4	2	6	7	8	9			10			11	5¹						1	12				39
3	11	4	5¹	6	7		9²	12	2	10	13	14	8³								1				40
3	11	4	5³	6	7		14	2	10²	9¹	13		8	12							1				41
3	11	4		7	6¹		9²	2	10	12	13		8	5							1				42
3	11	4³		7	6	9²		2	10¹	12	13		8	14	5						1				43
3²	11			6	7	4	9¹	13	2³	10	12	14	8	5			1								44
3	11	4¹	12	7	6		9²	2	10	13			8	5			1								45
3	11		14	7	6		9³	2	10				4	8¹	5		1				12²	13			46

FA Cup
First Round   Bury   (a)   0-2

Carling Cup
First Round   Ipswich T   (h)   2-3

J Paint Trophy
First Round   Yeovil T   (a)   3-1
Second Round   Hereford U   (a)   3-0
Southern Quarter-Final Plymouth Arg   (a)   2-1
Southern Semi-Final   Bristol R   (a)   2-2
Southern Final   Brentford   (a)   1-1
                                       (h)   1-2

FULHAM   FA Premiership

FOUNDATION

Churchgoers were responsible for the foundation of Fulham, which first saw the light of day as Fulham St Andrew's Church Sunday School FC in 1879. They won the West London Amateur Cup in 1887 and the championship of the West London League in its initial season of 1892–93. The name Fulham had been adopted in 1888.

Craven Cottage, Stevenage Road, London SW6 6HH
Telephone: 0870 442 1222.
Fax: 0870 442 0236 (Motspur Park).
Ticket Office: 0870 442 1234.
Website: www.fulhamfc.co.uk
Email: enquiries@fulhamfc.com
Ground Capacity: 26,600.
Record Attendance: 49,335 v Millwall, Division 2, 8 October 1938.
Pitch Measurements: 100m × 65m.
Chairman: Mohamed Al Fayed.
Chief Executive: Alistair Mackintosh.
Secretary: Darren Preston.
Manager: Martin Jol.
Head Coach: Michael Lindeman.
Head of Sports Medicine and Exercise Science: Mark Taylor.
Colours: White shirts with black trim, black shorts, white stockings.
Change Colours: Red shirts with black trim, black shorts, black stockings.
Year Formed: 1879.
Turned Professional: 1898.
Ltd Co.: 1903.
Reformed: 1987.
Previous Name: 1879, Fulham St Andrew's; 1888, Fulham.
Club Nickname: 'Cottagers'.
Grounds: 1879, Star Road, Fulham; c.1883, Eel Brook Common, 1884, Lillie Road; 1885, Putney Lower Common; 1886, Ranelagh House, Fulham; 1888, Barn Elms, Castelnau; 1889, Purser's Cross (Roskell's Field), Parsons Green Lane; 1891, Eel Brook Common; 1891, Half Moon, Putney; 1895, Captain James Field, West Brompton; 1896, Craven Cottage.
First Football League Game: 3 September 1907, Division 2, v Hull C (h) L 0–1 – Skene; Ross, Lindsay; Collins, Morrison, Goldie; Dalrymple, Freeman, Bevan, Hubbard, Threlfall.
Record League Victory: 10–1 v Ipswich T, Division 1, 26 December 1963 – Macedo; Cohen, Langley; Mullery (1), Keetch, Robson (1); Key, Cook (1), Leggat (4), Haynes, Howfield (3).
Record Cup Victory: 7–0 v Swansea C, FA Cup 1st rd, 11 November 1995 – Lange; Jupp (1), Herrera, Barkus (Brooker (1)), Moore, Angus, Thomas (1), Morgan, Brazil (Hamill), Conroy (3) (Bolt), Cusack (1).

HONOURS

Football League –
Division 1: *Champions* 2000–01;
Division 2: *Champions* 1948–49, 1998–99; *Runners-up* 1958–59;
Division 3 (S): *Champions* 1931–32;
Division 3: *Runners-up* 1970–71, 1996–97.

FA Cup: *Runners-up* 1975.

Football League Cup: Best season: 5th rd, 1968, 1971, 2000, 2005.

European Competitions
UEFA Cup: 2002–03.
Intertoto Cup: 2002 (*winners*).
Europa League: 2009–10 (*runners-up*).

sky SPORTS FACT FILE

Fulham was involved in an eventful FA Cup tie with Grimsby Town during 1953–54. The teams shared ten goals at Blundell Park but the replay at Craven Cottage was abandoned at half-time on a waterlogged pitch. Fulham prevailed in the third round tie at the third attempt 3-1.

Record Defeat: 0–10 v Liverpool, League Cup 2nd rd 1st leg, 23 September 1986.

Most League Points (2 for a win): 60, Division 2, 1958–59 and Division 3, 1970–71.

Most League Points (3 for a win): 101, Division 2, 1998–99. 101, Division 1, 2000–01.

Most League Goals: 111, Division 3 (S), 1931–32.

Highest League Scorer in Season: Frank Newton, 43, Division 3 (S), 1931–32.

Most League Goals in Total Aggregate: Gordon Davies, 159, 1978–84, 1986–91.

Most League Goals in One Match: 5, Fred Harrison v Stockport Co, Division 2, 5 September 1908; 5, Bedford Jezzard v Hull C, Division 2, 8 October 1955; 5, Jimmy Hill v Doncaster R, Division 2, 15 March 1958; 5, Steve Earle v Halifax T, Division 3, 16 September 1969.

Most Capped Player: Johnny Haynes, 56, England.

Most League Appearances: Johnny Haynes, 594, 1952–70.

Youngest League Player: Matthew Briggs, 16 years 65 days v Middlesbrough, 13 May 2007.

Record Transfer Fee Received: £11,500,000 from Manchester U for Louis Saha, January 2004.

Record Transfer Fee Paid: £11,500,000 to Lyon for Steve Marlet, August 2001.

Football League Record: 1907 Elected to Division 2; 1928–32 Division 3 (S); 1932–49 Division 2; 1949–52 Division 1; 1952–59 Division 2; 1959–68 Division 1; 1968–69 Division 2; 1969–71 Division 3; 1971–80 Division 2; 1980–82 Division 3; 1982–86 Division 2; 1986–92 Division 3; 1992–94 Division 2; 1994–97 Division 3; 1997–99 Division 2; 1999–2001 Division 1; 2001– FA Premier League.

LATEST SEQUENCES

Longest Sequence of League Wins: 12, 7.5.2000 – 18.10.2000.

Longest Sequence of League Defeats: 11, 2.12.1961 – 24.2.1962.

Longest Sequence of League Draws: 6, 14.10.1995 – 18.11.1995.

Longest Sequence of Unbeaten League Matches: 15, 26.1.1999 – 13.4.1999.

Longest Sequence Without a League Win: 15, 25.2.1950 – 23.8.1950.

Successive Scoring Runs: 26 from 28.3.1931.

Successive Non-scoring Runs: 6 from 21.8.1971.

MANAGERS

Harry Bradshaw 1904–09
Phil Kelso 1909–24
Andy Ducat 1924–26
Joe Bradshaw 1926–29
Ned Liddell 1929–31
Jim McIntyre 1931–34
Jimmy Hogan 1934–35
Jack Peart 1935–48
Frank Osborne 1948–64
(was Secretary-Manager or General Manager for most of this period and Team Manager 1953–56)
Bill Dodgin Snr 1949–53
Duggie Livingstone 1956–58
Bedford Jezzard 1958–64
(General Manager for last two months)
Vic Buckingham 1965–68
Bobby Robson 1968
Bill Dodgin Jnr 1968–72
Alec Stock 1972–76
Bobby Campbell 1976–80
Malcolm Macdonald 1980–84
Ray Harford 1984–96
Ray Lewington 1986–90
Alan Dicks 1990–91
Don Mackay 1991–94
Ian Branfoot 1994–96
(continued as General Manager)
Micky Adams 1996–97
Ray Wilkins 1997–98
Kevin Keegan 1998–99
(Chief Operating Officer)
Paul Bracewell 1999–2000
Jean Tigana 2000–03
Chris Coleman 2003–07
Lawrie Sanchez 2007
Roy Hodgson 2007–10
Mark Hughes 2010–11
Martin Jol June 2011–

TEN YEAR LEAGUE RECORD

		P	W	D	L	F	A	Pts	Pos
2001-02	PR Lge	38	10	14	14	36	44	44	13
2002-03	PR Lge	38	13	9	16	41	50	48	14
2003-04	PR Lge	38	14	10	14	52	46	52	9
2004-05	PR Lge	38	12	8	18	52	60	44	13
2005-06	PR Lge	38	14	6	18	48	58	48	12
2006-07	PR Lge	38	8	15	15	38	60	39	16
2007-08	PR Lge	38	8	12	18	38	60	36	17
2008-09	PR Lge	38	14	11	13	39	34	53	7
2009-10	PR Lge	38	12	10	16	39	46	46	12
2010-11	PR Lge	38	11	16	11	49	43	49	8

DID YOU KNOW ?

On 30 January 2011 Fulham defeated Tottenham Hotspur 4-0 in a fourth round FA Cup tie at Craven Cottage. Their first two goals were both scored from the penalty spot by Danny Murphy who had been transferred from the White Hart Lane club to Fulham in August 2007.

FULHAM 2010–11 LEAGUE RECORD

Match No.	Date	Venue	Opponents	Result	H/T Score	Lg Pos.	Goalscorers	Attendance
1	Aug 14	A	Bolton W	D	0-0	0-0	—	20,352
2	22	H	Manchester U	D	2-2	0-1	13	Davies [57], Hangeland [89]	25,643
3	28	A	Blackpool	D	2-2	1-0	14	Zamora [35], Etuhu [87]	15,529
4	Sept 11	H	Wolverhampton W	W	2-1	0-1	6	Dembele 2 [49, 90]	25,280
5	18	A	Blackburn R	D	1-1	0-1	7	Dempsey [56]	23,759
6	25	H	Everton	D	0-0	0-0	7		25,598
7	Oct 2	A	West Ham U	D	1-1	1-0	10	Dempsey [33]	34,589
8	16	H	Tottenham H	L	1-2	1-1	12	Kamara [30]	25,615
9	23	A	WBA	L	1-2	1-2	16	Carson (og) [9]	25,625
10	30	H	Wigan Ath	W	2-0	2-0	9	Dempsey 2 [30, 44]	25,448
11	Nov 6	H	Aston Villa	D	1-1	0-1	13	Hangeland [90]	23,654
12	10	A	Chelsea	L	0-1	0-1	—		41,593
13	13	A	Newcastle U	D	0-0	0-0	16		44,686
14	21	H	Manchester C	L	1-4	0-3	17	Gera [70]	25,694
15	27	H	Birmingham C	D	1-1	0-1	17	Dempsey [53]	24,391
16	Dec 4	A	Arsenal	L	1-2	1-1	17	Kamara [30]	60,049
17	11	H	Sunderland	D	0-0	0-0	17		24,462
18	26	H	West Ham U	L	1-3	1-2	18	Hughes [11]	25,332
19	28	A	Stoke C	W	2-0	2-0	17	Baird 2 [4, 10]	26,954
20	Jan 1	A	Tottenham H	L	0-1	0-1	18		35,603
21	4	H	WBA	W	3-0	1-0	14	Davies [45], Dempsey [56], Hangeland [65]	23,654
22	15	A	Wigan Ath	D	1-1	0-0	15	Johnson, A [86]	18,820
23	22	H	Stoke C	W	2-0	1-0	14	Dempsey 2 (1 pen) [33, 56 (p)]	23,766
24	26	A	Liverpool	L	0-1	0-0	—		40,466
25	Feb 2	H	Newcastle U	W	1-0	0-0	—	Duff [67]	25,620
26	5	A	Aston Villa	D	2-2	0-1	12	Johnson, A [52], Dempsey [78]	35,899
27	14	H	Chelsea	D	0-0	0-0	—		25,685
28	27	A	Manchester C	D	1-1	0-1	13	Duff [48]	43,077
29	Mar 5	H	Blackburn R	W	3-2	1-1	11	Duff 2 [37, 59], Zamora (pen) [89]	25,687
30	19	A	Everton	L	1-2	0-1	12	Dempsey [62]	33,239
31	Apr 3	H	Blackpool	W	3-0	2-0	10	Zamora 2 [23, 28], Etuhu [72]	25,692
32	9	A	Manchester U	L	0-2	0-2	11		75,339
33	23	A	Wolverhampton W	D	1-1	0-1	13	Johnson, A [80]	28,825
34	27	H	Bolton W	W	3-0	1-0	—	Dempsey 2 [15, 48], Hangeland [65]	23,222
35	30	A	Sunderland	W	3-0	1-0	9	Kakuta [33], Davies 2 [61, 73]	39,576
36	May 9	H	Liverpool	L	2-5	0-3	—	Dembele [57], Sidwell [86]	25,693
37	15	A	Birmingham C	W	2-0	1-0	8	Hangeland 2 [5, 49]	27,759
38	22	H	Arsenal	D	2-2	1-1	8	Sidwell [26], Zamora [57]	25,674

Final League Position: 8

GOALSCORERS

League (49): Dempsey 12 (1 pen), Hangeland 6, Zamora 5 (1 pen), Davies 4, Duff 4, Dembele 3, Johnson, A 3, Baird 2, Etuhu 2, Kamara 2, Sidwell 2, Gera 1, Hughes 1, Kakuta 1, own goal 1.
Carling Cup (6): Gera 2, Zamora 2, Dembele 1, Dempsey 1.
FA Cup (10): Kamara 3, Murphy 2 (2 pens), Dembele 1, Etuhu 1, Gera 1, Greening 1, Hangeland 1.

Stockdale D 7	Pantsil J 15 + 1	Kelly S 8 + 2	Murphy D 37	Hughes A 38	Hangeland B 37	Duff D 22 + 2	Etuhu D 23 + 5	Gera Z 10 + 17	Zamora B 9 + 5	Davies S 25 + 5	Dempsey C 35 + 2	Konchesky P 1	Dembele M 22 + 2	Greening J 6 + 4	Schwarzer M 31	Baird C 25 + 4	Johnson E 1 + 10	Salcido C 22 + 1	Kamara D 7 + 3	Riise B — + 3	Johnson A 15 + 12	Dikgacoi K — + 1	Briggs M 3	Sidwell S 10 + 2	Halliche R — + 1	Kakuta G 2 + 5	Gudjohnsen E 4 + 6	Senderos P 3	Match No.
1	2	3	4	5	6	7	8	9^1	10	11	12																		1
1	2		4^2	5	6	7	8	14	10	11^3	9^1	3	12	13															2
1	2	3	4^2	5	6	7^3	8	13	10^1	11	12		9	14															3
	2^2	3	4	5	6		8	12	10^1	11	7^3			9	1	13	14												4
	2		4^2	5	6	7	8	13		11	10^1		9		1		12	3											5
	2^1	4	5	6	7	8	9^2		11^3	10				1	12	13	3	14											6
		4	5	6	7^1	8	12		11^3	10				1	2	9^2	3	13	14										7
	12	4^1	5	6			13		7	11	9^2	8^2	1	2	14	3	10												8
	2		5	6		7		11		9	8	1	4^2		3	10^1	13	12											9
		4^2	5	6	8		11^1	10	9	7	11		2	3		12	13												10
	12	4	5	6	14		11		7	10		9	8^2	1	2^1	3^3		13											11
	2	4	5	6	7	8^1	13		11	10		9		1			12	3^2											12
	2	4	5	6	3	12	11^1		7	8		9		1		13		10^2											13
		4	5	6	7^1	8^2	12		11	10			1	2		3	13	9											14
12		4	5	6		8	9		7^2	11			1	2	13	3^1	10												15
	2		4^3	5	6		8	9		7	11		1	12	14		10^2	13	3^1										16
	2		4	5	6		8^2	9		7	11		1	14	13	3^2	10^1	12											17
	2		4	5	6	12	8^2	9		7	11^1		1		13	3	10												18
	2		4	5	6	7	8			11	10		1	3			9												19
	3		4	5	6	7^1	8	12		11	10		1	2			9												20
1	3		4	5	6	7	8	12		11^2	9^3			2	14		10^1	13											21
1	2		4	5	6	7	8			11^2	9	12		3			10^1	13											22
1	2		4	5^2	6	7	8^1	13		11		10^3		3			9			12	14								23
1	2		4	5	6	7^1		12		11		10		3			9			8									24
	2		4^2	5	6	7^3		13		14	11	10		1	3		9^1			8		12							25
	2^1		4	5	6	7^2				13	11	10		1	3	12	9^3			8			14					26
		4^2	5	6	7		13			12	11	10		1	2	3		9^1			8			14					27
		4	5	6	7	8				11	9		1	2	3		10^1						12					28
		4^1	5	0	7	8		12		11		10^4		1	2	3		9				13						29
		4	5	6	7^2	8^1	12		11		10		1	2	3		9^3					13	14					30
		4^2	5	6	7^3	8		10^1	14	11	9		1	2	3		12		13									31
		4^3	5	6		8^2	13	10		11	9^1	14	1	2	3				7	12								32
		4^1	5	6			13	7	11^3	9		1	2	3		14			8	12	10^2								33
		4^2	5	6	13		12	7	10	9^1		1	2	3		14			8		11^3							34
		4^2	5		14		10^3	11			12	1	2	3		13			8	7^1	9	6							35
		4	5	6			12	11^1	10	9^3		1	2	3		13			8	14	7^2								36
		4	5^2	6	13	14	10^1	11^3		7	1		3		9			8		12	2								37
		4^1	5	6	12	14^4	10^3	13	11		7^2	1				9		2	8				3					38

FA Cup

Third Round	Peterborough U	(h)	6-2	
Fourth Round	Tottenham H	(h)	4-0	
Fifth Round	Bolton W	(h)	0-1	

Carling Cup

Second Round	Port Vale	(h)	6-0	
Third Round	Stoke C	(a)	0-2	

GILLINGHAM   FL Championship 2

FOUNDATION

The success of the pioneering Royal Engineers of Chatham excited the interest of the residents of the Medway Towns and led to the formation of many clubs including Excelsior. After winning the Kent Junior Cup and the Chatham District League in 1893, Excelsior decided to go for bigger things and it was at a meeting in the Napier Arms, Brompton, in 1893 that New Brompton FC came into being, buying and developing the ground which is now Priestfield Stadium. Changed name to Gillingham in 1913, when they also changed their strip from black and white stripes to predominantly blue.

KRBS Priestfield Stadium, Redfern Avenue, Gillingham, Kent ME7 4DD.

Telephone: (01634) 300 000.

Fax: (01634) 850 986.

Ticket Office: (01634) 300 000 (option 3).

Website: www.gillinghamfootballclub.com

Email: info@priestfield.com

Ground Capacity: 11,440.

Record Attendance: 23,002 v QPR, FA Cup 3rd rd, 10 January 1948.

Pitch Measurements: 110yd × 70yd.

Chairman: Paul D. P. Scally.

Vice-chairman: Michael Anderson.

Secretary: Gwen Poynter.

Manager: Andy Hessenthaler.

Assistant Manager: Ian Hendon.

Physio: Steve Allen.

Colours: Blue shirts with white sleeves, blue shorts, blue stockings.

Change Colours: Yellow shirts with blue sleeves, yellow shorts, yellow stockings.

Year Formed: 1893.

Turned Professional: 1894.

Ltd Co.: 1893.

Previous Name: 1893, New Brompton; 1913, Gillingham.

Club Nickname: 'The Gills'.

Ground: 1893, Priestfield Stadium.

First Football League Game: 28 August 1920, Division 3, v Southampton (h) D 1–1 – Branfield; Robertson, Sissons; Battiste, Baxter, Wigmore; Holt, Hall, Gilbey (1), Roe, Gore.

HONOURS

Football League –
Division 1: 11th, 2002–03;
Division 3: *Runners-up* 1995–96;
Division 4: *Champions* 1963–64;
Runners-up 1973–74.

FA Cup: Best season: 6th rd, 2000.

Football League Cup: Best season: 4th rd, 1964, 1997.

sky SPORTS FACT FILE

In 1949–50, the season before Gillingham regained their Football League status, Harold Williams succeeded in scoring 18 Southern League goals in just 19 appearances. His achievement included six goals in the second game of the season, an 8-0 win over Hastings United.

Record League Victory: 10–0 v Chesterfield, Division 3, 5 September 1987 – Kite; Haylock, Pearce, Shipley (2) (Lillis), West, Greenall (1), Pritchard (2), Shearer (2), Lovell, Elsey (2), David Smith (1).

Record Cup Victory: 10–1 v Gorleston, FA Cup 1st rd, 16 November 1957 – Brodie; Parry, Hannaway; Riggs, Boswell, Laing; Payne, Fletcher (2), Saunders (5), Morgan (1), Clark (2).

Record Defeat: 2–9 v Nottingham F, Division 3 (S), 18 November 1950.

Most League Points (2 for a win): 62, Division 4, 1973–74.

Most League Points (3 for a win): 85, Division 2, 1999–2000.

Most League Goals: 90, Division 4, 1973–74.

Highest League Scorer in Season: Ernie Morgan, 31, Division 3 (S), 1954–55; Brian Yeo, 31, Division 4, 1973–74.

Most League Goals in Total Aggregate: Brian Yeo, 135, 1963–75.

Most League Goals in One Match: 6, Fred Cheesmur v Merthyr T, Division 3 (S), 26 April 1930.

Most Capped Player: Mamady Sidibe, 7 (14), Mali.

Most League Appearances: John Simpson, 571, 1957–72.

Youngest League Player: Luke Freeman, 15 years 247 days v Hartlepool U, 24 November 2007.

Record Transfer Fee Received: £1,500,000 from Manchester C for Robert Taylor, November 1999.

Record Transfer Fee Paid: £600,000 to Reading for Carl Asaba, August 1998.

Football League Record: 1920 Original Member of Division 3; 1921 Division 3 (S); 1938 Failed re-election; Southern League 1938–44; Kent League 1944–46; Southern League 1946–50; 1950 Re-elected to Division 3 (S); 1958–64 Division 4; 1964–71 Division 3; 1971–74 Division 4; 1974–89 Division 3; 1989–92 Division 4; 1992–96; Division 3; 1996–2000 Division 2; 2000–04 Division 1; 2004–05 FL C; 2005–08 FL 1; 2008–09 FL 2; 2009–10 FL 1; 2010– FL 2.

LATEST SEQUENCES

Longest Sequence of League Wins: 7, 18.12.1954 – 29.1.1955.

Longest Sequence of League Defeats: 10, 20.9.1988 – 5.11.1988.

Longest Sequence of League Draws: 5, 28.8.1993 – 18.9.1993.

Longest Sequence of Unbeaten League Matches: 20, 13.10.1973 – 10.2.1974.

Longest Sequence Without a League Win: 15, 1.4.1972 – 2.9.1972.

Successive Scoring Runs: 20 from 31.10.1959.

Successive Non-scoring Runs: 6 from 11.2.1961.

MANAGERS

W. Ironside Groombridge
1896–1906 *(Secretary-Manager)*
(previously Financial Secretary)
Steve Smith 1906–08
W. I. Groombridge 1908–19
(Secretary-Manager)
George Collins 1919–20
John McMillan 1920–23
Harry Curtis 1923–26
Albert Hoskins 1926–29
Dick Hendrie 1929–31
Fred Mavin 1932–37
Alan Ure 1937–38
Bill Harvey 1938–39
Archie Clark 1939–58
Harry Barratt 1958–62
Freddie Cox 1962–65
Basil Hayward 1966–71
Andy Nelson 1971–74
Len Ashurst 1974–75
Gerry Summers 1975–81
Keith Peacock 1981–87
Paul Taylor 1988
Keith Burkinshaw 1988–89
Damien Richardson 1989–92
Glenn Roeder 1992–93
Mike Flanagan 1993–95
Neil Smillie 1995
Tony Pulis 1995–99
Peter Taylor 1999–2000
Andy Hessenthaler 2000–04
Stan Ternent 2004–05
Neale Cooper 2005
Ronnie Jepson 2005–07
Mark Stimson 2007–10
Andy Hessenthaler May 2010–

TEN YEAR LEAGUE RECORD

		P	W	D	L	F	A	Pts	Pos
2001-02	Div 1	46	18	10	18	64	67	64	12
2002-03	Div 1	46	16	14	16	56	65	62	11
2003-04	Div 1	46	14	9	23	48	67	51	21
2004-05	FL C	46	12	14	20	45	66	50	22
2005-06	FL 1	46	16	12	18	50	64	60	14
2006-07	FL 1	46	17	8	21	56	77	59	16
2007-08	FL 1	46	11	13	22	44	73	46	22
2008-09	FL 2	46	21	12	13	58	55	75	5
2009-10	FL 1	46	12	14	20	48	64	50	21
2010-11	FL 2	46	17	17	12	67	57	68	8

DID YOU KNOW ?

A 5-1 win for Gillingham (as New Brompton) in the Test Match on 27 April 1895 against Swindon Town, gave them promotion after finishing top of the Southern League. Arthur Rule hit four of the goals after scoring no fewer than 18 in only nine League outings.

GILLINGHAM 2010–11 LEAGUE RECORD

Match No.	Date	Venue	Opponents	Result	H/T Score	Lg Pos.	Goalscorers	Attendance
1	Aug 7	H	Cheltenham T	D	1-1	0-0	—	Akinfenwa [76]	5655
2	14	A	Hereford U	D	0-0	0-0	12		2915
3	21	H	Lincoln C	L	0-1	0-1	17		4838
4	28	A	Morecambe	D	1-1	0-0	17	Spiller [84]	2325
5	Sept 4	A	Bury	L	4-5	0-2	21	Akinfenwa 2 [47, 58], Spiller [59], Palmer [66]	2700
6	11	H	Shrewsbury T	W	2-0	1-0	17	Palmer 2 (1 pen) [12, 59 (p)]	4815
7	18	A	Bradford C	L	0-1	0-0	20		10,722
8	25	H	Burton Alb	W	1-0	0-0	17	McDonald [50]	4823
9	28	H	Southend U	D	0-0	0-0	—		4925
10	Oct 2	A	Accrington S	L	4-7	2-3	18	Bentley 2 [29, 31], McDonald [55], Akinfenwa (pen) [79]	1933
11	9	H	Stockport Co	W	2-1	2-0	16	McDonald [3], Payne, J [37]	4755
12	16	A	Port Vale	D	0-0	0-0	16		6420
13	23	H	Torquay U	D	1-1	0-0	15	McDonald [80]	5345
14	30	A	Northampton T	L	1-2	1-2	18	Palmer [7]	4573
15	Nov 2	H	Wycombe W	L	0-2	0-1	—		4076
16	13	H	Crewe Alex	L	1-3	0-2	22	Whelpdale [47]	5292
17	20	A	Oxford U	W	1-0	1-0	20	McDonald [40]	7144
18	23	A	Barnet	W	2-1	0-1	—	Whelpdale [59], Lee [65]	2519
19	Dec 11	A	Macclesfield T	W	4-2	4-1	13	Whelpdale [9], Gowling [12], McDonald [19], Akinfenwa [33]	1507
20	28	H	Port Vale	W	3-0	2-0	—	McDonald 2 [1, 37], Akinfenwa [60]	5364
21	Jan 1	H	Stevenage	W	1-0	1-0	7	Akinfenwa [38]	5429
22	3	A	Wycombe W	L	0-1	0-0	9		4617
23	8	A	Stockport Co	W	5-1	1-0	9	McDonald 3 [32, 56, 79], Barcham [51], Weston [71]	3573
24	15	H	Northampton T	W	1-0	1-0	7	McDonald [32]	5613
25	22	A	Torquay U	D	1-1	0-1	8	Rooney [87]	2368
26	25	H	Chesterfield	L	0-2	0-1	—		4770
27	29	H	Aldershot T	W	2-1	0-0	—	McDonald 2 [53, 90]	4810
28	Feb 1	A	Stevenage	D	2-2	1-1	8	McDonald [45], Akinfenwa [50]	2424
29	5	H	Oxford U	D	0-0	0-0	7		5364
30	8	H	Rotherham U	W	3-1	2-1	—	McDonald 2 [5, 36], Oli [89]	4824
31	12	A	Crewe Alex	D	1-1	0-1	6	Weston [54]	4012
32	19	H	Bury	D	1-1	1-0	7	Weston [25]	5021
33	26	A	Shrewsbury T	D	0-0	0-0	7		5574
34	Mar 1	A	Aldershot T	D	1-1	0-0	—	Nutter [82]	2038
35	5	H	Bradford C	W	2-0	1-0	7	Akinfenwa [43], Weston [46]	5019
36	8	A	Southend U	D	2-2	2-1	—	McDonald [7], Akinfenwa (pen) [18]	5771
37	12	H	Accrington S	W	3-1	2-1	6	Barcham 2 [2, 45], McDonald [56]	5299
38	19	A	Burton Alb	D	1-1	0-1	5	McDonald [78]	3230
39	27	A	Cheltenham T	W	2-1	0-1	—	McDonald 2 [86, 90]	3157
40	Apr 2	H	Hereford U	D	0-0	0-0	7		5709
41	9	A	Lincoln C	W	4-0	2-0	7	Gowling [20], McDonald [41], Hone (og) [59], Akinfenwa [69]	3022
42	16	A	Morecambe	D	1-1	0-1	7	McDonald [88]	5545
43	23	H	Barnet	L	2-4	1-2	8	Barcham 2 [28, 80]	6170
44	25	A	Rotherham U	W	1-0	0-0	7	Barcham [79]	3455
45	30	H	Macclesfield T	L	2-4	1-3	8	Jackman [43], Martin [71]	6841
46	May 7	A	Chesterfield	L	1-3	0-0	8	McDonald [67]	10,023

Final League Position: 8

GOALSCORERS

League (67): McDonald 25, Akinfenwa 11 (2 pens), Barcham 6, Palmer 4 (1 pen), Weston 4, Whelpdale 3, Bentley 2, Gowling 2, Spiller 2, Jackman 1, Lee 1, Martin 1, Nutter 1, Oli 1, Payne, J 1, Rooney 1, own goal 1.
Carling Cup (1): Palmer 1.
FA Cup (0).
J Paint Trophy (0).

Match No.	Julian A 39	Sinclair T 17+3	Nutter J 32+2	Weston C 29+4	Gowling J 21+1	Bentley M 15+10	Spiller D 23+7	Palmer C 18	Payne S 1+15	Barcham A 18+6	Payne J 25+6	Akinfenwa A 40+4	Rooney L 2+21	Lawrence M 41+2	Maher K 36	Cronin L 7	Fuller B 40+2	McDonald C 41	McCammon M —+5	Oli D 3+18	Aborah S —+1	Inkango B 1+4	Miller Ashley —+1	Kennedy C 3	Lee C 4	Davies C 1	Whelpdale C 4	Jackman D 15+2	Martin J 12+5	Richards G 15+2	King S 3+1	White A —+1
1	1	2	3	4	5	6	7	8^1	9^2	10	11	12	13																			
2	1	2	3		5	6	7	8^1		12	10	9					4	11														
3	1	2	3	12	5	4^2	7	8^3	14	10		9	13				6	11^1														
4				4		6^2	7	3		11		8		9	13	5								1	2	10^1	12					
5		6	3^3		5	8^2	7	10	13		11	9	14	4^1			1	2		12												
6		6^1	3	14	12	4	7	8			11	9^3		5			1	2	10^2	13												
7			3	12	5	6	7	8^1			11	9^2		4			1	2	10^3		13	14										
8				4^1	5	8	7	3	13		11	9		6			1	2	10^2			12										
9				4	5		7	3			8	9	12	6			1	2	10			11^1										
10		13		4^1	5^2	8^1	7	3			11	9					1	2	10	12												
11	1	5	3	4^3		8			7		9^1	14	6	11			2	10^2	12	13												
12	1	6	3	4^2		7		8	12		10			5	11		2	13	9^1													
13	1	6	3	4^1		14	13	8^3		11	12			5	7^2		2	10	9													
14	1	6	3			4^2	13	8^3	14		7	9		5	11^1		2	10	12													
15	1	6	3				7	8^2	14		4	9^1		5			2	10	11^3		13	12										
16	1	6						8	14			9^3			11^1		2	10^2		13		3	4	5^1	7	12						
17	1	6					13	8^3	12			9^1		5	11^2		2	10				3	4		7	14						
18	1	6	12				13	8^3				9		5	11^2		2	10		14		3^1	4		7							
19	1	3		6		11					9		5	8			2	10	13						4^2		7^1	12				
20	1	3	4^1	6	12	7		13	14		9^2		5	8			2	10											11^3				
21	1	3^1	4	6	13	7		14	12		9^3		5	8^2			2	10											11				
22	1	3	4^2	8	13	7			12		9	14	5	8^2			2	10											11^1				
23	1	3	4^1	6		7		13	11			12	5^3	8			2	10^2										9		14		
24	1	3	4^1	6	13	7			11^3		12	14	5	8			7	10										9^2				
25	1	3	4	6	14	7^1			11^3		12	13	5	8			2	10										9^2				
26	1	3	4^1	6		7^3		14			13	9	12	5	8		2	10										11^2				
27	1	3	4^3	6	12						14	9	7^1	5	8		2	10										11^2	13			
28	1	3	6^1		4^2						14	9		5	8^3		2	10	13									7	11	12		
29	1	3	4^2							13		9	12	5	8		2	10	14									7^2	11^1	6		
30	1	3	4^2	14						11		9		5^1	8		2	10	13									7^3		6	12	
31	1	12	3	4^2	14					11		9		8			2	10^3	13									7		6	5^1	
32	1	3	4^2						12	11		9		5	8		2	10	13									7^1		6		
33	1	3	4^1						12	11		9		5	8		2	10	13									7^2		6		
34	1	3	4						12	11		9^3	14	5	8^2		2	10	13									7^1		6		
35	1	3	4^2						11^3	7		9^1	12	5	8		2	10	13										14	6		
36	1	3	4						11^2	7		9^1	13	5	8		2	10	12											6		
37	1	3^1	4						11	7		9		5	8		2	10^2	13										12	6		
38	1	3^1	4^2						11	7		9		5	8		2	10	13										12	6		
39	1		4		13				11^3	7^1		9	14	5	8^2		2	10	12										3	6		
40	1		4		13				11^3	7^2		9	14	5	8^1		2	10	12										3	6		
41	1		4^1	6			7^3		13	11	12	9^2	14	5	8		2	10											3			
42	1	12	4^3	6			7		11	14		9	13	5	8^2		2	10											3^1			
43	1	14	3		6^2	12	7^1		11	4		9^3	8	5			2	10														13
44	1	2			7	13			11^2		9		14	4		12		10										8^3	3	6	5^1	
45	1	2			4				11^1		9	12	14	8		13^3		10										7	3	6	5^2	
46	1	2^3		12			4^2	7^1	14			9	13	5	8			10										11	3	6		

FA Cup
First Round   Dover Ath   (h)   0-2

Carling Cup
First Round   Norwich C   (a)   1-4

J Paint Trophy
First Round   Southend U   (a)   0-0

HARTLEPOOL UNITED FL Championship 1

FOUNDATION

The inspiration for the launching of Hartlepool United was the West Hartlepool club which won the FA Amateur Cup in 1904–05. They had been in existence since 1881 and their Cup success led in 1908 to the formation of the new professional concern which first joined the North-Eastern League. In those days they were Hartlepools United and won the Durham Senior Cup in their first two seasons.

Victoria Park, Clarence Road, Hartlepool TS24 8BZ.
Telephone: (01429) 272 584.
Fax: (01429) 863 007.
Ticket Office: (01429) 272 584 (option 2).
Website: www.hartlepoolunited.co.uk
Email: enquires@hartlepoolunited.co.uk
Ground Capacity: 7,630.
Record Attendance: 17,426 v Manchester U, FA Cup 3rd rd, 5 January 1957.
Pitch Measurements: 110yd × 74yd.
Chairman: Ken Hodcroft.
Chief Executive: Russ Green.
Senior Administrator: Maureen Smith.
First Team Coach: Mick Wadsworth.
Physio: James Haycock.

HONOURS

Football League –
FL 2: *Runners-up* 2006–07;
Division 3: *Runners-up* 2002–03;
Division 3 (N): *Runners-up* 1956–57.
FA Cup: Best season: 4th rd, 1955, 1978, 1989, 1993, 2005, 2009.
Football League Cup: Best season: 4th rd, 1975.

Colours: Broad blue and white striped shirts with blue sleeves, blue shorts, white stockings.
Change Colours: Tangerine shirts with white trim, black shorts, tangerine stockings with white tops.
Year Formed: 1908.
Turned Professional: 1908.
Ltd Co.: 1908.
Previous Names: 1908, Hartlepools United; 1968, Hartlepool; 1977, Hartlepool United.
Club Nickname: 'The Pool'.
Ground: 1908, Victoria Park.
First Football League Game: 27 August 1921, Division 3 (N), v Wrexham (a) W 2–0 – Gill; Thomas, Crilly; Dougherty, Hopkins, Short; Kessler, Mulholland (1), Lister (1), Robertson, Donald.
Record League Victory: 10–1 v Barrow, Division 4, 4 April 1959 – Oakley; Cameron, Waugh; Johnson, Moore, Anderson; Scott (1), Langland (1), Smith (3), Clark (2), Luke (2), (1 og).
Record Cup Victory: 6–0 v North Shields, FA Cup 1st rd, 30 November 1946 – Heywood; Brown, Gregory; Spelman, Lambert, Jones; Price, Scott (2), Sloan (4), Moses, McMahon; 6–0 v Gainsborough Trinity (a), FA Cup 1st rd, 10 November 2007 – Budtz; McCunnie, Humphreys, Liddle (1) (Antwi), Nelson, Clark, Moore (1), Sweeney, Barker (2) (Monkhouse), Mackay (Porter 1), Brown (1).
Record Defeat: 1–10 v Wrexham, Division 4, 3 March 1962.

sky SPORTS FACT FILE

At the end of September 1954, Hartlepools United were 17th in the table. They went on an unbeaten 20-match run in League and Cup including playing neighbours Darlington five times in three weeks, winning three games and drawing the first two FA Cup matches.

Most League Points (2 for a win): 60, Division 4, 1967–68.

Most League Points (3 for a win): 88, FL 2, 2006–07.

Most League Goals: 90, Division 3 (N), 1956–57.

Highest League Scorer in Season: William Robinson, 28, Division 3 (N), 1927–28; Joe Allon, 28, Division 4, 1990–91.

Most League Goals in Total Aggregate: Ken Johnson, 98, 1949–64.

Most League Goals in One Match: 5, Harry Simmons v Wigan Borough, Division 3 (N), 1 January 1931; 5, Bobby Folland v Oldham Ath, Division 3 (N), 15 April 1961.

Most Capped Player: Ambrose Fogarty, 1 (11), Republic of Ireland.

Most League Appearances: Wattie Moore, 447, 1948–64.

Youngest League Player: David Foley, 16 years 105 days v Port Vale, 25 August 2003.

Record Transfer Fee Received: £750,000 from Ipswich T for Tommy Miller, July 2001.

Record Transfer Fee Paid: £75,000 to Northampton for Chris Freestone, March 1993; £75,000 to Notts Co for Gary Jones, March 1999; £75,000 to Mansfield T for Darrell Clarke, July 2001.

Football League Record: 1921 Original Member of Division 3 (N); 1958–68 Division 4; 1968–69 Division 3; 1969–91 Division 4; 1991–92 Division 3; 1992–94 Division 2; 1994–2003 Division 3; 2003–04 Division 2; 2004–06 FL 1; 2006–07 FL 2; 2007– FL 1.

LATEST SEQUENCES

Longest Sequence of League Wins: 9, 18.11.2006 – 1.1.2007.

Longest Sequence of League Defeats: 8, 27.1.1993 – 27.2.1993.

Longest Sequence of League Draws: 5, 24.2.2001 – 17.3.2001.

Longest Sequence of Unbeaten League Matches: 23, 18.11.2006 – 30.3.2007.

Longest Sequence Without a League Win: 18, 9.1.1993 – 3.4.1993.

Successive Scoring Runs: 27 from 18.11.2006.

Successive Non-scoring Runs: 11 from 9.1.1993.

MANAGERS

Alfred Priest 1908–12
Percy Humphreys 1912–13
Jack Manners 1913–20
Cecil Potter 1920–22
David Gordon 1922–24
Jack Manners 1924–27
Bill Norman 1927–31
Jack Carr 1932–35
(had been Player-Coach since 1931)
Jimmy Hamilton 1935–43
Fred Westgarth 1943–57
Ray Middleton 1957–59
Bill Robinson 1959–62
Allenby Chilton 1962–63
Bob Gurney 1963–64
Alvan Williams 1964–65
Geoff Twentyman 1965
Brian Clough 1965–67
Angus McLean 1967–70
John Simpson 1970–71
Len Ashurst 1971–74
Ken Hale 1974–76
Billy Horner 1976–83
Johnny Duncan 1983
Mike Docherty 1983
Billy Horner 1984–86
John Bird 1986–88
Bobby Moncur 1988–89
Cyril Knowles 1989–91
Alan Murray 1991–93
Viv Busby 1993
John MacPhail 1993–94
David McCreery 1994–95
Keith Houchen 1995–96
Mick Tait 1996–99
Chris Turner 1999–2002
Mike Newell 2002–03
Neale Cooper 2003–05
Martin Scott 2005–06
Danny Wilson 2006–08
Chris Turner 2008–10
Mick Wadsworth August 2010–

TEN YEAR LEAGUE RECORD

		P	W	D	L	F	A	Pts	Pos
2001-02	Div 3	46	20	11	15	74	48	71	7
2002-03	Div 3	46	24	13	9	71	51	85	2
2003-04	Div 2	46	20	13	13	76	61	73	6
2004-05	FL 1	46	21	8	17	76	66	71	6
2005-06	FL 1	46	11	17	18	44	59	50	21
2006-07	FL 2	46	26	10	10	65	40	88	2
2007-08	FL 1	46	15	9	22	63	66	54	15
2008-09	FL 1	46	13	11	22	66	79	50	19
2009-10	FL 1	46	14	11	21	59	67	50*	20
2010-11	FL 1	46	15	12	19	47	65	57	16

*3 pts deducted.

DID YOU KNOW ?

In 1938–39 during a difficult campaign for Hartlepools United (21st), Tommy McGarry was top scorer with twelve goals in twenty League games. He played in seven of the dozen victories achieved that season, but was allowed to leave in March for Bradford Park Avenue.

HARTLEPOOL UNITED 2010–11 LEAGUE RECORD

Match No.	Date		Venue	Opponents	Result	H/T Score	Lg Pos.	Goalscorers	Attendance
1	Aug	7	A	Rochdale	D 0-0	0-0	—		3706
2		14	H	Swindon T	D 2-2	2-0	15	Boyd [4], Sweeney [12]	2893
3		21	A	Yeovil T	W 2-0	1-0	8	Liddle [30], Monkhouse [54]	3537
4		28	H	Sheffield W	L 0-5	0-3	13		4084
5	Sept	4	A	Milton Keynes D	L 0-1	0-0	16		7656
6		11	H	Exeter C	L 2-3	2-1	20	Humphreys [38], Sweeney [42]	2641
7		18	A	Brentford	D 0-0	0-0	20		4710
8		25	H	Walsall	W 2-1	1-1	16	Sweeney [43], Monkhouse [56]	2552
9		28	H	Carlisle U	L 0-4	0-3	—		3419
10	Oct	2	A	Plymouth Arg	W 1-0	0-0	18	McSweeney [87]	7333
11		9	H	Peterborough U	W 2-0	1-0	15	Hartley [44], Liddle [90]	3047
12		16	A	Leyton Orient	L 0-1	0-0	17		3605
13		23	H	Bristol R	D 2-2	1-0	18	Gamble [29], Sweeney [79]	2792
14		30	A	Dagenham & R	D 1-1	0-0	17	Arber (og) [90]	2464
15	Nov	13	H	Brighton & HA	W 3-1	1-0	14	Austin [23], Liddle [71], Poole [84]	3073
16		20	A	Colchester U	L 2-3	1-0	19	Murray [28], Horwood [88]	3640
17		23	H	Tranmere R	W 1-0	0-0	—	Gulacsi (og) [77]	4340
18	Dec	11	A	Bournemouth	W 1-0	1-0	12	Brown [31]	6129
19		26	A	Huddersfield T	W 1-0	1-0	—	McSweeney [42]	14,813
20	Jan	1	A	Oldham Ath	W 4-2	2-1	7	Austin (pen) [27], Hartley [45], Humphreys [58], Sweeney [69]	3411
21		3	A	Notts Co	L 0-3	0-1	8		6285
22		15	H	Dagenham & R	L 0-1	0-0	13		2939
23		18	A	Bristol R	D 0-0	0-0	—		5285
24		22	A	Peterborough U	L 0-4	0-0	14		5800
25		25	H	Notts Co	D 1-1	1-0	—	Liddle [38]	2545
26	Feb	1	A	Oldham Ath	L 0-4	0-1	14		3056
27		5	H	Colchester U	W 1-0	0-0	11	Sweeney [88]	2646
28		12	A	Brighton & HA	L 1-4	0-2	13	Sweeney [63]	7296
29		15	H	Charlton Ath	W 2-1	1-0	—	Monkhouse [14], Liddle [62]	2289
30		19	H	Milton Keynes D	L 0-1	0-1	14		2620
31		22	H	Southampton	D 0-0	0-0	—		3301
32		26	A	Exeter C	W 2-1	2-0	12	Monkhouse 2 [21, 29]	4931
33	Mar	1	A	Huddersfield T	L 0-1	0-1	—		2857
34		5	H	Brentford	W 3-0	1-0	10	Monkhouse 2 [36, 57], Liddle [83]	2936
35		8	A	Carlisle U	L 0-1	0-0	—		3898
36		12	H	Plymouth Arg	W 2-0	1-0	8	Sweeney [20], Collins [64]	3059
37		15	H	Leyton Orient	L 0-1	0-1	—		2313
38		19	A	Walsall	L 2-5	1-0	10	Larkin 2 [21, 52]	4234
39		25	H	Rochdale	L 0-2	0-1	—		3081
40	Apr	2	A	Swindon T	D 1-1	1-0	14	Horwood [37]	7146
41		9	H	Yeovil T	W 3-1	1-1	13	Boyd [18], Collins [62], Larkin [69]	2834
42		16	A	Sheffield W	L 0-2	0-1	14		16,358
43		22	H	Tranmere R	D 1-1	1-0	—	Sweeney [14]	2969
44		25	A	Southampton	L 0-2	0-0	14		24,210
45		30	H	Bournemouth	D 2-2	0-2	18	Boyd (pen) [52], Flinders [90]	3159
46	May	7	A	Charlton Ath	D 0-0	0-0	16		15,804

Final League Position: 16

GOALSCORERS

League (47): Sweeney 9, Monkhouse 7, Liddle 6, Boyd 3 (1 pen), Larkin 3, Austin 2 (1 pen), Collins 2, Hartley 2, Horwood 2, Humphreys 2, McSweeney 2, Brown 1, Flinders 1, Gamble 1, Murray 1, Poole 1, own goals 2.
Carling Cup (2): Boyd 1 (pen), Brown 1.
FA Cup (6): Sweeney 4, Brown 1, Humphreys 1.
J Paint Trophy (6): Behan 1, Horwood 1, McSweeney 1, Monkhouse 1, Sweeney 1, Yantorno 1.

Flinders S 26	Austin N 24	Horwood E 44 + 1	Gamble J 25 + 5	Collins S 42	Hartley P 38 + 2	Sweeney A 38 + 2	Murray P 35 + 1	Bjornsson A 3 + 15	Brown J 17 + 9	Monkhouse A 43 + 1	Boyd A 9 + 10	McSweeney L 24 + 22	Haslam S 22 + 7	Liddle G 42	Yantorno F 9 + 8	Fredriksen J — + 1	Humphreys R 14 + 11	Behan D 1 + 12	Larkin C 15 + 15	Kean J 19	Poole J — + 3	Donaldson R 11 + 1	Mackay M 1 + 2	Rafferty A 1	Rowbotham J 1	Holden D 1	Johnson P 1	Match No.
1	2³	3	4	5	6	7	8	9¹	10²	11	12	13	14															1
1		3	4	5		7	8		10¹	11	9²	12	2	6	13													2
1		3	4¹	5	13	7	8		10³	11	9²	14	2	6		12												3
1		3	4	5	13	7	8¹		10³	11	9²	14	2	6	12													4
1		3		5		4	8		7	9¹	13	2	6	10³			11²	12	14									5
1	2	3		5		4	8		7	13	14		6		9³		11²	12	10¹									6
	2	3		5		4	8		7		12	13	6		9¹		11³	14	10²	1								7
	2	3	13	5		4	8		7		14		6		9²		11¹	12	10³	1								8
	2	3	4	5		7	8²	13		11	14	12		6¹			9¹		10	1								9
	2	3	4	5	7		8²	14		11				9³	13		6	12	10¹	1								10
	2	3	4	5	6		8²	14		11			9³	13	7			12	10¹	1								11
	2	3	4²	5	6	14	8	9³	13	11		9	7	12					10¹	1								12
	2	3¹	4²	5	6	13	8	12		11		9	7						10³	1			14					13
	2		4	5	6	7³	3	12		11		9²	8					13	10¹	1			14					14
	2	3	4¹	5	6	7	8³		9²	11		12	14	10						1	13							15
	2	3		5	6	7	8²	13	10³	11			4	9¹				12		1								16
	2	3	4³	5	6	7	14	13	12	11		9²	8				10¹			1								17
	2	3	13	5	6	4	8²	14	10¹	11		9³	7				12			1								18
	2	3		5	6	7	8²	14	10¹	11		9³	13	4				12		1								19
	2	3		5²	6	7	8¹	12	10	9	13	4		11³					14	1								20
	2	3	4¹		6	7		14	12	11	13	9²	5	8			10³			1								21
	2²	3			6	7	8³	5	10¹	11	14	9		4	13		12			1								22
	2	3	8		6	7		5		11		9		4			10¹	12		1								23
	2	3	8	5	6¹	7		12		11		9		4			10			1								24
	2	3	12	5	6	7	8		13	11	14	9³		4¹					10²	1								25
1	2	3		5	6	7	8		10¹	11	13			4			12		9²									26
1		3		5	6	7	8		9²	12	10¹	14	2	4			11³	13										27
1		3	8¹	5	6	7	10³	13	11			12	2	4			14	9²										28
1		3		5	0	7³	8		9¹	11	14		2	4			13	12	10²									29
1		3		5	6	7	8¹	12	11		14		2	4			9²	13	10³									30
1		3		5	6	7	8²	9¹	11	14	13		2	4				12	10³									31
1		3	8²	5	6	7			11	10			2	4			13	9¹	12									32
1		3		5	6	7	8¹	12	11		9		2	4			13		10²									33
1		3		5	6	7	8²	14	11		9³		2	4			13	12	10¹									34
1		3		5	6	7¹	8³	14	11		9		2	4			12		10²									35
1		3	14	5	6	7³		8¹	11		9		2	4			13	12	10²									36
1	3	13	5	6		8³	9¹		11	14	7	2	4				12		10²									37
1	3	10	5	6		8²	12		11	7	2¹	4	14	13			9³											38
1	3	8	5	6			11	13	14	2	4	7³		12			9²		10¹									39
1	3	8	5	6	7		13		11²	9	2	4▪		12					10¹									40
1	3	8	5	6	7³	4		11	10²		12	2	14		9¹		13											41
1	3	8	5	6	4	9³		11	10²	12	2	7¹					13							14				42
	14		8	5	6	4			11	10²	7		12	13					9¹	1		2		3³				43
1		3	8	5²	6	7			11	12	2	4		10¹			9²					13						44
1	2	3			6	8		9²	10³	7		4	14				11¹	13	12								5	45
1	2	3	8³	5	6	7			12	11	14	13		4					9¹			10²						46

FA Cup

First Round	Vauxhall Motors	(h)	0-0
		(a)	1-0
Second Round	Yeovil T	(h)	4-2
Third Round	Watford	(a)	1-4

Carling Cup

First Round	Sheffield U	(h)	2-0
Second Round	Wigan Ath	(h)	0-3

J Paint Trophy

First Round	Northampton T	(h)	4-0
Second Round	Bradford C	(h)	1-0
Northern Quarter-Final			
	Sheffield W	(a)	1-4

HEREFORD UNITED   FL Championship 2

FOUNDATION

Two local teams RAOC and St Martins amalgamated in 1924 under the chairmanship of Dr. E.W. Maples to form Hereford United and joined the Birmingham Combination. The first game at Edgar Street was against Atherstone Town on 24 August 1924, the visitors winnning 3-2. The players used the Wellington Hotel as a changing room. They graduated to the Birmingham League four years later and the Southern League in 1939.

Athletic Ground, Edgar Street, Hereford HR4 9JU.

Telephone: (08442) 761 939.

Fax: (08442) 761 982.

Ticket Office: (08442) 761 939.

Website: www.herefordunited.co.uk

Email: hufc1939@hotmail.com

Ground capacity: 7,149.

Record Attendance: 18,114 v Sheffield W, FA Cup 3rd rd, 4 January 1958.

Pitch measurements: 100m × 72m.

Chairman: David Keyte.

Vice-chairman: Tim Russon.

Manager: Jamie Pitman.

Assistant Manager: Russell Hoult.

Physio: Ian Rodgerson.

Colours: White shirts with black trim, black shorts, white stockings.

Change colours: All tangerine.

Year Formed: 1924.

Turned Professional: 1924.

Ltd Co.: 1939.

Club Nickname: 'United'.

Ground: 1924, Edgar Street.

First Football League game: 12 August 1972, Division 4, v Colchester U (a) L 0-1 – Potter; Mallender, Naylor; Jones, McLaughlin, Tucker; Slattery, Hollett, Owen, Radford, Wallace.

HONOURS

Football League –
Division 2: 22nd, 1976–77;
Division 3: *Champions* 1975–76;
Division 4: *Runners-up* 1972–73.
FA Cup: Best season: 4th rd, 1972, 1974, 1977, 1982, 1990, 1992, 2008, 2011.
Football League Cup: Best season: 3rd rd, 1975.
Welsh Cup: *Winners* 1990.
Conference: *Runners-up* 2003–04, 2004–05.

sky SPORTS FACT FILE

On 16 October 2010 Hereford United were trailing 3-0 at half-time away to Northampton Town. They reduced the arrears after 59 minutes and then scored three times in an eight minute spell to turn the match on its head for a 4-3 victory at Sixfields.

Record League Victory: 6–0 v Burnley (away), Division 4, 24 January 1987 – Rose; Rodgerson, Devine, Halliday, Pejic, Dalziel, Harvey (1p), Wells, Phillips (3), Kearns (2), Spooner.

Record Cup Victory: 6–1 v QPR, FA Cup 2nd rd, 7 December 1957 – Sewell; Tomkins, Wade; Masters, Niblett, Horton (2p); Reg Bowen (1), Clayton (1), Fidler, Williams (1), Cyril Beech (1).

Record Defeat: 0–7 v Middlesbrough, Coca-Cola Cup 2nd rd, 1st leg, 18 September 1996.

Most League Points (2 for a win): 63, Division 3, 1975–76.

Most League Points (3 for a win): 88, FL 2, 2007–08.

Most League Goals: 86, Division 3, 1975–76.

Highest League Scorer in Season: Dixie McNeil, 35, 1975–76.

Most League Goals in Total Aggregate: Stewart Phillips, 93, 1980–88, 1990–91.

Most League Goals in One Match: 4, Dixie McNeil v Chester C, Division 3, 10 March 1976; 4, Steve White v Cambridge U, Division 3, 13 January 1996.

Most Capped Player: Trevor Benjamin, 2, Jamaica.

Most League Appearances: Mel Pejic, 412, 1980–92.

Youngest League Player: Stewart Phillips, 16 years 112 days v Swindon T, 22 April 1979.

MANAGERS
Eric Keen 1939
George Tranter 1948–49
Alex Massie 1952
George Tranter 1953–55
Joe Wade 1956–62
Ray Daniels 1962–63
Bob Dennison 1963–67
John Charles 1967–71
Colin Addison 1971–74
John Sillett 1974–78
Mike Bailey 1978–79
Frank Lord 1979–82
Tommy Hughes 1982–83
Johnny Newman 1983–87
Ian Bowyer 1987–90
Colin Addison 1990–91
John Sillett 1991–92
Greg Downs 1992–94
John Layton 1994–95
Graham Turner 1995–2009
John Trewick 2009–10
Graham Turner 2010
Simon Davey 2010
Jamie Pitman October 2010–

Record Transfer Fee Received: £440,000 from QPR for Darren Peacock, December 1990.

Record Transfer Fee Paid: £80,000 to Walsall for Dean Smith, June 1994.

Football League Record: 1972 Elected to Division 4; 1973–76 Division 3; 1976–77 Division 2; 1977–78 Division 3; 1978–92 Division 4; 1992–97 Division 3; 1997–2006 Vauxhall Conference; 2006–08 FL 2; 2008–09 FL 1; 2009– FL 2.

LATEST SEQUENCES

Longest Sequence of League Wins: 6, 2.4.1996 – 20.4.1996.

Longest Sequence of League Defeats: 8, 7.2.1987 – 18.3.1987.

Longest Sequence of League Draws: 6, 12.4.1975 – 23.8.1975.

Longest Sequence of Unbeaten League Matches: 14, 21.10.1972 – 17.1.1973.

Longest Sequence Without a League Win: 13, 19.11.1977 – 25.2.1978.

Successive Scoring Runs: 23 from 20.9.1975.

Successive Non-scoring Runs: 6 from 10.3.2007.

TEN YEAR LEAGUE RECORD

		P	W	D	L	F	A	Pts	Pos
2001-02	Conf	42	14	10	18	50	53	52	17
2002-03	Conf	42	19	7	16	64	51	64	6
2003-04	Conf	42	28	7	7	103	44	91	2
2004-05	Conf	42	21	11	10	68	41	74	2
2005-06	Conf	42	22	14	6	59	33	80	2
2006-07	FL 2	46	14	13	19	45	53	55	16
2007-08	FL 2	46	26	10	10	72	41	88	3
2008-09	FL 1	46	9	7	30	42	79	34	24
2009-10	FL 2	46	17	8	21	54	65	59	16
2010-11	FL 2	46	12	17	17	50	66	50*	21

3 points deducted.

DID YOU KNOW ?

Such was the impact Miller Craddock had at Hereford United when signed from Newport County in 1947 that they received £5,000 from Aston Villa for this versatile forward. Tragically he was forced to retire in 1951 with a heart condition and died prematurely at 34.

HEREFORD UNITED 2010–11 LEAGUE RECORD

Match No.	Date	Venue	Opponents	Result	H/T Score	Lg Pos.	Goalscorers	Attendance
1	Aug 7	A	Crewe Alex	W	1-0	1-0	—	Kovacs [16]	4343
2	14	H	Gillingham	D	0-0	0-0	9		2915
3	21	A	Chesterfield	L	0-4	0-2	13		4970
4	28	H	Rotherham U	L	0-1	0-1	16		2166
5	Sept 4	A	Burton Alb	L	0-3	0-2	20		2556
6	11	H	Oxford U	L	0-2	0-1	23		2980
7	18	A	Bury	D	1-1	0-0	23	Bauza (pen) [46]	2753
8	25	H	Southend U	L	1-3	1-1	24	McQuilkin [4]	2104
9	28	H	Stevenage	L	1-4	0-1	—	Canham [49]	1444
10	Oct 2	A	Barnet	L	0-2	0-1	24		1745
11	9	H	Port Vale	D	1-1	1-1	24	Canham [15]	2651
12	16	A	Northampton T	W	4-3	0-3	24	Fleetwood 2 [59, 70], McQuilkin [72], Manset [78]	4333
13	23	H	Accrington S	D	1-1	0-1	24	Manset [54]	2434
14	30	A	Stockport Co	W	5-0	2-0	23	Purdie 2 [9, 12], Manset [52], Fleetwood [86], Assoumani (og) [90]	4017
15	Nov 2	H	Aldershot T	D	2-2	2-1	—	Rose [25], Colbeck [45]	2126
16	13	H	Cheltenham T	D	1-1	1-0	23	Manset [45]	3264
17	20	A	Lincoln C	L	1-3	0-2	24	Fleetwood [55]	3888
18	23	A	Shrewsbury T	L	0-4	0-1	—		6565
19	Dec 11	A	Bradford C	L	0-1	0-1	24		10,460
20	26	A	Wycombe W	L	1-2	0-0	24	Manset [79]	3792
21	Jan 1	H	Torquay U	D	2-2	1-2	24	Fleetwood [32], Manset [66]	2373
22	3	A	Aldershot T	W	2-1	1-0	23	Fleetwood [3], Colbeck [82]	2767
23	15	H	Stockport Co	W	3-0	2-0	23	Halls (og) [3], Manset [25], Bauza [86]	3154
24	25	H	Morecambe	W	2-1	1-0	—	Colbeck [44], Townsend [60]	1831
25	Feb 1	A	Torquay U	W	3-1	1-1	20	Fleetwood 2 [14, 46], Featherstone [80]	1680
26	5	H	Lincoln C	L	0-1	0-1	20		2776
27	8	H	Macclesfield T	D	2-2	1-1	—	Purdie (pen) [40], Fleetwood [70]	1975
28	12	A	Cheltenham T	W	3-0	1-0	20	Fairhurst 2 [23, 89], Kovacs [51]	3643
29	19	H	Burton Alb	D	0-0	0-0	20		2773
30	22	H	Northampton T	D	1-1	0-0	—	Fairhurst [67]	2125
31	26	A	Oxford U	W	2-0	1-0	17	Fleetwood 2 [8, 90]	7807
32	Mar 5	H	Bury	L	0-3	0-1	19		2650
33	8	A	Stevenage	W	1-0	0-0	—	Colbeck [83]	1670
34	12	H	Barnet	L	1-2	1-1	20	Rose [1]	2517
35	18	A	Southend U	L	0-4	0-1	—		5056
36	22	A	Port Vale	D	1-1	0-0	—	McQuilkin [76]	4869
37	27	H	Crewe Alex	W	1-0	1-0	—	Fleetwood [22]	2334
38	30	A	Accrington S	L	0-4	0-3	—		1632
39	Apr 2	A	Gillingham	D	0-0	0-0	19		5709
40	5	H	Wycombe W	D	0-0	0-0	—		1633
41	9	H	Chesterfield	W	3-0	1-0	19	Fleetwood [11], Leslie [76], Colbeck [81]	2492
42	16	H	Rotherham U	D	0-0	0-0	17		3770
43	23	H	Shrewsbury T	L	0-2	0-1	20		3942
44	25	A	Morecambe	D	1-1	1-0	20	Leslie [42]	2016
45	30	H	Bradford C	D	1-1	0-0	21	Fleetwood [87]	3219
46	May 7	A	Macclesfield T	D	1-1	1-0	21	Green [29]	2013

Final League Position: 21

GOALSCORERS

League (50): Fleetwood 14, Manset 7, Colbeck 5, Fairhurst 3, McQuilkin 3, Purdie 3 (1 pen), Bauza 2 (1 pen), Canham 2, Kovacs 2, Leslie 2, Rose 2, Featherstone 1, Green 1, Townsend 1, own goals 2.
Carling Cup (0).
FA Cup (13): Manset 6 (1 pen), Fleetwood 4, Purdie 2, Rose 1.
J Paint Trophy (0).

Bartlett A 46	Green R 40+1	Valentine R 16	Kovacs J 21+4	Townsend M 42+1	Thompson O 5+1	Fleetwood S 36+7	McQuilkin J 31+7	Manset M 18+3	Canham S 7+9	Colbeck J 40+4	Lunt K 38+4	Stratford D 2+5	Malsom S 1+3	Rose R 32+2	Rabihou A 1+2	Werling D 4+2	Kanoute S —+1	Bauza G 9+3	Gwynne S 3+3	James T 6	Purdie R 18+7	Weir T 2+2	Featherstone N 20+7	Webster B 2	Heath J 26	Lund M 1+1	Jervis J 3+1	Ngo Baheng W —+2	Pell H 5+2	Fairhurst W 10+6	Patulea A —+6	Leslie S 10+1	Stam S 10	Price J 1+3	Match No.
1	2	3	4	5	6	7	8	9	10¹	11	12	.																							1
1	2	3	4	5	6	7	8	9	10¹	11																									2
1	2	3	4	5		7	8²	9	10¹	11	6	12	13																						3
1	2	3	4	5	6	9	8		10	11	7																								4
1	2	3	4	6¹	14	8	9²		11	7		13		5	10³	12																			5
1	2	3		6¹	7³	9	12	11²	4	8	10			5	14			13																	6
1	2	3		5		7	8	9²	13	11	4⁸	12		6				10¹																	7
1	2	3		5		7²	8	9³	11		4¹	12		6	14			10	13																8
1	2	3		5		7	8	12	10		4¹			6				9	11																9
1		3		5		7¹	8	12	10²	13	4			2				9	11	6															10
1	2	3		5	12		8		10⁸	11	4¹			7²				9	13	6															11
1	2	3		5		13	8	12		11	4²			10	7¹			9		6															12
1	2	3		5		12	8	9¹	13	11	10			6	7²				4																13
1	2	3		5		12	8	9¹		11	4²			7				13		6	10³	14													14
1	2	3	12³	5		13	8	9		11	4²			7				6¹	10	14															15
1	4	3		5			9		12	11	8¹			6				10	2	7															16
1	2		5		10		9	12	11³		4¹			7		13		14			3²	8	6												17
1	2⁸		5		13		9³	14	11		4¹			7	3		12			10²		8	6												18
1		4	5		13	12	9		11¹	6								10	2				8				3	7²							19
1		4	5	7²	8	9		13	14					2				10			11¹		6³				3	12							20
1	2	4	5	7³	8	9		12	13	14				6				10⁷					11¹				3								21
1	2	4	5	7²	8	9			13	10¹	12			6									11				3								22
1		4	5	10²	8³	9¹	12	7		6	14			2				13					11				3								23
1	13	4	5	9¹	8		7		6					2							12		11¹				3	10							24
1	2	4	5	9¹	8		13	7	6¹					3							11		12					10²	14						25
1	2	4	5	9	8²		12	7	14					6							11³						3	10¹		13					26
1	2	4	5⁸	9	8¹			7	10					6							11						3		12						27
1	2	4		9				7¹	6					5							11		12				3		13	8	10²				28
1	2	4⁸	12	10⁸	14			7¹	6					5							11		13				3			8²	9				29
1	2			5				10	12					7	4						6		11¹				3			8	9				30
1	2	4	5					10						11	6						7						3			8	9				31
1	2	4	5					10	13					11²	8¹						6		12				3		14	7³	9				32
1	2	4	5					10	8²					7	11						6		13				3			9¹	12				33
1	2	4	5					10	13					7	11³						6		3		8²				14	9¹	12				34
1	2	4	5					10	12					7⁸	8²						6		13				3			9¹	14	11¹			35
1	2		5					10¹	8					6							9		11				3			12		7	4		36
1	2		5					9¹	10					11²	6						13		8				3			12		7	4		37
1	2		5					8						7				6¹			11		12				3		9¹	14	13	4	10²		38
1	2		5					9²	8					7¹	4						12		11				3			10		6	13		39
1	2		5					9²	8¹					7	4						12		11				3			10		6	13		40
1	2¹		5					9²	8³					7	4			14			12		11				3			13		10	6		41
1	14	5						9²	8¹					7	4³			12			2		11				3			13		10	6		42
1	2		5					9²	8¹					7	4			6			10		11				3			12			13		43
1	2		5					9¹						7	4						10		11				3			12		8	6		44
1	2	14	5					9						7²	4						10¹		11³				3			12	13	8	6		45
1	2	12	5⁸					9	14					7¹	4						13		11²				3			10		8¹	6		46

FA Cup

First Round	Hythe T	(h)	5-1
Second Round	Lincoln C	(h)	2-2
		(a)	4-3
Third Round	Wycombe W	(a)	1-0
Fourth Round	Sheffield W	(a)	1-4

Carling Cup

| First Round | Colchester U | (h) | 0-3 |

J Paint Trophy

| Second Round | Exeter C | (h) | 0-3 |

HUDDERSFIELD TOWN FL Championship 1

FOUNDATION

A meeting, attended largely by members of the Huddersfield & District FA, was held at the Imperial Hotel in 1906 to discuss the feasibility of establishing a football club in this rugby stronghold. However, it was not until a man with both the enthusiasm and the money to back the scheme came on the scene, that real progress was made. This benefactor was Mr Hilton Crowther and it was at a meeting at the Albert Hotel in 1908, that the club formally came into existence with a capital of £2,000 and joined the North-Eastern League.

The Galpharm Stadium, Stadium Way, Leeds Road, Huddersfield HD1 6PX.

Telephone: 0870 4444 677.

Fax: (01484) 484 101.

Ticket Office: 0870 4444 552.

Website: www.htafc.com

Email: info@htafc.com

Ground Capacity: 24,554.

Record Attendance: 67,037 v Arsenal, FA Cup 6th rd, 27 February 1932 (at Leeds Road); 23,678 v Liverpool, FA Cup 3rd rd, 12 December 1999 (at Alfred McAlpine Stadium).

Pitch Measurements: 115yd × 76yd.

Chairman: Dean Hoyle.

Operations Director: Ann Hough.

Secretary: Nicola Stead.

Manager: Lee Clark.

Assistant Manager: Terry McDermott.

Physios: Dave Buckby, Adam Hirst.

Colours: Blue and white striped shirts, white shorts, blue stockings.

Change Colours: Red and black striped shirts, red shorts, red stockings.

Year Formed: 1908. *Turned Professional:* 1908. *Ltd Co.:* 1908. *Club Nickname:* 'The Terriers'.

Grounds: 1908, Leeds Road; 1994, The Alfred McAlpine Stadium (renamed the Galpharm Stadium 2004).

First Football League Game: 3 September 1910, Division 2, v Bradford PA (a) W 1–0 – Mutch; Taylor, Morris; Beaton, Hall, Bartlett; Blackburn, Wood, Hamilton (1), McCubbin, Jee.

Record League Victory: 10–1 v Blackpool, Division 1, 13 December 1930 – Turner; Goodall, Spencer; Redfern, Wilson, Campbell; Bob Kelly (1), McLean (4), Robson (3), Davies (1), Smailes (1).

Record Cup Victory: 7–0 v Lincoln U, FA Cup 1st rd, 16 November 1991 – Clarke; Trevitt, Charlton, Donovan (2), Mitchell, Doherty, O'Regan (1), Stapleton (1) (Wright), Roberts (2), Onuora (1), Barnett (Ireland). *N.B.* 11–0 v Heckmondwike (a), FA Cup pr rd, 18 September 1909 – Doggart; Roberts, Ewing; Hooton, Stevenson, Randall; Kenworthy (2), McCreadie (1), Foster (4), Stacey (4), Jee.

HONOURS

Football League – Division 1: *Champions* 1923–24, 1924–25, 1925–26; *Runners-up* 1926–27, 1927–28, 1933–34; **Division 2:** *Champions* 1969–70; *Runners-up* 1919–20, 1952–53; **Division 4:** *Champions* 1979–80.

FA Cup: *Winners* 1922; *Runners-up* 1920, 1928, 1930, 1938.

Football League Cup: Semi-final 1968.

Autoglass Trophy: *Runners-up* 1994.

sky SPORTS FACT FILE

Before a then British record transfer fee of £8,750 took him to Chelsea in September 1930, right-winger Alex Jackson had scored 19 goals in only 24 FA Cup matches for Huddersfield Town. This Scottish "Wembley Wizard" scored three against England in 1928.

Record Defeat: 1–10 v Manchester C, Division 2, 7 November 1987.

Most League Points (2 for a win): 66, Division 4, 1979–80.

Most League Points (3 for a win): 87, FL 1, 2010–11.

Most League Goals: 101, Division 4, 1979–80.

Highest League Scorer in Season: Sam Taylor, 35, Division 2, 1919–20; George Brown, 35, Division 1, 1925–26.

Most League Goals in Total Aggregate: George Brown, 142, 1921–29; Jimmy Glazzard, 142, 1946–56.

Most League Goals in One Match: 5, Dave Mangnall v Derby Co, Division 1, 21 November 1931; 5, Alf Lythgoe v Blackburn R, Division 1, 13 April 1935.

Most Capped Player: Jimmy Nicholson, 31 (41), Northern Ireland.

Most League Appearances: Billy Smith, 520, 1914–34.

Youngest League Player: Denis Law, 16 years 303 days v Notts Co, 24 December 1956.

Record Transfer Fee Received: £2,750,000 from Ipswich T for Marcus Stewart, February 2000.

Record Transfer Fee Paid: £1,200,000 to Bristol R for Marcus Stewart, July 1996.

Football League Record: 1910 Elected to Division 2; 1920–52 Division 1; 1952–53 Division 2; 1953–56 Division 1; 1956–70 Division 2; 1970–72 Division 1; 1972–73 Division 2; 1973–75 Division 3; 1975–80 Division 4; 1980–83 Division 3; 1983–88 Division 2; 1988–92 Division 3; 1992–95 Division 2; 1995–2001 Division 1; 2001–03 Division 2; 2003–04 Division 3; 2004– FL 1.

LATEST SEQUENCES

Longest Sequence of League Wins: 11, 5.4.1920 – 4.9.1920.

Longest Sequence of League Defeats: 7, 8.10.1955 – 19.11.1955.

Longest Sequence of League Draws: 6, 3.3.1987 – 3.4.1987.

Longest Sequence of Unbeaten League Matches: 27, 24.1.1925 – 17.10.1925.

Longest Sequence Without a League Win: 22, 4.12.1971 – 29.4.1972.

Successive Scoring Runs: 27 from 12.3.2005.

Successive Non-scoring Runs: 7 from 22.1.1972.

MANAGERS

Fred Walker 1908–10
Richard Pudan 1910–12
Arthur Fairclough 1912–19
Ambrose Langley 1919–21
Herbert Chapman 1921–25
Cecil Potter 1925–26
Jack Chaplin 1926–29
Clem Stephenson 1929–42
Ted Magner 1942–43
David Steele 1943–47
George Stephenson 1947–52
Andy Beattie 1952–56
Bill Shankly 1956–59
Eddie Boot 1960–64
Tom Johnston 1964–68
Ian Greaves 1968–74
Bobby Collins 1974
Tom Johnston 1975–78
  (had been General Manager since 1975)
Mike Buxton 1978–86
Steve Smith 1986–87
Malcolm Macdonald 1987–88
Eoin Hand 1988–92
Ian Ross 1992–93
Neil Warnock 1993–95
Brian Horton 1995–97
Peter Jackson 1997–99
Steve Bruce 1999–2000
Lou Macari 2000–02
Mick Wadsworth 2002–03
Peter Jackson 2003–07
Andy Ritchie 2007–08
Stan Ternent 2008
Lee Clark December 2008–

TEN YEAR LEAGUE RECORD

		P	W	D	L	F	A	Pts	Pos
2001-02	Div 2	46	21	15	10	65	47	78	6
2002-03	Div 2	46	11	12	23	39	61	45	22
2003-04	Div 3	46	23	12	11	68	52	81	4
2004-05	FL 1	46	20	10	16	74	65	70	9
2005-06	FL 1	46	19	16	11	72	59	73	4
2006-07	FL 1	46	14	17	15	60	69	59	15
2007-08	FL 1	46	20	6	20	50	62	66	10
2008-09	FL 1	46	18	14	14	62	65	68	9
2009-10	FL 1	46	23	11	12	82	56	80	6
2010-11	FL 1	46	25	12	9	77	48	87	3

DID YOU KNOW ?

In 1919–20 versatile forward Sam Taylor was the only ever present in the Huddersfield Town team. He scored 35 League goals and six in as many FA Cup matches that season. Huddersfield won promotion to the First Division and finished Cup runners-up at Stamford Bridge.

HUDDERSFIELD TOWN 2010–11 LEAGUE RECORD

Match No.	Date	Venue	Opponents	Result	H/T Score	Lg Pos.	Goalscorers	Attendance
1	Aug 7	A	Notts Co	W 3-0	2-0	—	Pilkington 2 [32, 72], Rhodes [35]	10,342
2	14	H	Tranmere R	D 0-0	0-0	3		13,707
3	21	A	Peterborough U	L 2-4	2-1	10	Rhodes [22], Carey [33]	6647
4	28	H	Charlton Ath	W 3-1	2-0	6	Rhodes [39], McCombe [42], Roberts [82]	13,858
5	Sept 4	H	Bournemouth	D 2-2	1-1	8	Kay [45], Roberts (pen) [48]	12,426
6	11	A	Leyton Orient	W 2-1	1-0	4	Arfield [3], Rhodes [78]	3918
7	18	H	Yeovil T	W 4-2	0-2	1	Arfield [49], McCombe 2 [66, 68], Roberts (pen) [75]	13,479
8	25	A	Swindon T	L 0-1	0-0	4		8652
9	28	A	Rochdale	L 0-3	0-1	—		6121
10	Oct 2	H	Bristol R	L 0-1	0-0	11		12,344
11	9	A	Colchester U	W 3-0	2-0	6	Novak [34], Pilkington [42], Rhodes [78]	4211
12	16	H	Southampton	W 2-0	2-0	5	Pilkington [6], Gudjonsson [45]	14,769
13	23	A	Plymouth Arg	L 1-2	1-1	5	Pilkington [19]	7048
14	30	H	Walsall	W 1-0	1-0	2	Pilkington [35]	13,062
15	Nov 2	H	Sheffield W	W 2-0	2-0	—	Carey [23], Pilkington [34]	20,540
16	13	A	Oldham Ath	L 0-1	0-1	5		7723
17	20	H	Exeter C	L 0-1	0-1	9		13,108
18	23	H	Milton Keynes D	W 4-1	2-0	—	Kay [24], Roberts [36], Rhodes 2 [47, 66]	12,773
19	Dec 11	H	Brighton & HA	W 2-1	0-0	3	Rhodes [56], McCombe [84]	14,398
20	26	H	Hartlepool U	L 0-1	0-1	—		14,813
21	28	A	Southampton	L 1-4	1-2	—	Novak [15]	24,483
22	Jan 1	A	Carlisle U	D 2-2	1-0	6	Clarke, P [23], Arfield [63]	5904
23	3	H	Sheffield W	W 1-0	1-0	4	Pilkington [27]	17,024
24	11	H	Plymouth Arg	W 3-2	3-2	—	Arnason (og) [18], Rhodes [29], Clarke, P [32]	11,462
25	15	A	Walsall	W 4-2	2-1	2	Kilbane [19], McCombe [25], Clarke, P [77], Rhodes [90]	3827
26	22	H	Colchester U	D 0-0	0-0	3		12,689
27	Feb 1	H	Carlisle U	W 2-0	2-0	3	Roberts 2 [39, 45]	11,572
28	5	A	Exeter C	W 4-1	0-0	3	Cadamarteri [55], Roberts [67], Pilkington [81], Kilbane [88]	4786
29	12	H	Oldham Ath	D 0-0	0-0	3		16,176
30	19	A	Bournemouth	D 1-1	0-0	3	Cadamarteri [89]	7923
31	22	A	Dagenham & R	D 1-1	1-0	—	Clarke, T [28]	2336
32	26	H	Leyton Orient	D 2-2	1-0	3	Rhodes [3], Novak [49]	13,527
33	Mar 1	A	Hartlepool U	W 1-0	1-0	—	Pilkington [12]	2857
34	5	A	Yeovil T	D 1-1	0-1	3	Kay [58]	3620
35	8	H	Rochdale	W 2-1	2-0	—	Afobe [25], Roberts [33]	12,531
36	12	H	Bristol R	W 1-0	1-0	2	Rhodes [5]	7380
37	15	A	Brentford	W 1-0	0-0	—	Clarke, P [90]	4402
38	19	H	Swindon T	D 0-0	0-0	2		13,907
39	27	H	Notts Co	W 3-0	1-0	—	Rhodes 2 [36, 61], Roberts [58]	13,661
40	Apr 2	A	Tranmere R	W 2-0	1-0	2	Afobe [39], Novak [87]	6438
41	9	H	Peterborough U	D 1-1	0-1	3	Hunt [90]	16,431
42	16	A	Charlton Ath	W 1-0	0-0	3	Gudjonsson [83]	15,879
43	22	A	Milton Keynes D	W 3-1	2-0	—	Arfield [23], Peltier [35], Cadamarteri [70]	11,857
44	25	H	Dagenham & R	W 2-1	2-1	3	Rhodes 2 [9, 32]	14,072
45	30	A	Brighton & HA	W 3-2	1-0	3	Afobe 2 [8, 61], Ward [90]	8416
46	May 7	H	Brentford	D 4-4	2-1	3	Ward 2 [14, 15], Novak [52], Afobe [63]	13,977

Final League Position: 3

GOALSCORERS

League (77): Rhodes 16, Pilkington 10, Roberts 9 (2 pens), Afobe 5, McCombe 5, Novak 5, Arfield 4, Clarke, P 4, Cadamarteri 3, Kay 3, Ward 3, Carey 2, Gudjonsson 2, Kilbane 2, Clarke, T 1, Hunt 1, Peltier 1, own goal 1.
Carling Cup (2): Rhodes 1, own goal 1.
FA Cup (11): Roberts 3, Afobe 1, Arfield 1, Kay 1, Lee 1, McCombe 1, Peltier 1, Pilkington 1, Rhodes 1.
J Paint Trophy (13): Rhodes 4, Pilkington 3, Afobe 2, Lee 2, Arfield 1, Carey 1.
Play-Offs (4): Kay 1, Kilbane 1, Peltier 1, Ward 1.

Smithies A 22	Peltier L 38	Naysmith G 13+1	Gudjonsson J 29+8	Clarke P 46	McCombe J 31+3	Pilkington A 30+1	Arfield S 33+7	Rhodes J 27+10	Garner J 10+6	Roberts G 34+3	Johnson D 14+2	Novak L 12+19	Robinson T —+1	Carey G 18+1	Croft L —+3	Ridehalgh L 15+5	Kay A 21+6	Lee A 17+11	Bennett I 24	Afobe B 14+14	Clarke T 3+2	Clarke N 1	Kilbane K 23+1	Kadar T 2	Hunt J 14+5	Cadamarteri D 2+9	Atkinson C 2	Jordan S 6	Chippendale A —+1	Ward D 5+2	Match No.
1	2	3	4	5	6	7	8^1	9^2	10	11	12	13																			1
1	2	3^1	4	5	6	7	8^3	9^2	10^1	11	14	12		13																	2
1	2		4	5	6	7^3	8	9^2	10	12	11	13		3^1	14																3
1			4	5	6		2	9^1	13	11				12		7	3	8		10^2											4
1	2		4	5	6	7^2		9^1		11		13		12			3	8		10											5
1		14		5	6		2	13	10^1	7	12			4^3			3	8		9^2											6
1	2	12		5	6	4	13	11	7	10				3^3		14	8^1	9^2													7
1	2		4	5	6	12	8^2	9	14	11^1	7			3		13	10^3														8
1	2			5	6	7	8	9^1	10	11	12			4		13	3^2														9
1	2	14		5	6^4	7	8^3	9^1	10^2	11	13			4			3			12											10
	2		4	5	6		7^1	13	14	11	10^2			12^4			3	8	1	9^3											11
	2^1		4	5	6		7^2	12	14	13	11	10					3	8	1	9^3											12
	2		4	5		$7³$	13	8^3	14	12	10^1	11				6	3		1	9^2											13
	2		4	5		7	13	9^1	12	11	8^2					6	3		1	10^4											14
	2		4	5		7	13	9		10^1	11					6	3		1				12								15
	2		4	5		7^1	12	9^2	14	11	8^3					6	3		1		13		10								16
	2		4^1	5	14	7	8	9^2		11	10					6^3	3		1		12		13								17
1				5	6	7	8	9	10^2	11^1		3		2		13	4			12											18
1	2		12	5	6	7		9	10^3	11	8^1			3^2		13	4			14											19
1			4^2	5	6	7	2	9	10^1	11	13			3^3			8	14		12											20
1	2	14		5		7	8		11	10				3^1		12	4	9^2		13			6^1								21
1	2		4	5			12	13		10				3			9^1	8^2	7	6	11										22
1	2			5		7	4	9^2		11^1	10^2			3		6	13		14	12			8								23
1	2	13		5		7^3	4^2	9		11^1	10			12		6		14			8		3								24
1	2			5	6	7	11	14		13		10^2		12		4		9^3			8		3^1								25
	2		4	5	6	7	8	9^1		11^2	12					10	1			3	13										26
10	3	4^2	5	6		7^3	14		11	13				9^1		1	12				8	2									27
7	3	4^2	5	6	10				11					9^1		1				8	2	12									28
7	3			5	10	8			11^2					9^1		1	13			4	2	12									29
7	3^2	4	5	6	10^3				11					9^1		1	14			8	2	12									30
7		4	5		10			13		11						1	12	6		3	2	9^1	8^2								31
7			5	6	8	14	9^1		11^3	12				13		1	10			4	2		3								32
	2		4	5		7	8		11		9^1			6		1	12	10			3										33
	2^8			5	10	8		11	9^2					6		1	13			7	12		4^1		3						34
1			5	12	7^2	8	9^3		11					6^1	14		10			4	2		13		3						35
1		4	5	6	8	7^2	13		14	10^3		11								9^1	3		12		2						36
1	13	4	5	6	8	9^1	11			10^3		7					2	14			3^2		12								37
1	3		5	6	8	9^1	11		10^2	14		13		7			2	12												4^3	38
	2		4	5	6	8	9^2		11	13		3					1			10^1			12							7	39
	2		4	5	6	8	13		11	14		3^1					1			9^3	7		12							10^2	40
	2	3	12^5	5	6	8	9^2		11	13							1	10			4		14							7^1	41
	2	3	4	5	6	8	11^1		12	13							1	9^2			10		7								42
	2^1	3	4	5	6	8		11^3	13	14							1	9^2			10		7	12							43
	2	3	12	5	6	8	9^3		11	13							1	10^2			7		4^1	14							44
	2	3^3	4^2	5	6	8	13		11	14							1	10			9		7^1	12							45
	2	3	4	5	6	8	11^2		12								1	10^3			14		13	7							46

FA Cup

First Round	Cambridge U	(a)	0-0		Northern Quarter-Final		Rotherham U	(a)	5-2
		(h)	2-1		Northern Semi-Final				
Second Round	Macclesfield T	(h)	6-0				Tranmere R	(a)	2-0
Third Round	Dover Ath	(h)	2-0		Northern Final		Carlisle U	(a)	0-4
Fourth Round	Arsenal	(a)	1-2					(h)	3-0
Carling Cup					**Play-Offs**				
First Round	Carlisle U	(a)	1-0		Semi-Final		Bournemouth	(a)	1-1
Second Round	Everton	(a)	1-5					(h)	3-3
J Paint Trophy					Final		Peterborough U		0-3
Second Round	Peterborough U	(h)	3-2		*(at Old Trafford).*				

HULL CITY   FL Championship

FOUNDATION

The enthusiasts who formed Hull City in 1904 were brave men indeed. More than that they were audacious for they immediately put the club on the map in this Rugby League fortress by obtaining a three-year agreement with the Hull Rugby League club to rent their ground! They had obtained quite a number of conversions to the dribbling code, before the Rugby League forbade the use of any of their club grounds by Association Football clubs. By that time, Hull City were well away having entered the FA Cup in their initial season and the Football League, Second Division after only a year.

The Circle, The KC Stadium, Walton Street, Hull, East Yorkshire HU3 6HU.

Telephone: (01482) 504 600.

Fax: (01482) 304 882.

Ticket Office: (01482) 505 600.

Website: www.hullcityafc.net

Email: info@hulltigers.com

Ground Capacity: 25,404.

Record Attendance: 25,512 v Sunderland, FL C, 28 October 2007 (KC Stadium). 55,019 v Manchester U, FA Cup 6th rd, 26 February 1949 (Boothferry Park).

Pitch Measurements: 100.5m × 67.5m.

Chairman: Assem Allam.

Vice-Chairman: Ehab Allam.

Chief Executive: Mark McGuire.

Football Secretary: Phil Hough.

Manager: Nigel Pearson.

Assistant Manager: Craig Shakespeare.

Physio: Simon Maltby.

Colours: Black and amber striped shirts, black shorts, amber stockings with black hoops.

Change Colours: All blue with black trim.

Year Formed: 1904. *Turned Professional:* 1905.

Ltd Co.: 1905.

Club Nickname: 'The Tigers'.

Grounds: 1904, Boulevard Ground (Hull RFC); 1905, Anlaby Road (Hull CC); 1944, Boulevard Ground; 1946, Boothferry Park; 2002, Kingston Communications Stadium.

First Football League Game: 2 September 1905, Division 2, v Barnsley (h) W 4–1 – Spendiff; Langley, Jones; Martin, Robinson, Gordon (2); Rushton, Spence (1), Wilson (1), Howe, Raisbeck.

Record League Victory: 11–1 v Carlisle U, Division 3 (N), 14 January 1939 – Ellis; Woodhead, Dowen; Robinson (1), Blyth, Hardy; Hubbard (2), Richardson (2), Dickinson (2), Davies (2), Cunliffe (2).

HONOURS

FA Premier League: Best season 17th, 2008–09.

Football League – FL C: Best season 3rd, 2007–08;
FL 1: *Runners-up* 2004–05;
Division 3 (N): *Champions* 1932–33, 1948–49;
Division 3: *Champions* 1965–66;
Runners-up 1958–59, 2003–04;
Division 4: *Runners-up* 1982–83.

FA Cup: Semi-final 1930.

Football League Cup: Best season: 4th, 1974, 1976, 1978.

Associate Members' Cup: *Runners-up* 1984.

sky SPORTS FACT FILE

Inside-forward Eric Longden had two spells with Hull City. He played the first two games for Leeds United in 1930–31, moved to Hull in October, went to Blackpool in January 1931 and returned to Hull in December 1932 to help the Tigers win the Third Division (North) title.

Record Cup Victory: 8–2 v Stalybridge Celtic (a), FA Cup 1st rd, 26 November 1932 – Maddison; Goldsmith, Woodhead; Gardner, Hill (1), Denby; Forward (1), Duncan, McNaughton (1), Wainscoat (4), Sargeant (1).

Record Defeat: 0–8 v Wolverhampton W, Division 2, 4 November 1911.

Most League Points (2 for a win): 69, Division 3, 1965–66.

Most League Points (3 for a win): 90, Division 4, 1982–83.

Most League Goals: 109, Division 3, 1965–66.

Highest League Scorer in Season: Bill McNaughton, 39, Division 3 (N), 1932–33.

Most League Goals in Total Aggregate: Chris Chilton, 193, 1960–71.

Most League Goals in One Match: 5, Ken McDonald v Bristol C, Division 2, 17 November 1928; 5, Simon 'Slim' Raleigh v Halifax T, Division 3 (N), 26 December 1930.

Most Capped Player: Theo Whitmore, 28 (105), Jamaica.

Most League Appearances: Andy Davidson, 520, 1952–67.

Youngest League Player: Matthew Edeson, 16 years 63 days v Fulham, 10 October 1992.

Record Transfer Fee Received: £3,000,000 from Wolverhampton W for Stephen Hunt, August 2010.

Record Transfer Fee Paid: £5,000,000 to Fulham for Jimmy Bullard, January 2009.

Football League Record: 1905 Elected to Division 2; 1930–33 Division 3 (N); 1933–36 Division 2; 1936–49 Division 3 (N); 1949–56 Division 2; 1956–58 Division 3 (N); 1958–59 Division 3; 1959–60 Division 2; 1960–66 Division 3; 1966–78 Division 2; 1978–81 Division 3; 1981–83 Division 4; 1983–85 Division 3; 1985–91 Division 2; 1991–92 Division 3; 1992–96 Division 2; 1996–2004 Division 3; 2004–05 FL 1; 2005–08 FL C; 2008–10 FA Premier League; 2010– FL C.

LATEST SEQUENCES

Longest Sequence of League Wins: 10, 23.2.1966 – 20.4.1966.

Longest Sequence of League Defeats: 8, 7.4.1934 – 8.9.1934.

Longest Sequence of League Draws: 5, 30.3.1929 – 15.4.1929.

Longest Sequence of Unbeaten League Matches: 19, 13.3.2001 – 22.9.2001.

Longest Sequence Without a League Win: 27, 27.3.1989 – 4.11.1989.

Successive Scoring Runs: 26 from 10.4.1990.

Successive Non-scoring Runs: 6 from 13.11.1920.

MANAGERS

James Ramster 1904–05
(Secretary-Manager)
Ambrose Langley 1905–13
Harry Chapman 1913–14
Fred Stringer 1914–16
David Menzies 1916–21
Percy Lewis 1921–23
Bill McCracken 1923–31
Haydn Green 1931–34
John Hill 1934–36
David Menzies 1936
Ernest Blackburn 1936–46
Major Frank Buckley 1946–48
Raich Carter 1948–51
Bob Jackson 1952–55
Bob Brocklebank 1955–61
Cliff Britton 1961–70
(continued as General Manager to 1971)
Terry Neill 1970–74
John Kaye 1974–77
Bobby Collins 1977–78
Ken Houghton 1978–79
Mike Smith 1979–82
Bobby Brown 1982
Colin Appleton 1982–84
Brian Horton 1984–88
Eddie Gray 1988–89
Colin Appleton 1989
Stan Ternent 1989–91
Terry Dolan 1991–97
Mark Hateley 1997–98
Warren Joyce 1998–2000
Brian Little 2000–02
Jan Molby 2002
Peter Taylor 2002–06
Phil Parkinson 2006
Phil Brown *(after caretaker role December 2006)* 2007–10
Ian Dowie *(consultant)* 2010
Nigel Pearson June 2010–

TEN YEAR LEAGUE RECORD

		P	W	D	L	F	A	Pts	Pos
2001-02	Div 3	46	16	13	17	57	51	61	11
2002-03	Div 3	46	14	17	15	58	53	59	13
2003-04	Div 3	46	25	13	8	82	44	88	2
2004-05	FL 1	46	26	8	12	80	53	86	2
2005-06	FL C	46	12	16	18	49	55	52	18
2006-07	FL C	46	13	10	23	51	67	49	21
2007-08	FL C	46	21	12	13	65	47	75	3
2008-09	PR Lge	38	8	11	19	39	64	35	17
2009-10	PR Lge	38	6	12	20	34	75	30	19
2010-11	FL C	46	16	17	13	52	51	65	11

DID YOU KNOW ?

The highest win achieved by Hull City in any overseas match occurred on 14 May 1910 at The Hague in Holland when they defeated Solingen 16-0. Arthur Temple scored six of the goals and Joe Smith had a hat-trick.

HULL CITY 2010–11 LEAGUE RECORD

Match No.	Date	Venue	Opponents	Result	H/T Score	Lg Pos.	Goalscorers	Attendance
1	Aug 7	H	Swansea C	W 2-0	1-0	—	Bostock [23], Ashbee [50]	21,478
2	14	A	Millwall	L 0-4	0-2	14		13,292
3	21	H	Watford	D 0-0	0-0	12		20,426
4	28	A	Doncaster R	L 1-3	1-2	—	Barmby [9]	11,149
5	Sept 11	A	Cardiff C	L 0-2	0-1	19		24,083
6	14	H	Derby Co	W 2-0	1-0	—	Ayala [43], Koren [82]	19,714
7	18	H	Nottingham F	D 0-0	0-0	18		21,180
8	25	A	Norwich C	W 2-0	0-0	15	Koren [83], Cairney [88]	24,947
9	28	A	Burnley	L 0-4	0-2	—		14,458
10	Oct 2	H	Coventry C	D 0-0	0-0	16		20,626
11	16	A	Leicester C	D 1-1	0-1	16	Koren [52]	23,766
12	19	H	Sheffield U	L 0-1	0-0	—		20,276
13	23	H	Portsmouth	L 1-2	0-1	19	Barmby [62]	20,378
14	30	A	Barnsley	D 1-1	0-1	20	Kilbane [72]	10,566
15	Nov 6	H	Scunthorpe U	L 0-1	0-0	20		21,873
16	9	A	Leeds U	D 2-2	1-1	—	Bostock [14], Johnson (og) [82]	24,906
17	12	A	Preston NE	W 2-0	1-0	—	Garcia [20], Barmby [72]	9088
18	20	H	Ipswich T	W 1-0	0-0	19	Koren [77]	20,535
19	27	A	Middlesbrough	D 2-2	2-1	18	Koren [20], Gerrard [41]	15,075
20	Dec 11	A	Crystal Palace	D 0-0	0-0	19		13,341
21	18	H	Bristol C	W 2-0	1-0	18	Simpson 2 [13, 62]	20,299
22	26	A	Sheffield U	W 3-2	2-0	15	Simpson 2 (1 pen) [3, 45 (p)], Bullard [90]	22,688
23	28	H	Reading	D 1-1	1-0	15	Harper [39]	21,975
24	Jan 1	H	Leicester C	L 0-1	0-1	16		22,410
25	3	A	Portsmouth	W 3-2	1-0	15	Bullard (pen) [21], Fryatt [69], Barmby [72]	14,604
26	15	H	Barnsley	W 2-0	0-0	12	Fryatt (pen) [66], Koren [90]	21,222
27	22	A	Reading	D 1-1	0-0	12	Evans [51]	16,494
28	29	H	QPR	D 0-0	0-0	—		20,601
29	Feb 1	H	Leeds U	D 2-2	2-1	13	Fryatt [33], Chester [40]	24,110
30	5	A	Scunthorpe U	W 5-1	1-0	12	Fryatt 3 (1 pen) [5, 73 (p), 89], McLean 2 [50, 81]	6835
31	12	H	Preston NE	W 1-0	1-0	10	Gerrard [45]	21,566
32	19	A	Ipswich T	D 1-1	0-0	10	Simpson [85]	19,135
33	22	A	Derby Co	W 1-0	0-0	—	Gerrard [71]	24,533
34	26	H	Cardiff C	L 0-2	0-0	9		21,441
35	Mar 5	A	Nottingham F	W 1-0	0-0	8	Fryatt [64]	25,119
36	8	H	Burnley	L 0-1	0-1	—		20,218
37	12	A	Coventry C	W 1-0	1-0	8	McLean [33]	14,370
38	19	H	Norwich C	D 1-1	0-1	10	Barmby [73]	22,967
39	Apr 2	H	Millwall	L 0-1	0-1	11		19,852
40	9	A	Watford	W 2-1	1-0	10	Evans [3], Koren [90]	13,355
41	12	A	Swansea C	D 1-1	0-0	—	Evans [70]	14,822
42	16	H	Doncaster R	W 3-1	2-1	8	Garcia [9], Fryatt 2 (1 pen) [21 (p), 50]	21,395
43	23	H	Middlesbrough	L 2-4	1-4	10	Simpson [3], Gerrard [69]	21,937
44	25	A	QPR	D 1-1	0-1	10	Amoo [81]	17,399
45	30	H	Crystal Palace	D 1-1	1-0	10	Gerrard [31]	20,407
46	May 7	A	Bristol C	L 0-3	0-2	11		15,112

Final League Position: 11

GOALSCORERS

League (52): Fryatt 9 (3 pens), Koren 7, Simpson 6 (1 pen), Barmby 5, Gerrard 5, Evans 3, McLean 3, Bostock 2, Bullard 2 (1 pen), Garcia 2, Amoo 1, Ashbee 1, Ayala 1, Cairney 1, Chester 1, Harper 1, Kilbane 1, own goal 1.
Carling Cup (1): Cullen 1.
FA Cup (2): Barmby 2.

Duke M 20+1	Solano N 6+5	Dawson A 45	Ashbee I 19	Gardner A 2	Zayatte K 16	Atkinson W 3+1	Cairney T 16+6	Garcia R 16+9	Bostock J 8+3	Kilbane K 11+3	Devitt J 7+9	Cullen M 4+13	Barmby N 8+23	McShane P 13+6	Koren R 39+1	Cooper L 2	Simpson J 19+13	Ayala D 12	Gerrard A 41	Fagan C 4+1	Bullard J 5+3	Vine R 4+1	Folan C 2+1	Harper J 27+1	Rosenior L 26	Mannone V 10	Stewart C 14	Guzan B 16	McLean A 18+5	Fryatt M 21+1	Chester J 21	Evans C 17+1	Belaid T 3+5	Hobbs J 9+4	Amoo D 1+6	Akpan H 1+1	Match No.
1	2	3	4	5	6	7¹	8	9²	10³	11	12	13	14																								1
1	2¹	3	4	5	6	7²	8	9³	10	11		13		12	14																						2
1		3	4		6		8	13	10²	11¹		12	14	2	7	5	9³																				3
1	2	3	4		6		12	11	10¹			9		8²	7	5	13																				4
1		3	4				12	9		11¹		13		8²	5	7	14	2	6	10³																	5
1		3					4	12	11¹			13			2	7	9²	6	5	10	8																6
1		3			14		7	11¹				12	13	2	4	9³	6	5	10²	8																	7
1		3	4				7	14				12	13	2	11³	9²	6	5	10¹	8																	8
1		3	4¹			7	8					14	13	10³	2	11	9²	6	5	12																	9
1		3					4	7²				13	12	2	11	9¹	6	5	8	10																	10
1	12	3				7	8³	14		9	13	2¹	4	6	5	11²	10																				11
1		3				7	8¹	12	11	9³		2	4	13	6	5	14	10²																			12
1	7¹	3				8		11³	14	9	2	4²	13	6	5	10	12																				13
1		3	6		7	14	11	8²	12	9¹	4	5	10³	13	2																						14
1		3	6		8	12	13	11¹	9³	14	10²	4	5	7	2																						15
1		3	4		8¹	12	10	9⁴	11²	13	6	5	7	2																							16
12	3	4	10²	9	11³	13		7	14	6	5	8	2¹	1																							17
14	3	4	6	9³	10¹	11²	13	12		7	5	8	2	1																							18
14	3	4¹	6	9	10³	12	8	13		5	11	2	1	7²																							19
	3	4	6	9¹	14	10³	13	7	12	5²	8	2	1	11																							20
	3	4	6	11	7	9	5	8	2	1	10																										21
	4	6	14	3¹	11³	12	7²	9	5	13	8	2	1	10																							22
	3	4	6	13	11¹	12	5	7³	9²	14	8	2	1	10																							23
	3	4²	6	11¹	14	7	9³	5	13	8	2■	10	1	12																							24
2	3	4	6	13	9¹	5	7	8	10²	1	11	12																									25
2	3	4	13	12	7	5	8	11¹	1	9²	10	6																									26
	3	4	13	7	5	8	2	11¹	1	9²	10	6	12																								27
	3	13	12	7	5	8	2	11²	1	9¹	10	6	4																								28
	3	13	12	7	5	8¹	2	11²	1	9³	10	6	4	14																							29
14	3	8¹	12	2	7²	9	5	11³	1	9	10	6	4	13																							30
	3	13	12	7	5	2	11²	1	9	10	6	4	8¹																								31
	3	14	12	8	13	5	2	11³	1	9	10	6	4	7²																							32
	3	13	7	12	5	8	2	1	9²	10³	6	4	11¹	14																							33
	3	14	13	7	11	5¹	8²	2	1	9³	10	6	4	12																							34
	3	13	7³	11¹	5	8	2	1	9²	10	6	4	14	12																							35
	3	11¹	7	13	5	8²	2	1	9	10	6	4	12																								36
	3¹	11²	13	14	7	5	8	2	1	9³	10	6	4	12																							37
	3	14	11	5	8³	2²	1	9¹	10	6	7	12	4	13																							38
	3	11¹	7	12	5	8²	1	9³	10	2	4	13	6	14																							39
	3	14	13	11	12	5	8³	2	1	9¹	10²	4	7	6																							40
1	3	12	11	12	5	8²	2	1	9¹	10	4	7	6																								41
	3	8¹	12	11	9²	5	2	1	13	10	4	7	6																								42
15	3	13	8²	11	9	5	2¹	1⁶	12	10	4	7	6																								43
1	3	2²	7	9³	5	8	13	10	4	11¹	6	14	12																								44
1	3	7¹	13	8	11²	5	6	9³	10	2	14	4	12																								45
1	3	14	12	11²	9	5	8	13	10	2¹	6	7³	4																								46

FA Cup
Third Round   Wigan Ath   (h)   2-3

Carling Cup
Second Round   Brentford   (a)   1-2

IPSWICH TOWN FL Championship

FOUNDATION

Considering that Ipswich Town only reached the Football League in 1938, many people outside of East Anglia may be surprised to learn that this club was formed at a meeting held in the Town Hall as far back as 1878 when Mr T. C. Cobbold, MP, was voted president. Originally it was the Ipswich Association FC to distinguish it from the older Ipswich Football Club which played rugby. These two amalgamated in 1888 and the handling game was dropped in 1893.

Portman Road, Ipswich, Suffolk IP1 2DA.

Telephone: (01473) 400 500.

Fax: (01473) 400 040.

Ticket Office: 0844 8011 555.

Website: www.itfc.co.uk

Email: enquiries@itfc.co.uk

Ground Capacity: 30,311.

Record Attendance: 38,010 v Leeds U, FA Cup 6th rd, 8 March 1975.

Pitch Measurements: 102.46m × 66m.

Chief Executive: Simon Clegg CBE.

Secretary: Sally Webb.

Manager: Paul Jewell.

Assistant Manager: Chris Hutchings.

Physio: Matt Byard.

Colours: Blue shirts with white trim, white shorts, blue stockings.

Change Colours: Black shirts with white trim, black shorts and stockings.

Year Formed: 1878.

Turned Professional: 1936.

Ltd Co.: 1936.

Club Nicknames: 'Blues' or 'Town' or 'Tractor Boys'.

Grounds: 1878, Broom Hill and Brook's Hall; 1884, Portman Road.

Record League Victory: 7–0 v Portsmouth, Division 2, 7 November 1964 – Thorburn; Smith, McNeil; Baxter, Bolton, Thompson; Broadfoot (1), Hegan (2), Baker (1), Leadbetter, Brogan (3). 7–0 v Southampton, Division 1, 2 February 1974 – Sivell; Burley, Mills (1), Morris, Hunter, Beattie (1), Hamilton (2), Viljoen, Johnson, Whymark (2), Lambert (1) (Woods). 7–0 v WBA, Division 1, 6 November 1976 – Sivell; Burley, Mills, Talbot, Hunter, Beattie (1), Osborne, Wark (1), Mariner (1) (Bertschin), Whymark (4), Woods.

HONOURS

Football League – Division 1:
Champions 1961–62;
Runners-up 1980–81, 1981–82;
Division 2: *Champions* 1960–61, 1967–68, 1991–92;
Division 3 (S): *Champions* 1953–54, 1956–57.

FA Cup: *Winners* 1978.

Football League Cup: Semi-final 1982, 1985, 2001, 2011.

Texaco Cup: *Winners* 1973.

European Competitions
European Cup: 1962–63.
European Cup-Winners' Cup: 1978–79.
UEFA Cup: 1973–74, 1974–75, 1975–76, 1977–78, 1979–80, 1980–81 (*winners*), 1981–82, 1982–83, 2001–02, 2002–03.

sky SPORTS FACT FILE

Republic of Ireland international midfield player Matt Holland was turned down as too small by Arsenal, released by West Ham United but made skipper at Bournemouth. Sold to Ipswich Town for £800,000 in July 1997, he went on to make 223 consecutive appearances there.

First Football League Game: 27 August 1938, Division 3 (S), v Southend U (h) W 4–2 – Burns; Dale, Parry; Perrett, Fillingham, McLuckie; Williams, Davies (1), Jones (2), Alsop (1), Little.

Record Cup Victory: 10–0 v Floriana, European Cup prel. rd, 25 September 1962 – Bailey; Malcolm, Compton; Baxter, Laurel, Elsworthy (1); Stephenson, Moran (2), Crawford (5), Phillips (2), Blackwood.

Record Defeat: 1–10 v Fulham, Division 1, 26 December 1963.

Most League Points (2 for a win): 64, Division 3 (S), 1953–54 and 1955–56.

Most League Points (3 for a win): 87, Division 1, 1999–2000.

Most League Goals: 106, Division 3 (S), 1955–56.

Highest League Scorer in Season: Ted Phillips, 41, Division 3 (S), 1956–57.

MANAGERS
Mick O'Brien 1936–37
Scott Duncan 1937–55
(continued as Secretary)
Alf Ramsey 1955–63
Jackie Milburn 1963–64
Bill McGarry 1964–68
Bobby Robson 1969–82
Bobby Ferguson 1982–87
Johnny Duncan 1987–90
John Lyall 1990–94
George Burley 1994–2002
Joe Royle 2002–06
Jim Magilton 2006–09
Roy Keane 2009–11
Paul Jewell January 2011–

Most League Goals in Total Aggregate: Ray Crawford, 204, 1958–63 and 1966–69.

Most League Goals in One Match: 5, Alan Brazil v Southampton, Division 1, 16 February 1981.

Most Capped Player: Allan Hunter, 47 (53), Northern Ireland.

Most League Appearances: Mick Mills, 591, 1966–82.

Youngest League Player: Jason Dozzell, 16 years 56 days v Coventry C, 4 February 1984.

Record Transfer Fee Received: £6,000,000 from Newcastle U for Kieron Dyer, July 1999 and £6,000,000 from Arsenal for Richard Wright, July 2001.

Record Transfer Fee Paid: £5,000,000 to Sampdoria for Matteo Sereni, August 2001.

Football League Record: 1938 Elected to Division 3 (S), 1954–55 Division 2; 1955–57 Division 3 (S); 1957–61 Division 2; 1961–64 Division 1; 1964–68 Division 2; 1968–86 Division 1; 1986–92 Division 2; 1992–95 FA Premier League; 1995–2000 Division 1; 2000–02 FA Premier League; 2002–04 Division 1; 2004– FL C.

LATEST SEQUENCES

Longest Sequence of League Wins: 8, 23.9.1953 – 31.10.1953.

Longest Sequence of League Defeats: 10, 4.9.1954 – 16.10.1954.

Longest Sequence of League Draws: 7, 10.11.1990 – 21.12.1990.

Longest Sequence of Unbeaten League Matches: 23, 8.12.1979 – 26.4.1980.

Longest Sequence Without a League Win: 21, 28.8.1963 – 14.12.1963.

Successive Scoring Runs: 31 from 7.3.2004.

Successive Non-scoring Runs: 7 from 28.2.1995.

TEN YEAR LEAGUE RECORD

		P	W	D	L	F	A	Pts	Pos
2001-02	PR Lge	38	9	9	20	41	64	36	18
2002-03	Div 1	46	19	13	14	80	64	70	7
2003-04	Div 1	46	21	10	15	84	72	73	5
2004-05	FL C	46	24	13	9	85	56	85	3
2005-06	FL C	46	14	14	18	53	66	56	15
2006-07	FL C	46	18	8	20	64	59	62	14
2007-08	FL C	46	18	15	13	65	56	69	8
2008-09	FL C	46	17	15	14	62	53	66	9
2009-10	FL C	46	12	20	14	50	61	56	15
2010-11	FL C	46	18	8	20	62	68	62	13

DID YOU KNOW ?

On 12 January 2011, three days after losing 7-0 to Chelsea in a Premier League game at Stamford Bridge, Ipswich Town defeated Arsenal 1-0 at Portman Road in the first leg semi-final of the Carling Cup. The team was still in charge of caretaker-manager Charlie McParland.

IPSWICH TOWN 2010–11 LEAGUE RECORD

Match No.	Date	Venue	Opponents	Result	H/T Score	Lg Pos.	Goalscorers	Atten-dance
1	Aug 7	A	Middlesbrough	W 3-1	0-1	—	Smith [50], Priskin [51], Stead [77]	21,882
2	14	H	Burnley	D 1-1	0-0	4	Norris [86]	19,317
3	21	A	Crystal Palace	W 2-1	0-0	5	Leadbitter (pen) [51], Edwards [56]	15,781
4	28	H	Bristol C	W 2-0	0-0	3	Priskin [58], Scotland [74]	19,011
5	Sept 11	A	Portsmouth	D 0-0	0-0	3		15,445
6	14	H	QPR	L 0-3	0-2	—		19,931
7	18	H	Cardiff C	W 2-0	0-0	2	Matthews (og) [62], Scotland [74]	22,599
8	25	A	Scunthorpe U	D 1-1	0-1	4	Peters [57]	5931
9	28	A	Reading	L 0-1	0-0	—		15,763
10	Oct 2	H	Leeds U	W 2-1	1-0	5	Scotland [19], Smith [83]	23,105
11	16	H	Coventry C	L 1-2	0-1	6	Scotland [58]	19,100
12	19	A	Watford	L 1-2	0-2	—	Norris [69]	11,836
13	23	A	Nottingham F	L 0-2	0-2	14		22,935
14	30	H	Millwall	W 2-0	1-0	11	Scotland [5], Leadbitter (pen) [56]	19,020
15	Nov 6	A	Sheffield U	W 2-1	2-1	6	Priskin [6], McAuley [40]	19,207
16	9	H	Derby Co	L 0-2	0-0	—		17,572
17	13	H	Barnsley	L 1-3	0-2	12	Smith [80]	18,024
18	20	A	Hull C	L 0-1	0-0	13		20,535
19	28	A	Norwich C	L 1-4	1-2	16	Delaney [29]	26,532
20	Dec 4	H	Swansea C	L 1-3	0-0	—	Townsend [50]	16,978
21	11	A	Preston NE	L 0-1	0-0	18		9419
22	18	H	Leicester C	W 3-0	3-0	17	Norris [6], Scotland 2 [27, 39]	16,728
23	Jan 1	A	Coventry C	D 1-1	1-0	19	Fallon [44]	14,412
24	3	H	Nottingham F	L 0-1	0-1	19		19,455
25	15	A	Millwall	L 1-2	1-1	20	Priskin [25]	12,111
26	22	H	Doncaster R	W 3-2	0-1	19	Norris [48], Wickham [60], Edwards [64]	17,298
27	Feb 1	A	Derby Co	W 2-1	1-1	17	Bullard [28], Norris [68]	23,159
28	5	H	Sheffield U	W 3-0	1-0	14	Delaney [29], Norris [53], Wickham [87]	18,280
29	12	A	Barnsley	D 1-1	0-0	15	Scotland [82]	10,904
30	15	A	Doncaster R	W 6-0	3-0	—	Hird (og) [25], Healy [33], Wickham 3 (1 pen) [42, 61, 90 (p)], McAuley [65]	8448
31	19	H	Hull C	D 1-1	0-0	13	Scotland [58]	19,135
32	22	A	QPR	L 0-2	0-0	—		16,587
33	26	H	Portsmouth	L 0-2	0-0	14		23,345
34	Mar 5	A	Cardiff C	W 2-0	0-0	14	Bullard 2 [67, 86]	21,347
35	8	H	Reading	L 1-3	0-1	—	Wickham [90]	17,308
36	12	A	Leeds U	D 0-0	0-0	16		27,432
37	15	H	Watford	L 0-3	0-1	—		17,789
38	19	H	Scunthorpe U	W 2-0	1-0	15	Edwards [26], Bullard [53]	17,787
39	Apr 2	A	Burnley	W 2-1	2-0	15	Norris [17], Wickham [24]	14,483
40	9	H	Crystal Palace	W 2-1	1-0	13	Carson 2 [38, 66]	24,378
41	12	A	Middlesbrough	D 3-3	1-2	—	Leadbitter 2 (1 pen) [6, 76 (p)], Wickham [64]	17,286
42	16	A	Bristol C	W 1-0	0-0	12	Carson [52]	14,159
43	21	H	Norwich C	L 1-5	0-2	—	Bullard [78]	29,258
44	25	A	Swansea C	L 1-4	1-3	13	Healy [20]	16,001
45	30	H	Preston NE	W 2-1	2-0	12	Scotland [10], Norris [19]	18,431
46	May 7	A	Leicester C	L 2-4	0-3	13	Leadbitter (pen) [69], Wickham [70]	24,859

Final League Position: 13

GOALSCORERS

League (62): Scotland 10, Wickham 9 (1 pen), Norris 8, Bullard 5, Leadbitter 5 (4 pens), Priskin 4, Carson 3, Edwards 3, Smith 3, Delaney 2, Healy 2, McAuley 2, Fallon 1, Peters 1, Stead 1, Townsend 1, own goals 2.
Carling Cup (11): Norris 3, Priskin 3, Delaney 1, Edwards 1, Leadbitter 1 (pen), McAuley 1, Murray 1.
FA Cup (0).

Fulop M 35	Peters J 12 + 11	Kennedy M 24 + 2	Smith T 22	McAuley G 39	Leadbitter G 44	Edwards C 42 + 3	Hyam L 8 + 2	Priskin T 18 + 14	Walters J 1	Norris D 35 + 1	Lambe R — + 2	Stead J 2 + 1	Ainsley J — + 1	O'Connor S 2 + 3	Townsend A 11 + 2	Healy C 7 + 9	Murray R 1 + 7	O'Dea D 17 + 3	Eastman T 8 + 1	Scotland J 32 + 7	Wickham C 24 + 13	Brown T 6 + 6	Livermore J 8 + 4	Murphy B 4	Delaney D 32	Colback J 13	Zuiverloon G 4	Fallon R 4 + 2	Martin L 15 + 1	Bullard J 16	Civelli L — + 9	Drury A 4 + 8	Dyer K 1 + 3	Lee-Barrett A 7	Carson J 8 + 1	Match No.
1	2	3^3	4	5	6	7^1	8	9^2	10	11	12	13	14																							1
1	2		4	5	6^1		8	9		7				10	3	11^2	12	13																		2
1	2^2		4	5	6	7	8^3	12		9				10^1	13	11^8		3	14																	3
1	2		4	5	6	7	8^1	9		11					12			13	3	10^2																4
1	2	13	4	5	6	7	8	9^2		11							14		3^1	10^3	12															5
1	2	3	4	5	6	7^3	8^1	12		9						11^2				10	13	14														6
1	12		4	5	6	7		14		8						11^1	13	3	2	10^2	9^3															7
1	13		4	5	6	7	12	14		8						11^2		3	2	10^3	9^1															8
1	2			5	6	7^1	8^8	9				13				11^3		3		10^2	12	4	14													9
1	8	3	4	5	6	7^3		12		11								2^1		10^2	13	14	9													10
1	2^2	3	4	5	6	7	8^1	14		13						11^3				10	12	9														11
			4	5	6	14		9^2		7										10	12	2^3	8^1	1	3	11										12
1	2^2	3		5	6	7		9								11^3	14			10^1	12				13	4	8									13
1			4	5	6	7		9^1		8^3							13	2		10^2	12				14	3	11									14
1	13	3		5	6	7		9^2										2^3		10^1	12	14	8		4	11										15
1	13	3		5^2	6	7^3		9^2									14	2		10	12		8^1		4	11										16
1		3	4			7	12	9^3								11^1	13	2		10^2	14				6	5	8									17
	13	3				7	12	9^3									6	2		10^1	14		4^2	1	5	11										18
1			4		6	7		9^3		8					12			3		10^1	14				5^8	11	2^2	13								19
14			4		6	7		9^1							13	11^3		3^2		10				1	5	8	2	12								20
14	3^1		4		6	7^3									13	8		12		10^4				1	5	11	2	9								21
1	11		4		6	14				8				3^3						10^2	12				5	13	2		7		9^1					22
1	2^2		4	5	6	7				8							13	3		10^1	12	14							11^2		9					23
1	12	3		5^1	6^8	13		8												14	10	2	7^2			4			11		9^3					24
1	2	11^1		5		7		9		8							4	3		12	10				6											25
1				4	6	2		9		8							7	3		10					5				11							26
1		3		4	6	2		9		8										10					5				11		7					27
1		3		4	6	2		9^3		8					12			13		10					5				11^2		7^1	14				28
1		3		4	6	2		9^2		7^1					12		14	13		10					5				11		8^3					29
1	14	3		4	6^3	2									13		7			10^2	9				5				11^1		8	12				30
1		3		4	6	2				8					12					10^1	9				5				11^2		13	7				31
1		3		4	6	2									13		7^1			10^2	9				5				11^3		8	14	12			32
1		3		4	6	2				8^1					14					10^2	9				5				11^3		7	13	12			33
1		3^1		4	6	2				8					13		12			10^2	9^3				5				11		7	14				34
1				4	6	2				8					12			3		10^1	9				5				11		13	7^2				35
1				4	6	2					10^3							3		14	9				5				11^1	8	7^2	12	13			36
1		3		4	6	2									10²			13			9				5				11^1		8	7	12			37
	7			4	6^2	2					10							13			9				5				11		8	12		1	3^1	38
		3		4	6	7				11										10^1	9				5					8		12	13	1	2^2	39
		3		4	6	2				8					13					10^1	9				5					7^2		12		1	11	40
		3^2		4	6	2				8					13					10^1	9				5					12		7		1	11	41
				4	6^1	2				8					12			3		10^1	9				5					10^8		7		1	11	42
				4	6	2				8								3		10^1	9				5					7		12		1	11	43
	12			4^2	6	2				8					9			3^1		10	13				5						14	7^3		1	11	44
1	13	3			6	2				8					9^1					10^3					5	4					7	14	12		11^2	45
1	13	3		4	6	2				8					7					10^1	9				5						11^2				12	46

FA Cup

Third Round	Chelsea		(a)	0-7

Carling Cup

First Round	Exeter C	(a)	3-2
Second Round	Crewe Alex	(a)	1-0
Third Round	Millwall	(a)	2-1
Fourth Round	Northampton T	(h)	3-1
Quarter-Final	WBA	(h)	1-0
Semi-Final	Arsenal	(h)	1-0
		(a)	0-3

LEEDS UNITED   FL Championship

FOUNDATION

Immediately the Leeds City club (founded in 1904) was wound up
by the FA in October 1919, following allegations of illegal
payments to players, a meeting was called by a Leeds solicitor,
Mr Alf Masser, at which Leeds United was formed. They joined
the Midland League playing their first game in that competition in
November 1919. It was in this same month that the new club had
discussions with the directors of a virtually bankrupt Huddersfield
Town who wanted to move to Leeds in an amalgamation. But
Huddersfield survived even that crisis.

Elland Road, Leeds, West Yorkshire LS11 0ES.
Telephone: (0871) 334 1919.
Fax: (0113) 367 6050.
Ticket Office: 0871 334 1992.
Website: www.leedsunited.com
Email: reception@leedsunited.com
Ground Capacity: 39,457.
Record Attendance: 57,892 v Sunderland, FA Cup 5th rd
(replay), 15 March 1967.
Pitch Measurements: 115yd × 76yd.
Chairman: Ken Bates.
Chief Executive: Shaun Harvey.
Manager: Simon Grayson.
Assistant Managers: Glynn Snodin, Ian Miller.
Physio: Harvey Sharman.
Colours: White shirts, white shorts, white stockings with
yellow trim.
Change Colours: Yellow shirts with blue trim, yellow
shorts, yellow stockings.
Year Formed: 1919, as Leeds United after disbandment
(by FA order) of Leeds City (formed in 1904).
Turned Professional: 1920.
Ltd Co.: 1920.
Club Nickname: 'The Whites'.
Ground: 1919, Elland Road.

HONOURS

Football League – Division 1:
Champions 1968–69, 1973–74,
1991–92; *Runners-up* 1964–65,
1965–66, 1969–70, 1970–71, 1971–72;
Division 2: *Champions* 1923–24,
1963–64, 1989–90;
Runners-up 1927–28, 1931–32,
1955–56; **FL 1:** *Runners-up* 2009–10.
FA Cup: *Winners* 1972;
Runners-up 1965, 1970, 1973.
Football League Cup: *Winners* 1968;
Runners-up 1996.
European Competitions
European Cup: 1969–70, 1974–75
(*runners-up*).
Champions League: 1992–93, 2000–01
(*s-f*).
European Cup-Winners' Cup: 1972–73
(*runners-up*).
European Fairs Cup: 1965–66,
1966–67 (*runners-up*), 1967–68
(*winners*), 1968–69, 1970–71 (*winners*).
UEFA Cup: 1971–72, 1973–74,
1979–80, 1995–96, 1998–99, 1999–2000
(*s-f*), 2001–02, 2002–03.

First Football League Game: 28 August 1920, Division 2, v Port Vale (a) L 0–2 – Down; Duffield,
Tillotson; Musgrove, Baker, Walton; Mason, Goldthorpe, Thompson, Lyon, Best.

sky SPORTS FACT FILE

Charlie Keetley was the youngest of eight brothers who
all played professional football. He had to battle for a
Leeds United first team place in the 1920s. He not only
succeeded but scored his 100th League goal, the middle
one of a hat-trick against Wolves on 11 March 1933.

Record League Victory: 8–0 v Leicester C, Division 1, 7 April 1934 – Moore; George Milburn, Jack Milburn; Edwards, Hart, Copping; Mahon (2), Firth (2), Duggan (2), Furness (2), Cochrane.

Record Cup Victory: 10–0 v Lyn (Oslo), European Cup 1st rd 1st leg, 17 September 1969 – Sprake; Reaney, Cooper, Bremner (2), Charlton, Hunter, Madeley, Clarke (2), Jones (3), Giles (2) (Bates), O'Grady (1).

Record Defeat: 1–8 v Stoke C, Division 1, 27 August 1934.

Most League Points (2 for a win): 67, Division 1, 1968–69.

Most League Points (3 for a win): 86, FL 1, 2009–10.

Most League Goals: 98, Division 2, 1927–28.

Highest League Scorer in Season: John Charles, 42, Division 2, 1953–54.

Most League Goals in Total Aggregate: Peter Lorimer, 168, 1965–79 and 1983–86.

Most League Goals in One Match: 5, Gordon Hodgson v Leicester C, Division 1, 1 October 1938.

Most Capped Player: Lucas Radebe, 58 (70), South Africa.

Most League Appearances: Jack Charlton, 629, 1953–73.

Youngest League Player: Peter Lorimer, 15 years 289 days v Southampton, 29 September 1962.

Record Transfer Fee Received: £30,000,000 from Manchester U for Rio Ferdinand, July 2002.

Record Transfer Fee Paid: £18,000,000 to West Ham United for Rio Ferdinand, November 2000.

MANAGERS

Dick Ray 1919–20
Arthur Fairclough 1920–27
Dick Ray 1927–35
Bill Hampson 1935–47
Willis Edwards 1947–48
Major Frank Buckley 1948–53
Raich Carter 1953–58
Bill Lambton 1958–59
Jack Taylor 1959–61
Don Revie OBE 1961–74
Brian Clough 1974
Jimmy Armfield 1974–78
Jock Stein CBE 1978
Jimmy Adamson 1978–80
Allan Clarke 1980–82
Eddie Gray MBE 1982–85
Billy Bremner 1985–88
Howard Wilkinson 1988–96
George Graham 1996–98
David O'Leary 1998–2002
Terry Venables 2002–03
Peter Reid 2003
Eddie Gray *(Caretaker)* 2003–04
Kevin Blackwell 2004–06
Dennis Wise 2006–08
Gary McAllister 2008
Simon Grayson December 2008–

Football League Record: 1920 Elected to Division 2; 1924–27 Division 1; 1927–28 Division 2; 1928–31 Division 1; 1931–32 Division 2; 1932–47 Division 1; 1947–56 Division 2; 1956–60 Division 1; 1960–64 Division 2; 1964–82 Division 1; 1982–90 Division 2; 1990–92 Division 1; 1992–2004 FA Premier League; 2004–07 FL C; 2007–10 FL 1; 2010– FL C.

LATEST SEQUENCES

Longest Sequence of League Wins: 9, 26.9.1931 – 21.11.1931.

Longest Sequence of League Defeats: 6, 28.12.2003 – 7.2.2004.

Longest Sequence of League Draws: 5, 19.4.1997 – 9.8.1997.

Longest Sequence of Unbeaten League Matches: 34, 26.10.1968 – 26.8.1969.

Longest Sequence Without a League Win: 17, 1.2.1947 – 26.5.1947.

Successive Scoring Runs: 30 from 27.8.1927.

Successive Non-scoring Runs: 6 from 30.1.1982.

TEN YEAR LEAGUE RECORD

		P	W	D	L	F	A	Pts	Pos
2001-02	PR Lge	38	18	12	8	53	37	66	5
2002-03	PR Lge	38	14	5	19	58	57	47	15
2003-04	PR Lge	38	8	9	21	40	79	33	19
2004-05	FL C	46	14	18	14	49	52	60	14
2005-06	FL C	46	21	15	10	57	38	78	5
2006-07	FL C	46	13	7	26	46	72	36*	24
2007-08	FL 1	46	27	10	9	72	38	76†	5
2008-09	FL 1	46	26	6	14	77	49	84	4
2009-10	FL 1	46	25	11	10	77	44	86	2
2010-11	FL C	46	19	15	12	81	70	72	7

*10 pts deducted; †15 pts deducted.

DID YOU KNOW ?

Tom Jennings and Charlie Keetley were reliable marksmen for Leeds United in the years between the wars. Their scoring records were so similar that Jennings with 112 goals in 167 League games was just 0.01 of a goal ratio better than Keetley's 108 in 160 such games.

LEEDS UNITED 2010–11 LEAGUE RECORD

Match No.	Date	Venue	Opponents	Result	H/T Score	Lg Pos.	Goalscorers	Atten- dance
1	Aug 7	H	Derby Co	L 1-2	1-2	—	Becchio [16]	26,761
2	15	A	Nottingham F	D 1-1	1-1	16	Sam [36]	24,986
3	21	H	Millwall	W 3-1	1-1	9	Sam [32], Somma 2 [79, 90]	25,067
4	28	A	Watford	W 1-0	1-0	6	Naylor [6]	14,039
5	Sept 11	H	Swansea C	W 2-1	0-1	6	Johnson [56], Becchio [64]	26,453
6	14	A	Barnsley	L 2-5	1-1	—	Howson [3], Somma [88]	20,309
7	17	A	Doncaster R	D 0-0	0-0	—		13,293
8	25	H	Sheffield U	W 1-0	0-0	5	Johnson [83]	33,622
9	28	H	Preston NE	L 4-6	4-2	—	Becchio [15], Bruce [20], Somma 2 [27, 39]	22,727
10	Oct 2	A	Ipswich T	L 1-2	0-1	10	Snodgrass [77]	23,105
11	16	A	Middlesbrough	W 2-1	1-0	9	Somma [12], Becchio [63]	23,550
12	19	H	Leicester C	L 1-2	0-0	—	Becchio [83]	22,775
13	25	H	Cardiff C	L 0-4	0-1	—		20,747
14	30	A	Scunthorpe U	W 4-1	1-1	12	Gradel [8], Howson 3 [60, 74, 75]	8122
15	Nov 6	A	Coventry C	W 3-2	2-0	8	Howson [4], Snodgrass [40], Gradel (pen) [61]	28,184
16	9	A	Hull C	D 2-2	1-1	—	Johnson [33], O'Brien [71]	24,906
17	13	H	Bristol C	W 3-1	0-0	5	Becchio 3 [66, 70, 83]	27,567
18	20	A	Norwich C	D 1-1	1-0	5	Gradel [13]	26,315
19	27	A	Reading	D 0-0	0-0	8		23,677
20	Dec 4	H	Crystal Palace	W 2-1	0-1	—	Becchio 2 [81, 83]	25,476
21	11	A	Burnley	W 3-2	0-2	4	Gradel [52], Becchio [66], Howson [85]	20,453
22	18	H	QPR	W 2-0	1-0	2	Gradel 2 [25, 70]	29,426
23	26	A	Leicester C	D 2-2	1-0	3	Gradel [19], Snodgrass [55]	30,919
24	28	H	Portsmouth	D 3-3	2-1	4	Gradel [7], Howson [10], Johnson [62]	31,556
25	Jan 1	H	Middlesbrough	D 1-1	0-1	4	Becchio [90]	30,452
26	4	A	Cardiff C	L 1-2	0-1	—	Snodgrass [59]	25,010
27	15	H	Scunthorpe U	W 4-0	3-0	5	Watt [17], Gradel [20], Johnson [29], Somma [88]	25,446
28	22	A	Portsmouth	D 2-2	0-1	5	Becchio [47], Somma [63]	20,040
29	Feb 1	A	Hull C	D 2-2	1-2	6	Snodgrass [44], Somma [56]	24,110
30	5	H	Coventry C	W 1-0	0-0	6	Somma [56]	27,033
31	12	A	Bristol C	W 2-0	1-0	6	Snodgrass [17], Gradel [50]	18,000
32	19	H	Norwich C	D 2-2	1-1	6	Becchio [16], Somma [75]	31,601
33	22	H	Barnsley	D 3-3	2-1	—	Becchio [23], Gradel 2 (1 pen) [37 (pl), 70]	26,289
34	26	A	Swansea C	L 0-3	0-1	6		19,309
35	Mar 5	H	Doncaster R	W 5-2	1-1	6	Gradel 2 [12, 83], Howson 2 [50, 90], Becchio [75]	27,027
36	8	A	Preston NE	W 2-1	1-0	—	Kilkenny [29], Paynter [57]	15,269
37	12	H	Ipswich T	D 0-0	0-0	5		27,432
38	19	A	Sheffield U	L 0-2	0-0	5		23,728
39	Apr 2	H	Nottingham F	W 4-1	0-0	5	Howson [51], Becchio [58], Gradel 2 [73, 87]	29,524
40	9	A	Millwall	L 2-3	0-2	6	Becchio [51], O'Brien [90]	16,724
41	12	A	Derby Co	L 1-2	0-0	—	Gradel [58]	27,252
42	16	A	Watford	D 2-2	0-0	6	Becchio [72], Deeney (og) [88]	30,240
43	22	H	Reading	D 0-0	0-0	—		24,564
44	25	A	Crystal Palace	L 0-1	0-1	9		20,142
45	30	H	Burnley	W 1-0	1-0	7	McCormack [33]	31,186
46	May 7	A	QPR	W 2-1	1-1	7	Gradel [38], McCormack [68]	18,234

Final League Position: 7

GOALSCORERS

League (81): Becchio 19, Gradel 18 (2 pens), Somma 11, Howson 10, Snodgrass 6, Johnson 5, McCormack 2, O'Brien 2, Sam 2, Bruce 1, Kilkenny 1, Naylor 1, Paynter 1, Watt 1, own goal 1.
Carling Cup (5): Becchio 1, Howson 1, Kilkenny 1 (pen), Sam 1, Somma 1.
FA Cup (2): Johnson 1, Snodgrass 1 (pen).

Schmeichel K 37	Connolly P 30	Bessone F 6	Howson J 46	Collins N 20+1	Naylor R 13+2	Johnson B 40+5	Kilkenny N 29+8	Watt S 9+13	Becchio L 34+7	Sam L 7+11	White A 1+1	Clayton A —+4	Grella M —+1	Somma D 12+17	Hughes A 5+5	Gradel M 38+3	McCormack R 6+15	Higgs S 6	Bruce A 21	Snodgrass R 34+3	McCartney G 32	Faye A 6+2	Brown J 3+1	Bromby L 9+4	Nunez R —+2	O'Brien A 30	Paynter B 8+14	Parker B 1+1	Lichaj E 16	Bannan B 3+4	Livermore J 4+1	Kisnorbo P —+1	Match No.
1	2	3	4^3	5	6	7	8^2	9	10	11^1	12	13	14																				1
1	2	3	4	5	6	7	8	9	10	11^1	12																						2
1	2	3^1	4	5	6	7	8	9	10	11^2				12	13																		3
1	2	3^1	4	5	6	7	8	9^1	10	11^2					12	13	14																4
	2	3	4	5	6	7	8^2	9^1	10^3	12				14	11	13		1															5
	2	3^1	4	5	6	7^2	8		10	11^3				14	12	9		1															6
			4	5		7	8		13		3			10	2	11^2	9^1	1	6	12													7
			4	5		7			13	10	11^1			9^3	2	8^2	14	1	6	12^2	3												8
			4^3	5		7	12	14	10^2	11^1		13		9	2	8		1	6		3												9
			4	5	6	7^2	8^1		13	12				9	2	10		1		11	3	15											10
	2		4	5	6	7^2			13	10				9	12			1		11	3^1	8^3			14								11
	2		4	5	6	7^1	12	14	10					9	13			1		11^2	3	8^3											12
1	2		4	5		7^2			10	14				9^1	13				6	11	3	8^3	12										13
1	2		4				8		10^2		12			9	13	7^1	14		6	11^3	3					5							14
	2		4				12		10					9^1	14	7^2	13	1	6	11	3	8^3				5							15
1	2		4			7	8^2		10^3					9^1		12	13		6	11	3					5	14						16
1	2		4^3			7	8		10^1					9^2		12	13		6	11	3					5	14						17
1	2		4			7	8^2		10^3					9^1	14	12	13		6	11	3					5							18
1	2		4			7	8		10^2					9^1	14	12	13		6	11^3	3					5							19
1			4			7^2	8		10	13				9^1	2^3	12	14		6	11	3					5							20
1	2		4	5		7	8^1		10^2					9		12	13		6	11	3												21
1	2		4	5		7	8		10^3					9^2		13	12		6^1	11	3						14						22
1	2		4^1	5		7	8^3		10^2					9		13	14		6	11	3				12								23
1	2		4	5		7	8		10^1					9^4		12	13		6	11	3												24
1	2		4	5		7			10					9^2		12	13		6	11^3	3^1	8			14								25
1	2		4	5		7			10					9^1	13	8^3	12^2		6	11	3				14								26
1	2		4			7	8^2		10^1					9	14	13	12		6	11^3	3					5							27
1	2		4			7	8^1		10					9		12			6	11	3					5							28
1	2		4			7	8^3		10^2					9^1		12	14		6	11	3					5	13						29
1	2^2		4			7	8		10^3					9^1		12	13		6	11	3					5	14						30
1			4			7	8^1		10^2					9		12	13		6	11	3					5			2				31
1			4			7	8^1		10^2					9		12			6	11	3					5	13		2				32
1			4			7	8		10^2					9		12	13		6	11^1	3					5			2				33
1			4				8		10^1					9	14	7	12		6	11^3	3^2					5	13		2				34
1			4				8		10^1					9^3	14	7	13		6	11	3					5	12		2				35
1			4			7	8^2		10^3						14		12		6	11	3					5	9^1		2	13			36
1			4^1			7	8		10								12		6	11	3					5	9^2		2	13			37
1			4			7			10^3					9	13		12		6	11^2	3^1	8				5	14		2				38
1			4			7^2			10^3					9	13		14		6	11	3	8^1				5	12		2				39
1	2^2		4			7			10					9		12	14		6	11^1	3	8^3				5	13						40
1	2		4				8		10^2					9	12	7^1	13		6	11^3	3				14	5							41
1			4			7	8^1		10^3					9		13	12^2		6	11	3					5	14		2				42
1	2		4^2	5		7								9		12	13		6	11	3					10^3	14				8^1		43
1	2^1		4	5		7								9		12	13		6	11	3					10^3	14				8^2		44
1			4	5		7	8							9^2	13				6	11^3	3				12	10^1			2				45
1	2		4	5^2		7	8							9^3	14				6	11	3				12	10^1	13						46

FA Cup

Third Round	Arsenal	(a)	1-1
		(h)	1-3

Carling Cup

First Round	Lincoln C	(h)	4-0
Second Round	Leicester C	(h)	1-2

LEICESTER CITY   FL Championship

FOUNDATION

In 1884 a number of young footballers who were mostly old boys of Wyggeston School, held a meeting at a house on the Roman Fosse Way and formed Leicester Fosse FC. They collected 9d (less than 4p) towards the cost of a ball, plus the same amount for membership. Their first professional, Harry Webb from Stafford Rangers, was signed in 1888 for 2s 6d (12p) per week, plus travelling expenses.

King Power Stadium, Filbert Way, Leicester LE2 7FL.
Telephone: 0844 815 6000.
Fax: (0116) 229 4549.
Ticket Office: 0844 815 5000.
Website: www.lcfc.co.uk
Email: customer.relations@lcfc.co.uk
Ground Capacity: 32,500 (all seated).
Record Attendance: 47,298 v Tottenham H, FA Cup 5th rd, 18 February 1928 (at Filbert Street). 32,148 v Manchester U, FA Premier League, 26 December 2003 (at Walkers Stadium).
Pitch Measurements: 110yd × 74yd.
Chairman: Vichai Raksriaksorn.
Chief Executive: Lee Hoos.
Secretary: Andrew Neville.
Manager: Sven-Göran Eriksson.
Assistant Manager: Derek Fazackerley.
Physio: Dave Rennie.
Colours: Blue shirts with white trim, white shorts, blue stockings with white trim.
Change Colours: Black shirts with one diagonal light blue stripe, black shorts, black stockings.
Year Formed: 1884.
Turned Professional: 1888.   *Ltd Co:* 1897.
Previous Name: 1884, Leicester Fosse; 1919, Leicester City.
Club Nickname: 'Foxes'.
Grounds: 1884, Victoria Park; 1887, Belgrave Road; 1888, Victoria Park; 1891, Filbert Street; 2002, Walkers Stadium (now known as King Power Stadium from 2011).
First Football League Game: 1 September 1894, Division 2, v Grimsby T (a) L 3–4 – Thraves; Smith, Bailey; Seymour, Brown, Henrys; Hill, Hughes, McArthur (1), Skea (2), Priestman.
Record League Victory: 10–0 v Portsmouth, Division 1, 20 October 1928 – McLaren; Black, Brown; Findlay, Carr, Watson; Adcock, Hine (3), Chandler (6), Lochhead, Barry (1).
Record Cup Victory: 8–1 v Coventry C (a), League Cup 5th rd, 1 December 1964 – Banks; Sjoberg, Norman (2); Roberts, King, McDerment; Hodgson (2), Cross, Goodfellow, Gibson (1), Stringfellow (2), (1 og).

HONOURS

Football League – Division 1:
Runners-up 1928–29, 2002–03;
Division 2: *Champions* 1924–25, 1936–37, 1953–54, 1956–57, 1970–71, 1979–80; *Runners-up* 1907–08;
FL 1: *Champions* 2008–09.
FA Cup: *Runners-up* 1949, 1961, 1963, 1969.
Football League Cup: *Winners* 1964, 1997, 2000; *Runners-up* 1965, 1999.
European Competitions
European Cup-Winners' Cup: 1961–62.
UEFA Cup: 1997–98, 2000–01.

sky SPORTS FACT FILE

Arthur Rowley, the record goal scorer in a season for Leicester City, was actually discovered by the legendary pre-war Manchester United scout Louis Rocca. It was in 1939 and the youngster was then aged 12. His brother Jack was already an established United forward.

Record Defeat: 0–12 (as Leicester Fosse) v Nottingham F, Division 1, 21 April 1909.

Most League Points (2 for a win): 61, Division 2, 1956–57.

Most League Points (3 for a win): 96, FL 1, 2008–09.

Most League Goals: 109, Division 2, 1956–57.

Highest League Scorer in Season: Arthur Rowley, 44, Division 2, 1956–57.

Most League Goals in Total Aggregate: Arthur Chandler, 259, 1923–35.

Most League Goals in One Match: 6, John Duncan v Port Vale, Division 2, 25 December 1924; 6, Arthur Chandler v Portsmouth, Division 1, 20 October 1928.

Most Capped Player: John O'Neill, 39, Northern Ireland.

Most League Appearances: Adam Black, 528, 1920–35.

Youngest League Player: Dave Buchanan, 16 years 192 days v Oldham Ath, 1 January 1979.

Record Transfer Fee Received: £11,000,000 from Liverpool for Emile Heskey, March 2000.

Record Transfer Fee Paid: £5,000,000 to Wolverhampton W for Ade Akinbiyi, July 2000.

Football League Record: 1894 Elected to Division 2; 1908–09 Division 1; 1909–25 Division 2; 1925–35 Division 1; 1935–37 Division 2; 1937–39 Division 1; 1946–54 Division 2; 1954–55 Division 1; 1955–57 Division 2; 1957–69 Division 1; 1969–71 Division 2; 1971–78 Division 1; 1978–80 Division 2; 1980–81 Division 1; 1981–83 Division 2; 1983–87 Division 1; 1987–92 Division 2; 1992–94 Division 1; 1994–95 FA Premier League; 1995–96 Division 1; 1996–2002 FA Premier League; 2002–03 Division 1; 2003–04 FA Premier League; 2004–08 FL C; 2008–09 FL 1; 2009– FL C.

LATEST SEQUENCES

Longest Sequence of League Wins: 7, 28.2.1993 – 27.3.1993.

Longest Sequence of League Defeats: 8, 17.3.2001 – 28.4.2001.

Longest Sequence of League Draws: 6, 21.8.1976 – 18.9.1976.

Longest Sequence of Unbeaten League Matches: 23, 1.11.2008 – 7.3.2009.

Longest Sequence Without a League Win: 18, 12.4.1975 – 1.11.1975.

Successive Scoring Runs: 31 from 12.11.1932.

Successive Non-scoring Runs: 7 from 21.11.1987.

MANAGERS

Frank Gardner 1884–92
Ernest Marson 1892–94
J. Lee 1894–95
Henry Jackson 1895–97
William Clark 1897–98
George Johnson 1898–1912
Jack Bartlett 1912–14
Louis Ford 1914–15
Harry Linney 1915–19
Peter Hodge 1919–26
Willie Orr 1926–32
Peter Hodge 1932–34
Arthur Lochhead 1934–36
Frank Womack 1936–39
Tom Bromilow 1939–45
Tom Mather 1945–46
John Duncan 1946–49
Norman Bullock 1949–55
David Halliday 1955–58
Matt Gillies 1958–68
Frank O'Farrell 1968–71
Jimmy Bloomfield 1971–77
Frank McLintock 1977–78
Jock Wallace 1978–82
Gordon Milne 1982–86
Bryan Hamilton 1986–87
David Pleat 1987–91
Gordon Lee 1991
Brian Little 1991–94
Mark McGhee 1994–95
Martin O'Neill 1995–2000
Peter Taylor 2000–01
Dave Bassett 2001–02
Micky Adams 2002–04
Craig Levein 2004–06
Robert Kelly 2006–07
Martin Allen 2007
Gary Megson 2007
Ian Holloway 2007–08
Nigel Pearson 2008–10
Paulo Sousa 2010
Sven-Göran Eriksson October 2010–

TEN YEAR LEAGUE RECORD

		P	W	D	L	F	A	Pts	Pos
2001-02	PR Lge	38	5	13	20	30	64	28	20
2002-03	Div 1	46	26	14	6	73	40	92	2
2003-04	PR Lge	38	6	15	17	48	65	33	18
2004-05	FL C	46	12	21	13	49	46	57	15
2005-06	FL C	46	13	15	18	51	59	54	16
2006-07	FL C	46	13	14	19	49	64	53	19
2007-08	FL C	46	12	16	18	42	45	52	22
2008-09	FL 1	46	27	15	4	84	39	96	1
2009-10	FL C	46	21	13	12	61	45	76	5
2010-11	FL C	46	19	10	17	76	71	67	10

DID YOU KNOW ?

In the crucial battle for survival in 1957–58, Leicester City achieved a remarkable 8-4 win over Manchester City on 22 February. Jimmy Walsh scored four for Leicester. The win helped towards safety by just a point after they had scored 91 goals but conceded 112 during the season!

LEICESTER CITY 2010–11 LEAGUE RECORD

Match No.	Date	Venue	Opponents	Result	H/T Score	Lg Pos.	Goalscorers	Attendance
1	Aug 7	A	Crystal Palace	L	2-3	0-3	—	King, A [57], Campbell [84]	17,486
2	14	H	Middlesbrough	D	0-0	0-0	17		21,587
3	21	A	Burnley	L	0-3	0-1	23		15,516
4	28	H	Reading	L	1-2	0-1	23	Dyer [52]	19,611
5	Sept 11	A	Coventry C	D	1-1	0-1	23	King, A [76]	20,060
6	14	H	Cardiff C	W	2-1	0-1	—	King, A 2 [51, 68]	20,510
7	18	H	QPR	L	0-2	0-1	22		22,968
8	24	A	Portsmouth	L	1-6	0-2	—	Howard [71]	13,751
9	28	A	Norwich C	L	3-4	1-1	—	Waghorn [2], Fryatt 2 [65, 78]	25,091
10	Oct 2	H	Scunthorpe U	W	3-1	1-0	22	Waghorn [10], Dyer [54], Moussa [90]	20,652
11	16	H	Hull C	D	1-1	1-0	22	King, A [3]	23,766
12	19	A	Leeds U	W	2-1	0-0	—	Naughton [63], Howard [81]	22,775
13	23	A	Swansea C	L	0-2	0-0	21		14,651
14	30	H	Preston NE	W	1-0	1-0	19	Gallagher [36]	21,212
15	Nov 6	A	Barnsley	W	2-0	1-0	17	Miguel Vitor [18], King, A [85]	12,360
16	10	A	Sheffield U	D	2-2	1-2	—	Gallagher [8], Howard (pen) [90]	20,445
17	13	H	Derby Co	W	2-0	1-0	16	King, A [13], Howard (pen) [71]	25,930
18	20	A	Bristol C	L	0-2	0-0	17		14,517
19	29	H	Nottingham F	W	1-0	0-0	—	King, A [59]	24,659
20	Dec 4	A	Watford	L	2-3	0-2	—	Gallagher 2 (1 pen) [50 (pl), 69]	14,449
21	11	H	Doncaster R	W	5-1	1-1	13	Gallagher (pen) [45], Wellens [61], Naughton [69], Vassell [75], Waghorn [90]	27,549
22	18	A	Ipswich T	L	0-3	0-3	16		16,728
23	26	H	Leeds U	D	2-2	0-1	17	Gallagher (pen) [72], King, A [76]	30,919
24	28	A	Millwall	L	0-2	0-2	17		12,188
25	Jan 1	A	Hull C	W	1-0	1-0	14	Vassell [11]	22,410
26	3	H	Swansea C	W	2-1	2-1	12	Berner [6], Vassell [43]	21,656
27	15	A	Preston NE	D	1-1	0-0	13	Yakubu [60]	14,205
28	22	H	Millwall	W	4-2	3-1	10	Dyer [8], Yakubu [22], Bamba 2 [35, 74]	23,347
29	Feb 1	A	Sheffield U	W	1-0	1-0	10	King, A [4]	20,464
30	5	H	Barnsley	W	4-1	2-1	8	Gallagher [15], King, A 2 [43, 58], Naughton [89]	22,667
31	12	A	Derby Co	W	2-0	2-0	7	Yakubu [28], King, A [45]	26,142
32	18	A	Bristol C	W	2-1	1-0	—	Yakubu [21], Waghorn [90]	28,768
33	22	A	Cardiff C	L	0-2	0-1	—		22,410
34	26	H	Coventry C	D	1-1	1-1	7	Naughton [45]	25,356
35	Mar 5	A	QPR	L	0-1	0-0	9		18,068
36	8	H	Norwich C	L	2-3	1-1	—	Wellens [23], Gallagher [90]	23,398
37	12	A	Scunthorpe U	W	3-0	1-0	9	Miguel Vitor 2 [31, 72], Naughton [76]	6528
38	19	H	Portsmouth	L	0-1	0-1	11		26,645
39	Apr 2	A	Middlesbrough	D	3-3	2-1	12	Yakubu 3 [5, 45, 49]	14,500
40	9	H	Burnley	W	4-0	1-0	9	Kamara [23], Gallagher 2 (1 pen) [52 (pl), 71], Van Aanholt [81]	24,039
41	12	H	Crystal Palace	D	1-1	0-1	—	Oakley [58]	22,303
42	16	A	Reading	L	1-3	0-2	10	King, A [79]	19,199
43	22	A	Nottingham F	L	2-3	1-1	—	Oakley [20], Vassell [74]	24,217
44	25	H	Watford	W	4-2	1-2	11	Bruma 2 [39, 73], Yakubu 2 [62, 75]	21,473
45	30	A	Doncaster R	D	1-1	0-0	11	Yakubu [76]	11,757
46	May 7	H	Ipswich T	W	4-2	3-0	10	King, A [26], Yakubu [42], Abe [45], Kamara [72]	24,859

Final League Position: 10

GOALSCORERS

League (76): King, A 15, Yakubu 11, Gallagher 10 (4 pens), Naughton 5, Howard 4 (2 pens), Vassell 4, Waghorn 4, Dyer 3, Miguel Vitor 3, Bamba 2, Bruma 2, Fryatt 2, Kamara 2, Oakley 2, Wellens 2, Abe 1, Berner 1, Campbell 1, Moussa 1, Van Aanholt 1.
Carling Cup (9): Fryatt 2, Wellens 2, Dyer 1, Howard 1 (pen), Morrison 1, Neilson 1, own goal 1.
FA Cup (4): Bamba 1, Dyer 1, Gallagher 1 (pen), King 1.

Weale C 28+1	Neilson R 7	Berner B 15+2	King A 44+1	Morrison M 10+1	Hobbs J 23+3	N'Guessan D 3+2	Oakley M 22+12	Campbell D 3	Fryatt M 5+7	Dyer L 18+17	Wellens S 11+18	Howard S 11+18	Moreno J 3	Gallagher P 32+9	Lamey M 2+2	Moussa F 2+6	Logan C 2+1	Ikeme C 5	Waghorn M 11+19	Abe Y 25+11	Miguel Vitor 13+2	Kennedy T 1	Naughton K 34	Davies C 12	Cunningham G 13	Vassell D 26+5	Bednar R 4+1	Kirkland C 3	Bamba S 16	Yakubu A 19+1	Mee B 15	Van Aanholt P 12	Ricardo 8	Bruma J 10+1	Kamara D 5+2	Tunchev A —+2	Match No.
1	2	3	4	5	6	7^1	8	9	10^2	11	12	13																									1
1	2^2	5	4^1		6		8	9^3	13	11	7	10	3	12	14																						2
1^6	2^1	3	4		6	11	8^2	9		7		10	5	12	13	15																					3
		3		13	6	7^3	8^2			12	11	4	10	5	9^1	2	14	1																			4
	2	3	4	5	6	14	8		10^3	11^2	7	13		12				1	9^1																		5
	2	3	4^1	5	6		8			11	7	10		13				1	9^2	12																	6
	2	3	4	5	6		8^2		10	11^1	7	13		12				1	9																		7
	2	3	4	5	12		8		13	11^2		10					1		9	7^1	6^8																8
			4	5	6		8^1		12^4	11^2	7^3	10		13	2			1	9	14		3															9
		3	4	5	6		8			11^2		10		7^1	13			1	9	12	2																10
1		3	4		6		8^2				7	10^1		11	13				9	12			2	5													11
1		3	4		6		8				7	13		10^1	11^2				9	12			2	5													12
1			4^2	13	6		8			10	11	7		9^1	14					12			2	5^2	3												13
1			4		6	13	8		14	10^1	12			11^3					9^2	7			2	5	3												14
1			4				8			12	13			11^3	14				9^2	7	6		2	5	3	10^1											15
1			4		6	14	13			8	12			11					9^1	7^3			2	5	3	10^1											16
1			4		6		8			12		9^2		11					13	7			2	5	3	10^1											17
1			4^2		6	14	8			12		9^3		11					13	7			2	5	3	10^1											18
1			4		6		8			12	13			11^3					14	7			2	5	3	10^1	9^2										19
1			4^2		6				13	8		12		11					14	7			2	5	3	10^3	9^1										20
1			4		14					12		8		11^2					13	7	6		2	5	3	10^3	9^1										21
			4		14				13		11^1	8		12					9^2	7	6		2	5^2	3	10		1									22
			4		6		8			12		9^2		11						7^1			2	5	3	10		1	13								23
16			4	5	6					7		11		8^2	13				9	12			2		3	10^1		1^6									24
1	12		4	5	6	14	8			11^3				9					13	7			2		3^1	10^2											25
1		3	4	5	6		8			12	11^1			9					13	7			2			10^2											26
1		3	4		6		8			12	11^1	13		9^2	14					7			2						5	10^3							27
1		3	4				8			12	11^2				14				13	7			2			10^1			5	9^3	6						28
1			4				8		13	12	11^1				14					7^2			2		3	10		1	5	9^1	6	3					29
1			4			14	8			12		13		11						7^1			2		3	10^2			6^3	9	5	3					30
			4				8			7		12		11					13				2		3	10^2		1	6^3	9^1	5	3				14	31
			4				8^2			7		12		11^1	14				13				2		3	10^3		1	6	9	5	3			7		32
			4				8^1				11^3			10^2					12	13			2		3	14		1	6	9	5	3					33
			4			14	8			12				11^1	14				13	7^3			2		3	10^2		1	6	9		5					34
			4^2				8			7		13		11	14				12	11			2		3	10^1		1	5	9^3	6						35
		3	4				8^3			7^2		14		11					13	12			2			10^1		1	5	9	6						36
			4				8		13					11^2	14				12	7	6		2		3	10^1		1	5	9^1							37
			4				8					12		11					13	7^1			2		3	10^2		1	5	9	6						38
1			4				8					12		7^1	14				14	12	13		2		3	11			5	9^2		3		6^8	10^3		39
1			4				8			7^3		12		11					14		13		2		3				6	9^1	5				10^2		40
1			4				8		13	7				11^1	14				12				2		3				6	9^3	5				10^2		41
1			4				8			7				11	14				13	12			2			11^2			5^1	9	6				10^3		42
1			4				8			7^1				11	14				13	12	3		2			13			5	9^2	6				10^3		43
1	11		4							13		9		8^1					7	4			2	12	3	10^2	12		5	6^3		14					44
1	13		4				8					14		11^1					7^2	3			2			10			5^3	9	6			12			45
1			4							14		8^3		11					7	5^2			2		3	10^1				9	6			12	13		46

FA Cup
Third Round   Manchester C   (h)   2-2
    (a)   2-4

Carling Cup
First Round   Macclesfield T   (h)   4-3
Second Round   Leeds U   (a)   2-1
Third Round   Portsmouth   (a)   2-1
Fourth Round   WBA   (h)   1-4

LEYTON ORIENT FL Championship 1

FOUNDATION

There is some doubt about the foundation of Leyton Orient, and, indeed, some confusion with clubs like Leyton and Clapton over their early history. As regards the foundation, the most favoured version is that Leyton Orient was formed originally by members of Homerton Theological College who established Glyn Cricket Club in 1881 and then carried on through the following winter playing football. Eventually many employees of the Orient Shipping Line became involved and so the name Orient was chosen in 1888.

Matchroom Stadium, Brisbane Road, Leyton, London E10 5NF.

Telephone: 0871 310 1881.

Fax: 0871 310 1882.

Ticket Office: 0871 310 1883.

Website: www.leytonorient.com

Email: info@leytonorient.net

Ground Capacity: 9,300.

Record Attendance: 34,345 v West Ham U, FA Cup 4th rd, 25 January 1964.

Pitch Measurements: 110yd × 76yd.

Chairman: Barry Hearn.

Vice-chairman: Eddie Hearn.

Chief Executive: Matthew Porter.

Secretary: Lindsey Martin.

Manager: Russell Slade.

Assistant Manager: Kevin Nugent.

Physio: Dave Appanah.

Colours: Red shirts with white insert and striped sleeves, red shorts, red stockings.

Change Colours: All blue.

Year Formed: 1881. *Turned Professional:* 1903. *Ltd Co.:* 1906.

Previous Names: 1881, Glyn Cricket and Football Club; 1886, Eagle Football Club; 1888, Orient Football Club; 1898, Clapton Orient; 1946, Leyton Orient; 1966, Orient; 1987, Leyton Orient.

Club Nickname: 'The O's'.

Grounds: 1884, Glyn Road; 1896, Whittles Athletic Ground; 1900, Millfields Road; 1930, Lea Bridge Road; 1937, Brisbane Road.

First Football League Game: 2 September 1905, Division 2, v Leicester Fosse (a) L 1–2 – Butler; Holmes, Codling; Lamberton, Boden, Boyle; Kingaby (1), Wootten, Leigh, Evenson, Bourne.

Record League Victory: 8–0 v Crystal Palace, Division 3 (S), 12 November 1955 – Welton; Lee, Earl; Blizzard, Aldous, McKnight; White (1), Facey (3), Burgess (2), Heckman, Hartburn (2). 8–0 v Rochdale, Division 4, 20 October 1987 – Wells; Howard, Dickenson (1), Smalley (1), Day, Hull, Hales (2), Castle (Sussex), Shinners (2), Godfrey (Harvey), Comfort (2). 8–0 v Colchester U,

HONOURS

Football League – Division 1: 22nd, 1962–63;

Division 2: *Runners-up* 1961–62;

Division 3: *Champions* 1969–70;

Division 3 (S): *Champions* 1955–56; *Runners-up* 1954–55.

FA Cup: Semi-final 1978.

Football League Cup: Best season: 5th rd, 1963.

sky SPORTS FACT FILE

In the run up to Christmas 2010 Scott McGleish and other Leyton Orient players participated in a brain-teasing DS game advertisement on television. The same week he scored twice as Orient won their FA Cup first round replay against local rivals Dagenham & Redbridge 3-2.

Division 4, 15 October 1988 – Wells; Howard, Dickenson, Hales (1p), Day (1), Sitton (1), Baker (1), Ward, Hull (3), Juryeff, Comfort (1). 8–0 v Doncaster R, Division 3, 28 December 1997 – Hyde; Channing, Naylor, Smith (1p), Hicks, Clark, Ling, Roger Joseph, Griffiths (3) (Harris), Richards (2) (Baker (1)), Inglethorpe (1) (Simpson).

Record Cup Victory: 9–2 v Chester, League Cup 3rd rd, 15 October 1962 – Robertson; Charlton, Taylor; Gibbs, Bishop, Lea; Deeley (1), Waites (3), Dunmore (2), Graham (3), Wedge.

Record Defeat: 0–8 v Aston Villa, FA Cup 4th rd, 30 January 1929.

Most League Points (2 for a win): 66, Division 3 (S), 1955–56.

Most League Points (3 for a win): 81, FL 2, 2005–06.

Most League Goals: 106, Division 3 (S), 1955–56.

Highest League Scorer in Season: Tom Johnston, 35, Division 2, 1957–58.

Most League Goals in Total Aggregate: Tom Johnston, 121, 1956–58, 1959–61.

Most League Goals in One Match: 4, Wally Leigh v Bradford C, Division 2, 13 April 1906; 4, Albert Pape v Oldham Ath, Division 2, 1 September 1924; 4, Peter Kitchen v Millwall, Division 3, 21 April 1984.

Most Capped Players: Tunji Banjo, 7 (7), Nigeria; John Chiedozie, 7 (9), Nigeria; Tony Grealish, 7 (45), Republic of Ireland.

Most League Appearances: Peter Allen, 432, 1965–78.

Youngest League Player: Paul Went, 15 years 327 days v Preston NE, 4 September 1965.

Record Transfer Fee Received: £1,000,000 from Fulham for Gabriel Zakuani, July 2006.

Record Transfer Fee Paid: £175,000 to Wigan Ath for Paul Beesley, October 1989.

Football League Record: 1905 Elected to Division 2; 1929–56 Division 3 (S); 1956–62 Division 2; 1962–63 Division 1; 1963–66 Division 2; 1966–70 Division 3; 1970–82 Division 2; 1982–85 Division 3; 1985–89 Division 4; 1989–92 Division 3; 1992–95 Division 3; 1995–2004 Division 3; 2004–06 FL 2; 2006– FL 1.

LATEST SEQUENCES

Longest Sequence of League Wins: 10, 21.1.1956 – 30.3.1956.

Longest Sequence of League Defeats: 9, 1.4.1995 – 6.5.1995.

Longest Sequence of League Draws: 6, 30.11.1974 – 28.12.1974.

Longest Sequence of Unbeaten League Matches: 13, 30.10.1954 – 19.2.1955.

Longest Sequence Without a League Win: 23, 6.10.1962 – 13.4.1963.

Successive Scoring Runs: 24 from 3.5.2003.

Successive Non-scoring Runs: 8 from 19.11.1994.

MANAGERS

Sam Omerod 1905–06
Ike Ivenson 1906
Billy Holmes 1907–22
Peter Proudfoot 1922–29
Arthur Grimsdell 1929–30
Peter Proudfoot 1930–31
Jimmy Seed 1931–33
David Pratt 1933–34
Peter Proudfoot 1935–39
Tom Halsey 1939
Bill Wright 1939–45
Willie Hall 1945
Bill Wright 1945–46
Charlie Hewitt 1946–48
Neil McBain 1948–49
Alec Stock 1949–59
Les Gore 1959–61
Johnny Carey 1961–63
Benny Fenton 1963–64
Dave Sexton 1965
Dick Graham 1966–68
Jimmy Bloomfield 1968–71
George Petchey 1971–77
Jimmy Bloomfield 1977–81
Paul Went 1981
Ken Knighton 1981–83
Frank Clark 1983–91
(Managing Director)
Peter Eustace 1991–94
Chris Turner/John Sitton 1994–95
Pat Holland 1995–96
Tommy Taylor 1996–2001
Paul Brush 2001–03
Martin Ling 2003–09
Geraint Williams 2009–10
Russell Slade April 2010–

TEN YEAR LEAGUE RECORD

		P	W	D	L	F	A	Pts	Pos
2001-02	Div 3	46	13	13	20	55	71	52	18
2002-03	Div 3	46	14	11	21	51	61	53	18
2003-04	Div 3	46	13	14	19	48	65	53	19
2004-05	FL 2	46	16	15	15	65	67	63	11
2005-06	FL 2	46	22	15	9	67	51	81	3
2006-07	FL 1	46	12	15	19	61	77	51	20
2007-08	FL 1	46	16	12	18	49	63	60	14
2008-09	FL 1	46	15	11	20	45	57	56	14
2009-10	FL 1	46	13	12	21	53	63	51	17
2010-11	FL 1	46	19	13	14	71	62	70	7

DID YOU KNOW ?

On 7 December 2010, ten-man Leyton Orient were trailing 2-0 to Droylsden in an FA Cup replay after 54 minutes. In the 77th minute the O's reduced the score. Orient down to nine men forced extra time with Droylsden's ten and hit six in 26 minutes to win 8-2 in a nine-a-side finish!

LEYTON ORIENT 2010–11 LEAGUE RECORD

Match No.	Date	Venue	Opponents	Result	H/T Score	Lg Pos.	Goalscorers	Attendance
1	Aug 7	A	Yeovil T	L	1-2	1-2	—	Revell [41]	4126
2	13	H	Charlton Ath	L	1-3	0-1	—	McGleish [50]	5535
3	21	A	Southampton	D	1-1	1-1	21	Forbes [15]	21,468
4	28	H	Exeter C	W	3-0	1-0	15	Revell [39], McGleish [70], Cox [90]	4145
5	Sept 4	A	Dagenham & R	L	0-2	0-1	20		4195
6	11	H	Huddersfield T	L	1-2	0-1	23	Cox [79]	3918
7	18	A	Notts Co	L	2-3	1-2	23	Jarvis [22], Spring [54]	6256
8	24	H	Brentford	W	1-0	1-0	—	McGleish [25]	4485
9	28	H	Walsall	D	0-0	0-0	—		2963
10	Oct 2	A	Oldham Ath	D	1-1	0-1	22	McGleish [79]	3806
11	9	A	Sheffield W	L	0-1	0-0	23		17,445
12	16	H	Hartlepool U	W	1-0	0-0	20	Tehoue [89]	3605
13	23	A	Swindon T	D	2-2	0-0	21	Spring [60], Revell [76]	8384
14	30	H	Rochdale	W	2-1	0-1	18	Chorley (pen) [48], Cox [66]	4880
15	Nov 2	A	Colchester U	L	2-3	2-2	—	Revell 2 [10, 18]	3899
16	13	H	Bristol R	W	3-0	2-0	17	Cox [20], Revell 2 [27, 51]	5541
17	20	H	Bournemouth	D	2-2	0-1	18	Tehoue 2 [85, 90]	4531
18	23	A	Peterborough U	D	2-2	1-1	—	Revell [43], Smith [86]	4423
19	Dec 11	A	Tranmere R	W	2-1	2-0	16	Dawson [10], McGleish [45]	4291
20	Jan 1	A	Brighton & HA	L	0-5	0-2	19		7198
21	3	H	Colchester U	W	4-2	1-0	18	Smith [41], Revell [49], M'Poku [75], Tehoue [86]	4339
22	15	A	Rochdale	D	1-1	0-1	18	Chorley [60]	2731
23	22	H	Sheffield W	W	4-0	0-0	17	Chorley (pen) [51], Kane [57], Revell [79], McGleish [84]	6449
24	25	H	Milton Keynes D	D	2-2	2-1	—	McGleish [9], Forbes [14]	3131
25	Feb 1	H	Brighton & HA	D	0-0	0-0	15		5872
26	5	A	Bournemouth	D	1-1	0-1	16	Cox [90]	6717
27	8	H	Swindon T	W	3-0	3-0	—	Cox [12], Revell [31], Dawson [32]	4214
28	12	H	Bristol R	W	4-1	2-0	11	Smith [5], Whing [16], Kane 2 [77, 82]	4913
29	15	A	Milton Keynes D	W	3-2	2-2	—	Smith 2 [17, 39], Tehoue [74]	6469
30	26	A	Huddersfield T	D	2-2	0-1	11	Kane [73], Smith [88]	13,527
31	Mar 5	H	Notts Co	W	2-0	1-0	9	Cox [8], Whing [79]	4238
32	8	A	Walsall	W	2-0	1-0	—	Kane [43], Tehoue [56]	3019
33	12	H	Oldham Ath	W	1-0	0-0	7	M'Poku [87]	4349
34	15	H	Hartlepool U	W	1-0	1-0	—	Smith [28]	2313
35	19	A	Brentford	L	1-2	0-2	7	McGleish [55]	6368
36	22	H	Dagenham & R	D	1-1	0-1	—	McGleish (pen) [90]	4581
37	26	H	Yeovil T	L	1-5	0-3	—	Cox [70]	4258
38	Apr 2	A	Charlton Ath	L	1-3	1-0	8	McGleish [16]	15,875
39	5	H	Plymouth Arg	W	2-0	2-0	—	McGleish [4], Cox [13]	3255
40	9	H	Southampton	L	0-2	0-1	8		7714
41	12	H	Carlisle U	D	0-0	0-0	—		3228
42	16	A	Exeter C	L	1-2	1-1	8	Cox [12]	5036
43	22	H	Peterborough U	W	2-1	0-0	—	Zakuani (og) [67], Jarvis [90]	5476
44	25	A	Carlisle U	W	1-0	1-0	8	Tehoue [36]	4685
45	30	H	Tranmere R	L	0-3	0-2	7		5302
46	May 7	A	Plymouth Arg	W	4-1	2-0	7	McGleish (pen) [13], Cox [15], Revell 2 [77, 89]	11,501

Final League Position: 7

GOALSCORERS

League (71): Revell 13, McGleish 12 (2 pens), Cox 11, Smith 7, Tehoue 7, Kane 5, Chorley 3 (2 pens), Dawson 2, Forbes 2, Jarvis 2, M'Poku 2, Spring 2, Whing 2, own goal 1.
Carling Cup (2): Jarvis 1, Revell 1.
FA Cup (17): McGleish 6, Tehoue 4, Revell 2, Smith 2, Chorley 1 (pen), M'Poku 1, own goal 1.
J Paint Trophy (1): Cox 1.

Jones J 35	Omozusi E 39 + 1	Liddle M 1	Chambers A 23 + 6	Chorley B 28 + 1	Forbes T 32 + 2	Dawson S 39 + 1	Spring M 39	McGleish S 27 + 12	Revell A 35 + 4	Cox D 44 + 1	Tehoue J 9 + 23	Smith J 25 + 6	Cestor M 2	Daniels C 41 + 1	Porter G — + 1	Jarvis R 3 + 8	Patulea A — + 1	Frampton A 1	Walker J — + 11	Brown A 4 + 1	M'Poku P 9 + 18	Butcher L 8 + 1	Whing A 23 + 1	Brown J 3	Kane H 9 + 9	Crowe J 5 + 7	Carroll T 8 + 4	Barrett A 14	Match No.
1	2	3	4^1	5	6	7	8	9^2	10	11	12	13																	1
1	2		4^2	5	6	7	8	9	10^3	11				3^1	12	13	14												2
1	2		4	5	6	7	8		10	11^{12}	13			3	9^1	12													3
1	2		4	5	6	7	8	9^2	10	11	12			3^1		13													4
1	2		4^1	5	6	7	8	9	10^2	11		3				12	13												5
1	2		4	5	6	7	8^2	9^2	10	11	12		13	3^1	14														6
1	2		4	5		7	8		10	11		3		9^1		12	6												7
1	2		4^1	5	6	7	8	9	10	11	12	3																	8
1	2		4^1	5	6	7	8	9^2	10	11		3			13	12													9
1^6	2		4^2	5	6	7	8	12	10	11		13		3	9^1				15										10
	2		4	5	6	7	8	9	10^1	11^2	13			3		12				13	1								11
	2		4	5	6		8	9	10^2	11^1	12	7		3					13	1									12
	2		4	5	6		8	9^2	12	11		10		3		13			7^1	1									13
	2	13	5	6	7	8		10^3	11^2	14	4			3	9^1				12	1									14
	2		4	5	6		8		10^1	7	12	11^{12}	9	3		13^1			1	3									15
	2			5	6	7^1	8	14	10^3	11		4		3		13			9^2	1	12								16
	2			5	6		8	9^1	10	11	12	4		3^4		14	13	7^3			1								17
	2			6		8	13	10^3	11	9^2	4			3		14	5	12	7^1	1									18
	2				7	8	9	10	12	6				3		13	5	11^2	4	1									19
1	2	13	5		7	8	9^2	10	12	14	6			3			4^1	11^3											20
1	4	14	5		7	8^3	9	10^1	11^2	12	6			3		13	2												21
1			5	6	4	8^1	9^2	10	11		7	3				12	2	13											22
1			5	6	4	8	12^2	10	11^3	14	7	3				13	2	9^1											23
1			5	6	4^1	8	9	10	11^1	13	7	3				14	2	12											24
1	4^1		5	6	12	8^3		10	11	9^2	7	3				13	2				14								25
1	5			6	4		13	12	11	9^1	8	3				7^2	2			10^3	14								26
1			5	6	4	8^1	9^3	10^2	11	13	7	3					2	14	12										27
1			5	6	4		9	10	11^2		7^1	3				13	2	12	8	14									28
1			6		5	4		10^1	11	12	7	3				9^2	2		12	8	13								29
1	14		5	6	4^1			10	11	9^2	7	3^3				13	2	12		8									30
1	5			6	4	8	13	10^2	11^3	12		3				14	2	9^1		7									31
1	5	13		6	4	8	14	10^1	11	12		3					2	9^3		7^2									32
1	5				4	8	12	10^1	11	13		3				14	2	9^2		7^3	6								33
1	5	12			4^1	8	14	10^3	11		7	3				9^2	2	13			6								34
1	5		13			8	9	10^1	11	12	7	3				14	2^2			4^3	6								35
1	5	7^3		4	8	13		11	10^2			3^1				14	2	9	12		6								36
1	2		5	13	4^1	8^4	9	14	11	10^3	12									3	7^2	6							37
1	2			5	4		9^1	10^2	11	12	8	3				14		13		7^3	6								38
1	5	7		4		9^2	10^1	11	12	8	3				2	13			6										39
1	5	8^3		4	9		11	10^1	7^2		3				14	2	12	13		6									40
1	5	7		4	8	9^3		11	14		3				12	2^2	10^1	13		6									41
1	5	7		4^1	8	9^2		11	13		3		14			2	10^3	12		6									42
1	2	7		5	4	8	9^1		11	12	3^3	13				10^2	14			6									43
	2	7		5	4	10	12		11^2	9^1	3	13			1					8	6								44
1	2	7^1		5	4	8	12		11	9^2	3		14				10^3		13	6									45
	2	14	12	5	4	8^1	9^2	13	11		3		10	1					7^3	6									46

FA Cup		
First Round	Dagenham & R	(a) 1-1
		(h) 3-2
Second Round	Droylsden	(a) 1-1
		(h) 8-2
Third Round	Norwich C	(a) 1-0
Fourth Round	Swansea C	(a) 2-1
Fifth Round	Arsenal	(h) 1-1
		(a) 0-5
Carling Cup		
First Round	Swindon T	(a) 2-1
Second Round	WBA	(h) 0-2
J Paint Trophy		
First Round	Brighton & HA	(a) 1-0
Second Round	Brentford	(h) 0-0

LINCOLN CITY   Blue Square Premier

FOUNDATION

The original Lincoln Football Club was established in the early 1860s and was one of the first provisional clubs to affiliate to the Football Association. In their early years, they regularly played matches against the famous Sheffield Club and later became known as Lincoln Lindum. The present organisation was formed at a public meeting held in the Monson Arms Hotel in June 1884 and won the Lincolnshire Cup in only their third season. They were founder members of the Midland League in 1889 and that competition's first champions.

Sincil Bank Stadium, Sincil Bank, Lincoln LN5 8LD.
Telephone: (01522) 880 011.
Fax: (01522) 880 020.
Ticket Office: (01522) 880 011.
Website: www.redimps.com
Email: lcfc@redimps.com
Ground Capacity: 10,120.
Record Attendance: 23,196 v Derby Co, League Cup 4th rd, 15 November 1967.
Pitch Measurements: 100m × 65m.
Chairman: Bob Dorrian.
Football Secretary: Fran Martin.
Manager: Steve Tilson.
Assistant Manager: Paul Brush.
Physio: Kevin Oxby.
Colours: Red and white striped shirts, black shorts, red stockings.
Change Colours: Grey shirts with dark blue sleeves, dark blue shorts, dark blue stockings.
Year Formed: 1884. *Turned Professional:* 1892. *Ltd Co.:* 1895.
Club Nickname: 'The Red Imps'.
Grounds: 1883, John O'Gaunt's; 1894, Sincil Bank.
First Football League Game: 3 September 1892, Division 2, v Sheffield U (a) L 2–4 – William Gresham; Coulton, Neill; Shaw, Mettam, Moore; Smallman, Irving (1), Cameron (1), Kelly, James Gresham.
Record League Victory: 11–1 v Crewe Alex, Division 3 (N), 29 September 1951 – Jones; Green (1p), Varney; Wright, Emery, Grummett (1); Troops (1), Garvey, Graver (6), Whittle (1), Johnson (1).
Record Cup Victory: 8–1 v Bromley, FA Cup 2nd rd, 10 December 1938 – McPhail; Hartshorne, Corbett; Bean, Leach, Whyte (1); Hancock, Wilson (1), Ponting (3), Deacon (1), Clare (2).
Record Defeat: 3–11 v Manchester C, Division 2, 23 March 1895.
Most League Points (2 for a win): 74, Division 4, 1975–76.

HONOURS

Football League – Division 2:
Best season: 5th, 1901–02;
Division 3 (N): *Champions* 1931–32, 1947–48, 1951–52;
Runners-up 1927–28, 1930–31, 1936–37;
Division 4: *Champions* 1975–76;
Runners-up 1980–81.
FA Cup: Best season: 1st rd of Second Series (5th rd equivalent), 1887, 2nd rd (5th rd equivalent), 1890, 1902.
Football League Cup: Best season: 4th rd, 1968.
GM Vauxhall Conference:
Champions 1987–88.

sky SPORTS FACT FILE

Versatile George Whyte holds the Lincoln City record for the number of consecutive League appearances. Between April 1934 and September 1938 he made 183. His career total in League and Cup was 322, having played wing-half, inside-forward and on both wings.

Most League Points (3 for a win): 77, Division 3, 1981–82.

Most League Goals: 121, Division 3 (N), 1951–52.

Highest League Scorer in Season: Allan Hall, 41, Division 3 (N), 1931–32.

Most League Goals in Total Aggregate: Andy Graver, 143, 1950–55 and 1958–61.

Most League Goals in One Match: 6, Frank Keetley v Halifax T, Division 3 (N), 16 January 1932; 6, Andy Graver v Crewe Alex, Division 3 (N), 29 September 1951.

Most Capped Player: Gareth McAuley, 5 (30), Northern Ireland.

Most League Appearances: Grant Brown, 407, 1989–2002.

Youngest League Player: Shane Nicholson, 16 years 172 days v Burnley, 22 November 1986.

Record Transfer Fee Received: £750,000 from Liverpool for Jack Hobbs, August 2005.

Record Transfer Fee Paid: £75,000 to Carlisle U for Dean Walling, October 1997 and £75,000 to Bury for Tony Battersby, August 1998.

Football League Record: 1892 Founder member of Division 2. Remained in Division 2 until 1920 when they failed re-election but also missed seasons 1908–09 and 1911–12 when not re-elected. 1921–32 Division 3 (N); 1932–34 Division 2; 1934–48 Division 3 (N); 1948–49 Division 2; 1949–52 Division 3 (N); 1952–61 Division 2; 1961–62 Division 3; 1962–76 Division 4; 1976–79 Division 3; 1979–81 Division 4; 1981–86 Division 3; 1986–87 Division 4; 1987–88 GM Vauxhall Conference; 1988–92 Division 4; 1992–98 Division 3; 1998–99 Division 2; 1999–2004 Division 3; 2004–11 FL 2; 2011– Blue Square Premier.

LATEST SEQUENCES

Longest Sequence of League Wins: 10, 1.9.1930 – 18.10.1930.

Longest Sequence of League Defeats: 12, 21.9.1896 – 9.1.1897.

Longest Sequence of League Draws: 5, 21.2.1981 – 7.3.1981.

Longest Sequence of Unbeaten League Matches: 18, 11.3.1980 – 13.9.1980.

Longest Sequence Without a League Win: 19, 22.8.1978 – 23.12.1978.

Successive Scoring Runs: 37 from 1.3.1930.

Successive Non-scoring Runs: 5 from 15.11.1913.

MANAGERS

Alf Martin 1896–97
(Secretary/Manager)
David Calderhead 1900–07
John Henry Strawson 1907–14
(had been Secretary)
George Fraser 1919–21
David Calderhead Jnr. 1921–24
Horace Henshall 1924–27
Harry Parkes 1927–36
Joe McClelland 1936–46
Bill Anderson 1946–65
(General Manager to 1966)
Roy Chapman 1965–66
Ron Gray 1966–70
Bert Loxley 1970–71
David Herd 1971–72
Graham Taylor 1972–77
George Kerr 1977–78
Willie Bell 1977–78
Colin Murphy 1978–85
John Pickering 1985
George Kerr 1985–87
Peter Daniel 1987
Colin Murphy 1987–90
Allan Clarke 1990
Steve Thompson 1990–93
Keith Alexander 1993–94
Sam Ellis 1994–95
Steve Wicks (Head Coach) 1995
John Beck 1995–98
Shane Westley 1998
John Reames 1998–2000
Phil Stant 2000–01
Alan Buckley 2001–02
Keith Alexander 2002–06
John Schofield 2006–07
Peter Jackson 2007–09
Chris Sutton 2009–10
Steve Tilson October 2010–

TEN YEAR LEAGUE RECORD

		P	W	D	L	F	A	Pts	Pos
2001-02	Div 3	46	10	16	20	44	62	46	22
2002-03	Div 3	46	18	16	12	46	37	70	6
2003-04	Div 3	46	19	17	10	68	47	74	7
2004-05	FL 2	46	20	12	14	64	47	72	6
2005-06	FL 2	46	15	21	10	65	53	66	7
2006-07	FL 2	46	21	11	14	70	59	74	5
2007-08	FL 2	46	18	4	24	61	77	58	15
2008-09	FL 2	46	14	17	15	53	52	59	13
2009-10	FL 2	46	13	11	22	42	65	50	20
2010-11	FL 2	46	13	8	25	45	81	47	23

DID YOU KNOW ?

When Alex McCulloch arrived at Lincoln City as a forward in 1919 having played for Hearts in the Scottish Victory Cup final, he had been with twelve clubs making League outings for Middlesbrough, Newcastle United and Bradford Park Avenue. He then moved on to Merthyr and Llanelli!

LINCOLN CITY 2010–11 LEAGUE RECORD

Match No.	Date	Venue	Opponents	Result	H/T Score	Lg Pos.	Goalscorers	Attendance
1	Aug 7	A	Rotherham U	L 1-2	0-1	—	Carayol [52]	3772
2	14	H	Torquay U	L 0-2	0-1	24		3033
3	21	A	Gillingham	W 1-0	1-0	15	Hughton [9]	4838
4	28	H	Crewe Alex	D 1-1	1-1	15	Jarrett [40]	3024
5	Sept 4	A	Chesterfield	L 1-2	0-1	18	Hutchinson, B [88]	6429
6	11	H	Barnet	W 1-0	1-0	15	Hutchinson, B (pen) [16]	2884
7	17	A	Accrington S	L 0-3	0-2	—		1844
8	25	H	Stevenage	L 0-1	0-1	21		3215
9	28	H	Burton Alb	D 0-0	0-0	—		2510
10	Oct 2	A	Southend U	L 0-1	0-1	22		5154
11	9	H	Macclesfield T	W 2-1	0-0	20	Swaibu [38], Clapham [68]	3047
12	16	A	Shrewsbury T	L 0-2	0-2	21		5453
13	23	H	Stockport Co	D 0-0	0-0	21		4809
14	30	A	Wycombe W	D 2-2	1-2	22	Carayol [21], Hutchinson, B [69]	4325
15	Nov 2	H	Northampton T	L 0-2	0-1	—		4459
16	13	A	Morecambe	W 2-1	0-1	21	Swaibu [52], Grimes [57]	2085
17	20	H	Hereford U	W 3-1	2-0	17	Hutchinson, B [27], Facey [34], Carayol [57]	3888
18	23	H	Bury	L 0-5	0-3	—		3659
19	Jan 1	H	Bradford C	L 1-2	1-2	22	Grimes (pen) [25]	3225
20	3	A	Northampton T	L 1-2	0-0	22	O'Keefe [75]	4112
21	15	H	Wycombe W	L 1-2	1-2	24	McCallum [17]	2890
22	22	A	Stockport Co	W 4-3	2-1	24	Grimes 3 [5, 60, 65], Watts [45]	4348
23	25	A	Cheltenham T	W 2-1	2-1	—	Hunt [9], O'Keefe [22]	2292
24	29	H	Port Vale	W 1-0	0-0	—	Grimes [86]	3370
25	Feb 1	A	Bradford C	W 2-1	1-1	19	Facey [42], McCallum [79]	10,543
26	5	A	Hereford U	W 1-0	1-0	15	Facey [29]	2776
27	8	H	Shrewsbury T	L 1-5	1-5	—	Grimes [7]	3202
28	12	H	Morecambe	W 2-0	2-0	13	Grimes 2 [10, 42]	2884
29	15	A	Aldershot T	D 2-2	0-1	—	O'Keefe [65], Grimes [86]	1847
30	19	H	Chesterfield	L 0-2	0-1	15		4172
31	26	A	Barnet	L 2-4	0-3	16	Howell [47], Grimes [50]	2226
32	Mar 1	H	Oxford U	W 3-1	1-1	—	O'Keefe [5], Worley (og) [63], Tonkin (og) [67]	2261
33	5	H	Accrington S	D 0-0	0-0	15		2868
34	8	A	Burton Alb	L 1-3	0-1	—	Grimes [82]	2051
35	12	H	Southend U	W 2-1	1-0	15	Grimes 2 [38, 78]	3560
36	15	A	Macclesfield T	D 1-1	1-0	—	Hunt [19]	1067
37	19	A	Stevenage	L 1-2	1-1	16	Grimes (pen) [33]	2732
38	25	H	Rotherham U	L 0-6	0-2	—		3766
39	29	A	Port Vale	L 1-2	1-0	—	McCallum [3]	4636
40	Apr 2	A	Torquay U	L 0-2	0-0	18		2751
41	9	H	Gillingham	L 0-4	0-2	20		3022
42	16	A	Crewe Alex	D 1-1	0-0	20	Green [47]	3731
43	22	A	Bury	L 0-1	0-0	—		4248
44	25	H	Cheltenham T	L 0-2	0-0	21		3007
45	30	A	Oxford U	L 1-2	1-0	22	Hughton [5]	7485
46	May 7	H	Aldershot T	L 0-3	0-0	23		7932

Final League Position: 23

GOALSCORERS

League (45): Grimes 15 (2 pens), Hutchinson, B 4 (1 pen), O'Keefe 4, Carayol 3, Facey 3, McCallum 3, Hughton 2, Hunt 2, Swaibu 2, Clapham 1, Green 1, Howell 1, Jarrett 1, Watts 1, own goals 2.
Carling Cup (0).
FA Cup (6): Grimes 2, Carayol 1, Clapham 1, Facey 1, Jarrett 1.
J Paint Trophy (0).

Anyon J 21	Green P 14+3	Anderson J 19+3	Watts A 40	Swaibu M 12	Carayol M 24+9	O'Keefe J 33+4	Hughton C 17+5	Broughton D 9+14	Pearce I 3+1	Jarrett A 19+3	Keltie C 16+2	Kerr S 10+6	McCallum G 24+12	Clapham J 21+4	Facey D 26+6	Hutchinson A —+5	Hutchinson B 26+10	Musselwhite P —+1	Turner S —+2	Hoyte G 11+1	Howell L 23+2	Grimes A 24+3	Gowling J 4	Hone D 25+1	Kelly J 21	Carson T 16	Hunt S 14	Kanyuka P 2+4	Fuseini A 15+3	Spencer S 2+8	Parish E 9	Kilbey T 6+1	Match No.
1	2	3	4¹	5¹		7	8	9	10	12	11	13	6²	14																			1
1	2		4	5³		7	8	3	10²	11	6	9¹	14	12	13																		2
1	2	3	4			7	13	5	11¹	8		6	9		12		10²																3
1	2	3	4			7	12	5	11¹	8		6	9		13		10²																4
1	2	3	4		11		13	7	5³	8²	14	6	9¹		12		10																5
1	5	3	4			7		2	10²	11	8¹	12	6		13		9																6
1	2	3	4			7³	8	5	9²	11	12	6¹		14	13		10																7
1		3	4	5		7¹	8	2	13	11	10	12	6²		14		9³																8
1		3	4	5		12	8	2	10¹	7	6	13			11		9²																9
1⁶		3	4	5		12	8	2	10¹	7	6				11		9	15															10
1			4	5		7²	8¹	2	11³	6	12	13			10		9		14														11
1			4	5		7¹	8	2	11	10	6	13		3			9²		12														12
1			4	5		7	13	2	10	11¹	8	6²			12	3	9																13
1	12		4	5		7			10	11¹	8³	14			3		9²			2	6	13											14
1			4					7³	10¹	11	8	14			3	12	9²			2	6	13		5									15
1	14		5					7	13	11³		6			3	12	9¹			2	8²	10	4										16
1	13		4					7¹		8	12	14	9³	6	11²	3				2		10		5									17
1			4					7¹		8	12	14	9³	6	11²	3	13			2		10		5									18
1			4	5				7³		8		14	9	6¹	11²	12	3			2	10	13											19
1	14	3	4³			7				13	12		9		11²		8¹			2	6	10		5									20
1	2¹			5		7					4	3	9		11²	12	13			2	6	10											21
			4			7¹	8			13	12	11	9								6	10²		5	2	1	3						22
			4				8			12	11	7²	9		13						6	10¹		5	2	1	3						23
			4				8			13	12	11	7¹		9²		14				6	10⁴		5	2	1	3						24
						7	8			13	11		9²							2	6	10		5		1	14	3³	4¹	12			25
			4				8			12	11¹		9²							2	6	10³		5	7	1	3		14	13			26
			4				8			13	11		9²							2	6	10³		5	7	1	3¹	12		14			27
			4				13	7		11		3	9				14				6	10		5	2¹	1	12	8²					28
	2³		4				12	7	14	11		3	9²		13						6	10		5	1		8¹						29
			4				13	7		11³		9	14							2¹	6²	10		5	8	1	3	12					30
			4				12	7¹		11			9³	13							6	10²		5	2	1	3	8	14				31
			4				12	7		11			9²	13							6¹	10³		5	2	1	3	8	14				32
			4				6	7		11			9	12								10¹		5	2	1	3	8					33
			4				7	6		11²		12	9³	13								10		5	2	1	3	8¹	14				34
			4				7	8		6			9	11								10¹		5	2	1	3	12					35
			4				7¹	8		12		6²	9	11●	13					13	10³			5	2	1	3	14					36
			14				4	7	8	12				11						13	6¹	10²		5	2	1	3³		9				37
	3		4			7	13			11			9								12	2						5¹	8	10¹	1	6²	38
13	3		4			7	10	12		11			9								5²	2							8		1	6¹	39
	3		4			7¹	10	12	14	11			9³	13							6	10³		5	2				8		1	13	40
	3		4			7¹				12			11									9²		5	2				8	14	1	13	41
	2	3							10	11			9		7						5	6							8		1	4	42
	6	3				12	7¹	2	13	11			9³								10			5					8	14	1	4²	43
	6	3					2	13	12	11			9²		7						10			5					8		1	4¹	44
	2	3	4			7			10	11					6						9	5●							8		1		45
	5	3	4			2			7	11		10		12	6						9								8¹		1		46

FA Cup

First Round	Nuneaton Bor	(h)	1-0
Second Round	Hereford U	(a)	2-2
		(h)	3-4

Carling Cup

First Round	Leeds U	(a)	0-4

J Paint Trophy

First Round	Rotherham U	(a)	0-1

LIVERPOOL   FA Premiership

FOUNDATION

But for a dispute between Everton FC and their landlord at
Anfield in 1892, there may never have been a Liverpool club. This
dispute persuaded the majority of Evertonians to quit Anfield for
Goodison Park, leaving the landlord, Mr John Houlding, to form a
new club. He originally tried to retain the name 'Everton' but
when this failed, he founded Liverpool Association FC on
15 March 1892.

*Anfield Stadium, Anfield Road, Liverpool
L4 0TH.*

Telephone: (0151) 260 1433.

Fax: (0151) 260 8813.

Ticket Office: (0151) 260 8680.

Website: www.liverpoolfc.tv

Email: customercontact@liverpoolfc.tv or
customerservices@liverpoolfc.tv

Ground Capacity: 45,522.

Record Attendance: 61,905 v Wolverhampton
W, FA Cup 4th rd, 2 February 1952.

Pitch Measurements: 101m × 68m.

Chairman: Tom Werner.

Vice-Chairman: David Ginsberg.

Managing Director: Ian Ayre.

Secretary: Ian Silvester.

Manager: Kenny Dalglish.

Assistant Manager: Steve Clarke.

First Team Coach: Kevin Keen.

Physio: Rob Price.

Colours: All red with white trim.

Change Colours: All black with yellow trim.

Year Formed: 1892.

Turned Professional: 1892.

Ltd Co.: 1892.

Club Nicknames: 'Reds' or 'Pool'.

Ground: 1892, Anfield.

HONOURS

FA Premier League: *Runners-up* 2001–02,
2008–09.
Football League – Division 1:
Champions 1900–01, 1905–06, 1921–22, 1922–23,
1946–47, 1963–64, 1965–66, 1972–73, 1975–76,
1976–77, 1978–79, 1979–80, 1981–82, 1982–83,
1983–84, 1985–86, 1987–88, 1989–90; *Runners-up*
1898–99, 1909–10, 1968–69, 1973–74, 1974–75,
1977–78, 1984–85, 1986–87, 1988–89, 1990–91;
Division 2: *Champions* 1893–94, 1895–96,
1904–05, 1961–62.
FA Cup: *Winners* 1965, 1974, 1986, 1989, 1992,
2001, 2006; *Runners-up* 1914, 1950, 1971, 1977,
1988, 1996.
Football League Cup: *Winners* 1981, 1982, 1983,
1984, 1995, 2001, 2003; *Runners-up* 1978, 1987,
2005.
League Super Cup: *Winners* 1986.
European Competitions: European Cup: 1964–65,
1966–67, 1973–74, 1976–77 (*winners*), 1977–78
(*winners*), 1978–79, 1979–80, 1980–81 (*winners*),
1981–82, 1982–83, 1983–84 (*winners*), 1984–85
(*runners-up*). **Champions League:** 2001–02,
2002–03, 2004–05 (*winners*), 2005–06, 2006–07
(*runners-up*), 2007–08 (*s-f*), 2008–09 (*q-f*),
2009–10. **European Cup-Winners' Cup:** 1965–66
(*runners-up*), 1971–72, 1974–75, 1992–93, 1996–97
(*s-f*). **European Fairs Cup:** 1967–68, 1968–69,
1969–70, 1970–71. **UEFA Cup:** 1972–73 (*winners*),
1975–76 (*winners*), 1991–92, 1995–96, 1997–98,
1998–99, 2000–01 (*winners*), 2002–03, 2003–04.
Europa League: 2009–10, 2010–11. **Super Cup:**
1977 (*winners*), 1978, 1984, 2001 (*winners*), 2005
(*winners*). **World Club Championship:** 1981, 1984.
FIFA Club World Cup: 2005.

First Football League Game: 2 September 1893, Division 2, v Middlesbrough Ironopolis (a) W 2–0 –
McOwen; Hannah, McLean; Henderson, McQue (1), McBride; Gordon, McVean (1), Matt McQueen,
Stott, Hugh McQueen.

sky SPORTS FACT FILE

On 16 January 1926 Liverpool won 2-1 away to West
Ham United. They took the lead after 15 minutes with a
shot from full-back Donald McKinlay from fully 75 yards.
Ahead of his time as an attacking defender this Scottish
international had 19 successful seasons at Anfield.

Record League Victory: 10–1 v Rotherham T, Division 2, 18 February 1896 – Storer; Goldie, Wilkie; McCartney, McQue, Holmes; McVean (3), Ross (2), Allan (4), Becton (1), Bradshaw.

Record Cup Victory: 11–0 v Stromsgodset Drammen, ECWC 1st rd 1st leg, 17 September 1974 – Clemence; Smith (1), Lindsay (1p), Thompson (2), Cormack (1), Hughes (1), Boersma (2), Hall, Heighway (1), Kennedy (1), Callaghan (1).

Record Defeat: 1–9 v Birmingham C, Division 2, 11 December 1954.

Most League Points (2 for a win): 68, Division 1, 1978–79.

Most League Points (3 for a win): 90, Division 1, 1987–88.

Most League Goals: 106, Division 2, 1895–96.

Highest League Scorer in Season: Roger Hunt, 41, Division 2, 1961–62.

Most League Goals in Total Aggregate: Roger Hunt, 245, 1959–69.

Most League Goals in One Match: 5, Andy McGuigan v Stoke C, Division 1, 4 January 1902; 5, John Evans v Bristol R, Division 2, 15 September 1954; 5, Ian Rush v Luton T, Division 1, 29 October 1983.

Most Capped Player: Steven Gerrard, 89, England.

Most League Appearances: Ian Callaghan, 640, 1960–78.

Youngest League Player: Jack Robinson, 16 years 250 days v Hull C, 9 May 2010.

Record Transfer Fee Received: £50,000,000 from Chelsea for Fernando Torres, January 2011.

Record Transfer Fee Paid: £35,000,000 to Newcastle U for Andy Carroll, January 2011.

Football League Record: 1893 Elected to Division 2; 1894–95 Division 1; 1895–96 Division 2; 1896–1904 Division 1; 1904–05 Division 2; 1905–54 Division 1; 1954–62 Division 2; 1962–92 Division 1; 1992– FA Premier League.

MANAGERS
W. E. Barclay 1892–96
Tom Watson 1896–1915
David Ashworth 1920–23
Matt McQueen 1923–28
George Patterson 1928–36
(continued as Secretary)
George Kay 1936–51
Don Welsh 1951–56
Phil Taylor 1956–59
Bill Shankly 1959–74
Bob Paisley 1974–83
Joe Fagan 1983–85
Kenny Dalglish 1985–91
Graeme Souness 1991–94
Roy Evans 1994–98
(then Joint Manager)
Gerard Houllier 1998–2004
Rafael Benitez 2004–10
Roy Hodgson 2010–11
Kenny Dalglish January 2011–

LATEST SEQUENCES

Longest Sequence of League Wins: 12, 21.4.1990 – 6.10.1990.

Longest Sequence of League Defeats: 9, 29.4.1899 – 14.10.1899.

Longest Sequence of League Draws: 6, 19.2.1975 – 19.3.1975.

Longest Sequence of Unbeaten League Matches: 31, 4.5.1987 – 16.3.1988.

Longest Sequence Without a League Win: 14, 12.12.1953 – 20.3.1954.

Successive Scoring Runs: 29 from 27.4.1957.

Successive Non-scoring Runs: 5 from 22.12.1906.

TEN YEAR LEAGUE RECORD		P	W	D	L	F	A	Pts	Pos
2001-02	PR Lge	38	24	8	6	67	30	80	2
2002-03	PR Lge	38	18	10	10	61	41	64	5
2003-04	PR Lge	38	16	12	10	55	37	60	4
2004-05	PR Lge	38	17	7	14	52	41	58	5
2005-06	PR Lge	38	25	7	6	57	25	82	3
2006-07	PR Lge	38	20	8	10	57	27	68	3
2007-08	PR Lge	38	21	13	4	67	28	76	4
2008-09	PR Lge	38	25	11	2	77	27	86	2
2009-10	PR Lge	38	18	9	11	61	35	63	7
2010-11	PR Lge	38	17	7	14	59	44	58	6

DID YOU KNOW ?

The last weekend of the 1992–93 season, 8-9 May, was one of high scoring in the Premier League with the eleven matches producing no fewer than 53 goals. Top scorers on the day were Liverpool with a 6-2 victory over Tottenham Hotspur.

LIVERPOOL 2010–11 LEAGUE RECORD

Match No.	Date	Venue	Opponents	Result		H/T Score	Lg Pos.	Goalscorers	Atten- dance
1	Aug 15	H	Arsenal	D	1-1	0-0	—	N'Gog [46]	44,722
2	23	A	Manchester C	L	0-3	0-1	—		47,087
3	29	H	WBA	W	1-0	0-0	13	Torres [65]	41,194
4	Sept 12	A	Birmingham C	D	0-0	0-0	13		27,333
5	19	A	Manchester U	L	2-3	0-1	16	Gerrard 2 (1 pen) [64 (p), 70]	75,213
6	25	H	Sunderland	D	2-2	1-1	16	Kuyt [5], Gerrard [64]	43,626
7	Oct 3	H	Blackpool	L	1-2	0-2	18	Kyrgiakos [53]	43,156
8	17	A	Everton	L	0-2	0-1	19		39,673
9	24	H	Blackburn R	W	2-1	0-0	18	Kyrgiakos [48], Torres [53]	43,328
10	31	A	Bolton W	W	1-0	0-0	12	Rodriguez [86]	25,171
11	Nov 7	H	Chelsea	W	2-0	2-0	9	Torres 2 [11, 44]	44,238
12	10	A	Wigan Ath	D	1-1	1-0	—	Torres [7]	16,754
13	13	A	Stoke C	L	0-2	0-0	11		27,286
14	20	H	West Ham U	W	3-0	3-0	9	Johnson [18], Kuyt (pen) [27], Rodriguez [38]	43,024
15	28	A	Tottenham H	L	1-2	1-0	10	Skrtel [42]	35,962
16	Dec 6	A	Aston Villa	W	3-0	2-0	—	N'Gog [14], Babel [16], Rodriguez [55]	39,079
17	11	A	Newcastle U	L	1-3	0-1	9	Kuyt [49]	50,137
18	29	H	Wolverhampton W	L	0-1	0-0	—		41,614
19	Jan 1	H	Bolton W	W	2-1	0-1	9	Torres [49], Cole [90]	35,400
20	5	A	Blackburn R	L	1-3	0-2	12	Gerrard [81]	24,522
21	12	A	Blackpool	L	1-2	1-1	—	Torres [3]	16,089
22	16	H	Everton	D	2-2	1-0	13	Raul Meireles [29], Kuyt (pen) [68]	44,795
23	22	A	Wolverhampton W	W	3-0	1-0	11	Torres 2 [36, 90], Raul Meireles [50]	28,869
24	26	H	Fulham	W	1-0	0-0	—	Pantsil (og) [52]	40,466
25	Feb 2	H	Stoke C	W	2-0	0-0	—	Raul Meireles [47], Suarez [79]	40,254
26	6	A	Chelsea	W	1-0	0-0	6	Raul Meireles [69]	41,829
27	12	H	Wigan Ath	D	1-1	1-0	6	Raul Meireles [24]	44,609
28	27	A	West Ham U	L	1-3	0-2	6	Johnson [84]	34,941
29	Mar 6	H	Manchester U	W	3-1	2-0	6	Kuyt 3 [34, 39, 65]	44,753
30	20	A	Sunderland	W	2-0	1-0	6	Kuyt (pen) [34], Suarez [77]	47,207
31	Apr 2	A	WBA	L	1-2	0-0	6	Skrtel [50]	26,196
32	11	H	Manchester C	W	3-0	3-0	—	Carroll 2 [13, 35], Kuyt [34]	44,776
33	17	A	Arsenal	D	1-1	0-0	6	Kuyt (pen) [90]	60,029
34	23	H	Birmingham C	W	5-0	2-0	6	Rodriguez 3 [7, 66, 73], Kuyt [23], Cole [86]	44,734
35	May 1	H	Newcastle U	W	3-0	1-0	5	Rodriguez [10], Kuyt (pen) [59], Suarez [65]	44,923
36	9	A	Fulham	W	5-2	3-0	—	Rodriguez 3 [1, 7, 70], Kuyt [16], Suarez [75]	25,693
37	15	H	Tottenham H	L	0-2	0-1	6		44,893
38	22	A	Aston Villa	L	0-1	0-1	6		42,785

Final League Position: 6

GOALSCORERS

League (59): Kuyt 13 (5 pens), Rodriguez 10, Torres 9, Raul Meireles 5, Gerrard 4 (1 pen), Suarez 4, Carroll 2, Cole 2, Johnson 2, Kyrgiakos 2, N'Gog 2, Skrtel 2, Babel 1, own goal 1.
Carling Cup (2): Jovanovic 1, N'Gog 1.
FA Cup (0).
Europa League (16): N'Gog 5 (1 pen), Gerrard 4 (2 pens), Kuyt 2, Babel 1, Cole 1, Jovanovic 1, Lucas 1, own goal 1.

Reina J 38	Johnson G 28	Skrtel M 38	Mascherano J 1	Carragher J 28	Agger D 12+4	Jovanovic M 5+5	Gerrard S 20+1	N'Gog D 9+16	Cole J 9+11	Kuyt D 32+1	Rodriguez M 24+4	Torres F 22+1	Lucas 32+1	Babel R 1+8	Pacheco D —+1	Poulsen C 9+3	Konchesky P 15	Raul Meireles 32+1	Kyrgiakos S 10+6	Shelvey J —+15	Kelly M 10+1	Spearing J 10+1	Eccleston N —+1	Fabio Aurelio 7+7	Suarez L 12+1	Wilson D 1+1	Carroll A 5+2	Flanagan J 7	Robinson J 1+1	Match No.
1	2	3	4^3	5	6	7^1	8	9^2	10^8	11	12	13	14																	1
1	2	3		5	6	7^2	8	9		10	11^1	4	12	13																2
1	2	3		5	6	11^1	10			7	12	9^2	4	13		8														3
1	2	4		5	13	10	8			7		9	11^1			6	3^2	12												4
1	2	6		5	14	13	8	12	10		11^1	9				7	3^3	4^2												5
1	2	6		5	12		8	13	11	10		9				4^2	3^1	7												6
1		6		5	13	8	12	10^3	11	14	9^1					7^2	4	3												7
1		6		2	14		8	12	10^2	7^3	9	11^1	13				3	4	5											8
1		6		2			8	12	10^1	7	9	11					3	4^2	5	13										9
1		6		2			8	12	10^1	7	9	11	13				3	4^2	5											10
1		6		5			8	13	10^1	7	9^2	11						3	4^3		12	2	14							11
1		6		5			8	10^2		7^3	9	11	13					3	4^1		12	2	14							12
1	2	6					8	12	10		7^2	9	11^8	13				3	4^1		5									13
1	2	6		5				10¹		7	11	9^3	14			8		3	4^2		13			12						14
1	2	6		5^2				10^1		7	8	9	11					3	4		13			12						15
1	2	6				9	13			7^2	10^1	8	11					3	4		5^3	14		12						16
1	2	6					13	10^1		7	11^2	9	8	12				3	4		5									17
1	2	6					8	10^1	14	7	9	11	12				3^2	4^3	5	13										18
1	2	6		5^3			12	10^2	13	7	11	9	8					4^1	14	3										19
1	2	6				12	4	10^3	11	13	7^2	9	8	14			3	5^1												20
1	2	6		5	11		13	10^1		9	8	7^7					4	12	3											21
1	2	6		5^1				10	11	9	8						4^2	12	13	3	7									22
1	2	6		5				7	10^2	9	11					8^1		4	12	3		13								23
1	2	6		5				11^1	10	9						7^2		4	12	3		13								24
1	7	6		5		8		9					10			4^2	3	13	2					11^1	12					25
1	2	4		5	6	8				10	9^1	11			13	7^2		3				12								26
1	2	6		5		13			12	10^2	7		8				4^1		3		11	9								27
1	7	6		5			8	13	12	10			11				4^2		2^1			9	3							28
1	2	6		5				14	10	7			11				4^2	12			3^1	9^3	13							29
1	2	6		5	3		12	14	7	13			8				4^2				11			10^3	9^1					30
1	2^1	6		3	5^2			14	7^3				11				4	12			8			10	13	9				31
1		6		5			12		7				8				4				11	3	10	9^1	2					32
1		6		5^2					7				11				4	13	14		8	3^1	10	9^3	2	12				33
1		6		5			14	13	10		7^3		11				4^2	12			8			9		2	3^1			34
1	2	6		5				14	10	7^1			11				4	13			8			9^3	12	3^2				35
1	2	6		5				13	10	7^2			11				4^1	12			8			9		3				36
1	2	6		5			13	14	7	8^2			11				12	4^1			10			9^9	3					37
1		6		5			13	11^2	10				7				4	12			8^1	3	9			2				38

FA Cup
Third Round   Manchester U   (a)   0-1

Carling Cup
Third Round   Northampton T   (h)   2-2

Europa League
Third Qualifying Round

	Rabotnicki	(a)	2-0
		(h)	2-0
Play-Off	Trabzonspor	(h)	1-0
		(a)	2-1
Group K	Steaua	(h)	4-1
	Utrecht	(a)	0-0
	Napoli	(a)	0-0
		(h)	3-1
	Steaua	(a)	1-1
	Utrecht	(h)	0-0
Second Round	Sparta Prague	(a)	0-0
		(h)	1-0
Third Round	Braga	(a)	0-1
		(h)	0-0

MACCLESFIELD TOWN FL Championship 2

FOUNDATION

From the mid-19th Century until 1874, Macclesfield Town FC played under rugby rules. In 1891 they moved to the Moss Rose and finished champions of the Manchester & District League in 1906 and 1908. By 1911, they had carried off the Cheshire Senior Cup five times. Macclesfield were founder members of the Cheshire County League in 1919.

Moss Rose Ground, London Road, Macclesfield, Cheshire SK11 7SP.

Telephone: (01625) 264 686.

Fax: (01625) 264 692.

Ticket Office: (01625) 264 686.

Website: www.mtfc.co.uk

Email: office@mtfc.co.uk

Ground Capacity: 6,141.

Record Attendance: 9,008 v Winsford U, Cheshire Senior Cup 2nd rd, 4 February 1948.

Pitch Measurements: 100m × 60m.

Chairman: Mike Rance.

Vice-chairman: Andy Scott.

Company Secretary: Barrie Darcey.

Manager: Gary Simpson.

Assistant Manager: Glyn Chamberlain.

Physio: Nick Reid.

Colours: Blue shirts with white design, white shorts, blue stockings.

Change Colours: Black shirts with one yellow sleeve, black shorts, yellow stockings.

Year formed: 1874.

Club Nickname: 'The Silkmen'.

Grounds: 1874, Rostron Field; 1891, Moss Rose.

First Football League Game: 9 August 1997, Division 3, v Torquay U (h) W 2–1 – Price; Tinson, Rose, Payne (Edey), Howarth, Sodje (1), Askey, Wood, Landon (1) (Power), Mason, Sorvel.

HONOURS

Football League – Division 3: *Runners-up* 1997–98.

FA Cup: Best season: 3rd rd, 1968, 1988, 2002, 2003, 2004, 2007, 2009.

Football League Cup: never past 2nd rd.

Vauxhall Conference: *Champions* 1994–95, 1996–97.

FA Trophy: *Winners* 1969–70, 1995–96; *Runners-up* 1988–89.

Bob Lord Trophy: *Winners* 1993–94; *Runners-up* 1995–96, 1996–97.

Vauxhall Conference Championship Shield: *Winners* 1996, 1997, 1998.

Northern Premier League: *Winners* 1968–69, 1969–70, 1986–87; *Runners-up* 1984–85.

Northern Premier League Challenge Cup: *Winners* 1986–87; *Runners-up* 1969–70, 1970–71, 1982–83.

Northern Premier League Presidents Cup: *Winners* 1986–87; *Runners-up* 1984–85.

Cheshire Senior Cup: *Winners* 20 times; *Runners-up* 11.

sky SPORTS FACT FILE

The first floodlit match involving Macclesfield Town was at Ashton United on 1 November 1954 against Stalybridge Celtic. Fog delayed the start 100 minutes. The match ended at 10.20 pm, Macclesfield won 2-0 with goals from Malcolm Glazzard and Frank Monaghan.

Record League Victory: 6–0 v Stockport Co, FL 1, 26 December 2005 – Fettis; Harsley, Sandwith, Morley, Swailes (Teague), Navarro, Whitaker (Miles (1)), Bullock (1), Parkin (2), Wijnhard (2) (Townson), McIntyre.

Record Cup Victory: 15–0 v Chester St Mary's, Cheshire Senior Cup 3rd rd, 6 February 1886. 15–0 v Barnton Rovers, Cheshire Senior Cup 1st rd, 12 November 1887.

Record Win: 15–0 v Chester St Marys, Cheshire Senior Cup 2nd rd, 16 February 1886.

Record Defeat: 1–13 v Tranmere R reserves, 3 May 1929.

Most League Points (3 for a win): 82, Division 3, 1997–98.

Most League Goals: 66, Division 3, 1999–2000.

Highest League Scorer in Season: Jon Parkin, 22, FL 2, 2004–05.

Most League Goals in Total Aggregate: Matt Tipton, 50, 2002–05; 2006–07; 2009–10.

Most Capped Player: George Abbey, 10, Nigeria.

Most League Appearances: Darren Tinson, 263, 1997–2003.

Youngest League Player: Elliott Hewitt, 16 years 342 days v Hereford U, 7 May 2011.

Record Transfer Fee Received: £300,000 from Stockport Co for Rickie Lambert, April 2002.

Record Transfer Fee Paid: £40,000 to Bury for Danny Swailes, January 2005.

Football League Record: 1997 Promoted to Division 3; 1998–99 Division 2; 1999–2004 Division 3; 2004– FL 2.

MANAGERS

Since 1967
Keith Goalen 1967–68
Frank Beaumont 1968–72
Billy Haydock 1972–74
Eddie Brown 1974
John Collins 1974
Willie Stevenson 1974
John Collins 1975–76
Tony Coleman 1976
John Barnes 1976
Brian Taylor 1976
Dave Connor 1976–78
Derek Partridge 1978
Phil Staley 1978–80
Jimmy Williams 1980–81
Brian Booth 1981–85
Neil Griffiths 1985–86
Roy Campbell 1986
Peter Wragg 1986–93
Sammy McIlroy 1993–2000
Peter Davenport 2000
Gil Prescott 2000–01
David Moss 2001–03
John Askey 2003–04
Brian Horton 2004–06
Paul Ince 2006–07
Ian Brightwell 2007–08
Keith Alexander 2008–10
Gary Simpson April 2010–

LATEST SEQUENCES

Longest Sequence of League Wins: 6, 25.1.2005 – 26.2.2005.

Longest Sequence of League Defeats: 6, 26.12.1998 – 6.2.1999.

Longest Sequence of League Draws: 5, 5.5.2007 – 1.9.2007.

Longest Sequence of Unbeaten League Matches: 8, 16.10.1999 – 27.11.1999.

Longest Sequence Without a League Win: 19, 5.8.2006 – 25.11.2006.

Successive Scoring Runs: 14 from 11.10.2003.

Successive Non-scoring Runs: 5 from 18.12.1998.

TEN YEAR LEAGUE RECORD

		P	W	D	L	F	A	Pts	Pos
2001-02	Div 3	46	15	13	18	41	52	58	13
2002-03	Div 3	46	14	12	20	57	63	54	16
2003-04	Div 3	46	13	13	20	54	69	52	20
2004-05	FL 2	46	22	9	15	60	49	75	5
2005-06	FL 2	46	12	18	16	60	71	54	17
2006-07	FL 2	46	12	12	22	55	77	48	22
2007-08	FL 2	46	11	17	18	47	64	50	19
2008-09	FL 2	46	13	8	25	45	77	47	20
2009-10	FL 2	46	12	18	16	49	58	54	19
2010-11	FL 2	46	14	13	19	59	73	55	15

DID YOU KNOW ?

The last match Macclesfield Town played before the club packed up for the war period was the Cheshire Senior Cup final against Northwich Victoria at Crewe in 1940. The Silkmen just won 3-2 with goalkeeper Cliff Pitt virtually ending it with a last minute save to avoid extra time.

MACCLESFIELD TOWN 2010–11 LEAGUE RECORD

Match No.	Date	Venue	Opponents	Result	H/T Score	Lg Pos.	Goalscorers	Attendance
1	Aug 7	A	Stevenage	D	2-2	1-1	—	Brown [12], Barnett [53]	3553
2	14	H	Shrewsbury T	L	0-1	0-1	16		2302
3	21	A	Accrington S	L	0-3	0-2	23		1371
4	28	H	Chesterfield	D	1-1	0-0	22	Sinclair [74]	2176
5	Sept 4	H	Stockport Co	L	0-2	0-1	23		3683
6	11	A	Wycombe W	W	2-1	2-0	20	Daniel [11], Barnett [14]	3789
7	18	H	Port Vale	L	0-3	0-1	22		3915
8	25	A	Torquay U	W	3-1	1-1	19	Bencherif [12], Draper [76], Sinclair [78]	2551
9	28	A	Crewe Alex	D	1-1	0-0	—	Barnett [52]	3659
10	Oct 2	H	Northampton T	W	2-0	1-0	16	Bencherif [25], Brown [71]	1699
11	9	A	Lincoln C	L	1-2	0-1	18	Bencherif [55]	3047
12	16	H	Oxford U	W	3-2	0-2	13	Bolland 2 [51, 78], Hamshaw [67]	1395
13	23	A	Barnet	L	0-1	0-1	17		1594
14	30	H	Burton Alb	W	2-1	1-0	12	Bencherif 2 [29, 48]	1791
15	Nov 2	A	Rotherham U	D	1-1	0-0	—	Barnett [84]	2548
16	13	H	Aldershot T	W	2-0	1-0	10	Daniel [17], Barnett [77]	1519
17	20	A	Bradford C	W	1-0	1-0	8	Draper [23]	10,779
18	23	H	Cheltenham T	L	0-2	0-2	—		1870
19	Dec 11	H	Gillingham	L	2-4	1-4	10	Bencherif [7], Barnett [71]	1507
20	28	A	Oxford U	L	1-2	0-1	—	Sappleton [82]	9440
21	Jan 1	A	Bury	D	2-2	1-0	14	Butcher [29], Gray [69]	2860
22	3	H	Rotherham U	L	0-2	0-1	16		2316
23	22	H	Barnet	D	1-1	0-0	19	Daniel [70]	1655
24	25	A	Southend U	L	1-4	0-4	—	Daniel [79]	5011
25	Feb 1	H	Bury	L	2-4	2-3	21	Draper [37], Barnett [39]	1267
26	8	A	Hereford U	D	2-2	1-1	—	Diagne [18], Barnett [90]	1975
27	12	A	Aldershot T	D	0-0	0-0	21		2373
28	19	A	Stockport Co	W	4-1	1-1	21	Reid [33], Barnett [48], Turnbull (og) [60], Bencherif [67]	5470
29	22	H	Morecambe	W	2-0	2-0	—	Hamshaw [21], McCready (og) [26]	1286
30	26	H	Wycombe W	L	0-1	0-1	21		1622
31	Mar 5	A	Port Vale	L	1-2	0-1	21	Barnett [90]	5459
32	8	H	Crewe Alex	W	1-0	1-0	—	Draper [41]	1485
33	12	A	Northampton T	W	1-0	0-0	18	Daniel [54]	4707
34	15	H	Lincoln C	D	1-1	0-1	—	Wedgbury [90]	1067
35	19	H	Torquay U	D	3-3	2-0	18	Barnett [29], Daniel [35], Bencherif [57]	1556
36	22	A	Morecambe	W	2-1	1-0	—	Bencherif [43], Barnett [56]	1612
37	26	H	Stevenage	L	0-4	0-2	—		1346
38	30	A	Burton Alb	L	2-3	1-1	—	Sinclair 2 [1, 81]	1974
39	Apr 2	A	Shrewsbury T	L	1-4	1-1	17	Bencherif [19]	5396
40	5	H	Bradford C	L	0-1	0-1	—		1207
41	8	H	Accrington S	D	2-2	1-0	—	Bencherif [22], Mukendi [90]	1674
42	16	A	Chesterfield	L	1-2	1-0	18	Chalmers (pen) [45]	8206
43	23	A	Cheltenham T	W	1-0	1-0	16	Barnett [27]	2757
44	25	H	Southend U	D	0-0	0-0	16		1427
45	30	A	Gillingham	W	4-2	3-1	15	Draper [3], Daniel 2 [7, 17], Sinclair [48]	6841
46	May 7	H	Hereford U	D	1-1	0-1	15	Chalmers (pen) [57]	2013

Final League Position: 15

GOALSCORERS

League (59): Barnett 13, Bencherif 11, Daniel 8, Draper 5, Sinclair 5, Bolland 2, Brown 2, Chalmers 2 (2 pens), Hamshaw 2, Butcher 1, Diagne 1, Gray 1, Mukendi 1, Reid 1, Sappleton 1, Wedgbury 1, own goals 2.
Carling Cup (3): Brown 1, Daniel 1, Mukendi 1.
FA Cup (4): Brown 1, Daniel 1, Nsiala 1, Sinclair 1.
J Paint Trophy (3): Mukendi 1, own goals 2.

Veiga J 46	Reid I 34+3	Tremarco C 20+5	Bolland P 31+1	Brown N 44	Brisley S 12+2	Wedgbury S 13+10	Butcher C 5+2	Sinclair E 26+5	Barnett T 45	Hamshaw M 18+10	Daniel C 36+7	Chalmers L 22+8	Mukendi V 8+13	Bencherif H 36+5	Morgan P 27+1	Draper R 34+6	Nsiala A 10	Lowe M —+1	Sappleton R 1+9	Gray D 18+3	Diagne T 19+1	Roberts A —+2	Hewitt E 1	Match No.
1	2	3	4	5	6	7^2	8	9^1	10	11	12	13												1
1	2^3	3	4	5	6^2	12	8^1	9	10	7			14	11	13									2
1		3	4	5	2	8		9	10	7	13			11^2	6^1	12								3
1	2	3	4	5				9	10^1	7	11	12			6	8								4
1	2	3	4	5				9^1	10	7	11	12		13	6	8^2								5
1	2	3	4	5		13		9^2	10		11	12		7	6	8^1								6
1	2	3	4	5				9^1	10	13	11	12		7	6	8^2								7
1	2	3		5		12		9^3	10	13	11^2	7^1	14	4	6	8								8
1	2^1	3		5		12		9	10	13	11^2	7		4	6	8								9
1		3		5		12	14	9^2	10	7^1	11	2	13	4	6	8^3								10
1		3		5		13		9^2	10	7^1	11	2	12	4	8	6								11
1	12	3	4	5		13				7^2	11	8	9	6^1	10	2								12
1	2	3	4	5					10	7^1	11		9	12	8	6								13
1	2	3	4	5					10	7	9		11		8	6								14
1		3	4	5					10		12	7	9^1	11	6	8	2							15
1	12	3		5		13			10	7^1	9^2	8	11	6		2								16
1	2		4	5				9^1	10		11	7	12		6	8	3							17
1	2		4^2	5				9	10		11	7	13	12	6	8	3^1							18
1	2		4				14	9	10	13		7^1	11^2	5	6	8	3^3	12						19
1	2		4	5			8		10	12	9	7		11^2	6		3^1		13					20
1	2		4^1	5			8		10		9	7		11	6	12				3				21
1	2			5		11			10		9	7		4	6	8^1			12	3				22
1	2		4	5			12	9^2	10		7	13	11		6	8^1				3				23
1	2		4	5				9^2	8	12	10	7^1	13	11	6					3				24
1	2		4	5				9	14	11	7^3	10^2		6^1	8					13	3	12		25
1	2		4	5				9	10	7	13			11^2		8^1			12	3	6			26
1	2		4	5			14	9^1	10	7^3	12	13		11^2		8				3	6			27
1	2		4	5				9^1	8	7^2	12	13		11	6	14			10^3	3				28
1	2		4	5				9	8^2	7^1	10			11	6	13			12	3				29
1	2^2		4^3	5				9^4	10	7^1	12			11	6	14			13	3	8			30
1	2		4^2	5			12		10	7^1	9			11	6	13				3	8			31
1	2		4	5		7			10		9			11	6	8					3			32
1	2	12	4	5		7			10		9^1			11	6	8					3			33
1			4^1	5		7		13	10		9			11	6	8^2			12	2	3			34
1	12	13	4^3	5		7			10		9^1		14	11	6	8				2^2	3			35
1	7	12		5				9	10^2		11			4	6^1	8			13	2	3			36
1	3^1			5		13	7	12	10		11			4		8			9^2	2	6			37
1	2			5	6	11	8	9^1	10					4		12				7	3			38
1	2			5	6			9^1	10^3	13	11	7	14	4^2		8			12	7	3			39
1				5	6	7^3		9	10	14	11	13	12	4		8^2				2^1	3			40
1	2	3^4		5	6	11^2	13		10		9	7	12	4		8^1								41
1	2	13		5^1	6	11	12		10		9	7^2	14	4		8^3					3			42
1	14		4^1	5	6		13	9^3	10	7^1	11		12			8				2	3			43
1	2	3		5	6	11			10	12	9^1	7^2		4		8				13				44
1	2	12		5	6			9^1	10			11^2		4		8				7	3	13		45
1	3			5	4				10	11	9^1	7^3		8^2					13	14	6	12	2	46

FA Cup

First Round	Southend U	(h)	2-2	
		(a)	2-2	
Second Round	Huddersfield T	(a)	0-6	

Carling Cup

First Round	Leicester C	(a)	3-4

J Paint Trophy

First Round	Morecambe	(h)	1-0
Second Round	Crewe Alex	(h)	2-4

MANCHESTER CITY   FA Premiership

FOUNDATION

Manchester City was formed as a Limited Company in 1894 after their predecessors Ardwick had been forced into bankruptcy. However, many historians like to trace the club's lineage as far back as 1880 when St Mark's Church, West Gorton added a football section to their cricket club. They amalgamated with Gorton Athletic in 1884 as Gorton FC. Because of a change of ground they became Ardwick in 1887.

Etihad Stadium, SportCity, Manchester M11 3FF.
Telephone: 0870 062 1894.
Fax: (0161) 438 7999.
Ticket Office: 0870 062 1894 (option 2).
Website: www.mcfc.co.uk
Email: mcfc@mcfc.co.uk
Ground Capacity: 47,726.
Record Attendance: 84,569 v Stoke C, FA Cup 6th rd, 3 March 1934 (at Maine Road, British record for any game outside London or Glasgow). 47,370 v Tottenham H, FA Premier League, 5 May 2010 (at City of Manchester Stadium).
Pitch Measurements: 105m × 68m.
Chairman: Khaldoon Al Mubarak.
Chief Executive: Garry Cook.
Secretary: Rebecca Firth.
Manager: Roberto Mancini.
Assistant Manager: Brian Kidd.
Fitness Coach: Ivan Carminati.
Colours: Sky blue shirts with white detail, white shorts with sky blue detail, white stockings with sky blue tops.
Change Colours: Black shirts with yellow trim, black shorts, black stockings.
Year Formed: 1887 as Ardwick FC; 1894 as Manchester City.
Turned Professional: 1887 as Ardwick FC. *Ltd Co.:* 1894.
Previous Names: 1887, Ardwick FC (formed through the amalgamation of West Gorton and Gorton Athletic, the latter having been formed in 1880); 1894, Manchester City.
Club Nicknames: 'Blues' or 'The Citizens'.
Grounds: 1880, Clowes Street; 1881, Kirkmanshulme Cricket Ground; 1882, Queens Road; 1884, Pink Bank Lane; 1887, Hyde Road (1894–1923 as City); 1923, Maine Road; 2003, City of Manchester Stadium (now know as Etihad Stadium from 2011).
First Football League Game: 3 September 1892, Division 2, v Bootle (h) W 7–0 – Douglas; McVickers, Robson; Middleton, Russell, Hopkins; Davies (3), Morris (2), Angus (1), Weir (1), Milarvie.
Record League Victory: 10–1 v Huddersfield T, Division 2, 7 November 1987 – Nixon; Gidman, Hinchcliffe, Clements, Lake, Redmond, White (3), Stewart (3), Adcock (3), McNab (1), Simpson.

HONOURS

Football League – Division 1:
Champions 1936–37, 1967–68, 2001–02; *Runners-up* 1903–04, 1920–21, 1976–77, 1999–2000;
Division 2: *Champions* 1898–99, 1902–03, 1909–10, 1927–28, 1946–47, 1965–66; *Runners-up* 1895–96, 1950–51, 1988–89.
FA Cup: *Winners* 1904, 1934, 1956, 1969, 2011; *Runners-up* 1926, 1933, 1955, 1981.
Football League Cup: *Winners* 1970, 1976; *Runners-up* 1974.
Full Members Cup: *Runners-up* 1986.
European Competitions
European Cup: 1968–69.
European Cup-Winners' Cup: 1969–70 (*winners*), 1970–71.
UEFA Cup: 1972–73, 1976–77, 1977–78, 1978–79, 2003–04, 2008–09.
Europa League: 2010–11.

sky SPORTS FACT FILE

Perhaps it was not a surprise when Mario Balotelli scored on his bow for Manchester City against Timisoara in the Europa League on 19 August 2010. In 2008–09 other City debutant marksmen were Robinho on 13 September 2008 and Craig Bellamy on 28 January 2009.

Record Cup Victory: 10–1 v Swindon T, FA Cup 4th rd, 29 January 1930 – Barber; Felton, McCloy; Barrass, Cowan, Heinemann; Toseland, Marshall (5), Tait (3), Johnson (1), Brook (1).

Record Defeat: 1–9 v Everton, Division 1, 3 September 1906.

Most League Points (2 for a win): 62, Division 2, 1946–47.

Most League Points (3 for a win): 99, Division 1, 2001–02.

Most League Goals: 108, Division 2, 1926–27, 108, Division 1, 2001–02.

Highest League Scorer in Season: Tommy Johnson, 38, Division 1, 1928–29.

Most League Goals in Total Aggregate: Tommy Johnson, 158, 1919–30.

Most League Goals in One Match: 5, Fred Williams v Darwen, Division 2, 18 February 1899; 5, Tom Browell v Burnley, Division 2, 24 October 1925; 5, Tom Johnson v Everton, Division 1, 15 September 1928; 5, George Smith v Newport Co, Division 2, 14 June 1947.

Most Capped Player: Colin Bell, 48, England.

Most League Appearances: Alan Oakes, 565, 1959–76.

Youngest League Player: Glyn Pardoe, 15 years 314 days v Birmingham C, 11 April 1962.

Record Transfer Fee Received: £21,000,000 from Chelsea for Shaun Wright-Phillips, July 2005.

Record Transfer Fee Paid: £32,500,000 to Real Madrid for Robinho, September 2008.

Football League Record: 1892 Ardwick elected founder member of Division 2; 1894 Newly-formed Manchester C elected to Division 2; Division 1 1899–1902, 1903–09, 1910–26, 1928–38, 1947–50, 1951–63, 1966–83, 1985–87, 1989–92; Division 2 1902–03, 1909–10, 1926–28, 1938–47, 1950–51, 1963–66, 1983–85, 1987–89; 1992–96 FA Premier League; 1996–98 Division 1; 1998–99 Division 2; 1999–2000 Division 1; 2000–01 FA Premier League; 2001–02 Division 1; 2002– FA Premier League.

LATEST SEQUENCES

Longest Sequence of League Wins: 9, 8.4.1912 – 28.9.1912.

Longest Sequence of League Defeats: 8, 23.8.1995 – 14.10.1995.

Longest Sequence of League Draws: 6, 5.4.1913 – 6.9.1913.

Longest Sequence of Unbeaten League Matches: 22, 16.11.1946 – 19.4.1947.

Longest Sequence Without a League Win: 17, 26.12.1979 – 7.4.1980.

Successive Scoring Runs: 44 from 3.10.1936.

Successive Non-scoring Runs: 6 from 30.1.1971.

MANAGERS

Joshua Parlby 1893–95
 (Secretary-Manager)
Sam Omerod 1895–1902
Tom Maley 1902–06
Harry Newbould 1906–12
Ernest Magnall 1912–24
David Ashworth 1924–25
Peter Hodge 1926–32
Wilf Wild 1932–46
 (continued as Secretary to 1950)
Sam Cowan 1946–47
John 'Jock' Thomson 1947–50
Leslie McDowall 1950–63
George Poyser 1963–65
Joe Mercer 1965–71
 (continued as General Manager to 1972)
Malcolm Allison 1972–73
Johnny Hart 1973
Ron Saunders 1973–74
Tony Book 1974–79
Malcolm Allison 1979–80
John Bond 1980–83
John Benson 1983
Billy McNeill 1983–86
Jimmy Frizzell 1986–87
 (continued as General Manager)
Mel Machin 1987–89
Howard Kendall 1989–90
Peter Reid 1990–93
Brian Horton 1993–95
Alan Ball 1995–96
Steve Coppell 1996
Frank Clark 1996–98
Joe Royle 1998–2001
Kevin Keegan 2001–05
Stuart Pearce 2005–07
Sven-Göran Eriksson 2007–08
Mark Hughes 2008–09
Roberto Mancini December 2009–

TEN YEAR LEAGUE RECORD

		P	W	D	L	F	A	Pts	Pos
2001-02	Div 1	46	31	6	9	108	52	99	1
2002-03	PR Lge	38	15	6	17	47	54	51	9
2003-04	PR Lge	38	9	14	15	55	54	41	16
2004-05	PR Lge	38	13	13	12	47	39	52	8
2005-06	PR Lge	38	13	4	21	43	48	43	15
2006-07	PR Lge	38	11	9	18	29	44	42	14
2007-08	PR Lge	38	15	10	13	45	53	55	9
2008-09	PR Lge	38	15	5	18	58	50	50	10
2009-10	PR Lge	38	18	13	7	73	45	67	5
2010-11	PR Lge	38	21	8	9	60	33	71	3

DID YOU KNOW ?

When Manchester City produced its record attendance on 3 March 1934 (see above), the receipts were £5,426. This equated to the average cost of entry at sixpence in present currency (1s 2d in old money). Eric Brook scored the only goal against Stoke City.

MANCHESTER CITY 2010–11 LEAGUE RECORD

Match No.	Date	Venue	Opponents	Result	H/T Score	Lg Pos.	Goalscorers	Attendance
1	Aug 14	A	Tottenham H	D 0-0	0-0	—		35,928
2	23	H	Liverpool	W 3-0	1-0	—	Barry [13], Tevez 2 (1 pen) [52, 68 (p)]	47,087
3	29	A	Sunderland	L 0-1	0-0	9		38,610
4	Sept 11	H	Blackburn R	D 1-1	0-1	8	Vieira [55]	44,246
5	19	A	Wigan Ath	W 2-0	1-0	4	Tevez [43], Toure, Y [70]	15,525
6	25	H	Chelsea	W 1-0	0-0	4	Tevez [59]	47,203
7	Oct 3	H	Newcastle U	W 2-1	1-1	2	Tevez (pen) [18], Johnson, A [75]	46,067
8	17	A	Blackpool	W 3-2	0-0	2	Tevez 2 [67, 79], Silva [90]	16,116
9	24	H	Arsenal	L 0-3	0-1	4		47,393
10	30	A	Wolverhampton W	L 1-2	1-1	4	Adebayor (pen) [23]	25,971
11	Nov 7	A	WBA	W 2-0	2-0	4	Balotelli 2 [20, 26]	23,013
12	10	H	Manchester U	D 0-0	0-0	—		47,210
13	13	H	Birmingham C	D 0-0	0-0	4		44,321
14	21	A	Fulham	W 4-1	3-0	4	Tevez 2 [6, 56], Zabaleta [32], Toure, Y [35]	25,694
15	27	A	Stoke C	D 1-1	0-0	4	Richards [81]	27,405
16	Dec 4	H	Bolton W	W 1-0	1-0	4	Tevez [4]	46,860
17	11	A	West Ham U	W 3-1	1-0	2	Toure, Y 2 [30, 73], Johnson, A [81]	32,813
18	20	H	Everton	L 1-2	0-2	—	Toure, Y [72]	45,028
19	26	A	Newcastle U	W 3-1	2-0	2	Barry [2], Tevez [5], Coloccini (og) [81]	51,635
20	28	H	Aston Villa	W 4-0	3-0	2	Balotelli 3 (2 pens) [8 (p), 27, 55 (p)], Lescott [13]	46,716
21	Jan 1	H	Blackpool	W 1-0	1-0	2	Johnson, A [34]	47,296
22	5	A	Arsenal	D 0-0	0-0	2		60,085
23	15	H	Wolverhampton W	W 4-3	1-1	2	Toure, K [40], Tevez 2 [49, 66], Toure, Y [54]	46,672
24	22	A	Aston Villa	L 0-1	0-1	3		37,315
25	Feb 2	A	Birmingham C	D 2-2	2-1	—	Tevez [4], Kolarov [41]	24,379
26	5	H	WBA	W 3-0	3-0	3	Tevez 3 (2 pens) [17 (p), 22, 39 (p)]	46,846
27	12	A	Manchester U	L 1-2	0-1	3	Silva [65]	75,322
28	27	H	Fulham	D 1-1	1-0	3	Balotelli [26]	43,077
29	Mar 5	A	Wigan Ath	W 1-0	1-0	3	Silva [38]	44,864
30	20	A	Chelsea	L 0-2	0-0	4		41,741
31	Apr 3	H	Sunderland	W 5-0	2-0	3	Johnson, A [9], Tevez (pen) [15], Silva [63], Vieira [67], Toure, Y [73]	44,197
32	11	A	Liverpool	L 0-3	0-3	—		44,776
33	25	A	Blackburn R	W 1-0	0-0	—	Dzeko [75]	23,529
34	May 1	H	West Ham U	W 2-1	2-1	4	De Jong [10], Zabaleta [15]	44,511
35	7	A	Everton	L 1-2	1-0	4	Toure, Y [28]	37,351
36	10	H	Tottenham H	W 1-0	1-0	—	Crouch (og) [30]	47,029
37	17	H	Stoke C	W 3-0	1-0	—	Tevez 2 [14, 65], Lescott [53]	45,103
38	22	A	Bolton W	W 2-0	1-0	3	Lescott [43], Dzeko [62]	26,285

Final League Position: 3

GOALSCORERS

League (60): Tevez 20 (5 pens), Toure Y 8, Balotelli 6 (2 pens), Johnson, A 4, Silva 4, Lescott 3, Barry 2, Dzeko 2, Vieira 2, Zabaleta 2, Adebayor 1 (1 pen), De Jong 1, Kolarov 1, Richards 1, Toure K 1, own goals 2.
Carling Cup (1): Jo 1.
FA Cup (18): Tevez 3, Toure Y 3, Vieira 3, Dzeko 2, Richards 2, Balotelli 1, Johnson A 1, Kolarov 1, Milner 1, Silva 1.
Europa League (18): Adebayor 4, Balotelli 3, Dzeko 2, Jo 2, Johnson A 2, Boyata 1, Kolarov 1, Silva 1, Toure Y 1, Wright-Phillips 1.

Hart J 38	Richards M 16+2	Kolarov A 20+4	De Jong N 30+2	Toure K 21+1	Kompany V 37	Wright-Phillips S 2+5	Toure Y 35	Silva D 30+5	Tevez C 30+1	Barry G 31+2	Zabaleta P 21+5	Johnson A 15+16	Adebayor E 2+6	Lescott J 20+2	Milner J 23+9	Jo 3+9	Vieira P 4+11	Boyata A 5+2	Boateng W 14+2	Bridge W 1+2	Balotelli M 12+5	Santa Cruz R —+1	Dzeko E 8+7	Razak A —+1	McGivern R —+1	Wabara R —+1	Match No.
1	2	3^1	4	5	6	7^2	8	9	10^3	11	12	13	14														1
1	2		4	5	6		8^1		10^2	7	12	11		3	9	13											2
1	2		4	5	6		8	13	10^3	7		11^2	12	3^1	9	14											3
1	2			5	6	7^1	8	14	10	13		11^3		3	9	12	4^2										4
1	2		4	5	6	14	8^2	9^1	10^3	11		3	12		7	13											5
1			4	5	6		8	7^1	10^2	11		3	12	13	9			2^3	14								6
1			4	5	6		8^1	7	10^3	11^2		13	12	3	9		14		2								7
1	13		4		6			12	10	8		11^3	9^1	5	7		14		2^2	3							8
1	2		4		6		8^1	7	10^2	11^3			13		9			5^4	3	12	14						9
1	2^3			5	6		8	11		4^1	13	12	9^2		7	14			3	10							10
1		13	4	5	6		8	11^1	10	7	2^2	12						3	9^4								11
1		13	4	5	6		8	7	10^3	11	2	12	14		9^1			3^2									12
1		3^2	4	5	6		8	7	10^3	14	13	11			9^1			2		12							13
1		3	4	5	6		8	7^3	10^1	11^2	2	12		14	9	13											14
1	2	3	4	5	6			7	10	11		12		8^1	13				9^2								15
1	13	3^4	4	5^1	6		8	7^2	10^3	11	2			12	14			9									16
1			4	5	6		8	7^2		11	3	12		13	10			2	9^1								17
1		3		5^4	6		8	11	10	4	2	12			7^1	13			9^2								18
1		3	4		6		8^2	9^1	10^3	11		2		5	7		13		14								19
1	2		4^3		6		8^2	9^1				3	11	5	12	13	7		14	10							20
1		3^1	4		6		8^3	9^1	10	7	12	11		5	13		14	2									21
1	2		4	5	6		8		10^2	11	3^4	12		7	9^1			13									22
1		3	4	5^1	6		8	14	10^2	7	2	11^3		12	13						9						23
1		3	4	5	6		8	9	11	7^1		12						2			10						24
1	5^1	3	4^2	12	6			8	10	11				7			13	2			9						25
1		3			5	6	13	8^1	9^3	10^2	4	7			11				2			12	14				26
1	2	11^1			6	12	8	9	10	4	3				5	7^2							13				27
1		3^2		5			8		10	4	11			6	13			12	9^1								28
1	2	12	13		0		8	7^1	10^3	11	3			5		4			9^1	14							29
1	2	3	4		6		8^1	9		11		13		5	7^2					12	10						30
1		3	4		6	14	8	7^3	10			11^1		5			12	2^4		9					13		31
1		3	14		6		8	13	10^1	4		11		5	7^2			2		12^3	9						32
1		3	4		6		8	10^3		7	2	11^1		5			13	14		9^2	12						33
1		3	4^1		6		8	10		7^2	2	11		5	12		14			9^3	13						34
1		3	4^3		6		10	11			2^2	13		5	7	14	8^1			12	9						35
1	2	12	14		6		8	9^3	14	3^1	11^2			5	7	13					10						36
1	2		4		6	13	8	9^1	10^3		3	11^2		5			14				12						37
1			4		6		8	9^2	10	7	2^3	11^1		5	13			3			12		14				38

FA Cup

Third Round	Leicester C	(a)	2-2
		(h)	4-2
Fourth Round	Notts Co	(a)	1-1
		(h)	5-0
Fifth Round	Aston Villa	(h)	3-0
Sixth Round	Reading	(h)	1-0
Semi-Final	Manchester C		1-0
(at Wembley).			
Final	Stoke C		1-0
(at Wembley).			

Carling Cup

Third Round	WBA	(a)	1-2

Europa League

Play-Off	Timisoara	(a)	1-0
		(h)	2-0
Group A	Salzburg	(a)	2-0
	Juventus	(h)	1-1
	Lech	(h)	3-1
		(a)	1-3
	Salzburg	(h)	3-0
	Juventus	(a)	1-1
Second Round	Aris Salonika	(a)	0-0
		(h)	3-0
Third Round	Dynamo Kiev	(a)	0-2
		(h)	1-0

MANCHESTER UNITED   FA Premiership

FOUNDATION

Manchester United was formed as comparatively recently as 1902 after their predecessors, Newton Heath, went bankrupt. However, it is usual to give the date of the club's foundation as 1878 when the dining room committee of the carriage and waggon works of the Lancashire and Yorkshire Railway Company formed Newton Heath L and YR Cricket and Football Club. They won the Manchester Cup in 1886 and as Newton Heath FC were admitted to the Second Division in 1892.

Old Trafford, Sir Matt Busby Way, Manchester M16 0RA.

Telephone: (0161) 868 8000.

Fax: (0161) 868 8804.

Ticket Office: (0161) 868 8000.

Website: www.manutd.com

Email: enquiries@manutd.co.uk

Ground Capacity: 75,769.

Record Attendance: 76,962 Wolverhampton W v Grimsby T, FA Cup semi-final, 25 March 1939.

Club Record Attendance: 76,098 v Blackburn R, FA Premier League, 31 March 2007.

Pitch Measurements: 105m × 68m.

Co-Chairmen: Joel and Avram Glazer.

Chief Executive: David Gill.

Secretary: John Alexander.

Manager: Sir Alex Ferguson CBE.

Assistant Manager: Mick Phelan.

Fitness Coach: Tony Strudwick.

Colours: Red shirts with black chevron, white shorts with red side panels, black stockings.

Change Colours: All black with light blue chevron on shirts.

Year Formed: 1878 as Newton Heath LYR; 1902, Manchester United.

Turned Professional: 1885. *Ltd Co.:* 1907.

Previous Name: 1880, Newton Heath; 1902, Manchester United.

Club Nickname: 'Red Devils'.

Grounds: 1880, North Road, Monsall Road; 1893, Bank Street; 1910, Old Trafford (played at Maine Road 1941–49).

HONOURS

FA Premier League: *Champions* 1992–93, 1993–94, 1995–96, 1996–97, 1998–99, 1999–2000, 2000–01, 2002–03, 2006–07, 2007–08, 2008–09, 2010–11; *Runners-up* 1994–95, 1997–98, 2005–06, 2009–10.

Football League – Division 1: *Champions* 1907–08, 1910–11, 1951–52, 1955–56, 1956–57, 1964–65, 1966–67; *Runners-up* 1946–47, 1947–48, 1948–49, 1950–51, 1958–59, 1963–64, 1967–68, 1979–80, 1987–88, 1991–92. **Division 2:** *Champions* 1935–36, 1974–75; *Runners-up* 1896–97, 1905–06, 1924–25, 1937–38.

FA Cup: *Winners* 1909, 1948, 1963, 1977, 1983, 1985, 1990, 1994, 1996, 1999, 2004; *Runners-up* 1957, 1958, 1976, 1979, 1995, 2005, 2007.

Football League Cup: *Winners* 1992, 2006, 2009, 2010; *Runners-up* 1983, 1991, 1994, 2003.

European Competitions
European Cup: 1956–57 (*s-f*), 1957–58 (*s-f*), 1965–66 (*s-f*), 1967–68 (*winners*), 1968–69 (*s-f*). **Champions League:** 1993–94, 1994–95, 1996–97 (*s-f*), 1997–98, 1998–99 (*winners*), 1999–2000, 2000–01, 2001–02 (*s-f*), 2002–03, 2003–04, 2004–05, 2005–06, 2006–07 (*s-f*), 2007–08 (*winners*), 2008–09 (*runners-up*), 2009–10, 2010–11 (*runners-up*).
European Cup-Winners' Cup: 1963–64, 1977–78, 1983–84, 1990–91 (*winners*). 1991–92. **Inter Cities Fairs Cup:** 1964–65. **UEFA Cup:** 1976–77, 1980–81, 1982–83, 1984–85, 1992–93, 1995–96.
Super Cup: 1991 (*winners*), 1999, 2008. **World Club Championship:** 1968, 1999 (*winners*).
FIFA Club World Cup: 2008 (*winners*).
NB: In 1958–59 FA refused permission to compete in World Club Championship.

sky SPORTS FACT FILE

On 6 November 2010 Sir Alex Ferguson celebrated his 24th anniversary as manager of Manchester United in a 2-1 win over Wolverhampton Wanderers. It was his 1,351st overall match in charge with 798 wins, 314 draws and 239 defeats, goals for 2,464, against 1,207.

First Football League Game: 3 September 1892, Division 1, v Blackburn R (a) L 3–4 – Warner; Clements, Brown; Perrins, Stewart, Erentz; Farman (1), Coupar (1), Donaldson (1), Carson, Mathieson.

Record League Victory (as Newton Heath): 10–1 v Wolverhampton W, Division 1, 15 October 1892 – Warner; Mitchell, Clements; Perrins, Stewart (3), Erentz; Farman (1), Hood (1), Donaldson (3), Carson (1), Hendry (1).

Record League Victory (as Manchester U): 9–0 v Ipswich T, FA Premier League, 4 March 1995 – Schmeichel; Keane (1) (Sharpe), Irwin, Bruce (Butt), Kanchelskis, Pallister, Cole (5), Ince (1), McClair, Hughes (2), Giggs.

Record Cup Victory: 10–0 v RSC Anderlecht, European Cup prel. rd 2nd leg, 26 September 1956 – Wood; Foulkes, Byrne; Colman, Jones, Edwards; Berry (1), Whelan (2), Taylor (3), Viollet (4), Pegg.

Record Defeat: 0–7 v Blackburn R, Division 1, 10 April 1926; 0–7 v Aston Villa, Division 1, 27 December 1930; 0–7 v Wolverhampton W, Division 2, 26 December 1931.

Most League Points (2 for a win): 64, Division 1, 1956–57.

Most League Points (3 for a win): 92, FA Premier League, 1993–94.

Most League Goals: 103, Division 1, 1956–57 and 1958–59.

Highest League Scorer in Season: Dennis Viollet, 32, 1959–60.

Most League Goals in Total Aggregate: Bobby Charlton, 199, 1956–73.

Most Capped Player: Bobby Charlton, 106, England.

Most League Appearances: Ryan Giggs, 613, 1991–.

Youngest League Player: Jeff Whitefoot, 16 years 105 days v Portsmouth, 15 April 1950.

Record Transfer Fee Received: £80,000,000 from Real Madrid for Cristiano Ronaldo, June 2009.

Record Transfer Fee Paid: £30,750,000 to Tottenham H for Dimitar Berbatov, September 2008.

Football League Record: 1892 Newton Heath elected to Division 1; 1894–1906 Division 2; 1906–22 Division 1; 1922–25 Division 2; 1925–31 Division 1; 1931–36 Division 2; 1936–37 Division 1; 1937–38 Division 2; 1938–74 Division 1; 1974–75 Division 2; 1975–92 Division 1; 1992– FA Premier League.

LATEST SEQUENCES

Longest Sequence of League Wins: 14, 15.10.1904 – 3.1.1905.

Longest Sequence of League Defeats: 14, 26.4.1930 – 25.10.1930.

Longest Sequence of League Draws: 6, 30.10.1988 – 27.11.1988.

Longest Sequence of Unbeaten League Matches: 29, 26.12.1998 – 25.9.1999.

Longest Sequence Without a League Win: 16, 19.4.1930 – 25.10.1930.

Successive Scoring Runs: 36 from 3.12.2007.

Successive Non-scoring Runs: 5 from 22.2.1902.

MANAGERS

J. Ernest Mangnall 1903–12
John Bentley 1912–14
John Robson 1914–21
  (Secretary-Manager from 1916)
John Chapman 1921–26
Clarence Hilditch 1926–27
Herbert Bamlett 1927–31
Walter Crickmer 1931–32
Scott Duncan 1932–37
Walter Crickmer 1937–45
  (Secretary-Manager)
Matt Busby 1945–69
  (continued as General Manager then Director)
Wilf McGuinness 1969–70
Sir Matt Busby 1970–71
Frank O'Farrell 1971–72
Tommy Docherty 1972–77
Dave Sexton 1977–81
Ron Atkinson 1981–86
Sir Alex Ferguson November 1986–

TEN YEAR LEAGUE RECORD

		P	W	D	L	F	A	Pts	Pos
2001-02	PR Lge	38	24	5	9	87	45	77	3
2002-03	PR Lge	38	25	8	5	74	34	83	1
2003-04	PR Lge	38	23	6	9	64	35	75	3
2004-05	PR Lge	38	22	11	5	58	26	77	3
2005-06	PR Lge	38	25	8	5	72	34	83	2
2006-07	PR Lge	38	28	5	5	83	27	89	1
2007-08	PR Lge	38	27	6	5	80	22	87	1
2008-09	PR Lge	38	28	6	4	68	24	90	1
2009-10	PR Lge	38	27	4	7	86	28	85	2
2010-11	PR Lge	38	23	11	4	78	37	80	1

DID YOU KNOW ?

On 27 November 2010 Dimitar Berbatov scored five goals for Manchester United in the 7-1 win over Blackburn Rovers at Old Trafford, the team's second player and fourth overall to achieve this Premier League feat. Andy Cole hit five on 4 March 1995 against Ipswich Town.

MANCHESTER UNITED 2010–11 LEAGUE RECORD

Match No.	Date		Venue	Opponents	Result		H/T Score	Lg Pos.	Goalscorers	Atten- dance
1	Aug	16	H	Newcastle U	W	3-0	2-0	—	Berbatov [33], Fletcher [41], Giggs [85]	75,221
2		22	A	Fulham	D	2-2	1-0	3	Scholes [11], Hangeland (og) [84]	25,643
3		28	H	West Ham U	W	3-0	1-0	3	Rooney (pen) [33], Nani [50], Berbatov [69]	75,061
4	Sept	11	A	Everton	D	3-3	1-1	3	Fletcher [43], Vidic [47], Berbatov [66]	36,556
5		19	H	Liverpool	W	3-2	1-0	3	Berbatov 3 [42, 59, 84]	75,213
6		26	A	Bolton W	D	2-2	1-1	2	Nani [23], Owen [74]	23,926
7	Oct	2	A	Sunderland	D	0-0	0-0	3		41,709
8		16	H	WBA	D	2-2	2-0	4	Hernandez [5], Nani [25]	75,272
9		24	A	Stoke C	W	2-1	1-0	3	Hernandez 2 [27, 86]	27,372
10		30	H	Tottenham H	W	2-0	1-0	3	Vidic [31], Nani [84]	75,223
11	Nov	6	H	Wolverhampton W	W	2-1	1-0	2	Park 2 [45, 90]	75,285
12		10	A	Manchester C	D	0-0	0-0	—		47,210
13		13	A	Aston Villa	D	2-2	0-0	3	Macheda [81], Vidic [85]	40,073
14		20	H	Wigan Ath	W	2-0	1-0	2	Evra [45], Hernandez [77]	74,181
15		27	H	Blackburn R	W	7-1	3-0	1	Berbatov 5 [2, 27, 47, 62, 70], Park [23], Nani [48]	74,850
16	Dec	13	H	Arsenal	W	1-0	1-0	—	Park [41]	75,227
17		26	H	Sunderland	W	2-0	1-0	1	Berbatov [5], Ferdinand (og) [57]	75,269
18		28	A	Birmingham C	D	1-1	0-0	1	Berbatov [58]	28,242
19	Jan	1	A	WBA	W	2-1	1-1	1	Rooney [3], Hernandez [75]	25,499
20		4	H	Stoke C	W	2-1	1-0	1	Hernandez [27], Nani [62]	73,401
21		16	A	Tottenham H	D	0-0	0-0	1		35,828
22		22	H	Birmingham C	W	5-0	3-0	1	Berbatov 3 [2, 31, 53], Giggs [45], Nani [76]	75,326
23		25	A	Blackpool	W	3-2	0-2	—	Berbatov 2 [72, 88], Hernandez [74]	15,574
24	Feb	1	A	Aston Villa	W	3-1	2-0	—	Rooney 2 [1, 45], Vidic [63]	75,256
25		5	A	Wolverhampton W	L	1-2	1-2	1	Nani [3]	28,811
26		12	H	Manchester C	W	2-1	1-0	1	Nani [41], Rooney [78]	75,322
27		26	A	Wigan Ath	W	4-0	1-0	1	Hernandez 2 [17, 74], Rooney [84], Fabio [87]	18,140
28	Mar	1	A	Chelsea	L	1-2	1-0	—	Rooney [29]	41,825
29		6	A	Liverpool	L	1-3	0-2	1	Hernandez [90]	44,753
30		19	H	Bolton W	W	1-0	0-0	1	Berbatov [88]	75,486
31	Apr	2	A	West Ham U	W	4-2	0-2	1	Rooney 3 (1 pen) [65, 73, 79 (p)], Hernandez [84]	34,546
32		9	H	Fulham	W	2-0	2-0	1	Berbatov [12], Valencia [32]	75,339
33		19	A	Newcastle U	D	0-0	0-0	—		49,025
34		23	H	Everton	W	1-0	0-0	1	Hernandez [83]	75,300
35	May	1	A	Arsenal	L	0-1	0-0	1		60,107
36		8	H	Chelsea	W	2-1	2-0	1	Hernandez [1], Vidic [23]	75,445
37		14	A	Blackburn R	D	1-1	0-1	1	Rooney (pen) [73]	29,867
38		22	H	Blackpool	W	4-2	1-1	1	Park [21], Anderson [62], Evatt (og) [74], Owen [81]	75,400

Final League Position: 1

GOALSCORERS

League (78): Berbatov 20, Hernandez 13, Rooney 11 (3 pens), Nani 9, Park 5, Vidic 5, Fletcher 2, Giggs 2, Owen 2, Anderson 1, Evra 1, Fabio 1, Macheda 1, Scholes 1, Valencia 1, own goals 3.
Carling Cup (8): Owen 2, Park 2, Bebe 1, Gibson 1, Hernandez 1, Smalling 1.
FA Cup (6): Brown 1, Fabio 1, Giggs 1 (pen), Hernandez 1, Owen 1, Rooney 1.
Champions League (19): Hernandez 4, Rooney 4 (1 pen), Anderson 3, Fletcher 1, Gibson 1, Giggs 1, Nani 1, Obertan 1, Park 1, Valencia 1, own goal 1.
Community Shield (3): Berbatov 1, Hernandez 1, Valencia 1.

Van der Sar E 33	O'Shea J 18 + 2	Evra P 34 + 1	Fletcher D 24 + 2	Evans J 11 + 2	Vidic N 35	Valencia L 8 + 2	Scholes P 16 + 6	Berbatov D 24 + 8	Rooney W 25 + 3	Nani 31 + 2	Hernandez J 15 + 12	Giggs R 19 + 6	Rafael 15 + 1	Park J 13 + 2	Owen M 1 + 10	Smalling C 11 + 5	Carrick M 23 + 5	Neville G 3	Macheda F 2 + 5	Anderson 14 + 4	Gibson D 6 + 6	Ferdinand R 19	Bebe — + 2	Brown W 4 + 3	Obertan G 3 + 4	Hargreaves 0 1	Kuszczak T 5	Fabio 5 + 6	Match No.
1	2	3³	4	5	6	7	8	9	10¹	11²	12	13	14																1
1	2	3	4	5	6	7²	8	9	12	10³	13			11¹	14														2
1	2	3	4	5²	6		8³	9¹	10	7		11				12	13	14											3
1	4	3¹	10	5	6		8	9	7		11	12					2												4
1	2	3	4	5	6		8	9²	10	7²	11¹					12	13	14											5
1	2	3	4³	5	6		8	9	10²	7	11¹					12	14	13											6
1		3	4		6		8	12				7	13	2	9¹	10²	11³					5	14						7
1		3			6							14	9	13	7	10	11¹	2		4³	8²	12	5						8
1	4²	3	7		6		8³	9	11	10						13	2¹			5				12	14				9
1		3	8		6		13	9²	7	10³		2¹	11			4				5				12	14				10
1	7²	3	8		6		13			10		11				14			5	12³	2	9	4¹						11
1	13	3¹	7		6		8	9²	11	14		2¹	10			4			5	12									12
1		3	8		6			9²	11	10¹		7³		14	4	12			5	2	13								13
1		3	8		6		13		12	7	14	2	11¹			4³	9²		5		10								14
1		3	12		6¹			9	10	7		2	11²			4	8		5	13									15
1		3	9		6			10	7	12		2	11			4	8¹		5										16
1		3			6		9¹	10		14	11²	2	7			4	12	8¹	13	5									17
1		3	12		6		9	10		13	11	2				4	8¹	7²	5										18
1		3	8		6		9²	10		12						4	2³	11	13	5			7¹			1	14		19
1		3	4		6		9		7	10²	11	2		12	5	13			8¹							1			20
1		3	8		8		9²	10	7	13	11	2ᴺ				4			12	5									21
1	2	3²			6		9	10	7		11³				14	5	4¹			8	12				13				22
1		3	4		6		8	9	10²	11	13	12	2³			5				14	7¹								23
1	2	3	8¹		6		9	10	7		11					4	12	5											24
1		3	8	5²	6		12	9³	10	7	13	11	2			14	4¹												25
1	2	3	4		6		8²	12	10	7		11				5	13			9¹									26
1	2	3	7		6		8²	12	10	11³	9¹					5	4			13								14	27
1	2	3⁴	7		6⁴		8¹	12	10	11	9²	13				5	4											14	28
1	13	3	14		6		8³	9	10	7¹	12	11	2²			5	4					6							29
1		3	6⁴	7			12	10	8	9²	11					5	4					2¹						13	30
		3¹		6	7		13	10³	14	12	9		11²			5	4			8						1	2		31
	2	3		6	7¹	8	9		11³				12	5	14	4²	10									1	13		32
1	2	3		6	12			10	7²	9	11					13	5	4		8¹									33
1	2¹	12		6			7			10	11²	9	14			13				4	8³	5						3	34
1		3			6	12		13	10	11	9²			7	14	4³				8¹	5							2	35
1	3¹		12	6	7			10			9	8		11		13	4				5						2²		36
		3	6	7	12	13	10	11²	9	8						4				5					1	2¹			37
1		3	4	5	6³		10	9	14	7				2¹	11²	13	12			8									38

FA Cup

Third Round	Liverpool	(h)	1-0	
Fourth Round	Southampton	(a)	2-1	
Fifth Round	Crawley T	(h)	1-0	
Sixth Round	Arsenal	(h)	2-0	
Semi-Final	Manchester C		0-1	
(at Wembley).				

Carling Cup

Third Round	Scunthorpe U	(a)	5-2
Fourth Round	Wolverhampton W	(h)	3-2
Quarter-Final	West Ham U	(a)	0-4

Community Shield

	Chelsea	3-1
(at Wembley).		

Champions League

Group C	Rangers	(h)	0-0
	Valencia	(a)	1-0
	Bursa	(h)	1-0
		(a)	3-0
	Rangers	(a)	1-0
	Valencia	(h)	1-1
Knock-Out Round	Marseille	(a)	0-0
		(h)	2-1
Quarter-Final	Chelsea	(a)	1-0
		(h)	2-1
Semi-Final	Schalke	(a)	2-0
		(h)	4-1
Final	Barcelona		1-3
(at Wembley).			

MIDDLESBROUGH FL Championship

FOUNDATION

A previous belief that Middlesbrough Football Club was founded at a tripe supper at the Corporation Hotel has proved to be erroneous. In fact, members of Middlesbrough Cricket Club were responsible for forming it at a meeting in the gymnasium of the Albert Park Hotel in 1875.

Riverside Stadium, Middlesbrough TS3 6RS.
Telephone: (0844) 499 6789.
Fax: (01642) 757 690.
Ticket Office: (0844) 499 1234.
Website: www.mfc.co.uk
Email: enquiries@mfc.co.uk
Ground Capacity: 35,100.
Record Attendance: 53,536 v Newcastle U, Division 1, 27 December 1949 (at Ayresome Park). 34,814 v Newcastle U, FA Premier League, 5 March 2003 (at Riverside Stadium).
Pitch Measurements: 105m × 68m.
Chairman: Steve Gibson.
Secretary: Karen Nelson.
Manager: Tony Mowbray.
Assistant Manager: Mark Venus.
Head of Medical: Grant Downie.
Colours: Red shirts with white design and one white sleeve, white shorts with red trim, white stockings.

HONOURS

Football League – Division 1: *Champions* 1994–95; *Runners-up* 1997–98; **Division 2:** *Champions* 1926–27, 1928–29, 1973–74; *Runners-up* 1901–02, 1991–92; **Division 3:** *Runners-up* 1966–67, 1986–87.

FA Cup: *Runners-up* 1997.

Football League Cup: *Winners* 2004; *Runners-up* 1997, 1998.

Amateur Cup: *Winners* 1895, 1898.

Anglo-Scottish Cup: *Winners* 1976.

Zenith Data Systems Cup: *Runners-up* 1990.

European Competitions
UEFA Cup: 2004–05, 2005–06 (*runners-up*).

Change Colours: All light blue with white trim on shirts, black stockings.
Year Formed: 1876; reformed 1986.
Turned Professional: 1889; became amateur 1892, and professional again, 1899.
Ltd Co: 1892. *Club Nickname:* 'Boro'.
Grounds: 1877, Old Archery Ground, Albert Park; 1879, Breckon Hill; 1882, Linthorpe Road Ground; 1903, Ayresome Park; 1995, Riverside Stadium.
First Football League Game: 2 September 1899, Division 2, v Lincoln C (a) L 0–3 – Smith; Shaw, Ramsey; Allport, McNally, McCracken; Wanless, Longstaffe, Gettins, Page, Pugh.
Record League Victory: 9–0 v Brighton & HA, Division 2, 23 August 1958 – Taylor; Bilcliff, Robinson; Harris (2p), Phillips, Walley; Day, McLean, Clough (5), Peacock (2), Holliday.
Record Cup Victory: 7–0 v Hereford U, Coca-Cola Cup 2nd rd, 1st leg, 18 September 1996 – Miller; Fleming (1), Branco (1), Whyte, Vickers, Whelan, Emerson (1), Mustoe, Stamp, Juninho, Ravanelli (4).

sky SPORTS FACT FILE

But for Walter Tinsley, George Elliott might have been the leading goal scorer for Middlesbrough for seven consecutive seasons before and after the Great War. In 1914–15 Tinsley scored 26 League and Cup goals, nine more than Elliott's tally.

Record Defeat: 0–9 v Blackburn R, Division 2, 6 November 1954.

Most League Points (2 for a win): 65, Division 2, 1973–74.

Most League Points (3 for a win): 94, Division 3, 1986–87.

Most League Goals: 122, Division 2, 1926–27.

Highest League Scorer in Season: George Camsell, 59, Division 2, 1926–27 (Second Division record).

Most League Goals in Total Aggregate: George Camsell, 325, 1925–39.

Most League Goals in One Match: 5, John Wilkie v Gainsborough T, Division 2, 2 March 1901; 5, Andy Wilson v Nottingham F, Division 1, 6 October 1923; 5, George Camsell v Manchester C, Division 2, 25 December 1926; 5, George Camsell v Aston Villa, Division 1, 9 September 1935; 5, Brian Clough v Brighton & HA, Division 2, 22 August 1958.

Most Capped Player: Wilf Mannion, 26, England.

Most League Appearances: Tim Williamson, 563, 1902–23.

Youngest League Player: Stephen Bell, 16 years 323 days v Southampton, 30 January 1982; Sam Lawrie, 16 years 323 days v Arsenal, 3 November 1951.

Record Transfer Fee Received: £12,000,000 from Atletico Madrid for Juninho, July 1997; £12,000,000 from Aston Villa for Stewart Downing, July 2009.

Record Transfer Fee Paid: £12,000,000 to Heerenveen for Afonso Alves, January 2008.

Football League Record: 1899 Elected to Division 2; 1902–24 Division 1; 1924–27 Division 2; 1927–28 Division 1; 1928–29 Division 2; 1929–54 Division 1; 1954–66 Division 2; 1966–67 Division 3; 1967–74 Division 2; 1974–82 Division 1; 1982–86 Division 2; 1986–87 Division 3; 1987–88 Division 2; 1988–89 Division 1; 1989–92 Division 2; 1992–93 FA Premier League; 1993–95 Division 1; 1995–97 FA Premier League; 1997–98 Division 1; 1998–2009 FA Premier League; 2009– FL C.

MANAGERS

John Robson 1899–1905
Alex Mackie 1905–06
Andy Aitken 1906–09
J. Gunter 1908–10
  (Secretary-Manager)
Andy Walker 1910–11
Tom McIntosh 1911–19
Jimmy Howie 1920–23
Herbert Bamlett 1923–26
Peter McWilliam 1927–34
Wilf Gillow 1934–44
David Jack 1944–52
Walter Rowley 1952–54
Bob Dennison 1954–63
Raich Carter 1963–66
Stan Anderson 1966–73
Jack Charlton 1973–77
John Neal 1977–81
Bobby Murdoch 1981–82
Malcolm Allison 1982–84
Willie Maddren 1984–86
Bruce Rioch 1986–90
Colin Todd 1990–91
Lennie Lawrence 1991–94
Bryan Robson 1994–2001
Steve McClaren 2001–06
Gareth Southgate 2006–09
Gordon Strachan 2009–10
Tony Mowbray October 2010–

LATEST SEQUENCES

Longest Sequence of League Wins: 9, 16.2.1974 – 6.4.1974.

Longest Sequence of League Defeats: 8, 26.12.1995 – 17.2.1996.

Longest Sequence of League Draws: 8, 3.4.1971 – 1.5.1971.

Longest Sequence of Unbeaten League Matches: 24, 8.9.1973 – 19.1.1974.

Longest Sequence Without a League Win: 19, 3.10.1981 – 6.3.1982.

Successive Scoring Runs: 26 from 21.9.1946.

Successive Non-scoring Runs: 5 from 17.1.2009.

TEN YEAR LEAGUE RECORD

		P	W	D	L	F	A	Pts	Pos
2001-02	PR Lge	38	12	9	17	35	47	45	12
2002-03	PR Lge	38	13	10	15	48	44	49	11
2003-04	PR Lge	38	13	9	16	44	52	48	11
2004-05	PR Lge	38	14	13	11	53	46	55	7
2005-06	PR Lge	38	12	9	17	48	58	45	14
2006-07	PR Lge	38	12	10	16	44	49	46	12
2007-08	PR Lge	38	10	12	16	43	53	42	13
2008-09	PR Lge	38	7	11	20	28	57	32	19
2009-10	FL C	46	16	14	16	58	50	62	11
2010-11	FL C	46	17	11	18	68	68	62	12

DID YOU KNOW ?

Legendary Middlesbrough goalkeeper Tim Williamson was selected for his first England international cap against Ireland on 25 February 1905. The match finished 1-1 and it also was notable as the first international fixture to be staged at Ayresome Park.

MIDDLESBROUGH 2010–11 LEAGUE RECORD

Match No.	Date	Venue	Opponents	Result	H/T Score	Lg Pos.	Goalscorers	Attendance
1	Aug 7	H	Ipswich T	L 1-3	1-0	—	McDonald [22]	21,882
2	14	A	Leicester C	D 0-0	0-0	20		21,587
3	22	H	Sheffield U	W 1-0	0-0	10	Boyd [52]	14,633
4	28	A	Barnsley	L 0-2	0-1	16		11,767
5	Sept 11	A	QPR	L 0-3	0-0	20		14,784
6	14	H	Burnley	W 2-1	0-0	—	Kink 2 [79, 90]	15,033
7	18	H	Reading	W 3-1	2-1	13	Robson [1], Lita [41], Wheater [68]	· 15,158
8	25	A	Watford	L 1-3	0-3	17	Mariappa (og) [80]	12,185
9	28	A	Derby Co	L 1-3	1-1	—	Boyd [20]	24,739
10	Oct 2	H	Portsmouth	D 2-2	2-0	18	Bates [29], Robson (pen) [42]	13,749
11	16	H	Leeds U	L 1-2	0-1	20	Boyd [53]	23,550
12	19	A	Nottingham F	L 0-1	0-0	—		22,115
13	23	A	Norwich C	L 0-1	0-1	22		25,410
14	30	H	Bristol C	L 1-2	1-1	23	Boyd [30]	19,039
15	Nov 6	H	Crystal Palace	W 2-1	0-1	23	Kink [76], McCarthy (og) [85]	15,400
16	9	A	Scunthorpe U	W 2-0	2-0	—	Boyd [6], McDonald [23]	5475
17	14	A	Swansea C	L 0-1	0-0	21		14,906
18	20	H	Millwall	L 0-1	0-1	22		15,697
19	27	H	Hull C	D 2-2	1-2	23	Lita [29], McDonald [46]	15,075
20	Dec 4	A	Coventry C	L 0-1	0-0	—		15,768
21	11	H	Cardiff C	W 1-0	1-0	23	Arca (pen) [40]	14,250
22	17	A	Doncaster R	L 1-2	1-1	—	McDonald [4]	9543
23	28	A	Preston NE	W 3-1	1-1	21	Lita 2 [30, 59], Wheater [61]	11,946
24	Jan 1	A	Leeds U	D 1-1	1-0	20	Wheater [20]	30,452
25	3	H	Norwich C	D 1-1	1-1	20	Martin (og) [21]	16,853
26	15	A	Bristol C	W 4-0	1-0	19	Cisse (og) [43], Lita 2 (1 pen) [58, 90 (p)], Robson [77]	13,699
27	22	H	Preston NE	D 1-1	0-0	20	Bates [71]	16,157
28	Feb 1	H	Scunthorpe U	W 2-0	1-0	18	Boyd [8], McMahon [69]	14,364
29	5	A	Crystal Palace	L 0-1	0-1	19		14,060
30	12	H	Swansea C	L 3-4	2-1	20	Emnes [8], Grounds [34], Lita [53]	14,825
31	19	A	Millwall	W 3-2	0-1	19	McMahon [58], McDonald [62], Lita [83]	11,871
32	26	H	QPR	L 0-3	0-1	20		16,972
33	Mar 1	H	Nottingham F	D 1-1	0-0	—	McDonald [51]	15,341
34	5	A	Reading	L 2-5	1-2	20	Lita 2 (1 pen) [29, 72 (p)]	18,568
35	8	H	Derby Co	W 2-1	0-1	—	Hines [73], Zemmama [88]	13,712
36	12	A	Portsmouth	D 0-0	0-0	20		16,447
37	19	H	Watford	W 2-1	2-1	18	McDonald [33], Taylor [45]	16,090
38	Apr 2	H	Leicester C	D 3-3	1-2	18	Emnes [14], Williams, R [55], McManus [90]	14,500
39	9	A	Sheffield U	W 2-1	1-1	17	Bates [18], Emnes [89]	21,572
40	12	A	Ipswich T	D 3-3	2-1	—	Halliday [42], McDonald [43], Taylor [51]	17,286
41	16	H	Barnsley	D 1-1	0-1	18	McDonald [84]	16,107
42	19	A	Burnley	L 1-3	0-3	—	Taylor [81]	14,366
43	23	A	Hull C	W 4-2	4-1	17	McDonald 3 [11, 13, 45], Arca [26]	21,937
44	25	H	Coventry C	W 2-1	1-1	15	Arca [25], Kink [90]	15,817
45	May 2	A	Cardiff C	W 3-0	3-0	—	Lita [3], Robson [13], Smallwood [21]	25,183
46	7	H	Doncaster R	W 3-0	1-0	12	Robson [43], Lita [66], Reach [90]	19,978

Final League Position: 12

GOALSCORERS

League (68): Lita 12 (2 pens), McDonald 12, Boyd 6, Robson 5 (1 pen), Kink 4, Arca 3 (1 pen), Bates 3, Emnes 3, Taylor 3, Wheater 3, McMahon 2, Grounds 1, Halliday 1, Hines 1, McManus 1, Reach 1, Smallwood 1, Williams, R 1, Zemmama 1, own goals 4.
Carling Cup (3): McDonald 2, Arca 1.
FA Cup (1): O'Neil 1.

Coyne D 1	Bates M 31	Hoyte J 14+3	Bailey N 28+6	Wheater D 24	McManus S 22+2	Flood W 1+4	Thomson K 18+1	Boyd K 18+9	McDonald S 34+4	Robson B 29+3	Arca J 27+5	Kink T 8+13	Steele J 35	Williams L 5+1	O'Neil G 17+1	Lita L 28+10	Kilgallon M 2	Halliday A 5+7	Taylor A 20+1	Tavares M 10+3	McMahon T 28+6	Bennett J 28+3	Smallwood R 7+6	Miller L —+1	Emnes M 18+5	Hines S 14	Franks J 1+3	Park C —+4	Grounds J 5+1	Zemmama M 2+7	Davies A 5+1	Haas M 1+1	Williams R 10+2	Ripley C —+1	Smith P 10	Gibson B —+1	Reach A —+1	Match No.
1	2	3²	4	5	6	7¹	8	9	10	11	12	13																										1
	2	3	4	5	6		8²	9³	10	11		14	1		7¹	12	13																					2
	2		4	5	6			9²	10	8	12	11¹	1		13	3	7³	14																				3
	2		4	5	6			9	10	7	8	11¹	1		13	3²	12																					4
	2	12	4³	5	6			9²	10	7		11¹	1		8	13	14	3																				5
	2	3		6				12	10	7	8	13	1		4²	9		11¹	5																			6
	2²		4	5	6				10	7	3	11¹	1		9	12	8	13																				7
	2²			5	6			12	10	11	3	14	1		4	9³	8¹	7	13																			8
		4²	5	6				9		11	3¹	13	1		8	10	14	7³	2	12																		9
	2	13	5	6		8¹		9	10	11			1		4³	14	7²	12	3																			10
	2		4	5	6			9	10	3	11¹	1		8	12	13	7²																					11
	3	4³	5	6				9	10		1	8	11²	7¹	2	13	12	14																				12
	3		4	5	6	7¹	9²	13		1	11	8	10	2³	14	12																						13
	3	13	5	6		8¹	9	10	11		14	1	4²	12	7³	2																						14
	4	12	5	6¹	8	9²	10	11	14		1		7³	13	2	3																						15
	6	12	14	5	8	9²	10	11³	7¹		1	4	13		2	3																						16
	5	7³	12	6	8¹	14	10	11²	13		1	4	9		2	3																						17
	5	12		6		9³	11	8²	1		7	4¹	10	14	2	3	13																					18
	5		4	6	13	10²	11	12	1		9	7¹	2	3	8																							19
	5	12	4	6	13	10	11²	1		8	9	2¹	3	7																								20
	5	2	4		0	10	11	1	7	J		9	0																										21
	5	2		6	8	13	10¹	12	11³	14	1	4	9²	3	7																							22
	5	2		6	8	12	11	1	4	9	7²	13	3	10¹																								23
	5	2	4	6	8¹	13	10³	12	11	1	9²	14	3	7																								24
	5	2	4	6	13	11	8	7¹	1	9²	3	10	12																										25
	5	2¹	4	6		10²	7	1	8³	9	11	12	3	13	14																							26
	5		4			10²	7¹	12	1	8	9	11	2	3	13	6																						27
	5		4			10¹	12	8	1	9²	11	2	3	7	6	13																						28
	5¹		4			10³	14	7	1	9	11	2	3	6	8²	13	12																					29
			4			10²	11	8³	1	9¹	2	3	14	7	6	13	5	12																				30
			8			10²	7¹	1	9	6	2	11	13	4	3	12	5																					31
			4			10	13	8²	1	9	11	2	3	7¹	6	12	5³	14																				32
			4			10	7	8	1	9	11	2	3	6	5																							33
			4			12	7²	1⁶	9	11	2	3	10	6	5	8¹	13	15																				34
			4			10²	7	1	9	11	2	3	8¹	12	5	13	6	1																				35
			4			10¹	7	1	9²	11	2	3	8	12	5	13	6	1																				36
			4	12		10²	7	8¹	11	2	3	8	9	5	13	6	1																					37
				13		10	8	14	11³	2	3	7¹	9	6	12	5²	4	1																				38
	4	8¹		6		10²	12	13	11	14	2	3	9³	5	7	1																						39
	4			6	14	10	8	7³	12	11	2	3	5²	9¹	13	1																						40
				6	12	8³	10	7²	13	9¹	11	2	3	14	5	4	1																					41
	5			6	8³	9	7¹	11	12	13	10	2²	3	14	4	1																						42
	5			6¹	14	4	10²	7	8	13	11	2³	9	12	3	1																						43
	2			14	8²	7	11	13	9	3	6³	10	5¹	4	1	12																						44
	2			6	13	4	7²	1	9	3	8	11	10¹	12	5																							45
	2			6	4	10²	7¹	1	9	3	13	11³	8	14	5	12																						46

FA Cup
Third Round — Burton Alb — (a) — 1-2

Carling Cup
First Round — Chesterfield — (a) — 2-1
Second Round — Millwall — (a) — 1-2

MILLWALL   FL Championship

FOUNDATION

Formed in 1885 as Millwall Rovers by employees of Morton & Co, a jam and marmalade factory in West Ferry Road. The founders were predominantly Scotsmen. Their first headquarters was The Islanders pub in Tooke Street, Millwall. Their first trophy was the East End Cup in 1887.

The Den, Zampa Road, London SE16 3LN.

Telephone: (020) 7232 1222. *Fax:* (020) 7231 3663.

Ticket Office: (020) 7231 9999.

Website: www.millwallfc.co.uk

Email: questions@millwallplc.com

Ground Capacity: 19,734.

Record Attendance: 48,672 v Derby Co, FA Cup 5th rd, 20 February 1937 (at The Den, Cold Blow Lane). 20,093 v Arsenal, FA Cup 3rd rd, 10 January 1994 (at The Den, Bermondsey).

Pitch Measurements: 105m × 68m.

Chairman: John G Berylson.

Chief Executive: Andy Ambler.

Secretary: Yvonne Haines.

Manager: Kenny Jackett.

Assistant Manager: Joe Gallen. *Physio:* Bobby Bacic.

Colours: All blue with white detail on shirts.

Change Colours: Red and black striped shirts, black shorts, black stockings.

Year Formed: 1885. *Turned Professional:* 1893. *Ltd Co.:* 1894.

Previous Names: 1885, Millwall Rovers; 1889, Millwall Athletic; 1899, Millwall; 1985, Millwall Football & Athletic Company.

Club Nickname: 'The Lions'.

Grounds: 1885, Glengall Road, Millwall; 1886, Back of 'Lord Nelson'; 1890, East Ferry Road; 1901, North Greenwich; 1910, The Den, Cold Blow Lane; 1993, The Den, Bermondsey.

First Football League Game: 28 August 1920, Division 3, v Bristol R (h) W 2–0 – Lansdale; Fort, Hodge; Voisey (1), Riddell, McAlpine; Waterall, Travers, Broad (1), Sutherland, Dempsey.

Record League Victory: 9–1 v Torquay U, Division 3 (S), 29 August 1927 – Lansdale, Tilling, Hill, Amos, Bryant (3), Graham, Chance, Hawkins (3), Landells (1), Phillips (2), Black. 9–1 v Coventry C, Division 3 (S), 19 November 1927 – Lansdale, Fort, Hill, Amos, Collins (1), Graham, Chance, Landells (4), Cock (2), Phillips (2), Black.

Record Cup Victory: 7–0 v Gateshead, FA Cup 2nd rd, 12 December 1936 – Yuill; Ted Smith, Inns; Brolly, Hancock, Forsyth; Thomas (1), Mangnall (1), Ken Burditt (2), McCartney (2), Thorogood (1).

HONOURS

Football League – Division 1:
Best season: 3rd, 1993–94;
Division 2: *Champions* 1987–88,
2000–01; **Division 3 (S):**
Champions 1927–28, 1937–38;
Runners-up 1952–53;
Division 3: *Runners–up* 1965–66,
1984–85;
Division 4: *Champions* 1961–62;
Runners-up 1964–65.

FA Cup: *Runners-up* 2004; Semi-final
1900, 1903, 1937 (first Division 3 side to
reach semi-final).

Football League Cup: Best season:
5th rd, 1974, 1977, 1995.

Football League Trophy: *Winners* 1983.

Auto Windscreens Shield:
Runners-up 1999.

European Competitions
UEFA Cup: 2004–05.

sky SPORTS FACT FILE

The first Millwall player to score four goals in the FA Cup outside of the qualifying stages was centre-forward Billy Keen with all four against Swansea Town on 18 February 1922. The previous season he had been top scorer for the Lions with ten goals from only 22 League appearances.

Record Defeat: 1–9 v Aston Villa, FA Cup 4th rd, 28 January 1946.

Most League Points (2 for a win): 65, Division 3 (S), 1927–28 and Division 3, 1965–66.

Most League Points (3 for a win): 93, Division 2, 2000–01.

Most League Goals: 127, Division 3 (S), 1927–28.

Highest League Scorer in Season: Richard Parker, 37, Division 3 (S), 1926–27.

Most League Goals in Total Aggregate: Neil Harris, 124, 1995–2004; 2006–11.

Most League Goals in One Match: 5, Richard Parker v Norwich C, Division 3 (S), 28 August 1926.

Most Capped Player: Eamonn Dunphy, 22 (23), Republic of Ireland.

Most League Appearances: Barry Kitchener, 523, 1967–82.

Youngest League Player: Moses Ashikodi, 15 years 240 days v Brighton & HA, 22 February 2003.

Record Transfer Fee Received: £2,300,000 from Liverpool for Mark Kennedy, March 1995.

Record Transfer Fee Paid: £800,000 to Derby Co for Paul Goddard, December 1989.

Football League Record: 1920 Original Members of Division 3; 1921 Division 3 (S); 1928–34 Division 2; 1934–38 Division 3 (S); 1938–48 Division 2; 1948–58 Division 3 (S); 1958–62 Division 4; 1962–64 Division 3; 1964–65 Division 4; 1965–66 Division 3; 1966–75 Division 2; 1975–76 Division 3; 1976–79 Division 2; 1979–85 Division 3; 1985–88 Division 2; 1988–90 Division 1; 1990–92 Division 2; 1992–96 Division 1; 1996–2001 Division 2; 2001–04 Division 1; 2004–06 FL C; 2006–10 FL 1; 2010– FL C.

LATEST SEQUENCES

Longest Sequence of League Wins: 10, 10.3.1928 – 25.4.1928.

Longest Sequence of League Defeats: 11, 10.4.1929 – 16.9.1929.

Longest Sequence of League Draws: 5, 22.12.1973 – 12.1.1974.

Longest Sequence of Unbeaten League Matches: 19, 22.8.1959 – 31.10.1959.

Longest Sequence Without a League Win: 20, 26.12.1989 – 5.5.1990.

Successive Scoring Runs: 22 from 8.12.1923.

Successive Non-scoring Runs: 6 from 20.12.1947.

MANAGERS

F. B. Kidd 1894–99
 (Hon. Treasurer/Manager)
E. R. Stopher 1899–1900
 (Hon. Treasurer/Manager)
George Saunders 1900–11
 (Hon. Treasurer/Manager)
Herbert Lipsham 1911–19
Robert Hunter 1919–33
Bill McCracken 1933–36
Charlie Hewitt 1936–40
Bill Voisey 1940–44
Jack Cock 1944–48
Charlie Hewitt 1948–56
Ron Gray 1956–57
Jimmy Seed 1958–59
Reg Smith 1959–61
Ron Gray 1961–63
Billy Gray 1963–66
Benny Fenton 1966–74
Gordon Jago 1974–77
George Petchey 1978–80
Peter Anderson 1980–82
George Graham 1982–86
John Docherty 1986–90
Bob Pearson 1990
Bruce Rioch 1990–92
Mick McCarthy 1992–96
Jimmy Nicholl 1996–97
John Docherty 1997
Billy Bonds 1997–98
Keith Stevens 1998–2000
 (then Joint Manager)
(plus **Alan McLeary** 1999–2000)
Mark McGhee 2000–03
Dennis Wise 2003–05
Steve Claridge 2005
Colin Lee 2005
David Tuttle 2005–06
Nigel Spackman 2006
Willie Donachie 2006–07
Kenny Jackett November 2007–

TEN YEAR LEAGUE RECORD

		P	W	D	L	F	A	Pts	Pos
2001-02	Div 1	46	22	11	13	69	48	77	4
2002-03	Div 1	46	19	9	18	59	69	66	9
2003-04	Div 1	46	18	15	13	55	48	69	10
2004-05	FL C	46	18	12	16	51	45	66	10
2005-06	FL C	46	8	17	21	35	61	40	23
2006-07	FL 1	46	19	9	18	59	62	66	10
2007-08	FL 1	46	14	10	22	45	60	52	17
2008-09	FL 1	46	25	7	14	63	53	82	5
2009-10	FL 1	46	24	13	9	76	44	85	3
2010-11	FL C	46	18	13	15	62	48	67	9

DID YOU KNOW ?

In successive promotion seasons 1964–65 from Division Four and 1965–66 from Division Three, Millwall remained unbeaten at home in League matches. But whereas at The Den in the first of these they drew as many as ten games, it was just four in the subsequent campaign.

MILLWALL 2010–11 LEAGUE RECORD

Match No.	Date	Venue	Opponents	Result	H/T Score	Lg Pos.	Goalscorers	Attendance
1	Aug 7	A	Bristol C	W 3-0	1-0	—	Ward [42], Schofield [48], Robinson, P [60]	18,308
2	14	H	Hull C	W 4-0	2-0	1	Morison 2 [14, 52], Lisbie [29], Trotter [60]	13,292
3	21	A	Leeds U	L 1-3	1-1	6	Naylor (og) [15]	25,067
4	28	H	Coventry C	W 3-1	1-0	4	Cranie (og) [17], Trotter [75], Morison (pen) [79]	11,688
5	Sept 11	A	Nottingham F	D 1-1	1-0	4	Morison [5]	23,342
6	14	H	Reading	D 0-0	0-0	—		11,061
7	18	H	Watford	L 1-6	0-3	9	Trotter [56]	12,562
8	25	A	Cardiff C	L 1-2	1-1	12	Barron [10]	23,010
9	28	A	QPR	D 0-0	0-0	—		15,325
10	Oct 2	H	Burnley	D 1-1	1-1	12	Barron [26]	12,330
11	16	A	Crystal Palace	W 1-0	0-0	11	Robinson, T [53]	16,693
12	19	H	Portsmouth	L 0-1	0-0	—		12,095
13	23	H	Derby Co	W 2-0	1-0	9	Morison [11], Robinson, T [49]	12,024
14	30	A	Ipswich T	L 0-2	0-1	14		19,020
15	Nov 6	A	Doncaster R	L 1-2	1-0	16	Morison [11]	10,356
16	9	H	Norwich C	D 1-1	0-0	—	Marquis [90]	10,211
17	13	H	Sheffield U	L 0-1	0-1	17		11,312
18	20	A	Middlesbrough	W 1-0	1-0	15	Puncheon [25]	15,697
19	27	A	Preston NE	D 0-0	0-0	15		9579
20	Dec 4	H	Scunthorpe U	W 3-0	1-0	—	Henry [23], Morison 2 [81, 86]	8937
21	10	A	Swansea C	D 1-1	1-1	—	Mkandawire [26]	13,853
22	26	A	Portsmouth	D 1-1	1-0	13	Trotter [26]	17,521
23	28	H	Leicester C	W 2-0	2-0	10	Morison [12], Puncheon [25]	12,188
24	Jan 1	H	Crystal Palace	W 3-0	1-0	7	Puncheon 3 [8, 65, 71]	16,170
25	3	A	Derby Co	D 0-0	0-0	9		24,239
26	15	H	Ipswich T	W 2-1	1-1	9	Schofield [45], Morison [76]	12,111
27	22	A	Leicester C	L 2-4	1-3	9	Henry [9], Smith (pen) [69]	23,347
28	28	H	Barnsley	W 2-0	2-0	—	Morison [17], Henry [37]	10,087
29	Feb 1	A	Norwich C	L 1-2	0-0	9	Robinson, T [56]	24,571
30	5	H	Doncaster R	W 1-0	0-0	7	Lisbie [90]	11,427
31	12	A	Sheffield U	D 1-1	0-0	9	Lisbie [90]	19,793
32	19	H	Middlesbrough	L 2-3	1-0	9	Harris [15], Bouazza [78]	11,871
33	22	A	Reading	L 1-2	0-1	—	Harris [46]	15,934
34	26	H	Nottingham F	D 0-0	0-0	11		14,226
35	Mar 5	A	Watford	L 0-1	0-0	13		13,539
36	8	H	QPR	W 2-0	0-0	—	Morison [63], Trotter (pen) [73]	14,104
37	12	A	Burnley	W 3-0	0-0	12	Robinson, P 2 [52, 71], Townsend [87]	14,589
38	19	H	Cardiff C	D 3-3	0-0	12	Trotter (pen) [52], Lisbie [62], Morison [87]	15,039
39	Apr 2	A	Hull C	W 1-0	1-0	8	Morison [33]	19,852
40	9	H	Leeds U	W 3-2	2-0	7	Henry [24], Trotter [30], Morison [62]	16,724
41	12	H	Bristol C	D 0-0	0-0	—		11,108
42	16	A	Coventry C	L 1-2	1-1	9	Townsend [45]	16,354
43	23	H	Preston NE	W 4-0	2-0	9	Purse [42], McQuoid [44], Marquis [54], Henry (pen) [65]	10,426
44	25	A	Scunthorpe U	W 2-1	1-0	7	Marquis 2 [39, 51]	5190
45	30	H	Swansea C	L 0-2	0-1	8		15,101
46	May 7	A	Barnsley	L 0-1	0-0	9		11,136

Final League Position: 9

GOALSCORERS

League (62): Morison 15 (1 pen), Trotter 7 (2 pens), Henry 5 (1 pen), Puncheon 5, Lisbie 4, Marquis 4, Robinson, P 3, Robinson, T 3, Barron 2, Harris 2, Schofield 2, Townsend 2, Bouazza 1, McQuoid 1, Mkandawire 1, Purse 1, Smith 1 (1 pen), Ward 1, own goals 2.
Carling Cup (5): Morison 2 (1 pen), Dunne 1, Harris 1, Trotter 1.
FA Cup (1): Schofield 1.

Forde D 46	Dunne A 38 + 1	Barron S 35 + 3	Carter D 5 + 5	Robinson P 35 + 2	Ward D 28 + 3	Henry J 39 + 3	Trotter L 34 + 1	Morison S 40	Lisbie K 10 + 10	Schofield D 20 + 11	Hackett C 7 + 9	Harris N 7 + 19	Laird M — + 1	Abdou N 30 + 4	Mkandawire T 34 + 1	Robinson T 8 + 3	Craig T 21 + 3	Shittu D 9	Marquis J 5 + 6	Grabban L 1	Hughes-Mason K — + 1	Andrew C 3	Puncheon J 7	McQuoid J 7 + 4	Smith J 9	Berthel Askou J 1	Purse D 9 + 4	Eastmond C 4 + 2	Bouazza H 3 + 9	Townsend A 11	Rowlands M — + 1	Match No.
1	2	3	4[8]	5	6	7[1]	8[3]	9[2]	10	11	12	13	14																			1
1	2	3	12	5	6	7	8	9[2]	10[1]	11[3]	14	13		4																		2
1	2	3	12	5	6	7	8	9	10[1]	11				4																		3
1	2	3	13	5	6	7[1]	4	9	14	11[2]	12	10[3]		8																		4
1	2	3	4	5	6	7[1]		9	13	11	12	10[2]		8																		5
1	2	3		5	6	7		9	10[1]	11		12		8	4																	6
1	2	3		5	6	7[1]	8	9		11	12	10[2]		4[3]	14	13																7
1	2	3		5	6		8[4]	9	10[1]	12				7	4		11															8
1	2	3[1]		5	6			9		11	7	12		8	4		10															9
1	2	3	14	5	6			9		12	7	13		8[3]	4	10[2]	11[1]															10
1		2	11[2]	5	6	14		9		13	7[3]	12		8	4	10[1]	3															11
1	13	11	4	5	6			12	9	14		7		8	2[1]	10[3]	3[2]															12
1	2	3		5	13	7[3]	8	9		11	14			12	4	10[1]	6[2]															13
1	2	3	12	5		7	8	9		11				4[1]		10[2]	6	13														14
1	2	3	11[1]	5		7[2]	8	9	10	12				4			6	13														15
1	2	3		5	12	7	8			11				4			6	9	10[1]													16
1	2	3		5		7	8	9		11[2]	13[3]	12		4			6		10[1]		14											17
1	2			5		7	8	9		12				4		3	6						10[1]	11								18
1	2	3		5		7	8[1]	9						12	4	14	6	13					10[2]	11[3]								19
1	2	3		5		7		9		13				8	4		6						10	11[2]	12							20
1	2	3		5[1]	12	7		9		13				8	4		6						11	10[2]								21
1	2	3			6	7[1]	8	9		12				10	4		5						11									22
1	2[4]	3			6	7[1]	8	9		12	13			10	4		5						11[2]									23
1		3			6	13	10[3]	7		14				8	4		5		12				11[2]	9[1]	2							24
1		3		13	6	7	10	9[1]		11[2]				8	4		5							12	2							25
1	4	3			6	7		9		11	12	10[7]		8		13	5[1]								2							26
1	2	3			8			9		12	11[1]	7		4	10[2]								5	6	13							27
1	2	3				7	10	9		11		12		8	4									6	5[1]							28
1	2	3				7[2]	8	9[1]		13				11	4	12	5							6	10							29
1	2	3	14			7	8			13	11	12		10	4[3]	9[2]								6	5[1]							30
1	2	3		5		7	4	9	13	11[2]		12		8	10[1]									6								31
1	2	3		5		7	8	9		13	11[1]	10[2]		4										6			12					32
1	2	3[2]		5		7	10	9		11		12		6[3]	4	13											14	8[1]				33
1	2			5		7	8	9		13		12		10[2]	4		3										6		11[1]			34
1	2	12		5		7[3]	10	9		13	11	14		4			3[1]										6		8[2]			35
1	2			5	6	7	8	9		12		10[1]		4			3													11		36
1	2	13		5	6	7[3]	8	9		10[1]				4			3											14	11[2]	12		37
1	2[4]			5[1]	6	7	8	9		10[3]		14		4			3							12					13	11[2]		38
1				5	6	7	8	9[2]		10[1]		12		4			3							14	2				13	11[2]		39
1				5	6	7	8	9[2]		10[1]		12		4			3							14	2				13	11[2]		40
1	2	12		5	6	7	8	9		13				4			3[1]										10[2]		14	11[3]		41
1	2[3]	3			6	7	10					12		8[1]	4		14						9[2]				5		13	11		42
1	2[3]	3			6	7	8[1]					12		4			14						9	10[2]			5		13	11		43
1				5	6	7				13				8	4		3		9[2]					10[1]	2			14	12	11[3]		44
1		3		5	6	7	8	9[2]						14	4[3]		10[1]										13	2	12	11		45
1	2			5	6	12		9[3]				14		8	4		3		13								10[2]		7[1]	11		46

FA Cup

Third Round	Birmingham C	(h)	1-4

Carling Cup

First Round	Wycombe W	(a)	2-1
Second Round	Middlesbrough	(h)	2-1
Third Round	Ipswich T	(h)	1-2

MILTON KEYNES DONS   FL Championship 1

FOUNDATION

In July 2004 Wimbledon became MK Dons and relocated to Milton Keynes. In 2007 it recognised itself as a new club with no connection with the old Wimbledon FC. In August of that year the replica trophies and other Wimbledon FC memorabilia were returned to the London Borough of Merton.

*Stadium*mk, *Stadium Way West, Milton Keynes MK1 1ST.*

Telephone: (01908) 622 922.

Fax: (01908) 622 933.

Ticket Office: (01908) 622 900.

Website: www.mkdons.com

Email: info@mkdons.com

Ground Capacity: 21,189.

Record Attendance: 8,306 v Tottenham H, League Cup 3rd rd, 25 October 2006 (at National Hockey Stadium). 20,222 for England U21 v Bulgaria U21, 16 November 2007 and 17,717 v Leicester C, FL 1, 28 February 2009 (both at Stadiummk).

Pitch Measurements: 105m × 68m.

Chairman: Pete Winkelman.

Head of Football Operations: Kirstine Nicholson.

Manager: Karl Robinson.

Assistant Manager: John Gorman.

Physio: Simon Crampton.

Colours: White shirts with black sleeves, white shorts, white stockings with black tops.

Change Colours: Red shirts with white sleeves, red shorts, red stockings with white tops.

Year Formed: 2004.

Turned Professional: 2004.

Ltd Co.: 2004.

HONOURS

Football League – FL 2: *Champions* 2007–08.
Johnstone's Paint Trophy: *Winners* 2008.

sky SPORTS FACT FILE

MK Dons manager Karl Robinson was the youngest at 29 to achieve a UEFA Pro Licence before he was appointed as the club's manager. At 30 when appointed as manager of MK Dons he was the youngest in the Football League and is a former assistant manager at the club.

Grounds: 2003, The National Hockey Stadium; 2007, Stadiummk.

Club Nicknames: 'The Dons'.

Most League Points (3 for a win): 97, FL 2, 2007–08.

Most League Goals: 83, FL 1, 2008–09.

Highest League Scorer in Season: Izale McLeod, 21, 2006–07.

Most League Goals in Total Aggregate: Izale McLeod, 54, 2004–07.

Most Capped Player: Ali Gerba (29), Canada.

Most League Appearances: Dean Lewington, 301, 2004–.

Football League Record: 2004–06 FL 1; 2006–08 FL 2; 2008– FL 1.

MANAGERS

Stuart Murdock 2002–04
Danny Wilson 2004–06
Martin Allen 2006–07
Paul Ince 2007–08
Roberto Di Matteo 2008–09
Paul Ince 2009–10
Karl Robinson May 2010–

LATEST SEQUENCES

Longest Sequence of League Wins: 8, 7.9.2007 – 20.10.2007.

Longest Sequence of League Defeats: 4, 10.8.2004 – 28.8.2004.

Longest Sequence of League Draws: 4, 21.2.2009 – 10.3.2009.

Longest Sequence of Unbeaten League Matches: 18, 29.1.2008 – 3.5.2008.

Longest Sequence Without a League Win: 11, 13.3.2010 – 2.5.2010.

Successive Scoring Runs: 18 from 7.4.2007.

Successive Non-scoring Runs: 4, 17.12.2005–2.1.2006.

TEN YEAR LEAGUE RECORD

		P	W	D	L	F	A	Pts	Pos
2002-03*	Div 1	46	18	11	17	76	73	65	10
2003-04*	Div 1	46	8	5	33	41	89	29	24
2004-05	FL 1	46	12	15	19	54	68	51	20
2005-06	FL 1	46	12	14	20	45	66	50	22
2006-07	FL 2	46	25	9	12	76	58	84	4
2007-08	FL 2	46	29	10	7	82	37	97	1
2008-09	FL 1	46	26	9	11	83	47	87	3
2009-10	FL 1	46	17	9	20	60	68	60	12
2010-11	FL 1	46	23	8	15	67	60	77	5
*As Wimbledon.									

DID YOU KNOW

At the end of the 2007–08 season MK Dons made the decision to scrap its reserve team to concentrate on first team matters and the club's Academy. In 2006–07 they had won the Berks and Bucks Senior Cup defeating Maidenhead United 2-1 at Wycombe.

MILTON KEYNES DONS 2010–11 LEAGUE RECORD

Match No.	Date	Venue	Opponents	Result	H/T Score	Lg Pos.	Goalscorers	Attendance
1	Aug 7	A	Walsall	W 2-1	1-0	—	Baldock, S [42], Woodards [60]	4034
2	21	A	Carlisle U	L 1-4	0-2	14	Leven [64]	5205
3	28	H	Swindon T	W 2-1	0-1	11	Baldock, S 2 [72, 73]	7866
4	Sept 4	H	Hartlepool U	W 1-0	0-0	6	Guy [77]	7656
5	11	A	Brighton & HA	L 0-2	0-0	11		6683
6	15	H	Southampton	W 2-0	0-0	—	Balanta [72], Leven [87]	8133
7	18	H	Rochdale	D 1-1	1-1	4	Doumbe [28]	7034
8	25	A	Peterborough U	L 1-2	1-1	9	Lewington [37]	7838
9	28	A	Charlton Ath	L 0-1	0-0	—		13,155
10	Oct 2	H	Colchester U	D 1-1	0-1	13	Balanta [66]	11,280
11	9	H	Dagenham & R	W 2-0	0-0	8	Baldock, S [55], Doumbe [62]	7083
12	16	A	Bournemouth	L 2-3	1-0	11	O'Hanlon [45], Leven (pen) [86]	6715
13	23	H	Exeter C	W 1-0	0-0	7	Wilbraham [53]	8002
14	30	A	Tranmere R	L 2-4	1-3	11	Leven (pen) [14], Baldock, S [85]	4512
15	Nov 2	H	Yeovil T	W 3-2	1-1	—	Lewington [36], Johnson [50], Leven (pen) [87]	7281
16	13	A	Brentford	W 2-0	0-0	7	Doumbe [57], Balanta [59]	4789
17	20	H	Sheffield W	L 1-4	1-2	10	Carrington [6]	10,552
18	23	A	Huddersfield T	L 1-4	0-2	—	Wilbraham [56]	12,773
19	Dec 11	A	Notts Co	L 0-2	0-0	14		5172
20	28	H	Bournemouth	W 2-0	1-0	—	Guy [6], Doumbe [86]	7638
21	Jan 1	H	Bristol R	W 2-0	2-0	8	Powell, Daniel [10], Leven [13]	7185
22	3	A	Yeovil T	L 0-1	0-1	9		3508
23	8	A	Exeter C	D 1-1	0-1	—	Ibehre [73]	4544
24	15	H	Tranmere R	W 2-0	0-0	6	Powell, Daniel [46], Ibehre [70]	8014
25	18	H	Plymouth Arg	L 1-3	1-2	—	Bhasera (og) [39]	7189
26	22	A	Dagenham & R	W 1-0	0-0	6	Carrington [90]	4446
27	25	A	Leyton Orient	D 2-2	1-2	—	Gleeson [7], O'Hanlon [56]	3131
28	Feb 2	A	Bristol R	W 2-1	1-0	—	O'Hanlon [1], Powell, Daniel [61]	4829
29	5	A	Sheffield W	D 2-2	2-0	7	Leven (pen) [18], Powell, Daniel [27]	17,631
30	12	H	Brentford	D 1-1	0-0	7	Marsh-Brown [48]	8636
31	15	H	Leyton Orient	L 2-3	2-2	—	Lewington [7], Ibehre [23]	6469
32	19	A	Hartlepool U	W 1-0	1-0	6	Powell, Daniel [45]	2620
33	22	H	Oldham Ath	D 0-0	0-0	—		7806
34	26	H	Brighton & HA	W 1-0	1-0	6	Powell, Daniel [27]	9327
35	Mar 5	A	Rochdale	W 4-1	3-0	6	Vine [15], Powell, Daniel [19], Gleeson [45], Baldock, S (pen) [89]	2837
36	8	H	Charlton Ath	W 2-0	0-0	—	Powell, Daniel [55], Baldock, S [90]	7026
37	12	A	Colchester U	W 3-1	0-1	6	Baldock, S 3 [48, 62, 86]	4103
38	21	H	Peterborough U	W 1-0	0-0	—	MacKenzie [69]	10,019
39	25	H	Walsall	D 1-1	0-1	—	Leven (pen) [51]	8923
40	Apr 2	A	Southampton	L 2-3	1-0	5	MacKenzie [34], Baldock, S [52]	22,377
41	9	H	Carlisle U	W 3-2	1-1	5	Powell, Daniel [13], Balanta [81], Clayton [90]	10,795
42	16	A	Swindon T	W 1-0	1-0	5	O'Hanlon [17]	8305
43	22	H	Huddersfield T	L 1-3	0-2	—	Doumbe [89]	11,857
44	25	A	Plymouth Arg	L 0-1	0-1	5		8553
45	30	H	Notts Co	W 2-1	0-0	5	Baldock, S [52], Balanta [60]	10,013
46	May 7	A	Oldham Ath	W 2-1	1-1	5	Balanta [28], Marsh-Brown [50]	4063

Final League Position: 5

GOALSCORERS

League (67): Baldock, S 12 (1 pen), Powell, Daniel 9, Leven 8 (5 pens), Balanta 6, Doumbe 5, O'Hanlon 4, Ibehre 3, Lewington 3, Carrington 2, Gleeson 2, Guy 2, MacKenzie 2, Marsh-Brown 2, Wilbraham 2, Clayton 1, Johnson 1, Vine 1, Woodards 1, own goal 1.
Carling Cup (7): Easter 2, Ibehre 2, Baldock, S 1, Guy 1, Wilbraham 1.
FA Cup (1): Guy 1.
J Paint Trophy (1): Chadwick 1.
Play-Offs (3): Balanta 1, Baldock, S 1, Powell 1.

Martin D 43	Gleeson S 35+1	Lewington D 42	Carrington M 7+5	O'Hanlon S 28+4	Woodards D 36+1	Chadwick L 39+5	Hamann D 12	Easter J 11+3	Baldock S 20+10	Balanta A 12+6	Guy L 20+14	Howell L —+1	Ibehre J 19+23	Leven P 40	Doumbe S 42+2	Chicksen A 5+9	Johnson J 2+5	Wilbraham A 5+5	MacKenzie G 24+2	Searle S 3	Powell Daniel 23+6	McIndoe M 8	Vine R 12+5	Baldock G 1+1	Amoo D —+3	Marsh-Brown K 12+5	Stirling J —+4	Hughes S 2+4	Flanagan T 2	Clayton A 1+5	Collins C —+1	Match No.
1	2	3	4	5	6	7^1	8^2	9^3	10	11	12	13	14																			1
1	2^3	3		5	6	7		8^1	9	10	11^2	12	13																			2
1		3		5	2	7	8^2	9^1	10	11	13		12	4	6																	3
1	3^4	12		5	2^1	7	8^2	9^1	10	11	13		14	4	6																	4
1				5	2	7	8^1	9	10^2	11	12		13	4	6	3^3	14															5
1	3			5^2	2	7	8^2	9	10^1	13	11		12	4	6				14													6
1	3			5	2	7		9		11	8^1		10	4	6				12													7
1	3			2	7	8^1	9			11			10	4	6	13			12	5^2												8
1	3	13		2	7	8^2	12			11			10^1	4	6				9	5												9
1	3			2	7	8^2	9		13	11^3			14	4	6	12			10	5^1												10
1	3			5	2	7	8	9^2	10	11			13	4^1	6																	11
1	12			5	2^3	7	8^1	9^2	10	11^4	14		13	4	3				6													12
1	2	12		5	3	7		13	10		11^1		14		4			8^2	9^3	6												13
1	7^3	3		5	2^1	11	8^2		10		13			4	12			14	9	6^4												14
	2	3	4	5^1		7		13	10		9^3			8	6	12	11^2			1	14											15
1	2	3	4		5	7			10^3	9^1	13		12	8	6						14	11^2										16
1	2	3	4		5	7^4			10^1	12			9	8	6	13	14					11^2										17
1	2	3	4^1	5	6				10				9^2	8	7	14	12				13	11^3										18
1	7	3	4^3		2	13			10^2	12	8		6^1						9^4	5	14	11										19
1	7^3	3	14	5	2	13			10^2	9			4	6							8^1	11										20
1	7	3		5	7	13			10^1	12			9	4	6	14					0^7	11^3										21
1	7^3	3		5^2	2	12			10		8^1		9	4	6	14			13		11											22
1	7	3			2	12		9	10^3				13	4	6	14			5		8^2	11^1										23
1	7^1	3			2	10			11^1				9	4	6^2	13			5		8		12	14								24
1	7	3	14		2	10^1			11				9	4	6^2	13			5^3		8		12									25
1	7	3	14		2	10			12^2	11^3			9	4	5	6					8^1		13									26
1	7	3	4	12	2^1	11^3			10^2				9	8	5	6					14		13									27
1	7	3	5^9		2	11			10^1				9^3	4	6	12			8^2		13		14									28
1	7	3			2^1	11			13				9	4^4	6	12			5^9		10^3			8^2	14							29
1	7	3	5			11				13			9		2	6^1			4		10^2		14	8^3		12						30
1	7	3	5			11		9^1		4			2^3		12				10				14	8		13		6^2				31
1	7	3	6			11			13				4	2					5		9^3		10^1			8	14	12				32
1	7	3	6	12^2		11			14				4	2^1					5		9		10^3			8	13					33
1	7	3	6^9			11		14					12	4	2				5		9^1		10^3			8^2	13					34
1	7	3				2		11		14			12	4^2	6				5		9		10^3			8^1	13					35
1	7	3				2		11^3		12			13	6	14				5		9		10^2			8^1	4					36
	7	3	12			2		11^3	9		14		13		6				5^1	1	8		10^2				4					37
1	7	3	14			2^3		11^2	9				13	4	6				5		8		10^1		12							38
1	7	3				2		11		9	12		13	4	6				5		8^1		10^2									39
1	7	3				2		11		9^2			14	4	6				5		8^3		10^1		13				12			40
1	7	3	5			2^1		11^3		14			13	4	6				9		10^2		8						12			41
1	7	3	5			11			13	12			9	4	6				2		10^2		8^1									42
1	7	3	6^3	8^1		9			11^2	13			4	2	5				10		12						14					43
1	7	3	6^3			11			12	10^1			9	4	2				5		8^2		13					14				44
1	7	3	6			11^1			9^3	12			13	4	2				5		8		10^2					14				45
		6	2			12		7^3	10^2	9					3					1	13			4		11^1			5	8	14	46

FA Cup

First Round	Stevenage	(a)	0-0
		(h)	1-1

Carling Cup

First Round	Dagenham & R	(h)	2-1
Second Round	Blackpool	(h)	4-3
Third Round	Birmingham C	(a)	1-3

J Paint Trophy

Second Round	Charlton Ath	(h)	1-2

Play-Offs

Semi-Final	Peterborough U	(h)	3-2
		(a)	0-2

MORECAMBE   FL Championship 2

FOUNDATION

Several attempts to start a senior football club in a rugby stronghold finally succeeded on 7 May 1920 at the West View Hotel, Morecambe and a team competed in the Lancashire Combination for 1920–21. The club shared with a local cricket club at Woodhill Lane for the first season and a crowd of 3,000 watched the first game. The club moved to Roseberry Park the name of which was changed to Christie Park after J.B. Christie who as President had purchased the ground.

Globe Arena, Christie Way, Westgate, Morecambe LA4 4TB.

Telephone: (01524) 598 393.

Website: www.morecambefc.com

Email: info@globearena.co.uk

Ground Capacity: 6,402.

Record Attendance: 9,383 v Weymouth, FA Cup 3rd rd, 6 January 1962 (at Christie Park). 5,003 v Burnley, Lge Cup 2nd rd, 24 August 2010 (at Globe Arena).

Chairman: Peter McGuigan.

Vice-chairman: Graham Hodgson.

Chief Executive: Rod Taylor.

Secretary: Neil Marsdin.

Player-Manager: Jim Bentley.

Assistant Manager: Ken McKenna.

Physio: Simon Farnworth.

Colours: Red shirts with black trim, white shorts, red stockings.

Change Colours: All royal blue with black trim.

Year Formed: 1920.

Club Nickname: The Shrimps.

Grounds: 1920, Woodhill Lane; 1921, Christie Park; 2010, Globe Arena.

First Football League game: 11 August 2007, FL 2, v Barnet (h) D 0–0 – Lewis; Yates, Adams, Artell, Bentley, Stanley, Baker (Burns), Sorvel, Twiss (Newby), Curtis, Hunter (Thompson).

HONOURS

FA Cup: Best season: 3rd rd, 1962, 2001, 2003.

League Cup: Best season: 3rd rd, 2008.

Northern Premier League: *Runners-up* – 1994–95.

Presidents Cup: *Winners* – 1991–92.

FA Trophy: *Winners* 1973–74.

Lancs Senior Cup: *Winners* 1967–68.

Lancs Combination – *Champions* 1924–25, 1961–62, 1962–63, 1967–68. *Runners-up* 1925–26.

Lancs Combination Cup: *Winners* 1926–27, 1945–46, 1964–65, 1966–67, 1967–68. *Runners-up* 1923–24, 1924–25, 1962–63.

Lancs Junior Cup: *Winners* – 1927, 1928, 1962, 1963, 1969, 1986, 1987, 1994, 1996, 1999, 2004.

sky SPORTS FACT FILE

Arguably the most famous player to appear for Morecambe was centre-forward Ray Charnley. He had three seasons from 1954 and another two at the end of a career mostly at Blackpool where he won his England cap. He scored 98 goals in 177 Morecambe appearances.

Record League Victory: 5-0 v AFC Bournemouth, FL 2, 12 December 2009 – Roche; Parrish, Wilson (1), Artell, Haining, Stanley (1), Hunter (Duffy (1)), Twiss, Jevons (pen) (Wainwright), Mullin (Curtis), Drummond (1).

Record League Defeat: 2–7 v Port Vale, FL 2, 30 April 2011.

Most League Points (3 for a win): 73, FL 2, 2009–10.

Most League Goals: 73, FL 2, 2009–10.

Highest League Scorer in Season: Phil Jevons, 18, 2009–10.

Most League Goals in Total Aggregate: Stuart Drummond, 27, 2007–.

Most League Goals in One Match: 3, Jon Newby v Rotherham U, FL 2, 29 March 2008.

Most League Appearances: Jim Bentley, 146, 2007–.

Youngest League Player: James Spencer, 18 years 258 days v Gillingham, 28 August 2010.

Record Transfer Fee Received: undisclosed from Rushden & D for Justin Jackson, June 2000.

Record Transfer Fee Paid: undisclosed to Southport for Carl Baker, July 2007.

Football League Record: 2006–07 Promoted from Conference; 2007– FL 2.

MANAGERS

Jimmy Milne 1947–48
Albert Dainty 1955–56
Ken Horton 1956–61
Joe Dunn 1961–64
Geoff Twentyman 1964–65
Ken Waterhouse 1965–69
Ronnie Clayton 1969–70
Gerry Irving/Ronnie Mitchell 1970
Ken Waterhouse 1970–72
Dave Roberts 1972–75
Alan Spavin 1975–76
Johnny Johnson 1976–77
Tommy Ferber 1977–78
Mick Hogarth 1978–79
Don Curbage 1979–81
Jim Thompson 1981
Les Rigby 1981–84
Sean Gallagher 1984–85
Joe Wojciechowicz 1985–88
Eric Whalley 1988
Billy Wright 1988–89
Lawrie Milligan 1989
Bryan Griffiths 1989–93
Leighton James 1994
Jim Harvey 1994–2006
Sammy McIlroy 2006–11
Jim Bentley May 2011–

LATEST SEQUENCES

Longest Sequence of League Wins: 7, 31.10.2009 – 12.12.2009.

Longest Sequence of League Defeats: 4, 23.2.2008 – 12.3.2008.

Longest Sequence of League Draws: 4, 13.9.2008 – 4.10.2008.

Longest Sequence of Unbeaten League Matches: 12, 31.1.2009 – 21.3.2009.

Longest Sequence Without a League Win: 10, 5.4.2008 – 30.8.2008.

Successive Scoring Runs: 16 from 3.10.2009.

Successive Non-scoring Runs: 2 from 15.1.2008.

TEN YEAR LEAGUE RECORD

		P	W	D	L	F	A	Pts	Pos
2001-02	Conf	42	17	11	14	63	67	62	6
2002-03	Conf	42	23	9	10	86	42	78	2
2003-04	Conf	42	20	7	15	66	66	67	7
2004-05	Conf	42	19	14	9	69	50	71	7
2005-06	Conf	42	22	8	12	68	41	74	5
2006-07	Conf	46	23	12	11	64	46	81	3
2007-08	FL 2	46	16	12	18	59	63	60	11
2008-09	FL 2	46	15	18	13	53	56	63	11
2009-10	FL 2	46	20	13	13	73	64	73	4
2010-11	FL 2	46	13	12	21	54	73	51	20

DID YOU KNOW ?

Three Morecambe players have scored four-timers in various rounds in the FA Cup over the years. Tommy Ross in 1936 in a 5-1 win over Chorley, Bill Johnstone in 1953 in the 6-0 victory over Penrith and Ian Whitehead in the 8-1 drubbing of Burscough in 1961.

MORECAMBE 2010–11 LEAGUE RECORD

Match No.	Date		Venue	Opponents	Result		H/T Score	Lg Pos.	Goalscorers	Atten- dance
1	Aug	7	A	Wycombe W	L	0-2	0-1	—		4016
2		14	H	Rotherham U	D	0-0	0-0	21		3258
3		21	A	Burton Alb	L	2-3	1-1	21	Fleming 2 [8, 51]	2072
4		28	H	Gillingham	D	1-1	0-0	21	Stanley [60]	2325
5	Sept	4	A	Oxford U	L	0-4	0-2	24		6237
6		11	H	Chesterfield	D	1-1	1-0	24	Brown [26]	2323
7		18	A	Southend U	W	3-2	2-1	22	Drummond [21], Mullin [26], Spencer [73]	5106
8		25	H	Barnet	D	2-2	0-0	20	Drummond [70], Mullin [83]	2221
9		28	H	Bury	L	1-4	1-2	—	Drummond [45]	2607
10	Oct	2	A	Bradford C	W	1-0	1-0	20	Mullin [23]	10,640
11		9	H	Shrewsbury T	W	1-0	0-0	17	Stanley [83]	3239
12		16	A	Aldershot T	L	1-2	0-2	20	Brown [66]	2308
13		23	H	Stevenage	D	0-0	0-0	19		2254
14		30	A	Torquay U	L	1-3	1-1	20	McCready [30]	2172
15	Nov	2	H	Stockport Co	W	5-0	3-0	—	Jevons 3 (1 pen) [8 (p), 38, 66], Bentley [33], Brown [68]	2005
16		13	H	Lincoln C	L	1-2	1-0	19	Jevons [6]	2085
17		20	A	Cheltenham T	D	1-1	0-1	19	Jevons (pen) [80]	2524
18		27	H	Crewe Alex	L	1-2	0-2	—	Shuker [89]	1793
19	Dec	11	H	Port Vale	W	1-0	1-0	19	Charnock [27]	2326
20	Jan	1	H	Accrington S	L	1-2	1-1	21	McCready [27]	2702
21		3	A	Stockport Co	W	2-0	2-0	20	Shuker [29], Spencer [32]	3890
22		8	A	Shrewsbury T	W	3-1	2-0	16	Holden (og) [7], Spencer [28], Wilson (pen) [48]	4605
23		15	H	Torquay U	W	2-1	0-0	13	Wilson 2 (2 pens) [87, 90]	1643
24		22	A	Stevenage	L	0-2	0-2	17		2002
25		25	A	Hereford U	L	1-2	0-1	—	Drummond [52]	1831
26	Feb	1	A	Accrington S	D	1-1	0-0	17	Jevons [66]	1675
27		5	H	Cheltenham T	D	1-1	0-0	18	Drummond [58]	10,691
28		8	H	Aldershot T	D	1-1	0-0	—	Holdsworth [51]	1703
29		12	A	Lincoln C	L	0-2	0-2	19		2884
30		15	A	Northampton T	D	3-3	1-1	—	Hurst [22], Spencer [65], Mullin [88]	3522
31		19	H	Oxford U	L	0-3	0-2	18		2171
32		22	A	Macclesfield T	L	0-2	0-2	—		1286
33		26	A	Chesterfield	W	2-0	1-0	19	Hurst [22], Spencer [57]	6441
34	Mar	5	H	Southend U	W	2-1	1-0	17	McCready [28], Drummond [63]	1917
35		8	A	Bury	L	0-1	0-0	—		2480
36		12	H	Bradford C	L	0-1	0-1	21		3521
37		19	A	Barnet	W	2-1	2-1	19	Carlton 2 [35, 42]	2510
38		22	H	Macclesfield T	L	1-2	0-1	—	Spencer [59]	1612
39		26	H	Wycombe W	L	0-3	0-3	—		1940
40	Apr	2	A	Rotherham U	W	1-0	0-0	16	Spencer [82]	3661
41		9	H	Burton Alb	W	2-1	1-0	15	McCready [14], Carlton [67]	1877
42		16	A	Gillingham	D	1-1	1-0	15	Jevons (pen) [21]	5545
43		22	A	Crewe Alex	L	1-2	0-0	—	Hunter [58]	3614
44		25	H	Hereford U	D	1-1	0-1	15	Haining [71]	2016
45		30	A	Port Vale	L	2-7	1-4	17	Jevons [32], Spencer [79]	4134
46	May	7	H	Northampton T	L	1-2	0-1	20	Cowperthwaite [90]	2674

Final League Position: 20

GOALSCORERS

League (54): Jevons 8 (3 pens), Spencer 8, Drummond 6, McCready 4, Mullin 4, Brown 3, Carlton 3, Wilson 3 (3 pens), Fleming 2, Hurst 2, Shuker 2, Stanley 2, Bentley 1, Charnock 1, Cowperthwaite 1, Haining 1, Holdsworth 1, Hunter 1, own goal 1.
Carling Cup (3): Fleming 2, Jevons 1.
FA Cup (0).
J Paint Trophy (0).

Roche B 42	Moss D 4	Parrish A 41	Scott P 6+2	McCready C 35+1	Wilson L 37+1	Drummond S 39+2	Stanley C 21+1	Shuker C 12+15	Jevons P 27+11	Rundle A 8+9	Mullin P 15+11	Duffy M 16+6	Fleming A 23+7	Hunter G 27+6	Spencer J 20+12	Haining W 12	Brown S 19+13	Capaldi T 17+1	McLachlan F 1	Bentley J 7+1	Hendrie S 1+6	Charnock K 20+1	Wainwright N 1+4	Holdsworth A 12+3	Hurst K 21	Carlton D 11+5	Anyon J 4	Aley Z 1+1	Cowperthwaite N 6+1	Match No.
1	2^1	3	4	5	6	7	8	9^2	10	11	12	13																		1
1	2	3	4	5	6		8	9^1	10^3	11	13	12	7^2	14																2
1	2	3	4^2	5	6	12	8	9^1	10	11^3	13	14	7																	3
1	2^1	3	4	5	6	13	8	9^2	10^3		12	11	7		14															4
1		6	2	5	3^4	4	8	14	10^1	11^3	12	9	7^2	13																5
1		3	13	5		7		9^1		10	8	11	2	12	4	6^2														6
1		2		5		7		9^1		10	8	11	12	6	4	3														7
1		2	12			8	13		14	10	7	11	9^3	5^2	4	3	6^1													8
1		6	2	14	7	8		10^2	12	9	11		13		4^1	3^3	5													9
1		2			4	7	6	11^1	10	9	3	8		12		5														10
1		5	13	3	7	8	12	11^1	10	6^3	9	2^2		14		4														11
1		6		3	8	4	14	13	11^2	10	7^3	9^1	2		12	5														12
1		6	5	3	8	4		12	13	10	7	9^1	2	11^2																13
1		6^3	5	3	8	4	12^4	13	14	10^3	7^2	9^1	2		11															14
1			5	3	8^3	6^2		9	13	10^1	7	14	2	12		11														15
1			5	3			9	11^1	10^2	7		8	12	2	6		4	13												16
1	6		5	3		8		9	12	10^2		4	7	13	2	11^1														17
1	2		5^1	3		8	13	10		12	7^2	6	9		11		4													18
1	2		5	3	8	4	12	10^3		14	13	7	9^1	11^2		6														19
1	3		5	8	7	6	13		10^1	12	14	2	11^3		4^2															20
1	2		5	11^1	8	6	10		12	13	7		9^2		3		4													21
1	2		5	11	8	6^3	9^1		12	7^2		10^4	14	3		4	13													22
1	2		5	11	8	6^1	9		10^2	12	13		3		13	4	7^1													23
1	2		5	11	8	6	9^3	12	14	10^2			3		13	4	7^1													24
1	2		5	11	8	6	9^2	10	12	13	14		3^3		7^1	4														25
1		5		7	6		12	10		9^1	8	3		4		2	11													26
1		5		11^2	6	14	10		13	12	9^3	8	3		4		2	7^1												27
1		5	11	6		9^1	10	13		17		8^1	3		4		2	7												28
1		5			6		10^7	12	13	2	8	9^9	11^1	3		14	4	7												29
1		5		11	6		10^2	13	8^1	12	9^3		3		14	4	2	7												30
1		5		11	6	10^1		8^2	13	9^9		3		14	4	2	7	12												31
1		5	4	11^3	6	10		8	13	12	9^1	3		2^2	7	14														32
1	2		5	3	6	13		8	7	9^9	14		4	12	11^1	10^2														33
1	2		5	3	6	12		8	7^2	9^1	13		4	11	10															34
	2		5	3^2	6	13		8	7^1	9	14		4	12	11	10^3	1													35
	3		5	2	6	12	13		8	7^1	9^2	14		4	11	10^3	1													36
	2		5	11	6	13	12		8	9^2	14	3	4	7^3	10^1	1														37
	2		5	11	6^8		12	8	9^1	3	4	7^2	10	1	13															38
1		5	6	3^1		14	9	4^2	8	13	12	2	7	10	11^3															39
1	6	5	8	10^1	7	9	4	13	2	11	12	3^2																		40
1	6	5	4	14	10	8	9^1	2	13	7^3	11^1	12	3																	41
1	6	5	4	10^9	8	12	2	14	13	7	11^2	9^1	3																	42
1	6^1	5	4	10^9	8	9	2	12	13	7	11^2	14	3																	43
1		5	6	4	12	10^9	8	13	2	7	14	11^1	9^2	3																44
1		5	6	4	12	10	8^8	13	2	14	7	11^1	9^2	3																45
1		5^2	3	6	10^9	7	14	2^1	8	4	13	11	9	12																46

FA Cup
First Round   Cheltenham T   (a)   0-1

Carling Cup
First Round   Coventry C   (h)   2-0
Second Round   Burnley   (h)   1-3

J Paint Trophy
First Round   Macclesfield T   (a)   0-1

NEWCASTLE UNITED   FA Premiership

FOUNDATION

In October 1882 a club called Stanley, which had been formed in 1881, changed its name to Newcastle East End to avoid confusion with two other local clubs, Stanley Nops and Stanley Albion. Shortly afterwards another club Rosewood merged with them. Newcastle West End had been formed in August 1882 and they played on a pitch which was part of the Town Moor. Moved to Brandling Park 1885 and St James' Park 1886 (home of Newcastle Rangers). West End went out of existence after a bad run and the remaining committee men invited East End to move to St James' Park. They accepted and, at a meeting in Bath Lane Hall in 1892, changed their name to Newcastle United.

St James' Park, Newcastle-upon-Tyne NE1 4ST.
Telephone: (0191) 201 8400.
Fax: (0191) 201 8600.
Ticket Office: (0844) 372 1892.
Website: www.nufc.co.uk
Email: admin@nufc.co.uk
Ground Capacity: 52,387.
Record Attendance: 68,386 v Chelsea, Division 1, 3 September 1930.
Pitch Measurements: 105m × 68m.
Managing Director: Derek Llambias.
Manager: Alan Pardew.
Assistant Manager: John Carver.
Physio: Derek Wright.
Colours: Black and white striped shirts, black shorts with white trim, black stockings with white trim.
Change Colours: All blue with white trim.
Year Formed: 1881.
Turned Professional: 1889.
Ltd Co.: 1890.
Previous Names: 1881, Stanley; 1882, Newcastle East End; 1892, Newcastle United.
Club Nickname: 'The Magpies'.
Grounds: 1881, South Byker; 1886, Chillingham Road, Heaton; 1892, St James' Park.

HONOURS

FA Premier League:
Runners-up 1995–96, 1996–97.

Football League – Division 1:
Champions 1904–05, 1906–07, 1908–09, 1926–27, 1992–93;
Division 2: *Champions* 1964–65;
Runners-up 1897–98, 1947–48;
FL C: *Champions* 2009–10.

FA Cup: *Winners* 1910, 1924, 1932, 1951, 1952, 1955; *Runners-up* 1905, 1906, 1908, 1911, 1974, 1998, 1999.

Football League Cup:
Runners-up 1976.

Texaco Cup: *Winners* 1974, 1975.

European Competitions
Champions League: 1997–98, 2002–03, 2003–04. **European Fairs Cup:** 1968–69 (*winners*), 1969–70, 1970–71.
UEFA Cup: 1977–78, 1994–95, 1996–97, 1999–2000, 2003–04 (*s-f*), 2004–05, 2006–07.
European Cup Winners' Cup: 1998–99.
Anglo-Italian Cup: 1972–73 (*winners*).
Intertoto Cup: 2001 (*runners-up*), 2005, 2006 (*winners*).

First Football League Game: 2 September 1893, Division 2, v Royal Arsenal (a) D 2–2 – Ramsay; Jeffery, Miller; Crielly, Graham, McKane; Bowman, Crate (1), Thompson, Sorley (1), Wallace. Graham not Crate scored according to some reports.

sky SPORTS FACT FILE

On 21 September 2010, Newcastle United defeated Chelsea 4-3 in a third round League Cup tie. It was their first success at Stamford Bridge since 22 November 1986 when goals from Andy Thomas (two) and Peter Beardsley had given United a 3-1 Division One win.

Record League Victory: 13–0 v Newport Co, Division 2, 5 October 1946 – Garbutt; Cowell, Graham; Harvey, Brennan, Wright; Milburn (2), Bentley (1), Wayman (4), Shackleton (6), Pearson.

Record Cup Victory: 9–0 v Southport (at Hillsborough), FA Cup 4th rd, 1 February 1932 – McInroy; Nelson, Fairhurst; McKenzie, Davidson, Weaver (1); Boyd (1), Jimmy Richardson (3), Cape (2), McMenemy (1), Lang (1).

Record Defeat: 0–9 v Burton Wanderers, Division 2, 15 April 1895.

Most League Points (2 for a win): 57, Division 2, 1964–65.

Most League Points (3 for a win): 102, FL C, 2009–10.

Most League Goals: 98, Division 1, 1951–52.

Highest League Scorer in Season: Hughie Gallacher, 36, Division 1, 1926–27.

Most League Goals in Total Aggregate: Jackie Milburn, 177, 1946–57.

Most League Goals in One Match: 6, Len Shackleton v Newport Co, Division 2, 5 October 1946.

Most Capped Player: Shay Given, 82 (113), Republic of Ireland.

Most League Appearances: Jim Lawrence, 432, 1904–22.

Youngest League Player: Steve Watson, 16 years 223 days v Wolverhampton W, 10 November 1990.

Record Transfer Fee Received: £35,000,000 from Liverpool for Andy Carroll, January 2011.

Record Transfer Fee Paid: £16,000,000 to Real Madrid for Michael Owen, September 2005.

Football League Record: 1893 Elected to Division 2; 1898–1934 Division 1; 1934–48 Division 2; 1948–61 Division 1; 1961–65 Division 2; 1965–78 Division 1; 1978–84 Division 2; 1984–89 Division 1; 1989–92 Division 2; 1992–93 Division 1; 1993–2009 FA Premier League; 2009–10 FL C; 2010– FA Premier League.

MANAGERS

Frank Watt 1895–32
(Secretary-Manager)
Andy Cunningham 1930–35
Tom Mather 1935–39
Stan Seymour 1939–47
(Hon. Manager)
George Martin 1947–50
Stan Seymour 1950–54
(Hon. Manager)
Duggie Livingstone 1954–56
Stan Seymour 1956–58
(Hon. Manager)
Charlie Mitten 1958–61
Norman Smith 1961–62
Joe Harvey 1962–75
Gordon Lee 1975–77
Richard Dinnis 1977
Bill McGarry 1977–80
Arthur Cox 1980–84
Jack Charlton 1984
Willie McFaul 1985–88
Jim Smith 1988–91
Ossie Ardiles 1991–92
Kevin Keegan 1992–97
Kenny Dalglish 1997–98
Ruud Gullit 1998–99
Sir Bobby Robson 1999–2004
Graeme Souness 2004–06
Glenn Roeder 2006–07
Sam Allardyce 2007–08
Kevin Keegan 2008
Joe Kinnear 2008–09
Alan Shearer 2009
Chris Hughton 2009–10
Alan Pardew December 2010–

LATEST SEQUENCES

Longest Sequence of League Wins: 13, 25.4.1992 – 18.10.1992.

Longest Sequence of League Defeats: 10, 23.8.1977 – 15.10.1977.

Longest Sequence of League Draws: 4, 20.1.1990 – 24.2.1990.

Longest Sequence of Unbeaten League Matches: 17, 13.2.2010 – 2.5.2010.

Longest Sequence Without a League Win: 21, 14.1.1978 – 23.8.1978.

Successive Scoring Runs: 25 from 15.4.1939.

Successive Non-scoring Runs: 6 from 31.12.1938.

TEN YEAR LEAGUE RECORD

		P	W	D	L	F	A	Pts	Pos
2001-02	PR Lge	38	21	8	9	74	52	71	4
2002-03	PR Lge	38	21	6	11	63	48	69	3
2003-04	PR Lge	38	13	17	8	52	40	56	5
2004-05	PR Lge	38	10	14	14	47	57	44	14
2005-06	PR Lge	38	17	7	14	47	42	58	7
2006-07	PR Lge	38	11	10	17	38	47	43	13
2007-08	PR Lge	38	11	10	17	45	65	43	12
2008-09	PR Lge	38	7	13	18	40	59	34	18
2009-10	FL C	46	30	12	4	90	35	102	1
2010-11	PR Lge	38	11	13	14	56	57	46	12

DID YOU KNOW ?

On 5 February 2011 Newcastle United found themselves a goal down in 43 seconds, four adrift in 26 minutes to Arsenal at St James' Park. A second half revival enabled them to force a 4-4 draw, making Arsenal the first Premier League team to fail to defend a four goal lead.

NEWCASTLE UNITED 2010–11 LEAGUE RECORD

Match No.	Date		Venue	Opponents		Result	H/T Score	Lg Pos.	Goalscorers	Attendance
1	Aug	16	A	Manchester U	L	0-3	0-2	—		75,221
2		22	H	Aston Villa	W	6-0	3-0	8	Barton [12], Nolan 2 [31, 87], Carroll 3 [34, 67, 90]	43,546
3		28	A	Wolverhampton W	D	1-1	0-1	8	Carroll [62]	27,745
4	Sept	11	H	Blackpool	L	0-2	0-1	14		49,597
5		18	A	Everton	W	1-0	1-0	6	Ben Arfa [45]	38,019
6		26	H	Stoke C	L	1-2	1-0	10	Nolan (pen) [43]	41,915
7	Oct	3	A	Manchester C	L	1-2	1-1	15	Gutierrez [24]	46,067
8		16	H	Wigan Ath	D	2-2	0-2	14	Ameobi, Shola [72], Coloccini [90]	44,415
9		23	A	West Ham U	W	2-1	1-1	9	Nolan [23], Carroll [69]	34,486
10		31	H	Sunderland	W	5-1	3-0	7	Nolan 3 [26, 34, 75], Ameobi, Shola 2 (1 pen) [45 (p), 70]	51,988
11	Nov	7	A	Arsenal	W	1-0	1-0	5	Carroll [45]	60,059
12		10	H	Blackburn R	L	1-2	0-1	—	Carroll [47]	41,053
13		13	H	Fulham	D	0-0	0-0	8		44,686
14		20	A	Bolton W	L	1-5	0-2	10	Carroll [52]	22,203
15		28	H	Chelsea	D	1-1	1-1	9	Carroll [6]	46,469
16	Dec	5	A	WBA	L	1-3	0-1	11	Lovenkrands [90]	23,486
17		11	H	Liverpool	W	3-1	1-0	8	Nolan [15], Barton [80], Carroll [90]	50,137
18		26	A	Manchester C	L	1-3	0-2	9	Carroll [72]	51,635
19		28	A	Tottenham H	L	0-2	0-0	13		35,927
20	Jan	2	A	Wigan Ath	W	1-0	1-0	10	Ameobi, Shola [19]	15,277
21		5	H	West Ham U	W	5-0	3-0	8	Best 3 [18, 39, 60], Nolan [45], Lovenkrands [63]	42,387
22		16	A	Sunderland	D	1-1	0-0	9	Nolan [52]	47,864
23		22	H	Tottenham H	D	1-1	0-0	8	Coloccini [59]	51,010
24	Feb	2	A	Fulham	L	0-1	0-0	—		25,620
25		5	H	Arsenal	D	4-4	0-4	10	Barton 2 (2 pens) [68, 83], Best [75], Tiote [87]	51,561
26		12	A	Blackburn R	D	0-0	0-0	10		26,781
27		15	A	Birmingham C	W	2-0	1-0	—	Lovenkrands [2], Best [50]	28,270
28		26	H	Bolton W	D	1-1	1-1	9	Nolan [13]	48,062
29	Mar	5	A	Everton	L	1-2	1-2	9	Best [23]	50,128
30		19	A	Stoke C	L	0-4	0-1	11		27,505
31	Apr	2	H	Wolverhampton W	W	4-1	2-0	9	Nolan [22], Ameobi, Shola [45], Lovenkrands [50], Gutierrez [90]	49,939
32		10	A	Aston Villa	L	0-1	0-1	9		37,090
33		19	H	Manchester U	D	0-0	0-0	—		49,025
34		23	A	Blackpool	D	1-1	1-1	9	Lovenkrands [17]	16,003
35	May	1	A	Liverpool	L	0-3	0-1	12		44,923
36		7	H	Birmingham C	W	2-1	2-1	11	Ameobi, Shola (pen) [36], Taylor, S [43]	47,409
37		15	A	Chelsea	D	2-2	1-1	12	Gutierrez [10], Taylor, S [90]	41,739
38		22	H	WBA	D	3-3	2-0	12	Taylor, S [16], Lovenkrands [39], Olsson (og) [47]	51,678

Final League Position: 12

GOALSCORERS

League (56): Nolan 12 (1 pen), Carroll 11, Ameobi, Shola 6 (2 pens), Best 6, Lovenkrands 6, Barton 4 (2 pens), Gutierrez 3, Taylor, S 3, Coloccini 2, Ben Arfa 1, Tiote 1, own goal 1.
Carling Cup (7): Ameobi 3, Taylor, R 2, Lovenkrands 1, Ranger 1.
FA Cup (1): Barton 1.

Harper S 18	Perch J 9+4	Jose Enrique 36	Barton J 32	Coloccini F 35	Williamson M 28+1	Routledge W 10+7	Smith A 7+4	Carroll A 18+1	Nolan K 30	Gutierrez J 34+3	Ameobi Shola 21+7	Xisco —+2	Taylor R 3+2	Ben Arfa H 3+1	Lovenkrands P 18+7	Tiote C 26	Krul T 20+1	Campbell S 4+3	Guthrie D 11+3	Ranger N 1+23	Simpson D 30	Taylor S 12+2	Best L 9+2	Ferguson S 3+4	Gosling D —+1	Kuqi S —+6	Ireland S —+2	LuaLua K —+2	Ameobi Sam —+1	Match No.
1	2	3	4	5	6	7	8	9	10^1	11^2	12	13																		1
1	2	3	4	5	6	7^1	8^2	9	10	11^3	13	14	12																	2
1	2	3	4	5	6	7	8	9^1	10	11	12																			3
1	2	3	4	5	6	7^2	8^3	9	10	11^1	14			12	13															4
1^6	2	3	4	5	6	7		9	10		12				11^1		8	15												5
	2	3	4	5	6	7		9	10		12	13			11^1		8^2	1												6
	2	3	4	5^1	6		12	14	10^3	11	9				7^1		8	1	13											7
	2^3	3	4	5	6			13			9		11	12	10^1	7	1	8^2	14											8
		3	4	5	6			9	7	11	10^1					8	1				2									9
		3	4	5	6			9	8	11	10^1					7	1		12		2									10
		3	4	5	6			9	7	11	10^1					8	1		12		2									11
		3	4	5	6		13	9	7	11	10^1					8^2	1		12		2									12
		3		5	6		12	9	4	11	10^2					8	1		7^1	13	2									13
		3		5^1	6		12	8	9	11^3	10^2				13	4	1	14	7^1		2									14
		3	7					9		11	10^1					4	1	5	8	12	2	6								15
		3	7^3				13	9		11	10^1				12	4	1	5	8^2	14	2	6								16
		3	7^3			14	13	9	8^2	11	10^1					4	1	5	12		2	6								17
		3	4	5		7^1		9	10	11						8	1		12		2	6								18
	2	3	4	5		7			10	11^1					13		1	8^2	12			6	9							19
1		3	4	5			12			11	10^1			14	7^3	8					2	6	9^2	13						20
1		3	4	5		7	12			11^1	10				13	8		8^1		14	2									21
1		3	7	5	6			8^1	4	11^3	10				13				12		2		9^2	14						22
1	13	3	7	5	6				4	11	10^3							8^2	12		2		9^1	14						23
1		3	7	5	6				4	11	10^1				13	8			12		2		9^2							24
1		3	7	5	6				4	11	10^1				13	8			12		2		9^2							25
1	12	3	7	5	6				4	11	10^2				13	8					2^1		9^3	14						26
1		3	7	5	6				4	11^3	10^1				13	8			12	14	2		9^2							27
1		3		5	6				4	11^1	10^2		7			8			13		2	12	9^3		14					28
1		3^1		5	6				4	11	10			12		8			7		2^2		9^3	13	14					29
1		3^1	7	5	4					11	10^2			14	13	8		6^3	12		2		9							30
1	12		7^3	5	6				4	11	10^2				13	8			14		2				3^1					31
1		3	7	5	6				4^1	11	10			12		8					2		9^2				13			32
		3	7	5	6				4	11	10^1				13	8	1				2		9^2					12		33
	13	3	7	5	6				4^2	11	10^1					8	1				2		9^3				14	12		34
		3^1	7	5	6				4	11	10^1					8	1		12		2		9^2	13			14			35
		3	7	5					4	11	10^1					8	1		12		2	6	9							36
		3	7	5					4	11^2	10^3				13		1		8^1		2	6	9				14	12		37
		3	7	5			13		4	11^1	10^2						1	8^3			2	6	9				14	12		38

FA Cup

Third Round	Stevenage		(a)	1-3

Carling Cup

Second Round	Accrington S		(a)	3-2
Third Round	Chelsea		(a)	4-3
Fourth Round	Arsenal		(h)	0-4

NORTHAMPTON TOWN   FL Championship 2

FOUNDATION

Formed in 1897 by school teachers connected with the Northampton and District Elementary Schools' Association, they survived a financial crisis at the end of their first year when they were £675 in the red and became members of the Midland League – a fast move indeed for a new club. They achieved Southern League membership in 1901.

Sixfields Stadium, Upton Way, Northampton NN5 5QA.
Telephone: (01604) 683 700.
Fax: (01604) 751 613.
Ticket Office: (01604) 683 777.
Website: www.ntfc.co.uk
Email: gareth.willsher@ntfc.tv
Ground Capacity: 7,300.
Record Attendance: 24,523 v Fulham, Division 1, 23 April 1966 (at County Ground). 7,557 v Manchester C, Division 2, 26 September 1998 (at Sixfields Stadium).
Pitch Measurements: 116yd × 72yd.
Chairman: David Cardoza.
Secretary: Norman Howells.
Manager: Gary Johnson.
Assistant Manager: David Lee.
Physio: Stuart Barker.
Colours: Claret shirts, white shorts, white stockings.
Change Colours: Light blue shirts, white shorts, light blue stockings.
Year Formed: 1897.
Turned Professional: 1901.
Ltd Co.: 1901.
Grounds: 1897, County Ground; 1994, Sixfields Stadium.
Club Nickname: 'The Cobblers'.
First Football League Game: 28 August 1920, Division 3, v Grimsby T (a) L 0–2 – Thorpe; Sproston, Hewison; Jobey, Tomkins, Pease; Whitworth, Lockett, Thomas, Freeman, MacKechnie.
Record League Victory: 10–0 v Walsall, Division 3 (S), 5 November 1927 – Hammond; Watson, Jeffs; Allen, Brett, Odell; Daley, Smith (3), Loasby (3), Hoten (1), Wells (3).
Record Cup Victory: 10–0 v Sutton T, FA Cup prel rd, 7 December 1907 – Cooch; Drennan, Lloyd Davies, Tirrell (1), McCartney, Hickleton, Badenock (3), Platt (3), Lowe (1), Chapman (2), McDiarmid.
Record Defeat: 0–11 v Southampton, Southern League, 28 December 1901.

HONOURS

Football League – Division 1: 21st, 1965–66;
Division 2: *Runners-up* 1964–65;
Division 3: *Champions* 1962–63;
Division 3 (S): *Runners-up* 1927–28, 1949–50;
Division 4: *Champions* 1986–87; *Runners-up* 1975–76;
FL 2: *Runners-up* 2005–06.
FA Cup: Best season: 5th rd, 1934, 1950, 1970.
Football League Cup: Best season: 5th rd, 1965, 1967.

sky SPORTS FACT FILE

On 1 February 2011 Northampton Town beat Crewe 6-2 at Sixfields. Shaun Harrad scored after just eleven minutes of his debut after transfer from Burton Albion. It was the Cobblers' first six goals since defeating Aldershot 6-0 on 1 October 1988 when Paul Culpin scored three.

Most League Points (2 for a win): 68, Division 4, 1975–76.

Most League Points (3 for a win): 99, Division 4, 1986–87.

Most League Goals: 109, Division 3, 1962–63 and Division 3 (S), 1952–53.

Highest League Scorer in Season: Cliff Holton, 36, Division 3, 1961–62.

Most League Goals in Total Aggregate: Jack English, 135, 1947–60.

Most League Goals in One Match: 5, Ralph Hoten v Crystal Palace, Division 3 (S), 27 October 1928.

Most Capped Player: Edwin Lloyd Davies, 12 (16), Wales.

Most League Appearances: Tommy Fowler, 521, 1946–61.

Youngest League Player: Adrian Mann, 16 years 297 days v Bury, 5 May 1984.

Record Transfer Fee Received: £265,000 from Watford for Richard Hill, July 1987.

Record Transfer Fee Paid: £165,000 to Oldham Ath for Josh Low, July 2003.

Football League Record: 1920 Original Member of Division 3; 1921 Division 3 (S); 1958–61 Division 4; 1961–63 Division 3; 1963–65 Division 2; 1965–66 Division 1; 1966–67 Division 2; 1967–69 Division 3; 1969–76 Division 4; 1976–77 Division 3; 1977–87 Division 4; 1987–90 Division 3; 1990–92 Division 4; 1992–97 Division 3; 1997–99 Division 2; 1999–2000 Division 3; 2000–03 Division 2; 2003–04 Division 3; 2004–06 FL 2; 2006–09 FL 1; 2009– FL 2.

LATEST SEQUENCES

Longest Sequence of League Wins: 8, 27.8.1960 – 19.9.1960.

Longest Sequence of League Defeats: 8, 26.10.1935 – 21.12.1935.

Longest Sequence of League Draws: 6, 18.9.1983 – 15.10.1983.

Longest Sequence of Unbeaten League Matches: 21, 27.9.1986 – 6.2.1987.

Longest Sequence Without a League Win: 18, 26.3.1969 – 20.9.1969.

Successive Scoring Runs: 27 from 23.8.1986.

Successive Non-scoring Runs: 7 from 7.4.1939.

MANAGERS

Arthur Jones 1897–1907
(Secretary-Manager)
Herbert Chapman 1907–12
Walter Bull 1912–13
Fred Lessons 1913–19
Bob Hewison 1920–25
Jack Tresadern 1925–30
Jack English 1931–35
Syd Puddefoot 1935–37
Warney Cresswell 1937–39
Tom Smith 1939–49
Bob Dennison 1949–54
Dave Smith 1954–59
David Bowen 1959–67
Tony Marchi 1967–68
Ron Flowers 1968–69
Dave Bowen 1969–72
(continued as General Manager and Secretary to 1985 when joined the board)
Billy Baxter 1972–73
Bill Dodgin Jnr 1973–76
Pat Crerand 1976–77
By committee 1977
Bill Dodgin Jnr 1977
John Petts 1977–78
Mike Keen 1978–79
Clive Walker 1979–80
Bill Dodgin Jnr 1980–82
Clive Walker 1982–84
Tony Barton 1984–85
Graham Carr 1985–90
Theo Foley 1990–92
Phil Chard 1992–93
John Barnwell 1993–94
Ian Atkins 1995–99
Kevin Wilson 1999–2001
Kevan Broadhurst 2001–03
Terry Fenwick 2003
Martin Wilkinson 2003
Colin Calderwood 2003–06
John Gorman 2006
Stuart Gray 2007–09
Ian Sampson 2009–11
Gary Johnson March 2011–

TEN YEAR LEAGUE RECORD

		P	W	D	L	F	A	Pts	Pos
2001-02	Div 2	46	14	7	25	54	79	49	20
2002-03	Div 2	46	10	9	27	40	79	39	24
2003-04	Div 3	46	22	9	15	58	51	75	6
2004-05	FL 2	46	20	12	14	62	51	72	7
2005-06	FL 2	46	22	17	7	63	37	83	2
2006-07	FL 1	46	15	14	17	48	51	59	14
2007-08	FL 1	46	17	15	14	60	55	66	9
2008-09	FL 1	46	12	13	21	61	65	49	21
2009-10	FL 2	46	18	13	15	62	53	67	11
2010-11	FL 2	46	11	19	16	63	71	52	16

DID YOU KNOW ?

On 21 September 2010, Northampton Town forced Liverpool to extra time in a League Cup third round tie at Anfield. Extra time found the score at 2-2. Northampton won the shoot-out 4-2 avenging a 3-1 FA Cup defeat on 25 January 1958 at the same venue.

NORTHAMPTON TOWN 2010–11 LEAGUE RECORD

Match No.	Date	Venue	Opponents	Result	H/T Score	Lg Pos.	Goalscorers	Attendance
1	Aug 7	A	Torquay U	L	0-3	0-1	—	3567
2	14	H	Accrington S	D	0-0	0-0	22		4042
3	21	A	Bury	D	1-1	1-0	20	Guinan (pen) [33]	2845
4	28	H	Wycombe W	D	1-1	0-1	18	Thornton (pen) [87]	4202
5	Sept 4	A	Aldershot T	D	1-1	1-0	19	McKay [34]	2739
6	11	H	Southend U	W	2-1	0-0	16	Osman [63], Holt [76]	5720
7	18	A	Shrewsbury T	L	1-3	1-1	17	Thornton [44]	5527
8	25	H	Bradford C	W	2-0	0-0	13	McKay [61], Tozer [81]	4646
9	28	H	Chesterfield	L	1-2	1-0	—	Thornton [45]	4025
10	Oct 2	A	Macclesfield T	L	0-2	0-1	19		1699
11	9	A	Cheltenham T	L	0-1	0-0	22		3016
12	16	H	Hereford U	L	3-4	3-0	22	McKenzie 3 [24, 42, 45]	4333
13	23	A	Oxford U	L	1-3	1-2	23	McKenzie [16]	7647
14	30	H	Gillingham	W	2-1	2-1	21	Beckwith [21], McKenzie (pen) [40]	4573
15	Nov 2	A	Lincoln C	W	2-0	1-0	—	Beckwith [37], Johnson [74]	4459
16	13	H	Port Vale	D	0-0	0-0	20		4612
17	20	A	Barnet	L	1-4	1-2	22	McKenzie [6]	1918
18	23	A	Rotherham U	D	2-2	2-2	—	Osman [23], Holt [24]	2490
19	Dec 4	H	Stockport Co	W	2-0	1-0	—	Thornton [4], Jacobs [75]	4088
20	11	A	Stevenage	W	1-0	1-0	15	Gilligan [14]	3128
21	Jan 1	A	Crewe Alex	L	0-2	0-1	19		3835
22	3	H	Lincoln C	W	2-1	0-0	14	McKay [64], Johnson [88]	4112
23	8	H	Cheltenham T	D	1-1	1-0	14	McKay [9]	4031
24	15	A	Gillingham	L	0-1	0-1	16		5613
25	22	H	Oxford U	W	2-1	1-0	14	Holt [42], McKenzie [67]	6097
26	Feb 1	H	Crewe Alex	W	6-2	3-1	13	Harrad [11], Jacobs [14], Beckwith [44], Holt [46], Osman [48], McKay [80]	4021
27	5	H	Barnet	D	0-0	0-0	14		4573
28	12	A	Port Vale	D	1-1	0-0	14	McKenzie [58]	5321
29	15	A	Morecambe	D	3-3	1-1	—	Johnson [13], Thornton [50], McKenzie (pen) [71]	3522
30	19	H	Aldershot T	D	1-1	1-0	14	Tozer [18]	5011
31	22	A	Hereford U	D	1-1	0-0	—	Holt [47]	2125
32	26	A	Southend U	D	1-1	1-1	15	Johnson [27]	6384
33	Mar 1	H	Burton Alb	L	2-3	1-3	—	Johnson [45], Holt [61]	3423
34	5	A	Shrewsbury T	L	2-3	1-1	16	Jacobs 2 [6, 47]	5113
35	8	A	Chesterfield	L	1-2	0-0	—	Johnson [82]	5661
36	12	H	Macclesfield T	L	0-1	0-0	19		4707
37	19	A	Bradford C	D	1-1	0-1	20	Harrad (pen) [60]	10,684
38	25	H	Torquay U	D	2-2	1-1	—	Johnson [30], Bauza [90]	4553
39	Apr 2	A	Accrington S	L	1-3	0-3	21	Jacobs [67]	1876
40	5	A	Burton Alb	D	1-1	1-1	—	Bauza [39]	2536
41	9	H	Bury	L	2-4	0-3	21	Harrad 2 [59, 90]	5077
42	16	A	Wycombe W	D	2-2	2-0	21	Harrad (pen) [20], Bauza [37]	5161
43	22	H	Rotherham U	D	2-2	0-2	—	McKenzie [68], Davis [90]	5167
44	25	A	Stockport Co	D	2-2	1-1	22	Bauza [2], Harrad (pen) [78]	4807
45	30	H	Stevenage	W	2-0	1-0	20	Davis [3], Uwezu [59]	6257
46	May 7	A	Morecambe	W	2-1	1-0	16	Thornton [24], Tozer [84]	2674

Final League Position: 16

GOALSCORERS

League (63): McKenzie 10 (2 pens), Johnson 7, Harrad 6 (3 pens), Holt 6, Thornton 6 (1 pen), Jacobs 5, McKay 5, Bauza 4, Beckwith 3, Osman 3, Tozer 3, Davis 2, Gilligan 1, Guinan 1 (1 pen), Uwezu 1.
Carling Cup (8): Jacobs 2, McKay 2, Davis 1, Holt 1, Thornton 1, own goal 1.
FA Cup (5): Guinan 1, Jacobs 1, Johnson 1, McKay 1, Thornton 1.
J Paint Trophy (0).

Jansson O 4	Johnson J 38	Holt A 32 + 7	Rodgers P 15 + 10	Hall M 21 + 3	Beckwith D 35 + 2	Gilligan R 20 + 2	Osman A 37 + 1	Guinan S 5 + 6	McKay B 24 + 10	Davis L 32 + 1	Jacobs M 33 + 8	Herbert C 1 + 14	Purcell T 1 + 3	Wedderburn N 21 + 10	Thornton K 16 + 9	Harris S 1 + 3	Dunn C 39	McKenzie L 17 + 10	Tozer B 28 + 3	Parker J 3	King C 3 + 4	Jarvis R 3	Kaziboni G — + 2	Laurent F 3 + 3	Walker J 19	Harrad S 18	Ofori-Twumasi N 11	Reckord J 4 + 3	Bauza G 9 + 1	Webster B 8	Uwezu M 2 + 2	Collis S 3 + 1	Walker P — + 1	Match No.
1	2	3	4[1]	5	6	7	8		9[3]	10	11[2]	12	13	14																				1
1	2	3		5	6	7	8		9[3]	10[3]	11[1]		14	13	4	12																		2
1		3	2[3]	5	6	7[2]	8	9	10			4[1]		12	11	14	13																	3
1		3	2	5	6		8	9[2]	10[3]		12	13		7[1]	11	4	14																	4
	2[1]	5	7		6		8	9[2]	10	3	11[3]	12		4	14	13	1																	5
	2	5	7[1]		6	4	8	13	9	3	11[3]	14		12			1	10[2]																6
	2	5	12				7	8[3]		10	3	13	14	11[2]	4	6[1]	1	9																7
	2	5	7[2]		11		8	14	9[3]	3	10	13		4[1]			1	12	6															8
	2	5	7[3]		11[1]		8		10[2]	3	9	14		12	4		1	13	6															9
	2	5			11		8	13	10	3	9[2]			12	4[2]		1	14	6	7														10
	2	3			6[1]	7	8		10[2]	9	12			4[1]			1	13	5	11														11
	2	5	14			7	8[2]	12	10	3				13	4		1	9[1]	6[6]	11[3]														12
4[8]	12	2	5		7				10	3	8[1]			11	6		1	9																13
	2	5	14	4	6	7[3]	8	13	10[1]	3	12			11			1	9[2]																14
	2	5	13		6	7[2]	8	12	10	3				11			1	9[1]	4															15
	2	11	12	13	6		8[8]		10[2]	3	7			4			1		5		9[1]													16
	2	11	12		6	7	8[3]		3[8]	13				4[2]	14		1	9[1]	5		10													17
	2[1]	11	12	3	6	7	8		13					4			1	9	5		10[2]													18
	2[1]	11[1]			6	7	8		10[2]	3	12			4			1	9	5		13													19
	2[1]	11	12		6	7			10[2]	3				8	4		1	14	5		13	9[3]												20
	2	11			8		8		13	3	7	12		4			1	9[1]	5			10[2]												21
	2	11			6		8		9[2]	3	7	12		4			1		5		13	10[1]												22
	2	11			6	7[2]	8		9[1]	3	10	13		4[3]	14		1		5			12												23
	2	11	13	6	7	8			3	10	9[1]			4[2]			1		5				12											24
	2	11		3	6	13	8		12		7			4			1	9[2]	5					10[1]										25
2[3]	11[1]	14	3	6		4			13		7			12			1	9[2]	5							8	10							26
		2	3	6	12	8			9[2]		11						1	13	5						7[1]	4	10							27
	11[1]	2	3	6		8[8]		14	12		7			13			1								4	10[3]								28
	2	12	14	3	6				11[1]	8				13	4[3]		1	9[2]	5						7	10								29
	2	12			3	6			14		8[3]			11	4[1]		1	9[2]	5						13	7	10[8]							30
	5	10	2	3	6				9	11	8			4	12		1									7[1]								31
	2	10	12	6		7			9[2]	3[1]	8			11	4[3]		1	13	5						14									32
	2	10			3	6		4			12		8	13			1	9	5[2]						7[1]	11								33
	2	3	7		6		8		9[1]		11	12					1		5						4	10								34
	5	10			6[1]		7[3]			11				14	8[2]		1		12						13	4	9	2	3					35
	5	11[2]		3		7[1]	8		10	13					14		1								4	9	2[3]	6	12					36
	2		3	12		8[2]			11[3]	7				13			1								4	9	3	6	14	10	5[1]			37
	2		6[1]			8[2]			11[3]	7				14	13		1								4	9	3	12	10	5				38
	2		3[1]		8				11[2]	7							1	12							4	9[1]	6	14	10	5	13			39
		3	6	13		8			11					8[2]	14		1	12							4	9	2	7[3]	10[1]	5				40
6[1]		3	12	6		8			11	13				16			1								4[2]	9	2	7	10[1]	5		15		41
	14	2[3]	6		8				13	11	7				12		1								4	9[2]	3	10[1]	5		1		42
	14	7[1]	6						3	10				13	4			10[1]	5						11	9	2	8	5[2]	12[3]	1			43
	12	3	6	8		13			11					10[1]	5										4	9	2	7[2]			16	15		44
5	12		6				11		8					1	3										7	9	2		10[1]					45
2			6		12	3	11[3]			13	8		1		4[2]									14		9		7	5	10[1]				46

FA Cup

First Round	Forest Green R	(a)	3-0
Second Round	Sheffield W	(a)	2-3

Carling Cup

First Round	Brighton & HA	(h)	2-0
Second Round	Reading	(a)	3-3
Third Round	Liverpool	(a)	2-2
Fourth Round	Ipswich T	(a)	1-3

J Paint Trophy

First Round	Hartlepool U	(a)	0-4

NORWICH CITY
FA Premiership

FOUNDATION

Formed in 1902, largely through the initiative of two local schoolmasters who called a meeting at the Criterion Cafe, they were shocked by an FA Commission which in 1904 declared the club professional and ejected them from the FA Amateur Cup. However, this only served to strengthen their determination. New officials were appointed and a professional club established at a meeting in the Agricultural Hall in March 1905.

Carrow Road, Norwich NR1 1JE.

Telephone: (01603) 760 760.

Fax: (01603) 613 886.

Ticket Office: (0844) 826 1902.

Website: www.canaries.co.uk

Email: reception@ncfc-canaries.co.uk

Ground Capacity: 26,034.

Record Attendance: 25,037 v Sheffield W, FA Cup 5th rd, 16 February 1935 (at The Nest). 43,984 v Leicester C, FA Cup 6th rd, 30 March 1963 (at Carrow Road).

Pitch Measurements: 105m × 67m.

Joint Majority Shareholders: Delia Smith and Michael Wynn Jones.

Chairman: Alan Bowkett.

Deputy Chairman: Michael Foulger.

Chief Executive: David McNally.

Secretary: Kevan Platt.

Manager: Paul Lambert.

Assistant Manager: Ian Culverhouse.

Physio: Neal Reynolds.

Colours: Yellow shirts with green trim, green shorts, yellow stockings.

Change Colours: All white with green trim on shirts.

Year Formed: 1902. *Turned Professional:* 1905. *Ltd Co.:* 1905.

Club Nickname: 'The Canaries'.

Grounds: 1902, Newmarket Road; 1908, The Nest, Rosary Road; 1935, Carrow Road.

First Football League Game: 28 August 1920, Division 3, v Plymouth Arg (a) D 1–1 – Skermer; Gray, Gadsden; Wilkinson, Addy, Martin; Laxton, Kidger, Parker, Whitham (1), Dobson.

Record League Victory: 10–2 v Coventry C, Division 3 (S), 15 March 1930 – Jarvie; Hannah, Graham; Brown, O'Brien, Lochhead (1); Porter (1), Anderson, Hunt (5), Scott (2), Slicer (1).

HONOURS

FA Premier League: Best season: 3rd 1992–93.

Football League – Division 1: *Champions* 2003–04;

FL C: *Runners-up* 2010–11;

Division 2: *Champions* 1971–72, 1985–86;

FL 1: *Champions* 2009–10;

Division 3 (S): *Champions* 1933–34; *Runners-up* 1950–51;

Division 3: *Runners-up* 1959–60.

FA Cup: Semi-finals 1959, 1989, 1992.

Football League Cup: *Winners* 1962, 1985; *Runners-up* 1973, 1975.

European Competitions **UEFA Cup:** 1993–94.

sky SPORTS FACT FILE

Norwich City manager Tom Parker spotted Alf Kirchen as a centre-half but it was on the right wing he made his name. A carpenter by trade he was transferred to Arsenal in 1935 for £6,000, won England caps. Following injury, he became a successful farmer and clay pigeon champion.

Record Cup Victory: 8–0 v Sutton U, FA Cup 4th rd, 28 January 1989 – Gunn; Culverhouse, Bowen, Butterworth, Linighan, Townsend (Crook), Gordon, Fleck (3), Allen (4), Phelan, Putney (1).

Record Defeat: 2–10 v Swindon T, Southern League, 5 September 1908.

Most League Points (2 for a win): 64, Division 3 (S), 1950–51.

Most League Points (3 for a win): 95, FL 1, 2009–10.

Most League Goals: 99, Division 3 (S), 1952–53.

Highest League Scorer in Season: Ralph Hunt, 31, Division 3 (S), 1955–56.

Most League Goals in Total Aggregate: Johnny Gavin, 122, 1945–54, 1955–58.

Most League Goals in One Match: 5, Tommy Hunt v Coventry C, Division 3 (S), 15 March 1930; 5, Roy Hollis v Walsall, Division 3 (S), 29 December 1951.

Most Capped Player: Mark Bowen, 35 (41), Wales.

Most League Appearances: Ron Ashman, 592, 1947–64.

Youngest League Player: Ryan Jarvis, 16 years 282 days v Walsall, 19 April 2003.

Record Transfer Fee Received: £7,250,000 from West Ham U for Dean Ashton, January 2006.

Record Transfer Fee Paid: £3,800,000 to Crewe Alex for Dean Ashton, January 2005 (including sell-on).

Football League Record: 1920 Original Member of Division 3; 1921 Division 3 (S): 1934–39 Division 2; 1946–58 Division 3 (S); 1958–60 Division 3; 1960–72 Division 2; 1972–74 Division 1; 1974–75 Division 2; 1975–81 Division 1; 1981–82 Division 2; 1982–85 Division 1; 1985–86 Division 2; 1986–92 Division 1; 1992–95 FA Premier League; 1995–2004 Division 1; 2004–05 FA Premier League; 2005–09 FL C; 2009–10 FL 1; 2010–11 FL C; 2011– FA Premier League.

LATEST SEQUENCES

Longest Sequence of League Wins: 10, 23.11.1985 – 25.1.1986.

Longest Sequence of League Defeats: 7, 1.4.1995 – 6.5.1995.

Longest Sequence of League Draws: 7, 15.1.1994 – 26.2.1994.

Longest Sequence of Unbeaten League Matches: 20, 31.8.1950 – 30.12.1950.

Longest Sequence Without a League Win: 25, 22.9.1956 – 23.2.1957.

Successive Scoring Runs: 25 from 31.8.1963.

Successive Non-scoring Runs: 5 from 21.2.1925.

MANAGERS

John Bowman 1905–07
James McEwen 1907–08
Arthur Turner 1909–10
Bert Stansfield 1910–15
Major Frank Buckley 1919–20
Charles O'Hagan 1920–21
Albert Gosnell 1921–26
Bert Stansfield 1926
Cecil Potter 1926–29
James Kerr 1929–33
Tom Parker 1933–37
Bob Young 1937–39
Jimmy Jewell 1939
Bob Young 1939–45
Duggie Lochhead 1945–46
Cyril Spiers 1946–47
Duggie Lochhead 1947–50
Norman Low 1950–55
Tom Parker 1955–57
Archie Macaulay 1957–61
Willie Reid 1961–62
George Swindin 1962
Ron Ashman 1962–66
Lol Morgan 1966–69
Ron Saunders 1969–73
John Bond 1973–80
Ken Brown 1980–87
Dave Stringer 1987–92
Mike Walker 1992–94
John Deehan 1994–95
Martin O'Neill 1995
Gary Megson 1995–96
Mike Walker 1996–98
Bruce Rioch 1998–2000
Bryan Hamilton 2000
Nigel Worthington 2000–06
Peter Grant 2006–07
Glenn Roeder 2007–09
Bryan Gunn 2009
Paul Lambert August 2009–

TEN YEAR LEAGUE RECORD

		P	W	D	L	F	A	Pts	Pos
2001-02	Div 1	46	22	9	15	60	51	75	6
2002-03	Div 1	46	19	12	15	60	49	69	8
2003-04	Div 1	46	28	10	8	79	39	94	1
2004-05	PR Lge	38	7	12	19	42	77	33	19
2005-06	FL C	46	18	8	20	56	65	62	9
2006-07	FL C	46	16	9	21	56	71	57	16
2007-08	FL C	46	15	10	21	49	59	55	17
2008-09	FL C	46	12	10	24	57	70	46	22
2009-10	FL 1	46	29	8	9	89	47	95	1
2010-11	FL C	46	23	15	8	83	58	84	2

DID YOU KNOW ?

Last goal Norwich City became something of a regular event during 2010–11. On ten occasions, including an amazing five in the month of August alone, they scored goals in either the dying seconds or in added time as follows: 91, 92, 91, 94, 90, 92, 97, 90, 94 and 94 minutes.

NORWICH CITY 2010–11 LEAGUE RECORD

Match No.	Date	Venue	Opponents	Result	H/T Score	Lg Pos.	Goalscorers	Attendance
1	Aug 6	H	Watford	L	2-3	0-2	—	Crofts [52], Nelson [90]	24,348
2	14	A	Scunthorpe U	W	1-0	0-0	12	Holt [90]	6042
3	21	H	Swansea C	W	2-0	0-0	7	Williams (og) [87], Jackson [90]	23,852
4	28	A	Nottingham F	D	1-1	1-1	7	Crofts [42]	21,890
5	Sept 11	H	Barnsley	W	2-1	0-1	7	Foster (og) [71], Martin, C [80]	24,624
6	14	A	Doncaster R	L	1-3	0-1	—	Martin, R [64]	9314
7	18	A	Preston NE	W	1-0	0-0	4	Holt [62]	18,417
8	25	H	Hull C	L	0-2	0-0	6		24,947
9	28	H	Leicester C	W	4-3	1-1	—	Crofts [31], Hoolahan 2 (1 pen) [53 (p), 74], Drury [62]	25,091
10	Oct 2	A	Bristol C	W	3-0	2-0	3	Jackson 2 [23, 64], Hoolahan (pen) [35]	14,124
11	16	A	QPR	D	0-0	0-0	3		18,059
12	19	H	Crystal Palace	L	1-2	1-0	—	Holt [43]	24,975
13	23	H	Middlesbrough	W	1-0	1-0	4	Jackson [44]	25,410
14	30	A	Cardiff C	L	1-3	1-3	5	Hoolahan [34]	24,634
15	Nov 6	H	Burnley	D	2-2	0-2	7	Martin, C [71], Crofts [90]	24,519
16	9	A	Millwall	D	1-1	0-0	—	Fox [75]	10,211
17	13	A	Reading	D	3-3	3-1	8	Martin, R [16], Holt [26], Martin, C [32]	15,934
18	20	H	Leeds U	D	1-1	0-1	8	Barnett [65]	26,315
19	28	H	Ipswich T	W	4-1	2-1	5	Holt 3 [13, 35, 76], Hoolahan [78]	26,532
20	Dec 4	A	Derby Co	W	2-1	2-1	—	Barker (og) [11], Martin, C [13]	26,134
21	11	H	Portsmouth	L	0-2	0-0	6		25,215
22	18	A	Coventry C	W	2-1	0-0	5	Holt 2 [64, 87]	15,230
23	28	H	Sheffield U	W	4-2	1-2	5	Nelson [20], Hoolahan 3 (2 pens) [64 (p), 84 (p), 90]	25,809
24	Jan 1	H	QPR	W	1-0	1-0	3	Martin, R [10]	26,273
25	3	A	Middlesbrough	D	1-1	1-1	2	Holt [12]	16,853
26	15	H	Cardiff C	D	1-1	0-1	4	Martin, R [90]	25,270
27	22	A	Sheffield U	W	2-1	0-0	3	Crofts 2 [61, 80]	20,725
28	29	A	Crystal Palace	D	0-0	0-0	—		16,327
29	Feb 1	H	Millwall	W	2-1	0-0	2	Ward [77], Lansbury [90]	24,571
30	5	A	Burnley	L	1-2	0-1	4	Holt [65]	14,859
31	12	H	Reading	W	2-1	1-1	3	Lansbury [16], Holt [90]	25,560
32	19	A	Leeds U	D	2-2	1-1	5	Lansbury [45], Hoolahan [69]	31,601
33	22	H	Doncaster R	D	1-1	1-0	—	Holt [31]	25,529
34	26	A	Barnsley	W	2-0	2-0	4	Crofts 2 [34, 40]	12,461
35	Mar 5	H	Preston NE	D	1-1	0-0	4	Holt [62]	25,572
36	8	A	Leicester C	W	3-2	1-1	—	Hoolahan [21], Holt (pen) [49], Wilbraham [59]	23,398
37	14	H	Bristol C	W	3-1	1-0	—	Holt (pen) [2], Lansbury [89], Surman [90]	24,428
38	19	H	Hull C	D	1-1	1-0	2	Whitbread [27]	22,967
39	Apr 2	H	Scunthorpe U	W	6-0	2-0	2	Holt 3 (1 pen) [10, 32 (p), 61], Jackson 3 [75, 77, 90]	26,512
40	9	A	Swansea C	L	0-3	0-2	2		19,094
41	12	A	Watford	D	2-2	1-2	—	Vokes [2], Jackson [69]	13,777
42	15	H	Nottingham F	W	2-1	2-1	—	Holt [10], Surman [37]	26,188
43	21	A	Ipswich T	W	5-1	2-0	—	Surman [13], McAuley (og) [24], Jackson [73], Martin, R [80], Pacheco [90]	29,258
44	25	H	Derby Co	W	3-2	1-0	2	Jackson 3 [45, 60, 90]	26,078
45	May 2	A	Portsmouth	W	1-0	0-0	—	Jackson [50]	17,113
46	7	H	Coventry C	D	2-2	0-0	2	Holt [56], Pacheco [62]	26,268

Final League Position: 2

GOALSCORERS

League (83): Holt 21 (3 pens), Jackson 13, Hoolahan 10 (4 pens), Crofts 8, Martin, R 5, Lansbury 4, Martin, C 4, Surman 3, Nelson 2, Pacheco 2, Barnett 1, Drury 1, Fox 1, Vokes 1, Ward 1, Whitbread 1, Wilbraham 1, own goals 4.
Carling Cup (5): Holt 2, Martin, C 2, Berthel Askou 1.
FA Cup (0).

Note on goal markers: a bracketed number after a shirt number indicates goals scored in that match (e.g. 10[1] = shirt 10, 1 goal).

Ruddy J 45	Martin R 46	Drury A 19+1	Crofts A 44	Nelson M 7+1	Ward E 39	Surman A 19+3	Fox D 30+2	Jackson S 20+18	Hoolahan W 36+5	Holt G 44+1	McNamee A 5+12	Smith K 19+9	Lappin S 20+7	Berthel Askou J 2+3	Barnett L 25	Rudd D 1	Johnson O —+4	Hughes S —+1	Gill M —+4	Smith S 5+2	Daley L —+1	Lansbury H 15+8	Tudur Jones O 1+1	Whitbread Z 20+2	Wilbraham A 5+7	Tierney M 14+2	Edwards R —+3	Pacheco D 3+3	Vokes S 1+3	Match No
1	2	3	4	5	6	7[2]	8	9	10[1]	11	12	13																		1
1	2	3	4	5	6	7[3]		9[1]	12	11[2]	10	8	13	14																2
1	2	3	4	5[3]	6	7[1]		9	13	11[2]	10	12	8	14																3
1	2	3	4		6	7		9		11	10	8			5															4
	2	3	4		6			9	13	7[2]	10	12	8	11[1]	5	1														5
1	2	3	4		6			9	11	10[1]	7	8[2]			5		12	13												6
1	2	3	4		6			9[1]	12	7	10[2]	8	11		5				13											7
1	2	3	4		6			9[1]	12	7	10	13	8	11[2]	5															8
1	2	3	4		6			12	9[1]	7[2]	10	8	11		5					13										9
1	2		4		6			13	12	9[1]	7	10	8	11	5					3[2]										10
1	2	3[1]	4		6			13	9	7[2]	10	8	11		5					12										11
1	2		4		6[3]			12	9	7[2]	10	13	8	11[1]	5		14		3											12
1	2		4		6		8	12	9[1]	10	7[2]	13	11		5				3											13
1	2		4		6			12	9[2]	7[3]	10	13	8	11[1]	5		14		3											14
1	2		4[8]		6			13	14	9[3]	7	10	12	8	5				3[2]											15
1	2				6		8	9	13	7[2]	10	3[1]	4	11	5				12											16
1	2		4		6		8[2]	9[1]	12	10[1]	11[1]	7	3		5		13		14											17
1	2		4		6	7[2]	8	9	12	13	10	11[1]	3		5															18
1	2		4		6	7[2]	8	9	14	13	10[3]	12	3		5							11[1]								19
1	2		4		6		8	9[2]	13	11[1]	10	12	3		5							7[3]	14							20
1	2		4					9	10[1]	11	14	13	3[3]	5[2]			12					7[2]								21
1	2			5	6		8	9	11[1]	12[2]	10	13	4[3]	3			14					7								22
1	2		4	5			8[2]	9	11[1]	12	10	13[3]	7	3	6									14						23
1	2	3	4	5				9	11	10	8		12		6							7[1]								24
1	2	3	4	5				12	13	10[2]		7	11	6								8[1]		9						25
1	2	3	4[2]				8	9[3]		11	10	13	14		5							7[1]		6	12					26
1	2	3	4	14			8	9	11[2]	7[1]	10		12		5									6[3]	13					27
1	2	3[1]	4				8[2]	9[1]	12	14	10	13			5							7		6	14	13				28
1	2		4		6		8[3]	9[2]	14	10	13		11[1]		5							7		12	3					29
1	2	3	4		6			13	9[2]	11	10		12		5							7[3]		8[1]	14					30
1	2	3	4		6	12	8	9[3]		11	10				5[2]							7[1]		13	14					31
1	2	3[2]	4		6	12	8			11	10				5							7[1]		5	9	13				32
1	2	3	4		6	12	8[1]	14	11[2]	10	13											7[3]		5	9					33
1	2	9			6	11	4		7	10	8													5	3					34
1	2		4		6	11[2]	8	14	9	10	7[3]													5[1]	13	3	3	12		35
1	2		4		6	7	8		11[1]	10	12													5	9	3				36
1	2		4		6	7	8	9[1]	11[2]	10	13	12												5		3				37
1	2		4		6	7[1]	11[2]	13	9	10	12		8											5		3				38
1	2		4		6	7	8	14	11[1]	10[2]	12													5		3		9[3]	13	39
1	2		4[2]		6	7[1]	8	12	10	13	11													5		3		9[3]	14	40
1	2		4		6	7[3]	8	12	10	13	14													5		3		9[1]	11[2]	41
1	2		4		6	7	8[1]	9[3]	11[2]	10	13			13								12		5		3	14			42
1	2		4		6	7	8[1]	9	11[3]	10[2]	12													5		3	14	13		43
1	2		4		6	7[3]	8[2]	9	11	10	13													5[1]		3	12	14		44
1	2		4		6	7[2]	8[1]	9	11	10			13											5		3				45
1	2	14	4		6	7[2]	8	9	11	10[1]			13											5		3[3]	12			46

FA Cup
Third Round   Leyton Orient   (h)   0-1

Carling Cup
First Round   Gillingham   (h)   4-1
Second Round   Blackburn R   (a)   1-3

NOTTINGHAM FOREST   FL Championship

FOUNDATION

One of the oldest football clubs in the world, Nottingham Forest was formed at a meeting in the Clinton Arms in 1865. Known originally as the Forest Football Club, the game which first drew the founders together was 'shinney', a form of hockey. When they determined to change to football in 1865, one of their first moves was to buy a set of red caps to wear on the field.

The City Ground, Nottingham NG2 5FJ.
Telephone: (0115) 982 4444.
Fax: (0115) 982 4455.
Ticket Office: 0871 226 1980.
Website: www.nottinghamforest.co.uk
Email: info@nottinghamforest.co.uk
Ground Capacity: 30,576.
Record Attendance: 49,946 v Manchester U, Division 1, 28 October 1967.
Pitch Measurements: 112yd × 76yd.
Chairman: Nigel Doughty.
Chief Executive: Mark Arthur.
Finance Director: John Pelling.
Manager: Steve McClaren.
Assistant Manager: TBC.
Physios: Steve Devine, Andy Hunt.
Colours: Red shirt with white trim, white shorts, red stockings.
Change Colours: Black and blue halved shirts with red trim, blue shorts, blue stockings.
Year Formed: 1865.
Turned Professional: 1889. *Ltd Co.:* 1982.
Club Nickname: 'Reds'.
Grounds: 1865, Forest Racecourse; 1879, The Meadows; 1880, Trent Bridge Cricket Ground; 1882, Parkside, Lenton; 1885, Gregory, Lenton; 1890, Town Ground; 1898, City Ground.

HONOURS

Football League – Division 1:
Champions 1977–78, 1997–98;
Runners-up 1966–67, 1978–79,
1993–94; **FL 1:** *Runners-up* 2007–08;
Division 2: *Champions* 1906–07,
1921–22; *Runners-up* 1956–57;
Division 3 (S): *Champions* 1950–51.
FA Cup: *Winners* 1898, 1959;
Runners-up 1991.
Football League Cup: *Winners* 1978,
1979, 1989, 1990; *Runners-up* 1980,
1992.
Anglo-Scottish Cup: *Winners* 1977.
Simod Cup: *Winners* 1989.
Zenith Data Systems Cup:
Winners: 1992.
European Competitions
European Cup: 1978–79 (*winners*),
1979–80 (*winners*), 1980–81.
European Fairs Cup: 1961–62,
1967–68. **UEFA Cup:** 1983–84,
1984–85, 1995–96. **Super Cup:** 1979
(*winners*), 1980.
World Club Championship: 1980.

First Football League Game: 3 September 1892, Division 1, v Everton (a) D 2–2 – Brown; Earp, Scott; Hamilton, Albert Smith, McCracken; McCallum, 'Tich' Smith, Higgins (2), Pike, McInnes.
Record League Victory: 12–0 v Leicester Fosse, Division 1, 12 April 1909 – Iremonger; Dudley, Maltby; Hughes (1), Needham, Armstrong; Hooper (3), Marrison, West (3), Morris (2), Spouncer (3 incl. 1p).
Record Cup Victory: 14–0 v Clapton (away), FA Cup 1st rd, 17 January 1891 – Brown; Earp, Scott; Albert Smith, Russell, Jeacock; McCallum (2), 'Tich' Smith (1), Higgins (5), Lindley (4), Shaw (2).
Record Defeat: 1–9 v Blackburn R, Division 2, 10 April 1937.

sky SPORTS FACT FILE

Nottingham Forest have had their successes against Manchester United in FA Cup ties. On the first four such occasions they won a 1935 replay, had an away win in 1947, home victory in 1981 and a quarter-final success at Old Trafford courtesy of a Garry Parker goal.

Most League Points (2 for a win): 70, Division 3 (S), 1950–51.

Most League Points (3 for a win): 94, Division 1, 1997–98.

Most League Goals: 110, Division 3 (S), 1950–51.

Highest League Scorer in Season: Wally Ardron, 36, Division 3 (S), 1950–51.

Most League Goals in Total Aggregate: Grenville Morris, 199, 1898–1913.

Most League Goals in One Match: 4, Enoch West v Sunderland, Division 1, 9 November 1907; 4, Tommy Gibson v Burnley, Division 2, 25 January 1913; 4, Tom Peacock v Port Vale, Division 2, 23 December 1933; 4, Tom Peacock v Barnsley, Division 2, 9 November 1935; 4, Tom Peacock v Port Vale, Division 2, 23 November 1935; 4, Tom Peacock v Doncaster R, Division 2, 26 December 1935; 4, Tommy Capel v Gillingham, Division 3 (S), 18 November 1950; 4, Wally Ardron v Hull C, Division 2, 26 December 1952; 4, Tommy Wilson v Barnsley, Division 2, 9 February 1957; 4, Peter Withe v Ipswich T, Division 1, 4 October 1977; 4, Marlon Harewood v Stoke C, Division 1, 22 February 2003.

Most Capped Player: Stuart Pearce, 76 (78), England.

Most League Appearances: Bob McKinlay, 614, 1951–70.

Youngest League Player: Craig Westcarr, 16 years 257 days v Burnley, 13 October 2001.

Record Transfer Fee Received: £8,500,000 from Liverpool for Stan Collymore, June 1995.

Record Transfer Fee Paid: £3,500,000 to Celtic for Pierre van Hooijdonk, March 1997.

Football League Record: 1892 Elected to Division 1; 1906–07 Division 2; 1907–11 Division 1; 1911–22 Division 2; 1922–25 Division 1; 1925–49 Division 2; 1949–51 Division 3 (S); 1951–57 Division 2; 1957–72 Division 1; 1972–77 Division 2; 1977–92 Division 1; 1992–93 FA Premier League; 1993–94 Division 1; 1994–97 FA Premier League; 1997–98 Division 1; 1998–99 FA Premier League; 1999–2004 Division 1; 2004–05 FL C; 2005–08 FL 1; 2008– FL C.

MANAGERS

Harry Radford 1889–97
(Secretary-Manager)
Harry Haslam 1897–1909
(Secretary-Manager)
Fred Earp 1909–12
Bob Masters 1912–25
John Baynes 1925–29
Stan Hardy 1930–31
Noel Watson 1931–36
Harold Wightman 1936–39
Billy Walker 1939–60
Andy Beattie 1960–63
Johnny Carey 1963–68
Matt Gillies 1969–72
Dave Mackay 1972
Allan Brown 1973–75
Brian Clough 1975–93
Frank Clark 1993–96
Stuart Pearce 1996–97
Dave Bassett 1997–99
(previously General Manager)
Ron Atkinson 1999
David Platt 1999–2001
Paul Hart 2001–04
Joe Kinnear 2004
Gary Megson 2005–06
Colin Calderwood 2006–08
Billy Davies 2009–11
Steve McClaren June 2011–

LATEST SEQUENCES

Longest Sequence of League Wins: 7, 9.5.1979 – 1.9.1979.

Longest Sequence of League Defeats: 14, 21.3.1913 – 27.9.1913.

Longest Sequence of League Draws: 7, 29.4.1978 – 2.9.1978.

Longest Sequence of Unbeaten League Matches: 42, 26.11.1977 – 25.11.1978.

Longest Sequence Without a League Win: 19, 8.9.1998 – 16.1.1999.

Successive Scoring Runs: 22 from 28.3.1931.

Successive Non-scoring Runs: 7 from 13.12.2003.

TEN YEAR LEAGUE RECORD

		P	W	D	L	F	A	Pts	Pos
2001-02	Div 1	46	12	18	16	50	51	54	16
2002-03	Div 1	46	20	14	12	82	50	74	6
2003-04	Div 1	46	15	15	16	61	58	60	14
2004-05	FL C	46	9	17	20	42	66	44	23
2005-06	FL 1	46	19	12	15	67	52	69	7
2006-07	FL 1	46	23	13	10	65	41	82	4
2007-08	FL 1	46	22	16	8	64	32	82	2
2008-09	FL C	46	13	14	19	50	65	53	19
2009-10	FL C	46	22	13	11	65	40	79	3
2010-11	FL C	46	20	15	11	69	50	75	6

DID YOU KNOW ❓

Left-back Sandy Wood, though born in Scotland, became a US citizen and was capped for them in the 1930 World Cup. He came to England but was not allowed to play professionally and had to play as an amateur with Leicester City before joining Nottingham Forest in 1936.

NOTTINGHAM FOREST 2010–11 LEAGUE RECORD

Match No.	Date	Venue	Opponents	Result	H/T Score	Lg Pos.	Goalscorers	Attendance
1	Aug 7	A	Burnley	L 0-1	0-1	—	—	17,496
2	15	H	Leeds U	D 1-1	1-1	19	Blackstock [9]	24,986
3	21	A	Reading	D 1-1	0-1	20	Earnshaw [50]	17,324
4	28	H	Norwich C	D 1-1	1-1	19	Blackstock (pen) [35]	21,890
5	Sept 11	H	Millwall	D 1-1	0-1	17	Blackstock [80]	23,342
6	14	A	Preston NE	W 2-1	0-1	—	McGugan 2 [68, 81]	9779
7	18	H	Hull C	D 0-0	0-0	17		21,180
8	25	H	Swansea C	W 3-1	1-0	11	McGugan 2 (1 pen) [12 (p), 60], Majewski [84]	19,974
9	28	H	Sheffield U	D 1-1	0-1	—	McKenna [69]	19,782
10	Oct 2	A	Doncaster R	D 1-1	1-1	11	Blackstock [28]	10,759
11	16	A	Barnsley	L 1-3	0-1	15	McGugan [68]	12,844
12	19	H	Middlesbrough	W 1-0	0-0	—	McGugan [51]	22,115
13	23	H	Ipswich T	W 2-0	2-0	10	McGoldrick [13], McGugan [45]	22,935
14	30	A	Portsmouth	L 1-2	1-1	13	Anderson [27]	19,719
15	Nov 6	A	Watford	D 1-1	1-1	14	McGugan [20]	14,708
16	9	H	Coventry C	W 2-1	1-1	—	Majewski [41], Cohen [62]	19,501
17	13	H	QPR	D 0-0	0-0	10		22,859
18	20	A	Cardiff C	W 2-0	1-0	6	McGugan [23], Blackstock [84]	23,526
19	29	A	Leicester C	L 0-1	0-0	—		24,659
20	Dec 18	H	Crystal Palace	W 3-0	1-0	8	Chambers [31], Tudgay [46], McCleary [85]	22,359
21	29	H	Derby Co	W 5-2	3-1	—	Chambers [2], Tudgay 2 [24, 45], Earnshaw 2 [53, 90]	29,490
22	Jan 1	H	Barnsley	D 2-2	0-1	10	McGugan (pen) [68], Tyson [80]	22,179
23	3	A	Ipswich T	W 1-0	1-0	7	Delaney (og) [45]	19,455
24	15	H	Portsmouth	W 2-1	0-1	8	Sonko (og) [87], Tudgay [90]	21,856
25	22	A	Derby Co	W 1-0	0-0	6	Earnshaw [79]	33,010
26	25	H	Bristol C	W 1-0	0-0	—	Chambers [47]	19,694
27	Feb 1	A	Coventry C	W 2-1	2-1	4	McGugan [31], Earnshaw [36]	14,631
28	5	H	Watford	W 1-0	1-0	2	Tudgay [1]	23,393
29	13	A	QPR	D 1-1	1-1	4	McGoldrick [26]	17,227
30	16	A	Scunthorpe U	L 0-1	0-1	—		5578
31	19	H	Cardiff C	W 2-1	1-0	2	Morgan [32], Earnshaw [67]	26,019
32	22	H	Preston NE	D 2-2	0-1	—	Konchesky [54], Cohen [89]	28,310
33	26	A	Millwall	D 0-0	0-0	5		14,226
34	Mar 1	A	Middlesbrough	D 1-1	0-0	—	Adebola [90]	15,341
35	5	H	Hull C	L 0-1	0-0	5		25,119
36	8	A	Sheffield U	L 1-2	1-0	—	Adebola [42]	20,547
37	12	H	Doncaster R	D 0-0	0-0	6		25,442
38	19	A	Swansea C	L 2-3	1-2	6	Boyd [44], Anderson [90]	18,371
39	Apr 2	A	Leeds U	L 1-4	0-0	7	McCleary [65]	29,524
40	9	H	Reading	L 3-4	1-1	8	Boyd (pen) [38], Earnshaw [51], McGugan (pen) [88]	22,495
41	12	H	Burnley	W 2-0	0-0	—	McGoldrick 2 [73, 90]	19,411
42	15	A	Norwich C	L 1-2	1-2	—	Tyson [3]	26,188
43	22	H	Leicester C	W 3-2	1-1	—	Tudgay [15], Earnshaw [73], McKenna [84]	24,217
44	25	A	Bristol C	W 3-2	2-0	6	Boyd 2 (1 pen) [4, 43 (p)], Chambers [72]	14,867
45	30	H	Scunthorpe U	W 5-1	2-1	6	Boyd 2 [9, 90], Chambers 2 [25, 82], Anderson [48]	27,949
46	May 7	A	Crystal Palace	W 3-0	1-0	6	McGugan [17], Tudgay [70], McGoldrick [80]	18,443

Final League Position: 6

GOALSCORERS

League (69): McGugan 13 (3 pens), Earnshaw 8, Tudgay 7, Boyd 6 (2 pens), Chambers 6, Blackstock 5 (1 pen), McGoldrick 5, Anderson 3, Adebola 2, Cohen 2, Majewski 2, McCleary 2, McKenna 2, Tyson 2, Konchesky 1, Morgan 1, own goals 2.
Carling Cup (1): Thornhill 1.
FA Cup (4): Adebola 1, Anderson 1, Chambers 1, McGoldrick 1.
Play-Offs (1): Earnshaw 1.

Camp L 46	Gunter C 40+3	Bertrand R 19	Moussi G 25+6	Morgan W 46	Wilson K 8+2	Tyson N 11+19	McKenna P 30+2	Blackstock D 13+4	Earnshaw R 26+8	Cohen C 41+1	Chambers L 43+1	Anderson P 27+9	Majewski R 21+5	McCleary G 7+11	McGugan L 34+6	Adebola D 4+25	McGoldrick D 10+11	Lynch J 8+4	Rodney N —+3	Ramsey A 2+3	Tudgay M 19+3	Konchesky P 14+1	Moloney B 5+1	Boyd K 7+3	Bennett J —+3	Findlay R —+2	Darlow K —+1	Match No.
1	2	3	4^3	5	6^1	7	8	9^2	10	11	12	13	14															1
1	2	3	14	5	6	13	8	9^3	10	11					7^1	4^2	12											2
1		3	4	5	6	13		9^2	10^3	11	2	7	8^1		12	14												3
1		3	13	5	6	12	8^3	9	10	11	2	7^1	4^2		14													4
1		3		5	6	7^3	8^2	9	10^1	11	2	12	4		13	14												5
1	2	3	4^1	5	6	7^2	8	9		11		12		13	10^3	14												6
1	2	3	4	5		13	8^3	12	10^1	11	6	7^2	14		9													7
1	2	3	4	5			8	9^3		11	6	7^1	13		10^2	14	12											8
1	2	3	4^1	5		13	8	9		11	6	7^2		14	10^3	12												9
1	2	3	4	5		12	8	9^3		11^1	6	7			10^2	14	13											10
1	2	3	4^1	5			8^3	9		11	6	12	14		7	10^2	13											11
1	2	3	13	5			8	9^1		11	4	7	6^3		10^2	12	14											12
1	2		13	5	6	12	8			11	3	7	4^1		10^3	14	9^2											13
1	2			5	6		8	14	13	11	3	7^3	4^1		10	12	9^2											14
1	2	3	14	5		12	8^3	9	10^1	11	4	7			6^2	13												15
1	2	3	4	5		7		12	10^1	11	6	13	8^3		9^2	14												16
1	2	3		5		14	8	9^2	13	11	4	7	6^1		10^3	12												17
1	2	3	4	5				12^3	10^1	11	6		7^2	8	9			13	14									18
1	2	3	4	5		14			12	11^2	6	7		8	10^3	9^1			13									19
1	2	3	4	5		13		10			6	7^3	8^1	14	11^2						12	9						20
1	2	3^1	4	5	13	7^3		10	12	6	14	8									11^2	9						21
1	2		4	5		12		10^3	3	6		11^2	7^1	8	14						13	9						22
1	2		4	5	13	10^3			3	6	7			14	9^1	11^2					8	12						23
1	2		4	5		13		9^2	11	6	7^3	8^1	12	14				3			10							24
1	2		4	5		9		12	11	6	7		8^2	13				3			10^1							25
1	2		4	5		7^1		9^3	11	6		12	8	13	14			3			10^2							26
1	2		4^1	5			12	9^3	11	6	7		8^2	13		14					10	3						27
1	2			5		12	4	9^2	11	6	7^1	8^3		14	13						10	3						28
1	2			5		14	4		11	6	13	7^*		8^2		9^3	12				10^1	3						29
1	2			5		7^2	4	9^3	11	6			14	8^1	12	13					10	3						30
1	2			5		13	4	9^2	11	6	7^3			8	14	12					10^1	3						31
1	2			5			4		11	6	7			8	12	9^2	13	14			10^3	3^1						32
1	2			5			4	14	11	6	7^2	8^1	13	10		9^3	3				12							33
1	2			5			4	10	11	6	13		7	8^2	14	9^3	3^1							12				34
1	2			5				10^2	11	4	7^3	6	12	8^1	14			13			9	3						35
1	2			5			4	14	11	6	7		13		9^1	8^2					10^3	3		12				36
1	2			5		12	4	9^1	11	6		8^2	7	14							10^3	3		13				37
1	2			5		10	4		11	6	7	8^1	12		13						3^3			9^2	14			38
1	2			5		13			14	11^*	4	7^1	6	12	8			3			10^3			9^2				39
1	2	7^2	5		13			10		4		6	11	8	14		3^1				12			9^3				40
1	14	11^1	5			4	9		6	12	7	8		13							10^2	3	2^3					41
1	13	11^2	5	7^3	4	14	6			8	9			12	3^4	2	10^1											42
1	2	7	5		4	9^2	11	6			8^3	14			10^1		3	12								13		43
1	13	7	5		4	9	11	6			8^3					3	2^2	10^1	14	12								44
1	2	13	5		4^1	9^*	11	6	12		8^3	7^2				3		10	14									45
1^6	2	4^1	5		12			11	6	7			8	13			10			3	9^2		15				46

FA Cup
Third Round   Preston NE   (a)   2-1
Fourth Round   West Ham U   (a)   2-3

Carling Cup
First Round   Bradford C   (a)   1-2

Play-Offs
Semi-Final   Swansea C   (h)   0-0
                                       (a)   1-3

NOTTS COUNTY   FL Championship 1

FOUNDATION

According to the official history of Notts County 'the true date of Notts' foundation has to be the meeting at the George Hotel on 7 December 1864'. However, there is documented evidence of continuous play from 1862, when club members played organised matches amongst themselves in The Park in Nottingham.

Meadow Lane Stadium, Meadow Lane, Nottingham NG2 3HJ.

Telephone: (0115) 952 9000.

Fax: (0115) 955 3994.

Ticket Office: (0115) 955 7204.

Website: www.nottscountyfc.co.uk

Email: office@nottscountyfc.co.uk

Ground Capacity: 20,300.

Record Attendance: 47,310 v York C, FA Cup 6th rd, 12 March 1955.

Pitch Measurements: 113yd × 72yd.

Chairman: Ray Trew.

Chief Executive: James Rodwell.

Secretary: Tony Cuthbert.

Manager: Martin Allen.

Assistant Manager: Carl Muggleton.

Colours: Black and white striped shirts, black shorts, black stockings.

Change Colours: All blue.

Year Formed: 1862* (*see Foundation*). *Turned Professional:* 1885. *Ltd Co.:* 1890.

Club Nickname: 'Magpies'.

Grounds: 1862, The Park; 1864, The Meadows; 1877, Beeston Cricket Ground; 1880, Castle Ground; 1883, Trent Bridge; 1910, Meadow Lane.

First Football League Game: 15 September 1888, Football League, v Everton (a) L 1–2 – Holland; Guttridge, McLean; Brown, Warburton, Shelton; Hodder, Harker, Jardine, Albert Moore (1), Wardle.

Record League Victory: 11–1 v Newport Co, Division 3 (S), 15 January 1949 – Smith; Southwell, Purvis; Gannon, Baxter, Adamson; Houghton (1), Sewell (4), Lawton (4), Pimbley, Johnston (2).

Record Cup Victory: 15–0 v Rotherham T (at Trent Bridge), FA Cup 1st rd, 24 October 1885 – Sherwin; Snook, Henry Thomas Moore; Dobson (1), Emmett (1), Chapman; Gunn (1), Albert Moore (2), Jackson (3), Daft (2), Cursham (4), (1 og).

Record Defeat: 1–9 v Blackburn R, Division 1, 16 November 1889. 1–9 v Aston Villa, Division 1, 29 September 1888. 1–9 v Portsmouth, Division 2, 9 April 1927.

HONOURS

Football League – Division 1:
Best season: 3rd, 1890–91, 1900–01;
Division 2: *Champions* 1896–97, 1913–14, 1922–23;
Runners-up 1894–95, 1980–81;
Division 3 (S): *Champions* 1930–31, 1949–50; *Runners-up* 1936–37;
Division 3: *Champions* 1997–98;
Runners-up 1972–73;
Division 4: *Champions* 1970–71;
Runners-up 1959–60;
FL 2: *Champions* 2009–10.
FA Cup: *Winners* 1894;
Runners-up 1891.
Football League Cup: Best season: 5th rd, 1964, 1973, 1976.
Anglo-Italian Cup: *Winners* 1995;
Runners-up 1994.

---

sky SPORTS FACT FILE

Notts County were invited to play three matches in Denmark in June 1910. After a 2-2 in the first of these against a Danish XI, they followed it with a 4-2 win against similar opposition and a third 2-1 to complete a highly successful first overseas tour.

Most League Points (2 for a win): 69, Division 4, 1970–71.
Most League Points (3 for a win): 99, Division 3, 1997–98.
Most League Goals: 107, Division 4, 1959–60.
Highest League Scorer in Season: Tom Keetley, 39, Division 3 (S), 1930–31.
Most League Goals in Total Aggregate: Les Bradd, 125, 1967–78.
Most League Goals in One Match: 5, Robert Jardine v Burnley, Division 1, 27 October 1888; 5, Daniel Bruce v Port Vale, Division 2, 26 February 1895; 5, Bertie Mills v Barnsley, Division 2, 19 November 1927.
Most Capped Player: Kevin Wilson, 15 (42), Northern Ireland.
Most League Appearances: Albert Iremonger, 564, 1904–26.
Youngest League Player: Tony Bircumshaw, 16 years 54 days v Brentford, 3 April 1961.
Record Transfer Fee Received: £2,500,000 from Derby Co for Craig Short, September 1992.
Record Transfer Fee Paid: £800,000 to Manchester C for Kasper Schmeichel, July 2009.
Football League Record: 1888 Founder Member of the Football League; 1893–97 Division 2; 1897–1913 Division 1; 1913–14 Division 2; 1914–20 Division 1; 1920–23 Division 2; 1923–26 Division 1; 1926–30 Division 2; 1930–31 Division 3 (S); 1931–35 Division 2; 1935–50 Division 3 (S); 1950–58 Division 2; 1958–59 Division 3; 1959–60 Division 4; 1960–64 Division 3; 1964–71 Division 4; 1971–73 Division 3; 1973–81 Division 2; 1981–84 Division 1; 1984–85 Division 2; 1985–90 Division 3; 1990–91 Division 2; 1991–95 Division 1; 1995–97 Division 2; 1997–98 Division 3; 1998–2004 Division 2; 2004–10 FL 2; 2010– FL 1.

LATEST SEQUENCES

Longest Sequence of League Wins: 10, 3.12.1997 – 31.1.1998.
Longest Sequence of League Defeats: 7, 3.9.1983 – 16.10.1983.
Longest Sequence of League Draws: 6, 16.8.2008 – 20.9.2008.
Longest Sequence of Unbeaten League Matches: 19, 26.4.1930 – 6.12.1930.
Longest Sequence Without a League Win: 20, 3.12.1996 – 31.3.1997.
Successive Scoring Runs: 35 from 26.4.1930.
Successive Non-scoring Runs: 9 from 15.3.2011 – 16.4.2011.

MANAGERS

Edwin Browne 1883–93
Tom Featherstone 1893
Tom Harris 1893–1913
Albert Fisher 1913–27
Horace Henshall 1927–34
Charlie Jones 1934
David Pratt 1935
Percy Smith 1935–36
Jimmy McMullan 1936–37
Harry Parkes 1938–39
Tony Towers 1939–42
Frank Womack 1942–43
Major Frank Buckley 1944–46
Arthur Stollery 1946–49
Eric Houghton 1949–53
George Poyser 1953–57
Tommy Lawton 1957–58
Frank Hill 1958–61
Tim Coleman 1961–63
Eddie Lowe 1963–65
Tim Coleman 1965–66
Jack Burkitt 1966–67
Andy Beattie *(General Manager)* 1967
Billy Gray 1967–68
Jack Wheeler *(Caretaker Manager)* 1968–69
Jimmy Sirrel 1969–75
Ron Fenton 1975–77
Jimmy Sirrel 1978–82 *(continued as General Manager to 1984)*
Howard Wilkinson 1982–83
Larry Lloyd 1983–84
Richie Barker 1984–85
Jimmy Sirrel 1985–87
John Barnwell 1987–88
Neil Warnock 1989–93
Mick Walker 1993–94
Russell Slade 1994–95
Howard Kendall 1995
Colin Murphy 1995–96 *(General Manager)*
Steve Thompson 1995–96
Sam Allardyce 1997–99
Gary Brazil 1999–2000
Jocky Scott 2000–01
Gary Brazil 2001–02
Billy Dearden 2002–04
Gary Mills 2004
Ian Richardson 2004–05
Gudjon Thordarson 2005–06
Steve Thompson 2006–07
Ian McParland 2007–09
Hans Backe 2009
Steve Cotterill 2010
Craig Short 2010
Paul Ince 2010–11
Martin Allen April 2011–

TEN YEAR LEAGUE RECORD

		P	W	D	L	F	A	Pts	Pos
2001-02	Div 2	46	13	11	22	59	71	50	19
2002-03	Div 2	46	13	16	17	62	70	55	15
2003-04	Div 2	46	10	12	24	50	78	42	23
2004-05	FL 2	46	13	13	20	46	62	52	19
2005-06	FL 2	46	12	16	18	48	63	52	21
2006-07	FL 2	46	16	14	16	55	53	62	13
2007-08	FL 2	46	10	18	18	37	53	48	21
2008-09	FL 2	46	11	14	21	49	69	47	19
2009-10	FL 2	46	27	12	7	96	31	93	1
2010-11	FL 1	46	14	8	24	46	60	50	19

DID YOU KNOW ?

On 8 January 2011, Notts County beat Sunderland 2-1 at the Stadium of Light in a third round FA Cup tie. It was the eighth meeting between the two sides in the competition. Notts' previous win had been on 11 March 1891 when two Jimmy Oswald goals settled the semi-final.

NOTTS COUNTY 2010–11 LEAGUE RECORD

Match No.	Date		Venue	Opponents	Result		H/T Score	Lg Pos.	Goalscorers	Attendance
1	Aug	7	H	Huddersfield T	L	0-3	0-2	—		10,342
2		14	A	Oldham Ath	L	0-3	0-1	24		5037
3		21	H	Dagenham & R	W	1-0	0-0	16	Westcarr [53]	5210
4		28	A	Bournemouth	D	3-3	1-3	18	Burgess [30], Westcarr [89], Smith [90]	6447
5	Sept	4	H	Yeovil T	W	4-0	3-0	12	Westcarr [24], Davies 2 [29, 45], Hughes [73]	6288
6		11	A	Charlton Ath	L	0-1	0-0	13		14,436
7		18	H	Leyton Orient	W	3-2	2-1	12	Hughes 2 [14, 74], Westcarr [21]	6256
8		25	A	Bristol R	L	1-2	0-1	15	Davies [87]	5962
9		28	A	Peterborough U	W	3-2	3-1	—	Davies 2 [31, 34], Westcarr [43]	6136
10	Oct	2	H	Sheffield W	L	0-2	0-0	14		11,355
11		9	A	Carlisle U	L	0-1	0-0	17		5599
12		16	H	Plymouth Arg	W	2-0	1-0	13	Westcarr [35], Spicer [51]	6333
13		23	A	Colchester U	L	1-2	1-0	16	Westcarr [8]	3811
14		30	H	Southampton	L	1-3	1-0	19	Edwards [9]	9547
15	Nov	13	A	Exeter C	L	1-3	1-2	21	Hughes [45]	5302
16		20	H	Tranmere R	L	0-1	0-0	21		5782
17		23	H	Swindon T	W	1-0	0-0	—	Hughes [88]	4644
18	Dec	11	H	Milton Keynes D	W	2-0	0-0	19	Ince [86], Hughes [90]	5172
19		28	A	Plymouth Arg	D	1-1	1-1	—	Hughes [7]	9822
20	Jan	1	A	Walsall	W	3-0	2-0	16	Westcarr [9], Miller [16], Pearce [56]	4131
21		3	H	Hartlepool U	W	3-0	1-0	13	Ince [44], Miller [70], Westcarr [79]	6285
22		15	A	Southampton	D	0-0	0-0	16		20,201
23		22	H	Carlisle U	L	0-1	0-0	18		6327
24		25	A	Hartlepool U	D	1-1	0-1	—	Hughes [69]	2545
25	Feb	2	H	Walsall	D	1-1	0-0	—	Hughes [64]	4714
26		12	H	Exeter C	L	0-2	0-0	20		6176
27		15	H	Colchester U	W	2-0	2-0	—	Westcarr [21], Clarke (og) [37]	4041
28		25	H	Charlton Ath	W	1-0	0-0	—	Bishop [49]	8141
29	Mar	1	A	Brentford	D	1-1	1-0	—	Westcarr [44]	3795
30		5	A	Leyton Orient	L	0-2	0-1	17		4238
31		8	H	Peterborough U	L	0-1	0-0	—		5714
32		12	A	Sheffield W	W	1-0	1-0	17	Gow (pen) [27]	17,835
33		15	A	Rochdale	L	0-1	0-0	—		2019
34		19	H	Bristol R	L	0-1	0-0	17		5691
35		22	A	Brighton & HA	L	0-1	0-0	—		7264
36		27	A	Huddersfield T	L	0-3	0-1	—		13,661
37	Apr	2	H	Oldham Ath	L	0-2	0-0	19		5538
38		5	H	Rochdale	L	1-2	0-2	—	Hughes [54]	4689
39		9	A	Dagenham & R	L	1-3	0-3	21	Demba-Nyren [69]	2608
40		12	A	Yeovil T	L	1-2	0-1	—	Spicer [51]	3533
41		16	H	Bournemouth	L	0-2	0-0	22		6010
42		19	A	Tranmere R	W	1-0	1-0	—	Westcarr (pen) [42]	12,249
43		23	A	Swindon T	W	2-1	0-1	—	Judge [78], Hughes [85]	8064
44		25	H	Brentford	D	1-1	0-0	19	Hughes (pen) [82]	6879
45		30	A	Milton Keynes D	L	1-2	0-0	19	Hughes [62]	10,013
46	May	7	H	Brighton & HA	D	1-1	1-1	19	Greer (og) [36]	10,347

Final League Position: 19

GOALSCORERS

League (46): Hughes 13 (1 pen), Westcarr 12 (1 pen), Davies 5, Ince 2, Miller 2, Spicer 2, Bishop 1, Burgess 1, Demba-Nyren 1, Edwards 1, Gow 1 (1 pen), Judge 1, Pearce 1, Smith 1, own goals 2.
Carling Cup (5): Smith 2, Davies 1, Hughes 1, Spicer 1.
FA Cup (8): Hughes 2, Bishop 1, Davies 1 (pen), Pearce 1, Rodgers 1, Westcarr 1, own goal 1.
J Paint Trophy (1): Davies 1.

Burch R 14+1	Thompson J 23+2	Hunt S 3+1	Ravenhill R 31+3	Lee G 14+4	Chilvers L 17+4	Harley J 39	Bishop N 42+1	Hughes L 24+7	Burgess B 8+9	Davies B 22	Westcarr C 36+5	Jervis J 1+9	Spicer J 15+8	Nelson S 32+1	Pearce K 26+1	Edwards M 36+1	Smith K 6+7	Judge A 17+2	Hawley K 12+12	Rodgers L —+4	Darby S 23	Ince T 3+3	Miller L 5+1	Gow A 12+4	Gobern L —+5	Martin D 7+3	McDonald K 10+1	Clifford C 5+4	Regan C 4	Sproule I 4+1	Sodje S 5+6	Demba-Nyren N 5+7	Brandy F 5+4	Wholey J —+1	Nicholas G —+1	Match No.
1	2	3[1]	4[3]	5	6	7	8	9	10[2]	11	12	13	14																							1
	4[2]		6	3	8	9	10[1]	11[3]	7	13	14			1	2	5	12																			2
	2		4	5	3	8	10	9	7	11				1		6																				3
	2		4[1]	5	3	8	10[2]	11	9	12	7			1		6	13																			4
	2		4	5[3]	14	3	8	9	11	7[2]	12	13		1		6	10[1]																			5
	2		4[2]	5	3	8	9	13	11	10	12			1		6	7[1]																			6
	2		4	5	3	8	9[2]	13	11	7	10[1]	12		1		6																				7
	2		4	5[4]	3	8	11				7[2]	9[1]		1		6	12	13	10[3]	14																8
1	2		4■		3	8	11				7[2]	14	13		6	5	10[1]	9[3]	12																	9
1	2				3	8	9		11		7[2]				6	5	10[1]	4■	12	13																10
1	2		4		3	8[1]	13		11		7[2]				6	5	10[1]		9[2]	12																11
1	2		4		3	8[1]	9		11	10	7[2]				6	5	12		13																	12
1	2		4		3		9		11	8[1]	13	7			6	5	12[2]		10																	13
1	2■	3	4[3]	12		8			11			14	7		6	5		9[1]	10[2]	13																14
1	4[1]		6		3	12	9		11	14	7[2]					5		8	10[3]			2	13													15
1		3	4	6		8			11	9[2]						5		10[1]	14	13	2[3]	7	12													16
1			4[2]	6	3	8	12		11	9		13				5		10			2		7[1]													17
1	4			6[1]	3	8	13		11	7					12	5		10[3]			2	14	9[2]													18
1					3	8	9		11	10[1]					6	5		7[3]	13		2	12	4[2]													19
1	12				3	8		13	11	10[1]					6	5		7[3]	14		2	9	4[2]													20
1[5]	12				3	8	13		11	10[2]				15	6	5		7[1]			2	9	4													21
	2	13	4[3]		3	8		12	11	9		14		1	6	5		7[2]								10[1]										22
	2		4[2]	14	3	8				9		11[1]		1	6	5		7[3]	13							10	12									23
			4		5	3	8	10[2]		9				1	6[1]				7	12				14			11[3]									24
	12		4		3[1]	8	9			7[2]				1	6	5	14		10					2		13	11[3]									25
			4[1]		3	11	9			7				1	6	5			10[2]					2		8[3]	14	12	13							26
	12				3	8	9[2]	13		7				1	6	5			14					2		10[3]	11	4[1]								27
3	4					7	12			9				1	6	5			10[1]					2		11[2]	8	13	2							28
12	4	13	3■			7				9[3]				1	6	5■			10[1]					14		11	8	2[2]								29
	2		4		5		7			9				1	6[1]				10					14		3	8[2]	11[3]	12	13						30
			4[1]	6	3	7				9[2]				1	5				10		2			8		12	11			13						31
				6	14	3	7						12	1		5			10[2]		2			4[1]		8	11[3]	9		13						32
				6	13	3	7							11	1	5			10		2			4		8[1]	9[2]	12								33
					3[3]	7	9							1		5					2			8	12	4	11[1]	14	10[2]	13						34
	4[2]		6		3	7	9[1]			13				1		5					2			10	11	8[1]	12		14							35
	4[2]		6[1]		3	7	9			10				1		5■			10[1]		2			12	11[3]	8		13	14							36
	4		6		7		9			11				1		5■			10[1]		2[3]			12	3	14	13	8[2]								37
3	4[3]	5	6			7	9	12	8[1]					1							2			13	11[2]	14			10							38
	5■	12	13		3	7	9	8[2]		4				1							2			11[1]	6	13	10[3]									39
6			4	3	7	9	8[2]		13	11	1			5		2[3]					12	14	10[1]													40
3			4[3]		7	9	13	7	11			1		5[2]							12	2	6	10[1]	14											41
6[2]	8[■]	14	4	3	7	9[2]	13	10	11		1				12						2[1]	5														42
	6		4	3	7	13	9	8[2]		11[1]	1			5	12	10	2[3]							14												43
	4		3	7	9	13	12		1	6[2]	5	11[3]	8	2														14	10[1]								44
	4		3	7	12	9[2]	8		14	1	2	5[1]	11[3]	10														6	13							45
15	2			8[1]	9[2]		4		11	1[6]	3	5	7	10														6■	13		12					46

FA Cup

First Round	Gateshead	(h)	2-0
Second Round	Bournemouth	(h)	3-1
Third Round	Sunderland	(a)	2-1
Fourth Round	Manchester C	(h)	1-1
		(a)	0-5

Carling Cup

First Round	Plymouth Arg	(a)	1-0
Second Round	Watford	(a)	2-1
Third Round	Wolverhampton W	(a)	2-4

J Paint Trophy

First Round	Sheffield W	(a)	1-2

OLDHAM ATHLETIC   FL Championship 1

FOUNDATION

It was in 1895 that John Garland, the landlord of the Featherstall and Junction Hotel, decided to form a football club. As Pine Villa they played in the Oldham Junior League. In 1899 the local professional club, Oldham County, went out of existence and one of the liquidators persuaded Pine Villa to take over their ground at Sheepfoot Lane and change their name to Oldham Athletic.

Boundary Park, Furtherwood Road, Oldham OL1 2PA.

Telephone: (0161) 624 4972.

Fax: (0161) 627 5915.

Ticket Office: (0161) 785 5150.

Website: www.oldhamathletic.co.uk

Email: enquiries@oldhamathletic.co.uk

Ground Capacity: 13,624.

Record Attendance: 46,471 v Sheffield W, FA Cup 4th rd, 25 January 1930.

Pitch Measurements: 106yd × 72yd.

Chairman: Simon Corney.

Chief Executive/Secretary: Alan Hardy.

Manager: Paul Dickov.

Assistant Manager: Gerry Taggart.

Physio: Marc Czuczman.

Colours: Blue shirts with white sleeves, white shorts, white stockings.

Change Colours: Black shirts with tangerine sleeves, black shorts, black stockings.

Year Formed: 1895.

Turned Professional: 1899.

Ltd Co.: 1906.

Previous Name: 1895, Pine Villa; 1899, Oldham Athletic.

Club Nickname: 'The Latics'.

Grounds: 1895, Sheepfoot Lane; 1900, Hudson Field; 1906, Sheepfoot Lane; 1907, Boundary Park.

First Football League Game: 9 September 1907, Division 2, v Stoke (a) W 3–1 – Hewitson; Hodson, Hamilton; Fay, Walders, Wilson; Ward, Billy Dodds (1), Newton (1), Hancock, Swarbrick (1).

Record League Victory: 11–0 v Southport, Division 4, 26 December 1962 – Bollands; Branagan, Marshall; McCall, Williams, Scott; Ledger (1), Johnstone, Lister (6), Colquhoun (1), Whitaker (3).

Record Cup Victory: 10–1 v Lytham, FA Cup 1st rd, 28 November 1925 – Gray; Wynne, Grundy; Adlam, Heaton, Naylor (1), Douglas, Pynegar (2), Ormston (2), Barnes (3), Watson (2).

HONOURS

Football League – Division 1:
Runners-up 1914–15;
Division 2: *Champions* 1990–91;
Runners-up 1909–10;
Division 3 (N): *Champions* 1952–53;
Division 2: *Champions* 1973–74;
Division 4: *Runners-up* 1962–63.
FA Cup: Semi-final 1913, 1990, 1994.
Football League Cup:
Runners-up 1990.

sky SPORTS FACT FILE

On 27 September 1947 winless Oldham Athletic had scored only five goals in the opening eight matches. They then won 6-0 at Darlington, all the goals being scored in a 58 minute spell. Ray Haddington, formerly with both Bradford clubs, City and Park Avenue, hit a hat-trick.

Record Defeat: 4–13 v Tranmere R, Division 3 (N), 26 December 1935.

Most League Points (2 for a win): 62, Division 3, 1973–74.

Most League Points (3 for a win): 88, Division 2, 1990–91.

Most League Goals: 95, Division 4, 1962–63.

Highest League Scorer in Season: Tom Davis, 33, Division 3 (N), 1936–37.

Most League Goals in Total Aggregate: Roger Palmer, 141, 1980–94.

Most League Goals in One Match: 7, Eric Gemmell v Chester, Division 3 (N), 19 January 1952.

Most Capped Player: Gunnar Halle, 24 (64), Norway.

Most League Appearances: Ian Wood, 525, 1966–80.

Youngest League Player: Wayne Harrison, 15 years 11 months v Notts Co, 27 October 1984.

Record Transfer Fee Received: £1,700,000 from Aston Villa for Earl Barrett, February 1992.

Record Transfer Fee Paid: £750,000 to Aston Villa for Ian Olney, June 1992.

Football League Record: 1907 Elected to Division 2; 1910–23 Division 1; 1923–35 Division 2; 1935–53 Division 3 (N); 1953–54 Division 2; 1954–58 Division 3 (N); 1958–63 Division 4; 1963–69 Division 3; 1969–71 Division 4; 1971–74 Division 3; 1974–91 Division 2; 1991–92 Division 1; 1992–94 FA Premier League; 1994–97 Division 1; 1997–2004 Division 2; 2004– FL 1.

LATEST SEQUENCES

Longest Sequence of League Wins: 10, 12.1.1974 – 12.3.1974.

Longest Sequence of League Defeats: 8, 15.12.1934 – 2.2.1935.

Longest Sequence of League Draws: 5, 26.12.1982 – 15.1.1983.

Longest Sequence of Unbeaten League Matches: 20, 1.5.1990 – 10.11.1990.

Longest Sequence Without a League Win: 17, 4.9.1920 – 18.12.1920.

Successive Scoring Runs: 25 from 15.1.1927.

Successive Non-scoring Runs: 6 from 4.2.1922.

MANAGERS

David Ashworth 1906–14
Herbert Bamlett 1914–21
Charlie Roberts 1921–22
David Ashworth 1923–24
Bob Mellor 1924–27
Andy Wilson 1927–32
Bob Mellor 1932–33
Jimmy McMullan 1933–34
Bob Mellor 1934–45
   (continued as Secretary to 1953)
Frank Womack 1945–47
Billy Wootton 1947–50
George Hardwick 1950–56
Ted Goodier 1956–58
Norman Dodgin 1958–60
Danny McLennan 1960
Jack Rowley 1960–63
Les McDowall 1963–65
Gordon Hurst 1965–66
Jimmy McIlroy 1966–68
Jack Rowley 1968–69
Jimmy Frizzell 1970–82
Joe Royle 1982–94
Graeme Sharp 1994–97
Neil Warnock 1997–98
Andy Ritchie 1998–2001
Mick Wadsworth 2001–02
Iain Dowie 2002–03
Brian Talbot 2004–05
Ronnie Moore 2005–06
John Sheridan 2006–09
Joe Royle 2009
Dave Penney 2009–10
Paul Dickov June 2010–

TEN YEAR LEAGUE RECORD

		P	W	D	L	F	A	Pts	Pos
2001-02	Div 2	46	18	16	12	77	65	70	9
2002-03	Div 2	46	22	16	8	68	38	82	5
2003-04	Div 2	46	12	21	13	66	60	57	15
2004-05	FL 1	46	14	10	22	60	73	52	19
2005-06	FL 1	46	18	11	17	58	60	65	10
2006-07	FL 1	46	21	12	13	69	47	75	6
2007-08	FL 1	46	18	13	15	58	46	67	8
2008-09	FL 1	46	16	17	13	66	65	65	10
2009-10	FL 1	46	13	13	20	39	57	52	16
2010-11	FL 1	46	13	17	16	53	60	56	17

DID YOU KNOW ?

John Clarke was an amateur outside-right on the books of Oldham Athletic in the mid-1930s. He made just one first team appearance but had the satisfaction of scoring the first goal against Barrow on 17 April 1937 in what turned out to be a 4-3 win for the Latics.

OLDHAM ATHLETIC 2010–11 LEAGUE RECORD

Match No.	Date	Venue	Opponents	Result	H/T Score	Lg Pos.	Goalscorers	Attendance
1	Aug 7	A	Tranmere R	W 2-1	1-0	—	Stephens 2 [27, 81]	7270
2	14	H	Notts Co	W 3-0	1-0	1	Furman [31], Tounkara [66], Lee [87]	5037
3	21	A	Charlton Ath	D 1-1	1-1	2	Furman [45]	14,842
4	28	H	Yeovil T	D 0-0	0-0	4		4180
5	Sept 4	H	Bristol R	D 1-1	1-1	3	Taylor [45]	4039
6	11	A	Peterborough U	L 2-5	2-1	10	Jones [19], Taylor [38]	6337
7	18	H	Bournemouth	W 2-1	1-0	6	Lee [78], Tounkara [81]	3912
8	25	A	Brighton & HA	L 1-2	1-1	10	Alessandra [30]	7148
9	28	A	Sheffield W	D 0-0	0-0	—		16,609
10	Oct 2	H	Leyton Orient	D 1-1	1-0	12	Taylor [40]	3806
11	9	A	Brentford	W 3-1	1-1	7	Furman [14], Taylor [46], Stephens (pen) [65]	5339
12	16	H	Colchester U	D 0-0	0-0	8		4136
13	23	A	Southampton	L 1-2	1-1	13	Furman [22]	20,968
14	30	H	Plymouth Arg	W 4-2	1-1	8	Stephens (pen) [5], Tounkara [64], M'Voto [89], Kelly [90]	4080
15	Nov 13	H	Huddersfield T	W 1-0	1-0	11	Tounkara [24]	7723
16	20	A	Dagenham & R	W 1-0	0-0	7	White [57]	2239
17	23	H	Exeter C	D 3-3	3-0	—	White [8], Tounkara [17], Taylor [42]	3561
18	27	A	Rochdale	D 1-1	1-1	—	Evina [16]	6483
19	Jan 1	A	Hartlepool U	L 2-4	1-2	12	Stephens [18], M'Voto [81]	3411
20	3	H	Rochdale	L 1-2	0-0	12	Furman [87]	7251
21	8	H	Swindon T	W 2-0	1-0	—	Taylor [4], Stephens (pen) [88]	3573
22	11	H	Southampton	L 0-6	0-2	—		3767
23	15	A	Plymouth Arg	W 2-0	0-0	8	Stephens [47], Tounkara [72]	8106
24	22	H	Brentford	W 2-1	1-0	8	Tounkara [40], Morais [70]	3759
25	25	A	Walsall	D 1-1	1-0	—	Morais [39]	3247
26	29	A	Carlisle U	D 2-2	2-0	—	White [8], Taylor [33]	5389
27	Feb 1	H	Hartlepool U	W 4-0	1-0	5	White [7], Taylor [51], Evina [69], Reid [90]	3056
28	5	H	Dagenham & R	D 1-1	0-0	6	Stephens [50]	4121
29	12	A	Huddersfield T	D 0-0	0-0	6		16,176
30	15	H	Carlisle U	L 0-1	0-0	—		8564
31	19	A	Bristol R	L 0-1	0-0	8		5379
32	22	A	Milton Keynes D	D 0-0	0-0	—		7806
33	26	H	Peterborough U	L 0-5	0-0	8		4263
34	Mar 5	A	Bournemouth	L 0-3	0-1	11		7075
35	8	H	Sheffield W	L 2-3	2-2	—	Morais [22], Stephens [45]	4133
36	12	A	Leyton Orient	L 0-1	0-0	13		4349
37	19	A	Brighton & HA	L 0-1	0-0	15		3863
38	22	A	Colchester U	L 0-1	0-0	—		2892
39	28	H	Tranmere R	D 0-0	0-0	—		3114
40	Apr 2	A	Notts Co	W 2-0	0-0	15	Lowe (pen) [87], Reid [90]	5538
41	9	H	Charlton Ath	D 0-0	0-0	15		3562
42	16	A	Yeovil T	D 1-1	1-0	16	Taylor [17]	3350
43	22	A	Exeter C	L 0-2	0-2	—		5458
44	25	H	Walsall	D 1-1	0-0	16	Lowe [88]	3463
45	30	A	Swindon T	W 2-0	1-0	16	Taylor 2 [17, 65]	7420
46	May 7	H	Milton Keynes D	L 1-2	1-1	17	Winchester [34]	4063

Final League Position: 17

GOALSCORERS

League (53): Taylor 11, Stephens 9 (3 pens), Tounkara 7, Furman 5, White 4, Morais 3, Evina 2, Lee 2, Lowe 2 (1 pen), M'Voto 2, Reid 2, Alessandra 1, Jones 1, Kelly 1, Winchester 1.
Carling Cup (1): Bembo-Leta 1.
FA Cup (2): Feeney 1, Stephens 1 (pen).
J Paint Trophy (0).

Note: superscript figures denote goals scored; they are shown here as bracketed values (e.g. 9[1] = shirt 9, 1 goal).

Brill D 30	Lee K 43	Black P 28+1	Furman D 42	Jarrett J 7+1	Hazell R 33	Jones R 21+10	Stephens D 34	Tounkara O 40+4	Feeney W 13+10	Alessandra L 10+9	Kelly D 1+12	Bembo-Lita D 2+1	Taylor C 41+1	Millar K —+5	Smalley D —+3	M'Voto J 25+2	Dikaba R 1	Jacobson J —+1	Dickov P —+2	Brooke R 2+11	Gregan S —+1	Evina C 24+3	Christophe J —+1	Morais F 20+3	Winchester C 5+1	White A 19+5	Trotman N 15+3	Amos B 16	Tarkowski J 7+2	Todd A 5+1	Reid R 11+8	Mantom S 3+1	Lowe J 7	Burns R 1	McGrath P —+1	Match No.
1	2	3	4	5	6	7	8	9[1]	10	11	12																									1
1	2	3	4	5	6	7[3]	8	9		11[2]	12		10[1]	13	14																					2
1	2	3	4	5[4]	6	7	8	9[3]	13				10[1]	11[1]																						3
1	2	3	4[3]		6	7	8	9	10[1]			14	12	11[2]	13	5																				4
1	2	3	4	5			8	9					10[2]			11	6	7[1]	12	13																5
1	2	3[1]	4	5	6	7	8[2]	9	10			13				11			12																	6
1	2		4[2]	14	6	7[1]	8	9	10[3]		12	13	11			5																				7
1	2	3	4		6	7	8	9	10[1]		12		11			5																				8
1	2	3	4		6	7	8	9[1]	10				11			5			12																	9
1	2	3	4	5[3]		7[1]	8	9[2]	10		12		11			6			13	14																10
1	2		4	5		7	8	9[2]	10			13	11[1]				6		12	3																11
1	2	13	4		6	7	8	9	10[2]		12		11			5					3[1]															12
1	2	3	4		6	7[2]	8	9[1]	10[3]		12	13	11			5						14														13
1	2		4		6	7[2]	8	9	10[1]			13	11		14	5						3[3]		12												14
1	2	3	4		6	12	8	9				13	11			5								10[2]		7[1]										15
1		3			6	7	8	9					11			5								10	2	4										16
1		3	4		6	12	8	9				13	11[2]		14	5								10[3]	2	7[1]										17
1	2	3	4		6		8	9			12		11			5								10[1]		7										18
1	2	3	4[2]		6	12	8	9					11			5						14		13		7[1]	10[3]									19
1	2		4		6		8	9			12		11[3]		14	5[1]				13		3				7	10[2]									20
	2	3	4		6		8	9					11						12	13				10[1]		7[1]	5	1								21
	2	3	4[3]		6		8	9					11		14				12	13				10[1]		7[2]	5	1								22
	2	3	4		6		8	9					11											10		7	5	1								23
	2	3	4		6		8	9					11											10[1]	12	7	5[2]	1	13							24
	2	3	4		6		8	9					11							13				10[2]	12	7[1]	5	1								25
	2	3	4		6		8	9[2]					11											10[1]		7	5	1	12	13						26
	2		4		6		8	9[3]					11							13		3		10[1]	12	7[2]	5	1	14							27
	2		4		6		8	9					11									3		10		7[1]	5	1	12							28
	2		4		6		8	9					11[1]							13		3		10[2]	12	7	5	1								29
	2		4					9					11							13		3		10[1]	12	7	5	1	6			8[2]				30
	2		4[3]					9[2]					11		14							3		10	12	7[1]	5	1	6	13		8				31
	2		4										11		14					13		3		10[1]	12	7	5	1	6		9[2]	8[3]				32
	2						8	9[1]					11[2]		14							3		10[3]	12	7	5	1	6	13		4				33
	2	3	4[2]				8	9					11							13				10[1]		7	5	1	6	12						34
	2	3	4		6		8	9					11[2]											10[1]	12	7	5	1		13						35
	2	3	4[1]		6		8	9					11											10[2]		7	13	1	5	12						36
1	2	3	4		6		8					13	11[2]		14									10[1]	12		5				9		7[3]			37
1	2	3	4		6		8						11		14									10[1]	12	5[2]				13	9		7[3]			38
1	2	3[1]	4		6			9[2]					11											10	12	7	5				13	8				39
1	2		4		6			9					11							13		3[2]		10	2	7[1]	5			12		8				40
1	2		4		6			9					11									3		10	12	7	5					8[1]				41
1	2		4					9					11							13		3		10[2]	12		5		6			8	7[1]			42
1	2		4					9[2]					11[3]							13		3		10	12		5		6			8	7[1]	14		43
1	2[2]		4										11[1]		14					13		3		10[3]	12[4]	7	5		6		9	8				44
1			4										11							13		3		10[3]	2		5		12	6[1]	9	8	7[2]		14	45
1	2		4										11							13		3		10[1]	12		5		6		9[2]	8	7[3]		14	46

FA Cup					J Paint Trophy			
First Round	Accrington S	(a)	2-3		First Round	Shrewsbury T	(h)	0-1

Carling Cup			
First Round	Scunthorpe U	(a)	1-2

OXFORD UNITED
FL Championship 2

The Kassam Stadium, Grenoble Road, Oxford OX4 4XP.

Telephone: (01865) 337 500.

Fax: (01865) 337 501.

Ticket Office: (01865) 337 533.

Website: www.oufc.co.uk

Email: admin@oufc.co.uk

Ground Capacity: 12,500.

Record Attendance: 22,730 v Preston NE, FA Cup 6th rd, 29 February 1964 (at Manor Ground). 12,243 v Leyton Orient, FL 2, 6 May 2006 (at The Kassam Stadium).

Pitch Measurements: 115yd × 71yd.

Chairman: Kelvin Thomas.

General Manager/Club Secretary: Mick Brown.

Manager: Chris Wilder.

First Team Coach: Mickey Lewis.

Physios: Charlie Greig, Jon Brown.

Colours: Yellow shirts, blue shorts, blue stockings.

Change Colours: All white.

Year Formed: 1893.

Turned Professional: 1949.

Ltd Co.: 1949.

Club Nickname: 'The U's'.

HONOURS

Football League – Division 1: Best season: 12th, 1997–98; **Division 2: *Champions*** 1984–85; ***Runners-up*** 1995–96; **Division 3: *Champions*** 1967–68, 1983–84.

FA Cup: Best season: 6th rd, 1964 (shared record for 4th Division club).

Football League Cup: *Winners* 1986.

Previous Names: 1893, Headington; 1894, Headington United; 1960, Oxford United.

Grounds: 1893, Headington Quarry; 1894, Wootten's Field; 1898, Sandy Lane Ground; 1902, Britannia Field; 1909, Sandy Lane; 1910, Quarry Recreation Ground; 1914, Sandy Lane; 1922, The Paddock Manor Road; 1925, Manor Ground; 2001, The Kassam Stadium.

First Football League Game: 18 August 1962, Division 4, v Barrow (a) L 2–3 – Medlock; Beavon, Quartermain; Ron Atkinson, Kyle, Jones; Knight, Graham Atkinson (1), Houghton (1), Cornwell, Colfar.

Record League Victory: 7–0 v Barrow, Division 4, 19 December 1964 – Fearnley; Beavon, Quartermain; Ron Atkinson (1), Kyle, Jones; Morris, Booth (3), Willey (1), Graham Atkinson (1), Harrington (1).

sky SPORTS FACT FILE

On 8 November 1986 Oxford United entertained Manchester United and took the lead after 17 minutes through a John Aldridge penalty. The home team added a second goal in the second half through Dave Leworthy. It was Alex Ferguson's first game in charge of the visitors.

Record Cup Victory: 9–1 v Dorchester T, FA Cup 1st rd, 11 November 1995 – Whitehead; Wood (2), Mike Ford (1), Smith, Elliott, Gilchrist, Rush (1), Massey (Murphy), Moody (3), Bobby Ford (1), Angel (Beauchamp (1)).

Record Defeat: 0–7 v Sunderland, Division 1, 19 September 1998.

Most League Points (2 for a win): 61, Division 4, 1964–65.

Most League Points (3 for a win): 95, Division 3, 1983–84.

Most League Goals: 91, Division 3, 1983–84.

Highest League Scorer in Season: John Aldridge, 30, Division 2, 1984–85.

Most League Goals in Total Aggregate: Graham Atkinson, 77, 1962–73.

Most League Goals in One Match: 4, Tony Jones v Newport Co, Division 4, 22 September 1962; 4, Arthur Longbottom v Darlington, Division 4, 26 October 1963; 4, Richard Hill v Walsall, Division 2, 26 December 1988; 4, John Durnin v Luton T, 14 November 1992.

Most Capped Player: Jim Magilton, 18 (52), Northern Ireland.

Most League Appearances: John Shuker, 478, 1962–77.

Youngest League Player: Jason Seacole, 16 years 149 days v Mansfield T, 7 September 1976.

Record Transfer Fee Received: £1,600,000 from Leicester C for Matt Elliott, January 1997.

Record Transfer Fee Paid: £475,000 to Aberdeen for Dean Windass, August 1998.

Football League Record: 1962 Elected to Division 4; 1965–68 Division 3; 1968–76 Division 2; 1976–84 Division 3; 1984–85 Division 2; 1985–88 Division 1; 1988–92 Division 2; 1992–94 Division 1; 1994–96 Division 2; 1996–99 Division 1; 1999–2001 Division 2; 2001–04 Division 3; 2004–06 FL2; 2006–10 Conference; 2010– FL 2.

MANAGERS

Harry Thompson 1949–58
  (Player-Manager) 1949-51
Arthur Turner 1959–69
  (continued as General Manager to 1972)
Ron Saunders 1969
Gerry Summers 1969–75
Mick Brown 1975–79
Bill Asprey 1979–80
Ian Greaves 1980–82
Jim Smith 1982–85
Maurice Evans 1985–88
Mark Lawrenson 1988
Brian Horton 1988–93
Denis Smith 1993–97
Malcolm Crosby 1997–98
Malcolm Shotton 1998–99
Micky Lewis 1999–2000
Denis Smith 2000
David Kemp 2000–01
Mark Wright 2001
Ian Atkins 2001–04
Graham Rix 2004
Ramon Diaz 2004–05
Brian Talbot 2005–2006
Darren Patterson 2006
Jim Smith 2006–07
Darren Patterson 2007–08
Chris Wilder December 2008–

LATEST SEQUENCES

Longest Sequence of League Wins: 6, 6.4.1985 – 24.4.1985.

Longest Sequence of League Defeats: 7, 4.5.1991 – 7.9.1991.

Longest Sequence of League Draws: 5, 7.10.1978 – 28.10.1978.

Longest Sequence of Unbeaten League Matches: 20, 17.3.1984 – 29.9.1984.

Longest Sequence Without a League Win: 27, 14.11.1987 – 27.8.1988.

Successive Scoring Runs: 17 from 10.9.1983.

Successive Non-scoring Runs: 6 from 26.3.1988.

TEN YEAR LEAGUE RECORD

		P	W	D	L	F	A	Pts	Pos
2001-02	Div 3	46	11	14	21	53	62	47	21
2002-03	Div 3	46	19	12	15	57	47	69	8
2003-04	Div 3	46	18	17	11	55	44	71	9
2004-05	FL 2	46	16	11	19	50	63	59	15
2005-06	FL 2	46	11	16	19	43	57	49	23
2006-07	Conf	46	22	15	9	66	33	81	2
2007-08	B Sq Pr	46	20	11	15	56	48	71	9
2008-09	B Sq Pr	46	24	10	12	72	51	77*	7
2009-10	B Sq Pr	44	25	11	8	64	31	86	3
2010-11	FL 2	46	17	12	17	58	60	63	12

* 5 points deducted.

DID YOU KNOW ?

In 1964–65 Oxford United had an average home attendance in Division Four of 8,744. The club's reserve side in the Football Combination had some encouraging crowds at the Manor Ground too, and the visit of Brighton & Hove Albion "stiffs" attracted a gate of 4,003.

OXFORD UNITED 2010–11 LEAGUE RECORD

Match No.	Date		Venue	Opponents	Result		H/T Score	Lg Pos.	Goalscorers	Atten- dance
1	Aug	7	A	Burton Alb	D	0-0	0-0	—		4321
2		14	H	Bury	L	1-2	1-1	19	Midson [31]	7552
3		21	A	Wycombe W	D	0-0	0-0	18		6983
4		28	H	Accrington S	D	0-0	0-0	18		6428
5	Sept	4	H	Morecambe	W	4-0	2-0	13	Heslop [21], Constable 3 [25, 82, 90]	6237
6		11	A	Hereford U	W	2-0	1-0	7	Constable [35], Craddock [65]	2980
7		18	H	Stockport Co	L	0-1	0-1	10		7033
8		25	A	Crewe Alex	D	1-1	0-1	9	Constable [71]	4584
9		28	A	Cheltenham T	D	1-1	0-1	—	Midson [60]	4349
10	Oct	2	H	Port Vale	W	2-1	0-0	9	Craddock [61], Green [90]	7947
11		9	H	Aldershot T	L	0-1	0-0	11		7808
12		16	A	Macclesfield T	L	2-3	2-0	14	Constable [6], Craddock [45]	1395
13		23	H	Northampton T	W	3-1	2-1	11	Potter [4], Payne [45], Craddock (pen) [90]	7647
14		30	A	Bradford C	L	0-5	0-0	14		11,376
15	Nov	2	H	Torquay U	L	0-2	0-1	—		6401
16		13	A	Rotherham U	L	1-2	1-2	18	Clist [45]	3891
17		20	H	Gillingham	L	0-1	0-1	21		7144
18		23	A	Chesterfield	W	2-1	0-1	—	Craddock [58], MacLean [69]	5929
19	Dec	4	H	Barnet	W	2-1	0-1	—	Uddin (og) [64], Constable [83]	6004
20		28	H	Macclesfield T	W	2-1	1-0	—	Heslop [17], Constable [70]	9440
21	Jan	1	H	Southend U	L	0-2	0-2	13		7362
22		3	A	Torquay U	W	4-3	2-1	12	Craddock [35], Midson 3 [42, 64, 90]	3021
23		8	A	Aldershot T	W	2-1	1-0	10	Charles (og) [8], Craddock [85]	3129
24		15	H	Bradford C	W	2-1	0-1	9	MacLean [77], Craddock [82]	7068
25		22	A	Northampton T	L	1-2	0-1	10	Craddock [47]	6097
26		25	H	Shrewsbury T	W	3-1	1-1	—	Hall [11], Constable 2 [59, 76]	6264
27		29	H	Cheltenham T	D	1-1	1-1	—	Craddock [33]	7738
28	Feb	1	A	Southend U	L	1-2	1-2	10	Constable [14]	4944
29		5	A	Gillingham	D	0-0	0-0	9		5364
30		12	H	Rotherham U	W	2-1	1-1	8	Heslop [18], MacLean (pen) [63]	6615
31		15	A	Stevenage	D	0-0	0-0	—		2590
32		19	A	Morecambe	W	3-0	2-0	8	Hall 2 [30, 66], McLaren [36]	2171
33		26	H	Hereford U	L	0-2	0-1	9		7807
34	Mar	1	A	Lincoln C	L	1-3	1-1	—	MacLean [40]	2261
35		5	A	Stockport Co	L	1-2	0-0	10	Craddock [49]	4119
36		12	H	Port Vale	W	2-1	1-1	9	Midson [33], Worley [58]	5661
37		15	H	Stevenage	L	1-2	1-1	—	Craddock (pen) [45]	6018
38		19	H	Crewe Alex	W	2-1	1-0	10	Constable 2 [29, 67]	6751
39		27	H	Burton Alb	W	3-0	1-0	—	MacLean 2 [5, 90], Craddock (pen) [57]	7127
40	Apr	2	A	Bury	L	0-3	0-1	11		3515
41		9	H	Wycombe W	D	2-2	1-0	11	Potter [35], Winfield (og) [54]	9309
42		16	A	Accrington S	D	0-0	0-0	11		2066
43		23	H	Chesterfield	D	0-0	0-0	13		8195
44		25	A	Barnet	D	2-2	1-1	12	Constable 2 [16, 78]	3425
45		30	H	Lincoln C	W	2-1	0-1	11	Hall [61], Craddock [75]	7485
46	May	7	A	Shrewsbury T	L	0-3	0-0	12		8817

Final League Position: 12

GOALSCORERS

League (58): Constable 15, Craddock 14 (3 pens), MacLean 6 (1 pen), Midson 6, Hall 4, Heslop 3, Potter 2, Clist 1, Green 1, McLaren 1, Payne 1, Worley 1, own goals 3.
Carling Cup (6): Constable 2, Heslop 2, Green 1, Midson 1.
FA Cup (0).
J Paint Trophy (0).

Clarke R 46	Batt D 27+1	Tonkin A 37+2	Bulman D 4+1	Worley H 41+2	Wright J 33+2	Hall A 34+7	Heslop S 30+8	Constable J 35+9	Midson J 11+10	Green M 9+8	Dering S —+6	Philliskirk D —+1	Cole M —+4	Potter A 16+22	Purkiss B 19+4	Baker R —+6	Payne J 23+5	Craddock T 36+3	Creighton M 5+2	Kinniburgh W 10+1	Franks L 4+1	Clist S 16+7	Futcher B 6	Wotton P 4	MacLeane S 26+5	McLaren P 24	Sangare 2+2	Hackney S 2+11	Burge R 5	Doble R 1+2	Hanson M —+2	Match No.
1	2	3	4	5	6	7	8	9	10²	11¹	12	13																				1
1	2	3	4¹	5	6	7	8	9	10¹	11¹²	12		13	14																		2
1	2¹	3	4²	5	6	7	8	9	10	11³				14	12	13																3
1		3	4³	5	6	7	8	9	10²	11¹			13	12	2		14															4
1		3		5	6³	7	8	9	10²	13				12	2		4	11¹	14													5
1		3	13	5		7	8	9³	14	11¹				12	2		4²	10	6													6
1		3		5		7	8	9		11¹			13	12	2	14	4²	10	6³													7
1		3		5		7	8³	9¹	13	14				4²	2	12	11¹	10	6													8
1		3		5		7¹	8	10³	14					11	2	4	9	6¹	3	12	13											9
1	13			5		7¹	8	9²		12				11³	2		4	10	3	6	14											10
1		3		5		4²	8³	9	13				14	7	2		11	10		6¹	12											11
1		3		5		4³	8	9	13				14	7²	2	12	11¹	10	6													12
1		3		5¹	6	7²	8	9³		14				11	2		4	10	12			13										13
1		3		14	6²	7²	8	9		13				11³	2	12	4¹	10	5²													14
1	2	3		5		7¹	8	9	14	11¹²		13		12			4	10		6³												15
1		3		5			12	13						11²	2		4¹	10³				7	6	8	9							16
1					6		13	12		14				7³	2		4¹	10	3			11	5	8²	9							17
1	2		12		6¹	7	8³		13					14				10²	3			11	5		9	4						18
1	2			5		7¹	8		13					12		14		10²	3			11	6		9	4³						19
1	2	13		5		12	14	8	9					7¹				10	3²			11	6			4³						20
1				5		14	12	8	9					7	2		4¹	10	3²			11										21
1	2	3		5	6	8	13		7¹					12				10³				11			9	4²		14				22
1	2	3		5	6	7²	14	12	8¹					13				10				11			9³	4						23
1	2	3		5	6	7	12	13	8²									10¹				11			9	4		14				24
1	2	3		5	6³	7¹	12	8		13				14				10				11			9	4²						25
1	2	3		5	6	7¹		8³	14					12				10²				11			9	4		13				26
1	2	3		5	6	7¹	12	8						13				10²				11			9	4						27
1	2⁴	3		5	6	7¹	0²	11						13				10³				12			9	4		14				28
1		3		5	6	7¹⁴	8							12	2			10²				11			9¹	4		13				29
1		3		5	6	7²	8³	11	10¹					14	2							13			9	4		12				30
1		3		5	6	12		9¹	14						2		8¹	10				11			13	4		7²				31
1	2	3		5	6	7	8	11³	14					12				10²							9¹	4		13				32
1	2	3		5	6	7²	8	11	14					13				10¹							9	4	11					33
1	2	3		5	6	7²	8	11	14					13				10¹							9³	4		12				34
1	2	3⁴		5	6	7	8	11						13				10³					12		9²	4¹		14				35
1	13			5	6			12	10¹					7	2		8			3²		11			14	4		9³				36
1				5	6		14	8³						12	2		7¹	10²		3		11			9	4		13				37
1	2	3		5	6		8	11						12				13	10²						9³	4¹		14	7			38
1	2	3		5	6	13	8	11³									12	10							9	4¹		14	7²			39
1	2	3		5	6	12	8³	11									4¹	10²							9			14	7	13		40
1	2	3		5	6	14	8	10²						7				12							9¹	4³		11		13		41
1	2	3		6		12	8¹	13						7²				10							14	4	5	11		9³		42
1	2	3			6	7		10						11	13		8	14							9	4³	5¹			12²		43
1	2¹	3		5	6	7		10						13	12		8	11							9²	4						44
1	2²	3		5	6³	7		9						11	13		8	10		14					12	4¹						45
1	2	6		5²		7		11						12			8	10¹		3					9	4					13	46

FA Cup
First Round Burton Alb (a) 0-1

Carling Cup
First Round Bristol R (h) 6-1
Second Round West Ham U (a) 0-1

J Paint Trophy
First Round Aldershot T (a) 0-2

PETERBOROUGH UNITED   FL Championship

FOUNDATION

The old Peterborough & Fletton club, founded in 1923, was suspended by the FA during season 1932–33 and disbanded. Local enthusiasts determined to carry on and in 1934 a new professional club, Peterborough United, was formed and entered the Midland League the following year. Peterborough's first success came in 1939–40, but from 1955–56 to 1959–60 they won five successive titles. During the 1958–59 season they were undefeated in the Midland League. They reached the third round of the FA Cup, won the Northamptonshire Senior Cup, the Maunsell Cup and were runners-up in the East Anglian Cup.

London Road Stadium, London Road, Peterborough PE2 8AL.

Telephone: (01733) 563 947. *Fax:* (01733) 344 140.

Ticket Office: (01733) 865 674.

Website: www.theposh.com

Email: info@theposh.com

Ground Capacity: 15,460.

Record Attendance: 30,096 v Swansea T, FA Cup 5th rd, 20 February 1965.

Pitch Measurements: 112yd × 71yd.

Chairman: Darragh MacAnthony.

Chief Executive: Bob Symns.

Director of Football and Club Secretary: Barry Fry.

Manager: Darren Ferguson.

Assistant Manager: Kevin Russell.

Physio: Peter Corder.

Colours: Blue shirts with white design, white shorts, white stockings.

Change Colours: Green and white striped shirts with green sleeves, black shorts, green stockings.

Year Formed: 1934. *Turned Professional:* 1934. *Ltd Co.:* 1934.

Club Nickname: 'The Posh'.

Ground: 1934, London Road Stadium.

First Football League Game: 20 August 1960, Division 4, v Wrexham (h) W 3–0 – Walls; Stafford, Walker; Rayner, Rigby, Norris; Hails, Emery (1), Bly (1), Smith, McNamee (1).

Record League Victory: 9–1 v Barnet (a) Division 3, 5 September 1998 – Griemink; Hooper (1), Drury (Farell), Gill, Bodley, Edwards, Davies, Payne, Grazioli (5), Quinn (2) (Rowe), Houghton (Etherington) (1).

Record Cup Victory: 9–1 v Rushden T, FA Cup 1st qual rd, 6 October 1945 – Hilliard; Bryan, Parrott, Warner, Hobbs, Woods, Polhill (1), Fairchild, Laxton (6), Tasker (1), Rodgers (1); 9–1 v Kingstonian, FA Cup 1st rd, 25 November 1992. Match ordered to be replayed by FA. Peterborough won replay 1–0.

HONOURS

Football League – Division 1: Best season: 10th, 1992–93;
Division 2: 1991–92 (play-offs);
FL 1: *Runners-up* 2008–09;
FL 2: *Runners-up* 2007–08;
Division 4: *Champions* 1960–61, 1973–74.
FA Cup: Best season: 6th rd, 1965.
Football League Cup: Semi-final 1966.

sky SPORTS FACT FILE

On 5 February 2011 Peterborough United twice found themselves two goals in arrears to visiting Southampton. Two penalties, one by Grant McCann and other in added time from Lee Tomlin, enabled Posh to level the scores at 4-4 with their 60th League goal of the season.

Record Defeat: 1–8 v Northampton T, FA Cup 2nd rd (2nd replay), 18 December 1946.

Most League Points (2 for a win): 66, Division 4, 1960–61.

Most League Points (3 for a win): 92, FL 2, 2007–08.

Most League Goals: 134, Division 4, 1960–61.

Highest League Scorer in Season: Terry Bly, 52, Division 4, 1960–61.

Most League Goals in Total Aggregate: Jim Hall, 122, 1967–75.

Most League Goals in One Match: 5, Guiliano Grazioli v Barnet, Division 3, 5 September 1998.

Most Capped Player: Craig Morgan, 19 (23), Wales.

Most League Appearances: Tommy Robson, 482, 1968–81.

Youngest League Player: Matthew Etherington, 15 years 262 days v Brentford, 3 May 1997.

Record Transfer Fee Received: £1,300,000 from Hull C for Aaron McLean, January 2011.

Record Transfer Fee Paid: £500,000 to Grimsby T for Ryan Bennett, January 2010.

Football League Record: 1960 Elected to Division 4; 1961–68 Division 3, when they were demoted for financial irregularities; 1968–74 Division 4; 1974–79 Division 3; 1979–91 Division 4; 1991–92 Division 3; 1992–94 Division 1; 1994–97 Division 2; 1997–2000 Division 3; 2000–04 Division 2; 2004–05 FL 1; 2005–08 FL 2; 2008–09 FL 1; 2009–10 FL C; 2010–11 FL 1; 2011– FL C.

LATEST SEQUENCES

Longest Sequence of League Wins: 9, 1.2.1992 – 14.3.1992.

Longest Sequence of League Defeats: 8, 12.1.2008 – 12.4.2008.

Longest Sequence of League Draws: 8, 18.12.1971 – 12.2.1972.

Longest Sequence of Unbeaten League Matches: 17, 17.12.1960 – 8.4.1961.

Longest Sequence Without a League Win: 17, 23.9.1978 – 30.12.1978.

Successive Scoring Runs: 33 from 20.9.1960.

Successive Non-scoring Runs: 6 from 13.8.2002.

MANAGERS

Jock Porter 1934–36
Fred Taylor 1936–37
Vic Poulter 1937–38
Sam Haden 1938–48
Jack Blood 1948–50
Bob Gurney 1950–52
Jack Fairbrother 1952–54
George Swindin 1954–58
Jimmy Hagan 1958–62
Jack Fairbrother 1962–64
Gordon Clark 1964–67
Norman Rigby 1967–69
Jim Iley 1969–72
Noel Cantwell 1972–77
John Barnwell 1977–78
Billy Hails 1978–79
Peter Morris 1979–82
Martin Wilkinson 1982–83
John Wile 1983–86
Noel Cantwell 1986–88 *(continued as General Manager)*
Mick Jones 1988–89
Mark Lawrenson 1989–90
Dave Booth 1990–91
Chris Turner 1991–92
Lil Fuccillo 1992–93
Chris Turner 1993–94
John Still 1994–95
Mick Halsall 1995–96
Barry Fry 1996–2005
Mark Wright 2005–06
Steve Bleasdale 2006
Keith Alexander 2006–07
Darren Ferguson 2007–09
Mark Cooper 2009–10
Jim Gannon 2010
Gary Johnson 2010–11
Darren Ferguson January 2011–

TEN YEAR LEAGUE RECORD

		P	W	D	L	F	A	Pts	Pos
2001-02	Div 2	46	15	10	21	64	59	55	17
2002-03	Div 2	46	14	16	16	51	54	58	11
2003-04	Div 2	46	12	16	18	58	58	52	18
2004-05	FL 1	46	9	12	25	49	73	39	23
2005-06	FL 2	46	17	11	18	57	49	62	9
2006-07	FL 2	46	18	11	17	70	61	65	10
2007-08	FL 2	46	28	8	10	84	43	92	2
2008-09	FL 1	46	26	11	9	78	54	89	2
2009-10	FL C	46	8	10	28	46	80	34	24
2010-11	FL 1	46	23	10	13	106	75	79	4

DID YOU KNOW ❓

In successive home League matches during 2010–11, Peterborough United came back from being two goals in arrears to win. On 21 August they recovered to beat Huddersfield Town 4-2 and on 11 September they defeated Oldham Athletic 5-2.

PETERBOROUGH UNITED 2010–11 LEAGUE RECORD

Match No.	Date	Venue	Opponents	Result	H/T Score	Lg Pos.	Goalscorers	Attendance
1	Aug 7	H	Bristol R	W 3-0	0-0	—	Boyd [57], McLean [73], McCann [88]	7113
2	14	A	Bournemouth	L 1-5	0-2	12	Langmead [61]	5949
3	21	H	Huddersfield T	W 4-2	1-2	6	Boyd [45], McLean 2 [50, 67], Mackail-Smith [52]	6647
4	28	A	Plymouth Arg	W 3-0	0-0	2	Mackail-Smith 2 [61, 75], McLean [77]	7712
5	Sept 4	A	Tranmere R	L 0-1	0-1	4		4636
6	11	H	Oldham Ath	W 5-2	1-2	1	Wesolowski [45], McLean [62], Boyd [71], Hibbert [82], McCann (pen) [90]	6337
7	18	A	Exeter C	D 2-2	1-0	2	Archibald-Henville (og) [29], Tomlin [82]	5146
8	25	H	Milton Keynes D	W 2-1	1-1	2	Mackail-Smith [36], McLean [48]	7838
9	28	H	Notts Co	L 2-3	1-3	—	Zakuani [36], Mackail-Smith [59]	6136
10	Oct 2	A	Carlisle U	W 1-0	1-0	2	Mackail-Smith [32]	5735
11	9	A	Hartlepool U	L 0-2	0-1	3		3047
12	16	H	Swindon T	W 5-4	3-3	2	Mackail-Smith 2 [3, 5], Frecklington [22], Boyd [58], Amankwaah (og) [90]	7077
13	23	A	Brentford	L 1-2	1-1	3	McCann (pen) [19]	6543
14	30	H	Brighton & HA	L 0-3	0-2	5		10,116
15	Nov 2	A	Walsall	W 3-1	2-0	—	Bennett [15], Davies [17], Langmead [55]	3294
16	13	A	Charlton Ath	L 1-5	0-4	8	McCann [54]	7477
17	20	A	Southampton	L 1-4	0-1	11	McLean [76]	22,177
18	23	H	Leyton Orient	D 2-2	1-1	—	McLean 2 (1 pen) [18 (p), 61]	4423
19	Dec 10	H	Rochdale	W 2-1	1-0	—	McLean [19], Mackail-Smith [50]	4233
20	28	A	Swindon T	D 1-1	1-0	—	Tomlin [17]	8592
21	Jan 3	H	Walsall	W 4-1	1-1	7	Mackail-Smith 2 [36, 71], Mendez-Laing [81], Bennett [90]	5517
22	11	H	Brentford	W 2-1	1-0	—	McCann (pen) [5], Obika [90]	4667
23	15	A	Brighton & HA	L 1-3	0-2	5	Tomlin [66]	7233
24	22	H	Hartlepool U	W 4-0	0-0	5	Mackail-Smith [62], Rowe [64], Tomlin [68], Wesolowski [90]	5800
25	28	A	Colchester U	L 1-2	1-1	—	Rowe [1]	4645
26	Feb 1	H	Sheffield W	W 5-3	2-3	6	Mackail-Smith 2 [16, 90], Boyd 2 [26, 74], Mendez-Laing [84]	6480
27	5	H	Southampton	D 4-4	2-2	8	Mackail-Smith [39], Whelpdale [45], McCann (pen) [55], Tomlin (pen) [90]	6905
28	12	A	Charlton Ath	L 2-3	1-0	9	Tomlin [29], Mackail-Smith [90]	15,909
29	15	A	Yeovil T	W 2-0	0-0	—	Mackail-Smith [85], Basey [88]	3351
30	19	H	Tranmere R	W 2-1	0-1	4	McCann [53], Showunmi (og) [70]	5774
31	22	H	Colchester U	D 1-1	1-1	—	Boyd [6]	5758
32	26	A	Oldham Ath	W 5-0	0-0	4	Rowe [49], Ball [52], Zakuani [61], Mackail-Smith 2 [68, 83]	4263
33	Mar 5	H	Exeter C	W 3-0	1-0	4	Boyd 2 [10, 74], Mackail-Smith [87]	6174
34	8	A	Notts Co	W 1-0	0-0	—	Lee [57]	5714
35	12	H	Carlisle U	W 6-0	3-0	3	Rowe [2], Mackail-Smith [24], Boyd 2 [45, 83], Bennett [77], Ball [90]	6467
36	15	A	Sheffield W	W 4-1	3-0	—	Mackail-Smith [25], Tomlin [35], Boyd 2 [41, 81]	16,014
37	21	A	Milton Keynes D	L 0-1	0-0	—		10,019
38	25	A	Bristol R	D 2-2	1-1	—	Anthony (og) [23], Boyd [53]	6589
39	Apr 1	H	Bournemouth	D 3-3	3-1	4	Mackail-Smith 2 [11, 42], Rowe [15]	6670
40	5	A	Dagenham & R	W 2-0	2-0	—	Ball 2 [3, 8]	2063
41	9	A	Huddersfield T	D 1-1	1-0	4	McCann (pen) [41]	16,431
42	16	H	Plymouth Arg	W 2-1	0-1	4	Bennett [55], Mackail-Smith [70]	6723
43	22	A	Leyton Orient	L 1-2	0-0	—	Mendez-Laing [75]	5476
44	25	H	Yeovil T	D 2-2	0-1	4	Langmead [87], Mackail-Smith [89]	6489
45	30	A	Rochdale	D 2-2	1-1	4	Mendez-Laing [45], Tomlin [46]	3147
46	May 7	H	Dagenham & R	W 5-0	1-0	4	Mendez-Laing [11], McCann [65], Boyd [82], Mackail-Smith [84], Ball [90]	7519

Final League Position: 4

GOALSCORERS

League (106): Mackail-Smith 27, Boyd 15, McLean 10 (1 pen), McCann 9 (5 pens), Tomlin 8 (1 pen), Ball 5, Mendez-Laing 5, Rowe 5, Bennett 4, Langmead 3, Wesolowski 2, Zakuani 2, Basey 1, Davies 1, Frecklington 1, Hibbert 1, Lee 1, Obika 1, Whelpdale 1, own goals 4.
Carling Cup (7): Mackail-Smith 3, Boyd 2, Bennett 1, McLean 1.
FA Cup (9): Tomlin 3, Mackail-Smith 2, McLean 2, Langmead 1, McCann 1 (pen).
J Paint Trophy (2): Little 1, McLean 1.
Play-Offs (7): Mackail-Smith 3, McCann 3 (1 pen), Rowe 1.

Lewis J 45	Little M 32+3	Ofori-Twumasi N 6+5	McCann G 34+4	Bennett R 32+2	Langmead K 28+4	Wesolowski J 23+9	Mendez-Laing N 8+25	Mackail-Smith C 44+1	McLean A 19	Boyd G 42+1	Davies A 12+10	Lee C 26+8	Tomlin L 31+6	Rowe T 32+3	Hibbert D —+7	Whelpdale D 16+6	Zakuani G 29+1	Gill M 4	Frecklington L 3+6	Nyatanga L 3	Williams M 3	Clayton A 6+1	Piergianni C —+1	Obika J —+1	Kennedy T 14	Ball D 7+12	Bassey G 5+2	Jones P 1	Newell J 1+1	Taylor P —+1	Match No.
1	2	3	4	5	6	7^2	8^1	9	10^3	11	12	13	14																		1
1	2	3^1	4	5^1	6	7	8^2	9	10	11	12	13	14																		2
1	2	3^1	4	5	6	7^3	8	9	10^2	11	12	13	14																		3
1	2	3	4	5	6	7	8^1	9	10^3	11^2	12	13	14																		4
1	2	3	4^2	5	6	7	8^1	9	10^3	11	12	13	14																		5
1	2	3	4	5^1	6	7	8^2	9	10^3	11	12	13	14																		6
1	2	3	4	5	6	7^1	8^2	9	10^3	11	12	13	14																		7
1	2	3^1	4	5	6	7^3	8^2	9	10	11	12	13	14																		8
1	2^1	3	4▪	5	6	7^3	8^2	9	10	11	12	13	14																		9
1	2	3^1	4^2	5	6	7	8	9	10^3	11	12	13	14																		10
1	2	3^2	4^1	5	6	7▪	8^3	9	10	11	12	13	14																		11
1	2	3	4	5^1	6	7^3	8^2	9	10	11	12	13	14																		12
1	2	3^3	4	5	6	7^1	8^2	9	10	11	12	13	14																		13
1	2	3	4	5	6	7^3	8	9	10^1	11▪	12^2	13	14																		14
1	2	3	4		6	7	8	9	10^1	11	12									5											15
1	2	3^1	4		6	7^2	8	9^3	10	11	12	13	14							5											16
1	2	3	4^3		6	7^1	8	9	10	11^2	12	13	14							5											17
1	2			5	6	7	8^1	9	10	11	12										3	4									18
1	2	3	4	5	6	7^1		9	10	11^2	12	13										8									19
1	2	3	4^3	5	6	7^1		9	10^2	11	12	13	14									8									20
1	2	3	4	5	6	7^1		9	10^3	11^2	12	13	14									8									21
1	2	3	4	5^1	6	7^3		9	10^2	11	12		14									8			13						22
1	2	3	4▪	5	6	7		9	10	11	12								2			8									23
1	2		4		6			9	10	11			7				5		8						3						24
1	2		4^1		6			9	10	11			7^2			13	5		8						3	12					25
1	2^3		4		6			9	10	11			7^1			13	5		8^2						3	12	14				26
1	2		4		6			9	10	11			7^1			13	5		8^2						3	12					27
1	2		4		6			9	10	11			7^1			13	5		8^1						3^3	12					28
1	2		4					9	10^3	11			7^2			13	5		8^1						3	12	14				29
1	2		4		6			9	10^3	11^2			7^1			13	5		8						3	12	14				30
1	2		4		6			9	10^2	11			7^1			13	5		8						3	12					31
1	2		4^3		6			9	10^1	11			7^2			13	5		8						3	12	14				32
1	2		4		6			9	10^1	11			7^3			13	5		8						3^2	12	14				33
1	2		4^2		6			9	10^1	11			7			13	5		8						3	12					34
1	2		4		6			9^2	10	11			7^1			13	5		8^2						3	12	14				35
1	2		4		6			9	10^1	11			7^3			13	5		8^2						3	12	14				36
1	2		4		6			9	10^2	11			7^3			13	5		8^1						3	12	14				37
1	2▪		4					9	10^2	11			7			13	5		8						3	12	6^1				38
1	2		4		6			9	10	11			7^1			13	5		8^2						3^1	12					39
1	2		4		6			9	10	11			7^2			13	5		8						3^1	12					40
1	2		4^1		6			9	10^3	11			7			13	5		8^2						3	12	14				41
1	2		4		6			9	10^3	11			7^2			13	5		8						3^1	12	14				42
1	2		4		6			9	10^2	11			7^1			13	5		8						3^3	12	14				43
	2		4		6			9	10^3	11^2	12		7			13	5								3^1			1	8	14	44
1	2^1		4		6			9	10^2	11			7			13	5		8						3	12					45
1	2		4		6			9^2	10	11			7^2			13	5		8						3^1		14		12		46

FA Cup		
First Round	Stockport Co	(a) 1-1
		(h) 4-1
Second Round	Bury	(a) 2-1
Third Round	Fulham	(a) 2-6
Carling Cup		
First Round	Rotherham U	(h) 4-1
Second Round	Cardiff C	(h) 2-1
Third Round	Swansea C	(h) 1-3
J Paint Trophy		
Second Round	Huddersfield T	(a) 2-3
Play-Offs		
Semi-Final	Milton Keynes D	(a) 2-3
		(h) 2-0
Final	Huddersfield T	3-0
(at Old Trafford).		

PLYMOUTH ARGYLE   FL Championship 2

FOUNDATION

The club was formed in September 1886 as the Argyle Football Club by former public and private school pupils who wanted to continue playing the game. The meeting was held in a room above the Borough Arms (a Coffee House), Bedford Street, Plymouth. It was common then to choose a local street/terrace as a club name and Argyle or Argyll was a fashionable name throughout the land due to Queen Victoria's great interest in Scotland.

Home Park, Plymouth, Devon PL2 3DQ.

Telephone: (01752) 562 561.

Fax: (01752) 606 167.

Ticket Office: 0845 338 7232.

Website: www.pafc.co.uk

Email: argyle@pafc.co.uk

Ground Capacity: 21,118.

Record Attendance: 43,596 v Aston Villa, Division 2, 10 October 1936.

Pitch Measurements: 112yd × 73yd.

Interim Chairman: Peter Ridsdale.

Manager: Peter Reid.

Physio: Paul Atkinson.

HONOURS

Football League – Division 2: *Champions* 2003–04;
Division 3 (S): *Champions* 1929–30, 1951–52; *Runners-up* 1921–22, 1922–23, 1923–24, 1924–25, 1925–26, 1926–27 (record of six consecutive years);
Division 3: *Champions* 1958–59, 2001–02; *Runners-up* 1974–75, 1985–86.
FA Cup: Semi-final 1984.
Football League Cup: Semi-final 1965, 1974.

Colours: Dark green shirts with white design, white shorts, white stockings with green design.

Change Colours: White shirts with dark green design, green shorts, green stockings with white design.

Year Formed: 1886.

Turned Professional: 1903.

Ltd Co.: 1903.

Previous Name: 1886, Argyle Athletic Club; 1903, Plymouth Argyle.

Club Nickname: 'The Pilgrims'.

Ground: 1886, Home Park.

First Football League Game: 28 August 1920, Division 3, v Norwich C (h) D 1–1 – Craig; Russell, Atterbury; Logan, Dickinson, Forbes; Kirkpatrick, Jack, Bowler, Heeps (1), Dixon.

Record League Victory: 8–1 v Millwall, Division 2, 16 January 1932 – Harper; Roberts, Titmuss; Mackay, Pullan, Reed; Grozier, Bowden (2), Vidler (3), Leslie (1), Black (1), (1 og). 8–1 v Hartlepool U (a), Division 2, 7 May 1994 – Nicholls; Patterson (Naylor), Hill, Burrows, Comyn, McCall (1), Barlow, Castle (1), Landon (3), Marshall (1), Dalton (2).

sky SPORTS FACT FILE

Wales Under-23 cap George Baker had the distinction, while on the books of Plymouth Argyle, of being a member of the national team which reached the 1958 World Cup finals in Sweden and reached the quarter-finals. He was twelfth man for all five matches as a midfield player.

Record Cup Victory: 6–0 v Corby T, FA Cup 3rd rd, 22 January 1966 – Leiper; Book, Baird; Williams, Nelson, Newman; Jones (1), Jackson (1), Bickle (3), Piper (1), Jennings.

Record Defeat: 0–9 v Stoke C, Division 2, 17 December 1960.

Most League Points (2 for a win): 68, Division 3 (S), 1929–30.

Most League Points (3 for a win): 102, Division 3, 2001–02.

Most League Goals: 107, Division 3 (S), 1925–26 and 1951–52.

Highest League Scorer in Season: Jack Cock, 32, Division 3 (S), 1926–27.

Most League Goals in Total Aggregate: Sammy Black, 180, 1924–38.

Most League Goals in One Match: 5, Wilf Carter v Charlton Ath, Division 2, 27 December 1960.

Most Capped Player: Moses Russell, 20 (23), Wales.

Most League Appearances: Kevin Hodges, 530, 1978–92.

Youngest League Player: Lee Phillips, 16 years 43 days v Gillingham, 29 October 1996.

Record Transfer Fee Received: £3,000,000 from Hull C for Peter Halmosi, July 2008.

Record Transfer Fee Paid: £500,000 to Cardiff C for Steve MacLean, January 2008; £500,000 to QPR for Simon Walton, August 2008.

Football League Record: 1920 Original Member of Division 3; 1921–30 Division 3 (S); 1930–50 Division 2; 1950–52 Division 3 (S); 1952–56 Division 2; 1956–58 Division 3 (S); 1958–59 Division 3; 1959–68 Division 2; 1968–75 Division 3; 1975–77 Division 2; 1977–86 Division 3; 1986–95 Division 2; 1995–96 Division 3; 1996–98 Division 2; 1998–2002 Division 3; 2002–04 Division 2; 2004–10 FL C; 2010–11 FL 1; 2011– FL 2.

LATEST SEQUENCES

Longest Sequence of League Wins: 9, 8.3.1986 – 12.4.1986.

Longest Sequence of League Defeats: 9, 12.10.1963 – 7.12.1963.

Longest Sequence of League Draws: 5, 26.2.2000 – 14.3.2000.

Longest Sequence of Unbeaten League Matches: 22, 20.4.1929 – 21.12.1929.

Longest Sequence Without a League Win: 13, 27.4.1963 – 2.10.1963.

Successive Scoring Runs: 39 from 15.4.1939.

Successive Non-scoring Runs: 5 from 20.9.1947.

MANAGERS

Frank Brettell 1903–05
Bob Jack 1905–06
Bill Fullerton 1906–07
Bob Jack 1910–38
Jack Tresadern 1938–47
Jimmy Rae 1948–55
Jack Rowley 1955–60
Neil Dougall 1961
Ellis Stuttard 1961–63
Andy Beattie 1963–64
Malcolm Allison 1964–65
Derek Ufton 1965–68
Billy Bingham 1968–70
Ellis Stuttard 1970–72
Tony Waiters 1972–77
Mike Kelly 1977–78
Malcolm Allison 1978–79
Bobby Saxton 1979–81
Bobby Moncur 1981–83
Johnny Hore 1983–84
Dave Smith 1984–88
Ken Brown 1988–90
David Kemp 1990–92
Peter Shilton 1992–95
Steve McCall 1995
Neil Warnock 1995–97
Mick Jones 1997–98
Kevin Hodges 1998–2000
Paul Sturrock 2000–04
Bobby Williamson 2004–05
Tony Pulis 2005–06
Ian Holloway 2006–07
Paul Sturrock 2007–09
Paul Mariner 2009–10
Peter Reid June 2010–

TEN YEAR LEAGUE RECORD

		P	W	D	L	F	A	Pts	Pos
2001-02	Div 3	46	31	9	6	71	28	102	1
2002-03	Div 2	46	17	14	15	63	52	65	8
2003-04	Div 2	46	26	12	8	85	41	90	1
2004-05	FL C	46	14	11	21	52	64	53	17
2005-06	FL C	46	13	17	16	39	46	56	14
2006-07	FL C	46	17	16	13	63	62	67	11
2007-08	FL C	46	17	13	16	60	50	64	10
2008-09	FL C	46	13	12	21	44	57	51	21
2009-10	FL C	46	11	8	27	43	68	41	23
2010-11	FL 1	46	15	7	24	51	74	42*	23

*10 points deducted.

DID YOU KNOW ?

During the 1920s when Plymouth Argyle famously finished runners-up in Division Three (South) six years in a row, their strong point was at home. In three of these seasons they were undefeated at Home Park and again in 1929–30 when they finally won promotion to Division Two.

PLYMOUTH ARGYLE 2010–11 LEAGUE RECORD

Match No.	Date	Venue	Opponents	Result	H/T Score	Lg Pos.	Goalscorers	Attendance
1	Aug 7	A	Southampton	W 1-0	0-0	—	Summerfield [47]	21,727
2	14	H	Carlisle U	D 1-1	0-0	7	Patterson [90]	7782
3	21	A	Walsall	L 1-2	1-0	12	Mason [29]	3966
4	28	H	Peterborough U	L 0-3	0-0	17		7712
5	Sept 11	A	Colchester U	D 1-1	0-1	18	Johnson, R [48]	4201
6	18	H	Sheffield W	W 3-2	1-1	16	Fletcher [19], Wright-Phillips [46], Noone [77]	7916
7	21	H	Brighton & HA	L 0-2	0-2	—		7079
8	25	A	Rochdale	D 1-1	1-0	17	Wright-Phillips [18]	3294
9	28	A	Swindon T	W 3-2	2-1	—	Johnson, R [4], Wright-Phillips 2 [8, 90]	9346
10	Oct 2	H	Hartlepool U	L 0-1	0-0	17		7333
11	9	H	Charlton Ath	D 2-2	1-1	18	Wright-Phillips [4], Bolasie [82]	7738
12	16	A	Notts Co	L 0-2	0-1	19		6333
13	23	H	Huddersfield T	W 2-1	1-1	17	Wright-Phillips 2 [16, 66]	7048
14	30	A	Oldham Ath	L 2-4	1-1	21	Noone [7], Wright-Phillips [48]	4080
15	Nov 2	H	Bristol R	W 3-1	0-0	—	Parrett [64], Wright-Phillips 2 [77, 90]	7413
16	13	A	Tranmere R	L 0-1	0-0	19		4840
17	20	A	Brentford	L 1-2	1-1	20	Fallon [38]	6939
18	23	H	Dagenham & R	W 2-1	0-1	—	Noone [62], Patterson [83]	4960
19	Dec 11	H	Exeter C	W 2-0	1-0	15	Wright-Phillips 2 [28, 57]	14,347
20	28	H	Notts Co	D 1-1	1-1	—	Zubar [4]	9822
21	Jan 1	H	Yeovil T	D 0-0	0-0	15		9720
22	4	A	Bristol R	W 3-2	0-2	—	Wright-Phillips [58], Mason [69], Zubar [81]	5943
23	8	A	Bournemouth	L 0-3	0-2	—		7589
24	11	A	Huddersfield T	L 2-3	2-3	—	Mason 2 [1, 15]	11,462
25	15	H	Oldham Ath	L 0-2	0-0	17		8106
26	18	A	Milton Keynes D	W 3-1	2-1	—	Bhasera [22], Arnason [29], Clark [80]	7189
27	22	A	Charlton Ath	L 0-2	0-0	15		16,607
28	29	H	Bournemouth	L 1-2	0-1	—	Fallon [71]	8836
29	Feb 1	A	Yeovil T	L 0-1	0-0	16		5208
30	5	A	Brentford	L 0-2	0-1	18		5613
31	12	H	Tranmere R	L 1-3	0-1	19	Mason [90]	8015
32	22	A	Brighton & HA	L 0-4	0-2	—		7261
33	26	H	Colchester U	W 2-1	1-1	24	Fallon [8], Bolasie (pen) [74]	8982
34	Mar 5	A	Sheffield W	W 4-2	2-0	24	N'Gala [12], Mason 2 [31, 65], Bolasie [79]	18,474
35	8	H	Swindon T	W 1-0	1-0	—	Fallon [10]	8830
36	12	A	Hartlepool U	L 0-2	0-1	24		3059
37	15	A	Carlisle U	D 1-1	0-1	—	Bolasie [84]	3354
38	19	H	Rochdale	L 0-1	0-0	24		8361
39	Apr 5	A	Leyton Orient	L 0-2	0-2	—		3255
40	9	H	Walsall	W 2-0	0-0	24	Bolasie [51], Patterson [88]	7995
41	16	A	Peterborough U	L 1-2	1-0	24	Fletcher [38]	6723
42	22	A	Dagenham & R	W 1-0	0-0	—	Patterson [48]	3559
43	25	H	Milton Keynes D	W 1-0	1-0	23	Walton [21]	8553
44	30	A	Exeter C	L 0-1	0-0	23		7869
45	May 2	H	Southampton	L 1-3	0-1	—	Bolasie [90]	13,118
46	7	H	Leyton Orient	L 1-4	0-2	23	Bolasie [63]	11,501

Final League Position: 23

GOALSCORERS

League (51): Wright-Phillips 13, Bolasie 7 (1 pen), Mason 7, Fallon 4, Patterson 4, Noone 3, Fletcher 2, Johnson, R 2, Zubar 2, Arnason 1, Bhasera 1, Clark 1, N'Gala 1, Parrett 1, Summerfield 1, Walton 1.
Carling Cup (0).
FA Cup (0).
J Paint Trophy (3): Clark 1, MacLean 1, Noone 1.

Button D 29+1	N'Gala B 23+3	Molyneux L 7+2	Fletcher C 37+1	Timar K 7+2	Arnason K 39+1	Summerfield L 4+3	Peterlin A 9+3	Fallon R 25+3	MacLean S 4+3	Bhasera O 28+1	Johnson R 15+2	Patterson R 21+14	Clark C 18+4	Parrett D 5+3	Mason J 26+8	Noone C 16+1	Duguid K 19+7	Paterson J 21+7	Larrieu R 17+1	Wright-Phillips B 17	Seip M 16+1	Stephens J 2+3	Bolasie Y 25+10	Nelson C 32+3	Clifford C 7	Zubar S 29	Rickard M —+1	Young L 2+3	Walton S 6+1	Harper-Penman G —+2	Match No.
1	2	3	4	5	6[1]	7[3]	8	9	10[2]	11	12	13	14																		1
1	2	3	4	5	6	7[2]	8	9[1]	10[3]	11	12	13	14																		2
1	2	3[1]	4	5[2]	6[8]	7[3]		14	11	13	10	12	8	9																	3
1	2	3[8]					13	12	11	5	10	4	8[2]	9[1]	6	7	14														4
16	2	3[8]		5	6		8			11[2]	4	9		7[1]	10	12		13	15												5
	2[8]		4	5	6		13	11	3	9[1]	7[3]	8					1	10[2]	12	14											6
			4	5	6			11[1]	3	9		12	7		8		1	10	2												7
	2	14	4		6		9[1]	11[2]	5	12			7		8[3]		1	10	3	13											8
	2	13	4		6		11[2]	5[8]		9[1]		7			8		1	10	3	12											9
	2		8	5[1]	6		3[3]		14	9[2]	7		11		1	10	4	12	13												10
	2	3	8		6		9[2]	5[1]		12	11	14			1	10	4	7[3]	13												11
	2	3[1]	4		6		12	11		9[2]	8[3]	7			1	10	5	13	14												12
1	5[1]		6				9	3	4	13		7	2		10[2]		11	12	8												13
1	5[8]		6[8]				9[1]	3	4	13		7	2		10[2]		11	12	8												14
1							9	3		13	8[2]	12	7	2	10	5	14	11[1]	6	4[3]											15
	5						12	3	6	4[1]		13	9	2		1	10	11[2]	7	8											16
			6				9	3	5	12		7				1	10	11[1]	4	8	2										17
			6				9[1]	3	5	12	7[2]	13	11			1	10		4	8	2										18
1	12		6				3	4	9[3]	13	11[1]	7			10[2]		14	5	8	2											19
1	13	8	6				3[1]	4	9	11[2]	7	12			10		14	5[3]	2												20
1	8		6				11[1]	4	8	7	3				10		12	5	2												21
1	12	4	6[3]				3	9[2]	7	11	14	8[1]			10		13	5	2												22
1	11	4	6[1]				3	9	7	10[2]	12	13						8	5	2											23
1		4	6				3	9	7	11[2]	12						5	8[1]	13	10[8]	2[8]										24
1	8		6				3	9	7	11	2[1]						5	10	4	12											25
1	8		6				9	3[1]		13	7	11[2]					12	5	10	4	2										26
1	8		6				10			9	7						3	5	11	4	2										27
1	8		6				9			10[1]	7						3	5	11	4	2	12									28
1	8		6				9			10	3				7			5	11[8]	4	2										29
1	8	13	6				9[1]			10[2]	7	11			3			5		4	2	12									30
1	12	8	6				9			10[2]	7	11			3[1]			5		4	2	13									31
1	3	8	6[2]				12			9		11	13	10				5		4	2	7[1]									32
5	8		6				9	12		7[8]		10	3[1]	1				11	4	2											33
5	8		6				9	11			10		3	1				7	4	2											34
5	8		6[1]				9	11			10	12	3	1				7	4	2											35
5	8		4				9	11[1]		13		10	12	3[2]		1		7	6	2											36
5[3]	8		6[2]				13	9		12	7[1]	10		3	14			11	4	2											37
5[1]	8		4				9			12	7[2]	10		3	13		1	11	6	2											38
1	5	8	4				9			7[1]	10[2]			3				11	6	2								12	13		39
1		8	6				9[1]			12	10[2]			3	4			11	5	2								7	13		40
	8[1]		6	12	10[3]	9				13	14			5	3			11	4	2								7[2]			41
1	8	13	6	12	10[2]		9[8]							5	3			11	4	2								7[1]			42
1	8		6	12	13	9				10[1]				5	3			11	4	2								7[2]			43
1	8		6	10[2]	9		13			12				5	3			11	4	2								7[1]			44
1	8		6		9		10			12				5	3			11	4	2								7[1]			45
15	8		12	4	9[1]		10							5	3	1[8]		11	6	2								7[6]			46

FA Cup
First Round   Swindon T   (h)   0-4

Carling Cup
First Round   Notts Co   (h)   0-1

J Paint Trophy
Second Round   Cheltenham T   (a)   2-0
Southern Quarter-Final   Exeter C   (h)   1-2

PORTSMOUTH
FL Championship

FOUNDATION

At a meeting held in his High Street, Portsmouth offices in 1898, solicitor Alderman J. E. Pink and five other business and professional men agreed to buy some ground close to Goldsmith Avenue for £4,950 which they developed into Fratton Park in record breaking time. A team of professionals was signed up by manager Frank Brettell and entry to the Southern League obtained for the new club's September 1899 kick-off.

Fratton Park, Frogmore Road, Portsmouth, Hampshire PO4 8RA.

Telephone: (02392) 731 204.

Fax: (02392) 734 129.

Ticket Office: (0844) 847 1898.

Website: www.pompeyfc.co.uk

Email: info@pompeyfc.co.uk

Ground Capacity: 20,688.

Record Attendance: 51,385 v Derby Co, FA Cup 6th rd, 26 February 1949.

Pitch Measurements: 100m × 65m.

Chairman: Vladimir Antonov.

Chief Executive: David Lampitt.

Secretary: Paul Weld.

Manager: Steve Cotterill.

Assistant Manager: Guy Whittingham.

First Team Coach: Stuart Gray.

Head of Sports Performance: Steve Allen.

Colours: Blue shirts with white trim, white shorts, red stockings.

Change Colours: White shirts with maroon trim, maroon shorts, maroon stockings.

Year Formed: 1898.

Turned Professional: 1898.

Ltd Co.: 1898.

Club Nickname: 'Pompey'.

Ground: 1898, Fratton Park.

First Football League Game: 28 August 1920, Division 3, v Swansea T (h) W 3–0 – Robson; Probert, Potts; Abbott, Harwood, Turner; Thompson, Stringfellow (1), Reid (1), James (1), Beedie.

Record League Victory: 9–1 v Notts Co, Division 2, 9 April 1927 – McPhail; Clifford, Ted Smith; Reg Davies (1), Foxall, Moffat; Forward (1), Mackie (2), Haines (3), Watson, Cook (2).

Record Cup Victory: 7–0 v Stockport Co, FA Cup 3rd rd, 8 January 1949 – Butler; Rookes, Ferrier;

HONOURS

Football League – Division 1: *Champions* 1948–49, 1949–50, 2002–03;
Division 2: *Runners-up* 1926–27, 1986–87;
Division 3 (S): *Champions* 1923–24;
Division 3: *Champions* 1961–62, 1982–83.
FA Cup: Winners 1939, 2008; *Runners-up* 1929, 1934, 2010.
Football League Cup: Best season: 5th rd, 1961, 1986, 1994, 2010.
European Competitions
UEFA Cup: 2008–09.

sky SPORTS FACT FILE

Portsmouth had a club record seven players at the 2010 World Cup finals in South Africa: David James (England), Nadir Belhadj and Hassan Yebda (Algeria), Kevin-Prince Boateng (Ghana), Nwankwo Kanu and John Utaka (Nigeria) and Aaron Mokoena (South Africa).

Scoular, Flewin, Dickinson; Harris (3), Barlow, Clarke (2), Phillips (2), Froggatt.

Record Defeat: 0–10 v Leicester C, Division 1, 20 October 1928.

Most League Points (2 for a win): 65, Division 3, 1961–62.

Most League Points (3 for a win): 98, Division 1, 2002–03.

Most League Goals: 97, Division 1, 2002–03.

Highest League Scorer in Season: Guy Whittingham, 42, Division 1, 1992–93.

Most League Goals in Total Aggregate: Peter Harris, 194, 1946–60.

Most League Goals in One Match: 5, Alf Strange v Gillingham, Division 3, 27 January 1923; 5, Peter Harris v Aston Villa, Division 1, 3 September 1958.

Most Capped Player: Jimmy Dickinson, 48, England.

Most League Appearances: Jimmy Dickinson, 764, 1946–65.

Youngest League Player: Clive Green, 16 years 259 days v Wrexham, 21 August 1976.

Record Transfer Fee Received: £20,000,000 from Real Madrid for Lassana Diarra, January 2009.

Record Transfer Fee Paid: Reported fee of £11,000,000 to Liverpool for Peter Crouch, July 2008.

Football League Record: 1920 Original Member of Division 3; 1921 Division 3 (S); 1924–27 Division 2; 1927–59 Division 1; 1959–61 Division 2; 1961–62 Division 3; 1962–76 Division 2; 1976–78 Division 3; 1978–80 Division 4; 1980–83 Division 3; 1983–87 Division 2; 1987–88 Division 1; 1988–92 Division 2; 1992–2003 Division 1; 2003–10 FA Premier League; 2010– FL C.

MANAGERS

Frank Brettell 1898–1901
Bob Blyth 1901–04
Richard Bonney 1905–08
Bob Brown 1911–20
John McCartney 1920–27
Jack Tinn 1927–47
Bob Jackson 1947–52
Eddie Lever 1952–58
Freddie Cox 1958–61
George Smith 1961–70
Ron Tindall 1970–73
 (General Manager to 1974)
John Mortimore 1973–74
Ian St John 1974–77
Jimmy Dickinson 1977–79
Frank Burrows 1979–82
Bobby Campbell 1982–84
Alan Ball 1984–89
John Gregory 1989–90
Frank Burrows 1990–91
Jim Smith 1991–95
Terry Fenwick 1995–98
Alan Ball 1998–99
Tony Pulis 2000
Steve Claridge 2000–01
Graham Rix 2001–02
Harry Redknapp 2002–04
Velimir Zajec 2004–05
Alain Perrin 2005
Harry Redknapp 2005–08
Tony Adams 2008–09
Paul Hart 2009
Avram Grant 2009–10
Steve Cotterill June 2010–

LATEST SEQUENCES

Longest Sequence of League Wins: 7, 17.8.2002 – 17.9.2002.

Longest Sequence of League Defeats: 9, 21.10.1975 – 6.12.1975.

Longest Sequence of League Draws: 5, 16.12.2000 – 13.1.2001.

Longest Sequence of Unbeaten League Matches: 15, 18.4.1924 – 18.10.1924.

Longest Sequence Without a League Win: 25, 29.11.1958 – 22.8.1959.

Successive Scoring Runs: 23 from 30.8.1930.

Successive Non-scoring Runs: 6 from 14.1.1939.

TEN YEAR LEAGUE RECORD

		P	W	D	L	F	A	Pts	Pos
2001-02	Div 1	46	13	14	19	60	72	53	17
2002-03	Div 1	46	29	11	6	97	45	98	1
2003-04	PR Lge	38	12	9	17	47	54	45	13
2004-05	PR Lge	38	10	9	19	43	59	39	16
2005-06	PR Lge	38	10	8	20	37	62	38	17
2006-07	PR Lge	38	14	12	12	45	42	54	9
2007-08	PR Lge	38	16	9	13	48	40	57	8
2008-09	PR Lge	38	10	11	17	38	57	41	14
2009-10	PR Lge	38	7	7	24	34	66	19*	20
2010-11	FL C	46	15	13	18	53	60	58	16

9 pts deducted.

DID YOU KNOW ?

Despite failing to win a match between October and December 1927 in their debut season in the First Division, Portsmouth survived chiefly thanks to a run of seven matches from 25 February in which they managed 13 points. Remarkably, too, they did not concede one goal.

PORTSMOUTH 2010–11 LEAGUE RECORD

Match No.	Date		Venue	Opponents	Result		H/T Score	Lg Pos.	Goalscorers	Attendance
1	Aug	7	A	Coventry C	L	0-2	0-1	—		18,814
2		14	H	Reading	D	1-1	1-0	21	Ciftci [8]	16,497
3		21	A	Preston NE	L	0-1	0-1	22		9666
4		28	H	Cardiff C	L	0-2	0-1	24		15,866
5	Sept	11	H	Ipswich T	D	0-0	0-0	24		15,445
6		14	A	Crystal Palace	L	1-4	1-1	—	Kitson [24]	14,219
7		18	A	Sheffield U	L	0-1	0-0	24		20,712
8		24	H	Leicester C	W	6-1	2-0	—	Lawrence 2 (1 pen) [10 (pl. 33], Nugent [58], Kitson 2 [59, 83], Brown [90]	13,751
9		28	H	Bristol C	W	3-1	0-0	—	Utaka [51], Mokoena [58], Mullins [90]	14,417
10	Oct	2	A	Middlesbrough	D	2-2	0-2	21	Nugent [60], Lawrence (pen) [88]	13,749
11		16	H	Watford	W	3-2	1-0	17	Mullins [17], Kitson [72], Brown [80]	16,606
12		19	A	Millwall	W	1-0	0-0	—	Lawrence (pen) [78]	12,095
13		23	A	Hull C	W	2-1	1-0	13	Nugent [45], Halford [47]	20,378
14		30	H	Nottingham F	W	2-1	1-1	10	Sonko [18], Lawrence [62]	19,719
15	Nov	6	A	Derby Co	L	0-2	0-1	13		29,086
16		9	H	QPR	D	1-1	0-0	—	Lawrence (pen) [71]	17,818
17		13	H	Doncaster R	L	2-3	0-2	14	Ward [66], Nugent [74]	14,828
18		20	A	Barnsley	L	0-1	0-1	16		10,908
19		26	A	Swansea C	W	2-1	1-1	—	Nugent [43], Halford [65]	17,584
20	Dec	11	A	Norwich C	W	2-0	0-0	12	Kitson [73], Halford (pen) [90]	25,215
21		26	H	Millwall	D	1-1	0-1	14	Nugent [73]	17,521
22		28	A	Leeds U	D	3-3	1-2	13	Nugent [33], O'Brien (2 ogs) [63, 90]	31,556
23	Jan	1	A	Watford	L	0-3	0-1	15		12,577
24		3	H	Hull C	L	2-3	0-1	18	Lawrence (pen) [57], Halford [76]	14,604
25		15	A	Nottingham F	L	1-2	1-0	18	Kanu [26]	21,856
26		22	H	Leeds U	D	2-2	1-0	18	Ward [26], Utaka [61]	20,040
27		25	H	Burnley	L	1-2	1-2	—	Utaka [33]	13,345
28	Feb	1	A	QPR	L	0-2	0-0	20		14,078
29		5	H	Derby Co	D	1-1	0-1	20	Nugent [90]	14,555
30		12	A	Doncaster R	W	2-0	1-0	18	Kitson [42], Ward [52]	10,288
31		19	H	Barnsley	W	1-0	0-0	16	Kanu [84]	14,318
32		22	H	Crystal Palace	W	1-0	0-0	—	Nugent [65]	15,641
33		26	A	Ipswich T	W	2-0	0-0	13	Nugent [55], Cotterill [77]	23,345
34	Mar	1	H	Scunthorpe U	W	2-0	0-0	—	Kitson [62], Mokoena [80]	14,252
35		5	H	Sheffield U	W	1-0	1-0	11	Hreidarsson [24]	15,096
36		8	A	Bristol C	L	1-2	0-1	—	Kitson [90]	13,886
37		12	H	Middlesbrough	D	0-0	0-0	13		16,447
38		19	A	Leicester C	W	1-0	1-0	13	Nugent [13]	26,645
39	Apr	2	A	Reading	L	0-2	0-2	13		21,896
40		9	H	Preston NE	D	1-1	0-1	14	Halford [62]	14,349
41		12	H	Coventry C	L	0-3	0-1	—		13,132
42		16	A	Cardiff C	L	0-3	0-2	14		24,007
43		23	H	Swansea C	D	0-0	0-0	14		15,907
44		25	A	Burnley	D	1-1	0-0	14	Nugent [57]	14,927
45	May	2	H	Norwich C	L	0-1	0-0	—		17,113
46		7	A	Scunthorpe U	D	1-1	0-1	16	Nugent [81]	5142

Final League Position: 16

GOALSCORERS

League (53): Nugent 13, Kitson 8, Lawrence 7 (5 pens), Halford 5 (1 pen), Utaka 3, Ward 3, Brown 2, Kanu 2, Mokoena 2, Mullins 2, Ciftci 1, Cotterill 1, Hreidarsson 1, Sonko 1, own goals 2.
Carling Cup (4): Brown 1, Ciftci 1, Lawrence 1, Nugent 1.
FA Cup (1): Kilbey 1.

Ashdown J 46	Mullins H 45	Ritchie M 2+3	Mokoena A 29+8	Sonko I 16+7	Wilson M 4	Utaka J 23+2	Hughes R 5+6	Smith T 3	Nugent D 44	Brown M 20+1	Ciftci N 4+15	Gregory P —+1	Dickinson C 23+13	Ward J 33+9	Pack M —+1	Ricardo Rocha 26+3	Lawrence L 28+3	Kitson D 35	Kanu N 13+19	Halford G 33	Hreidarsson H 20+8	Kilbey T —+2	De Laet R 22	Hogg J 19	Cotterill D 12+3	Webber D 1+7	Match No.
1	2	3	4	5	6	7²	8¹	9	10	11	12	13															1
1	4	3	5	6		9¹	8		10	11	7		2	12													2
1	2	12	4	5	6		8¹	9	10	11²	7		3	13													3
1	2	14	4	5	6	7³	8¹	9	10	11²	12		3	13													4
1	8		4¹	5		14			10	12	13		3	2		6	7	9³	11²								5
1	4			5		12			10	11			3	2		6	7	9	8¹								6
1	6		4			11	8		10¹		13		3	2		5	7	9	12								7
1	6¹		4	14			8		10²	11	12		3	2		5³	7	9	13								8
1	6	14	4				8³		10²	11	13		3	2		5	7	9¹	12								9
1	6		4			13	8		10	11			3	2¹		5²	7	9	12								10
1	6		4			13	8¹	12	10³	11			3	2²		5	7	9	14								11
1	4		6			14	8²		10³	11	12		3	2		5¹	7	9	13								12
1	6³		4	5		12	8¹		10²	11	13		3	2			7	9	14								13
1	6		4	5			8¹		10	11	12		3	2			7	9²	13								14
1	6		4	5			8		10	11²	13		3	2¹			7	9	12								15
1	6		4	5		14	8²		10³	11	13		3	2¹		7		9	12								16
1	6		4	5¹		14	8		10³	11	12		3⁴	2			7²	9	13								17
1	6		4			13	8³		10	11²	14		3	2		5	7	9¹	12								18
1	6		4			12	8³		10	11¹	14		3	2		5	7	9²	13								19
1	6		4			13	8²		10	11	12		3	2		5	7¹	9³	14								20
1	6		4			13	8		10	11	12		3²	2		5¹	7	9³	14								21
1	6		4			13	8³		10	11	14		3	2		5²	7¹	9	12								22
1	6		4	5²			8		10				3				7¹		9	2	13	12			11		23
1	6		4			14	8³		10		13		3	2		5¹	7	9	11²		12						24
1	6		4	5			8¹		10				3	2			7		9²		13	12			11		25
1	6			5			8		10	11	12						7		9	4	3		2¹				26
1	6			5			8		10		12						7	13	9¹	4	3		2		11²		27
1	6								10		12					4	7		9	5	3		2	8	11¹		28
1	6								10							4	7	12	9	5	3		2	8	11¹		29
1	6								10	11	12					4	7		9¹	5	3		2	8⁴			30
1	6	12							10							4	7¹	13	9	5	3		2	8²	11		31
1	6	12							10							4	7¹		9	5	3		2	8	11		32
1	6²	12							10³							4	7¹	13	9	5	3	14	2	8	11		33
1	6¹	12							10²							4		13	9	5	3	14	2	8	11	7³	34
1	6	12							10							4		13	9	5	3	14	2	8²	11¹	7³	35
1	6	13							10		12					4²			9	5	3¹	14	2	8	11³	7	36
1	6								10		12					4		13	9	5	3		2	8	11¹	7²	37
1	6								10²		12					4	7	13	9	5	3		2	8	11¹		38
1	6	12							10³							4⁴	7	13	9	5	3²	14	2	8	11¹		39
1	6		4¹						10³		12							13	9	5	3	14	2	8	11	7²	40
1	6								10³		12					4		13	9	5	3	14	2	8	11¹	7²	41
1	6	12							10²							4⁴	7	13	9	5	3¹	14	2	8	11³		42
1									10		13					4	7	6	9¹	5	3	12	2²	8	11		43
1	6								10³		12					4		13	9	5	3	14	2¹	8²	11	7	44
1	6								10		12					4	7²	13	9³	5	3	14	2	8	11¹		45
1	6								10		12					4³	7	13	9	5	3	14	2	8¹	11²		46

FA Cup
Third Round — Brighton & HA — (a) 1-3

Carling Cup
First Round — Stevenage — (a) 2-1
Second Round — Crystal Palace — (h) 1-1
Third Round — Leicester C — (h) 1-2

PORT VALE

FL Championship 2

FOUNDATION

Formed in 1876 as Port Vale, adopting the prefix 'Burslem' in 1884 upon moving to that part of the city. It was dropped in 1909.

Vale Park, Hamil Road, Burslem, Stoke-on-Trent ST6 1AW.

Telephone: (01782) 655 800.

Fax: (01782) 834 981.

Ticket Office: (01782) 655 832.

Website: www.port-vale.co.uk

Email: enquiries@port-vale.co.uk

Ground Capacity: 18,982.

Record Attendance: 22,993 v Stoke C, Division 2, 6 March 1920 (at Recreation Ground). 49,768 v Aston Villa, FA Cup 5th rd, 20 February 1960 (at Vale Park).

Pitch Measurements: 114yd × 75yd.

Chairman: Bill Bratt MBE.

Chief Executive: Perry Deakin.

Secretary: Bill Lodey.

Manager: Micky Adams.

Assistant Manager: Mark Grew.

Physio: Andrew Foster.

Colours: White shirts with black trim, black shorts with white trim, white stockings.

Change Colours: Black shirts with black and white sleeves, white shorts, black stockings.

Year Formed: 1876.

Turned Professional: 1885.

Ltd Co.: 1911.

Previous Names: 1876, Port Vale; 1884, Burslem Port Vale; 1909, Port Vale.

Club Nickname: 'Valiants'.

Grounds: 1876, Limekin Lane, Longport; 1881, Westport; 1884, Moorland Road, Burslem; 1886, Athletic Ground, Cobridge; 1913, Recreation Ground, Hanley; 1950, Vale Park.

First Football League Game: 3 September 1892, Division 2, v Small Heath (a) L 1–5 – Frail; Clutton, Elson; Farrington, McCrindle, Delves; Walker, Scarratt, Bliss (1), Jones. (Only 10 men).

Record League Victory: 9–1 v Chesterfield, Division 2, 24 September 1932 – Leckie; Shenton, Poyser; Sherlock, Round, Jones; McGrath, Mills, Littlewood (6), Kirkham (2), Morton (1).

Record Cup Victory: 7–1 v Irthlingborough, FA Cup 1st rd, 12 January 1907 – Matthews; Dunn, Hamilton; Eardley, Baddeley, Holyhead; Carter, Dodds (2), Beats, Mountford (2), Coxon (3).

Record Defeat: 0–10 v Sheffield U, Division 2, 10 December 1892. 0–10 v Notts Co, Division 2, 26 February 1895.

HONOURS

Football League – Division 2: *Runners-up* 1993–94;
Division 3 (N): *Champions* 1929–30, 1953–54; *Runners-up* 1952–53;
Division 4: *Champions* 1958–59.
FA Cup: Semi-final 1954, when in Division 3.
Football League Cup: Best season: 4th rd 2007.
Autoglass Trophy: Winners 1993.
Anglo-Italian Cup: *Runners-up* 1996.
LDV Vans Trophy: *Winners* 2001.

sky SPORTS FACT FILE

Goalkeeper George Hepple had already played in two Cup ties when he let in seven goals on his League debut for Port Vale on 4 December 1937! But he became first choice making over 200 League and Cup appearances. Ex-Wolves he starred in Army football during WWII.

Most League Points (2 for a win): 69, Division 3 (N), 1953–54.

Most League Points (3 for a win): 89, Division 2, 1992–93.

Most League Goals: 110, Division 4, 1958–59.

Highest League Scorer in Season: Wilf Kirkham 38, Division 2, 1926–27.

Most League Goals in Total Aggregate: Wilf Kirkham, 154, 1923–29, 1931–33.

Most League Goals in One Match: 6, Stewart Littlewood v Chesterfield, Division 2, 24 September 1922.

Most Capped Player: Chris Birchall, 22 (37), Trinidad & Tobago.

Most League Appearances: Roy Sproson, 761, 1950–72.

Youngest League Player: Malcolm McKenzie, 15 years 347 days v Newport Co, 12 April 1966.

Record Transfer Fee Received: £2,000,000 from Wimbledon for Gareth Ainsworth, October 1998.

Record Transfer Fee Paid: £500,000 to Lincoln C for Gareth Ainsworth, September 1997.

Football League Record: 1892 Original Member of Division 2. Failed re-election in 1896; Re-elected 1898; Resigned 1907; Returned in Oct, 1919, when they took over the fixtures of Leeds City; 1929–30 Division 3 (N); 1930–36 Division 2; 1936–38 Division 3 (N); 1938–52 Division 3 (S); 1952–54 Division 3 (N); 1954–57 Division 2; 1957–58 Division 3 (S); 1958–59 Division 4; 1959–65 Division 3; 1965–70 Division 4; 1970–78 Division 3; 1978–83 Division 4; 1983–84 Division 3; 1984–86 Division 4; 1986–89 Division 3; 1989–94 Division 2; 1994–2000 Division 1; 2000–04 Division 2; 2004–08 FL 1; 2008– FL 2.

LATEST SEQUENCES

Longest Sequence of League Wins: 8, 8.4.1893 – 30.9.1893.

Longest Sequence of League Defeats: 9, 9.3.1957 – 20.4.1957.

Longest Sequence of League Draws: 6, 26.4.1981 – 12.9.1981.

Longest Sequence of Unbeaten League Matches: 19, 5.5.1969 – 8.11.1969.

Longest Sequence Without a League Win: 17, 7.12.1991 – 21.3.1992.

Successive Scoring Runs: 22 from 12.9.1992.

Successive Non-scoring Runs: 4 from 10.2.1896.

MANAGERS

Sam Gleaves 1896–1905
(Secretary-Manager)
Tom Clare 1905–11
A. S. Walker 1911–12
H. Myatt 1912–14
Tom Holford 1919–24
(continued as Trainer)
Joe Schofield 1924–30
Tom Morgan 1930–32
Tom Holford 1932–35
Warney Cresswell 1936–37
Tom Morgan 1937–38
Billy Frith 1945–46
Gordon Hodgson 1946–51
Ivor Powell 1951
Freddie Steele 1951–57
Norman Low 1957–62
Freddie Steele 1962–65
Jackie Mudie 1965–67
Sir Stanley Matthews
(General Manager) 1965–68
Gordon Lee 1968–74
Roy Sproson 1974–77
Colin Harper 1977
Bobby Smith 1977–78
Dennis Butler 1978–79
Alan Bloor 1979
John McGrath 1980–83
John Rudge 1983–99
Brian Horton 1999–2004
Martin Foyle 2004–07
Lee Sinnott 2007–08
Dean Glover 2008–09
Micky Adams 2009–10
Jim Gannon 2011
Micky Adams May 2011–

TEN YEAR LEAGUE RECORD

		P	W	D	L	F	A	Pts	Pos
2001-02	Div 2	46	16	10	20	51	62	58	14
2002-03	Div 2	46	14	11	21	54	70	53	17
2003-04	Div 2	46	21	10	15	73	63	73	7
2004-05	FL 1	46	17	5	24	49	59	56	18
2005-06	FL 1	46	16	12	18	49	54	60	13
2006-07	FL 1	46	18	6	22	64	65	60	12
2007-08	FL 1	46	9	11	26	47	81	38	23
2008-09	Fl 2	46	13	9	24	44	66	48	18
2009-10	FL 2	46	17	17	12	61	50	68	10
2010-11	FL 2	46	17	14	15	54	49	65	11

DID YOU KNOW ?

The most goals scored by a Port Vale player was seven achieved by Chris "Sandy" Young with seven of the goals in the 14-1 first round win in the Birmingham Senior Cup on 21 September 1914 against Burton Rangers. He scored 40 League and Cup goals in the season.

PORT VALE 2010–11 LEAGUE RECORD

Match No.	Date	Venue	Opponents	Result	H/T Score	Lg Pos.	Goalscorers	Attendance
1	Aug 7	A	Bury	W 1-0	0-0	—	Collins [66]	4681
2	14	H	Chesterfield	D 1-1	1-0	6	Richards, M [12]	6444
3	21	A	Southend U	W 3-1	1-0	4	Richards, J [5], Dodds [54], Richards, M [83]	4946
4	28	H	Torquay U	L 1-2	1-2	5	Griffith [37]	5750
5	Sept 4	A	Bradford C	W 2-0	1-0	4	Richards, M [32], Richards, J [75]	10,834
6	11	H	Aldershot T	W 1-0	1-0	3	Roberts [10]	5360
7	18	A	Macclesfield T	W 3-0	1-0	2	Richards, M 2 [30, 87], Rigg [71]	3915
8	25	H	Accrington S	W 2-0	1-0	1	Richards, M [31], Dodds [81]	5777
9	28	H	Shrewsbury T	W 1-0	0-0	—	Roberts [73]	8443
10	Oct 2	A	Oxford U	L 1-2	0-0	1	Owen [89]	7947
11	9	A	Hereford U	D 1-1	1-1	1	Richards, M (pen) [28]	2651
12	16	H	Gillingham	D 0-0	0-0	2		6420
13	23	A	Cheltenham T	D 0-0	0-0	2		3167
14	30	H	Crewe Alex	W 2-1	1-0	2	Dodds [13], Richards, M (pen) [74]	8607
15	Nov 2	A	Burton Alb	D 0-0	0-0	—		4027
16	13	A	Northampton T	D 0-0	0-0	2		4612
17	20	H	Wycombe W	W 2-1	1-1	2	McCombe 2 [11, 61]	5587
18	23	A	Stockport Co	W 5-0	2-0	—	Rigg [23], Richards, M 2 (2 pens) [44, 62], Richards, J [89], Speight [90]	4571
19	Dec 11	A	Morecambe	L 0-1	0-1	2		2326
20	28	A	Gillingham	L 0-3	0-2	—		5364
21	Jan 1	A	Rotherham U	L 0-5	0-2	4		3994
22	3	H	Burton Alb	W 2-1	2-0	4	McCombe [4], Richards, J [6]	5681
23	15	A	Crewe Alex	L 1-2	0-1	4	Richards, J (pen) [58]	7183
24	22	H	Cheltenham T	L 0-1	0-0	5		5163
25	25	H	Barnet	D 0-0	0-0	—		4112
26	29	A	Lincoln C	L 0-1	0-0	—		3370
27	Feb 1	H	Rotherham U	W 1-0	0-0	5	O'Shea [53]	4515
28	5	A	Wycombe W	D 1-1	0-0	5	Johnson (og) [47]	4173
29	12	H	Northampton T	D 1-1	0-0	7	Richards, J (pen) [55]	5321
30	18	H	Bradford C	W 2-1	0-0	—	Pope 2 [49, 64]	4775
31	22	H	Stevenage	L 1-3	0-2	—	Morsy [56]	4588
32	26	A	Aldershot T	W 2-1	1-0	6	McCombe [26], Richards, M [51]	2506
33	Mar 5	A	Macclesfield T	W 2-1	1-0	6	Collins [28], Dodds [87]	5459
34	8	A	Shrewsbury T	D 2-2	1-1	—	Richards, M 2 (1 pen) [29, 83 (p)]	6402
35	12	H	Oxford U	L 1-2	1-1	7	Richards, M [27]	5661
36	19	A	Accrington S	L 0-3	0-1	8		2413
37	22	H	Hereford U	D 1-1	0-0	—	Pope [90]	4869
38	26	H	Bury	D 0-0	0-0	—		5510
39	29	H	Lincoln C	W 2-1	0-1	—	Richards, M [59], Loft [70]	4636
40	Apr 2	A	Chesterfield	L 0-2	0-0	9		8606
41	9	H	Southend U	D 1-1	1-0	9	Taylor, R [25]	5108
42	16	A	Torquay U	D 0-0	0-0	9		3726
43	23	H	Stockport Co	L 1-2	0-1	10	Rigg [55]	5334
44	25	A	Stevenage	L 0-1	0-0	10		3146
45	30	H	Morecambe	W 7-2	4-1	9	Dodds 3 [17, 58, 67], Richards, M [21], Richards, J 3 [40, 45, 90]	4134
46	May 7	A	Barnet	L 0-1	0-0	11		4478

Final League Position: 11

GOALSCORERS

League (54): Richards, M 16 (5 pens), Richards, J 9 (2 pens), Dodds 7, McCombe 4, Pope 3, Rigg 3, Collins 2, Roberts 2, Griffith 1, Loft 1, Morsy 1, O'Shea 1, Owen 1, Speight 1, Taylor, R 1, own goal 1.
Carling Cup (3): Richards, J 2, Rigg 1.
FA Cup (8): Richards, J 2, Richards, M 2 (1 pen), Taylor, R 2, McCombe 1, Rigg 1.
J Paint Trophy (4): Richards, M 2, Richards, J 1, own goal 1.

Tomlinson S 34+2	Yates A 45+1	Collins L 41+1	Griffith A 36+4	McCombe J 42	Owen G 35+1	Rigg S 16+9	Roberts G 30+5	Richards M 37+3	Richards J 37+5	Loft D 24+5	Taylor R 21+15	Dodds L 14+19	Bell-Baggie A —+3	Malbon A —+2	Taylor K 15+5	Morsy S 12+4	Fraser T 7+5	Sutton R 5+6	Johnson J 1+5	Speight J 1+3	Haldane L 14+9	Martin C 12+2	Cox K —+1	O'Shea J 5	Brown K —+4	Sawyers R —+1	Geohaghon E 11+1	Pope T 10+3	Blizzard D 1	Davis J —+1	Lloyd R —+1	Match No.
1	2	3	4	5	6	7^1	8	9	10	11^2	12	13																				1
1	2	3	4	5	6	7^3	8	9^1	10	11^2	13	12	14																			2
1	2	3	4	5	6	7^1	8	9^3	10		12	11^2	13	14																		3
1	12	2	4	5	6^1	7^2	8	9	10		13	11^3				3	14															4
1	2	3	4	5	6	7^2	8	9^1	10		12	13								11^3	14											5
1	2	3	4	5	6	7^2	8	9	10		13	12								11^1												6
1	2	3	4	5	6	7^2		9^1	10		12	11^1	14			8				13												7
1	2	3	4	5	6	7^1	8^3	9	10^2	14	13				11	12																8
1	2	3	4	5	6	7^2	8	9^3	10	14	12					11^1	13															9
1	2	3	4^2	5	6	7^3	8	9	10		13	14				11^1	12															10
1	2	3	4^3	5	6	7^2	8	9	10	14	13	12					11^1															11
1	2	3	4		6	13	8	9	10^3	14	11^1					7^2	5	12														12
1	2	3	4	5	6	12	8	9	10	7						11^1																13
1	2	3	4^4	5	6	13	8	9	10^1	11		7^2				12																14
1	2	3		5	6	12	4^2	9	10	11		7^3	14	13			8^1															15
1	2		4^1	5	6	7^3	8	9	12	11	13	14	3			10^2																16
1	2			5	6	7^1	4	9	10^3	11	8^2	12	3				14	13														17
1	2		5^2	6		7^3	4	9^1	10	11	8	14	3				13	12														18
1	2	14		5	6^3	7^2	4	9	10	11	8	13	3^1				12															19
1	2	3	4	5	6	8^3	9	10^2	11	7^1	13					14	12															20
1^8	2	3	4	5^1	6	13	8	9	10^6	11^2		7			17							15										21
1	2	3	4	5	6	12	8	9^4	10^3		11^2	7^1				14						13										22
1	2	3	4	5	6	8^2		9^1	10			14	11^3	13			7		12													23
1	2^3	3	4	5	6^8		10	9^2			12		8		7^1			11	13	14												24
1	2	6	4	5			10	9		3		8^2				7			11^1	12	13											25
	2	6	4	5	12		8	10	14	9		3^1				7^3	1					11^2	13									26
	2	3	4	5	6			10^2	7	9	14				12				1		8^3	13	11^1									27
	2	5	4		6^1			10^3	7	9			3			12		13	1		8^2		11	14								28
	7	6	12	5		14	13	10	7	8^1		3							1		11^2		4^3	9								29
	2	3	4	5			8	13	10^7	11					8				14	7^3	1		12	6	9^2							30
	2	3	4	5			13	10^7	11^1	12	14					8				7^3	1			6	9							31
1^6	2	3	13	5			9		7^2	12					11	4				8^1	15			6	10							32
	2	3	13	5			9		8^1	12					11	6				7^2	1			4	10							33
	2	6^3		5			13	9	14		12	11			3^1	8				7^2	1			4	10							34
15	2	6		5^2			8	9	13			12			3	11				7^1	1^6			4	10							35
1	2	12	5		13^8		9	14	11	10					3^1	8				7^3				4		-6^2						36
1	2	3	4	5	6		8	9	10^1	7	13	11^2	14													12						37
1	2	3^1	4	5	6		9		8^2	12	13					11				7							10					38
1	2	3	4	5	6^1	14	9		8	13					12	11^3				7^2							10					39
1	2	6	4	5			8	9	13	7^1	11				3					12							10^2					40
1	2	3	4	5^1	6		8^2	9	10	7	11^3					13	12			14												41
1	2	3	4	5	6	13	12	9	10	11^2	7^3					8^1				14												42
1	2	3	4	5	6	12	8	9	10	11^2	7^1									13												43
	2	3	4^2	5	6	7^1	8	9	10	11	12				13							1										44
	2	5	4		6^1			9	10	11^2	7				8	3				1										12	13	45
15	2	3	4		6		12	9	10^2		11	7				8^1	5			13	1^6											46

FA Cup

First Round	Dartford	(a)	1-1
		(h)	4-0
Second Round	Accrington S	(h)	1-0
Third Round	Burnley	(a)	2-4

Carling Cup

First Round	QPR	(a)	3-1
Second Round	Fulham	(a)	0-6

J Paint Trophy

First Round	Rochdale	(h)	2-1
Second Round	Carlisle U	(a)	2-2

PRESTON NORTH END   FL Championship 1

FOUNDATION

North End Cricket and Rugby Club which was formed in 1863, indulged in most sports before taking up soccer in about 1879. In 1881 they decided to stick to football to the exclusion of other sports and even a 16–0 drubbing by Blackburn Rovers in an invitation game at Deepdale, a few weeks after taking this decision, did not deter them for they immediately became affiliated to the Lancashire FA.

Deepdale Stadium, Sir Tom Finney Way, Deepdale, Preston PR1 6RU.
Telephone: (0844) 856 1964.
Fax: (01772) 693 366.
Ticket Office: (0844) 856 1966.
Website: www.pne.com
Email: enquiries@pne.com
Ground Capacity: 23,408.
Record Attendance: 42,684 v Arsenal, Division 1, 23 April 1938.
Pitch Measurements: 110yd × 77yd.
Chairman: Maurice Lindsay.
Deputy Chairman: David Taylor.
Secretary: Janet Parr.
Manager: Phil Brown.
Assistant Manager: Brian Horton.
Head Physio: Matthew Jackson.
Colours: White shirts, blue shorts, white stockings.
Change Colours: Red shirts with blue sleeves, red shorts, red stockings.
Year Formed: 1880.
Turned Professional: 1885. *Ltd Co.:* 1893.
Club Nicknames: 'The Lilywhites' or 'North End'.
Ground: 1881, Deepdale.
First Football League Game: 8 September 1888, Football League, v Burnley (h) W 5–2 – Trainer; Howarth, Holmes; Robertson, William Graham, Johnny Graham; Gordon (1), Jimmy Ross (2), Goodall, Dewhurst (2), Drummond.
Record League Victory: 10–0 v Stoke, Division 1, 14 September 1889 – Trainer; Howarth, Holmes; Kelso, Russell (1), Johnny Graham; Gordon, Jimmy Ross (2), Nick Ross (3), Thomson (2), Drummond (2).
Record Cup Victory: 26–0 v Hyde, FA Cup 1st rd, 15 October 1887 – Addison; Howarth, Nick Ross; Russell (1), Thomson (5), Johnny Graham (1); Gordon (5), Jimmy Ross (8), John Goodall (1), Dewhurst (3), Drummond (2).
Record Defeat: 0–7 v Blackpool, Division 1, 1 May 1948.
Most League Points (2 for a win): 61, Division 3, 1970–71.

HONOURS

Football League – Division 1:
Champions 1888–89 (first champions) 1889–90; *Runners-up* 1890–91, 1891–92, 1892–93, 1905–06, 1952–53, 1957–58;
Division 2: *Champions* 1903–04, 1912–13, 1950–51, 1999–2000; *Runners-up* 1914–15, 1933–34;
Division 3: *Champions* 1970–71, 1995–96;
Division 4: *Runners-up* 1986–87.
FA Cup: *Winners* 1889, 1938; *Runners-up* 1888, 1922, 1937, 1954, 1964.
Football League Cup: Best season: 4th rd, 2003.
Double Performed: 1888–89.
Football League Cup: Best season: 4th rd, 1963, 1966, 1972, 1981.

sky SPORTS FACT FILE

On 28 September 2010, Preston North End scored first away to Leeds United then conceded four goals in 24 minutes to trail 4-1. The revival began in the 39th minute and with Jon Parkin completing his hat-trick they ran out 6-4 winners at Elland Road.

Most League Points (3 for a win): 95, Division 2, 1999–2000.

Most League Goals: 100, Division 2, 1927–28 and Division 1, 1957–58.

Highest League Scorer in Season: Ted Harper, 37, Division 2, 1932–33.

Most League Goals in Total Aggregate: Tom Finney, 187, 1946–60.

Most League Goals in One Match: 4, Jimmy Ross v Stoke, Division 1, 6 October 1888; 4, Nick Ross v Derby Co, Division 1, 11 January 1890; 4, George Drummond v Notts Co, Division 1, 12 December 1891; 4, Frank Becton v Notts Co, Division 1, 31 March 1893; 4, George Harrison v Grimsby T, Division 2, 3 November 1928; 4, Alex Reid v Port Vale, Division 2, 23 February 1929; 4, James McClelland v Reading, Division 2, 6 September 1930; 4, Dick Rowley v Notts Co, Division 2, 16 April 1932; 4, Ted Harper v Burnley, Division 2, 29 August 1932; 4, Ted Harper v Lincoln C, Division 2, 11 March 1933; 4, Charlie Wayman v QPR, Division 2, 25 December 1950; 4, Alex Bruce v Colchester U, Division 3, 28 February 1978.

Most Capped Player: Tom Finney, 76, England.

Most League Appearances: Alan Kelly, 447, 1961–75.

Youngest League Player: Steve Doyle, 16 years 166 days v Tranmere R, 15 November 1974.

Record Transfer Fee Received: £6,000,000 from Portsmouth for David Nugent, August 2007.

Record Transfer Fee Paid: £1,500,000 to Manchester U for David Healy, December 2000.

Football League Record: 1888 Founder Member of League; 1901–04 Division 2; 1904–12 Division 1; 1912–13 Division 2; 1913–14 Division 1; 1914–15 Division 2; 1919–25 Division 1; 1925–34 Division 2; 1934–49 Division 1; 1949–51 Division 2; 1951–61 Division 1; 1961–70 Division 2; 1970–71 Division 3; 1971–74 Division 2; 1974–78 Division 3; 1978–81 Division 2; 1981–85 Division 3; 1985–87 Division 4; 1987–92 Division 3; 1992–93 Division 2; 1993–96 Division 3; 1996–2000 Division 2; 2000–04 Division 1; 2004–11 FL C; 2011– FL 1.

LATEST SEQUENCES

Longest Sequence of League Wins: 14, 25.12.1950 – 27.3.1951.

Longest Sequence of League Defeats: 8, 22.9.1984 – 27.10.1984.

Longest Sequence of League Draws: 6, 24.2.1979 – 20.3.1979.

Longest Sequence of Unbeaten League Matches: 23, 8.9.1888 – 14.9.1889.

Longest Sequence Without a League Win: 15, 14.4.1923 – 20.10.1923.

Successive Scoring Runs: 30 from 15.11.1952.

Successive Non-scoring Runs: 6 from 8.4.1897.

MANAGERS

Charlie Parker 1906–15
Vincent Hayes 1919–23
Jim Lawrence 1923–25
Frank Richards 1925–27
Alex Gibson 1927–31
Lincoln Hayes 1931–32
Run by committee 1932–36
Tommy Muirhead 1936–37
Run by committee 1937–49
Will Scott 1949–53
Scot Symon 1953–54
Frank Hill 1954–56
Cliff Britton 1956–61
Jimmy Milne 1961–68
Bobby Seith 1968–70
Alan Ball Snr 1970–73
Bobby Charlton 1973–75
Harry Catterick 1975–77
Nobby Stiles 1977–81
Tommy Docherty 1981
Gordon Lee 1981–83
Alan Kelly 1983–85
Tommy Booth 1985–86
Brian Kidd 1986
John McGrath 1986–90
Les Chapman 1990–92
Sam Allardyce 1992 (*Caretaker*)
John Beck 1992–94
Gary Peters 1994–98
David Moyes 1998–2002
Kelham O'Hanlon 2002
     (*Caretaker*)
Craig Brown 2002–04
Billy Davies 2004–06
Paul Simpson 2006–07
Alan Irvine 2007–09
Darren Ferguson 2010
Phil Brown January 2011–

TEN YEAR LEAGUE RECORD

		P	W	D	L	F	A	Pts	Pos
2001-02	Div 1	46	20	12	14	71	59	72	8
2002-03	Div 1	46	16	13	17	68	70	61	12
2003-04	Div 1	46	15	14	17	69	71	59	15
2004-05	FL C	46	21	12	13	67	58	75	5
2005-06	FL C	46	20	20	6	59	30	80	4
2006-07	FL C	46	22	8	16	64	53	74	7
2007-08	FL C	46	15	11	20	50	56	56	15
2008-09	FL C	46	21	11	14	66	54	74	6
2009-10	FL C	46	13	15	18	58	73	54	17
2010-11	FL C	46	10	12	24	54	79	42	22

DID YOU KNOW ?

On 17 January 1987 Preston North End drew 1-1 away to Swansea City. The match provided Les Chapman with the last of the then 92 Football League club grounds on which he had played. Preston also went on that season to clinch promotion as runners-up in Division Four.

PRESTON NORTH END 2010–11 LEAGUE RECORD

Match No.	Date		Venue	Opponents	Result		H/T Score	Lg Pos.	Goalscorers	Atten- dance
1	Aug	7	H	Doncaster R	L	0-2	0-2	—		12,190
2		14	A	Swansea C	L	0-4	0-3	24		14,010
3		21	H	Portsmouth	W	1-0	1-0	18	Hayes [18]	9666
4		28	A	Sheffield U	L	0-1	0-0	21		19,602
5	Sept	11	A	Burnley	L	3-4	2-1	22	Barton [23], Treacy [32], Parkin [70]	15,509
6		14	H	Nottingham F	L	1-2	1-0	—	Parkin [42]	9779
7		18	H	Norwich C	L	0-1	0-0	23		18,417
8		25	A	Coventry C	W	2-1	2-0	22	Jones [35], Hume [45]	14,945
9		28	A	Leeds U	W	6-4	2-4	—	Parkin 3 [5, 40, 64], Treacy [54], Davidson (pen) [58], Hume [79]	22,727
10	Oct	2	H	Reading	D	1-1	1-0	20	Treacy [23]	10,269
11		16	A	Derby Co	L	0-3	0-2	21		26,117
12		19	H	Scunthorpe U	L	2-3	0-1	—	Morgan [58], Jones [64]	11,179
13		23	H	Crystal Palace	W	4-3	3-1	20	Parkin 2 [13, 25], Treacy [38], Davidson (pen) [66]	10,116
14		30	A	Leicester C	L	0-1	0-1	21		21,212
15	Nov	6	A	Bristol C	D	1-1	1-0	21	Hume [2]	14,429
16		9	H	Barnsley	L	1-2	1-1	—	Morgan [4]	8994
17		12	H	Hull C	L	0-2	0-1	—		9088
18		20	A	QPR	L	1-3	0-1	24	Connolly (og) [88]	13,505
19		27	H	Millwall	D	0-0	0-0	24		9579
20	Dec	4	A	Cardiff C	D	1-1	1-0	—	Tonge [26]	21,151
21		11	H	Ipswich T	W	1-0	0-0	24	Hume [50]	9419
22		28	H	Middlesbrough	L	1-3	1-1	24	Jones [27]	11,946
23	Jan	1	H	Derby Co	L	1-2	0-0	24	Davidson (pen) [90]	11,198
24		3	A	Crystal Palace	L	0-1	0-0	24		14,961
25		15	H	Leicester C	D	1-1	0-0	24	Hume [90]	14,205
26		22	A	Middlesbrough	D	1-1	0-0	24	Jones [88]	16,157
27	Feb	1	A	Barnsley	L	0-2	0-1	24		10,740
28		5	H	Bristol C	L	0-4	0-1	24		11,784
29		12	A	Hull C	L	0-1	0-1	24		21,566
30		15	A	Watford	D	2-2	2-0	—	St Ledger-Hall [1], Clarke [37]	10,620
31		19	H	QPR	D	1-1	0-1	24	Nicholson [64]	10,521
32		22	A	Nottingham F	D	2-2	1-0	—	Nicholson [16], Jones [90]	28,310
33		26	H	Burnley	L	1-2	1-1	24	Nicholson [23]	17,136
34	Mar	5	A	Norwich C	D	1-1	0-0	24	Brown, C [60]	25,572
35		8	H	Leeds U	L	1-2	0-1	—	Hume [63]	15,269
36		15	A	Scunthorpe U	W	3-0	3-0	—	Treacy [32], Jones [37], Hume [43]	4190
37		19	H	Coventry C	W	2-1	1-0	24	Hume [24], Ellington [90]	12,269
38	Apr	2	H	Swansea C	W	2-1	1-1	23	Hume 2 (1 pen) [3 (p), 83]	11,791
39		5	A	Reading	L	1-2	0-1	—	McCarthy (og) [52]	14,844
40		9	A	Portsmouth	D	1-1	1-0	23	Hume [32]	14,349
41		12	A	Doncaster R	D	1-1	0-0	—	Hayes [80]	9456
42		16	H	Sheffield U	W	3-1	0-0	23	Treacy 2 [55, 68], Ellington [90]	12,076
43		23	A	Millwall	L	0-4	0-2	23		10,426
44		25	H	Cardiff C	L	0-1	0-1	24		12,818
45		30	A	Ipswich T	L	1-2	0-2	24	Coutts [52]	18,431
46	May	7	H	Watford	W	3-1	1-1	22	Nicholson [28], Hume [56], Proctor [88]	10,953

Final League Position: 22

GOALSCORERS

League (54): Hume 12 (1 pen), Parkin 7, Treacy 7, Jones 6, Nicholson 4, Davidson 3 (3 pens), Ellington 2, Hayes 2, Morgan 2, Barton 1, Brown, C 1, Clarke 1, Coutts 1, Proctor 1, St Ledger-Hall 1, Tonge 1, own goals 2.
Carling Cup (8): Hayes 2 (1 pen), Treacy 2, Coutts 1, Davidson 1 (pen), James 1, King 1.
FA Cup (1): Carter 1.

Lonergan A 29	Gray D 12+10	Davidson C 17+1	Jones B 43	Morgan C 30+1	James M 10	Mayor D 5+16	Russell D 21+4	Brown C 12+4	Hayes P 11+12	Treacy K 33+5	Coutts P 17+6	King J 6+2	Devine D 2	Barton A 24+9	Parry P 6+17	Parkin J 16+3	St Ledger-Hall S 31	Brown W 12+1	Hume I 29+2	McLaughlin C 5+2	Middleton D —+2	De Laet R 5	Tonge M 5	Miller G —+1	Pugh D 5	Cort L 13	Nicholson B 18+4	Douglas J —+2	Carter D 13+1	Linganzi A 1	Ellington N 7+11	Ashbee I 19	Clarke L 5+1	Johnson E 15+1	Turner I 17	Proctor J —+5	Wright B —+2	Gardner R 4	Khumalo B 6	Leather S 2	Match No.
1	2	3	4	5	6	7	8¹	9	10²	11	12	13																													1
1	4	3	8	5	6	7¹			9²	10³	11			12	2	13	14																								2
1	13	3	2	5	6	7²		12	10¹	11	8	9						4																							3
1	7³	3	2	5	6	12			10²	11¹	8	9		14				13	4																						4
1		3	2⁴	5	6²		13	14	11	8³	10¹	7		12	9			4																							5
1	2	3		5		12	8	13		11¹	4²			9	7	10			6																						6
1	2		4				13	3	14	10³	11¹			8	7²	9	6	5	12																						7
1	14	3	2	12			8			11³	4²			7	13	9	6	5¹	10																						8
1	13	3	2	5			8		12	11¹	4			7		9²	6		10																						9
1	14	3	2	12			8	13		11²	4			7¹		9³	5	6	10																						10
1	12	3	2	5				14		11¹	4			7¹	8²	13	9³	6	10																						11
1		3	2	5		7	8		9²		4	11¹		12	13		6		10																						12
1	12	3	2		6		8¹			11²				7	13	9	4	5	10																						13
1	13	3²	2		6		8¹	14		11	12			7		9³	4	5	10																						14
1	13	3	2	5	6		8			11²				7¹	12	9	4		10																						15
1	12	3	2¹	5	6²		14	8		11³				7	13	10	9	4																							16
1		3¹	2		6²		14	8		11³		13		7		9	4	5	10	12																					17
1	2						8							7		9	6	5	10			3	4		11																18
1	14		2				13	8¹			12			7		9		5	10			3³	4		11²	6															19
1	12		2				8							7	13	9²		5	10¹			3	4		11	6															20
1			2				8							7	12	9		5	10¹			3	4		11	6															21
1			2	5			8¹			13	12	10		7	14	9³		6				3	4		11²																22
1	3		2			14		9		11	4³			8	10²			6	5¹		12						7		13												23
1			2	5			13		9		8¹	11²	12	4				6	10³		3						7	14													24
1			2	5			13		7		9						6		10		3²				4	12	8³		11¹	14											25
1			2	5			13	8³	9¹					14	11				10²		3				4		7		12												26
1			2	5¹			14				12			13				6	11		3						8		7²			10	4	9³							27
1	3						14	8³	12					7	13			6		2¹							5				9	11	4	10²							28
	3		2					14	8²		12			7				6		5							13					11	4	9³	10						29
	3		2					14	13	11²				7³				6									5		8			4		9	10¹	1	12				30
	2	3								12	11			7²	13			6									5		8			9¹	4	10¹		1	14				31
	2	3							14	11				7²	13			6											8			9³	4	12	10¹	1					32
	2	3	5							13				7¹				6	12								8		14			10	4	9³	13	1					33
	2	3	5						13	8²	12							6	9								8	14				10	4	9³	13	1		14			34
1	6	2				10¹		11	13					14				5	9										7			12	4²	8				3³			35
	2	5				9		11²							13			6	10¹										14			8	12	4	7³	1		3			36
	2	5				9		11³						13				6	10										12			8²	14	4	7¹	1		3			37
	2	5						11						13	14			10										7			8²	12	4³	9¹	1		3	6		38
	2	5							13	11³				8¹	14			10										7			6	12	4	9²				3		39
	5	2			12					11	14			7¹				10										3			8³	13	4	9²				6		40
	5	2							9	12	11²							10³										3			8	13	4	7¹	1	14		6		41
	5	2						14	9³	11²	12							10										3			8	13	4	7¹				6		42
	5	2							9²	13	11							10³										7			6	14	4	8	1	12	3¹		43
	3	5				12		9	14	11				13				10¹								6²	2					7	8³	4		1					44
	3	5			10			9²	13	11¹	7	6		8³								14					4									1	12		3	2	45
	3	5						9³	11		6							10²		12	14						7		8			4¹				1			13	2	46

QUEENS PARK RANGERS   FA Premiership

FOUNDATION

There is an element of doubt about the date of the foundation of this club, but it is believed that in either 1885 or 1886 it was formed through the amalgamation of Christchurch Rangers and St Jude's Institute FC. The leading light was George Wodehouse, whose family maintained a connection with the club until comparatively recent times. Most of the players came from the Queen's Park district so this name was adopted after a year as St Jude's Institute.

Loftus Road Stadium, South Africa Road, Shepherds Bush, London W12 7PJ.

Telephone: (020) 8743 0262.

Fax: (020) 8749 0994.

Ticket Office: 08444 777007.

Website: www.qpr.co.uk

Ground Capacity: 18,682.

Record Attendance: 41,097 v Leeds U, FA Cup 3rd rd, 9 January 1932 (at White City). 35,353 v Leeds U, Division 1, 27 April 1974 (at Loftus Road).

Pitch Measurements: 110yd × 73yd.

Chairman: Gianni Paladini.

Finance Director: Rebecca Caplehorn.

Manager: Neil Warnock.

Assistant Manager: Mick Jones.

Physio: Nigel Cox.

Colours: Blue and white hooped shirts, white shorts, white stockings.

Change Colours: All red with blue design on shirts.

Year Formed: 1885* (*see Foundation*). *Turned Professional:* 1898. *Ltd Co.:* 1899.

Previous Name: 1885, St Jude's; 1887, Queens Park Rangers. *Club Nicknames:* 'Rangers' or 'Rs'.

Grounds: 1885* (*see Foundation*), Welford's Fields; 1888–99; London Scottish Ground, Brondesbury, Home Farm, Kensal Rise Green, Gun Club Wormwood Scrubs, Kilburn Cricket Ground; 1899, Kensal Rise Athletic Ground; 1901, Latimer Road, Notting Hill; 1904, Agricultural Society, Park Royal; 1907, Park Royal Ground; 1917, Loftus Road; 1931, White City; 1933, Loftus Road; 1962, White City; 1963, Loftus Road.

First Football League Game: 28 August 1920, Division 3, v Watford (h) L 1–2 – Price; Blackman, Wingrove; McGovern, Grant, O'Brien; Faulkner, Birch (1), Smith, Gregory, Middlemiss.

Record League Victory: 9–2 v Tranmere R, Division 3, 3 December 1960 – Drinkwater; Woods, Ingham; Keen, Rutter, Angell; Lazarus (2), Bedford (2), Evans (2), Andrews (1), Clark (2).

Record Cup Victory: 8–1 v Bristol R (away), FA Cup 1st rd, 27 November 1937 – Gilfillan; Smith, Jefferson; Lowe, James, March; Cape, Mallett, Cheetham (3), Fitzgerald (3) Bott (2). 8–1 v Crewe Alex, Milk Cup 1st rd, 3 October 1983 – Hucker; Neill, Dawes, Waddock (1), McDonald (1), Fenwick, Micklewhite (1), Stewart (1), Allen (1), Stainrod (3), Gregory.

HONOURS

Football League – Division 1:
Runners-up 1975–76;
FL C: *Champions* 2010–11;
Division 2: *Champions* 1982–83;
Runners-up 1967–68, 1972–73, 2003–04;
Division 3 (S): *Champions* 1947–48;
Runners-up 1946–47;
Division 3: *Champions* 1966–67.
FA Cup: *Runners-up* 1982.
Football League Cup: *Winners* 1967;
Runners-up 1986. (In 1966–67 won Division 3 and Football League Cup).
European Competitions
UEFA Cup: 1976–77, 1984–85.

sky SPORTS FACT FILE

Queens Park Rangers started 1937–38 with a full-back pairing of Sam Abel and Reg Swinfen, both former centre-forwards. Abel, despite twice topping Chesterfield's scorers, failed in attack at Rangers and Swinfen had already had a handful of outings leading their line.

Record Defeat: 1–8 v Mansfield T, Division 3, 15 March 1965. 1–8 v Manchester U, Division 1, 19 March 1969.

Most League Points (2 for a win): 67, Division 3, 1966–67.

Most League Points (3 for a win): 88, FL C, 2010–11.

Most League Goals: 111, Division 3, 1961–62.

Highest League Scorer in Season: George Goddard, 37, Division 3 (S), 1929–30.

Most League Goals in Total Aggregate: George Goddard, 172, 1926–34.

Most League Goals in One Match: 4, George Goddard v Merthyr T, Division 3 (S), 9 March 1929; 4, George Goddard v Swindon T, Division 3 (S), 12 April 1930; 4, George Goddard v Exeter C, Division 3 (S), 20 December 1930; 4, George Goddard v Watford, Division 3 (S), 19 September 1931; 4, Tom Cheetham v Aldershot, Division 3 (S), 14 September 1935; 4, Tom Cheetham v Aldershot, Division 3 (S), 12 November 1938.

Most Capped Player: Alan McDonald, 52, Northern Ireland.

Most League Appearances: Tony Ingham, 519, 1950–63.

Youngest League Player: Frank Sibley, 16 years 97 days v Bristol C, 10 March 1964.

Record Transfer Fee Received: £6,000,000 from Newcastle U for Les Ferdinand, June 1995.

Record Transfer Fee Paid: £3,500,000 to Instituto for Alejandro Faurlin, July 2009.

Football League Record: 1920 Original Members of Division 3; 1921–48 Division 3 (S); 1948–52 Division 2; 1952–58 Division 3 (S); 1958–67 Division 3; 1967–68 Division 2; 1968–69 Division 1; 1969–73 Division 2; 1973–79 Division 1; 1979–83 Division 2; 1983–92 Division 1; 1992–96 FA Premier League; 1996–2001 Division 1; 2001–04 Division 2; 2004–11 FL C; 2011– FA Premier League.

LATEST SEQUENCES

Longest Sequence of League Wins: 8, 7.11.1931 – 28.12.1931.

Longest Sequence of League Defeats: 9, 25.2.1969 – 5.4.1969.

Longest Sequence of League Draws: 6, 29.1.2000 – 5.3.2000.

Longest Sequence of Unbeaten League Matches: 20, 11.3.1972 – 23.9.1972.

Longest Sequence Without a League Win: 20, 7.12.1968 – 7.4.1969.

Successive Scoring Runs: 33 from 9.12.1961.

Successive Non-scoring Runs: 6 from 18.3.1939.

MANAGERS

James Cowan 1906–13
Jimmy Howie 1913–20
Ned Liddell 1920–24
Will Wood 1924–25
  (had been Secretary since 1903)
Bob Hewison 1925–31
John Bowman 1931
Archie Mitchell 1931–33
Mick O'Brien 1933–35
Billy Birrell 1935–39
Ted Vizard 1939–44
Dave Mangnall 1944–52
Jack Taylor 1952–59
Alec Stock 1959–65
  (General Manager to 1968)
Bill Dodgin Jnr 1968
Tommy Docherty 1968
Les Allen 1968–71
Gordon Jago 1971–74
Dave Sexton 1974–77
Frank Sibley 1977–78
Steve Burtenshaw 1978–79
Tommy Docherty 1979–80
Terry Venables 1980–84
Gordon Jago 1984
Alan Mullery 1984
Frank Sibley 1984–85
Jim Smith 1985–88
Trevor Francis 1988–89
Don Howe 1989–91
Gerry Francis 1991–94
Ray Wilkins 1994–96
Stewart Houston 1996–97
Ray Harford 1997–98
Gerry Francis 1998–2001
Ian Holloway 2001–06
Gary Waddock 2006
John Gregory 2006–07
Luigi Di Canio 2007–08
Iain Dowie 2008
Paulo Sousa 2008–09
Jim Magilton 2009
Paul Hart 2009–10
Neil Warnock March 2010–

TEN YEAR LEAGUE RECORD

		P	W	D	L	F	A	Pts	Pos
2001-02	Div 2	46	19	14	13	60	49	71	8
2002-03	Div 2	46	24	11	11	69	45	83	4
2003-04	Div 2	46	22	17	7	80	45	83	2
2004-05	FL C	46	17	11	18	54	58	62	11
2005-06	FL C	46	12	14	20	50	65	50	21
2006-07	FL C	46	14	11	21	54	68	53	18
2007-08	FL C	46	14	16	16	60	66	58	14
2008-09	FL C	46	15	16	15	42	44	61	11
2009-10	FL C	46	14	15	17	58	65	57	13
2010-11	FL C	46	24	16	6	71	32	88	1

DID YOU KNOW

In 1975–76 when Queens Park Rangers finished runners-up in the First Division, they were unbeaten at home for the first time in their Football League history. Only four points were dropped at Loftus Road during the campaign.

QUEENS PARK RANGERS 2010–11 LEAGUE RECORD

Match No.	Date	Venue	Opponents	Result	H/T Score	Lg Pos.	Goalscorers	Attendance
1	Aug 7	H	Barnsley	W 4-0	1-0	—	Helguson (pen) [41], Mackie [53], Taarabt (pen) [63], Hall [81]	13,445
2	14	A	Sheffield U	W 3-0	3-0	2	Ephraim [11], Mackie [20], Taarabt (pen) [23]	22,651
3	21	H	Scunthorpe U	W 2-0	2-0	1	Orr [17], Helguson [41]	12,046
4	28	A	Derby Co	D 2-2	0-1	1	Agyemang [69], Mackie [90]	25,874
5	Sept 11	H	Middlesbrough	W 3-0	0-0	1	Helguson (pen) [49], Ephraim [53], Mackie [59]	14,784
6	14	A	Ipswich T	W 3-0	2-0	—	Mackie 2 [31, 42], Helguson (pen) [68]	19,931
7	18	A	Leicester C	W 2-0	1-0	1	Mackie 2 [12, 86]	22,968
8	25	H	Doncaster R	W 3-0	0-0	1	Gorkss 2 [53, 88], Taarabt (pen) [81]	13,990
9	28	H	Millwall	D 0-0	0-0	—		15,325
10	Oct 2	A	Crystal Palace	W 2-1	0-0	1	Taarabt [49], Helguson [90]	17,171
11	16	H	Norwich C	D 0-0	0-0	1		18,059
12	19	A	Swansea C	D 0-0	0-0	—		16,742
13	22	A	Bristol C	D 1-1	0-1	—	Agyemang [84]	14,552
14	30	H	Burnley	D 1-1	1-1	2	Taarabt [32]	15,620
15	Nov 6	H	Reading	W 3-1	1-0	1	Taarabt (pen) [27], Faurlin [61], Smith [71]	15,692
16	9	A	Portsmouth	D 1-1	0-0	1	Smith (pen) [90]	17,818
17	13	A	Nottingham F	D 0-0	0-0	2		22,859
18	20	H	Preston NE	W 3-1	1-0	1	Hulse [4], Taarabt 2 [56, 84]	13,505
19	27	H	Cardiff C	W 2-1	1-1	1	Gorkss [18], Taarabt [68]	17,316
20	Dec 10	H	Watford	L 1-3	0-2	1	Smith [89]	14,079
21	18	A	Leeds U	L 0-2	0-1	1		29,426
22	26	H	Swansea C	W 4-0	1-0	1	Mackie [16], Helguson (pen) [62], Taarabt 2 [70, 80]	15,963
23	28	A	Coventry C	W 2-0	0-0	1	Westwood (og) [49], Smith [61]	17,678
24	Jan 1	A	Norwich C	L 0-1	0-1	1		26,273
25	3	H	Bristol C	D 2-2	0-0	1	Faurlin [53], Taarabt (pen) [85]	15,618
26	15	A	Burnley	D 0-0	0-0	1		14,819
27	23	A	Coventry C	W 2-1	1-1	1	Taarabt [45], Routledge [79]	13,185
28	29	A	Hull C	D 0-0	0-0	—		20,601
29	Feb 1	H	Portsmouth	W 2-0	0-0	1	Taarabt [59], Hill [73]	14,078
30	4	A	Reading	W 1-0	0-0	—	Routledge [82]	18,982
31	13	H	Nottingham F	D 1-1	1-1	1	Smith [16]	17,227
32	19	A	Preston NE	D 1-1	1-0	1	Helguson [37]	10,521
33	22	H	Ipswich T	W 2-0	0-0	1	Hill [77], Helguson [83]	16,587
34	26	A	Middlesbrough	W 3-0	1-0	1	Helguson 2 [41, 61], Taarabt (pen) [68]	16,972
35	Mar 5	H	Leicester C	W 1-0	0-0	1	Miller [88]	18,068
36	8	A	Millwall	L 0-2	0-0	—		14,104
37	12	H	Crystal Palace	W 2-1	1-1	1	Helguson 2 (1 pen) [20, 54 (p)]	18,116
38	19	A	Doncaster R	W 1-0	0-0	1	Ephraim [47]	11,747
39	Apr 4	H	Sheffield U	W 3-0	1-0	—	Routledge 2 [29, 66], Faurlin [52]	14,535
40	9	A	Scunthorpe U	L 1-4	1-1	1	Hulse [7]	6061
41	12	A	Barnsley	W 1-0	1-0	—	Taarabt [1]	11,381
42	18	H	Derby Co	D 0-0	0-0	—		16,745
43	23	A	Cardiff C	D 2-2	1-2	1	Taarabt 2 [10, 71]	26,058
44	25	H	Hull C	D 1-1	1-0	1	Routledge [9]	17,399
45	30	A	Watford	W 2-0	0-0	1	Taarabt [77], Smith [90]	15,538
46	May 7	H	Leeds U	L 1-2	1-1	1	Helguson [1]	18,234

Final League Position: 1

GOALSCORERS

League (71): Taarabt 19 (6 pens), Helguson 13 (5 pens), Mackie 9, Smith 6 (1 pen), Routledge 5, Ephraim 3, Faurlin 3, Gorkss 3, Agyemang 2, Hill 2, Hulse 2, Hall 1, Miller 1, Orr 1, own goal 1.
Carling Cup (1): German 1.
FA Cup (0).

Kenny P 44	Orr B 29 + 4	Hill C 44	Derry S 45	Hall F 12 + 7	Gorkss K 42	Ephraim H 19 + 9	Mackie J 25	Helguson H 32 + 2	Taarabt A 43 + 1	Faurlin A 40	Parker J — + 1	Leigertwood M — + 9	German A — + 2	Ramage P — + 4	Clarke L 2 + 11	Connolly M 33 + 3	Buzsaky A 9 + 10	Agyemang P — + 19	Smith T 23 + 10	Walker K 20	Hulse R 12 + 9	Borrowdale G — + 1	Rowlands M — + 4	Andrade B — + 1	Tofas G — + 1	Vaagan Moen P 1 + 6	Routledge W 20	Miller I 4 + 8	Chimbonda P — + 3	Shittu D 5 + 2	Cerny R 2	Match No.
1	2	3	4[2]	5	6	7	8	9[3]	10[1]	11	12	13	14																			1
1	2	3	4	5[1]	6	7[3]	8	9	10[2]	11			14		12	13																2
1	2	3	4[2]		6	7	8	9[3]	10[1]	11		13	14			5	12															3
1	2	3	4[1]		6	7	8	9[2]	10[2]	11			14			5	12	13														4
1	2[1]	3	4		6	7	8[3]	9	10[2]	11			12			5	13		14													5
1		3	4		6	7	8[3]	9	10[2]	11[1]		13				5	12		14	2												6
1		3	4		6	7	8[3]	9[1]	10[2]			13				5	11	12	14	2												7
1		3	4[1]		6	7	8[3]	9[2]	10		12					5	11	13	14	2												8
1		3	4		6	7[2]	8	9	10		12					5	11[1]	13		2												9
1		3	4		6	7	8	9	10[1]			13				5	11[2]		12	2												10
1		3	4		6	7[2]	8	9	10[3]		12					5	11[1]	13		2												11
1		3	4		6	7[3]	8	9[2]	10[1]	11					14	5	12	13		2												12
1		3	4		6	7[1]	8	9[2]	10[3]	11						5	14	12		2	13											13
1		3	4		6	7[1]	8		10[3]	11					13	5	12	14		2	9[2]											14
1		3[s]	4		6	14	8		7[1]	11					12	5		13	10[3]	2	9[2]											15
1		3	4[3]		6		8		7[1]	11					14	5[s]	12	10		2	9[2]	13										16
1		3	4		6	7[2]	8		10[3]	11					13	12	5		2		9[1]	14										17
1		3	5[2]		6		8[3]	7		11						10	4	12	2		9[1]		13	14								18
1		3	4	13	6		8[2]		7[1]	11					12	5	14	10[3]	2		9											19
1	12	3	4		6		8	9[3]	7[2]	11[1]		13				5		10	2		14											20
1	2	3[1]	4	17	6	14	8	13	7							6			10[7]	11	0[9]											21
1	12	3[s]	4		6		8	9[3]	7[2]	11						5		10[1]	2		14		13									22
1	14	3	4		6		8	9[3]	7[2]	11					12	5		10[1]	2				13									23
1	12	3[1]	4		6		8	9[7]	10[1]	11					7	5[s]	13		2						14							24
1	2	5	4		6		8		7[1]	11						10	3		9							12						25
1	2	3	4	14	6		13	7[3]	11[1]						12	5		10		9[2]							8					26
1	2	3	4	12	6	13	8	9[3]		11						5		10[1]								7[2]		14				27
1	2	3	4		6	14	8		11[1]							5		10[2]					13			12		7	9[3]			28
1	2	3	4	13	6	11	8	10[3]								5										12		14	7[2]	9[1]		29
1	2	3	4	14	6		8	10[2]	11[s]							5					9[1]						13	7[3]	12			30
1	2	3	4		6[2]		8		11[3]							5		10[1]			9					14	7	12	13			31
1	2	3	4		6		8	9[2]	11							5	14									12	13	7[3]	10[1]			32
1	2	3	4	5			8	9	11							13	12									7			10[1]	6[2]		33
1	2[2]	3	4	5	12			9[3]	10	11						13	8[1]		14							7				6		34
1	2	3	4	5[1]	14			9	10[2]	11						12	8[3]									7		13		6		35
1	2	3	4		6			9[3]	10[1]	11							8[2]	12								7		13	14	5[s]		36
1	2	3	4	5	6	12	8[2]	9	11							13		10[1]								7						37
1	2	3	4	5	6	11[1]	8	9[2]								12		10								7	13					38
1	2	3	4[3]	5	6		8[1]	9	11							14	12	10[2]								7		13				39
1	2	3	4[3]	5			8			11						14	10		9[2]							7		13	12	6[1]		40
1	2	3	4		6	12	8[1]	9	11							5		10								7						41
1	2	3	4		6		8[1]	9[3]	11							5	12	10	14							7[2]	13					42
1	2	3	4	13	6		8	9	11							5[2]	12	10[1]								7						43
1	2	3	4	5	6	12	8	9[2]	11							13		10[1]								7						44
	2		4	5[1]	6		8[3]	9	11				14			3	13	10								7[2]				12	1	45
	2	3[2]	4		6		12	9[3]	11			13				5	8[1]	10								7				14	1	46

FA Cup
Third Round   Blackburn R   (a)   0-1

Carling Cup
First Round   Port Vale   (h)   1-3

READING

FL Championship

Madejski Stadium, Junction 11, M4, Reading, Berkshire RG2 0FL.

Telephone: (0118) 968 1100.

Fax: (0118) 968 1101.

Ticket Office: (0844) 249 1871.

Website: www.readingfc.co.uk

Email: customerservice@readingfc.co.uk

Ground Capacity: 24,082.

Record Attendance: 33,042 v Brentford, FA Cup 5th rd, 19 February 1927 (at Elm Park). 24,122 v Aston Villa, FA Premier League, 10 February 2007 (at Madejski Stadium).

Pitch Measurements: 105m × 68m.

Chairman: Sir John Madejski OBE, DL.

Vice-chairman: Ian Wood-Smith.

Chief Executive: Nigel Howe.

Secretary: Sue Hewett.

Director of Football: Nick Hammond.

Manager: Brian McDermott.

First Team Coach: Nigel Gibbs.

Physio: Luke Anthony.

Colours: Blue and white hooped shirts, blue shorts, blue stockings.

Change Colours: White shirts, green shorts, white stockings.

Year Formed: 1871. *Turned Professional:* 1895. *Ltd Co.:* 1895.

Club Nickname: 'The Royals'.

Grounds: 1871, Reading Recreation; Reading Cricket Ground; 1882, Coley Park; 1889, Caversham Cricket Ground; 1896, Elm Park; 1998, Madejski Stadium.

First Football League Game: 28 August 1920, Division 3, v Newport Co (a) W 1–0 – Crawford; Smith, Horler; Christie, Mavin, Getgood; Spence, Weston, Yarnell, Bailey (1), Andrews.

Record League Victory: 10–2 v Crystal Palace, Division 3 (S), 4 September 1946 – Groves; Glidden, Gulliver; McKenna, Ratcliffe, Young; Chitty, Maurice Edelston (3), McPhee (4), Barney (1), Deverell (2).

HONOURS

FA Premier League: Best season: 8th 2006–07.

Football League – FL C:
Champions 2005–06;
Division 1: *Runners-up* 1994–95;
Division 2: *Champions* 1993–94;
Runners-up 2001–02;
Division 3: *Champions* 1985–86;
Division 3 (S): *Champions* 1925–26;
Runners-up 1931–32, 1934–35, 1948–49, 1951–52;
Division 4: *Champions* 1978–79.

FA Cup: Semi-final 1927.

Football League Cup: Best season: 5th rd, 1996, 1998.

Simod Cup: *Winners* 1988.

sky SPORTS FACT FILE

On 13 January 2010, Reading defeated Liverpool 2-1 at Anfield in a third round FA Cup replay. Shane Long scored the winner in the 100th minute. The Reading striker has a framed photograph at his home depicting the goal which put his team into the fourth round.

Record Cup Victory: 6–0 v Leyton, FA Cup 2nd rd, 12 December 1925 – Duckworth; Eggo, McConnell; Wilson, Messer, Evans; Smith (2), Braithwaite (1), Davey (1), Tinsley, Robson (2).

Record Defeat: 0–18 v Preston NE, FA Cup 1st rd, 1893–94.

Most League Points (2 for a win): 65, Division 4, 1978–79.

Most League Points (3 for a win): 106, Championship, 2005–06.

Most League Goals: 112, Division 3 (S), 1951–52.

Highest League Scorer in Season: Ronnie Blackman, 39, Division 3 (S), 1951–52.

Most League Goals in Total Aggregate: Ronnie Blackman, 158, 1947–54.

Most League Goals in One Match: 6, Arthur Bacon v Stoke C, Division 2, 3 April 1931.

Most Capped Player: Kevin Doyle, 26 (41), Republic of Ireland.

Most League Appearances: Martin Hicks, 500, 1978–91.

Youngest League Player: Peter Castle, 16 years 49 days v Watford, 30 April 2003.

Record Transfer Fee Received: £6,500,000 from Wolverhampton W for Kevin Doyle, June 2009.

Record Transfer Fee Paid: Undisclosed to Nantes for Emerse Fae, August 2007.

Football League Record: 1920 Original Member of Division 3; 1921–26 Division 3 (S); 1926–31 Division 2; 1931–58 Division 3 (S); 1958–71 Division 3; 1971–76 Division 4; 1976–77 Division 3; 1977–79 Division 4; 1979–83 Division 3; 1983–84 Division 4; 1984–86 Division 3; 1986–88 Division 2; 1988–92 Division 3; 1992–94 Division 2; 1994–98 Division 1; 1998–2002 Division 2; 2002–04 Division 1; 2004–06 FL C; 2006–08 FA Premier League; 2008– FL C.

MANAGERS

Thomas Sefton 1897–1901
  (Secretary-Manager)
James Sharp 1901–02
Harry Matthews 1902–20
Harry Marshall 1920–22
Arthur Chadwick 1923–25
H. S. Bray 1925–26
  (Secretary only since 1922 and 1926–35)
Andrew Wylie 1926–31
Joe Smith 1931–35
Billy Butler 1935–39
John Cochrane 1939
Joe Edelston 1939–47
Ted Drake 1947–52
Jack Smith 1952–55
Harry Johnston 1955–63
Roy Bentley 1963–69
Jack Mansell 1969–71
Charlie Hurley 1972–77
Maurice Evans 1977–84
Ian Branfoot 1984–89
Ian Porterfield 1989–91
Mark McGhee 1991–94
Jimmy Quinn/Mick Gooding 1994–97
Terry Bullivant 1997–98
Tommy Burns 1998–99
Alan Pardew 1999–2003
Steve Coppell 2003–09
Brendan Rodgers 2009
Brian McDermott December 2009–

LATEST SEQUENCES

Longest Sequence of League Wins: 13, 17.8.1985 – 19.10.1985.

Longest Sequence of League Defeats: 8, 29.12.2007 – 24.2.2008.

Longest Sequence of League Draws: 6, 23.3.2002 – 20.4.2002.

Longest Sequence of Unbeaten League Matches: 33, 9.8.2005 – 14.2.2006.

Longest Sequence Without a League Win: 14, 30.4.1927 – 29.10.1927.

Successive Scoring Runs: 32 from 1.10.1932.

Successive Non-scoring Runs: 6 from 13.4.1925.

TEN YEAR LEAGUE RECORD

		P	W	D	L	F	A	Pts	Pos
2001-02	Div 2	46	23	15	8	70	43	84	2
2002-03	Div 1	46	25	4	17	61	46	79	4
2003-04	Div 1	46	20	10	16	55	57	70	9
2004-05	FL C	46	19	13	14	51	44	70	7
2005-06	FL C	46	31	13	2	99	32	106	1
2006-07	PR Lge	38	16	7	15	52	47	55	8
2007-08	PR Lge	38	10	6	22	41	66	36	18
2008-09	FL C	46	21	14	11	72	40	77	4
2009-10	FL C	46	17	12	17	68	63	63	9
2010-11	FL C	46	20	17	9	77	51	77	5

DID YOU KNOW ?

Although Archie Summerfield's official record while playing for Reading consisted of two FA Cup appearances in 1945–46 against neighbours Aldershot, he had the satisfaction of playing in a two-legged tie which produced a total of fourteen goals of which he contributed two.

READING 2010–11 LEAGUE RECORD

Match No.	Date	Venue	Opponents	Result	H/T Score	Lg Pos.	Goalscorers	Attendance
1	Aug 7	H	Scunthorpe U	L	1-2	1-1	—	Sigurdsson [26]	15,914
2	14	A	Portsmouth	D	1-1	0-1	18	Kebe [87]	16,497
3	21	H	Nottingham F	D	1-1	1-0	19	Pearce [15]	17,324
4	28	A	Leicester C	W	2-1	1-0	13	Sigurdsson [22], Mills [86]	19,611
5	Sept 11	H	Crystal Palace	W	3-0	1-0	8	Long (pen) [37], Harte (pen) [65], Kebe [90]	17,921
6	14	A	Millwall	D	0-0	0-0	—		11,061
7	18	A	Middlesbrough	L	1-3	1-2	15	Kebe [44]	15,158
8	25	H	Barnsley	W	3-0	0-0	7	Kebe [78], Harte [89], Robson-Kanu [90]	14,830
9	28	H	Ipswich T	W	1-0	0-0	—	Church [88]	15,763
10	Oct 2	A	Preston NE	D	1-1	0-1	7	Karacan [55]	10,269
11	16	H	Swansea C	L	0-1	0-1	10		18,418
12	19	A	Bristol C	L	0-1	0-1	—		13,519
13	23	A	Burnley	W	4-0	1-0	8	Long (pen) [8], McAnuff [64], Antonio [85], Church [90]	14,895
14	30	H	Doncaster R	W	4-3	1-2	6	Mills [9], Karacan [60], Harte [74], Church [88]	15,553
15	Nov 6	A	QPR	L	1-3	0-1	10	Long [68]	15,692
16	10	H	Cardiff C	D	1-1	1-0	—	Hunt [5]	17,960
17	13	H	Norwich C	D	3-3	1-3	9	Harte [29], Hunt [59], Long (pen) [62]	15,934
18	20	A	Watford	D	1-1	1-1	11	Hunt [15]	12,196
19	27	H	Leeds U	D	0-0	0-0	11		23,677
20	Dec 11	A	Coventry C	D	0-0	0-0	14		14,029
21	18	A	Derby Co	W	2-1	1-0	7	Long 2 (1 pen) [43 (p), 88]	24,514
22	26	H	Bristol C	W	4-1	2-1	7	McAnuff [31], Hunt [43], Long 2 [66, 89]	19,293
23	28	A	Hull C	D	1-1	0-1	6	Church [82]	21,975
24	Jan 1	A	Swansea C	L	0-1	0-0	11		14,329
25	3	H	Burnley	W	2-1	1-1	8	Long 2 [31, 68]	16,151
26	15	A	Doncaster R	W	3-0	1-0	16	Long [29], Kebe [67], McAnuff [74]	9496
27	22	H	Hull C	D	1-1	0-0	8	Harte (pen) [80]	16,494
28	Feb 1	A	Cardiff C	D	2-2	1-0	8	Leigertwood [21], Manset [90]	21,405
29	4	H	QPR	L	0-1	0-0	—		18,982
30	12	A	Norwich C	L	1-2	1-1	12	Long [26]	25,560
31	15	A	Sheffield U	D	1-1	0-0	—	Long [81]	19,271
32	19	H	Watford	D	1-1	0-1	12	Hunt [50]	16,934
33	22	H	Millwall	W	2-1	1-0	—	Hunt [3], Long [55]	15,934
34	26	A	Crystal Palace	D	3-3	1-2	10	Long (pen) [30], Kebe [49], Hunt [73]	13,845
35	Mar 5	H	Middlesbrough	W	5-2	2-1	10	Robson-Kanu [14], Harte 2 [35, 48], Long 2 [53, 68]	18,568
36	8	A	Ipswich T	W	3-1	1-0	—	Long [18], Harte [86], Hunt [89]	17,308
37	19	A	Barnsley	W	1-0	0-0	7	Manset [71]	10,284
38	Apr 2	H	Portsmouth	W	2-0	2-0	6	Long 2 (1 pen) [30, 37 (p)]	21,896
39	5	H	Preston NE	W	2-1	1-0	—	Kebe [21], Robson-Kanu [82]	14,844
40	9	A	Nottingham F	W	4-3	1-1	5	Harte [19], Karacan [54], Kebe [62], Church [90]	22,495
41	12	A	Scunthorpe U	W	2-0	0-0	—	Long [57], Harte (pen) [63]	4458
42	16	H	Leicester C	W	3-1	2-0	4	Kebe [19], McAnuff [21], Hunt [67]	19,199
43	22	A	Leeds U	D	0-0	0-0	—		24,564
44	25	H	Sheffield U	L	2-3	2-2	5	Hunt [9], Robson-Kanu [20]	19,165
45	30	A	Coventry C	D	0-0	0-0	5		22,436
46	May 7	H	Derby Co	W	2-1	1-1	5	Harte (pen) [24], Robson-Kanu [72]	21,902

Final League Position: 5

GOALSCORERS

League (77): Long 21 (6 pens), Harte 11 (4 pens), Hunt 10, Kebe 9, Church 5, Robson-Kanu 5, McAnuff 4, Karacan 3, Manset 2, Mills 2, Sigurdsson 2, Antonio 1, Pearce 1.
Carling Cup (4): Mills 2, Rasiak 1, Robson-Kanu 1.
FA Cup (4): Long 2, Leigertwood 1, Mills 1.
Play-Offs (5): Long 2 (1 pen), McAnuff 1, Mills 1, own goal 1.

Federici A 34	Griffin A 33	Williams M 3	Karacan J 39 + 1	Mills M 38	Pearce A 20 + 1	Kebe J 34 + 2	Gunnarsson B 10 + 2	Long S 44	Sigurdsson G 4	McAnuff J 40	Tabb J 15 + 6	Church S 14 + 23	Antonio M 2 + 19	Howard B 19 + 5	Hunt N 19 + 14	Rasiak G — + 1	Cummings S 10	Harte I 40	Khizanishvili Z 21 + 1	Armstrong C 6 + 1	Robson-Kanu H 12 + 15	Leigertwood M 21 + 1	Ingimarsson I 12 + 1	Manset M 4 + 9	McCarthy A 12 + 1	Taylor J — + 1	Match No.
1	2	3	4^2	5	6	7	8^1	9	10	11^3	12	13	14														1
1	2^3	3	4^1	5		7	8		10	11	9^2	12	6	13	14	14											2
1	2^2	3	4	5	6	7	13	9^1	10	11	8	12															3
1			4^2	5	6	7	2^1	9	10	11	13	12	8				3										4
1			4	5	6	7	8	9^1		11		12	10				2	3									5
1			4	5	6	7		9		11	10^1	13	8	12			2^2	3									6
1			4	5	6	7	8	9^3		11^2	14	13	10^4	12			2^1	3									7
1			4	5	12	7		9^3		8		10^2	14				2	3	6^8	11^1	13						8
1			4	5^8	6	7^2		9^3		8		14	12	13			2	3		11	10^1						9
1			4		6	7		9		8		10^1		12			2	3	5	11							10
1	2		4	5		7		9^2		8		13		12				3	6	11	10^1						11
1	2		4	5		7^3		9^2		8		13		12			10	3^1	6	11	14						12
1	2		4^1	5		7^2		9		11		13		12				3	6		10	8					13
1	2		4	5		7^1		9^2		11		13	14	12				3	6		10^3	8					14
1	2		4^1	5		7^3		9		11		12	14	13				3	6		10^2	8					15
1	2		4	5		7		9				12^1		10				3	6		11^2	13					16
1	2		4	5				9		11		10	12	8^1	7			3	6								17
1	2		4	5	6	13		9		11		7^2	10^3	14				3^1		12		8					18
1	2		4^1		5	13		9		11	12	10^2	14	8				3	6			7^3					19
1	2		4^1	5	6	7^3		9		11	14	13	10^2					3			12	8					20
1	2		4^3	5	6	7^2		9		11		12		14	10^1			3			13	8					21
1	2		4	5	6	7^1		9		11					10			3			12	8					22
1	2		4^1	5	6	7		9		11		12	14	13	10^2			3			8^3						23
1	2			5	6	7		9		11^2	10	12	4	13				3		8^1							24
1	2			5	6	7		9		11		13		10^2				3			12	8					25
1	2		4^1		6	7		9		11	12	13		10^2				3			8	5					26
1	2		4^2	5	6	7		9		11		10^1						3			13	8	12				27
1	2		4	5		7		9^1		11		10^2		12				3			8	6	13				28
1	2		4	5		7		0		11^2	10^1							3			13	6	12				29
1	2		4^8	5		7		9		11			12	8				3			10^1	6					30
1	2			5		7	4^1	9		10	11^2		12	8				3				6	13				31
1^6	2			5	11		9		7		12		4^2	10^1				3			13	8	6	15			32
	2			5	7		9	8		11	12			10^1			3	4	6						1		33
	13		5		7		9	8		11			10				2^2	3	12			4	6^1		1		34
			5		7^2	2	9^1			11	12	13	10^3				3	6			8	4	14	1		35
	4		5^1		2		9^2			13			8	10				3	6		11	7	12	1		36
	4				7	2	9			11	10^1	12	8^2					3	5			6	13	1		37
	4				7	2	9	10^1		11	13		8^2					3	5		12	6		1		38
	2		4		7		9	10^2		11^1			8^3					3	5		13	14	6	12	1		39
	2		4		7^1		9	11		12								3	5		13	8	6	10^2	1		40
	2		4^2	5	7		9	11		13		12						3	6		13	8	10^1	1			41
	2		4	5	7^2		9	11		12								3	6		13	8	10^1	1			42
	2		4	5			9	11		12		10^1						3	6		7^2	8	13	1			43
	2		4^3	5			9	11		12		14	10^2					3	6		7^1	8	13	1			44
1	2		4	5			9	11		7^1	12	10^2						3	6		13	8					45
1				5	6	13		11	9	7^1		14					2	3			8	4^2	10^3		12		46

FA Cup

Third Round	WBA	(h)	1-0	
Fourth Round	Stevenage	(a)	2-1	
Fifth Round	Everton	(a)	1-0	
Sixth Round	Manchester C	(a)	0-1	

Carling Cup

First Round	Torquay U	(a)	1-0
Second Round	Northampton T	(h)	3-3

Play-Offs

Semi-Final	Cardiff C	(h)	0-0
		(a)	3-0
Final	Swansea C		2-4
(at Wembley).			

ROCHDALE   FL Championship 1

FOUNDATION

Considering the love of rugby in their area, it is not surprising that Rochdale had difficulty in establishing an Association Football club. The earlier Rochdale Town club formed in 1900 went out of existence in 1907 when the present club was immediately established and joined the Manchester League, before graduating to the Lancashire Combination in 1908.

Spotland Stadium, Willbutts Lane, Rochdale OL11 5DS.

Telephone: (0844) 826 1907.

Ticket Office: (0844) 826 1907.

Website: www.rochdaleafc.co.uk

Email: office@rochdaleafc.co.uk

Ground Capacity: 9,223.

Record Attendance: 24,231 v Notts Co, FA Cup 2nd rd, 10 December 1949.

Pitch Measurements: 114yd × 76yd.

Chairman: Chris Dunphy.

Chief Executive/Secretary: Colin Garlick.

Manager: Steve Eyre.

Assistant Manager: Frankie Bunn.

Physio: Andy Thorpe.

Colours: Black and blue striped shirts, white shorts, blue stockings with black tops.

Change Colours: Purple shirts with white sleeves and purple trim, purple shorts, purple stockings with white tops.

Year Formed: 1907.

Turned Professional: 1907.

Ltd Co.: 1910.

Club Nickname: 'The Dale'.

Ground: 1907, St Clements Playing Fields (original name Spotland).

First Football League Game: 27 August 1921, Division 3 (N), v Accrington Stanley (h) W 6–3 – Crabtree; Nuttall, Sheehan; Hill, Farrer, Yarwood; Hoad, Sandiford, Dennison (2), Owens (3), Carney (1).

Record League Victory: 8–1 v Chesterfield, Division 3 (N), 18 December 1926 – Hill; Brown, Ward; Hillhouse, Parkes, Braidwood; Hughes, Bertram, Whitehurst (5), Schofield (2), Martin (1).

Record Cup Victory: 8–2 v Crook T, FA Cup 1st rd, 26 November 1927 – Moody; Hopkins, Ward; Braidwood, Parkes, Barker; Tompkinson, Clennell (3) Whitehurst (4), Hall, Martin (1).

HONOURS

Football League – Division 3:
Best season: 9th, 1969–70;
Division 3 (N): *Runners-up* 1923–24, 1926–27.
FA Cup: Best season: 5th rd, 1990, 2003.
Football League Cup:
***Runners-up* 1962 (record for 4th Division club).**

sky SPORTS FACT FILE

Despite failing to score in no fewer than 17 Football League matches in 1968–69, Rochdale finished third and won promotion to Division Three. Their goal drought even included five successive goalless draws!

Record Defeat: 1–9 v Tranmere R, Division 3 (N), 25 December 1931.

Most League Points (2 for a win): 62, Division 3 (N), 1923–24.

Most League Points (3 for a win): 82, FL 2, 2009–10.

Most League Goals: 105, Division 3 (N), 1926–27.

Highest League Scorer in Season: Albert Whitehurst, 44, Division 3 (N), 1926–27.

Most League Goals in Total Aggregate: Reg Jenkins, 119, 1964–73.

Most League Goals in One Match: 6, Tommy Tippett v Hartlepools U, Division 3 (N), 21 April 1930.

Most Capped Player: Leo Bertos, 6 (39), New Zealand.

Most League Appearances: Gary Jones, 379, 1998–2001; 2003–.

Youngest League Player: Zac Hughes, 16 years 105 days v Exeter C, 19 September 1987.

Record Transfer Fee Received: £400,000 from West Ham U for Stephen Bywater, August 1998.

Record Transfer Fee Paid: £150,000 to Stoke C for Paul Connor, March 2001.

Football League Record: 1921 Elected to Division 3 (N); 1958–59 Division 3; 1959–69 Division 4; 1969–74 Division 3; 1974–92 Division 4; 1992–2004 Division 3; 2004–10 FL 2; 2010– FL 1.

LATEST SEQUENCES

Longest Sequence of League Wins: 8, 29.9.1969 – 3.11.1969.

Longest Sequence of League Defeats: 17, 14.11.1931 – 12.3.1932.

Longest Sequence of League Draws: 6, 17.8.1968 – 14.9.1968.

Longest Sequence of Unbeaten League Matches: 20, 15.9.1923 – 19.1.1924.

Longest Sequence Without a League Win: 28, 14.11.1931 – 29.8.1932.

Successive Scoring Runs: 29 from 8.1.1927.

Successive Non-scoring Runs: 9 from 14.3.1980.

MANAGERS

Billy Bradshaw 1920
Run by committee 1920–22
Tom Wilson 1922–23
Jack Peart 1923–30
Will Cameron 1930–31
Herbert Hopkinson 1932–34
Billy Smith 1934–35
Ernest Nixon 1935–37
Sam Jennings 1937–38
Ted Goodier 1938–52
Jack Warner 1952–53
Harry Catterick 1953–58
Jack Marshall 1958–60
Tony Collins 1960–68
Bob Stokoe 1967–68
Len Richley 1968–70
Dick Conner 1970–73
Walter Joyce 1973–76
Brian Green 1976–77
Mike Ferguson 1977–78
Doug Collins 1979
Bob Stokoe 1979–80
Peter Madden 1980–83
Jimmy Greenhoff 1983–84
Vic Halom 1984–86
Eddie Gray 1986–88
Danny Bergara 1988–89
Terry Dolan 1989–91
Dave Sutton 1991–94
Mick Docherty 1994–96
Graham Barrow 1996–99
Steve Parkin 1999–2001
John Hollins 2001–02
Paul Simpson 2002–03
Alan Buckley 2003
Steve Parkin 2003–06
Keith Hill 2007–11
   (caretaker from December 2006)
Steve Eyre June 2011–

TEN YEAR LEAGUE RECORD

		P	W	D	L	F	A	Pts	Pos
2001-02	Div 3	46	21	15	10	65	52	78	5
2002-03	Div 3	46	12	16	18	63	70	52	19
2003-04	Div 3	46	12	14	20	49	58	50	21
2004-05	FL 2	46	16	18	12	54	48	66	9
2005-06	FL 2	46	14	14	18	66	69	56	14
2006-07	FL 2	46	18	12	16	70	50	66	9
2007-08	FL 2	46	23	11	12	77	54	80	5
2008-09	FL 2	46	19	13	14	70	59	70	6
2009-10	FL 2	46	25	7	14	82	48	82	3
2010-11	FL 1	46	18	14	14	63	55	68	9

DID YOU KNOW ?

Joe Hargreaves was aged 30 when Rochdale signed him from Rossendale United in 1945. He scored twice in each of his first four games, finished with 26 goals in 28 League and FA Cup matches. Never took a penalty because he was stone deaf!

ROCHDALE 2010–11 LEAGUE RECORD

Match No.	Date		Venue	Opponents	Result		H/T Score	Lg Pos.	Goalscorers	Attendance
1	Aug	7	H	Hartlepool U	D	0-0	0-0	—		3706
2		14	A	Brighton & HA	D	2-2	0-0	16	Jones 2 (1 pen) [53 (p), 90]	6602
3		21	H	Colchester U	L	1-2	0-1	19	Dawson [47]	3016
4		28	A	Brentford	W	3-1	1-1	12	Elding [11], O'Grady [60], Kennedy, J [62]	4636
5	Sept	4	A	Southampton	W	2-0	1-0	9	O'Grady [45], Jones [68]	18,169
6		11	H	Walsall	W	3-2	2-2	5	Thompson, Josh [27], Elding [44], Jones (pen) [65]	3174
7		18	A	Milton Keynes D	D	1-1	1-1	5	Kennedy, J [20]	7034
8		25	H	Plymouth Arg	D	1-1	0-1	6	Dawson [64]	3294
9		28	H	Huddersfield T	W	3-0	1-0	—	Kennedy, J [7], Akpa Akpro [88], O'Grady [90]	6121
10	Oct	2	A	Exeter C	L	0-1	0-0	5		5363
11		9	H	Yeovil T	L	0-1	0-0	9		3150
12		16	A	Bristol R	L	1-2	0-1	12	Anthony (og) [86]	5872
13		23	H	Dagenham & R	W	3-2	2-0	9	O'Grady [22], Elding [35], Jones [58]	2650
14		30	A	Leyton Orient	L	1-2	1-0	13	O'Grady [45]	4880
15	Nov	13	A	Sheffield W	L	0-2	0-0	16		16,520
16		20	H	Swindon T	D	3-3	1-1	14	Jones 2 (1 pen) [20 (p), 85], Grant [64]	2866
17		23	A	Carlisle U	D	1-1	0-1	—	Jones (pen) [62]	7412
18		27	H	Oldham Ath	D	1-1	1-1	—	Done [36]	6483
19	Dec	10	A	Peterborough U	L	1-2	0-1	—	Akpa Akpro [79]	4233
20	Jan	1	H	Tranmere R	W	3-2	2-1	17	Jones 2 (1 pen) [26 (p), 44], Grant [84]	5500
21		3	A	Oldham Ath	W	2-1	0-0	16	O'Grady 2 [64, 76]	7251
22		8	A	Dagenham & R	W	1-0	0-0	—	O'Grady [74]	1948
23		15	H	Leyton Orient	D	1-1	1-0	11	Forbes (og) [35]	2731
24		18	H	Bournemouth	D	0-0	0-0	—		2312
25		22	A	Yeovil T	W	1-0	1-0	9	Jones [17]	3711
26	Feb	1	A	Tranmere R	D	1-1	0-1	10	Jones [90]	4766
27		5	A	Swindon T	D	1-1	0-0	9	Dawson [81]	7386
28		8	H	Bristol R	W	3-1	0-0	—	Dawson [72], Akpa Akpro [89], Done [90]	2372
29		12	H	Sheffield W	W	2-1	2-0	8	Done [15], Jones (pen) [27]	6154
30		26	A	Walsall	D	0-0	0-0	9		3830
31	Mar	5	H	Milton Keynes D	L	1-4	0-3	13	Dawson [81]	2837
32		8	A	Huddersfield T	L	1-2	0-2	—	Jones [90]	12,531
33		12	H	Exeter C	L	0-1	0-1	15		2726
34		15	H	Notts Co	W	1-0	0-0	—	Dawson [46]	2019
35		19	A	Plymouth Arg	W	1-0	0-0	9	Jones [49]	8361
36		25	H	Hartlepool U	W	2-0	1-0	—	Jones [23], Dawson [56]	3081
37		29	H	Charlton Ath	W	2-0	1-0	—	Kennedy, J [35], Dawson [76]	2589
38	Apr	2	H	Brighton & HA	D	2-2	1-1	7	Atkinson [22], Jones (pen) [71]	3959
39		5	A	Notts Co	W	2-1	2-0	—	Dawson [7], Atkinson [16]	4689
40		9	A	Colchester U	L	0-1	0-0	7		4052
41		12	H	Southampton	W	2-0	2-0	—	Thompson, Joe [28], O'Grady [41]	3825
42		16	H	Brentford	L	0-1	0-0	7		2963
43		23	H	Carlisle U	L	2-3	1-1	—	Thompson, Joe [30], Done [49]	3762
44		25	A	Charlton Ath	L	1-3	0-1	7	Holness [51]	13,253
45		30	H	Peterborough U	D	2-2	1-1	9	Akpa Akpro [1], Dawson [87]	3147
46	May	7	A	Bournemouth	W	2-1	1-1	9	Done [35], Gray [80]	9005

Final League Position: 9

GOALSCORERS

League (63): Jones 17 (7 pens), Dawson 10, O'Grady 9, Done 5, Akpa Akpro 4, Kennedy, J 4, Elding 3, Atkinson 2, Grant 2, Thompson, Joe 2, Gray 1, Holness 1, Thompson, Josh 1, own goals 2.
Carling Cup (3): Jones 2, Elding 1.
FA Cup (2): Dawson 1, Elding 1.
J Paint Trophy (1): Done 1.

Lillis J 23	Wiseman S 37	Widdowson J 30 + 4	Jones G 45 + 1	Holness M 46	Dawson C 44 + 1	Kennedy J 44 + 1	Barry-Murphy B 31 + 1	O'Grady C 45 + 1	Akpa Akpro J 8 + 24	Thompson Joe 19 + 13	Elding A 9 + 8	Andre H — + 1	Done M 16 + 17	Redshaw J — + 2	Tutte A 5 + 2	Thompson Josh 11 + 1	Goodall A 3 + 2	Smalley D — + 3	Flynn M — + 1	Adams N 25 + 5	Gray R — + 2	Kennedy T 6	Grant R 5 + 1	Edwards M — + 1	Daniels L 1	Dickinson L 7 + 7	Atkinson W 15 + 6	Williams O 22	Williams R 9	Match No.
1	2	3	4	5	6	7	8	9	10^1	11^2	12		13																	1
1	2	3	4	5	6	7	8^3	9	10^1	11^2	12	13	14																	2
1	2	3	4	5	6	7^2	8	9	12	11^1	10^3		14	13																3
1	2	3	4	5	6	7	8	9	12		10^1									11										4
1	2	3	4	5	6	7	8	9	12		10									11^1										5
1		3	4	5	6	7	8	9	12		10^1				2					11										6
1		3^1	4	5	6	7	8	9	14	13	10^2		11^3		2	12														7
1		3	4	5	6	7	8	9	12		10^2		11^1		2	13														8
1			4	5	6	7	8	9	14	11^3	10^2		13		2	12	3^1													9
1			4	5	6	7^2	8^3	9	12	11	10		14		2	13	3^1													10
1		3	4	5	6	7	8	9	10^3	11^1	14		13		2^2	12														11
1	2	3	4	5	6	7^2	8	9	12		10^1		13							11										12
1	2	3	4	5	6	7	8	9	12		10^1									11										13
1	2	3^1	4	5	6	7	8^2	9	13	11	10^3		14							12										14
1	2	3	4^1	5	6	7	8	9^3	13	11	14		12							10^2										15
1	2	3	4	5	6	7		9	13	11	12									8^2			3				10^1			16
1	2	3	4	5	12	7^3	8^1	9	11	14	13												3				10^2			17
1	2	3	4	5	6	7	8	9	13	11^1	12											3	15				10^2			18
	2	3	4	5	6	7	8^1	9	13	11	12											3			1		10^2			19
1	2	3	4	5	6	7	8	9	10^1	11^2			13										12							20
1	2	3	4	5	6	7	8^2	9	14	11^1	10^3		13										12							21
1		3	4	5^2	6	7	8	9	10^1				13		2											11	12			22
1		3	4	5	6	7	8^3	9	14				13		2^1								12			11^2	10			23
1	2		4	5	6	7		9	13	11	12												3			10^2	8^1			24
	2	3	4	5	6	7^2	8	9		11			13							10^1							12	1		25
	2	3	4	5	6		8	9	14	11^2			7^1							10^3						13	12	1		26
	2	3	4	5	6	7	8	9		11^1			13													12	10^2	1		27
	2	3	4	5	6	7	8^3	9	14				13							12						10^1	11^1	1		28
	2	3	4	5	0	7	8^1	9					13							12						10	11^2	1		29
	2	3	4	5	6	7^2	8	9		11										10^1						13	12	1		30
	2	3	4	5	6	7		9		11			10^2							8^1						12	13	1		31
	2	3	4	5	6	7	8	9	12											10^1							11	1		32
	2	3	4	5	6	7	8^3	9	12				14							13						10^1	11^2	1		33
	2		4	5	6	7	8	9	12											11^2						10^1	13	1	3	34
	2	13	4	5	6	7	8	9^3	12											10						14	11^1	1	3^2	35
	2		4	5	6	7		9	12	11										8						10^1		1	3	36
	2		4	5	6	7		9	12	11			13							8^2						10^1		1	3	37
	2^2	13	4	5	6	7^1		9	12	11										8						10		1	3	38
	2	13	4	5	6	7		9	12	11										8^1						10		1	3^2	39
	2	12	4	5	6	7		9	13	11			14							8^3						10^2		1	3^1	40
	2		4	5	6	7		9	10	11										8								1	3	41
	2		4	5	6	7		9	12	11^3			14							8^2						13	10^1	1	3	42
	2	3	4	5	6	7^1		9	12	11			10							8^2						13		1		43
	2	3	4	5	6	7^1	8	9	14	11^2	12									10^3						13		1		44
	2	3	12	5		7^1	8	9	13	11			14							10^2							4^3	1		45
	2	3	4	5	6		8	9^3	10^1	11	12		13							7^2							14	1		46

FA Cup
First Round　　FC United of Manchester (h)　　2-3

Carling Cup
First Round　　Barnsley　　(a)　　1-0
Second Round　　Birmingham C　　(a)　　2-3

J Paint Trophy
First Round　　Port Vale　　(a)　　1-2

ROTHERHAM UNITED   FL Championship 2

FOUNDATION

Rotherham were formed in 1870 before becoming Town in the late 1880s. Thornhill United were founded in 1877 and changed their name to Rotherham County in 1905. The Town amalgamated with Rotherham County to form Rotherham United in 1925.

Don Valley Stadium, Worksop Road, Sheffield, South Yorkshire S9 3TL.
Telephone: (08444) 140 737.
Fax: (08444) 140 744.
Ticket Office: (08444) 140 737.
Website: www.themillers.co.uk
Email: office@rotherhamunited.net
Ground Capacity: 25,000.
Record Attendance: 25,170 v Sheffield U, Division 2, 13 December 1952 (at Millmoor); 7,082 v Aldershot T, FL 2 Play-offs semi-final 2nd leg, 19 May 2010 (at Don Valley).
Pitch Measurements. 108yd × 72yd.
Chairman: Tony Stewart.
Chief Operating Officer: Paul Douglas.
Manager: Andy Scott.
Assistant Manager: Darren Patterson.
Physio: Denis Circuit.

HONOURS

Football League – Division 2:
Runners-up 2000–01;
Division 3: *Champions* 1980–81;
Runners-up 1999–2000;
Division 3 (N): *Champions* 1950–51;
Runners-up 1946–47, 1947–48, 1948–49;
Division 4: *Champions* 1988–89;
Runners-up 1991–92.

FA Cup: Best season: 5th rd, 1953, 1968.

Football League Cup:
Runners-up 1961.

Auto Windscreens Shield:
Winners 1996.

Colours: Red shirts with white design, white shorts, red stockings.
Change Colours: All sky blue with white trim.
Year Formed: 1870. *Turned Professional:* 1905. *Ltd Co.:* 1920.
Club Nickname: 'The Merry Millers'.
Previous Names: 1877, Thornhill United; 1905, Rotherham County; 1925, amalgamated with Rotherham Town under Rotherham United.
Grounds: 1870, Red House Ground; 1907, Millmoor; 2008, Don Valley Stadium.
First Football League Game: 2 September 1893, Division 2, Rotherham T v Lincoln C (a) D 1–1 – McKay; Thickett, Watson; Barr, Brown, Broadhead; Longden, Cutts, Leatherbarrow, McCormick, Pickering, (1 og). 30 August 1919, Division 2, Rotherham Co v Nottingham F (h) W 2–0 – Branston; Alton, Baines; Bailey, Coe, Stanton; Lee (1), Cawley (1), Glennon, Lees, Lamb.
Record League Victory: 8–0 v Oldham Ath, Division 3 (N), 26 May 1947 – Warnes; Selkirk, Ibbotson; Edwards, Horace Williams, Danny Williams; Wilson (2), Shaw (1), Ardron (3), Guest (1), Hainsworth (1).
Record Cup Victory: 6–0 v Spennymoor U, FA Cup 2nd rd, 17 December 1977 – McAlister; Forrest, Breckin, Womble, Stancliffe, Green, Finney, Phillips (3), Gwyther (2) (Smith), Goodfellow, Crawford (1). 6–0 v Wolverhampton W, FA Cup 1st rd, 16 November 1985 – O'Hanlon; Forrest, Dungworth, Gooding (1), Smith (1), Pickering, Birch (2), Emerson, Tynan (1), Simmons (1), Pugh. 6–0 v Kings Lynn, FA Cup 2nd rd, 6 December 1997 – Mimms; Clark, Hurst (Goodwin), Garner (1) (Hudson) (1), Warner (Bass), Richardson (1), Berry (1), Thompson, Druce (1), Glover (1), Roscoe.
Record Defeat: 1–11 v Bradford C, Division 3 (N), 25 August 1928.

sky SPORTS FACT FILE

On 21 August 2010 Rotherham United were losing 3-1 at home to Cheltenham Town after 36 minutes. They fought back to be leading 6-3 in the 66th minute with Adam Le Fondre scoring four times. Andy Warrington then saved a penalty for the Millers in the eventual 6-4 win.

Most League Points (2 for a win): 71, Division 3 (N), 1950–51.

Most League Points (3 for a win): 91, Division 2, 2000–01.

Most League Goals: 114, Division 3 (N), 1946–47.

Highest League Scorer in Season: Wally Ardron, 38, Division 3 (N), 1946–47.

Most League Goals in Total Aggregate: Gladstone Guest, 130, 1946–56.

Most League Goals in One Match: 4, Roland Bastow v York C, Division 3 (N), 9 November 1935; 4, Roland Bastow v Rochdale, Division 3 (N), 7 March 1936; 4, Wally Ardron v Crewe Alex, Division 3 (N), 5 October 1946; 4, Wally Ardron v Carlisle U, Division 3 (N), 13 September 1947; 4, Wally Ardron v Hartlepools U, Division 3 (N), 13 October 1948; 4, Ian Wilson v Liverpool, Division 2, 2 May 1955; 4, Carl Gilbert v Swansea C, Division 3, 28 September 1971; 4, Carl Airey v Chester, Division 3, 31 August 1987; 4, Shaun Goater v Hartlepool U, Division 3, 9 April 1994; 4, Lee Glover v Hull C, Division 3, 28 December 1997; 4, Darren Byfield v Millwall, Division 1, 10 August 2002; 4, Adam Le Fondre v Cheltenham T, FL 2, 21 August 2010.

Most Capped Player: Shaun Goater, 14 (36), Bermuda.

Most League Appearances: Danny Williams, 459, 1946–62.

Youngest League Player: Kevin Eley, 16 years 72 days v Scunthorpe U, 15 May 1984.

Record Transfer Fee Received: £850,000 from Cardiff C for Alan Lee, August 2003.

Record Transfer Fee Paid: £150,000 to Millwall for Tony Towner, August 1980; £150,000 to Port Vale for Lee Glover, August 1996; £150,000 to Burnley for Alan Lee, September 2000; £150,000 to Reading for Martin Butler, September 2003. £150,000 to Crewe Alex for Tom Pope, June 2009; £150,000 to Burnley for John Mullin, October 2001.

MANAGERS

Billy Heald 1925–29 *(Secretary only for long spell)*
Stanley Davies 1929–30
Billy Heald 1930–33
Reg Freeman 1934–52
Andy Smailes 1952–58
Tom Johnston 1958–62
Danny Williams 1962–65
Jack Mansell 1965–67
Tommy Docherty 1967–68
Jimmy McAnearney 1968–73
Jimmy McGuigan 1973–79
Ian Porterfield 1979–81
Emlyn Hughes 1981–83
George Kerr 1983–85
Norman Hunter 1985–87
Dave Cusack 1987–88
Billy McEwan 1988–91
Phil Henson 1991–94
Archie Gemmill/John McGovern 1994–96
Danny Bergara 1996–97
Ronnie Moore 1997–2005
Mick Harford 2005
Alan Knill 2005–07
Mark Robins 2007–09
Ronnie Moore 2009–11
Andy Scott May 2011

Football League Record: 1893 Rotherham Town elected to Division 2; 1896 Failed re-election; 1919 Rotherham County elected to Division 2; 1923–51 Division 3 (N); 1951–68 Division 2; 1968–73 Division 3; 1973–75 Division 4; 1975–81 Division 3; 1981–83 Division 2; 1983–88 Division 3; 1988–89 Division 4; 1989–91 Division 3; 1991–92 Division 4; 1992–97 Division 2; 1997–2000 Division 3; 2000–01 Division 2; 2001–04 Division 1; 2004–05 FL C; 2005–07 FL 1; 2007– FL 2.

LATEST SEQUENCES

Longest Sequence of League Wins: 9, 2.2.1982 – 6.3.1982.

Longest Sequence of League Defeats: 8, 7.4.1956 – 18.8.1956.

Longest Sequence of League Draws: 6, 13.10.1969 – 22.11.1969.

Longest Sequence of Unbeaten League Matches: 18, 13.10.1969 – 7.2.1970.

Longest Sequence Without a League Win: 21, 9.5.2004 – 20.11.2004.

Successive Scoring Runs: 30 from 3.4.1954.

Successive Non-scoring Runs: 6 from 21.8.2004.

TEN YEAR LEAGUE RECORD

		P	W	D	L	F	A	Pts	Pos
2001-02	Div 1	46	10	19	17	52	66	49	21
2002-03	Div 1	46	15	14	17	62	62	59	15
2003-04	Div 1	46	13	15	18	53	61	54	17
2004-05	FL C	46	5	14	27	35	69	29	24
2005-06	FL 1	46	12	16	18	52	62	52	20
2006-07	FL 1	46	13	9	24	58	75	38	23
2007-08	FL 2	46	21	11	14	62	58	64*	9
2008-09	FL 2	46	21	12	13	60	46	58†	14
2009-10	FL 2	46	21	10	15	55	52	73	5
2010-11	FL 2	46	17	15	14	75	60	66	9

*10 pts deducted; †17 points deducted.

DID YOU KNOW ?

In February 1982 due to earlier postponements, Rotherham United were forced to play eight League games and won them all, scoring fifteen goals and conceding just three. It also moved them from the relegation zone into fifth place by the end of the month.

ROTHERHAM UNITED 2010–11 LEAGUE RECORD

Match No.	Date	Venue	Opponents	Result	H/T Score	Lg Pos.	Goalscorers	Attendance
1	Aug 7	H	Lincoln C	W 2-1	1-0	—	Le Fondre [9], Cresswell [88]	3772
2	14	A	Morecambe	D 0-0	0-0	7		3258
3	21	H	Cheltenham T	W 6-4	2-3	3	Le Fondre 4 [16, 48, 50, 66], Harrison [41], Cresswell [55]	3072
4	28	A	Hereford U	W 1-0	1-0	3	Warne [45]	2166
5	Sept 4	A	Shrewsbury T	L 0-1	0-1	5		6206
6	11	H	Burton Alb	D 3-3	3-0	5	Ellison [1], Cresswell [34], Le Fondre [38]	3516
7	18	A	Barnet	W 4-1	0-0	5	Ellison [69], Pope [72], Harrison [76], Le Fondre [89]	1731
8	25	A	Chesterfield	W 1-0	0-0	3	Le Fondre [53]	5365
9	28	H	Bradford C	D 0-0	0-0	—		3872
10	Oct 2	A	Bury	D 1-1	0-1	3	Le Fondre [47]	3788
11	9	H	Stevenage	D 1-1	1-0	3	Law [45]	4037
12	16	A	Accrington S	W 3-2	1-1	3	Le Fondre (pen) [18], Geohaghon [81], Cresswell [90]	2256
13	23	H	Wycombe W	L 3-4	2-3	4	Le Fondre 2 (1 pen) [23, 69 (p)], Taylor, J [39]	3651
14	30	A	Southend U	L 0-1	0-1	5		5533
15	Nov 2	H	Macclesfield T	D 1-1	0-0	—	Le Fondre [85]	2548
16	13	A	Oxford U	W 2-1	2-1	6	Le Fondre 2 [25, 37]	3891
17	20	A	Crewe Alex	W 1-0	1-0	4	Dugdale (og) [2]	4301
18	23	H	Northampton T	D 2-2	2-2	—	Taylor, R [4], Marshall [19]	2490
19	Dec 11	H	Aldershot T	W 1-0	1-0	4	Le Fondre [40]	2754
20	Jan 1	H	Port Vale	W 5-0	2-0	2	Law [10], Taylor, R 2 [18, 68], Atkinson [46], Randall [85]	3994
21	3	A	Macclesfield T	W 2-0	1-0	2	Taylor, J [28], Fenton [84]	2316
22	11	A	Stockport Co	D 3-3	1-1	—	Ellison [34], Grieve (og) [84], Taylor, R [90]	3612
23	15	H	Southend U	L 1-2	0-2	3	Fenton [61]	4310
24	22	A	Wycombe W	L 0-1	0-1	3		4181
25	25	A	Stevenage	L 0-3	0-1	—		1549
26	29	H	Stockport Co	W 4-0	3-0	—	Brown (og) [12], Taylor, R 2 [21, 57], Le Fondre [34]	4876
27	Feb 1	A	Port Vale	L 0-1	0-0	3		4515
28	5	H	Crewe Alex	W 3-1	1-0	3	Fenton [43], Le Fondre [84], Taylor, R [89]	3750
29	8	A	Gillingham	L 1-3	1-2	—	Law [7]	4824
30	12	A	Oxford U	L 1-2	1-1	4	Law [36]	6615
31	15	H	Accrington S	W 2-0	0-0	—	Daley [58], Le Fondre [90]	2529
32	26	A	Burton Alb	W 4-2	1-2	3	Mullins [6], Marshall [75], Le Fondre [89], Taylor, J [90]	3596
33	Mar 1	A	Torquay U	D 1-1	0-1	—	Taylor, R [73]	1514
34	5	H	Barnet	D 0-0	0-0	4		3566
35	8	A	Bradford C	L 1-2	1-1	—	Marshall [38]	10,910
36	12	H	Bury	D 0-0	0-0	4		4620
37	18	A	Chesterfield	L 0-5	0-3	—		10,089
38	25	A	Lincoln C	W 6-0	2-0	—	Thomas-Moore 3 (1 pen) [9, 50, 63 (p)], Harrison [14], Taylor, R [53], Taylor, J [87]	3766
39	29	H	Shrewsbury T	L 1-3	0-2	—	Le Fondre [70]	3471
40	Apr 2	H	Morecambe	L 0-1	0-0	10		3661
41	9	A	Cheltenham T	D 1-1	1-0	10	Taylor, J [11]	2413
42	16	A	Hereford U	D 0-0	0-0	10		3770
43	22	H	Northampton T	D 2-2	2-0	—	Rodgers (og) [5], Taylor, R [45]	5167
44	25	H	Gillingham	L 0-1	0-0	9		3455
45	30	A	Aldershot T	D 2-2	1-2	10	Le Fondre 2 [32, 55]	2107
46	May 7	H	Torquay U	W 3-1	2-1	9	Taylor, R [10], Harrison [33], Banks [80]	3379

Final League Position: 9

GOALSCORERS

League (75): Le Fondre 23 (2 pens), Taylor, R 11, Taylor, J 5, Cresswell 4, Harrison 4, Law 4, Ellison 3, Fenton 3, Marshall 3, Thomas-Moore 3 (1 pen), Atkinson 1, Banks 1, Daley 1, Geohaghon 1, Mullins 1, Pope 1, Randall 1, Warne 1, own goals 4.
Carling Cup (1): Marshall 1.
FA Cup (0).
J Paint Trophy (5): Bradley 1, Cresswell 1, Ellison 1 (pen), Le Fondre 1, Taylor, R 1.

Warrington A 38	Holden D 4 + 2	Newey T 38	Harrison D 23 + 7	Cresswell R 21 + 1	Geohaghon E 14	Law N 44	Taylor J 37 + 5	Elliott T 4 + 2	Le Fondre A 40 + 5	Ellison K 20 + 3	Bradley M 14 + 7	Marshall M 26 + 10	Warne P 3 + 8	Mullins J 35	Fenton N 31 + 1	Pope T 9 + 9	Taylor R 30 + 4	Ashworth L 3 + 6	Randall M 3 + 7	Coid D 9	Brogan S 1	Annerson J 8 + 1	Green J 5 + 2	Atkinson W 3	Tonge D 21 + 2	Thomas-Moore I 11 + 1	Kennedy C 4 + 1	Daley O 2 + 6	Henderson L 5 + 6	Banks 0 — + 1	Match No.
1	2	3	4^1	5	6	7	8	9	10	11	12																				1
1	2	3	4	5	6	7	8	9^1	10	11		12																			2
1	2	3	4	5	6	7	8	9^1	10	11^2		12	13																		3
1	2	3	4	5	6	7	8		10	11^2	13	12	9^1																		4
1		3	4	5	6	7	8	9^1	10	11			12	2^2	13																5
1	12	3	4^2	5	6	7^3	8		10	11	13		9	2^1	14																6
1		3	4	5	6	7	8^1		10	11	13		9^2	2	12																7
1		3	4^1	5	6	7	8		10	11	12			2		9															8
1		3	4^1	5	6	7^2	8		10	11	12		13	2		9^3	14														9
1		3	4		6	7	8		10	11	9^1	12		2	5																10
1	12	3	14		6	7	8		10	11	4^3			2	5^1	9^2	13														11
1		3	12	5	6	7	8^1		10	11	4^2			2		9	13														12
1		3	12		6	7^1	8		10	11	4^2	13		2		9^3	14	5													13
1		3	14		6	7^2	8		10	11^1		12		2	5	13	9	4^3													14
1		3	4	6		7^1	8	13	10	11^2	14	12		2	5	9^3															15
1		3		5^1		7	14	10	13	4	8				6	9^3	12					2	11^2								16
		3				7	12	10	11^2	4	8	13		6	5^1	9						2	1								17
	13					7	12	10	11^1	4^2	8			6	5	9						2	1	3							18
1		3		5^1		7	8	10	13		11			6	9	12								4^2							19
1		3				7^2	8	10^3		11				6	5	14	9	12	13	2^1		4									20
1		3				7	8	10		11				5	6	13	9^2	12					4^1	2							21
1		3				7	8	10	11^2			7		6	5	12	9							2							22
1		3				7	8	10	11^2		4^1	13		6	5	9	12							2							23
1						7	8^4	10^1		11				6	5	12	9	4					3		2						24
1		4^1				7		10^1	11^2		8^3	13		6	5	14	9	12						3		2					25
1	3	4				7^2		10	12		8^1			6	5^3		9	14	13						2	11					26
1	3	4				7		10	12		8^1			6	5		9								2	11					27
1	3		4	8				10			7^1			6	5		9	12							2	11					28
1^6	3		4	8				10			7^1			6	5		9	13	12		15				2	11					29
1			4	8				10						6	5	9^1	7								2	11	3^8	12			30
1	3	12	4	8				10			7^1			6	5										2			11	9		31
1		3	4	8				10			7			6	5	9					2							11^1	12		32
1		3	4	8				10			7			6^1	5	9	12				2								11		33
1		3^4	4	8				10			7^2			6	5	9					2						13	12	11^1		34
1			4	8				10			7			6	5	9					2^1					12	11	3	10		35
1		12	5	4	8^1		10				7			6		9					2					11^2	3	13			36
1		5		4	8		10				7^3			6		9					2					12	11^2	3^1	13	14	37
1	3	4	12		7	14		13		8^3	11			6	5^1	9									2	10^2					38
1	3	4			7	12		13		8	11^2			6		9	5^1								2	10^3		14			39
1	3	4^3			11	14		10		8^1	7			6	5		9^2								2			12	13		40
	3	4	5		7	8		12				11^2			6	10^1	9				1				2			13		41
	3	4	5		7	8		12			11^1	13			6	10^2	9				1				2					42
	3	4	5		7^1	8		10^3		11					6	14	9^2				1	12			2	13					43
	3	4	5			8		13			7^1	14			6^3	10					1	11			2	9^2		12			44
	3^1	4	5			8		10			7	13			6	9					1	12			2			11^2			45
		4	5			7^3	8		10			11	13			9^1	6^2				1	3			2			12	14		46

FA Cup
First Round — York C — (h) 0-0 / (a) 0-3

Carling Cup
First Round — Peterborough U — (a) 1-4

J Paint Trophy
First Round — Lincoln C — (h) 1-0
Second Round — Burton Alb — (a) 2-1
Northern Quarter-Final — Huddersfield T — (h) 2-5

SCUNTHORPE UNITED FL Championship 1

FOUNDATION

The year of foundation for Scunthorpe United has often been quoted as 1910, but the club can trace its history back to 1899 when Brumby Hall FC, who played on the Old Showground, consolidated their position by amalgamating with some other clubs and changing their name to Scunthorpe United. The year 1910 was when that club amalgamated with North Lindsey United as Scunthorpe and Lindsey United. The link is Mr W. T. Lockwood whose chairmanship covers both years.

Glanford Park, Doncaster Road, Scunthorpe DN15 8TD.
Telephone: (0871) 221 1899.
Fax: (01724) 857 986.
Ticket Office: (0871) 221 1899 (option 1).
Website: www.scunthorpe-united.co.uk
Email: admin@scunthorpe-united.co.uk
Ground Capacity: 9,088.
Record Attendance: 23,935 v Portsmouth, FA Cup 4th rd, 30 January 1954 (at Old Showground). 9,077 v Manchester U, League Cup 3rd rd, 22 September 2010 (at Glanford Park).
Pitch Measurements: 112yd × 72yd.
Chairman: Steve Wharton.
Vice-chairman: Rex Garton.
Manager: Alan Knill.
Assistant Manager: Chris Brass.
Physio: Alex Dalton.
Colours: Claret shirts with light blue sleeves, white shorts, claret stockings.
Change Colours: White shirts with blue inserts and claret cuffs on sleeves, white shorts, white stockings.
Year Formed: 1899. *Turned Professional:* 1912. *Ltd Co.:* 1912.
Club Nickname: 'The Iron'.
Previous Names: Amalgamated first with Brumby Hall then North Lindsey United to become Scunthorpe & Lindsey United, 1910; 1958 Scunthorpe United.
Grounds: 1899, Old Showground; 1988, Glanford Park.
First Football League Game: 19 August 1950, Division 3 (N), v Shrewsbury T (h) D 0–0 – Thompson; Barker, Brownsword; Allen, Taylor, McCormick; Mosby, Payne, Gorin, Rees, Boyes.
Record League Victory: 8–1 v Luton T, Division 3, 24 April 1965 – Sidebottom; Horstead, Hemstead; Smith, Neale, Lindsey; Bramley (1), Scott, Thomas (5), Mahy (1), Wilson (1). 8–1 v Torquay U (a), Division 3, 28 October 1995 – Samways; Housham, Wilson, Ford (1), Knill (1), Hope (Nicholson), Thornber, Bullimore (Walsh), McFarlane (4) (Young), Eyre (2), Paterson.

HONOURS

Football League – FL 1: *Champions* 2006–07;
FL 2: *Runners-up* 2004–05;
Division 3 (N): *Champions* 1957–58.
FA Cup: Best season: 5th rd, 1958, 1970.
Football League Cup: Best season: 4th rd, 2010.
Johnstone's Paint Trophy: *Runners-up* 2008–09.

sky SPORTS FACT FILE

Paul Stanley made just two first team appearances for Scunthorpe United in his career. Both were in the FA Cup during 1984–85. He led the attack against Nuneaton Borough in a 1-1 draw and kept his place for the replay which produced a 2-1 win for United.

Record Cup Victory: 9–0 v Boston U, FA Cup 1st rd, 21 November 1953 – Malan; Hubbard, Brownsword; Sharpe, White, Bushby; Mosby (1), Haigh (3), Whitfield (2), Gregory (1), Mervyn Jones (2).

Record Defeat: 0–8 v Carlisle U, Division 3 (N), 25 December 1952.

Most League Points (2 for a win): 66, Division 3 (N), 1956–57, 1957–58.

Most League Points (3 for a win): 91, FL 1, 2006–07.

Most League Goals: 88, Division 3 (N), 1957–58.

Highest League Scorer in Season: Barrie Thomas, 31, Division 2, 1961–62.

Most League Goals in Total Aggregate: Steve Cammack, 110, 1979–81, 1981–86.

Most League Goals in One Match: 5, Barrie Thomas v Luton T, Division 3, 24 April 1965.

Most Capped Player: Grant McCann, 10 (33), Northern Ireland.

Most League Appearances: Jack Brownsword, 595, 1950–65.

Youngest League Player: Mike Farrell, 16 years 240 days v Workington, 8 November 1975.

Record Transfer Fee Received: £2,500,000 from Celtic for Gary Hooper, August 2010.

Record Transfer Fee Paid: £700,000 to Hibernian for Rob Jones, July 2009.

Football League Record: 1950 Elected to Division 3 (N); 1958–64 Division 2; 1964–68 Division 3; 1968–72 Division 4; 1972–73 Division 3; 1973–83 Division 4; 1983–84 Division 3; 1984–92 Division 4; 1992–99 Division 3; 1999–2000 Division 2; 2000–04 Division 3; 2004–05 FL 2; 2005–07 FL 1; 2007–08 FL C; 2008–09 FL 1; 2009–11 FL C; 2011– FL 1.

MANAGERS

Harry Allcock 1915–53
(Secretary-Manager)
Tom Crilly 1936–37
Bernard Harper 1946–48
Leslie Jones 1950–51
Bill Corkhill 1952–56
Ron Suart 1956–58
Tony McShane 1959
Bill Lambton 1959
Frank Soo 1959–60
Dick Duckworth 1960–64
Fred Goodwin 1964–66
Ron Ashman 1967–73
Ron Bradley 1973–74
Dick Rooks 1974–76
Ron Ashman 1976–81
John Duncan 1981–83
Allan Clarke 1983–84
Frank Barlow 1984–87
Mick Buxton 1987–91
Bill Green 1991–93
Richard Money 1993–94
David Moore 1994–96
Mick Buxton 1996–97
Brian Laws 1997–2004; 2004–06
Nigel Adkins 2006–10
Ian Baraclough 2010–11
Alan Knill March 2011–

LATEST SEQUENCES

Longest Sequence of League Wins: 7, 27.1.2007 – 3.3.2007.

Longest Sequence of League Defeats: 8, 29.11.1997 – 20.1.1998.

Longest Sequence of League Draws: 6, 2.1.1984 – 25.2.1984.

Longest Sequence of Unbeaten League Matches: 19, 22.12.2006 – 6.4.2007.

Longest Sequence Without a League Win: 14, 22.3.1975 – 6.9.1975.

Successive Scoring Runs: 24 from 13.1.2007.

Successive Non-scoring Runs: 7 from 19.4.1975.

TEN YEAR LEAGUE RECORD

		P	W	D	L	F	A	Pts	Pos
2001-02	Div 3	46	19	14	13	74	56	71	8
2002-03	Div 3	46	19	15	12	68	49	72	5
2003-04	Div 3	46	11	16	19	69	72	49	22
2004-05	FL 2	46	22	14	10	69	42	80	2
2005-06	FL 1	46	15	15	16	68	73	60	12
2006-07	FL 1	46	26	13	7	73	35	91	1
2007-08	FL C	46	11	13	22	46	69	46	23
2008-09	FL 1	46	22	10	14	82	63	76	6
2009-10	FL C	46	14	10	22	62	84	52	20
2010-11	FL C	46	12	6	28	43	87	42	24

DID YOU KNOW ?

Although their record FA Cup victory in the competition proper is 9-0, Scunthorpe United can claim to have twice beaten Hull Holderness 10-0! The first occasion was in a first qualifying round on 8 October 1921, the second a preliminary round tie on 18 September 1926.

SCUNTHORPE UNITED 2010–11 LEAGUE RECORD

Match No.	Date	Venue	Opponents	Result	H/T Score	Lg Pos.	Goalscorers	Attendance
1	Aug 7	A	Reading	W 2-1	1-1	—	Thompson [9], Jones [60]	15,914
2	14	H	Norwich C	L 0-1	0-0	13		6042
3	21	A	QPR	L 0-2	0-2	17		12,046
4	28	H	Crystal Palace	W 3-0	2-0	11	Forte 2 [33, 45], O'Connor (pen) [71]	5292
5	Sept 11	H	Bristol C	L 0-2	0-1	15		5185
6	14	A	Sheffield U	W 4-0	1-0	—	Dagnall 2 [33, 73], Mirfin [63], Woolford [90]	19,390
7	18	A	Swansea C	L 0-2	0-0	16		13,597
8	25	H	Ipswich T	D 1-1	1-0	16	Mirfin [30]	5931
9	28	H	Barnsley	D 0-0	0-0	—		5421
10	Oct 2	A	Leicester C	L 1-3	0-1	17	O'Connor [60]	20,652
11	16	H	Doncaster R	L 1-3	1-1	19	Woolford [11]	7005
12	19	A	Preston NE	W 3-2	1-0	—	Dagnall [4], O'Connor [85], Woolford [82]	11,179
13	23	A	Watford	W 2-0	2-0	15	Byrne [28], Woolford [45]	12,366
14	30	H	Leeds U	L 1-4	1-1	16	Byrne [27]	8122
15	Nov 6	A	Hull C	W 1-0	0-0	15	O'Connor [89]	21,873
16	9	H	Middlesbrough	L 0-2	0-2	—		5475
17	13	H	Cardiff C	L 2-4	1-3	18	McDonald [45], N'Guessan [73]	5333
18	20	A	Derby Co	L 2-3	1-2	20	Forte [27], O'Connor (pen) [75]	25,189
19	27	H	Coventry C	L 0-2	0-1	21		4397
20	Dec 4	A	Millwall	L 0-3	0-1	—		8937
21	28	A	Burnley	W 2-0	1-0	22	Woolford [14], Dagnall [84]	15,043
22	Jan 1	A	Doncaster R	L 0-3	0-3	22		9447
23	3	H	Watford	L 1-2	0-0	23	Woolford [60]	4498
24	15	A	Leeds U	L 0-4	0-3	23		25,446
25	22	H	Burnley	D 0-0	0-0	23		4334
26	Feb 1	A	Middlesbrough	L 0-2	0-1	23		14,364
27	5	H	Hull C	L 1-5	0-1	23	Garner [55]	6835
28	12	A	Cardiff C	L 0-1	0-0	23		21,604
29	16	H	Nottingham F	W 1-0	1-0	—	Dagnall [19]	5578
30	19	H	Derby Co	D 0-0	0-0	23		5696
31	22	H	Sheffield U	W 3-2	2-2	—	Garner 2 (1 pen) [37 (p), 44], Miller [53]	6281
32	26	A	Bristol C	L 0-2	0-1	22		14,423
33	Mar 1	A	Portsmouth	L 0-2	0-0	—		14,252
34	5	H	Swansea C	W 1-0	0-0	22	Garner (pen) [71]	4608
35	8	A	Barnsley	L 1-2	0-0	—	Collins [90]	10,250
36	12	H	Leicester C	L 0-3	0-1	22		6528
37	15	H	Preston NE	L 0-3	0-3	—		4190
38	19	A	Ipswich T	L 0-2	0-1	23		17,787
39	Apr 2	A	Norwich C	L 0-6	0-2	24		26,512
40	9	H	QPR	W 4-1	1-1	22	Garner 2 [28, 48], O'Connor [58], Duffy [79]	6061
41	12	H	Reading	L 0-2	0-0	—		4458
42	16	A	Crystal Palace	W 2-1	1-0	22	Mirfin [25], Nunez [57]	17,810
43	22	A	Coventry C	D 1-1	1-1	—	Nunez [38]	16,705
44	25	H	Millwall	L 1-2	0-1	23	O'Connor (pen) [88]	5190
45	30	A	Nottingham F	L 1-5	1-2	23	O'Connor (pen) [36]	27,949
46	May 7	H	Portsmouth	D 1-1	1-0	24	Nunez [27]	5142

Final League Position: 24

GOALSCORERS

League (43): O'Connor 8 (4 pens), Garner 6 (2 pens), Woolford 6, Dagnall 5, Forte 3, Mirfin 3, Nunez 3, Byrne 2, Collins 1, Duffy 1, Jones 1, McDonald 1, Miller 1, N'Guessan 1, Thompson 1.
Carling Cup (8): Dagnall 2, Woolford 2, Collins 1, Forte 1, O'Connor 1 (pen), Wright, J 1.
FA Cup (1): Collins 1.

Murphy J 29	Nolan E 32 + 3	McNulty J 5 + 1	Togwell S 34 + 2	Mirfin D 23	Jones R 13 + 1	Wright J 31 + 5	O'Connor M 25 + 7	Dagnall C 31 + 6	Forte J 18 + 6	Thompson G 4 + 8	Raynes M 15 + 1	Woolford M 18 + 6	Wright A 16 + 4	Collins N 19 + 13	Canavan N 6 + 2	Grant R 7 + 20	Byrne C 20 + 1	Sears F 9	Slocombe S — + 2	Warner T 2	McDonald K 3 + 2	N'Guessan D 3	McClenahan T — + 1	Godden M — + 5	Cowan-Hall P — + 1	Reid P 12	Ibrahim A 4 + 7	Lillis J 15	Hughes A 18 + 1	Duffy M 19 + 3	Garner J 17 + 1	Nelson M 20	Miller L 12 + 6	Gordon B 13 + 1	Nunez R 8	Williams M 5	Match No.
1	2	3		4	5¹	6	7	8³	9²	10	11	12	13	14																							1
1	2	3		5	6	4¹	8²	9	10	7		11	12	13																							2
1	2	3²	4			7	8	9	10			5	11¹		6	12	13																				3
1	3			4	5	6	7	8¹	9²	10		12		11		13	2																				4
1	2			4²	5	6¹	7	8	9	10		13		11	12	14	3³																				5
1	2			4	5		7³	8¹	9²	10	14	12		11	6	13	3																				6
1	2			4²	5	14	7	8	9³	10		12		11¹	6	13	3																				7
1	2			4	5	6	7²	12	9	10		11		8¹		13	3																				8
1	2			4	5	6	7²	13	9	10		11		8¹		12	3																				9
1	2			4²	5		7	12	9	10		11		13	6	8¹	3																				10
1	2			4²	5	6	7	13	9	10¹	12	11		8³		14	3																				11
1⁰	2			5	6¹	7	8	9²	13	12	11		4			3	10		15																		12
	2			4	5		7	8	9¹	13	12	6	11			3	10²			1																	13
	2			4	5¹		7³	8	9²	14	13	6	11		12	3	10			1																	14
1	2			4			7	8	9¹	12		6	11²	14	5	13	3	10³																			15
1	2						7³	8	9¹²	12		6	11	4¹	5	14	3	10				13															16
1	2	14				6³		8	12	9			5	11¹		13	3	10²			4	7															17
1		3				6	7	8	9				14	5¹	13	2	10				4	11²	12														18
1	2	3				6	7²	8	12	9			13	5			10¹				4	11															19
1	2			4		6	7³	8¹	9	13	12			11		3					5	10²	14														20
1	2			4		6	14	8	9³	10²	7¹			11		3	12				5				13												21
1	2			4	5	13	8²	9³	10¹	14				11		3	7				6				12												22
1	2	13		5		4	8²	9	10¹	7²				11		3					6				12	14											23
1	3			4				9²		12				5	11	2	7	10¹							13		6	8									24
	13			4				9¹	10³					5	11	2			12						14	6	8	1	3	7²							25
	3			4				13		9²						2	12	8¹								5	6⁴	1	11	7	10						26
	3			4						2	12	11¹														5		1	8	7	9	6	10				27
	2			4				8³			12	14														5	13	1	11	7¹	9²	6	10	3			28
	2¹			4				8	9³		12	13	14													5		1	11	7¹		6	10	3			29
				4				8¹								2	12	13								5	14	1	11	7³	9²	6	10	3			30
				4²				8					14			2	12									5	13	1	11¹	7³	9	6	10	3			31
				4				8				12	14			2										5¹	13	1	11	7²	9	6	10³	3			32
	2				5			8¹					4			9											11²	1	12	7	13	6	10	3			33
				4				8					5			2	7²	14									12	1	11¹	13	9³	6	10	3			34
				4¹				8²					14	5		2	7										13	1	11	12	9	6	10³	3			35
	12			4				9³						5		2	13										14	1	11²	8	7	6	10	3¹			36
	3					7	13	14				6	12	4												5²	1	11	10³	9	2	8					37
	2			5			8	4	14					13	12												1	11	7²	9	6	10³	3¹			38
1	2	12					4	14					5			8²									3⁴		11	13	9³	6	7		10¹		39
1				4²	5		12	8¹	9		13					2										11	10³	6	14	3	7				40
1				4	5		12	8¹	9							2										7²	10	6	13	3	11				41
1				4	5			9²				8	12			2										7¹	10⁴	6	13	11	3			42
1				4	5		12	9²		8¹	10					2										7³	6	13	14	11	3			43
1	2¹			4	5		12	9		8	13															7²	10	6		11	3			44
1	14			4	5		8	9¹		2³	13	10													7²	6	12		11	3			45
				4			8			2	12	10¹		15		5	1⁰		7²	9	6	13		11	3								46

FA Cup
Third Round   Everton   (h)   1-5

Carling Cup
First Round   Oldham Ath   (h)   2-1
Second Round   Sheffield W   (h)   4-2
Third Round   Manchester U   (h)   2-5

SHEFFIELD UNITED   FL Championship 1

Bramall Lane Ground, Cherry Street, Bramall Lane, Sheffield S2 4SU.

Telephone: (0871) 995 1899.

Fax: 0871 663 2430.

Ticket Office: (0871) 995 1889.

Website: www.sufc.co.uk

Email: info@sufc.co.uk

Ground Capacity: 32,500.

Record Attendance: 68,287 v Leeds U, FA Cup 5th rd, 15 February 1936.

Pitch Measurements: 101.1m × 62.2m.

Chairman (PLC): Kevin McCabe.

Chairman (Football Club): Chris Steer.

Chief Executive: Trevor Birch.

Secretary: Donna Fletcher.

Manager: Danny Wilson.

Assistant Manager: Frank Barlow.

Physio: Paul Teather.

Colours: Red and white striped shirts with red sleeves, black shorts, black stockings.

Change Colours: White shirts with red trim, white shorts, white stockings.

Year Formed: 1889. *Turned Professional:* 1889. *Ltd Co.:* 1899.

Club Nickname: 'The Blades'.

Ground: 1889, Bramall Lane.

First Football League Game: 3 September 1892, Division 2, v Lincoln C (h) W 4–2 – Lilley; Witham, Cain; Howell, Hendry, Needham (1); Wallace, Dobson, Hammond (3), Davies, Drummond.

Record League Victory: 10–0 v Burslem Port Vale (a), Division 2, 10 December 1892 – Howlett; Witham, Lilley; Howell, Hendry, Needham; Drummond (1), Wallace (1), Hammond (4), Davies (2), Watson (2).

Record Cup Victory: 6–1 v Scarborough (a), FA Cup 1st qualifying rd, 5 October 1889 – Howlett; Stringer, Gilmartin, Mack, Hobson, Hudson, Galbraith (2), Robertson (1), Fraser (2), Duncan, Mosforth (1). 6–1 v Loughborough, FA Cup 4th qualifying rd, 6 December 1890. 6–1 v Lincoln C, League Cup, 22 August 2000 – Tracey; Uhlenbeek, Weber, Woodhouse (Ford), Murphy, Sandford, Devlin (pen), Ribeiro (Santos), Bent (3), Kelly (1) (Thompson), Jagielka, og (1).

HONOURS

Football League – FL C:
Runners-up 2005–06;
Division 1: *Champions* 1897–98;
Runners-up 1896–97, 1899–1900;
Division 2: *Champions* 1952–53;
Runners-up 1892–93, 1938–39, 1960–61, 1970–71, 1989–90;
Division 3: *Runners-up* 1988–89;
Division 4: *Champions* 1981–82.
FA Cup: *Winners* 1899, 1902, 1915, 1925; *Runners-up* 1901, 1936.
Football League Cup: semi-final 2003.

sky SPORTS FACT FILE

On 28 August 2010 right-back Jean Calve, playing for Sheffield United against Preston North End on a year's loan from Nancy, scored on his debut with a shot from 30 yards. It ended the club's 410-minute goal drought. For Calve it was his first ever goal.

Record Defeat: 0–13 v Bolton W, FA Cup 2nd rd, 1 February 1890.

Most League Points (2 for a win): 60, Division 2, 1952–53.

Most League Points (3 for a win): 96, Division 4, 1981–82.

Most League Goals: 102, Division 1, 1925–26.

Highest League Scorer in Season: Jimmy Dunne, 41, Division 1, 1930–31.

Most League Goals in Total Aggregate: Harry Johnson, 205, 1919–30.

Most League Goals in One Match: 5, Harry Hammond v Bootle, Division 2, 26 November 1892; 5, Harry Johnson v West Ham U, Division 1, 26 December 1927.

Most Capped Player: Billy Gillespie, 25, Northern Ireland.

Most League Appearances: Joe Shaw, 629, 1948–66.

Youngest League Player: Steve Hawes, 17 years 47 days v WBA, 2 September 1995.

Record Transfer Fee Received: £4,000,000 from Everton for Phil Jagielka, July 2007.

Record Transfer Fee Paid: £4,000,000 to Everton for James Beattie, August 2007.

Football League Record: 1892 Elected to Division 2; 1893–1934 Division 1; 1934–39 Division 2; 1946–49 Division 1; 1949–53 Division 2; 1953–56 Division 1; 1956–61 Division 2; 1961–68 Division 1; 1968–71 Division 2; 1971–76 Division 1; 1976–79 Division 2; 1979–81 Division 3; 1981–82 Division 4; 1982–84 Division 3; 1984–88 Division 2; 1988–89 Division 3; 1989–90 Division 2; 1990–92 Division 1; 1992–94 FA Premier League; 1994–2004 Division 1; 2004–06 FL C; 2006–07 FA Premier League; 2007–11 FL C; 2011– FL 1.

MANAGERS

J. B. Wostinholm 1889–99 *(Secretary-Manager)*
John Nicholson 1899–1932
Ted Davison 1932–52
Reg Freeman 1952–55
Joe Mercer 1955–58
Johnny Harris 1959–68 *(continued as General Manager to 1970)*
Arthur Rowley 1968–69
Johnny Harris *(General Manager resumed Team Manager duties)* 1969–73
Ken Furphy 1973–75
Jimmy Sirrel 1975–77
Harry Haslam 1978–81
Martin Peters 1981
Ian Porterfield 1981–86
Billy McEwan 1986–88
Dave Bassett 1988–95
Howard Kendall 1995–97
Nigel Spackman 1997–98
Steve Bruce 1998–99
Adrian Heath 1999
Neil Warnock 1999–2007
Bryan Robson 2007–08
Kevin Blackwell 2008–10
Gary Speed 2010
Micky Adams 2010–11
Danny Wilson May 2011–

LATEST SEQUENCES

Longest Sequence of League Wins: 8, 14.9.1960 – 22.10.1960.

Longest Sequence of League Defeats: 7, 19.8.1975 – 20.9.1975.

Longest Sequence of League Draws: 6, 6.5.2001 – 8.9.2001.

Longest Sequence of Unbeaten League Matches: 22, 2.9.1899 – 13.1.1900.

Longest Sequence Without a League Win: 19, 27.9.1975 – 7.2.1976.

Successive Scoring Runs: 34 from 30.3.1956.

Successive Non-scoring Runs: 6 from 4.12.1993.

TEN YEAR LEAGUE RECORD

		P	W	D	L	F	A	Pts	Pos
2001-02	Div 1	46	15	15	16	53	54	60	13
2002-03	Div 1	46	23	11	12	72	52	80	3
2003-04	Div 1	46	20	11	15	65	56	71	8
2004-05	FL C	46	18	13	15	57	56	67	8
2005-06	FL C	46	26	12	8	76	46	90	2
2006-07	PR Lge	38	10	8	20	32	55	38	18
2007-08	FL C	46	17	15	14	56	51	66	9
2008-09	FL C	46	22	14	10	64	39	80	3
2009-10	FL C	46	17	14	15	62	55	65	8
2010-11	FL C	46	11	9	26	44	79	42	23

DID YOU KNOW ?

When Sheffield United won the First Division Championship in 1897–98 they gave League debuts to as many as eight players: John Blair, David Martin, Henry White, John Cunningham, George Simpson, Ralph Gaudie, George Hedley and Harry Howard.

SHEFFIELD UNITED 2010–11 LEAGUE RECORD

Match No.	Date	Venue	Opponents	Result	H/T Score	Lg Pos.	Goalscorers	Atten-dance
1	Aug 8	A	Cardiff C	D 1-1	1-0	—	Evans [24]	20,573
2	14	H	QPR	L 0-3	0-3	23		22,651
3	22	A	Middlesbrough	L 0-1	0-0	24		14,633
4	28	H	Preston NE	W 1-0	0-0	17	Calve [74]	19,692
5	Sept 11	A	Derby Co	W 1-0	1-0	12	Cresswell [15]	25,749
6	14	H	Scunthorpe U	L 0-4	0-1	—		19,390
7	18	H	Portsmouth	W 1-0	0-0	14	Evans [77]	20,712
8	25	A	Leeds U	L 0-1	0-0	18		33,622
9	28	A	Nottingham F	D 1-1	1-0	—	Cresswell [6]	19,782
10	Oct 2	H	Watford	L 0-1	0-1	19		22,433
11	16	H	Burnley	D 3-3	0-0	18	Bogdanovic [57], Lowton [82], Yeates [90]	22,936
12	19	A	Hull C	W 1-0	0-0	—	Yeates [53]	20,276
13	23	A	Doncaster R	L 0-2	0-2	18		8985
14	30	H	Coventry C	L 0-1	0-1	18		20,059
15	Nov 6	H	Ipswich T	L 1-2	1-2	19	Quinn [29]	19,207
16	10	A	Leicester C	D 2-2	2-1	—	Yeates 2 [29, 41]	20,445
17	13	A	Millwall	W 1-0	1-0	19	Reid [29]	11,312
18	20	H	Crystal Palace	W 3-2	1-1	18	Cresswell (pen) [39], Evans [85], Bogdanovic (pen) [87]	20,240
19	27	A	Bristol C	L 0-3	0-2	20		13,376
20	Dec 11	A	Barnsley	L 0-1	0-1	20		12,976
21	18	H	Swansea C	W 1-0	1-0	20	Evans [44]	17,496
22	26	H	Hull C	L 2-3	0-2	20	Evans 2 [62, 73]	22,688
23	28	A	Norwich C	L 2-4	2-1	20	Reid [17], Cresswell [29]	25,809
24	Jan 1	A	Burnley	L 2-4	1-3	21	Yeates [9], Evans (pen) [47]	14,897
25	3	H	Doncaster R	D 2-2	0-0	21	Bogdanovic [86], Kozluk [90]	21,102
26	15	H	Coventry C	D 0-0	0-0	21		14,854
27	22	H	Norwich C	L 1-2	0-0	21	Evans [69]	20,725
28	Feb 1	H	Leicester C	L 0-1	0-1	22		20,464
29	5	A	Ipswich T	L 0-3	0-1	22		18,280
30	12	H	Millwall	D 1-1	0-0	22	Bogdanovic (pen) [77]	19,793
31	15	H	Reading	D 1-1	0-0	—	Bogdanovic (pen) [88]	19,271
32	19	A	Crystal Palace	L 0-1	0-0	22		14,214
33	22	A	Scunthorpe U	L 2-3	2-2	—	Evans [6], Cresswell [7]	6281
34	26	H	Derby Co	L 0-1	0-1	23		21,084
35	Mar 5	A	Portsmouth	L 0-1	0-1	23		15,096
36	8	H	Nottingham F	W 2-1	0-1	—	Vokes [74], Lowton [80]	20,547
37	12	A	Watford	L 0-3	0-1	23		12,441
38	19	H	Leeds U	W 2-0	0-0	22	Lichaj (og) [55], Riise [74]	23,728
39	Apr 4	A	QPR	L 0-3	0-1	—		14,535
40	9	H	Middlesbrough	L 1-2	1-1	24	Lowton [28]	21,572
41	12	H	Cardiff C	L 0-2	0-1	—		18,230
42	16	A	Preston NE	L 1-3	0-0	24	Slew [72]	12,076
43	23	H	Bristol C	W 3-2	2-1	24	Williamson [40], McAllister [43], Slew [80]	18,151
44	25	A	Reading	W 3-2	2-2	22	Henderson 2 [30, 51], Williamson [45]	19,165
45	30	H	Barnsley	D 2-2	1-1	22	Lowton [39], Williamson [59]	22,366
46	May 7	A	Swansea C	L 0-4	0-1	23		17,584

Final League Position: 23

GOALSCORERS

League (44): Evans 9 (1 pen), Bogdanovic 5 (3 pens), Cresswell 5 (1 pen), Yeates 5, Lowton 4, Williamson 3, Henderson 2, Reid 2, Slew 2, Calve 1, Kozluk 1, McAllister 1, Quinn 1, Riise 1, Vokes 1, own goal 1.
Carling Cup (0).
FA Cup (1): Ward 1 (pen).

Simonsen S 43+2	Taylor A 7+2	Lowton M 21+11	Montgomery N 34+1	Morgan C 8	Ertl J 25+3	Ward J 13+6	Britton L 22+2	Evans C 26+8	Cresswell R 30+5	Quinn S 33+4	Bogdanovic D 12+20	Kozluk R 2+6	Yeates M 18+17	Long G 1	Bartley K 21	Nosworthy N 31+1	Calve J 16+2	Jordan S 14+1	De Laet R 4+2	Slew J 5+2	Reid A 8+1	Wright R 2	Bath D —+1	Kennedy T —+1	Williamson L 14+2	Parrino E 7+1	Harriott M —+2	Mattock J 12+1	Lowry S 17	Bent M 4+7	Doyle M 16	Collins N 14	Vokes S 4+2	Riise B 9+4	Henderson D 8	Tonne E —+2	Maguire H 4+1	Philliskirk D —+3	McAllister D 1+1	Match No.
1	2	3^4	4	5	6	7^3	8^1	9^2	10	11	12	13	14																											1
1		3^2	4	5	6	7	8	9^1	10	11^3	12	13	14																											2
1		3	4	5	6	7	8	9^1	10	13	12				2	11^2																								3
1		13	4		11	7	8	9^1	10				12		6	5	2^2	3																						4
1		13	4		11	7^3	8	9^1	10	12			14		6	5	2^2	3																						5
1			4^1		11	7	8	9^2	10		13		12		6	5	2	3																						6
1			4^1	5	11	7	8	9^2	10	12			13		6	14	2	3																						7
1			4		7	13^8	8	9^2	10	11^2			14		6	5	2^1	3	12																					8
1		13	4		11		8	12	10	9^1			7		6^2	5	14	3	2^3																					9
1			4		11^1		12	10	8^2	9			7			5	2	3	6	13																				10
1		13		5	6^2		8	12	10	11	9^1		7			4	2	14	3^3																					11
1		14		5	6	13	8	9^2	10	11			7^3			4	2	3^1	12																					12
1		13		5	6^2	12	8	9^1	10^3	11			7			4	2	3	14																					13
1	3^1	12		5	6^3	9	8	14	10	11^2			7		4	2			13																					14
1		3	4		6^2	9^1	8	12	10	11	13		7			5	2																							15
1		3	4		12		8	9^1	10^2	11	13		7		6	5	2																							16
1	14	3	4		13		8	9			12				11^3	6	5	7^2	2	10																				17
1		13	4				8	9	10^1	12^8			7		6	5	2^2	3		11																				18
1	12	2	4		13		8	9	10^8	11^2					6	5	14	3^1			7^3																			19
1		3	4		11^1	13	8	9			12		7		6	5	2^2			10		1^6																		20
1	3		4				8	9^2		11	12		7		6	5	2^2			10					13															21
1	3^1	12	4				8	9		11^2	13		7		6	5	2			10																				22
1		3	4				8	9	10	11^8	12		7		6	5	2^1					8																		23
1		3			6	7	8	9	10	11	13					5^1	2					1^6			4^2	12														24
1			4		2	7^1	12	9	10^2	11	13	3			6										8^3	5	14													25
1			4		6^1	10^2		9	13	11	12					5									8^3	2	3	7												26
1			4			7		9	10^3	11^2	14	12	13		6											2	3	5	8^1											27
1			4		6			9	11		14	12	13		7											2	3^1	5	10^3	8^2										28
1			4		6			11	12	9	14^8		13													7	2^3	3	10^2	8^1	5									29
1			4					9^2	13	11	12		7													3	2	6	10^1	8	5									30
1	12		6			10	11	13	7^7							3^1										8	2	4	5	9^3	14									31
1		3							10	11^2	12	2	9^3		7												14	6		13	4^1	5	8							32
1		3			6^1			9	10^2	11	12	2^3	14																		5^8	13	4	7	8					33
1		3			6			9	10^1	11^3	12	2																			7	14	4^2	5	13	8				34
1		3			6			9	10^3	11	13	2^2																			7	14	8^1	5	12	4				35
1	3							7^2	11	9^3	12	2^1													14						13	6	8	5	10					36
1	4^2			12	11^3	13	14	2																	7^8		3	6		8	5	10^1	9^8							37
1	2	4^1			9^2	13	11	8^3	14	5																					3	6	7	10	12					38
1	2	4			9^3		11		10^2			13					5^1														3	14	8	6	12	7				39
1			4		11				10^2		13	2^1																			3	6	12	8^3	5	7	9	14		40
1			4	12	11				10			2^1																			3^8	6	14	8	5	7	9^3	13		41
1	2		4		11			14								10									12						3^3	8^1	5	7^2	9		6	13		42
1	2		4		11^2						12					10^3									7^1						3	6		13	9	8		5^8	14	43
1	2		4		11											10^1									7						3	6		5	8		9	12		44
1	2		4		12		14			11						10^2									7						3^3	6	8^1				9	5	13	45
	2	4^3						9					3	1		10^2									12	7	14	11^1			6^8	8		5				13		46

FA Cup
Third Round   Aston Villa   (h)   1-3

Carling Cup
First Round   Hartlepool U   (a)   0-2

SHEFFIELD WEDNESDAY FL Championship 1

FOUNDATION

Sheffield being one of the principal centres of early Association Football, this club was formed as long ago as 1867 by the Sheffield Wednesday Cricket Club (formed 1825) and their colours from the start were blue and white. The inaugural meeting was held at the Adelphi Hotel and the original committee included Charles Stokes who was subsequently a founder member of Sheffield United.

Hillsborough, Sheffield S6 1SW.
Telephone: (0871) 995 1867.
Fax: (0114) 221 2122.
Ticket Office: (0871) 900 1867.
Website: www.swfc.co.uk
Email: enquiries@swfc.co.uk
Ground Capacity: 39,812.
Record Attendance: 72,841 v Manchester C, FA Cup 5th rd, 17 February 1934.
Pitch Measurements: 110yd × 71yd.
Chairman: Milan Mandaric.
Chief Executive: Paul Aldridge.
Secretary: Lindsey Taylor-Higgins.
Manager: Gary Megson.
Assistant Manager: Chris Evans.
Physio: Dean Taylor.
Colours: Blue and white striped shirts, black shorts, blue stockings.
Change Colours: Yellow shirts, blue shorts, blue stockings.
Year Formed: 1867 (fifth oldest League club).
Turned Professional: 1887.
Ltd Co.: 1899.
Former Names: The Wednesday until 1929.
Club Nickname: 'The Owls'.

HONOURS

Football League – Division 1:
Champions 1902–03, 1903–04, 1928–29, 1929–30;
Runners-up 1960–61;
Division 2: *Champions* 1899–1900, 1925–26, 1951–52, 1955–56, 1958–59;
Runners-up 1949–50, 1983–84.
FA Cup: *Winners* 1896, 1907, 1935;
Runners-up 1890, 1966, 1993.
Football League Cup: *Winners* 1991;
Runners-up 1993.
European Competitions
European Fairs Cup: 1961–62, 1963–64. **UEFA Cup:** 1992–93.
Intertoto Cup: 1995.

Grounds: 1867, Highfield; 1869, Myrtle Road; 1877, Sheaf House; 1887, Olive Grove; 1899, Owlerton (since 1912 known as Hillsborough). Some games were played at Endcliffe in the 1880s. Until 1895 Bramall Lane was used for some games.
First Football League Game: 3 September 1892, Division 1, v Notts Co (a) W 1–0 – Allan; Tom Brandon (1), Mumford; Hall, Betts, Harry Brandon; Spiksley, Brady, Davis, Bob Brown, Dunlop.
Record League Victory: 9–1 v Birmingham, Division 1, 13 December 1930 – Brown; Walker, Blenkinsop; Strange, Leach, Wilson; Hooper (3), Seed (2), Ball (2), Burgess (1), Rimmer (1).
Record Cup Victory: 12–0 v Halliwell, FA Cup 1st rd, 17 January 1891 – Smith; Thompson, Brayshaw; Harry Brandon (1), Betts, Cawley (2); Winterbottom, Mumford (2), Bob Brandon (1), Woolhouse (5), Ingram (1).

sky SPORTS FACT FILE

In 1939 Sheffield Wednesday manager Jimmy McMullan split the £165 First Division third place talent money between the 21 players depending on their number of appearances. It worked out at around seven old pence a match (3p!). Two ever present players each received £15.

Record Defeat: 0–10 v Aston Villa, Division 1, 5 October 1912.

Most League Points (2 for a win): 62, Division 2, 1958–59.

Most League Points (3 for a win): 88, Division 2, 1983–84.

Most League Goals: 106, Division 2, 1958–59.

Highest League Scorer in Season: Derek Dooley, 46, Division 2, 1951–52.

Most League Goals in Total Aggregate: Andrew Wilson, 199, 1900–20.

Most League Goals in One Match: 6, Doug Hunt v Norwich C, Division 2, 19 November 1938.

Most Capped Player: Nigel Worthington, 50 (66), Northern Ireland.

Most League Appearances: Andrew Wilson, 501, 1900–20.

Youngest League Player: Peter Fox, 15 years 269 days v Orient, 31 March 1973.

Record Transfer Fee Received: £2,750,000 from Blackburn R for Paul Warhurst, September 1993.

Record Transfer Fee Paid: £4,500,000 to Celtic for Paolo Di Canio, August 1997.

Football League Record: 1892 Elected to Division 1; 1899–1900 Division 2; 1900–20 Division 1; 1920–26 Division 2; 1926–37 Division 1; 1937–50 Division 2; 1950–51 Division 1; 1951–52 Division 2; 1952–55 Division 1; 1955–56 Division 2; 1956–58 Division 1; 1958–59 Division 2; 1959–70 Division 1; 1970–75 Division 1; 1975–80 Division 3; 1980–84 Division 2; 1984–90 Division 1; 1990–91 Division 2; 1991–92 Division 1; 1992–2000 FA Premier League; 2000–03 Division 1; 2003–04 Division 2; 2004–05 FL 1; 2005–10 FL C; 2010– FL 1.

LATEST SEQUENCES

Longest Sequence of League Wins: 9, 23.4.1904 – 15.10.1904.

Longest Sequence of League Defeats: 8, 9.9.2000 – 17.10.2000.

Longest Sequence of League Draws: 7, 15.3.2008 – 14.4.2008.

Longest Sequence of Unbeaten League Matches: 19, 10.12.1960 – 8.4.1961.

Longest Sequence Without a League Win: 20, 11.1.1975 – 30.8.1975.

Successive Scoring Runs: 40 from 14.11.1959.

Successive Non-scoring Runs: 8 from 8.3.1975.

MANAGERS

Arthur Dickinson 1891–1920
(Secretary-Manager)
Robert Brown 1920–33
Billy Walker 1933–37
Jimmy McMullan 1937–42
Eric Taylor 1942–58
(continued as General Manager to 1974)
Harry Catterick 1958–61
Vic Buckingham 1961–64
Alan Brown 1964–68
Jack Marshall 1968–69
Danny Williams 1969–71
Derek Dooley 1971–73
Steve Burtenshaw 1974–75
Len Ashurst 1975–77
Jackie Charlton 1977–83
Howard Wilkinson 1983–88
Peter Eustace 1988–89
Ron Atkinson 1989–91
Trevor Francis 1991–95
David Pleat 1995–97
Ron Atkinson 1997–98
Danny Wilson 1998–2000
Peter Shreeves (Acting) 2000
Paul Jewell 2000–01
Peter Shreeves 2001
Terry Yorath 2001–02
Chris Turner 2002–04
Paul Sturrock 2004–06
Brian Laws 2006–09
Alan Irvine 2010–11
Gary Megson February 2011–

TEN YEAR LEAGUE RECORD

		P	W	D	L	F	A	Pts	Pos
2001-02	Div 1	46	12	14	20	49	71	50	20
2002-03	Div 1	46	10	16	20	56	73	46	22
2003-04	Div 2	46	13	14	19	48	64	53	16
2004-05	FL 1	46	19	15	12	77	59	72	5
2005-06	FL C	46	13	13	20	39	52	52	19
2006-07	FL C	46	20	11	15	70	66	71	9
2007-08	FL C	46	14	13	19	54	55	55	16
2008-09	FL C	46	16	13	17	51	58	61	12
2009-10	FL C	46	11	14	21	49	69	47	22
2010-11	FL 1	46	16	10	20	67	67	58	15

DID YOU KNOW ?

Though he spent ten years with Sheffield Wednesday as a half-back from 1882, Jack Dungworth was better known as a long-distance runner who won some 125 medals in athletics. However between 1885 and 1890 he played 17 consecutive FA Cup games for Wednesday.

SHEFFIELD WEDNESDAY 2010–11 LEAGUE RECORD

Match No.	Date	Venue	Opponents	Result	H/T Score	Lg Pos.	Goalscorers	Attendance
1	Aug 7	H	Dagenham & R	W 2-0	2-0	—	Doe (og) [13], Morrison, C [15]	23,081
2	14	A	Colchester U	D 1-1	0-0	5	Mellor [83]	6011
3	21	H	Brighton & HA	W 1-0	1-0	4	Coke [38]	18,674
4	28	A	Hartlepool U	W 5-0	3-0	1	Murray (og) [8], Coke [10], Mellor [23], Tudgay (pen) [71], Morrison, C [90]	4084
5	Sept 5	A	Brentford	L 0-1	0-1	1		5396
6	11	H	Carlisle U	L 0-1	0-1	6		20,282
7	18	A	Plymouth Arg	L 2-3	1-1	11	O'Connor [38], Miller [75]	7916
8	25	H	Southampton	L 0-1	0-0	14		18,198
9	28	H	Oldham Ath	D 0-0	0-0	—		16,609
10	Oct 2	A	Notts Co	W 2-0	0-0	10	Tudgay [52], Potter [90]	11,355
11	9	H	Leyton Orient	W 1-0	0-0	5	Buxton [52]	17,445
12	16	A	Yeovil T	W 2-0	0-0	4	Johnson, J [72], Miller (pen) [84]	5927
13	23	H	Bournemouth	D 1-1	0-1	4	Mellor [82]	17,868
14	30	A	Charlton Ath	L 0-1	0-1	7		17,365
15	Nov 2	H	Huddersfield T	L 0-2	0-2	—		20,540
16	13	H	Rochdale	W 2-0	0-0	9	Coke [62], Morrison, C [82]	16,520
17	20	A	Milton Keynes D	W 4-1	2-1	5	Mellor 3 [22, 71, 83], Chadwick (og) [27]	10,552
18	23	H	Walsall	W 3-0	1-0	—	Potter [7], Beevers [75], Morrison, C [83]	15,228
19	Dec 4	A	Swindon T	L 1-2	1-1	—	Morrison, C [30]	9123
20	11	H	Bristol R	W 6-2	4-1	2	Sedgwick [10], Miller [23], Teale [26], Johnson, J [32], O'Connor [71], Heffernan [81]	19,242
21	18	A	Exeter C	L 1-5	1-1	—	Miller [31]	5524
22	Jan 3	A	Huddersfield T	L 0-1	0-1	6		17,024
23	15	H	Charlton Ath	D 2-2	0-2	9	Heffernan [47], Johnson, R [51]	19,051
24	22	A	Leyton Orient	L 0-4	0-0	12		6449
25	25	H	Yeovil T	D 2-2	1-1	—	Madine [36], Johnson, R [86]	16,618
26	Feb 1	A	Peterborough U	L 3-5	3-2	12	Johnson, J [5], Madine [21], Sedgwick [35]	6480
27	5	H	Milton Keynes D	D 2-2	0-2	12	Mellor [69], Morrison, C [83]	17,631
28	12	A	Rochdale	L 1-2	0-2	14	Madine [90]	6154
29	15	A	Tranmere R	L 0-3	0-0	—		5941
30	22	A	Bournemouth	D 0-0	0-0	—		7268
31	26	A	Carlisle U	W 1-0	1-0	16	Miller [20]	6834
32	Mar 5	H	Plymouth Arg	L 2-4	0-2	16	Coke [61], Johnson, R [83]	18,474
33	8	A	Oldham Ath	W 3-2	2-2	—	Beevers [3], Sedgwick 2 [13, 52]	4133
34	12	H	Notts Co	L 0-1	0-1	16		17,835
35	15	H	Peterborough U	L 1-4	0-3	—	Heffernan [52]	16,014
36	19	A	Southampton	L 0-2	0-0	16		20,234
37	26	A	Dagenham & R	D 1-1	1-0	—	Teale [17]	3549
38	29	H	Brentford	L 1-3	1-2	—	Jones, R [12]	14,797
39	Apr 2	H	Colchester U	W 2-1	1-0	16	Mellor 2 [25, 51]	15,663
40	5	H	Tranmere R	W 4-0	3-0	—	Miller 2 (1 pen) [10, 22 (p)], Madine [14], Mellor [90]	15,235
41	9	A	Brighton & HA	L 0-2	0-1	16		8107
42	16	H	Hartlepool U	W 2-0	1-0	15	Miller (pen) [45], Madine [65]	16,358
43	23	A	Walsall	D 1-1	1-1	—	Mellor [26]	2072
44	25	H	Swindon T	W 3-1	2-1	15	Potter [17], Mellor 2 [28, 53]	17,348
45	30	A	Bristol R	D 1-1	1-1	13	Miller (pen) [3]	8340
46	May 7	H	Exeter C	L 1-2	1-0	15	Johnson, J [13]	21,085

Final League Position: 15

GOALSCORERS

League (67): Mellor 13, Miller 9 (4 pens), Morrison, C 6, Madine 5, Coke 4, Johnson, J 4, Sedgwick 4, Heffernan 3, Johnson, R 3, Potter 3, Beevers 2, O'Connor 2, Teale 2, Tudgay 2 (1 pen), Buxton 1, Jones, R 1, own goals 3.
Carling Cup (3): Coke 1, Mellor 1, Tudgay 1.
FA Cup (15): Morrison, C 5 (2 pens), Mellor 2, Miller 2 (2 pens), Teale 2, Beevers 1, Johnson, J 1, Potter 1, Spurr 1.
J Paint Trophy (9): Mellor 4 (1 pen), O'Connor 2, Purse 1, Teale 1, Tudgay 1.

Weaver N 36	Buxton L 29 + 1	Spurr T 26	O'Connor J 25 + 11	Beevers M 27 + 1	Purse D 22	Sedgwick C 24 + 9	Coke G 22 + 5	Morrison C 22 + 13	Mellor N 24 + 9	Tudgay M 15 + 2	Teale G 37 + 4	Potter D 22 + 11	Jones D 13 + 12	Heffernan P 3 + 14	Palmer L 4 + 5	Miller T 29 + 5	Otsemobor J 13 + 2	Johnson J 15 + 11	Jameson A 2	Johnson R 15 + 1	Morrison M 12	Madine G 20 + 2	Reynolds M 7	Osbourne 19 + 1	Hinds R 4	O'Donnell R 8 + 1	Bath D 10	Jones R 8	O'Brien J 3 + 1	Match No.
1	2	3	4[2]	5	6	7	8	9[1]	12	10	11[3]	13	14																	1
1	2	3[3]	4[2]	5	6	7	8	9	12	10	11[1]	13	14																	2
1	2	3	13	5	6	7[2]	8[3]	9[1]	10	11		4				12	14													3
1	2	3	12	5	6	7	8[3]	13	9[2]	10	11[1]	4					14													4
1	2	3	12	5	6	7[1]	8	13	9[2]	10	11[3]	4				14														5
1	2	3	13	5	6	7[2]	8	9[1]	10	11[3]		4				12	14													6
1	2	3[3]	4	5	6	7	8	13	9	10		11[2]	14			12														7
1	2		4[1]	5	6[1]		8	13	9	10	11[3]	7[2]	3			14	12													8
1		3[1]	4[3]	5	6	7[2]	8	9		10	13			12	14	11	2													9
1		3	4	5	6		8	9[2]	13	10			12		7[1]	11	2													10
1	5	3	4		6			9[1]	12	10	11	8				7	2													11
1	5		4		6	14		9[1]	13	10[2]	11[1]	8	3			7	2[ ]	12												12
1	2		4[1]	5	6		8	9[2]	13	10[3]	12	11	3	14		7														13
1	5	3		6			8	13	9	10[2]	11[1]	4	2			7		12												14
1	2		12	5	6	7[3]	8	13	9	10[2]	14	4[1]	3			11														15
1	2	3	4	5	6	12	8	9[2]	10	13	11[1]					7														16
	2	3		5	6	7[1]		9	10[3]	12	11	4		13	14	8[2]			1											17
1		3		5	6	7[1]		9	10	11	4	2		13		8[2]		12												18
1	2[1]	3		5	6	7[2]	13	9		11	4	12	14			8		10[3]												19
1		3	13	5	6	7[1]		9		11	4[3]	2	12	14		8[1]		10[2]												20
1		3		5	6	7[1]		9	12	11	4	2				8		10												21
1		3	4[3]	5	6	12		9	10	11[1]		13	14			8	2[2]	7												22
1		8		6	7			9	10[2]		11	3	12			4		13		2	5									23
1	2[1]		8		12		7	9	13	11		3				4[3]		14		6	5	10[2]								24
1		3				14	8	13	10	11		6				7				6	5[3]	9	2[2]							25
1	2		13				7[3]	8		10[2]		12		4[4]	14			11[1]		6	5	9	3							26
	2		4				8	9	13			11[1]			3	12			7	1	6	5	10[2]							27
1	2		7	3			14	8[3]	9	10[1]				6[5]	11					5	12	4	13							28
							8[4]	9				11[1]	13	12						6	5	10	2[2]	4						29
1		3	12	2				9			11			7[1]	8			6			10			4	5					30
1		3		2				9	13			11[3]	12	14		7[1]	8			6		10[2]			4	5				31
1		3		2				7[1]	12	14		11			9[3]	8		13		6		10			4[2]	5				32
1		3	10	2				7		12		11	13			8				6	5	9[1]			4[2]					33
1		3	14	2				7[1]		9	10[2]	11		12		8		13		6	5				4[3]					34
1			6[1]			10					11	14	12	13		8		7[2]		2	9	3	4	5[3]						35
		14				7					11[3]	13		9		8[2]		12		2	10	3	4[1]		1	5	6			36
	12	13				10					11	4				8[2]				2	9	3[1]			1	5	6	7		37
	2	3									13	11	7[3]		10[2]		12	14			9		4		1	5	6[1]	8		38
	3	4				12	13		10		11[2]					8	2	7[1]		6		9			1	5				39
	3	4				13			14	10	11[1]					8[2]	2	7		6		9[3]			1	5		12		40
	3	4				7[2]	12	9	10		13					2	11[3]			6		14			1	5		8[1]		41
	3	8				13	14	10	11		12					4[1]	2	7[2]				9			1	5	6			42
	3	7						8[1]			10	11				4	2	12	13			9			1	5	6[2]			43
1	3	8		12				10			4	11[3]		14	13	2	7[1]		5			9[2]					6			44
1	2	8[1]		13				10			11[2]	14		7[3]	4	3	12					9					5	6		45
1[6]	3	4						10			11[2]	13	12		8	2	7					9		15			5	6[1]		46

SHREWSBURY TOWN   FL Championship 2

FOUNDATION

Shrewsbury School having provided a number of the early England and Wales international players it is not surprising that there was a Town club as early as 1876 which won the Birmingham Senior Cup in 1879. However, the present Shrewsbury Town club was formed in 1886 and won the Welsh FA Cup as early as 1891.

Greenhous Meadow, Oteley Road, Shrewsbury SY2 6ST.

Telephone: (01743) 289 177.

Fax: (01743) 246 972.

Ticket Office: (01743) 273 943.

Website: www.shrewsburytown.com

Email: ian@shrewsburytown.co.uk

Ground Capacity: 10,000.

Record Attendance: 18,917 v Walsall, Division 3, 26 April 1961 (at Gay Meadow). 8,429 v Bury, FL 2 Play-off semi-final, 7 May 2009 (at ProStar Stadium).

Pitch Measurements: 114yd × 73yd.

Chairman: Roland Wycherley.

Vice-chairman: Keith Sayfritz.

Manager: Graham Turner.

First Team Coach: John Trewick.

Physio: Nathan Ring.

Colours: All blue with yellow and red design.

Change Colours: All black with red and white design on shirts.

Year Formed: 1886.

Turned Professional: 1896.

Ltd Co.: 1936.

HONOURS

Football League – Division 2: Best season: 8th, 1983–84, 1984–85; **Division 3:** *Champions* 1978–79, 1993–94; **Division 4:** *Runners-up* 1974–75.

FA Cup: Best season: 6th rd, 1979, 1982.

Football League Cup: Semi-final 1961.

Welsh Cup: *Winners* 1891, 1938, 1977, 1979, 1984, 1985; *Runners-up* 1931, 1948, 1980.

Auto Windscreens Shield: *Runners-up* 1996.

Club Nickname: 'Town', 'Blues' or 'Salop'. The name 'Salop' is a colloquialism for the county of Shropshire. Since Shrewsbury is the only club in Shropshire, cries of 'Come on Salop' are frequently used!

Grounds: 1886, Old Racecourse Ground; 1889, Ambler's Field; 1893, Sutton Lane; 1895, Barracks Ground; 1910, Gay Meadow; 2007, New Meadow.

First Football League Game: 19 August 1950, Division 3 (N), v Scunthorpe U (a) D 0–0 – Egglestone; Fisher, Lewis; Wheatley, Depear, Robinson; Griffin, Hope, Jackson, Brown, Barker.

Record League Victory: 7–0 v Swindon T, Division 3 (S), 6 May 1955 – McBride; Bannister, Skeech; Wallace, Maloney, Candlin; Price, O'Donnell (1), Weigh (4), Russell, McCue (2); 7-0 v Gillingham, FL 2, 13 September 2008 – Daniels; Herd, Tierney, Davies (2), Jackson (1) (Langmead), Coughlan (1), Cansdell-Sherriff (1), Thornton, Hibbert (1) (Hindmarch), Holt (pen), McIntyre (Ashton).

sky SPORTS FACT FILE

In 1945–46 former England international Billy "Ginger" Richardson scored all seven Midland League goals for Shrewsbury Town against Notts County Reserves. It equalled seven by Alf Ellis of an amazing 21 on 27 October 1894 against Mold Alyn Stars in the Welsh Cup.

Record Cup Victory: 11–2 v Marine, FA Cup 1st rd, 11 November 1995 – Edwards, Seabury (Dempsey (1)), Withe (1), Evans (1), Whiston (2), Scott (1), Woods, Stevens (1), Spink (3) (Anthrobus), Walton, Berkley, (1 og).

Record Defeat: 1–8 v Norwich C, Division 3 (S), 13 September 1952; 1–8 v Coventry C, Division 3, 22 October 1963.

Most League Points (2 for a win): 62, Division 4, 1974–75.

Most League Points (3 for a win): 79, Division 3, 1993–94; 79, FL 2, 2010–11.

Most League Goals: 101, Division 4, 1958–59.

Highest League Scorer in Season: Arthur Rowley, 38, Division 4, 1958–59.

Most League Goals in Total Aggregate: Arthur Rowley, 152, 1958–65 (thus completing his League record of 434 goals).

Most League Goals in One Match: 5, Alf Wood v Blackburn R, Division 3, 2 October 1971.

Most Capped Player: Jimmy McLaughlin, 5 (12), Northern Ireland; Bernard McNally, 5, Northern Ireland.

Most League Appearances: Mickey Brown, 418, 1986–91; 1992–94; 1996–2001.

Youngest League Player: Graham French, 16 years 177 days v Reading, 30 September 1961.

Record Transfer Fee Received: £600,000 from Manchester C for Joe Hart, May 2006.

Record Transfer Fee Paid: £170,000 to Nottingham F for Grant Holt, June 2008.

Football League Record: 1950 Elected to Division 3 (N); 1951–58 Division 3 (S); 1958–59 Division 4; 1959–74 Division 3; 1974–75 Division 4; 1975–79 Division 3; 1979–89 Division 2; 1989–94 Division 3; 1994–97 Division 2; 1997–2003 Division 3; 2003–04 Conference; 2004– FL 2.

MANAGERS

W. Adams 1905–12
 (Secretary-Manager)
A. Weston 1912–34
 (Secretary-Manager)
Jack Roscamp 1934–35
Sam Ramsey 1935–36
Ted Bousted 1936–40
Leslie Knighton 1945–49
Harry Chapman 1949–50
Sammy Crooks 1950–54
Walter Rowley 1955–57
Harry Potts 1957–58
Johnny Spuhler 1958
Arthur Rowley 1958–68
Harry Gregg 1968–72
Maurice Evans 1972–73
Alan Durban 1974–78
Richie Barker 1978
Graham Turner 1978–84
Chic Bates 1984–87
Ian McNeill 1987–90
Asa Hartford 1990–91
John Bond 1991–93
Fred Davies 1994–97
 (previously Caretaker-Manager 1993–94)
Jake King 1997–99
Kevin Ratcliffe 1999 2003
Jimmy Quinn 2003–04
Gary Peters 2004–08
Paul Simpson 2008–10
Graham Turner June 2010–

LATEST SEQUENCES

Longest Sequence of League Wins: 7, 28.10.1995 – 16.12.1995.

Longest Sequence of League Defeats: 11, 9.4.2003 – 14.8.2004.

Longest Sequence of League Draws: 6, 30.10.1963 – 14.12.1963.

Longest Sequence of Unbeaten League Matches: 16, 30.10.1993 – 26.2.1994.

Longest Sequence Without a League Win: 18, 8.3.2003 – 14.8.2004.

Successive Scoring Runs: 28 from 7.9.1960.

Successive Non-scoring Runs: 6 from 1.1.1991.

TEN YEAR LEAGUE RECORD

		P	W	D	L	F	A	Pts	Pos
2001-02	Div 3	46	20	10	16	64	53	70	9
2002-03	Div 3	46	9	14	23	62	92	41	24
2003-04	Conf.	42	20	14	8	67	42	74	3
2004-05	FL 2	46	11	16	19	48	53	49	21
2005-06	FL 2	46	16	13	17	55	55	61	10
2006-07	FL 2	46	18	17	11	68	46	71	7
2007-08	FL 2	46	12	14	20	56	65	50	18
2008-09	FL 2	46	17	18	11	61	44	69	7
2009-10	FL 2	46	17	12	17	55	54	63	12
2010-11	FL 2	46	22	13	11	72	49	79	4

DID YOU KNOW ?

Billy Scarratt was a leading goal scorer for Shrewsbury Town in 1906–07 with 14 Birmingham League goals. He eventually appeared in all eleven positions on the field. This included keeping goal in three successive FA Cup ties in which he conceded only one goal.

SHREWSBURY TOWN 2010–11 LEAGUE RECORD

Match No.	Date	Venue	Opponents	Result	H/T Score	Lg Pos.	Goalscorers	Attendance
1	Aug 7	H	Bradford C	W 3-1	1-1	—	Robinson 3 [34, 51, 56]	6993
2	14	A	Macclesfield T	W 1-0	1-0	2	Harrold [3]	2302
3	21	H	Aldershot T	D 1-1	1-1	5	Sharps [29]	5353
4	28	A	Stockport Co	W 4-0	1-0	2	Robinson [41], Harrold [58], Wright 2 [63, 82]	4350
5	Sept 4	H	Rotherham U	W 1-0	1-0	1	Ainsworth [5]	6206
6	11	A	Gillingham	L 0-2	0-1	2		4815
7	18	H	Northampton T	W 3-1	1-1	1	Harrold [12], Robinson 2 [49, 53]	5527
8	25	A	Wycombe W	D 2-2	0-0	2	Bradshaw [76], Ainsworth [87]	4208
9	28	A	Port Vale	L 0-1	0-0	—		8443
10	Oct 2	H	Torquay U	D 1-1	1-1	4	Robinson [5]	6034
11	9	A	Morecambe	L 0-1	0-0	5		3239
12	16	H	Lincoln C	W 2-0	2-0	5	Wright [39], Robinson [42]	5453
13	23	A	Chesterfield	L 3-4	0-3	5	Wright [80], McIntyre [89], Disley [90]	7777
14	30	H	Barnet	W 2-1	2-0	4	Disley [39], Harrold [41]	5331
15	Nov 2	A	Crewe Alex	W 2-1	1-0	—	Wright 2 [5, 90]	4594
16	13	A	Stevenage	D 1-1	0-1	3	Harrold [55]	2765
17	20	H	Southend U	D 1-1	0-0	5	Wright [49]	5406
18	23	H	Hereford U	W 4-0	1-0	—	Wright 3 [14, 64, 77], Cansdell-Sherriff [72]	6565
19	Dec 11	H	Cheltenham T	D 1-1	0-1	5	Bradshaw [89]	4901
20	Jan 1	A	Burton Alb	D 0-0	0-0	6		3594
21	3	H	Crewe Alex	L 0-1	0-0	6		6561
22	8	H	Morecambe	L 1-3	0-2	7	Cansdell-Sherriff [67]	4605
23	15	A	Barnet	D 1-1	1-0	8	Hughes (og) [27]	2164
24	18	A	Accrington S	W 3-1	0-0	—	Collins 2 [50, 71], Wright [83]	1362
25	22	H	Chesterfield	D 0-0	0-0	4		6483
26	25	A	Oxford U	L 1-3	1-1	—	Wright [26]	6264
27	28	A	Bury	L 0-1	0-1	—		2917
28	Feb 1	H	Burton Alb	W 3-0	0-0	6	Taylor, J 2 [55, 70], Harrold [72]	4343
29	5	A	Southend U	W 2-0	1-0	4	Taylor, J [43], Harrold [60]	5396
30	8	A	Lincoln C	W 5-1	5-1	—	Taylor, J [6], Kelly (og) [13], Ainsworth 3 [22, 24, 35]	3202
31	12	H	Stevenage	W 1-0	1-0	2	Wroe [38]	5261
32	26	H	Gillingham	D 0-0	0-0	4		5574
33	Mar 1	H	Bury	L 0-3	0-1	—		5298
34	5	A	Northampton T	W 3-2	1-1	5	Davis [8], Collins [51], Taylor, J [87]	5113
35	8	H	Port Vale	D 2-2	1-1	—	Ainsworth [30], Collins [72]	6402
36	12	A	Torquay U	L 0-5	0-1	5		2861
37	19	H	Wycombe W	D 1-1	1-0	4	Collins [31]	5886
38	26	A	Bradford C	W 2-1	0-0	—	Bradshaw 2 [77, 87]	10,735
39	29	A	Rotherham U	W 3-1	2-0	—	Collins 2 [20, 48], Wroe (pen) [43]	3471
40	Apr 2	H	Macclesfield T	W 4-1	1-1	3	Taylor, J [22], Ainsworth 2 [67, 70], Harrold [90]	5396
41	9	A	Aldershot T	L 0-3	0-2	4		2371
42	16	H	Stockport Co	W 2-0	2-0	4	Bradshaw [17], Wroe (pen) [20]	5711
43	23	A	Hereford U	W 2-0	1-0	3	Collins [27], Bradshaw [56]	3942
44	25	A	Accrington S	D 0-0	0-0	4		7038
45	30	A	Cheltenham T	W 1-0	1-0	4	Wright [10]	4288
46	May 7	H	Oxford U	W 3-0	0-0	4	Wright [52], Davis [77], Ainsworth [89]	8817

Final League Position: 4

GOALSCORERS
League (72): Wright 14, Ainsworth 9, Collins 8, Harrold 8, Robinson 8, Bradshaw 6, Taylor, J 6, Wroe 3 (2 pens), Cansdell-Sherriff 2, Davis 2, Disley 2, McIntyre 1, Sharps 1, own goals 2.
Carling Cup (5): Harrold 1, Leslie 1, O'Donnell 1, Robinson 1, own goal 1.
FA Cup (0).
J Paint Trophy (1): Leslie 1.
Play-Offs (0).

Smith B 25	Raven D 22+2	Sadler M 46	McIntyre K 18+13	Sharps I 43	O'Donnell D 4+1	Wright M 43+2	Disley C 22+2	Harrold M 28+13	Robinson J 20+2	Ainsworth L 21+12	McAllister S 15+3	Van den Broek B —+11	Cansdell-Sheriff S 39+2	Neal C 21+1	Leslie S 9+9	Neal L —+2	Bradshaw T 13+13	Bright K —+1	Holden D 11+2	Obadeyi T 7+2	Geohaghon E 2	Tutte A 2	Collins J 22+2	Grandison J 13	Taylor J 19+1	Davis D 19	Wroe N 18	Goldson C 1+2	Lomax K —+1	Canavan N 3	Match No.
1	2	3	4⁴	5	6	7	8³	9	10¹	11²	12	13	14																		1
1⁶	2	3		5	6	7	8	9	10¹	11	4	12			15																2
	2	3		5	6²	7	8	9⁴	10¹	11³	4	14	13	1	12																3
	2	3	14	5		7	8²	9	10¹		4	12	6	1			11³	13													4
	2	3	13	5		7	8	9	10¹	11²	4	12	6	1																	5
	2	3		5		7	8²	9	10¹	11	4	12	6	1		13															6
	2	3		5		7	8	9²	10¹		4		6	1	11		12	13													7
	2	3	12	5		7	8	9	10³	13	4¹		6	1	11²		14														8
	2	3	4³	5		7	8	9	10²	11¹			6	1	12	14	13														9
	2	3	12	5		7	8	9	10	11			6	1	4¹																10
	2	3	4	5	6	7		9³	10¹	11²	8	14		1	13		12														11
	2	3		5		7	8	9	10	11	4		6	1																	12
		3	12	5		7	8		10³	11¹	4²	14	6	1	13				2	9											13
	2¹	3	4	5²	13	7	8	9³	10			14	6	1					12	11											14
		3	11			7	8¹		10		4		6	1	12				2	9	5										15
		3	11			7	8	12	10²		4	13	5	1					2	9¹	6										16
		3	11	5		7	8		10		4¹		8	1					2	12											17
		3	4	5		7	8¹	9	10			12	6	1					2	11											18
		3	11	5		7		9³	10¹	13	4²	14	6	1			12		2	8											19
		3	4	5		7		9	13	11¹			6	1			10²		2	12		8									20
		3	4	5		7		9³	10²	12			6	1	14		13		2	11¹		8									21
12		3	11³	5¹		8		14		7²	4		6	1	13		9		2				10								22
		3	4	5		7	8	12	13				6	1	11		9¹		2				10²								23
1		3	4	5		7	8						6		11		9						10	2							24
1		3	4	5		7	8²	12				13	6		11		9¹						10	2							25
1		3	4	5		7	8²					13	6		11		9³		12				10	2¹							26
1		3	4	5		7	8	12	9²				6		11¹		14		2				10³		13						27
1		3	4	5		7	12	9²					6		13								10	2	11	8¹					28
1		3	12	5		7							6		13								10²	2	11	8¹	4				29
1		3	12	5		7	14	9³	10				6											2²	11	8¹	4	13			30
1		3	13	5		7		9	10¹				6										12	2	11	8²	4				31
1		3		5⁴		7		9	10¹				6										12	2	11²	8	4	13			32
1		3				7		9		12			6		13								10²	2³	11¹	8	4	5	14		33
1		3		5		7		9¹		12			6										10	2	11	8	4				34
1		3		5		7		9¹					6						12				10	2	11	8	4				35
1	12	3		5		7¹		13		9²			6										10	2⁴	11	8	4				36
1	2	3		5		7		9					6						12				10¹		11	8	4				37
1	2	3		5		7²		9		13			6						12				10¹		11	8	4				38
1	2	3		5		7				12			6						9				10		11¹	8	4			6	39
1	2	3	13	5		7²		14		12			6						9³				10		11¹	8	4			6	40
1	2	3		5		7²		9		12			6						13				10		11¹	8	4			6	41
1	2	3	12	5			13			7			6						9²				10¹		11	8	4				42
1	2	3	14	5			12	13		7³			6						9²				10		11¹	8	4				43
1	2	3		5			12	13		7¹			6						9				10²		11	8	4				44
1	2	3	14	5		7³		12		13			6						9¹				10²		11	8	4				45
1		3	14	5		7		12		13			6						9¹				10²	2	11	8³	4				46

FA Cup

First Round	Southampton	(a)	0-2

Carling Cup

First Round	Charlton Ath	(h)	4-3
Second Round	Stoke C	(a)	1-2

J Paint Trophy

First Round	Oldham Ath	(a)	1-0
Second Round	Bury	(a)	0-0

Play-Offs

Semi-Final	Torquay U	(a)	0-2
		(h)	0-0

SOUTHAMPTON FL Championship

FOUNDATION

The club was formed by members of the St Mary's Church of England Young Men's Association at a meeting of the Y.M.A. in November 1885 and it was named as such. For the sake of brevity this was usually shortened to St Mary's Y.M.A. The rector Canon Albert Basil Orme Wilberforce was elected president. The name was changed to plain St Mary's during 1887–88 and did not become Southampton St Mary's until 1894, the inaugural season in the Southern League.

St Mary's Stadium, Britannia Road, Southampton SO14 5FP.

Telephone: (0845) 688 9448.

Fax: (0845) 688 9445.

Ticket Office: (0845) 688 9288.

Website: www.saintsfc.co.uk

Email: sfc@saintsfc.co.uk

Ground Capacity: 32,689.

Record Attendance: 31,044 v Manchester U, Division 1, 8 October 1969 (at The Dell). 32,151 v Arsenal, FA Premier League, 29 December 2003 (at St Mary's).

Pitch Measurements: 112yd × 72yd.

Chairman: Nicola Cortese.

Football Secretary: Ros Wheeler.

Manager: Nigel Adkins B.Sc (Hons).

Assistant Manager: Andy Crosby.

Physio: Mo Gimpel.

Colours: White shirts with diagonal red stripe, white shorts, black stockings.

Change Colours: Dark blue shirts, yellow shorts, yellow stockings.

HONOURS

Football League – Division 1:
Runners-up 1983–84;
Division 2: *Runners-up* 1965–66, 1977–78;
Division 3 (S): *Champions* 1921–22;
Division 3: *Champions* 1959–60:
Runners-up 1920–21.

FA Cup: *Winners* 1976;
Runners-up 1900, 1902, 2003.

Football League Cup:
Runners-up 1979.

Zenith Data Systems Cup:
Runners-up 1992.

Johnstone's Paint Trophy:
Winners 2009–10.

European Competitions
European Fairs Cup: 1969–70.
UEFA Cup: 1971–72, 1981–82, 1982–83, 1984–85, 2003–04.
European Cup-Winners' Cup: 1976–77.

Year Formed: 1885. *Turned Professional:* 1894. *Ltd Co.:* 1897.

Previous Name: 1885, St Mary's Young Men's Association; 1887–88, St Mary's; 1894–95 Southampton St Mary's; 1897, Southampton.

Club Nickname: 'The Saints'.

Grounds: 1885, 'The Common' (from 1887 also used the County Cricket Ground and Antelope Cricket Ground); 1889, Antelope Cricket Ground; 1896 The County Cricket Ground; 1898, The Dell; 2001, St Mary's.

First Football League Game: 28 August 1920, Division 3, v Gillingham (a) D 1–1 – Allen; Parker, Titmuss; Shelley, Campbell, Turner; Barratt, Dominy (1), Rawlings, Moore, Foxall.

Record League Victory: 9–3 v Wolverhampton W, Division 2, 18 September 1965 – Godfrey; Jones, Williams; Walker, Knapp, Huxford; Paine (2), O'Brien (1), Melia, Chivers (4), Sydenham (2).

sky SPORTS FACT FILE

On 5 December 1960 an FA Cup fourth round tie at The Dell between Southampton and Leeds United started at 7.30 pm and ended at 10.10 pm because of 62 minutes floodlight failure. A see-saw score line during the game ended with a Saints winner 25 seconds from time at 5-4.

Record Cup Victory: 7–1 v Ipswich T, FA Cup 3rd rd, 7 January 1961 – Reynolds; Davies, Traynor, Conner, Page, Huxford, Paine (1), O'Brien (3 incl. 1p), Reeves, Mulgrew (2), Penk (1).

Record Defeat: 0–8 v Tottenham H, Division 2, 28 March 1936; 0–8 v Everton, Division 1, 20 November 1971.

Most League Points (2 for a win): 61, Division 3 (S), 1921–22 and Division 3, 1959–60.

Most League Points (3 for a win): 92, FL 1, 2010–11.

Most League Goals: 112, Division 3 (S), 1957–58.

Highest League Scorer in Season: Derek Reeves, 39, Division 3, 1959–60.

Most League Goals in Total Aggregate: Mike Channon, 185, 1966–77, 1979–82.

Most League Goals in One Match: 5, Charlie Wayman v Leicester C, Division 2, 23 October 1948.

Most Capped Player: Peter Shilton, 49 (125), England.

Most League Appearances: Terry Paine, 713, 1956–74.

Youngest League Player: Theo Walcott, 16 years 143 days v Wolverhampton W, 6 August 2005.

Record Transfer Fee Received: Up to £10,000,000 from Arsenal for Theo Walcott, January 2006.

Record Transfer Fee Paid: £4,000,000 to Derby Co for Rory Delap, July 2001.

Football League Record: 1920 Original Member of Division 3; 1921–22 Division 3 (S); 1922–53 Division 2; 1953–58 Division 3 (S); 1958–60 Division 3; 1960–66 Division 2; 1966–74 Division 1; 1974–78 Division 2; 1978–92 Division 1; 1992–2005 FA Premier League; 2005–09 FL C; 2009–11 FL 1; 2011– FL C.

LATEST SEQUENCES

Longest Sequence of League Wins: 6, 3.3.1992 – 4.4.1992.

Longest Sequence of League Defeats: 5, 16.8.1998 – 12.9.1998.

Longest Sequence of League Draws: 8, 29.8.2005 – 15.10.2005.

Longest Sequence of Unbeaten League Matches: 19, 5.9.1921 – 31.12.1921.

Longest Sequence Without a League Win: 20, 30.8.1969 – 27.12.1969.

Successive Scoring Runs: 28 from 10.2.2008.

Successive Non-scoring Runs: 5 from 1.9.1937.

MANAGERS

Cecil Knight 1894–95
  (Secretary-Manager)
Charles Robson 1895–97
Er Arnfield 1897–1911
  (Secretary-Manager)
  (continued as Secretary)
George Swift 1911–12
Er Arnfield 1912–19
Jimmy McIntyre 1919–24
Arthur Chadwick 1925–31
George Kay 1931–36
George Gross 1936–37
Tom Parker 1937–43
J. R. Sarjantson stepped down
  from the board to act as
  Secretary-Manager 1943–47
  with the next two listed being
  team Managers during this
  period
Arthur Dominy 1943–46
Bill Dodgin Snr 1946–49
Sid Cann 1949–51
George Roughton 1952–55
Ted Bates 1955–73
Lawrie McMenemy 1973–85
Chris Nicholl 1985–91
Ian Branfoot 1991–94
Alan Ball 1994–95
Dave Merrington 1995–96
Graeme Souness 1996–97
Dave Jones 1997–2000
Glenn Hoddle 2000–01
Stuart Gray 2001
Gordon Strachan 2001–04
Paul Sturrock 2004
Steve Wigley 2004
Harry Redknapp 2004–05
George Burley 2005–08
Nigel Pearson 2008
Jan Poortvliet 2008–09
Mark Wotte 2009
Alan Pardew 2009–10
Nigel Adkins September 2010–

TEN YEAR LEAGUE RECORD

		P	W	D	L	F	A	Pts	Pos
2001-02	PR Lge	38	12	9	17	46	54	45	11
2002-03	PR Lge	38	13	13	12	43	46	52	8
2003-04	PR Lge	38	12	11	15	44	45	47	12
2004-05	PR Lge	38	6	14	18	45	66	32	20
2005-06	FL C	46	13	19	14	49	50	58	12
2006-07	FL C	46	21	12	13	77	53	75	6
2007-08	FL C	46	13	15	18	56	72	54	20
2008-09	FL C	46	10	15	21	46	69	45	23
2009-10	FL 1	46	23	14	9	85	47	73*	7
2010-11	FL 1	46	28	8	10	86	38	92	2

10 pts deducted.

DID YOU KNOW

In 1905–06 Southampton, then in the Southern League, beat Middlesbrough 6-1 in a third round FA Cup tie on 24 February. At the time it was the heaviest defeat inflicted on a Football League club. Their opponents were members of the First Division that season.

SOUTHAMPTON 2010–11 LEAGUE RECORD

Match No.	Date	Venue	Opponents	Result	H/T Score	Lg Pos.	Goalscorers	Attendance
1	Aug 7	H	Plymouth Arg	L 0-1	0-0	—		21,727
2	21	H	Leyton Orient	D 1-1	1-1	20	Lambert [12]	21,468
3	28	A	Bristol R	W 4-0	2-0	14	Fonte [10], Lallana [34], Lambert (pen) [59], Barnard [90]	8226
4	Sept 4	H	Rochdale	L 0-2	0-1	18		18,169
5	11	A	Swindon T	L 0-1	0-0	22		11,087
6	15	A	Milton Keynes D	L 0-2	0-0	—		8133
7	18	H	Colchester U	D 0-0	0-0	22		17,857
8	25	A	Sheffield W	W 1-0	0-0	18	Barnard [61]	18,198
9	28	A	Yeovil T	D 1-1	0-0	—	Do Prado [56]	5854
10	Oct 2	H	Bournemouth	W 2-0	1-0	15	Lambert 2 (2 pens) [19, 55]	26,289
11	9	H	Tranmere R	W 2-0	1-0	13	Lambert [42], Lallana [56]	19,293
12	16	A	Huddersfield T	L 0-2	0-2	15		14,769
13	23	H	Oldham Ath	W 2-1	1-1	14	Fonte [45], Oxlade-Chamberlain [73]	20,968
14	30	A	Notts Co	W 3-1	0-1	9	Lambert (pen) [68], Barnard [73], Lallana [90]	9547
15	Nov 2	H	Dagenham & R	W 4-0	2-0	—	Oxlade-Chamberlain 2 [11, 37], Barnard [56], Fonte [69]	20,161
16	13	A	Carlisle U	L 2-3	0-2	10	Oxlade-Chamberlain [49], Hammond [81]	6578
17	20	H	Peterborough U	W 4-1	1-0	6	Barnard [28], Fonte [46], Chaplow [50], Do Prado [80]	22,177
18	23	H	Brighton & HA	D 0-0	0-0	—		26,237
19	Dec 11	H	Brentford	L 0-2	0-2	9		19,641
20	28	H	Huddersfield T	W 4-1	2-1	—	Lambert [28], Oxlade-Chamberlain [32], Jaidi [51], Chaplow [72]	24,483
21	Jan 1	H	Exeter C	W 4-0	1-0	2	Do Prado 2 [19, 51], Lallana [66], Barnard [90]	22,465
22	3	A	Dagenham & R	W 3-1	0-0	2	Lallana [47], Do Prado [75], Lambert [90]	3585
23	11	A	Oldham Ath	W 6-0	2-0	—	Oxlade-Chamberlain [9], Lallana [38], Do Prado [52], Chaplow [69], Lambert [74], Barnard [86]	3767
24	15	H	Notts Co	D 0-0	0-0	3		20,201
25	22	A	Tranmere R	L 0-2	0-1	4		5504
26	Feb 1	A	Exeter C	W 2-1	0-1	4	Lambert 2 [70, 90]	6370
27	5	A	Peterborough U	D 4-4	2-2	4	Chaplow [18], Lambert 2 (2 pens) [31, 47], Hammond [50]	6905
28	12	H	Carlisle U	W 1-0	1-0	4	Lambert [43]	25,076
29	22	A	Hartlepool U	D 0-0	0-0	—		3301
30	26	H	Swindon T	W 4-1	1-0	5	Lallana [15], Lambert [60], Jaidi [61], Barnard [90]	22,627
31	Mar 1	A	Walsall	L 0-1	0-0	—		4684
32	5	A	Colchester U	W 2-0	1-0	5	Oxlade-Chamberlain [30], Hammond [50]	6523
33	8	H	Yeovil T	W 3-0	1-0	—	Barnard 2 [15, 55], Oxlade-Chamberlain [67]	18,623
34	12	A	Bournemouth	W 3-1	1-1	4	Barnard [11], Hammond [71], Lambert [88]	10,008
35	19	H	Sheffield W	W 2-0	0-0	4	Fonte [60], Lambert [66]	20,234
36	22	A	Charlton Ath	D 1-1	0-0	—	Jaidi [64]	16,550
37	Apr 2	H	Milton Keynes D	W 3-2	0-1	3	Forte 2 [66, 67], Barnard [77]	22,377
38	5	H	Charlton Ath	W 2-0	1-0	—	Do Prado [11], Barnard [58]	20,112
39	9	A	Leyton Orient	W 2-0	1-0	2	Lambert [26], Barnard [88]	7714
40	12	A	Rochdale	L 0-2	0-2	—		3825
41	16	H	Bristol R	W 1-0	0-0	2	Do Prado [82]	23,647
42	23	A	Brighton & HA	W 2-1	0-1	—	Connolly [84], Fonte [89]	8169
43	25	H	Hartlepool U	W 2-0	0-0	2	Lambert (pen) [50], Fonte [82]	24,210
44	30	A	Brentford	W 3-0	2-0	2	Lallana [16], Connolly [30], Gobern [90]	7015
45	May 2	H	Plymouth Arg	W 3-1	1-0	—	Lambert 2 (1 pen) [45, 59 (p)], Dickson [49]	13,118
46	7	H	Walsall	W 3-1	2-1	2	Do Prado [26], Connolly [29], Oxlade-Chamberlain [68]	31,653

Final League Position: 2

GOALSCORERS

League (86): Lambert 21 (8 pens), Barnard 14, Do Prado 9, Oxlade-Chamberlain 9, Lallana 8, Fonte 7, Chaplow 4, Hammond 4, Connolly 3, Jaidi 3, Forte 2, Dickson 1, Gobern 1.
Carling Cup (2): Lallana 1, Oxlade-Chamberlain 1.
FA Cup (8): Do Prado 2, Lallana 2, Barnard 1, Chaplow 1, Connolly 1, Gobern 1.
J Paint Trophy (0).

Davis K 46	Butterfield D 32 + 2	Harding D 35 + 1	Schneiderlin M 23 + 4	Jaidi R 31	Fonte J 43	Puncheon J 15	Hammond D 40 + 1	Barnard L 24 + 12	Connolly D 8 + 7	Dickson R 15 + 8	Lallana A 30 + 6	Holmes L — + 7	Lambert R 45	Oxlade-Chamberlain A 27 + 7	Martin A 4 + 4	Do Prado G 23 + 11	Mills J — + 2	Seaborne D 14 + 10	Wotton P — + 2	Chaplow R 27 + 6	Bignall N — + 3	Richardson F 14 + 7	Gobern O 1 + 10	N'Guessan D 2 + 4	Forte J 2 + 8	Stephens D 5 + 1	Match No.
1	2	3¹	4	5	6	7²	8	9	10	11	12	13															1
1	2	3	4	5	6	7	8²	9¹	12		11		10	13													2
1	2	3	4³		6	7	8	9	13	12	11¹		10²		5	14											3
1	2	3	4		6	7	8		10¹				9	11²	5	12	13										4
1	2	3	4		6	7¹	8		10				9	11²	5	12	13										5
1	2	3	4		6	7	8		10¹			13	9	11²		5	12										6
1	2	3¹	4		6	7²	8	9		12		13	10	11³		14	5										7
1	2	3	4	5		7³	8	9¹	13	12	14	10	11²		6												8
1	2	3	4	5		7	8	9²	13				10	11¹	12	6											9
1	2	3	4		6	7	8	9²		11¹			10³	12	14	5	13										10
1	2	3			6	7²	8	12		11³	14	9	13	10¹	5	4											11
1	2	3	14		6	7³	8	12		11			10²	9¹	5		4	13									12
1	2	3	4		6	7¹		13		11			10²	12	9³	5	14	8									13
1		3	4²		6	7¹	8	9³		11			10	12	5	13	14	2									14
1		3	14		6		8	9¹		11			10²	7³	13	5	4	12	2								15
1		3¹	4²	5	6		8	13		12	10		9	11	7		2										16
1			5	6		8	9¹	14	3	7	13	10⁵	11²	12		4	2										17
1	14		4¹	5	6	8	9²		3	7	12	10	11³	13		2											18
1	2		4	5		8		12	3	7		10¹	11	9	6												19
1	2¹	3	4²	5	6	8		14	7			10	11³	9		13	12										20
1		3	4		6		13	12	7			10	11¹	9²	5	8³	2	14									21
1	2		5	6		8	12	3	7			10³	11¹	9²	14	4	13										22
1		4	5³	6			14	3	7¹			10	11²	9	13	8	2	12									23
1		4	5	6	11²		13	3				10	7	9		8¹	2	12									24
1		4	5	6			12	11¹				10	7	9		8	2										25
1	2	3	8³	5²	6	12	9					10	11		13	4				14	7¹						26
1	2	3¹			6	8	9¹	12				10	11	7²	5	4		13			14						27
1	2	3		5	6	8	13			12		10²	11	9		4¹				7³	14						28
1	2	3		5	6	8	12			7		10	11¹	9		4											29
1	2	3	12	5	6	8	13			7		10	11³	9²		4¹		14									30
1	2	3	11¹	5	6	8	9			7		10	13			4		12²									31
1	2	3		5¹	6	8	9²			7		10	11³	12		4		14	13								32
1	2	3			6	8	9			7²		10	11³	5		4¹		14	12		13						33
1	2	3¹		5	6	8	9²			7		10	11	12		4³		14	13●								34
1	2	3		5	6	8	9²			7³		10	11¹	12	14	4			13								35
1	2	3		5	6	8	9³			7¹		10	11²	13		4			12	14							36
1	2³	3		5	6	8	9			7		10		11²		4¹		14			12	13					37
1			5	6	4	9	14	3	7²		10		11³			12		2	13			8⁶					38
1	2³	3²		5	6	8	9			7		10		14	11¹	13		4			12						39
1		3¹		5²	6	8	9			4	14	10			11	13		2				12	7³				40
1	2		5¹	6	8	9²	13	3			10		11			12			14	7³	4						41
1	2		5	6	8		13	3³	12		9		11			14		4		7²	10¹						42
1	3				6²	8		10		7³		9	14	11¹	5	12		2		13	4						43
1	14	3²		5	6	8		10³	13	7		9	11¹			4		2	12								44
1	2		14	5²	6	8		10	3	11³		9	13		12	4¹						7					45
1		13	4³	5	6	8		9	3²	7		10	12	11¹		14		2									46

FA Cup

First Round	Shrewsbury T	(h)	2-0
Second Round	Cheltenham T	(h)	3-0
Third Round	Blackpool	(h)	2-0
Fourth Round	Manchester U	(h)	1-2

Carling Cup

First Round	Bournemouth	(h)	2-0
Second Round	Bolton W	(h)	0-1

J Paint Trophy

First Round	Swindon T	(h)	0-3

SOUTHEND UNITED   FL Championship 2

FOUNDATION

The leading club in Southend around the turn of the century was Southend Athletic, but they were an amateur concern. Southend United was a more ambitious professional club when they were founded in 1906, employing Bob Jack as secretary-manager and immediately joining the Second Division of the Southern League.

Roots Hall Stadium, Victoria Avenue, Southend-on-Sea, Essex SS2 6NQ.

Telephone: (01702) 304 050.

Fax: (01702) 304 124.

Ticket Office: (08444) 770 077.

Website: www.southendunited.co.uk

Email: info@southend-united.co.uk

Ground Capacity: 12,260.

Record Attendance: 22,862 v Tottenham H, FA Cup 3rd rd replay, 11 January 1936 (at Southend Stadium). 31,090 v Liverpool, FA Cup 3rd rd, 10 January 1979 (at Roots Hall).

Pitch Measurements: 110yd × 76yd.

Chairman: Ronald Martin.

Chief Executive: Tara Brady.

Secretary: Mrs Helen Norbury.

Manager: Paul Sturrock.

Physio: Ben Clarkson.

Club Nickname: 'The Blues' or 'The Shrimpers'.

Colours: Navy blue shirts with white collar, navy blue shorts, white stockings.

Change Colours: Maroon shirts with white trim, maroon shorts, maroon stockings.

Year Formed: 1906.

Turned Professional: 1906. *Ltd Co.:* 1919.

Grounds: 1906, Roots Hall, Prittlewell; 1920, Kursaal; 1934, Southend Stadium; 1955, Roots Hall Football Ground.

First Football League Game: 28 August 1920, Division 3, v Brighton & HA (a) W 2–0 – Capper; Reid, Newton; Wileman, Henderson, Martin; Nicholls, Nuttall, Fairclough (2), Myers, Dorsett.

Record League Victory: 9–2 v Newport Co, Division 3 (S), 5 September 1936 – McKenzie; Nelson, Everest (1); Deacon, Turner, Carr; Bolan, Lane (1), Goddard (4), Dickinson (2), Oswald (1).

Record Cup Victory: 10–1 v Golders Green, FA Cup 1st rd, 24 November 1934 – Moore; Morfitt, Kelly; Mackay, Joe Wilson, Carr (1); Lane (1), Johnson (5), Cheesmuir (2), Deacon (1), Oswald. 10–1 v Brentwood, FA Cup 2nd rd, 7 December 1968 – Roberts; Bentley, Birks; McMillan (1) Beesley, Kurila; Clayton, Chisnall, Moore (4), Best (5), Hamilton. 10–1 v Aldershot, Leyland Daf Cup Prel rd, 6 November 1990 – Sansome; Austin, Powell, Cornwell, Prior (1), Tilson (3), Cawley, Butler, Ansah (1), Benjamin (1), Angell (4).

Record Defeat: 1–9 v Brighton & HA, Division 3, 27 November 1965.

HONOURS

Football League – Division 1:
Best season: 13th, 1994–95;

FL 1: *Champions* 2005–06;

Division 3: *Runners-up* 1990–91;

Division 4: *Champions* 1980–81;
Runners-up 1971–72, 1977–78.

FA Cup: Best season: old 3rd rd, 1921; 5th rd, 1926, 1952, 1976, 1993.

Football League Cup: Quarter final 2007.

LDV Vans Trophy: *Runners-up* 2004, 2005.

sky|SPORTS FACT FILE

Southend United can claim to have had international players from as wide a range as Congo DR, Jamaica, Montserrat, Northern Ireland, the Republic of Ireland and Wales. Northern Ireland inside-forward Jimmy McAlinden had also played for the Republic before joining United.

Most League Points (2 for a win): 67, Division 4, 1980–81.

Most League Points (3 for a win): 85, Division 3, 1990–91.

Most League Goals: 92, Division 3 (S), 1950–51.

Highest League Scorer in Season: Jim Shankly, 31, 1928–29; Sammy McCrory, 1957–58, both in Division 3 (S).

Most League Goals in Total Aggregate: Roy Hollis, 122, 1953–60.

Most League Goals in One Match: 5, Jim Shankly v Merthyr T, Division 3 (S), 1 March 1930.

Most Capped Player: George Mackenzie, 9, Eire.

Most League Appearances: Sandy Anderson, 452, 1950–63.

Youngest League Player: Phil O'Connor, 16 years 76 days v Lincoln C, 26 December 1969.

Record Transfer Fee Received: £4,200,000 from Nottingham F for Stan Collymore, June 1993.

Record Transfer Fee Paid: £750,000 to Crystal Palace for Stan Collymore, November 1992.

Football League Record: 1920 Original Member of Division 3; 1921–58 Division 3 (S); 1958–66 Division 3; 1966–72 Division 4; 1972–76 Division 3; 1976–78 Division 4; 1978–80 Division 3; 1980–81 Division 4; 1981–84 Division 3; 1984–87 Division 4; 1987–89 Division 3; 1989–90 Division 4; 1990–91 Division 3; 1991–92 Division 2; 1992–97 Division 1; 1997–98 Division 2; 1998–2004 Division 3; 2004–05 FL 2; 2005–06 FL 1; 2006–07 FL C; 2007–10 FL 1; 2010– FL 2.

LATEST SEQUENCES

Longest Sequence of League Wins: 8, 29.8.2005 – 9.10.2005.

Longest Sequence of League Defeats: 6, 29.8.1987 – 19.9.1987.

Longest Sequence of League Draws: 6, 30.1.1982 – 19.2.1982.

Longest Sequence of Unbeaten League Matches: 16, 20.2.1932 – 29.8.1932.

Longest Sequence Without a League Win: 17, 31.12.1983 – 14.4.1984.

Successive Scoring Runs: 24 from 23.3.1929.

Successive Non-scoring Runs: 6 from 28.10.1933.

MANAGERS

Bob Jack 1906–10
George Molyneux 1910–11
O. M. Howard 1911–12
Joe Bradshaw 1912–19
Ned Liddell 1919–20
Tom Mather 1920–21
Ted Birnie 1921–34
David Jack 1934–40
Harry Warren 1946–56
Eddie Perry 1956–60
Frank Broome 1960
Ted Fenton 1961–65
Alvan Williams 1965–67
Ernie Shepherd 1967–69
Geoff Hudson 1969–70
Arthur Rowley 1970–76
Dave Smith 1976–83
Peter Morris 1983–84
Bobby Moore 1984–86
Dave Webb 1986–87
Dick Bate 1987
Paul Clark 1987–88
Dave Webb *(General Manager)* 1988–92
Colin Murphy 1992–93
Barry Fry 1993
Peter Taylor 1993–95
Steve Thompson 1995
Ronnie Whelan 1995–97
Alvin Martin 1997–99
Alan Little 1999–2000
David Webb 2000–01
Rob Newman 2001–03
Steve Wignall 2003
Steve Tilson 2003–10
Paul Sturrock July 2010–

TEN YEAR LEAGUE RECORD

		P	W	D	L	F	A	Pts	Pos
2001-02	Div 3	46	15	13	18	51	54	58	12
2002-03	Div 3	46	17	3	26	47	59	54	17
2003-04	Div 3	46	14	12	20	51	63	54	17
2004-05	FL 2	46	22	12	12	65	46	78	4
2005-06	FL 1	46	23	13	10	72	43	82	1
2006-07	FL C	46	10	12	24	47	80	42	22
2007-08	FL 1	46	22	10	14	70	55	76	6
2008-09	FL 1	46	21	8	17	58	61	71	8
2009-10	FL 1	46	10	13	23	51	72	43	23
2010-11	FL 2	46	16	13	17	62	56	61	13

DID YOU KNOW ?

On 15 January 2010, a goal after 32 seconds scored by Ryan Hall helped Southend United to defeat Rotherham United 2-1 at the Don Valley Stadium and thus complete the first double for them in the season. On 30 October 2010, Southend had won 1-0 at Roots Hall.

SOUTHEND UNITED 2010–11 LEAGUE RECORD

Match No.	Date	Venue	Opponents	Result	H/T Score	Lg Pos.	Goalscorers	Attendance
1	Aug 7	H	Stockport Co	D 1-1	0-0	—	Sturrock [90]	5589
2	14	A	Aldershot T	L 0-1	0-0	20		3011
3	21	H	Port Vale	L 1-3	0-1	22	Owen (og) [88]	4946
4	27	A	Bradford C	W 2-0	1 0	—	Corr [16], Grant [54]	10,752
5	Sept 4	H	Torquay U	W 2-1	2-0	11	Grant [15], Simpson [43]	5505
6	11	A	Northampton T	L 1-2	0-0	14	Grant [57]	5720
7	18	H	Morecambe	L 2-3	1-2	16	Grant [22], Corr [50]	5106
8	25	A	Hereford U	W 3-1	1-1	12	Corr [27], Timlin [52], Sturrock [67]	2104
9	28	A	Gillingham	D 0-0	0-0	—		4925
10	Oct 2	H	Lincoln C	W 1-0	1-0	11	Corr [3]	5154
11	9	A	Chesterfield	L 1-2	1-1	14	Grant [36]	6557
12	16	H	Crewe Alex	L 0-2	0-0	17		5506
13	23	A	Bury	L 0-1	0-1	18		3531
14	30	H	Rotherham U	W 1-0	1-0	15	Sturrock [5]	5533
15	Nov 13	H	Accrington S	D 1-1	0-1	15	Mohsni [65]	4748
16	20	A	Shrewsbury T	D 1-1	0-0	15	Grant [87]	5406
17	23	A	Stevenage	D 1-1	0-1	—	Corr [84]	2544
18	Dec 11	A	Burton Alb	L 1-3	0-2	20	Sturrock [51]	2604
19	14	A	Cheltenham T	W 2-0	2-0	—	Midson 2 [8, 14]	2229
20	Jan 1	A	Oxford U	W 2-0	2-0	12	Corr [18], Clohessy [44]	7362
21	3	H	Cheltenham T	L 1-2	0-2	15	Corr [77]	4942
22	8	H	Chesterfield	L 2-3	0-2	17	Easton [58], Corr (pen) [83]	5021
23	15	A	Rotherham U	W 2-1	2-0	15	Hall [1], Sturrock [13]	4310
24	21	H	Bury	D 1-1	0-0	—	Mohsni [90]	5175
25	25	H	Macclesfield T	W 4-1	4-0	—	Mohsni 2 [17, 39], Hall [33], Easton [43]	5011
26	29	A	Barnet	W 2-0	1-0	—	Grant [25], Corr [67]	2867
27	Feb 1	H	Oxford U	W 2-1	2-1	9	Hall [43], Mohsni [45]	4944
28	5	H	Shrewsbury T	L 0-2	0-1	10		5396
29	15	A	Wycombe W	W 3-2	0-1	—	Corr [50], Ferdinand [59], Easton [90]	4499
30	19	A	Torquay U	D 1-1	0-0	10	Corr [81]	2880
31	22	H	Barnet	W 2-1	2-0	—	Easton [11], Hall [16]	5501
32	26	H	Northampton T	D 1-1	1-1	8	Corr [34]	6384
33	Mar 5	A	Morecambe	L 1-2	0-1	9	Corr (pen) [50]	1917
34	8	H	Gillingham	D 2-2	1-2	—	Hall 2 [15, 52]	5771
35	12	A	Lincoln C	L 1-2	0-1	12	Sturrock [60]	3560
36	15	A	Crewe Alex	L 0-1	0-0	—		3319
37	18	H	Hereford U	W 4-0	1-0	—	Crawford 2 (1 pen) [36, 90 (p)], Corr 2 [65, 67]	5056
38	26	A	Stockport Co	L 1-2	0-1	—	Asante [81]	3335
39	Apr 2	H	Aldershot T	D 0-0	0-0	14		5557
40	5	A	Accrington S	L 1-3	0-1	—	Hall [58]	2222
41	9	A	Port Vale	D 1-1	0-1	14	Prosser [90]	5108
42	15	H	Bradford C	W 4-0	2-0	—	Corr (pen) [29], Hall 2 [43, 70], Ferdinand [66]	5217
43	22	A	Stevenage	W 1-0	0-0	—	Corr [81]	6622
44	25	A	Macclesfield T	D 0-0	0-0	11		1427
45	30	H	Burton Alb	D 1-1	1-1	13	Corr [3]	5730
46	May 7	A	Wycombe W	L 1-3	1-2	13	Grant [15]	8567

Final League Position: 13

GOALSCORERS
League (62): Corr 18 (3 pens), Hall 9, Grant 8, Sturrock 6, Mohsni 5, Easton 4, Crawford 2 (1 pen), Ferdinand 2, Midson 2, Asante 1, Clohessy 1, Prosser 1, Simpson 1, Timlin 1, own goal 1.
Carling Cup (4): Paterson 2 (1 pen), Corr 1, Easton 1.
FA Cup (4): Corr 2, German 1 (pen), Simpson 1.
J Paint Trophy (3): Paterson 2, Soares 1.

Morris G 33	Clohessy S 46	Barker C 43	Simpson J 17	Phillips M 3+2	Prosser L 14+3	Grant A 41+2	Easton C 32	Spencer S 1+4	Corr B 32+9	Soares L 17+14	Zaabout S 2+1	Sturrock B 34+9	Paterson M 4+7	Hall R 36+5	Coughlan G 28+5	Gilbert P 26	Mohsni B 21+2	Timlin M 8	Herd J 6+3	Jarvis N —+6	Crawford H 5+18	Fairhurst W 2+1	German A 3+1	Midson J 4	Woodyard A 3	Evans R 13	Ferdinand K 19+3	Comminges M 4+3	Sawyer L 7+10	Asante K 1+8	Stevens J 1	Nesbitt T —+2	Match No.
1	2	3	4¹	5	6	7	8	9²	10	11³	12	13	14																				1
1	2	3	4	5	6	7	8	14	10³	11²		9¹	12	13																			2
1	2	3	12		6¹	7	8	14	13	11	4²	9³	10	5																			3
1	2*	5	4		14	7	8		10²	12		9¹	13	11³	3	6																	4
1	2	5	4			7	8		10¹			9	12	11²	13	3	6																5
1	2	5	4			7	8	14	12	10¹		9³	13	11²	3	6																	6
1	2	5	4³			7		14	10	12		9²		11	3¹	6	8	13															7
1	2	5	4		14	7			10³	13		9¹		11²	3	6	8		12														8
1	2	5	4			7²			10	11		9¹		12	3	6	8		13														9
1	2	5	4			7			10¹	13		9³		11²	3	6	8		12	14													10
1	2	5	4			7				11		10¹	13	6	3		8		12		9²												11
1	2	5			6²	7				11		10¹	13	4		8	3	14	12	9³													12
1	2	5	4			7			10	12		9²		11	6³	3	8		13	14													13
1	2	5¹	4			7			10	13		9²		11²	12	3	6	8		14													14
1	2		4		5	7	8		12		11				3	6			13		9²	10¹											15
1	2		4²			7	8		13	11		9¹			5	3	6		14		12	10³											16
1	2		4		12	7	8		14	11³		13			5¹	3⁴	6				9	10²											17
1	2	3	4		6		8		10³	11		13		12	5				14		9²		7¹										18
1	2	5	4¹			7	8		14	12		9		11	13		6²	3				10³											19
	2	5					8		10¹	7		9	12	11	4			3									1	6					20
	2	5				12	8		10	7²		9³	13	11	4			3									1	6¹	14				21
1	2	5				7	8		10			13	9²	11	4			3									12	6¹					22
1	2	5				4	8		10	7¹		9		11	6	3											12						23
1	2	5				4	8		10			9²		11	6	3³	13		14								7¹		12				24
	2	5	13			7³	8		12			9		11	6²	3	10¹									1	4	14					25
	2	5				7³	8		12	13		9²		11	6¹	3	10									1	4	14					26
	2	5				7	8		10			9²		11³	3¹	6		12	13							1	4	14					27
	2	5				7	8		10	14		9²		11	3³	6¹			13							1	4	12					28
	2	5		6		7	8		10¹			9		11²	3			12								1	4	13					29
	2	5				7¹	8		10			9²		11	6	3										1	4	12	13				30
	2	5					8		14	11²		9³		10	6	3	13									1	4	7¹	12				31
	2	5				7	8		10	13		9¹		11³	6	3		12								1	14	4²					32
	2	5				4	8		10	7¹		9²		11	6	3³		14								1		12	13				33
	2	5				4	8		10			9¹		11	6	3		12								1		7					34
	2	5				13	8²		10			9		11³	6	3¹										1	4	12	7	14			35
1	2	5				3	7		10	13		9¹		11³	6			12									4²		8	14			36
1	2	5				7			10²	13		9		11	6		3¹	12									4	8					37
1	2	5				7				11²		9		3	6			10		8									13	4¹	12		38
1	2	3				7			10			12		11	5	6		9¹		8							4						39
1	2	3		5		7			10	13		12		11		6⁸											4	8²	9¹				40
1	2	5		4		7			10	12		9¹		11	6			13									8	3²					41
1	2	5		3²	7	8³			10			12		11	6			9¹									4		14	13			42
1	2	5		3¹	7	8			10			14		11	6		12	9³									4²	13					43
1	2	5²		3	4	8			10			12		11³	13		6	9¹									14	7					44
1	2	5		3	7¹	8³			10			9²		11	14		6	13									4	12⁸					45
1	2	5		3	7	8						9¹		11	6		10	12									4²		13				46

FA Cup

First Round	Macclesfield T	(a)	2-2	
		(h)	2-2	

Carling Cup

First Round	Bristol C	(h)	3-2	
Second Round	Wolverhampton W	(a)	1-2	

J Paint Trophy

First Round	Gillingham	(h)	0-0	
Second Round	Barnet	(a)	3-1	
Southern Quarter-Final	Charlton Ath	(h)	0-1	

STEVENAGE   FL Championship 1

FOUNDATION

There have been several clubs associated with town of Stevenage. Stevenage Town was formed in 1884. They absorbed Stevenage Rangers in 1955 and later played at Broadhall Way. The club went into liquidation in 1968 and Stevenage Athletic was formed, but they, too, followed a similar path in 1976. Then Stevenage Borough was founded. The Broadhall Way pitch was dug up and remained unused for three years. Thus the new club started its life in the modest surrounds of the King George V playing fields with a roped-off ground in the Chiltern League. A change of competition followed to the Wallspan Southern Combination and by 1980 the club returned to the council-owned Broadhall Way when "Borough" was added to the name. Entry into the United Counties League was so successful the League and Cup were won in the first season. On to the Isthmian League Division Two and the climb up the pyramid continued. In 1995–96 Stevenage Borough won the Conference but was denied a place in the Football League as the ground did not measure up to the competition's standards. Subsequent improvements changed this and the 7,100 capacity venue became one of the best appointed grounds in non-league football. After winning elevation to the Football League the club dropped Borough from its title.

Lamex Stadium, Broadhall Way, Stevenage, Herts SG2 8RH.

Telephone: 01438 223223.

Fax: 01438 743611.

Website: stevenageboro.fc.com

Ground Capacity: 6,546.

Record Attendance: 6,489 v Kidderminster H, Conference, 25 January 1997.

Chairman: Phil Wallace.

Chief Executive: Bob Makin.

Secretary: Roger Austin.

Manager: Graham Westley.

MANAGERS

Derek Montgomery 1976–83
Frank Cornwell 1983–87
John Bailey 1987–88
Brian Wilcox 1988–90
Paul Fairclough 1990–98
Richard Hill 1998–2000
Steve Wignall 2000
Paul Fairclough 2000–02
Wayne Turner 2002–03
Graham Westley 2003–06
Mark Stimson 2006–07
Peter Taylor 2007–08
Graham Westley May 2008–

sky SPORTS FACT FILE

On 8 January 2011 Stevenage gained revenge against Newcastle United in the FA Cup when they beat them 3-0 in a third round tie. On 25 January 1998 they had lost in controversial circumstances 2-1 in a replay (see 40th edition for further details).

Assistant Manager: John Dreyer.

Sports Therapist: Paul Dando.

Nickname: The Boro.

Grounds: 1976, King George V playing fields; 1980, Broadhall Way.

First Football League Game: 7 August 2010, FL 2, v Macclesfield T (h) D 2–2 – Day; Henry, Laird, Bostwick, Roberts, Foster, Wilson (Sinclair), Byrom, Griffin (1), Winn (Odubade), Vincenti (1) (Beardsley).

Colours: White shirts, red shorts, red stockings with white tops.

Change Colours: All blue.

Year Formed: 1976.

Record Victory: 11-1 v British Timken Ath 1980–81.

Record Defeat: 0-7 v Southwick 1987–88.

Most League Appearances: Chris Day, 46, 2010–11.

Most League Goals: Byron Harrison, 8, 2010–11.

Most Goals in One Season: Martin Gittings, 40, 1991–92.

Most Goals in Total Aggregate: Byron Harrison, 9, 2010–11.

Record Transfer Fee Received: £260,000 from Peterborough U for George Boyd, January 2007.

Record Transfer Fee Paid: £20,000 to Hereford United for Richard Leadbetter, February 1999.

Football League Record: 2010–11 FL 2; 2011– FL 1.

HONOURS
Football League – FL 2: Best season: 6th 2010–11 promoted to FL 1.
FA Cup: Never past fourth round.
Blue Square Premier League: *Champions* 2009–10.
Conference: *Champions* 1995–96.
FA Trophy: *Winners* 2007, 2009; *Runners-up* 2002, 2010.
Herts Senior Cup: *Winners* 2009.
Isthmian League Premier Division: *Champions* 1993–94.
Isthmian League Division 1: *Champions*: 1991–92.
Isthmian League Division 2 (N): *Champions*: 1985–86, 1990–91.
United Counties League Division 1: *Champions* 1980–81.
United Counties League Cup: *Winners* 1981.

LATEST SEQUENCES

Longest Sequence of League Wins: 6, 12.3.2011 – 2.4.2011.

Longest Sequence of League Defeats: 2, 5.3.2011 – 8.3.2011.

Longest Sequence of League Draws: 2, 28.8.2010 – 4.9.2010.

Longest Sequence of Unbeaten League Matches: 8, 12.3.2011 – 16.4.2011.

Longest Sequence Without a League Win: 5, 13.11.2010 – 1.1.2011.

Successive Scoring Runs: 8 from 12.3.2011 – 16.4.2011.

Successive Non-scoring Runs: 8.2.2011 – 15.2.2011.

TEN YEAR LEAGUE RECORD

		P	W	D	L	F	A	Pts	Pos
2001-02	Conf	42	15	10	17	57	60	55	11
2002-03	Con	42	14	10	18	61	55	52	12
2003-04	Conf	42	18	9	15	58	52	63	8
2004-05	Conf	42	22	6	14	65	52	72	5
2005-06	Conf	42	19	12	11	62	47	69	6
2006-07	Conf	46	20	10	16	76	66	70	8
2007-08	B Sq Pr	46	24	7	15	82	55	79	6
2008-09	B Sq Pr	46	23	12	11	73	54	81	5
2009-10	B Sq Pr	44	30	9	5	79	24	99	1
2010-11	FL 2	46	18	15	13	62	45	69	6

DID YOU KNOW ?

Stevenage Borough became the first club to win a competitive final at the new Wembley Stadium when on 12 May 2007 they defeated Kidderminster Harriers 3-2 in the FA Trophy. The attendance for the match was 53,262, a record for the competition.

STEVENAGE 2010–11 LEAGUE RECORD

Match No.	Date		Venue	Opponents	Result		H/T Score	Lg Pos.	Goalscorers	Atten- dance
1	Aug	7	H	Macclesfield T	D	2-2	1-1	—	Vincenti [7], Griffin [69]	3553
2		14	A	Bradford C	L	0-1	0-1	17		10,967
3		21	H	Stockport Co	W	3-1	2-0	10	Griffin 2 [29, 71], Bostwick [43]	2726
4		28	A	Aldershot T	D	1-1	0-0	10	Beardsley [50]	2525
5	Sept	4	H	Crewe Alex	D	1-1	1-0	14	Odubade [45]	3431
6		11	A	Cheltenham T	L	0-1	0-0	18		2805
7		18	H	Torquay U	D	0-0	0-0	15		3049
8		25	A	Lincoln C	W	1-0	1-0	11	Holroyd [40]	3215
9		28	A	Hereford U	W	4-1	1-0	—	Holroyd 3 [13, 69, 82], Ashton [62]	1444
10	Oct	2	H	Wycombe W	L	0-2	0-2	13		3384
11		9	A	Rotherham U	D	1-1	0-1	13	Mousinho [82]	4037
12		16	H	Burton Alb	W	2-1	1-0	8	Laird (pen) [34], Holroyd [58]	2550
13		23	A	Morecambe	D	0-0	0-0	8		2254
14		30	H	Chesterfield	D	0-0	0-0	10		3556
15	Nov	2	A	Barnet	W	3-0	2-0	—	Mousinho 2 (1 pen) [27, 78 (p)], Roberts [33]	2722
16		13	H	Shrewsbury T	D	1-1	1-0	8	Holroyd [8]	2765
17		20	A	Accrington S	L	0-1	0-0	9		1370
18		23	H	Southend U	D	1-1	1-0	—	Long [26]	2544
19	Dec	11	H	Northampton T	L	0-1	0-1	11		3128
20	Jan	1	A	Gillingham	L	0-1	0-1	17		5429
21		3	A	Barnet	W	4-2	3-0	13	Foster [4], Basey (og) [8], Long [27], Roberts [46]	3744
22		15	A	Chesterfield	L	0-1	0-1	17		6219
23		22	H	Morecambe	W	2-0	2-0	15	Laird [5], Charnock (og) [9]	2002
24		25	H	Rotherham U	W	3-0	1-0	—	Winn [44], Harrison [85], Laird [90]	1549
25	Feb	1	H	Gillingham	D	2-2	1-1	12	Harrison 2 [25, 75]	2424
26		5	H	Accrington S	D	2-2	1-0	13	Harrison [7], Wilson [78]	2265
27		8	A	Bury	L	0-3	0-1	—		2080
28		12	A	Shrewsbury T	L	0-1	0-1	15		5261
29		15	H	Oxford U	D	0-0	0-0	—		2590
30		19	A	Crewe Alex	W	1-0	0-0	13	Harrison [87]	3793
31		22	A	Port Vale	W	3-1	2-0	—	Griffith (og) [33], Winn [40], Bridges [67]	4588
32		26	A	Cheltenham T	W	4-0	2-0	10	Roberts [16], Harrison 2 [33, 54], Bostwick [52]	2733
33	Mar	5	A	Torquay U	L	0-2	0-0	12		2197
34		8	H	Hereford U	L	0-1	0-0	—		1670
35		12	A	Wycombe W	W	1-0	0-0	11	Mousinho [47]	4453
36		15	A	Oxford U	W	2-1	1-1	—	Worley (og) [20], Reid [48]	6018
37		19	H	Lincoln C	W	2-1	1-1	9	Wilson 2 [37, 60]	2732
38		22	A	Burton Alb	W	2-0	1-0	—	Mousinho 2 (1 pen) [4, 88 (p)]	1962
39		26	A	Macclesfield T	W	4-0	2-0	—	Roberts 2 [29, 46], Sinclair 2 [34, 61]	1346
40	Apr	2	H	Bradford C	W	2-1	1-0	5	Mousinho (pen) [37], Charles [77]	3079
41		9	A	Stockport Co	D	2-2	0-0	6	Roberts [56], Wilson [90]	3449
42		16	H	Aldershot T	D	2-2	1-1	6	Charles [9], Harrison [72]	3031
43		22	A	Southend U	L	0-1	0-0	—		6622
44		25	A	Port Vale	W	1-0	0-0	6	Wilson [72]	3146
45		30	A	Northampton T	L	0-2	0-1	7		6257
46	May	7	H	Bury	D	3-3	2-2	6	Laird [8], Reid (pen) [19], May [73]	5016

Final League Position: 6

GOALSCORERS

League (62): Mousinho 7 (3 pens), Harrison 8, Holroyd 6, Roberts 6, Laird 4 (1 pen), Wilson 5, Griffin 3, Bostwick 2, Charles 2, Long 2, Reid 2 (1 pen), Sinclair 2, Winn 2, Ashton 1, Beardsley 1, Bridges 1, Foster 1, May 1, Odubade 1, Vincenti 1, own goals 4.
Carling Cup (1): Murphy 1.
FA Cup (7): Charles 2, Bostwick 1, Odubade 1, Walker 1, Winn 1, own goal 1.
J Paint Trophy (0).
Play-Offs (4): Beardsley 1, Byrom 1, Long 1, Mousinho 1.

Day C 46	Henry R 42	Laird S 42+2	Bostwick M 41	Roberts M 42	Foster L 16+7	Wilson L 39+3	Byrom J 5+2	Griffin C 13+2	Winn P 13+15	Vincenti P 1+4	Odubade Y 5+10	Beardsley C 14+9	Sinclair R 14+13	Mousinho J 36+2	Boylan L -+1	Ashton J 37+1	Charles D 20+8	Kuqi N -+1	Bridges D 8+11	Long S 19+3	Sills T 1	Holroyd C 12	Williams M -+1	May B 7+13	O'Shea J 5	Walker J 1	Dixon T -+1	Harrison B 11+9	Daley L -+2	Reid C 14+6	Atieno 1	Murphy D 1+4	Match No.
1	2	3	4	5	6	7^3	8	9	10^1	11^2	12	13	14																				1
1	2	3	4	5			8	9	12	13	11^1	10^2	7^3	6	14																		2
1	2	3	4	5		14		9^2	12		10^3	7	8		6	11^1	13																3
1	2	12	4	5		14		9^1		11	10	7^3	8		6	3^2	13																4
1	2	3	4	5		12	14	9^3		13	10		7^1	8^2	6		$11^■$																5
1	2	3	4	5^2		$7^■$	8	9	12	14	11^3	13		6			10^1																6
1	2	3	4	5				9	12	11^1				8		6	7		10														7
1	2	3^1	4		13	7		9^{12^2}			14	8		6	5		11^3	10															8
1	2	3^1	4		7		9^2	12	13			14	8		6	5		11^3	10														9
1	2	3^1	4		7		9^2		12		8	6	5	13	11^3	10	14																10
1	2	3	4	5	7^1		9	12	8	6	13	11^2	10																				11
1	2	3	4	5^2	$13^■$	7	10^1	12^3	8	6	14	11	9																				12
1	2	3	4	5	7	10^2	8	6	13	12^3	11^1	9	14																				13
1	2	3	4	5	7	13	8	6^1		14	10	12^9	9^2																				14
1	2	3	4	5	12	7	13	8	6^1	14	10	9^2	11^3																				15
1	2	3	4	5	7^3	12	13	8	6	14	10	9^2	11^1																				16
1	2		4	5	6^1	7	12	9^2	8^3	3	13	10	14	11																			17
1		3	4	5	13	2	7^3	12			6	14	8^1	11	9^2																		18
1	2	3	4	5^1	7^3	13	8	$6^{12^■}$			10	9^2	11	14																			19
1		3	4	5	6	9	13	10	12	8	7^1	14	11^3	2^2																			20
1		3	4	2	5	6	9^1	12^2	14	10	11^3	8	7	13																			21
1	2	3	6	4^3	7	13	9^1	10	8	5	12	14	11^2																				22
1	2	11	6	4	7	9^2	10	12	8^3	5	3^1																13	14					23
1	2	3	6	4	11	9^3	10	12	0^1	5	13	7^2															14						24
1	2	11		4	6	7	13	10^1	8	5	3^2		12													9						25
1	2	3	6	4	7	11^1	12	13	8	5																9	10^2					26
1		3	7	4^2	6	2	14	13	10^1	11	8^3	5														9	12					27
1	2	3	4	7	6	9^1	$8^■$	5	13	12	11														13	12	11	10^2			28
1	2	3	8	4	7	14	12	5	8	11^1	9^2											13	10^3						29
1	2	3		4	6	7	12	14	5	8	11^1	9^3											13	10^2						30
1	2	3	6	4	14	11	7^3		8^1	5	9	13											12	10^2						31
1	2	3	6	4	7	10^3	13	5	14	8^2	11^1											9	12							32
1	2	3	6	$4^■$	7	10	11^1	12	8^3	12	9^2										13	14								33
1	2	3	6	4	7	13	12	5^1	8	11^2	14											9	10^3							34
1	2	$3^■$	6	4	12	7	13	11^3	10	5	14	9^2												8^1						35
1	2		6	4	5	7	10^1	13	11	8	3^2	12		14										9^3						36
1	2	3^1	6	4	5	7	13	8	12	10	11^2	14												9^3						37
1	2	3^1	6^2	4	8	7	12	10	5	11	14													9^3	13					38
1	2	13	11^1	4	6	7	14	9	8	5	3^3	10^2																	12	39
1	2	3	6	4	5	7	13	8	10^2	11^1	14													9^3	12					40
1	2	3	11^1	4	6^3	7	13	12	8	5	10									14	9^2									41
1	2	3		4	6	7	12	11^1	8	5	9^3	14												13	10^2					42
1	2	3	6	4^1	7	$11^■$	8	5	10^2	13														9	12					43
1	2	3	6	4	13	7^2	10^1	11^2	8	5	14													9	12					44
1	2	3	7	4^2	$6^■$	10^1	13	$8^■$	5	11														9	12					45
1	2	3	6	4	7^3	13	8	5	11	12^2														9^1	10	14				46

FA Cup

First Round	Milton Keynes D	(h)	0-0
		(a)	1-1
Second Round	AFC Wimbledon	(a)	2-0
Third Round	Newcastle U	(h)	3-1
Fourth Round	Reading	(h)	1-2

Carling Cup

First Round	Portsmouth	(h)	1-2

J Paint Trophy

First Round	Brentford	(h)	0-1

Play-Offs

Semi-Final	Accrington S	(h)	2-0
		(a)	1-0
Final	Torquay U		1-0
(at Old Trafford).			

STOCKPORT COUNTY   Blue Square Premier

FOUNDATION

Formed at a meeting held at Wellington Road South by members of Wycliffe Congregational Chapel in 1883, they called themselves Heaton Norris Rovers until changing to Stockport County in 1890, a year before joining the Football Combination.

Edgeley Park, Hardcastle Road, Edgeley, Stockport, Cheshire SK3 9DD.

Telephone: (0161) 286 8888 (ext 257).

Fax: (0161) 429 7392.

Ticket Office: 0845 688 5799.

Website: www.stockportcounty.com

Email: stockport.county@btinternet.com

Ground Capacity: 10,641.

Record Attendance: 27,833 v Liverpool, FA Cup 5th rd, 11 February 1950.

Pitch Measurements: 104m × 66m.

Chairman: Lord Snape.

Secretary: Tony Whiteside.

Manager: Dietmar Hamman.

Assistant Manager: Willie McStay.

Physio: Rodger Wylde.

HONOURS

Football League – Division 1: Best season: 8th, 1997–98; **Division 2:** *Runners-up* 1996–97; **Division 3 (N):** *Champions* 1921–22, 1936–37; *Runners-up* 1928–29, 1929–30; **Division 4:** *Champions* 1966–67; *Runners-up* 1990–91.

FA Cup: Best season: 5th rd, 1935, 1950, 2001.

Football League Cup: Semi-final 1997.

Autoglass Trophy: *Runners-up* 1992, 1993.

Colours: Reflex blue shirts with one broad white band, reflex blue shorts, white stockings.

Change Colours: All black.

Year Formed: 1883.

Turned Professional: 1891.

Ltd Co.: 1908.

Previous Names: 1883, Heaton Norris Rovers; 1888, Heaton Norris; 1890, Stockport County.

Club Nicknames: 'County' or 'Hatters'.

Grounds: 1883, Heaton Norris Recreation Ground; 1884, Heaton Norris Wanderers Cricket Ground; 1885, Chorlton's Farm, Chorlton's Lane; 1886, Heaton Norris Cricket Ground; 1887, Wilkes' Field, Belmont Street; 1889, Nursery Inn, Green Lane; 1902, Edgeley Park.

First Football League Game: 1 September 1900, Division 2, v Leicester Fosse (a) D 2–2 – Moores; Earp, Wainwright; Pickford, Limond, Harvey; Stansfield, Smith (1), Patterson, Foster, Betteley (1).

Record League Victory: 13–0 v Halifax T, Division 3 (N), 6 January 1934 – McGann; Vincent (1p), Jenkinson; Robinson, Stevens, Len Jones; Foulkes (1), Hill (3), Lythgoe (2), Stevenson (2), Downes (4).

Record Cup Victory: 5–0 v Lincoln C, FA Cup 1st rd, 11 November 1995 – Edwards; Connelly, Todd, Bennett, Flynn, Gannon (Dinning), Beaumont, Oliver (Ware), Eckhardt (3), Armstrong (1) (Mike), Chalk, (1 og).

Record Defeat: 1–8 v Chesterfield, Division 2, 19 April 1902.

sky SPORTS FACT FILE

One of the first renowned players to join Stockport County was right-back Jack Earp who had skippered Sheffield Wednesday in the 1896 FA Cup final. He cost £100 in 1900 but always changed alone in a room at the George Hotel, travelling by cab to home matches!

Most League Points (2 for a win): 64, Division 4, 1966–67.

Most League Points (3 for a win): 85, Division 2, 1993–94.

Most League Goals: 115, Division 3 (N), 1933–34.

Highest League Scorer in Season: Alf Lythgoe, 46, Division 3 (N), 1933–34.

Most League Goals in Total Aggregate: Jack Connor, 132, 1951–56.

Most League Goals in One Match: 5, Joe Smith v Southport, Division 3 (N), 7 January 1928; 5, Joe Smith v Lincoln C, Division 3 (N), 15 September 1928; 5, Frank Newton v Nelson, Division 3 (N), 21 September 1929; 5, Alf Lythgoe v Southport, Division 3 (N), 25 August 1934; 5, Billy McNaughton v Mansfield T, Division 3 (N), 14 December 1935; 5, Jack Connor v Workington, Division 3 (N), 8 November 1952; 5, Jack Connor v Carlisle U, Division 3 (N), 7 April 1956.

Most Capped Player: Jarkko Wiss, 9 (45), Finland.

Most League Appearances: Andy Thorpe, 489, 1978–86, 1988–92.

Youngest League Player: Paul Turnbull, 16 years 97 days v Wrexham, 30 April 2005.

Record Transfer Fee Received: £1,600,000 from Middlesbrough for Alun Armstrong, February 1998.

Record Transfer Fee Paid: £800,000 to Nottingham F for Ian Moore, July 1998.

Football League Record: 1900 Elected to Division 2; 1904 Failed re-election; 1905–21 Division 2; 1921–22 Division 3 (N); 1922–26 Division 2; 1926–37 Division 3 (N); 1937–38 Division 2; 1938–58 Division 3 (N); 1958–59 Division 3; 1959–67 Division 4; 1967–70 Division 3; 1970–91 Division 4; 1991–92 Division 3; 1992–97 Division 2; 1997–2002 Division 1; 2002–04 Division 2; 2004–05 FL 1; 2005–08 FL 2; 2008–10 FL 1; 2010–11 FL 2; 2011– Blue Square Premier.

LATEST SEQUENCES

Longest Sequence of League Wins: 9, 13.1.2007 – 3.3.2007.

Longest Sequence of League Defeats: 10, 24.11.2001 – 13.01.2002.

Longest Sequence of League Draws: 7, 17.3.1989 – 14.4.1989.

Longest Sequence of Unbeaten League Matches: 18, 28.1.1933 – 28.8.1933.

Longest Sequence Without a League Win: 19, 28.12.1999 – 22.4.2000.

Successive Scoring Runs: 27 from 20.10.2007.

Successive Non-scoring Runs: 7 from 10.3.1923.

MANAGERS

Fred Stewart 1894–1911
Harry Lewis 1911–14
David Ashworth 1914–19
Albert Williams 1919–24
Fred Scotchbrook 1924–26
Lincoln Hyde 1926–31
Andrew Wilson 1932–33
Fred Westgarth 1934–36
Bob Kelly 1936–38
George Hunt 1938–39
Bob Marshall 1939–49
Andy Beattie 1949–52
Dick Duckworth 1952–56
Billy Moir 1956–60
Reg Flewin 1960–63
Trevor Porteous 1963–65
Bert Trautmann
  (General Manager) 1965–66
Eddie Quigley *(Team
  Manager)* 1965–66
Jimmy Meadows 1966–69
Wally Galbraith 1969–70
Matt Woods 1970–71
Brian Doyle 1972–74
Jimmy Meadows 1974–75
Roy Chapman 1975–76
Eddie Quigley 1976–77
Alan Thompson 1977–78
Mike Summerbee 1978–79
Jimmy McGuigan 1979–82
Eric Webster 1982–85
Colin Murphy 1985
Les Chapman 1985–86
Jimmy Melia 1986
Colin Murphy 1986–87
Asa Hartford 1987–89
Danny Bergara 1989–95
Dave Jones 1995–97
Gary Megson 1997–99
Andy Kilner 1999–2001
Carlton Palmer 2001–03
Sammy McIlroy 2003–04
Chris Turner 2004–05
Jim Gannon 2005–09
Gary Ablett 2009–10
Paul Simpson 2010–11
Ray Mathias 2011
Dietmar Hamman July 2011–

TEN YEAR LEAGUE RECORD

		P	W	D	L	F	A	Pts	Pos
2001-02	Div 1	46	6	8	32	42	102	26	24
2002-03	Div 2	46	15	10	21	65	70	55	14
2003-04	Div 2	46	11	19	16	62	70	52	19
2004-05	FL 1	46	6	8	32	49	98	26	24
2005-06	FL 2	46	11	19	16	57	78	52	22
2006-07	FL 2	46	21	8	17	65	54	71	8
2007-08	FL 2	46	24	10	12	72	54	82	4
2008-09	FL 1	46	16	12	18	59	57	50*	18
2009-10	FL 1	46	5	10	31	35	95	25	24
2010-11	FL 2	46	9	14	23	48	96	41	24

* 10 points deducted.

DID YOU KNOW ❓

The first Stockport County player to achieve parity between goals and appearances was centre-forward Jack Everest in 1930 when he scored seven times in as many League games. This included a four-timer against Carlisle United on 18 January.

STOCKPORT COUNTY 2010–11 LEAGUE RECORD

Match No.	Date	Venue	Opponents	Result	H/T Score	Lg Pos.	Goalscorers	Attendance
1	Aug 7	A	Southend U	D 1-1	0-0	—	Donnelly [83]	5589
2	14	H	Wycombe W	D 0-0	0-0	13		3837
3	21	A	Stevenage	L 1-3	0-2	19	Donnelly [90]	2726
4	28	H	Shrewsbury T	L 0-4	0-1	23		4350
5	Sept 4	A	Macclesfield T	W 2-0	1-0	16	Donnelly [45], Assoumani [59]	3683
6	11	H	Bradford C	D 1-1	0-0	19	Donnelly [78]	4277
7	18	A	Oxford U	W 1-0	1-0	12	Donnelly [41]	7033
8	25	H	Aldershot T	D 2-2	0-2	14	Turnbull 2 [73, 82]	4231
9	28	H	Accrington S	D 2-2	0-1	—	Fisher [78], Donnelly [84]	3584
10	Oct 2	A	Burton Alb	L 1-2	1-0	17	Turnbull [19]	3107
11	9	A	Gillingham	L 1-2	0-2	19	Pulis [81]	4755
12	16	H	Barnet	W 2-1	0-0	18	Donnelly [52], Williams, R [79]	4177
13	23	A	Lincoln C	D 0-0	0-0	16		4809
14	30	H	Hereford U	L 0-5	0-2	19		4017
15	Nov 2	A	Morecambe	L 0-5	0-3	—		2005
16	13	H	Bury	W 1-0	1-0	16	Fletcher [15]	4244
17	20	H	Torquay U	D 1-1	0-0	18	Tansey [75]	3772
18	23	H	Port Vale	L 0-5	0-2	—		4571
19	Dec 4	A	Northampton T	L 0-2	0-1	—		4088
20	11	H	Crewe Alex	D 3-3	1-1	21	Tansey 2 (1 pen) [24, 72 (p)], Poole [54]	4036
21	28	A	Barnet	W 3-1	0-0	—	Donnelly [51], Tansey 2 (1 pen) [73, 79 (p)]	2045
22	Jan 1	A	Chesterfield	L 1-4	1-1	20	Mattis (og) [19]	7542
23	3	H	Morecambe	L 0-2	0-2	21		3890
24	8	H	Gillingham	L 1-5	0-1	21	Demontagnac [70]	3573
25	11	H	Rotherham U	D 3-3	1-1	—	Demontagnac [33], Husband 2 [50, 68]	3612
26	15	A	Hereford U	L 0-3	0-2	21		3154
27	22	H	Lincoln C	L 3-4	1-2	22	Griffin [25], Watts (og) [74], Poole [63]	4348
28	29	A	Rotherham U	L 0-4	0-3	—		4876
29	Feb 1	H	Chesterfield	D 1-1	0-0	24	Turnbull [72]	4092
30	5	A	Torquay U	L 0-2	0-1	24		1954
31	12	H	Bury	W 2-1	0-0	23	Paterson [66], Elding [84]	4903
32	19	H	Macclesfield T	L 1-4	1-1	23	Wallace [25]	5470
33	26	A	Bradford C	L 2-3	2-1	24	Turnbull [27], Doble [40]	15,332
34	Mar 1	A	Cheltenham T	L 1-2	1-1	—	Brown [39]	2191
35	5	H	Oxford U	W 2-1	0-0	24	Paterson [76], Tansey [90]	4119
36	8	A	Accrington S	L 0-3	0-3	—		1831
37	12	H	Burton Alb	D 0-0	0-0	24		4278
38	19	A	Aldershot T	L 0-1	0-0	24		2263
39	26	H	Southend U	W 2-1	1-0	—	Tansey (pen) [28], Rowe [90]	3335
40	Apr 2	A	Wycombe W	L 0-2	0-2	24		6836
41	9	H	Stevenage	D 2-2	0-0	24	Tansey (pen) [67], Paterson [70]	3449
42	16	A	Shrewsbury T	L 0-2	0-2	24		5711
43	23	A	Port Vale	W 2-1	1-0	24	Elding 2 [20, 87]	5334
44	25	H	Northampton T	D 2-2	1-1	24	Rodgers (og) [23], Tansey [88]	4807
45	30	A	Crewe Alex	L 0-2	0-0	24		4799
46	May 7	H	Cheltenham T	D 1-1	0-1	24	Tansey (pen) [90]	5027

Final League Position: 24

GOALSCORERS

League (48): Tansey 10 (5 pens), Donnelly 8, Turnbull 5, Elding 3, Paterson 3, Demontagnac 2, Husband 2, Poole 2, Assoumani 1, Brown 1, Doble 1, Fisher 1, Fletcher 1, Griffin 1, Pulis 1, Rowe 1, Wallace 1, Williams, R 1, own goals 3.
Carling Cup (0).
FA Cup (2): Griffin 1, Tansey 1.
J Paint Trophy (0).

Williams O 5	Lynch M 30+1	Williams R 19+3	Turnbull P 39+2	Swailes D 13	Assoumani M 34+2	Poole D 22+7	Tansey G 30+8	Conlon B 5+4	Donnelly G 23	Griffin A 42+3	Vincent J 13+6	Rowe D 7+10	Proctor J 4+3	Pilkington D 1+5	Fisher T 6+20	Mainwaring M 9+2	Glennon M 36	Simpson J 11+8	Pulis A 9+1	Fletcher W 8+1	Darkwah C —+6	Rose J 13+2	Salem Y 2+3	Aldred T 7	Halls A 17+2	Grieve M 3	Husband S 5	Elding A 18+3	Demontagnac 17	O'Donnell D 7	Brown A 17	Goodall A 13	Paterson M 9+1	Doble R 3	Wallace J 14	McLoughlin 15	Match No.
1	2	3^1	4	5	6	7	8	9^2	10	11	12	13																									1
1	2	3^2	4	5	6	7^3	8	9	10	13	11^1	12	14																								2
1	2		4	5	6	7	8	9^2	10	3		11^1	13	12																							3
1	2		4	5	6		8	13	10	3	12	14	9^3	7^2	11^1																						4
	2		4	5	6		8	9^1	10^2	3	7				12	11	1	13																			5
	2^3		4	5	6		8	9^1	10	3	7^2			12	13	11	1	14																			6
	2		4	5	6		8		10	3	7^1			12	9^2	11	1	13																			7
	2	14	4	5	6		8		10	3	7^1			12	9^3	11^2	1	13																			8
	2	3	4	5	6	13	8^1		10	11			9		12		1	7^2																			9
	2	3	4	5	6		8		10	11^1		12	9				1	7																			10
	2^2	3	4	5	6	7^1			10	11		13	12		9	8	1																				11
	2	3	4	5	6				10	11^2		13			7^1	8	1	9	12																		12
	2	3	4	5^1	6				13	10	11				7^2		1	9^3	8	14	12																13
	2	3	4		6				13	10	11			12			1	7	8^2	9		5^1															14
	2	3	4		6		12			10^2	11	9^1					1	7^4	8		5	13															15
	2	3	4		6	7^2	13			10	11^1						1	12	8	9	5																16
	2	3	4		6				13	10	11^2		14				1	7^1	8	12		9^3	5														17
	2	3	4		6^4	7^2	8^3			10	11	14					1	13	12		9^1	5															18
		3	4			7	8	12		10	11^2			13^3			1	14	9^1		5	6	2														19
			4		6	7	8			10	11						1	3		9^1		12	5	2													20
		12	4		6	7	8			10	11						1	3^1		9			5	2													21
		3	4^1		6	7				10	11	12					1	13	8^2	9^3		14	5	2													22
		3			6^2	7^2	4			10	11		12				1	8^1		9		13	5	2													23
	2	3^1	12		6^1	14	8			13							1		7		6			4	9^2	10	11										24
1		3	4		6		8			7	12														2	5	9^1	10	11									25
	5	3	4		6	13	8			7	12						1								2^1		9^4	10	11^2									26
	13	4			6	9	8			3	11^1		12				1								2		5^2	10	7								27
	2	3^1	4				8			7			12				1										9	10	11	5	6							28
	2		4				8			3							1				10^1					12	7	9	11	5	6							29
	2		4				13	8		7^3							1				10^2						12	11	5	6	3						30
	2		4		13	7^1	8			11							1										12	10	5	6	3	9^2					31
	2		4		13	8^1				12							1										9^2	5	6	3	10	7	11				32
		4			13	7^1	12			11^4															2		14	5	6	3	10^3	9^4	8^2				33
		4			8	7^3	12			11	14		13				1								2		9^2	5^1	6	3	10					1	34
		4			5^3	7^1	14			11		13	12				1								2		9		6	3^2	10		8			1	35
		4			12	8				11		14	13				5^1								2		9^2		6	3^3	10	7				1	36
	2		4			7^1				11			12				5								2			6		3	10^2	9	8			1	37
	2		4			7^1	12			11^3			13				5								14		9	6		3^4	10^2		8			1	38
	2		4				8^1			3	10	7			12		1								5		9	6			11						39
	2		4^1				8			3	11	9^2			13		1								5		10	6			12		7				40
	2		4^1	5			8			3	11^2		12				1								13			6			10		7				41
	14		4		12					3	11	8			9^1	13	1							5^2	2^3		10	6					7				42
				5	8^1					9^2	11				12	7	1		13						2			10			6	3	4				43
				5	8^2	12				9	11^1				13	7	1		14						2			10			6	3^3	4				44
				6	7^2	8				5		4^1			13	11	1		12						2			10			3		9				45
		13		5	7^2	8				3		9			12	11^1	1								2			10			6		4				46

FA Cup
First Round Peterborough U (h) 1-1
  (a) 1-4

Carling Cup
First Round Preston NE (h) 0-5

J Paint Trophy
Second Round Tranmere R (a) 0-0

STOKE CITY   FA Premiership

FOUNDATION

The date of the formation of this club has long been in doubt. The year 1863 was claimed, but more recent research by Wade Martin has uncovered nothing earlier than 1868, when a couple of Old Carthusians, who were apprentices at the local works of the old North Staffordshire Railway Company, met with some others from that works, to form Stoke Ramblers. It should also be noted that the old Stoke club went bankrupt in 1908 when a new club was formed.

Britannia Stadium, Stanley Matthews Way, Stoke-on-Trent, Staffs ST4 4EG.

Telephone: (0871) 663 2008.

Fax: (01782) 592 210.

Ticket Office: (0871) 663 2008.

Website: www.stokecityfc.com

Email: info@stokecityfc.com

Ground Capacity: 28,383.

Record Attendance: 51,380 v Arsenal, Division 1, 29 March 1937 (at Victoria Ground). 28,218 v Everton, Division 2, 5 January 2002 (at Britannia Stadium).

Pitch Measurements: 100m × 64m.

Chairman: Peter Coates.

Chief Executive: Tony Scholes.

Club Secretary: Eddie Harrison.

Manager: Tony Pulis.

Assistant Manager: Dave Kemp.

Physio: Chris Banks.

Colours: Red and white striped shirts with red sleeves and shoulders, white shorts, white stockings.

Change Colours: All black with red trim on shirt.

Year Formed: 1863* (*see Foundation*). *Turned Professional:* 1885. *Ltd Co.:* 1908.

Previous Names: 1868, Stoke Ramblers; 1870, Stoke; 1925, Stoke City.

Club Nickname: 'The Potters'.

Grounds: 1875, Sweeting's Field; 1878, Victoria Ground (previously known as the Athletic Club Ground); 1997, Britannia Stadium.

First Football League Game: 8 September 1888, Football League, v WBA (h) L 0–2 – Rowley; Clare, Underwood; Ramsey, Shutt, Smith; Sayer, McSkimming, Staton, Edge, Tunnicliffe.

Record League Victory: 10–3 v WBA, Division 1, 4 February 1937 – Doug Westland; Brigham, Harbot; Tutin, Turner (1p), Kirton; Matthews, Antonio (2), Freddie Steele (5), Jimmy Westland, Johnson (2).

Record Cup Victory: 7–1 v Burnley, FA Cup 2nd rd (replay), 20 February 1896 – Clawley; Clare, Eccles; Turner, Grewe, Robertson; Willie Maxwell, Dickson, Alan Maxwell (3), Hyslop (4), Schofield.

HONOURS

Football League – Division 1:
Best season: 4th, 1935–36, 1946–47;
FL C: *Runners-up* 2007–08;
Division 2: *Champions* 1932–33, 1962–63, 1992–93;
Runners-up 1921–22;
Division 3 (N): *Champions* 1926–27.

FA Cup: *Runners-up* 2011.

Football League Cup: *Winners* 1972;
Runners-up 1964.

Autoglass Trophy: *Winners*: 1992.

Auto Windscreens Shield:
Winners: 2000.

European Competitions
UEFA Cup: 1972–73, 1974–75.

sky SPORTS FACT FILE

Goalkeeper Billy Rowley had been the subject of protracted legal proceedings before joining Stoke from Port Vale in 1887. Twice capped by England he made more than a century of League appearances despite several injuries including a broken breastbone and numerous ribs.

Record Defeat: 0–10 v Preston NE, Division 1, 14 September 1889.

Most League Points (2 for a win): 63, Division 3 (N), 1926–27.

Most League Points (3 for a win): 93, Division 2, 1992–93.

Most League Goals: 92, Division 3 (N), 1926–27.

Highest League Scorer in Season: Freddie Steele, 33, Division 1, 1936–37.

Most League Goals in Total Aggregate: Freddie Steele, 142, 1934–49.

Most League Goals in One Match: 7, Neville Coleman v Lincoln C, Division 2, 23 February 1957.

Most Capped Player: Gordon Banks, 36 (73), England.

Most League Appearances: Eric Skeels, 506, 1958–76.

Youngest League Player: Peter Bullock, 16 years 163 days v Swansea C, 19 April 1958.

Record Transfer Fee Received: £3,000,000 from Manchester U for Ritchie De Laat, January 2009; £3,000,000 from Hull C for Seyi Olofinjana, August 2009.

Record Transfer Fee Paid: £8,000,000 to Sunderland for Kenwyne Jones, August 2010.

Football League Record: 1888 Founder Member of Football League; 1890 Not re-elected; 1891 Re-elected; relegated in 1907, and after one year in Division 2, resigned for financial reasons; 1919 re-elected to Division 2; 1922–23 Division 1; 1923–26 Division 2; 1926–27 Division 3 (N); 1927–33 Division 2; 1933–53 Division 1; 1953–63 Division 2; 1963–77 Division 1; 1977–79 Division 2; 1979–85 Division 1; 1985–90 Division 2; 1990–92 Division 2; 1992–93 Division 2; 1993–98 Division 1; 1998–2002 Division 2; 2002–04 Division 1; 2004–08 FL C; 2008– FA Premier League.

LATEST SEQUENCES

Longest Sequence of League Wins: 8, 30.3.1895 – 21.9.1895.

Longest Sequence of League Defeats: 11, 6.4.1985 – 17.8.1985.

Longest Sequence of League Draws: 5, 21.3.1987 – 11.4.1987.

Longest Sequence of Unbeaten League Matches: 25, 5.9.1992 – 20.2.1993.

Longest Sequence Without a League Win: 17, 22.4.1989 – 14.10.1989.

Successive Scoring Runs: 21 from 24.12.1921.

Successive Non-scoring Runs: 8 from 29.12.1984.

MANAGERS

Tom Slaney 1874–83
(Secretary-Manager)
Walter Cox 1883–84
(Secretary-Manager)
Harry Lockett 1884–90
Joseph Bradshaw 1890–92
Arthur Reeves 1892–95
William Rowley 1895–97
H. D. Austerberry 1897–1908
A. J. Barker 1908–14
Peter Hodge 1914–15
Joe Schofield 1915–19
Arthur Shallcross 1919–23
John 'Jock' Rutherford 1923
Tom Mather 1923–35
Bob McGrory 1935–52
Frank Taylor 1952–60
Tony Waddington 1960–77
George Eastham 1977–78
Alan A'Court 1978
Alan Durban 1978–81
Richie Barker 1981–83
Bill Asprey 1984–85
Mick Mills 1985–89
Alan Ball 1989–91
Lou Macari 1991–93
Joe Jordan 1993–94
Lou Macari 1994–97
Chic Bates 1997–98
Chris Kamara 1998
Brian Little 1998–99
Gary Megson 1999
Gudjon Thordarson 1999–2002
Steve Cotterill 2002
Tony Pulis 2002–05
Johan Boskamp 2005–06
Tony Pulis June 2006–

TEN YEAR LEAGUE RECORD

		P	W	D	L	F	A	Pts	Pos
2001-02	Div 2	46	23	11	12	67	40	80	5
2002-03	Div 1	46	12	14	20	45	69	50	21
2003-04	Div 1	46	18	12	16	58	55	66	11
2004-05	FL C	46	17	10	19	36	38	61	12
2005-06	FL C	46	17	7	22	54	63	58	13
2006-07	FL C	46	19	16	11	62	41	73	8
2007-08	FL C	46	21	16	9	69	55	79	2
2008-09	PR Lge	38	12	9	17	38	55	45	12
2009-10	PR Lge	38	11	14	13	34	48	47	11
2010-11	PR Lge	38	13	7	18	46	48	46	13

DID YOU KNOW ?

Stoke-on-Trent born Alf Edge was the first player to score a hat-trick against Everton in 1890. It was for Stoke City on 1 February 1890 in a 4-2 second round FA Cup win. He can also claim to have played for both Manchester clubs' forerunners Newton Heath and Ardwick.

STOKE CITY 2010–11 LEAGUE RECORD

Match No.	Date	Venue	Opponents	Result		H/T Score	Lg Pos.	Goalscorers	Attendance
1	Aug 14	A	Wolverhampton W	L	1-2	0-2	—	Diagne-Faye [55]	27,850
2	21	H	Tottenham H	L	1-2	1-2	18	Fuller [25]	27,243
3	28	A	Chelsea	L	0-2	0-1	19		40,931
4	Sept 13	H	Aston Villa	W	2-1	0-1	—	Jones [80], Huth [90]	25,899
5	18	H	West Ham U	D	1-1	0-1	17	Jones [48]	27,028
6	26	A	Newcastle U	W	2-1	0-1	14	Jones [67], Perch (og) [85]	41,915
7	Oct 2	H	Blackburn R	W	1-0	0-0	7	Walters [48]	25,515
8	16	A	Bolton W	L	1-2	0-1	9	Delap [48]	22,975
9	24	H	Manchester U	L	1-2	0-1	13	Tuncay [81]	27,372
10	30	A	Everton	L	0-1	0-0	15		35,513
11	Nov 6	A	Sunderland	L	0-2	0-1	17		36,541
12	9	H	Birmingham C	W	3-2	1-0	—	Huth [44], Fuller [71], Whitehead [85]	26,381
13	13	H	Liverpool	W	2-0	0-0	10	Fuller [56], Jones [90]	27,286
14	20	A	WBA	W	3-0	0-0	8	Etherington (pen) [55], Walters 2 (1 pen) [85 (p), 90]	24,164
15	27	H	Manchester C	D	1-1	0-0	8	Etherington [90]	27,405
16	Dec 4	A	Wigan Ath	D	2-2	2-2	9	Huth [18], Etherington [31]	15,100
17	11	H	Blackpool	L	0-1	0-0	12		26,879
18	26	A	Blackburn R	W	2-0	0-0	8	Huth [51], Wilson [90]	25,440
19	28	H	Fulham	L	0-2	0-2	10		26,954
20	Jan 1	H	Everton	W	2-0	1-0	8	Jones [23], Jagielka (og) [69]	27,418
21	4	A	Manchester U	L	1-2	0-1	10	Whitehead [50]	73,401
22	15	H	Bolton W	W	2-0	1-0	8	Higginbotham [37], Etherington (pen) [63]	26,809
23	22	A	Fulham	L	0-2	0-1	10		23,766
24	Feb 2	A	Liverpool	L	0-2	0-0	—		40,254
25	5	H	Sunderland	W	3-2	1-1	9	Carew [32], Huth 2 [83, 90]	26,008
26	12	A	Birmingham C	L	0-1	0-0	9		23,660
27	23	A	Arsenal	L	0-1	0-1	—		60,041
28	28	H	WBA	D	1-1	0-0	—	Delap [53]	25,019
29	Mar 5	A	West Ham U	L	0-3	0-2	12		33,066
30	19	H	Newcastle U	W	4-0	1-0	10	Walters [28], Pennant [46], Higginbotham [49], Fuller [90]	27,505
31	Apr 2	H	Chelsea	D	1-1	1-1	11	Walters [8]	27,508
32	9	A	Tottenham H	L	2-3	2-3	12	Etherington [27], Jones [41]	32,702
33	23	A	Aston Villa	D	1-1	1-1	14	Jones [20]	35,235
34	26	H	Wolverhampton W	W	3-0	2-0	12	Jones [16], Shawcross [45], Pennant [51]	27,030
35	30	A	Blackpool	D	0-0	0-0	10		16,003
36	May 8	H	Arsenal	W	3-1	2-0	8	Jones [28], Pennant [40], Walters [82]	27,478
37	17	A	Manchester C	L	0-3	0-1	—		45,103
38	22	H	Wigan Ath	L	0-1	0-0	13		27,566

Final League Position: 13

GOALSCORERS

League (46): Jones 9, Huth 6, Walters 6 (1 pen), Etherington 5 (2 pens), Fuller 4, Pennant 3, Delap 2, Higginbotham 2, Whitehead 2, Carew 1, Diagne-Faye 1, Shawcross 1, Tuncay 1, Wilson 1, own goals 2.
Carling Cup (5): Jones 2, Higginbotham 1, Tuncay 1, Walters 1.
FA Cup (14): Walters 5, Huth 3, Carew 1, Etherington 1, Higginbotham 1, Jones 1, Shawcross 1, Tuncay 1.

Sorensen T 10	Huth R 35	Higginbotham D 9+1	Whitehead D 31+6	Shawcross R 36	Diagne-Faye A 12+2	Delap R 33+4	Whelan G 14+15	Jones K 33+1	Fuller R 9+19	Etherington M 30+2	Sidibe M —+2	Tuncay S 5+9	Tonge M —+2	Collins D 23+2	Walters J 27+9	Wilkinson A 21+1	Pugh D 5+5	Wilson M 21+7	Pennant J 26+3	Gudjohnsen E —+4	Diao S 3+5	Begovic A 28	Carew J 7+3	Shotton R —+2	Match No.
1	2	3	4	5	6	7	8³	9¹	10	11	12²	13	14												1
1	2		4	5	6	7²	8¹		10	11	13³	12	14	3	9										2
1	2		4	5	6	7³	12	9²	13	11				3	10	8¹	14								3
1	2		4	5	6	7³	14	9	12	11				3	10¹			8²	13						4
1	2		4	5	6	8	14	9²	12	11				3	10¹				7³	13					5
1	6		4	5		13	8¹	9	12³	11				3	10	2		14	7²						6
1	2		4	5	6	8³	14	9	12	11²				3	10			13	7¹						7
1	2		4	5	6	8	14	9	12²	11				3	10³			7¹	13						8
1	2	12		5	6	8		9		11		13		3¹	10²		4	7³	14						9
	2		4	5	6		13	9	12	11			7	3	10¹	8²	12					1			10
	2		4²	5	6	13		9	12	11			10	3	7¹	8						1			11
	2	3	4		6	8	12	9	10¹	11³				5	13	14	7¹					1			12
	2		4	5		8		9	10¹	11²				6	12	3	13	7				1			13
	6		4	5		8		9	10³	11²		12		3	13	2	14	7¹				1			14
	6		4	5		8		9	10³	11		12		3	14	2²	13	7¹				1			15
	2	3	4	5		8	12	9	10²	11		13		6	7¹							1			16
	6		4	5		8		9²	10	11		12		3	13	2³		7¹				1			17
	2		4	5		8	12	9³	13	11¹				6	10	3	14	7²				1			18
	6		4	5		8		9	12	11²		13		3	10¹	2³	14	7				1			19
		3		4	5		8	12	9	10²	11¹		14	6	13	2		7³				1			20
	6		4	5		0³		9¹	14	11¹		10		3	13	2		7	12			1			21
	4	3	6	5		8	12	9²		11³		10		13	2	14	7¹					1			22
	6		4	5⁴	13	8	14	9		11³		10²		3¹		2		7				1	12		23
	5	3	4	6²	12			14			13	9	2	11³	7		8¹	1	10						24
	4	3	6	5		8		9		11		12	2¹		7				1	10					25
	4		6	5		2	12	9²	13			11		3	8	7¹			1	10					26
	4		6	5		8	11		12			9¹	13	3	2²	7 .			1	10					27
	4		6	5		8	13	9³	14	12			11	3	2	7²			1	10¹					28
	4		6	5		8²	11	14	13	12			9	3	2	7¹			1	10³					29
	4	3	13	5		8	6	9³	14	11¹			10	12	2	7²			1						30
	4	3²	12	5		8	6¹	9	14	11		13	10		2	7³			1						31
	4		14	5		8³	6¹	9	12	11			10	3	2	7²	13	1							32
	4		12	5		8²	6	9³	13	11¹			10	2	3	7	14	1							33
	4		12	5		8³	6	9		11¹			10	2	13	3	7²	14	1						34
	4		11	5		8²	6	9					10	2¹		3	7³	14	1		13	12			35
	4¹		11	5	12	8	6	9³					10	2	13	3	7²	14	1						36
1			11	5		12	6²					4	9	2	7	3		8		10¹	13				37
			12	5		8	6	9²		11¹			4	10	2		3	7		1	13				38

FA Cup

Third Round	Cardiff C	(h)	1-1	
		(a)	2-0	
Fourth Round	Wolverhampton W	(a)	1-0	
Fifth Round	Brighton & HA	(h)	3-0	
Sixth Round	West Ham U	(h)	2-1	
Semi-Final	Bolton W		5-0	
(at Wembley).				
Final	Manchester C		0-1	
(at Wembley).				

Carling Cup

Second Round	Shrewsbury T	(h)	2-1
Third Round	Fulham	(h)	2-0
Fourth Round	West Ham U	(a)	1-3

SUNDERLAND FA Premiership

FOUNDATION

A Scottish schoolmaster named James Allan, working at Hendon Board School, took the initiative in the foundation of Sunderland in 1879 when they were formed as The Sunderland and District Teachers' Association FC at a meeting in the Adults School, Norfolk Street. Due to financial difficulties, they quickly allowed members from outside the teaching profession and so became Sunderland AFC in October 1880.

Stadium of Light, Sunderland, Tyne and Wear SR5 1SU.
Telephone: (0871) 911 1200.
Fax: (0191) 551 5123.
Ticket Office: (0871) 911 1973.
Website: www.safc.com
Email: enquiries@safc.com
Ground Capacity: 49,000.
Record Attendance: 75,118 v Derby Co, FA Cup 6th rd replay, 8 March 1933 (at Roker Park). 48,353 v Liverpool, FA Premier League, 13 April 2002 (at Stadium of Light). FA Premier League figure (46,062).
Pitch Measurements: 105m × 68m.
Chairman: Niall Quinn.
Chief Executive: Margaret Byrne.
Finance Director: Angela Lowes.
Manager: Steve Bruce.
Assistant Manager: Eric Black.
Physio: Pete Friar.

HONOURS

Football League: FL C:
Champions 2004–05, 2006–07;
Division 1: *Champions* 1891–92, 1892–93, 1894–95, 1901–02, 1912–13, 1935–36, 1995–96, 1998–99;
Runners-up 1893–94, 1897–98, 1900–01, 1922–23, 1934–35;
Division 2: *Champions* 1975–76;
Runners-up 1963–64, 1979–80.
Division 3: *Champions* 1987–88.
FA Cup: *Winners* 1937, 1973;
Runners-up 1913, 1992.
Football League Cup:
Runners-up 1985.
European Competitions
European Cup-Winners' Cup:
1973–74.

Colours: Red and white striped shirts, black shorts, black stockings with red tops.
Change Colours: Stone shirts with burgundy trim, stone shorts, stone stockings with burgundy tops.
Year Formed: 1879. *Turned Professional:* 1886. *Ltd Co.:* 1906.
Club Nickname: Black Cats.
Previous Name: 1879, Sunderland and District Teacher's AFC; 1880, Sunderland.
Grounds: 1879, Blue House Field, Hendon; 1882, Groves Field, Ashbrooke; 1883, Horatio Street; 1884, Abbs Field, Fulwell; 1886, Newcastle Road; 1898, Roker Park; 1997, Stadium of Light.
First Football League Game: 13 September 1890, Football League, v Burnley (h) L 2–3 – Kirtley; Porteous, Oliver; Wilson, Auld, Gibson; Spence (1), Miller, Campbell (1), Scott, Davy Hannah.
Record League Victory: 9–1 v Newcastle U (a), Division 1, 5 December 1908 – Roose; Forster, Melton; Daykin, Thomson, Low; Mordue (1), Hogg (3), Brown, Holley (3), Bridgett (2).
Record Cup Victory: 11–1 v Fairfield, FA Cup 1st rd, 2 February 1895 – Doig; McNeill, Johnston; Dunlop, McCreadie (1), Wilson; Gillespie (1), Millar (5), Campbell, Jimmy Hannah (3), Scott (1).

sky SPORTS FACT FILE

On 24 April 1915 Charlie Buchan scored Sunderland's last goal against Tottenham Hotspur in the last game before official football ended for the Great War. On 30 August 1919 when the competition resumed, he scored the first goal for Sunderland against Aston Villa.

Record Defeat: 0–8 v Sheff Wed, Division 1, 26 December 1911. 0–8 v West Ham U, Division 1, 19 October 1968. 0–8 v Watford, Division 1, 25 September 1982.

Most League Points (2 for a win): 61, Division 2, 1963–64.

Most League Points (3 for a win): 105, Division 1, 1998–99 (Football League Record).

Most League Goals: 109, Division 1, 1935–36.

Highest League Scorer in Season: Dave Halliday, 43, Division 1, 1928–29.

Most League Goals in Total Aggregate: Charlie Buchan, 209, 1911–25.

Most League Goals in One Match: 5, Charlie Buchan v Liverpool, Division 1, 7 December 1919; 5, Bobby Gurney v Bolton W, Division 1, 7 December 1935; 5, Dominic Sharkey v Norwich C, Division 2, 20 February 1962.

Most Capped Player: Charlie Hurley, 38 (40), Republic of Ireland.

Most League Appearances: Jim Montgomery, 537, 1962–77.

Youngest League Player: Derek Forster, 15 years 184 days v Leicester C, 22 August 1964.

Record Transfer Fee Received: £19,000,000 from Aston Villa for Darren Bent, January 2011.

Record Transfer Fee Paid: £13,250,000 to Rennes for Asamoah Gyan, August 2010.

Football League Record: 1890 Elected to Division 1; 1958–64 Division 2; 1964–70 Division 1; 1970–76 Division 2; 1976–77 Division 1; 1977–80 Division 2; 1980–85 Division 1; 1985–87 Division 2; 1987–88 Division 3; 1988–90 Division 2; 1990–91 Division 1; 1991–92 Division 2; 1992–96 Division 1; 1996–97 FA Premier League; 1997–99 Division 1; 1999–2003 FA Premier League; 2003–04 Division 1; 2004–05 FL C; 2005–06 FA Premier League; 2006–07 FL C; 2007– FA Premier League.

MANAGERS

Tom Watson 1888–96
Bob Campbell 1896–99
Alex Mackie 1899–1905
Bob Kyle 1905–28
Johnny Cochrane 1928–39
Bill Murray 1939–57
Alan Brown 1957–64
George Hardwick 1964–65
Ian McColl 1965–68
Alan Brown 1968–72
Bob Stokoe 1972–76
Jimmy Adamson 1976–78
Ken Knighton 1979–81
Alan Durban 1981–84
Len Ashurst 1984–85
Lawrie McMenemy 1985–87
Denis Smith 1987–91
Malcolm Crosby 1991–93
Terry Butcher 1993
Mick Buxton 1993–95
Peter Reid 1995–2002
Howard Wilkinson 2002–03
Mick McCarthy 2003–06
Niall Quinn 2006
Roy Keane 2006–08
Ricky Sbragia 2008–09
Steve Bruce June 2009–

LATEST SEQUENCES

Longest Sequence of League Wins: 13, 14.11.1891 – 2.4.1892.

Longest Sequence of League Defeats: 17, 18.1.2003 – 16.8.2003.

Longest Sequence of League Draws: 6, 26.3.1949 – 19.4.1949.

Longest Sequence of Unbeaten League Matches: 19, 3.5.1998 – 14.11.1998.

Longest Sequence Without a League Win: 22, 21.12.2002 – 16.8.2003.

Successive Scoring Runs: 29 from 8.11.1997.

Successive Non-scoring Runs: 10 from 27.11.1976.

TEN YEAR LEAGUE RECORD

		P	W	D	L	F	A	Pts	Pos
2001-02	PR Lge	38	10	10	18	29	51	40	17
2002-03	PR Lge	38	4	7	27	21	65	19	20
2003-04	Div 1	46	22	13	11	62	45	79	3
2004-05	FL C	46	29	7	10	76	41	94	1
2005-06	PR Lge	38	3	6	29	26	69	15	20
2006-07	FL C	46	27	7	12	76	47	88	1
2007-08	PR Lge	38	11	6	21	36	59	39	15
2008-09	PR Lge	38	9	9	20	34	54	36	16
2009-10	PR Lge	38	11	11	16	48	56	44	13
2010-11	PR Lge	38	12	11	15	45	56	47	10

DID YOU KNOW ?

On 11 May 1968 Sunderland won 2-1 at Old Trafford and helped towards preventing Manchester United winning the First Division championship. On the same day Manchester City won 4-3 at Newcastle United to take the title by two points from their Mancunian neighbours.

SUNDERLAND 2010–11 LEAGUE RECORD

Match No.	Date	Venue	Opponents	Result	H/T Score	Lg Pos.	Goalscorers	Attendance
1	Aug 14	H	Birmingham C	D	2-2	1-0	—	Bent (pen) [24], Carr (og) [56]	38,390
2	21	A	WBA	L	0-1	0-0	16		23,624
3	29	H	Manchester C	W	1-0	0-0	10	Bent (pen) [90]	38,610
4	Sept 11	A	Wigan Ath	D	1-1	0-0	10	Gyan [66]	15,844
5	18	H	Arsenal	D	1-1	0-1	11	Bent [90]	38,950
6	25	A	Liverpool	D	2-2	1-1	11	Bent 2 (1 pen) [25 (p), 48]	43,626
7	Oct 2	H	Manchester U	D	0-0	0-0	11		41,709
8	18	A	Blackburn R	D	0-0	0-0	—		21,894
9	23	H	Aston Villa	W	1-0	1-0	7	Dunne (og) [25]	41,506
10	31	A	Newcastle U	L	1-5	0-3	11	Bent [90]	51,988
11	Nov 6	H	Stoke C	W	2-0	1-0	8	Gyan 2 [9, 86]	36,541
12	9	A	Tottenham H	D	1-1	0-0	—	Gyan [67]	35,843
13	14	A	Chelsea	W	3-0	1-0	6	Onuoha [45], Gyan [52], Welbeck [87]	41,072
14	22	H	Everton	D	2-2	1-1	—	Welbeck 2 [23, 70]	37,331
15	27	A	Wolverhampton W	L	2-3	0-0	7	Bent [67], Welbeck [77]	25,112
16	Dec 5	H	West Ham U	W	1-0	1-0	7	Henderson [34]	36,940
17	11	A	Fulham	D	0-0	0-0	7		24,462
18	18	H	Bolton W	W	1-0	1-0	—	Welbeck [32]	35,101
19	26	A	Manchester U	L	0-2	0-1	7		75,269
20	28	H	Blackpool	L	0-2	0-0	7		42,892
21	Jan 1	H	Blackburn R	W	3-0	2-0	6	Welbeck [11], Bent [19], Gyan [89]	36,242
22	5	A	Aston Villa	W	1-0	0-0	6	Bardsley [80]	32,627
23	16	H	Newcastle U	D	1-1	0-0	6	Gyan [90]	47,864
24	22	A	Blackpool	W	2-1	2-0	6	Richardson 2 [15, 36]	16,037
25	Feb 1	H	Chelsea	L	2-4	2-2	—	Bardsley [4], Richardson [26]	37,855
26	5	A	Stoke C	L	2-3	1-1	7	Richardson [2], Gyan [48]	26,008
27	12	A	Tottenham H	L	1-2	1-1	7	Gyan [11]	40,986
28	26	H	Everton	L	0-2	0-2	8		37,776
29	Mar 5	A	Arsenal	D	0-0	0-0	8		60,081
30	20	H	Liverpool	L	0-2	0-1	9		47,207
31	Apr 3	A	Manchester C	L	0-5	0-2	12		44,197
32	9	H	WBA	L	2-3	2-1	13	Shorey (og) [10], Bardsley [31]	41,586
33	16	A	Birmingham C	L	0-2	0-1	15		28,108
34	23	H	Wigan Ath	W	4-2	0-0	10	Gyan [55], Henderson 2 [66, 77], Sessegnon (pen) [73]	39,650
35	30	H	Fulham	L	0-3	0-1	14		39,576
36	May 7	A	Bolton W	W	2-1	1-0	12	Zenden [45], Muntari [90]	22,597
37	14	H	Wolverhampton W	L	1-3	1-1	14	Sessegnon [34]	41,273
38	22	A	West Ham U	W	3-0	1-0	10	Zenden [17], Sessegnon [51], Riveros [90]	32,792

Final League Position: 10

GOALSCORERS

League (45): Gyan 10, Bent 8 (3 pens), Welbeck 6, Richardson 4, Bardsley 3, Henderson 3, Sessegnon 3 (1 pen), Zenden 2, Muntari 1, Onuoha 1, Riveros 1, own goals 3.
Carling Cup (3): Bent 2, Gyan 1.
FA Cup (1): Bent 1 (pen).

Mignolet S 23	Onuoha N 31	Richardson K 23 + 3	Bramble T 22 + 1	Mensah J 15 + 3	Cattermole L 22 + 1	Al-Muhammadi A 26 + 10	Henderson J 37	Campbell F 3	Bent D 20	Malbranque S 24 + 11	Riveros C 5 + 7	Welbeck D 21 + 5	Waghorn M — + 2	Da Silva P 1	Zenden B 10 + 17	Ferdinand A 23 + 4	Turner M 15	Bardsley P 32 + 2	Gyan A 20 + 11	Reid A — + 2	Gordon C 15	Meyler D 4 + 1	Cook J — + 3	Angeleri M — + 2	Colback J 6 + 5	Sessegnon S 13 + 1	Muntari S 7 + 2	Noble R — + 3	Lynch C — + 2	Laing L — + 1	Match No.
1	2	3	4	5	6⁸	7³	8	9	10²	11¹	12	13	14																		1
1	2	3	4		7²		8	9	10	11¹	6³	12	14	5	13																2
1		3	4		6	7	8	9²	10	11		13			2	5¹	12														3
1	2	3³	4	14	6⁸	7¹	8		10	11	12	9²			13	5															4
1	2²	3	4			7	8		10	11³	6¹	9			13	5			12	14											5
1	2		4		6	7	8		10³	11²	13	9¹	14			5		3	12												6
1	2		4		6	7	8		10	11¹		9²				5		3	13			12									7
1	2¹		4		6	7	8		10	11²		9			13	5		3	12												8
1	2		4	13	6	7³	8		10	11²		9¹	14			5		3	12												9
1	2	13	4⁸	14	6³	7¹	8		10	11		9²				5		3	12												10
1	2	12		5²	6	7³	8			11¹		9	14		13	4		3	10												11
	2	11³	4		6		8			14	7²	13			10	3¹	5	12	9		1										12
	2	11	4		6²	14	8			12	13	9³			7	5		3	10¹		1										13
	2	11			6	13	8²		10	12		9			7¹	5	4	3			1										14
	2	11			4³	6	14	8¹	10	12		9			7²	5		3	13		1										15
	2	11			5	6	13	8²	10¹	12		9			14	4		3	7³		1										16
1	2	11			4	6	12	8	10			9³			14	5¹		3	13			7²									17
	2	11			5¹	6	12	8	10			9			13	4		3	7²		1										18
	2					6	8	10	11²	4		7³	5			3		9			1	12	13	14							19
	2¹	13	12			6	4	8	10	14		9			5	3		11³			1	7²									20
		11	4			2³	8	10²	7			9¹			12	5		3	13		1	6		14							21
		3	4			7	8	10	11²	14	9³				12⁸	5		2	13		1	6¹									22
	2¹	11	6			7²	4	10	8			12			5			3	9		1				13						23
	2	11	4			7	8			6²	13				10	5		3¹	9		1				12						24
	2²	11	4			7	8			6¹					5			3	9		1		13		12	10					25
	2	11	4	5			8¹			12					13	6		3	9		1				10	7²					26
	2²	11	4	5		12	8			6¹					13			3	9		1				10	7					27
1		11	4	5		2	8			13					6¹			3	9						10	7²	12				28
1		11	6	5		13	0³			4¹	12				2			3	9²						14	10	/				29
1		11²	6	5¹	12	14	4			13	10³				2			3	9							8	7¹				30
1				5	6	12	8⁷					9			13	3	4	2¹	10						14	11	7³				31
1	2	11²		5¹	6	7		8	9						13	12³	4	3	10							14					32
1	5				6	2	7			13		9¹				4	3	10							11²	8		12			33
1	5				6	2	7			13		9²			12	4	3¹	10³							11	8	14				34
1	5				6	2	7³					9²			13	12	4	3							11	10	8¹	14			35
1	5		4			2	7			8¹					9	6		3							11	10	12				36
1	5		4³			2	7²			8¹	6				9			3							11	10		12	13	14	37
1	5					2	7			4	12				8	6		3¹	9²						13	11	10				38

FA Cup
Third Round   Notts Co   (h)   1-2

Carling Cup
Second Round   Colchester U   (h)   2-0
Third Round   West Ham U   (h)   1-2

SWANSEA CITY   FA Premiership

FOUNDATION

The earliest Association Football in Wales was played in the
Northern part of the country and no international took place in
the South until 1894, when a local paper still thought it necessary
to publish an outline of the rules and an illustration of the pitch
markings. There had been an earlier Swansea club, but this has no
connection with Swansea Town (now City) formed at a public
meeting in June 1912.

Liberty Stadium, Morfa, Landore, Swansea SA1 2FA.
Telephone: (01792) 616 600.
Fax: (01792) 616 606.
Ticket Office: (0870) 040 0004.
Website: www.swanseacity.net
Email: info@swanseacityfc.co.uk
Ground Capacity: 20,520.
Record Attendance: 32,796 v Arsenal, FA Cup 4th rd,
17 February 1968 (at Vetch Field). 19,288 v Yeovil T, FL 1,
11 November 2005 (at Liberty Stadium).
Pitch Measurements: 115yd × 74yd.
Chairman: Huw Jenkins.
Vice-chairman: Leigh Dineen.
Secretary: Jackie Rockey.
Manager: Brendan Rodgers.
First Team Coaches: Colin Pascoe, Alan Curtis.
Physio: Dave Galley.
Colours: All white.
Change Colours: All black with white and black hooped
stockings.
Year Formed: 1912. *Turned Professional:* 1912.
Ltd Co.: 1912.
Previous Name: 1912, Swansea Town; 1970, Swansea City.
Club Nicknames: 'The Swans', 'The Jacks'.
Grounds: 1912, Vetch Field; 2005, Liberty Stadium.
First Football League Game: 28 August 1920, Division 3, v Portsmouth (a) L 0–3 – Crumley; Robson,
Evans; Smith, Holdsworth, Williams; Hole, Ivor Jones, Edmundson, Rigsby, Spottiswood.
Record League Victory: 8–0 v Hartlepool U, Division 4, 1 April 1978 – Barber; Evans, Bartley, Lally (1)
(Morris), May, Bruton, Kevin Moore, Robbie James (3 incl. 1p), Curtis (3), Toshack (1), Chappell.
Record Cup Victory: 12–0 v Sliema W (Malta), ECWC 1st rd 1st leg, 15 September 1982 – Davies;
Marustik, Hadziabdic (1), Irwin (1), Kennedy, Rajkovic (1), Loveridge (2) (Leighton James), Robbie
James, Charles (2), Stevenson (1), Latchford (1) (Walsh (3)).

HONOURS

Football League – Division 1:
Best season: 6th, 1981–82;
FL 1: *Champions* 2007–08;
Division 35(S): *Champions* 1924–25,
1948–49; **Division 3:**
Champions 1999–2000.
FA Cup: Semi-finals 1926, 1964.
Football League Cup: Best season:
4th rd, 1965, 1977, 2009, 2011.
Welsh Cup: *Winners* 11 times;
Runners-up 8 times.
Autoglass Trophy: *Winners* 1994,
2006.
Football League Trophy:
Winners 2006.
European Competitions
European Cup-Winners' Cup:
1961–62, 1966–67, 1981–82, 1982–83,
1983–84, 1989–90, 1991–92.

sky SPORTS FACT FILE

In 2009–10 Swansea City goalkeeper Dorus de Vries
beat the club record for the number of clean sheets in
League matches when he remained unbeaten for the
23rd occasion against Scunthorpe United on 5 April.
Roger Freestone had been the previous holder.

Record Defeat: 0–8 v Liverpool, FA Cup 3rd rd, 9 January 1990. 0–8 v Monaco, ECWC, 1st rd 2nd leg, 1 October 1991.

Most League Points (2 for a win): 62, Division 3 (S), 1948–49.

Most League Points (3 for a win): 92, FL 1, 2007–08.

Most League Goals: 90, Division 2, 1956–57.

Highest League Scorer in Season: Cyril Pearce, 35, Division 2, 1931–32.

Most League Goals in Total Aggregate: Ivor Allchurch, 166, 1949–58, 1965–68.

Most League Goals in One Match: 5, Jack Fowler v Charlton Ath, Division 3S, 27 December 1924.

Most Capped Player: Ivor Allchurch, 42 (68), Wales.

Most League Appearances: Wilfred Milne, 585, 1919–37.

Youngest League Player: Nigel Dalling, 15 years 289 days v Southport, 6 December 1974.

Record Transfer Fee Received: £2,000,000 from Wigan Ath for Jason Scotland, July 2009.

Record Transfer Fee Paid: £3,500,000 to Watford for Danny Graham, June 2011.

Football League Record: 1920 Original Member of Division 3; 1921–25 Division 3 (S); 1925–47 Division 2; 1947–49 Division 3 (S); 1949–65 Division 2; 1965–67 Division 3; 1967–70 Division 4; 1970–73 Division 3; 1973–78 Division 4; 1978–79 Division 3; 1979–81 Division 2; 1981–83 Division 1; 1983–84 Division 2; 1984–86 Division 3; 1986–88 Division 4; 1988–92 Division 3; 1992–96 Division 2; 1996 2000 Division 3; 2000–01 Division 2; 2001–04 Division 3; 2004–05 FL 2; 2005–08 FL 1; 2008–11 FL C; 2011– FA Premier League.

LATEST SEQUENCES

Longest Sequence of League Wins: 9, 27.11.1999 – 22.01.2000.

Longest Sequence of League Defeats: 9, 26.1.1991 – 19.3.1991.

Longest Sequence of League Draws: 8, 25.11.2008 – 28.12.2008.

Longest Sequence of Unbeaten League Matches: 19, 19.10.1970 – 9.3.1971.

Longest Sequence Without a League Win: 15, 25.3.1989 – 2.9.1989.

Successive Scoring Runs: 27 from 28.8.1947.

Successive Non-scoring Runs: 6 from 6.2.1996.

MANAGERS

Walter Whittaker 1912–14
William Bartlett 1914–15
Joe Bradshaw 1919–26
Jimmy Thomson 1927–31
Neil Harris 1934–39
Haydn Green 1939–47
Bill McCandless 1947–55
Ron Burgess 1955–58
Trevor Morris 1958–65
Glyn Davies 1965–66
Billy Lucas 1967–69
Roy Bentley 1969–72
Harry Gregg 1972–75
Harry Griffiths 1975–77
John Toshack 1978–83
  (resigned October re-appointed in December) 1983–84
Colin Appleton 1984
John Bond 1984–85
Tommy Hutchison 1985–86
Terry Yorath 1986–89
Ian Evans 1989–90
Terry Yorath 1990–91
Frank Burrows 1991–95
Bobby Smith 1995
Kevin Cullis 1996
Jan Molby 1996–97
Micky Adams 1997
Alan Cork 1997–98
John Hollins 1998–2001
Colin Addison 2001–02
Nick Cusack 2002
Brian Flynn 2002–04
Kenny Jackett 2004–07
Roberto Martinez 2007–09
Paulo Sousa 2009–10
Brendan Rodgers July 2010–

TEN YEAR LEAGUE RECORD

		P	W	D	L	F	A	Pts	Pos
2001-02	Div 3	46	13	12	21	53	77	51	20
2002-03	Div 3	46	12	13	21	48	65	49	21
2003-04	Div 3	46	15	14	17	58	61	59	10
2004-05	FL 2	46	24	8	14	62	43	80	3
2005-06	FL 1	46	18	17	11	78	55	71	6
2006-07	FL 1	46	20	12	14	69	53	72	7
2007-08	FL 1	46	27	11	8	82	42	92	1
2008-09	FL C	46	16	20	10	63	50	68	8
2009-10	FL C	46	17	18	11	40	37	69	7
2010-11	FL C	46	24	8	14	69	42	80	3

DID YOU KNOW ?

In 1957–58 six Swansea Town players were selected to play for Wales against East Germany on 25 September. Five actually played: Len Allchurch, Mel Charles, Cliff Jones, Des Palmer and Dai Thomas. Wales won 4-1 and Palmer was man of the match with a hat-trick.

SWANSEA CITY 2010–11 LEAGUE RECORD

Match No.	Date		Venue	Opponents	Result		H/T Score	Lg Pos.	Goalscorers	Attendance
1	Aug	7	A	Hull C	L	0-2	0-1	—		21,478
2		14	H	Preston NE	W	4-0	3-0	9	Dobbie [23], Pratley [40], Dyer [43], Cotterill (pen) [56]	14,010
3		21	A	Norwich C	L	0-2	0-0	14		23,852
4		28	H	Burnley	W	1-0	1-0	12	Sinclair [8]	15,135
5	Sept	11	A	Leeds U	L	1-2	1-0	14	Dobbie [13]	26,453
6		14	H	Coventry C	W	2-1	1-0	—	Pratley [19], Sinclair [47]	12,411
7		18	H	Scunthorpe U	W	2-0	0-0	6	Sinclair [83], Dobbie [85]	13,597
8		25	A	Nottingham F	L	1-3	0-1	9	Van der Gun [90]	19,974
9		28	A	Watford	W	3-2	2-0	—	Sinclair [11], Dobbie [30], Nouble [69]	11,485
10	Oct	2	H	Derby Co	D	0-0	0-0	8		15,071
11		16	A	Reading	W	1-0	1-0	4	Sinclair [35]	18,418
12		19	H	QPR	D	0-0	0-0	—		16,742
13		23	H	Leicester C	W	2-0	0-0	3	Emnes [50], Sinclair [90]	14,651
14		30	A	Crystal Palace	W	3-0	1-0	3	Sinclair [6], Pratley [71], Allen [80]	16,223
15	Nov	7	A	Cardiff C	W	1-0	0-0	3	Emnes [75]	26,049
16		10	H	Bristol C	L	0-1	0-1	—		14,741
17		14	H	Middlesbrough	W	1-0	0-0	3	Sinclair [84]	14,906
18		20	A	Doncaster R	D	1-1	0-1	3	Rangel [90]	13,614
19		26	H	Portsmouth	L	1-2	1-1	—	Beattie [2]	17,584
20	Dec	4	A	Ipswich T	W	3-1	0-0	—	Beattie 2 [64, 86], Allen [90]	16,978
21		10	H	Millwall	D	1-1	1-1	—	Rangel [18]	13,853
22		18	A	Sheffield U	L	0-1	0-1	4		17,496
23		26	A	QPR	L	0-4	0-1	4		15,963
24		28	H	Barnsley	W	1-0	1-0	3	Easter [27]	15,093
25	Jan	1	H	Reading	W	1-0	0-0	2	Pratley [65]	14,329
26		3	A	Leicester C	L	1-2	1-2	3	Sinclair [12]	21,656
27		15	H	Crystal Palace	W	3-0	1-0	2	Pratley [43], Sinclair 2 (2 pens) [56, 61]	13,369
28		22	A	Barnsley	D	1-1	0-1	4	Sinclair (pen) [86]	10,481
29	Feb	1	A	Bristol C	W	2-0	1-0	3	Pratley 2 [10, 67]	14,366
30		6	H	Cardiff C	L	0-1	0-0	5		18,280
31		12	A	Middlesbrough	W	4-3	1-2	5	Dyer [14], Sinclair (pen) [60], Williams [68], Beattie [90]	14,825
32		19	H	Doncaster R	W	3-0	2-0	3	Sinclair [6], Williams [39], Moore [78]	13,309
33		22	A	Coventry C	W	1-0	0-0	—	Dobbie [76]	13,481
34		26	H	Leeds U	W	3-0	1-0	2	Sinclair 2 (1 pen) [13, 55 (p)], Moore [72]	19,309
35	Mar	5	A	Scunthorpe U	L	0-1	0-0	2		4608
36		8	H	Watford	D	1-1	1-0	—	Dobbie [26]	14,410
37		12	A	Derby Co	L	1-2	0-1	2	Pratley [65]	25,341
38		19	H	Nottingham F	W	3-2	2-1	3	Sinclair [21], Borini 2 [26, 56]	18,371
39	Apr	2	A	Preston NE	L	1-2	1-1	4	Williams [24]	11,791
40		9	H	Norwich C	W	3-0	2-0	4	Borini [5], Gower [29], Priskin [90]	19,094
41		12	H	Hull C	D	1-1	0-0	—	Gower [63]	14,822
42		16	A	Burnley	L	1-2	0-0	5	Borini [53]	13,675
43		23	A	Portsmouth	D	0-0	0-0	5		15,907
44		25	H	Ipswich T	W	4-1	3-1	4	Borini 2 [9, 30], Moore [14], Sinclair (pen) [71]	16,001
45		30	A	Millwall	W	2-0	1-0	4	Pratley [30], Dobbie [47]	15,101
46	May	7	H	Sheffield U	W	4-0	1-0	3	Dobbie 2 [30, 60], Sinclair (pen) [55], Britton [90]	17,584

Final League Position: 3

GOALSCORERS

League (69): Sinclair 19 (7 pens), Dobbie 9, Pratley 9, Borini 6, Beattie 4, Moore 3, Williams 3, Allen 2, Dyer 2, Emnes 2, Gower 2, Rangel 2, Britton 1, Cotterill 1 (1 pen), Easter 1, Nouble 1, Priskin 1, Van der Gun 1.
Carling Cup (9): Sinclair 4, Kuqi 2, Van der Gun 2, Pratley 1.
FA Cup (5): Van der Gun 2, Monk 1, Pratley 1, Sinclair 1.
Play-Offs (7): Sinclair 3 (2 pens), Dobbie 2, Britton 1, Pratley 1.

De Vries D 46	Serran A 5 + 6	Tate A 39 + 1	Lopez J 1 + 2	Monk G 27 + 2	Williams A 46	Gower M 37 + 3	Pratley D 28 + 6	Dobbie S 23 + 18	Dyer N 45 + 1	Cotterill D 10 + 4	Orlandi A 13 + 7	Kuqi S — + 2	Pintado G — + 1	Rangel A 37 + 1	Sinclair S 39 + 4	Allen J 30 + 10	Taylor N 25 + 4	Van der Gun C 1 + 9	Nouble F 2 + 4	Beattie C 9 + 13	Emnes M 3 + 1	Agustien K 3 + 5	Donnelly S — + 1	Easter J 2 + 4	Richards J 6	Moore L 11 + 4	Alfei D — + 1	Britton L 10 + 7	Borini F 8 + 1	Priskin T — + 4	Lucas L — + 1	Match No.
1	2	3	4³	5	6	7¹	8	9²	10	11	12	13	14																			1
1	13	3		5	6	7	4	9	10²	11¹	14			2²	8³	12																2
1	2¹	3		5	6	7	4	9	10²	11	13				8	12																3
1	3			5	6	7	4⁴	9³	10²	8¹	13	14			11	12	2															4
1	2			5	6	7	8	9	10²		4¹				11	12	3	13														5
1	3	13		5	6	7	8	9¹	10						11	4²	2	12														6
1	14	3		5	6	7	8	12	10³	13					11	4²	2	9¹														7
1	2			5	6	7	8		10	11¹	13				4	3²	12	9														8
1	4	2		5	6	7		9²	10					12	11³	8	3¹	14	13													9
1	3	13		5	6	7²		9	10	11¹				2	4	8³	12	14														10
1	14	3		5	6	7¹	8	9²	10³	12				2	11		13															11
1	3			5	6		8	9²	10	11¹	4³			2	7	12		13	14													12
1	13	3		5	6		8	9¹	10		4³			2	11	7²		12	14													13
1				5	6	7²	8	12	10					2	11	4	3			9¹		13										14
1				5	6	7	8²	12	10³					2	11	4		14		9¹		13										15
1	3			5	6	7²	8¹	13	10	14				2	11	12		9				4³										16
1	3			5³	6	7¹	8	13	10	12				2	11	4		14		9²												17
1	5²				6	7³	8	14	10¹	11				2	12	4	3			9		13										18
1	3³			5	6	7¹	8	12	10					2	11	4		13		9²		14										19
1				5	6	7	8¹	12	10²	13				2	11	4	3			9												20
1	3			5	6	7²	8³	13	10	14				2	11	4				9¹						12						21
1	3			5	6	7¹	8	12	10³	14				2	11	4				9²						13						22
1	3⁴			5	6		8	13	10¹					2	11	4		12		9³	7²					14						23
1				5	6	7²	8	9³	13	4	11			2	14	12	3							10¹								24
1	13			5	6	7¹	8	9¹	10	12				2	11	4	3²									14						25
1				5	6	7³	8	14	11					2	10		3	13				12				4²			9¹			26
1				5	6	7	8	13	10¹					2	11	4						12			3³			14	9²			27
1				5	6	7¹	8	12	10²					2	11	4³						13			3			14	9			28
1				5	6	7	0		10²					2	11	12		14				13			3			4	9²			29
1				5	6	7	8	14	10					2	11	12						13			3			4³	9²			30
1				5	6	7	8²	12	10					2	11	13						14			3			4¹	9¹			31
1				5	6	7¹	8	13	10²					2	11	4	3					14						12	9³			32
1				5	6	7	8¹	12	10³					2	11		3					9²						4		14	13	33
1				5	6	7		10¹	8					2	11	4	3					13						12	9²			34
1				5	6	7		12	10					2	11	8	3²			9								4¹	13			35
1				5	6	7	8		10					2	11	4	3					12						9¹				36
1				5	6	7¹		12	10	8³				2	11	4	3					14						9²	13			37
1		13		5	6	7			10¹	8³				2²	11	4	3	14								12			9			38
1	2			5	6	7³	8		10²	14					11	4¹	3					13						9		12		39
1	13			5	6	7			10¹	8²				2	11	4	3					14						9³		12		40
1				5	6	7			10³	8¹				2	11	4	3	14				12						9²		13		41
1				5	6	7	8¹	14	10³					2	11²	3						12						4	9	13		42
1	3			5	6	7	8	13	10					2	11¹							12						4	9²			43
1				5	6		11²	7³	13					2	12	8	3	14								10		4	9¹			44
1	14			5	6	7			10¹	11				2	12	8	3			9²								4³	13			45
1	5¹	13			6	12			10		7³			2	11	8²	3											4	9	14		46

FA Cup

Third Round	Colchester U	(h)	4-0
Fourth Round	Leyton Orient	(h)	1-2

Carling Cup

First Round	Barnet	(h)	3-0
Second Round	Tranmere R	(a)	3-1
Third Round	Peterborough U	(a)	3-1
Fourth Round	Wigan Ath	(a)	0-2

Play-Offs

Semi-Final	Nottingham F	(a)	0-0
		(h)	3-1
Final	Reading		4-2
(at Wembley).			

SWINDON TOWN   FL Championship 2

FOUNDATION

It is generally accepted that Swindon Town came into being in 1881, although there is no firm evidence that the club's founder, Rev. William Pitt, captain of the Spartans (an offshoot of a cricket club) changed his club's name to Swindon Town before 1883, when the Spartans amalgamated with St Mark's Young Men's Friendly Society.

The County Ground, County Road, Swindon, Wiltshire SN1 2ED.

Telephone: 0871 423 6433.

Fax: (0844) 880 1112.

Ticket Office: 0871 223 2300.

Website: www.swindontownfc.co.uk

Email: brianp@swindontownfc.co.uk

Ground Capacity: 14,700.

Record Attendance: 32,000 v Arsenal, FA Cup 3rd rd, 15 January 1972.

Pitch Measurements: 110yd × 75yd.

Chairman: Jeremy Wray (interim).

Chief Executive: Nicholas Watkins.

Secretary: Louise Fletcher.

Manager: Paulo Di Canio.

Assistant Manager: Fabrizio Piccareta.

Head of Sports Therapy: Kate Cady.

Colours: Red shirts with white inserts, red shorts with white inserts, red stockings with white inserts.

Change Colours: All white with blue inserts.

Year Formed: 1881* (*see Foundation*). *Turned Professional:* 1894. *Ltd Co.:* 1894.

Club Nickname: 'Robins'.

Grounds: 1881, The Croft; 1896, County Ground.

First Football League Game: 28 August 1920, Division 3, v Luton T (h) W 9–1 – Nash; Kay, Macconachie; Langford, Hawley, Wareing; Jefferson (1), Fleming (4), Rogers, Batty (2), Davies (1), (1 og).

Record League Victory: 9–1 v Luton T, Division 3 (S), 28 August 1920 – Nash; Kay, Macconachie; Langford, Hawley, Wareing; Jefferson (1), Fleming (4), Rogers, Batty (2), Davies (1), (1 og).

Record Cup Victory: 10–1 v Farnham U Breweries (away), FA Cup 1st rd (replay), 28 November 1925 – Nash; Dickenson, Weston, Archer, Bew, Adey; Denyer (2), Wall (1), Richardson (4), Johnson (3), Davies.

HONOURS

Football League: Best season: 1992–93. **Division 2:** *Champions* 1995–96; **Division 3:** *Runners-up* 1962–63, 1968–69; **Division 4:** *Champions* 1985–86 (with record 102 points). **FA Cup:** Semi-finals 1910, 1912. **Football League Cup:** *Winners* 1969. **Anglo-Italian Cup:** *Winners* 1970.

sky SPORTS FACT FILE

On 12 April 1993 Swindon Town were trailing 2-1 at half-time away to Birmingham City. Six minutes into the second half the Robins were 4-1 in arrears. But they rallied to score five times in 30 minutes to win 6-4. David Mitchell scored three times.

Record Defeat: 1–10 v Manchester C, FA Cup 4th rd (replay), 25 January 1930.

Most League Points (2 for a win): 64, Division 3, 1968–69.

Most League Points (3 for a win): 102, Division 4, 1985–86.

Most League Goals: 100, Division 3 (S), 1926–27.

Highest League Scorer in Season: Harry Morris, 47, Division 3 (S), 1926–27.

Most League Goals in Total Aggregate: Harry Morris, 216, 1926–33.

Most League Goals in One Match: 5, Harry Morris v QPR, Division 3 (S), 18 December 1926; 5, Harry Morris v Norwich C, Division 3 (S), 26 April 1930; 5, Keith East v Mansfield T, Division 3, 20 November 1965.

Most Capped Player: Rod Thomas, 30 (50), Wales.

Most League Appearances: John Trollope, 770, 1960–80.

Youngest League Player: Paul Rideout, 16 years 107 days v Hull C, 29 November 1980.

Record Transfer Fee Received: £1,500,000 from Manchester C for Kevin Horlock, January 1997; £1,500,000 from WBA for Simon Cox, July 2009.

Record Transfer Fee Paid: £800,000 to West Ham U for Joey Beauchamp, August 1994.

Football League Record: 1920 Original Member of Division 3; 1921–58 Division 3 (S); 1958–63 Division 3; 1963–65 Division 2; 1965–69 Division 3; 1969–74 Division 2; 1974–82 Division 3; 1982–86 Division 4; 1986–87 Division 3; 1987–92 Division 2; 1992–93 Division 1; 1993–94 FA Premier League; 1994–95 Division 1; 1995–96 Division 2; 1996–2000 Division 1; 2000–04 Division 2; 2004–06 FL 1; 2006–07 FL 2; 2007–11 FL 1; 2011– FL 2.

MANAGERS

Sam Allen 1902–33
Ted Vizard 1933–39
Neil Harris 1939–41
Louis Page 1945–53
Maurice Lindley 1953–55
Bert Head 1956–65
Danny Williams 1965–69
Fred Ford 1969–71
Dave Mackay 1971–72
Les Allen 1972–74
Danny Williams 1974–78
Bobby Smith 1978–80
John Trollope 1980–83
Ken Beamish 1983–84
Lou Macari 1984–89
Ossie Ardiles 1989–91
Glenn Hoddle 1991–93
John Gorman 1993–94
Steve McMahon 1994–98
Jimmy Quinn 1998–2000
Colin Todd 2000
Andy King 2000–01
Roy Evans 2001
Andy King 2001–05
Iffy Onuora 2005–06
Dennis Wise 2006
Paul Sturrock 2006–07
Maurice Malpas 2008
Danny Wilson 2008–11
Paul Hart 2011
Paulo Di Canio May 2011–

LATEST SEQUENCES

Longest Sequence of League Wins: 8, 12.1.1986 – 15.3.1986.

Longest Sequence of League Defeats: 8, 29.8.2005 – 8.10.2005.

Longest Sequence of League Draws: 6, 22.11.1991 – 28.12.1991.

Longest Sequence of Unbeaten League Matches: 22, 12.1.1986 – 23.8.86.

Longest Sequence Without a League Win: 19, 30.10.1999 – 4.3.2000.

Successive Scoring Runs: 31 from 17.4.1926.

Successive Non-scoring Runs: 5 from 16.11.1963.

TEN YEAR LEAGUE RECORD

		P	W	D	L	F	A	Pts	Pos
2001-02	Div 2	46	15	14	17	46	56	59	13
2002-03	Div 2	46	16	12	18	59	63	60	10
2003-04	Div 2	46	20	13	13	76	58	73	5
2004-05	FL 1	46	17	12	17	66	68	63	12
2005-06	FL 1	46	11	15	20	46	65	48	23
2006-07	FL 2	46	25	10	11	58	38	85	3
2007-08	FL 1	46	16	13	17	63	56	61	13
2008-09	FL 1	46	12	17	17	68	71	53	15
2009-10	FL 1	46	22	16	8	73	57	82	5
2010-11	FL 1	46	9	14	23	50	72	41	24

DID YOU KNOW ?

Frank Richardson was the first Swindon Town player to score four times in successive FA Cup ties. Initially in the record victory against Farnham United Breweries, then in the 7-0 win over Sittingbourne on 12 December 1925, during his first of two spells with the club.

SWINDON TOWN 2010–11 LEAGUE RECORD

Match No.	Date		Venue	Opponents	Result		H/T Score	Lg Pos.	Goalscorers	Atten- dance
1	Aug	7	H	Brighton & HA	L	1-2	0-1	—	Austin [80]	10,392
2		14	A	Hartlepool U	D	2-2	0-2	18	Dossevi [72], Austin [74]	2893
3		21	H	Brentford	D	1-1	1-1	18	Prutton [40]	8132
4		28	A	Milton Keynes D	L	1-2	1-0	20	Cuthbert [45]	7866
5	Sept	4	A	Carlisle U	D	0-0	0-0	24		5689
6		11	H	Southampton	W	1-0	0-0	15	Austin [65]	11,087
7		18	A	Walsall	W	2-1	1-0	13	Sheehan [10], Pericard [74]	4580
8		25	H	Huddersfield T	W	1-0	0-0	12	Morrison [90]	8652
9		28	H	Plymouth Arg	L	2-3	1-2	—	Prutton [37], Rose [74]	9346
10	Oct	2	A	Dagenham & R	L	1-2	1-0	16	Dossevi [1]	2767
11		11	H	Bristol R	W	2-1	1-0	—	Morrison [45], Pericard [57]	9065
12		16	A	Peterborough U	L	4-5	3-3	16	Ball 2 [24, 43], Ritchie [30], Austin (pen) [73]	7077
13		23	H	Leyton Orient	D	2-2	0-0	15	Austin [62], Rose [84]	8384
14		30	A	Yeovil T	D	3-3	1-1	16	Austin [23], Morrison [87], McGovern [88]	4671
15	Nov	2	H	Charlton Ath	L	0-3	0-1	—		7939
16		13	H	Colchester U	W	2-1	1-1	13	Dossevi [29], Austin [54]	7679
17		20	A	Rochdale	D	3-3	1-1	15	Timlin [1], Austin [78], Rose [80]	2866
18		23	A	Notts Co	L	0-1	0-0	—		4644
19	Dec	4	H	Sheffield W	W	2-1	1-1	—	Austin [24], McGovern [70]	9123
20		28	H	Peterborough U	D	1-1	0-1	—	Austin (pen) [72]	8592
21	Jan	1	H	Bournemouth	L	1-2	1-1	18	Ritchie [21]	8874
22		3	A	Charlton Ath	W	4-2	1-1	17	Ritchie [41], Austin 2 [56, 81], Morrison [77]	14,740
23		8	A	Oldham Ath	L	0-2	0-1	—		3573
24		15	H	Yeovil T	L	0-1	0-0	19		7950
25		22	A	Bristol R	L	1-3	0-1	20	McGovern [66]	6972
26		25	H	Tranmere R	D	0-0	0-0	—		6912
27		29	H	Exeter C	D	0-0	0-0	—		8132
28	Feb	1	A	Bournemouth	L	2-3	1-2	21	Caddis [21], Ritchie [58]	7212
29		5	H	Rochdale	D	1-1	0-0	20	Benyon [90]	7386
30		8	A	Leyton Orient	L	0-3	0-3	—		4214
31		12	A	Colchester U	L	1-2	0-1	21	Cuthbert [51]	3624
32		19	A	Carlisle U	L	0-1	0-1	21		7592
33		26	A	Southampton	L	1-4	0-1	20	Ritchie [54]	22,627
34	Mar	5	H	Walsall	D	0-0	0-0	22		10,489
35		8	A	Plymouth Arg	L	0-1	0-1	—		8830
36		12	H	Dagenham & R	D	1-1	1-0	22	Grella [44]	7864
37		19	A	Huddersfield T	D	0-0	0-0	23		13,907
38		26	A	Brighton & HA	L	1-2	1-1	—	Prutton [22]	7562
39		29	A	Exeter C	L	0-1	0-0	—		4174
40	Apr	2	H	Hartlepool U	D	1-1	0-1	23	Ritchie [67]	7146
41		9	A	Brentford	W	1-0	0-0	23	Andrew [80]	4593
42		16	H	Milton Keynes D	L	0-1	0-1	23		8305
43		23	A	Notts Co	L	1-2	1-0	—	Ritchie [18]	8064
44		25	A	Sheffield W	L	1-3	1-2	24	Douglas [43]	17,348
45		30	H	Oldham Ath	L	0-2	0-1	24		7420
46	May	7	A	Tranmere R	W	2-0	2-0	24	Lescinel [10], Timlin [38]	5302

Final League Position: 24

GOALSCORERS

League (50): Austin 12 (2 pens), Ritchie 7, Morrison 4, Dossevi 3, McGovern 3, Prutton 3, Rose 3, Ball 2, Cuthbert 2, Pericard 2, Timlin 2, Andrew 1, Benyon 1, Caddis 1, Douglas 1, Grella 1, Lescinel 1, Sheehan 1.
Carling Cup (1): McGovern 1.
FA Cup (7): Austin 3, McGovern 1, Morrison 1, Pericard 1, Ritchie 1.
J Paint Trophy (6): Pericard 3, Austin 2, Ball 1.

Smith P 26+1	Amankwaah K 17+2	Rose M 27+8	Douglas J 38+1	Cuthbert S 38+3	Lescinel J 16+2	McGovern J 30+8	Ball D 7+11	Dossevi T 16+11	Austin C 20+1	Prutton D 31+10	Pericard V 11+7	O'Brien A 8+13	Ferry S 18+3	Lucas D 20+1	Caddis P 36+2	Morrison S 19	Kennedy C 2+1	Timlin M 18+4	Sheehan A 17+4	Bodin B 2+3	Ritchie M 35+1	Frampton A 23	Thompson N 2+1	Flint A 2+1	Benyon E 7+5	Obika J 3+2	Grella M 6+1	Andrew C 9+1	N'Diaye A 2+4	Storey M —+2	Clark M —+1	Match No.
1	2	3	4	5	6	7	8²	9¹	10	11³	12	13	14																			1
	3	4	5	6	7¹		13	10	11	12	9	8²		1	2																	2
	3¹	4	5		7		13	9²	10	11	14	8³		1	2	6	12															3
13	3	4	5		7²	14		9¹	10	11⁸	12	8³		1	2	6																4
	2		4	5	7		13		10		9²	14	8	1		6	3¹	11³	12													5
1	2		4	5	13	7	14	12	10³	11	9¹		8			6	3²															6
	2		4	5	7	12		9¹		11	10			1	8	6		3														7
	2		4	5	7			9¹		11	10	12		1	8	6		3														8
	2	12	4	5	7²			9³		11⁸	10	13	14	1	8	6		3¹														9
	2²	3	4	5		12	8¹	9³	10	13	11			1	7	6			14													10
	2	3	4	5	7¹	8²		12	10	13	11			1		6			9													11
15	2	3	4²	5		7	8	12	13	10¹	11	1⁶			6				9													12
	2²	12		5	7	8¹	14	10		13	11	1	4	6					3⁸		9³											13
	3			5	12	8³	10	11	14	13	7¹	1	2²	4					9	6												14
1	3			5	7	14	13	10	11	9²	12	4¹	6						8³		2											15
1	3	4	2	6	13	12	9¹	10	11			5				8			7²													16
1	3	4	2³	6		13	9²	10	11			12	5			7¹	14	8														17
1	3	4¹	2	6²	12	14	9³	10	11			13	5			7	8															18
1⁰	3	4	5		7	12	13	10	11	9²			15	2	6			8¹														19
1		3		5	7			12	10	11	9¹	13	4		2			3	8²	6												20
	13			5	7	8¹		10	11	12		4³		2		14		3²	9	6												21
1	3	13			12		14	10¹	11			8²	4		2	5	7³	9	6													22
1	3	13	14		12			10	11			8¹	4		2	5	7²	9	6³													23
1	3⁸	4	5	6	7²		9¹	10	11	12					7	14	13	8³														24
1		4	5	6	7		12	10	11			8¹	2			3	9															25
1	2	4	5	3²	7¹		9	10		12		11	13	8	6																	26
1	2	4	5	7¹		9		12		11		8	3	10	6																	27
1	2	13	4	5	12		9		14	11		7	8³	3²	10¹	6																28
1	2²	3	4		14		9	13	11¹	7		8⁸	12	6	5	10																29
1	2	11	4	3¹	14	9²	12	7	8³		10	6	5	13																		30
	3	4	5	7	12		13	1	2	8	10²	6	9	11¹																		31
	3	4	5	7	12²		13	14	1	2	8³	10	6	9¹	11																	32
	3	4	5	7¹		12	13	8	1	2	14	10²	6	11³	9																	33
	3	4	5	7²		11	8¹	1	2	12	10	6	13	9																		34
1	3	4	5	7²	12	11	13	2	8¹	10³	6	14	9																			35
1	12	4	5	11	2	8²	3	10	6	13	7¹	9																				36
12	13	4	5	14	11	1	2	8	3³	10²	6	7¹	9																			37
	2	4	5	11	1	7	3	8¹	6	12	10¹	9	13																			38
	2	4	5	11	1	7	3	8¹	6	10	9	12																				39
1	4	5	7¹	11	2	3	8	6	10²	13	9	12																				40
1	13	4	3	7²	11	2	10¹	5	8	6	9	12																				41
1	13	4	11	2	3²	10	6⁸	12	9	8¹																						42
10	4	5	6	7²	11	1	2	12	3	8¹	13	9																				43
1	3	4	12	6	11	8	2	13	10	5¹	9²	14	7³																			44
1	3	4²	5	6	7¹	12	8	2	10	11	13	9³	14																			45
1	3	5	6²	4	7	8	11	10	2³	13	9¹	12	14																			46

FA Cup

First Round	Plymouth Arg	(a)	4-0
Second Round	Crawley T	(a)	1-1
		(h)	2-3

Carling Cup

First Round	Leyton Orient	(h)	1-2

J Paint Trophy

First Round	Southampton	(a)	3-0
Second Round	Torquay U	(h)	2-0
Southern Quarter-Final	Brentford	(h)	1-1

TORQUAY UNITED — FL Championship 2

FOUNDATION

The idea of establishing a Torquay club was agreed by old boys of Torquay College and Torbay College, while sitting in Princess Gardens listening to the band. A proper meeting was subsequently held at Tor Abbey Hotel at which officers were elected. This was on 1 May 1899 and the club's first competition was the Eastern League (later known as the East Devon League). As an amateur club it played at Teignmouth Road, Torquay Recreation Ground and Cricket Field Road before settling down for four years at Torquay Cricket Ground where the rugby club now plays. They became Torquay United in 1921 after merging with Babbacombe FC.

Plainmoor Ground, Torquay, Devon TQ1 3PS.
Telephone: (01803) 328 666.
Fax: (01803) 323 976.
Ticket Office: (01803) 328 666.
Website: www.torquayunited.com
Email: reception@torquayunited.com
Ground Capacity: 6,117.
Record Attendance: 21,908 v Huddersfield T, FA Cup 4th rd, 29 January 1955.
Pitch Measurements: 110yd × 74yd.
Chairman: Simon Baker.
Secretary: Kerry Haggan.
Manager: Martin Ling.
First Team Coach: Shaun Taylor.
Physio: Damian Davey.
Colours: All yellow with blue inserts.
Change Colours: All white with blue design, tangerine cuffs and stocking tops.
Year Formed: 1899.
Turned Professional: 1921.
Ltd Co.: 1921.
Previous Name: 1910, Torquay Town; 1921, Torquay United.
Club Nickname: 'The Gulls'.
Grounds: 1899, Teignmouth Road; 1900, Torquay Recreation Ground; 1904, Cricket Field Road; 1906, Torquay Cricket Ground; 1910, Plainmoor Ground.
First Football League Game: 27 August 1927, Division 3 (S), v Exeter C (h) D 1–1 – Millsom; Cook, Smith; Wellock, Wragg, Connor, Mackey, Turner (1), Jones, McGovern, Thomson.

HONOURS

Football League – Division 3 (S): *Runners-up* 1956–57.
FA Cup: Best season: 4th rd, 1949, 1955, 1971, 1983, 1990, 2009, 2011.
Football League Cup: never past 3rd rd.
Sherpa Van Trophy: *Runners-up* 1989.

sky SPORTS FACT FILE

Tommy Tait, a prolific goal scorer with 200 League and Cup goals for half a dozen League clubs pre-war, signed for Torquay United from Reading in 1939. Yet his only official first team games for them were the three pre-war aborted matches and two FA Cup games in 1945.

Record League Victory: 9–0 v Swindon T, Division 3 (S), 8 March 1952 – George Webber; Topping, Ralph Calland; Brown, Eric Webber, Towers; Shaw (1), Marchant (1), Tommy Northcott (2), Collins (3), Edds (2).

Record Cup Victory: 7–1 v Northampton T, FA Cup 1st rd, 14 November 1959 – Gill; Penford, Downs; Bettany, George Northcott, Rawson; Baxter, Cox, Tommy Northcott (1), Bond (3), Pym (3).

Record Defeat: 2–10 v Fulham, Division 3 (S), 7 September 1931. 2–10 v Luton T, Division 3 (S), 2 September 1933.

Most League Points (2 for a win): 60, Division 4, 1959–60.

Most League Points (3 for a win): 81, Division 3, 2003–04.

Most League Goals: 89, Division 3 (S), 1956–57.

Highest League Scorer in Season: Sammy Collins, 40, Division 3 (S), 1955–56.

Most League Goals in Total Aggregate: Sammy Collins, 204, 1948–58.

Most League Goals in One Match: 5, Robin Stubbs v Newport Co, Division 4, 19 October 1963.

Most Capped Player: Tony Bedeau, 4, Grenada.

Most League Appearances: Dennis Lewis, 443, 1947–59.

Youngest League Player: David Byng, 16 years 36 days v Walsall, 14 August 1993.

Record Transfer Fee Received: £650,000 from Crewe Alex for Rodney Jack, June 1998.

Record Transfer Fee Paid: £75,000 to Peterborough U for Leon Constantine, December 2004.

Football League Record: 1927 Elected to Division 3 (S); 1958–60 Division 4; 1960–62 Division 3; 1962–66 Division 4; 1966–72 Division 3; 1972–91 Division 4; 1991–2004 Division 3; 2004–05 FL 1; 2005–07 FL 2; 2007–09 Blue Square Pr; 2009– FL 2.

LATEST SEQUENCES

Longest Sequence of League Wins: 8, 24.1.1998 – 3.3.1998.

Longest Sequence of League Defeats: 8, 30.9.1995 – 18.11.1995.

Longest Sequence of League Draws: 8, 25.10.1969 – 13.12.1969.

Longest Sequence of Unbeaten League Matches: 15, 5.5.1990 – 3.11.1990.

Longest Sequence Without a League Win: 19, 23.9.2006 – 20.1.2007.

Successive Scoring Runs: 19 from 3.10.1953.

Successive Non-scoring Runs: 7 from 8.1.1972.

MANAGERS

Percy Mackrill 1927–29
A. H. Hoskins 1929
  (Secretary-Manager)
Frank Womack 1929–32
Frank Brown 1932–38
Alf Steward 1938–40
Billy Butler 1945–46
Jack Butler 1946–47
John McNeil 1947–50
Bob John 1950
Alex Massie 1950–51
Eric Webber 1951–65
Frank O'Farrell 1965–68
Alan Brown 1969–71
Jack Edwards 1971–73
Malcolm Musgrove 1973–76
Frank O'Farrell 1976–77
Mike Green 1977–81
Frank O'Farrell 1981–82
  (continued as General Manager to 1983)
Bruce Rioch 1982–84
Dave Webb 1984–85
John Sims 1985
Stuart Morgan 1985–87
Cyril Knowles 1987–89
Dave Smith 1989–91
John Impey 1991
Ivan Golac 1992
Paul Compton 1992–93
Don O'Riordan 1993–95
Eddie May 1995–96
Kevin Hodges *(Head Coach)* 1996–98
Wes Saunders 1998–2001
Roy McFarland 2001–02
Leroy Rosenior 2002–06
Ian Atkins 2006
John Cornforth 2006
Lubos Kubik 2006–07
Keith Curle 2007
Leroy Rosenior 2007
Paul Buckle 2007–11
Martin Ling June 2011–

TEN YEAR LEAGUE RECORD

		P	W	D	L	F	A	Pts	Pos
2001-02	Div 3	46	12	15	19	46	63	51	19
2002-03	Div 3	46	16	18	12	71	71	66	9
2003-04	Div 3	46	23	12	11	68	44	81	3
2004-05	FL 1	46	12	15	19	55	79	51	21
2005-06	FL 2	46	13	13	20	53	66	52	20
2006-07	FL 2	46	7	14	25	36	63	35	24
2007-08	B Sq Pr	46	26	8	12	83	57	86	3
2008-09	B Sq Pr	46	23	14	9	72	47	83	4
2009-10	FL 2	46	14	15	17	64	55	57	17
2010-11	FL 2	46	17	18	11	74	53	68*	7

*1 point deducted.

DID YOU KNOW ?

In 1910–11 Torquay United (as Torquay Town) entered the FA Cup for the first time. In the first qualifying round on 1 October they were drawn away against Green Waves. They caused a ripple winning 2-0 and were successfully to meet the same team three times in the early 1920s.

TORQUAY UNITED 2010–11 LEAGUE RECORD

Match No.	Date	Venue	Opponents	Result	H/T Score	Lg Pos.	Goalscorers	Attendance
1	Aug 7	H	Northampton T	W 3-0	1-0	—	Nicholson [44], Zebroski [47], Benyon [50]	3567
2	14	A	Lincoln C	W 2-0	1-0	1	Benyon 2 [26, 71]	3033
3	21	H	Bradford C	W 2-0	1-0	1	Stevens [2], Zebroski [66]	2941
4	28	A	Port Vale	W 2 1	2-1	1	Wroe (pen) [5], Zebroski [28]	5750
5	Sept 4	A	Southend U	L 1-2	0-2	2	Zebroski [78]	5505
6	11	H	Accrington S	D 0-0	0-0	1		2598
7	18	A	Stevenage	D 0-0	0-0	4		3049
8	25	H	Macclesfield T	L 1-3	1-1	5	Benyon [40]	2551
9	28	H	Aldershot T	L 0-1	0-0	—		2167
10	Oct 2	A	Shrewsbury T	D 1-1	1-1	8	Benyon (pen) [34]	6034
11	9	A	Crewe Alex	D 3-3	2-1	8	Ellis 2 [8, 16], O'Kane [67]	4445
12	16	H	Bury	L 3-4	2-2	11	Robertson [18], Zebroski 2 [20, 56]	2553
13	23	A	Gillingham	D 1-1	0-0	13	Nicholson [90]	5345
14	30	H	Morecambe	W 3-1	1-1	8	Benyon 2 [11, 75], Rose [69]	2172
15	Nov 2	A	Oxford U	W 2-0	1-0	—	Batt (og) [5], Kee [89]	6401
16	13	H	Barnet	D 1-1	1-1	7	Benyon [11]	2257
17	20	A	Stockport Co	D 1-1	0-0	7	O'Kane [61]	3772
18	23	A	Wycombe W	W 3-1	1-1	—	Wroe 2 [27, 49], Benyon [88]	2273
19	Dec 11	A	Chesterfield	L 0-1	0-1	7		4801
20	Jan 1	A	Hereford U	D 2-2	2-1	10	O'Kane [25], Benyon [45]	2373
21	3	H	Oxford U	L 3-4	1-2	11	Benyon 2 [43, 73], Kee [79]	3021
22	11	H	Crewe Alex	W 2-1	2-0	—	O'Kane [7], Zebroski [16]	1955
23	15	A	Morecambe	L 1-2	0-0	11	Kee [78]	1643
24	22	H	Gillingham	D 1-1	1-0	11	Benyon [7]	2368
25	Feb 1	A	Hereford U	L 1-3	1-1	14	Robinson [10]	1680
26	5	H	Stockport Co	W 2-0	1-0	12	Zebroski [13], Kee [73]	1954
27	12	A	Barnet	W 3-0	1-0	10	Rowe-Turner [25], Kee [75], Zebroski [90]	2168
28	15	H	Burton Alb	W 1-0	0-0	—	Robertson [56]	1602
29	19	H	Southend U	D 1-1	0-0	9	Kee [73]	2880
30	22	A	Cheltenham T	D 2-2	1-0	—	Robinson [14], Stevens [65]	2977
31	26	A	Accrington S	L 0-1	0-0	11		1543
32	Mar 1	H	Rotherham U	D 1-1	1-0	—	O'Kane [17]	1514
33	5	H	Stevenage	W 2-0	0-0	8	Stevens [46], Robinson [85]	2197
34	8	A	Aldershot T	L 0-1	0-0	—		1939
35	12	H	Shrewsbury T	W 5-0	1-0	8	Tomlin [5], Robinson 2 (1 pen) [54 (p), 56], Zebroski [70], Sharps (og) [85]	2861
36	15	A	Bury	W 2-1	0-1	—	Stanley [61], Zebroski [70]	2757
37	19	A	Macclesfield T	D 3-3	0-2	7	Robinson 2 (1 pen) [52, 74 (p)], Branston [90]	1556
38	22	H	Cheltenham T	W 2-1	1-0	—	Branston [28], Murray [71]	2186
39	25	H	Northampton T	D 2-2	1-1	—	O'Kane [14], Kee [89]	4553
40	Apr 2	H	Lincoln C	W 2-0	0-0	6	Zebroski [74], Tomlin [84]	2751
41	9	A	Bradford C	W 3-0	1-0	5	Nicholson [31], Tomlin [59], Kee [78]	10,894
42	16	H	Port Vale	D 0-0	0-0	5		3726
43	22	H	Wycombe W	D 0-0	0-0	—		4009
44	25	A	Burton Alb	D 3-3	2-2	8	Zebroski [10], Tomlin [14], Kee [73]	3280
45	29	H	Chesterfield	D 0-0	0-0	—		5002
46	May 7	A	Rotherham U	L 1-3	1-2	7	Zebroski [31]	3379

Final League Position: 7

GOALSCORERS

League (74): Zebroski 14, Benyon 13 (1 pen), Kee 9, Robinson 7 (2 pens), O'Kane 6, Tomlin 4, Nicholson 3, Stevens 3, Wroe 3 (1 pen), Branston 2, Ellis 2, Robertson 2, Murray 1, Rose 1, Rowe-Turner 1, Stanley 1, own goals 2.
Carling Cup (0).
FA Cup (3): Benyon 1, Kee 1 (pen), O'Kane 1.
J Paint Trophy (0).
Play-Offs (2): O'Kane 1, Zebroski 1.

Bevan S 37	Robertson C 40+3	Nicholson K 42+2	Ellis M 24+3	Branston G 45	Wroe N 20	Mansell L 45	Gritton M 3+9	Benyon E 22+1	Zebroski C 44	Stevens D 19+18	Kee B 17+23	Macklin L 3+7	O'Kane E 31+14	Carlisle W 3+7	Charnock K 1+3	Senda D 2	Lathrope D 10+8	Oastler J 17+8	Rose R 2+3	Hemmings A 4+5	Stanley C 19	Robinson J 22	Halpin S —+4	Potter D 9	Rowe-Turner L 4+4	Gilligan R —+5	Pringle B 5	Murray R 4+3	Tomlin G 12	Match No.
1	2	3	4	5	6	7	8^1	9^2	10	11	12	13																		1
1	2	3	4	5^3	6	8		9	11	7^2	10^1		12	13	14															2
1	2	3	4	5	6	8	13	9^3	11	7^2	10^1		14	12																3
1	2	3	4	5	6	8	13	9^2	10^3	7^1	14		12	11																4
1	2	3	4	5	6	8	12	9^2	10	11^1	14		13	7^3																5
1	2	3	4	5	6	8	9^3		10	11^1	14	12	13	7^2																6
1	2	3	4^2	5	6	7	9^1	14	10	11	12		8^3		13															7
1	4	3		5	6	7	14	9	10	11^1		12	8^3	13		2^2														8
1	2	3		5		7	13	9^2	10	11^2	14		4	12	6		8^1													9
1	2	3	4	5	6	7		9^1	10^2	11		13	8	12																10
1	2	3	4	5		7	14	9	10	11^1	8^2		6^3	12			13													11
1	2	3	4	5^1		8		9	11	7^3	10^2	14	6	13	12															12
1	2	3	4	5		7^4	14	9^3	10		13		6^1				11	8^2	12											13
1		3	4	5	6		9	11		10^2	8^1	14				2^3		7	12	13										14
1	12	3	4	5	6	8		9^3	10^2		14	11^4	13					7	2^1											15
1	2	3	4	5	6	7	14	9	11^2	10^3	8^1							12	13											16
1		3	4	5	6			9^2		11			13		8			7	12	10^1										17
1	14	3	4	5	6	2		9^3		11	12	13	8^1					7		10^2										18
1		3	4	5	6	2	13	9	10	11^3		14	8^2					7		10^2										19
1	13	3	4	5^2	6	2		9		11	12	14	8^1					7		10^3										20
1	5	3	4		6	2		9		11	12		13				8^3	7^2	14	10^1										21
1	2	3	4	5	6	7		9^3	10	11^1			12				8^2	13	14											22
1	2	3	4	5	6	7		9^3	10	11^1			13				8^2	14	12											23
1	2	3	4	5	6^1	7		9^2	10	11			13				8	12												24
1	2	3	4^1	5		7				11^2	10		8				12				6	9	13							25
	2	3		5		4				11	12		9^2				8	7			6	10^1	13	1						26
	4			5		2				11	14	13	9^3				8^2	7			6	10^1		1	3	12				27
	4	13		5		2				11^3	12		9				8	7			6	10^1		1	3^2	14				28
	4	12		5		2				11	14	0	0^7					7			6	10^1		1	3^1	13				29
	4			5		2				11	12		9^3	8^1	13			7			6	10^2		1	3	14				30
	2	3	4^4	5		8				11			9^2	14				7^3			6	10^1		1	13	12				31
	4	3		5		2				11	14		9^2	13	8^1		12	7			6	10^3		1						32
	4	3		5		2				11	12		9^1	8^3			14	13			6	10		1			7^2			33
	4	3	14	5		2				9	11^3	12	8^1								6	10	13	1			7^2			34
1	4	3		5		2				11	12		13					14			6	10^2					7^3	8^1	9	35
1	4	3		5		2				11			13					12			6	10^2					7	8^1	9	36
1	4	3^1		5		2				11^3				8^2							6	10		12			7	13	9	37
1	4	3		5		2				11	14	13	12				7				6	10^3					8^2		9^1	38
1	4	3	13	5		2				11	12		8^2				7	14			6	10^3							9^1	39
1	4	3		5		2				11	14	12	13				8^2				6	10^3					7^1		9	40
1	4	3		5		2				11^2	13	12	8					6	7							10^3	14		9^1	41
1	4	3		5		2				11	12	9	8					6^3	14							7^1	13		10^2	42
1	4	3		5		2				11		12	8					7^1				6	10				13		9^2	43
1	4	3^2		5		2				11	14	12	8					7^1				6	10^3				13		9	44
1	4	3^2		5		2				11	14	7^3	8				12				6	10				13		9^1	45
1	4	3	13	5		2				11	14	12	8				6^3	7^1				10							9^2	46

FA Cup

First Round	Mansfield T	(a)	1-0
Second Round	Walsall	(h)	1-0
Third Round	Carlisle U	(h)	1-0
Fourth Round	Crawley T	(h)	0-1

Carling Cup

First Round	Reading	(h)	0-1

J Paint Trophy

First Round	Bournemouth	(a)	0-0
Second Round	Swindon T	(a)	0-2

Play-Offs

Semi-Final	- Shrewsbury T	(h)	2-0
		(a)	0-0
Final	Stevenage		0-1
(at Old Trafford).			

TOTTENHAM HOTSPUR   FA Premiership

FOUNDATION

The Hotspur Football Club was formed from an older cricket club in 1882. Most of the founders were old boys of St John's Presbyterian School and Tottenham Grammar School. The Casey brothers were well to the fore as the family provided the club's first goalposts (painted blue and white) and their first ball. They soon adopted the local YMCA as their meeting place, but after a couple of moves settled at the Red House, which is still their headquarters, although now known simply as 748 High Road.

White Hart Lane, Bill Nicholson Way, 748 High Road, Tottenham, London N17 0AP.

Telephone: (0844) 499 5000.

Fax: (020) 8365 5005.

Ticket Office: 0844 844 0102.

Website: www.tottenhamhotspur.com

Email: website@tottenhamhotspur.com

Ground Capacity: 36,534.

Record Attendance: 75,038 v Sunderland, FA Cup 6th rd. 5 March 1938.

Pitch Measurements: 100m × 67m.

Executive Chairman: Daniel Levy.

Secretary: Darren Eales.

Manager: Harry Redknapp.

Assistant Manager: Kevin Bond.

Head of Medical Services: Wayne Diesel.

Colours: White shirts with black and yellow trim, black shorts, white stockings.

Change Colours: All black with yellow trim.

Year Formed: 1882.

Turned Professional: 1895.

Ltd Co.: 1898.

Previous Name: 1882, Hotspur Football Club; 1884, Tottenham Hotspur.

Club Nickname: 'Spurs'.

Grounds: 1882, Tottenham Marshes; 1888, Northumberland Park; 1899, White Hart Lane.

First Football League Game: 1 September 1908, Division 2, v Wolverhampton W (h) W 3–0 – Hewitson; Coquet, Burton; Morris (1), Danny Steel, Darnell; Walton, Woodward (2), Macfarlane, Bobby Steel, Middlemiss.

Record League Victory: 9–0 v Bristol R, Division 2, 22 October 1977 – Daines; Naylor, Holmes, Hoddle (1), McAllister, Perryman, Pratt, McNab, Moores (3), Lee (4), Taylor (1).

HONOURS

Football League – Division 1:
Champions 1950–51, 1960–61;
Runners-up 1921–22, 1951–52,
1956–57, 1962–63;
Division 2: *Champions* 1919–20,
1949–50; *Runners-up* 1908–09,
1932–33.

FA Cup: *Winners* 1901 (as non-League club), 1921, 1961, 1962, 1967, 1981, 1982, 1991; *Runners-up* 1987.

Football League Cup: *Winners* 1971, 1973, 1999, 2008; *Runners-up* 1982, 2002, 2009.

European Competitions
European Cup: 1961–62.
Champions League: 2010–11.
European Cup-Winners' Cup:
1962–63 (*winners*), 1963–64, 1967–68,
1981–82, 1982–83, 1991–92.
UEFA Cup: 1971–72 (*winners*),
1972–73, 1973–74 (*runners-up*),
1983–84 (*winners*), 1984–85,
1999–2000, 2006–07, 2007–08,
2008–09. **Intertoto Cup:** 1995.

sky SPORTS FACT FILE

On 26 January 1935 in the FA Cup fourth round, Tottenham Hotspur defeated Newcastle United 2-0 at White Hart Lane. George Hunt scored both second half goals. The attendance was a then club record (since beaten, see above) of 61,195 who paid £5,162.

Record Cup Victory: 13–2 v Crewe Alex, FA Cup 4th rd (replay), 3 February 1960 – Brown; Hills, Henry; Blanchflower, Norman, Mackay; White, Harmer (1), Smith (4), Allen (5), Jones (3 incl. 1p).

Record Defeat: 0–8 v Cologne, UEFA Intertoto Cup, 22 July 1995.

Most League Points (2 for a win): 70, Division 2, 1919–20.

Most League Points (3 for a win): 77, Division 1, 1984–85.

Most League Goals: 115, Division 1, 1960–61.

Highest League Scorer in Season: Jimmy Greaves, 37, Division 1, 1962–63.

Most League Goals in Total Aggregate: Jimmy Greaves, 220, 1961–70.

Most League Goals in One Match: 5, Ted Harper v Reading, Division 2, 30 August 1930; 5, Alf Stokes v Birmingham C, Division 1, 18 September 1957; 5, Bobby Smith v Aston Villa, Division 1, 29 March 1958; 5, Jermain Defoe v Wigan Ath, FA Premier League, 22 November 2009.

Most Capped Player: Pat Jennings, 74 (119), Northern Ireland.

Most League Appearances: Steve Perryman, 655, 1969–86.

Youngest League Player: Ally Dick, 16 years 301 days v Manchester C, 20 February 1982.

Record Transfer Fee Received: £30,750,000 from Manchester U for Dimitar Berbatov, September 2008.

Record Transfer Fee Paid: £17,000,000 to Blackburn R for David Bentley, July 2008.

Football League Record: 1908 Elected to Division 2; 1909–15 Division 1; 1919–20 Division 2; 1920–28 Division 1; 1928–33 Division 2; 1933–35 Division 1; 1935–50 Division 2; 1950–77 Division 1; 1977–78 Division 2; 1978–92 Division 1; 1992– FA Premier League.

MANAGERS

Frank Brettell 1898–99
John Cameron 1899–1906
Fred Kirkham 1907–08
Peter McWilliam 1912–27
Billy Minter 1927–29
Percy Smith 1930–35
Jack Tresadern 1935–38
Peter McWilliam 1938–42
Arthur Turner 1942–46
Joe Hulme 1946–49
Arthur Rowe 1949–55
Jimmy Anderson 1955–58
Bill Nicholson 1958–74
Terry Neill 1974–76
Keith Burkinshaw 1976–84
Peter Shreeves 1984–86
David Pleat 1986–87
Terry Venables 1987–91
Peter Shreeves 1991–92
Doug Livermore 1992–93
Ossie Ardiles 1993–94
Gerry Francis 1994–97
Christian Gross *(Head Coach)* 1997–98
George Graham 1998–2001
Glenn Hoddle 2001–03
David Pleat *(Caretaker)* 2003–04
Jacques Santini 2004
Martin Jol 2004–07
Juande Ramos 2007–08
Harry Redknapp October 2008–

LATEST SEQUENCES

Longest Sequence of League Wins: 13, 23.4.1960 – 1.10.1960.

Longest Sequence of League Defeats: 7, 1.1.1994 – 27.2.1994.

Longest Sequence of League Draws: 6, 9.1.1999 – 27.2.1999.

Longest Sequence of Unbeaten League Matches: 22, 31.8.1949 – 31.12.1949.

Longest Sequence Without a League Win: 16, 29.12.1934 – 13.4.1935.

Successive Scoring Runs: 32 from 24.2.1962.

Successive Non-scoring Runs: 6 from 28.12.1985.

TEN YEAR LEAGUE RECORD ·

		P	W	D	L	F	A	Pts	Pos
2001-02	PR Lge	38	14	8	16	49	53	50	9
2002-03	PR Lge	38	14	8	16	51	62	50	10
2003-04	PR Lge	38	13	6	19	47	57	45	14
2004-05	PR Lge	38	14	10	14	47	41	52	9
2005-06	PR Lge	38	18	11	9	53	38	65	5
2006-07	PR Lge	38	17	9	12	57	54	60	5
2007-08	PR Lge	38	11	13	14	66	61	46	11
2008-09	PR Lge	38	14	9	15	45	45	51	8
2009-10	PR Lge	38	21	7	10	67	41	70	4
2010-11	PR Lge	38	16	14	8	55	46	62	5

DID YOU KNOW ?

In 1936–37 no fewer than five players scored hat-tricks or more for Tottenham Hotspur in League and FA Cup matches: Johnny Morrison who had five including one four, Les Miller also one four, plus single threesomes for Andy Duncan, George Hunt and Jimmy McCormick.

TOTTENHAM HOTSPUR 2010–11 LEAGUE RECORD

Match No.	Date	Venue	Opponents	Result	H/T Score	Lg Pos.	Goalscorers	Attendance
1	Aug 14	H	Manchester C	D 0-0	0-0	—		35,928
2	21	A	Stoke C	W 2-1	2-1	7	Bale 2 [19, 30]	27,243
3	28	H	Wigan Ath	L 0-1	0-0	11		35,101
4	Sept 11	A	WBA	D 1-1	1-1	11	Modric [27]	23,642
5	18	H	Wolverhampton W	W 3-1	0-1	5	Van der Vaart (pen) [77], Pavlyuchenko [87], Hutton [90]	35,940
6	25	A	West Ham U	L 0-1	0-1	8		34,190
7	Oct 2	A	Aston Villa	W 2-1	1-1	5	Van der Vaart 2 [45, 75]	35,871
8	16	A	Fulham	W 2-1	1-1	5	Pavlyuchenko [31], Huddlestone [63]	25,615
9	23	H	Everton	D 1-1	1-1	5	Van der Vaart [20]	35,967
10	30	A	Manchester U	L 0-2	0-1	5		75,223
11	Nov 6	A	Bolton W	L 2-4	0-1	7	Hutton [79], Pavlyuchenko [87]	20,255
12	9	H	Sunderland	D 1-1	0-0	—	Van der Vaart [64]	35,843
13	13	H	Blackburn R	W 4-2	2-0	7	Bale 2 [16, 75], Pavlyuchenko [42], Crouch [69]	35,700
14	20	A	Arsenal	W 3-2	0-2	6	Bale [50], Van der Vaart (pen) [67], Kaboul [85]	60,102
15	28	H	Liverpool	W 2-1	0-1	5	Skrtel (og) [65], Lennon [90]	35,962
16	Dec 4	A	Birmingham C	D 1-1	1-0	5	Bassong [19]	25,770
17	12	H	Chelsea	D 1-1	1-0	5	Pavlyuchenko [15]	35,787
18	26	A	Aston Villa	W 2-1	1-0	5	Van der Vaart 2 [23, 67]	39,411
19	28	H	Newcastle U	W 2-0	0-0	4	Lennon [57], Bale [81]	35,927
20	Jan 1	H	Fulham	W 1-0	1-0	4	Bale [42]	35,603
21	5	A	Everton	L 1-2	1-1	4	Van der Vaart [11]	34,124
22	16	H	Manchester U	D 0-0	0-0	5		35,828
23	22	A	Newcastle U	D 1-1	0-0	5	Lennon [90]	51,010
24	Feb 2	A	Blackburn R	W 1-0	1-0	—	Crouch [3]	23,253
25	5	H	Bolton W	W 2-1	1-0	5	Van der Vaart (pen) [6], Kranjcar [90]	36,197
26	12	A	Sunderland	W 2-1	1-1	4	Dawson [44], Kranjcar [57]	40,986
27	22	A	Blackpool	L 1-3	0-2	—	Cathcart (og) [90]	16,069
28	Mar 6	A	Wolverhampton W	D 3-3	2-2	5	Defoe 2 [30, 35], Pavlyuchenko [48]	28,669
29	19	H	West Ham U	D 0-0	0-0	5		36,010
30	Apr 2	A	Wigan Ath	D 0-0	0-0	5		18,578
31	9	H	Stoke C	W 3-2	3-2	5	Crouch 2 [11, 34], Modric [18]	32,702
32	20	H	Arsenal	D 3-3	2-3	—	Van der Vaart 2 (1 pen) [7, 70 (p)], Huddlestone [44]	36,138
33	23	H	WBA	D 2-2	1-1	5	Pavlyuchenko [27], Defoe [66]	36,160
34	30	A	Chelsea	L 1-2	1-1	6	Sandro [19]	41,681
35	May 7	H	Blackpool	D 1-1	0-0	5	Defoe [89]	35,585
36	10	A	Manchester C	L 0-1	0-1	—		47,029
37	15	A	Liverpool	W 2-0	1-0	5	Van der Vaart [9], Modric (pen) [56]	44,893
38	22	H	Birmingham C	W 2-1	0-0	5	Pavlyuchenko 2 [49, 90]	36,119

Final League Position: 5

GOALSCORERS

League (55): Van der Vaart 13 (4 pens), Pavlyuchenko 9, Bale 7, Crouch 4, Defoe 4, Lennon 3, Modric 3 (1 pen), Huddlestone 2, Hutton 2, Kranjcar 2, Bassong 1, Dawson 1, Kaboul 1, Sandro 1, own goals 2.
Carling Cup (1): Keane 1.
FA Cup (3): Defoe 2, Townsend 1.
Champions League (25): Crouch 7 (1 pen), Pavlyuchenko 4 (2 pens), Bale 4, Defoe 3, Van der Vaart 2, Bassong 1, Kaboul 1, Modric 1, own goals 2.

Gomes H 30	Corluka V 13+2	Assou-Ekotto B 30	Huddlestone T 13+1	Dawson M 24	King L 6	Lennon A 25+9	Modric L 32	Crouch P 20+14	Defoe J 16+6	Pavlyuchenko R 18+11	Keane R 2+5	Giovani —+3	Palacios W 16+5	Kaboul Y 19+2	Jenas J 14+5	Walker K —+1	Cudicini C 8	Kranjcar N 2+11	Gallas W 26+1	Van der Vaart R 28	Hutton A 19+2	Bassong S 7+5	Sandro 11+8	Bentley D 1+1	Plenaar S 5+3	Rose D 4	Match No.
1	2	3	4	5	6	7³	8	9¹	10²	11	12	13	14														1
1	2	3	10	5		7¹		9		11				4	6		8	12									2
		3¹	8	5	6	7³		9²	10	11	12		14	4	2		1	13									3
	2	8				7²	10¹	14		3	9³	13		4	5		1	12	6	11							4
	3	4			6	14		9		11	13	10²		2¹	8		1		5	7³	12						5
5		4				7¹	11	9³		3	14	12	13		8		1		10²	2	6						6
1		3	4			12	6²	9		11	10¹			13	8				7³	2	5	14					7
1		3	4		6¹	13	8	14		11	9³								5	7	2	12	10²				8
1		3				7²	8	9		11	13			4¹	6				5	10	2		12				9
1		3				7	4	14		11	12	10¹		13	6	8²			5	9³	2						10
1		3	13			8	9			11	12			4¹	6		7³	5		2		10²	14				11
1		3	4			8	12			11	9¹				6				5	10	2		7				12
1		3				8	9			11	10²		12	6	4				5	7¹	2	13					13
1		3				7¹	4	13	12	11	9²		14	6	8				5	10³	2						14
1		3				7	8	9	12²	11				4	6³				5	10¹	2	14	13				15
1		3				7	8	9	10¹	11	12			4					5		2	6					16
1		3	5			7	8	12	10¹	11	9²	13		4³						2	6	14					17
1	14	3	5			7²	8³	12	10⁴	11				4	6	13				9¹	2						18
1		3	5			7	8	14		11	9²			4¹	6⁴	12				10³	2	13					19
1	12	3	5			7	8	13		11	9²			4	14				5	7²	2						20
1		3	5			7²	4	9		11¹		13			8				12	6	10	7					21
1		3	6			7	8	9	12	11				4¹					5	10	2						22
			6			7	4	13	10	3¹					8²		1	14	5	9	2	12		11³			23
1	2	3				7		9	10¹					4	8				5	11		6	12				24
1	2	3	6			7		9²	10		13			4³	8	14			5	11¹			12				25
1	2	3	6			12			10²	9		13		8			11	5			4		7¹				26
1		3	6			7	11	14	10	9				4¹	12			13	5			2³	8²				27
1		3	6			13	4³		10	12	9²				8			14	5	2		11	7¹				28
1	7²	3	6			7	4		10	11	12							5	9	13	8						29
1	2	3	6			13	4³	12	10¹	9					8			14	7²		5	11					30
1	2	3¹	4	5		8	10		11	9			6						12	7							31
1	2¹	3	4	6		13	8	10		11²	9³		12						5	7		14					32
1	3¹	4²		6		13	8	14	10	11	9³		2						5	7		12					33
1	2²			6		7	4		12	11	9¹		3	14					5	10³		8	13				34
1				6		12	4	13	10	3²	9¹		2				14	5	7		8		11³				35
	2			6		7	11	9²	13			4¹	14		1		5³	10		8		12	3				36
		5	6	7		4	9	12			2			1	14		10¹		13	8	11³	3²					37
	4²	5	6	7		11	9¹	10		12			2		1	13			8		3						38

FA Cup

Third Round	Charlton Ath	(h)	3-0
Fourth Round	Fulham	(a)	0-4

Carling Cup

Third Round	Arsenal	(h)	1-4

Champions League

Play-Off	Young Boys	(a)	2-3
		(h)	4-0
Group A	Werder Bremen	(a)	2-2
	Twente	(h)	4-1
	Internazionale	(a)	3-4
		(h)	3-1
	Werder Bremen	(h)	3-0
	Twente	(a)	3-3
Knock-Out Round	AC Milan	(a)	1-0
		(h)	0-0
Quarter-Final	Real Madrid	(a)	0-4
		(h)	0-1

TRANMERE ROVERS FL Championship 1

FOUNDATION

Formed in 1884 as Belmont they adopted their present title the following year and eventually joined their first league, the West Lancashire League in 1889–90, the same year as their first success in the Wirral Challenge Cup. The club almost folded in 1899–1900 when all the players left en bloc to join a rival club, but they survived the crisis and went from strength to strength winning the 'Combination' title in 1907–08 and the Lancashire Combination in 1913–14. They joined the Football League in 1921 from the Central League.

Prenton Park, Prenton Road West, Birkenhead, Merseyside CH42 9PY.

Telephone: (0871) 221 2001.

Fax: (0151) 608 6144.

Ticket Office: (0871) 221 2001.

Website: www.tranmererovers.co.uk

Email: info@tranmererovers.co.uk

Ground Capacity: 16,587.

Record Attendance: 24,424 v Stoke C, FA Cup 4th rd, 5 February 1972.

Pitch Measurements: 100yd × 70yd.

Chairman: Peter Johnson.

Chief Executive/Secretary: Mick Horton.

Manager: Les Parry.

Assistant Manager: Kevin Summerfield.

Head of Youth/Centre of Excellence Manager: Shaun Garnett.

Physio: Steve Walker.

Colours: White shirts, white shorts, blue and white hooped stockings.

Change Colours: Light green shirts, light green shorts, black and light green hooped stockings.

Year Formed: 1884.

Turned Professional: 1912.

Ltd Co.: 1920.

Previous Name: 1884, Belmont AFC; 1885, Tranmere Rovers.

Club Nickname: 'The Rovers'.

Grounds: 1884, Steeles Field; 1887, Ravenshaws Field/Old Prenton Park; 1912, Prenton Park.

First Football League Game: 27 August 1921, Division 3 (N), v Crewe Alex (h) W 4–1 – Bradshaw; Grainger, Stuart (1); Campbell, Milnes (1), Heslop; Moreton, Groves (1), Hyam, Ford (1), Hughes.

Record League Victory: 13–4 v Oldham Ath, Division 3 (N), 26 December 1935 – Gray; Platt, Fairhurst; McLaren, Newton, Spencer; Eden, MacDonald (1), Bell (9), Woodward (2), Urmson (1).

HONOURS

Football League Division 1: Best season: 4th, 1992–93;

Division 3 (N): *Champions* 1937–38; **Division 4:** *Runners-up* 1988–89.

FA Cup: Best season: 6th rd, 2000, 2001, 2004.

Football League Cup: *Runners-up* 2000.

Welsh Cup: *Winners* 1935; *Runners-up* 1934.

Leyland Daf Cup: *Winners* 1990; *Runners-up* 1991.

sky SPORTS FACT FILE

In October 1919, Tranmere Rovers resigned from the Cheshire County League and took over the Central League fixtures of Leeds City reserves, expelled from the Football League. The beneficial effect on attendances saw the visit of Bolton's "stiffs" attract an 11,000 gate.

Record Cup Victory: 13–0 v Oswestry U, FA Cup 2nd prel rd, 10 October 1914 – Ashcroft; Stevenson, Bullough, Hancock, Taylor, Holden (1), Moreton (1), Cunningham (2), Smith (5), Leck (3), Gould (1).

Record Defeat: 1–9 v Tottenham H, FA Cup 3rd rd (replay), 14 January 1953.

Most League Points (2 for a win): 60, Division 4, 1964–65.

Most League Points (3 for a win): 80, Division 4, 1988–89; Division 3, 1989–90; Division 2, 2002–03.

Most League Goals: 111, Division 3 (N), 1930–31.

Highest League Scorer in Season: Bunny Bell, 35, Division 3 (N), 1933–34.

Most League Goals in Total Aggregate: Ian Muir, 142, 1985–95.

Most League Goals in One Match: 9, Bunny Bell v Oldham Ath, Division 3 (N), 26 December 1935.

Most Capped Player: John Aldridge, 30 (69), Republic of Ireland.

Most League Appearances: Harold Bell, 595, 1946–64 (incl. League record 401 consecutive appearances).

Youngest League Player: Iain Hume, 16 years 167 days v Swindon T, 15 April 2000.

Record Transfer Fee Received: £3,300,000 from Everton for Steve Simonsen, September 1998.

Record Transfer Fee Paid: £500,000 to Aston Villa for Shaun Teale, July 1995.

Football League Record: 1921 Original Member of Division 3 (N): 1938–39 Division 2; 1946–58 Division 3 (N); 1958–61 Division 3; 1961–67 Division 4; 1967–75 Division 3; 1975–76 Division 4; 1976–79 Division 3; 1979–89 Division 4; 1989–91 Division 3; 1991–92 Division 2; 1992–2001 Division 1; 2001–04 Division 2; 2004– FL 1.

MANAGERS

Bert Cooke 1912–35
Jackie Carr 1935–36
Jim Knowles 1936–39
Bill Ridding 1939–45
Ernie Blackburn 1946–55
Noel Kelly 1955–57
Peter Farrell 1957–60
Walter Galbraith 1961
Dave Russell 1961–69
Jackie Wright 1969–72
Ron Yeats 1972–75
John King 1975–80
Bryan Hamilton 1980–85
Frank Worthington 1985–87
Ronnie Moore 1987
John King 1987–96
John Aldridge 1996–2001
Dave Watson 2001–02
Ray Mathias 2002–03
Brian Little 2003–06
Ronnie Moore 2006–09
John Barnes 2009
Les Parry October 2009–

LATEST SEQUENCES

Longest Sequence of League Wins: 9, 9.2.1990 – 19.3.1990.

Longest Sequence of League Defeats: 8, 29.10.1938 – 17.12.1938.

Longest Sequence of League Draws: 5, 26.12.1997 – 31.1.1998.

Longest Sequence of Unbeaten League Matches: 18, 16.3.1970 – 4.9.1970.

Longest Sequence Without a League Win: 16, 8.11.1969 – 14.3.1970.

Successive Scoring Runs: 32 from 24.2.1934.

Successive Non-scoring Runs: 7 from 20.12.1997.

TEN YEAR LEAGUE RECORD

		P	W	D	L	F	A	Pts	Pos
2001-02	Div 2	46	16	15	15	63	60	63	12
2002-03	Div 2	46	23	11	12	66	57	80	7
2003-04	Div 2	46	17	16	13	59	56	67	8
2004-05	FL 1	46	22	13	11	73	55	79	3
2005-06	FL 1	46	13	15	18	50	52	54	18
2006-07	FL 1	46	18	13	15	58	53	67	9
2007-08	FL 1	46	18	11	17	52	47	65	11
2008-09	FL 1	46	21	11	14	62	49	74	7
2009-10	FL 1	46	14	9	23	45	72	51	19
2010-11	FL 1	46	15	11	20	53	60	56	17

DID YOU KNOW ?

The longest unbeaten home run achieved by Tranmere Rovers started on 24 October 1988 and ended on 10 November 1989 for twenty-six League matches, of which twenty produced wins and six draws. The sequence also coincided with promotion from the Fourth Division.

TRANMERE ROVERS 2010–11 LEAGUE RECORD

Match No.	Date		Venue	Opponents		Result	H/T Score	Lg Pos.	Goalscorers	Atten- dance
1	Aug	7	H	Oldham Ath	L	1-2	0-1	—	Thomas-Moore [89]	7270
2		14	A	Huddersfield T	D	0-0	0-0	19		13,707
3		21	H	Bournemouth	L	0-3	0-2	23		4847
4		28	A	Dagenham & R	D	2-2	0-0	22	Showunmi [78], Cresswell [88]	2256
5	Sept	4	H	Peterborough U	W	1-0	1-0	15	Mendy [44]	4636
6		11	A	Yeovil T	L	1-3	0-3	21	Thomas-Moore (pen) [89]	3364
7		18	H	Charlton Ath	D	1-1	0-1	21	Showunmi [53]	4735
8		25	A	Colchester U	L	1-3	0-3	24	Showunmi [81]	3637
9		28	A	Bristol R	W	1-0	1-0	—	Jennings [45]	5589
10	Oct	2	H	Brighton & HA	D	1-1	0-1	21	Cresswell [87]	5421
11		9	A	Southampton	L	0-2	0-1	22		19,293
12		16	H	Brentford	L	0-3	0-1	24		4929
13		23	A	Walsall	W	4-1	1-0	22	Welsh 2 [34, 88], Showunmi [59], Thomas-Moore (pen) [78]	3362
14		30	H	Milton Keynes D	W	4-2	3-1	20	Jennings 2 [3, 25], Thomas-Moore 2 (1 pen) [22 (p), 76]	4512
15	Nov	2	A	Carlisle U	L	0-2	0-1	—		3744
16		13	H	Plymouth Arg	W	1-0	0-0	20	Jennings [60]	4840
17		20	A	Notts Co	W	1-0	0-0	14	Showunmi [50]	5782
18		23	H	Hartlepool U	L	0-1	0-0	—		4340
19	Dec	11	H	Leyton Orient	L	1-2	0-2	20	Wootton [61]	4291
20	Jan	1	A	Rochdale	L	2-3	1-2	20	Labadie [42], Thomas-Moore (pen) [81]	5500
21		3	A	Carlisle U	W	2-1	1-0	20	Goodison [39], Thomas-Moore [80]	5128
22		8	H	Walsall	D	3-3	2-1	—	Richards (og) [41], Cresswell [45], Elford-Alliyu [56]	4602
23		15	A	Milton Keynes D	L	0-2	0-0	20		8014
24		22	H	Southampton	W	2-0	1-0	19	Welsh [13], Jennings [60]	5504
25		25	A	Swindon T	D	0-0	0-0	—		6912
26	Feb	1	H	Rochdale	D	1-1	1-0	20	Elford-Alliyu [4]	4766
27		12	A	Plymouth Arg	W	3-1	1-0	17	Elford-Alliyu 2 [22, 64], Showunmi [80]	8015
28		15	H	Sheffield W	W	3-0	0-0	—	Elford-Alliyu [60], Goodison [85], Showunmi [81]	5941
29		19	A	Peterborough U	L	1-2	1-0	15	Welsh [24]	5774
30		22	A	Brentford	L	1-2	0-1	—	Labadie [65]	4192
31		26	H	Yeovil T	L	0-1	0-0	18		8016
32	Mar	1	A	Exeter C	D	1-1	1-0	—	Bakayogo [16]	3456
33		5	A	Charlton Ath	D	1-1	1-0	18	Showunmi [26]	14,015
34		8	H	Bristol R	L	0-1	0-1	—		4110
35		12	A	Brighton & HA	L	0-2	0-0	18		7461
36		19	H	Colchester U	W	1-0	0-0	18	Showunmi [53]	4292
37		28	A	Oldham Ath	D	0-0	0-0	—		3114
38	Apr	2	H	Huddersfield T	L	0-2	0-1	18		6438
39		5	A	Sheffield W	L	0-4	0-3	—		15,235
40		9	A	Bournemouth	W	2-1	1-0	18	Goodison [41], McGurk [90]	6004
41		16	H	Dagenham & R	W	2-0	2-0	18	Showunmi [12], Goodison [34]	4562
42		19	H	Notts Co	L	0-1	0-1	—		12,249
43		22	A	Hartlepool U	D	1-1	0-1	—	Jennings [81]	2969
44		25	H	Exeter C	W	4-0	1-0	18	Kay [44], Akins 2 [67, 90], Showunmi [71]	5017
45		30	A	Leyton Orient	W	3-0	2-0	15	Cresswell [8], McGurk 2 [45, 49]	5302
46	May	7	H	Swindon T	L	0-2	0-2	18		5302

Final League Position: 17

GOALSCORERS

League (53): Showunmi 11, Thomas-Moore 7 (4 pens), Jennings 6, Elford-Alliyu 5, Cresswell 4, Goodison 4, Welsh 4, McGurk 3, Akins 2, Labadie 2, Bakayogo 1, Kay 1, Mendy 1, Wootton 1, own goal 1.
Carling Cup (2): Goodison 1, Showunmi 1.
FA Cup (3): Cresswell 1, Goodison 1, Thomas-Moore 1.
J Paint Trophy (2): Showunmi 1, Thomas-Moore 1.

Nielsen G 2	Darville L 8+1	Cresswell A 42+1	Wood N 5+6	Goodison I 40	McLaren P 6	Welsh J 41	Labadie J 29+5	Thomas-Moore I 15+4	Showunmi E 43	Gornell T 3	Fraughan R 4+10	Collister J 7	Blanchard M 14+6	Brown K 1+3	McGurk A 3+18	Bakayogo Z 15+12	Akins L 23+10	Grandison J 6+2	Mendy A 11+1	Morrow S 2+3	Gulacsi P 12	Jennings D 25+4	Cathalina T 6+1	Wootton S 7	Broomes M 5	Manton S 2	Elford-Alliyu L 13+3	Taylor A 23+3	Warner T 25	Kay M 22	McChrystal M 21+2	Robinson A 9+6	Weir R 16+2	Match No.
1	2	3	4	5	6¹	7	8	9	10	11	12																							1
	2	3	4	5	6¹	7	8	9	10²	11		1	12	13																				2
	2	3	4	5	6¹	7	8²	9³	10	11		13		1	12	14																		3
	2	3		5	6¹	7	8³		10				9	1	4	11²	13	12	14															4
	2	3		5				9	10				8	1	6	12	11¹		4	7														5
	2	3		5			12	9	10				11³	1	7¹	14	13	6	4	8²														6
		3		5		7	8		*10					2	11	6	4		9¹		1	12												7
		3		5		7	8	12	10			13		2		9¹	6	4²			1	11³												8
		3	12	5		7	8		10					2		14	9²	6¹	4		1	11³	13											9
		3		5		7	8		10			12		2			9		6¹		1	11		4										10
		3	4	5		7	8		10			12		2			9¹	8²	14		1	11³	5											11
	2	3		5	6²	7			10			13				8	9¹	12			1	11		4										12
	2	3¹		5		7	8³		10			13			6	12					1	11²	2	4										13
14				5		7	8	9	10²			13		6		3⁴	12				1	11¹	2³	4										14
		3		5		7	8	9	10					6		12					1	11	2¹	4										15
				5		7		9	10¹					3	8	13	6	12			1	11	2	4²										16
	12			5		7	8⁴	9	10²					6		3¹	13	4			1	11	2											17
		3	12	5				9			7		6	13		10	4				1	11	2¹				8²							18
1		3		5		7		9²	10		14	4¹	13			6						11	2				8¹	12						19
		3		5		7	8	9	10		1					12						13	2	4⁴			11²	6¹						20
		3		5		4	8	9	10		1	12										11	2¹	6			7							21
		3		5¹		4	8	9²	10		14		13									11³					7	6	1	2	12			22
		3				4	8	12	10	13					14	9²						11³					7¹	6	1	2	5			23
		3	12			4	8		9						12		13					10²			5¹		7	11	1	2	6			24
		3	5			7	8	13	9					12								10²					11¹	4	1	2	6			25
		3	12	5¹		4	8		10													9²					7	11	1	2	6	13		26
		3	14	5		7	8		10						13	9¹											11²	4³	1	2	6	12		27
		3		5		7	8		10							9											11	4	1	2	6			28
		3		5		4	8³		10						12	9¹											11	7⁴	1	2	6	14	13	29
		3¹		5		7	8²		10						12	9											11	4	1	2	6		13	30
				5		8			10					13	3	9²											11	4	1	2	6	12	7¹	31
		3		5		8			10						2												11	4	1		6	9¹	7	32
		3		5		8	11		10						2												12	4	1		6	9¹	7	33
		3		5		7	8²		10					12	2³	14											13	4¹	1		6	9	11	34
		3		5		7			10					12	2¹	9²											13	1	4	6	11	8		35
		3		5		4	13		10					12	9²						11¹						14	1	2	6	8³	7		36
		3		5		4	12		10					13	9³						11²						14	1	2	6	8¹	7		37
		3				4	8		10					12	9¹	13					11²						5	1	2	6		7		38
		3				4	8		10					12	9	13					11¹						5	1	2	6		7²		39
		3¹	14				8		10		13			12	9	11											4	1	2	6		7²		40
		3¹	14	5³			8		10		13			12	9	11											4	1	2	6		7²		41
		3		5		8			10					13	9¹	11³					12						4	1	2	6	14	7²		42
		3		5		8			10					13	9²	11³					14						4	1	2	6	12	7¹		43
		3		5		4			10²				14	12	13	9					11¹						6	1	2		8³	7		44
		3		5		4	12						14	10¹	13	8					11²						6	1	2		9³	7		45
		3		5		4	12							10	14	8¹					11						6	1	2	13	9²	7³		46

FA Cup
First Round — Bournemouth — (a) 3-5

Carling Cup
First Round — Walsall — (a) 1-0
Second Round — Swansea C — (h) 1-3

J Paint Trophy
First Round — Accrington S — (h) 1-1
Second Round — Stockport Co — (h) 0-0
Northern Quarter-Final — Bury — (a) 1-0
Northern Semi-Final — Huddersfield T — (h) 0-2

WALSALL   FL Championship 1

FOUNDATION

Two of the leading clubs around Walsall in the 1880s were Walsall Swifts (formed 1877) and Walsall Town (formed 1879). The Swifts were winners of the Birmingham Senior Cup in 1881, while the Town reached the 4th round (5th round modern equivalent) of the FA Cup in 1883. These clubs amalgamated as Walsall Town Swifts in 1888, becoming simply Walsall in 1895.

Banks's Stadium, Bescot Crescent, Walsall WS1 4SA.
Telephone: (01922) 622 791. *Fax:* (01922) 613 202.
Ticket Office: (01922) 651 414/416.
Website: www.saddlers.co.uk
Email: info@walsallfc.co.uk
Ground Capacity: 11,300.
Record Attendance: 25,453 v Newcastle U, Division 2, 29 August 1961 (at Fellows Park). 11,049 v Rotherham U, Division 1, 9 May 2004 (at Bescot Stadium).
Pitch Measurements: 110yd × 73yd.
Chairman: Jeff Bonser.
Secretary: Roy Whalley.
Manager: Dean Smith.
Assistant Manager and Physio: Jon Whitney.
Colours: Red shirts with black trim, red shorts, red stockings with black tops.
Change Colours: Laser green shirts with red trim and blue sleeves, laser green shorts, laser green stockings.
Year Formed: 1888. *Turned Professional:* 1888. *Ltd Co.:* 1921.
Previous Names: Walsall Swifts (founded 1877) and Walsall Town (founded 1879) amalgamated in 1888 as Walsall Town Swifts; 1895, Walsall.
Club Nickname: 'The Saddlers'.
Grounds: 1888, Fellows Park; 1990, Bescot Stadium.
First Football League Game: 3 September 1892, Division 2, v Darwen (h) L 1–2 – Hawkins; Withington, Pinches; Robinson, Whitrick, Forsyth; Marshall, Holmes, Turner, Gray (1), Pangbourn.
Record League Victory: 10–0 v Darwen, Division 2, 4 March 1899 – Tennent; Ted Peers (1), Davies; Hickinbotham, Jenkyns, Taggart; Dean (3), Vail (2), Aston (4), Martin, Griffin.
Record Cup Victory: 7–0 v Macclesfield T (a), FA Cup 2nd rd, 6 December 1997 – Walker; Evans, Marsh, Viveash (1), Ryder, Peron, Boli (2 incl. 1p) (Ricketts), Porter (2), Keates, Watson (Platt), Hodge (2 incl. 1p).
Record Defeat: 0–12 v Small Heath, 17 December 1892. 0–12 v Darwen, 26 December 1896, both Division 2.
Most League Points (2 for a win): 65, Division 4, 1959–60.
Most League Points (3 for a win): 89, FL 2, 2006–07.
Most League Goals: 102, Division 4, 1959–60.

HONOURS

Football League –
Division 2: *Runners-up*, 1998–99;
FL 2: *Champions* 2006–07;
Division 3: *Runners-up* 1960–61, 1994–95;
Division 4: *Champions* 1959–60; *Runners-up* 1979–80.

FA Cup: Best season: 5th rd, 1939, 1975, 1978, 1987, 2002, 2003 and last 16 1889.

Football League Cup: Semi-final 1984.

sky SPORTS FACT FILE

Scorer of four goals in the record League victory by Walsall (see above) was Jack "Soldier" Aston. Signed by the Saddlers during the 1895–96 season, the club bought him out of the Army when he was arrested and about to be put on a charge by the Military Police!

Highest League Scorer in Season: Gilbert Alsop, 40, Division 3 (N), 1933–34 and 1934–35.

Most League Goals in Total Aggregate: Tony Richards, 184, 1954–63; Colin Taylor, 184, 1958–63, 1964–68, 1969–73.

Most League Goals in One Match: 5, Gilbert Alsop v Carlisle U, Division 3 (N), 2 February 1935; 5, Bill Evans v Mansfield T, Division 3 (N), 5 October 1935; 5, Johnny Devlin v Torquay U, Division 3 (S), 1 September 1949.

Most Capped Player: Mick Kearns, 15 (18), Republic of Ireland.

Most League Appearances: Colin Harrison, 467, 1964–82.

Youngest League Player: Geoff Morris, 16 years 218 days v Scunthorpe U, 14 September 1965.

Record Transfer Fee Received: £820,000 from Bolton W for Michael Ricketts, July 2000 (including sell-on).

Record Transfer Fee Paid: £175,000 to Birmingham C for Alan Buckley, June 1979.

Football League Record: 1892 Elected to Division 2; 1895 Failed re-election; 1896–1901 Division 2; 1901 Failed re-election; 1921 Original Member of Division 3 (N); 1927–31 Division 3 (S); 1931–36 Division 3 (N); 1936–58 Division 3 (S); 1958–60 Division 4; 1960–61 Division 3; 1961–63 Division 2; 1963–79 Division 3; 1979–80 Division 4; 1980–88 Division 3; 1988–89 Division 2; 1989–90 Division 3; 1990–92 Division 4; 1992–95 Division 3; 1995–99 Division 2; 1999–2000 Division 1; 2000–01 Division 2; 2001–04 Division 1; 2004–06 FL 1; 2006–07 FL 2; 2007– FL 1.

LATEST SEQUENCES

Longest Sequence of League Wins: 7, 10.10.1959 – 21.11.1959.

Longest Sequence of League Defeats: 15, 29.10.1988 – 4.2.1989.

Longest Sequence of League Draws: 5, 7.5.1988 – 17.9.1988.

Longest Sequence of Unbeaten League Matches: 21, 6.11.1979 – 22.3.1980.

Longest Sequence Without a League Win: 18, 15.10.1988 – 4.2.1989.

Successive Scoring Runs: 27 from 9.2.1928.

Successive Non-scoring Runs: 5 from 8.10.1927.

MANAGERS

H. Smallwood 1888–91 *(Secretary-Manager)*
A. G. Burton 1891–93
J. H. Robinson 1893–95
C. H. Ailso 1895–96 *(Secretary-Manager)*
A. E. Parsloe 1896–97 *(Secretary-Manager)*
L. Ford 1897–98 *(Secretary-Manager)*
G. Hughes 1898–99 *(Secretary-Manager)*
L. Ford 1899–1901 *(Secretary-Manager)*
J. E. Shutt 1908–13 *(Secretary-Manager)*
Haydn Price 1914–20
Joe Burchell 1920–26
David Ashworth 1926–27
Jack Torrance 1927–28
James Kerr 1928–29
Sid Scholey 1929–30
Peter O'Rourke 1930–32
Bill Slade 1932–34
Andy Wilson 1934–37
Tommy Lowes 1937–44
Harry Hibbs 1944–51
Tony McPhee 1951
Brough Fletcher 1952–53
Major Frank Buckley 1953–55
John Love 1955–57
Billy Moore 1957–64
Alf Wood 1964
Reg Shaw 1964–68
Dick Graham 1968
Ron Lewin 1968–69
Billy Moore 1969–72
John Smith 1972–73
Ronnie Allen 1973
Doug Fraser 1973–77
Dave Mackay 1977–78
Alan Ashman 1978
Frank Sibley 1979
Alan Buckley 1979–86
Neil Martin *(Joint Manager with Buckley)* 1981–82
Tommy Coakley 1986–88
John Barnwell 1989–90
Kenny Hibbitt 1990–94
Chris Nicholl 1994–97
Jan Sorensen 1997–98
Ray Graydon 1998–2002
Colin Lee 2002–04
Paul Merson 2004–06
Kevin Broadhurst 2006
Richard Money 2006–08
Jimmy Mullen 2008–09
Chris Hutchings 2009–10
Dean Smith January 2011–

TEN YEAR LEAGUE RECORD

		P	W	D	L	F	A	Pts	Pos
2001-02	Div 1	46	13	12	21	51	71	51	18
2002-03	Div 1	46	15	9	22	57	69	54	17
2003-04	Div 1	46	13	12	21	45	65	51	22
2004-05	FL 1	46	16	12	18	65	69	60	14
2005-06	FL 1	46	11	14	21	47	70	47	24
2006-07	FL 2	46	25	14	7	66	34	89	1
2007-08	FL 1	46	16	16	14	52	46	64	12
2008-09	FL 1	46	17	10	19	61	66	61	13
2009-10	FL 1	46	16	14	16	60	63	62	10
2010-11	FL 1	46	12	12	22	56	75	48	20

DID YOU KNOW ?

The first Walsall player to be ever present in the Football League for the club was full-back Wally Webster in 1922–23 when he appeared in all 38 League matches. In three and a half seasons with the Saddlers he made 137 League and Cup appearances.

WALSALL 2010–11 LEAGUE RECORD

Match No.	Date	Venue	Opponents	Result	H/T Score	Lg Pos.	Goalscorers	Attendance
1	Aug 7	H	Milton Keynes D	L	1-2	0-1	—	Smith [48]	4034
2	14	A	Brentford	W	2-1	1-1	10	Nicholls [12], Gray [54]	4544
3	21	H	Plymouth Arg	W	2-1	0-1	7	Marshall [53], Reid [69]	3966
4	28	A	Brighton & HA	L	1-2	0-0	10	Macken [90]	6474
5	Sept 4	H	Colchester U	L	0-1	0-0	13		3416
6	11	A	Rochdale	L	2-3	2-2	16	Macken [4], Byfield [45]	3174
7	18	H	Swindon T	L	1-2	0-1	18	Reid [70]	4580
8	25	A	Hartlepool U	L	1-2	1-1	21	Gray [9]	2552
9	28	A	Leyton Orient	D	0-0	0-0	—		2963
10	Oct 2	H	Yeovil T	L	0-1	0-0	24		3172
11	9	H	Exeter C	W	2-1	2-0	20	Reid [32], Richards [43]	3776
12	16	A	Dagenham & R	D	1-1	0-1	22	Devaney [50]	2666
13	23	H	Tranmere R	L	1-4	0-1	23	Macken [65]	3362
14	30	A	Huddersfield T	L	0-1	0-1	24		13,062
15	Nov 2	H	Peterborough U	L	1-3	0-2	—	Gray [53]	3294
16	13	A	Bournemouth	L	0-3	0-1	24		5601
17	20	H	Carlisle U	W	2-1	1-1	24	Richards 2 [37, 53]	4256
18	23	A	Sheffield W	L	0-3	0-1	—		15,228
19	Dec 12	A	Charlton Ath	W	1-0	0-0	23	Richards [69]	14,938
20	Jan 1	H	Notts Co	L	0-3	0-2	24		4131
21	3	A	Peterborough U	L	1-4	1-1	24	Nicholls [10]	5517
22	8	A	Tranmere R	D	3-3	1-2	—	Richards [32], Macken [85], Butler [90]	4602
23	11	A	Bristol R	D	2-2	1-0	—	Grigg [5], Lescott [83]	5369
24	15	H	Huddersfield T	L	2-4	1-2	24	Nicholls [14], Richards [47]	3827
25	22	A	Exeter C	L	1-2	0-1	24	Gray [85]	4853
26	25	H	Oldham Ath	D	1-1	0-1	—	Westlake [61]	3247
27	29	H	Bristol R	W	6-1	3-0	—	Butler 2 [17, 73], Gill [34], Gray [45], Richards [50], Nicholls [69]	4023
28	Feb 2	A	Notts Co	D	1-1	0-0	—	Nicholls [88]	4714
29	5	A	Carlisle U	W	3-1	1-0	22	Gill [37], Gray 2 [59, 73]	4332
30	12	H	Bournemouth	L	0-1	0-0	23		4103
31	15	H	Dagenham & R	W	1-0	0-0	—	Grigg [81]	3174
32	19	A	Colchester U	L	0-2	0-1	22		3439
33	26	H	Rochdale	D	0-0	0-0	21		3830
34	Mar 1	H	Southampton	W	1-0	0-0	—	Macken [69]	4684
35	5	A	Swindon T	D	0-0	0-0	20		10,489
36	8	H	Leyton Orient	L	0-2	0-1	—		3019
37	12	A	Yeovil T	D	1-1	1-1	21	Macken [18]	3737
38	19	H	Hartlepool U	W	5-2	0-1	21	Grigg [59], Byfield [64], Gray [77], Smith [83], Ledesma [90]	4234
39	25	A	Milton Keynes D	D	1-1	1-0	—	Richards [29]	8923
40	Apr 9	A	Plymouth Arg	L	0-2	0-0	22		7995
41	12	H	Brentford	W	3-2	1-1	—	Macken 2 [40, 64], Cook [57]	3154
42	16	H	Brighton & HA	L	1-3	1-1	20	Butler [11]	6015
43	23	A	Sheffield W	D	1-1	1-1	—	Macken [10]	2072
44	25	H	Oldham Ath	D	1-1	0-0	21	Williams [58]	3463
45	30	H	Charlton Ath	W	2-0	1-0	20	Grigg [34], Gray [78]	5088
46	May 7	A	Southampton	L	1-3	1-2	20	Gray [45]	31,653

Final League Position: 20

GOALSCORERS

League (56): Gray 10, Macken 9, Richards 8, Nicholls 5, Butler 4, Grigg 4, Reid 3, Byfield 2, Gill 2, Smith 2, Cook 1, Devaney 1, Ledesma 1, Lescott 1, Marshall 1, Westlake 1, Williams 1.
Carling Cup (0).
FA Cup (3): Reid 2, Richards 1.
J Paint Trophy (1): Reid 1.

Brain J 16	Lescott A 34	McGivern R 15	Taundry R 26+2	Lancashire O 28+1	Smith M 23+2	Jones S 9+4	Richards M 46	Byfield D 8+11	Nicholls A 26+11	Gray J 42+1	McDonald C 7+7	Grigg W 8+20	Reid R 13+5	Marshall P 12+6	Macken J 35+4	Westlake B 26+2	Paterson J 2+12	Davis D 7	Davies A 3	Devaney M 4	Walker J 26	Dickinson L 2+2	Butler A 31	Bevan D 4	Gill M 8	Price J 4+1	Williams T 14	Ledesma E 5+5	Gbarssin M 8+1	Laird M 8	Cook J 6+2	Match No.
1	2	3	4	5¹	6	7	8	9	10	11	12																					1
1	3	2	4	5	6	7	8	9¹	10	11	12																					2
1	2	3	4	5	6³	7¹	8		10	11	14	13		9²	12																	3
1	2	3	4	5	6		8			10⁸	11¹			9	7	12																4
1	3				6		8	12		11¹		5		9	4	10		2	7													5
1	2	3			6		8	9		11²		5		12	4¹		10		13	7												6
1	2	3			6		8	9¹	14	11		5		12	4¹		10		13	7²												7
1	2	3		5	6		8			7	11¹			12	9	10		4														8
1	2	3		5²	6		8			7	11	13		12	9	10¹		4														9
1	2	3		5²	6		8			7²	11	14	12		9¹	10	13	4														10
1	2	3			6	13	8²		12	11³				9	14	10¹		4			5	7										11
1	2	3			6		12	8		11¹	13			9		10		4			5²	7										12
1	2	3	4		6	7	8		12			13	14	9¹		10³					5²	11										13
	5¹	3	4		6	7	8		12	11	9		13	10²		2					1											14
		3	4		6	13	8			11	5	12		10¹	2						7²	1	9									15
	5		4		6	13	8		12	11¹	9	7²		2	1	10	3															16
	3		4	5		8		11			13	9²	7	10¹	2						1	12	6									17
	3		4	5		8		11			13	9²	7	10¹	2						1	12	6									18
1	3		4	5		7	8		10	11			9¹			2	12						6									19
1	4	3		5		7	8		10¹	11³			9²		13	12					2		6									20
1	3			5		7²	8		10	11			9¹	4	12	2	13						6									21
	3			5	9¹	0			11	13		12		4	10	2	7²						6	1								22
	3					6	8		9¹	11		7		4	10	2	12						5	1								23
	3					6	8		7¹	11		9		4	10	2	12						5	1								24
	3	4				6	8		9¹	11		13			10	2	12				1		5		7²							25
	3			5			8		7	11		9		12	10	2					1		6		4¹							26
	3			5			8		7	11		12			10²	2	13						6	1	4	9¹						27
	3	12		5			8		7	11		13			10³	2	14						1	6	4¹	9²						28
	3		4	5			8	9		11		13		12	10²	2							1	6	7¹							29
	3	13		5			8		7	11		12			10¹	2							1	6	4	9²						30
	3		4	5			8		9¹	11		12			10	2							1	6	7							31
	3		4	5			8		9¹	11		13		14	10²	2							1	6	7³	12						32
	2		4	5			8	13	7³	11		9¹	14		12						1		6		10²	3						33
	2		4	5	14		8	13	12	11				7¹	10³						1		6			3	9²					34
	2³		4	5			8	13	12	11¹				10	14						1		6			3	9²	7				35
			4¹	5			8	13	12	11				10	2						1		6			3	9²	7				36
			4²	5¹	12		8	13	9	11				10³	2						1		6			3	14	7				37
				5			8	9¹	4²	11	14	12		10¹	2						1		6			3	13	7				38
				5			8	10²		11	13				2						1		6			3	7¹	9	4	12		39
				5			8	9²	14	11	12				2						1		6			3	10¹	7³	4	13		40
	2						8¹	9²		11	6	14		10³							1		5			3	13	12	4	7		41
	2	13					8¹	14		11	5²			10							1		6			3	12⁸	9	4	7³		42
	7			5			8	12	13	11				10	2¹						1		6			3			4	9²		43
	2			5			8	13		11	9			10²	12						1		6			3			4	7¹		44
	2			5			8	12	13	11		9¹		10²							1		6			3			4	7		45
	2			5			8	14		11		12		10³							1		6			3	13	9¹	4	7²		46

FA Cup

First Round	Fleetwood T	(a)	1-1
		(h)	2-0
Second Round	Torquay U	(a)	0-1

Carling Cup

First Round	Tranmere R	(h)	0-1

J Paint Trophy

First Round	Chesterfield	(h)	1-2

WATFORD — FL Championship

FOUNDATION

The club was formed as Watford Rovers in 1881. The name was changed to West Herts in 1893 and then the name Watford was adopted after rival club Watford St Mary's was absorbed in 1898.

Vicarage Road Stadium, Vicarage Road, Watford, Hertsfordshire, WD18 0ER.

Telephone: 0844 856 1881.

Fax: (01923) 496 001.

Ticket Office: 0844 856 1881.

Website: www.watfordfc.com

Email: yourvoice@watfordfc.com

Ground Capacity: 19,920.

Record Attendance: 34,099 v Manchester U, FA Cup 4th rd (replay), 3 February 1969.

Pitch Measurements: 114 yd × 73yd.

Chairman: Graham Taylor OBE.

Chief Executive: Julian Winter.

Secretary: Michelle Ives.

Manager: Sean Dyche.

Assistant Manager: Ian Woan.

First Team Coach: Tony Loughlan.

Head of Medicine: Richard Collinge.

Colours: Yellow shirts with red and black trim, black shorts, yellow stockings.

Change Colours: All black.

Year Formed: 1881.

Turned Professional: 1897.

Ltd Co.: 1909.

Club Nickname: 'The Hornets'.

Previous Names: 1881, Watford Rovers; 1893, West Herts; 1898, Watford.

Grounds: 1883, Vicarage Meadow, Rose and Crown Meadow; 1889, Colney Butts; 1890, Cassio Road; 1922, Vicarage Road.

First Football League Game: 28 August 1920, Division 3, v QPR (a) W 2–1 – Williams; Horseman, Fred Gregory; Bacon, Toone, Wilkinson; Bassett, Ronald (1), Hoddinott, White (1), Waterall.

Record League Victory: 8–0 v Sunderland, Division 1, 25 September 1982 – Sherwood; Rice, Rostron, Taylor, Terry, Bolton, Callaghan (2), Blissett (4), Jenkins (2), Jackett, Barnes.

Record Cup Victory: 10–1 v Lowestoft T, FA Cup 1st rd, 27 November 1926 – Yates; Prior, Fletcher (1); Frank Smith, Bert Smith, Strain; Stephenson, Warner (3), Edmonds (3), Swan (1), Daniels (1), (1 og).

HONOURS

Football League – Division 1:
Runners-up 1982–83;
Division 2: *Champions* 1997–98;
Runners-up 1981–82;
Division 3: *Champions* 1968–69;
Runners-up 1978–79;
Division 4: *Champions* 1977–78.

FA Cup: *Runners-up* 1984, semi-finals 1970, 1984, 1987, 2003, 2007.

Football League Cup: Semi-final 1979, 2005.

European Competitions
UEFA Cup: 1983–84.

sky SPORTS FACT FILE

On 21 September 2010 Watford won 6-1 at Millwall in a Football League Championship match. It was the club's best away victory since when they were still known as West Herts and defeated Old St Stephens an amateur club in the Southern League by the same score.

Record Defeat: 0–10 v Wolverhampton W, FA Cup 1st rd (replay), 24 January 1912.

Most League Points (2 for a win): 71, Division 4, 1977–78.

Most League Points (3 for a win): 88, Division 2, 1997–98.

Most League Goals: 92, Division 4, 1959–60.

Highest League Scorer in Season: Cliff Holton, 42, Division 4, 1959–60.

Most League Goals in Total Aggregate: Luther Blissett, 148, 1976–83, 1984–88, 1991–92.

Most League Goals in One Match: 5, Eddie Mummery v Newport Co, Division 3 (S), 5 January 1924.

Most Capped Player: John Barnes, 31 (79), England and Kenny Jackett, 31, Wales.

Most League Appearances: Luther Blissett, 415, 1976–83, 1984–88, 1991–92.

Youngest League Player: Keith Mercer, 16 years 125 days v Tranmere R, 16 February 1973.

Record Transfer Fee Received: £9,600,000 from Aston V for Ashley Young, January 2007.

Record Transfer Fee Paid: £3,250,000 to WBA for Nathan Ellington, August 2007.

Football League Record: 1920 Original Member of Division 3; 1921–58 Division 3 (S); 1958–60 Division 4; 1960–69 Division 3; 1969–72 Division 2; 1972–75 Division 3; 1975–78 Division 4; 1978–79 Division 3; 1979–82 Division 2; 1982–88 Division 1; 1988–92 Division 2; 1992–96 Division 1; 1996–98 Division 2; 1998–99 Division 1; 1999–2000 FA Premier League; 2000–04 Division 1; 2004–06 FL C; 2006–07 FA Premier League; 2007– FL C.

MANAGERS

John Goodall 1903–10
Harry Kent 1910–26
Fred Pagnam 1926–29
Neil McBain 1929–37
Bill Findlay 1938–47
Jack Bray 1947–48
Eddie Hapgood 1948–50
Ron Gray 1950–51
Haydn Green 1951–52
Len Goulden 1952–55
  (General Manager to 1956)
Johnny Paton 1955–56
Neil McBain 1956–59
Ron Burgess 1959–63
Bill McGarry 1963–64
Ken Furphy 1964–71
George Kirby 1971–73
Mike Keen 1973–77
Graham Taylor 1977–87
Dave Bassett 1987–88
Steve Harrison 1988–90
Colin Lee 1990
Steve Perryman 1990–93
Glenn Roeder 1993–96
Kenny Jackett 1996–97
Graham Taylor 1997–2001
Gianluca Vialli 2001–02
Ray Lewington 2002–05
Adrian Boothroyd 2005–08
Brendan Rodgers 2008–09
Malky Mackay 2009–11
Sean Dyche June 2011

LATEST SEQUENCES

Longest Sequence of League Wins: 7, 28.8.2000 – 14.10.2000.

Longest Sequence of League Defeats: 9, 26.12.1972 – 27.2.1973.

Longest Sequence of League Draws: 7, 30.11.1996 – 27.1.1997.

Longest Sequence of Unbeaten League Matches: 22, 1.10.1996 – 1.3.1997.

Longest Sequence Without a League Win: 19, 27.11.1971 – 8.4.1972.

Successive Scoring Runs: 22 from 20.8.1985.

Successive Non-scoring Runs: 7 from 18.12.1971.

TEN YEAR LEAGUE RECORD

		P	W	D	L	F	A	Pts	Pos
2001-02	Div 1	46	16	11	19	62	56	59	14
2002-03	Div 1	46	17	9	20	54	70	60	13
2003-04	Div 1	46	15	12	19	54	68	57	16
2004-05	FL C	46	12	16	18	52	59	52	18
2005-06	FL C	46	22	15	9	77	53	81	3
2006-07	PR Lge	38	5	13	20	29	59	28	20
2007-08	FL C	46	18	16	12	62	56	70	6
2008-09	FL C	46	16	10	20	68	72	58	13
2009-10	FL C	46	14	12	20	61	68	54	16
2010-11	FL C	46	16	13	17	77	71	61	14

DID YOU KNOW ?

On 15 January 2011, Danny Graham playing for Watford against Derby County scored for the seventh successive match, equalling the feat of Frank "Leftie" McPherson, who began his sequence for the club on 2 February 1929 against Plymouth Argyle.

WATFORD 2010–11 LEAGUE RECORD

Match No.	Date	Venue	Opponents	Result	H/T Score	Lg Pos.	Goalscorers	Attendance
1	Aug 6	A	Norwich C	W 3-2	2-0	—	Eustace [14], Graham 2 [24, 81]	24,348
2	14	H	Coventry C	D 2-2	1-0	6	Buckley [45], Eustace [58]	12,813
3	21	A	Hull C	D 0-0	0-0	8		20,426
4	28	H	Leeds U	L 0-1	0-1	14		14,039
5	Sept 11	H	Doncaster R	D 2-2	0-1	13	Sordell 2 [63, 70]	15,101
6	14	A	Bristol C	W 2-0	1-0	—	Sordell [3], Graham [47]	13,998
7	18	A	Millwall	W 6-1	3-0	5	Eustace [7], Mutch [13], Sordell [45], Mariappa [54], Graham [77], Taylor, M [90]	12,562
8	25	H	Middlesbrough	W 3-1	3-0	3	Graham 2 [1, 20], Mutch [11]	12,185
9	28	H	Swansea C	L 2-3	0-2	—	Deeney [76], Taylor, M [85]	11,485
10	Oct 2	A	Sheffield U	W 1-0	1-0	4	Sordell [16]	22,433
11	16	A	Portsmouth	L 2-3	0-1	5	Taylor, M [67], McGinn [70]	16,606
12	19	H	Ipswich T	W 2-1	2-0	—	McGinn [41], Sordell [43]	11,836
13	23	H	Scunthorpe U	L 0-2	0-2	5		12,366
14	30	A	Derby Co	L 1-4	0-2	9	Whichelow [55]	27,119
15	Nov 6	H	Nottingham F	D 1-1	1-1	11	Mutch [3]	14,708
16	9	A	Crystal Palace	L 2-3	0-1	—	Graham [48], Mutch [52]	12,353
17	13	A	Burnley	L 2-3	1-1	13	Cowie [30], Taylor, M [57]	14,160
18	20	H	Reading	D 1-1	1-1	14	Deeney [40]	12,196
19	27	A	Barnsley	D 0-0	0-0	14		10,653
20	Dec 4	H	Leicester C	W 3-2	2-0	—	Eustace [15], Buckley [22], Graham [85]	14,449
21	10	A	QPR	W 3-1	2-0	—	Graham 2 [26, 48], Mutch [30]	14,079
22	28	H	Cardiff C	W 4-1	1-1	8	Graham 2 (1 pen) [24, 84 (p)], Sordell [57], Eustace [64]	14,560
23	Jan 1	H	Portsmouth	W 3-0	1-0	6	Taylor, A [42], Sordell [52], Graham [69]	12,577
24	3	A	Scunthorpe U	W 2-1	0-0	6	Graham [64], Whichelow [85]	4498
25	15	H	Derby Co	W 3-0	3-0	6	Buckley [36], Graham [43], Sordell [45]	12,917
26	22	A	Cardiff C	L 2-4	1-3	7	Buckley [33], Sordell [48]	23,702
27	Feb 1	H	Crystal Palace	D 1-1	1-1	7	Weimann [10]	12,664
28	5	A	Nottingham F	L 0-1	0-1	9		23,393
29	12	H	Burnley	L 1-3	1-1	11	Graham [13]	13,103
30	15	H	Preston NE	D 2-2	0-2	—	Whichelow [69], Thompson [79]	10,620
31	19	A	Reading	D 1-1	1-0	11	Weimann [27]	16,934
32	22	H	Bristol C	L 1-3	1-1	—	Cowie [19]	12,125
33	26	A	Doncaster R	D 1-1	1-1	12	Graham [22]	8954
34	Mar 5	H	Millwall	W 1-0	0-0	12	Graham [51]	13,539
35	8	A	Swansea C	D 1-1	0-1	—	Graham [78]	14,410
36	12	H	Sheffield U	W 3-0	1-0	11	Graham [10], Taylor, M [57], Jenkins [86]	12,441
37	15	A	Ipswich T	W 3-0	1-0	—	Deeney [3], Graham [61], Cowie [90]	17,789
38	19	A	Middlesbrough	L 1-2	1-2	9	Graham [28]	16,090
39	Apr 2	A	Coventry C	L 0-2	0-1	10		16,519
40	9	H	Hull C	L 1-2	0-1	12	Taylor, M [90]	13,355
41	12	H	Norwich C	D 2-2	2-1	—	Graham [26], Cowie [36]	13,777
42	16	A	Leeds U	D 2-2	0-0	13	Hodson [78], Weimann [86]	30,240
43	23	H	Barnsley	W 1-0	1-0	14	Eustace [2]	14,098
44	25	A	Leicester C	L 2-4	2-1	12	Sordell 2 [28, 41]	21,473
45	30	H	QPR	L 0-2	0-0	13		15,538
46	May 7	A	Preston NE	L 1-3	1-1	14	Weimann [13]	10,953

Final League Position: 14

GOALSCORERS

League (77): Graham 23 (1 pen), Sordell 12, Eustace 6, Taylor, M 6, Mutch 5, Buckley 4, Cowie 4, Weimann 4, Deeney 3, Whichelow 3, McGinn 2, Hodson 1, Jenkins 1, Mariappa 1, Taylor, A 1, Thompson 1.
Carling Cup (4): Graham 2, Deeney 1, Sordell 1.
FA Cup (4): Sordell 2, Graham 1, Mingoia 1.

Loach S 46	Hodson L 26 + 3	Doyley L 36	Eustace J 41	Taylor M 46	Mariappa A 45	Cowie D 37	McGinn S 24 + 5	Sordell M 25 + 18	Graham D 45	Buckley W 27 + 6	Deeney T 17 + 19	Jenkins R 13 + 6	Mutch J 21 + 2	Walker J — + 5	Taylor A 19	Bryan M 4 + 1	Whichelow M 4 + 15	Massey G — + 3	Bennett D 5 + 5	Mingoia P 2 + 3	Townsend A 2 + 1	Weimann A 10 + 8	Drinkwater D 3 + 9	Thompson A 7 + 3	Murray S 1 + 1	Hoban T — + 1	Match No.
1	2	3	4	5	6	7	8	9¹	10	11²	12	13															1
1	2	3	4	5	6	7	8	9²	10	11¹	13		12														2
1	2	3	4	5	6	7	8³	9²	10	11¹	12	13	14														3
1	2	3	4	5	6	7	8¹	9		12	10		11														4
1	2		4	5	6	7	8¹	12	10	11²		13	9³	14	3												5
1	2		4	5	6	7	13	9	10¹	11²	12		8		3												6
1	14	2	4	5	6	7	12	9	10	11¹	13		8		3³												7
1	2	3	4	5	6	7	12	9²	10³	11¹	13		8	14													8
1		2	4	5	6	7		9	10	11¹	12		8		3												9
1	14	2	4	5	6	7	13	9¹	10	11²	12		8		3³												10
1		2	4	5	6	7¹	12	9³	10	11²	14		8		3	13											11
1		2	4	5	6		8	9¹	10	13	12		11		3	7²											12
1		2	4	5	6		8	9²	10¹		12	11³	14		3	7	13										13
1		2	4	5	6		8	9¹	10²		12	11			3	7	13										14
1		2	4	5	6		8	13	10		9²	11			3	7¹	12										15
1		2	4	5	6		8	13	10²	12	9	11			3	7¹											16
1		2	4	5	6	7	8¹	12	10²	13	9	11			3												17
1		2		5	6	7	8	9	10		4	11			3												18
1		2	4	5	6	7	8	12	10		9¹	11			3												19
1		2	4	5	6	7	8²	13³	10	11¹	12		9		3			14									20
1		2	4	5	6	7	8¹	12	10	11²	13		9		3												21
1		2	4	5	6	7		9	10³	11¹		13	8²	12	3			14									22
1		2	4¹	5	6	7		9³	10	11²	12	8			3		13	14									23
1		2		5	6	7¹	8	9	10	11²	12	4			8		3²	14	13								24
1		3		5	2	7¹	8	9	10	11²	12	4					13		6	14							25
1	12	3		5	2		8	9	10	7		4							13	6¹	11²						26
1	2	3	4	5	6		8		10	11²	14								13		7¹	9³	12				27
1	2	3	4	5	6		8	9²	10	11									12			13	7¹				28
1	2		4		5	6		8	9²	10	11									6¹		14	13	7¹	12		29
1	2	3¹	4³	5	6	7	8	14	10				12									9	11²	13			30
1	2		4	5	6	7	8²	12	10			14					11³					9¹	13	3			31
1	2		4	5	6	7	8¹	13	10			14					11³					9²	12	3			32
1	2		4	5	6	7	8¹	13	10			14					11					9²	12³	3			33
1	2			5	6	7		12	10	11³	8				4				13	14		9¹		3²			34
1	2		4	5	6	7		12	10	11¹	9	8				3											35
1	2¹	3	4	5	6	7		14	10³	11	9²	8							13					12			36
1		3	4	5	6	7		13	10³	11¹	9²	8				12			14	2							37
1	2		4	5	6⁴	7		13	10	11²	9³	8							12			14	3¹				38
1	2		4	5		7		10	12	14	8¹					11²			6			9³	13	3			39
1	2	3	4	5	6	7		12	10	11¹	14	8³				13						9²					40
1	2	3	4	5	6	7		9¹	10		11	8²											12	13			41
1	2	3	4	5	6	7		9²	10³		11	8¹									14		13	12			42
1	2	3	4	5	6	7		9¹	10		11										8²		12	13			43
1	2	3	4	5¹	6	7		12	10		11								14		8²	9¹	13				44
1	2	3	4	5¹	6	7		9²	10	11³	8								13				12		14		45
1	2	3	4	5¹	6	7		10	14	11²									13				9		8³	12	46

FA Cup
Third Round   Hartlepool U   (h)   4-1
Fourth Round   Brighton & HA   (h)   0-1

Carling Cup
First Round   Aldershot T   (a)   3-0
Second Round   Notts Co   (h)   1-2

WEST BROMWICH ALBION   FA Premiership

FOUNDATION

There is a well known story that when employees of Salter's Spring Works in West Bromwich decided to form a football club, they had to send someone to the nearby Association Football stronghold of Wednesbury to purchase a football. A weekly subscription of 2d (less than 1p) was imposed and the name of the new club was West Bromwich Strollers.

The Hawthorns, West Bromwich, West Midlands B71 4LF.

Telephone: 0871 271 1100.

Fax: 0871 271 9861.

Ticket Office: 0871 271 9780.

Website: www.wbafc.co.uk

Email: enquiries@wbafc.co.uk

Ground Capacity: 28,003.

Record Attendance: 64,815 v Arsenal, FA Cup 6th rd, 6 March 1937.

Pitch Measurements: 115yd × 74yd.

Chairman: Jeremy Peace.

Legal Counsel/Secretary: Richard Garlick.

Head Coach: Roy Hodgson.

First Team Coach: Michael Appleton.

Physio: Richie Rawlins.

Colours: Navy blue and white striped shirts, white shorts, white stockings.

Change Colours: Red shirts with blue trim, blue shorts, blue stockings.

Year Formed: 1878. *Turned Professional:* 1885.

Ltd Co.: 1892.

Plc: 1996.

Previous Name: 1878, West Bromwich Strollers; 1881, West Bromwich Albion.

Club Nicknames: 'Throstles', 'Baggies', 'Albion'.

Grounds: 1878, Coopers Hill; 1879, Dartmouth Park; 1881, Bunns Field, Walsall Street; 1882, Four Acres (Dartmouth Cricket Club); 1885, Stoney Lane; 1900, The Hawthorns.

First Football League Game: 8 September 1888, Football League, v Stoke (a) W 2–0 – Roberts; Jack Horton, Green; Ezra Horton, Perry, Bayliss; Bassett, Woodhall (1), Hendry, Pearson, Wilson (1).

Record League Victory: 12–0 v Darwen, Division 1, 4 April 1892 – Reader; Jack Horton, McCulloch; Reynolds (2), Perry, Groves; Bassett (3), McLeod, Nicholls (1), Pearson (4), Geddes (1), (1 og).

HONOURS

Football League – Division 1:
Champions 1919–20;
Runners-up 1924–25, 1953–54, 2001–02, 2003–04.
FL C: *Champions* 2007–08;
Runners-up 2009–10.
Division 2: *Champions* 1901–02, 1910–11; *Runners-up* 1930–31, 1948–49.
FA Cup: *Winners* 1888, 1892, 1931, 1954, 1968; *Runners-up* 1886, 1887, 1895, 1912, 1935.
Football League Cup: *Winners* 1966; *Runners-up* 1967, 1970.
European Competitions
European Cup-Winners' Cup:
1968–69.
European Fairs Cup: 1966–67.
UEFA Cup: 1978–79, 1979–80, 1981–82.

sky SPORTS FACT FILE

On 21 August 2010 Uzbekistan born Peter Odemwingie, signed from Lokomotiv Moscow, scored the only goal against Sunderland. He was the 24th Nigerian to play in the Premier League and third for West Bromwich Albion after Nwankwo Kanu and Ifeanyi Udeze.

Record Cup Victory: 10–1 v Chatham (away), FA Cup 3rd rd, 2 March 1889 – Roberts; Jack Horton, Green; Timmins (1), Charles Perry, Ezra Horton; Bassett (2), Walter Perry (1), Bayliss (2), Pearson, Wilson (3), (1 og).

Record Defeat: 3–10 v Stoke C, Division 1, 4 February 1937.

Most League Points (2 for a win): 60, Division 1, 1919–20.

Most League Points (3 for a win): 91, FL C, 2009–10.

Most League Goals: 105, Division 2, 1929–30.

Highest League Scorer in Season: William 'Ginger' Richardson, 39, Division 1, 1935–36.

Most League Goals in Total Aggregate: Tony Brown, 218, 1963–79.

Most League Goals in One Match: 6, Jimmy Cookson v Blackpool, Division 2, 17 September 1927.

Most Capped Player: Stuart Williams, 33 (43), Wales.

Most League Appearances: Tony Brown, 574, 1963–80.

Youngest League Player: Charlie Wilson, 16 years 73 days v Oldham Ath, 1 October 1921.

Record Transfer Fee Received: £8,000,000 from Aston Villa for Curtis Davies, July 2008.

Record Transfer Fee Paid: £4,700,000 to Mallorca for Borja Valero, August 2008.

Football League Record: 1888 Founder Member of Football League; 1901–02 Division 2; 1902–04 Division 1; 1904–11 Division 2; 1911–27 Division 1; 1927–31 Division 2; 1931–38 Division 1; 1938–49 Division 2; 1949–73 Division 1; 1973–76 Division 2; 1976–86 Division 1; 1986–91 Division 2; 1991–92 Division 3; 1992–93 Division 2; 1993–2002 Division 1; 2002–03 FA Premier League; 2003–04 Division 1; 2004–06 FA Premier League; 2006–08 FL C; 2008–09 FA Premier League; 2009–10 FL C; 2010 FA Premier League.

LATEST SEQUENCES

Longest Sequence of League Wins: 11, 5.4.1930 – 8.9.1930.

Longest Sequence of League Defeats: 11, 28.10.1995 – 26.12.1995.

Longest Sequence of League Draws: 5, 30.8.1999 – 3.10.1999.

Longest Sequence of Unbeaten League Matches: 17, 7.9.1957 – 7.12.1957.

Longest Sequence Without a League Win: 15, 16.10.2004 – 25.9.2004.

Successive Scoring Runs: 36 from 26.4.1958.

Successive Non-scoring Runs: 4 from 15.2.1913.

MANAGERS

Louis Ford 1890–92
(Secretary-Manager)
Henry Jackson 1892–94
(Secretary-Manager)
Edward Stephenson 1894–95
(Secretary-Manager)
Clement Keys 1895–96
(Secretary-Manager)
Frank Heaven 1896–1902
(Secretary-Manager)
Fred Everiss 1902–48
Jack Smith 1948–52
Jesse Carver 1952
Vic Buckingham 1953–59
Gordon Clark 1959–61
Archie Macaulay 1961–63
Jimmy Hagan 1963–67
Alan Ashman 1967–71
Don Howe 1971–75
Johnny Giles 1975–77
Ronnie Allen 1977
Ron Atkinson 1978–81
Ronnie Allen 1981–82
Ron Wylie 1982–84
Johnny Giles 1984–85
Nobby Stiles 1985–86
Ron Saunders 1986–87
Ron Atkinson 1987–88
Brian Talbot 1988–91
Bobby Gould 1991–92
Ossie Ardiles 1992–93
Keith Burkinshaw 1993–94
Alan Buckley 1994–97
Ray Harford 1997
Denis Smith 1997–1999
Brian Little 1999–2000
Gary Megson 2000–04
Bryan Robson 2004–06
Tony Mowbray 2006–09
Roberto Di Matteo 2009–11
Roy Hodgson February 2011–

TEN YEAR LEAGUE RECORD

		P	W	D	L	F	A	Pts	Pos
2001-02	Div 1	46	27	8	11	61	29	89	2
2002-03	PR Lge	38	6	8	24	29	65	26	19
2003-04	Div 1	46	25	11	10	64	42	86	2
2004-05	PR Lge	38	6	16	16	36	61	34	17
2005-06	PR Lge	38	7	9	22	31	58	30	19
2006-07	FL C	46	22	10	14	81	55	76	4
2007-08	FL C	46	23	12	11	88	55	81	1
2008-09	PR Lge	38	8	8	22	36	67	32	20
2009-10	FL C	46	26	13	7	89	48	91	2
2010-11	PR Lge	38	12	11	15	56	71	47	11

DID YOU KNOW ?

On 25 September 2010, West Bromwich Albion won 3-2 at the Emirates. It was their first win against Arsenal in London since 3 December 1983 when they were successful at Highbury. The only goal was scored by Derek Monaghan, one of his only two goals for the Baggies.

WEST BROMWICH ALBION 2010–11 LEAGUE RECORD

Match No.	Date	Venue	Opponents	Result	H/T Score	Lg Pos.	Goalscorers	Atten- dance
1	Aug 14	A	Chelsea	L 0-6	0-2	—		41,589
2	21	H	Sunderland	W 1-0	0-0	12	Odemwingie [81]	23,624
3	29	A	Liverpool	L 0-1	0-0	16		41,194
4	Sept 11	H	Tottenham H	D 1-1	1-1	16	Brunt [41]	23,642
5	18	H	Birmingham C	W 3-1	0-1	10	Dann (og) [51], Odemwingie [59], Olsson [69]	23,062
6	25	A	Arsenal	W 3-2	0-0	6	Odemwingie [50], Jara [52], Thomas [73]	60,025
7	Oct 2	H	Bolton W	D 1-1	0-0	6	Morrison [78]	22,846
8	16	A	Manchester U	D 2-2	0-2	6	Evra (og) [50], Tchoyi [55]	75,272
9	23	H	Fulham	W 2-1	2-1	6	Mulumbu [17], Fortune [40]	25,625
10	Nov 1	A	Blackpool	L 1-2	0-1	—	Mulumbu [85]	15,210
11	7	H	Manchester C	L 0-2	0-2	10		23,013
12	10	A	West Ham U	D 2-2	1-1	—	Odemwingie (pen) [38], Pablo [71]	33,023
13	13	A	Wigan Ath	L 0-1	0-0	12		16,085
14	20	H	Stoke C	L 0-3	0-0	15		24,164
15	27	A	Everton	W 4-1	2-1	12	Scharner [16], Brunt [26], Tchoyi [76], Mulumbu [87]	35,237
16	Dec 5	H	Newcastle U	W 3-1	1-0	8	Tchoyi [32], Odemwingie 2 [71, 89]	23,486
17	11	A	Aston Villa	L 1-2	0-1	11	Scharner [89]	37,015
18	26	A	Bolton W	L 0-2	0-1	12		23,413
19	28	H	Blackburn R	L 1-3	1-1	14	Thomas [17]	24,440
20	Jan 1	H	Manchester U	L 1-2	1-1	14	Morrison [14]	25,499
21	4	A	Fulham	L 0-3	0-1	16		23,654
22	15	H	Blackpool	W 3-2	1-1	14	Odemwingie 2 [37, 87], Morrison [52]	25,316
23	23	A	Blackburn R	L 0-2	0-1	15		24,057
24	Feb 1	H	Wigan Ath	D 2-2	1-2	—	Odemwingie [5], Fortune [79]	25,358
25	5	A	Manchester C	L 0-3	0-3	17		46,846
26	12	H	West Ham U	D 3-3	3-0	17	Dorrans [3], Thomas [8], Reid (og) [32]	23,916
27	20	H	Wolverhampton W	D 1-1	0-1	—	Vela [90]	26,170
28	28	A	Stoke C	D 1-1	0-0	16	Vela [87]	25,019
29	Mar 5	A	Birmingham C	W 3-1	0-0	16	Mulumbu [47], Morrison [58], Scharner [72]	27,013
30	19	H	Arsenal	D 2-2	1-0	16	Reid [3], Odemwingie [58]	25,729
31	Apr 2	H	Liverpool	W 2-1	0-0	13	Brunt 2 (2 pens) [62, 88]	26,196
32	9	A	Sunderland	W 3-2	1-2	10	Odemwingie [28], Mulumbu [54], Scharner [72]	41,586
33	16	H	Chelsea	L 1-3	1-3	11	Odemwingie [17]	25,163
34	23	A	Tottenham H	D 2-2	1-1	12	Odemwingie [5], Cox [81]	36,160
35	30	H	Aston Villa	W 2-1	0-1	11	Odemwingie [60], Mulumbu [84]	25,889
36	May 8	A	Wolverhampton W	L 1-3	0-2	13	Odemwingie (pen) [55]	28,510
37	14	H	Everton	W 1-0	1-0	11	Mulumbu [10]	25,838
38	22	A	Newcastle U	D 3-3	0-2	11	Tchoyi 3 [62, 71, 90]	51,678

Final League Position: 11

GOALSCORERS

League (56): Odemwingie 15 (2 pens), Mulumbu 7, Tchoyi 6, Brunt 4 (2 pens), Morrison 4, Scharner 4, Thomas 3, Fortune 2, Vela 2, Cox 1, Dorrans 1, Jara 1, Olsson 1, Pablo 1, Reid 1, own goals 3.
Carling Cup (8): Cox 3, Pablo 1, Reid 1, Tchoyi 1, Wood 1, Zuiverloon 1.
FA Cup (0).

Carson S 32	Jara G 24 + 5	Cech M 14 + 1	Mulumbu Y 34	Tamas G 22 + 4	Pablo 8 + 2	Thomas J 32 + 1	Morrison J 26 + 5	Bednar R 1 + 3	Brunt C 34	Dorrans G 16 + 5	Miller I — + 6	Cox S 8 + 11	Barnes G 1 + 13	Olsson J 24	Odemwingie P 29 + 3	Reid S 13 + 10	Shorey N 25 + 3	Fortune M 14 + 11	Tchoyi S 7 + 16	Wood C — + 1	Scharner P 33	Zuiverloon G 1 + 1	Hurst J 1	Myhill B 6	Vela C 3 + 5	Meite A 10	Thorne G — + 1	Match No.
1	2	3	4	5	6	7³	8	9²	10	11¹	12	13	14															1
1	2	3	4³	5		7¹	8		10	11²	12			6	9	13	14											2
1	2		4	5		7	8⁴			11¹				6	9		3	10²	12		13							3
1	2		4	5		7				11²		13		6	9	12	3	10³	14		8¹							4
1	2		4²	5		7³				11	12		14	6	9	13	3	10¹			8							5
1	2		4		6	7³	8²		11			13		5	9	12	3	14			10¹							6
1	2		4	5		7³			10	11¹		13	12	6	9		3	14			8²							7
1	2		4	5		12	8³		13	11		14		6	9²		3	7¹			10							8
1	2		4	5	12	7³	8		13	11				6¹	9²		3	14			10							9
1	2		4	5	6	7³			11	10¹		13	14		9²	12	3				8							10
1		3¹	4¹	5	6	7			10	11	12	13	14		9²	2					8³							11
1	2			5	6	7³	8		10	11¹	12	13			9³		3	14			4							12
1	2		4³	5	6	7	8²		10	11¹		13			9	2	3	12	14									13
1	2	3	4³	5	6	7	8¹			11		13	14		9			10²	12									14
1	2	3	4⁸	5		7¹	8		10³	11²		13	14		9			12			6							15
1	2	3		5		7¹	8²		10	11	12	13			9		4				6							16
1	2³	3		5		7	8¹		10	11	12	13	14		9²		4				6							17
1	2	3	4²	5			8¹		10	11	12	13			9		7				6							18
1	2²		4	5⁸		7	8¹			11	12	13			9		3	10			6							19
1		3	4³	5²		7	8		10	11					9	2¹		14	13		6	12						20
1		3¹	4²	5		7	8³		10	11			14		9	12		13			6	2						21
	2	3	4³	5		7	8¹		10	11²	12				9			14	13		6			1				22
	2	3	4¹	5		7			10	11²		13		6	9			12			8			1				23
	2³	3	4			7	8		10²					5	9	12		14	13		6			1	11¹			24
	13		4			7¹	8			11²				5	9²	2	3	10	14		6			1	12			25
	2	14	4¹			7²	8		12	11³		13		5	9		3	10			6			1				26
	2³		5			7¹	8		12	11²				6	9		3	14	10		4			1	13			27
1				5		7¹	9³		8	11		13				2	3	10²	12		4	14				6		28
1	13		4	5		7²			10	11³					9¹	2	3	12			8					6		29
1	12		4	5		7			10	11					9²	2	3	13			8¹					6		30
1	13		4	5		7²			10¹	11					9	2	3	12			8					6		31
1	14		4	5		7			10²	11¹					9³	2	3	13	12		8					6		32
1	13		4	5		7³			10²	11					9	2	3	14			8¹				12	6		33
1	12		4	5		7²			13	11		14			9	2¹	3				8³				10	6		34
1	2¹		4	5		12			10	11					9³		3	13	14		8				7²	6		35
1	2¹		4	5		7³			10²	11		13			9		3	12			8				14	6		36
1			4	5	6	7²			10¹	11³					9	2	3	14	13		8							37
1			4	5		7			10	11			14		9³	2	3				8²					6¹	13	38

FA Cup

Third Round	Reading	(a)	0-1	

Carling Cup

Second Round	Leyton Orient	(a)	2-0
Third Round	Manchester C	(h)	2-1
Fourth Round	Leicester C	(a)	4-1
Quarter-Final	Ipswich T	(a)	0-1

WEST HAM UNITED   FL Championship

FOUNDATION

Thames Iron Works FC was formed by employees of this famous shipbuilding company in 1895 and entered the FA Cup in their initial season at Chatham and the London League in their second. The committee wanted to introduce professional players, so Thames Iron Works was wound up in June 1900 and relaunched a month later as West Ham United.

The Boleyn Ground, Upton Park, Green Street, London E13 9AZ.

Telephone: (020) 8548 2748.

Fax: (020) 8548 2758.

Ticket Office: 0871 222 2700.

Website: www.whufc.co.uk

Email: yourcomments@westhamunited.co.uk

Ground Capacity: 35,303.

Record Attendance: 42,322 v Tottenham H, Division 1, 17 October 1970.

Pitch Measurements: 100.58m × 66.84m.

Joint Chairmen: David Sullivan and David Gold.

Vice-chairman: Karren Brady.

Secretary: Peter Barnes.

Manager: Sam Allardyce.

Assistant Manager: Neil McDonald.

Physio: Stijn Vandenbroucke.

Colours: Claret shirts with blue trim, white shorts, claret stockings.

Change Colours: Dark blue shirts with broad royal blue stripe, dark blue shorts, dark blue stockings.

Year Formed: 1895.

Turned Professional: 1900.

Ltd Co.: 1900.

Previous Name: 1895, Thames Iron Works FC; 1900, West Ham United.

Club Nicknames: 'The Hammers', 'The Irons'.

Grounds: 1895, Memorial Recreation Ground, Canning Town; 1904, Boleyn Ground.

First Football League Game: 30 August 1919, Division 2, v Lincoln C (h) D 1–1 – Hufton; Cope, Lee; Lane, Fenwick, McCrae; David Smith, Moyes (1), Puddefoot, Morris, Bradshaw.

HONOURS

Football League – Division 1:
Runners-up 1992–93
Division 2: *Champions* 1957–58, 1980–81; *Runners-up* 1922–23, 1990–91.

FA Cup: *Winners* 1964, 1975, 1980; *Runners-up* 1923, 2006.

Football League Cup:
Runners-up 1966, 1981.

European Competitions
European Cup-Winners' Cup:
1964–65 (*winners*), 1965–66, 1975–76 (*runners-up*), 1980–81.
UEFA Cup: 1999–2000; 2006–07.
Intertoto Cup: 1999 (*winners*).

sky SPORTS FACT FILE

Even before the Second World War, West Ham United had toured a dozen different European countries, but the Football Association had refused to sanction a trip to the Soviet Union. It was not until the 1975–76 Cup Winners' Cup that they finally made it against Ararat Erevan.

Record League Victory: 8–0 v Rotherham U, Division 2, 8 March 1958 – Gregory; Bond, Wright; Malcolm, Brown, Lansdowne; Grice, Smith (2), Keeble (2), Dick (4), Musgrove. 8–0 v Sunderland, Division 1, 19 October 1968 – Ferguson; Bonds, Charles; Peters, Stephenson, Moore (1); Redknapp, Boyce, Brooking (1), Hurst (6), Sissons.

Record Cup Victory: 10–0 v Bury, League Cup 2nd rd (2nd leg), 25 October 1983 – Parkes; Stewart (1), Walford, Bonds (Orr), Martin (1), Devonshire (2), Allen, Cottee (4), Swindlehurst, Brooking (2), Pike.

Record Defeat: 2–8 v Blackburn R, Division 1, 26 December 1963.

Most League Points (2 for a win): 66, Division 2, 1980–81.

Most League Points (3 for a win): 88, Division 1, 1992–93.

Most League Goals: 101, Division 2, 1957–58.

Highest League Scorer in Season: Vic Watson, 42, Division 1, 1929–30.

Most League Goals in Total Aggregate: Vic Watson, 298, 1920–35.

MANAGERS
Syd King 1902–32
Charlie Paynter 1932–50
Ted Fenton 1950–61
Ron Greenwood 1961–74
(continued as General Manager to 1977)
John Lyall 1974–89
Lou Macari 1989–90
Billy Bonds 1990–94
Harry Redknapp 1994–2001
Glenn Roeder 2001–03
Alan Pardew 2003–06
Alan Curbishley 2006–08
Gianfranco Zola 2008–10
Avram Grant 2010–11
Sam Allardyce June 2011–

Most League Goals in One Match: 6, Vic Watson v Leeds U, Division 1, 9 February 1929; 6, Geoff Hurst v Sunderland, Division 1, 19 October 1968.

Most Capped Player: Bobby Moore, 108, England.

Most League Appearances: Billy Bonds, 663, 1967–88.

Youngest League Player: Billy Williams, 16 years 221 days v Blackpool, 6 May 1922.

Record Transfer Fee Received: £18,000,000 from Leeds U for Rio Ferdinand, November 2000.

Record Transfer Fee Paid: £7,500,000 to Liverpool for Craig Bellamy, July 2007.

Football League Record: 1919 Elected to Division 2; 1923–32 Division 1; 1932–58 Division 2; 1958–78 Division 1; 1978–81 Division 2; 1981–89 Division 1; 1989–91 Division 2; 1991–93 Division 1; 1993–2003 FA Premier League; 2003–04 Division 1; 2004–05 FL C; 2005–11 FA Premier League; 2011– FL C.

LATEST SEQUENCES

Longest Sequence of League Wins: 9, 19.10.1985 – 14.12.1985.

Longest Sequence of League Defeats: 9, 28.3.1932 – 29.8.1932.

Longest Sequence of League Draws: 5, 15.10.2003 – 1.11.2003.

Longest Sequence of Unbeaten League Matches: 27, 27.12.80 – 10.10.81.

Longest Sequence Without a League Win: 17, 31.1.1976 – 21.8.1976.

Successive Scoring Runs: 27 from 5.10.1957.

Successive Non-scoring Runs: 5 from 1.5.1971.

TEN YEAR LEAGUE RECORD

		P	W	D	L	F	A	Pts	Pos
2001-02	PR Lge	38	15	8	15	48	57	53	7
2002-03	PR Lge	38	10	12	16	42	59	42	18
2003-04	Div 1	46	19	17	10	67	45	74	4
2004-05	FL C	46	21	10	15	66	56	73	6
2005-06	PR Lge	38	16	7	15	52	55	55	9
2006-07	PR Lge	38	12	5	21	35	59	41	15
2007-08	PR Lge	38	13	10	15	42	50	49	10
2008-09	PR Lge	38	14	9	15	42	45	51	9
2009-10	PR Lge	38	8	11	19	47	66	35	17
2010-11	PR Lge	38	7	12	19	43	70	33	20

DID YOU KNOW ?

On 30 November 2010, West Ham United, bottom of the Premier League, defeated the holders and League leaders Manchester United 4-0 in a Carling Cup quarter-final. It was the first defeat for the Old Trafford club following a run of 30 overall matches dating back to April.

WEST HAM UNITED 2010–11 LEAGUE RECORD

Match No.	Date	Venue	Opponents	Result	H/T Score	Lg Pos.	Goalscorers	Attendance
1	Aug 14	A	Aston Villa	L	0-3	0-2	—	36,604
2	21	H	Bolton W	L	1-3	0-0	19	Noble (pen) [79]	32,533
3	28	A	Manchester U	L	0-3	0-1	20		75,061
4	Sept 11	H	Chelsea	L	1-3	0-2	20	Parker [85]	33,014
5	18	A	Stoke C	D	1-1	1-0	20	Parker [32]	27,028
6	25	H	Tottenham H	W	1-0	1-0	19	Piquionne [29]	34,190
7	Oct 2	H	Fulham	D	1-1	0-1	20	Piquionne [51]	34,589
8	16	A	Wolverhampton W	D	1-1	0-1	20	Noble (pen) [53]	28,582
9	23	H	Newcastle U	L	1-2	1-1	20	Cole [12]	34,486
10	30	A	Arsenal	L	0-1	0-0	20		60,086
11	Nov 6	A	Birmingham C	D	2-2	0-0	20	Piquionne [48], Behrami [58]	26,474
12	10	H	WBA	D	2-2	1-1	—	Parker [43], Piquionne (pen) [50]	33,023
13	13	H	Blackpool	D	0-0	0-0	20		31,194
14	20	A	Liverpool	L	0-3	0-3	20		43,024
15	27	H	Wigan Ath	W	3-1	1-0	20	Behrami [34], Obinna [56], Parker [75]	34,178
16	Dec 5	A	Sunderland	L	0-1	0-1	20		36,940
17	11	H	Manchester C	L	1-3	0-1	20	Tomkins [89]	32,813
18	18	A	Blackburn R	D	1-1	0-0	—	Stanislas [78]	21,934
19	26	A	Fulham	W	3-1	2-1	19	Cole 2 [37, 73], Piquionne [45]	25,332
20	28	H	Everton	D	1-1	1-1	20	Hibbert (og) [16]	33,422
21	Jan 1	H	Wolverhampton W	W	2-0	0-0	15	Zubar (og) [51], Sears [79]	33,500
22	5	A	Newcastle U	L	0-5	0-3	20		42,387
23	15	H	Arsenal	L	0-3	0-2	20		32,682
24	22	A	Everton	D	2-2	1-0	20	Spector [26], Piquionne [84]	34,179
25	Feb 2	A	Blackpool	W	3-1	3-1	—	Obinna 2 [24, 44], Keane [37]	15,095
26	6	H	Birmingham C	L	0-1	0-0	20		32,927
27	12	A	WBA	D	3-3	0-3	19	Ba 2 [50, 83], Cole [58]	23,916
28	27	H	Liverpool	W	3-1	2-0	18	Parker [22], Ba [45], Cole [90]	34,941
29	Mar 5	H	Stoke C	W	3-0	2-0	17	Ba [21], Da Costa [29], Hitzlsperger [83]	33,066
30	19	A	Tottenham H	D	0-0	0-0	17		36,010
31	Apr 2	H	Manchester U	L	2-4	2-0	18	Noble 2 (2 pens) [11, 25]	34,546
32	9	A	Bolton W	L	0-3	0-2	18		25,857
33	16	H	Aston Villa	L	1-2	1-1	19	Keane [2]	34,672
34	23	A	Chelsea	L	0-3	0-1	20		41,656
35	May 1	A	Manchester C	L	1-2	1-2	20	Ba [33]	44,511
36	7	H	Blackburn R	D	1-1	0-1	20	Hitzlsperger [78]	33,789
37	15	A	Wigan Ath	L	2-3	2-0	20	Ba 2 [12, 26]	22,043
38	22	H	Sunderland	L	0-3	0-1	20		32,792

Final League Position: 20

GOALSCORERS

League (43): Ba 7, Piquionne 6 (1 pen), Cole 5, Parker 5, Noble 4 (4 pens), Obinna 3, Behrami 2, Hitzlsperger 2, Keane 2, Da Costa 1, Sears 1, Spector 1, Stanislas 1, Tomkins 1, own goals 2.
Carling Cup (13): Cole 4, Obinna 2, Parker 2, Spector 2, Da Costa 1, Noble 1, Piquionne 1.
FA Cup (11): Obinna 3 (1 pen), Cole 2, Piquionne 2, Hitzlsperger 1, Reid 1, Sears 1, Spector 1.

Green R 37	Reid W 3 + 4	Ilunga H 10 + 1	Parker S 30 + 2	Tomkins J 18 + 1	Upson M 30	Faubert J 7 + 2	Kovac R 7 + 6	Cole C 21 + 14	Boa Morte L 19 + 3	Noble M 25 + 1	Barrera P 6 + 8	Piquionne F 26 + 8	Diamanti A — + 1	Gabbidon D 24 + 2	Dyer K 8 + 3	McCarthy B — + 6	Sears F 9 + 2	Spector J 10 + 4	Stanislas J 4 + 2	Jacobsen L 22 + 2	Ben Haim T 8	Behrami V 6 + 1	Obinna V 17 + 8	Da Costa M 14 + 2	Hines Z 4 + 5	Boffin R 1	Nouble F — + 2	Bridge W 15	O'Neil G 7 + 1	Keane R 5 + 4	Ba D 10 + 2	Hitzlsperger T 11	Collison J 2 + 1	Spence J 2	Match No.
1	2	3	4	5^3	6	7	8^1	9	10^2	11	12	13	14																						1
1	12	3	4		6^1	2		9^3		8	11	10		5	7^2		13	14																	2
1		3	4		6	7^1		9	10^3	8	12	13		5	11^2			2	14																3
1		3	4		6			9	11^1	8		13		12						2	5	7^2	10												4
1			4		6		12	9	13	8		10		3						2		7^1	11^2	5											5
1			4		6		14	13	11	8	12	10^2		3	7^1					2			9^3	5											6
1			4		6			12	11	8		7^1	10	3						2			9	5											7
1			4					12	11	8		10		3	7^1					2	5		9	6											8
1	12		4		6^1			9		8	14	10^2		3	13					2		7^3	11	5											9
1		3	4	13				12	11	8	14	10^1		6						2		7^3	9^2	5											10
1		3	4		6			13	9	11^1		10		5	12					2		7	8^2												11
1		3	4		6		12	9^2	11^1		8^3	10		5	7	14				2			13												12
1		3	4		6			13	11^2	8	12	10^3		5	7^1	14				2			9												13
1		3^1		14	6			8	9^2	11	4	12	10	5		13				2		7^1													14
1	12		4^3	5	6		14	13		8		10^2						11			2^1	7	9												15
1			4	5	6		14	9	11^2			13		2	7^1			8				3^3	10		12										16
1			4	5	6	2		13				7^2	10^3		12			8			11^1	· 3	9	14											17
1			4	5	6			13	9			7^1	10	3		11^3	14				8^2	12		2		1									18
1			4	5	6		8	9				10^1						7			11			2			12								19
1		3^1	4	5	6	2	8	13		11		10^2						7			12		9^3	14											20
1			4	5	6		8	9			12	10		3				7			11^1			2											21
1			4	5	6		8^1	9				11^3	10^2	3				7				2		12	13		14								22
1				5	6	2	8	9			12		4^1	13				7^2			11						14	3^3	10						23
1	13		4	5	6	2		9		8			10^4					12^2			11	7^1						3							24
1	12		8	5				14	13	4		10			6^1					2	11^2							3	7	9^3					25
1	5		8	6^1				13		4		10^2								2	11	12						3	7	9^3	14				26
1	5		8					9	11^1	4	12							13		2		6						3	7^2	10					27
1	8		5		6			13		4		10^1						12		2								3	7	9^2	11				28
1	8^3	2			6			0^7		4		11	14									13	5					3	12	10^1	7				29
1	8				6			9^1		4										2		12		5				3	7	10	11				30
1	8				6			9^1		4^3	12									2		13		5				3	7^2	14	10	11			31
1	8^3	2			6^1			12		4		11^2			14							13		5				3	10	9	7				32
1					6			9		4	12									2	8^2			5^1	13			3	7^3	10	14	11			33
1								9^2		4^1		13		6				7^3			8	2		14	5				12	10	11				34
1			5	6^1				13				11^3		3				7	4			2		14	12				10^2	9	8				35
1								9	11^1				14	6				7^2	4			2^3		5				3	12	10	8	13			36
1	12	5						13				8^2		6		4^1						3			9^2			3		14	10	11	7^3	2	37
1	14	5^1										11^3		10		6	7					13			12			3		9^2		8	4	2	38

FA Cup

Third Round	Barnsley	(h)	2-0
Fourth Round	Nottingham F	(h)	3-2
Fifth Round	Burnley	(h)	5-1
Sixth Round	Stoke C	(a)	1-2

Carling Cup

Second Round	Oxford U	(h)	1-0
Third Round	Sunderland	(a)	2-1
Fourth Round	Stoke C	(h)	3-1
Sixth Round	Manchester U	(h)	4-0
Semi-Final	Birmingham C	(h)	2-1
		(a)	1-3

WIGAN ATHLETIC   FA Premiership

FOUNDATION

Following the demise of Wigan Borough and their resignation from the Football League in 1931, a public meeting was called in Wigan at the Queen's Hall in May 1932 at which a new club, Wigan Athletic, was founded in the hope of carrying on in the Football League. With this in mind, they bought Springfield Park for £2,250, but failed to gain admission to the Football League until 46 years later.

The DW Stadium, Robin Park Complex, Newtown, Wigan, Lancashire WN5 0UZ.

Telephone: (01942) 774 000.

Fax: (01942) 770 477.

Ticket Office: (0871) 663 3552.

Website: www.wiganathletic.tv

Email: s.hayton@wiganathletic.com

Ground Capacity: 25,138.

Record Attendance: 27,526 v Hereford U, 12 December 1953 (at Springfield Park). 25,133 v Manchester U, FA Premier League, 11 May 2008 (at DW Stadium).

Pitch Measurements: 105m × 68m.

Chairman: David Whelan.

Vice-chairman: Phillip Williams.

Chief Executive: Brenda Spencer.

Secretary: Stuart Hayton.

Manager: Roberto Martinez.

Assistant Manager: Graeme Jones.

Physios: Alex Cribley and Neil Fitzhenry.

Colours: Blue and white striped shirts with blue sleeves, blue shorts, white stockings.

Change Colours: Orange shirts with black trim, black shorts, black stockings.

Year Formed: 1932.

Grounds: 1932, Springfield Park; 1999, JJB Stadium (renamed the DW Stadium in 2009).

Club Nickname: 'The Latics'.

First Football League Game: 19 August 1978, Division 4, v Hereford U (a) D 0–0 – Brown; Hinnigan, Gore, Gillibrand, Ward, Davids, Corrigan, Purdie, Houghton, Wilkie, Wright.

Record League Victory: 7–1 v Scarborough, Division 3, 11 March 1997 – Lee Butler; John Butler, Sharp (Morgan), Greenall, McGibbon (Biggins (1)), Martinez (1), Diaz (2), Jones (Lancashire (1)), Lowe (2), Rogers, Kilford.

Record Cup Victory: 6–0 v Carlisle U (away), FA Cup 1st rd, 24 November 1934 – Caunce; Robinson, Talbot; Paterson, Watson, Tufnell; Armes (2), Robson (1), Roberts (2), Felton, Scott (1).

HONOURS

Football League – FL C:
Runners-up 2004–05;
Division 2: *Champions,* 2002–03;
Division 3: *Champions,* 1996–97.

FA Cup: Best season: 6th rd, 1987.

Football League Cup:
Runners-up 2006.

Freight Rover Trophy: *Winners* 1985.

Auto Windscreens Shield:
Winners 1999.

sky SPORTS FACT FILE

In 1967–68 Wigan Athletic signed central defender Ian Gillibrand when in the Cheshire League. He subsequently turned out in the Northern Premier for them and survived when the club entered the Football League in 1978. In all, he made a club record 621 League and Cup appearances.

Record Defeat: 1–9 v Tottenham H, FA Premier League, 22 November 2009.

Most League Points (2 for a win): 55, Division 4, 1978–79 and 1979–80.

Most League Points (3 for a win): 100, Division 2, 2002–03.

Most League Goals: 84, Division 3, 1996–97.

Highest League Scorer in Season: Graeme Jones, 31, Division 3, 1996–97.

Most League Goals in Total Aggregate: Andy Liddell, 70, 1998–2004.

Most League Goals in One Match: Not more than three goals by one player.

Most Capped Players: Kevin Kilbane, 22 (110), Republic of Ireland; Henri Camara, 22 (99), Senegal.

Most League Appearances: Kevin Langley, 317, 1981–86, 1990–94.

Youngest League Player: Steve Nugent, 16 years 132 days v Leyton Orient, 16 September 1989.

Record Transfer Fee Received: £15,250,000 from Manchester U for Antonio Valencia, June 2009.

Record Transfer Fee Paid: £6,000,000 to Newcastle U for Charles N'Zogbia, February 2009; £6,000,000 to Estudiantes for Mauro Boselli, August 2010.

Football League Record: 1978 Elected to Division 4; 1982–92 Division 3; 1992–93 Division 2; 1993–97 Division 3; 1997–2003 Division 2; 2003–04 Division 1; 2004–05 FL C; 2005– FA Premier League.

LATEST SEQUENCES

Longest Sequence of League Wins: 11, 2.11.2002 – 18.1.2003.

Longest Sequence of League Defeats: 8, 13.12.2006 – 30.1.2007.

Longest Sequence of League Draws: 6, 11.12.2001 – 5.1.2002.

Longest Sequence of Unbeaten League Matches: 25, 8.5.1999 – 3.1.2000.

Longest Sequence Without a League Win: 14, 9.5.1989 – 17.10.1989.

Successive Scoring Runs: 24 from 27.4.1996.

Successive Non-scoring Runs: 4 from 15.4.1995.

MANAGERS

Charlie Spencer 1932–37
Jimmy Milne 1946–47
Bob Pryde 1949–52
Ted Goodier 1952–54
Walter Crook 1954–55
Ron Suart 1955–56
Billy Cooke 1956
Sam Barkas 1957
Trevor Hitchen 1957–58
Malcolm Barrass 1958–59
Jimmy Shirley 1959
Pat Murphy 1959–60
Allenby Chilton 1960
Johnny Ball 1961–63
Allan Brown 1963–66
Alf Craig 1966–67
Harry Leyland 1967–68
Alan Saunders 1968
Ian McNeill 1968–70
Gordon Milne 1970–72
Les Rigby 1972–74
Brian Tiler 1974–76
Ian McNeill 1976–81
Larry Lloyd 1981–83
Harry McNally 1983–85
Bryan Hamilton 1985–86
Ray Mathias 1986–89
Bryan Hamilton 1989–93
Dave Philpotts 1993
Kenny Swain 1993–94
Graham Barrow 1994–95
John Deehan 1995–98
Ray Mathias 1998–99
John Benson 1999–2000
Bruce Rioch 2000–01
Steve Bruce 2001
Paul Jewell 2001–07
Chris Hutchings 2007
Steve Bruce 2007–09
Roberto Martinez June 2009–

TEN YEAR LEAGUE RECORD

		P	W	D	L	F	A	Pts	Pos
2001-02	Div 2	46	16	16	14	66	51	64	10
2002-03	Div 2	46	29	13	4	68	25	100	1
2003-04	Div 1	46	18	17	11	60	45	71	7
2004-05	FL C	46	25	12	9	79	35	87	2
2005-06	PR Lge	38	15	6	17	45	52	51	10
2006-07	PR Lge	38	10	8	20	37	59	38	17
2007-08	PR Lge	38	10	10	18	34	51	40	14
2008-09	PR Lge	38	12	9	17	34	45	45	11
2009-10	PR Lge	38	9	9	20	37	79	36	16
2010-11	PR Lge	38	9	15	14	40	61	42	16

DID YOU KNOW ?

On 28 August 2010 Wigan Athletic won 1-0 at Tottenham Hotspur ending the home team's run of 17 unbeaten League and Cup matches and three days after Spurs had beaten Young Boys in a Champions League match. Wigan thus avenged their 9-1 defeat there in 2009–10.

WIGAN ATHLETIC 2010–11 LEAGUE RECORD

Match No.	Date		Venue	Opponents		Result	H/T Score	Lg Pos.	Goalscorers	Attendance
1	Aug	14	H	Blackpool	L	0-4	0-3	—		16,152
2		21	H	Chelsea	L	0-6	0-1	20		14,476
3		28	A	Tottenham H	W	1-0	0-0	17	Rodallega [80]	35,101
4	Sept	11	H	Sunderland	D	1-1	0-0	17	Alcaraz [87]	15,844
5		19	H	Manchester C	L	0-2	0-1	18		15,525
6		25	A	Birmingham C	D	0-0	0-0	18		22,186
7	Oct	2	H	Wolverhampton W	W	2-0	0-0	14	Gomez [65], Rodallega [85]	14,042
8		16	A	Newcastle U	D	2-2	2-0	13	N'Zogbia 2 [22, 23]	44,415
9		23	H	Bolton W	D	1-1	0-0	15	Rodallega [59]	17,100
10		30	A	Fulham	L	0-2	0-2	17		25,448
11	Nov	6	A	Blackburn R	L	1-2	0-0	18	N'Zogbia [74]	24,413
12		10	H	Liverpool	D	1-1	0-1	—	Rodallega [52]	16,754
13		13	H	WBA	W	1-0	0-0	17	Moses [70]	16,085
14		20	A	Manchester U	L	0-2	0-1	18		74,181
15		27	A	West Ham U	L	1-3	0-1	18	Cleverley [86]	34,178
16	Dec	4	H	Stoke C	D	2-2	2-2	18	Collins (og) [30], Delap (og) [40]	15,100
17		11	A	Everton	D	0-0	0-0	18		32,853
18		26	A	Wolverhampton W	W	2-1	2-0	16	Rodallega [9], Cleverley [20]	26,901
19		29	H	Arsenal	D	2-2	1-2	—	Watson (pen) [18], Squillaci (og) [81]	17,014
20	Jan	2	H	Newcastle U	L	0-1	0-1	17		15,277
21		5	A	Bolton W	D	1-1	0-0	19	Stam [80]	18,852
22		15	H	Fulham	D	1-1	0-0	18	Rodallega [57]	18,820
23		22	A	Arsenal	L	0-3	0-1	18		59,552
24		25	H	Aston Villa	L	1-2	0-0	—	McCarthy [80]	16,442
25	Feb	1	A	WBA	D	2-2	2-1	—	N'Zogbia [20], Watson [43]	25,358
26		5	H	Blackburn R	W	4-3	1-1	18	McCarthy 2 [35, 56], Rodallega [50], Watson (pen) [65]	18,567
27		12	A	Liverpool	D	1-1	0-1	18	Gohouri [65]	44,609
28		26	H	Manchester U	L	0-4	0-1	20		18,140
29	Mar	5	A	Manchester C	L	0-1	0-1	20		44,864
30		19	H	Birmingham C	W	2-1	1-1	20	Cleverley [25], Figueroa [90]	16,421
31	Apr	2	H	Tottenham H	D	0-0	0-0	20		18,578
32		9	A	Chelsea	L	0-1	0-0	20		40,734
33		16	A	Blackpool	W	3-1	2-0	17	Rodallega [3], N'Zogbia [45], Eardley (og) [67]	16,030
34		23	A	Sunderland	L	2-4	0-0	18	Diame [52], Di Santo [90]	39,650
35		30	H	Everton	D	1-1	1-0	18	N'Zogbia [21]	17,051
36	May	7	A	Aston Villa	D	1-1	1-1	19	N'Zogbia [10]	36,293
37		15	H	West Ham U	W	3-2	0-2	19	N'Zogbia 2 [57, 90], Sammon [68]	22,043
38		22	A	Stoke C	W	1-0	0-0	16	Rodallega [78]	27,566

Final League Position: 16

GOALSCORERS

League (40): N'Zogbia 9, Rodallega 9, Cleverley 3, McCarthy 3, Watson 3 (2 pens), Alcaraz 1, Di Santo 1, Diame 1, Figueroa 1, Gohouri 1, Gomez 1, Moses 1, Sammon 1, Stam 1, own goals 4.
Carling Cup (7): Gomez 2, Boselli 1, Moses 1, N'Zogbia 1, Watson 1 (pen), own goal 1.
FA Cup (3): Diame 2, McManaman 1.

Kirkland C 4	Boyce E 20 + 2	Figueroa M 32 + 1	Diame M 30 + 6	Gohouri S 26 + 1	Alcaraz A 34	McCarthy J 24	Watson B 23 + 6	Boselii M 5 + 3	Rodallega H 34 + 2	Moses V 8 + 13	Thomas H 22 + 2	Stam R 17 + 8	McArthur J 3 + 15	N'Zogbia C 32 + 2	Al-Habsi A 34	Gomez J 9 + 4	Di Santo F 9 + 16	Cleverley T 19 + 6	Caldwell S 8 + 2	Caldwell G 23	McManaman C — + 3	Pollitt M — + 1	Piscu 1	Sammon C 1 + 6	Match No.
1	2¹	3	4²	5	6	7	8	9	10	11³	12	13	14												1
1	14	3³	4²	5	6	7¹	12	9	10		8	2	13	11											2
	11	3	4	5	6	7		9¹	10		8	2²	13		1	12									3
	11	3	4	5	6	7		9³	10		8²	2¹		12	1		13	14							4
	2¹	3	4³	5	6	7	13		10	14	8	12		11²	1		9								5
	2	3	4²	5	6	7	13		10	14	8	11¹		9	1		12³								6
	2	3¹	13	5	6	7	14		10		4²	12	11	1		8	9³								7
	2	3	14		6	7		12		4	8²	11³	1	10	9¹	13	5								8
1	2²	3	12		6	7¹		10		4	13	11		8³	9	14	5								9
		3	4²		6			10	13	8	2		7	1	12	9¹	11	5							10
		3	4²	2	6		12	10		8	7¹	11	1	9	13		5								11
		3	4		6		10²	8	2	11	1	9¹	13	7	5										12
		4	5	3		10³	13	8	2	11	1	9²	14	7	12	6¹									13
		3	4	2	6⁸		10⁸	12	8	7³	14	11²	1	9¹	13	5									14
		3	4	5	14	12	13	8³	2	11	1	10¹	9²	7	6										15
		3¹	4	2	6	8	9	10	12	7	1	11	5												16
		3	4	2	6	8	10	11²	12	13	9	1	7¹	5											17
			4	2	6	8	10	3	7	9	1	11	5												18
	13	4¹	2	6	8	10	7	3²	12	9⁴	1	11	5												19
		4	3	6	8	13	10	7¹	2³	12	1	9²	11	5	14										20
1⁰			3	12	4	6	8	10	7	2⁸	9	11¹	5	13	15										21
	11	4	3	6	8²	10	7	2¹	12	9	1	13	5												22
14	3	4²	2	8	10	11	7¹	13	9³	1	12	6	5⁹												23
5¹	3	2	8³	12	10	4²	13	7	11	1	9	6	14												24
2	3²	4	6	7¹	8	10	9¹	13	11³	1	14	12	5												25
2	3	4	5	6	7²	8	10	9¹	13	11³	1	14	12												26
	3	4	2	6	7	8²	10	9¹	13	11	1	12	5												27
	3	4	2	6	7	8²	10	9¹	14	11³	1	13	12	5											28
	3	4³	13	6	7	8	10	0¹	12	1	11	5	2²	14											29
2	3	14	6	4	8	13	10¹	11³	1	9²	7	5	12												30
2	3	14	6	4	8	10³	9¹	11²	1	13	7	5	12												31
2	3	4³	6	11	8	10²	14	9¹	1	13	7	5	12												32
2	4²	3	6	7	8	10	9¹	1	13	11	5	12													33
2²	4	3	6	7¹	8	10	12	13	9³	1	14	11	5												34
2	3	4¹	6	7	8	10	13	12	9²	1	14	11³	5												35
2	3		6	4	8	10	9²	13	11¹	1	12	7	5												36
2	3	4	6	7¹	8	9³	12	14	10	1	11²	5	13												37
2	3	4	6	7	8	10²	14	11³	1	13	12	5	9¹												38

FA Cup

Third Round	Hull C	(a)	3-2
Fourth Round	Bolton W	(a)	0-0
		(h)	0-1

Carling Cup

Second Round	Hartlepool U	(a)	3-0
Third Round	Preston NE	(h)	2-1
Fourth Round	Swansea C	(h)	2-0
Quarter-Final	Arsenal	(a)	0-2

WOLVERHAMPTON WANDERERS   FA Premiership

FOUNDATION

Enthusiasts of the game at St Luke's School, Blakenhall formed a club in 1877. In the same neighbourhood a cricket club called Blakenhall Wanderers had a football section. Several St Luke's footballers played cricket for them and shortly before the start of the 1879–80 season the two amalgamated and Wolverhampton Wanderers FC was brought into being.

Molineux Stadium, Waterloo Road, Wolverhampton WV1 4QR.

Telephone: (0871) 222 2220.

Fax: (01902) 687 006.

Ticket Office: (0871) 222 1877.

Website: wolves.co.uk

Email: info@wolves.co.uk

Ground Capacity: 28,565.

Record Attendance: 61,315 v Liverpool, FA Cup 5th rd, 11 February 1939.

Pitch Measurements: 110yd × 75yd.

Chairman: Steve Morgan OBE.

Chief Executive: Jez Moxey.

Secretary: Richard Skirrow.

Manager: Mick McCarthy.

Assistant Manager: Terry Connor.

Physio: Alan Peauchamp.

Colours: Gold shirts with black trim, black shorts, gold stockings.

Change Colours: All black with gold trim.

Year Formed: 1877* (*see Foundation*).

Turned Professional: 1888.

Ltd Co.: 1923 (but current club is WWFC (1986) Ltd).

HONOURS

Football League – Division 1: *Champions* 1953–54, 1957–58, 1958–59; *Runners-up* 1937–38, 1938–39, 1949–50, 1954–55, 1959–60; **Division 2:** *Champions* 1931–32, 1976–77; *Runners-up* 1966–67, 1982–83; **FL C:** *Champions* 2008–09; **Division 3 (N):** *Champions* 1923–24; **Division 3:** *Champions* 1988–89; **Division 4:** *Champions* 1987–88.

FA Cup: *Winners* 1893, 1908, 1949, 1960; *Runners-up* 1889, 1896, 1921, 1939.

Football League Cup: *Winners* 1974, 1980.

Texaco Cup: *Winners* 1971.

Sherpa Van Trophy: *Winners* 1988.

European Competitions
European Cup: 1958–59, 1959–60. **European Cup-Winners' Cup:** 1960–61. **UEFA Cup:** 1971–72 (*runners-up*), 1973–74, 1974–75, 1980–81.

Previous Names: 1879, St Luke's combined with Wanderers Cricket Club to become Wolverhampton Wanderers (1923) Ltd. New limited companies followed in 1982 and 1986 (current).

Club Nickname: 'Wolves'.

Grounds: 1877, Windmill Field; 1879, John Harper's Field; 1881, Dudley Road; 1889, Molineux.

First Football League Game: 8 September 1888, Football League, v Aston Villa (h) D 1–1 – Baynton; Baugh, Mason; Fletcher, Allen, Lowder; Hunter, Cooper, Anderson, White, Cannon, (1 og).

Record League Victory: 10–1 v Leicester C, Division 1, 15 April 1938 – Sidlow; Morris, Dowen; Galley, Cullis, Gardiner; Maguire (1), Horace Wright, Westcott (4), Jones (1), Dorsett (4).

sky SPORTS FACT FILE

On 4 March 1939 Wolverhampton Wanderers defeated Everton 2-0 in a sixth round FA Cup tie at Molineux with goals by Dennis Westcott. As a lad he had trained evenings at Everton but found the two shillings (10p) fare too much and – unbeknown to the club – quit for that reason.

Record Cup Victory: 14–0 v Crosswell's Brewery, FA Cup 2nd rd, 13 November 1886 – Ike Griffiths; Baugh, Mason; Pearson, Allen (1), Lowder; Hunter (4), Knight (2), Brodie (4), Bernie Griffiths (2), Wood. Plus one goal 'scrambled through'.

Record Defeat: 1–10 v Newton Heath, Division 1, 15 October 1892.

Most League Points (2 for a win): 64, Division 1, 1957–58.

Most League Points (3 for a win): 92, Division 3, 1988–89.

Most League Goals: 115, Division 2, 1931–32.

Highest League Scorer in Season: Dennis Westcott, 38, Division 1, 1946–47.

Most League Goals in Total Aggregate: Steve Bull, 250, 1986–99.

Most League Goals in One Match: 5, Joe Butcher v Accrington, Division 1, 19 November 1892; 5, Tom Phillipson v Barnsley, Division 2, 26 April 1926; 5, Tom Phillipson v Bradford C, Division 2, 25 December 1926; 5, Billy Hartill v Notts Co, Division 2, 12 October 1929; 5, Billy Hartill v Aston Villa, Division 1, 3 September 1934.

Most Capped Player: Billy Wright, 105, England (70 consecutive).

Most League Appearances: Derek Parkin, 501, 1967–82.

Youngest League Player: Jimmy Mullen, 16 years 43 days v Leeds U, 18 February 1939.

Record Transfer Fee Received: £6,000,000 from Coventry C for Robbie Keane, August 1999.

Record Transfer Fee Paid: £6,500,000 to Reading for Kevin Doyle, June 2009; £6,500,000 to Burnley for Steven Fletcher, June 2010.

MANAGERS

George Worrall 1877–85
(Secretary-Manager)
John Addenbrooke 1885–1922
George Jobey 1922–24
Albert Hoskins 1924–26
(had been Secretary since 1922)
Fred Scotchbrook 1926–27
Major Frank Buckley 1927–44
Ted Vizard 1944–48
Stan Cullis 1948–64
Andy Beattie 1964–65
Ronnie Allen 1966–68
Bill McGarry 1968–76
Sammy Chung 1976–78
John Barnwell 1978–81
Ian Greaves 1982
Graham Hawkins 1982–84
Tommy Docherty 1984–85
Bill McGarry 1985
Sammy Chapman 1985–86
Brian Little 1986
Graham Turner 1986–94
Graham Taylor 1994–95
Mark McGhee 1995–98
Colin Lee 1998–2000
Dave Jones 2001–04
Glenn Hoddle 2004–06
Mick McCarthy July 2006–

Football League Record: 1888 Founder Member of Football League: 1906–23 Division 2; 1923–24 Division 3 (N); 1924–32 Division 2; 1932–65 Division 1; 1965–67 Division 2; 1967–76 Division 1; 1976–77 Division 2; 1977–82 Division 1; 1982–83 Division 2; 1983–84 Division 1; 1984–85 Division 2; 1985–86 Division 3; 1986–88 Division 4; 1988–89 Division 3; 1989–92 Division 2; 1992–2003 Division 1; 2003–04 FA Premier League; 2004–09 FL C; 2009– FA Premier League.

LATEST SEQUENCES

Longest Sequence of League Wins: 8, 15.10.1988 – 26.11.1988.
Longest Sequence of League Defeats: 8, 5.12.1981 – 13.2.1982.
Longest Sequence of League Draws: 6, 22.4.1995 – 20.8.1995.
Longest Sequence of Unbeaten League Matches: 21, 15.1.2005 – 13.8.2005.
Longest Sequence Without a League Win: 19, 1.12.1984 – 6.4.1985.
Successive Scoring Runs: 41 from 20.12.1958.
Successive Non-scoring Runs: 7 from 2.2.1985.

TEN YEAR LEAGUE RECORD

		P	W	D	L	F	A	Pts	Pos
2001-02	Div 1	46	25	11	10	76	43	86	3
2002-03	Div 1	46	20	16	10	81	44	76	5
2003-04	PR Lge	38	7	12	19	38	77	33	20
2004-05	FL C	46	15	21	10	72	59	66	9
2005-06	FL C	46	16	19	11	50	42	67	7
2006-07	FL C	46	22	10	14	59	56	76	5
2007-08	FL C	46	18	16	12	53	48	70	7
2008-09	FL C	46	27	9	10	80	52	90	1
2009-10	PR Lge	38	9	11	18	32	56	38	15
2010-11	PR Lge	38	11	7	20	46	66	40	17

DID YOU KNOW ?

On 5 February 2011 Wolverhampton Wanderers were a goal down in three minutes to Manchester United at Molineux. They drew level in ten minutes, and took the lead five minutes before half-time with the season's 700th Premier League goal inflicting United's first League defeat.

WOLVERHAMPTON WANDERERS 2010–11 LEAGUE RECORD

Match No.	Date	Venue	Opponents	Result	H/T Score	Lg Pos.	Goalscorers	Attendance
1	Aug 14	H	Stoke C	W 2-1	2-0	—	Jones [37], Fletcher [39]	27,850
2	21	A	Everton	D 1-1	0-1	6	Ebanks-Blake [74]	37,767
3	28	H	Newcastle U	D 1-1	1-0	7	Ebanks-Blake [43]	27,745
4	Sept 11	A	Fulham	L 1-2	1-0	9	Van Damme [10]	25,280
5	18	A	Tottenham H	L 1-3	1-0	15	Fletcher [45]	35,940
6	26	H	Aston Villa	L 1-2	0-1	17	Jarvis [61]	27,511
7	Oct 2	A	Wigan Ath	L 0-2	0-0	19		14,042
8	16	H	West Ham U	D 1-1	1-0	18	Jarvis [10]	28,582
9	23	A	Chelsea	L 0-2	0-1	19		41,752
10	30	H	Manchester C	W 2-1	1-1	19	Milijas [30], Edwards [57]	25,971
11	Nov 6	A	Manchester U	L 1-2	0-1	19	Ebanks-Blake [66]	75,285
12	10	A	Arsenal	L 0-2	0-1	—		27,329
13	13	H	Bolton W	L 2-3	0-1	19	Foley [69], Fletcher [77]	27,508
14	20	A	Blackpool	L 1-2	0-2	19	Doyle [86]	15,922
15	27	H	Sunderland	W 3-2	0-0	19	Foley [50], Hunt [81], Ebanks-Blake [89]	25,112
16	Dec 4	A	Blackburn R	L 0-3	0-2	19		22,314
17	12	H	Birmingham C	W 1-0	1-0	16	Hunt [45]	25,150
18	26	H	Wigan Ath	L 1-2	0-2	20	Fletcher [87]	26,901
19	29	A	Liverpool	W 1-0	0-0	—	Ward [56]	41,614
20	Jan 1	A	West Ham U	L 0-2	0-0	20		33,500
21	5	H	Chelsea	W 1-0	1-0	17	Bosingwa (og) [5]	26,432
22	15	A	Manchester C	L 3-4	1-1	19	Milijas [12], Doyle (pen) [68], Zubar [86]	46,672
23	22	H	Liverpool	L 0-3	0-1	19		28,869
24	Feb 2	A	Bolton W	L 0-1	0-0	—		18,944
25	5	H	Manchester U	W 2-1	2-1	19	Elokobi [10], Doyle [40]	28,811
26	12	A	Arsenal	L 0-2	0-1	20		60,050
27	20	A	WBA	D 1-1	1-0	—	O'Hara [39]	26,170
28	26	H	Blackpool	W 4-0	1-0	17	Jarvis [2], O'Hara [54], Ebanks-Blake 2 [78, 90]	29,086
29	Mar 6	A	Tottenham H	D 3-3	2-2	19	Doyle 2 (1 pen) [20, 40 (p)], Fletcher [87]	28,669
30	19	A	Aston Villa	W 1-0	1-0	18	Jarvis [38]	38,965
31	Apr 2	A	Newcastle U	L 1-4	0-2	19	Ebanks-Blake [58]	49,939
32	9	H	Everton	L 0-3	0-3	19		28,352
33	23	H	Fulham	D 1-1	1-0	19	Fletcher [22]	28,825
34	26	A	Stoke C	L 0-3	0-2	—		27,030
35	May 1	A	Birmingham C	D 1-1	1-1	19	Fletcher (pen) [7]	26,072
36	8	H	WBA	W 3-1	2-0	17	Fletcher 2 [15, 47], Guedioura [28]	28,510
37	14	A	Sunderland	W 3-1	1-1	16	Craddock [22], Fletcher [54], Elokobi [78]	41,273
38	22	H	Blackburn R	L 2-3	0-3	17	O'Hara [73], Hunt [87]	29,009

Final League Position: 17

GOALSCORERS

League (46): Fletcher 10 (1 pen), Ebanks-Blake 7, Doyle 5 (2 pens), Jarvis 4, Hunt 3, O'Hara 3, Elokobi 2, Foley 2, Milijas 2, Craddock 1, Edwards 1, Guedioura 1, Jones 1, Van Damme 1, Ward 1, Zubar 1, own goal 1.
Carling Cup (8): Doyle 2, Milijas 2 (2 pens), Elokobi 1, Fletcher 1, Foley 1, Stearman 1.
FA Cup (7): Bia 1, Doyle 1, Fletcher 1, Hunt 1 (pen), Jarvis 1, Jones 1, Milijas 1.

Hahnemann M 14	Foley K 30 + 3	Van Damme J 4 + 2	Jones D 11 + 1	Berra C 31 + 1	Craddock J 14 + 1	Jarvis M 34 + 3	Henry K 28 + 1	Ebanks-Blake S 11 + 19	Fletcher S 15 + 14	Ward S 27 + 7	Keogh A — + 1	Halford G — + 2	Elokobi G 23 + 4	Doyle K 25 + 1	Guedioura A 4 + 6	Stearman R 27 + 4	Zubar R 14 + 1	Mancienne M 13 + 3	Edwards D 12 + 3	Bent M — + 3	Milijas N 20 + 3	Hunt S 14 + 6	Mouyokolo S 2 + 2	Hennessey W 24	Mujangi Bia G — + 1	Hammill A 7 + 3	O'Hara J 13 + 1	Kightly M 1 + 3	Vokes S — + 2	Match No.
1	2	3^3	4	5	6	7	8	9	10^1	11	12^2	13	14																	1
1	2	3^1	4^2	5	6	7	8	9^3	10	11	12	13	14																	2
1	2	3^1	4^2	5	6	7	8	9	10^3	11	12	13	14																	3
1	2	3^1	13	5^4	6	7	8	9^3	12	11	10^2	14						4												4
1	2	12	4	5	6	7^1	8	9	10^2	11		13	14	9		5			3^3		14									5
1	2^2		4	5	6	7	8		10	3^1				12		9		14	13		11^3									6
1	2			5	6	7	8^8	13	10^1	3^2				12		9		4	11^3	14										7
1	2	13	4	5	6^1	7		14	10^2	11				9	12	3		8^3												8
1	2	3^1	4	5		7^3		13	14	11				9^2		6			8		10	12								9
1	2			5		7^3	8			3				12	9	6	13	4			11^2	10^1	14							10
1	2			5			8		12	13				3	9	6	14	4^2			11^3	10^1								11
1	2			5			10		8	13			14	3^3	9	6		7^2	4^1		11	12								12
1	2					7	8		10	12				3	9	6					4	11^1	5							13
1	2^1		4	5		7	8^3	13	14	3				9		6					11	12	10^2							14
	4^1					7	8	13		3				5	9	6	2				10^2	11	12	1						15
	5					7	8		12	3				4	9	6	2				10^2	11	13	1		6^1				16
	5					7			12	11				3	9	6	2	4^1	8			10		1						17
	5					7			12	11				3^2	9	6	2	4^1	8		13	10		1						18
	5					7	8^2		12					3	9	6	2	4	13		11^1	10		1						19
	5					7			13					3^1	9	6	2	4	12	14	11	10^2	8^3	1						20
	5					7	8		12^2					3	9^2	6	2	4	13		11	10^1	14	1						21
	5		4			7^3	8		12					3^2	9	6	2		13		11	10^1		1	14					22
	5					7	8							3	9	6	2	4			11^1	10		1		12				23
	5		4				8		10^2					3	9	6	2					12	7^1	1	14	11^3	13			24
	5						8		10					3	9	6	2	4^3			11^2	13		1	14	12	7^1			25
	5					7	8							3	9^3	6	2	4^1			11	12		1	14		13 / 10^2			26
	5					7^7	8		10^3					3	9	6	2	4^1			11	12		1	14		13			27
	5					7	8		10					3	9	6	2^2	4^3			11^3	12		1	14	12	13			28
2	5					7^1	8		10					3	9	6		4			11^1	12		1			13			29
2	5					7^1	8		10^2	11				3	9	6		4				12		1			13			30
2	5					7	8	9	10	11^2				3^3		6		4^1				12		1	14			13		31
2	5					7^2	8	9^1	10^3	11			14	4		6			13		12			1						32
	5				6	7	8	9^2	10	11^1			14	3		2^3		4	12					1						33
	5				6	7^2	8	9^1	10	11				3^3		2		4	13			12		1	14					34
2	6			5		7	8	9	10^2	11^3			14	3				4^1	13			12		1						35
2	6			5		7^2	8	9	10^3	11			14	3				4^1	13			12		1						36
2	6			5		7^1	8	9^2	10	11				3				4	13			12		1						37
2	6			5^1		7	8^2	9^3	10	11			14	3				4	13			12		1						38

FA Cup

Third Round	Doncaster R	(a)	2-2	
		(h)	5-0	
Fourth Round	Stoke C	(h)	0-1	

Carling Cup

Second Round	Southend U	(h)	2-1	
Third Round	Notts Co	(h)	4-2	
Fourth Round	Manchester U	(a)	2-3	

WYCOMBE WANDERERS FL Championship 1

FOUNDATION

In 1887 a group of young furniture trade workers called a meeting at the Steam Engine public house with the aim of forming a football club and entering junior football. It is thought that they were named after the famous FA Cup winners, The Wanderers who had visited the town in 1877 for a tie with the original High Wycombe club. It is also possible that they played informally before their formation, although there is no proof of this.

Adams Park, Hillbottom Road, Sands, High Wycombe HP12 4HJ.

Telephone: (01494) 472 100. *Fax:* (01494) 527 633.

Ticket Office: (01494) 472 100.

Website: www.wwfc.com

Email: wwfc@wwfc.com

Ground Capacity: 10,000.

Record Attendance: 15,850 v St Albans C, FA Amateur Cup 4th rd, 25 February 1950 (at Loakes Park). 9,921 v Fulham, FA Cup 3rd rd, 9 January 2002 (at Adams Park).

Pitch Measurements: 115yd × 75yd.

Owner: Steve Hayes.

Chairman: Ivor L. Beeks.

Vice-chairman: Brian Kane.

Secretary: Keith Allen.

Manager: Gary Waddock.

Head of Medical and Sports Science: Stuart Ayles.

Colours: Light blue and dark blue quartered shirts, dark blue shorts, light blue stockings.

Change Colours: All black with white trim.

Year Formed: 1887. *Turned Professional:* 1974.

Club Nicknames: 'Chairboys' (after High Wycombe's tradition of furniture making), 'The Blues'.

Grounds: 1887, The Rye; 1893, Spring Meadow; 1895, Loakes Park; 1899, Daws Hill Park; 1901, Loakes Park; 1990, Adams Park.

First Football League Game: 14 August 1993, Division 3 v Carlisle U (a) D 2–2: Hyde; Cousins, Horton (Langford), Kerr, Crossley, Ryan, Carroll, Stapleton, Thompson, Scott, Guppy (1) (Hutchinson), (1 og).

Record League Victory: 5–0 v Burnley, Division 2, 15 April 1997 – Parkin; Cousins, Bell, Kavanagh, McCarthy, Forsyth, Carroll (2p) (Simpson), Scott (Farrell), Stallard (1), McGavin (1) (Read (1)), Brown. 5–0 v Northampton T, Division 2, 4 January 2003 – Talia; Senda, Ryan, Thomson, McCarthy, Johnson, Bulman, Simpson (1), Faulconbridge (Harris), Dixon (1) (Roberts 3), Brown (Currie).

Record Cup Victory: 5–0 v Hitchin T (a), FA Cup 2nd rd, 3 December 1994 – Hyde; Cousins, Brown, Crossley, Evans, Ryan (1), Carroll, Bell (1), Thompson, Garner (3) (Hemmings), Stapleton (Langford).

HONOURS

Football League – Division 2: Best season: 6th, 1994–95.

FA Amateur Cup: *Winners* 1931.

FA Trophy: *Winners* 1991, 1993.

GM Vauxhall Conference: *Winners* 1992–93.

FA Cup: semi-final 2001.

Football League Cup: semi-final 2007.

sky SPORTS FACT FILE

One of the outstanding performances by Wycombe Wanderers in Isthmian League days came in the 1974–75 FA Cup. Having beaten Cheltenham Town and Bournemouth after a replay, they held First Division Middlesbrough to a draw and only lost narrowly away 1-0.

Record Defeat: 0–7 v Shrewsbury T, Johnstone's Paint Trophy, 7 October 2008.

Most League Points (3 for a win): 80, FL 2, 2010-11.

Most League Goals: 72, FL 2, 2005–06.

Highest League Goalscorer in Season: Scott McGleish, 25, 2007–08.

Most League Goals in Total Aggregate: Nathan Tyson, 42, 2004–06.

Most League Goals in One Match: 3, Miquel Desouza v Bradford C, Division 2, 2 September 1995; 3, John Williams v Stockport Co, Division 2, 24 February 1996; 3, Mark Stallard v Walsall, Division 2, 21 October 1997; 3, Sean Devine v Reading, Division 2, 2 October 1999; 3, Sean Divine v Bury, Division 2, 26 February 2000; 3, Stuart Roberts v Northampton T, Division 2, 4 January 2003; 3, Nathan Tyson v Lincoln C, FL 2, 5 March 2005; 3, Nathan Tyson v Kidderminster H, FL 2, 2 April 2005; 3, Nathan Tyson v Stockport Co, FL 2, 10 September 2005; 3, Kevin Betsy v Mansfield T, FL 2, 24 September 2005; 3, Scott McGleish v Mansfield T, FL 2, 8 January 2008; 3, Stuart Roberts v Northampton T, Division 2, 4 January 2003.

Most Capped Player: Mark Rogers, 7, Canada.

Most League Appearances: Steve Brown, 371, 1994–2004.

Youngest League Player: Ikechi Anya, 16 years 279 days v Scunthorpe U, 8 October 2004.

Record Transfer Fee Received: £600,000 from Nottingham F for Nathan Tyson, January 2006.

Record Transfer Fee Paid: £200,000 to Barnet for Sean Devine, 15 April 1999.

Football League Record: 1993 Promoted to Division 3 from GM Vauxhall Conference; 1993–94 Division 3; 1994–2004 Division 2; 2004–09 FL 2; 2009–10 FL 1; 2010–11 FL 2; 2011– FL 1.

MANAGERS

First coach appointed 1951.
Prior to Brian Lee's appointment in 1969 the team was selected by a Match Committee which met every Monday evening.

James McCormack 1951–52
Sid Cann 1952–61
Graham Adams 1961–62
Don Welsh 1962–64
Barry Darvill 1964–68
Brian Lee 1969–76
Ted Powell 1976–77
John Reardon 1977–78
Andy Williams 1978–80
Mike Keen 1980–84
Paul Bence 1984–86
Alan Gane 1986–87
Peter Suddaby 1987–88
Jim Kelman 1988–90
Martin O'Neill 1990–95
Alan Smith 1995–96
John Gregory 1996–98
Neil Smillie 1998–99
Lawrie Sanchez 1999–2003
Tony Adams 2003–04
John Gorman 2004–06
Paul Lambert 2006–08
Peter Taylor 2008–09
Gary Waddock October 2009–

LATEST SEQUENCES

Longest Sequence of League Wins: 6, 19.8.2006 – 16.9.2006.
Longest Sequence of League Defeats: 6, 18.3.2006 – 17.4.2006.
Longest Sequence of League Draws: 5, 24.1.2004 – 21.2.2004.
Longest Sequence of Unbeaten League Matches: 21, 6.8.2005 – 10.12.2005.
Longest Sequence Without a League Win: 13, 16.8.2003 – 18.10.2003 and 10.1.2004 – 20.3.2004.
Successive Scoring Runs: 15 from 28.12.2004.
Successive Non-scoring Runs: 5 from 15.10.1996.

TEN YEAR LEAGUE RECORD

		P	W	D	L	F	A	Pts	Pos
2001-02	Div 2	46	17	13	16	58	64	64	11
2002-03	Div 2	46	13	13	20	59	66	52	18
2003-04	Div 2	46	6	19	21	50	75	37	24
2004-05	FL 2	46	17	14	15	58	52	65	10
2005-06	FL 2	46	18	17	11	72	56	71	6
2006-07	FL 2	46	16	14	16	52	47	62	12
2007-08	FL 2	46	22	12	12	56	42	78	7
2008-09	FL 2	46	20	18	8	54	33	78	3
2009-10	FL 1	46	10	15	21	56	76	45	22
2010-11	FL 2	46	22	14	10	69	50	80	3

DID YOU KNOW ?

During World War II Wycombe Wanderers successfully managed to keep playing in the Great Western Combination. On Boxing Day 1939 they also won the Berks and Bucks Emergency Senior Cup beating Wycombe Redfords 4-0 before a crowd of 5,000 at Loakes Park.

WYCOMBE WANDERERS 2010–11 LEAGUE RECORD

Match No.	Date	Venue	Opponents	Result	H/T Score	Lg Pos.	Goalscorers	Attendance
1	Aug 7	H	Morecambe	W 2-0	1-0	—	Rendell (pen) 36, Pittman 84	4016
2	14	A	Stockport Co	D 0-0	0-0	3		3837
3	21	H	Oxford U	D 0-0	0-0	7		6983
4	28	A	Northampton T	D 1-1	1-0	8	Sandell 30	4202
5	Sept 4	A	Accrington S	D 1-1	0-0	9	Bloomfield 67	1610
6	11	H	Macclesfield T	L 1-2	0-2	12	Rendell (pen) 65	3789
7	18	A	Aldershot T	D 0-0	0-0	13		3722
8	25	H	Shrewsbury T	D 2-2	0-0	16	Sandell 63, Montrose 90	4208
9	28	H	Barnet	W 4-2	3-0	—	Sandell 2 19, 41, Montrose 24, Bloomfield 85	3518
10	Oct 2	A	Stevenage	W 2-0	2-0	7	Betsy 35, Beavon 45	3384
11	9	A	Burton Alb	W 2-1	0-0	6	Ainsworth 16, Sandell 41	3042
12	16	H	Chesterfield	L 1-2	0-1	6	Strevens 64	5211
13	23	A	Rotherham U	W 4-3	3-2	6	Betsy 9, Bloomfield 18, Strevens 45, Rendell (pen) 84	3651
14	30	H	Lincoln C	D 2-2	2-1	6	Betsy 1, Davies 38	4325
15	Nov 2	A	Gillingham	W 2-0	1-0	—	Ainsworth 23, Betsy 49	4076
16	13	H	Bradford C	W 1-0	0-0	4	Betsy 82	4077
17	20	A	Port Vale	L 1-2	1-1	6	Winfield 16	5587
18	23	H	Torquay U	L 1-3	1-1	—	Beavon 7	2273
19	Dec 11	H	Bury	W 1-0	0-0	6	Rendell 69	3673
20	26	H	Hereford U	W 2-1	1-0	—	Ainsworth 41, Strevens 87	3792
21	Jan 1	A	Cheltenham T	W 2-1	1-1	3	Beavon 44, Ainsworth 58	3326
22	3	H	Gillingham	W 1-0	0-0	3	Winfield 64	4617
23	8	A	Crewe Alex	L 0-3	0-0	3		3727
24	15	A	Lincoln C	W 2-1	2-1	2	Sandell 2 19, 39	2890
25	22	H	Rotherham U	W 1-0	1-0	2	Ainsworth 28	4181
26	Feb 1	H	Cheltenham T	W 2-1	1-0	2	Strevens 28, Ainsworth 54	3409
27	5	H	Port Vale	D 1-1	0-0	2	Donnelly 57	4173
28	12	A	Bradford C	L 0-1	0-0	3		10,897
29	15	A	Southend U	L 2-3	1-0	—	Pittman 31, Rendell (pen) 89	4499
30	19	H	Accrington S	L 1-2	0-1	4	Rendell 52	3747
31	22	H	Burton Alb	W 4-1	3-0	—	Lewis 2 10, 40, Montrose 30, Rendell (pen) 63	3345
32	26	A	Macclesfield T	W 1-0	1-0	2	Ainsworth 39	1622
33	Mar 1	A	Chesterfield	L 1-4	0-2	—	Pittman 81	6392
34	5	H	Aldershot T	D 2-2	1-1	3	Foster 44, Betsy 48	4421
35	8	A	Barnet	W 1-0	1-0	—	Westwood 45	1520
36	12	H	Stevenage	L 0-1	0-0	3		4453
37	19	A	Shrewsbury T	D 1-1	0-1	3	Ainsworth 50	5886
38	26	A	Morecambe	W 3-0	3-0	—	Rendell 2 (1 pen) 35 (p), 45, Ainsworth 37	1940
39	Apr 2	H	Stockport Co	W 2-0	2-0	2	Montrose 10, Rendell (pen) 41	6836
40	5	A	Hereford U	D 0-0	0-0	—		1633
41	9	A	Oxford U	D 2-2	0-1	2	Rendell 63, Pittman 66	9309
42	16	H	Northampton T	D 2-2	0-2	3	Donnelly 51, Johnson 82	5161
43	22	A	Torquay U	D 0-0	0-0	—		4009
44	25	H	Crewe Alex	W 2-0	2-0	3	Rendell 2 (1 pen) 42, 45 (p)	4615
45	30	A	Bury	W 3-1	1-1	3	Ainsworth 20, Strevens 2 63, 88	6238
46	May 7	H	Southend U	W 3-1	2-1	3	Donnelly 20, Strevens 26, Rendell 53	8567

Final League Position: 3

GOALSCORERS

League (69): Rendell 14 (8 pens), Ainsworth 10, Sandell 7, Strevens 7, Betsy 6, Montrose 4, Pittman 4, Beavon 3, Bloomfield 3, Donnelly 3, Lewis 2, Winfield 2, Davies 1, Foster 1, Johnson 1, Westwood 1.
Carling Cup (1): Strevens 1.
FA Cup (5): Beavon 2, Rendell 2, Ainsworth 1.
J Paint Trophy (5): Rendell 3, Betsy 1, Davies 1.

Bull N 46	Foster D 37 + 1	Westwood C 24 + 3	Bennett A 16 + 1	Winfield D 34 + 3	Montrose L 27 + 9	Ainsworth G 39 + 4	Bloomfield M 30 + 4	Rendell S 24 + 13	Strevens B 36 + 4	Betsy K 41 + 4	Pittman J 6 + 13	Phillips M 1 + 2	Murtagh K 1 + 6	Sandell A 30 + 2	Johnson L 22 + 1	Beavon S 30 + 7	Davies S 5 + 3	McClure M — + 8	Federico J — + 1	Parker J — + 1	Lewis S 24 + 1	McCoy M 18 + 3	Donnelly S 11 + 7	Straker A 2 + 2	Kiernan R 2	Scowen J — + 2	Match No.
1	2	3	4	5	6^1	7	8^3	9^2	10	11	12	13	14														1
1	2		4		6^3	7	8^1	9^2	10	11	12	13	14	3	5												2
1	2		4^1	5	6^2	13	8	14	10	11		9^3	7	3	12												3
1	2			5	4	7^1	8	9^2	10	11	12			13	3	6											4
1	2			5	6	7	8	9^1	10^2	11	12			3	4	13											5
1	2		4	5	13	12	8^1	9	10^3	11			4^2	3	6	14	7										6
1	2		4	5	6	7	10	12	9^1	11				3		8											7
1	2		4	5	6	7^2	10		11					3		12	8^1	13									8
1	2	5	4		6	7^1	8	12	10^3	11				3		9^2	13	14									9
1	2	5	4	14	6	7^1	8	13	10^3	11				3		9^2	12										10
1	2	5	4		6	7^1	8		10	11				3		9	12										11
1	2	5	4		6	7^1	8		10	11				3		9	12										12
1	2^3	5	4	14	6	7^2	8^1	13	10	11				3		9	12										13
1	2	5	4^1	12	6	7			10	11				3		9	8^2	13									14
1	2	4		5	6	7^1		12	10	11				3		9	8										15
1	2	4		5	6	7	8	12	10^1	11				3		9											16
1	2	4		5	6	7	8		10	11				3		9											17
1	2^1	4		5	6^3	7	8	12	10^2	11				3		9			13	14							18
1		2	5	13		7^1	8	9^2	12	11				3	6	10					4						19
1		2	5			7	8		10	11				3	6	9					4						20
1		2	5	13		7^1	0	12	10	11				3	6	9^3					4						21
1		2^1	5			8	7	10	11					3	6	9					4	12					22
1		2^1	5	6^2	7^3		10	14	11					3	4	9					8	12	13				23
1		6	5	13	7^4	8		10	11^1					3		9					4	2	12				24
1	12	2		5		7^2	8		10	11				3^1		9					4	6					25
1	3	5	6		12	7^1	8^3		10	11^2						9					4	2	14	13			26
1	3	5			7^1		12	10	11	13				6	9^2					4	2	8					27
1	6^1	12	5		7^2	8	13	10	11					9^1	14					4	2		3				28
1		6	5		13	8^1	11		12	10				$0^?$	9					4	2	7	3				29
1	3		6	5	7		11	10	12					9^1						4	2	8					30
1	6		3	5	8	7^1		11	10	13	9^2					12					4^3	2	14				31
1	3		5^8	8	7^3		11	10	13	9^2						12					4	2		14	6^1		32
1	3	12	5		8^3	7^2	13	11	10	14	9										4	2	14		6^1		33
1	3	5			12	8^2	7^1	10	11	13				6	9^3					4	2	14				34
1	3	5			14	7^1	8	13	10	11				6	9^2	12					4^3	2					35
1	3	6		5	12	7^3	8	13	10	11	14				9^2						4^1	2					36
1	3		5	4	7^3	8^2	10^1	14	11	12				6	9							2	13				37
1	3		5	4	7^1	10		11^3	13		12			6	9							2	8^2		14		38
1	3		5	4	7^1		10^3	11		12	14			6	9							2	8^2		13		39
1	3		5	4	7^1		10^2	11	13		14		12	6	9							2	8^3				40
1	3	14	5	4		10		7	12		11^3	6	9^1								8	2^2	13				41
1	2^3	12	5^1	7^2	14	10		11	9			3	6	13						4		8				42
1	2		5	13	7^1	8^2	9	12	11				3	6							4		10				43
1	2		5		7^1	13	9^3	10	11				3	6		14					4	12	8^2				44
1	2		5	13	7^1	12	9^2	10	11				3	6							4		8				45
1	2		5		7^1		9^2	10	11	13			3	6	12						4		8				46

FA Cup

First Round	Hayes & Yeading U	(a)	2-1
Second Round	Chelmsford C	(h)	3-1
Third Round	Hereford U	(h)	0-1

Carling Cup

First Round	Millwall	(h)	1-2

J Paint Trophy

Second Round	Colchester U	(a)	2-0
Southern Quarter-Final	Bristol R	(h)	3-6

YEOVIL TOWN FL Championship 1

FOUNDATION

One of the prime movers of Yeovil football was Ernest J. Sercombe. His association with the club began in 1895 as a playing member of Yeovil Casuals, of which team he became vice-captain and in his last season 1899–1900, he was chosen to play for Somerset against Devon. Upon the reorganisation of the club, he became secretary of the old Yeovil Town FC and with the amalgamation with Petters United in 1914, he continued to serve until his resignation in 1930.

Huish Park, Lufton Way, Yeovil, Somerset BA22 8YF.

Telephone: (01935) 423 662.

Fax: (01935) 473 956.

Ticket Office: (01935) 847 888.

Website: www.ytfc.net

Email: jcotton@ytfc.net

Ground Capacity: 9,665.

Record Attendance: 16,318 v Sunderland, FA Cup 4th rd, 29 January 1949 (at Huish). 9,527 v Leeds U, FL 1, 25 April 2008 (at Huish Park).

Pitch Measurements: 110m × 69m.

Chairman: John R. Fry.

Chief Executive: Martyn Starnes.

Secretary: Jean Cotton.

Manager: Terry Skiverton.

Assistant Manager: Nathan Jones.

Physio: Simon Baker.

Colours: Green and white hooped shirts with green sleeves and black trim, white shorts, white stockings.

Change Colours: Black shirts with one green sleeve, green shorts, black stockings.

Year Formed: 1895. *Turned Professional:* 1921. *Ltd Co.:* 1923.

Club Nickname: 'Glovers'.

Previous Names: 1895, Yeovil Casuals; 1907, Yeovil Town; 1915, Yeovil & Petters United; 1946, Yeovil Town.

Grounds: 1895, Pen Mill Ground; 1921, Huish; 1990, Huish Park.

First Football League Game: 9 August 2003, Division 3 v Rochdale (a) W 3-1: Weale; Williams (Lindegaard), Crittenden, Lockwood, O'Brien, Pluck (Rodrigues), Gosling (El Kholti), Way, Jackson, Gall (2), Johnson (1).

HONOURS

Football League – FL 2: *Winners* 2004–05.

Conference: *Champions* 2002–03.

FA Cup: 5th rd 1949.

League Cup: never past 2nd rd.

Southern League: *Champions* 1954–55, 1963–64, 1970–71; *Runners-up:* 1923–24, 1931–32, 1934–35, 1969–70, 1972–73.

Southern League Cup: *Winners* 1948–49, 1954–55, 1960–61, 1965–66; *Runners-up:* 1946–47, 1955–56.

Isthmian League: *Winners* 1987–88; *Runners-up:* 1985–86, 1986–87, 1996–97.

AC Delco Cup: *Winners* 1987–88.

Bob Lord Trophy: *Winners* 1989–90.

FA Trophy: *Winners* 2002.

London Combination: *Runners-up* 1930–31, 1932–33.

sky SPORTS FACT FILE

In 1964–65 the official match day programme of Yeovil Town, produced by the Supporters Club, was judged the tenth best in the entire country. Those considered better were all from the First Division of the Football League with the exception of Manchester City and Middlesbrough.

Record League Victory: 6–1 v Oxford U, FL 2, 18 September 2004 – Weale; Rose, O'Brien, Way, Skiverton, Fontaine, Caceres (Tarachulski), Johnson, Jevons (3), Stoicers (2) (Mirza), Terry (Gall 1).

Record Cup Victory: 12–1 v Westbury United, FA Cup 1st qual rd, 1923–24.

Record Defeat: 0–8 v Manchester United, FA Cup 5th rd, 12 February 1949.

Most League Points (3 for a win): 83, FL 2, 2004–05.

Most League Goals: 90, FL 2, 2004–05.

Highest League Goalscorer in Season: Phil Jevons, 27, 2004–05.

Most League Goals in Total Aggregate: Phil Jevons, 42, 2004–06.

Most League Goals in One Match: 3, Phil Jevons v Oxford U, FL 2, 18 September 2004; 3, Phil Jevons v Chester C, FL 2, 30 October 2004; 3, Phil Jevons v Bristol R, FL 2, 12 February 2005; 3, Arron Davies v Chesterfield, FL 1, 4 March 2006.

Most Capped Player: Andrejs Stolcers, 1 (81), Latvia; Arron Davies, 1, Wales.

Most League Appearances: Terry Skiverton, 195, 2003–09.

Record Transfer Fee Received: £1,200,000 from Nottingham F for Arron Davies and Chris Cohen, July 2007.

Record Transfer Fee Paid: £250,000 to Quilmes AC for Pablo Bastianini, August 2005.

Football League Record: 2003 Promoted to Division 3 from Conference; 2003–04 Division 3; 2004–05 FL 2; 2005– FL 1.

LATEST SEQUENCES

Longest Sequence of League Wins: 7, 7.12.2004 – 15.1.2005.

Longest Sequence of League Defeats: 5, 29.10.05 – 6.12.05.

Longest Sequence of Unbeaten League Matches: 7, 7.12.2004 – 15.1.2005.

Longest Sequence Without a League Win: 9, 16.10.2010 – 1.1.2011.

Successive Scoring Runs: 22 from 30.10.2004.

Successive Non-scoring Runs: 3 from 21.1.2006.

MANAGERS

Jack Gregory 1922–28
Tommy Lawes 1928–29
Dave Pratt 1929–33
Louis Page 1933–35
Dave Halliday 1935–38
Billy Kingdon 1938–46
Alec Stock 1946–49
George Patterson 1949–51
Harry Lowe 1951–53
Ike Clarke 1953–57
Norman Dodgin 1957
Jimmy Baldwin 1957–60
Basil Hayward 1960–64
Glyn Davies 1964–65
Joe McDonald 1965–67
Ron Saunders 1967–69
Mike Hughes 1969–72
Cecil Irwin 1972–75
Stan Harland 1975–81
Barry Lloyd 1978–81
Malcolm Allison 1981
Jimmy Giles 1981–83
Trevor Finnigan/Mike Hughes 1983
Steve Coles 1983–84
Ian McFarlane 1984
Gerry Gow 1984–87
Brian Hall 1987–90
Clive Whitehead 1990–91
Steve Rutter 1991–93
Brian Hall 1994–95
Graham Roberts 1995–98
Colin Lippiatt 1998–99
Steve Thompson 1999–2000
Dave Webb 2000
Gary Johnson 2001–05
Steve Thompson 2005–06
Russell Slade 2006–09
Terry Skiverton February 2009–

TEN YEAR LEAGUE RECORD

		P	W	D	L	F	A	Pts	Pos
2001-02	Conf.	42	19	13	10	66	53	70	3
2002-03	Conf.	42	28	11	3	100	37	95	1
2003-04	Div 3	46	23	5	18	70	57	74	8
2004-05	FL 2	46	25	8	13	90	65	83	1
2005-06	FL 1	46	15	11	20	54	62	56	15
2006-07	FL 1	46	23	10	13	55	39	79	5
2007-08	FL 1	46	14	10	22	38	59	52	18
2008-09	FL 1	46	12	15	19	41	66	51	17
2009-10	FL 1	46	13	14	19	55	59	53	15
2010-11	FL 1	46	16	11	19	56	66	59	14

DID YOU KNOW ?

West Country rivalry with Cheltenham Town during the days in the Southern League saw Yeovil Town suffer a 7-3 defeat at Cheltenham during 1957–58. Moreover, it was not until 22 January 1966 that Yeovil gained revenge, winning 8-0 at Huish.

YEOVIL TOWN 2010–11 LEAGUE RECORD

Match No.	Date	Venue	Opponents	Result	H/T Score	Lg Pos.	Goalscorers	Attendance
1	Aug 7	H	Leyton Orient	W 2-1	2-1	—	Bowditch [12], Freeman [45]	4126
2	14	A	Bristol R	L 1-2	0-1	11	Virgo [89]	6438
3	21	H	Hartlepool U	L 0-2	0-1	15		3537
4	28	A	Oldham Ath	D 0-0	0-0	16		4180
5	Sept 4	A	Notts Co	L 0-4	0-3	23		6288
6	11	H	Tranmere R	W 3-1	3-0	14	Bowditch [7], Welsh [11], Huntington [27]	3364
7	18	A	Huddersfield T	L 2-4	2-0	17	Bowditch [9], Huntington [15]	13,479
8	25	H	Exeter C	L 1-3	0-1	20	Williams, S [57]	5886
9	28	H	Southampton	D 1-1	0-0	—	Virgo (pen) [65]	5854
10	Oct 2	A	Walsall	W 1-0	0-0	19	Virgo [70]	3172
11	9	A	Rochdale	W 1-0	0-0	16	Freeman [66]	3150
12	16	H	Sheffield W	L 0-2	0-0	18		5927
13	23	A	Brighton & HA	L 0-2	0-1	20		7253
14	30	H	Swindon T	D 3-3	1-1	22	Williams, G [45], Bowditch 2 [50, 61]	4671
15	Nov 2	A	Milton Keynes D	L 2-3	1-1	—	Bowditch [19], Virgo [75]	7281
16	13	H	Dagenham & R	L 1-3	1-1	23	Williams, A [45]	3586
17	20	A	Charlton Ath	L 2-3	1-2	23	Williams, A [17], Doherty (og) [55]	15,184
18	23	A	Bournemouth	L 0-2	0-2	—		6465
19	Dec 11	A	Colchester U	D 0-0	0-0	24		3748
20	Jan 1	A	Plymouth Arg	D 0-0	0-0	23		9720
21	3	H	Milton Keynes D	W 1-0	1-0	22	Huntington [11]	3508
22	8	H	Brentford	W 2-0	1-0	—	Huntington [32], Williams, A [59]	3688
23	15	A	Swindon T	W 1-0	0-0	21	Bowditch [65]	7950
24	22	H	Rochdale	L 0-1	0-1	22		3711
25	25	A	Sheffield W	D 2-2	1-1	—	Bowditch [15], Huntington [57]	16,618
26	29	A	Brentford	W 2-1	1-1	—	Johnson [22], Wotton [83]	4753
27	Feb 1	H	Plymouth Arg	W 1-0	0-0	17	Williams, A [66]	5208
28	5	H	Charlton Ath	L 0-1	0-0	17		4651
29	12	A	Dagenham & R	L 1-2	1-1	18	Johnson [33]	2119
30	15	H	Peterborough U	L 0-2	0-0	—		3351
31	26	A	Tranmere R	W 1-0	0-0	19	Johnson [77]	8016
32	Mar 1	H	Brighton & HA	L 0-1	0-1	—		3832
33	5	A	Huddersfield T	D 1-1	1-0	19	Williams, A [39]	3620
34	8	A	Southampton	L 0-3	0-1	—		18,623
35	12	H	Walsall	D 1-1	1-1	19	Williams, A [45]	3737
36	19	A	Exeter C	W 3-2	1-2	19	Williams, S [43], Bowditch 2 [58, 64]	5841
37	26	A	Leyton Orient	W 5-1	3-0	—	Macdonald 3 (1 pen) [9, 18, 42 (p)], Welsh [47], Bowditch [88]	4258
38	29	H	Carlisle U	W 1-0	0-0	—	Obika [59]	3331
39	Apr 2	H	Bristol R	L 0-1	0-0	17		6281
40	9	A	Hartlepool U	L 1-3	1-1	17	Obika [10]	2834
41	12	H	Notts Co	W 2-1	1-0	—	Bowditch 2 [32, 57]	3533
42	16	H	Oldham Ath	D 1-1	0-1	17	Welsh [85]	3350
43	23	A	Bournemouth	D 2-2	0-0	—	Virgo (pen) [86], Macdonald [90]	6150
44	25	A	Peterborough U	D 2-2	1-0	17	Wotton (pen) [23], Tutte [87]	6489
45	30	H	Colchester U	W 4-2	3-1	17	Alcock [15], Tutte [22], Bowditch [44], Welsh [64]	3797
46	May 7	A	Carlisle U	W 2-0	1-0	14	Obika [26], Bowditch [69]	6473

Final League Position: 14

GOALSCORERS

League (56): Bowditch 15, Williams, A 6, Huntington 5, Virgo 5 (2 pens), Macdonald 4 (1 pen), Welsh 4, Johnson 3, Obika 3, Freeman 2, Tutte 2, Williams, S 2, Wotton 2 (1 pen), Alcock 1, Williams, G 1, own goal 1.
Carling Cup (0).
FA Cup (3): Williams, A 2, Upson 1.
J Paint Trophy (1): Welsh 1.

Sullivan J 13	Alcock C 19+7	Jones N 7+1	Ayling L 31+6	Huntington P 40	Virgo A 28+5	Williams A 27+10	Kalala J 13+2	Williams S 23+13	Bowditch D 40+1	Freeman L 5+8	Stewart C 1+4	Kiernan R 1+2	Smith N 35+5	Upson E 15+8	Welsh A 31+3	Tudur Jones O 12+2	Stam S 3	Calver C —+6	Macdonald S 26	Williams G 11+1	Henderson S 33	Gibson B —+4	Roberts B —+1	Phillip A —+3	Sproule I 2	Parkes T —+1	Wotton P 23	Ehmer M 26+1	Russell A 2+12	Johnson O 16+1	Tutte A 12+3	German A —+4	Obika J 11	Gritton M —+2	Match No.
1	2	3	4	5	6	7	8	9	10^1	11^2	12	13																							1
1	2	3^3	4	5	6	7	8^8	9	10^2	11^1			14	12	13																				2
1	2	3^2	4	5	6	7		9	10	11^1			14	8^3	13	12																			3
1	2		14	5	6	7^3	8	9^2	10		13	12	3		11^1	4																			4
1	2		7^1	5	6		8	9^2		12			3		11	10	4	13																	5
1	2	13		5	6	7^1	8		10^3	12			3	11^1	8^2			4	9																6
	2	12		5	6	7			10	13			3	14	11^1	8^2		4	9^3		1														7
		14	5	6	7^1				12	10	13		3		11^2	8	2	4^3	9		1														8
		4	5	6	7^3			13	10		12		3		11^1	2		8	9^2		1	14													9
	13	4	5	6	12				9	10			3		11^1	2		8	7^2		1														10
	14	2	5	6	12			9	10^3	13			3		11^2	4		8	7^1		1														11
	12	2	5	6^1	14			9	10^3	13			3		11^2	4		8	7		1														12
		2	5		12	8	9		10^3	11^1			3	6^2	13	4	14		7		1														13
	3	2	5	6	13	8	12	10						11^1	4			7	9^2	16		15													14
1	3	2^3	5	6	13	8		9^1	10^2	12			14	4		7	11																		15
1	3^3		5	6	7	2		9	10^2	13			14	11^1	4		8	12																	16
1	2		5^4	6	7^1	8	9	10					3		4	11					12														17
1	2	13		6^2	7	8		9^3	10				3				12	5	4^1		14	11														18
1	2	4	5^1	6	7	8	14		10^2				3				9			13	11^3	12													19
1			2	5		7	12	9	10				3		11^1		8										4	6							20
1			2	5		7	12^8	9^1	10^2				3		11		13	8									4	6							21
			2	5		7		9	10^1				3	4	11				1	12							8	6							22
			2	5	14	7^1		9	10^2				3	6^3	11		12		1								8	4	13						23
			2	5		7^3		9^1	10				3	6^3	11	14			1								8	4	13	12					24
			2^8	5	12^8	7		13	10^1				3	6^3	11				1								8	4	14	9^2					25
				5		7	8	13	10				3	6^1	11^2				1								4	2	12	9					26
			2	5		7		14	10^3				3	6^1	11				1								8	4	12	9^2	13				27
			2	5	14	10		13					3	6^2	11				1								8	4	12	9^3	7^1				28
			2	5		7		9^2					3	6					1	12							8	4	10	11^1	13				29
			2	5	14	7		9^1					3	6^3					1								8	4	12	10^2	11	13			30
	13		2	5		7^1		9	12				3	6					1								8	4		10	11^2				31
			2	5	13	7^2	9^3						3	6^1					1								8^1	4	6	9	11	14			32
			2	5		7^3	13		10				3	12					1								8^1	4	6	9^3	11	14			33
	13		2		5	7		12	10				3	6			14		1								4	8^2	9^3	11^1					34
			2	5	8			12	10				3	6	11				1								4	9^1	7						35
	2		5	13				9^1	10				3^2		11		6		1								4	12		8		7			36
	2^2		14	5	3	13			10					12	11^3		8		1								6^2	4	13	9^1		7			37
	2^2	14	5	3	13				10					12	11^3		8		1								6	4		9^1		7			38
	2		5	3	12			14	10					11			8		1								6^2	4^3	13	9^1		7			39
	2		5	3		9^1			10^2				6	13			8		1								4	14		11^3		7	12	40
	12		2	5	3				10						11		8		1								6	4		9^1		7		41
	14		2^8	5^1	3				10				12	11	11^3		8		1								6	4		9^2		7		42
	2		5^1	6				14	10				3	9^2			8		1		13						11^1	4		12		7^3		43
	2	3							10^1				5	13	9^2		8		1								6	4		11		7	12	44
	2		5						10				3	9			8		1								6	4		11		7		45
	2^2	14	4		5				10^3				3	6^1	9		8		1								11	13		12		7		46

FA Cup
First Round   Rushden & D   (a)   1-0
Second Round   Hartlepool U   (a)   2-4

Carling Cup
First Round   Crystal Palace   (h)   0-1

J Paint Trophy
First Round   Exeter C   (h)   1-3

ENGLISH LEAGUE PLAYERS DIRECTORY

Players listed represent those with their clubs during the 2010–11 season.

Players are listed alphabetically on pages 561–568.
The number alongside each player corresponds to the team number heading. (Abalimba, Medi 59 = team 59 (Oldham Ath))

ACCRINGTON S (1)

BARNETT, Charlie (M)   **76 6**
H: 5 7   W: 11 07   b.Liverpool 19-9-88
Source: Scholar.

2006–07	Liverpool	0	0		
2007–08	Liverpool	0	0		
2008–09	Tranmere R	29	3		
2009–10	Tranmere R	7	1	**36**	**4**
2010–11	Accrington S	40	2	**40**	**2**

BATESON, Jonathan (D)   **33 0**
H: 6 1   W: 12 04   b.Preston 20-9-89
Source: Scholar.

2008–09	Blackburn R	0	0		
2009–10	Blackburn R	0	0		
2009–10	Bradford C	21	0	**21**	**0**
2010–11	Accrington S	12	0	**12**	**0**

BLACK, Adam (F)   **1 0**
H: 6 1   W: 11 00   b.Liverpool 24-5-92
Source: Scholar.

2009–10	Accrington S	1	0		
2010–11	Accrington S	0	0	**1**	**0**

BOULDING, Rory (F)   **38 2**
H: 6 0   W: 12 02   b.Sheffield 21-7-88
Source: Ilkeston T.

2006–07	Mansfield T	9	0		
2007–08	Mansfield T	11	0	**20**	**0**
2008–09	Bradford C	1	0		
2009–10	Bradford C	2	0	**3**	**0**
2010–11	Accrington S	15	2	**15**	**2**

BURTON, Alan (M)   **1 0**
H: 6 0   W: 11 00   b.Blackpool 22-2-91
Source: Scholar.

2009–10	Accrington S	0	0		
2010–11	Accrington S	1	0	**1**	**0**

CISAK, Aleksander (G)   **21 0**
H: 6 3   W: 14 11   b.Krakow 19-5-89
Source: Scholar. *Honours:* Australia Under-20.

2006–07	Leicester C	0	0		
2007–08	Leicester C	0	0		
2008–09	Leicester C	0	0		
2009–10	Leicester C	0	0		
2010–11	Accrington S	21	0	**21**	**0**

CRANEY, Ian (M)   **154 27**
H: 5 10   W: 12 00   b.Liverpool 21-7-82
Source: Runcorn, Altrincham.

2006–07	Accrington S	18	5		
2006–07	Swansea C	27	0		
2007–08	Swansea C	1	0	**28**	**0**
2007–08	Accrington S	34	7		
2008–09	Accrington S	2	1		
2008–09	Huddersfield T	34	5		
2009–10	Huddersfield T	0	0	**34**	**5**
2009–10	Morecambe	16	2	**16**	**2**
From Fleetwood T.					
2010–11	Accrington S	22	7	**76**	**20**

DUNBAVIN, Ian (G)   **198 0**
H: 6 1   W: 12 10   b.Knowsley 27-5-80
Source: Trainee.

1998–99	Liverpool	0	0		
1999–2000	Liverpool	0	0		
1999–2000	Shrewsbury T	7	0		
2000–01	Shrewsbury T	22	0		
2001–02	Shrewsbury T	34	0		
2002–03	Shrewsbury T	33	0		
2003–04	Shrewsbury T	0	0	**96**	**0**
From Halifax T.					
2006–07	Accrington S	23	0		
2007–08	Accrington S	23	0		
2008–09	Accrington S	4	0		
2009–10	Accrington S	27	0		
2010–11	Accrington S	25	0	**102**	**0**

EDWARDS, Phil (D)   **200 23**
H: 5 8   W: 11 03   b.Bootle 8-11-85
Source: Scholar.

2005–06.	Wigan Ath	0	0		
2006–07	Accrington S	33	1		
2007–08	Accrington S	31	1		
2008–09	Accrington S	46	0		
2009–10	Accrington S	46	8		
2010–11	Accrington S	44	13	**200**	**23**

GORNELL, Terry (F)   **91 20**
H: 5 11   W: 12 04   b.Liverpool 16-12-89
Source: Scholar.

2008–09	Tranmere R	10	1		
2008–09	*Accrington S*	11	4		
2009–10	Tranmere R	27	2		
2010–11	Tranmere R	3	0	**40**	**3**
2010–11	Accrington S	40	13	**51**	**17**

HESSEY, Sean (D)   **267 3**
H: 5 10   W: 12 08   b.Prescot 19-9-78
Source: Liverpool Trainee.

1997–98	Wigan Ath	0	0		
1997–98	Leeds U	0	0		
1997–98	Huddersfield T	1	0		
1998–99	Huddersfield T	10	0	**11**	**0**
1999–2000	Kilmarnock	11	0		
2000–01	Kilmarnock	6	0		
2001–02	Kilmarnock	15	0		
2002–03	Kilmarnock	5	0		
2003–04	Kilmarnock	7	1	**44**	**1**
2003–04	Blackpool	6	0	**6**	**0**
2004–05	Chester C	34	1		
2005–06	Chester C	19	0		
2006–07	Chester C	26	0		
2007–08	Chester C	0	0	**79**	**1**
2007–08	*Macclesfield T*	26	0		
2008–09	Macclesfield T	33	0		
2009–10	Macclesfield T	27	0	**86**	**0**
2010–11	Accrington S	41	1	**41**	**1**

JACOBSON, Joe (D)   **122 4**
H: 5 11   W: 12 06   b.Cardiff 17-11-86
Source: Scholar. *Honours:* Wales Under-21.

2005–06	Cardiff C	1	0		
2006–07	Cardiff C	0	0	**1**	**0**
2006–07	*Accrington S*	6	1		
2006–07	*Bristol R*	11	0		
2007–08	Bristol R	40	1		
2008–09	Bristol R	22	0	**73**	**1**
2009–10	Oldham Ath	15	0		
2010–11	Oldham Ath	1	0	**16**	**0**
2010–11	Accrington S	26	2	**32**	**3**

JOYCE, Luke (M)   **94 4**
H: 5 11   W: 12 03   b.Bolton 9-7-87
Source: Scholar.

2005–06	Wigan Ath	0	0		
2005–06	Carlisle U	0	0		
2006–07	Carlisle U	16	1		
2007–08	Carlisle U	3	1		
2008–09	Carlisle U	7	0	**26**	**2**
2009–10	Accrington S	41	1		
2010–11	Accrington S	27	1	**68**	**2**

LINDFIELD, Craig (F)   **67 6**
H: 6 0   W: 10 05   b.Greasby 7-9-88
Source: Scholar. *Honours:* England Youth.

2006–07	Liverpool	0	0		
2007–08	Liverpool	0	0		
2007–08	*Notts Co*	3	1	**3**	**1**
2007–08	*Chester C*	7	0	**7**	**0**
2008–09	Liverpool	0	0		
2008–09	Bournemouth	3	1	**3**	**1**
2008–09	*Accrington S*	20	2		
2009–10	Liverpool	0	0		
2009–10	Macclesfield T	18	2	**18**	**2**
2010–11	Accrington S	16	0	**36**	**2**

McCONVILLE, Sean (F)   **76 14**
H: 5 11   W: 11 09   b.Burscough 6-3-89
Source: Skelmersdale U.

2008–09	Accrington S	5	0		
2009–10	Accrington S	28	1		
2010–11	Accrington S	43	13	**76**	**14**

MURPHY, Peter (D)   **28 0**
H: 6 0   W: 11 10   b.Liverpool 13-2-90
Source: Scholar.

2007–08	Accrington S	2	0		
2008–09	Accrington S	3	0		
2009–10	Accrington S	10	0		
2010–11	Accrington S	13	0	**28**	**0**

OWENS, Andrew (D)   **3 0**
H: 6 3   W: 13 05   b.Liverpool 15-10-89
Source: Stoke C Schools, Stafford R, Rhyl.

2010–11	Accrington S	3	0	**3**	**0**

PARKINSON, Andy (M)   **356 40**
H: 5 8   W: 10 12   b.Liverpool 27-5-79
Source: Liverpool Trainee.

1996–97	Tranmere R	0	0		
1997–98	Tranmere R	18	1		
1998–99	Tranmere R	29	2		
1999–2000	Tranmere R	37	7		
2000–01	Tranmere R	39	6		
2001–02	Tranmere R	31	2		
2002–03	Tranmere R	10	0	**164**	**18**
2003–04	Sheffield U	7	0	**7**	**0**
2003–04	*Notts Co*	14	3		
2004–05	Grimsby T	45	8		
2005–06	Grimsby T	40	4	**85**	**12**
2006–07	Notts Co	45	5		
2007–08	Notts Co	23	0	**82**	**8**
From Cambridge U, Gateshead.					
2010–11	Accrington S	18	2	**18**	**2**

PROCTER, Andy (M)   **210 27**
H: 6 0   W: 12 04   b.Blackburn 13-3-83
Source: Great Harwood T.

2006–07	Accrington S	43	3		
2007–08	Accrington S	43	10		
2008–09	Accrington S	37	3		
2009–10	Accrington S	44	5		
2010–11	Accrington S	43	6	**210**	**27**

PUTTERILL, Ray (M)   **24 0**
H: 5 8   W: 12 03   b.Liverpool 2-3-89
Source: Scholar.

2007–08	Liverpool	0	0		
2008–09	Liverpool	0	0		
From Halewood T.					
2010–11	Accrington S	24	0	**24**	**0**

RICHARDSON, Leam (D)   **204 2**
H: 5 7   W: 11 04   b.Leeds 19-11-79
Source: Trainee.

1997–98	Blackburn R	0	0		
1998–99	Blackburn R	0	0		
1999–2000	Blackburn R	0	0		
2000–01	Bolton W	12	0		
2001–02	Bolton W	1	0		
2001–02	Notts Co	21	0	**21**	**0**
2002–03	Bolton W	0	0	**13**	**0**
2002–03	*Blackpool*	20	0		
2003–04	Blackpool	28	0		
2004–05	Blackpool	23	0	**71**	**0**
2006–07	Accrington S	38	0		
2007–08	Accrington S	37	1		
2008–09	Accrington S	11	0		
2009–10	Accrington S	2	0		
2010–11	Accrington S	11	1	**99**	**2**

RYAN, James (M)   **133 22**
H: 5 8   W: 11 08   b.Maghull 6-9-88
Source: Scholar. *Honours:* Eire Youth, Under-21.

2006–07	Liverpool	0	0		
2007–08	Liverpool	0	0		
2007–08	*Shrewsbury T*	4	0	**4**	**0**

2008–09	Accrington S	44	10
2009–10	Accrington S	39	3
2010–11	Accrington S	46	9	129	22

SMYTH, Tom (D)   4 0
H: 5 11 W: 12 08 b.Southport 18-3-91
Source: Preston NE.

2009–10	Preston NE	0	0
2010–11	Accrington S	4	0	4	0

TURNER, Chris (M)   60 2
H: 5 10 W: 11 10 b.Burnley 26-8-90
Source: Scholar.

2007–08	Accrington S	1	0
2008–09	Accrington S	22	0
2009–10	Accrington S	24	2
2010–11	Accrington S	13	0	60	2

WINNARD, Dean (D)   89 1
H: 5 9 W: 10 04 b.Wigan 20-8-89

2006–07	Blackburn R	0	0
2007–08	Blackburn R	0	0
2008–09	Blackburn R	0	0
2009–10	Accrington S	44	0
2010–11	Accrington S	45	1	89	1

ALDERSHOT T (2)

BERGQVIST, Doug (D)   1 0
H: 6 0 W: 13 07 b.Stockholm 29-3-93
Source: Scholar.

2010–11	Aldershot T	1	0	1	0

BREIMYR, Henrik (D)   0 0
H: 6 1 W: 12 02 b.Stavanger 20-7-93
Source: Scholar. *Honours:* Norway Youth.

2010–11	Aldershot T	0	0

CHARLES, Anthony (D)   172 11
H: 6 1 W: 12 07 b.Isleworth 11-3-81
Source: Brook House.

1999–2000	Crewe Alex	0	0

From Brookhouse

2000–01	Crewe Alex	0	0

From Hayes, Aldershot T, Farnborough T

2004–05	Barnet	0	0
2005–06	Barnet	40	0
2006–07	Barnet	17	0	57	0
2008–09	Aldershot T	41	2
2009–10	Aldershot T	33	4
2010–11	Aldershot T	41	5	115	11

CLEMENT, Jordan (G)   0 0
H: 6 1 W: 12 00 b.Chertsey 6-12-93
Honours: Frpm Scholar.

2009–10	Aldershot T	0	0
2010–11	Aldershot T	0	0

CONNOLLY, Reece (F)   8 0
H: 6 0 W: 11 09 b.Frimley 22-1-92
Source: Scholar.

2009–10	Aldershot T	3	0
2010–11	Aldershot T	5	0	8	0

FORTUNE, Clayton (D)   115 2
H: 6 3 W: 13 10 b.Forest Gate 10-11-82
Source: Tottenham H Scholar.

2000–01	Bristol C	0	0
2001–02	Bristol C	1	0
2002–03	Bristol C	10	0
2003–04	Bristol C	6	0
2004–05	Bristol C	30	0
2005–06	Bristol C	6	0	53	0
2005–06	*Port Vale*	25	2
2006–07	Leyton Orient	9	0
2006–07	*Port Vale*	13	0	38	2
2007–08	Leyton Orient	1	0	10	0
2008–09	Darlington	7	0	7	0

From Weston-Super-Mare.

2010–11	Aldershot T	7	0	7	0

GRAND, Simon (D)   71 5
H: 6 0 W: 10 03 b.Chorley 23-2-84
Source: Scholar.

2002–03	Rochdale	23	2
2003–04	Rochdale	17	0	40	2
2004–05	Carlisle U	0	0
2005–06	Carlisle U	8	2
2006–07	Carlisle U	4	0	12	2
2006–07	Grimsby T	7	0	7	0
2007–08	Morecambe	6	1	6	1

From Northwich Vic, Fleetwood T.

2010–11	Aldershot T	6	0	6	0

GUTTRIDGE, Luke (M)   328 37
H: 5 6 W: 9 07 b.Barnstaple 27-3-82
Source: Trainee.

1999–2000	Torquay U	1	0
2000–01	Torquay U	0	0	1	0
2000–01	Cambridge U	1	1
2001–02	Cambridge U	29	2
2002–03	Cambridge U	43	3
2003–04	Cambridge U	46	11
2004–05	Cambridge U	17	0	136	17
2004–05	Southend U	5	0
2005–06	Southend U	41	5
2006–07	Southend U	17	0	63	5
2006–07	Leyton Orient	17	1	17	1
2007–08	Colchester U	14	0	14	0
2008–09	Northampton T	25	2
2009–10	Northampton T	31	4	56	6
2010–11	Aldershot T	41	8	41	8

HALLS, John (M)   154 4
H: 6 0 W: 11 11 b.Islington 14-2-82
Source: Scholar. *Honours:* England Youth, Under-20.

2000–01	Arsenal	0	0
2001–02	Arsenal	0	0
2001–02	*Colchester U*	6	0	6	0
2002–03	Arsenal	0	0
2003–04	Arsenal	0	0
2003–04	Stoke C	34	0
2004–05	Stoke C	22	0
2005–06	Stoke C	13	2	69	2
2005–06	Reading	1	1
2006–07	Reading	0	0
2007–08	Reading	1	0
2007–08	*Preston NE*	4	0	4	0
2007–08	*Crystal Palace*	5	0	5	0
2007–08	*Sheffield U*	6	0	6	0
2008–09	Reading	0	0	2	1
2008–09	Brentford	23	0	23	0
2009–10	Aldershot T	16	0
2010–11	Aldershot T	23	1	39	1

HARDING, Ben (M)   148 12
H: 5 10 W: 11 02 b.Carshalton 6-9-84
Source: Scholar.

2001–02	Wimbledon	0	0
2002–03	Wimbledon	0	0
2003–04	Wimbledon	15	0	15	0
2004–05	Milton Keynes D	26	4
2005–06	Milton Keynes D	10	2
2006–07	Milton Keynes D	0	0	36	6
2007–08	Aldershot T	29	3
2009–10	Aldershot T	33	1
2010–11	Aldershot T	35	2	97	6

HERD, Ben (D)   220 4
H: 5 9 W: 10 12 b.Welwyn 21-6-85
Source: Scholar.

2002–03	Watford	0	0
2003–04	Watford	0	0
2004–05	Watford	0	0
2005–06	Shrewsbury T	46	2
2007–08	Shrewsbury T	31	1
2007–08	Shrewsbury T	45	0
2008–09	Shrewsbury T	21	0	143	3
2009–10	Aldershot T	34	0
2010–11	Aldershot T	43	1	77	1

HYLTON, Danny (F)   83 13
H: 6 0 W: 11 13 b.Camden 25-2-89
Source: Youth.

2008–09	Aldershot T	29	5
2009–10	Aldershot T	21	3
2010–11	Aldershot T	33	5	83	13

JAIMEZ-RUIZ, Mikhael (G)   44 0
H: 6 0 W: 12 02 b.Merida 12-7-84
Source: Northwood. *Honours:* Venezuela 1 full cap.

2008–09	Aldershot T	14	0
2009–10	Aldershot T	30	0

From Varacuyanos.

2010–11	Aldershot T	0	0	44	0

JONES, Darren (D)   100 5
H: 6 0 W: 14 12 b.Newport 28-8-83
Source: Scholar. *Honours:* Wales Schools, Youth.

2000–01	Bristol C	0	0
2001–02	Bristol C	2	0
2002–03	Bristol C	0	0

2003–04	Bristol C	0	0	2	0
2003–04	*Cheltenham T*	14	1	14	1

From Forest Green R.

2009–10	Hereford U	41	3	41	3
2010–11	Aldershot T	43	1	43	1

LITTLE, Glen (M)   437 54
H: 6 3 W: 13 00 b.Wimbledon 15-10-75
Source: Trainee.

1994–95	Crystal Palace	0	0
1994–95	Glentoran	14	4
1995–96	Glentoran	22	9
1996–97	Glentoran	6	2	42	15
1996–97	Burnley	9	0
1997–98	Burnley	24	4
1998–99	Burnley	34	5
1999–2000	Burnley	41	3
2000–01	Burnley	34	3
2001–02	Burnley	37	9
2002–03	Burnley	33	5
2002–03	*Reading*	6	1
2003–04	Burnley	34	3	246	32
2003–04	*Bolton W*	4	0	4	0
2004–05	Reading	35	0
2005–06	Reading	35	5
2006–07	Reading	24	0
2007–08	Reading	2	0
2008–09	Portsmouth	5	0
2008–09	*Reading*	8	0	110	6
2009–10	Portsmouth	0	0	5	0
2009–10	Sheffield U	16	0	16	0
2010–11	Aldershot T	14	1	14	1

McGLASHAN, Jermaine (M)   38 1
H: 5 7 W: 10 00 b.Croydon 14-4-88
Source: Ashford T (Middlesex).

2010–11	Aldershot T	38	1	38	1

MEDLEY, Luke (F)   32 3
H: 6 1 W: 13 03 b.Greenwich 21-6-89
Source: Tottenham H Scholar.

2007–08	Bradford C	9	2	9	2
2008–09	Barnet	18	1
2009–10	Barnet	1	0	19	1

On loan from Mansfield T

2010–11	Aldershot T	4	0	4	0

MEKKI, Adam (M)   8 0
H: 5 9 W: 11 00 b.Chester 24-12-91
Source: Scholar.

2009–10	Aldershot T	0	0
2010–11	Aldershot T	8	0	8	0

MORGAN, Marvin (F)   103 26
H: 6 4 W: 12 08 b.Manchester 13-4-83
Source: Wealdstone, Yeading, Woking.

2008–09	Aldershot T	32	6
2009–10	Aldershot T	40	15
2010–11	Aldershot T	19	5	91	26
2010–11	*Dagenham & R*	12	0	12	0

MORRIS, Aaron (D)   23 0
H: 6 1 W: 12 05 b.Cardiff 30-12-89
Source: Scholar. *Honours:* Wales Youth, Under-21.

2008–09	Cardiff C	0	0
2009–10	Cardiff C	1	0	1	0
2010–11	Aldershot T	22	0	22	0

PANTHER, Manny (F)   105 5
H: 6 0 W: 13 07 b.Glasgow 11-5-84

2001–02	St Johnstone	7	0
2002–03	St Johnstone	4	0	11	0
2003–04	Partick T	8	0
2004–05	Partick T	14	2	22	2
2004–05	*Brechin C*	8	1	8	1

From York C.

2008–09	Exeter C	22	2
2009–10	Exeter C	0	0	22	2
2009–10	Morecambe	19	0	19	0
2010–11	Aldershot T	23	0	23	0

RANDALL, Jack (F)   1 0
H: 5 9 W: 11 00 b.Bromley 7-7-92
Source: Crystal Palace Scholar.

2010–11	Aldershot T	1	0	1	0

RODMAN, Alex (F)   39 14
H: 6 2 W: 12 08 b.Sutton Coldfield 15-12-87
Source: Leamington, Grantham T, Lincoln U, Gainsborough T, Tamworth.

2010–11	Tamworth	25	9	25	9
2010–11	Aldershot T	14	5	14	5

SILLS, Tim (F)   87   7
H: 6 1   W: 14 00   b.Romsey 10-9-79
Source: Camberley T, Basingstoke T, Kingstonian, Aldershot T.

2005–06	Oxford U	13	1	13	1
2006–07	Hereford U	36	2	36	2
2009–10	Torquay U	18	2	18	2
2010–11	Stevenage	1	0	1	0
2010–11	Aldershot T	19	2	19	2

SMALL, Wade (M)   228   29
H: 5 8   W: 11 05   b.Croydon 23-2-84
Source: Scholar.

2003–04	Wimbledon	27	1	27	1
2004–05	Milton Keynes D	44	10		
2005–06	Milton Keynes D	28	1	72	11
2006–07	Sheffield W	20	2		
2007–08	Sheffield W	29	4		
2008–09	Sheffield W	19	1		
2008–09	*Blackpool*	5	1	5	1
2009–10	Sheffield W	0	0	68	7
2009–10	Chesterfield	27	4	27	4
2010–11	Aldershot T	29	5	29	5

SPENCER, Damien (F)   278   41
H: 6 1   W: 14 00   b.Ascot 19-9-81
Source: Scholarship.

1999–2000	Bristol C	9	1		
2000–01	Bristol C	4	0		
2000–01	*Exeter C*	6	0	6	0
2001–02	Bristol C	0	0	13	1
2002–03	Cheltenham T	30	6		
2003–04	Cheltenham T	36	9		
2004–05	Cheltenham T	41	8		
2005–06	Cheltenham T	46	3		
2006–07	Cheltenham T	27	3		
2007–08	Cheltenham T	30	3		
2008–09	Cheltenham T	14	3		
2008–09	*Brentford*	5	1	5	1
2009–10	Cheltenham T	0	0	224	35

From Kettering T.

2009–10	*Aldershot T*	12	0		
2010–11	Aldershot T	18	4	30	4

STRAKER, Anthony (D)   111   4
H: 5 9   W: 11 11   b.Ealing 23-9-88
Source: Crystal Palace Scholar.

2008–09	Aldershot T	32	0		
2009–10	Aldershot T	37	2		
2010–11	Aldershot T	38	2	107	4
2010–11	*Wycombe W*	4	0	4	0

VINCENT, Jamie (D)   443   10
H: 5 10   W: 11 08   b.Wimbledon 18-6-75
Source: Trainee.

1993–94	Crystal Palace	0	0		
1994–95	Crystal Palace	0	0		
1994–95	*Bournemouth*	8	0		
1995–96	Crystal Palace	25	0		
1996–97	Crystal Palace	0	0	25	0
1996–97	Bournemouth	29	0		
1997–98	Bournemouth	44	3		
1998–99	Bournemouth	32	2	113	5
1998–99	Huddersfield T	7	0		
1999–2000	Huddersfield T	36	2		
2000–01	Huddersfield T	16	0	59	2
2000–01	Portsmouth	14	0		
2001–02	Portsmouth	34	1		
2002–03	Portsmouth	0	0		
2003–04	Portsmouth	0	0	48	1
2003–04	*Walsall*	12	0		
2003–04	Derby Co	7	1		
2004–05	Derby Co	15	1	22	2
2005–06	Millwall	19	0	19	0
2005–06	Yeovil T	0	0		
2006–07	Swindon T	34	0		
2007–08	Swindon T	32	0		
2008–09	Swindon T	18	0	84	0
2009–10	Walsall	38	0	50	0
2010–11	Aldershot T	23	0	23	0

VINCENTI, Peter (F)   28   7
H: 6 2   W: 11 13   b.St Peter 7-7-86
Source: St Peter.

2007–08	Millwall	0	0		
2010–11	Stevenage	5	1	5	1
2010–11	Aldershot T	23	6	23	6

YOUNG, Jamie (G)   115   0
H: 5 11   W: 13 00   b.Brisbane 25-8-85
Source: Scholar. *Honours:* England Youth, Under-20.

2003–04	Reading	1	0		
2004–05	Reading	0	0		
2005–06	Reading	0	0	1	0
2005–06	*Rushden & D*	20	0	20	0
2006–07	Wycombe W	19	0		
2007–08	Wycombe W	4	0		
2008–09	Wycombe W	15	0		
2009–10	Wycombe W	1	0	39	0
2009–10	Aldershot T	9	0		
2010–11	Aldershot T	46	0	55	0

ARSENAL (3)

AFOBE, Benik (F)   28   5
H: 5 10   W: 11 00   b.Leyton 12-2-93
Source: Scholar. *Honours:* England Youth.

2009–10	Arsenal	0	0		
2010–11	Arsenal	0	0		
2010–11	*Huddersfield T*	28	5	28	5

ALMUNIA, Manuel (G)   244   0
H: 6 3   W: 13 00   b.Pamplona 19-5-77

1996–97	Osasuna B	2	0		
1997–98	Osasuna B	31	0		
1998–99	Osasuna B	13	0	46	0
1999–2000	*Cartagena*	3	0	3	0
2000–01	Sabadell	25	0	25	0
2000–01	Celta Vigo	0	0		
2001–02	Celta Vigo	0	0		
2001–02	Eibar	35	0	35	0
2002–03	Recreativo	2	0	2	0
2003–04	Albacete	24	0	24	0
2004–05	Arsenal	10	0		
2005–06	Arsenal	0	0		
2006–07	Arsenal	1	0		
2007–08	Arsenal	29	0		
2008–09	Arsenal	32	0		
2009–10	Arsenal	29	0		
2010–11	Arsenal	8	0	109	0

ANEKE, Chuks (M)   0   0
b.Newham 3-7-93
Source: Scholar.

2010–11	Arsenal	0	0		

ANGHA, Martin (D)   0   0
b.Switzerland 22-1-94
Source: Zurich.

2010–11	Arsenal	0	0		

ANSAH, Zak (F)   0   0
b. 4-5-94
Source: Scholar.

2010–11	Arsenal	0	0		

ARSHAVIN, Andrei (F)   317   73
H: 5 8   W: 9 11   b.St Petersburg 29-5-81
Honours: Russia 61 full caps, 16 goals.

1999	Zenit	0	0		
2000	Zenit	10	0		
2001	Zenit	29	4		
2002	Zenit	30	4		
2003	Zenit	27	5		
2004	Zenit	28	6		
2005	Zenit	29	9		
2006	Zenit	28	7		
2007	Zenit	30	10		
2008	Zenit	27	6	238	51
2008–09	Arsenal	12	6		
2009–10	Arsenal	30	10		
2010–11	Arsenal	37	6	79	22

BARTLEY, Kyle (D)   35   0
H: 5 11   W: 11 00   b.Stockport 22-5-91
Source: Scholar.

2008–09	Arsenal	0	0		
2009–10	Arsenal	0	0		
2009–10	*Sheffield U*	14	0		
2010–11	Arsenal	0	0		
2010–11	*Sheffield U*	21	0	35	0

BENDTNER, Nicklas (F)   140   33
H: 6 2   W: 13 00   b.Copenhagen 16-1-88
Source: Scholar. *Honours:* Denmark Youth, Under-21, 38 full caps, 12 goals.

2005–06	Arsenal	0	0		
2006–07	Arsenal	0	0		
2006–07	*Birmingham C*	42	11	42	11
2007–08	Arsenal	27	5		
2008–09	Arsenal	31	9		
2009–10	Arsenal	23	6		
2010–11	Arsenal	17	2	98	22

BOATENG, Daniel (D)   0   0
b.London 2-9-92
Source: Scholar.

2010–11	Arsenal	0	0		

BOTHELO, Pedro (D)   102   5
H: 6 2   W: 13 00   b.Salvador 14-12-89
Source: Salamanca.

2007–08	Arsenal	0	0		
2008–09	Arsenal	0	0		
2008–09	*Salamanca*	36	0	36	0
2009–10	Arsenal	0	0		
2009–10	*Celta Vigo*	27	1	27	1
2010–11	Arsenal	0	0		
2010–11	*Cartagena*	39	4	39	4

CHAMAKH, Marouane (F)   259   63
H: 6 1   W: 11 00   b.Tonnens 10-1-84
Honours: Morocco 59 full caps, 16 goals.

2002–03	Bordeaux	10	1		
2003–04	Bordeaux	25	6		
2004–05	Bordeaux	33	10		
2005–06	Bordeaux	29	7		
2006–07	Bordeaux	29	5		
2007–08	Bordeaux	32	4		
2008–09	Bordeaux	34	13		
2009–10	Bordeaux	38	10	230	56
2010–11	Arsenal	29	7	29	7

CLICHY, Gael (D)   187   1
H: 5 9   W: 10 04   b.Toulouse 26-7-85
Source: Cannes. *Honours:* France Under-21, B, 10 full caps.

2003–04	Arsenal	12	0		
2004–05	Arsenal	15	0		
2005–06	Arsenal	7	0		
2006–07	Arsenal	27	0		
2007–08	Arsenal	38	0		
2008–09	Arsenal	31	1		
2009–10	Arsenal	24	0		
2010–11	Arsenal	33	0	187	1

COQUELIN, Francis (M)   0   0
H: 5 10   W: 11 08   b.Laval 13-5-91
Source: Laval.

2008–09	Arsenal	0	0		
2009–10	Arsenal	0	0		
2010–11	Arsenal	0	0		

CRUISE, Tom (D)   3   0
H: 6 1   W: 12 08   b.Camden 9-3-91
Source: Scholar. *Honours:* England Youth.

2008–09	Arsenal	0	0		
2009–10	Arsenal	0	0		
2010–11	Arsenal	0	0		
2010–11	*Carlisle U*	3	0	3	0

DEACON, Roarie (F)   0   0
b.London 12-10-91
Source: Scholar.

2010–11	Arsenal	0	0		

DENILSON (M)   108   6
H: 5 10   W: 10 10   b.Sao Paulo 16-2-88
Honours: Brazil Youth, Under-20.

2005	Sao Paulo	10	0		
2006	Sao Paulo	2	0	12	0
2006–07	Arsenal	10	0		
2007–08	Arsenal	13	0		
2008–09	Arsenal	37	3		
2009–10	Arsenal	20	3		
2010–11	Arsenal	16	0	96	6

DIABY, Abu (M)   118   15
H: 6 2   W: 12 04   b.Paris 11-5-86
Honours: France Youth, Under-21, 15 full caps.

2004–05	Auxerre	5	0		
2005–06	Auxerre	5	1	10	1
2005–06	Arsenal	12	1		
2006–07	Arsenal	12	1		
2007–08	Arsenal	15	1		
2008–09	Arsenal	24	3		
2009–10	Arsenal	29	6		
2010–11	Arsenal	16	2	108	14

DJOUROU, Johan (D) 81 1
H: 6 2 W: 12 05 b.Ivory Coast 18-1-87
Source: Scholar. *Honours:* Switzerland Youth, Under-20, Under-21, 26 full caps, 1 goal.

2004–05	Arsenal	0	0		
2005–06	Arsenal	7	0		
2006–07	Arsenal	21	0		
2007–08	Arsenal	2	0		
2007–08	*Birmingham C*	13	0	13	0
2008–09	Arsenal	15	0		
2009–10	Arsenal	1	0		
2010–11	Arsenal	22	1	68	1

EASTMOND, Craig (D) 10 0
H: 6 0 W: 11 11 b.Wandsworth 9-12-90
Source: Scholar.

2009–10	Arsenal	4	0		
2010–11	Arsenal	0	0	4	0
2010–11	*Millwall*	6	0	6	0

EBECILIO, Kyle (M) 0 0
b. 17-2-94
Source: Feyenoord. *Honours:* Holland Youth.

2010–11	Arsenal	0	0		

EBOUE, Emmanuel (D) 202 9
H: 5 10 W: 11 08 b.Abidjan 4-6-83
Source: Academie JM Guillou. *Honours:* Ivory Coast 64 full caps, 2 goals.

2002–03	Beveren	23	0		
2003–04	Beveren	30	2		
2004–05	Beveren	17	2	70	4
2004–05	Arsenal	1	0		
2005–06	Arsenal	18	0		
2006–07	Arsenal	24	0		
2007–08	Arsenal	23	0		
2008–09	Arsenal	28	3		
2009–10	Arsenal	25	1		
2010–11	Arsenal	13	1	132	5

EDGE, Jamie (M) 0 0
b. 9-9-93
Source: Scholar.

2010–11	Arsenal	0	0		

EMMANUEL-THOMAS, Jay (M) 40 8
H: 5 9 W: 11 05 b.Forest Gate 27-12-90
Source: Scholar. *Honours:* England Youth.

2008–09	Arsenal	0	0		
2009–10	Arsenal	0	0		
2009–10	*Blackpool*	11	1	11	1
2009–10	*Doncaster R*	14	5	14	5
2010–11	Arsenal	1	0	1	0
2010–11	*Cardiff C*	14	2	14	2

FABIANSKI, Lukasz (G) 90 0
H: 6 3 W: 13 01 b.Costrzyn nad Odra 18-4-85
Honours: Poland Under-21, 18 full caps.

2005–06	Legia	30	0		
2006–07	Legia	23	0	53	0
2007–08	Arsenal	3	0		
2008–09	Arsenal	6	0		
2009–10	Arsenal	4	0		
2010–11	Arsenal	14	0	27	0

FABREGAS, Francesc (M) 212 35
H: 5 11 W: 11 01 b.Vilessoc de Mar 4-5-87
Source: Barcelona. *Honours:* Spain Youth, Under-21, 58 full caps, 6 goals.

2003–04	Arsenal	0	0		
2004–05	Arsenal	33	2		
2005–06	Arsenal	35	3		
2006–07	Arsenal	38	2		
2007–08	Arsenal	32	7		
2008–09	Arsenal	22	3		
2009–10	Arsenal	27	15		
2010–11	Arsenal	25	3	212	35

FREEMAN, Luke (F) 14 2
H: 6 0 W: 10 00 b.Dartford 22-3-92
Source: Scholar.

2007–08	Gillingham	1	0	1	0
2008–09	Arsenal	0	0		
2009–10	Arsenal	0	0		
2010–11	Arsenal	0	0		
2010–11	*Yeovil T*	13	2	13	2

FRIMPONG, Emmanuel (M) 0 0
H: 5 11 W: 10 07 b.Ghana 10-1-92
Source: Scholar.

2008–09	Arsenal	0	0		
2009–10	Arsenal	0	0		
2010–11	Arsenal	0	0		

GALINDO, Samuel (M) 0 0
H: 6 3 W: 12 00 b.Santa Cruz 18-4-92
Source: Real America.

2010–11	Arsenal	0	0		

GIBBS, Kieran (M) 25 0
H: 5 10 W: 10 02 b.Lambeth 26-9-89
Source: Scholar. *Honours:* England Youth, Under-21, 2 full caps.

2007–08	Arsenal	0	0		
2007–08	*Norwich C*	7	0	7	0
2008–09	Arsenal	8	0		
2009–10	Arsenal	3	0		
2010–11	Arsenal	7	0	18	0

HAJROVIC, Sead (D) 0 0
b.Brugg 4-6-93
Source: Scholar.

2010–11	Arsenal	0	0		

HENDERSON, Conor (M) 0 0
H: 6 1 W: 11 13 b.Sidcup 8-9-91
Source: Scholar. *Honours:* Eire Youth, Under-21.

2008–09	Arsenal	0	0		
2009–10	Arsenal	0	0		
2010–11	Arsenal	0	0		

HOYTE, Gavin (D) 38 0
H: 5 11 W: 11 00 b.Waltham Forest 6-6-90
Source: Scholar. *Honours:* England Youth, Under-20.

2007–08	Arsenal	0	0		
2008–09	Arsenal	1	0		
2008–09	*Watford*	7	0	7	0
2009–10	Arsenal	0	0		
2009–10	*Brighton & HA*	18	0	18	0
2010–11	Arsenal	0	0	1	0
2010–11	*Lincoln C*	12	0	12	0

JENKINSON, Carl (D) 8 0
H: 6 1 W: 12 02 b.Buckhurst Hill 8-2-92
Source: Scholar.

2010–11	*Charlton Ath*	8	0	8	0
2010–11	Arsenal	0	0		

KOSCIELNY, Laurent (D) 173 11
H: 6 1 W: 11 11 b.Tulle 10-9-85

2004–05	Guingamp	11	0		
2005–06	Guingamp	9	0		
2006–07	Guingamp	21	0	41	0
2007–08	Tours	33	1		
2008–09	Tours	34	5	67	6
2009–10	Lorient	35	3	35	3
2010–11	Arsenal	30	2	30	2

LANSBURY, Henri (M) 77 13
H: 6 0 W: 13 06 b.Enfield 12-10-90
Source: Scholar. *Honours:* England Youth, Under-21.

2007–08	Arsenal	0	0		
2008–09	Arsenal	0	0		
2008–09	*Scunthorpe U*	16	4	16	4
2009–10	Arsenal	1	0		
2009–10	*Watford*	37	5	37	5
2010–11	Arsenal	0	0	1	0
2010–11	*Norwich C*	23	4	23	4

LEHMANN, Jens (G) 482 2
H: 6 4 W: 13 05 b.Essen 10-11-69
Honours: Germany Youth, Under-21, 61 full caps.

1991–92	Schalke	37	0		
1992–93	Schalke	8	0		
1993–94	Schalke	21	0		
1994–95	Schalke	34	1		
1995–96	Schalke	32	0		
1996–97	Schalke	34	0		
1997–98	Schalke	34	1	200	2
1998–99	*AC Milan*	5	0	5	0
1998–99	Borussia Dortmd	13	0		
1999–2000	Borussia Dortmd	31	0		
2000–01	Borussia Dortmd	31	0		
2001–02	Borussia Dortmd	30	0		
2002–03	Borussia Dortmd	24	0	129	0
2003–04	Arsenal	38	0		
2004–05	Arsenal	28	0		
2005–06	Arsenal	38	0		
2006–07	Arsenal	36	0		
2007–08	Arsenal	7	0		
2008–09	Arsenal	0	0		
2010–11	Arsenal	1	0	148	0

MANNONE, Vito (G) 18 0
H: 6 0 W: 11 08 b.Milan 2-3-88
Source: Atalanta.

2005–06	Arsenal	0	0		
2006–07	Arsenal	0	0		
2006–07	*Barnsley*	2	0	2	0
2007–08	Arsenal	0	0		
2008–09	Arsenal	1	0		
2009–10	Arsenal	5	0		
2010–11	Arsenal	0	0	6	0
2010–11	*Hull C*	10	0	10	0

MARTINEZ, Damian (G) 0 0
H: 6 3
Source: Independiente.

2010–11	Arsenal	0	0		

McDERMOTT, Sean (G) 0 0
b.Kristiansand 30-5-93
Source: Scholar. *Honours:* Eire Youth.

2009–10	Arsenal	0	0		
2010–11	Arsenal	0	0		

MIQUEL, Ignasi (D) 0 0
H: 6 4 W: 13 05 b.Barcelona 28-9-92
Source: Scholar.

2009–10	Arsenal	0	0		
2010–11	Arsenal	0	0		

MIYAICHI, Ryo (F) 0 0
H: 6 0 W: 11 02 b.Okazaki 14-12-92
Source: Chukyodai Chuyo High School.
Honours: Japan Youth.

2010–11	Arsenal	0	0		

MONTEIRO, Elton (D) 0 0
b.Switzerland 22-2-94
Source: Scholar.

2010–11	Arsenal	0	0		

MURPHY, Rhys (F) 5 0
H: 6 1 W: 11 13 b.Shoreham 6-11-90
Honours: England Youth.

2007–08	Arsenal	0	0		
2008–09	Arsenal	0	0		
2009–10	Arsenal	0	0		
2009–10	*Brentford*	5	0	5	0
2010–11	Arsenal	0	0		

NASRI, Samir (M) 206 29
H: 5 9 W: 11 11 b.Marseille 26-6-87
Honours: France Youth, Under-21, 22 full caps, 2 goals.

2004–05	Marseille	24	1		
2005–06	Marseille	30	1		
2006–07	Marseille	37	3		
2007–08	Marseille	30	6	121	11
2008–09	Arsenal	29	6		
2009–10	Arsenal	26	2		
2010–11	Arsenal	30	10	85	18

NORDTVEIT, Havard (D) 48 0
H: 6 2 W: 11 09 b.Haugesund 21-6-90
Honours: Norway Youth, Under-21.

2007	Haugesund	9	0	9	0
2007–08	Arsenal	0	0		
2008–09	Arsenal	0	0		
2008–09	*Salamanca*	3	0	3	0
2009	*Lillestrom*	17	0	17	0
2009–10	*Nuremberg*	19	0	19	0
2010–11	Arsenal	0	0		

Transferred to Moenchengladbach December 2010.

OZYAKUP, Oguzhan (M) 0 0
H: 5 10 W: 11 00 b.Zaandam 23-9-92
Source: Scholar.

2009–10	Arsenal	0	0		
2010–11	Arsenal	0	0		

RAMSEY, Aaron (M) 61 6
H: 5 9 W: 10 07 b.Caerphilly 26-12-90
Source: School. *Honours:* Wales Youth, Under-21, 14 full caps, 3 goals.

2006–07	Cardiff C	1	0		
2007–08	Cardiff C	15	1		
2008–09	Arsenal	9	0		
2009–10	Arsenal	18	3		
2010–11	Arsenal	7	1	34	4
2010–11	*Nottingham F*	5	0	5	0
2010–11	*Cardiff C*	6	1	22	2

RANDALL, Mark (M)   38   1
H: 6 0   W: 12 12   b.Milton Keynes 28-9-89
Source: Scholar. *Honours:* England Youth.

2006–07	Arsenal	0	0	
2007–08	Arsenal	1	0	
2007–08	*Burnley*	10	0	10 0
2008–09	Arsenal	1	0	
2009–10	Arsenal	0	0	
2009–10	*Milton Keynes D*	16	0	16 0
2010–11	Arsenal	0	0	2 0
2010–11	*Rotherham U*	10	1	10 1

ROSICKY, Tomas (M)   280   39
H: 5 10   W: 10 10   b.Prague 4-10-80
Honours: Czech Republic Under-21, 80 full caps, 20 goals.

1998–99	Sparta Prague	3	0	
1999–2000	Sparta Prague	24	5	
2000–01	Sparta Prague	14	3	41 8
2000–01	Borussia Dortmund	15	0	
2001–02	Borussia Dortmund	30	5	
2002–03	Borussia Dortmund	30	3	
2003–04	Borussia Dortmund	19	2	
2004–05	Borussia Dortmund	27	4	
2005–06	Borussia Dortmund	25	5	149 19
2006–07	Arsenal	26	3	
2007–08	Arsenal	18	6	
2008–09	Arsenal	0	0	
2009–10	Arsenal	25	3	
2010–11	Arsenal	21	0	90 12

SAGNA, Bakari (D)   219   2
H: 5 10   W: 11 05   b.Sens 14-2-83
Source: Auxerre B. *Honours:* France Under-21, 30 full caps.

2003–04	Auxerre	0	0	
2004–05	Auxerre	26	0	
2005–06	Auxerre	23	0	
2006–07	Auxerre	38	0	87 0
2007–08	Arsenal	29	1	
2008–09	Arsenal	35	0	
2009–10	Arsenal	35	0	
2010–11	Arsenal	33	1	132 2

SHEA, James (G)   0   0
H: 5 11   W: 12 00   b.Islington 16-6-91
Source: Scholar.

2009–10	Arsenal	0	0
2010–11	Arsenal	0	0

SILVA, Wellington (M)   2   0
H: 5 6   W: 10 00   b.Rio de Janeiro 6-1-93
Source: Fluminense.

2010–11	Arsenal	0	0	
2010–11	*Levante*	2	0	2 0

SONG BILLONG, Alexandre (M)   116   6
H: 5 11   W: 12 04   b.Douala 9-9-87
Source: Bastia. *Honours:* France Youth, Cameroon Youth. Cameroon 24 full caps.

2005–06	Arsenal	5	0	
2006–07	Arsenal	2	0	
2006–07	*Charlton Ath*	12	0	12 0
2007–08	Arsenal	9	0	
2008–09	Arsenal	31	1	
2009–10	Arsenal	26	1	
2010–11	Arsenal	31	4	104 6

SQUILLACI, Sebastien (D)   322   22
H: 6 0   W: 11 13   b.Toulon 11-8-80
Honours: France 21 full caps.

1997–98	Toulon	6	0	6 0
1998–99	Monaco	0	0	
1999–2000	Monaco	0	0	
2000–01	Ajaccio	36	2	
2001–02	Ajaccio	33	5	69 7
2002–03	Monaco	34	2	
2003–04	Monaco	27	5	
2004–05	Monaco	28	2	
2005–06	Monaco	26	1	115 10
2006–07	Lyon	28	3	
2007–08	Lyon	34	0	62 3
2008–09	Sevilla	32	0	
2009–10	Sevilla	16	1	48 1
2010–11	Arsenal	22	1	22 1

SUNU, Gilles (F)   18   1
H: 5 11   W: 11 00   b.Chateauroux 30-3-91
Source: Scholar. *Honours:* France Youth.

2007–08	Arsenal	0	0	
2008–09	Arsenal	0	0	
2009–10	Arsenal	0	0	
2009–10	*Derby Co*	9	1	9 1

2010–11	Arsenal	0	0	
2010–11	*Lorient*	9	0	9 0

SZCZESNY, Wojciech (G)   43   0
H: 5 10   W: 11 11   b.Warsaw 18-4-90
Source: Scholar. *Honours:* Poland 4 full caps.

2007–08	Arsenal	0	0	
2008–09	Arsenal	0	0	
2009–10	Arsenal	0	0	
2009–10	*Brentford*	28	0	28 0
2010–11	Arsenal	15	0	15 0

TRAORE, Armand (D)   41   1
H: 6 1   W: 12 12   b.Paris 8-10-89
Source: Monaco. *Honours:* France Youth.

2006–07	Arsenal	0	0	
2007–08	Arsenal	3	0	
2008–09	Arsenal	0	0	
2008–09	*Portsmouth*	19	1	19 1
2009–10	Arsenal	9	0	
2010–11	Arsenal	0	0	12 0
2010–11	*Juventus*	10	0	10 0

VAN PERSIE, Robin (F)   217   80
H: 6 0   W: 11 00   b.Rotterdam 6-8-83
Source: Excelsior. *Honours:* Holland Under-21, 56 full caps, 21 goals.

2001–02	Feyenoord	10	0	
2002–03	Feyenoord	23	8	
2003–04	Feyenoord	28	6	61 14
2004–05	Arsenal	26	5	
2005–06	Arsenal	24	5	
2006–07	Arsenal	22	11	
2007–08	Arsenal	15	7	
2008–09	Arsenal	28	11	
2009–10	Arsenal	16	9	
2010–11	Arsenal	25	18	156 66

VELA, Carlos (F)   101   16
H: 5 9   W: 10 05   b.Cancun 1-3-89
Source: Guadalajara. *Honours:* Mexico Youth, Under-20, 34 full caps, 9 goals.

2005–06	Arsenal	0	0	
2006–07	Arsenal	0	0	
2006–07	*Salamanca*	31	8	31 8
2007–08	*Osasuna*	33	3	33 3
2007–08	Arsenal	0	0	
2008–09	Arsenal	14	1	
2009–10	Arsenal	11	1	
2010–11	Arsenal	4	1	29 3
2010–11	*WBA*	8	2	8 2

VERMAELEN, Thomas (D)   150   16
H: 6 0   W: 11 11   b.Antwerp 14-11-85
Source: Ekeren, Antwerp. *Honours:* Belgium Under-21, 32 full caps, 1 goal.

2003–04	Ajax	1	0	
2004–05	*RKC Waalwijk*	13	2	13 2
2005–06	Ajax	24	3	
2006–07	Ajax	23	0	
2007–08	Ajax	20	0	
2008–09	Ajax	31	4	99 7
2009–10	Arsenal	33	7	
2010–11	Arsenal	5	0	38 7

WALCOTT, Theo (F)   135   22
H: 5 9   W: 11 01   b.Stanmore 16-3-89
Source: Scholar. *Honours:* England Youth, Under-21, B, 17 full caps, 3 goals.

2005–06	Southampton	21	4	21 4
2005–06	Arsenal	0	0	
2006–07	Arsenal	16	0	
2007–08	Arsenal	25	4	
2008–09	Arsenal	22	2	
2009–10	Arsenal	23	3	
2010–11	Arsenal	28	9	114 18

WATT, Sanchez (M)   32   1
H: 5 11   W: 12 00   b.Hackney 14-2-91
Source: Scholar. *Honours:* England Youth.

2008–09	Arsenal	0	0	
2009–10	Arsenal	0	0	
2009–10	*Southend U*	4	0	4 0
2009–10	*Leeds U*	6	0	
2010–11	Arsenal	0	0	
2010–11	*Leeds U*	22	1	28 1

WILSHERE, Jack (M)   51   2
H: 5 7   W: 11 03   b.Stevenage 1-1-92
Source: Scholar. *Honours:* England Youth, Under-21, 5 full caps.

2008–09	Arsenal	1	0	
2009–10	Arsenal	1	0	
2009–10	*Bolton W*	14	1	14 1
2010–11	Arsenal	35	1	37 1

YENNARIS, Nicholas (D)   0   0
b.Leytonstone 23-5-93
Source: Scholar.

2010–11	Arsenal	0	0

Scholars
Bihmoutine Samir; Brislen-Hall George; Bunjaku Alban; Campbell James Andrew; Charles-Cook Reice Jordan; Glasgow Benjamin Luke; Meade Jernade Ronnel; Monakana Jeffrey; Oldfield Spence-Neita Nigel Paul; Rees Joshua David; Roberts Philip James; Smith Steven Robert; Webb Callum Taylor; Wynter Jordan James Cecil

ASTON VILLA (4)

AGBONLAHOR, Gabriel (F)   192   48
H: 5 11   W: 12 05   b.Birmingham 13-10-86
Source: Scholar. *Honours:* England Under-20, Under-21, 3 full caps.

2005–06	Aston Villa	9	1	
2005–06	*Watford*	2	0	2 0
2005–06	*Sheffield W*	8	0	8 0
2006–07	Aston Villa	38	9	
2007–08	Aston Villa	37	11	
2008–09	Aston Villa	36	11	
2009–10	Aston Villa	36	13	
2010–11	Aston Villa	26	3	182 48

ALBRIGHTON, Marc (M)   32   5
H: 6 2   W: 12 06   b.Tamworth 18-11-89
Source: Scholar. *Honours:* England Youth, Under-20, Under-21.

2008–09	Aston Villa	0	0	
2009–10	Aston Villa	3	0	
2010–11	Aston Villa	29	5	32 5

BAKER, Nathan (D)   22   0
H: 6 2   W: 11 11   b.Worcester 23-4-91
Source: Scholar. *Honours:* England Youth, Under-21.

2008–09	Aston Villa	0	0	
2009–10	Aston Villa	0	0	
2009–10	*Lincoln C*	18	0	18 0
2010–11	Aston Villa	4	0	4 0

BANNAN, Barry (D)   49   2
H: 5 10   W: 10 08   b.Glasgow 1-12-89
Source: Scholar. *Honours:* Scotland Under-21, 5 full caps.

2008–09	Aston Villa	0	0	
2008–09	*Derby Co*	10	1	10 1
2009–10	Aston Villa	0	0	
2009–10	*Blackpool*	20	1	20 1
2010–11	Aston Villa	12	0	12 0
2010–11	*Leeds U*	7	0	7 0

BENT, Darren (F)   324   139
H: 5 11   W: 12 07   b.Wandsworth 6-2-84
Source: Scholar. *Honours:* England Youth, Under-21, 10 full caps, 3 goals.

2001–02	Ipswich T	5	1	
2002–03	Ipswich T	35	12	
2003–04	Ipswich T	37	16	
2004–05	Ipswich T	45	20	122 49
2005–06	Charlton Ath	36	18	
2006–07	Charlton Ath	32	13	68 31
2007–08	Tottenham H	27	6	
2008–09	Tottenham H	33	12	
2009–10	Tottenham H	0	0	60 18
2009–10	Sunderland	38	24	
2010–11	Sunderland	20	8	58 32
2010–11	Aston Villa	16	9	16 9

BERRY, Durrell (M)   0   0
b. 27-5-92

2010–11	Aston Villa	0	0

BEYE, Habib (D)   323   11
H: 6 0   W: 12 06   b.Paris 19-10-77
Honours: Senegal 45 full caps, 1 goal.

1997–98	Paris St Germain	0	0	
1998–99	Strasbourg	23	0	
1999–2000	Strasbourg	33	1	
2000–01	Strasbourg	31	3	
2001–02	Strasbourg	20	3	
2002–03	Strasbourg	26	1	
2003–04	Strasbourg	1	0	134 8
2003–04	Marseille	22	0	
2004–05	Marseille	37	1	

Season	Club	Apps	Gls	Tot A	Tot G
2005–06	Marseille	29	1		
2006–07	Marseille	36	0		
2007–08	Marseille	4	0	128	2
2007–08	Newcastle U	29	1		
2008–09	Newcastle U	23	0	52	1
2009–10	Aston Villa	6	0		
2010–11	Aston Villa	3	0	9	0

BRADLEY, Michael (M)   166 27
H: 6 1 W: 12 13 b.Princeton 31-7-87.
Source: Chicago Sockers, IMG Academy.
Honours: USA 55 full caps, 8 goals.

Season	Club	Apps	Gls	Tot A	Tot G
2004	MetroStars	0	0		
2005	MetroStars	30	1	30	1
2005–06	Heerenveen	6	0		
2006–07	Heerenveen	21	0		
2007–08	Heerenveen	30	16	57	16
2008–09	Mgladbach	28	5		
2009–10	Mgladbach	29	2		
2010–11	Mgladbach	19	3	76	10
2010–11	Aston Villa	3	0	3	0

On loan from Moenchengladbach.

BURKE, Graham (F)   0 0
b. 21-9-93
Honours: Eire Youth.

Season	Club	Apps	Gls
2010–11	Aston Villa	0	0

CAREW, John (F)   337 121
H: 6 5 W: 14 11 b.Oslo 5-9-79
Source: Lorenskog. *Honours:* Norway Youth, Under-21, 88 full caps, 23 goals.

Season	Club	Apps	Gls	Tot A	Tot G
1998	Valerenga	18	7		
1999	Valerenga	15	7	33	14
1999	Rosenborg	8	10		
2000	Rosenborg	10	8	18	18
2000–01	Valencia	37	11		
2001–02	Valencia	15	1		
2002–03	Valencia	32	8	84	20
2003–04	Roma	20	8	20	8
2004–05	Besiktas	24	13	24	13
2005–06	Lyon	26	9		
2006–07	Lyon	9	1	35	10
2006–07	Aston Villa	11	3		
2007–08	Aston Villa	32	13		
2008–09	Aston Villa	27	11		
2009–10	Aston Villa	33	10		
2010–11	Aston Villa	10	0	113	37
2010–11	Stoke C	10	1	10	1

CLARK, Ciaran (D)   20 3
H: 6 2 W: 12 00 b.Harrow 26-9-89
Source: Scholar. *Honours:* England Youth, Under-20. Eire 2 full caps.

Season	Club	Apps	Gls	Tot A	Tot G
2008–09	Aston Villa	0	0		
2009–10	Aston Villa	1	0		
2010–11	Aston Villa	19	3	20	3

COLLINS, James M (D)   179 9
H: 6 2 W: 14 05 b.Newport 23-8-83
Source: Scholar. *Honours:* Wales Youth, Under-21, 39 full caps, 2 goals.

Season	Club	Apps	Gls	Tot A	Tot G
2000–01	Cardiff C	3	0		
2001–02	Cardiff C	7	1		
2002–03	Cardiff C	2	0		
2003–04	Cardiff C	20	1		
2004–05	Cardiff C	34	1	66	3
2005–06	West Ham U	14	2		
2006–07	West Ham U	16	0		
2007–08	West Ham U	3	0		
2008–09	West Ham U	18	0		
2009–10	West Ham U	3	0	54	2
2009–10	Aston Villa	27	1		
2010–11	Aston Villa	32	3	59	4

CUELLAR, Carlos (D)   272 12
H: 6 2 W: 13 03 b.Madrid 23-8-81

Season	Club	Apps	Gls	Tot A	Tot G
2000–01	Calahorra	27	0	27	0
2001–02	Numancia	23	1		
2002–03	Numancia	39	3	62	4
2003–04	Osasuna	5	0		
2004–05	Osasuna	14	0		
2005–06	Osasuna	29	1		
2006–07	Osasuna	23	1	71	2
2007–08	Rangers	36	4	36	4
2008–09	Aston Villa	28	0		
2009–10	Aston Villa	36	2		
2010–11	Aston Villa	12	0	76	2

DEENEY, Ellis (D)   0 0
b. 19-10-91

Season	Club	Apps	Gls
2010–11	Aston Villa	0	0

DELFOUNESO, Nathan (F)   35 3
H: 6 1 W: 12 04 b.Birmingham 2-2-91
Source: Scholar. *Honours:* England Youth, Under-21.

Season	Club	Apps	Gls	Tot A	Tot G
2007–08	Aston Villa	0	0		
2008–09	Aston Villa	4	0		
2009–10	Aston Villa	9	1		
2010–11	Aston Villa	11	1	24	2
2010–11	*Burnley*	11	1	11	1

DELPH, Fabian (D)   59 6
H: 5 8 W: 11 00 b.Bradford 21-11-89
Source: Scholar. *Honours:* England Youth, Under-21.

Season	Club	Apps	Gls	Tot A	Tot G
2006–07	Leeds U	1	0		
2007–08	Leeds U	1	0		
2008–09	Leeds U	42	6	44	6
2009–10	Aston Villa	8	0		
2010–11	Aston Villa	7	0	15	0

DEVINE, Daniel (M)   0 0
b.Dublin 8-5-93
Source: Scholar.

Season	Club	Apps	Gls
2009–10	Aston Villa	0	0
2010–11	Aston Villa	0	0

DOWNING, Stewart (M)   251 29
H: 5 11 W: 10 04 b.Middlesbrough 22-7-84
Source: Scholar. *Honours:* England Youth, Under-21, B, 27 full caps.

Season	Club	Apps	Gls	Tot A	Tot G
2001–02	Middlesbrough	3	0		
2002–03	Middlesbrough	2	0		
2003–04	Middlesbrough	20	0		
2003–04	*Sunderland*	7	3	7	3
2004–05	Middlesbrough	35	5		
2005–06	Middlesbrough	12	1		
2006–07	Middlesbrough	34	2		
2007–08	Middlesbrough	38	9		
2008–09	Middlesbrough	37	0	181	17
2009–10	Aston Villa	25	2		
2010–11	Aston Villa	38	7	63	9

DRENNAN, Michael (F)   0 0
b.Kilkenny 1-1-94
Source: Scholar.

Season	Club	Apps	Gls
2010–11	Aston Villa	0	0

DUNNE, Richard (D)   423 11
H: 6 2 W: 15 10 b.Dublin 21-9-79
Source: Trainee. *Honours:* Eire Schools, Youth, Under-21, B, 65 full caps, 7 goals.

Season	Club	Apps	Gls	Tot A	Tot G
1996–97	Everton	7	0		
1997–98	Everton	3	0		
1998–99	Everton	16	0		
1999–2000	Everton	31	0		
2000–01	Everton	3	0	60	0
2000–01	Manchester C	25	0		
2001–02	Manchester C	43	1		
2002–03	Manchester C	25	0		
2003–04	Manchester C	29	0		
2004–05	Manchester C	35	2		
2005–06	Manchester C	32	3		
2006–07	Manchester C	38	1		
2007–08	Manchester C	36	0		
2008–09	Manchester C	31	1		
2009–10	Manchester C	2	0	296	0
2009–10	Aston Villa	35	3		
2010–11	Aston Villa	32	0	67	3

FLANAGAN, Callum (D)   0 0
b. 30-12-91

Season	Club	Apps	Gls
2010–11	Aston Villa	0	0

FORRESTER, Harry (F)   0 0
H: 5 9 W: 11 03 b.Milton Keynes 2-1-91

Season	Club	Apps	Gls
2007–08	Aston Villa	0	0
2008–09	Aston Villa	0	0
2009–10	Aston Villa	0	0
2010–11	Aston Villa	0	0

FRIEDEL, Brad (G)   465 1
H: 6 3 W: 14 00 b.Lakewood 18-5-71
Honours: USA 82 full caps.

Season	Club	Apps	Gls	Tot A	Tot G
1996	Columbus Crew	9	0		
1997	Columbus Crew	29	0	38	0
1997–98	Liverpool	11	0		
1998–99	Liverpool	12	0		
1999–2000	Liverpool	2	0		
2000–01	Liverpool	0	0	25	0
2000–01	Blackburn R	27	0		
2001–02	Blackburn R	36	0		
2002–03	Blackburn R	37	0		
2003–04	Blackburn R	36	1		
2004–05	Blackburn R	38	0		
2005–06	Blackburn R	38	0		
2006–07	Blackburn R	38	0		
2007–08	Blackburn R	38	0	288	1
2008–09	Aston Villa	38	0		
2009–10	Aston Villa	38	0		
2010–11	Aston Villa	38	0	114	0

GARDNER, Gary (M)   0 0
b.Solihull 29-6-92
Source: Scholar. *Honours:* England Youth, Under-20.

Season	Club	Apps	Gls
2009–10	Aston Villa	0	0
2010–11	Aston Villa	0	0

GUZAN, Brad (G)   96 0
H: 6 4 W: 14 11 b.Chicago 9-9-84
Honours: USA 19 full caps.

Season	Club	Apps	Gls	Tot A	Tot G
2005	Chivas USA	24	0		
2006	Chivas USA	13	0		
2007	Chivas USA	27	0		
2008	Chivas USA	15	0	79	0
2008–09	Aston Villa	1	0		
2009–10	Aston Villa	0	0		
2010–11	Aston Villa	0	0	1	0
2010–11	*Hull C*	16	0	16	0

HALFHUID, Arsenio (D)   0 0
H: 6 2 b.Voorburg 9-11-91
Source: Excelsior.

Season	Club	Apps	Gls
2008–09	Aston Villa	0	0
2009–10	Aston Villa	0	0
2010–11	Aston Villa	0	0

HERD, Chris (M)   41 6
H: 5 9 W: 11 04 b.Perth 4-4-89
Source: Scholar.

Season	Club	Apps	Gls	Tot A	Tot G
2007–08	Aston Villa	0	0		
2007–08	*Port Vale*	11	2	11	2
2007–08	*Wycombe W*	4	0	4	0
2008–09	Aston Villa	0	0		
2009–10	Aston Villa	0	0		
2009–10	*Lincoln C*	20	4	20	4
2010–11	Aston Villa	6	0	6	0

HESKEY, Emile (F)   518 116
H: 6 2 W: 13 12 b.Leicester 11-1-78
Source: Trainee. *Honours:* England Youth, Under-21, B, 62 full caps, 7 goals.

Season	Club	Apps	Gls	Tot A	Tot G
1994–95	Leicester C	1	0		
1995–96	Leicester C	30	7		
1996–97	Leicester C	35	10		
1997–98	Leicester C	35	10		
1998–99	Leicester C	30	6		
1999–2000	Leicester C	23	7	154	40
1999–2000	Liverpool	12	3		
2000–01	Liverpool	36	14		
2001–02	Liverpool	35	9		
2002–03	Liverpool	32	6		
2003–04	Liverpool	37	7	150	39
2004–05	Birmingham C	34	10		
2005–06	Birmingham C	34	4	68	14
2006–07	Wigan Ath	34	8		
2007–08	Wigan Ath	28	4		
2008–09	Wigan Ath	20	3	82	15
2008–09	Aston Villa	14	2		
2009–10	Aston Villa	31	3		
2010–11	Aston Villa	19	3	64	8

HOGG, Jonathan (M)   29 1
H: 5 7 W: 10 05 b.Middlesbrough 6-12-88
Source: Scholar.

Season	Club	Apps	Gls	Tot A	Tot G
2007–08	Aston Villa	0	0		
2008–09	Aston Villa	0	0		
2009–10	Aston Villa	0	0		
2009–10	*Darlington*	5	1	5	1
2010–11	Aston Villa	5	0	5	0
2010–11	*Portsmouth*	19	0	19	0

IRELAND, Stephen (F)   150 16
H: 5 8 W: 10 07 b.Cork 22-8-86
Source: Scholar. *Honours:* Eire Youth, Under-21, 6 full caps, 4 goals.

Season	Club	Apps	Gls	Tot A	Tot G
2005–06	Manchester C	24	0		
2006–07	Manchester C	24	1		
2007–08	Manchester C	33	4		
2008–09	Manchester C	35	9		
2009–10	Manchester C	22	2		
2010–11	Manchester C	0	0	138	16
2010–11	Aston Villa	10	0	10	0
2010–11	*Newcastle U*	2	0	2	0

JOHNSON, Daniel (M)   0   0
H: 5 8   W: 10 07   b.Kingston, Jam 8-10-92
Source: Scholar.

2010–11	Aston Villa	0	0

LAMPKIN, Jason (M)   0   0
b. 24-4-92
Honours: England Youth.

2010–11	Aston Villa	0	0

LICHAJ, Eric (D)   36   1
H: 5 11   W: 12 07   b.Chicago 17-11-88
Source: Univ of North Carolina, Chicago Magic. *Honours:* USA 4 full caps.

2007–08	Aston Villa	0	0		
2008–09	Aston Villa	0	0		
2009–10	Aston Villa	0	0		
2009–10	*Lincoln C*	6	0	6	0
2009–10	*Leyton Orient*	9	1	9	1
2010–11	Aston Villa	5	0	5	0
2010–11	*Leeds U*	16	0	16	0

LOWRY, Shane (D)   41   0
H: 6 1   W: 13 01   b.Perth 12-6-89
Source: Scholar. *Honours:* Eire Under-21.

2007–08	Aston Villa	0	0		
2008–09	Aston Villa	0	0		
2009–10	Aston Villa	0	0		
2009–10	*Plymouth Arg*	13	0	13	0
2009–10	*Leeds U*	11	0	11	0
2010–11	Aston Villa	0	0		
2010–11	*Sheffield U*	17	0	17	0

MAKOUN, Jean II (M)   281   26
H: 5 8   W: 10 12   b.Yaounde 29-5-83
Honours: Cameroon 55 full caps, 3 goals.

2001–02	Lille B	20	9		
2002–03	Lille B	13	0	33	9
2002–03	Lille	10	0		
2003–04	Lille	32	1		
2004–05	Lille	33	0		
2005–06	Lille	31	5		
2006–07	Lille	33	1		
2007–08	Lille	26	2	165	9
2008–09	Lyon	35	6		
2009–10	Lyon	28	1		
2010–11	Lyon	13	1	76	8
2010–11	Aston Villa	7	0	7	0

MARSHALL, Andy (G)   390   0
H: 6 3   W: 14 08   b.Bury St Edmunds 14-4-75
Source: Trainee. *Honours:* England Youth, Under-21.

1993–94	Norwich C	0	0		
1994–95	Norwich C	21	0		
1995–96	Norwich C	3	0		
1996–97	Norwich C	7	0		
1996–97	*Bournemouth*	11	0	11	0
1996–97	*Gillingham*	5	0	5	0
1997–98	Norwich C	42	0		
1998–99	Norwich C	37	0		
1999–2000	Norwich C	44	0		
2000–01	Norwich C	41	0	195	0
2001–02	Ipswich T	13	0		
2002–03	Ipswich T	40	0		
2003–04	Ipswich T	0	0	53	0
2003–04	Millwall	16	0		
2004–05	Millwall	22	0		
2005–06	Millwall	29	0	67	0
2006–07	Coventry C	41	0		
2007–08	Coventry C	16	0		
2008–09	Coventry C	2	0	59	0
2009–10	Aston Villa	0	0		
2010–11	Aston Villa	0	0		

OSBOURNE, Isaiah (M)   46   0
H: 6 2   W: 12 07   b.Birmingham 5-11-87
Source: Scholar.

2005–06	Aston Villa	0	0		
2006–07	Aston Villa	11	0		
2007–08	Aston Villa	8	0		
2008–09	Aston Villa	0	0		
2008–09	*Nottingham F*	8	0	8	0
2009–10	Aston Villa	0	0		
2009–10	*Middlesbrough*	9	0	9	0
2010–11	Aston Villa	0	0	19	0
2010–11	*Sheffield W*	10	0	10	0

PARISH, Elliot (G)   9   0
H: 6 2   W: 13 00   b.Towcester 20-5-90
Source: Scholar. *Honours:* England Youth, Under-20.

2008–09	Aston Villa	0	0		
2009–10	Aston Villa	0	0		
2010–11	Aston Villa	0	0		
2010–11	*Lincoln C*	9	0	9	0

PETROV, Stilian (M)   424   61
H: 5 11   W: 11 09   b.Sofia 5-7-79
Source: FC Montana. *Honours:* Bulgaria 101 full caps, 8 goals.

1997–98	CSKA Sofia	10	0		
1998–99	CSKA Sofia	29	3	39	3
1999–2000	Celtic	29	1		
2000–01	Celtic	28	7		
2001–02	Celtic	27	6		
2002–03	Celtic	34	12		
2003–04	Celtic	35	6		
2004–05	Celtic	37	11		
2005–06	Celtic	37	10	227	53
2006–07	Aston Villa	30	2		
2007–08	Aston Villa	28	1		
2008–09	Aston Villa	36	1		
2009–10	Aston Villa	37	0		
2010–11	Aston Villa	27	1	158	5

PIRES, Robert (M)   529   126
H: 6 1   W: 12 09   b.Reims 29-10-73
Honours: France 79 full caps, 14 goals.

1992–93	Metz	2	0		
1993–94	Metz	24	1		
1994–95	Metz	35	9		
1995–96	Metz	38	11		
1996–97	Metz	32	11		
1997–98	Metz	31	11	162	43
1998–99	Marseille	34	6		
1999–2008	Marseille	32	2	66	8
2000–01	Arsenal	33	4		
2001–02	Arsenal	28	9		
2002–03	Arsenal	26	14		
2003–04	Arsenal	36	14		
2004–05	Arsenal	33	14		
2005–06	Arsenal	33	7	189	62
2006–07	Villarreal	11	3		
2007–08	Villarreal	32	3		
2008–09	Villarreal	32	3		
2009–10	Villarreal	28	4	103	13
2010–11	Aston Villa	9	0	9	0

REO-COKER, Nigel (M)   280   18
H: 5 8   W: 12 03   b.Southwark 14-5-84
Source: Scholar. *Honours:* England Youth, Under-20, Under-21.

2001–02	Wimbledon	1	0		
2002–03	Wimbledon	32	2		
2003–04	Wimbledon	25	4	58	6
2003–04	West Ham U	15	2		
2004–05	West Ham U	39	3		
2005–06	West Ham U	31	5		
2006–07	West Ham U	35	1	120	11
2007–08	Aston Villa	36	0		
2008–09	Aston Villa	26	1		
2009–10	Aston Villa	10	0		
2010–11	Aston Villa	30	0	102	1

SALIFOU, Moustapha (M)   67   3
H: 5 11   W: 10 12   b.Lome 1-6-83
Source: Modele de Lome. *Honours:* Togo 51 full caps, 6 goals.

2002–03	Oberhausen	11	1		
2003–04	Oberhausen	6	0		
2004–05	Oberhausen	16	0	33	1
2005–06	Stade Brest	7	0	7	0
2006–07	FC Wil	19	2		
2007–08	FC Wil	4	0	23	2
2007–08	Aston Villa	4	0		
2008–09	Aston Villa	0	0		
2009–10	Aston Villa	0	0		
2010–11	Aston Villa	0	0	4	0

SERRANO, Juan (M)   0   0
b.Spain 17-1-94
Source: Espanyol.

2010–11	Aston Villa	0	0

SIEGRIST, Benjamin (G)   0   0
H: 6 4   W: 13 05   b.Basle 31-1-92
Source: Scholar. *Honours:* Switzerland Youth.

2008–09	Aston Villa	0	0
2009–10	Aston Villa	0	0
2010–11	Aston Villa	0	0

STIEBER, Andras (M)   0   0
b. 8-10-91

2010–11	Aston Villa	0	0

WARNOCK, Stephen (D)   233   10
H: 5 7   W: 11 09   b.Ormskirk 12-12-81
Source: Trainee. *Honours:* England Schools, Youth, 2 full caps.

1998–99	Liverpool	0	0		
1999–2000	Liverpool	0	0		
2000–01	Liverpool	0	0		
2001–02	Liverpool	0	0		
2002–03	Liverpool	0	0		
2002–03	*Bradford C*	12	1	12	1
2003–04	Liverpool	0	0		
2003–04	*Coventry C*	44	3	44	3
2004–05	Liverpool	19	0		
2005–06	Liverpool	20	1		
2006–07	Liverpool	1	0	40	1
2006–07	Blackburn R	13	1		
2007–08	Blackburn R	37	1		
2008–09	Blackburn R	37	3		
2009–10	Blackburn R	1	0	88	5
2009–10	Aston Villa	30	0		
2010–11	Aston Villa	19	0	49	0

WEIMANN, Andreas (F)   19   4
H: 5 9   W: 11 09   b.Vienna 5-8-91
Source: Scholar. *Honours:* Austria Under-21.

2008–09	Aston Villa	0	0		
2009–10	Aston Villa	0	0		
2010–11	Aston Villa	1	0	1	0
2010–11	*Watford*	18	4	18	4

WILLIAMS, Derrick (D)   0   0
b.Germany 17-1-93
Source: Scholar. *Honours:* Eire Youth.

2009–10	Aston Villa	0	0
2010–11	Aston Villa	0	0

YOUNG, Ashley (M)   255   49
H: 5 10   W: 10 03   b.Stevenage 9-7-85
Source: Juniors. *Honours:* England Under-21, 15 full caps, 2 goals.

2002–03	Watford	0	0		
2003–04	Watford	5	3		
2004–05	Watford	34	0		
2005–06	Watford	39	13		
2006–07	Watford	20	3	98	19
2006–07	Aston Villa	13	2		
2007–08	Aston Villa	37	9		
2008–09	Aston Villa	36	7		
2009–10	Aston Villa	37	5		
2010–11	Aston Villa	34	7	157	30

YOUNG, Luke (D)   353   7
H: 6 0   W: 12 04   b.Harlow 19-7-79
Source: Trainee. *Honours:* England Youth, Under-21, 7 full caps.

1997–98	Tottenham H	0	0		
1998–99	Tottenham H	15	0		
1999–2000	Tottenham H	20	0		
2000–01	Tottenham H	23	0	58	0
2001–02	Charlton Ath	34	0		
2002–03	Charlton Ath	32	0		
2003–04	Charlton Ath	24	0		
2004–05	Charlton Ath	36	2		
2005–06	Charlton Ath	32	1		
2006–07	Charlton Ath	29	1	187	4
2007–08	Middlesbrough	35	1	35	1
2008–09	Aston Villa	34	1		
2009–10	Aston Villa	16	0		
2010–11	Aston Villa	23	1	73	2

Scholars
Barrett Calum Alastair; Barton Joshua; Bryan Richard; Caira Reece; Cameron Courtney Lee; Carruthers Samir Badre; Coton Matthew James; Darkin Darious Paul; Jenkins Sebastian Stephen; Nelson-Addy Ebby; Taylor Connor; Ward Charles Patrick

BARNET (5)

ADJEMAN-PAMBOE, Kwame (F)   31   5
H: 5 8   W: 11 00   b.London 24-10-87
Source: St Francis Red Flash, George Patriots.

2009	Vikingit	9	4	9	4
2010	Tampa Bay	21	1	21	1
2010–11	Barnet	1	0	1	0

COLE, Jake (G) 93 0
H: 6 2 W: 13 00 b.Hammersmith 11-9-85
Source: Scholar.

2005–06	QPR	3	0		
2006–07	QPR	3	0		
2007–08	QPR	0	0		
2008–09	QPR	0	0	6	0
2008–09	Barnet	10	0		
2009–10	Barnet	46	0		
2010–11	Barnet	31	0	87	0

COULTON, Tom (G) 1 0
b. 15-11-92
Source: Arsenal.

| 2010–11 | Barnet | 1 | 0 | 1 | 0 |

COX, Sam (D) 14 0
H: 5 7 W: 10 00 b.Edgware 10-10-90
Source: Scholar.

2009–10	Tottenham H	0	0		
2009–10	Cheltenham T	1	0		
2009–10	Torquay U	3	0	3	0
2010–11	Barnet	10	0	10	0

DENNEHY, Darren (D) 34 0
H: 6 3 W: 11 11 b.Tralee 21-9-88
Source: Scholar. *Honours:* Eire Under-21.

2005–06	Everton	0	0		
2006–07	Everton	0	0		
2007–08	Everton	0	0		
2008–09	Cardiff C	0	0		
2008–09	Hereford U	3	0		
2009–10	Cardiff C	0	0		
2009–10	Hereford U	7	0	10	0
2009–10	Gillingham	19	0	19	0
2010–11	Barnet	5	0	5	0

DEVERA, Joe (D) 177 2
H: 6 2 W: 12 00 b.Southgate 6-2-87

2005–06	Barnet	0	0		
2006–07	Barnet	26	0		
2007–08	Barnet	41	0		
2008–09	Barnet	34	1		
2009–10	Barnet	33	0		
2010–11	Barnet	43	1	177	2

DOBSON, Craig (M) 4 0
H: 5 7 W: 10 06 b.Chingford 23-1-84
Source: Crystal Palace scholar. *Honours:* Jamaica 1 full cap.

| 2003–04 | Cheltenham T | 2 | 0 | 2 | 0 |

From Barnet, Camb C, Stevenage.

2007–08	Milton Keynes D	1	0		
2008–09	Milton Keynes D	0	0		
2008–09	Wycombe W	0	0		
2009–10	Milton Keynes D	0	0	1	0
2010–11	Barnet	1	0	1	0

FRASER, Tom (M) 144 3
H: 5 10 W: 11 02 b.Brighton 5-12-87
Source: Bognor Regis T.

2006–07	Brighton & HA	28	1		
2007–08	Brighton & HA	24	0		
2008–09	Brighton & HA	27	1	79	2
2009–10	Port Vale	38	1		
2010–11	Port Vale	12	0	50	1
2010–11	Barnet	15	0	15	0

GALLEN, Kevin (F) 523 132
H: 5 11 W: 13 05 b.Hammersmith 21-9-75
Source: Trainee. *Honours:* England Schools, Youth, Under-21.

1992–93	QPR	0	0		
1993–94	QPR	0	0		
1994–95	QPR	37	10		
1995–96	QPR	30	8		
1996–97	QPR	2	3		
1997–98	QPR	27	3		
1998–99	QPR	44	8		
1999–2000	QPR	31	4		
2000–01	Huddersfield T	38	10	38	10
2001–02	Barnsley	9	2	9	2
2001–02	QPR	25	7		
2002–03	QPR	42	13		
2003–04	QPR	45	17		
2004–05	QPR	46	10		
2005–06	QPR	18	4		
2006–07	QPR	18	3	365	90
2006–07	Plymouth Arg	13	1	13	1
2007–08	Milton Keynes D	24	8		
2008–09	Milton Keynes D	6	1	30	9
2008–09	Luton T	29	3		
2009–10	Luton T	32	16	61	19

On loan from Luton T.

| 2010–11 | Barnet | 7 | 1 | 7 | 1 |

HOLMES, Ricky (F) 25 2
H: 6 2 W: 11 11 b.Southend 19-6-87
Source: Southend U, Chelmsford C.

| 2010–11 | Barnet | 25 | 2 | 25 | 2 |

HUGHES, Mark (M) 217 10
H: 5 10 W: 12 05 b.Dungannon 16-9-83
Source: Scholar. *Honours:* Northern Ireland Schools, Youth, Under-21, Under-23, 2 full caps.

2001–02	Tottenham H	0	0		
2002–03	Tottenham H	0	0		
2003–04	Tottenham H	0	0		
2004–05	Tottenham H	0	0		
2004–05	Northampton T	3	0	3	0
2004–05	Oldham Ath	27	0		
2005–06	Oldham Ath	33	1		
2006–07	Oldham Ath	0	0	60	1

From Thurrock.

| 2006–07 | Chesterfield | 2 | 1 | 2 | 1 |

From Stevenage B.

2007–08	Chester C	43	4		
2008–09	Chester C	26	0	69	4
2008–09	Barnet	9	0		
2009–10	Barnet	41	2		
2010–11	Barnet	33	2	83	4

JARVIS, Rossi (D) 106 3
H: 5 11 W: 11 12 b.Fakenham 11-3-88
Source: Scholar. *Honours:* England Youth.

2005–06	Norwich C	3	0		
2006–07	Norwich C	0	0		
2006–07	Torquay U	4	0	4	0
2006–07	Rotherham U	10	0	10	0
2007–08	Norwich C	4	0	7	0
2008–09	Luton T	35	1		
2009–10	Luton T	28	2	63	3
2010–11	Barnet	22	0	22	0

KABBA, Steven (F) 210 45
H: 5 10 W: 11 03 b.Lambeth 7-3-81
Source: Trainee.

1999–2000	Crystal Palace	1	0		
2000–01	Crystal Palace	1	0		
2001–02	Crystal Palace	4	0		
2001–02	Luton T	3	0	3	0
2002–03	Crystal Palace	4	1	10	1
2002–03	Grimsby T	13	6	13	6
2002–03	Sheffield U	25	7		
2003–04	Sheffield U	1	0		
2004–05	Sheffield U	11	2		
2005–06	Sheffield U	34	9		
2006–07	Sheffield U	7	0	78	18
2006–07	Watford	11	0		
2007–08	Watford	14	1		
2008–09	Watford	0	0	25	1
2008–09	Blackpool	17	2	17	2
2008–09	Oldham Ath	8	0	8	0
2009–10	Brentford	10	0	10	0
2009–10	Burton Alb	23	6	23	6
2010–11	Barnet	23	11	23	11

KAMDJO, Clovis (D) 47 1
H: 5 11 W: 12 02 b.Cameroon 15-12-90
Source: Reading Youth. *Honours:* Cameroon Youth.

| 2009–10 | Barnet | 15 | 0 | | |
| 2010–11 | Barnet | 32 | 1 | 47 | 1 |

KELLY, Danny (F) 3 0
H: 6 1 W: 12 12 b.Huntingdon 18-10-90
Source: Scholar.

| 2009–10 | Norwich C | 0 | 0 | | |
| 2010–11 | Barnet | 3 | 0 | 3 | 0 |

LEACH, Daniel (D) 27 1
H: 6 3 W: 12 10 b.Perth 5-1-86
Source: Queensland Academy, Brisbane Toro, Brisbane Strikers, Oregon State Univ, Portland Timbers.

| 2009–10 | Barnet | 13 | 0 | | |
| 2010–11 | Barnet | 14 | 1 | 27 | 1 |

LOCKHART-ADAMS, Kofi (F) 1 0
H: 6 1 W: 12 13 b.London 9-10-92
Source: Scholar.

| 2009–10 | Barnet | 1 | 0 | | |
| 2010–11 | Barnet | 0 | 0 | 1 | 0 |

MARSHALL, Mark (M) 73 6
H: 5 7 W: 10 07 b.Jamaica 9-5-86
Source: Carshalton Ath, Grays Ath, Eastleigh.

2008–09	Swindon T	12	0		
2009–10	Swindon T	7	0	19	0
2009–10	Hereford U	8	0	8	0
2010–11	Barnet	46	6	46	6

McLEOD, Izale (F) 235 77
H: 6 1 W: 11 02 b.Birmingham 15-10-84
Source: Scholar. *Honours:* England Under-21.

2002–03	Derby Co	29	3		
2003–04	Derby Co	10	1	39	4
2003–04	Sheffield U	7	0	7	0
2004–05	Milton Keynes D	43	16		
2005–06	Milton Keynes D	39	17		
2006–07	Milton Keynes D	34	21	116	54
2007–08	Charlton Ath	18	1		
2007–08	Colchester U	2	0	2	0
2008–09	Charlton Ath	2	0		
2008–09	Millwall	7	2	7	2
2009–10	Charlton Ath	11	2		
2009–10	Peterborough U	4	0	4	0
2010–11	Charlton Ath	31	3		
2010–11	Barnet	29	14	29	14

O'BRIEN, Liam (G) 8 0
H: 6 1 W: 12 06 b.Ruislip 30-11-91
Source: Scholar. *Honours:* England Youth.

2008–09	Portsmouth	0	0		
2009–10	Portsmouth	0	0		
2010–11	Barnet	8	0	8	0

PARKES, Jordan (D) 52 1
H: 6 0 W: 12 00 b.Watford 26-7-89
Source: Scholar. *Honours:* England Youth, Under-20.

2006–07	Watford	0	0		
2007–08	Watford	0	0		
2007–08	Brentford	1	0	1	0
2007–08	Barnet	10	0		
2008–09	Watford	1	0		
2009–10	Watford	0	0	1	0
2010–11	Barnet	40	1	50	1

POOLE, Glenn (M) 87 20
H: 5 7 W: 11 04 b.Barking 3-2-81
Source: Tottenham H Trainee, Yeovil T, Ford U, Thurrock, Grays Ath.

2006–07	Rochdale	6	0	6	0
2007–08	Brentford	45	14		
2008–09	Brentford	26	5	71	19

From Grays Ath.

| 2010–11 | Barnet | 10 | 1 | 10 | 1 |

SOUTHAM, Glen (M) 114 4
H: 5 7 W: 11 10 b.Enfield 27-8-80
Source: Hereford T, Bishop's Stortford, Histon.

2007–08	Dagenham & R	45	2		
2008–09	Dagenham & R	30	1	75	3
2009–10	Hereford U	6	0	6	0
2010–11	Barnet	33	1	33	1

STIMSON, Charlie (F) 6 0
H: 5 11 W: 13 10 b.Newcastle 1-3-92
Source: Scholar.

| 2010–11 | Barnet | 6 | 0 | 6 | 0 |

TAYLOR, Charlie (F) 18 1
H: 6 2 W: 11 13 b.Lewisham 28-12-85
Source: Charlton Ath, Crystal Palace, Nottingham F, Welling U, AFC Hornchurch, Fisher Ath, Margate, Dulwich Hamlet, Grays Ath, Sutton U.

| 2010–11 | Barnet | 18 | 1 | 18 | 1 |

UDDIN, Anwar (D) 113 3
H: 5 11 W: 11 10 b.Whitechapel 1-11-81
Source: West Ham U Scholar.

2001–02	West Ham U	0	0		
2001–02	Sheffield W	0	0		
2002–03	Bristol R	18	1		
2003–04	Bristol R	1	0		
2004–05	Bristol R	0	0		
2005–06	Bristol R	0	0		
2006–07	Bristol R	0	0	19	1
2007–08	Dagenham & R	41	1		
2008–09	Dagenham & R	17	0		
2009–10	Dagenham & R	6	0	64	1
2010–11	Barnet	30	1	30	1

VILHETE, Mauro (M) 22 0
H: 5 8 W: 11 09 b.Sintra 10-5-93
Source: Scholar.

2009–10	Barnet	2	0	
2010–11	Barnet	20	0	22 0

YORKE, Reece (D) 0 0
b.Hillingdon 22-8-92
Source: Wealdstone.

2010–11	Barnet	0	0

BARNSLEY (6)

BENNETT, Steven (F) 4 0
H: 5 11 W: 11 00 b.Barnsley 21-11-91
Source: Scholar.

2010–11	Barnsley	4	0	4 0

BRANSON, Conor (D) 0 0
H: 6 2 W: 11 13 b.Pontefract 14-11-91
Source: Scholar.

2010–11	Barnsley	0	0

BUTTERFIELD, Jacob (D) 66 3
H: 5 10 W: 11 00 b.Bradford 10-6-90
Source: Scholar.

2007–08	Barnsley	3	0	
2008–09	Barnsley	3	0	
2009–10	Barnsley	20	1	
2010–11	Barnsley	40	2	66 3

CLARK, Jordan (F) 4 0
b.Barnsley 22-9-93
Source: Scholar.

2010–11	Barnsley	4	0	4 0

COLACE, Hugo (M) 101 8
H: 5 10 W: 11 07 b.Buenos Aires 6-1-84
Honours: Argentina Youth.

2008–09	Barnsley	34	0	
2009–10	Barnsley	41	7	
2010–11	Barnsley	26	1	101 8

DEVANEY, Martin (M) 368 50
H: 5 11 W: 12 00 b.Cheltenham 1-6-80
Source: Trainee.

1997–98	Coventry C	0	0	
1998–99	Coventry C	0	0	
1999–2000	Cheltenham T	26	6	
2000–01	Cheltenham T	34	10	
2001–02	Cheltenham T	25	1	
2002–03	Cheltenham T	40	6	
2003–04	Cheltenham T	40	5	
2004–05	Cheltenham T	38	10	203 38
2005–06	Watford	0	0	
2005–06	Barnsley	38	6	
2006–07	Barnsley	41	5	
2007–08	Barnsley	34	4	
2008–09	Barnsley	26	0	
2009–10	Barnsley	11	0	
2009–10	*Milton Keynes D*	5	0	5 0
2010–11	Barnsley	6	0	156 15
2010–11	*Walsall*	4	1	4 1

DICKINSON, Liam (F) 179 50
H: 6 4 W: 11 07 b.Salford 4-10-85
Source: Woodley Sports.

2005–06	Stockport Co	21	7	
2006–07	Stockport Co	33	7	
2007–08	Stockport Co	40	19	94 33
2008–09	*Huddersfield T*	13	6	13 6
2008–09	*Blackpool*	7	4	7 4
2008–09	*Leeds U*	8	0	8 0
2008–09	Derby Co	0	0	
2009–10	*Brighton & HA*	27	4	27 4
2009–10	*Peterborough U*	9	3	9 3
2010–11	Barnsley	3	0	3 0
2010–11	*Walsall*	4	0	4 0
2010–11	*Rochdale*	14	0	14 0

DOYLE, Nathan (M) 131 2
H: 5 11 W: 12 06 b.Derby 12-1-87
Source: Scholar. *Honours:* England Youth, Under-20.

2003–04	Derby Co	2	0	
2004–05	Derby Co	3	0	
2005–06	Derby Co	4	0	
2005–06	*Notts Co*	12	0	12 0
2006–07	Derby Co	0	0	9 0
2006–07	*Bradford C*	28	0	28 0
2006–07	Hull C	1	0	
2007–08	Hull C	1	0	
2008–09	Hull C	3	0	
2009–10	Hull C	0	0	5 0
2009–10	Barnsley	34	0	
2010–11	Barnsley	43	2	77 2

FEARNEHOUGH, Danny (M) 0 0
H: 5 10 W: 11 00 b.Liverpool 23-11-91
Source: Scholar.

2010–11	Barnsley	0	0

FOSTER, Stephen (D) 389 22
H: 6 0 W: 11 05 b.Warrington 10-9-80
Source: Trainee. *Honours:* England Schools.

1998–99	Crewe Alex	1	0	
1999–2000	Crewe Alex	0	0	
2000–01	Crewe Alex	30	0	
2001–02	Crewe Alex	34	5	
2002–03	Crewe Alex	35	4	
2003–04	Crewe Alex	45	2	
2004–05	Crewe Alex	34	1	
2005–06	Crewe Alex	39	3	218 15
2006–07	Burnley	17	0	
2007–08	Burnley	0	0	17 0
2007–08	Barnsley	41	1	
2008–09	Barnsley	38	3	
2009–10	Barnsley	42	2	
2010–11	Barnsley	33	1	154 7

GRAY, Andy (F) 435 98
H: 6 1 W: 13 00 b.Harrogate 15-11-77
Source: Trainee. *Honours:* Scotland Youth, B, 2 full caps.

1995–96	Leeds U	15	0	
1996–97	Leeds U	7	0	
1997–98	Leeds U	0	0	
1997–98	*Bury*	6	1	6 1
1998–99	Leeds U	0	0	22 0
1998–99	Nottingham F	8	0	
1998–99	*Preston NE*	5	0	5 0
1998–99	*Oldham Ath*	4	0	4 0
1999–2000	Nottingham F	22	0	
2000–01	Nottingham F	18	0	
2001–02	Nottingham F	16	1	64 1
2002–03	Bradford C	44	15	
2003–04	Bradford C	33	5	77 20
2003–04	Sheffield U	14	9	
2004–05	Sheffield U	43	15	
2005–06	Sheffield U	1	1	58 25
2005–06	Sunderland	21	1	21 1
2005–06	Burnley	9	3	
2006–07	Burnley	35	14	
2007–08	Burnley	25	11	69 28
2007–08	Charlton Ath	16	2	
2008–09	Charlton Ath	27	7	
2009–10	Charlton Ath	2	0	45 9
2009–10	Barnsley	30	6	
2010–11	Barnsley	34	7	64 13

HASSELL, Bobby (D) 387 9
H: 5 10 W: 12 00 b.Derby 4-6-80
Source: Trainee.

1997–98	Mansfield T	9	0	
1998–99	Mansfield T	3	0	
1999–2000	Mansfield T	11	1	
2000–01	Mansfield T	40	1	
2001–02	Mansfield T	43	1	
2002–03	Mansfield T	20	0	
2003–04	Mansfield T	34	0	160 3
2004–05	Barnsley	39	0	
2005–06	Barnsley	28	2	
2006–07	Barnsley	39	2	
2007–08	Barnsley	20	0	
2008–09	Barnsley	40	0	
2009–10	Barnsley	24	1	
2010–11	Barnsley	37	1	227 6

HAYNES, Danny (F) 190 33
H: 5 11 W: 12 04 b.Peckham 19-1-88
Source: Scholar. *Honours:* England Youth.

2005–06	Ipswich T	19	3	
2006–07	Ipswich T	31	7	
2006–07	*Millwall*	5	2	5 2
2007–08	Ipswich T	40	7	
2008–09	Ipswich T	24	0	114 17
2009–10	Bristol C	38	7	
2010–11	Bristol C	13	1	51 8
2010–11	Barnsley	20	6	20 6

HILL, Matt (D) 357 8
H: 5 7 W: 12 06 b.Bristol 26-3-81
Source: Trainee.

1998–99	Bristol C	3	0	
1999–2000	Bristol C	14	0	
2000–01	Bristol C	34	0	
2001–02	Bristol C	40	1	
2002–03	Bristol C	42	3	
2003–04	Bristol C	42	2	
2004–05	Bristol C	23	0	198 6
2004–05	Preston NE	14	0	
2005–06	Preston NE	26	0	
2006–07	Preston NE	38	0	
2007–08	Preston NE	26	0	
2008–09	Preston NE	1	0	105 0
2008–09	Wolverhampton W	13	0	
2009–10	Wolverhampton W	2	0	
2009–10	*QPR*	16	0	16 0
2010–11	Wolverhampton W	0	0	15 0
2010–11	Barnsley	23	2	23 2

LOVRE, Goran (M) 200 31
H: 6 3 W: 12 13 b.Zagreb 23-3-82
Source: Partizan Belgrade. *Honours:* Serbia Under-21.

2001–02	Anderlecht	1	0	
2002–03	Anderlecht	15	2	
2003–04	Anderlecht	10	1	
2004–05	Anderlecht	18	2	
2005–06	Anderlecht	2	0	46 5
2006–07	Groningen	30	8	
2007–08	Groningen	33	9	
2008–09	Groningen	36	5	
2009–10	Groningen	34	2	133 24
2010–11	Barnsley	21	2	21 2

McEVELEY, James (D) 173 7
H: 6 1 W: 13 03 b.Liverpool 11-2-85
Source: Trainee. *Honours:* England Under-20, Under-21. Scotland B, 3 full caps.

2002–03	Blackburn R	9	0	
2003–04	Blackburn R	0	0	
2003–04	*Burnley*	4	0	4 0
2004–05	Blackburn R	5	0	
2004–05	*Gillingham*	10	1	10 1
2005–06	Blackburn R	0	0	
2005–06	*Ipswich T*	19	1	19 1
2006–07	Blackburn R	4	0	18 0
2006–07	Derby Co	15	0	
2007–08	Derby Co	29	2	
2008–09	Derby Co	15	0	
2008–09	*Preston NE*	7	0	7 0
2008–09	*Charlton Ath*	6	0	6 0
2009–10	Derby Co	33	2	92 4
2010–11	Barnsley	17	1	17 1

MILLER, Kern (D) 1 0
H: 5 9 W: 11 03 b.Skegness 2-9-91
Source: Scholar.

2008–09	Lincoln C	1	0	
2009–10	Lincoln C	0	0	
2010–11	Lincoln C	0	0	1 0
2010–11	Barnsley	0	0	

NEWMANN, Jeronimo Morales (F) 5 0
H: 5 8 W: 11 00 b.Godoy Cruz 3-6-86
Source: River Plate, San Lorenzo, Instituto, Estudiantes.

2010–11	Barnsley	5	0	5 0

NOBLE-LAZARUS, Reuben (F) 11 1
H: 5 11 W: 13 07 b.Huddersfield 16-8-93
Source: Youth.

2008–09	Barnsley	2	0	
2009–10	Barnsley	2	0	
2010–11	Barnsley	7	1	11 1

O'BRIEN, Jim (F) 126 6
H: 6 0 W: 11 11 b.Glasgow 28-9-87

2006–07	Celtic	0	0	
2006–07	*Dunfermline Ath*	18	1	18 1
2007–08	Celtic	1	0	1 0
2007–08	*Dundee U*	10	0	10 0
2008–09	Motherwell	29	1	
2009–10	Motherwell	35	3	64 4
2010–11	Barnsley	33	1	33 1

O'CONNOR, Garry (F) 214 61
H: 6 1 W: 12 02 b.Edinburgh 7-5-83
Honours: Scotland Under-21, 16 full caps, 4 goals.

2000–01	Hibernian	1	0	
2001–02	Hibernian	4	1	
2002–03	Hibernian	19	10	
2003–04	Hibernian	24	6	
2004–05	Hibernian	35	13	
2005–06	Hibernian	24	11	107 41
2006	Lokomotiv Moscow	24	7	

2007	Lokomotiv Moscow	9	0	33	7
2007–08	Birmingham C	23	2		
2008–09	Birmingham C	16	6		
2009–10	Birmingham C	10	1		
2010–11	Birmingham C	3	0	52	9
2010–11	Barnsley	22	4	22	4

POTTER, Luke (D)   **19 0**
H: 6 2   W: 12 07   b.Barnsley 17-7-89
Source: Scholar.

2006–07	Barnsley	1	0		
2007–08	Barnsley	0	0		
2008–09	Barnsley	0	0		
2009–10	Barnsley	14	0		
2010–11	Barnsley	4	0	19	0

PREECE, David (G)   **260 0**
H: 6 2   W: 11 11   b.Sunderland 26-8-76
Source: Sunderland Scholar.

1994–95	Sunderland	0	0		
1995–96	Sunderland	0	0		
1996–97	Sunderland	0	0		
1997–98	Darlington	45	0		
1998–99	Darlington	46	0	91	0
1999–2000	Aberdeen	10	0		
2000–01	Aberdeen	2	0		
2001–02	Aberdeen	8	0		
2002–03	Aberdeen	16	0		
2003–04	Aberdeen	36	0		
2004–05	Aberdeen	17	0	89	0
2005–06	Silkeborg	32	0		
2006–07	Silkeborg	23	0		
2007–08	Silkeborg	19	0	74	0
2008–09	Odense	0	0		
2009–10	Barnsley	6	0		
2010–11	Barnsley	0	0	6	0

ROSE, Danny (F)   **1 0**
b.Barnsley 10-12-93
Source: Scholar.

2010–11	Barnsley	1	0	1	0

SHACKELL, Jason (D)   **210 7**
H: 6 4   W: 13 06   b.Stevenage 27-9-83
Source: Scholar.

2002–03	Norwich C	2	0		
2003–04	Norwich C	6	0		
2004–05	Norwich C	11	0		
2005–06	Norwich C	17	0		
2006–07	Norwich C	43	3		
2007–08	Norwich C	39	0		
2008–09	Norwich C	15	0	133	3
2008–09	Wolverhampton W	12	0		
2009–10	Wolverhampton W	0	0	12	0
2009–10	Doncaster R	21	1	21	1
2010–11	Barnsley	44	3	44	3

STEELE, Luke (G)   **150 0**
H: 6 2   W: 12 00   b.Peterborough 24-9-84
Source: Scholar. *Honours:* England Youth,
Under-20.

2001–02	Peterborough U	2	0	2	0
2001–02	Manchester U	0	0		
2002–03	Manchester U	0	0		
2003–04	Manchester U	0	0		
2004–05	Manchester U	0	0		
2004–05	Coventry C	32	0		
2005–06	Manchester U	0	0		
2006–07	WBA	0	0		
2006–07	Coventry C	5	0	37	0
2007–08	WBA	2	0	2	0
2007–08	Barnsley	14	0		
2008–09	Barnsley	10	0		
2009–10	Barnsley	39	0		
2010–11	Barnsley	46	0	109	0

TAYLOR, Alistair (M)   **3 0**
H: 6 1   W: 10 06   b.Sheffield 13-9-91
Source: Scholar.

2009–10	Barnsley	1	0		
2010–11	Barnsley	2	0	3	0

THOMPSON, O'Neil (D)   **55 1**
H: 6 4   W: 13 00   b.Kingston 11-8-83
Source: Boys Town. *Honours:* Jamaica 21 full
caps, 1 goal.

2007	Notodden	22	1		
2008	Notodden	14	0		
2009	Notodden	10	0	46	1
2009–10	Barnsley	1	0		
2009–10	Burton Alb	2	0	2	0
2010–11	Barnsley	0	0	1	0
2010–11	Hereford U	6	0	6	0
Transferred to Boys Town January 2011.

BIRMINGHAM C (7)

ASANTE, Akwasi (F)   **0 0**
H: 5 7   W: 10 00   b.Amsterdam 6-9-92

2010–11	Birmingham C	0	0		

BEAUSEJOUR, Jean (M)   **232 32**
H: 5 10   W: 12 08   b.Santiago 1-6-84
Honours: Chile 32 full caps, 3 goals.

2002	Univ Catolica	1	0		
2003	Univ Concepcion	30	3	30	3
2004	Univ Catolica	15	3	16	3
2004–05	Servette	11	1	11	1
2005–06	Gremio	55	7	55	7
2006–07	Gent	0	0		
2007–08	Cobreloa	22	0	22	0
2008	O'Higgins	34	13	34	13
2008–09	America	17	0		
2009–10	America	28	3		
2010–11	America	2	0	47	3
2010–11	Birmingham C	17	2	17	2

BENT, Marcus (F)   **489 93**
H: 6 2   W: 13 03   b.Hammersmith 19-5-78
Source: Trainee. *Honours:* England
Under-21.

1995–96	Brentford	12	1		
1996–97	Brentford	34	3		
1997–98	Brentford	24	4	70	8
1997–98	Crystal Palace	16	5		
1998–99	Crystal Palace	12	0	28	5
1998–99	Port Vale	15	0		
1999–2000	Port Vale	8	1	23	1
1999–2000	Sheffield U	32	15		
2000–01	Sheffield U	16	5		
2000–01	Blackburn R	28	8		
2001–02	Blackburn R	9	0	37	8
2001–02	Ipswich T	25	9		
2002–03	Ipswich T	32	11		
2003–04	Ipswich T	4	1	61	21
2003–04	Leicester C	33	9	33	9
2004–05	Everton	37	6		
2005–06	Everton	18	1	55	7
2005–06	Charlton Ath	13	2		
2006–07	Charlton Ath	30	1		
2007–08	Charlton Ath	3	1	46	4
2007–08	Wigan Ath	31	7	31	7
2008–09	Birmingham C	33	3		
2009–10	Birmingham C	0	0		
2009–10	Middlesbrough	7	0	7	0
2009–10	QPR	3	0	3	0
2010–11	Birmingham C	0	0	33	3
2010–11	Wolverhampton W	3	0	3	0
2010–11	Sheffield U	11	0	59	20

BOWYER, Lee (M)   **460 66**
H: 5 9   W: 10 12   b.Canning Town 3-1-77
Source: Trainee. *Honours:* England Youth,
Under-21, 1 full cap.

1993–94	Charlton Ath	0	0		
1994–95	Charlton Ath	5	0		
1995–96	Charlton Ath	41	8	46	8
1996–97	Leeds U	32	4		
1997–98	Leeds U	25	3		
1998–99	Leeds U	35	9		
1999–2000	Leeds U	33	5		
2000–01	Leeds U	38	9		
2001–02	Leeds U	25	5		
2002–03	Leeds U	15	3	203	38
2002–03	West Ham U	10	0		
2003–04	Newcastle U	24	2		
2004–05	Newcastle U	27	3		
2005–06	Newcastle U	28	1	79	6
2006–07	West Ham U	20	0		
2007–08	West Ham U	15	4		
2008–09	West Ham U	6	0	51	4
2008–09	Birmingham C	17	1		
2009–10	Birmingham C	35	5		
2010–11	Birmingham C	29	4	81	10

BUTLAND, Jack (G)   **0 0**
H: 6 4   W: 12 00   b.Clevedon 10-3-93
Source: Scholar. *Honours:* England Youth.

2009–10	Birmingham C	0	0		
2010–11	Birmingham C	0	0		

CARR, Stephen (D)   **390 8**
H: 5 9   W: 11 13   b.Dublin 29-8-76
Source: Trainee. *Honours:* Eire Schools,
Youth, Under-21, 44 full caps.

1993–94	Tottenham H	1	0		
1994–95	Tottenham H	0	0		
1995–96	Tottenham H	0	0		
1996–97	Tottenham H	26	0		
1997–98	Tottenham H	38	0		
1998–99	Tottenham H	37	0		
1999–2000	Tottenham H	34	3		
2000–01	Tottenham H	28	3		
2001–02	Tottenham H	0	0		
2002–03	Tottenham H	30	0		
2003–04	Tottenham H	32	1	226	7
2004–05	Newcastle U	26	1		
2005–06	Newcastle U	19	0		
2006–07	Newcastle U	23	0		
2007–08	Newcastle U	10	0		
2008–09	Newcastle U	0	0	78	1
2008–09	Birmingham C	13	0		
2009–10	Birmingham C	35	0		
2010–11	Birmingham C	38	0	86	0

DANN, Scott (D)   **156 12**
H: 6 2   W: 12 00   b.Liverpool 14-2-87
Source: Scholar. *Honours:* England Under-21.

2004–05	Walsall	1	0		
2005–06	Walsall	0	0		
2006–07	Walsall	30	4		
2007–08	Walsall	28	3	59	7
2007–08	Coventry C	16	0		
2008–09	Coventry C	31	3	47	3
2009–10	Birmingham C	30	0		
2010–11	Birmingham C	20	2	50	2

DAVIES, Curtis (D)   **188 7**
H: 6 2   W: 11 13   b.Waltham Forest 15-3-85
Source: Scholar. *Honours:* England Under-21.

2003–04	Luton T	6	0		
2004–05	Luton T	44	1		
2005–06	Luton T	6	1	56	2
2005–06	WBA	33	2		
2006–07	WBA	32	0		
2007–08	WBA	0	0	65	2
2007–08	Aston Villa	12	1		
2008–09	Aston Villa	35	1		
2009–10	Aston Villa	2	1		
2010–11	Aston Villa	0	0	49	3
2010–11	Leicester C	12	0	12	0
2010–11	Birmingham C	6	0	6	0

DERBYSHIRE, Matt (F)   **130 31**
H: 5 10   W: 11 01   b.Gt Harwood 14-4-86
Source: Gt Harwood T. *Honours:* England
Under-21.

2003–04	Blackburn R	0	0		
2004–05	Blackburn R	1	0		
2005–06	Blackburn R	0	0		
2005–06	Plymouth Arg	12	0	12	0
2005–06	Wrexham	16	10	16	10
2006–07	Blackburn R	22	5		
2007–08	Blackburn R	23	3		
2008–09	Blackburn R	17	2	63	10
2008–09	Olympiakos	7	5		
2009–10	Olympiakos	19	6		
2010–11	Olympiakos	0	0	26	11
2010–11	Birmingham C	13	0	13	0
On loan from Olympiakos.

DOYLE, Colin (G)   **42 0**
H: 6 5   W: 14 05   b.Cork 12-8-85
Honours: Eire Youth, Under-21, 1 full cap.

2004–05	Birmingham C	0	0		
2004–05	Chester C	0	0		
2004–05	Nottingham F	3	0	3	0
2005–06	Birmingham C	0	0		
2005–06	Millwall	14	0	14	0
2006–07	Birmingham C	19	0		
2007–08	Birmingham C	3	0		
2008–09	Birmingham C	2	0		
2009–10	Birmingham C	0	0		
2010–11	Birmingham C	1	0	25	0

FAHEY, Keith (M)   **221 27**
H: 5 10   W: 12 07   b.Dublin 15-1-83
Source: Arsenal Trainee. *Honours:* Eire 11
full caps, 3 goals.

1999–2000	Aston Villa	0	0		
2000–01	Aston Villa	0	0		
2001–02	Aston Villa	0	0		
2002–03	Aston Villa	0	0		
2003	St Patrick's Ath	0	0		
2004	St Patrick's Ath	33	5		
2005	St Patrick's Ath	14	3		
2005	Drogheda U	14	2		
2006	Drogheda U	8	0	22	2

2006	St Patrick's Ath	13	3		
2007	St Patrick's Ath	32	1		
2008	St Patrick's Ath	30	8	122	20
2008–09	Birmingham C	19	4		
2009–10	Birmingham C	34	0		
2010–11	Birmingham C	24	1	77	5

FERGUSON, Barry (M) — 398 47
H: 5 7 W: 9 10 b.Glasgow 2-2-78
Source: Rangers SABC. *Honours:* Scotland Under-21, 45 full caps, 3 goals.

1994–95	Rangers	0	0		
1995–96	Rangers	0	0		
1996–97	Rangers	1	0		
1997–98	Rangers	7	0		
1998–99	Rangers	23	1		
1999–2000	Rangers	31	4		
2000–01	Rangers	30	2		
2001–02	Rangers	22	1		
2002–03	Rangers	36	16		
2003–04	Rangers	3	0		
2003–04	Blackburn R	15	1		
2004–05	Blackburn R	21	2	36	3
2004–05	Rangers	13	2		
2005–06	Rangers	32	5		
2006–07	Rangers	32	4		
2007–08	Rangers	38	7		
2008–09	Rangers	22	2	290	44
2009–10	Birmingham C	37	0		
2010–11	Birmingham C	35	0	72	0

FOSTER, Ben (G) — 142 0
H: 6 2 W: 12 08 b.Leamington Spa 3-4-83
Source: Racing Club Warwick. *Honours:* England 5 full caps.

2000–01	Stoke C	0	0		
2001–02	Stoke C	0	0		
2002–03	Stoke C	0	0		
2003–04	Stoke C	0	0		
2004–05	Stoke C	0	0		
2004–05	Kidderminster H	2	0	2	0
2004–05	Wrexham	17	0	17	0
2005–06	Manchester U	0	0		
2005–06	Watford	44	0		
2006–07	Manchester U	0	0		
2006–07	Watford	29	0	73	0
2007–08	Manchester U	1	0		
2008–09	Manchester U	2	0		
2009–10	Manchester U	9	0	12	0
2010–11	Birmingham C	38	0	38	0

GARDNER, Craig (M) — 101 14
H: 5 10 W: 11 13 b.Solihull 25-11-86
Source: Scholar. *Honours:* England Under-21.

2004–05	Aston Villa	0	0		
2005–06	Aston Villa	8	0		
2006–07	Aston Villa	13	2		
2007–08	Aston Villa	23	3		
2008–09	Aston Villa	14	0		
2009–10	Aston Villa	1	0	59	5
2009–10	Birmingham C	13	1		
2010–11	Birmingham C	29	8	42	9

HLEB, Aleksandr (M) — 333 29
H: 5 10 W: 11 07 b.Minsk 1-5-81
Honours: Belarus 55 full caps, 4 goals.

1999	BATE	13	1		
2000	BATE	12	3	25	4
2000–01	Stuttgart B	17	4	17	4
2000–01	Stuttgart	6	0		
2001–02	Stuttgart	32	2		
2002–03	Stuttgart	34	4		
2003–04	Stuttgart	31	5		
2004–05	Stuttgart	34	2		
2005–06	Arsenal	25	3		
2006–07	Arsenal	33	2		
2007–08	Arsenal	31	2	89	7
2008–09	Barcelona	19	0		
2009–10	Barcelona	0	0	19	0
2009–10	*Stuttgart*	27	0	164	13
2010–11	Birmingham C	19	1	19	1

On loan from Barcelona.

HUBBINS, Luke (M) — 0 0
b.Birmingham 11-9-91
Source: Scholar.

| 2010–11 | Birmingham C | 0 | 0 | | |

JEROME, Cameron (F) — 253 61
H: 6 1 W: 13 06 b.Huddersfield 14-8-86
Honours: England Under-21.

2004–05	Cardiff C	29	6		
2005–06	Cardiff C	44	18	73	24
2005–06	Birmingham C	0	0		
2006–07	Birmingham C	38	7		
2007–08	Birmingham C	33	7		
2008–09	Birmingham C	43	9		
2009–10	Birmingham C	32	11		
2010–11	Birmingham C	34	3	180	37

JERVIS, Jake (F) — 21 2
H: 6 3 W: 12 13 b.Birmingham 17-9-91
Source: Scholar.

2009–10	Birmingham C	0	0		
2009–10	*Hereford U*	7	2		
2010–11	Birmingham C	0	0		
2010–11	*Notts Co*	10	0	10	0
2010–11	*Hereford U*	4	0	11	2

JIRANEK, Martin (D) — 323 11
H: 6 2 W: 14 02 b.Liberec 25-5-79
Honours: Czech Republic 31 full caps.

1995–96	Bohemians	1	0		
1996–97	Bohemians	4	0		
1997–98	Bohemians	16	4		
1998–99	Bohemians	18	0		
1999–2000	Bohemians	16	0	55	4
1999–2000	Slovan Liberec	13	0		
2000–01	Slovan Liberec	9	0	22	0
2000–01	Reggina	14	0		
2001–02	Reggina	30	3		
2002–03	Reggina	29	0		
2003–04	Reggina	27	0	100	3
2004	Spartak Moscow	12	0		
2005	Spartak Moscow	22	0		
2006	Spartak Moscow	26	2		
2007	Spartak Moscow	11	0		
2008	Spartak Moscow	26	0		
2009	Spartak Moscow	29	1		
2010	Spartak Moscow	10	1	136	4
2010–11	Birmingham C	10	0	10	0

JOHNSON, Roger (D) — 352 33
H: 6 3 W: 11 00 b.Ashford (Middlesex) 28-4-83
Source: Trainee.

1999–2000	Wycombe W	1	0		
2000–01	Wycombe W	1	0		
2001–02	Wycombe W	7	1		
2002–03	Wycombe W	33	3		
2003–04	Wycombe W	28	2		
2004–05	Wycombe W	42	6		
2005–06	Wycombe W	45	7	157	19
2006–07	Cardiff C	32	2		
2007–08	Cardiff C	42	5		
2008–09	Cardiff C	45	5	119	12
2009–10	Birmingham C	38	0		
2010–11	Birmingham C	38	2	76	2

JOYCE, David (D) — 0 0
H: 5 10 W: 12 13 b.Castlebar 8-8-90
Source: Scholar. *Honours:* Eire Youth.

2007–08	Birmingham C	0	0		
2008–09	Birmingham C	0	0		
2009–10	Birmingham C	0	0		
2010–11	Birmingham C	0	0		

KERR, Fraser (D) — 0 0
H: 6 3 W: 13 03 b.Motherwell 17-1-93
Source: Scholar.

| 2010–11 | Birmingham C | 0 | 0 | | |

LARSSON, Sebastian (M) — 187 19
H: 5 11 W: 11 02 b.Eskilstuna 6-6-85
Source: Trainee. *Honours:* Sweden Under-21, 31 full caps, 1 goal.

2002–03	Arsenal	0	0		
2003–04	Arsenal	0	0		
2004–05	Arsenal	3	0		
2005–06	Arsenal	0	0		
2006–07	Arsenal	0	0	3	0
2006–07	Birmingham C	43	4		
2007–08	Birmingham C	35	6		
2008–09	Birmingham C	38	1		
2009–10	Birmingham C	33	4		
2010–11	Birmingham C	35	4	184	19

MARTINS, Obafemi (F) — 210 63
H: 5 9 W: 10 07 b.Lagos 28-10-84
Honours: Nigeria 37 full caps, 18 goals.

2000–01	Reggiana	2	0	2	0
2001–02	Internazionale	4	1		
2002–03	Internazionale	25	7		
2003–04	Internazionale	31	11		
2004–05	Internazionale	28	8	88	27
2006–07	Newcastle U	33	11		
2007–08	Newcastle U	31	9		
2008–09	Newcastle U	24	8	88	28
2009–10	Wolfsburg	16	6	16	6
2010–11	Rubin	12	2	12	2

On loan from Rubin.

| 2010–11 | Birmingham C | 4 | 0 | 4 | 0 |

McFADDEN, James (M) — 254 50
H: 6 0 W: 12 11 b.Glasgow 14-4-83
Honours: Scotland Under-21, B, 48 full caps, 15 goals.

2000–01	Motherwell	6	0		
2001–02	Motherwell	24	10		
2002–03	Motherwell	30	13		
2003–04	Motherwell	3	3	63	26
2003–04	Everton	23	0		
2004–05	Everton	23	1		
2005–06	Everton	32	6		
2006–07	Everton	19	2		
2007–08	Everton	12	2	109	11
2007–08	Birmingham C	12	4		
2008–09	Birmingham C	30	4		
2009–10	Birmingham C	36	5		
2010–11	Birmingham C	4	0	82	13

McPIKE, Mitchell (M) — 0 0
b.Birmingham 21-9-91
Source: Scholar.

| 2009–10 | Birmingham C | 0 | 0 | | |
| 2010–11 | Birmingham C | 0 | 0 | | |

MICHEL (M) — 196 9
H: 6 0 W: 11 05 b.Pola de Lena 9-11-85

2004–05	Gijon B	33	2	33	2
2005–06	Gijon	24	1		
2006–07	Gijon	35	3		
2007–08	Gijon	36	3		
2008–09	Gijon	30	0		
2009–10	Gijon	14	0	139	7
2009–10	Birmingham C	9	0		
2010–11	Birmingham C	0	0	9	0
2010–11	*AEK Athens*	15	0	15	0

MURPHY, David (D) — 184 7
H: 6 1 W: 12 03 b.Hartlepool 1-3-84
Source: Scholar. *Honours:* England Youth.

2001–02	Middlesbrough	5	0		
2002–03	Middlesbrough	8	0		
2003–04	Middlesbrough	0	0	13	0
2003–04	*Barnsley*	10	2	10	2
2004–05	Hibernian	27	1		
2005–06	Hibernian	30	1		
2006–07	Hibernian	33	0		
2007–08	Hibernian	17	2	107	4
2007–08	Birmingham C	14	1		
2008–09	Birmingham C	30	0		
2009–10	Birmingham C	0	0		
2010–11	Birmingham C	10	0	54	1

MUTCH, Jordon (M) — 46 7
H: 5 9 W: 10 03 b.Derby 2-12-91
Source: Scholar. *Honours:* England Youth, Under-21.

2007–08	Birmingham C	0	0		
2008–09	Birmingham C	0	0		
2009–10	Birmingham C	0	0		
2009–10	*Hereford U*	3	0	3	0
2009–10	*Doncaster R*	17	2	17	2
2010–11	Birmingham C	3	0	3	0
2010–11	*Watford*	23	5	23	5

O'SHEA, Jay (M) — 88 16
H: 5 9 W: 12 00 b.Dun Laoghaire 10-8-88
Honours: Eire Under-21.

2007	Bray Wanderers	27	4	27	4
2008	Galway United	29	8		
2009	Galway United	19	3	48	11
2009–10	Birmingham C	1	0		
2009–10	*Middlesbrough*	2	0	2	0
2010–11	Birmingham C	0	0	1	0
2010–11	*Stevenage*	5	0	5	0
2010–11	*Port Vale*	5	1	5	1

PARNABY, Stuart (D) — 144 2
H: 5 11 W: 11 00 b.Bishop Auckland 19-7-82
Source: Trainee. *Honours:* England Youth, Under-20, Under-21.

1999–2000	Middlesbrough	0	0		
2000–01	Middlesbrough	0	0		
2000–01	*Halifax T*	6	0	6	0
2001–02	Middlesbrough	0	0		

2002–03	Middlesbrough	21	0		
2003–04	Middlesbrough	13	0		
2004–05	Middlesbrough	19	0		
2005–06	Middlesbrough	20	2		
2006–07	Middlesbrough	18	0	91	2
2007–08	Birmingham C	13	0		
2008–09	Birmingham C	21	0		
2009–10	Birmingham C	8	0		
2010–11	Birmingham C	5	0	47	0

PHILLIPS, Kevin (F)   494 220
H: 5 7 W: 11 00 b.Hitchin 25-7-73
Source: Baldock T. *Honours:* England B, 8 full caps.

1994–95	Watford	16	9		
1995–96	Watford	27	11		
1996–97	Watford	16	4	59	24
1997–98	Sunderland	43	29		
1998–99	Sunderland	26	23		
1999–2000	Sunderland	36	30		
2000–01	Sunderland	34	14		
2001–02	Sunderland	37	11		
2002–03	Sunderland	32	6	208	113
2003–04	Southampton	34	12		
2004–05	Southampton	30	10	64	22
2005–06	Aston Villa	23	4		
2006–07	Aston Villa	0	0	23	4
2006–07	WBA	36	16		
2007–08	WBA	35	22	71	38
2008–09	Birmingham C	36	14		
2009–10	Birmingham C	19	4		
2010–11	Birmingham C	14	1	69	19

PRESTON, Dan (D)   4 0
H: 5 11 W: 12 04 b.Birmingham 26-9-91
Source: Scholar.

2009–10	Birmingham C	0	0		
2009–10	Hereford U	4	0	4	0
2010–11	Birmingham C	0	0		

RIDGEWELL, Liam (D)   222 15
H: 5 10 W: 10 03 b.Bexley 21-7-84
Source: Scholar. *Honours:* England Youth, Under-20, Under-21.

2001–02	Aston Villa	0	0		
2002–03	Aston Villa	0	0		
2002–03	Bournemouth	5	0	5	0
2003–04	Aston Villa	11	0		
2004–05	Aston Villa	15	0		
2005–06	Aston Villa	32	5		
2006–07	Aston Villa	21	1	79	6
2007–08	Birmingham C	35	1		
2008–09	Birmingham C	36	1		
2009–10	Birmingham C	31	3		
2010–11	Birmingham C	36	4	138	9

ROWE, Luke (D)   0 0

2010–11	Birmingham C	0	0	

SAMMONS, Ashley (M)   0 0
b.Solihull 10-11-91
Source: Scholar. *Honours:* England Youth.

2008–09	Birmingham C	0	0	
2009–10	Birmingham C	0	0	
2010–11	Birmingham C	0	0	

SHROOT, Robin (M)   19 1
H: 5 9 W: 11 05 b.Hammersmith 26-3-88
Source: Staines T, AFC Wimbledon, Harrow Borough. *Honours:* Northern Ireland Under-21.

2008–09	Birmingham C	0	0		
2008–09	Walsall	5	0	5	0
2009–10	Birmingham C	0	0		
2009–10	Burton Alb	7	0	7	0
2010–11	Birmingham C	0	0		
2010–11	Cheltenham T	7	1	7	1

TAYLOR, Maik (G)   486 0
H: 6 4 W: 14 02 b.Hildesheim 4-9-71
Source: Farnborough T. *Honours:* Northern Ireland Under-21, B, 87 full caps.

1995–96	Barnet	45	0		
1996–97	Barnet	25	0	70	0
1996–97	Southampton	18	0		
1997–98	Southampton	0	0	18	0
1997–98	Fulham	28	0		
1998–99	Fulham	46	0		
1999–2000	Fulham	46	0		
2000–01	Fulham	44	0		
2001–02	Fulham	1	0		
2002–03	Fulham	19	0		
2003–04	Fulham	0	0	184	0

2003–04	Birmingham C	34	0		
2004–05	Birmingham C	38	0		
2005–06	Birmingham C	34	0		
2006–07	Birmingham C	27	0		
2007–08	Birmingham C	34	0		
2008–09	Birmingham C	45	0		
2009–10	Birmingham C	2	0		
2010–11	Birmingham C	0	0	214	0

VALLES, Enric (M)   4 0
H: 6 2 W: 13 01 b.Barcelona 1-3-90

2008–09	NAC Breda	3	0		
2009–10	NAC Breda	1	0	4	0
2010–11	Birmingham C	0	0		

ZIGIC, Nikola (F)   301 181
H: 6 8 W: 14 02 b.Backa Topola 25-9-80
Honours: Serbia 54 full caps, 20 goals.

1998–99	Backa Topola	14	8		
1999–2000	Backa Topola	28	8		
2000–01	Backa Topola	30	30		
2001–02	Backa Topola	4	2	76	68
2001–02	Mornar Bar	23	15	23	15
2002–03	Kolubara	8	3	8	3
2002–03	Spartak Subotica	11	14	11	14
2003–04	Red Star Belgrade	28	19		
2004–05	Red Star Belgrade	25	15		
2005–06	Red Star Belgrade	23	11		
2006–07	Red Star Belgrade	3	2	79	47
2006–07	Santander	32	11		
2007–08	Valencia	15	1		
2008–09	Santander	19	13	51	24
2009–10	Valencia	13	4	28	5
2010–11	Birmingham C	25	5	25	5

Scholars
Delfouneso Emmitt Daniel; Gascoigne Brad Lee; Gnahore Vhakka Eddy Stelh; Hancox Mitchell John; Hawker Joshua Michael; Hutchison Graham William Robert McDonald; Newell Leon James; Ntambwe Brice; Redmond Nathan Daniel Jerome; Reilly Callum

BLACKBURN R (8)

ALEY, Zach (M)   2 0
b.Fazakerley 17-8-91
Source: Scholar.

2009–10	Blackburn R	0	0		
2010–11	Blackburn R	0	0		
2010–11	Morecambe	2	0	2	0

ANDREWS, Keith (M)   270 26
H: 6 0 W: 12 04 b.Dublin 13-9-80
Source: Trainee. *Honours:* Eire Youth, 20 full caps, 2 goals.

1997–98	Wolverhampton W	0	0		
1998–99	Wolverhampton W	0	0		
1999–2000	Wolverhampton W	2	0		
2000–01	Wolverhampton W	22	0		
2000–01	Oxford U	4	1	4	1
2001–02	Wolverhampton W	11	0		
2002–03	Wolverhampton W	9	0		
2003–04	Wolverhampton W	1	0		
2003–04	Stoke C	16	0	16	0
2003–04	Walsall	10	2	10	2
2004–05	Wolverhampton W	20	0	65	0
2005–06	Hull C	26	0		
2006–07	Hull C	3	0	29	0
2006–07	Milton Keynes D	34	6		
2007–08	Milton Keynes D	41	12		
2008–09	Milton Keynes D	1	0	76	18
2008–09	Blackburn R	33	4		
2009–10	Blackburn R	32	1		
2010–11	Blackburn R	5	0	70	5

BASTURK, Yildiray (M)   280 39
H: 5 6 W: 10 12 b.Herne 24-12-78
Honours: Turkey 49 full caps, 3 goals.

1996–97	Wattenscheid	0	0		
1997–98	Bochum	17	1		
1998–99	Bochum	28	1		
1999–2000	Bochum	30	7		
2000–01	Bochum	29	4	104	13
2001–02	Leverkusen	30	3		
2002–03	Leverkusen	26	3		
2003–04	Leverkusen	17	2	73	8
2004–05	Hertha Berlin	25	7		
2005–06	Hertha Berlin	27	6		
2006–07	Hertha Berlin	19	1	71	14

2007–08	Stuttgart	26	4		
2008–08	Stuttgart	4	0		
2009–10	Stuttgart	1	0	31	4
2009–10	Blackburn R	1	0		
2010–11	Blackburn R	0	0	1	0

BLACKMAN, Nick (F)   62 15
H: 6 2 W: 11 08 b.Whitefield 11-11-89
Source: Scholar.

2006–07	Macclesfield T	1	0		
2007–08	Macclesfield T	11	1		
2008–09	Macclesfield T	0	0	12	1
2008–09	Blackburn R	0	0		
2008–09	Blackpool	5	1	5	1
2009–10	Blackburn R	0	0		
2009–10	Oldham Ath	12	1	12	1
2010–11	Blackburn R	0	0		
2010–11	Motherwell	18	10	18	10
2010–11	Aberdeen	15	2	15	2

BOWEN, Jordan (M)   0 0
b.Preston 27-3-92
Source: Scholar.

2008–09	Blackburn R	0	0	
2009–10	Blackburn R	0	0	
2010–11	Blackburn R	0	0	

BROWN, Jason (G)   142 0
H: 6 0 W: 15 07 b.Southwark 18-5-82
Source: Charlton Ath Scholar. *Honours:* Wales Youth, Under-21, 2 full caps.

2000–01	Gillingham	9	0		
2001–02	Gillingham	10	0		
2002–03	Gillingham	39	0		
2003–04	Gillingham	22	0		
2004–05	Gillingham	16	0		
2005–06	Gillingham	39	0	126	0
2006–07	Blackburn R	1	0		
2007–08	Blackburn R	0	0		
2008–09	Blackburn R	4	0		
2009–10	Blackburn R	0	0		
2010–11	Blackburn R	0	0	9	0
2010–11	Leeds U	4	0	4	0
2010–11	Leyton Orient	3	0	3	0
2010–11	Cardiff C	0	0		

BUNN, Mark (G)   128 0
H: 6 0 W: 12 02 b.Southgate 16-11-84
Source: Scholar.

2004–05	Northampton T	0	0		
2005–06	Northampton T	0	0		
2006–07	Northampton T	42	0		
2007–08	Northampton T	45	0		
2008–09	Northampton T	3	0	90	0
2008–09	Blackburn R	0	0		
2008–09	Leicester C	3	0	3	0
2009–10	Blackburn R	0	0		
2009–10	Sheffield U	32	0	32	0
2010–11	Blackburn R	3	0	3	0

DIOUF, El Hadji (F)   355 48
H: 5 11 W: 11 11 b.Dakar 15-1-81
Honours: Senegal 57 full caps, 16 goals.

1998–99	Sochaux	15	0	15	0
1999–2000	Rennes	28	1	28	1
2000–01	Lens	28	8		
2001–02	Lens	26	10	54	18
2002–03	Liverpool	29	3		
2003–04	Liverpool	26	0		
2004–05	Liverpool	0	0	55	3
2004–05	Bolton W	27	9		
2005–06	Bolton W	20	3		
2006–07	Bolton W	33	5		
2007–08	Bolton W	34	4	114	21
2008–09	Sunderland	14	0	14	0
2008–09	Blackburn R	14	1		
2009–10	Blackburn R	26	3		
2010–11	Blackburn R	20	0	60	4
2010–11	Rangers	15	1	15	1

DORAN-COGAN, Aaron (M)   27 0
H: 5 7 W: 11 13 b.Dublin 13-5-91
Source: Scholar. *Honours:* Eire Youth, Under-21.

2007–08	Blackburn R	0	0		
2008–09	Blackburn R	3	0		
2009–10	Blackburn R	0	0		
2009–10	Milton Keynes D	4	0	4	0
2009–10	Leyton Orient	6	0	6	0
2010–11	Blackburn R	0	0	3	0
2010–11	Inverness CT	14	0	14	0

DUNN, David (M)   301 50
H: 5 9   W: 12 03   b.Gt Harwood 27-12-79
Source: Trainee. *Honours:* England Youth,
Under-21, 1 full cap.

1997–98	Blackburn R	0	0	
1998–99	Blackburn R	15	1	
1999–2000	Blackburn R	22	2	
2000–01	Blackburn R	42	12	
2001–02	Blackburn R	29	7	
2002–03	Blackburn R	28	8	
2003–04	Birmingham C	21	2	
2004–05	Birmingham C	11	2	
2005–06	Birmingham C	15	2	
2006–07	Birmingham C	11	1	58 7
2006–07	Blackburn R	11	0	
2007–08	Blackburn R	31	1	
2008–09	Blackburn R	15	1	
2009–10	Blackburn R	23	9	
2010–11	Blackburn R	27	2	243 43

EMERTON, Brett (M)   431 40
H: 6 1   W: 13 05   b.Bankstown 22-2-79
Honours: Australia Youth, Under-20,
Under-23, 86 full caps, 19 goals.

1996–97	Sydney Olympic	18	2	
1997–98	Sydney Olympic	24	3	
1998–99	Sydney Olympic	21	2	
1999–2000	Sydney Olympic	31	9	94 16
2000–01	Feyenoord	28	2	
2001–02	Feyenoord	31	6	
2002–03	Feyenoord	33	3	92 11
2003–04	Blackburn R	37	2	
2004–05	Blackburn R	37	4	
2005–06	Blackburn R	30	1	
2006–07	Blackburn R	34	0	
2007–08	Blackburn R	33	1	
2008–09	Blackburn R	20	1	
2009–10	Blackburn R	24	0	
2010–11	Blackburn R	30	4	245 13

FORMICA, Mauro (M)   75 17
H: 5 9   W: 10 01   b.Rosario 4-4-88
Honours: Argentina Youth.

2007–08	Newell's Old Boys	4	0	
2008–09	Newell's Old Boys	19	7	
2009–10	Newell's Old Boys	36	8	
2010–11	Newell's Old Boys	16	2	75 17
2010–11	Blackburn R	0	0	

GIVET, Gael (D)   284 11
H: 5 11   W: 11 11   b.Arles 9-10-81
Honours: France 13 full caps.

2000–01	Monaco	1	0	
2001–02	Monaco	23	2	
2002–03	Monaco	23	1	
2003–04	Monaco	33	2	
2004–05	Monaco	34	0	
2005–06	Monaco	32	2	
2006–07	Monaco	32	1	178 8
2007–08	Marseille	29	0	
2008–09	Marseille	0	0	29 0
2008–09	Blackburn R	14	0	
2009–10	Blackburn R	34	2	
2010–11	Blackburn R	29	1	77 3

GOULON, Herold (M)   41 0
H: 6 4   W: 14 07   b.Paris 12-6-88
Source: Soltaires Paris, Esperance Paris,
Bourget. *Honours:* France Under-21.

2005–06	Lyon	0	0	
2006–07	Middlesbrough	0	0	
2007–08	Middlesbrough	0	0	
2008–09	Le Mans	11	0	
2009–10	Le Mans	26	0	37 0
2010–11	Blackburn R	4	0	4 0

GRELLA, Vince (M)   305 7
H: 6 0   W: 12 06   b.Melbourne 5-10-79
Honours: Australia Under-20, Under-23, 46
full caps.

1996–97	Canberra Cosmos	14	1	14 1
1997–98	Carlton SC	22	2	
1998–99	Carlton SC	1	0	23 2
1998–99	Empoli	5	0	
1999–2000	Empoli	0	0	
1999–2000	Ternana	9	0	
2000–01	Ternana	18	0	27 0
2001–02	Empoli	32	0	
2002–03	Empoli	31	1	
2003–04	Empoli	24	0	
2004–05	Empoli	0	0	92 1
2004–05	Parma	23	0	

2005–06	Parma	35	1	
2006–07	Parma	26	1	84 2
2007–08	Torino	28	1	28 1
2008–09	Blackburn R	17	0	
2009–10	Blackburn R	15	0	
2010–11	Blackburn R	5	0	37 0

GUNNING, Gavin (D)   43 0
H: 6 0   W: 12 06   b.Dublin 26-1-91
Source: Scholar. *Honours:* Eire Youth,
Under-21.

2007–08	Blackburn R	0	0	
2008–09	Blackburn R	0	0	
2009–10	Blackburn R	0	0	
2009–10	Tranmere R	6	0	6 0
2009–10	Rotherham U	21	0	21 0
2010–11	Blackburn R	0	0	
2010–11	Bury	2	0	2 0
2010–11	Motherwell	14	0	14 0

HANLEY, Grant (D)   8 0
H: 6 2   W: 12 00   b.Dumfries 20-11-91
Source: Scholar. *Honours:* Scotland Youth,
Under-21, 2 full caps.

2008–09	Blackburn R	0	0	
2009–10	Blackburn R	1	0	
2010–11	Blackburn R	7	0	8 0

HITCHCOCK, Tom (F)   0 0
b.Hemel Hempstead 1-10-92
Source: Scholar.

2009–10	Blackburn R	0	0	
2010–11	Blackburn R	0	0	

HOILETT, David (M)   47 5
H: 5 8   W: 11 00   b.Ottowa 5-6-90
Source: Scholar.

2008–09	Blackburn R	0	0	
2009–10	Blackburn R	23	0	
2010–11	Blackburn R	24	5	47 5

JONES, Phil (D)   35 0
H: 5 11   W: 11 02   b.Preston 21-2-92
Source: Scholar. *Honours:* England Youth,
Under-21.

2009–10	Blackburn R	9	0	
2010–11	Blackburn R	26	0	35 0

JONES, Jermaine (M)   174 17
H: 6 0   W: 12 04   b.Frankfurt am Main
3-11-81
Honours: Germany Youth, 3 full caps, USA
10 full caps.

2000–01	Eintracht Frankfurt	2	0	
2001–02	Eintracht Frankfurt	22	1	
2002–03	Eintracht Frankfurt	17	6	
2003–04	Eintracht Frankfurt	5	0	
2004–05	Leverkusen	5	0	5 0
2004–05	Eintracht Frankfurt	14	3	
2005–06	Eintracht Frankfurt	20	2	
2006–07	Eintracht Frankfurt	4	0	84 12
2007–08	Schalke	30	1	
2008–09	Schalke	30	3	
2009–10	Schalke	0	0	
2010–11	Schalke	10	1	70 5
2010–11	Blackburn R	15	0	15 0

KALINIC, Nikola (F)   123 45
H: 6 2   W: 12 11   b.Split 5-1-88
Honours: Croatia Youth, Under-21, 8 full
caps, 4 goals.

2005–06	Hajduk Split	6	0	
2006–07	Sibenik	8	3	8 3
2006–07	Pula 1856	12	3	12 3
2007–08	Hajduk Split	25	17	
2008–09	Hajduk Split	28	15	59 32
2009–10	Blackburn R	26	2	
2010–11	Blackburn R	18	5	44 7

KEAN, Jake (G)   19 0
H: 6 4   W: 11 13   b.Derby 4-2-91
Source: Derby Co Scholar.

2010–11	Blackburn R	0	0	
2010–11	Hartlepool U	19	0	19 0

KHIZANISHVILI, Zurab (D)   235 6
H: 6 1   W: 12 08   b.Tbilisi 6-10-81
Honours: Georgia 67 full caps, 1 goal.

1998–99	Dynamo Tbilisi B	17	3	17 3
1998–99	Dynamo Tbilisi	2	1	2 1
1999–2000	Tbilisi	9	0	9 0
1999–2000	Lokomotivi	5	1	
2000–01	Lokomotivi	11	0	16 1
2000–01	Dundee	6	0	

2001–02	Dundee	18	0	
2002–03	Dundee	19	0	43 0
2003–04	Rangers	26	0	
2004–05	Rangers	16	0	
2005–06	Rangers	0	0	42 0
2005–06	*Blackburn R*	26	1	
2006–07	Blackburn R	18	0	
2007–08	Blackburn R	13	0	
2008–09	Blackburn R	5	0	
2009–10	Blackburn R	0	0	
2009–10	*Newcastle U*	7	0	7 0
2009–10	*Reading*	15	0	
2010–11	Blackburn R	0	0	62 1
2010–11	*Reading*	22	0	37 0

KNOWLES, James (M)   0 0
H: 5 9   W: 11 00   b.Lisburn 6-4-93
Source: Scholar.

2009–10	Blackburn R	0	0	
2010–11	Blackburn R	0	0	

LINDSAY, Cameron (D)
b.New Zealand 21-12-92
Source: Scholar.

2010–11	Blackburn R	0	0	

LINGANZI, Amine (M)   6 0
H: 6 1   W: 10 00   b.Algiers 16-11-89

2008–09	St Etienne	3	0	
2009–10	St Etienne	0	0	3 0
2009–10	Blackburn R	1	0	
2010–11	Blackburn R	1	0	2 0
2010–11	*Preston NE*	1	0	1 0

LOWE, Jason (M)   8 2
b.Wigan 2-9-91
Source: Scholar.

2009–10	Blackburn R	0	0	
2010–11	Blackburn R	1	0	1 0
2010–11	*Oldham Ath*	7	2	7 2

MORRIS, Josh (D)   4 0
b. 30-9-91
Source: Scholar.

2010–11	Blackburn R	4	0	4 0

MWARUWARI, Benjamin (F)   261 66
H: 6 2   W: 12 03   b.Harare 13-8-78
Honours: Zimbabwe 31 full caps, 8 goals.

1999–2000	Jomo Cosmos	15	7	
2000–01	Jomo Cosmos	30	13	45 20
2001–02	Grasshoppers	25	1	25 1
2002–03	Auxerre	27	7	
2003–04	Auxerre	3	0	
2004–05	Auxerre	31	11	
2005–06	Auxerre	11	1	72 19
2005–06	Portsmouth	16	1	
2006–07	Portsmouth	31	6	
2007–08	Portsmouth	23	12	70 19
2007–08	Manchester C	13	3	
2008–09	Manchester C	8	1	
2009–10	Manchester C	2	0	23 4
2009–10	*Sunderland*	8	0	8 0
2010–11	Blackburn R	18	3	18 3

N'ZONZI, Steven (M)   91 4
H: 6 3   W: 11 11   b.Paris 15-12-88
Honours: France Under-21.

2007–08	Amiens	3	0	
2008–09	Amiens	34	1	37 1
2009–10	Blackburn R	33	2	
2010–11	Blackburn R	21	1	54 3

NELSEN, Ryan (D)   252 15
H: 5 11   W: 14 02   b.Christchurch, NZ
18-10-77
Honours: New Zealand Under-23, 45 full
caps, 7 goals.

2001	DC United	19	0	
2002	DC United	20	4	
2003	DC United	25	1	
2004	DC United	17	2	81 7
2004–05	Blackburn R	15	0	
2005–06	Blackburn R	31	0	
2006–07	Blackburn R	12	0	
2007–08	Blackburn R	22	0	
2008–09	Blackburn R	35	1	
2009–10	Blackburn R	28	4	
2010–11	Blackburn R	28	3	171 8

O'CONNOR, Anthony (D)   0 0
Honours: Eire Youth.

2010–11	Blackburn R	0	0	

OLSSON, Martin (D) — 61 3
H: 5 7 W: 12 12 b.Gavle 17-5-88
Source: Hogaborg. *Honours:* Sweden Under-21, 3 full caps, 2 goals.

2005–06	Blackburn R	0	0		
2006–07	Blackburn R	0	0		
2007–08	Blackburn R	2	0		
2008–09	Blackburn R	9	0		
2009–10	Blackburn R	21	1		
2010–11	Blackburn R	29	2	61	3

PEDERSEN, Morten (F) — 390 76
H: 5 11 W: 11 00 b.Vadso 8-9-81
Honours: Norway Youth, Under-21, 68 full caps, 15 goals.

1997	Norlid	21	0		
1998	Pola	20	4	20	4
1999	Norlid	19	0	40	0
2000	Tromso	10	3		
2001	Tromso	26	5		
2002	Tromso	23	18		
2003	Tromso	26	8		
2004	Tromso	18	7	103	41
2004–05	Blackburn R	19	4		
2005–06	Blackburn R	34	9		
2006–07	Blackburn R	36	6		
2007–08	Blackburn R	37	4		
2008–09	Blackburn R	33	1		
2009–10	Blackburn R	33	3		
2010–11	Blackburn R	35	4	227	31

PIVKOVSKI, Filip (M) — 0 0
b.Sweden 31-1-94
Source: Scholar.

2010–11	Blackburn R	0	0

POTTS, Michael (M) — 0 0
H: 5 6 W: 10 00 b.Gravesend 26-11-91
Source: Scholar.

2008–09	Blackburn R	0	0
2009–10	Blackburn R	0	0
2010–11	Blackburn R	0	0

RIGTERS, Maceo (F) — 107 10
H: 5 10 W: 14 07 b.Amsterdam 22-1-84
Honours: Holland Under-21.

2005–06	NAC Breda	24	2		
2006–07	NAC Breda	32	3	56	5
2007–08	Blackburn R	2	0		
2007–08	Norwich C	2	0	2	0
2008–09	Blackburn R	0	0		
2008–09	Barnsley	19	0	19	0
2009–10	Blackburn R	0	0		
2010–11	Blackburn R	0	0	2	0
2010–11	Willem II	28	5	28	5

ROBERTS, Jason (F) — 411 131
H: 6 0 W: 14 01 b.Acton 25-1-78
Source: Hayes. *Honours:* Grenada 22 full caps, 12 goals.

1997–98	Wolverhampton W	0	0		
1997–98	Torquay U	14	6	14	6
1997–98	Bristol C	3	1	3	1
1998–99	Bristol R	37	16		
1999–2000	Bristol R	41	22	78	38
2000–01	WBA	43	14		
2001–02	WBA	14	7		
2002–03	WBA	32	3		
2003–04	WBA	0	0	89	24
2003–04	Portsmouth	10	1	10	1
2003–04	Wigan Ath	14	8		
2004–05	Wigan Ath	45	21		
2005–06	Wigan Ath	34	8	93	37
2006–07	Blackburn R	18	4		
2007–08	Blackburn R	26	3		
2008–09	Blackburn R	26	7		
2009–10	Blackburn R	29	5		
2010–11	Blackburn R	25	5	124	24

ROBINSON, Paul (G) — 338 1
H: 6 1 W: 14 07 b.Beverley 15-10-79
Source: Trainee. *Honours:* England Under-21, 41 full caps.

1996–97	Leeds U	0	0		
1997–98	Leeds U	0	0		
1998–99	Leeds U	5	0		
1999–2000	Leeds U	0	0		
2000–01	Leeds U	16	0		
2001–02	Leeds U	0	0		
2002–03	Leeds U	38	0		
2003–04	Leeds U	36	0	95	0
2003–04	Tottenham H				
2004–05	Tottenham H	36	0		
2005–06	Tottenham H	38	0		
2006–07	Tottenham H	38	1		
2007–08	Tottenham H	25	0	137	1
2008–09	Blackburn R	35	0		
2009–10	Blackburn R	35	0		
2010–11	Blackburn R	36	0	106	0

ROCHINA, Ruben (F) — 17 2
H: 5 11 W: 11 00 b.Sagunto 23-3-91
Honours: Spain Youth.

2008–09	Barcelona B	10	2		
2009–10	Barcelona B	3	0	13	2
2010–11	Blackburn R	4	0	4	0

SALGADO, Michel (D) — 457 9
H: 5 9 W: 11 11 b.Pontevedra 22-10-75
Honours: Spain Youth, Under-20, Under-21, 53 full caps.

1992–93	Celta Vigo B	20	1		
1993–94	Celta Vigo B	0	0	20	1
1994–95	Celta Vigo	14	0		
1995–96	Celta Vigo	18	0		
1996–97	Salamanque	36	1	36	1
1997–98	Celta Vigo	25	0		
1998–99	Celta Vigo	35	3	92	3
1999–2000	Real Madrid	29	0		
2000–01	Real Madrid	28	1		
2001–02	Real Madrid	35	0		
2002–03	Real Madrid	35	0		
2003–04	Real Madrid	35	1		
2004–05	Real Madrid	30	2		
2005–06	Real Madrid	27	0		
2006–07	Real Madrid	16	0		
2007–08	Real Madrid	8	0		
2008–09	Real Madrid	9	0	252	4
2009–10	Blackburn R	21	0		
2010–11	Blackburn R	36	0	57	0

SAMBA, Christopher (D) — 199 18
H: 6 5 W: 13 03 b.Creteil 28-3-84
Source: Issy-les-Moulineaux, Rouen.
Honours: Congo 5 full caps.

2001–02	Sedan	1	0		
2002–03	Sedan	0	0		
2003–04	Sedan	3	0	4	0
2004–05	Hertha Berlin	0	0		
2004–05	Hertha Berlin II	16	3		
2005–06	Hertha Berlin	12	0		
2005–06	Hertha Berlin II	12	1		
2006–07	Hertha Berlin	8	0	20	0
2006–07	Hertha Berlin II	2	0	30	4
2006–07	Blackburn R	14	2		
2007–08	Blackburn R	33	2		
2008–09	Blackburn R	35	2		
2009–10	Blackburn R	30	4		
2010–11	Blackburn R	33	4	145	14

VASTIC, Tony (F) — 0 0
b.St Polten 17-1-93
Source: Blackburn R Academy. *Honours:* Austria Youth.

2009–10	Blackburn R	0	0
2010–11	Blackburn R	0	0

Scholars
Dilo Christopher Jean-Louis; Edwards Ryan Christopher; Evans Micah; Hall Jadan; Hands Reece; Hanley Raheem Shaquille Rushan; Henley Adam David; James William Sebastian Graveson; MacLaren Jamie; Molina Huge Fernandez; Osawe Osayamen; O'Sullivan John Anthony James; Pearson Matthew Joe; Ramm Jackson Wayne; Urwin Matthew William; Wylie Peter James John

BLACKPOOL (9)

ADAM, Charlie (M) — 189 50
H: 6 1 W: 12 00 b.Dundee 10-12-85
Honours: Scotland Under-21, B, 11 full caps.

2004–05	Rangers	1	0		
2004–05	Ross Co	10	2	10	2
2005–06	Rangers	1	0		
2005–06	St Mirren	29	5	29	5
2006–07	Rangers	32	11		
2007–08	Rangers	16	2		
2008–09	Rangers	9	0	59	13
2008–09	Blackpool	13	2		
2009–10	Blackpool	43	16		
2010–11	Blackpool	35	12	91	30

ALMOND, Louis (F) — 4 0
H: 5 11 W: 12 00 b.Blackburn 10-1-92
Source: Scholar.

2009–10	Blackpool	0	0		
2009–10	Cheltenham T	4	0	4	0
2010–11	Blackpool	0	0		

BASHAM, Chris (M) — 34 1
H: 5 11 W: 12 08 b.Hebburn 20-7-88
Source: Scholar.

2007–08	Bolton W	0	0		
2007–08	Rochdale	13	0	13	0
2008–09	Bolton W	11	1		
2009–10	Bolton W	8	0	19	1
2010–11	Blackpool	2	0	2	0

BEATTIE, James (F) — 400 125
H: 6 1 W: 13 06 b.Lancaster 27-2-78
Source: Trainee. *Honours:* England Under-21, 5 full caps.

1994–95	Blackburn R	0	0		
1995–96	Blackburn R	0	0		
1996–97	Blackburn R	1	0		
1997–98	Blackburn R	3	0	4	0
1998–99	Southampton	35	5		
1999–2000	Southampton	18	0		
2000–01	Southampton	37	11		
2001–02	Southampton	28	12		
2002–03	Southampton	38	23		
2003–04	Southampton	37	14		
2004–05	Southampton	11	3	204	68
2004–05	Everton	11	1		
2005–06	Everton	32	10		
2006–07	Everton	33	2	76	13
2007–08	Sheffield U	39	22		
2008–09	Sheffield U	23	12	62	34
2008–09	Stoke C	16	7		
2009–10	Stoke C	22	3	38	10
2010–11	Rangers	7	0	7	0

On loan from Rangers.

2010–11	Blackpool	9	0	9	0

CAMPBELL, Dudley (F) — 181 56
H: 5 10 W: 11 00 b.Hammersmith 12-11-81
Source: Aston Villa Trainee, QPR, Chesham U, Stevenage B, Yeading.

2005–06	Brentford	23	9	23	9
2005–06	Birmingham C	11	0		
2006–07	Birmingham C	32	9	43	9
2007–08	Leicester C	28	4		
2008–09	Leicester C	7	0		
2008–09	Blackpool	20	9		
2009–10	Leicester C	3	0		
2009–10	Derby Co	8	3	8	3
2009–10	Blackpool	15	8		
2010–11	Leicester C	3	1	41	5
2010–11	Blackpool	31	13	66	30

CARNEY, David (M) — 87 9
H: 5 11 W: 11 00 b.Sydney 30-11-83
Source: Scholar. *Honours:* Australia Under-20, 39 full caps, 6 goals.

2000–01	Everton	0	0		
2001–02	Everton	0	0		
2002–03	Everton	0	0		
2003–04	Oldham Ath	0	0		
2004–05	Hamilton A	8	0	8	0
2005–06	Sydney FC	24	6		
2006–07	Sydney FC	14	1	38	7
2007–08	Sheffield U	21	2		
2008–09	Sheffield U	0	0		
2008–09	Norwich C	9	0	9	0
2009–10	Sheffield U	0	0	21	2
2010–11	Blackpool	11	0	11	0

CATHCART, Craig (D) — 86 4
H: 6 2 W: 11 06 b.Belfast 6-2-89
Source: Scholar. *Honours:* Northern Ireland Youth, Under-21, 5 full caps.

2005–06	Manchester U	0	0		
2006–07	Manchester U	0	0		
2007–08	Manchester U	0	0		
2007–08	Antwerp	13	2	13	2
2008–09	Manchester U	0	0		
2008–09	Plymouth Arg	31	1	31	1
2009–10	Manchester U	0	0		
2009–10	Watford	12	0	12	0
2010–11	Blackpool	30	1	30	1

CLARKE, Billy (F)   114 22
H: 5 7   W: 10 01   b.Cork 13-12-87
Source: Scholar. Honours: Eire Youth, Under-21.

2004–05	Ipswich T	0	0		
2005–06	Ipswich T	2	0		
2005–06	Colchester U	6	0	6	0
2006–07	Ipswich T	27	3		
2007–08	Ipswich T	20	0		
2007–08	Falkirk	8	1	8	1
2008–09	Ipswich T	0	0	49	3
2008–09	Darlington	20	8	20	8
2008–09	Northampton T	5	3	5	3
2008–09	Brentford	8	6	8	6
2009–10	Blackpool	18	1		
2010–11	Blackpool	0	0	18	1

COID, Danny (D)   273 9
H: 5 11   W: 11 07   b.Liverpool 3-10-81
Source: Trainee.

1998–99	Blackpool	1	0		
1999–2000	Blackpool	21	1		
2000–01	Blackpool	46	1		
2001–02	Blackpool	27	3		
2002–03	Blackpool	36	1		
2003–04	Blackpool	35	3		
2004–05	Blackpool	35	0		
2005–06	Blackpool	13	0		
2006–07	Blackpool	18	0		
2007–08	Blackpool	13	0		
2008–09	Blackpool	18	0		
2009–10	Blackpool	1	0		
2010–11	Blackpool	0	0	264	9
2010–11	Rotherham U	9	0	9	0

CRAINEY, Stephen (D)   227 1
H: 5 9   W: 9 11   b.Glasgow 22-6-81
Honours: Scotland B, Under-21, 9 full caps.

1999–2000	Celtic	9	0		
2000–01	Celtic	2	0		
2001–02	Celtic	15	0		
2002–03	Celtic	13	0		
2003–04	Celtic	2	0	41	0
2003–04	Southampton	5	0	5	0
2004–05	Leeds U	9	0		
2005–06	Leeds U	24	0		
2006–07	Leeds U	19	0	52	0
2007–08	Blackpool	40	1		
2008–09	Blackpool	17	0		
2009–10	Blackpool	41	0		
2010–11	Blackpool	31	0	129	1

DEMONTAGNAC, Ishmel (F)   109 14
H: 5 10   W: 11 05   b.Newham 15-6-88
Source: Charlton Ath Scholar. Honours: England Youth.

2005–06	Walsall	24	2		
2006–07	Walsall	19	1		
2007–08	Walsall	30	3		
2008–09	Walsall	10	3		
2009–10	Walsall	0	0	83	9
2009–10	Blackpool	8	0		
2009–10	Chesterfield	10	3	10	3
2010–11	Blackpool	1	0	9	0
2010–11	Stockport Co	7	2	7	2

EARDLEY, Neal (M)   168 11
H: 5 11   W: 11 00   b.Llandudno 6-11-88
Source: Scholar. Honours: Wales Under-21, 16 full caps.

2005–06	Oldham Ath	1	0		
2006–07	Oldham Ath	36	2		
2007–08	Oldham Ath	42	6		
2008–09	Oldham Ath	34	2		
2009–10	Oldham Ath	0	0	113	10
2009–10	Blackpool	24	0		
2010–11	Blackpool	31	1	55	1

EASTHAM, Ashley (D)   30 0
H: 6 3   W: 12 06   b.Preston 22-3-91
Source: Scholar.

2009–10	Blackpool	1	0		
2009–10	Cheltenham T	20	0		
2010–11	Blackpool	0	0	1	0
2010–11	Cheltenham T	9	0	29	0
2010–11	Carlisle U	1	0		

EDWARDS, Rob (D)   188 5
H: 6 1   W: 11 10   b.Telford 25-12-82
Source: Trainee. Honours: Wales Youth, 15 full caps.

1999–2000	Aston Villa	0	0		
2000–01	Aston Villa	0	0		
2001–02	Aston Villa	0	0		
2002–03	Aston Villa	8	0		
2003–04	Aston Villa	0	0	8	0
2003–04	Crystal Palace	7	1	7	1
2003–04	Derby Co	11	1	11	1
2004–05	Wolverhampton W	17	0		
2005–06	Wolverhampton W	42	0		
2006–07	Wolverhampton W	33	0		
2007–08	Wolverhampton W	8	1	100	1
2008–09	Blackpool	36	2		
2009–10	Blackpool	21	0		
2010–11	Blackpool	2	0	59	2
2010–11	Norwich C	3	0	3	0

EUELL, Jason (F)   407 87
H: 5 11   W: 11 13   b.Lambeth 6-2-77
Source: Trainee. Honours: England Youth, Under-21, Jamaica 3 full caps, 1 goal.

1995–96	Wimbledon	9	2		
1996–97	Wimbledon	7	2		
1997–98	Wimbledon	19	4		
1998–99	Wimbledon	33	10		
1999–2000	Wimbledon	37	4		
2000–01	Wimbledon	36	19	141	41
2001–02	Charlton Ath	36	11		
2002–03	Charlton Ath	36	10		
2003–04	Charlton Ath	31	10		
2004–05	Charlton Ath	26	2		
2005–06	Charlton Ath	10	1		
2006–07	Charlton Ath	0	0	139	34
2006–07	Middlesbrough	17	0		
2007–08	Middlesbrough	0	0	17	0
2007–08	Southampton	38	3		
2008–09	Southampton	24	2	62	5
2009–10	Blackpool	33	4		
2010–11	Blackpool	3	0	36	4
2010–11	Doncaster R	12	3	12	3

EVATT, Ian (D)   336 15
H: 6 3   W: 13 12   b.Coventry 19-11-81
Source: Trainee.

1998–99	Derby Co	0	0		
1999–2000	Derby Co	0	0		
2000–01	Derby Co	1	0		
2001–02	Northampton T	11	0	11	0
2001–02	Derby Co	3	0		
2002–03	Derby Co	30	0	34	0
2003–04	Chesterfield	43	5		
2004–05	Chesterfield	41	4	84	9
2005–06	QPR	27	0		
2006–07	QPR	0	0	27	0
2006–07	Blackpool	44	0		
2007–08	Blackpool	29	0		
2008–09	Blackpool	33	1		
2009–10	Blackpool	36	4		
2010–11	Blackpool	38	1	180	6

GILKS, Matthew (G)   229 0
H: 6 3   W: 13 12   b.Rochdale 4-6-82
Source: Scholar.

2000–01	Rochdale	3	0		
2001–02	Rochdale	19	0		
2002–03	Rochdale	20	0		
2003–04	Rochdale	12	0		
2004–05	Rochdale	30	0		
2005–06	Rochdale	46	0		
2006–07	Rochdale	46	0	176	0
2007–08	Norwich C	0	0		
2008–09	Blackpool	5	0		
2008–09	Shrewsbury T	4	0	4	0
2009–10	Blackpool	26	0		
2010–11	Blackpool	18	0	49	0

GRANDIN, Elliot (F)   113 13
H: 5 10   W: 10 07   b.Caen 17-10-87

2004–05	Caen	1	0		
2005–06	Caen	19	3		
2006–07	Caen	23	2		
2007–08	Caen	12	1	55	6
2007–08	Marseille	8	0		
2008–09	Marseille	8	2	16	2
2008–09	Grenoble	8	0	8	0
2009–10	CSKA Sofia	10	4		
2010–11	CSKA Sofia	1	0	11	4
2010–11	Blackpool	23	1	23	1

HALSTEAD, Mark (G)   1 0
H: 6 3   W: 14 00   b.Blackpool 1-1-90
Source: Scholar.

2009–10	Blackpool	0	0		
2010–11	Blackpool	1	0	1	0

HAREWOOD, Marlon (F)   405 118
H: 6 1   W: 13 07   b.Hampstead 25-8-79
Source: Trainee.

1996–97	Nottingham F	0	0		
1997–98	Nottingham F	1	0		
1998–99	Nottingham F	23	1		
1998–99	Ipswich T	6	1	6	1
1999–2000	Nottingham F	34	4		
2000–01	Nottingham F	33	3		
2001–02	Nottingham F	28	11		
2002–03	Nottingham F	44	20		
2003–04	Nottingham F	19	12	182	51
2003–04	West Ham U	28	13		
2004–05	West Ham U	45	17		
2005–06	West Ham U	37	14		
2006–07	West Ham U	32	3	142	47
2007–08	Aston Villa	23	5		
2008–09	Aston Villa	6	0		
2008–09	Wolverhampton W	5	0	5	0
2009–10	Aston Villa	0	0	29	5
2009–10	Newcastle U	15	5	15	5
2010–11	Blackpool	16	5	16	5
2010–11	Barnsley	10	4	10	4

HUSBAND, Stephen (M)   20 2
H: 6 0   W: 12 13   b.Dunfermline 29-10-90

2006–07	Cowdenbeath	5	0	5	0
2007–08	Hearts	0	0		
2008–09	Hearts	0	0		
2009–10	Hearts	0	0		
2009–10	Livingston	7	0	7	0
2009–10	Blackpool	3	0		
2010–11	Blackpool	0	0	3	0
2010–11	Stockport Co	5	2	5	2

JOHN-BAPTISTE, Alex (D)   258 11
H: 6 0   W: 11 11   b.Sutton-in-Ashfield 31-1-86
Source: Scholar.

2002–03	Mansfield T	4	0		
2003–04	Mansfield T	17	0		
2004–05	Mansfield T	41	1		
2005–06	Mansfield T	41	1		
2006–07	Mansfield T	46	3		
2007–08	Mansfield T	25	0	174	5
2008–09	Blackpool	21	1		
2009–10	Blackpool	42	3		
2010–11	Blackpool	21	2	84	6

KINGSON, Richard (G)   126 0
H: 6 3   W: 13 10   b.Accra 13-6-78
Honours: Ghana 90 full caps, 1 goal.

1998–99	Sakarya	21	0	21	0
1999–2000	Goztepe	19	0		
2000–01	Goztepe	10	0	29	0
2001–02	Antalya	15	0	15	0
2002–03	Elazig	20	0	20	0
2003–04	Ankara	0	0		
2004–05	Galatasaray	1	0	1	0
2005–06	Ankara	1	0		
2006–07	Ankara	3	0	4	0
2007	Hammarby	11	0	11	0
2007–08	Birmingham C	1	0		
2008–09	Birmingham C	0	0	1	0
2008–09	Wigan Ath	4	0		
2009–10	Wigan Ath	0	0	4	0
2010–11	Blackpool	20	0	20	0

KORNILENKO, Sergei (F)   218 80
H: 6 1   W: 12 04   b.Vitebsk 14-6-83
Honours: Belarus 46 full caps, 10 goals.

2000	Lyakamatyu	4	0	4	0
2001	Dynamo Minsk	16	5		
2002	Dynamo Minsk	16	5		
2003	Dynamo Minsk	30	18	46	23
2003–04	Dynamo Kiev II	15	9	15	9
2003–04	Dynamo Kiev	10	2		
2004–05	Dynamo Kiev	2	0	12	2
2004–05	Dnepr	14	7		
2005–06	Dnepr	35	7		
2006–07	Dnepr	26	10		
2007–08	Dnepr	9	0		
2008	Tomsk	3	0		
2008–09	Dnepr	4	1	88	25
2009	Tomsk	10	6		
2009	Zenit	11	1	11	1
2010	Tomsk	15	11	28	17
2010	Rubin	8	3	8	3
2010–11	Blackpool	6	0	6	0

On loan from Zenit.

MARTIN, Malaury (M) 22 0
b.Nice 25-8-88
Honours: France Youth, Under-21.

2005–06	Monaco	1	0		
2006–07	Monaco	0	0		
2007–08	Monaco	7	0		
2008–09	*Nimes*	14	0	14	0
2009–10	Monaco	0	0	8	0
2010–11	Blackpool	0	0		

ORMEROD, Brett (F) 389 88
H: 5 11 W: 11 12 b.Blackburn 18-10-76
Source: Blackburn R Trainee, Accrington S.

1996–97	Blackpool	4	0		
1997–98	Blackpool	9	2		
1998–99	Blackpool	40	8		
1999–2000	Blackpool	13	5		
2000–01	Blackpool	41	17		
2001–02	Blackpool	21	13		
2001–02	Southampton	18	1		
2002–03	Southampton	31	5		
2003–04	Southampton	22	5		
2004–05	Southampton	9	0		
2004–05	*Leeds U*	6	0	6	0
2004–05	*Wigan Ath*	6	2	6	2
2005–06	Southampton	19	1	99	12
2005–06	Preston NE	15	4		
2006–07	Preston NE	29	8		
2007–08	Preston NE	18	1		
2007–08	*Nottingham F*	13	2	13	2
2008–09	Preston NE	0	0	62	13
2008–09	*Oldham Ath*	5	0	5	0
2008–09	Blackpool	15	2		
2009–10	Blackpool	36	11		
2010–11	Blackpool	19	1	198	59

PHILLIPS, Matthew (M) 105 9
H: 6 0 W: 12 10 b.Aylesbury 13-3-91
Source: Scholar. *Honours:* England Youth.

2007–08	Wycombe W	2	0		
2008–09	Wycombe W	37	3		
2009–10	Wycombe W	36	5		
2010–11	Wycombe W	3	0	78	8
2010–11	Blackpool	27	1	27	1

RACHUBKA, Paul (G) 229 0
H: 6 1 W: 13 05 b.San Luis Opispo 21-5-81
Source: Trainee. *Honours:* England Youth, Under-20.

1999–2000	Manchester U	0	0		
2000–01	Manchester U	1	0		
2001–02	Manchester U	0	0	1	0
2001–02	*Oldham Ath*	16	0	16	0
2001–02	Charlton Ath	0	0		
2002–03	Charlton Ath	0	0		
2003–04	Charlton Ath	0	0		
2003–04	*Huddersfield T*	13	0		
2004–05	Charlton Ath	0	0		
2004–05	*Milton Keynes D*	4	0	4	0
2004–05	*Northampton T*	10	0	10	0
2004–05	Huddersfield T	29	0		
2005–06	Huddersfield T	34	0		
2006–07	Huddersfield T	0	0	76	0
2006–07	*Peterborough U*	4	0	4	0
2006–07	*Blackpool*	8	0		
2007–08	Blackpool	46	0		
2008–09	Blackpool	42	0		
2009–10	Blackpool	20	0		
2010–11	Blackpool	2	0	118	0

REID, Andy (M) 290 35
H: 5 9 W: 12 08 b.Dublin 29-7-82
Source: Trainee. *Honours:* Eire Youth, Under-21, 27 full caps, 4 goals.

1999–2000	Nottingham F	0	0		
2000–01	Nottingham F	14	2		
2001–02	Nottingham F	29	0		
2002–03	Nottingham F	30	1		
2003–04	Nottingham F	46	13		
2004–05	Nottingham F	25	5	144	21
2004–05	Tottenham H	13	1		
2005–06	Tottenham H	13	0	26	1
2006–07	Charlton Ath	16	2		
2007–08	Charlton Ath	22	5	38	7
2007–08	Sunderland	13	1		
2008–09	Sunderland	32	1		
2009–10	Sunderland	21	2		
2010–11	Sunderland	2	0	68	4
2010–11	*Sheffield U*	9	2	9	2
2010–11	Blackpool	5	0	5	0

SBAI, Salaheddine (D) 109 1
H: 5 10 W: 11 07 b.Sidi Kacem 21-8-85
Honours: Morocco 2 full caps.

2004–05	Ronse	5	0	5	0
2005–06	Tubize	25	1		
2006–07	Tubize	23	0	48	1
2007–08	Charleroi	26	0		
2008–09	Charleroi	15	0	41	0
2009–10	Nimes	13	0		
2010–11	Nimes	2	0	15	0
2010–11	Blackpool	0	0		

On loan from Nimes.

SOUTHERN, Keith (M) 305 24
H: 5 10 W: 12 06 b.Gateshead 24-4-81
Source: Trainee.

1998–99	Everton	0	0		
1999–2000	Everton	0	0		
2000–01	Everton	0	0		
2001–02	Everton	0	0		
2002–03	Everton	0	0		
2002–03	Blackpool	38	1		
2003–04	Blackpool	28	2		
2004–05	Blackpool	27	6		
2005–06	Blackpool	42	2		
2006–07	Blackpool	39	5		
2007–08	Blackpool	30	3		
2008–09	Blackpool	35	3		
2009–10	Blackpool	45	2		
2010–11	Blackpool	21	0	305	24

SYLVESTRE, Ludovic (M) 129 15
H: 6 0 W: 11 09 b.Le Blanc-Mesnil 5-2-84

2005–06	Barcelona B	20	0	20	0
2005–06	Barcelona	2	0	2	0
2006–07	Sparta Prague	19	0		
2007–08	Sparta Prague	6	0	25	0
2007–08	*Viktoria Plzen*	14	3	14	3
2008–09	Mlada Boleslav	29	4		
2009–10	Mlada Boleslav	27	7		
2010–11	Mlada Boleslav	4	1	60	12
2010–11	Blackpool	8	0	8	0

TAYLOR-FLETCHER, Gary (F) 331 72
H. 6 0 W. 11 00 b.Widnes 4-6-81
Source: Northwich Vic. *Honours:* England Schools.

2000–01	Hull C	5	0	5	0
2001–02	Leyton Orient	9	0		
2002–03	Leyton Orient	12	1	21	1
2003–04	Lincoln C	42	16		
2004–05	Lincoln C	38	11	80	27
2005–06	Huddersfield T	43	10		
2006–07	Huddersfield T	39	11	82	21
2007–08	Blackpool	42	6		
2008–09	Blackpool	38	5		
2009–10	Blackpool	32	6		
2010–11	Blackpool	31	6	143	23

VAUGHAN, David (M) 301 23
H: 5 7 W: 11 00 b.Abergele 18-2-83
Source: Scholar. *Honours:* Wales Youth, Under-21, 25 full caps, 1 goal.

2000–01	Crewe Alex	1	0		
2001–02	Crewe Alex	13	0		
2002–03	Crewe Alex	32	3		
2003–04	Crewe Alex	31	0		
2004–05	Crewe Alex	44	6		
2005–06	Crewe Alex	34	5		
2006–07	Crewe Alex	29	4		
2007–08	Crewe Alex	1	0	185	18
2007–08	Real Sociedad	7	1	7	1
2008–09	Blackpool	33	1		
2009–10	Blackpool	41	1		
2010–11	Blackpool	35	2	109	4

Scholars
Barkhuizen Thomas John; Challoner Matthew David; Dodd Adam John; Gratton Ryan; Kettings Christopher David; Menagh Jamie; O'Connor Dillan Ryan; Tarney Elliott Preston; Tchobanian Garen Hagop; Thompson Curtis Stephen

BOLTON W (10)

AL-HABSI, Ali (G) 106 0
H: 6 4 W: 12 06 b.Oman 30-12-81
Source: Al-Nasser, Al-Mudhaibi. *Honours:* Oman 70 full caps.

2003	Lyn	13	0
2004	Lyn	24	0
2005	Lyn	25	0	62	0
2005–06	Bolton W	0	0
2006–07	Bolton W	0	0
2007–08	Bolton W	10	0
2008–09	Bolton W	0	0
2009–10	Bolton W	0	0
2010–11	Bolton W	0	0	10	0
2010–11	*Wigan Ath*	34	0	34	0

ALONSO, Marcus (D) 44 3
H: 6 2 W: 13 05 b.Madrid 28-12-90

2008–09	RM Castilla	11	0		
2009–10	RM Castilla	28	3	39	3
2009–10	Real Madrid	1	0	1	0
2010–11	Bolton W	4	0	4	0

BLAKE, Robbie (F) 570 145
H: 5 9 W: 12 00 b.Middlesbrough 4-3-76
Source: Trainee.

1994–95	Darlington	9	0		
1995–96	Darlington	29	11		
1996–97	Darlington	30	10	68	21
1996–97	Bradford C	5	0		
1997–98	Bradford C	34	8		
1998–99	Bradford C	39	16		
1999–2000	Bradford C	28	2		
2000–01	Bradford C	21	4		
2001–02	*Nottingham F*	11	1	11	1
2001–02	Bradford C	26	10	153	40
2001–02	Burnley	10	0		
2002–03	Burnley	41	13		
2003–04	Burnley	45	19		
2004–05	Burnley	24	10		
2004–05	Birmingham C	11	2	11	2
2005–06	Leeds U	41	11		
2006–07	Leeds U	36	8	77	19
2007–08	Burnley	45	9		
2008–09	Burnley	46	8		
2009–10	Burnley	31	2	242	61
2010–11	Bolton W	8	1	8	1

BOGDAN, Adam (G) 5 0
H: 6 4 W: 14 02 b.Budapest 27-9-87
Source: Vasas. *Honours:* Hungary 1 full cap.

2007–08	Bolton W	0	0		
2008–09	Bolton W	0	0		
2009–10	Bolton W	0	0		
2009–10	*Crewe Alex*	1	0	1	0
2010–11	Bolton W	4	0	4	0

CAHILL, Gary (D) 182 15
H: 6 2 W: 12 06 b.Dronfield 19-12-85
Source: Trainee. *Honours:* England Youth, Under-20, Under-21, 3 full caps.

2003–04	Aston Villa	0	0		
2004–05	Aston Villa	0	0		
2004–05	*Burnley*	27	1	27	1
2005–06	Aston Villa	7	1		
2006–07	Aston Villa	20	0		
2007–08	Aston Villa	1	0	28	1
2007–08	*Sheffield U*	16	2	16	2
2007–08	Bolton W	13	0		
2008–09	Bolton W	33	3		
2009–10	Bolton W	29	5		
2010–11	Bolton W	36	3	111	11

COHEN, Tamir (M) 161 12
H: 5 11 W: 11 09 b.Tel Aviv 4-3-84
Honours: Israel Youth, Under-21, 18 full caps.

2002–03	Maccabi Tel Aviv	13	0		
2003–04	Maccabi Tel Aviv	30	2		
2004–05	Maccabi Tel Aviv	22	2		
2005–06	Maccabi Tel Aviv	16	0		
2006–07	Maccabi Tel Aviv	3	0	84	4
2006–07	Maccabi Netanya	13	1		
2007–08	Maccabi Netanya	13	1	28	2
2007–08	Bolton W	10	1		
2008–09	Bolton W	4	1		
2009–10	Bolton W	27	3		
2010–11	Bolton W	8	1	49	6

CONNOLLY, Mark (D) 0 0
H: 6 1 W: 12 01 b.Monaghan 16-12-91
Source: Wolverhampton W Scholar. *Honours:* Eire Youth, Under-21.

2009–10	Bolton W	0	0
2010–11	Bolton W	0	0

DAVIES, Kevin (F)   553 106
H: 6 0 W: 12 10 b.Sheffield 26-3-77
Source: Trainee. *Honours:* England Youth, Under-21, 1 full cap.

Season	Club				
1993–94	Chesterfield	24	4		
1994–95	Chesterfield	41	11		
1995–96	Chesterfield	30	4		
1996–97	Chesterfield	34	3	129	22
1996–97	Southampton	0	0		
1997–98	Southampton	25	9		
1998–99	Blackburn R	21	1		
1999–2000	Blackburn R	2	0	23	1
1999–2000	Southampton	23	6		
2000–01	Southampton	27	1		
2001–02	Southampton	23	2		
2002–03	Southampton	9	1	107	19
2002–03	*Millwall*	9	3	9	3
2003–04	Bolton W	38	9		
2004–05	Bolton W	35	8		
2005–06	Bolton W	37	7		
2006–07	Bolton W	30	8		
2007–08	Bolton W	32	3		
2008–09	Bolton W	38	11		
2009–10	Bolton W	37	7		
2010–11	Bolton W	38	8	285	61

DAVIES, Mark (M)   85 3
H: 5 11 W: 11 08 b.Wolverhampton 18-2-88
Source: Scholar. *Honours:* England Youth.

Season	Club				
2004–05	Wolverhampton W	0	0		
2005–06	Wolverhampton W	20	1		
2006–07	Wolverhampton W	7	0		
2007–08	Wolverhampton W	0	0		
2008–09	Wolverhampton W	0	0	27	1
2008–09	*Leicester C*	7	1	7	1
2008–09	Bolton W	10	0		
2009–10	Bolton W	17	0		
2010–11	Bolton W	24	1	51	1

DAVIS, Sean (M)   275 16
H: 5 10 W: 12 00 b.Clapham 20-9-79
Source: Trainee. *Honours:* England Under-21.

Season	Club				
1996–97	Fulham	1	0		
1997–98	Fulham	0	0		
1998–99	Fulham	6	0		
1999–2000	Fulham	26	0		
2000–01	Fulham	40	6		
2001–02	Fulham	30	0		
2002–03	Fulham	28	3		
2003–04	Fulham	24	5	155	14
2004–05	Tottenham H	15	0		
2005–06	Tottenham H	0	0	15	0
2005–06	Portsmouth	17	1		
2006–07	Portsmouth	31	0		
2007–08	Portsmouth	22	0		
2008–09	Portsmouth	32	1		
2009–10	Portsmouth	0	0	102	2
2009–10	Bolton W	3	0		
2010–11	Bolton W	0	0	3	0

EAVES, Tom (M)   15 0
H: 6 3 W: 13 07 b.Liverpool 14-1-92
Source: Scholar.

Season	Club				
2009–10	Oldham Ath	15	0		
2010–11	Bolton W	0	0		
2010–11	*Oldham Ath*	0	0	15	0

ELMANDER, Johan (F)   366 93
H: 6 1 W: 11 13 b.Alingsas 27-5-81
Honours: Sweden Under-21, 55 full caps, 16 goals.

Season	Club				
1997	Holmalund	5	0		
1998	Holmalund	19	5	24	5
1999	Orgryte	18	2		
2000	Orgryte	21	2	39	4
2000–01	Feyenoord	16	2		
2001–02	Feyenoord	22	1		
2002	Djurgaarden	8	5		
2002–03	Feyenoord	1	0	39	3
2003	Djurgaarden	11	7	19	12
2003–04	NAC Breda	31	7	31	7
2004–05	Brondby	27	9		
2005–06	Brondby	31	13	58	22
2006–07	Toulouse	32	11		
2007–08	Toulouse	32	11	64	22
2008–09	Bolton W	30	5		
2009–10	Bolton W	25	3		
2010–11	Bolton W	37	10	92	18

GARDNER, Ricardo (D)   342 20
H: 5 9 W: 11 00 b.St Andrews 25-9-78
Source: Harbour View. *Honours:* Jamaica 109 full caps, 9 goals.

Season	Club				
1998–99	Bolton W	30	2		
1999–2000	Bolton W	29	5		
2000–01	Bolton W	32	3		
2001–02	Bolton W	31	3		
2002–03	Bolton W	32	2		
2003–04	Bolton W	22	0		
2004–05	Bolton W	33	0		
2005–06	Bolton W	30	0		
2006–07	Bolton W	18	0		
2007–08	Bolton W	26	0		
2008–09	Bolton W	29	4		
2009–10	Bolton W	21	1		
2010–11	Bolton NE	5	0	338	20
2010–11	*Preston NE*	4	0	4	0

HOLDEN, Stuart (M)   115 17
H: 5 10 W: 11 07 b.Aberdeen 1-8-85
Source: Clemson Tigers. *Honours:* USA 17 full caps, 2 goals.

Season	Club				
2005–06	Sunderland	0	0		
2006	Houston Dynamo	13	1		
2007	Houston Dynamo	21	5		
2008	Houston Dynamo	27	3		
2009	Houston Dynamo	26	6	87	15
2009–10	Bolton W	2	0		
2010–11	Bolton W	26	2	28	2

JAASKELAINEN, Jussi (G)   574 0
H: 6 3 W: 12 10 b.Vaasa 19-4-75
Honours: Finland Youth, Under-21, 56 full caps.

Season	Club				
1992	MP	6	0		
1993	MP	6	0		
1994	MP	26	0		
1995	MP	26	0	64	0
1996	VPS	27	0		
1997	VPS	27	0	54	0
1997–98	Bolton W	0	0		
1998–99	Bolton W	34	0		
1999–2000	Bolton W	34	0		
2000–01	Bolton W	27	0		
2001–02	Bolton W	34	0		
2002–03	Bolton W	38	0		
2003–04	Bolton W	38	0		
2004–05	Bolton W	36	0		
2005–06	Bolton W	38	0		
2006–07	Bolton W	38	0		
2007–08	Bolton W	28	0		
2008–09	Bolton W	38	0		
2009–10	Bolton W	38	0		
2010–11	Bolton W	35	0	456	0

KLASNIC, Ivan (F)   324 93
H: 6 1 W: 12 00 b.Hamburg 29-1-80
Honours: Croatia Under-21, 40 full caps, 12 goals.

Season	Club				
1997–98	St Pauli	8	0		
1998–99	St Pauli	24	8		
1999–2000	St Pauli	32	8		
2000–01	St Pauli	31	10	95	26
2001–02	Werder Bremen	23	1		
2002–03	Werder Bremen	13	2		
2003–04	Werder Bremen	29	13		
2004–05	Werder Bremen	28	10		
2005–06	Werder Bremen	30	15		
2006–07	Werder Bremen	13	1		
2007–08	Werder Bremen	16	7	152	49
2008–09	Nantes	28	6	28	6
2009–10	Bolton W	27	8		
2010–11	Bolton W	22	4	49	12

KNIGHT, Zat (D)   267 7
H: 6 6 W: 15 02 b.Solihull 2-5-80
Source: Rushall Olympic. *Honours:* England Under-21, 2 full caps.

Season	Club				
1998–99	Fulham	0	0		
1999–2000	Fulham	0	0		
1999–2000	*Peterborough U*	8	0	8	0
2000–01	Fulham	0	0		
2001–02	Fulham	10	0		
2002–03	Fulham	17	0		
2003–04	Fulham	31	0		
2004–05	Fulham	35	1		
2005–06	Fulham	30	0		
2006–07	Fulham	23	2		
2007–08	Fulham	4	0	150	3
2007–08	Aston Villa	27	1		
2008–09	Aston Villa	13	1		
2009–10	Aston Villa	0	0	40	2
2009–10	Bolton W	35	1		
2010–11	Bolton W	34	1	69	2

LAINTON, Robert (G)   0 0
H: 6 2 W: 12 06 b.Ashton-under-Lyne 12-10-89
Source: Scholar.

Season	Club		
2009–10	Bolton W	0	0
2010–11	Bolton W	0	0

LEE, Chung Yong (M)   116 17
H: 5 11 W: 10 09 b.Seoul 2-7-88
Honours: South Korea 41 full caps, 5 goals.

Season	Club				
2006	FC Seoul	2	0		
2007	FC Seoul	15	3		
2008	FC Seoul	20	5		
2009	FC Seoul	14	2	51	10
2009–10	Bolton W	34	4		
2010–11	Bolton W	31	3	65	7

MORENO, Rodrigo (F)   39 7
H: 5 11 W: 11 09 b.Rio de Janeiro 6-3-91

Season	Club				
2009–10	RM Castilla	4	1	4	1
2009–10	Real Madrid B	18	5	18	5
2010–11	Bolton W	17	1	17	1

On loan from Benfica.

MUAMBA, Fabrice (M)   181 4
H: 6 1 W: 11 10 b.DR Congo 6-4-88
Source: Scholar. *Honours:* England Youth, Under-21.

Season	Club				
2005–06	Arsenal	0	0		
2006–07	Arsenal	0	0		
2006–07	Birmingham C	34	0		
2007–08	Birmingham C	37	2	71	2
2008–09	Bolton W	38	0		
2009–10	Bolton W	36	1		
2010–11	Bolton W	36	1	110	2

MUSTAPHA, Riga (F)   230 55
H: 5 10 W: 11 00 b.Accra 10-10-81
Honours: Holland Under-21.

Season	Club				
1998–99	Vitesse	1	0		
1999–2000	Vitesse	7	0		
2000–01	Roosendaal	8	0	8	0
2001–02	Vitesse	6	1		
2002–03	Vitesse	17	0	31	1
2003–04	Sparta Rotterdam	32	4		
2004–05	Sparta Rotterdam	36	22	68	26
2005–06	Levante	38	11		
2006–07	Levante	33	9		
2007–08	Levante	34	8	105	28
2007–08	Bolton W	17	0		
2009–10	Bolton W	1	0		
2010–11	Bolton W	0	0	18	0

Transferred to Cartagena January 2011.

O'BRIEN, Joey (M)   69 2
H: 5 11 W: 10 13 b.Dublin 17-2-86
Source: Scholar. *Honours:* Eire Youth, Under-21, 3 full caps.

Season	Club				
2004–05	Bolton W	1	0		
2004–05	Sheffield W	15	2		
2005–06	Bolton W	23	0		
2006–07	Bolton W	0	0		
2007–08	Bolton W	19	0		
2008–09	Bolton W	7	0		
2009–10	Bolton W	0	0		
2009–10	Bolton W	0	0	50	0
2010–11	Bolton W	0	0		
2010–11	*Sheffield W*	4	0	19	2

O'HALLORAN, Michael (F)   0 0
H: 6 2 W: 12 06 b.Glasgow 6-1-91
Source: Scholar.

Season	Club		
2009–10	Bolton W	0	0
2010–11	Bolton W	0	0

OBADEYI, Temitope (F)   35 3
H: 5 10 W: 11 09 b.Birmingham 29-10-89
Source: Coventry C. *Honours:* England Youth, Under-20.

Season	Club				
2006–07	Bolton W	0	0		
2007–08	Bolton W	0	0		
2008–09	Bolton W	3	0		
2009–10	Bolton W	0	0		
2009–10	Swindon T	12	2	12	2
2009–10	Rochdale	11	1	11	1
2010–11	Bolton W	0	0	3	0
2010–11	*Shrewsbury T*	9	0	9	0

PETROV, Martin (F) 334 65
H: 6 0 W: 12 02 b.Vzatza 15-1-79
Honours: Bulgaria 88 full caps, 19 goals.

1996–97	CSKA Sofia	3	0	
1997–98	CSKA Sofia	4	0	7 0
1998–99	Servette	12	2	
1999–2000	Servette	31	9	
2000–01	Servette	32	11	75 22
2001–02	Wolfsburg	32	6	
2002–03	Wolfsburg	26	2	
2003–04	Wolfsburg	28	8	
2004–05	Wolfsburg	30	12	116 28
2005–06	Atletico Madrid	36	1	
2006–07	Atletico Madrid	13	2	49 3
2007–08	Manchester C	34	5	
2008–09	Manchester C	9	0	
2009–10	Manchester C	16	4	59 9
2010–11	Bolton W	28	3	28 3

RICKETTS, Sam (D) 288 3
H: 6 1 W: 12 01 b.Aylesbury 11-10-81
Source: Trainee. *Honours:* Wales 42 full caps.

1999–2000	Oxford U	0	0	
2000–01	Oxford U	14	0	
2001–02	Oxford U	29	1	
2002–03	Oxford U	2	0	45 1
From Telford U				
2004–05	Swansea C	42	0	
2005–06	Swansea C	44	1	86 1
2006–07	Hull C	40	1	
2007–08	Hull C	44	0	
2008–09	Hull C	29	0	
2009–10	Hull C	0	0	113 1
2009–10	Bolton W	27	0	
2010–11	Bolton W	17	0	44 0

ROBINSON, Paul (D) 493 12
H: 5 9 W: 11 12 b.Watford 14-12-78
Source: Trainee. *Honours:* England Under-21.

1996–97	Watford	12	0	
1997–98	Watford	22	2	
1998–99	Watford	29	0	
1999–2000	Watford	32	0	
2000–01	Watford	39	0	
2001–02	Watford	38	3	
2002–03	Watford	37	3	
2003–04	Watford	10	0	219 8
2003–04	WBA	31	0	
2004–05	WBA	30	1	
2005–06	WBA	33	0	
2006–07	WBA	42	2	
2007–08	WBA	43	1	
2008–09	WBA	35	0	
2009–10	WBA	0	0	214 4
2009–10	Bolton W	25	0	
2010–11	Bolton W	35	0	60 0

SAMPSON, Jack (F) 0 0
b.Wigan 14-4-93
Source: Scholar.

2010–11	Bolton W	0	0

SAMUEL, JLloyd (D) 254 2
H: 5 11 W: 11 04 b.Trinidad 29-3-81
Source: Charlton Ath Trainee. *Honours:* England Youth, Under-20, Under-21.

1998–99	Aston Villa	0	0	
1999–2000	Aston Villa	9	0	
2000–01	Aston Villa	3	0	
2001–02	*Gillingham*	8	0	8 0
2001–02	Aston Villa	23	0	
2002–03	Aston Villa	38	0	
2003–04	Aston Villa	38	2	
2004–05	Aston Villa	35	0	
2005–06	Aston Villa	19	0	
2006–07	Aston Villa	4	0	169 2
2007–08	Bolton W	20	0	
2008–09	Bolton W	38	0	
2009–10	Bolton W	13	0	
2010–11	Bolton W	0	0	71 0
2010–11	*Cardiff C*	6	0	6 0

SHERIDAN, Sam (M) 0 0
H: 5 11 W: 11 10 b.Stockport 30-11-89
Source: Scholar. *Honours:* Eire Youth.

2009–10	Bolton W	0	0
2010–11	Bolton W	0	0

STEINSSON, Gretar Rafn (D) 261 26
H: 6 2 W: 12 04 b.Siglufjordur 9-1-82
Honours: Iceland 41 full caps, 4 goals.

1999	IA Akranes	0	0	
2000	IA Akranes	13	0	
2001	IA Akranes	18	6	
2002	IA Akranes	17	2	
2003	IA Akranes	11	2	
2004	IA Akranes	17	2	76 12
2004–05	Young Boys	14	3	
2005–06	Young Boys	7	0	21 3
2005–06	AZ	20	4	
2006–07	AZ	25	1	
2007–08	AZ	16	2	61 7
2007–08	Bolton W	16	0	
2008–09	Bolton W	37	3	
2009–10	Bolton W	27	0	
2010–11	Bolton W	23	1	103 4

TAYLOR, Matthew (D) 431 62
H: 5 11 W: 12 03 b.Oxford 27-11-81
Source: Trainee. *Honours:* England Youth, Under-21.

1998–99	Luton T	0	0	
1999–2000	Luton T	41	4	
2000–01	Luton T	45	1	
2001–02	Luton T	43	11	129 16
2002–03	Portsmouth	35	7	
2003–04	Portsmouth	30	0	
2004–05	Portsmouth	32	1	
2005–06	Portsmouth	34	6	
2006–07	Portsmouth	35	8	
2007–08	Portsmouth	13	1	179 23
2007–08	Bolton W	16	3	
2008–09	Bolton W	34	10	
2009–10	Bolton W	37	8	
2010–11	Bolton W	36	2	123 23

VAZ TE, Ricardo (F) 64 3
H: 6 2 W: 12 07 b.Lisbon 1-10-86
Source: Trainee. *Honours:* Portugal Youth, Under-20, Under-21.

2003–04	Bolton W	1	0	
2004–05	Bolton W	7	0	
2005–06	Bolton W	22	3	
2006–07	Bolton W	25	0	
2006–07	Hull C	6	0	6 0
2007–08	Bolton W	1	0	
2008–09	Bolton W	2	0	
2009–10	Bolton W	0	0	
2010–11	Bolton W	0	0	58 3

VELA, Joshua (M) 0 0
b. 14-12-93
Source: Scholar

2010–11	Bolton W	0	0

WARD, Danny (M) 42 10
H: 5 11 W: 12 05 b.Bradford 11-12-91
Source: Leeds U.

2008–09	Bolton W	0	0	
2009–10	Bolton W	2	0	
2009–10	*Swindon T*	28	7	28 7
2010–11	Bolton W	0	0	2 0
2010–11	*Coventry C*	5	0	5 0
2010–11	*Huddersfield T*	7	3	7 3

WHEATER, David (D) 170 12
H: 6 5 W: 12 12 b.Redcar 14-2-87
Source: Scholar. *Honours:* England Youth, Under-21.

2004–05	Middlesbrough	0	0	
2005–06	Middlesbrough	6	0	
2005–06	*Doncaster R*	7	1	7 1
2006–07	Middlesbrough	2	1	
2006–07	*Wolverhampton W*	1	0	1 0
2006–07	*Darlington*	15	2	15 2
2007–08	Middlesbrough	34	3	
2008–09	Middlesbrough	32	1	
2009–10	Middlesbrough	42	1	
2010–11	Middlesbrough	24	3	140 9
2010–11	Bolton W	7	0	7 0

Scholars
Battersby Nathan Paul; Bennett Rhys Gordon; Blakeman Adam John; Caton James Alan Kenneth; Dennis Elliott Ben; Fielding Lewis; Hampson Benjamin Christopher; Irwin Liam Joseph; Kellett Andrew Paul; Lynch Jay; MacGregor Graeme Douglas; McQuade Alexander Michael; Odelusi Oluwasanmi; Proudfoot Lewis Steven; Riley Joseph; Stayte Ryan; Threlkeld Oscar George

BOURNEMOUTH (11)

ARTER, Harry (M) 23 1
H: 5 9 W: 11 07 b.Sidcup 28-12-89
Source: Scholar.

2007–08	Charlton Ath	0	0	
2008–09	Charlton Ath	0	0	
From Woking.				
2010–11	Bournemouth	18	0	18 0
2010–11	*Carlisle U*	5	1	5 1

BAUDRY, Mathieu (D) 29 2
H: 6 2 W: 12 08 b.Le Havre 24-2-88

2007–08	Troyes	2	1	
2008–09	Troyes	17	0	
2009–10	Troyes	7	0	26 1
2010–11	Bournemouth	3	1	3 1

BRADBURY, Lee (F) 509 92
H: 6 0 W: 12 07 b.Cowes 3-7-75
Source: Cowes. *Honours:* England Under-21.

1995–96	Portsmouth	12	0	
1995–96	*Exeter C*	14	5	14 5
1996–97	Portsmouth	42	15	
1997–98	Manchester C	27	7	
1998–99	Manchester C	13	3	40 10
1998–99	Crystal Palace	22	4	
1998–99	*Birmingham C*	7	0	7 0
1999–2000	Crystal Palace	10	2	32 6
1999–2000	Portsmouth	35	10	
2000–01	Portsmouth	39	10	
2001–02	Portsmouth	22	7	
2002–03	Portsmouth	3	1	
2002–03	*Sheffield W*	11	3	11 3
2003–04	Portsmouth	0	0	153 43
2003–04	*Derby Co*	7	0	7 0
2003–04	*Walsall*	8	1	8 1
2004–05	Oxford U	41	4	
2005–06	Oxford U	22	5	63 9
2005–06	Southend U	15	1	
2006–07	Southend U	31	4	
2007–08	Southend U	1	0	47 5
2007–08	Bournemouth	35	3	
2008–09	Bournemouth	34	6	
2009–10	Bournemouth	44	1	
2010–11	Bournemouth	14	0	127 10

CONNELL, Alan (F) 214 41
H: 6 0 W: 12 00 b.Enfield 5-2-83
Source: Ipswich T Trainee.

2002–03	Bournemouth	13	6	
2003–04	Bournemouth	7	0	
2004–05	Bournemouth	34	2	
2005–06	*Torquay U*	22	7	22 7
2006–07	*Hereford U*	44	9	44 9
2007–08	Brentford	42	12	
2008–09	Brentford	2	0	44 12
2008–09	Bournemouth	12	0	
2009–10	Bournemouth	38	5	
2010–11	Bournemouth	0	0	104 13

COOPER, Shaun (D) 211 1
H: 5 10 W: 10 05 b.Newport (IW) 5-10-83
Source: School.

2000–01	Portsmouth	0	0	
2001–02	Portsmouth	7	0	
2002–03	Portsmouth	0	0	
2003–04	Portsmouth	0	0	
2003–04	*Leyton Orient*	9	0	9 0
2004–05	Portsmouth	0	0	
2004–05	*Kidderminster H*	10	0	10 0
2005–06	Portsmouth	0	0	7 0
2005–06	Bournemouth	35	0	
2006–07	Bournemouth	33	0	
2007–08	Bournemouth	38	1	
2008–09	Bournemouth	37	0	
2009–10	Bournemouth	6	0	
2010–11	Bournemouth	36	0	185 1

CUMMINGS, Warren (D) 262 7
H: 5 9 W: 11 05 b.Aberdeen 15-10-80
Source: Trainee. *Honours:* Scotland Under-21, 1 full cap.

1999–2000	Chelsea	0	0	
2000–01	Chelsea	0	0	
2000–01	*Bournemouth*	10	1	
2000–01	*WBA*	3	0	
2001–02	Chelsea	0	0	
2001–02	*WBA*	14	0	17 0
2002–03	Chelsea	0	0	
2002–03	Bournemouth	20	0	

2003–04	Bournemouth	42	2		
2004–05	Bournemouth	30	2		
2005–06	Bournemouth	0	0		
2006–07	Bournemouth	31	0		
2007–08	Bournemouth	32	2		
2008–09	Bournemouth	32	0		
2009–10	Bournemouth	34	0		
2010–11	Bournemouth	14	0	245	7

FEENEY, Liam (M)   105 12
H: 5 10 W: 12 02 b.Hammersmith 21-1-87
Source: Salisbury C.
On loan from Salisbury C.

2008–09	Southend U	1	0	1	0
2008–09	Bournemouth	14	3		
2009–10	Bournemouth	44	5		
2010–11	Bournemouth	46	4	104	12

FLETCHER, Steve (F)   667 111
H: 6 2 W: 14 09 b.Hartlepool 26-7-72
Source: Trainee.

1990–91	Hartlepool U	14	2		
1991–92	Hartlepool U	18	2	32	4
1992–93	Bournemouth	31	4		
1993–94	Bournemouth	36	6		
1994–95	Bournemouth	40	6		
1995–96	Bournemouth	7	1		
1996–97	Bournemouth	35	7		
1997–98	Bournemouth	42	12		
1998–99	Bournemouth	39	8		
1999–2000	Bournemouth	36	7		
2000–01	Bournemouth	45	9		
2001–02	Bournemouth	2	0		
2002–03	Bournemouth	35	5		
2003–04	Bournemouth	41	9		
2004–05	Bournemouth	36	9		
2005–06	Bournemouth	27	4		
2006–07	Bournemouth	41	1		
2007–08	Chesterfield	38	5	38	5

From Crawley T.

2008–09	Bournemouth	21	4		
2009–10	Bournemouth	45	4		
2010–11	Bournemouth	38	6	597	102

GARRY, Ryan (D)   78 3
H: 6 0 W: 11 05 b.Hornchurch 29-9-83
Source: Scholar. Honours: England Youth, Under-20.

2001–02	Arsenal	0	0		
2002–03	Arsenal	1	0		
2003–04	Arsenal	0	0		
2004–05	Arsenal	0	0		
2005–06	Arsenal	0	0		
2006–07	Arsenal	0	0	1	0
2007–08	Bournemouth	8	0		
2008–09	Bournemouth	25	0		
2009–10	Bournemouth	34	1		
2010–11	Bournemouth	10	2	77	3

HOLLANDS, Danny (M)   203 25
H: 6 0 W: 11 11 b.Ashford (Middlesex) 6-11-85
Source: Trainee.

2003–04	Chelsea	0	0		
2004–05	Chelsea	0	0		
2005–06	Chelsea	0	0		
2005–06	Torquay U	10	1	10	1
2006–07	Bournemouth	33	1		
2007–08	Bournemouth	37	4		
2008–09	Bournemouth	42	6		
2009–10	Bournemouth	39	6		
2010–11	Bournemouth	42	7	193	24

INGS, Danny (F)   26 7
H: 5 10 W: 11 07 b.Winchester 16-3-92
Source: Youth.

| 2009–10 | Bournemouth | 0 | 0 | | |
| 2010–11 | Bournemouth | 26 | 7 | 26 | 7 |

JALAL, Shwan (G)   148 0
H: 6 2 W: 14 02 b.Baghdad 14-8-83
Source: Hastings T.

2001–02	Tottenham H	0	0		
2002–03	Tottenham H	0	0		
2003–04	Tottenham H	0	0		

From Woking.

2006–07	*Sheffield W*	0	0		
2006–07	Peterborough U	1	0		
2007–08	Peterborough U	7	0		
2007–08	*Morecambe*	12	0	12	0
2008–09	Peterborough U	0	0	8	0
2008–09	Bournemouth	41	0		
2009–10	Bournemouth	44	0		
2010–11	Bournemouth	43	0	128	0

LOVELL, Stephen (F)   259 65
H: 5 11 W: 11 08 b.Amersham 6-12-80
Source: Trainee.

1998–99	Bournemouth	7	0		
1999–2000	Bournemouth	1	0		
1999–2000	Portsmouth	3	0		
1999–2000	*Exeter C*	5	1	5	1
2000–01	Portsmouth	9	1		
2001–02	Portsmouth	20	2	32	3
2001–02	*Sheffield U*	5	1	5	1
2002–03	Dundee	28	11		
2003–04	Dundee	21	5		
2004–05	Dundee	33	12	82	28
2005–06	Aberdeen	27	8		
2006–07	Aberdeen	27	9		
2007–08	Aberdeen	22	3	76	20
2008–09	Falkirk	28	8	28	8
2009–10	Partick Th	16	3	16	3
2010–11	Bournemouth	7	1	15	1

MOLESLEY, Mark (M)   41 5
H: 6 1 W: 12 07 b.Hillingdon 11-3-81
From Hayes, Cam C, Ald T, Steve B, Grays

2008–09	Bournemouth	29	4		
2009–10	Bournemouth	10	1		
2010–11	Bournemouth	2	0	41	5

NELSON, Mitchell (D)   0 0
b.Camberwell 31-8-89
Source: Colchester U, Scholar, Tooting & Mitcham U.

| 2010–11 | Bournemouth | 0 | 0 | | |

PARTINGTON, Joe (M)   33 2
H: 5 11 W: 11 13 b.Portsmouth 1-4-90
Source: Scholalr. Honours: Wales Youth, Under-21.

2007–08	Bournemouth	6	1		
2008–09	Bournemouth	11	1		
2009–10	Bournemouth	11	0		
2010–11	Bournemouth	5	0	33	2

PEARCE, Jason (D)   162 7
H: 5 11 W: 12 00 b.Hillingdon 6-12-87
Source: Scholar.

2006–07	Portsmouth	0	0		
2007–08	Bournemouth	33	1		
2008–09	Bournemouth	44	2		
2009–10	Bournemouth	39	1		
2010–11	Bournemouth	46	3	162	7

PUGH, Marc (M)   179 34
H: 5 11 W: 11 04 b.Bacup 2-4-87
Source: Scholar.

2005–06	Burnley	0	0		
2005–06	Bury	6	1		
2006–07	Bury	35	3	41	4
2007–08	Shrewsbury T	37	4		
2008–09	Shrewsbury T	7	0	44	4
2008–09	*Luton T*	4	0	4	0
2008–09	*Hereford U*	9	1		
2009–10	Hereford U	40	13	49	14
2010–11	Bournemouth	41	12	41	12

PURCHES, Stephen (D)   363 15
H: 5 11 W: 11 13 b.Ilford 14-1-80

1998–99	West Ham U	0	0		
1999–2000	West Ham U	0	0		
2000–01	Bournemouth	34	0		
2001–02	Bournemouth	41	2		
2002–03	Bournemouth	44	3		
2003–04	Bournemouth	42	3		
2004–05	Bournemouth	14	1		
2005–06	Bournemouth	26	0		
2006–07	Bournemouth	43	1		
2007–08	Leyton Orient	37	1		
2008–09	Leyton Orient	42	3		
2009–10	Leyton Orient	31	1	110	5
2010–11	Bournemouth	9	0	253	10

ROBINSON, Anton (M)   106 10
H: 5 9 W: 10 03 b.Harrow 17-2-86
Source: Millwall Scholar.

| 2004–05 | Millwall | 0 | 0 | | |
| 2005–06 | Millwall | 0 | 0 | | |

From Ex C, Eastb B, Fish A, Weymouth.

2008–09	Bournemouth	17	1		
2009–10	Bournemouth	44	4		
2010–11	Bournemouth	45	5	106	10

STEPHENSON, Tim (D)   0 0
b.Southampton
Source: Youth.

| 2010–11 | Bournemouth | 0 | 0 | | |

STEWART, Jon (G)   4 0
H: 6 2 W: 13 01 b.Hayes 13-3-89
Source: Swindon T Scholar, Weymouth.

2008–09	Portsmouth	0	0		
2009–10	Portsmouth	0	0		
2010–11	Bournemouth	4	0	4	0

STOCKLEY, Jayden (F)   6 0
H: 6 2 W: 12 07 b.Poole 10-10-93
Source: School.

| 2009–10 | Bournemouth | 2 | 0 | | |
| 2010–11 | Bournemouth | 4 | 0 | 6 | 0 |

SYMES, Michael (F)   171 41
H: 6 3 W: 12 04 b.Gt Yarmouth 31-10-83
Source: Scholar.

2001–02	Everton	0	0		
2002–03	Everton	0	0		
2003–04	Everton	0	0		
2003–04	*Crewe Alex*	4	1	4	1
2004–05	Bradford C	12	2		
2004–05	*Darlington*	0	0		
2005–06	Bradford C	3	1		
2005–06	*Stockport Co*	1	0	1	0
2006–07	Bradford C	0	0	15	3
2006–07	Shrewsbury T	33	9		
2007–08	Shrewsbury T	21	3		
2007–08	*Macclesfield T*	14	1	14	1
2008–09	Shrewsbury T	8	2	62	14
2008–09	*Bournemouth*	5	0		
2008–09	Accrington S	7	1		
2009–10	Accrington S	41	13	48	14
2010–11	Bournemouth	22	8	27	8

TAYLOR, Lyle (F)   11 0
H: 6 2 W: 12 00 b.Greenwich 29-3-90
Source: Staines T.

| 2007–08 | Millwall | 0 | 0 | | |

From Concord R.

| 2008–09 | Millwall | 0 | 0 | | |

From Concord R.

| 2010–11 | Bournemouth | 11 | 0 | 11 | 0 |

THOMAS, Dan (G)   2 0
H: 6 2 W: 13 01 b.Poole 1-9-91
Source: School.

| 2009–10 | Bournemouth | 2 | 0 | | |
| 2010–11 | Bournemouth | 0 | 0 | 2 | 0 |

WIGGINS, Rhoys (D)   68 2
H: 5 8 W: 11 05 b.Uxbridge 4-11-87
Source: Scholar. Honours: Wales Youth, Under-21.

2006–07	Crystal Palace	0	0		
2007–08	Crystal Palace	0	0		
2008–09	Crystal Palace	1	0	1	0
2008–09	*Bournemouth*	13	0		
2009–10	Norwich C	0	0		
2009–10	*Bournemouth*	19	0		
2010–11	Bournemouth	35	2	67	2

WILLIAMSON, Ben (F)   4 0
H: 5 11 W: 11 13 b.Lambeth 25-12-88
Source: Worthing, Jerez Industrial.

| 2010–11 | Bournemouth | 4 | 0 | 4 | 0 |

BRADFORD C (12)

BULLOCK, Lee (M)   375 40
H: 6 0 W: 11 04 b.Stockton 22-5-81
Source: Trainee.

1999–2000	York C	24	0		
2000–01	York C	33	3		
2001–02	York C	40	8		
2002–03	York C	39	6		
2003–04	York C	35	7	171	24
2003–04	*Cardiff C*	11	3		
2004–05	Cardiff C	21	3	32	6
2005–06	Hartlepool U	31	4		
2006–07	Hartlepool U	25	1		
2007–08	Hartlepool U	1	0	57	5
2007–08	*Mansfield T*	5	0	5	0
2007–08	*Bury*	8	0	8	0
2007–08	Bradford C	12	1		
2008–09	Bradford C	23	3		
2009–10	Bradford C	41	1		
2010–11	Bradford C	26	0	102	5

CHILAKA, Chibuzor (M)   4   0
H: 5 9   W: 13 01   b.Nigeria 21-10-86
Source: Notts Co, Hinckley U, Bridlington T, Leeds Carnegie.

2010–11	Bradford C	4	0	4 0

DALEY, Omar (M)   151   16
H: 5 10   W: 11 03   b.Kingston, Jamaica 25-4-81
Source: Portmore U. *Honours:* Jamaica Under-20, 65 full caps, 7 goals.

2003–04	Reading	6	0	6 0
2004–05	Preston NE	14	0	14 0
From Charleston B, Portmore U.				
2006–07	Bradford C	14	2	
2007–08	Bradford C	41	4	
2008–09	Bradford C	28	3	
2009–10	Bradford C	14	1	
2010–11	Bradford C	26	5	123 15
2010–11	*Rotherham U*	8	1	8 1

DEAN, Luke (F)   2   0
H: 5 9   W: 11 00   b.Cleckheaton 1-8-89
Source: Scholar.

2009–10	Bradford C	1	0	
2010–11	Bradford C	1	0	2 0

DOBIE, Scott (F)   410   63
H: 6 1   W: 12 05   b.Workington 10-10-78
Source: Trainee. *Honours:* Scotland 6 full caps, 1 goal.

1996–97	Carlisle U	2	1	
1997–98	Carlisle U	23	0	
1998–99	Carlisle U	33	6	
1998–99	*Clydebank*	6	0	6 0
1999–2000	Carlisle U	34	7	
2000–01	Carlisle U	44	0	
2001–02	WBA	43	10	
2002–03	WBA	31	5	
2003–04	WBA	31	5	
2004–05	WBA	5	1	110 21
2004–05	Millwall	16	3	16 3
2004–05	Nottingham F	12	1	
2005–06	Nottingham F	8	2	
2006–07	Nottingham F	19	0	
2007–08	Nottingham F	2	0	41 3
2007–08	Carlisle U	15	4	
2008–09	Carlisle U	30	3	
2009–10	Carlisle U	39	5	220 36
2010–11	St Johnstone	4	0	4 0
On loan from St Johnstone.				
2010–11	Bradford C	13	0	13 0

DOHERTY, Tom (M)   318   9
H: 5 8   W: 10 06   b.Bristol 17-3-79
Source: Trainee. *Honours:* Northern Ireland 9 full caps.

1997–98	Bristol C	30	2	
1998–99	Bristol C	23	1	
1999–2000	Bristol C	1	0	
2000–01	Bristol C	0	0	
2001–02	Bristol C	34	1	
2002–03	Bristol C	38	0	
2003–04	Bristol C	33	2	
2004–05	Bristol C	29	1	188 7
2005–06	QPR	15	0	
2005–06	*Yeovil T*	1	0	1 0
2006–07	QPR	0	0	
2006–07	*Wycombe W*	26	2	
2007–08	QPR	0	0	15 0
2007–08	Wycombe W	24	0	
2008–09	Wycombe W	34	0	
2009–10	Wycombe W	12	0	96 2
2010–11	Bradford C	18	0	18 0

DUFF, Shane (D)   207   3
H: 6 1   W: 12 10   b.Swindon 2-4-82
Source: Juniors. *Honours:* Northern Ireland Under-21.

2000–01	Cheltenham T	0	0	
2001–02	Cheltenham T	0	0	
2002–03	Cheltenham T	18	0	
2003–04	Cheltenham T	15	1	
2004–05	Cheltenham T	45	1	
2005–06	Cheltenham T	20	0	
2006–07	Cheltenham T	34	0	
2007–08	Cheltenham T	30	0	
2008–09	Cheltenham T	20	0	
2009–10	Cheltenham T	11	0	193 2
2010–11	Bradford C	14	1	14 1

ELLIOTT, Chris (G)   0   0
b.Newcastle 17-7-92
Source: Scholar.

2010–11	Bradford C	0	0	

EVANS, Gary (F)   161   33
H: 6 0   W: 12 08   b.Stockport 26-4-88
Source: Crewe Alex.

2007–08	Macclesfield T	42	7	
2008–09	Macclesfield T	40	12	82 19
2009–10	Bradford C	43	11	
2010–11	Bradford C	36	3	79 14

FLETT, Alex (M)   1   0
Source: Scholar.

2010–11	Bradford C	1	0	1 0

FLYNN, Michael (M)   255   34
H: 5 10   W: 13 04   b.Newport 17-10-80
Source: Barry T.

2002–03	Wigan Ath	17	1	
2003–04	Wigan Ath	8	0	
2004–05	Wigan Ath	13	1	38 2
2004–05	*Blackpool*	6	0	
2004–05	Gillingham	16	3	
2005–06	Gillingham	36	6	
2006–07	Gillingham	45	10	97 19
2007–08	Blackpool	28	3	34 3
2008–09	*Darlington*	0	0	
2008–09	Huddersfield T	25	4	25 4
2009–10	Bradford C	42	6	
2010–11	Bradford C	19	0	61 6

GRANT, Gavin (F)   35   1
H: 5 11   W: 11 00   b.Middlesex 27-3-84
Source: Tooting & Mitcham U.

2005–06	Gillingham	10	1	10 1
2005–06	Millwall	0	0	
2006–07	Millwall	4	0	
2007–08	Millwall	0	0	4 0
2008–09	Wycombe W	10	0	
2009–10	Wycombe W	0	0	10 0
2009–10	Bradford C	11	0	
2010–11	Bradford C	0	0	11 0

HANSON, James (F)   70   18
H: 6 4   W: 12 04   b.Bradford 9-11-87
Source: Eccleshill U, Guiseley.

2009–10	Bradford C	34	12	
2010–11	Bradford C	36	6	70 18

HARRISON, Ryan (M)   1   0
H: 5 10   W: 12 02   b.Leeds 13-10-91
Source: Scholar.

2009–10	Bradford C	1	0	
2010–11	Bradford C	0	0	1 0

HENDRIE, Lee (M)   340   34
H: 5 10   W: 11 00   b.Birmingham 18-5-77
Source: Trainee. *Honours:* England Youth, Under-21, B, 1 full cap.

1993–94	Aston Villa	0	0	
1994–95	Aston Villa	0	0	
1995–96	Aston Villa	3	0	
1996–97	Aston Villa	4	0	
1997–98	Aston Villa	17	3	
1998–99	Aston Villa	32	3	
1999–2000	Aston Villa	29	1	
2000–01	Aston Villa	32	6	
2001–02	Aston Villa	29	2	
2002–03	Aston Villa	27	4	
2003–04	Aston Villa	32	2	
2004–05	Aston Villa	29	5	
2005–06	Aston Villa	16	1	
2006–07	Aston Villa	1	0	251 27
2006–07	*Stoke C*	28	3	28 3
2007–08	Sheffield U	12	1	
2007–08	*Leicester C*	9	1	9 1
2008–09	Sheffield U	5	0	
2008–09	*Blackpool*	6	0	6 0
2009–10	Sheffield U	0	0	17 1
2009–10	Derby Co	9	0	9 0
2009–10	*Brighton & HA*	8	0	8 0
2010–11	Bradford C	12	2	12 2

HORNE, Louis (M)   1   0
H: 6 2   W: 12 07   b.Bradford 28-5-91
Source: Scholar.

2009–10	Bradford C	1	0	
2010–11	Bradford C	0	0	1 0

HUNT, Lewis (D)   228   4
H: 5 11   W: 12 09   b.Birmingham 25-8-82
Source: Scholar.

2000–01	Derby Co	0	0	
2001–02	Derby Co	0	0	
2002–03	Derby Co	10	0	
2003–04	Derby Co	1	0	11 0
2003–04	*Southend U*	26	0	
2004–05	Southend U	31	0	
2005–06	Southend U	30	0	
2006–07	Southend U	35	2	
2007–08	Southend U	24	0	146 2
2008–09	Wycombe W	20	1	
2009–10	Wycombe W	27	0	47 1
2010–11	Bradford C	24	1	24 1

McLAUGHLIN, Jon (G)   33   0
H: 6 2   W: 13 00   b.Edinburgh 9-9-87
Source: Harrogate T.

2008–09	Bradford C	1	0	
2009–10	Bradford C	7	0	
2010–11	Bradford C	25	0	33 0

NEILSON, Scott (M)   24   1
H: 6 0   W: 12 10   b.Enfield 15-5-87
Source: Cambridge C.

2009–10	Bradford C	23	1	
2010–11	Bradford C	1	0	24 1

O'BRIEN, Luke (D)   122   2
H: 5 9   W: 12 01   b.Halifax 11-9-88
Source: Scholar.

2007–08	Bradford C	2	0	
2008–09	Bradford C	35	1	
2009–10	Bradford C	43	1	
2010–11	Bradford C	42	0	122 2

OLIVER, Luke (D)   87   3
H: 6 6   W: 14 05   b.Acton 1-5-84
Source: Brook House.

2002–03	Wycombe W	2	0	
2003–04	Wycombe W	2	0	
From Woking				
2005–06	*Yeovil T*	3	0	3 0
From Stevenage B.				
2008–09	Wycombe W	8	0	
2009–10	Wycombe W	23	0	35 0
2009–10	*Bradford C*	7	2	
2010–11	Bradford C	42	1	49 3

OSBORNE, Leon (F)   37   1
H: 5 10   W: 10 10   b.Doncaster 28-10-89
Source: Scholar.

2006–07	Bradford C	1	0	
2007–08	Bradford C	0	0	
2008–09	Bradford C	2	0	
2009–10	Bradford C	12	0	
2010–11	Bradford C	22	1	37 1

PIDGELEY, Lenny (G)   122   0
H: 6 4   W: 14 09   b.Twickenham 7-2-84
Source: Scholar. *Honours:* England Under-20.

2003–04	Chelsea	0	0	
2003–04	*Watford*	27	0	27 0
2004–05	Chelsea	1	0	
2005–06	Chelsea	1	0	2 0
2005–06	*Millwall*	0	0	
2006–07	Millwall	42	0	
2007–08	Millwall	13	0	
2008–09	Millwall	0	0	55 0
2009–10	Carlisle U	17	0	17 0
From Woking.				
2010–11	Bradford C	21	0	21 0

RAMSDEN, Simon (D)   214   7
H: 6 0   W: 12 06   b.Bishop Auckland 17-12-81
Source: Scholar.

2000–01	Sunderland	0	0	
2001–02	Sunderland	0	0	
2002–03	Sunderland	0	0	
2002–03	*Notts Co*	32	0	32 0
2003–04	Sunderland	0	0	
2004–05	Grimsby T	25	0	
2005–06	Grimsby T	12	0	37 0
2005–06	Rochdale	15	1	
2006–07	Rochdale	34	3	
2007–08	Rochdale	35	2	
2008–09	Rochdale	28	0	112 6
2009–10	Bradford C	31	1	
2010–11	Bradford C	2	0	33 1

REHMAN, Zesh (D)　157 4
H: 6 2　W: 12 08　b.Birmingham 14-10-83
Source: Scholar. *Honours:* England Youth, Pakistan 6 full caps.

Season	Club				
2001–02	Fulham	0	0		
2002–03	Fulham	0	0		
2003–04	Fulham	1	0		
2003–04	*Brighton & HA*	11	2		
2004–05	Fulham	17	0		
2005–06	Fulham	3	0	21	0
2005–06	*Norwich C*	5	0	5	0
2006–07	QPR	25	0		
2006–07	*Brighton & HA*	8	0	19	2
2007–08	QPR	21	0		
2008–09	QPR	0	0	46	0
2008–09	*Blackpool*	3	0	3	0
2008–09	*Bradford C*	17	0		
2009–10	Bradford C	38	2		
2010–11	Bradford C	8	0	63	2

ROWE, Dominic (M)　2 0
Source: Scholar.

2010–11	Bradford C	2	0	2	0

SAXTON, Lloyd (G)　0 0
H: 5 11　W: 12 03　b.Alsager 18-4-90
Source: Scholar.

2008–09	Plymouth Arg	0	0		
2009–10	Plymouth Arg	0	0		
2010–11	Bradford C	0	0		

SPEIGHT, Jake (F)　62 7
H: 5 7　W: 11 02　b.Sheffield 28-9-83
Source: Bury, Northwich Vic, Droylsden, Mansfield T.
From Scarborough.

2005–06	Bury	17	2		
2006–07	Bury	13	0		
2007–08	Bury	0	0		
2008–09	Bury	0	0	30	2
2010–11	Bradford C	28	4	28	4
2010–11	*Port Vale*	4	1	4	1

STEPHENSON, Darren (F)　1 0
b. 6-3-93
Source: Scholar.

2010–11	Bradford C	1	0	1	0

SYERS, Dave (M)　37 8
b.Leeds 30-11-87
Source: Ossett Alb, Farsley C, Harrogate T.

2010–11	Bradford C	37	8	37	8

THRELFALL, Robbie (D)　55 2
H: 5 11　W: 11 00　b.Liverpool 25-11-88
Source: Scholar. *Honours:* England Youth.

2006–07	Liverpool	0	0		
2007–08	Liverpool	0	0		
2007–08	*Hereford U*	9	0		
2008–09	Liverpool	0	0		
2008–09	*Hereford U*	3	0	12	0
2008–09	*Stockport Co*	2	0	2	0
2009–10	Liverpool	0	0		
2009–10	*Northampton T*	4	0	4	0
2009–10	*Bradford C*	17	2		
2010–11	Bradford C	20	0	37	2

WETHERALL, David (D)　506 30
H: 6 3　W: 13 12　b.Sheffield 14-3-71
Source: School. *Honours:* England Schools.

1989–90	Sheffield W	0	0		
1990–91	Sheffield W	0	0		
1991–92	Leeds U	1	0		
1992–93	Leeds U	13	1		
1993–94	Leeds U	32	1		
1994–95	Leeds U	38	3		
1995–96	Leeds U	34	4		
1996–97	Leeds U	29	0		
1997–98	Leeds U	34	3		
1998–99	Leeds U	21	0	202	12
1999–2000	Bradford C	38	2		
2000–01	Bradford C	18	1		
2001–02	Bradford C	19	2		
2002–03	Bradford C	17	0		
2003–04	Bradford C	34	1		
2004–05	Bradford C	45	4		
2005–06	Bradford C	46	5		
2006–07	Bradford C	41	1		
2007–08	Bradford C	46	2		
2008–09	Bradford C	0	0		
2009–10	Bradford C	0	0		
2010–11	Bradford C	0	0	304	18

WILLIAMS, Steve (D)　67 7
H: 6 4　W: 13 06　b.Preston 24-4-87
Source: Charnock Richard, Chorley, Bamber Bridge, Hyde U, Fleetwood T, Bamber Bridge.

2009–10	Bradford C	39	4		
2010–11	Bradford C	28	3	67	7

WORTHINGTON, Jon (M)　254 12
H: 5 9　W: 11 05　b.Dewsbury 16-4-83
Source: Scholar.

2001–02	Huddersfield T	0	0		
2002–03	Huddersfield T	22	0		
2003–04	Huddersfield T	39	3		
2004–05	Huddersfield T	39	3		
2005–06	Huddersfield T	41	4		
2006–07	Huddersfield T	28	2		
2007–08	Huddersfield T	25	0		
2008–09	Huddersfield T	19	0	213	12
2008–09	*Yeovil T*	9	0	9	0
2009–10	Oldham Ath	16	0		
2010–11	Oldham Ath	0	0	16	0
2010–11	Bradford C	16	0	16	0

BRENTFORD (13)

ALEXANDER, Gary (F)　445 126
H: 6 0　W: 13 04　b.Lambeth 15-8-79
Source: Trainee.

1998–99	West Ham U	0	0		
1999–2000	West Ham U	0	0		
1999–2000	*Exeter C*	37	16	37	16
2000–01	Swindon T	37	7	37	7
2001–02	Hull C	43	17		
2002–03	Hull C	25	6	68	23
2002–03	Leyton Orient	17	2		
2003–04	Leyton Orient	44	15		
2004–05	Leyton Orient	28	9		
2005–06	Leyton Orient	46	14		
2006–07	Leyton Orient	44	12	179	52
2007–08	Millwall	36	7		
2008–09	Millwall	35	11		
2009–10	Millwall	15	1	86	19
2010–11	Brentford	38	9	38	9

BALKESTEIN, Pim (D)　63 2
H: 6 3　W: 12 00　b.Gouda 29-4-87
Source: Heerenveen.

2008–09	Ipswich T	20	0		
2009–10	Ipswich T	9	0	29	0
2009–10	*Brentford*	14	1		
2010–11	Brentford	20	1	34	2

BEAN, Marcus (M)　231 17
H: 5 11　W: 11 06　b.Hammersmith 2-11-84
Source: Scholar.

2002–03	QPR	7	0		
2003–04	QPR	31	1		
2004–05	QPR	20	1		
2004–05	*Swansea C*	8	0		
2005–06	QPR	9	0	67	2
2005–06	*Swansea C*	9	1	17	1
2005–06	Blackpool	17	1		
2006–07	Blackpool	6	0		
2007–08	Blackpool	0	0	23	1
2007–08	*Rotherham U*	12	1	12	1
2008–09	Brentford	44	9		
2009–10	Brentford	31	0		
2010–11	Brentford	37	3	112	12

BLAKE, Ryan (D)　1 0
H: 5 10　W: 10 10　b.Weybridge 8-12-91
Source: Scholar. *Honours:* Northern Ireland Youth, Under-21.

2009–10	Brentford	1	0		
2010–11	Brentford	0	0	1	0

CORT, Carl (D)　252 62
H: 6 4　W: 12 04　b.Southwark 1-11-77
Source: Trainee. *Honours:* England Under-21.

1996–97	Wimbledon	1	0		
1996–97	*Lincoln C*	6	1	6	1
1997–98	Wimbledon	22	4		
1998–99	Wimbledon	16	3		
1999–2000	Wimbledon	34	9	73	16
2000–01	Newcastle U	13	6		
2001–02	Newcastle U	8	1		
2002–03	Newcastle U	1	0		
2003–04	Newcastle U	0	0	22	7
2003–04	Wolverhampton W	16	5		
2004–05	Wolverhampton W	37	15		
2005–06	Wolverhampton W	31	11		
2006–07	Wolverhampton W	10	0	94	31
2007–08	Leicester C	14	0		
2008–09	Leicester C	0	0	14	0
2008–09	*Norwich C*	12	1	12	1
2009–10	Brentford	28	6		
2010–11	Brentford	3	0	31	6

DIAGOURAGA, Toumani (M)　173 5
H: 6 2　W: 11 05　b.Paris 10-6-87
Source: Scholar.

2004–05	Watford	0	0		
2005–06	Watford	1	0		
2005–06	*Swindon T*	8	0	8	0
2006–07	Watford	0	0		
2006–07	*Rotherham U*	7	0	7	0
2007–08	Watford	0	0	1	0
2007–08	*Hereford U*	41	2		
2008–09	Hereford U	45	2	86	4
2009–10	Peterborough U	19	0	19	0
2009–10	*Brentford*	20	0		
2010–11	Brentford	32	1	52	1

FORSTER, Nicky (F)　614 190
H: 5 9　W: 11 05　b.Caterham 8-9-73
Source: Horley T. *Honours:* England Under-21.

1992–93	Gillingham	26	6		
1993–94	Gillingham	41	18	67	24
1994–95	Brentford	46	24		
1995–96	Brentford	38	5		
1996–97	Brentford	25	10		
1996–97	Birmingham C	7	3		
1997–98	Birmingham C	28	3		
1998–99	Birmingham C	33	5	68	11
1999–2000	Reading	36	10		
2000–01	Reading	9	1		
2001–02	Reading	42	19		
2002–03	Reading	40	16		
2003–04	Reading	30	7		
2004–05	Reading	30	7	187	60
2005–06	Ipswich T	20	7		
2006–07	Ipswich T	4	1	24	8
2006–07	Hull C	35	5	35	5
2007–08	Brighton & HA	41	15		
2008–09	Brighton & HA	30	12		
2009–10	Brighton & HA	27	13	98	40
2009–10	*Charlton Ath*	8	2	8	2
2010–11	Brentford	18	1	127	40

GRABBAN, Lewis (F)　110 17
H: 6 0　W: 11 03　b.Croydon 12-1-88
Source: Scholar.

2005–06	Crystal Palace	0	0		
2006–07	Crystal Palace	8	1		
2006–07	*Oldham Ath*	9	0	9	0
2007–08	Crystal Palace	2	0	10	1
2007–08	*Motherwell*	6	0	6	0
2007–08	Millwall	13	3		
2008–09	Millwall	31	6		
2009–10	Millwall	11	0		
2009–10	*Brentford*	7	2		
2010–11	Millwall	1	0	56	9
2010–11	Brentford	22	5	29	7

HACKER, Luke (F)　1 0
H: 6 0　W: 12 08
Source: Hitchin T.

2010–11	Brentford	1	0	1	0

HUDSON, Kirk (F)　80 15
H: 5 8　W: 10 00　b.Southend 12-12-86
Source: Ipswich T Scholar, Celtic.

2005–06	Bournemouth	1	0	1	0
2008–09	Aldershot T	6	0		
2009–10	Aldershot T	34	4	77	15
2010–11	Brentford	2	0	2	0

HUNT, David (M)　216 11
H: 5 11　W: 11 09　b.Dulwich 10-9-82
Source: Scholar.

2002–03	Crystal Palace	2	0	2	0
2003–04	Leyton Orient	38	1		
2004–05	Leyton Orient	27	0	65	1
2004–05	Northampton T	4	0		
2005–06	Northampton T	40	3		
2006–07	Northampton T	29	0	73	3
2007–08	Shrewsbury T	27	2		
2008–09	Shrewsbury T	2	0	29	2
2008–09	*Brentford*	20	2		
2009–10	Brentford	24	3		
2010–11	Brentford	3	0	47	5

LEE, Richard (G) — 114 0
H: 6 0 W: 12 06 b.Oxford 5-10-82
Source: Scholar. *Honours:* England Under-20.

Season	Club				
2000–01	Watford	0	0		
2001–02	Watford	0	0		
2002–03	Watford	4	0		
2003–04	Watford	0	0		
2004–05	Watford	33	0		
2005–06	Watford	0	0		
2005–06	*Blackburn R*	0	0		
2006–07	Watford	10	0		
2007–08	Watford	35	0		
2008–09	Watford	10	0		
2009–10	Watford	0	0	92	0
2010–11	Brentford	22	0	22	0

LEGGE, Leon (D) — 59 5
H: 6 1 W: 11 02 b.Bexhill 28-4-85
Source: Eastbourne UA, Hailsham T, Lewes, Tonbridge Angels.

Season	Club				
2009–10	Brentford	29	2		
2010–11	Brentford	30	3	59	5

MACDONALD, Charlie (F) — 158 45
H: 5 8 W: 12 10 b.Southwark 13-2-81
Source: Trainee.

Season	Club				
1998–99	Charlton Ath	0	0		
1999–2000	Charlton Ath	3	0		
2000–01	Charlton Ath	0	0		
2000–01	*Cheltenham T*	8	2	8	2
2001–02	Charlton Ath	2	1	8	1
2001–02	*Torquay U*	5	0	5	0
2001–02	*Colchester U*	4	1	4	1

From Margate, Stevenage, Crawley T, Gravesend & N.

Season	Club				
2007–08	Southend U	25	1	25	1
2008–09	Brentford	38	16		
2009–10	Brentford	40	15		
2010–11	Brentford	30	9	108	40

McCRACKEN, David (D) — 307 11
H: 6 2 W: 11 06 b.Glasgow 16-10-81
Source: Dundee U BC. *Honours:* Scotland Under-21.

Season	Club				
1999–2000	Dundee U	2	0		
2000–01	Dundee U	9	1		
2001–02	Dundee U	19	0		
2002–03	Dundee U	25	1		
2003–04	Dundee U	32	1		
2004–05	Dundee U	24	2		
2005–06	Dundee U	34	2		
2006–07	Dundee U	33	1	178	8
2007–08	Wycombe W	37	1		
2008–09	Wycombe W	39	1	76	2
2009–10	Milton Keynes D	41	1	41	1
2010–11	Brentford	2	0	2	0
2010–11	*Bristol R*	10	0	10	0

MOORE, Simon (G) — 11 0
H: 6 3 W: 12 02 b.Sandown 19-5-90
Source: Farnborough T.

Season	Club				
2009–10	Brentford	1	0		
2010–11	Brentford	10	0	11	0

O'CONNOR, Kevin (F) — 385 31
H: 5 11 W: 12 00 b.Blackburn 24-2-82
Source: Trainee. *Honours:* Eire Youth, Under-21.

Season	Club				
1999–2000	Brentford	6	0		
2000–01	Brentford	11	1		
2001–02	Brentford	25	0		
2002–03	Brentford	45	5		
2003–04	Brentford	43	1		
2004–05	Brentford	37	2		
2005–06	Brentford	30	7		
2006–07	Brentford	39	6		
2007–08	Brentford	37	3		
2008–09	Brentford	28	0		
2009–10	Brentford	43	4		
2010–11	Brentford	41	2	385	31

OSBORNE, Karleigh (D) — 136 6
H: 6 2 W: 12 04 b.Southall 19-3-88
Source: Scholar.

Season	Club				
2004–05	Brentford	1	0		
2005–06	Brentford	1	0		
2006–07	Brentford	21	0		
2007–08	Brentford	29	1		
2008–09	Brentford	23	4		
2009–10	Brentford	19	0		
2010–11	Brentford	42	1	136	6

REEVES, Jake (M) — 1 0
H: 5 8 W: 11 11 b.Lewisham 30-6-93
Source: Scholar.

Season	Club				
2010–11	Brentford	1	0	1	0

ROYCE, Simon (G) — 361 0
H: 6 2 W: 12 10 b.Forest Gate 9-9-71
Source: Heybridge Swifts.

Season	Club				
1991–92	Southend U	1	0		
1992–93	Southend U	3	0		
1993–94	Southend U	6	0		
1994–95	Southend U	13	0		
1995–96	Southend U	46	0		
1996–97	Southend U	43	0		
1997–98	Southend U	37	0	149	0
1998–99	Charlton Ath	8	0		
1999–2000	Charlton Ath	0	0		
2000–01	Leicester C	19	0		
2001–02	Leicester C	0	0		
2001–02	*Brighton & HA*	6	0	6	0
2001–02	*Manchester C*	0	0		
2002–03	Leicester C	0	0	19	0
2002–03	*QPR*	16	0		
2003–04	Charlton Ath	1	0		
2004–05	Charlton Ath	0	0	9	0
2004–05	*Luton T*	2	0	2	0
2004–05	*QPR*	13	0		
2005–06	QPR	30	0		
2006–07	QPR	20	0	79	0
2006–07	*Gillingham*	3	0		
2007–08	Gillingham	33	0		
2008–09	Gillingham	42	0		
2009–10	Gillingham	17	0	95	0
2010–11	Brentford	2	0	2	0

SAUNDERS, Sam (M) — 109 17
H: 5 6 W: 11 04 b.Erith 29-8-83
Source: Welling U, Hastings T, Ashford T, Carshalton Ath.

Season	Club				
2007–08	Dagenham & R	22	0		
2008–09	Dagenham & R	40	14	62	14
2009–10	Brentford	26	1		
2010–11	Brentford	21	2	47	3

SPILLANE, Michael (M) — 89 5
H: 5 9 W: 11 10 b.Jersey 23-3-89
Source: Scholar. *Honours:* Eire Youth, Under-21.

Season	Club				
2005–06	Norwich C	2	0		
2006–07	Norwich C	5	0		
2007 08	Norwich C	6	0		
2008–09	Norwich C	0	0		
2008–09	*Luton T*	39	3	39	3
2009–10	Norwich C	13	1	26	1
2010–11	Brentford	24	1	24	1

WESTON, Myles (M) — 155 14
H: 5 11 W: 12 05 b.Lewisham 12-3-88
Source: Scholar.

Season	Club				
2006–07	Charlton Ath	0	0		
2006–07	Notts Co	4	0		
2007–08	Notts Co	25	0		
2008–09	Notts Co	44	3	73	3
2009–10	Brentford	40	8		
2010–11	Brentford	42	3	82	11

WOOD, Sam (M) — 103 4
H: 6 0 W: 11 05 b.Sidcup 9-8-86
Source: Bromley.

Season	Club				
2008–09	Brentford	40	1		
2009–10	Brentford	43	2		
2010–11	Brentford	20	1	103	4

WOODMAN, Craig (D) — 282 6
H: 5 9 W: 10 11 b.Tiverton 22-12-82
Source: Trainee.

Season	Club				
1999–2000	Bristol C	0	0		
2000–01	Bristol C	2	0		
2001–02	Bristol C	6	0		
2002–03	Bristol C	10	0		
2003–04	Bristol C	21	0		
2004–05	Bristol C	3	0		
2004–05	*Mansfield T*	8	1	8	1
2004–05	*Torquay U*	22	1		
2005–06	Bristol C	37	1		
2005–06	*Torquay U*	2	0	24	1
2006–07	Bristol C	11	0	90	1
2007–08	Wycombe W	29	0		
2008–09	Wycombe W	46	1		
2009–10	Wycombe W	44	1	119	2
2010–11	Brentford	41	1	41	1

WRIGHT, Stephen (D) — 211 2
H: 6 0 W: 12 06 b.Liverpool 8-2-80
Source: Trainee. *Honours:* England Youth, Under-21.

Season	Club				
1997–98	Liverpool	0	0		
1998–99	Liverpool	0	0		
1999–2000	Liverpool	0	0		
1999–2000	*Crewe Alex*	23	0	23	0
2000–01	Liverpool	2	0		
2001–02	Liverpool	12	0	14	0
2002–03	Sunderland	26	0		
2003–04	Sunderland	22	1		
2004–05	Sunderland	39	1		
2005–06	Sunderland	2	0		
2006–07	Sunderland	3	0		
2007–08	Sunderland	0	0	92	2
2007–08	*Stoke C*	16	0	16	0
2008–09	Coventry C	17	0		
2009–10	Coventry C	38	0		
2010–11	Coventry C	0	0	55	0
2010–11	Brentford	11	0	11	0

BRIGHTON & HA (14)

AGDESTEIN, Torbjorn (F) — 0 0
H: 6 0 W: 12 10 b.Norway 18-9-91
Source: Stord.

Season	Club				
2010–11	Brighton & HA	0	0		

ANKERGREN, Casper (G) — 250 0
H: 6 3 W: 14 07 b.Koge 9-11-79
Source: Koge. *Honours:* Denmark Youth, Under-21.

Season	Club				
2001–02	Brondby	1	0		
2002–03	Brondby	16	0		
2003–04	Brondby	1	0		
2004–05	Brondby	32	0		
2005–06	Brondby	18	0		
2006–07	Brondby	18	0	86	0
2006–07	Leeds U	14	0		
2007–08	Leeds U	43	0		
2008–09	Leeds U	33	0		
2009–10	Leeds U	29	0	119	0
2010–11	Brighton & HA	45	0	45	0

BARKER, George (F) — 0 0
Source: Scholar.

Season	Club				
2010–11	Brighton & HA	0	0		

BARNES, Ashley (F) — 78 24
H: 6 0 W: 12 00 b.Bath 30-10-89
Source: Paulton R.

Season	Club				
2006 07	Plymouth Arg	0	0		
2007–08	Plymouth Arg	0	0		
2008–09	Plymouth Arg	15	1		
2009–10	Plymouth Arg	7	1	22	2
2009–10	*Torquay U*	6	0	6	0
2009–10	*Brighton & HA*	8	4		
2010–11	Brighton & HA	42	18	50	22

BATTIPIEDI, Agustin (M) — 8 0
b.Capital Federal 1-9-90
Source: Comunicaciones.

Season	Club				
2010–11	Brighton & HA	8	0	8	0

BAZ, Cristian (M) — 7 0
b. 5-5-87
Source: Olimpo, Comunicaciones.

Season	Club				
2010–11	Brighton & HA	7	0	7	0

BENNETT, Elliott (M) — 163 18
H: 5 9 W: 10 11 b.Telford 18-12-88
Source: Scholar.

Season	Club				
2006–07	Wolverhampton W	0	0		
2007–08	Wolverhampton W	0	0		
2007–08	*Crewe Alex*	9	1	9	1
2007–08	*Bury*	19	1		
2008–09	Wolverhampton W	0	0		
2008–09	*Bury*	46	3	65	4
2009–10	Wolverhampton W	0	0		
2009–10	*Brighton & HA*	43	7		
2010–11	Brighton & HA	46	6	89	13

BREZOVAN, Peter (G) — 115 0
H: 6 6 W: 14 13 b.Bratislava 9-12-79
Source: PS Bratislava, Vinohrady, Devin, Slovan Breclav, Zigma Olomouc. *Honours:* Slovakia U-21.

Season	Club				
2002–03	Brno	10	0		
2003–04	Brno	2	0		
2004–05	Inter Bratislava	8	0	8	0

2005–06	Brno	7	0	19	0
2006–07	Swindon T	14	0		
2007–08	Swindon T	31	0		
2008–09	Swindon T	21	0	66	0
2009–10	Brighton & HA	20	0		
2010–11	Brighton & HA	2	0	22	0

BRIDCUTT, Liam (M) 67 2
H: 5 9 W: 11 07 b.Reading 8-5-89
Source: Scholar.

2007–08	Chelsea	0	0		
2007–08	Yeovil T	9	0	9	0
2008–09	Chelsea	0	0		
2008–09	Watford	6	0	6	0
2009–10	Chelsea	0	0		
2009–10	Stockport Co	15	0	15	0
2010–11	Chelsea	0	0		
2010–11	Brighton & HA	37	2	37	2

CALDERON, Inigo (D) 268 16
H: 5 10 W: 12 02 b.Vitoria 4-1-82

2002–03	Alaves B	35	1		
2003–04	Alaves B	33	0	68	1
2004–05	Alicante	25	0		
2005–06	Alicante	31	4		
2006–07	Alicante	28	1	84	5
2007–08	Alaves	20	0		
2008–09	Alaves	33	2	53	2
2009–10	Brighton & HA	19	1		
2010–11	Brighton & HA	44	7	63	8

CASKEY, Jake (M) 1 0
H: 5 10 W: 10 00 b.Southend 25-4-94
Source: Scholar.

| 2009–10 | Brighton & HA | 1 | 0 | | |
| 2010–11 | Brighton & HA | 0 | 0 | 1 | 0 |

COOK, Steve (D) 2 0
H: 6 1 W: 12 13 b.Hastings 19-4-91
Source: Scholar.

2008–09	Brighton & HA	2	0		
2009–10	Brighton & HA	0	0		
2010–11	Brighton & HA	0	0	2	0

DICKER, Gary (M) 220 11
H: 6 0 W: 12 00 b.Dublin 31-7-86
Honours: Eire Under-21.

2004	UCD	9	1		
2005	UCD	31	2		
2006	UCD	28	2	68	5
2006–07	Birmingham C	0	0		
2007–08	Stockport Co	30	0		
2008–09	Stockport Co	25	0	55	0
2008–09	Brighton & HA	9	1		
2009–10	Brighton & HA	42	2		
2010–11	Brighton & HA	46	3	97	6

DUNK, Lewis (D) 6 0
H: 6 3 W: 12 02 b.Brighton 1-12-91
Source: Scholar.

| 2009–10 | Brighton & HA | 1 | 0 | | |
| 2010–11 | Brighton & HA | 5 | 0 | 6 | 0 |

EL-ABD, Adam (D) 236 4
H: 5 10 W: 13 05 b.Brighton 11-9-84
Source: Scholar.

2003–04	Brighton & HA	11	0		
2004–05	Brighton & HA	16	0		
2005–06	Brighton & HA	29	0		
2006–07	Brighton & HA	42	1		
2007–08	Brighton & HA	35	1		
2008–09	Brighton & HA	31	0		
2009–10	Brighton & HA	35	1		
2010–11	Brighton & HA	37	1	236	4

ELPHICK, Tommy (M) 153 7
H: 5 11 W: 11 07 b.Brighton 7-9-87
Source: Scholar.

2005–06	Brighton & HA	1	0		
2006–07	Brighton & HA	3	0		
2007–08	Brighton & HA	39	2		
2008–09	Brighton & HA	39	1		
2009–10	Brighton & HA	44	3		
2010–11	Brighton & HA	27	1	153	7

GREER, Gordon (D) 249 7
H: 6 2 W: 12 05 b.Glasgow 14-12-80
Source: Port Glasgow. Honours: Scotland B.

2000–01	Clyde	30	0	30	0
2000–01	Blackburn R	0	0		
2001–02	Blackburn R	0	0		
2002–03	Blackburn R	0	0		
2002–03	Stockport Co	5	1	5	1
2003–04	Kilmarnock	25	0		
2004–05	Kilmarnock	22	1		
2005–06	Kilmarnock	27	2		
2006–07	Kilmarnock	33	0	107	3
2007–08	Doncaster R	11	1		
2008–09	Doncaster R	1	0	12	1
2008–09	Swindon T	19	1		
2009–10	Swindon T	44	1	63	2
2010–11	Brighton & HA	32	0	32	0

HALL, Grant (D) 0 0
b.Brighton 1-9-92
Source: Lewes.

| 2009–10 | Brighton & HA | 0 | 0 | | |
| 2010–11 | Brighton & HA | 0 | 0 | | |

HART, Gary (F) 373 44
H: 5 9 W: 12 03 b.Harlow 21-9-76
Source: Stansted.

1998–99	Brighton & HA	44	12		
1999 2000	Brighton & HA	43	9		
2000–01	Brighton & HA	45	7		
2001–02	Brighton & HA	39	4		
2002–03	Brighton & HA	36	4		
2003–04	Brighton & HA	42	3		
2004–05	Brighton & HA	26	2		
2005–06	Brighton & HA	35	1		
2006–07	Brighton & HA	25	2		
2007–08	Brighton & HA	7	0		
2008–09	Brighton & HA	11	0		
2009–10	Brighton & HA	17	0		
2010–11	Brighton & HA	3	0	373	44

HOLROYD, Chris (F) 79 11
H: 5 11 W: 12 03 b.Macclesfield 24-10-86
Source: Crewe Alex Scholar.

2005–06	Chester C	0	0		
2006–07	Chester C	22	0		
2007–08	Chester C	25	4		
2008–09	Chester C	0	0	47	4
From Cambridge U.					
2009–10	Brighton & HA	13	0		
From Cambridge U.					
2010–11	Brighton & HA	3	0	16	0
2010–11	Stevenage	12	6	12	6
2010–11	Bury	4	1	4	1

KASIM, Yaser (M) 1 0
b.Bagdad 10-5-91
Source: Tottenham H Scholar.

| 2010–11 | Brighton & HA | 1 | 0 | 1 | 0 |

KISHISHEV, Radostin (D) 463 20
H: 5 11 W: 12 03 b.Bourgas 30-7-74
Honours: Bulgaria 78 full caps.

1991–92	Chernomorets	6	1		
1992–93	Chernomorets	23	2		
1993–94	Chernomorets	23	1	52	4
1994–95	Neftochimik	14	0		
1995–96	Neftochimik	30	0		
1996–97	Neftochimik	30	6		
1997–98	Neftochimik	1	0	75	6
1997–98	Bursaspor	20	3	20	3
1997–98	Litets Lovech	5	0		
1998–99	Litets Lovech	26	2		
1999–2000	Litets Lovech	15	2	46	4
2000–01	Charlton Ath	27	0		
2001–02	Charlton Ath	3	0		
2002–03	Charlton Ath	34	2		
2003–04	Charlton Ath	33	0		
2004–05	Charlton Ath	31	0		
2005–06	Charlton Ath	37	0		
2006–07	Charlton Ath	14	0	179	2
2006–07	Leeds U	10	0		
2007–08	Leicester C	7	0	7	0
2007–08	Leeds U	7	0	17	0
2008–09	Litex	15	1		
2009–10	Litex	20	0	35	1
2010–11	Brighton & HA	32	0	32	0

MATUTU, Luc (D) 0 0
b.Paris 8-9-90
Source: Wolfsburg, Nantes.

| 2010–11 | Brighton & HA | 0 | 0 | | |

McNULTY, Jim (D) 93 3
H: 6 1 W: 12 00 b.Runcorn 13-2-85
Source: Wrexham Scholar, Caernarfon T.
Honours: Scotland Youth.

2006–07	Macclesfield T	15	0		
2007–08	Macclesfield T	19	1	34	1
2007–08	Stockport Co	11	0		
2008–09	Stockport Co	26	1	37	1
2008–09	Brighton & HA	5	1		
2009–10	Brighton & HA	8	0		
2009–10	Scunthorpe U	3	0		
2010–11	Brighton & HA	0	0	13	1
2010–11	Scunthorpe U	6	0	9	0

MURRAY, Glenn (F) 210 85
H: 6 1 W: 12 12 b.Maryport 25-9-83
Source: Wilmington Hammerheads,
Workington.

2005–06	Carlisle U	26	3		
2006–07	Carlisle U	1	0	27	3
2006–07	Stockport Co	11	3	11	3
2006–07	Rochdale	31	16		
2007–08	Rochdale	23	9	54	25
2007–08	Brighton & HA	21	9		
2008–09	Brighton & HA	23	11		
2009–10	Brighton & HA	32	12		
2010–11	Brighton & HA	42	22	118	54

NAVARRO, Alan (M) 250 9
H: 5 10 W: 11 07 b.Liverpool 31-5-81
Source: Trainee.

1998–99	Liverpool	0	0		
1999–2000	Liverpool	0	0		
2000–01	Liverpool	0	0		
2000–01	Crewe Alex	8	1		
2001–02	Liverpool	0	0		
2001–02	Crewe Alex	7	0	15	1
2001–02	Tranmere R	21	1		
2002–03	Tranmere R	5	0		
2003–04	Tranmere R	19	0		
2004–05	Tranmere R	0	0		
2004–05	Chester C	3	0	3	0
2004–05	Macclesfield T	11	1		
2005–06	Tranmere R	0	0	45	1
From Accrington S.					
2005–06	Macclesfield T	27	0		
2006–07	Macclesfield T	32	2	70	3
2007–08	Milton Keynes D	39	3		
2008–09	Milton Keynes D	38	1	77	4
2009–10	Brighton & HA	36	0		
2010–11	Brighton & HA	4	0	40	0

NOONE, Craig (M) 85 9
H: 6 3 W: 12 07 b.Kirkby 17-11-87
Source: Skelmersdale U, Burscough,
Southport.

2008–09	Plymouth Arg	21	1		
2009–10	Plymouth Arg	17	1		
2009–10	Exeter C	7	2	7	2
2010–11	Plymouth Arg	17	3	55	5
2010–11	Brighton & HA	23	2	23	2

PAINTER, Marcos (D) 138 1
H: 5 11 W: 12 04 b.Solihull 17-8-86
Source: Scholar. Honours: Eire Youth,
Under-21.

2005–06	Birmingham C	4	0		
2006–07	Birmingham C	1	0	5	0
2006–07	Swansea C	23	0		
2007–08	Swansea C	30	0		
2008–09	Swansea C	11	0		
2009–10	Swansea C	4	0	68	0
2009–10	Brighton & HA	19	0		
2010–11	Brighton & HA	46	1	65	1

POKE, Michael (G) 33 0
H: 6 1 W: 13 12 b.Staines 21-11-85
Source: Trainee.

2003–04	Southampton	0	0		
2004–05	Southampton	0	0		
2005–06	Southampton	0	0		
2005–06	Oldham Ath	0	0		
2005–06	Northampton T	0	0		
2006–07	Southampton	0	0		
2007–08	Southampton	4	0		
2008–09	Southampton	0	0		
2009–10	Southampton	0	0	4	0
2009–10	Torquay U	29	0	29	0
2010–11	Brighton & HA	0	0		

REDWOOD, Leon (M) 0 0
b. 23-9-91
Source: Scholar.

| 2010–11 | Brighton & HA | 0 | 0 | | |

SANDAZA, Fran (F) 53 13
H: 6 2 W: 12 08 b.Toledo 30-11-84
Source: Toledo, Valencia, Onda, Puzol.

2008–09	Dundee	31	10		
2009–10	Dundee U	7	1	38	11
2010–11	Brighton & HA	15	2	15	2

SIMMONDS, Ryan (M) 0 0
b.Sutton Coldfield 30-10-91
Source: Aston Villa Schools.

| 2010–11 | Brighton & HA | 0 | 0 | | |

SMITH, Jamie (M) 10 0
H: 5 6 W: 10 07 b.Leytonstone 16-9-89
Source: Leytonstone.

| 2009–10 | Brighton & HA | 2 | 0 | | |
| 2010–11 | Brighton & HA | 8 | 0 | 10 | 0 |

SMITH, James (D) 0 0
b.Eastbourne
Source: Scholar.

| 2010–11 | Brighton & HA | 0 | 0 | | |

SPARROW, Matt (M) 365 41
H: 5 11 W: 10 06 b.Wembley 3-10-81
Source: Scholar.

1999–2000	Scunthorpe U	11	0		
2000–01	Scunthorpe U	11	4		
2001–02	Scunthorpe U	24	1		
2002–03	Scunthorpe U	42	9		
2003–04	Scunthorpe U	38	3		
2004–05	Scunthorpe U	44	5		
2005–06	Scunthorpe U	39	5		
2006–07	Scunthorpe U	29	4		
2007–08	Scunthorpe U	32	1		
2008–09	Scunthorpe U	36	4		
2009–10	Scunthorpe U	30	1	336	37
2010–11	Brighton & HA	29	4	29	4

TARICCO, Mauricio (D) 293 6
H: 5 8 W: 11 07 b.Buenos Aires 10-3-73
Honours: Argentina Under-23.

1993–94	Argentinos Juniors	21	0	21	0
1994–95	Ipswich T	0	0		
1995–96	Ipswich T	39	0		
1996–97	Ipswich T	41	3		
1997–98	Ipswich T	41	0		
1998–99	Ipswich T	16	1	137	4
1998–99	Tottenham H	13	0		
1999–2000	Tottenham H	29	0		
2000–01	Tottenham H	5	0		
2001–02	Tottenham H	30	0		
2002–03	Tottenham H	21	1		
2003–04	Tottenham H	32	1		
2004–05	Tottenham H	0	0	130	2
2004–05	West Ham U	1	0		
2005–06	West Ham U	0	0		
2006–07	West Ham U	0	0		
2007–08	West Ham U	0	0		
2008–09	West Ham U	0	0	1	0
2010–11	Brighton & HA	4	0	4	0

THOMSON, Ryan (M) 0 0
b. 26-7-92
Source: Scholar.

| 2010–11 | Brighton & HA | 0 | 0 | | |

TUNNICLIFFE, James (D) 92 3
H: 6 4 W: 12 03 b.Denton 17-1-89
Source: Scholar.

2005–06	Stockport Co	1	0		
2006–07	Stockport Co	5	0		
2007–08	Stockport Co	5	0		
2008–09	Stockport Co	30	0	41	0
2009–10	Brighton & HA	17	2		
2009–10	Milton Keynes D	9	1	9	1
2010–11	Brighton & HA	0	0	17	2
2010–11	Bristol R	25	0	25	0

WALKER, Mitch (G) 1 0
H: 6 2 W: 13 00 b.St Albans 24-9-91
Source: Scholar.

| 2009–10 | Brighton & HA | 1 | 0 | | |
| 2010–11 | Brighton & HA | 0 | 0 | 1 | 0 |

BRISTOL C (15)

ADOMAH, Albert (F) 158 24
H: 6 1 W: 11 08 b.Lambeth 13-12-87
Source: Harrow Borough.

2007–08	Barnet	22	5		
2008–09	Barnet	45	9		
2009–10	Barnet	45	5	112	19
2010–11	Bristol C	46	5	46	5

AKINDE, John (F) 58 11
H: 6 2 W: 10 01 b.Camberwell 8-7-89
Source: Ebbsfleet U.

2008–09	Bristol C	7	1		
2008–09	Wycombe W	11	7		
2009–10	Bristol C	7	0		
2009–10	Wycombe W	6	1	17	8
2009–10	Brentford	2	0	2	0
2010–11	Bristol C	2	0	16	1
2010–11	Bristol R	14	0	14	0
2010–11	Dagenham & R	9	2	9	2

BALL, Danny (D) 0 0
b. 21-11-91
Source: Scholar.

| 2010–11 | Bristol C | 0 | 0 | | |

CAMPBELL-RYCE, Jamal (M) 266 18
H: 5 7 W: 12 03 b.Lambeth 6-4-83
Source: Scholar. *Honours:* Jamaica 20 full caps.

2002–03	Charlton Ath	1	0		
2002–03	Leyton Orient	17	2	17	2
2003–04	Charlton Ath	2	0		
2003–04	Wimbledon	4	0	4	0
2004–05	Charlton Ath	0	0	3	0
2004–05	Chesterfield	14	0	14	0
2004–05	Rotherham U	24	0		
2005–06	Rotherham U	7	0	31	0
2005–06	Southend U	13	0		
2005–06	Colchester U	4	0	4	0
2006–07	Southend U	43	2		
2007–08	Southend U	2	0	58	2
2007–08	Barnsley	37	3		
2008–09	Barnsley	40	9		
2009–10	Barnsley	13	0	90	12
2009–10	Bristol C	14	0		
2010–11	Bristol C	31	2	45	2

CAREY, Louis (D) 544 12
H: 5 10 W: 11 00 b.Bristol 20-1-77
Source: Trainee. *Honours:* Scotland Under-21.

1995–96	Bristol C	23	0		
1996–97	Bristol C	42	0		
1997–98	Bristol C	38	0		
1998–99	Bristol C	41	0		
1999–2000	Bristol C	22	0		
2000–01	Bristol C	46	3		
2001–02	Bristol C	35	0		
2002–03	Bristol C	24	1		
2003–04	Bristol C	41	1		
2004–05	Coventry C	23	0	23	0
2004–05	Bristol C	14	0		
2005–06	Bristol C	38	3		
2006–07	Bristol C	38	2		
2007–08	Bristol C	33	0		
2008–09	Bristol C	37	2		
2009–10	Bristol C	37	2		
2010–11	Bristol C	21	0	521	12

CISSE, Kalifa (M) 152 7
H: 6 2 W: 12 11 b.Dreux 1-9-84
Source: Toulouse. *Honours:* Mali 4 full caps.

2004–05	Estoril	6	0	6	0
2005–06	Boavista	15	0		
2006–07	Boavista	27	0	42	0
2007–08	Reading	22	1		
2008–09	Reading	36	5		
2009–10	Reading	17	1	75	7
2010–11	Bristol C	29	0	29	0

CLARKSON, David (F) 281 60
H: 5 10 W: 10 03 b.Airdrie 10-9-85
Honours: Scotland Under 21, B.

2002–03	Motherwell	19	3		
2003–04	Motherwell	38	12		
2004–05	Motherwell	35	3		
2005–06	Motherwell	32	4		
2006–07	Motherwell	29	2		
2007–08	Motherwell	35	12		
2008–09	Motherwell	33	13	221	49
2009–10	Bristol C	26	4		
2010–11	Bristol C	34	7	60	11

EDWARDS, Joe (D) 2 0
H: 5 8 W: 11 07 b.Gloucester 31-10-90
Source: Scholar.

| 2009–10 | Bristol C | 0 | 0 | | |
| 2010–11 | Bristol C | 2 | 0 | 2 | 0 |

ELLIOTT, Marvin (M) 302 20
H: 6 0 W: 12 02 b.Wandsworth 15-9-84
Source: Scholar.

2001–02	Millwall	0	0		
2002–03	Millwall	1	0		
2003–04	Millwall	21	0		
2004–05	Millwall	41	1		
2005–06	Millwall	39	2		
2006–07	Millwall	42	0	144	3
2007–08	Bristol C	45	5		
2008–09	Bristol C	28	3		
2009–10	Bristol C	39	1		
2010–11	Bristol C	46	8	158	17

FONTAINE, Liam (D) 218 5
H: 5 11 W: 11 09 b.Beckenham 7-1-86
Source: Trainee. *Honours:* England Youth, Under-20.

2003–04	Fulham	0	0		
2004–05	Fulham	1	0		
2004–05	Yeovil T	15	0		
2005–06	Fulham	0	0	1	0
2005–06	Yeovil T	10	0	25	0
2005–06	Bristol C	15	0		
2006–07	Bristol C	30	0		
2007–08	Bristol C	38	1		
2008–09	Bristol C	42	2		
2009–10	Bristol C	36	2		
2010–11	Bristol C	31	0	192	5

GERKEN, Dean (G) 156 0
H: 6 3 W: 12 08 b.Southend 22-5-85
Source: Scholar.

2003–04	Colchester U	1	0		
2004–05	Colchester U	13	0		
2005–06	Colchester U	7	0		
2006–07	Colchester U	27	0		
2007–08	Colchester U	40	0		
2008–09	Colchester U	21	0	109	0
2008–09	Darlington	7	0	7	0
2009–10	Bristol C	39	0		
2010–11	Bristol C	1	0	40	0

HENDERSON, Stephen (G) 46 0
H: 6 3 W: 11 00 b.Dublin 2-5-88
Source: Scholar. *Honours:* Eire Under-21.

2005–06	Aston Villa	0	0		
2006–07	Aston Villa	0	0		
2007–08	Bristol C	1	0		
2008–09	Bristol C	1	0		
2009–10	Bristol C	3	0		
2009–10	Aldershot T	8	0	8	0
2010–11	Bristol C	0	0	5	0
2010–11	Yeovil T	33	0	33	0

HOBAN, Patrick (M) 0 0
b.Galway 28-7-91
Source: Mervue U.

| 2010–11 | Bristol C | 0 | 0 | | |

HUNT, Nicky (D) 167 1
H: 6 1 W: 13 07 b.Westhoughton 3-9-03
Source: Scholar. *Honours:* England Under-21.

2000–01	Bolton W	1	0		
2001–02	Bolton W	0	0		
2002–03	Bolton W	0	0		
2003–04	Bolton W	31	1		
2004–05	Bolton W	29	0		
2005–06	Bolton W	20	0		
2006–07	Bolton W	33	0		
2007–08	Bolton W	14	0		
2008–09	Bolton W	0	0		
2008–09	Birmingham C	11	0	11	0
2009–10	Bolton W	0	0	128	1
2009–10	Derby Co	21	0	21	0
2010–11	Bristol C	7	0	7	0

JACKSON, Marlon (F) 40 1
H: 5 11 W: 11 12 b.Bristol 6-12-90
Source: Scholar.

2009–10	Bristol C	0	0		
2009–10	Hereford U	5	0	5	0
2009–10	Aldershot T	22	1		
2010–11	Bristol C	4	0	4	0
2010–11	Aldershot T	9	0	31	1

JAMES, David (G) 733 0
H: 6 5 W: 15 07 b.Welwyn 1-8-70
Source: Trainee. *Honours:* England Youth, Under-21, B, 53 full caps.

1988–89	Watford	0	0		
1989–90	Watford	0	0		
1990–91	Watford	46	0		
1991–92	Watford	43	0	89	0
1992–93	Liverpool	29	0		
1993–94	Liverpool	14	0		
1994–95	Liverpool	42	0		
1995–96	Liverpool	38	0		
1996–97	Liverpool	38	0		

1997–98	Liverpool	27	0
1998–99	Liverpool	26	0	214	0
1999–2000	Aston Villa	29	0
2000–01	Aston Villa	38	0	67	0
2001–02	West Ham U	26	0
2002–03	West Ham U	38	0
2003–04	West Ham U	27	0	91	0
2003–04	Manchester C	17	0
2004–05	Manchester C	38	0
2005–06	Manchester C	38	0	93	0
2006–07	Portsmouth	38	0
2007–08	Portsmouth	35	0
2008–09	Portsmouth	36	0
2009–10	Portsmouth	25	0	134	0
2010–11	Bristol C	45	0	45	0

JOHNSON, Lee (M)   297 25
H: 5 6   W: 10 07   b.Newmarket 7-6-81
Source: Trainee.

1998–99	Watford	0	0
1999–2000	Watford	0	0
2000–01	Brighton & HA	0	0
2000–01	Brentford	0	0
2001–02	Brentford	0	0
2003–04	Yeovil T	45	5
2004–05	Yeovil T	44	7
2005–06	Yeovil T	26	2	115	14
2005–06	Hearts	4	0	4	0
2006–07	Bristol C	42	5
2007–08	Bristol C	40	1
2008–09	Bristol C	44	3
2009–10	Bristol C	28	1
2009–10	*Derby Co*	4	0	4	0
2010–11	Bristol C	20	1	174	11

KEOHANE, Jimmy (M)   0 0
b.Wexford 22-1-91
Source: Wexford.

2010–11	Bristol C	0	0

LENNOX, Joe (M)   0 0
b. 22-11-91
Source: Scholar.

2010–11	Bristol C	0	0

MAYNARD, Nicky (F)   157 68
H: 5 11   W: 11 00   b.Winsford 11-12-86
Source: Scholar.

2005–06	Crewe Alex	1	1
2006–07	Crewe Alex	31	16
2007–08	Crewe Alex	27	14	59	31
2008–09	Bristol C	43	11
2009–10	Bristol C	42	20
2010–11	Bristol C	13	6	98	37

McALLISTER, Jamie (D)   422 4
H: 5 10   W: 11 00   b.Glasgow 26-4-78
Honours: Scotland 1 full cap.

1995–96	Q of S	2	0
1996–97	Q of S	6	0
1997–98	Q of S	15	0
1998–99	Q of S	27	0	50	0
1999–2000	Aberdeen	34	0
2000–01	Aberdeen	25	0
2001–02	Aberdeen	29	0
2002–03	Aberdeen	29	0	117	0
2003–04	Livingston	34	1	34	1
2004–05	Hearts	30	0
2005–06	Hearts	17	0	47	0
2006–07	Bristol C	31	1
2007–08	Bristol C	41	0
2008–09	Bristol C	35	1
2009–10	Bristol C	33	0
2010–11	Bristol C	34	1	174	3

NYATANGA, Lewin (D)   185 8
H: 6 2   W: 12 08   b.Burton 18-8-88
Source: Scholar. *Honours:* Wales Under-21,
34 full caps.

2005–06	Derby Co	24	1
2006–07	Derby Co	7	1
2006–07	*Sunderland*	11	0	11	0
2006–07	*Barnsley*	10	1
2007–08	Derby Co	2	1
2007–08	*Barnsley*	41	1	51	2
2008–09	Derby Co	30	1	63	4
2009–10	Bristol C	37	1
2010–11	Bristol C	20	1	57	2
2010–11	*Peterborough U*	3	0	3	0

PITMAN, Brett (F)   213 71
H: 6 0   W: 11 00   b.Jersey 31-1-88
Source: St Pauls (Jersey).

2005–06	Bournemouth	19	1
2006–07	Bournemouth	29	5
2007–08	Bournemouth	39	6
2008–09	Bournemouth	39	17
2009–10	Bournemouth	46	26
2010–11	Bournemouth	2	3	174	58
2010–11	Bristol C	39	13	39	13

REID, Bobby (M)   1 0
Source: Scholar.

2010–11	Bristol C	1	0	1	0

RIBEIRO, Christian (D)   23 0
H: 5 11   W: 12 02   b.Neath 14-12-89
Source: Scholar. *Honours:* Wales Youth,
Under-21, 2 full caps.

2006–07	Bristol C	0	0
2007–08	Bristol C	0	0
2008–09	Bristol C	0	0
2009–10	Bristol C	5	0
2009–10	*Stockport Co*	7	0	7	0
2009–10	*Colchester U*	2	0	2	0
2010–11	Bristol C	9	0	14	0

SKUSE, Cole (M)   218 7
H: 6 1   W: 11 05   b.Bristol 29-3-86
Source: Scholar.

2004–05	Bristol C	7	0
2005–06	Bristol C	38	2
2006–07	Bristol C	42	0
2007–08	Bristol C	25	0
2008–09	Bristol C	33	2
2009–10	Bristol C	43	2
2010–11	Bristol C	30	1	218	7

SPROULE, Ivan (M)   190 17
H: 5 8   W: 11 09   b.Omagh 18-2-81
Source: Omagh Town, Institute. *Honours:*
Northern Ireland 11 full caps, 1 goal.

2005–06	Hibernian	32	4
2006–07	Hibernian	32	7	64	11
2007–08	Bristol C	40	2
2008–09	Bristol C	38	3
2009–10	Bristol C	30	1
2010–11	Bristol C	11	0	119	6
2010–11	*Yeovil T*	2	0	2	0
2010–11	*Notts Co*	5	0	5	0

STEAD, Jon (F)   302 73
H: 6 3   W: 13 03   b.Huddersfield 7-4-83
Source: Scholar. *Honours:* England Under-21.

2001–02	Huddersfield T	0	0
2002–03	Huddersfield T	42	6
2003–04	Huddersfield T	26	16	68	22
2003–04	Blackburn R	13	6
2004–05	Blackburn R	29	2	42	8
2005–06	Sunderland	30	1
2006–07	Sunderland	5	1	35	2
2006–07	*Derby Co*	17	3	17	3
2006–07	Sheffield U	14	5
2007–08	Sheffield U	24	3
2008–09	Sheffield U	1	0	39	8
2008–09	Ipswich T	39	12
2009–10	Ipswich T	22	6
2009–10	*Coventry U*	10	2	10	2
2010–11	Ipswich T	3	1	64	19
2010–11	Bristol C	27	9	27	9

STEWART, Damion (D)   195 11
H: 6 3   W: 13 10   b.Jamaica 18-8-80
Source: Harbour View. *Honours:* Jamaica 55
full caps, 3 goals.

2005–06	Bradford C	23	1	23	1
2006–07	QPR	45	1
2007–08	QPR	39	5
2008–09	QPR	37	2
2009–10	QPR	30	1	151	9
2010–11	Bristol C	21	1	21	1

WILSON, James (D)   31 0
H: 6 2   W: 11 05   b.Chepstow 26-2-89
Source: Scholar. *Honours:* Wales Youth,
Under-21.

2005–06	Bristol C	0	0
2006–07	Bristol C	0	0
2007–08	Bristol C	0	0
2008–09	*Brentford*	14	0
2009–10	Bristol C	0	0
2009–10	*Brentford*	13	0	27	0
2010–11	Bristol C	2	0	4	0

WOOLFORD, Martyn (M)   118 15
H: 6 0   W: 11 09   b.Castleford 13-10-85
Source: Glasshoughton W, Frickley Ath,
York C.

2008–09	Scunthorpe U	39	4
2009–10	Scunthorpe U	40	5
2010–11	Scunthorpe U	24	6	103	15
2010–11	Bristol C	15	0	15	0

BRISTOL R (16)

ANTHONY, Byron (D)   147 6
H: 6 1   W: 11 02   b.Newport 20-9-84
Source: Scholar. *Honours:* Wales Youth,
Under-21.

2003–04	Cardiff C	0	0
2004–05	Cardiff C	0	0
2005–06	Cardiff C	0	0
2006–07	Bristol R	23	0
2007–08	Bristol R	20	1
2008–09	Bristol R	30	2
2009–10	Bristol R	37	0
2010–11	Bristol R	37	3	147	6

BLIZZARD, Dominic (M)   142 7
H: 6 2   W: 12 04   b.High Wycombe 2-9-83
Source: Scholar.

2001–02	Watford	0	0
2002–03	Watford	0	0
2003–04	Watford	2	1
2004–05	Watford	17	1
2005–06	Watford	10	0
2006–07	Watford	0	0	29	2
2006–07	*Stockport Co*	7	0
2006–07	*Milton Keynes D*	8	0	8	0
2007–08	Stockport Co	27	1
2008–09	Stockport Co	31	3	65	4
2009–10	Bristol R	34	1
2010–11	Bristol R	5	0	39	1
2010–11	*Port Vale*	1	0	1	0

BROWN, Wayne (M)   66 13
H: 5 9   W: 12 05   b.Kingston 6-8-88
Source: Scholar.

2006–07	Fulham	0	0
2007–08	Fulham	0	0
2007–08	*Brentford*	11	1	11	1
2008–09	Fulham	1	0
2009	*TPS Turku*	25	9	25	9
2009–10	Fulham	0	0	1	0
2009–10	*Bristol R*	4	0
2010–11	Bristol R	25	3	29	3

CAMPBELL, Stuart (M)   471 14
H: 5 10   W: 10 08   b.Corby 9-12-77
Source: Trainee. *Honours:* Scotland
Under-21.

1996–97	Leicester C	10	0
1997–98	Leicester C	11	0
1998–99	Leicester C	12	0
1999–2000	Leicester C	4	0
1999–2000	*Birmingham C*	2	0	2	0
2000–01	Leicester C	0	0	37	0
2000–01	*Grimsby T*	38	2
2001–02	Grimsby T	33	3
2002–03	Grimsby T	45	6
2003–04	Grimsby T	39	1	155	12
2004–05	Bristol R	25	0
2005–06	Bristol R	38	1
2006–07	Bristol R	41	1
2007–08	Bristol R	46	0
2008–09	Bristol R	44	0
2009–10	Bristol R	46	0
2010–11	Bristol R	37	0	277	2

CLARKE, Ollie (M)   1 0
b.Bristol 29-6-92

2009–10	Bristol R	0	0
2010–11	Bristol R	1	0	1	0

CLOUGH, Charlie (M)   2 0
H: 6 2   W: 12 08   b.Taunton 4-9-90
Source: Scholar.

2010–11	Bristol R	2	0	2	0

COLES, Danny (D)   284 8
H: 6 1   W: 11 05   b.Bristol 31-10-81
Source: Scholarship.

1999–2000	Bristol C	1	0
2000–01	Bristol C	2	0
2001–02	Bristol C	23	0

Season	Club				
2002–03	Bristol C	39	2		
2003–04	Bristol C	45	2		
2004–05	Bristol C	38	1	148	5
2005–06	Hull C	9	0		
2006–07	Hull C	21	0		
2007–08	Hull C	1	0	31	0
2007–08	*Hartlepool U*	3	0	3	0
2007–08	Bristol R	24	1		
2008–09	Bristol R	5	1		
2009–10	Bristol R	36	1		
2010–11	Bristol R	37	0	102	3

DUFFY, Darryl (F)   218 61
H: 5 11 W: 12 01 b.Glasgow 16-4-84
Honours: Scotland Under-21, B.

Season	Club				
2003–04	Rangers	1	0	1	0
2003–04	*Brechin C*	8	3	8	3
2004–05	Falkirk	35	17		
2005–06	Falkirk	21	9	56	26
2005–06	Hull C	15	3		
2006–07	Hull C	9	0	24	3
2006–07	*Hartlepool U*	10	5	10	5
2006–07	Swansea C	8	5		
2007–08	Swansea C	20	1	28	6
2008–09	Bristol R	43	13		
2009–10	Bristol R	30	4		
2009–10	*Carlisle U*	8	1	8	1
2010–11	Bristol R	3	0	76	17
2010–11	*Hibernian*	7	0	7	0

GREEN, Mike (G)   2 0
H: 6 1 W: 13 01 b.Bristol 23-7-89
Source: Scholar.

Season	Club				
2006–07	Bristol R	0	0		
2007–08	Bristol R	0	0		
2008–09	Bristol R	0	0		
2009–10	Bristol R	0	0		
2010–11	Bristol R	2	0	2	0

HARRISON, Ellis (F)   1 0
Source: Scholar.

Season	Club				
2010–11	Bristol R	1	0	1	0

HOSKINS, Will (F)   188 49
H: 5 11 W: 11 02 b.Nottingham 6-5-86
Source: Scholar. Honours: England Youth, Under-20.

Season	Club				
2003–04	Rotherham U	4	2		
2004–05	Rotherham U	22	2		
2005–06	Rotherham U	23	4		
2006–07	Rotherham U	24	15	73	23
2006–07	Watford	9	0		
2007–08	Watford	1	0		
2007–08	Millwall	10	2	10	2
2007–08	*Nottingham F*	2	0	2	0
2008–09	Watford	32	4		
2009–10	Watford	18	3	60	7
2010–11	Bristol R	43	17	43	17

HUGHES, Jeff (D)   259 38
H: 6 1 W: 11 00 b.Larne 29-5-85
Source: Larne Tech Old Boys. Honours: Northern Ireland Under-21, 2 full caps.

Season	Club				
2003–04	Larne	21	1		
2004–05	Larne	29	0	50	1
2005–06	Lincoln C	22	2		
2006–07	Lincoln C	41	6	63	8
2007–08	Crystal Palace	10	0		
2007–08	*Peterborough U*	7	1	7	1
2008–09	Bristol R	43	6		
2009–10	Bristol R	44	12		
2010–11	Bristol R	42	10	129	28

IFIL, Jerel (D)   266 3
Source: Academy.

Season	Club				
1999–2000	Watford	0	0		
2000–01	Watford	0	0		
2001–02	Watford	0	0		
2001–02	*Huddersfield T*	2	0	2	0
2002–03	Watford	1	0		
2002–03	*Swindon T*	9	0		
2003–04	Watford	10	0	11	0
2003–04	*Swindon T*	16	0		
2004–05	Swindon T	35	0		
2005–06	Swindon T	36	0		
2006–07	Swindon T	40	1		
2007–08	Swindon T	40	1		
2008–09	Swindon T	30	1		
2009–10	Swindon T	0	0	206	3
2009–10	Aberdeen	27	0		
2010–11	Aberdeen	17	0	44	0

On loan from Aberdeen.

Season	Club				
2010–11	*Bristol R*	3	0	3	0

JEFFERIES, Darren (M)   0 0
b.Swindon 25-10-93
Source: Scholar.

Season	Club				
2010–11	Bristol R	0	0		

KALALA, Jean-Paul (M)   162 9
H: 5 10 W: 12 02 b.Lubumbashi 16-2-82
Honours: DR Congo 6 full caps.

Season	Club				
2003–04	Nice	2	0		
2004–05	Nice	0	0	2	0
2005–06	Grimsby T	21	5		
2006–07	Yeovil T	38	1		
2007–08	Oldham Ath	20	0		
2008–09	Oldham Ath	0	0		
2008–09	*Grimsby T*	21	2	42	7
2009–10	Oldham Ath	0	0	20	0
2009–10	Yeovil T	34	1		
2010–11	Yeovil T	15	0	87	2
2010–11	Bristol R	11	0	11	0

LINES, Chris (M)   167 20
H: 6 2 W: 12 00 b.Bristol 30-11-88
Source: Youth.

Season	Club				
2005–06	Bristol R	4	0		
2006–07	Bristol R	7	0		
2007–08	Bristol R	27	3		
2008–09	Bristol R	45	4		
2009–10	Bristol R	42	10		
2010–11	Bristol R	42	3	167	20

OSEI-KUFFOUR, Jo (F)   367 86
H: 5 8 W: 11 11 b.Edmonton 17-11-81
Source: Scholar.

Season	Club				
2000–01	Arsenal	0	0		
2001–02	Arsenal	0	0		
2001–02	*Swindon T*	11	2	11	2
2002–03	Torquay U	30	5		
2003–04	Torquay U	41	10		
2004–05	Torquay U	34	6		
2005–06	Torquay U	43	8	148	29
2006–07	Brentford	39	12	39	12
2007–08	Bournemouth	42	12		
2008–09	Bournemouth	2	0	44	12
2008–09	Bristol R	41	11		
2009–10	Bristol R	42	14		
2010–11	Bristol R	42	6	125	31

PELL, Harry (M)   17 0
b.Tilbury 21-10-91
Source: Charlton Ath Scholar.

Season	Club				
2010–11	Bristol R	10	0	10	0
2010–11	*Hereford U*	7	0	7	0

POWELL, Lamar (F)   1 0
b.Bristol 3-9-93
Source: Scholar.

Season	Club				
2010–11	Bristol R	1	0	1	0

REECE, Charlie (M)   30 0
H: 5 11 W: 11 03 b.Birmingham 8-9-88
Source: Scholar.

Season	Club				
2007–08	Bristol R	1	0		
2008–09	Bristol R	1	0		
2009–10	Bristol R	14	0		
2010–11	Bristol R	14	0	30	0

REGAN, Carl (D)   276 3
H: 5 11 W: 11 12 b.Liverpool 14-1-80
Source: Trainee. Honours: England Youth.

Season	Club				
1997–98	Everton	0	0		
1998–99	Everton	0	0		
1999–2000	Everton	0	0		
2000–01	Barnsley	27	0		
2001–02	Barnsley	10	0		
2002–03	Barnsley	0	0	37	0
2002–03	Hull C	38	0		
2003–04	Hull C	0	0	38	0

From Droylsden.

Season	Club				
2004–05	Chester C	6	0		
2005–06	Chester C	41	0	47	0
2006–07	Macclesfield T	38	2		
2007–08	Macclesfield T	20	0	58	2
2007–08	Milton Keynes D	9	1		
2008–09	Milton Keynes D	27	0	36	1
2009–10	Bristol R	35	0		
2010–11	Bristol R	21	0	56	0
2010–11	*Notts Co*	4	0	4	0

RICHARDS, Eliot (M)   18 1
H: 5 9 W: 11 09 b.New Tredegar 1-9-91
Source: Scholar. Honours: Wales Youth.

Season	Club				
2009–10	Bristol R	5	0		
2010–11	Bristol R	13	1	18	1

SAWYER, Gary (D)   134 5
H: 6 0 W: 11 08 b.Bideford 5-7-85
Source: Trainee.

Season	Club				
2004–05	Plymouth Arg	0	0		
2005–06	Plymouth Arg	0	0		
2006–07	Plymouth Arg	22	0		
2007–08	Plymouth Arg	31	1		
2008–09	Plymouth Arg	13	3		
2009–10	Plymouth Arg	29	1	95	5
2009–10	*Bristol C*	2	0	2	0
2010–11	Bristol R	37	0	37	0

SENDA, Danny (D)   369 10
H: 5 10 W: 10 02 b.Harrow 17-4-81
Source: Southampton Trainee. Honours: England Youth.

Season	Club				
1998–99	Wycombe W	6	0		
1999–2000	Wycombe W	27	1		
2000–01	Wycombe W	31	2		
2001–02	Wycombe W	43	0		
2002–03	Wycombe W	41	2		
2003–04	Wycombe W	40	0		
2004–05	Wycombe W	44	4		
2005–06	Wycombe W	44	0	276	9
2006–07	Millwall	36	0		
2007–08	Millwall	40	1		
2008–09	Millwall	0	0	76	1
2009–10	Inactive	0	0		
2010–11	Torquay U	2	0	2	0
2010–11	Bristol R	15	0	15	0

SWALLOW, Ben (M)   40 0
H: 5 8 W: 10 10 b.Barry 20-10-89
Source: Scholar.

Season	Club				
2008–09	Bristol R	0	0		
2009–10	Bristol R	23	0		
2010–11	Bristol R	17	0	40	0

WILLIAMS, Gavin (M)   210 26
H: 5 10 W: 11 05 b.Pontypridd 20-6-80
Source: Hereford U. Honours: Wales 2 full caps.

Season	Club				
2003–04	Yeovil T	42	9		
2004–05	Yeovil T	13	2		
2004–05	West Ham U	10	1		
2005–06	West Ham U	0	0	10	1
2005–06	Ipswich T	12	1		
2006–07	Ipswich T	29	2		
2007–08	Ipswich T	13	0	54	3
2008–09	Bristol C	35	3		
2009–10	Bristol C	14	0		
2009–10	*Yeovil T*	8	5		
2010–11	Bristol C	3	0	52	3
2010–11	*Yeovil T*	12	1	75	17
2010–11	Bristol R	19	2	19	2

BURNLEY (17)

ALEXANDER, Graham (D)   815 105
H: 5 10 W: 12 07 b.Coventry 10-10-71
Source: Trainee. Honours: Scotland B, 40 full caps.

Season	Club				
1989–90	Scunthorpe U	0	0		
1990–91	Scunthorpe U	1	0		
1991–92	Scunthorpe U	36	5		
1992–93	Scunthorpe U	41	5		
1993–94	Scunthorpe U	41	4		
1994–95	Scunthorpe U	40	4	159	18
1995–96	Luton T	37	1		
1996–97	Luton T	45	2		
1997–98	Luton T	39	8		
1998–99	Luton T	29	4	150	15
1998–99	Preston NE	10	0		
1999–2000	Preston NE	46	6		
2000–01	Preston NE	34	5		
2001–02	Preston NE	45	6		
2002–03	Preston NE	45	10		
2003–04	Preston NE	45	9		
2004–05	Preston NE	42	7		
2005–06	Preston NE	40	3		
2006–07	Preston NE	42	6		
2007–08	Preston NE	3	0	352	52
2007–08	Burnley	43	1		
2008–09	Burnley	46	9		
2009–10	Burnley	33	7		
2010–11	Burnley	32	3	154	20

ANDERSON, Chris (M)   0 0
H: 5 11 W: 10 02 b.Burnley 2-10-90
Source: Scholar.

Season	Club				
2009–10	Burnley	0	0		
2010–11	Burnley	0	0		

AUSTIN, Charlie (F)   58 31
H: 6 2 W: 13 03 b.Hungerford 5-7-89
Source: Poole T.

2009–10	Swindon T	33	19		
2010–11	Swindon T	21	12	54	31
2010–11	Burnley	4	0	4	0

BARTLEY, Marvyn (M)   118 3
H: 6 1 W: 12 04 b.Reading 4-7-86
Source: Hampton & Richmond B.

2007–08	Bournemouth	20	1		
2008–09	Bournemouth	33	1		
2009–10	Bournemouth	34	0		
2010–11	Bournemouth	26	1	113	3
2010–11	Burnley	5	0	5	0

BIKEY, Andre (D)   145 10
H: 6 0 W: 12 08 b.Douala 8-1-85
Source: Espanyol, Marco. *Honours:*
Cameroon 25 full caps, 1 goal.

2003–04	Pacos de Ferreira	2	0	2	0
2004–05	Dep Aves	0	0		
2005	Shinnik	11	1	11	1
2005	Loko Moscow	9	0		
2006	Loko Moscow	5	0	14	0
2006–07	Reading	15	0		
2007–08	Reading	22	3		
2008–09	Reading	25	3		
2009–10	Reading	0	0	62	6
2009–10	Burnley	28	1		
2010–11	Burnley	28	2	56	3

CARLISLE, Clarke (D)   396 26
H: 6 2 W: 14 11 b.Preston 14-10-79
Source: Trainee. *Honours:* England
Under-21.

1997–98	Blackpool	11	2		
1998–99	Blackpool	39	1		
1999–2000	Blackpool	43	4	93	7
2000–01	QPR	27	3		
2001–02	QPR	0	0		
2002–03	QPR	36	2		
2003–04	QPR	33	1	96	6
2004–05	Leeds U	35	4	35	4
2005–06	Watford	32	3		
2006–07	Watford	4	0		
2006–07	Luton T	5	0	5	0
2007–08	Watford	0	0	36	3
2007–08	Burnley	33	2		
2008–09	Burnley	36	3		
2009–10	Burnley	27	0		
2010–11	Burnley	35	1	131	6

CORT, Leon (D)   348 36
H: 6 3 W: 13 01 b.Bermondsey 11-9-79
Source: Dulwich H.

1997–98	Millwall	0	0		
1998–99	Millwall	0	0		
1999–2000	Millwall	0	0		
2000–01	Millwall	0	0		
2001–02	Southend U	45	4		
2002–03	Southend U	46	6		
2003–04	Southend U	46	1	137	11
2004–05	Hull C	44	6		
2005–06	Hull C	42	4	86	10
2006–07	Crystal Palace	37	7		
2007–08	Crystal Palace	12	0	49	7
2007–08	Stoke C	33	8		
2008–09	Stoke C	11	0		
2009–10	Stoke C	0	0	44	8
2009–10	Burnley	15	0		
2010–11	Burnley	4	0	19	0
2010–11	Preston NE	13	0	13	0

DUFF, Michael (D)   402 17
H: 6 1 W: 11 08 b.Belfast 11-1-78
Source: Trainee. *Honours:* Northern Ireland
22 full caps.

1999–2000	Cheltenham T	31	2		
2000–01	Cheltenham T	39	5		
2001–02	Cheltenham T	45	3		
2002–03	Cheltenham T	44	2		
2003–04	Cheltenham T	42	0	201	12
2004–05	Burnley	42	0		
2005–06	Burnley	41	0		
2006–07	Burnley	44	2		
2007–08	Burnley	8	1		
2008–09	Burnley	27	1		
2009–10	Burnley	11	0		
2010–11	Burnley	28	1	201	5

EAGLES, Chris (M)   196 30
H: 5 10 W: 11 07 b.Hemel Hempstead
19-11-85
Source: Trainee. *Honours:* England Youth.

2003–04	Manchester U	0	0		
2004–05	Manchester U	0	0		
2004–05	Watford	13	1		
2005–06	Manchester U	0	0		
2005–06	Sheffield W	25	3	25	3
2005–06	Watford	17	3	30	4
2006–07	Manchester U	2	1		
2006–07	NEC Nijmegen	15	1	15	1
2007–08	Manchester U	4	0	6	1
2008–09	Burnley	43	8		
2009–10	Burnley	34	2		
2010–11	Burnley	43	11	120	21

EASTON, Brian (D)   126 3
H: 6 0 W: 12 00 b.Glasgow 5-3-88
Honours: Scotland Under-21, B.

2006–07	Hamilton A	31	1		
2007–08	Hamilton A	36	0		
2008–09	Hamilton A	35	1		
2009–10	Burnley	0	0		
2009–10	Hamilton A	12	0	114	2
2010–11	Burnley	12	1	12	1

ECKERSLEY, Richard (D)   36 0
H: 5 9 W: 11 09 b.Worsley 12-3-89
Source: Scholar.

2006–07	Manchester U	0	0		
2007–08	Manchester U	0	0		
2008–09	Manchester U	2	0		
2009–10	Manchester U	0	0	2	0
2009–10	Burnley	0	0		
2009–10	Plymouth Arg	7	0	7	0
2010–11	Burnley	0	0		
2010–11	Toronto	12	0	12	0
2010–11	Bradford C	12	0	12	0
2010–11	Bury	3	0	3	0

EDGAR, David (D)   35 3
H: 6 2 W: 12 13 b.Ontario 19-5-87
Source: Scholar. *Honours:* Canada Youth,
Under-20, 2 full caps.

2005–06	Newcastle U	0	0		
2006–07	Newcastle U	3	1		
2007–08	Newcastle U	8	0		
2008–09	Newcastle U	11	1		
2009–10	Newcastle U	0	0	19	2
2009–10	Burnley	0	0		
2009–10	Swansea C	5	1	5	1
2010–11	Burnley	7	0	11	0

ELLIOTT, Wade (M)   468 50
H: 5 10 W: 10 03 b.Eastleigh 14-12-78
Source: Bashley.

1999–2000	Bournemouth	12	3		
2000–01	Bournemouth	36	9		
2001–02	Bournemouth	46	8		
2002–03	Bournemouth	44	4		
2003–04	Bournemouth	39	3		
2004–05	Bournemouth	43	4	220	31
2005–06	Burnley	36	3		
2006–07	Burnley	42	4		
2007–08	Burnley	46	2		
2008–09	Burnley	42	4		
2009–10	Burnley	38	4		
2010–11	Burnley	44	2	248	19

FLETCHER, Wes (F)   15 2
H: 5 11 W: 12 06 b.Ormskirk 28-2-90
Source: Scholar.

2008–09	Burnley	0	0		
2009–10	Burnley	0	0		
2009–10	Grimsby T	6	1	6	1
2010–11	Burnley	0	0		
2010–11	Stockport Co	9	1	9	1

FOX, Danny (D)   231 14
H: 5 11 W: 12 06 b.Winsford 29-5-86
Source: Scholar. *Honours:* England Under-21,
Scotland 1 full cap.

2004–05	Everton	0	0		
2004–05	Stranraer	11	1	11	1
2005–06	Walsall	33	0		
2006–07	Walsall	44	3		
2007–08	Walsall	22	3	99	6
2007–08	Coventry C	18	1		
2008–09	Coventry C	39	5		
2009–10	Coventry C	0	0	57	6
2009–10	Celtic	15	0	15	0
2009–10	Burnley	14	1		
2010–11	Burnley	35	0	49	1

GRANT, Lee (G)   252 0
H: 6 3 W: 13 01 b.Hemel Hempstead
27-1-83
Source: Scholar. *Honours:* England Youth,
Under-21.

2000–01	Derby Co	0	0		
2001–02	Derby Co	0	0		
2002–03	Derby Co	29	0		
2003–04	Derby Co	36	0		
2004–05	Derby Co	2	0		
2005–06	Derby Co	0	0		
2005–06	Burnley	1	0		
2005–06	Oldham Ath	16	0	16	0
2006–07	Derby Co	7	0	74	0
2007–08	Sheffield W	44	0		
2008–09	Sheffield W	46	0		
2009–10	Sheffield W	46	0	136	0
2010–11	Burnley	25	0	26	0

HARVEY, Alex-Ray (M)   0 0
H: 5 7 W: 10 09 b.Burnley 4-4-90
Source: Scholar.

| 2009–10 | Burnley | 0 | 0 | | |
| 2010–11 | Burnley | 0 | 0 | | |

IWELUMO, Chris (F)   408 99
H: 6 3 W: 15 03 b.Coatbridge 1-8-78
Source: Juniors. *Honours:* Scotland B, 4 full
caps.

1996–97	St Mirren	14	0		
1997–98	St Mirren	12	0	26	0
1998–99	Aarhus Fremad	27	4	27	4
1999–2000	Stoke C	3	0		
2000–01	Stoke C	2	1		
2000–01	York C	12	2	12	2
2000–01	Cheltenham T	4	1	4	1
2001–02	Stoke C	38	10		
2002–03	Stoke C	32	5		
2003–04	Stoke C	9	0	84	16
2003–04	Brighton & HA	10	4	10	4
2004–05	Aachen	9	0	9	0
2005–06	Colchester U	46	17		
2006–07	Colchester U	46	18	92	35
2007–08	Charlton Ath	46	10	46	10
2008–09	Wolverhampton W	31	14		
2009–10	Wolverhampton W	15	0	46	14
2009–10	Bristol C	7	2	7	2
2010–11	Burnley	45	11	45	11

JENSEN, Brian (G)   313 0
H: 6 1 W: 12 04 b.Copenhagen 8-6-75
Source: Hvidovre, B93.

1997–98	AZ	0	0		
1998–99	AZ	1	0	1	0
1999–2000	WBA	12	0		
2000–01	WBA	33	0		
2001–02	WBA	1	0		
2002–03	WBA	0	0	46	0
2003–04	Burnley	46	0		
2004–05	Burnley	27	0		
2005–06	Burnley	39	0		
2006–07	Burnley	31	0		
2007–08	Burnley	19	0		
2008–09	Burnley	45	0		
2009–10	Burnley	38	0		
2010–11	Burnley	21	0	266	0

KING, Michael (M)   0 0
b.Aughton 26-9-91

| 2010–11 | Burnley | 0 | 0 | | |

KNOWLES, Dominic (F)   0 0
b. 13-2-92

| 2010–11 | Burnley | 0 | 0 | | |

KUDIERSKY, Nikolaus (D)   0 0
H: 6 1 W: 13 04 b.Glossop 15-2-91
Source: Scholar.

| 2009–10 | Burnley | 0 | 0 | | |
| 2010–11 | Burnley | 0 | 0 | | |

LONG, Kevin (D)   31 0
H: 6 3 W: 13 01 b.Cork 18-8-90

2009	Cork City	16	0	16	0
2009–10	Burnley	0	0		
2010–11	Burnley	0	0		
2010–11	Accrington S	15	0	15	0

LYNCH, Chris (D) 10 0
H: 6 3 W: 15 06 b.Blackburn 31-1-91
Source: Scholar.

2009–10	Burnley	0	0		
2009–10	*Chester C*	10	0	**10**	**0**
2010–11	Burnley	0	0		

MACDONALD, Alex (F) 26 1
H: 5 7 W: 11 04 b.Warrington 14-4-90
Source: Scholar. Honours: Scotland Youth, Under-21.

2007–08	Burnley	2	0		
2008–09	Burnley	3	0		
2009–10	Burnley	0	0		
2009–10	*Falkirk*	11	1	**11**	**1**
2010–11	Burnley	0	0	**5**	**0**
2010–11	*Inverness CT*	10	0	**10**	**0**

MARNEY, Dean (M) 196 14
H: 5 10 W: 11 09 b.Barking 31-1-84
Source: Scholar. Honours: England Under-21.

2002–03	Tottenham H	0	0		
2002–03	*Swindon T*	9	0	**9**	**0**
2003–04	Tottenham H	3	0		
2003–04	*QPR*	2	0	**2**	**0**
2004–05	Tottenham H	5	2		
2004–05	*Gillingham*	3	0	**3**	**0**
2005–06	Tottenham H	0	0	**8**	**2**
2005–06	*Norwich C*	13	0	**13**	**0**
2006–07	Hull C	37	2		
2007–08	Hull C	41	6		
2008–09	Hull C	31	0		
2009–10	Hull C	16	1	**125**	**9**
2009–10	Burnley	0	0		
2010–11	Burnley	36	3	**36**	**3**

McCANN, Chris (M) 151 19
H: 6 1 W: 11 11 b.Dublin 21-7-87
Source: Scholar. Honours: Eire Youth.

2005–06	Burnley	23	2		
2006–07	Burnley	38	5		
2007–08	Burnley	35	5		
2008–09	Burnley	44	6		
2009–10	Burnley	7	0		
2010–11	Burnley	4	1	**151**	**19**

McDONALD, Kevin (M) 158 17
H: 6 2 W: 13 03 b.Carnoustie 4-11-88
Honours: Scotland Youth, Under-21.

2005–06	Dundee	26	3		
2006–07	Dundee	31	2		
2007–08	Dundee	34	9	**91**	**14**
2008–09	Burnley	25	1		
2009–10	Burnley	26	1		
2010–11	Burnley	0	0	**51**	**2**
2010–11	*Scunthorpe U*	5	1	**5**	**1**
2010–11	*Notts Co*	11	0	**11**	**0**

MEARS, Tyrone (D) 203 7
H: 5 11 W: 11 10 b.Stockport 18-2-83
Source: Manchester C Juniors. Honours: Jamaica 1 full cap.

2000–01	Manchester C	0	0		
2001–02	Manchester C	1	0	**1**	**0**
2002–03	Preston NE	22	1		
2003–04	Preston NE	12	1		
2004–05	Preston NE	4	0		
2005–06	Preston NE	32	2	**70**	**4**
2006–07	West Ham U	5	0	**5**	**0**
2006–07	Derby Co	13	1		
2007–08	Derby Co	25	1		
2008–09	Derby Co	3	0	**41**	**2**
2008–09	*Marseille*	4	0	**4**	**0**
2009–10	Burnley	38	0		
2010–11	Burnley	44	1	**82**	**1**

PATERSON, Martin (F) 147 38
H: 5 9 W: 10 11 b.Tunstall 13-5-87
Source: Scholar. Honours: Northern Ireland Youth, Under-21,12 full caps.

2004–05	Stoke C	3	0		
2005–06	Stoke C	3	0		
2006–07	Stoke C	9	1	**15**	**1**
2006–07	*Grimsby T*	15	6	**15**	**6**
2007–08	Scunthorpe U	40	13	**40**	**13**
2008–09	Burnley	43	12		
2009–10	Burnley	23	4		
2010–11	Burnley	11	2	**77**	**18**

RODRIGUEZ, Jay (F) 85 20
H: 6 0 W: 12 00 b.Burnley 29-7-89
Source: Scholar. Honours: England Under-21.

2007–08	Burnley	1	0		
2007–08	*Stirling Alb*	11	3	**11**	**3**
2008–09	Burnley	25	2		
2009–10	Burnley	0	0		
2009–10	*Barnsley*	6	1	**6**	**1**
2010–11	Burnley	42	14	**68**	**16**

THOMPSON, Steven (F) 371 64
H: 6 2 W: 12 05 b.Paisley 14-10-78
Source: Dundee U BC. Honours: Scotland Under-21, 16 full caps, 3 goals.

1996–97	Dundee U	1	0		
1997–98	Dundee U	8	0		
1998–99	Dundee U	15	1		
1999–2000	Dundee U	27	1		
2000–01	Dundee U	31	4		
2001–02	Dundee U	32	6		
2002–03	Dundee U	20	6	**134**	**18**
2002–03	Rangers	8	2		
2003–04	Rangers	16	8		
2004–05	Rangers	19	5		
2005–06	Rangers	14	2	**57**	**17**
2005–06	Cardiff C	14	4		
2006–07	Cardiff C	43	6		
2007–08	Cardiff C	36	5		
2008–09	Cardiff C	4	1	**97**	**16**
2008–09	Burnley	34	7		
2009–10	Burnley	20	4		
2010–11	Burnley	29	2	**83**	**13**

VAN DER SCHAAF, Remco (D) 240 14
H: 6 01 W: 12 02 b.Groningen 28-2-79
Honours: Holland Under-21.

1997–98	Vitesse	3	0		
1998–99	Vitesse	22	0		
1999–2000	Vitesse	14	1		
1999–2000	*Fortuna Sittard*	4	0	**4**	**0**
2000–01	Vitesse	26	0		
2001 02	Vitesse	27	4		
2002–03	PSV Eindhoven	17	0		
2003–04	PSV Eindhoven	18	0		
2004–05	PSV Eindhoven	4	0	**39**	**0**
2005–06	Vitesse	27	2		
2006–07	Vitesse	14	0		
2007–08	Vitesse	29	3	**162**	**10**
2008–09	Burnley	0	0		
2008–09	*Brondby*	10	0		
2009–10	Burnley	0	0		
2009–10	*Brondby*	14	0		
2010–11	Burnley	0	0	**1**	**0**
2010–11	*Brondby*	10	4	**34**	**4**

WALLACE, Ross (M) 210 24
H: 5 6 W: 9 12 b.Dundee 23-5-85
Source: Celtic S Form. Honours: Scotland Youth, Under 21, B, 1 full cap.

2001–02	Celtic	0	0		
2002–03	Celtic	0	0		
2003–04	Celtic	8	1		
2004–05	Celtic	16	0		
2005–06	Celtic	11	0		
2006–07	Celtic	2	0	**37**	**1**
2006–07	Sunderland	32	6		
2007–08	Sunderland	21	2		
2008–09	Sunderland	0	0	**53**	**8**
2008–09	*Preston NE*	39	5		
2009–10	Preston NE	41	7	**80**	**12**
2010–11	Burnley	40	3	**40**	**3**

BURTON ALB (18)

AUSTIN, Ryan (D) 42 2
H: 6 2 W: 12 09 b.Stoke 15-11-84
Source: Scholar.

2004–05	Crewe Alex	0	0		
2009–10	Burton Alb	18	2		
2010–11	Burton Alb	24	0	**42**	**2**

BOERTIEN, Paul (D) 243 4
H: 5 10 W: 11 02 b.Haltwhistle 21-1-79
Source: Trainee.

1996–97	Carlisle U	0	0		
1997–98	Carlisle U	9	0		
1998–99	Carlisle U	8	1	**17**	**1**
1998–99	Derby Co	1	0		
1999–2000	Derby Co	2	0		
1999–2000	*Crewe Alex*	2	0	**2**	**0**
2000–01	Derby Co	8	1		
2001–02	Derby Co	32	0		
2002–03	Derby Co	42	1		
2003–04	Derby Co	18	0		
2003–04	Notts Co	5	0	**5**	**0**
2004–05	Derby Co	0	0		
2005–06	Derby Co	0	0		
2006–07	Derby Co	11	0	**114**	**2**
2006–07	*Chesterfield*	4	0	**4**	**0**
2007–08	Walsall	20	0		
2008–09	Walsall	31	0	**51**	**0**
2009–10	Burton Alb	34	1		
2010–11	Burton Alb	16	0	**50**	**1**

BOLDER, Adam (M) 329 17
H: 5 9 W: 10 08 b.Hull 25-10-80
Source: Trainee.

1998–99	Hull C	1	0		
1999–2000	Hull C	19	0	**20**	**0**
1999–2000	Derby Co	0	0		
2000–01	Derby Co	2	0		
2001–02	Derby Co	11	0		
2002–03	Derby Co	45	6		
2003–04	Derby Co	24	1		
2004–05	Derby Co	36	2		
2005–06	Derby Co	35	2		
2006–07	Derby Co	13	0	**166**	**11**
2006–07	QPR	16	0		
2007–08	QPR	24	2		
2007–08	*Sheffield W*	13	2	**13**	**2**
2008–09	QPR	0	0	**40**	**2**
2008–09	Millwall	28	0		
2009–10	Millwall	10	0	**39**	**0**
2009–10	*Bradford C*	14	1	**14**	**1**
2010–11	Burton Alb	37	1	**37**	**1**

CORBETT, Andy (F) 82 2
H: 6 0 W: 11 07 b.Worcester 20-2-82

2000–01	Kidderminster H	6	0		
2001–02	Kidderminster H	2	0	**8**	**0**

From Solihull B, Nuneaton B.

2009–10	Burton Alb	34	1		

From Solihull B, Nuneaton B.

2010–11	Burton Alb	40	1	**74**	**2**

DYER, Jack (M) 5 0
b.Sutton Coldfield 11-12-91
Source: Aston Villa Scholar.

2010–11	Burton Alb	5	0	**5**	**0**

ELLISON, James (F) 2 0
H: 5 10 W: 12 08 b.Liverpool 25-10-91
Source: Scholar.

2009–10	Liverpool	0	0		
2010–11	Liverpool	0	0		
2010–11	Burton Alb	2	0	**2**	**0**

GILROY, Keith (F) 17 1
H: 5 10 W: 11 04 b.Sligo 8-7-83
Honours: Eire Youth, Under-21.

2001–02	Sligo R	6	1	**6**	**1**
2002–03	Middlesbrough	0	0		
2003–04	Middlesbrough	0	0		
2004–05	Middlesbrough	0	0		

From Scarborough.

2004–05	Darlington	2	0	**2**	**0**
2009–10	Burton Alb	8	0		
2010–11	Burton Alb	1	0	**9**	**0**

GROCOTT, Kevin (D) 2 0
H: 5 11 W: 12 04 b.Derby 31-7-92
Source: Notts Co Youth.

2010–11	Burton Alb	2	0	**2**	**0**

HUGHES, Bryan (M) 461 52
H: 5 10 W: 11 08 b.Liverpool 19-6-76
Source: Trainee.

1993–94	Wrexham	11	0		
1994–95	Wrexham	38	9		
1995–96	Wrexham	22	0		
1996–97	Wrexham	23	3	**94**	**12**
1996–97	Birmingham C	11	0		
1997–98	Birmingham C	40	5		
1998–99	Birmingham C	28	3		
1999–2000	Birmingham C	45	10		
2000–01	Birmingham C	45	4		
2001–02	Birmingham C	31	7		
2002–03	Birmingham C	22	2		
2003–04	Birmingham C	26	3	**248**	**34**
2004–05	Charlton Ath	17	1		
2005–06	Charlton Ath	33	3		
2006–07	Charlton Ath	24	1	**74**	**5**
2007–08	Hull C	35	1		
2008–09	Hull C	6	0		
2009–10	Hull C	0	0		
2009–10	*Derby Co*	3	0	**3**	**0**
2010–11	Hull C	0	0	**41**	**1**
2010–11	Burton Alb	1	0	**1**	**0**

JAMES, Tony (D)　　75　1
H: 5 10　W: 13 06　b.Abergavenny 9-10-78
Source: WBA Scholar, Hereford U, Weymouth.

Season	Club				
2009–10	Burton Alb	42	1		
2010–11	Burton Alb	27	0	69	1
2010–11	*Hereford U*	6	0	6	0

LEGZDINS, Adam (G)　　52　0
H: 6 1　W: 14 02　b.Penkridge 28-11-86
Source: Scholar.

Season	Club				
2006–07	Birmingham C	0	0		
2007–08	Birmingham C	0	0		
2008–09	Crewe Alex	0	0		
2009–10	Crewe Alex	6	0	6	0
2010–11	Burton Alb	46	0	46	0

MAGHOMA, Jacques (M)　　76　7
H: 5 9　W: 11 06　b.Lubumbashi 23-10-87
Source: Scholar. *Honours:* DR Congo 2 full caps.

Season	Club				
2005–06	Tottenham H	0	0		
2006–07	Tottenham H	0	0		
2007–08	Tottenham H	0	0		
2008–09	Tottenham H	0	0		
2009–10	Burton Alb	35	3		
2010–11	Burton Alb	41	4	76	7

McGRATH, John (M)　　127　4
H: 5 10　W: 10 04　b.Limerick 27-3-80
Source: Belvedere. *Honours:* Eire Under-21.

Season	Club				
1999–2000	Aston Villa	0	0		
2000–01	Aston Villa	3	0		
2001–02	Aston Villa	0	0		
2002–03	Aston Villa	0	0	3	0
2003–04	Doncaster R	11	0		
2004–05	Doncaster R	0	0	11	0
2004–05	*Shrewsbury T*	8	0	8	0
2004–05	*Kidderminster H*	19	0	19	0
From Weymouth, Tamworth.					
2005–06	*Limerick*	0	0		
2009–10	Burton Alb	45	1		
2010–11	Burton Alb	41	3	86	4

MOORE, Darren (D)　　591　31
H: 6 2　W: 15 07　b.Birmingham 22-4-74
Source: Trainee. *Honours:* Jamaica 3 full caps.

Season	Club				
1991–92	Torquay U	5	1		
1992–93	Torquay U	31	2		
1993–94	Torquay U	37	2		
1994–95	Torquay U	30	3	103	8
1995–96	Doncaster R	35	2		
1996–97	Doncaster R	41	5	76	7
1997–98	Bradford C	18	0		
1998–99	Bradford C	44	3		
1999–2000	Bradford C	0	0	62	3
1999–2000	Portsmouth	25	1		
2000–01	Portsmouth	32	1		
2001–02	Portsmouth	2	0	59	2
2001–02	WBA	32	2		
2002–03	WBA	29	2		
2003–04	WBA	22	2		
2004–05	WBA	16	0		
2005–06	WBA	5	0	104	6
2005–06	Derby Co	14	1		
2006–07	Derby Co	35	2		
2007–08	Derby Co	31	0	80	3
2008–09	Barnsley	38	1		
2009–10	Barnsley	35	1	73	2
2010–11	Burton Alb	34	0	34	0

PEARSON, Greg (F)　　102　20
H: 6 0　W: 12 00　b.Birmingham 3-4-85
Source: Trainee.

Season	Club				
2003–04	West Ham U	0	0		
2004–05	West Ham U	0	0		
2004–05	*Lincoln C*	3	0	3	0
2005–06	*Rushden & D*	22	1	22	1
From Bishop's Stortford.					
2009–10	Burton Alb	42	14		
From Bishop's Stortford.					
2010–11	Burton Alb	35	5	77	19

PENN, Russ (M)　　81　7
H: 5 11　W: 12 13　b.Dudley 8-11-85
Source: Scunthorpe U, Kidderminster H.
Honours: England C.

Season	Club				
2009–10	Burton Alb	40	4		
2010–11	Burton Alb	41	3	81	7

PHILLIPS, Jimmy (M)　　47　1
H: 5 7　W: 10 00　b.Stoke 20-9-89
Source: Scholar.

Season	Club				
2008–09	Stoke C	0	0		
2009–10	Burton Alb	24	1		
2010–11	Burton Alb	23	0	47	1

POOLE, Kevin (G)　　313　0
H: 5 10　W: 12 11　b.Bromsgrove 21-7-63
Source: Apprentice.

Season	Club				
1981–82	Aston Villa	0	0		
1982–83	Aston Villa	0	0		
1983–84	Aston Villa	7	0		
1984–85	Aston Villa	0	0		
1984–85	*Northampton T*	3	0	3	0
1985–86	Aston Villa	11	0		
1986–87	Aston Villa	10	0	28	0
1987–88	Middlesbrough	1	0		
1988–89	Middlesbrough	12	0		
1989–90	Middlesbrough	21	0		
1990–91	Middlesbrough	0	0	34	0
1990–91	*Hartlepool U*	12	0	12	0
1991–92	Leicester C	42	0		
1992–93	Leicester C	19	0		
1993–94	Leicester C	14	0		
1994–95	Leicester C	36	0		
1995–96	Leicester C	45	0		
1996–97	Leicester C	7	0	163	0
1997–98	Birmingham C	1	0		
1998–99	Birmingham C	36	0		
1999–2000	Birmingham C	18	0		
2000–01	Birmingham C	1	0		
2001–02	Birmingham C	0	0	56	0
2001–02	Bolton W	3	0		
2002–03	Bolton W	0	0		
2003–04	Bolton W	0	0		
2004–05	Bolton W	2	0	5	0
2005–06	Derby Co	6	0	6	0
2009–10	Burton Alb	6	0		
2010–11	Burton Alb	0	0	6	0

PREEN, Garyn (M)　　1　0
H: 5 11　W: 12 06　b.Tredegar 25-10-91
Source: Southampton Scholar. *Honours:* Wales Youth.

Season	Club				
2010–11	Burton Alb	1	0	1	0

STANTON, Nathan (D)　　399　0
H: 5 9　W: 12 06　b.Nottingham 6-5-81
Source: Trainee. *Honours:* England Youth.

Season	Club				
1997–98	Scunthorpe U	1	0		
1998–99	Scunthorpe U	4	0		
1999–2000	Scunthorpe U	34	0		
2000–01	Scunthorpe U	38	0		
2001–02	Scunthorpe U	42	0		
2002–03	Scunthorpe U	42	0		
2003–04	Scunthorpe U	33	0		
2004–05	Scunthorpe U	21	0		
2005–06	Scunthorpe U	22	0	237	0
2006–07	Rochdale	35	0		
2007–08	Rochdale	27	0		
2008–09	Rochdale	39	0		
2009–10	Rochdale	38	0	139	0
2010–11	Burton Alb	23	0	23	0

WALKER, Richard (F)　　340　82
H: 6 0　W: 12 04　b.Sutton Coldfield 8-11-77
Source: Trainee.

Season	Club				
1995–96	Aston Villa	0	0		
1996–97	Aston Villa	0	0		
1997–98	Aston Villa	1	0		
1998–99	Aston Villa	0	0		
1998–99	*Cambridge U*	21	3	21	3
1999–2000	Aston Villa	5	2		
2000–01	Aston Villa	0	0		
2000–01	*Blackpool*	18	3		
2001–02	Aston Villa	0	0	6	2
2001–02	*Wycombe W*	12	3	12	3
2001–02	Blackpool	21	8		
2002–03	Blackpool	32	4		
2003–04	Blackpool	9	0	80	15
2003–04	*Northampton T*	12	4	12	4
2003–04	*Oxford U*	4	0	4	0
2004–05	Bristol R	27	10		
2005–06	Bristol R	46	20		
2006–07	Bristol R	46	12		
2007–08	Bristol R	24	4		
2008–09	Bristol R	0	0	143	46
2008–09	*Shrewsbury T*	5	5	27	5
2009–10	Burton Alb	17	3		
2010–11	Burton Alb	18	1	35	4

WEBSTER, Aaron (D)　　66　15
H: 6 1　W: 12 00　b.Burton-on-Trent 19-12-80
Source: Youth.

Season	Club				
2009–10	Burton Alb	24	4		
2010–11	Burton Alb	42	11	66	15

WHALEY, Simon (M)　　224　30
H: 5 10　W: 11 11　b.Bolton 7-6-85
Source: Scholar.

Season	Club				
2002–03	Bury	2	0		
2003–04	Bury	10	1		
2004–05	Bury	38	3		
2005–06	Bury	23	7	73	11
2005–06	Preston NE	16	3		
2006–07	Preston NE	40	6		
2007–08	Preston NE	43	4		
2008–09	Preston NE	21	1	120	14
2008–09	*Barnsley*	4	1	4	1
2009–10	*Norwich C*	3	0	3	0
2009–10	*Rochdale*	9	2	9	2
2009–10	*Bradford C*	6	1	6	1
2009–10	*Chesterfield*	6	1	6	1
2010–11	Doncaster R	0	0		
2010–11	Burton Alb	3	0	3	0

YOUNG, Lewis (M)　　26　0
H: 5 10　W: 11 02　b.Stevenage 27-9-89
Source: Scholar.

Season	Club				
2008–09	Watford	1	0		
2009–10	Watford	0	0	1	0
2009–10	*Hereford U*	6	0	6	0
2010–11	Burton Alb	19	0	19	0

BURY (19)

BELFORD, Cameron (G)　　48　0
H: 6 1　W: 11 10　b.Nuneaton 16-10-88
Source: Coventry C Scholar.

Season	Club				
2007–08	Bury	1	0		
2008–09	Bury	1	0		
2009–10	Bury	7	0		
2010–11	Bury	39	0	48	0

BENNETT, Kyle (F)　　32　2
H: 5 5　W: 9 08　b.Telford 9-9-90
Source: Scholar. *Honours:* England Youth.

Season	Club				
2007–08	Wolverhampton W	0	0		
2008–09	Wolverhampton W	0	0		
2009–10	Wolverhampton W	0	0		
2010–11	Bury	32	2	32	2

BISHOP, Andy (F)　　228　67
H: 6 0　W: 10 10　b.Cannock 19-10-82
Source: Scholar.

Season	Club				
2002–03	Walsall	0	0		
2002–03	*Kidderminster H*	29	5		
2003–04	*Kidderminster H*	11	2	40	7
2003–04	*Rochdale*	10	1	10	1
2003–04	*Yeovil T*	5	2	5	2
From York C.					
2006–07	Bury	43	15		
2007–08	Bury	44	19		
2008–09	Bury	42	16		
2009–10	Bury	25	3		
2010–11	Bury	19	4	173	57

BRANAGAN, Richie (G)　　2　0
H: 5 11　W: 12 10　b.Gravesend 20-10-91
Source: Bolton W. *Honours:* Eire Under-21.

Season	Club				
2010–11	Bury	2	0	2	0

FUTCHER, Ben (D)　　312　21
H: 6 7　W: 12 05　b.Manchester 20-2-81
Source: Trainee.

Season	Club				
1999–2000	Oldham Ath	5	0		
2000–01	Oldham Ath	5	0		
2001–02	Oldham Ath	0	0	10	0
From Stalybridge C, Doncaster R.					
2002–03	Lincoln C	43	8		
2003–04	Lincoln C	43	2		
2004–05	Lincoln C	35	3	121	13
2005–06	Boston U	14	0	14	0
2005–06	Grimsby T	15	2		
2006–07	Grimsby T	4	0	19	2
2006–07	*Peterborough U*	25	3	25	3
2007–08	Bury	40	0		
2008–09	Bury	34	2		
2009–10	Bury	32	0		
2010–11	Bury	11	1	117	3
2010–11	*Oxford U*	6	0	6	0

HARROP, Max (M) 3 0
H: 5 8 W: 10 00 b.Oldham 30-6-93
Source: Scholar.
2010–11	Bury	3	0	3 0

HAWORTH, Andrew (M) 47 3
H: 5 11 W: 11 10 b.Lancaster 28-11-88
Source: Scholar.
2007–08	Blackburn R	0	0	
2008–09	Blackburn R	0	0	
2009–10	Blackburn R	0	0	
2009–10	Rochdale	7	0	7 0
2010–11	Bury	40	3	40 3

JOHN-LEWIS, Leneli (M) 111 10
H: 5 10 W: 11 10 b.Hammersmith 17-5-89
Source: Scholar.
2006–07	Lincoln C	0	0	
2007–08	Lincoln C	21	3	
2008–09	Lincoln C	27	4	
2009–10	Lincoln C	24	1	72 8
2010–11	Bury	39	2	39 2

JONES, Mike (M) 152 19
H: 5 11 W: 12 04 b.Birkenhead 15-8-87
Source: Scholar.
2005–06	Tranmere R	1	0	
2006–07	Tranmere R	0	0	
2006–07	Shrewsbury T	13	1	13 1
2007–08	Tranmere R	9	1	10 1
2008–09	Bury	46	4	
2009–10	Bury	41	5	
2010–11	Bury	42	8	129 17

JONES, Andrai (M) 1 0
H: 5 11 W: 10 10 b.Liverpool 1-1-92
Source: Scholar.
2010–11	Bury	1	0	1 0

LOWE, Ryan (F) 375 110
H: 5 10 W: 12 08 b.Liverpool 18-9-78
Source: Burscough.
2000–01	Shrewsbury T	30	4	
2001–02	Shrewsbury T	38	7	
2002–03	Shrewsbury T	39	9	
2003–04	Shrewsbury T	30	3	137 23
2004–05	Chester C	8	4	
2005–06	Chester C	32	10	
2005–06	Crewe Alex	0	0	
2006–07	Crewe Alex	37	8	
2007–08	Crewe Alex	27	4	64 12
2007–08	Stockport Co	4	0	4 0
2008–09	Chester C	45	16	85 30
2009–10	Bury	39	18	
2010–11	Bury	46	27	85 45

McCARTHY, Luke (M) 1 0
H: 5 9 W: 10 10 b.Bolton 7-7-93
Source: Scholar.
2010–11	Bury	1	0	1 0

MORRELL, Andy (F) 359 96
H: 5 11 W: 12 00 b.Doncaster 28-9-74
Source: Newcastle Blue Star.
1998–99	Wrexham	7	0	
1999–2000	Wrexham	13	1	
2000–01	Wrexham	20	3	
2001–02	Wrexham	25	2	
2002–03	Wrexham	45	34	110 40
2003–04	Coventry C	30	9	
2004–05	Coventry C	34	6	
2005–06	Coventry C	34	2	
2006–07	Coventry C	0	0	98 17
2006–07	Blackpool	40	16	
2007–08	Blackpool	38	5	78 21
2008–09	Bury	41	9	
2009–10	Bury	32	9	
2010–11	Bury	0	0	73 18

MOZIKA, Damien (M) 83 4
H: 6 0 W: 11 13 b.Corbell-Essonnes 15-4-87
2006–07	Nancy	0	0	
2007–08	Louhans	28	0	28 0
2008–09	Chester C	22	2	22 2
From Tarbiat Yazd.
2010–11	Bury	33	2	33 2

PATEL, Krishnan (M) 0 0
H: 5 7 W: 11 00 b.Bolton 17-12-91
Source: Scholar.
2010–11	Bury	0	0	

PICKEN, Phil (D) 200 2
H: 5 9 W: 10 07 b.Droylsden 12-11-85
Source: Scholar.
2004–05	Manchester U	0	0	
2005–06	Manchester U	0	0	
2005–06	Chesterfield	32	1	
2006–07	Chesterfield	39	1	
2007–08	Chesterfield	37	0	
2008–09	Chesterfield	11	0	
2008–09	Notts Co	22	0	22 0
2009–10	Chesterfield	21	0	140 2
2010–11	Bury	38	0	38 0

ROTHWELL, Zach (M) 0 0
H: 6 1 W: 11 07 b.Bury 16-7-92
Source: Scholar.
2010–11	Bury	0	0	

SCHUMACHER, Steven (M) 237 29
H: 5 10 W: 11 00 b.Liverpool 30-4-84
Source: Scholar. Honours: England Youth.
2000–01	Everton	0	0	
2001–02	Everton	0	0	
2002–03	Everton	0	0	
2003–04	Everton	0	0	
2003–04	Carlisle U	4	0	4 0
2004–05	Bradford C	43	6	
2005–06	Bradford C	30	1	
2006–07	Bradford C	44	6	117 13
2007–08	Crewe Alex	26	1	
2008–09	Crewe Alex	15	2	
2009–10	Crewe Alex	32	4	73 7
2010–11	Bury	43	9	43 9

SKARZ, Joe (D) 141 2
H: 5 10 W: 11 04 b.Huddersfield 13-7-89
Source: Scholar.
2006–07	Huddersfield T	17	0	
2007–08	Huddersfield T	27	0	
2008–09	Huddersfield T	9	1	
2008–09	Hartlepool U	7	0	7 0
2009–10	Huddersfield T	15	0	68 1
2009–10	Shrewsbury T	20	0	20 0
2010–11	Bury	46	1	46 1

SODJE, Efe (D) 471 32
H: 6 1 W: 12 00 b.Greenwich 5-10-72
Source: Delta Steel Pioneer, Stevenage Bor.
Honours: Nigeria 9 full caps, 1 goal.
1997–98	Macclesfield T	41	3	
1998–99	Macclesfield T	42	3	83 6
1999–2000	Luton T	9	0	9 0
1999–2000	Colchester U	3	0	3 0
2000–01	Crewe Alex	32	0	
2001–02	Crewe Alex	36	2	
2002–03	Crewe Alex	30	1	98 3
2003–04	Huddersfield T	39	4	
2004–05	Huddersfield T	28	1	67 5
2004–05	Yeovil T	6	2	
2005–06	Yeovil T	19	1	25 3
2005–06	Southend U	1	0	
2006–07	Southend U	24	1	37 2
2007–08	Gillingham	13	0	13 0
2007–08	Bury	16	1	
2008–09	Bury	41	7	
2009–10	Bury	39	2	
2010–11	Bury	40	3	136 13

SWEENEY, Peter (M) 191 11
H: 6 0 W: 12 11 b.Glasgow 25-9-84
Source: Scholar. Honours: Scotland Youth, Under-21, B.
2001–02	Millwall	1	0	
2002–03	Millwall	5	1	
2003–04	Millwall	29	2	
2004–05	Millwall	24	2	59 5
2005–06	Stoke C	17	1	
2006–07	Stoke C	13	1	
2006–07	Yeovil T	8	0	8 0
2007–08	Stoke C	5	0	35 2
2007–08	Walsall	7	0	7 0
2007–08	Leeds U	9	0	
2008–09	Leeds U	0	0	9 0
2008–09	Grimsby T	8	0	
2009–10	Grimsby T	40	4	48 4
2010–11	Bury	25	0	25 0

WORRALL, David (M) 94 6
H: 6 0 W: 11 03 b.Manchester 12-6-90
Source: Scholar.
2006–07	Bury	1	0	
2007–08	Bury	0	0	

2007–08	WBA	0	0	
2008–09	Accrington S	4	0	4 0
2008–09	Shrewsbury T	9	0	9 0
2009–10	WBA	0	0	
2009–10	Bury	40	4	
2010–11	Bury	40	2	81 6

CARDIFF C (20)

BLAKE, Darcy (M) 77 0
H: 5 10 W: 12 05 b.New Tredegar 13-12-88
Source: Scholar. Honours: Wales Youth, Under-21, 2 full caps.
2005–06	Cardiff C	1	0	
2006–07	Cardiff C	10	0	
2007–08	Cardiff C	8	0	
2008–09	Cardiff C	7	0	
2009–10	Cardiff C	18	0	
2009–10	Plymouth Arg	7	0	7 0
2010–11	Cardiff C	26	0	70 0

BOTHROYD, Jay (F) 302 74
H: 6 3 W: 14 13 b.Islington 7-5-82
Source: Trainee. Honours: England Schools, Youth, Under-20, Under-21, 1 full cap.
1999–2000	Arsenal	0	0	
2000–01	Coventry C	8	0	
2001–02	Coventry C	31	6	
2002–03	Coventry C	33	8	72 14
2003–04	Perugia	26	4	26 4
2004–05	Blackburn R	11	1	11 1
2005–06	Charlton Ath	18	2	18 2
2006–07	Wolverhampton W	33	9	
2007–08	Wolverhampton W	22	3	55 12
2007–08	Stoke C	4	0	4 0
2008–09	Cardiff C	39	12	
2009–10	Cardiff C	40	11	
2010–11	Cardiff C	37	18	116 41

BURKE, Chris (M) 197 26
H: 5 9 W: 10 10 b.Glasgow 2-12-83
Honours: Scotland Under-21, B, 2 full caps.
2001–02	Rangers	2	1	
2002–03	Rangers	0	0	
2003–04	Rangers	20	3	
2004–05	Rangers	12	0	
2005–06	Rangers	21	3	
2006–07	Rangers	22	2	
2007–08	Rangers	11	2	
2008–09	Rangers	1	0	95 11
2008–09	Cardiff C	14	1	
2009–10	Cardiff C	44	9	
2010–11	Cardiff C	44	5	102 15

CHOPRA, Michael (F) 251 87
H: 5 9 W: 10 10 b.Newcastle 23-12-83
Source: Scholar. Honours: England Youth, Under-21, Under-21.
2000–01	Newcastle U	0	0	
2001–02	Newcastle U	0	0	
2002–03	Newcastle U	1	0	
2002–03	Watford	5	5	5 5
2003–04	Newcastle U	6	0	
2003–04	Nottingham F	5	0	5 0
2004–05	Newcastle U	1	0	
2004–05	Barnsley	39	17	39 17
2005–06	Newcastle U	13	1	21 1
2006–07	Cardiff C	42	22	
2007–08	Sunderland	33	6	
2008–09	Sunderland	6	2	39 8
2008–09	Cardiff C	27	9	
2009–10	Cardiff C	41	16	
2010–11	Cardiff C	32	9	142 56

GERRARD, Anthony (D) 243 14
H: 6 2 W: 13 07 b.Huyton 2-8-86
Source: Scholar. Honours: Eire Youth.
2004–05	Everton	0	0	
2004–05	Walsall	8	0	
2005–06	Walsall	34	0	
2006–07	Walsall	35	1	
2007–08	Walsall	44	3	
2008–09	Walsall	42	3	163 7
2009–10	Cardiff C	39	2	
2010–11	Cardiff C	0	0	39 2
2010–11	Hull C	41	5	41 5

GYEPES, Gabor (D) 213 16
H: 6 3 W: 13 01 b.Hungary 26-6-81
Honours: Hungary 26 full caps, 1 goal.
1999–2000	Ferencvaros	2	0	

2000–01	Ferencvaros	29	2		
2001–02	Ferencvaros	33	3		
2002–03	Ferencvaros	17	2		
2003–04	Ferencvaros	7	0		
2004–05	Ferencvaros	26	5	114	12
2005–06	Wolverhampton W	20	0		
2006–07	Wolverhampton W	0	0	20	0
2007–08	Northampton T	13	0		
2008–09	Northampton T	2	0	15	0
2008–09	Cardiff C	27	2		
2009–10	Cardiff C	16	1		
2010–11	Cardiff C	21	1	64	4

HEATON, Tom (G)   **90 0**
H: 6 1   W: 13 12   b.Chester 15-4-86
Source: Trainee. *Honours:* England Youth, Under-21:

2003–04	Manchester U	0	0		
2004–05	Manchester U	0	0		
2005–06	Manchester U	0	0		
2005–06	*Swindon T*	14	0	14	0
2006–07	Manchester U	0	0		
2007–08	Manchester U	0	0		
2008–09	Manchester U	0	0		
2008–09	*Cardiff C*	21	0		
2009–10	Manchester U	0	0		
2009–10	*Rochdale*	12	0	12	0
2009–10	*Wycombe W*	16	0	16	0
2010–11	Cardiff C	27	0	48	0

HUDSON, Mark (D)   **245 12**
H: 6 1   W: 12 01   b.Guildford 30-3-82
Source: Trainee.

1998–99	Fulham	0	0		
1999–2000	Fulham	0	0		
2000–01	Fulham	0	0		
2001–02	Fulham	0	0		
2002–03	Fulham	0	0		
2003–04	Fulham	0	0		
2003–04	*Oldham Ath*	15	0	15	0
2003–04	*Crystal Palace*	14	0		
2004–05	*Crystal Palace*	7	1		
2005–06	*Crystal Palace*	15	0		
2006–07	*Crystal Palace*	39	4		
2007–08	*Crystal Palace*	45	2	120	7
2008–09	*Charlton Ath*	43	3	43	3
2009–10	Cardiff C	27	2		
2010–11	Cardiff C	40	0	67	2

JARVIS, Nathaniel (F)   **6 0**
H: 6 0   W: 12 06   b.Cardiff 20-10-91
Source: Scholar.

2010–11	Cardiff C	0	0		
2010–11	*Southend U*	6	0	6	0

JOHN, Martin (D)   **12 2**
b.Camden 1-8-88
Source: Welling U.

2008	Ottawa Fury	12	2	12	2

From Argentinos Juniors.

2010–11	Cardiff C	0	0		

KEINAN, Dekel (D)   **204 13**
H: 6 0   W: 11 09   b.Rosh Hanikra 15-9-84
Honours: Israel 17 full caps.

2002–03	Maccabi Haifa	7	0		
2003–04	Maccabi Haifa	13	0		
2004–05	Maccabi Haifa	1	0		
2004–05	*Hapoel Bnei Sakhnin*	23	3	23	3
2005–06	Maccabi Haifa	1	0		
2005–06	*Maccabi Netanya*	21	2	21	2
2006–07	Maccabi Haifa	28	0		
2007–08	Maccabi Haifa	24	2		
2008–09	Maccabi Haifa	28	3		
2009–10	Maccabi Haifa	34	1	136	6
2010–11	*Blackpool*	6	0	6	0
2010–11	Cardiff C	18	2	18	2

MARSHALL, David (G)   **183 0**
H: 6 3   W: 13 04   b.Glasgow 5-3-85
Source: Celtic Youth. *Honours:* Scotland Youth, Under-21, B, 5 full caps.

2003–04	Celtic	11	0		
2004–05	Celtic	18	0		
2005–06	Celtic	4	0		
2006–07	Celtic	2	0	35	0
2006–07	Norwich C	2	0		
2007–08	Norwich C	46	0		
2008–09	Norwich C	46	0	94	0
2008–09	Cardiff C	0	0		
2009–10	Cardiff C	43	0		
2010–11	Cardiff C	11	0	54	0

MATTHEWS, Adam (M)   **40 1**
H: 5 10   W: 11 02   b.Gorseinon 13-1-92
Source: Scholar. *Honours:* Wales Youth, Under-21, 2 full caps.

2008–09	Cardiff C	0	0		
2009–10	Cardiff C	32	1		
2010–11	Cardiff C	8	0	40	1

McNAUGHTON, Kevin (D)   **356 4**
H: 5 10   W: 10 06   b.Dundee 28-8-82
Source: Trainee. *Honours:* Scotland Under-21, 4 full caps.

1999–2000	Aberdeen	0	0		
2000–01	Aberdeen	33	0		
2001–02	Aberdeen	34	0		
2002–03	Aberdeen	22	1		
2003–04	Aberdeen	17	0		
2004–05	Aberdeen	35	2		
2005–06	Aberdeen	34	0	175	3
2006–07	Cardiff C	42	0		
2007–08	Cardiff C	35	1		
2008–09	Cardiff C	39	0		
2009–10	Cardiff C	21	0		
2010–11	Cardiff C	44	0	181	1

McPHAIL, Stephen (M)   **332 10**
H: 5 8   W: 11 04   b.Westminster 9-12-79
Source: Trainee. *Honours:* Eire Youth, B, Under-21, 10 full caps, 1 goal.

1996–97	Leeds U	0	0		
1997–98	Leeds U	4	0		
1998–99	Leeds U	17	0		
1999–2000	Leeds U	24	2		
2000–01	Leeds U	7	0		
2001–02	Leeds U	1	0		
2001–02	*Millwall*	3	0	3	0
2002–03	Leeds U	13	0		
2003–04	Leeds U	12	1	78	3
2003–04	*Nottingham F*	14	0	14	0
2004–05	Barnsley	36	2		
2005–06	Barnsley	34	2	70	4
2006–07	Cardiff C	43	0		
2007–08	Cardiff C	43	3		
2008–09	Cardiff C	32	0		
2009–10	Cardiff C	21	0		
2010–11	Cardiff C	28	0	167	3

MEADES, Jonathan (D)   **0 0**
H: 6 1   W: 13 00   b.Cardiff 2-3-92
Source: Scholar.

2010–11	Cardiff C	0	0		

NAYLOR, Lee (D)   **420 12**
H: 5 9   W: 11 03   b.Walsall 19-3-80
Source: Trainee. *Honours:* England Youth, Under-21.

1997–98	Wolverhampton W	16	0		
1998–99	Wolverhampton W	23	1		
1999–2000	Wolverhampton W	30	2		
2000–01	Wolverhampton W	46	1		
2001–02	Wolverhampton W	27	0		
2002–03	Wolverhampton W	32	1		
2003–04	Wolverhampton W	38	0		
2004–05	Wolverhampton W	38	1		
2005–06	Wolverhampton W	40	1		
2006–07	Wolverhampton W	3	0	293	7
2006–07	Celtic	32	0		
2007–08	Celtic	33	1		
2008–09	Celtic	23	1		
2009–10	Celtic	12	1	100	3
2010–11	Cardiff C	27	2	27	2

PARKIN, Jon (F)   **344 89**
H: 6 4   W: 13 07   b.Barnsley 30-12-81
Source: Scholarship.

1998–99	Barnsley	2	0		
1999–2000	Barnsley	0	0		
2000–01	Barnsley	4	0		
2001–02	Barnsley	4	0	10	0
2001–02	*Hartlepool U*	1	0	1	0
2001–02	Barnsley	18	2		
2002–03	York C	41	10		
2003–04	York C	15	2	74	14
2003–04	Macclesfield T	12	1		
2004–05	Macclesfield T	42	22		
2005–06	Macclesfield T	1	0	65	30
2005–06	Hull C	18	5		
2006–07	Hull C	29	6	47	11
2006–07	Stoke C	6	3		
2007–08	Stoke C	29	2		
2008–09	Stoke C	0	0	35	5
2008–09	Preston NE	39	11		
2009–10	Preston NE	43	10		
2010–11	Preston NE	19	7	101	28
2010–11	Cardiff C	11	1	11	1

QUINN, Paul (D)   **206 4**
H: 6 0   W: 11 04   b.Wishaw 21-7-85
Honours: Scotland Under-21.

2002–03	Motherwell	4	0		
2003–04	Motherwell	26	0		
2004–05	Motherwell	23	0		
2005–06	Motherwell	18	0		
2006–07	Motherwell	26	0		
2007–08	Motherwell	31	2		
2008–09	Motherwell	33	1	161	3
2009–10	Cardiff C	22	0		
2010–11	Cardiff C	23	1	45	1

RAE, Gavin (D)   **370 33**
H: 5 11   W: 10 04   b.Aberdeen 28-11-77
Source: Hermes J. *Honours:* Scotland Under-21, 14 full caps.

1995–96	Dundee	6	0		
1996–97	Dundee	17	2		
1997–98	Dundee	6	0		
1998–99	Dundee	30	1		
1999–2000	Dundee	35	4		
2000–01	Dundee	32	4		
2001–02	Dundee	36	6		
2002–03	Dundee	37	4		
2003–04	Dundee	13	2	212	23
2003–04	Rangers	10	2		
2004–05	Rangers	8	0		
2005–06	Rangers	8	0		
2006–07	Rangers	10	1	28	3
2007–08	Cardiff C	45	4		
2008–09	Cardiff C	41	0		
2009–10	Cardiff C	37	1		
2010–11	Cardiff C	7	1	130	7

RIGGOTT, Chris (D)   **206 10**
H: 6 2   W: 13 09   b.Derby 1-9-80
Source: Trainee. *Honours:* England Youth, Under-21.

1998–99	Derby Co	0	0		
1999–2000	Derby Co	1	0		
2000–01	Derby Co	31	3		
2001–02	Derby Co	37	0		
2002–03	Derby Co	22	2	91	5
2002–03	Middlesbrough	5	2		
2003–04	Middlesbrough	17	0		
2004–05	Middlesbrough	21	2		
2005–06	Middlesbrough	22	0		
2006–07	Middlesbrough	6	0		
2007–08	Middlesbrough	10	1		
2007–08	*Stoke C*	9	0	9	0
2008–09	Middlesbrough	17	0		
2009–10	Middlesbrough	6	0	104	5
2010–11	Cardiff C	2	0	2	0

SANTIAGO, Jordan (G)   **0 0**
b.Calgary 3-4-91
Source: Scholar.

2010–11	Cardiff C	0	0		

TAIWO, Soloman (M)   **80 4**
H: 6 1   W: 13 02   b.Lagos 29-4-85
Source: Sutton U.

2007–08	Dagenham & R	10	0		
2008–09	Dagenham & R	40	4		
2009–10	Dagenham & R	4	0		
2009–10	Cardiff C	8	0		
2010–11	Cardiff C	0	0	8	0
2010–11	*Dagenham & R*	18	0	72	4

WHITTINGHAM, Peter (M)   **253 44**
H: 5 10   W: 9 13   b.Nuneaton 8-9-84
Source: Trainee. *Honours:* England Youth, Under-20, Under-21.

2002–03	Aston Villa	4	0		
2003–04	Aston Villa	32	0		
2004–05	Aston Villa	13	1		
2004–05	*Burnley*	7	0	7	0
2005–06	Aston Villa	4	0		
2005–06	*Derby Co*	11	0	11	0
2006–07	Aston Villa	3	0	56	1
2006–07	Cardiff C	19	4		
2007–08	Cardiff C	41	5		
2008–09	Cardiff C	33	3		
2009–10	Cardiff C	41	20		
2010–11	Cardiff C	45	11	179	43

WILDIG, Aaron (M)   **16 1**
H: 5 9   W: 11 02   b.Hereford 15-4-92
Source: Scholar.

2009–10	Cardiff C	11	1	
2010–11	Cardiff C	2	0	**13 1**
2010–11	Hamilton A	3	0	**3 0**

CARLISLE U (21)

BERRETT, James (M)   **81 12**
H: 5 10   W: 10 13   b.Halifax 13-1-89
Source: Scholar. Honours: Eire Youth, Under-21.

2006–07	Huddersfield T	2	0	
2007–08	Huddersfield T	15	1	
2008–09	Huddersfield T	9	1	
2009–10	Huddersfield T	9	0	**35 2**
2010–11	Carlisle U	46	10	**46 10**

BOWMAN, Ryan (F)   **9 0**
H: 6 2   W: 12 00   b.Carlisle 30-11-91
Source: Scholar.

2009–10	Carlisle U	6	0	
2010–11	Carlisle U	3	0	**9 0**

BRIDGE-WILKINSON, Marc (M)   **331 56**
H: 5 6   W: 11 00   b.Coventry 16-3-79
Source: Trainee.

1996–97	Derby Co	0	0	
1997–98	Derby Co	0	0	
1998–99	Derby Co	1	0	
1998–99	Carlisle U	7	0	
1999–2000	Derby Co	0	0	**1 0**
2000–01	Port Vale	42	9	
2001–02	Port Vale	19	6	
2002–03	Port Vale	31	9	
2003–04	Port Vale	32	7	**124 31**
2004–05	Stockport Co	22	2	**22 2**
2004–05	Bradford C	12	3	
2005–06	Bradford C	36	5	
2006–07	Bradford C	39	4	**87 12**
2007–08	Carlisle U	45	6	
2008–09	Carlisle U	23	5	
2009–10	Carlisle U	19	0	
2010–11	Carlisle U	3	0	**97 11**

COLLIN, Adam (G)   **75 0**
H: 6 2   W: 12 00   b.Penrith 9-12-84
Source: Trainee.

2003–04	Newcastle U	0	0	
2003–04	Oldham Ath	0	0	
2003–04	Doncaster R	0	0	
2004–05	Doncaster R	0	0	
2005–06	Doncaster R	0	0	
2006–07	Doncaster R	0	0	
2007–08	Doncaster R	0	0	
2008–09	Doncaster R	0	0	
2009–10	Carlisle U	29	0	
2010–11	Carlisle U	46	0	**75 0**

CURRAN, Craig (F)   **142 22**
H: 5 9   W: 11 09   b.Liverpool 23-9-89
Source: Scholar.

2006–07	Tranmere R	4	4	
2007–08	Tranmere R	35	2	
2008–09	Tranmere R	15	3	
2009–10	Tranmere R	43	5	**97 14**
2010–11	Carlisle U	45	8	**45 8**

GBARSSIN, Marc-Antoine (M)   **102 5**
H: 5 11   W: 12 04   b.Bordeaux 11-12-84

2004–05	Loombeek	0	0	
2005–06	Excelsior	12	0	
2006–07	Excelsior	31	1	**43 1**
2007–08	Antwerp	16	1	
2008–09	Antwerp	23	2	
2009–10	Antwerp	5	0	**44 3**
2010–11	Fredericia	6	1	**6 1**
2010–11	Carlisle U	0	0	
2010–11	Walsall	9	0	**9 0**

GILLESPIE, Mark (G)   **1 0**
H: 6 3   W: 13 07   b.Newcastle 27-3-92
Source: Scholar.

2009–10	Carlisle U	1	0	
2010–11	Carlisle U	0	0	**1 0**

HURST, Kevan (M)   **206 16**
H: 5 10   W: 11 07   b.Chesterfield 27-8-85
Source: Sheffield U Scholar.

2003–04	Boston U	7	1	**7 1**

2004–05	Sheffield U	1	0	
2004–05	Stockport Co	14	1	**14 1**
2005–06	Sheffield U	0	0	
2005–06	Chesterfield	37	4	
2006–07	Sheffield U	0	0	**1 0**
2006–07	Chesterfield	25	3	**62 7**
2006–07	Scunthorpe U	13	0	
2007–08	Scunthorpe U	33	1	
2008–09	Scunthorpe U	20	2	**66 3**
2009–10	Carlisle U	33	2	
2010–11	Carlisle U	2	0	**35 2**
2010–11	Morecambe	21	2	**21 2**

KANE, Tony (D)   **25 0**
H: 5 11   W: 11 00   b.Belfast 29-8-87
Source: Scholar. Honours: Eire Under-21, Northern Ireland Youth, Under-21.

2004–05	Blackburn R	0	0	
2005–06	Blackburn R	0	0	
2006–07	Blackburn R	0	0	
2006–07	Stockport Co	4	0	
2007–08	Blackburn R	0	0	
2008–09	Blackburn R	0	0	
2008–09	Stockport Co	3	0	**7 0**
2008–09	Carlisle U	9	0	
2009–10	Carlisle U	4	0	
2009–10	Darlington	4	0	**4 0**
2010–11	Carlisle U	1	0	**14 0**
Transferred to Cliftonville January 2011.

KAVANAGH, Graham (M)   **537 76**
H: 5 10   W: 13 03   b.Dublin 2-12-73
Source: Home Farm. Honours: Eire Schools, Youth, Under-21, B, 16 full caps, 1 goal.

1991–92	Middlesbrough	0	0	
1992–93	Middlesbrough	10	0	
1993–94	Middlesbrough	11	2	
1993–94	Darlington	5	0	**5 0**
1994–95	Middlesbrough	7	0	
1995–96	Middlesbrough	7	1	
1996–97	Middlesbrough	0	0	**35 3**
1996–97	Stoke C	38	4	
1997–98	Stoke C	44	5	
1998–99	Stoke C	36	11	
1999–2000	Stoke C	45	7	
2000–01	Stoke C	43	8	**206 35**
2001–02	Cardiff C	43	13	
2002–03	Cardiff C	44	5	
2003–04	Cardiff C	27	7	
2004–05	Cardiff C	28	3	**142 28**
2005–06	Wigan Ath	11	0	
2006–07	Wigan Ath	35	0	
2006–07	Wigan Ath	2	0	**48 0**
2006–07	Sunderland	14	1	
2007–08	Sunderland	0	0	
2007–08	Sheffield W	23	2	**23 2**
2008–09	Sunderland	0	0	**14 1**
2008–09	Carlisle U	34	5	
2009–10	Carlisle U	29	2	
2010–11	Carlisle U	1	0	**64 7**

LIVESEY, Danny (D)   **214 13**
H: 6 3   W: 13 01   b.Salford 31-12-84
Source: Trainee.

2002–03	Bolton W	2	0	
2003–04	Bolton W	0	0	
2003–04	Notts Co	11	0	**11 0**
2003–04	Rochdale	13	0	**13 0**
2004–05	Bolton W	0	0	**2 0**
2004–05	Blackpool	1	0	**1 0**
2005–06	Carlisle U	36	4	
2006–07	Carlisle U	31	1	
2007–08	Carlisle U	45	6	
2008–09	Carlisle U	27	0	
2009–10	Carlisle U	38	2	
2010–11	Carlisle U	10	0	**187 13**

LOY, Rory (F)   **45 4**
H: 5 10   W: 10 07   b.Dumfries 19-3-88
Honours: Scotland Under-21.

2008–09	Rangers	1	0	
2008–09	Dunfermline Ath	18	3	**18 3**
2009–10	Rangers	0	0	
2009–10	St Mirren	8	0	**8 0**
2010–11	Rangers	1	0	**2 0**
2010–11	Carlisle U	17	1	**17 1**

MADDEN, Patrick (F)   **80 20**
b.Dublin 4-3-90
Honours: Eire Youth, Under-21.

2008	Bohemians	18	4	
2009	Bohemians	2	0	

2009	Shelbourne	13	6	**13 6**
2010	Bohemians	34	10	**54 14**
2010–11	Carlisle U	13	0	**13 0**

McDAID, Sean (M)   **92 1**
H: 5 6   W: 9 08   b.Harrogate 6-3-86
Source: Trainee.

2002–03	Leeds U	0	0	
2003–04	Leeds U	0	0	
2004–05	Leeds U	0	0	
2005–06	Doncaster R	35	0	
2006–07	Doncaster R	20	0	
2007–08	Doncaster R	24	1	
2008–09	Doncaster R	0	0	
2009–10	Doncaster R	1	0	**80 1**
2010–11	Carlisle U	12	0	**12 0**

McKENNA, Ben (M)   **1 0**
b.Burnley 16-1-93
Source: Scholar. Honours: Northern Ireland Youth.

2010–11	Carlisle U	1	0	**1 0**

MICHALIK, Lubomir (D)   **119 7**
H: 6 4   W: 13 00   b.Cadca 13-8-83
Source: Cadca, Martin. Honours: Slovakia 4 full caps, 2 goals.

2005–06	Senec	8	1	
2006–07	Senec	12	1	**20 2**
2006–07	Leeds U	7	1	
2006–07	Bolton W	4	1	
2007–08	Bolton W	7	0	**11 1**
2007–08	Leeds U	17	0	
2008–09	Leeds U	19	0	
2009–10	Leeds U	13	1	
2010–11	Leeds U	0	0	**56 2**
2010–11	Carlisle U	32	2	**32 2**

MURPHY, Peter (M)   **334 14**
H: 5 10   W: 12 10   b.Dublin 27-10-80
Source: Trainee. Honours: Eire Youth, Under-21, 1 full cap.

1998–99	Blackburn R	0	0	
1999–2000	Blackburn R	0	0	
2000–01	Blackburn R	0	0	
2000–01	Halifax T	21	1	**21 1**
2001–02	Blackburn R	0	0	
2001–02	Carlisle U	40	0	
2002–03	Carlisle U	40	2	
2003–04	Carlisle U	35	1	
2004–05	Carlisle U	0	0	
2005–06	Carlisle U	44	2	
2006–07	Carlisle U	40	2	
2007–08	Carlisle U	36	3	
2008–09	Carlisle U	28	0	
2009–10	Carlisle U	16	0	
2010–11	Carlisle U	34	3	**313 13**

PRICE, Jason (M)   **437 69**
H: 6 2   W: 11 05   b.Pontypridd 12-4-77
Source; Aberaman Ath. Honours: Wales Under-21.

1995–96	Swansea C	0	0	
1996–97	Swansea C	2	0	
1997–98	Swansea C	34	3	
1998–99	Swansea C	28	4	
1999–2000	Swansea C	39	6	
2000–01	Swansea C	41	4	**144 17**
2001–02	Brentford	15	1	**15 1**
2001–02	Tranmere R	24	7	
2002–03	Tranmere R	25	4	**49 11**
2003–04	Hull C	33	9	
2004–05	Hull C	27	2	
2005–06	Hull C	15	2	**75 13**
2005–06	Doncaster R	11	4	
2006–07	Doncaster R	31	6	
2007–08	Doncaster R	29	7	
2008–09	Doncaster R	22	0	**93 17**
2008–09	Millwall	8	3	
2009–10	Millwall	15	1	**23 4**
2009–10	Oldham Ath	7	1	**7 1**
2010–11	Carlisle U	9	4	
2010–11	Carlisle U	3	0	**12 4**
2010–11	Bradford C	10	1	**10 1**
2010–11	Walsall	5	0	**5 0**
2010–11	Hereford U	4	0	**4 0**

ROBSON, Matty (D)   **216 15**
H: 5 10   W: 11 02   b.Spennymoor 23-1-85
Source: Scholar.

2002–03	Hartlepool U	0	0	
2003–04	Hartlepool U	23	1	
2004–05	Hartlepool U	27	2	

2005–06	Hartlepool U	19	1		
2006–07	Hartlepool U	20	2		
2007–08	Hartlepool U	17	1		
2008–09	Hartlepool U	29	2	135	9
2009–10	Carlisle U	39	4		
2010–11	Carlisle U	42	2	81	6

SIMEK, Frankie (D) 178 2
H: 6 0 W: 11 06 b.St Louis 13-10-84
Source: Trainee. Honours: USA 5 full caps.

2002–03	Arsenal	0	0		
2003–04	Arsenal	0	0		
2004–05	Arsenal	0	0		
2004–05	QPR	5	0	5	0
2004–05	Bournemouth	8	0	8	0
2005–06	Sheffield W	43	1		
2006–07	Sheffield W	41	1		
2007–08	Sheffield W	17	0		
2008–09	Sheffield W	6	0		
2009–10	Sheffield W	12	0	119	2
2010–11	Carlisle U	46	0	46	0

TAIWO, Tom (M) 85 3
H: 5 8 W: 10 07 b.Leeds 27-2-90
Source: Scholar.

2007–08	Chelsea	0	0		
2008–09	Chelsea	0	0		
2008–09	Port Vale	4	0	4	0
2009–10	Chelsea	0	0		
2009–10	Carlisle U	35	1		
2010–11	Carlisle U	46	2	81	3

THIRLWELL, Paul (M) 268 7
H: 5 11 W: 12 08 b.Washington 13-2-79
Source: Trainee. Honours: England Under-21.

1996–97	Sunderland	0	0		
1997–98	Sunderland	0	0		
1998–99	Sunderland	2	0		
1999–2000	Sunderland	8	0		
1999–2000	Swindon T	12	0	12	0
2000–01	Sunderland	5	0		
2001–02	Sunderland	14	0		
2002–03	Sunderland	19	0		
2003–04	Sunderland	29	0	77	0
2004–05	Sheffield U	30	1	30	1
2005–06	Derby Co	21	0		
2006–07	Derby Co	0	0	21	0
2006–07	Carlisle U	30	0		
2007–08	Carlisle U	13	0		
2008–09	Carlisle U	34	4		
2009–10	Carlisle U	28	1		
2010–11	Carlisle U	23	1	128	6

WELLS, Nahki (F) 3 0
b.Bermuda 1-6-90
Source: Dandy T Hornets, Bermuda Hogges.
Honours: Bermuda 1 full cap.

2010–11	Carlisle U	3	0	3	0

ZOKO, Francois (F) 268 40
H: 6 0 W: 11 05 b.Daloa 13-9-83

2001–02	Nancy	24	3		
2002–03	Nancy	28	2		
2003–04	Nancy	19	3	71	8
2004–05	Laval	27	7		
2005–06	Laval	33	2	60	9
2006–07	Mons	23	4		
2007–08	Mons	32	8	55	12
2008–09	Hacettepe	27	1	27	1
2009–10	Ostend	11	4	11	4
2010–11	Carlisle U	44	6	44	6

CHARLTON ATH (22)

ABBOTT, Pawel (F) 269 93
H: 6 2 W: 13 10 b.York 5-5-82
Source: LKS Lodz. Honours: Poland Under-21.

2000–01	Preston NE	0	0		
2001–02	Preston NE	0	0		
2002–03	Preston NE	16	4		
2002–03	Bury	17	6	17	6
2003–04	Preston NE	9	2	25	6
2003–04	Huddersfield T	13	5		
2004–05	Huddersfield T	44	26		
2005–06	Huddersfield T	36	12		
2006–07	Huddersfield T	18	5	111	48
2006–07	Swansea C	18	1	18	1
2007–08	Darlington	24	9		
2008–09	Darlington	18	8	42	17
2009–10	Oldham Ath	39	13	39	13
2010–11	Charlton Ath	17	2	17	2

Transferred to Ruch Chorzow February 2011.

ANYINSAH, Joe (M) 113 19
H: 5 8 W: 11 00 b.Bristol 8-10-84
Source: Scholar.

2001–02	Bristol C	0	0		
2002–03	Bristol C	0	0		
2003–04	Bristol C	0	0		
2004–05	Bristol C	7	0	7	0
2005–06	Preston NE	3	0		
2005–06	Bury	3	0	3	0
2006–07	Preston NE	3	0		
2007–08	Preston NE	0	0		
2007–08	Carlisle U	12	3		
2007–08	Crewe Alex	8	0	8	0
2008–09	Preston NE	0	0	6	0
2008–09	Brighton & HA	11	0	11	0
2009–10	Carlisle U	19	4		
2009–10	Carlisle U	28	9		
2010–11	Carlisle U	0	0	59	16
2010–11	Charlton Ath	19	3	19	3

BENSON, Paul (F) 135 50
H: 6 1 W: 11 01 b.Southend 12-10-79
Source: White Notley.

2007–08	Dagenham & R	22	6		
2008–09	Dagenham & R	33	17		
2009–10	Dagenham & R	45	17		
2010–11	Dagenham & R	3	0	103	40
2010–11	Charlton Ath	32	10	32	10

DAILLY, Christian (D) 545 31
H: 6 1 W: 12 10 b.Dundee 23-10-73
Source: 'S' Form. Honours: Scotland Schools, Youth, Under-21, B, 67 full caps, 6 goals.

1990–91	Dundee U	18	5		
1991–92	Dundee U	8	0		
1992–93	Dundee U	14	4		
1993–94	Dundee U	38	4		
1994–95	Dundee U	33	4		
1995–96	Dundee U	30	1	141	18
1996–97	Derby Co	36	3		
1997–98	Derby Co	30	1		
1998–99	Derby Co	1	0	67	4
1998–99	Blackburn R	17	0		
1999–2000	Blackburn R	43	4		
2000–01	Blackburn R	10	0	70	4
2000–01	West Ham U	12	0		
2001–02	West Ham U	38	0		
2002–03	West Ham U	26	0		
2003–04	West Ham U	43	2		
2004–05	West Ham U	3	0		
2005–06	West Ham U	22	0		
2006–07	West Ham U	14	0		
2007–08	West Ham U	0	0	158	2
2007–08	Southampton	11	0	11	0
2007–08	Rangers	13	2		
2008–09	Rangers	9	0	22	2
2009–10	Charlton Ath	44	1		
2010–11	Charlton Ath	32	0	76	1

DAVISSON, Benjamin (M) 0 0
H: 5 7 W: 11 00 b.Sidcup 23-10-91
Source: Scholar.

2010–11	Charlton Ath	0	0

DOHERTY, Gary (D) 374 27
H: 6 3 W: 13 13 b.Co. Donegal 31-1-80
Source: Trainee. Honours: Eire Youth, Under-20, Under-21, 34 full caps, 4 goals.

1997–98	Luton T	10	0		
1998–99	Luton T	20	6		
1999–2000	Luton T	40	6	70	12
1999–2000	Tottenham H	2	0		
2000–01	Tottenham H	22	3		
2001–02	Tottenham H	7	0		
2002–03	Tottenham H	15	1		
2003–04	Tottenham H	10	0		
2004–05	Tottenham H	1	0	64	4
2004–05	Norwich C	20	2		
2005–06	Norwich C	42	1		
2006–07	Norwich C	34	0		
2007–08	Norwich C	34	0		
2008–09	Norwich C	34	3		
2009–10	Norwich C	38	5	202	11
2010–11	Charlton Ath	38	0	38	0

ELLIOT, Rob (G) 103 0
H: 6 3 W: 14 10 b.Chatham 30-4-86
Source: Scholar.

2004–05	Charlton Ath	0	0		
2004–05	Notts Co	4	0	4	0
2005–06	Charlton Ath	0	0		
2006–07	Charlton Ath	0	0		
2006–07	Accrington S	7	0	7	0
2007–08	Charlton Ath	1	0		
2008–09	Charlton Ath	23	0		
2009–10	Charlton Ath	33	0		
2010–11	Charlton Ath	35	0	92	0

FORTUNE, Jon (D) 219 9
H: 6 2 W: 12 12 b.Islington 23-8-80
Source: Trainee.

1998–99	Charlton Ath	0	0		
1999–2000	Charlton Ath	0	0		
1999–2000	Mansfield T	4	0		
2000–01	Charlton Ath	0	0		
2000–01	Mansfield T	14	0	18	0
2001–02	Charlton Ath	19	0		
2002–03	Charlton Ath	26	1		
2003–04	Charlton Ath	28	2		
2004–05	Charlton Ath	31	2		
2005–06	Charlton Ath	11	0		
2006–07	Charlton Ath	8	0		
2006–07	Stoke C	14	1	14	1
2007–08	Charlton Ath	26	2		
2008–09	Charlton Ath	17	0		
2009–10	Charlton Ath	0	0		
2009–10	Sheffield U	5	1		
2010–11	Sheffield U	0	0	5	1
2010–11	Charlton Ath	16	0	182	7

FRANCIS, Simon (D) 280 6
H: 6 0 W: 12 06 b.Nottingham 16-2-85
Source: Scholar. Honours: England Youth, Under-20.

2002–03	Bradford C	25	1		
2003–04	Bradford C	30	0	55	1
2003–04	Sheffield U	5	0		
2004–05	Sheffield U	6	0		
2005–06	Sheffield U	1	0	12	0
2005–06	Grimsby T	5	0	5	0
2005–06	Tranmere R	17	1	17	1
2006–07	Southend U	40	1		
2007–08	Southend U	27	2		
2008–09	Southend U	45	0		
2009–10	Southend U	45	1	157	4
2010–11	Charlton Ath	34	0	34	0

HARRIOTT, Callum (M) 3 0
H: 5 5 W: 10 05 b.Norbury 4-3-94
Source: Scholar.

2010–11	Charlton Ath	3	0	3	0

JACKSON, Johnnie (M) 232 32
H: 6 1 W: 12 00 b.Camden 15-8-82
Source: Trainee. Honours: England Youth, Under-20.

1999–2000	Tottenham H	0	0		
2000–01	Tottenham H	0	0		
2001–02	Tottenham H	0	0		
2002–03	Tottenham H	0	0		
2002–03	Swindon T	13	1	13	1
2002–03	Colchester U	8	0		
2003–04	Tottenham H	11	1		
2003–04	Coventry C	5	2	5	2
2004–05	Tottenham H	8	0		
2004–05	Watford	15	0	15	0
2005–06	Tottenham H	1	0	20	1
2005–06	Derby Co	6	0	6	0
2006–07	Colchester U	32	2		
2007–08	Colchester U	46	7		
2008–09	Colchester U	29	4		
2009–10	Colchester U	0	0	115	13
2009–10	Notts Co	24	2	24	2
2009–10	Charlton Ath	4	0		
2010–11	Charlton Ath	30	13	34	13

LLERA, Miguel (D) 126 13
H: 6 3 W: 13 12 b.Seville 7-8-79
Source: Recretivo B, San Fernando (loan), Alicante.

2005–06	Gimnastic	27	3		
2006–07	Gimnastic	12	0	39	5
2007–08	Heracles	13	1	13	1
2008–09	Milton Keynes D	34	2	34	2
2009–10	Charlton Ath	25	4		
2010–11	Charlton Ath	15	1	40	5

MAMBO, Yado (D) 0 0
H: 6 3 W: 13 01 b.Kilburn 22-10-91
Source: Scholar.

2009–10	Charlton Ath	0	0
2010–11	Charlton Ath	0	0

McCORMACK, Alan (M) 215 21
H: 5 8 W: 11 00 b.Dublin 10-1-84
Source: Stella Maris BC.

Season	Club				
2002–03	Preston NE	0	0		
2003–04	Preston NE	5	0		
2003–04	Leyton Orient	10	0	10	0
2004–05	Preston NE	3	0		
2004–05	Southend U	7	2		
2005–06	Preston NE	0	0		
2005–06	*Motherwell*	24	2	24	2
2006–07	Preston NE	3	0	11	0
2006–07	Southend U	22	3		
2007–08	Southend U	42	8		
2008–09	Southend U	34	2		
2009–10	Southend U	41	3	146	18
2010–11	Charlton Ath	24	1	24	1

PERKINS, Lewis (F) 0 0
b.Hornchurch 26-9-91
Source: Scholar.

Season	Club		
2010–11	Charlton Ath	0	0

RACON, Therry (M) 134 10
H: 5 10 W: 10 02 b.Paris 1-5-84

Season	Club				
2004–05	Lorient	28	3	28	3
2005–06	Guingamp	0	0		
2006–07	Guingamp	0	0		
2007–08	Charlton Ath	4	0		
2007–08	*Brighton & HA*	8	0	8	0
2008–09	Charlton Ath	19	3		
2009–10	Charlton Ath	36	1		
2010–11	Charlton Ath	39	3	98	7

REID, Kyel (M) 102 8
H: 5 10 W: 12 05 b.Deptford 26-11-87
Source: Scholar. *Honours:* England Youth.

Season	Club				
2004–05	West Ham U	0	0		
2005–06	West Ham U	2	0		
2006–07	West Ham U	0	0		
2006–07	*Barnsley*	26	2	26	2
2007–08	West Ham U	1	0		
2007–08	*Crystal Palace*	2	0	2	0
2008–09	West Ham U	0	0		
2008–09	*Blackpool*	7	0	7	0
2008–09	*Wolverhampton W*	8	1	8	1
2009–10	Sheffield U	7	0	7	0
2009–10	*Charlton Ath*	17	4		
2010–11	Charlton Ath	32	1	49	5

SEMEDO, Jose (D) 190 4
H: 6 0 W: 12 08 b.Setubal 11-1-85
Honours: Portugal Under-21.

Season	Club				
2004–05	Sporting Lisbon	0	0		
2004–05	*Casa Pia*	34	2	34	2
2005–06	*Feirense*	18	0	18	0
2006–07	*Cagliari*	3	0	3	0
2007–08	Charlton Ath	37	0		
2008–09	Charlton Ath	18	0		
2009–10	Charlton Ath	38	1		
2010–11	Charlton Ath	42	1	135	2

SODJE, Akpo (F) 177 38
H: 6 2 W: 12 08 b.Greenwich 31-1-81
Source: QPR, Stevenage B, Margate, Gravesend & N, Erith & Belvedere.

Season	Club				
2000–01	QPR	0	0		
2004–05	Huddersfield T	7	0	7	0
2004–05	*Darlington*	7	1		
2005–06	Darlington	36	8	43	9
2006–07	Port Vale	43	14		
2007–08	Port Vale	3	0	46	14
2007–08	Sheffield W	19	7		
2008–09	Sheffield W	11	2		
2009–10	Sheffield W	11	0	41	9
2009–10	Charlton Ath	25	5		
2010–11	Charlton Ath	15	1	40	6

Transferred to Hibernian January 2011.

SOLLY, Chris (D) 24 1
H: 5 8 W: 10 07 b.Rochester 20-1-91
Source: Scholar.

Season	Club				
2008–09	Charlton Ath	1	0		
2009–10	Charlton Ath	9	0		
2010–11	Charlton Ath	14	1	24	1

STAVRINOU, Alex (M) 0 0
H: 5 9 W: 11 12 b.Harlow 13-9-90
Source: Scholar. *Honours:* Cyprus Youth.

Season	Club		
2009–10	Charlton Ath	0	0
2010–11	Charlton Ath	0	0

STEWART, Michael (M) 186 14
H: 5 11 W: 11 11 b.Edinburgh 26-2-81
Source: Trainee. *Honours:* Scotland Schools, Under-21, 4 full caps.

Season	Club				
1997–98	Manchester U	0	0		
1998–99	Manchester U	0	0		
1999–2000	Manchester U	0	0		
2000–01	Manchester U	3	0		
2001–02	Manchester U	3	0		
2002–03	Manchester U	1	0		
2003–04	Manchester U	0	0	7	0
2003–04	*Nottingham F*	13	0	13	0
2004–05	Hearts	17	0		
2005–06	Hibernian	25	1		
2006–07	Hibernian	29	1	54	2
2007–08	Hearts	27	3		
2008–09	Hearts	34	4		
2009–10	Hearts	25	5	103	12
2010–11	Genclerbirligi	0	0		
2010–11	Charlton Ath	9	0	9	0

TUNA, Tamer (F) 3 0
H: 5 9 W: 11 05 b.Bexley 19-10-91
Source: Scholar.

Season	Club				
2008–09	Charlton Ath	2	0		
2009–10	Charlton Ath	1	0		
2010–11	Charlton Ath	0	0	3	0

WAGSTAFF, Scott (M) 79 12
H: 5 10 W: 10 03 b.Maidstone 31-3-90
Source: Scholar.

Season	Club				
2007–08	Charlton Ath	2	0		
2008–09	Charlton Ath	2	0		
2008–09	*Bournemouth*	5	0	5	0
2009–10	Charlton Ath	30	4		
2010–11	Charlton Ath	40	8	74	12

WORNER, Ross (G) 8 0
H: 6 1 W: 12 05 b.Hindhead 3-10-89
Source: Woking.

Season	Club				
2010–11	Charlton Ath	8	0	8	0

WRIGHT-PHILLIPS, Bradley (F) 196 50
H: 5 10 W: 10 07 b.Lewisham 12-3-85
Source: Scholar. *Honours:* England Youth, Under-20.

Season	Club				
2002–03	Manchester C	0	0		
2003–04	Manchester C	0	0		
2004–05	Manchester C	14	1		
2005–06	Manchester C	18	1	32	2
2006–07	Southampton	39	8		
2007–08	Southampton	39	8		
2008–09	Southampton	33	6	111	22
2009–10	Plymouth Arg	15	4		
2010–11	Plymouth Arg	17	13	32	17
2010–11	Charlton Ath	21	9	21	9

YOUGA, Kelly (D) 96 2
H: 6 1 W: 12 00 b.Bangui 22-9-85
Source: Lyon.

Season	Club				
2005–06	Charlton Ath	0	0		
2005–06	*Bristol C*	4	0	4	0
2006–07	Charlton Ath	0	0		
2006–07	*Bradford C*	11	0	11	0
2007–08	Charlton Ath	11	0		
2007–08	*Scunthorpe U*	19	1	19	1
2008–09	Charlton Ath	33	1		
2009–10	Charlton Ath	18	0		
2010–11	Charlton Ath	0	0	62	1

CHELSEA (23)

ALEX (D) 230 30
H: 6 2 W: 14 00 b.Niteroi 17-6-82
Honours: Brazil 17 full caps.

Season	Club				
2002	Santos	25	3		
2003	Santos	34	9		
2004	Santos	4	0	63	12
2004–05	PSV Eindhoven	27	3		
2005–06	PSV Eindhoven	28	2		
2006–07	PSV Eindhoven	29	6	84	11
2007–08	Chelsea	28	2		
2008–09	Chelsea	24	2		
2009–10	Chelsea	16	1		
2010–11	Chelsea	15	2	83	7

ANELKA, Nicolas (F) 450 149
H: 6 1 W: 13 03 b.Versailles 14-3-79
Honours: France Youth, Under-21, 69 full caps, 14 goals.

Season	Club				
1995–96	Paris St Germain	2	0		
1996–97	Paris St Germain	8	1		
1996–97	Arsenal	4	0		
1997–98	Arsenal	26	6		
1998–99	Arsenal	35	17	65	23
1999–2000	Real Madrid	19	2	19	2
2000–01	Paris St Germain	27	8		
2001–02	Paris St Germain	12	2	49	11
2001–02	Liverpool	20	4	20	4
2002–03	Manchester C	38	14		
2003–04	Manchester C	32	16		
2004–05	Manchester C	19	7	89	37
2004–05	Fenerbahce	14	4		
2005–06	Fenerbahce	25	10	39	14
2006–07	Bolton W	35	11		
2007–08	Bolton W	18	10	53	21
2007–08	Chelsea	14	1		
2008–09	Chelsea	37	19		
2009–10	Chelsea	33	11		
2010–11	Chelsea	32	6	116	37

ASHTON, James (D) 0 0
b.Gravesend 2-10-92
Source: Scholar.

Season	Club		
2010–11	Chelsea	0	0

BENAYOUN, Yossi (M) 383 108
H: 5 10 W: 11 00 b.Beer Sheva 6-6-80
Honours: Israel 82 full caps, 24 goals.

Season	Club				
1997–98	Hapoel Beer Sheva	25	15	25	15
1998–99	Maccabi Haifa	29	16		
1999–2000	Maccabi Haifa	38	19		
2000–01	Maccabi Haifa	37	13		
2001–02	Maccabi Haifa	26	7	130	55
2002–03	Santander	31	4		
2003–04	Santander	35	7		
2004–05	Santander	0	0	66	11
2005–06	West Ham U	34	5		
2006–07	West Ham U	29	3	63	8
2007–08	Liverpool	30	4		
2008–09	Liverpool	32	8		
2009–10	Liverpool	30	6	92	18
2010–11	Chelsea	7	1	7	1

BERTRAND, Ryan (D) 146 1
H: 5 10 W: 11 00 b.Southwark 5-8-89
Source: Scholar. *Honours:* England Youth, Under-21.

Season	Club				
2006–07	Chelsea	0	0		
2006–07	*Bournemouth*	5	0	5	0
2007–08	Chelsea	0	0		
2007–08	*Oldham Ath*	21	0	21	0
2007–08	*Norwich C*	18	0		
2008–09	Chelsea	0	0		
2008–09	*Norwich C*	38	0	56	0
2009–10	Chelsea	0	0		
2009–10	*Reading*	44	1	44	1
2010–11	Chelsea	1	0	1	0
2010–11	*Nottingham F*	19	0	19	0

BORINI, Fabio (F) 13 6
H: 5 10 W: 11 02 b.Bologna 23-3-91
Source: Scholar. *Honours:* Italy Youth, Under-21.

Season	Club				
2008–09	Chelsea	0	0		
2009–10	Chelsea	4	0		
2010–11	Chelsea	0	0	4	0
2010–11	*Swansea C*	9	6	9	6

BOSINGWA, Jose (D) 221 5
H: 6 0 W: 12 08 b.Kinshasa 24-8-82
Honours: Portugal Under-21, 24 full caps.

Season	Club				
2000–01	Freamunde	11	0	11	0
2001–02	Boavista	15	0		
2002–03	Boavista	26	0	41	0
2003–04	Porto	13	1		
2004–05	Porto	25	1		
2005–06	Porto	21	0		
2006–07	Porto	25	0		
2007–08	Porto	23	1	107	3
2008–09	Chelsea	34	2		
2009–10	Chelsea	8	0		
2010–11	Chelsea	20	0	62	2

BRUMA, Jeffrey (D) 15 2
H: 6 1 W: 12 00 b.Rotterdam 13-11-91
Source: Feyenoord. *Honours:* Holland Under-21, 2 full caps.

Season	Club				
2009–10	Chelsea	2	0		
2010–11	Chelsea	2	0	4	0
2010–11	*Leicester C*	11	2	11	2

CECH, Petr (G) — 350 0
H: 6 5 W: 14 07 b.Plzen 20-5-82
Honours: Czech Republic Youth, Under-20, Under-21, 83 full caps.

Season	Club	App	Gls	Tot App	Tot Gls
1998–99	Viktoria Plzen	0	0		
1999–2000	Chmel	1	0		
2000–01	Chmel	26	0	27	0
2001–02	Sparta Prague	26	0	26	0
2002–03	Rennes	37	0		
2003–04	Rennes	38	0	75	0
2004–05	Chelsea	35	0		
2005–06	Chelsea	34	0		
2006–07	Chelsea	20	0		
2007–08	Chelsea	26	0		
2008–09	Chelsea	35	0		
2009–10	Chelsea	34	0		
2010–11	Chelsea	38	0	222	0

CHALOBAH, Nathaniel (D) — 0 0
b.Freetown 12-12-94
Source: Scholar. Honours: England Youth.

Season	Club	App	Gls
2010–11	Chelsea	0	0

CLIFFORD, Conor (M) — 16 0
H: 5 8 W: 10 08 b.Dublin 1-10-91
Source: Scholar. Honours: Eire Youth, Under-21.

Season	Club	App	Gls	Tot App	Tot Gls
2008–09	Chelsea	0	0		
2009–10	Chelsea	0	0		
2010–11	Chelsea	0	0		
2010–11	Plymouth Arg	7	0	7	0
2010–11	Notts Co	9	0	9	0

CLIFFORD, Billy (M) — 0 0
b.Slough 18-10-92
Source: Scholar.

Season	Club	App	Gls
2010–11	Chelsea	0	0

COLE, Ashley (D) — 319 15
H: 5 8 W: 10 05 b.Stepney 20-12-80
Source: Trainee. Honours: England Schools, Youth, Under-21, B, 89 full caps, 1 goal.

Season	Club	App	Gls	Tot App	Tot Gls
1998–99	Arsenal	0	0		
1999–2000	Arsenal	1	0		
1999–2000	Crystal Palace	14	1	14	1
2000–01	Arsenal	17	3		
2001–02	Arsenal	29	2		
2002–03	Arsenal	31	1		
2003–04	Arsenal	32	0		
2004–05	Arsenal	35	2		
2005–06	Arsenal	11	0		
2006–07	Arsenal	0	0	156	8
2006–07	Chelsea	23	0		
2007–08	Chelsea	27	1		
2008–09	Chelsea	34	1		
2009–10	Chelsea	27	4		
2010–11	Chelsea	38	0	149	6

CORK, Jack (D) — 155 6
H: 6 0 W: 10 12 b.Carshalton 25-6-89
Source: Scholar. Honours: England Youth, Under-20, Under-21.

Season	Club	App	Gls	Tot App	Tot Gls
2006–07	Chelsea	0	0		
2006–07	Bournemouth	7	0	7	0
2007–08	Chelsea	0	0		
2007–08	Scunthorpe U	34	2	34	2
2008–09	Chelsea	0	0		
2008–09	Southampton	23	0	23	0
2008–09	Watford	19	0	19	0
2009–10	Chelsea	0	0		
2009–10	Coventry C	21	0	21	0
2009–10	Burnley	11	1		
2010–11	Chelsea	0	0		
2010–11	Burnley	40	3	51	4

DEEN-CONTEH, Aziz (D) — 0 0
b.Bumpeh 14-1-93
Source: Scholar.

Season	Club	App	Gls
2010–11	Chelsea	0	0

DELAC, Matej (G) — 0 0
b.Vakuf-Uskoplje 20-8-92
Source: Vitesse.

Season	Club	App	Gls
2010–11	Chelsea	0	0

DJALO, Aliu (M) — 0 0
b.Guinea-Bissau 5-2-92
Source: Scholar.

Season	Club	App	Gls
2009–10	Chelsea	0	0
2010–11	Chelsea	0	0

DROGBA, Didier (F) — 346 144
H: 6 2 W: 14 05 b.Abidjan 11-3-78
Honours: Ivory Coast 72 full caps, 42 goals.

Season	Club	App	Gls	Tot App	Tot Gls
1998–99	Le Mans	2	0		
1999–2000	Le Mans	30	6		
2000–01	Le Mans	11	0		
2001–02	Le Mans	21	5	64	11
2001–02	Guingamp	11	3		
2002–03	Guingamp	34	17	45	20
2003–04	Marseille	35	18	35	18
2004–05	Chelsea	26	10		
2005–06	Chelsea	29	12		
2006–07	Chelsea	36	20		
2007–08	Chelsea	19	8		
2008–09	Chelsea	24	5		
2009–10	Chelsea	32	29		
2010–11	Chelsea	36	11	202	95

ESSIEN, Michael (M) — 286 35
H: 6 1 W: 13 06 b.Accra 3-12-82
Source: Liberty Accra. Honours: Ghana 52 full caps, 9 goals.

Season	Club	App	Gls	Tot App	Tot Gls
2000–01	Bastia	13	1		
2001–02	Bastia	24	4		
2002–03	Bastia	29	6	66	11
2003–04	Lyon	34	3		
2004–05	Lyon	37	4	71	7
2005–06	Chelsea	31	2		
2006–07	Chelsea	33	2		
2007–08	Chelsea	27	6		
2008–09	Chelsea	11	1		
2009–10	Chelsea	14	3		
2010–11	Chelsea	33	3	149	17

GORDON, Ben (D) — 18 0
H: 5 11 W: 12 06 b.Bradford 2-3-91
Source: Scholar.

Season	Club	App	Gls	Tot App	Tot Gls
2008–09	Chelsea	0	0		
2009–10	Chelsea	0	0		
2009–10	Tranmere R	4	0	4	0
2010–11	Chelsea	0	0		
2010–11	Scunthorpe U	14	0	14	0

HILARIO (G) — 251 2
H: 6 2 W: 13 05 b.San Pedro da Cova 21-10-75
Honours: Portugal Under-21, B, 1 full cap.

Season	Club	App	Gls	Tot App	Tot Gls
1994–95	Naval	27	0	27	0
1995–96	Academica	33	2		
1996–97	Porto	18	0		
1997–98	Porto	3	0		
1998–99	Amadora	27	0	27	0
1999–2000	Porto	19	0		
2000–01	Porto	0	0		
2001–02	Varzim	24	0	24	0
2002–03	Porto	0	0	40	0
2002–03	Academica	10	0	43	2
2003–04	Nacional	29	0		
2004–05	Nacional	32	0		
2005–06	Nacional	11	0	72	0
2006–07	Chelsea	11	0		
2007–08	Chelsea	3	0		
2008–09	Chelsea	1	0		
2009–10	Chelsea	3	0		
2010–11	Chelsea	0	0	18	0

HUTCHINSON, Sam (M) — 3 0
H: 6 0 W: 11 07 b.Windsor 3-8-89
Source: Scholar. Honours: England Youth.

Season	Club	App	Gls	Tot App	Tot Gls
2006–07	Chelsea	1	0		
2007–08	Chelsea	0	0		
2008–09	Chelsea	0	0		
2009–10	Chelsea	2	0		
2010–11	Chelsea	0	0	3	0

INCE, Rohan (D) — 0 0
b.Whitechapel 8-11-92
Source: Scholar.

Season	Club	App	Gls
2010–11	Chelsea	0	0

IVANOVIC, Branislav (M) — 206 17
H: 6 0 W: 12 04 b.Sremska Mitreovica 22-2-84
Honours: Serbia Under-21, 41 full caps, 4 goals.

Season	Club	App	Gls	Tot App	Tot Gls
2002–03	Sremska	19	2	19	2
2003–04	OFK Belgrade	13	0		
2004–05	OFK Belgrade	27	2		
2005–06	OFK Belgrade	15	3	55	5
2006	Lokomotiv Moscow	28	2		
2007	Lokomotiv Moscow	26	3	54	5
2007–08	Chelsea	0	0		
2008–09	Chelsea	16	0		
2009–10	Chelsea	28	1		
2010–11	Chelsea	34	4	78	5

KAKUTA, Gael (F) — 13 1
H: 5 8 W: 10 03 b.Lille 21-6-91
Source: Lens. Honours: Chelsea Scholar. France Youth.

Season	Club	App	Gls	Tot App	Tot Gls
2008–09	Chelsea	0	0		
2009–10	Chelsea	1	0		
2010–11	Chelsea	5	0	6	0
2010–11	Fulham	7	1	7	1

KALAS, Tomas (D) — 0 0
H: 6 0 W: 12 00 b.Olomouc 15-5-93
Source: Sigma Olomouc.

Season	Club	App	Gls
2010–11	Chelsea	0	0

KALOU, Salomon (F) — 222 74
H: 6 0 W: 12 02 b.Oume 5-8-85
Source: Feyenoord. Honours: Ivory Coast 37 full caps, 13 goals.

Season	Club	App	Gls	Tot App	Tot Gls
2003–04	Excelsior	11	4	11	4
2003–04	Feyenoord	2	0		
2004–05	Feyenoord	31	20		
2005–06	Feyenoord	34	15	67	35
2006–07	Chelsea	33	7		
2007–08	Chelsea	30	7		
2008–09	Chelsea	27	6		
2009–10	Chelsea	23	5		
2010–11	Chelsea	31	10	144	35

LALKOVIC, Milan (F) — 0 0
b.Kosice 9-12-92
Source: Scholar. Honours: Slovakia Under-21.

Season	Club	App	Gls
2010–11	Chelsea	0	0

LAMPARD, Frank (M) — 501 140
H: 6 0 W: 14 02 b.Romford 20-6-78
Source: Trainee. Honours: England Youth, Under-21, B, 86 full caps, 22 goals.

Season	Club	App	Gls	Tot App	Tot Gls
1994–95	West Ham U	0	0		
1995–96	West Ham U	2	0		
1995–96	Swansea C	9	1	9	1
1996–97	West Ham U	13	0		
1997–98	West Ham U	31	5		
1998–99	West Ham U	38	5		
1999–2000	West Ham U	34	7		
2000–01	West Ham U	30	7	148	24
2001–02	Chelsea	37	5		
2002–03	Chelsea	38	6		
2003–04	Chelsea	38	10		
2004–05	Chelsea	38	13		
2005–06	Chelsea	35	16		
2006–07	Chelsea	37	11		
2007–08	Chelsea	24	10		
2008–09	Chelsea	37	12		
2009–10	Chelsea	36	22		
2010–11	Chelsea	24	10	344	115

LUIZ, David (D) — 120 7
H: 6 2 W: 13 03 b.Sao Paulo 22-4-87
Honours: Brazil Youth, 6 full caps.

Season	Club	App	Gls	Tot App	Tot Gls
2005	Vitoria	0	0		
2006	Vitoria	26	1	26	1
2006–07	Benfica	10	0		
2007–08	Benfica	8	0		
2008–09	Benfica	19	2		
2009–10	Benfica	29	2		
2010–11	Benfica	16	0	82	4
2010–11	Chelsea	12	2	12	2

MAGNAY, Carl (D) — 4 0
H: 6 0 W: 11 13 b.Gateshead 27-1-89
Honours: Northern Ireland Under-21.

Season	Club	App	Gls	Tot App	Tot Gls
2006–07	Chelsea	0	0		
2007–08	Chelsea	0	0		
2008–09	Chelsea	0	0		
2008–09	Milton Keynes D	2	0	2	0
2008–09	Northampton T	2	0	2	0
2009–10	Chelsea	0	0		
2010–11	Chelsea	0	0		

MALOUDA, Florent (M) — 412 78
H: 6 0 W: 11 06 b.Guyane 13-6-80
Honours: France 68 full caps, 6 goals.

Season	Club	App	Gls	Tot App	Tot Gls
1996–97	Chateauroux	2	0		
1997–98	Chateauroux	1	0		
1998–99	Chateauroux	28	3		
1999–2000	Chateauroux	28	2	59	5
2000–01	Guingamp	23	1		
2001–02	Guingamp	32	4		
2002–03	Guingamp	37	10	92	15
2003–04	Lyon	35	4		

2004–05	Lyon	37	5		
2005–06	Lyon	31	6		
2006–07	Lyon	35	10	138	25
2007–08	Chelsea	21	2		
2008–09	Chelsea	31	6		
2009–10	Chelsea	33	12		
2010–11	Chelsea	38	13	123	33

MANCIENNE, Michael (D) 118 0
H: 6 0 W: 11 09 b.Feltham 8-1-88
Source: Scholar. Honours: England Youth, Under-21.

2005–06	Chelsea	0	0		
2006–07	Chelsea	0	0		
2006–07	QPR	28	0		
2007–08	Chelsea	0	0		
2007–08	QPR	30	0	58	0
2008–09	Chelsea	4	0		
2008–09	Wolverhampton W	10	0		
2009–10	Chelsea	0	0		
2009–10	Wolverhampton W	30	0		
2010–11	Chelsea	0	0	4	0
2010–11	Wolverhampton W	16	0	56	0

MATIC, Nemanja (M) 112 6
H: 6 4 W: 12 13 b.Sabac 1-8-88
Source: Kolubara, Kosice. Honours: Serbia Under-21, 2 full caps.

2005–06	Jedinstvo	7	0		
2006–07	Jedinstvo	9	0	16	0
2006–07	Kosice	13	1		
2007–08	Kosice	25	1		
2008–09	Kosice	29	2	67	4
2009–10	Chelsea	2	0		
2010–11	Chelsea	0	0	2	0
2010–11	Vitesse	27	2	27	2

McEACHRAN, Josh (D) 9 0
H: 5 10 b.Oxford 1-3-93
Source: Scholar. Honours: England Under-21.

2010–11	Chelsea	9	0	9	0

MELLIS, Jacob (D) 27 2
H: 6 0 W: 11 08 b.Nottingham 8-1-91
Source: Scholar. Honours: England Youth.

2008–09	Chelsea	0	0		
2009–10	Chelsea	0	0		
2009–10	Southampton	12	0	12	0
2010–11	Chelsea	0	0		
2010–11	Barnsley	15	2	15	2

MIKEL, John Obi (M) 144 1
H: 6 0 W: 13 05 b.Plateau State 22-4-87
Source: Plateau U. Honours: Nigeria Youth, 34 full caps, 2 goals.

2005	Lyn	6	1	6	1
2006–07	Chelsea	22	0		
2007–08	Chelsea	29	0		
2008–09	Chelsea	34	0		
2009–10	Chelsea	25	0		
2010–11	Chelsea	28	0	138	0

MITROVIC, Marko (F) 0 0
b.Malmo 27-6-92
Source: Malmo.

2009–10	Chelsea	0	0		
2010–11	Chelsea	0	0		

PAULO FERREIRA (D) 298 4
H: 6 0 W: 11 13 b.Cascais 18-1-79
Honours: Portugal Under-21, 62 full caps.

1997–98	Estoril	1	0		
1998–99	Estoril	16	0		
1999–2000	Estoril	18	2	35	2
2000–01	Vitoria Setubal	34	2		
2001–02	Vitoria Setubal	34	0	68	2
2002–03	Porto	30	0		
2003–04	Porto	32	0	62	0
2004–05	Chelsea	29	0		
2005–06	Chelsea	21	0		
2006–07	Chelsea	24	0		
2007–08	Chelsea	18	0		
2008–09	Chelsea	7	0		
2009–10	Chelsea	13	0		
2010–11	Chelsea	21	0	133	0

PHILLIP, Adam (F) 3 0
H: 5 10 W: 11 00 b.Carshalton 19-6-91
Source: Scholar.

2009–10	Chelsea	0	0		
2010–11	Chelsea	0	0		
2010–11	Yeovil T	3	0	3	0

PHILLISKIRK, Daniel (M) 4 0
H: 5 10 W: 11 05 b.Oldham 10-4-91
Source: Scholar.

2008–09	Chelsea	0	0		
2009–10	Chelsea	0	0		
2010–11	Chelsea	0	0		
2010–11	Oxford U	1	0	1	0
2010–11	Sheffield U	3	0	3	0

PROSENIK, Philipp (F) 0 0
b.Vienna 1-3-93
Source: Scholar.

2010–11	Chelsea	0	0		

RAJKOVIC, Slobodan (D) 121 3
H: 6 5 W: 14 00 b.Belgrade 3-3-89
Honours: Serbia Under-21, 2 full caps.

2004–05	OFK Belgrade	26	1		
2005–06	Chelsea	0	0		
2005–06	OFK Belgrade	25	0		
2006–07	Chelsea	0	0		
2006–07	OFK Belgrade	11	0	62	1
2007–08	Chelsea	0	0		
2007–08	PSV Eindhoven	13	0	13	0
2008–09	Chelsea	0	0		
2008–09	Twente	8	1		
2009–10	Chelsea	0	0		
2009–10	Twente	14	1	22	2
2010–11	Chelsea	0	0		
2010–11	Vitesse	24	0	24	0

RAMIRES (M) 130 19
H: 5 11 W: 10 03 b.Rio de Janeiro 24-3-87
Honours: Brazil 22 full caps, 2 goals.

2006	Joinville	14	3	14	3
2007	Cruzeiro	32	3		
2008	Cruzeiro	25	6		
2009	Cruzeiro	4	1	61	10
2009–10	Benfica	26	4	26	4
2010–11	Chelsea	29	2	29	2

SALA, Jacopo (M) 0 0
H: 6 0 W: 11 08 b.Bergamo 5-12-91
Source: Scholar.

2009–10	Chelsea	0	0		
2010–11	Chelsea	0	0		

SAVILLE, George (M) 0 0
b.Camberley 1-6-93
Source: Scholar.

2010–11	Chelsea	0	0		

SEBEK, Jan (G) 0 0
H: 6 4 W: 12 13 b.Plana 31-1-91
Source: Scholar.

2009–10	Chelsea	0	0		
2010–11	Chelsea	0	0		

STURRIDGE, Daniel (F) 59 14
H: 6 2 W: 12 00 b.Birmingham 1-9-89
Source: Scholar. Honours: England Youth, Under-21.

2006–07	Manchester C	0	0		
2007–08	Manchester C	3	1		
2008–09	Manchester C	16	4		
2009–10	Chelsea	0	0	21	5
2009–10	Chelsea	13	1		
2010–11	Chelsea	13	0	26	1
2010–11	Bolton W	12	8	12	8

TAYLOR, Rhys (G) 44 0
H: 6 2 W: 12 08 b.Neath 7-4-90
Honours: Wales Under-21.

2007–08	Chelsea	0	0		
2008–09	Chelsea	0	0		
2009–10	Chelsea	0	0		
2010–11	Chelsea	0	0		
2010–11	Crewe Alex	44	0	44	0

TERRY, John (D) 348 22
H: 6 1 W: 14 02 b.Barking 7-12-80
Source: Trainee. Honours: England Under-21, 68 full caps, 6 goals.

1997–98	Chelsea	0	0		
1998–99	Chelsea	2	0		
1999–2000	Chelsea	4	0		
1999–2000	Nottingham F	6	0	6	0
2000–01	Chelsea	22	1		
2001–02	Chelsea	33	1		
2002–03	Chelsea	20	3		
2003–04	Chelsea	33	2		
2004–05	Chelsea	36	3		
2005–06	Chelsea	36	4		
2006–07	Chelsea	28	1		

2007–08	Chelsea	23	1		
2008–09	Chelsea	35	1		
2009–10	Chelsea	37	2		
2010–11	Chelsea	33	3	342	22

TORE, Gokhan (M) 0 0
H: 5 9 W: 11 09 b.Cologne 20-1-92
Source: Leverkusen.

2008–09	Chelsea	0	0		
2009–10	Chelsea	0	0		
2010–11	Chelsea	0	0		

TORRES, Fernando (F) 290 141
H: 5 9 W: 12 03 b.Madrid 20-3-84
Honours: Spain 86 full caps, 27 goals.

2002–03	Atletico Madrid	29	13		
2003–04	Atletico Madrid	35	19		
2004–05	Atletico Madrid	38	16		
2005–06	Atletico Madrid	36	13		
2006–07	Atletico Madrid	36	14	174	75
2007–08	Liverpool	33	24		
2008–09	Liverpool	24	14		
2009–10	Liverpool	22	18		
2010–11	Liverpool	23	9	102	65
2010–11	Chelsea	14	1	14	1

TURNBULL, Ross (G) 93 0
H: 6 4 W: 15 00 b.Bishop Auckland 4-1-85
Source: Trainee. Honours: England Youth, Under-20.

2002–03	Middlesbrough	0	0		
2003–04	Middlesbrough	0	0		
2003–04	Darlington	1	0	1	0
2003–04	Barnsley	3	0		
2004–05	Middlesbrough	0	0		
2004–05	Bradford C	2	0	2	0
2004–05	Barnsley	23	0	26	0
2005–06	Middlesbrough	2	0		
2005–06	Crewe Alex	29	0	29	0
2006–07	Middlesbrough	0	0		
2007–08	Middlesbrough	3	0		
2007–08	Cardiff C	6	0	6	0
2008–09	Middlesbrough	22	0		
2009–10	Middlesbrough	0	0	27	0
2009–10	Chelsea	2	0		
2010–11	Chelsea	0	0	2	0

VAN AANHOLT, Patrick (D) 41 1
H: 5 9 W: 10 08 b.Den Bosch 3-7-88
Honours: Holland Youth, Under-21.

2007–08	Chelsea	0	0		
2008–09	Chelsea	0	0		
2009–10	Chelsea	2	0		
2009–10	Coventry C	20	0	20	0
2009–10	Newcastle U	7	0	7	0
2010–11	Chelsea	0	0	2	0
2010–11	Leicester C	12	1	12	1

WALKER, Sam (G) 7 0
H: 6 5 W: 14 00 b.Gravesend 2-10-91
Source: Scholar.

2009–10	Chelsea	0	0		
2010–11	Chelsea	0	0		
2010–11	Barnet	7	0	7	0

WOODS, Michael (M) 0 0
H: 6 0 W: 12 07 b.Pocklington 6-4-90
Source: Scholar. Honours: England Youth.

2006–07	Chelsea	0	0		
2007–08	Chelsea	0	0		
2008–09	Chelsea	0	0		
2009–10	Chelsea	0	0		
2010–11	Chelsea	0	0		
2010–11	Notts Co	0	0		

ZHIRKOV, Yuri (M) 169 15
H: 6 1 W: 11 11 b.Tambov 20-8-83
Honours: Russia 43 full caps.

2004	CSKA Moscow	25	6		
2005	CSKA Moscow	20	2		
2006	CSKA Moscow	27	1		
2007	CSKA Moscow	29	2		
2008	CSKA Moscow	28	3		
2009	CSKA Moscow	11	1	140	15
2009–10	Chelsea	17	0		
2010–11	Chelsea	12	0	29	0

Scholars
Affane Amin; Blackman Jamal Clint-Ross; Kane Todd Arthur Lucien; Loudon Reece; Na Bangna Buomesca Tue; Nkumu Archange; Pappoe Daniel Mills; Stenning Daniel

CHELTENHAM T (24)

ANDREW, Danny (D)   55   4
H: 5 11 W: 11 06 b.Holbeach 23-12-90

Season	Club	App	Gls	Tot	Tot
2009–10	Peterborough U	2	0	2	0
2009–10	*Cheltenham T*	10	0		
2010–11	Cheltenham T	43	4	53	4

ARTUS, Frankie (M)   49   6
H: 6 0 W: 11 02 b.Bristol 27-9-88
Source: Scholar.

Season	Club	App	Gls	Tot	Tot
2005–06	Bristol C	0	0		
2006–07	Bristol C	0	0		
2007–08	Bristol C	0	0		
2008–09	Bristol C	0	0		
2008–09	*Brentford*	1	0	1	0
2008–09	*Cheltenham T*	9	3		
2009–10	Bristol C	0	0		
2009–10	*Cheltenham T*	7	0		
2009–10	*Chesterfield*	3	0	3	0
2010–11	Cheltenham T	29	3	45	6

BIRD, David (M)   288   8
H: 5 9 W: 12 00 b.Gloucester 26-12-84
Source: Cinderford T.

Season	Club	App	Gls	Tot	Tot
2001–02	Cheltenham T	0	0		
2002–03	Cheltenham T	14	0		
2003–04	Cheltenham T	24	0		
2004–05	Cheltenham T	34	0		
2005–06	Cheltenham T	36	1		
2006–07	Cheltenham T	31	2		
2007–08	Cheltenham T	46	4		
2008–09	Cheltenham T	27	1		
2009–10	Cheltenham T	37	0		
2010–11	Cheltenham T	39	0	288	8

BROWN, Scott P (G)   139   0
H: 6 2 W: 13 01 b.Wolverhampton 26-4-85
Source: Wolverhampton W Trainee.
From Welshpool T

Season	Club	App	Gls	Tot	Tot
2003–04	Bristol C	0	0		
2004–05	Cheltenham T	0	0		
2005–06	Cheltenham T	1	0		
2006–07	Cheltenham T	11	0		
2007–08	Cheltenham T	0	0		
2008–09	Cheltenham T	35	0		
2009–10	Cheltenham T	46	0		
2010–11	Cheltenham T	46	0	139	0

ELLIOTT, Steve (D)   360   18
H: 6 1 W: 14 00 b.Derby 29-10-78
Source: Trainee. Honours: England Under-21.

Season	Club	App	Gls	Tot	Tot
1996–97	Derby Co	0	0		
1997–98	Derby Co	3	0		
1998–99	Derby Co	11	0		
1999–2000	Derby Co	20	0		
2000–01	Derby Co	6	0		
2001–02	Derby Co	6	0		
2002–03	Derby Co	23	1		
2003–04	Derby Co	4	0	73	1
2003–04	Blackpool	28	0	28	0
2004–05	Bristol R	41	2		
2005–06	Bristol R	45	2		
2006–07	Bristol R	39	5		
2007–08	Bristol R	33	3		
2008–09	Bristol R	39	3		
2009–10	Bristol R	21	1	218	16
2010–11	Cheltenham T	41	1	41	1

GALLINAGH, Andy (D)   130   4
H: 5 8 W: 11 08 b.Sutton Coldfield 16-3-85
Source: Stratford T.

Season	Club	App	Gls	Tot	Tot
2004–05	Cheltenham T	0	0		
2005–06	Cheltenham T	1	0		
2006–07	Cheltenham T	1	0		
2007–08	Cheltenham T	26	0		
2008–09	Cheltenham T	39	1		
2009–10	Cheltenham T	39	1		
2010–11	Cheltenham T	24	2	130	4

GOULDING, Jeff (F)   83   14
H: 6 2 W: 11 11 b.Sutton 13-5-82
Source: Croydon, Egham T, Aldershot T, Hayes, Yeading, Fisher Ath.

Season	Club	App	Gls	Tot	Tot
2008–09	Bournemouth	27	3		
2009–10	Bournemouth	17	1	44	4
2010–11	Cheltenham T	39	10	39	10

HAYNES, Kyle (D)   18   0
H: 5 11 W: 11 02 b.Wolverhampton 29-12-91
Source: Scholar.

Season	Club	App	Gls	Tot	Tot
2008–09	Cheltenham T	4	0		
2009–10	Cheltenham T	13	0		
2010–11	Cheltenham T	1	0	18	0

LEE, Jake (F)   4   0
H: 6 0 W: 12 07 b.Cirencester 18-9-91
Source: Scholar.

Season	Club	App	Gls	Tot	Tot
2008–09	Cheltenham T	3	0		
2009–10	Cheltenham T	1	0		
2010–11	Cheltenham T	0	0	4	0

LEWIS, Theo (F)   39   0
H: 5 10 W: 10 12 b.Oxford 10-8-91
Source: Scholar.

Season	Club	App	Gls	Tot	Tot
2008–09	Cheltenham T	2	0		
2009–10	Cheltenham T	15	0		
2010–11	Cheltenham T	22	0	39	0

LLOYD-WESTON, Daniel (G)   0   0
H: 6 1 W: 12 12 b.Manchester 17-8-91
Source: Scholar.

Season	Club	App	Gls	Tot	Tot
2009–10	Port Vale	0	0		
2010–11	Cheltenham T	0	0		

LOW, Josh (M)   358   39
H: 6 2 W: 14 03 b.Bristol 15-2-79
Source: Trainee. Honours: Wales Youth, Under-21.

Season	Club	App	Gls	Tot	Tot
1995–96	Bristol R	1	0		
1996–97	Bristol R	3	0		
1997–98	Bristol R	10	0		
1998–99	Bristol R	8	0	22	0
1999–2000	Leyton Orient	5	1	5	1
1999–2000	Cardiff C	17	2		
2000–01	Cardiff C	36	4		
2001–02	Cardiff C	22	0		
2002–03	Cardiff C	0	0	75	6
2002–03	Oldham Ath	21	3	21	3
2003–04	Northampton T	33	3		
2004–05	Northampton T	34	7		
2005–06	Northampton T	35	5	102	15
2006–07	Leicester C	16	0	16	0
2006–07	Peterborough U	19	1		
2007–08	Peterborough U	15	2		
2008–09	Peterborough U	0	0	34	3
2008–09	Cheltenham T	14	0		
2009–10	Cheltenham T	39	4		
2010–11	Cheltenham T	30	7	83	11

LOWE, Keith (D)   134   6
H: 6 2 W: 13 03 b.Wolverhampton 13-9-85
Source: Scholar.

Season	Club	App	Gls	Tot	Tot
2004–05	Wolverhampton W	11	0		
2005–06	Wolverhampton W	3	0		
2005–06	*Burnley*	16	0	16	0
2005–06	*QPR*	1	0	1	0
2005–06	*Swansea C*	4	0	4	0
2006–07	Wolverhampton W	0	0		
2006–07	*Brighton & HA*	0	0		
2006–07	*Cheltenham T*	16	1		
2007–08	Wolverhampton W	0	0		
2007–08	*Port Vale*	28	3	28	3
2008–09	Wolverhampton W	0	0	14	0
2009–10	Hereford U	19	1	19	1
2010–11	Cheltenham T	36	1	52	2

MELLIGAN, John (M)   304   37
H: 5 9 W: 11 02 b.Dublin 11-2-82
Source: Trainee. Honours: Eire Youth, Under-21.

Season	Club	App	Gls	Tot	Tot
2000–01	Wolverhampton W	0	0		
2001–02	Wolverhampton W	0	0		
2001–02	*Bournemouth*	8	0	8	0
2002–03	Wolverhampton W	2	0		
2002–03	*Kidderminster H*	29	10		
2003–04	Wolverhampton W	0	0	2	0
2003–04	*Kidderminster H*	5	1	34	11
2003–04	*Doncaster R*	21	2	21	2
2004–05	Cheltenham T	29	2		
2005–06	Cheltenham T	42	6		
2006–07	Cheltenham T	43	7		
2007–08	Leyton Orient	32	3		
2008–09	Leyton Orient	35	2		
2009–10	Leyton Orient	16	1	83	6
2010	Dundalk	15	3	15	3
2010–11	Cheltenham T	27	0	141	15

POOK, Michael (M)   173   9
H: 5 11 W: 11 10 b.Swindon 22-10-85
Source: Scholar.

Season	Club	App	Gls	Tot	Tot
2003–04	Swindon T	0	0		
2004–05	Swindon T	5	0		
2005–06	Swindon T	30	0		
2006–07	Swindon T	38	2		
2007–08	Swindon T	22	1		
2008–09	Swindon T	14	0	109	3
2009–10	Cheltenham T	35	5		
2010–11	Cheltenham T	29	1	64	6

RILEY, Martin (D)   26   0
H: 6 0 W: 12 01 b.Wolverhampton 5-12-86
Source: Scholar. Honours: England Under-20.

Season	Club	App	Gls	Tot	Tot
2004–05	Wolverhampton W	0	0		
2005–06	Wolverhampton W	0	0		
2006–07	Wolverhampton W	0	0		
2007–08	Wolverhampton W	0	0		
2007–08	Shrewsbury T	0	0		
	From Kidderminster H.				
2010–11	Cheltenham T	26	0	26	0

SMIKLE, Brian (M)   46   4
b.Tipton 3-11-85
Source: Scholar.
From Kidderminster H.

Season	Club	App	Gls	Tot	Tot
2005–06	WBA	0	0		
	From Kidderminster H.				
2010–11	Cheltenham T	46	4	46	4

THOMAS, Wesley (F)   69   21
H: 5 10 W: 11 00 b.Barking 23-1-87
Source: QPR Youth, Waltham Forest, Thurrock, Fisher Ath.

Season	Club	App	Gls	Tot	Tot
2008–09	Dagenham & R	5	0		
2009–10	Dagenham & R	23	3	28	3
2010–11	Cheltenham T	41	18	41	18

WATKINS, Marley (M)   26   1
H: 5 10 W: 10 04 b.Lewisham 17-10-90
Source: Scholar.

Season	Club	App	Gls	Tot	Tot
2008–09	Cheltenham T	12	0		
2009–10	Cheltenham T	13	1		
2010–11	Cheltenham T	1	0	26	1

CHESTERFIELD (25)

ALLOTT, Mark (M)   543   51
H: 5 11 W: 11 07 b.Middleton 3-10-77
Source: Trainee.

Season	Club	App	Gls	Tot	Tot
1995–96	Oldham Ath	0	0		
1996–97	Oldham Ath	5	1		
1997–98	Oldham Ath	22	2		
1998–99	Oldham Ath	41	7		
1999–2000	Oldham Ath	32	10		
2000–01	Oldham Ath	39	7		
2001–02	Oldham Ath	15	4		
2001–02	Chesterfield	21	4		
2002–03	Chesterfield	33	0		
2003–04	Chesterfield	40	2		
2004–05	Chesterfield	45	2		
2005–06	Chesterfield	43	3		
2006–07	Chesterfield	39	0		
2007–08	Chesterfield	42	4		
2008–09	Oldham Ath	45	3	241	38
2009–10	Chesterfield	45	2		
2010–11	Chesterfield	36	0	302	13

BODEN, Scott (F)   69   11
H: 5 11 W: 11 00 b.Sheffield 19-12-89
Source: IFK Marlehamn.

Season	Club	App	Gls	Tot	Tot
2008–09	Chesterfield	11	2		
2009–10	Chesterfield	35	6		
2010–11	Chesterfield	23	3	69	11

BOWERY, Jordan (F)   40   1
H: 6 1 W: 12 00 b.Nottingham 2-7-91
Source: Scholar.

Season	Club	App	Gls	Tot	Tot
2008–09	Chesterfield	3	0		
2009–10	Chesterfield	10	0		
2010–11	Chesterfield	27	1	40	1

BRECKIN, Ian (D)   650   26
H: 6 2 W: 13 05 b.Rotherham 24-2-75

Season	Club	App	Gls	Tot	Tot
1993–94	Rotherham U	10	0		
1994–95	Rotherham U	41	2		
1995–96	Rotherham U	39	1		
1996–97	Rotherham U	42	3	132	6
1997–98	Chesterfield	43	1		

Season	Club	Apps	Gls	Tot A	Tot G
1998–99	Chesterfield	44	2		
1999–2000	Chesterfield	38	1		
2000–01	Chesterfield	45	3		
2001–02	Chesterfield	42	1		
2002–03	Wigan Ath	9	0		
2003–04	Wigan Ath	45	0		
2004–05	Wigan Ath	42	0	96	0
2005–06	Nottingham F	46	8		
2006–07	Nottingham F	46	3		
2007–08	Nottingham F	28	1		
2008–09	Nottingham F	23	0	143	12
2009–10	Chesterfield	42	0		
2010–11	Chesterfield	25	0	279	8

CLAY, Craig (M) 3 1
H: 5 11 W: 11 07 b.Nottingham 5-5-92
Source: Scholar.

Season	Club	Apps	Gls	Tot A	Tot G
2010–11	Chesterfield	3	1	3	1

CROSSLEY, Mark (G) 451 1
H: 6 3 W: 15 09 b.Barnsley 16-6-69
Source: Trainee. *Honours:* England Under-21, B, Wales B, 8 full caps.

Season	Club	Apps	Gls	Tot A	Tot G
1987–88	Nottingham F	0	0		
1988–89	Nottingham F	2	0		
1989–90	Nottingham F	8	0		
1989–90	*Manchester U*	0	0		
1990–91	Nottingham F	38	0		
1991–92	Nottingham F	36	0		
1992–93	Nottingham F	37	0		
1993–94	Nottingham F	37	0		
1994–95	Nottingham F	42	0		
1995–96	Nottingham F	38	0		
1996–97	Nottingham F	33	0		
1997–98	Nottingham F	0	0		
1997–98	*Millwall*	13	0	13	0
1998–99	Nottingham F	12	0		
1999–2000	Nottingham F	20	0	303	0
2000–01	Middlesbrough	5	0		
2001–02	Middlesbrough	18	0		
2002–03	Middlesbrough	0	0	23	0
2002–03	*Stoke C*	12	0	12	0
2003–04	Fulham	1	0		
2004–05	Fulham	6	0		
2005–06	Fulham	13	0		
2006–07	Fulham	0	0	20	0
2006–07	*Sheffield W*	17	1	17	1
2007–08	Oldham Ath	38	0		
2008–09	Oldham Ath	21	0	59	0
2009–10	Chesterfield	4	0		
2010–11	Chesterfield	0	0	4	0

DARIKWAH, Tendayi (M) 0 0
b.Nottingham 13 12 91
Source: Scholar.

Season	Club	Apps	Gls	Tot A	Tot G
2010–11	Chesterfield	0	0		

DAVIES, Craig (F) 214 54
H: 6 2 W: 13 05 b.Burton-on-Trent 9-1-86
Source: Manchester C. *Honours:* Wales Youth, Under-21, 5 full caps.

Season	Club	Apps	Gls	Tot A	Tot G
2004–05	Oxford U	28	6		
2005–06	Oxford U	20	2	48	8
2005–06	Verona	0	0		
2006–07	Wolverhampton W	23	0	23	0
2007–08	Oldham Ath	32	10		
2008–09	Oldham Ath	12	0	44	10
2008–09	*Stockport Co*	9	5	9	5
2008–09	Brighton & HA	16	1		
2009–10	Brighton & HA	5	0	21	1
2009–10	*Yeovil T*	4	0	4	0
2009–10	Port Vale	24	7	24	7
2010–11	Chesterfield	41	23	41	23

DOWNES, Aaron (D) 165 10
H: 6 2 W: 13 02 b.Mudgee 15-5-85
Honours: Australia Youth, Under-20, Under-21, Under-23.

Season	Club	Apps	Gls	Tot A	Tot G
2004–05	Chesterfield	9	2		
2005–06	Chesterfield	22	0		
2006–07	Chesterfield	45	3		
2007–08	Chesterfield	40	2		
2008–09	Chesterfield	42	2		
2009–10	Chesterfield	7	1		
2010–11	Chesterfield	0	0	165	10

FORD, Simon (D) 253 11
H: 6 1 W: 12 04 b.Lincoln 17-11-81
Source: Charlton Ath Scholar. *Honours:* Jamaica 3 full caps.

Season	Club	Apps	Gls	Tot A	Tot G
2001–02	Grimsby T	13	1		
2002–03	Grimsby T	39	2		
2003–04	Grimsby T	26	1	78	4
2004–05	Kilmarnock	18	1		
2005–06	Kilmarnock	32	2		
2006–07	Kilmarnock	16	0		
2007–08	Kilmarnock	28	1		
2008–09	Kilmarnock	27	1		
2009–10	Kilmarnock	23	1	144	6
2010–11	Chesterfield	31	1	31	1

GRAY, Dan (M) 67 1
H: 6 0 W: 11 00 b.Mansfield 23-11-89
Source: Scholar.

Season	Club	Apps	Gls	Tot A	Tot G
2008–09	Chesterfield	25	0		
2009–10	Chesterfield	19	0		
2010–11	Chesterfield	2	0	46	0
2010–11	*Macclesfield T*	21	1	21	1

HOLDEN, Dean (D) 305 19
H: 6 1 W: 12 04 b.Swinton 15-9-79
Source: Trainee. *Honours:* England Youth.

Season	Club	Apps	Gls	Tot A	Tot G
1997–98	Bolton W	0	0		
1998–99	Bolton W	0	0		
1999–2000	Bolton W	12	0		
2000–01	Bolton W	1	1	13	1
2001	Valur	7	0	7	0
2001–02	Oldham Ath	23	2		
2002–03	Oldham Ath	6	2		
2003–04	Oldham Ath	39	4		
2004–05	Oldham Ath	40	2	108	10
2005–06	Peterborough U	35	3		
2006–07	Peterborough U	21	1	56	4
2006–07	Falkirk	9	1		
2007–08	Falkirk	20	0		
2008–09	Falkirk	19	1	48	2
2009–10	Shrewsbury T	37	0		
2010–11	Shrewsbury T	13	0	50	0
2010–11	*Rotherham U*	6	0	6	0
2010–11	Chesterfield	17	2	17	2

LEE, Tommy (G) 190 0
H: 6 2 W: 12 00 b.Keighley 3-1-86
Source: Scholar.

Season	Club	Apps	Gls	Tot A	Tot G
2005–06	Manchester U	0	0		
2005–06	*Macclesfield T*	11	0		
2006–07	Macclesfield T	34	0		
2007–08	Macclesfield T	18	0	63	0
2007–08	*Rochdale*	11	0	11	0
2008–09	Chesterfield	28	0		
2009–10	Chesterfield	42	0		
2010–11	Chesterfield	46	0	116	0

LESTER, Jack (F) 505 134
H: 5 9 W: 12 08 b.Sheffield 8-10-75
Source: Trainee. *Honours:* England Schools.

Season	Club	Apps	Gls	Tot A	Tot G
1994–95	Grimsby T	7	0		
1995–96	Grimsby T	5	0		
1996–97	Grimsby T	22	5		
1996–97	*Doncaster R*	11	1	11	1
1997–98	Grimsby T	40	4		
1998–99	Grimsby T	33	4		
1999–2000	Grimsby T	26	4	133	17
1999–2000	Nottingham F	15	2		
2000–01	Nottingham F	19	7		
2001–02	Nottingham F	32	5		
2002–03	Nottingham F	33	7		
2003–04	Sheffield U	32	12		
2004–05	Sheffield U	12	0	44	12
2004–05	Nottingham F	3	1		
2005–06	Nottingham F	38	5		
2006–07	Nottingham F	35	6	175	33
2007–08	Chesterfield	36	23		
2008–09	Chesterfield	37	20		
2009–10	Chesterfield	29	11		
2010–11	Chesterfield	40	17	142	71

LOWRY, Jamie (D) 108 11
H: 6 0 W: 12 00 b.Newquay 18-3-87
Source: Scholar.

Season	Club	Apps	Gls	Tot A	Tot G
2006–07	Chesterfield	8	0		
2007–08	Chesterfield	42	6		
2008–09	Chesterfield	42	0		
2009–10	Chesterfield	13	5		
2010–11	Chesterfield	3	0	108	11

MATTIS, Dwayne (M) 283 22
H: 6 1 W: 11 12 b.Huddersfield 31-7-81
Source: Trainee. *Honours:* Eire Youth, Under-21.

Season	Club	Apps	Gls	Tot A	Tot G
1998–99	Huddersfield T	2	0		
1999–2000	Huddersfield T	0	0		
2000–01	Huddersfield T	0	0		
2001–02	Huddersfield T	29	1		
2002–03	Huddersfield T	33	1		
2003–04	Huddersfield T	5	0	69	2
2004–05	Bury	39	5		
2005–06	Bury	36	5		
2006–07	Bury	22	1	97	11
2006–07	Barnsley	3	0		
2007–08	Barnsley	1	0	4	0
2007–08	*Walsall*	4	0		
2008–09	Walsall	37	4		
2009–10	Walsall	34	2	75	6
2010–11	Chesterfield	38	3	38	3

MORGAN, Dean (M) 278 32
H: 5 11 W: 13 00 b.Enfield 3-10-83
Source: Scholar.

Season	Club	Apps	Gls	Tot A	Tot G
2000–01	Colchester U	4	0		
2001–02	Colchester U	30	0		
2002–03	Colchester U	37	6		
2003–04	Colchester U	0	0	71	6
2003–04	Reading	13	1		
2004–05	Reading	18	2	31	3
2005–06	Luton T	36	6		
2006–07	Luton T	36	4		
2007–08	Luton T	16	1		
2007–08	*Southend U*	8	0	8	0
2007–08	*Crewe Alex*	9	1	9	1
2008–09	Luton T	0	0		
2008–09	*Leyton Orient*	32	5	32	5
2009–10	Luton T	0	0	88	11
2009–10	*Milton Keynes D*	9	1	9	1
2009–10	*Aldershot T*	9	4	9	4
2010–11	Chesterfield	21	1	21	1

NIVEN, Derek (M) 291 18
H: 5 11 W: 12 05 b.Falkirk 12-12-83
Source: Stenhousemuir.

Season	Club	Apps	Gls	Tot A	Tot G
2000–01	Raith R	1	0	1	0
2001–02	Bolton W	0	0		
2002–03	Bolton W	0	0		
2003–04	Bolton W	0	0		
2003–04	Chesterfield	22	1		
2004–05	Chesterfield	38	1		
2005–06	Chesterfield	42	5		
2006–07	Chesterfield	45	3		
2007–08	Chesterfield	38	3		
2008–09	Chesterfield	31	2		
2009–10	Chesterfield	39	2		
2010–11	Chesterfield	35	1	290	18

PAGE, Robert (D) 476 6
H: 6 0 W: 12 05 b.Llwynpia 3-9-74
Source: Trainee. *Honours:* Wales Schools, Youth, Under-21, B, 41 full caps.

Season	Club	Apps	Gls	Tot A	Tot G
1992–93	Watford	0	0		
1993–94	Watford	4	0		
1994–95	Watford	5	0		
1995–96	Watford	19	0		
1996–97	Watford	36	0		
1997–98	Watford	41	0		
1998–99	Watford	39	0		
1999–2000	Watford	36	1		
2000–01	Watford	36	1		
2001–02	Watford	0	0	216	2
2001–02	Sheffield U	43	0		
2002–03	Sheffield U	34	0		
2003–04	Sheffield U	30	1	107	1
2004–05	*Cardiff C*	9	0	9	0
2004–05	Coventry C	9	0		
2005–06	Coventry C	32	1		
2006–07	Coventry C	29	0		
2007–08	Coventry C	0	0	70	1
2007–08	*Huddersfield T*	18	1	18	1
2008–09	Chesterfield	16	0		
2009–10	Chesterfield	39	1		
2010–11	Chesterfield	1	0	56	1

REDMOND, Shane (G) 22 0
H: 6 0 W: 12 10 b.Dublin 23-3-89
Source: Scholar. *Honours:* Eire Youth, Under-21.

Season	Club	Apps	Gls	Tot A	Tot G
2006–07	Nottingham F	0	0		
2007–08	Nottingham F	0	0		
2008–09	Nottingham F	0	0		
2009–10	Nottingham F	0	0		
2009–10	*Burton Alb*	3	0	3	0
2009–10	*Darlington*	19	0	19	0
2010–11	Chesterfield	0	0		

ROBERTSON, Gregor (D) 193 4
H: 6 0 W: 12 04 b.Edinburgh 19-1-84
Honours: Scotland Under-21.

Season	Club	Apps	Gls	Tot A	Tot G
2000–01	Nottingham F	0	0		
2001–02	Nottingham F	0	0		
2002–03	Nottingham F	0	0		

Season	Club	Apps	Gls	Tot A	Tot G
2003–04	Nottingham F	16	0		
2004–05	Nottingham F	20	0	36	0
2005–06	Rotherham U	35	1		
2006–07	Rotherham U	18	0	53	1
2007–08	Chesterfield	35	1		
2008–09	Chesterfield	38	2		
2009–10	Chesterfield	10	0		
2010–11	Chesterfield	21	0	104	3

TALBOT, Drew (F) 172 19
H: 5 10 W: 11 00 b.Barnsley 19-7-86
Source: Dodworth Colliery.

Season	Club	Apps	Gls	Tot A	Tot G
2003–04	Sheffield W	0	0		
2004–05	Sheffield W	21	4		
2005–06	Sheffield W	0	0		
2006–07	Sheffield W	8	0	29	4
2006–07	*Scunthorpe U*	3	1	3	1
2006–07	Luton T	15	3		
2007–08	Luton T	27	0		
2008–09	Luton T	7	0	49	3
2008–09	*Chesterfield*	17	2		
2009–10	Chesterfield	30	6		
2010–11	Chesterfield	44	3	91	11

WHITAKER, Danny (M) 383 60
H: 5 10 W: 11 00 b.Wilmslow 14-11-80
Source: Wilmslow Sports.

Season	Club	Apps	Gls	Tot A	Tot G
2000–01	Macclesfield T	0	0		
2001–02	Macclesfield T	16	2		
2002–03	Macclesfield T	41	10		
2003–04	Macclesfield T	36	5		
2004–05	Macclesfield T	36	2		
2005–06	Macclesfield T	42	4	171	23
2006–07	Port Vale	45	7		
2007–08	Port Vale	41	7	86	14
2008–09	Oldham Ath	39	6		
2009–10	Oldham Ath	41	2	80	8
2010–11	Chesterfield	46	15	46	15

COLCHESTER U (26)

BALDWIN, Pat (D) 227 2
H: 6 3 W: 12 07 b.City of London 12-11-82
Source: Chelsea Academy.

Season	Club	Apps	Gls	Tot A	Tot G
2002–03	Colchester U	19	0		
2003–04	Colchester U	4	0		
2004–05	Colchester U	38	0		
2005–06	Colchester U	25	0		
2006–07	Colchester U	26	0		
2007–08	Colchester U	35	0		
2008–09	Colchester U	7	0		
2009–10	*Bristol R*	6	0	6	0
2009–10	*Southend U*	18	1	18	1
2010–11	Colchester U	11	0	203	1

BEEVERS, Lee (D) 261 12
H: 6 2 W: 11 07 b.Doncaster 4-12-83
Source: Scholar. *Honours:* Wales Youth, Under-21.

Season	Club	Apps	Gls	Tot A	Tot G
2000–01	Ipswich T	0	0		
2001–02	Ipswich T	0	0		
2002–03	Ipswich T	0	0		
2002–03	*Boston U*	1	0		
2003–04	Boston U	40	2		
2004–05	Boston U	31	1	72	3
2004–05	Lincoln C	8	0		
2005–06	Lincoln C	33	1		
2006–07	Lincoln C	44	5		
2007–08	Lincoln C	37	1		
2008–09	Lincoln C	44	2	166	9
2009–10	Colchester U	19	0		
2010–11	Colchester U	19	0	23	0

BENDER, Tom (M) 1 0
H: 6 3 W: 12 00 b.Harlow 19-1-93
Source: Scholar. *Honours:* Wales Youth, Under-21.

Season	Club	Apps	Gls	Tot A	Tot G
2009–10	Colchester U	1	0		
2010–11	Colchester U	0	0	1	0

BOND, Andy (M) 43 7
H: 5 10 W: 11 07 b.Wigan 16-3-86
Source: Crewe Alex Scholar, Barrow.

Season	Club	Apps	Gls	Tot A	Tot G
2010–11	Colchester U	43	7	43	7

COKER, Ben (D) 20 0
H: 5 11 W: 11 09 b.Hatfield 17-6-89
Source: Bury T.

Season	Club	Apps	Gls	Tot A	Tot G
2010–11	Colchester U	20	0	20	0

COUSINS, Mark (G) 25 0
H: 6 2 W: 12 02 b.Chelmsford 9-1-87
Source: Scholar.

Season	Club	Apps	Gls	Tot A	Tot G
2005–06	Colchester U	0	0		
2006–07	Colchester U	0	0		
2007–08	Colchester U	2	0		
2008–09	Colchester U	9	0		
2009–10	Colchester U	0	0		
2010–11	Colchester U	14	0	25	0

ELITO, Medy (M) 43 6
H: 6 2 W: 13 00 b.Kinshasa 20-3-90
Source: Scholar. *Honours:* England Youth.

Season	Club	Apps	Gls	Tot A	Tot G
2007–08	Colchester U	11	1		
2008–09	Colchester U	5	0		
2009–10	Colchester U	3	0		
2009–10	*Cheltenham T*	12	3		
2010–11	Colchester U	0	0	19	1
2010–11	*Dagenham & R*	10	2	10	2
2010–11	*Cheltenham T*	2	0	14	3

GILLESPIE, Steven (F) 163 44
H: 5 9 W: 11 02 b.Liverpool 4-6-84
Source: Liverpool Scholar.

Season	Club	Apps	Gls	Tot A	Tot G
2004–05	Bristol C	8	0		
2004–05	*Cheltenham T*	12	5		
2005–06	Bristol C	4	1	12	1
2005–06	Cheltenham T	14	5		
2006–07	Cheltenham T	23	5		
2007–08	Cheltenham T	37	14	86	29
2008–09	Colchester U	17	4		
2009–10	Colchester U	30	1		
2010–11	Colchester U	18	9	65	14

HACKNEY, Simon (M) 169 19
H: 5 8 W: 9 13 b.Manchester 5-2-84
Source: Woodley Sports.

Season	Club	Apps	Gls	Tot A	Tot G
2005–06	Carlisle U	30	6		
2006–07	Carlisle U	18	2		
2007–08	Carlisle U	43	8		
2008–09	Carlisle U	22	1	113	17
2008–09	Colchester U	17	0		
2009–10	Colchester U	17	1		
2009–10	*Morecambe*	8	1	8	1
2010–11	Colchester U	1	0	35	1
2010–11	*Oxford U*	13	0	13	0

HEATH, Matt (D) 217 14
H: 6 4 W: 13 13 b.Leicester 1-11-81
Source: Scholar.

Season	Club	Apps	Gls	Tot A	Tot G
2000–01	Leicester C	0	0		
2001–02	Leicester C	5	0		
2002–03	Leicester C	11	3		
2003–04	Leicester C	13	0		
2003–04	*Stockport Co*	8	0	8	0
2004–05	Leicester C	22	3	51	6
2005–06	Coventry C	25	1		
2006–07	Coventry C	7	0	32	1
2006–07	Leeds U	26	3		
2007–08	Leeds U	26	1	52	4
2007–08	*Colchester U*	5	0		
2008–09	Colchester U	14	0		
2008–09	*Brighton & HA*	6	1	6	1
2009–10	Colchester U	18	0		
2009–10	*Southend U*	4	0	4	0
2010–11	Colchester U	27	2	64	2

HENDERSON, Ian (F) 182 20
H: 5 10 W: 11 06 b.Thetford 25-1-85
Source: Scholar. *Honours:* England Youth, Under-20.

Season	Club	Apps	Gls	Tot A	Tot G
2002–03	Norwich C	20	1		
2003–04	Norwich C	19	4		
2004–05	Norwich C	3	0		
2005–06	Norwich C	24	1		
2006–07	Norwich C	2	0	68	6
2006–07	*Rotherham U*	18	1	18	1
2007–08	Northampton T	23	0		
2008–09	Northampton T	3	0	26	0
2008–09	*Luton T*	19	1	19	1
2009–10	Colchester U	13	2		
2009–10	*Ankaragucu*	2	0	2	0
2010–11	Colchester U	36	10	49	12

IZZET, Kem (M) 377 18
H: 5 7 W: 10 05 b.Mile End 29-9-80
Source: Trainee.

Season	Club	Apps	Gls	Tot A	Tot G
1998–99	Charlton Ath	0	0		
1999–2000	Charlton Ath	0	0		
2000–01	Charlton Ath	0	0		
2000–01	Colchester U	6	1		
2001–02	Colchester U	40	3		
2002–03	Colchester U	45	8		
2003–04	Colchester U	44	3		
2004–05	Colchester U	4	0		
2005–06	Colchester U	33	0		
2006–07	Colchester U	45	1		
2007–08	Colchester U	39	1		
2008–09	Colchester U	43	1		
2009–10	Colchester U	37	0		
2010–11	Colchester U	41	0	377	18

JAMES, Lloyd (M) 99 2
H: 5 11 W: 11 01 b.Bristol 16-2-88
Source: Scholar. *Honours:* Wales Youth, Under-21.

Season	Club	Apps	Gls	Tot A	Tot G
2005–06	Southampton	0	0		
2006–07	Southampton	0	0		
2007–08	Southampton	0	0		
2008–09	Southampton	41	0		
2009–10	Southampton	30	2	71	2
2010–11	Colchester U	28	0	28	0

KNUDSEN, Morten (D) 17 0
b.Norway 27-10-86

Season	Club	Apps	Gls	Tot A	Tot G
2009	Notodden	17	0	17	0
2009–10	Colchester U	0	0		
2010–11	Colchester U	0	0		

O'TOOLE, John (M) 108 13
H: 6 2 W: 13 07 b.Harrow 30-9-88
Honours: Eire Under-21.

Season	Club	Apps	Gls	Tot A	Tot G
2007–08	Watford	35	3		
2008–09	Watford	22	7		
2008–09	*Sheffield U*	9	1	9	1
2009–10	Watford	0	0	57	10
2009–10	Colchester U	31	2		
2010–11	Colchester U	11	0	42	2

ODEJAYI, Kayode (F) 304 48
H: 6 2 W: 12 02 b.Ibadon 21-2-82
Source: Scholar. *Honours:* Nigeria 1 full cap.

Season	Club	Apps	Gls	Tot A	Tot G
1999–2000	Bristol C	3	0		
2000–01	Bristol C	3	0		
2001–02	Bristol C	0	0		
2002–03	Bristol C	0	0	6	0
2003–04	Cheltenham T	30	5		
2004–05	Cheltenham T	32	1		
2005–06	Cheltenham T	41	11		
2006–07	Cheltenham T	45	13	148	30
2007–08	Barnsley	39	3		
2008–09	Barnsley	28	1		
2008–09	*Scunthorpe U*	6	1	6	1
2009–10	Barnsley	5	0	72	4
2009–10	Colchester U	28	9		
2010–11	Colchester U	44	4	72	13

OKUONGHAE, Magnus (D) 135 5
H: 6 3 W: 13 04 b.Nigeria 16-2-86
Source: Scholar.

Season	Club	Apps	Gls	Tot A	Tot G
2003–04	Rushden & D	1	0		
2004–05	Rushden & D	0	0		
2005–06	Rushden & D	21	1		
2006–07	Rushden & D	0	0	22	1
2007–08	Dagenham & R	10	0		
2008–09	Dagenham & R	45	2	55	2
2009–10	Colchester U	44	0		
2010–11	Colchester U	14	2	58	2

PENTNEY, Carl (G) 1 0
H: 6 0 W: 12 00 b.Colchester 3-2-89

Season	Club	Apps	Gls	Tot A	Tot G
2007–08	Leicester C	0	0		
2008–09	Leicester C	1	0		
2009–10	Leicester C	0	0	1	0
2010–11	Colchester U	0	0		

PERKINS, David (D) 172 12
H: 5 6 W: 11 06 b.Heysham 21-6-82

Season	Club	Apps	Gls	Tot A	Tot G
2006–07	Rochdale	18	0		
2007–08	Rochdale	40	4	58	4
2008–09	Colchester U	38	5		
2009–10	Colchester U	5	1		
2009–10	*Chesterfield*	13	1	13	1
2009–10	*Stockport Co*	22	0	22	0
2010–11	Colchester U	36	1	79	7

POWELL, Conor (D) 121 1
H: 5 10 W: 11 13 b.Dublin 26-8-87
Honours: Eire Under-21.

Season	Club	Apps	Gls	Tot A	Tot G
2005	Bohemians	5	0		
2006	Bohemians	15	0		
2007	Bohemians	23	0		
2008	Bohemians	20	0		
2009	Bohemians	29	1		
2010	Bohemians	27	0	119	1
2010–11	Colchester U	2	0	2	0

ROSE, Michael (D)   210   13
H: 5 11   W: 12 04   b.Salford 28-7-82
Source: Trainee.

1999–2000	Manchester U	0	0		
2000–01	Manchester U	0	0		
2001–02	Manchester U	0	0		
From Hereford U					
2004–05	Yeovil T	40	1		
2005–06	Yeovil T	1	0	41	1
2005–06	*Cheltenham T*	3	0	3	0
2005–06	*Scunthorpe U*	15	0	15	0
2006–07	Stockport Co	25	3		
2007–08	Stockport Co	28	3		
2008–09	Stockport Co	27	0		
2009–10	Stockport Co	24	2	104	8
2009–10	*Norwich C*	12	1	12	1
2010–11	Swindon T	35	3	35	3
2010–11	Colchester U	0	0		

SANDERSON, Jordan (M)   1   0
Source: Scholar.

2010–11	Colchester U	1	0	1	0

VILHJALMSSON, Matthias (F)   110   31
H: 6 2   W: 12 13   b.Isafjordur 30-1-87
Honours: Iceland 6 full caps, 1 goal.

2002	Bolungarvik	2	0		
2003	Bolungarvik	11	4		
2004	Bolungarvik	0	0	13	4
2005	Hafnarfjordur	1	0		
2006	Hafnarfjordur	14	0		
2007	Hafnarfjordur	17	6		
2008	Hafnarfjordur	19	5	51	11
2009	Harfnarfjordur	22	10		
2010	Harfnarfjordur	21	6	43	16
On loan from Hafnarfjordur.					
2010–11	Colchester U	3	0	3	0

VINCENT, Ashley (M)   172   17
H: 5 10   W: 11 08   b.Oldbury 26-5-85
Source: Wolverhampton W Scholar.

2004–05	Cheltenham T	26	1		
2005–06	Cheltenham T	13	2		
2006–07	Cheltenham T	5	0		
2007–08	Cheltenham T	37	2		
2008–09	Cheltenham T	29	3	110	8
2008–09	Colchester U	6	1		
2009–10	Colchester U	19	3		
2010–11	Colchester U	37	5	62	9

WHITE, John (D)   184   0
H: 6 0   W: 12 01   b.Maldon 26-7-86
Source: Scholar.

2004–05	Colchester U	20	0		
2005–06	Colchester U	33	0		
2006–07	Colchester U	16	0		
2007–08	Colchester U	21	0		
2008–09	Colchester U	26	0		
2009–10	Colchester U	39	0		
2009–10	*Southend U*	5	0	5	0
2010–11	Colchester U	22	0	179	0

WILLIAMS, Ben (G)   259   0
H: 6 0   W: 13 01   b.Manchester 27-8-82
Source: Scholar. *Honours:* England Schools.

2001–02	Manchester U	0	0		
2002–03	Manchester U	0	0		
2002–03	*Coventry C*	0	0		
2002–03	*Chesterfield*	14	0	14	0
2003–04	Manchester U	0	0		
2003–04	*Crewe Alex*	10	0		
2004–05	Crewe Alex	23	0		
2005–06	Crewe Alex	17	0		
2006–07	Crewe Alex	39	0		
2007–08	Crewe Alex	46	0	135	0
2008–09	Carlisle U	31	0	31	0
2009–10	Colchester U	46	0		
2010–11	Colchester U	33	0	79	0

WILSON, Brian (D)   217   16
H: 5 10   W: 11 00   b.Manchester 9-5-83
Source: Scholar.

2001–02	Stoke C	1	0		
2002–03	Stoke C	3	0		
2003–04	Stoke C	2	0	6	0
2003–04	Cheltenham T	14	0		
2004–05	Cheltenham T	43	3		
2005–06	Cheltenham T	43	9		
2006–07	Cheltenham T	25	2	125	14
2006–07	Bristol C	19	0		
2007–08	Bristol C	18	1		
2008–09	Bristol C	20	0		

2009–10	Bristol C	3	0	60	1
2010–11	Colchester U	26	1	26	1

WORDSWORTH, Anthony (M)   109   19
H: 6 1   W: 12 00   b.Camden 3-1-89
Source: Scholar.

2007–08	Colchester U	3	0		
2008–09	Colchester U	30	3		
2009–10	Colchester U	41	11		
2010–11	Colchester U	35	5	109	19

COVENTRY C (27)

BAKER, Carl (M)   138   23
H: 6 2   W: 12 06   b.Prescot 26-12-82
Source: Southport.

2007–08	Morecambe	42	10	42	10
2008–09	Stockport Co	22	3		
2009–10	Stockport Co	20	9	42	12
2009–10	Coventry C	22	0		
2010–11	Coventry C	32	1	54	1

BELL, David (M)   280   22
H: 5 10   W: 11 05   b.Wellingborough 21-4-84
Source: Trainee. *Honours:* Eire Youth, Under-21.

2001–02	Rushden & D	0	0		
2002–03	Rushden & D	30	3		
2003–04	Rushden & D	37	1		
2004–05	Rushden & D	40	3		
2005–06	Rushden & D	14	3	121	10
2005–06	Luton T	9	0		
2006–07	Luton T	34	3		
2007–08	Luton T	32	4	75	7
2007–08	*Leicester C*	6	0	6	0
2008–09	Norwich C	19	0	19	0
2008–09	Coventry C	9	1		
2009–10	Coventry C	28	2		
2010–11	Coventry C	22	2	59	5

CAMERON, Nathan (D)   25   0
H. 6 2   W: 12 04   b.Birmingham 21-11-91
Source: Scholar.

2009–10	Coventry C	0	0		
2010–11	Coventry C	25	0	25	0

CARSLEY, Lee (M)   470   33
H: 5 10   W: 12 04   b.Birmingham 28-2-74
Source: Trainee. *Honours:* Eire 39 full caps.

1992–93	Derby Co	0	0		
1993–94	Derby Co	0	0		
1994–95	Derby Co	23	2		
1995–96	Derby Co	35	1		
1996–97	Derby Co	24	0		
1997–98	Derby Co	34	1		
1998–99	Derby Co	22	1	138	5
1998–99	Blackburn R	8	0		
1999–2000	Blackburn R	30	10		
2000–01	Blackburn R	8	0	46	10
2000–01	Coventry C	21	2		
2001–02	Coventry C	26	2		
2001–02	Everton	8	1		
2002–03	Everton	24	3		
2003–04	Everton	21	2		
2004–05	Everton	36	4		
2005–06	Everton	5	0		
2006–07	Everton	38	1		
2007–08	Everton	34	1	166	12
2008–09	Birmingham C	41	2		
2009–10	Birmingham C	7	0	48	2
2010–11	Coventry C	25	0	72	4

CLARKE, Jordan (D)   33   1
H: 6 0   W: 11 02   b.Coventry 19-11-91
Source: Scholar. *Honours:* England Youth.

2009–10	Coventry C	12	0		
2010–11	Coventry C	21	1	33	1

CLINGAN, Sammy (M)   223   15
H: 5 11   W: 11 06   b.Belfast 13-1-84
Source: Scholar. *Honours:* Northern Ireland Schools, Youth, Under-21, Under-23, 28 full caps.

2001–02	Wolverhampton W	0	0		
2002–03	Wolverhampton W	0	0		
2003–04	Wolverhampton W	0	0		
2004–05	Wolverhampton W	0	0		
2004–05	*Chesterfield*	15	2		
2005–06	Wolverhampton W	0	0		
2005–06	*Chesterfield*	21	1	36	3

2005–06	Nottingham F	15	0		
2006–07	Nottingham F	28	0		
2007–08	Nottingham F	42	1	85	1
2008–09	Norwich C	40	6		
2009–10	Norwich C	0	0	40	6
2009–10	Coventry C	34	5		
2010–11	Coventry C	28	0	62	5

CRANIE, Martin (D)   134   1
H: 6 1   W: 12 09   b.Yeovil 23-9-86
Source: Scholar. *Honours:* England Youth, Under-20, Under-21.

2003–04	Southampton	1	0		
2004–05	Southampton	3	0		
2004–05	*Bournemouth*	3	0	3	0
2005–06	Southampton	11	0		
2006–07	Southampton	1	0	16	0
2006–07	*Yeovil T*	12	0	12	0
2007–08	Portsmouth	2	0		
2007–08	*QPR*	6	0	6	0
2008–09	Portsmouth	0	0		
2008–09	*Charlton Ath*	19	0	19	0
2009–10	Portsmouth	0	0	2	0
2009–10	Coventry C	40	1		
2010–11	Coventry C	36	0	76	1

DEEGAN, Gary (M)   118   14
H: 5 9   W: 11 11   b.Dublin 28-9-87

2005–06	Shelbourne	0	0		
2006	*Kilkenny City*	18	4	18	4
2007	Longford Town	30	3	30	3
2008	Galway U	17	0	17	0
2008	Bohemians	12	3	12	3
2009	Bohemians	23	2	23	2
2009–10	Coventry C	17	2		
2010–11	Coventry C	1	0	18	2

EASTWOOD, Freddy (F)   255   73
H: 5 11   W: 12 04   b.Epsom 29-10-83
Source: West Ham U Trainee, Grays Ath.
Honours: Wales 11 full caps, 4 goals.

2004–05	Southend U	33	19		
2005–06	Southend U	40	23		
2006–07	*Southend U*	42	11	115	53
2007–08	Wolverhampton W	31	3	31	3
2008–09	Coventry C	46	4		
2009–10	Coventry C	36	8		
2010–11	Coventry C	27	5	109	17

GUNNARSSON, Aron (M)   123   6
H: 5 9   W: 11 00   b.Akureyri 22-9-89
Honours: Iceland Under-21, 22 full caps.

2007–08	AZ	1	0	1	0
2008–09	Coventry C	40	2		
2009–10	Coventry C	40	1		
2010–11	Coventry C	42	4	122	6

HUSSEY, Chris (D)   19   0
H: 5 10   W: 10 03   b.Hammersmith 2-1-89
Source: AFC Wimbledon.

2009–10	Coventry C	8	0		
2010–11	Coventry C	11	0	19	0
2010–11	*Crewe Alex*	0	0		

IRELAND, Daniel (G)   1   0
H: 6 2   W: 13 00   b.Sydney 30-9-90
Source: Academy.

2007–08	Coventry C	0	0		
2008–09	Coventry C	0	0		
2009–10	Coventry C	0	0		
2010–11	Coventry C	1	0	1	0

JEFFERS, Shaun (F)   26   1
H: 6 1   W: 11 03   b.Bedford 14-4-92
Source: Scholar.

2009–10	Coventry C	4	0		
2010–11	Coventry C	0	0	4	0
2010–11	*Cheltenham T*	22	1	22	1

JUTKIEWICZ, Lucas (F)   124   26
H: 6 1   W: 12 11   b.Southampton 20-3-89
Source: Scholar.

2005–06	Swindon T	5	0		
2006–07	Swindon T	33	5	38	5
2006–07	Everton	0	0		
2007–08	Everton	0	0		
2007–08	*Plymouth Arg*	3	0	3	0
2008–09	Everton	1	0		
2008–09	*Huddersfield T*	7	0	7	0
2009–10	Everton	0	0	1	0
2009–10	*Motherwell*	33	12	33	12
2010–11	Coventry C	42	9	42	9

KEOGH, Richard (D) 188 9
H: 6 0　W: 11 02　b.Harlow 11-8-86
Source: Scholar. Honours: Eire Under-21.

2004–05	Stoke C	0	0	
2005–06	Bristol C	9	1	
2005–06	*Wycombe W*	3	0	3 0
2006–07	Bristol C	31	2	
2007–08	Bristol C	0	0	40 3
2007–08	*Huddersfield T*	9	1	9 1
2007–08	*Carlisle U*	7	0	
2007–08	*Cheltenham T*	10	0	10 0
2008–09	Carlisle U	32	1	
2009–10	Carlisle U	41	3	80 4
2010–11	Coventry C	46	1	46 1

KING, Marlon (F) 373 120
H: 5 10　W: 12 10　b.Dulwich 26-4-80
Source: Trainee. Honours: Jamaica 19 full caps, 12 goals.

1998 99	Barnet	22	6	
1999–2000	Barnet	31	8	53 14
2000–01	Gillingham	38	15	
2001–02	Gillingham	42	17	
2002–03	Gillingham	10	4	
2003–04	Gillingham	11	4	101 40
2003–04	Nottingham F	24	5	
2004–05	Nottingham F	26	5	
2004–05	*Leeds U*	9	0	9 0
2005–06	Nottingham F	0	0	50 10
2005–06	Watford	41	21	
2006–07	Watford	13	4	
2007–08	Watford	27	11	81 36
2007–08	Wigan Ath	15	1	
2008–09	Wigan Ath	0	0	
2008–09	*Hull C*	20	5	20 5
2008–09	*Middlesbrough*	13	2	13 2
2009–10	Wigan Ath	3	0	18 1
2010–11	Coventry C	28	12	28 12

McINDOE, Michael (M) 358 48
H: 5 8　W: 11 00　b.Edinburgh 2-12-79
Source: Trainee. Honours: Scotland B.

1997–98	Luton T	0	0	
1998–99	Luton T	22	0	
1999–2000	Luton T	17	0	39 0
From Hereford, Yeovil.				
2003–04	Doncaster R	45	10	
2004–05	Doncaster R	44	10	
2005–06	Doncaster R	33	8	122 28
2005–06	*Derby Co*	8	0	8 0
2006–07	Barnsley	18	4	18 4
2006–07	Wolverhampton W	27	3	27 3
2007–08	Bristol C	45	6	
2008–09	Bristol C	45	6	
2009–10	Bristol C	0	0	90 12
2009–10	Coventry C	40	1	
2010–11	Coventry C	6	0	46 1
2010–11	*Milton Keynes D*	8	0	8 0

McPAKE, James (D) 145 10
H: 6 2　W: 12 08　b.Airdrie 2-6-84
Source: Trainee.

2003–04	Livingston	1	0	
2004–05	Livingston	15	2	
2005–06	Livingston	15	0	
2005–06	*Morton*	11	2	11 2
2006–07	Livingston	33	3	
2007–08	Livingston	19	0	
2008–09	Livingston	18	2	101 7
2008–09	Coventry C	4	0	
2009–10	Coventry C	17	1	
2010–11	Coventry C	12	0	33 1

McSHEFFREY, Gary (F) 301 80
H: 5 8　W: 10 06　b.Coventry 13-8-82
Source: Trainee. Honours: England Youth, Under-20.

1998–99	Coventry C	1	0	
1999–2000	Coventry C	3	0	
2000–01	Coventry C	0	0	
2001–02	*Stockport Co*	5	1	5 1
2001–02	Coventry C	8	1	
2002–03	Coventry C	29	4	
2003–04	Coventry C	19	11	
2003–04	*Luton T*	18	9	
2004–05	Coventry C	37	12	
2004–05	*Luton T*	5	1	23 10
2005–06	Coventry C	43	15	
2006–07	Coventry C	3	1	
2006–07	Birmingham C	40	13	
2007–08	Birmingham C	32	3	
2008–09	Birmingham C	3	1	
2008–09	*Nottingham F*	4	0	4 0
2009–10	Birmingham C	5	0	83 16
2009–10	*Leeds U*	10	1	10 1
2010–11	Coventry C	33	8	176 52

O'DONOVAN, Roy (F) 135 42
H: 5 10　W: 11 07　b.Cork 10-8-85
Source: Scholar. Honours: Eire Under-21, B.

2002–03	Coventry C	0	0	
2003–04	Coventry C	0	0	
2004–05	Coventry C	0	0	
2005	Cork C	26	6	
2006	Cork C	29	11	
2007	Cork C	19	14	74 31
2007–08	Sunderland	17	0	
2008–09	Sunderland	0	0	
2008–09	*Dundee U*	11	1	11 1
2008–09	*Blackpool*	12	0	12 0
2009–10	Sunderland	0	0	17 0
2009 10	*Southend U*	4	1	4 1
2009–10	*Hartlepool U*	15	9	15 9
2010–11	Coventry C	2	0	2 0

O'HALLORAN, Stephen (D) 25 0
H: 6 0　W: 11 07　b.Cork 29-11-87
Source: Scholar. Honours: Eire Under-21, 2 full caps.

2005–06	Aston Villa	0	0	
2006–07	Aston Villa	0	0	
2006–07	*Wycombe W*	11	0	11 0
2007–08	Aston Villa	0	0	
2007–08	*Southampton*	1	0	1 0
2008–09	Aston Villa	0	0	
2008–09	*Swansea C*	2	0	2 0
2009–10	Aston Villa	0	0	
2010–11	Coventry C	11	0	11 0

OSBOURNE, Isaac (M) 124 0
H: 5 10　W: 11 11　b.Birmingham 22-6-86
Source: Scholar.

2002–03	Coventry C	2	0	
2003–04	Coventry C	0	0	
2004–05	Coventry C	9	0	
2005–06	Coventry C	10	0	
2006–07	Coventry C	19	0	
2006–07	*Crewe Alex*	2	0	2 0
2007–08	Coventry C	42	0	
2008–09	Coventry C	25	0	
2009–10	Coventry C	15	0	
2010–11	Coventry C	0	0	122 0

PLATT, Clive (F) 518 98
H: 6 4　W: 12 07　b.Wolverhampton 27-10-77
Source: Trainee.

1995–96	Walsall	4	2	
1996–97	Walsall	1	0	
1997–98	Walsall	20	1	
1998–99	Walsall	7	1	
1999–2000	Walsall	0	0	32 4
1999–2000	Rochdale	41	9	
2000–01	Rochdale	43	8	
2001–02	Rochdale	43	7	
2002–03	Rochdale	42	6	169 30
2003–04	Notts Co	19	3	19 3
2003–04	Peterborough U	18	2	
2004–05	Peterborough U	19	4	37 6
2004–05	Milton Keynes D	20	3	
2005–06	Milton Keynes D	40	6	
2006–07	Milton Keynes D	42	18	102 27
2007–08	Colchester U	41	8	
2008–09	Colchester U	43	10	
2009–10	Colchester U	41	7	125 25
2010–11	Coventry C	34	3	34 3

QUIRKE, Michael (G) 4 0
b.Coventry 10-9-91
Source: Scholar. Honours: Eire Under-21.

2010–11	Coventry C	4	0	4 0

THOMAS, Conor (M) 0 0
b.Coventry 29-10-93
Source: Scholar.

2010–11	*Liverpool*	0	0	
2010–11	Coventry C	0	0	

TURNER, Ben (D) 81 4
H: 6 4　W: 14 04　b.Birmingham 21-1-88
Source: Scholar. Honours: England Youth.

2005–06	Coventry C	1	0	
2006–07	Coventry C	1	0	
2006–07	*Peterborough U*	8	0	8 0
2006–07	*Oldham Ath*	1	0	1 0
2007–08	Coventry C	19	0	
2008–09	Coventry C	24	0	
2009–10	Coventry C	13	0	
2010–11	Coventry C	14	4	72 4

WESTWOOD, Keiren (G) 258 0
H: 6 1　W: 13 10　b.Manchester 23-10-84
Source: Scholar. Honours: Eire 7 full caps.

2001–02	Manchester C	0	0	
2002–03	Manchester C	0	0	
2003–04	Manchester C	0	0	
2003–04	*Oldham Ath*	0	0	
2004–05	Manchester C	0	0	
2005–06	Manchester C	0	0	
2005–06	Carlisle U	35	0	
2006–07	Carlisle U	46	0	
2007–08	Carlisle U	46	0	127 0
2008–09	Coventry C	46	0	
2009–10	Coventry C	44	0	
2010–11	Coventry C	41	0	131 0

WILSON, Callum (M) 1 0
H: 5 11　W: 10 06　b.Coventry 27-2-92
Source: Scholar.

2009–10	Coventry C	0	0	
2010–11	Coventry C	1	0	1 0

WOOD, Richard (D) 235 11
H: 6 3　W: 12 13　b.Ossett 5-7-85
Source: Scholar.

2002–03	Sheffield W	3	1	
2003–04	Sheffield W	12	0	
2004–05	Sheffield W	34	1	
2005–06	Sheffield W	30	1	
2006–07	Sheffield W	12	0	
2007–08	Sheffield W	27	2	
2008–09	Sheffield W	42	0	
2009–10	Sheffield W	11	2	171 7
2009–10	Coventry C	24	3	
2010–11	Coventry C	40	1	64 4

WORBY, Alistair (G) 0 0
b.Reading

2010–11	Coventry C	0	0	

CREWE ALEX (28)

ADA, Patrick (D) 58 1
H: 6 0　W: 13 05　b.Yaounde 14-1-85
Source: Redbridge, Barnet, St Albans C, Exeter C, Histon.

2009–10	Crewe Alex	18	0	
2010–11	Crewe Alex	40	1	58 1

ARTELL, Dave (D) 340 30
H: 6 3　W: 14 01　b.Rotherham 22-11-80
Source: Trainee.

1999–2000	Rotherham U	1	0	
2000–01	Rotherham U	36	4	
2001–02	Rotherham U	0	0	
2002–03	Rotherham U	0	0	37 4
2002–03	*Shrewsbury T*	28	1	28 1
2003–04	Mansfield T	26	3	
2004–05	Mansfield T	19	2	45 5
2005–06	Chester C	37	2	
2006–07	Chester C	43	1	80 3
2007–08	Morecambe	36	3	
2008–09	Morecambe	37	3	
2009–10	Morecambe	37	7	110 13
2010–11	Crewe Alex	40	4	40 4

BELL, Lee (M) 205 8
H: 5 11　W: 12 04　b.Alsager 26-1-83
Source: Scholar.

2000–01	Crewe Alex	0	0	
2001–02	Crewe Alex	0	0	
2002–03	Crewe Alex	17	1	
2003–04	Crewe Alex	3	0	
2004–05	Crewe Alex	17	0	
2005–06	Crewe Alex	17	2	
2006–07	Crewe Alex	0	0	
2007–08	*Mansfield T*	23	1	23 1
2008–09	Macclesfield T	41	1	
2009–10	Macclesfield T	42	2	83 3
2010–11	Crewe Alex	45	1	99 4

BLANCHETT, Danny (D) 59 1
H: 5 11　W: 11 12　b.Wembley 12-3-88
Source: Northwood, Hendon, Harrow Borough, Cambridge C.

2006–07	Peterborough U	3	1	
2007–08	Peterborough U	1	0	

Season	Club	Apps	Gls	Tot A	Tot G
2008–09	Peterborough U	3	0		
2009–10	Peterborough U	0	0	7	1
2009–10	*Hereford U*	13	0	13	0
2010–11	Crewe Alex	39	0	39	0

CLAYTON, Max (F) — 2 0
b.Crewe 9-8-94
Source: Scholar.

Season	Club	Apps	Gls	Tot A	Tot G
2010–11	Crewe Alex	2	0	2	0

CONNERTON, Jordan (F) — 1 0
b.Lancaster 2-10-89
Source: Lancaster C, Chorley, Kendal, Lancaster C.

Season	Club	Apps	Gls	Tot A	Tot G
2009–10	Crewe Alex	0	0		
2010–11	Crewe Alex	1	0	1	0

DAVIS, Harry (D) — 2 0
H:6 2 W:12 04 b.Burnley 24-9-91
Source: Scholar.

Season	Club	Apps	Gls	Tot A	Tot G
2009–10	Crewe Alex	1	0		
2010–11	Crewe Alex	1	0	2	0

DONALDSON, Clayton (F) — 136 52
H:6 1 W:11 07 b.Bradford 7-2-84
Source: Scholar.

Season	Club	Apps	Gls	Tot A	Tot G
2002–03	Hull C	2	0		
2003–04	Hull C	0	0		
2004–05	Hull C	0	0	2	0
From York C					
2007–08	Hibernian	17	5	17	5
2008–09	Crewe Alex	37	6		
2009–10	Crewe Alex	37	13		
2010–11	Crewe Alex	43	28	117	47

DUGDALE, Adam (D) — 22 1
H:6 3 W:12 07 b.Liverpool 12-9-87
Source: Scholar.

Season	Club	Apps	Gls	Tot A	Tot G
2006–07	Crewe Alex	0	0		
2006–07	*Accrington S*	2	0	2	0
From Southport, Droylsden, Montagnee, Barrow, AFC Telford U.					
2010–11	Crewe Alex	20	1	20	1

FOGLER, Bartok (G) — 0 0
H:6 2 W:13 12 b.Warsaw 7-2-85
Source: Swit Nowy Dwor.

Season	Club	Apps	Gls	Tot A	Tot G
2010–11	Crewe Alex	0	0		

GRANT, Joel (F) — 103 16
H:6 0 W:12 01 b.Acton 26-8-87
Source: Scholar.

Season	Club	Apps	Gls	Tot A	Tot G
2005–06	Watford	7	0		
2006–07	Watford	0	0	7	0
From Aldershot T.					
2008–09	Crewe Alex	28	2		
2009–10	Crewe Alex	43	9		
2010–11	Crewe Alex	25	5	96	16

HUGHES, Caspar (M) — 1 0
b.Crewe 9-6-93
Source: Scholar.

Season	Club	Apps	Gls	Tot A	Tot G
2010–11	Crewe Alex	1	0	1	0

LEITCH-SMITH, AJ (F) — 35 10
H:5 11 W:12 04 b.Crewe 6-3-90
Source: Scholar.

Season	Club	Apps	Gls	Tot A	Tot G
2008–09	Crewe Alex	0	0		
2009	*IBV*	18	5	18	5
2009–10	Crewe Alex	1	0		
2010–11	Crewe Alex	16	5	17	5

MARTIN, Carl (D) — 6 1
H:5 8 W:10 07 b.Camden 24-10-86
Source: Wealdstone.

Season	Club	Apps	Gls	Tot A	Tot G
2009–10	Crewe Alex	6	1		
2010–11	Crewe Alex	0	0	6	1

MELLOR, Kelvin (D) — 1 0
H:5 10 W:11 09 b.Copenhagen 25-1-91
Source: Nantwich T.

Season	Club	Apps	Gls	Tot A	Tot G
2007–08	Crewe Alex	0	0		
2008–09	Crewe Alex	0	0		
2009–10	Crewe Alex	0	0		
2010–11	Crewe Alex	1	0	1	0

MILLER, Shaun (F) — 130 33
H:5 10 W:11 08 b.Alsager 25-9-87
Source: Scholar.

Season	Club	Apps	Gls	Tot A	Tot G
2006–07	Crewe Alex	7	3		
2007–08	Crewe Alex	15	1		
2008–09	Crewe Alex	33	4		
2009–10	Crewe Alex	33	7		
2010–11	Crewe Alex	42	18	130	33

MITCHEL-KING, Mat (D) — 46 0
H:6 4 W:13 00 b.Reading 12-9-83
Source: Cambridge C, Mildenhall T, Histon.

Season	Club	Apps	Gls	Tot A	Tot G
2009–10	Crewe Alex	32	0		
2010–11	Crewe Alex	14	0	46	0

MOORE, Byron (M) — 139 15
H:6 0 W:10 06 b.Stoke 24-8-88
Source: Scholar.

Season	Club	Apps	Gls	Tot A	Tot G
2006–07	Crewe Alex	0	0		
2007–08	Crewe Alex	33	3		
2008–09	Crewe Alex	36	3		
2009–10	Crewe Alex	32	3		
2010–11	Crewe Alex	38	6	139	15

MURPHY, Luke (M) — 80 7
H:6 1 W:11 05 b.Alsager 21-10-89
Source: Scholar.

Season	Club	Apps	Gls	Tot A	Tot G
2008–09	Crewe Alex	9	1		
2009–10	Crewe Alex	32	3		
2010–11	Crewe Alex	39	3	80	7

PHILLIPS, Steve (G) — 435 0
H:6 1 W:11 10 b.Bath 6-5-78
Source: Paulton R.

Season	Club	Apps	Gls	Tot A	Tot G
1996–97	Bristol C	0	0		
1997–98	Bristol C	0	0		
1998–99	Bristol C	15	0		
1999–2000	Bristol C	21	0		
2000–01	Bristol C	42	0		
2001–02	Bristol C	22	0		
2003–04	Bristol C	46	0		
2004–05	Bristol C	46	0		
2005–06	Bristol C	19	0	257	0
2006–07	Bristol R	44	0		
2007–08	Bristol R	46	0		
2008–09	Bristol R	46	0		
2009–10	Bristol R	0	0	136	0
2009–10	*Shrewsbury T*	11	0	11	0
2009–10	*Crewe Alex*	28	0		
2010–11	Crewe Alex	3	0	31	0

POWELL, Nick (M) — 17 0
H:6 0 W:10 05 b.Crewe 23-3-94
Source: Scholar.

Season	Club	Apps	Gls	Tot A	Tot G
2010–11	Crewe Alex	17	0	17	0

SARCEVIC, Antoni (M) — 6 1
H:5 10 W:11 00 b. 13-3-92
Source: Woodley Sports.

Season	Club	Apps	Gls	Tot A	Tot G
2009–10	Crewe Alex	0	0		
2010–11	Crewe Alex	6	1	6	1

SHELLEY, Danny (D) — 47 7
H:5 9 W:10 08 b.Stoke 29-12-90
Source: Scholar.

Season	Club	Apps	Gls	Tot A	Tot G
2008–09	Crewe Alex	3	0		
2009–10	Crewe Alex	19	1		
2010–11	Crewe Alex	25	6	47	7

SHORT, Lewis (M) — 0 0
H:5 9 W:11 07 b. 11-6-90
Source: Congleton T.

Season	Club	Apps	Gls	Tot A	Tot G
2010–11	Crewe Alex	0	0		

TOOTLE, Matt (D) — 67 1
H:5 9 W:11 00 b.Widnes 11-10-90
Source: Scholar.

Season	Club	Apps	Gls	Tot A	Tot G
2009–10	Crewe Alex	28	1		
2010–11	Crewe Alex	39	0	67	1

TURTON, Oliver (D) — 1 0
b.Manchester 6-12-92
Source: Scholar.

Season	Club	Apps	Gls	Tot A	Tot G
2010–11	Crewe Alex	1	0	1	0

WESTWOOD, Ashley M (D) — 285 21
H:6 0 W:12 09 b.Bridgnorth 31-8-76
Source: Trainee. Honours: England Youth.

Season	Club	Apps	Gls	Tot A	Tot G
1994–95	Manchester U	0	0		
1995–96	Crewe Alex	33	4		
1996–97	Crewe Alex	44	2		
1997–98	Crewe Alex	21	3		
1998–99	Bradford C	19	2		
1999–2000	Bradford C	5	0		
2000–01	Bradford C	0	0	24	2
2000–01	Sheffield W	33	2		
2001–02	Sheffield W	26	1		
2002–03	Sheffield W	23	2	82	5
2003–04	Northampton T	9	0		
2004–05	Northampton T	19	2		
2005–06	Northampton T	3	0	31	2
2006–07	Chester C	21	3		
2006–07	*Swindon T*	9	0	9	0
2007–08	Chester C	0	0	21	3
2007–08	*Port Vale*	12	0	12	0
From Stevenage B, Wrexham, Kettering T.					
2010–11	Crewe Alex	8	0	106	9

WESTWOOD, Ashley (M) — 84 11
H:5 10 W:11 00 b.Nantwich 1-4-90
Source: Scholar.

Season	Club	Apps	Gls	Tot A	Tot G
2008–09	Crewe Alex	2	0		
2009–10	Crewe Alex	36	6		
2010–11	Crewe Alex	46	5	84	11

ZOLA, Calvin (F) — 206 45
H:6 3 W:14 06 b.Kinshasa 31-12-84
Source: Scholar.

Season	Club	Apps	Gls	Tot A	Tot G
2001–02	Newcastle U	0	0		
2002–03	Newcastle U	0	0		
2003–04	Newcastle U	0	0		
2003–04	*Oldham Ath*	25	5	25	5
2004–05	Tranmere R	15	2		
2005–06	Tranmere R	22	4		
2006–07	Tranmere R	29	5		
2007–08	Tranmere R	30	5	96	16
2008–09	Crewe Alex	27	5		
2009–10	Crewe Alex	34	15		
2010–11	Crewe Alex	6	1	67	21
2010–11	*Burton Alb*	18	3	18	3

CRYSTAL PALACE (29)

AMBROSE, Darren (M) — 262 48
H:6 0 W:11 00 b.Harlow 29-2-84
Source: Scholar. Honours: England Youth, Under-20, Under-21.

Season	Club	Apps	Gls	Tot A	Tot G
2001–02	Ipswich T	1	0		
2002–03	Ipswich T	29	8		
2002–03	Newcastle U	1	0		
2003–04	Newcastle U	24	2		
2004–05	Newcastle U	12	3	37	5
2005–06	Charlton Ath	28	3		
2006–07	Charlton Ath	26	3		
2007–08	Charlton Ath	37	7		
2008–09	Charlton Ath	21	0	112	13
2008–09	*Ipswich T*	9	0	39	8
2009–10	Crystal Palace	46	15		
2010–11	Crystal Palace	28	7	74	22

ANDREW, Calvin (F) — 135 9
H:6 0 W:12 11 b.Luton 19-12-86
Source: Scholar.

Season	Club	Apps	Gls	Tot A	Tot G
2004–05	Luton T	8	0		
2005–06	Luton T	1	1		
2005–06	*Grimsby T*	8	1	8	1
2005–06	*Bristol C*	3	0	3	0
2006–07	Luton T	7	1		
2007–08	Luton T	39	2	55	4
2008–09	Crystal Palace	7	0		
2008–09	*Brighton & HA*	9	2	9	2
2009–10	Crystal Palace	27	1		
2010–11	Crystal Palace	13	0	47	1
2010–11	*Millwall*	3	0	3	0
2010–11	Swindon T	10	1	10	1

BARRETT, Adam (D) — 447 36
H:5 10 W:12 00 b.Dagenham 29-11-79
Source: Leyton Orient Trainee.

Season	Club	Apps	Gls	Tot A	Tot G
1998–99	Plymouth Arg	1	0		
1999–2000	Plymouth Arg	42	3		
2000–01	Plymouth Arg	9	0	52	3
2000–01	Mansfield T	8	1		
2001–02	Mansfield T	29	0	37	1
2002–03	Bristol R	45	1		
2003–04	Bristol R	45	4	90	5
2004–05	Southend U	43	11		
2005–06	Southend U	45	3		
2006–07	Southend U	28	3		
2007–08	Southend U	45	6		
2008–09	Southend U	45	2		
2009–10	Southend U	41	2	247	27
2010–11	Crystal Palace	7	0	7	0
2010–11	*Leyton Orient*	14	0	14	0

CADOGAN, Kieron (M) — 22 2
H:6 4 W:12 07 b.Tooting 3-8-90
Source: Scholar.

Season	Club	Apps	Gls	Tot A	Tot G
2007–08	Crystal Palace	0	0		
2008–09	Crystal Palace	4	1		
2009–10	Crystal Palace	0	0		
2009–10	*Burton Alb*	2	0	2	0
2010–11	Crystal Palace	16	1	20	2

CLYNE, Nathaniel (D) 94 1
H: 5 9 W: 10 07 b.Stockwell 5-4-91
Source: Scholar. Honours: England Youth.
2008–09	Crystal Palace	26	0		
2009–10	Crystal Palace	22	1		
2010–11	Crystal Palace	46	0	94	1

DANNS, Neil (M) 231 43
H: 5 10 W: 10 12 b.Liverpool 23-11-82
Source: Scholar.
2000–01	Blackburn R	0	0		
2001–02	Blackburn R	0	0		
2002–03	Blackburn R	2	0		
2003–04	Blackpool	12	2	12	2
2003–04	Blackburn R	1	0		
2003–04	*Hartlepool U*	9	1	9	1
2004–05	Blackburn R	0	0	3	0
2004–05	Colchester U	32	11		
2005–06	Colchester U	41	8	73	19
2006–07	Birmingham C	29	3		
2007–08	Birmingham C	2	0	31	3
2007–08	Crystal Palace	4	0		
2008–09	Crystal Palace	20	2		
2009–10	Crystal Palace	42	8		
2010–11	Crystal Palace	37	8	103	18

DAVIDS, Edgar (M) 361 34
H: 5 7 W: 10 10 b.Paramaribo 13-3-73
Honours: Holland Under-21, 74 full caps, 6 goals.
1991–92	Ajax	13	9		
1992–93	Ajax	28	1		
1993–94	Ajax	15	2		
1994–95	Ajax	22	5		
1995–96	Ajax	28	7	106	24
1996–97	AC Milan	15	0		
1997–98	AC Milan	3	0	18	0
1997–98	Juventus	20	1		
1998–99	Juventus	27	2		
1999–2000	Juventus	27	1		
2000–01	Juventus	26	1		
2001–02	Juventus	28	2		
2002–03	Juventus	26	1		
2003–04	Juventus	5	0	159	8
2003–04	Barcelona	18	1	18	1
2004–05	Internazionale	14	0	14	0
2005–06	Tottenham H	31	1		
2006–07	Tottenham H	9	0		
2007–08	Tottenham H	0	0		
2008–09	Tottenham H	0	0	40	1
2010–11	Crystal Palace	6	0	6	0

DAVIS, Claude (D) 194 4
H: 6 3 W: 14 04 b.Kingston, Jam 6-3-79
Source: Portmore U. Honours: Jamaica 65 full caps, 2 goals.
2003–04	Preston NE	22	1		
2004–05	Preston NE	32	0		
2005–06	Preston NE	40	3	94	4
2006–07	Sheffield U	21	0	21	0
2007–08	Derby Co	19	0		
2008–09	Derby Co	8	0		
2008–09	*Crystal Palace*	7	0		
2009–10	Derby Co	0	0	27	0
2009–10	Crystal Palace	21	0		
2010–11	Crystal Palace	24	0	52	0

DE SILVA, Kyle (F) 0 0
b.Croydon
Source: Scholar.
| 2010–11 | Crystal Palace | 0 | 0 | | |

DJILALI, Kieran (M) 46 3
H: 6 3 W: 13 02 b.Lambeth 1-1-91
Source: Scholar.
2008–09	Crystal Palace	6	0		
2009–10	Crystal Palace	8	1		
2009–10	*Chesterfield*	8	1		
2010–11	Crystal Palace	14	0	28	1
2010–11	*Chesterfield*	10	1	18	2

DORMAN, Andy (M) 220 37
H: 6 0 W: 10 10 b.Chester 1-5-82
Honours: Wales 3 full caps.
2004	New England Rev	20	2		
2005	New England Rev	30	2		
2006	New England Rev	30	7		
2007	New England Rev	30	7	112	17
2007–08	St Mirren	18	3		
2008–09	St Mirren	36	10		
2009–10	St Mirren	34	6	88	19
2010–11	Crystal Palace	20	1	20	1

EASTER, Jermaine (F) 269 67
H: 5 9 W: 12 02 b.Cardiff 15-1-82
Source: Trainee. Honours: Wales Youth, 10 full caps.
2000–01	Wolverhampton W	0	0		
2000–01	Hartlepool U	4	0		
2001–02	Hartlepool U	12	2		
2002–03	Hartlepool U	8	0		
2003–04	Hartlepool U	3	0	27	2
2003–04	*Cambridge U*	15	2		
2004–05	Cambridge U	24	6	39	8
2004–05	Boston U	9	3	9	3
2005–06	Stockport Co	19	8	19	8
2005–06	Wycombe W	15	2		
2006–07	Wycombe W	38	17		
2007–08	Wycombe W	6	2	59	21
2007–08	Plymouth Arg	32	6		
2008–09	Plymouth Arg	4	0	36	6
2008–09	*Millwall*	5	1	5	1
2008–09	*Colchester U*	5	2	5	2
2009–10	Milton Keynes D	36	14		
2010–11	Milton Keynes D	14	0	50	14
2010–11	*Swansea C*	6	1	6	1
2010–11	Crystal Palace	14	1	14	1

FODERINGHAM, Wesley (G) 0 0
H: 6 1 W: 12 00 b.Hammersmith 14-1-91
Source: Scholar.
| 2009–10 | Fulham | 0 | 0 | | |
| 2010–11 | Crystal Palace | 0 | 0 | | |

GARVAN, Owen (M) 190 16
H: 6 0 W: 10 07 b.Dublin 29-1-88
Source: Scholar. Honours: Eire Youth, Under-21.
2005–06	Ipswich T	32	3		
2006–07	Ipswich T	27	1		
2007–08	Ipswich T	43	2		
2008–09	Ipswich T	37	7		
2009–10	Ipswich T	25	0	164	13
2010–11	Crystal Palace	26	3	26	3

HILLS, Lee (D) 50 1
H: 5 10 W: 11 11 b.Croydon 13-4-90
Source: Scholar. Honours: England Youth.
2007–08	Crystal Palace	12	1		
2008–09	Crystal Palace	14	0		
2008–09	*Colchester U*	2	0	2	0
2009–10	Crystal Palace	19	0		
2009–10	*Oldham Ath*	3	0	3	0
2010–11	Crystal Palace	0	0	45	1

HOLLAND, Jack (D) 0 0
H: 6 3 W: 12 02 b.Bromley 1-3-92
Source: Scholar.
| 2010–11 | Crystal Palace | 0 | 0 | | |

HOLNESS, Charlie (D) 0 0
H: 5 11 W: 13 01 b.Lewisham 9-2-92
Source: Scholar.
| 2010–11 | Crystal Palace | 0 | 0 | | |

IVERSEN, Steffen (F) 361 125
H: 6 1 W: 12 07 b.Oslo 10-11-76
Honours: Norway 79 full caps, 21 goals.
1996	Rosenborg	25	10		
1996–97	Tottenham H	16	6		
1997–98	Tottenham H	13	0		
1998–99	Tottenham H	27	8		
1999–2000	Tottenham H	36	14		
2000–01	Tottenham H	14	2		
2001–02	Tottenham H	18	4		
2002–03	Tottenham H	19	1	143	35
2003–04	Wolverhampton W	16	4	16	4
2004	Valerenga	11	4		
2005	Valerenga	21	7	32	11
2006	Rosenborg	24	17		
2007	Rosenborg	23	13		
2008	Rosenborg	22	10		
2009	Rosenborg	29	9		
2010	Rosenborg	30	14	153	73
2010–11	Crystal Palace	17	2	17	2

MANN, Charlie (G) 0 0
H: 6 2 W: 11 07 b.Harlow 17-9-92
Source: Scholar.
| 2010–11 | Crystal Palace | 0 | 0 | | |

MARROW, Alex (M) 53 1
H: 6 1 W: 13 00 b.Tyldesley 21-1-90
Source: Ashton Ath.
| 2007–08 | Blackburn R | 0 | 0 | | |
| 2008–09 | Blackburn R | 0 | 0 | | |

2009–10	Blackburn R	0	0		
2009–10	*Oldham Ath*	32	1	32	1
2010–11	Blackburn R	0	0		
2010–11	Crystal Palace	21	0	21	0

McCARTHY, Patrick (D) 209 9
H: 6 2 W: 13 07 b.Dublin 31-5-83
Source: Scholar. Honours: Eire Youth, B, Under-21.
2000–01	Manchester C	0	0		
2001–02	Manchester C	0	0		
2002–03	Manchester C	0	0		
2002–03	*Boston U*	12	0	12	0
2002–03	*Notts Co*	6	0	6	0
2003–04	Manchester C	0	0		
2004–05	Manchester C	0	0		
2004–05	Leicester C	12	0		
2005–06	Leicester C	38	2		
2006–07	Leicester C	22	1	72	3
2007–08	Charlton Ath	29	2	29	2
2008–09	Crystal Palace	27	3		
2009–10	Crystal Palace	20	0		
2010–11	Crystal Palace	43	1	90	4

MOXEY, Dean (D) 112 7
H: 6 2 W: 11 00 b.Exeter 14-1-86
Source: Scholar.
2008–09	Exeter C	43	4	43	4
2009–10	Derby Co	30	0		
2010–11	Derby Co	22	2	52	2
2010–11	Crystal Palace	17	1	17	1

N'DIAYE, Alassane (M) 44 3
H: 6 4 W: 14 02 b.Montbeliard 25-2-90
Source: Scholar.
2008–09	Crystal Palace	0	0		
2009–10	Crystal Palace	26	3		
2010–11	Crystal Palace	12	0	38	3
2010–11	*Swindon T*	6	0	6	0

NNAMANI, Jerry (D) 0 0
H: 6 2 W: 13 12 b.Deptford 12-10-91
Source: Scholar.
| 2010–11 | Crystal Palace | 0 | 0 | | |

O'KEEFE, Stuart (M) 14 0
H: 5 8 W: 10 00 b.Eye 4-3-91
Source: Ipswich T Scholar.
2008–09	Southend U	3	0		
2009–10	Southend U	7	0		
2009–10	Southend U	0	0	10	0
2010–11	Crystal Palace	4	0	4	0

PARSONS, Matthew (D) 10 0
H: 5 10 W: 11 09 b.London 25-12-91
Source: Scholar.
| 2010–11 | Crystal Palace | 2 | 0 | 2 | 0 |
| 2010–11 | *Barnet* | 8 | 0 | 8 | 0 |

PINNEY, Nathaniel (F) 2 0
H: 6 0 W: 12 05 b.South Norwood 16-11-90
Source: Scholar.
2008–09	Crystal Palace	1	0		
2009–10	Crystal Palace	0	0		
2010–11	Crystal Palace	0	0	1	0
2010–11	*Dagenham & R*	1	0	1	0

PRICE, Lewis (G) 97 0
H: 6 3 W: 13 05 b.Bournemouth 19-7-84
Source: Southampton Academy. Honours: Wales Youth, Under-21, 8 full caps.
2002–03	Ipswich T	0	0		
2003–04	Ipswich T	1	0		
2004–05	Ipswich T	8	0		
2004–05	*Cambridge U*	6	0	6	0
2005–06	Ipswich T	25	0		
2006–07	Ipswich T	34	0	68	0
2007–08	Derby Co	6	0		
2008–09	Derby Co	0	0		
2008–09	*Milton Keynes D*	2	0	2	0
2008–09	*Luton T*	1	0	1	0
2009–10	Derby Co	0	0	6	0
2009–10	*Brentford*	13	0	13	0
2010–11	Crystal Palace	1	0	1	0

SCANNELL, Sean (F) 93 8
H: 5 9 W: 11 07 b.Croydon 19-9-90
Source: Scholar. Honours: Eire Youth, Under-21.
2007–08	Crystal Palace	23	2		
2008–09	Crystal Palace	25	2		
2009–10	Crystal Palace	26	2		
2010–11	Crystal Palace	19	2	93	8

SEKAJJA, Ibra (F) 1 1
b. 31-10-92
Source: Scholar.

2010–11	Crystal Palace	1	1	1	1

SPERONI, Julian (G) 290 0
H: 6 0 W: 11 00 b.Buenos Aires 18-5-79
Honours: Argentina Under-20, Under-21.

1999–2000	Platense	2	0		
2000–01	Platense	0	0	2	0
2001–02	Dundee	17	0		
2002–03	Dundee	38	0		
2003–04	Dundee	37	0	92	0
2004–05	Crystal Palace	6	0		
2005–06	Crystal Palace	4	0		
2006–07	Crystal Palace	5	0		
2007–08	Crystal Palace	46	0		
2008–09	Crystal Palace	45	0		
2009–10	Crystal Palace	45	0		
2010–11	Crystal Palace	45	0	196	0

TAYLOR, Quade (M) 0 0
Source: Dulwich H.

2010–11	Crystal Palace	0	0		

WILLIAMS, Jon (M) 0 0
b.Pembury 9-10-93
Source: Scholar. *Honours:* Wales Youth, Under-21.

2010–11	Crystal Palace	0	0		

WRIGHT, David (D) 409 8
H: 5 11 W: 11 01 b.Warrington 1-5-80
Source: Trainee. *Honours:* England Youth.

1997–98	Crewe Alex	3	0		
1998–99	Crewe Alex	20	1		
1999–2000	Crewe Alex	45	0		
2000–01	Crewe Alex	42	0		
2001–02	Crewe Alex	30	0		
2002–03	Crewe Alex	31	1		
2003–04	Crewe Alex	40	1	211	3
2004–05	Wigan Ath	31	0		
2005–06	Wigan Ath	2	0		
2005–06	*Norwich C*	5	0	5	0
2006–07	Wigan Ath	12	0	45	0
2006–07	Ipswich T	19	1		
2007–08	Ipswich T	41	2		
2008–09	Ipswich T	34	1		
2009–10	Ipswich T	26	1	120	5
2010–11	Crystal Palace	28	0	28	0

WYNTER, Alex (M) 0 0
H: 6 0 W: 13 04 b.Camberwell 15-9-93
Source: Scholar.

2009–10	Crystal Palace	0	0		
2010–11	Crystal Palace	0	0		

ZAHA, Wilfred (F) 42 1
H: 5 11 W: 10 05 b.Ivory Coast 10-11-92
Source: Scholar.

2009–10	Crystal Palace	1	0		
2010–11	Crystal Palace	41	1	42	1

DAGENHAM & R (30)

ANTWI, Will (D) 76 3
H: 6 2 W: 12 08 b.Epsom 19-10-82
Source: Scholar. *Honours:* Ghana 1 full cap.

2002–03	Crystal Palace	4	0		
2003–04	Crystal Palace	0	0	4	0

From Aldershot T

2005–06	Wycombe W	5	0		
2006–07	Wycombe W	25	1		
2007–08	Wycombe W	6	0		
2008–09	Wycombe W	6	0	42	1
2009–10	Dagenham & R	19	1		
2010–11	Dagenham & R	11	1	30	2

ARBER, Mark (D) 452 34
H: 6 1 W: 11 09 b.Johannesburg 9-10-77
Source: Trainee.

1995–96	Tottenham H	0	0		
1996–97	Tottenham H	0	0		
1997–98	Tottenham H	0	0		
1998–99	Tottenham H	0	0		
1998–99	Barnet	35	2		
1999–2000	Barnet	45	6		
2000–01	Barnet	45	7		
2001–02	Barnet	0	0	125	15
2002–03	Peterborough U	25	2		
2003–04	Peterborough U	44	3		

2004–05	Oldham Ath	14	1	14	1
2004–05	Peterborough U	21	0		
2005–06	Peterborough U	46	2		
2006–07	Peterborough U	34	1		
2007–08	Peterborough U	0	0	170	8
2007–08	*Dagenham & R*	16	1		
2008–09	Dagenham & R	42	3		
2009–10	Dagenham & R	41	4		
2010–11	Dagenham & R	44	2	143	10

BATES, Jon-Jo (F) 0 0
b. 29-3-91

2010–11	Dagenham & R	0	0		

BINGHAM, Billy (D) 8 0
H: 5 11 W: 11 02 b.London 15-7-90
Source: Crystal Palace.

2008–09	Dagenham & R	0	0		
2009–10	Dagenham & R	2	0		
2010–11	Dagenham & R	6	0	8	0

CURRIE, Darren (M) 573 61
H: 5 11 W: 12 07 b.Hampstead 29-11-74
Source: Trainee.

1993–94	West Ham U	0	0		
1994–95	West Ham U	0	0		
1994–95	*Shrewsbury T*	17	2		
1995–96	West Ham U	0	0		
1995–96	*Leyton Orient*	10	0	10	0
1995–96	*Shrewsbury T*	13	2		
1996–97	Shrewsbury T	37	2		
1997–98	Shrewsbury T	16	4	83	10
1997–98	Plymouth Arg	7	0	7	0
1998–99	Barnet	38	4		
1999–2000	Barnet	44	5		
2000–01	Barnet	45	10	127	19
2001–02	Wycombe W	46	3		
2002–03	Wycombe W	38	4		
2003–04	Wycombe W	42	7	126	14
2004–05	Brighton & HA	22	2	22	2
2004–05	Ipswich T	24	3		
2005–06	Ipswich T	46	5		
2006–07	Ipswich T	13	1	83	9
2006–07	*Coventry C*	8	0	8	0
2006–07	*Derby Co*	7	1	7	1
2007–08	Luton T	31	2	31	2
2008–09	Chesterfield	27	3		
2009–10	*Chesterfield*	4	0	31	3
2009–10	Dagenham & R	16	0		
2010–11	Dagenham & R	22	1	38	1

DEMETRIOU, Stephen (M) 0 0
b.Redbridge

2009–10	Dagenham & R	0	0		
2010–11	Dagenham & R	0	0		

DOE, Scott (D) 80 0
H: 6 0 W: 11 06 b.Reading 6-11-88
Source: Weymouth.

2009–10	Dagenham & R	42	0		
2010–11	Dagenham & R	38	0	80	0

GAIN, Peter (M) 427 34
H: 5 9 W: 11 07 b.Hammersmith 11-11-76
Source: Trainee.

1995–96	Tottenham H	0	0		
1996–97	Tottenham H	0	0		
1997–98	Tottenham H	0	0		
1998–99	Tottenham H	0	0		
1998–99	Lincoln C	4	0		
1999–2000	Lincoln C	32	2		
2000–01	Lincoln C	24	5		
2001–02	Lincoln C	42	2		
2002–03	Lincoln C	43	5		
2003–04	Lincoln C	42	7		
2004–05	Lincoln C	40	0	227	21
2005–06	Peterborough U	37	3		
2006–07	Peterborough U	34	6		
2007–08	Peterborough U	0	0	71	9
2007–08	*Dagenham & R*	18	1		
2008–09	Dagenham & R	31	0		
2009–10	Dagenham & R	43	3		
2010–11	Dagenham & R	37	0	129	4

GREEN, Danny (M) 87 24
H: 5 11 W: 12 00 b.Harlow 9-7-88
Source: Bishop's Stortford.

2006–07	Northampton T	0	0		
2007–08	Nottingham F	0	0		

From Bishop's Stortford.

2009–10	Dagenham & R	46	13		
2010–11	Dagenham & R	41	11	87	24

GREEN, Danny J (M) 3 0
b. 4-8-90
Source: Billericay T.

2010–11	Dagenham & R	3	0	3	0

GWILLIM, Gareth (M) 2 0
b.Bromley 9-2-83
Source: Welling U.

2000–01	Crystal Palace	0	0		
2001–02	Crystal Palace	0	0		

From Ashford T, Farnborough T, Bishop's Stortford, Histon.

2010–11	Dagenham & R	2	0	2	0

IFIL, Phil (D) 98 2
H: 5 10 W: 12 02 b.Willesden 18-11-86
Honours: England Youth, Under-20.

2004–05	Tottenham H	2	0		
2005–06	Tottenham H	0	0		
2005–06	*Millwall*	16	0	16	0
2006–07	Tottenham H	1	0		
2007–08	Tottenham H	0	0	3	0
2007–08	*Southampton*	12	0	12	0
2007–08	Colchester U	20	0		
2008–09	Colchester U	6	0		
2009–10	Colchester U	27	2	53	2
2010–11	Dagenham & R	14	0	14	0

ILESANMI, Femi (D) 25 0
b.Southwark 18-4-91
Source: QPR Scholar, Ashford T (M'sex).

2010–11	Dagenham & R	25	0	25	0

LEWINGTON, Chris (G) 3 0
H: 6 1 W: 12 00 b.Sidcup 23-8-88
Source: Erith & B, Dulwich H, Fisher Ath, Sittingbourne, Leatherhead.

2009–10	Dagenham & R	0	0		
2010–11	Dagenham & R	3	0	3	0

McCRORY, Damien (M) 70 0
H: 6 2 W: 12 10 b.Limerick 22-2-90
Honours: Eire Youth.

2008–09	Plymouth Arg	0	0		
2008–09	*Port Vale*	12	0		
2009–10	Plymouth Arg	0	0		
2009–10	*Port Vale*	5	0	17	0
2009–10	*Grimsby T*	10	0	10	0
2009–10	Dagenham & R	20	0		
2010–11	Dagenham & R	23	0	43	0

MONTGOMERY, Graeme (M) 22 2
H: 6 1 W: 12 00 b.Enfield 3-3-88
Source: Wealdstone.

2008–09	Dagenham & R	5	0		
2009–10	Dagenham & R	17	2		
2010–11	Dagenham & R	0	0	22	2

NURSE, Jon (M) 140 22
H: 5 9 W: 12 04 b.Barbados 1-3-81
Source: Stevenage B. *Honours:* Barbados 4 full caps.

2007–08	Dagenham & R	30	1		
2008–09	Dagenham & R	34	4		
2009–10	Dagenham & R	38	7		
2010–11	Dagenham & R	38	10	140	22

OGOGO, Abu (D) 72 4
H: 5 8 W: 10 02 b.Epsom 3-11-89
Source: Scholar.

2007–08	Arsenal	0	0		
2008–09	Arsenal	0	0		
2008–09	*Barnet*	9	1	9	1
2009–10	Dagenham & R	30	2		
2010–11	Dagenham & R	33	1	63	3

OKUS, Conor (M) 0 0
b.London 15-9-91
Source: West Ham U.

2010–11	Dagenham & R	0	0		

OSBORN, Alex (F) 0 0
b.Walthamstow 29-7-93
Source: Grays Ath.

2010–11	Dagenham & R	0	0		

REYNOLDS, Duran-Rhys (D) 0 0
b.Skegness 27-9-91
Source: Southend U Scholar.

2010–11	Dagenham & R	0	0		

ROBERTS, Tony (G)   305   0
H: 6 0   W: 13 11   b.Holyhead 4-8-69
Source: Trainee. *Honours:* Wales Under-21, 2 full caps.

1987–88	QPR	1	0	
1988–89	QPR	0	0	
1989–90	QPR	5	0	
1990–91	QPR	12	0	
1991–92	QPR	1	0	
1992–93	QPR	28	0	
1993–94	QPR	16	0	
1994–95	QPR	31	0	
1995–96	QPR	5	0	
1996–97	QPR	13	0	
1997–98	QPR	10	0	122 0
1998–99	Millwall	8	0	8 0

From St Albans C.

2007–08	Dagenham & R	43	0	
2008–09	Dagenham & R	43	0	
2009–10	Dagenham & R	46	0	
2010–11	Dagenham & R	43	0	175 0

SAVAGE, Bas (F)   200   25
H: 6 3   W: 13 08   b.Wandsworth 7-1-82
Source: Walton & Hersham.

2001–02	Reading	1	0	
2002–03	Reading	0	0	
2003–04	Reading	15	0	
2004–05	Reading	0	0	16 0
2004–05	Wycombe W	4	0	4 0
2004–05	Bury	5	0	5 0
2005–06	Bristol C	23	1	23 1
2006–07	Gillingham	14	1	14 1
2006–07	Brighton & HA	15	6	
2007–08	Brighton & HA	21	3	36 9
2007–08	Millwall	11	2	11 2
2008–09	Tranmere R	42	9	
2009–10	Tranmere R	13	0	55 9
2010–11	Dagenham & R	36	3	36 3

SCANNELL, Damian (M)   75   4
H: 5 10   W: 11 07   b.Croydon 28-4-85
Source: Eastleigh.

2007–08	Southend U	9	0	
2008–09	Southend U	19	1	
2008–09	Brentford	2	0	2 0
2009–10	Southend U	25	1	53 2
2010–11	Dagenham & R	20	2	20 2

SCOTT, Josh (F)   56   11
H: 6 1   W: 12 00   b.Camden 10-5-85
Source: Hayes, Hayes & Yeading U.

2009–10	Dagenham & R	40	10	
2010–11	Dagenham & R	16	1	56 11

TEJAN-SIE, Thomas (M)   4   0
H: 5 6   W: 11 08   b.Camden 23-11-88
Source: Leicester C Scholar, Wingate & Finchley.

2007–08	Dagenham & R	0	0	
2008–09	Dagenham & R	1	0	
2009–10	Dagenham & R	3	0	
2010–11	Dagenham & R	0	0	4 0

TOMLIN, Gavin (F)   120   20
H: 6 0   W: 12 02   b.Gillingham 13-1-83
Source: Staines T, Yeading.

2006–07	Brentford	12	0	
2007–08	Brentford	0	0	12 0

From Fisher Ath.

2008–09	Yeovil T	42	7	
2009–10	Yeovil T	35	7	77 14
2010–11	Dagenham & R	19	2	19 2
2010–11	Torquay U	12	4	12 4

VINCELOT, Romain (M)   121   14
H: 5 9   W: 11 02   b.Poitiers 29-10-85
Source: Chamois Niortais.

2004–05	Chamois Niortais	3	0	3 0
2005–06	Chamois Niortais	28	1	
2006–07	Chamois Niortais	9	0	
2007–08	Chamois Niortais	6	0	43 1
2008–09	Gueugnon	20	0	20 0
2009–10	Dagenham & R	9	1	
2010–11	Dagenham & R	46	12	55 13

WALSH, Phil (F)   25   3
H: 6 3   W: 13 04   b.Hartlepool 4-2-84
Source: Dorchester T.

2009–10	Dagenham & R	9	0	
2010–11	Dagenham & R	3	0	12 0
2010–11	Barnet	9	3	9 3
2010–11	Cheltenham T	4	0	4 0

WILKINSON, Luke (D)   0   0
H: 6 2   W: 11 09   b.Wells 2-12-92
Source: Bristol C Scholar.

2009–10	Portsmouth	0	0
2010–11	Dagenham & R	0	0

WOOTTON, Lee (M)   0   0
b.Hackney 23-8-92
Source: Youth.

2010–11	Dagenham & R	0	0

DERBY CO (31)

ADDISON, Miles (D)   65   3
H: 6 2   W: 13 03   b.Newham 7-1-89
Source: Scholar. *Honours:* England Under-21.

2005–06	Derby Co	2	0	
2006–07	Derby Co	0	0	
2007–08	Derby Co	1	0	
2008–09	Derby Co	28	1	
2009–10	Derby Co	13	2	
2010–11	Derby Co	21	0	65 3

ANDERSON, Russell (D)   319   19
H: 5 11   W: 10 09   b.Aberdeen 25-10-78
Source: Dyce J. *Honours:* Scotland Under-21, 11 full caps.

1996–97	Aberdeen	14	0	
1997–98	Aberdeen	26	0	
1998–99	Aberdeen	16	0	
1999–2000	Aberdeen	34	1	
2000–01	Aberdeen	0	0	
2001–02	Aberdeen	24	1	
2002–03	Aberdeen	33	2	
2003–04	Aberdeen	25	5	
2004–05	Aberdeen	31	1	
2005–06	Aberdeen	36	6	
2006–07	Aberdeen	35	2	274 18
2007–08	Sunderland	1	0	
2007–08	Plymouth Arg	14	0	14 0
2008–09	Sunderland	0	0	
2008–09	Burnley	4	0	4 0
2009–10	Sunderland	0	0	1 0
2009–10	Derby Co	15	1	
2010–11	Derby Co	11	0	26 1

ATKINS, Ross (G)   1   0
H: 6 0   W: 13 00   b.Derby 3-11-89
Source: Scholar.

2008–09	Derby Co	0	0	
2009–10	Derby Co	0	0	
2010–11	Derby Co	1	0	1 0

BAILEY, James (M)   82   1
H: 6 0   W: 12 05   b.Bollington 18-9-88
Source: Scholar.

2006–07	Crewe Alex	0	0	
2007–08	Crewe Alex	1	0	
2008–09	Crewe Alex	24	0	
2009–10	Crewe Alex	21	0	46 0
2010–11	Derby Co	36	1	36 1

BALL, Callum (F)   6   0
H: 6 1   W: 10 03   b.Leicester 8-10-92
Source: Scholar.

2009–10	Derby Co	1	0	
2010–11	Derby Co	5	0	6 0

BARKER, Shaun (D)   335   18
H: 6 2   W: 12 08   b.Nottingham 19-9-82
Source: Scholar.

2002–03	Rotherham U	11	0	
2003–04	Rotherham U	36	2	
2004–05	Rotherham U	33	2	
2005–06	Rotherham U	43	3	123 7
2006–07	Blackpool	45	3	
2007–08	Blackpool	46	2	
2008–09	Blackpool	43	0	134 5
2009–10	Derby Co	35	5	
2010–11	Derby Co	43	1	78 6

BRAYFORD, John (D)   127   3
H: 5 8   W: 11 02   b.Stoke 29-12-87
Source: Burton Alb.

2008–09	Crewe Alex	36	2	
2009–10	Crewe Alex	45	0	81 2
2010–11	Derby Co	46	1	46 1

BUENO, Alberto (F)   148   28
H: 5 10   W: 10 03   b.Madrid 20-3-88
Source: Youth.

2006–07	Real Madrid B	31	2

2007–08	Real Madrid B	31	4	
2008–09	Real Madrid B	34	16	96 22
2008–09	Real Madrid	3	0	3 0
2009–10	Valladolid	20	1	20 1
2010–11	Derby Co	29	5	29 5

BUXTON, Jake (D)   171   6
H: 6 1   W: 13 05   b.Sutton-in-Ashfield 4-3-85
Source: Scholar.

2002–03	Mansfield T	3	0	
2003–04	Mansfield T	9	1	
2004–05	Mansfield T	30	1	
2005–06	Mansfield T	39	0	
2006–07	Mansfield T	30	1	
2007–08	Mansfield T	40	2	
2008–09	Mansfield T	0	0	151 5

From Burton Alb.

2008–09	Derby Co	0	0	
2009–10	Derby Co	19	1	
2010–11	Derby Co	1	0	20 1

BYWATER, Steve (G)   254   0
H: 6 2   W: 12 10   b.Manchester 7-6-81
Source: Trainee. *Honours:* England Youth, Under-20, Under-21.

1997–98	Rochdale	0	0	
1998–99	West Ham U	0	0	
1999–2000	West Ham U	4	0	
1999–2000	Wycombe W	2	0	2 0
1999–2000	Hull C	4	0	4 0
2000–01	West Ham U	1	0	
2001–02	West Ham U	0	0	
2001–02	Wolverhampton W	0	0	
2001–02	Cardiff C	0	0	
2002–03	West Ham U	0	0	
2003–04	West Ham U	17	0	
2004–05	West Ham U	36	0	
2005–06	West Ham U	1	0	
2005–06	Coventry C	14	0	14 0
2006–07	West Ham U	0	0	59 0
2006–07	Derby Co	37	0	
2007–08	Derby Co	18	0	
2007–08	Ipswich T	17	0	17 0
2008–09	Derby Co	31	0	
2009–10	Derby Co	42	0	
2010–11	Derby Co	22	0	150 0
2010–11	Cardiff C	8	0	8 0

COMMONS, Kris (M)   259   58
H: 5 6   W: 9 08   b.Mansfield 30-8-83
Source: Scholar. *Honours:* Scotland 9 full caps, 2 goals.

2000–01	Stoke C	0	0	
2001–02	Stoke C	0	0	
2002–03	Stoke C	8	1	
2003–04	Stoke C	33	4	41 5
2004–05	Nottingham F	30	6	
2005–06	Nottingham F	37	8	
2006–07	Nottingham F	32	9	
2007–08	Nottingham F	39	9	138 32
2008–09	Derby Co	34	5	
2009–10	Derby Co	20	3	
2010–11	Derby Co	26	13	80 21

Transferred to Celtic January 2011.

CONNOLLY, Ryan (M)   1   0
H: 5 10   W: 10 04   b.Castlebar 13-1-92
Source: Scholar. *Honours:* Eire Youth.

2009–10	Derby Co	1	0	
2010–11	Derby Co	0	0	1 0

CROFT, Lee (F)   180   11
H: 5 11   W: 13 00   b.Wigan 21-6-85
Source: Scholar. *Honours:* England Youth, Under-20.

2002–03	Manchester C	0	0	
2003–04	Manchester C	0	0	
2004–05	Manchester C	7	0	
2004–05	Oldham Ath	12	0	12 0
2005–06	Manchester C	21	1	28 1
2006–07	Norwich C	36	3	
2007–08	Norwich C	41	1	
2008–09	Norwich C	41	5	118 9
2009–10	Derby Co	19	1	
2010–11	Derby Co	0	0	19 1
2010–11	Huddersfield T	3	0	3 0

CYWKA, Thomasz (M)   40   4
H: 5 10   W: 11 09   b.Gliwice 27-6-88
Source: Gwarek Zabrze. *Honours:* Poland Youth, Under-21.

2006–07	Wigan Ath	0	0

2006–07	Oldham Ath	4	0	4	0
2007–08	Wigan Ath	0	0		
2008–09	Wigan Ath	0	0		
2009–10	Wigan Ath	0	0		
2009–10	Derby Co	5	0		
2010–11	Derby Co	31	4	36	4

DAVIES, Ben (M) 293 60
H: 5 7 W: 12 03 b.Birmingham 27-5-81
Source: Walsall trainee.

2000–01	Kidderminster H	3	0		
2001–02	Kidderminster H	9	0	12	0
2004–05	Chester C	44	2		
2005–06	Chester C	45	7	89	9
2006–07	Shrewsbury T	43	12		
2007–08	Shrewsbury T	27	6		
2008–09	Shrewsbury T	42	12	112	30
2009–10	Notts Co	45	15		
2010–11	Notts Co	22	5	67	20
2010–11	Derby Co	13	1	13	1

DAVIES, Steve (F) 117 14
H: 6 0 W: 12 00 b.Liverpool 29-12-87
Source: Scholar.

2005–06	Tranmere R	22	2		
2006–07	Tranmere R	28	1		
2007–08	Tranmere R	10	2	60	5
2008–09	Derby Co	19	3		
2009–10	Derby Co	18	1		
2010–11	Derby Co	20	5	57	9

DEENEY, Saul (G) 52 0
H: 6 0 W: 12 13 b.Londonderry 12-3-83
Source: Scholar. *Honours:* Eire Youth, Under-21.

2000–01	Notts Co	0	0		
2001–02	Notts Co	0	0		
2002–03	Notts Co	7	0		
2003–04	Notts Co	3	0		
2004–05	Notts Co	32	0		
2005–06	Notts Co	0	0		
2006–07	Notts Co	7	0		
2007–08	Notts Co	0	0		
2008–09	Notts Co	0	0	49	0
2009–10	Derby Co	3	0		
2010–11	Derby Co	0	0	3	0

DILLON, Kealan (F) 0 0
b.Mullingar 21-2-94
Source: Scholar. *Honours:* Eire Youth.

2010–11	Derby Co	0	0		

DOYLE, Conor (F) 14 0
H: 6 2 W: 12 04 b.Mckinney 13-10-91
Source: Creighton Univ. *Honours:* Eire Under-21.

2010–11	Derby Co	14	0	14	0

FIELDING, Frank (G) 105 0
H: 5 11 W: 12 00 b.Blackburn 4-4-88
Source: Scholar. *Honours:* England Youth, Under-21.

2006–07	Blackburn R	0	0		
2007–08	Blackburn R	0	0		
2007–08	Wycombe W	36	0	36	0
2008–09	Blackburn R	0	0		
2008–09	Northampton T	12	0	12	0
2008–09	Rochdale	23	0		
2009–10	Blackburn R	0	0		
2009–10	Rochdale	18	0	41	0
2010–11	Blackburn R	0	0		
2010–11	Derby Co	16	0	16	0

GREEN, Paul (M) 296 32
H: 5 9 W: 10 02 b.Pontefract 10-4-83
Source: Scholar. *Honours:* Eire 9 full caps, 1 goal.

2003–04	Doncaster R	43	8		
2004–05	Doncaster R	42	7		
2005–06	Doncaster R	34	3		
2006–07	Doncaster R	41	2		
2007–08	Doncaster R	38	5	198	25
2008–09	Derby Co	29	3		
2009–10	Derby Co	33	2		
2010–11	Derby Co	36	2	98	7

HENDRICK, Jeff (M) 4 0
H: 6 1 W: 11 11 b.Dublin 31-1-92
Source: Scholar. *Honours:* Eire Youth.

2010–11	Derby Co	4	0	4	0

LEACOCK, Dean (D) 139 1
H: 6 2 W: 12 04 b.Croydon 10-6-84
Source: Trainee. *Honours:* England Youth, Under-20.

2002–03	Fulham	0	0		
2003–04	Fulham	4	0		
2004–05	Fulham	0	0		
2004–05	Coventry C	13	0	13	0
2005–06	Fulham	5	0		
2006–07	Fulham	0	0	9	0
2006–07	Derby Co	38	0		
2007–08	Derby Co	26	0		
2008–09	Derby Co	11	0		
2009–10	Derby Co	17	0		
2010–11	Derby Co	25	1	117	1

MARTIN, David J (M) 112 10
H: 5 9 W: 10 10 b.Erith 3-6-85
Source: Dartford.

2006–07	Crystal Palace	5	0		
2007–08	Crystal Palace	9	0	14	0
2007–08	Millwall	11	2		
2008–09	Millwall	44	4		
2009–10	Millwall	20	3	75	9
2009–10	Derby Co	11	1		
2010–11	Derby Co	2	0	13	1
2010–11	Notts Co	10	0	10	0

MENDY, Arnaud (F) 14 1
H: 6 3 W: 13 10 b.Evreux 10-2-90
Source: Rouen. *Honours:* Guinea-Bissau 1 full cap.

2008–09	Derby Co	0	0		
2009–10	Derby Co	1	0		
2009–10	Grimsby T	1	0	1	0
2010–11	Derby Co	0	0	1	0
2010–11	Tranmere R	12	1	12	1

MILLS, Greg (F) 3 0
H: 6 2 W: 13 01 b.Derby 18-9-90
Source: Scholar.

2009–10	Derby Co	2	0		
2009–10	Macclesfield T	1	0	1	0
2010–11	Derby Co	0	0	2	0

MORCH, Mats (G) 0 0
b.Norway

2010–11	Derby Co	0	0		

O'BRIEN, Mark (D) 3 0
H: 5 11 W: 12 02 b.Dublin 20-11-92
Source: Cherry Orchard. *Honours:* Eire Youth

2008–09	Derby Co	1	0		
2009–10	Derby Co	0	0		
2010–11	Derby Co	2	0	3	0

PEARSON, Stephen (M) 252 21
H: 6 0 W: 11 01 b.Lanark 2-10-82
Honours: Scotland Under-21, B, 10 full caps.

2000–01	Motherwell	6	0		
2001–02	Motherwell	27	2		
2002–03	Motherwell	29	6		
2003–04	Motherwell	18	4	80	12
2003–04	Celtic	17	3		
2004–05	Celtic	8	0		
2005–06	Celtic	18	2		
2006–07	Celtic	13	1	56	6
2006–07	Derby Co	9	0		
2007–08	Derby Co	24	0		
2007–08	Stoke C	4	0	4	0
2008–09	Derby Co	12	1		
2009–10	Derby Co	37	1		
2010–11	Derby Co	30	1	112	3

PORTER, Chris (F) 240 78
H: 6 1 W: 12 09 b.Wigan 12-12-83
Source: School.

2002–03	Bury	2	0		
2003–04	Bury	37	9		
2004–05	Bury	32	9	71	18
2005–06	Oldham Ath	31	7		
2006–07	Oldham Ath	35	21	66	28
2007–08	Motherwell	37	14		
2008–09	Motherwell	22	9	59	23
2008–09	Derby Co	5	3		
2009–10	Derby Co	21	4		
2010–11	Derby Co	18	2	44	9

PRINGLE, Ben (M) 25 0
H: 5 8 W: 11 10 b.Whitley Bay 25-7-88
Source: WBA Scholar, Newcastle Blue Star, Morpeth T, Ilkeston T.

2009–10	Derby Co	5	0		
2010–11	Derby Co	15	0	20	0
2010–11	Torquay U	5	0	5	0

ROBERTS, Gareth (D) 463 21
H: 5 8 W: 11 12 b.Wrexham 6-2-78
Source: Trainee. *Honours:* Wales Under-21, B, 9 full caps.

1995–96	Liverpool	0	0		
1996–97	Liverpool	0	0		
1997–98	Liverpool	0	0		
1998–99	Liverpool	0	0		
1998–99	Panionios	15	0	15	0
1999–2000	Tranmere R	37	1		
2000–01	Tranmere R	34	0		
2001–02	Tranmere R	45	2		
2002–03	Tranmere R	37	4		
2003–04	Tranmere R	44	1		
2004–05	Tranmere R	40	3		
2005–06	Tranmere R	44	2	281	13
2006–07	Doncaster R	30	1		
2007–08	Doncaster R	37	3		
2008–09	Doncaster R	32	1		
2009–10	Doncaster R	42	3	141	8
2010–11	Derby Co	26	0	26	0

SAVAGE, Robbie (M) 537 37
H: 5 11 W: 11 00 b.Wrexham 18-10-74
Source: Trainee. *Honours:* Wales Schools, Youth, Under-21, 39 full caps, 2 goals.

1993–94	Manchester U	0	0		
1994–95	Crewe Alex	6	2		
1995–96	Crewe Alex	30	7		
1996–97	Crewe Alex	41	1	77	10
1997–98	Leicester C	35	2		
1998–99	Leicester C	34	1		
1999–2000	Leicester C	35	1		
2000–01	Leicester C	33	4		
2001–02	Leicester C	35	0	172	8
2002–03	Birmingham C	33	4		
2003–04	Birmingham C	31	3		
2004–05	Birmingham C	18	4	82	11
2004–05	Blackburn R	9	0		
2005–06	Blackburn R	34	1		
2006–07	Blackburn R	21	0		
2007–08	Blackburn R	12	0	76	1
2007–08	Derby Co	16	0		
2008–09	Derby Co	22	1		
2008–09	Brighton & HA	6	0	6	0
2009–10	Derby Co	46	2		
2010–11	Derby Co	40	4	124	7

SEVERN, James (G) 1 0
H: 6 4 W: 14 11 b.Nottingham 10-10-91
Source: Scholar.

2010–11	Derby Co	1	0	1	0

VARNEY, Luke (F) 237 54
H: 5 11 W: 11 00 b.Leicester 28-9-82
Source: Quorn.

2002–03	Crewe Alex	0	0		
2003–04	Crewe Alex	8	1		
2004–05	Crewe Alex	26	4		
2005–06	Crewe Alex	27	5		
2006–07	Crewe Alex	34	17	95	27
2007–08	Charlton Ath	39	8		
2008–09	Charlton Ath	18	2	57	10
2008–09	Sheffield W	4	2		
2008–09	Derby Co	10	1		
2009–10	Derby Co	1	0		
2009–10	Sheffield W	39	9	43	11
2010–11	Derby Co	1	0	12	1
2010–11	Blackpool	30	5	30	5

WARD, Jamie (M) 177 53
H: 5 5 W: 9 04 b.Birmingham 12-5-86
Source: Scholar. *Honours:* Northern Ireland Youth, Under-21.

2003–04	Aston Villa	0	0		
2004–05	Aston Villa	0	0		
2005–06	Aston Villa	0	0		
2005–06	Stockport Co	9	1	9	1
2006–07	Torquay U	25	9	25	9
2006–07	Chesterfield	9	3		
2007–08	Chesterfield	35	12		
2008–09	Chesterfield	23	14	67	29
2008–09	Sheffield U	16	2		
2009–10	Sheffield U	28	7		

2010–11	Sheffield U	19	0	**63**	**9**
2010–11	Derby Co	13	5	**13**	**5**

DONCASTER R (32)

BROOKER, Stephen (F)   **261**   **79**
H: 6 0   W: 14 00   b.Newport Pagnell 21-5-81
Source: Trainee.

1999–2000	Watford	1	0		
2000–01	Watford	0	0	**1**	**0**
2000–01	Port Vale	23	8		
2001–02	Port Vale	41	9		
2002–03	Port Vale	26	5		
2003–04	Port Vale	32	8		
2004–05	Port Vale	9	5	**131**	**35**
2004–05	Bristol C	33	16		
2005–06	Bristol C	37	16		
2006–07	Bristol C	23	2		
2007–08	Bristol C	4	1		
2007–08	Cheltenham T	14	5	**14**	**5**
2008–09	Bristol C	4	2	**101**	**37**
2008–09	Doncaster R	1	1		
2009–10	Doncaster R	0	0		
2010–11	Doncaster R	13	1	**14**	**2**

BURGE, Ryan (M)   **8**   **0**
H: 5 10   W: 10 03   b.Cheltenham 12-10-88
Source: Scholar.

2005–06	Birmingham C	0	0		
2006–07	Birmingham C	0	0		
2007–08	Birmingham C	0	0		
2008–09	Barnet	2	0	**2**	**0**
From Jerez Industrial.					
2010–11	Doncaster R	1	0	**1**	**0**
2010–11	Oxford U	5	0	**5**	**0**

CHAMBERS, James (D)   **281**   **0**
H: 5 10   W: 11 11   b.West Bromwich 20-11-80
Source: Trainee. *Honours:* England Youth.

1998–99	WBA	0	0		
1999–2000	WBA	12	0		
2000–01	WBA	31	0		
2001–02	WBA	5	0		
2002–03	WBA	8	0		
2003–04	WBA	17	0		
2004–05	WBA	0	0	**73**	**0**
2004–05	Watford	40	0		
2005–06	Watford	38	0		
2006–07	Watford	12	0	**90**	**0**
2006–07	Cardiff C	7	0	**7**	**0**
2007–08	Leicester C	24	0	**24**	**0**
2008–09	Doncaster R	37	0		
2009–10	Doncaster R	43	0		
2010–11	Doncaster R	7	0	**87**	**0**

COPPINGER, James (F)   **324**   **38**
H: 5 7   W: 10 03   b.Middlesbrough 10-1-81
Source: Darlington Trainee. *Honours:*
England Youth.

1997–98	Newcastle U	0	0		
1998–99	Newcastle U	0	0		
1999–2000	Newcastle U	0	0		
1999–2000	Hartlepool U	10	3		
2000–01	Newcastle U	1	0		
2001–02	Newcastle U	0	0	**1**	**0**
2001–02	Hartlepool U	14	2	**24**	**5**
2002–03	Exeter C	43	5		
2003–04	Exeter C	0	0	**43**	**5**
2004–05	Doncaster R	31	0		
2005–06	Doncaster R	36	5		
2006–07	Doncaster R	39	4		
2007–08	Doncaster R	39	3		
2008–09	Doncaster R	32	5		
2009–10	Doncaster R	39	4		
2010–11	Doncaster R	40	7	**256**	**28**

DUMBUYA, Mustapha (D)   **26**   **0**
H: 5 7   W: 11 00   b.Sierra Leone 7-8-87
Source: Potters Bar T.

2009–10	Doncaster R	3	0		
2010–11	Doncaster R	23	0	**26**	**0**

FAIRHURST, Waide (F)   **40**   **9**
H: 5 10   W: 10 07   b.Sheffield 7-5-89
Source: Scholar.

2008–09	Doncaster R	3	0		
2009–10	Doncaster R	6	2		
2009–10	Shrewsbury T	10	4	**10**	**4**
2010–11	Doncaster R	2	0	**11**	**2**
2010–11	Southend U	3	0	**3**	**0**
2010–11	Hereford U	16	3	**16**	**3**

FRIEND, George (D)   **72**   **3**
H: 6 2   W: 13 01   b.Barnstaple 19-10-87

2008–09	Exeter C	4	0		
2008–09	Wolverhampton W	6	0		
2009–10	Wolverhampton W	1	0	**7**	**0**
2009–10	Millwall	6	0	**6**	**0**
2009–10	Southend U	6	1	**6**	**1**
2009–10	Scunthorpe U	4	0	**4**	**0**
2009–10	Exeter C	13	1	**17**	**1**
2010–11	Doncaster R	32	1	**32**	**1**

GILLETT, Simon (M)   **108**   **3**
H: 5 6   W: 11 07   b.Oxford 6-11-85
Source: Trainee. *Honours:*

2003–04	Southampton	0	0		
2004–05	Southampton	0	0		
2005–06	Southampton	0	0		
2005–06	Walsall	2	0	**2**	**0**
2006–07	Southampton	0	0		
2006–07	Blackpool	31	1	**31**	**1**
2006–07	Bournemouth	7	1	**7**	**1**
2007–08	Southampton	2	0		
2007–08	Yeovil T	4	0	**4**	**0**
2008–09	Southampton	27	0		
2009–10	Southampton	2	0	**31**	**0**
2009–10	Doncaster R	11	0		
2010–11	Doncaster R	22	1	**33**	**1**

HAYTER, James (F)   **489**   **123**
H: 5 9   W: 10 13   b.Sandown 9-4-79
Source: Trainee.

1996–97	Bournemouth	2	0		
1997–98	Bournemouth	5	0		
1998–99	Bournemouth	20	2		
1999–2000	Bournemouth	31	2		
2000–01	Bournemouth	40	11		
2001–02	Bournemouth	44	7		
2002–03	Bournemouth	45	9		
2003–04	Bournemouth	44	14		
2004–05	Bournemouth	39	19		
2005–06	Bournemouth	46	20		
2006–07	Bournemouth	42	10	**358**	**94**
2007–08	Doncaster R	34	7		
2008–09	Doncaster R	27	4		
2009–10	Doncaster R	38	9		
2010–11	Doncaster R	32	9	**131**	**29**

HIRD, Samuel (D)   **131**   **1**
H: 5 7   W: 10 12   b.Askern 7-9-87
Source: Scholar.

2005–06	Leeds U	0	0		
2006–07	Leeds U	0	0		
2006–07	Doncaster R	5	0		
2007–08	Doncaster R	4	0		
2007–08	Grimsby T	17	0	**17**	**0**
2008–09	Doncaster R	37	1		
2009–10	Doncaster R	36	0		
2010–11	Doncaster R	32	0	**114**	**1**

KEEGAN, Paul (M)   **171**   **12**
H: 5 11   W: 11 05   b.Dublin 5-7-84
Source: Home Farm. *Honours:* Eire Youth,
Under-21.

2000–01	Leeds U	0	0		
2001–02	Leeds U	0	0		
2002–03	Leeds U	0	0		
2003–04	Leeds U	0	0		
2003–04	Scunthorpe U	2	0	**2**	**0**
2004–05	Leeds U	0	0		
2005	Drogheda	11	0		
2006	Drogheda	25	4		
2007	Drogheda	30	1		
2008	Drogheda	27	1	**93**	**6**
2009	Bohemians	34	2		
2010	Bohemians	32	4	**66**	**6**
2010–11	Doncaster R	10	0	**10**	**0**

LOCKWOOD, Adam (D)   **219**   **15**
H: 6 0   W: 12 07   b.Wakefield 26-10-81
Source: Reading Trainee.

2003–04	Yeovil T	43	4		
2004–05	Yeovil T	10	0		
2005–06	Yeovil T	20	0	**73**	**4**
2005–06	Torquay U	9	3	**9**	**3**
2006–07	Doncaster R	44	2		
2007–08	Doncaster R	39	3		
2008–09	Doncaster R	22	0		
2009–10	Doncaster R	16	2		
2010–11	Doncaster R	16	1	**137**	**8**

MARTIS, Shelton (D)   **192**   **7**
H: 6 0   W: 11 11   b.Willemstad 29-11-82
Honours: Netherlands Antilles 1 full cap.

2002–03	Excelsior	12	0		
2003–04	Excelsior	10	0	**22**	**0**
2004–05	Eindhoven	32	0	**32**	**0**
2005–06	Darlington	40	2		
2006–07	Darlington	2	0	**42**	**2**
2006–07	Hibernian	26	0	**26**	**0**
2007–08	WBA	2	0		
2007–08	Scunthorpe U	3	0	**3**	**0**
2008–09	WBA	7	0		
2008–09	Doncaster R	5	1		
2009–10	WBA	13	2	**22**	**2**
2009–10	Doncaster R	14	1		
2010–11	Doncaster R	26	1	**45**	**3**

O'CONNOR, James (D)   **242**   **5**
H: 5 10   W: 12 05   b.Birmingham 20-11-84
Source: Scholar.

2003–04	Aston Villa	0	0		
2004–05	Aston Villa	0	0		
2004–05	Port Vale	13	0	**13**	**0**
2004–05	Bournemouth	6	0		
2005–06	Bournemouth	39	1	**45**	**1**
2006–07	Doncaster R	40	1		
2007–08	Doncaster R	40	0		
2008–09	Doncaster R	32	1		
2009–10	Doncaster R	38	0		
2010–11	Doncaster R	34	2	**184**	**4**

OSTER, John (M)   **362**   **23**
H: 5 9   W: 10 08   b.Boston 8-12-78
Source: Trainee. *Honours:* Wales Youth,
Under-21, B, 13 full caps.

1996–97	Grimsby T	24	3		
1997–98	Everton	31	1		
1998–99	Everton	9	0	**40**	**1**
1999–2000	Sunderland	10	0		
2000–01	Sunderland	8	0		
2001–02	Sunderland	0	0		
2001–02	Barnsley	2	0	**2**	**0**
2002–03	Sunderland	3	0		
2002–03	Grimsby T	17	6	**41**	**9**
2003–04	Sunderland	38	5		
2004–05	Sunderland	9	0	**68**	**5**
2004–05	Leeds U	8	1	**8**	**1**
2004–05	Burnley	15	1	**15**	**1**
2005–06	Reading	33	1		
2006–07	Reading	25	1		
2007–08	Reading	18	0	**76**	**2**
2008–09	Crystal Palace	31	3	**31**	**3**
2009–10	Doncaster R	40	1		
2010–11	Doncaster R	41	0	**81**	**1**

SHARP, Billy (F)   **213**   **100**
H: 5 9   W: 11 00   b.Sheffield 5-2-86
Source: Scholar.

2004–05	Sheffield U	0	0		
2004–05	Rushden & D	16	9	**16**	**9**
2005–06	Sheffield U	0	0		
2005–06	Scunthorpe U	37	23		
2006–07	Scunthorpe U	45	30	**82**	**53**
2007–08	Sheffield U	29	4		
2008–09	Sheffield U	22	4		
2009–10	Sheffield U	0	0	**53**	**8**
2009–10	Doncaster R	33	15		
2010–11	Doncaster R	29	15	**62**	**30**

SHIELS, Dean (F)   **201**   **34**
H: 5 11   W: 9 10   b.Magherfelt 1-2-85
Source: Arsenal Scholar. *Honours:* Northern
Ireland Under-21, 9 full caps.

2002–03	Arsenal	0	0		
2003–04	Arsenal	0	0		
2004–05	Hibernian	37	5		
2005–06	Hibernian	16	2		
2006–07	Hibernian	24	7		
2007–08	Hibernian	22	7		
2008–09	Hibernian	19	3	**118**	**24**
2008–09	Doncaster R	12	1		
2009–10	Doncaster R	38	6		
2010–11	Doncaster R	33	3	**83**	**10**

SOUZA, Dennis (M)   **182**   **6**
H: 6 3   W: 13 05   b.Sao Paulo 9-1-80
Source: Matsubara, Roda JC.

2000–01	Harelbeke	0	0		
2002–03	RAEC Mons	25	1		
2003–04	KBHZ	31	0	**31**	**0**
2004–05	Standard	0	0		
2004–05	RAEC Mons	8	0		

2005–06	RAEC Mons	16	1	49	2
2006–07	Charleroi	16	2	16	2
2007–08	Barnsley	45	2		

From Al-Sailiya.

| 2008–09 | Barnsley | 33 | 0 | 78 | 2 |

From Al-Saliya.

| 2010–11 | Doncaster R | 8 | 0 | 8 | 0 |

STOCK, Brian (M) 317 33
H: 5 11 W: 11 02 b.Winchester 24-12-81
Source: Trainee. *Honours:* Wales Under-21, 3 full caps.

1999–2000	Bournemouth	5	0		
2000–01	Bournemouth	1	0		
2001–02	Bournemouth	26	2		
2002–03	Bournemouth	27	2		
2003–04	Bournemouth	19	3		
2004–05	Bournemouth	41	6		
2005–06	Bournemouth	26	3	145	16
2005–06	Preston NE	6	1		
2006–07	Preston NE	2	0	8	1
2006–07	Doncaster R	36	3		
2007–08	Doncaster R	40	5		
2008–09	Doncaster R	36	6		
2009–10	Doncaster R	15	0		
2010–11	Doncaster R	37	2	164	16

SULLIVAN, Neil (G) 529 0
H: 6 2 W: 12 00 b.Sutton 24-2-70
Source: Trainee. *Honours:* Scotland 28 full caps.

1988–89	Wimbledon	0	0		
1989–90	Wimbledon	0	0		
1990–91	Wimbledon	1	0		
1991–92	Wimbledon	1	0		
1991–92	*Crystal Palace*	1	0	1	0
1992–93	Wimbledon	1	0		
1993–94	Wimbledon	2	0		
1994–95	Wimbledon	11	0		
1995–96	Wimbledon	16	0		
1996–97	Wimbledon	36	0		
1997–98	Wimbledon	38	0		
1998–99	Wimbledon	38	0		
1999–2000	Wimbledon	37	0	181	0
2000–01	Tottenham H	35	0		
2001–02	Tottenham H	29	0		
2002–03	Tottenham H	0	0	64	0
2003–04	Chelsea	4	0	4	0
2004–05	Leeds U	46	0		
2005–06	Leeds U	42	0		
2006–07	Leeds U	7	0	95	0
2006–07	*Doncaster R*	16	0		
2007–08	*Doncaster R*	46	0		
2008–09	Doncaster R	46	0		
2009–10	Doncaster R	45	0		
2010–11	Doncaster R	31	0	184	0

THOMAS, Wayne (D) 428 13
H: 6 2 W: 14 12 b.Gloucester 17-5-79
Source: Trainee.

1995–96	Torquay U	6	0		
1996–97	Torquay U	12	0		
1997–98	Torquay U	21	1		
1998–99	Torquay U	44	1		
1999–2000	Torquay U	40	3	123	5
2000–01	Stoke C	34	0		
2001–02	Stoke C	40	2		
2002–03	Stoke C	41	0		
2003–04	Stoke C	39	3		
2004–05	Stoke C	35	2	189	7
2005–06	Burnley	16	1		
2006–07	Burnley	33	0		
2007–08	Burnley	1	0	50	1
2007–08	Southampton	30	0		
2008–09	Southampton	0	0		
2009–10	Southampton	15	0	45	0
2010–11	Doncaster R	21	0	21	0

WEBSTER, Byron (D) 45 4
H: 6 5 W: 12 07 b.Sherburn-in-Elmet 31-3-87
Source: York C, Harrogate T, Whitby T.

2007–08	Siad Most	23	4		
2008–09	Siad Most	0	0	23	4
2009–10	Doncaster R	5	0		
2010–11	Doncaster R	7	0	12	0
2010–11	*Hereford U*	2	0	2	0
2010–11	*Northampton T*	8	0	8	0

WILSON, Mark (M) 222 10
H: 5 10 W: 12 07 b.Scunthorpe 9-2-79
Source: Trainee. *Honours:* England Schools, Youth, Under-21.

1995–96	Manchester U	0	0		
1996–97	Manchester U	0	0		
1997–98	Manchester U	0	0		
1997–98	*Wrexham*	13	4	13	4
1998–99	Manchester U	0	0		
1999–2000	Manchester U	3	0		
2000–01	Manchester U	0	0	3	0
2001–02	Middlesbrough	10	0		
2002–03	Middlesbrough	6	0		
2002–03	*Stoke C*	4	0	4	0
2003–04	Middlesbrough	0	0		
2003–04	*Swansea C*	12	2	12	2
2003–04	*Sheffield W*	3	0	3	0
2004–05	Middlesbrough	0	0	16	0
2004–05	*Doncaster R*	3	0		
2004–05	*Livingston*	5	0	5	0
2005	Dallas	8	0		
2006	Dallas	12	1	20	1
2006–07	Doncaster R	22	1		
2007–08	Doncaster R	31	1		
2008–09	Doncaster R	22	1		
2008–09	*Tranmere R*	5	0	5	0
2009–10	Doncaster R	35	0		
2010–11	Doncaster R	28	0	141	3

WOODS, Gary (G) 17 0
H: 6 1 W: 11 00 b.Kettering 1-10-90
Source: Manchester U Scholar.

2008–09	Doncaster R	1	0		
2009–10	Doncaster R	0	0		
2010–11	Doncaster R	16	0	17	0

WOODS, Martin (M) 148 11
H: 5 11 W: 11 13 b.Airdrie 1-1-86
Source: Trainee. *Honours:* Scotland Youth, Under-21.

2002–03	Leeds U	0	0		
2003–04	Leeds U	0	0		
2004–05	Leeds U	1	0	1	0
2004–05	*Hartlepool U*	6	0	6	0
2005–06	Sunderland	7	0	7	0
2006–07	Rotherham U	36	4	36	4
2007–08	Doncaster R	15	0		
2007–08	*Yeovil T*	3	0	3	0
2008–09	Doncaster R	41	2		
2009–10	Doncaster R	24	4		
2010–11	Doncaster R	15	1	95	7

EVERTON (33)

AGARD, Kieran (F) 9 0
H: 5 10 W: 10 10 b.Newham 10-10-89
Source: Scholar.

2006–07	Everton	0	0		
2007–08	Everton	0	0		
2008–09	Everton	0	0		
2009–10	Everton	1	0		
2010–11	Everton	0	0	1	0
2010–11	*Kilmarnock*	8	0	8	0
2010–11	*Peterborough U*	0	0		

AKPAN, Hope (M) 2 0
H: 6 0 W: 10 08 b.Liverpool 14-8-91
Source: Scholar.

2007–08	Everton	0	0		
2008–09	Everton	0	0		
2009–10	Everton	0	0		
2010–11	Everton	0	0		
2010–11	*Hull C*	2	0	2	0

ANICHEBE, Victor (F) 92 7
H: 6 1 W: 13 00 b.Nigeria 23-4-88
Source: Scholar. *Honours:* Nigeria Under-23, 8 full caps, 1 goal.

2005–06	Everton	2	1		
2006–07	Everton	19	3		
2007–08	Everton	27	1		
2008–09	Everton	17	1		
2009–10	Everton	11	1		
2010–11	Everton	16	0	92	7

ARTETA, Mikel (M) 309 44
H: 5 9 W: 10 08 b.San Sebastian 26-3-82
Honours: Spain Youth, Under-21.

| 1999–2000 | Barcelona B | 26 | 1 | | |
| 2000–01 | Barcelona B | 16 | 2 | 42 | 3 |

2000–01	Paris St Germain	6	1		
2001–02	Paris St Germain	25	1	31	2
2002–03	Rangers	27	4		
2003–04	Rangers	23	8	50	12
2004–05	Real Sociedad	14	1	14	1
2004–05	Everton	12	1		
2005–06	Everton	29	1		
2006–07	Everton	35	9		
2007–08	Everton	28	1		
2008–09	Everton	26	5		
2009–10	Everton	13	6		
2010–11	Everton	29	3	172	26

BAINES, Leighton (D) 273 11
H: 5 8 W: 11 00 b.Liverpool 11-12-84
Source: Trainee. *Honours:* England Under-21, 5 full caps.

2002–03	Wigan Ath	6	0		
2003–04	Wigan Ath	26	0		
2004–05	Wigan Ath	41	1		
2005–06	Wigan Ath	37	0		
2006–07	Wigan Ath	35	3		
2007–08	Wigan Ath	0	0	145	4
2007–08	Everton	22	0		
2008–09	Everton	31	1		
2009–10	Everton	37	1		
2010–11	Everton	38	5	128	7

BARKLEY, Ross (M) 0 0
H: 6 2 W: 12 00 b.Liverpool 5-12-93
Source: Scholar.

| 2010–11 | Everton | 0 | 0 | | |

BAXTER, Jose (F) 6 0
H: 5 10 W: 11 07 b.Bootle 7-2-92
Source: Academy. *Honours:* England Youth.

2008–09	Everton	3	0		
2009–10	Everton	2	0		
2010–11	Everton	1	0	6	0

BECKFORD, Jermaine (F) 180 88
H: 6 2 W: 13 02 b.Ealing 9-12-83
Source: Wealdstone.

2005–06	Leeds U	5	0		
2006–07	Leeds U	5	0		
2006–07	*Carlisle U*	4	1	4	1
2006–07	*Scunthorpe U*	18	8	18	8
2007–08	Leeds U	40	20		
2008–09	Leeds U	34	26		
2009–10	Leeds U	42	25	126	71
2010–11	Everton	32	8	32	8

BIDWELL, Jake (D) 0 0
H: 6 0 W: 11 00 b.Southport 21-3-93
Source: Scholar. *Honours:* England Youth.

| 2009–10 | Everton | 0 | 0 | | |
| 2010–11 | Everton | 0 | 0 | | |

BILYALETDINOV, Diniyar (F) 199 39
H: 6 1 W: 11 11 b.Moscow 27-2-85
Honours: Russia 41 full caps, 5 goals.

2003	Lokomotiv Moscow	0	0		
2004	Lokomotiv Moscow	25	5		
2004	*Neftekhlmik*	0	0		
2005	Lokomotiv Moscow	29	8		
2006	Lokomotiv Moscow	29	3		
2007	Lokomotiv Moscow	28	3		
2008	Lokomotiv Moscow	26	9		
2009	Lokomotiv Moscow	13	3	150	31
2009–10	Everton	23	6		
2010–11	Everton	26	2	49	8

CAHILL, Tim (M) 408 106
H: 5 10 W: 10 12 b.Sydney 6-12-79
Source: Sydney U. *Honours:* Western Samoa Youth, Australia Under-23, 52 full caps, 23 goals.

1997–98	Millwall	1	0		
1998–99	Millwall	36	6		
1999–2000	Millwall	45	12		
2000–01	Millwall	41	9		
2001–02	Millwall	43	13		
2002–03	Millwall	11	3		
2003–04	Millwall	40	9	217	52
2004–05	Everton	33	11		
2005–06	Everton	32	6		
2006–07	Everton	18	5		
2007–08	Everton	18	7		
2008–09	Everton	30	8		
2009–10	Everton	33	8		
2010–11	Everton	27	9	191	54

COLEMAN, Seamus (D)   **46 5**
H: 6 4   W: 10 07   b.Donegal 11-10-88
Source: Sligo R. *Honours:* Eire Under-21, Under-23, 4 full caps.

Season	Club				
2008–09	Everton	0	0		
2009–10	Everton	3	0		
2009–10	*Blackpool*	9	1	**9**	**1**
2010–11	Everton	34	4	**37**	**4**

CRAIG, Nathan (M)   **0 0**
H: 6 0   W: 11 06   b.Bangor 25-10-91
Source: Scholar. *Honours:* Wales Under-21.

Season	Club		
2008–09	Everton	0	0
2009–10	Everton	0	0
2010–11	Everton	0	0

DAVIES, Adam (G)   **0 0**
b.Rinteln 17-7-92
Source: Scholar.

Season	Club		
2009–10	Everton	0	0
2010–11	Everton	0	0

DISTIN, Sylvain (D)   **437 11**
H: 6 3   W: 14 06   b.Bagnolet 16-12-77

Season	Club				
1998–99	Tours	26	3	**26**	**3**
1999–2000	Gueugnon	33	1	**33**	**1**
2000–01	Paris St Germain	28	0	**28**	**0**
2001–02	Newcastle U	28	0	**28**	**0**
2002–03	Manchester C	34	0		
2003–04	Manchester C	38	2		
2004–05	Manchester C	38	1		
2005–06	Manchester C	31	0		
2006–07	Manchester C	37	2	**178**	**5**
2007–08	Portsmouth	36	0		
2008–09	Portsmouth	38	0		
2009–10	Portsmouth	3	0	**77**	**0**
2009–10	Everton	29	0		
2010–11	Everton	38	2	**67**	**2**

DUFFY, Shane (D)   **1 0**
H: 6 4   W: 12 00   b.Derry 1-1-92
Source: Scholar. *Honours:* Northern Ireland Under-21, Eire Under-21.

Season	Club				
2008–09	Everton	0	0		
2009–10	Everton	0	0		
2010–11	Everton	0	0		
2010–11	*Burnley*	1	0	**1**	**0**

FELLAINI, Marouane (M)   **135 17**
H: 6 4   W: 13 05   b.Brussels 22-11-87
Honours: Belgium 26 full caps, 4 goals.

Season	Club				
2006–07	Standard Liege	29	0		
2007–08	Standard Liege	30	6		
2008–09	Standard Liege	3	0	**62**	**6**
2008–09	Everton	30	8		
2009–10	Everton	23	2		
2010–11	Everton	20	1	**73**	**11**

FORRESTER, Anton (F)   **0 0**
b.Liverpool 11-2-94

Season	Club		
2010–11	Everton	0	0

FORSHAW, Adam (M)   **1 0**
H: 6 1   W: 11 02   b.Liverpool 8-10-91
Source: Scholar.

Season	Club				
2009–10	Everton	0	0		
2010–11	Everton	1	0	**1**	**0**

GARBUTT, Luke (D)   **0 0**
H: 5 10   W: 11 07   b.Harrogate 21-5-93
Source: Scholar.

Season	Club		
2010–11	Everton	0	0

GUEYE, Magaye (F)   **32 9**
H: 5 10   W: 11 07   b.Nogent-sur-Marne 6-7-90
Honours: France Youth, Under-21.

Season	Club				
2008–09	Strasbourg	3	0		
2009–10	Strasbourg	24	9	**27**	**9**
2010–11	Everton	5	0	**5**	**0**

HAMMAR, Johan (D)   **0 0**
b.Malmo 22-2-94
Source: Malmo.

Season	Club		
2010–11	Everton	0	0

HEITINGA, Johnny (D)   **237 9**
H: 5 11   W: 11 05   b.Alphen aan den Rijn 15-11-83
Honours: Holland 70 full caps, 6 goals.

Season	Club			
2000–01	Ajax	0	0	
2001–02	Ajax	15	0	
2002–03	Ajax	1	0	
2003–04	Ajax	26	3	
2004–05	Ajax	26	1	
2005–06	Ajax	19	1	
2006–07	Ajax	32	0	
2007–08	Ajax	33	0	**152 5**
2008–09	Atletico Madrid	27	3	**27 3**
2009–10	Everton	31	0	
2010–11	Everton	27	1	**58 1**

HIBBERT, Tony (D)   **221 0**
H: 5 9   W: 11 05   b.Liverpool 20-2-81
Source: Trainee.

Season	Club			
1998–99	Everton	0	0	
1999–2000	Everton	0	0	
2000–01	Everton	3	0	
2001–02	Everton	10	0	
2002–03	Everton	24	0	
2003–04	Everton	25	0	
2004–05	Everton	36	0	
2005–06	Everton	29	0	
2006–07	Everton	13	0	
2007–08	Everton	24	0	
2008–09	Everton	17	0	
2009–10	Everton	20	0	
2010–11	Everton	20	0	**221 0**

HOPE, Hallam (F)   **0 0**
b.Manchester 17-3-94
Source: Scholar.

Season	Club		
2010–11	Everton	0	0

HOWARD, Tim (G)   **316 0**
H: 6 3   W: 14 12   b.North Brunswick 6-3-79
Honours: USA Under-21, Under-23, 61 full caps.

Season	Club			
1998	NY/NJ MetrStars	1	0	
1999	NY/NJ MetrStars	9	0	
2000	NY/NJ MetrStars	9	0	
2001	NY/NJ MetrStars	26	0	
2002	NY/NJ MetrStars	27	0	
2003	NY/NJ MetrStars	13	0	**85 0**
2003–04	Manchester U	32	0	
2004–05	Manchester U	12	0	
2005–06	Manchester U	1	0	
2006–07	Manchester U	0	0	**45 0**
2006–07	Everton	36	0	
2007–08	Everton	36	0	
2008–09	Everton	38	0	
2009–10	Everton	38	0	
2010–11	Everton	38	0	**186 0**

JAGIELKA, Phil (D)   **367 20**
H: 6 0   W: 13 01   b.Manchester 17-8-82
Source: Scholar. *Honours:* England Youth, Under-20, Under-21, B, 9 full caps.

Season	Club			
1999–2000	Sheffield U	1	0	
2000–01	Sheffield U	15	0	
2001–02	Sheffield U	23	3	
2002–03	Sheffield U	42	0	
2003–04	Sheffield U	43	3	
2004–05	Sheffield U	46	0	
2005–06	Sheffield U	46	8	
2006–07	Sheffield U	38	4	**254 18**
2007–08	Everton	34	1	
2008–09	Everton	34	0	
2009–10	Everton	12	0	
2010–11	Everton	33	1	**113 2**

KINSELLA, Gerard (M)   **0 0**
b.Liverpool 13-11-91
Source: Scholar.

Season	Club		
2008–09	Everton	0	0
2009–10	Everton	0	0
2010–11	Everton	0	0

McALENY, Conor (F)   **0 0**
b.Liverpool 12-8-92
Source: Scholar.

Season	Club		
2009–10	Everton	0	0
2010–11	Everton	0	0

McARDLE, Lee (M)   **0 0**
Source: Scholar.

Season	Club		
2008–09	Everton	0	0
2009–10	Everton	0	0
2010–11	Everton	0	0

MUCHA, Jan (G)   **127 0**
H: 6 2   W: 12 00   b.Bela nad Cirochou 5-12-82
Honours: Slovakia 27 full caps.

Season	Club			
2002–03	Zilina	8	0	
2003–04	Zilina	12	0	
2004–05	Zilina	12	0	**32 0**
2005–06	Legia	0	0	
2006–07	Legia	7	0	
2007–08	Legia	29	0	
2008–09	Legia	29	0	
2009–10	Legia	30	0	**95 0**
2010–11	Everton	0	0	

MUSTAFI, Shkodran (D)   **0 0**
H: 6 0   W: 11 07   b.Bad Hersfeld 17-4-92
Source: Hamburg.

Season	Club		
2009–10	Everton	0	0
2010–11	Everton	0	0

NEVILLE, Phil (M)   **460 9**
H: 5 11   W: 12 00   b.Bury 21-1-77
Source: Trainee. *Honours:* England Schools, Youth, B, Under-21, 59 full caps.

Season	Club			
1994–95	Manchester U	2	0	
1995–96	Manchester U	24	0	
1996–97	Manchester U	18	0	
1997–98	Manchester U	30	1	
1998–99	Manchester U	28	0	
1999–2000	Manchester U	29	0	
2000–01	Manchester U	29	1	
2001–02	Manchester U	28	2	
2002–03	Manchester U	25	1	
2003–04	Manchester U	31	0	
2004–05	Manchester U	19	0	**263 5**
2005–06	Everton	34	0	
2006–07	Everton	35	1	
2007–08	Everton	37	2	
2008–09	Everton	37	0	
2009–10	Everton	23	0	
2010–11	Everton	31	1	**197 4**

NSIALA, Aristote (D)   **10 0**
H: 6 4   W: 14 09   b.DR Congo 25-3-92
Source: Scholar.

Season	Club				
2009–10	Everton	0	0		
2010–11	Everton	0	0		
2010–11	*Macclesfield T*	10	0	**10**	**0**

ORENUGA, Femi (M)   **0 0**
b.Lewisham 18-3-93
Source: Southend U.

Season	Club		
2009–10	Everton	0	0
2010–11	Everton	0	0

OSMAN, Leon (F)   **247 33**
H: 5 8   W: 10 09   b.Billinge 17-5-81
Source: Trainee. *Honours:* England Schools, Youth.

Season	Club				
1998–99	Everton	0	0		
1999–2000	Everton	0	0		
2000–01	Everton	0	0		
2001–02	Everton	0	0		
2002–03	Everton	2	0		
2002–03	*Carlisle U*	12	1	**12**	**1**
2003–04	Everton	4	1		
2003–04	*Derby Co*	17	3	**17**	**3**
2004–05	Everton	29	6		
2005–06	Everton	35	3		
2006–07	Everton	34	3		
2007–08	Everton	28	4		
2008–09	Everton	34	6		
2009–10	Everton	26	2		
2010–11	Everton	26	4	**218**	**29**

ROBERTS, Connor (G)   **0 0**
b.Wrexham 8-12-92
Source: Scholar. *Honours:* Wales Youth.

Season	Club		
2009–10	Everton	0	0
2010–11	Everton	0	0

RODWELL, Jack (D)   **71 2**
H: 6 2   W: 12 08   b.Southport 11-3-91
Source: Scholar. *Honours:* England Youth, Under-21.

Season	Club				
2007–08	Everton	2	0		
2008–09	Everton	19	0		
2009–10	Everton	26	2		
2010–11	Everton	24	0	**71**	**2**

SAHA, Louis (F)   **340 113**
H: 6 1   W: 12 08   b.Paris 8-8-78
Honours: France Youth, Under-21, 19 full caps, 4 goals.

Season	Club				
1997–98	Metz	21	1		
1998–99	Metz	3	0		
1998–99	Newcastle U	11	1	**11**	**1**
1999–2000	Metz	23	4	**47**	**5**
2000–01	Fulham	43	27		
2001–02	Fulham	36	8		
2002–03	Fulham	17	5		
2003–04	Fulham	21	13	**117**	**53**
2003–04	Manchester U	12	7		

2004–05	Manchester U	14	1		
2005–06	Manchester U	19	7		
2006–07	Manchester U	24	8		
2007–08	Manchester U	17	5		
2008–09	Manchester U	0	0	86	28
2008–09	Everton	24	6		
2009–10	Everton	33	13		
2010–11	Everton	22	7	79	26

SILVA, Joao (F)   **42 17**
H: 6 2   W: 12 08   b.Vila das Aves 21-5-90
Honours: Portugal Youth, Under-21.

2009–10	Aves	30	13	30	13
2010–11	Everton	0	0		
2010–11	*Leiria*	12	4	12	4

TURNER, Iain (G)   **67 0**
H: 6 3   W: 12 10   b.Stirling 26-1-84
Source: Riverside BC. *Honours:* Scotland Youth, Under-21, B.

2002–03	Stirling A	14	0	14	0
2002–03	Everton	0	0		
2003–04	Everton	0	0		
2004–05	Everton	0	0		
2004–05	Doncaster R	8	0	8	0
2005–06	Everton	3	0		
2005–06	Wycombe W	3	0	3	0
2006–07	Everton	1	0		
2006–07	Crystal Palace	5	0	5	0
2006–07	Sheffield W	11	0	11	0
2007–08	Everton	0	0		
2008–09	Everton	0	0		
2008–09	Nottingham F	3	0	3	0
2009–10	Everton	0	0		
2010–11	Everton	0	0	4	0
2010–11	Coventry C	2	0	2	0
2010–11	Preston NE	17	0	17	0

VAUGHAN, James (F)   **79 16**
H: 5 11   W: 13 00   b.Birmingham 14-7-88
Source: Scholar. *Honours:* England Youth, Under-21.

2004–05	Everton	2	1		
2005–06	Everton	1	0		
2006–07	Everton	14	4		
2007–08	Everton	8	1		
2008–09	Everton	13	0		
2009–10	Everton	8	1		
2009–10	Derby Co	2	0	2	0
2010–11	Everton	1	0	47	7
2010–11	Crystal Palace	30	9	30	9

VELLIOS, Apostolos (F)   **25 4**
H: 6 3   W: 12 06   b.Salonika 8-1-92
Honours: Greece Youth.

2008–09	Iraklis	1	0		
2009–10	Iraklis	9	2		
2010–11	Iraklis	12	2	22	4
2010–11	Everton	3	0	3	0

WALLACE, James (M)   **14 1**
H: 5 11   W: 12 08   b.Fazackerly 19-12-91
Source: Scholar. *Honours:* England Youth.

2008–09	Everton	0	0		
2009–10	Everton	0	0		
2010–11	Everton	0	0		
2010–11	Stockport Co	14	1	14	1
2010–11	*Bury*	0	0		

YAKUBU, Ayegbeni (F)   **315 118**
H: 6 0   W: 14 07   b.Benin City 22-11-82
Source: Julius Berger. *Honours:* Nigeria Under-21, Under-23, 54 full caps, 21 goals.

1999–2000	Gil Vicente	0	0		
1999–2000	Hapoel Kfar-Sava	23	6	23	6
2000–01	Maccabi Haifa	14	3		
2001–02	Maccabi Haifa	22	13	36	16
2002–03	Portsmouth	14	7		
2003–04	Portsmouth	37	16		
2004–05	Portsmouth	32	12	81	35
2005–06	Middlesbrough	34	13		
2006–07	Middlesbrough	37	12		
2007–08	Middlesbrough	2	0	73	25
2007–08	Everton	29	15		
2008–09	Everton	14	4		
2009–10	Everton	25	5		
2010–11	Everton	14	1	82	25
2010–11	*Leicester C*	20	11	20	11

YOBO, Joseph (D)   **321 11**
H: 6 1   W: 13 00   b.Kano 6-9-80
Source: Mechelen. *Honours:* Nigeria B, 70 full caps, 4 goals.

1998–99	Standard Liege	0	0		
1999–2000	Standard Liege	18	0		
2000–01	Standard Liege	30	2	48	2
2001–02	Marseille	23	0	23	0
2002–03	Everton	24	0		
2003–04	Everton	28	2		
2004–05	Everton	27	0		
2005–06	Everton	29	1		
2006–07	Everton	38	2		
2007–08	Everton	30	1		
2008–09	Everton	27	1		
2009–10	Everton	17	1		
2010–11	Everton	0	0	220	8
2010–11	*Fenerbahce*	30	1	30	1

Scholars
Barrow Jordan Joseph; Browning Tyias; Donegan Thomas David; Fitzgibbon James Thomas; Harris Matthew Bret Stephen; Heneghan Benjamin John; Higgins Ryan Leslie; Lundstram John David; Thomas Adam Christopher

EXETER C (34)

ARCHIBALD-HENVILLE, Troy (D) 70   1
H: 6 2   W: 13 03   b.Newham 4-11-88
Source: Scholar.

2007–08	Tottenham H	0	0		
2008–09	Tottenham H	0	0		
2008–09	Norwich C	0	0		
2008–09	*Exeter C*	19	0		
2009–10	Tottenham H	0	0		
2009–10	Exeter C	15	0		
2010–11	Exeter C	36	1	70	1

BENNETT, Scott (D)   **1 0**
H: 5 10   W: 12 10   b.Truro 30-11-90
Source: Scholar.

2008–09	Exeter C	0	0		
2009–10	Exeter C	0	0		
2010–11	Exeter C	1	0	1	0

COZIC, Bertrand (M)   **96 3**
H: 5 10   W: 12 06   b.Quimper 18-5-78
Source: Team Bath.

2003–04	Cheltenham T	7	1	7	1
From Hereford U					
2004–05	Northampton T	14	0	14	0
2004–05	Kidderminster H	15	0	15	0
From Aldershot T.					
2008–09	Exeter C	20	0		
2009–10	Exeter C	29	2		
2010–11	Exeter C	11	0	60	2

CURETON, Jamie (F)   **571 203**
H: 5 8   W: 10 07   b.Bristol 28-8-75
Source: Trainee. *Honours:* England Youth.

1992–93	Norwich C	0	0		
1993–94	Norwich C	0	0		
1994–95	Norwich C	17	4		
1995–96	Norwich C	12	2		
1995–96	*Bournemouth*	5	0	5	0
1996–97	Norwich C	0	0		
1996–97	*Bristol R*	38	11		
1997–98	Bristol R	43	13		
1998–99	Bristol R	46	25		
1999–2000	Bristol R	46	22		
2000–01	Bristol R	1	1	174	72
2000–01	Reading	43	26		
2001–02	Reading	38	15		
2002–03	Reading	27	9	108	50
From Busan Icons.					
2003–04	QPR	13	2		
2004–05	QPR	30	4	43	6
2005–06	Swindon T	30	7	30	7
2005–06	*Colchester U*	8	4		
2006–07	Colchester U	44	23	52	27
2007–08	Norwich C	41	12		
2008–09	Norwich C	22	2		
2008–09	*Barnsley*	8	2	8	2
2009–10	Norwich C	6	2	98	22
2009–10	*Shrewsbury T*	12	0	12	0
2010–11	Exeter C	41	17	41	17

DAWSON, Aaron (M)   **0 0**
H: 5 10   W: 10 10   b. 24-3-92
Source: Scholar.

2010–11	Exeter C	0	0		

DUFFY, Richard (D)   **194 5**
H: 5 9   W: 10 03   b.Swansea 30-8-85
Source: Scholar. *Honours:* Wales Youth, Under-21, 13 full caps.

2002–03	Swansea C	0	0		
2003–04	Swansea C	18	1		
2003–04	Portsmouth	1	0		
2004–05	Portsmouth	0	0		
2004–05	*Burnley*	7	1	7	1
2004–05	*Coventry C*	14	0		
2005–06	Portsmouth	0	0		
2005–06	*Coventry C*	32	0		
2006–07	Portsmouth	0	0		
2006–07	*Coventry C*	13	0		
2006–07	*Swansea C*	11	0	29	1
2007–08	Portsmouth	0	0		
2007–08	*Coventry C*	2	0	61	0
2008–09	Portsmouth	0	0	1	0
2008–09	Millwall	12	0	12	0
2009–10	Exeter C	42	1		
2010–11	Exeter C	42	2	84	3

DUNNE, James (M)   **65 4**
H: 5 11   W: 10 12   b.Bromley 18-9-89
Source: Scholar.

2007–08	Arsenal	0	0		
2008–09	Arsenal	0	0		
2008–09	*Nottingham F*	0	0		
2009–10	Exeter C	23	3		
2010–11	Exeter C	42	1	65	4

EDWARDS, Rob (D)   **565 15**
H: 6 0   W: 12 02   b.Kendal 1-4-73
Source: Trainee. *Honours:* Wales Youth, Under-21, B, 4 full caps.

1989–90	Carlisle U	12	0		
1990–91	Carlisle U	36	5	48	5
1990–91	Bristol C	12	0		
1991–92	Bristol C	20	1		
1992–93	Bristol C	18	0		
1993–94	Bristol C	38	2		
1994–95	Bristol C	30	0		
1995–96	Bristol C	19	0		
1996–97	Bristol C	31	0		
1997–98	Bristol C	37	2		
1998–99	Bristol C	23	0	216	5
1999–2000	Preston NE	41	2		
2000–01	Preston NE	42	0		
2001–02	Preston NE	36	2		
2002–03	Preston NE	26	0		
2003–04	Preston NE	24	0	169	4
2004–05	Blackpool	26	1		
2005–06	Blackpool	32	0	58	1
2008–09	Exeter C	44	0		
2009–10	Exeter C	21	0		
2010–11	Exeter C	9	0	74	0

FREAR, Elliott (F)   **0 0**
H: 5 8   W: 10 01   b.Exeter 11-9-90
Source: Scholar.

2009–10	Exeter C	0	0		
2010–11	Exeter C	0	0		

FURZER, Jack (D)   **0 0**
H: 5 11   W: 12 02   b.Exeter 17-2-92
Source: Scholar.

2010–11	Exeter C	0	0		

GOLBOURNE, Scott (M)   **141 3**
H: 5 8   W: 11 08   b.Bristol 29-2-88
Source: Scholar. *Honours:* England Youth.

2004–05	Bristol C	9	0		
2005–06	Bristol C	5	0	14	0
2005–06	Reading	1	0		
2006–07	Reading	0	0		
2006–07	*Wycombe W*	34	1	34	1
2007–08	Reading	1	0		
2007–08	*Bournemouth*	5	0	5	0
2008–09	Reading	0	0	2	0
2008–09	*Oldham Ath*	8	0	8	0
2009–10	Exeter C	34	0		
2010–11	Exeter C	44	2	78	2

HEATH, Joe (D)   **40 0**
H: 5 11   W: 11 11   b.Birkenhead 4-10-88
Source: Scholar.

2005–06	Nottingham F	0	0		
2006–07	Nottingham F	0	0		
2007–08	Nottingham F	0	0		

2008–09 Nottingham F 10 0
2009–10 Nottingham F 0 0 10 0
2009–10 Lincoln C 4 0 4 0
2010–11 Exeter C 0 0
2010–11 *Hereford U* 26 0 26 0

JONES, Billy (D) 184 8
H: 6 1 W: 11 05 b.Chatham 26-3-83
Source: Trainee.
2000–01 Leyton Orient 1 0
2001–02 Leyton Orient 16 0
2002–03 Leyton Orient 24 0
2003–04 Leyton Orient 31 0
2004–05 Leyton Orient 0 0 72 0
2004–05 Kidderminster H 12 0
2005–06 Kidderminster H 0 0
2006–07 Kidderminster H 0 0 12 0
2007–08 Crewe Alex 22 0
2008–09 Crewe Alex 38 6
2009–10 Crewe Alex 11 2 71 8
2010–11 Exeter C 29 0 29 0

JONES, Paul (G) 91 0
H: 6 3 W: 13 00 b.Maidstone 28-6-86
Source: Leyton Orient Scholar.
2008–09 Exeter C 46 0
2009–10 Exeter C 26 0
2010–11 Exeter C 18 0 90 0
2010–11 Peterborough U 1 0 1 0

KEATS, Noah (M) 0 0
H: 5 9 W: 11 05 b.Weymouth 17-2-92
Source: Scholar.
2010–11 Exeter C 0 0

KRYSIAK, Artur (G) 55 0
H: 6 1 W: 12 00 b.Lodz 11-8-89
Source: LKS Lodz. Honours: Poland Youth.
2006–07 Birmingham C 0 0
2007–08 *Gretna* 4 0 4 0
2007–08 Birmingham C 0 0
2008–09 Birmingham C 0 0
2008–09 *Motherwell* 1 0 1 0
2008–09 *Swansea C* 2 0 2 0
2009–10 Birmingham C 0 0
2009–10 *Burton Alb* 38 0 38 0
2010–11 Exeter C 10 0 10 0

LOGAN, Richard (F) 259 52
H: 6 1 W: 12 05 b.Bury St Edmunds 4-1-82
Source: Trainee. Honours: England Youth.
1998–99 Ipswich T 2 0
1999–2000 Ipswich T 1 0
2000–01 Ipswich T 0 0
2000–01 *Cambridge U* 5 1 5 1
2001–02 Ipswich T 0 0
2001–02 *Torquay U* 16 4 16 4
2002–03 Ipswich T 0 0 3 0
2002–03 Boston U 27 10
2003–04 Boston U 8 0 35 10
2003–04 Peterborough U 29 7
2004–05 Peterborough U 26 4
2004–05 *Shrewsbury T* 5 1 5 1
2005–06 Peterborough U 28 4 83 15
2005–06 *Lincoln C* 8 2 8 2
From Weymouth.
2008–09 Exeter C 30 4
2009–10 Exeter C 34 4
2010–11 Exeter C 40 11 104 19

NARDIELLO, Daniel (F) 188 47
H: 5 11 W: 11 04 b.Coventry 22-10-82
Source: Trainee. Honours: Wales 3 full caps.
1999–2000 Manchester U 0 0
2000–01 Manchester U 0 0
2001–02 Manchester U 0 0
2002–03 Manchester U 0 0
2003–04 Manchester U 0 0
2003–04 *Swansea C* 4 0 4 0
2003–04 Barnsley 16 7
2004–05 Manchester U 0 0
2004–05 *Barnsley* 28 7
2005–06 Barnsley 34 5
2006–07 Barnsley 30 9
2007–08 QPR 8 0 8 0
2007–08 *Barnsley* 11 2 119 30
2008–09 Blackpool 2 0
2008–09 *Hartlepool U* 12 3 12 3
2009–10 Blackpool 5 0 7 0
2009–10 *Bury* 6 4 6 4
2009–10 *Oldham Ath* 2 0 2 0
2010–11 Exeter C 30 10 30 10

NICHOLS, Tom (F) 1 0
b. 1-9-93
Source: Scholar.
2010–11 Exeter C 1 0 1 0

NOBLE, David (M) 198 13
H: 6 0 W: 12 04 b.Hitchin 2-2-82
Source: Scholar. Honours: England Youth, Under-20. Scotland Under-21, B.
2000–01 Arsenal 0 0
2001–02 Arsenal 0 0
2001–02 *Watford* 15 1 15 1
2002–03 Arsenal 0 0
2002–03 West Ham U 0 0
2003–04 West Ham U 3 0 3 0
2003–04 Boston U 14 2
2004–05 Boston U 32 3
2005–06 Boston U 11 0 57 5
2005–06 Bristol C 24 1
2006–07 Bristol C 26 3
2007–08 Bristol C 26 2
2008–09 Bristol C 9 1 85 7
2008–09 *Yeovil T* 2 0 2 0
2009–10 Exeter C 0 0
2010–11 Exeter C 36 0 36 0

NORWOOD, James (F) 4 0
H: 5 9 W: 11 07 b.Eastbourne 5-9-90
Source: Eastbourne T. Honours: England Schools.
2009–10 Exeter C 3 0
2010–11 Exeter C 1 0 4 0

O'FLYNN, John (F) 259 103
H: 5 11 W: 11 11 b.Cobh 11-7-82
Source: Scholar, Cork C. Honours: Eire Under-21.
2001–02 Peterborough U 0 0
2002–03 Cork C 27 15
2003 Cork C 23 15
2004 Cork C 28 12
2005 Cork C 21 11
2006 Cork C 15 6
2007 Cork C 25 5
2008 Cork C 19 4 158 68
2008–09 Barnet 34 17
2009–10 Barnet 36 12 70 29
2010–11 Exeter C 31 6 31 6

SAUNDERS, Neil (M) 23 3
H: 5 11 W: 11 02 b.Dagenham 7-5-83
Source: Watford Scholar, Harlow T.
2001–02 Watford 0 0
2002–03 Watford 0 0
From Barnet, Team Bath.
2008–09 Exeter C 17 3
2009–10 Exeter C 6 0
2010–11 Exeter C 0 0 23 3

SERCOMBE, Liam (M) 99 6
H: 5 10 W: 10 10 b.Exeter 25-4-90
Source: Scholar.
2008–09 Exeter C 29 2
2009–10 Exeter C 28 1
2010–11 Exeter C 42 3 99 6

SHEPHARD, Chris (M) 2 0
H: 6 3 W: 13 03 b.Exeter 25-12-88
Source: Scholar.
2008–09 Exeter C 2 0
2009–10 Exeter C 0 0
2010–11 Exeter C 0 0 2 0

STEWART, Marcus (F) 664 199
H: 5 10 W: 10 10 b.Bristol 7-11-72
Source: Trainee. Honours: England Schools, Football League.
1991–92 Bristol R 33 5
1992–93 Bristol R 38 11
1993–94 Bristol R 29 5
1994–95 Bristol R 27 15
1995–96 Bristol R 44 21 171 57
1996–97 Huddersfield T 20 7
1997–98 Huddersfield T 40 16
1998–99 Huddersfield T 43 22
1999–2000 Huddersfield T 29 14 133 58
1999–2000 Ipswich T 10 2
2000–01 Ipswich T 34 19
2001–02 Ipswich T 28 6
2002–03 Ipswich T 3 0 75 27
2002–03 Sunderland 19 1
2003–04 Sunderland 40 14
2004–05 Sunderland 43 16 102 31

2005–06 Bristol C 27 5
2005–06 *Preston NE* 4 0 4 0
2006–07 Bristol C 0 0 27 5
2006–07 Yeovil T 31 8
2007–08 Yeovil T 36 4 67 12
2008–09 Exeter C 36 7
2009–10 Exeter C 41 2
2010–11 Exeter C 8 0 85 9

TAYLOR, Matthew (D) 105 9
H: 6 0 W: 12 04 b.Chorley 30-1-82
Source: Burscough, Rossendale U, Matlock T, Hucknall T, Guiseley, Team Bath.
2008–09 Exeter C 31 2
2009–10 Exeter C 46 5
2010–11 Exeter C 28 2 105 9

THOMSON, Jake (M) 56 3
H: 5 11 W: 11 05 b.Southsea 12-5-89
Source: Scholar.
2006–07 Southampton 0 0
2007–08 Southampton 0 0
2008–09 Southampton 10 0
2008–09 *Bournemouth* 6 1 6 1
2009–10 Southampton 4 0 14 0
2009–10 *Torquay U* 15 1 15 1
2010–11 Exeter C 16 0 16 0
2010–11 *Cheltenham T* 5 1 5 1

TISDALE, Paul (M) 1 0
H: 5 9 W: 11 13 b.Valletta 14-1-73
Source: out of retirement.
2010–11 Exeter C 1 0 1 0

TULLY, Steve (D) 223 5
H: 5 8 W: 11 02 b.Paignton 10-2-80
Source: Trainee.
1997–98 Torquay U 9 0
1998–99 Torquay U 37 2
1999–2000 Torquay U 13 0
2000–01 Torquay U 29 1
2001–02 Torquay U 18 0 106 3
From Weymouth.
2008–09 Exeter C 36 0
2009–10 Exeter C 38 1
2010–11 Exeter C 43 1 117 2

WATSON, Ben (F) 13 2
H: 5 10 W: 10 11 b.Shoreham 6-12-85
Source: Bognor Regis T, Grays Ath.
2008–09 Exeter C 12 2
2009–10 Exeter C 1 0
2010–11 Exeter C 0 0 13 2

WESTERN, Dan (M) 0 0
H: 5 8 W: 11 07 b.Exeter 14-12-91
Source: Scholar.
2010–11 Exeter C 0 0

FULHAM (35)

BAIRD, Chris (D) 175 5
H: 5 10 W: 11 11 b.Ballymoney 25-2-82
Source: Scholar. Honours: Northern Ireland Youth, Under-21, 51 full caps.
2000–01 Southampton 0 0
2001–02 Southampton 0 0
2002–03 Southampton 3 0
2003–04 Southampton 4 0
2003–04 *Walsall* 10 0 10 0
2003–04 *Watford* 8 0 8 0
2004–05 Southampton 0 0
2005–06 Southampton 17 0
2006–07 Southampton 44 3 68 3
2007–08 Fulham 18 0
2008–09 Fulham 10 0
2009–10 Fulham 32 0
2010–11 Fulham 29 2 89 2

BARROILHET, Richard (F) 0 0
H: 6 2 W: 11 13 b.Westminster 29-8-92
Source: Academy.
2010–11 Fulham 0 0

BETTINELLI, Marcus (G) 0 0
b.London 24-5-92
Source: Academy.
2010–11 Fulham 0 0

BRIGGS, Matthew (D) 5 0
H: 6 1 W: 11 12 b.Wandsworth 6-3-91
Source: School. Honours: England Youth, Under-20.

2006–07	Fulham	1	0		
2007–08	Fulham	0	0		
2008–09	Fulham	0	0		
2009–10	Fulham	0	0		
2009–10	Leyton Orient	1	0	1	0
2010–11	Fulham	3	0	4	0

BURN, Dan (D) 4 0
H: 6 6 W: 13 00 b.Blyth 9-5-92
Source: Scholar.

| 2009–10 | Darlington | 4 | 0 | 4 | 0 |
| 2010–11 | Fulham | 0 | 0 | | |

COSGROVE, Jonathan (F) 0 0
b.Northern Ireland 12-1-93
Source: Scholar.

| 2010–11 | Fulham | 0 | 0 | | |

DALLA VALLE, Lauri (F) 16 2
H: 5 9 W: 11 03 b.Kontiolahti 14-9-91
Honours: Finland Youth, Under-21.

2007	JIPPO	8	0	8	0
2008–09	Liverpool	0	0		
2009–10	Liverpool	0	0		
2010–11	Fulham	0	0		
2010–11	Bournemouth	8	2	8	2

DAVIES, Simon (M) 362 33
H: 5 10 W: 11 07 b.Haverfordwest 23-10-79
Source: Trainee. Honours: Wales Youth, Under-21, B, 58 full caps, 6 goals.

1997–98	Peterborough U	6	0		
1998–99	Peterborough U	43	4		
1999–2000	Peterborough U	16	2	65	6
1999–2000	Tottenham H	3	0		
2000–01	Tottenham H	13	2		
2001–02	Tottenham H	31	4		
2002–03	Tottenham H	36	5		
2003–04	Tottenham H	17	2		
2004–05	Tottenham H	21	0	121	13
2005–06	Everton	30	1		
2006–07	Everton	15	0	45	1
2006–07	Fulham	14	2		
2007–08	Fulham	37	5		
2008–09	Fulham	33	2		
2009–10	Fulham	17	0		
2010–11	Fulham	30	4	131	13

DEMBELE, Moussa (F) 195 37
H: 5 9 W: 10 01 b.Wilrijk 17-7-87
Honours: Belgium 33 full caps, 5 goals.

2003–04	Beerschot	1	0		
2004–05	Beerschot	19	1	20	1
2005–06	Willem II	33	9	33	9
2006–07	AZ	33	6		
2007–08	AZ	33	4		
2008–09	AZ	23	10		
2009–10	AZ	29	4	118	24
2010–11	Fulham	24	3	24	3

DEMPSEY, Clint (M) 224 59
H: 6 1 W: 12 02 b.Nacogdoches 9-3-83
Source: Furman Univ. Honours: USA Under-21, 73 full caps, 20 goals.

2004	New England Rev	24	7		
2005	New England Rev	30	11		
2006	New England Rev	23	8	77	26
2006–07	Fulham	10	1		
2007–08	Fulham	36	6		
2008–09	Fulham	35	7		
2009–10	Fulham	29	7		
2010–11	Fulham	37	12	147	33

DIKGACOI, Kagisho (M) 116 9
H: 5 11 W: 12 10 b.Brandfort 24-11-84
Honours: South Africa 41 full caps, 2 goals.

2004–05	Bloemfontein YT	10	0	10	0
2005–06	Lamontville GA	9	0		
2006–07	Lamontville GA	23	4		
2007–08	Lamontville GA	23	4		
2008–09	Lamontville GA	23	4	80	8
2009–10	Fulham	12	0		
2010–11	Fulham	1	0	13	0
2010–11	Crystal Palace	13	1	13	1

DUFF, Damien (F) 390 56
H: 5 9 W: 12 06 b Ballyboden 2-3-79
Source: Lourdes Celtic. Honours: Eire Schools, Youth, Under-20, B, 87 full caps, 8 goals.

1995–96	Blackburn R	0	0		
1996–97	Blackburn R	1	0		
1997–98	Blackburn R	26	4		
1998–99	Blackburn R	28	1		
1999–2000	Blackburn R	39	5		
2000–01	Blackburn R	32	1		
2001–02	Blackburn R	32	7		
2002–03	Blackburn R	26	9	184	27
2003–04	Chelsea	23	5		
2004–05	Chelsea	30	6		
2005–06	Chelsea	28	3	81	14
2006–07	Newcastle U	22	1		
2007–08	Newcastle U	16	0		
2008–09	Newcastle U	30	3		
2009–10	Newcastle U	1	1	69	5
2009–10	Fulham	32	6		
2010–11	Fulham	24	4	56	10

ETHERIDGE, Neil (G) 0 0
H: 6 3 W: 14 00 b.Enfield 7-2-90
Source: Scholar.

2008–09	Fulham	0	0		
2009–10	Fulham	0	0		
2010–11	Fulham	0	0		

ETUHU, Dickson (M) 297 27
H: 6 2 W: 13 04 b.Kano 8-6-82
Source: Scholar. Honours: Nigeria 17 full caps.

1999–2000	Manchester C	0	0		
2000–01	Manchester C	0	0		
2001–02	Manchester C	12	0	12	0
2001–02	Preston NE	16	3		
2002–03	Preston NE	39	6		
2003–04	Preston NE	31	3		
2004–05	Preston NE	35	3		
2005–06	Preston NE	13	2	134	17
2005–06	Norwich C	19	0		
2006–07	Norwich C	43	6	62	6
2007–08	Sunderland	20	1		
2008–09	Sunderland	0	0	20	1
2008–09	Fulham	21	1		
2009–10	Fulham	20	0		
2010–11	Fulham	28	2	69	3

FREI, Kerim (M) 0 0
b.Fledkirch 19-11-93
Source: Scholar.

| 2010–11 | Fulham | 0 | 0 | | |

GAMEIRO, Corey (F) 0 0
b.Wollongong 7-2-93
Source: Academy.

| 2010–11 | Fulham | 0 | 0 | | |

GERA, Zoltan (M) 352 62
H: 6 0 W: 11 11 b.Pecs 22-4-79
Source: Hakarny. Honours: Hungary 71 full caps, 21 goals.

1999–2000	Pecsi	15	4	15	4
2000–01	Ferencvaros	32	7		
2001–02	Ferencvaros	27	8		
2002–03	Ferencvaros	26	6		
2003–04	Ferencvaros	30	11	115	32
2004–05	WBA	38	6		
2005–06	WBA	15	2		
2006–07	WBA	40	5		
2007–08	WBA	43	8	136	31
2008–09	Fulham	32	2		
2009–10	Fulham	27	2		
2010–11	Fulham	27	1	86	5

GREENING, Jonathan (M) 367 14
H: 5 11 W: 11 00 b.Scarborough 2-1-79
Source: Trainee. Honours: England Youth, Under-21.

1996–97	York C	5	0		
1997–98	York C	20	2	25	2
1997–98	Manchester U	0	0		
1998–99	Manchester U	3	0		
1999–2000	Manchester U	4	0		
2000–01	Manchester U	7	0	14	0
2001–02	Middlesbrough	36	1		
2002–03	Middlesbrough	35	0		
2003–04	Middlesbrough	25	1	99	4
2004–05	WBA	34	0		
2005–06	WBA	38	2		

2006–07	WBA	42	2		
2007–08	WBA	46	1		
2008–09	WBA	34	2		
2009–10	WBA	2	0	196	7
2009–10	Fulham	23	1		
2010–11	Fulham	10	0	33	1

HALLICHE, Rafik (D) 79 1
H: 6 2 W: 12 02 b.Algiers 2-9-86
Honours: Algeria Under-23, 21 full caps, 1 goal.

2006–07	Hussein Dey	28	1		
2007–08	Hussein Dey	16	0	44	1
2007–08	Benfica	0	0		
2007–08	Nacional	3	0		
2008–09	Nacional	15	0		
2009–10	Nacional	16	0	34	0
2010–11	Fulham	1	0	1	0

HANGELAND, Brede (D) 298 17
H: 6 4 W: 13 05 b.Houston 20-6-81
Honours: Norway Under-21, 70 full caps, 1 goal.

2000	Vidar	0	0		
2001	Viking	22	0		
2002	Viking	26	2		
2003	Viking	26	1		
2004	Viking	14	3		
2005	Viking	26	0	114	6
2005–06	FC Copenhagen	13	1		
2006–07	FC Copenhagen	32	0		
2007–08	FC Copenhagen	18	2	63	3
2007–08	Fulham	15	0		
2008–09	Fulham	37	1		
2009–10	Fulham	32	1		
2010–11	Fulham	37	6	121	8

HARRIS, Courtney (M) 0 0
b.London 7-9-91
Source: Scholar.

| 2010–11 | Fulham | 0 | 0 | | |

HOESEN, Danny (F) 0 0
H: 6 1 W: 12 00 b.Kerkrade 15-1-91
Source: Fortuna Sittard.

2008–09	Fulham	0	0		
2009–10	Fulham	0	0		
2010–11	Fulham	0	0		

HUGHES, Aaron (D) 399 5
H: 6 0 W: 11 02 b.Cookstown 8-11-79
Source: Trainee. Honours: Northern Ireland Youth, B, 76 full caps.

1996–97	Newcastle U	0	0		
1997–98	Newcastle U	4	0		
1998–99	Newcastle U	14	0		
1999–2000	Newcastle U	27	2		
2000–01	Newcastle U	35	0		
2001–02	Newcastle U	34	0		
2002–03	Newcastle U	35	1		
2003–04	Newcastle U	34	0		
2004–05	Newcastle U	32	1	205	4
2005–06	Aston Villa	35	0		
2006–07	Aston Villa	19	0	54	0
2007–08	Fulham	30	0		
2008–09	Fulham	38	0		
2009–10	Fulham	34	0		
2010–11	Fulham	38	1	140	1

JOHNSON, Andy (F) 350 109
H: 5 7 W: 10 09 b.Bedford 10-2-81
Source: Trainee. Honours: England Youth, Under-20, 8 full caps.

1997–98	Birmingham C	0	0		
1998–99	Birmingham C	4	0		
1999–2000	Birmingham C	22	1		
2000–01	Birmingham C	34	4		
2001–02	Birmingham C	23	3	83	8
2002–03	Crystal Palace	28	11		
2003–04	Crystal Palace	42	27		
2004–05	Crystal Palace	37	21		
2005–06	Crystal Palace	33	15	140	74
2006–07	Everton	32	11		
2007–08	Everton	29	6	61	17
2008–09	Fulham	31	7		
2009–10	Fulham	8	0		
2010–11	Fulham	27	3	66	10

JOHNSON, Eddie (F) 195 43
H: 6 0 W: 12 02 b.Bunnell 31-3-84
Honours: USA 41 full caps, 12 goals.

| 2001 | Dallas Burn | 10 | 2 | | |
| 2002 | Dallas Burn | 14 | 2 | | |

2003	Dallas Burn	22	3		
2004	Dallas Burn	26	12		
2005	Dallas Burn	15	5	87	24
2006	Kansas City Wizards	19	2		
2007	Kansas City Wizards	24	15	43	17
2007–08	Fulham	6	0		
2008–09	Fulham	0	0		
2008–09	*Cardiff C*	30	2	30	2
2009–10	Fulham	2	0		
2010–11	Fulham	11	0	19	0
2010–11	*Preston NE*	16	0	16	0

JORENEN, Jesse (G)   0   0
b.Finland 21-3-93
Source: Scholar.

| 2010–11 | Fulham | 0 | 0 | | |

KACANIKLIC, Alex (M)   0   0
H: 5 11   W: 10 05   b.Helsingborg 13-8-91
Source: Scholar.

2008–09	Liverpool	0	0		
2009–10	Liverpool	0	0		
2010–11	Fulham	0	0		

KAMARA, Diomansy (F)   271   63
H: 6 0   W: 11 05   b.Paris 8-11-80
Honours: Senegal 49 full caps, 9 goals.

1998–99	Red Star 93	4	0	4	0
1999–2000	Catanzaro	11	4		
2000–01	Catanzaro	23	5	34	9
2001–02	Chievo	0	0		
2001–02	Modena	24	4		
2002–03	Modena	29	5		
2003–04	Modena	29	6	82	15
2004–05	Portsmouth	25	4	25	4
2005–06	WBA	26	1		
2006–07	WBA	34	20	60	21
2007–08	Fulham	28	5		
2008–09	Fulham	12	4		
2009–10	Fulham	9	1		
2010–11	Fulham	10	2	59	12
2010–11	*Leicester C*	7	2	7	2

KELLY, Stephen (D)   170   2
H: 6 0   W: 12 04   b.Dublin 6-9-83
Source: Juniors. *Honours:* Eire Youth,
Under-21, 25 full caps.

2000–01	Tottenham H	0	0		
2001–02	Tottenham H	0	0		
2002–03	Tottenham H	0	0		
2002–03	*Southend U*	10	0	10	0
2002–03	*QPR*	7	0	7	0
2003–04	Tottenham H	11	0		
2003–04	*Watford*	13	0	13	0
2004–05	Tottenham H	17	2		
2005–06	Tottenham H	9	0	37	2
2006–07	Birmingham C	36	0		
2007–08	Birmingham C	38	0		
2008–09	Birmingham C	5	0		
2008–09	*Stoke C*	6	0	6	0
2009–10	Birmingham C	0	0	79	0
2009–10	Fulham	8	0		
2010–11	Fulham	10	0	18	0

MARQUEZ-SANCHEZ, Christian (D) 0   0
b.Barcelona 13-1-93
Source: Scholar.

| 2009–10 | Fulham | 0 | 0 | | |
| 2010–11 | Fulham | 0 | 0 | | |

MARSH-BROWN, Keanu (F)   17   2
H: 5 11   W: 12 04   b.Hammersmith 10-8-92
Source: Scholar.

2009–10	Fulham	0	0		
2010–11	Fulham	0	0		
2010–11	*Milton Keynes D*	17	2	17	2

MILSOM, Robert (D)   27   0
H: 5 10   W: 11 05   b.Redhill 2-1-87
Source: Scholar.

2005–06	Fulham	0	0		
2006–07	Fulham	0	0		
2007–08	Fulham	0	0		
2007–08	*Brentford*	6	0	6	0
2008–09	Fulham	1	0		
2008–09	*Southend U*	6	0	6	0
2009–10	Fulham	0	0		
2010	*TPS Turku*	14	0	14	0
2010–11	Fulham	0	0	1	0

Transferred to Aberdeen January 2011.

MINKWITZ, Ronny (M)   0   0
b.Duisburg 9-12-93
Source: Stuttgart.

| 2010–11 | Fulham | 0 | 0 | | |

MURPHY, Danny (M)   531   76
H: 5 10   W: 11 09   b.Chester 18-3-77
Source: Trainee. *Honours:* England Schools,
Youth, Under-21, 9 full caps, 1 goal.

1993–94	Crewe Alex	12	2		
1994–95	Crewe Alex	35	5		
1995–96	Crewe Alex	42	10		
1996–97	Crewe Alex	45	10		
1997–98	Liverpool	16	0		
1998–99	Liverpool	1	0		
1998–99	*Crewe Alex*	16	1	150	28
1999–2000	Liverpool	23	3		
2000–01	Liverpool	27	4		
2001–02	Liverpool	36	6		
2002–03	Liverpool	36	7		
2003–04	Liverpool	31	5	170	25
2004–05	Charlton Ath	38	3		
2005–06	Charlton Ath	18	4	56	7
2005–06	Tottenham H	10	0		
2006–07	Tottenham H	12	1		
2007–08	Tottenham H	0	0	22	1
2007–08	Fulham	33	5		
2008–09	Fulham	38	5		
2009–10	Fulham	25	5		
2010–11	Fulham	37	0	133	15

PANTSIL, John (D)   223   5
H: 5 10   W: 12 08   b.Berekum 15-6-81
Source: Liberty Professionals, Berkum
Arsenals. *Honours:* Ghana Youth, Under-20,
72 full caps.

2000–01	Liberty Pros	10	0	10	0
2001–02	Berekum Arsenal	12	1	12	1
2001–02	Widzew Lodz	19	1	19	1
2002–03	Maccabi Tel Aviv	17	0		
2003–04	Maccabi Tel Aviv	22	0		
2004–05	Maccabi Tel Aviv	7	0	46	0
2004–05	Hapoel Tel Aviv	15	1		
2005–06	Hapoel Tel Aviv	27	2	42	3
2006–07	West Ham U	5	0		
2007–08	West Ham U	14	0	19	0
2008–09	Fulham	37	0		
2009–10	Fulham	22	0		
2010–11	Fulham	16	0	75	0

PENIKET, Richard (F)   0   0
b.Bromsgrove 4-3-93
Source: Scholar. *Honours:* Wales Youth.

| 2010–11 | Fulham | 0 | 0 | | |

RIISE, Bjorn Helge (M)   162   13
H: 5 10   W: 11 11   b.Alesund 21-6-83
Honours: Norway Under-21, 31 full caps, 1
goal.

2002	*Viking*	0	0		
2002–03	Standard Liege	9	0		
2003–04	Standard Liege	8	0	17	0
2004–05	*FC Brussels*	31	2	31	2
2005	Lillestrom	13	0		
2006	Lillestrom	25	1		
2007	Lillestrom	24	3		
2008	Lillestrom	9	0		
2009	Lillestrom	15	6	86	10
2009–10	Fulham	12	0		
2010–11	Fulham	3	0	15	0
2010–11	*Sheffield U*	13	1	13	1

SALCIDO, Carlos (D)   282   9
H: 5 8   W: 11 00   b.Ocotlan 2-4-80
Honours: Mexico 88 full caps, 6 goals.

2000–01	Gallos	0	0		
2001–02	Guadalajara	1	0		
2002–03	Tapatio	42	4	42	4
2003–04	Guadalajara	35	1		
2004–05	Guadalajara	31	1		
2005–06	Guadalajara	29	0	96	2
2006–07	PSV Eindhoven	33	1		
2007–08	PSV Eindhoven	33	0		
2008–09	PSV Eindhoven	29	0		
2009–10	PSV Eindhoven	27	0	121	3
2010–11	Fulham	23	0	23	0

SAUNDERS, Matthew (M)   18   3
H: 5 11   W: 11 05   b.Chertsey 12-9-89
Source: Scholar.

2008–09	Fulham	0	0		
2009–10	Fulham	0	0		
2009–10	*Lincoln C*	18	3	18	3
2010–11	Fulham	0	0		

SCHWARZER, Mark (G)   550   0
H: 6 4   W: 14 07   b.Sydney 6-10-72
Honours: Australia Youth, Under-20,
Under-23, 88 full caps.

1990–91	Marconi Stallions	1	0		
1991–92	Marconi Stallions	9	0		
1992–93	Marconi Stallions	23	0		
1993–94	Marconi Stallions	25	0	58	0
1994–95	Dynamo Dresden	2	0	2	0
1995–96	Kaiserslautern	4	0		
1996–97	Kaiserslautern	0	0	4	0
1996–97	Bradford C	13	0	13	0
1996–97	Middlesbrough	7	0		
1997–98	Middlesbrough	35	0		
1998–99	Middlesbrough	34	0		
1999–2000	Middlesbrough	37	0		
2000 01	Middlesbrough	31	0		
2001–02	Middlesbrough	21	0		
2002–03	Middlesbrough	38	0		
2003–04	Middlesbrough	36	0		
2004–05	Middlesbrough	31	0		
2005–06	Middlesbrough	27	0		
2006–07	Middlesbrough	36	0		
2007–08	Middlesbrough	34	0	367	0
2008–09	Fulham	38	0		
2009–10	Fulham	37	0		
2010–11	Fulham	31	0	106	0

SENDEROS, Philippe (D)   109   7
H: 6 1   W: 13 10   b.Geneva 14-2-85
Honours: Switzerland Youth, Under-20,
Under-21, 42 full caps, 5 goals.

2001–02	Servette	3	0		
2002–03	Servette	23	3	26	3
2003–04	Arsenal	0	0		
2004–05	Arsenal	13	0		
2005–06	Arsenal	20	2		
2006–07	Arsenal	14	0		
2007–08	Arsenal	17	2		
2008–09	Arsenal	0	0		
2008–09	*AC Milan*	14	0	14	0
2009–10	Arsenal	0	0	64	4
2009–10	*Everton*	2	0	2	0
2010–11	Fulham	3	0	3	0

SIDWELL, Steve (M)   282   43
H: 5 10   W: 11 00   b.Wandsworth 14-12-82
Source: Scholar. *Honours:* England Under-20,
Under-21.

2001–02	Arsenal	0	0		
2001–02	*Brentford*	30	4	30	4
2002–03	Arsenal	0	0		
2002–03	*Brighton & HA*	12	5	12	5
2002–03	Reading	13	2		
2003–04	Reading	43	8		
2004–05	Reading	44	5		
2005–06	Reading	33	10		
2006–07	Reading	35	4	168	29
2007–08	Chelsea	15	0	15	0
2008–09	Aston Villa	16	3		
2009–10	Aston Villa	25	0		
2010–11	Aston Villa	4	0	45	3
2010–11	Fulham	12	2	12	2

SMITH, Alex (D)   0   0
H: 5 9   W: 8 09   b.Clapham 31-10-91
Source: Scholar.

| 2009–10 | Fulham | 0 | 0 | | |
| 2010–11 | Fulham | 0 | 0 | | |

STOCKDALE, David (G)   93   0
H: 6 3   W: 13 04   b.Leeds 20-9-85
Source: Scholar.

2002–03	York C	1	0		
2003–04	York C	0	0	1	0
2006–07	Darlington	6	0		
2007–08	Darlington	41	0	47	0
2008–09	Fulham	0	0		
2008–09	*Rotherham U*	8	0	8	0
2009–10	*Leicester C*	8	0	8	0
2009–10	Fulham	1	0		
2009–10	*Plymouth Arg*	21	0	21	0
2010–11	Fulham	7	0	8	0

STOOR, Fredrik (D)   87   2
H: 6 0   W: 12 06   b.Stockholm 28-2-84
Honours: Sweden 11 full caps.

2002	Hammarby	0	0		
2003	Hammarby	1	0		
2004	Hammarby	7	0		

2005	Hammarby	20	1		
2006	Hammarby	23	1	51	2
2007	Rosenborg	21	0	21	0
2008-09	Fulham	2	0		
2009-10	Fulham	2	0		
2009-10	*Derby Co*	11	0	11	0
2010-11	Fulham	0	0	4	0

Transferred to Valerenga January 2011.

TROTTA, Marcello (F)   0 0
b.Santa Maria Capua 29-9-92
Source: Napoli.

| 2009-10 | Fulham | 0 | 0 | | |
| 2010-11 | Fulham | 0 | 0 | | |

ZAMORA, Bobby (F)   351 121
H:6 1   W:11 11   b.Barking 16-1-81
Source: Trainee. *Honours:* England Under-21, 1 full cap.

1999-2000	Bristol R	4	0	4	0
1999-2000	*Brighton & HA*	6	6		
2000-01	Brighton & HA	43	28		
2001-02	Brighton & HA	41	28		
2002-03	Brighton & HA	35	14	125	76
2003-04	Tottenham H	16	0	16	0
2003-04	West Ham U	17	5		
2004-05	West Ham U	34	7		
2005-06	West Ham U	34	6		
2006-07	West Ham U	32	11		
2007-08	West Ham U	13	1	130	30
2008-09	Fulham	35	2		
2009-10	Fulham	27	8		
2010-11	Fulham	14	5	76	15

Scholars
Banya Charles; Brister Alexander Keith; Dean Jack; Maloney Robert John; Monguel Oliver; Pritchard Joshua Philip; Smith Grant Ashley; Toure Cheick Sekou

GILLINGHAM (36)

ABORAH, Stanley (M)   66 9
H:5 7   W:11 05   b.Kumasi 23-6-87
Honours: Belgium Youth.

2004-05	Ajax	4	0		
2005-06	Ajax	0	0	4	0
2005-06	Den Bosch	21	3		
2006-07	Dender	3	0	3	0
2007-08	Den Bosch	16	3		
2008-09	Den Bosch	21	3	58	9
2009-10	Trencin	0	0		
2010-11	Gillingham	1	0	1	0

AKINFENWA, Adebayo (F)   271 85
H:5 11   W:13 07   b.Nigeria 10 5 82

| 2001 | Atlantas | 19 | 4 | | |
| 2002 | Atlantas | 4 | 1 | 23 | 5 |

From Barry T

2003-04	Boston U	3	0	3	0
2003-04	Leyton Orient	1	0	1	0
2003-04	Rushden & D	0	0		
2003-04	Doncaster R	9	4	9	4
2004-05	Torquay U	37	14	37	14
2005-06	Swansea C	34	9		
2006-07	Swansea C	25	5		
2007-08	Swansea C	0	0	59	14
2007-08	Millwall	7	0	7	0
2007-08	Northampton T	15	7		
2008-09	Northampton T	33	13		
2009-10	Northampton T	40	17	88	37
2010-11	Gillingham	44	11	44	11

BARCHAM, Andy (F)   124 20
H:5 8   W:11 10   b.Basildon 16-12-86
Source: Scholar.

2005-06	Tottenham H	0	0		
2006-07	Tottenham H	0	0		
2007-08	Tottenham H	0	0		
2007-08	*Leyton Orient*	25	1	25	1
2008-09	Tottenham H	0	0		
2008-09	Gillingham	33	6		
2009-10	Gillingham	42	7		
2010-11	Gillingham	24	6	99	19

BENTLEY, Mark (M)   267 23
H:6 2   W:13 04   b.Hertford 7-1-78
Source: Enfield, Aldershot;T, Gravesend & N, Dagenham & R.

2003-04	Southend U	21	2		
2004-05	Southend U	39	5		
2005-06	Southend U	33	5	93	12

2006-07	Gillingham	41	4		
2007-08	Gillingham	33	2		
2008-09	Gillingham	39	1		
2009-10	Gillingham	36	2		
2010-11	Gillingham	25	2	174	11

CRONIN, Lance (G)   8 0
H:6 1   W:12 00   b.Brighton 11-9-85
Source: Scholar. *Honours:* England Youth.

2002-03	Crystal Palace	0	0		
2003-04	Crystal Palace	0	0		
2004-05	Crystal Palace	0	0		
2004-05	Wycombe W	1	0	1	0
2005-06	Crystal Palace	0	0		
2005-06	Oldham Ath	0	0		

From Ebbsfleet U.

| 2010-11 | Gillingham | 7 | 0 | 7 | 0 |

DAVIES, Callum (D)   1 0
b. 8-2-93
Source: Scholar.

| 2010-11 | Gillingham | 1 | 0 | 1 | 0 |

ESSAM, Connor (D)   0 0
H:6 0   W:12 00   b.Chatham 9-7-92
Source: Scholar.

| 2010-11 | Gillingham | 0 | 0 | | |

FULLER, Barry (D)   140 1
H:5 10   W:11 10   b.Ashford 25-9-84
Source: Scholar.

2004-05	Charlton Ath	0	0		
2005-06	Charlton Ath	0	0		
2005-06	Barnet	15	1	15	1

From Stevenage B.

2007-08	Gillingham	10	0		
2008-09	Gillingham	37	0		
2009-10	Gillingham	36	0		
2010-11	Gillingham	42	0	125	0

GOWLING, Josh (D)   169 5
H:6 3   W:12 08   b.Coventry 29-11-83
Source: WBA Scholar.

2004-05	Herfolge	13	0	13	0
2005-06	Bournemouth	13	0		
2006-07	Bournemouth	33	1		
2007-08	Bournemouth	37	0	83	1
2008-09	Carlisle U	4	0		
2008-09	*Hereford U*	13	0	13	0
2009-10	Carlisle U	0	0	4	0
2009-10	Gillingham	30	2		
2010-11	Gillingham	22	2	52	4
2010-11	*Lincoln C*	4	0	4	0

INKANGO, Bruce (F)   5 0
H:5 8   W:10 07   b.Poitiers 18-5-84
Source: Cannes, Neuchatel Xamax, Angers, RCF Paris (loan), Poitiers, Cherbourg, Paris Red Star.

| 2010-11 | Gillingham | 5 | 0 | 5 | 0 |

Transferred to Kastroiti January 2011.

JACKMAN, Danny (D)   261 16
H:5 4   W:10 00   b.Worcester 3-1-83
Source: Scholar.

2000-01	Aston Villa	0	0		
2001-02	Aston Villa	0	0		
2001-02	*Cambridge U*	7	1	7	1
2002-03	Aston Villa	0	0		
2003-04	Aston Villa	0	0		
2003-04	Stockport Co	27	2		
2004-05	Stockport Co	33	2	60	4
2005-06	Gillingham	42	0		
2006-07	Gillingham	31	1		
2007-08	Northampton T	39	1		
2008-09	Northampton T	43	8		
2009-10	Northampton T	0	0	82	9
2009-10	Gillingham	22	0		
2010-11	Gillingham	17	1	112	2

JULIAN, Alan (G)   89 0
H:6 2   W:13 07   b.Ashford 11-3-83
Source: Trainee. *Honours:* Northern Ireland Youth, Under-21.

2001-02	Brentford	0	0		
2002-03	Brentford	3	0		
2003-04	Brentford	13	0		
2004-05	Brentford	0	0	16	0

From Stevenage B.

2008-09	Gillingham	4	0		
2009-10	Gillingham	30	0		
2010-11	Gillingham	39	0	73	0

KING, Simon (D)   168 4
H:6 0   W:13 00   b.Oxford 11-4-83
Source: Scholar.

2000-01	Oxford U	2	0		
2001-02	Oxford U	2	0		
2002-03	Oxford U	0	0		
2003-04	Oxford U	0	0		
2004-05	Oxford U	0	0	4	0
2005-06	Barnet	32	0		
2006-07	Barnet	43	2	75	2
2007-08	Gillingham	42	0		
2008-09	Gillingham	43	2		
2009-10	Gillingham	0	0		
2010-11	Gillingham	4	0	89	2

LAWRENCE, Matt (D)   526 6
H:6 1   W:12 12   b.Northampton 19-6-74
Source: Grays Ath. *Honours:* England Schools.

1995-96	Wycombe W	3	0		
1996-97	Wycombe W	13	1		
1996-97	Fulham	15	0		
1997-98	Fulham	43	0		
1998-99	Fulham	1	0	59	0
1998-99	Wycombe W	34	2		
1999-2000	Wycombe W	29	2	79	5
1999-2000	Millwall	9	0		
2000-01	Millwall	45	0		
2001-02	Millwall	26	0		
2002-03	Millwall	33	0		
2003-04	Millwall	36	0		
2004-05	Millwall	44	0		
2005-06	Millwall	31	0	224	0
2006-07	Crystal Palace	34	0		
2007-08	Crystal Palace	37	1		
2008-09	Crystal Palace	32	0		
2009-10	Crystal Palace	18	0	121	1
2010-11	Gillingham	43	0	43	0

MAHER, Kevin (M)   480 23
H:6 0   W:12 13   b.Ilford 17-10-76
Source: Trainee. *Honours:* Eire Under-21.

1995-96	Tottenham H	0	0		
1996-97	Tottenham H	0	0		
1997-98	Tottenham H	0	0		
1997-98	Southend U	18	1		
1998-99	Southend U	34	4		
1999-2000	Southend U	24	0		
2000-01	Southend U	41	2		
2001-02	Southend U	36	5		
2002-03	Southend U	42	2		
2003-04	Southend U	42	1		
2004-05	Southend U	42	1		
2005-06	Southend U	44	1		
2006-07	Southend U	41	5		
2007-08	Southend U	19	0	383	22
2007-08	*Gillingham*	7	0		
2008-09	Oldham Ath	28	1	28	1
2009-10	Gillingham	26	0		
2010-11	Gillingham	36	0	69	0

MARTIN, Joe (M)   39 1
H:6 0   W:12 13   b.Dagenham 29-11-88
Source: Scholar. *Honours:* England Youth.

2005-06	Tottenham H	0	0		
2006-07	Tottenham H	0	0		
2007-08	Tottenham H	0	0		
2007-08	*Blackpool*	1	0		
2008-09	Blackpool	15	0		
2009-10	Blackpool	6	0	22	0
2010-11	Gillingham	17	1	17	1

McCAMMON, Mark (F)   253 30
H:6 2   W:14 05   b.Barnet 7-8-78
Source: Cambridge C. *Honours:* Barbados 5 full caps, 4 goals.

1997-98	Cambridge U	2	0		
1998-99	Cambridge U	2	0	4	0
1998-99	Charlton Ath	0	0		
1999-2000	Charlton Ath	4	0	4	0
1999-2000	*Swindon T*	4	0	4	0
2000-01	Brentford	24	3		
2001-02	Brentford	14	0		
2002-03	Brentford	37	7	75	10
2002-03	Millwall	7	2		
2003-04	Millwall	7	0		
2004-05	Millwall	8	0	22	2
2004-05	Brighton & HA	18	3		
2005-06	Brighton & HA	7	0	25	3
2005-06	*Bristol C*	11	4	11	4
2006-07	Doncaster R	22	2		

2007–08	Doncaster R	32	4	54	6
2008–09	Gillingham	31	5		
2009–10	Gillingham	14	0		
2009–10	*Bradford C*	4	0	4	0
2010–11	Gillingham	5	0	50	5

MILLER, Ashley (F) 1 0
b.Dover 8-6-94

| 2010–11 | Gillingham | 1 | 0 | 1 | 0 |

NUTTER, John (D) 139 3
H: 6 2 W: 12 10 b.Burnham 13-6-82
Source: Blackburn R Scholar.

| 2000–01 | Wycombe W | 1 | 0 | 1 | 0 |

From Aldershot T, Grays Ath, Stevenage B

2007–08	Gillingham	24	1		
2008–09	Gillingham	45	0		
2009–10	Gillingham	35	1		
2010–11	Gillingham	34	1	138	3

OLI, Dennis (M) 138 13
H: 6 0 W: 12 00 b.Newham 28-1-84

2001–02	QPR	2	0		
2002–03	QPR	18	0		
2003–04	QPR	3	0	23	0
2004–05	Swansea C	1	0	1	0
2004–05	Cambridge U	4	1	4	1

From Grays Ath.

2007–08	Gillingham	22	4		
2008–09	Gillingham	31	4		
2009–10	Gillingham	36	3		
2010–11	Gillingham	21	1	110	12

PALMER, Chris (D) 173 11
H: 5 7 W: 11 00 b.Derby 16-10-83
Source: Scholar.

2003–04	Derby Co	0	0		
2004–05	Notts Co	25	4		
2005–06	Notts Co	29	1	54	5
2006–07	Wycombe W	32	0		
2007–08	Wycombe W	1	0	33	0
2007–08	*Darlington*	4	0	4	0
2008–09	Walsall	44	1	44	1
2009–10	Gillingham	20	1		
2010–11	Gillingham	18	4	38	5

PAYNE, Jack (M) 52 1
H: 5 9 W: 9 02 b.Gravesend 5-12-91
Source: Scholar.

2008–09	Gillingham	2	0		
2009–10	Gillingham	19	0		
2010–11	Gillingham	31	1	52	1

PAYNE, Stefan (F) 16 0
b.Lambeth 10-8-91
Source: Sutton U.

| 2009–10 | Fulham | 0 | 0 | | |
| 2010–11 | Gillingham | 16 | 0 | 16 | 0 |

RANCE, Dean (M) 0 0
b.Maidstone 14-5-91
Source: Scholar.

| 2010–11 | Gillingham | 0 | 0 | | |

RICHARDS, Garry (D) 123 5
H: 6 3 W: 13 00 b.Romford 11-6-86
Source: Scholar.

2005–06	Colchester U	15	0		
2006–07	Colchester U	5	1	20	1
2006–07	*Brentford*	10	1	10	1
2007–08	Southend U	10	0	10	0
2007–08	Gillingham	14	1		
2008–09	Gillingham	36	2		
2009–10	Gillingham	16	0		
2010–11	Gillingham	17	0	83	3

ROONEY, Luke (M) 36 3
H: 5 8 W: 11 07 b.Southwark 28-12-90
Source: Scholar.

| 2009–10 | Gillingham | 13 | 2 | | |
| 2010–11 | Gillingham | 23 | 1 | 36 | 3 |

SINCLAIR, Tony (D) 20 0
b.Lewisham 5-3-85
Source: Beckenham T, Fisher Ath, Welling U, Woking.

| 2010–11 | Gillingham | 20 | 0 | 20 | 0 |

SPILLER, Danny (M) 177 9
H: 5 8 W: 11 00 b.Maidstone 10-10-81
Source: Trainee.

2000–01	Gillingham	0	0		
2001–02	Gillingham	1	0		
2002–03	Gillingham	10	0		
2003–04	Gillingham	39	6		
2004–05	Gillingham	22	0		
2005–06	Gillingham	32	0		
2006–07	Gillingham	25	0		
2007–08	Millwall	6	1		
2008–09	Millwall	2	0	8	1
2009–10	Dagenham & R	10	0	10	0
2010–11	Gillingham	30	2	159	8

WESTON, Curtis (M) 162 17
H: 5 11 W: 11 09 b.Greenwich 24-1-87
Source: Scholar.

2003–04	Millwall	1	0		
2004–05	Millwall	3	0		
2005–06	Millwall	0	0	4	0
2006–07	Swindon T	27	1	27	1
2007–08	Leeds U	7	1		
2007–08	*Scunthorpe U*	7	0	7	0
2008–09	Leeds U	0	0	7	1
2008–09	Gillingham	45	5		
2009–10	Gillingham	39	6		
2010–11	Gillingham	33	4	117	15

WHITE, Andy (F) 1 0
H: 6 0 b.Reading 11-9-91
Source: Reading Scholar.

| 2010–11 | Gillingham | 1 | 0 | 1 | 0 |

HARTLEPOOL U (37)

AUSTIN, Neil (D) 273 10
H: 5 10 W: 11 09 b.Barnsley 26-4-83
Source: Trainee. *Honours:* England Youth, Under-20.

1999–2000	Barnsley	0	0		
2000–01	Barnsley	0	0		
2001–02	Barnsley	0	0		
2002–03	Barnsley	34	0		
2003–04	Barnsley	37	0		
2004–05	Barnsley	15	0		
2005–06	Barnsley	38	0		
2006–07	Barnsley	24	0	148	0
2007–08	Darlington	29	2		
2008–09	Darlington	33	3	62	5
2009–10	Hartlepool U	39	3		
2010–11	Hartlepool U	24	2	63	5

BEHAN, Denis (F) 194 37
H: 6 0 W: 13 04 b.Tralee 2-1-84
Honours: Eire Under-21.

2004	Cork C	21	1		
2005	Cork C	22	4		
2006	Cork C	28	6		
2007	Cork C	30	8		
2008	Cork C	31	7		
2009	Cork C	20	5	152	31
2009–10	Hartlepool U	29	6		
2010–11	Hartlepool U	13	0	42	6

BJORNSSON, Armann (F) 155 26
H: 6 5 W: 14 00 b.Hafnarfjordur 7-1-81
Source: Sindri, Lillestrom (loan).

2001	Valur	14	4		
2002	Valur	14	1		
2002	*Brann*	7	3		
2003	Valur	14	4	42	0
2004	Hafnafjordur	12	3		
2005	Hafnafjordur	9	2		
2006	Hafnafjordur	15	2	36	7
2006	Brann	2	0		
2007	Brann	15	2		
2008	Brann	8	0		
2009	Brann	9	2	41	7
2009–10	Hartlepool U	18	3		
2010–11	Hartlepool U	18	0	36	3

BLACKFORD, Williams (M) 0 0
b. 23-1-92
Source: Scholar.

| 2010–11 | Hartlepool U | 0 | 0 | | |

BOYD, Adam (F) 313 91
H: 5 9 W: 10 12 b.Hartlepool 25-5-82
Source: Scholarship.

1999–2000	Hartlepool U	4	1		
2000–01	Hartlepool U	5	0		
2001–02	Hartlepool U	29	9		
2002–03	Hartlepool U	22	5		
2003–04	Hartlepool U	18	12		
2003–04	*Boston U*	14	4	14	4
2004–05	Hartlepool U	45	22		
2005–06	Hartlepool U	21	4		
2006–07	Luton T	19	1	19	1
2007–08	Leyton Orient	44	14		
2008–09	Leyton Orient	33	9	77	23
2009–10	Hartlepool U	40	7		
2010–11	Hartlepool U	19	3	203	63

BROWN, James (F) 151 28
H: 5 11 W: 11 00 b.Cramlington 3-1-87
Source: Cramlington Jun.

2004–05	Hartlepool U	0	0		
2005–06	Hartlepool U	4	1		
2006–07	Hartlepool U	36	6		
2007–08	Hartlepool U	35	10		
2008–09	Hartlepool U	18	6		
2009–10	Hartlepool U	32	4		
2010–11	Hartlepool U	26	1	151	28

COLLINS, Sam (D) 417 18
H: 6 2 W: 14 03 b.Pontefract 5-6-77
Source: Trainee.

1994–95	Huddersfield T	0	0		
1995–96	Huddersfield T	0	0		
1996–97	Huddersfield T	4	0		
1997–98	Huddersfield T	1	0		
1998–99	Huddersfield T	23	0	37	0
1999–2000	Bury	19	0		
2000–01	Bury	34	2		
2001–02	Bury	29	0	82	2
2002–03	Port Vale	44	5		
2003–04	Port Vale	43	4		
2004–05	Port Vale	33	2		
2005–06	Port Vale	15	0	135	11
2005–06	Hull C	17	0		
2006–07	Hull C	6	0		
2007–08	Hull C	0	0	23	0
2007–08	*Swindon T*	4	0	4	0
2007–08	Hartlepool U	10	2		
2008–09	Hartlepool U	40	1		
2009–10	Hartlepool U	44	0		
2010–11	Hartlepool U	42	2	136	5

FLINDERS, Scott (G) 124 1
H: 6 4 W: 13 00 b.Rotherham 12-6-86
Source: Scholar. *Honours:* England Youth, Under-20.

2004–05	Barnsley	11	0		
2005–06	Barnsley	3	0	14	0
2006–07	Crystal Palace	8	0		
2006–07	*Gillingham*	9	0	9	0
2006–07	*Brighton & HA*	12	0	12	0
2007–08	Crystal Palace	0	0		
2007–08	*Yeovil T*	9	0	9	0
2008–09	Crystal Palace	0	0	8	0
2009–10	Hartlepool U	46	0		
2010–11	Hartlepool U	26	1	72	1

FREDRIKSEN, Jon-Andre (M) 182 26
H: 5 11 W: 12 00 b.Moss 5-4-82

2002	Moss	10	0		
2003	Moss	21	1		
2004	Moss	25	4		
2005	Moss	29	7		
2006	Moss	27	8		
2007	Moss	27	6		
2008	Moss	17	0	156	26
2009	Sarpsborg	13	0	13	0
2009–10	Hartlepool U	12	0		
2010–11	Hartlepool U	1	0	13	0

Transferred to Moss October 2010.

GAMBLE, Joe (M) 199 7
H: 5 7 W: 11 00 b.Cork 14-1-82
Honours: Eire Under-21, B, 2 full caps.

2000–01	Reading	1	0		
2001–02	Reading	6	0		
2002–03	Reading	0	0		
2003–04	Reading	0	0	7	0
2004	Cork C	16	0		
2005	Cork C	25	2		
2006	Cork C	24	0		
2007	Cork C	27	1		
2008	Cork C	25	1		
2009	Cork C	23	0	140	4
2009–10	Hartlepool U	22	2		
2010–11	Hartlepool U	30	1	52	3

GREULICH, Billy (F) 4 0
H: 6 3 W: 11 13 b.Sunderland 24-4-91
Source: Brandon U.

| 2009–10 | Hartlepool U | 4 | 0 | | |
| 2010–11 | Hartlepool U | 0 | 0 | 4 | 0 |

HARTLEY, Peter (D) 91 4
H: 6 0 W: 12 06 b.Hartlepool 3-4-88
Source: Scholar.

2006-07	Sunderland	1	0		
2007-08	Sunderland	0	0		
2007-08	*Chesterfield*	12	0	12	0
2008-09	Sunderland	0	0	1	0
2009-10	Hartlepool U	38	2		
2010-11	Hartlepool U	40	2	78	4

HASLAM, Steven (M) 241 3
H: 5 11 W: 10 10 b.Sheffield 6-9-79
Source: Trainee. *Honours:* England Schools, Youth.

1996-97	Sheffield W	0	0		
1997-98	Sheffield W	0	0		
1998-99	Sheffield W	2	0		
1999-2000	Sheffield W	23	0		
2000-01	Sheffield W	27	1		
2001-02	Sheffield W	41	0		
2002-03	Sheffield W	26	1		
2003-04	Sheffield W	25	0	144	2
2004-05	Northampton T	3	0		
2005-06	Northampton T	0	0		
2006-07	Northampton T	0	0	3	0

From Halifax T.

2007-08	Bury	37	1		
2008-09	Bury	13	0	50	1
2009-10	Hartlepool U	15	0		
2010-11	Hartlepool U	29	0	44	0

HOLDEN, Darren (D) 1 0
b.Krugersdorp 27-8-93
Source: Scholar.

2010-11	Hartlepool U	1	0	1	0

HORWOOD, Evan (D) 166 3
H: 6 0 W: 10 06 b.Billingham 10-3-86
Source: Scholar.

2004-05	Sheffield U	0	0		
2004-05	*Stockport Co*	10	0	10	0
2005-06	Sheffield U	0	0		
2005-06	*Scunthorpe U*	0	0		
2005-06	*Chester C*	1	0	1	0
2006-07	Sheffield U	0	0		
2006-07	*Darlington*	20	0	20	0
2007-08	Sheffield U	0	0		
2007-08	Gretna	15	1	15	1
2007-08	Carlisle U	19	0		
2008-09	Carlisle U	24	0		
2009-10	Carlisle U	32	0	75	0
2010-11	Hartlepool U	45	2	45	2

HUMPHREYS, Richie (M) 517 43
H: 5 11 W: 12 07 b.Sheffield 30-11-77
Source: Trainee. *Honours:* England Youth, Under-21.

1995-96	Sheffield W	5	0		
1996-97	Sheffield W	29	3		
1997-98	Sheffield W	7	0		
1998-99	Sheffield W	19	1		
1999-2000	Sheffield W	0	0		
1999-2000	*Scunthorpe U*	6	2	6	2
1999-2000	*Cardiff C*	9	2	9	2
2000-01	Sheffield W	7	0	67	4
2000-01	Cambridge U	7	3	7	3
2001-02	Hartlepool U	46	5		
2002-03	Hartlepool U	46	11		
2003-04	Hartlepool U	46	3		
2004-05	Hartlepool U	46	3		
2005-06	Hartlepool U	46	2		
2006-07	Hartlepool U	38	3		
2006-07	*Port Vale*	7	0	7	0
2007-08	Hartlepool U	45	3		
2008-09	Hartlepool U	45	0		
2009-10	Hartlepool U	38	0		
2010-11	Hartlepool U	25	2	421	32

JOHNSON, Paul (D) 1 0
b.Sunderland 5-4-92
Source: Scholar.

2010-11	Hartlepool U	1	0	1	0

LARKIN, Colin (F) 314 49
H: 5 9 W: 11 07 b.Dundalk 27-4-82
Source: Trainee.

1998-99	Wolverhampton W	0	0		
1999-2000	Wolverhampton W	1	0		
2000-01	Wolverhampton W	2	0		
2001-02	Wolverhampton W	0	0	3	0
2001-02	*Kidderminster H*	33	6	33	6
2002-03	Mansfield T	22	7		
2003-04	Mansfield T	37	7		
2004-05	Mansfield T	33	11	92	25
2005-06	Chesterfield	41	7		
2006-07	Chesterfield	39	4	80	11
2007-08	Northampton T	33	2		
2008-09	Northampton T	21	1		
2009-10	Northampton T	0	0	54	3
2009-10	Hartlepool U	22	1		
2010-11	Hartlepool U	30	3	52	4

LIDDLE, Gary (D) 208 14
H: 6 1 W: 12 06 b.Middlesbrough 15-6-86
Source: Trainee. *Honours:* England Youth.

2003-04	Middlesbrough	0	0		
2004-05	Middlesbrough	0	0		
2005-06	Middlesbrough	0	0		
2006-07	Hartlepool U	42	3		
2007-08	Hartlepool U	41	2		
2008-09	Hartlepool U	43	0		
2009-10	Hartlepool U	40	3		
2010-11	Hartlepool U	42	6	208	14

MACKAY, Michael (F) 52 7
H: 6 0 W: 11 06 b.Durham 11-10-82
Source: Consett.

2006-07	Hartlepool U	1	0		
2007-08	Hartlepool U	24	5		
2008-09	Hartlepool U	23	2		
2009-10	Hartlepool U	1	0		
2010-11	Hartlepool U	3	0	52	7

MARTIN, Callum (M) 0 0
b. 15-9-91
Source: Hibernian.

2010-11	Hartlepool U	0	0		

McSWEENEY, Leon (F) 142 13
H: 5 10 W: 10 11 b.Cork 19-2-83
Source: Cork C.

2001-02	Leicester C	0	0		
2002-03	Leicester C	0	0		

From Scarborough, Hucknall T, Hednesford T, Ilkeston T.

2007	Cork C	18	5	18	5
2007-08	Stockport Co	11	1		
2008-09	Stockport Co	36	4	47	5
2009-10	Hartlepool U	31	1		
2010-11	Hartlepool U	46	2	77	3

MONKHOUSE, Andy (M) 320 44
H: 6 1 W: 11 06 b.Leeds 23-10-80
Source: Trainee.

1998-99	Rotherham U	5	1		
1999-2000	Rotherham U	0	0		
2000-01	Rotherham U	12	0		
2001-02	Rotherham U	38	2		
2002-03	Rotherham U	20	0		
2003-04	Rotherham U	27	3		
2004-05	Rotherham U	14	2		
2005-06	Rotherham U	12	1	128	9
2006-07	Swindon T	10	2	10	2
2006-07	Hartlepool U	26	7		
2007-08	Hartlepool U	25	2		
2008-09	Hartlepool U	44	6		
2009-10	Hartlepool U	43	11		
2010-11	Hartlepool U	44	7	182	33

MURRAY, Paul (M) 435 30
H: 5 9 W: 10 08 b.Carlisle 31-8-76
Source: Trainee. *Honours:* England Youth, Under-21, B.

1993-94	Carlisle U	8	0		
1994-95	Carlisle U	5	0		
1995-96	Carlisle U	28	1		
1995-96	QPR	1	0		
1996-97	QPR	32	5		
1997-98	QPR	32	1		
1997-98	QPR	0	0		
1998-99	QPR	39	1		
1999-2000	QPR	30	0		
2000-01	QPR	6	0	140	7
2001-02	Southampton	1	0	1	0
2001-02	Oldham Ath	24	5		
2002-03	Oldham Ath	30	1		
2003-04	Oldham Ath	41	9	95	15
2004-05	Beira Mar	17	2	17	2
2005-06	Carlisle U	0	0		
2006-07	Carlisle U	14	1	55	2
2007-08	Gretna	32	1	32	1
2008-09	Shrewsbury T	32	2		
2009-10	Shrewsbury T	27	0	59	2
2010-11	Hartlepool U	36	1	36	1

PURVIS, Dylan (D) 0 0
b.Sunderland 18-12-91
Source: Scholar.

2010-11	Hartlepool U	0	0		

RAFFERTY, Andy (G) 1 0
b.Sidcup 27-5-88
Source: Guisborough T.

2010-11	Hartlepool U	1	0	1	0

ROWBOTHAM, Josh (M) 1 0
b.Stockton 7-1-94
Source: Scholar.

2010-11	Hartlepool U	1	0	1	0

ROWELL, Jonny (M) 12 0
H: 5 7 W: 11 02 b.Newcastle 10-9-89

2007-08	Hartlepool U	0	0		
2008-09	Hartlepool U	6	0		
2009-10	Hartlepool U	6	0		
2010-11	Hartlepool U	0	0	12	0

SWEENEY, Anthony (M) 293 43
H: 6 0 W: 11 07 b.Stockton 5-9-83
Source: Scholar.

2001-02	Hartlepool U	2	0		
2002-03	Hartlepool U	4	0		
2003-04	Hartlepool U	11	1		
2004-05	Hartlepool U	44	13		
2005-06	Hartlepool U	35	5		
2006-07	Hartlepool U	35	4		
2007-08	Hartlepool U	36	4		
2008-09	Hartlepool U	44	5		
2009-10	Hartlepool U	42	2		
2010-11	Hartlepool U	40	9	293	43

YANTORNO, Fabian (M) 70 3
H: 5 8 W: 11 05 b.Montevideo 4-9-82
Source: Miramar.

2005-06	Sambenedettese	16	0	16	0
2007-08	Gretna	21	3	21	3
2008-09	Hibernian	7	0	7	0
2009-10	Atenas San Carlos	9	0	9	0
2010-11	Hartlepool U	17	0	17	0

HEREFORD U (38)

BARTLETT, Adam (G) 92 0
H: 6 0 W: 11 11 b.Newcastle-upon-Tyne 27-2-86
Source: Blyth Spartans, Kidderminster H, Cambridge U (loan). *Honours:* England C.

From Kidderminster H.

2009-10	Hereford U	46	0		

From Kidderminster H.

2010-11	Hereford U	46	0	92	0

CANHAM, Sean (F) 40 5
H: 6 1 W: 13 01 b.Exeter 26-9-84
Source: Exeter City Scholar, Team Bath.

2008-09	Notts Co	23	3		
2009-10	Notts Co	1	0	24	3
2010-11	Hereford U	16	2	16	2

COLBECK, Joe (M) 186 16
H: 5 10 W: 10 12 b.Bradford 29-11-86
Source: Scholar.

2004-05	Bradford C	0	0		
2005-06	Bradford C	11	0		
2006-07	Bradford C	32	0		
2007-08	Bradford C	33	6		
2007-08	*Darlington*	6	2	6	2
2008-09	Bradford C	28	2		
2009-10	Bradford C	50	0	109	8
2009-10	Oldham Ath	27	1	27	1
2010-11	Hartlepool U	44	5	44	5

CONNOR, Dan (G) 152 0
H: 6 2 W: 13 04 b.Dublin 31-1-81
Source: Trainee.

1997-98	Peterborough U	0	0		
1998-99	Peterborough U	2	0		
1999-2000	Peterborough U	1	0		
2000-01	Peterborough U	0	0		
2001-02	Peterborough U	1	0		
2002-03	Peterborough U	4	0	8	0
2003	Waterford U	0	0		
2004	Waterford U	29	0	29	0
2005	Drogheda U	29	0		
2006	Drogheda U	30	0		
2007	Drogheda U	22	0		
2008	Drogheda U	1	0	82	0

2009	Cork C	28	0	28	0
2010	St Patrick's Ath	5	0	5	0
2010–11	Hereford U	0	0		

EVANS, Zac (M) 0 0
b.Presteigne 3-5-91
Source: Cardiff C Scholar.

2010–11	Hereford U	0	0

FEATHERSTONE, Nicky (F) 43 1
H: 5 6 W: 11 02 b.Goole 22-9-88
Source: Scholar.

2006–07	Hull C	2	0		
2007–08	Hull C	6	0		
2008–09	Hull C	0	0		
2009–10	Hull C	0	0		
2009–10	*Grimsby T*	8	0	8	0
2010–11	Hull C	0	0	8	0
2010–11	Hereford U	27	1	27	1

FLEETWOOD, Stuart (F) 134 27
H: 5 10 W: 12 07 b.Chepstow 23-4-86
Source: Scholar. *Honours:* Wales Youth, Under-21.

2003–04	Cardiff C	2	0		
2004–05	Cardiff C	6	0		
2005–06	Cardiff C	0	0	8	0
2006–07	Hereford U	27	3		
2006–07	*Accrington S*	3	0	3	0
2008–09	Charlton Ath	0	0		
From Forest Green R.					
2008–09	*Cheltenham T*	6	2	6	2
2008–09	*Brighton & HA*	11	1	11	1
2008–09	*Exeter C*	9	3		
2009–10	Charlton Ath	0	0		
2009–10	*Exeter C*	27	4	36	7
2010–11	Hereford U	43	14	70	17

GREEN, Ryan (D) 178 2
H: 5 7 W: 10 10 b.Cardiff 20-10-80
Source: Danes Court. *Honours:* Wales Youth, Under-21, 2 full caps.

1997–98	Wolverhampton W	0	0		
1998–99	Wolverhampton W	1	0		
1999–2000	Wolverhampton W	0	0		
2000–01	Wolverhampton W	7	0		
2000–01	*Torquay U*	10	0	10	0
2001–02	Wolverhampton W	0	0	8	0
2001–02	Millwall	13	0	13	0
2002–03	Cardiff C	0	0		
2002–03	Sheffield W	4	0	4	0
From Hereford U.					
2006–07	Bristol R	33	0		
2007–08	Bristol R	12	0		
2008–09	Bristol R	26	0	71	0
2009–10	Hereford U	31	1		
2010–11	Hereford U	41	1	72	2

GWYNNE, Sam (M) 68 1
H: 5 9 W: 11 11 b.Hereford 17-12-87
Source: Scholar.

2006–07	Hereford U	0	0		
2007–08	Hereford U	15	0		
2008–09	Hereford U	21	1		
2009–10	Hereford U	26	0		
2010–11	Hereford U	6	0	68	1

KANOUTE, Samba (D) 1 0
b.Paris 30-7-91
Source: Auxerre Youth.

2010–11	Hereford U	1	0	1	0

KOVACS, Janos (D) 141 8
H: 6 4 W: 14 10 b.Budapest 11-9-85
Source: MTK. *Honours:* Hungary Under-20.

2005–06	Chesterfield	9	0		
2006–07	Chesterfield	7	0		
2007–08	Chesterfield	41	2	57	2
2008–09	Lincoln C	45	3		
2009–10	Lincoln C	14	1	59	4
2010–11	Hereford U	25	2	25	2

LUNT, Kenny (M) 515 36
H: 5 10 W: 10 05 b.Runcorn 20-11-79
Source: Trainee. *Honours:* England Schools, Youth.

1997–98	Crewe Alex	41	2
1998–99	Crewe Alex	18	1
1999–2000	Crewe Alex	43	3
2000–01	Crewe Alex	46	1
2001–02	Crewe Alex	45	5
2002–03	Crewe Alex	46	7
2003–04	Crewe Alex	45	7
2004–05	Crewe Alex	46	5
2005–06	Crewe Alex	43	4		
2006–07	Sheffield W	37	0		
2007–08	Sheffield W	4	0		
2007–08	*Crewe Alex*	14	0		
2008–09	Sheffield W	0	0	41	0
2008–09	*Crewe Alex*	3	0	390	35
2009–10	Hereford U	42	1		
2010–11	Hereford U	42	0	84	1

MALSOM, Sam (F) 43 12
H: 5 10 W: 11 11 b.Teignmouth 10-1-87
Source: Scholar.

2006–07	Plymouth Arg	0	0		
2008	B36	12	3		
2009	B36	12	4	24	7
2009	Throttur	10	4	10	4
2010	Motala	5	1	5	1
2010–11	Hereford U	4	0	4	0

McQUILKIN, James (F) 66 5
H: 5 8 W: 11 10 b.Tipton 9-1-89
Source: WBA Scholar. *Honours:* Northern Ireland Youth, Under-21.

2007–08	Zlin	4	0		
2008–09	Zlin	2	0	6	0
2009–10	Hereford U	22	2		
2010–11	Hereford U	38	3	60	5

NGO BAHENG, Wesley (F) 5 0
H: 5 11 W: 11 06 b.Dieppe 23-9-89
Source: Le Havre.

2007–08	Newcastle U	0	0		
2008–09	Newcastle U	0	0		
2009–10	Newcastle U	0	0		
2010–11	Aldershot T	3	0	3	0
2010–11	Hereford U	2	0	2	0

PATULEA, Adrian (F) 59 12
H: 5 10 W: 11 04 b.Targoviste 10-11-84
Source: Petrolul Ploesti.

2008–09	Lincoln C	31	11	31	11
2009–10	Leyton Orient	21	1		
2010–11	Leyton Orient	1	0	22	1
2010–11	Hereford U	6	0	6	0

PURDIE, Rob (M) 148 15
H: 5 9 W: 11 06 b.Leicester 28-9-82
Source: Leicester C.

2006–07	Hereford U	44	6		
2007–08	Darlington	39	0		
2008–09	Darlington	40	6	79	6
2008–09	Oldham Ath	0	0		
2009–10	Oldham Ath	0	0		
2010–11	Oldham Ath	0	0		
2010–11	Hereford U	25	3	69	9

RABIHOU, Amadou (F) 118 21
H: 6 1 W: 12 04 b.Douala 2-12-84
Source: Lustenau.

2003–04	Sturm Graz	20	4		
2004–05	Sturm Graz	11	2		
2005–06	Sturm Graz	27	2		
2006–07	Sturm Graz	31	7		
2007–08	Sturm Graz	7	3	96	18
2008–09	Dunajska	3	0	3	0
2009–10	Lusteneau	16	3	16	3
2010–11	Hereford U	3	0	3	0

ROSE, Richard (D) 232 4
H: 6 0 W: 12 04 b.Tonbridge 8-9-82
Source: Trainee.

2000–01	Gillingham	4	0		
2001–02	Gillingham	3	0		
2002–03	Gillingham	2	0		
2002–03	*Bristol R*	9	0	9	0
2003–04	Gillingham	17	0		
2004–05	Gillingham	18	0		
2005–06	Gillingham	14	0	58	0
2006–07	Hereford U	33	1		
2007–08	Hereford U	31	1		
2008–09	Hereford U	42	0		
2009–10	Hereford U	25	0		
2010–11	Hereford U	34	2	165	4

STRATFORD, Dan (M) 26 1
H: 5 11 W: 11 13 b.Sutton 29-5-85
Source: Fulham, West Virginia Univ.

2008	DC United	5	0	5	0
2009–10	Inverness CT	14	1	14	1
2010–11	Hereford U	7	0	7	0

THOMAS, Aidan (M) 0 0
b.Hereford 1-12-91
Source: Youth.

2010–11	Hereford U	0	0

TOWNSEND, Michael (D) 190 7
H: 6 1 W: 13 12 b.Walsall 17-5-86
Source: Wolverhampton W scholar.

2004–05	Cheltenham T	0	0		
2005–06	Cheltenham T	31	0		
2006–07	Cheltenham T	30	1		
2007–08	Cheltenham T	13	1		
2008–09	Cheltenham T	26	1		
2008–09	*Barnet*	13	0	13	0
2009–10	Cheltenham T	34	3	134	6
2010–11	Hereford U	43	1	43	1

VALENTINE, Ryan (D) 314 10
H: 5 10 W: 11 05 b.Wrexham 19-8-82
Source: Trainee. *Honours:* Wales Youth, Under-21.

1999–2000	Everton	0	0		
2000–01	Everton	0	0		
2001–02	Everton	0	0		
2002–03	Darlington	43	1		
2003–04	Darlington	40	2		
2004–05	Darlington	36	1		
2005–06	Darlington	43	0		
2006–07	Wrexham	34	2		
2007–08	Wrexham	14	0	48	2
2007–08	Darlington	17	0		
2008–09	Darlington	31	0	210	4
2009–10	Hereford U	40	4		
2010–11	Hereford U	16	0	56	4

WEIR, Tyler (D) 7 0
H: 5 10 W: 11 10 b.Hereford 21-12-90
Source: Youth.

2009–10	Hereford U	3	0		
2010–11	Hereford U	4	0	7	0

WERLING, Dominik (M) 81 4
H: 5 8 W: 12 08 b.Ludwigshafen 13-12-82

2003–04	Bielefeld II	20	0	20	0
2004–05	Union Berlin	9	0	9	0
2005–06	Crailsheim	26	3	26	3
2006–07	Sakarya	0	0		
2007–08	Barnsley	17	1		
2008–09	Barnsley	0	0	17	1
2008–09	Huddersfield T	3	0		
2009–10	Huddersfield T	0	0	3	0
2010–11	Hereford U	6	0	6	0

HUDDERSFIELD T (39)

ALLINSON, Lloyd (G) 0 0
H: 6 2 W: 13 00 b.Rothwell 7-9-93
Source: Scholar.

2010–11	Huddersfield T	0	0

ARFIELD, Scott (M) 148 17
H: 5 10 W: 10 01 b.Dechmont 1-11-88
Honours: Scotland Under-21.

2007–08	Falkirk	35	3		
2008–09	Falkirk	37	7		
2009–10	Falkirk	36	3	108	13
2010–11	Huddersfield T	40	4	40	4

ATKINSON, Chris (M) 2 0
H: 6 1 W: 11 13 b. 13-2-92
Source: Scholar.

2010–11	Huddersfield T	2	0	2	0

BENNETT, Ian (G) 414 0
H: 6 0 W: 12 10 b.Worksop 10-10-71
Source: Newcastle U Trainee.

1991–92	Peterborough U	7	0		
1992–93	Peterborough U	46	0		
1993–94	Peterborough U	19	0	72	0
1993–94	Birmingham C	22	0		
1994–95	Birmingham C	46	0		
1995–96	Birmingham C	24	0		
1996–97	Birmingham C	40	0		
1997–98	Birmingham C	45	0		
1998–99	Birmingham C	10	0		
1999–2000	Birmingham C	21	0		
2000–01	Birmingham C	45	0		
2001–02	Birmingham C	18	0		
2002–03	Birmingham C	10	0		
2003–04	Birmingham C	6	0		
2004–05	Birmingham C	0	0	287	0

2004–05	*Sheffield U*	5	0		
2004–05	*Coventry C*	6	0	6	0
2005–06	Leeds U	4	0		
2006–07	Leeds U	0	0	4	0
2006–07	Sheffield U	2	0		
2007–08	Sheffield U	7	0		
2008–09	Sheffield U	2	0		
2009–10	Sheffield U	5	0	21	0
2010–11	Huddersfield T	24	0	24	0

CADAMARTERI, Danny (F)   309 35
H: 5 7 W: 13 05 b.Cleckheaton 12-10-79
Source: Trainee. *Honours:* England Youth, Under-21.

1996–97	Everton	1	0		
1997–98	Everton	26	4		
1998–99	Everton	30	4		
1999–2000	Everton	17	1		
1999–2000	*Fulham*	5	1	5	1
2000–01	Everton	16	4		
2001–02	Everton	3	0	93	13
2001–02	Bradford C	14	2		
2002–03	Bradford C	20	0		
2003–04	Bradford C	18	3		
2004–05	Leeds U	0	0		
2004–05	Sheffield U	21	1	21	0
2005–06	Bradford C	39	2		
2006–07	Bradford C	0	0	91	7
2006–07	*Doncaster R*	6	1	6	1
2006–07	Leicester C	9	0	9	0
2007–08	Huddersfield T	12	3		
2008–09	Huddersfield T	32	2		
2009–10	Huddersfield T	0	0		
2009–10	Dundee U	21	4		
2010–11	Dundee U	8	0	29	4
2010–11	Huddersfield T	11	3	55	8

CAREY, Graham (M)   19 2
H: 6 0 W: 10 12 b.Dublin 2-5-89
Honours: Eire Under-21.

2010–11	Huddersfield T	19	2	19	2

On loan from Celtic.

CHIPPENDALE, Aiden (M)   1 0
H: 5 8 W: 10 10 b.Bradford 24-5-92
Source: Scholar.

2010–11	Huddersfield T	1	0	1	0

CLARKE, Nathan (D)   282 8
H: 6 2 W: 12 00 b.Halifax 30-11 83
Source: Scholar.

2001–02	Huddersfield T	36	1		
2002–03	Huddersfield T	3	0		
2003–04	Huddersfield T	26	1		
2004–05	Huddersfield T	37	0		
2005–06	Huddersfield T	46	0		
2006 07	Huddersfield T	16	0		
2007–08	Huddersfield T	44	2		
2008–09	Huddersfield T	38	3		
2009–10	Huddersfield T	17	1		
2010–11	Huddersfield T	1	0	264	8
2010–11	*Colchester U*	18	0	18	0

CLARKE, Peter (D)   345 34
H: 6 0 W: 12 00 b.Southport 3-1-82
Source: Trainee. *Honours:* England Schools, Youth, Under-20, Under-21.

1998–99	Everton	0	0		
1999–2000	Everton	0	0		
2000–01	Everton	1	0		
2001–02	Everton	7	0		
2002–03	Everton	0	0		
2002–03	*Blackpool*	16	3		
2002–03	*Port Vale*	13	1	13	1
2003–04	Everton	1	0		
2003–04	*Coventry C*	5	0	5	0
2004–05	Everton	0	0	9	0
2004–05	Blackpool	38	5		
2005–06	Blackpool	46	6	100	14
2006–07	Southend U	38	2		
2007–08	Southend U	45	4		
2008–09	Southend U	43	4	126	10
2009–10	Huddersfield T	46	5		
2010–11	Huddersfield T	46	4	92	9

CLARKE, Tom (D)   88 3
H: 6 0 W: 11 02 b.Sowerby Bridge 21-12-87
Source: Scholar. *Honours:* England Youth.

2004–05	Huddersfield T	5	0		
2005–06	Huddersfield T	17	1		
2006–07	Huddersfield T	9	0		
2007–08	Huddersfield T	3	0		

2008–09	Huddersfield T	15	1		
2008–09	*Bradford C*	6	0	6	0
2009–10	Huddersfield T	21	0		
2010–11	Huddersfield T	5	1	82	3

FRANKS, Lee (D)   5 0
H: 5 11 W: 12 00 b. 7-3-91
Source: Scholar.

2009–10	Huddersfield T	0	0		
2010–11	Huddersfield T	0	0		
2010–11	*Oxford U*	5	0	5	0

GUDJONSSON, Joey (M)   295 30
H: 5 9 W: 12 04 b.Akranes 25-5-80
Honours: Iceland Youth, Under-21, 34 full caps, 1 goal.

1998–99	Genk	5	0	5	0
1999–2000	MVV	19	5	19	5
2000–01	RKC	31	4	31	4
2001–02	Betis	11	0	11	0
2002–03	Aston Villa	11	2	11	2
2003–04	Wolverhampton W	11	0	11	0
2004–05	Leicester C	35	2		
2005–06	Leicester C	42	8	77	10
2006–07	AZ	5	0	5	0
2006–07	Burnley	11	0		
2007–08	Burnley	28	1		
2008–09	Burnley	39	6		
2009–10	Burnley	10	0	88	7
2010–11	Huddersfield T	37	2	37	2

HUNT, Jack (D)   39 1
H: 5 9 W: 11 02 b.Rothwell 6-12-90
Source: Scholar.

2009–10	Huddersfield T	0	0		
2010–11	Huddersfield T	19	1	19	1
2010–11	*Chesterfield*	20	0	20	0

KAY, Antony (D)   323 37
H: 5 11 W: 11 08 b.Barnsley 21-10-82
Source: Trainee. *Honours:* England Youth.

1999–2000	Barnsley	0	0		
2000–01	Barnsley	7	0		
2001–02	Barnsley	1	0		
2002–03	Barnsley	16	0		
2003–04	Barnsley	43	3		
2004–05	Barnsley	39	6		
2005–06	Barnsley	36	1		
2006–07	Barnsley	32	1	174	11
2007–08	Tranmere R	38	6		
2008–09	Tranmere R	44	11	82	17
2009–10	Huddersfield T	40	6		
2010–11	Huddersfield T	27	3	67	9

LEE, Alan (F)   429 94
H: 6 2 W: 13 09 b.Galway 21-8-78
Source: Trainee. *Honours:* Eire Under-21, 10 full caps.

1995–96	Aston Villa	0	0		
1996–97	Aston Villa	0	0		
1997–98	Aston Villa	0	0		
1998–99	Aston Villa	0	0		
1998–99	*Torquay U*	7	2	7	2
1998–99	*Port Vale*	11	2	11	2
1999–2000	Burnley	15	0		
2000–01	Burnley	0	0	15	0
2000–01	Rotherham U	31	13		
2001–02	Rotherham U	38	9		
2002–03	Rotherham U	41	15		
2003–04	Rotherham U	1	0	111	37
2003–04	Cardiff C	23	3		
2004–05	Cardiff C	38	5		
2005–06	Cardiff C	25	2	86	10
2005–06	Ipswich T	14	4		
2006–07	Ipswich T	41	16		
2007–08	Ipswich T	45	11		
2008–09	Ipswich T	3	0	103	31
2008–09	Crystal Palace	16	3		
2008–09	*Norwich C*	7	2	7	2
2009–10	Crystal Palace	42	6		
2010–11	Crystal Palace	3	1	61	10
2010–11	Huddersfield T	28	0	28	0

McCOMBE, Jamie (D)   303 22
H: 6 5 W: 12 05 b.Scunthorpe 1-1-83
Source: Scholar.

2001–02	Scunthorpe U	17	0		
2002–03	Scunthorpe U	31	1		
2003–04	Scunthorpe U	15	0	63	1
2003–04	Lincoln C	8	0		
2004–05	Lincoln C	41	3		
2005–06	Lincoln C	38	4	87	7
2006–07	Bristol C	41	4		

2007–08	Bristol C	34	3		
2008–09	Bristol C	28	1		
2009–10	Bristol C	16	1	119	9
2010–11	Huddersfield T	34	5	34	5

NAYSMITH, Gary (D)   324 9
H: 5 9 W: 12 01 b.Edinburgh 16-11-78
Source: Whitehill Welfare Colts. *Honours:* Scotland Schools, Under-21, B, 46 full caps, 1 goal.

1995–96	Hearts	1	0		
1996–97	Hearts	10	0		
1997–98	Hearts	16	2		
1998–99	Hearts	26	0		
1999–2000	Hearts	35	1		
2000–01	Hearts	9	0	97	3
2000–01	Everton	20	2		
2001–02	Everton	24	0		
2002–03	Everton	28	1		
2003–04	Everton	29	2		
2004–05	Everton	11	0		
2005–06	Everton	7	0		
2006–07	Everton	15	1	134	6
2007–08	Sheffield U	38	0		
2008–09	Sheffield U	39	0		
2009–10	Sheffield U	2	0	79	0
2010–11	Huddersfield T	14	0	14	0

NOVAK, Lee (F)   68 17
H: 6 0 W: 12 04 b.Newcastle 28-9-88
Source: Gateshead.

2008–09	Huddersfield T	0	0		
2009–10	Huddersfield T	37	12		
2010–11	Huddersfield T	31	5	68	17

PELTIER, Lee (D)   156 2
H: 5 10 W: 12 00 b.Liverpool 11-12-86
Source: Scholar.

2004–05	Liverpool	0	0		
2005–06	Liverpool	0	0		
2006–07	Liverpool	0	0		
2006–07	*Hull C*	7	0	7	0
2007–08	Liverpool	0	0		
2007–08	Yeovil T	34	0		
2008 09	*Yeovil T*	35	1	69	1
2009–10	Huddersfield T	42	0		
2010–11	Huddersfield T	38	1	80	1

PILKINGTON, Anthony (M)   167 35
H: 5 11 W: 12 00 b.Blackburn 3-11-87
Source: Atherton Collieries. *Honours:* Eire Under-21.

2006–07	Stockport Co	24	5		
2007–08	Stockport Co	29	6		
2008 09	Stockport Co	24	5	77	16
2008 09	*Huddersfield T*	16	2		
2009–10	Huddersfield T	43	7		
2010–11	Huddersfield T	31	10	90	19

RHODES, Jordan (F)   111 45
H: 6 1 W: 11 03 b.Oldham 5-2-90
Source: Academy. *Honours:* Scotland Under-21.

2007–08	Ipswich T	8	1		
2008–09	Ipswich T	2	0	10	1
2008–09	*Rochdale*	5	2	5	2
2008–09	*Brentford*	14	7	14	7
2009–10	Huddersfield T	45	19		
2010–11	Huddersfield T	37	16	82	35

RIDEHALGH, Liam (D)   20 0
H: 5 10 W: 11 05 b.Halifax 20-4-91
Source: Scholar.

2009–10	Huddersfield T	0	0		
2010–11	Huddersfield T	20	0	20	0

ROBERTS, Gary (F)   195 36
H: 5 10 W: 11 09 b.Chester 18-3-84
Source: Denbigh T, Bangor C.

2006–07	Accrington S	14	8	14	8
2006–07	Ipswich T	33	2		
2007–08	Ipswich T	21	1	54	3
2007–08	*Crewe Alex*	4	0	4	0
2008–09	Huddersfield T	43	9		
2009–10	Huddersfield T	43	8		
2010–11	Huddersfield T	37	9	123	25

ROBINSON, Theo (F)   131 38
H: 5 9 W: 10 03 b.Birmingham 22-1-89
Source: Scholar.

2005–06	Watford	1	0		
2006–07	Watford	1	0		
2007–08	Watford	0	0		
2007–08	*Hereford U*	43	13	43	13

Season	Club	Apps	Gls	Tot A	Tot G
2008–09	Watford	3	0	5	0
2008–09	*Southend U*	21	7	21	7
2009–10	Huddersfield T	37	13		
2010–11	Huddersfield T	1	0	38	13
2010–11	Millwall	11	3	11	3
2010–11	*Derby Co*	13	2	13	2

SIMPSON, Robbie (F)   101 8
H: 6 1 W: 11 11 b.Poole 15-3-85
Source: Cambridge U.

Season	Club	Apps	Gls	Tot A	Tot G
2007–08	Coventry C	28	1		
2008–09	Coventry C	33	3	61	4
2009–10	Huddersfield T	13	0		
2010–11	Huddersfield T	0	0	13	0
2010–11	*Brentford*	27	4	27	4

SMITHIES, Alex (G)   97 0
H: 6 1 W: 10 01 b.Huddersfield 25-3-90
Source: Scholar. Honours: England Youth.

Season	Club	Apps	Gls	Tot A	Tot G
2006–07	Huddersfield T	0	0		
2007–08	Huddersfield T	2	0		
2008–09	Huddersfield T	27	0		
2009–10	Huddersfield T	46	0		
2010–11	Huddersfield T	22	0	97	0

SPENCER, James (F)   32 8
H: 6 1 W: 13 00 b.Leeds 13-12-91
Source: Scholar.

Season	Club	Apps	Gls	Tot A	Tot G
2008–09	Huddersfield T	0	0		
2009–10	Huddersfield T	0	0		
2010–11	Huddersfield T	0	0		
2010–11	*Morecambe*	32	8	32	8

HULL C (40)

ATKINSON, Will (M)   61 7
H: 5 10 W: 10 07 b.Beverley 14-10-88
Source: Scholar.

Season	Club	Apps	Gls	Tot A	Tot G
2006–07	Hull C	0	0		
2007–08	Hull C	0	0		
2007–08	*Port Vale*	4	0	4	0
2007–08	*Mansfield T*	12	0	12	0
2008–09	Hull C	0	0		
2009–10	Hull C	2	1		
2009–10	*Rochdale*	15	3		
2010–11	Hull C	4	0	6	1
2010–11	*Rotherham U*	3	1	3	1
2010–11	*Rochdale*	21	2	36	5

BARMBY, Nick (F)   480 78
H: 5 7 W: 11 03 b.Hull 11-2-74
Source: Trainee. Honours: England Schools, Youth, Under-21, B, 23 full caps, 4 goals.

Season	Club	Apps	Gls	Tot A	Tot G
1991–92	Tottenham H	0	0		
1992–93	Tottenham H	22	6		
1993–94	Tottenham H	27	5		
1994–95	Tottenham H	38	9	87	20
1995–96	Middlesbrough	32	7		
1996–97	Middlesbrough	10	1	42	8
1996–97	Everton	25	4		
1997–98	Everton	30	2		
1998–99	Everton	24	3		
1999–2000	Everton	37	9	116	18
2000–01	Liverpool	26	2		
2001–02	Liverpool	6	0	32	2
2002–03	Leeds U	19	4		
2003–04	*Nottingham F*	6	1	6	1
2003–04	Leeds U	6	0	25	4
2004–05	Hull C	39	9		
2005–06	Hull C	26	5		
2006–07	Hull C	20	4		
2007–08	Hull C	15	1		
2008–09	Hull C	21	1		
2009–10	Hull C	20	0		
2010–11	Hull C	31	5	172	25

BELAID, Tijani (M)   73 15
H: 5 9 W: 11 09 b.Paris 6-9-87
Honours: Tunisia 18 full caps, 3 goals.

Season	Club	Apps	Gls	Tot A	Tot G
2004–05	Internazionale	1	0		
2005–06	Internazionale	0	0	1	0
2006–07	*PSV Eindhoven*	0	0		
2007–08	Slavia Prague	15	4		
2008–09	Slavia Prague	24	9		
2009–10	Slavia Prague	14	2		
2010–11	Slavia Prague	11	0	64	15
2010–11	Hull C	8	0	8	0

BULLARD, Jimmy (M)   289 39
H: 5 10 W: 11 05 b.Newham 23-10-78
Source: Corinthian, Dartford, Gravesend & N.

Season	Club	Apps	Gls	Tot A	Tot G
1998–99	West Ham U	0	0		
1999–2000	West Ham U	0	0		
2000–01	West Ham U	0	0		
2001–02	Peterborough U	40	8		
2002–03	Peterborough U	26	3	66	11
2002–03	Wigan Ath	17	1		
2003–04	Wigan Ath	46	2		
2004–05	Wigan Ath	46	3		
2005–06	Wigan Ath	36	4	145	10
2005–06	Fulham	0	0		
2006–07	Fulham	4	2		
2007–08	Fulham	17	2		
2008–09	Fulham	18	2	39	6
2008–09	Hull C	1	0		
2009–10	Hull C	14	5		
2010–11	Hull C	8	2	23	7
2010–11	*Ipswich T*	16	5	16	5

CAIRNEY, Tom (M)   33 2
H: 6 0 W: 11 05 b.Nottingham 20-1-91
Source: Scholar. Honours: Scotland Youth, Under-21.

Season	Club	Apps	Gls	Tot A	Tot G
2009–10	Hull C	11	1		
2010–11	Hull C	22	1	33	2

CHESTER, James (D)   47 3
H: 5 11 W: 11 04 b.Warrington 23-1-89
Source: Scholar.

Season	Club	Apps	Gls	Tot A	Tot G
2007–08	Manchester U	0	0		
2008–09	Manchester U	0	0		
2008–09	*Peterborough U*	5	0	5	0
2009–10	Manchester U	0	0		
2009–10	*Plymouth Arg*	3	0	3	0
2010–11	Manchester U	0	0		
2010–11	*Carlisle U*	18	2	18	2
2010–11	Hull C	21	1	21	1

COOPER, Liam (D)   10 1
H: 6 2 W: 13 07 b.Hull 30-8-91
Source: Scholar. Honours: Scotland Youth.

Season	Club	Apps	Gls	Tot A	Tot G
2008–09	Hull C	0	0		
2009–10	Hull C	2	0		
2010–11	Hull C	2	0	4	0
2010–11	*Carlisle U*	6	1	6	1

CULLEN, Mark (F)   24 1
H: 5 9 W: 11 11 b.Ashington 24-4-92
Source: Scholar.

Season	Club	Apps	Gls	Tot A	Tot G
2009–10	Hull C	3	1		
2010–11	Hull C	17	0	20	1
2010–11	*Bradford C*	4	0	4	0

DAWSON, Andy (D)   – 452 16
H: 5 9 W: 11 02 b.Northallerton 20-10-78
Source: Trainee.

Season	Club	Apps	Gls	Tot A	Tot G
1995–96	Nottingham F	0	0		
1996–97	Nottingham F	0	0		
1997–98	Nottingham F	0	0		
1998–99	Nottingham F	0	0		
1998–99	Scunthorpe U	24	0		
1999–2000	Scunthorpe U	43	2		
2000–01	Scunthorpe U	41	4		
2001–02	Scunthorpe U	44	0		
2002–03	Scunthorpe U	43	2	195	8
2003–04	Hull C	33	3		
2004–05	Hull C	34	0		
2005–06	Hull C	18	0		
2006–07	Hull C	38	2		
2007–08	Hull C	29	1		
2008–09	Hull C	25	1		
2009–10	Hull C	35	1		
2010–11	Hull C	45	0	257	8

DEAGLE, Dean (D)   0 0
b.Cramlington 26-12-91
Source: Scholar.

Season	Club	Apps	Gls	Tot A	Tot G
2010–11	Hull C	0	0		

DEVITT, Jamie (F)   46 8
H: 5 10 W: 10 05 b.Dublin 6-7-90
Source: Cherry Orchard BC, Hull C Scholar.
Honours: Eire Youth, Under-21.

Season	Club	Apps	Gls	Tot A	Tot G
2007–08	Hull C	0	0		
2008–09	Hull C	0	0		
2009–10	Hull C	0	0		
2009–10	*Darlington*	6	1	6	1
2009–10	*Shrewsbury T*	9	2	9	2
2009–10	*Grimsby T*	15	5	15	5
2010–11	Hull C	16	0	16	0

DUKE, Matt (G)   58 0
H: 6 5 W: 13 04 b.Sheffield 16-7-77
Source: Alfreton T.

Season	Club	Apps	Gls	Tot A	Tot G
1999–2000	Sheffield U	0	0		
2000–01	Sheffield U	0	0		
2001–02	Sheffield U	0	0		
2004–05	Hull C	2	0		
2005–06	Hull C	2	0		
2005–06	*Stockport Co*	3	0	3	0
2005–06	*Wycombe W*	5	0	5	0
2006–07	Hull C	1	0		
2007–08	Hull C	3	0		
2008–09	Hull C	10	0		
2009–10	Hull C	11	0		
2010–11	Hull C	21	0	50	0

EMERTON, Danny (F)   0 0
b.Beverley
Source: Scholar.

Season	Club	Apps	Gls	Tot A	Tot G
2010–11	Hull C	0	0		

FAGAN, Craig (F)   249 39
H: 5 11 W: 11 11 b.Birmingham 11-12-82
Source: Scholar.

Season	Club	Apps	Gls	Tot A	Tot G
2001–02	Birmingham C	0	0		
2002–03	Birmingham C	1	0		
2002–03	*Bristol C*	6	1	6	1
2003–04	Birmingham C	0	0	1	0
2003–04	Colchester U	37	9		
2004–05	Colchester U	26	8	63	17
2004–05	Hull C	12	4		
2005–06	Hull C	41	5		
2006–07	Hull C	27	6		
2006–07	Derby Co	17	1		
2007–08	Derby Co	22	0	39	1
2007–08	*Hull C*	8	0		
2008–09	Hull C	22	3		
2009–10	Hull C	25	2		
2010–11	Hull C	5	0	140	20

FOLAN, Caleb (F)   180 28
H: 6 2 W: 14 07 b.Leeds 26-10-82
Source: Trainee. Honours: Eire 7 full caps.

Season	Club	Apps	Gls	Tot A	Tot G
1999–2000	Leeds U	0	0		
2000–01	Leeds U	0	0		
2001–02	Leeds U	0	0		
2001–02	*Rushden & D*	6	0	6	0
2001–02	*Hull C*	1	0		
2002–03	Leeds U	0	0		
2002–03	Chesterfield	13	1		
2003–04	Chesterfield	7	0		
2004–05	Chesterfield	32	6		
2005–06	Chesterfield	27	0		
2006–07	Chesterfield	23	8	102	15
2006–07	Wigan Ath	13	2		
2007–08	Wigan Ath	2	0	15	2
2007–08	Hull C	29	8		
2008–09	Hull C	15	1		
2009–10	Hull C	8	2		
2009–10	*Middlesbrough*	1	0	1	0
2010–11	Hull C	3	0	56	11

FOX, Joe (D)   0 0
b.York
Source: Scholar.

Season	Club	Apps	Gls	Tot A	Tot G
2010–11	Hull C	0	0		

FRYATT, Matty (F)   270 88
H: 5 10 W: 11 00 b.Nuneaton 5-3-86
Source: Scholar. Honours: England Youth.

Season	Club	Apps	Gls	Tot A	Tot G
2002–03	Walsall	0	0		
2003–04	Walsall	11	1		
2003–04	*Carlisle U*	10	1	10	1
2004–05	Walsall	36	15		
2005–06	Walsall	23	11	70	27
2005–06	Leicester C	19	6		
2006–07	Leicester C	32	3		
2007–08	Leicester C	30	2		
2008–09	Leicester C	46	27		
2009–10	Leicester C	29	11		
2010–11	Leicester C	12	2	168	51
2010–11	Hull C	22	9	22	9

GARCIA, Richard (F)   220 28
H: 5 11 W: 12 01 b.Perth 4-9-81
Source: Trainee. Honours: Australia Under-23, 13 full caps.

Season	Club	Apps	Gls	Tot A	Tot G
1998–99	West Ham U	0	0		
1999–2000	West Ham U	0	0		
2000–01	West Ham U	0	0		
2000–01	*Leyton Orient*	18	4	18	4
2001–02	West Ham U	8	0		

2002–03	West Ham U	0	0		
2003–04	West Ham U	7	0		
2004–05	West Ham U	1	0	16	0
2004–05	Colchester U	24	4		
2005–06	Colchester U	22	5		
2006–07	Colchester U	36	7	82	16
2007–08	Hull C	38	5		
2008–09	Hull C	23	1		
2009–10	Hull C	18	0		
2010–11	Hull C	25	2	104	8

GARDNER, Anthony (D) 215 7
H: 6 3 W: 14 00 b.Stone 19-9-80
Source: Trainee. *Honours:* England Under-21, 1 full cap.

1998–99	Port Vale	15	1		
1999–2000	Port Vale	26	3	41	4
1999–2000	Tottenham H	0	0		
2000–01	Tottenham H	8	0		
2001–02	Tottenham H	15	0		
2002–03	Tottenham H	12	1		
2003–04	Tottenham H	33	0		
2004–05	Tottenham H	17	0		
2005–06	Tottenham H	17	0		
2006–07	Tottenham H	8	0		
2007–08	*Everton*	0	0		
2007–08	Tottenham H	4	1	114	2
2008–09	Hull C	6	0		
2009–10	Hull C	24	0		
2010–11	Hull C	2	0	32	0
2010–11	*Crystal Palace*	28	1	28	1

GHILAS, Kamel (F) 208 54
H: 5 10 W: 11 00 b.Marseille 9-3-84
Honours: Algeria 16 full caps, 3 goals.

2003–04	Cannes	18	0		
2004–05	Cannes	31	7		
2005–06	Cannes	35	13	84	20
2006–07	Guimaraes	29	12		
2007–08	Guimaraes	30	6	59	18
2008–09	Celta Vigo	33	13	33	13
2009–10	Hull C	13	1		
2010–11	Hull C	0	0	13	1
2010–11	*Arles-Avignon*	19	2	19	2

HALMOSI, Peter (M) 271 39
H: 5 10 W: 10 12 b.Szombathely 25-9-79
Honours: Hungary 30 full caps.

1998–99	Haladas	2	0		
1999–2000	Haladas	26	2		
2000–01	Haladas	14	2		
2001–02	Haladas	38	2	80	6
2002–03	Graz	17	3	17	3
2003–04	Debrecen	29	5		
2004–05	Debrecen	28	5		
2005–06	Debrecen	26	7		
2006–07	Debrecen	14	1	97	18
2006–07	Plymouth Arg	16	4		
2007–08	Plymouth Arg	43	8	59	12
2008–09	Hull C	18	0		
2009–10	Hull C	0	0		
2010–11	Hull C	0	0	18	0

Transferred to Haladas January 2011.

HARPER, James (M) 377 30
H: 5 10 W: 11 02 b.Chelmsford 9-11-80
Source: Trainee.

1999–2000	Arsenal	0	0		
2000–01	Arsenal	0	0		
2000–01	*Cardiff C*	3	0	3	0
2000–01	Reading	12	1		
2001–02	Reading	26	1		
2002–03	Reading	36	2		
2003–04	Reading	39	1		
2004–05	Reading	41	3		
2005–06	Reading	45	7		
2006–07	Reading	38	3		
2007–08	Reading	38	6		
2008–09	Reading	34	1		
2009–10	Reading	3	0	312	25
2009–10	Sheffield U	34	4	34	4
2010–11	Hull C	28	1	28	1

HOLOHAN, Gavan (M) 0 0
b.Republic of Ireland 15-12-91
Source: Scholar.

2010–11	Hull C	0	0		

KILBANE, Kevin (M) 521 36
H: 6 1 W: 13 05 b.Preston 1-2-77
Source: Trainee. *Honours:* Eire Under-21, 110 full caps, 8 goals.

1993–94	Preston NE	0	0		
1994–95	Preston NE	0	0		
1995–96	Preston NE	11	1		
1996–97	Preston NE	36	2	47	3
1997–98	WBA	43	4		
1998–99	WBA	44	6		
1999–2000	WBA	19	5	106	15
1999–2000	Sunderland	20	1		
2000–01	Sunderland	30	4		
2001–02	Sunderland	28	2		
2002–03	Sunderland	30	1		
2003–04	Sunderland	5	0	113	8
2003–04	Everton	30	3		
2004–05	Everton	38	1		
2005–06	Everton	34	0		
2006–07	Everton	2	0	104	4
2006–07	Wigan Ath	31	1		
2007–08	Wigan Ath	35	1		
2008–09	Wigan Ath	10	0	76	2
2008–09	Hull C	16	0		
2009–10	Hull C	21	1		
2010–11	Hull C	14	1	51	2
2010–11	*Huddersfield T*	24	2	24	2

KOREN, Robert (M) 382 75
H: 5 10 W: 11 03 b.Ljubljana 20-9-80
Honours: Slovenia Under-21, 58 full caps, 5 goals.

1999–2000	Dravograd	31	2		
2000–01	Dravograd	31	9	62	11
2001–02	Publikum	31	5		
2002–03	Publikum	32	12		
2003–04	Publikum	15	5	78	22
2004	Lillestrom	23	1		
2005	Lillestrom	26	8		
2006	Lillestrom	26	10	75	19
2006–07	WBA	18	1		
2007–08	WBA	40	9		
2008–09	WBA	35	1		
2009–10	WBA	34	5	127	16
2010–11	Hull C	40	7	40	7

LISLES, Dean (D) 0 0
b.York 5-5-92
Source: York C Scholar, Ossett T.

2010–11	Hull C	0	0		

McLEAN, Aaron (F) 220 76
H: 5 9 W: 10 10 b.Hammersmith 25-5-83
Source: Trainee.

1999–2000	Leyton Orient	3	0		
2000–01	Leyton Orient	2	1		
2001–02	Leyton Orient	27	1		
2002–03	Leyton Orient	8	0	40	2

From Aldershot T, Grays Ath.

2006–07	Peterborough U	16	7		
2007–08	Peterborough U	45	29		
2008–09	Peterborough U	42	18		
2009–10	Peterborough U	35	7		
2010–11	Peterborough U	19	10	157	71
2010–11	Hull C	23	3	23	3

McSHANE, Paul (D) 171 8
H: 6 0 W: 11 05 b.Wicklow 6-1-86
Source: Trainee. *Honours:* Eire Youth, Under-21, 26 full caps.

2002–03	Manchester U	0	0		
2003–04	Manchester U	0	0		
2004–05	Manchester U	0	0		
2004–05	*Walsall*	4	1	4	1
2005–06	Manchester U	0	0		
2005–06	*Brighton & HA*	38	3	38	3
2006–07	WBA	32	2	32	2
2007–08	Sunderland	21	0		
2008–09	Sunderland	3	0		
2008–09	*Hull C*	17	1		
2009–10	Sunderland	0	0	24	0
2009–10	Hull C	27	0		
2010–11	Hull C	19	0	63	1
2010–11	*Barnsley*	10	1	10	1

OLOFINJANA, Seyi (M) 245 36
H: 6 4 W: 11 10 b.Lagos 30-6-80
Source: Kwara United Ilorin. *Honours:* Nigeria 44 full caps.

2003	Brann	25	9		
2004	Brann	9	2	34	11
2004–05	Wolverhampton W	42	5		
2005–06	Wolverhampton W	13	0		
2006–07	Wolverhampton W	44	8		
2007–08	Wolverhampton W	36	3	135	16
2008–09	Stoke C	18	2		
2009–10	Stoke C	0	0	18	2
2009–10	Hull C	19	1		
2010–11	Hull C	0	0	19	1
2010–11	*Cardiff C*	39	6	39	6

OXLEY, Mark (G) 3 0
H: 5 11 W: 11 05 b.Aston 2-6-90
Source: Rotherham U Scholar. *Honours:* England Youth.

2008–09	Hull C	0	0		
2009–10	Hull C	0	0		
2009–10	*Grimsby T*	3	0	3	0
2010–11	Hull C	0	0		

ROSENIOR, Liam (D) 230 3
H: 5 10 W: 11 05 b.Wandsworth 9-7-84
Source: Scholar. *Honours:* England Youth, Under-20, Under-21.

2001–02	Bristol C	1	0		
2002–03	Bristol C	21	2		
2003–04	Bristol C	0	0	22	2
2003–04	Fulham	0	0		
2003–04	*Torquay U*	10	0	10	0
2004–05	Fulham	17	0		
2005–06	Fulham	24	0		
2006–07	Fulham	38	0		
2007–08	Fulham	0	0	79	0
2007–08	Reading	17	0		
2008–09	Reading	42	0		
2009–10	Reading	5	0		
2009–10	*Ipswich T*	29	1	29	1
2010–11	Reading	0	0	64	0
2010–11	Hull C	26	0	26	0

SIMPSON, Jay (F) 125 25
H: 5 11 W: 13 04 b.Enfield 1-12-88
Source: Scholar. *Honours:* England Youth.

2007–08	Arsenal	0	0		
2007–08	*Millwall*	41	6	41	6
2008–09	Arsenal	0	0		
2008–09	*WBA*	13	1	13	1
2009–10	Arsenal	0	0		
2009–10	*QPR*	39	12	39	12
2010–11	Hull C	32	6	32	6

SOLANO, Nolberto (M) 490 98
H: 5 8 W: 10 07 b.Callao 12-12-74
Honours: Peru 95 full caps, 20 goals.

1994–95	Sporting Cristal	38	12		
1995–96	Sporting Cristal	26	13		
1996–97	Sporting Cristal	11	7	75	32
1997–98	Boca Juniors	32	5	32	5
1998–99	Newcastle U	29	6		
1999–2000	Newcastle U	30	3		
2000–01	Newcastle U	33	6		
2001–02	Newcastle U	37	7		
2002–03	Newcastle U	31	7		
2003–04	Newcastle U	12	0		
2003–04	Aston Villa	19	0		
2004–05	Aston Villa	36	8		
2005–06	Aston Villa	3	0	49	8
2005–06	Newcastle U	29	6		
2006–07	Newcastle U	28	2		
2007–08	Newcastle U	1	0	230	37
2007–08	West Ham U	23	4	23	4
2008–09	Larissa	17	2	17	2
2009	Universitario	32	10	32	10
2009–10	Leicester C	11	0	11	0
2010–11	Hull C	11	0	11	0

STEWART, Cameron (M) 19 0
H: 5 8 W: 11 05 b.Manchester 8-4-91
Source: Scholar. *Honours:* England Youth.

2009–10	Manchester U	0	0		
2010–11	Manchester U	0	0		
2010–11	*Yeovil T*	5	0	5	0
2010–11	Hull C	14	0	14	0

WILKINSON, Danny (D) 0 0
H: 6 1 W: 12 08 b.Hull 2-10-91
Source: Scholar.

2010–11	Hull C	0	0		

ZAYATTE, Kamil (D) 113 4
H: 6 2 W: 13 10 b.Conakry 7-3-85
Honours: Guinea 30 full caps, 4 goals.

2005–06	Lens	1	0		
2006–07	Lens	1	0	1	0
2006–07	Young Boys	18	0		
2007–08	Young Boys	23	1	41	1
2008–09	Hull C	32	1		
2009–10	Hull C	23	2		
2010–11	Hull C	16	0	71	3

Transferred to Konya January 2011.

IPSWICH T (41)

AINSLEY, Jack (D)   1   0
H: 5 11 W: 11 00 b.Ipswich 17-9-90
Source: Scholar.

2009–10	Ipswich T	0	0		
2010–11	Ipswich T	1	0	1	0

BROWN, Troy (D)   13   0
H: 6 1 W: 12 01 b.Croydon 17-9-90
Source: Fulham Scholar. *Honours:* Wales Under-21.

2009–10	Ipswich T	1	0		
2010–11	Ipswich T	12	0	13	0

CARSON, Josh (M)   9   3
H: 5 9 W: 11 00 b.Ballymena 3-6-93
Source: Scholar. *Honours:* Northern Ireland Under-21, 2 full caps.

2010–11	Ipswich T	9	3	9	3

CAWLEY, David (M)   0   0
H: 5 10 W: 11 13 b.Mayo 19-9-91
Source: Scholar.

2010–11	Ipswich T	0	0		

CIVELLI, Luciano (M)   87   8
H: 6 2 W: 13 01 b.Buenos Aires 6-10-86

2005–06	Banfield	1	0		
2006–07	Banfield	18	0		
2007–08	Banfield	34	6		
2008–09	Banfield	17	2	70	8
2008–09	Ipswich T	8	0		
2009–10	Ipswich T	0	0		
2010–11	Ipswich T	9	0	17	0

CLARK, Billy (M)   3   0
H: 5 10 W: 11 11 b.Ipswich 20-10-91
Source: Scholar.

2009–10	Ipswich T	3	0		
2010–11	Ipswich T	0	0	3	0

COUNAGO, Pablo (F)   340   71
H: 5 11 W: 11 06 b.Pontevedra 9-8-79

1998–99	Numancia	13	1	13	1
1998–99	Celta Vigo	1	0		
1999–2000	Huelva	26	4	26	4
2000–01	Celta Vigo	8	0	9	0
2001–02	Ipswich T	13	0		
2002–03	Ipswich T	39	17		
2003–04	Ipswich T	29	11		
2004–05	Ipswich T	19	3		
2005–06	Malaga	27	3		
2006–07	Malaga	21	7	48	10
2007–08	Ipswich T	43	12		
2008–09	Ipswich T	44	9		
2009–10	Ipswich T	27	2		
2010–11	Ipswich T	0	0	214	54
2010–11	Crystal Palace	30	2	30	2

DELANEY, Damien (D)   375   10
H: 6 3 W: 14 00 b.Cork 20-7-81
Source: Cork C. *Honours:* Eire 5 full caps.

2000–01	Leicester C	5	0		
2001–02	Leicester C	3	0		
2001–02	Stockport Co	12	1	12	1
2001–02	Huddersfield T	2	0	2	0
2002–03	Leicester C	0	0	8	0
2002–03	Mansfield T	7	0	7	0
2002–03	Hull C	30	1		
2003–04	Hull C	46	2		
2004–05	Hull C	43	1		
2005–06	Hull C	46	0		
2006–07	Hull C	37	1		
2007–08	Hull C	22	0	224	5
2007–08	QPR	17	1		
2008–09	QPR	37	1		
2009–10	QPR	0	0	54	2
2009–10	Ipswich T	36	0		
2010–11	Ipswich T	32	2	68	2

DRURY, Andy (M)   35   6
H: 5 11 W: 12 06 b.Sittingbourne 28-11-83
Source: Sittingbourne, Ebbsfleet U, Lewes, Stevenage Bor, Luton T.

2010–11	Luton T	23	6	23	6
2010–11	Ipswich T	12	0	12	0

EASTMAN, Tom (D)   10   0
H: 6 3 W: 13 12 b.Clacton 21-10-91
Source: Scholar.

2009–10	Ipswich T	1	0		
2010–11	Ipswich T	9	0	10	0

EDWARDS, Carlos (M)   363   41
H: 5 8 W: 11 02 b.Port of Spain 24-10-78
Source: Defence Force. *Honours:* Trinidad & Tobago 78 full caps, 4 goals.

2000–01	Wrexham	36	4		
2001–02	Wrexham	26	5		
2002–03	Wrexham	44	8		
2003–04	Wrexham	42	5		
2004–05	Wrexham	18	1	166	23
2005–06	Luton T	42	2		
2006–07	Luton T	26	6	68	8
2006–07	Sunderland	15	5		
2007–08	Sunderland	13	0		
2008–09	Sunderland	22	0		
2008–09	Wolverhampton W	6	0	6	0
2009–10	Sunderland	0	0	50	5
2009–10	Ipswich T	28	2		
2010–11	Ipswich T	45	3	73	5

FULOP, Marton (G)   145   0
H: 6 6 W: 14 07 b.Budapest 3-5-83
Source: MTK, Elore, Bodajk. *Honours:* Hungary Under-21, 24 full caps.

2004–05	Tottenham H	0	0		
2004–05	Chesterfield	7	0	7	0
2005–06	Tottenham H	0	0		
2005–06	Coventry C	31	0	31	0
2006–07	Tottenham H	0	0		
2006–07	Sunderland	5	0		
2007–08	Sunderland	1	0		
2007–08	Leicester C	24	0	24	0
2007–08	Stoke C	0	0		
2008–09	Sunderland	26	0		
2009–10	Sunderland	13	0	45	0
2009–10	Manchester C	3	0	3	0
2010–11	Ipswich T	35	0	35	0

GRIFFITHS, Jamie (M)   0   0
H: 5 11 W: 9 13 b.Bury St Edmunds 4-1-92
Source: Scholar.

2010–11	Ipswich T	0	0		

HEALY, Colin (M)   185   10
H: 6 1 W: 12 13 b.Cork 14-3-80
Source: Wilton U. *Honours:* Eire Youth, Under-21, 13 full caps, 1 goal.

1998–99	Celtic	3	0		
1999–2000	Celtic	10	1		
2000–01	Celtic	11	0		
2001–02	Celtic	4	0		
2001–02	Coventry C	17	2	17	2
2002–03	Celtic	0	0	28	1
2003–04	Sunderland	20	0		
2004–05	Sunderland	0	0	20	0
2005–06	Livingston	10	2	10	2
2006–07	Barnsley	8	0	8	0
2006–07	Bradford C	2	0	2	0
2007	Cork C	18	0		
2008	Cork C	24	0		
2009	Cork C	20	2	62	2
2009–10	Ipswich T	3	0		
2009–10	Falkirk	19	1	19	1
2010–11	Ipswich T	16	2	19	2

HOURIHANE, Conor (M)   0   0
H: 5 11 W: 9 11 b.Cork 2-2-91
Source: Scholar. *Honours:* Eire Under-21.

2008–09	Sunderland	0	0		
2009–10	Sunderland	0	0		
2010–11	Ipswich T	0	0		

HYAM, Luke (M)   10   0
H: 5 10 W: 11 05 b.Ipswich 24-10-91
Source: Scholar.

2010–11	Ipswich T	10	0	10	0

KENNEDY, Mark (D)   459   32
H: 5 11 W: 11 09 b.Dublin 15-5-76
Source: Belvedere, Trainee. *Honours:* Eire Schools, Youth, Under-21, 34 full caps, 3 goals.

1992–93	Millwall	1	0		
1993–94	Millwall	12	4		
1994–95	Millwall	30	5	43	9
1994–95	Liverpool	6	0		
1995–96	Liverpool	4	0		
1996–97	Liverpool	5	0		
1997–98	Liverpool	1	0	16	0
1997–98	QPR	8	2	8	2
1997–98	Wimbledon	4	0		
1998–99	Wimbledon	17	0	21	0
1999–2000	Manchester C	41	8		

2000–01	Manchester C	25	0	66	8
2001–02	Wolverhampton W	35	5		
2002–03	Wolverhampton W	31	3		
2003–04	Wolverhampton W	31	2		
2004–05	Wolverhampton W	30	0		
2005–06	Wolverhampton W	40	2	167	12
2006–07	Crystal Palace	38	1		
2007–08	Crystal Palace	8	0	46	1
2008–09	Cardiff C	36	0		
2009–10	Cardiff C	30	0	66	0
2010–11	Ipswich T	26	0	26	0

LAMBE, Reggie (M)   9   0
H: 5 7 W: 10 09 b.Bermuda 4-2-91
Source: Scholar. *Honours:* Bermuda 9 full caps, 4 goals.

2009–10	Ipswich T	0	0		
2010–11	Ipswich T	2	0	2	0
2010–11	Bristol R	7	0	7	0

LEADBITTER, Grant (M)   198   20
H: 5 9 W: 11 06 b.Chester-le-Street 7-1-86
Source: Trainee. *Honours:* FA Schools, England Youth, Under-20, Under-21.

2002–03	Sunderland	0	0		
2003–04	Sunderland	0	0		
2004–05	Sunderland	0	0		
2005–06	Sunderland	12	0		
2005–06	Rotherham U	5	1	5	1
2006–07	Sunderland	44	7		
2007–08	Sunderland	31	2		
2008–09	Sunderland	23	2		
2009–10	Sunderland	1	0	111	11
2009–10	Ipswich T	38	3		
2010–11	Ipswich T	44	5	82	8

LEE-BARRETT, Arran (G)   75   0
H: 6 2 W: 14 01 b.Ipswich 28-2-84
Source: Norwich C Scholar.

2002–03	Cardiff C	0	0		
2003–04	Cardiff C	0	0		
2004–05	Cardiff C	0	0		
2005–06	Cardiff C	0	0		
From Weymouth					
2006–07	Coventry C	0	0		
2007–08	Hartlepool U	18	0		
2008–09	Hartlepool U	37	0		
2009–10	Hartlepool U	0	0	55	0
2009–10	Ipswich T	13	0		
2010–11	Ipswich T	7	0	20	0

LISBIE, Kevin (F)   323   62
H: 5 10 W: 11 06 b.Hackney 17-10-78
Source: Trainee. *Honours:* England Youth. Jamaica 10 full caps, 2 goals.

1996–97	Charlton Ath	25	1		
1997–98	Charlton Ath	17	1		
1998–99	Charlton Ath	1	0		
1998–99	Gillingham	7	4	7	4
1999–2000	Charlton Ath	0	0		
1999–2000	Reading	2	0	2	0
2000–01	Charlton Ath	18	0		
2000–01	QPR	2	0	2	0
2001–02	Charlton Ath	22	5		
2002–03	Charlton Ath	32	4		
2003–04	Charlton Ath	9	4		
2004–05	Charlton Ath	17	1		
2005–06	Charlton Ath	6	0		
2005–06	Norwich C	6	1	6	1
2005–06	Derby Co	7	1	7	1
2006–07	Charlton Ath	8	0	155	16
2007–08	Colchester U	42	17		
2008–09	Ipswich T	41	6		
2009–10	Ipswich T	0	0		
2009–10	Colchester U	41	13	83	30
2010–11	Ipswich T	0	0	41	6
2010–11	Millwall	20	4	20	4

MARTIN, Lee (M)   104   7
H: 5 10 W: 10 03 b.Taunton 9-2-87
Source: Scholar. *Honours:* England Youth.

2004–05	Manchester U	0	0		
2005–06	Manchester U	0	0		
2006–07	Manchester U	0	0		
2006–07	Rangers	7	0	7	0
2006–07	Stoke C	13	1	13	1
2007–08	Manchester U	0	0		
2007–08	Plymouth Arg	12	2	12	2
2007–08	Sheffield U	6	0	6	0
2008–09	Manchester U	1	0		
2008–09	Nottingham F	13	1	13	1
2009–10	Manchester U	0	0	1	0

2009–10	Ipswich T	16	1		
2010–11	Ipswich T	16	0	32	1
2010–11	*Charlton Ath*	20	2	20	2

McAULEY, Gareth (D)   **261 20**
H: 6 3 W: 13 00 b.Larne 5-12-79
Source: Coleraine. *Honours:* Northern Ireland Schools, B, 30 full caps, 2 goals.

2004–05	Lincoln C	37	3		
2005–06	Lincoln C	35	5	72	8
2006–07	Leicester C	30	3		
2007–08	Leicester C	44	2	74	5
2008–09	Ipswich T	35	0		
2009–10	Ipswich T	41	5		
2010–11	Ipswich T	39	2	115	7

McLOUGHLIN, Ian (G)   **5 0**
H: 6 3 W: 13 08 b.Dublin 9-8-91
Source: St Francis. *Honours:* Eire Under-21.

2008–09	Ipswich T	0	0		
2009–10	Ipswich T	0	0		
2010–11	Ipswich T	0	0		
2010–11	*Stockport Co*	5	0	5	0

MURPHY, Brian (G)   **131 0**
H: 6 0 W: 13 00 b.Waterford 7-5-83
Honours: Eire Under-21.

2000–01	Manchester C	0	0		
2001–02	Manchester C	0	0		
2002–03	Manchester C	0	0		
2002–03	*Oldham Ath*	0	0		
2002–03	*Peterborough U*	1	0	1	0

From Waterford

2003–04	Swansea C	11	0		
2004–05	Swansea C	2	0		
2005–06	Swansea C	0	0		
2006–07	Swansea C	0	0	13	0
2007	Bohemians	29	0		
2008	Bohemians	33	0		
2009	Bohemians	35	0	97	0
2009–10	Ipswich T	16	0		
2010–11	Ipswich T	4	0	20	0

MURRAY, Ronan (F)   **15 1**
H: 5 7 W: 11 00 b.Mayo 12-9-91
Source: Scholar. *Honours:* Eire Under-21.

2010–11	Ipswich T	8	0	8	0
2010–11	*Torquay U*	7	1	7	1

NORRIS, David (M)   **338 41**
H: 5 7 W: 11 06 b.Stamford 22-2-81
Source: Boston U.

1999–2000	Bolton W	0	0		
2000–01	Bolton W	0	0		
2001–02	Bolton W	0	0		
2001–02	*Hull C*	6	1	6	1
2002–03	Bolton W	0	0		
2002–03	Plymouth Arg	33	6		
2003–04	Plymouth Arg	45	5		
2004–05	Plymouth Arg	35	3		
2005–06	Plymouth Arg	45	2		
2006–07	Plymouth Arg	41	6		
2007–08	Plymouth Arg	27	5	226	27
2007–08	Ipswich T	9	1		
2008–09	Ipswich T	37	3		
2009–10	Ipswich T	24	1		
2010–11	Ipswich T	36	8	106	13

O'CONNOR, Shane (M)   **17 0**
H: 5 9 W: 11 08 b.Cork 14-4-90
Source: Liverpool Academy. *Honours:* Eire Youth, Under-21.

2009–10	Ipswich T	12	0		
2010–11	Ipswich T	5	0	17	0

O'DEA, Darren (D)   **77 4**
H: 6 1 W: 13 01 b.Dublin 4-2-87
Honours: Eire Under-21, 9 full caps.

2006–07	Celtic	14	2		
2007–08	Celtic	6	0		
2008–09	Celtic	10	1		
2009–10	Celtic	19	1	49	4
2009–10	*Reading*	8	0	8	0

On loan from Celtic.

2010–11	Ipswich T	20	0	20	0

PETERS, Jaime (M)   **116 5**
H: 5 7 W: 10 12 b.Ontario 4-5-87
Source: Kaiserslautern. *Honours:* Canada Youth, Under-20, Under-23, 26 full caps, 1 goal.

2005–06	Ipswich T	13	0		
2006–07	Ipswich T	23	2		
2007–08	Ipswich T	5	0		
2007–08	*Yeovil T*	14	1	14	1
2008–09	Ipswich T	3	0		
2008–09	*Gillingham*	3	0	3	0
2009–10	Ipswich T	32	1		
2010–11	Ipswich T	23	1	99	4

PRISKIN, Tamas (F)   **205 48**
H: 6 2 W: 13 03 b.Komarno 27-9-86
Honours: Hungary Under-21, 33 full caps, 8 goals.

2002–03	Gyor	3	0		
2003–04	Gyor	17	5		
2004–05	Gyor	23	8		
2005–06	Gyor	25	11	68	24
2006–07	Watford	16	2		
2007–08	Watford	14	1		
2007–08	*Preston NE*	5	2	5	2
2008–09	Watford	36	12		
2009–10	Watford	0	0	66	15
2009–10	Ipswich T	17	1		
2009–10	*QPR*	13	1	13	1
2010–11	Ipswich T	32	4	49	5
2010–11	*Swansea C*	4	1	4	1

QUINN, Alan (M)   **329 30**
H: 5 9 W: 10 06 b.Dublin 13-6-79
Source: Cherry Orchard. *Honours:* Eire Youth, Under-21, 8 full caps.

1997–98	Sheffield W	1	0		
1998–99	Sheffield W	1	0		
1999–2000	Sheffield W	19	3		
2000–01	Sheffield W	37	2		
2001–02	Sheffield W	38	2		
2002–03	Sheffield W	37	5		
2003–04	Sheffield W	24	4	157	16
2003–04	*Sunderland*	6	0	6	0
2004–05	Sheffield U	43	7		
2005–06	Sheffield U	27	4		
2006–07	Sheffield U	19	0		
2007–08	Sheffield U	8	0	97	11
2007–08	Ipswich T	16	1		
2008–09	Ipswich T	34	2		
2009–10	Ipswich T	19	0		
2010–11	Ipswich T	0	0	69	3

SCOTLAND, Jason (F)   **277 96**
H: 5 8 W: 11 10 b.Morvant 18-2-79
Source: San Juan Jabloteh, Defence Force. *Honours:* Trinidad & Tobago 41 full caps, 8 goals.

2003–04	Dundee U	21	4		
2004–05	Dundee U	29	3	50	7
2005–06	St Johnstone	31	15		
2006–07	St Johnstone	35	18	66	33
2007–08	Swansea C	45	24		
2008–09	Swansea C	45	21		
2009–10	Swansea C	0	0	90	45
2009–10	Wigan Ath	32	1		
2010–11	Wigan Ath	0	0	32	1
2010–11	Ipswich T	39	10	39	10

SMITH, Tommy (D)   **52 3**
H: 6 2 W: 12 02 b.Macclesfield 31-3-90
Source: Scholar. *Honours:* England Youth. New Zealand 8 full caps.

2007–08	Ipswich T	0	0		
2008–09	Ipswich T	2	0		
2009–10	Ipswich T	14	0		
2009–10	*Brentford*	8	0	8	0
2010–11	Ipswich T	22	3	38	3
2010–11	*Colchester U*	6	0	6	0

WICKHAM, Connor (F)   **65 13**
H: 6 0 W: 14 01 b.Hereford 31-3-93
Source: School. *Honours:* England Youth, Under-21.

2008–09	Ipswich T	2	0		
2009–10	Ipswich T	26	4		
2010–11	Ipswich T	37	9	65	13

LEEDS U (42)

BECCHIO, Luciano (F)   **223 81**
H: 6 2 W: 13 05 b.Cordoba 28-12-83
Source: Boca Juniors.

2003–04	Mallorca B	0	0		
2004–05	Mallorca B	0	0		
2004–05	Murcia	16	3	16	3
2005–06	Terrassa	24	2	24	2
2006–07	Barcelona Athletic	10	0	10	0
2006–07	Merida	12	5		
2007–08	Merida	38	22	50	27
2008–09	Leeds U	45	15		
2009–10	Leeds U	37	15		
2010–11	Leeds U	41	19	123	49

BESSONE, Fede (D)   **65 1**
H: 5 11 W: 11 13 b.Cordoba 23-1-84
Source: Barcelona B, Espanyol B.

2007–08	Gimnastic	10	0	10	0
2008–09	Swansea C	15	0		
2009–10	Swansea C	21	1	36	1
2010–11	Leeds U	6	0	6	0
2010–11	*Charlton Ath*	13	0	13	0

BROMBY, Leigh (D)   **319 12**
H: 5 11 W: 11 06 b.Dewsbury 2-6-80
Honours: England Schools.

1998–99	Sheffield W	0	0		
1999–2000	Sheffield W	0	0		
1999–2000	*Mansfield T*	10	1	10	1
2000–01	Sheffield W	18	0		
2001–02	Sheffield W	26	1		
2002–03	Sheffield W	27	0		
2002–03	*Norwich C*	5	0	5	0
2003–04	Sheffield W	29	1	100	2
2004–05	Sheffield U	46	5		
2005–06	Sheffield U	35	1		
2006–07	Sheffield U	17	0		
2007–08	Sheffield U	11	0		
2007–08	Watford	16	1		
2008–09	Watford	22	0	38	1
2008–09	*Sheffield U*	12	1	121	7
2009–10	Leeds U	32	1		
2010–11	Leeds U	13	0	45	1

BRUCE, Alex (D)   **174 3**
H: 6 0 W: 11 06 b.Norwich 28-9-84
Source: Trainee. *Honours:* Eire B, Under-21, 2 full caps.

2002–03	Blackburn R	0	0		
2003–04	Blackburn R	0	0		
2004–05	Blackburn R	0	0		
2004–05	*Oldham Ath*	12	0	12	0
2004–05	Birmingham C	0	0		
2004–05	*Sheffield W*	6	0	6	0
2005–06	Birmingham C	0	0	6	0
2005–06	*Tranmere R*	11	0	11	0
2006–07	Ipswich T	41	0		
2007–08	Ipswich T	36	0		
2008–09	Ipswich T	25	1		
2009–10	*Leicester C*	3	0	3	0
2009–10	Ipswich T	0	0	115	2
2010–11	Ipswich T	21	1	21	1

CLAYTON, Adam (M)   **45 2**
H: 5 9 W: 11 11 b.Manchester 14-1-89
Source: Scholar. *Honours:* England Under-20.

2007–08	Manchester C	0	0		
2008–09	Manchester C	0	0		
2009–10	Manchester C	0	0		
2009–10	*Carlisle U*	28	1	28	1
2010–11	Leeds U	4	0	4	0
2010–11	*Peterborough U*	7	0	7	0
2010–11	*Milton Keynes D*	6	1	6	1

CONNOLLY, Paul (D)   **260 2**
H: 6 0 W: 11 09 b.Liverpool 29-9-83
Source: Scholar.

2000–01	Plymouth Arg	1	0		
2001–02	Plymouth Arg	0	0		
2002–03	Plymouth Arg	2	0		
2003–04	Plymouth Arg	29	0		
2004–05	Plymouth Arg	19	0		
2005–06	Plymouth Arg	31	0		
2006–07	Plymouth Arg	38	0		
2007–08	Plymouth Arg	42	1	162	1
2008–09	Derby Co	40	1		
2009–10	Derby Co	21	0	61	1
2009–10	*Sheffield U*	7	0	7	0
2010–11	Leeds U	30	0	30	0

DARVILLE, Liam (D)   **9 0**
b.Leyburn 26-10-90
Source: Scholar. *Honours:* England Youth.

2008–09	Leeds U	0	0		
2009–10	Leeds U	0	0		
2010–11	Leeds U	0	0		
2010–11	*Tranmere R*	9	0	9	0
2010–11	*Rotherham U*	0	0		

ELLIOTT, Tom (F) 31 1
H: 5 10 W: 11 02 b.Leeds 9-9-89
Source: School.
2006–07	Leeds U	3	0	
2007–08	Leeds U	0	0	
2008–09	Leeds U	0	0	
2008–09	*Macclesfield T*	6	0	6	0
2009–10	Leeds U	0	0	
2009–10	*Bury*	16	1	16	1
2010–11	Leeds U	0	0	3	0
2010–11	*Rotherham U*	6	0	6	0

Transferred to Hamilton A January 2011.

FAYE, Amdy (M) 220 3
H: 6 1 W: 12 06 b.Dakar 12-3-77
Source: Frejus. *Honours:* Senegal 18 full caps.
1998–99	Auxerre	0	0		
1999–2000	Auxerre	3	0		
2000–01	Auxerre	23	0		
2001–02	Auxerre	20	0		
2002–03	Auxerre	34	2	80	2
2003–04	Portsmouth	27	0		
2004–05	Portsmouth	20	0	47	0
2004–05	Newcastle U	9	0		
2005–06	Newcastle U	22	0	31	0
2006–07	Charlton Ath	28	1		
2007–08	Charlton Ath	1	0	29	1
2007–08	*Rangers*	4	0	4	0
2008–09	Stoke C	21	0		
2009–10	Stoke C	0	0	21	0
2010–11	Leeds U	8	0	8	0

GRADEL, Max (M) 134 34
H: 5 8 W: 12 03 b.Ivory Coast 30-9-87
Honours: Ivory Coast 1 full cap.
2005–06	Leicester C	0	0		
2006–07	Leicester C	0	0		
2007–08	Leicester C	0	0		
2007–08	*Bournemouth*	34	9	34	9
2008–09	Leicester C	27	1		
2009–10	Leicester C	0	0	27	1
2009–10	Leeds U	32	6		
2010–11	Leeds U	41	18	73	24

GRELLA, Mike (F) 46 5
H: 5 11 W: 12 02 b.New York 23-1-87
Source: Duke University. *Honours:* USA Youth.
2008–09	Leeds U	11	0		
2009–10	Leeds U	17	1		
2010–11	Leeds U	1	0	29	1
2010–11	*Carlisle U*	10	3	10	3
2010–11	*Swindon T*	7	1	7	1

HATFIELD, Will (M) 0 0
b.Liversedge 10-10-91
Source: Scholar.
2009–10	Leeds U	0	0
2010–11	Leeds U	0	0

HIGGS, Shane (G) 272 0
H: 6 3 W: 14 06 b.Oxford 13-5-77
Source: Trainee.
1994–95	Bristol R	0	0		
1995–96	Bristol R	0	0		
1996–97	Bristol R	2	0		
1997–98	Bristol R	8	0	10	0

From Worcester C.
1999–2000	Cheltenham T	0	0		
2000–01	Cheltenham T	1	0		
2001–02	Cheltenham T	1	0		
2002–03	Cheltenham T	10	0		
2003–04	Cheltenham T	42	0		
2004–05	Cheltenham T	46	0		
2005–06	Cheltenham T	45	0		
2006–07	Cheltenham T	36	0		
2007–08	Cheltenham T	46	0		
2008–09	Cheltenham T	10	0	237	0
2008–09	*Wolverhampton W*	0	0		
2009–10	Leeds U	19	0		
2010–11	Leeds U	6	0	25	0

HOWSON, Jonathan (M) 166 22
H: 5 11 W: 12 01 b.Morley 21-5-88
Source: Scholar. *Honours:* England Under-21.
2006–07	Leeds U	9	1	
2007–08	Leeds U	26	3	
2008–09	Leeds U	40	4	
2009–10	Leeds U	45	4	
2010–11	Leeds U	46	10	166	22

JOHNSON, Brad (M) 181 27
H: 6 0 W: 12 10 b.Hackney 28-4-87
Source: Cambridge U Juniors.
2004–05	Cambridge U	1	0	1	0
2005–06	Northampton T	3	0		
2006–07	Northampton T	27	5		
2007–08	Northampton T	23	2	53	7
2007–08	Leeds U	21	3		
2008–09	Leeds U	15	1		
2008–09	*Brighton & HA*	10	4	10	4
2009–10	Leeds U	36	7		
2010–11	Leeds U	45	5	117	16

KILKENNY, Neil (M) 191 13
H: 5 8 W: 10 08 b.Enfield 19-12-85
Source: Arsenal Trainee. *Honours:* England Youth, Under-20, Australia Under-23, 9 full caps.
2003–04	Birmingham C	0	0		
2004–05	Birmingham C	0	0		
2004–05	*Oldham Ath*	27	4		
2005–06	Birmingham C	18	0		
2006–07	Birmingham C	8	0		
2007–08	Birmingham C	0	0	26	0
2007–08	*Oldham Ath*	20	1	47	5
2007–08	Leeds U	16	1		
2008–09	Leeds U	30	4		
2009–10	Leeds U	35	2		
2010–11	Leeds U	37	1	118	8

KISNORBO, Patrick (D) 271 14
H: 6 1 W: 11 11 b.Melbourne 24-3-81
Honours: Australia Schools, Under-20, Under-23, 18 full caps, 1 goal.
2000–01	South Melbourne	25	0		
2001–02	South Melbourne	23	2		
2002–03	South Melbourne	19	1	67	3
2003–04	Hearts	31	0		
2004–05	Hearts	17	1	48	1
2005–06	Leicester C	37	1		
2006–07	Leicester C	40	5		
2007–08	Leicester C	41	3		
2008–09	Leicester C	8	0	126	9
2009–10	Leeds U	29	1		
2010–11	Leeds U	1	0	30	1

LEES, Tom (D) 84 4
H: 6 1 W: 12 04 b.Warwick 28-11-90
2008–09	Leeds U	0	0		
2009–10	Leeds U	0	0		
2009–10	*Accrington S*	39	0	39	0
2010–11	Leeds U	0	0		
2010–11	*Bury*	45	4	45	4

MARTIN, Alan (G) 7 0
H: 6 0 W: 11 11 b.Glasgow 1-1-89
Source: Motherwell. *Honours:* Scotland Youth, Under-21.
2007–08	Leeds U	0	0		
2008–09	Leeds U	0	0		
2009–10	Leeds U	0	0		
2009–10	*Accrington S*	7	0	7	0
2010–11	Leeds U	0	0		

Transferred to Ayr U January 2011.

McCANN, Joe (M) 0 0
b.Leeds 11-10-92
Source: Scholar. *Honours:* England Youth.
2009–10	Leeds U	0	0
2010–11	Leeds U	0	0

McCORMACK, Ross (F) 173 44
H: 5 9 W: 11 00 b.Glasgow 18-8-86
Honours: Scotland Youth, Under-21, B, 7 full caps, 1 goal.
2003–04	Rangers	2	1		
2004–05	Rangers	1	0		
2005–06	Rangers	8	1	11	2
2005–06	*Doncaster R*	19	4	19	4
2006–07	Motherwell	12	2		
2007–08	Motherwell	36	9	48	11
2008–09	Cardiff C	38	21		
2009–10	Cardiff C	34	4		
2010–11	Cardiff C	2	0	74	25
2010–11	Leeds U	21	2	21	2

NAYLOR, Richard (D) 401 41
H: 6 1 W: 13 07 b.Leeds 28-2-77
Source: Trainee.
1995–96	Ipswich T	0	0
1996–97	Ipswich T	27	4
1997–98	Ipswich T	5	2
1998–99	Ipswich T	30	5

1999–2000	Ipswich T	36	8		
2000–01	Ipswich T	13	1		
2001–02	Ipswich T	14	1		
2001–02	*Millwall*	3	0	3	0
2001–02	*Barnsley*	8	0	8	0
2002–03	Ipswich T	17	2		
2003–04	Ipswich T	39	5		
2004–05	Ipswich T	46	6		
2005–06	Ipswich T	42	3		
2006–07	Ipswich T	25	0		
2007–08	Ipswich T	7	0		
2008–09	Ipswich T	23	0	324	37
2008–09	Leeds U	22	1		
2009–10	Leeds U	29	2		
2010–11	Leeds U	15	1	66	4

NUNEZ, Ramon (M) 161 30
H: 5 7 W: 10 00 b.Tegucigalpa 14-11-85
Honours: Honduras 42 full caps, 5 goals.
2004	Dallas	8	0		
2005	Dallas	21	5		
2006	Dallas	25	6		
2007	Dallas	13	3	67	14
2007	Chivas	8	0	8	0
2007–08	Olimpia	34	3		
2008–09	Olimpia	11	5	45	8
2008–09	Puebla	20	5	20	5
2009–10	Cruz Azul	11	0	11	0
2010–11	Leeds U	2	0	2	0
2010–11	*Scunthorpe U*	8	3	8	3

O'BRIEN, Andy (D) 389 12
H: 6 2 W: 11 13 b.Harrogate 29-6-79
Source: Trainee. *Honours:* England Youth, Under-21, Eire Under-21, 26 full caps, 1 goal.
1996–97	Bradford C	22	2		
1997–98	Bradford C	26	0		
1998–99	Bradford C	31	0		
1999–2000	Bradford C	36	1		
2000–01	Bradford C	18	0	133	3
2000–01	Newcastle U	9	1		
2001–02	Newcastle U	34	2		
2002–03	Newcastle U	26	0		
2003–04	Newcastle U	28	1		
2004–05	Newcastle U	23	2	120	6
2005–06	Portsmouth	29	0		
2006–07	Portsmouth	3	0		
2007–08	Portsmouth	0	0	32	0
2007–08	Bolton W	32	0		
2008–09	Bolton W	34	1		
2009–10	Bolton W	6	0		
2010–11	Bolton W	2	0	74	1
2010–11	Leeds U	30	2	30	2

PARKER, Ben (D) 91 0
H: 5 11 W: 11 06 b.Pontefract 8-11-87
Source: Scholar. *Honours:* England Youth.
2004–05	Leeds U	0	0		
2005–06	Leeds U	0	0		
2006–07	Leeds U	0	0		
2006–07	*Bradford C*	39	0	39	0
2007–08	Leeds U	9	0		
2007–08	*Darlington*	13	0	13	0
2008–09	Leeds U	24	0		
2009–10	Leeds U	4	0		
2010–11	Leeds U	2	0	39	0

PAYNE, Sanchez (M) 0 0
b.Leeds 31-1-92
Source: Scholar.
2010–11	Leeds U	0	0

PAYNTER, Billy (F) 332 83
H: 6 1 W: 14 01 b.Liverpool 13-7-84
Source: Schoolboy.
2000–01	Port Vale	1	0		
2001–02	Port Vale	7	0		
2002–03	Port Vale	31	5		
2003–04	Port Vale	44	13		
2004–05	Port Vale	45	10		
2005–06	Port Vale	16	2	144	30
2005–06	Hull C	22	3	22	3
2006–07	Southend U	9	0		
2006–07	*Bradford C*	15	4	15	4
2007–08	Southend U	0	0	9	0
2007–08	Swindon T	36	8		
2008–09	Swindon T	42	11		
2009–10	Swindon T	42	26	120	45
2010–11	Leeds U	22	1	22	1

RUI MARQUES, Manuel (D) 206 4
H: 5 11 W: 11 13 b.Luanda 3-9-77
Source: Benfica *Honours:* Angola 19 full caps.

Season	Club	App	Gls	Tot App	Tot Gls
1998–99	Baden	27	0	27	0
1999–2000	SSV Ulm	32	0	32	0
2000–01	Hertha	1	0	1	0
2000–01	Stuttgart	12	0		
2001–02	Stuttgart	23	0		
2002–03	Stuttgart	12	0		
2003–04	Stuttgart	0	0	47	0
2004–05	Maritimo	8	0	8	0
2005–06	Leeds U	0	0		
2005–06	*Hull C*	1	0	1	0
2006–07	Leeds U	17	0		
2007–08	Leeds U	36	3		
2008–09	Leeds U	32	1		
2009–10	Leeds U	5	0		
2010–11	Leeds U	0	0	90	4

SAM, Lloyd (F) 153 8
H: 5 10 W: 11 00 b.Leeds 27-9-84
Source: Scholar. *Honours:* England Youth, Under-20.

Season	Club	App	Gls	Tot App	Tot Gls
2002–03	Charlton Ath	0	0		
2003–04	Charlton Ath	0	0		
2003–04	*Leyton Orient*	10	0	10	0
2004–05	Charlton Ath	1	0		
2005–06	Charlton Ath	2	0		
2006–07	Charlton Ath	7	0		
2006–07	*Sheffield W*	4	0	4	0
2006–07	*Southend U*	2	0	2	0
2007–08	Charlton Ath	28	2		
2008–09	Charlton Ath	38	0		
2009–10	Charlton Ath	43	4	119	6
2010–11	Leeds U	18	2	18	2

SCHMEICHEL, Kasper (G) 159 0
H: 6 1 W: 13 00 b.Copenhagen 5-11-86
Source: Scholar. *Honours:* Denmark Youth, Under-20, Under-21.

Season	Club	App	Gls	Tot App	Tot Gls
2003–04	Manchester C	0	0		
2004–05	Manchester C	0	0		
2005–06	Manchester C	0	0		
2005–06	*Darlington*	4	0	4	0
2005–06	Bury	15	0		
2006–07	Manchester C	0	0		
2006–07	*Falkirk*	15	0	15	0
2006–07	*Bury*	14	0	29	0
2007–08	Manchester C	7	0		
2007–08	*Cardiff C*	14	0	14	0
2007–08	*Coventry C*	9	0	9	0
2008–09	Manchester C	1	0		
2009–10	Manchester C	0	0	8	0
2009–10	Notts Co	43	0	43	0
2010–11	Leeds U	37	0	37	0

SNODGRASS, Robert (M) 216 42
H: 6 0 W: 12 02 b.Glasgow 7-9-87
Honours: Scotland Youth, Under-21, 2 full caps.

Season	Club	App	Gls	Tot App	Tot Gls
2003–04	Livingston	0	0		
2004–05	Livingston	17	2		
2005–06	Livingston	27	4		
2006–07	Livingston	6	0		
2006–07	*Stirling A*	12	5	12	5
2007–08	Livingston	31	9	81	15
2008–09	Leeds U	42	9		
2009–10	Leeds U	44	7		
2010–11	Leeds U	37	6	123	22

SOMMA, Davide (F) 103 23
H: 6 1 W: 12 13 b.Johannesburg 26-3-85
Honours: South Africa 3 full caps, 1 goal.

Season	Club	App	Gls	Tot App	Tot Gls
2005–06	Pro Vasto	20	2		
2006–07	Pro Vasto	19	0	39	2
2007–08	Olbia	15	1	15	1
2008	San Jose Eq	3	0	3	0
2009–10	Leeds U	0	0		
2009–10	*Chesterfield*	3	0	3	0
2009–10	*Lincoln C*	14	9	14	9
2010–11	Leeds U	29	11	29	11

THOMPSON, Zac (M) 0 0
b.Billinge 5-1-93
Source: Everton Scholar.

Season	Club	App	Gls
2010–11	Leeds U	0	0

WHITE, Aidan (D) 39 4
H: 5 7 W: 10 00 b.Otley 10-10-91
Source: Scholar. *Honours:* England Youth.

Season	Club	App	Gls
2008–09	Leeds U	5	0
2009–10	Leeds U	8	0
2010–11	Leeds U	2	0
2010–11	*Oldham Ath*	24	4

(2010–11 Leeds U 15 0; 2010–11 Oldham Ath 24 4)

LEICESTER C (43)

ABE, Yuki (M) 370 51
H: 5 9 W: 12 02 b.Ichikawa 6-9-81
Honours: Japan 50 full caps, 3 goals.

Season	Club	App	Gls	Tot App	Tot Gls
1998	JEF United	1	0		
1999	JEF United	30	1		
2000	JEF United	25	0		
2001	JEF United	17	3		
2002	JEF United	24	1		
2003	JEF United	27	3		
2004	JEF United	24	5		
2005	JEF United	33	12		
2006	JEF United	33	11	214	36
2007	Urawa	33	3		
2008	Urawa	33	6		
2009	Urawa	34	2		
2010	Urawa	20	3	120	14
2010–11	Leicester C	36	1	36	1

AMBROSICS, Robert (G) 0 0
H: 6 3 W: 13 00 b.Hungary 22-1-92
Honours: Hungary Youth.

Season	Club	App	Gls
2009–10	Leicester C	0	0
2010–11	Leicester C	0	0

BAMBA, Souleymane (D) 131 6
H: 6 3 W: 14 02 b.Ivry-sur-Seine 13-1-85
Honours: Ivory Coast 18 full caps, 2 goals.

Season	Club	App	Gls	Tot App	Tot Gls
2004–05	Paris St Germain	1	0		
2005–06	Paris St Germain	0	0	1	0
2006–07	Dunfermline Ath	23	0		
2007–08	Dunfermline Ath	15	0		
2008–09	Dunfermline Ath	1	0	39	0
2008–09	Hibernian	29	0		
2009–10	Hibernian	30	2		
2010–11	Hibernian	16	2	75	4
2010–11	Leicester C	16	2	16	2

BERNER, Bruno (M) 268 14
H: 6 1 W: 12 13 b.Zurich 21-11-77
Honours: Switzerland Youth, Under-20, Under-21, 16 full caps.

Season	Club	App	Gls	Tot App	Tot Gls
1997–98	Grasshoppers	2	0		
1998–99	Grasshoppers	21	0		
1999–2000	Grasshoppers	6	1		
1999–2000	*Oviedo*	1	1	1	1
2000–01	Grasshoppers	27	1		
2001–02	Grasshoppers	16	0	72	2
2002–03	Freiburg	31	2		
2003–04	Freiburg	33	1		
2004–05	Freiburg	12	0	76	3
2005–06	Basle	17	0		
2006–07	Basle	15	0	32	0
2006–07	Blackburn R	1	0		
2007–08	Blackburn R	2	0		
2008–09	Blackburn R	0	0	3	0
2008–09	Leicester C	32	3		
2009–10	Leicester C	35	4		
2010–11	Leicester C	17	1	84	8

BOLGER, Cian (D) 6 0
b.Co. Kildare 12-3-92
Source: Scholar.

Season	Club	App	Gls	Tot App	Tot Gls
2009–10	Leicester C	0	0		
2010–11	Leicester C	0	0		
2010–11	*Bristol R*	6	0	6	0

BYRNE, Shane (M) 0 0
b.Republic of Ireland 25-4-93
Honours: Eire Youth.

Season	Club	App	Gls
2010–11	Leicester C	0	0

CHAMBERLAIN, Elliott (M) 0 0
b.Wales 29-4-92
Source: Scholar. *Honours:* Wales Youth, Under-21.

Season	Club	App	Gls
2009–10	Leicester C	0	0
2010–11	Leicester C	0	0

CHAMBERS, Ashley (F) 13 3
H: 5 10 W: 11 06 b.Leicester 1-3-90
Source: Scholar. *Honours:* England Schools, Youth.

Season	Club	App	Gls	Tot App	Tot Gls
2005–06	Leicester C	0	0		
2006–07	Leicester C	0	0		
2007–08	Leicester C	5	0		
2008–09	Leicester C	1	0		
2009–10	Leicester C	0	0		
2009–10	*Wycombe W*	3	1	3	1
2009–10	*Grimsby T*	4	2	4	2
2010–11	Leicester C	0	0	6	0

CRNCIC, Leon (F) 0 0
H: 6 1 W: 11 09 b.Slovenia 2-3-90
Source: Aluminij. *Honours:* Slovenia Under-21.

Season	Club	App	Gls
2010–11	Leicester C	0	0

DYER, Lloyd (M) 253 35
H: 5 8 W: 10 03 b.Birmingham 13-9-82
Source: Aston Villa Juniors.

Season	Club	App	Gls	Tot App	Tot Gls
2001–02	WBA	0	0		
2002–03	WBA	0	0		
2003–04	WBA	17	2		
2003–04	*Kidderminster H*	7	1	7	1
2004–05	WBA	4	0		
2004–05	*Coventry C*	6	0	6	0
2005–06	WBA	0	0	21	2
2005–06	*QPR*	15	0	15	0
2005–06	*Millwall*	6	0	6	0
2006–07	Milton Keynes D	41	5		
2007–08	Milton Keynes D	45	11	86	16
2008–09	Leicester C	44	10		
2009–10	Leicester C	33	3		
2010–11	Leicester C	35	3	112	16

GALLAGHER, Paul (F) 246 48
H: 6 1 W: 11 00 b.Glasgow 9-8-84
Source: Trainee. *Honours:* Scotland Under-21, B, 1 full cap.

Season	Club	App	Gls	Tot App	Tot Gls
2002–03	Blackburn R	1	0		
2003–04	Blackburn R	26	3		
2004–05	Blackburn R	16	2		
2005–06	Blackburn R	1	0		
2005–06	Stoke C	37	11		
2006–07	Blackburn R	16	1		
2007–08	Blackburn R	0	0		
2007–08	*Preston NE*	19	1	19	1
2007–08	*Stoke C*	7	0	44	11
2008–09	Blackburn R	0	0		
2008–09	*Plymouth Arg*	40	13	40	13
2009–10	Blackburn R	1	0	61	6
2009–10	Leicester C	41	7		
2010–11	Leicester C	41	10	82	17

HICKS, Nathan (F) 0 0
Source: Scholar.

Season	Club	App	Gls
2010–11	Leicester C	0	0

HOBBS, Jack (D) 139 2
H: 6 3 W: 13 05 b.Portsmouth 18-8-88
Source: Scholar. *Honours:* England Youth.

Season	Club	App	Gls	Tot App	Tot Gls
2004–05	Lincoln C	1	0	1	0
2005–06	Liverpool	0	0		
2006–07	Liverpool	0	0		
2007–08	Liverpool	2	0		
2007–08	*Scunthorpe U*	9	1	9	1
2008–09	Liverpool	0	0	2	0
2008–09	Leicester C	44	1		
2009–10	Leicester C	44	0		
2010–11	Leicester C	26	0	114	1
2010–11	*Hull C*	13	0	13	0

HOWARD, Steve (F) 630 185
H: 6 3 W: 15 00 b.Durham 10-5-76
Source: Tow Law T. *Honours:* Scotland B.

Season	Club	App	Gls	Tot App	Tot Gls
1995–96	Hartlepool U	39	7		
1996–97	Hartlepool U	32	8		
1997–98	Hartlepool U	43	7		
1998–99	Hartlepool U	28	5	142	27
1998–99	Northampton T	12	0		
1999–2000	Northampton T	41	10		
2000–01	Northampton T	33	8	86	18
2000–01	Luton T	12	3		
2001–02	Luton T	42	24		
2002–03	Luton T	41	22		
2003–04	Luton T	34	14		
2004–05	Luton T	40	18		
2005–06	Luton T	43	14	212	95
2006–07	Derby Co	43	16		
2007–08	Derby Co	20	1	63	17
2007–08	Leicester C	21	6		
2008–09	Leicester C	41	13		
2009–10	Leicester C	36	5		
2010–11	Leicester C	29	4	127	28

JOHN, Jorrin (F) 0 0
b.Leicester 6-11-91
Source: Scholar.

Season	Club	App	Gls
2009–10	Leicester C	0	0
2010–11	Leicester C	0	0

KENNEDY, Tom (D) 296 14
H: 5 10 W: 11 01 b.Bury 24-6-85
Source: Scholar.
2002–03	Bury	0	0		
2003–04	Bury	27	0		
2004–05	Bury	46	1		
2005–06	Bury	33	4		
2006–07	Bury	37	0	143	5
2007–08	Rochdale	43	2		
2008–09	Rochdale	45	4		
2009–10	Rochdale	44	3		
2010–11	Leicester C	1	0	1	0
2010–11	*Rochdale*	6	0	138	9
2010–11	*Peterborough U*	14	0	14	0

KERMORGANT, Yann (F) 200 47
H: 6 0 W: 13 03 b.Vannes 8-11-81
Source: Vannes.
2004–05	Chatellerault	29	14	29	14
2005–06	Grenoble	26	6		
2006–07	Grenoble	32	10	58	16
2007–08	Reims	33	4		
2008–09	Reims	34	9	67	13
2009–10	Leicester C	20	1		
2010–11	Leicester C	0	0	20	1
2010–11	*Arles-Avignon*	26	3	26	3

KING, Andy (M) 144 34
H: 6 0 W: 11 10 b.Barnstaple 29-10-88
Source: Scholar. *Honours:* Wales Youth, Under-21, 9 full caps, 1 goal.
2007–08	Leicester C	11	1		
2008–09	Leicester C	45	9		
2009–10	Leicester C	43	9		
2010–11	Leicester C	45	15	144	34

KING, Craig (F) 33 3
H: 5 11 W: 11 12 b.Chesterfield 6-10-90
Source: Scholar. *Honours:* Scotland Youth.
2008–09	Leicester C	0	0		
2009–10	Leicester C	0	0		
2009–10	*Hereford U*	26	3	26	3
2010–11	Leicester C	0	0		
2010–11	*Northampton T*	7	0	7	0

LAMEY, Michael (D) 194 9
H: 6 1 W: 12 06 b.Amsterdam 29-11-79
2000–01	RKC	26	2		
2001–02	RKC	21	1	47	3
2002–03	PSV Eindhoven	0	0		
2002–03	*AZ*	14	1	14	1
2003–04	*Utrecht*	17	1	17	1
2004–05	PSV Eindhoven	5	1		
2005–06	PSV Eindhoven	26	1		
2006–07	PSV Eindhoven	7	0	38	2
2007–08	Duisburg	25	1	25	1
2008–09	Arminia Bielfeld	23	0		
2009–10	Arminia Bielfeld	26	1	49	1
2010–11	Leicester C	4	0	4	0

LOGAN, Conrad (G) 115 0
H: 6 2 W: 14 00 b.Letterkenny 18-4-86
Source: Scholar. *Honours:* Eire Youth.
2003–04	Leicester C	0	0		
2004–05	Leicester C	0	0		
2005–06	Leicester C	0	0		
2005–06	*Boston U*	13	0	13	0
2006–07	Leicester C	18	0		
2007–08	Leicester C	0	0		
2007–08	*Stockport Co*	34	0		
2008–09	Leicester C	0	0		
2008–09	*Luton T*	22	0	22	0
2008–09	*Stockport Co*	7	0	41	0
2009–10	Leicester C	2	0		
2010–11	Leicester C	3	0	23	0
2010–11	*Bristol R*	16	0	16	0

MIGUEL VITOR (D) 42 3
H: 6 0 W: 12 08 b.Torres Vedras 30-6-89
2007–08	Benfica	2	0		
2007–08	*Aves*	7	0	7	0
2008–09	Benfica	16	0		
2009–10	Benfica	2	0	20	0
2010–11	Leicester C	15	3	15	3

MILNES, Ben (D) 0 0
Source: Scholar.
| 2010–11 | Leicester C | 0 | 0 | | |

MORENO, Joao (D) 185 6
H: 6 1 W: 12 10 b.Urgeses 19-8-81
Source: Amigos Urgezes, Felgueiras, Macedo Cavaleiros.
2002–03	Taipas	37	1		
2003–04	Taipas	28	2	65	3
2004–05	Guimaraes	16	2		
2005–06	Guimaraes	22	0		
2006–07	Guimaraes	17	1		
2007–08	Guimaraes	14	0		
2008–09	Guimaraes	25	0		
2009–10	Guimaraes	23	0	117	3
2010–11	Leicester C	3	0	3	0

MOUSSA, Franck (M) 121 10
H: 5 8 W: 10 08 b.Brussels 24-7-89
Source: Scholar.
2005–06	Southend U	1	0		
2006–07	Southend U	4	0		
2007–08	Southend U	16	0		
2008–09	Southend U	26	2		
2008–09	*Wycombe W*	9	0	9	0
2009–10	Southend U	43	5	90	7
2010–11	Leicester C	8	1	8	1
2010–11	*Doncaster R*	14	2	14	2

N'GUESSAN, Dany (M) 155 24
H: 6 0 W: 12 13 b.Paris 11-8-87
Source: Auxerre, Rangers.
2006–07	Boston U	23	5	23	5
2006–07	Lincoln C	9	0		
2007–08	Lincoln C	37	7		
2008–09	Lincoln C	45	8	91	15
2009–10	Lincoln C	27	3		
2010–11	Leicester C	5	0	32	3
2010–11	*Scunthorpe U*	3	1	3	1
2010–11	*Southampton*	6	0	6	0

NEILSON, Robbie (D) 262 1
H: 6 0 W: 13 01 b.Paisley 19-6-80
Honours: Scotland Under-21, 1 full cap.
1999–2000	Cowdenbeath	8	0	8	0
2000–01	Hearts	18	0		
2001–02	Hearts	2	0		
2002–03	Hearts	5	0		
2002–03	*Queen of the S*	13	0	13	0
2003–04	Hearts	29	0		
2004–05	Hearts	35	1		
2005–06	Hearts	37	0		
2006–07	Hearts	14	0		
2007–08	Hearts	33	0		
2008–09	Hearts	27	0	200	1
2009–10	Leicester C	19	0		
2010–11	Leicester C	7	0	26	0
2010–11	*Brentford*	15	0	15	0

O'NEILL, Luke (D) 5 0
H: 6 0 W: 11 04 b.Slough 20-8-91
Source: Scholar. *Honours:* England Youth.
2008–09	Leicester C	0	0		
2009–10	Leicester C	1	0		
2009–10	*Tranmere R*	4	0	4	0
2010–11	Leicester C	0	0	1	0

OAKLEY, Matthew (M) 454 33
H: 5 10 W: 12 06 b.Peterborough 17-8-77
Source: Trainee. *Honours:* England Under-21.
1994–95	Southampton	1	0		
1995–96	Southampton	10	0		
1996–97	Southampton	28	3		
1997–98	Southampton	33	1		
1998–99	Southampton	22	2		
1999–2000	Southampton	31	3		
2000–01	Southampton	35	1		
2001–02	Southampton	27	1		
2002–03	Southampton	31	0		
2003–04	Southampton	7	0		
2004–05	Southampton	7	1		
2005–06	Southampton	29	2	261	14
2006–07	Derby Co	37	6		
2007–08	Derby Co	19	3	56	9
2007–08	Leicester C	20	0		
2008–09	Leicester C	45	8		
2009–10	Leicester C	38	0		
2010–11	Leicester C	34	2	137	10

PARKES, Tom (D) 28 1
H: 6 3 W: 12 05 b.Sutton-in-Ashfield 15-1-92
Source: Scholar.
| 2008–09 | Leicester C | 0 | 0 | | |

2009–10	Leicester C	0	0		
2009–10	*Burton Alb*	22	1		
2010–11	Leicester C	0	0		
2010–11	*Yeovil T*	1	0	1	0
2010–11	*Burton Alb*	5	0	27	1

RICARDO (G) 335 1
H: 6 1 W: 12 05 b.Montijo 11-2-76
Honours: Portugal 79 full caps.
1995–96	Boavista	0	0		
1996–97	Boavista	16	0		
1997–98	Boavista	34	0		
1998–99	Boavista	5	0		
1999–2000	Boavista	9	0		
2000–01	Boavista	28	0		
2001–02	Boavista	29	0		
2002–03	Boavista	33	1	154	1
2003–04	Sporting	34	0		
2004–05	Sporting	33	0		
2005–06	Sporting	30	0		
2006–07	Sporting	28	0	125	0
2007–08	Betis	28	0		
2008–09	Betis	20	0		
2009–10	Betis	0	0	48	0
2010–11	Leicester C	8	0	8	0

SCHLUPP, Jeffrey (M) 9 6
H: 5 8 W: 11 00 b.Hamburg 23-12-92
Source: Scholar.
| 2010–11 | Leicester C | 0 | 0 | | |
| 2010–11 | *Brentford* | 9 | 6 | 9 | 6 |

SMITH, Adam (G) 0 0
b.Sunderland 23-1-92
Source: Scholar.
| 2010–11 | Leicester C | 0 | 0 | | |

TAFT, George (D) 0 0
b.Leicester 29-7-93
Source: Scholar. *Honours:* England Youth.
| 2010–11 | Leicester C | 0 | 0 | | |

TUNCHEV, Aleksandar (D) 235 25
H: 6 2 W: 13 03 b.Pazardzhik 10-7-81
Honours: Bulgaria 25 full caps, 1 goal.
1998–99	Pazardzhik	6	0		
1999–2000	Pazardzhik	14	2		
1999–2000	Iskar	15	1	15	1
2000–01	Pazardzhik	18	3	38	5
2001–02	Belasitsa	30	3	30	3
2002–03	Lokomotiv Plovdiv	4	1		
2003–04	Lokomotiv Plovdiv	25	1		
2004–05	Lokomotiv Plovdiv	28	1		
2005–06	Lokomotiv Plovdiv	11	2	65	4
2005–06	CSKA Sofia	10	1		
2006–07	CSKA Sofia	27	7		
2007–08	CSKA Sofia	26	3	63	11
2008–09	Leicester C	20	1		
2009–10	Leicester C	2	0		
2010–11	Leicester C	2	0	24	1

UCHECHI, Danny (F) 0 0
b.Abia State 14-9-89
Source: Charlton Ath Scholar, West Ham U, FC Dender. *Honours:* Nigeria Youth, Under-23.
| 2010–11 | Leicester C | 0 | 0 | | |
On loan from FC Dender.

VASSELL, Darius (F) 318 60
H: 5 9 . W: 13 00 b.Birmingham 13-6-80
Source: Trainee. *Honours:* England Youth, Under-21, 22 full caps, 6 goals.
1998–99	Aston Villa	6	0		
1999–2000	Aston Villa	11	0		
2000–01	Aston Villa	23	4		
2001–02	Aston Villa	36	12		
2002–03	Aston Villa	33	8		
2003–04	Aston Villa	32	9		
2004–05	Aston Villa	21	2	162	35
2005–06	Manchester C	36	8		
2006–07	Manchester C	32	3		
2007–08	Manchester C	27	6		
2008–09	Manchester C	8	0	103	17
2009–10	Ankaragucu	22	4	22	4
2010–11	Leicester C	31	4	31	4

VERMA, Aman (M) 7 0
H: 6 1 W: 13 00 b.Leicester 3-1-87
Source: Bedworth U, Redditch U.
2008–09	Leicester C	0	0		
2009–10	Leicester C	0	0		
2009–10	*Crewe Alex*	7	0	7	0
2010–11	Leicester C	0	0		

WAGHORN, Martyn (F) 86 17
H: 5 9 W: 13 01 b.South Shields 23-1-90
Source: Scholar. Honours: England Youth.

2007–08	Sunderland	3	0
2008–09	Sunderland	1	0
2008–09	*Charlton Ath*	7	1	7 1
2009–10	Sunderland	0	0
2009–10	*Leicester C*	43	12
2010–11	Sunderland	2	0	6 0
2010–11	Leicester C	30	4	73 16

WARBURTON, Jack (M) 0 0
b.Enfield 27-4-93
Source: Watford Scholar.

2010–11	Leicester C	0	0

WEALE, Chris (G) 193 1
H: 6 2 W: 13 03 b.Chard 9-2-82
Source: Juniors.

2003–04	Yeovil T	35	0
2004–05	Yeovil T	38	0
2005–06	Yeovil T	25	0
2006–07	Bristol C	1	0
2007–08	Hereford U	1	0
2007–08	Bristol C	3	0
2008–09	Bristol C	5	0	9 0
2008–09	*Hereford U*	1	0	2 0
2008–09	*Yeovil T*	10	1	108 1
2009–10	Leicester C	45	0
2010–11	Leicester C	29	0	74 0

WELLENS, Richard (M) 445 36
H: 5 9 W: 11 06 b.Manchester 26-3-80
Source: Trainee. Honours: England Youth.

1996–97	Manchester U	0	0
1997–98	Manchester U	0	0
1998–99	Manchester U	0	0
1999–2000	Manchester U	0	0
1999–2000	Blackpool	8	0
2000–01	Blackpool	36	8
2001–02	Blackpool	36	1
2002–03	Blackpool	39	1
2003–04	Blackpool	41	3
2004–05	Blackpool	28	3	188 16
2005–06	Oldham Ath	45	4
2006–07	Oldham Ath	42	4	87 8
2007–08	Doncaster R	45	6
2008–09	Doncaster R	39	3	84 9
2009–10	Leicester C	41	1
2010–11	Leicester C	45	2	86 3

YUSSUF, Abdi (F) 0 0
Source: Scholar.

2010–11	Leicester C	0	0

LEYTON ORIENT (44)

ARGENT, Jake (F) 0 0
b.Enfield 9-12-91
Source: Scholar.

2010–11	Leyton Orient	0	0

BEAUTYMAN, Harry (M) 0 0
b.Newham 1-4-92
Source: Youth.

2010–11	Leyton Orient	0	0

BROWN, Aaron (D) 62 5
H: 6 4 W: 14 07 b.Birmingham 23-6-83
Source: Stafford R, Tamworth.

2005–06	Reading	0	0
2005–06	*Bournemouth*	4	0	4 0
2006–07	Reading	0	0
2007–08	Walsall	0	0
2007–08	Reading	0	0
From Redditch U.			
2008–09	Yeovil T	23	3	23 3
From AFC Telford U, Truro C.			
2009–10	Burton Alb	1	0	1 0
2009–10	*Aldershot T*	12	1	12 1
2010–11	Leyton Orient	5	0	5 0
2010–11	*Stockport Co*	17	1	17 1

BUTCHER, Lee (G) 9 0
b.Waltham Forest 11-10-88
Source: Tottenham H.

2010–11	Leyton Orient	9	0	9 0

CESTOR, Mike (D) 2 0
b.Paris 30-4-92
Source: Youth.

2009–10	Leyton Orient	0	0
2010–11	Leyton Orient	2	0	2 0

CHAMBERS, Adam (D) 243 10
H: 5 10 W: 11 12 b.Sandwell 20-11-80
Source: Trainee. Honours: England Youth.

1998–99	WBA	0	0
1999–2000	WBA	0	0
2000–01	WBA	11	1
2001–02	WBA	32	0
2002–03	WBA	13	0
2003–04	WBA	0	0
2003–04	*Sheffield W*	11	0	11 0
2004–05	WBA	0	0	56 1
2004–05	Kidderminster H	2	0	2 0
2006–07	Leyton Orient	38	4
2007–08	Leyton Orient	45	3
2008–09	Leyton Orient	33	1
2009–10	Leyton Orient	29	1
2010–11	Leyton Orient	29	0	174 9

CHORLEY, Ben (D) 301 12
H: 6 3 W: 13 02 b.Sidcup 30-9-82
Source: Scholar.

2001–02	Arsenal	0	0
2002–03	Arsenal	0	0
2002–03	*Brentford*	2	0	2 0
2002–03	Wimbledon	10	0
2003–04	Wimbledon	35	2	45 2
2004–05	Milton Keynes D	41	2
2005–06	Milton Keynes D	26	0
2006–07	Milton Keynes D	13	1	80 3
2006–07	Gillingham	27	1	27 1
2007–08	Tranmere R	31	1
2008–09	Tranmere R	45	1	76 2
2009–10	Leyton Orient	42	1
2010–11	Leyton Orient	29	3	71 4

COX, Dean (M) 191 27
H: 5 4 W: 9 08 b.Cuckfield 12-8-87
Source: Scholar.

2005–06	Brighton & HA	1	0
2006–07	Brighton & HA	42	6
2007–08	Brighton & HA	42	6
2008–09	Brighton & HA	40	4
2009–10	Brighton & HA	21	0	146 16
2010–11	Leyton Orient	45	11	45 11

CROWE, Jason (D) 372 23
H: 5 9 W: 10 09 b.Sidcup 30-9-78
Source: Trainee. Honours: England Schools,
Youth.

1995–96	Arsenal	0	0
1996–97	Arsenal	0	0
1997–98	Arsenal	0	0
1998–99	Arsenal	0	0
1998–99	*Crystal Palace*	8	0	8 0
1999–2000	Portsmouth	25	0
2000–01	Portsmouth	23	0
2000–01	*Brentford*	9	0	9 0
2001–02	Portsmouth	22	1
2002–03	Portsmouth	16	4	86 5
2003–04	Grimsby T	32	0
2004–05	Grimsby T	37	4	69 4
2005–06	Northampton T	41	2
2006–07	Northampton T	43	3
2007–08	Northampton T	44	4
2008–09	Northampton T	43	5	171 14
2009–10	Leeds U	17	0
2010–11	Leeds U	0	0	17 0
2010–11	Leyton Orient	12	0	12 0

DANIELS, Charlie (M) 142 5
H: 6 1 W: 12 12 b.Harlow 7-9-86
Source: Scholar.

2005–06	Tottenham H	0	0
2006–07	Tottenham H	0	0
2006–07	*Chesterfield*	2	0	2 0
2007–08	Tottenham H	0	0
2007–08	*Leyton Orient*	31	2
2008–09	Tottenham H	0	0
2008–09	*Gillingham*	5	1	5 1
2008–09	Leyton Orient	21	2
2009–10	Leyton Orient	41	0
2010–11	Leyton Orient	42	0	135 4

DAWSON, Stephen (M) 245 12
H: 5 9 W: 11 09 b.Dublin 4-12-85
Source: Scholar. Honours: Eire Under-21.

2003–04	Leicester C	0	0
2004–05	Leicester C	0	0
2005–06	Mansfield T	40	1
2006–07	Mansfield T	34	1
2007–08	Mansfield T	43	2	117 4
2008–09	Bury	43	2

2009–10	Bury	45	4	88 6
2010–11	Leyton Orient	40	2	40 2

FORBES, Terrell (D) 386 3
H: 5 11 W: 12 07 b.Southwark 17-8-81
Source: Trainee.

1999–2000	West Ham U	0	0
1999–2000	*Bournemouth*	3	0	3 0
2000–01	West Ham U	0	0
2001–02	QPR	43	0
2002–03	QPR	38	0
2003–04	QPR	30	0
2004–05	QPR	3	0	114 0
2004–05	Grimsby T	33	0	33 0
2005–06	Oldham Ath	39	0	39 0
2006–07	Yeovil T	46	0
2007–08	Yeovil T	41	0
2008–09	Yeovil T	38	0
2009–10	Yeovil T	38	1	163 1
2010–11	Leyton Orient	34	2	34 2

JARVIS, Ryan (F) 162 22
H: 6 1 W: 11 11 b.Fakenham 11-7-86
Source: Scholar. Honours: FA Schools,
England Youth.

2002–03	Norwich C	3	0
2003–04	Norwich C	12	1
2004–05	Norwich C	4	1
2004–05	*Colchester U*	6	0	6 0
2005–06	Norwich C	4	1
2006–07	Norwich C	5	0
2006–07	*Leyton Orient*	14	6
2007–08	Norwich C	1	0	29 3
2007–08	*Kilmarnock*	9	1	9 1
2007–08	Notts Co	17	2	17 2
2008–09	Leyton Orient	31	0
2009–10	Leyton Orient	42	8
2010–11	Leyton Orient	11	2	98 16
2010–11	*Northampton T*	3	0	3 0

JONES, Jamie (G) 91 0
H: 6 2 W: 14 05 b.Kirkby 18-2-89
Source: Scholar.

2007–08	Everton	0	0
2008–09	Leyton Orient	20	0
2009–10	Leyton Orient	36	0
2010–11	Leyton Orient	35	0	91 0

McGLEISH, Scott (F) 656 201
H: 5 9 W: 11 09 b.Barnet 10-2-74
Source: Edgware T.

1994–95	Charlton Ath	6	0	6 0
1994–95	*Leyton Orient*	6	1
1995–96	Peterborough U	12	0
1995–96	*Colchester U*	15	6
1996–97	Peterborough U	1	0	13 0
1996–97	*Cambridge U*	10	7	10 7
1996–97	Leyton Orient	28	7
1997–98	Leyton Orient	8	0
1997–98	*Barnet*	37	13
1998–99	Barnet	36	8
1999–2000	Barnet	42	10
2000–01	Barnet	19	5	134 36
2000–01	Colchester U	21	5
2001–02	Colchester U	46	15
2002–03	Colchester U	43	8
2003–04	Colchester U	34	10	159 44
2004–05	Northampton T	44	13
2005–06	Northampton T	42	17
2006–07	Northampton T	25	12
2006–07	Wycombe W	14	5
2007–08	Wycombe W	46	25
2008–09	Wycombe W	15	3	75 33
2008–09	*Northampton T*	9	1	120 43
2008–09	Leyton Orient	16	6
2009–10	Leyton Orient	42	12
2010–11	Leyton Orient	39	12	139 38

OMOZUSI, Elliot (D) 78 0
H: 5 11 W: 12 09 b.Hackney 15-12-88
Source: Scholar. Honours: England Youth.

2005–06	Fulham	0	0
2006–07	Fulham	8	0
2007–08	Fulham	0	0
2008–09	Fulham	0	0
2008–09	*Norwich C*	21	0	21 0
2009–10	Fulham	0	0	8 0
2009–10	*Charlton Ath*	9	0	9 0
2010–11	Leyton Orient	40	0	40 0

PORTER, George (F) 1 0
H: 5 10 b.Sidcup 27-6-92
Source: Cray W.
| 2010–11 | Leyton Orient | 1 | 0 | 1 | 0 |

REVELL, Alex (F) 214 43
H: 6 3 W: 13 00 b.Cambridge 7-7-83
Source: Scholar.
2000–01	Cambridge U	4	0		
2001–02	Cambridge U	24	2		
2002–03	Cambridge U	9	0		
2003–04	Cambridge U	20	3	57	5
From Braintree T.
2006–07	Brighton & HA	38	7		
2007–08	Brighton & HA	21	6	59	13
2007–08	Southend U	8	0		
2008–09	Southend U	23	4		
2009–10	Southend U	3	0	34	4
2009 10	*Swindon T*	10	2	10	2
2009–10	Wycombe W	15	6	15	6
2010–11	Leyton Orient	39	13	39	13

SMITH, Jimmy (M) 138 15
H: 6 0 W: 10 03 b.Newham 7-1-87
Source: Scholar. Honours: England Youth.
2004–05	Chelsea	0	0		
2005–06	Chelsea	1	0		
2006–07	Chelsea	0	0		
2006–07	*QPR*	29	6	29	6
2007–08	Chelsea	0	0		
2007–08	*Norwich C*	9	0	9	0
2008–09	Chelsea	0	0	1	0
2008–09	*Sheffield W*	12	0	12	0
2008–09	*Leyton Orient*	16	0		
2009–10	Leyton Orient	40	2		
2010–11	Leyton Orient	31	7	87	9

SPRING, Matthew (M) 441 49
H: 5 11 W: 12 05 b.Harlow 17-11-79
Source: Trainee.
1997–98	Luton T	12	0		
1998–99	Luton T	45	3		
1999–2000	Luton T	45	6		
2000–01	Luton T	41	4		
2001–02	Luton T	42	6		
2002–03	Luton T	41	5		
2003–04	Luton T	24	1		
2004–05	Leeds U	13	1		
2005–06	Leeds U	0	0	13	1
2005–06	Watford	39	8		
2006–07	Watford	6	0	45	8
2006–07	Luton T	14	1		
2007–08	Luton T	44	9		
2008–09	Luton T	0	0	308	35
2008–09	*Sheffield U*	11	1	11	1
2008–09	Charlton Ath	13	2		
2009–10	Charlton Ath	12	0	25	2
2010–11	Leyton Orient	39	2	39	2

TEHOUE, Jonathan (F) 142 34
H: 5 8 W: 11 06 b.Paris 3-5-84
2003–04	Bastia	7	0	7	0
2004–05	Apoel	0	0		
2005–06	Virton	13	4	13	4
2006–07	FC Brussels	15	5	19	5
2007–08	Kasimpasa	15	6	15	6
2008–09	Konya	38	9	38	9
2009–10	Alfortville	2	1	2	1
2009–10	Leyton Orient	16	2		
2010–11	Leyton Orient	32	7	48	9

WALKER, James (F) 110 13
H: 5 10 W: 11 10 b.Hackney 25-11-87
Source: Scholar. Honours: England Youth.
2004–05	Charlton Ath	0	0		
2005–06	Charlton Ath	0	0		
2005–06	*Hartlepool U*	4	0	4	0
2006–07	Charlton Ath	0	0		
2006–07	*Bristol R*	4	1	4	1
2006–07	*Leyton Orient*	14	2		
2006–07	*Notts Co*	8	0	8	0
2007–08	Charlton Ath	0	0		
2007–08	*Yeovil T*	13	3	13	3
2007–08	*Southend U*	15	4		
2008–09	Southend U	17	2		
2009–10	Southend U	13	0	45	6
2009–10	*Hereford U*	6	1	6	1
2009–10	Gillingham	5	0		
2010–11	Gillingham	0	0	5	0
2010–11	Leyton Orient	11	0	25	2

WHING, Andrew (D) 244 4
H: 6 0 W: 12 00 b.Birmingham 20-9-84
Source: Scholar.
2002–03	Coventry C	14	0		
2003–04	Coventry C	28	1		
2004–05	Coventry C	16	1		
2005–06	Coventry C	32	0		
2006–07	Coventry C	16	0	106	2
2006–07	Brighton & HA	12	0		
2007–08	Brighton & HA	42	0		
2008–09	Brighton & HA	40	0		
2009–10	Brighton & HA	9	0		
2009–10	*Chesterfield*	11	0	11	0
2010–11	Brighton & HA	0	0	103	0
2010–11	Leyton Orient	24	2	24	2

LINCOLN C (45)

ANDERSON, Joe (D) 45 0
H: 5 11 W: 11 05 b.Stepney 13-10-89
Source: Scholar.
2008–09	Fulham	0	0		
2009–10	Fulham	0	0		
2009–10	Lincoln C	23	0		
2010–11	Lincoln C	22	0	45	0

ANYON, Joe (G) 134 0
H: 6 1 W: 12 11 b.Poulton-le-Fylde 29-12-86
Source: Scholar.
2005–06	Port Vale	0	0		
2006–07	Port Vale	22	0		
2007–08	Port Vale	44	0		
2008–09	Port Vale	36	0		
2009–10	Port Vale	7	0	109	0
2010–11	Lincoln C	21	0	21	0
2010–11	Morecambe	4	0	4	0

BROUGHTON, Drewe (F) 402 67
H: 6 3 W: 12 01 b.Hitchin 25-10-78
Source: Trainee.
1996–97	Norwich C	8	1		
1997–98	Norwich C	1	0		
1997–98	*Wigan Ath*	4	0	4	0
1998–99	Norwich C	0	0	9	1
1998–99	Brentford	1	0	1	0
1998–99	Peterborough U	25	7		
1999–2000	Peterborough U	10	1		
2000–01	Peterborough U	0	0	35	8
2000–01	Kidderminster H	19	7		
2001–02	Kidderminster H	38	8		
2002–03	Kidderminster H	37	4	94	19
2003–04	Southend U	35	2		
2004–05	Southend U	9	0	44	2
2004–05	Rushden & D	21	6		
2004–05	*Wycombe W*	3	0	3	0
2005–06	Rushden & D	37	10	58	16
2006–07	Chester C	14	2	14	2
2006–07	*Boston U*	25	8	25	8
2007–08	Milton Keynes D	13	0	13	0
2007–08	*Wrexham*	16	2	16	2
2008–09	Rotherham U	40	6		
2009–10	Rotherham U	16	3	56	9
2009–10	*Lincoln C*	7	0		
2010–11	Lincoln C	23	0	30	0

CARAYOL, Mustapha (F) 53 9
H: 5 10 W: 11 11 b.Gambia 10-6-89
Source: Scholar.
2007–08	Milton Keynes D	0	0		
2009–10	Torquay U	20	6	20	6
2010–11	Lincoln C	33	3	33	3

CLAPHAM, Jamie (M) 448 15
H: 5 9 W: 11 09 b.Lincoln 7-12-75
Source: Trainee.
1994–95	Tottenham H	0	0		
1995–96	Tottenham H	0	0		
1996–97	Tottenham H	1	0		
1996–97	*Leyton Orient*	6	0	6	0
1996–97	*Bristol R*	5	0	5	0
1997–98	Tottenham H	0	0	1	0
1997–98	Ipswich T	22	0		
1998–99	Ipswich T	46	3		
1999–2000	Ipswich T	46	2		
2000–01	Ipswich T	35	2		
2001–02	Ipswich T	32	2		
2002–03	Ipswich T	26	1	207	10
2002–03	Birmingham C	16	0		
2003–04	Birmingham C	25	0		
2004–05	Birmingham C	27	0		
2005–06	Birmingham C	16	1	84	1
2006–07	Wolverhampton W	26	0		
2007–08	Wolverhampton W	0	0	26	0
2007–08	*Leeds U*	13	0	13	0
2007–08	Leicester C	11	0		
2008–09	Leicester C	0	0	11	0
2008–09	Notts Co	40	2		
2009–10	Notts Co	30	1	70	3
2010–11	Lincoln C	25	1	25	1

FACEY, Delroy (F) 368 63
H: 6 0 W: 15 02 b.Huddersfield 22-4-80
Source: Trainee.
1996–97	Huddersfield T	3	0		
1997–98	Huddersfield T	3	0		
1998–99	Huddersfield T	20	3		
1999–2000	Huddersfield T	2	0		
2000–01	Huddersfield T	34	10		
2001–02	Huddersfield T	13	2		
2002–03	Huddersfield T	0	0		
2002–03	*Bradford C*	6	1	6	1
2002–03	Bolton W	9	1		
2003–04	Bolton W	1	0	10	1
2003–04	*Burnley*	14	5	14	5
2003–04	WBA	9	0	9	0
2004–05	Hull C	21	4	21	4
2004–05	*Huddersfield T*	4	0	79	15
2004–05	Oldham Ath	6	0		
2005–06	Oldham Ath	3	0	9	0
2005–06	Tranmere R	37	8	37	8
2006–07	Rotherham U	40	10	40	10
2007–08	Gillingham	32	3	32	3
2007–08	*Wycombe W*	6	1	6	1
2008–09	Notts Co	45	9		
2009–10	Notts Co	18	2	63	11
2009–10	*Lincoln C*	10	1		
2010–11	Lincoln C	32	3	42	4

FUSEINI, Ali (M) 94 2
H: 5 6 W: 9 10 b.Ghana 7-12-88
Source: Scholar.
2006–07	Millwall	7	0		
2007–08	Millwall	37	2		
2008–09	Millwall	17	0		
2009–10	Millwall	15	0		
2010–11	Millwall	0	0	76	2
2010–11	Lincoln C	18	0	18	0

GREEN, Paul (D) 117 4
H: 5 8 W: 10 04 b.Birmingham 15-4-87
Source: Scholar.
2005–06	Aston Villa	0	0		
2006–07	Aston Villa	0	0		
2006–07	Lincoln C	16	1		
2007–08	Lincoln C	36	1		
2008–09	Lincoln C	33	1		
2009–10	Lincoln C	15	0		
2010–11	Lincoln C	17	1	117	4

HONE, Daniel (D) 85 3
H: 6 2 W: 12 00 b.Croydon 15-9-90
Source: Scholar.
2007–08	Lincoln C	23	1		
2008–09	Lincoln C	19	1		
2009–10	Lincoln C	17	1		
2010–11	Lincoln C	26	0	85	3

HOWELL, Luke (D) 79 2
H: 5 10 W: 10 05 b.Heathfield 5-1-87
Source: Scholar.
2006–07	Gillingham	1	0	1	0
2007–08	Milton Keynes D	8	0		
2008–09	Milton Keynes D	15	1		
2009–10	Milton Keynes D	29	0		
2010–11	Milton Keynes D	1	0	53	1
2010–11	Lincoln C	25	1	25	1

HUGHTON, Cian (D) 63 6
H: 5 8 W: 10 05 b.Enfield 25-1-89
Source: Tottenham H Scholar. Honours: Eire Under-21.
2007–08	Tottenham H	0	0		
2008–09	Tottenham H	0	0		
2009–10	Lincoln C	41	4		
2010–11	Lincoln C	22	2	63	6

HUTCHINSON, Andrew (F) 19 1
H: 5 7 W: 12 00 b.Lincoln 10-3-92
Source: Scholar.
2008–09	Lincoln C	4	1		
2009–10	Lincoln C	10	0		
2010–11	Lincoln C	5	0	19	1

HUTCHINSON, Ben (F)   68   8
H: 5 11 W: 12 07 b.Nottingham 27-11-87
Source: Arnold T.
2005–06	Middlesbrough	0	0		
2006–07	Middlesbrough	0	0		
2007–08	Middlesbrough	8	1	8	1
2008–09	Celtic	5	0		
2009–10	Celtic	0	0	5	0
2009–10	Swindon T	10	1	10	1
2009–10	*Dundee*	9	2	9	2

On loan from Celtic.
| 2010–11 | Lincoln C | 36 | 4 | 36 | 4 |

JARRETT, Albert (M)   136   6
H: 6 1 W: 10 07 b.Sierra Leone 23-10-84
Source: Dulwich Hamlet. *Honours:* Sierra
Leone 5 full caps.
2002–03	Wimbledon	0	0		
2003–04	Wimbledon	9	0	9	0
2004–05	Brighton & HA	12	1		
2005–06	Brighton & HA	11	0	23	1
2005–06	Swindon T	6	0	6	0
2006–07	Watford	1	0		
2006–07	Boston U	5	2	5	2
2006–07	Milton Keynes D	5	0	5	0
2007–08	Watford	0	0		
2008–09	Watford	0	0	1	0
2008–09	Gillingham	16	0	16	0
2009–10	Barnet	45	2	45	2
2010–11	Lincoln C	22	1	22	1
2010–11	*Aldershot T*	4	0	4	0

KANYUKA, Patrick (D)   44   1
H: 6 0 W: 12 06 b.Kinshasa 19-7-87
Source: Scholar.
2004–05	QPR	1	0		
2005–06	QPR	0	0		
2006–07	QPR	11	0		
2007–08	QPR	0	0	12	0
2007–08	Swindon T	4	0		
2008–09	Swindon T	16	1		
2009–10	Swindon T	0	0	20	1
2009–10	Northampton T	3	0	3	0
2010–11	Cluj	0	0		
2010–11	*Unirea*	3	0	3	0
2010–11	Lincoln C	6	0	6	0

KELTIE, Clark (M)   221   10
H: 5 11 W: 11 08 b.Newcastle 31-8-83
Source: Walker Central.
2001–02	Darlington	1	0		
2002–03	Darlington	30	3		
2003–04	Darlington	31	1		
2004–05	Darlington	21	0		
2005–06	Darlington	24	0		
2006–07	Darlington	27	1		
2007–08	Darlington	27	4	161	9
2008–09	Rochdale	31	1		
2009–10	Rochdale	0	0	31	1
2009–10	Lincoln C	11	0		
2010–11	Lincoln C	18	0	29	0

KERR, Scott (M)   222   8
H: 5 9 W: 10 07 b.Leeds 11-12-81
Source: Scholar.
2000–01	Bradford C	1	0	1	0
2001–02	Hull C	0	0		
2002–03	Hull C	0	0		
2003–04	Hull C	0	0		
2004–05	Hull C	0	0		

From Scarborough.
2005–06	Lincoln C	41	2		
2006–07	Lincoln C	44	3		
2007–08	Lincoln C	36	1		
2008–09	Lincoln C	45	2		
2009–10	Lincoln C	39	0		
2010–11	Lincoln C	16	0	221	8

McCALLUM, Gavin (M)   63   11
H: 5 9 W: 12 00 b.Toronto 24-8-87
Honours: Canada 1 full cap, 1 goal.
| 2005–06 | Yeovil T | 0 | 0 | | |
| 2006–07 | Yeovil T | 0 | 0 | | |

From Weymouth, Havant & W, Sutton U.
| 2009–10 | Hereford U | 27 | 8 | 27 | 8 |

From Weymouth, Havant & W, Sutton U.
| 2010–11 | Lincoln C | 36 | 3 | 36 | 3 |

MUSSELWHITE, Paul (G)   614   0
H: 6 2 W: 14 02 b.Portsmouth 22-12-68
Source: Apprentice.
1987–88	Portsmouth	0	0		
1988–89	Scunthorpe U	41	0		
1989–90	Scunthorpe U	29	0		
1990–91	Scunthorpe U	38	0		
1991–92	Scunthorpe U	24	0		
1992–93	Port Vale	41	0		
1993–94	Port Vale	46	0		
1994–95	Port Vale	44	0		
1995–96	Port Vale	39	0		
1996–97	Port Vale	33	0		
1997–98	Port Vale	41	0		
1998–99	Port Vale	38	0		
1999–2000	Port Vale	30	0	312	0
2000–01	Sheffield W	0	0		
2000–01	Hull C	37	0		
2001–02	Hull C	20	0		
2002–03	Hull C	20	0		
2003–04	Hull C	18	0	95	0
2004–05	Scunthorpe U	46	0		
2005–06	Scunthorpe U	28	0		
2006–07	Scunthorpe U	0	0		
2007–08	Scunthorpe U	0	0		
2008–09	Scunthorpe U	0	0	206	0
2009–10	Lincoln C	0	0		
2010–11	Lincoln C	1	0	1	0

O'KEEFE, Josh (M)   50   4
H: 6 1 W: 11 05 b.Whalley 22-12-88
Source: Scholar. *Honours:* Eire Under-21.
2005–06	Blackburn R	0	0		
2006–07	Blackburn R	0	0		
2007–08	Blackburn R	0	0		
2008–09	Blackburn R	0	0		
2009–10	Walsall	13	0	13	0
2010–11	Lincoln C	37	4	37	4

PEARCE, Ian (D)   280   12
H: 6 3 W: 15 06 b.Bury St Edmunds 7-5-74
Source: School. *Honours:* England Youth,
Under-21.
1990–91	Chelsea	1	0		
1991–92	Chelsea	2	0		
1992–93	Chelsea	1	0		
1993–94	Chelsea	0	0	4	0
1993–94	Blackburn R	5	1		
1994–95	Blackburn R	28	0		
1995–96	Blackburn R	12	1		
1996–97	Blackburn R	12	0		
1997–98	Blackburn R	5	0	62	2
1997–98	West Ham U	30	1		
1998–99	West Ham U	33	2		
1999–2000	West Ham U	30	0		
2000–01	West Ham U	15	1		
2001–02	West Ham U	9	2		
2002–03	West Ham U	30	2		
2003–04	West Ham U	24	1	142	9
2003–04	Fulham	13	0		
2004–05	Fulham	11	0		
2005–06	Fulham	10	0		
2006–07	Fulham	22	1		
2007–08	Fulham	1	0		
2007–08	*Southampton*	1	0	1	0
2008–09	Fulham	0	0	57	1
2009–10	Lincoln C	10	0		
2010–11	Lincoln C	4	0	14	0

SPENCER, Scott (F)   34   4
H: 5 11 W: 12 08 b.Oldham 1-1-89
Source: Oldham Ath Scholar.
2006–07	Everton	0	0		
2007–08	Everton	0	0		
2007–08	Yeovil T	0	0		
2007–08	*Macclesfield T*	3	0	3	0
2008–09	Everton	0	0		
2009–10	Everton	0	0		
2009–10	Rochdale	4	0	4	0
2009–10	Southend U	12	4		
2010–11	Southend U	5	0	17	4
2010–11	Lincoln C	10	0	10	0

SWAIBU, Moses (D)   56   3
H: 6 2 W: 11 11 b.Southwark 9-5-89
Source: Scholar.
| 2007–08 | Crystal Palace | 0 | 0 | | |

From Bromley.
2008–09	Lincoln C	10	0		
2009–10	Lincoln C	34	1		
2010–11	Lincoln C	12	2	56	3

TURNER, Sam (F)   2   0
b.Lincoln 30-8-93
Source: Scholar.
| 2010–11 | Lincoln C | 2 | 0 | 2 | 0 |

WATTS, Adam (D)   65   1
H: 6 1 W: 11 09 b.Hackney 4-3-88
Source: Scholar. *Honours:* England Youth.
2006–07	Fulham	0	0		
2006–07	*Milton Keynes D*	2	0	2	0
2007–08	Fulham	0	0		
2008–09	Fulham	0	0		
2008–09	*Northampton T*	5	0	5	0
2009–10	Fulham	0	0		
2009–10	Lincoln C	18	0		
2010–11	Lincoln C	40	1	58	1

LIVERPOOL (46)

ADORJAN, Krisztian (F)   0   0
b.Budapest 19-1-93
Source: Scholar.
| 2010–11 | Liverpool | 0 | 0 | | |

AGGER, Daniel (D)   127   8
H: 6 2 W: 12 06 b.Hvidovre 12-12-84
Honours: Denmark Youth, Under-20,
Under-21, 40 full caps, 4 goals.
2004–05	Brondby	26	5		
2005–06	Brondby	8	0	34	5
2005–06	Liverpool	4	0		
2006–07	Liverpool	27	2		
2007–08	Liverpool	5	0		
2008–09	Liverpool	18	1		
2009–10	Liverpool	23	0		
2010–11	Liverpool	16	0	93	3

AMOO, David (F)   10   1
H: 5 10 W: 12 03 b.London 23-4-91
Source: Millwall.
2007–08	Liverpool	0	0		
2008–09	Liverpool	0	0		
2009–10	Liverpool	0	0		
2010–11	Liverpool	0	0		
2010–11	*Milton Keynes D*	3	0	3	0
2010–11	*Hull C*	7	1	7	1

AQUILANI, Alberto (M)   184   16
H: 6 0 W: 12 03 b.Rome 7-7-84
Honours: Italy 11 full caps, 2 goals.
2002–03	Roma	1	0		
2003–04	Triestina	31	4	31	4
2004–05	Roma	29	0		
2005–06	Roma	24	3		
2006–07	Roma	13	1		
2007–08	Roma	21	3		
2008–09	Roma	14	2	102	9
2009–10	Liverpool	18	1		
2010–11	Liverpool	0	0	18	1
2010–11	*Juventus*	33	2	33	2

AYALA, Daniel (M)   34   1
H: 6 3 W: 13 03 b.Sevilla 7-11-90
Honours: Spain Under-21.
2007–08	Liverpool	0	0		
2008–09	Liverpool	0	0		
2009–10	Liverpool	5	0		
2010–11	Liverpool	0	0	5	0
2010–11	*Hull C*	12	1	12	1
2010–11	*Derby Co*	17	0	17	0

BABEL, Ryan (F)   164   26
H: 6 1 W: 12 04 b.Amsterdam 19-12-86
Honours: Holland Under-21, 39 full caps, 5
goals.
2003–04	Ajax	1	0		
2004–05	Ajax	20	7		
2005–06	Ajax	25	2		
2006–07	Ajax	27	5	73	14
2007–08	Liverpool	30	4		
2008–09	Liverpool	27	3		
2009–10	Liverpool	25	4		
2010–11	Liverpool	9	1	91	12

Transferred to Hoffenheim January 2011.

BANTON, Jason (F)   0   0
b.Tottenham 15-12-92
Source: Scholar.
2009–10	Blackburn R	0	0		
2010–11	Blackburn R	0	0		
2010–11	Liverpool	0	0		

BOUZANIS, Dean (G)   14   0
H: 6 1 W: 13 06 b.Sydney 2-10-90
Source: St George Saints, Sydney.
| 2007–08 | Liverpool | 0 | 0 | | |

2008–09	Liverpool	0	0		
2009–10	Liverpool	0	0		
2009–10	*Accrington S*	14	0	14	0
2010–11	*Liverpool*	0	0		

BRUNA, Gerardo (M)   0   0
H: 5 8   W: 10 02   b.Mendoza 29-1-91
Source: Real Madrid.

2007–08	Liverpool	0	0		
2008–09	Liverpool	0	0		
2009–10	Liverpool	0	0		
2010–11	Liverpool	0	0		

CARRAGHER, Jamie (D)   463   3
H: 5 9   W: 12 01   b.Liverpool 28-1-78
Source: Trainee. *Honours:* England Youth, Under-21, B, 38 full caps.

1995–96	Liverpool	0	0		
1996–97	Liverpool	2	1		
1997–98	Liverpool	20	0		
1998–99	Liverpool	34	1		
1999–2000	Liverpool	36	0		
2000–01	Liverpool	34	0		
2001–02	Liverpool	33	0		
2002–03	Liverpool	35	0		
2003–04	Liverpool	22	0		
2004–05	Liverpool	38	0		
2005–06	Liverpool	36	0		
2006–07	Liverpool	35	1		
2007–08	Liverpool	35	0		
2008–09	Liverpool	38	0		
2009–10	Liverpool	37	0		
2010–11	Liverpool	28	0	463	3

CARROLL, Andy (F)   98   34
H: 6 4   W: 11 00   b.Gateshead 6-1-89
Source: Scholar. *Honours:* England Youth, Under-21, 2 full caps, 1 goal.

2006–07	Newcastle U	4	0		
2007–08	Newcastle U	4	0		
2007–08	*Preston NE*	11	1	11	1
2008–09	Newcastle U	14	3		
2009–10	Newcastle U	39	17		
2010–11	Newcastle U	19	11	80	31
2010–11	Liverpool	7	2	7	2

CHAMBERLAIN, Deale (G)   0   0
b.Burton 10-4-92
Source: Scholar.

2010–11	Liverpool	0	0		

COADY, Conor (D)   0   0
H: 6 1   W: 11 05   b.Liverpool 25-2-93
Source: Scholar.

2010–11	Liverpool	0	0		

COLE, Joe (M)   329   39
H: 5 9   W: 11 09   b.Camden 8-11-81
Source: Trainee. *Honours:* England Schools, Youth, Under-21, B, 56 full caps, 10 goals.

1998–99	West Ham U	8	0		
1999–2000	West Ham U	22	1		
2000–01	West Ham U	30	5		
2001–02	West Ham U	30	5		
2002–03	West Ham U	36	4	126	10
2003–04	Chelsea	35	1		
2004–05	Chelsea	28	8		
2005–06	Chelsea	34	7		
2006–07	Chelsea	13	0		
2007–08	Chelsea	33	7		
2008–09	Chelsea	14	2		
2009–10	Chelsea	26	2	183	27
2010–11	Liverpool	20	2	20	2

COOPER, Alex (M)   0   0
H: 5 8   W: 11 08   b.Edinburgh 4-11-91

2008–09	Liverpool	0	0		
2009–10	Liverpool	0	0		
2010–11	Liverpool	0	0		

DARBY, Stephen (D)   36   0
H: 5 9   W: 10 00   b.Liverpool 6-10-88
Source: Scholar. *Honours:* England Youth.

2006–07	Liverpool	0	0		
2007–08	Liverpool	0	0		
2008–09	Liverpool	0	0		
2009–10	Liverpool	1	0		
2009–10	*Swindon T*	12	0	12	0
2010–11	Liverpool	0	0	1	0
2010–11	*Notts Co*	23	0	23	0

DEGEN, Philipp (D)   174   5
H: 6 0   W: 12 10   b.Holstein 15-2-83
Honours: Switzerland Under-21, 30 full caps.

2001–02	Basle	3	0		
2002–03	Basle	16	0		
2002–03	*Aarau*	16	0	16	0
2003–04	Basle	33	4		
2004–05	Basle	31	0	83	4
2005–06	Bor Dortmund	31	1		
2006–07	Bor Dortmund	27	0		
2007–08	Bor Dortmund	10	0	68	1
2008–09	Liverpool	0	0		
2009–10	Liverpool	7	0		
2010–11	Liverpool	0	0	7	0

ECCLESTON, Nathan (F)   34   4
H: 5 10   W: 12 00   b.Manchester 30-12-90
Source: Scholar.

2007–08	Liverpool	0	0		
2008–09	Liverpool	0	0		
2009–10	Liverpool	1	0		
2009–10	*Huddersfield T*	11	1	11	1
2010–11	Liverpool	1	0	2	0
2010–11	*Charlton Ath*	21	3	21	3

EL ZHAR, Nabil (F)   33   3
H: 5 9   W: 11 05   b.Ales 27-8-86
Source: St Etienne. *Honours:* France Youth, Morocco Under-20, 8 full caps, 2 goals.

2006–07	Liverpool	3	0		
2007–08	Liverpool	0	0		
2008–09	Liverpool	15	0		
2009–10	Liverpool	3	0		
2010–11	Liverpool	0	0	21	0
2010–11	*PAOK Salonika*	12	3	12	3

EMILSSON, Kristjan (M)   0   0
b.Sweden 26-4-93
Source: Scholar.

2009–10	Liverpool	0	0		
2010–11	Liverpool	0	0		

FABIO AURELIO (M)   233   17
H: 5 10   W: 11 11   b.Sao Carlos 24-9-79
Honours: Brazil Youth, Under-20, Under-21.

1997	Sao Paulo	15	1		
1998	Sao Paulo	11	1		
1998	Santos	0	0		
1999	Sao Paulo	23	1		
2000	Sao Paulo	4	0	53	3
2000–01	Valencia	7	0		
2001–02	Valencia	15	1		
2002–03	Valencia	26	8		
2003–04	Valencia	2	0		
2004–05	Valencia	21	0		
2005–06	Valencia	24	2	95	11
2006–07	Liverpool	17	0		
2007–08	Liverpool	16	1		
2008–09	Liverpool	24	2		
2009–10	Liverpool	14	0		
2010–11	Liverpool	14	0	85	3

FLANAGAN, John (D)   7   0
b.Liverpool 1-1-93
Source: Scholar.

2010–11	Liverpool	7	0	7	0

GERRARD, Steven (M)   387   84
H: 6 0   W: 12 05   b.Huyton 30-5-80
Source: Trainee. *Honours:* England Youth, Under-21, 89 full caps, 19 goals.

1997–98	Liverpool	0	0		
1998–99	Liverpool	12	0		
1999–2000	Liverpool	29	1		
2000–01	Liverpool	33	7		
2001–02	Liverpool	28	3		
2002–03	Liverpool	34	5		
2003–04	Liverpool	34	4		
2004–05	Liverpool	30	7		
2005–06	Liverpool	32	10		
2006–07	Liverpool	36	7		
2007–08	Liverpool	34	11		
2008–09	Liverpool	31	16		
2009–10	Liverpool	33	9		
2010–11	Liverpool	21	4	387	84

GULACSI, Peter (G)   35   0
H: 6 3   W: 13 01   b.Budapest 6-5-90
Source: MTK. *Honours:* Hungary Youth, Under-21.

2007–08	Liverpool	0	0		
2008–09	Liverpool	0	0		
2008–09	*Hereford U*	18	0	18	0

2009–10	Liverpool	0	0		
2009–10	*Tranmere R*	5	0		
2010–11	Liverpool	0	0		
2010–11	*Tranmere R*	12	0	17	0

HANSEN, Martin (G)   0   0
H: 6 2   W: 12 07   b.Glostrup 15-6-90
Source: Brondby. *Honours:* Denmark Under-21.

2007–08	Liverpool	0	0		
2008–09	Liverpool	0	0		
2009–10	Liverpool	0	0		
2010–11	Liverpool	0	0		

HIGHDALE, Sean (M)   0   0
b.Liverpool 4-3-91

2007–08	Liverpool	0	0		
2008–09	Liverpool	0	0		
2009–10	Liverpool	0	0		
2010–11	Liverpool	0	0		
2010–11	*Oldham Ath*	0	0		

INCE, Thomas (F)   6   2
H: 5 10   W: 10 05   b.Liverpool 30-1-92
Source: Scholar.

2009–10	Liverpool	0	0		
2010–11	Liverpool	0	0		
2010–11	*Notts Co*	6	2	6	2

INSUA, Emiliano (D)   46   0
H: 5 10   W: 12 08   b.Buenos Aires 7-1-89
Source: Boca Juniors. *Honours:* Argentina Youth, Under-20, Under-23, 1 full cap.

2006–07	Liverpool	2	0		
2007–08	Liverpool	3	0		
2008–09	Liverpool	10	0		
2009–10	Liverpool	31	0		
2010–11	Liverpool	0	0	46	0

IRWIN, Steven (D)   0   0
H: 5 8   W: 10 06   b.Liverpool 29-9-90
Source: Scholar.

2007–08	Liverpool	0	0		
2008–09	Liverpool	0	0		
2009–10	Liverpool	0	0		
2010–11	Liverpool	0	0		

ITANDJE, Charles (G)   198   0
H: 6 3   W: 13 01   b.Paris 2-11-82
Honours: France Under-21.

2000–01	Red Star 93	9	0	9	0
2001–02	Lens	0	0		
2002–03	Lens	22	0		
2003–04	Lens	35	0		
2004–05	Lens	38	0		
2005–06	Lens	37	0		
2006–07	Lens	38	0	170	0
2007–08	Liverpool	0	0		
2008–09	Liverpool	0	0		
2009–10	Liverpool	0	0		
2009–10	*Kavala*	19	0	19	0
2010–11	Liverpool	0	0		

Transferred to Atromitos Janaury 2011.

JOHNSON, Glen (D)   202   12
H: 6 0   W: 13 04   b.Greenwich 23-8-84
Source: Scholar. *Honours:* England Youth, Under-20, Under-21, 34 full caps, 1 goal.

2001–02	West Ham U	0	0		
2002–03	West Ham U	15	0	15	0
2002–03	*Millwall*	8	0	8	0
2003–04	Chelsea	19	3		
2004–05	Chelsea	17	0		
2005–06	Chelsea	4	0		
2006–07	Chelsea	0	0		
2006–07	*Portsmouth*	26	0		
2007–08	Chelsea	2	0	42	3
2007–08	Portsmouth	29	1		
2008–09	Portsmouth	29	3		
2009–10	Portsmouth	0	0	84	4
2009–10	Liverpool	25	3		
2010–11	Liverpool	28	2	53	5

JONES, Brad (G)   100   0
H: 6 3   W: 12 01   b.Armidale 19-3-82
Source: Trainee. *Honours:* Australia Under-23, 3 full caps.

1998–99	Middlesbrough	0	0		
1999–2000	Middlesbrough	0	0		
2000–01	Middlesbrough	0	0		
2001–02	Middlesbrough	0	0		
2002	*Shelbourne*	2	0	2	0
2002–03	Middlesbrough	0	0		
2002–03	*Stockport Co*	1	0	1	0

2003–04	Middlesbrough	1	0		
2003–04	*Blackpool*	5	0		
2003–04	*Rotherham U*	0	0		
2004–05	Middlesbrough	5	0		
2004–05	*Blackpool*	12	0	17	0
2005–06	Middlesbrough	9	0		
2006–07	Middlesbrough	2	0		
2006–07	*Sheffield W*	15	0	15	0
2007–08	Middlesbrough	1	0		
2008–09	Middlesbrough	16	0		
2009–10	Middlesbrough	24	0	58	0
2010–11	Liverpool	0	0		
2010–11	*Derby Co*	7	0	7	0

JOVANOVIC, Milan (M)   180 63
H: 6 0   W: 11 07   b.Belgrade 18-4-83
Honours: Serbia 35 full caps, 10 goals.

1999–2000	Vojvodina	9	0		
2000–01	Vojvodina	15	3		
2001–02	Vojvodina	7	0		
2002–03	Vojvodina	12	7	43	10
2002–03	Shakhtar Donetsk	6	1		
2003–04	Shakhtar Donetsk	1	0	7	1
2004	Lokomotiv Moscow	3	0		
2005	Lokomotiv Moscow	1	0	4	0
2006–07	Standard Liege	29	14		
2007–08	Standard Liege	31	16		
2008–09	Standard Liege	30	12		
2009–10	Standard Liege	26	10	116	52
2010–11	Liverpool	10	0	10	0

KELLY, Martin (D)   19 1
H: 6 3   W: 12 02   b.Bolton 27-4-90
Source: Scholar. *Honours:* England Youth, Under-20, Under-21.

2007–08	Liverpool	0	0		
2008–09	Liverpool	0	0		
2008–09	*Huddersfield T*	7	1	7	1
2009–10	Liverpool	1	0		
2010–11	Liverpool	11	0	12	0

KOHLERT, Nicolaj (F)   0 0
H: 5 10   W: 11 00   b.Esbjerg 21-1-93
Honours: Denmark Youth.

2009 10	Liverpool	0	0		
2010–11	Liverpool	0	0		

KONCHESKY, Paul (D)   347 9
H: 5 10   W: 11 07   b.Barking 15-5-81
Source: Trainee. *Honours:* England Youth, Under-20, Under-21, 2 full caps.

1997–98	Charlton Ath	3	0		
1998–99	Charlton Ath	2	0		
1999–2000	Charlton Ath	8	0		
2000 01	Charlton Ath	23	0		
2001 02	Charlton Ath	34	1		
2002–03	Charlton Ath	30	3		
2003–04	Charlton Ath	21	0		
2003–04	*Tottenham H*	12	0	12	0
2004–05	Charlton Ath	28	1	149	5
2005–06	West Ham U	37	1		
2006 07	West Ham U	22	0	59	1
2007–08	Fulham	33	0		
2008–09	Fulham	36	1		
2009–10	Fulham	27	1		
2010–11	Fulham	1	0	97	2
2010–11	Liverpool	15	0	15	0
2010–11	*Nottingham F*	15	1	15	1

KUYT, Dirk (F)   435 171
H: 6 0   W: 12 02   b.Katwijk 22-7-80
Source: Quick Boys. *Honours:* Holland 78 full caps, 22 goals.

1998–99	Utrecht	28	5		
1999–2000	Utrecht	32	6		
2000–01	Utrecht	32	13		
2001–02	Utrecht	34	7		
2002–03	Utrecht	34	20	160	51
2003–04	Feyenoord	34	20		
2004–05	Feyenoord	34	29		
2005–06	Feyenoord	33	22	101	71
2006–07	Liverpool	34	12		
2007–08	Liverpool	32	3		
2008–09	Liverpool	38	12		
2009–10	Liverpool	37	9		
2010–11	Liverpool	33	13	174	40

KYRGIAKOS, Sotirios (D)   256 20
H: 6 3   W: 14 06   b.Trikala 23-7-79
Honours: Greece 61 full caps, 4 goals.

1998–99	Panathinaikos	0	0		
1999–2000	Agios	28	1		
2000–01	Agios	25	2	53	3
2001–02	Panathinaikos	18	1		
2002–03	Panathinaikos	24	0		
2003–04	Panathinaikos	6	1		
2004–05	Panathinaikos	12	3	60	5
2004–05	Rangers	15	0		
2005–06	Rangers	28	1	43	1
2006–07	Eintracht Frankfurt	27	5		
2007–08	Eintracht Frankfurt	24	3	51	8
2008–09	AEK Athens	19	0	19	0
2009–10	Liverpool	14	1		
2010–11	Liverpool	16	2	30	3

LUCAS (M)   144 5
H: 5 10   W: 11 09   b.Dourados 9-1-87
Honours: Brazil Under-20, 12 full caps.

2005	Gremio	3	0		
2006	Gremio	30	4	33	4
2007–08	Liverpool	18	0		
2008–09	Liverpool	25	1		
2009–10	Liverpool	35	0		
2010–11	Liverpool	33	0	111	1

MASCHERANO, Javier (M)   152 1
H: 5 7   W: 10 05   b.San Lorenzo 8-6-84
Honours: Argentina Youth, Under-20, Under-23, 61 full caps, 2 goals.

2003–04	River Plate	21	0		
2004–05	River Plate	25	0	46	0
2005	Corinthians	7	0	7	0
2006–07	West Ham U	5	0	5	0
2006–07	Liverpool	7	0		
2007–08	Liverpool	25	1		
2008–09	Liverpool	27	0		
2009–10	Liverpool	34	0		
2010–11	Liverpool	10	0	94	1

Transferred to Barcelona August 2010.

MAVINGA, Chrys (D)   9 0
H: 5 10   W: 10 03   b.Meaux 26-5-91
Source: Paris St Germain.

2009–10	Liverpool	0	0		
2010–11	Liverpool	0	0		
2010–11	*Genk*	9	0	9	0

MENDY, Emmanuel (D)   0 0
H: 5 7   W: 11 09   b.Medina Gounass 30-3-90
Source: Murcia.

2008–09	Liverpool	0	0		
2009–10	Liverpool	0	0		
2010–11	Liverpool	0	0		

N'GOG, David (F)   81 10
H: 6 3   W: 12 04   b.Paris 1-4-89
Honours: France Youth, Under-21.

2006–07	Paris St Germain	4	0		
2007 08	Paris St Germain	14	1	18	1
2008–09	Liverpool	14	2		
2009–10	Liverpool	24	5		
2010–11	Liverpool	25	2	63	9

NGOO, Michael (F)   0 0
b.Walthamstow 23-10-92
Source: Southend U Scholar.

2009–10	Liverpool	0	0		
2010–11	Liverpool	0	0		

PACHECO, Daniel (F)   11 2
H: 5 6   W: 10 07   b.Malaga 5-1-91
Honours: Spain Youth, Under-21.

2007–08	Liverpool	0	0		
2008–09	Liverpool	0	0		
2009–10	Liverpool	4	0		
2010–11	Liverpool	1	0	5	0
2010–11	*Norwich C*	6	2	6	2

PALSSON, Victor (M)   2 0
H: 6 1   W: 12 09   b.Reykjavik 30-4-91
Source: Aarhus. *Honours:* Iceland Youth.

2008–09	Liverpool	0	0		
2009–10	Liverpool	0	0		
2010–11	Liverpool	0	0		
2010–11	*Dagenham & R*	2	0	2	0

Transferred to Hibernian January 2011.

POULSEN, Christian (M)   277 19
H: 5 9   W: 12 04   b.Asnaes 28-2-80
Honours: Denmark 83 full caps, 6 goals.

2000–01	FC Copenhagen	14	2		
2001–02	FC Copenhagen	30	9	44	11
2002–03	Schalke	24	1		
2003–04	Schalke	27	0		
2004–05	Schalke	32	0		
2005–06	Schalke	28	2	111	3
2006–07	Sevilla	33	1		
2007–08	Sevilla	29	3	62	4
2008–09	Juventus	23	1		
2009–10	Juventus	25	0	48	1
2010–11	Liverpool	12	0	12	0

RAUL MEIRELES (M)   241 21
H: 5 10   W: 10 12   b.Oporto 17-3-83
Honours: Portugal Under-21, 47 full caps, 8 goals.

2001–02	Aves	16	0		
2002–03	Aves	26	1	42	1
2003–04	Boavista	29	0	29	0
2004–05	Porto	13	0		
2005–06	Porto	18	2		
2006–07	Porto	25	3		
2007–08	Porto	28	4		
2008–09	Porto	28	4		
2009–10	Porto	25	2	137	15
2010–11	Liverpool	33	5	33	5

REINA, Jose (G)   389 0
H: 6 2   W: 14 06   b.Madrid 31-8-82
Honours: Spain Youth, Under-21, 22 full caps.

1999–2000	Barcelona	30	0	30	0
2000–01	Barcelona	19	0		
2001–02	Barcelona	11	0	30	0
2002–03	Villarreal	33	0		
2003–04	Villarreal	38	0		
2004–05	Villarreal	38	0	109	0
2005–06	Liverpool	33	0		
2006–07	Liverpool	35	0		
2007–08	Liverpool	38	0		
2008–09	Liverpool	38	0		
2009–10	Liverpool	38	0		
2010–11	Liverpool	38	0	220	0

ROBERTS, Michael (M)   0 0
b.Liverpool 5-12-91

2008–09	Liverpool	0	0		
2009–10	Liverpool	0	0		
2010–11	Liverpool	0	0		

ROBINSON, Jack (D)   3 0
H: 5 11   W: 10 08   b.Warrington 1-9-93
Source: Scholar. *Honours:* England Youth.

2009–10	Liverpool	1	0		
2010–11	Liverpool	2	0	3	0

RODRIGUEZ, Maxi (M)   334 88
H: 5 11   W: 12 06   b.Rosario 2-1-81
Honours: Argentina 41 full caps, 12 goals.

1999–2000	Newell's Old Boys	6	0		
2000 01	Newell's Old Boys	18	3		
2001–02	Newell's Old Boys	33	15	57	20
2002–03	Espanyol	37	7		
2003–04	Espanyol	37	4		
2004–05	Espanyol	37	15	111	26
2005–06	Atletico Madrid	29	10		
2006–07	Atletico Madrid	10	5		
2007–08	Atletico Madrid	35	8		
2008–09	Atletico Madrid	33	6		
2009–10	Atletico Madrid	14	2	121	31
2009–10	Liverpool	17	1		
2010–11	Liverpool	28	10	45	11

SAMA, Stephen (D)   0 0
b.Cameroon 5-3-93
Source: Scholar.

2009–10	Liverpool	0	0		
2010–11	Liverpool	0	0		

SARIC, Nikola (F)   0 0
H: 6 0   W: 11 08   b.Sarajevo 6-1-91
Source: Herfolge. *Honours:* Denmark Youth.

2008–09	Liverpool	0	0		
2009–10	Liverpool	0	0		
2010–11	Liverpool	0	0		

SHELVEY, Jonjo (M)   57 7
H: 6 1   W: 11 02   b.Romford 27-2-92
Source: Scholar. *Honours:* England Youth.

2007–08	Charlton Ath	2	0		
2008–09	Charlton Ath	16	3		
2009–10	Charlton Ath	24	4	42	7
2010–11	Liverpool	15	0	15	0

SILVA, Toni (M)   0 0
b.Guinea-Bissau 15-9-93
Honours: Portugal Youth.

2010–11	Liverpool	0	0		

SKRTEL, Martin (D)   201   6
H: 6 3   W: 12 10   b.Handlova 15-12-84
Honours: Slovakia 49 full caps, 5 goals.

2002–03	Trencin	1	0	
2003–04	Trencin	34	0	35	0
2004	Zenit	7	0	
2005	Zenit	18	1	
2006	Zenit	26	1	
2007	Zenit	23	1	74	3
2007–08	Liverpool	14	0	
2008–09	Liverpool	21	0	
2009–10	Liverpool	19	1	
2010–11	Liverpool	38	2	92	3

SOKOLIK, Jakub (D)   0   0
H: 5 6   b.Prague 28-8-93
Source: Scholar.
2010–11   Liverpool   0   0

SPEARING, Jay (M)   21   1
H: 5 6   W: 11 01   b.Wallasey 25-11-88
Source: Scholar.

2006–07	Liverpool	0	0	
2007–08	Liverpool	0	0	
2008–09	Liverpool	0	0	
2009–10	Liverpool	3	0	
2009–10	*Leicester C*	7	1	7	1
2010–11	Liverpool	11	0	14	0

STEPHENS, James (G)   0   0
b.Wotton-under-Edge 24-8-93
Source: Scholar.
2010–11   Liverpool   0   0

SUAREZ, Luis (F)   179   105
H: 5 11   W: 12 10   b.Salto 24-1-87
Honours: Uruguay 41 full caps, 17 goals.

2005–06	Nacional	27	10	27	10
2006–07	Groningen	29	10	29	10
2007–08	Ajax	33	17	
2008–09	Ajax	31	22	
2009–10	Ajax	33	35	
2010–11	Ajax	13	7	110	81
2010–11	Liverpool	13	4	13	4

SUSO (M)   20   7
H: 5 8   W: 10 12   b.Cadiz 19-11-93
2010–11   Cadiz B   20   7   20   7
2010–11   Liverpool   0   0

WILSON, Danny (D)   16   1
H: 6 2   W: 12 06   b.Livingston 27-12-91
Honours: Scotland Youth, Under-21, 3 full caps, 1 goal.
2009–10   Rangers   14   1   14   1
2010–11   Liverpool   2   0   2   0

WISDOM, Andre (D)   0   0
H: 6 1   W: 12 04   b.Leeds 9-5-93
Source: Scholar. *Honours:* England Youth.
2009–10   Liverpool   0   0
2010–11   Liverpool   0   0

Scholars
Aylmer Peter; Belford Tyrell; Hatch Lewis William; King Tom Fredrik; Morgan Adam Joseph; Mukendi Henoc John; Poor Patrik Peter; Rafferty Joseph Gerad; Regan Matthew George; Smith Bradley Shaun; Sumner Joshua Andrew; Walsh Thomas

MACCLESFIELD T (47)

BARNETT, Tyrone (F)   45   13
b.Stevenage 28-10-83
Source: Rushall Olympic, AFC Telford U, Willenhall T, Hednesford T.
2010–11   Macclesfield T   45   13   45   13

BEARDSLEY, Jason (D)   11   0
H: 6 0   W: 11 00   b.Uttoxeter 12-7-89

2007–08	Derby Co	0	0	
2008–09	Derby Co	0	0	
2008–09	*Notts Co*	11	0	11	0
2009–10	Tampa Bay	0	0	
2010–11	Macclesfield T	0	0	

BENCHERIF, Hamza (D)   72   17
H: 5 9   W: 12 03   b.Paris 9-2-88
Source: Scholar.
2006–07   Nottingham F   0   0
2007–08   *Lincoln C*   12   1   12   1
2008–09   Nottingham F   0   0

2009–10   Macclesfield T   19   5
2010–11   Macclesfield T   41   11   60   16

BOLLAND, Paul (D)   361   22
H: 5 10   W: 10 12   b.Bradford 23-12-79
Source: Trainee.

1997–98	Bradford C	10	0	
1998–99	Bradford C	2	0	12	0
1998–99	Notts Co	13	0	
1999–2000	Notts Co	25	1	
2000–01	Notts Co	7	0	
2001–02	Notts Co	19	0	
2002–03	Notts Co	29	3	
2003–04	Notts Co	39	1	
2004–05	Notts Co	40	1	172	6
2005–06	Grimsby T	44	4	
2006–07	Grimsby T	39	5	
2007–08	Grimsby T	35	4	
2008–09	Grimsby T	0	0	118	13
2009–10	Macclesfield T	27	1	
2010–11	Macclesfield T	32	2	59	3

BRISLEY, Shaun (M)   95   3
H: 6 2   W: 12 02   b.Macclesfield 6-5-90
Source: Scholar.
2007–08   Macclesfield T   10   2
2008–09   Macclesfield T   38   0
2009–10   Macclesfield T   33   1
2010–11   Macclesfield T   14   0   95   3

BROWN, Nat (D)   282   20
H: 6 2   W: 12 05   b.Sheffield 15-6-81
Source: Trainee.

1999–2000	Huddersfield T	0	0	
2000–01	Huddersfield T	0	0	
2001–02	Huddersfield T	0	0	
2002–03	Huddersfield T	38	0	
2003–04	Huddersfield T	21	0	
2004–05	Huddersfield T	17	0	76	0
2005–06	Lincoln C	39	7	
2006–07	Lincoln C	28	1	
2007–08	Lincoln C	27	0	94	8
2008–09	Macclesfield T	30	6	
2009–10	Macclesfield T	38	4	
2010–11	Macclesfield T	44	2	112	12

BUTCHER, Richard (M)   297   45
H: 6 0   W: 13 01   b.Peterborough 22-1-81
Source: Kettering T.

2002–03	Lincoln C	26	3	
2003–04	Lincoln C	32	6	
2004–05	Lincoln C	46	2	
2005–06	Oldham Ath	36	4	36	4
2005–06	*Lincoln C*	4	1	
2006–07	Peterborough U	43	4	43	4
2007–08	Notts Co	46	12	
2008–09	Notts Co	34	6	80	18
2009–10	Lincoln C	15	0	123	12
2009–10	*Macclesfield T*	8	2	
2010–11	Macclesfield T	7	1	15	3

Deceased - See Obituary.

CHALMERS, Lewis (M)   76   3
H: 6 0   W: 12 04   b.Manchester 4-2-86
Source: Altrincham.
2008–09   Aldershot T   23   1
2009–10   Aldershot T   23   0   46   1
2010–11   Macclesfield T   30   2   30   2

CUDWORTH, Jack (G)   0   0
b.Preston 11-9-90
Source: Preston NE Scholar, Welshpool, Rhyl.
2010–11   Macclesfield T   0   0

DANIEL, Colin (M)   103   12
H: 5 11   W: 11 06   b.Eastwood 15-2-88
Source: Eastwood T.
2006–07   Crewe Alex   0   0
2007–08   Crewe Alex   1   0
2008–09   Crewe Alex   13   1   14   1
2008–09   *Macclesfield T*   8   0
2009–10   Macclesfield T   38   3
2010–11   Macclesfield T   43   8   89   11

DIAGNE, Tony (D)   20   1
b.Meulan 17-9-90
Source: Scholar.
2008–09   Nottingham F   0   0
2009–10   Nottingham F   0   0
2010–11   Macclesfield T   20   1   20   1

DRAPER, Ross (M)   69   6
H: 6 3   W: 15 05   b.Wolverhampton 20-10-88
Source: Shrewsbury T, Stafford R, Hednesford T.
2009–10   Macclesfield T   29   1
2010–11   Macclesfield T   40   5   69   6

HAMSHAW, Matt (M)   287   18
H: 5 10   W: 11 08   b.Rotherham 1-1-82
Source: Trainee. *Honours:* England Youth, Under-20.

1998–99	Sheffield W	0	0	
1999–2000	Sheffield W	0	0	
2000–01	Sheffield W	18	0	
2001–02	Sheffield W	21	0	
2002–03	Sheffield W	15	1	
2003–04	Sheffield W	0	0	
2004–05	Sheffield W	20	1	74	2
2005–06	Stockport Co	39	5	39	5
2006–07	Mansfield T	40	4	
2007–08	Mansfield T	45	2	85	6
2008–09	Notts Co	41	3	
2009–10	Notts Co	20	0	61	3
2010–11	Macclesfield T	28	2	28	2

HEWITT, Elliott (D)   1   0
Source: Scholar.
2010–11   Macclesfield T   1   0   1   0

LOWE, Matt (M)   11   0
H: 5 8   W: 10 12   b.Stoke 20-10-90
Source: Scholar.
2009–10   Macclesfield T   10   0
2010–11   Macclesfield T   1   0   11   0

MORGAN, Paul (D)   335   3
H: 6 0   W: 11 05   b.Belfast 23-10-78
Source: Trainee. *Honours:* Northern Ireland Under-21.

1997–98	Preston NE	0	0	
1998–99	Preston NE	0	0	
1999–2000	Preston NE	0	0	
2000–01	Preston NE	0	0	
2001–02	Lincoln C	34	1	
2002–03	Lincoln C	45	0	
2003–04	Lincoln C	41	0	
2004–05	Lincoln C	39	0	
2005–06	Lincoln C	20	0	
2006–07	Lincoln C	33	1	212	2
2007–08	Bury	20	0	
2008–09	Bury	0	0	20	0
2008–09	*Macclesfield T*	39	1	
2009–10	Macclesfield T	36	0	
2010–11	Macclesfield T	28	0	103	1

MUKENDI, Vinny (F)   31   2
H: 6 2   W: 12 00   b.Manchester 12-3-92
Source: Scholar.
2008–09   Macclesfield T   1   0
2009–10   Macclesfield T   9   1
2010–11   Macclesfield T   21   1   31   2

REID, Izak (M)   145   5
H: 5 5   W: 10 05   b.Stafford 8-7-87
Source: Scholar.
2006–07   Macclesfield T   8   0
2007–08   Macclesfield T   25   2
2008–09   Macclesfield T   38   2
2009–10   Macclesfield T   37   0
2010–11   Macclesfield T   37   1   145   5

ROBERTS, Adam (M)   2   0
H: 5 9   W: 10 07   b.Manchester 30-12-91
Source: Scholar.
2010–11   Macclesfield T   2   0   2   0

SAPPLETON, Reneil (M)   38   9
H: 5 10   W: 11 13   b.Kingston, Jam 8-12-89
Source: QPR Scholar.
2007–08   Leicester C   1   0
2008–09   Leicester C   0   0
2008–09   *Bournemouth*   3   1   3   1
2009–10   Leicester C   0   0   1   0
2010–11   Macclesfield T   24   7
2010–11   Macclesfield T   10   1   34   8

SINCLAIR, Emile (F)   109   14
H: 6 0   W: 11 04   b.Leeds 29-12-87
Source: Scholar.
2007–08   Nottingham F   12   1
2007–08   *Brentford*   4   0   4   0
2008–09   Nottingham F   3   0   15   1
2008–09   *Macclesfield T*   17   1

2009–10	Macclesfield T	42	7		
2010–11	Macclesfield T	31	5	**90**	**13**

THOMAS, Michael (M) 4 0
H: 6 1 W: 11 00 b.Manchester 12-8-92
Source: Scholar.

2009–10	Macclesfield T	4	0		
2010–11	Macclesfield T	0	0	**4**	**0**

TREMARCO, Carl (D) 118 1
H: 5 8 W: 11 11 b.Liverpool 11-10-85
Source: Scholar.

2003–04	Tranmere R	0	0		
2004–05	Tranmere R	3	0		
2005–06	Tranmere R	18	1		
2006–07	Tranmere R	23	0		
2007–08	Tranmere R	8	0	**52**	**1**
2007–08	Wrexham	10	0	**10**	**0**
2008–09	*Darlington*	2	0	**2**	**0**
2009–10	Macclesfield T	29	0		
2010–11	Macclesfield T	25	0	**54**	**0**

VEIGA, Jose Manuel (G) 323 0
H: 6 2 W: 12 13 b.Lisbon 18-12-76
Source: Benfica. *Honours:* Cape Verde full caps.

1996–97	Alverca	14	0		
1997–98	Alverca	33	0	**47**	**0**
1998–99	Levante	38	0		
1999–2000	Levante	40	0		
2000–01	Levante	30	0		
2001–02	Levante	22	0	**130**	**0**
2001–02	Valladolid	0	0		
2002–03	Amadora	33	0		
2003–04	Amadora	28	0		
2004–05	Amadora	31	0	**92**	**0**
2005–06	Olhanense	2	0	**2**	**0**

From Tamworth, Atherstone T.

2008–09	Hereford U	1	0		
2009–10	Hereford U	0	0	**1**	**0**
2009–10	Macclesfield T	5	0		
2010–11	Macclesfield T	46	0	**51**	**0**

WEDGBURY, Sam (M) 29 2
b.Oldbury 26-2-89
Source: Scholar.

2006–07	Sheffield U	0	0		
2007–08	Sheffield U	0	0		
2008–09	Sheffield U	0	0		
2009–10	Sheffield U	0	0		
2009–10	*Ferencvaros*	6	1	**6**	**1**
2010–11	Macclesfield T	23	1	**23**	**1**

MANCHESTER C (48)

ABU, Mohammed (M) 0 0
b.Ghana 14-11-91
Source: SC Accra.

2010–11	Manchester C	0	0

ADEBAYOR, Emmanuel (F) 274 99
H: 6 4 W: 11 08 b.Lome 26-2-84
Source: Lome. *Honours:* Togo 42 full caps, 18 goals.

2001–02	Metz	10	2		
2002–03	Metz	34	13	**44**	**15**
2003–04	Monaco	31	8		
2004–05	Monaco	34	9		
2005–06	Monaco	13	1	**78**	**18**
2005–06	Arsenal	13	4		
2006–07	Arsenal	29	8		
2007–08	Arsenal	36	24		
2008–09	Arsenal	26	10	**104**	**46**
2009–10	Manchester C	26	14		
2010–11	Manchester C	8	1	**34**	**15**
2010–11	*Real Madrid*	14	5	**14**	**5**

ASSULIN, Gai (M) 67 13
b.Nahariya 9-4-91
Honours: Israel Under-21, 1 full cap.

2007–08	Barcelona B	22	10		
2008–09	Barcelona B	20	1		
2009–10	Barcelona B	25	2	**67**	**13**
2009–10	Barcelona	0	0		
2010–11	Manchester C	0	0		

BALOTELLI, Mario (F) 78 26
H: 6 2 W: 13 08 b.Palermo 12-8-90
Honours: Italy Under-21, 2 full caps.

2005–06	Lumezzane	2	0	**2**	**0**
2006–07	Internazionale	0	0		
2007–08	Internazionale	11	3		
2008–09	Internazionale	22	8		
2009–10	Internazionale	26	9	**59**	**20**
2010–11	Manchester C	17	6	**17**	**6**

BARRY, Gareth (M) 432 45
H: 5 11 W: 12 06 b.Hastings 23-2-81
Source: Trainee. *Honours:* England Youth, B, Under-21, 46 full caps, 2 goals.

1997–98	Aston Villa	2	0		
1998–99	Aston Villa	32	2		
1999–2000	Aston Villa	30	1		
2000–01	Aston Villa	30	0		
2001–02	Aston Villa	20	0		
2002–03	Aston Villa	35	3		
2003–04	Aston Villa	36	3		
2004–05	Aston Villa	34	7		
2005–06	Aston Villa	36	3		
2006–07	Aston Villa	35	8		
2007–08	Aston Villa	37	9		
2008–09	Aston Villa	38	5	**365**	**41**
2009–10	Manchester C	34	2		
2010–11	Manchester C	33	2	**67**	**4**

BELLAMY, Craig (F) 376 123
H: 5 9 W: 10 12 b.Cardiff 13-7-79
Source: Trainee. *Honours:* Wales Schools, Youth, Under-21, 62 full caps, 18 goals.

1996–97	Norwich C	3	0		
1997–98	Norwich C	36	13		
1998–99	Norwich C	40	17		
1999–2000	Norwich C	4	2		
2000–01	Norwich C	1	0	**84**	**32**
2000–01	Coventry C	34	6	**34**	**6**
2001–02	Newcastle U	27	9		
2002–03	Newcastle U	29	7		
2003–04	Newcastle U	16	4		
2004–05	Newcastle U	21	7	**93**	**27**
2004–05	*Celtic*	12	7		
2005–06	Blackburn R	27	13	**27**	**13**
2006–07	Liverpool	27	7	**27**	**7**
2007–08	West Ham U	8	2		
2008–09	West Ham U	16	5	**24**	**7**
2008–09	Manchester C	8	3		
2009–10	Manchester C	32	10		
2010–11	Manchester C	0	0	**40**	**13**
2010–11	*Cardiff C*	35	11	**35**	**11**

BENALI, Ahmed (M) 0 0
b.Libya 7-2-92
Source: Scholar.

2008–09	Manchester C	0	0
2009–10	Manchester C	0	0
2010–11	Manchester C	0	0

BOATENG, Jerome (D) 101 0
H: 6 3 W: 14 02 b.Berlin 3-9-88
Honours: Germany Under-21, 13 full caps.

2006–07	Hertha Berlin	10	0	**10**	**0**
2007–08	Hamburg	27	0		
2008–09	Hamburg	21	0		
2009–10	Hamburg	27	0	**75**	**0**
2010–11	Manchester C	16	0	**16**	**0**

BOYATA, Dedryck (M) 10 0
H: 6 2 W: 12 00 b.Brussels 8-9-90
Source: Scholar. *Honours:* Belgium Under-21.

2008–09	Manchester C	0	0		
2009–10	Manchester C	3	0		
2010–11	Manchester C	7	0	**10**	**0**

BRIDGE, Wayne (D) 308 3
H: 5 10 W: 12 13 b.Southampton 5-8-80
Source: Trainee. *Honours:* England Youth, Under-21, 36 full caps, 1 goal.

1997–98	Southampton	0	0		
1998–99	Southampton	23	0		
1999–2000	Southampton	19	1		
2000–01	Southampton	38	0		
2001–02	Southampton	38	0		
2002–03	Southampton	34	1	**152**	**2**
2003–04	Chelsea	33	1		
2004–05	Chelsea	15	0		
2005–06	Chelsea	0	0		
2005–06	Fulham	12	0	**12**	**0**
2006–07	Chelsea	22	0		
2007–08	Chelsea	11	0		
2008–09	Chelsea	6	0	**87**	**1**
2008–09	Manchester C	16	0		
2009–10	Manchester C	23	0		
2010–11	Manchester C	3	0	**42**	**0**
2010–11	*West Ham U*	15	0	**15**	**0**

BUNN, Harry (F) 0 0
b.Oldham 25-11-92
Source: Scholar.

2010–11	Manchester C	0	0

CAICEDO, Felipe (F) 124 32
H: 6 1 W: 12 08 b.Guayaquil 5-9-88
Source: Rocafuerte. *Honours:* Ecuador 28 full caps, 3 goals.

2006–07	Basle	27	7		
2007–08	Basle	18	4	**45**	**11**
2007–08	Manchester C	10	0		
2008–09	Manchester C	17	4		
2009–10	*Sporting Lisbon*	7	0	**7**	**0**
2009–10	*Malaga*	18	4	**18**	**4**
2010–11	Manchester C	0	0	**27**	**4**
2010–11	*Levante*	27	13	**27**	**13**

CHANTLER, Chris (M) 0 0
H: 5 8 W: 11 00 b.Cheadle Hulme 16-12-90
Source: Scholar.

2009–10	Manchester C	0	0
2010–11	Manchester C	0	0

CUNNINGHAM, Greg (D) 15 0
H: 6 0 W: 11 00 b.Galway 31-1-91
Source: Scholar. *Honours:* Eire 3 full caps.

2008–09	Manchester C	0	0		
2009–10	Manchester C	2	0		
2010–11	Manchester C	0	0	**2**	**0**
2010–11	*Leicester C*	13	0	**13**	**0**

DE JONG, Nigel (D) 244 12
H: 5 8 W: 11 05 b.Amsterdam 30-11-84
Honours: Holland 54 full caps, 1 goal.

2002–03	Ajax	17	0		
2003–04	Ajax	32	1		
2004–05	Ajax	31	5		
2005–06	Hamburg	12	1		
2005–06	Ajax	16	2	**96**	**8**
2006–07	Hamburg	18	1		
2007–08	Hamburg	29	1		
2008–09	Hamburg	7	0	**66**	**3**
2008–09	Manchester C	16	0		
2009–10	Manchester C	34	0		
2010–11	Manchester C	32	1	**82**	**1**

DRURY, Adam (M) 0 0
Source: Scholar.

2010–11	Manchester C	0	0

DZEKO, Edin (F) 197 91
H: 6 3 W: 12 08 b.Doboj 17-3-86
Honours: Bosnia Youth, Under-21, 34 full caps, 18 goals.

2004–05	Zeljeznicar	13	1	**13**	**1**
2005–06	Usti nad Labem	15	6	**15**	**6**
2005–06	Teplice	13	3		
2006–07	Teplice	30	13	**43**	**16**
2007–08	Wolfsburg	28	8		
2008–09	Wolfsburg	32	26		
2009–10	Wolfsburg	34	22		
2010–11	Wolfsburg	17	10	**111**	**66**
2010–11	Manchester C	15	2	**15**	**2**

ELABDELLAOUI, Omar (M) 0 0
b.Norway 5-12-91
Source: Scholar.

2009–10	Manchester C	0	0
2010–11	Manchester C	0	0

GIVEN, Shay (G) 428 0
H: 6 0 W: 13 03 b.Lifford 20-4-76
Source: Celtic. *Honours:* Eire Youth, Under-21, 113 full caps.

1994–95	Blackburn R	0	0		
1994–95	*Swindon T*	0	0		
1995–96	Blackburn R	0	0		
1995–96	*Swindon T*	5	0	**5**	**0**
1995–96	*Sunderland*	17	0	**17**	**0**
1996–97	Blackburn R	2	0	**2**	**0**
1997–98	Newcastle U	24	0		
1998–99	Newcastle U	31	0		
1999–2000	Newcastle U	14	0		
2000–01	Newcastle U	34	0		
2001–02	Newcastle U	38	0		
2002–03	Newcastle U	38	0		
2003–04	Newcastle U	38	0		
2004–05	Newcastle U	36	0		
2005–06	Newcastle U	38	0		
2006–07	Newcastle U	22	0		
2007–08	Newcastle U	19	0		
2008–09	Newcastle U	22	0	**354**	**0**

2008–09	Manchester C	15	0		
2009–10	Manchester C	35	0		
2010–11	Manchester C	0	0	50	0

GONZALEZ, David (G)   238   0
H: 6 4   W: 13 01   b.Medellin 20-7-82
Honours: Colombia 2 full caps.

2001	At Nacional	0	0		
2002	Independiente	21	0		
2003	Independiente	38	0		
2004	Independiente	46	0		
2005	Independiente	22	0	127	0
2006	Dep Cali	35	0		
2007	Dep Cali	22	0	57	0
2007–08	Rize	24	0	24	0
2009	Huracan	30	0	30	0
2009–10	Manchester C	0	0		
2010–11	Manchester C	0	0		
2010–11	Leeds U	0	0		
2010–11	Aberdeen	0	0		

GUIDETTI, John (F)   13   4
H: 5 11   W: 12 06   b.Stockholm 15-4-92
Source: Scholar. *Honours:* Sweden Youth, Under-21.

2009–10	Manchester C	0	0		
2009–10	*Brommapojkana*	8	3	8	3
2010–11	Manchester C	0	0		
2010–11	*Burnley*	5	1	5	1

HART, Joe (G)   187   0
H: 6 3   W: 13 03   b.Shrewsbury 19-4-87
Source: Scholar. *Honours:* England Youth, Under-21, 11 full caps.

2004–05	Shrewsbury T	6	0		
2005–06	Shrewsbury T	46	0	52	0
2006–07	Manchester C	1	0		
2006–07	*Tranmere R*	6	0	6	0
2006–07	*Blackpool*	5	0	5	0
2007–08	Manchester C	26	0		
2008–09	Manchester C	23	0		
2009–10	Manchester C	0	0		
2009–10	*Birmingham C*	36	0	36	0
2010–11	Manchester C	38	0	88	0

HELAN, Jeremy (M)   0   0
b.France 9-5-92
Source: Rennes.

| 2009–10 | Manchester C | 0 | 0 | | |
| 2010–11 | Manchester C | 0 | 0 | | |

HENSHALL, Alex (M)   0   0
b.Swindon 15-2-94
Source: Swindon T.

| 2010–11 | Manchester C | 0 | 0 | | |

HUWS, Emyr (M)   0   0
Source: Scholar.

| 2010–11 | Manchester C | 0 | 0 | | |

IBRAHIM, Abdisalam (M)   12   0
H: 6 0   W: 11 02   b.Guricent 4-5-91
Source: Scholar. *Honours:* Norway Under-21.

2008–09	Manchester C	0	0		
2009–10	Manchester C	1	0		
2010–11	Manchester C	0	0	1	0
2010–11	*Scunthorpe U*	11	0	11	0

JO (F)   182   49
H: 5 9   W: 11 00   b.Sao Paulo 20-3-87
Honours: Brazil Under-23, 3 full caps.

2003	Corinthians	14	1		
2004	Corinthians	42	8		
2005	Corinthians	25	4	81	13
2006	CSKA Moscow	18	14		
2007	CSKA Moscow	27	13		
2008	CSKA Moscow	8	3	53	30
2008–09	Manchester C	9	1		
2008–09	*Everton*	12	5		
2009–10	Manchester C	0	0		
2009–10	*Everton*	15	0	27	5
2010–11	Manchester C	12	0	21	1

JOHANSEN, Eirik (G)   0   0
b.Norway 12-7-92
Honours: Norway Youth.

| 2010–11 | Manchester C | 0 | 0 | | |

JOHNSON, Adam (M)   160   23
H: 5 8   W: 10 00   b.Sunderland 14-7-87
Source: Scholar. *Honours:* England Youth, Under-21, 6 full caps, 2 goals.

| 2004–05 | Middlesbrough | 0 | 0 | | |
| 2005–06 | Middlesbrough | 13 | 1 | | |

2006–07	Middlesbrough	12	0		
2006–07	*Leeds U*	5	0	5	0
2007–08	Middlesbrough	19	1		
2007–08	*Watford*	12	5	12	5
2008–09	Middlesbrough	26	0		
2009–10	Middlesbrough	26	11	96	13
2009–10	Manchester C	16	1		
2010–11	Manchester C	31	4	47	5

JOHNSON, Michael (M)   37   2
H: 6 1   W: 12 07   b.Urmston 3-3-88
Source: Scholar. *Honours:* England Youth, Under-21.

2005–06	Manchester C	0	0		
2006–07	Manchester C	10	0		
2007–08	Manchester C	23	2		
2008–09	Manchester C	3	0		
2009–10	Manchester C	1	0		
2010–11	Manchester C	0	0	37	2

KARIUS, Loris (G)   0   0
H: 6 2   W: 11 11   b.Biberach 22-6-93
Source: Scholar.

| 2010–11 | Manchester C | 0 | 0 | | |

KAY, Scott (M)   0   0
b.Denton 18-9-89
Source: Scholar.

2007–08	Manchester C	0	0		
2008–09	Manchester C	0	0		
2009–10	Manchester C	0	0		
2010–11	Manchester C	0	0		

KOLAROV, Aleksandar (D)   188   14
H: 6 2   W: 13 05   b.Belgrade 10-11-85
Honours: Serbia 21 full caps.

2004–05	Cukaricki	27	2		
2005–06	Cukaricki	17	0	44	2
2005–06	OFK Belgrade	11	1		
2006–07	OFK Belgrade	27	4	38	5
2007–08	Lazio	24	1		
2008–09	Lazio	25	2		
2009–10	Lazio	33	3	82	6
2010–11	Manchester C	24	1	24	1

KOMPANY, Vincent (D)   186   8
H: 6 3   W: 13 05   b.Brussels 10-4-86
Honours: Belgium 39 full caps, 1 goal.

2004–05	Anderlecht	29	2		
2005–06	Anderlecht	32	2	61	4
2006–07	Hamburg	6	0		
2007–08	Hamburg	22	1		
2008–09	Hamburg	1	0	29	1
2008–09	Manchester C	34	1		
2009–10	Manchester C	25	2		
2010–11	Manchester C	37	0	96	3

LESCOTT, Joleon (D)   365   31
H: 6 2   W: 13 00   b.Birmingham 16-8-82
Source: Trainee. *Honours:* England Youth, Under-20, Under-21, B, 13 full caps.

1999–2000	Wolverhampton W	0	0		
2000–01	Wolverhampton W	37	2		
2001–02	Wolverhampton W	44	5		
2002–03	Wolverhampton W	44	1		
2003–04	Wolverhampton W	0	0		
2004–05	Wolverhampton W	41	4		
2005–06	Wolverhampton W	46	1	212	13
2006–07	Everton	38	2		
2007–08	Everton	38	8		
2008–09	Everton	36	4		
2009–10	Everton	1	0	113	14
2010–11	Manchester C	18	1		
2010–11	Manchester C	22	3	40	4

LOGAN, Shaleum (D)   50   2
H: 5 11   W: 12 07   b.Wythenshawe 29-1-88
Source: Scholar.

2006–07	Manchester C	0	0		
2007–08	Manchester C	0	0		
2007–08	*Grimsby T*	5	2	5	2
2007–08	*Scunthorpe U*	4	0	4	0
2007–08	*Stockport Co*	7	0	7	0
2008–09	Manchester C	1	0		
2009–10	Manchester C	0	0		
2009–10	*Tranmere R*	33	0	33	0
2010–11	Manchester C	0	0	1	0

McDERMOTT, Donal (F)   34   6
H: 6 6   W: 12 00   b.Dublin 19-10-89
Source: Scholar. *Honours:* Eire Youth.

2007–08	Manchester C	0	0		
2008–09	Manchester C	0	0		
2008–09	*Milton Keynes D*	1	0	1	0

2009–10	Manchester C	0	0		
2009–10	*Chesterfield*	15	5	15	5
2009–10	*Scunthorpe U*	9	0	9	0
2010–11	Manchester C	0	0		
2010–11	*Bournemouth*	9	1	9	1

McGIVERN, Ryan (D)   33   1
H: 5 10   W: 11 07   b.Newry 8-1-90
Source: Scholar. *Honours:* Northern Ireland Youth, Under-21, B, 13 full caps.

2007–08	Manchester C	0	0		
2008–09	Manchester C	0	0		
2008–09	*Morecambe*	5	1	5	1
2009–10	Manchester C	0	0		
2009–10	*Leicester C*	12	0	12	0
2010–11	Manchester C	1	0	1	0
2010–11	*Walsall*	15	0	15	0

MEE, Ben (D)   15   0
H: 5 11   W: 11 09   b.Sale 21 9 89
Source: Scholar. *Honours:* England Youth, Under-20, Under-21.

2007–08	Manchester C	0	0		
2008–09	Manchester C	0	0		
2009–10	Manchester C	0	0		
2010–11	Manchester C	0	0		
2010–11	*Leicester C*	15	0	15	0

MILNER, James (M)   280   25
H: 5 9   W: 11 00   b.Leeds 4-1-86
Source: Trainee. *Honours:* FA Schools, Youth, England Under-20, Under-21, 19 full caps.

2002–03	Leeds U	18	2		
2003–04	Leeds U	30	3	48	5
2003–04	*Swindon T*	6	2	6	2
2004–05	Newcastle U	25	1		
2005–06	Newcastle U	3	0		
2005–06	*Aston Villa*	27	1		
2006–07	Newcastle U	35	3		
2007–08	Newcastle U	29	2		
2008–09	Newcastle U	2	0	94	6
2008–09	Aston Villa	36	3		
2009–10	Aston Villa	36	7		
2010–11	Aston Villa	1	1	100	12
2010–11	Manchester C	32	0	32	0

MORRISSEY, Conor (D)   0   0
b.Republic of Ireland 13-4-93
Source: Scholar.

| 2010–11 | Manchester C | 0 | 0 | | |

NIELSEN, Gunnar (G)   3   0
H: 6 3   W: 14 00   b.Faeroes 7-10-86
Source: Frem. *Honours:* Faeroes Under-21, 7 full caps.

2007–08	Blackburn R	0	0		
2008–09	Manchester C	0	0		
2009–10	Manchester C	1	0		
2010–11	Manchester C	0	0	1	0
2010–11	*Tranmere R*	2	0	2	0

NIMELY-TCHUIMENI, Alex (F)   1   0
H: 5 11   W: 11 03   b.Monrovia 11-5-91
Source: Mighty Barolle, Cotonsport Garoua, Manchester C Scholar. *Honours:* Liberia Youth. England Under-20.

2008–09	Manchester C	0	0		
2009–10	Manchester C	1	0		
2010–11	Manchester C	0	0	1	0

ONUOHA, Nedum (D)   125   4
H: 6 2   W: 12 04   b.Warri 12-11-86
Source: Scholar. *Honours:* England Youth, Under-20, Under-21.

2004–05	Manchester C	17	0		
2005–06	Manchester C	10	0		
2006–07	Manchester C	18	0		
2007–08	Manchester C	16	1		
2008–09	Manchester C	23	1		
2009–10	Manchester C	10	1		
2010–11	Manchester C	0	0	94	3
2010–11	*Sunderland*	31	1	31	1

POOLE, James (F)   12   1
H: 5 11   W: 12 05   b.Stockport 20-3-90
Source: Scholar.

2008–09	Manchester C	0	0		
2009–10	Manchester C	0	0		
2009–10	*Bury*	9	0	9	0
2010–11	Manchester C	0	0		
2010–11	*Hartlepool U*	3	1	3	1

RAZAK, Abdul (M)   1   0
b.Abidjan 11-11-92

2010–11	Manchester C	1 0	1 0

RICHARDS, Micah (D)   141   6
H: 5 11 W: 13 00 b.Birmingham 24-6-88
Source: Scholar. *Honours:* England Youth,
Under-21, 12 full caps, 1 goal.

2005–06	Manchester C	13 0	
2006–07	Manchester C	28 1	
2007–08	Manchester C	25 0	
2008–09	Manchester C	34 1	
2009–10	Manchester C	23 3	
2010–11	Manchester C	18 1	141 6

SANTA CRUZ, Roque (F)   249 60
H: 6 2 W: 13 12 b.Asuncion 16-8-81
Honours: Paraguay Under-20, 82 full caps, 24
goals.

1998–99	Olimpia	9 3	9 3
1999–2000	Bayern Munich	28 5	
2000–01	Bayern Munich	19 5	
2001–02	Bayern Munich	22 5	
2002–03	Bayern Munich	14 5	
2003–04	Bayern Munich	28 5	
2004–05	Bayern Munich	4 0	
2005–06	Bayern Munich	13 4	
2006–07	Bayern Munich	26 2	154 31
2007–08	Blackburn R	37 19	
2008–09	Blackburn R	20 4	
2009–10	Blackburn R	0 0	
2009–10	Manchester C	19 3	
2010–11	Manchester C	1 0	20 3
2010–11	*Blackburn R*	9 0	66 23

SILVA, David (F)   237 34
H: 5 7 W: 10 07 b.Arguineguin 8-1-86
Honours: Spain 48 full caps, 11 goals.

2003–04	Mestalla	14 1	14 1
2004–05	Eibar	35 5	35 5
2005–06	Celta Vigo	34 3	34 3
2006–07	Valencia	36 5	
2007–08	Valencia	34 4	
2008–09	Valencia	19 4	
2009–10	Valencia	30 8	119 21
2010–11	Manchester C	35 4	35 4

SMITH, Tom (D)   0   0
Source: Scholar.

2010–11	Manchester C	0 0	

TAYLOR, Stuart (G)   68   0
H: 6 5 W: 13 07 b.Romford 28-11-80
Source: Trainee. *Honours:* FA Schools,
England Youth, Under-21.

1998–99	Arsenal	0 0	
1999–2000	Arsenal	0 0	
1999–2000	*Bristol R*	4 0	4 0
2000–01	Arsenal	0 0	
2000–01	*Crystal Palace*	10 0	10 0
2000–01	*Peterborough U*	6 0	6 0
2001–02	Arsenal	10 0	
2002–03	Arsenal	8 0	
2003–04	Arsenal	0 0	
2004–05	Arsenal	0 0	18 0
2004–05	*Leicester C*	10 0	10 0
2005–06	Aston Villa	2 0	
2006–07	Aston Villa	6 0	
2007–08	Aston Villa	4 0	
2008–09	Aston Villa	0 0	
2008–09	*Cardiff C*	8 0	8 0
2009–10	Aston Villa	0 0	12 0
2009–10	Manchester C	0 0	
2010–11	Manchester C	0 0	

TEVEZ, Carlos (F)   259 115
H: 5 8 W: 11 11 b.Buenos Aires 5-2-84
Source: All Boys. *Honours:* Argentina Youth,
Under-20, Under-23, 58 full caps, 12 goals.

2001–02	Boca Juniors	11 1	
2002–03	Boca Juniors	32 11	
2003–04	Boca Juniors	23 12	
2004–05	Boca Juniors	9 2	75 26
2005	Corinthians	29 20	29 20
2006–07	West Ham U	26 7	26 7
2007–08	Manchester U	34 14	
2008–09	Manchester U	29 5	
2009–10	Manchester U	0 0	63 19
2009–10	Manchester C	35 23	
2010–11	Manchester C	31 20	66 43

TOURE, Kolo (D)   278 11
H: 5 10 W: 13 08 b.Sokuora Bouakc
19-3-81
Source: ASEC Mimosas. *Honours:* Ivory
Coast 86 full caps, 4 goals.

2001–02	Arsenal	0 0	
2002–03	Arsenal	26 2	
2003–04	Arsenal	37 1	
2004–05	Arsenal	35 0	
2005–06	Arsenal	33 0	
2006–07	Arsenal	35 3	
2007–08	Arsenal	30 2	
2008–09	Arsenal	29 1	
2009–10	Arsenal	0 0	225 9
2009–10	Manchester C	31 1	
2010–11	Manchester C	22 1	53 2

TOURE, Yaya (M)   259 26
H: 6 3 W: 14 02 b.Sokoura Bouake 13-5-83
Honours: Ivory Coast 57 full caps, 7 goals.

2001–02	Beveren	28 0	
2002–03	Beveren	30 3	
2003–04	Beveren	12 0	70 3
2003–04	Metalurgs Donetsk	11 1	
2004–05	Metalurgs Donetsk	22 2	33 3
2005–06	Olympiakos	20 3	20 3
2006–07	Monaco	27 5	27 5
2007–08	Barcelona	26 1	
2008–09	Barcelona	25 2	
2009–10	Barcelona	23 1	74 4
2010–11	Manchester C	35 8	35 8

TRIPPIER, Keiran (D)   42   2
H: 5 10 W: 11 00 b.Bury 19-9-90
Source: Scholar. *Honours:* England Youth,
Under-20, Under-21.

2007–08	Manchester C	0 0	
2008–09	Manchester C	0 0	
2009–10	Manchester C	0 0	
2009–10	*Barnsley*	3 0	
2010–11	Manchester C	0 0	
2010–11	*Barnsley*	39 2	42 2

TSE, Sean (D)   0   0
Source: Scholar.

2010–11	Manchester C	0 0	

TUTTE, Andrew (M)   24   2
II: 5 9 W: 10 10 b.Huyton 21-9-90
Source: Scholar. *Honours:* England Youth,
Under-20.

2007–08	Manchester C	0 0	
2008–09	Manchester C	0 0	
2009–10	Manchester C	0 0	
2010–11	Manchester C	0 0	
2010–11	*Rochdale*	7 0	7 0
2010–11	*Shrewsbury T*	2 0	2 0
2010–11	*Yeovil T*	15 2	15 2

VESELI, Frederic (D)   0   0
H: 6 0 W: 12 08 b.Kosovo 20-11-92
Source: Scholar. *Honours:* Switzerland Youth.

2009–10	Manchester C	0 0	
2010–11	Manchester C	0 0	

VIDAL, Javan (D)   23   0
H: 5 10 W: 10 10 b.Manchester 10-5-89
Source: Scholar. *Honours:* England Youth,
Under-20.

2007–08	Manchester C	0 0	
2008–09	Manchester C	0 0	
2008–09	*Grimsby T*	3 0	3 0
2008–09	*Aberdeen*	13 0	13 0
2009–10	Manchester C	0 0	
2009–10	*Derby Co*	1 0	1 0
2010–11	Manchester C	0 0	
2010–11	*Chesterfield*	6 0	6 0

VIEIRA, Patrick (M)   456 44
H: 6 4 W: 13 09 b.Dakar 23-6-76
Honours: France Under-21, 107 full caps, 6
goals.

1993–94	Cannes	5 0	
1994–95	Cannes	31 2	
1995–96	Cannes	13 0	49 2
1995–96	AC Milan	2 0	2 0
1996–97	Arsenal	31 2	
1997–98	Arsenal	33 2	
1998–99	Arsenal	34 3	
1999–2000	Arsenal	30 2	
2000–01	Arsenal	30 5	
2001–02	Arsenal	36 2	
2002–03	Arsenal	24 3	

2003–04	Arsenal	29 3	
2004–05	Arsenal	32 6	279 28
2005–06	Juventus	31 5	31 5
2006–07	Inter Milan	20 1	
2007–08	Inter Milan	16 3	
2008–09	Inter Milan	19 1	
2009–10	Inter Milan	12 1	67 6
2009–10	Manchester C	13 1	
2010–11	Manchester C	15 2	28 3

WABARA, Reece (D)   1   0
b. 28-12-91

2008–09	Manchester C	0 0	
2009–10	Manchester C	0 0	
2010–11	Manchester C	1 0	1 0

WEISS, Vladimir (M)   37   0
H: 5 9 W: 10 10 b.Bratislava 30-11-89
Source: Scholar. *Honours:* Slovakia Under-21,
18 full caps, 1 goal.

2007–08	Manchester C	0 0	
2008–09	Manchester C	1 0	
2009–10	Manchester C	0 0	
2009–10	*Bolton W*	13 0	13 0
2010–11	Manchester C	0 0	1 0
2010–11	*Rangers*	23 0	23 0

WOOD, James (G)   0   0
H: 6 0 W: 13 01 b.Church Village 10-11-91
Source: Scholar. *Honours:* Scotland Youth.

2009–10	Manchester C	0 0	
2010–11	Manchester C	0 0	
2010–11	*Exeter C*	0 0	

WRIGHT-PHILLIPS, Shaun (M)   299 39
H: 5 5 W: 10 01 b.Lewisham 25-10-81
Source: Scholar. *Honours:* England Under-21,
36 full caps, 6 goals.

1998–99	Manchester C	0 0	
1999–2000	Manchester C	4 0	
2000–01	Manchester C	15 0	
2001–02	Manchester C	35 8	
2002–03	Manchester C	31 1	
2003–04	Manchester C	34 7	
2004–05	Manchester C	34 10	
2005–06	Chelsea	27 0	
2006–07	Chelsea	27 2	
2007–08	Chelsea	27 2	
2008–09	Chelsea	1 0	82 4
2008–09	Manchester C	27 5	
2009–10	Manchester C	30 4	
2010–11	Manchester C	7 0	217 35

ZABALETA, Pablo (D)   228 14
H: 5 8 W: 10 12 b.Buenos Aires 16-1-85
Honours: Argentina Youth, Under-23, 11 full
caps.

2002–03	San Lorenzo	11 0	
2003–04	San Lorenzo	27 3	
2004–05	San Lorenzo	28 5	66 8
2005–06	Espanyol	27 2	
2006–07	Espanyol	21 0	
2007–08	Espanyol	32 1	80 3
2008–09	Manchester C	29 1	
2009–10	Manchester C	27 0	
2010–11	Manchester C	26 2	82 3

Scholars
Clowes Paul Allan; Coulson Luke; Halsall
Thomas Charles; Kennedy Kieran; King
George Liam; Meppen-Walters Courtney;
Rusnak Albert

MANCHESTER U (49)

AJOSE, Nicholas (F)   28 13
H: 5 8 W: 11 00 b.Bury 7-10-91
Source: Scholar.

2009–10	Manchester U	0 0	
2010–11	Manchester U	0 0	
2010–11	*Bury*	28 13	28 13

AMOS, Ben (G)   17   0
H: 6 1 W: 13 00 b.Macclesfield 10-4-90
Source: Scholar. *Honours:* England Youth.

2007–08	Manchester U	0 0	
2008–09	Manchester U	0 0	
2009–10	Manchester U	0 0	
2009–10	*Peterborough U*	1 0	1 0
2010–11	Manchester U	0 0	
2010–11	*Oldham Ath*	16 0	16 0

ANDERSON (M) 96 5
H: 5 8 W: 10 07 b.Porto Alegre 13-4-88
Honours: Brazil Youth, Under-23, 8 full caps.

2004–05	Gremio	5	1	5	1
2005–06	Porto	3	0		
2006–07	Porto	15	2	18	2
2007–08	Manchester U	24	0		
2008–09	Manchester U	17	0		
2009–10	Manchester U	14	1		
2010–11	Manchester U	18	1	73	2

BEBE (F) 28 4
H: 6 3 W: 11 11 b.Agualva-cacem 12-7-90
Honours: Portugal Under-21.

2009–10	Amadora	26	4	26	4
2010–11	Guimaraes	0	0		
2010–11	Manchester U	2	0	2	0

BERBATOV, Dimitar (F) 370 162
H: 6 2 W: 12 06 b.Blagoevgrad 30-1-81
Honours: Bulgaria Under-21, 78 full caps, 48 goals.

1998–99	CSKA Sofia	11	3		
1999–2000	CSKA Sofia	27	14		
2000–01	CSKA Sofia	12	8	50	25
2000–01	Leverkusen	6	0		
2001–02	Leverkusen	24	8		
2002–03	Leverkusen	24	4		
2003–04	Leverkusen	33	16		
2004–05	Leverkusen	33	20		
2005–06	Leverkusen	34	21	154	69
2006–07	Tottenham H	33	12		
2007–08	Tottenham H	36	15		
2008–09	Tottenham H	1	0	70	27
2008–09	Manchester U	31	9		
2009–10	Manchester U	33	12		
2010–11	Manchester U	32	20	96	41

BRADY, Robert (F) 0 0
b.Belfast 14-1-92
Source: Scholar. *Honours:* Eire Youth, Under-21.

2008–09	Manchester U	0	0		
2009–10	Manchester U	0	0		
2010–11	Manchester U	0	0		

BROWN, Wes (D) 232 3
H: 6 1 W: 13 08 b.Manchester 13-10-79
Source: Trainee. *Honours:* England Schools, Youth, Under-21, 23 full caps, 1 goal.

1996–97	Manchester U	0	0		
1997–98	Manchester U	2	0		
1998–99	Manchester U	14	0		
1999–2000	Manchester U	0	0		
2000–01	Manchester U	28	0		
2001–02	Manchester U	17	0		
2002–03	Manchester U	22	0		
2003–04	Manchester U	17	0		
2004–05	Manchester U	21	1		
2005–06	Manchester U	19	0		
2006–07	Manchester U	22	0		
2007–08	Manchester U	36	1		
2008–09	Manchester U	8	1		
2009–10	Manchester U	19	0		
2010–11	Manchester U	7	0	232	3

BROWN, Reece (D) 3 0
b.Manchester 1-11-91

2010–11	Bradford C	3	0	3	0
2010–11	Manchester U	0	0		

CARRICK, Michael (M) 358 22
H: 6 1 W: 11 10 b.Wallsend 28-7-81
Source: Trainee. *Honours:* England Youth, Under-21, B, 22 full caps.

1998–99	West Ham U	0	0		
1999–2000	West Ham U	8	1		
1999–2000	Swindon T	6	2	6	2
1999–2000	Birmingham C	2	0	2	0
2000–01	West Ham U	33	1		
2001–02	West Ham U	30	2		
2002–03	West Ham U	30	1		
2003–04	West Ham U	35	1		
2004–05	West Ham U	0	0	136	6
2004–05	Tottenham H	29	0		
2005–06	Tottenham H	35	2	64	2
2006–07	Manchester U	33	3		
2007–08	Manchester U	31	2		
2008–09	Manchester U	28	4		
2009–10	Manchester U	30	3		
2010–11	Manchester U	28	0	150	12

CLEVERLEY, Tom (M) 73 16
H: 5 9 W: 10 07 b.Basingstoke 12-8-89
Source: Scholar. *Honours:* England Youth, Under-20, Under-21.

2007–08	Manchester U	0	0		
2008–09	Manchester U	0	0		
2008–09	Leicester C	15	2	15	2
2009–10	Manchester U	0	0		
2009–10	Watford	33	11	33	11
2010–11	Manchester U	0	0		
2010–11	Wigan Ath	25	3	25	3

COFIE, John (F) 0 0
b.Aboso 21-1-93
Source: Scholar.

2010–11	Manchester U	0	0		

DE LAET, Ritchie (D) 36 0
H: 6 1 W: 12 02 b.Antwerp 28-11-88
Source: Antwerp. *Honours:* Belgium Under-21, 2 full caps.

2007–08	Stoke C	0	0		
2008–09	Stoke C	0	0		
2008–09	Manchester U	1	0		
2009–10	Manchester U	2	0		
2010–11	Manchester U	0	0	3	0
2010–11	Sheffield U	6	0	6	0
2010–11	Preston NE	5	0	5	0
2010–11	Portsmouth	22	0	22	0

DEVLIN, Conor (G) 0 0
b. 23-9-91
Source: Scholar. *Honours:* Northern Ireland Under-21.

2010–11	Manchester U	0	0		
2010–11	Hartlepool U	0	0		

DIOUF, Mame Biram (F) 104 36
H: 6 1 W: 11 13 b.Dakar 16-12-87
Source: Diaraf. *Honours:* Senegal 9 full caps, 2 goals.

2007	Molde	21	9		
2008	Molde	23	7		
2009	Molde	29	16	73	32
2009–10	Manchester U	5	1		
2010–11	Manchester U	0	0	5	1
2010–11	Blackburn R	26	3	26	3

DRINKWATER, Daniel (M) 54 2
H: 5 10 W: 11 00 b.Manchester 5-3-90
Source: Scholar. *Honours:* England Youth.

2008–09	Manchester U	0	0		
2009–10	Manchester U	0	0		
2009–10	Huddersfield T	33	2	33	2
2010–11	Manchester U	0	0		
2010–11	Cardiff C	9	0	9	0
2010–11	Watford	12	0	12	0

DUDGEON, Joe (D) 2 0
b.Leeds 26-11-90
Source: Scholar. *Honours:* Northern Ireland Under-21.

2009–10	Manchester U	0	0		
2010–11	Manchester U	0	0		
2010–11	Carlisle U	2	0	2	0

EIKREM, Magnus (M) 0 0
H: 5 8 W: 10 12 b.Molde 8-8-90
Source: Scholar.

2008–09	Manchester U	0	0		
2009–10	Manchester U	0	0		
2010–11	Manchester U	0	0		

Transferred to Molde January 2011.

EVANS, Corry (M) 19 3
H: 5 8 W: 10 12 b.Belfast 30-7-90
Source: Scholar. *Honours:* Northern Ireland Under-21, B, 11 full caps, 1 goal.

2007–08	Manchester U	0	0		
2008–09	Manchester U	0	0		
2009–10	Manchester U	0	0		
2010–11	Manchester U	0	0		
2010–11	Carlisle U	1	0	1	0
2010–11	Hull C	18	3	18	3

EVANS, Jonny (D) 95 3
H: 6 2 W: 12 02 b.Belfast 3-1-88
Source: Scholar. *Honours:* Northern Ireland Schools, Youth, Under-21, 26 full caps, 1 goal.

2004–05	Manchester U	0	0		
2005–06	Manchester U	0	0		
2006–07	Manchester U	0	0		
2006–07	Antwerp	14	2	14	2
2006–07	Sunderland	18	1		
2007–08	Manchester U	0	0		
2007–08	Sunderland	15	0	33	1
2008–09	Manchester U	17	0		
2009–10	Manchester U	18	0		
2010–11	Manchester U	13	0	48	0

EVRA, Patrice (D) 355 7
H: 5 8 W: 11 10 b.Dakar 15-5-81
Honours: France 35 full caps.

1998–99	Marsala	24	3	24	3
1999–2000	Monza	3	0	3	0
2000–01	Nice	5	0		
2001–02	Nice	34	1	39	1
2002–03	Monaco	36	1		
2003–04	Monaco	33	0		
2004–05	Monaco	36	0		
2005–06	Monaco	15	0	120	1
2005–06	Manchester U	11	0		
2006–07	Manchester U	24	1		
2007–08	Manchester U	33	0		
2008–09	Manchester U	28	0		
2009–10	Manchester U	38	0		
2010–11	Manchester U	35	1	169	2

FABIO (M) 16 1
H: 5 8 W: 10 03 b.Rio de Janeiro 9-7-90
Source: Fluminense.

2008–09	Manchester U	0	0		
2009–10	Manchester U	5	0		
2010–11	Manchester U	11	1	16	1

FERDINAND, Rio (D) 431 10
H: 6 2 W: 13 12 b.Peckham 7-11-78
Source: Trainee. *Honours:* England Youth, Under-21, B, 81 full caps, 3 goals.

1995–96	West Ham U	1	0		
1996–97	West Ham U	15	2		
1996–97	Bournemouth	10	0	10	0
1997–98	West Ham U	35	0		
1998–99	West Ham U	31	0		
1999–2000	West Ham U	33	0		
2000–01	West Ham U	12	0	127	2
2001–02	Leeds U	23	2		
2001–02	Leeds U	31	0	54	2
2002–03	Manchester U	28	0		
2003–04	Manchester U	20	0		
2004–05	Manchester U	31	0		
2005–06	Manchester U	37	3		
2006–07	Manchester U	33	1		
2007–08	Manchester U	35	2		
2008–09	Manchester U	24	0		
2009–10	Manchester U	13	0		
2010–11	Manchester U	19	0	240	6

FLETCHER, Darren (M) 189 16
H: 6 0 W: 11 09 b.Edinburgh 1-2-84
Source: Scholar. *Honours:* Scotland Under-21, B, 53 full caps, 4 goals.

2000–01	Manchester U	0	0		
2001–02	Manchester U	0	0		
2002–03	Manchester U	0	0		
2003–04	Manchester U	22	0		
2004–05	Manchester U	18	3		
2005–06	Manchester U	27	1		
2006–07	Manchester U	24	3		
2007–08	Manchester U	16	0		
2008–09	Manchester U	26	3		
2009–10	Manchester U	30	4		
2010–11	Manchester U	26	2	189	16

FORNASIER, Michele (D) 0 0
b.Vittorio Veneto 22-8-93
Source: Scholar.

2010–11	Manchester U	0	0		

GIBSON, Darron (M) 51 4
H: 6 0 W: 12 04 b.Derry 25-10-87
Source: Scholar. *Honours:* Eire Youth, Under-21, 16 full caps, 1 goal.

2005–06	Manchester U	0	0		
2006–07	Manchester U	0	0		
2007–08	Manchester U	0	0		
2007–08	Wolverhampton W	21	1	21	1
2008–09	Manchester U	3	1		
2009–10	Manchester U	15	2		
2010–11	Manchester U	12	0	30	3

GIGGS, Ryan (F) 613 110
H: 5 11 W: 11 02 b.Cardiff 29-11-73
Source: School. *Honours:* England Schools, Wales Youth, Under-21, 64 full caps, 12 goals.

1990–91	Manchester U	2	1		
1991–92	Manchester U	38	4		

1992–93	Manchester U	41	9		
1993–94	Manchester U	38	13		
1994–95	Manchester U	29	1		
1995–96	Manchester U	33	11		
1996–97	Manchester U	26	3		
1997–98	Manchester U	29	8		
1998–99	Manchester U	24	3		
1999–2000	Manchester U	30	6		
2000–01	Manchester U	31	5		
2001–02	Manchester U	25	7		
2002–03	Manchester U	36	8		
2003–04	Manchester U	33	7		
2004–05	Manchester U	32	5		
2005–06	Manchester U	27	3		
2006–07	Manchester U	30	4		
2007–08	Manchester U	31	3		
2008–09	Manchester U	28	2		
2009–10	Manchester U	25	5		
2010–11	Manchester U	25	2	613	110

GILL, Oliver (D) 4 0
b.Frimley 15-9-90
Source: Scholar.

2009–10	Manchester U	0	0		
2010–11	Manchester U	0	0		
2010–11	*Bradford C*	4	0	4	0

HARGREAVES, Owen (M) 172 7
H: 5 11 W: 11 07 b.Calgary 20-1-81
Source: Calgary Foothills. *Honours:* England Under-21, B, 42 full caps.

2000–01	Bayern Munich	14	0		
2001–02	Bayern Munich	29	0		
2002–03	Bayern Munich	25	1		
2003–04	Bayern Munich	25	2		
2004–05	Bayern Munich	27	1		
2005–06	Bayern Munich	16	1		
2006–07	Bayern Munich	9	0	145	5
2007–08	Manchester U	23	2		
2008–09	Manchester U	2	0		
2009–10	Manchester U	1	0		
2010–11	Manchester U	1	0	27	2

HERNANDEZ, Javier (F) 134 50
H: 5 8 W: 9 11 b.Guadalajara 1-6-88
Honours: Mexico Youth, 26 full caps, 18 goals.

2005–06	Tapatio	11	0		
2006–07	Tapatio	12	3		
2006–07	Guadalajara	7	1		
2007–08	Guadalajara	5	0		
2007–08	Tapatio	15	6		
2008–09	Tapatio	7	2	45	11
2008–09	Guadalajara	22	4		
2009–10	Guadalajara	28	21	62	26
2010–11	Manchester U	27	13	27	13

JAMES, Matthew (M) 28 2
H: 6 0 W: 11 12 b.Bacup 22-7-91
Source: Scholar. *Honours:* England Youth, Under-20.

2007–08	Manchester U	0	0		
2008–09	Manchester U	0	0		
2009–10	Manchester U	0	0		
2009–10	*Preston NE*	18	2		
2010–11	Manchester U	0	0		
2010–11	*Preston NE*	10	0	28	2

JOHNSTONE, Samuel (G) 0 0
b.Preston 25-3-93
Source: Scholar. *Honours:* England Youth.

2009–10	Manchester U	0	0		
2010–11	Manchester U	0	0		

KEANE, William (F) 0 0
b.Stockport 11-11-93
Source: Scholar. *Honours:* England Youth.

2009–10	Manchester U	0	0		
2010–11	Manchester U	0	0		

KING, Josh (F) 8 0
H: 5 11 W: 11 09 b.Oslo 15-1-92
Source: Scholar.

2008–09	Manchester U	0	0		
2009–10	Manchester U	0	0		
2010–11	Manchester U	0	0		
2010–11	*Preston NE*	8	0	8	0

KUSZCZAK, Tomasz (G) 63 0
H: 6 3 W: 13 03 b.Krosno Odrzansia 20-3-82
Source: Uerdingen. *Honours:* Poland Youth, Under-21, 10 full caps.

2001–02	Hertha Berlin	0	0		
2002–03	Hertha Berlin	0	0		
2003–04	Hertha Berlin	0	0		
2004–05	WBA	3	0		
2005–06	WBA	28	0		
2006–07	WBA	0	0	31	0
2006–07	*Manchester U*	6	0		
2007–08	Manchester U	9	0		
2008–09	Manchester U	4	0		
2009–10	Manchester U	8	0		
2010–11	Manchester U	5	0	32	0

LINDEGAARD, Anders (G) 72 0
H: 6 4 W: 12 08 b.Odense 13-4-84
Honours: Denmark Youth, 4 full caps.

2003–04	Odense	0	0		
2004–05	Odense	0	0		
2005–06	Odense	0	0		
2006–07	Odense	1	0		
2007–08	Odense	1	0		
2008–09	Kolding	10	0	10	0
2009	Aalesund	26	0		
2009	Odense	4	0	6	0
2010	Aalesund	30	0	56	0
2010–11	Manchester U	0	0		

MACHEDA, Federico (F) 30 4
H: 6 0 W: 11 13 b.Rome 22-8-91
Source: Scholar. *Honours:* Italy Under-21.

2008–09	Manchester U	4	2		
2009–10	Manchester U	5	1		
2010–11	Manchester U	7	1	16	4
2010–11	*Sampdoria*	14	0	14	0

MASSACCI, Alberto (D) 0 0
b. 27-5-93
Source: Scholar.

2010–11	Manchester U	0	0		

McGINTY, Sean (D) 0 0
b. 11-8-93
Source: Scholar. *Honours:* Eire Youth.

2010–11	Manchester U	0	0		

MORRISON, Ravel (M) 0 0
b.Wythenshawe 2-2-93
Source: Scholar.

2009–10	Manchester U	0	0		
2010 11	Manchester U	0	0		

NANI (M) 153 26
H: 5 9 W: 10 04 b.Cape Verde 17-11-86
Honours: Portugal Under-21, 45 full caps, 9 goals.

2005–06	Sporting Lisbon	29	4		
2006–07	Sporting Lisbon	29	5	58	9
2007–08	Manchester U	26	3		
2008–09	Manchester U	13	1		
2009–10	Manchester U	23	4		
2010–11	Manchester U	33	9	95	17

NEVILLE, Gary (D) 400 5
H: 5 11 W: 12 10 b.Bury 18-2-75
Source: Trainee. *Honours:* England Youth, 85 full caps.

1992–93	Manchester U	0	0		
1993–94	Manchester U	1	0		
1994–95	Manchester U	18	0		
1995–96	Manchester U	31	0		
1996–97	Manchester U	31	1		
1997–98	Manchester U	34	0		
1998–99	Manchester U	34	1		
1999–2000	Manchester U	22	0		
2000–01	Manchester U	32	1		
2001–02	Manchester U	34	0		
2002–03	Manchester U	26	0		
2003–04	Manchester U	30	2		
2004–05	Manchester U	22	0		
2005–06	Manchester U	25	0		
2006–07	Manchester U	24	0		
2007–08	Manchester U	0	0		
2008–09	Manchester U	16	0		
2009–10	Manchester U	17	0		
2010–11	Manchester U	3	0	400	5

NORWOOD, Oliver (M) 6 0
b.Burnley 12-4-91
Source: Scholar. *Honours:* Northern Ireland Youth, Under-21, 4 full caps.

2009–10	Manchester U	0	0		
2010–11	Manchester U	0	0		
2010–11	*Carlisle U*	6	0	6	0

O'SHEA, John (D) 266 11
H: 6 3 W: 13 07 b.Waterford 30-4-81
Source: Waterford. *Honours:* Eire Youth, Under-21, 70 full caps, 1 goal.

1998–99	Manchester U	0	0		
1999–2000	Manchester U	0	0		
1999–2000	*Bournemouth*	10	1	10	1
2000–01	Manchester U	9	0		
2001–02	Manchester U	9	0		
2002–03	Manchester U	32	0		
2003–04	Manchester U	33	2		
2004–05	Manchester U	23	2		
2005–06	Manchester U	34	1		
2006–07	Manchester U	32	4		
2007–08	Manchester U	28	0		
2008–09	Manchester U	30	0		
2009–10	Manchester U	15	1		
2010–11	Manchester U	20	0	256	10

OBERTAN, Gabriel (F) 83 4
H: 6 1 W: 12 06 b.Paris 26-2-89
Honours: France Youth, Under-21.

2006–07	Bordeaux	17	1		
2007–08	Bordeaux	26	2		
2008–09	Bordeaux	11	0	54	3
2008–09	*Lorient*	15	1	15	1
2009–10	Manchester U	7	0		
2010–11	Manchester U	7	0	14	0

OWEN, Michael (F) 353 162
H: 5 8 W: 10 12 b.Chester 14-12-79
Source: Trainee. *Honours:* England Schools, Youth, Under-21, B, 89 full caps, 40 goals.

1996–97	Liverpool	2	1		
1997–98	Liverpool	36	18		
1998–99	Liverpool	30	18		
1999–2000	Liverpool	27	11		
2000–01	Liverpool	28	16		
2001–02	Liverpool	29	19		
2002–03	Liverpool	35	19		
2003–04	Liverpool	29	16	216	118
2004–05	Real Madrid	36	13	36	13
2005–06	Newcastle U	11	7		
2006 07	Newcastle U	3	0		
2007–08	Newcastle U	29	11		
2008–09	Newcastle U	28	8		
2009–10	Newcastle U	0	0	71	26
2009–10	Manchester U	19	3		
2010–11	Manchester U	11	2	30	5

PARK, Ji-Sung (M) 256 41
H: 5 9 W: 11 06 b.Seoul 25-2-81
Honours: South Korea 101 full caps, 13 goals.

2000	Kyoto Purple S	13	1		
2001	Kyoto Purple S	38	3		
2002	Kyoto Purple S	25	7	76	11
2002–03	PSV Eindhoven	8	0		
2003–04	PSV Eindhoven	28	6		
2004–05	PSV Eindhoven	28	7	64	13
2005–06	Manchester U	33	1		
2006–07	Manchester U	14	5		
2007–08	Manchester U	12	1		
2008–09	Manchester U	25	2		
2009–10	Manchester U	17	3		
2010–11	Manchester U	15	5	116	17

PETRUCCI, Davide (M) 0 0
b.Rome 5-10-91
Source: Scholar.

2008–09	Manchester U	0	0		
2009–10	Manchester U	0	0		
2010–11	Manchester U	0	0		

POGBA, Paul (M) 0 0
b.Lagny-sur-Marne 15-3-93
Source: Scholar.

2009–10	Manchester U	0	0		
2010–11	Manchester U	0	0		

RAFAEL (D) 40 2
H: 5 8 W: 10 03 b.Rio de Janeiro 9-7-90
Source: Fluminense. *Honours:* Brazil Youth.

2008–09	Manchester U	16	1		
2009–10	Manchester U	8	1		
2010–11	Manchester U	16	0	40	2

ROONEY, Wayne (F) 284 117
H: 5 10 W: 12 13 b.Liverpool 24-10-85
Source: Scholar. *Honours:* FA Schools, England Youth, 70 full caps, 26 goals.

2002–03	Everton	33	6		
2003–04	Everton	34	9	67	15
2004–05	Manchester U	29	11		

2005–06	Manchester U	36	16		
2006–07	Manchester U	35	14		
2007–08	Manchester U	27	12		
2008–09	Manchester U	30	12		
2009–10	Manchester U	32	26		
2010–11	Manchester U	28	11	217	102

SCHOLES, Paul (M) 466 102
H: 5 7　W: 11 00　b.Salford 16-11-74
Source: Trainee. *Honours:* England Youth, 66 full caps, 14 goals.

1992–93	Manchester U	0	0		
1993–94	Manchester U	0	0		
1994–95	Manchester U	17	5		
1995–96	Manchester U	26	10		
1996–97	Manchester U	24	3		
1997–98	Manchester U	31	8		
1998–99	Manchester U	31	6		
1999 2000	Manchester U	31	9		
2000–01	Manchester U	32	6		
2001–02	Manchester U	35	8		
2002–03	Manchester U	33	14		
2003–04	Manchester U	28	9		
2004–05	Manchester U	33	9		
2005–06	Manchester U	20	2		
2006–07	Manchester U	30	6		
2007–08	Manchester U	24	1		
2008–09	Manchester U	21	2		
2009–10	Manchester U	28	3		
2010–11	Manchester U	22	1	466	102

SMALLING, Chris (D) 29 0
H: 6 4　W: 14 02　b.Greenwich 22-11-89
Source: Maidstone U. *Honours:* England Youth, Under-21.

2008–09	Fulham	1	0		
2009–10	Fulham	12	0	13	0
2010–11	Manchester U	16	0	16	0

THORPE, Tom (D) 0 0
b.Manchester 13-1-93
Source: Scholar.

2010–11	Manchester U	0	0	

TUNNICLIFFE, Ryan (M) 0 0
b.Bury 30-12-92
Source: Scholar.

2009–10	Manchester U	0	0	
2010–11	Manchester U	0	0	

VALENCIA, Antonio (M) 217 24
H: 5 10　W: 12 04　b.Lago Agrio 5-8-85
Honours: Ecuador Under-21, Under-23, 44 full caps, 6 goals.

2002	El Nacional	1	0		
2003	El Nacional	26	2		
2004	El Nacional	42	5		
2005	El Nacional	14	4	83	11
2005–06	Villarreal	2	0	2	0
2005–06	*Recreativo*	4	0	4	0
2006–07	Wigan Ath	22	1		
2007–08	Wigan Ath	31	3		
2008–09	Wigan Ath	31	3	84	7
2009–10	Manchester U	34	5		
2010–11	Manchester U	10	1	44	6

VAN DER SAR, Edwin (G) 605 1
H: 6 5　W: 14 11　b.Voorhout 29-10-70
Honours: Holland 130 full caps.

1990–91	Ajax	9	0		
1991–92	Ajax	0	0		
1992–93	Ajax	19	0		
1993–94	Ajax	32	0		
1994–95	Ajax	33	0		
1995–96	Ajax	33	0		
1996–97	Ajax	33	0		
1997–98	Ajax	33	1	192	1
1998–99	Juventus	34	0		
1999–2000	Juventus	32	0		
2000–01	Juventus	34	0	100	0
2001–02	Fulham	37	0		
2002–03	Fulham	19	0		
2003–04	Fulham	37	0		
2004–05	Fulham	34	0	127	0
2005–06	Manchester U	38	0		
2006–07	Manchester U	32	0		
2007–08	Manchester U	29	0		
2008–09	Manchester U	33	0		
2009–10	Manchester U	21	0		
2010–11	Manchester U	33	0	186	0

VAN VELZEN, Gyliano (F) 0 0
b.Holland 14-4-94
Source: Scholar.

2010–11	Manchester U	0	0	

VERMIJL, Marnick (D) 0 0
H: 5 11　W: 11 12　b.Belgium 13-1-92
Honours: Belgium Youth.

2010–11	Manchester U	0	0	

VIDIC, Nemanja (D) 295 36
H: 6 1　W: 13 02　b.Uzice 21-10-81
Honours: Serbia 54 full caps, 2 goals.

2000–01	Subotica	27	6	27	6
2001–02	Red Star Belgrade	22	2		
2002–03	Red Star Belgrade	26	5		
2003–04	Red Star Belgrade	20	5	68	12
2004	Spartak Moscow	12	2		
2005	Spartak Moscow	27	2	39	4
2005–06	Manchester U	11	0		
2006–07	Manchester U	25	3		
2007–08	Manchester U	32	1		
2008–09	Manchester U	34	4		
2009–10	Manchester U	24	1		
2010–11	Manchester U	35	5	161	14

WELBECK, Danny (F) 42 9
H: 6 1　W: 11 07　b.Manchester 26-11-90
Source: Scholar. *Honours:* England Youth, Under-21, 1 full cap.

2007–08	Manchester U	0	0		
2008–09	Manchester U	3	1		
2009–10	Manchester U	5	0		
2009–10	*Preston NE*	8	2	8	2
2010–11	Manchester U	0	0	8	1
2010–11	*Sunderland*	26	6	26	6

WOOTTON, Scott (D) 7 1
b.Birkenhead 12-9-91
Source: Scholar.

2009–10	Manchester U	0	0		
2010–11	Manchester U	0	0		
2010–11	*Tranmere R*	7	1	7	1

Scholars
Blackett Tyler Nathan; Cole Larnell James; Coll Joseph Aloysious; Ekangamene Charni; Fryers Ezekiel David; Hendrie Luke John; Jacob Liam David; Lawrence Thomas Morris; Lingard Jesse Ellis; McCullough Luke

MIDDLESBROUGH (50)

ARCA, Julio (M) 322 25
H: 5 9　W: 11 13　b.Quilmes 31-1-81
Honours: Argentina Youth, Under-21.

1999–2000	Argentinos Jun	19	0		
2000–01	Argentinos Jun	17	1	36	1
2000–01	Sunderland	27	2		
2001–02	Sunderland	22	1		
2002–03	Sunderland	13	0		
2003–04	Sunderland	31	4		
2004–05	Sunderland	40	9		
2005–06	Sunderland	24	1	157	17
2006–07	Middlesbrough	21	2		
2007–08	Middlesbrough	24	2		
2008–09	Middlesbrough	18	0		
2009–10	Middlesbrough	34	0		
2010–11	Middlesbrough	32	3	129	7

ATKINSON, David (D) 0 0
b.Shildon 27-4-93
Source: Scholar. *Honours:* England Youth.

2010–11	Middlesbrough	0	0	

BAILEY, Nicky (M) 255 46
H: 5 10　W: 12 06　b.Hammersmith 10-6-84
Source: Sutton U.

2005–06	Barnet	45	7		
2006–07	Barnet	44	5	89	12
2007–08	Southend U	44	9		
2008–09	Southend U	1	0	45	9
2008–09	Charlton Ath	43	13		
2009–10	Charlton Ath	44	12	87	25
2010–11	Middlesbrough	34	0	34	0

BATES, Matthew (D) 76 4
H: 5 10　W: 12 03　b.Stockton 10-12-86
Source: Scholar. *Honours:* England Youth, Under-20.

2003–04	Middlesbrough	0	0	
2004–05	Middlesbrough	2	0	

2004–05	*Darlington*	4	0	4	0
2005–06	Middlesbrough	16	0		
2006–07	Middlesbrough	1	0		
2006–07	*Ipswich T*	2	0	2	0
2007–08	Middlesbrough	0	0		
2007–08	*Norwich C*	3	0	3	0
2008–09	Middlesbrough	17	1		
2009–10	Middlesbrough	0	0		
2010–11	Middlesbrough	31	3	67	4

BENNETT, Joe (D) 44 0
H: 5 10　W: 10 04　b.Rochdale 28-3-90
Source: Scholar. *Honours:* England Under-20, Under-21.

2008–09	Middlesbrough	1	0		
2009–10	Middlesbrough	12	0		
2010–11	Middlesbrough	31	0	44	0

BOYD, Kris (F) 333 176
H: 6 0　W: 13 01　b Irvine 18-8-83
Honours: Scotland 18 full caps, 7 goals.

2000–01	Kilmarnock	1	0		
2001–02	Kilmarnock	28	4		
2002–03	Kilmarnock	38	12		
2003–04	Kilmarnock	37	15		
2004–05	Kilmarnock	30	17		
2005–06	Kilmarnock	19	15	153	63
2005–06	Rangers	17	17		
2006–07	Rangers	32	20		
2007–08	Rangers	28	14		
2008–09	Rangers	35	27		
2009–10	Rangers	31	23	143	101
2010–11	Middlesbrough	27	6	27	6
2010–11	*Nottingham F*	10	6	10	6

COYNE, Danny (G) 440 0
H: 6 0　W: 13 00　b.Prestatyn 27-8-73
Source: Trainee. *Honours:* Wales Schools, Youth, Under-21, B, 16 full caps.

1991–92	Tranmere R	0	0		
1992–93	Tranmere R	1	0		
1993–94	Tranmere R	5	0		
1994–95	Tranmere R	5	0		
1995–96	Tranmere R	46	0		
1996–97	Tranmere R	21	0		
1997–98	Tranmere R	16	0		
1998–99	Tranmere R	17	0		
1999–2000	Grimsby T	44	0		
2000–01	Grimsby T	46	0		
2001–02	Grimsby T	45	0		
2002–03	Grimsby T	46	0	181	0
2003–04	Leicester C	4	0	4	0
2004–05	Burnley	20	0		
2005–06	Burnley	8	0		
2006–07	Burnley	12	0	40	0
2007–08	Tranmere R	41	0		
2008–09	Tranmere R	39	0	191	0
2009–10	Middlesbrough	23	0		
2010–11	Middlesbrough	1	0	24	0

DIGARD, Didier (M) 120 3
H: 6 0　W: 11 13　b.Gisors 12-7-86
Honours: France Under-21.

2004–05	Le Havre	15	0		
2005–06	Le Havre	30	2		
2006–07	Le Havre	27	1	72	3
2007–08	Paris St Germain	16	0	16	0
2008–09	Middlesbrough	23	0		
2009–10	Middlesbrough	9	0		
2010–11	Middlesbrough	0	0	32	0

DOLAN, Matthew (M) 0 0
b.Hartlepool 11-2-93
Source: Scholar.

2010–11	Middlesbrough	0	0	

EMNES, Marvin (M) 114 15
H: 5 11　W: 10 06　b.Rotterdam 27-5-88
Honours: Holland Under-21.

2005–06	Sparta Rotterdam	11	1		
2006–07	Sparta Rotterdam	16	0		
2007–08	Sparta Rotterdam	29	8	56	9
2008–09	Middlesbrough	15	0		
2009–10	Middlesbrough	16	1		
2010–11	Middlesbrough	23	3	54	4
2010–11	*Swansea C*	4	2	4	2

FLOOD, Willo (M) 131 5
H: 5 7　W: 10 05　b.Dublin 10-4-85
Source: Trainee. *Honours:* Eire Youth, Under-21.

2001–02	Manchester C	0	0	
2002–03	Manchester C	0	0	

2003–04	Manchester C	0	0		
2003–04	*Rochdale*	6	0	6	0
2004–05	Manchester C	9	1		
2005–06	Manchester C	5	0	14	1
2005–06	*Coventry C*	8	1	8	1
2006–07	Cardiff C	25	1		
2007–08	Cardiff C	0	0		
2007–08	*Dundee U*	36	1		
2008–09	*Dundee U*	20	0	56	1
2008–09	Cardiff C	0	0	25	1
2009–10	Celtic	6	0	6	0
2009–10	Middlesbrough	11	1		
2010–11	Middlesbrough	5	0	16	1

FRANKS, Jonathan (M) 28 3
H: 5 9 W: 11 03 b.Stockton 8-4-90
Source: Scholar. *Honours:* England Youth.

2007–08	Middlesbrough	0	0		
2008–09	Middlesbrough	1	0		
2009–10	Middlesbrough	23	3		
2010–11	Middlesbrough	4	0	28	3

GIBSON, Ben (D) 1 0
b.Nunthorpe 15-1-93
Source: Scholar. *Honours:* England Youth.

| 2010–11 | Middlesbrough | 1 | 0 | 1 | 0 |

GROUNDS, Jonathan (D) 49 4
H: 6 1 W: 13 10 b.Thornaby 2-2-88
Source: Scholar.

2007–08	Middlesbrough	5	0		
2008–09	Middlesbrough	2	0		
2008–09	*Norwich C*	16	3	16	3
2009–10	Middlesbrough	20	0		
2010–11	Middlesbrough	6	1	33	1

HAAS, Maximilian (D) 64 4
H: 6 3 W: 11 11 b.Freising 7-12-85
Source: Freising.

2007–08	Bayern Munich II	5	0		
2008–09	Bayern Munich II	15	2		
2009–10	Bayern Munich II	29	1		
2010–11	Bayern Munich II	18	1	62	4
2010–11	Middlesbrough	2	0	2	0

HALLIDAY, Andrew (M) 56 16
H: 5 8 W: 10 07 b.Glasgow 11-10-91

2008–09	Livingston	12	1		
2009–10	Livingston	32	14	44	15
2010–11	Middlesbrough	12	1	12	1

HINES, Seb (D) 22 1
H: 6 1 W: 12 02 b.Wetherby 29-5-88
Source: Scholar. *Honours:* England Youth.

2005–06	Middlesbrough	0	0		
2006–07	Middlesbrough	0	0		
2007–08	Middlesbrough	0	0		
2008–09	Middlesbrough	1	0		
2008–09	*Derby Co*	0	0		
2008–09	*Oldham Ath*	4	0	4	0
2009–10	Middlesbrough	2	0		
2010–11	Middlesbrough	14	1	18	1

HOYTE, Justin (D) 130 3
H: 5 11 W: 11 00 b.Waltham Forest 20-11-84
Source: Scholar. *Honours:* England Youth, Under-20, Under-21.

2002–03	Arsenal	1	0		
2003–04	Arsenal	1	0		
2004–05	Arsenal	5	0		
2005–06	Arsenal	0	0		
2005–06	*Sunderland*	27	1	27	1
2006–07	Arsenal	22	1		
2007–08	Arsenal	5	0	34	1
2008–09	Middlesbrough	22	0		
2009–10	Middlesbrough	30	1		
2010–11	Middlesbrough	17	0	69	1

KINK, Tarmo (F) 188 135
H: 6 0 W: 11 09 b.Tallinn 6-10-85
Honours: Estonia 53 full caps, 4 goals.

2001	Real Tallinn	9	30		
2002	Viimsi	6	31	6	31
2002	Trans	24	4	24	4
2003	Real Tallinn	6	16	15	46
2003	Spartak Moscow	2	0		
2004	Spartak Moscow	0	0		
2005	Spartak Moscow	0	0		
2006	Spartak Moscow	0	0	2	0
2006	Levadia	16	3		
2007	Levadia	31	16		
2008	Levadia	33	16	80	35
2008–09	Gyor	12	3		
2009–10	Gyor	28	12	40	15
2010–11	Middlesbrough	21	4	21	4

LITA, Leroy (F) 270 81
H: 5 7 W: 11 12 b.DR Congo 28-12-84
Source: Scholar. *Honours:* England Under-21.

2002–03	Bristol C	15	2		
2003–04	Bristol C	26	5		
2004–05	Bristol C	44	24	85	31
2005–06	Reading	26	11		
2006–07	Reading	33	7		
2007–08	Reading	14	1		
2007–08	*Charlton Ath*	8	3	8	3
2008–09	Reading	10	1	83	20
2008–09	*Norwich C*	16	7	16	7
2009–10	Middlesbrough	40	8		
2010–11	Middlesbrough	38	12	78	20

McDONALD, Scott (F) 275 112
H: 5 7 W: 12 07 b.Melbourne 21-8-83
Honours: Australia Youth, Under-20, Under-23, 24 full caps.

1998–99	Eastern Pride	3	0	3	0
1999–2000	Southampton	0	0		
2000–01	Southampton	0	0		
2001–02	Southampton	2	0		
2002–03	Southampton	0	0	2	0
2002–03	*Huddersfield T*	13	1	13	1
2002–03	*Bournemouth*	7	1	7	1
2003–04	*Wimbledon*	2	0	2	0
2003–04	Motherwell	15	2		
2004–05	Motherwell	27	15		
2005–06	Motherwell	35	11		
2006–07	Motherwell	32	15	109	43
2007–08	Celtic	36	25		
2008–09	Celtic	34	16		
2009–10	Celtic	18	10	88	51
2009–10	Middlesbrough	13	4		
2010–11	Middlesbrough	38	12	51	16

McMAHON, Tony (D) 102 3
H: 5 10 W: 11 04 b.Bishop Auckland 24-3-86
Source: Scholar. *Honours:* England Youth.

2003–04	Middlesbrough	0	0		
2004–05	Middlesbrough	13	0		
2005–06	Middlesbrough	3	0		
2006–07	Middlesbrough	0	0		
2007–08	Middlesbrough	1	0		
2007–08	*Blackpool*	2	0	2	0
2008–09	Middlesbrough	13	0		
2008–09	*Sheffield W*	15	1	15	1
2009–10	Middlesbrough	21	0		
2010–11	Middlesbrough	34	2	85	2

McMANUS, Stephen (D) 190 19
H: 6 2 W: 13 00 b.Lanark 10-9-82
Honours: Scotland 26 full caps, 2 goals.

2003–04	Celtic	5	0		
2004–05	Celtic	2	0		
2005–06	Celtic	36	7		
2006–07	Celtic	31	2		
2007–08	Celtic	37	4		
2008–09	Celtic	31	4		
2009–10	Celtic	8	0	150	17
2009–10	Middlesbrough	16	1		
2010–11	Middlesbrough	24	1	40	2

MILLER, Lee (F) 320 84
H: 6 0 W: 11 04 b.Lanark 18-5-83
Source: Form S. *Honours:* Scotland 3 full caps.

2000–01	Falkirk	0	0		
2001–02	Falkirk	27	11		
2002–03	Falkirk	34	17	61	28
2003–04	Bristol C	42	8		
2004–05	Bristol C	7	0	49	8
2004–05	Hearts	18	8	18	8
2005–06	Dundee U	34	8		
2006–07	Dundee U	3	0	37	8
2006–07	Aberdeen	32	4		
2007–08	Aberdeen	36	12		
2008–09	Aberdeen	34	10		
2009–10	Aberdeen	18	3	120	29
2009–10	Middlesbrough	10	0		
2010–11	Middlesbrough	1	0	11	0
2010–11	*Notts Co*	6	2	6	2
2010–11	*Scunthorpe U*	18	1	18	1

PARK, Cameron (M) 4 0
b.Marske 6-7-92
Source: Scholar.

| 2010–11 | Middlesbrough | 4 | 0 | 4 | 0 |

PILATOS, Bruno (D) 0 0
b.Angola 30-3-93
Source: Scholar. *Honours:* England Youth.

| 2010–11 | Middlesbrough | 0 | 0 | | |

REACH, Adam (D) 1 1
b.Gateshead 3-2-93
Source: Scholar.

| 2010–11 | Middlesbrough | 1 | 1 | 1 | 1 |

RIPLEY, Connor (G) 1 0
b.Middlesbrough 13-2-93
Source: Scholar.

| 2010–11 | Middlesbrough | 1 | 0 | 1 | 0 |

ROBSON, Barry (M) 392 75
H: 5 11 W: 12 00 b.Inverurie 7-11-78
Honours: Scotland B, 14 full caps.

1997–98	Inverness CT	23	3		
1998–99	Inverness CT	16	0		
1999–2000	Inverness CT	4	0		
1999–2000	*Forfar Ath*	25	9	25	9
2000–01	Inverness CT	34	5		
2001–02	Inverness CT	24	2		
2002–03	Inverness CT	34	10	135	20
2003–04	Dundee U	28	3		
2004–05	Dundee U	36	6		
2005–06	Dundee U	31	1		
2006–07	Dundee U	29	11		
2007–08	Dundee U	21	11	145	32
2007–08	Celtic	15	2		
2008–09	Celtic	12	1		
2009–10	Celtic	10	1	37	4
2009–10	Middlesbrough	18	5		
2010–11	Middlesbrough	32	5	50	10

SMALLWOOD, Richard (M) 13 1
b.Redcar 29-12-90
Source: Scholar. *Honours:* England Youth.

2008–09	Middlesbrough	0	0		
2009–10	Middlesbrough	0	0		
2010–11	Middlesbrough	13	1	13	1

STEELE, Jason (G) 48 0
H: 6 2 W: 12 07 b.Newton Aycliffe 18-8-90
Source: Scholar. *Honours:* England Youth, Under-21.

2007–08	Middlesbrough	0	0		
2008–09	Middlesbrough	0	0		
2009–10	Middlesbrough	0	0		
2009–10	*Northampton T*	13	0	13	0
2010–11	Middlesbrough	35	0	35	0

TAVARES, Mickael (M) 171 19
H: 6 1 W: 12 04 b.Villeneuve-St-Georges 25-10-82
Honours: Senegal 8 full caps.

2002–03	Abbeville	26	9	26	9
2003–04	Nantes B	24	1		
2004–05	Nantes B	19	1	43	2
2005–06	Tours	22	4		
2006–07	Tours	5	0	27	4
2007–08	Slavia Prague	22	2		
2008–09	Slavia Prague	14	1	36	3
2008–09	Hamburg	12	0		
2009–10	Hamburg	3	0	15	0
2009–10	Nuremberg	11	1	11	1
2010–11	Middlesbrough	13	0	13	0

On loan from Hamburg.

TAYLOR, Andrew (D) 168 4
H: 5 10 W: 11 04 b.Hartlepool 1-8-86
Source: Trainee. *Honours:* England Youth, Under-20, Under-21.

2003–04	Middlesbrough	0	0		
2004–05	Middlesbrough	0	0		
2005–06	Middlesbrough	13	0		
2005–06	*Bradford C*	24	0	24	0
2006–07	Middlesbrough	34	0		
2007–08	Middlesbrough	19	0		
2008–09	Middlesbrough	26	0		
2009–10	Middlesbrough	12	0		
2010–11	Middlesbrough	21	3	125	3
2010–11	*Watford*	19	1	19	1

THOMSON, Kevin (M) 170 4
H: 6 2 W: 11 05 b.Edinburgh 14-10-84
Honours: Scotland 3 full caps.

2003–04	Hibernian	23	1		
2004–05	Hibernian	3	0		
2005–06	Hibernian	31	0		
2006–07	Hibernian	23	1	80	2
2006–07	Rangers	9	0		

2007–08	Rangers	26	1		
2008–09	Rangers	11	1		
2009–10	Rangers	25	0	71	2
2010–11	Middlesbrough	19	0	19	0

WELDON, Paul (D)   0 0
b.Sunderland 27-11-91
Source: Scholar.

| 2010–11 | Middlesbrough | 0 | 0 | | |

WILLIAMS, Rhys (M)   61 3
H: 6 2 W: 11 05 b.Perth 14-7-88
Source: Scholar. *Honours:* Wales Under-21. Australia 5 full caps.

2006–07	Middlesbrough	0	0		
2007–08	Middlesbrough	0	0		
2008–09	Middlesbrough	0	0		
2008–09	*Burnley*	17	0	17	0
2009–10	Middlesbrough	32	2		
2010-11	Middlesbrough	12	1	44	3

WILLIAMS, Luke (F)   10 0
H: 6 1 W: 11 08 b.Middlesbrough 11-6-93
Source: Scholar. *Honours:* England Youth.

| 2009–10 | Middlesbrough | 4 | 0 | | |
| 2010–11 | Middlesbrough | 6 | 0 | 10 | 0 |

ZEMMAMA, Merouane (M)   109 13
H: 5 8 W: 10 05 b.Rabat 7-10-83
Source: Chabab Tabriquet.
Honours: Morocco 7 full caps, 1 goal.

2003–04	Raja	23	2		
2004–05	Qatar SC	0	0		
2005–06	Raja	0	0	23	2
2006–07	Hibernian	23	2		
2007–08	Hibernian	28	6		
2008–09	Hibernian	1	0		
2008–09	Al-Sha'ab	0	0		
2009–10	Hibernian	21	2		
2010–11	Hibernian	4	0	77	10
2010–11	Middlesbrough	9	1	9	1

MILLWALL (51)

ABDOU, Nadjim (M)   250 8
H: 5 10 W: 11 02 b.Martigues 13-7-84

2002–03	Martigues	26	1	26	1
2003–04	Sedan	17	0		
2004–05	Sedan	32	2		
2005–06	Sedan	14	0		
2006–07	Sedan	17	0	80	2
2007–08	Plymouth Arg	31	1	31	1
2008–09	Millwall	36	3		
2009–10	Millwall	43	1		
2010–11	Millwall	34	0	113	4

BARRON, Scott (D)   105 2
H: 5 9 W: 9 08 b.Preston 2-9-85
Source: Scholar.

2003–04	Ipswich T	0	0		
2004–05	Ipswich T	0	0		
2005–06	Ipswich T	15	0		
2006–07	Ipswich T	0	0	15	0
2006–07	*Wrexham*	3	0	3	0
2007–08	Millwall	12	0		
2008–09	Millwall	14	0		
2009–10	Millwall	23	0		
2010–11	Millwall	38	2	87	2

BATT, Shaun (M)   66 7
H: 6 3 W: 12 08 b.Harlow 22-2-87
Source: Stevenage B, Dagenham & R, Fisher Ath.

2008–09	Peterborough U	30	2		
2009–10	Peterborough U	20	2	50	4
2009–10	*Millwall*	16	3		
2010–11	Millwall	0	0	16	3

BOUAZZA, Hameur (M)   197 20
H: 5 10 W: 12 01 b.Evry 22-2-85
Source: Scholar. *Honours:* Algeria 15 full caps, 2 goals.

2003–04	Watford	9	1		
2004–05	Watford	28	1		
2005–06	Watford	14	1		
2005–06	*Swindon T*	13	2	13	2
2006–07	Watford	32	6	83	9
2007–08	Fulham	20	1		
2008–09	Fulham	0	0	20	1
2008–09	*Charlton Ath*	25	4	25	4
2008–09	*Birmingham C*	16	1	16	1
2009–10	Sivas	0	0		
2009–10	Blackpool	19	1	19	1
2010–11	Arles-Avignon	9	1	9	1
2010–11	Millwall	12	1	12	1

CRAIG, Tony (D)   209 7
H: 6 0 W: 10 03 b.Greenwich 20-4-85
Source: Scholar.

2002–03	Millwall	2	1		
2003–04	Millwall	9	0		
2004–05	Millwall	10	0		
2004–05	*Wycombe W*	14	0	14	0
2005–06	Millwall	28	0		
2006–07	Millwall	30	1		
2007–08	Crystal Palace	13	0	13	0
2007–08	*Millwall*	5	1		
2008–09	Millwall	44	2		
2009–10	Millwall	30	2		
2010–11	Millwall	24	0	182	7

DUNNE, Alan (D)   218 14
H: 5 10 W: 10 13 b.Dublin 23-8-82
Source: Trainee.

1999–2000	Millwall	0	0		
2000–01	Millwall	0	0		
2001–02	Millwall	1	0		
2002–03	Millwall	4	0		
2003–04	Millwall	8	0		
2004–05	Millwall	19	3		
2005–06	Millwall	40	0		
2006–07	Millwall	32	6		
2007–08	Millwall	19	3		
2008–09	Millwall	24	0		
2009–10	Millwall	32	2		
2010–11	Millwall	39	0	218	14

FORDE, David (G)   234 0
H: 6 3 W: 13 06 b.Galway 20-12-79
Source: Barry T. *Honours:* Eire 2 full caps.

2001–02	West Ham U	0	0		
2002–03	West Ham U	0	0		
2003–04	West Ham U	0	0		
2004	Derry C	11	0		
2005	Derry C	33	0		
2006	Derry C	29	0	73	0
2006–07	Cardiff C	7	0		
2007–08	Cardiff C	0	0	7	0
2007–08	*Luton T*	5	0	5	0
2007–08	*Bournemouth*	11	0	11	0
2008–09	Millwall	46	0		
2009–10	Millwall	46	0		
2010–11	Millwall	46	0	138	0

FRAMPTON, Andrew (D)   274 8
H: 5 11 W: 10 10 b.Wimbledon 3-9-79
Source: Trainee.

1998–99	Crystal Palace	6	0		
1999–2000	Crystal Palace	9	0		
2000–01	Crystal Palace	10	0		
2001–02	Crystal Palace	2	0		
2002–03	Crystal Palace	1	0	28	0
2002–03	Brentford	15	0		
2003–04	Brentford	16	0		
2004–05	Brentford	35	0		
2005–06	Brentford	36	3		
2006–07	Brentford	32	1	134	4
2007–08	Millwall	30	1		
2008–09	Millwall	37	1		
2009–10	Millwall	21	2		
2010–11	Millwall	0	0	88	4
2010–11	*Leyton Orient*	1	0	1	0
2010–11	*Swindon T*	23	0	23	0

GRIMES, Ashley (M)   52 17
H: 6 0 W: 11 02 b.Swinton 9-12-86
Source: Scholar.

2006–07	Manchester C	0	0		
2006–07	*Swindon T*	4	0	4	0
2007–08	Manchester C	0	0		
2008–09	Millwall	17	2		
2009–10	Millwall	4	0		
2010–11	Millwall	0	0	21	2
2010–11	*Lincoln C*	27	15	27	15

HACKETT, Chris (M)   244 14
H: 6 0 W: 12 08 b.Oxford 1-3-83
Source: Scholarship.

1999–2000	Oxford U	2	0		
2000–01	Oxford U	16	2		
2001–02	Oxford U	15	0		
2002–03	Oxford U	12	0		
2003–04	Oxford U	22	1		
2004–05	Oxford U	37	4		
2005–06	Oxford U	21	2	125	9
2005–06	Hearts	2	0	2	0
2006–07	Millwall	33	3		
2007–08	Millwall	6	0		
2008–09	Millwall	22	0		
2009–10	Millwall	40	2		
2010–11	Millwall	16	0	117	5

HARRIS, Neil (F)   446 132
H: 5 10 W: 12 08 b.Thurrock 12-7-77
Source: Cambridge C.

1997–98	Millwall	3	0		
1998–99	Millwall	39	15		
1999–2000	Millwall	38	25		
2000–01	Millwall	42	27		
2001–02	Millwall	21	4		
2002–03	Millwall	40	12		
2003–04	Millwall	38	9		
2004–05	Millwall	12	1		
2004–05	*Cardiff C*	3	1	3	1
2004–05	Nottingham F	13	0		
2005–06	Nottingham F	1	0		
2005–06	*Gillingham*	36	6	36	6
2006–07	Nottingham F	19	1	33	1
2006–07	Millwall	21	5		
2007–08	Millwall	27	3		
2008–09	Millwall	35	8		
2009–10	Millwall	32	13		
2010–11	Millwall	26	2	374	124

HENRY, James (M)   92 17
H: 6 1 W: 11 11 b.Reading 10-6-89
Source: Scholar. *Honours:* England Youth.

2006–07	Reading	0	0		
2006–07	*Nottingham F*	1	0	1	0
2007–08	Reading	0	0		
2007–08	*Bournemouth*	11	4	11	4
2007–08	*Norwich C*	3	0	3	0
2008–09	Reading	7	0		
2008–09	*Millwall*	16	3		
2009–10	Reading	3	0	10	0
2009–10	*Millwall*	9	5		
2010–11	Millwall	42	5	67	13

HUGHES-MASON, Kiernon (F)   2 0
H: 5 8 W: 10 05 b.Hackney 22-10-91
Source: Scholar.

2009–10	Millwall	1	0		
2009–10	*Cheltenham T*	0	0		
2010–11	Millwall	1	0	2	0

LAIRD, Marc (M)   101 8
H: 6 1 W: 10 07 b.Edinburgh 23-1-86
Source: Trainee.

2003–04	Manchester C	0	0		
2004–05	Manchester C	0	0		
2005–06	Manchester C	0	0		
2006–07	Manchester C	0	0		
2006–07	*Northampton T*	6	0	6	0
2007–08	Manchester C	0	0		
2007–08	*Port Vale*	7	1	7	1
2007–08	*Millwall*	17	1		
2008–09	Millwall	38	5		
2009–10	Millwall	20	0		
2010–11	Millwall	1	0	76	6
2010–11	*Brentford*	4	1	4	1
2010–11	*Walsall*	8	0	8	0

MARQUIS, John (M)   12 4
H: 6 1 W: 11 03 b.Lewisham 16-5-92
Source: Scholar.

| 2009–10 | Millwall | 1 | 0 | | |
| 2010–11 | Millwall | 11 | 4 | 12 | 4 |

McQUOID, Josh (F)   80 11
H: 5 9 W: 10 10 b.Southampton 15-12-89
Source: Scholar. *Honours:* Northern Ireland Under-21, B, 3 full caps.

2006–07	Bournemouth	2	0		
2007–08	Bournemouth	5	0		
2008–09	Bournemouth	16	0		
2009–10	Bournemouth	29	1		
2010–11	Bournemouth	17	9	69	10
2010–11	*Millwall*	11	1	11	1

MILDENHALL, Steve (G)   314 1
H: 6 4 W: 14 01 b.Swindon 13-5-78
Source: Trainee.

1996–97	Swindon T	1	0		
1997–98	Swindon T	4	0		
1998–99	Swindon T	0	0		
1999–2000	Swindon T	5	0		
2000–01	Swindon T	23	0	33	0
2001–02	Notts Co	26	0		

2002–03	Notts Co	21	0	
2003–04	Notts Co	28	0	
2004–05	Notts Co	1	0	76 0
2004–05	Oldham Ath	6	0	6 0
2005–06	Grimsby T	46	1	46 1
2006–07	Yeovil T	46	0	
2007–08	Yeovil T	29	0	75 0
2008–09	Southend U	34	0	
2009–10	Southend U	44	0	
2010–11	Southend U	0	0	78 0
2010–11	Southend U	0	0	

MKANDAWIRE, Tamika (D) 188 18
H: 6 1 W: 12 03 b.Malawi 28-5-83
Source: Scholar.

2002–03	WBA	0	0	
2003–04	WBA	0	0	
2006–07	Hereford U	39	2	39 2
2007–08	Leyton Orient	35	3	
2008–09	Leyton Orient	36	5	
2009–10	Leyton Orient	43	7	114 15
2010–11	Leyton Orient	35	1	35 1

MORISON, Steven (F) 106 38
H: 6 2 W: 13 07 b.Enfield 29-8-83
Source: Scholar. *Honours:* Wales 1 full caps.

2001–02	Northampton T	1	0	
2002–03	Northampton T	13	1	
2003–04	Northampton T	5	1	
2004–05	Northampton T	4	1	23 3
From Stevenage B.				
2008–09	Millwall	0	0	
2009–10	Millwall	43	20	
2010–11	Millwall	40	15	83 35

O'BRIEN, Aiden (F) 0 0
b.Islington 4-10-93
Source: Scholar. *Honours:* Eire Youth.

2010–11	Millwall	0	0	

O'CONNOR, Patrick (D) 0 0
H: 6 1 W: 13 00 b.Croydon 5-9-90
Source: Scholar.

2008–09	Millwall	0	0	
2009–10	Millwall	0	0	
2010–11	Millwall	0	0	

PURSE, Darren (D) 489 30
H: 6 2 W: 12 08 b.Stepney 14-2-77
Source: Trainee. *Honours:* England Under-21.

1993–94	Leyton Orient	5	0	
1994–95	Leyton Orient	38	3	
1995–96	Leyton Orient	12	0	55 3
1996–97	Oxford U	31	1	
1997–98	Oxford U	28	4	59 5
1997–98	Birmingham C	8	0	
1998–99	Birmingham C	20	0	
1999–2000	Birmingham C	38	2	
2000–01	Birmingham C	37	3	
2001–02	Birmingham C	36	3	
2002–03	Birmingham C	20	1	
2003–04	Birmingham C	9	0	168 9
2004–05	WBA	22	0	22 0
2005–06	Cardiff C	39	5	
2006–07	Cardiff C	31	4	
2007–08	Cardiff C	18	1	
2008–09	Cardiff C	23	0	111 10
2009–10	Sheffield W	39	2	
2010–11	Sheffield W	22	0	61 2
2010–11	Millwall	13	1	13 1

ROBINSON, Paul (D) 247 15
H: 6 1 W: 11 09 b.Barnet 7-1-82
Source: Scholar.

2000–01	Millwall	0	0	
2001–02	Millwall	0	0	
2002–03	Millwall	14	0	
2003–04	Millwall	9	0	
2004–05	Millwall	0	0	
2004–05	Torquay U	12	0	12 0
2005–06	Millwall	32	0	
2006–07	Millwall	38	3	
2007–08	Millwall	45	3	
2008–09	Millwall	26	2	
2009–10	Millwall	34	4	
2010–11	Millwall	37	3	235 15

SCHOFIELD, Danny (M) 358 53
H: 5 10 W: 11 02 b.Doncaster 10-4-80
Source: Brodsworth MW.

1998–99	Huddersfield T	1	0	
1999–2000	Huddersfield T	2	0	
2000–01	Huddersfield T	1	0	
2001–02	Huddersfield T	40	8	
2002–03	Huddersfield T	30	2	
2003–04	Huddersfield T	40	8	
2004–05	Huddersfield T	33	5	
2005–06	Huddersfield T	41	9	
2006–07	Huddersfield T	35	5	
2007–08	Huddersfield T	25	2	248 39
2008–09	Yeovil T	39	4	
2009–10	Yeovil T	4	1	43 5
2009–10	Millwall	36	7	
2010–11	Millwall	31	2	67 9

SMITH, Jack (D) 203 12
H: 5 11 W: 11 05 b.Hemel Hempstead 14-10-83
Source: Scholar.

2001–02	Watford	0	0	
2002–03	Watford	1	0	
2003–04	Watford	17	2	
2004–05	Watford	7	0	25 2
2005–06	Swindon T	38	0	
2006–07	Swindon T	41	3	
2007–08	Swindon T	21	1	
2008–09	Swindon T	38	5	138 9
2009–10	Millwall	31	0	
2010–11	Millwall	9	1	40 1

SULLIVAN, John (G) 30 0
H: 5 10 W: 11 04 b.Brighton 8-3-88
Source: Scholar.

2005–06	Brighton & HA	0	0	
2006–07	Brighton & HA	0	0	
2007–08	Brighton & HA	0	0	
2008–09	Brighton & HA	13	0	13 0
2009–10	Millwall	0	0	
2010–11	Millwall	0	0	
2010–11	*Yeovil T*	13	0	13 0
2010–11	*Charlton Ath*	4	0	4 0

TROTTER, Liam (M) 107 13
H: 6 2 W: 12 02 b.Ipswich 24-8-88
Source: Scholar.

2005–06	Ipswich T	1	0	
2006–07	Ipswich T	0	0	
2006–07	Millwall	2	0	
2007–08	Ipswich T	7	1	
2008–09	Ipswich T	3	1	
2008–09	Grimsby T	15	2	15 2
2008–09	Scunthorpe U	12	1	12 1
2009–10	Ipswich T	12	0	23 2
2009–10	*Millwall*	20	1	
2010–11	Millwall	35	7	57 8

WARD, Darren (D) 396 14
H: 6 3 W: 11 04 b.Harrow 13-9-78
Source: Trainee.

1995–96	Watford	1	0	
1996–97	Watford	7	0	
1997–98	Watford	0	0	
1998–99	Watford	1	0	
1999–2000	Watford	9	1	
1999–2000	QPR	14	0	14 0
2000–01	Watford	40	1	
2001–02	Watford	1	0	
2001–02	Millwall	14	0	
2002–03	Millwall	39	1	
2003–04	Millwall	46	3	
2004–05	Millwall	43	0	
2005–06	Crystal Palace	43	5	
2006–07	Crystal Palace	20	0	63 5
2007–08	Wolverhampton W	30	0	
2008–09	Wolverhampton W	1	0	
2008–09	*Watford*	9	1	68 3
2008–09	*Charlton Ath*	16	0	16 0
2009–10	Wolverhampton W	0	0	31 0
2009–10	Millwall	31	1	
2010–11	Millwall	31	1	204 6

MILTON KEYNES D (52)

BALDOCK, Sam (F) 96 29
H: 5 7 W: 10 07 b.Buckingham 15-3-89
Source: Scholar. *Honours:* England Under-20.

2005–06	Milton Keynes D	0	0	
2006–07	Milton Keynes D	1	0	
2007–08	Milton Keynes D	5	0	
2008–09	Milton Keynes D	40	12	
2009–10	Milton Keynes D	20	5	
2010–11	Milton Keynes D	30	12	96 29

BALDOCK, George (M) 3 0
H: 5 9 W: 10 07 b.Buckingham 26 1 93
Source: Youth.

2009–10	Milton Keynes D	1	0	
2010–11	Milton Keynes D	2	0	3 0

CARRINGTON, Mark (M) 61 8
H: 6 0 W: 11 00 b.Warrington 4-5-87
Source: Scholar.

2006–07	Crewe Alex	3	0	
2007–08	Crewe Alex	9	0	
2008–09	Crewe Alex	17	2	29 2
2009–10	Milton Keynes D	20	4	
2010–11	Milton Keynes D	12	2	32 6
Transferred to Hamilton A January 2011.				

CHADWICK, Luke (M) 284 24
H: 5 11 W: 11 08 b.Cambridge 18-11-80
Source: Trainee. *Honours:* England Youth, Under-21.

1998–99	Manchester U	0	0	
1999–2000	Manchester U	0	0	
2000–01	Manchester U	16	2	
2001–02	Manchester U	8	0	
2002–03	Manchester U	1	0	
2002–03	*Reading*	15	1	15 1
2003–04	Manchester U	0	0	25 2
2003–04	*Burnley*	36	5	36 5
2004–05	West Ham U	32	1	
2005–06	West Ham U	0	0	32 1
2005–06	Stoke C	36	2	
2006–07	Stoke C	15	3	51 5
2006–07	Norwich C	4	1	
2007–08	Norwich C	13	1	
2008–09	Norwich C	0	0	17 2
2008–09	Milton Keynes D	24	6	
2009–10	Milton Keynes D	40	2	
2010–11	Milton Keynes D	44	0	108 8

CHICKSEN, Adam (D) 21 0
H: 5 8 W: 11 09 b.Milton Keynes 27-9-91
Source: Scholar.

2008–09	Milton Keynes D	1	0	
2009–10	Milton Keynes D	6	0	
2010–11	Milton Keynes D	14	0	21 0

COLLINS, Charlie (F) 3 0
H: 6 0 W: 11 11 b.Hammersmith 22-11-91
Source: Scholar. *Honours:* Eire Youth.

2009–10	Milton Keynes D	2	0	
2010–11	Milton Keynes D	1	0	3 0

DOUMBE, Stephen (D) 256 12
H: 6 1 W: 12 05 b.Paris 28-10-79
Source: Paris St Germain. *Honours:* France Youth.

2001–02	Hibernian	0	0	
2002–03	Hibernian	12	0	
2003–04	Hibernian	33	2	45 2
2004–05	Plymouth Arg	26	2	
2005–06	Plymouth Arg	43	1	
2006–07	Plymouth Arg	29	0	
2007–08	Plymouth Arg	12	0	
2008–09	Plymouth Arg	24	1	134 4
2009–10	Milton Keynes D	33	1	
2010–11	Milton Keynes D	44	5	77 6

FLANAGAN, Tom (D) 3 0
H: 6 2 W: 11 05 b.Hammersmith 21-10-91
Source: Scholar.

2009–10	Milton Keynes D	1	0	
2010–11	Milton Keynes D	2	0	3 0

GLEESON, Stephen (M) 118 6
H: 6 2 W: 11 00 b.Dublin 3-8-88
Source: Scholar. *Honours:* Eire Youth, Under-21, 2 full caps.

2006–07	Wolverhampton W	3	0	
2006–07	*Stockport Co*	14	2	
2007–08	Wolverhampton W	0	0	
2007–08	*Hereford U*	4	0	4 0
2008–09	Wolverhampton W	0	0	3 0
2008–09	*Stockport Co*	21	2	41 4
2009–10	Milton Keynes D	5	0	
2009–10	Milton Keynes D	29	0	
2010–11	Milton Keynes D	36	2	70 2

GUY, Lewis (F) 197 23
H: 5 10 W: 10 07 b.Penrith 27-8-85
Source: Trainee. *Honours:* England Youth, Under-20.

2002–03	Newcastle U	0	0	

2003–04	Newcastle U	0	0		
2004–05	Newcastle U	0	0		
2004–05	Doncaster R	9	3		
2005–06	Doncaster R	31	3		
2006–07	Doncaster R	36	4		
2007–08	Doncaster R	29	6		
2008–09	Doncaster R	29	2		
2008–09	*Hartlepool U*	4	0	4	0
2009–10	Doncaster R	13	0	147	18
2009–10	*Oldham Ath*	12	3	12	3
2010–11	Milton Keynes D	34	2	34	2

HAMANN, Dietmar (M) 385 18
H: 6 2 W: 13 00 b.Waldasson 27-8-73
Source: Wacker Munich. *Honours:* Germany
Youth, Under-21, 59 full caps, 5 goals.

1993–94	Bayern Munich	5	1		
1994–95	Bayern Munich	30	0		
1995–96	Bayern Munich	20	2		
1996–97	Bayern Munich	22	1		
1997–98	Bayern Munich	28	2	105	6
1998–99	Newcastle U	23	4	23	4
1999–2000	Liverpool	28	1		
2000–01	Liverpool	30	2		
2001–02	Liverpool	31	1		
2002–03	Liverpool	30	2		
2003–04	Liverpool	25	2		
2004–05	Liverpool	30	0		
2005–06	Liverpool	17	0	191	0
2006–07	Manchester C	16	0		
2007–08	Manchester C	29	0		
2008–09	Manchester C	9	0	54	0
2010–11	Milton Keynes D	12	0	12	0

IBEHRE, Jabo (F) 324 55
H: 6 2 W: 13 13 b.Islington 28-1-83
Source: Trainee.

1999–2000	Leyton Orient	3	0		
2000–01	Leyton Orient	5	2		
2001–02	Leyton Orient	28	4		
2002–03	Leyton Orient	25	5		
2003–04	Leyton Orient	35	4		
2004–05	Leyton Orient	19	2		
2005–06	Leyton Orient	33	8		
2006–07	Leyton Orient	30	4		
2007–08	Leyton Orient	31	7	209	36
2008–09	Walsall	39	10	39	10
2009–10	Milton Keynes D	10	1		
2009–10	*Southend U*	4	0	4	0
2009–10	*Stockport Co*	20	5	20	5
2010–11	Milton Keynes D	42	3	52	4

JOHNSON, Jemal (F) 161 21
H: 5 8 W: 11 09 b.New Jersey 3-5-84
Source: Scholar.

2001–02	Blackburn R	0	0		
2002–03	Blackburn R	0	0		
2003–04	Blackburn R	0	0		
2004–05	Blackburn R	3	0		
2005–06	Blackburn R	3	0		
2005–06	*Preston NE*	3	1	3	1
2005–06	*Darlington*	9	3	9	3
2006–07	Blackburn R	0	0	6	0
2006–07	Wolverhampton W	20	3		
2006–07	*Leeds U*	5	0	5	0
2007–08	Wolverhampton W	0	0	20	3
2007–08	Milton Keynes D	39	5		
2008–09	Milton Keynes D	33	5		
2009–10	Milton Keynes D	17	1		
2009–10	*Stockport Co*	16	2	16	2
2010–11	Milton Keynes D	7	1	96	12
2010–11	*Port Vale*	6	0	6	0

Transferred to Lokomotiv Sofia January
2011.

LEVEN, Peter (M) 218 33
H: 5 11 W: 12 13 b.Glasgow 27-9-83
Source: Rangers.

2004–05	Kilmarnock	32	4		
2005–06	Kilmarnock	6	0		
2006–07	Kilmarnock	27	1	65	5
2007–08	Chesterfield	42	6	42	6
2008–09	Milton Keynes D	40	10		
2009–10	Milton Keynes D	31	4		
2010–11	Milton Keynes D	40	8	111	22

LEWINGTON, Dean (D) 330 11
H: 5 11 W: 11 07 b.Kingston 18-5-84
Source: Scholar.

2002–03	Wimbledon	1	0		
2003–04	Wimbledon	28	1	29	1
2004–05	Milton Keynes D	43	2		
2005–06	Milton Keynes D	44	1		
2006–07	Milton Keynes D	45	1		
2007–08	Milton Keynes D	45	0		
2008–09	Milton Keynes D	40	2		
2009–10	Milton Keynes D	42	1		
2010–11	Milton Keynes D	42	3	301	10

MACKENZIE, Gary (D) 126 4
H: 6 3 W: 13 01 b.Lanark 15-10-85

2003–04	Rangers	2	0		
2004–05	Rangers	0	0		
2005–06	Rangers	0	0	2	0
2006–07	Dundee	21	0		
2007–08	Dundee	33	1		
2008–09	Dundee	19	0		
2009–10	Dundee	25	1	98	2
2010–11	Milton Keynes D	26	2	26	2

MARTIN, David E (G) 100 0
H: 6 1 W: 13 04 b.Romford 22 1 86
Source: Scholar. *Honours:* England Youth,
Under-20.

2003–04	Wimbledon	2	0	2	0
2004–05	Milton Keynes D	15	0		
2005–06	Milton Keynes D	0	0		
2005–06	Liverpool	0	0		
2006–07	Liverpool	0	0		
2006–07	*Accrington S*	10	0	10	0
2007–08	Liverpool	0	0		
2008–09	Liverpool	0	0		
2008–09	*Leicester C*	25	0	25	0
2009–10	Liverpool	0	0		
2009–10	*Tranmere R*	3	0	3	0
2009–10	Leeds U	0	0		
2009–10	*Derby Co*	2	0	2	0
2010–11	Milton Keynes D	43	0	58	0

O'HANLON, Sean (D) 256 24
H: 6 1 W: 12 05 b.Southport 2-1-83
Honours: England Schools, Youth, Under-20.

1999–2000	Everton	0	0		
2000–01	Everton	0	0		
2001–02	Everton	0	0		
2002–03	Everton	0	0		
2003–04	Everton	0	0		
2003–04	Swindon T	19	2		
2004–05	Swindon T	40	3		
2005–06	Swindon T	40	4	99	9
2006–07	Milton Keynes D	36	4		
2007–08	Milton Keynes D	43	4		
2008–09	Milton Keynes D	40	3		
2009–10	Milton Keynes D	6	0		
2010–11	Milton Keynes D	32	4	157	15

POWELL, Daniel (F) 38 11
H: 5 11 W: 13 03 b.Luton 12-3-91
Source: Scholar.

2008–09	Milton Keynes D	7	1		
2009–10	Milton Keynes D	2	1		
2010–11	Milton Keynes D	29	9	38	11

SEARLE, Stuart (G) 6 0
H: 6 3 W: 12 04 b.Wimbledon 27-2-79
Source: Basingstoke T.

2008–09	Watford	0	0		
2009–10	Milton Keynes D	3	0		
2010–11	Milton Keynes D	3	0	6	0

STIRLING, Jude (D) 153 5
H: 6 2 W: 11 12 b.Enfield 29-6-82
Source: Trainee.

1999–2000	Luton T	0	0		
2000–01	Luton T	9	0		
2001–02	Luton T	1	0	10	0

From Tamworth.

2005–06	Oxford U	10	0	10	0

From Stevenage B, Hornchurch, Tamworth

2005–06	Lincoln C	6	0	6	0
2006–07	Peterborough U	22	0	22	0
2006–07	Milton Keynes D	16	1		
2007–08	Milton Keynes D	34	2		
2008–09	Milton Keynes D	32	2		
2009–10	Milton Keynes D	9	0		
2009–10	*Grimsby T*	4	0	4	0
2010–11	Milton Keynes D	4	0	95	5
2010–11	*Barnet*	6	0	6	0

WOODARDS, Danny (D) 150 1
H: 5 11 W: 11 01 b.Forest Gate 7-10-83
Source: Trainee.

2003–04	Chelsea	0	0		
2004–05	Chelsea	0	0		
2005–06	Chelsea	0	0		

From Exeter C.

2006–07	Crewe Alex	11	0		
2007–08	Crewe Alex	36	0		
2008–09	Crewe Alex	37	0	84	0
2009–10	Milton Keynes D	29	0		
2010–11	Milton Keynes D	37	1	66	1

MORECAMBE (53)

BENTLEY, Jim (D) 124 13
H: 6 1 W: 13 00 b.Liverpool 11-6-76
Source: Trainee.

1993–94	Manchester C	0	0		
1994–95	Manchester C	0	0		
1995–96	Manchester C	0	0		
1996–97	Manchester C	0	0		
1997–98	Manchester C	0	0		
1998–99	Manchester C	0	0		
2007–08	Morecambe	43	6		
2008–09	Morecambe	45	3		
2009–10	Morecambe	28	3		
2010–11	Morecambe	8	1	124	13

BROWN, Scott (M) 138 9
H: 5 9 W: 10 03 b.Runcorn 8-5-85
Source: Scholar. *Honours:* England Youth.

2001–02	Everton	0	0		
2002–03	Everton	0	0		
2003–04	Everton	0	0		
2004–05	Bristol C	19	0		
2005–06	Bristol C	29	1		
2006–07	Bristol C	15	4	63	5
2006–07	Cheltenham T	4	0		
2007–08	Cheltenham T	20	0		
2008–09	Cheltenham T	0	0		
2008–09	Port Vale	18	1		
2009–10	Port Vale	0	0	18	1
2009–10	Cheltenham T	1	0	25	0
2010–11	Morecambe	32	3	32	3

CAPALDI, Tony (D) 224 12
H: 6 0 W: 11 08 b.Porsgrunn 12-8-81
Source: Trainee. *Honours:* Northern Ireland
Youth, Under-21, 22 full caps.

1999–2000	Birmingham C	0	0		
2000–01	Birmingham C	0	0		
2001–02	Birmingham C	0	0		
2002–03	Birmingham C	0	0		
2003–04	Plymouth Arg	33	7		
2004–05	Plymouth Arg	35	2		
2005–06	Plymouth Arg	41	3		
2006–07	Plymouth Arg	31	0	141	12
2007–08	Cardiff C	44	0		
2008–09	Cardiff C	3	0		
2009–10	Cardiff C	15	0	62	0
2009–10	*Leeds U*	3	0	3	0
2010–11	Morecambe	18	0	18	0

CARLTON, Danny (F) 94 12
H: 5 11 W: 12 04 b.Leeds 22-12-83
Source: Morecambe.

2007–08	Carlisle U	31	0		
2008–09	Carlisle U	12	3	43	3
2008–09	*Morecambe*	8	2		
2008–09	*Darlington*	17	4	17	4
2009–10	Bury	7	0		
2010–11	Bury	3	0	10	0
2010–11	Morecambe	16	3	24	5

CHARNOCK, Kieran (D) 95 1
H: 6 1 W: 13 07 b.Preston 3-8-84
Source: Scholar.

2002–03	Wigan Ath	0	0		

From Southport, Northwich Vic.

2007–08	Peterborough U	10	0		
2008–09	Peterborough U	2	0	12	0
2008–09	*Accrington S*	34	0	34	0
2009–10	Torquay U	24	0		
2010–11	Torquay U	4	0	28	0
2010–11	Morecambe	21	1	21	1

COWPERTHWAITE, Niall (D) 7 1
H: 5 11 W: 11 00 b.Barrow 28-1-92
Source: Youth.

2010–11	Morecambe	7	1	7	1

DRUMMOND, Stuart (M) 300 46
H: 6 2 W: 13 08 b.Preston 11-12-75
Source: Morecambe.

2004–05	Chester C	45	6		

(continued)

Season	Club	Apps	Gls	Tot Apps	Tot Gls
2005–06	Chester C	42	6	87	12
2006–07	Shrewsbury T	44	4		
2007–08	Shrewsbury T	23	3	67	7
2007–08	Morecambe	18	2		
2008–09	Morecambe	44	10		
2009–10	Morecambe	43	9		
2010–11	Morecambe	41	6	146	27

FLEMING, Andy (M) 36 2
H: 6 1 W: 12 00 b.Liverpool 18-2-89
Source: Scholar.

Season	Club	Apps	Gls	Tot Apps	Tot Gls
2006–07	Wrexham	2	0		
2007–08	Wrexham	4	0	6	0
2010–11	Morecambe	30	2	30	2

HAINING, Will (D) 247 14
H: 6 0 W: 11 02 b.Glasgow 2-10-82
Source: Scholar.

Season	Club	Apps	Gls	Tot Apps	Tot Gls
2001–02	Oldham Ath	4	0		
2002–03	Oldham Ath	26	2		
2003–04	Oldham Ath	31	2		
2004–05	Oldham Ath	35	5		
2005–06	Oldham Ath	15	0		
2006–07	Oldham Ath	44	2	155	11
2007–08	St Mirren	29	1		
2008–09	St Mirren	19	0	48	1
2009–10	Morecambe	32	1		
2010–11	Morecambe	12	1	44	2

HENDRIE, Stuart (M) 7 0
H: 5 9 W: 11 00 b.Solihull 1-11-89
Source: Atherstone T.

Season	Club	Apps	Gls	Tot Apps	Tot Gls
2010–11	Morecambe	7	0	7	0

HOLDSWORTH, Andy (D) 258 7
H: 5 9 W: 11 02 b.Pontefract 29-1-84
Source: Scholar.

Season	Club	Apps	Gls	Tot Apps	Tot Gls
2003–04	Huddersfield T	36	0		
2004–05	Huddersfield T	40	0		
2005–06	Huddersfield T	42	1		
2006–07	Huddersfield T	35	2		
2007–08	Huddersfield T	44	3		
2008–09	Huddersfield T	34	0	231	6
2009–10	Oldham Ath	12	0		
2010–11	Oldham Ath	0	0	12	0
2010–11	Morecambe	15	1	15	1

HUNTER, Garry (M) 131 5
H: 5 7 W: 10 03 b.Morecambe 1-1-85
Source: Scholar.

Season	Club	Apps	Gls	Tot Apps	Tot Gls
2007–08	Morecambe	38	1		
2008–09	Morecambe	29	1		
2009–10	Morecambe	31	2		
2010–11	Morecambe	33	1	131	5

JEVONS, Phil (F) 351 111
H: 5 11 W: 12 00 b.Liverpool 1-8-79
Source: Trainee.

Season	Club	Apps	Gls	Tot Apps	Tot Gls
1996–97	Everton	0	0		
1997–98	Everton	0	0		
1998–99	Everton	1	0		
1999–2000	Everton	3	0		
2000–01	Everton	4	0	8	0
2001–02	Grimsby T	31	6		
2002–03	Grimsby T	3	0		
2002–03	Hull C	24	3	24	3
2003–04	Grimsby T	29	12	63	18
2004–05	Yeovil T	46	27		
2005–06	Yeovil T	38	15	84	42
2006–07	Bristol C	41	11		
2007–08	Bristol C	2	0	43	11
2007–08	Huddersfield T	21	7		
2008–09	Huddersfield T	23	2		
2008–09	Bury	7	2	7	2
2009–10	Huddersfield T	0	0	44	9
2009–10	Morecambe	40	18		
2010–11	Morecambe	38	8	78	26

McCREADY, Chris (D) 215 7
H: 6 1 W: 12 05 b.Ellesmere Port 5-9-81
Source: Scholar.

Season	Club	Apps	Gls	Tot Apps	Tot Gls
2000–01	Crewe Alex	0	0		
2001–02	Crewe Alex	1	0		
2002–03	Crewe Alex	8	0		
2003–04	Crewe Alex	22	0		
2004–05	Crewe Alex	20	0		
2005–06	Crewe Alex	25	0		
2006–07	Tranmere R	42	1		
2007–08	Crewe Alex	34	1		
2008–09	Crewe Alex	5	1	115	2
2009–10	Northampton T	14	0	14	0
2009–10	Tranmere R	8	0	50	1
2010–11	Morecambe	36	4	36	4

McLACHLAN, Fraser (M) 112 4
H: 5 11 W: 12 07 b.Manchester 9-11-82
Source: Scholar.

Season	Club	Apps	Gls	Tot Apps	Tot Gls
2001–02	Stockport Co	11	1		
2002–03	Stockport Co	22	0		
2003–04	Stockport Co	20	3		
2004–05	Stockport Co	0	0	53	4
2004–05	Mansfield T	21	0		
2005–06	Mansfield T	8	0	29	0
2007–08	Morecambe	1	0		
2008–09	Morecambe	27	0		
2009–10	Morecambe	1	0		
2010–11	Morecambe	1	0	30	0

MOSS, Darren (D) 278 15
H: 5 10 W: 11 00 b.Wrexham 24-5-81
Source: Trainee. *Honours:* Wales Youth, Under-21.

Season	Club	Apps	Gls	Tot Apps	Tot Gls
1998–99	Chester C	7	0		
1999–2000	Chester C	35	0		
2000–01	Chester C	0	0	42	0
2001–02	Shrewsbury T	31	2		
2002–03	Shrewsbury T	40	2		
2003–04	Shrewsbury T	0	0		
2004–05	Shrewsbury T	26	6		
2004–05	Crewe Alex	6	0		
2005–06	Crewe Alex	31	0		
2006–07	Crewe Alex	22	2	59	2
2007–08	Shrewsbury T	31	2		
2008–09	Shrewsbury T	29	0	157	12
2009–10	Morecambe	16	1		
2010–11	Morecambe	4	0	20	1

MULLIN, Paul (F) 199 49
H: 6 0 W: 12 01 b.Bury 16-3-74
Source: Clitheroe, Darwen, Radcliffe Borough.

Season	Club	Apps	Gls	Tot Apps	Tot Gls
2006–07	Accrington S	46	14		
2007–08	Accrington S	43	12		
2008–09	Accrington S	36	7		
2008–09	Bradford C	6	0	6	0
2009–10	Accrington S	4	0	129	33
2009–10	Morecambe	38	12		
2010–11	Morecambe	26	4	64	16

PARRISH, Andy (D) 132 1
H: 6 0 W: 11 00 b.Bolton 22-6-88
Source: Scholar.

Season	Club	Apps	Gls	Tot Apps	Tot Gls
2005–06	Bury	8	0		
2006–07	Bury	9	0		
2007–08	Bury	26	1	43	1
2008–09	Morecambe	13	0		
2009–10	Morecambe	35	0		
2010–11	Morecambe	41	0	89	0

ROCHE, Barry (G) 269 0
H: 6 5 W: 14 08 b.Dublin 6-4-82
Source: Trainee.

Season	Club	Apps	Gls	Tot Apps	Tot Gls
1999–2000	Nottingham F	0	0		
2000–01	Nottingham F	2	0		
2001–02	Nottingham F	0	0		
2002–03	Nottingham F	1	0		
2003–04	Nottingham F	8	0		
2004–05	Nottingham F	2	0	13	0
2005–06	Chesterfield	41	0		
2006–07	Chesterfield	40	0		
2007–08	Chesterfield	45	0	126	0
2008–09	Morecambe	46	0		
2009–10	Morecambe	42	0		
2010–11	Morecambe	42	0	130	0

RUNDLE, Adam (M) 278 27
H: 5 8 W: 11 02 b.Durham 8-7-84
Source: Scholar.

Season	Club	Apps	Gls	Tot Apps	Tot Gls
2001–02	Darlington	12	0		
2002–03	Darlington	5	0	17	0
2002–03	Carlisle U	21	1		
2003–04	Carlisle U	23	0		
2004–05	Carlisle U	0	0	44	1
2004–05	Mansfield T	18	4		
2005–06	Mansfield T	35	5	53	9
2006–07	Rochdale	29	4		
2007–08	Rochdale	42	5		
2008–09	Rochdale	44	7		
2009–10	Rochdale	12	1	127	17
2009–10	Rotherham U	4	0	4	0
2009–10	Chesterfield	16	0	16	0
2010–11	Morecambe	17	0	17	0

SCOTT, Paul (D) 253 15
H: 5 11 W: 12 00 b.Wakefield 5-11-79
Source: Trainee.

Season	Club	Apps	Gls	Tot Apps	Tot Gls
1998–99	Huddersfield T	0	0		
1999–2000	Huddersfield T	0	0		
2000–01	Huddersfield T	0	0		
2001–02	Huddersfield T	0	0		
2002–03	Huddersfield T	13	0		
2003–04	Huddersfield T	19	2		
2004–05	Huddersfield T	0	0	32	2
2004–05	Bury	23	0		
2005–06	Bury	41	2		
2006–07	Bury	46	2		
2007–08	Bury	40	6		
2008–09	Bury	33	3		
2009–10	Bury	30	0	213	13
2010–11	Morecambe	8	0	8	0

SHUKER, Chris (M) 297 36
H: 5 5 W: 9 03 b.Liverpool 9-5-82
Source: Scholarship.

Season	Club	Apps	Gls	Tot Apps	Tot Gls
1999–2000	Manchester C	0	0		
2000–01	Manchester C	0	0		
2000–01	Macclesfield T	9	1	9	1
2001–02	Manchester C	2	0		
2002–03	Manchester C	3	0		
2002–03	Walsall	5	0	5	0
2003–04	Manchester C	0	0	5	0
2003–04	Rochdale	14	1	14	1
2003–04	Hartlepool U	14	1	14	1
2003–04	Barnsley	9	0		
2004–05	Barnsley	45	7		
2005–06	Barnsley	46	10	100	17
2006–07	Tranmere R	46	6		
2007–08	Tranmere R	23	3		
2008–09	Tranmere R	28	3		
2009–10	Tranmere R	26	2	123	14
2010–11	Morecambe	27	2	27	2

STANLEY, Craig (M) 166 15
H: 5 8 W: 10 08 b.Bedworth 3-3-83
Source: Scholar.

Season	Club	Apps	Gls	Tot Apps	Tot Gls
2002–03	Walsall	0	0		
2003–04	Walsall	0	0		
2003–04	Raith R	20	1	20	1

From Hereford U.

Season	Club	Apps	Gls	Tot Apps	Tot Gls
2007–08	Morecambe	41	2		
2008–09	Morecambe	24	5		
2009–10	Morecambe	40	4		
2010–11	Morecambe	22	2	127	13
2010–11	Torquay U	19	1	19	1

WAINWRIGHT, Neil (M) 346 32
H: 6 0 W: 12 00 b.Warrington 4-11-77
Source: Trainee.

Season	Club	Apps	Gls	Tot Apps	Tot Gls
1996–97	Wrexham	0	0		
1997–98	Wrexham	11	3	11	3
1998–99	Sunderland	2	0		
1999–2000	Sunderland	0	0		
1999–2000	Darlington	17	4		
2000–01	Sunderland	0	0		
2000–01	Halifax T	13	0	13	0
2001–02	Sunderland	0	0	2	0
2001–02	Darlington	35	4		
2002–03	Darlington	33	1		
2003–04	Darlington	35	7		
2004–05	Darlington	38	4		
2005–06	Darlington	39	3		
2006–07	Darlington	41	5		
2007–08	Darlington	14	0	252	28
2007–08	Shrewsbury T	3	0	3	0
2007–08	Mansfield T	5	0	5	0
2008–09	Morecambe	38	1		
2009–10	Morecambe	17	0		
2010–11	Morecambe	5	0	60	1

WALKER, Laurie (G) 0 0
H: 6 5 W: 11 09 b.Bedford 8-2-90
Source: Milton Keynes D Scholar, Cambridge U.

Season	Club	Apps	Gls	Tot Apps	Tot Gls
2008–09	Millwall	0	0		
2010–11	Morecambe	0	0		

WILSON, Laurence (D) 209 11
H: 5 10 W: 10 09 b.Huyton 10-10-86
Source: Scholar. *Honours:* England Youth.

Season	Club	Apps	Gls	Tot Apps	Tot Gls
2004–05	Everton	0	0		
2005–06	Everton	0	0		
2005–06	Mansfield T	15	1	15	1
2006–07	Chester C	41	1		
2007–08	Chester C	40	2		
2008–09	Chester C	34	1	115	4

2009–10	Morecambe	41	3
2010–11	Morecambe	38	3	79	6

NEWCASTLE U (54)

ADJEI, Samuel (M) 0 0
H: 6 1   W: 12 00   b.Ghana 18-1-92
Source: Jonkoping.

2008–09	Newcastle U	0	0
2009–10	Newcastle U	0	0
2010–11	Newcastle U	0	0

AIREY, Philip (F) 0 0
H: 5 11   W: 10 05   b.Newcastle 14-11-91
Source: Scholar.

2009–10	Newcastle U	0	0
2010–11	Newcastle U	0	0

ALNWICK, Jak (G) 0 0
b.Hexham 17-6-93
Source: Scholar.

2010–11	Newcastle U	0	0

AMEOBI, Shola (F) 242 48
H: 6 3   W: 11 13   b.Zaria 12-10-81
Source: Trainee. *Honours:* England
Under-21.

1998–99	Newcastle U	0	0
1999–2000	Newcastle U	0	0
2000–01	Newcastle U	20	2
2001–02	Newcastle U	15	0
2002–03	Newcastle U	28	5
2003–04	Newcastle U	26	7
2004–05	Newcastle U	31	2
2005–06	Newcastle U	30	9
2006–07	Newcastle U	12	3
2007–08	Newcastle U	6	0
2007–08	*Stoke C*	6	0	6	0
2008–09	Newcastle U	22	4
2009–10	Newcastle U	18	10
2010–11	Newcastle U	28	6	236	48

AMEOBI, Sam (F) 1 0
H: 6 3   W: 10 04   b.Newcastle 1-5-92
Source: Scholar.

2010–11	Newcastle U	1	0	1	0

BARTON, Joey (M) 209 22
H: 5 11   W: 12 05   b.Huyton 2-9-82
Source: Scholar. *Honours:* England Under-21,
1 full cap.

2001–02	Manchester C	0	0
2002–03	Manchester C	7	1
2003–04	Manchester C	28	1
2004–05	Manchester C	31	1
2005–06	Manchester C	31	6
2006–07	Manchester C	33	6	130	15
2007–08	Newcastle U	23	1
2008–09	Newcastle U	9	1
2009–10	Newcastle U	15	1
2010–11	Newcastle U	32	4	79	7

BEN ARFA, Hatem (M) 163 26
H: 5 8   W: 10 08   b.Clamart 7-3-87
Honours: France Youth, Under-21, 8 full
caps, 2 goals.

2003–04	Lyon B	3	2
2004–05	Lyon B	10	3
2004–05	Lyon	9	0
2005–06	Lyon	12	0
2005–06	Lyon B	10	1
2006–07	Lyon B	9	3	32	9
2006–07	Lyon	13	1
2007–08	Lyon	30	6	64	7
2008–09	Marseille	33	6
2009–10	Marseille	29	3
2010–11	Marseille	1	0	63	9
2010–11	Newcastle U	4	1	4	1

BEST, Leon (F) 179 44
H: 6 1   W: 13 03   b.Nottingham 19-9-86
Source: Scholar. *Honours:* Eire Youth,
Under-21, 7 full caps.

2004–05	Southampton	3	0
2004–05	*QPR*	5	0	5	0
2005–06	Southampton	3	0
2005–06	*Sheffield W*	13	2	13	2
2006–07	Southampton	9	4	15	4
2006–07	*Bournemouth*	15	3	15	3
2006–07	*Yeovil T*	15	10	15	10
2007–08	Coventry C	34	8
2008–09	Coventry C	31	2

2009–10	Coventry C	27	9	92	19
2009–10	Newcastle U	13	0
2010–11	Newcastle U	11	6	24	6

CAMPBELL, Sol (D) 504 20
H: 6 2   W: 15 07   b.Plaistow 18-9-74
Source: Trainee. *Honours:* England Youth,
Under-21, B, 73 full caps, 1 goal.

1992–93	Tottenham H	1	1
1993–94	Tottenham H	34	0
1994–95	Tottenham H	30	0
1995–96	Tottenham H	31	1
1996–97	Tottenham H	38	0
1997–98	Tottenham H	34	0
1998–99	Tottenham H	37	6
1999–2000	Tottenham H	29	0
2000–01	Tottenham H	21	2	255	10
2001–02	Arsenal	31	2
2002–03	Arsenal	33	2
2003–04	Arsenal	35	1
2004–05	Arsenal	16	1
2005–06	Arsenal	20	2
2006–07	Portsmouth	32	1
2007–08	Portsmouth	31	1
2008–09	Portsmouth	32	0
2009–10	Portsmouth	0	0	95	2
2009–10	Notts Co	1	0	1	0
2009–10	Arsenal	11	0	146	8
2010–11	Newcastle U	7	0	7	0

COLOCCINI, Fabricio (D) 324 20
H: 6 0   W: 12 04   b.Cordoba 22-1-82
Honours: Argentina 34 full caps, 1 goal.

1998–99	Boca Juniors	1	1
1999–2000	Boca Juniors	1	0	2	1
1999–2000	AC Milan	0	0
2000–01	AC Milan	0	0
2000–01	San Lorenzo	19	3	19	3
2001–02	Alaves	33	6	33	6
2002–03	Atletico Madrid	27	0	27	0
2003–04	Villarreal	31	1	31	1
2004–05	AC Milan	1	0	1	0
2004–05	La Coruna	15	1
2005–06	La Coruna	26	0
2006–07	La Coruna	26	0
2007–08	La Coruna	38	4	105	5
2008–09	Newcastle U	34	0
2009–10	Newcastle U	37	2
2010–11	Newcastle U	35	2	106	4

DONALDSON, Ryan (F) 14 0
H: 5 9   W: 11 00   b.Newcastle 1-5-91
Source: Scholar. *Honours:* England Youth.

2008–09	Newcastle U	0	0
2009–10	Newcastle U	2	0
2010–11	Newcastle U	0	0	2	0
2010–11	*Hartlepool U*	12	0	12	0

DUMMETT, Paul (D) 0 0
H: 5 10   W: 10 02   b.Newcastle 26-9-91
Source: Scholar. *Honours:* Wales Under-21.

2010–11	Newcastle U	0	0

EDMUNDSSON, Joan (F) 49 10
b.Faeroes 26-7-91
Honours: Faeroes Under-21, 9 full caps, 1
goal.

2008	B68	24	4
2009	B68	25	6	49	10
2009–10	Newcastle U	0	0
2010–11	Newcastle U	0	0

FERGUSON, Shane (D) 7 0
H: 5 9   W: 10 01   b.Limavady 12-7-91
Source: Scholar. *Honours:* Northern Ireland
Under-21, B, 1 full cap.

2008–09	Newcastle U	0	0
2009–10	Newcastle U	0	0
2010–11	Newcastle U	7	0	7	0

FOLAN, Stephen (M) 0 0
H: 6 1   W: 12 01   b.Galway 14-1-92
Source: Scholar.

2010–11	Newcastle U	0	0

FORSTER, Fraser (G) 84 0
H: 6 0   W: 12 00   b.Hexham 17-3-88
Source: Scholar.

2007–08	Newcastle U	0	0
2008–09	Newcastle U	0	0
2008–09	*Stockport Co*	6	0	6	0
2009–10	Newcastle U	0	0
2009–10	*Bristol R*	4	0	4	0
2009–10	*Norwich C*	38	0	38	0

2010–11	Newcastle U	0	0
2010–11	*Celtic*	36	0	36	0

GOSLING, Dan (M) 45 6
H: 6 0   W: 11 00   b.Brixham 2-2-90
Source: Scholar. *Honours:* England Youth,
Under-21.

2006–07	Plymouth Arg	12	2
2007–08	Plymouth Arg	10	0	22	2
2007–08	Everton	11	2
2008–09	Everton	11	2
2009–10	Everton	11	2	22	4
2010–11	Newcastle U	1	0	1	0

GRIEVE, Matthew (D) 3 0
H: 6 3   W: 12 00   b.Ashington 8-11-90

2010–11	Newcastle U	0	0
2010–11	*Stockport Co*	3	0	3	0

GUTHRIE, Danny (M) 114 6
H: 5 9   W: 11 06   b.Shrewsbury 18-4-87
Source: Scholar. *Honours:* England Schools,
Youth.

2004–05	Liverpool	0	0
2005–06	Liverpool	0	0
2006–07	Liverpool	3	0
2006–07	*Southampton*	10	0	10	0
2007–08	Liverpool	0	0	3	0
2007–08	*Bolton W*	25	0	25	0
2008–09	Newcastle U	24	2
2009–10	Newcastle U	38	4
2010–11	Newcastle U	14	0	76	6

GUTIERREZ, Jonas (M) 298 13
H: 6 0   W: 11 07   b.Buenos Aires 5-7-82
Honours: Argentina 20 full caps, 1 goal.

2001–02	Velez Sarsfield	17	0
2002–03	Velez Sarsfield	21	1
2003–04	Velez Sarsfield	27	0
2004–05	Velez Sarsfield	33	0	98	1
2005–06	Mallorca	30	2
2006–07	Mallorca	36	3
2007–08	Mallorca	30	0	96	5
2008–09	Newcastle U	30	0
2009–10	Newcastle U	37	4
2010–11	Newcastle U	37	3	104	7

HARPER, Steve (G) 191 0
H: 6 2   W: 13 10   b.Easington 14-3-75
Source: Seaham Red Star.

1993–94	Newcastle U	0	0
1994–95	Newcastle U	0	0
1995–96	Newcastle U	0	0
1995–96	*Bradford C*	1	0	1	0
1996–97	Newcastle U	0	0
1996–97	*Stockport Co*	0	0
1997–98	Newcastle U	0	0
1997–98	*Hartlepool U*	15	0	15	0
1997–98	*Huddersfield T*	24	0	24	0
1998–99	Newcastle U	8	0
1999–2000	Newcastle U	18	0
2000–01	Newcastle U	5	0
2001–02	Newcastle U	0	0
2002–03	Newcastle U	0	0
2003–04	Newcastle U	0	0
2004–05	Newcastle U	2	0
2005–06	Newcastle U	0	0
2006–07	Newcastle U	18	0
2007–08	Newcastle U	21	0
2008–09	Newcastle U	16	0
2009–10	Newcastle U	45	0
2010–11	Newcastle U	18	0	151	0

HENDERSON, Jeff (D) 0 0
H: 6 1   W: 12 01   b.Ashington 9-12-91
Source: Scholar.

2010–11	Newcastle U	0	0

INMAN, Bradden (M) 0 0
H: 5 9   W: 11 03   b.Adelaide 10-12-91
Source: Scholar. *Honours:* Scotland Youth,
Under-21.

2009–10	Newcastle U	0	0
2010–11	Newcastle U	0	0

IONS, Billy (F) 0 0
b. 11-3-94
Source: Scholar.

2010–11	Newcastle U	0	0

JOSE ENRIQUE (D) 175 2
H: 6 0   W: 12 00   b.Valencia 23-1-86
Honours: Spain Under-21.

2004–05	Levante	19	1	19	1

2005–06 Valencia 0 0
2005–06 *Celta Vigo* 14 0 **14 0**
2006–07 *Villarreal* 23 0 **23 0**
2007–08 Newcastle U 23 0
2008–09 Newcastle U 26 0
2009–10 Newcastle U 34 1
2010–11 Newcastle U 36 0 **119 1**

KADAR, Tamas (D) **15 0**
H: 6 0 W: 12 10 b.Veszprem 14-3-90
Honours: Hungary Youth, Under-21.
2007–08 Newcastle U 0 0
2008–09 Newcastle U 0 0
2009–10 Newcastle U 13 0
2010–11 Newcastle U 0 0 **13 0**
2010–11 *Huddersfield T* 2 0 **2 0**

KRUL, Tim (G) **55 0**
H: 6 2 W: 11 08 b.Den Haag 3-4-88
Source: Academy. *Honours:* Holland Youth, Under-21, 2 full caps.
2005–06 Newcastle U 0 0
2006–07 Newcastle U 0 0
2007–08 *Falkirk* 22 0 **22 0**
2007–08 Newcastle U 0 0
2008–09 Newcastle U 0 0
2008–09 *Carlisle U* 9 0 **9 0**
2009–10 Newcastle U 3 0
2010–11 Newcastle U 21 0 **24 0**

KUQI, Shefki (F) **516 145**
H: 6 2 W: 13 13 b.Vushtrri 10-11-76
Source: Trepka, Miki. *Honours:* Albania 8 full caps, 1 goal, Finland 62 full caps, 8 goals.
1995 MP 24 3
1996 MP 26 7 **50 10**
1997 HJK Helsinki 25 6
1998 HJK Helsinki 22 1
1999 HJK Helsinki 25 11 **72 18**
2000 Jokerit 33 19 **33 19**
From Jokerit
2000–01 Stockport Co 17 6
2001–02 Stockport Co 18 5 **35 11**
2001–02 Sheffield W 17 6
2002–03 Sheffield W 40 8
2003–04 Sheffield W 7 5 **64 19**
2003–04 Ipswich T 36 11
2004–05 Ipswich T 43 19
2005–06 Blackburn R 33 7
2006–07 Blackburn R 1 0 **34 7**
2006–07 Crystal Palace 35 7
2007–08 Crystal Palace 8 0
2007–08 *Fulham* 10 0 **10 0**
2007–08 *Ipswich T* 4 0 **83 30**
2008–09 Crystal Palace 35 10 **78 17**
2009–10 Koblenz 17 7 **17 7**
2009–10 Swansea C 20 5
2010–11 Swansea C 2 0 **22 5**
2010–11 *Derby Co* 12 2 **12 2**
2010–11 Newcastle U 6 0 **6 0**

LOVENKRANDS, Peter (F) **274 73**
H: 5 11 W: 11 02 b.Copenhagen 29-1-80
Honours: Denmark Youth, 22 full caps, 1 goal.
1998–99 AB Copenhagen 18 2
1999–2000 AB Copenhagen 14 5 **32 7**
2000–01 Rangers 8 0
2001–02 Rangers 18 2
2002–03 Rangers 28 9
2003–04 Rangers 25 8
2004–05 Rangers 17 3
2005–06 Rangers 33 14 **129 36**
2006–07 Schalke 24 6
2007–08 Schalke 20 0 **44 6**
2008–09 Schalke B 3 2 **3 2**
2008–09 Newcastle U 12 3
2009–10 Newcastle U 29 13
2010–11 Newcastle U 25 6 **66 22**

LUALUA, Kazenga (F) **34 4**
H: 5 11 W: 12 00 b.Kinshasa 10-12-90
Source: Scholar.
2007–08 Newcastle U 2 0
2008–09 Newcastle U 3 0
2008–09 *Doncaster R* 4 0 **4 0**
2009–10 Newcastle U 1 0
2009–10 Brighton & HA 11 0
2010–11 Newcastle U 2 0 **8 0**
2010–11 *Brighton & HA* 11 4 **22 4**

McDERMOTT, Greg (M) **0 0**
H: 5 10 W: 10 00 b.Liverpool 18-10-91
Source: Scholar.
2010–11 Newcastle U 0 0

McLAUGHLIN, Patrick (M) **0 0**
H: 5 11 W: 12 01 b.Larne 14-1-91
Honours: Northern Ireland Under-21.
2007–08 Newcastle U 0 0
2008–09 Newcastle U 0 0
2009–10 Newcastle U 0 0
2010–11 Newcastle U 0 0

MOYO, Yven (M) **0 0**
b.France 15-3-92
Source: Sochaux.
2010–11 Newcastle U 0 0

NEWTON, Conor (M) **0 0**
H: 5 11 W: 11 00 b.Newcastle 17-10-91
Source: Scholar.
2010–11 Newcastle U 0 0

NOLAN, Kevin (M) **381 69**
H: 6 0 W: 14 00 b.Liverpool 24-6-82
Source: Scholar. *Honours:* England Youth, Under-20, Under-21.
1999–2000 Bolton W 4 0
2000–01 Bolton W 31 1
2001–02 Bolton W 35 8
2002–03 Bolton W 33 1
2003–04 Bolton W 37 9
2004–05 Bolton W 36 4
2005–06 Bolton W 36 9
2006–07 Bolton W 31 3
2007–08 Bolton W 33 5
2008–09 Bolton W 20 0 **296 40**
2008–09 Newcastle U 11 0
2009–10 Newcastle U 44 17
2010–11 Newcastle U 30 12 **85 29**

PERCH, James (D) **203 12**
H: 5 11 W: 11 05 b.Mansfield 29-9-85
Source: Scholar.
2002–03 Nottingham F 0 0
2003–04 Nottingham F 0 0
2004–05 Nottingham F 22 0
2005–06 Nottingham F 38 3
2006–07 Nottingham F 46 5
2007–08 Nottingham F 35 0
2008–09 Nottingham F 37 3
2009–10 Nottingham F 17 1 **190 12**
2010–11 Newcastle U 13 0 **13 0**

RANGER, Nile (F) **49 2**
H: 6 2 W: 13 03 b.Wood Green 11-4-91
Source: Southampton Scholar. *Honours:* England Youth.
2008–09 Newcastle U 0 0
2009–10 Newcastle U 25 2
2010–11 Newcastle U 24 0 **49 2**

RICHARDSON, Michael (M) **0 0**
b. 17-3-92
Source: Walker Central.
2010–11 Newcastle U 0 0

ROUTLEDGE, Wayne (M) **261 23**
H: 5 6 W: 11 02 b.Sidcup 7-1-85
Source: Scholar. *Honours:* England Youth, Under-20, Under-21.
2001–02 Crystal Palace 2 0
2002–03 Crystal Palace 26 4
2003–04 Crystal Palace 44 6
2004–05 Crystal Palace 38 0 **110 10**
2005–06 Tottenham H 3 0
2005–06 Portsmouth 13 0 **13 0**
2006–07 Tottenham H 0 0
2006–07 *Fulham* 24 0 **24 0**
2007–08 Tottenham H 2 0 **5 0**
2007–08 Aston Villa 1 0
2008–09 Aston Villa 1 0 **2 0**
2008–09 *Cardiff C* 9 2 **9 2**
2008–09 QPR 19 1
2009–10 QPR 25 2
2009–10 Newcastle U 17 3
2010–11 Newcastle U 17 0 **34 3**
2010–11 *QPR* 20 5 **64 8**

SIMPSON, Danny (D) **106 1**
H: 5 9 W: 11 05 b.Eccles 4-1-87
Source: Scholar.
2005–06 Manchester U 0 0
2006–07 Manchester U 0 0

2006–07 *Sunderland* 14 0 **14 0**
2007–08 Manchester U 3 0
2007–08 *Ipswich T* 8 0 **8 0**
2008–09 Manchester U 0 0
2008–09 *Blackburn R* 12 0 **12 0**
2009–10 Manchester U 0 0 **3 0**
2009–10 Newcastle U 39 1
2010–11 Newcastle U 30 0 **69 1**

SMITH, Alan (F) **315 45**
H: 5 10 W: 12 04 b.Rothwell 28-10-80
Source: Trainee. *Honours:* England Youth, Under-21, B, 19 full caps, 1 goal.
1997–98 Leeds U 0 0
1998–99 Leeds U 22 7
1999–2000 Leeds U 26 4
2000–01 Leeds U 33 11
2001–02 Leeds U 23 4
2002–03 Leeds U 33 3
2003–04 Leeds U 35 9 **172 38**
2004–05 Manchester U 31 6
2005–06 Manchester U 21 1
2006–07 Manchester U 9 0 **61 7**
2007–08 Newcastle U 33 0
2008–09 Newcastle U 6 0
2009–10 Newcastle U 32 0
2010–11 Newcastle U 11 0 **82 0**

SODERBERG, Ole (G) **0 0**
H: 6 4 W: 14 07 b.Norrkoping 20-7-90
Source: BK Hacken. *Honours:* Sweden Youth.
2007–08 Newcastle U 0 0
2008–09 Newcastle U 0 0
2009–10 Newcastle U 0 0
2010–11 Newcastle U 0 0

SPEAR, Aaron (F) **0 0**
b.Plymouth 29-4-93
Source: Scholar.
2010–11 Newcastle U 0 0

TAVERNIER, James (D) **0 0**
H: 5 9 W: 11 00 b.Bradford 31-10-91
Source: Scholar.
2009–10 Newcastle U 0 0
2010–11 Newcastle U 0 0

TAYLOR, Ryan (M) **200 24**
H: 5 8 W: 10 04 b.Liverpool 19-8-84
Source: Scholar. *Honours:* England Youth, Under-21.
2001–02 Tranmere R 0 0
2002–03 Tranmere R 25 1
2003–04 Tranmere R 30 5
2004–05 Tranmere R 43 8 **98 14**
2005–06 Wigan Ath 11 0
2006–07 Wigan Ath 16 1
2007–08 Wigan Ath 17 3
2008–09 Wigan Ath 12 2 **56 6**
2008–09 Newcastle U 10 0
2009–10 Newcastle U 31 4
2010–11 Newcastle U 5 0 **46 4**

TAYLOR, Steven (D) **152 11**
H: 6 2 W: 13 01 b.Greenwich 23-1-86
Source: Trainee. *Honours:* FA Schools, Youth, England Under-20, Under-21, B.
2002–03 Newcastle U 0 0
2003–04 Newcastle U 1 0
2003–04 *Wycombe W* 6 0 **6 0**
2004–05 Newcastle U 13 0
2005–06 Newcastle U 12 0
2006–07 Newcastle U 27 2
2007–08 Newcastle U 31 1
2008–09 Newcastle U 27 4
2009–10 Newcastle U 21 1
2010–11 Newcastle U 14 3 **146 11**

TIOTE, Cheik (M) **114 4**
H: 5 11 W: 12 06 b.Yamoussoukro 21-6-86
Honours: Ivory Coast 20 full caps.
2005–06 Anderlecht 2 0
2006–07 Anderlecht 2 0 **4 0**
2007–08 Roda JC 26 2 **26 2**
2008–09 Twente 28 0
2009–10 Twente 28 1
2010–11 Twente 2 0 **58 1**
2010–11 Newcastle U 26 1 **26 1**

TOLAND, Lee-Ryan (D) **0 0**
b.Derry 2-10-93
Source: Ballymoor.
2010–11 Newcastle U 0 0

TOZER, Ben (D)   34   3
H: 6 1   W: 12 11   b.Plymouth 1-3-90
Source: Scholar.

2007–08	Swindon T	2	0	2	0	
2007–08	Newcastle U	0	0			
2008–09	Newcastle U	0	0			
2009–10	Newcastle U	1	0			
2010–11	Newcastle U	0	0	1	0	
2010–11	*Northampton T*	31	3	31	3	

VUCKIC, Haris (F)   7   0
H: 6 2   W: 12 02   b.Ljubljana 21-8-92
Source: Scholar. *Honours:* Slovenia Youth.

2007–08	Domzale	1	0			
2008–09	Domzale	4	0	5	0	
2009–10	Newcastle U	2	0			
2010–11	Newcastle U	0	0	2	0	

WILLIAMSON, Mike (D)   223   13
H: 6 4   W: 13 03   b.Stoke 8-11-83
Source: Trainee.

2001–02	Torquay U	3	0			
2001–02	Southampton	0	0			
2002–03	Southampton	0	0			
2003–04	Southampton	0	0			
2003–04	*Torquay U*	11	0	14	0	
2003–04	*Doncaster R*	0	0			
2004–05	Southampton	0	0			
2004–05	Wycombe W	37	2			
2005–06	Wycombe W	39	5			
2006–07	Wycombe W	33	1			
2007–08	Wycombe W	12	0			
2008–09	Wycombe W	22	3	143	11	
2008–09	Watford	17	1			
2009–10	Watford	4	1	21	2	
2009–10	Portsmouth	0	0			
2009–10	Newcastle U	16	0			
2010–11	Newcastle U	29	0	45	0	

XISCO (F)   112   31
H: 6 0   W: 13 03   b.Palma 26-6-86
Honours: Spain Under-21.

2004–05	La Coruna	7	2			
2005–06	La Coruna	12	1			
2006–07	*Vecindario*	27	13	27	13	
2007–08	La Coruna	25	9			
2008–09	Newcastle U	5	1			
2009–10	Newcastle U	2	0			
2009–10	*Santander*	23	3	23	3	
2010–11	Newcastle U	2	0	9	1	
2010–11	*La Coruna*	9	2	53	14	

ZAMBLERA, Fabio (F)   0   0
H: 6 3   W: 14 09   b.Bergamo 7-4-90
Source: Atalanta. *Honours:* Italy Youth.

2007–08	Newcastle U	0	0	
2008–09	Newcastle U	0	0	
2009–10	Newcastle U	0	0	
2010–11	Newcastle U	0	0	
2010–11	*Sampdoria*	0	0	

Scholars
Baird Alex James; Evans Nathan; Henderson Liam Alexander; Hoganson Michael George; Ions William; Knight Dennis Peter; Maddison Marcus Harley; McGorrigan Ryan Anthony; Miele Brandon; Nicholson Alex Jack; Nzuzi Patrick Nime; Riley Michael Liam; Sayer Ben; Smith Jamie Paul; Storey Louis Alan; Taylor Daniel Scott; Toland Lee

NORTHAMPTON T (55)

BAUZA, Guillem (F)   71   15
H: 5 11   W: 12 01   b.Palma de Mallorca 25-10-84
Source: Mallorca, Espanyol.

2007–08	Swansea C	28	7			
2008–09	Swansea C	15	2			
2009–10	Swansea C	6	0	49	9	
2010–11	Hereford U	12	2	12	2	
2010–11	Northampton T	10	4	10	4	

BECKWITH, Dean (D)   171   6
H: 6 3   W: 13 04   b.Southwark 18-9-83
Source: Scholar.

2003–04	Gillingham	0	0			
2004–05	Gillingham	1	0	1	0	
2006–07	Hereford U	32	0			
2007–08	Hereford U	38	2			
2008–09	Hereford U	25	1	95	3	

2009–10	Northampton T	38	0			
2010–11	Northampton T	37	3	75	3	

BUILT, Michael (D)   0   0
H: 5 10   W: 11 00   b.Hamilton (NZ) 12-11-92
Source: Youth.

2010–11	Northampton T	0	0	

DAVIS, Liam (M)   97   8
H: 5 9   W: 11 07   b.Wandsworth 23-11-86
Source: Scholar.

2005–06	Coventry C	2	0			
2006–07	Coventry C	3	0			
2006–07	*Peterborough U*	7	0	7	0	
2007–08	Coventry C	6	0	11	0	
2008–09	Northampton T	29	4			
2009–10	Northampton T	17	2			
2010–11	Northampton T	33	2	79	8	

DUNN, Chris (G)   98   0
H: 6 5   W: 13 11   b.Brentwood 23-10-87
Source: Scholar.

2006–07	Northampton T	0	0	
2007–08	Northampton T	1	0	
2008–09	Northampton T	29	0	
2009–10	Northampton T	29	0	
2010–11	Northampton T	39	0	98 0

GILLIGAN, Ryan (M)   185   20
H: 5 10   W: 11 07   b.Swindon 18-1-87
Source: Watford Scholar.

2005–06	Northampton T	23	4			
2006–07	Northampton T	24	0			
2007–08	Northampton T	38	4			
2008–09	Northampton T	31	3			
2009–10	Northampton T	42	8			
2010–11	Northampton T	22	1	180	20	
2010–11	*Torquay U*	5	0	5	0	

GUINAN, Stephen (F)   304   57
H: 6 1   W: 13 02   b.Birmingham 24-12-75
Source: Trainee.

1992–93	Nottingham F	0	0			
1993–94	Nottingham F	0	0			
1994–95	Nottingham F	0	0			
1995–96	Nottingham F	2	0			
1995–96	*Darlington*	3	1	3	1	
1996–97	Nottingham F	2	0			
1996–97	*Burnley*	6	0	6	0	
1997–98	Nottingham F	2	0			
1997–98	*Crewe Alex*	3	0	3	0	
1998–99	Nottingham F	0	0			
1998–99	*Halifax T*	12	2	12	2	
1998–99	*Plymouth Arg*	11	7			
1999–2000	Nottingham F	1	0	7	0	
1999–2000	*Scunthorpe U*	3	1	3	1	
1999–2000	*Cambridge U*	6	0	6	0	
1999–2000	Plymouth Arg	8	2			
2000–01	Plymouth Arg	22	1			
2001–02	Plymouth Arg	0	0	41	10	
2001–02	Shrewsbury T	5	0			
2002–03	Shrewsbury T	0	0			
2003–04	Shrewsbury T	0	0	5	0	
2004–05	Cheltenham T	43	6			
2005–06	Cheltenham T	30	7			
2006–07	Cheltenham T	19	0	92	13	
2006–07	Hereford U	16	7			
2007–08	Hereford U	28	3			
2008–09	Hereford U	43	15	87	25	
2009–10	Northampton T	28	4			
2010–11	Northampton T	11	1	39	5	

HALL, Marcus (D)   374   3
H: 6 1   W: 12 02   b.Coventry 24-3-76
Source: Trainee. *Honours:* England Under-21, B.

1994–95	Coventry C	5	0			
1995–96	Coventry C	25	0			
1996–97	Coventry C	13	0			
1997–98	Coventry C	25	1			
1998–99	Coventry C	5	0			
1999–2000	Coventry C	9	0			
2000–01	Coventry C	21	0			
2001–02	Coventry C	29	1			
2002–03	Nottingham F	1	0	1	0	
2002–03	Stoke C	24	0			
2003–04	Stoke C	35	0			
2004–05	Stoke C	20	1	79	1	
2004–05	Coventry C	15	0			
2005–06	Coventry C	39	0			
2006–07	Coventry C	40	0			
2007–08	Coventry C	18	0			

2008–09	Coventry C	23	0			
2009–10	Coventry C	8	0	270	2	
2010–11	Northampton T	24	0	24	0	

HARRAD, Shaun (F)   109   38
H: 5 10   W: 12 04   b.Nottingham 11-12-84
Source: Scholar.

2002–03	Notts Co	5	0			
2003–04	Notts Co	8	0			
2004–05	Notts Co	16	1	29	1	
2009–10	Burton Alb	42	21			
2010–11	Burton Alb	20	10	62	31	
2010–11	Northampton T	18	6	18	6	

HARRIS, Seb (D)   27   2
H: 6 3   W: 12 12   b.Michigan 5-10-87
Source: Oakland Univ.

2009	Michigan Bucks	14	1	14	1	
2009–10	Northampton T	9	1			
2010–11	Northampton T	4	0	13	1	

HERBERT, Courtney (F)   38   2
H: 6 2   W: 12 08   b.Northampton 25-10-88
Source: Long Buckby.

2009–10	Northampton T	23	2			
2010–11	Northampton T	15	0	38	2	

HOLT, Andy (M)   474   37
H: 6 1   W: 12 07   b.Stockport 21-5-78
Source: Trainee.

1996–97	Oldham Ath	1	0			
1997–98	Oldham Ath	14	1			
1998–99	Oldham Ath	43	5			
1999–2000	Oldham Ath	46	3			
2000–01	Oldham Ath	20	1	124	10	
2000–01	*Hull C*	10	2			
2001–02	*Hull C*	30	0			
2002–03	*Hull C*	6	0			
2002–03	*Barnsley*	7	0	7	0	
2002–03	*Shrewsbury T*	9	0	9	0	
2003–04	Hull C	25	1	71	3	
2004–05	Wrexham	45	6			
2005–06	Wrexham	36	3	81	9	
2006–07	Northampton T	35	2			
2007–08	Northampton T	36	2			
2008–09	Northampton T	41	2			
2009–10	Northampton T	31	3			
2010–11	Northampton T	39	6	182	15	

JACOBS, Michael (M)   41   5
H: 5 9   W: 11 08   b.Rothwell 23-3-92
Source: Scholar.

2009–10	Northampton T	0	0			
2010–11	Northampton T	41	5	41	5	

JOHNSON, John (D)   79   12
H: 6 0   W: 12 00   b.Middlesbrough 16-9-88
Source: Scholar.

2007–08	Middlesbrough	0	0			
2008–09	Middlesbrough	1	0			
2008–09	*Tranmere R*	4	0	4	0	
2009–10	Middlesbrough	0	0	1	0	
2009–10	*Northampton T*	36	5			
2010–11	Northampton T	38	7	74	12	

KAZIBONI, Greg (M)   2   0
H: 5 9   W: 11 00   b.Northampton 16-5-92
Source: Gregory Celtic.

2010–11	Northampton T	2	0	2	0	

LAURENT, Francis (F)   62   9
H: 6 3   W: 14 00   b.Paris 6-1-86
Source: Mainz.

2008–09	Southend U	21	3			
2009–10	Southend U	35	6			
2010–11	Southend U	0	0	56	9	
2010–11	Northampton T	6	0	6	0	

McKAY, Billy (F)   74   13
H: 5 9   W: 10 01   b.Corby 22-10-88
Honours: Northern Ireland Under-21.

2007–08	Leicester C	0	0			
2008–09	Leicester C	0	0			
2009–10	Northampton T	40	8			
2010–11	Northampton T	34	5	74	13	

McKENZIE, Leon (F)   372   102
H: 5 11   W: 12 11   b.Croydon 17-5-78
Source: Trainee.

1995–96	Crystal Palace	12	0			
1996–97	Crystal Palace	21	2			
1997–98	Crystal Palace	3	0			
1997–98	*Fulham*	3	0	3	0	
1998–99	Crystal Palace	16	1			

1998–99	*Peterborough U*	14	8		
1999–2000	Crystal Palace	25	4		
2000–01	Crystal Palace	8	0	85	7
2000–01	Peterborough U	30	13		
2001–02	Peterborough U	30	18		
2002–03	Peterborough U	11	5		
2003–04	Peterborough U	19	9	104	53
2003–04	Norwich C	18	9		
2004–05	Norwich C	37	7		
2005–06	Norwich C	20	4		
2006–07	Norwich C	4	0	79	20
2006–07	Coventry C	31	7		
2007–08	Coventry C	11	2		
2008–09	Coventry C	19	3		
2009–10	Coventry C	1	0	62	12
2009–10	Charlton Ath	12	0		
2010–11	Charlton Ath	0	0	12	0
2010–11	Northampton T	27	10	27	10

OSMAN, Abdul (M)   122 8
H: 6 0   W: 11 00   b.Accra 27-2-87
Source: Hampton & Richmond B,
Maidenhead U.

2007–08	Gretna	18	1	18	1
2008–09	Northampton T	36	2		
2009–10	Northampton T	30	2		
2010–11	Northampton T	38	3	104	7

PURCELL, Tadhg (F)   106 27
H: 5 11   W: 11 08   b.Dublin 9-2-85
Source: UCD, Kilkenny City.

2007	Shamrock R	28	12		
2008	Shamrock R	28	4		
2009	Shamrock R	24	2	80	18
2009–10	Darlington	22	9	22	9
2010–11	Northampton T	4	0	4	0

RODGERS, Paul (D)   67 0
H: 5 10   W: 10 10   b.Edmonton 6-10-89
Source: Scholar.

2007–08	Arsenal	0	0		
2008–09	Arsenal	0	0		
2008–09	*Northampton T*	11	0		
2009–10	Northampton T	31	0		
2010–11	Northampton T	25	0	67	0

THORNTON, Kevin (M)   98 9
H: 5 7   W: 11 00   b.Drogheda 9-7-86
Source: Scholar. *Honours:* Eire Youth.

2003–04	Coventry C	0	0		
2004–05	Coventry C	0	0		
2005–06	Coventry C	16	0		
2006–07	Coventry C	11	1		
2007–08	Coventry C	19	1		
2008–09	Coventry C	4	0	50	2
2008–09	*Brighton & HA*	12	0	12	0
From Nuneaton T.					
2009–10	Northampton T	11	1		
2010–11	Northampton T	25	6	36	7

UWEZU, Michael (M)   6 1
H: 5 6   W: 12 02   b.Nigeria 12-12-90

2008–09	Fulham	0	0		
2009–10	Fulham	0	0		
2009–10	*Lincoln C*	2	0	2	0
2010–11	Northampton T	4	1	4	1

WALKER, Paul (G)   1 0
H: 5 10   W: 10 10   b.Wales 18-4-92
Source: Scholar.

2010–11	Northampton T	1	0	1	0

WEDDERBURN, Nathanial (M)   43 0
H: 6 1   W: 13 05   b.Wolverhampton 30-6-91
Source: Scholar. *Honours:* England Youth.

2008–09	Stoke C	0	0		
2008–09	*Notts Co*	9	0	9	0
2009–10	Stoke C	0	0		
2009–10	*Hereford U*	3	0	3	0
2010–11	Northampton T	31	0	31	0

NORWICH C (56)

ADEYEMI, Tom (M)   45 5
H: 6 1   W: 12 04   b.Milton Keynes 24-10-91
Source: Scholar.

2008–09	Norwich C	0	0		
2009–10	Norwich C	11	0		
2010–11	Norwich C	0	0	11	0
2010–11	*Bradford C*	34	5	34	5

BARNETT, Leon (D)   149 7
H: 6 0   W: 12 04   b.Stevenage 30-11-85
Source: Scholar.

2003–04	Luton T	0	0		
2004–05	Luton T	0	0		
2005–06	Luton T	20	0		
2006–07	Luton T	39	3	59	3
2007–08	WBA	32	3		
2008–09	WBA	11	0		
2009–10	WBA	2	0		
2009–10	*Coventry C*	20	0	20	0
2010–11	WBA	0	0	45	3
2010–11	Norwich C	25	1	25	1

BERTHEL ASKOU, Jens (D)   159 8
H: 6 2   W: 13 00   b.Videbaek 19-8-82

2002	Holstebro	0	0		
2003	Silkeborg	0	0		
2004	Silkeborg	29	2		
2005	Silkeborg	33	2		
2006	Silkeborg	31	2		
2006–07	Silkeborg	27	0	120	6
2007–08	Kasimpasa	11	0		
2008–09	Kasimpasa	0	0	11	0
2009–10	Norwich C	22	2		
2010–11	Norwich C	5	0	27	2
2010–11	*Millwall*	1	0	1	0

CROFTS, Andrew (D)   271 30
H: 5 10   W: 12 09   b.Chatham 29-5-84
Source: Trainee. *Honours:* Wales Youth,
Under-21, 17 full caps.

2000–01	Gillingham	1	0		
2001–02	Gillingham	0	0		
2002–03	Gillingham	0	0		
2003–04	Gillingham	8	0		
2004–05	Gillingham	27	2		
2005–06	Gillingham	45	2		
2006–07	Gillingham	43	8		
2007–08	Gillingham	41	5		
2008–09	Gillingham	9	0	174	17
2008–09	*Peterborough U*	9	0	9	0
2009–10	Brighton & HA	44	5	44	5
2010–11	Norwich C	44	8	44	8

DALEY, Luke (F)   13 0
H: 5 11   W: 11 00   b.Northampton 10-11-89
Source: Scholar.

2007–08	Norwich C	0	0		
2008–09	Norwich C	3	0		
2009–10	Norwich C	7	0		
2010–11	Norwich C	1	0	11	0
2010–11	*Stevenage*	2	0	2	0

DAWKIN, Josh (M)   0 0
H: 5 9   W: 10 12   b.Huntingdon 16-1-92
Source: Scholar. *Honours:* Wales Youth.

2009–10	Norwich C	0	0		
2010–11	Norwich C	0	0		

DRURY, Adam (D)   462 6
H: 5 10   W: 11 09   b.Cambridge 29-8-78
Source: Trainee.

1995–96	Peterborough U	1	0		
1996–97	Peterborough U	5	1		
1997–98	Peterborough U	31	0		
1998–99	Peterborough U	40	0		
1999–2000	Peterborough U	42	1		
2000–01	Peterborough U	29	0	148	2
2000–01	Norwich C	6	0		
2001–02	Norwich C	35	0		
2002–03	Norwich C	45	2		
2003–04	Norwich C	42	0		
2004–05	Norwich C	33	1		
2005–06	Norwich C	39	0		
2006–07	Norwich C	39	0		
2007–08	Norwich C	9	0		
2008–09	Norwich C	11	0		
2009–10	Norwich C	35	0		
2010–11	Norwich C	20	1	314	4

FOX, David (M)   148 11
H: 5 9   W: 11 08   b.Leek 13-12-83
Source: Scholar. *Honours:* England Youth,
Under-20.

2000–01	Manchester U	0	0		
2001–02	Manchester U	0	0		
2002–03	Manchester U	0	0		
2003–04	Manchester U	0	0		
2004–05	*Shrewsbury T*	4	1	4	1
2005–06	Manchester U	0	0		

2005–06	Blackpool	7	1		
2006–07	Blackpool	37	4		
2007–08	Blackpool	28	1		
2008–09	Blackpool	22	0	94	6
2009–10	Colchester U	18	3	18	3
2010–11	Norwich C	32	1	32	1

FRANCOMB, George (D)   15 0
H: 5 11   W: 11 07   b.Hackney 8-9-91
Source: Scholar.

2009–10	Norwich C	2	0		
2010–11	Norwich C	0	0	2	0
2010–11	*Barnet*	13	0	13	0

GILL, Matthew (M)   275 16
H: 5 11   W: 11 10   b.Cambridge 8-11-80
Source: Trainee.

1997–98	Peterborough U	2	0		
1998–99	Peterborough U	26	0		
1999–2000	Peterborough U	20	1		
2000–01	Peterborough U	17	1		
2001–02	Peterborough U	12	2		
2002–03	Peterborough U	41	1		
2003–04	Peterborough U	33	0		
2004–05	Notts Co	43	0		
2005–06	Notts Co	14	0	57	0
2008–09	Exeter C	43	9	43	9
2009–10	Norwich C	8	0		
2010–11	Norwich C	4	0	12	0
2010–11	*Peterborough U*	4	0	155	5
2010–11	Walsall	8	2	8	2

HABERGHAM, Sam (D)   0 0
H: 6 1   W: 11 07   b.Rotherham 20-2-92
Source: Scholar.

2009–10	Norwich C	0	0		
2010–11	Norwich C	0	0		

HOLT, Grant (F)   332 124
H: 6 1   W: 14 02   b.Carlisle 12-4-81
Source: Workington.

1999–2000	Halifax T	4	0		
2000–01	Halifax T	2	0	6	0
From Sengkang,Barrow					
2002–03	Sheffield W	7	1		
2003–04	Sheffield W	17	2	24	3
2003–04	Rochdale	14	4		
2004–05	Rochdale	40	17		
2005–06	Rochdale	21	14	75	35
2005–06	Nottingham F	19	4		
2006–07	Nottingham F	45	14		
2007–08	Nottingham F	32	3	96	21
2007–08	*Blackpool*	4	0		
2008–09	Shrewsbury T	43	20	43	20
2009–10	Norwich C	39	24		
2010–11	Norwich C	45	21	84	45

HOOLAHAN, Wes (M)   316 45
H: 5 6   W: 10 03   b.Dublin 10-8-83
Honours: Eire Under-21, 1 full cap.

2001–02	Shelbourne	20	3		
2002–03	Shelbourne	23	0		
2004	Shelbourne	31	2		
2005	Shelbourne	29	4	103	9
2005–06	Livingston	16	0	16	0
2006–07	Blackpool	42	8		
2007–08	Blackpool	45	5	87	13
2008–09	Norwich C	32	2		
2009–10	Norwich C	37	11		
2010–11	Norwich C	41	10	110	23

HUGHES, Stephen (M)   256 19
H: 5 10   W: 11 04   b.Motherwell 14-11-82
Honours: Scotland Youth, Under-21, 1 full
cap.

2000–01	Rangers	1	0		
2001–02	Rangers	17	1		
2002–03	Rangers	12	1		
2003–04	Rangers	22	3		
2004–05	Rangers	11	2	63	7
2004–05	Leicester C	16	1		
2005–06	Leicester C	34	3		
2006–07	Leicester C	41	3	91	7
2007–08	Motherwell	31	1		
2008–09	Motherwell	35	1	66	2
2009–10	Norwich C	29	3		
2010–11	Norwich C	1	0	30	3
2010–11	*Milton Keynes D*	6	0	6	0

JACKSON, Simeon (M)   156 53
H: 5 10   W: 10 12   b.Kingston, Jamaica 28-3-87
Source: Scholar. *Honours:* Canada Youth, 18 full caps, 2 goals.

2004–05	Rushden & D	3	0		
2005–06	Rushden & D	14	5		
2006–07	Rushden & D	0	0		
2007–08	Rushden & D	0	0	17	5
2007–08	Gillingham	18	4		
2008–09	Gillingham	41	17		
2009–10	Gillingham	42	14	101	35
2010–11	Norwich C	38	13	38	13

JOHNSON, Oli (F)   78 14
H: 5 11   W: 12 04   b.Wakefield 6-11-87
Source: Nostell MW.

2008–09	Stockport Co	24	6		
2009–10	Stockport Co	16	1	40	7
2009–10	Norwich C	17	4		
2010–11	Norwich C	4	0	21	4
2010–11	Yeovil T	17	3	17	3

LAPPIN, Simon (M)   271 13
H: 5 11   W: 9 06   b.Glasgow 25-1-83
Honours: Scotland Under-21.

2001–02	St Mirren	1	0		
2002–03	St Mirren	34	0		
2003–04	St Mirren	24	4		
2004–05	St Mirren	34	1		
2005–06	St Mirren	35	3		
2006–07	St Mirren	24	1	152	9
2006–07	Norwich C	14	1		
2007–08	*Motherwell*	14	2	14	2
2007–08	Norwich C	15	1		
2008–09	Norwich C	5	0		
2009–10	Norwich C	44	0		
2010–11	Norwich C	27	0	105	2

MARTIN, Chris (F)   137 36
H: 6 2   W: 12 06   b.Beccles 4-11-88
Source: Scholar. *Honours:* England Youth.

2006–07	Norwich C	18	4		
2007–08	Norwich C	7	0		
2008–09	Norwich C	0	0		
2008–09	*Luton T*	40	11	40	11
2009–10	Norwich C	42	17		
2010–11	Norwich C	30	4	97	25

MARTIN, Russell (M)   244 11
H: 6 0   W: 11 08   b.Brighton 4-1-86
Source: Lewes. *Honours:* Scotland 1 full cap.

2004–05	Wycombe W	7	0		
2005–06	Wycombe W	23	3		
2006–07	Wycombe W	42	2		
2007–08	Wycombe W	44	0	116	5
2008–09	Peterborough U	46	1		
2009–10	Peterborough U	10	0	56	1
2009–10	Norwich C	26	0		
2010–11	Norwich C	46	5	72	5

McDONALD, Cody (F)   65 29
H: 5 10   W: 11 03   b.Witham 30-5-86
Source: Dartford.

2008–09	Norwich C	7	1		
2009–10	Norwich C	17	3		
2010–11	Norwich C	0	0	24	4
2010–11	*Gillingham*	41	25	41	25

McNAMEE, Anthony (M)   209 6
H: 5 6   W: 10 03   b.Kensington 13-7-84
Source: Scholar. *Honours:* England Youth, Under-20.

2001–02	Watford	7	1		
2002–03	Watford	23	0		
2003–04	Watford	2	0		
2004–05	Watford	14	0		
2005–06	Watford	38	1		
2006–07	Watford	7	0		
2006–07	*Crewe Alex*	5	0	5	0
2007–08	Watford	0	0	91	2
2007–08	Swindon T	19	2		
2008–09	Swindon T	43	0		
2009–10	Swindon T	17	1	79	3
2009–10	Norwich C	17	1		
2010–11	Norwich C	17	0	34	1

RUDD, Declan (G)   8 0
H: 6 3   W: 12 06   b.Diss 16-1-91
Source: Scholar. *Honours:* England Youth, Under-20.

2008–09	Norwich C	0	0		
2009–10	Norwich C	7	0		
2010–11	Norwich C	1	0	8	0

RUDDY, John (G)   179 0
H: 6 3   W: 12 07   b.St Ives 24-10-86
Source: Scholar. *Honours:* England Youth.

2003–04	Cambridge U	1	0		
2004–05	Cambridge U	38	0	39	0
2005–06	Everton	1	0		
2005–06	*Walsall*	5	0	5	0
2005–06	*Rushden & D*	3	0	3	0
2005–06	*Chester C*	4	0	4	0
2006–07	Everton	0	0		
2006–07	*Stockport Co*	11	0		
2006–07	*Wrexham*	5	0	5	0
2006–07	*Bristol C*	1	0	1	0
2007–08	Everton	0	0		
2007–08	*Stockport Co*	12	0	23	0
2008–09	Everton	0	0		
2009–10	*Crewe Alex*	19	0	19	0
2009–10	Everton	0	0	1	0
2009–10	*Motherwell*	34	0	34	0
2010–11	Norwich C	45	0	45	0

SMITH, Korey (M)   67 4
H: 5 9   W: 11 01   b.Hatfield 31-1-91
Source: Scholar.

2008–09	Norwich C	2	0		
2009–10	Norwich C	37	4		
2010–11	Norwich C	28	0	67	4

SMITH, Steven (D)   79 1
H: 5 8   W: 10 08   b.Bellshill 30-4-85

2004–05	Rangers	4	0		
2005–06	Rangers	18	0		
2006–07	Rangers	17	1		
2007–08	Rangers	0	0		
2008–09	Rangers	5	0		
2009–10	Rangers	12	0	56	1
2010–11	Norwich C	7	0	7	0
2010–11	*Aberdeen*	16	0	16	0

STEER, Jed (G)   0 0
H: 6 2   W: 14 00   b.Norwich 23-9-92
Source: Scholar.

2009–10	Norwich C	0	0	
2010–11	Norwich C	0	0	

SURMAN, Andrew (M)   200 26
H: 5 10   W: 11 06   b.Johannesburg 20-8-86
Source: Trainee. *Honours:* England Under-21.

2003–04	Southampton	0	0		
2004–05	Southampton	0	0		
2004–05	*Walsall*	14	2	14	2
2005–06	Southampton	12	2		
2005–06	*Bournemouth*	24	6	24	6
2006–07	Southampton	37	4		
2007–08	Southampton	40	2		
2008–09	Southampton	44	7		
2009–10	Southampton	0	0	133	15
2009–10	Wolverhampton W	7	0	7	0
2010–11	Norwich C	22	3	22	3

TIERNEY, Marc (D)   212 2
H: 5 11   W: 11 04   b.Prestwich 23-8-85
Source: Trainee.

2003–04	Oldham Ath	2	0		
2004–05	Oldham Ath	11	0		
2005–06	Oldham Ath	19	0		
2006–07	Oldham Ath	5	0	37	0
2006–07	Shrewsbury T	18	0		
2007–08	Shrewsbury T	43	1		
2008–09	Shrewsbury T	18	0	79	1
2008–09	Colchester U	26	1		
2009–10	Colchester U	41	0		
2010–11	Colchester U	13	0	80	1
2010–11	Norwich C	16	0	16	0

TUDUR JONES, Owain (M)   84 6
H: 6 2   W: 12 00   b.Bangor 15-10-84
Source: Bangor C. *Honours:* Wales Under-21, 6 full caps.

2005–06	Swansea C	21	3		
2006–07	Swansea C	4	0		
2007–08	Swansea C	8	0		
2008–09	Swansea C	9	0	42	3
2008–09	*Swindon T*	11	1	11	1
2009–10	Norwich C	3	1		
2009–10	*Yeovil T*	6	1		
2010–11	Norwich C	2	0	5	1
2010–11	*Yeovil T*	14	0	20	1
2010–11	*Brentford*	6	0	6	0

WARD, Elliot (D)   200 17
H: 6 2   W: 13 00   b.Harrow 19-1-85
Source: Scholar.

2001–02	West Ham U	0	0		
2002–03	West Ham U	0	0		
2003–04	West Ham U	0	0		
2004–05	West Ham U	11	0		
2004–05	*Bristol R*	3	0	3	0
2005–06	West Ham U	4	0	15	0
2005–06	*Plymouth Arg*	16	1	16	1
2006–07	Coventry C	39	3		
2007–08	Coventry C	37	6		
2008–09	Coventry C	33	5		
2009–10	Coventry C	8	0	117	14
2009–10	*Doncaster R*	6	1	6	1
2009–10	*Preston NE*	4	0	4	0
2010–11	Norwich C	39	1	39	1

WHITBREAD, Zak (D)   126 4
H: 6 2   W: 12 07   b.Houston 4-3-84
Honours: USA Under-23.

2002–03	Liverpool	0	0		
2003–04	Liverpool	0	0		
2004–05	Liverpool	0	0		
2005–06	Liverpool	0	0		
2005–06	Millwall	25	0		
2006–07	Millwall	14	0		
2007–08	Millwall	23	3		
2008–09	Millwall	38	0		
2009–10	Millwall	0	0	100	3
2009–10	Norwich C	4	0		
2010–11	Norwich C	22	1	26	1

WILBRAHAM, Aaron (F)   388 90
H: 6 3   W: 12 04   b.Knutsford 21-10-79
Source: Trainee.

1997–98	Stockport Co	7	1		
1998–99	Stockport Co	26	0		
1999–2000	Stockport Co	26	4		
2000–01	Stockport Co	36	12		
2001–02	Stockport Co	21	3		
2002–03	Stockport Co	15	7		
2003–04	Stockport Co	41	8	172	35
2004–05	Hull C	19	2	19	2
2004–05	*Oldham Ath*	4	2	4	2
2005–06	Milton Keynes D	31	4		
2005–06	*Bradford C*	5	1	5	1
2006–07	Milton Keynes D	32	7		
2007–08	Milton Keynes D	35	10		
2008–09	Milton Keynes D	33	16		
2009–10	Milton Keynes D	33	16		
2010–11	Milton Keynes D	10	2	176	49
2010–11	Norwich C	12	1	12	1

NOTTINGHAM F (57)

ADEBOLA, Dele (F)   596 131
H: 6 3   W: 12 08   b.Lagos 23-6-75
Source: Trainee.

1992–93	Crewe Alex	6	0		
1993–94	Crewe Alex	0	0		
1994–95	Crewe Alex	30	8		
1995–96	Crewe Alex	29	8		
1996–97	Crewe Alex	32	16		
1997–98	Crewe Alex	27	7	124	39
1997–98	Birmingham C	17	7		
1998–99	Birmingham C	39	13		
1999–2000	Birmingham C	42	5		
2000–01	Birmingham C	31	6		
2001–02	Birmingham C	0	0	129	31
2001–02	*Oldham Ath*	5	0	5	0
2002–03	Crystal Palace	39	5	39	5
2003–04	Coventry C	28	2		
2003–04	*Burnley*	3	1	3	1
2004–05	Coventry C	25	5		
2004–05	*Bradford C*	15	3	15	3
2005–06	Coventry C	44	12		
2006–07	Coventry C	40	8		
2007–08	Coventry C	26	4	163	31
2007–08	Bristol C	17	6		
2008–09	Bristol C	39	10	56	16
2009–10	Nottingham F	33	3		
2010–11	Nottingham F	29	2	62	5

ANDERSON, Paul (M)   130 16
H: 5 9   W: 10 04   b.Leicester 23-7-88
Source: Scholar. *Honours:* England Youth.

2005–06	Hull C	0	0	
2005–06	Liverpool	0	0	

2006–07	Liverpool	0	0		
2007–08	Liverpool	0	0		
2007–08	Swansea C	31	7	31	7
2008–09	Liverpool	0	0		
2008–09	Nottingham F	26	2		
2009–10	Nottingham F	37	4		
2010–11	Nottingham F	36	3	99	9

BAMFORD, Patrick (F) 0 0
b.Newark 5-9-93
Source: Scholar. *Honours:* England Youth.

| 2010–11 | Nottingham F | 0 | 0 | | |

BENNETT, Julian (D) 161 12
H: 6 1 W: 13 00 b.Nottingham 17-12-84
Source: Scholar.

2003–04	Walsall	1	0		
2004–05	Walsall	31	2		
2005–06	Walsall	19	1	51	3
2005–06	Nottingham F	18	2		
2006–07	Nottingham F	30	2		
2007–08	Nottingham F	34	4		
2008–09	Nottingham F	12	0		
2009–10	Nottingham F	0	0		
2010–11	Nottingham F	3	0	97	8
2010–11	*Crystal Palace*	13	1	13	1

BLACKSTOCK, Dexter (F) 223 60
H: 6 2 W: 13 00 b.Oxford 20-5-86
Source: Scholar. *Honours:* England Youth, Under-20, Under-21.

2004–05	Southampton	9	1		
2004–05	*Plymouth Arg*	14	4	14	4
2005–06	Southampton	19	3	28	4
2005–06	*Derby Co*	9	3	9	3
2006–07	QPR	39	13		
2007–08	QPR	35	6		
2008–09	QPR	36	11	110	30
2008–09	*Nottingham F*	6	2		
2009–10	Nottingham F	39	12		
2010–11	Nottingham F	17	5	62	19

BYRNE, Mark (M) 30 6
H: 5 9 W: 11 00 b.Dublin 9-11-88
Source: Crumlin U.

2006 07	Nottingham F	0	0		
2007–08	Nottingham F	1	0		
2008–09	Nottingham F	1	0		
2009–10	Nottingham F	0	0		
2010–11	Nottingham F	0	0	2	0
2010–11	*Barnet*	28	6	28	6

BYRNE, Neil (D) 0 0
b.Portmarnock 2-2-93
Source: Scholar. *Honours:* Eire Youth.

| 2010 11 | Nottingham F | 0 | 0 | | |

CAMP, Lee (G) 271 0
H: 5 11 W: 11 11 b.Derby 22-8-84
Source: Scholar. *Honours:* England Youth, Under-20, Under-21. Northern Ireland 2 full caps.

2002–03	Derby Co	1	0		
2003–04	Derby Co	0	0		
2004–05	*QPR*	12	0		
2004–05	Derby Co	45	0		
2005–06	Derby Co	40	0		
2006–07	Derby Co	3	0	89	0
2006–07	*Norwich C*	3	0	3	0
2006–07	*QPR*	11	0		
2007–08	QPR	46	0		
2008–09	QPR	4	0	73	0
2008–09	*Nottingham F*	15	0		
2009–10	Nottingham F	45	0		
2010–11	Nottingham F	46	0	106	0

CHAMBERS, Luke (D) 286 18
H: 6 1 W: 11 13 b.Kettering 29-8-85
Source: Scholar.

2002–03	Northampton T	1	0		
2003–04	Northampton T	24	0		
2004–05	Northampton T	27	0		
2005–06	Northampton T	43	0		
2006–07	Northampton T	29	1	124	1
2006–07	Nottingham F	14	0		
2007–08	Nottingham F	42	6		
2008–09	Nottingham F	39	2		
2009–10	Nottingham F	23	3		
2010–11	Nottingham F	44	6	162	17

COHEN, Chris (M) 260 16
H: 5 11 W: 10 11 b.Norwich 5-3-87
Source: Scholar. *Honours:* England Youth.

2003–04	West Ham U	7	0		
2004–05	West Ham U	11	0		
2005–06	West Ham U	0	0	18	0
2005–06	*Yeovil T*	30	1		
2006–07	Yeovil T	44	6	74	7
2007–08	Nottingham F	41	2		
2008–09	Nottingham F	41	2		
2009–10	Nottingham F	44	3		
2010–11	Nottingham F	42	2	168	9

DARLOW, Karl (G) 1 0
H: 6 1 W: 12 05 b.Northampton 8-10-90
Source: Scholar.

| 2009–10 | Nottingham F | 0 | 0 | | |
| 2010–11 | Nottingham F | 1 | 0 | 1 | 0 |

EARNSHAW, Robert (F) 389 162
H: 5 6 W: 9 09 b.Mulfulira 6-4-81
Source: Trainee. *Honours:* Wales Youth, Under-21, 54 full caps, 16 goals.

1997–98	Cardiff C	5	0		
1998–99	Cardiff C	5	1		
1998–99	*Middlesbrough*	0	0		
1999–2000	Cardiff C	6	1		
1999–2000	*Morton*	3	2	3	2
2000–01	Cardiff C	36	19		
2001–02	Cardiff C	30	11		
2002–03	Cardiff C	46	31		
2003–04	Cardiff C	46	21		
2004–05	Cardiff C	4	1	178	85
2004–05	WBA	31	11		
2005–06	WBA	12	1	43	12
2005–06	Norwich C	15	8		
2006–07	Norwich C	30	19	45	27
2007–08	Derby Co	22	1	22	1
2008–09	Nottingham F	32	12		
2009–10	Nottingham F	32	15		
2010–11	Nottingham F	34	8	98	35

FINDLEY, Robbie (F) 124 46
H: 5 9 W: 11 11 b.Phoenix 4-8-85
Source: Oregon State Beavers. *Honours:* USA 11 full caps.

2005	Boulder Rapids	9	10		
2006	Boulder Rapids	8	5	17	15
2007	LA Galaxy	9	2	9	2
2007	Real Salt Lake	16	6		
2008	Real Salt Lake	29	6		
2009	Real Salt Lake	27	12		
2010	Real Salt Lake	24	5	96	29
2010–11	Nottingham F	2	0	2	0

FREEMAN, Kieron (D) 0 0
b.Bestwood 21 3 92
Source: Scholar. *Honours:* Wales Youth.

| 2010–11 | Nottingham F | 0 | 0 | | |

GARNER, Joe (F) 129 34
H: 5 10 W: 11 02 b.Blackburn 12-4-88
Source: Scholar. *Honours:* England Schools, Youth.

2004–05	Blackburn R	0	0		
2005–06	Blackburn R	0	0		
2006–07	Blackburn R	0	0		
2006–07	*Carlisle U*	18	5		
2007–08	Carlisle U	31	14	49	19
2008–09	Nottingham F	28	7		
2009–10	Nottingham F	18	2		
2010–11	Nottingham F	0	0	46	9
2010–11	*Huddersfield T*	16	0	16	0
2010–11	*Scunthorpe U*	18	6	18	6

GIBBONS, Robert (M) 0 0
b.Dublin 8-10-91
Source: Scholar.

2008–09	Nottingham F	0	0		
2009–10	Nottingham F	0	0		
2010–11	Nottingham F	0	0		

Transferred to Alki December 2010.

GUNTER, Chris (D) 128 1
H: 5 11 W: 11 02 b.Newport 21-7-89
Source: Scholar. *Honours:* Wales Youth, Under-21, 29 full caps.

2006–07	Cardiff C	15	0		
2007–08	Cardiff C	13	0	28	0
2007–08	Tottenham H	2	0		
2008–09	Tottenham H	3	0	5	0
2008–09	*Nottingham F*	8	0		
2009–10	Nottingham F	44	1		
2010–11	Nottingham F	43	0	95	1

LASCELLES, Jamaal (D) 0 0
H: 6 2 W: 13 01 b.Derby 11-11-93
Source: Scholar. *Honours:* England Youth.

| 2010–11 | Nottingham F | 0 | 0 | | |

LYNCH, Joel (D) 124 2
H: 6 1 W: 12 10 b.Eastbourne 3-10-87
Source: Scholar. *Honours:* England Youth.

2005–06	Brighton & HA	16	1		
2006–07	Brighton & HA	39	0		
2007–08	Brighton & HA	22	1		
2008–09	Brighton & HA	2	0	79	2
2008–09	*Nottingham F*	23	0		
2009–10	Nottingham F	10	0		
2010–11	Nottingham F	12	0	45	0

MAJEWSKI, Radoslaw (M) 132 10
H: 5 7 W: 10 06 b.Pruszkow 15-12-86
Source: Znicz Pruszkow. *Honours:* Poland 9 full caps.

2006–07	Groclin	14	0		
2007–08	Groclin	28	4	42	4
2008–09	Polonia Warsaw	29	1	29	1
2009–10	Nottingham F	35	3		
2010–11	Nottingham F	26	2	61	5

McCLEARY, Garath (M) 89 4
H: 5 10 W: 12 06 b.Oxford 15-5-87
Source: Bromley.

2007–08	Nottingham F	8	1		
2008–09	Nottingham F	39	1		
2009–10	Nottingham F	24	0		
2010–11	Nottingham F	18	2	89	4

McGOLDRICK, David (F) 157 28
H: 6 1 W: 11 10 b.Nottingham 29-11-87
Source: Schoolboy.

2003–04	Notts Co	4	0		
2004–05	Notts Co	0	0		
2005–06	Southampton	1	0		
2005–06	*Notts Co*	6	0	10	0
2006–07	Southampton	9	0		
2006–07	*Bournemouth*	12	6	12	6
2007–08	Southampton	8	0		
2007–08	*Port Vale*	17	2	17	2
2008–09	Southampton	46	12	64	12
2009–10	Nottingham F	33	3		
2010–11	Nottingham F	21	5	54	8

McGUGAN, Lewis (M) 137 29
H: 5 9 W: 11 06 b.Long Eaton 25-10-88
Source: Scholar.

2006–07	Nottingham F	13	2		
2007–08	Nottingham F	33	6		
2008–09	Nottingham F	33	5		
2009–10	Nottingham F	18	3		
2010–11	Nottingham F	40	13	137	29

McKENNA, Paul (M) 489 33
H: 5 7 W: 11 12 b.Eccleston 20-10-77
Source: Trainee.

1995–96	Preston NE	0	0		
1996–97	Preston NE	5	1		
1997–98	Preston NE	5	0		
1998–99	Preston NE	36	0		
1999–2000	Preston NE	24	2		
2000–01	Preston NE	44	5		
2001–02	Preston NE	38	4		
2002–03	Preston NE	41	3		
2003–04	Preston NE	39	6		
2004–05	Preston NE	39	3		
2005–06	Preston NE	41	2		
2006–07	Preston NE	33	2		
2007–08	Preston NE	33	0		
2008–09	Preston NE	44	2	422	30
2009–10	Nottingham F	35	1		
2010–11	Nottingham F	32	2	67	3

MOLONEY, Brendan (M) 51 2
H: 6 1 W: 11 12 b.Killarney 18-1-89
Source: Scholar. *Honours:* Eire Under-21.

2005–06	Nottingham F	0	0		
2006–07	Nottingham F	1	0		
2007–08	Nottingham F	2	0		
2007–08	*Chesterfield*	9	1	9	1
2008–09	Nottingham F	12	0		
2009–10	Nottingham F	0	0		
2009–10	*Notts Co*	18	1	18	1
2009–10	*Scunthorpe U*	3	0	3	0
2010–11	Nottingham F	6	0	21	0

MORGAN, Wes (D) 335 12
H: 6 2 W: 14 00 b.Nottingham 21-1-84
Source: Dunkirk.
2002-03 Nottingham F 0 0
2002-03 *Kidderminster H* 5 1 5 1
2003-04 Nottingham F 32 2
2004-05 Nottingham F 43 1
2005-06 Nottingham F 43 2
2006-07 Nottingham F 38 0
2007-08 Nottingham F 42 1
2008-09 Nottingham F 42 1
2009-10 Nottingham F 44 3
2010-11 Nottingham F 46 1 330 11

MOUSSI, Guy (M) 164 5
H: 6 1 W: 12 11 b.Paris 23-1-85
2004-05 Angers 15 1
2005-06 Angers 9 0
2006-07 Angers 32 0
2007-08 Angers 35 1 91 2
2008-09 Nottingham F 15 0
2009-10 Nottingham F 27 3
2010-11 Nottingham F 31 0 73 3

RODNEY, Nialle (F) 6 0
H: 6 1 W: 11 11 b.Nottingham 28-2-91
Source: Scholar.
2008-09 Nottingham F 0 0
2009-10 Nottingham F 0 0
2010-11 Nottingham F 3 0 3 0
2010-11 *Burton Alb* 3 0 3 0

SMITH, Paul (G) 232 0
H: 6 3 W: 14 00 b.Epsom 17-12-79
Source: Walton & Hersham.
1998-99 Charlton Ath 0 0
1998-99 *Brentford* 0 0
1999-2000 Charlton Ath 0 0
From Carshalton Ath.
2000-01 Brentford 2 0
2001-02 Brentford 18 0
2002-03 Brentford 43 0
2003-04 Brentford 24 0 87 0
2003-04 Southampton 0 0
2004-05 Southampton 6 0
2005-06 Southampton 9 0 15 0
2006-07 Nottingham F 45 0
2007-08 Nottingham F 46 0
2008-09 Nottingham F 28 0
2009-10 Nottingham F 0 0
2010-11 Nottingham F 0 0 120 0
2010-11 *Middlesbrough* 10 0 10 0

THORNHILL, Matt (M) 62 8
H: 5 9 W: 12 00 b.Nottingham 11-10-88
Source: Scholar.
2007-08 Nottingham F 14 2
2008-09 Nottingham F 24 3
2009-10 Nottingham F 0 0
2009-10 *Brighton & HA* 7 0 7 0
2009-10 *Cheltenham T* 17 3 17 3
2010-11 Nottingham F 0 0 38 5
Transferred to Hibernian January 2011.

TUDGAY, Marcus (F) 309 73
H: 5 10 W: 12 04 b.Shoreham 3-2-83
Source: Trainee.
2002-03 Derby Co 8 0
2003-04 Derby Co 29 6
2004-05 Derby Co 34 9
2005-06 Derby Co 21 2 92 17
2005-06 Sheffield W 18 5
2006-07 Sheffield W 40 11
2007-08 Sheffield W 35 7
2008-09 Sheffield W 42 14
2009-10 Sheffield W 43 10
2010-11 Sheffield W 17 2 195 49
2010-11 Nottingham F 22 7 22 7

TYSON, Nathan (F) 314 80
H: 5 10 W: 10 02 b.Reading 4-5-82
Source: Trainee. *Honours:* England Under-20.
1999-2000 Reading 1 0
2000-01 Reading 0 0
2001-02 Reading 1 0
2001-02 *Swansea C* 11 1 11 1
2001-02 *Cheltenham T* 8 1 8 1
2002-03 Reading 23 1
2003-04 Reading 8 0 33 1
2003-04 Wycombe W 21 9
2004-05 Wycombe W 42 22
2005-06 Wycombe W 15 11 78 42
2005-06 Nottingham F 28 10
2006-07 Nottingham F 24 7
2007-08 Nottingham F 34 9
2008-09 Nottingham F 35 5
2009-10 Nottingham F 33 2
2010-11 Nottingham F 30 2 184 35

WATSON, Karlton (D) 0 0
b.Peterborough 30-4-92
Source: Scholar.
2010-11 Nottingham F 0 0

WILSON, Kelvin (D) 228 4
H: 6 2 W: 12 11 b.Nottingham 3-9-85
Source: Scholar.
2003-04 Notts Co 3 0
2004-05 Notts Co 41 2
2005-06 Notts Co 34 1 78 3
2005-06 *Preston NE* 6 0
2006-07 *Preston NE* 21 1 27 1
2007-08 Nottingham F 42 0
2008-09 Nottingham F 36 0
2009-10 Nottingham F 35 0
2010-11 Nottingham F 10 0 123 0

NOTTS CO (58)

BISHOP, Neil (M) 169 5
H: 6 1 W: 12 10 b.Stockton 7-8-81
Source: Billingham T, Gateshead, Spennymoor U, Whitby T, Scarborough, York C.
2007-08 Barnet 39 2
2008-09 Barnet 44 1 83 3
2009-10 Notts Co 43 1
2010-11 Notts Co 43 1 86 2

BRANDY, Febian (F) 64 8
H: 5 5 W: 10 00 b.Manchester 4-2-89
Source: Scholar. *Honours:* England Youth, Under-20.
2006-07 Manchester U 0 0
2007-08 Manchester U 0 0
2007-08 *Swansea C* 19 3
2008-09 Manchester U 0 0
2008-09 *Swansea C* 14 0 33 3
2008-09 *Hereford U* 15 4 15 4
2009-10 Manchester U 0 0
2009-10 *Gillingham* 7 1 7 1
2010-11 Notts Co 9 0 9 0

BURCH, Rob (G) 115 0
H: 6 2 W: 12 13 b.Yeovil 8-10-83
Source: Trainee. *Honours:* England Under-20.
2002-03 Tottenham H 0 0
2003-04 Tottenham H 0 0
2004-05 Tottenham H 0 0
2004-05 *West Ham U* 0 0
2005-06 Tottenham H 0 0
2006-07 *Bristol C* 0 0
2006-07 Tottenham H 0 0
2007-08 *Barnet* 6 0 6 0
2007-08 *Sheffield W* 2 0 2 0
2008-09 Lincoln C 46 0
2009-10 Lincoln C 46 0 92 0
2010-11 Notts Co 15 0 15 0

BURGESS, Ben (F) 311 85
H: 6 3 W: 14 04 b.Buxton 9-11-81
Source: Trainee. *Honours:* Eire Youth, Under-21.
1998-99 Blackburn R 0 0
1999-2000 Blackburn R 2 0
2000-01 Blackburn R 0 0
2000-01 *Northern Spirit* 27 16 27 16
2001-02 Blackburn R 0 0
2001-02 *Brentford* 43 17 43 17
2002-03 *Stockport Co* 19 4 19 4
2002-03 *Oldham Ath* 7 0 7 0
2002-03 Hull C 7 4
2003-04 Hull C 44 18
2004-05 Hull C 2 0
2005-06 Hull C 14 2
2006-07 Hull C 3 0 70 24
2006-07 Blackpool 27 2
2007-08 Blackpool 35 9
2008-09 Blackpool 29 6
2009-10 Blackpool 35 6 126 23
2010-11 Notts Co 17 1 17 1

CHILVERS, Liam (D) 247 6
H: 6 2 W: 12 03 b.Chelmsford 6-11-81
Source: Scholar.
2000-01 Arsenal 0 0
2000-01 *Northampton T* 7 0 7 0
2001-02 Arsenal 0 0
2001-02 *Notts Co* 9 1
2002-03 Arsenal 0 0
2002-03 *Colchester U* 6 0
2003-04 Arsenal 0 0
2003-04 *Colchester U* 32 0
2004-05 Colchester U 41 1
2005-06 Colchester U 34 2 113 3
2006-07 Preston NE 45 2
2007-08 Preston NE 28 0
2008-09 Preston NE 1 0
2009-10 Preston NE 23 0 97 2
2010-11 Notts Co 21 0 30 1

DEMBA-NYREN, Njogu (F) 258 79
H: 6 2 W: 12 08 b.Banjul 26-6-79
Honours: Gambia 11 full caps, 2 goals.
1998 Falu 10 1
1999 Falu 21 19 31 20
2000 Hacken 11 1
2001 Hacken 18 3 29 4
2001-02 Giannina 15 5 15 5
2002-03 Aris Salonika 22 12 22 12
2003-04 Levski 10 0 10 0
2003-04 Panathinaikos 5 0
2004-05 Panathinaikos 4 0 9 0
2004-05 Kerkyra 7 1 7 1
2005-06 Esbjerg 19 6
2006-07 Esbjerg 25 8
2007-08 Esbjerg 17 7 61 21
2008 Brann 16 3 16 3
2008-09 Odense 16 8
2009-10 Odense 30 4
2010-11 Odense 0 0 46 12
2010-11 Notts Co 12 1 12 1

EDWARDS, Mike (D) 455 26
H: 6 0 W: 12 10 b.Hessle 25-4-80
Source: Trainee.
1997-98 Hull C 21 0
1998-99 Hull C 30 0
1999-2000 Hull C 40 1
2000-01 Hull C 42 4
2001-02 Hull C 39 1
2002-03 Hull C 6 0 178 6
2002-03 *Colchester U* 5 0 5 0
2003-04 Grimsby T 33 1 33 1
2004-05 Notts Co 9 0
2005-06 Notts Co 46 7
2006-07 Notts Co 45 3
2007-08 Notts Co 19 1
2008-09 Notts Co 43 2
2009-10 Notts Co 40 5
2010-11 Notts Co 37 1 239 19

FOX, Nathan (M) 1 0
H: 5m 10 W: 12 02 b.Leicester 14-11-92
Source: Scholar.
2009-10 Notts Co 1 0
2010-11 Notts Co 0 0 1 0

GOBERN, Lewis (M) 66 4
H: 5 10 W: 11 07 b.Birmingham 28-1-85
Source: Scholar.
2003-04 Wolverhampton W 0 0
2004-05 Wolverhampton W 0 0
2004-05 *Hartlepool U* 1 0 1 0
2005-06 Wolverhampton W 1 0
2005-06 *Blackpool* 8 1 8 1
2005-06 *Bury* 7 1 7 1
2006-07 Wolverhampton W 12 2
2007-08 Wolverhampton W 0 0
2008-09 Wolverhampton W 0 0 13 2
2008-09 *Colchester U* 12 0 12 0
2009-10 Milton Keynes D 20 0
2010-11 Milton Keynes D 0 0 20 0
2010-11 *Notts Co* 5 0 5 0

GOW, Alan (M) 239 48
H: 6 0 W: 11 00 b.Clydebank 9-10-82
Honours: Scotland B.
2000-01 Clydebank 3 0
2001-02 Clydebank 5 0 8 0
2002-03 Airdrie U 27 5
2003-04 Airdrie U 32 12
2004-05 Airdrie U 26 9 85 26
2005-06 Falkirk 34 6

2006–07 Falkirk 36 7 **70 13**
2007–08 Rangers 0 0
On loan from Rangers.
2008–09 Blackpool 17 5 **17 5**
2008–09 Norwich C 13 0 **13 0**
2009–10 Plymouth Arg 14 2 **14 2**
2009–10 *Hibernian* 7 0 **7 0**
2010–11 Motherwell 9 1 **9 1**
2010–11 Notts Co 16 1 **16 1**

GROF, David (G) **0 0**
H: 6 3 W: 14 02 b.Budapest 17-4-89
2008–09 Hibernian 0 0
2009–10 Hibernian 0 0
2010–11 Notts Co 0 0

HARLEY, Jon (D) **371 14**
H: 5 8 W: 10 03 b.Maidstone 26-9-79
Source: Trainee. *Honours:* England Under-21.
1996–97 Chelsea 0 0
1997–98 Chelsea 3 0
1998–99 Chelsea 0 0
1999–2000 Chelsea 17 2
2000–01 Chelsea 10 0 **30 2**
2000–01 *Wimbledon* 6 2 **6 2**
2001–02 Fulham 10 0
2002–03 Fulham 11 1
2002–03 *Sheffield U* 9 1
2003–04 Fulham 4 0 **25 1**
2003–04 *Sheffield U* 5 0
2003–04 West Ham U 15 1 **15 1**
2004–05 Sheffield U 44 2
2005–06 Sheffield U 4 0 **62 3**
2005–06 Burnley 41 2
2006–07 Burnley 45 1
2007–08 Burnley 33 0 **119 3**
2008–09 Watford 37 1
2009–10 Watford 38 1 **75 2**
2010–11 Notts Co 39 0 **39 0**

HAWLEY, Karl (F) **207 51**
H: 5 8 W: 12 02 b.Walsall 6-12-81
Source: Scholar.
2000–01 Walsall 0 0
2001–02 Walsall 1 0
2002–03 Walsall 0 0
2002–03 *Raith R* 17 7
2003–04 Walsall 0 0 **1 0**
2003–04 *Raith R* 11 2 **28 9**
2004–05 Carlisle U 0 0
2005–06 Carlisle U 46 22
2006–07 Carlisle U 32 12 **78 34**
2007–08 Preston NE 25 3
2008–09 Preston NE 5 0 **30 3**
2008–09 *Northampton T* 11 2 **11 2**
2008–09 *Colchester U* 4 0 **4 0**
2009–10 Notts Co 31 3
2010–11 Notts Co 24 0 **55 3**

HUGHES, Lee (F) **381 173**
H: 5 10 W: 12 00 b.Smethwick 22-5-76
Source: Kidderminster H.
1997–98 WBA 37 14
1998–99 WBA 42 31
1999–2000 WBA 36 12
2000–01 WBA 41 21
2001–02 Coventry C 38 14
2002–03 Coventry C 4 1 **42 15**
2002–03 WBA 23 0
2003–04 WBA 32 11 **211 89**
2007–08 Oldham Ath 18 7
2008–09 Oldham Ath 37 18 **55 25**
2008–09 *Blackpool* 3 1 **3 1**
2009–10 Notts Co 39 30
2010–11 Notts Co 31 13 **70 43**

HUNT, Stephen (D) **152 7**
H: 6 2 W: 13 00 b.Southampton 11-11-84
Source: Southampton Scholar.
2004–05 Colchester U 20 1
2005–06 Colchester U 2 0 **22 1**
2006–07 Notts Co 32 1
2007–08 Notts Co 37 2
2008–09 Notts Co 11 0
2009–10 Notts Co 32 1
2010–11 Notts Co 4 0 **116 4**
2010–11 *Lincoln C* 14 2 **14 2**

JUDGE, Alan (F) **73 8**
H: 5 6 W: 11 03 b.Dublin 11-11-88
Honours: Eire Under-21.
2006–07 Blackburn R 0 0

2007–08 Blackburn R 0 0
2008–09 Blackburn R 0 0
2008–09 *Plymouth Arg* 17 2
2009–10 Blackburn R 0 0
2009–10 *Plymouth Arg* 37 5 **54 7**
2010–11 Blackburn R 0 0
2010–11 Notts Co 19 1 **19 1**

LEE, Graeme (D) **448 35**
H: 6 2 W: 13 07 b.Middlesbrough 31-5-78
Source: Trainee.
1995–96 Hartlepool U 6 0
1996–97 Hartlepool U 24 0
1997–98 Hartlepool U 37 3
1998–99 Hartlepool U 24 3
1999–2000 Hartlepool U 38 7
2000–01 Hartlepool U 6 0
2001–02 Hartlepool U 39 4
2002–03 Hartlepool U 45 2
2003–04 Sheffield W 30 3
2004–05 Sheffield W 22 1
2005–06 Sheffield W 15 1 **67 5**
2005–06 Doncaster R 20 1
2006–07 Doncaster R 39 4
2007–08 Doncaster R 1 0 **60 5**
2007–08 *Hartlepool U* 3 0 **222 19**
2007–08 *Shrewsbury T* 5 0 **5 0**
2008–09 Bradford C 44 2 **44 2**
2009–10 Notts Co 32 4
2010–11 Notts Co 18 0 **50 4**

NELSON, Stuart (G) **179 0**
H: 6 1 W: 12 12 b.Stroud 17-9-81
Source: Doncaster R, Hucknall T.
2003–04 Brentford 9 0
2004–05 Brentford 43 0
2005–06 Brentford 45 0
2006–07 Brentford 19 0 **116 0**
2007–08 Leyton Orient 30 0 **30 0**
2008–09 Norwich C 0 0
2010–11 Notts Co 33 0 **33 0**

NICHOLAS, George (M) **1 0**
Source: Scholar.
2010–11 Notts Co 1 0 **1 0**

PEARCE, Krystian (D) **89 2**
H: 6 1 W: 13 05 b.Birmingham 5-1-90
Source: Scholar. *Honours:* England Youth.
2006–07 Birmingham C 0 0
2007–08 Birmingham C 0 0
2007–08 *Port Vale* 12 0 **12 0**
2007–08 *Notts Co* 8 1
2008–09 Birmingham C 0 0
2008–09 *Scunthorpe U* 39 0 **39 0**
2009–10 Birmingham C 0 0
2009–10 *Peterborough U* 2 0 **2 0**
2009–10 *Huddersfield T* 1 0 **1 0**
2010–11 Notts Co 27 1 **35 2**

RAVENHILL, Ricky (M) **280 20**
H: 5 10 W: 11 02 b.Doncaster 16-1-81
Source: Barnsley Trainee.
2003–04 Doncaster R 36 3
2004–05 Doncaster R 35 3
2005–06 Doncaster R 27 3 **98 9**
2006–07 Chester C 3 0 **3 0**
2006–07 Grimsby T 17 2 **17 2**
2006–07 Darlington 15 1
2007–08 Darlington 35 3
2008–09 Darlington 38 2 **88 6**
2008–09 Notts Co 0 0
2009–10 Notts Co 40 3
2010–11 Notts Co 34 0 **74 3**

RODGERS, Luke (F) **307 92**
H: 5 8 W: 11 00 b.Birmingham 1-1-82
Source: Trainee.
1999–2000 Shrewsbury T 6 1
2000–01 Shrewsbury T 26 7
2001–02 Shrewsbury T 38 22
2002–03 Shrewsbury T 36 16
2003–04 Shrewsbury T 0 0
2004–05 Shrewsbury T 36 6 **142 52**
2005–06 Crewe Alex 26 6
2006–07 Crewe Alex 12 3 **38 9**
2006–07 Port Vale 8 3
2007–08 Port Vale 36 9
2008–09 Port Vale 15 3 **59 15**
2008–09 Yeovil T 22 3 **22 3**
2009–10 Notts Co 42 13
2010–11 Notts Co 4 0 **46 13**
Transferred to NY Red Bulls December 2010.

SMITH, Kevin (F) **65 22**
H: 5 11 W: 11 09 b.Edinburgh 20-8-87
Source: Scholar.
2003–04 Leeds U 0 0
2004–05 Leeds U 0 0
2005–06 Leeds U 0 0
2005–06 Sunderland 0 0
2006–07 Sunderland 0 0
2006–07 Dundee 8 0 **8 0**
2006–07 Wrexham 8 1 **8 1**
2007–08 Sunderland 0 0
2008–09 Dundee U 0 0
2008–09 *Raith R* 28 18
2009–10 Dundee U 3 0 **3 0**
2009–10 *Raith R* 5 2 **33 20**
2010–11 Notts Co 13 1 **13 1**

SODJE, Sam (D) **164 19**
H: 6 0 W: 12 00 b.Greenwich 29-5-79
Source: Stevenage B, Margate. *Honours:* Nigeria 5 full caps.
2004–05 Brentford 40 7
2005–06 Brentford 43 5 **83 12**
2006–07 Reading 3 0
2006–07 WBA 7 1 **7 1**
2007–08 Reading 0 0
2007–08 *Charlton Ath* 27 2
2008–09 Reading 0 0
2008–09 *Watford* 1 0 **1 0**
2008–09 *Leeds U* 5 0 **5 0**
2009–10 Reading 0 0 **3 0**
2009–10 *Charlton Ath* 27 4 **54 6**
2010–11 Notts Co 11 0 **11 0**

SPICER, John (M) **194 14**
H: 5 11 W: 11 07 b.Romford 13-9-83
Source: Scholar. *Honours:* England Schools, Youth, Under-20.
2001–02 Arsenal 0 0
2002–03 Arsenal 0 0
2003–04 Arsenal 0 0
2004–05 Arsenal 0 0
2004–05 Bournemouth 39 6
2005–06 Bournemouth 4 0 **43 6**
2005–06 Burnley 34 3
2006–07 Burnley 11 1
2007–08 Burnley 24 0 **69 4**
2008–09 Doncaster R 30 1
2009–10 Doncaster R 20 0 **50 1**
2009–10 *Leyton Orient* 9 1 **9 1**
2010–11 Notts Co 23 2 **23 2**

THOMPSON, John (D) **248 9**
H: 6 0 W: 12 01 b.Dublin 12-10-81
Source: Home Farm. *Honours:* Eire Youth, Under-21, 1 full cap.
1999–2000 Nottingham F 0 0
2000–01 Nottingham F 0 0
2001–02 Nottingham F 8 0
2002–03 Nottingham F 20 3
2003–04 Nottingham F 32 1
2004–05 Nottingham F 20 0
2005–06 Nottingham F 35 3
2006–07 Nottingham F 14 0 **129 7**
2006–07 Tranmere R 12 0 **12 0**
2007–08 Oldham Ath 7 0
2008–09 Oldham Ath 0 0 **7 0**
2008–09 Notts Co 35 2
2009–10 Notts Co 40 0
2010–11 Notts Co 25 0 **100 2**

WESTCARR, Craig (F) **116 23**
H: 5 11 W: 11 04 b.Nottingham 29-1-85
Source: Scholar. *Honours:* England Youth.
2001–02 Nottingham F 8 0
2002–03 Nottingham F 11 1
2003–04 Nottingham F 3 0
2004–05 Nottingham F 1 0 **23 1**
2004–05 *Lincoln C* 6 1 **6 1**
2004–05 *Milton Keynes D* 4 0 **4 0**
From Cambridge U, Kettering T.
2009–10 Notts Co 42 9
From Cambridge U, Kettering T.
2010–11 Notts Co 41 12 **83 21**

WHOLEY, Jake (D) **1 0**
b.Nottingham 1-12-93
Source: Scholar.
2010–11 Notts Co 1 0 **1 0**

OLDHAM ATH (59)

ABALIMBA, Medi (M)　0　0
b. 14-10-92
Source: Southend U.

| 2009–10 | Derby Co | 0 | 0 | | |
| 2010–11 | Oldham Ath | 0 | 0 | | |

ALESSANDRA, Lewis (F)　67　8
H: 5 9　W: 11 07　b.Heywood 8-2-89
Source: Scholar.

2007–08	Oldham Ath	15	2		
2008–09	Oldham Ath	32	5		
2009–10	Oldham Ath	1	0		
2010–11	Oldham Ath	19	1	67	8

BEMBO-LITA, Djenny (F)　3　0
H: 5 10　W: 11 05　b.Kinshasa 9-11-91
Source: Scholar.

| 2009–10 | Oldham Ath | 0 | 0 | | |
| 2010–11 | Oldham Ath | 3 | 0 | 3 | 0 |

BLACK, Paul (D)　47　1
H: 6 0　W: 12 10　b.Middleton 18-5-90
Source: Scholar.

2007–08	Oldham Ath	2	0		
2008–09	Oldham Ath	3	0		
2009–10	Oldham Ath	13	1		
2010–11	Oldham Ath	29	0	47	1

BRILL, Dean (G)　147　0
H: 6 2　W: 14 05　b.Luton 2-12-85
Source: Scholar.

2003–04	Luton T	5	0		
2004–05	Luton T	0	0		
2005–06	Luton T	5	0		
2006–07	Luton T	11	0		
2006–07	Gillingham	8	0	8	0
2007–08	Luton T	37	0		
2008–09	Luton T	23	0	81	0
2009–10	Oldham Ath	28	0		
2010–11	Oldham Ath	30	0	58	0

BROOKE, Ryan (F)　29　2
H: 6 1　W: 11 07　b.Congleton 4-10-90
Source: Scholar.

2008–09	Oldham Ath	1	1		
2009–10	Oldham Ath	15	1		
2010–11	Oldham Ath	13	0	29	2

BURNS, Ryan (M)　1　0
b.Belfast 8-9-92
Source: Scholar.

| 2010–11 | Oldham Ath | 1 | 0 | 1 | 0 |

CHRISTOPHE, Jean-Francois (M)　85　6
H: 6 1　W: 13 01　b.Creil 13-6-82
Source: Lens.

2007–08	Portsmouth	0	0		
2007–08	*Bournemouth*	10	1	10	1
2007–08	*Yeovil T*	5	0	5	0
2008–09	Portsmouth	0	0		
2008–09	Southend U	33	4		
2009–10	Southend U	36	1		
2010–11	Southend U	0	0	69	5
2010–11	Oldham Ath	1	0	1	0

Transferred to Compiegne November 2010.

DICKOV, Paul (F)　418　98
H: 5 6　W: 10 06　b.Livingston 1-11-72
Source: Trainee. *Honours:* Scotland Schools, Youth, Under-21, 10 full caps, 1 goal.

1992–93	Arsenal	3	2		
1993–94	Arsenal	1	0		
1993–94	*Luton T*	15	1	15	1
1993–94	*Brighton & HA*	8	5	8	5
1994–95	Arsenal	9	0		
1995–96	Arsenal	7	1		
1996–97	Arsenal	1	0	21	3
1996–97	Manchester C	29	5		
1997–98	Manchester C	30	9		
1998–99	Manchester C	35	10		
1999–2000	Manchester C	34	5		
2000–01	Manchester C	21	4		
2001–02	Manchester C	7	0		
2001–02	Leicester C	12	4		
2002–03	Leicester C	42	17		
2003–04	Leicester C	35	11		
2004–05	Blackburn R	29	9		
2005–06	Blackburn R	21	5	50	14
2006–07	Manchester C	16	0		
2007–08	Manchester C	0	0	172	33
2007–08	*Crystal Palace*	9	0	9	0
2007–08	*Blackpool*	11	6	11	6
2008–09	Leicester C	20	2		
2009–10	Leicester C	1	0	110	34
2009–10	*Derby Co*	16	2	16	2
2009–10	*Leeds U*	4	0	4	0
2010–11	Oldham Ath	2	0	2	0

DIKABA, Rodrigue (D)　95　1
H: 5 8　W: 11 09　b.Toulouse 29-10-85
Source: Arras. *Honours:* DR Congo 11 full caps.

2006–07	Beauvais	22	0		
2007–08	Beauvais	36	1		
2008–09	Beauvais	29	0	87	1
2009–10	Ceahlaul	7	0	7	0
2010–11	Oldham Ath	1	0	1	0

EVINA, Cedric (D)　27　2
H: 5 11　W: 12 08　b.Cameroon 16-11-91
Source: Scholar.

2009–10	Arsenal	0	0		
2010–11	Arsenal	0	0		
2010–11	Oldham Ath	27	2	27	2

FEENEY, Warren (F)　293　70
H: 5 8　W: 12 04　b.Belfast 17-1-81
Source: Trainee. *Honours:* Northern Ireland Schools, Youth, Under-21, 42 full caps, 5 goals.

1997–98	Leeds U	0	0		
1998–99	Leeds U	0	0		
1999–2000	Leeds U	0	0		
2000–01	Leeds U	0	0		
2000–01	Bournemouth	10	4		
2001–02	Bournemouth	37	13		
2002–03	Bournemouth	21	7		
2003–04	Bournemouth	40	12	108	36
2004–05	Stockport Co	31	15	31	15
2004–05	Luton T	6	0		
2005–06	Luton T	42	6		
2006–07	Luton T	29	2	77	8
2006–07	*Cardiff C*	6	0		
2007–08	Cardiff C	5	0		
2007–08	*Swansea C*	10	5	10	5
2008–09	*Dundee U*	23	6	23	6
2008–09	Cardiff C	0	0		
2009–10	Cardiff C	9	0	20	0
2009–10	*Sheffield W*	1	0	1	0
2010–11	Oldham Ath	23	0	23	0

FLEMING, Greg (G)　48　0
H: 5 11　W: 12 09　b.Dunfermline 27-9-86
Source: Livingston. *Honours:* Scotland Under-21.

2006–07	Gretna	2	0		
2007–08	Gretna	28	0	30	0
2008–09	Oldham Ath	18	0		
2009–10	Oldham Ath	0	0		
2010–11	Oldham Ath	0	0	18	0

Transferred to Galway U January 2011.

FURMAN, Dean (M)　113　9
H: 6 0　W: 11 08　b.Cape Town 22-6-88
Source: Chelsea Scholar.

2007–08	Rangers	1	0	1	0
2008–09	*Bradford C*	32	4	32	4
2009–10	Oldham Ath	38	0		
2010–11	Oldham Ath	42	5	80	5

GREGAN, Sean (M)　620　19
H: 6 2　W: 14 00　b.Guisborough 29-3-74
Source: Trainee.

1991–92	Darlington	17	0		
1992–93	Darlington	17	1		
1993–94	Darlington	23	1		
1994–95	Darlington	25	2		
1995–96	Darlington	38	0		
1996–97	Darlington	16	0	136	4
1996–97	Preston NE	21	1		
1997–98	Preston NE	35	2		
1998–99	Preston NE	41	3		
1999–2000	Preston NE	33	3		
2000–01	Preston NE	41	2		
2001–02	Preston NE	41	1	212	12
2002–03	WBA	36	1		
2003–04	WBA	43	1		
2004–05	WBA	0	0	79	2
2004–05	Leeds U	35	0		
2005–06	Leeds U	28	0		
2006–07	Leeds U	1	0	64	0
2006–07	Oldham Ath	27	0		
2007–08	Oldham Ath	15	0		
2008–09	Oldham Ath	40	0		
2009–10	Oldham Ath	46	1		
2010–11	Oldham Ath	1	0	129	1

HAZELL, Reuben (D)　349　12
H: 5 11　W: 12 05　b.Birmingham 24-4-79
Source: Trainee.

1996–97	Aston Villa	0	0		
1997–98	Aston Villa	0	0		
1998–99	Aston Villa	0	0		
1999–2000	Tranmere R	23	1		
2000–01	Tranmere R	13	0		
2001–02	Tranmere R	6	0	42	1
2001–02	Torquay U	19	0		
2002–03	Torquay U	46	1		
2003–04	Torquay U	19	1		
2004–05	Torquay U	0	0	84	2
2005–06	Chesterfield	33	0		
2006–07	Chesterfield	39	2		
2007–08	Chesterfield	0	0	72	2
2007–08	Oldham Ath	34	1		
2008–09	Oldham Ath	43	3		
2009–10	Oldham Ath	41	3		
2010–11	Oldham Ath	33	0	151	7

JARRETT, Jason (M)　261　9
H: 6 1　W: 13 10　b.Bury 14-9-79
Source: Trainee.

1998–99	Blackpool	2	0		
1999–2000	Blackpool	0	0	2	0
1999–2000	Wrexham	1	0	1	0
2000–01	Bury	25	2		
2001–02	Bury	37	2	62	4
2001–02	Wigan Ath	5	0		
2002–03	Wigan Ath	35	0		
2003–04	Wigan Ath	41	1		
2004–05	Wigan Ath	14	0	95	1
2004–05	*Stoke C*	2	0	2	0
2005–06	Norwich C	11	0	11	0
2005–06	*Plymouth Arg*	7	0	7	0
2006–07	Preston NE	10	1		
2006–07	Preston NE	5	0		
2006–07	*Hull C*	3	0	3	0
2006–07	*Leicester C*	13	0	13	0
2007–08	Preston NE	0	0		
2007–08	*QPR*	2	0	2	0
2007–08	*Oldham Ath*	15	3		
2008–09	Preston NE	3	0	18	1
2008–09	Brighton & HA	13	0	13	0
2009–10	Port Vale	9	0	9	0
2010–11	Oldham Ath	8	0	23	3

JONES, Richie (M)　119　8
H: 6 0　W: 11 00　b.Manchester 26-9-86
Source: Scholar. *Honours:* England Youth.

2004–05	Manchester U	0	0		
2005–06	Manchester U	0	0		
2006–07	Manchester U	0	0		
2006–07	*Colchester U*	6	0	6	0
2006–07	*Barnsley*	4	0	4	0
2007–08	Manchester U	0	0		
2007–08	*Yeovil T*	9	0	9	0
2008–09	Hartlepool U	36	3		
2009–10	Hartlepool U	33	4	69	7
2010–11	Oldham Ath	31	1	31	1

KELLY, Dean (F)　13　1
H: 5 9　W: 11 00　b.Dublin 18-9-91
Source: Tolkar R, Crumlin U.

| 2010–11 | Oldham Ath | 13 | 1 | 13 | 1 |

LEE, Kieran (D)　82　3
H: 6 1　W: 12 00　b.Stalybridge 22-6-88
Source: Scholar.

2006–07	Manchester U	1	0		
2006–07	Manchester U	0	0	1	0
2007–08	*QPR*	7	0	7	0
2008–09	Oldham Ath	7	0		
2009–10	Oldham Ath	24	1		
2010–11	Oldham Ath	43	2	74	3

McDONALD, Rodney (D)　0　0
b.Liverpool 11-4-92
Source: Stoke C Scholar.

| 2010–11 | Oldham Ath | 0 | 0 | | |

McGRATH, Phillip (M)　1　0
H: 5 9　W: 10 01　b. 7-4-92
Source: Glenavon.

| 2009–10 | Oldham Ath | 0 | 0 | | |
| 2010–11 | Oldham Ath | 1 | 0 | 1 | 0 |

MILLAR, Kirk (M) 12 0
H: 5 9 W: 10 07 b.Belfast 7-7-92
Source: Scholar. Honours: Northern Ireland Under-21.

2008–09	Linfield	1	0	1	0
2009–10	Oldham Ath	6	0		
2010–11	Oldham Ath	5	0	11	0

MORAIS, Filipe (M) 133 11
H: 5 9 W: 11 10 b.Lisbon 21-11-85
Source: Trainee. Honours: Portugal Youth, Under-21.

2003–04	Chelsea	0	0		
2004–05	Chelsea	0	0		
2005–06	Chelsea	0	0		
2005–06	Milton Keynes D	13	0	13	0
2006–07	Millwall	12	1	12	1
2006–07	St Johnstone	13	1		
2007–08	Hibernian	28	1		
2008–09	Hibernian	2	0	30	1
2008–09	Inverness CT	12	3	12	3
2009–10	St Johnstone	30	2	43	3
2010–11	Oldham Ath	23	3	23	3

OLLERENSHAW, Josh (G) 0 0
H: 6 5 W: 12 10 b.Manchester 5-10-90
Source: Scholar.

| 2009–10 | Oldham Ath | 0 | 0 | | |
| 2010–11 | Oldham Ath | 0 | 0 | | |

REID, Reuben (F) 132 27
H: 6 0 W: 12 02 b.Bristol 26-7-88
Source: Millfield School.

2005–06	Plymouth Arg	1	0		
2006–07	Plymouth Arg	6	0		
2006–07	Rochdale	2	0	2	0
2006–07	Torquay U	7	2	7	2
2007–08	Plymouth Arg	0	0	7	0
2007–08	Wycombe W	11	1	11	1
2007–08	Brentford	10	1	10	1
2008–09	Rotherham U	41	18	41	18
2009–10	WBA	4	0		
2009–10	Peterborough U	13	0	13	0
2010–11	WBA	0	0	4	0
2010–11	Walsall	18	3	18	3
2010–11	Oldham Ath	19	2	19	2

SMALLEY, Deane (M) 136 22
H: 6 0 W: 11 10 b.Chadderton 5-9-88
Source: Scholar.

2006–07	Oldham Ath	2	0		
2007–08	Oldham Ath	37	2		
2008–09	Oldham Ath	34	5		
2009–10	Oldham Ath	29	3		
2010–11	Oldham Ath	3	0	105	10
2010–11	Rochdale	3	0		
2010–11	Chesterfield	28	12	28	12

STEPHENS, Dale (M) 81 13
H: 5 7 W: 11 04 b.Bolton 12-6-89
Source: Scholar.

2006–07	Bury	3	0		
2007–08	Bury	6	1	9	1
2008–09	Oldham Ath	0	0		
2009–10	Oldham Ath	26	2		
2009–10	Rochdale	6	1	6	1
2010–11	Oldham Ath	34	9	60	11
2010–11	Southampton	6	0	6	0

TARKOWSKI, James (D) 9 0
b.Manchester 19-11-92
Source: Scholar.

| 2010–11 | Oldham Ath | 9 | 0 | 9 | 0 |

TAYLOR, Chris (M) 216 31
H: 5 11 W: 11 00 b.Oldham 20-12-86
Source: Scholar.

2005–06	Oldham Ath	14	0		
2006–07	Oldham Ath	44	4		
2007–08	Oldham Ath	42	5		
2008–09	Oldham Ath	42	10		
2009–10	Oldham Ath	32	1		
2010–11	Oldham Ath	42	11	216	31

TODD, Andy (D) 336 11
H: 5 11 W: 13 04 b.Derby 21-9-74
Source: Trainee.

1991–92	Middlesbrough	0	0		
1992–93	Middlesbrough	0	0		
1993–94	Middlesbrough	3	0		
1994–95	Middlesbrough	5	0	8	0
1994–95	Swindon T	13	0	13	0
1995–96	Bolton W	12	2		
1996–97	Bolton W	15	0		
1997–98	Bolton W	25	0		
1998–99	Bolton W	20	0		
1999–2000	Bolton W	12	0	84	2
1999–2000	Charlton Ath	12	0		
2000–01	Charlton Ath	23	1		
2001–02	Charlton Ath	5	0	40	1
2001–02	Grimsby T	12	3	12	3
2002–03	Blackburn R	12	1		
2003–04	Blackburn R	19	0		
2003–04	Burnley	7	0	7	0
2004–05	Blackburn R	26	1		
2005–06	Blackburn R	22	2		
2006–07	Blackburn R	9	0	88	4
2007–08	Derby Co	19	1		
2008–09	Derby Co	11	0	30	1
2008–09	Northampton T	7	0	7	0
2009–10	Perth Glory	25	0		
2010–11	Perth Glory	16	0	41	0
2010–11	Oldham Ath	6	0	6	0

WINCHESTER, Carl (D) 6 1
b.Belfast 12-4-93
Source: Scholar. Honours: Northern Ireland Under-21, 1 full cap.

| 2010–11 | Oldham Ath | 6 | 1 | 6 | 1 |

OXFORD U (60)

BAKER, Richie (M) 113 7
H: 5 10 W: 11 05 b.Burnley 29-12-87
Source: Preston NE Scholar.

2006–07	Bury	39	5		
2007–08	Bury	32	1		
2008–09	Bury	22	0		
2009–10	Bury	14	1	107	7
2010–11	Oxford U	6	0	6	0

BATT, Damian (D) 50 0
H: 5 10 W: 11 06 b.Hoddesdon 16-9-84
Source: Norwich C Trainee.

| 2005–06 | Barnet | 22 | 0 | 22 | 0 |

From St Albans C, Stevenage, Woking, Fisher Ath, Grays Ath.

| 2010–11 | Oxford U | 28 | 0 | 28 | 0 |

BULMAN, Dannie (M) 207 14
H: 5 9 W: 11 12 b.Ashford 24-1-79
Source: Ashford T.

1998–99	Wycombe W	11	1		
1999–2000	Wycombe W	29	1		
2000–01	Wycombe W	36	4		
2001–02	Wycombe W	46	5		
2002–03	Wycombe W	42	3		
2003–04	Wycombe W	38	0	202	14

From Stevenage, Crawley T.

| 2010–11 | Oxford U | 5 | 0 | 5 | 0 |

Transferred to Crawley T January 2011.

CHAPMAN, Adam (M) 0 0
H: 5 10 W: 11 00 b.Doncaster 29-11-89
Source: Scholar. Honours: Northern Ireland Under-21.

2008–09	Sheffield U	0	0		
2009–10	Sheffield U	0	0		
2010–11	Oxford U	0	0		

CLARKE, Ryan (G) 120 0
H: 6 3 W: 13 00 b.Bristol 30-4-82
Source: Scholar.

2001–02	Bristol R	1	0		
2002–03	Bristol R	2	0		
2003–04	Bristol R	2	0		
2004–05	Bristol R	18	0	23	0
2004–05	Southend U	1	0	1	0
2004–05	Kidderminster H	6	0	6	0

From Salisbury C.

| 2009–10 | Oxford U | 44 | 0 | | |
| 2010–11 | Oxford U | 46 | 0 | 90 | 0 |

CLIST, Simon (D) 119 9
H: 5 9 W: 11 09 b.Bournemouth 13-6-81
Source: Tottenham H Trainee.

1999–2000	Bristol C	9	0		
2000–01	Bristol C	38	4		
2001–02	Bristol C	20	1		
2002–03	Bristol C	3	1		
2002–03	Torquay U	11	2	11	2
2003–04	Bristol C	1	0	71	6
2005–06	Barnet	14	0	14	0

From Forest Green R.

| 2010–11 | Oxford U | 23 | 1 | 23 | 1 |

COLE, Mitchell (M) 45 2
H: 5 11 W: 11 05 b.London 6-10-85
Source: Trainee. Honours: England Youth.

2002–03	West Ham U	0	0		
2003–04	West Ham U	0	0		
2004–05	West Ham U	0	0		

From Grays Ath.

2005–06	Southend U	29	1		
2006–07	Southend U	4	0	33	1
2006–07	Northampton T	8	1	8	1

From Stevenage.

| 2010–11 | Oxford U | 4 | 0 | 4 | 0 |

CONSTABLE, James (F) 81 22
H: 6 2 W: 12 12 b.Malmesbury 4-10-84
Source: Chippenham T.

| 2005–06 | Walsall | 17 | 3 | | |
| 2006–07 | Walsall | 6 | 0 | 23 | 3 |

From Kidderminster H.

2007–08	Shrewsbury T	14	4		
2008–09	Shrewsbury T	0	0	14	4
2010–11	Oxford U	44	15	44	15

CRADDOCK, Tom (F) 121 47
H: 5 11 W: 11 10 b.Durham 14-10-86
Source: Scholar.

2005–06	Middlesbrough	1	0		
2006–07	Middlesbrough	0	0		
2006–07	Wrexham	1	1	1	1
2007–08	Middlesbrough	3	0		
2007–08	Hartlepool U	4	0	4	0
2008–09	Middlesbrough	0	0	4	0
2008–09	Luton T	27	10		
2009–10	Luton T	46	22	73	32
2010–11	Oxford U	39	14	39	14

CREIGHTON, Mark (D) 7 0
H: 6 4 W: 12 02 b.Burton-on-Trent 8-10-81
Source: Moor Green, Paget R, Halesowen T, Redditch U, Bromsgrove R, Willenhall T, Redditch U, Kidderminster H.

| 2010–11 | Oxford U | 7 | 0 | 7 | 0 |

DEERING, Sam (M) 22 2
H: 5 5 W: 10 00 b.Tower Hamlets 26-2-91
Source: Charlton Ath.

| 2010–11 | Oxford U | 6 | 0 | 6 | 0 |
| 2010–11 | Barnet | 16 | 2 | 16 | 2 |

EASTWOOD, Simon (G) 23 0
H: 6 2 W: 13 00 b.Luton 26-6-89
Source: Scholar. Honours: England Youth.

2005–06	Huddersfield T	0	0		
2006–07	Huddersfield T	0	0		
2007–08	Huddersfield T	0	0		
2008–09	Huddersfield T	1	0		
2009–10	Huddersfield T	0	0	1	0
2009–10	Bradford C	22	0	22	0
2010–11	Oxford U	0	0		

GREEN, Matt (M) 78 12
H: 5 8 W: 10 05 b.Bath 2-1-87

2009–10	Torquay U	0	0		
2009–10	Oxford U	42	11		
2010–11	Oxford U	17	1	59	12
2010–11	Cheltenham T	19	0	19	0

HALL, Asa (M) 143 22
H: 6 2 W: 11 09 b.Sandwell 29-11-86
Source: Scholar. Honours: England Youth, Under-20.

2004–05	Birmingham C	0	0		
2005–06	Birmingham C	0	0		
2005–06	Boston U	12	0	12	0
2006–07	Birmingham C	0	0		
2007–08	Birmingham C	0	0		
2007–08	Shrewsbury T	15	3	15	3
2008–09	Luton T	42	10		
2009–10	Luton T	33	5	75	15
2010–11	Oxford U	41	4	41	4

HANSON, Mitch (D) 7 0
H: 6 1 W: 13 07 b.Derby 2-9-88
Source: Scholar.

2007–08	Derby Co	0	0		
2008–09	Derby Co	0	0		
2008–09	Notts Co	5	0	5	0
2009–10	Derby Co	0	0		
2010–11	Derby Co	0	0		
2010–11	Oxford U	2	0	2	0

HESLOP, Simon (M)   47   3
H: 5 11 W: 11 00 b.York 1-5-87
Source: Scholar.

2005–06	Barnsley	0	0		
2006–07	Barnsley	1	0		
2007–08	Barnsley	0	0		
2008–09	Barnsley	0	0		
2008–09	*Grimsby T*	8	0	8	0
2009–10	Barnsley	0	0		
2010–11	Oxford U	38	3	38	3

KINNIBURGH, Steve (D)   17   0
H: 6 0 W: 11 00 b.Glasgow 13-6-89

2007–08	Rangers	0	0		
2008–09	Rangers	0	0		
2008–09	*Queen of the S*	2	0	2	0
2008–09	*St Johnstone*	0	0		
2010–11	Partick Th	4	0	4	0
2010–11	Oxford U	11	0	11	0

McLAREN, Paul (M)   522   25
H: 6 0 W: 13 04 b.High Wycombe 17-11-76
Source: Trainee.

1993–94	Luton T	1	0		
1994–95	Luton T	0	0		
1995–96	Luton T	12	1		
1996–97	Luton T	24	0		
1997–98	Luton T	43	0		
1998–99	Luton T	23	0		
1999–2000	Luton T	29	1		
2000–01	Luton T	35	2	167	4
2001–02	Sheffield W	35	2		
2002–03	Sheffield W	36	4		
2003–04	Sheffield W	25	2	96	8
2004–05	Rotherham U	33	1		
2005–06	Rotherham U	39	3	72	4
2006–07	Tranmere R	42	1		
2007–08	Tranmere R	43	4		
2008–09	Bradford C	34	3	34	3
2009–10	Tranmere R	38	0		
2010–11	Tranmere R	6	0	129	5
2010–11	Oxford U	24	1	24	1

MIDSON, Jack (F)   30   8
H: 5 8 W: 11 07 b.Stevenage 21-7-83
Source: Stevenage B, Chelmsford C (loan), Dagenham & R, Hemel Hempstead (loan), Bishop's Stortford, Histon.

2010–11	Oxford U	21	6	21	6
2010–11	*Southend U*	4	2	4	2
2010–11	*Barnet*	5	0	5	0

PAYNE, Josh (M)   47   3
H: 6 0 W: 11 09 b.Basingstoke 25-11-90
Source: Scholar.

2008–09	West Ham U	2	0		
2008–09	*Cheltenham T*	11	1	11	1
2009–10	West Ham U	0	0		
2009–10	*Colchester U*	3	0	3	0
2009–10	*Wycombe W*	3	1	3	1
2010–11	West Ham U	0	0	2	0
2010–11	*Doncaster R*	0	0		
2010–11	Oxford U	28	1	28	1

POTTER, Alfie (M)   40   2
H: 5 7 W: 9 06 b.Islington 9-1-89
Source: Millwall.

2007–08	Peterborough U	2	0	2	0
From Kettering T.					
2010–11	Oxford U	38	2	38	2

PURKISS, Ben (D)   23   0
H: 6 2 W: 11 00 b.Sheffield 1-4-84

2001–02	Sheffield U	0	0		
2002–03	Sheffield U	0	0		
From Gainsborough T, York C.					
2010–11	Oxford U	23	0	23	0

SANGARE, Djourmin (D)   8   0
H: 6 1 W: 12 08 b.Dunkerque 16-12-83

2003–04	Wasquehal	4	0	4	0
From Redbridge, Chelmsford C, Lewes, St Albans C (loan), Grays Ath, Stafford R, Salisbury C, York C.					
2010–11	Oxford U	4	0	4	0

TONKIN, Anthony (D)   156   0
H: 5 11 W: 12 02 b.Newlyn 17-1-80
Source: Yeovil T.

2002–03	Stockport Co	24	0		
2003–04	Stockport Co	0	0	24	0
2003–04	Crewe Alex	26	0		
2004–05	Crewe Alex	35	0		
2005–06	Crewe Alex	27	0	88	0
2006–07	Yeovil T	5	0	5	0
From Forest Green R, Cambridge U.					
2010–11	Oxford U	39	0	39	0

WOODLEY, Aaron (F)   0   0
b.Oxford 13-10-92
Source: Scholar.

2010–11	Oxford U	0	0		

WORLEY, Harry (D)   87   2
H: 6 3 W: 13 00 b.Warrington 25-11-88
Source: Scholar.

2005–06	Chelsea	0	0		
2006–07	Chelsea	0	0		
2006–07	*Doncaster R*	10	0	10	0
2007–08	Chelsea	0	0		
2007–08	*Carlisle U*	1	0	1	0
2007–08	*Leicester C*	2	0		
2008–09	Leicester C	0	0		
2008–09	*Luton T*	8	0	8	0
2009–10	Leicester C	0	0	2	0
2009–10	*Crewe Alex*	23	1	23	1
2010–11	Oxford U	43	1	43	1

WRIGHT, Jake (D)   42   0
H: 5 10 W: 11 07 b.Keighley 11-3-86
Source: Scholar.

2005–06	Bradford C	1	0	1	0
From Halifax T, Crawley T.					
2009–10	Brighton & HA	6	0	6	0
2010–11	Oxford U	35	0	35	0

PETERBOROUGH U (61)

BALL, David (F)   37   7
H: 6 0 W: 11 08 b.Whitefield 14-12-89
Source: Scholar.

2007–08	Manchester C	0	0		
2008–09	Manchester C	0	0		
2009–10	Manchester C	0	0		
2010–11	Manchester C	0	0		
2010–11	*Swindon T*	18	2	18	2
2010–11	Peterborough U	19	5	19	5

BASEY, Grant (D)   72   3
H: 6 2 W: 13 12 b.Bromley 30-11-88
Source: Scholar. *Honours:* Wales Under-21.

2007–08	Charlton Ath	8	1		
2007–08	*Brentford*	8	0	8	0
2008–09	Charlton Ath	19	0		
2009–10	Charlton Ath	19	0		
2010–11	Charlton Ath	0	0	46	1
2010–11	*Barnet*	11	1	11	1
2010–11	Peterborough U	7	1	7	1

BENNETT, Ryan (M)   159   11
H: 6 2 W: 11 00 b.Thurrock 6-3-90
Source: Scholar. *Honours:* England Youth.

2006–07	Grimsby T	5	0		
2007–08	Grimsby T	40	1		
2008–09	Grimsby T	45	5		
2009–10	Grimsby T	13	0	103	6
2009–10	Peterborough U	22	1		
2010–11	Peterborough U	34	4	56	5

BOYD, George (M)   193   52
H: 5 10 W: 11 07 b.Chatham 2-10-85
Source: Stevenage B. *Honours:* Scotland B.

2006–07	Peterborough U	20	6		
2007–08	Peterborough U	46	12		
2008–09	Peterborough U	46	9		
2009–10	Peterborough U	32	9		
2009–10	*Nottingham F*	6	1	6	1
2010–11	Peterborough U	43	15	187	51

BREEZE, Matthew (M)   0   0
b.Worcester 6-2-93
Source: Scholar.

2010–11	Peterborough U	0	0		

COLLIS, Steve (G)   88   0
H: 6 3 W: 12 05 b.Harrow 18-3-81
Source: Barnet Juniors.

1999–2000	Barnet	0	0		
2000–01	Nottingham F	0	0		
2001–02	Nottingham F	0	0		
2003–04	Yeovil T	11	0		
2004–05	Yeovil T	9	0		
2005–06	Yeovil T	23	0	43	0
2006–07	Southend U	1	0		
2007–08	Southend U	20	0	21	0
2008–09	*Crewe Alex*	18	0		
2009–10	*Crewe Alex*	1	0	19	0
2009–10	Bristol C	0	0		
2009–10	*Torquay U*	1	0	1	0
2010–11	Peterborough U	0	0		
2010–11	*Northampton T*	4	0	4	0

DAVIES, Arron (M)   176   24
H: 5 9 W: 11 00 b.Cardiff 22-6-84
Source: Trainee. *Honours:* Wales Under-21, 1 full cap.

2002–03	Southampton	0	0		
2003–04	Southampton	0	0		
2003–04	*Barnsley*	4	0	4	0
2004–05	Southampton	0	0		
2004–05	Yeovil T	23	8		
2005–06	Yeovil T	39	8		
2006–07	Yeovil T	39	6		
2007–08	Nottingham F	19	1		
2008–09	Nottingham F	13	0		
2009–10	Nottingham F	0	0	32	1
2009–10	*Brighton & HA*	7	0	7	0
2009–10	*Yeovil T*	10	0	111	22
2010–11	Peterborough U	22	1	22	1

FRECKLINGTON, Lee (M)   175   24
H: 5 8 W: 11 00 b.Lincoln 8-9-85
Source: Scholar. *Honours:* Eire B.

2003–04	Lincoln C	0	0		
2004–05	Lincoln C	3	0		
2005–06	Lincoln C	18	2		
2006–07	Lincoln C	42	8		
2007–08	Lincoln C	34	4		
2008–09	Lincoln C	27	7	124	21
2008–09	Peterborough U	7	0		
2009–10	Peterborough U	35	2		
2010–11	Peterborough U	9	1	51	3

GEOHAGHON, Exodus (D)   47   2
H: 6 7 W: 11 11 b.Birmingham 27-2-85
Source: Sutton Coldfield T, Bromsgrove R, Redditch U, Kettering T, England C.

2009–10	Peterborough U	19	1		
2010–11	Peterborough U	0	0	19	1
2010–11	*Rotherham U*	14	1	14	1
2010–11	*Shrewsbury T*	2	0	2	0
2010–11	*Port Vale*	12	0	12	0

GREEN, Dominic (F)   51   5
H: 5 6 W: 11 02 b.Newham 5-7-89
Source: Scholar.

2007–08	Dagenham & R	12	0		
2008–09	Dagenham & R	2	1	14	1
2008–09	Peterborough U	16	1		
2009–10	Peterborough U	11	1		
2009–10	*Chesterfield*	10	2	10	2
2010–11	Peterborough U	0	0	27	2

GRIFFITHS, Scott (D)   147   1
H: 5 9 W: 11 08 b.Westminster 27-11-85
Source: Aveley.

2007–08	Dagenham & R	41	0		
2008–09	Dagenham & R	44	0		
2009–10	Dagenham & R	13	1	98	1
2009–10	Peterborough U	20	0		
2010–11	Peterborough U	0	0	20	0
2010–11	*Chesterfield*	29	0	29	0

HIBBERT, Dave (F)   160   34
H: 6 2 W: 12 00 b.Eccleshall 28-1-86
Source: Scholar.

2004–05	Port Vale	9	2	9	2
2005–06	Preston NE	10	0		
2006–07	Preston NE	0	0	10	0
2006–07	*Rotherham U*	21	2	21	2
2006–07	*Bradford C*	8	0	8	0
2007–08	Shrewsbury T	44	12		
2008–09	Shrewsbury T	23	3		
2009–10	Shrewsbury T	38	14	105	29
2010–11	Peterborough U	7	1	7	1

HOWE, Rene (F)   119   28
H: 6 0 W: 14 03 b.Bedford 22-10-86
Source: Kettering T.

2007–08	Peterborough U	15	1		
2007–08	*Rochdale*	20	9	20	9
2008–09	Peterborough U	0	0		
2008–09	*Morecambe*	37	10	37	10
2009–10	Peterborough U	0	0		
2009–10	*Lincoln C*	17	5	17	5
2009–10	*Gillingham*	18	2	18	2
2010–11	Peterborough U	0	0	15	1
2010–11	*Bristol R*	12	1	12	1

LANGMEAD, Kelvin (D) 285 24
H: 6 1 W: 12 00 b.Coventry 23-3-85
Source: Scholar.

2003–04	Preston NE	0	0	
2003–04	Carlisle U	11	1	11 1
2004–05	Preston NE	1	0	1 0
2004–05	Kidderminster H	10	1	10 1
2004–05	Shrewsbury T	28	3	
2005–06	Shrewsbury T	42	9	
2006–07	Shrewsbury T	45	3	
2007–08	Shrewsbury T	39	1	
2008–09	Shrewsbury T	33	0	
2009–10	Shrewsbury T	44	3	231 19
2010–11	Peterborough U	32	3	32 3

LEE, Charlie (M) 162 15
H: 5 11 W: 11 07 b.Whitechapel 5-1-87
Source: Scholar.

2005–06	Tottenham H	0	0	
2006–07	Tottenham H	0	0	
2006–07	Millwall	5	0	5 0
2007–08	Peterborough U	42	6	
2008–09	Peterborough U	44	5	
2009–10	Peterborough U	33	2	
2010–11	Peterborough U	34	1	153 14
2010–11	Gillingham	4	1	4 1

LEWIS, Joe (G) 180 0
H: 6 5 W: 12 10 b.Bungay 6-10-87
Source: Scholar. *Honours:* England Youth, Under-21.

2004–05	Norwich C	0	0	
2005–06	Norwich C	0	0	
2006–07	Norwich C	0	0	
2006–07	Stockport Co	5	0	5 0
2007–08	Norwich C	0	0	
2007–08	Morecambe	19	0	19 0
2007–08	Peterborough U	22	0	
2008–09	Peterborough U	46	0	
2009–10	Peterborough U	43	0	
2010–11	Peterborough U	45	0	156 0

LITTLE, Mark (D) 109 0
H: 6 1 W: 12 10 b.Worcester 20-8-88
Source: Scholar. *Honours:* England Youth.

2005–06	Wolverhampton W	0	0	
2006–07	Wolverhampton W	26	0	
2007–08	Wolverhampton W	1	0	
2007–08	Northampton T	17	0	
2008–09	Wolverhampton W	0	0	
2008–09	Northampton T	9	0	26 0
2009–10	Wolverhampton W	0	0	27 0
2009–10	Chesterfield	12	0	12 0
2009–10	Peterborough U	9	0	
2010–11	Peterborough U	45	0	44 0

MACKAIL-SMITH, Craig (F) 185 80
H: 6 3 W: 12 04 b.Watford 25-2-84
Source: Dagenham & R. *Honours:* Scotland 1 full cap.

2006–07	Peterborough U	15	8	
2007–08	Peterborough U	36	12	
2008–09	Peterborough U	46	23	
2009–10	Peterborough U	43	10	
2010–11	Peterborough U	45	27	185 80

McCANN, Grant (M) 377 65
H: 5 10 W: 11 00 b.Belfast 14-4-80
Source: Trainee. *Honours:* Northern Ireland Youth, Under-21, 33 full caps, 4 goals.

1998–99	West Ham U	0	0	
1999–2000	West Ham U	0	0	
2000–01	West Ham U	1	0	
2000–01	Notts Co	2	0	2 0
2000–01	Cheltenham T	30	3	
2001–02	West Ham U	3	0	
2002–03	West Ham U	0	0	4 0
2002–03	Cheltenham T	27	6	
2003–04	Cheltenham T	43	8	
2004–05	Cheltenham T	39	4	
2005–06	Cheltenham T	39	8	
2006–07	Cheltenham T	15	5	193 34
2006–07	Barnsley	22	1	
2007–08	Barnsley	39	3	41 4
2007–08	Scunthorpe U	14	1	
2008–09	Scunthorpe U	43	9	
2009–10	Scunthorpe U	42	8	99 18
2010–11	Peterborough U	38	9	38 9

McCRAE, Romone (M) 2 0
H: 6 1 W: 12 07 b.Southwark 25-8-91
Source: Crawley T.

2009–10	Peterborough U	2	0	
2010–11	Peterborough U	0	0	2 0

MILLS, Danny (F) 5 0
H: 6 4 W: 13 02 b.Croydon 27-11-91
Source: Crawley T.

2009–10	Peterborough U	3	0	
2009–10	Torquay U	2	0	2 0
2010–11	Peterborough U	0	0	3 0

NEWELL, Joe (M) 2 0
b.Tamworth 15-3-93
Source: Scholar.

2010–11	Peterborough U	2	0	2 0

NTLHE, Kgosietsile (M) 0 0
Source: Scholar.

2010–11	Peterborough U	0	0	

OFORI-TWUMASI, Nana (D) 30 2
H: 5 8 W: 11 09 b.Accra 15-5-90
Source: Scholar. *Honours:* England Under-20.

2007–08	Chelsea	0	0	
2008–09	Chelsea	0	0	
2009–10	Chelsea	0	0	
2009–10	Dagenham & R	8	2	8 2
2010–11	Peterborough U	11	0	11 0
2010–11	Northampton T	11	0	11 0

PIERGIANNI, Carl (D) 1 0
b.Peterborough 3-5-92
Source: Scholar.

2010–11	Peterborough U	1	0	1 0

ROWE, Tommy (M) 139 20
H: 5 11 W: 12 11 b.Manchester 1-5-89
Source: Scholar.

2006–07	Stockport Co	4	0	
2007–08	Stockport Co	24	6	
2008–09	Stockport Co	44	7	72 13
2008–09	Peterborough U	0	0	
2009 10	Peterborough U	32	2	
2010–11	Peterborough U	35	5	67 7

SIMPSON, Josh (M) 38 3
H: 5 10 W: 12 02 b.Cambridge 6-3-87
Source: Cambridge C, Cambridge U, Histon.

2009–10	Peterborough U	21	2	
2010–11	Peterborough U	0	0	21 2
2010–11	Southend U	17	1	17 1

TAYLOR, Paul (F) 12 0
H: 5 11 W: 11 02 b.Liverpool 4 11 87
Source: Vauxhall M.
on loan from Vauxhall M.

2008–09	Chester C	9	0	9 0
2009–10	Montegnee	1	0	1 0
2010–11	Anderlecht	0	0	
2010–11	Charleroi	1	0	1 0
2010–11	Peterborough U	1	0	1 0

TOMLIN, Lee (F) 37 8
H: 5 11 W: 11 09 b.Leicester 12-1-89
Source: Leicester C, Rushden & D.

2010–11	Peterborough U	37	8	37 8

WESOLOWSKI, James (M) 119 6
H: 5 8 W: 11 11 b.Sydney 25-8-87
Source: Scholar. *Honours:* Australia Youth, Under-20.

2004–05	Leicester C	0	0	
2005–06	Leicester C	5	0	
2006–07	Leicester C	19	0	
2007–08	Leicester C	22	0	
2008–09	Leicester C	0	0	
2008–09	Dundee U	8	0	8 0
2008–09	Cheltenham T	4	0	4 0
2009–10	Leicester C	0	0	46 0
2009–10	Hamilton A	29	4	29 4
2010–11	Peterborough U	32	2	32 2

WHELPDALE, Chris (M) 129 15
H: 6 0 W: 12 08 b.Harold Wood 27-1-87
Source: Billericay T.

2007–08	Peterborough U	33	3	
2008–09	Peterborough U	39	7	
2009–10	Peterborough U	29	1	
2010–11	Peterborough U	22	1	125 12
2010–11	Gillingham	4	3	4 3

ZAKUANI, Gaby (D) 206 6
H: 6 1 W: 12 13 b.DR Congo 31-5-86
Source: Scholar. *Honours:* DR Congo 1 full cap.

2002–03	Leyton Orient	1	0	
2003–04	Leyton Orient	10	2	
2004–05	Leyton Orient	33	0	
2005–06	Leyton Orient	43	1	87 3
2006–07	Fulham	0	0	
2006–07	Stoke C	9	0	
2007–08	Fulham	0	0	
2007–08	Stoke C	19	0	28 0
2008–09	Fulham	0	0	
2008–09	Peterborough U	32	1	
2009–10	Peterborough U	29	0	
2010–11	Peterborough U	30	2	91 3

PLYMOUTH ARG (62)

ARNASON, Kari (M) 207 9
H: 6 3 W: 13 10 b.Reykjavik 13-10-82
Honours: Iceland 17 full caps, 1 goal.

2001	Vikingur	5	2	
2002	Vikingur	5	1	
2003	Vikingur	16	0	
2004	Vikingur	15	0	41 3
2005	Djurgaarden	21	0	
2006	Djurgaarden	14	0	35 0
2006–07	Aarhus	14	2	
2007–08	Aarhus	25	0	
2008–09	Aarhus	12	1	51 3
2008–09	Esbjerg	8	0	8 0
2009–10	Plymouth Arg	32	2	
2010–11	Plymouth Arg	40	1	72 3

BHASERA, Onismor (D) 154 3
H: 5 9 W: 11 13 b.Mutare 7-12-86
Honours: Zimbabwe 15 full caps.

2004	Harare S	0	0	
2004–05	Tembisa Classic	14	0	14 0
2005–06	Maritzburg U	27	0	
2006–07	Maritzburg U	26	1	53 1
2007–08	Kaizer Chiefs	26	1	
2008–09	Kaizer Chiefs	25	0	51 1
2009–10	Plymouth Arg	7	0	
2010–11	Plymouth Arg	29	1	36 1

BOLASIE, Yannick (M) 93 13
H: 6 2 W: 13 02 b.DR Congo 24-5-89

2008–09	Plymouth Arg	0	0	
2008–09	Barnet	20	3	
2009–10	Plymouth Arg	16	1	
2009–10	Barnet	22	2	42 6
2010–11	Plymouth Arg	35	7	51 8

CHENOWETH, Oliver (M) 0 0
Source: Scholar.

2010–11	Plymouth Arg	0	0	

CLARK, Chris (F) 288 10
H: 5 7 W: 10 05 b.Aberdeen 15-9-80

1999–2000	Aberdeen	2	0	
2000–01	Aberdeen	24	0	
2001–02	Aberdeen	8	0	
2002–03	Aberdeen	25	1	
2003–04	Aberdeen	23	1	
2004–05	Aberdeen	31	2	
2005–06	Aberdeen	31	3	
2006–07	Aberdeen	37	1	181 8
2007–08	Plymouth Arg	12	0	
2008–09	Plymouth Arg	36	0	
2009–10	Plymouth Arg	37	1	
2010–11	Plymouth Arg	22	1	107 2

DONNELLY, George (F) 44 12
H: 6 2 W: 13 03 b.Liverpool 28-5-88
Source: Skelmersdale U.

2008–09	Plymouth Arg	2	0	
2009–10	Plymouth Arg	0	0	
2009–10	Stockport Co	19	4	
2010–11	Plymouth Arg	0	0	2 0
2010–11	Stockport Co	23	8	42 12

DUGUID, Karl (M) 492 44
H: 5 11 W: 11 06 b.Letchworth 21-3-78
Source: Trainee.

1995–96	Colchester U	16	1	
1996–97	Colchester U	20	3	
1997–98	Colchester U	21	3	
1998–99	Colchester U	33	4	
1999–2000	Colchester U	41	12	

2000–01	Colchester U	41	5		
2001–02	Colchester U	41	4		
2002–03	Colchester U	27	3		
2003–04	Colchester U	30	2		
2004–05	Colchester U	0	0		
2005–06	Colchester U	35	0		
2006–07	Colchester U	43	5		
2007–08	Colchester U	37	0	385	42
2008–09	Plymouth Arg	39	1		
2009–10	Plymouth Arg	42	1		
2010–11	Plymouth Arg	26	0	107	2

FALLON, Rory (F) 340 68
H: 6 2 W: 11 09 b.Gisborne 20-3-82
Source: North Shore U. Honours: England Youth. New Zealand 11 full caps, 3 goals.

1998–99	Barnsley	0	0		
1999–2000	Barnsley	0	0		
2000–01	Barnsley	1	0		
2001–02	Barnsley	9	0		
2001–02	*Shrewsbury T*	11	0	11	0
2002–03	Barnsley	26	7		
2003–04	Barnsley	16	4	52	11
2003–04	Swindon T	19	6		
2004–05	Swindon T	31	3		
2004–05	*Yeovil T*	6	1	6	1
2005–06	Swindon T	25	12	75	21
2005–06	Swansea C	17	4		
2006–07	Swansea C	24	8	41	12
2006–07	Plymouth Arg	15	1		
2007–08	Plymouth Arg	29	7		
2008–09	Plymouth Arg	44	5		
2009–10	Plymouth Arg	33	5		
2010–11	Plymouth Arg	28	4	149	22
2010–11	*Ipswich T*	6	1	6	1

FLETCHER, Carl (M) 405 33
H: 5 10 W: 11 07 b.Camberley 7-4-80
Source: Trainee. Honours: Wales 36 full caps, 1 goal.

1997–98	Bournemouth	1	0		
1998–99	Bournemouth	1	0		
1999–2000	Bournemouth	25	3		
2000–01	Bournemouth	43	6		
2001–02	Bournemouth	35	5		
2002–03	Bournemouth	42	1		
2003–04	Bournemouth	40	2		
2004–05	Bournemouth	6	2	193	19
2004–05	West Ham U	32	2		
2005–06	West Ham U	12	1	44	3
2005–06	Watford	3	0	3	0
2006–07	Crystal Palace	37	3		
2007–08	Crystal Palace	28	1		
2008–09	Crystal Palace	3	0	68	4
2008–09	*Nottingham F*	5	0	5	0
2008–09	Plymouth Arg	13	1		
2009–10	Plymouth Arg	41	4		
2010–11	Plymouth Arg	38	2	92	7

HARPER-PENMAN, Ged (M) 2 0
b.Bideford 2-2-94
Source: Scholar.

2010–11	Plymouth Arg	2	0	2	0

HEAD, Liam (F) 0 0
H: 6 1 W: 13 05 b.Bovey Tracey 26-1-92
Source: Scholar.

2008–09	Plymouth Arg	0	0	
2009–10	Plymouth Arg	0	0	
2010–11	Plymouth Arg	0	0	

JOHNSON, Damien (M) 295 9
H: 5 9 W: 11 09 b.Lisburn 18-11-78
Source: Trainee. Honours: Northern Ireland Youth, Under-21, 56 full caps.

1995–96	Blackburn R	0	0		
1996–97	Blackburn R	0	0		
1997–98	Blackburn R	0	0		
1997–98	*Nottingham F*	6	0	6	0
1998–99	Blackburn R	21	1		
1999–2000	Blackburn R	16	1		
2000–01	Blackburn R	16	0		
2001–02	Blackburn R	7	1	60	3
2001–02	Birmingham C	8	1		
2002–03	Birmingham C	30	1		
2003–04	Birmingham C	35	1		
2004–05	Birmingham C	36	0		
2005–06	Birmingham C	31	0		
2006–07	Birmingham C	26	1		
2007–08	Birmingham C	17	0		
2008–09	Birmingham C	9	0		
2009–10	Birmingham C	1	0	193	4

2009–10	Plymouth Arg	20	2		
2010–11	Plymouth Arg	0	0	20	2
2010–11	*Huddersfield T*	16	0	16	0

KINSELLA, Sean (M) 0 0
H: 5 9 W: 13 01 b.Stone 25-10-91
Source: Scholar.

2010–11	Plymouth Arg	0	0	

Transferred to Hibernian January 2011.

LARRIEU, Romain (G) 302 0
Source: Montpellier, ASOA Valence.
Honours: France Youth.

2000–01	Plymouth Arg	15	0		
2001–02	Plymouth Arg	45	0		
2002–03	Plymouth Arg	43	0		
2003–04	Plymouth Arg	6	0		
2004–05	Plymouth Arg	23	0		
2005–06	Plymouth Arg	45	0		
2006–07	Plymouth Arg	6	0		
2006–07	Gillingham	14	0	14	0
2007–08	Plymouth Arg	15	0		
2007–08	*Yeovil T*	6	0	6	0
2008–09	Plymouth Arg	41	0		
2009–10	Plymouth Arg	25	0		
2010–11	Plymouth Arg	18	0	282	0

LEONARD, Ryan (D) 1 0
H: 6 0 W: 11 01 b.Plympton 24-5-92
Source: Scholar.

2009–10	Plymouth Arg	1	0		
2010–11	Plymouth Arg	0	0	1	0

MACLEAN, Steve (F) 238 72
H: 5 11 W: 12 06 b.Edinburgh 23-8-82
Honours: Scotland Under-21.

2002–03	Rangers	3	0	3	0
2003–04	Scunthorpe U	42	23	42	23
2004–05	Sheffield W	36	18		
2005–06	Sheffield W	6	2		
2006–07	Sheffield W	41	12	83	32
2007–08	Cardiff C	15	1	15	1
2007–08	Plymouth Arg	17	3		
2008–09	Plymouth Arg	21	2		
2009–10	Plymouth Arg	3	0		
2009–10	*Aberdeen*	16	5	16	5
2010–11	Plymouth Arg	7	0	48	5
2010–11	*Oxford U*	31	6	31	6

MASON, Joe (F) 53 10
H: 5 9 W: 11 11 b.Plymouth 13-5-91
Honours: Eire Youth, Under-21.

2009–10	Plymouth Arg	19	3		
2010–11	Plymouth Arg	34	7	53	10

MOLYNEUX, Lee (D) 13 0
H: 5 10 W: 11 07 b.Liverpool 24-2-89
Source: Scholar. Honours: England Schools, Youth.

2005–06	Everton	0	0		
2006–07	Everton	0	0		
2007–08	Everton	0	0		
2008–09	Everton	0	0		
2008–09	Southampton	4	0		
2009–10	Southampton	0	0	4	0
2010–11	Plymouth Arg	9	0	9	0

N'GALA, Bondz (D) 40 1
H: 6 0 W: 12 03 b.Forest Gate 13-9-89
Source: Scholar.

2007–08	West Ham U	0	0		
2008–09	West Ham U	0	0		
2008–09	*Milton Keynes D*	3	0	3	0
2009–10	West Ham U	0	0		
2009–10	*Scunthorpe U*	2	0	2	0
2009–10	*Plymouth Arg*	9	0		
2010–11	Plymouth Arg	26	1	35	1

NELSON, Curtis (D) 35 0
b.Newcastle-u-Lyme 21-5-93
Source: Scholar.

2010–11	Plymouth Arg	35	0	35	0

PATERSON, Jim (M) 285 11
H: 5 11 W: 12 13 b.Airdrie 25-9-79
Source: Dundee U BC. Honours: Scotland Under-21.

1998–99	Dundee U	15	0		
1999–2000	Dundee U	8	1		
2000–01	Dundee U	6	1		
2001–02	Dundee U	27	2		
2002–03	Dundee U	33	1		
2003–04	Dundee U	16	0	105	5

2004–05	Motherwell	35	3		
2005–06	Motherwell	19	1		
2006–07	Motherwell	34	1		
2007–08	Motherwell	20	0	108	5
2007–08	Plymouth Arg	8	1		
2008–09	Plymouth Arg	17	0		
2009–10	Plymouth Arg	12	0		
2009–10	*Aberdeen*	7	0	7	0
2010–11	Plymouth Arg	28	0	65	1

PATTERSON, Rory (F) 50 4
H: 5 10 W: 10 13 b.Strabane 16-7-84
Source: Scholar. Honours: Northern Ireland 5 full caps, 1 goal.

2002–03	Rochdale	8	0		
2003–04	Rochdale	7	0	15	0

From Radcliffe B, Mossley, FC United of Manchester, Bradford PA, Droylsden.

2010–11	Plymouth Arg	35	4	35	4

PETERLIN, Anton (D) 64 5
H: 5 11 W: 11 05 b.San Francisco 4-4-87

2007	Cal Poly Mustangs	12	0	12	0
2007	San Francisco Seals	16	3	16	3
2008	Ventura CF	16	2		
2009	Ventura CF	8	0	24	2
2009–10	Everton	0	0		
2010–11	Plymouth Arg	12	0	12	0

RICKARD, Matt (F) 1 0
b.Exeter 29-1-93
Source: Scholar.

2010–11	Plymouth Arg	1	0	1	0

SEIP, Marcel (D) 269 10
H: 6 0 W: 11 03 b.Winschoten 5-4-82
Honours: Holland Under-21.

1999–2000	Veendam	9	0		
2000–01	Veendam	18	0	27	0
2001–02	Heerenveen	0	0		
2002–03	Heerenveen	6	0		
2003–04	Heerenveen	31	1		
2004–05	Heerenveen	30	1		
2005–06	Heerenveen	28	0	95	2
2006–07	Plymouth Arg	37	2		
2007–08	Plymouth Arg	34	1		
2008–09	Plymouth Arg	41	3		
2009–10	Plymouth Arg	5	0		
2009–10	*Blackpool*	7	2	7	2
2009–10	*Sheffield U*	6	0	6	0
2010–11	Plymouth Arg	17	0	134	6
2010–11	*Charlton Ath*	0	0		

SUMMERFIELD, Luke (M) 101 5
H: 6 0 W: 11 00 b.Ivybridge 6-12-87
Source: Scholar.

2004–05	Plymouth Arg	1	0		
2005–06	Plymouth Arg	0	0		
2006–07	Plymouth Arg	23	1		
2006–07	*Bournemouth*	8	1	8	1
2007–08	Plymouth Arg	7	0		
2008–09	Plymouth Arg	29	2		
2009–10	Plymouth Arg	12	0		
2009–10	*Leyton Orient*	14	0	14	0
2010–11	Plymouth Arg	7	1	79	4

TIMAR, Krisztian (D) 167 12
H: 6 3 W: 13 08 b.Budapest 4-10-79
Source: Ferencvaros, MTK, Elore. Honours: Hungary Youth, Under-21, Under-23, 4 full caps.

2001–02	Videoton	31	4		
2002–03	Videoton	15	0	46	4
2003	Jokerit	0	0		
2003–04	Tatabanya	0	0		
2004–05	Nyiregyhaza	12	0	12	0
2005–06	Ferencvaros	23	3	23	3
2006–07	Plymouth Arg	9	1		
2007–08	Plymouth Arg	38	3		
2008–09	Plymouth Arg	21	0		
2009–10	Plymouth Arg	7	1		
2009–10	*Oldham Ath*	2	0	2	0
2010–11	Plymouth Arg	9	0	84	5

WALTON, Simon (M) 126 8
H: 6 1 W: 13 05 b.Sherburn-in-Elmet 13-9-87
Source: Scholar. Honours: England Youth.

2004–05	Leeds U	30	3		
2005–06	Leeds U	4	0	34	3
2006–07	Charlton Ath	0	0		
2006–07	*Ipswich T*	19	3	19	3
2006–07	*Cardiff C*	6	0	6	0

2007-08	QPR	5	0	5	0
2007-08	*Hull C*	10	0	10	0
2008-09	Plymouth Arg	13	0		
2008-09	*Blackpool*	1	0	1	0
2009-10	Plymouth Arg	0	0		
2009-10	*Crewe Alex*	31	1	31	1
2010-11	Plymouth Arg	7	1	20	1
2010-11	*Sheffield U*	0	0		

YOUNG, Luke (M) 5 0
b.Plymouth 22-2-93
Source: Scholar.

| 2010-11 | Plymouth Arg | 5 | 0 | 5 | 0 |

ZUBAR, Stephane (D) 86 3
b.Guadeloupe 9-10-86
Honours: Guadeloupe 2 full caps.

2006-07	Caen	0	0		
2006-07	*Pau*	10	0	10	0
2007-08	Caen	0	0		
2007-08	*FC Brussels*	11	0	11	0
2008-09	Vaslui	10	0		
2009-10	Vaslui	26	1	36	1
2010-11	Plymouth Arg	29	2	29	2

PORT VALE (63)

BELL, Matty (D) 0 0
H: 5 10 W: 11 03 b.Stoke 3-1-92
Source: Scholar.

| 2010-11 | Port Vale | 0 | 0 | | |

COLLINS, Lee (D) 142 4
H: 6 1 W: 11 10 b.Telford 23-9-83
Source: Scholar. *Honours:* England Youth.

2006-07	Wolverhampton W	0	0		
2007-08	Wolverhampton W	0	0		
2007-08	*Hereford U*	16	0	16	0
2008-09	Wolverhampton W	0	0		
2008-09	Port Vale	39	1		
2009-10	Port Vale	45	1		
2010-11	Port Vale	42	2	126	4

COX, Kristian (F) 1 0
H: 5 11 W: 12 06 b.Birmingham 28-9-92
Source: Scholar.

| 2010-11 | Port Vale | 1 | 0 | 1 | 0 |

DAVIS, Joe (D) 1 0
b.Burnley 10-11-93
Source: Scholar.

| 2010-11 | Port Vale | 1 | 0 | 1 | 0 |

DODDS, Louis (M) 174 31
H: 5 10 W: 12 04 b.Leicester 8-10-86
Source: Scholar.

2005-06	Leicester C	0	0		
2006-07	Leicester C	0	0		
2006-07	*Rochdale*	12	2	12	2
2007-08	Leicester C	0	0		
2007-08	*Lincoln C*	41	9	41	9
2008-09	Port Vale	44	7		
2009-10	Port Vale	44	6		
2010-11	Port Vale	33	7	121	20

GRIFFITH, Anthony (M) 128 1
H: 6 0 W: 12 00 b.Huddersfield 28-10-86
Source: Glasshoughton W.

2005-06	Doncaster R	4	0		
2005-06	*Oxford U*	0	0		
2006-07	Doncaster R	2	0		
2006-07	*Darlington*	4	0	4	0
2007-08	Doncaster R	0	0	6	0
2007-08	Port Vale	0	0		
2008-09	Port Vale	38	0		
2009-10	Port Vale	40	0		
2010-11	Port Vale	40	1	118	1

HALDANE, Lewis (F) 207 18
H: 6 0 W: 11 03 b.Trowbridge 13-3-85
Source: Scholar. *Honours:* Wales Under-21.

2003-04	Bristol R	27	5		
2004-05	Bristol R	13	0		
2005-06	Bristol R	30	3		
2006-07	Bristol R	45	6		
2007-08	Bristol R	32	1		
2008-09	Bristol R	0	0	147	15
2009-10	Port Vale	37	3		
2010-11	Port Vale	23	0	60	3

LLOYD, Ryan (M) 1 0
b.Newcastle-under-Lyme 1-2-94
Source: Scholar.

| 2010-11 | Port Vale | 1 | 0 | 1 | 0 |

LOFT, Doug (M) 111 6
H: 6 0 W: 12 01 b.Maidstone 25-12-86
Source: Hastings U.

2005-06	Brighton & HA	3	1		
2006-07	Brighton & HA	11	1		
2007-08	Brighton & HA	13	0		
2008-09	Brighton & HA	12	0	39	2
2008-09	*Dagenham & R*	11	0	11	0
2009-10	Port Vale	32	3		
2010-11	Port Vale	29	1	61	4

MALBON, Anthony (M) 3 0
H: 5 8 W: 11 00 b.Stoke 14-10-91
Source: Scholar.

2008-09	Port Vale	1	0		
2009-10	Port Vale	0	0		
2010-11	Port Vale	2	0	3	0

MARTIN, Chris (G) 66 0
H: 6 0 W: 13 05 b.Mansfield 21-7-90
Source: Scholar.

2007-08	Port Vale	2	0		
2008-09	Port Vale	11	0		
2009-10	Port Vale	39	0		
2010-11	Port Vale	14	0	66	0

McCOMBE, John (D) 154 9
H: 6 2 W: 13 00 b.Pontefract 7-5-85
Source: Scholar.

2002-03	Huddersfield T	1	0		
2003-04	Huddersfield T	0	0		
2004-05	Huddersfield T	5	0		
2005-06	Huddersfield T	1	0		
2005-06	*Torquay U*	0	0		
2006-07	Huddersfield T	7	0	14	0
2007-08	*Hereford U*	27	0	27	0
2008-09	Port Vale	31	2		
2009-10	Port Vale	40	3		
2010-11	Port Vale	42	4	113	9

MORSY, Sam (M) 17 1
H: 5 9 W: 12 06 b.Wolverhampton 10-9-91
Source: Scholar.

| 2009-10 | Port Vale | 1 | 0 | | |
| 2010-11 | Port Vale | 16 | 1 | 17 | 1 |

OWEN, Gareth (D) 229 2
H: 6 1 W: 11 07 b.Cheadle 21-9-82
Source: Scholar. *Honours:* Wales Youth.

2001-02	Stoke C	0	0		
2002-03	Stoke C	0	0		
2003-04	Stoke C	3	0		
2003-04	*Oldham Ath*	15	1		
2004-05	Stoke C	2	0	5	0
2004-05	*Torquay U*	5	0	5	0
2004-05	*Oldham Ath*	9	0		
2005-06	Oldham Ath	17	0		
2006-07	Oldham Ath	0	0	41	1
2006-07	*Stockport Co*	39	0		
2007-08	Stockport Co	36	0		
2008-09	Stockport Co	8	0	83	0
2008-09	*Yeovil T*	7	0	7	0
2008-09	Port Vale	12	0		
2009-10	Port Vale	40	0		
2010-11	Port Vale	36	1	88	1

RICHARDS, Justin (F) 121 25
H: 5 11 W: 11 00 b.Sandwell 16-10-80
Source: Trainee.

1998-99	WBA	1	0		
1999-2000	WBA	0	0		
2000-01	WBA	0	0	1	0
2000-01	*Bristol R*	7	0		
2001-02	Bristol R	1	0		
2002-03	Bristol R	8	0	16	0
2002-03	*Colchester U*	2	0	2	0

From Stevenage B, Woking.

| 2006-07 | Peterborough U | 13 | 1 | 13 | 1 |
| 2006-07 | *Boston U* | 3 | 0 | 3 | 0 |

From Kidderminster H.

| 2009-10 | Cheltenham T | 44 | 15 | 44 | 15 |
| 2010-11 | Port Vale | 42 | 9 | 42 | 9 |

RICHARDS, Marc (F) 303 88
H: 6 2 W: 12 06 b.Wolverhampton 8-7-82
Source: Trainee. *Honours:* England Youth, Under-20.

1999-2000	Blackburn R	0	0		
2000-01	Blackburn R	0	0		
2001-02	Blackburn R	0	0		
2001-02	*Crewe Alex*	4	0	4	0
2001-02	*Oldham Ath*	5	0	5	0
2001-02	*Halifax T*	5	0	5	0
2002-03	Blackburn R	0	0		
2002-03	*Swansea C*	17	7	17	7
2003-04	Northampton T	41	8		
2004-05	Northampton T	12	2		
2004-05	*Rochdale*	5	2	5	2
2005-06	Northampton T	0	0	53	10
2005-06	*Barnsley*	38	12		
2006-07	Barnsley	31	6	69	18
2007-08	Port Vale	29	5		
2008-09	Port Vale	30	10		
2009-10	Port Vale	46	20		
2010-11	Port Vale	40	16	145	51

RIGG, Sean (F) 108 8
H: 5 9 W: 12 01 b.Bristol 1-10-88
Source: Forest Green R.

2006-07	Bristol R	18	1		
2007-08	Bristol R	31	1		
2008-09	Bristol R	8	0		
2009-10	Bristol R	0	0	57	2
2009-10	*Port Vale*	26	3		
2010-11	Port Vale	25	3	51	6

ROBERTS, Gary (M) 200 18
H: 5 8 W: 10 05 b.Chester 4-2-87
Source: Scholar. *Honours:* England Youth.

2003-04	Crewe Alex	2	0		
2004-05	Crewe Alex	2	0		
2005-06	Crewe Alex	33	2		
2006-07	Crewe Alex	43	3		
2007-08	Crewe Alex	42	6		
2008-09	Crewe Alex	0	0	122	11
2008 09	Yeovil T	30	2		
2009-10	Yeovil T	0	0	30	2
2009-10	*Rotherham U*	13	3	13	3
2010-11	Port Vale	35	2	35	2

SUTTON, Ritchie (D) 0 0
H: 6 0 W: 11 05 b.Stoke 29-4-86
Source: Scholar.

| 2005-06 | Crewe Alex | 0 | 0 | | |

From Stafford R, Northwich Vic, FC Halifax T, Nantwich T.

| 2010-11 | Port Vale | 0 | 0 | | |

SUTTON, Richard (D) 11 0
H: 5 8 W: 11 05 b.Stoke 28-4-92
Source: Stafford R, Nantwich T.

| 2010-11 | Port Vale | 11 | 0 | 11 | 0 |

TAYLOR, Kris (M) 211 11
H: 5 9 W: 11 05 b.Stafford 12-1-84
Source: Scholar. *Honours:* England Schools, Youth.

2000-01	Manchester U	0	0		
2001-02	Manchester U	0	0		
2002-03	Manchester U	0	0		
2002-03	*Walsall*	0	0		
2003-04	Walsall	11	1		
2004-05	Walsall	12	2		
2005-06	Walsall	22	2		
2006-07	Walsall	35	1	80	6
2007-08	Hereford U	31	1		
2008-09	Hereford U	39	1	70	2
2009-10	Port Vale	41	3		
2010-11	Port Vale	20	0	61	3

TAYLOR, Rob (D) 95 12
H: 6 0 W: 12 08 b.Shrewsbury 16-1-85
Source: Ludlow T, Stourport Swifts, Solihull B, Redditch U, Nuneaton B.

2008-09	Port Vale	20	3		
2009-10	Port Vale	39	8		
2010-11	Port Vale	36	1	95	12

TOMLINSON, Stuart (G) 56 0
H: 6 1 W: 11 02 b.Ellesmere Port 10-5-85
Source: Scholar.

2002-03	Crewe Alex	1	0		
2003-04	Crewe Alex	1	0		
2004-05	Crewe Alex	0	0		
2005-06	Crewe Alex	2	0		
2006-07	Crewe Alex	7	0		
2007-08	Crewe Alex	0	0		
2008-09	Crewe Alex	9	0		
2009-10	Crewe Alex	0	0	20	0

From Barrow.

| 2010-11 | Port Vale | 36 | 0 | 36 | 0 |

YATES, Adam (D)   154   0
H: 5 10   W: 10 07   b.Stoke 28-5-83
Source: Scholar.

2000–01	Crewe Alex	0	0
2001–02	Crewe Alex	0	0
2002–03	Crewe Alex	0	0
2003–04	Crewe Alex	0	0
2004–05	Crewe Alex	0	0
2005–06	Crewe Alex	0	0
2006–07	Crewe Alex	0	0
2007–08	Morecambe	44	0
2008–09	Morecambe	32	0	76	0
2009–10	Port Vale	32	0
2010–11	Port Vale	46	0	78	0

PORTSMOUTH (64)

ASHDOWN, Jamie (G)   124   0
H: 6 1   W: 13 05   b.Reading 30-11-80
Source: Scholar.

1999–2000	Reading	0	0
2000–01	Reading	1	0
2001–02	Reading	1	0
2001–02	*Arsenal*	0	0
2002–03	Reading	1	0
2002–03	*Bournemouth*	2	0	2	0
2003–04	Reading	10	0	13	0
2003–04	*Rushden & D*	19	0	19	0
2004–05	Portsmouth	16	0
2005–06	Portsmouth	17	0
2006–07	Portsmouth	0	0
2006–07	*Norwich C*	2	0	2	0
2007–08	Portsmouth	3	0
2008–09	Portsmouth	0	0
2009–10	Portsmouth	6	0
2010–11	Portsmouth	46	0	88	0

BEN HAIM, Tal (D)   231   3
H: 5 11   W: 11 09   b.Rishon Le Zion 31-3-82
Source: Maccabi Tel Aviv. *Honours:* Israel
Under-21, 61 full caps, 1 goal.

2000–01	Maccabi Tel Aviv	1	0
2001–02	Maccabi Tel Aviv	29	1
2002–03	Maccabi Tel Aviv	30	0
2003–04	Maccabi Tel Aviv	26	1	86	2
2004–05	Bolton W	21	1
2005–06	Bolton W	35	0
2006–07	Bolton W	32	0	88	1
2007–08	Chelsea	13	0	13	0
2008–09	Manchester C	9	0
2008–09	*Sunderland*	5	0	5	0
2009–10	Manchester C	0	0	9	0
2009–10	Portsmouth	22	0
2010–11	Portsmouth	0	0	22	0
2010–11	*West Ham U*	8	0	8	0

BROWN, Michael (M)   444   36
H: 5 9   W: 12 04   b.Hartlepool 25-1-77
Source: Trainee. *Honours:* England
Under-21.

1994–95	Manchester C	0	0
1995–96	Manchester C	21	0
1996–97	Manchester C	11	0
1996–97	*Hartlepool U*	6	1	6	1
1997–98	Manchester C	26	0
1998–99	Manchester C	31	2
1999–2000	Manchester C	0	0	89	2
1999–2000	*Portsmouth*	4	0
1999–2000	Sheffield U	24	3
2000–01	Sheffield U	36	1
2001–02	Sheffield U	36	5
2002–03	Sheffield U	40	16
2003–04	Sheffield U	15	2	151	27
2003–04	Tottenham H	17	1
2004–05	Tottenham H	24	1
2005–06	Tottenham H	9	0	50	2
2005–06	Fulham	7	0
2006–07	Fulham	34	0	41	0
2007–08	Wigan Ath	31	0
2008–09	Wigan Ath	25	0
2009–10	Wigan Ath	2	0	58	0
2009–10	Portsmouth	24	2
2010–11	Portsmouth	21	2	49	4

CIFTCI, Nadir (F)   19   1
H: 6 1   W: 13 00   b.Den Haag 12-2-92
Source: Scholar. *Honours:* Holland Youth.

2008–09	Portsmouth	0	0
2009–10	Portsmouth	0	0
2010–11	Portsmouth	19	1	19	1

GODDARD, Billy (M)   0   0
b. 18-12-91
Source: Scholar.

2010–11	Portsmouth	0	0

GREGORY, Pete (D)   1   0
H: 5 7   W: 11 05   b.Eastbourne 25-7-92
Source: Scholar.

2010–11	Portsmouth	1	0	1	0

HREIDARSSON, Hermann (D)   503   26
H: 6 3   W: 12 12   b.Reykjavik 11-7-74
Honours: Iceland Under-21, 87 full caps, 5
goals.

1993	IBV	2	0
1994	IBV	18	2
1995	IBV	18	1
1996	IBV	17	2
1997	IBV	11	0	66	5
1997–98	Crystal Palace	30	2
1998–99	Crystal Palace	7	0	37	2
1998–99	Brentford	33	4
1999–2000	Brentford	8	2	41	6
1999–2000	Wimbledon	24	1
2000–01	Wimbledon	1	0	25	1
2000–01	Ipswich T	36	1
2001–02	Ipswich T	38	1
2002–03	Ipswich T	28	0	102	2
2002–03	Charlton Ath	0	0
2003–04	Charlton Ath	33	2
2004–05	Charlton Ath	34	1
2005–06	Charlton Ath	34	0
2006–07	Charlton Ath	31	0	132	3
2007–08	Portsmouth	32	3
2008–09	Portsmouth	23	2
2009–10	Portsmouth	17	1
2010–11	Portsmouth	28	1	100	7

HUGHES, Richard (M)   274   15
H: 6 0   W: 13 03   b.Glasgow 25-6-79
Source: Atalanta. *Honours:* Scotland Youth,
Under-21, 5 full caps.

1997–98	Arsenal	0	0
1998–99	Bournemouth	44	2
1999–2000	Bournemouth	21	2
2000–01	Bournemouth	44	8
2001–02	Bournemouth	22	2	131	14
2002–03	Portsmouth	6	0
2002–03	*Grimsby T*	12	1	12	1
2003–04	Portsmouth	11	0
2004–05	Portsmouth	16	0
2005–06	Portsmouth	26	0
2006–07	Portsmouth	18	0
2007–08	Portsmouth	13	0
2008–09	Portsmouth	20	0
2009–10	Portsmouth	10	0
2010–11	Portsmouth	11	0	131	0

KANU, Nwankwo (F)   431   97
H: 6 5   W: 12 08   b.Owerri 1-8-76
Honours: Nigeria 86 full caps, 13 goals.

1991–92	Federation Works	30	9	30	9
1992–93	Iwanyanwu	30	6	30	6
1993–94	Ajax	6	2
1994–95	Ajax	18	10
1995–96	Ajax	30	13	54	25
1996–97	Internazionale	0	0
1997–98	Internazionale	11	1
1998–99	Internazionale	1	0	12	1
1998–99	Arsenal	12	6
1999–2000	Arsenal	31	12
2000–01	Arsenal	27	3
2001–02	Arsenal	23	3
2002–03	Arsenal	16	5
2003–04	Arsenal	10	1	119	30
2004–05	WBA	28	2
2005–06	WBA	25	5	53	7
2006–07	Portsmouth	36	10
2007–08	Portsmouth	25	4
2008–09	Portsmouth	17	1
2009–10	Portsmouth	23	2
2010–11	Portsmouth	32	2	133	19

KILBEY, Tom (M)   9   0
H: 6 3   W: 13 08   b.Waltham Forest
19-10-90
Source: Millwall.

2007–08	Portsmouth	0	0
2008–09	Portsmouth	0	0
2009–10	Portsmouth	0	0
2010–11	Portsmouth	2	0	2	0
2010–11	*Lincoln C*	7	0	7	0

KITSON, Dave (F)   322   110
H: 6 3   W: 12 07   b.Hitchin 21-1-80
Source: Arlesey.

2000–01	Cambridge U	8	1
2001–02	Cambridge U	33	9
2002–03	Cambridge U	44	20
2003–04	Cambridge U	17	10	102	40
2003–04	Reading	17	5
2004–05	Reading	37	19
2005–06	Reading	34	18
2006–07	Reading	13	2
2007–08	Reading	34	10
2008–09	Stoke C	16	0
2008–09	*Reading*	10	2	145	56
2009–10	Stoke C	18	3
2009–10	*Middlesbrough*	6	3	6	3
2010–11	Stoke C	0	0	34	3
2010–11	Portsmouth	35	8	35	8

LAWRENCE, Liam (M)   353   74
H: 5 11   W: 12 06   b.Retford 14-12-81
Source: Trainee. *Honours:* Eire 15 full caps, 2
goals.

1999–2000	Mansfield T	2	0
2000–01	Mansfield T	18	4
2001–02	Mansfield T	32	2
2002–03	Mansfield T	43	10
2003–04	Mansfield T	41	18	136	34
2004–05	Sunderland	32	7
2005–06	Sunderland	29	3
2006–07	Sunderland	12	0	73	10
2006–07	Stoke C	27	5
2007–08	Stoke C	41	14
2008–09	Stoke C	20	3
2009–10	Stoke C	25	1
2010–11	Stoke C	0	0	113	23
2010–11	Portsmouth	31	7	31	7

MAGRI, Sam (D)   0   0
b.Portsmouth 30-3-94
Source: Scholar.

2010–11	Portsmouth	0	0

MARTIN, Ellis (D)   0   0
b. 18-10-91
Source: Scholar.

2010–11	Portsmouth	0	0

MOKOENA, Aaron (D)   239   4
H: 6 2   W: 14 00   b.Johannesburg 25-11-80
Honours: South Africa 106 full caps, 1 goal.

2000–01	Ajax	6	0
2000–01	Antwerp	13	1
2001–02	Antwerp	29	1	48	2
2002–03	Antwerp	18	0
2003–04	Genk	18	0
2004–05	Genk	12	0	30	0
2004–05	Blackburn R	16	0
2005–06	Blackburn R	22	0
2006–07	Blackburn R	27	0
2007–08	Blackburn R	18	0
2008–09	Blackburn R	18	0
2009–10	Blackburn R	0	0	101	0
2009–10	Portsmouth	23	0
2010–11	Portsmouth	37	2	60	2

MULLINS, Hayden (D)   482   24
H: 5 11   W: 11 12   b.Reading 27-3-79
Source: Trainee. *Honours:* England
Under-21.

1996–97	Crystal Palace	0	0
1997–98	Crystal Palace	0	0
1998–99	Crystal Palace	40	5
1999–2000	Crystal Palace	45	10
2000–01	Crystal Palace	41	1
2001–02	Crystal Palace	43	0
2002–03	Crystal Palace	43	2
2003–04	Crystal Palace	10	0	222	18
2003–04	West Ham U	27	0
2004–05	West Ham U	37	1
2005–06	West Ham U	35	0
2006–07	West Ham U	30	2
2007–08	West Ham U	34	0
2008–09	West Ham U	17	1	180	4
2008–09	Portsmouth	17	0
2009–10	Portsmouth	18	0
2010–11	Portsmouth	45	2	80	2

NUGENT, Dave (F) 290 73
H: 5 11 W: 12 13 b.Liverpool 2-5-85
Source: Scholar. *Honours:* England Youth,
Under-20, Under-21, 1 full cap, 1 goal.

2001–02	Bury	5	0		
2002–03	Bury	31	4		
2003–04	Bury	26	3		
2004–05	Bury	26	11	88	18
2004–05	Preston NE	18	8		
2005–06	Preston NE	32	10		
2006–07	Preston NE	44	15	94	33
2007–08	Portsmouth	15	0		
2008–09	Portsmouth	16	3		
2009–10	Portsmouth	3	0		
2009–10	*Burnley*	30	6	30	6
2010–11	Portsmouth	44	13	78	16

PACK, Marlon (M) 64 3
H: 6 2 W: 11 09 b.Portsmouth 25-3-91
Source: Scholar.

2008–09	Portsmouth	0	0		
2009–10	Portsmouth	0	0		
2009–10	*Wycombe W*	8	0	8	0
2009–10	*Dagenham & R*	17	1	17	1
2010–11	Portsmouth	1	0	1	0
2010–11	*Cheltenham T*	38	2	38	2

RICARDO ROCHA (D) 280 8
H: 6 0 W: 12 08 b.Santo Tirso 3-10-78
Honours: Portugal 6 full caps.

1998–99	Famalicao	28	2	28	2
1999–2000	Braga	25	1		
2000–01	Braga	19	0		
2000–01	Braga B	8	0	8	0
2001–02	Braga	25	2	69	3
2002–03	Benfica	27	0		
2003–04	Benfica	25	0		
2004–05	Benfica	25	0		
2005–06	Benfica	26	0		
2006–07	Benfica	12	3	115	3
2006–07	Tottenham H	9	0		
2007–08	Tottenham H	5	0		
2008–09	Tottenham H	0	0	14	0
2009–10	*Standard Liege*	7	0	7	0
2009–10	Portsmouth	10	0		
2010–11	Portsmouth	29	0	39	0

RYAN, Perry (D) 0 0
b. 10-4-92
Source: Scholar.

2010–11	Portsmouth	0	0

TSOVOLOS, Billy (M) 0 0
b.New South Wales 1-8-93
Source: Scholar.

2010–11	Portsmouth	0	0

UTAKA, John (F) 255 56
H: 5 9 W: 11 02 b.Enugu 8-1-82
Source: Ismaily, Al Saad. *Honours:* Nigeria 45
full caps, 6 goals.

2002–03	Lens	36	8		
2003–04	Lens	32	4		
2004–05	Lens	34	12	102	24
2005–06	Rennes	28	11		
2006–07	Rennes	35	11	63	22
2007–08	Portsmouth	29	5		
2008–09	Portsmouth	18	1		
2009–10	Portsmouth	18	1		
2010–11	Portsmouth	25	3	90	10

Transferred to Montpellier January 2011.

WALSHE, Carl (F) 0 0
b.Dublin 7-10-92
Source: Scholar.

2010–11	Portsmouth	0	0

WARD, Joel (D) 66 4
H: 6 2 W: 11 13 b.Emsworth 29-10-89
Source: Scholar.

2008–09	Portsmouth	0	0		
2008–09	*Bournemouth*	21	1	21	1
2009–10	Portsmouth	3	0		
2010–11	Portsmouth	42	3	45	3

WEBBER, Danny (F) 215 45
H: 5 10 W: 11 04 b.Manchester 28-12-81
Source: Trainee. *Honours:* England Youth,
Under-20.

1998–99	Manchester U	0	0
1999–2000	Manchester U	0	0
2000–01	Manchester U	0	0
2001–02	Manchester U	0	0

2001–02	*Port Vale*	4	0	4	0
2001–02	*Watford*	5	2		
2002–03	Manchester U	0	0		
2002–03	*Watford*	12	2		
2003–04	Watford	27	5		
2004–05	Watford	28	12	72	21
2004–05	*Sheffield U*	7	3		
2005–06	Sheffield U	35	10		
2006–07	Sheffield U	22	3		
2007–08	Sheffield U	14	3		
2008–09	Sheffield U	36	4		
2009–10	Sheffield U	0	0	114	23
2009–10	Portsmouth	17	1		
2010–11	Portsmouth	8	0	25	1

PRESTON NE (65)

ARESTIDOU, Andreas (G) 2 0
H: 6 2 W: 13 00 b.Lambeth 6-12-89
Source: Scholar.

2007–08	Blackburn R	0	0
2008–09	Blackburn R	0	0
2009–10	Shrewsbury T	2	0	2	0
2010–11	Preston NE	0	0

ASHBEE, Ian (M) 466 21
H: 6 1 W: 13 07 b.Birmingham 6-9-76
Source: Trainee. *Honours:* England Youth.

1994–95	Derby Co	1	0		
1995–96	Derby Co	0	0		
1996–97	Derby Co	0	0	1	0
1996–97	Cambridge U	18	0		
1997–98	Cambridge U	27	1		
1998–99	Cambridge U	31	4		
1999–2000	Cambridge U	45	1		
2000–01	Cambridge U	44	3		
2001–02	Cambridge U	38	2	203	11
2002–03	Hull C	31	1		
2003–04	Hull C	39	2		
2004–05	Hull C	40	1		
2005–06	Hull C	6	0		
2006–07	Hull C	35	1		
2007–08	Hull C	42	3		
2008–09	Hull C	31	1		
2009–10	Hull C	0	0		
2010–11	Hull C	19	1	243	10
2010–11	Preston NE	19	0	19	0

BARTON, Adam (M) 34 1
H: 5 11 W: 12 01 b.Clitheroe 7-1-91
Source: Scholar. *Honours:* Eire Under-21.
Northern Ireland 1 full cap.

2008–09	Preston NE	0	0		
2009–10	Preston NE	1	0		
2010–11	Preston NE	33	1	34	1

BROWN, Chris (F) 225 39
H: 6 3 W: 13 01 b.Doncaster 11-12-84
Source: Trainee. *Honours:* England Youth.

2002–03	Sunderland	0	0		
2003–04	Sunderland	0	0		
2003–04	*Doncaster R*	22	10	22	10
2004–05	Sunderland	37	5		
2005–06	Sunderland	13	1		
2005–06	*Hull C*	13	1	13	1
2006–07	Sunderland	16	3	66	9
2006–07	Norwich C	4	0		
2007–08	Norwich C	14	1	18	1
2007–08	Preston NE	17	5		
2008–09	Preston NE	30	6		
2009–10	Preston NE	43	6		
2010–11	Preston NE	16	1	106	18

BROWN, Wayne (D) 350 11
H: 6 0 W: 12 06 b.Barking 20-8-77
Source: Trainee.

1995–96	Ipswich T	0	0		
1996–97	Ipswich T	0	0		
1997–98	Ipswich T	1	0		
1997–98	*Colchester U*	2	0		
1998–99	Ipswich T	1	0		
1999–2000	Ipswich T	25	0		
2000–01	Ipswich T	4	0		
2000–01	*QPR*	2	0	2	0
2001–02	Ipswich T	0	0		
2001–02	*Wimbledon*	17	1	17	1
2001–02	*Watford*	11	3		
2002–03	Ipswich T	9	0	40	0
2002–03	Watford	13	1		
2003–04	Watford	12	0	36	4

2003–04	Gillingham	4	1	4	1
2003–04	Colchester U	16	0		
2004–05	Colchester U	40	1		
2005–06	Colchester U	38	2		
2006–07	Colchester U	46	1	142	4
2007–08	Hull C	41	1		
2008–09	Hull C	1	0	42	1
2008–09	Preston NE	6	0		
2008–09	*Leicester C*	9	0		
2009–10	Leicester C	39	0	48	0
2010–11	Preston NE	13	0	19	0

CARTER, Darren (M) 212 12
H: 6 2 W: 12 11 b.Solihull 18-12-83
Source: Scholar. *Honours:* England Youth,
Under-20.

2001–02	Birmingham C	13	1		
2002–03	Birmingham C	12	0		
2003–04	Birmingham C	5	0		
2004–05	Birmingham C	15	2	45	3
2004–05	*Sunderland*	10	1	10	1
2005–06	WBA	20	1		
2006–07	WBA	33	3	53	4
2007–08	Preston NE	39	4		
2008–09	Preston NE	18	0		
2009–10	Preston NE	23	0		
2010–11	Preston NE	14	0	94	4
2010–11	*Millwall*	10	0	10	0

COLLINS, Dominic (D) 0 0
b.Blackpool 15-4-91
Source: Scholar.

2008–09	Preston NE	0	0
2009–10	Preston NE	0	0
2010–11	Preston NE	0	0

COUTTS, Paul (M) 89 2
H: 5 9 W: 11 11 b.Aberdeen 22-7-88
Source: Cove R. *Honours:* Scotland
Under-21.

2008–09	Peterborough U	37	0		
2009–10	Peterborough U	16	0	53	0
2009–10	Preston NE	13	1		
2010–11	Preston NE	23	1	36	2

DAVIDSON, Callum (D) 376 28
H: 5 10 W: 11 08 b.Stirling 25-6-76
Source: 'S' Form. *Honours:* Scotland
Under-21, 19 full caps.

1994–95	St Johnstone	7	1		
1995–96	St Johnstone	2	0		
1996–97	St Johnstone	20	2		
1997–98	St Johnstone	15	1	44	4
1997–98	Blackburn R	1	0		
1998–99	Blackburn R	34	1		
1999–2000	Blackburn R	30	0	65	1
2000–01	Leicester C	28	1		
2001–02	Leicester C	30	0		
2002–03	Leicester C	30	1		
2003–04	Leicester C	13	0	101	2
2004–05	Preston NE	19	1		
2005–06	Preston NE	27	4		
2006–07	Preston NE	15	0		
2007–08	Preston NE	40	4		
2008–09	Preston NE	20	4		
2009–10	Preston NE	27	5		
2010–11	Preston NE	18	3	166	21

DEVINE, Daniel (D) 2 0
H: 6 0 W: 11 00 b.Belfast 7-9-92
Source: Scholar.

2010–11	Preston NE	2	0	2	0

DOUGAN, Neil (M) 0 0
H: 5 6 W: 10 02 b.Newtownards 8-3-92
Source: Scholar.

2009–10	Preston NE	0	0
2010–11	Preston NE	0	0

DOUGLAS, Jamie (M) 2 0
H: 5 11 W: 12 00 b.Belfast 4-7-92
Source: Scholar.

2010–11	Preston NE	2	0	2	0

GRAY, David (F) 49 0
H: 5 11 W: 11 02 b.Edinburgh 4-5-88
Source: Scholar. *Honours:* Scotland
Under-21.

2005–06	Manchester U	0	0		
2006–07	Manchester U	0	0		
2007–08	Manchester U	0	0		
2007–08	*Crewe Alex*	1	0	1	0
2008–09	Manchester U	0	0		
2008–09	*Plymouth Arg*	14	0		

2009–10	Manchester U	0	0		
2009–10	*Plymouth Arg*	12	0	26	0
2010–11	Preston NE	22	0	22	0

HART, Sam (D)   0 0
H: 5 11 W: 12 04 b.Chester 29-11-91
Source: Scholar.

2010–11	Preston NE	0	0		

HAYES, Paul (F)   337 76
H: 6 0 W: 12 12 b.Dagenham 20-9-83
Source: Norwich C Scholar.

2002–03	Scunthorpe U	18	8		
2003–04	Scunthorpe U	35	2		
2004–05	Scunthorpe U	46	18		
2005–06	Barnsley	45	6		
2006–07	Barnsley	30	5		
2006–07	*Huddersfield T*	4	1	4	1
2007–08	Scunthorpe U	40	8		
2008–09	Scunthorpe U	44	17		
2009–10	Scunthorpe U	45	9	228	62
2010–11	Preston NE	23	2	23	2
2010–11	*Barnsley*	7	0	82	11

HUME, Iain (F)   354 86
H: 5 7 W: 11 02 b.Ontario 31-10-83
Source: Juniors. *Honours:* Canada Youth, Under-20, 29 full caps, 2 goals.

1999–2000	Tranmere R	3	0		
2000–01	Tranmere R	10	0		
2001–02	Tranmere R	14	0		
2002–03	Tranmere R	35	6		
2003–04	Tranmere R	40	10		
2004–05	Tranmere R	42	15		
2005–06	Tranmere R	6	1	150	32
2005–06	Leicester C	37	9		
2006–07	Leicester C	45	13		
2007–08	Leicester C	40	11	122	33
2008–09	Barnsley	15	4		
2009–10	Barnsley	35	5		
2010–11	Barnsley	1	0	51	9
2010–11	Preston NE	31	12	31	12

JONES, Billy (M)   292 21
H: 5 11 W: 13 00 b.Shrewsbury 24-3-87
Source: Scholar. *Honours:* England Youth, Under-20.

2003–04	Crewe Alex	27	1		
2004–05	Crewe Alex	20	0		
2005–06	Crewe Alex	44	6		
2006–07	Crewe Alex	41	1	132	8
2007–08	Preston NE	29	0		
2008–09	Preston NE	44	3		
2009–10	Preston NE	44	4		
2010–11	Preston NE	43	6	160	13

LEATHER, Scott (D)   2 0
H: 6 1 W: 10 12 b.Manchester 30-9-92
Source: Scholar.

2010–11	Preston NE	2	0	2	0

LONERGAN, Andrew (G)   213 1
H: 6 4 W: 13 02 b.Preston 19-10-83
Source: Scholar. *Honours:* Eire Youth, England Youth, Under-20.

2000–01	Preston NE	1	0		
2001–02	Preston NE	0	0		
2002–03	Preston NE	0	0		
2002–03	*Darlington*	2	0	2	0
2003–04	Preston NE	8	0		
2004–05	Preston NE	23	1		
2005–06	Preston NE	0	0		
2005–06	*Wycombe W*	2	0	2	0
2006–07	Preston NE	13	0		
2006–07	*Swindon T*	1	0	1	0
2007–08	Preston NE	43	0		
2008–09	Preston NE	46	0		
2009–10	Preston NE	45	0		
2010–11	Preston NE	29	0	208	1

MAYOR, Danny (M)   31 0
H: 6 0 W: 11 12 b.Leyland 18-10-90
Source: Scholar.

2008–09	Preston NE	0	0		
2008–09	*Tranmere R*	3	0	3	0
2009–10	Preston NE	7	0		
2010–11	Preston NE	21	0	28	0

McLAUGHLIN, Conor (D)   7 0
H: 6 0 W: 11 02 b.Belfast 26-7-91
Source: Scholar. *Honours:* Northern Ireland Under-21.

2009–10	Preston NE	0	0		
2010–11	Preston NE	7	0	7	0

MELLOR, Neil (F)   177 48
H: 6 0 W: 13 05 b.Sheffield 4-11-82
Source: Scholar.

2001–02	Liverpool	0	0		
2002–03	Liverpool	3	0		
2003–04	Liverpool	0	0		
2003–04	*West Ham U*	16	2	16	2
2004–05	Liverpool	9	2		
2005–06	Liverpool	0	0		
2005–06	*Wigan Ath*	3	1	3	1
2006–07	Liverpool	0	0	12	2
2006–07	Preston NE	5	1		
2007–08	Preston NE	36	9		
2008–09	Preston NE	33	10		
2009–10	Preston NE	39	10		
2010–11	Preston NE	0	0	113	30
2010–11	*Sheffield W*	33	13	33	13

MIDDLETON, Doyle (M)   2 0
H: 5 6 W: 10 10 b.Sefton 11-4-94
Source: Scholar.

2010–11	Preston NE	2	0	2	0

MILLER, George (M)   1 0
H: 5 9 W: 12 02 b.Eccleston 25-11-91
Source: Scholar.

2009–10	Preston NE	0	0		
2010–11	Preston NE	1	0	1	0

MORGAN, Craig (D)   252 7
H: 6 0 W: 11 04 b.Flint 18-6-85
Source: Scholar. *Honours:* Wales Youth, Under-21, 23 full caps.

2001–02	Wrexham	2	0		
2002–03	Wrexham	6	1		
2003–04	Wrexham	18	0		
2004–05	Wrexham	26	0		
2005–06	Milton Keynes D	40	0		
2006–07	Milton Keynes D	3	0	43	0
2006–07	*Wrexham*	1	0	53	1
2006–07	Peterborough U	23	1		
2007–08	Peterborough U	41	2		
2008–09	Peterborough U	27	0		
2009–10	Peterborough U	34	1	125	4
2010–11	Preston NE	31	2	31	2

NICHOLSON, Barry (M)   347 43
H: 5 7 W: 9 01 b.Dumfries 24-8-78
Honours: Scotland Under-21, 3 full caps.

1995–96	Rangers	0	0		
1996–97	Rangers	0	0		
1997–98	Rangers	0	0		
1998–99	Rangers	6	0		
1999–2000	Rangers	2	0	8	0
2000–01	Dunfermline Ath	36	3		
2001–02	Dunfermline Ath	37	7		
2002–03	Dunfermline Ath	38	5		
2003–04	Dunfermline Ath	36	5		
2004–05	Dunfermline Ath	27	3	174	23
2005–06	Aberdeen	33	2		
2006–07	Aberdeen	31	6		
2007–08	Aberdeen	38	5	102	13
2008–09	Preston NE	37	3		
2009–10	Preston NE	4	0		
2010–11	Preston NE	22	4	63	7

PARRY, Paul (M)   231 26
H: 5 11 W: 12 12 b.Chepstow 19-8-80
Source: Hereford U. *Honours:* Wales 12 full caps, 1 goal.

2003–04	Cardiff C	17	1		
2004–05	Cardiff C	24	4		
2005–06	Cardiff C	27	1		
2006–07	Cardiff C	42	6		
2007–08	Cardiff C	41	10		
2008–09	Cardiff C	40	2	191	24
2009–10	Preston NE	17	2		
2010–11	Preston NE	23	0	40	2

PROCTOR, Jamie (F)   13 1
H: 6 2 W: 12 03 b.Preston 25-3-92
Source: Scholar.

2009–10	Preston NE	1	0		
2010–11	Preston NE	5	1	6	1
2010–11	*Stockport Co*	7	0	7	0

RUSSELL, Darel (M)   440 34
H: 5 10 W: 11 09 b.Mile End 22-10-80
Source: Trainee. *Honours:* England Youth.

1997–98	Norwich C	1	0		
1998–99	Norwich C	13	1		
1999–2000	Norwich C	33	4		
2000–01	Norwich C	41	2		
2001–02	Norwich C	23	0		
2002–03	Norwich C	21	0		
2003–04	Stoke C	46	4		
2004–05	Stoke C	45	2		
2005–06	Stoke C	37	3		
2006–07	Stoke C	43	7	171	16
2007–08	Norwich C	39	4		
2008–09	Norwich C	38	4		
2009–10	Norwich C	35	3	244	18
2010–11	Preston NE	25	0	25	0

ST LEDGER-HALL, Sean (D)   279 13
H: 6 0 W: 11 09 b.Solihull 28-12-84
Source: Scholar. *Honours:* Eire 18 full caps, 2 goals.

2002–03	Peterborough U	1	0		
2003–04	Peterborough U	2	0		
2004–05	Peterborough U	33	0		
2005–06	Peterborough U	43	1	79	1
2006–07	Preston NE	41	1		
2007–08	Preston NE	37	1		
2008–09	Preston NE	46	5		
2009–10	Preston NE	30	2		
2009–10	*Middlesbrough*	15	2	15	2
2010–11	Preston NE	31	1	185	10

TREACY, Keith (M)   87 10
H: 6 0 W: 13 02 b.Dublin 13-9-88
Source: Scholar. *Honours:* Eire Youth, Under-21, 5 full caps.

2005–06	Blackburn R	0	0		
2006–07	Blackburn R	0	0		
2006–07	*Stockport Co*	4	0	4	0
2007–08	Blackburn R	0	0		
2008–09	Blackburn R	12	0		
2009–10	Blackburn R	0	0	12	0
2009–10	*Sheffield U*	16	1	16	1
2009–10	Preston NE	17	2		
2010–11	Preston NE	38	7	55	9

TROTMAN, Neal (D)   84 5
H: 6 3 W: 13 08 b.Manchester 11-3-87
Source: Burnley Scholar.

2006–07	Oldham Ath	1	0		
2007–08	Oldham Ath	17	1		
2007–08	Preston NE	3	0		
2008–09	Preston NE	0	0		
2008–09	*Colchester U*	6	0	6	0
2009–10	Preston NE	0	0		
2009–10	*Southampton*	18	2	18	2
2009–10	*Huddersfield T*	21	2	21	2
2010–11	Preston NE	0	0	3	0
2010–11	*Oldham Ath*	18	0	36	1

WRIGHT, Bailey (D)   2 0
H: 5 9 W: 13 05 b.Melbourne 28-7-92
Source: Scholar.

2010–11	Preston NE	2	0	2	0

QPR (66)

AGYEMANG, Patrick (F)   368 64
H: 6 1 W: 12 00 b.Walthamstow 29-9-80
Source: Trainee. *Honours:* Ghana 3 full caps, 1 goal.

1998–99	Wimbledon	0	0		
1999–2000	Wimbledon	0	0		
1999–2000	*Brentford*	12	0	12	0
2000–01	Wimbledon	29	4		
2001–02	Wimbledon	33	4		
2002–03	Wimbledon	33	5		
2003–04	Wimbledon	26	7	121	20
2003–04	Gillingham	20	6		
2004–05	Gillingham	13	2	33	8
2004–05	Preston NE	27	4		
2005–06	Preston NE	42	6		
2006–07	Preston NE	31	7		
2007–08	Preston NE	22	4	122	21
2007–08	QPR	17	8		
2008–09	QPR	20	2		
2009–10	QPR	17	3		
2009–10	*Bristol C*	7	0	7	0
2010–11	QPR	19	2	73	15

ALBERTI, Matteo (M)   12 2
H: 5 10 W: 11 05 b.Chievo Verona 4-8-88
Source: Chievo Verona.

2008–09	QPR	12	2		
2009–10	QPR	0	0		
2010–11	QPR	0	0	12	2

ANDRADE, Bruno (M) — 1 0
H: 5 9 W: 11 09 b.Sao Bernardo 2-10-93
Source: Scholar.

Season	Club	A	G	Tot A	Tot G
2010–11	QPR	1	0	1	0

BALANTA, Angelo (F) — 54 11
H: 5 10 W: 11 11 b.Colombia 1-7-90
Source: Scholar.

Season	Club	A	G	Tot A	Tot G
2007–08	QPR	11	1		
2008–09	QPR	10	1		
2008–09	Wycombe W	11	3	11	3
2009–10	QPR	4	0		
2010–11	QPR	0	0	25	2
2010–11	Milton Keynes D	18	6	18	6

BORROWDALE, Gary (D) — 168 0
H: 6 0 W: 12 01 b.Sutton 16-7-85
Source: Scholar. *Honours:* England Youth, Under-20.

Season	Club	A	G	Tot A	Tot G
2002–03	Crystal Palace	13	0		
2003–04	Crystal Palace	23	0		
2004–05	Crystal Palace	30	0		
2005–06	Crystal Palace	7	0		
2006–07	Crystal Palace	25	0	98	0
2007–08	Coventry C	21	0		
2008–09	Coventry C	0	0	21	0
2008–09	Colchester U	4	0	4	0
2008–09	QPR	0	0		
2008–09	Brighton & HA	12	0	12	0
2009–10	QPR	21	0		
2009–10	Charlton Ath	10	0	10	0
2010–11	QPR	1	0	22	0
2010–11	Carlisle U	1	0	1	0

BROWN, Lee (M) — 1 0
H: 6 0 W: 12 06 b.Bromley 10-8-90
Source: Scholar.

Season	Club	A	G	Tot A	Tot G
2008–09	QPR	0	0		
2009–10	QPR	1	0		
2010–11	QPR	0	0	1	0

BUZSAKY, Akos (M) — 192 29
H: 5 11 W: 11 09 b.Hungary 7-5-82
Source: MTK, Porto. *Honours:* Hungary Under-21, 19 full caps, 2 goals.

Season	Club	A	G	Tot A	Tot G
2004–05	Plymouth Arg	15	1		
2005–06	Plymouth Arg	34	4		
2006–07	Plymouth Arg	36	3		
2007–08	Plymouth Arg	11	0	96	8
2007–08	QPR	27	10		
2008–09	QPR	11	1		
2009–10	QPR	39	10		
2010–11	QPR	19	0	96	21

CERNY, Radek (G) — 293 1
H: 6 1 W: 14 02 b.Prague 10-2-74
Honours: Czech Republic 3 full caps.

Season	Club	A	G	Tot A	Tot G
1992–93	Slavia Prague	0	0		
1993–94	Ceske	4	0		
1994–95	Ceske	3	0	7	0
1995–96	Union Cheb	12	0	12	0
1995–96	Tatran	8	0	8	0
1996–97	Slavia Prague	7	0		
1997–98	Slavia Prague	6	0		
1998–99	Slavia Prague	25	0		
1999–2000	Slavia Prague	30	1		
2000–01	Slavia Prague	30	0		
2001–02	Slavia Prague	16	0		
2002–03	Slavia Prague	25	0		
2003–04	Slavia Prague	22	0		
2004–05	Tottenham H	3	0		
2004–05	Slavia Prague	16	0	177	1
2005–06	Tottenham H	0	0		
2006–07	Tottenham H	0	0		
2007–08	Tottenham H	13	0	16	0
2008–09	QPR	42	0		
2009–10	QPR	29	0		
2010–11	QPR	2	0	73	0

CHIMBONDA, Pascal (D) — 304 15
H: 5 10 W: 11 05 b.Les Abymes 21-2-79
Source: Port Louis. *Honours:* Guadeloupe 3 full caps, France 1 full cap.

Season	Club	A	G	Tot A	Tot G
1999–2000	Le Havre	2	0		
2000–01	Le Havre	32	1		
2001–02	Le Havre	27	2		
2002–03	Le Havre	24	2	85	5
2003–04	Bastia	31	1		
2004–05	Bastia	36	3	67	4
2005–06	Wigan Ath	37	2		
2006–07	Wigan Ath	1	0	38	2
2006–07	Tottenham H	33	1		
2007–08	Tottenham H	32	2		
2008–09	Sunderland	13	0	13	0
2008–09	Tottenham H	3	0	68	3
2009–10	Blackburn R	24	1		
2010–11	Blackburn R	6	0	30	1
2010–11	QPR	3	0	3	0

CLARKE, Leon (F) — 207 43
H: 6 2 W: 14 02 b.Birmingham 10-2-85
Source: Scholar.

Season	Club	A	G	Tot A	Tot G
2003–04	Wolverhampton W	0	0		
2003–04	Kidderminster H	4	0	4	0
2004–05	Wolverhampton W	28	7		
2005–06	Wolverhampton W	24	1		
2005–06	QPR	1	0		
2005–06	Plymouth Arg	5	0	5	0
2006–07	Wolverhampton W	22	5	74	13
2006–07	Sheffield W	10	1		
2006–07	Oldham Ath	5	3	5	3
2007–08	Sheffield W	8	3		
2007–08	Southend U	16	8	16	8
2008–09	Sheffield W	29	8		
2009–10	Sheffield W	36	6	83	18
2010–11	QPR	13	0	14	0
2010–11	Preston NE	6	1	6	1

CONNOLLY, Matthew (D) — 131 5
H: 6 1 W: 11 03 b.Barnet 24-9-87
Source: Scholar. *Honours:* England Youth.

Season	Club	A	G	Tot A	Tot G
2005–06	Arsenal	0	0		
2006–07	Arsenal	0	0		
2006–07	Bournemouth	5	1	5	1
2007–08	Arsenal	0	0		
2007–08	Colchester U	16	2	16	2
2007–08	QPR	20	0		
2008–09	QPR	35	0		
2009–10	QPR	19	2		
2010 11	QPR	36	0	110	2

COOK, Lee (M) — 257 20
H: 5 8 W: 11 10 b.Hammersmith 3-8-82
Source: Aylesbury U.

Season	Club	A	G	Tot A	Tot G
1999–2000	Watford	0	0		
2000–01	Watford	4	0		
2001–02	Watford	10	0		
2002–03	Watford	4	0		
2002–03	York C	7	1	7	1
2002–03	QPR	13	1		
2003–04	Watford	41	7	59	7
2004–05	QPR	42	2		
2005–06	QPR	40	4		
2006–07	QPR	37	3		
2007–08	Fulham	0	0		
2007–08	Charlton Ath	9	0	9	0
2008 09	Fulham	0	0		
2008–09	QPR	34	1		
2009–10	QPR	16	1		
2010–11	QPR	0	0	182	12

COX, Elliott (M) — 0 0
Source: Scholar.

Season	Club	A	G	Tot A	Tot G
2010–11	QPR	0	0		

DERRY, Shaun (M) — 521 11
H: 5 10 W: 10 13 b.Nottingham 6-12-77
Source: Trainee.

Season	Club	A	G	Tot A	Tot G
1995–96	Notts Co	12	0		
1996–97	Notts Co	39	2		
1997–98	Notts Co	28	2	79	4
1997–98	Sheffield U	12	0		
1998–99	Sheffield U	26	0		
1999–2000	Sheffield U	34	0	72	0
1999–2000	Portsmouth	9	1		
2000–01	Portsmouth	28	0		
2001–02	Portsmouth	12	0	49	1
2002–03	Crystal Palace	39	1		
2003–04	Crystal Palace	37	2		
2004–05	Crystal Palace	7	0		
2004–05	Nottingham F	7	0	7	0
2004–05	Leeds U	7	2		
2005–06	Leeds U	41	0		
2006–07	Leeds U	23	1		
2007–08	Leeds U	0	0	71	3
2007–08	Crystal Palace	30	0		
2008–09	Crystal Palace	39	0		
2009–10	Crystal Palace	46	0	198	3
2010–11	QPR	45	0	45	0

DOUGHTY, Michael (M) — 0 0
b.Westminster 20-11-92
Source: Scholar. *Honours:* Wales Youth.

Season	Club	A	G	Tot A	Tot G
2010–11	QPR	0	0		

EHMER, Max (M) — 27 0
b.Frankfurt 3-2-92
Source: Scholar.

Season	Club	A	G	Tot A	Tot G
2009–10	QPR	0	0		
2010–11	QPR	0	0		
2010–11	Yeovil T	27	0	27	0

EPHRAIM, Hogan (F) — 130 8
H: 5 9 W: 10 06 b.Islington 31-3-88
Source: Scholar. *Honours:* England Youth.

Season	Club	A	G	Tot A	Tot G
2004–05	West Ham U	0	0		
2005–06	West Ham U	0	0		
2006–07	West Ham U	0	0		
2006–07	Colchester U	21	1	21	1
2007–08	West Ham U	0	0		
2007–08	QPR	29	3		
2008–09	QPR	27	1		
2009–10	QPR	22	0		
2009–10	Leeds U	3	0	3	0
2010–11	QPR	28	3	106	7

FAURLIN, Alejandro (M) — 149 12
H: 6 1 W: 12 06 b.Argentina 9-8-86

Season	Club	A	G	Tot A	Tot G
2004	Rosario Central	1	0		
2005	Rosario Central	0	0		
2006	Rosario Central	0	0	1	0
2007	Atletico Rafaela	40	1	40	1
2008–09	Instituto	27	7	27	7
2009–10	QPR	41	1		
2010–11	QPR	40	3	81	4

GERMAN, Antonio (F) — 29 2
H: 5 10 W: 12 03 b.Wembley 26-12-91
Source: Scholar.

Season	Club	A	G	Tot A	Tot G
2008–09	QPR	3	0		
2009–10	QPR	13	2		
2009–10	Aldershot T	3	0	3	0
2010–11	QPR	2	0	18	2
2010–11	Southend U	4	0	4	0
2010–11	Yeovil T	4	0	4	0

GORKSS, Kaspars (D) — 275 17
H: 6 3 W: 13 05 b.Riga 6-11-81
Honours: Latvia 37 full caps, 4 goals.

Season	Club	A	G	Tot A	Tot G
2002	Auda Riga	28	0	28	0
2003	Oster	8	0		
2004	Oster	24	1	32	1
2005	Assyriska	23	0	23	0
2006	Ventspils	28	5	28	5
2006–07	Blackpool	10	0		
2007–08	Blackpool	40	5	50	5
2008–09	QPR	31	0		
2009–10	QPR	41	3		
2010–11	QPR	42	3	114	6

HALL, Fitz (D) — 233 11
H: 6 3 W: 13 00 b.Leytonstone 20-12-80
Source: Barnet Trainee, Chesham U.

Season	Club	A	G	Tot A	Tot G
2001–02	Oldham Ath	4	1		
2002–03	Oldham Ath	40	4	44	5
2003–04	Southampton	11	0	11	0
2004–05	Crystal Palace	36	2		
2005–06	Crystal Palace	39	1	75	3
2006–07	Wigan Ath	24	0		
2007–08	Wigan Ath	1	0	25	0
2007–08	QPR	14	0		
2008–09	QPR	24	2		
2009–10	QPR	14	0		
2009–10	Newcastle U	7	0	7	0
2010–11	QPR	19	1	71	3

HARRIMAN, Michael (D) — 0 0
b.Chichester 23-10-92
Source: Scholar.

Season	Club	A	G	Tot A	Tot G
2010–11	QPR	0	0		

HELGUSON, Heidar (F) — 370 117
H: 5 10 W: 12 09 b.Akureyri 22-8-77
Source: Throttur. *Honours:* Iceland Youth, Under-21, 53 full caps, 12 goals.

Season	Club	A	G	Tot A	Tot G
1998	Lillestrom	19	2		
1999	Lillestrom	25	16	44	18
1999–2000	Watford	16	6		
2000–01	Watford	33	8		
2001–02	Watford	34	6		
2002–03	Watford	30	11		
2003–04	Watford	22	8		
2004–05	Watford	39	16		
2005–06	Fulham	27	8		
2006–07	Fulham	30	4	57	12
2007–08	Bolton W	6	2		
2008–09	Bolton W	1	0	7	2
2008–09	QPR	20	5		

2009–10	QPR	5	1	
2009–10	*Watford*	29	11	203 66
2010–11	QPR	34	13	59 19

HEWITT, Troy (F)　0　0
b. 10-2-90
Source: Clapton, Ilford, Harrow B.

2010–11	QPR	0	0

HIBBERT, Jordan (M)　0　0
H: 5 10　W: 11 05　b.Hampstead 25-10-90
Source: Scholar.

2007–08	Chelsea	0	0
2008–09	Chelsea	0	0
2009–10	Barnsley	0	0
2010–11	QPR	0	0

HILL, Clint (D)　395　27
H: 6 0　W: 11 06　b.Liverpool 19-10-78
Source: Trainee.

1997–98	Tranmere R	14	0	
1998–99	Tranmere R	33	4	
1999–2000	Tranmere R	29	5	
2000–01	Tranmere R	34	5	
2001–02	Tranmere R	30	2	140 16
2002–03	Oldham Ath	17	1	17 1
2003–04	Stoke C	12	0	
2004–05	Stoke C	32	1	
2005–06	Stoke C	13	0	
2006–07	Stoke C	18	2	
2007–08	Stoke C	5	0	80 3
2007–08	Crystal Palace	28	3	
2008–09	Crystal Palace	43	1	
2009–10	Crystal Palace	43	1	114 5
2010–11	QPR	44	2	44 2

HULSE, Rob (F)　359　112
H: 6 1　W: 12 04　b.Crewe 25-10-79
Source: Trainee.

1998–99	Crewe Alex	0	0	
1999–2000	Crewe Alex	4	1	
2000–01	Crewe Alex	33	11	
2001–02	Crewe Alex	41	12	
2002–03	Crewe Alex	38	22	116 46
2003–04	WBA	33	10	
2004–05	WBA	5	0	38 10
2004–05	*Leeds U*	13	6	
2005–06	Leeds U	39	12	52 18
2006–07	Sheffield U	29	8	
2007–08	Sheffield U	21	0	50 8
2008–09	Derby Co	44	15	
2009–10	Derby Co	37	12	
2010–11	Derby Co	1	1	82 28
2010–11	QPR	21	2	21 2

KENNY, Paddy (G)　455　0
H: 6 1　W: 14 01　b.Halifax 17-5-78
Source: Bradford PA. *Honours:* Eire 7 full caps.

1998–99	Bury	0	0	
1999–2000	Bury	46	0	
2000–01	Bury	46	0	
2001–02	Bury	41	0	
2002–03	Bury	0	0	133 0
2002–03	Sheffield U	45	0	
2003–04	Sheffield U	27	0	
2004–05	Sheffield U	40	0	
2005–06	Sheffield U	46	0	
2006–07	Sheffield U	34	0	
2007–08	Sheffield U	40	0	
2008–09	Sheffield U	44	0	
2009–10	Sheffield U,	2	0	278 0
2010–11	QPR	44	0	44 0

LEIGERTWOOD, Mikele (D)　297　16
H: 6 1　W: 11 04　b.Enfield 12-11-82
Source: Scholar.

2001–02	Wimbledon	1	0	
2001–02	*Leyton Orient*	8	0	8 0
2002–03	Wimbledon	28	0	
2003–04	Wimbledon	27	2	56 2
2003–04	Crystal Palace	12	0	
2004–05	Crystal Palace	20	1	
2005–06	Crystal Palace	27	0	59 1
2006–07	Sheffield U	19	0	
2007–08	Sheffield U	2	0	21 0
2007–08	QPR	40	5	
2008–09	QPR	42	2	
2009–10	QPR	40	5	
2010–11	QPR	9	0	131 12
2010–11	*Reading*	22	1	22 1

MACKIE, Jamie (F)　139　25
H: 5 8　W: 11 00　b.Dorking 22-9-85
Source: Leatherhead. *Honours:* Scotland 3 full caps, 1 goal.

2003–04	Wimbledon	13	0	13 0
2004–05	Milton Keynes D	3	0	3 0
From Exeter C				
2007–08	Plymouth Arg	13	3	
2008–09	Plymouth Arg	43	5	
2009–10	Plymouth Arg	42	8	98 16
2010–11	QPR	25	9	25 9

MAHON, Gavin (M)　399　19
H: 5 11　W: 13 07　b.Birmingham 2-1-77
Source: Trainee.

1995–96	Wolverhampton W	0	0	
1996–97	Hereford U	11	1	
1997–98	Hereford U	0	0	
1998–99	Hereford U	0	0	11 1
1998–99	Brentford	29	4	
1999–2000	Brentford	37	3	
2000–01	Brentford	40	1	
2001–02	Brentford	35	0	141 8
2001–02	Watford	6	0	
2002–03	Watford	17	0	
2003–04	Watford	32	2	
2004–05	Watford	43	0	
2005–06	Watford	38	3	
2006–07	Watford	34	1	
2007–08	Watford	19	0	189 6
2007–08	QPR	16	1	
2008–09	QPR	35	2	
2009–10	QPR	7	1	
2010–11	QPR	0	0	58 4
2010–11	*Crystal Palace*	0	0	

OASTLER, Joe (D)　26　0
H: 5 10　W: 11 03　b.Portsmouth 3-7-90
Source: Portsmouth Scholar.

2008–09	QPR	0	0	
2009–10	QPR	1	0	
2010–11	QPR	0	0	1 0
2010–11	*Torquay U*	25	0	25 0

ORR, Bradley (D)　266　13
H: 6 0　W: 11 11　b.Liverpool 1-11-82
Source: Scholar.

2001–02	Newcastle U	0	0	
2002–03	Newcastle U	0	0	
2003–04	Newcastle U	0	0	
2003–04	*Burnley*	4	0	4 0
2004–05	Bristol C	37	0	
2005–06	Bristol C	38	1	
2006–07	Bristol C	35	4	
2007–08	Bristol C	42	4	
2008–09	Bristol C	38	1	
2009–10	Bristol C	39	2	229 12
2010–11	QPR	33	1	33 1

PARKER, Josh (F)　9　0
H: 5 11　W: 12 00　b.Slough 1-12-90
Source: Scholar.

2009–10	QPR	4	0	
2010–11	QPR	1	0	5 0
2010–11	*Northampton T*	3	0	3 0
2010–11	*Wycombe U*	1	0	1 0

PARMENTER, Taylor (D)　0　0
b.Bromley 9-9-92
Source: Scholar.

2009–10	QPR	0	0
2010–11	QPR	0	0

PELLICORI, Alessandro (F)　239　67
H: 5 11　W: 11 11　b.Cosenza 22-7-81

1999–2000	Cosenza	1	0	1 0
2000–01	Lecce	1	0	
2001–02	Lecce	3	0	4 0
2002–03	*Avellino*	18	7	
2002–03	*Varese*	9	1	9 1
2003–04	*Foggia*	15	2	15 2
2003–04	*Benevento*	14	1	14 1
2004–05	Grosseto	35	12	
2005–06	Grosseto	18	10	
2005–06	*Catanzaro*	7	0	7 0
2006–07	*Piacenza*	9	0	9 0
2006–07	*Cesena*	12	3	12 3
2007–08	*Avellino*	38	18	56 25
2008–09	*Grosseto*	19	4	72 26
2009–10	QPR	8	0	
2009–10	*Mantova*	17	8	17 8
2010–11	QPR	0	0	8 0

2010–11	*Torino*	15	1	15 1

PUTNINS, Elvijs (G)　0　0
b.Latvia 12-6-91
Source: FK Auda. *Honours:* Latvia Youth.

2008–09	QPR	0	0
2009–10	QPR	0	0
2010–11	QPR	0	0

RAMAGE, Peter (D)　119　2
H: 6 3　W: 11 02　b.Whitley Bay 22-11-83
Source: Trainee.

2003–04	Newcastle U	0	0	
2004–05	Newcastle U	4	0	
2005–06	Newcastle U	23	0	
2006–07	Newcastle U	21	0	
2007–08	Newcastle U	3	0	51 0
2008–09	QPR	31	0	
2009–10	QPR	33	2	
2010–11	QPR	4	0	68 2

ROSE, Romone (M)　11　1
H: 5 9　W: 11 05　b.Reading 19-1-90
Source: Scholar.

2007–08	QPR	1	0	
2008–09	QPR	2	0	
2009–10	QPR	1	0	
2009–10	*Northampton T*	1	0	1 0
2009–10	*Cheltenham T*	1	0	1 0
2010–11	QPR	0	0	4 0
2010–11	*Torquay U*	5	1	5 1

ROWLANDS, Martin (M)　348　53
H: 5 9　W: 10 10　b.Hammersmith 8-2-79
Source: Farnborough T. *Honours:* Eire Under-21, 5 full caps.

1998–99	Brentford	36	4	
1999–2000	Brentford	40	6	
2000–01	Brentford	32	2	
2001–02	Brentford	23	7	
2002–03	Brentford	18	1	149 20
2003–04	QPR	42	10	
2004–05	QPR	35	3	
2005–06	QPR	14	2	
2006–07	QPR	29	10	
2007–08	QPR	44	6	
2008–09	QPR	24	2	
2009–10	QPR	6	0	
2010–11	QPR	4	0	198 33
2010–11	*Millwall*	1	0	1 0

SHARIFF, Abdulla (D)　0　0
b.Newham
Source: Youth.

2010–11	QPR	0	0

SHITTU, Dan (D)　281　27
H: 6 2　W: 16 03　b.Lagos 2-9-80
Honours: Nigeria 32 full caps.

1999–2000	Charlton Ath	0	0	
2000–01	Charlton Ath	0	0	
2000–01	*Blackpool*	17	2	17 2
2001–02	Charlton Ath	0	0	
2001–02	QPR	27	2	
2002–03	QPR	43	7	
2003–04	QPR	20	0	
2004–05	QPR	34	4	
2005–06	QPR	45	4	
2006–07	Watford	30	1	
2007–08	Watford	39	7	69 8
2008–09	Bolton W	10	0	
2009–10	Bolton W	0	0	
2010–11	Bolton W	0	0	10 0
2010–11	*Millwall*	9	0	9 0
2010–11	QPR	7	0	176 17

SMITH, Tommy (F)　450　91
H: 5 8　W: 11 04　b.Hemel Hempstead 22-5-80
Source: Trainee. *Honours:* England Youth, Under-21.

1997–98	Watford	1	0	
1998–99	Watford	8	2	
1999–2000	Watford	22	2	
2000–01	Watford	43	11	
2001–02	Watford	40	11	
2002–03	Watford	35	7	
2003–04	Watford	0	0	
2003–04	*Sunderland*	35	4	35 4
2004–05	Derby Co	42	11	
2005–06	Derby Co	43	8	
2006–07	Derby Co	5	1	90 20
2006–07	Watford	32	1	

2007–08	Watford	44	7		
2008–09	Watford	44	17		
2009–10	Watford	4	2	273	60
2009–10	Portsmouth	16	1		
2010–11	Portsmouth	3	0	19	1
2010–11	QPR	33	6	33	6

SUTHERLAND, Frankie (M) 0 0
H: 5 9 W: 10 00 b.Hillingdon 6-12-93
Source: Scholar. *Honours:* Eire Youth.

| 2010–11 | QPR | 0 | 0 | | |

TAARABT, Adel (M) 102 27
H: 5 9 W: 10 12 b.Marseille 24-5-89
Honours: France Youth. Morocco 10 full caps, 3 goals.

2006–07	Lens	1	0	1	0
2006–07	Tottenham H	2	0		
2007–08	Tottenham H	6	0		
2008–09	Tottenham H	1	0		
2008–09	QPR	7	1		
2009–10	Tottenham H	0	0	9	0
2009–10	QPR	41	7		
2010–11	QPR	44	19	92	27

TOFAS, Giorgos (M) 41 5
H: 5 11 W: 11 02 b.Larnaca 17-6-89
Honours: Cyprus Under-21.

2006–07	Paralimni	9	0	9	0
2007–08	AEK Athens	4	1		
2008–09	AEK Athens	0	0	4	1
2008–09	Anagennisi	3	1	3	1
2008–09	Anorthosis	8	2		
2009–10	Anorthosis	16	1	24	3
2010–11	QPR	1	0	1	0

VAAGAN MOEN, Petter (M) 226 41
H: 5 11 W: 11 13 b.Hamar 5-2-84
Honours: Norway 9 full caps, 1 goal.

2001	HamKam	4	0		
2002	HamKam	16	3		
2003	HamKam	28	3		
2004	HamKam	25	1		
2005	HamKam	23	3	96	10
2006	Brann	24	3		
2007	Brann	25	5		
2008	Brann	22	3		
2009	Brann	25	6		
2010	Brann	27	14	123	31
2010–11	QPR	7	0	7	0

VINE, Rowan (F) 300 57
H: 5 11 W: 12 10 b.Basingstoke 21-9-82
Source: Scholar.

2000–01	Portsmouth	2	0		
2001–02	Portsmouth	11	0		
2002–03	Portsmouth	0	0		
2002–03	Brentford	42	10		
2003–04	Portsmouth	0	0		
2003–04	Colchester U	35	6	35	6
2004–05	Portsmouth	0	0	13	0
2004–05	Luton T	45	9		
2005–06	Luton T	31	10		
2006–07	Luton T	26	12	102	31
2006–07	Birmingham C	17	1		
2007–08	Birmingham C	0	0	17	1
2007–08	QPR	33	6		
2008–09	QPR	5	1		
2009–10	QPR	31	1		
2010–11	QPR	0	0	69	8
2010–11	Hull C	5	0	5	0
2010–11	Milton Keynes D	17	1	17	1
2010–11	Brentford	0	0	42	10

READING (67)

ANDERSEN, Mikkel (G) 64 0
H: 6 5 W: 12 08 b.Copenhagen 17-12-88
Source: AB Copenhagen. *Honours:* Denmark Youth, Under-21.

2006–07	Reading	0	0		
2007–08	Reading	0	0		
2008–09	Reading	0	0		
2008–09	Brentford	1	0	1	0
2008–09	Brighton & HA	5	0	5	0
2009–10	Reading	0	0		
2009–10	Bristol R	39	0		
2010–11	Reading	0	0		
2010–11	Bristol R	19	0	58	0

ANTONIO, Michael (M) 59 4
H: 6 0 W: 11 11 b.Wandsworth 28-3-90
Source: Tooting & M.

2008–09	Reading	0	0		
2008–09	Cheltenham T	9	0	9	0
2009–10	Reading	1	0		
2009–10	Southampton	28	3	28	3
2010–11	Reading	21	1	22	1

ARMSTRONG, Chris (D) 245 9
H: 5 9 W: 11 00 b.Newcastle 5-8-82
Source: Scholar. *Honours:* England Under-20. Scotland B.

2000–01	Bury	22	1		
2001–02	Bury	11	0	33	1
2001–02	Oldham Ath	32	0		
2002–03	Oldham Ath	33	1	65	1
2003–04	Sheffield U	12	1		
2004–05	Sheffield U	0	0		
2005–06	Sheffield U	24	2		
2005–06	Blackpool	5	0	5	0
2006–07	Sheffield U	27	0		
2007–08	Sheffield U	32	3		
2008–09	Sheffield U	0	0	95	6
2008–09	Reading	40	1		
2009–10	Reading	0	0		
2010–11	Reading	7	0	47	1

BELL-BAGGIE, Abdulai (F) 14 0
H: 5 4 W: 9 10 b.Sierra Leone 28-4-92
Source: Scholar.

2009–10	Reading	0	0		
2009–10	Rotherham U	11	0	11	0
2010–11	Reading	0	0		
2010–11	Port Vale	3	0	3	0

BIGNALL, Nicholas (F) 44 4
H: 5 10 W: 11 12 b.Reading 11-7-90
Source: Scholar.

2008–09	Reading	0	0		
2008–09	Northampton T	5	1	5	1
2008–09	Cheltenham T	13	1	13	1
2009–10	Reading	0	0		
2009–10	Stockport Co	11	2	11	2
2010–11	Reading	0	0	1	0
2010–11	Southampton	3	0	3	0
2010–11	Bournemouth	5	0	5	0
2010–11	Brentford	6	0	6	0

CHURCH, Simon (F) 113 21
H: 6 0 W: 13 04 b.Amersham 10-12-88
Source: Scholar. *Honours:* Wales Under-21, 12 full caps, 1 goal.

2007 08	Reading	0	0		
2007–08	Crewe Alex	12	1	12	1
2007–08	Yeovil T	6	0	6	0
2008–09	Reading	0	0		
2008–09	Wycombe W	9	0	9	0
2008–09	Leyton Orient	13	5	13	5
2009–10	Reading	36	10		
2010–11	Reading	37	5	73	15

CUMMINGS, Shaun (D) 53 0
H: 6 0 W: 11 10 b.Hammersmith 25-2-89

2007–08	Chelsea	0	0		
2008–09	Chelsea	0	0		
2008–09	Milton Keynes D	32	0	32	0
2009–10	Chelsea	0	0		
2009–10	WBA	3	0	3	0
2009–10	Reading	8	0		
2010–11	Reading	10	0	18	0

D'ATH, Lawson (M) 0 0
H: 5 9 W: 12 02 b.Witney 24-12-92
Source: Scholar.

| 2010–11 | Reading | 0 | 0 | | |

DAVIES, Scott (M) 79 17
H: 5 11 W: 12 00 b.Aylesbury 10-3-88
Source: Scholar. *Honours:* Eire Under-21.

2006–07	Reading	0	0		
2007–08	Reading	0	0		
2008–09	Reading	0	0		
2008–09	Aldershot T	41	13	41	13
2009–10	Reading	0	0		
2009–10	Wycombe W	15	3		
2009–10	Yeovil T	4	0	4	0
2010–11	Reading	0	0	4	0
2010–11	Wycombe W	8	1	23	4
2010–11	Bristol R	7	0	7	0

FEDERICI, Adam (G) 107 1
H: 6 2 W: 14 02 b.Nowra 31-1-85
Honours: Australia Youth, Under-20, Under-21, 4 full caps.

2005–06	Reading	0	0		
2006–07	Reading	2	0		
2007–08	Reading	0	0		
2008–09	Reading	15	1		
2008–09	Southend U	10	0	10	0
2009–10	Reading	46	0		
2010–11	Reading	34	0	97	1

GAGE, Ethan (D) 60 2
H: 5 11 b.Calgary 8-5-91
Honours: Canada Youth.

2007–08	Whitecaps Res	16	2		
2008	Vancouver W'Caps	6	0		
2009	Vancouver W'Caps	17	0		
2009	Whitecaps Res	1	0		
2010	Vancouver W'Caps	7	0	30	0
2010	Whitecaps Res	13	0	30	2
2010–11	Reading	0	0		

GRIFFIN, Andy (D) 314 6
H: 5 9 W: 10 10 b.Billinge 7-3-79
Source: Trainee. *Honours:* England Youth, Under-21.

1996–97	Stoke C	34	1		
1997–98	Stoke C	23	1		
1997–98	Newcastle U	4	0		
1998–99	Newcastle U	14	0		
1999–2000	Newcastle U	3	1		
2000–01	Newcastle U	19	0		
2001–02	Newcastle U	4	0		
2002–03	Newcastle U	27	1		
2003–04	Newcastle U	5	0	76	2
2004–05	Portsmouth	22	0		
2005–06	Portsmouth	22	0		
2006–07	Portsmouth	0	0	44	0
2006–07	Stoke C	33	2		
2007–08	Derby Co	15	0	15	0
2007–08	Stoke C	15	0		
2008–09	Stoke C	20	0		
2009–10	Stoke C	0	0	125	4
2009–10	Reading	21	0		
2010–11	Reading	33	0	54	0

GUNNARSSON, Brynjar (M) 375 31
H: 6 1 W: 12 01 b.Reykjavik 16-10-75
Honours: Iceland Youth, Under-21, 74 full caps, 4 goals.

1995	KR	16	1		
1996	KR	18	0		
1997	KR	16	0	50	1
1998	Moss	3	2	3	2
1999–2000	Stoke C	22	1		
2000–01	Stoke C	46	5		
2001–02	Stoke C	23	5		
2002–03	Stoke C	40	5		
2003–04	Nottingham F	13	0	13	0
2003–04	Stoke C	3	0	134	16
2004–05	Watford	36	3	36	3
2005–06	Reading	29	4		
2006–07	Reading	23	3		
2007–08	Reading	20	0		
2008–09	Reading	27	2		
2009–10	Reading	26	0		
2010–11	Reading	12	0	137	9

HAMER, Ben (G) 93 0
H: 5 11 W: 12 04 b.Chard 20-11-87
Source: Crawley T.

2006–07	Reading	0	0		
2007–08	Reading	0	0		
2007–08	Brentford	20	0		
2008–09	Reading	0	0		
2008–09	Brentford	45	0		
2009–10	Reading	0	0		
2010–11	Reading	0	0		
2010–11	Brentford	10	0	75	0
2010–11	Exeter C	18	0	18	0

HARTE, Ian (D) 347 59
H: 5 11 W: 12 06 b.Drogheda 31-8-77
Source: Trainee. *Honours:* Eire 63 full caps, 11 goals.

1995–96	Leeds U	4	0		
1996–97	Leeds U	14	2		
1997–98	Leeds U	12	0		
1998–99	Leeds U	35	4		
1999–2000	Leeds U	33	6		
2000–01	Leeds U	29	7		

2001–02	Leeds U	36	5		
2002–03	Leeds U	27	3		
2003–04	Leeds U	23	1	213	28
2004–05	Levante	24	1		
2005–06	Levante	0	0		
2006–07	Levante	6	0	30	1
2007–08	Sunderland	8	0	8	0
2008–09	Blackpool	4	0	4	0
2008–09	Carlisle U	3	1		
2009–10	Carlisle U	45	16		
2010–11	Carlisle U	4	2	52	19
2010–11	Reading	40	11	40	11

HECTOR, Michael (D)   11 2
b.Newham 19-7-92
Source: Scholar.

2009–10	Reading	0	0		
2010–11	Reading	0	0		
2011	*Dundalk*	11	2	11	2

HOWARD, Brian (M)   279 40
H: 5 8 W: 11 00 b.Winchester 23-1-83
Source: Trainee. Honours: England Schools, Youth, Under-20.

1999–2000	Southampton	0	0		
2000–01	Southampton	0	0		
2001–02	Southampton	0	0		
2002–03	Southampton	0	0		
2003–04	Swindon T	35	4		
2004–05	Swindon T	35	5	70	9
2005–06	Barnsley	31	5		
2006–07	Barnsley	42	8		
2007–08	Barnsley	41	13		
2008–09	Barnsley	7	1	121	27
2008–09	Sheffield U	26	2		
2009–10	Sheffield U	4	0	30	2
2009–10	Reading	34	2		
2010–11	Reading	24	0	58	2

HUNT, Noel (F)   224 54
H: 5 8 W: 11 05 b.Waterford 26-12-82
Honours: Eire Under-21, B, 3 full caps.

2002–03	Dunfermline Ath	12	1		
2003–04	Dunfermline Ath	13	2		
2004–05	Dunfermline Ath	23	1		
2005–06	Dunfermline Ath	32	4	80	8
2006–07	Dundee U	28	10		
2007–08	Dundee U	36	13	64	23
2008–09	Reading	37	11		
2009–10	Reading	10	2		
2010–11	Reading	33	10	80	23

INGIMARSSON, Ivar (D)   477 34
H: 6 0 W: 12 07 b.Reykjavik 20-8-77
Honours: Iceland Youth, Under-21, 30 full caps.

1995	Valur	12	0		
1996	Valur	17	2		
1997	Valur	16	3	45	5
1998	IBV	18	1		
1999	IBV	18	4	36	5
1999–2000	Torquay U	4	1	4	1
1999–2000	Brentford	25	1		
2000–01	Brentford	42	3		
2001–02	Brentford	46	6	113	10
2002–03	Wolverhampton W	13	2		
2002–03	*Brighton & HA*	15	0	15	0
2003–04	Wolverhampton W	0	0	13	2
2003–04	Reading	25	1		
2004–05	Reading	44	3		
2005–06	Reading	46	2		
2006–07	Reading	38	2		
2007–08	Reading	34	2		
2008–09	Reading	26	1		
2009–10	Reading	25	0		
2010–11	Reading	13	0	251	11

JOYCE, Danny (D)   4 0
b.Dublin 5-6-92
Source: Scholar.

2009–10	Reading	0	0		
2010–11	Reading	0	0		
2011	*Bohemians*	4	0	4	0

KARACAN, Jem (M)   102 5
H: 5 10 W: 11 13 b.Lewisham 21-2-89
Source: Scholar. Honours: Turkey Youth, Under-21.

2007–08	Reading	0	0		
2007–08	*Bournemouth*	13	1	13	1
2007–08	*Millwall*	7	0	7	0
2008–09	Reading	15	1		
2009–10	Reading	27	0		
2010–11	Reading	40	3	82	4

KEBE, Jimmy (M)   158 28
H: 6 2 W: 11 07 b.Paris 19-1-84
Honours: Mali 8 full caps, 3 goals.

2005–06	Lens	0	0		
2006–07	*Chateauroux*	18	2	18	2
2007–08	Lens	0	0		
2007–08	*Boulogne*	16	5	16	5
2007–08	Reading	5	0		
2008–09	Reading	41	2		
2009–10	Reading	42	10		
2010–11	Reading	36	9	124	21

KELLY, Julian (D)   37 1
H: 5 8 W: 11 04 b.Enfield 6-9-89
Source: Arsenal Scholar.

2008–09	Reading	7	0		
2009–10	Reading	0	0		
2009–10	Wycombe W	9	1	9	1
2010–11	Reading	0	0	7	0
2010–11	*Lincoln C*	21	0	21	0

LOCKE, Simon (G)   0 0
b.Newbury 15-10-91
Source: Scholar.

2010–11	Reading	0	0		

LONG, Shane (F)   174 44
H: 5 10 W: 11 02 b.Co. Tipperary 22-1-87
Honours: Eire Youth, B, Under-21, 21 full caps, 6 goals.

2005	Cork C	1	0	1	0
2005–06	Reading	11	3		
2006–07	Reading	21	2		
2007–08	Reading	29	3		
2008–09	Reading	37	9		
2009–10	Reading	31	6		
2010–11	Reading	44	21	173	44

MANSET, Mathieu (F)   63 12
H: 6 1 W: 13 08 b.Metz 5-8-89
Source: Le Havre.

2009–10	Hereford U	29	3		
2010–11	Hereford U	21	7	50	10
2010–11	Reading	13	2	13	2

McANUFF, Jobi (M)   385 41
H: 5 11 W: 11 05 b.Edmonton 9-11-81
Source: Scholar. Honours: Jamaica 1 full cap.

2000–01	Wimbledon	0	0		
2001–02	Wimbledon	38	4		
2002–03	Wimbledon	31	4		
2003–04	Wimbledon	27	5	96	13
2003–04	West Ham U	12	1		
2004–05	West Ham U	1	0	13	1
2004–05	Cardiff C	43	2	43	2
2005–06	Crystal Palace	41	8		
2006–07	Crystal Palace	34	5	75	13
2007–08	Watford	39	2		
2008–09	Watford	40	3		
2009–10	Watford	3	0	82	5
2009–10	Reading	36	3		
2010–11	Reading	40	4	76	7

McCARTHY, Alex (G)   64 0
H: 6 4 W: 11 12 b.Guildford 3-12-89
Source: Scholar. Honours: England Under-21.

2008–09	Reading	0	0		
2008–09	*Aldershot T*	4	0	4	0
2009–10	Reading	0	0		
2009–10	*Yeovil T*	44	0	44	0
2010–11	Reading	13	0	13	0
2010–11	*Brentford*	3	0	3	0

MILLS, Matthew (D)   167 10
H: 6 3 W: 12 12 b.Swindon 14-7-86
Source: Scholar. Honours: England Youth.

2004–05	Southampton	0	0		
2004–05	*Coventry C*	4	0	4	0
2004–05	*Bournemouth*	12	3	12	3
2005–06	Southampton	4	0	4	0
2005–06	Manchester C	1	0		
2006–07	Manchester C	1	0		
2006–07	*Colchester U*	9	0	9	0
2006–07	Manchester C	0	0	2	0
2007–08	Doncaster R	34	3		
2008–09	Doncaster R	41	0		
2009–10	Doncaster R	0	0	75	3
2009–10	Reading	23	2		
2010–11	Reading	38	2	61	4

MILLS, Jack (D)   7 0
b. 26-3-92
Source: Scholar.

2010–11	Reading	0	0		
2010–11	*Telstar*	7	0	7	0

MOONEY, David (F)   180 60
H: 6 2 W: 12 06 b.Dublin 30-10-84
Source: Shamrock R, Longford T. Honours: Eire Under-23.

2005	Longford T	13	4		
2005	Shamrock R	14	2	14	2
2006	Longford T	21	3		
2007	Longford T	32	19	66	26
2008	Cork City	22	15	22	15
2008–09	Reading	0	0		
2008–09	*Stockport Co*	2	0	2	0
2008–09	*Norwich C*	9	3	9	3
2009–10	Reading	0	0		
2009–10	*Charlton Ath*	28	5	28	5
2010–11	Reading	0	0		
2010–11	*Colchester U*	39	9	39	9

MORRISON, Sean (D)   58 6
H: 6 4 W: 14 00 b.Plymouth 8-1-91
Source: Plymouth Arg.

2007–08	Swindon T	2	0		
2008–09	Swindon T	20	1		
2009–10	Swindon T	9	1		
2009–10	*Southend U*	8	0	8	0
2010–11	Swindon T	19	4	50	6
2010–11	Reading	0	0		
2010–11	*Huddersfield T*	0	0		

OBITA, Jordan (M)   0 0
H: 5 11 W: 11 08 b.Oxford 8-12-93
Source: Scholar.

2010–11	Reading	0	0		

OPSAHL, Erik (M)   0 0
H: 5 10 b.Rockville

2010–11	Reading	0	0		

PEARCE, Alex (D)   108 9
H: 6 0 W: 11 10 b.Wallingford 9-11-88
Source: Scholar. Honours: Scotland Youth, Under-21.

2006–07	Reading	0	0		
2006–07	*Northampton T*	15	1	15	1
2007–08	Reading	0	0		
2007–08	*Bournemouth*	11	0	11	0
2007–08	*Norwich C*	11	0	11	0
2008–09	Reading	16	1		
2008–09	*Southampton*	9	2	9	2
2009–10	Reading	25	4		
2010–11	Reading	21	1	62	6

RASIAK, Grzegorz (F)   279 106
H: 6 3 W: 13 03 b.Szczecin 12-1-79
Source: Warta, GKS. Honours: Poland 37 full caps, 8 goals.

2000–01	Odra	28	9	28	9
2001–02	Groclin	26	14		
2002–03	Groclin	22	10		
2003–04	Groclin	18	10	66	34
2003–04	Siena	0	0		
2004–05	Derby Co	35	16		
2005–06	Derby Co	6	2	41	18
2005–06	Tottenham H	8	0	8	0
2005–06	Southampton	13	4		
2006–07	Southampton	39	18		
2007–08	Southampton	23	6		
2007–08	Bolton W	7	0	7	0
2008–09	Southampton	0	0		
2008–09	*Watford*	21	8	21	8
2009–10	Southampton	3	0	78	28
2009–10	Reading	29	9		
2010–11	Reading	1	0	30	9

Transferred to AEL August 2010.

RAYMOND, Frankie (M)   0 0
Source: Scholar.

2010–11	Reading	0	0		

ROBSON-KANU, Hal (F)   86 14
H: 5 7 W: 11 08 b.Acton 21-5-89
Honours: England Youth, Under-20. Wales Under-21, 3 full caps.

2007–08	Reading	0	0		
2007–08	*Southend U*	8	3		
2008–09	Reading	0	0		
2008–09	*Southend U*	14	2	22	5
2008–09	*Swindon T*	20	4	20	4

2009–10	Reading	17	0		
2010–11	Reading	27	5	44	5

ROWE, James (M)   0 0
Source: Scholar.

2010–11	Reading	0	0		

SIGURDSSON, Gylfi (M)   62 22
H: 6 1 W: 12 02 b.Reykjavik 9-9-89
Source: Scholar. *Honours:* Iceland Youth, Under-21, 4 full caps.

2007–08	Reading	0	0		
2008–09	Reading	0	0		
2008–09	*Shrewsbury T*	5	1	5	1
2008–09	*Crewe Alex*	15	3	15	3
2009–10	Reading	38	16		
2010–11	Reading	4	2	42	18

Transferred to Hoffenheim August 2010.

TABB, Jay (M)   281 31
H: 5 7 W: 10 00 b.Tooting 21-2-84
Source: Trainee. *Honours:* Eire Under-21.

2000–01	Brentford	2	0		
2001–02	Brentford	3	0		
2002–03	Brentford	5	0		
2003–04	Brentford	36	9		
2004–05	Brentford	40	5		
2005–06	Brentford	42	6	128	20
2006–07	Coventry C	31	3		
2007–08	Coventry C	42	5		
2008–09	Coventry C	22	3	95	11
2008–09	Reading	9	0		
2009–10	Reading	28	0		
2010–11	Reading	21	0	58	0

TAYLOR, Jake (M)   1 0
H: 5 10 W: 12 01 b.Ascot 1-12-91
Source: Scholar. *Honours:* Wales Under-21.

2010–11	Reading	1	0	1	0

WALCOTT, Jacob (F)   14 2
b.Abingdon 26-6-92
Source: Scholar.

2010–11	Reading	0	0		
2010–11	*Telstar*	14	2	14	2

WILLIAMS, Marcus (D)   177 0
H: 5 8 W: 10 07 b.Doncaster 8-4-86
Source: Scholar.

2003–04	Scunthorpe U	1	0		
2004–05	Scunthorpe U	4	0		
2005–06	Scunthorpe U	29	0		
2006–07	Scunthorpe U	35	0		
2007–08	Scunthorpe U	34	0		
2008–09	Scunthorpe U	26	0		
2009–10	Scunthorpe U	37	0		
2010–11	Reading	3	0	3	0
2010–11	*Peterborough U*	3	0	3	0
2010–11	*Scunthorpe U*	5	0	171	0

WILLIAMS, Brett (F)   0 0
b.Southampton 1-12-87
Source: Eastleigh.

2010–11	Reading	0	0		

ROCHDALE (68)

ADAMS, Nicky (F)   164 15
H: 5 10 W: 11 00 b.Bolton 16-10-86
Source: Scholar. *Honours:* Wales Under-21.

2005–06	Bury	15	1		
2006–07	Bury	19	1		
2007–08	Bury	43	12	77	14
2008–09	Leicester C	12	0		
2008–09	*Rochdale*	14	1		
2009–10	Leicester C	18	0	30	0
2009–10	*Leyton Orient*	6	0	6	0
2010–11	Brentford	7	0	7	0
2010–11	Rochdale	30	0	44	1

AKPA AKPRO, Jean-Louis (F)   133 17
H: 6 0 W: 10 12 b.Toulouse 4-1-85

2004–05	Toulouse	13	0		
2005–06	Toulouse	14	3	27	3
2006–07	Brest	15	2	15	2
2007–08	FC Brussels	3	0	3	0
2008–09	Grimsby T	20	3		
2009–10	Grimsby T	36	5	56	8
2010–11	Rochdale	32	4	32	4

ANDRE, Helio (F)   1 0
b.Angola 3-12-92
Source: Scholar.

2010–11	Rochdale	1	0	1	0

BARRY-MURPHY, Brian (M)   424 16
H: 5 10 W: 13 01 b.Cork 27-7-78
Honours: Eire Youth, Under-21.

1995–96	Cork City	13	0		
1996–97	Cork City	25	0		
1997–98	Cork City	15	1		
1998–99	Cork City	27	1	80	2
1999–2000	Preston NE	1	0		
2000–01	Preston NE	14	0		
2001–02	Preston NE	4	0		
2001–02	*Southend U*	8	1	8	1
2002–03	Preston NE	2	0	21	0
2002–03	*Hartlepool U*	7	0	7	0
2002–03	Sheffield W	17	0		
2003–04	Sheffield W	41	0	58	0
2004–05	Bury	45	6		
2005–06	Bury	40	3		
2006–07	Bury	14	0		
2007–08	Bury	31	1		
2008–09	Bury	42	2		
2009–10	Bury	46	1	218	13
2010–11	Rochdale	32	0	32	0

BROWN, Chris (D)   0 0
H: 6 3 W: 12 04 b.Hazel Grove 21-2-92
Source: Scholar.

2009–10	Rochdale	0	0		
2010–11	Rochdale	0	0		

BYRNE, Callum (M)   0 0
b. 5-2-92
Source: Scholar.

2010–11	Rochdale	0	0		

DONE, Matt (D)   155 6
H: 5 10 W: 10 04 b.Oswestry 22-6-88
Source: Scholar.

2005–06	Wrexham	6	0		
2006–07	Wrexham	34	1		
2007–08	Wrexham	26	0	66	1
2008–09	Hereford U	36	0		
2009–10	Hereford U	20	0	56	0
2010–11	Rochdale	33	5	33	5

EDWARDS, Matty (G)   1 0
H: 6 2 W: 12 11 b.Birkenhead 22-8-90
Source: Leeds U.

2008–09	Leeds U	0	0		
2009–10	Rochdale	0	0		
2010–11	Rochdale	1	0	1	0

ELDING, Anthony (F)   160 40
H: 6 1 W: 12 02 b.Boston 16-4-82
Source: Trainee.

2002–03	Boston U	8	0		

From Stevenage B, Kettering T.

2006–07	Boston U	19	5	27	5
2006–07	Stockport Co	20	11		
2007–08	Stockport Co	25	13		
2007–08	*Leeds U*	9	1	9	1
2008–09	Crewe Alex	16	1		
2008–09	*Lincoln C*	15	3	15	3
2009–10	Crewe Alex	10	0	26	1
2009–10	Rochdale	17	3	17	3
2010–11	*Stockport Co*	21	3	66	27

FLYNN, Matthew (D)   39 0
H: 6 0 W: 11 08 b.Preston 10-5-89
Source: Scholar.

2007–08	Macclesfield T	0	0		
2008–09	Macclesfield T	28	0		
2009–10	Macclesfield T	0	0	28	0
2009–10	Rochdale	10	0		
2010–11	Rochdale	1	0	11	0

GRAY, Reece (F)   4 1
H: 5 7 W: 8 08 b.Oldham 1-9-92
Source: Scholar.

2009–10	Rochdale	2	0		
2010–11	Rochdale	2	1	4	1

HOLNESS, Marcus (D)   84 1
H: 6 0 W: 12 02 b.Swinton 8-12-88
Source: Scholar.

2007–08	Oldham Ath	0	0		
2007–08	*Rochdale*	19	0		
2008–09	Rochdale	8	0		
2009–10	Rochdale	11	0		
2010–11	Rochdale	46	1	84	1

JONES, Gary (M)   489 71
H: 5 11 W: 12 05 b.Birkenhead 3-6-77
Source: Caernarfon T.

1997–98	Swansea C	8	0	8	0
1997–98	Rochdale	17	2		
1998–99	Rochdale	20	0		
1999–2000	Rochdale	39	7		
2000–01	Rochdale	44	8		
2001–02	Rochdale	20	5		
2001–02	Barnsley	25	1		
2002–03	Barnsley	31	1		
2003–04	Barnsley	0	0	56	2
2003–04	Rochdale	26	4		
2004–05	Rochdale	39	8		
2005–06	Rochdale	42	4		
2006–07	Rochdale	27	3		
2007–08	Rochdale	43	7		
2008–09	Rochdale	28	0		
2009–10	Rochdale	34	4		
2010–11	Rochdale	46	17	425	69

KENNEDY, Jason (M)   193 14
H: 6 1 W: 13 02 b.Stockton 11-9-86
Source: Scholar.

2004–05	Middlesbrough	1	0		
2005–06	Middlesbrough	3	0		
2006–07	Middlesbrough	0	0		
2006–07	*Boston U*	13	1	13	1
2006–07	*Bury*	12	0	12	0
2007–08	Middlesbrough	0	0	4	0
2007–08	*Livingston*	18	2	18	2
2007–08	*Darlington*	13	2		
2008–09	Darlington	46	5	59	7
2009–10	Rochdale	42	0		
2010–11	Rochdale	45	4	87	4

O'GRADY, Chris (F)   234 51
H: 6 3 W: 12 04 b.Nottingham 25-1-86
Source: Trainee. *Honours:* England Youth.

2002–03	Leicester C	1	0		
2003–04	Leicester C	0	0		
2004–05	Leicester C	0	0		
2004–05	*Notts Co*	9	0	9	0
2005–06	Leicester C	13	1		
2005–06	*Rushden & D*	22	4	22	4
2006–07	Leicester C	10	0	24	1
2006–07	Rotherham U	13	4		
2007–08	Rotherham U	38	9	51	13
2008–09	Oldham Ath	13	0		
2008–09	*Bury*	6	0	6	0
2008–09	*Bradford C*	2	0	2	0
2008–09	*Stockport Co*	18	2	18	2
2009–10	Oldham Ath	0	0	13	0
2009–10	Rochdale	43	22		
2010–11	Rochdale	46	9	89	31

REDSHAW, Jack (F)   2 0
H: 5 6 W: 10 00 b.Salford 20-11-90
Source: Scholar.

2009–10	Manchester C	0	0		
2010–11	Rochdale	2	0	2	0

THOMPSON, Joe (M)   123 14
H: 6 0 W: 9 07 b.Rochdale 5-3-89
Source: Scholar.

2005–06	Rochdale	1	0		
2006–07	Rochdale	13	0		
2007–08	Rochdale	11	1		
2008–09	Rochdale	30	5		
2009–10	Rochdale	36	6		
2010–11	Rochdale	32	2	123	14

THOMPSON, Josh (D)   39 4
H: 6 4 W: 12 00 b.Bolton 25-2-91
Source: Scholar. *Honours:* England Youth.

2008–09	Stockport Co	9	0	9	0
2009–10	Celtic	18	3	18	3

On loan from Celtic.

2010–11	Rochdale	12	1	12	1

WIDDOWSON, Joe (D)   95 1
H: 6 0 W: 12 00 b.Forest Gate 28-3-89
Source: Scholar.

2007–08	West Ham U	0	0		
2007–08	*Rotherham U*	3	0	3	0
2008–09	West Ham U	0	0		
2008–09	*Grimsby T*	20	1		
2009–10	Grimsby T	38	0	58	1
2010–11	Rochdale	34	0	34	0

WILLIAMS, Owain fon (G) 110 0
H: 6 1 W: 12 09 b.Penygroes 17-3-87
Source: Scholar. Honours: Wales Youth, Under-21.

2005–06	Crewe Alex	0	0	
2006–07	Crewe Alex	0	0	
2007–08	Crewe Alex	0	0	
2008–09	Stockport Co	33	0	
2009–10	Stockport Co	44	0	
2010–11	Stockport Co	5	0	82 0
2010–11	*Bury*	6	0	6 0
2010–11	Rochdale	22	0	22 0

WILLIAMS, Robbie (D) 183 13
H: 5 10 W: 11 13 b.Pontefract 2-10-84
Source: Scholar.

2002–03	Barnsley	8	0	
2003–04	Barnsley	4	1	
2004–05	Barnsley	17	1	
2005–06	Barnsley	22	2	
2006–07	Barnsley	15	0	
2006–07	*Blackpool*	9	4	9 4
2007–08	Barnsley	0	0	66 4
2007–08	Huddersfield T	25	2	
2008–09	Huddersfield T	35	0	
2009–10	Huddersfield T	17	2	77 4
2010–11	Stockport Co	22	1	22 1
2010–11	Rochdale	9	0	9 0

WISEMAN, Scott (D) 158 2
H: 6 0 W: 11 06 b.Hull 9-10-85
Source: Scholar. Honours: England Youth, Under-20.

2003–04	Hull C	2	0	
2004–05	Hull C	3	0	
2004–05	*Boston U*	2	0	2 0
2005–06	Hull C	11	0	
2006–07	Hull C	0	0	16 0
2006–07	*Rotherham U*	18	1	18 1
2006–07	Darlington	10	0	
2007–08	Darlington	7	0	17 0
2008–09	Rochdale	32	0	
2009–10	Rochdale	36	1	
2010–11	Rochdale	37	0	105 1

ROTHERHAM U (69)

ANI, Jeremiah (F) 41 20
H: 6 0 W: 12 00 b.Kaduna 7-10-85
Source: Adamawa U, Naxxar Lions. Honours: Nigeria Youth.

2005–06	Valletta	8	1	8 1
2006–07	Kercem Ajax	16	17	16 17
2007–08	Amadora	5	0	5 0
2008	Gondomar	3	0	3 0
2009	Sichuan Guandong	3	0	3 0
2009	Rovaniemi	6	2	6 2
2010–11	Rotherham U	0	0	

ANNERSON, Jamie (G) 9 0
H: 6 2 W: 13 02 b.Sheffield 1-11-88
Source: Scholar. Honours: England Youth.

2005–06	Sheffield U	0	0	
2006–07	Sheffield U	0	0	
2007–08	*Rotherham U*	0	0	
2007–08	*Chesterfield*	0	0	
2007–08	Sheffield U	0	0	
2008–09	Sheffield U	0	0	
2008–09	*Rotherham U*	0	0	
2009–10	Rotherham U	0	0	
2010–11	Rotherham U	9	0	9 0

ASHWORTH, Luke (D) 22 0
H: 6 2 W: 12 08 b.Bolton 4-12-89

2008–09	Wigan Ath	0	0	
2008–09	Leyton Orient	3	0	
2009–10	Leyton Orient	10	0	13 0
2010–11	Rotherham U	9	0	9 0

BANKS, Oliver (M) 1 1
Source: Scholar.

2010–11	Rotherham U	1	1	1 1

BRADLEY, Mark (D) 117 5
H: 6 0 W: 11 05 b.Dudley 14-1-88
Source: Scholar. Honours: Wales Youth, Under-21, 1 full cap.

2004–05	Walsall	1	0	
2005–06	Walsall	3	0	
2006–07	Walsall	1	0	
2007–08	Walsall	35	3	

2008–09	Walsall	28	2	
2009–10	Walsall	28	0	96 5
2010–11	Rotherham U	21	0	21 0

BROGAN, Stephen (D) 62 4
H: 5 7 W: 10 04 b.Rotherham 12-4-88
Source: Scholar.

2005–06	Rotherham U	3	0	
2006–07	Rotherham U	23	0	
2007–08	Rotherham U	29	3	
2008–09	Rotherham U	1	0	
2009–10	Rotherham U	5	1	
2010–11	Rotherham U	1	0	62 4

CRESSWELL, Ryan (D) 99 6
H: 5 9 W: 10 05 b.Rotherham 22-12-87
Source: Scholar.

2006–07	Sheffield U	0	0	
2007–08	Sheffield U	0	0	
2007 08	*Rotherham U*	3	0	
2007–08	*Morecambe*	2	0	2 0
2007–08	*Macclesfield T*	19	1	19 1
2008–09	Bury	25	1	
2009–10	Bury	28	0	53 1
2010–11	Rotherham U	22	4	25 4

DARLEY, Grant (M) 0 0
b. 25-2-90
Source: Scholar.

2010–11	Rotherham U	0	0	

ELLISON, Kevin (M) 301 48
H: 6 0 W: 12 00 b.Liverpool 23-2-79
Source: Altrincham.

2000–01	Leicester C	1	0	
2001–02	Leicester C	0	0	1 0
2001–02	Stockport Co	11	0	
2002–03	Stockport Co	23	1	
2003–04	Stockport Co	14	1	48 2
2003–04	*Lincoln C*	11	0	11 0
2004–05	Chester C	24	9	
2004–05	Hull C	16	1	
2005–06	Hull C	23	1	39 2
2006–07	Tranmere R	34	4	34 4
2007–08	Chester C	36	11	
2008–09	Chester C	39	8	99 28
2008–09	Rotherham U	0	0	
2009–10	Rotherham U	39	8	
2010–11	Rotherham U	23	3	62 11
2010–11	*Bradford C*	7	1	7 1

FENTON, Nick (D) 451 23
H: 6 0 W: 10 02 b.Preston 23-11-79
Source: Trainee. Honours: England Youth.

1996–97	Manchester C	0	0	
1997–98	Manchester C	0	0	
1998–99	Manchester C	15	0	
1999–2000	Manchester C	0	0	
1999–2000	*Notts Co*	13	1	
1999–2000	*Bournemouth*	8	0	
2000–01	Manchester C	0	0	15 0
2000–01	*Bournemouth*	5	0	13 0
2000–01	Notts Co	30	2	
2001–02	Notts Co	42	3	
2002–03	Notts Co	40	3	
2003–04	Notts Co	43	1	168 10
2004–05	Doncaster R	38	1	
2005–06	Doncaster R	25	2	
2006–07	Doncaster R	8	0	63 3
2006–07	Grimsby T	38	4	
2007–08	Grimsby T	42	2	80 6
2008–09	Rotherham U	45	1	
2009–10	Rotherham U	35	0	
2010–11	Rotherham U	32	3	112 4

GREEN, Jamie (F) 66 2
H: 5 7 W: 10 07 b.Rossington 18-8-89
Source: Scholar.

2007–08	Rotherham U	9	1	
2008–09	Rotherham U	31	1	
2009–10	Rotherham U	19	0	
2010–11	Rotherham U	7	0	66 2

HARRISON, Danny (M) 268 18
H: 5 11 W: 12 04 b.Liverpool 4-11-82
Source: Scholar.

2001–02	Tranmere R	1	0	
2002–03	Tranmere R	12	0	
2003–04	Tranmere R	32	2	
2004–05	Tranmere R	32	0	
2005–06	Tranmere R	35	2	
2006–07	Tranmere R	12	1	124 5
2007–08	Rotherham U	44	4	

2008–09	Rotherham U	33	1	
2009–10	Rotherham U	37	4	
2010–11	Rotherham U	30	4	144 13

LAW, Nicky (M) 140 11
H: 5 10 W: 11 06 b.Nottingham 29-3-88
Source: Scholar. Honours: England Youth.

2005–06	Sheffield U	0	0	
2006–07	Sheffield U	4	0	
2006–07	*Yeovil T*	6	0	6 0
2007–08	Sheffield U	1	0	
2007–08	*Bradford C*	10	2	
2008–09	Sheffield U	0	0	5 0
2008–09	*Bradford C*	33	3	43 5
2009–10	Rotherham U	42	2	
2010–11	Rotherham U	44	4	86 6

LE FONDRE, Adam (F) 250 103
H: 5 9 W: 11 04 b.Stockport 2-12-86
Source: Trainee.

2004–05	Stockport Co	20	4	
2005–06	Stockport Co	22	6	
2006–07	Stockport Co	21	7	63 17
2006–07	*Rochdale*	7	4	
2007–08	Rochdale	46	16	
2008–09	Rochdale	44	18	
2009–10	Rochdale	1	0	98 38
2009–10	Rotherham U	44	25	
2010–11	Rotherham U	45	23	89 48

MARSHALL, Marcus (F) 58 3
H: 5 10 W: 11 06 b.Hammersmith 7-10-89
Source: Scholar.

2007–08	Blackburn R	0	0	
2008–09	Blackburn R	0	0	
2009–10	Blackburn R	0	0	
2009–10	*Rotherham U*	22	0	
2010–11	Rotherham U	36	3	58 3

MULLINS, John (D) 211 11
H: 5 11 W: 12 07 b.Hampstead 6-11-85
Source: Scholar.

2004–05	Reading	0	0	
2004–05	*Kidderminster H*	21	2	21 2
2005–06	Reading	0	0	
2006–07	Mansfield T	43	2	
2007–08	Mansfield T	43	2	86 4
2008–09	Stockport Co	33	3	
2009–10	Stockport Co	36	1	69 4
2010–11	Rotherham U	35	1	35 1

NEWEY, Tom (D) 302 7
H: 5 10 W: 10 02 b.Sheffield 31-10-82
Source: Scholar.

2000–01	Leeds U	0	0	
2001–02	Leeds U	0	0	
2002–03	Leeds U	0	0	
2002–03	*Cambridge U*	6	0	
2002–03	*Darlington*	7	1	7 1
2003–04	Leyton Orient	34	2	
2004–05	Leyton Orient	20	1	54 3
2004–05	*Cambridge U*	16	0	22 0
2005–06	Grimsby T	38	1	
2006–07	Grimsby T	43	1	
2007–08	Grimsby T	42	1	
2008–09	Grimsby T	24	0	
2008–09	*Rochdale*	2	0	2 0
2009–10	Grimsby T	0	0	147 3
2009–10	Bury	32	0	32 0
2010–11	Rotherham U	38	0	38 0

POPE, Tom (F) 122 24
H: 6 3 W: 11 03 b.Stoke 27-8-85
Source: Biddulph Vic.

2005–06	Crewe Alex	0	0	
2006–07	Crewe Alex	4	0	
2007–08	Crewe Alex	26	7	
2008–09	Crewe Alex	26	10	56 17
2009–10	Rotherham U	35	3	
2010–11	Rotherham U	18	1	53 4
2010–11	*Port Vale*	13	3	13 3

TAYLOR, Jason (M) 186 13
H: 6 1 W: 11 03 b.Ashton-under-Lyne 28-1-87
Source: Scholar.

2005–06	Oldham Ath	0	0	
2005–06	*Stockport Co*	9	0	
2006–07	Stockport Co	45	1	
2007–08	Stockport Co	42	4	
2008–09	Stockport Co	8	1	104 6
2008–09	Rotherham U	15	1	
2009–10	Rotherham U	2	0	

2009–10	Rochdale	23 1	23	1
2010–11	Rotherham U	42 5	59	6

TAYLOR, Ryan (F)   139 21
H: 6 2   W: 10 10   b.Rotherham 4-5-88
Source: Scholar.

2005–06	Rotherham U	1 0		
2006–07	Rotherham U	10 0		
2007–08	Rotherham U	35 6		
2008–09	Rotherham U	33 4		
2009–10	Rotherham U	19 0		
2009–10	*Exeter C*	7 0	7	0
2010–11	Rotherham U	34 11	132	21

THOMAS-MOORE, Ian (F)   581 114
H: 5 11   W: 12 00   b.Birkenhead 26-8-76
Source: Trainee. *Honours:* England Youth, Under-21.

1994–95	Tranmere R	1 0		
1995–96	Tranmere R	36 9		
1996–97	Tranmere R	21 3		
1996–97	*Bradford C*	6 0	6	0
1996–97	Nottingham F	5 0		
1997–98	Nottingham F	10 1	15	1
1997–98	*West Ham U*	1 0	1	0
1998–99	Stockport Co	38 3		
1999–2000	Stockport Co	38 10		
2000–01	Stockport Co	17 7	93	20
2000–01	Burnley	27 5		
2001–02	Burnley	46 11		
2002–03	Burnley	44 8		
2003–04	Burnley	40 9		
2004–05	Burnley	35 4	192	37
2004–05	Leeds U	6 0		
2005–06	Leeds U	20 0		
2006–07	Leeds U	33 2	59	2
2007–08	Hartlepool U	24 6	24	6
2007–08	Tranmere R	17 3		
2008–09	Tranmere R	42 10		
2009–10	Tranmere R	43 13		
2010–11	Tranmere R	19 7	179	45
2010–11	Rotherham U	12 3	12	3

TONGE, Dale (D)   168 1
H: 5 10   W: 10 06   b.Doncaster 7-5-85
Source: Scholar.

2003–04	Barnsley	1 0		
2004–05	Barnsley	14 0		
2005–06	Barnsley	24 0		
2006–07	Barnsley	6 0	45	0
2006–07	*Gillingham*	3 0	3	0
2007–08	Rotherham U	37 0		
2008–09	Rotherham U	39 1		
2009–10	Rotherham U	21 0		
2010–11	Rotherham U	23 0	120	1

WARNE, Paul (M)   461 58
H: 5 10   W: 11 07   b.Norwich 8-5-73
Source: Wroxham.

1997–98	Wigan Ath	25 2		
1998–99	Wigan Ath	11 1	36	3
1998–99	Rotherham U	19 8		
1999–2000	Rotherham U	43 10		
2000–01	Rotherham U	44 7		
2001–02	Rotherham U	25 0		
2002–03	Rotherham U	40 1		
2003–04	Rotherham U	35 1		
2004–05	Rotherham U	24 1		
2004–05	*Mansfield T*	7 1	7	1
2005–06	Oldham Ath	40 9		
2006–07	Oldham Ath	46 9	86	18
2007–08	Yeovil T	33 1		
2008–09	Yeovil T	44 4	77	5
2009–10	Rotherham U	14 2		
2010–11	Rotherham U	11 1	255	31

WARRINGTON, Andy (G)   338 0
H: 6 3   W: 12 13   b.Sheffield 10-6-76
Source: Trainee.

1994–95	York C	0 0		
1995–96	York C	6 0		
1996–97	York C	27 0		
1997–98	York C	17 0		
1998–99	York C	11 0	61	0
2003–04	Doncaster R	46 0		
2004–05	Doncaster R	34 0		
2005–06	Doncaster R	9 0		
2006–07	Doncaster R	0 0	89	0
2006–07	*Bury*	20 0	20	0
2007–08	Rotherham U	46 0		
2008–09	Rotherham U	38 0		
2009–10	Rotherham U	46 0		
2010–11	Rotherham U	38 0	168	0

SCUNTHORPE U (70)

BYRNE, Cliff (D)   262 9
H: 6 0   W: 12 11   b.Dublin 27-4-82
Honours: Eire Youth, Under-21.

1999–2000	Sunderland	0 0		
2000–01	Sunderland	0 0		
2001–02	Sunderland	0 0		
2002–03	Sunderland	0 0		
2002–03	*Scunthorpe U*	13 0		
2003–04	Scunthorpe U	39 1		
2004–05	Scunthorpe U	29 1		
2005–06	Scunthorpe U	32 1		
2006–07	Scunthorpe U	24 0		
2007–08	Scunthorpe U	25 0		
2008–09	Scunthorpe U	43 2		
2009–10	Scunthorpe U	36 2		
2010–11	Scunthorpe U	21 2	262	9

CANAVAN, Niall (D)   18 1
H: 6 3   W: 12 00   b.Guiseley 11-4-91
Source: Scholar. *Honours:* Eire Under-21.

2009–10	Scunthorpe U	7 1		
2010–11	Scunthorpe U	8 0	15	1
2010–11	*Shrewsbury T*	3 0	3	0

COLEMAN, Rory (D)   0 0
H: 6 0   W: 11 09   b.Rotherham 22-12-90
Source: Scholar.

2009–10	Scunthorpe U	0 0		
2010–11	Scunthorpe U	0 0		

COLLINS, Michael (M)   205 20
H: 6 0   W: 11 00   b.Halifax 30-4-86
Source: Scholar. *Honours:* Eire Youth, Under-21.

2004–05	Huddersfield T	8 0		
2005–06	Huddersfield T	17 1		
2006–07	Huddersfield T	43 4		
2007–08	Huddersfield T	41 2		
2008–09	Huddersfield T	36 9		
2009–10	Huddersfield T	28 3	173	19
2010–11	Scunthorpe U	32 1	32	1

COWAN-HALL, Paris (F)   4 0
H: 5 8   W: 11 08   b.Hillingdon 5 10 90
Source: Scholar.

2008–09	Portsmouth	0 0		
2009–10	Portsmouth	0 0		
2009–10	*Grimsby T*	3 0	3	0
2010–11	Portsmouth	0 0		
2010–11	Scunthorpe U	1 0	1	0

DAGNALL, Chris (F)   233 66
H: 5 8   W: 12 03   b.Liverpool 15-4-86
Source: Scholar.

2003–04	Tranmere R	10 1		
2004–05	Tranmere R	23 6		
2005–06	Tranmere R	6 0	39	7
2005–06	Rochdale	21 3		
2006–07	Rochdale	37 17		
2007–08	Rochdale	14 7		
2008–09	Rochdale	40 7		
2009–10	Rochdale	45 20	157	54
2010–11	Rochdale	37 5	37	5

DUFFY, Mark (M)   88 6
H: 5 9   W: 11 05   b.Liverpool 7-10-85
Source: Vauxhall M, Prescot C, Southport.

2008–09	Morecambe	9 1		
2009–10	Morecambe	35 4		
2010–11	Morecambe	22 0	66	5
2010–11	Scunthorpe U	22 1	22	1

GODDEN, Matthew (F)   5 0
H: 6 1   W: 12 03   b.Canterbury 29-7-91
Source: Scholar.

2009–10	Scunthorpe U	0 0		
2010–11	Scunthorpe U	5 0	5	0

GRANT, Robert (M)   98 17
H: 5 11   W: 12 00   b.Liverpool 1-7-90
Source: Scholar.

2006–07	Accrington S	1 0		
2007–08	Accrington S	7 0		
2008–09	Accrington S	15 1		
2009–10	Accrington S	42 14	65	15
2010–11	Scunthorpe U	27 0	27	0
2010–11	*Rochdale*	6 2	6	2

HUGHES, Andy (M)   516 39
H: 5 11   W: 12 01   b.Stockport 2-1-78
Source: Trainee.

1995–96	Oldham Ath	15 1		
1996–97	Oldham Ath	8 0		
1997–98	Oldham Ath	10 0	33	1
1997–98	Notts Co	15 2		
1998–99	Notts Co	30 3		
1999–2000	Notts Co	35 7		
2000–01	Notts Co	30 5	110	17
2001–02	Reading	39 6		
2002–03	Reading	43 9		
2003–04	Reading	43 3		
2004–05	Reading	41 0	166	18
2005–06	Norwich C	36 2		
2006–07	Norwich C	36 0	72	2
2007–08	Leeds U	40 1		
2008–09	Leeds U	27 0		
2009–10	Leeds U	39 0		
2010–11	Leeds U	10 0	116	1
2010–11	Scunthorpe U	19 0	19	0

JONES, Rob (D)   223 18
H: 6 7   W: 12 02   b.Stockton 30-11-79
Source: Gateshead.

2002–03	Stockport Co	0 0		
2003–04	Stockport Co	16 2	16	2
2003–04	*Macclesfield T*	1 0	1	0
2004–05	Grimsby T	20 1		
2005–06	Grimsby T	40 4	60	5
2006–07	Hibernian	34 4		
2007–08	Hibernian	30 0		
2008–09	Hibernian	32 4	96	8
2009–10	Scunthorpe U	28 1		
2010–11	Scunthorpe U	14 1	42	2
2010–11	*Sheffield W*	8 1	8	1

LILLIS, Josh (G)   65 0
H: 6 0   W: 12 08   b.Derby 24-6-87
Source: Scholar.

2006–07	Scunthorpe U	1 0		
2007–08	Scunthorpe U	3 0		
2008–09	Scunthorpe U	5 0		
2008–09	*Notts Co*	5 0	5	0
2009–10	Scunthorpe U	8 0		
2009–10	*Grimsby T*	4 0	4	0
2009–10	*Rochdale*	1 0		
2010–11	Scunthorpe U	15 0	32	0
2010–11	*Rochdale*	23 0	24	0

McCLENAHAN, Trent (D)   154 2
H: 5 11   W: 12 00   b.Sydney 4-2-83
Source: Scholar. *Honours:* Australia Under-20, Under-23.

2004–05	West Ham U	? 0		
2004–05	*Milton Keynes D*	8 0		
2005–06	West Ham U	0 0	2	0
2005–06	*Milton Keynes D*	29 0	37	0
2006–07	Hereford U	26 1		
2007–08	Hereford U	38 1	64	2
2008–09	Hamilton A	23 0		
2009–10	Hamilton A	27 0	50	0
2010–11	Scunthorpe U	1 0	1	0

MIRFIN, David (D)   254 13
H: 6 3   W: 13 00   b.Sheffield 18-4-85
Source: Scholar.

2002–03	Huddersfield T	1 0		
2003–04	Huddersfield T	21 2		
2004–05	Huddersfield T	41 4		
2005–06	Huddersfield T	31 1		
2006–07	Huddersfield T	38 1		
2007–08	Huddersfield T	29 1	161	9
2008–09	Scunthorpe U	33 0		
2009–10	Scunthorpe U	37 1		
2010–11	Scunthorpe U	23 3	93	4

MORRIS, Ian (D)   138 11
H: 6 0   W: 11 05   b.Dublin 27-2-87
Source: Scholar. *Honours:* Eire Under-21.

2003–04	Leeds U	0 0		
2004–05	Leeds U	0 0		
2005–06	Leeds U	0 0		
2005–06	*Blackpool*	30 3	30	3
2006–07	Leeds U	0 0		
2006–07	Scunthorpe U	28 3		
2007–08	Scunthorpe U	25 3		
2008–09	Scunthorpe U	20 1		
2008–09	*Carlisle U*	6 0	6	0
2009–10	Scunthorpe U	3 0		
2009–10	*Chesterfield*	7 0		
2010–11	Scunthorpe U	0 0	76	7
2010–11	*Chesterfield*	19 1	26	1

MURPHY, Joe (G) 308 0
H: 6 2 W: 13 06 b.Dublin 21-8-81
Source: Trainee. *Honours:* Eire Youth, Under-21, 2 full caps.

Season	Club				
1999-2000	Tranmere R	21	0		
2000-01	Tranmere R	20	0		
2001-02	Tranmere R	22	0	63	0
2002-03	WBA	2	0		
2003-04	WBA	3	0		
2004-05	WBA	0	0	5	0
2004-05	*Walsall*	25	0		
2005-06	Sunderland	0	0		
2005-06	*Walsall*	14	0	39	0
2006-07	Scunthorpe U	45	0		
2007-08	Scunthorpe U	45	0		
2008-09	Scunthorpe U	42	0		
2009-10	Scunthorpe U	40	0		
2010-11	Scunthorpe U	29	0	201	0

NELSON, Michael (D) 390 27
H: 6 2 W: 13 03 b.Gateshead 15-3-82
Source: Bishop Auckland.

Season	Club				
2000-01	Bury	2	1		
2001-02	Bury	31	2		
2002-03	Bury	39	5	72	8
2003-04	Hartlepool U	40	3		
2004-05	Hartlepool U	43	1		
2005-06	Hartlepool U	43	2		
2006-07	Hartlepool U	42	1		
2007-08	Hartlepool U	45	2		
2008-09	Hartlepool U	46	5	259	14
2009-10	Norwich C	31	3		
2010-11	Norwich C	8	2	39	5
2010-11	Scunthorpe U	20	0	20	0

NOLAN, Eddie (D) 104 1
H: 6 0 W: 13 05 b.Waterford 5-8-88
Source: Scholar. *Honours:* Eire Under-21, 3 full caps.

Season	Club				
2005-06	Blackburn R	0	0		
2006-07	Blackburn R	0	0		
2006-07	*Stockport Co*	4	0	4	0
2007-08	Blackburn R	0	0		
2007-08	*Hartlepool U*	11	0	11	0
2008-09	Blackburn R	0	0		
2008-09	Preston NE	21	0		
2009-10	Preston NE	19	0		
2009-10	*Sheffield W*	14	1	14	1
2010-11	Preston NE	0	0	40	0
2010-11	Scunthorpe U	35	0	35	0

O'CONNOR, Michael (M) 151 14
H: 6 1 W: 11 08 b.Belfast 6-10-87
Source: Scholar. *Honours:* Northern Ireland Youth, Under-21, B, 10 full caps.

Season	Club				
2005-06	Crewe Alex	2	0		
2006-07	Crewe Alex	29	0		
2007-08	Crewe Alex	23	0		
2008-09	Crewe Alex	23	3	77	3
2008-09	*Lincoln C*	10	1	10	1
2009-10	Scunthorpe U	32	2		
2010-11	Scunthorpe U	32	8	64	10

PALMER, Ashley (D) 0 0
H: 6 1 W: 11 13 b.Pontefract 9-11-92
Source: Scholar.

Season	Club		
2010-11	Scunthorpe U	0	0

RAYNES, Michael (D) 174 5
H: 6 4 W: 12 00 b.Wythenshawe 15-10-87
Source: Scholar.

Season	Club				
2004-05	Stockport Co	19	0		
2005-06	Stockport Co	25	1		
2006-07	Stockport Co	9	0		
2007-08	Stockport Co	27	0		
2008-09	Stockport Co	35	3		
2009-10	Stockport Co	25	1	140	5
2009-10	Scunthorpe U	12	0		
2010-11	Scunthorpe U	22	0	34	0

REID, Paul (D) 255 7
H: 6 2 W: 11 08 b.Carlisle 18-2-82
Source: Trainee. *Honours:* England Youth, Under-20.

Season	Club				
1998-99	Carlisle U	0	0		
1999-2000	Carlisle U	19	0		
2000-01	Rangers	0	0		
2001-02	Rangers	0	0		
2001-02	*Preston NE*	1	1	1	1
2002-03	Rangers	0	0		
2002-03	*Northampton T*	19	0		
2003-04	Northampton T	33	2	52	2
2004-05	Barnsley	41	3		
2005-06	Barnsley	33	0		
2006-07	Barnsley	37	0		
2007-08	Barnsley	3	0	114	3
2007-08	*Carlisle U*	1	0	20	0
2008-09	Colchester U	26	1		
2009-10	Colchester U	12	0		
2010-11	Colchester U	18	0	56	1
2010-11	Scunthorpe U	12	0	12	0

SLOCOMBE, Sam (G) 3 0
H: 6 0 W: 11 11 b.Scunthorpe 5-6-88
Source: Bottesford T.

Season	Club				
2008-09	Scunthorpe U	0	0		
2009-10	Scunthorpe U	1	0		
2010-11	Scunthorpe U	2	0	3	0

THOMPSON, Gary (M) 112 20
H: 6 0 W: 14 02 b.Kendal 24-11-80
Source: Scholar.

Season	Club				
2007-08	Morecambe	40	7	40	7
2008-09	Scunthorpe U	24	3		
2009-10	Scunthorpe U	36	9		
2010-11	Scunthorpe U	12	1	72	13

TOGWELL, Sam (M) 223 8
H: 5 11 W: 12 04 b.Beaconsfield 14-10-84
Source: Scholar.

Season	Club				
2002-03	Crystal Palace	1	0		
2003-04	Crystal Palace	0	0		
2004-05	Crystal Palace	0	0		
2004-05	*Oxford U*	4	0	4	0
2004-05	*Northampton T*	8	0	8	0
2005-06	Crystal Palace	0	0	1	0
2005-06	*Port Vale*	27	2	27	2
2006-07	Barnsley	44	1		
2007-08	Barnsley	22	1	66	2
2008-09	Scunthorpe U	40	2		
2009-10	Scunthorpe U	41	2		
2010-11	Scunthorpe U	36	0	117	4

TURNER, Jake (G) 0 0
H: 6 1 W: 11 13 b.Retford 19-1-93
Source: Scholar.

Season	Club		
2010-11	Scunthorpe U	0	0

WILLIAMS, Johnathan (D) 0 0
b.Sheffield 26-3-92
Source: Scholar.

Season	Club		
2010-11	Scunthorpe U	0	0

WRIGHT, Andrew (M) 69 0
H: 6 1 W: 13 07 b.Formby 15-1-85
Source: Liverpool Scholar.

Season	Club				
2006-07	Liverpool	0	0		

From West Virginia Univ.

Season	Club				
2007-08	Scunthorpe U	2	0		
2008-09	Scunthorpe U	28	0		
2009-10	Scunthorpe U	19	0		
2010-11	Scunthorpe U	20	0	69	0

WRIGHT, Josh (M) 115 1
H: 6 1 W: 11 07 b.Bethnal Green 6-11-89
Source: Scholar. *Honours:* England Youth.

Season	Club				
2007-08	Charlton Ath	0	0		
2007-08	*Barnet*	32	1	32	1
2008-09	Charlton Ath	2	0	2	0
2008-09	*Brentford*	5	0	5	0
2008-09	*Gillingham*	5	0	5	0
2009-10	Scunthorpe U	35	0		
2010-11	Scunthorpe U	36	0	71	0

SHEFFIELD U (71)

AKSALU, Mihkel (G) 117 0
H: 6 3 W: 12 06 b.Kuressaare 7-11-84
Honours: Estonia Under-21, 9 full caps.

Season	Club				
2000	Kuressaare	1	0		
2001	Kuressaare	0	0		
2002	Kuressaare	0	0	1	0
2003	Emmaste	0	0		
2003	Flora	1	0		
2004	Flora	1	0		
2005	Flora	8	0		
2006	Flora	15	0		
2007	Flora	30	0		
2008	Flora	30	0		
2009	Flora	31	0	116	0
2009-10	Sheffield U	0	0		
2010-11	Sheffield U	0	0		

BOGDANOVIC, Daniel (F) 77 21
H: 6 2 W: 11 02 b.Misurata 26-3-80
Source: Sliema W, Naxxar Lions, Valletta, Marsaxlokk, Cisco Roma, Lokomotiv Sofia.
Honours: Malta 33 full caps, 1 goal.

Season	Club				
2008-09	Barnsley	16	5		
2009-10	Barnsley	29	11	45	16
2010-11	Sheffield U	32	5	32	5

BROWN, Connor (M) 0 0
Source: Scholar.

Season	Club		
2010-11	Sheffield U	0	0

CALVE, Jean (D) 18 1
H: 6 0 W: 12 04 b.Cormeilles-en-Parisis 30-4-84

Season	Club				
	Sheffield U	18	1	18	1

On loan from Nancy.

CHAPPLE, Jordan (M) 0 0
Source: Scholar.

Season	Club		
2010-11	Sheffield U	0	0

COLLINS, Neill (D) 286 15
H: 6 3 W: 12 07 b.Irvine 2-9-83
Honours: Scoland Under-21, B.

Season	Club				
2000-01	Queen's Park	4	0		
2001-02	Queen's Park	28	0	32	0
2002-03	Dumbarton	33	2		
2003-04	Dumbarton	30	2	63	4
2004-05	Sunderland	11	0		
2005-06	Sunderland	0	0		
2005-06	*Hartlepool U*	22	0	22	0
2005-06	*Sheffield U*	2	0		
2006-07	Sunderland	7	1	18	1
2007-08	Wolverhampton W	22	2		
2008-09	Wolverhampton W	39	3		
2008-09	Wolverhampton W	23	4		
2009-10	Wolverhampton W	0	0	84	9
2009-10	Preston NE	21	1	21	1
2009-10	*Leeds U*	9	0		
2010-11	Leeds U	21	0	30	0
2010-11	Sheffield U	14	0	16	0

CONNEELY, Seamus (D) 86 2
b.Galway 9-7-88
Honours: Eire Under-21.

Season	Club				
2008	Galway U	20	0		
2009	Galway U	34	2		
2010	Galway U	32	0	86	2
2010-11	Sheffield U	0	0		

CRESSWELL, Richard (F) 504 110
H: 6 0 W: 11 08 b.Bridlington 20-9-77
Source: Trainee. *Honours:* England Under-21.

Season	Club				
1995-96	York C	16	1		
1996-97	York C	17	0		
1996-97	*Mansfield T*	5	1	5	1
1997-98	York C	26	4		
1998-99	York C	36	16	95	21
1998-99	Sheffield W	7	1		
1999-2000	Sheffield W	20	1		
2000-01	Sheffield W	4	0	31	2
2000-01	Leicester C	8	0	8	0
2000-01	*Preston NE*	11	2		
2001-02	Preston NE	40	13		
2002-03	Preston NE	42	16		
2003-04	Preston NE	45	2		
2004-05	Preston NE	46	16		
2005-06	Preston NE	3	0	187	49
2005-06	Leeds U	16	5		
2006-07	Leeds U	22	4	38	9
2007-08	Stoke C	43	11		
2008-09	Stoke C	29	0		
2009-10	Stoke C	2	0	74	11
2009-10	Sheffield U	31	12		
2010-11	Sheffield U	35	5	66	17

DOYLE, Micky (M) 323 20
H: 5 10 W: 11 00 b.Dublin 8-7-81
Source: Celtic. *Honours:* Eire Under-21, 1 full cap.

Season	Club				
2003-04	Coventry C	40	5		
2004-05	Coventry C	44	2		
2005-06	Coventry C	44	0		
2006-07	Coventry C	40	3		
2007-08	Coventry C	42	7		
2008-09	Coventry C	37	2		
2009-10	Coventry C	0	0		
2009-10	*Leeds U*	42	0	42	0
2010-11	Coventry C	18	1	265	20
2010-11	Sheffield U	16	0	16	0

ERTL, Johannes (D)   190 6
H: 6 2   W: 12 08   b.Graz 13-11-82
Honours: Austria 7 full caps.

Season	Club				
2003-04	*Kalzdorf*	11	3	11	3
2004-05	Sturm Graz	26	0		
2005-06	Sturm Graz	27	0		
2006-07	Sturm Graz	5	0	58	0
2006-07	FK Austria	24	1		
2007-08	FK Austria	24	2	48	3
2008-09	Crystal Palace	12	0		
2009-10	Crystal Palace	33	0	45	0
2010-11	Sheffield U	28	0	28	0

EVANS, Ched (F)   111 24
H: 6 0   W: 12 00   b.Rhyl 28-12-88
Source: Scholar. *Honours:* Wales Under-21, 13 full caps, 2 goals.

2006-07	Manchester C	0	0		
2007-08	Manchester C	0	0		
2007-08	*Norwich C*	28	10	28	10
2008-09	*Manchester C*	16	1	16	1
2009-10	Sheffield U	33	4		
2010-11	Sheffield U	34	9	67	13

FRANCE, Ryan (M)   142 6
H: 5 11   W: 11 11   b.Sheffield 13-12-80
Source: Alfreton T.

2003-04	Hull C	28	2		
2004-05	Hull C	31	2		
2005-06	Hull C	35	2		
2006-07	Hull C	24	0		
2007-08	Hull C	13	0		
2008-09	Hull C	2	0	133	6
2009-10	Sheffield U	9	0		
2010-11	Sheffield U	0	0	9	0

GARDOS, Andros (M)   1 1
b.Budapest 9-1-91

2010-11	Ferencvaros	1	1	1	1
2010-11	Sheffield U	0	0		

HARRIOTT, Matty (M)   2 0
b.Luton 23-9-92
Source: Scholar.

2010-11	Sheffield U	2	0	2	0

HENDERSON, Darius (F)   300 76
H: 6 3   W: 14 03   b.Sutton 7-9-81
Source: Trainee.

1999-2000	Reading	6	0		
2000-01	Reading	4	0		
2001-02	Reading	38	7		
2002-03	Reading	22	4		
2003-04	Reading	1	0	71	11
2003-04	*Brighton & HA*	10	2	10	2
2003-04	Gillingham	4	0		
2004-05	Gillingham	32	9	36	9
2004-05	*Swindon T*	6	5	6	5
2005-06	Watford	30	14		
2006-07	Watford	35	3		
2007-08	Watford	40	12	105	29
2008-09	Sheffield U	32	6		
2009-10	Sheffield U	32	12		
2010-11	Sheffield U	8	2	72	20

JAMES, Kingsley (D)   0 0
H: 6 1   W: 11 09   b.Rotherham 17-2-92
Source: Scholar.

2010-11	Sheffield U	0	0		

JORDAN, Stephen (D)   158 0
H: 6 1   W: 13 00   b.Warrington 6-3-82
Source: Scholarship.

1998-99	Manchester C	0	0		
1999-2000	Manchester C	0	0		
2000-01	Manchester C	0	0		
2001-02	Manchester C	0	0		
2002-03	Manchester C	1	0		
2002-03	*Cambridge U*	11	0	11	0
2003-04	Manchester C	2	0		
2004-05	Manchester C	19	0		
2005-06	Manchester C	18	0		
2006-07	Manchester C	13	0	53	0
2007-08	Burnley	21	0		
2008-09	Burnley	27	0		
2009-10	Burnley	25	0		
2010-11	Burnley	0	0	73	0
2010-11	Sheffield U	15	0	15	0
2010-11	*Huddersfield T*	6	0	6	0

KENNEDY, Terry (D)   1 0
b.Barnsley 14-11-93
Source: Scholar.

2010-11	Sheffield U	1	0	1	0

KOZLUK, Rob (D)   327 3
H: 5 8   W: 10 02   b.Mansfield 5-8-77
Source: Trainee. *Honours:* England Under-21.

1995-96	Derby Co	0	0		
1996-97	Derby Co	0	0		
1997-98	Derby Co	9	0		
1998-99	Derby Co	7	0	16	0
1998-99	Sheffield U	10	0		
1999-2000	Sheffield U	39	0		
2000-01	Sheffield U	27	0		
2000-01	*Huddersfield T*	14	0	14	0
2001-02	Sheffield U	8	0		
2002-03	Sheffield U	32	1		
2003-04	Sheffield U	42	1		
2004-05	Sheffield U	9	0		
2004-05	*Preston NE*	1	0	1	0
2005-06	Sheffield U	27	0		
2006-07	Sheffield U	19	0		
2007-08	Barnsley	24	0		
2008-09	Barnsley	37	0		
2009-10	Barnsley	14	0	75	0
2010-11	Sheffield U	8	1	221	3

LOKBERG, Kristoffer (M)   0 0
b.Norway 22-1-92
Source: Strindheim. *Honours:* Norway Youth.

2010-11	Sheffield U	0	0		

LONG, George (G)   1 0
H: 6 0   W: 12 05   b.Sheffield 5-11-93
Source: Scholar.

2010-11	Sheffield U	1	0	1	0

LOWTON, Matt (M)   39 4
H: 5 11   W: 12 04   b.Chesterfield 9-6-89
Source: Scholar.

2008-09	Sheffield U	0	0		
2009-10	Sheffield U	2	0		
2009-10	*Ferencvaros*	5	0	5	0
2010-11	Sheffield U	32	4	34	4

MAGUIRE, Harry (D)   5 0
H: 6 2   W: 12 06   b.Mexborough 5-3-93
Source: Scholar.

2010-11	Sheffield U	5	0	5	0

McALLISTER, David (M)   80 27
H: 5 10   W: 11 09   b.Dublin 29-12-88

2008	Drogheda U	0	0		
2008	Shelbourne	16	7		
2009	Shelbourne	30	16	46	23
2010	St Patrick's Ath	32	3	32	3
2010-11	Sheffield U	2	1	2	1

McFADZEAN, Callum (D)   0 0
b.Waterthorpe
Source: Scholar.

2010-11	Sheffield U	0	0		

MONTGOMERY, Nick (M)   329 8
H: 5 9   W: 11 08   b.Leeds 28-10-81
Source: Scholar. *Honours:* Scotland Under-21, B.

2000-01	Sheffield U	27	0		
2001-02	Sheffield U	31	2		
2002-03	Sheffield U	23	0		
2003-04	Sheffield U	36	3		
2004-05	Sheffield U	25	1		
2005-06	Sheffield U	39	1		
2006-07	Sheffield U	26	0		
2007-08	Sheffield U	20	0		
2008-09	Sheffield U	28	0		
2009-10	Sheffield U	39	1		
2010-11	Sheffield U	35	0	329	8

MORGAN, Chris (D)   432 20
H: 6 1   W: 12 03   b.Barnsley 9-11-77
Source: Trainee.

1996-97	Barnsley	0	0		
1997-98	Barnsley	11	0		
1998-99	Barnsley	19	0		
1999-2000	Barnsley	37	0		
2000-01	Barnsley	40	1		
2001-02	Barnsley	42	4		
2002-03	Barnsley	36	2	185	7
2003-04	Sheffield U	32	1		
2004-05	Sheffield U	41	2		
2005-06	Sheffield U	39	3		
2006-07	Sheffield U	24	1		
2007-08	Sheffield U	25	2		
2008-09	Sheffield U	41	2		
2009-10	Sheffield U	37	2		
2010-11	Sheffield U	8	0	247	13

PARRINO, Elian (D)   8 0
H: 5 10   W: 12 04   b.Perez 3-9-88

2010-11	Sheffield U	8	0	8	0

On loan from Estudiantes.

POMARES, Carlos (D)   0 0
b.Albaraya 5-12-92
Source: Scholar.

2009-10	Sheffield U	0	0		
2010-11	Sheffield U	0	0		

QUINN, Stephen (M)   189 16
H: 5 6   W: 9 08   b.Dublin 4-4-86
Source: Trainee. *Honours:* Eire Under-21.

2005-06	Sheffield U	0	0		
2005-06	*Milton Keynes D*	15	0	15	0
2005-06	*Rotherham U*	16	0	16	0
2006-07	Sheffield U	15	2		
2007-08	Sheffield U	19	2		
2008-09	Sheffield U	43	7		
2009-10	Sheffield U	44	4		
2010-11	Sheffield U	37	1	158	16

ROBERTSON, Jordan (F)   65 14
H: 6 0   W: 12 06   b.Sheffield 12-2-88
Source: Scholar.

2006-07	Sheffield U	0	0		
2006-07	*Torquay U*	9	2	9	2
2006-07	*Northampton T*	17	3	17	3
2007-08	Sheffield U	0	0		
2007-08	*Dundee U*	14	3	14	3
2007-08	*Oldham Ath*	3	1	3	1
2008-09	Sheffield U	0	0		
2008-09	*Southampton*	10	1	10	1
2008-09	*Ferencvaros*	8	3	8	3
2009-10	Sheffield U	0	0		
2009-10	*Bury*	4	1	4	1
2010-11	Sheffield U	0	0		

Transferred to St Johnstone March 2011.

ROE, Philip (M)   0 0
Source: Scholar.

2010-11	Sheffield U	0	0		

SIMONSEN, Steve (G)   283 0
H: 6 2   W: 12 08   b.South Shields 3-4-79
Source: Trainee. *Honours:* England Youth, Under-21.

1996-97	Tranmere R	9	0		
1997-98	Tranmere R	30	0		
1998-99	Tranmere R	5	0	35	0
1998-99	Everton	0	0		
1999-2000	Everton	1	0		
2000-01	Everton	1	0		
2001-02	Everton	25	0		
2002-03	Everton	2	0		
2003-04	Everton	1	0	30	0
2004-05	Stoke C	31	0		
2005-06	Stoke C	45	0		
2006-07	Stoke C	46	0		
2007-08	Stoke C	36	0		
2008-09	Stoke C	5	0		
2009-10	Stoke C	3	0	166	0
2009-10	*Sheffield U*	7	0		
2010-11	Sheffield U	45	0	52	0

SLEW, Jordan (F)   7 2
H: 6 3   W: 12 11   b.Sheffield 7-9-92
Source: Scholar.

2010-11	Sheffield U	7	2	7	2

TAYLOR, Andy (D)   122 3
H: 5 11   W: 11 07   b.Blackburn 14-3-86
Source: Scholar. *Honours:* England Youth, Under-20, Under-21.

2004-05	Blackburn R	0	0		
2005-06	Blackburn R	0	0		
2005-06	QPR	3	0	3	0
2005-06	*Blackpool*	3	0	3	0
2006-07	Blackburn R	0	0		
2006-07	*Crewe Alex*	4	0	4	0
2006-07	*Huddersfield T*	8	0	8	0
2007-08	Blackburn R	0	0		
2007-08	Tranmere R	30	2		
2008-09	Tranmere R	39	1	69	3
2009-10	Sheffield U	26	0		
2010-11	Sheffield U	9	0	35	0

THOMAS, Lawrence (G)   0 0
b.Australia

Season	Club				
2010–11	Sheffield U	0	0		

TONNE, Erik (M)   2 0
b.Trondheim 7-5-91
Source: Strindheim.

2010–11	Sheffield U	2	0	2	0

WARREN, Mark (D)   0 0
b.Sydney 11-2-92
Source: Central Coast Mariners.

2010–11	Sheffield U	0	0		

WARREN, Marc (M)   0 0

2010–11	Sheffield U	0	0		

WILLIAMSON, Lee (M)   349 23
H: 5 10 W: 10 04 b.Derby 7-6-82
Source: Trainee.

Season	Club				
1999–2000	Mansfield T	4	0		
2000–01	Mansfield T	15	0		
2001–02	Mansfield T	46	3		
2002–03	Mansfield T	40	0		
2003–04	Mansfield T	35	0		
2004–05	Mansfield T	4	0	144	3
2004–05	Northampton T	37	0	37	0
2005–06	Rotherham U	37	4		
2006–07	Rotherham U	19	5	56	9
2006–07	Watford	5	0		
2007–08	Watford	32	2		
2008–09	Watford	34	2	71	4
2008–09	*Preston NE*	5	1	5	1
2009–10	Sheffield U	20	3		
2010–11	Sheffield U	16	3	36	6

WRIGHT, Richard (G)   379 0
H: 6 2 W: 14 04 b.Ipswich 5-11-77
Source: Trainee. Honours: England Schools, Youth, Under-21, 2 full caps.

Season	Club				
1994–95	Ipswich T	3	0		
1995–96	Ipswich T	23	0		
1996–97	Ipswich T	40	0		
1997–98	Ipswich T	46	0		
1998–99	Ipswich T	46	0		
1999–2000	Ipswich T	46	0		
2000–01	Ipswich T	36	0		
2001–02	Arsenal	12	0	12	0
2002–03	Everton	33	0		
2003–04	Everton	4	0		
2004–05	Everton	7	0		
2005–06	Everton	15	0		
2006–07	Everton	1	0	60	0
2007–08	West Ham U	0	0		
2007–08	Southampton	7	0	7	0
2008–09	Ipswich T	46	0		
2009–10	Ipswich T	12	0		
2010–11	Ipswich T	0	0	298	0
2010–11	Sheffield U	2	0	2	0

YEATES, Mark (F)   220 34
H: 5 8 W: 13 03 b.Dublin 11-1-85
Source: Trainee. Honours: Eire Youth, Under-21.

Season	Club				
2002–03	Tottenham H	0	0		
2003–04	Tottenham H	1	0		
2003–04	*Brighton & HA*	9	0	9	0
2004–05	Tottenham H	2	0		
2004–05	*Swindon T*	4	0	4	0
2005–06	Tottenham H	0	0		
2005–06	*Colchester U*	44	5		
2006–07	Tottenham H	0	0	3	0
2006–07	*Hull C*	5	0	5	0
2006–07	*Leicester C*	9	1	9	1
2007–08	Colchester U	29	8		
2008–09	Colchester U	43	12	116	25
2009–10	Middlesbrough	19	1	19	1
2009–10	Sheffield U	20	2		
2010–11	Sheffield U	35	5	55	7

SHEFFIELD W (72)

BARNETT, Jack (M)   0 0
b. 27-12-91
Source: Scholar.

2010–11	Sheffield W	0	0		

BEEVERS, Mark (D)   127 2
H: 6 4 W: 13 00 b.Barnsley 21-11-89
Source: Scholar. Honours: England Youth.

Season	Club				
2006–07	Sheffield W	2	0		
2007–08	Sheffield W	28	0		
2008–09	Sheffield W	34	0		
2009–10	Sheffield W	35	0		
2010–11	Sheffield W	28	2	127	2

BODEN, Luke (F)   23 0
H: 6 1 W: 12 00 b.Sheffield 26-11-88
Source: Scholar.

Season	Club				
2006–07	Sheffield W	1	0		
2007–08	Sheffield W	2	0		
2008–09	Sheffield W	12	0		
2008–09	*Chesterfield*	4	0	4	0
2009–10	Sheffield W	0	0		
2009–10	*Northampton T*	4	0	4	0
2010–11	Sheffield W	0	0	15	0

Transferred to Orlando C January 2011.

BUXTON, Lewis (D)   220 3
H: 6 1 W: 13 11 b.Newport (IW) 10-12-83
Source: School.

Season	Club				
2000–01	Portsmouth	0	0		
2001–02	Portsmouth	29	0		
2002–03	Portsmouth	1	0		
2002–03	*Exeter C*	4	0	4	0
2002–03	Bournemouth	17	0		
2003–04	Portsmouth	0	0		
2003–04	Bournemouth	26	0	43	0
2004–05	Portsmouth	0	0	30	0
2004–05	Stoke C	16	0		
2005–06	Stoke C	32	1		
2006–07	Stoke C	1	0		
2007–08	Stoke C	4	0		
2008–09	Stoke C	0	0	53	1
2009–10	Sheffield W	28	0		
2010–11	Sheffield W	30	1	90	2

COKE, Gilles (M)   181 18
H: 6 0 W: 11 11 b.Westminster 3-6-86
Source: Kingstonian.

Season	Club				
2004–05	Mansfield T	9	0		
2005–06	Mansfield T	40	4		
2006–07	Mansfield T	21	1	70	5
2007–08	Northampton T	20	5		
2008–09	Northampton T	32	2	52	7
2009–10	Motherwell	32	2	32	2
2010–11	Sheffield W	27	4	27	4

COTTINGHAM, James (M)   0 0
b.London 3-6-86
Source: Scholar.

2010–11	Sheffield W	0	0		

HEFFERNAN, Paul (F)   286 85
H: 5 10 W: 11 00 b.Dublin 29-12-81
Source: Newton.

Season	Club				
1999–2000	Notts Co	2	0		
2000–01	Notts Co	1	0		
2001–02	Notts Co	23	6		
2002–03	Notts Co	36	10		
2003–04	Notts Co	38	20	100	36
2004–05	Bristol C	27	5	27	5
2005–06	Doncaster R	26	8		
2006–07	Doncaster R	29	11		
2007–08	Doncaster R	27	7		
2008–09	Doncaster R	28	10		
2009–10	Doncaster R	17	0	127	36
2009–10	*Oldham Ath*	4	1	4	1
2009–10	*Bristol R*	11	4	11	4
2010–11	Sheffield W	17	3	17	3

HINDS, Richard (D)   260 11
H: 6 2 W: 12 02 b.Sheffield 22-8-80
Source: Schoolboy.

Season	Club				
1998–99	Tranmere R	2	0		
1999–2000	Tranmere R	6	0		
2000–01	Tranmere R	29	0		
2001–02	Tranmere R	10	0		
2002–03	Tranmere R	8	0	55	0
2003–04	Hull C	39	1		
2004–05	Hull C	6	0	45	1
2004–05	*Scunthorpe U*	7	0		
2005–06	Scunthorpe U	42	6		
2006–07	Scunthorpe U	44	2	93	8
2007–08	Sheffield W	38	2		
2008–09	Sheffield W	14	0		
2009–10	Sheffield W	11	0		
2010–11	Sheffield W	4	0	67	2

JAMESON, Arron (G)   2 0
H: 6 3 W: 13 01 b.Sheffield 7-11-89
Source: Scholar.

Season	Club				
2008–09	Sheffield W	0	0		
2009–10	Sheffield W	0	0		
2010–11	Sheffield W	2	0	2	0

JOHNSON, Jermaine (M)   217 28
H: 5 11 W: 11 05 b.Kingston, Jamaica 25-6-80
Source: Tivoli Gardens. Honours: Jamaica 62 full caps, 9 goals.

Season	Club				
2001–02	Bolton W	10	0		
2002–03	Bolton W	2	0		
2003–04	Bolton W	0	0	12	0
2003–04	Oldham Ath	20	5		
2004–05	Oldham Ath	19	4		
2005–06	Oldham Ath	0	0	39	9
2006–07	Bradford C	27	4	27	4
2006–07	Sheffield W	7	2		
2007–08	Sheffield W	35	1		
2008–09	Sheffield W	37	3		
2009–10	Sheffield W	34	5		
2010–11	Sheffield W	26	4	139	15

JOHNSON, Reda (D)   73 5
H: 6 2 W: 13 10 b.Marseille 21-3-88
Honours: Benin 6 full caps.

Season	Club				
2005–06	Gueugnon	0	0		
2006–07	Gueugnon	0	0		
2007–08	Amiens	8	0		
2008–09	Amiens	7	0	15	0
2009–10	Plymouth Arg	25	0		
2010–11	Plymouth Arg	17	2	42	2
2010–11	Sheffield W	16	3	16	3

JONES, Daniel (D)   115 4
H: 6 2 W: 13 00 b.Rowley Regis 14-7-86
Source: Scholar.

Season	Club				
2005–06	Wolverhampton W	1	0		
2006–07	Wolverhampton W	8	0		
2007–08	Wolverhampton W	1	0		
2007–08	*Northampton T*	33	3	33	3
2008–09	Wolverhampton W	0	0		
2008–09	*Oldham Ath*	23	1	23	1
2009–10	Wolverhampton W	0	0	10	0
2009–10	*Notts Co*	7	0	7	0
2009–10	*Bristol R*	17	0	17	0
2010–11	Sheffield W	25	0	25	0

MADINE, Gary (F)   104 18
H: 6 1 W: 12 00 b.Gateshead 24-8-90
Source: Scholar.

Season	Club				
2007–08	Carlisle U	11	0		
2008–09	Carlisle U	14	1		
2008–09	*Rochdale*	3	0	3	0
2009–10	Carlisle U	20	4		
2009–10	*Coventry C*	9	0	9	0
2009–10	*Chesterfield*	4	0	4	0
2010–11	Carlisle U	21	8	66	13
2010–11	Sheffield W	22	5	22	5

MILLER, Tommy (M)   417 88
H: 6 0 W: 11 07 b.Shotton 8-1-79
Source: Trainee.

Season	Club				
1997–98	Hartlepool U	13	1		
1998–99	Hartlepool U	34	4		
1999–2000	Hartlepool U	44	14		
2000–01	Hartlepool U	46	16		
2001–02	Hartlepool U	0	0	137	35
2001–02	Ipswich T	8	0		
2002–03	Ipswich T	30	6		
2003–04	Ipswich T	34	11		
2004–05	Ipswich T	45	13		
2005–06	Sunderland	29	3		
2006–07	Sunderland	4	0	33	3
2006–07	*Preston NE*	7	0	7	0
2007–08	Ipswich T	37	5		
2008–09	Ipswich T	32	5	186	40
2009–10	Sheffield W	20	1		
2010–11	Sheffield W	34	9	54	10

MODEST, Nathan (F)   4 0
H: 5 9 W: 12 02 b.Sheffield 29-9-91
Source: Scholar.

Season	Club				
2008–09	Sheffield W	4	0		
2009–10	Sheffield W	0	0		
2010–11	Sheffield W	0	0	4	0

MORRISON, Clinton (F)   494 144
H: 6 0 W: 12 00 b.Tooting 14-5-79
Source: Trainee. Honours: Eire Under-21, 36 full caps, 9 goals.

Season	Club				
1996–97	Crystal Palace	0	0		
1997–98	Crystal Palace	1	1		
1998–99	Crystal Palace	37	12		
1999–2000	Crystal Palace	29	13		

2000–01	Crystal Palace	45	14		
2001–02	Crystal Palace	45	22		
2002–03	Birmingham C	28	6		
2003–04	Birmingham C	32	4		
2004–05	Birmingham C	26	4		
2005–06	Birmingham C	1	0	87	14
2005–06	Crystal Palace	40	13		
2006–07	Crystal Palace	41	12		
2007–08	Crystal Palace	43	16	281	103
2008–09	Coventry C	45	10		
2009–10	Coventry C	46	11	91	21
2010–11	Sheffield W	35	6	35	6

MORRISON, Michael (D) 89 5
H: 6 0 W: 12 00 b.Bury St Edmunds 3-3-88
Source: Cambridge U.

2008–09	Leicester C	35	3		
2009–10	Leicester C	31	2		
2010–11	Leicester C	11	0	77	5
2010–11	Sheffield W	12	0	12	0

O'CONNOR, James (M) 466 32
H: 5 8 W: 11 00 b.Dublin 1-9-79
Source: Trainee. Honours: Eire Youth, Under-21.

1996–97	Stoke C	0	0		
1997–98	Stoke C	0	0		
1998–99	Stoke C	4	0		
1999–2000	Stoke C	42	6		
2000–01	Stoke C	44	8		
2001–02	Stoke C	43	2		
2002–03	Stoke C	43	0	176	16
2003–04	WBA	30	0		
2004–05	WBA	0	0	30	0
2004–05	Burnley	21	2		
2005–06	Burnley	46	3		
2006–07	Burnley	43	3		
2007–08	Burnley	29	3	139	11
2008–09	Sheffield W	41	0		
2009–10	Sheffield W	44	3		
2010–11	Sheffield W	36	2	121	5

O'DONNELL, Richard (G) 13 0
H: 6 2 W: 13 05 b.Sheffield 12-9-88
Source: Scholar.

2007–08	Sheffield W	0	0		
2007–08	*Rotherham U*	0	0		
2007–08	*Oldham Ath*	4	0	4	0
2008–09	Sheffield W	0	0		
2009–10	Sheffield W	0	0		
2010–11	Sheffield W	9	0	9	0

OLIVER, Vadaine (F) 0 0
b.Sheffield 21-10-91
Source: Scholar.

2010–11	Sheffield W	0	0

OTSEMOBOR, John (D) 208 6
H: 5 10 W: 12 07 b.Liverpool 23-3-83
Source: Trainee. Honours: England Youth, Under-20.

1999–2000	Liverpool	0	0		
2000–01	Liverpool	0	0		
2001–02	Liverpool	0	0		
2002–03	Liverpool	0	0		
2002–03	*Hull C*	9	3	9	3
2003–04	Liverpool	4	0		
2003–04	*Bolton W*	1	0	1	0
2004–05	Liverpool	0	0	4	0
2004–05	Crewe Alex	14	1		
2005–06	*Rotherham U*	10	0	10	0
2005–06	Crewe Alex	16	0		
2006–07	Crewe Alex	27	0	57	1
2007–08	Norwich C	43	1		
2008–09	Norwich C	37	0		
2009–10	Norwich C	13	1	93	2
2009–10	Southampton	19	0	19	0
2010–11	Sheffield W	15	0	15	0

PALMER, Liam (M) 9 0
b.Worksop 19-9-91
Source: Scholar. Honours: Scotland Under-21.

2010–11	Sheffield W	9	0	9	0

POTTER, Darren (M) 164 8
H: 6 0 W: 10 08 b.Liverpool 21-12-84
Source: Scholar. Honours: Eire Youth, B, Under-21, 5 full caps.

2001–02	Liverpool	0	0
2002–03	Liverpool	0	0
2003–04	Liverpool	0	0
2004–05	Liverpool	2	0
2005–06	Liverpool	0	0		
2005–06	*Southampton*	10	0	10	0
2006–07	Liverpool	0	0	2	0
2006–07	Wolverhampton W	38	0		
2007–08	Wolverhampton W	18	0		
2008–09	Wolverhampton W	0	0	56	0
2008–09	*Sheffield W*	17	2		
2009–10	Sheffield W	46	3		
2010–11	Sheffield W	33	3	96	8

REYNOLDS, Mark (D) 162 4
H: 5 11 W: 10 07 b.Motherwell 7-5-87

2005–06	Motherwell	1	0		
2006–07	Motherwell	35	2		
2007–08	Motherwell	38	0		
2008–09	Motherwell	36	0		
2009–10	Motherwell	26	2		
2010–11	Motherwell	19	0	155	4
2010–11	Sheffield W	7	0	7	0

SEDGWICK, Chris (M) 505 33
H: 5 11 W: 11 10 b.Sheffield 28-4-80
Source: Trainee.

1997–98	Rotherham U	4	0		
1998–99	Rotherham U	33	4		
1999–2000	Rotherham U	38	5		
2000–01	Rotherham U	21	2		
2001–02	Rotherham U	44	1		
2002–03	Rotherham U	43	1		
2003–04	Rotherham U	40	2		
2004–05	Rotherham U	20	2	243	17
2004–05	Preston NE	24	3		
2005–06	Preston NE	46	4		
2006–07	Preston NE	43	1		
2007–08	Preston NE	42	2		
2008–09	Preston NE	40	1		
2009–10	Preston NE	34	1	229	12
2010–11	Sheffield W	33	4	33	4

SPURR, Tommy (D) 192 5
H: 6 1 W: 11 05 b.Leeds 13-9-87
Source: Scholar.

2005–06	Sheffield W	2	0		
2006–07	Sheffield W	36	0		
2007–08	Sheffield W	41	2		
2008–09	Sheffield W	41	2		
2009–10	Sheffield W	46	1		
2010–11	Sheffield W	26	0	192	5

TEALE, Gary (F) 475 41
H: 5 11 W: 12 02 b.Glasgow 21-7-78
Honours: Scotland Under-21, B, 13 full caps.

1996–97	Clydebank	33	6		
1997–98	Clydebank	27	6		
1998–99	Clydebank	8	2	68	14
1998–99	Ayr U	23	4		
1999–2000	Ayr U	32	0		
2000–01	Ayr U	29	5		
2001–02	Ayr U	18	4	102	13
2001–02	Wigan Ath	23	1		
2002–03	Wigan Ath	38	2		
2003–04	Wigan Ath	28	2		
2004–05	Wigan Ath	37	3		
2005–06	Wigan Ath	24	0		
2006–07	Wigan Ath	12	0	162	8
2006–07	Derby Co	16	1		
2007–08	Derby Co	18	0		
2007–08	*Plymouth Arg*	12	0	12	0
2008–09	Derby Co	25	1		
2008–09	*Barnsley*	3	0	3	0
2009–10	Derby Co	28	2	87	4
2010–11	Sheffield W	41	2	41	2

WEAVER, Nick (G) 308 0
H: 6 4 W: 14 07 b.Sheffield 2-3-79
Source: Trainee. Honours: England Under-21.

1995–96	Mansfield T	1	0		
1996–97	Mansfield T	0	0	1	0
1996–97	Manchester C	0	0		
1997–98	Manchester C	0	0		
1998–99	Manchester C	45	0		
1999–2000	Manchester C	45	0		
2000–01	Manchester C	31	0		
2001–02	Manchester C	25	0		
2002–03	Manchester C	0	0		
2003–04	Manchester C	0	0		
2004–05	Manchester C	1	0		
2005–06	Manchester C	0	0		
2005–06	*Sheffield W*	14	0		
2006–07	Manchester C	25	0	172	0
2007–08	Charlton Ath	45	0		
2008–09	Charlton Ath	22	0	67	0
2009–10	Dundee U	18	0	18	0
2009–10	Burnley	0	0		
2010–11	Sheffield W	36	0	50	0

SHREWSBURY T (73)

AINSWORTH, Lionel (F) 120 16
H: 5 9 W: 9 10 b.Nottingham 1-10-87
Source: Scholar. Honours: England Youth.

2005–06	Derby Co	2	0		
2006–07	Derby Co	0	0	2	0
2006–07	*Bournemouth*	7	0	7	0
2006–07	*Wycombe W*	7	0	7	0
2007–08	Hereford U	15	4		
2007–08	Watford	8	0		
2008–09	Watford	7	0	15	0
2008–09	*Hereford U*	7	3	22	7
2008–09	Huddersfield T	14	0		
2009–10	Huddersfield T	11	0		
2009–10	*Brentford*	9	0	9	0
2010–11	Shrewsbury T	33	9	33	9
2010–11	*Huddersfield T*	0	0	25	0

BRADSHAW, Tom (F) 32 9
H: 5 5 W: 11 02 b.Shrewsbury 27-7-92
Source: Aberystwyth T. Honours: Wales Youth.

2009–10	Shrewsbury T	6	3		
2010–11	Shrewsbury T	26	6	32	9

BRIGHT, Kris (F) 96 53
H: 6 2 W: 12 10 b.Auckland 5-9-86
Honours: New Zealand 4 full caps, 1 goal.

2005	Waitakere C	21	29	21	29
2005–06	New Zealand K	12	0	12	0
2006–07	Fortuna Sittard	11	1	11	1
2007	Kristiansund	7	11		
2008	Kristiansund	12	10	19	21
2008–09	Panserraikos	6	0	6	0
2009–10	Shrewsbury T	2	0		
2010–11	Shrewsbury T	1	0	27	2

Transferred to Honved January 2011.

CANSDELL SHERRIFF, Shane (D) 285 18
H: 5 11 W: 11 08 b.Sydney 10-11-82
Source: NSW Academy. Honours: Australia Youth, Under-23.

1999–2000	Leeds U	0	0		
2000–01	Leeds U	0	0		
2001–02	Leeds U	0	0		
2002–03	Leeds U	0	0		
2002–03	*Rochdale*	3	0	3	0
2003–04	Aarhus	29	4		
2004–05	Aarhus	26	2		
2005–06	Aarhus	27	1	82	7
2006–07	Tranmere R	43	3		
2007–08	Tranmere R	44	3	87	6
2008–09	Shrewsbury T	31	2		
2009–10	Shrewsbury T	41	1		
2010–11	Shrewsbury T	41	2	113	5

COLLINS, James S (F) 41 14
H: 6 2 W: 13 08 b.Coventry 1-12-90
Source: Scholar. Honours: Eire Under-21.

2008–09	Aston Villa	0	0		
2009–10	Aston Villa	0	0		
2009–10	*Darlington*	7	2	7	2
2010–11	Aston Villa	0	0		
2010–11	*Burton Alb*	10	4	10	4
2010–11	Shrewsbury T	24	8	24	8

DISLEY, Craig (M) 386 44
H: 5 10 W: 10 13 b.Worksop 24-8-81
Source: Trainee.

1999–2000	Mansfield T	5	0		
2000–01	Mansfield T	24	0		
2001–02	Mansfield T	36	7		
2002–03	Mansfield T	42	4		
2003–04	Mansfield T	34	5	141	16
2004–05	Bristol R	28	4		
2005–06	Bristol R	42	8		
2006–07	Bristol R	45	4		
2007–08	Bristol R	44	6		
2008–09	Bristol R	44	3	203	25
2009–10	Shrewsbury T	18	1		
2010–11	Shrewsbury T	24	2	42	3

ELDER, Nathan (F)   85   14
H: 6 1   W: 13 12   b.Hornchurch 5-4-85
Source: Billericay T.

Season	Club				
2006–07	Brighton & HA	13	1		
2007–08	Brighton & HA	9	1	22	2
2007–08	Brentford	17	4		
2008–09	Brentford	27	6	44	10
2009–10	Shrewsbury T	19	2		
2010–11	Shrewsbury T	0	0	19	2

GOLDSON, Connor (D)   3   0
b.York 18-12-92
Source: Youth.

Season	Club				
2010–11	Shrewsbury T	3	0	3	0

GRANDISON, Jermaine (D)   26   0
H: 6 4   W: 13 03   b.Birmingham 15-12-90
Source: Scholar.

Season	Club				
2008–09	Coventry C	2	0		
2009–10	Coventry C	3	0		
2010–11	Coventry C	0	0	5	0
2010–11	Tranmere R	8	0	8	0
2010–11	Shrewsbury T	13	0	13	0

HARROLD, Matt (F)   251   41
H: 6 1   W: 11 10   b.Leyton 25-7-84
Source: Harlow T.

Season	Club				
2003–04	Brentford	13	2		
2004–05	Brentford	19	0	32	2
2004–05	*Grimsby T*	6	2	6	2
2005–06	Yeovil T	42	9		
2006–07	Yeovil T	5	0	47	9
2006–07	Southend U	36	3		
2007–08	Southend U	16	0		
2008–09	Southend U	0	0	52	3
2008–09	Wycombe W	37	9		
2009–10	Wycombe W	36	8	73	17
2010–11	Shrewsbury T	41	8	41	8

HOOMAN, Harry (D)   2   0
H: 5 11   W: 12 06   b.Worcester 27-4-91
Source: Scholar.

Season	Club				
2009–10	Shrewsbury T	2	0		
2010–11	Shrewsbury T	0	0	2	0

LESLIE, Steven (M)   113   9
H: 5 10   W: 11 02   b.Glasgow 5-11-87
Source: Scholar.

Season	Club				
2005–06	Shrewsbury T	1	0		
2006–07	Shrewsbury T	5	0		
2007–08	Shrewsbury T	17	1		
2008–09	Shrewsbury T	27	0		
2009–10	Shrewsbury T	34	6		
2010–11	Shrewsbury T	18	0	102	7
2010–11	Hereford U	11	2	11	2

LOMAX, Kelvin (D)   97   0
H: 5 11   W: 12 03   b.Bury 12-11-86
Source: Scholar.

Season	Club				
2003–04	Oldham Ath	1	0		
2004–05	Oldham Ath	9	0		
2005–06	Oldham Ath	9	0		
2006–07	Oldham Ath	9	0		
2007–08	Oldham Ath	21	0		
2007–08	*Rochdale*	10	0	10	0
2008–09	Oldham Ath	27	0		
2009–10	Oldham Ath	15	0		
2010–11	Oldham Ath	0	0	82	0
2010–11	*Chesterfield*	4	0	4	0
2010–11	Shrewsbury T	1	0	1	0

McALLISTER, Sean (M)   93   4
H: 5 8   W: 10 07   b.Bolton 15-8-87
Source: Scholar.

Season	Club				
2005–06	Sheffield W	2	0		
2006–07	Sheffield W	6	1		
2007–08	Sheffield W	8	0		
2007–08	*Mansfield T*	7	0	7	0
2007–08	*Bury*	0	0		
2008–09	Sheffield W	40	3		
2009–10	Sheffield W	12	0	68	4
2010–11	Shrewsbury T	18	0	18	0

McINTYRE, Kevin (M)   270   20
H: 6 0   W: 11 10   b.Liverpool 23-12-77
Source: Trainee.

Season	Club				
1996–97	Tranmere R	0	0		
1997–98	Tranmere R	2	0		
1998–99	Tranmere R	0	0		
1999–2000	Tranmere R	0	0		
2000–01	Tranmere R	0	0		
2001–02	Tranmere R	0	0	2	0
2004–05	Chester C	10	0	10	0
2004–05	Macclesfield T	23	0		
2005–06	Macclesfield T	44	5		
2006–07	Macclesfield T	44	9		
2007–08	Macclesfield T	23	2	134	16
2007–08	Shrewsbury T	22	2		
2008–09	Shrewsbury T	26	0		
2009–10	Shrewsbury T	45	1		
2010–11	Shrewsbury T	31	1	124	4

NEAL, Chris (G)   30   0
H: 6 2   W: 12 04   b.St Albans 23-10-85
Source: Scholar.

Season	Club				
2004–05	Preston NE	1	0		
2005–06	Preston NE	0	0		
2006–07	Preston NE	0	0		
2006–07	*Shrewsbury T*	0	0		
2007–08	*Morecambe*	0	0		
2007–08	Preston NE	0	0		
2008–09	Preston NE	0	0	1	0
2009–10	Shrewsbury T	7	0		
2010–11	Shrewsbury T	22	0	29	0

NEAL, Lewis (M)   186   11
H: 5 10   W: 11 02   b.Leicester 14-7-81
Source: Juniors.

Season	Club				
1998–99	Stoke C	0	0		
1999–2000	Stoke C	0	0		
2000–01	Stoke C	1	0		
2001–02	Stoke C	11	0		
2002–03	Stoke C	16	0		
2003–04	Stoke C	19	1		
2004–05	Stoke C	23	1	70	2
2005–06	Preston NE	24	2		
2006–07	Preston NE	24	1		
2007–08	Preston NE	17	2		
2008–09	Preston NE	0	0	65	5
2008–09	*Notts Co*	4	0	4	0
2008–09	*Carlisle U*	16	2	16	2
2009–10	Shrewsbury T	29	2		
2010–11	Shrewsbury T	2	0	31	2

Transferred to Orlando C January 2011.

RAVEN, David (D)   172   1
H: 6 0   W: 11 04   b.West Kirby 10-3-85
Source: Scholar. *Honours:* England Youth, Under-20.

Season	Club				
2001–02	Liverpool	0	0		
2002–03	Liverpool	0	0		
2003–04	Liverpool	0	0		
2004–05	Liverpool	1	0		
2005–06	Liverpool	0	0	1	0
2005–06	*Tranmere R*	11	0	11	0
2006–07	Carlisle U	36	0		
2007–08	Carlisle U	43	1		
2008–09	Carlisle U	41	0		
2009–10	Carlisle U	16	0	136	1
2010–11	Shrewsbury T	24	0	24	0

ROBINSON, Jake (F)   220   35
H: 5 7   W: 10 10   b.Brighton 23-10-86
Source: Scholar.

Season	Club				
2003–04	Brighton & HA	9	0		
2004–05	Brighton & HA	10	1		
2005–06	Brighton & HA	27	1		
2006–07	Brighton & HA	38	6		
2007–08	Brighton & HA	34	4		
2008–09	Brighton & HA	5	1	123	13
2008–09	*Aldershot T*	19	4	19	4
2009–10	Shrewsbury T	34	3		
2010–11	Shrewsbury T	22	8	56	11
2010–11	*Torquay U*	22	7	22	7

SHARPS, Ian (D)   373   15
H: 6 3   W: 14 07   b.Warrington 23-10-80
Source: Trainee.

Season	Club				
1998–99	Tranmere R	1	0		
1999–2000	Tranmere R	0	0		
2000–01	Tranmere R	0	0		
2001–02	Tranmere R	29	0		
2002–03	Tranmere R	30	3		
2003–04	Tranmere R	27	1		
2004–05	Tranmere R	44	1		
2005–06	Tranmere R	39	1	170	6
2006–07	Rotherham U	38	2		
2007–08	Rotherham U	33	2		
2008–09	Rotherham U	45	4		
2009–10	Rotherham U	44	0	160	8
2010–11	Shrewsbury T	43	1	43	1

SMITH, Benjamin (G)   52   0
H: 6 1   W: 12 11   b.Newcastle 5-9-86
Source: Newcastle U Scholar.

Season	Club				
2006–07	Stockport Co	0	0		
2006–07	Doncaster R	13	0		
2007–08	Doncaster R	0	0		
2007–08	*Lincoln C*	9	0	9	0
2008–09	Doncaster R	0	0		
2009–10	Doncaster R	2	0	15	0
2009–10	*Morecambe*	3	0	3	0
2010–11	Shrewsbury T	25	0	25	0

TAYLOR, Danny (D)   3   0
H: 5 10   W: 9 06   b.Chester 1-9-91
Source: Youth.

Season	Club				
2009–10	Shrewsbury T	3	0		
2010–11	Shrewsbury T	0	0	3	0

TAYLOR, Jon (M)   22   6
H: 5 11   W: 12 04   b.Liverpool 23-12-89
Source: Youth.

Season	Club				
2009–10	Shrewsbury T	2	0		
2010–11	Shrewsbury T	20	6	22	6

VAN DEN BROEK, Benjamin (M)   79   11
H: 6 0   W: 13 03   b.Geleen 21-9-87

Season	Club				
2008–09	Haarlem	35	9		
2009–10	Haarlem	22	1	57	10
2009–10	Shrewsbury T	11	1		
2010–11	Shrewsbury T	11	0	22	1

WRIGHT, Mark (M)   263   41
H: 5 11   W: 11 00   b.Wolverhampton 24-2-82
Source: Scholar.

Season	Club				
2000–01	Walsall	4	0		
2001–02	Walsall	0	0		
2002–03	Walsall	5	0		
2003–04	Walsall	11	2		
2004–05	Walsall	37	2		
2005–06	Walsall	30	2		
2006–07	Walsall	37	3	124	9
2007–08	Milton Keynes D	34	13		
2008–09	Milton Keynes D	32	5	66	18
2009–10	*Brighton & HA*	4	0	4	0
2009–10	Bristol R	24	0		
2010–11	Bristol R	0	0	24	0
2010–11	Shrewsbury T	45	14	45	14

WROE, Nicky (M)   137   16
H: 5 11   W: 10 02   b.Sheffield 28-9-85
Source: Scholar.

Season	Club				
2002–03	Barnsley	1	0		
2003–04	Barnsley	2	1		
2004–05	Barnsley	31	0		
2005–06	Barnsley	12	0		
2006–07	Barnsley	3	0	49	1
2006–07	*Bury*	5	0	5	0

From York C.

Season	Club				
2009–10	Torquay U	45	9		

From York C.

Season	Club				
2010–11	Torquay U	20	3	65	12
2010–11	Shrewsbury T	18	3	18	3

SOUTHAMPTON (74)

ARGENT, Sam (D)   0   0
b.Basingstoke 17-10-91
Source: Scholar.

Season	Club				
2008–09	Southampton	0	0		
2009–10	Southampton	0	0		
2010–11	Southampton	0	0		

BARNARD, Lee (F)   160   61
H: 5 10   W: 10 10   b.Romford 18-7-84
Source: Trainee.

Season	Club				
2002–03	Tottenham H	0	0		
2002–03	*Exeter C*	3	0	3	0
2003–04	Tottenham H	0	0		
2004–05	Tottenham H	0	0		
2004–05	*Leyton Orient*	8	0	8	0
2004–05	*Northampton T*	5	0	5	0
2005–06	Tottenham H	3	0		
2006–07	Tottenham H	0	0		
2007–08	Tottenham H	0	0	3	0
2007–08	*Crewe Alex*	10	3	10	3
2007–08	Southend U	15	9		
2008–09	Southend U	35	11		
2009–10	Southend U	25	15	75	35
2009–10	Southampton	20	9		
2010–11	Southampton	36	14	56	23

BIALKOWSKI, Bartosz (G)   30   0
H: 6 3   W: 12 10   b.Braniewo 6-7-87
Honours: Poland Under-20, Under-21.

Season	Club				
2004–05	Gornik Zabrze	7	0	7	0
2005–06	Southampton	5	0		

Season	Club				
2006–07	Southampton	8	0		
2007–08	Southampton	1	0		
2008–09	Southampton	0	0		
2009–10	Southampton	7	0		
2009–10	*Barnsley*	2	0	2	0
2010–11	Southampton	0	0	21	0

BUTTERFIELD, Danny (D)   402   9
H: 5 10 W: 11 06 b.Boston 21-11-79
Source: Trainee. *Honours:* England Youth.

Season	Club				
1997–98	Grimsby T	7	0		
1998–99	Grimsby T	12	0		
1999–2000	Grimsby T	29	0		
2000–01	Grimsby T	30	1		
2001–02	Grimsby T	46	2	124	3
2002–03	Crystal Palace	46	1		
2003–04	Crystal Palace	45	4		
2004–05	Crystal Palace	7	0		
2005–06	Crystal Palace	13	0		
2006–07	Crystal Palace	28	0		
2007–08	Crystal Palace	30	0		
2008–09	Crystal Palace	26	1		
2008–09	*Charlton Ath*	12	0	12	0
2009–10	Crystal Palace	37	0	232	6
2010–11	Southampton	34	0	34	0

CHAPLOW, Richard (M)   221   21
H: 5 9 W: 9 03 b.Accrington 2-2-85
Source: Scholar. *Honours:* England Youth, Under-20, Under-21.

Season	Club				
2002–03	Burnley	5	0		
2003–04	Burnley	39	5		
2004–05	Burnley	21	2	65	7
2004–05	WBA	4	0		
2005–06	WBA	7	0		
2005–06	Southampton	11	1		
2006–07	WBA	28	1		
2007–08	WBA	5	0	44	1
2007–08	Preston NE	12	3		
2008–09	Preston NE	25	3		
2009–10	Preston NE	31	2		
2010–11	Preston NE	0	0	68	8
2010–11	Southampton	33	4	44	5

CONNOLLY, David (F)   359 143
H: 5 9 W: 11 00 b.Willesden 6-6-77
Source: Trainee. *Honours:* Eire Under-21, 41 full caps, 9 goals.

Season	Club				
1994–95	Watford	2	0		
1995–96	Watford	11	8		
1996–97	Watford	13	2	26	10
1997–98	Feyenoord	10	2		
1998–99	Wolverhampton W	32	6	32	6
1999–2000	*Excelsior*	32	29	32	29
2000–01	Feyenoord	15	5	25	7
2001–02	Wimbledon	33	13		
2002–03	Wimbledon	28	24	63	42
2003–04	West Ham U	39	10	39	10
2004–05	Leicester C	44	13		
2005–06	Leicester C	5	4	49	17
2005–06	Wigan Ath	17	1		
2006–07	Wigan Ath	2	0	19	1
2006–07	Sunderland	36	13		
2007–08	Sunderland	3	0		
2008–09	Sunderland	0	0	39	13
2009–10	Southampton	20	5		
2010–11	Southampton	15	3	35	8

DAVIS, Kelvin (G)   549   0
H: 6 1 W: 11 05 b.Bedford 29-9-76
Source: Trainee. *Honours:* England Youth, Under-21.

Season	Club				
1993–94	Luton T	1	0		
1994–95	Luton T	9	0		
1994–95	*Torquay U*	2	0	2	0
1995–96	Luton T	6	0		
1996–97	Luton T	0	0		
1997–98	Luton T	32	0		
1997–98	*Hartlepool U*	2	0	2	0
1998–99	Luton T	44	0	92	0
1999–2000	Wimbledon	0	0		
2000–01	Wimbledon	45	0		
2001–02	Wimbledon	40	0		
2002–03	Wimbledon	46	0	131	0
2003–04	Ipswich T	45	0		
2004–05	Ipswich T	39	0	84	0
2005–06	Sunderland	33	0	33	0
2006–07	Southampton	38	0		
2007–08	Southampton	35	0		
2008–09	Southampton	46	0		
2009–10	Southampton	40	0		
2010–11	Southampton	46	0	205	0

DEAN, Harlee (M)   1   0
H: 6 0 W: 11 10 b.Basingstoke 26-7-91
Source: Scholar.

Season	Club				
2008–09	Dagenham & R	0	0		
2009–10	Dagenham & R	1	0	1	0
2010–11	Southampton	0	0		

DICKSON, Ryan (M)   134   5
H: 5 10 W: 11 05 b.Saltash 14-12-86
Source: Scholar.

Season	Club				
2004–05	Plymouth Arg	3	0		
2005–06	Plymouth Arg	0	0		
2006–07	Plymouth Arg	2	0		
2006–07	*Torquay U*	9	1	9	1
2007–08	Plymouth Arg	0	0	5	0
2007–08	Brentford	31	0		
2008–09	Brentford	39	1		
2009–10	Brentford	27	2	97	3
2010–11	Southampton	23	1	23	1

DO PRADO, Guilherme (F)   170   39
H: 6 2 W: 12 04 b.Sao Paulo 31-12-81

Season	Club				
2002	Portuguese Santista	22	7	22	7
2002–03	Catania	6	0	6	0
2003–04	Perugia	17	0		
2004–05	Perugia	17	4	34	4
2005–06	Fiorentina	0	0		
2006–07	Fiorentina	0	0		
2006–07	Spezia	12	1	12	1
2007–08	Mantoba	14	2	14	2
2008–09	Pro Patria	14	7	14	7
2009–10	Cesena	34	9	34	9
2010–11	Southampton	34	9	34	9

On loan from Cesena.

DOBLE, Ryan (M)   6   1
b.Blaenavon 1-2-91
Source: Scholar. *Honours:* Wales Under-21.

Season	Club				
2008–09	Southampton	0	0		
2009–10	Southampton	0	0		
2010–11	Southampton	0	0		
2010–11	*Stockport Co*	3	1	3	1
2010–11	*Oxford U*	3	0	3	0

FONTE, Jose (D)   226   16
H: 6 2 W: 12 08 b.Penafiel 22-12-83
Source: Sporting Lisbon, Salgueiros.
Honours: Portugal Under-21.

Season	Club				
2004–05	Felgueiros	28	1	28	1
2005–06	Setubal	15	0	15	0
2005–06	Benfica	1	0	1	0
2005–06	Pacos	11	1	11	1
2006–07	Amadora	25	1	25	1
2007–08	Crystal Palace	22	1		
2008–09	Crystal Palace	38	4		
2009–10	Crystal Palace	22	1	82	6
2009–10	Southampton	21	0		
2010–11	Southampton	43	7	64	7

FORECAST, Tommy (G)   4   0
H: 6 2 W: 11 10 b.Newham 15-10-86
Source: Scholar.

Season	Club				
2005–06	Tottenham H	0	0		
2006–07	Tottenham H	0	0		
2007–08	Tottenham H	0	0		
2008–09	Southampton	0	0		
2009–10	Southampton	0	0		
2009–10	*Grimsby T*	4	0	4	0
2010–11	Southampton	0	0		

FORTE, Jonathan (M)   221   33
H: 6 0 W: 12 02 b.Sheffield 25-7-86
Source: Scholar. *Honours:* England Youth.
Barbados 2 full caps.

Season	Club				
2003–04	Sheffield U	7	0		
2004–05	Sheffield U	22	1		
2005–06	Sheffield U	1	0		
2005–06	Doncaster R	13	4		
2005–06	*Rotherham U*	11	4	11	4
2006–07	Sheffield U	0	0	30	1
2006–07	*Doncaster R*	41	5	54	9
2007–08	Scunthorpe U	38	4		
2008–09	Scunthorpe U	8	0		
2008–09	*Notts Co*	18	8	18	8
2009–10	Scunthorpe U	3	0		
2010–11	Scunthorpe U	24	3	98	9
2010–11	Southampton	10	2	10	2

GARROD, Tony (F)   0   0
H: 6 2 W: 11 09 b.Crawley 14-9-91
Source: Scholar.

Season	Club				
2010–11	Southampton	0	0		

GOBERN, Oscar (M)   22   1
H: 5 11 W: 10 10 b.Birmingham 26-1-91
Source: Scholar. *Honours:* England Youth.

Season	Club				
2008–09	Southampton	6	0		
2009–10	Southampton	4	0		
2009–10	*Milton Keynes D*	1	0	1	0
2010–11	Southampton	11	1	21	1

HAMMOND, Dean (M)   281   35
H: 6 0 W: 11 09 b.Hastings 7-3-83
Source: Scholar.

Season	Club				
2002–03	Brighton & HA	4	0		
2003–04	Brighton & HA	0	0		
2003–04	*Leyton Orient*	8	0	8	0
2004–05	Brighton & HA	30	4		
2005–06	Brighton & HA	41	4		
2006–07	Brighton & HA	37	8		
2007–08	Brighton & HA	24	5	136	21
2007–08	Colchester U	13	0		
2008–09	Colchester U	41	5		
2009–10	Colchester U	2	0	56	5
2009–10	Southampton	40	5		
2010–11	Southampton	41	4	81	9

HARDING, Dan (D)   260   6
H: 6 0 W: 11 11 b.Gloucester 23-12-83
Source: Scholar. *Honours:* England Under-21.

Season	Club				
2002–03	Brighton & HA	1	0		
2003–04	Brighton & HA	23	0		
2004–05	Brighton & HA	43	1	67	1
2005–06	Leeds U	20	0	20	0
2006–07	Ipswich T	42	0		
2007–08	Ipswich T	30	1		
2008–09	Ipswich T	1	0	73	1
2008–09	*Southend U*	19	1	19	1
2008–09	*Reading*	3	0	3	0
2009–10	Southampton	42	3		
2010–11	Southampton	36	0	78	3

HOLMES, Lee (M)   119   7
H: 5 8 W: 10 06 b.Mansfield 2-4-87
Source: Scholar. *Honours:* FA Schools, England Youth.

Season	Club				
2002–03	Derby Co				
2003–04	Derby Co	23	2		
2004–05	Derby Co	3	0		
2004–05	*Swindon T*	15	1	15	1
2005–06	Derby Co	18	0		
2006–07	Derby Co	0	0		
2006–07	*Bradford C*	16	0	16	0
2007–08	Derby Co	0	0	46	2
2007–08	*Walsall*	19	4	19	4
2008–09	Southampton	11	0		
2009–10	Southampton	5	0		
2010–11	Southampton	7	0	23	0

JAIDI, Radhi (D)   187   18
H: 6 2 W: 14 00 b.Tunis 30-8-75
Source: Esperance. *Honours:* Tunisia 101 full caps, 7 goals.

Season	Club				
2004–05	Bolton W	27	5		
2005–06	Bolton W	16	3	43	8
2006–07	Birmingham C	38	6		
2007–08	Birmingham C	18	0		
2008–09	Birmingham C	30	0		
2009–10	Birmingham C	0	0	86	6
2009–10	Southampton	27	1		
2010–11	Southampton	31	3	58	4

LALLANA, Adam (M)   129   25
H: 5 8 W: 11 06 b.St Albans 10-5-88
Source: Scholar. *Honours:* England Youth, Under-21.

Season	Club				
2005–06	Southampton	0	0		
2006–07	Southampton	1	0		
2007–08	Southampton	5	1		
2007–08	*Bournemouth*	3	0	3	0
2008–09	Southampton	40	1		
2009–10	Southampton	44	15		
2010–11	Southampton	36	8	126	25

LAMBERT, Ricky (F)   427 157
H: 6 2 W: 14 08 b.Liverpool 16-2-82
Source: Trainee.

Season	Club				
1999–2000	Blackpool	3	0		
2000–01	Blackpool	0	0	3	0
2000–01	Macclesfield T	9	0		
2001–02	Macclesfield T	35	8	44	8
2001–02	Stockport Co	5	0		
2002–03	Stockport Co	29	2		
2003–04	Stockport Co	40	12		
2004–05	Stockport Co	29	4	98	18

2004–05	Rochdale	15	6		
2005–06	Rochdale	46	22		
2006–07	Rochdale	3	0	64	28
2006–07	Bristol R	36	8		
2007–08	Bristol R	46	14		
2008–09	Bristol R	45	29		
2009–10	Bristol R	1	1	128	52
2009–10	Southampton	45	30		
2010–11	Southampton	45	21	90	51

MARTIN, Aaron (D)   10   0
H: 6 3 W: 11 13 b.Newport (IW) 29-9-89
Source: Eastleigh.

| 2009–10 | Southampton | 2 | 0 | | |
| 2010–11 | Southampton | 8 | 0 | 10 | 0 |

McNISH, Callum (M)   1   0
H: 6 2 W: 12 06 b.Oxford 25-5-92
Source: Scholar.

2008–09	Southampton	0	0		
2009–10	Southampton	1	0		
2010–11	Southampton	0	0	1	0

MILLS, Joseph (D)   58   2
H: 5 9 W: 11 00 b.Swindon 30-10-89
Source: Scholar.

2006–07	Southampton	0	0		
2007–08	Southampton	0	0		
2008–09	Southampton	8	0		
2008–09	*Scunthorpe U*	14	0	14	0
2009–10	Southampton	16	0		
2010–11	Southampton	2	0	26	0
2010–11	*Doncaster R*	18	2	18	2

OXLADE-CHAMBERLAIN, Alex (M) 36   9
H: 5 11 W: 11 00 b.Portsmouth 15-8-93
Source: Scholar. *Honours:* England Under-21.

| 2009–10 | Southampton | 2 | 0 | | |
| 2010–11 | Southampton | 34 | 9 | 36 | 9 |

PULIS, Anthony (M)   41   1
H: 5 10 W: 10 10 b.Bristol 21-7-84
Source: Scholar. *Honours:* Wales Under-21.

2002–03	Portsmouth	0	0		
2003–04	Portsmouth	0	0		
2004–05	Portsmouth	0	0		
2004–05	Stoke C	0	0		
2004–05	*Torquay U*	3	0	3	0
2005–06	Stoke C	0	0		
2005–06	*Plymouth Arg*	5	0	5	0
2006–07	Stoke C	1	0		
2006–07	*Grimsby T*	9	0	9	0
2007–08	Stoke C	1	0		
2007–08	*Bristol R*	1	0	1	0
2008–09	Stoke C	0	0	2	0
2008–09	Southampton	0	0		
2009–10	Southampton	0	0		
2009–10	*Lincoln C*	7	0	7	0
2010–11	Southampton	0	0		
2010–11	*Stockport Co*	10	1	10	1
2010–11	*Barnet*	4	0	4	0

PUNCHEON, Jason (M)   221   38
H: 5 9 W: 12 05 b.Croydon 26-6-86
Source: Scholar.

2003–04	Wimbledon	8	0	8	0
2004–05	Milton Keynes D	25	1		
2005–06	Milton Keynes D	1	0		
2006–07	Barnet	37	5		
2007–08	Barnet	41	10	78	15
2008–09	Plymouth Arg	6	0		
2008–09	*Milton Keynes D*	27	4		
2009–10	Plymouth Arg	0	0	6	0
2009–10	*Milton Keynes D*	24	7	77	12
2009–10	Southampton	19	3		
2010–11	Southampton	15	0	34	3
2010–11	*Millwall*	7	5	7	5
2010–11	*Blackpool*	11	3	11	3

RACINE, Aaron (D)   0   0
b.Littlehampton 30-10-91
Source: Scholar.

2008–09	Southampton	0	0		
2009–10	Southampton	0	0		
2010–11	Southampton	0	0		

REEVES, Ben (D)   0   0
H: 5 10 W: 10 07 b.Verwood 19-11-91
Source: Scholar.

2008–09	Southampton	0	0		
2009–10	Southampton	0	0		
2010–11	Southampton	0	0		

RICHARDSON, Frazer (D)   221   5
H: 5 11 W: 11 12 b.Rotherham 29-10-82
Source: Trainee. *Honours:* England Youth, Under-20.

1999–2000	Leeds U	0	0		
2000–01	Leeds U	0	0		
2001–02	Leeds U	0	0		
2002–03	Leeds U	0	0		
2002–03	*Stoke C*	7	0		
2003–04	Leeds U	4	0		
2003–04	*Stoke C*	6	1	13	1
2004–05	Leeds U	38	1		
2005–06	Leeds U	23	1		
2006–07	Leeds U	22	0		
2007–08	Leeds U	39	1		
2008–09	Leeds U	23	0	149	3
2009–10	Charlton Ath	38	1	38	1
2010–11	Southampton	21	0	21	0

SAVILLE, Jack (D)   0   0
H: 6 3 W: 12 00 b.Camberley 2-4-91
Source: Chelsea Scholar.

| 2009–10 | Southampton | 0 | 0 | | |
| 2010–11 | Southampton | 0 | 0 | | |

SCHNEIDERLIN, Morgan (M)   99   1
H: 5 11 W: 11 11 b.Obernai 8-11-89
Honours: France Youth.

2007–08	Strasbourg	5	0	5	0
2008–09	Southampton	30	0		
2009–10	Southampton	37	1		
2010–11	Southampton	27	0	94	1

SEABORNE, Danny (D)   92   1
H: 6 0 W: 11 10 b.Barnstaple 5-3-87
Source: Scholar.

2008–09	Exeter C	33	1		
2009–10	Exeter C	19	0	52	1
2009–10	Southampton	16	0		
2010–11	Southampton	24	0	40	0

SEIDI, Alberto (M)   0   0
b.Guinea-Bissau 20-11-92
Source: Guinea-Bissau.

| 2010–11 | Southampton | 0 | 0 | | |

STEPHENS, Jack (D)   5   0
b.Torpoint 27-1-94
Source: Scholar.

| 2010–11 | Plymouth Arg | 5 | 0 | 5 | 0 |
| 2010–11 | Southampton | 0 | 0 | | |

TAFAZOLLI, Ryan (D)   0   0
H: 6 5 W: 12 04 b.Sutton 28-9-91
Source: Scholar.

| 2010–11 | Southampton | 0 | 0 | | |

SOUTHEND U (75)

ASANTE, Kyle (M)   9   1
H: 5 9 W: 10 10 b.Chelmsford 13-11-91
Source: Scholar.

| 2009–10 | Southend U | 0 | 0 | | |
| 2010–11 | Southend U | 9 | 1 | 9 | 1 |

BARKER, Chris (D)   436   3
H: 6 2 W: 13 08 b.Sheffield 2-3-80
Source: Alfreton.

1998–99	Barnsley	0	0		
1999–2000	Barnsley	29	0		
2000–01	Barnsley	40	0		
2001–02	Barnsley	44	3	113	3
2002–03	Cardiff C	40	0		
2003–04	Cardiff C	39	0		
2004–05	*Stoke C*	4	0	4	0
2004–05	Cardiff C	39	0		
2005–06	Cardiff C	41	0		
2006–07	Cardiff C	0	0	159	0
2006–07	*Colchester U*	38	0	38	0
2007–08	QPR	25	0	25	0
2008–09	Plymouth Arg	40	0		
2009–10	Plymouth Arg	14	0		
2010–11	Plymouth Arg	0	0	54	0
2010–11	Southend U	43	0	43	0

BOUZID, Adam (M)   0   0
b.Nancy 30-11-89
Source: Mc Oujda.

| 2010–11 | Southend U | 0 | 0 | | |

CLOHESSY, Sean (D)   89   2
H: 5 11 W: 12 07 b.Croydon 12-12-86
Source: Arsenal Scholar.

2005–06	Gillingham	20	1		
2006–07	Gillingham	6	0		
2007–08	Gillingham	17	0	43	1

From Salisbury C.

| 2010–11 | Southend U | 46 | 1 | 46 | 1 |

COMMINGES, Miguel (D)   164   0
H: 5 9 W: 11 03 b.Guadeloupe 16-3-82

2002–03	Amiens	12	0	12	0
2003–04	Reims	29	0		
2004–05	Reims	21	0		
2005–06	Reims	11	0		
2006–07	Reims	13	0	74	0
2007–08	Swindon T	40	0	40	0
2008–09	Cardiff C	30	0		
2009–10	Cardiff C	1	0		
2010–11	Cardiff C	0	0	31	0
2010–11	*Carlisle U*	0	0		
2010–11	Southend U	7	0	7	0

CORR, Barry (F)   131   31
H: 6 3 W: 12 07 b.Co Wicklow 2-4-85
Honours: Eire Youth.

2001–02	Leeds U	0	0		
2002–03	Leeds U	0	0		
2003–04	Leeds U	0	0		
2004–05	Leeds U	0	0		
2005–06	Sheffield W	16	0		
2006–07	Sheffield W	1	0	17	0
2006–07	*Bristol C*	3	0	3	0
2006–07	*Swindon T*	8	3		
2007–08	Swindon T	17	5		
2008–09	Swindon T	11	2	36	10
2009–10	Exeter C	34	3	34	3
2010–11	Southend U	41	18	41	18

COUGHLAN, Graham (D)   445   39
H: 6 2 W: 13 07 b.Dublin 18-11-74
Source: Bray Wanderers.

1995–96	Blackburn R	0	0		
1996–97	Blackburn R	0	0		
1996–97	*Swindon T*	3	0	3	0
1997–98	Blackburn R	0	0		
1998–99	Livingston	6	0		
1999–2000	Livingston	29	0		
2000–01	Livingston	21	2	56	2
2001–02	Plymouth Arg	46	11		
2002–03	Plymouth Arg	42	5		
2003–04	Plymouth Arg	46	7		
2004–05	Plymouth Arg	43	2	177	25
2005–06	Sheffield W	33	4		
2006–07	Sheffield W	18	1	51	5
2006–07	*Burnley*	2	0	2	0
2007–08	Rotherham U	45	1	45	1
2008–09	Shrewsbury T	42	4		
2009–10	Shrewsbury T	36	2	78	6
2010–11	Southend U	33	0	33	0

CRAWFORD, Harry (F)   30   3
H: 6 1 W: 12 04 b.Watford 10-12-91
Source: Scholar.

| 2009–10 | Southend U | 7 | 1 | | |
| 2010–11 | Southend U | 23 | 2 | 30 | 3 |

EASTON, Craig (M)   239   19
H: 5 11 W: 11 03 b.Airdrie 26-2-79
Source: Dundee U BC. *Honours:* Scotland Youth, Under-21.

1995–96	Dundee U	0	0		
1996–97	Dundee U	2	0		
1997–98	Dundee U	29	1		
1998–99	Dundee U	30	1		
1999–2000	Dundee U	0	0		
2000–01	Dundee U	0	0		
2001–02	Dundee U	0	0	61	2
2005–06	Leyton Orient	41	4		
2006–07	Leyton Orient	30	1	71	5
2007–08	Swindon T	40	6		
2008–09	Swindon T	23	2		
2009–10	Swindon T	12	0	75	8
2010–11	Southend U	32	4	32	4

EVANS, Rhys (G)   258   0
H: 6 1 W: 13 12 b.Swindon 27-1-82
Source: Trainee. *Honours:* England Schools, Youth, Under-20, Under-21.

1998–99	Chelsea	0	0		
1999–2000	Chelsea	0	0		
1999–2000	*Bristol R*	4	0		

2000–01	Chelsea	0	0
2001–02	Chelsea	0	0
2001–02	*QPR*	11	0	11	0
2002–03	Chelsea	0	0
2002–03	*Leyton Orient*	7	0	7	0
2003–04	Swindon T	41	0
2004–05	Swindon T	45	0
2005–06	Swindon T	32	0	118	0
2006–07	Blackpool	32	0
2007–08	Blackpool	0	0	32	0
2007–08	*Bradford C*	4	0
2007–08	Millwall	21	0	21	0
2008–09	Bradford C	45	0
2009–10	Bradford C	0	0	49	0
2009–10	Bristol R	3	0	7	0
2010–11	Southend U	13	0	13	0

FERDINAND, Kane (D) 22 2
H: 6 1 W: 13 07 b.Newham 7-10-92
Source: Scholar. Honours: Eire Youth.

2010–11	Southend U	22	2	22	2

GILBERT, Peter (D) 189 1
H: 5 11 W: 12 00 b.Newcastle 31-7-83
Source: Scholar. Honours: Wales Under-21.

2001–02	Birmingham C	0	0
2002–03	Birmingham C	0	0
2003–04	Birmingham C	0	0
2003–04	Plymouth Arg	40	1
2004–05	Plymouth Arg	38	0	78	1
2005–06	Leicester C	5	0	5	0
2005–06	Sheffield W	17	0
2006–07	Sheffield W	6	0
2006–07	Doncaster R	4	0	4	0
2007–08	Sheffield W	10	0
2008–09	Sheffield W	8	0	41	0
2009–10	Oldham Ath	5	0	5	0
2009–10	Northampton T	30	0	30	0
2010–11	Southend U	26	0	26	0

GRANT, Anthony (M) 173 9
H: 5 10 W: 11 01 b.Lambeth 4-6-87
Source: Scholar. Honours: England Youth.

2004–05	Chelsea	1	0
2005–06	Chelsea	0	0
2005–06	*Oldham Ath*	2	0	2	0
2006–07	Chelsea	0	0
2006–07	*Wycombe W*	40	0	40	0
2007–08	Chelsea	0	0	1	0
2007–08	*Luton T*	4	0	4	0
2007–08	*Southend U*	10	0
2008–09	Southend U	35	1
2009–10	Southend U	38	0
2010–11	Southend U	43	8	126	9

HALL, Ryan (M) 50 11
H: 5 10 W: 10 04 b.Dulwich 4-1-88
Source: Scholar.

2005–06	Crystal Palace	0	0
2006–07	Crystal Palace	0	0
2007–08	Crystal Palace	1	0	1	0
2007–08	*Dagenham & R*	8	2	8	2
From Bromley.			
2010–11	Southend U	41	9	41	9

HAZELL, Justin (M) 0 0
H: 5 9 W: 11 06 b.Leigh-on-Sea 12-1-92
Source: Scholar.

2008–09	Southend U	0	0
2009–10	Southend U	0	0
2010–11	Southend U	0	0

HERD, Johnny (D) 35 0
H: 5 9 W: 12 00 b.Huntingdon 3-10-89
Source: Welling United.

2008–09	Southend U	6	0
2009–10	Southend U	20	0
2010–11	Southend U	9	0	35	0

JAMES-LEWIS, Merrick (M) 0 0
b.Southend 21-5-92
Source: Scholar.

2010–11	Southend U	0	0

MILNER, Marcus (M) 1 0
H: 5 10 W: 12 03 b.Kingston (Jam)
28-11-91
Source: Scholar.

2009–10	Southend U	1	0
2010–11	Southend U	0	0	1	0

MOHSNI, Bilel (D) 23 5
H: 6 3 W: 11 11 b.Paris 21-7-87
Source: Les Ulis, Saint-Georges, Sainte
Genevieve Sp.

2010–11	Southend U	23	5	23	5

MORRIS, Glenn (G) 157 0
H: 6 0 W: 12 03 b.Woolwich 20-12-83
Source: Scholar.

2001–02	Leyton Orient	2	0
2002–03	Leyton Orient	23	0
2003–04	Leyton Orient	27	0
2004–05	Leyton Orient	12	0
2005–06	Leyton Orient	4	0
2006–07	Leyton Orient	3	0
2007–08	Leyton Orient	16	0
2008–09	Leyton Orient	26	0
2009–10	Leyton Orient	11	0	124	0
2010–11	Southend U	33	0	33	0

NESBITT, Teddy (D) 2 0
b. 6-9-93
Source: Scholar.

2010–11	Southend U	2	0	2	0

OKAI, Julian (M) 0 0
H: 5 6 W: 9 11 b.Rochford 26-2-93
Source: Scholar.

2009–10	Southend U	0	0
2010–11	Southend U	0	0

PATERSON, Matthew (F) 55 7
H: 5 10 W: 10 10 b.Dunfermline 18-10-89
Source: Scholar. Honours: Scotland Youth.

2008–09	Southampton	11	1
2009–10	Southampton	7	1	18	2
2009–10	Southend U	16	2
2010–11	*Southend U*	11	0	27	2
2010–11	*Stockport Co*	10	3	10	3

PHILLIPS, Mark (D) 135 2
H: 6 2 W: 11 00 b.Lambeth 27-1-82
Source: Scholarship.

1999–2000	Millwall	0	0
2000–01	Millwall	0	0
2001–02	Millwall	1	0
2002–03	Millwall	7	0
2003–04	Millwall	0	0
2004–05	Millwall	25	1
2005–06	Millwall	22	0
2006–07	Millwall	12	0	67	1
2006–07	*Darlington*	8	0	8	0
2007–08	Inactive	0	0
2008–09	Brentford	33	1
2009–10	Brentford	22	0	55	1
2010–11	Southend U	5	0	5	0

PROSSER, Luke (D) 50 3
H: 6 2 W: 12 04 b.Waltham Cross 28-5-88
Source: Scholar.

2005–06	Port Vale	0	0
2006–07	Port Vale	0	0
2007–08	Port Vale	5	0
2008–09	Port Vale	26	1
2009–10	Port Vale	2	1	33	2
2010–11	Southend U	17	1	17	1

SAWYER, Lee (M) 53 3
H: 5 10 W: 10 03 b.Leytonstone 10-9-89
Source: Scholar. Honours: England Youth.

2007–08	Chelsea	0	0
2008–09	Chelsea	0	0
2008–09	*Southend U*	2	1
2008–09	*Coventry C*	2	0	2	0
2008–09	*Wycombe W*	9	1	9	1
2009–10	Chelsea	0	0
2009–10	*Southend U*	6	0
2009–10	*Barnet*	7	1	7	1
From Woking.			
2010–11	Southend U	17	0	35	1

SOARES, Louie (M) 123 11
H: 5 11 W: 13 05 b.Reading 8-1-85
Source: Scholar. Honours: Barbados 3 full
caps.

2003–04	Reading	0	0
2004–05	Bristol R	1	0	1	0
2005–06	Barnet	20	1	20	1
2008–09	Aldershot T	35	3
2009–10	Aldershot T	36	7	71	10
2010–11	Southend U	31	0	31	0

STEVENS, James (M) 1 0
Source: Scholar. Honours: Northern Ireland
Youth.

2010–11	Southend U	1	0	1	0

STURROCK, Blair (F) 240 31
H: 5 10 W: 12 09 b.Dundee 25-8-81
Source: Dundee U.

2000–01	Brechin C	27	6	27	6
2001–02	Plymouth Arg	19	1
2002–03	Plymouth Arg	20	1
2003–04	Plymouth Arg	24	0
2004–05	Plymouth Arg	0	0	63	2
2004–05	Kidderminster H	22	5	22	5
2005–06	Rochdale	31	6
2006–07	Rochdale	0	0	31	6
2006–07	Swindon T	19	3
2007–08	Swindon T	21	3
2008–09	Swindon T	10	0	50	6
2008–09	*Bournemouth*	4	0	4	0
From Mansfield T.			
2010–11	Southend U	43	6	43	6

WOODYARD, Alex (M) 3 0
Source: Scholar.

2010–11	Southend U	3	0	3	0

ZAABOUB, Sofiane (D) 108 2
H: 5 11 W: 11 09 b.Melun 23-1-83
Source: Montereau, St Etienne, Modena,
Sora, Real Jaen.

2005–06	FC Brussels	20	1	20	1
2006–07	Swindon T	27	1
2007–08	Swindon T	29	0	56	1
2008–09	Walsall	29	0	29	0
2010–11	Southend U	3	0	3	0

Transferred to Setif January 2011.

STEVENAGE (76)

ASHTON, Jon (D) 146 2
H: 6 2 W: 13 12 b.Nuneaton 4-10-82
Source: Scholar.

2000–01	Leicester C	0	0
2001–02	Leicester C	7	0
2002–03	*Notts Co*	4	0	4	0
2003–04	Leicester C	0	0	7	0
2003–04	Oxford U	34	0
2004–05	Oxford U	30	0
2005–06	Oxford U	33	1	97	1
From Rushden & D, Grays Ath.			
2010–11	Stevenage	38	1	38	1

ATIENO, Taiwo (F) 88 17
H: 6 2 W: 12 13 b.Brixton 6-8-85
Source: Scholar.

2003–04	Walsall	3	0
2004–05	Walsall	0	0
2004–05	*Rochdale*	13	2	13	2
2004–05	*Chester C*	4	1	4	1
2005–06	Walsall	2	0	5	0
2005–06	*Darlington*	3	0	3	0
2007	Puerto Rico Is	10	5
2008	Puerto Rico Is	22	4	32	9
From Charleston Battery.			
2009	Rochester Rhinos	17	2	17	2
2010–11	Luton T	3	1	13	3
2010–11	Stevenage	1	0	1	0

BEARDSLEY, Chris (F) 85 7
H: 6 0 W: 12 12 b.Derby 28-2-84
Source: Scholar.

2002–03	Mansfield T	5	0
2003–04	Mansfield T	15	1
2004–05	Doncaster R	4	0	4	0
2004–05	Kidderminster H	25	5	25	5
2005–06	Mansfield T	3	0
2006–07	Mansfield T	10	0	33	1
From Rushden & D, York C, Kettering T.			
2010–11	Stevenage	23	1	23	1

BOSTWICK, Michael (D) 41 2
H: 6 4 W: 14 00 b.Eltham 17-5-88
Source: Scholar.

2005–06	Millwall	0	0
2006–07	Millwall	0	0
From Rushden & D, Ebbsfleet U.			
2010–11	Stevenage	41	2	41	2

BOYLAN, Lee (F)   10   2
H: 5 6   W: 11 05   b.Witham 2-9-78
Honours: Eire Under-21.
1996–97	West Ham U	1	0		
1997–98	West Ham U	0	0		
1998–99	West Ham U	0	0	1	0
1999	Trelleborg	2	1	2	1
1999–2000	Exeter C	6	1	6	1
From Kingstonian, Hayes, Stevenage, Canvey Island, Grays Ath, Cambridge U.
2010–11	Stevenage	1	0	1	0

BRIDGES, David (M)   64   6
H: 6 0   W: 12 00   b.Huntingdon 22-9-82
Source: Scholar.
2001–02	Cambridge U	7	1
2002–03	Cambridge U	17	2
2003–04	Cambridge U	21	2	45	5
From Riga, Braintree T, Histon, Cambridge U, Kettering T.
2010–11	Stevenage	19	1	19	1

BYROM, Joel (M)   8   0
H: 6 0   W: 12 04   b.Accrington 14-9-86
Source: Scholar.
2004–05	Blackburn R	0	0
2005–06	Blackburn R	0	0
2006–07	Accrington S	1	0	1	0
From Clitheroe, Southport, Clitheroe, Northwich Vic.
2010–11	Stevenage	7	0	7	0

CHARLES, Darius (M)   65   3
H: 6 1   W: 13 05   b.Ealing 10-12-87
Source: Scholar.
2004–05	Brentford	1	0
2005–06	Brentford	2	0
2006–07	Brentford	17	1
2007–08	Brentford	17	0
2008–09	Brentford	0	0	37	1
From Ebbsfleet U.
2010–11	Stevenage	28	2	28	2

DAY, Chris (G)   228   0
H: 6 2   W: 13 07   b.Whipps Cross 7-7-75
Source: Trainee. *Honours:* England Youth, Under-21.
1992–93	Tottenham H	0	0
1993–94	Tottenham H	0	0
1994–95	Tottenham H	0	0
1995–96	Tottenham H	0	0
1996–97	Crystal Palace	24	0	24	0
1997–98	Watford	0	0
1998–99	Watford	0	0
1999–2000	Watford	11	0
2000–01	Watford	0	0	11	0
2000–01	Lincoln C	14	0	14	0
2001–02	QPR	16	0
2002–03	QPR	12	0
2003–04	QPR	29	0
2004–05	QPR	30	0	87	0
2004–05	Preston NE	6	0	6	0
2005–06	Oldham Ath	30	0	30	0
2006–07	Millwall	5	0
2007–08	Millwall	5	0	10	0
2010–11	Stevenage	46	0	46	0

DIXON, Terry (F)   1   0
H: 6 1   W: 11 13   b.Holloway 15-1-90
Honours: Eire Youth, Under-21.
2006–07	Tottenham H	0	0
2007–08	Tottenham H	0	0
2008–09	West Ham U	0	0
2009–10	West Ham U	0	0
2010–11	Stevenage	1	0	1	0

FOSTER, Luke (D)   39   2
H: 6 2   W: 12 08   b.Mexborough 8-9-85
Source: Scholar.
2004–05	Sheffield W	0	0
2005–06	Lincoln C	16	1
2006–07	Lincoln C	0	0	16	1
From Stalybridge C, Oxford U, Mansfield T.
2010–11	Stevenage	23	1	23	1

GRIFFIN, Charlie (F)   65   8
H: 6 0   W: 12 07   b.Bath 25-6-79
Source: Bristol R Schoolboy, Chippenham T.
1998–99	Swindon T	5	1
1999–2000	Swindon T	21	1
2000–01	Swindon T	2	0	28	2
From Forest Green R.
2005–06	Wycombe W	22	3	22	3

From Woking, Chippenham T, Wycombe W, Newport Co, Salisbury C.
2010–11	Stevenage	15	3	15	3

HARRISON, Byron (F)   20   8
b.Wandsworth 15-6-87
Source: Havant & Waterlooville, Worthing, Boreham Wood, Harrow B, Ashford T, Carshalton Ath.
2010–11	Stevenage	20	8	20	8

HENRY, Ronnie (D)   57   0
H: 5 11   W: 11 10   b.Hemel Hempstead 2-1-84
Source: Trainee.
2002–03	Tottenham H	0	0		
2002–03	Southend U	3	0	3	0
2004	Dublin C	12	0	12	0
2010–11	Stevenage	42	0	42	0

KUQI, Njazi (F)   6   0
H: 6 3   W: 13 05   b.Vushtrri 25-3-83
Source: Lahti. *Honours:* Finland Under-21.
2004–05	Birmingham C	0	0		
2005–06	Birmingham C	0	0		
2005–06	Blackpool	4	0	4	0
2005–06	Peterborough U	1	0	1	0
From Groningen, Carl Zeiss Jena, Koblenz.
2010–11	Stevenage	1	0	1	0
Transferred to Dundee August 2010.

LAIRD, Scott (D)   44   4
H: 5 11   W: 11 05   b.Taunton 15-5-88
Source: Scholar.
2006–07	Plymouth Arg	0	0		
2007–08	Plymouth Arg	0	0		
2010–11	Stevenage	44	4	44	4

LONG, Stacy (M)   41   3
H: 5 8   W: 10 00   b.Farnborough 11-1-85
Source: Scholar. *Honours:* England Under-20, Youth.
2001–02	Charlton Ath	0	0		
2002–03	Charlton Ath	0	0		
2003–04	Charlton Ath	0	0		
2004–05	Charlton Ath	0	0		
2005–06	Notts Co	19	1	19	1
From Ebbsfleet U.
2010–11	Stevenage	22	2	22	2

MAY, Ben (F)   214   27
H: 6 3   W: 12 12   b.Gravesend 10-3-84
Source: Juniors.
2000–01	Millwall	0	0		
2001–02	Millwall	0	0		
2002–03	Millwall	10	1		
2002–03	Colchester U	6	0		
2003–04	Millwall	0	0		
2003–04	Brentford	41	7		
2004–05	Millwall	8	1		
2004–05	Colchester U	14	1	20	1
2004–05	Brentford	10	1	51	8
2005–06	Millwall	39	10		
2006–07	Millwall	13	2		
2007–08	Millwall	8	0	78	14
2007–08	Scunthorpe U	21	1		
2008–09	Scunthorpe U	23	2		
2009–10	Scunthorpe U	1	0	45	3
2010–11	Stevenage	20	1	20	1

MOUSINHO, John (M)   175   12
H: 6 1   W: 12 07   b.Hounslow 30-4-86
Source: Univ of Notre Dame.
2005–06	Brentford	7	0		
2006–07	Brentford	34	0		
2007–08	Brentford	23	2	64	2
2008–09	Wycombe W	34	2		
2009–10	Wycombe W	39	1	73	3
2010–11	Stevenage	38	7	38	7

MURPHY, Darren (M)   37   2
H: 6 0   W: 11 11   b.Cork 28-7-85
Source: Cobh Ramblers.
2007	Cork C	9	1		
2008	Cork C	23	1	32	2
2010–11	Stevenage	5	0	5	0

ODUBADE, Yemi (F)   27   2
H: 5 7   W: 11 07   b.Lagos 4-7-84
Source: Eastbourne B.
2004–05	Yeovil T	4	0	4	0
From Eastbourne B.
2005–06	Oxford U	8	1	8	1
2010–11	Stevenage	15	1	15	1

REID, Craig (F)   34   2
H: 5 10   W: 11 10   b.Coventry 17-12-85
Honours: Ipswich T Scholar.
2004–05	Coventry C	0	0		
2005–06	Coventry C	0	0		
2006–07	Cheltenham T	6	0		
2007–08	Cheltenham T	8	0	14	0
From Grays Ath, Newport Co.
2010–11	Stevenage	20	2	20	2

ROBERTS, Mark (D)   83   6
H: 6 1   W: 12 00   b.Northwich 16-10-83
Source: Scholar.
2002–03	Crewe Alex	0	0		
2003–04	Crewe Alex	0	0		
2004–05	Crewe Alex	6	0		
2005–06	Crewe Alex	0	0		
2005–06	Chester C	1	0	1	0
2006–07	Crewe Alex	0	0	6	0
From Northwich Vic.
2007–08	Accrington S	34	0	34	0
From Northwich Vic.
2010–11	Stevenage	42	6	42	6

SINCLAIR, Robert (D)   27   2
H: 5 10   W: 11 02   b.Bedford 29-8-89
Source: Scholar.
2007–08	Luton T	0	0		
From Salisbury C.
2010–11	Stevenage	27	2	27	2

WILLIAMS, Marvin (M)   122   9
H: 5 11   W: 11 06   b.London 12-8-87
Source: Scholar.
2005–06	Millwall	22	4		
2006–07	Millwall	29	3	51	7
2006–07	Torquay U	2	1		
2007–08	Yeovil T	23	0	23	0
2008–09	Brentford	34	0	34	0
2009–10	Torquay U	4	0	6	1
2010	Ostersund	7	1	7	1
2010–11	Stevenage	1	0	1	0

WILSON, Lawrie (D)   42   5
H: 5 11   W: 11 06   b.London 11-9-87
Source: Charlton Ath.
2006–07	Colchester U	0	0		
2010–11	Stevenage	42	5	42	5

WINN, Peter (M)   32   2
H: 6 0   W: 11 09   b.Cleethorpes 19-12-88
Source: Scholar.
2006–07	Scunthorpe U	0	0		
2007–08	Scunthorpe U	4	0		
2008–09	Scunthorpe U	0	0		
2009–10	Scunthorpe U	0	0	4	0
2010–11	Stevenage	28	2	28	2

STOCKPORT CO (77)

ASSOUMANI, Mansour (D)   111   5
H: 6 2   W: 11 13   b.Nice 30-1-83
2001–02	Montpellier	2	0		
2002–03	Montpellier	15	1		
2003–04	Montpellier	27	1		
2004–05	Montpellier	15	2		
2005–06	Montpellier	15	0	74	4
2006–07	Saarebruck	0	0		
2007–08	Siegen	0	0		
2008–09	Leeds U	1	0	1	0
From Wrexham.
2010–11	Stockport Co	36	1	36	1

CONLON, Barry (F)   441   121
H: 6 3   W: 14 00   b.Drogheda 1-10-78
Source: QPR Trainee. *Honours:* Eire Under-21.
1997–98	Manchester C	7	0		
1997–98	Plymouth Arg	13	2	13	2
1998–99	Manchester C	0	0	7	0
1998–99	Southend U	34	7	34	7
1999–2000	York C	40	11		
2000–01	York C	8	0	48	11
2000–01	Colchester U	26	8	26	8
2001–02	Darlington	35	10		
2002–03	Darlington	41	15		
2003–04	Darlington	39	14		
2004–05	Barnsley	24	6		
2005–06	Barnsley	11	1	35	7
2005–06	Rotherham U	3	1	3	1
2006–07	Darlington	19	6	134	45

2006–07	Mansfield T	17	6	17	6
2007–08	Bradford C	42	7		
2008–09	Bradford C	30	10	72	17
2008–09	*Grimsby T*	8	5		
2009–10	Grimsby T	16	5	24	10
2009–10	Chesterfield	19	7	19	7
2010–11	Stockport Co	9	0	9	0

Transferred to Charleroi December 2010.

DARKWAH, Cameron (F) 6 0
b.Manchester 2-9-92
Source: Scholar.

2010–11	Stockport Co	6	0	6	0

FISHER, Tom (F) 28 1
H: 5 10 W: 11 07 b.Wythenshawe 28-6-92
Source: Scholar.

2008–09	Stockport Co	1	0		
2009–10	Stockport Co	1	0		
2010–11	Stockport Co	26	1	28	1

GLENNON, Matty (G) 315 0
H: 6 2 W: 14 08 b.Stockport 8-10-78
Source: Trainee.

1997–98	Bolton W	0	0		
1998–99	Bolton W	0	0		
1999–2000	Bolton W	0	0		
1999–2000	*Port Vale*	0	0		
1999–2000	*Stockport Co*	0	0		
2000–01	Bolton W	0	0		
2000–01	*Bristol R*	1	0	1	0
2000–01	Carlisle U	29	0		
2001–02	Hull C	26	0		
2002–03	Hull C	9	0	35	0
2002–03	Carlisle U	32	0		
2003–04	Carlisle U	44	0		
2004–05	Carlisle U	0	0	105	0
2005–06	St Johnstone	12	0	12	0
2006–07	Huddersfield T	46	0		
2007–08	Huddersfield T	45	0		
2008–09	Huddersfield T	18	0		
2009–10	Huddersfield T	0	0	109	0
2009–10	Bradford C	17	0	17	0
2010–11	Stockport Co	36	0	36	0

GOODALL, Alan (D) 212 12
H: 5 7 W: 11 08 b.Birkenhead 2-12-81
Source: Bangor C.

2004–05	Rochdale	34	2		
2005–06	Rochdale	40	3		
2006–07	Rochdale	46	3		
2007–08	Luton T	29	1	29	1
2008–09	Chesterfield	28	3		
2009–10	Chesterfield	17	0	45	3
2010–11	Rochdale	5	0	125	8
2010–11	Stockport Co	13	0	13	0

GRIFFIN, Adam (D) 242 10
H: 5 7 W: 10 04 b.Salford 26-8-84
Source: Scholar.

2001–02	Oldham Ath	1	0		
2002–03	Oldham Ath	0	0		
2003–04	Oldham Ath	26	1		
2004–05	Oldham Ath	35	2		
2005–06	Oldham Ath	0	0	62	3
2005–06	*Oxford U*	9	0	9	0
2005–06	*Stockport Co*	21	2		
2006–07	Stockport Co	42	3		
2007–08	Stockport Co	28	1		
2008–09	Darlington	17	0		
2009–10	Darlington	0	0	17	0
2009–10	Stockport Co	18	0		
2010–11	Stockport Co	45	1	154	7

HALLS, Andy (D) 35 0
H: 6 0 W: 12 02 b.Urmston 20-4-92
Source: Scholar.

2008–09	Stockport Co	5	0		
2009–10	Stockport Co	11	0		
2010–11	Stockport Co	19	0	35	0

KOSYLO, Matty (F) 0 0
Source: Scholar.

2010–11	Stockport Co	0	0		

LYNCH, Mark (D) 140 2
H: 5 11 W: 11 03 b.Manchester 2-9-81
Source: Trainee.

1999–2000	Manchester U	0	0		
2000–01	Manchester U	0	0		
2001–02	Manchester U	0	0		
2001–02	*St Johnstone*	20	0	20	0
2002–03	Manchester U	0	0		
2003–04	Manchester U	0	0		

2004–05	Sunderland	11	0	11	0
2005–06	Hull C	16	0		
2006–07	Hull C	0	0	16	0
2006–07	Yeovil T	17	0		
2007–08	Yeovil T	14	0	31	0
2008–09	Rotherham U	8	2		
2009–10	Rotherham U	23	0	31	2
2010–11	Stockport Co	31	0	31	0

MAINWARING, Matty (M) 32 1
H: 5 11 W: 12 02 b.Salford 28-3-90
Source: Preston NE Scholar.

2008–09	Stockport Co	21	1		
2009–10	Stockport Co	0	0		
2010–11	Stockport Co	11	0	32	1

O'DONNELL, Daniel (D) 115 3
H: 6 2 W: 11 11 b.Rainford 10-3-86
Source: Scholar.

2004–05	Liverpool	0	0		
2005–06	Liverpool	0	0		
2006–07	Liverpool	0	0		
2006–07	*Crewe Alex*	25	1		
2007–08	Crewe Alex	27	1		
2008–09	Crewe Alex	24	1		
2009–10	Crewe Alex	27	0	103	3
2010–11	Shrewsbury T	5	0	5	0
2010–11	Stockport Co	7	0	7	0

PILKINGTON, Danny (M) 38 1
H: 5 9 W: 11 10 b.Blackburn 25-5-90
Source: Chorley.

2008–09	Stockport Co	3	0		
2009–10	Stockport Co	29	1		
2010–11	Stockport Co	6	0	38	1

POOLE, David (M) 173 11
H: 5 8 W: 12 00 b.Manchester 25-11-84
Source: Trainee.

2002–03	Manchester U	0	0		
2003–04	Manchester U	0	0		
2004–05	Manchester U	0	0		
2005–06	Yeovil T	25	2		
2006–07	Yeovil T	4	0	29	2
2006–07	*Stockport Co*	31	4		
2007–08	Stockport Co	22	2		
2008–09	Darlington	26	1	26	1
2009–10	Stockport Co	36	0		
2010–11	Stockport Co	29	2	118	8

ROBERTS, Craig (M) 0 0
b.Bangor 28-10-91
Honours: Wales Youth.

2009–10	Stockport Co	0	0		
2010–11	Stockport Co	0	0		

ROSE, Jordan (D) 15 0
b.Southampton 22-11-89
Source: Salisbury C, Weymouth, Paulton R.

2010–11	Stockport Co	15	0	15	0

ROWE, Daniel (M) 24 1
H: 6 0 W: 11 12 b.Wythenshawe 9-3-92
Source: Bolton W.

2008–09	Stockport Co	3	0		
2009–10	Stockport Co	4	0		
2010–11	Stockport Co	17	1	24	1

SALEM, Yannick (F) 5 0
H: 5 11 W: 11 07 b.Amiens 29-3-83
Source: Chateauroux, Creteil, Grenoble, De Graafschap, Apeldoorn, Beveren, Eintracht Trier. *Honours:* Congo 3 full caps.

2010–11	Stockport Co	5	0	5	0

SIMPSON, Jake (M) 37 0
H: 5 11 W: 12 03 b.Oxford 27-10-90
Source: Blackburn R Academy.

2009–10	Shrewsbury T	18	0	18	0
2010–11	Stockport Co	19	0	19	0

SWAILES, Danny (D) 337 22
H: 6 3 W: 12 06 b.Bolton 1-4-79
Source: Trainee.

1997–98	Bury	0	0		
1998–99	Bury	0	0		
1999–2000	Bury	24	3		
2000–01	Bury	11	0		
2001–02	Bury	28	1		
2002–03	Bury	39	3		
2003–04	Bury	42	5		
2004–05	Bury	20	1	164	13
2004–05	Macclesfield T	17	0		
2005–06	Macclesfield T	39	2		

2006–07	Macclesfield T	38	3		
2007–08	Macclesfield T	0	0	94	5
2007–08	Milton Keynes D	40	4		
2008–09	Milton Keynes D	1	0		
2009–10	Milton Keynes D	2	0	43	4
2009–10	*Northampton T*	3	0	3	0
2009–10	Stockport Co	20	0		
2010–11	Stockport Co	13	0	33	0

TANSEY, Greg (M) 98 13
H: 6 1 W: 12 03 b.Huyton 21-11-88
Source: Scholar.

2006–07	Stockport Co	3	0		
2007–08	Stockport Co	13	0		
2008–09	Stockport Co	12	1		
2009–10	Stockport Co	32	2		
2010–11	Stockport Co	38	10	98	13

TURNBULL, Paul (M) 125 6
H: 6 0 W: 12 07 b.Handforth 23-1-89
Source: Scholar.

2004–05	Stockport Co	1	0		
2005–06	Stockport Co	0	0		
2006–07	Stockport Co	0	0		
2007–08	Stockport Co	19	0		
2008–09	Stockport Co	34	1		
2009–10	Stockport Co	30	0		
2010–11	Stockport Co	41	5	125	6

VINCENT, James (M) 70 2
H: 5 11 W: 11 00 b.Glossop 27-9-89
Source: Scholar.

2007–08	Stockport Co	1	0		
2008–09	Stockport Co	16	2		
2009–10	Stockport Co	34	0		
2010–11	Stockport Co	19	0	70	2

STOKE C (78)

ARISMENDI, Diego (M) 92 3
H: 6 2 W: 12 13 b.Montevideo 25-1-88
Honours: Uruguay 2 full caps.

2006–07	Nacional	10	0		
2007–08	Nacional	21	1		
2008–09	Nacional	24	1	55	2
2009–10	Stoke C	0	0		
2009–10	*Brighton & HA*	6	0	6	0
2010–11	Stoke C	0	0		
2010–11	*Barnsley*	31	1	31	1

BEGOVIC, Asmir (G) 76 0
H: 6 5 W: 13 01 b.Trebinje 20-6-87
Source: La Louviere. *Honours:* Canada Under-20, Bosnia 4 full caps.

2006–07	Portsmouth	0	0		
2006–07	Macclesfield T	3	0	3	0
2007–08	Portsmouth	0	0		
2007–08	Bournemouth	8	0	8	0
2007–08	Yeovil T	2	0		
2008–09	Portsmouth	2	0		
2008–09	Yeovil T	14	0	16	0
2009–10	Portsmouth	9	0	11	0
2009–10	Ipswich T	6	0	6	0
2009–10	Stoke C	4	0		
2010–11	Stoke C	28	0	32	0

COLLINS, Danny (D) 211 4
H: 6 2 W: 11 13 b.Buckley 6-8-80
Source: Buckley T. *Honours:* Wales 12 full caps.

2004–05	Chester C	12	1	12	1
2004–05	Sunderland	14	0		
2005–06	Sunderland	23	1		
2006–07	Sunderland	38	0		
2007–08	Sunderland	36	1		
2008–09	Sunderland	35	1		
2009–10	Sunderland	3	0	149	3
2009–10	Stoke C	25	0		
2010–11	Stoke C	25	0	50	0

CUVELIER, Florent (M) 0 0
b.Brussels 12-9-92
Source: Scholar.

2009–10	Portsmouth	0	0		
2010–11	Stoke C	0	0		

DAVIES, Andrew (D) 132 3
H: 6 3 W: 14 08 b.Stockton 17-12-84
Source: Scholar. *Honours:* England Youth, Under-20, Under-21.

2002–03	Middlesbrough	1	0		
2003–04	Middlesbrough	10	0		

2004–05	Middlesbrough	3	0	
2004–05	QPR	9	0	9 0
2005–06	Middlesbrough	12	0	
2005–06	Derby Co	23	3	23 3
2006–07	Middlesbrough	23	0	
2007–08	Middlesbrough	4	0	
2007–08	Southampton	23	0	
2008–09	Southampton	0	0	23 0
2008–09	Stoke C	2	0	
2008–09	Preston NE	5	0	5 0
2009–10	Stoke C	0	0	
2009–10	Sheffield U	8	0	8 0
2010–11	Stoke C	0	0	2 0
2010–11	Walsall	3	0	3 0
2010–11	Middlesbrough	6	0	59 0

DELAP, Rory (M)   465 30
H: 6 3   W: 13 00   b.Sutton Coldfield 6-7-76
Source: Trainee. *Honours:* Eire Under-21, B, 11 full caps.

1992–93	Carlisle U	1	0	
1993–94	Carlisle U	1	0	
1994–95	Carlisle U	3	0	
1995–96	Carlisle U	19	3	
1996–97	Carlisle U	32	4	
1997–98	Carlisle U	9	0	65 7
1997–98	Derby Co	13	0	
1998–99	Derby Co	23	0	
1999–2000	Derby Co	34	8	
2000–01	Derby Co	33	3	103 11
2001–02	Southampton	28	2	
2002–03	Southampton	24	0	
2003–04	Southampton	27	1	
2004–05	Southampton	37	2	
2005–06	Southampton	16	0	132 5
2005–06	Sunderland	6	1	
2006–07	Sunderland	6	0	12 1
2006–07	Stoke C	2	0	
2007–08	Stoke C	44	2	
2008–09	Stoke C	34	2	
2009–10	Stoke C	36	0	
2010–11	Stoke C	37	2	153 6

DIAO, Salif (M)   209 2
H: 6 1   W: 12 08   b.Kedougou 10-2-77
Honours: Senegal 39 full caps, 4 goals.

1996–97	Epinal	2	0	2 0
1996–97	Monaco	0	0	
1997–98	Monaco	12	0	
1998–99	Monaco	14	0	
1999–2000	Monaco	1	0	27 0
2000–01	Sedan	26	0	
2001–02	Sedan	22	0	48 0
2002–03	Liverpool	26	1	
2003–04	Liverpool	3	0	
2004–05	Liverpool	8	0	
2004–05	Birmingham C	2	0	2 0
2005–06	Liverpool	0	0	
2005–06	Portsmouth	11	0	11 0
2006–07	Liverpool	0	0	37 1
2006–07	Stoke C	27	0	
2007–08	Stoke C	11	0	
2008–09	Stoke C	20	0	
2009–10	Stoke C	16	1	
2010–11	Stoke C	8	0	82 1

DICKINSON, Carl (D)   129 1
H: 6 1   W: 12 04   b.Swadlincote 31-3-87
Source: Scholar.

2004–05	Stoke C	1	0	
2005–06	Stoke C	5	0	
2006–07	Stoke C	13	0	
2006–07	Blackpool	7	0	7 0
2007–08	Stoke C	27	0	
2008–09	Stoke C	5	0	
2008–09	Leeds U	7	0	7 0
2009–10	Stoke C	0	0	
2009–10	Barnsley	28	1	28 1
2010–11	Stoke C	0	0	51 0
2010–11	Portsmouth	36	0	36 0

ETHERINGTON, Matthew (M)   354 34
H: 5 10   W: 10 12   b.Truro 14-8-81
Source: School. *Honours:* England Youth, Under-21.

1996–97	Peterborough U	1	0	
1997–98	Peterborough U	2	0	
1998–99	Peterborough U	29	3	
1999–2000	Peterborough U	19	3	51 6
1999–2000	Tottenham H	5	0	
2000–01	Tottenham H	6	0	
2001–02	Bradford C	13	1	13 1

2001–02	Tottenham H	11	0	
2002–03	Tottenham H	23	1	45 1
2003–04	West Ham U	35	5	
2004–05	West Ham U	39	4	
2005–06	West Ham U	33	2	
2006–07	West Ham U	27	0	
2007–08	West Ham U	18	3	
2008–09	West Ham U	13	2	165 16
2008–09	Stoke C	14	0	
2009–10	Stoke C	34	5	
2010–11	Stoke C	32	5	80 10

FAYE, Aboulaye (M)   257 14
H: 6 2   W: 13 10   b.Dakar 26-2-78
Source: Ndiambour Louga. *Honours:* Senegal 35 full caps, 3 goals.

2001–02	Jeanne D'Arc	32	4	32 4
2002–03	Lens	15	0	
2003–04	Lens	19	0	34 0
2004–05	Istrea	28	0	28 0
2005–06	Bolton W	27	1	
2006–07	Bolton W	32	2	
2007–08	Bolton W	1	0	60 3
2007–08	Newcastle U	22	1	22 1
2008–09	Stoke C	36	3	
2009–10	Stoke C	31	2	
2010–11	Stoke C	14	1	81 6

FULLER, Ricardo (F)   327 90
H: 6 3   W: 12 10   b.Kingston, Jamaica 31-10-79
Source: Tivoli Gardens. *Honours:* Jamaica 60 full caps, 11 goals.

2000–01	Crystal Palace	8	0	8 0
2001–02	Hearts	27	8	27 8
From Tivoli Gardens.				
2002–03	Preston NE	18	9	
2003–04	Preston NE	38	17	
2004–05	Preston NE	2	1	58 27
2004–05	Portsmouth	31	1	31 1
2005–06	Southampton	30	9	
2005–06	Ipswich T	3	2	3 2
2006–07	Southampton	1	0	31 9
2006–07	Stoke C	30	10	
2007–08	Stoke C	42	15	
2008–09	Stoke C	34	11	
2009–10	Stoke C	35	3	
2010–11	Stoke C	28	4	169 43

GUDJOHNSEN, Eidur (F)   383 93
H: 6 1   W: 14 02   b.Reykjavik 15-9-78
Honours: Iceland Youth, Under-21, 63 full caps, 24 goals.

1994–95	Valur	17	7	17 7
1995–96	PSV Eindhoven	13	3	
1996–97	PSV Eindhoven	0	0	13 3
1998	KR	6	0	6 0
1998–99	Bolton W	14	5	
1999–2000	Bolton W	41	13	55 18
2000–01	Chelsea	30	10	
2001–02	Chelsea	32	14	
2002–03	Chelsea	35	10	
2003–04	Chelsea	26	6	
2004–05	Chelsea	37	12	
2005–06	Chelsea	26	2	186 54
2006–07	Barcelona	25	5	
2007–08	Barcelona	23	2	
2008–09	Barcelona	24	3	72 10
2009–10	Monaco	9	0	9 0
2009–10	Tottenham H	11	1	11 1
2010–11	Stoke C	4	0	4 0
2010–11	Fulham	10	0	10 0

HIGGINBOTHAM, Danny (D)   313 21
H: 6 2   W: 13 01   b.Manchester 29-12-78
Source: Trainee.

1997–98	Manchester U	1	0	
1998–99	Manchester U	0	0	
1999–2000	Manchester U	3	0	4 0
2000–01	Derby Co	26	0	
2001–02	Derby Co	37	1	
2002–03	Derby Co	23	2	86 3
2002–03	Southampton	9	0	
2003–04	Southampton	27	0	
2004–05	Southampton	21	1	
2005–06	Southampton	37	3	94 4
2006–07	Stoke C	44	7	
2007–08	Stoke C	1	0	
2007–08	Sunderland	21	3	
2008–09	Sunderland	1	0	22 3
2008–09	Stoke C	28	1	
2009–10	Stoke C	24	1	
2010–11	Stoke C	10	2	107 11

HUTH, Robert (D)   162 11
H: 6 3   W: 14 07   b.Berlin 18-8-84
Source: Scholar. *Honours:* Germany Youth, Under-21, 19 full caps, 2 goals.

2001–02	Chelsea	1	0	
2002–03	Chelsea	2	0	
2003–04	Chelsea	16	0	
2004–05	Chelsea	10	0	
2005–06	Chelsea	13	0	42 0
2006–07	Middlesbrough	12	1	
2007–08	Middlesbrough	13	1	
2008–09	Middlesbrough	24	0	
2009–10	Middlesbrough	4	0	53 2
2009–10	Stoke C	32	3	
2010–11	Stoke C	35	6	67 9

JONES, Kenwyne (F)   219 64
H: 6 2   W: 13 06   b.Trinidad & Tobago 5-10-84
Source: W Connection. *Honours:* Trinidad & Tobago Youth, Under-23, 45 full caps, 5 goals.

2004–05	Southampton	2	0	
2004–05	Sheffield W	7	7	7 7
2004–05	Stoke C	13	3	
2005–06	Southampton	34	4	
2006–07	Southampton	34	14	
2007–08	Southampton	1	1	71 19
2007–08	Sunderland	33	7	
2008–09	Sunderland	29	10	
2009–10	Sunderland	32	9	94 26
2010–11	Stoke C	34	9	47 12

LUND, Matthew (M)   2 0
H: 6 0   W: 11 13   b.Manchester 21-11-90
Source: Crewe Alex. *Honours:* Northern Ireland Under-21.

2009–10	Stoke C	0	0	
2010–11	Stoke C	0	0	
2010–11	Hereford U	2	0	2 0

MARSHALL, Ben (F)   74 10
H: 5 11   W: 11 13   b.Salford 29-3-91
Source: Crewe Alex Scholar.

2009–10	Stoke C	0	0	
2009–10	Northampton T	15	2	15 2
2009–10	Cheltenham T	6	2	6 2
2009–10	Carlisle U	20	3	
2010–11	Stoke C	0	0	
2010–11	Carlisle U	33	3	53 6

MOULT, Louis (F)   12 1
H: 6 0   W: 13 05   b.Stoke 14-5-92
Source: Scholar.

2009–10	Stoke C	1	0	
2010–11	Stoke C	0	0	1 0
2010–11	Bradford C	11	1	11 1

NASH, Carlo (G)   243 0
H: 6 5   W: 14 01   b.Bolton 13-9-73
Source: Clitheroe.

1996–97	Crystal Palace	21	0	
1997–98	Crystal Palace	0	0	21 0
1998–99	Stockport Co	43	0	
1999–2000	Stockport Co	38	0	
2000–01	Stockport Co	8	0	89 0
2000–01	Manchester C	6	0	
2001–02	Manchester C	23	0	
2002–03	Manchester C	9	0	38 0
2003–04	Middlesbrough	1	0	
2004–05	Middlesbrough	2	0	3 0
2004–05	Preston NE	7	0	
2005–06	Preston NE	46	0	
2006–07	Preston NE	29	0	82 0
2007–08	Wigan Ath	0	0	
2007–08	Stoke C	10	0	
2008–09	Wigan Ath	0	0	
2008–09	Everton	0	0	
2009–10	Everton	0	0	
2010–11	Stoke C	0	0	10 0

PENNANT, Jermaine (M)   241 15
H: 5 9   W: 10 06   b.Nottingham 15-1-83
Honours: England Schools, Youth, Under-21.

1998–99	Notts Co	0	0	
1998–99	Arsenal	0	0	
1999–2000	Arsenal	0	0	
2000–01	Arsenal	0	0	
2001–02	Arsenal	0	0	
2001–02	Watford	9	2	
2002–03	Arsenal	5	3	
2002–03	Watford	12	0	21 2

Season	Club	Apps	Gls	Tot Apps	Tot Gls
2003–04	Arsenal	0	0		
2003–04	*Leeds U*	36	2	**36**	**2**
2004–05	Arsenal	7	0	**12**	**3**
2004–05	Birmingham C	12	0		
2005–06	Birmingham C	38	2	**50**	**2**
2006–07	Liverpool	34	1		
2007–08	Liverpool	18	2		
2008–09	Liverpool	3	0	**55**	**3**
2008–09	*Portsmouth*	13	0	**13**	**0**
2009–10	Zaragoza	25	0	**25**	**0**
2010–11	Stoke C	29	3	**29**	**3**

PUGH, Danny (M)   **172 10**
H: 6 0   W: 12 10   b.Cheadle Hulme 19-10-82
Source: Scholar.

Season	Club	Apps	Gls	Tot Apps	Tot Gls
2000–01	Manchester U	0	0		
2001–02	Manchester U	0	0		
2002–03	Manchester U	1	0		
2003–04	Manchester U	0	0	**1**	**0**
2004–05	Leeds U	38	5		
2005–06	Leeds U	12	0	**50**	**5**
2006–07	Preston NE	45	4		
2007–08	Preston NE	7	0		
2007–08	Stoke C	30	0		
2008–09	Stoke C	17	0		
2009–10	Stoke C	7	1		
2010–11	Stoke C	10	0	**64**	**1**
2010–11	*Preston NE*	5	0	**57**	**4**

SHAWCROSS, Ryan (D)   **135 13**
H: 6 3   W: 13 13   b.Buckley 4-10-87
Source: Scholar. *Honours:* England Under-21.

Season	Club	Apps	Gls	Tot Apps	Tot Gls
2006–07	Manchester U	0	0		
2007–08	Manchester U	0	0		
2007–08	Stoke C	41	7		
2008–09	Stoke C	30	3		
2009–10	Stoke C	28	2		
2010–11	Stoke C	36	1	**135**	**13**

SHOTTON, Ryan (D)   **65 5**
H: 6 3   W: 13 05   b.Stoke 30-9-88
Source: Scholar.

Season	Club	Apps	Gls	Tot Apps	Tot Gls
2006–07	Stoke C	0	0		
2007–08	Stoke C	0	0		
2008–09	Stoke C	0	0		
2008–09	*Tranmere R*	33	5	**33**	**5**
2009–10	Stoke C	0	0		
2009–10	*Barnsley*	30	0	**30**	**0**
2010–11	Stoke C	2	0	**2**	**0**

SIDIBE, Mamady (F)   **305 41**
H: 6 4   W: 12 02   b.Bamako 18-12-79
Source: CA Paris. *Honours:* Mali 14 full caps, 3 goals.

Season	Club	Apps	Gls	Tot Apps	Tot Gls
2001–02	Swansea C	31	7	**31**	**7**
2002–03	Gillingham	30	3		
2003–04	Gillingham	41	5		
2004–05	Gillingham	35	2	**106**	**10**
2005–06	Stoke C	42	6		
2006–07	Stoke C	43	9		
2007–08	Stoke C	35	4		
2008–09	Stoke C	22	3		
2009–10	Stoke C	24	2		
2010–11	Stoke C	2	0	**168**	**24**

SOARES, Tom (M)   **192 14**
H: 6 0   W: 11 04   b.Reading 10-7-86
Source: Scholar. *Honours:* England Youth, Under-20, Under-21.

Season	Club	Apps	Gls	Tot Apps	Tot Gls
2003–04	Crystal Palace	3	0		
2004–05	Crystal Palace	22	0		
2005–06	Crystal Palace	44	1		
2006–07	Crystal Palace	37	3		
2007–08	Crystal Palace	39	6		
2008–09	Crystal Palace	4	1	**149**	**11**
2008–09	Stoke C	7	0		
2008–09	*Charlton Ath*	11	1	**11**	**1**
2009–10	Stoke C	0	0		
2009–10	*Sheffield W*	25	2	**25**	**2**
2010–11	Stoke C	0	0	**7**	**0**

SONKO, Ibrahima (D)   **253 17**
H: 6 3   W: 13 07   b.Bignola 22-1-81
Source: St Etienne, Grenoble. *Honours:* Senegal Under-21, 5 full caps, 1 goal.

Season	Club	Apps	Gls	Tot Apps	Tot Gls
2002–03	Brentford	37	5		
2003–04	Brentford	43	3	**80**	**8**
2004–05	Reading	39	1		
2005–06	Reading	46	3		
2006–07	Reading	23	1		
2007–08	Reading	16	0		
2008–09	Reading	3	3	**127**	**8**
2008–09	Stoke C	14	0		
2009–10	Stoke C	0	0		
2009–10	*Hull C*	9	0	**9**	**0**
2010–11	Stoke C	0	0	**14**	**0**
2010–11	*Portsmouth*	23	1	**23**	**1**

SORENSEN, Thomas (G)   **389 0**
H: 6 4   W: 13 10   b.Fredericia 12-6-76
Source: Odense. *Honours:* Denmark Youth, Under-21, B, 94 full caps.

Season	Club	Apps	Gls	Tot Apps	Tot Gls
1998–99	Sunderland	45	0		
1999–2000	Sunderland	37	0		
2000–01	Sunderland	34	0		
2001–02	Sunderland	34	0		
2002–03	Sunderland	21	0	**171**	**0**
2003–04	Aston Villa	38	0		
2004–05	Aston Villa	36	0		
2005–06	Aston Villa	36	0		
2006–07	Aston Villa	29	0		
2007–08	Aston Villa	0	0	**139**	**0**
2008–09	Stoke C	36	0		
2009–10	Stoke C	33	0		
2010–11	Stoke C	10	0	**79**	**0**

TONGE, Michael (M)   **304 24**
H: 6 0   W: 11 10   b.Manchester 7-4-83
Source: Scholar. *Honours:* England Youth, Under-20, Under-21.

Season	Club	Apps	Gls	Tot Apps	Tot Gls
2000–01	Sheffield U	1	0		
2001–02	Sheffield U	30	3		
2002–03	Sheffield U	44	6		
2003–04	Sheffield U	46	4		
2004–05	Sheffield U	34	2		
2005–06	Sheffield U	30	3		
2006–07	Sheffield U	27	2		
2007–08	Sheffield U	45	1		
2008–09	Sheffield U	4	0	**262**	**21**
2008–09	Stoke C	10	0		
2009–10	Stoke C	0	0		
2009–10	*Preston NE*	7	0		
2009–10	*Derby Co*	18	2	**18**	**2**
2010–11	Stoke C	2	0	**12**	**0**
2010–11	*Preston NE*	5	1	**12**	**1**

TUNCAY, Sanli (F)   **331 111**
H: 5 10   W: 11 00   b.Sakarya 16-1-82
Honours: Turkey 79 full caps, 20 goals.

Season	Club	Apps	Gls	Tot Apps	Tot Gls
2000–01	Sakarya	31	16		
2001–02	Sakarya	35	16	**66**	**32**
2002–03	Fenerbahce	29	9		
2003–04	Fenerbahce	31	19		
2004–05	Fenerbahce	31	7		
2005–06	Fenerbahce	27	13		
2006–07	Fenerbahce	33	9	**151**	**57**
2007–08	Middlesbrough	34	8		
2008–09	Middlesbrough	33	7		
2009–10	Middlesbrough	3	2	**70**	**17**
2009–10	Stoke C	30	4		
2010–11	Stoke C	14	1	**44**	**5**

Transferred to Wolfsburg January 2011.

WALTERS, Jon (F)   **299 57**
H: 6 0   W: 12 06   b.Birkenhead 20-9-83
Source: Blackburn R. *Honours:* Eire Youth, Under-21, B, 2 full caps.

Season	Club	Apps	Gls	Tot Apps	Tot Gls
2001–02	Bolton W	0	0		
2002–03	Bolton W	4	0		
2002–03	*Hull C*	11	5		
2003–04	Bolton W	0	0	**4**	**0**
2003–04	*Crewe Alex*	0	0		
2003–04	*Barnsley*	8	0	**8**	**0**
2003–04	*Hull C*	16	1		
2004–05	Hull C	21	1	**48**	**7**
2004–05	*Scunthorpe U*	3	0	**3**	**0**
2005–06	Wrexham	38	5	**38**	**5**
2006–07	Chester C	26	9	**26**	**9**
2006–07	Ipswich T	16	4		
2007–08	Ipswich T	40	13		
2008–09	Ipswich T	36	5		
2009–10	Ipswich T	43	8		
2010–11	Ipswich T	1	0	**136**	**30**
2010–11	Stoke C	36	6	**36**	**6**

WHELAN, Glenn (M)   **257 16**
H: 5 11   W: 12 07   b.Dublin 13-1-84
Source: Scholar. *Honours:* Eire Youth, Under-21, B, 29 full caps, 2 goals.

Season	Club	Apps	Gls	Tot Apps	Tot Gls
2000–01	Manchester C	0	0		
2001–02	Manchester C	0	0		
2002–03	Manchester C	0	0		
2003–04	Manchester C	0	0		
2003–04	*Bury*	13	0	**13**	**0**
2004–05	Sheffield W	36	2		
2005–06	Sheffield W	43	1		
2006–07	Sheffield W	38	7		
2007–08	Sheffield W	25	2	**142**	**12**
2007–08	Stoke C	14	1		
2008–09	Stoke C	26	1		
2009–10	Stoke C	33	2		
2010–11	Stoke C	29	0	**102**	**4**

WHITEHEAD, Dean (M)   **380 24**
H: 5 11   W: 12 06   b.Abingdon 12-1-82
Source: Trainee.

Season	Club	Apps	Gls	Tot Apps	Tot Gls
1999–2000	Oxford U	0	0		
2000–01	Oxford U	20	0		
2001–02	Oxford U	40	1		
2002–03	Oxford U	18	1		
2003–04	Oxford U	44	7	**122**	**9**
2004–05	Sunderland	42	5		
2005–06	Sunderland	37	3		
2006–07	Sunderland	45	4		
2007–08	Sunderland	27	1		
2008–09	Sunderland	34	0		
2009–10	Sunderland	0	0	**185**	**13**
2009–10	Stoke C	36	0		
2010–11	Stoke C	37	2	**73**	**2**

WILKINSON, Andy (D)   **122 0**
H: 5 11   W: 11 00   b.Stone 6-8-84
Source: Scholar.

Season	Club	Apps	Gls	Tot Apps	Tot Gls
2001–02	Stoke C	0	0		
2002–03	Stoke C	0	0		
2003–04	Stoke C	3	0		
2004–05	Stoke C	1	0		
2004–05	*Shrewsbury T*	9	0	**9**	**0**
2005–06	Stoke C	6	0		
2006–07	Stoke C	4	0		
2006–07	*Blackpool*	7	0	**7**	**0**
2007–08	Stoke C	23	0		
2008–09	Stoke C	22	0		
2009–10	Stoke C	25	0		
2010–11	Stoke C	22	0	**106**	**0**

WILSON, Marc (M)   **95 4**
H: 6 2   W: 12 07   b.Lisburn 17-8-87
Source: Scholar. *Honours:* Eire Under-21, 1 full cap.

Season	Club	Apps	Gls	Tot Apps	Tot Gls
2005–06	Portsmouth	0	0		
2005–06	*Yeovil T*	2	0	**2**	**0**
2006–07	Portsmouth	0	0		
2006–07	*Bournemouth*	19	3		
2007–08	Portsmouth	0	0		
2007–08	*Bournemouth*	7	0	**26**	**3**
2007–08	*Luton T*	4	0	**4**	**0**
2008–09	Portsmouth	3	0		
2009–10	Portsmouth	28	0		
2010–11	Portsmouth	4	0	**35**	**0**
2010–11	Stoke C	28	1	**28**	**1**

Scholars
Agbaje Jordan Patrick Adetunji Adewale; Bossman Allen; Brunt Ryan Samuel; Clarkson Michael Thomas; Dawson Lucas Jay; Galloway Jordan; Gray Travis Edwin; Hall Andrew Stephen; Koroma Unpha; Musungun Andrew; Richardson Jordan; Roberts Nurse Connor; Sinclair Craig; Whitehurst Sam Ashley

SUNDERLAND (79)

ADAMS, Blair (D)   **0 0**
H: 5 11   W: 11 05   b.South Shields 8-9-91
Source: Scholar.

Season	Club	Apps	Gls	Tot Apps	Tot Gls
2010–11	Sunderland	0	0		

ANGELERI, Marcos (D)   **161 3**
H: 6 0   W: 10 10   b.La Plata 4-7-83
Honours: Argentina 4 full caps.

Season	Club	Apps	Gls	Tot Apps	Tot Gls
2005–06	Estudiantes	29	1		
2006–07	Estudiantes	29	1		
2007–08	Estudiantes	34	0		
2008–09	Estudiantes	49	1		
2009–10	Estudiantes	18	0	**159**	**3**
2010–11	Sunderland	2	0	**2**	**0**

BAGNALL, Liam (D)   **0 0**
H: 5 11   W: 10 04   b.Newry 17-5-92
Source: Scholar. *Honours:* Northern Ireland Under-21.

Season	Club	Apps	Gls	Tot Apps	Tot Gls
2009–10	Sunderland	0	0		
2010–11	Sunderland	0	0		

BARDSLEY, Phillip (D) 147 4
H: 5 11 W: 11 13 b.Salford 28-6-85
Source: Trainee. *Honours:* Scotland 5 full caps.

2003–04	Manchester U	0	0		
2004–05	Manchester U	0	0		
2005–06	Manchester U	8	0		
2005–06	Burnley	6	0	6	0
2006–07	Manchester U	0	0		
2006–07	Rangers	5	1	5	1
2006–07	Aston Villa	13	0	13	0
2007–08	Manchester U	0	0	8	0
2007–08	Sheffield U	16	0	16	0
2007–08	Sunderland	11	0		
2008–09	Sunderland	28	0		
2009–10	Sunderland	26	0		
2010–11	Sunderland	34	3	99	3

BRAMBLE, Titus (D) 274 9
H: 6 2 W: 13 10 b.Ipswich 31-7-81
Source: Trainee. *Honours:* England Under-21.

1998–99	Ipswich T	4	0		
1999–2000	Ipswich T	0	0		
1999–2000	Colchester U	2	0	2	0
2000–01	Ipswich T	26	1		
2001–02	Ipswich T	18	0	48	1
2002–03	Newcastle U	16	0		
2003–04	Newcastle U	29	0		
2004–05	Newcastle U	19	1		
2005–06	Newcastle U	24	2		
2006–07	Newcastle U	17	0	105	3
2007–08	Wigan Ath	26	2		
2008–09	Wigan Ath	35	1		
2009–10	Wigan Ath	35	2	96	5
2010–11	Sunderland	23	0	23	0

CAMPBELL, Frazier (F) 80 20
H: 5 11 W: 12 04 b.Huddersfield 13-9-87
Source: Scholar. *Honours:* England Youth, Under-21.

2005–06	Manchester U	0	0		
2006–07	Manchester U	0	0		
2007–08	Manchester U	1	0		
2007–08	Hull C	34	15	34	15
2008–09	Manchester U	1	0		
2008–09	Tottenham H	10	1	10	1
2009–10	Manchester U	0	0	2	0
2009–10	Sunderland	31	4		
2010–11	Sunderland	3	0	34	4

CARSON, Trevor (G) 35 0
H: 6 0 W: 14 11 b.Downpatrick 5-3-88
Source: Scholar. *Honours:* Northern Ireland Youth, Under-21, B.

2004–05	Sunderland	0	0		
2005–06	Sunderland	0	0		
2006–07	Sunderland	0	0		
2007–08	Sunderland	0	0		
2008–09	Sunderland	0	0		
2008–09	Chesterfield	18	0	18	0
2009–10	Sunderland	0	0		
2010–11	Sunderland	0	0		
2010–11	Lincoln C	16	0	16	0
2010–11	Brentford	1	0	1	0

CATTERMOLE, Lee (M) 147 4
H: 5 10 W: 11 13 b.Stockton 21-3-88
Source: Scholar. *Honours:* England Youth, Under-21.

2005–06	Middlesbrough	14	1		
2006–07	Middlesbrough	31	1		
2007–08	Middlesbrough	24	1	69	3
2008–09	Wigan Ath	33	1		
2009–10	Wigan Ath	0	0	33	1
2009–10	Sunderland	22	0		
2010–11	Sunderland	23	0	45	0

COLBACK, Jack (M) 62 4
H: 5 9 W: 11 05 b.Killingworth 24-10-89
Source: Scholar. *Honours:* England Youth.

2007–08	Sunderland	0	0		
2008–09	Sunderland	0	0		
2009–10	Sunderland	1	0		
2009–10	Ipswich T	37	4		
2010–11	Sunderland	11	0	12	0
2010–11	Ipswich T	13	0	50	4

COOK, Jordan (F) 16 1
H: 5 10 W: 10 10 b.Hetton-le-Hole 20-3-90
Source: Scholar.

| 2007–08 | Sunderland | 0 | 0 | | |

2008–09	Sunderland	0	0		
2009–10	Sunderland	0	0		
2009–10	Darlington	5	0	5	0
2010–11	Sunderland	3	0	3	0
2010–11	Walsall	8	1	8	1

DA SILVA, Paulo (D) 325 16
H: 6 0 W: 13 12 b.Asuncion 1-2-80
Honours: Paraguay 76 full caps, 2 goals.

1996–97	Atlantida SC	29	0	29	0
1997–98	Cerro Porteno	30	1	30	1
1998–99	Perugia	2	0	2	0
1999–2000	Lanus	12	1	12	1
2000–01	Venezia	7	0	7	0
2001–02	Cosenza	2	0	2	0
2002	Libertad	30	2		
2003	Libertad	0	0	30	2
2003–04	Toluca	36	2		
2004–04	Toluca	34	2		
2005–06	Toluca	34	1		
2006–07	Toluca	28	3		
2007–08	Toluca	32	4		
2008–09	Toluca	32	0	196	12
2009–10	Sunderland	16	0		
2010–11	Sunderland	1	0	17	0

Transferred to Zaragoza January 2011.

EGAN, John (D) 0 0
H: 6 1 W: 11 11 b.Cork 20-10-92
Source: Scholar. *Honours:* Eire Youth.

| 2009–10 | Sunderland | 0 | 0 | | |
| 2010–11 | Sunderland | 0 | 0 | | |

ELMOHAMADY, Ahmed (M) 111 14
H: 5 11 W: 12 10 b.El Mahalla El-Kubra 9-9-87
Honours: Egypt 44 full caps, 1 goal.

2003–04	Ghazi Al-Mehalla	0	0		
2004–05	Ghazi Al-Mehalla	14	4		
2005–06	Ghazi Al-Mehalla	3	0	17	4
2006–07	ENPPI	12	2		
2007–08	ENPPI	6	1		
2008–09	ENPPI	28	6		
2009–10	ENPPI	12	1	58	10
2010–11	Sunderland	36	0	36	0

On loan from ENPPI.

FERDINAND, Anton (D) 220 5
H: 6 2 W: 11 00 b.Peckham 18-2-85
Source: Trainee. *Honours:* England Youth, Under-20, Under-21.

2002–03	West Ham U	0	0		
2003–04	West Ham U	20	0		
2004–05	West Ham U	29	1		
2005–06	West Ham U	33	2		
2006–07	West Ham U	31	0		
2007–08	West Ham U	25	2		
2008–09	West Ham U	0	0	138	5
2008–09	Sunderland	31	0		
2009–10	Sunderland	24	0		
2010–11	Sunderland	27	0	82	0

FLETCHER, Matthew (F) 0 0
H: 6 0 W: 12 00 b.Sydney 1-6-92
Source: Scholar.

| 2009–10 | Sunderland | 0 | 0 | | |
| 2010–11 | Sunderland | 0 | 0 | | |

GORDON, Craig (G) 225 0
H: 6 4 W: 12 02 b.Edinburgh 31-12-82
Honours: Scotland Under-21, 40 full caps.

2000–01	Hearts	0	0		
2001–02	Hearts	0	0		
2002–03	Hearts	1	0		
2003–04	Hearts	29	0		
2004–05	Hearts	38	0		
2005–06	Hearts	36	0		
2006–07	Hearts	34	0	138	0
2007–08	Sunderland	34	0		
2008–09	Sunderland	12	0		
2009–10	Sunderland	26	0		
2010–11	Sunderland	15	0	87	0

GYAN, Asamoah (F) 170 50
H: 5 11 W: 12 08 b.Accra 22-11-85
Honours: Ghana 51 full caps, 9 goals.

2003–04	Udinese	1	0		
2004–05	Modena	27	7		
2005–06	Modena	25	8	52	15
2006–07	Udinese	25	8		
2007–08	Udinese	13	3	39	11
2008–09	Rennes	16	1		
2009–10	Rennes	29	13		

| 2010–11 | Rennes | 3 | 0 | 48 | 14 |
| 2010–11 | Sunderland | 31 | 10 | 31 | 10 |

HEALY, David (F) 343 86
H: 5 8 W: 10 09 b.Downpatrick 5-8-79
Source: Trainee. *Honours:* Northern Ireland Schools, Youth, Under-21, B, 86 full caps, 35 goals.

1997–98	Manchester U	0	0		
1998–99	Manchester U	0	0		
1999–2000	Manchester U	0	0		
1999–2000	Port Vale	16	3	16	3
2000–01	Manchester U	1	0	1	0
2000–01	Preston NE	22	9		
2001–02	Preston NE	44	10		
2002–03	Preston NE	24	5		
2002–03	Norwich C	13	2	13	2
2003–04	Preston NE	38	15		
2004–05	Preston NE	11	5	139	44
2004–05	Leeds U	28	7		
2005–06	Leeds U	42	12		
2006–07	Leeds U	41	10	111	29
2007–08	Fulham	30	4		
2008–09	Fulham	0	0	30	4
2008–09	Sunderland	10	1		
2009–10	Sunderland	3	0		
2009–10	Ipswich T	12	1	12	1
2010–11	Sunderland	0	0	13	1
2010–11	Doncaster R	8	2	8	2

Transferred to Rangers January 2011.

HENDERSON, Jordan (M) 81 5
H: 6 0 W: 10 07 b.Sunderland 17-6-90
Source: Scholar. *Honours:* England Youth, Under-20, Under-21, 1 full cap.

2008–09	Sunderland	1	0		
2008–09	Coventry C	10	1	10	1
2009–10	Sunderland	33	1		
2010–11	Sunderland	37	3	71	4

KAY, Michael (D) 22 1
H: 6 0 W: 11 05 b.Consett 12-9-89
Source: Scholar.

2007–08	Sunderland	0	0		
2008–09	Sunderland	0	0		
2009–10	Sunderland	0	0		
2010–11	Sunderland	0	0		
2010–11	Tranmere R	22	1	22	1

KILGALLON, Matthew (D) 211 7
H: 6 1 W: 12 10 b.York 8-1-84
Source: Scholar. *Honours:* England Youth, Under-20, Under-21.

2000–01	Leeds U	0	0		
2001–02	Leeds U	0	0		
2002–03	Leeds U	2	0		
2003–04	Leeds U	8	2		
2003–04	West Ham U	3	0	3	0
2004–05	Leeds U	26	0		
2005–06	Leeds U	25	1		
2006–07	Leeds U	19	0	80	3
2006–07	Sheffield U	6	0		
2007–08	Sheffield U	40	2		
2008–09	Sheffield U	40	1		
2009–10	Sheffield U	21	1	107	4
2009–10	Sunderland	7	0		
2010–11	Sunderland	0	0	7	0
2010–11	Middlesbrough	2	0	2	0
2010–11	Doncaster R	12	0	12	0

KNOTT, Billy (M) 0 0
H: 5 8 W: 11 02 b.Canvey Island 28-11-92
Source: Scholar.

| 2010–11 | Sunderland | 0 | 0 | | |

LAING, Louis (D) 1 0
H: 5 11 W: 12 00 b.Newcastle 6-3-93
Source: Scholar. *Honours:* England Youth.

| 2009–10 | Sunderland | 0 | 0 | | |
| 2010–11 | Sunderland | 1 | 0 | 1 | 0 |

LIDDLE, Michael (D) 23 0
H: 5 6 W: 11 00 b.Hounslow 25-12-89
Source: Scholar. *Honours:* Eire Under-21.

2007–08	Sunderland	0	0		
2008–09	Sunderland	0	0		
2008–09	Carlisle U	22	0	22	0
2009–10	Sunderland	0	0		
2010–11	Sunderland	0	0		
2010–11	Leyton Orient	1	0	1	0

LUSCOMBE, Nathan (M) 0 0
H: 5 8 W: 11 07 b.Gateshead 6-11-89
Source: Scholar.

2008–09	Sunderland	0	0	
2009–10	Sunderland	0	0	
2010–11	Sunderland	0	0	

LYNCH, Craig (F) 2 0
H: 5 9 W: 10 01 b.Durham 25-3-92
Source: Scholar.

2010–11	Sunderland	2	0	2	0

M'VOTO, Jean-Yves (D) 44 3
H: 6 4 W: 14 00 b.Paris 6-9-88
Source: Paris St Germain. *Honours:* France Youth.

2007–08	Sunderland	0	0		
2008–09	Sunderland	0	0		
2009–10	Sunderland	0	0		
2009–10	*Southend U*	17	1	17	1
2010–11	Sunderland	0	0		
2010–11	*Oldham Ath*	27	2	27	2

MADDEN, Daniel (D) 0 0
H: 5 10 W: 14 02 b.Sunderland 10-9-90
Source: Scholar.

2008–09	Sunderland	0	0	
2009–10	Sunderland	0	0	
2010–11	Sunderland	0	0	

MALBRANQUE, Steed (M) 413 44
H: 5 7 W: 11 07 b.Mouscron 6-1-80
Honours: France Under-21.

1997–98	Lyon	2	0		
1998–99	Lyon	21	0		
1999–2000	Lyon	28	3		
2000–01	Lyon	26	2	77	5
2001–02	Fulham	37	8		
2002–03	Fulham	37	6		
2003–04	Fulham	38	6		
2004–05	Fulham	26	6		
2005–06	Fulham	34	6	172	32
2006–07	Tottenham H	25	2		
2007–08	Tottenham H	37	4	62	6
2008–09	Sunderland	36	1		
2009–10	Sunderland	31	0		
2010–11	Sunderland	35	0	102	1

McCARTNEY, George (D) 268 1
H: 5 11 W: 11 02 b.Belfast 29-4-81
Source: Trainee. *Honours:* Northern Ireland Schools, Youth, Under-21, 34 full caps, 1 goal.

1998–99	Sunderland	0	0		
1999–2000	Sunderland	0	0		
2000–01	Sunderland	2	0		
2001–02	Sunderland	18	0		
2002–03	Sunderland	24	0		
2003–04	Sunderland	41	0		
2004–05	Sunderland	36	0		
2005–06	Sunderland	13	0		
2006–07	West Ham U	22	0		
2007–08	West Ham U	38	1		
2008–09	West Ham U	1	0	61	1
2008–09	Sunderland	16	0		
2009–10	Sunderland	25	0		
2010–11	Sunderland	0	0	175	0
2010–11	*Leeds U*	32	0	32	0

MENSAH, John (D) 180 0
H: 5 9 W: 11 05 b.Obuasi 29-11-82
Honours: Ghana 73 full caps.

1999–2000	Bologne	0	0		
1999–2000	Bellinzona	0	0		
2000–01	Bellinzona	8	0	8	0
2001–02	Genoa	24	3	24	3
2002–03	Verona	11	0		
2003–04	Verona	2	0		
2003–04	Modena	6	0	6	0
2004–05	Verona	9	0	22	0
2005–06	Cremonese	14	0	14	0
2005–06	Rennes	12	1		
2006–07	Rennes	23	0		
2007–08	Rennes	25	1	60	2
2008–09	Lyon	12	0	12	0
2009–10	*Sunderland*	16	1		

On loan from Lyon.

2010–11	Sunderland	18	0	34	1

MEYLER, David (M) 17 0
H: 6 3 W: 11 09 b.Cork 29-5-89
Honours: Eire Under-21.

2008	Cork C	2	0	2	0
2008–09	Sunderland	0	0		
2009–10	Sunderland	10	0		
2010–11	Sunderland	5	0	15	0

MIGNOLET, Simon (G) 145 1
H: 6 4 W: 13 10 b.St Truiden 6-3-88
Honours: Belgium Under-21, 3 full caps.

2006–07	St Truiden	2	0		
2007–08	St Truiden	25	0		
2008–09	St Truiden	35	1		
2009–10	St Truiden	37	0		
2010–11	St Truiden	23	0	122	1
2010–11	Sunderland	23	0	23	0

MUNTARI, Sulley Ali (M) 225 20
H: 5 10 W: 12 00 b.Konongo 27-8-84
Honours: Ghana 62 full caps, 17 goals.

2002–03	Udinese	12	0		
2003–04	Udinese	23	0		
2004–05	Udinese	33	2		
2005–06	Udinese	29	3		
2006–07	Udinese	28	3	125	8
2007–08	Portsmouth	29	4	29	4
2008–09	Internazionale	27	4		
2009–10	Internazionale	27	2		
2010–11	Internazionale	8	1	62	7
2010–11	Sunderland	9	1	9	1

On loan from Internazionale.

NOBLE, Liam (M) 21 3
H: 5 9 W: 10 05 b.Newcastle 8-5-91
Source: Scholar.

2009–10	Sunderland	0	0		
2010–11	Sunderland	0	0		
2010–11	*Carlisle U*	21	3	21	3

NOBLE, Ryan (F) 4 0
H: 6 0 W: 11 00 b.Sunderland 6-11-91
Source: Scholar. *Honours:* England Youth.

2008–09	Sunderland	0	0		
2009–10	*Watford*	0	0		
2009–10	Sunderland	3	0	3	0
2010–11	*Derby Co*	1	0	1	0

NOSWORTHY, Nyron (D) 339 5
H: 6 0 W: 12 08 b.Brixton 11-10-80
Source: Trainee.

1998–99	Gillingham	3	0		
1999–2000	Gillingham	29	1		
2000–01	Gillingham	10	0		
2001–02	Gillingham	29	0		
2002–03	Gillingham	39	2		
2003–04	Gillingham	27	2		
2004–05	Gillingham	37	0	174	5
2005–06	Sunderland	30	0		
2006–07	Sunderland	29	0		
2007–08	Sunderland	29	0		
2008–09	Sunderland	16	0		
2009–10	Sunderland	10	0		
2009–10	*Sheffield U*	19	0		
2010–11	Sunderland	0	0	114	0
2010–11	*Sheffield U*	32	0	51	0

PICKFORD, Jordan (G) 0 0
b.Washington 7-3-94
Source: Scholar. *Honours:* England Youth.

2010–11	Sunderland	0	0	

REED, Adam (M) 11 0
H: 5 5 W: 10 03 b.Hartlepool 8-5-91
Source: Scholar.

2009–10	Sunderland	0	0		
2010–11	Sunderland	0	0		
2010–11	*Brentford*	11	0	11	0

RICHARDSON, Kieran (M) 157 17
H: 5 9 W: 11 13 b.Greenwich 21-10-84
Source: Scholar. *Honours:* England Under-21, 8 full caps, 2 goals.

2002–03	Manchester U	2	0		
2003–04	Manchester U	0	0		
2004–05	Manchester U	2	0		
2004–05	*WBA*	12	3	12	3
2005–06	Manchester U	21	0		
2006–07	Manchester U	15	1	41	2
2007–08	Sunderland	17	3		
2008–09	Sunderland	32	4		
2009–10	Sunderland	20	0		
2010–11	Sunderland	26	4	104	12

RIVEROS, Cristian (M) 244 31
H: 5 10 W: 11 13 b.Saldivar 16-10-81
Honours: Paraguay 60 full caps, 12 goals.

2002	Sportivo San Lorenzo	14	0	14	0
2003	Tacuary	29	1		
2004	Tacuary	30	3		
2005	Tacuary	18	3	77	7
2005	Libertad	17	4		
2006	Libertad	24	4		
2007	Libertad	7	1	48	9
2007–08	Cruz Azul	32	5		
2008–09	Cruz Azul	31	5		
2009–10	Cruz Azul	30	4	93	14
2010–11	Sunderland	12	1	12	1

SESSEGNON, Stephane (M) 222 27
H: 5 8 W: 11 05 b.Allahe 1-6-84
Honours: Benin 39 full caps, 8 goals.

2003–04	Requins	2	0	2	0
2004–05	Creteil	35	5		
2005–06	Creteil	33	5	68	10
2006–07	Le Mans	31	1		
2007–08	Le Mans	30	5	61	6
2008–09	Paris St Germain	34	5		
2009–10	Paris St Germain	29	3		
2010–11	Paris St Germain	14	0	77	8
2010–11	Sunderland	14	3	14	3

TOUNKARA, Oumare (F) 44 7
H: 6 1 W: 12 08 b.Paris 25-5-90
Source: Sedan.

2009–10	Sunderland	0	0		
2010–11	Sunderland	0	0		
2010–11	*Oldham Ath*	44	7	44	7

TURNER, Michael (D) 271 18
H: 6 4 W: 13 05 b.Lewisham 9-11-83
Source: Scholar.

2001–02	Charlton Ath	0	0		
2002–03	Charlton Ath	0	0		
2002–03	*Leyton Orient*	7	1	7	1
2003–04	Charlton Ath	0	0		
2004–05	Charlton Ath	0	0		
2004–05	Brentford	45	1		
2005–06	Brentford	46	2	91	3
2006–07	Hull C	43	3		
2007–08	Hull C	44	5		
2008–09	Hull C	38	4		
2009–10	Hull C	4	0	129	12
2009–10	Sunderland	29	2		
2010–11	Sunderland	15	0	44	2

WATSON, Jordan (M) 0 0
b.Cyprus 7-4-93
Honours: Northern Ireland Youth.

2009–10	Sunderland	0	0	
2010–11	Sunderland	0	0	

WEIR, Robbie (M) 18 0
H: 5 9 W: 11 07 b.Belfast 9-12-88
Source: Scholar. *Honours:* Northern Ireland Under-21, B.

2007–08	Sunderland	0	0		
2008–09	Sunderland	0	0		
2009–10	Sunderland	0	0		
2010–11	Sunderland	0	0		
2010–11	*Tranmere R*	18	0	18	0

WILSON, Ben (G) 0 0
Source: Scholar.

2010–11	Sunderland	0	0	

WILSON, Nathan (M) 0 0
b.Darlington
Source: Scholar.

2010–11	Sunderland	0	0	

ZENDEN, Boudewijn (M) 409 51
H: 5 8 W: 11 01 b.Maastricht 15-8-76
Honours: Holland 54 full caps, 7 goals.

1994–95	PSV Eindhoven	27	5		
1995–96	PSV Eindhoven	25	0		
1996–97	PSV Eindhoven	34	8		
1997–98	PSV Eindhoven	25	3	111	23
1998–99	Barcelona	25	0		
1999–2000	Barcelona	29	2		
2000–01	Barcelona	10	1	64	3
2001–02	Chelsea	22	3		
2002–03	Chelsea	21	1		
2003–04	Chelsea	0	0	43	4
2003–04	*Middlesbrough*	17	2		
2004–05	Middlesbrough	36	5	67	9
2005–06	Liverpool	7	2		
2006–07	Liverpool	16	0	23	2
2007–08	Marseille	27	2		
2008–09	Marseille	27	4	54	6
2009–10	Sunderland	20	2		
2010–11	Sunderland	27	2	47	4

Scholars
Armstrong James; Brace James Henry; Callaghan Anthony; Dixon Joel Stephen; Elliott Brett; Gorrin Alejandro Rodriguez; King Lewis Andrew John; Laidler Jordan Lee; Lavender Jordan; Marrs Liam; Mitchell Adam John; Oliver Connor

SWANSEA C (80)

AGUSTIEN, Kemy (M)   164 8
H: 5 10 W: 11 05 b.Tilburg 20-8-86
Honours: Holland Under-21.
2004–05 Willem II   21 1
2005–06 Willem II   34 2 55 3
2006–07 Roda JC   31 2 31 2
2007–08 AZ   25 2 25 2
2008–09 Birmingham C   18 0 18 0
2009–10 RKC Waalwijk   19 1 19 1
2010–11 Swansea C   8 0   8 0
2010–11 *Crystal Palace* 8 0   8 0

ALFEI, Daniel (D)   1 0
H: 5 11 W: 12 02 b.Swansea 23-2-92
Source: Scholar. *Honours:* Wales Youth, Under-21.
2010–11 Swansea C   1 0   1 0

ALLEN, Joe (M)   91 3
H: 5 6 W: 9 10 b.Carmarthen 14-3-90
Source: Scholar. *Honours:* Wales Under-21, 2 full caps.
2006–07 Swansea C   1 0
2007–08 Swansea C   6 0
2008–09 Swansea C   23 1
2009–10 Swansea C   21 0
2010–11 Swansea C   40 2 91 3

BEATTIE, Craig (F)   157 30
H: 6 0 W: 11 07 b.Glasgow 16-1-84
Honours: Scotland Under-21, 7 full caps, 1 goal.
2003–04 Celtic   10 1
2004–05 Celtic   11 4
2005–06 Celtic   14 6
2006–07 Celtic   16 2 51 13
2007–08 WBA   21 3
2007–08 *Preston NE*   2 0   2 0
2008–09 WBA   7 1
2008–09 *Crystal Palace* 15 5 15 5
2008–09 *Sheffield U*   13 1 13 1
2009–10 WBA   3 0 31 4
2009–10 Swansea C   23 3
2010–11 Swansea C   22 4 45 7

BODDE, Ferrie (M)   215 24
H: 5 10 W: 12 06 b.Delft 4-5-82
2000–01 Den Haag   4 0
2001–02 Den Haag   27 3
2002–03 Den Haag   28 2
2003–04 Den Haag   27 1
2004–05 Den Haag   29 2
2005–06 Den Haag   19 2
2006–07 Den Haag   27 1 161 11
2007–08 Swansea C   33 6
2008–09 Swansea C   17 7
2009–10 Swansea C   4 0
2010–11 Swansea C   0 0   54 13

BOND, Chad (F)   1 0
H: 6 0 W: 11 00 b.Neath 20-4-87
Source: Scholar. *Honours:* Wales Youth.
2005–06 Swansea C   0 0
From Port Talbot T.
2008–09 Swansea C   0 0
2009–10 Swansea C   1 0
2010–11 Swansea C   0 0   1 0

BRITTON, Leon (M)   336 11
H: 5 6 W: 10 00 b.Merton 16-9-82
Source: Trainee. *Honours:* England Youth.
1999–2000 West Ham U   0 0
2000–01 West Ham U   0 0
2001–02 West Ham U   0 0
2002–03 West Ham U   0 0
2002–03 *Swansea C*   25 0
2003–04 Swansea C   42 3
2004–05 Swansea C   30 1
2005–06 Swansea C   38 4
2006–07 Swansea C   41 2
2007–08 Swansea C   40 0
2008–09 Swansea C   43 0
2009–10 Swansea C   36 0
2010–11 Sheffield U   24 0 24 0
2010–11 Swansea C   17 1 312 11

BUTLER, Thomas (M)   214 11
H: 5 7 W: 12 00 b.Dublin 25-4-81
Source: Trainee. *Honours:* Eire Youth, Under-21, 2 full caps.
1998–99 Sunderland   0 0
1999–2000 Sunderland   1 0
2000–01 Sunderland   4 0
2000–01 *Darlington*   8 0   8 0
2001–02 Sunderland   7 0
2002–03 Sunderland   7 0
2003–04 Sunderland   12 0 31 0
2004–05 Dunfermline Ath 12 0 12 0
2004–05 Hartlepool U   9 1
2005–06 Hartlepool U   28 1 37 2
2006–07 Swansea C   30 1
2007–08 Swansea C   42 6
2008–09 Swansea C   29 1
2009–10 Swansea C   25 1
2010–11 Swansea C   0 0 126 9

CORNELL, David (G)   0 0
H: 5 11 W: 11 07 b.Gorseinon 28-3-91
Source: Scholar. *Honours:* Wales Under-21.
2009–10 Swansea C   0 0
2010–11 Swansea C   0 0

COTTERILL, David (F)   184 20
H: 5 9 W: 11 02 b.Cardiff 4-12-87
Source: Scholar. *Honours:* Wales Youth, Under-21, 19 full caps, 1 goal.
2004–05 Bristol C   12 0
2005–06 Bristol C   45 7
2006–07 Bristol C   5 1 62 8
2006–07 Wigan Ath   16 1
2007–08 Wigan Ath   2 0 18 1
2007–08 *Sheffield U*   16 0
2008–09 Sheffield U   24 4
2009–10 Sheffield U   14 2 54 6
2009–10 Swansea C   21 3
2010–11 Swansea C   14 1 35 4
2010–11 Portsmouth   15 1 15 1

DE VRIES, Dorus (G)   336 0
H: 6 1 W: 12 08 b.Beverwijk 29-12-80
1999–2000 Telstar   1 0
2000–01 Telstar   27 0
2001–02 Telstar   27 0
2002–03 Telstar   26 0 81 0
2003–04 Den Haag   18 0
2004–05 Den Haag   32 0
2005–06 Den Haag   0 0 50 0
2006–07 Dunfermline Ath 27 0 27 0
2007–08 Swansea C   46 0
2008–09 Swansea C   40 0
2009–10 Swansea C   46 0
2010–11 Swansea C   46 0 178 0

DOBBIE, Stephen (F)   229 80
H: 5 10 W: 11 00 b.Glasgow 5-12-82
2002–03 Rangers   0 0
2002–03 *Northern Spirit* 3 3   3 3
2003–04 Hibernian   28 2
2004–05 Hibernian   7 0 35 2
2004–05 *St Johnstone*   8 2
2005–06 St Johnstone   20 1 28 3
2006–07 *Dumbarton*   17 10 17 10
2006–07 Queen of the S   15 10
2007–08 Queen of the S   36 16
2008–09 Queen of the S   32 23 83 49
2009–10 Swansea C   6 0
2009–10 *Blackpool*   16 4 16 4
2010–11 Swansea C   41 9 47 9

DONNELLY, Scott (M)   95 17
H: 5 8 W: 11 10 b.Hammersmith 25-12-87
Source: Scholar.
2004–05 QPR   2 0
2005–06 QPR   8 0
2006–07 QPR   3 0 13 0
From Wealdstone.
2008–09 Aldershot T   20 1
2009–10 Aldershot T   43 13 63 14
2010–11 Swansea C   1 0   1 0
2010–11 *Wycombe W*   18 3 18 3

DYER, Nathan (M)   171 10
H: 5 5 W: 9 00 b.Trowbridge 29-11-87
Source: Scholar. *Honours:* England Youth.
2005–06 Southampton   17 0
2005–06 *Burnley*   5 2   5 2
2006–07 Southampton   18 0
2007–08 Southampton   17 1
2008–09 Southampton   4 0 56 1
2008–09 *Sheffield U*   7 1   7 1
2008–09 Swansea C   17 2
2009–10 Swansea C   40 2
2010–11 Swansea C   46 2 103 6

GOWER, Mark (M)   333 40
H: 5 11 W: 11 12 b.Edmonton 5-10-78
Source: Trainee. *Honours:* England Schools, Youth.
1996–97 Tottenham H   0 0
1997–98 Tottenham H   0 0
1998–99 Tottenham H   0 0
1998–99 *Motherwell*   9 1   9 1
1999–2000 Tottenham H   0 0
2000–01 Tottenham H   0 0
2000–01 Barnet   14 1
2001–02 Barnet   0 0
2002–03 Barnet   0 0 14 1
2003–04 Southend U   40 6
2004–05 Southend U   38 6
2005–06 Southend U   40 6
2006–07 Southend U   43 8
2007–08 Southend U   42 9 203 35
2008–09 Swansea C   36 0
2009–10 Swansea C   31 1
2010–11 Swansea C   40 2 107 3

GRIMES, Jamie (D)   0 0
H: 6 2 W: 13 00 b.Shepshed 22-12-90
Source: Scholar.
2009–10 Swansea C   0 0
2010–11 Swansea C   0 0

HARLEY, Ryan (M)   119 24
H: 5 11 W: 11 00 b.Bristol 22-1-85
Source: Scholar.
2004–05 Bristol C   2 0
2005–06 Bristol C   0 0   2 0
2008–09 Exeter C   31 4
2009–10 Exeter C   44 10
2010–11 Exeter C   21 6
2010–11 Swansea C   0 0
2010–11 *Exeter C*   21 4 117 24

LOPEZ, Jordi (M)   101 3
H: 6 0 W: 12 02 b.Barcelona 28-2-81
2003–04 Real Madrid   2 0   2 0
2004–05 Sevilla   18 1
2005–06 Sevilla   19 1 37 2
2006–07 Mallorca   23 0 23 0
2007–08 Santander   14 0 14 0
2008–09 QPR   10 1 10 1
2009–10 Swansea C   12 0
2010–11 Swansea C   3 0 15 0
Transferred to Vitesse January 2011.

LUCAS, Lee (M)   1 0
H: 5 11 W: 11 08 b.Aberdare 10-6-92
Source: Scholar. *Honours:* Wales Youth, Under-21.
2010–11 Swansea C   1 0   1 0

MA KALAMBAY, Yves (G)   57 0
H: 6 5 W: 14 10 b.Brussels 31-1-86
Source: PSV Eindhoven. *Honours:* Belgium Youth, Under-21.
2003–04 Chelsea   0 0
2004–05 Chelsea   0 0
2005–06 Chelsea   0 0
2005–06 *Watford*   0 0
2006–07 Chelsea   0 0
2007–08 Hibernian   29 0
2008–09 Hibernian   21 0
2009–10 Hibernian   7 0 57 0
2010–11 Swansea C   0 0

MACDONALD, Shaun (M)   85 9
H: 6 1 W: 11 04 b.Swansea 17-6-88
Source: Scholar. *Honours:* Wales Youth, Under-21, 1 full cap.
2005–06 Swansea C   7 0
2006–07 Swansea C   8 0
2007–08 Swansea C   1 0
2008–09 Swansea C   5 0
2008–09 *Yeovil T*   4 2
2009–10 Swansea C   3 0
2009–10 *Yeovil T*   31 3
2010–11 Swansea C   0 0 24 0
2010–11 *Yeovil T*   26 4 61 9

MONK, Garry (D)   254 3
H: 6 0 W: 12 10 b.Bedford 6-3-79
Source: Trainee.

Season	Club	A	G	T A	T G
1995–96	Torquay U	5	0		
1996–97	Southampton	0	0		
1997–98	Southampton	0	0		
1998–99	Southampton	4	0		
1998–99	Torquay U	6	0	11	0
1999–2000	Southampton	2	0		
1999–2000	Stockport Co	2	0	2	0
2000–01	Southampton	2	0		
2000–01	Oxford U	5	0	5	0
2001–02	Southampton	2	0		
2002–03	Southampton	1	0		
2002–03	Sheffield W	15	0	15	0
2003–04	Southampton	0	0	11	0
2003–04	Barnsley	17	0	17	0
2004–05	Swansea C	34	0		
2005–06	Swansea C	33	1		
2006–07	Swansea C	2	0		
2007–08	Swansea C	32	1		
2008–09	Swansea C	40	1		
2009–10	Swansea C	23	0		
2010–11	Swansea C	29	0	193	3

MOORE, Luke (F)   178 30
H: 5 11 W: 11 13 b.Birmingham 13-2-86
Source: Trainee. *Honours:* FA Schools, England Youth, Under-21.

Season	Club	A	G	T A	T G
2002–03	Aston Villa	0	0		
2003–04	Aston Villa	7	0		
2003–04	Wycombe W	6	4	6	4
2004–05	Aston Villa	25	1		
2005–06	Aston Villa	27	8		
2006–07	Aston Villa	13	4		
2007–08	Aston Villa	15*	1	87	14
2007–08	WBA	10	0		
2008–09	WBA	21	1		
2009–10	WBA	26	4		
2010–11	WBA	0	0	57	5
2010–11	Derby Co	13	4	13	4
2010–11	Swansea C	15	3	15	3

MORGAN, Kerry (M)   3 0
H: 5 10 W: 11 03 b.Merthyr Tydfil 31-10-88
Source: Scholar.

Season	Club	A	G	T A	T G
2008–09	Swansea C	0	0		
2009–10	Swansea C	3	0		
2010–11	Swansea C	0	0	3	0

ORLANDI, Andrea (M)   137 7
H: 6 0 W: 12 01 b.Barcelona 3-8-84

Season	Club	A	G	T A	T G
2005–06	Alaves	0	0		
2005–06	Barcelona	1	0	1	0
2005 06	Barcelona B	32	4		
2006–07	Barcelona B	35	1	67	5
2007–08	Swansea C	8	0		
2008–09	Swansea C	11	1		
2009–10	Swansea C	30	1		
2010–11	Swansea C	20	0	69	2

PINTADO, Gorka (F)   306 83
H: 5 11 W: 11 11 b.San Sebastian 24-3-78

Season	Club	A	G	T A	T G
2000–01	Union Irun	28	2	28	2
2001–02	Osasuna	35	10	35	10
2002–03	Leganes	12	0		
2003–04	Leganes	4	0	16	0
2003–04	Figures	3	0		
2004–05	Figures	34	7	37	7
2005–06	Gramenet	37	17		
2006–07	Gramenet	36	18	73	35
2007–08	Granada	38	18	38	18
2008–09	Swansea C	40	5		
2009–10	Swansea C	32	2		
2010–11	Swansea C	0	0	73	7
2010–11	AEK Larnaca	6	4	6	4

PRATLEY, Darren (M)   224 31
H: 6 1 W: 10 12 b.Barking 22-4-85
Source: Scholar.

Season	Club	A	G	T A	T G
2001–02	Fulham	0	0		
2002–03	Fulham	0	0		
2003–04	Fulham	1	0		
2004–05	Fulham	0	0		
2004–05	Brentford	14	1		
2005–06	Fulham	0	0	1	0
2005–06	Brentford	32	4	46	5
2006–07	Swansea C	28	1		
2007–08	Swansea C	42	5		
2008–09	Swansea C	37	4		
2009–10	Swansea C	36	7		
2010–11	Swansea C	34	9	177	26

RANGEL, Angel (D)   193 7
H: 5 11 W: 11 09 b.Barcelona 28-10-82
Source: Tortosa, Reus Deportiu, Girona, Sant Andreu.

Season	Club	A	G	T A	T G
2006–07	Terrassa	34	2	34	2
2007–08	Swansea C	43	2		
2008–09	Swansea C	40	1		
2009–10	Swansea C	38	0		
2010–11	Swansea C	38	2	159	5

RICHARDS, Jazz (M)   21 0
H: 6 1 W: 12 04 b.Swansea 12-4-91
Source: Scholar. *Honours:* Wales Under-21.

Season	Club	A	G	T A	T G
2009–10	Swansea C	15	0		
2010–11	Swansea C	6	0	21	0

SERRAN, Albert (D)   33 0
H: 6 0 W: 12 10 b.Barcelona 17-7-84

Season	Club	A	G	T A	T G
2006–07	Espanyol	2	0		
2007–08	Espanyol	1	0	3	0
2008–09	Swansea C	13	0		
2009–10	Swansea C	6	0		
2010–11	Swansea C	11	0	30	0

SINCLAIR, Scott (F)   115 25
H: 5 10 W: 10 00 b.Bath 26-3-89
Source: Bristol R Schoolboy, England Youth, Under-11.

Season	Club	A	G	T A	T G
2004–05	Bristol R	2	0	2	0
2005–06	Chelsea	0	0		
2006–07	Chelsea	2	0		
2006–07	Plymouth Arg	15	2	15	2
2007–08	Chelsea	1	0		
2007–08	QPR	9	1	9	1
2007–08	Charlton Ath	3	0	3	0
2007–08	Crystal Palace	6	2	6	2
2008–09	Chelsea	2	0		
2008–09	Birmingham C	14	0	14	0
2009–10	Chelsea	0	0	5	0
2009–10	Wigan Ath	18	1	18	1
2010–11	Swansea C	43	19	43	19

TATE, Alan (D)   282 5
H: 6 1 W: 13 05 b.Seaham 2-9-82
Source: Scholar.

Season	Club	A	G	T A	T G
2000–01	Manchester U	0	0		
2001–02	Manchester U	0	0		
2002–03	Manchester U	0	0		
2002–03	Swansea C	27	0		
2003–04	Manchester U	0	0		
2003–04	Swansea C	26	1		
2004–05	Swansea C	23	0		
2005–06	Swansea C	43	0		
2006–07	Swansea C	38	1		
2007–08	Swansea C	21	1		
2008–09	Swansea C	25	1		
2009–10	Swansea C	39	1		
2010–11	Swansea C	40	0	282	5

TAYLOR, Neil (D)   55 0
H: 5 9 W: 10 02 b.Ruthin 7-2-89
Source: Scholar. *Honours:* Wales Youth, Under-21, 3 full caps.

Season	Club	A	G	T A	T G
2007–08	Wrexham	26	0	26	0
2010–11	Swansea C	29	0	29	0

THOMAS, Casey (M)   1 0
H: 5 9 W: 10 09 b.Port Talbot 14-11-90
Source: Scholar. *Honours:* Wales Youth, Under-21.

Season	Club	A	G	T A	T G
2009–10	Swansea C	1	0		
2010–11	Swansea C	0	0	1	0

VAN DER GUN, Cedric (M)   223 47
H: 5 9 W: 11 00 b.Den Haag 5-5-79
Honours: Holland Under-21.

Season	Club	A	G	T A	T G
1999–2000	Den Bosch	10	0	10	0
2000–01	Ajax	33	9		
2001–02	Ajax	2	0		
2002–03	Ajax	0	0	35	9
2002–03	Willem II	30	6	30	6
2003–04	Den Haag	26	6		
2004–05	Den Haag	32	6	58	12
2005–06	Borussia Dortmund	3	0	3	0
2006 07	Utrecht	18	4		
2007–08	Utrecht	13	3		
2008–09	Utrecht	21	10	52	17
2009–10	Swansea C	25	2		
2010–11	Swansea C	10	1	223	3

WALSH, Joe (D)   0 0
H: 5 11 W: 11 00 b.Cardiff 15-5-92
Source: Scholar. *Honours:* Wales Youth.

Season	Club	A	G	T A	T G
2010–11	Swansea C	0	0		

WILLIAMS, Ashley (D)   303 13
H: 6 0 W: 11 02 b.Wolverhampton 23-8-84
Source: Hednesford T. *Honours:* Wales 25 full caps, 2 goals.

Season	Club	A	G	T A	T G
2003–04	Stockport Co	10	0		
2004–05	Stockport Co	44	1		
2005–06	Stockport Co	36	1		
2006–07	Stockport Co	46	1		
2007–08	Stockport Co	26	0	162	3
2007–08	Swansea C	3	0		
2008–09	Swansea C	46	2		
2009–10	Swansea C	46	5		
2010–11	Swansea C	46	3	141	10

SWINDON T (81)

AMANKWAAH, Kevin (D)   240 7
H: 6 1 W: 12 12 b.Harrow 19-5-82
Source: Scholar. *Honours:* England Youth.

Season	Club	A	G	T A	T G
1999–2000	Bristol C	5	0		
2000–01	Bristol C	14	0		
2001–02	Bristol C	24	1		
2002–03	Bristol C	1	0		
2002–03	Torquay U	6	0	6	0
2003–04	Bristol C	5	0		
2003–04	Cheltenham T	12	0	12	0
2004–05	Bristol C	5	0	54	1
2004–05	Yeovil	15	0		
2005–06	Yeovil	38	1	53	1
2006–07	Swansea C	29	0		
2007–08	Swansea C	0	0	29	0
2008–09	Swindon T	31	2		
2009–10	Swindon T	36	3		
2010–11	Swindon T	19	0	86	5

BENYON, Elliot (F)   80 25
H: 5 9 W: 10 01 b.High Wycombe 29-8-87
Source: Scholar.

Season	Club	A	G	T A	T G
2005–06	Bristol C	0	0		
2006–07	Bristol C	0	0		
2009–10	Torquay U	45	11		
2010–11	Torquay U	23	13	68	24
2010–11	Swindon T	12	1	12	1

BODIN, Billy (F)   5 0
b.Swindon 24-3-92
Honours: Wales Youth, Under-21.

Season	Club	A	G	T A	T G
2009–10	Swindon T	0	0		
2010–11	Swindon T	5	0	5	0

CADDIS, Paul (D)   66 1
H: 5 7 W: 10 07 b.Irvine 19-4-88

Season	Club	A	G	T A	T G
2007–08	Celtic	2	0		
2008–09	Celtic	5	0		
2008–09	Dundee U	11	0	11	0
2009–10	Celtic	10	0	17	0
2010–11	Swindon T	38	1	38	1

CLARK, Matt (M)   1 0
b.Swindon 16-11-92
Source: Scholar.

Season	Club	A	G	T A	T G
2010–11	Swindon T	1	0	1	0

CUTHBERT, Scott (D)   113 6
H: 6 2 W: 14 00 b.Alexandria 15-6-87
Honours: Scotland Youth, Under-21, B.

Season	Club	A	G	T A	T G
2004–05	Celtic	0	0		
2005–06	Celtic	0	0		
2006–07	Celtic	0	0		
2006–07	Livingston	4	1	4	1
2007–08	Celtic	0	0		
2008–09	Celtic	0	0		
2008–09	St Mirren	29	0	29	0
2009–10	Swindon T	39	3		
2010–11	Swindon T	41	2	80	5

DOSSEVI, Thomas (F)   228 44
H: 6 0 W: 12 13 b.Tours 6-3-79
Honours: Togo 27 full caps, 1 goal.

Season	Club	A	G	T A	T G
2000–01	ASOA Valence	28	7	28	7
2001–02	Chateauroux	6	0		
2002–03	Chateauroux	22	3		
2003–04	Chateauroux	1	1	34	4
2003–04	Reims	12	4		
2004–05	Reims	35	9	47	13
2005–06	Valenciennes	31	6		

2006–07	Valenciennes	20	2	51	8
2007–08	Nantes	24	9		
2008–09	Nantes	10	0		
2009–10	Nantes	7	0	41	9
2010–11	Swindon T	27	3	27	3

DOUGLAS, Jonathan (M) 273 16
H: 5 11   W: 11 11   b.Monaghan 22-11-81
Source: Trainee. *Honours:* Eire Under-21, 8 full caps.

1999–2000	Blackburn R	0	0		
2000–01	Blackburn R	0	0		
2001–02	Blackburn R	1	0		
2002–03	Blackburn R	1	0		
2002–03	*Chesterfield*	7	1	7	1
2003–04	Blackpool	16	3	16	3
2003–04	Blackburn R	14	1		
2004–05	Blackburn R	1	0		
2004–05	*Gillingham*	10	0	10	0
2005–06	Blackburn R	0	0		
2005–06	*Leeds U*	40	5		
2006–07	Blackburn R	0	0	16	1
2006–07	Leeds U	35	1		
2007–08	Leeds U	24	3		
2008–09	Leeds U	43	1	142	10
2009–10	Swindon T	43	0		
2010–11	Swindon T	39	1	82	1

EVANS, Will (D) 0 0
b.Cricklade 19-10-91
Source: Scholar.

| 2010–11 | Swindon T | 0 | 0 | | |

FERRY, Simon (M) 61 2
H: 5 8   W: 11 00   b.Dundee 11-1-88

2005–06	Celtic	0	0		
2006–07	Celtic	0	0		
2007–08	Celtic	0	0		
2008–09	Celtic	0	0		
2009–10	Celtic	0	0		
2009–10	Swindon T	40	2		
2010–11	Swindon T	21	0	61	2

FLINT, Aiden (D) 3 0
H: 6 2   W: 12 00   b.Pinxton 11-7-89
Source: Alfreton T.

| 2010–11 | Swindon T | 3 | 0 | 3 | 0 |

JESIONKOWSKI, Jakub (G) 23 0
H: 6 3   W: 13 01   b.Poznan 7-3-89
Honours: Poland Youth, Under-21.

2007–08	Zaglebie	1	0		
2008–09	Zaglebie	22	0	23	0
2009–10	Swindon T	0	0		
2010–11	Swindon T	0	0		

KENNEDY, Callum (D) 23 0
H: 6 1   W: 12 10   b.Chertsey 9-11-89
Source: Scholar.

2007–08	Swindon T	0	0		
2008–09	Swindon T	4	0		
2009–10	Swindon T	8	0		
2010–11	Swindon T	3	0	15	0
2010–11	*Gillingham*	3	0	3	0
2010–11	*Rotherham U*	5	0	5	0

LESCINEL, Jean-Francois (M) 76 1
H: 6 2   W: 12 04   b.Guyane 2-10-86
Source: Paris St Germain, Sedan. *Honours:* Haiti 1 full cap.

2006–07	Falkirk	8	0	8	0
2006–07	Guingamp	12	0	12	0
2008–09	Swindon T	5	0		
2009–10	Swindon T	33	0		
2010–11	Swindon T	18	1	56	1

LUCAS, David (G) 290 0
H: 6 1   W: 13 07   b.Preston 23-11-77
Source: Trainee. *Honours:* England Youth.

1995–96	Preston NE	1	0		
1995–96	*Darlington*	6	0		
1996–97	Preston NE	2	0		
1996–97	*Darlington*	7	0	13	0
1996–97	*Scunthorpe U*	6	0	6	0
1997–98	Preston NE	6	0		
1998–99	Preston NE	30	0		
1999–2000	Preston NE	6	0		
2000–01	Preston NE	29	0		
2001–02	Preston NE	24	0		
2002–03	Preston NE	21	0		
2003–04	Preston NE	2	0	121	0
2003–04	Sheffield W	17	0		
2004–05	Sheffield W	34	0		
2005–06	Sheffield W	18	0		

2006–07	Sheffield W	0	0	69	0
2006–07	Barnsley	3	0		
2007–08	Barnsley	0	0	3	0
2007–08	Leeds U	3	0		
2008–09	Leeds U	13	0	16	0
2009–10	Swindon T	41	0		
2010–11	Swindon T	21	0	62	0

McGOVERN, John-Paul (M) 265 18
H: 5 10   W: 12 02   b.Glasgow 3-10-80
Source: Celtic BC.

2001–02	Celtic	0	0		
2002–03	Celtic	0	0		
2002–03	*Sheffield U*	15	1	15	1
2003–04	Celtic	0	0		
2004–05	Sheffield W	46	6		
2005–06	Sheffield W	7	0	53	6
2006–07	Milton Keynes D	44	3		
2007–08	Milton Keynes D	3	0	47	3
2007–08	Swindon T	41	2		
2008–09	Swindon T	26	2		
2009–10	Swindon T	45	1		
2010–11	Swindon T	38	3	150	8

O'BRIEN, Alan (M) 87 1
H: 5 10   W: 10 10   b.Dublin 20-2-85
Source: Scholar. *Honours:* Eire Youth, B, Under-21, 5 full caps.

2001–02	Newcastle U	0	0		
2002–03	Newcastle U	0	0		
2003–04	Newcastle U	0	0		
2004–05	Newcastle U	0	0		
2005–06	Newcastle U	3	0		
2005–06	Carlisle U	5	1	5	1
2006–07	Newcastle U	2	0	5	0
2007–08	Hibernian	23	0	23	0
2008–09	Hibernian	24	0	24	0
2009–10	Swindon T	9	0		
2010–11	Swindon T	21	0	30	0

PAVETT, Jordan (F) 0 0
b.Maldon 16-12-91
Source: Colchester U Scholar, Histon, Redbridge.

| 2010–11 | Swindon T | 0 | 0 | | |

PERICARD, Vincent de Paul (F) 157 23
H: 6 1   W: 13 08   b.Efok 3 10 82
Source: St Etienne. *Honours:* France Under-21.

2000–01	Juventus	0	0		
2001–02	Juventus	0	0		
2002–03	Portsmouth	32	9		
2003–04	Portsmouth	6	0		
2004–05	Portsmouth	0	0		
2005–06	Portsmouth	6	0	44	9
2005–06	*Sheffield U*	11	2	11	2
2005–06	*Plymouth Arg*	15	4	15	4
2006–07	Stoke C	29	2		
2007–08	Stoke C	5	0		
2007–08	*Southampton*	5	0	5	0
2008–09	Stoke C	4	0		
2008–09	*Millwall*	2	0	2	0
2009–10	Stoke C	0	0	38	2
2009–10	Carlisle U	10	4	10	4
2009–10	Swindon T	14	0		
2010–11	Swindon T	18	2	32	2

PRUTTON, David (M) 362 22
H: 5 10   W: 13 00   b.Hull 12-9-81
Source: Trainee. *Honours:* England Youth, Under-21.

1998–99	Nottingham F	0	0		
1999–2000	Nottingham F	34	2		
2000–01	Nottingham F	42	1		
2001–02	Nottingham F	43	3		
2002–03	Nottingham F	24	1		
2002–03	Southampton	12	0		
2003–04	Southampton	27	1		
2004–05	Southampton	23	1		
2005–06	Southampton	17	0		
2006–07	Southampton	3	1	82	3
2006–07	*Nottingham F*	12	2	155	9
2007–08	Leeds U	43	4		
2008–09	Leeds U	16	0		
2009–10	Leeds U	6	0	65	4
2009–10	Colchester U	19	3	19	3
2010–11	Swindon T	41	3	41	3

RITCHIE, Matt (M) 100 21
H: 5 8   W: 11 00   b.Gosport 10-9-89
Source: Scholar.

| 2008–09 | Portsmouth | 0 | 0 | | |

2008–09	*Dagenham & R*	37	11	37	11
2009–10	Portsmouth	2	0		
2009–10	*Notts Co*	16	3	16	3
2009–10	*Swindon T*	4	0		
2010–11	Portsmouth	5	0	7	0
2010–11	Swindon T	36	7	40	7

SCOTT, Mark (G) 0 0
H: 5 9   W: 12 04   b.Fleet 3-1-91
Source: Scholar.

2007–08	Swindon T	0	0		
2008–09	Swindon T	0	0		
2009–10	Swindon T	0	0		
2010–11	Swindon T	0	0		

SHEEHAN, Alan (D) 108 6
H: 5 11   W: 11 02   b.Athlone 14-9-86
Source: Scholar. *Honours:* Eire Youth, Under-21.

2004–05	Leicester C	1	0		
2005–06	Leicester C	2	0		
2006–07	Leicester C	0	0		
2006–07	*Mansfield T*	10	0	10	0
2007–08	Leicester C	20	1	23	1
2007–08	Leeds U	10	1		
2008–09	Leeds U	11	1		
2008–09	*Crewe Alex*	3	0	3	0
2009–10	Leeds U	0	0		
2009–10	*Oldham Ath*	8	1	8	1
2009–10	*Swindon T*	22	1		
2010–11	Leeds U	0	0	21	2
2010–11	Swindon T	21	1	43	2

SMITH, Phil (G) 109 0
H: 6 1   W: 13 11   b.Harrow 14-12-79
Source: Trainee.

| 1997–98 | Millwall | 0 | 0 | | |
| 1998–99 | Millwall | 5 | 0 | 5 | 0 |

From Folkestone, Dover, Margate, Crawley

2006–07	Swindon T	31	0		
2007–08	Swindon T	15	0		
2008–09	Swindon T	25	0		
2009–10	Swindon T	6	0		
2010–11	Swindon T	27	0	104	0

STOREY, Miles (F) 2 0
b.Sandwell
Source: Scholar.

| 2010–11 | Swindon T | 2 | 0 | 2 | 0 |

THOMPSON, Nathan (D) 3 0
b.Chester 9-11-90
Source: Scholar.

| 2009–10 | Swindon T | 0 | 0 | | |
| 2010–11 | Swindon T | 3 | 0 | 3 | 0 |

TIMLIN, Michael (M) 130 7
H: 5 8   W: 11 08   b.New Cross 19-3-85
Source: Trainee. *Honours:* Eire Youth, Under-21.

2002–03	Fulham	0	0		
2003–04	Fulham	0	0		
2004–05	Fulham	0	0		
2005–06	Fulham	0	0		
2005–06	*Scunthorpe U*	1	0	1	0
2005–06	*Doncaster R*	3	0	3	0
2006–07	Fulham	0	0		
2006–07	*Swindon T*	24	1		
2007–08	Fulham	0	0		
2007–08	*Swindon T*	10	1		
2008–09	Swindon T	41	2		
2009–10	Swindon T	21	0		
2010–11	Swindon T	22	2	118	6
2010–11	*Southend U*	8	1	8	1

TORQUAY U (82)

BEVAN, Scott (G) 112 0
H: 6 6   W: 15 10   b.Southampton 16-9-79
Source: Trainee.

1997–98	Southampton	0	0		
1998–99	Southampton	0	0		
1999	*Ayr U*	0	0		
1999–2000	Southampton	0	0		
2000–01	Southampton	0	0		
2001–02	Southampton	0	0		
2001–02	*Stoke C*	0	0		
2002–03	Southampton	0	0		
2002–03	*Huddersfield T*	30	0	30	0
2003–04	Southampton	0	0		
2003–04	*Wycombe W*	5	0	5	0

2003–04 Wimbledon 10 0 **10 0**
2004–05 Milton Keynes D 7 0
2005–06 Milton Keynes D 0 0 **7 0**
From Kidderminster H.
2007–08 Shrewsbury T 5 0 **5 0**
2009–10 Torquay U 18 0
2010–11 Torquay U 37 0 **55 0**

BRANSTON, Guy (D) 325 20
H: 6 1 W: 15 01 b.Leicester 9-1-79
Source: Trainee.
1997–98 Leicester C 0 0
1997–98 *Colchester U* 12 1
1998–99 Leicester C 0 0
1998–99 *Colchester U* 1 0 **13 1**
1998–99 *Plymouth Arg* 7 1 **7 1**
1999–2000 Leicester C 0 0
1999–2000 *Lincoln C* 4 0 **4 0**
1999–2000 Rotherham U 30 4
2000–01 Rotherham U 41 6
2001–02 Rotherham U 10 1
2002–03 Rotherham U 15 2
2003–04 Rotherham U 8 0 **104 13**
2003–04 *Wycombe W* 9 0 **9 0**
2003–04 *Peterborough U* 14 0
2004–05 Sheffield W 11 0 **11 0**
2004–05 *Peterborough U* 4 1
2004–05 Oldham Ath 7 1
2005–06 Oldham Ath 38 1 **45 2**
2006–07 Peterborough U 24 0
2007–08 Peterborough U 2 0 **44 1**
2007–08 *Rochdale* 4 0 **4 0**
2007–08 *Northampton T* 3 0 **3 0**
2007–08 Notts Co 1 0 **1 0**
2009–10 Burton Alb 19 0 **19 0**
From Kettering T.
2009–10 *Torquay U* 16 0
2010–11 *Torquay U* 45 2 **61 2**

CARLISLE, Wayne (M) 202 24
H: 5 11 W: 11 06 b.Lisburn 9-9-79
Source: Trainee. *Honours:* Northern Ireland Schools, Youth, Under-21.
1996–97 Crystal Palace 0 0
1997–98 Crystal Palace 0 0
1998–99 Crystal Palace 6 0
1999–2000 Crystal Palace 26 3
2000–01 Crystal Palace 14 0
2001–02 Crystal Palace 0 0 **46 3**
2001–02 *Swindon T* 11 2 **11 2**
2001–02 Bristol R 5 0
2002–03 Bristol R 41 7
2003–04 Bristol R 25 7 **71 14**
2004–05 Leyton Orient 28 3
2005–06 Leyton Orient 12 0 **40 3**
From Exeter C.
2009–10 Torquay U 24 2
From Exeter C.
2010–11 Torquay U 10 0 **34 2**

ELLIS, Mark (D) 54 5
H: 6 2 W: 12 04 b.Kingsbridge 30-9-88
Source: Exeter C.
2007–08 Bolton W 0 0
2009–10 Torquay U 27 3
2010–11 Torquay U 27 2 **54 5**

HALPIN, Saul (M) 4 0
H: 6 1 W: 12 00 b.Truro 31-5-91
Source: Scholar.
2009–10 Torquay U 0 0
2010–11 Torquay U 4 0 **4 0**

KEE, Billy (F) 77 18
H: 5 9 W: 11 04 b.Loughborough 1-12-90
Honours: Northern Ireland Youth, Under-21.
2009–10 Leicester C 0 0
2009–10 *Accrington S* 37 9 **37 9**
2010–11 Torquay U 40 9 **40 9**

LATHROPE, Damon (M) 18 0
H: 5 8 W: 10 02 b.Stevenage 28-10-89
Source: Scholar.
2007–08 Norwich C 0 0
2008–09 Norwich C 0 0
2009–10 Norwich C 0 0
2010–11 Torquay U 18 0 **18 0**

MACKLIN, Lloyd (M) 25 0
H: 5 9 W: 12 03 b.Camberley 2-8-91
Source: Scholar.
2007–08 Swindon T 0 0
2008–09 Swindon T 2 0

2009–10 Swindon T 9 0 **11 0**
2009–10 *Torquay U* 4 0
2010–11 Torquay U 10 0 **14 0**

MANSELL, Lee (D) 220 15
H: 5 10 W: 11 10 b.Gloucester 28-10-82
Source: Scholar.
2000–01 Luton T 18 5
2001–02 Luton T 11 1
2002–03 Luton T 1 0
2003–04 Luton T 16 2
2004–05 Luton T 1 0 **47 8**
2005–06 Oxford U 44 1 **44 1**
2006–07 Torquay U 45 4
2009–10 Torquay U 39 2
2010–11 Torquay U 45 0 **129 6**

NICHOLSON, Kevin (D) 174 6
H: 5 8 W: 12 05 b.Derby 2-10-80
Source: Trainee. *Honours:* England Schools.
1997–98 Sheffield W 0 0
1998–99 Sheffield W 0 0
1999–2000 Sheffield W 0 0
2000–01 Sheffield W 1 0 **1 0**
From Forest Green R.
2000–01 Northampton T 7 0 **7 0**
2000–01 Notts Co 11 2
2001–02 Notts Co 24 1
2002–03 Notts Co 37 0
2003–04 Notts Co 23 0 **95 3**
From Scarborough, Forest Green R.
2009–10 *Torquay U* 27 0
From Scarborough, Forest Green R.
2010–11 Torquay U 44 3 **71 3**

O'KANE, Eunan (M) 74 11
II: 5 8 W. 13 04 b.Derry 10-7-90
Honours: Northern Ireland Schools, Youth, Under-21.
2007–08 Everton 0 0
2008–09 Everton 0 0
2009–10 Coleraine 13 4 **13 4**
2009–10 *Torquay U* 16 1
2010–11 Torquay U 45 6 **61 7**

PALMER, Ed (D) 0 0
b. 13-11-91
Source: Scholar.
2010–11 Torquay U 0 0

POTTER, Danny (G) 9 0
H: 5 11 W: 13 01 b.Ipswich 18-3-79
Source: Colchester U, Exeter C, Chelmsford C, Weymouth, Canvey Island, Stevenage Bor, Cambridge U.
2010–11 Torquay U 9 0 **9 0**

ROBERTSON, Chris (D) 98 5
H: 6 3 W: 11 08 b.Dundee 11-10-85
Source: Scholar.
2005–06 Sheffield U 0 0
2005–06 *Chester C* 1 0 **1 0**
2006–07 Sheffield U 0 0
2006–07 Torquay U 9 1
2009–10 Torquay U 45 2
2010–11 Torquay U 43 2 **97 5**

ROWE-TURNER, Lathanial (D) 15 1
H: 6 1 W: 13 00 b.Leicester 12-11-89
Source: Scholar.
2007–08 Leicester C 0 0
2008–09 Leicester C 0 0
2008–09 *Cheltenham T* 1 0 **1 0**
2009–10 Leicester C 0 0
2009–10 Torquay U 6 0
2010–11 Torquay U 8 1 **14 1**

STEVENS, Danny (M) 65 4
H: 5 5 W: 9 09 b.Enfield 26-11-86
Source: Tottenham H Scholar.
2004–05 Luton T 0 0
2005–06 Luton T 1 0
2006–07 Luton T 0 0 **1 0**
2009–10 Torquay U 27 1
2010–11 Torquay U 37 3 **64 4**

YEOMAN, Ashley (M) 0 0
H: 5 10 W: 12 01 b.London 25-2-92
Source: Scholar.
2010–11 Torquay U 0 0

ZEBROSKI, Chris (F) 151 32
H: 6 1 W: 11 08 b.Swindon 29-10-86
Source: Cirencester T, Scholar.
2005–06 Plymouth Arg 4 0
2006–07 Plymouth Arg 0 0 **4 0**
2006–07 Millwall 25 3
2007–08 Millwall 0 0 **25 3**
2008–09 Wycombe W 33 7
2009–10 Wycombe W 15 2 **48 9**
2009–10 Torquay U 30 6
2010–11 Torquay U 44 14 **74 20**

TOTTENHAM H (83)

ALNWICK, Ben (G) 41 0
H: 6 2 W: 13 12 b.Prudhoe 1-1-87
Source: Scholar. *Honours:* England Youth, Under-21.
2003–04 Sunderland 0 0
2004–05 Sunderland 3 0
2005–06 Sunderland 5 0
2006–07 Sunderland 11 0 **19 0**
2006–07 Tottenham H 0 0
2007–08 Tottenham H 0 0
2007–08 *Luton T* 4 0 **4 0**
2007–08 *Leicester C* 8 0 **8 0**
2008–09 Tottenham H 0 0
2008–09 *Carlisle U* 6 0 **6 0**
2009–10 Tottenham H 1 0
2009–10 *Norwich C* 3 0 **3 0**
2010–11 Tottenham H 0 0 **1 0**
2010–11 *Leeds U* 0 0
2010–11 *Doncaster R* 0 0

ASSOU-EKOTTO, Benoit (M) 172 1
H: 5 10 W: 10 12 b.Arras 24-3-84
Honours: Cameroon B, 16 full caps.
2003–04 Lens 3 0
2004–05 Lens 29 0
2005–06 Lens 34 0 **66 0**
2006–07 Tottenham H 16 0
2007–08 Tottenham H 1 0
2008–09 Tottenham H 29 0
2009–10 Tottenham H 30 1
2010–11 Tottenham H 30 0 **106 1**

BALE, Gareth (D) 117 17
H: 6 0 W: 11 10 b.Cardiff 16-7-89
Source: Scholar. *Honours:* Wales Youth, Under-21, 27 full caps, 3 goals.
2005–06 Southampton 2 0
2006–07 Southampton 38 5 **40 5**
2007–08 Tottenham H 8 2
2008–09 Tottenham H 16 0
2009–10 Tottenham H 23 3
2010–11 Tottenham H 30 7 **77 12**

BASSONG, Sebastien (D) 149 3
H: 6 2 W: 11 07 b.Paris 9-7-86
Honours: France Under-21. Cameroon 14 full caps.
2005–06 Metz 23 0
2006–07 Metz 37 1
2007–08 Metz 19 0 **79 1**
2008–09 Newcastle U 30 0
2009–10 Newcastle U 0 0 **30 0**
2009–10 Tottenham H 28 1
2010–11 Tottenham H 12 1 **40 2**

BENTLEY, David (F) 184 18
H: 5 10 W: 11 03 b.Peterborough 27-8-84
Source: Scholar. *Honours:* England Youth, Under-20, Under-21, B, 7 full caps.
2001–02 Arsenal 0 0
2002–03 Arsenal 0 0
2003–04 Arsenal 1 0
2004–05 Arsenal 0 0
2004–05 *Norwich C* 26 2 **26 2**
2005–06 Arsenal 0 0 **1 0**
2005–06 Blackburn R 29 3
2006–07 Blackburn R 36 4
2007–08 Blackburn R 37 6 **102 13**
2008–09 Tottenham H 25 1
2009–10 Tottenham H 15 2
2010–11 Tottenham H 2 0 **42 3**
2010–11 *Birmingham C* 13 0 **13 0**

BOSTOCK, John (M)   **24   4**
H: 5 10   W: 11 11   b.Camberwell 13-10-91
Honours: England Youth.

2007–08	Crystal Palace	4	0	**4**	**0**
2008–09	Tottenham H	0	0		
2009–10	Tottenham H	0	0		
2009–10	Brentford	9	2	**9**	**2**
2010–11	Tottenham H	0	0		
2010–11	*Hull C*	11	2	**11**	**2**

BUTTON, David (G)   **73   0**
H: 6 3   W: 13 00   b.Stevenage 27-2-89
Source: Scholar. *Honours:* England Youth.

2005–06	Tottenham H	0	0		
2006–07	Tottenham H	0	0		
2007–08	*Rochdale*	0	0		
2007–08	Tottenham H	0	0		
2008–09	Tottenham H	0	0		
2008–09	*Bournemouth*	4	0	**4**	**0**
2008–09	*Luton T*	0	0		
2008–09	*Dagenham & R*	3	0	**3**	**0**
2009–10	Tottenham H	0	0		
2009–10	*Crewe Alex*	10	0	**10**	**0**
2009–10	*Shrewsbury T*	26	0	**26**	**0**
2010–11	Tottenham H	0	0		
2010–11	*Plymouth Arg*	30	0	**30**	**0**

BYRNE, Nathan (D)   **11   0**
b.St Albans 5-6-92
Source: Scholar.

2010–11	Tottenham H	0	0		
2010–11	*Brentford*	11	0	**11**	**0**

CARROLL, Tommy (M)   **12   0**
b.Watford 28-5-92
Source: Scholar.

2010–11	Tottenham H	0	0		
2010–11	*Leyton Orient*	12	0	**12**	**0**

CAULKER, Steven (D)   **73   2**
H: 6 3   W: 12 00   b.Feltham 29-12-91
Honours: England Youth. Under-21.

2009–10	Tottenham H	0	0		
2009–10	*Yeovil T*	44	0	**44**	**0**
2010–11	Tottenham H	0	0		
2010–11	*Bristol C*	29	2	**29**	**2**

CORLUKA, Vedran (D)   **204   13**
H: 6 3   W: 13 03   b.Zagreb 9-2-86
Honours: Croatia 46 full caps, 1 goal.

2003–04	Dynamo Zagreb	0	0		
2004–05	Inter Zapresic	27	4	**27**	**4**
2005–06	Dynamo Zagreb	32	3		
2006–07	Dynamo Zagreb	29	4	**61**	**7**
2007–08	Manchester C	35	0		
2008–09	Manchester C	3	1	**38**	**1**
2008–09	Tottenham H	34	0		
2009–10	Tottenham H	29	1		
2010–11	Tottenham H	15	0	**78**	**1**

CROUCH, Peter (F)   **353   95**
H: 6 7   W: 13 03   b.Macclesfield 30-1-81
Source: Trainee. *Honours:* England Youth, Under-20, Under-21, B, 42 full caps, 22 goals.

1998–99	Tottenham H	0	0		
1999–2000	Tottenham H	0	0		
2000–01	QPR	42	10	**42**	**10**
2001–02	Portsmouth	37	18		
2001–02	Aston Villa	7	2		
2002–03	Aston Villa	14	0		
2003–04	Aston Villa	16	4	**37**	**6**
2003–04	*Norwich C*	15	4	**15**	**4**
2004–05	Southampton	27	12	**27**	**12**
2005–06	Liverpool	32	8		
2006–07	Liverpool	32	9		
2007–08	Liverpool	21	5	**85**	**22**
2008–09	Portsmouth	38	11		
2009–10	Portsmouth	0	0	**75**	**29**
2009–10	Tottenham H	38	8		
2010–11	Tottenham H	34	4	**72**	**12**

CUDICINI, Carlo (G)   **244   0**
H: 6 1   W: 12 08   b.Milan 6-9-73
Honours: Italy Youth, Under-21.

1991–92	AC Milan	0	0		
1992–93	AC Milan	0	0		
1993–94	Como	6	0	**6**	**0**
1994–95	AC Milan	0	0		
1995–96	AC Milan	0	0		
1995–96	Prato	30	0	**30**	**0**
1996–97	Lazio	1	0	**1**	**0**
1997–98	Castel di Sangro	14	0		
1998–99	Castel di Sangro	32	0	**46**	**0**

1999–2000	Chelsea	1	0		
2000–01	Chelsea	24	0		
2001–02	Chelsea	28	0		
2002–03	Chelsea	36	0		
2003–04	Chelsea	26	0		
2004–05	Chelsea	3	0		
2005–06	Chelsea	4	0		
2006–07	Chelsea	8	0		
2007–08	Chelsea	10	0		
2008–09	Chelsea	2	0	**142**	**0**
2008–09	Tottenham H	4	0		
2009–10	Tottenham H	7	0		
2010–11	Tottenham H	8	0	**19**	**0**

DAWKINS, Simon (F)   **11   0**
H: 5 10   W: 11 01   b.Edgware 1-12-87
Source: Scholar.

2005–06	Tottenham H	0	0		
2006–07	Tottenham H	0	0		
2007–08	Tottenham H	0	0		
2008–09	Tottenham H	0	0		
2008–09	*Leyton Orient*	11	0	**11**	**0**
2009–10	Tottenham H	0	0		
2010–11	Tottenham H	0	0		

DAWSON, Michael (D)   **253   13**
H: 6 2   W: 12 02   b.Northallerton 18-11-83
Source: School. *Honours:* England Youth, Under-21, B, 4 full caps.

2000–01	Nottingham F	0	0		
2001–02	Nottingham F	1	0		
2002–03	Nottingham F	38	5		
2003–04	Nottingham F	30	1		
2004–05	Nottingham F	14	1	**83**	**7**
2004–05	Tottenham H	5	0		
2005–06	Tottenham H	32	0		
2006–07	Tottenham H	37	1		
2007–08	Tottenham H	27	1		
2008–09	Tottenham H	16	1		
2009–10	Tottenham H	29	2		
2010–11	Tottenham H	24	1	**170**	**6**

DEFOE, Jermain (F)   **356   130**
H: 5 7   W: 10 04   b.Beckton 7-10-82
Source: Charlton Ath. *Honours:* England Youth, Under-21, B, 46 full caps, 15 goals.

1999–2000	West Ham U	0	0		
2000–01	West Ham U	1	0		
2000–01	*Bournemouth*	29	18	**29**	**18**
2001–02	West Ham U	35	10		
2002–03	West Ham U	38	8		
2003–04	West Ham U	19	11	**93**	**29**
2003–04	Tottenham H	15	7		
2004–05	Tottenham H	35	13		
2005–06	Tottenham H	36	9		
2006–07	Tottenham H	34	10		
2007–08	Tottenham H	19	4		
2007–08	Portsmouth	12	8		
2008–09	Portsmouth	19	7	**31**	**15**
2008–09	Tottenham H	8	3		
2009–10	Tottenham H	34	18		
2010–11	Tottenham H	22	4	**203**	**68**

FREDERICKS, Ryan (M)   **0   0**
b.London 10-10-92
Source: Scholar.

2010–11	Tottenham H	0	0		

GALLAS, William (D)   **390   26**
H: 6 0   W: 12 12   b.Asnieres 17-8-77
Honours: France Under-21, 84 full caps, 5 goals.

1996–97	Caen	18	0	**18**	**0**
1997–98	Marseille	3	0		
1998–99	Marseille	30	0		
1999–2000	Marseille	22	0		
2000–01	Chelsea	30	2	**85**	**2**
2001–02	Chelsea	30	1		
2002–03	Chelsea	38	4		
2003–04	Chelsea	29	0		
2004–05	Chelsea	28	2		
2005–06	Chelsea	34	5		
2006–07	Chelsea	0	0	**159**	**12**
2006–07	Arsenal	21	3		
2007–08	Arsenal	31	4		
2008–09	Arsenal	23	2		
2009–10	Arsenal	26	3		
2010–11	Arsenal	0	0	**101**	**12**
2010–11	Tottenham H	27	0	**27**	**0**

GIOVANI (F)   **76   12**
H: 5 8   W: 12 03   b.Monterrey 11-5-89
Honours: Mexico Youth, 29 full caps, 5 goals.

2006–07	Barcelona B	0	0		
2007–08	Barcelona	28	3	**28**	**3**
2008–09	Tottenham H	6	0		
2008–09	*Ipswich T*	8	4	**8**	**4**
2009–10	Tottenham H	1	0		
2009–10	*Galatasaray*	14	0	**14**	**0**
2010–11	Tottenham H	3	0	**10**	**0**
2010–11	*Santander*	16	5	**16**	**5**

GOMES, Heurelho (G)   **282   0**
H: 6 3   W: 12 13   b.Minas Gerais 15-2-81
Source: Democrata. *Honours:* Brazil Under-23, 11 full caps.

2001	Cruzeiro	0	0		
2002	Cruzeiro	14	0		
2003	Cruzeiro	40	0		
2004	Cruzeiro	5	0	**59**	**0**
2004–05	PSV Eindhoven	30	0		
2005–06	PSV Eindhoven	32	0		
2006–07	PSV Eindhoven	32	0		
2007–08	PSV Eindhoven	34	0	**128**	**0**
2008–09	Tottenham H	34	0		
2009–10	Tottenham H	31	0		
2010–11	Tottenham H	30	0	**95**	**0**

HUDDLESTONE, Tom (M)   **223   9**
H: 6 2   W: 11 02   b.Nottingham 28-12-86
Source: Scholar. *Honours:* England Youth, Under-20, Under-21, 3 full caps.

2003–04	Derby Co	43	0		
2004–05	Derby Co	45	0	**88**	**0**
2005–06	Tottenham H	4	0		
2005–06	*Wolverhampton W*	13	1	**13**	**1**
2006–07	Tottenham H	21	1		
2007–08	Tottenham H	28	3		
2008–09	Tottenham H	22	0		
2009–10	Tottenham H	33	2		
2010–11	Tottenham H	14	2	**122**	**8**

HUTTON, Alan (D)   **144   3**
H: 6 1   W: 11 05   b.Glasgow 30-11-84
Honours: Scotland Under-21, 20 full caps.

2004–05	Rangers	10	0		
2005–06	Rangers	19	0		
2006–07	Rangers	33	1		
2007–08	Rangers	20	0	**82**	**1**
2007–08	Tottenham H	14	0		
2008–09	Tottenham H	8	0		
2009–10	Tottenham H	4	0		
2009–10	*Sunderland*	11	0	**11**	**0**
2010–11	Tottenham H	21	2	**51**	**2**

JANSSON, Oscar (G)   **11   0**
H: 6 0   W: 12 13   b.Orebro 23-12-90
Source: Scholar.

2007–08	Tottenham H	0	0		
2008–09	Tottenham H	0	0		
2009–10	Tottenham H	0	0		
2009–10	*Exeter C*	7	0	**7**	**0**
2010–11	Tottenham H	0	0		
2010–11	*Northampton T*	4	0	**4**	**0**

JENAS, Jermaine (M)   **293   34**
H: 5 11   W: 11 00   b.Nottingham 18-2-83
Source: Scholar. *Honours:* England Youth, Under-21, B, 21 full caps, 1 goal.

1999–2000	Nottingham F	0	0		
2000–01	Nottingham F	1	0		
2001–02	Nottingham F	28	4	**29**	**4**
2001–02	Newcastle U	12	0		
2002–03	Newcastle U	32	6		
2003–04	Newcastle U	31	2		
2004–05	Newcastle U	31	1		
2005–06	Newcastle U	4	0	**110**	**9**
2005–06	Tottenham H	30	6		
2006–07	Tottenham H	25	6		
2007–08	Tottenham H	29	4		
2008–09	Tottenham H	32	4		
2009–10	Tottenham H	19	1		
2010–11	Tottenham H	19	0	**154**	**21**

KABOUL, Younes (D)   **143   11**
H: 6 2   W: 13 07   b.Annemasse 4-1-86
Honours: France Under-21, 2 full caps, 1 goal.

2004–05	Auxerre	12	1		
2005–06	Auxerre	9	0		
2006–07	Auxerre	31	2	**52**	**3**
2007–08	Tottenham H	21	3		
2008–09	Portsmouth	20	1		

	2009–10	Portsmouth	19	3	39	4
	2009–10	Tottenham H	10	0		
	2010–11	Tottenham H	21	1	52	4

KANE, Harry (F)   18   5
b.Walthamstow 28-7-93
Source: Scholar.

2010–11	Tottenham H	0	0		
2010–11	*Leyton Orient*	18	5	18	5

KEANE, Robbie (F)   438   159
H: 5 9   W: 12 02   b.Dublin 8-7-80
Source: Trainee. Honours: Eire Youth, B, 108 full caps, 51 goals.

1997–98	Wolverhampton W	38	11		
1998–99	Wolverhampton W	33	11		
1999–2000	Wolverhampton W	2	2	73	24
1999–2000	Coventry C	31	12	31	12
2000–01	Internazionale	6	0	6	0
2000–01	Leeds U	18	9		
2001–02	Leeds U	25	3		
2002–03	Leeds U	3	1	46	13
2002–03	Tottenham H	29	13		
2003–04	Tottenham H	34	14		
2004–05	Tottenham H	35	11		
2005–06	Tottenham H	36	16		
2006–07	Tottenham H	27	11		
2007–08	Tottenham H	36	15		
2008–09	Liverpool	19	5	19	5
2008–09	Tottenham H	14	5		
2009–10	Tottenham H	20	6		
2009–10	Celtic	16	12	16	12
2010–11	Tottenham H	7	0	238	91
2010–11	*West Ham U*	9	2	9	2

KHUMALO, Bongani (D)   137   12
H: 6 2   W: 12 13   b.Manzini 6-1-87
Honours: South Africa 22 full caps, 1 goal.

2005–06	Pretoria Univ	22	0		
2006–07	Pretoria Univ	28	4	50	4
2007–08	Supersport U	25	4		
2008–09	Supersport U	23	3		
2009–10	Supersport U	26	1		
2010–11	Supersport U	7	0	81	8
2010–11	Tottenham H	0	0		
2010–11	*Preston NE*	6	0	6	0

KING, Ledley (D)   247   10
H: 6 2   W: 14 05   b.Bow 12-10-80
Source: Trainee. Honours: England Youth, B, Under-21, 21 full caps, 2 goals.

1998–99	Tottenham H	1	0		
1999–2000	Tottenham H	3	0		
2000–01	Tottenham H	18	1		
2001–02	Tottenham H	32	0		
2002–03	Tottenham H	25	0		
2003–04	Tottenham H	29	1		
2004–05	Tottenham H	38	2		
2005–06	Tottenham H	26	3		
2006–07	Tottenham H	21	0		
2007–08	Tottenham H	4	0		
2008–09	Tottenham H	24	1		
2009–10	Tottenham H	20	2		
2010–11	Tottenham H	6	0	247	10

KRANJCAR, Niko (M)   255   50
H: 6 1   W: 12 13   b.Zagreb 13-8-84
Honours: Croatia Youth, Under-21, 64 full caps, 5 goals.

2001–02	Dynamo Zagreb	24	3		
2002–03	Dynamo Zagreb	21	4		
2003–04	Dynamo Zagreb	24	10		
2004–05	Dynamo Zagreb	16	2	85	19
2004–05	Hajduk Split	13	1		
2005–06	Hajduk Split	32	10		
2006–07	Hajduk Split	5	3	50	14
2006–07	Portsmouth	24	2		
2007–08	Portsmouth	34	4		
2008–09	Portsmouth	21	3		
2009–10	Portsmouth	4	0	83	9
2009–10	Tottenham H	24	6		
2010–11	Tottenham H	13	2	37	8

LANCASTER, Cameron (F)   4   0
b.Camden 5-11-92
Source: Scholar.

2010–11	Tottenham H	0	0		
2010–11	*Dagenham & R*	4	0	4	0

LENNON, Aaron (M)   211   19
H: 5 6   W: 10 03   b.Leeds 16-4-87
Source: Trainee. Honours: England Youth, Under-21, B, 19 full caps.

2003–04	Leeds U	11	0		
2004–05	Leeds U	27	1	38	1
2005–06	Tottenham H	27	2		
2006–07	Tottenham H	26	3		
2007–08	Tottenham H	29	2		
2008–09	Tottenham H	35	5		
2009–10	Tottenham H	22	3		
2010–11	Tottenham H	34	3	173	18

LIVERMORE, Jake (M)   48   2
H: 5 9   W: 12 08   b.Enfield 14-11-89
Source: Scholar.

2006–07	Tottenham H	0	0		
2007–08	Tottenham H	0	0		
2007–08	*Milton Keynes D*	5	0	5	0
2008–09	Tottenham H	0	0		
2008–09	*Crewe Alex*	0	0		
2009–10	Tottenham H	1	0		
2009–10	*Derby Co*	16	1	16	1
2009–10	*Peterborough U*	9	1	9	1
2010–11	Tottenham H	0	0	1	0
2010–11	*Ipswich T*	12	0	12	0
2010–11	*Leeds U*	5	0	5	0

LOUNGO, Massimo (F)   0   0
b.Australia 25-9-92
Source: Rushden & D.

2010–11	Tottenham H	0	0		

M'POKU, Paul-Jose (M)   27   2
H: 5 8   W: 10 03   b.Kinshasa 19-4-92
Source: Scholar.

2008–09	Tottenham H	0	0		
2009–10	Tottenham H	0	0		
2010–11	*Leyton Orient*	27	2	27	2

MASON, Ryan (F)   43   6
H: 5 9   W: 10 00   b.Enfield 13-6-91
Source: Scholar. Honours: England Youth.

2007–08	Tottenham H	0	0		
2008–09	Tottenham H	0	0		
2009–10	Tottenham H	0	0		
2009–10	*Yeovil T*	28	6	28	6
2010–11	Tottenham H	0	0		
2010–11	*Doncaster R*	15	0	15	0

MODRIC, Luka (M)   202   40
H: 5 8   W: 10 03   b.Zadar 9-9-85
Honours: Croatia Youth, Under-21, 47 full caps, 7 goals.

2004–05	Inter Zapresic	18	4	18	4
2004–05	Dinamo Zagreb	6	0		
2005–06	Dinamo Zagreb	32	8		
2006–07	Dinamo Zagreb	30	6		
2007–08	Dinamo Zagreb	25	13	93	27
2008–09	Tottenham H	34	3		
2009–10	Tottenham H	25	3		
2010–11	Tottenham H	32	3	91	9

NAUGHTON, Kyle (M)   108   6
H: 5 11   W: 11 07   b.Sheffield 11-11-88
Honours: England Under-21.

2006–07	Sheffield U	0	0		
2007–08	*Gretna*	18	0	18	0
2007–08	Sheffield U	0	0		
2008–09	Sheffield U	40	1		
2009–10	Sheffield U	0	0	40	1
2009–10	Tottenham H	1	0		
2009–10	*Middlesbrough*	15	0	15	0
2010–11	Tottenham H	0	0	1	0
2010–11	*Leicester C*	34	5	34	5

NICHOLSON, Jake (M)   2   0
b.Harrow 19-7-92
Source: Scholar.

2010–11	Tottenham H	0	0		
2010–11	*MyPa*	2	0	2	0

O'HARA, Jamie (M)   107   14
H: 5 11   W: 12 04   b.Dartford 25-9-86
Source: Scholar. Honours: England Youth, Under-21.

2004–05	Tottenham H	0	0		
2005–06	Tottenham H	0	0		
2005–06	*Chesterfield*	19	5	19	5
2006–07	Tottenham H	0	0		
2007–08	Tottenham H	17	1		
2007–08	*Millwall*	14	2	14	2

2008–09	Tottenham H	15	1		
2009–10	Tottenham H	2	0		
2009–10	*Portsmouth*	26	2	26	2
2010–11	Tottenham H	0	0	34	2
2010–11	Wolverhampton W	14	3	14	3

OBIKA, Jonathan (F)   68   16
H: 6 0   W: 12 00   b.Enfield 12-9-90
Source: Scholar. Honours: England Youth, Under-20.

2008–09	Tottenham H	0	0		
2008–09	*Yeovil T*	10	4		
2009–10	Tottenham H	0	0		
2009–10	*Yeovil T*	22	6		
2009–10	*Millwall*	12	2	12	2
2010–11	Tottenham H	0	0		
2010–11	*Crystal Palace*	7	0	7	0
2010–11	*Peterborough U*	1	1	1	1
2010–11	*Swindon T*	5	0	5	0
2010–11	*Yeovil T*	11	3	43	13

OYENUGA, Kudus (F)   0   0
H: 5 9   W: 11 00   b.Walthamstow 18-3-93
Source: Scholar.

2010–11	Tottenham H	0	0		

PALACIOS, Wilson (D)   109   1
H: 5 11   W: 11 11   b.La Ceiba 29-7-84
Source: Olimpia. Honours: Honduras 74 full caps, 5 goals.

2007–08	Birmingham C	7	0	7	0
2007–08	Wigan Ath	16	0		
2008–09	Wigan Ath	21	0	37	0
2008–09	Tottenham H	11	0		
2009–10	Tottenham H	33	1		
2010–11	Tottenham H	21	0	65	1

PARRETT, Dean (M)   21   2
H: 5 10   W: 11 04   b.Hampstead 16-11-91
Source: Scholar. Honours: England Youth.

2008–09	Tottenham H	0	0		
2009–10	Tottenham H	0	0		
2009–10	*Aldershot T*	4	0	4	0
2010–11	Tottenham H	0	0		
2010–11	*Plymouth Arg*	8	1	8	1
2010–11	*Charlton Ath*	9	1	9	1

PAVLYUCHENKO, Roman (F)   310   100
H: 6 2   W: 12 04   b.Mostovskoy 15-12-81
Honours: Russia 40 full caps, 19 goals.

1999	Dinamo Stavropol	3	1	31	1
2000	Rotor Volgograd II	13	3	13	3
2000	Rotor Volgograd	16	5		
2001	Rotor Volgograd	28	5		
2002	Rotor Volgograd	22	4	66	14
2003	Spartak Moscow	27	10		
2004	Spartak Moscow	26	10		
2005	Spartak Moscow	25	11		
2006	Spartak Moscow	27	18		
2007	Spartak Moscow	22	14	127	63
2008–09	Tottenham H	28	5		
2009–10	Tottenham H	16	5		
2010–11	Tottenham H	29	9	73	19

PIENAAR, Steven (M)   231   24
H: 5 10   W: 10 06   b.Westbury 17-3-82
Honours: South Africa 57 full caps, 3 goals.

2001–02	Ajax	8	1		
2002–03	Ajax	31	5		
2003–04	Ajax	16	3		
2004–05	Ajax	24	4		
2005–06	Ajax	15	2	94	15
2006–07	Bor Dortmund	25	0	25	0
2007–08	Everton	28	2		
2008–09	Everton	28	2		
2009–10	Everton	30	4		
2010–11	Everton	18	1	104	9
2010–11	Tottenham H	8	0	8	0

PLETIKOSA, Stipe (G)   257   4
H: 6 4   W: 14 05   b.Split 8-1-79
Honours: Croatia Youth, Under-21, 82 full caps.

1996–97	Hajduk Split	1	0		
1997–98	Hajduk Split	1	0		
1998–99	Hajduk Split	19	0		
1999–2000	Hajduk Split	32	0		
2000–01	Hajduk Split	31	1		
2001–02	Hajduk Split	27	0		
2002–03	Hajduk Split	30	3		
2003–04	Shakhtar Donetsk	23	0		
2004–05	Shakhtar Donetsk	6	0		
2005–06	Hajduk Split	21	0	162	4

2006–07	Shakhtar Donetsk	3	0	**32**	**0**
2007	Spartak Moscow	29	0		
2008	Spartak Moscow	30	0		
2009	Spartak Moscow	4	0	**63**	**0**
2010–11	Tottenham H	0	0		

On loan from Spartak Moscow

RANIERI, Mirko (G) **0 0**
b.Assisi 8-2-92
Source: Perugia.

2008–09	Tottenham H	0	0
2009–10	Tottenham H	0	0
2010–11	Tottenham H	0	0

ROSE, Danny (M) **29 1**
H: 5 8 W: 11 11 b.Doncaster 2-6-90
Source: Leeds U. *Honours:* England Youth, Under-21.

2007–08	Tottenham H	0	0		
2008–09	Tottenham H	0	0		
2008–09	*Watford*	7	0	**7**	**0**
2009–10	Tottenham H	1	1		
2010–11	Tottenham H	4	0	**5**	**1**
2010–11	*Bristol C*	17	0	**17**	**0**

SANDRO (M) **62 5**
H: 6 2 W: 11 11 b.Riachinho 15-3-89
Honours: Brazil 7 full caps.

2008	Internacional	7	2		
2009	Internacional	27	1		
2010	Internacional	9	1	**43**	**4**
2010–11	Tottenham H	19	1	**19**	**1**

SMITH, Adam (D) **57 1**
H: 5 8 W: 10 07 b.Leytonstone 29-4-91
Source: Scholar. *Honours:* England Youth.

2007–08	Tottenham H	0	0		
2008–09	Tottenham H	0	0		
2009–10	Tottenham H	0	0		
2009–10	*Wycombe W*	3	0	**3**	**0**
2009–10	*Torquay U*	16	0	**16**	**0**
2010–11	Tottenham H	0	0		
2010–11	*Bournemouth*	38	1	**38**	**1**

TAPPING, Callum (M) **0 0**
b.London
Source: Scholar.

2010–11	Tottenham H	0	0

TOWNSEND, Andros (M) **68 8**
H: 6 0 W: 12 00 b.Chingford 16-7-91
Source: Scholar. *Honours:* England Youth.

2008–09	Tottenham H	0	0		
2008–09	*Yeovil T*	10	1	**10**	**1**
2009–10	Tottenham H	0	0		
2009–10	*Leyton Orient*	22	2	**22**	**2**
2009–10	*Milton Keynes D*	9	2	**9**	**2**
2010–11	Tottenham H	0	0		
2010–11	*Ipswich T*	13	1	**13**	**1**
2010–11	*Watford*	3	0	**3**	**0**
2010–11	*Millwall*	11	2	**11**	**2**

VAN DER VAART, Rafael (M) **277 105**
H: 5 9 W: 11 09 b.Heemskerk 11-2-83
Honours: Holland 90 full caps, 17 goals.

1999–2000	Ajax	1	0		
2000–01	Ajax	27	7		
2001–02	Ajax	20	14		
2002–03	Ajax	21	18		
2003–04	Ajax	26	7		
2004–05	Ajax	22	6	**117**	**52**
2005–06	Hamburg	19	9		
2006–07	Hamburg	26	8		
2007–08	Hamburg	29	12	**74**	**29**
2008–09	Real Madrid	32	5		
2009–10	Real Madrid	26	6	**58**	**11**
2010–11	Tottenham H	28	13	**28**	**13**

WALKER, Kyle (D) **75 1**
H: 5 10 W: 11 07 b.Sheffield 28-5-90
Source: Scholar. *Honours:* England Youth, Under-21.

2008–09	Sheffield U	2	0		
2008–09	*Northampton T*	9	0	**9**	**0**
2009–10	Tottenham H	2	0		
2009–10	*Sheffield U*	26	0	**28**	**0**
2010–11	Tottenham H	1	0	**3**	**0**
2010–11	*QPR*	20	0	**20**	**0**
2010–11	*Aston Villa*	15	1	**15**	**1**

WOODGATE, Jonathan (D) **236 6**
H: 6 2 W: 12 06 b.Middlesbrough 22-1-80
Source: Trainee. *Honours:* England Youth, Under-21, 8 full caps.

1996–97	Leeds U	0	0		
1997–98	Leeds U	0	0		
1998–99	Leeds U	25	2		
1999–2000	Leeds U	34	1		
2000–01	Leeds U	14	1		
2001–02	Leeds U	13	0		
2002–03	Leeds U	18	0	**104**	**4**
2003–04	Newcastle U	10	0		
2004–05	Newcastle U	18	0	**28**	**0**
2004–05	Real Madrid	0	0		
2005–06	Real Madrid	9	0	**9**	**0**
2006–07	Middlesbrough	30	0		
2007–08	Middlesbrough	16	0	**46**	**0**
2007 08	Tottenham H	12	1		
2008–09	Tottenham H	34	1		
2009–10	Tottenham H	3	0		
2010–11	Tottenham H	0	0	**49**	**2**

Scholars
Angol Lee Anthony; Archer Jordan Gideon; Barthram Jack Patrick; Champion Frederick; Day Daniel; Ekong William Paul; Hawkins Ronnie; Lancaster Cameron Paul; Lassen Jesse Waller; McBride Paul; Miles Jonathan David; Munns Jack Frederick; Pritchard Alex David; Sheriff Ramil; Stewart Kevin Linford; Yeboah James

TRANMERE R (84)

AKINS, Lucas (F) **58 3**
H: 5 10 W: 11 07 b.Huddersfield 25-2-89
Source: Scholar.

2006–07	Huddersfield T	2	0		
2007–08	Huddersfield T	3	0	**5**	**0**
2008–09	Hamilton A	11	0		
2008–09	*Partick Th*	9	1	**9**	**1**
2009–10	Hamilton A	0	0	**11**	**0**
2010 11	Tranmere R	33	2	**33**	**2**

BAKAYOGO, Zaoumana (D) **71 1**
H: 5 9 W: 10 08 b.Paris 11-8-86
Source: Paris St Germain. *Honours:* Ivory Coast Under-23.

2006–07	Millwall	5	0		
2007–08	Millwall	10	0	**15**	**0**

From Alfortville.

2009–10	Tranmere R	29	0		
2010–11	Tranmere R	27	1	**56**	**1**

BLANCHARD, Maximo (D) **116 2**
H: 5 11 W: 11 13 b.Alencon 27-9-86

2006–07	Laval	4	0		
2007–08	Laval	22	0	**26**	**0**
2008–09	Entente	35	1	**35**	**1**
2009–10	Moulins	35	1	**35**	**1**
2010–11	Tranmere R	20	0	**20**	**0**

BROOMES, Marlon (D) **244 5**
H: 6 0 W: 12 12 b.Birmingham 28-11-77
Source: Trainee. *Honours:* England Schools, Youth, Under-21.

1994–95	Blackburn R	0	0		
1995–96	Blackburn R	0	0		
1996–97	Blackburn R	0	0		
1996–97	*Swindon T*	12	1	**12**	**1**
1997–98	Blackburn R	4	0		
1998–99	Blackburn R	13	0		
1999–2000	Blackburn R	13	1		
2000–01	Blackburn R	1	0		
2000–01	*QPR*	5	0	**5**	**0**
2001–02	Blackburn R	0	0	**31**	**1**
2001–02	*Grimsby T*	15	0	**15**	**0**
2001–02	*Sheffield W*	19	0	**19**	**0**
2002–03	Preston NE	28	0		
2003–04	Preston NE	30	0		
2004–05	Preston NE	11	0	**69**	**0**
2005–06	Stoke C	37	2		
2006–07	Stoke C	0	0		
2007–08	Stoke C	0	0	**37**	**2**
2008–09	Blackpool	1	0	**1**	**0**
2008–09	*Crewe Alex*	19	0	**19**	**0**
2009–10	Tranmere R	31	1		
2010–11	Tranmere R	5	0	**36**	**1**

CATHALINA, Timothy (D) **133 5**
H: 5 11 W: 12 02 b.Willemstad 24-1-85

2005–06	Apeldoorn	29	2		
2006–07	Apeldoorn	25	0		
2007–08	Apeldoorn	33	0		
2008–09	Apeldoorn	23	3	**110**	**5**
2009–10	Emmen	16	0	**16**	**0**
2010–11	Tranmere R	7	0	**7**	**0**

COLLISTER, Joe (G) **10 0**
H: 6 0 W: 13 10 b.Hoylake 15-12-91
Source: Scholar.

2009–10	Tranmere R	3	0		
2010–11	Tranmere R	7	0	**10**	**0**

COUGHLIN, Andy (G) **0 0**
H: 6 3 W: 14 04 b.Bootle 31-1-93
Source: Scholar.

2010–11	Tranmere R	0	0

CRESSWELL, Aaron (D) **70 5**
H: 5 7 W: 10 05 b.Liverpool 15-12-89
Source: Scholar.

2008–09	Tranmere R	13	1		
2009–10	Tranmere R	14	0		
2010–11	Tranmere R	43	4	**70**	**5**

FRAUGHAN, Ryan (M) **20 0**
H: 5 7 W: 11 02 b.Liverpool 11-2-91
Source: Scholar.

2008–09	Tranmere R	0	0		
2009–10	Tranmere R	6	0		
2010–11	Tranmere R	14	0	**20**	**0**

GOODISON, Ian (D) **363 11**
H: 6 1 W: 13 04 b.St James, Jamaica 21-11-72
Source: Olympic Gardens. *Honours:* Jamaica 113 full caps, 9 goals.

1999–2000	Hull C	18	0		
2000–01	Hull C	36	1		
2001–02	Hull C	16	0		
2002–03	Hull C	0	0	**70**	**1**

From Seba U.

2003–04	Tranmere R	12	0		
2004–05	Tranmere R	44	1		
2005–06	Tranmere R	38	1		
2006–07	Tranmere R	40	0		
2007–08	Tranmere R	42	0		
2008–09	Tranmere R	33	1		
2009–10	Tranmere R	44	3		
2010–11	Tranmere R	40	4	**293**	**10**

JENNINGS, Dale (M) **29 6**
H: 5 7 W: 11 00 b.Liverpool 21-12-92
Source: Scholar.

2010–11	Tranmere R	29	6	**29**	**6**

LABADIE, Joss (M) **68 10**
H: 5 7 W: 11 02 b.Croydon 31-8-90

2008–09	WBA	0	0		
2008–09	*Shrewsbury T*	1	0		
2009–10	WBA	0	0		
2009–10	*Shrewsbury T*	13	5	**14**	**5**
2009–10	*Cheltenham T*	11	0	**11**	**0**
2009–10	*Tranmere R*	9	3		
2010–11	Tranmere R	34	2	**43**	**5**

MAHON, Alan (M) **314 31**
H: 5 8 W: 12 03 b.Dublin 4-4-78
Source: Crumplin U. *Honours:* Eire School, Youth, Under-21, 2 full caps.

1994–95	Tranmere R	0	0		
1995–96	Tranmere R	2	0		
1996–97	Tranmere R	25	2		
1997–98	Tranmere R	18	1		
1998–99	Tranmere R	39	6		
1999–2000	Tranmere R	36	4		
2000–01	Sporting Lisbon	1	0	**1**	**0**
2000–01	Blackburn R	18	0		
2001–02	Blackburn R	13	1		
2002–03	Blackburn R	2	0		
2002–03	*Cardiff C*	15	2	**15**	**2**
2003–04	Blackburn R	3	0	**36**	**1**
2003–04	*Ipswich T*	11	1	**11**	**1**
2003–04	Wigan Ath	14	1		
2004–05	Wigan Ath	27	7		
2005–06	Wigan Ath	6	1	**47**	**9**
2005–06	Burnley	8	0		
2006–07	Burnley	25	2		
2007–08	Burnley	26	1		
2008–09	Burnley	8	1	**67**	**4**
2008–09	*Blackpool*	1	0	**1**	**0**

2009–10 Tranmere R 16 1
2010–11 Tranmere R 0 0 **136 14**

McCHRYSTAL, Mark (D) 97 2
H: 6 1 W: 13 07 b.Derry 26-6-84
Source: Scholar. *Honours:* Northern Ireland Under-21.
2001–02 Wolverhampton W 0 0
2003 Derry C 5 0
2003 *Institute* 6 0 **6 0**
2004 Derry C 9 1
2005 Derry C 9 0
2006–07 Partick Th 15 1 **15 1**
2007 Derry C 3 0
2008 Derry C 11 0
2009 Derry C 13 0 **50 1**
2009–10 Lisburn Distillery 3 0 **3 0**
2010–11 Tranmere R 23 0 **23 0**

McGURK, Adam (F) 21 3
H: 5 9 W: 12 13 b.St Helier 24-1-89
Source: Scholar. *Honours:* Northern Ireland Under-21.
2005–06 Aston Villa 0 0
2006–07 Aston Villa 0 0
2007–08 Aston Villa 0 0
2008–09 Aston Villa 0 0
2009–10 Aston Villa 0 0
2010–11 Tranmere R 21 3 **21 3**

MORROW, Sam (F) 101 11
H: 6 0 W: 12 10 b.Derry 3-3-85
Source: Trainee. *Honours:* Northern Ireland Youth, Under-21.
2002–03 Ipswich T 0 0
2003–04 Ipswich T 0 0
2003–04 *Boston U* 2 0 **2 0**
2004–05 Hibernian 22 1
2005–06 Hibernian 8 0
2005–06 *Livingston* 11 2 **11 2**
2006–07 Hibernian 0 0 **30 1**
2006–07 Partick Th 8 1 **8 1**
2007 Derry C 8 3
2008 Derry C 14 1
2009 Derry C 19 3 **41 7**
2009–10 Coleraine 4 0 **4 0**
2010–11 Tranmere R 5 0 **5 0**

POWER, Max (D) 0 0
b. 27-7-93
Source: Scholar.
2010–11 Tranmere R 0 0

ROBINSON, Andy (M) 250 46
H: 5 8 W: 11 04 b.Birkenhead 3-11-79
Source: Cammell Laird.
2002–03 Tranmere R 0 0
2003–04 Swansea C 37 8
2004–05 Swansea C 37 8
2005–06 Swansea C 39 12
2006–07 Swansea C 39 7
2007–08 Swansea C 40 8 **192 43**
2008–09 Leeds U 32 2
2009–10 Leeds U 6 0
2009–10 *Tranmere R* 5 1
2010–11 Leeds U 0 0 **38 2**
2010–11 Tranmere R 15 0 **20 1**

SHOWUNMI, Enoch (F) 220 40
H: 6 3 W: 14 11 b.Kilburn 21-4-82
Source: Willesden Constantine. *Honours:* Nigeria 2 full caps.
2003–04 Luton T 26 7
2004–05 Luton T 35 6
2005–06 Luton T 41 1 **102 14**
2006–07 Bristol C 33 10
2007–08 Bristol C 17 3 **50 13**
2007–08 *Sheffield W* 10 0 **10 0**
2008–09 Leeds U 8 2
2009–10 Leeds U 7 0 **15 2**
2010–11 Tranmere R 43 11 **43 11**

TAYLOR, Ash (M) 60 1
H: 6 0 W: 12 00 b.Bromborough 2-9-90
Source: Scholar. *Honours:* Wales Youth.
2008–09 Tranmere R 1 0
2009–10 Tranmere R 33 1
2010–11 Tranmere R 26 0 **60 1**

WARNER, Tony (G) 318 0
H: 6 4 W: 15 06 b.Liverpool 11-5-74
Source: School. *Honours:* Trinidad & Tobago 1 full cap.
1993–94 Liverpool 0 0

1994–95 Liverpool 0 0
1995–96 Liverpool 0 0
1996–97 Liverpool 0 0
1997–98 Liverpool 0 0
1997–98 *Swindon T* 2 0 **2 0**
1998–99 Liverpool 0 0
1998–99 *Celtic* 3 0 **3 0**
1998–99 *Aberdeen* 6 0 **6 0**
1999–2000 Millwall 45 0
2000–01 Millwall 35 0
2001–02 Millwall 46 0
2002–03 Millwall 46 0
2003–04 Millwall 28 0 **200 0**
2004–05 Cardiff C 26 0
2005–06 Cardiff C 0 0 **26 0**
2005–06 Fulham 18 0
2006–07 Fulham 0 0
2006–07 Leeds U 13 0 **13 0**
2006–07 *Norwich C* 13 0 **13 0**
2007–08 Fulham 3 0 **21 0**
2007–08 *Barnsley* 3 0 **3 0**
2008–09 Hull C 0 0
2008–09 *Leicester C* 4 0 **4 0**
2009–10 Hull C 0 0
2010–11 Scunthorpe U 2 0 **2 0**
2010–11 Tranmere R 25 0 **25 0**

WELSH, John (M) 155 11
H: 5 7 W: 12 02 b.Liverpool 10-1-84
Source: Scholar. *Honours:* England Youth, Under-20, Under-21.
2000–01 Liverpool 0 0
2001–02 Liverpool 0 0
2002–03 Liverpool 0 0
2003–04 Liverpool 1 0
2004–05 Liverpool 3 0
2005–06 Liverpool 0 0 **4 0**
2005–06 Hull C 32 2
2006–07 Hull C 18 1
2007–08 Hull C 0 0
2007–08 *Chester C* 6 0 **6 0**
2008–09 Hull C 0 0 **50 3**
2008–09 *Carlisle U* 4 0 **4 0**
2008–09 *Bury* 5 0 **5 0**
2009–10 Tranmere R 45 4
2010–11 Tranmere R 41 4 **86 8**

WOOD, Nick (D) 11 0
H: 6 1 W: 12 02 b.Ossett 9-11-90
Source: Scholar.
2009–10 Sheffield W 0 0
2010–11 Tranmere R 11 0 **11 0**

WALSALL (85)

BEVAN, David (G) 4 0
H: 6 2 W: 13 00 b.Cork 24-6-89
Source: Scholar.
2007–08 Aston Villa 0 0
2008–09 Aston Villa 0 0
2009–10 Aston Villa 0 0
2010–11 Walsall 4 0 **4 0**

BOWERMAN, George (F) 0 0
H: 5 10 W: 10 07 b.Wordsley 6-11-91
Source: Scholar.
2010–11 Walsall 0 0

BRAIN, Jonny (G) 200 0
H: 6 3 W: 13 05 b.Carlisle 11-2-83
Source: Newcastle U Trainee.
2003–04 Port Vale 32 0
2004–05 Port Vale 27 0
2005–06 Port Vale 0 0 **59 0**
2006–07 Macclesfield T 9 0
2007–08 Macclesfield T 29 0
2008–09 Macclesfield T 46 0
2009–10 Macclesfield T 41 0 **125 0**
2010–11 Walsall 16 0 **16 0**

BUTLER, Andy (D) 230 24
H: 6 0 W: 13 00 b.Doncaster 4-11-83
Source: Scholar.
2003–04 Scunthorpe U 35 2
2004–05 Scunthorpe U 37 10
2005–06 Scunthorpe U 16 1
2006–07 Scunthorpe U 11 1
2006–07 *Grimsby T* 4 0 **4 0**
2007–08 Scunthorpe U 36 2 **135 16**
2008–09 Huddersfield T 42 4
2009–10 Huddersfield T 11 0 **53 4**

2009–10 *Blackpool* 7 0 **7 0**
2010–11 Walsall 31 4 **31 4**

BYFIELD, Darren (F) 400 98
H: 5 11 W: 12 07 b.Sutton Coldfield 29-9-76
Source: Trainee. *Honours:* Jamaica 7 full caps.
1993–94 Aston Villa 0 0
1994–95 Aston Villa 0 0
1995–96 Aston Villa 0 0
1996–97 Aston Villa 0 0
1997–98 Aston Villa 7 0
1998–99 Aston Villa 0 0
1998–99 *Preston NE* 5 1 **5 1**
1999–2000 Aston Villa 0 0 **7 0**
1999–2000 *Northampton T* 6 1 **6 1**
1999–2000 *Cambridge U* 4 0 **4 0**
1999–2000 *Blackpool* 3 0 **3 0**
2000–01 Walsall 40 9
2001–02 Walsall 37 4
2001–02 Rotherham U 3 2
2002–03 Rotherham U 37 13
2003–04 Rotherham U 28 7 **68 22**
2003–04 Sunderland 17 5 **17 5**
2004–05 Gillingham 38 6
2005–06 Gillingham 29 13 **67 19**
2006–07 Millwall 31 16
2007–08 Millwall 0 0 **31 16**
2007–08 *Bristol C* 33 8 **33 8**
2008–09 Doncaster R 15 0 **15 0**
2008–09 Oldham Ath 8 1
2009–10 Oldham Ath 3 0 **11 1**
2009–10 Walsall 37 10
2010–11 Walsall 19 2 **133 25**

GEDDES, Sean (M) 0 0
H: 5 6 W: 10 02 b.West Bromwich 13-2-92
Source: Scholar.
2009–10 Walsall 0 0
2010–11 Walsall 0 0

GRAY, Julian (M) 291 31
H: 6 1 W: 11 00 b.Lewisham 21-9-79
Source: Trainee.
1998–99 Arsenal 0 0
1999–2000 Arsenal 1 0 **1 0**
2000–01 Crystal Palace 23 1
2001–02 Crystal Palace 43 2
2002–03 Crystal Palace 35 5
2003–04 Crystal Palace 24 2 **125 10**
2003–04 *Cardiff C* 9 0 **9 0**
2004–05 Birmingham C 32 2
2005–06 Birmingham C 21 1
2006–07 Birmingham C 7 0 **60 3**
2007–08 Coventry C 26 3
2008–09 Coventry C 3 1 **29 4**
2008–09 Fulham 1 0
2009–10 Fulham 0 0 **1 0**
2009–10 Barnsley 5 0 **5 0**
2009–10 Walsall 18 4
2010–11 Walsall 43 10 **61 14**

GRIGG, Will (M) 29 4
H: 5 11 W: 11 00 b.Solihull 3-7-91
Source: Scholar. *Honours:* Northern Ireland Youth, Under-21.
2008–09 Walsall 1 0
2009–10 Walsall 0 0
2010–11 Walsall 28 4 **29 4**

HICKMAN, Alex (D) 0 0
H: 6 1 W: 12 00 b.Dudley 4-12-91
Source: Scholar.
2010–11 Walsall 0 0

JONES, Steve (F) 316 59
H: 5 10 W: 10 05 b.Derry 25-10-76
Source: Leigh RMI. *Honours:* Northern Ireland B, 29 full caps, 1 goal.
2001–02 *Rochdale* 9 1 **9 1**
2001–02 Crewe Alex 6 0
2002–03 Crewe Alex 31 9
2003–04 Crewe Alex 45 15
2004–05 Crewe Alex 36 10
2005–06 Crewe Alex 41 5
2006–07 Burnley 41 5
2007–08 Burnley 17 1
2007–08 *Crewe Alex* 4 1 **163 40**
2008–09 Burnley 0 0 **58 6**
2008–09 *Huddersfield T* 4 0 **4 0**
2008–09 *Bradford C* 27 3 **27 3**
2009–10 Walsall 30 9
2010–11 Walsall 13 0 **43 9**
2010–11 *Motherwell* 12 0 **12 0**

LANCASHIRE, Oliver (D)   67   1
H: 6 1 W: 11 10 b.Basingstoke 13-12-88
Source: Scholar.

2006–07	Southampton	0	0	
2007–08	Southampton	0	0	
2008–09	Southampton	11	0	
2009–10	Southampton	2	0	13 0
2009–10	*Grimsby T*	25	1	25 1
2010–11	Walsall	29	0	29 0

LEDESMA, Emmanuel (M)   54   4
H: 5 11 W: 12 02 b.Quilmes 24-5-88

2007–08	Genoa	1	0	1 0
2008–09	Salernitana	8	1	8 1
2008–09	*QPR*	17	1	17 1
2009–10	Novara	8	1	8 1
2010–11	Crotone	10	0	10 0
2010–11	Walsall	10	1	10 1

LESCOTT, Aaron (M)   363   7
H: 5 8 W: 10 09 b.Birmingham 2-12-78
Source: Trainee. Honours: England Schools.

1996–97	Aston Villa	0	0	
1997–98	Aston Villa	0	0	
1998–99	Aston Villa	0	0	
1999–2000	Aston Villa	0	0	
1999–2000	*Lincoln C*	5	0	5 0
2000–01	Aston Villa	0	0	
2000–01	Sheffield W	30	0	
2001–02	Sheffield W	7	0	37 0
2001–02	Stockport Co	17	0	
2002–03	Stockport Co	41	1	
2003–04	Stockport Co	14	0	72 1
2003–04	*Bristol R*	8	0	
2004–05	Bristol R	26	0	
2005–06	Bristol R	37	0	
2006–07	Bristol R	34	0	
2007–08	Bristol R	34	0	
2008–09	Bristol R	44	3	
2009–10	Bristol R	24	2	207 5
2009–10	*Cheltenham T*	8	0	8 0
2010–11	Walsall	34	1	34 1

MACKEN, Jon (F)   429   105
H: 5 11 W: 12 04 b.Manchester 7-9-77
Source: Trainee. Honours: England Youth.
Eire 1 full cap.

1996–97	Manchester U	0	0	
1997–98	Preston NE	29	6	
1998–99	Preston NE	42	8	
1999–2000	Preston NE	44	22	
2000–01	Preston NE	38	19	
2001–02	Preston NE	31	8	184 63
2001–02	Manchester C	8	5	
2002–03	Manchester C	5	0	
2003–04	Manchester C	15	1	
2004–05	Manchester C	23	1	51 7
2005–06	Crystal Palace	24	2	
2006–07	Crystal Palace	1	0	25 2
2006–07	*Ipswich T*	14	4	14 4
2006–07	Derby Co	8	0	
2007–08	Derby Co	3	0	11 0
2007–08	Barnsley	29	7	
2008–09	Barnsley	45	9	
2009–10	Barnsley	31	4	
2010–11	Barnsley	0	0	105 20
2010–11	Walsall	39	9	39 9

MARSHALL, Paul (M)   42   2
H: 6 1 W: 12 03 b.Manchester 9-7-89
Source: Scholar. Honours: England Under-20.

2007–08	Manchester C	0	0	
2008–09	Manchester C	0	0	
2008–09	*Blackpool*	2	0	2 0
2008–09	*Port Vale*	13	1	13 1
2009–10	Manchester C	0	0	
2009–10	*Aberdeen*	9	0	9 0
2010–11	Walsall	18	1	18 1

McDONALD, Clayton (D)   44   1
H: 6 6 W: 16 05 b.Liverpool 26-12-88
Source: Scholar.

2007–08	Manchester C	0	0	
2008–09	Manchester C	0	0	
2008–09	*Macclesfield T*	2	0	2 0
2008–09	*Chesterfield*	2	0	2 0
2009–10	Manchester C	0	0	
2009–10	Walsall	26	1	
2010–11	Walsall	14	0	40 1

NICHOLLS, Alex (M)   146   17
H: 5 10 W: 11 00 b.Stourbridge 9-12-87
Source: Scholar.

2005–06	Walsall	8	0	
2006–07	Walsall	0	0	
2007–08	Walsall	19	2	
2008–09	Walsall	45	6	
2009–10	Walsall	37	4	
2010–11	Walsall	37	5	146 17

PATERSON, Jamie (F)   14   0
H: 5 9 W: 10 07 b.Coventry 20-12-91
Source: Scholar.

2010–11	Walsall	14	0	14 0

RICHARDS, Matt (D)   286   21
H: 5 8 W: 11 00 b.Harlow 26-12-84
Source: Scholar. Honours: England Under-21.

2001–02	Ipswich T	0	0	
2002–03	Ipswich T	13	0	
2003–04	Ipswich T	44	1	
2004–05	Ipswich T	24	1	
2005–06	Ipswich T	38	4	
2006–07	Ipswich T	28	2	
2007–08	Ipswich T	0	0	
2007–08	*Brighton & HA*	28	0	
2008–09	*Brighton & HA*	23	1	51 1
2008–09	Wycombe W	0	0	
2008–09	*Notts Co*	1	0	1 0
2008–09	Ipswich T	1	0	148 8
2009–10	Walsall	40	4	
2010–11	Walsall	46	8	86 12

SMITH, Manny (D)   91   6
H: 6 2 W: 12 03 b.Birmingham 8-11-88
Source: Scholar.

2005–06	Walsall	0	0	
2006–07	Walsall	3	0	
2007–08	Walsall	4	0	
2008–09	Walsall	26	0	
2009–10	Walsall	33	4	
2010–11	Walsall	25	2	91 6

TAUNDRY, Richard (D)   117   3
H: 5 9 W: 12 10 b.Walsall 15-2-89
Source: Scholar.

2007–08	Walsall	21	0	
2008–09	Walsall	38	0	
2009–10	Walsall	30	3	
2010–11	Walsall	28	0	117 3

WALKER, Jim (G)   458   0
H: 5 11 W: 13 04 b.Sutton-in-Ashfield 9-7-73
Source: Trainee.

1991–92	Notts Co	0	0	
1992–93	Notts Co	0	0	
1993–94	Walsall	31	0	
1994–95	Walsall	4	0	
1995–96	Walsall	26	0	
1996–97	Walsall	36	0	
1997–98	Walsall	46	0	
1998–99	Walsall	46	0	
1999–2000	Walsall	43	0	
2000–01	Walsall	44	0	
2001–02	Walsall	43	0	
2002–03	Walsall	41	0	
2003–04	Walsall	43	0	
2004–05	West Ham U	10	0	
2005–06	West Ham U	3	0	
2006–07	West Ham U	0	0	
2007–08	West Ham U	0	0	
2008–09	West Ham U	0	0	
2008–09	*Colchester U*	16	0	16 0
2009–10	West Ham U	0	0	13 0
2010–11	Walsall	26	0	429 0

WESTLAKE, Darryl (D)   50   1
H: 5 9 W: 11 00 b.Sutton Coldfield 1-3-91
Source: Scholar.

2009–10	Walsall	22	0	
2010–11	Walsall	28	1	50 1

WILLIAMS, Tom (M)   284   6
H: 5 11 W: 12 06 b.Carshalton 8-7-80
Source: Walton & Hersham. Honours: Cyprus 1 full cap.

1999–2000	West Ham U	0	0	
2000–01	West Ham U	0	0	
2000–01	*Peterborough U*	2	0	
2001–02	*Peterborough U*	34	2	
2001–02	Birmingham C	0	0	
2002–03	Birmingham C	0	0	
2002–03	*QPR*	26	1	
2003–04	Birmingham C	0	0	4 0
2003–04	*QPR*	5	0	
2003–04	*Peterborough U*	21	1	
2004–05	Barnsley	39	0	39 0
2005–06	Gillingham	13	0	13 0
2005–06	Swansea C	17	0	
2006–07	Swansea C	29	0	46 0
2007–08	Wycombe W	10	0	10 0
2007–08	Peterborough U	7	0	
2008–09	Peterborough U	25	0	
2009–10	Peterborough U	15	0	104 3
2009–10	*QPR*	5	0	36 1
2009–10	*Preston NE*	10	0	10 0
2010–11	Bristol C	1	0	1 0
2010–11	*Colchester U*	7	1	7 1
2010–11	Walsall	14	1	14 1

WATFORD (86)

ALDRED, Tom (D)   12   0
H: 6 2 W: 13 02 b.Bolton 11-9-90
Source: Scholar.

2008–09	Carlisle U	0	0	
2009–10	Carlisle U	5	0	5 0
2010–11	Watford	0	0	
2010–11	*Stockport Co*	7	0	7 0

ASSOMBALONGA, Britt (M)   0   0
b. 6-12-92
Source: Youth.

2010–11	Watford	0	0	

BENNETT, Dale (D)   20   0
H: 5 11 W: 12 02 b.Enfield 6-1-90
Source: Scholar.

2008–09	Watford	0	0	
2009–10	Watford	10	0	
2010–11	Watford	10	0	20 0

BOND, Jonathan (G)   0   0
b.Hemel Hempstead 19-5-93
Source: Scholar. Honours: Wales Youth, Under-21.

2010–11	Watford	0	0	

BONHAM, Jack (G)   0   0
b.Republic of Ireland 14-9-93
Source: Scholar. Honours: Eire Youth.

2010–11	Watford	0	0	

BRYAN, Michael (M)   12   0
H: 5 8 W: 10 00 b.Hayes 21-2-90
Honours: Northern Ireland Under-21, 2 full caps.

2008–09	Watford	0	0	
2009–10	Watford	7	0	
2010–11	Watford	5	0	12 0

BUCKLEY, Will (F)   98   18
H: 6 0 W: 13 00 b.Oldham 12-8-88
Source: Curzon Ashton.

2007–08	Rochdale	7	0	
2008–09	Rochdale	37	10	
2009–10	Rochdale	15	3	59 13
2009–10	Watford	6	1	
2010–11	Watford	33	4	39 5

COWIE, Don (M)   313   38
H: 5 5 W: 8 05 b.Inverness 15-2-83
Honours: Scotland 3 full caps.

2000–01	Ross Co	1	0	
2001–02	Ross Co	18	0	
2002–03	Ross Co	30	1	
2003–04	Ross Co	23	0	
2004–05	Ross Co	34	5	
2005–06	Ross Co	32	4	
2006–07	Ross Co	28	7	166 17
2007–08	Inverness CT	37	9	
2008–09	Inverness CT	22	3	59 12
2008–09	Watford	10	3	
2009–10	Watford	41	2	
2010–11	Watford	37	4	88 9

DEENEY, Troy (F)   159   30
H: 5 11 W: 12 00 b.Birmingham 29-6-88
Source: Chelmsley T.

2006–07	Walsall	1	0	
2007–08	Walsall	35	1	
2008–09	Walsall	45	12	
2009–10	Walsall	42	14	123 27
2010–11	Watford	36	3	36 3

DOYLEY, Lloyd (D)   298 1
H: 5 10 W: 12 13 b.Whitechapel 1-12-82
Source: Scholar.

2000–01	Watford	0	0		
2001–02	Watford	20	0		
2002–03	Watford	22	0		
2003–04	Watford	9	0		
2004–05	Watford	29	0		
2005–06	Watford	44	0		
2006–07	Watford	21	0		
2007–08	Watford	36	0		
2008–09	Watford	37	0		
2009–10	Watford	44	1		
2010–11	Watford	36	0	298	1

ELLINGTON, Nathan (F)   424 122
H: 5 10 W: 13 01 b.Bradford 2-7-81
Source: Walton & Hersham.

1998–99	Bristol R	10	1		
1999–2000	Bristol R	37	4		
2000–01	Bristol R	42	15		
2001–02	Bristol R	27	15	116	35
2001–02	Wigan Ath	3	2		
2002–03	Wigan Ath	42	15		
2003–04	Wigan Ath	44	18		
2004–05	Wigan Ath	45	24	134	59
2005–06	WBA	31	5		
2006–07	WBA	34	9		
2007–08	WBA	3	0	68	14
2007–08	Watford	34	4		
2008–09	Watford	0	0		
2008–09	*Derby Co*	27	3	27	3
2009–10	Watford	17	1		
2009–10	*Xanthi*	10	4	10	4
2010–11	Watford	0	0	51	5
2010–11	*Preston NE*	18	2	18	2

EUSTACE, John (M)   302 26
H: 5 11 W: 11 12 b.Solihull 3-11-79
Source: Trainee.

1996–97	Coventry C	0	0		
1997–98	Coventry C	0	0		
1998–99	Coventry C	0	0		
1998–99	Dundee U	11	1	11	1
1999–2000	Coventry C	16	1		
2000–01	Coventry C	32	2		
2001–02	Coventry C	6	0		
2002–03	Coventry C	32	4	86	7
2002–03	*Middlesbrough*	1	0	1	0
2003–04	Stoke C	26	5		
2004–05	Stoke C	7	0		
2005–06	Stoke C	0	0		
2006–07	Stoke C	15	0		
2006–07	*Hereford U*	8	0	8	0
2007–08	Stoke C	26	0	74	5
2007–08	Watford	13	0		
2008–09	Watford	17	2		
2008–09	*Derby Co*	9	1	9	1
2009–10	Watford	42	4		
2010–11	Watford	41	6	113	12

GILMARTIN, Rene (G)   35 0
H: 6 5 W: 13 06 b.Dublin 31-5-87
Source: St Patrick's BC. *Honours:* Eire Youth, Under-21.

2005–06	Walsall	2	0		
2006–07	Walsall	0	0		
2007–08	Walsall	0	0		
2008–09	Walsall	11	0		
2009–10	Walsall	22	0	35	0
2010–11	Watford	0	0		

GRAHAM, Danny (F)   236 77
H: 5 11 W: 12 05 b.Gateshead 12-8-85
Source: Trainee. *Honours:* England Youth, Under-20.

2003–04	Middlesbrough	0	0		
2003–04	*Darlington*	9	2	9	2
2004–05	Middlesbrough	11	1		
2005–06	Middlesbrough	3	0		
2005–06	*Derby Co*	14	0	14	0
2005–06	*Leeds U*	3	0	3	0
2006–07	Middlesbrough	1	0	15	1
2006–07	*Blackpool*	4	1	4	1
2006–07	*Carlisle U*	11	7		
2007–08	Carlisle U	45	14		
2008–09	Carlisle U	44	15	100	36
2009–10	Watford	46	14		
2010–11	Watford	45	23	91	37

HENDERSON, Liam (F)   46 0
H: 5 11 W: 12 02 b.Gateshead 28-12-89
Source: Hartlepool U.

2008–09	Watford	5	0		
2008–09	*Hartlepool U*	8	0	8	0
2009–10	Watford	13	0		
2010–11	Watford	0	0	18	0
2010–11	*Colchester U*	8	0	8	0
2010–11	*Aldershot T*	1	0	1	0
2010–11	*Rotherham U*	11	0	11	0

HOBAN, Tommie (D)   1 0
b. 24-1-94
Source: Scholar.

2010–11	Watford	1	0	1	0

HODSON, Lee (D)   61 1
H: 5 11 W: 11 02 b.Boreham Wood 2-10-91
Source: Scholar. *Honours:* Northern Ireland Under-21, 4 full caps.

2008–09	Watford	1	0		
2009–10	Watford	31	0		
2010–11	Watford	29	1	61	1

JENKINS, Ross (M)   72 2
H: 5 11 W: 12 06 b.Watford 9-11-90
Source: Scholar. *Honours:* England Under-20.

2008–09	Watford	29	1		
2009–10	Watford	24	0		
2010–11	Watford	19	1	72	2

KIERNAN, Rob (D)   13 0
H: 6 1 W: 11 13 b.Rickmansworth 13-1-91
Source: Scholar. *Honours:* Eire Under-21.

2008–09	Watford	0	0		
2009–10	Watford	0	0		
2010–11	Watford	0	0		
2010–11	*Yeovil T*	3	0	3	0
2010–11	*Bradford C*	8	0	8	0
2010–11	*Wycombe W*	2	0	2	0

LOACH, Scott (G)   145 0
H: 6 1 W: 13 01 b.Nottingham 27-5-88
Source: Lincoln C Scholar. *Honours:* England Under-21.

2006–07	Watford	0	0		
2007–08	Watford	0	0		
2007–08	*Morecambe*	2	0	2	0
2007–08	*Bradford C*	20	0	20	0
2008–09	Watford	31	0		
2009–10	Watford	46	0		
2010–11	Watford	46	0	123	0

MARIAPPA, Adrian (D)   177 3
H: 5 10 W: 11 12 b.Harrow 3 10 86
Source: Scholar.

2005–06	Watford	3	0		
2006–07	Watford	19	0		
2007–08	Watford	25	0		
2008–09	Watford	39	1		
2009–10	Watford	46	1		
2010–11	Watford	45	1	177	3

MASSEY, Gavin (F)   4 0
H: 5 11 W: 11 06 b.Watford 14-9-92
Source: Scholar.

2009–10	Watford	1	0		
2010–11	Watford	3	0	4	0

McGINN, Stephen (M)   111 9
H: 5 9 W: 10 01 b.Glasgow 2-12-88
Honours: Scotland Under-21.

2006–07	St Mirren	4	1		
2007–08	St Mirren	25	2		
2008–09	St Mirren	26	1		
2009–10	St Mirren	18	3	73	7
2009–10	Watford	9	0		
2010–11	Watford	29	2	38	2

MINGOIA, Piero (M)   5 0
b.Enfield 20-10-91
Source: Scholar.

2010–11	Watford	5	0	5	0

MURRAY, Sean (M)   2 0
b.Abbots Langley 11-10-93
Source: Scholar. *Honours:* Eire Youth.

2010–11	Watford	2	0	2	0

OSHODI, Eddie (D)   1 0
H: 6 3 W: 12 07 b.Wembley 14-1-92
Source: Scholar.

2008–09	Watford	0	0		
2009–10	Watford	1	0		
2010–11	Watford	0	0	1	0
2010–11	*Dagenham & R*	0	0		

SADLER, Matthew (D)   154 0
H: 5 11 W: 11 08 b.Birmingham 26-2-85
Source: Scholar. *Honours:* England Youth.

2001–02	Birmingham C	0	0		
2002–03	Birmingham C	2	0		
2003–04	Birmingham C	0	0		
2003–04	*Northampton T*	7	0	7	0
2004–05	Birmingham C	0	0		
2005–06	Birmingham C	8	0		
2006–07	Birmingham C	36	0		
2007–08	Birmingham C	5	0	51	0
2007–08	Watford	15	0		
2008–09	Watford	15	0		
2009–10	Watford	0	0		
2009–10	*Stockport Co*	20	0	20	0
2010–11	Watford	0	0	30	0
2010–11	*Shrewsbury T*	46	0	46	0

SORDELL, Marvin (F)   57 14
H: 5 9 W: 12 06 b.Pinner 17-2-91
Source: Scholar.

2009–10	Watford	6	1		
2009–10	*Tranmere R*	8	1	8	1
2010–11	Watford	43	12	49	13

TAYLOR, Martin (D)   271 16
H: 6 4 W: 15 00 b.Ashington 9-11-79
Source: Trainee. *Honours:* England Youth, Under-21.

1997–98	Blackburn R	0	0		
1998–99	Blackburn R	3	0		
1999–2000	Blackburn R	6	0		
1999–2000	*Darlington*	4	0	4	0
1999–2000	*Stockport Co*	7	0	7	0
2000–01	Blackburn R	16	3		
2001–02	Blackburn R	19	0		
2002–03	Blackburn R	33	2		
2003–04	Blackburn R	11	0	88	5
2003–04	Birmingham C	12	1		
2004–05	Birmingham C	7	0		
2005–06	Birmingham C	21	0		
2006–07	Birmingham C	31	0		
2007–08	Birmingham C	4	0		
2007–08	*Norwich C*	8	1	8	1
2008–09	Birmingham C	24	1		
2009–10	Birmingham C	0	0	99	2
2009–10	Watford	19	2		
2010–11	Watford	46	6	65	8

THOMPSON, Adam (D)   10 1
H: 6 2 W: 12 10 b.Harlow 28-9-92
Source: Scholar. *Honours:* Northern Ireland Under-21, 2 full caps.

2010–11	Watford	10	1	10	1

TRAVNER, Jure (D)   141 2
H: 5 11 W: 12 08 b.Celje 28-9-85

2004–05	Publikum Celje	2	0		
2004–05	*Smartno*	20	1	20	1
2005–06	Publikum Celje	25	0		
2005–06	*Dravograd*	6	0	6	0
2006–07	Publikum Celje	31	0	58	0
2007–08	Celje	28	0		
2008–09	Celje	29	1	57	1
2009–10	Watford	0	0		
2010–11	Watford	0	0		

Transferred to St Mirren January 2011.

WALKER, Josh (M)   65 3
H: 5 11 W: 11 13 b.Newcastle 21-2-89
Source: Scholar. *Honours:* England Schools, Youth, Under-20.

2005–06	Middlesbrough	1	0		
2006–07	Middlesbrough	0	0		
2006–07	*Bournemouth*	6	0	6	0
2007–08	*Aberdeen*	8	0	8	0
2007–08	Middlesbrough	0	0		
2008–09	Middlesbrough	6	0		
2009–10	Middlesbrough	1	0	8	0
2009–10	*Northampton T*	3	0		
2009–10	*Rotherham U*	15	3	15	3
2010–11	Watford	5	0	5	0
2010–11	*Stevenage*	1	0	1	0
2010–11	*Northampton T*	19	0	22	0

WHICHELOW, Matt (M)   19 3
b.Islington 28-9-91
Source: Scholar.

2010–11	Watford	19	3	19	3

WBA (87)

BARNES, Giles (M) 105 10
H: 6 0 W: 12 10 b.Barking 5-8-88
Source: Scholar. Honours: England Youth.

2005–06	Derby Co	19	1		
2006–07	Derby Co	39	8		
2007–08	Derby Co	21	1		
2008–09	Derby Co	3	0		
2008–09	Fulham	0	0		
2009–10	Derby Co	0	0	82	10
2009–10	WBA	9	0		
2010–11	WBA	14	0	23	0

BEDNAR, Roman (F) 164 48
H: 6 3 W: 13 03 b.Prague 26-3-83
Honours: Czech Republic Under-21, 8 full caps, 1 goal.

2001–02	Mlada Boleslav	0	0		
2002–03	Mlada Boleslav	0	0		
2003–04	Mlada Boleslav	0	0		
2004–05	Mlada Boleslav	25	6	25	6
2004–05	Kaunas	0	0		
2005–06	Hearts	22	7		
2006–07	Hearts	18	4	40	11
2007–08	WBA	29	13		
2008–09	WBA	26	6		
2009–10	WBA	27	11		
2010–11	WBA	4	0	86	30
2010–11	Leicester C	5	0	5	0
2010–11	Ankaragucu	8	1	8	1

BERAHINO, Saido (F) 0 0
b.Burundi 4-8-93
Source: Scholar.

2010–11	WBA	0	0		

BORJA VALERO (M) 209 16
H: 5 9 W: 11 07 b.Madrid 12-1-85
Honours: Spain Youth.

2005–06	R M Castilla	0	0		
2005–06	R M Castilla	39	2		
2006–07	R M Castilla	37	2	76	4
2007–08	Mallorca	34	4		
2008–09	WBA	30	0		
2009–10	WBA	1	0		
2009–10	Mallorca	33	5	67	9
2010–11	WBA	0	0	31	0
2010–11	Villarreal	35	3	35	3

BROWN, Kayleden (M) 11 0
b.Derry 15-4-92
Source: Scholar. Honours: Wales Youth.

2010–11	WBA	0	0		
2010–11	Tranmere R	4	0	4	0
2010–11	Dagenham & R	3	0	3	0
2010–11	Port Vale	4	0	4	0

BRUNT, Chris (M) 282 53
H: 6 1 W: 13 04 b.Belfast 14-12-84
Source: Trainee. Honours: Northern Ireland Under-21, Under-23, 33 full caps, 1 goal.

2002–03	Middlesbrough	0	0		
2003–04	Middlesbrough	0	0		
2003–04	Sheffield W	9	2		
2004–05	Sheffield W	42	4		
2005–06	Sheffield W	44	7		
2006–07	Sheffield W	44	11		
2007–08	Sheffield W	1	0	140	24
2007–08	WBA	34	4		
2008–09	WBA	34	8		
2009–10	WBA	40	13		
2010–11	WBA	34	4	142	29

CARSON, Scott (G) 197 0
H: 6 3 W: 14 00 b.Whitehaven 3-9-85
Source: Scholar. Honours: England Youth, Under-21, B, 3 full caps.

2002–03	Leeds U	0	0		
2003–04	Leeds U	3	0		
2004–05	Leeds U	0	0	3	0
2004–05	Liverpool	4	0		
2005–06	Liverpool	0	0		
2005–06	Sheffield W	9	0	9	0
2006–07	Liverpool	0	0		
2006–07	Charlton Ath	36	0	36	0
2007–08	Liverpool	0	0	4	0
2007–08	Aston Villa	35	0	35	0
2008–09	WBA	35	0		
2009–10	WBA	43	0		
2010–11	WBA	32	0	110	0

CECH, Marek (D) 196 5
H: 6 0 W: 11 09 b.Trebisov 26-1-83
Honours: Slovakia 44 full caps, 5 goals.

2000–01	Inter Bratislava	2	0		
2001–02	Inter Bratislava	13	0		
2002–03	Inter Bratislava	30	0		
2003–04	Inter Bratislava	26	1	71	1
2004–05	Sparta Prague	17	0		
2005–06	Sparta Prague	0	0	17	0
2005–06	Porto	14	1		
2006–07	Porto	22	1		
2007–08	Porto	16	0	52	2
2008–09	WBA	8	0		
2009–10	WBA	33	2		
2010–11	WBA	15	0	56	2

COX, Simon (F) 151 57
H: 5 10 W: 10 12 b.Reading 28-4-87
Source: Scholar. Honours: Eire 4 full caps, 2 goals.

2005–06	Reading	2	0		
2006–07	Reading	0	0		
2006–07	Brentford	13	0	13	0
2006–07	Northampton T	8	3	8	3
2007–08	Reading	0	0	2	0
2007–08	Swindon T	36	15		
2008–09	Swindon T	45	29	81	44
2009–10	WBA	28	9		
2010–11	WBA	19	1	47	10

DANIELS, Luke (G) 87 0
H: 6 1 W: 12 10 b.Bolton 5-1-88
Source: Manchester U Scholar. Honours: England Youth.

2006–07	WBA	0	0		
2007–08	Motherwell	2	0	2	0
2007–08	WBA	0	0		
2008–09	WBA	0	0		
2008–09	Shrewsbury T	38	0	38	0
2009–10	WBA	0	0		
2009–10	Tranmere R	37	0	37	0
2010–11	WBA	0	0		
2010–11	Charlton Ath	0	0		
2010–11	Rochdale	1	0	1	0
2010–11	Bristol R	9	0	9	0

DAWSON, Craig (D) 87 19
H: 6 0 W: 12 04 b.Rochdale 6-5-90
Source: Radcliffe B.

2008–09	Rochdale	0	0		
2009–10	Rochdale	42	9		
2010–11	WBA	0	0		
2010–11	Rochdale	45	10	87	19

DORRANS, Graham (F) 165 35
H: 5 9 W: 11 07 b.Glasgow 5-5-87
Honours: Scotland Youth, Under-21, 5 full caps.

2006–07	Livingston	8	0		
2006–07	Partick T	15	5	15	5
2006–07	Livingston	34	5		
2007–08	Livingston	34	11	76	16
2008–09	WBA	8	0		
2009–10	WBA	45	13		
2010–11	WBA	21	1	74	14

DOWNING, Paul (D) 6 0
H: 6 1 W: 12 06 b.Taunton 26-10-91
Source: Scholar.

2009–10	WBA	0	0		
2009–10	Hereford U	6	0		
2010–11	WBA	0	0		
2010–11	Hereford U	0	0	6	0
2010–11	Swansea C	0	0		

ELFORD-ALLIYU, Lateef (F) 17 5
H: 5 8 W: 10 12 b.Ibadan 1-6-92
Source: Scholar.

2009–10	WBA	0	0		
2009–10	Hereford U	1	0	1	0
2010–11	WBA	0	0		
2010–11	Tranmere R	16	5	16	5

FORTUNE, Marc-Antoine (F) 336 71
H: 6 0 W: 11 13 b.Cayenne 2-7-81

2000–01	Angouleme	18	3		
2001–02	Angouleme	36	12	54	15
2002–03	Nancy	19	1		
2002–03	Lille	15	0	15	0
2003–04	Rouen	34	10	34	10
2004–05	Brest	33	10	33	10
2005–06	Utrecht	31	6		
2006–07	Utrecht	22	5	53	11

2006–07	Nancy	15	5		
2007–08	Nancy	37	6		
2008–09	Nancy	19	1	90	13
2009–10	Celtic	30	10		
2010–11	Celtic	2	0	32	10
2010–11	WBA	25	2	25	2

GAYLE, Cameron (D) 0 0
b.Birmingham 22-11-92
Source: Scholar.

2010–11	WBA	0	0		

HABER, Marcus (F) 5 0
H: 6 3 W: 13 05 b.Vancouver 11-1-89
Source: Vancouver W. Honours: Canada Youth, Under-23.

2009–10	WBA	0	0		
2009–10	Exeter C	5	0	5	0
2010–11	WBA	0	0		

HURST, James (D) 1 0
b.Sutton Coldfield 31-1-92
Source: Scholar.

2008–09	Portsmouth	0	0		
2009–10	Portsmouth	0	0		
2010–11	Portsmouth	0	0		
2010–11	WBA	1	0	1	0

JARA, Gonzalo (D) 184 5
H: 5 10 W: 12 02 b.Chile 29-8-85
Honours: Chile 40 full caps, 3 goals.

2002	Huachipato	0	0		
2003	Huachipato	17	1		
2004	Huachipato	11	0		
2005	Huachipato	23	0		
2006	Huachipato	18	1	69	2
2007	Colo Colo	23	1		
2008	Colo Colo	25	0		
2009	Colo Colo	16	0	64	1
2009–10	WBA	22	1		
2010–11	WBA	29	1	51	2

KIELY, Dean (G) 664 0
H: 6 1 W: 13 10 b.Salford 10-10-70
Source: WBA School. Honours: England Schools, FA Schools, Youth, Eire B, 11 full caps.

1987–88	Coventry C	0	0		
1988–89	Coventry C	0	0		
1989–90	Coventry C	0	0		
1989–90	Ipswich T	0	0		
1989–90	York C	0	0		
1990–91	York C	17	0		
1991–92	York C	21	0		
1992–93	York C	40	0		
1993–94	York C	46	0		
1994–95	York C	46	0		
1995–96	York C	40	0	210	0
1996–97	Bury	46	0		
1997–98	Bury	46	0		
1998–99	Bury	45	0	137	0
1999–2000	Charlton Ath	45	0		
2000–01	Charlton Ath	25	0		
2001–02	Charlton Ath	38	0		
2002–03	Charlton Ath	38	0		
2003–04	Charlton Ath	37	0		
2004–05	Charlton Ath	36	0		
2005–06	Charlton Ath	3	0	222	0
2005–06	Portsmouth	15	0		
2006–07	Portsmouth	0	0	15	0
2006–07	Luton T	11	0	11	0
2006–07	WBA	17	0		
2007–08	WBA	44	0		
2008–09	WBA	3	0		
2009–10	WBA	5	0		
2010–11	WBA	0	0	69	0

MANTOM, Sam (M) 6 0
b.Stourbridge 20-2-92
Source: Scholar.

2010–11	WBA	0	0		
2010–11	Tranmere R	2	0	2	0
2010–11	Oldham Ath	4	0	4	0

MATTOCK, Joe (D) 108 1
H: 5 11 W: 12 05 b.Leicester 15-5-90
Source: Scholar. Honours: England Youth, Under-21.

2006–07	Leicester C	4	0		
2007–08	Leicester C	31	0		
2008–09	Leicester C	31	1		
2009–10	Leicester C	0	0	66	1
2009–10	WBA	29	0		

2010–11	WBA	0	0	**29**	**0**
2010–11	Sheffield U	13	0	**13**	**0**

MEITE, Abdoulaye (D) 224 2
H: 6 1 W: 12 13 b.Paris 6-10-80
Honours: Ivory Coast 49 full caps, 1 goal.

1998–99	Red Star 93	4	1		
1999–2000	Red Star 93	0	0	**4**	**1**
2000–01	Marseille	1	0		
2001–02	Marseille	10	0		
2002–03	Marseille	28	0		
2003–04	Marseille	30	0		
2004–05	Marseille	34	1		
2005–06	Marseille	13	0	**116**	**1**
2006–07	Bolton W	35	0		
2007–08	Bolton W	21	0	**56**	**0**
2008–09	WBA	18	0		
2009–10	WBA	20	0		
2010–11	WBA	10	0	**48**	**0**

MILLER, Ishmael (F) 99 15
H: 6 3 W: 14 00 b.Manchester 5-3-87
Source: Scholar.

2005–06	Manchester C	1	0		
2006–07	Manchester C	16	0		
2007–08	Manchester C	0	0	**17**	**0**
2007–08	WBA	34	9		
2008–09	WBA	15	3		
2009–10	WBA	15	2		
2010–11	WBA	6	0	**70**	**14**
2010–11	QPR	12	1	**12**	**1**

MORRISON, James (M) 174 15
H: 5 10 W: 10 06 b.Darlington 25-5-86
Source: Trainee. *Honours:* England Youth,
Under-20. Scotland 13 full caps, 1 goal.

2003–04	Middlesbrough	1	0		
2004–05	Middlesbrough	14	0		
2005–06	Middlesbrough	24	1		
2006–07	Middlesbrough	28	2	**67**	**3**
2007–08	WBA	35	4		
2008–09	WBA	30	3		
2009–10	WBA	11	1		
2010–11	WBA	31	4	**107**	**12**

MULUMBU, Youssef (M) 116 11
H: 5 9 W: 10 03 b.Kinshasa 25-1-87
Honours: France Youth, Under-21. DR
Congo 2 full caps.

2006–07	Paris St Germain	12	0		
2007–08	Paris St Germain	1	0		
2007–08	Amiens	23	1	**23**	**1**
2008–09	Paris St Germain	0	0	**13**	**0**
2008–09	WBA	6	0		
2009–10	WBA	40	3		
2010–11	WBA	34	7	**80**	**10**

MYHILL, Boaz (G) 282 0
H: 6 3 W: 14 06 b.California 9-11-82
Source: Scholar. *Honours:* England Youth,
Under-20. Wales 10 full caps.

2000–01	Aston Villa	0	0		
2001–02	Aston Villa	0	0		
2001–02	Stoke C	0	0		
2002–03	Aston Villa	0	0		
2002–03	Bristol C	0	0		
2002–03	Bradford C	2	0	**2**	**0**
2003–04	Aston Villa	0	0		
2003–04	Macclesfield T	15	0	**15**	**0**
2003–04	Stockport Co	2	0	**2**	**0**
2003–04	Hull C	23	0		
2004–05	Hull C	45	0		
2005–06	Hull C	45	0		
2006–07	Hull C	46	0		
2007–08	Hull C	43	0		
2008–09	Hull C	28	0		
2009–10	Hull C	27	0	**257**	**0**
2010–11	WBA	6	0	**6**	**0**

NABI, Adil (F) 0 0
b. 28-2-94
Source: Scholar.

2010–11	WBA	0	0		

ODEMWINGIE, Peter (F) 226 68
H: 6 0 W: 12 11 b.Tashkent 15-7-81
Honours: Nigeria 53 full caps, 9 goals.

2002–03	La Louviere	14	2		
2003–04	La Louviere	27	5		
2004–05	La Louviere	3	2	**44**	**9**
2004–05	Lille	20	4		
2005–06	Lille	26	14		
2006–07	Lille	29	5	**75**	**23**

2007	Lokomotiv Moscow	14	4		
2008	Lokomotiv Moscow	26	10		
2009	Lokomotiv Moscow	25	7		
2010	Lokomotiv Moscow	10	0	**75**	**21**
2010–11	WBA	32	15	**32**	**15**

OLSSON, Jonas (D) 244 13
H: 6 4 W: 12 08 b.Landskrona 10-3-83
Honours: Sweden Under-21, 2 full caps.

2002	Landskrona	0	0		
2003	Landskrona	22	0		
2004	Landskrona	22	1		
2005	Landskrona	12	0	**56**	**1**
2005–06	NEC Nijmegen	34	0		
2006–07	NEC Nijmegen	32	2		
2007–08	NEC Nijmegen	27	3	**93**	**5**
2008–09	WBA	28	2		
2009–10	WBA	43	4		
2010–11	WBA	24	1	**95**	**7**

PABLO (D) 240 12
H: 6 3 W: 13 07 b.Madrigueras 3-8-81
Honours: Spain Under-21, 23 full caps.

2002–03	Albacete	38	1		
2003–04	Albacete	36	1	**74**	**2**
2004–05	Atletico Madrid	35	3		
2005–06	Atletico Madrid	35	2		
2006–07	Atletico Madrid	24	2		
2007–08	Atletico Madrid	34	1		
2008–09	Atletico Madrid	21	1		
2009–10	Atletico Madrid	7	0	**156**	**9**
2010–11	WBA	10	1	**10**	**1**

REID, Steven (M) 287 26
H: 6 0 W: 12 07 b.Kingston 10-3-81
Source: Trainee. *Honours:* England Youth.
Eire Under-21, 23 full caps, 2 goals.

1997–98	Millwall	1	0		
1998–99	Millwall	25	0		
1999–2000	Millwall	21	0		
2000–01	Millwall	37	7		
2001–02	Millwall	35	5		
2002–03	Millwall	20	6	**139**	**18**
2003–04	Blackburn R	16	0		
2004–05	Blackburn R	28	2		
2005–06	Blackburn R	34	4		
2006–07	Blackburn R	3	0		
2007–08	Blackburn R	24	0		
2008–09	Blackburn R	4	0		
2009–10	Blackburn R	4	0	**113**	**6**
2009–10	QPR	2	0	**2**	**0**
2009–10	WBA	10	1		
2010–11	WBA	23	1	**33**	**2**

SAWYERS, Romaine (M) 1 0
H: 5 9 W: 11 00 b.Birmingham 2-11-91
Source: Scholar.

2009–10	WBA	0	0		
2010–11	WBA	0	0		
2010–11	Port Vale	1	0	**1**	**0**

SCHARNER, Paul (D) 312 31
H: 6 3 W: 12 09 b.Scheibbs 11-3-80
Source: St Polten. *Honours:* Austria Youth,
Under-21, 35 full caps.

1998–99	FK Austria	4	0		
1999–2000	FK Austria	12	0		
2000–01	FK Austria	14	0		
2001–02	FK Austria	16	1		
2002–03	FK Austria	29	1		
2003–04	FK Austria	9	1	**84**	**3**
2003–04	Salzburg	13	2		
2004	Brann	7	1		
2004–05	Salzburg	5	1	**18**	**3**
2005	Brann	25	6	**32**	**7**
2005–06	Wigan Ath	16	3		
2006–07	Wigan Ath	25	3		
2007–08	Wigan Ath	37	4		
2008–09	Wigan Ath	29	0		
2009–10	Wigan Ath	38	4		
2010–11	Wigan Ath	0	0	**145**	**14**
2010–11	WBA	33	4	**33**	**4**

SHOREY, Nicky (D) 352 12
H: 5 9 W: 10 08 b.Romford 19-2-81
Source: Trainee. *Honours:* England B, 2 full caps.

1999–2000	Leyton Orient	7	0		
2000–01	Leyton Orient	8	0	**15**	**0**
2000–01	Reading	0	0		
2001–02	Reading	32	0		
2002–03	Reading	43	2		
2003–04	Reading	35	2		
2004–05	Reading	44	3		
2005–06	Reading	40	2		
2006–07	Reading	37	1		
2007–08	Reading	36	2	**267**	**12**
2008–09	Aston Villa	21	0		
2009–10	Aston Villa	3	0	**24**	**0**
2009–10	Nottingham F	9	0	**9**	**0**
2009–10	Fulham	9	0	**9**	**0**
2010–11	WBA	28	0	**28**	**0**

TAMAS, Gabriel (D) 243 12
H: 6 2 W: 12 02 b.Brasov 9-11-83
Honours: Romania 55 full caps, 3 goals.

1998–99	Brasov	1	0		
1999–2000	Brasov	0	0	**1**	**0**
2000–01	Tractorul	15	1		
2001–02	Tractorul	19	2	**34**	**3**
2002–03	Dinamo Bucharest	19	4		
2003–04	Galatasaray	6	0	**6**	**0**
2004	Spartak Moscow	14	0		
2004–05	Dinamo Bucharest	13	0		
2005–06	Dinamo Bucharest	14	1		
2006	Spartak Moscow	3	0	**17**	**0**
2006–07	Celta Vigo	29	0	**29**	**0**
2007–08	Auxerre	27	0	**27**	**0**
2008–09	Dinamo Bucharest	22	0		
2009–10	Dinamo Bucharest	12	2	**80**	**7**
2009–10	WBA	23	2		
2010–11	WBA	26	0	**49**	**2**

TCHOYI, Somen (M) 170 29
H: 6 3 W: 13 10 b.Douala 29-3-83
Honours: Cameroon 15 full caps, 2 goals.

2005	Odd	22	1		
2006	Odd	8	0	**30**	**1**
2006	Stabaek	15	3		
2007	Stabaek	26	4		
2008	Stabaek	8	1	**49**	**8**
2008–09	Salzburg	32	6		
2009–10	Salzburg	36	8	**68**	**14**
2010–11	WBA	23	6	**23**	**6**

THOMAS, Jerome (M) 176 20
H: 5 9 W: 11 09 b.Wembley 23-3-83
Source: Scholar. *Honours:* England Youth,
Under-20, Under-21.

2001–02	Arsenal	0	0		
2001–02	QPR	4	1		
2002–03	Arsenal	0	0		
2002–03	QPR	6	2	**10**	**3**
2003–04	Arsenal	0	0		
2003–04	Charlton Ath	1	0		
2004–05	Charlton Ath	24	3		
2005–06	Charlton Ath	25	1		
2006–07	Charlton Ath	20	3		
2007–08	Charlton Ath	32	0		
2008–09	Charlton Ath	1	0	**103**	**7**
2008–09	Portsmouth	3	0		
2009–10	Portsmouth	0	0	**3**	**0**
2009–10	WBA	27	7		
2010–11	WBA	33	3	**60**	**10**

THORNE, George (M) 2 0
H: 6 2 W: 13 01 b.Chatham 4-1-93
Source: Scholar. *Honours:* England Youth.

2009–10	WBA	1	0		
2010–11	WBA	1	0	**2**	**0**

WOOD, Chris (F) 57 9
H: 6 3 W: 12 10 b.Auckland 7-12-91
Honours: New Zealand Youth, 17 full caps, 1 goal.

2008–09	WBA	2	0		
2009–10	WBA	18	1		
2010–11	WBA	1	0	**21**	**1**
2010–11	Barnsley	7	0	**7**	**0**
2010–11	Brighton & HA	29	8	**29**	**8**

ZUIVERLOON, Gianni (D) 166 8
H: 5 10 W: 11 00 b.Rotterdam 30-12-86
Honours: Holland Under-21.

2004–05	Feyenoord	9	0	**9**	**0**
2005–06	RKC Waalwijk	28	1	**28**	**1**
2006–07	Heerenveen	30	1		
2007–08	Heerenveen	30	2	**60**	**3**
2008–09	WBA	33	0		
2009–10	WBA	30	4		
2010–11	WBA	2	0	**65**	**4**
2010–11	Ipswich T	4	0	**4**	**0**

Scholars
Amenku Elikem; Brown Kayleden; Daniels
Donervorn Joseph; Garmston Bradley;
Goldsmith David; Hingley Mark David;

Lewis Shane; Manesio Sergio; O'Neil Liam
Christian James; O'Sullivan Mani; Roofe
Kemar; Tunnicliffe Jordan; Turton Thomas
Dale; Wellington Niall

WEST HAM U (88)

ABDULLAH, Ahmad (F) 0　0
b.Saudi Arabia 12-11-91
Source: Scholar.
2008–09	West Ham U	0	0
2009–10	West Ham U	0	0
2010–11	West Ham U	0	0

BA, Demba (F) 147　74
H: 6 2　W: 12 13　b.Sevres 25-5-85
Honours: Senegal 10 full caps, 3 goals.
2005–06	Rouen	26 22	26 22
2006–07	Mouscron	10 8	
2007–08	Mouscron	2 0	12 8
2007–08	Hoffenheim	30 12	
2008–09	Hoffenheim	33 14	
2009–10	Hoffenheim	17 5	
2010–11	Hoffenheim	17 6	97 37
2010–11	West Ham U	12 7	12 7

BARRERA, Pablo (M) 86　17
H: 5 9　W: 10 03　b.Tlalnepantla de Baz
21-6-87
Honours: Mexico Youth, 36 full caps, 4 goals.
2005–06	UNAM	1 0	
2006–07	UNAM	5 0	
2007–08	UNAM	24 4	
2008–09	UNAM	14 2	
2009–10	UNAM	28 11	72 17
2010–11	West Ham U	14 0	14 0

BEHRAMI, Valon (M) 183　11
H: 6 0　W: 11 02　b.Kosovo 19-4-85
Honours: Switzerland 30 full caps, 2 goals.
2002–03	Lugano	2 0	2 0
2003–04	Genoa	24 0	24 0
2004–05	Verona	33 3	33 3
2005–06	Lazio	26 2	
2006–07	Lazio	17 1	
2007–08	Lazio	23 1	66 4
2008–09	West Ham U	24 1	
2009–10	West Ham U	27 1	
2010–11	West Ham U	7 2	58 4
Transferred to Fiorentina January 2011.

BOA MORTE, Luis (F) 335　47
H: 5 9　W: 12 06　b.Lisbon 4-8-77
Source: Sporting Lisbon, Lourihanense
(loan). *Honours:* Portugal Youth, Under-21,
28 full caps, 1 goal.
1997–98	Arsenal	15 0	
1998–99	Arsenal	8 0	
1999–2000	Arsenal	2 0	25 0
1999–2000	Southampton	14 1	
2000–01	Southampton	0 0	14 1
2000–01	*Fulham*	39 18	
2001–02	Fulham	23 1	
2002–03	Fulham	29 2	
2003–04	Fulham	33 9	
2004–05	Fulham	31 8	
2005–06	Fulham	35 6	
2006–07	Fulham	15 0	205 44
2006–07	West Ham U	14 1	
2007–08	West Ham U	27 0	
2009–10	West Ham U	1 1	
2010–11	West Ham U	22 0	91 2

BOFFIN, Ruud (G) 1　0
H: 6 5　W: 13 07　b.St Truiden 5-11-87
2010–11	West Ham U	1 0	1 0

BROWN, Jordan (D) 0　0
b.Southend 11-10-91
Source: Scholar.
2010–11	West Ham U	0 0	

COLE, Carlton (F) 220　43
H: 6 3　W: 14 02　b.Croydon 12-11-83
Source: Scholar. *Honours:* England Youth,
Under-20, Under-21, 7 full caps.
2000–01	Chelsea	0 0	
2001–02	Chelsea	3 1	
2002–03	Chelsea	3 3	
2002–03	Wolverhampton W	7 1	7 1
2003–04	Chelsea	0 0	

2003–04	*Charlton Ath*	21 4	21 4
2004–05	Chelsea	0 0	
2004–05	*Aston Villa*	27 3	27 3
2005–06	Chelsea	9 0	25 4
2006–07	West Ham U	17 2	
2007–08	West Ham U	31 4	
2008–09	West Ham U	27 10	
2009–10	West Ham U	30 10	
2010–11	West Ham U	35 5	140 31

COLLISON, Jack (M) 47　5
H: 6 0　W: 13 10　b.Watford 2-10-88
Source: Scholar. *Honours:* Wales Under-21, 8
full caps.
2007–08	West Ham U	2 0	
2008–09	West Ham U	20 3	
2009–10	West Ham U	22 2	
2010–11	West Ham U	3 0	47 5

DA COSTA, Manuel (D) 60　4
H: 6 1　W: 12 12　b.Nancy 6-5-86
2005–06	Nancy	10 0	10 0
2006–07	PSV Eindhoven	15 1	
2007–08	PSV Eindhoven	1 0	16 1
2007–08	Fiorentina	1 0	1 0
2008–09	Sampdoria	2 0	2 0
2009–10	West Ham U	15 2	
2010–11	West Ham U	16 1	31 3

DIAMANTI, Alessandro (F) 140　30
H: 5 9　W: 11 09　b.Prato 2-5-83
2002–03	Prato	2 0	
2003–04	Prato	20 4	
2004–05	Albinoleffe	18 0	
2005–06	Prato	13 5	
2005–06	Albinoleffe	8 0	26 0
2006–07	Prato	25 10	60 19
2007–08	Livorno	26 4	26 4
2009–10	West Ham U	27 7	
2010–11	West Ham U	1 0	28 7
Transferred to Brescia August 2010.

DYER, Kieron (M) 315　32
H: 5 8　W: 10 01　b.Ipswich 29-12-78
Source: Trainee. *Honours:* England Youth,
Under-21, B, 33 full caps.
1996–97	Ipswich T	13 0	
1997–98	Ipswich T	41 4	
1998–99	Ipswich T	37 5	
1999–2000	Newcastle U	30 3	
2000–01	Newcastle U	26 5	
2001–02	Newcastle U	18 3	
2002–03	Newcastle U	35 2	
2003–04	Newcastle U	25 1	
2004–05	Newcastle U	23 4	
2005–06	Newcastle U	11 0	
2006–07	Newcastle U	22 5	
2007–08	Newcastle U	0 0	190 23
2007–08	West Ham U	2 0	
2008–09	West Ham U	7 0	
2009–10	West Ham U	10 0	
2010–11	West Ham U	11 0	30 0
2010–11	*Ipswich T*	4 0	95 9

EDGAR, Anthony (M) 3　0
H: 5 8　W: 11 00　b.Newham 30-9-90
Source: Scholar.
2008–09	West Ham U	0 0	
2009–10	*Bournemouth*	3 0	3 0
2010–11	West Ham U	0 0	

EYJOLFSSON, Holmar (D) 4　0
H: 6 2　W: 11 08　b.Iceland 6-8-90
Honours: Iceland Under-21.
2008–09	West Ham U	0 0	
2009–10	West Ham U	0 0	
2009–10	*Cheltenham T*	4 0	4 0
2010–11	West Ham U	0 0	

FAUBERT, Julien (M) 212　14
H: 5 10　W: 11 08　b.Le Havre 1-8-83
Honours: France 1 full cap, 1 goal.
2002–03	Cannes	5 0	
2003–04	Cannes	19 3	45 4
2004–05	Bordeaux	36 1	
2005–06	Bordeaux	34 5	
2006–07	Bordeaux	26 3	96 9
2007–08	West Ham U	7 0	
2008–09	West Ham U	20 0	
2008–09	*Real Madrid*	2 0	2 0
2009–10	West Ham U	33 1	
2010–11	West Ham U	9 0	69 1

FRY, Matt (D) 36　1
H: 6 1　W: 12 02　b.Longfield 26-9-90
Source: Scholar.
2009–10	West Ham U	0 0	
2009–10	*Gillingham*	11 0	11 0
2010–11	West Ham U	0 0	
2010–11	*Charlton Ath*	25 1	25 1

GABBIDON, Daniel (D) 313　10
H: 6 0　W: 13 05　b.Cwmbran 8-8-79
Source: Trainee. *Honours:* Wales Youth,
Under-21, 44 full caps.
1998–99	WBA	2 0	
1999–2000	WBA	18 0	
2000–01	WBA	0 0	20 0
2000–01	Cardiff C	43 3	
2001–02	Cardiff C	44 3	
2002–03	Cardiff C	24 0	
2003–04	Cardiff C	41 3	
2004–05	Cardiff C	45 1	197 10
2005–06	West Ham U	32 0	
2006–07	West Ham U	18 0	
2007–08	West Ham U	10 0	
2008–09	West Ham U	0 0	
2009–10	West Ham U	10 0	
2010–11	West Ham U	26 0	96 0

GREEN, Rob (G) 400　0
H: 6 3　W: 14 09　b.Chertsey 18-1-80
Source: Trainee. *Honours:* England Youth, B,
11 full caps.
1997–98	Norwich C	2 0	
1998–99	Norwich C	0 0	
1999–2000	Norwich C	3 0	
2000–01	Norwich C	5 0	
2001–02	Norwich C	41 0	
2002–03	Norwich C	46 0	
2003–04	Norwich C	46 0	
2004–05	Norwich C	38 0	
2005–06	Norwich C	42 0	223 0
2006–07	West Ham U	26 0	
2007–08	West Ham U	38 0	
2008–09	West Ham U	38 0	
2009–10	West Ham U	38 0	
2010–11	West Ham U	37 0	177 0

HALL, Robert (F) 0　0
b. 20-10-93
Source: Academy.
2010–11	West Ham U	0 0	

HINES, Zavon (F) 29　2
H: 5 10　W: 10 07　b.Jamaica 27-12-88
Source: Scholar. *Honours:* England Under-21.
2007–08	West Ham U	0 0	
2007–08	*Coventry C*	7 1	7 1
2008–09	West Ham U	0 0	
2009–10	West Ham U	13 1	
2010–11	West Ham U	9 0	22 1

HITZLSPERGER, Thomas (M) 246　31
H: 6 0　W: 11 12　b.Munich 5-4-82
Source: Bayern Munich. *Honours:* Germany
Youth, Under-21, 52 full caps, 6 goals.
2000–01	Aston Villa	1 0	
2001–02	*Chesterfield*	5 0	5 0
2001–02	Aston Villa	12 1	
2002–03	Aston Villa	26 2	
2003–04	Aston Villa	32 3	
2004–05	Aston Villa	28 2	99 6
2005–06	Stuttgart	26 2	
2006–07	Stuttgart	30 7	
2007–08	Stuttgart	25 5	
2008–09	Stuttgart	32 5	
2009–10	Stuttgart	12 1	125 20
2009–10	Lazio	6 1	6 1
2010–11	West Ham U	11 2	11 2

ILUNGA, Herita (D) 232　2
H: 5 11　W: 11 09　b.Kinshasa 25-2-82
Honours: DR Congo 31 full caps, 1 goal.
2002–03	Espanyol B	0 0	
2003–04	St Etienne	32 0	
2004–05	St Etienne	37 1	
2005–06	St Etienne	30 1	
2006–07	St Etienne	36 0	135 2
2007–08	Toulouse	35 0	35 0
2008–09	West Ham U	35 0	
2009–10	West Ham U	16 0	
2010–11	West Ham U	11 0	62 0

JACOBSEN, Lars (D) 291 6
H: 5 11 W: 12 02 b.Odense 29-9-79
Honours: Denmark Youth, Under-21, 41 full caps.

Season	Club				
1996–97	Odense	5	0		
1997–98	Odense	15	0		
1998–99	Odense	0	0		
1999–2000	Odense	27	1		
2000–01	Odense	32	0		
2001–02	Odense	32	1	111	2
2002–03	Hamburg II	5	0		
2002–03	Hamburg	12	1		
2003–04	Hamburg II	1	0	6	0
2003–04	Hamburg	10	0	22	1
2003–04	FC Copenhagen	13	0		
2004–05	FC Copenhagen	27	0		
2005–06	FC Copenhagen	33	3		
2006–07	FC Copenhagen	30	0	103	3
2007–08	Nuremberg	7	0	7	0
2008–09	Everton	5	0	5	0
2009–10	Blackburn R	13	0		
2010–11	Blackburn R	0	0	13	0
2010–11	West Ham U	24	0	24	0

KOVAC, Radoslav (D) 327 18
H: 6 2 W: 12 04 b.Sumperk 27-11-79
Honours: Czech Republic Under-21, 31 full caps, 2 goals.

Season	Club				
1997–98	Olomouc	1	0		
1998–99	Olomouc	20	0		
1999–2000	Olomouc	28	0		
2000–01	Olomouc	27	0		
2001–02	Olomouc	23	1		
2002–03	Olomouc	28	2	127	3
2003–04	Sparta Prague	29	3		
2004–05	Sparta Prague	17	0	46	3
2005	Spartak Moscow	27	4		
2006	Spartak Moscow	27	2		
2007	Spartak Moscow	26	1		
2008	Spartak Moscow	21	2	101	9
2008–09	West Ham U	9	1		
2009–10	West Ham U	31	2		
2010–11	West Ham U	13	0	53	3

KURUCZ, Peter (G) 10 0
H: 6 2 W: 13 09 b.Budapest 30-5-88
Honours: Hungary Under-21.

Season	Club				
2008–09	Ujpest	0	0		
2008–09	Tatabanya	9	0	9	0
2009–10	West Ham U	1	0		
2010–11	West Ham U	0	0	1	0

LARKINS, Jake (G) 0 0
b.Barking 11-1-94
Source: Scholar.

Season	Club		
2010–11	West Ham U	0	0

LEE, Oliver (M) 5 0
H: 5 11 W: 12 07 b.London 11-7-91
Source: Scholar.

Season	Club				
2009–10	West Ham U	0	0		
2010–11	West Ham U	0	0		
2010–11	Dagenham & R	5	0	5	0

LLETGET, Sebastian (M) 0 0
H: 5 10 W: 10 11 b.San Francisco 3-9-92
Honours: USA Youth.

Season	Club		
2010–11	West Ham U	0	0

McCALLUM, Paul (F) 0 0
H: 6 3 b. 28-7-93
Source: Dulwich Hamlet.

Season	Club		
2010–11	West Ham U	0	0

McCARTHY, Benni (F) 364 156
H: 6 0 W: 12 08 b.Cape Town 11-12-77
Honours: South Africa 83 caps, 31 goals.

Season	Club				
1995–96	Seven Stars	29	27		
1996–97	Seven Stars	20	12	49	39
1997–98	Cape Town Spurs	7	4	7	4
1997–98	Ajax	17	9		
1998–99	Ajax	19	11	36	20
1999–2000	Celta Vigo	31	8		
2000–01	Celta Vigo	19	0		
2001–02	Celta Vigo	2	0		
2001–02	Porto	11	12		
2002–03	Celta Vigo	14	2	66	10
2003–04	Porto	29	20		
2004–05	Porto	23	11		
2005–06	Porto	23	3	86	46
2006–07	Blackburn R	36	18		
2007–08	Blackburn R	31	8		
2008–09	Blackburn R	28	10		
2009–10	Blackburn R	14	1	109	37
2009–10	West Ham U	5	0		
2010–11	West Ham U	6	0	11	0

McNAUGHTON, Callum (D) 0 0
b. 25-10-91
Source: Scholar.

Season	Club		
2010–11	West Ham U	0	0

MODELSKI, Filip (D) 0 0
b.Gdynia 28-9-92
Source: Scholar.

Season	Club		
2009–10	West Ham U	0	0
2010–11	West Ham U	0	0

MONCUR, George (M) 0 0
b. 18-8-93
Source: Scholar. *Honours:* England Youth.

Season	Club		
2010–11	West Ham U	0	0

MONTANO, Cristian (F) 0 0
H: 5 11 W: 12 00 b.Colombia 11-12-91
Source: Scholar.

Season	Club		
2010–11	West Ham U	0	0

NOBLE, Mark (M) 159 15
H: 5 11 W: 12 00 b.West Ham 8-5-87
Source: Scholar. *Honours:* England Youth, Under-21.

Season	Club				
2004–05	West Ham U	13	0		
2005–06	West Ham U	5	0		
2005–06	Hull C	5	0	5	0
2006–07	West Ham U	10	2		
2006–07	Ipswich T	13	1	13	1
2007–08	West Ham U	31	3		
2008–09	West Ham U	29	3		
2009–10	West Ham U	27	2		
2010–11	West Ham U	26	4	141	14

NOUBLE, Frank (F) 40 2
H: 6 3 W: 12 08 b.Lewisham 24-9-91
Source: Chelsea Scholar. *Honours:* England Youth.

Season	Club				
2009–10	West Ham U	8	0		
2009–10	WBA	3	0	3	0
2009–10	Swindon T	8	0	8	0
2010–11	West Ham U	2	0	10	0
2010–11	Swansea C	6	1	6	1
2010–11	Barnsley	4	0	4	0
2010–11	Charlton Ath	9	1	9	1

O'NEIL, Gary (M) 308 25
H: 5 10 W: 11 00 b.Beckenham 18-5-83
Source: Scholar. *Honours:* England Youth, Under-20, Under-21.

Season	Club				
1999–2000	Portsmouth	1	0		
2000–01	Portsmouth	10	1		
2001–02	Portsmouth	33	1		
2002–03	Portsmouth	31	3		
2003–04	Portsmouth	3	2		
2003–04	Walsall	7	0	7	0
2004–05	Portsmouth	24	2		
2004–05	Cardiff C	9	1	9	1
2005–06	Portsmouth	36	6		
2006–07	Portsmouth	35	1		
2007–08	Portsmouth	2	0	175	16
2007–08	Middlesbrough	26	0		
2008–09	Middlesbrough	29	4		
2009–10	Middlesbrough	36	4		
2010–11	Middlesbrough	18	0	109	8
2010–11	West Ham U	8	0	8	0

OBINNA, Victor (F) 142 27
H: 5 10 W: 12 04 b.Jos 25-3-87
Honours: Nigeria 39 full caps, 9 goals.

Season	Club				
2005–06	Chievo	26	6		
2006–07	Chievo	24	5		
2007–08	Chievo	32	8	82	19
2008–09	Internazionale	9	1	9	1
2009–10	Malaga	26	4	26	4
On loan from Internazionale.					
2010–11	West Ham U	25	3	25	3

PARKER, Scott (M) 313 24
H: 5 9 W: 11 10 b.Lambeth 13-10-80
Source: Trainee. *Honours:* England Schools, Youth, Under-21, 6 full caps.

Season	Club				
1997–98	Charlton Ath	3	0		
1998–99	Charlton Ath	4	0		
1999–2000	Charlton Ath	15	1		
2000–01	Charlton Ath	20	1		
2000–01	Norwich C	6	1	6	1
2001–02	Charlton Ath	38	1		
2002–03	Charlton Ath	28	4		
2003–04	Charlton Ath	20	2	128	9
2003–04	Chelsea	11	1		
2004–05	Chelsea	4	0	15	1
2005–06	Newcastle U	26	1		
2006–07	Newcastle U	29	3	55	4
2007–08	West Ham U	18	1		
2008–09	West Ham U	28	1		
2009–10	West Ham U	31	2		
2010–11	West Ham U	32	5	109	9

PIQUIONNE, Frederic (F) 313 69
H: 6 2 W: 12 00 b.New Caledonia 8-12-78
Source: Martinique. *Honours:* France B, 1 full cap.

Season	Club				
2000–01	Nimes	8	3	8	3
2001–02	Rennes	20	3		
2002–03	Rennes	31	10		
2003–04	Rennes	32	5	83	18
2004–05	St Etienne	37	11		
2005–06	St Etienne	34	6		
2006–07	St Etienne	18	6	89	23
2006–07	Monaco	14	5		
2007–08	Monaco	32	7	46	12
2008–09	Lyon	19	2	19	2
On loan from Lyon.					
2009–10	Portsmouth	34	5	34	5
On loan from Lyon.					
2010–11	West Ham U	34	6	34	6

REID, Winston (D) 90 2
H: 6 3 W: 13 10 b.North Shore 3-7-88
Honours: Denmark Youth, Under-21. New Zealand 9 full caps, 1 goal.

Season	Club				
2005–06	Midtjylland	9	0		
2006–07	Midtjylland	11	0		
2007–08	Midtjylland	9	0		
2008–09	Midtjylland	25	2		
2009–10	Midtjylland	29	0	83	2
2010–11	West Ham U	7	0	7	0

SANCHEZ, Sergio (D) 0 0
b.Spain 20-9-92
Source: Barcelona.

Season	Club		
2010–11	West Ham U	0	0

SEARS, Freddie (F) 73 2
H: 5 8 W: 10 01 b.Hornchurch 27-11-89
Source: Scholar. *Honours:* England Youth, Under-21.

Season	Club				
2007–08	West Ham U	7	1		
2008–09	West Ham U	17	0		
2009–10	West Ham U	1	0		
2009–10	Crystal Palace	18	0	18	0
2009–10	Coventry C	10	0	10	0
2010–11	West Ham U	11	1	36	2
2010–11	Scunthorpe U	9	0	9	0

SPECTOR, Jonathan (D) 124 1
H: 6 0 W: 12 08 b.Chicago 1-3-86
Source: Chicago Sockers. *Honours:* USA Youth, 31 full caps.

Season	Club				
2003–04	Manchester U	0	0		
2004–05	Manchester U	3	0		
2005–06	Manchester U	0	0	3	0
2005–06	Charlton Ath	20	0	20	0
2006–07	West Ham U	25	0		
2007–08	West Ham U	26	0		
2008–09	West Ham U	9	0		
2009–10	West Ham U	27	0		
2010–11	West Ham U	14	1	101	1

SPENCE, Jordan (D) 43 0
H: 6 2 W: 12 07 b.Woodford 24-5-90
Source: Scholar. *Honours:* England Youth, Under-21.

Season	Club				
2007–08	West Ham U	0	0		
2008–09	West Ham U	0	0		
2008–09	Leyton Orient	20	0	20	0
2009–10	West Ham U	1	0		
2009–10	Scunthorpe U	9	0	9	0
2010–11	West Ham U	2	0	3	0
2010–11	Bristol C	11	0	11	0

STANISLAS, Junior (M) 47 7
H: 6 0 W: 12 00 b.Kidbrooke 26-11-89
Source: Scholar. *Honours:* England Youth, Under-21.

Season	Club				
2007–08	West Ham U	0	0		
2008–09	West Ham U	9	2		
2008–09	Southend U	6	1	6	1
2009–10	West Ham U	26	3		
2010–11	West Ham U	6	1	41	6

STECH, Marek (G)　　　**3　0**
H: 6 3　W: 14 00　b.Prague 28-1-90
Source: Sparta Prague, West Ham U Scholar.
Honours: Czech Republic Youth, Under-21.

2008–09	West Ham U	0	0	
2008–09	*Wycombe W*	2	0	**2　0**
2009–10	West Ham U	0	0	
2009–10	*Bournemouth*	1	0	**1　0**
2010–11	West Ham U	0	0	

STREET, Adam (G)　　　**0　0**
b.Canada 7-7-91

2008–09	West Ham U	0	0
2009–10	West Ham U	0	0
2010–11	West Ham U	0	0

TOMKINS, James (D)　　　**67　2**
H: 6 3　W: 11 10　b.Basildon 29-3-89
Source: Scholar. *Honours:* England Schools, Youth, Under-21.

2005–06	West Ham U	0	0	
2006–07	West Ham U	0	0	
2007–08	West Ham U	6	0	
2008–09	West Ham U	12	1	
2008–09	*Derby Co*	7	0	**7　0**
2009–10	West Ham U	23	0	
2010–11	West Ham U	19	1	**60　2**

UPSON, Matthew (D)　　　**301　9**
H: 6 1　W: 11 04　b.Eye 18-4-79
Source: Trainee. *Honours:* England Youth, Under-21, 21 full caps, 2 goals.

1995–96	Luton T	0	0	
1996–97	Luton T	1	0	**1　0**
1996–97	Arsenal	0	0	
1997–98	Arsenal	5	0	
1998–99	Arsenal	5	0	
1999–2000	Arsenal	8	0	
2000–01	Arsenal	2	0	
2000–01	*Nottingham F*	1	0	**1　0**
2000–01	*Crystal Palace*	7	0	**7　0**
2001–02	Arsenal	14	0	
2002–03	Arsenal	0	0	**34　0**
2002–03	*Reading*	14	0	**14　0**
2002–03	Birmingham C	14	0	
2003–04	Birmingham C	30	0	
2004–05	Birmingham C	36	2	
2005–06	Birmingham C	24	1	
2006–07	Birmingham C	9	2	**113　5**
2006–07	West Ham U	2	0	
2007–08	West Ham U	29	1	
2008–09	West Ham U	37	0	
2009–10	West Ham U	33	3	
2010–11	West Ham U	30	0	**131　4**

VOSE, Dominic (M)　　　**0　0**
b. 23-11-93
Source: Academy.

2010–11	West Ham U	0	0

WEAREN, Eoin Patrick (M)　　　**0　0**
b. 2-10-92
Source: Scholar.

2009–10	West Ham U	0	0
2010–11	West Ham U	0	0

Scholars
Cowler Samuel Paul; Driver Callum; Fanimo Matthias Olubori; Hunt Declan; Hurley Lamar Aaron; Larkins Jake; Lee Kenzer; Potts Daniel; Powell Jack Patrick; Tombides Dylan James; Turgott Blair Sebastian; Wootton David; Young Jake

WIGAN ATH (89)

ALCARAZ, Antolin (D)　　　**214　11**
H: 6 0　W: 12 08　b.Roque Gonzalez 30-7-82
Honours: Paraguay 16 full caps, 1 goal.

2002–03	Beira-Mar	7	0	
2003–04	Beira-Mar	24	1	
2004–05	Beira-Mar	24	1	
2005–06	Beira-Mar	31	0	
2006–07	Beira-Mar	26	3	**112　5**
2007–08	Club Brugge	10	1	
2008–09	Club Brugge	29	3	
2009–10	Club Brugge	29	1	**68　5**
2010–11	Wigan Ath	34	1	**34　1**

AMAYA, Antonio (D)　　　**191　7**
H: 6 3　W: 13 07　b.Madrid 31-5-83

2002–03	Rayo Vallecano B	23	2	**23　2**
2003–04	*SS Reyes*	15	0	**15　0**
2004–05	Rayo Vallecano	22	0	
2005–06	Rayo Vallecano	22	0	
2006–07	Rayo Vallecano	34	1	
2007–08	Rayo Vallecano	29	3	
2008–09	Rayo Vallecano	18	1	
2009–10	Wigan Ath	0	0	
2010–11	Wigan Ath	0	0	
2010–11	*Rayo Vallecano*	28	0	**153　5**

BOSELLI, Mauro (F)　　　**147　49**
H: 6 0　W: 11 11　b.Capital Federal 22-5-85
Honours: Argentina Youth, 3 full caps, 1 goal.

2002–03	Boca Juniors	1	0	
2003–04	Boca Juniors	0	0	
2004–05	Boca Juniors	10	2	
2005–06	Malaga	32	5	**32　5**
2006–07	Boca Juniors	12	4	
2007–08	Boca Juniors	21	4	**44　10**
2008–09	Estudiantes	25	10	
2009–10	Estudiantes	31	22	**56　32**
2010–11	Wigan Ath	8	0	**8　0**
2010–11	*Genoa*	7	2	**7　2**

BOYCE, Emmerson (D)　　　**387　14**
H: 6 0　W: 12 03　b.Aylesbury 24-9-79
Source: Trainee. *Honours:* Barbados 2 full caps.

1997–98	Luton T	0	0	
1998–99	Luton T	1	0	
1999–2000	Luton T	30	1	
2000–01	Luton T	42	3	
2001–02	Luton T	37	0	
2002–03	Luton T	34	0	
2003–04	Luton T	42	4	**186　8**
2004–05	Crystal Palace	27	0	
2005–06	Crystal Palace	42	2	**69　2**
2006–07	Wigan Ath	34	0	
2007–08	Wigan Ath	25	0	
2008–09	Wigan Ath	27	1	
2009–10	Wigan Ath	24	3	
2010–11	Wigan Ath	22	0	**132　4**

BREEZE, Jonathan (M)　　　**0　0**
b.Birkenhead 22-10-91
Source: Scholar. *Honours:* Northern Ireland Under-21.

2010–11	Wigan Ath	0	0

BUXTON, Adam (D)　　　**0　0**
H: 6 1　W: 12 10　b.Liverpool 12-5-92
Source: Scholar.

2010–11	Wigan Ath	0	0

CALDWELL, Steven (D)　　　**246　11**
H: 6 2　W: 13 12　b.Stirling 12-9-80
Source: Trainee. *Honours:* Scotland Youth, Under-21, B, 12 full caps.

1997–98	Newcastle U	0	0	
1998–99	Newcastle U	0	0	
1999–2000	Newcastle U	0	0	
2000–01	Newcastle U	9	0	
2001–02	Newcastle U	0	0	
2001–02	*Blackpool*	6	0	**6　0**
2001–02	*Bradford C*	9	0	**9　0**
2002–03	Newcastle U	14	1	
2003–04	Newcastle U	5	0	**28　1**
2003–04	*Leeds U*	13	1	**13　1**
2004–05	Sunderland	41	4	
2005–06	Sunderland	24	0	
2006–07	Sunderland	11	0	**76　4**
2006–07	Burnley	17	0	
2007–08	Burnley	29	2	
2008–09	Burnley	45	2	
2009–10	Burnley	13	1	
2010–11	Burnley	10	0	**104　5**
2010–11	Wigan Ath	10	0	**10　0**

CALDWELL, Gary (D)　　　**293　12**
H: 5 11　W: 11 10　b.Stirling 12-4-82
Source: Trainee. *Honours:* Scotland Under-21, 4 full caps, 2 goals.

1998–99	Newcastle U	0	0	
1999–2000	Newcastle U	0	0	
2000–01	Newcastle U	0	0	
2001–02	Newcastle U	0	0	
2001–02	*Darlington*	4	0	**4　0**
2001–02	*Hibernian*	11	0	
2002–03	Newcastle U	0	0	
2002–03	*Coventry C*	36	0	**36　0**
2003–04	Newcastle U	0	0	
2003–04	*Derby Co*	9	0	**9　0**
2003–04	Hibernian	17	1	
2004–05	Hibernian	37	3	
2005–06	Hibernian	34	1	**99　5**
2006–07	Celtic	21	0	
2007–08	Celtic	35	1	
2008–09	Celtic	36	3	
2009–10	Celtic	14	1	**106　5**
2009–10	Wigan Ath	16	2	
2010–11	Wigan Ath	23	0	**39　2**

CHO, Won-Hee (M)　　　**25　1**
H: 5 10　W: 11 07　b.South Korea 17-4-83
Honours: South Korea 36 full caps, 1 goal.

2008–09	Wigan Ath	1	0	
2009–10	Wigan Ath	4	0	
2010–11	Wigan Ath	0	0	**5　0**
2010–11	*Blue Wings*	20	1	**20　1**

DE RIDDER, Daniel (M)　　　**89　6**
H: 5 11　W: 10 12　b.Amsterdam 6-3-84
Honours: Holland Under-21.

2003–04	Ajax	15	1	
2004–05	Ajax	15	2	**30　3**
2005–06	Celta Vigo	17	1	
2006–07	Celta Vigo	3	0	**20　1**
2007–08	Birmingham C	10	0	**10　0**
2008–09	Wigan Ath	18	0	
2009–10	Wigan Ath	0	0	
2010–11	Wigan Ath	0	0	**18　0**
2010–11	*Hapoel Tel Aviv*	11	2	**11　2**

DI SANTO, Franco (F)　　　**110　15**
H: 6 4　W: 13 01　b.Mendoza 7-4-89
Source: Audax Italiano. *Honours:* Argentina Under-20.

2006	Audax Italiano	18	6	
2007	Audax Italiano	37	7	**55　13**
2007–08	Chelsea	0	0	
2008–09	Chelsea	8	0	
2009–10	Chelsea	0	0	
2009–10	*Blackburn R*	22	1	**22　1**
2010–11	Chelsea	0	0	**8　0**
2010–11	Wigan Ath	25	1	**25　1**

DIAME, Mohamed (M)　　　**136　5**
H: 6 1　W: 11 02　b.Creteil 14-6-87
Honours: Senegal 2 full caps.

2006–07	Lens	0	0	
2007–08	Linares	31	1	**31　1**
2008–09	Rayo Vallecano	35	2	**35　2**
2009–10	Wigan Ath	34	1	
2010–11	Wigan Ath	36	1	**70　2**

FIGUEROA, Maynor (D)　　　**132　5**
H: 5 11　W: 12 02　b.Jutiapa 2-5-83
Honours: Honduras 77 full caps, 2 goals.

2000–01	Victoria La Ceiba	2	0	
2001–02	Victoria La Ceiba	22	2	**24　2**
2007–08	Wigan Ath	2	0	
2008–09	Wigan Ath	38	1	
2009–10	Wigan Ath	35	1	
2010–11	Wigan Ath	33	1	**108　3**

GOHOURI, Steve (D)　　　**256　38**
H: 6 2　W: 13 01　b.Treichville 8-2-81
Honours: Ivory Coast 13 full caps, 3 goals.

1999–2000	Paris St Germain B	1	0	**1　0**
1999–2000	Bnei Yehuda	13	4	**13　4**
2000–01	Yverdon	34	9	
2001–02	Yverdon	18	2	
2002–03	Yverdon	20	1	**72　12**
2002–03	Bologna	0	0	
2003–04	Vaduz	18	5	
2004–05	Vaduz	28	5	
2005–06	Vaduz	7	0	**53　10**
2005–06	Young Boys	20	5	
2006–07	Young Boys	16	3	**36　8**
2006–07	Mgladbach	14	0	
2007–08	Mgladbach	17	0	
2008–09	Mgladbach	15	2	**46　2**
2009–10	Mgladbach II	3	0	**3　0**
2009–10	Wigan Ath	5	1	
2010–11	Wigan Ath	27	1	**32　2**

GOLOBART, Roman (D)　　　**0　0**
H: 6 4　W: 13 10　b.Barcelona 21-3-92
Source: Espanyol.

2010–11	Wigan Ath	0	0

GOMEZ, Jordi (M)　　　**103　14**
H: 5 10　W: 11 09　b.Barcelona 24-5-85

2006–07	Espanyol B	21	0	**21　0**
2007–08	Espanyol	2	0	**2　0**

On loan from Espanyol.

2008–09	Swansea C	44	12

2009–10	Swansea C	0	0	44	12
2009–10	Wigan Ath	23	1		
2010–11	Wigan Ath	13	1	36	2

HOLT, Joe (M)   6 2
H: 5 10 W: 10 05 b.Huyton 1-2-90
Source: Scholar.

2008–09	Wigan Ath	0	0		
2009–10	Wigan Ath	0	0		
2010	Ostersund	6	2	6	2
2010–11	Wigan Ath	0	0		

KIRKLAND, Chris (G)   193 0
H: 6 5 W: 14 08 b.Barwell 2-5-81
Source: Trainee. *Honours:* England Youth, Under-21, 1 full cap.

1997–98	Coventry C	0	0		
1998–99	Coventry C	0	0		
1999–2000	Coventry C	0	0		
2000–01	Coventry C	23	0		
2001–02	Coventry C	1	0	24	0
2001–02	Liverpool	1	0		
2002–03	Liverpool	8	0		
2003–04	Liverpool	6	0		
2004–05	Liverpool	10	0		
2005–06	Liverpool	0	0		
2005–06	WBA	10	0	10	0
2006–07	Liverpool	0	0	25	0
2006–07	Wigan Ath	26	0		
2007–08	Wigan Ath	37	0		
2008–09	Wigan Ath	32	0		
2009–10	Wigan Ath	32	0		
2010–11	Wigan Ath	4	0	131	0
2010–11	Leicester C	3	0	3	0

KOUMAS, Jason (M)   371 64
H: 5 10 W: 11 02 b.Wrexham 25-9-79
Source: Trainee. *Honours:* Wales 34 full caps, 10 goals.

1997–98	Tranmere R	0	0		
1998–99	Tranmere R	23	3		
1999–2000	Tranmere R	23	2		
2000–01	Tranmere R	39	10		
2001–02	Tranmere R	38	8		
2002–03	Tranmere R	4	2	127	25
2002–03	WBA	32	4		
2003–04	WBA	42	10		
2004–05	WBA	10	0		
2005–06	WBA	0	0		
2005–06	Cardiff C	44	12		
2006–07	WBA	39	9	123	23
2007–08	Wigan Ath	30	1		
2008–09	Wigan Ath	16	0		
2009–10	Wigan Ath	8	1		
2010–11	Wigan Ath	0	0	54	2
2010–11	Cardiff C	23	2	67	14

LANGLEY, Josh (M)   0 0
b.Warrington 13-8-92
Source: Scholar.

2010–11	Wigan Ath	0	0		

McARTHUR, James (M)   186 9
H: 5 9 W: 9 13 b.Glasgow 7-10-87
Honours: Scotland 4 full caps, 1 goal.

2004–05	Hamilton A	6	0		
2005–06	Hamilton A	20	1		
2006–07	Hamilton A	36	1		
2007–08	Hamilton A	34	4		
2008–09	Hamilton A	37	2		
2009–10	Hamilton A	35	1	168	8
2010–11	Wigan Ath	18	0	18	0

McCARTHY, James (M)   139 18
H: 5 11 W: 11 05 b.Glasgow 12-11-90
Honours: Eire Youth, Under-21, 3 full caps.

2006–07	Hamilton A	23	1		
2007–08	Hamilton A	35	7		
2008–09	Hamilton A	37	6	95	14
2009–10	Wigan Ath	20	1		
2010–11	Wigan Ath	24	3	44	4

McMANAMAN, Callum (F)   4 0
H: 5 9 W: 11 03 b.Huyton 25-4-91
Source: Everton.

2008–09	Wigan Ath	1	0		
2009–10	Wigan Ath	0	0		
2010–11	Wigan Ath	3	0	4	0

MOSES, Victor (M)   93 13
H: 5 10 W: 11 07 b.Lagos 12-12-90
Source: Scholar. *Honours:* England Youth, Under-21.

2007–08	Crystal Palace	13	3		

2008–09	Crystal Palace	27	2		
2009–10	Crystal Palace	18	6	58	11
2009–10	Wigan Ath	14	1		
2010–11	Wigan Ath	21	1	35	2

MUSTOE, Jordan (M)   0 0
b.Birkenhead 28-1-91
Source: Scholar.

2009–10	Wigan Ath	0	0		
2010–11	Wigan Ath	0	0		

N'ZOGBIA, Charles (M)   200 24
H: 5 9 W: 11 00 b.Le Havre 28-5-86
Honours: France Youth, Under-21, 2 full caps, 1 goal.

2004–05	Newcastle U	14	0		
2005–06	Newcastle U	32	5		
2006–07	Newcastle U	22	0		
2007–08	Newcastle U	31	3		
2008–09	Newcastle U	18	1	117	9
2008–09	Wigan Ath	13	1		
2009–10	Wigan Ath	36	5		
2010–11	Wigan Ath	34	9	83	15

NICHOLLS, Lee (G)   0 0
b.Huyton 5-10-92
Source: Scholar.

2009–10	Wigan Ath	0	0		
2010–11	Wigan Ath	0	0		
2010–11	Hartlepool U	0	0		
2010–11	Shrewsbury T	0	0		
2010–11	Sheffield W	0	0		

OAKES, Thomas (M)   0 0
b.Wigan 3-2-93
Source: Scholar.

2010–11	Wigan Ath	0	0		

PISCU (D)   39 1
H: 6 0 W: 12 00 b.As Pontes 25-2-87

2006–07	La Coruna	0	0		
2007–08	La Coruna B	12	0	12	0
2007–08	La Coruna	15	0		
2008–09	La Coruna	8	1		
2009–10	La Coruna	3	0	26	1
2010–11	Wigan Ath	1	0	1	0

POLLITT, Mike (G)   503 0
H: 6 4 W: 15 03 b.Farnworth 29-2-72
Source: Trainee.

1990–91	Manchester U	0	0		
1990–91	Oldham Ath	0	0		
1991–92	Bury	0	0		
1992–93	Lincoln C	27	0		
1993–94	Lincoln C	30	0	57	0
1994–95	Darlington	40	0		
1995–96	Darlington	15	0	55	0
1995–96	Notts Co	0	0		
1996–97	Notts Co	8	0		
1997–98	Notts Co	2	0	10	0
1997–98	Oldham Ath	16	0	16	0
1997–98	Gillingham	6	0	6	0
1997–98	Brentford	5	0	5	0
1997–98	Sunderland	0	0		
1998–99	Rotherham U	46	0		
1999–2000	Rotherham U	46	0		
2000–01	Chesterfield	46	0	46	0
2001–02	Rotherham U	46	0		
2002–03	Rotherham U	41	0		
2003–04	Rotherham U	43	0		
2004–05	Rotherham U	45	0	267	0
2005–06	Wigan Ath	24	0		
2006–07	Wigan Ath	3	0		
2006–07	Ipswich T	1	0	1	0
2006–07	Burnley	4	0	4	0
2007–08	Wigan Ath	1	0		
2008–09	Wigan Ath	3	0		
2009–10	Wigan Ath	4	0		
2010–11	Wigan Ath	1	0	36	0

REDMOND, Daniel (D)   0 0
b.Liverpool 2-3-91
Source: Scholar.

2009–10	Wigan Ath	0	0		
2010–11	Wigan Ath	0	0		

ROBINSON, Jordan (D)   0 0
b.Yarm 28-4-91
Source: Middlesbrough.

2010–11	Wigan Ath	0	0		

RODALLEGA, Hugo (F)   246 99
H: 5 11 W: 11 05 b.Valle del Cauca 25-7-85
Honours: Colombia 38 full caps, 8 goals.

2004	Quindio	32	31	32	31
2005	Dep Cali	26	12	26	12
2005–06	Monterrey	14	3		
2006–07	Atlas	17	5	17	5
2006–07	Monterrey	15	1	29	4
2007–08	Necaxa	36	16		
2008–09	Necaxa	17	9	53	25
2008–09	Wigan Ath	15	3		
2009–10	Wigan Ath	38	10		
2010–11	Wigan Ath	36	9	89	22

ROUTLEDGE, Jon (M)   15 1
H: 5 7 W: 11 05 b.Liverpool 23-11-89
Source: Liverpool.

2008–09	Wigan Ath	1	0		
2009–10	Wigan Ath	0	0		
2010–11	Wigan Ath	0	0	1	0
2010–11	Hamilton A	14	1	14	1

Transferred to Hamilton A February 2011.

RUGG, Jordan (M)   0 0
b.Liverpool 15-9-91
Source: Scholar.

2010–11	Wigan Ath	0	0		

SAMMON, Conor (F)   157 34
H: 5 10 W: 11 11 b.Dublin 13-4-87
Honours: Eire Under-21.

2005	UCD	7	0		
2006	UCD	31	7		
2007	UCD	31	6	69	13
2008	Derry C	16	3	16	3
2008–09	Kilmarnock	17	1		
2009–10	Kilmarnock	25	1		
2010–11	Kilmarnock	23	15	65	17
2010–11	Wigan Ath	7	1	7	1

SERRANO, Abian (M)   0 0
Source: Las Palmas.

2009–10	Wigan Ath	0	0		
2010–11	Wigan Ath	0	0		

STAM, Ronnie (M)   203 7
H: 5 9 W: 9 11 b.Breda 18-6-84

2002–03	NAC Breda	1	0		
2003–04	NAC Breda	21	1		
2004–05	NAC Breda	14	0		
2005–06	NAC Breda	28	1		
2006–07	NAC Breda	27	2		
2007–08	NAC Breda	29	0		
2008–09	NAC Breda	1	0	121	4
2008–09	Twente	24	1		
2009–10	Twente	33	1	57	2
2010–11	Wigan Ath	25	1	25	1

THOMAS, Hendry (M)   55 0
H: 5 11 W: 12 08 b.La Ceiba 23-2-85
Source: Club Olimpija. *Honours:* Honduras 48 full caps, 2 goals.

2009–10	Wigan Ath	31	0		
2010–11	Wigan Ath	24	0	55	0

WATSON, Ben (M)   236 27
H: 5 10 W: 10 11 b.Camberwell 9-7-85
Source: Scholar. *Honours:* England Under-21.

2002–03	Crystal Palace	5	0		
2003–04	Crystal Palace	16	1		
2004–05	Crystal Palace	21	0		
2005–06	Crystal Palace	42	4		
2006–07	Crystal Palace	25	3		
2007–08	Crystal Palace	42	5		
2008–09	Crystal Palace	18	5	169	18
2008–09	Wigan Ath	10	2		
2009–10	Wigan Ath	5	1		
2009–10	QPR	16	2	16	2
2009–10	WBA	7	1	7	1
2010–11	Wigan Ath	29	3	44	6

Scholars
Astles Ryan Stephen; Bingham Rakish; Boothman Steven Geoffrey; Chow Timothy Alexander; Girvan Michael; Lynch Jonathon Paul; Morris Callum Neil; Myler Sean Francis; Phillips Jack; Sheego Abubakar Ahmed; Waters Darius Josef; Watson Ryan; Willis Liam

WOLVERHAMPTON W (90)

BASSO, Adriano (G) 165 0
H: 6 1 W: 11 07 b.Jundiai 18-4-75
Source: Woking.

2005–06	Bristol C	29	0	
2006–07	Bristol C	45	0	
2007–08	Bristol C	44	0	
2008–09	Bristol C	43	0	
2009–10	Bristol C	4	0	
2010–11	Bristol C	0	0	165 0
2010–11	Wolverhampton W	0	0	

BATTH, Danny (D) 28 1
H: 6 3 W: 13 05 b.Brierley Hill 21-9-90
Source: Scholar.

2009–10	Wolverhampton W	0	0	
2009–10	*Colchester U*	17	1	17 1
2010–11	Wolverhampton W	0	0	
2010–11	*Sheffield U*	1	0	1 0
2010–11	*Sheffield W*	10	0	10 0

BERRA, Christophe (D) 202 4
H: 6 1 W: 12 10 b.Edinburgh 31-1-85
Honours: Scotland Under-21, B, 13 full caps, 1 goal.

2003–04	Hearts	6	0	
2004–05	Hearts	12	0	
2005–06	Hearts	12	1	
2006–07	Hearts	35	1	
2007–08	Hearts	35	2	
2008–09	Hearts	23	0	123 4
2008–09	Wolverhampton W	15	0	
2009–10	Wolverhampton W	32	0	
2010–11	Wolverhampton W	32	0	79 0

CASSIDY, Jake (F) 0 0
b. 9-2-93
Source: Airbus UK. *Honours:* Wales Youth, Under-21.

2010–11	Wolverhampton W	0	0

CRADDOCK, Jody (D) 519 20
H: 6 0 W: 12 04 b.Redditch 25-7-75
Source: Christchurch.

1993–94	Cambridge U	20	0	
1994–95	Cambridge U	38	0	
1995–96	Cambridge U	46	3	
1996–97	Cambridge U	41	1	145 4
1997–98	Sunderland	32	0	
1998–99	Sunderland	6	0	
1999–2000	Sunderland	19	0	
1999–2000	*Sheffield U*	10	0	10 0
2000–01	Sunderland	34	0	
2001–02	Sunderland	30	1	
2002–03	Sunderland	25	1	146 2
2003–04	Wolverhampton W	32	1	
2004–05	Wolverhampton W	42	1	
2005–06	Wolverhampton W	18	0	
2006–07	Wolverhampton W	34	4	
2007–08	Wolverhampton W	23	1	
2007–08	*Stoke C*	4	0	4 0
2008–09	Wolverhampton W	17	1	
2009–10	Wolverhampton W	33	5	
2010–11	Wolverhampton W	15	1	214 14

DAVIS, David (M) 31 2
H: 5 8 W: 12 03 b.Smethwick 20-2-91
Source: Scholar.

2009–10	Wolverhampton W	0	0	
2009–10	*Darlington*	5	0	5 0
2010–11	Wolverhampton W	0	0	
2010–11	*Walsall*	7	0	7 0
2010–11	*Shrewsbury T*	19	2	19 2

DOHERTY, Matthew (M) 0 0
b.Dublin 16-1-92
Source: Portsmouth.

2010–11	Wolverhampton W	0	0

DOYLE, Kevin (F) 257 89
H: 5 11 W: 12 06 b.Adamstown 18-9-83
Source: Adamstown, Wexford, St Patrick's Ath. *Honours:* Eire Under-21, 41 full caps, 9 goals.

2004	Cork C	32	13	
2005	Cork C	11	7	43 20
2005–06	Reading	45	18	
2006–07	Reading	32	13	
2007–08	Reading	36	6	
2008–09	Reading	41	18	154 55
2009–10	Wolverhampton W	34	9	
2010–11	Wolverhampton W	26	5	60 14

DUNLEAVY, Johnny (D) 3 0
H: 6 0 W: 11 02 b.Donegal 3-7-91
Source: Scholar. *Honours:* Eire Under-21.

2009–10	Wolverhampton W	0	0	
2010–11	Wolverhampton W	0	0	
2010–11	*Barnet*	3	0	3 0

EBANKS-BLAKE, Sylvan (F) 180 67
H: 5 10 W: 13 04 b.Cambridge 29-3-86
Source: Scholar. *Honours:* England Under-21.

2004–05	Manchester U	0	0	
2005–06	Manchester U	0	0	
2006–07	Plymouth Arg	41	10	
2007–08	Plymouth Arg	25	11	66 21
2007–08	Wolverhampton W	20	12	
2008–09	Wolverhampton W	41	25	
2009–10	Wolverhampton W	23	2	
2010–11	Wolverhampton W	30	7	114 46

EBANKS-LANDELL, Ethan (M) 0 0
H: 5 6 W: 11 02 b.Oldbury 16-12-92
Source: Scholar.

2009–10	Wolverhampton W	0	0
2010–11	Wolverhampton W	0	0

EDWARDS, Dave (M) 211 22
H: 5 11 W: 11 04 b.Shrewsbury 3-2-86
Source: Scholar. *Honours:* Wales Youth, Under-21, 22 full caps, 3 goals.

2002–03	Shrewsbury T	1	0	
2003–04	Shrewsbury T	0	0	
2004–05	Shrewsbury T	27	5	
2005–06	Shrewsbury T	30	2	
2006–07	Shrewsbury T	45	5	103 12
2007–08	Luton T	19	4	19 4
2007–08	Wolverhampton W	10	1	
2008–09	Wolverhampton W	44	3	
2009–10	Wolverhampton W	20	1	
2010–11	Wolverhampton W	15	1	89 6

ELOKOBI, George (D) 112 4
H: 5 10 W: 13 02 b.Cameroon 31-1-86
Source: Dulwich Hamlet.

2004–05	Colchester U	0	0	
2004–05	*Chester C*	5	0	5 0
2005–06	Colchester U	12	1	
2006–07	Colchester U	10	0	
2007–08	Colchester U	17	1	39 2
2007–08	Wolverhampton W	15	0	
2008–09	Wolverhampton W	4	0	
2009–10	Wolverhampton W	22	0	
2010–11	Wolverhampton W	27	2	68 2

FLETCHER, Steven (F) 220 61
H: 6 1 W: 12 00 b.Shrewsbury 26-3-87
Honours: Scotland Under-20, Under-21, B, 8 full caps, 1 goal.

2003–04	Hibernian	5	0	
2004–05	Hibernian	20	5	
2005–06	Hibernian	34	8	
2006–07	Hibernian	31	6	
2007–08	Hibernian	32	13	
2008–09	Hibernian	34	11	156 43
2009–10	Burnley	35	8	35 8
2010–11	Wolverhampton W	29	10	29 10

FOLEY, Kevin (D) 298 7
H: 5 9 W: 11 11 b.Luton 1-11-84
Source: Scholar. *Honours:* Eire B, Under-21, 8 full caps.

2002–03	Luton T	2	0	
2003–04	Luton T	33	1	
2004–05	Luton T	39	2	
2005–06	Luton T	38	0	
2006–07	Luton T	39	0	
2007–08	Luton T	0	0	151 3
2007–08	Wolverhampton W	44	1	
2008–09	Wolverhampton W	45	1	
2009–10	Wolverhampton W	25	0	
2010–11	Wolverhampton W	33	2	147 4

GORMAN, Johnny (M) 0 0
H: 5 9 W: 11 00 b.Sheffield 26-10-92
Honours: Northern Ireland 8 full caps.

2009–10	Wolverhampton W	0	0
2010–11	Wolverhampton W	0	0

GRIFFITHS, Leigh (F) 96 44
H: 5 07 W: 10 01 b.Leith 20-8-90
Honours: Scotland Youth, Under-21, B.

2006–07	Livingston	4	1	
2007–08	Livingston	18	5	
2008–09	Livingston	27	17	49 23
2009–10	Dundee	29	13	
2010–11	Dundee	18	8	47 21
2010–11	Wolverhampton W	0	0	

GUEDIOURA, Adlene (M) 119 13
H: 6 1 W: 12 08 b.La Roche-sur-Yon 12-11-85
Honours: Algeria 7 full caps, 1 goal.

2004–05	Sedan	0	0	
2005–06	Noisy-Le-Sec	15	1	15 1
2006–07	L'Entente	21	3	21 3
2007–08	Creteil	24	6	24 6
2008–09	Kortrijk	10	0	10 0
2008–09	Charleroi	12	0	
2009–10	Charleroi	13	1	25 1
2009–10	Wolverhampton W	14	1	
2010–11	Wolverhampton W	10	1	24 2

HAHNEMANN, Marcus (G) 394 0
H: 6 3 W: 13 03 b.Seattle 15-6-72
Honours: USA 9 full caps.

1997	Colorado Rapids	25	0	
1998	Colorado Rapids	28	0	
1999	Colorado Rapids	13	0	66 0
1999–2000	Fulham	0	0	
2000–01	Fulham	2	0	
2001–02	Fulham	0	0	2 0
2001–02	*Rochdale*	5	0	5 0
2001–02	*Reading*	6	0	
2002–03	Reading	41	0	
2003–04	Reading	36	0	
2004–05	Reading	46	0	
2005–06	Reading	45	0	
2006–07	Reading	38	0	
2007–08	Reading	38	0	
2008–09	Reading	32	0	
2009–10	Reading	0	0	282 0
2009–10	Wolverhampton W	25	0	
2010–11	Wolverhampton W	14	0	39 0

HALFORD, Greg (D) 254 29
H: 6 4 W: 12 10 b.Chelmsford 8-12-84
Source: Scholar. *Honours:* England Youth, Under-20.

2002–03	Colchester U	1	0	
2003–04	Colchester U	18	4	
2004–05	Colchester U	44	4	
2005–06	Colchester U	45	7	
2006–07	Colchester U	28	3	136 18
2006–07	*Reading*	3	0	3 0
2007–08	Sunderland	8	0	
2007–08	*Charlton Ath*	16	2	16 2
2008–09	Sunderland	0	0	
2008–09	*Sheffield U*	41	4	41 4
2009–10	Sunderland	0	0	8 0
2009–10	Wolverhampton W	15	0	
2010–11	Wolverhampton W	2	0	17 0
2010–11	*Portsmouth*	33	5	33 5

HAMMILL, Adam (M) 148 15
H: 5 11 W: 11 07 b.Liverpool 25-1-88
Source: Scholar. *Honours:* England Youth, Under-21.

2005–06	Liverpool	0	0	
2006–07	Liverpool	0	0	
2006–07	*Dunfermline Ath*	13	1	13 1
2007–08	Liverpool	0	0	
2007–08	*Southampton*	25	0	25 0
2008–09	Liverpool	0	0	
2008–09	*Blackpool*	22	1	22 1
2008–09	*Barnsley*	14	1	
2009–10	Liverpool	0	0	
2009–10	Barnsley	39	4	
2010–11	Barnsley	25	8	78 13
2010–11	Wolverhampton W	10	0	10 0

HEMMINGS, Ashley (M) 12 0
H: 5 8 W: 11 06 b.Lewisham 3-3-91
Source: Scholar.

2008–09	Wolverhampton W	2	0	
2008–09	*Cheltenham T*	1	0	1 0
2009–10	Wolverhampton W	0	0	
2010–11	Wolverhampton W	0	0	2 0
2010–11	*Torquay U*	9	0	9 0

HENNESSEY, Wayne (G) 133 0
H: 6 0 W: 11 06 b.Anglesey 24-1-87
Source: Scholar. *Honours:* Wales Schools, Youth, Under-21, 32 full caps.

2004–05	Wolverhampton W	0	0
2005–06	Wolverhampton W	0	0
2006–07	Wolverhampton W	0	0
2006–07	*Bristol C*	0	0

2006–07	Stockport Co	15	0	15	0
2007–08	Wolverhampton W	46	0		
2008–09	Wolverhampton W	35	0		
2009–10	Wolverhampton W	13	0		
2010–11	Wolverhampton W	24	0	118	0

HENRY, Karl (M)   309 8
H: 6 0   W: 12 00   b.Wolverhampton 26-11-82
Source: Trainee. *Honours:* England Youth, Under-20.

1999–2000	Stoke C	0	0		
2000–01	Stoke C	0	0		
2001–02	Stoke C	24	0		
2002–03	Stoke C	18	1		
2003–04	Stoke C	20	0		
2003–04	*Cheltenham T*	9	1	9	1
2004–05	Stoke C	34	0		
2005–06	Stoke C	24	0	120	1
2006–07	Wolverhampton W	34	3		
2007–08	Wolverhampton W	40	3		
2008–09	Wolverhampton W	43	0		
2009–10	Wolverhampton W	34	0		
2010–11	Wolverhampton W	29	0	180	6

HUNT, Steve (M)   342 51
H: 5 9   W: 10 10   b.Port Laoise 1-8-80
Source: Trainee. *Honours:* Eire Under-21, B, 30 full caps, 1 goal.

1999–2000	Crystal Palace	3	0		
2000–01	Crystal Palace	0	0	3	0
2001–02	Brentford	35	4		
2002–03	Brentford	42	7		
2003–04	Brentford	40	11		
2004–05	Brentford	19	3	136	25
2005–06	Reading	38	2		
2006–07	Reading	35	4		
2007–08	Reading	37	5		
2008–09	Reading	46	6		
2009–10	Reading	0	0	156	17
2009–10	Hull C	27	6	27	6
2010–11	Wolverhampton W	20	3	20	3

IKEME, Carl (G)   50 0
H: 6 2   W: 13 09   b.Sutton Coldfield 8-6-86
Source: Scholar.

2005–06	Wolverhampton W	0	0		
2005–06	*Stockport Co*	9	0	9	0
2006–07	Wolverhampton W	1	0		
2007–08	Wolverhampton W	0	0		
2008–09	Wolverhampton W	12	0		
2009–10	Wolverhampton W	0	0		
2009–10	*Charlton Ath*	4	0	4	0
2009–10	*Sheffield U*	2	0	2	0
2009–10	*QPR*	17	0	17	0
2010–11	Wolverhampton W	0	0	13	0
2010–11	*Leicester C*	5	0	5	0

ISMAIL, Zeli (M)   0 0
b.Serbia
Source: Scholar.

| 2010–11 | Wolverhampton W | 0 | 0 | | |

JARVIS, Matthew (M)   235 23
H: 5 8   W: 11 10   b.Middlesbrough 22-5-86
Source: Scholar. *Honours:* England 1 full cap.

2003–04	Gillingham	10	0		
2004–05	Gillingham	30	3		
2005–06	Gillingham	35	3		
2006–07	Gillingham	35	6	110	12
2007–08	Wolverhampton W	26	1		
2008–09	Wolverhampton W	28	3		
2009–10	Wolverhampton W	34	3		
2010–11	Wolverhampton W	37	4	125	11

JONES, David (M)   149 22
H: 5 11   W: 10 10   b.Southport 4-11-84
Source: Trainee. *Honours:* England Youth, Under-21.

2003–04	Manchester U	0	0		
2004–05	Manchester U	0	0		
2005–06	Manchester U	0	0		
2005–06	*Preston NE*	24	3	24	3
2005–06	*NEC Nijmegen*	17	6	17	6
2006–07	Manchester U	0	0		
2006–07	Derby Co	28	6		
2007–08	Derby Co	14	1	42	7
2008–09	Wolverhampton W	34	4		
2009–10	Wolverhampton W	20	1		
2010–11	Wolverhampton W	12	1	66	6

KEOGH, Andy (F)   243 45
H: 6 0   W: 11 00   b.Dublin 16-5-86
Source: Scholar. *Honours:* Eire Youth, B, Under-21, 21 full caps, 1 goal.

2003–04	Leeds U	0	0		
2004–05	Leeds U	0	0		
2004–05	*Bury*	4	2	4	2
2004–05	Scunthorpe U	25	3		
2005–06	Scunthorpe U	45	11		
2006–07	Scunthorpe U	28	7	98	21
2006–07	Wolverhampton W	17	5		
2007–08	Wolverhampton W	43	8		
2008–09	Wolverhampton W	42	5		
2009–10	Wolverhampton W	13	1		
2010–11	Wolverhampton W	1	0	116	19
2010–11	*Cardiff C*	16	2	16	2
2010–11	*Bristol C*	9	1	9	1

KIGHTLY, Michael (F)   109 20
H: 5 10   W: 10 10   b.Basildon 24-1-86
Source: Scholar. *Honours:* England Under-21.

2002–03	Southend U	1	0		
2003–04	Southend U	11	0		
2004–05	Southend U	1	0	13	0

From Grays Ath.

2006–07	Wolverhampton W	24	8		
2007–08	Wolverhampton W	21	4		
2008–09	Wolverhampton W	38	8		
2009–10	Wolverhampton W	9	0		
2010–11	Wolverhampton W	4	0	96	20

MAIERHOFER, Stefan (F)   208 92
H: 6 8   W: 14 11   b.Vienna 16-8-82
Honours: Austria 10 full caps, 1 goal.

2002–03	First Vienna	0	0		
2003–04	Langenrohr	28	10		
2004–05	Langenrohr	25	16	53	26
2005–06	Bayern Munich II	28	10		
2006–07	Bayern Munich II	14	11	42	21
2006–07	Bayern Munich	2	0	2	0
2006–07	Koblenz	14	3	14	3
2007–08	Furth	10	2	10	2
2007–08	Rapid Vienna	11	7		
2008–09	Rapid Vienna	35	23		
2009–10	Rapid Vienna	3	1	49	31
2009–10	Wolverhampton W	8	1		
2009–10	*Bristol C*	3	0	3	0
2010–11	Wolverhampton W	0	0	8	1
2010–11	*Duisburg*	27	8	27	8

MALONE, Scott (D)   46 2
H: 6 2   W: 11 11   b.Rowley Regis 25-3-91
Source: Scholar. *Honours:* England Youth.

2008–09	Wolverhampton W	0	0		
2008–09	*Ujpest*	7	1	7	1
2009–10	Wolverhampton W	0	0		
2009–10	*Southend U*	17	0	17	0
2010–11	Wolverhampton W	0	0		
2010–11	*Burton Alb*	22	1	22	1

McALINDEN, Liam (F)   0 0
b.Stafford
Source: Scholar. *Honours:* Northern Ireland Youth.

| 2010–11 | Wolverhampton W | 0 | 0 | | |

McCAREY, Aaron (G)   0 0
b.Monaghan 14-1-92
Source: Monaghan U. *Honours:* Eire Youth.

| 2009–10 | Wolverhampton W | 0 | 0 | | |
| 2010–11 | Wolverhampton W | 0 | 0 | | |

McGROARY, Brian (M)   0 0
b.Letterbarrow
Source: Scholar.

| 2010–11 | Wolverhampton W | 0 | 0 | | |

MENDEZ-LAING, Nathaniel (M)   33 5
H: 5 10   W: 11 12   b.Birmingham 15-4-92
Source: Scholar.

2009–10	Wolverhampton W	0	0		
2010–11	Wolverhampton W	0	0		
2010–11	*Peterborough U*	33	5	33	5

MILIJAS, Nenad (M)   268 59
H: 6 2   W: 13 09   b.Belgrade 30-4-83
Honours: Serbia 23 full caps, 4 goals.

1999–2000	Zemun	2	0		
2000–01	Zemun	10	0		
2001–02	Zemun	28	1		
2002–03	Zemun	27	2		
2003–04	Zemun	26	3		
2004–05	Zemun	22	3		
2005–06	Zemun	15	9	130	18
2005–06	Red Star Belgrade	10	4		
2006–07	Red Star Belgrade	25	5		
2007–08	Red Star Belgrade	28	10		
2008–09	Red Star Belgrade	33	18	96	37
2009–10	Wolverhampton W	19	2		
2010–11	Wolverhampton W	23	2	42	4

MOUYOKOLO, Steven (D)   60 1
H: 6 3   W: 13 08   b.Melun 24-1-87
From Chateauroux B.

2008–09	Boulogne	13	0	13	0
2009–10	Hull C	21	1	21	1
2010–11	Wolverhampton W	4	0	4	0

MUJANGI BIA, Geoff (M)   62 9
H: 5 9   W: 11 02   b.Kinshasa 12-8-89
Honours: Belgium Under-21, 2 full caps.

2006–07	Charleroi	3	0		
2007–08	Charleroi	17	3		
2008–09	Charleroi	28	4		
2009–10	Charleroi	10	2	58	9
2009–10	Wolverhampton W	3	0		
2010–11	Wolverhampton W	1	0	4	0

RECKORD, Jamie (D)   7 0
b. 9-3-92
Source: Scholar.

| 2010–11 | Wolverhampton W | 0 | 0 | | |
| 2010–11 | *Northampton T* | 7 | 0 | 7 | 0 |

ROONEY, Nathan (M)   0 0
b.Telford
Source: Scholar.

| 2010–11 | Wolverhampton W | 0 | 0 | | |

SPRAY, James (F)   0 0
H: 6 0   W: 12 01   b.Halesowen 2-12-92
Source: Scholar.

| 2009–10 | Wolverhampton W | 0 | 0 | | |
| 2010–11 | Wolverhampton W | 0 | 0 | | |

STEARMAN, Richard (D)   200 9
H: 6 2   W: 10 08   b.Wolverhampton 19-8-87
Source: Scholar. *Honours:* England Youth, Under-21.

2004–05	Leicester C	8	1		
2005–06	Leicester C	34	3		
2006–07	Leicester C	35	1		
2007–08	Leicester C	39	2	116	7
2008–09	Wolverhampton W	37	1		
2009–10	Wolverhampton W	16	1		
2010–11	Wolverhampton W	31	0	84	2

VAN DAMME, Jelle (D)   133 19
H: 6 4   W: 13 01   b.Lokeren 10-10-83
Honours: Belgium 28 full caps.

2001–02	Beerschot	7	0	7	0
2001–02	Ajax	1	0		
2002–03	Ajax	11	0		
2003–04	Ajax	6	0	18	0
2004–05	Southampton	6	0		
2005–06	Southampton	0	0	6	0
2005–06	*Werder Bremen*	8	1	8	1
2006–07	Anderlecht	25	0		
2007–08	Anderlecht	29	7		
2008–09	Anderlecht	22	3		
2009–10	Anderlecht	34	7	110	17
2010–11	Wolverhampton W	6	1	6	1

Transferred to Standard Liege January 2011.

VOKES, Sam (F)   116 25
H: 6 1   W: 13 10   b.Lymington 21-10-89
Source: Scholar. *Honours:* Wales Under-21, 18 full caps, 2 goals.

2006–07	Bournemouth	13	4		
2007–08	Bournemouth	41	12	54	16
2008–09	Wolverhampton W	36	6		
2009–10	Wolverhampton W	5	0		
2009–10	*Leeds U*	8	1	8	1
2010–11	Wolverhampton W	2	0	43	6
2010–11	*Bristol C*	1	0	1	0
2010–11	*Sheffield U*	6	1	6	1
2010–11	*Norwich C*	4	1	4	1

WARD, Stephen (D)   217 15
H: 5 11   W: 12 02   b.Dublin 20-8-85
Honours: Eire Youth, Under-21, B, 3 full caps, 1 goal.

2003	Bohemians	6	0		
2004	Bohemians	16	2		
2005	Bohemians	29	7		
2006	Bohemians	21	2	72	11

2006–07	Wolverhampton W	18	3	
2007–08	Wolverhampton W	29	0	
2008–09	Wolverhampton W	42	0	
2009–10	Wolverhampton W	22	0	
2010–11	Wolverhampton W	34	1	145 4

WINNALL, Sam (F)   19   7
H: 5 9   W: 11 04   b.Wolverhampton 19-1-91
Source: Scholar.

2009–10	Wolverhampton W	0	0	
2010–11	Wolverhampton W	0	0	
2010–11	*Burton Alb*	19	7	19 7

ZUBAR, Ronald (D)   206   6
H: 6 1   W: 12 08   b.Guadeloupe 20-9-85
Honours: France Under-21, Guadeloupe 1
full cap.

2002–03	Caen	7	0	
2003–04	Caen	24	1	
2004–05	Caen	34	1	
2005–06	Caen	31	0	96 2
2006–07	Marseille	34	0	
2007–08	Marseille	21	1	
2008–09	Marseille	17	1	72 2
2009–10	Wolverhampton W	23	1	
2010–11	Wolverhampton W	15	1	38 2

Scholars
Bashford Oliver; Cotman Aljaz; Cranston
Jordan Christopher; Forde Anthony; Harris
Louis David; Ihiekwe Michael; Keane Jordan
Michael; Kempton Jake Anthony; Kostrna
Kristian; Price Jack Alexander; Shepherd
Josh Liam; Whittall Sam

WYCOMBE W (91)

AINSWORTH, Gareth (M)   482 101
H: 5 10   W: 12 05   b.Blackburn 10-5-73
Source: Blackburn R Trainee.

1991–92	Preston NE	5	0	
1992–93	Cambridge U	4	1	4 1
1992–93	Preston NE	26	0	
1993–94	Preston NE	38	11	
1994–95	Preston NE	16	1	
1995–96	Preston NE	2	0	
1995–96	Lincoln C	31	12	
1996–97	Lincoln C	46	22	
1997–98	Lincoln C	6	3	83 37
1997–98	Port Vale	40	5	
1998–99	Port Vale	15	5	55 10
1998–99	Wimbledon	8	0	
1999–2000	Wimbledon	2	2	
2000–01	Wimbledon	12	2	
2001–02	Wimbledon	2	0	
2001–02	*Preston NE*	5	1	92 13
2002–03	Wimbledon	12	2	36 6
2002–03	Walsall	5	1	5 1
2002–03	Cardiff C	9	0	9 0
2003–04	QPR	29	6	
2004–05	QPR	22	2	
2005–06	QPR	43	9	
2006–07	QPR	22	1	
2007–08	QPR	24	3	
2008–09	QPR	0	0	
2009–10	QPR	1	0	141 21
2009–10	Wycombe W	14	2	
2010–11	Wycombe W	43	10	57 12

ARNOLD, Steven (G)   0   0
H: 6 1   W: 13 02   b.Welham Green 22-8-89
Source: Scholar.

2007–08	Norwich C	0	0
2008–09	Norwich C	0	0
From Grays Ath.			
2009–10	Wycombe W	0	0
From Grays Ath.			
2010–11	Wycombe W	0	0

BEAVON, Stuart (F)   70   6
H: 5 7   W: 10 10   b.Reading 5-5-84
Source: Dicot T, Weymouth.

2008–09	Wycombe W	8	0	
2009–10	Wycombe W	25	3	
2010–11	Wycombe W	37	3	70 6

BELCHER, Sam (M)   0   0
b. 5-1-92
Source: Scholar.

2010–11	Wycombe W	0	0

BENNETT, Alan (D)   101   3
H: 6 2   W: 12 08   b.Cork 4-10-81
Honours: Eire Under-21, B, 2 full caps.

2006–07	Reading	0	0	
2007–08	Reading	0	0	
2007–08	*Southampton*	10	0	10 0
2007–08	*Brentford*	11	1	
2008–09	Reading	0	0	
2008–09	*Brentford*	44	1	
2009–10	Brentford	13	0	68 2
2009–10	*Wycombe W*	6	1	
2010–11	Wycombe W	17	0	23 1

BETSY, Kevin (M)   395 53
H: 6 1   W: 12 00   b.Woking 20-3-78
Source: Woking.

1998–99	Fulham	7	1	
1999–2000	Fulham	2	0	
1999–2000	*Bournemouth*	5	0	5 0
1999–2000	*Hull C*	2	0	2 0
2000–01	Fulham	5	0	
2001–02	Fulham	1	0	15 1
2001–02	Barnsley	10	0	
2002–03	Barnsley	39	5	
2003–04	Barnsley	45	10	
2004–05	Barnsley	0	0	94 15
2004–05	*Hartlepool U*	6	1	6 1
2004–05	Oldham Ath	36	5	36 5
2005–06	Wycombe W	42	8	
2006–07	Wycombe W	29	5	
2006–07	Bristol C	17	1	
2007–08	Bristol C	1	0	18 1
2007–08	*Yeovil T*	5	1	5 1
2007–08	Walsall	16	2	16 2
2008–09	Southend U	41	3	
2009–10	Southend U	2	0	43 3
2009–10	Wycombe W	39	5	
2010–11	Wycombe W	45	6	155 24

BLOOMFIELD, Matt (M)   221 21
H: 5 9   W: 11 00   b.Felixstowe 8-2-84
Source: Scholar. *Honours:* England Youth,
Under-20.

2001–02	Ipswich T	0	0	
2002–03	Ipswich T	0	0	
2003–04	Ipswich T	0	0	
2003–04	Wycombe W	12	1	
2004–05	Wycombe W	26	2	
2005–06	Wycombe W	39	5	
2006–07	Wycombe W	41	4	
2007–08	Wycombe W	35	4	
2008–09	Wycombe W	20	0	
2009–10	Wycombe W	14	2	
2010–11	Wycombe W	34	3	221 21

BULL, Nikki (G)   82   0
H: 6 2   W: 12 08   b.Hastings 2-10-81
Source: Scholarship.

1999–2000	QPR	0	0	
2000–01	QPR	0	0	
2001–02	QPR	0	0	
2008–09	Aldershot T	30	0	30 0
2009–10	Brentford	6	0	6 0
2010–11	Wycombe W	46	0	46 0

FEDERICO, Jerome (M)   1   0
b.Watford 14-5-92
Source: Scholar.

2010–11	Wycombe W	1	0	1 0

FITCHETT, Dan (F)   0   0
b.Stevenage 28-3-91
Source: Scholar.

2009–10	Wycombe W	0	0
2010–11	Wycombe W	0	0

FOSTER, Danny (D)   144   4
H: 5 10   W: 12 10   b.Enfield 23-9-84
Source: Trainee.

2002–03	Tottenham H	0	0	
2003–04	Tottenham H	0	0	
2004–05	Tottenham H	0	0	
2005–06	Tottenham H	0	0	
2006–07	Tottenham H	0	0	
2007–08	Dagenham & R	32	1	
2008–09	Dagenham & R	38	2	70 3
2009–10	Brentford	36	0	36 0
2010–11	Wycombe W	38	1	38 1

HARRIS, Kedeem (M)   2   0
H: 5 9   W: 10 08   b.Westminster 8-6-93
Source: Scholar.

2009–10	Wycombe W	2	0	
2010–11	Wycombe W	0	0	2 0

JOHNSON, Leon (D)   248   8
H: 6 1   W: 13 05   b.Shoreditch 10-5-81
Source: Scholarship.

1999–2000	Southend U	0	0	
2000–01	Southend U	20	1	
2001–02	Southend U	28	2	48 3
2002–03	Gillingham	18	0	
2003–04	Gillingham	20	0	
2004–05	Gillingham	8	0	
2005–06	Gillingham	28	1	
2006–07	Gillingham	24	1	98 2
2007–08	Wycombe W	45	0	
2008–09	Wycombe W	29	2	
2009–10	Wycombe W	5	0	
2010–11	Wycombe W	23	1	102 3

LEWIS, Stuart (M)   90   3
H: 5 10   W: 11 06   b.Welwyn 15-10-87
Source: Scholar. *Honours:* England Youth.

2005–06	Tottenham H	0	0	
2006–07	Tottenham H	0	0	
2006–07	Barnet	4	0	4 0
From Stevenage B.				
2007–08	Gillingham	10	0	
2008–09	Gillingham	21	0	
2009–10	Gillingham	20	1	51 1
2010–11	Dagenham & R	10	0	10 0
2010–11	Wycombe W	25	2	25 2

McCLURE, Matt (F)   8   0
b.Slough 17-11-91
Source: Crystal Palace.

2010–11	Wycombe W	8	0	8 0

McCOY, Marvin (D)   21   0
b.Walthamstow 2-10-88
Source: Watford Scholar. *Honours:*

2007–08	Hereford U	0	0	
From Leyton, Wealdstone.				
2010–11	Wycombe W	21	0	21 0

MONTROSE, Lewis (M)   67   4
H: 6 0   W: 12 00   b.Manchester 17-11-88
Source: Scholar.

2006–07	Wigan Ath	0	0	
2007–08	Wigan Ath	0	0	
2008–09	Wigan Ath	0	0	
2008–09	*Cheltenham T*	5	0	5 0
2008–09	*Chesterfield*	12	0	12 0
2009–10	Wycombe W	14	0	
2010–11	Wycombe W	36	4	50 4

MURTAGH, Kieran (M)   60   3
H: 6 0   W: 12 00   b.Wapping 29-10-88
Source: Charlton Ath Academy, Fisher Ath.

2008–09	Yeovil T	26	0	
2009–10	Yeovil T	27	3	53 3
2010–11	Wycombe W	7	0	7 0

PITTMAN, Jon-Paul (F)   89 15
H: 5 9   W: 11 00   b.Oklahoma City 24-10-86
Source: Scholar.

2005–06	Nottingham F	0	0	
2005–06	*Hartlepool U*	3	0	3 0
2006–07	*Bury*	9	1	9 1
2006–07	Doncaster R	0	0	
From Crawley T.				
2008–09	Wycombe W	17	3	
2009–10	Wycombe W	41	7	
2010–11	Wycombe W	19	4	77 14

RENDELL, Scott (F)   90 30
H: 6 1   W: 13 00   b.Ashford (Middlesex)
21-10-86
Source: Aldershot T, Reading, Crawley T,
Cambridge U.
On loan from Cambridge U.

2007–08	Peterborough U	10	3	
2008–09	Peterborough U	3	1	
2008–09	*Yeovil T*	5	0	5 0
2009–10	Peterborough U	0	0	13 4
2009–10	*Torquay U*	35	12	35 12
2010–11	Wycombe W	37	14	37 14

SANDELL, Andy (D)   126 17
H: 5 11   W: 11 09   b.Calne 8-9-83
Source: Bath C.

2005–06	Bristol R	0	0	
2006–07	Bristol R	36	3	
2008–09	Bristol R	0	0	36 3
From Salisbury C.				
2008–09	Aldershot T	29	2	

| 2009–10 | Aldershot T | 29 | 5 | 58 | 7 |
| 2010–11 | Wycombe W | 32 | 7 | 32 | 7 |

SCOWEN, Josh (M)   2   0
b.Wycombe 28-3-93
Source: Scholar.

| 2010–11 | Wycombe W | 2 | 0 | 2 | 0 |

STREVENS, Ben (M)   226   51
H: 6 1 W: 12 00 b.Edgware 24-5-80
Source: Wingate & Finchley.

1998–99	Barnet	0	0		
1999–2000	Barnet	6	0		
2000–01	Barnet	28	4		
2005–06	Barnet	35	5	69	9
From Crawley T.					
2007–08	Dagenham & R	46	15		
2008–09	Dagenham & R	46	14	92	29
2009–10	Brentford	25	6	25	6
2010–11	Wycombe W	40	7	40	7

WESTWOOD, Chris (D)   440   18
H: 5 11 W: 12 10 b.Dudley 13-2-77
Source: Trainee.

1995–96	Wolverhampton W	0	0		
1996–97	Wolverhampton W	0	0		
1997–98	Wolverhampton W	4	1		
1998–99	Wolverhampton W	0	0	4	1
1998–99	Hartlepool U	4	0		
1999–2000	Hartlepool U	37	0		
2000–01	Hartlepool U	46	1		
2001–02	Hartlepool U	35	1		
2002–03	Hartlepool U	46	1		
2003–04	Hartlepool U	45	0		
2004–05	Hartlepool U	37	4	250	7
2005–06	Walsall	29	3		
2006–07	Walsall	40	2	69	5
2007–08	Peterborough U	37	0		
2008–09	Peterborough U	16	0	53	0
2008–09	*Cheltenham T*	9	2	9	2
2009–10	Wycombe W	28	2		
2010–11	Wycombe W	27	1	55	3

WINFIELD, Dave (D)   72   4
H: 6 3 W: 13 08 b.Aldershot 24-3-88
Source: Youth.

2008–09	Aldershot T	10	0		
2009–10	Aldershot T	25	2	35	2
2010–11	Wycombe W	37	2	37	2

YEOVIL T (92)

ALCOCK, Craig (D)   107   3
H: 5 8 W: 11 00 b.Cornwall 8-12-87
Source: Youth.

2006–07	Yeovil T	1	0		
2007–08	Yeovil T	8	0		
2008–09	Yeovil T	30	1		
2009–10	Yeovil T	42	0		
2010–11	Yeovil T	26	1	107	3

AYLING, Luke (D)   41   0
H: 5 11 W: 10 08 b.Lambeth 25-8-91

2009–10	Arsenal	0	0		
2009–10	*Yeovil T*	4	0		
2010–11	Yeovil T	37	0	41	0

BOWDITCH, Dean (F)   192   40
H: 5 11 W: 11 05 b.Bishops Stortford
15-6-86
Source: Trainee. *Honours:* FA Schools,
England Youth.

2002–03	Ipswich T	5	0		
2003–04	Ipswich T	16	4		
2004–05	Ipswich T	21	3		
2004–05	*Burnley*	10	1	10	1
2005–06	Ipswich T	21	0		
2005–06	*Wycombe W*	11	1	11	1
2006–07	Ipswich T	9	1		
2006–07	*Brighton & HA*	3	1		
2007–08	Ipswich T	0	0		
2007–08	*Northampton T*	10	2	10	2
2007–08	*Brighton & HA*	5	0	8	1
2008–09	Ipswich T	1	0	73	8
2008–09	*Brentford*	2	9	2	9
2009–10	Yeovil T	30	10		
2010–11	Yeovil T	41	15	71	25

CALVER, Craig (F)   6   0
H: 5 10 W: 12 00 b.Cambridge 20-1-91
Source: Scholar.

| 2009–10 | Southend U | 0 | 0 | | |

From AFC Sudbury.

| 2010–11 | Yeovil T | 6 | 0 | 6 | 0 |

GIBSON, Billy (M)   4   0
H: 6 2 W: 11 07 b.Harrow 30-9-90
Source: Scholar.

2008–09	Watford	0	0		
2009–10	Watford	0	0		
2010–11	Yeovil T	4	0	4	0

GRITTON, Martin (F)   327   63
H: 6 1 W: 12 02 b.Glasgow 1-6-78
Source: Porthleven.

1998–99	Plymouth Arg	2	0		
1999–2000	Plymouth Arg	30	6		
2000–01	Plymouth Arg	10	1		
2001–02	Plymouth Arg	2	0		
2002–03	Plymouth Arg	0	0	44	7
2002–03	Torquay U	43	13		
2003–04	Torquay U	31	4		
2004–05	Torquay U	19	6		
2004–05	Grimsby T	23	4		
2005–06	Grimsby T	26	2	49	6
2005–06	Lincoln C	10	1		
2006–07	Lincoln C	17	2	27	3
2006–07	*Mansfield T*	19	6	19	6
2007–08	Macclesfield T	31	8		
2008–09	Macclesfield T	21	5	52	13
2008–09	Chesterfield	20	4		
2009–10	Chesterfield	9	1		
2010–11	Chesterfield	0	0	29	5
2010–11	*Torquay U*	12	0	105	23
From Chester.					
2010–11	Yeovil T	2	0	2	0

HUNTINGTON, Paul (D)   98   8
H: 6 3 W: 12 08 b.Carlisle 17-9-87
Source: Scholar. *Honours:* England Youth.

2005–06	Newcastle U	0	0		
2006–07	Newcastle U	11	1		
2007–08	Newcastle U	0	0	11	1
2007–08	Leeds U	17	2		
2008–09	Leeds U	4	0		
2009–10	Leeds U	0	0	21	2
2009–10	Stockport Co	26	0	26	0
2010–11	Yeovil T	40	5	40	5

JONES, Nathan (M)   430   11
H: 5 6 W: 10 06 b.Rhondda 28-5-73
Source: Cardiff C Trainee, Maesteg Park, Ton
Pentre, Merthyr T.

| 1995–96 | Luton T | 0 | 0 | | |

From Badajoz, Numaicia

1997–98	Southend U	39	0		
1998–99	Southend U	17	0		
1998–99	*Scarborough*	9	0	9	0
1999–2000	Southend U	43	2	99	2
2000–01	Brighton & HA	40	4		
2001–02	Brighton & HA	36	2		
2002–03	Brighton & HA	28	1		
2003–04	Brighton & HA	36	0		
2004–05	Brighton & HA	19	0	159	7
2005–06	Yeovil T	43	0		
2006–07	Yeovil T	42	1		
2007–08	Yeovil T	31	1		
2008–09	Yeovil T	21	0		
2009–10	Yeovil T	18	0		
2010–11	Yeovil T	8	0	163	2

MARTIN, Richard (G)   3   0
H: 6 2 W: 12 13 b.Chelmsford 1-9-87
Source: Scholar.

2005–06	Brighton & HA	0	0		
2006–07	Brighton & HA	0	0		
2007–08	Manchester C	0	0		
2008–09	Manchester C	0	0		
2009–10	Yeovil T	3	0		
From Havant & Waterlooville, Crawley T.					
2010–11	Yeovil T	0	0	3	0

Transferred to Puerto Rico Islanders March
2011.

RUSSELL, Alex (M)   491   53
H: 5 10 W: 11 07 b.Crosby 17-3-73
Source: Burscough.

1994–95	Rochdale	7	1		
1995–96	Rochdale	25	0		
1996–97	Rochdale	39	9		
1997–98	Rochdale	31	4	102	14
1998–99	Cambridge U	37	6		
1999–2000	Cambridge U	15	0		
2000–01	Cambridge U	29	2	81	8
2001–02	Torquay U	33	7		
2002–03	Torquay U	39	9		
2003–04	Torquay U	43	2		
2004–05	Torquay U	38	3	153	21
2005–06	Bristol C	27	4		
2006–07	Bristol C	28	2		
2007–08	Bristol C	1	0	56	6
2007–08	*Northampton T*	13	1	13	1
2007–08	*Cheltenham T*	13	2		
2008–09	Cheltenham T	23	0	36	2
2008–09	Exeter C	7	0		
2009–10	Exeter C	29	1	36	1
From Bath C.					
2010–11	Yeovil T	14	0	14	0

SMITH, Nathan (D)   114   1
H: 5 11 W: 12 00 b.Enfield 11-1-87
Source: Potters Bar T.

2007–08	Yeovil T	7	0		
2008–09	Yeovil T	33	1		
2009–10	Yeovil T	34	0		
2010–11	Yeovil T	40	0	114	1

STAM, Stefan (D)   128   2
H: 6 2 W: 13 02 b.Amersfoort 14-9-79
Honours: Holland Under-21.

2004–05	Oldham Ath	13	0		
2005–06	Oldham Ath	13	0		
2006–07	Oldham Ath	22	1		
2007–08	Oldham Ath	36	0		
2008–09	Oldham Ath	13	0	97	1
2009–10	Yeovil T	18	1		
2010–11	Yeovil T	3	0	21	1
2010–11	*Hereford U*	10	0	10	0

UPSON, Edward (M)   32   1
H: 5 10 W: 11 07 b.Bury St Edmunds
21-11-89
Source: Scholar. *Honours:* England Youth.

2006–07	Ipswich T	0	0		
2007–08	Ipswich T	0	0		
2008–09	Ipswich T	0	0		
2009–10	Ipswich T	0	0		
2009–10	*Barnet*	9	1	9	1
2010–11	Yeovil T	23	0	23	0

VIRGO, Adam (D)   237   20
H: 6 2 W: 13 12 b.Brighton 25-1-83
Source: Juniors. *Honours:* Scotland B.

2000–01	Brighton & HA	6	0		
2001–02	Brighton & HA	6	0		
2002–03	Brighton & HA	3	0		
2002–03	*Exeter C*	9	0	9	0
2003–04	Brighton & HA	22	1		
2004–05	Brighton & HA	36	8		
2005–06	Celtic	10	0		
2006–07	Celtic	0	0	10	0
2006–07	Coventry C	15	1		
2007–08	Coventry C	0	0	15	1
2007–08	*Colchester U*	36	1	36	1
2008–09	Brighton & HA	36	3		
2009–10	Brighton & HA	25	1	134	13
2010–11	Yeovil T	33	5	33	5

WELSH, Andy (M)   273   14
H: 5 8 W: 10 03 b.Manchester 24-11-83
Source: Scholar. *Honours:* Scotland Youth.

2001–02	Stockport Co	15	0		
2002–03	Stockport Co	13	2		
2002–03	*Macclesfield T*	6	2	6	2
2003–04	Stockport Co	34	1		
2004–05	Stockport Co	13	0	75	3
2004–05	Sunderland	7	1		
2005–06	Sunderland	14	0		
2005–06	*Leicester C*	10	1		
2006–07	Sunderland	0	0	21	1
2006–07	*Leicester C*	7	0	17	1
2007	Toronto Lynx	20	1	20	1
2007–08	Blackpool	21	0		
2008–09	Blackpool	0	0	21	0
2008–09	Yeovil T	37	0		
2009–10	Yeovil T	42	2		
2010–11	Yeovil T	34	4	113	6

WILLIAMS, Andy (F)   192   24
H: 5 11 W: 11 09 b.Hereford 14-8-86
Source: Pershore College.

2006–07	Hereford U	41	8		
2007–08	Bristol R	41	4		
2008–09	Bristol R	4	1		
2008–09	*Hereford U*	26	2	67	10
2009–10	Bristol R	43	3	88	8
2010–11	Yeovil T	37	6	37	6

WILLIAMS, Sam (F)		**105**	**12**
H: 5 11 W: 10 08 b.Solihull 9-6-87			
Source: Scholar.			
2004–05	Aston Villa	0	0
2005–06	Aston Villa	0	0
2005–06	*Wrexham*	15	2	**15**	**2**
2006–07	Aston Villa	0	0
2006–07	*Brighton & HA*	3	1	**3**	**1**
2007–08	Aston Villa	0	0
2008–09	Aston Villa	0	0
2008–09	*Colchester U*	1	0	**1**	**0**
2008–09	*Walsall*	5	1	**5**	**1**
2008–09	*Brentford*	11	2	**11**	**2**

2009–10	Yeovil T	34	4		
2010–11	Yeovil T	36	2	**70**	**6**
WOTTON, Paul (D)				**478**	**56**
H: 5 11 W: 12 00 b.Plymouth 17-8-77					
Source: Trainee.					
1994–95	Plymouth Arg	7	0		
1995–96	Plymouth Arg	1	0		
1996–97	Plymouth Arg	9	1		
1997–98	Plymouth Arg	34	1		
1998–99	Plymouth Arg	36	1		
1999–2000	Plymouth Arg	23	0		
2000–01	Plymouth Arg	42	4		
2001–02	Plymouth Arg	46	5		

2002–03	Plymouth Arg	43	8		
2003–04	Plymouth Arg	38	9		
2004–05	Plymouth Arg	40	12		
2005–06	Plymouth Arg	45	8		
2006–07	Plymouth Arg	22	4		
2007–08	Plymouth Arg	8	1	**394**	**54**
2008–09	Southampton	29	0		
2009–10	Southampton	26	0		
2010–11	Southampton	2	0	**57**	**0**
2010–11	*Oxford U*	4	0	**4**	**0**
2010–11	Yeovil T	23	2	**23**	**2**

BLUE SQUARE PREMIER ROLL-CALL

CRAWLEY TOWN

Player	H	W	Birthplace	DOB	Source
Brodie Richard (F)	6 2	12 13	Gateshead	8 7 87	York C
Bulman Dannie (M)	5 9	11 11	Ashford	24 1 79	Oxford U
Dance James (M)			Coleshill	15 3 87	Kettering T
Dempster John (D)	6 1	11 07	Kettering	1 4 83	Kettering T
Gibson Willie (M)	5 10	10 01	Dumfries	6 8 84	Dunfermline Ath
Howell Dean (M)	6 1	12 04	Burton-on-Trent	29 11 80	Aldershot T
Kuipers Michel (G)	6 2	14 02	Amsterdam	26 6 74	Brighton & HA
McFadzean Kyle (D)	6 1	13 03	Sheffield	20 2 87	Alfreton T
Mills Pablo (D)	5 11	11 05	Birmingham	27 5 84	Rotherham U
Neilson Scott (M)	6 2	12 10	Enfield	15 5 87	Bradford C
Shearer Scott (G)	6 3	11 09	Glasgow	15 2 81	Wrexham
Simpson Josh (M)	5 10	12 02	Cambridge	6 3 87	Peterborough U
Smith Ben (M)	5 9	11 09	Chelmsford	23 11 78	Hereford U
Torres Sergio (M)	6 2	12 04	Mar del Plata	11 7 81	Peterborough U
Tubbs Matt (F)	5 9	11 00	Bournemouth	15 7 84	Salisbury C
Wassmer Charlie (D)			London	21 3 91	Hayes & Yeading U
Wilson Glenn (D)	6 1	12 08	Lewisham	16 3 86	Rushden & D

AFC WIMBLEDON

Player	H	W	Birthplace	DOB	Source
Blackman Andre (D)	5 11	11 05	Lambeth	10 11 90	Bristol C
Brown Seb (G)	6 0	12 13	Sutton	24 11 89	Brentford
Gregory Steven (M)	6 1	12 08	Aylesbury	19 3 87	Hayes & Yeading U
Harris Ed (D)	6 1	13 05	Roehampton	3 11 90	QPR
Hatton Sam (M)	5 11	11 02	St Albans	7 2 88	Stevenage
Jackson Ryan (D)			Streatham	31 7 90	Youth
Johnson Brett (D)	6 1	13 01	Hammersmith	15 8 85	Brentford
Jolley Christian (M)			Aldershot	12 5 88	Kingstonian
Jones Reece (M)	6 1	11 09	London	22 7 92	Fulham
Kedwell Danny (F)	5 11	12 13	Gillingham	22 10 85	Grays Ath
Main Jon (F)	5 10	12 02	Greenwich	7 3 81	Tonbridge Angels
Minshull Lee (M)	6 2	14 07	Chatham	11 11 85	Tonbridge Angels
Moore Luke (F)	5 11	11 07	Gravesend	27 4 88	Ebbsfleet U
Moore Sammy (M)	5 8	10 00	Deal	7 9 87	Dover Ath
Nwokeji Mark (F)	5 11	11 05	London	30 1 82	Dagenham & R
Stuart Jamie (D)	5 10	11 00	Southwark	15 10 76	Rushden & D
Wellard Ricky (M)	5 11	9 13	Hammersmith	9 5 88	Ashford T
Yakubu Ismail (D)	5 11	11 13	Kano	8 4 85	Barnet
Yussuf Rashid (M)	6 1	12 06	Poplar	23 9 89	Gillingham

ENGLISH LEAGUE PLAYERS – INDEX

REFEREEING AND THE LAWS OF THE GAME

Of all the problems that beset Referees last season through unfair allegations against them in the Premier and Football Leagues (especially the former) and the banning of Managers from the touchline for matches, the most radical change that is occurring for this season in the domestic game is at grass roots levels. From the beginning of season 2011–12 the FA has brought discipline for all open age players (not youths) in line with senior football. This will mean all suspensions will be a on a match basis rather than a suspension for a number of days. The FA rightly felt that players were playing the same game under the same Laws so that disciplinary punishments especially suspensions should also be the same. Also like professional football there will be no more standard charge appeals against dismissals except in the cases of mistaken identity or wrongful dismissal in which case video evidence must be produced (hardly a likely scenario on the park pitches and wastelands on which the grass roots game is normally played). The move is intended to bring all football in line, to stop fruitless appeals and to be fairer to junior players who if banned for a number of days could actually miss more games than on a match based suspension. Also a player now banned from Saturday football will be able to play on a Sunday or midweek and Sunday players banned on that day will be able to play on a Saturday or midweek. However those who commit a dismissal offence and follow it with misconduct will be banned from ALL football until their suspension is served and more serious offences will lead to longer periods of suspension.

There have for universal consumption been numerous changes (but of a minor nature) in the Laws of the Game. So in Law 1 – "The Field of Play" – there has been added an additional paragraph as follows "where artificial surfaces are used other lines are permitted provided that they are of a different colour and are clearly distinguishable from the lines used for football". Because of the demand for pitches, especially the synthetic variety, various lines have been marked for different sports, and there has been a problem in allowing the use of such variously marked pitches used for those multiple sports, to be permitted for competitive football. This change should cure that problem. In addition there are new regulations regarding the position of goalposts dependent on whether they are square, elliptical or rectangular so that viewed from above in relation to the goal line they do not cause inconsistencies between one field of play and any other.

In Law 2 where it is necessary to cover the situation of the ball bursting, the rule was that the new ball had to be dropped, to restart play, at the place where the original ball had become defective, except in the goal area where different rules applied. However it also encompassed the taking of a penalty kick but this caused certain unfairness so now if the ball bursts or becomes defective after it is struck and before it touches another player, the posts or bar the penalty kick is retaken.

Law 3 has been altered to redefine who is a "Team Official" especially in regard to entering the field of play to avoid the possibility of that person being treated as an outside agent which would bring into play the relevant punishments. Another provision relating to outside agents has been inserted in the "Guidelines for Referees" in their powers and duties section to clarify what in English football has become known as the "beach-ball incident". As a result the Law has now been altered to include any "other object or animal" and as before the game must be stopped to take care of this problem but only if the object etc. is interfering with play.

In Law 4 relating to players' equipment, the new phenomenon of players wearing tights has been recognised. Now not only undershorts, but tights too, must be of the same main colour as the shorts. Whilst dealing with equipment, FIFA have also outlawed "Snoods "and other similar clothing. These do not meet the appropriate definitions under this Law and are now not permitted.

In Law 8 specifying starts and restarts of play, there has been felt a need to define what is a "dropped ball". As a result this has now been rectified to deal with the how, when and why this procedure occurs. However nothing has been done now to avoid the ridiculous situation of players demanding who kicks the dropped ball when it hits the ground, where it is possible to inadvertently score a goal whilst trying to be sporting. That can lead to all kinds of problems because the Law does not allow the Referee to make a decision on a number of factors relating to this restart, including having a contested "drop". It is understood that this problem is being looked at in England and hopefully something can be sorted out for next season

The International Board have completed minor structural amendments to Laws 3 and 8 and have made some other interesting decisions. They have approved the use of vanishing spray on a trial basis and more importantly have also agreed to trial Goal Line technology a decision on which will be made after the conclusion of Euro 2012. Finally there is the question of those Additional Assistant Referees (AARs). Firstly it has been agreed they will be used in the Euro 2012 final tournament despite considerable disenchantment and perplexity in this country. The lack of certainty in their usefulness has been shown by the second proposition, that of moving them from the left side of the goal-line to the right. The object is to allow the Referee to return to his "traditional" position in the diagonal system run by him or her. This does not take into account that now there will be an Assistant Referee patrolling the right touchline who can be distracted by an AAR on his side of the field and who is actually permitted to step on to the pitch. The whole experiment will be permitted to continue until it has run its recommended course after which the International Board will make its final decision on its success or otherwise and whether to continue with it. There will be many who hope that it does not.

In the world of Referees and other officials, statistics recently produced show that referees make on average between 500 and 550 decisions per game which over the regulation 90 minutes equates to a decision approximately every ten seconds. So it is hardly any wonder that the FA who are working hard on the area of development have over the past 4 years been structuring what they term the "National Referee Development Programme". This is intended to assist with the recruitment, retention and development of referees involved with 11-a-side football, the area in which most of the problems for officials occur especially at grass roots levels. The programme was formally launched in March 2011 and aims to ensure support and coaching in a safe, constructive learning environment. There are no age restrictions involved and it aspires to offer something for everybody who takes part, from the trainee referee to the much more experienced down the line. Another of its aims is to make certain the target of 8,000 new referees by 2012 is achieved and from there to feed successful participants through to semi professional and professional football in what it calls "a clear pathway". In this concept all the County Associations have a very important role to play in the implementation of the scheme.

It is very pleasant to confirm that two of the most celebrated Referees have been inducted into the new Professional Game Match Officials Ltd (PGMOL) Hall of Fame. Both are ex-international referees at the highest level of the game who have contributed so much to it. Jack Taylor was the referee for the World Cup Final in 1974 between Holland and West Germany and still at the age of 80 is promoting his side of the game up and down the country. Ken Ridden is a UEFA refereeing representative and was previously awarded the Order of Merit for services to European Football. He was also primarily responsible for the last recodifying of the Laws of the Game. They both well deserve being the first to be inducted, and in June 2011 other World Cup Officials namely Howard Webb, Darren Cann, Mike Mullarky, Phil Sharp and Mark Warren were also all inducted into the PGMOL Hall of Fame. Jack Taylor was further honoured by the Football Association at a FIFA Officials' Meeting when both he and Howard Webb were formally recognised for their part in "elevating the status of referees and assistant referees in England by their personal efforts" and trying to be the best in their field of endeavour and especially for their respective attainments in the 1974 and 2010 World Cup Finals. Three other former top officials, Gordon Kew, Norman Burtenshaw and Pat Partridge were awarded special England Caps, whilst Webb was again honoured alongside his Assistants Darren Cann and Mike Mullarky with a framed image of themselves at the 2010 World Cup Final; they being the first "team" of officials from the same country to take charge of the Final.

KEN GOLDMAN

NATIONAL LIST OF REFEREES FOR SEASON 2011–12

So far as the current list of Referees and Assistant Referees on the National List is concerned the full such list appears below. However it is worth mentioning that the oldest Referee there, Peter Walton is retained for another season.

REFEREES

Adcock, James
Atkinson, Martin
Attwell, Stuart
Bates, Anthony
Berry, Carl
Booth, Russell
Boyeson, Carl
Brown, Mark
Clattenburg, Mark
Collins, Lee
Coote, David
Deadman, Darren
Dean, Mike
Dowd, Phil
Drysdale, Darren
D'Urso, Andrew
East, Roger
Eltringham, Geoff
Foster, David
Foy, Chris
Friend, Kevin
Gibbs, Philip
Graham, Frederick
Haines, Andy
Hall, Andrew
Halsey, Mark

Haywood, Mark
Hegley, Grant
Heywood, Mark
Hooper, Simon
Ilderton, Eddie
Jones, Michael
Kettle, Trevor
Langford, Oliver
Lewis, Robert
Linington, James
Madley, Andrew
Madley, Robert
Malone, Brendan
Marriner, Andre
Mason, Lee
Mathieson, Scott
McDermid, Danny
Miller, Nigel
Miller, Patrick
Mohareb, Dean
Moss, Jonathan
Naylor, Michael
Oliver, Michael
Pawson, Craig
Penn, Andrew
Phillips, David

Probert, Lee
Quinn, Peter
Rushton, Steven
Russell, Michael
Salisbury, Graham
Sarginson, Christopher
Scott, Graham
Sheldrake, Darren
Shoebridge, Robert
Stroud, Keith
Sutton, Gary
Swarbrick, Neil
Tanner, Stephen
Taylor, Anthony
Tierney, Paul
Walton, Peter
Ward, Gavin
Waugh, Jock
Webb, David
Webb, Howard
Webster, Colin
Whitestone, Dean
Williamson, Iain
Woolmer, Andy
Wright, Kevin

ASSISTANT REFEREES

Akers, Christopher
Amey, Justin
Amphlett, Marvyn
Artis, Stephen
Astley, Mark
Atkin, Robert
Atkin, Ryan
Atkin, Warren
Backhouse, Anthony
Bankes, Peter
Barratt, Wayne
Barrow, Simon
Bartlett, Richard
Beck, Simon
Bennett, Andrew
Bennett, Simon
Benton, David
Beswick, Gary
Betts, Lee
Blackledge, Mike
Blunden, Darren
Bond, Darren
Bratt, Stephen
Breakspear, Charles
Bristow, Matthew
Brook, Carl

Brooks, John
Bryan, David
Bull, Michael
Bull, Will
Buonassisi, Matthew
Burt, Stuart
Busby, John
Bushell, Dave
Butler, Stuart
Cairns, Michael
Cann, Darren
Child, Stephen
Clark, Richard
Clayton, Alan
Clayton, Simon
Coggins, Antony
Collin, Jake
Cook, Stephen
Cooper, Ian
Copeland, Steven
Corp, Richard
Coy, Martin
Creighton, Stephen
Crouch, Ian
Crysell, Adam
Curry, Paul

Daly, Stephen
Davies, Andy
Davies, Peter
Davison, Paul
Denton, Michael
Dermott, Philip
Dexter, Martin
Dudley, Ian
Duncan, Mark
Duncan, Scott
Dunn, Carl
Eaton, Derek
Ellis, Robert
England, Darren
Evetts, Gary
Farries, John
Fearn, Amy
Fitch, Carl
Fletcher, Russell
Flynn, John
Foley, Matt
Ford, Declan
Ganfield, Ronald
Garratt, Andrew
George, Mike
Gooch, Peter

Gordon, Barry
Gosling, Ian
Graham, Paul
Gratton, Danny
Greenhalgh, Nicholas
Greenwood, Alf
Griffiths, Mark
Grunnill, Wayne
Hair, Neil
Halliday, Andrew
Handley, Darren
Harrington, Tony
Harwood, Colin
Haycock, Ken
Hayward, Kevin
Hendley, Andy
Hicks, Craig
Hillier, Jake
Hilton, Gary
Hobbis, Nick
Hobday, Paul
Hodskinson, Paul
Holderness, Barry
Holmes, Adrian
Hopkins, Adam
Hopkins, John
Horton, Tony
Howes, Mark
Hull, Joe
Hunt, Jonathan
Hussin, Ian
Hutchinson, Andrew
Huxtable, Brett
Hyde, Robert
Ihringova, Sasa
Jerden, Gary
Johnson, Gordon
Johnson, Kevin
Johnson, Ryan
Jones, Mark
Jones, Robert
Joyce, Ross
Kavanagh, Christopher
Kaye, Elliott
Keane, Patrick
Kelly, Paul
Kendall, Richard
Kettlewell, Paul
Khatib, Billy
Kinseley, Nicholas
Kirkup, Peter
Knapp, Simon
Knight, Philip
Knowles, Chris

Laver, Andy
Law, Geoff
Lawrence, David
Lawson, Keith
Leach, Daniel
Ledger, Scott
Lennard, Harry
Linden, Wes
Long, Simon
Lucas, Simeon
Lugg, Nigel
Lymer, Colin
Mackay, Robert
Magill, John
Margetts, Dave
Markham, Danny
Marsden, Paul
Martin, Richard
Martin, Stephen
Mason, Tony
Massey, Sian
Mattocks, Kevin
McCallum, Dave
McDonough, Mick
Meeson, Daniel
Merchant, Rob
Metcalfe, Lee
Muge, Gavin
Mullarkey, Michael
Murphy, Nigel
Naylor, Dave
Newbold, Andrew
Newman, Ryan
Norcott, Wade
Norris, Paul
Nunn, Adam
O'Brien, John
O'Donnell, Christopher
Oldham, Scott
Parker, Alan
Parry, Matthew
Peart, Tony
Perry, Marc
Plowright, Dave
Pollock, Robert
Porter, Wayne
Pottage, Mark
Powell, Christopher
Radford, Neil
Rathbone, Ian
Rees, Paul
Richards, Ceri
Richardson, David
Robathan, Daniel

Roberts, Bob
Robinson, Tim
Rock, David
Rodda, Andrew
Ross, Stephen
Rubery, Steve
Russell, Geoff
Russell, Mark
Salisbury, Michael
Saliy, Oleksandr
Sannerude, Adrian
Scholes, Mark
Scott, John
Scregg, Andy
Siddall, Iain
Simpson, Jeremy
Slaughter, Ashley
Smallwood, William
Smith, Nigel
Smith, Stephen
Stewart, Matthew
Stockbridge, Sebastian
Storrie, Dave
Stott, Gary
Street, Duncan
Stretton, Guy
Sutton, Mark
Swabey, Lee
Tankard, Anthony
Thompson, Marvin
Toner, Ben
Tranter, Adrian
Treleaven, Dean
Trott, Wayne
Turner, Andy
Turner, Glenn
Tyas, Jason
Watts, Adam
Weaver, Mark
Webb, Michael
West, Richard
Whiteley, Jason
Whitton, Robert
Wigglesworth, Richard
Wilkes, Matthew
Wood, Tim
Woolford, David
Wootton, Ricky
Wright, Peter
Yates, Ollie
Yerby, Martin
Young, Gary

TRANSFERS 2010–11

	From	To	Fee in £
JUNE 2010			
7 Bailey, James J.	Crewe Alex	Derby Co	undisclosed
18 Batt, Shaun A.S.P.	Peterborough U	Millwall	1,000,000 joint fee
9 Brayford, John R.	Crewe Alex	Derby Co	1,000,000 joint fee
16 Connolly, Paul	Derby Co	Leeds U	Free
24 Crofts, Andrew L.	Brighton & HA	Norwich C	300,000
4 Foster, Benjamin A.	Manchester U	Birmingham C	6,000,000
7 Fox, David L.	Colchester U	Norwich C	undisclosed
21 Hunt, Stephen	Hull C	Wolverhampton W	3,000,000
10 Kenny, Patrick	Sheffield U	QPR	750,000
29 Langmead, Kelvin S.	Shrewsbury T	Peterborough U	undisclosed
30 Little, Mark D.	Wolverhampton W	Peterborough U	undisclosed
19 Mackie, James C.	Plymouth Arg	QPR	undisclosed
26 Marney, Dean E.	Hull C	Burnley	500,000
1 Martin, David J.	Millwall	Derby Co	200,000
18 Mouyokolo, Steven	Hull C	Wolverhampton W	2,500,000
18 Shackell, Jason	Wolverhampton W	Barnsley	700,000
17 Sodje, Akpo	Sheffield W	Charlton Ath	Free
24 Surman, Andrew R.E.	Wolverhampton W	Norwich C	1,200,000
25 Trotter, Liam A.	Ipswich T	Millwall	Free
JULY 2010			
14 Adomah, Albert	Barnet	Bristol C	150,000
14 Aldred, Thomas M.	Carlisle U	Watford	undisclosed
22 Ashworth, Luke A.	Leyton Orient	Rotherham U	Free
1 Ayling, Luke D.	Arsenal	Yeovil T	undisclosed
12 Bailey, Nicky F.	Charlton Ath	Middlesbrough	1,400,000
9 Barnes, Ashley L.	Plymouth Arg	Brighton & HA	undisclosed
9 Benayoun, Yossi S.	Liverpool	Chelsea	5,000,000
26 Berrett, James T.	Huddersfield T	Carlisle U	Free
26 Bramble, Titus M.	Wigan Ath	Sunderland	1,000,000
30 Bruce, Alex S.	Ipswich T	Leeds U	200,000
13 Cisse, Kalifa	Reading	Bristol C	400,000
9 Collins, Michael A.	Huddersfield T	Scunthorpe U	50,000
7 Collins, Neill	Preston NE	Leeds U	undisclosed
21 Cresswell, Ryan A.	Bury	Rotherham U	undisclosed
1 Cuvelier, Florent	Portsmouth	Stoke C	undisclosed
16 Diagouraga, Toumani	Peterborough U	Brentford	undisclosed
2 Dickinson, Liam M.	Brighton & HA	Barnsley	150,000
9 Dickson, Ryan A.	Brentford	Southampton	Free
14 Donnelly, Scott P.	Aldershot T	Swansea C	200,000
14 Eastwood, Simon C.	Huddersfield T	Oxford U	Free
23 Fleetwood, Stuart K.W.	Charlton Ath	Hereford U	undisclosed
1 Fletcher, Steven K.	Burnley	Wolverhampton W	6,500,000
27 Foster, Danny	Brentford	Wycombe W	Free
30 Francis, Simon C.	Southend U	Charlton Ath	35,000
7 Gilmartin, Rene	Walsall	Watford	undisclosed
1 Grant, Robert	Accrington S	Scunthorpe U	260,000
29 Gray, David P.	Manchester U	Preston NE	Free
14 Green, Matthew J.	Torquay U	Oxford U	undisclosed
13 Greer, Gordon	Swindon T	Brighton & HA	undisclosed
27 Griffin, Andrew	Stoke C	Reading	250,000
22 Haworth, Andrew A.D.	Blackburn R	Bury	Free
30 Henry, James	Reading	Millwall	200,000
23 Hourihane, Conor	Sunderland	Ipswich T	undisclosed
23 Hudson, Kirk I.	Aldershot T	Brentford	undisclosed
28 Huntington, Paul D.	Stockport Co	Yeovil T	Free
8 Iwelumo, Christopher R.	Wolverhampton W	Burnley	500,000
16 Jackson, Simeon A.	Gillingham	Norwich C	800,000
29 Jutkiewicz, Lukas I.P.	Everton	Coventry C	200,000
1 Keogh, Richard J.	Carlisle U	Coventry C	undisclosed

9 Labadie, Joss C.	WBA	Tranmere R	Free
24 McCallum, Gavin K.	Hereford U	Lincoln C	undisclosed
2 McCombe, Jamie P.	Bristol C	Huddersfield T	undisclosed
6 McCracken, David	Milton Keynes D	Brentford	undisclosed
26 McCready, Christopher J.	Northampton T	Morecambe	Free
6 Morgan, Craig	Peterborough U	Preston NE	400,000
5 Perch, James R.	Nottingham F	Newcastle U	1,500,000
30 Platt, Clive L.	Colchester U	Coventry C	nominal
14 Potter, Alfie J.	Peterborough U	Oxford U	undisclosed
30 Pugh, Marc A.	Hereford U	AFC Bournemouth	Free
20 Rendell, Scott D.	Peterborough U	Wycombe W	undisclosed
7 Richardson, Frazer	Charlton Ath	Southampton	undisclosed
5 Ruddy, John T.G.	Everton	Norwich C	Free
9 Sharp, Billy L.	Sheffield U	Doncaster R	1,150,000
23 Skarz, Joseph P.	Huddersfield T	Bury	undisclosed
1 Smalling, Chris	Fulham	Manchester U	10,000,000
5 Spillane, Michael E.	Norwich C	Brentford	undisclosed
27 Strevens, Ben J.	Brentford	Wycombe W	Free
20 Thomas, Wesley A.N.	Dagenham & R	Cheltenham T	5000
5 Wallace, Ross	Preston NE	Burnley	1,900,000
23 Wesolowski, James	Leicester C	Peterborough U	undisclosed
6 Woodman, Craig A.	Wycombe W	Brentford	undisclosed

TEMPORARY TRANSFERS

14 Adeyemi, Thomas O. – Norwich C – Bradford C; 15 Al Habsi, Ali – Bolton W – Wigan Ath; 13 Arismendi, Hugo D. – Stoke C – Barnsley; 18 Balanta, Angelo J. – QPR – Milton Keynes D; 20 Ball, David M. – Manchester C – Swindon T; 15 Byrne, Mark – Nottingham F – Barnet; 2 Croft, Lee D. – Derby Co – Huddersfield T; 20 Daniels, Luke M. – WBA – Bristol R; 15 Elliott, Thomas J. – Leeds U – Rotherham U; 27 Franks, Leigh D. – Huddersfield T – Oxford U; 2 Freeman, Luke A. – Arsenal – Yeovil T; 21 Garner, Joseph A. – Nottingham F – Huddersfield T; 30 Gritton, Martin – Chesterfield – Torquay U; 15 Hatch, Liam M.A. – Peterborough U – Darlington; 16 Hone, Daniel – Lincoln C – Darlington; 2 James, Matthew – Manchester U – Preston NE; 28 Kiernan, Robert S. – Watford – Yeovil T; 6 Lillis, Joshua M. – Scunthorpe U – Rochdale; 28 Lisbie, Kevin A. – Ipswich T – Millwall; 16 McDonald, Cody – Norwich C – Gillingham; 16 McNulty, Jimmy – Brighton & HA – Scunthorpe U; 2 Mellor, Neil A. – Preston NE – Sheffield W; 5 Mendez-Laing, Nathaniel – Wolverhampton W – Peterborough U; 15 Morris, Ian – Scunthorpe U – Chesterfield; 21 Nielsen, Gunnar – Manchester C – Tranmere R; 7 Nolan, Edward W. – Preston NE – Scunthorpe U; 22 Nosworthy, Nyron – Sunderland – Sheffield U; 6 Sadler, Matthew – Watford – Shrewsbury T; 30 Soncko, Ibrahima – Stoke C – Portsmouth; 15 Spencer, James C. – Huddersfield T – Morecambe; 28 Sullivan, John D. – Millwall – Yeovil T; 5 Taylor, Rhys F. – Chelsea – Crewe Alex; 8 Thompson, O'Neil A.M.T. – Barnsley – Hereford U; 15 Tunnicliffe, James M. – Brighton & HA – Bristol R; 6 Walton, Simon W. – Plymouth Arg – Sheffield U; 16 Wright, Mark A. – Bristol R – Shrewsbury T

AUGUST 2010

2 Abbott, Pawel T.H.	Oldham Ath	Charlton Ath	undisclosed
20 Adams, Nicholas W.	Leicester C	Brentford	undisclosed
7 Ainsworth, Lionel G.R.	Huddersfield T	Shrewsbury T	undisclosed
6 Alexander, Gary G.	Millwall	Brentford	undisclosed
12 Basham, Christopher P.	Bolton W	Blackpool	500,000
31 Benson, Paul A.	Dagenham & R	Charlton Ath	undisclosed
5 Caddis, Paul	Celtic	Swindon T	undisclosed
31 Campbell, Dudley J.	Leicester C	Blackpool	undisclosed
6 Carayol, Mustapha L.	Torquay U	Lincoln C	undisclosed
12 Cathcart, Craig G.	Manchester U	Blackpool	500,000
31 Clayton, Adam S.	Manchester C	Leeds U	undisclosed
31 Dalla Valle, Lauri	Liverpool	Fulham	exch.
31 Dawson, Craig	Rochdale	WBA	500,000
27 Dean, Harlee J.	Dagenham & R	Southampton	undisclosed
7 Deeney, Troy M.	Walsall	Watford	undisclosed
31 Di Santo, Francis M.	Chelsea	Wigan Ath	4,000,000
17 Doherty, Matthew J.	Portsmouth	Wolverhampton W	undisclosed
12 Eaves, Thomas J.	Oldham Ath	Bolton W	350,000
5 Ferry, Simon W.	Celtic	Swindon T	undisclosed
5 Fulop, Marton	Sunderland	Ipswich T	750,000
6 Garvan, Owen W.	Ipswich T	Crystal Palace	250,000

27 Gornell, Terence M.	Tranmere R	Accrington S	undisclosed
3 Grant, Lee A.	Sheffield W	Burnley	1,000,000
31 Harte, Ian P.	Carlisle U	Reading	undisclosed
31 Hulse, Robert W.	Derby Co	QPR	undisclosed
31 Hurst, James	Portsmouth	WBA	undisclosed
16 Ireland, Stephen	Manchester C	Aston Villa	8,000,000+exch.
31 Jacobsen, Lars	Blackburn R	West Ham U	undisclosed
6 Johnson, John J.	Middlesbrough	Northampton T	Free
16 Jones, Bradley	Middlesbrough	Liverpool	2,300,000
30 Jones, Kenwyne J.	Sunderland	Stoke C	8,000,000
31 Kacaniklic, Alexander	Liverpool	Fulham	exch.
6 Kennedy, Mark J.	Cardiff C	Ipswich T	75,000
31 Konchesky, Paul M.	Fulham	Liverpool	4,000,000+exch.
25 Lee Alan D.	Crystal Palace	Huddersfield T	undisclosed
27 McCormack, Ross	Cardiff C	Leeds U	300,000
18 Milner, James P.	Aston Villa	Manchester C	24,000,000+exch.
2 Myhill, Boaz	Hull C	WBA	1,500,000
17 O'Keefe, Stuart A.A.	Southend U	Crystal Palace	Free
3 Orr, Bradley J.	Bristol C	QPR	500,000
3 Payne, Stefan S.	Fulham	Gillingham	undisclosed
31 Phillips, Matthew	Wycombe W	Blackpool	325,000
23 Pitman, Brett D.	Bournemouth	Bristol C	800,000
3 Reid, Kyel R.	Sheffield U	Charlton Ath	undisclosed
23 Scotland, Jason K.	Wigan Ath	Ipswich T	750,000
9 Shorey, Nicholas	Aston Villa	WBA	1,500,000
19 Simpson, Jay-Alistaire F.	Arsenal	Hull C	1,200,000
11 Sinclair, Scott A.	Chelsea	Swansea C	500,000
26 Stead, Jonathan G.	Ipswich T	Bristol C	225,000
3 Stewart, Damion D.	QPR	Bristol C	undisclosed
6 Taarabt, Adel	Tottenham H	QPR	1,000,000
31 Waghorn, Martyn T.	Sunderland	Leicester C	3,000,000
23 Walker, Joshua	Middlesbrough	Watford	Free
18 Walters, Jonathan R.	Ipswich T	Stoke C	2,750,000
5 Wiggins, Rhoys B.	Norwich C	AFC Bournemouth	undisclosed
31 Wilson, Marc D.	Portsmouth	Stoke C	3,000,000
3 Winfield, David T.	Aldershot T	Wycombe W	undisclosed

TEMPORARY TRANSFERS

27 Akinde, John J.A. – Bristol C – Bristol R; 31, Akinde, John J.A. – Ebbsfleet U – Bristol R; 3 Andersen, Mikkel – Reading – Bristol R; 13 Atkins, Ross M. – Derby Co – Tamworth; 5 Barker, Christopher A. – Plymouth Arg – Southend U; 26 Barnett, Leon P. – WBA – Norwich C; 10 Bartley, Kyle – Arsenal – Sheffield U; 20 Bell, Matthew – Port Vale – Newcastle T; 13 Bell-Baggie, Abdulai H. – Reading – Port Vale; 19 Bellamy, Craig D. – Manchester C – Cardiff C; 6 Bennett, Julian L. – Nottingham F – Crystal Palace; 31 Bent, Marcus N. – Birmingham C – Wolverhampton W; 5 Bertrand, Ryan – Chelsea – Nottingham F; 5 Bostock, John – Tottenham H – Hull C; 27 Brown, Christopher R. – Rochdale – Ashton U; 14 Brown, Kayledene – WBA – Tranmere R; 4 Button, David R.E. – Tottenham H – Plymouth Arg; 6 Carter, Darren A. – Preston NE – Millwall; 4 Chester, James G. – Manchester U – Carlisle U; 6 Clayton, Adam S. – Manchester C – Leeds U; 31 Cleverley, Thomas W. – Manchester U – Wigan Ath; 6 Cook, Andrew E. – Carlisle U – Barrow; 12 Cork, Jack F.P. – Chelsea – Burnley; 20 Counago, Pablo G. – Ipswich T – Crystal Palace; 26 Crawford, Harrison – Southend U – Dover Ath; 5 Darville, Liam T. – Leeds U – Tranmere R; 13 Davis, Harry S. – Crewe Alex – Stafford R; 31 Dawson, Craig – Bolton W – Rochdale; 6 Deeney, Troy M. – Walsall – Watford; 20 Demetriou, Stephen – Dagenham & R – Grays Ath; 13 Dickinson, Carl M. – Stoke City – Portsmouth; 6 Diouf, Mame Biram – Manchester U – Blackburn R; 6 Donnelly, Georgie J. – Plymouth Arg – Stockport Co; 10 Doyle, Colin – Birmingham C – Coventry C; 5 Drinkwater, Daniel N. – Manchester U – Cardiff C; 18 Fodor, Ferenc – Oldham Ath – Northwich Vic; 19 Foderingham, Wesley – Crystal Palace – Bromley; 5 Fry, Matthew – West Ham U – Charlton Ath; 31 Gardner, Anthony – Tottenham H – Crystal Palace; 3 Geohaghon, Exodus I. – Peterborough U – Rotherham U; 31 Gerrard, Anthony – Walsall – Hull C; 31 Grandison, Jermaine M. – Coventry C – Tranmere R; 14 Green, Daniel J. – Fulham – Braintree T; 13 Green, Dominic A. – Peterborough U – Rushden & D; 7 Griffiths, Scott R. – Peterborough U – Chesterfield; 13 Grimes, Jamie N. – Swansea C – Forest Green R; 5 Grof, David – Notts Co – Tamworth; 31 Hamer, Benjamin J. – Reading – Brentford; 23 Hart, Danny – Barnet – Thurrock; 20 Hector, Michael A.J. – Reading – Oxford C; 9 Highdale, Sean – Liverpool – Oldham Ath; 5 Holden, Dean T.J. – Shrewsbury T – Rotherham U; 13 Howe, Jermaine R. – Peterborough U – Rushden & D; 20 Hubbins, Luke A. – Birmingham C – Notts Co; 11 Hughes-Mason, Kiernan P. –

Millwall – Tooting & Mitcham U; 1 Hunt, Jack P. – Huddersfield T – Chesterfield; 26 Ikeme, Carl – WolverhamptonW – Leicester C; 14 Ilesanmi, Oluwafemi A.A. – Dagenham & R – Histon; 6 Jansson, Oscar – Tottenham H – Northampton T; 6 Jeffers, Shaun E. – Coventry C – Cheltenham T; 6 Jervis, Jake M. – Birmingham C – Notts Co; 5 Johnson, Damian M. – Plymouth Arg – Huddersfield T; 31 Judge, Alan – Blackburn R – Notts Co; 25 Keogh, Andrew D. – Wolverhampton W – Cardiff C; 31 Khizanishvili, Zurab – Blackburn R – Reading; 25 Kiernan, Robert S. – Watford – Yeovil T; 20 Kilgallon, Matthew – Sunderland – Middlesbrough; 7 King, Joshua C.K. – Manchester U – Preston NE; 27 Kinsella, Sean W. – Plymouth Arg – Bridgwater T; 23 Koranteng, Nathan P.K.T. – Peterborough U – Rushden & D; 5 Koumas, Jason – Wigan Ath – Cardiff C; 3 Lees, Thomas J. – Leeds U – Bury; 5 Liddle, Michael W. – Sunderland – Leyton Orient; 31 LuaLua, Kazenga – Newcastle U – Brighton & HA; 13 Lynch, Christopher M. – Burnley – Hyde U; 27 MacDonald, Shaun B. – Swansea C – Yeovil T; 26 Mancienne, Michael I. – Chelsea – Wolverhampton W; 21 Marrow, Alexander J. – Blackburn R – Crystal Palace; 31 Marshall, Ben – Stoke C – Carlisle U; 5 Martin, Alan – Leeds U – Barrow; 7 Martin, Lee R. – Ipswich T – Charlton Ath; 13 Mason, Ryan G. – Tottenham Hotspur – Doncaster R; 12 McCarthy, Alex S. – Reading – Brentford; 12 McCrae, Romone C.A. – Barnet – Histon; 2 McGivern, Ryan – Manchester C – Walsall; 12 McKeown, James K. – Peterborough U – Boston U; 13 Mellor, Kelvin – Crewe Alex – Stafford R; 31 Mendy, Arnaud – Derby Co – Tranmere R; 31 Michalik, Lubomir – Bolton W – Carlisle U; 12 Mills, Daniel P. – Peterborough U – Histon; 23 Mills, Gregory A. – Derby Co – Telford U; 20 Mills, Jack I.A. – Reading – Oxford C; 5 Mooney, David – Reading – Colchester U; 20 Morgan, Kerry D. – Swansea C – Newport Co; 2 Moult, Louis E. – Stoke C – Bradford C; 14 Mutch, Jordon J.E.S. – Birmingham C – Watford; 6 Mvoto, Yves J.O. – Sunderland – Oldham Ath; 13 Norwood, James T. – Exeter C – Forest Green R; 20 Obika, Jonathan – Tottenham H – Crystal Palace; 12 Offiong, Richard – Carlisle U – Darlington; 24 Okus, Conor E. – Dagenham & R – Thurrock; 10 Olofinjana, Seyi G. – Hull C – Cardiff C; 12 Onuoha, Chinedum – Manchester C – Sunderland; 20 Osborn, Alexander S. – Dagenham & R – Grays Ath; 31 Pack, Marlon – Portsmouth – Cheltenham T; 13 Parrett, Dean G. – Tottenham H – Plymouth Arg; 31 Payne, Joshua J. – West Ham U – Oxford U; 19 Perkins, Lewis C. – Charlton Ath – Cray W; 5 Philliskirk, Daniel – Chelsea – Oxford U; 13 Proctor, Jamie T. – Preston NE – Stockport Co; 19 Reid, Ruben J. – WBA – Walsall; 20 Reynolds, Duran-Rhys – Dagenham & R – Grays Ath; 11 Scott, Mark J. – Swindon T – Swindon Super'e; 7 Shroot, Robin – Birmingham C – Cheltenham T; 5 Simpson, Joshua R – Peterborough U – Southend U; 6 Simpson, Robbie – Coventry C – Brenford; 2 Stewart, Cameron R. – Manchester U – Yeovil T; 30 Sullivan, John D. – Millwall – Yeovil T; 31 Taylor, Andrew D. – Middlesbrough – Watford; 6 Tomlin, Lee M. – Rushden & D – Peterborough U; 6 Tounkara, Oumare – Sunderland – Oldham Ath; 13 Townsend, Andros – Tottenham H – Ipswich T; 6 Trippier, Kieran J. – Manchester C – Barnsley; 27 Trott, Jordan R. – Plymouth Arg – Bridgwater T; 27 Tudur Jones, Owain – Norwich C – Yeovil T; 14 Turner, Iain – Everton – Coventry C; 13 Tutte, Andrew W. – Manchester C – Rochdale; 27 Varney, Luke I. – Charlton Ath – Blackpool; 5 Vokes, Samuel M. – Wolverhampton W – Bristol C; 20 Walker, Joshua – Middlesbrough – Watford; 13 Walsh, Phillip – Dagenham & R – Barnet; 21 Waters, Aaron L.J. – QPR – Thurrock; 3 Watt, Herschel O.S. – Arsenal – Leeds U; 13 Welbeck, Daniel N.T.M. – Manchester U – Sunderland; 12 Wootton, Lee S. – Dagenham & R – Histon

SEPTEMBER 2010 TEMPORARY TRANSFERS

25 Ajose, Nicholas – Manchester U – Bury; 11 Ayala, Daniel S. – Liverpool – Hull C; 10 Brown, Jason R. – Blackburn R – Leeds U; 10 Brown, Lee J. – QPR – Hayes & Yeading U; 28 Brown, Reece – Manchester U – Bradford C; 30 Bulman, Dannie M. – Oxford U – Crawley T; 20 Byrne, Callum – Rochdale – Trafford; 24 Carlton, Daniel – Bury – Grimsby T; 27 Caulker, Steven R. – Tottenham H – Bristol C; 30 Chaplow, Richard D. – WBA – Southampton; 2 Clark, Gavin E. – Morecambe – Kendal T; 10 Clarke, Oliver A. – Bristol R – Gloucster C; 27 Clough, Charlie – Bristol R – Newport Co; 27 Connerton, James – Crewe Alex – Nantwich T; 17 Cook, Steve A. – Brighton & HA – Eastbourne Bor; 2 Cox, Elliott J. – QPR – Tooting & Mitcham U; 17 Daniels, Luke M. – WBA – Charlton Ath; 10 Davies, Scott M.E. – Reading – Wycombe W; 17 Davisson, Benjamin J. – Charlton Ath – Bromley; 9 Davis, David L. – Wolverhampton W – Walsall; 25 De Laet, Ritchie R.A. – Manchester U – Sheffield U; 28 Devlin, Conor – Manchester U – Hartlepool U; 10 Edwards, Joseph R. – Bristol C – Bath C; 17 Elliott, Christopher M. – Bradford C – Harrogate Rail; 6 Emery, Joshua S. – Cheltenham T – Cirencester T; 3 Fitchett, Daniel O. – Wycombe W – Oxford C; 24 Fitzsimons, Danny – QPR – Histon; 24 Fodor, Ferenc – Oldham Ath – Northwich Vic; 10 Frampton, Andrew J.K. – Millwall – Leyton Orient; 24 Gill, Matthew J. – Norwich C – Peterborough U; 28 Gill, Oliver D. – Manchester U – Bradford C; 17 Gulacsi, Peter – Liverpool – Tranmere R; 24 Harrison, Ryan A. – Bradford C – Harrogate Rail; 16 Henderson, Liam M. – Watford – Colchester U; 17 Henderson, Stephen – Bristol C – Yeovil T; 24 Holroyd, Christopher – Brighton & HA – Stevenage; 17 Hume, Iain E. – Barnsley – Preston NE; 10 Ings, Daniel W.J. – Bournemouth – Dorchester T; 16 Jackson, Marlon M. – Bristol C – Aldershot T; 24 Jarvis, Nathaniel S. – Cardiff C – Southend U; 10 John, Martin – Cardiff C – Newport Co; 16 Johnson, Jemal P. – Milton Keynes D – Port Vale; 28 Jones, Andrai R. – Bury – Altrincham; 10 Kean, Jacob K. – Blackburn R – Hartlepool U; 13 Kuqi, Shefki – Swansea C – Derby Co; 10 Lawrence,

Liam – Stoke C – Portsmouth; 6 Lee, Jake A. – Cheltenham T – Cirencester T; 23 Livermore, Jake C.
– Tottenham H – Ipswich T; 23 Mackreth, Jack – Tranmere R – Burscough; 23 McCartney, George –
Sunderland – Leeds U; 17 Mambo, Yado M. – Charlton Ath – Eastbourne Bor; 13 Mills, Gregory A. –
Derby Co – Telford U; 24 Moore, Luke I. – WBA – Derby Co; 24 M'Poku, Paul-Jose – Tottenham H –
Leyton Orient; 27 Noble, Ryan – Sunderland – Derby Co; 16 Norwood, Oliver J. – Manchester U –
Carlisle U; 17 Nouble, Frank H. – West Ham U – Swansea C; 10 O'Brien, Liam D. – Portsmouth –
Eastbourne Bor; 11 O'Connor, Garry L.J. – Birmingham C – Barnsley; 3 O'Connor, Patrick J. –
Millwall – Tooting & Mitcham U; 13 O'Donnell, Richard M. – Sheffield W – Grimsby T; 10 Patulea,
Adrian M. – Leyton Orient – Hayes & Yeading U; 10 Robinson, Theo L.R. – Huddersfield T –
Millwall; 13 Rose, Daniel L. – Tottenham H – Bristol C; 24 Sills, Timothy – Stevenage – Rushden & D;
23 Smalley, Deane A.M. – Oldham Ath – Rochdale; 23 Smith, Adam J. – Tottenham H –
Bournemouth; 11 Smith, Thomas W. – Portsmouth – QPR; 16 Timlin, Michael A. – Swindon T –
Southend U; 22 Tozer, Ben P.A. – Newcastle U – Northampton T; 7 Verma, Aman K. – Leicester C –
Kidderminster H; 10 Vaughan, James O. – Everton – Crystal Palace; 28 Wainwright, Neil –
Morecambe – Barrow; 17 Walcott, Jacob D. – Reading – Staines T; 14 Walker, Kyle A. – Tottenham H
– QPR; 10 Ward, Daniel C. – Bolton W – Coventry C; 23 Waters, Aaron L.J. – QPR – Thurrock; 24
Watkins, Marley J. – Cheltenham T – Bath C; 17 Watson, Ben C. – Exeter C – Forest Green R; 9
Williams, Gavin J. – Bristol C – Yeovil T; 23 Wood, Christopher – WBA – Barnsley; 28 Woodley,
Aaron R. – Oxford U – Oxford C; 30 Wootton, Scott J. – Manchester U – Tranmere R; 3 Yorke,
Reece – Barnet – Harlow T

OCTOBER 2010 TEMPORARY TRANSFERS

15 Adams, Nicholas W. – Brentford – Rochdale; 7 Aksalu, Mihkel – Sheffield U – Mansfield T; 15
Alnwick, Ben R. – Tottenham H – Leeds U; 25 Beardsley, Jason C. – Macclesfield T – Eastwood T; 21
Beautyman, Harry H. – Leyton Orient – St Albans C; 8 Bignall, Nicholas C. – Reading –
Southampton; 2 Blake, Ryan G. – Brentford – Woking; 22 Bowman, Ryan M. – Carlisle U –
Workington; 15 Bridge-Wilkinson, Marc – Carlisle U – Darlington; 29 Bulmer, Niki-Lee – QPR –
Hayes & Yeading U; 1 Chamberlain, Deale – Liverpool – Leeds U; 8 Clark, Robert J. – Doncaster R –
Sheffield; 28 Clay, Craig W. – Chesterfield – Barrow; 22 Clifford, Conor – Chelsea – Plymouth Arg; 1
Coker, Ben – Colchester U – Chelmsford C; 18 Colback, Jack R. – Sunderland – Ipswich T; 15 Colgan,
Nicholas V. – Grimsby T – Huddersfield T; 1 Collins, Dominic – Preston NE – Northwich Vic; 15
Collins, James S. – Aston Villa – Burton Alb; 22 Connolly, Reece W. – Aldershot T – Didcot T; 19
Cook, Steve A. – Brighton & HA – Mansfield T; 21 Cunningham, Gregory R. – Manchester C –
Leicester C; 28 Darkwa, Tendayi D. – Chesterfield – Barrow; 6 Davies, Andrew J. – Stoke C – Walsall;
15 Davies, Curtis – Aston Villa – Leicester C; 18 Day, Rhys – Oxford U – Mansfield T; 7 Devaney,
Martin T. – Barnsley – Walsall; 18 Emnes, Marvin – Middlesbrough – Swansea C; 29 Essam, Connor –
Gillingham – Bishop's Stortford; 22 Evans, Corry J. – Manchester U – Carlisle U; 5 Evina, Cedric D. –
Arsenal – Oldham Ath; 7 Fairhurst, Waide S. – Doncaster R – Southend U; 15 Fielding, Francis D. –
Blackburn R – Derby Co; 15 Fletcher, Wesleigh J. – Burnley – Stockport Co; 29 Frampton, Andrew
J.K. – Millwall – Swindon T; 9 Francomb, Georgie – Norwich C – Barnet; 22 Gallen, Kevin A. – Luton
T – Barnet; 22 Gardner, Steven A. – Hull C – Harrogate T; 15 Gillespie, Mark J. – Carlisle U – Blyth
Spartans; 28 Gowling, Joshua A.I. – Carlisle U – Lincoln C; 8 Grabban, Lewis J. – Millwall –
Brentford; 29 Grandison, Jermaine M. – Coventry C – Tranmere R; 12 Grella, Michele – Leeds U –
Carlisle U; 29 Grimes, Ashley J. – Millwall – Lincoln C; 19 Halford, Gregory – Wolverhampton W –
Portsmouth; 22 Hall, Grant T. – Brighton & HA – Whitehawk; 29 Harris, Sebastian – Northampton T
– Stafford R; 28 Hayes, Paul E. – Preston NE – Barnsley; 15 Head, Liam T. – Plymouth Arg – Forest
Green R; 22 Hemmings, Ashley J. – Wolverhampton W – Torquay U; 21 Hill, Matthew C. –
Wolverhampton W – Barnsley; 28 Howell, Luke A. – Milton Keynes D – Lincoln C; 29 Hoyte, Gavin
A. – Arsenal – Lincoln C; 22 Jackson, Marlon M. – Bristol C – Aldershot T; 1 James, Anthony –
Burton Alb – Hereford U; 1 Joyce, Daniel D. – Reading – Bedford T; 21 Kosylo, Matthew S.P. –
Stockport Co – Woodley SP; 16 Lawrence, Liam – Stoke C – Portsmouth; 1 Locke, Simon J. – Reading
– Croydon Ath; 15 Long, Kevin F. – Burnley – Accrington S; 30 McCartney, George – Sunderland –
Leeds U; 14 McDonald, Kevin – Burnley – Scunthorpe U; 29 McDonald, Rodney T. – Oldham Ath –
Stafford R; 29 McLoughlin, Ian M. – Ipswich T – Lowestoft T; 19 Mills, Joseph N. – Southampton –
Doncaster R; 29 Moore, Luke I. – WBA – Derby Co; 7 Moore, Simon W. – Brentford – Basingstoke T;
14 Naughton, Kyle – Tottenham H – Leicester C; 8 Nsiala, Aristote – Everton – Macclesfield T; 8
Oastler, Joseph J. – QPR – Torquay U; 22 Obadeyi, Temitope – Bolton W – Shrewsbury T; 29
O'Brien, Andrew J. – Bolton W – Leeds U; 27 Ollerenshaw, Joshua D. – Oldham Ath – Mossley; 27
O'Shea, James – Birmingham C – Stevenage; 1 Parker, Joshua K.S. – QPR – Northampton T; 29
Partington, Joseph M. – Bournemouth – Eastbourne Bor; 14 Pinney, Nathaniel B. – Crystal Palace –
Dagenham & R; 14 Poole, James A. – Manchester C – Hartlepool U; 29 Porter, George – Leyton
Orient – Lewes; 12 Price, Jason J. – Carlisle U – Bradford C; 8 Pulis, Anthony J. – Southampton –
Stockport Co; 29 Purdie, Robert J. – Oldham Ath – Hereford U; 27 Randall, Mark – Arsenal –
Rotherham U; 29 Reid, Andrew M. – Sunderland – Sheffield U; 5 Ritchie, Matthew T. – Portsmouth –
Swindon T; 6 Roe, Phillip M. – Sheffield U – Retford T; 22 Rooney, Luke W. – Gillingham –

Eastbourne Bor; 22 Rose, Romone A. – QPR – Torquay U; 22 Sarcevic, Antoni – Crewe Alex – Chester; 19 Sears, Fred – West Ham U – Scunthorpe U; 15 Severn, James A. – Derby Co – Tamworth; 16 Smith, Thomas W. – Portsmouth – QPR; 29 Speight, Jake C. – Bradford C – Port Vale; 8 Stavrinou, Alexander M. – Charlton Ath – Cambridge U; 28 Taiwo, Soloman O. – Cardiff C – Dagenham & R; 29 Thomas, Michael D. – Macclesfield T – Mossley; 22 Vincenti, Peter I. – Stevenage – Mansfield T; 1 Vine, Rowan L. – QPR – Hull C; 21 Walcott, Jacob D. – Reading – Staines T; 28 Whing, Andrew J. – Brighton & HA – Leyton Orient; 26 White, Andrew J. – Gillingham – Margate; 29 Williams, Owain fon – Stockport Co – Bury; 1 Williams, Thomas A. – Bristol C – Colchester U

NOVEMBER 2010 TEMPORARY TRANSFERS
5 Adams, Nathan M. – Lincoln C – Stamford; 2 Afobe, Benik – Arsenal – Huddersfield T; 20 Ainsley, Jack W. – Ipswich T – Histon; 12 Aldred, Thomas M. – Carlisle U – Stockport Co; 2 Allsop, Ryan – WBA – Stockport Co; 19 Andrew, Calvin H. – Crystal Palace – Millwall; 11 Atkins, Ross M. – Derby Co – Tamworth; 25 Atkinson, William H. – Hull C – Rotherham U; 13 Bassett, Kyle L. – Exeter C – Bideford; 25 Batth, Daniel T. – Wolverhampton W – Sheffield U; 24 Bednar, Roman – WBA – Leicester C; 5 Belcher, Samuel M. – Wycombe W – Hinckley U; 25 Bell-Baggie, Abdulai H. – Reading – Crawley T; 12 Bignall, Nicholas C. – Reading – Bournemouth; 19 Brown, Jason R. – Blackburn R – Leyton Orient; 8 Brown, Kayledene – WBA – Dagenham & R; 4 Byrne, Callum – Rochdale – Mossley; 12 Chambers, Ashley R. – Leicester C – York C; 24 Charnock, Kieran J. – Peterborough U – Morecambe; 12 Chilaka, Chibuzor – Bradford C – Bradford PA; 19 Clayton, Adam S. – Leeds U – Peterborough U; 12 Coid, Daniel J. – Blackpool – Rotherham U; 4 Coleman, Rory C. – Scunthorpe U – Boston U; 24 Comminges, Miguel – Cardiff C – Carlisle U; 24 Cort, Leon T.A. – Burnley – Preston NE; 25 Craney, Ian T.W. – Huddersfield T – Accrington S; 12 Creighton, Mark A. – Oxford U – Wrexham; 3 Cruise, Thomas D. – Arsenal – Carlisle U; 2 Darby, Stephen – Liverpool – Notts Co; 5 Davisson, Benjamin J. – Charlton Ath – Thurrock; 18 Deering, Sam – Oxford U – Newport Co; 17 De Laet, Ritchie R.A. – Manchester U – Preston NE; 2 Dickinson, Liam M. – Brighton & HA – Walsall; 25 Downing, Paul – WBA – Rotherham U; 25 Easter, Jermaine M. – Milton Keynes D – Swansea C; 25 Eastham, Ashley – Blackpool – Carlisle U; 12 Eckersley, Richard J. – Burnley – Bradford C; 25 Elford-Alliyu, Lateef – WBA – Tranmere R; 11 Elito, Medy E. – Colchester U – Dagenham & R; 26 Ellison, James – Burton Alb – Stafford R; 25 Fallon, Rory M. – Plymouth Arg – Ipswich T; 4 Featherstone, Nicky L. – Hull C – Hereford U; 10 Federico, Jerome J. – Wycombe W – Woking; 4 Fitchett, Daniel O. – Wycombe W – Salisbury C; 11 Futcher, Benjamin P. – Bury – Oxford U; 2 Geohaghon, Exodus I. – Peterborough U – Shrewsbury T; 9 German, Antonio T. – QPR – Southend U; 4 Goodall, Alan J. – Rochdale – Newport Co; 16 Grant, Robert – Scunthorpe U – Rochdale; 25 Guidetti, John A. – Manchester C – Burnley; 26 Guinan, Stephen A. – Northampton – Forest Green R; 12 Gunning, Gavin – Blackburn R – Bury; 4 Healy MBE, David J. – Sunderland – Doncaster R; 25 Heath, Joseph – Exeter C – Hereford U; 12 Hector, Michael A.J. – Reading – Horsham; 24 Henderson, Liam M. – Watford – Colchester U; 24 Hill, Matthew C. – Wolverhampton W – Barnsley; 26 Hinton, Craig – Northampton T – Luton T; 16 Hoban, Patrick J. – Bristol C – Cleveland T; 18 Hooman, Harry J. – Shrewsbury T – Hinckley U; 26 Horne, Louis – Bradford C – Halifax T; 25 Hughes-Mason, Kiernan P. – Millwall – Tooting & Mitcham U; 24 Hussey, Christopher I. – Coventry C – Crewe Alex; 2 Ince, Thomas – Liverpool – Notts Co; 25 Jacobson, Joseph M. – Oldham Ath – Accrington S; 16 James-Lewis, Merrick A. – Southend U – Tooting & Mitcham U; 25 Jarvis, Ryan R. – Leyton Orient – Northampton T; 9 Jenkinson, Carl D. – Charlton Ath – Eastbourne Bor; 11 Jesionkowski, Jakub – Swindon T – Oxford C; 25 Johnson, Paul A. – Hartlepool U – Whitby T; 13 Keats, Noah J. – Exeter C – Bideford; 9 Kennedy, Callum E. – Swindon T – Gillingham; 1 Kennedy, Thomas G. – Leicester C – Rochdale; 16 Keohane, James C.J. – Bristol C – Cleveland T; 12 Kiernan, Robert S. – Watford – Bradford C; 12 King, Craig S. – Leicester C – Northampton T; 25 King, Joshua C.K. – Manchester U – Preston NE; 26 Kinsella, Sean – Plymouth Arg – Stafford R; 25 Kirkland, Christopher E. – Wigan Ath – Leicester C; 22 Lansbury, Henri G. – Arsenal – Norwich C; 20 Lawrence, Liam – Stoke C – Portsmouth; 12 Lee, Charlie – Peterborough U – Gillingham; 26 Lee, Jake A. – Cheltenham T – Bishop's Cleeve; 22 Leigertwood, Mikele B. – QPR – Reading; 22 Lewis, Stuart A. – Dagenham & R – Wycombe W; 26 Lindfield, Craig A. – Accrington S – Kidderminster H; 15 Livermore, Jake C. – Tottenham H – Ipswich T; 25 Locke, Simon J. – Reading – Dagenham & R; 2 Lomax, Kelvin – Oldham Ath – Chesterfield; 25 Lund, Matthew C. – Stoke C – Hereford U; 11 MacLean, Steven – Plymouth Arg – Oxford U; 12 McIndoe, Michael – Coventry C – Milton Keynes D; 23 McKenna, Jack S. – Bristol R – Chippenham T; 27 McPike, Mitchell L. – Birmingham C – Kidderminster H; 25 McQuoid, Joshua J.B. – Bournemouth – Millwall; 23 Mantom, Samuel S. – WBA – Tranmere R; 9 Midson, Jack W. – Oxford U – Southend U; 19 Miller, Lee A. – Middlesbrough – Notts Co; 19 Montgomery, Graeme – Dagenham & R – Hayes & Yeading U; 11 Nelson, Mitchell A. – Bournemouth – Eastbourne Bor; 12 N'Guessen, Diombo D-G. – Leicester C – Scunthorpe U; 9 Nicholls, Lee A. – Wigan Ath – Hartlepool U; 1 Nyatanga, Lewin J. – Bristol C – Peterborough U; 8 Oastler, Joseph J. – QPR – Torquay U; 8 O'Connor, Garry L.J. – Birmingham C – Barnsley; 25 O'Connor, Patrick J. – Millwall – Hampton & Richmond Bor; 25 Oshodi, Edward A.M.O.A. – Watford – Dagenham & R; 4 Palsson, Gudlaugur V. – AGF Aarhus – Dagenham & R; 23 Parker,

Joshua K.S. – QPR – Wycombe W; 25 Parkes, Thomas P.W. – Leicester C – Yeovil T; 4 Pentney, Carl – Colchester U – Bath C; 15 Perkins, Lewis C. – Charlton Ath – Cray W; 15 Phillip, Adam – Chelsea – Yeovil T; 26 Preen, Garyn V. – Burton Alb – Stafford R; 18 Pugh, Daniel A. – Stoke C – Preston NE; 19 Puncheon, Jason D.I. – Southampton – Millwall; 25 Ramsey, Aaron J. – Arsenal – Nottingham F; 26 Roberts, Adam J. – Macclesfield T – Northwich Vic; Roe, Philip – Sheffield W – Retford U; 12 Rowe, Daniel – Stockport Co – Northwich Vic; 5 Saville, Jack W. – Southampton – Stockport Co; 22 Seip, Marcel – Plymouth Arg – Charlton Ath; 19 Short, Lewis G.T. – Crewe Alex – Nantwich T; 2 Smalley, Deane A.M. – Oldham Ath – Chesterfield; 25 Smith, Thomas W. – Portsmouth – QPR; 26 Smyth, Thomas J. – Accrington S – Workington; 22 Sproule, Ivan – Bristol C – Yeovil T; 20 Stavrinou, Alexander M. – Charlton Ath – Cambridge U; 25 Stewart, Cameron R. – Manchester U – Hull C; 18 Tonge, Michael W.E. – Stoke C – Preston NE; 2 Tozer, Ben P.A. – Newcastle U – Northampton T; 25 Trotman, Neal A. – Preston NE – Oldham Ath; 4 Trott, Jordan R. – Plymouth Arg – Tiverton T; 25 Tudgay, Marcus – Sheffield W – Nottingham F; 5 Tuna, Tamer H. – Charlton Ath – Thurrock; 25 Tutte, Andrew W. – Manchester C – Shrewsbury T; 19 Verma, Aman K. – Leicester C – Darlington; 25 Vine, Rowan L. – QPR – Brentford; 25 Walker, Joshua – Watford – Stevenage; 25 Wallace, James R. – Everton – Bury; 2 Waters, Aaron L.J. – QPR – Thurrock; 18 Webster, Byron C. – Doncaster R – Hereford U; 12 Whelpdale, Christopher M. – Peterborough U – Gillingham; 18 White, Aidan P. – Leeds U – Oldham Ath; 12 Wilkinson, Luke A. – Dagenham & R – Boreham Wood; 19 Williams, Jonathan J. – Scunthorpe U – Boston U; 13 Williams, Marcus V. – Reading – Peterborough U; 4 Williams, Tom – Bristol C – Colchester U; 19 Wood, Chris – WBA – Brighton & HA; 25 Woods, Michael J. – Chelsea – Notts Co; 25 Wootton, Scott J. – Manchester U – Tranmere R; 9 Wotton, Paul A. – Southampton – Oxford U; 9 Wraighte, Christopher G. – Morecambe – Kendal T; 5 Yorke, Reece C. – Barnet – Wealdstone; 27 Zuiverloon, Gianni – Heerenveen – Ipswich T

DECEMBER 2010

31 Simpson, Joshua R.	Peterborough U	Crawley T	undisclosed

TEMPORARY TRANSFERS

10 Ambrusics, Robert – Leicester C – Stafford R; 31 Booth, George – Bristol R – Longwell Green; 23 Byrne, Callum – Rochdale – Mossley; 24 Clarke, Oliver A. – Bristol R – Mangotsfield U; 17 Collins, Dominic – Preston NE – Northwich Vic; 31 Cooper, Mark J. – Bristol R – Frome T; 3 Daniels, Luke M. – WBA – Rochdale; 11 Davisson, Benjamin J. – Charlton Ath – Hastings U; 10 Fitchett, Daniel O. – Wycombe W – Salisbury C; 28 Green, Daniel J. – Dagenham & R – Chelmsford C; 28 Green, Daniel J. – Dagenham & R – Boreham Wood; 2 Haynes, Kyle J. – Cheltenham T – Salisbury C; 10 Leonard, Ryan I. – Plymouth Arg – Weston-Super-Mare; 16 Mackreth, Jack – Tranmere R – Colwyn Bay; 17 Mambo, Yado M. – Charlton Ath – Staines T; 31 McKenna, Jack – Bristol R – Chippenham T; 18 Palmer, Edward G. – Torquay U – Tiverton T; 24 Raymond, Frankie J. – Reading – Horsham; 10 Ryan, Perry D. – Portsmouth – Bognor Regis T; 17 Wilkinson, Daniel P. – Hull C – Harrogate T; 18 Yeoman, Ashley S. – Torquay U – Tiverton T; 10 Yorke, Reece C. – Barnet – Harlow T

JANUARY 2011

1 Adams, Nicholas W.	Brentford	Rochdale	undisclosed
31 Austin, Charlie	Swindon T	Burnley	undisclosed
31 Ball, David M.	Manchester C	Peterborough U	undisclosed
1 Barnett, Leon P.	WBA	Norwich C	undisclosed
31 Bartley, Marvin C.	Bournemouth	Burnley	310,000
18 Bent, Darren A.	Sunderland	Aston Villa	18,000,000
31 Benyon, Elliot P.	Torquay U	Swindon T	150,000
20 Britton, Leon J.	Sheffield U	Swansea C	undisclosed
31 Carroll, Andrew T.	Newcastle U	Liverpool	35,000,000
1 Chaplow, Richard D.	Preston NE	Southampton	undisclosed
7 Charnock, Kieran J.	Torquay U	Morecambe	undisclosed
12 Chester, James G.	Manchester C	Hull C	300,000
7 Collins, James S.	Aston Villa	Shrewsbury T	undisclosed
31 Collins, Neill	Leeds U	Sheffield U	undisclosed
20 Davies, Benjamin J.	Notts Co	Derby Co	350,000
31 Davies, Curtis E.	Aston Villa	Birmingham C	3,500,000
26 Doyle, Michael P.	Coventry C	Sheffield U	Free
20 Duffy, Mark J.	Morecambe	Scunthorpe U	undisclosed
14 Easter, Jermaine M.	Milton Keynes D	Crystal Palace	undisclosed
28 Evina, Cedric D.	Arsenal	Oldham Ath	Free
31 Forte, Jonathan R.	Scunthorpe U	Southampton	undisclosed
2 Fryatt, Matthew C.	Leicester C	Hull C	1,200,000
31 Grandison, Jermaine M.	Coventry C	Shrewsbury T	undisclosed
20 Hammill, Adam	Barnsley	Wolverhampton W	500,000
26 Harley, Ryan	Exeter C	Swansea C	Free

25 Harrad, Shaun	Burton Alb	Northampton T	undisclosed
20 Haynes, Danny L.	Bristol C	Barnsley	undisclosed
21 Hughes, Andrew J.	Leeds U	Scunthorpe U	undisclosed
1 Hume, Iain E.	Barnsley	Preston NE	undisclosed
5 Johnson, Reda	Plymouth Arg	Sheffield W	undisclosed
12 Judge, Alan	Blackburn R	Notts Co	undisclosed
31 Kalala, Jean-Paul K.	Yeovil T	Bristol R	undisclosed
22 Keinan, Dekel	Blackpool	Cardiff C	undisclosed
1 Lawrence, Liam	Stoke C	Portsmouth	undisclosed
17 Madine, Gary L.	Carlisle U	Sheffield W	undisclosed
24 Manset, Mathieu	Hereford U	Reading	undisclosed
5 Marrow, Alexander J.	Blackburn R	Crystal Palace	undisclosed
1 McLean, Aaron	Peterborough U	Hull C	1,000,000
5 McQuoid, Joshua J.	Bournemouth	Millwall	undisclosed
12 Moore, Luke I.	WBA	Swansea C	undisclosed
6 Morrison, Michael B.	Leicester C	Sheffield W	undisclosed
18 Morrison, Sean J.	Swindon T	Reading	undisclosed
31 Moxey, Dean	Derby Co	Crystal Palace	undisclosed
31 Nelson, Michael J.	Norwich C	Scunthorpe U	undisclosed
7 Nolan, Edward W.	Preston NE	Scunthorpe U	undisclosed
1 Noone, Craig	Plymouth Arg	Brighton & HA	300,000
4 O'Brien, Andrew J.	Bolton W	Leeds U	undisclosed
25 O'Neil, Gary P.	Middlesbrough	West Ham U	1,500,000
5 Parkin, Jonathan	Preston NE	Cardiff C	100,000
23 Payne, Joshua J.	Doncaster R	Oxford U	undisclosed
18 Pienaar, Steven	Everton	Tottenham H	3,000,000
31 Reid, Andrew M.	Sunderland	Blackpool	1,000,000
14 Reid, Paul M.	Colchester U	Scunthorpe U	undisclosed
28 Reid, Reuben J.	WBA	Oldham Ath	Free
6 Ritchie, Matthew T.	Portsmouth	Swindon T	undisclosed
15 Robinson, Theo L.	Huddersfield T	Millwall	300,000
7 Sidwell, Steven J.	Aston Villa	Fulham	500,000
1 Smith, Thomas W.	Portsmouth	QPR	1,500,000
31 Stewart, Cameron R.	Manchester U	Hull C	undisclosed
27 Thomas-Moore, Ian R.	Tranmere R	Rotherham U	undisclosed
13 Tierney, Marc P.	Colchester U	Norwich C	undisclosed
31 Torres, Fernando J.	Liverpool	Chelsea	50,000,000
5 Tudgay, Marcus	Sheffield W	Nottingham F	500,000
13 Vincent, Peter I.	Stevenage	Aldershot T	undisclosed
20 Wheater, David J.	Middlesbrough	Bolton W	2,300,000
1 Wilbraham, Aaron T.	Milton Keynes D	Norwich C	undisclosed
31 Woolford, Martyn	Scunthorpe U	Bristol C	undisclosed
7 Wright, Mark A.	Bristol R	Shrewsbury T	undisclosed
25 Wright-Phillips, Bradley	Plymouth Arg	Charlton Ath	undisclosed
31 Wroe, Nicholas	Torquay U	Shrewsbury T	undisclosed

TEMPORARY TRANSFERS

13 Adeyemi, Thomas O. – Norwich C – Bradford C; 27 Afobe, Benik – Arsenal – Huddersfield T; 6 Agard, Kieran R. – Everton – Peterborough U; 17 Akinde, John J.A. – Bristol C – Dagenham & R; 25 Amoo, David O. – Liverpool – Milton Keynes D; 7 Amos, Benjamin P. – Manchester U – Oldham Ath; 8 Atkinson, William H. – Hull C – Rochdale; 14 Barker, George J. – Brighton & HA – Lewes; 19 Bent, Marcus N. – Birmingham C – Sheffield U; 19 Berthel-Askou, Jens – Norwich C – Millwall; 31 Bessone, Federico L. – Leeds U – Charlton Ath; 31 Bignall, Nicholas C. – Reading – Brentford; 10 Blake, Ryan G. – Brentford – Ebbsfleet U; 18 Bolger, Cian T. – Leicester C – Bristol R; 7 Brogan, Stephen P. – Rotherham U – Stalybridge C; 24 Brown, Aaron A. – Leyton Orient – Stockport C; 27 Brown, Christopher R. – Rochdale – Bamber Bridge; 21 Brown, Kayleden – WBA – Port Vale; 29 Brown, Lee J. – QPR – Hayes & Yeading; 27 Bullard, James R. – Hull C – Ipswich T; 27 Carroll, Thomas J. – Tottenham H – Leyton Orient; 21 Carson, Trevor – Sunderland – Lincoln C; 11 Cestor, Mike B. – Leyton Orient – Boreham Wood; 10 Chambers, Ashley R. – Leicester C – York C; 24 Clark, Gavin E. – Morecambe – Bamber Bridge; 28 Clarke, Leon M. – QPR – Preston NE; 27 Clarke, Nathan – Huddersfield T – Colchester U; 28 Clough, Charlie – Bristol R – Weymouth; 10 Coleman, Rory C. – Scunthorpe U – Boston U; 10 Cooper, Liam D.I. – Hull C – Carlisle U; 25 Cort, Leon T.A. – Burnley – Preston NE; 6 Cornell, David J. – Swansea C – Port Talbot; 6 Cullen, Mark – Hull C – Bradford C; 21 Daley, Luke A. – Norwich C – Stevenage; 5 Daniels, Luke M. – WBA – Bristol R; 21 Darby, Stephen – Liverpool – Notts Co; 21 Darley, Grant L.W. – Rotherham U – Ossett T; 28 Davies, Scott M.E. –

Reading – Bristol R; 31 Davis, David L. – Wolverhampton W – Shrewsbury T; 13 De Laet, Ritchie R.A. – Manchester U – Portsmouth; 7 Demontagnac, Ishmel – Blackpool – Stockport Co; 6 Dickinson, Liam M. – Barnsley – Rochdale; 24 Donaldson, Ryan M. – Newcastle U – Hartlepool U; 1 Donnelly, Scott P. – Swansea C – Wycombe W; 31 Downing, Paul – WBA – Shrewsbury T; 28 Drinkwater, Daniel N. – Manchester U – Watford; 27 Dudgeon, Joseph P. – Manchester U – Carlisle U; 12 Dunleavy, John F. – Wolverhampton W – Barnet; 7 Eastham, Ashley – Blackpool – Cheltenham T; 25 Eastmond, Craig L. – Arsenal – Millwall; 14 Eccleston, Nathan – Liverpool – Charlton Ath; 1 Ehmer, Maximillian A. – QPR – Yeovil T; 7 Elding, Anthony L. – Rochdale – Stockport Co; 13 Ellington, Nathan L. – Watford – Preston NE; 18 Emmanuel-Thomas, Jay-Aston – Arsenal – Cardiff C; 7 Essam, Connor – Gillingham – Bishop's Stortford; 14 Evans, Corry J. – Manchester U – Hull C; 7 Evina, Cedric D. – Arsenal – Oldham Ath; 28 Federico, Jerome J. – Wycombe W – Wealdstone; 6 Fitchett, Daniel O. – Wycombe W – Salisbury C; 31 Forecast, Tommy S. – Southampton – Eastbourne Bor; 6 Frampton, Andrew J. – Millwall – Swindon T; 7 Gardner, Anthony – Hull C – Crystal Palace; 31 Garner, Joseph A. – Nottingham F – Scunthorpe U; 24 Geohaghan, Exodus I. – Peterborough U – Port Vale; 21 Gill, Matthew J. – Norwich C – Walsall; 31 Gonzalez, David G. – Manchester C – Leeds U; 6 Gordon, Benjamin L. – Chelsea – Scunthorpe U; 20 Grand, Simon – Morecambe – Aldershot T; 14 Grandison, Jermaine M. – Coventry C – Shrewsbury T; 1 Gray, Daniel E. – Chesterfield – Macclesfield T; 31 Green, Matthew J. – Oxford U – Cheltenham T; 24 Greulich, Corey P. – Hartlepool U – Workington; 7 Grieve, Matthew A. – Newcastle U – Stockport Co; 31 Griffin, Charlie J. – Stevenage – Newport Co; 7 Griffiths, Scott R. – Peterborough U – Chesterfield; 14 Grimes, Ashley J. – Millwall – Lincoln C; 31 Grof, David A. – Notts Co – Mansfield T; 1 Guzan, Bradley E. – Aston Villa – Hull C; 31 Hackney, Simon J. – Colchester U – Oxford U; 28 Haining, William W. – Oldham Ath – Fleetwood T; 12 Halford, Gregory – Wolverhampton W – Portsmouth; 21 Hall, Grant T. – Brighton & HA – Lewes; 21 Hamer, Benjamin J. – Reading – Exeter C; 27 Harley, Ryan – Swansea C – Exeter C; 28 Hatfield, William H. – Leeds U – York C; 30 Heath, Joseph – Exeter C – Hereford U; 7 Henderson, Liam M. – Watford – Aldershot T; 4 Henderson, Stephen – Bristol C – Yeovil T; 25 Hogg, Jonathan – Aston Villa – Portsmouth; 17 Hooman, Harry J. – Shrewsbury T – Hinckley U; 28 Howe, Jermaine R. – Peterborough U – Bristol R; 11 Hudson, Kirk I. – Brentford – AFC Wimbledon; 1 Hunt, David J. – Brentford – Crawley T; 21 Hunt, Stephen J. – Notts Co – Lincoln C; 28 Hurst, Kevan – Carlisle U – Morecambe; 7 Husband, Stephen – Blackpool – Stockport Co; 7 Hutchinson, Andrew L. – Lincoln C – Harrogate T; 14 Ibrahim, Abdisalam – Manchester C – Scunthorpe U; 21 Jervis, Jake M. – Birmingham C – Hereford U; 14 Jesionkowski, Jakub – Swindon T – Oxford C; 31 Johnson, Edward – Fulham – Preston NE; 14 Johnson, Oliver T. – Norwich C – Yeovil T; 31 Jones, Paul – Exeter C – Peterborough U; 7 Judge, Alan – Blackburn R – Notts Co; 10 Kadar, Tamas – Newcastle U – Huddersfield T; 7 Kane, Harry – Tottenham H – Leyton Orient; 6 Kay, Michael J. – Sunderland – Tranmere R; 15 Keats, Noah J. – Exeter C – Barnstaple T; 21 Kelly, Danny M. – Barnet – Dover Ath; 14 Kelly, Julian J. – Reading – Lincoln C; 20 Kennedy, Thomas G. – Leicester C – Peterborough U; 31 Keogh, Andrew D. – Wolverhampton W – Bristol C; 1 Kilbane, Kevin D. – Hull C – Huddersfield T; 12 Kilgallon, Matthew – Sunderland – Doncaster R; 31 Konchesky, Paul M. – Liverpool – Nottingham F; 2 Koranteng, Nathan T. – Peterborough U – Boston U; 4 Laird, Marc J.P. – Millwall – Brentford; 25 Lansbury, Henri G. – Arsenal – Norwich C; 4 Lees, Thomas J. – Leeds U – Bury; 11 Leigertwood, Mikele – QPR – Reading; 27 Leonard, Ryan I. – Plymouth Arg – Tiverton T; 6 Lillis, Joshua M. – Scunthorpe U – Rochdale; 13 Linganzi, Amine K. – Blackburn R – Preston NE; 7 Locke, Simon J. – Reading – Basingstoke T; 31 Long, Kevin F. – Burnley – Accrington S; 13 Lowry, Shane T. – Aston Villa – Sheffield; 19 MacLean, Steven – Plymouth Arg – Oxford U; 7 Malone, Scott L. – Wolverhampton W – Burton Alb; 5 Malsom, Samual A. – Hereford U – Redditch U; 4 Mannone, Vito – Arsenal – Hull C; 21 Manset, Mathieu – Hereford U – Reading; 31 Marsh-Brown, Keanu – Fulham – Milton Keynes D; 7 Marshall, Ben – Stoke C – Carlisle U; 21 Martin, David J. – Derby Co – Notts Co; 21 Martin, Ellis – Portsmouth – Havant & W'Ville; 21 Mason, Ryan G. – Tottenham H – Doncaster R; 13 Mattock, Joseph W. – WBA – Sheffield U; 14 McCartney, George – Sunderland – Leeds U; 18 McCracken, David – Brentford – Bristol R; 3 McCrae, Romone C. – Histon – Peterborough U; 31 McKenna, Jack S. – Bristol R – Chippenham T; 1 McLean, Aaron – Peterborough U – Hull C; 2 Mee, Benjamin – Manchester C – Leicester C; 31 Mellis, Jacob A. – Chelsea – Barnsley; 22 Miller, Ishmael A. – WBA – QPR; 28 Miller, Lee A. – Middlesbrough – Scunthorpe U; 3 Mills, Daniel P. – Histon – Peterborough U; 31 Mills, Joseph N. – Southampton – Doncaster R; 14 Modest, Nathan D. – Sheffield W – Darlington; 1 Montgomery, Graeme – Dagenham & R – Newport Co; 7 Mooney, David – Reading – Colchester U; 14 Morgan, Kerry D. – Swansea C – Newport Co; 7 Morgan, Marvin N. – Aldershot T – Dagenham & R; 31 Murtagh, Keiran Z. – Yeovil T – Woking; 11 Naughton, Kyle – Tottenham H – Leicester C; 26 N'Guessen, Diombo – Leicester C – Southampton; 31 Nicholls, Lee A. – Wigan Ath – Shrewsbury T; 11 Noble, Liam T. – Sunderland – Carlisle U; 1 Norwood, James T. – Exeter C – Eastbourne Bor; 31 Nouble, Frank H. – West Ham U – Barnsley; 7 Obika, Jonathan – Tottenham H – Peterborough U; 7 O'Connor, Patrick J. – Millwall – Hampton & Richmond Bor; 31 O'Donnell, Richard M. – Sheffield W – Alfreton T; 7 Okus, Conor E. – Dagenahm & R – Ebbsfleet U; 17 Ollerenshaw, Joshua D. – Oldham Ath – Salford C; 31 O'Neill, Luke M. – Leicester C – Kettering

T; 20 O'Shea, James – Birmingham C – Port Vale; 30 Osbourne, Isaiah G. – Aston Villa – Sheffield W; 28 Oshodi, Edward A.M.O.A. – Watford – Rushden & D; 31 Pell, Harry D.B. – Bristol R – Hereford U; 31 Perkins, Lewis C. – Charlton Ath – Hastings U; 10 Philliskirk, Daniel – Chelsea – Sheffield U; 28 Pope, Thomas J. – Rotherham U – Port Vale; 31 Porter, George – Leyton Orient – Hastings U; 27 Preston, Daniel S. – Birmingham C – Hereford U; 28 Price, Jason J. – Carlisle U – Walsall; 7 Prosser, Luke B. – Southend U – Rushden & D; 31 Puncheon, Jason D.I. – Plymouth Arg – Blackpool; 15 Putnins, Elvijs – QPR – Boreham Wood; 28 Quirke, Michael J. – Coventry C – Nuneaton T; 24 Ramsey, Aaron J. – Arsenal – Cardiff C; 25 Rance, Dean J. – Gillingham – Maidstone U; 20 Roberts, Craig – Stockport Co – Lancaster C; 3 Rowe, James M. – Reading – Lewes; 31 Robinson, Jake D. – Brighton & HA – Torquay U; 21 Routledge, Wayne N. – Newcastle U – QPR; 11 Ryan, Perry D. – Portsmouth – Bognor Regis T; 6 Sadler, Matthew – Watford – Shrewsbury T; 21 Sawyers, Romaine – WBA – Port Vale; 30 Smalley, Deane A.M. – Oldham Ath – Chesterfield; 21 Smyth, Thomas J. – Accrington S – Workington; 28 Spencer, Damian M. – Cheltenham T – Eastbourne Bor; 5 Spencer, James C. – Huddersfield T – Morecambe; 31 Stanley, Craig – Morecambe – Torquay U; 7 Stockley, Jayden C. – Bournemouth – Dorchester T; 31 Straker, Anthony – Aldershot T – Wycombe W; 6 Tafazolli, Ryan S. – Southampton – Salisbury C; 1 Taiwo, Soloman O. – Cardiff C – Dagenham & R; 31 Taylor, Lyle J.A. – Bournemouth – Lewes; 7 Tejan-Sie, Thomas M. – Dagenham & R – Thurrock; 21 Thomas, Casey E. – Swansea C – Port Talbot; 20 Townsend, Andros – Tottenham H – Watford; 6 Tozer, Ben P.A. – Newcastle U – Northampton T; 11 Trippier, Kieran J. – Manchester C – Barnsley; 6 Trotman, Neal A. – Preston NE – Oldham Ath; 21 Tudur Jones, Owain – Norwich C – Brentford; 21 Tuna, Tamer H. – Charlton Ath – Aveley; 31 Tutte, Andrew W. – Manchester C – Yeovil T; 31 Van Aanholt, Patrick J. – Chelsea – Leicester C; 26 Vaughan, James O. – Everton – Crystal Palace; 31 Verma, Aman K. – Leicester C – Darlington; 20 Vidal, Javan – Manchester C – Chesterfield; 15 Vine, Rowan L. – QPR – Milton Keynes D; 28 Walker, Joshua – Watford – Northampton T; 14 Walker, Mitchell C. – Brighton & HA – Welling U; 7 Walsh, Phillip – Dagenham & R – Cheltenham T; 18 Watson, Ben C. – Exeter C – Bath C; 24 Wedgbury, Samuel – Macclesfield T – Altrincham; 20 Weimann, Andreas – Aston Villa – Watford; 27 White, Aidan P. – Leeds U – Oldham Ath; 7 White, Andrew J. – Gillingham – Bishop's Stortford; 1 Wilbraham, Aaron T. – Milton Keynes D – Norwich C; 28 Wilson, Callum E. – Coventry C – Kettering T; 6 Wood, Chris – WBA – Brighton & HA; 25 Worthington, Jonathan A. – Oldham Ath – Bradford C; 1 Wotton, Paul A. – Southampton – Yeovil T; 14 Yakubu, Ayegbeni – Everton Leicester C; 1 Yussuf, Abdillahic – Leicester C – Tamworth; 18 Zola, Calvin M. – Crewe Alex – Burton Alb

FEBRUARY 2011 TEMPORARY TRANSFERS

14 Allen-Djilali, Kieran S.L. – Crystal Palace – Chesterfield; 1 Almond, Louis J. – Blackpool – Barrow; 11 Ayala, Daniel S. – Liverpool – Derby Co; 8 Borrowdale, Gary I. – Coventry C – Carlisle U; 23 Broughton, Drewe O. – Lincoln C – AFC Wimbledon; 11 Bruma, Jeffrey K. – Chelsea – Leicester C; 21 Burton, Alan M. – Accrington S – Marine; 21 Byrne, Nathan W. – Tottenham H – Brentford; 12 Canham, Sean – Notts Co – Kidderminster H; 11 Chilaka, Chibuzor – Bradford C – Harrogate T; 11 Clifford, Conor – Chelsea – Notts Co; 28 Clough, Charlie – Bristol R – Bath C; 25 Coid, Daniel J. – Blackpool – Rotherham U; 21 Connolly, Reece W. – Aldershot T – Dorchester T; 18 Cotterill, David R.G.B. – Swansea C – Portsmouth; 15 Cowan-Hall, Paris D.J. – Scunthorpe U – Rushden & D; 10 Daley, Omar – Bradford C – Rotherham U; 22 Darley, Grant L.W. – Rotherham U – Boston U; 18 Davies, Andrew J. – Stoke C – Middlesbrough; 21 Davis, Harry S. – Crewe Alex – Curzon Ashton; 11 Dean, Harlee J. – Dagenham & R – Bishop's Stortford; 8 Deering, Sam – Oxford U – Barnet; 16 Dikagcoi, Kagisho – Fulham – Crystal Palace; 17 Doble, Ryan A. – Southampton – Stockport Co; 21 Edwards, Robert O. – Blackpool – Norwich C; 25 Elito, Medy E. – Colchester U – Cheltenham T; 10 Ellison, Kevin – Rotherham U – Bradford C; 18 Elliott, Christopher M. – Bradford C – Harrogate T; 17 Euell, Jason J. – Blackpool – Doncaster R; 11 Fairhurst, Waide S. – Doncaster R – Hereford U; 25 Fielding, Francis D. – Blackburn R – Derby Co; 22 Flanagan, Calum R. – Aston Villa – Kettering T; 1 Flanagan, Thomas M. – Milton Keynes D – Kettering T; 17 Foderingham, Wesley A. – Fulham – Boreham Wood; 26 Furzer, Jack L. – Exeter C – Bideford; 11 Garrod, Tony R. – Southampton – Bishop's Stortford; 10 German, Antonio T. – QPR – Yeovil T; 10 Gilligan, Ryan J. – Northampton T – Torquay U; 21 Green, Jamie P. – Rotherham U – Boston U; 25 Grella, Michele – Leeds U – Swindon T; 1 Grocutt, Kevin J. – Burton Alb – Vauxhall Motors; 4 Gwynne, Sam – Hereford U – Telford U; 26 Harewood, Marlon A. – Aston Villa – Barnsley; 28 Haynes, Kyle – Cheltenham T – Salisbury C; 15 Henderson, Liam M. – Watford – Rotherham U; 16 Hobbs, Jack – Leicester C – Hull C; 18 Holness, Charlie H.V. – Crystal Palace – Hampton & Richmond Bor; 25 Hooman, Harry J. – Shrewsbury T – Hinckley U; 11 Hughes, Stephen – Norwich C – Milton Keynes D; 25 Hughes-Mason, Kiernan P. – Millwall – Chelmsford C; 18 Jarrett, Albert O. – Lincoln C – Aldershot T; 16 Jeffers, Shaun E. – Coventry C – Cambridge U; 26 Jordan, Stephen R. – Sheffield U – Huddersfield T; 23 Kiernan, Robert S. – Watford – Wycombe W; 11 Kennedy, Callum E. – Swindon T – Rotherham U; 11 Lichaj, Eric J. – Aston Villa – Leeds U; 3 Locke, Simon J. – Reading – Basingstoke T; 18 Logan, Conrad J. – Leicester C – Bristol R; 21 Mackreth, Jack – Tranmere R – Hyde U; 11 Malsom, Samual A. – Hereford U – Gloucester C; 17 Mantom, Samuel S. – WBA – Oldham Ath; 14 McCrae, Romone C.A. –

Peterborough U – Kettering T; 11 McDonald, Kevin – Burnley – Notts Co; 22 McDonald, Rodney T. – Oldham Ath – Nantwich T; 25 McLoughlin, Ian M. – Ipswich T – Stockport Co; 17 McShane, Paul D. – Hull C – Barnsley; 28 Medley, Luke A.C. – Mansfield T – Aldershot T; 8 Mellor, Kelvin – Crewe Alex – Leek T; 14 Mills, Daniel P. – Peterborough U – Kettering T; 4 Mills, Gregory A. – Derby Co – Telford U; 19 Moussa, Franck – Leicester C – Doncaster R; 17 Neilson, Robbie – Leicester C – Brentford; 18 Nnamani, Jerry O. – Crystal Palace – Bromley; 8 Obika, Jonathan – Tottenham H – Swindon T; 11 O'Connor, Patrick J. – Millwall – Hampton & Richmond Bor; 9 Odubade, Yemi E. – Stevenage – Newport Co; 1 O'Neill, Luke M. – Leicester C – Kettering T; 25 Palmer, Edward G. – Torquay U – Weymouth; 10 Paterson, Matthew – Southend U – Stockport Co; 19 Payne, Stefan S. – Gillingham – Braintree T; 8 Pulis, Anthony J. – Southampton – Barnet; 4 Randall, Jack D. – Aldershot T – Didcot T; 11 Raymond, Frankie J. – Reading – Basingstoke T; 21 Reed, Adam M. – Sunderland – Brentford; 24 Regan, Carl A. – Bristol R – Notts Co; 15 Riise, Bjorn H.S. – Fulham – Sheffield U; 18 Roberts, Adam J. – Macclesfield T – Northwich Vic; 22 Robinson, Theo L.R. – Millwall – Derby Co; 25 Rowlands, Martin C. – QPR – Millwall; 23 Scott, Mark J. – Swindon T – Didcot T; 18 Shea, James – Arsenal – Southampton; 25 Shephard, Christopher J. – Exeter C – Salisbury C; 1 Smyth, Thomas J. – Accrington S – Workington; 15 Stockley, Jayden C. – AFC Bournemouth – Dorchester T; 7 Tavernier, James H. – Newcastle U – Gateshead; 11 Tejan-Sie, Thomas M. – Dagenham & R – Thurrock; 5 Thomas, Daniel – AFC Bournemouth – Dorchester T; 26 Thomson, Jake S. – Exeter C – Cheltenham T; 11 Turner, Iain – Everton – Preston NE; 15 Vokes, Samuel M. – Wolverhampton W – Sheffield U; 18 Wallace, James R. – Everton – Stockport Co; 16 Ward, Jamie J. – Sheffield U – Derby Co; 14 Weir, Robert J. – Sunderland – Tranmere R; 28 Weir, Tyler C. – Hereford U – Gloucester C; 10 Winnall, Sam T. – Wolverhampton W – Burton Alb

MARCH 2011 TEMPORARY TRANSFERS

10 Agustien, Germaine – Swansea C – Crystal Palace; 21 Akpan, Hope – Everton – Hull C; 17 Aley, Zachery G. – Blackburn R – Morecambe; 4 Alnwick, Ben R. – Tottenham H – Doncaster R; 1 Amoo, David O.S. – Liverpool – Hull C; 9 Andrew, Calvin H. – Crystal Palace – Swindon T; 7 Anyon, Joseph – Lincoln C – Morecambe; 4 Arter, Harry N. – AFC Bournemouth – Carlisle U; 7 Bannan, Barry – Aston Villa – Leeds U; 11 Barrett, Adam N. – Crystal Palace – Leyton Orient; 11 Bates, Jon-Jo D. – Dagenham & R – Maidenhead U; 3 Bateson, Jonathan A. – Accrington S – Altrincham; 16 Batth, Daniel T. – Wolverhampton W – Sheffield W; 23 Bell, Matthew – Port Vale – Newcastle T; 8 Bentley, Mark J. – Gillingham – Cambridge U; 18 Blizzard, Dominic J. – Bristol R – Port Vale; 17 Bond, Jonathan H. – Watford – Brackley T; 18 Borini, Fabio – Chelsea – Swansea C; 15 Bowerman, George O. – Walsall – Redditch U; 8 Boyd, Kris – Middlesbrough – Nottingham F; 31 Brown, Christopher R. – Rochdale – Hyde U; 3 Brown, Jason R. – Blackburn R – Cardiff C; 17 Burge, Ryan J. – Doncaster R – Oxford U; 31 Byrne, Callum – Rochdale – Hyde U; 2 Byrne, Mark – Nottingham F – Barnet; 4 Bywater Stephen – Derby Co – Cardiff C; 14 Calver, Craig – Yeovil T – Braintree T; 23 Canavan, Niall D.S. – Scunthorpe U – Shrewsbury T; 24 Canham, Sean – Hereford U – Kidderminster H; 24 Carson, Trevor – Sunderland – Brentford; 4 Cestor, Mike B. – Leyton Orient – Boreham Wood; 24 Clayton, Adam S. – Leeds U – Milton Keynes D; 8 Collis, Stephen P. – Peterborough U – Northampton T; 24 Cook, Jordan A. – Sunderland – Walsall; 4 Cooper, Liam D.I. – Hull C – Carlisle U; 11 Corcoran, Samuel A. – Colchester U – Lowestoft T; 24 Cosgrove, Jonathan G. – Fulham – Brentford; 25 Cox, Elliott J. – QPR – Histon; 4 Dalla Valle, Lauri – Liverpool – AFC Bournemouth; 31 Darley, Grant L.W. – Rotherham U – Frickley Ath; 31 Dean, Harlee J. – Southampton – Bishop's Stortofrd; 18 Dean, Luke A. – Bradford C – Ossett T; 8 Delfouneso, Nathan – Aston Villa – Burnley; 2 Doble, Ryan A. – Southampton – Oxford U; 31 Doughty, Michael E. – QPR – Woking; 24 Duffy, Shane P.M. – Everton – Burnley; 4 Duke, Matthew – Hull C – Derby Co; 11 Dyer, Kieron C. – West Ham U – Ipswich T; 14 Eckersley, Richard J. – Burnley – Bury; 18 Ellison, James – Burton Alb – Hednesford T – ; 21 Essam, Connor – Gillingham – Dover Ath; 8 Etheridge, Neil – Fulham – Charlton Ath; 3 Federico, Jerome J. – Wycombe W – Maidenhead U; 22 Flint, Aden – Swindon T – Alfreton T; 25 Foderingham, Wesley A. – Crystal Palace – Histon; 8 Gardner, Ricardo – Bolton W – Preston NE; 4 Gbarssin, Marc-Antoine – Carlisle U – Walsall; 15 Geddes, Sean A. – Walsall – Redditch U; 26 Green, Dominic A. – Dagenham & R – St Neots T; 8 Guzan, Bradley E. – Aston Villa – Hull C; 19 Harvey, Alex-Ray – Burnley – Fleetwood T; 8 Haynes, Kyle J. – Cheltenham T – Hednesford T; 11 Hendrie, Stuart S. – Morecambe – Tamworth; 22 Hickman, Alexander W. – Walsall – Redditch U; 25 Holland, Jack – Crystal Palace – Eastbourne Bor; 19 Holness, Charlie H.V. – Crystal Palace – Lewes; 11 Holroyd, Christopher – Brighton & HA – Bury; 31 Hutchinson, Andrew L. – Lincoln C – Lewes; 25 James-Lewis, Merrick – Southend U – Braintree T; 24 Jones, Bradley – Liverpool – Derby Co; 17 Jones, Robert W. – Scunthorpe U – Sheffield W; 21 Kamara, Diomansy – Fulham – Leicester C; 8 Kelly, Danny M. – Barnet – Eastbourne Bor; 24 Khumalo, Bongani – Tottenham H – Preston NE; 24 Kilbey, Thomas C. – Portsmouth – Lincoln C; 31 Kosylo, Matthew S.P. – Stockport Co – Salford C; 24 Laird, Marc J.P. – Millwall – Walsall; 22 Lancaster, Cameron P. – Tottenham H – Dagenham & R; 25 Lee, Jake A. – Cheltenham T – Thurrock; 24 Lee, Oliver R. – West Ham U – Dagenham & R; 24 Lennox, Joe M. – Bristol C – Bath C; 17 Leslie, Steven – Shrewsbury T – Hereford U; 24 Livermore, Jake C. – Tottenham H – Leeds U; 24 Lowe, Jason J. – Blackburn R – Oldham Ath; 10 Lowe,

Matthew T. – Macclesfield T – Kidderminster H; 17 MacDonald, Shaun B. – Swansea C – Yeovil T; 30 Mackreth, Jack – Tranmere R – Chester C; 24 Mahon, Gavin A. – QPR – Crystal Palace; 7 Massey, Gavin A. – Watford – Wealdstone; 24 McDermott, Donal – Manchester C – AFC Bournemouth; 21 Midson, Jack W. – Oxford U – Barnet; 23 Morrison, Sean J. – Reading – Huddersfield T; 11 Murray, Ronan M. – Ipswich T – Torquay U; 18 Mvoto, Jean Y.O. – Sunderland – Oldham Ath; 14 N'Diaye, Alassane – Crystal Palace – Swindon T; 31 Nelson, Mitchell A. – AFC Bournemouth – Lewes; 24 Nicholls, Lee A. – Wigan Ath – Sheffield W; 11 Nouble, Frank H. – West Ham U – Charlton Ath; 24 Nunez, Ramon F. – Leeds U – Scunthorpe U; 17 Obika, Jonathan – Tottenham H – Yeovil T; 24 O'Brian, Joseph M. – Bolton W – Sheffield W; 29 O'Connor, Patrick J. – Millwall – Lewes; 8 Ofori-Twumasi, Seth N. – Peterborough U – Northampton T; 24 Pacheco, Daniel L. – Liverpool – Norwich C; 24 Parish, Elliott C. – Aston Villa – Lincoln C; 24 Parkes, Thomas P.W. – Leicester C – Burton Alb; 11 Parrett, Dean G. – Tottenham H – Charlton Ath; 3 Parsons, Matthew J. – Crystal Palace – Barnet; 11 Pentney, Carl – Colchester U – Chelmsford C; 25 Perkins, Lewis C. – Charlton Ath – Aveley; 18 Pinney, Nathanel B. – Crystal Palace – Braintree T; 24 Price, Jason J. – Carlisle U – Hereford U; 4 Pringle, Ben P. – Derby Co – Torquay U; 24 Priskin, Tamas – Ipswich T – Swansea C; 31 Rance, Dean J.R. – Gillingham – Bishop's Stortford; 25 Raymond, Frankie J. – Reading – Basingstoke T; 8 Reckord, Jamie – Wolverhampton W – Northampton T; 29 Roberts, Craig – Stockport Co – Hyde U; 8 Rodney, Nialle – Nottingham F – Burton Alb; 1 Rundle, Adam – Morecambe – Gateshead; 24 Samuel, Jlloyd – Bolton W – Cardiff C; 14 Schlupp, Jeffrey – Leicester C – Brentford; 23 Short, Lewis G.T. – Crewe Alex – Northwich Vic; 29 Simpson, Jacob D. – Stockport Co – Hyde U; 8 Smith, Paul D. – Nottingham F – Middlesbrough; 17 Smith, Thomas J. – Ipswich T – Colchester U; 3 Spence, Jordan – West Ham U – Bristol C; 4 Sproule, Ivan – Bristol C – Notts Co; 21 Stam, Stefan – Yeovil T – Hereford U; 24 Stephens, Dale C. – Oldham Ath – Southampton; 24 Stirling, Jude B. – Milton Keynes D – Barnet; 17 Sullivan, John D. – Millwall – Charlton Ath; 31 Taylor, Lyle J.A. – AFC Bournemouth – Woking; 22 Taylor, Rhys F. – Chelsea – Crewe Alex; 31 Thomas, Aidan – Hereford U – Telford U; 31 Thomas, Daniel – AFC Bournemouth – Dorchester T; 24 Thompson-Lambe, Reginald – Ipswich T – Bristol R; 11 Tomlin, Gavin G. – Dagenham & R – Torquay U; 7 Townsend, Andros – Tottenham H – Millwall; 21 Vine, Rowan L. – QPR – Milton Keynes D; 24 Vokes, Samuel M. – Wolverhampton W – Norwich C; 24 Walker, Samuel C. – Chelsea – Barnet; 14 Ward, Daniel C. – Bolton W – Huddersfield T; 17 Webster, Byron C. – Doncaster R – Northampton T; 24 Welch, Joe – Histon – Stevenage; 30 Wilkinson, Daniel P. – Hull C – North Ferriby U; 5 Williams, Jonathan J. – Scunthorpe U – Brigg T; 24 Williams, Marcus V. – Reading – Scunthorpe U; 24 Wood, James R.F. – Manchester C – Exeter C; 11 Young, Lewis J. – Burton Alb – Forest Green R

APRIL 2011 TEMPORARY TRANSFERS

18 Byrne, Nathan – Tottenham H – Brentford; 3 Clough, Charlie – Bristol R – Bath C; 18 Connolly, Reece W. – Aldershot T – Dorchester T; 1 Davis, Harry S. – Crewe Alex – Curzon Ashton; 17 Djilai, Kieran – Crystal Palace – Chesterfield; 17 Fairhurst, Waide S. – Doncaster R – Hereford U; 27 Gwynne, Sam – Hereford U – AFC Telford U; 26 Moussa, Franck N. – Leicester C – Doncaster R; 17 Neilson, Robbie – Leicester C – Brentford; 1 O'Neill, Luke M. – Leicester C – Kettering T; 18 Reed, Adam – Sunderland – Brentford; 27 Shephard, Christopher – Exeter C – Salisbury C; 11 Turner, Iain R. – Everton – Preston NE; 3 Weir, Tyler – Hereford U – Gloucester C

MAY 2011

10 Fielding, Francis D.	Blackburn R	Derby Co	undisclosed
9 Ward, Jamie J.	Sheffield U	Derby Co	undisclosed

THE NEW FOREIGN LEGION 2010–11

JULY/AUGUST 2010	From	To	Fee in £
Alcaraz, Antolin	Club Brugge	Wigan Ath	undisclosed
Al-Muhammadi, Ahmed	ENPPI	Sunderland	Loan
Barrera, Pablo	UNAM	West Ham U	4,000,000
Beausejour, Jean	America	Birmingham C	3,300,000
Ben Arfa, Hatem	Marseille	Newcastle U	Loan
Boateng, Jerome	Hamburg	Manchester C	10,500,000
Boselli, Mauro	Estudiantes	Wigan Ath	6,000,000
Chamakh, Marouane	Bordeaux	Arsenal	undisclosed
Dembele, Moussa	AZ	Fulham	5,000,000
Gohouri, Steve	Moenchengladbach	Wigan Ath	undisclosed
Grandin, Elliot	CSKA Sofia	Blackpool	undisclosed
Gyan, Asamoah	Rennes	Sunderland	13,250,000
Hernandez, Javier	Guadalajara	Manchester U	6,000,000
Jovanovic, Milan	Standard Liege	Liverpool	undisclosed
Keinan, Dekel	Maccabi Haifa	Blackpool	undisclosed
Kolarov, Aleksandar	Lazio	Manchester C	16,000,000
Koscielny, Laurent	Lorient	Arsenal	8,500,000
Linganzi, Amine	St Etienne	Blackburn Rovers	undisclosed
Mignolet, Simon	St Truiden	Sunderland	2,000,000
Mujangi Bia, Geoffrey	Charleroi	Wolverhampton W	Loan
Obinna, Victor	Internazionale	West Ham U	Loan
Odemwingie, Peter	Lokomotiv Moscow	WBA	2,500,000
Pablo	Atletico Madrid	WBA	undisclosed
Poulsen, Christian	Juventus	Liverpool	4,500,000
Ramires	Benfica	Chelsea	16,300,000
Raul Meireles	Porto	Liverpool	11,500,000
Reid, Winston	Midtjylland	West Ham U	3,000,000
Riveros, Cristian	Cruz Azul	Sunderland	undisclosed
Salcido, Carlos	PSV Eindhoven	Fulham	1,600,000
Silva, David	Valencia	Manchester C	25,000,000
Squillaci, Sebastien	Sevilla	Arsenal	3,200,000
Stam, Ronnie	Twente	Wigan Ath	3,000,000
Sylvestre, Ludovic	Mlada Boleslav	Blackpool	undisclosed
Tchoyi, Somen	Salzburg	WBA	undisclosed
Tiote, Cheik Ismael	Twente	Newcastle U	3,500,000
Toure, Yaya	Barcelona	Manchester C	28,000,000
Van der Vaart, Rafael	Real Madrid	Tottenham H	8,000,000
Zigic, Nikola	Valencia	Birmingham C	6,000,000
JANUARY/FEBRUARY 2011			
Ba, Demba	Hoffenheim	West Ham U	500,000
Ben Arfa, Hatem	Marseille	Newcastle U	5,750,000
Dzeko, Edin	Wolfsburg	Manchester C	27,000,000
Jones, Jermaine	Schalke	Blackburn R	Loan
Kornilenko, Sergei	Zenit	Blackpool	undisclosed
Lindegaard, Anders	Aalesund	Manchester U	3,500,000
Lopez, Adrian	La Coruna	Wigan Ath	Free
Luiz, David	Benfica	Chelsea	25,000,000
Makoun, Jean	Lyon	Aston Villa	6,000,000
Rochina, Ruben	Barcelona	Blackburn R	Loan
Sessegnon, Stephane	Paris St Germain	Sunderland	6,000,000
Suarez, Luis	Ajax	Liverpool	23,000,000

THE THINGS THEY SAID . . .

Blackpool manager Ian Holloway watched videos of Arsenal before the start of the club's first season in the Premier League:
"I didn't sleep for two nights. Some of Arsenal's football and you're thinking 'Good gracious me.'"

Six weeks after the drama of his officiating at the 2010 World Cup final, referee Howard Webb had two regrets:
"I should have red-carded De Jong. I knew it was a high foot, but I didn't realise how bad it was until later. Van Bommel was to the right of Alonso so I didn't have a good enough view at the time. Then for the other regret, I gave a goal kick instead of a corner to Holland shortly before the goal was scored."

The controversy which surrounded Wayne Rooney and his much publicised request to move from Manchester United was eventually put to rest:
"I've spoken with the manager, David Gill and the owners and all of them have confirmed to me that this is the right club for me to be at and that the club is going to continue to be successful and win things."

Sir Alex Ferguson commenting on the Rooney situation which became known as Rooneygate and expecting mere mortals to understand perhaps:
"Sometimes you look in a field and see a cow. You think it is a better cow than the one you see in your field. It never really works out that way."

Before the dust settled at Old Trafford and when it seemed departure was inevitable, there were other opinions, as revealed by an ex-Manchester United favourite, Lou Macari:
"I have never known a player have the cheek to do what Rooney has done. Does he not think his team-mates are capable of winning things? It's a slight on them and I would think they are raging in the dressing room."

Rafa Benitez, erstwhile Liverpool and Internazionale manager, in one of his wistful moods:
"We have a saying in Spain – white liquid in a bottle has to be milk. This means that after 86 points and finishing second in the league. What changed? The Americans."

In the wake of England's failure to secure the 2018 World Cup finals, there were many and varied reasons put forward on the outcome. Mike Lee, the Englishman who assisted in the campaign to bring the 2012 Olympics to London and who helped Qatar secure the 2022 vote, had his own ideas:
"International legacy is very important and Russia and Qatar both presented something very strong in that. But if I'm being absolutely brutal about it and I look at international campaigns from across the world, I think this England bid campaign was not Premier League, it was relegation and League One."

Sir Alex defending Wayne Rooney who escaped a card for his elbow on James McCarthy of Wigan Athletic:
"Because it's Rooney, people will raise a campaign to get him hung by Tuesday or electrocuted or something like that. It is unbelievable people will try and get him up before the FA because that's what they always do in these situations when it's Wayne Rooney. The incident was nothing. Referee Mark Clattenburg saw it and said it was an accident, there's nothing to it."

Sports Minister Hugh Robertson represented the Coalition government's view of just how well or badly the sport is controlled in this country:
"Issues of football governance need attention and need action and that is precisely why the select committee has

responded to levels of anxiety across the House and announced their investigation.
"If you look across sport, it is very clear to me that football is the worst governed sport in this country without a shadow of a doubt. The levels of corporate governance that apply to football lag far behind other sports and other sports are by no means beacons in this regard."

Alex McLeish commenting after Birmingham City had upset the form book and the bookies by beating Arsenal in the Carling Cup final:
"Relatively speaking, it is my greatest achievement. At Rangers I was expected to win trophies, albeit it is difficult against Celtic. No one gave us a prayer but it shows the bookies do sometimes get it wrong. To come to England, to win my first trophy – and for a small club like Birmingham to beat the might of Arsenal – is a dream come true."

From the other camp at the Emirates, Arsène Wenger had an entirely different view as one would have expected:
"The Premier League is over 38 matches and the Carling Cup is only four or five. We will not throw 38 games away because of one game. I'm confident my players have enough character but they have to show it.
"I'm bitterly disappointed like the whole team. We had problems starting as the number of games we play is catching up with us. We will face a lot of questions after this, but we have to be strong enough. We have to show we have the mental strength."

Sir Geoff Hurst, goal scoring hero of the 1966 World Cup victory and his views on the present set up as far as England is concerned, in particular club v country:
"It's nonsense to say the Champions League is bigger than the World Cup. There cannot be anything better than representing England. I find it astounding when players don't turn up for England. There cannot be anything better than representing your country, but it's clear players don't feel that way."

Sir Geoff on Fabio Capello in relation to the 2010 World Cup finals:
"At the World Cup there was no camaraderie, no friendship or togetherness. I don't think Fabio Capello understood that."

Sir Geoff on selling his memorabilia:
"My family wanted the money then, to get them on the property ladder, so everything went to auction apart from the medal."

Sir Geoff on West Ham United's move to the Olympic Stadium:
"I'm not sure a top-class club should have a running track and I'm not sure whether an athletics stadium will get the use."

Arsène Wenger the Arsenal manager showing that the buck stops with the manager:
"When a guy tackles with one leg and closes like scissors with the second, that is putting another player's career under threat. All managers are responsible for the behaviour of our teams."

Thirteen days in which Arsenal lost out in three different cup competitions had manager Arsène Wenger ruefully looking at the season as it went into its last stage with just the Premier League title left for honours:
"Things aren't going our way at the moment but what happened on Tuesday night [losing in Barcelona] played a part in this game [losing to Manchester United].
"This is a good test of our resolve but I am convinced that if our home game against United is decisive, we will win it."

Sir Alex Ferguson received a five-game touchline ban and £30,000 fine for his comments on referee Martin Atkinson following the defeat at Chelsea on 1 March which included the following:
"You want a fair referee, or a strong referee anyway – and we didn't get that."

The FA's independent commission said in its report:
"No clarification or retraction of any of his comments has been made by Sir Alex and no apology given to Mr Atkinson, even after the charges had been brought. The Commission regarded this as a serious aggravating feature."

Gordon Taylor, PFA Chief Executive, rarely goes into print but he did have some observations on current affairs. Firstly on controversial decisions:
"Why don't officials look at monitors on big decisions? Robin van Persie was sent off. Why not have a sin bin?"

On players caring about England:
"Of course the players care about England. It's a fragile squad, psychologically. Some get screwed up."

On the PFA's stance:
"People say what have the PFA done that is altruistic. Edwin van der Sar talks to local schools about diet."

On Rooney's elbowgate:
"With Wayne Rooney, it didn't need me to say he was fortunate to stay on after the elbow incident with James McCarthy."

On players' behaviour off the field:
"It doesn't help when you see Ashley Cole with an air gun. That is an accident waiting to happen."

Fabio Capello speaking about his maximum requirement to carry out his duties as England manager:
"If I need to speak about the economy, I can't speak. But when you speak about tactics, you don't use a lot of words. Maximum 100."

The England manager talking about the highest priced England footballer, £35m Andy Carroll – and using up some more of those precious 100 words:
"He needs to improve, to drink less. His behaviour now is really, really important. He needs to be careful at every moment."

Sir Alex responding to the Premier League's intention of beefing up its respect campaign over referees:
"Richard Scudamore has not got a lot to do, has he? He is trying to elevate the Premier League and that's fine. That's good and that's his job, but I don't think managers disrespect referees. I do think Richard is jumping off the high diving board here without thinking about it.
   "I got done for what I consider to be fair comment, they [the Football Association] didn't and I got a five-match ban and that's fine. But that is not to say we don't respect referees.
   "It's a difficult job and we all know that. You wouldn't referee a game, would you? Neither would I."

Arsenal manager Arsène Wenger commenting on his team's failure to defeat Blackburn Rovers and slipping out of the race for the title:
"We can't speak about the title after a performance like this. We were flat and I don't know why because I didn't see this coming when the team trained on Friday.
   "It was frustrating to watch, we didn't have pace or direction. To see what I saw today is a big concern. We didn't have the resources to beat Blackburn. It is difficult to identify the problem, but that is my job."

The day before he was sent off in the FA Cup semi-final against Manchester City, the Manchester United midfield player Paul Scholes gave his opinion of the opposition:
"City will be classed as a genuine threat only when they win a trophy. That's what I think. Our main rivals are obviously Arsenal and Chelsea. City are just a rival because of where they are [geographically]. Liverpool are the same."

Jose Mourinho has long held the view that while he may be considered the Special One as a coach, Barcelona are given special treatment by officials. After receiving a red card, he repeated the inference when listing referees at important games involving Barcelona, following Real's defeat in the Champions League:
"I didn't say anything to the referee. I simply laughed and showed my thumbs up. That was it. If I say to him and UEFA what I think, my career ends today. I can't say what I feel. I only leave one question. Why? Why? Ovrebo, Busacca, Frisk, Stark? Why to all these people?"

Arsenal finally came good when it was too late for them but opened up the title race that had looked a one horse affair until the Gunners beat Manchester United. Arsène Wenger sorted his mixed emotions about it:
"I prefer to be more frustrated than to lose the game today. You look at the age of the team and it's a big encouragement for the club and the team. The midfield was very young and it was a positive display."

As Manchester United headed for the climax to the season with a title race duel against Chelsea and a Wembley Champions League final with Barcelona, Wayne Rooney put the record straight about his earlier statement about wanting to leave Old Trafford:
"I understood that I made a mistake. I have wanted to prove myself to the fans."

Accusations were made alleging undercover, underhand methods used by the FA's WC 2018 bid team. Sepp Blatter was not slow to add his opinion:
"Fair play is one of the matters that has been invented by British football."

A draw at Blackburn Rovers gave Manchester United their 19th overall championship and the club's 12th in Premier League terms alone. Sir Alex reflected on the past and present:
"They don't give in, that is their great quality. There are good ages in the team, a lot of good legs and a lot of speed.
   "The 1994 team and the one in 1999 stand out, but all the teams we have had here have risen to the challenge – which is to win things."

Sir Alex Ferguson was gracious and appreciative after Manchester United lost the Champions League final to Barcelona:
"In my time as a manager, it's the best team we've faced. Everyone acknowledges that and I accept that. It's not easy when you've been well beaten like that to think another way. No one has given us a hiding like that. It's a great moment for them. They deserve it because they play the right way and enjoy their football."

Following the farce of the one candidate re-election of Sepp Blatter to head FIFA, Prime Minister David Cameron, who had been one of the three-pronged attack hoping to win WC 2018 along with HRH Prince William and David Beckham, had a swipe at the situation affecting the world governing body of football:
"They have got to prove that they are actually capable of doing the job that they are meant to. But ultimately change has got to come from within football and I am sure the [English] FA will want to play a very major role in helping to bring that about."

ENGLISH LEAGUE HONOURS 1888 TO 2011

FA PREMIER LEAGUE

MAXIMUM POINTS: a 126; b 114.
*Won or placed on goal average (ratio), goal difference or most goals scored. ††Not promoted after play-offs.

	First	Pts	Second	Pts	Third	Pts
1992–93a	Manchester U	84	Aston Villa	74	Norwich C	72
1993–94a	Manchester U	92	Blackburn R	84	Newcastle U	77
1994–95a	Blackburn R	89	Manchester U	88	Nottingham F	77
1995–96b	Manchester U	82	Newcastle U	78	Liverpool	71
1996–97b	Manchester U	75	Newcastle U*	68	Arsenal*	68
1997–98b	Arsenal	78	Manchester U	77	Liverpool	65
1998–99b	Manchester U	79	Arsenal	78	Chelsea	75
1999–2000b	Manchester U	91	Arsenal	73	Leeds U	69
2000–01b	Manchester U	80	Arsenal	70	Liverpool	69
2001–02b	Arsenal	87	Liverpool	80	Manchester U	77
2002–03b	Manchester U	83	Arsenal	78	Newcastle U	69
2003–04b	Arsenal	90	Chelsea	79	Manchester U	75
2004–05b	Chelsea	95	Arsenal	83	Manchester U	77
2005–06b	Chelsea	91	Manchester U	83	Liverpool	82
2006–07b	Manchester U	89	Chelsea	83	Liverpool*	68
2007–08b	Manchester U	87	Chelsea	85	Arsenal	83
2008–09b	Manchester U	90	Liverpool	86	Chelsea	83
2009–10b	Chelsea	86	Manchester U	85	Arsenal	75
2010–11b	Manchester U	80	Chelsea*	71	Manchester C	71

FOOTBALL LEAGUE CHAMPIONSHIP

MAXIMUM POINTS: 138

	First	Pts	Second	Pts	Third	Pts
2004–05	Sunderland	94	Wigan Ath	87	Ipswich T††	85
2005–06	Reading	106	Sheffield U	90	Watford	81
2006–07	Sunderland	88	Birmingham C	86	Derby Co	84
2007–08	WBA	81	Stoke C	79	Hull C	75
2008–09	Wolverhampton W	90	Birmingham C	83	Sheffield U††	80
2009–10	Newcastle U	102	WBA	91	Nottingham F††	79
2010–11	QPR	88	Norwich C	84	Swansea C*	80

FIRST DIVISION

MAXIMUM POINTS: 138

	First	Pts	Second	Pts	Third	Pts
1992–93	Newcastle U	96	West Ham U*	88	Portsmouth††	88
1993–94	Crystal Palace	90	Nottingham F	83	Millwall††	74
1994–95	Middlesbrough	82	Reading††	79	Bolton W	77
1995–96	Sunderland	83	Derby Co	79	Crystal Palace††	75
1996–97	Bolton W	98	Barnsley	80	Wolverhampton W††	76
1997–98	Nottingham F	94	Middlesbrough	91	Sunderland††	90
1998–99	Sunderland	105	Bradford C	87	Ipswich T††	86
1999–2000	Charlton Ath	91	Manchester C	89	Ipswich T	87
2000–01	Fulham	101	Blackburn R	91	Bolton W	87
2001–02	Manchester C	99	WBA	89	Wolverhampton W††	86
2002–03	Portsmouth	98	Leicester C	92	Sheffield U††	80
2003–04	Norwich C	94	WBA	86	Sunderland††	79

FOOTBALL LEAGUE CHAMPIONSHIP 1

MAXIMUM POINTS: 138

	First	Pts	Second	Pts	Third	Pts
2004–05	Luton T	98	Hull C	86	Tranmere R††	79
2005–06	Southend U	82	Colchester U	79	Brentford††	76
2006–07	Scunthorpe U	91	Bristol C	85	Blackpool	83
2007–08	Swansea C	92	Nottingham F	82	Doncaster R	80
2008–09	Leicester C	96	Peterborough U	89	Milton Keynes D††	87
2009–10	Norwich C	95	Leeds U	86	Millwall	85
2010–11	Brighton & HA	95	Southampton	92	Huddersfield T††	87

SECOND DIVISION

MAXIMUM POINTS: 138

	First	Pts	Second	Pts	Third	Pts
1992–93	Stoke C	93	Bolton W	90	Port Vale††	89
1993–94	Reading	89	Port Vale	88	Plymouth Arg*††	85
1994–95	Birmingham C	89	Brentford††	85	Crewe Alex††	83
1995–96	Swindon T	92	Oxford U	83	Blackpool††	82
1996–97	Bury	84	Stockport Co	82	Luton T††	78
1997–98	Watford	88	Bristol C	85	Grimsby T	72
1998–99	Fulham	101	Walsall	87	Manchester C	82
1999–2000	Preston NE	95	Burnley	88	Gillingham	85
2000–01	Millwall	93	Rotherham U	91	Reading††	86
2001–02	Brighton & HA	90	Reading	84	Brentford*††	83
2002–03	Wigan Ath	100	Crewe Alex	86	Bristol C††	83
2003–04	Plymouth Arg	90	QPR	83	Bristol C††	82

FOOTBALL LEAGUE CHAMPIONSHIP 2

MAXIMUM POINTS: 138

	First	Pts	Second	Pts	Third	Pts
2004–05	Yeovil T	83	Scunthorpe U*	80	Swansea C	80
2005–06	Carlisle U	86	Northampton T	83	Leyton Orient	81
2006–07	Walsall	89	Hartlepool U	88	Swindon T	85
2007–08	Milton Keynes D	97	Peterborough U	92	Hereford U	88
2008–09	Brentford	85	Exeter C	79	Wycombe W*	78
2009–10	Notts Co	93	Bournemouth	83	Rochdale	82
2010–11	Chesterfield	86	Bury	81	Wycombe W	80

THIRD DIVISION

MAXIMUM POINTS: a 126; b 138.

	First	Pts	Second	Pts	Third	Pts
1992–93a	Cardiff C	83	Wrexham	80	Barnet	79
1993–94a	Shrewsbury T	79	Chester C	74	Crewe Alex	73
1994–95a	Carlisle U	91	Walsall	83	Chesterfield	81
1995–96b	Preston NE	86	Gillingham	83	Bury	79
1996–97b	Wigan Ath*	87	Fulham	87	Carlisle U	84

	First	Pts	Second	Pts	Third	Pts
1997–98b	Notts Co	99	Macclesfield T	82	Lincoln C	72
1998–99b	Brentford	85	Cambridge U	81	Cardiff C	80
1999–2000b	Swansea C	85	Rotherham U	84	Northampton T	82
2000–01	Brighton & HA	92	Cardiff C	82	Chesterfield¶	80
2001–02	Plymouth Arg	102	Luton T	97	Mansfield T	79
2002–03	Rushden & D	87	Hartlepool U	85	Wrexham	84
2003–04	Doncaster R	92	Hull C	88	Torquay U*	81

¶9pts deducted for irregularities.

FOOTBALL LEAGUE

MAXIMUM POINTS: a 44; b 60

	First	Pts	Second	Pts	Third	Pts
1888–89a	Preston NE	40	Aston Villa	29	Wolverhampton W	28
1889–90a	Preston NE	33	Everton	31	Blackburn R	27
1890–91a	Everton	29	Preston NE	27	Notts Co	26
1891–92b	Sunderland	42	Preston NE	37	Bolton W	36

FIRST DIVISION to 1991–92

MAXIMUM POINTS: a 44; b 52; c 60; d 68; e 76; f 84; g 126; h 120; k 114.

	First	Pts	Second	Pts	Third	Pts
1892–93c	Sunderland	48	Preston NE	37	Everton	36
1893–94c	Aston Villa	44	Sunderland	38	Derby Co	36
1894–95c	Sunderland	47	Everton	42	Aston Villa	39
1895–96c	Aston Villa	45	Derby Co	41	Everton	39
1896–97c	Aston Villa	47	Sheffield U*	36	Derby Co	36
1897–98c	Sheffield U	42	Sunderland	37	Wolverhampton W*	35
1898–99d	Aston Villa	45	Liverpool	43	Burnley	39
1899–1900d	Aston Villa	50	Sheffield U	48	Sunderland	41
1900–01d	Liverpool	45	Sunderland	43	Notts Co	40
1901–02d	Sunderland	44	Everton	41	Newcastle U	37
1902–03d	The Wednesday	42	Aston Villa*	41	Sunderland	41
1903–04d	The Wednesday	47	Manchester C	44	Everton	43
1904–05d	Newcastle U	48	Everton	47	Manchester C	46
1905–06e	Liverpool	51	Preston NE	47	The Wednesday	44
1906–07e	Newcastle U	51	Bristol C	48	Everton*	45
1907–08e	Manchester U	52	Aston Villa*	43	Manchester C	43
1908–09e	Newcastle U	53	Everton	46	Sunderland	44
1909–10e	Aston Villa	53	Liverpool	48	Blackburn R*	45
1910–11e	Manchester U	52	Aston Villa	51	Sunderland*	45
1911–12e	Blackburn R	49	Everton	46	Newcastle U	44
1912–13e	Sunderland	54	Aston Villa	50	Sheffield W	49
1913–14e	Blackburn R	51	Aston Villa	44	Middlesbrough*	43
1914–15e	Everton	46	Oldham Ath	45	Blackburn R*	43
1919–20f	WBA	60	Burnley	51	Chelsea	49
1920–21f	Burnley	59	Manchester C	54	Bolton W	52
1921–22f	Liverpool	57	Tottenham H	51	Burnley	49
1922–23f	Liverpool	60	Sunderland	54	Huddersfield T	53
1923–24f	Huddersfield T*	57	Cardiff C	57	Sunderland	53
1924–25f	Huddersfield T	58	WBA	56	Bolton W	55
1925–26f	Huddersfield T	57	Arsenal	52	Sunderland	48
1926–27f	Newcastle U	56	Huddersfield T	51	Sunderland	49
1927–28f	Everton	53	Huddersfield T	51	Leicester C	48
1928–29f	Sheffield W	52	Leicester C	51	Aston Villa	50
1929–30f	Sheffield W	60	Derby Co	50	Manchester C*	47
1930–31f	Arsenal	66	Aston Villa	59	Sheffield W	52
1931–32f	Everton	56	Arsenal	54	Sheffield W	50
1932–33f	Arsenal	58	Aston Villa	54	Sheffield W	51
1933–34f	Arsenal	59	Huddersfield T	56	Tottenham H	49
1934–35f	Arsenal	58	Sunderland	54	Sheffield W	49
1935–36f	Sunderland	56	Derby Co*	48	Huddersfield T	48
1936–37f	Manchester C	57	Charlton Ath	54	Arsenal	52
1937–38f	Arsenal	52	Wolverhampton W	51	Preston NE	49
1938–39f	Everton	59	Wolverhampton W	55	Charlton Ath	50
1946–47f	Liverpool	57	Manchester U*	56	Wolverhampton W	56
1947–48f	Arsenal	59	Manchester U*	52	Burnley	52
1948–49f	Portsmouth	58	Manchester U*	53	Derby Co	53
1949–50f	Portsmouth*	53	Wolverhampton W	53	Sunderland	52
1950–51f	Tottenham H	60	Manchester U	56	Blackpool	50
1951–52f	Manchester U	57	Tottenham H*	53	Arsenal	53
1952–53f	Arsenal*	54	Preston NE	54	Wolverhampton W	51
1953–54f	Wolverhampton W	57	WBA	53	Huddersfield T	51
1954–55f	Chelsea	52	Wolverhampton W*	48	Portsmouth*	48
1955–56f	Manchester U	60	Blackpool*	49	Wolverhampton W	49
1956–57f	Manchester U	64	Tottenham H*	56	Preston NE	56
1957–58f	Wolverhampton W	64	Preston NE	59	Tottenham H	51
1958–59f	Wolverhampton W	61	Manchester U	55	Arsenal*	50
1959–60f	Burnley	55	Wolverhampton W	54	Tottenham H	53

	First	Pts	Second	Pts	Third	Pts
1960–61f	Tottenham H	66	Sheffield W	58	Wolverhampton W	57
1961–62f	Ipswich T	56	Burnley	53	Tottenham H	52
1962–63f	Everton	61	Tottenham H	55	Burnley	54
1963–64f	Liverpool	57	Manchester U	53	Everton	52
1964–65f	Manchester U*	61	Leeds U	61	Chelsea	56
1965–66f	Liverpool	61	Leeds U*	55	Burnley	55
1966–67f	Manchester U	60	Nottingham F*	56	Tottenham H	56
1967–68f	Manchester C	58	Manchester U	56	Liverpool	55
1968–69f	Leeds U	67	Liverpool	61	Everton	57
1969–70f	Everton	66	Leeds U	57	Chelsea	55
1970–71f	Arsenal	65	Leeds U	64	Tottenham H*	52
1971–72f	Derby Co	58	Leeds U*	57	Liverpool*	57
1972–73f	Liverpool	60	Arsenal	57	Leeds U	53
1973–74f	Leeds U	62	Liverpool	57	Derby Co	48
1974–75f	Derby Co	53	Liverpool*	51	Ipswich T	51
1975–76f	Liverpool	60	QPR	59	Manchester U	56
1976–77f	Liverpool	57	Manchester C	56	Ipswich T	52
1977–78f	Nottingham F	64	Liverpool	57	Everton	55
1978–79f	Liverpool	68	Nottingham F	60	WBA	59
1979–80f	Liverpool	60	Manchester U	58	Ipswich T	52
1980–81f	Aston Villa	60	Ipswich T	56	Arsenal	53
1981–82g	Liverpool	87	Ipswich T	83	Manchester U	78
1982–83g	Liverpool	82	Watford	71	Manchester U	70
1983–84g	Liverpool	80	Southampton	77	Nottingham F*	74
1984–85g	Everton	90	Liverpool*	77	Tottenham H	77
1985–86g	Liverpool	88	Everton	86	West Ham U	84
1986–87g	Everton	86	Liverpool	77	Tottenham H	71
1987–88h	Liverpool	90	Manchester U	81	Nottingham F	73
1988–89k	Arsenal*	76	Liverpool	76	Nottingham F	64
1989–90k	Liverpool	79	Aston Villa	70	Tottenham H	63
1990–91k	Arsenal†	83	Liverpool	76	Crystal Palace	69
1991–92g	Leeds U	82	Manchester U	78	Sheffield W	75

No official competition during 1915–19 and 1939–46; Regional Leagues operated. †2 pts deducted.

SECOND DIVISION to 1991–92

MAXIMUM POINTS: a 44; b 56; c 60; d 68; e 76; f 84; g 126; h 132; k 138.

	First	Pts	Second	Pts	Third	Pts
1892–93a	Small Heath	36	Sheffield U	35	Darwen	30
1893–94b	Liverpool	50	Small Heath	42	Notts Co	39
1894–95c	Bury	48	Notts Co	39	Newton Heath*	38
1895–96c	Liverpool*	46	Manchester C	46	Grimsby T*	42
1896–97c	Notts Co	42	Newton Heath	39	Grimsby T	38
1897–98c	Burnley	48	Newcastle U	45	Manchester C	39
1898–99d	Manchester C	52	Glossop NE	46	Leicester Fosse	45
1899–1900d	The Wednesday	54	Bolton W	52	Small Heath	46
1900–01d	Grimsby T	49	Small Heath	48	Burnley	44
1901–02d	WBA	55	Middlesbrough	51	Preston NE*	42
1902–03d	Manchester C	54	Small Heath	51	Woolwich A	48
1903–04d	Preston NE	50	Woolwich A	49	Manchester U	48
1904–05d	Liverpool	58	Bolton W	56	Manchester U	53
1905–06e	Bristol C	66	Manchester U	62	Chelsea	53
1906–07e	Nottingham F	60	Chelsea	57	Leicester Fosse	48
1907–08e	Bradford C	54	Leicester Fosse	52	Oldham Ath	50
1908–09e	Bolton W	52	Tottenham H*	51	WBA	51
1909–10e	Manchester C	54	Oldham Ath*	53	Hull C*	53
1910–11e	WBA	53	Bolton W	51	Chelsea	49
1911–12e	Derby Co*	54	Chelsea	54	Burnley	52
1912–13e	Preston NE	53	Burnley	50	Birmingham	46
1913–14e	Notts Co	53	Bradford PA*	49	Woolwich A	49
1914–15e	Derby Co	53	Preston NE	50	Barnsley	47
1919–20f	Tottenham H	70	Huddersfield T	64	Birmingham	56
1920–21f	Birmingham*	58	Cardiff C	58	Bristol C	51
1921–22f	Nottingham F	56	Stoke C*	52	Barnsley	52
1922–23f	Notts Co	53	West Ham U*	51	Leicester C	51
1923–24f	Leeds U	54	Bury*	51	Derby Co	51
1924–25f	Leicester C	59	Manchester U	57	Derby Co	55
1925–26f	Sheffield W	60	Derby Co	57	Chelsea	52
1926–27f	Middlesbrough	62	Portsmouth*	54	Manchester C	54
1927–28f	Manchester C	59	Leeds U	57	Chelsea	54
1928–29f	Middlesbrough	55	Grimsby T	53	Bradford PA*	48
1929–30f	Blackpool	58	Chelsea	55	Oldham Ath	53
1930–31f	Everton	61	WBA	54	Tottenham H	51
1931–32f	Wolverhampton W	56	Leeds U	54	Stoke C	52
1932–33f	Stoke C	56	Tottenham H	55	Fulham	50
1933–34f	Grimsby T	59	Preston NE	52	Bolton W*	51
1934–35f	Brentford	61	Bolton W*	56	West Ham U	56
1935–36f	Manchester U	56	Charlton Ath	55	Sheffield U*	52
1936–37f	Leicester C	56	Blackpool	55	Bury	52
1937–38f	Aston Villa	57	Manchester U*	53	Sheffield U	53
1938–39f	Blackburn R	55	Sheffield U	54	Sheffield W	53
1946–47f	Manchester C	62	Burnley	58	Birmingham C	55
1947–48f	Birmingham C	59	Newcastle U	56	Southampton	52
1948–49f	Fulham	57	WBA	56	Southampton	55
1949–50f	Tottenham H	61	Sheffield W*	52	Sheffield U*	52

	First	Pts	Second	Pts	Third	Pts
1950–51f	Preston NE	57	Manchester C	52	Cardiff C	50
1951–52f	Sheffield W	53	Cardiff C*	51	Birmingham C	51
1952–53f	Sheffield U	60	Huddersfield T	58	Luton T	52
1953–54f	Leicester C*	56	Everton	56	Blackburn R	55
1954–55f	Birmingham C*	54	Luton T*	54	Rotherham U	54
1955–56f	Sheffield W	55	Leeds U	52	Liverpool*	48
1956–57f	Leicester C	61	Nottingham F	54	Liverpool	53
1957–58f	West Ham U	57	Blackburn R	56	Charlton Ath	55
1958–59f	Sheffield W	62	Fulham	60	Sheffield U*	53
1959–60f	Aston Villa	59	Cardiff C	58	Liverpool*	50
1960–61f	Ipswich T	59	Sheffield U	58	Liverpool	52
1961–62f	Liverpool	62	Leyton Orient	54	Sunderland	53
1962–63f	Stoke C	53	Chelsea*	52	Sunderland	52
1963–64f	Leeds U	63	Sunderland	61	Preston NE	56
1964–65f	Newcastle U	57	Northampton T	56	Bolton W	50
1965–66f	Manchester C	59	Southampton	54	Coventry C	53
1966–67f	Coventry C	59	Wolverhampton W	58	Carlisle U	52
1967–68f	Ipswich T	59	QPR*	58	Blackpool	58
1968–69f	Derby Co	63	Crystal Palace	56	Charlton Ath	50
1969–70f	Huddersfield T	60	Blackpool	53	Leicester C	51
1970–71f	Leicester C	59	Sheffield U	56	Cardiff C*	53
1971–72f	Norwich C	57	Birmingham C	56	Millwall	55
1972–73f	Burnley	62	QPR	61	Aston Villa	50
1973–74f	Middlesbrough	65	Luton T	50	Carlisle U	49
1974–75f	Manchester U	61	Aston Villa	58	Norwich C	53
1975–76f	Sunderland	56	Bristol C*	53	WBA	53
1976–77f	Wolverhampton W	57	Chelsea	55	Nottingham F	52
1977–78f	Bolton W	58	Southampton	57	Tottenham H*	56
1978–79f	Crystal Palace	57	Brighton & HA*	56	Stoke C	56
1979–80f	Leicester C	55	Sunderland	54	Birmingham C*	53
1980–81f	West Ham U	66	Notts Co	53	Swansea C*	50
1981–82g	Luton T	88	Watford	80	Norwich C	71
1982–83g	QPR	85	Wolverhampton W	75	Leicester C	70
1983–84g	Chelsea*	88	Sheffield W	88	Newcastle U	80
1984–85g	Oxford U	84	Birmingham C	82	Manchester C	74
1985–86g	Norwich C	84	Charlton Ath	77	Wimbledon	76
1986–87g	Derby Co	84	Portsmouth	78	Oldham Ath††	75
1987–88h	Millwall	82	Aston Villa*	78	Middlesbrough	78
1988–89k	Chelsea	99	Manchester C	82	Crystal Palace	81
1989–90k	Leeds U*	85	Sheffield U	85	Newcastle U††	80
1990–91k	Oldham Ath	88	West Ham U	87	Sheffield W	82
1991–92k	Ipswich T	84	Middlesbrough	80	Derby Co	78

No official competition during 1915–19 and 1939–46; Regional Leagues operated.

THIRD DIVISION to 1991–92

MAXIMUM POINTS: 92; 138 FROM 1981–82.

	First	Pts	Second	Pts	Third	Pts
1958–59	Plymouth Arg	62	Hull C	61	Brentford*	57
1959–60	Southampton	61	Norwich C	59	Shrewsbury T*	52
1960–61	Bury	68	Walsall	62	QPR	60
1961–62	Portsmouth	65	Grimsby T	62	Bournemouth*	59
1962–63	Northampton T	62	Swindon T	58	Port Vale	54
1963–64	Coventry C*	60	Crystal Palace	60	Watford	58
1964–65	Carlisle U	60	Bristol C*	59	Mansfield T	59
1965–66	Hull C	69	Millwall	65	QPR	57
1966–67	QPR	67	Middlesbrough	55	Watford	54
1967–68	Oxford U	57	Bury	56	Shrewsbury T	55
1968–69	Watford*	64	Swindon T	64	Luton T	61
1969–70	Orient	62	Luton T	60	Bristol R	56
1970–71	Preston NE	61	Fulham	60	Halifax T	56
1971–72	Aston Villa	70	Brighton & HA	65	Bournemouth*	62
1972–73	Bolton W	61	Notts Co	57	Blackburn R	55
1973–74	Oldham Ath	62	Bristol R*	61	York C	61
1974–75	Blackburn R	60	Plymouth Arg	59	Charlton Ath	55
1975–76	Hereford U	63	Cardiff C	57	Millwall	56
1976–77	Mansfield T	64	Brighton & HA	61	Crystal Palace*	59
1977–78	Wrexham	61	Cambridge U	58	Preston NE*	56
1978–79	Shrewsbury T	61	Watford*	60	Swansea C	60
1979–80	Grimsby T	62	Blackburn R	59	Sheffield W	58
1980–81	Rotherham U	61	Barnsley*	59	Charlton Ath	59
1981–82	Burnley*	80	Carlisle U	80	Fulham	78
1982–83	Portsmouth	91	Cardiff C	86	Huddersfield T	82
1983–84	Oxford U	95	Wimbledon	87	Sheffield U*	83
1984–85	Bradford C	94	Millwall	90	Hull C	87
1985–86	Reading	94	Plymouth Arg	87	Derby Co	84
1986–87	Bournemouth	97	Middlesbrough	94	Swindon T	87
1987–88	Sunderland	93	Brighton & HA	84	Walsall	82
1988–89	Wolverhampton W	92	Sheffield U*	84	Port Vale	84
1989–90	Bristol R	93	Bristol C	91	Notts Co	87
1990–91	Cambridge U	86	Southend U	85	Grimsby T*	83
1991–92	Brentford	82	Birmingham C	81	Huddersfield T	78

FOURTH DIVISION (1958–1992)

MAXIMUM POINTS: 92; 138 FROM 1981–82.

	First	Pts	Second	Pts	Third	Pts	Fourth	Pts
1958–59	Port Vale	64	Coventry C*	60	York C	60	Shrewsbury T	58
1959–60	Walsall	65	Notts Co*	60	Torquay U	60	Watford	57
1960–61	Peterborough U	66	Crystal Palace	64	Northampton T*	60	Bradford PA	60
1961–62†	Millwall	56	Colchester U	55	Wrexham	53	Carlisle U	52
1962–63	Brentford	62	Oldham Ath*	59	Crewe Alex	59	Mansfield T*	57
1963–64	Gillingham*	60	Carlisle U	60	Workington	59	Exeter C	58
1964–65	Brighton & HA	63	Millwall*	62	York C	62	Oxford U	61
1965–66	Doncaster R*	59	Darlington	59	Torquay U	58	Colchester U*	56
1966–67	Stockport Co	64	Southport*	59	Barrow	59	Tranmere R	58
1967–68	Luton T	66	Barnsley	61	Hartlepools U	60	Crewe Alex	58
1968–69	Doncaster R	59	Halifax T	57	Rochdale*	56	Bradford C	56
1969–70	Chesterfield	64	Wrexham	61	Swansea C	60	Port Vale	59
1970–71	Notts Co	69	Bournemouth	60	Oldham Ath	59	York C	56
1971–72	Grimsby T	63	Southend U	60	Brentford	59	Scunthorpe U	57
1972–73	Southport	62	Hereford U	58	Cambridge U	57	Aldershot*	56
1973–74	Peterborough U	65	Gillingham	62	Colchester U	60	Bury	59
1974–75	Mansfield T	68	Shrewsbury T	62	Rotherham U	59	Chester*	57
1975–76	Lincoln C	74	Northampton T	68	Reading	60	Tranmere R	58
1976–77	Cambridge U	65	Exeter C	62	Colchester U*	59	Bradford C	59
1977–78	Watford	71	Southend U	60	Swansea C*	56	Brentford	56
1978–79	Reading	65	Grimsby T*	61	Wimbledon*	61	Barnsley	61
1979–80	Huddersfield T	66	Walsall	64	Newport Co	61	Portsmouth*	60
1980–81	Southend U	67	Lincoln C	65	Doncaster R	56	Wimbledon	55
1981–82	Sheffield U	96	Bradford C*	91	Wigan Ath	91	Bournemouth	88
1982–83	Wimbledon	98	Hull C	90	Port Vale	88	Scunthorpe U	83
1983–84	York C	101	Doncaster R	85	Reading*	82	Bristol C	82
1984–85	Chesterfield	91	Blackpool	86	Darlington	85	Bury	84
1985–86	Swindon T	102	Chester C	84	Mansfield T	81	Port Vale	79
1986–87	Northampton T	99	Preston NE	90	Southend U	80	Wolverhampton W††	79
1987–88	Wolverhampton W	90	Cardiff C	85	Bolton W	78	Scunthorpe U††	77
1988–89	Rotherham U	82	Tranmere R	80	Crewe Alex	78	Scunthorpe U††	77
1989–90	Exeter C	89	Grimsby T	79	Southend U	75	Stockport Co††	74
1990–91	Darlington	83	Stockport Co*	82	Hartlepool U	82	Peterborough U	80
1991–92†*	Burnley	83	Rotherham U*	77	Mansfield T	77	Blackpool	76

†*Maximum points:* 88 owing to Accrington Stanley's resignation.
†**Maximum points:* 126 owing to Aldershot being expelled (and only 23 teams started the competition).

THIRD DIVISION—SOUTH (1920–1958)

1920–21 SEASON AS THIRD DIVISION. MAXIMUM POINTS: *a* 84; *b* 92.

	First	Pts	Second	Pts	Third	Pts
1920–21*a*	Crystal Palace	59	Southampton	54	QPR	53
1921–22*a*	Southampton*	61	Plymouth Arg	61	Portsmouth	53
1922–23*a*	Bristol C	59	Plymouth Arg*	53	Swansea T	53
1923–24*a*	Portsmouth	59	Plymouth Arg	55	Millwall	54
1924–25*a*	Swansea T	57	Plymouth Arg	56	Bristol C	53
1925–26*a*	Reading	57	Plymouth Arg	56	Millwall	53
1926–27*a*	Bristol C	62	Plymouth Arg	60	Millwall	56
1927–28*a*	Millwall	65	Northampton T	55	Plymouth Arg	53
1928–29*a*	Charlton Ath*	54	Crystal Palace	54	Northampton T*	52
1929–30*a*	Plymouth Arg	68	Brentford	61	QPR	51
1930–31*a*	Notts Co	59	Crystal Palace	51	Brentford	50
1931–32*a*	Fulham	57	Reading	55	Southend U	53
1932–33*a*	Brentford	62	Exeter C	58	Norwich C	57
1933–34*a*	Norwich C	61	Coventry C*	54	Reading*	54
1934–35*a*	Charlton Ath	61	Reading	53	Coventry C	51
1935–36*a*	Coventry C	57	Luton T	56	Reading	54
1936–37*a*	Luton T	58	Notts Co	56	Brighton & HA	53
1937–38*a*	Millwall	56	Bristol C	55	QPR*	53
1938–39*a*	Newport Co	55	Crystal Palace	52	Brighton & HA	49
1939–46	Competition cancelled owing to war. Regional Leagues operated.					
1946–47*a*	Cardiff C	66	QPR	57	Bristol C	51
1947–48*a*	QPR	61	Bournemouth	57	Walsall	51
1948–49*a*	Swansea T	62	Reading	55	Bournemouth	52
1949–50*a*	Notts Co	58	Northampton T*	51	Southend U	51
1950–51*b*	Nottingham F	70	Norwich C	64	Reading*	57
1951–52*b*	Plymouth Arg	66	Reading*	61	Norwich C	61
1952–53*b*	Bristol R	64	Millwall*	62	Northampton T	62
1953–54*b*	Ipswich T	64	Brighton & HA	61	Bristol C	56
1954–55*b*	Bristol C	70	Leyton Orient	61	Southampton	59
1955–56*b*	Leyton Orient	66	Brighton & HA	65	Ipswich T	64
1956–57*b*	Ipswich T*	59	Torquay U	59	Colchester U	58
1957–58*b*	Brighton & HA	60	Brentford*	58	Plymouth Arg	58

THIRD DIVISION—NORTH (1921–1958)

MAXIMUM POINTS: *a* 76; *b* 84; *c* 80; *d* 92.

	First	Pts	Second	Pts	Third	Pts
1921–22*a*	Stockport Co	56	Darlington*	50	Grimsby T	50
1922–23*a*	Nelson	51	Bradford PA	47	Walsall	46
1923–24*b*	Wolverhampton W	63	Rochdale	62	Chesterfield	54
1924–25*b*	Darlington	58	Nelson*	53	New Brighton	53
1925–26*b*	Grimsby T	61	Bradford PA	60	Rochdale	59

	First	Pts	Second	Pts	Third	Pts
1926–27b	Stoke C	63	Rochdale	58	Bradford PA	55
1927–28b	Bradford PA	63	Lincoln C	55	Stockport Co	54
1928–29b	Bradford C	63	Stockport Co	62	Wrexham	52
1929–30b	Port Vale	67	Stockport Co	63	Darlington*	50
1930–31b	Chesterfield	58	Lincoln C	57	Wrexham*	54
1931–32c	Lincoln C*	57	Gateshead	57	Chester	50
1932–33b	Hull C	59	Wrexham	57	Stockport Co	54
1933–34b	Barnsley	62	Chesterfield	61	Stockport Co	59
1934–35b	Doncaster R	57	Halifax T	55	Chester	54
1935–36b	Chesterfield	60	Chester*	55	Tranmere R	55
1936–37b	Stockport Co	60	Lincoln C	57	Chester	53
1937–38b	Tranmere R	56	Doncaster R	54	Hull C	53
1938–39b	Barnsley	67	Doncaster R	56	Bradford C	52
1939–46	Competition cancelled owing to war. Regional Leagues operated.					
1946–47b	Doncaster R	72	Rotherham U	64	Chester	56
1947–48b	Lincoln C	60	Rotherham U	59	Wrexham	50
1948–49b	Hull C	65	Rotherham U	62	Doncaster R	50
1949–50b	Doncaster R	55	Gateshead	53	Rochdale*	51
1950–51d	Rotherham U	71	Mansfield T	64	Carlisle U	62
1951–52d	Lincoln C	69	Grimsby T	66	Stockport Co	59
1952–53d	Oldham Ath	59	Port Vale	58	Wrexham	56
1953–54d	Port Vale	69	Barnsley	58	Scunthorpe U	57
1954–55d	Barnsley	65	Accrington S	61	Scunthorpe U*	58
1955–56d	Grimsby T	68	Derby Co	63	Accrington S	59
1956–57d	Derby Co	63	Hartlepools U	59	Accrington S*	58
1957–58d	Scunthorpe U	66	Accrington S	59	Bradford C	57

PROMOTED AFTER PLAY-OFFS

(NOT ACCOUNTED FOR IN PREVIOUS SECTION)

1986–87	Aldershot to Division 3.
1987–88	Swansea C to Division 3.
1988–89	Leyton Orient to Division 3.
1989–90	Sunderland to Division 1; Notts Co to Division 2; Cambridge U to Division 3.
1990–91	Notts Co to Division 1; Tranmere R to Division 2; Torquay U to Division 3.
1991–92	Blackburn R to Premier League; Peterborough U to Division 1.
1992–93	Swindon T to Premier League; WBA to Division 1; York C to Division 2.
1993–94	Leicester C to Premier League; Burnley to Division 1; Wycombe W to Division 2.
1994–95	Huddersfield T to Division 1.
1995–96	Leicester C to Premier League; Bradford C to Division 1; Plymouth Arg to Division 2.
1996–97	Crystal Palace to Premier League; Crewe Alex to Division 1; Northampton T to Division 2.
1997–98	Charlton Ath to Premier League; Colchester U to Division 2.
1998–99	Watford to Premier League; Scunthorpe U to Division 2.
1999–2000	Peterborough U to Division 2
2000–01	Walsall to Division 1; Blackpool to Division 2
2001–02	Birmingham C to Premier League; Stoke C to Division 1; Cheltenham T to Division 2
2002–03	Wolverhampton W to Premier League; Cardiff C to Division 1; Bournemouth to Division 2
2003–04	Crystal Palace to Premier League; Brighton & HA to Division 1; Huddersfield T to Division 2
2004–05	West Ham U to Premier League; Sheffield W to Championship; Southend U to Championship 1
2005–06	Watford to Premier League; Barnsley to Championship; Cheltenham T to Championship 1
2006–07	Derby Co to Premier League; Blackpool to Championship; Bristol R to Championship 1
2007–08	Hull C to Premier League; Doncaster R to Championship; Stockport Co to Championship 1
2008–09	Burnley to Premier League; Scunthorpe U to Championship; Gillingham to Championship 1
2009–10	Blackpool to Premier League; Millwall to Championship; Dagenham & R to Championship 1
2010–11	Swansea C to Premier League; Peterborough U to Championship; Stevenage to Championship 1

LEAGUE TITLE WINS

FA PREMIER LEAGUE – Manchester U 12, Arsenal 3, Chelsea 3, Blackburn R 1.

FOOTBALL LEAGUE CHAMPIONSHIP – Sunderland 2, Newcastle U 1, QPR 1, Reading 1, WBA 1, Wolverhampton W 1.

LEAGUE DIVISION 1 – Liverpool 18, Arsenal 10, Everton 9, Sunderland 8, Aston Villa 7, Manchester U 7, Newcastle U 5, Sheffield W 4, Huddersfield T 3, Leeds U 3, Manchester C 3, Portsmouth 3, Wolverhampton W 3, Blackburn R 2, Burnley 2, Derby Co 2, Nottingham F 2, Preston NE 2, Tottenham H 2; Bolton W, Charlton Ath, Chelsea, Crystal Palace, Fulham, Ipswich T, Middlesbrough, Norwich C, Sheffield U, WBA 1 each.

FOOTBALL LEAGUE CHAMPIONSHIP 1 – Brighton & HA 1, Leicester C 1, Luton T 1, Norwich C 1, Scunthorpe U 1, Southend U 1, Swansea C 1.

LEAGUE DIVISION 2 – Leicester C 6, Manchester C 6, Birmingham C (one as Small Heath) 5, Sheffield W 5, Derby Co 4, Liverpool 4, Preston NE 4, Ipswich T 3, Leeds U 3, Middlesbrough 3, Notts Co 3, Stoke C 3, Aston Villa 2, Bolton W 2, Burnley 2, Bury 2, Chelsea 2, Fulham 2, Grimsby T 2, Manchester U 2, Millwall 2, Norwich C 2, Nottingham F 2, Tottenham H 2, WBA 2, West Ham U 2, Wolverhampton W 2; Blackburn R, Blackpool, Bradford C, Brentford, Brighton & HA, Bristol C, Coventry C, Crystal Palace, Everton, Huddersfield T, Luton T, Newcastle U, QPR, Oldham Ath, Oxford U, Plymouth Arg, Reading, Sheffield U, Sunderland, Swindon T, Watford, Wigan Ath 1 each.

FOOTBALL LEAGUE CHAMPIONSHIP 2 – Brentford 1, Carlisle U 1, Chesterfield 1, Milton Keynes D 1, Notts Co 1, Walsall 1, Yeovil T 1.

LEAGUE DIVISION 3 – Brentford 2, Carlisle U 2, Oxford U 2, Plymouth Arg 2, Portsmouth 2, Preston NE 2, Shrewsbury T 2; Aston Villa, Blackburn R, Bolton W, Bournemouth, Bradford C, Brighton & HA, Bristol R, Burnley, Bury, Cambridge U, Cardiff C, Coventry C, Doncaster R. Grimsby T, Hereford U, Hull C, Leyton Orient, Mansfield T, Northampton T, Notts Co, Oldham Ath, QPR, Reading, Rotherham U, Rushden & D Southampton, Sunderland, Swansea C, Watford, Wigan Ath, Wolverhampton W, Wrexham 1 each.

LEAGUE DIVISION 4 – Chesterfield 2, Doncaster R 2, Peterborough U 2; Brentford, Brighton & HA, Burnley, Cambridge U, Darlington, Exeter C, Gillingham, Grimsby T, Huddersfield T, Lincoln C, Luton T, Mansfield T, Millwall, Northampton T, Notts Co, Port Vale, Reading, Rotherham U, Sheffield U, Southend U, Southport, Stockport Co, Swindon T, Walsall, Watford, Wimbledon, Wolverhampton W, York C 1 each.

LEAGUE TITLE WINS TO 1957–58

DIVISION 3 (South) – Bristol C 3, Charlton Ath 2, Ipswich T 2, Millwall 2, Notts Co 2, Plymouth Arg 2, Swansea T 2; Brentford, Brighton & HA, Bristol R, Cardiff C, Coventry C, Crystal Palace, Fulham, Leyton Orient, Luton T, Newport Co, Norwich C, Nottingham F, Portsmouth, QPR, Reading, Southampton 1 each.

DIVISION 3 (North) – Barnsley 3, Doncaster R 3, Lincoln C 3, Chesterfield 2, Grimsby T 2, Hull C 2, Port Vale 2, Stockport Co 2; Bradford C, Bradford PA, Darlington, Derby Co, Nelson, Oldham Ath, Rotherham U, Scunthorpe U, Stoke C, Tranmere R, Wolverhampton W 1 each.

RELEGATED CLUBS

1891–92 League extended. Newton Heath, Sheffield W and Nottingham F admitted. *Second Division formed* including Darwen.
1892–93 In Test matches, Sheffield U and Darwen won promotion in place of Notts Co and Accrington S.
1893–94 In Tests, Liverpool and Small Heath won promotion. Newton Heath and Darwen relegated.
1894–95 After Tests, Bury promoted, Liverpool relegated.
1895–96 After Tests, Liverpool promoted, Small Heath relegated.
1896–97 After Tests, Notts Co promoted, Burnley relegated.
1897–98 Test system abolished after success of Stoke C and Burnley. League extended. Blackburn R and Newcastle U elected to First Division. *Automatic promotion and relegation introduced.*

FA PREMIER LEAGUE TO DIVISION 1

1992–93 Crystal Palace, Middlesbrough, Nottingham F
1993–94 Sheffield U, Oldham Ath, Swindon T
1994–95 Crystal Palace, Norwich C, Leicester C, Ipswich T
1995–96 Manchester C, QPR, Bolton W
1996–97 Sunderland, Middlesbrough, Nottingham F
1997–98 Bolton W, Barnsley, Crystal Palace

1998–99 Charlton Ath, Blackburn R, Nottingham F
1999–2000 Wimbledon, Sheffield W, Watford
2000–01 Manchester C, Coventry C, Bradford C
2001–02 Ipswich T, Derby Co, Leicester C
2002–03 West Ham U, WBA, Sunderland
2003–04 Leicester C, Leeds U, Wolverhampton W.

FA PREMIER LEAGUE TO CHAMPIONSHIP

2004–05 Crystal Palace, Norwich C, Southampton
2005–06 Birmingham C, WBA, Sunderland
2006–07 Sheffield U, Charlton Ath, Watford
2007–08 Reading, Birmingham C, Derby Co

2008–09 Newcastle U, Middlesbrough, WBA
2009–10 Burnley, Hull C, Portsmouth
2010–11 Birmingham C, Blackpool, West Ham U

DIVISION 1 TO DIVISION 2

1898–99 Bolton W and Sheffield W
1899–1900 Burnley and Glossop
1900–01 Preston NE and WBA
1901–02 Small Heath and Manchester C
1902–03 Grimsby T and Bolton W
1903–04 Liverpool and WBA
1904–05 League extended. Bury and Notts Co, two bottom clubs in First Division, re-elected.
1905–06 Nottingham F and Wolverhampton W
1906–07 Derby Co and Stoke C
1907–08 Bolton W and Birmingham C
1908–09 Manchester C and Leicester Fosse
1909–10 Bolton W and Chelsea
1910–11 Bristol C and Nottingham F
1911–12 Preston NE and Bury
1912–13 Notts Co and Woolwich Arsenal
1913–14 Preston NE and Derby Co
1914–15 Tottenham H and Chelsea*
1919–20 Notts Co and Sheffield W
1920–21 Derby Co and Bradford PA
1921–22 Bradford C and Manchester U
1922–23 Stoke C and Oldham Ath
1923–24 Chelsea and Middlesbrough
1924–25 Preston NE and Nottingham F
1925–26 Manchester C and Notts Co
1926–27 Leeds U and WBA
1927–28 Tottenham H and Middlesbrough
1928–29 Bury and Cardiff C
1929–30 Burnley and Everton
1930–31 Leeds U and Manchester U
1931–32 Grimsby T and West Ham U
1932–33 Bolton W and Blackpool
1933–34 Newcastle U and Sheffield U
1934–35 Leicester C and Tottenham H
1935–36 Aston Villa and Blackburn R
1936–37 Manchester U and Sheffield W
1937–38 Manchester C and WBA
1938–39 Birmingham C and Leicester C
1946–47 Brentford and Leeds U
1947–48 Blackburn R and Grimsby T
1948–49 Preston NE and Sheffield U
1949–50 Manchester C and Birmingham C
1950–51 Sheffield W and Everton
1951–52 Huddersfield T and Fulham
1952–53 Stoke C and Derby Co
1953–54 Middlesbrough and Liverpool
1954–55 Leicester C and Sheffield W
1955–56 Huddersfield T and Sheffield U
1956–57 Charlton Ath and Cardiff C
1957–58 Sheffield W and Sunderland

1958–59 Portsmouth and Aston Villa
1959–60 Luton T and Leeds U
1960–61 Preston NE and Newcastle U
1961–62 Chelsea and Cardiff C
1962–63 Manchester C and Leyton Orient
1963–64 Bolton W and Ipswich T
1964–65 Wolverhampton W and Birmingham C
1965–66 Northampton T and Blackburn R
1966–67 Aston Villa and Blackpool
1967–68 Fulham and Sheffield U
1968–69 Leicester C and QPR
1969–70 Sunderland and Sheffield W
1970–71 Burnley and Blackpool
1971–72 Huddersfield T and Nottingham F
1972–73 Crystal Palace and WBA
1973–74 Southampton, Manchester U, Norwich C
1974–75 Luton T, Chelsea, Carlisle U
1975–76 Wolverhampton W, Burnley, Sheffield U
1976–77 Sunderland, Stoke C, Tottenham H
1977–78 West Ham U, Newcastle U, Leicester C
1978–79 QPR, Birmingham C, Chelsea
1979–80 Bristol C, Derby Co, Bolton W
1980–81 Norwich C, Leicester C, Crystal Palace
1981–82 Leeds U, Wolverhampton W, Middlesbrough
1982–83 Manchester C, Swansea C, Brighton & HA
1983–84 Birmingham C, Notts Co, Wolverhampton W
1984–85 Norwich C, Sunderland, Stoke C
1985–86 Ipswich T, Birmingham C, WBA
1986–87 Leicester C, Manchester C, Aston Villa
1987–88 Chelsea**, Portsmouth, Watford, Oxford U
1988–89 Middlesbrough, West Ham U, Newcastle U
1989–90 Sheffield W, Charlton Ath, Millwall
1990–91 Sunderland and Derby Co
1991–92 Luton T, Notts Co, West Ham U
1992–93 Brentford, Cambridge U, Bristol R
1993–94 Birmingham C, Oxford U, Peterborough U
1994–95 Swindon T, Burnley, Bristol C, Notts Co
1995–96 Millwall, Watford, Luton T
1996–97 Grimsby T, Oldham Ath, Southend U
1997–98 Manchester C, Stoke C, Reading
1998–99 Bury, Oxford U, Bristol C
1999–2000 Walsall, Port Vale, Swindon T
2000–01 Huddersfield T, QPR, Tranmere R
2001–02 Crewe Alex, Barnsley, Stockport Co
2002–03 Sheffield W, Brighton & HA, Grimsby T
2003–04 Walsall, Bradford C, Wimbledon
**Relegated after play-offs.
*Subsequently re-elected to Division 1 when League was extended after the War.

FOOTBALL LEAGUE CHAMPIONSHIP TO FOOTBALL LEAGUE CHAMPIONSHIP 1

2004–05 Gillingham, Nottingham F, Rotherham U
2005–06 Crewe Alex, Millwall, Brighton & HA
2006–07 Southend U, Luton T, Leeds U
2007–08 Leicester C, Scunthorpe U, Colchester U

2008–09 Norwich C, Southampton, Charlton Ath
2009–10 Sheffield W, Plymouth Arg, Peterborough U
2010–11 Preston NE, Sheffield U, Scunthorpe U

DIVISION 2 TO DIVISION 3

1920–21 Stockport Co
1921–22 Bradford PA and Bristol C
1922–23 Rotherham Co and Wolverhampton W
1923–24 Nelson and Bristol C
1924–25 Crystal Palace and Coventry C
1925–26 Stoke C and Stockport Co
1926–27 Darlington and Bradford C
1927–28 Fulham and South Shields
1928–29 Port Vale and Clapton Orient
1929–30 Hull C and Notts Co
1930–31 Reading and Cardiff C
1931–32 Barnsley and Bristol C
1932–33 Chesterfield and Charlton Ath
1933–34 Millwall and Lincoln C
1934–35 Oldham Ath and Notts Co
1935–36 Port Vale and Hull C
1936–37 Doncaster R and Bradford C
1937–38 Barnsley and Stockport Co
1938–39 Norwich C and Tranmere R
1946–47 Swansea T and Newport Co
1947–48 Doncaster R and Millwall
1948–49 Nottingham F and Lincoln C
1949–50 Plymouth Arg and Bradford PA
1950–51 Grimsby T and Chesterfield
1951–52 Coventry C and QPR
1952–53 Southampton and Barnsley
1953–54 Brentford and Oldham Ath
1954–55 Ipswich T and Derby Co
1955–56 Plymouth Arg and Hull C
1956–57 Port Vale and Bury
1957–58 Doncaster R and Notts Co
1958–59 Barnsley and Grimsby T
1959–60 Bristol C and Hull C
1960–61 Lincoln C and Portsmouth
1961–62 Brighton & HA and Bristol R
1962–63 Walsall and Luton T
1963–64 Grimsby T and Scunthorpe U
1964–65 Swindon T and Swansea T
1965–66 Middlesbrough and Leyton Orient
1966–67 Northampton T and Bury
1967–68 Plymouth Arg and Rotherham U

1968–69 Fulham and Bury
1969–70 Preston NE and Aston Villa
1970–71 Blackburn R and Bolton W
1971–72 Charlton Ath and Watford
1972–73 Huddersfield T and Brighton & HA
1973–74 Crystal Palace, Preston NE, Swindon T
1974–75 Millwall, Cardiff C, Sheffield W
1975–76 Oxford U, York C, Portsmouth
1976–77 Carlisle U, Plymouth Arg, Hereford U
1977–78 Blackpool, Mansfield T, Hull C
1978–79 Sheffield U, Millwall, Blackburn R
1979–80 Fulham, Burnley, Charlton Ath
1980–81 Preston NE, Bristol C, Bristol R
1981–82 Cardiff C, Wrexham, Orient
1982–83 Rotherham U, Burnley, Bolton W
1983–84 Derby Co, Swansea C, Cambridge U
1984–85 Notts Co, Cardiff C, Wolverhampton W
1985–86 Carlisle U, Middlesbrough, Fulham
1986–87 Sunderland**, Grimsby T, Brighton & HA
1987–88 Huddersfield T, Reading, Sheffield U**
1988–89 Shrewsbury T, Birmingham C, Walsall
1989–90 Bournemouth, Bradford C, Stoke C
1990–91 WBA and Hull C
1991–92 Plymouth Arg, Brighton & HA, Port Vale
1992–93 Preston NE, Mansfield T, Wigan Ath, Chester C
1993–94 Fulham, Exeter C, Hartlepool U, Barnet
1994–95 Cambridge U, Plymouth Arg, Cardiff C,
         Chester C, Leyton Orient
1995–96 Carlisle U, Swansea C, Brighton & HA, Hull C
1996–97 Peterborough U, Shrewsbury T, Rotherham U,
         Notts Co
1997–98 Brentford, Plymouth Arg, Carlisle U, Southend U
1998–99 York C, Northampton T, Lincoln C,
         Macclesfield T
1999–2000 Cardiff C, Blackpool, Scunthorpe U,
         Chesterfield
2000–01 Bristol R, Luton T, Swansea C, Oxford U
2001–02 Bournemouth, Bury, Wrexham, Cambridge U
2002–03 Cheltenham T, Huddersfield T, Mansfield T
         Northampton T
2003–04 Grimsby T, Rushden & D, Notts Co, Wycombe W

FOOTBALL LEAGUE CHAMPIONSHIP 1 TO FOOTBALL LEAGUE CHAMPIONSHIP 2

2004–05 Torquay U, Wrexham, Peterborough U,
         Stockport Co
2005–06 Hartlepool U, Milton Keynes D, Swindon T,
         Walsall
2006–07 Chesterfield, Bradford C, Rotherham U,
         Brentford
2007–08 Bournemouth, Gillingham, Port Vale, Luton T

2008–09 Northampton T, Crewe Alex, Cheltenham T,
         Hereford U
2009–10 Gillingham, Wycombe W, Southend U,
         Stockport Co
2010–11 Dagenham & R, Bristol R, Plymouth Arg,
         Swindon T

DIVISION 3 TO DIVISION 4

1958–59 Stockport Co, Doncaster R, Notts Co, Rochdale
1959–60 York C, Mansfield T, Wrexham, Accrington S
1960–61 Tranmere R, Bradford C, Colchester U,
         Chesterfield
1961–62 Torquay U, Lincoln C, Brentford, Newport Co
1962–63 Bradford PA, Brighton & HA, Carlisle U,
         Halifax T
1963–64 Millwall, Crewe Alex, Wrexham, Notts Co
1964–65 Luton T, Port Vale, Colchester U, Barnsley
1965–66 Southend U, Exeter C, Brentford, York C
1966–67 Swansea T, Darlington, Doncaster R, Workington
1967–68 Grimsby T, Colchester U, Scunthorpe U,
         Peterborough U (demoted)
1968–69 Northampton T, Hartlepool, Crewe Alex,
         Oldham Ath
1969–70 Bournemouth, Southport, Barrow, Stockport Co
1970–71 Reading, Bury, Doncaster R, Gillingham
1971–72 Mansfield T, Barnsley, Torquay U, Bradford C
1972–73 Rotherham U, Brentford, Swansea C,
         Scunthorpe U
1973–74 Cambridge U, Shrewsbury T, Southport,
         Rochdale

1974–75 Bournemouth, Tranmere R, Watford,
         Huddersfield T
1975–76 Aldershot, Colchester U, Southend U, Halifax T
1976–77 Reading, Northampton T, Grimsby T, York C
1977–78 Port Vale, Bradford C, Hereford U, Portsmouth
1978–79 Peterborough U, Walsall, Tranmere R, Lincoln C
1979–80 Bury, Southend U, Mansfield T, Wimbledon
1980–81 Sheffield U, Colchester U, Blackpool, Hull C
1981–82 Wimbledon, Swindon T, Bristol C, Chester
1982–83 Reading, Wrexham, Doncaster R, Chesterfield
1983–84 Scunthorpe U, Southend U, Port Vale, Exeter C
1984–85 Burnley, Orient, Preston NE, Cambridge U
1985–86 Lincoln C, Cardiff C, Wolverhampton W,
         Swansea C
1986–87 Bolton W**, Carlisle U, Darlington, Newport Co
1987–88 Rotherham U**, Grimsby T, York C, Doncaster R
1988–89 Southend U, Chesterfield, Gillingham, Aldershot
1989–90 Cardiff C, Northampton T, Blackpool, Walsall
1990–91 Crewe Alex, Rotherham U, Mansfield T
1991–92 Bury, Shrewsbury T, Torquay U, Darlington

** *Relegated after play-offs.*

APPLICATIONS FOR RE-ELECTION

FOURTH DIVISION
Eleven: Hartlepool U.
Seven: Crewe Alex.
Six: Barrow (lost League place to Hereford U 1972), Halifax T, Rochdale, Southport (lost League place to Wigan Ath 1978), York C.
Five: Chester C, Darlington, Lincoln C, Stockport Co, Workington (lost League place to Wimbledon 1977).
Four: Bradford PA (lost League place to Cambridge U 1970), Newport Co, Northampton T.
Three: Doncaster R, Hereford U.
Two: Bradford C, Exeter C, Oldham Ath, Scunthorpe U, Torquay U.
One: Aldershot, Colchester U, Gateshead (lost League place to Peterborough U 1960), Grimsby T, Swansea C, Tranmere R, Wrexham, Blackpool, Cambridge U, Preston NE.
Accrington S resigned and Oxford U were elected 1962.
Port Vale were forced to re-apply following expulsion in 1968.
Aldershot expelled March 1992. Maidstone U resigned August 1992.

THIRD DIVISIONS NORTH & SOUTH
Seven: Walsall.
Six: Exeter C, Halifax T, Newport Co.
Five: Accrington S, Barrow, Gillingham, New Brighton, Southport.
Four: Rochdale, Norwich C.
Three: Crystal Palace, Crewe Alex, Darlington, Hartlepool U, Merthyr T, Swindon T.
Two: Aberdare Ath, Aldershot, Ashington, Brentford, Bournemouth, Chester, Colchester U, Durham C, Millwall, Nelson, QPR, Rotherham U, Southend U, Tranmere R, Watford, Workington.
One: Bradford C, Bradford PA, Brighton & HA, Bristol R, Cardiff C, Carlisle U, Charlton Ath, Gateshead, Grimsby T, Mansfield T, Shrewsbury T, Torquay U, York C.

LEAGUE STATUS FROM 1986–87

RELEGATED FROM LEAGUE

1986–87 Lincoln C	1987–88 Newport Co
1988–89 Darlington	1989–90 Colchester U
1990–91 —	1991–92 —
1992–93 Halifax T	1993–94 —
1994–95 —	1995–96 —
1996–97 Hereford U	1997–98 Doncaster R
1998–99 Scarborough	1999–2000 Chester C
2000–01 Barnet	2001–02 Halifax T
2002–03 Shrewsbury T, Exeter C	
2003–04 Carlisle U, York C	
2004–05 Kidderminster H, Cambridge U	
2005–06 Oxford U, Rushden & D	
2006–07 Boston U, Torquay U	
2007–08 Mansfield T, Wrexham	
2008–09 Chester C, Luton T	
2009–10 Grimsby T, Darlington	
2010–11 Lincoln C, Stockport Co	

PROMOTED TO LEAGUE

1986–87 Scarborough	1987–88 Lincoln C
1988–89 Maidstone U	1989–90 Darlington
1990–91 Barnet	1991–92 Colchester U
1992–93 Wycombe W	1993–94 —
1994–95 —	1995–96 —
1996–97 Macclesfield T	1997–98 Halifax T
1998–99 Cheltenham T	1999–2000 Kidderminster H
2000–01 Rushden & D	2001–02 Boston U
2002–03 Yeovil T, Doncaster R	
2003–04 Chester C, Shrewsbury T	
2004–05 Barnet, Carlisle U	
2005–06 Accrington S, Hereford U	
2006–07 Dagenham & R, Morecambe	
2007–08 Aldershot T, Exeter C	
2008–09 Burton Alb, Torquay U	
2009–10 Stevenage B, Oxford U	
2010–11 Crawley T, AFC Wimbledon	

Liverpool manager Roy Hodgson (right) and Manchester City manager Roberto Mancini react during their Premier League encounter at The City of Manchester Stadium. (PA Photos)

LEAGUE ATTENDANCES SINCE 1946–47

Season	Matches	Total	Div. 1	Div. 2	Div. 3 (S)	Div. 3 (N)
1946–47	1848	35,604,606	15,005,316	11,071,572	5,664,004	3,863,714
1947–48	1848	40,259,130	16,732,341	12,286,350	6,653,610	4,586,829
1948–49	1848	41,271,414	17,914,667	11,353,237	6,998,429	5,005,081
1949–50	1848	40,517,865	17,278,625	11,694,158	7,104,155	4,440,927
1950–51	2028	39,584,967	16,679,454	10,780,580	7,367,884	4,757,109
1951–52	2028	39,015,866	16,110,322	11,066,189	6,958,927	4,880,428
1952–53	2028	37,149,966	16,050,278	9,686,654	6,704,299	4,708,735
1953–54	2028	36,174,590	16,154,915	9,510,053	6,311,508	4,198,114
1954–55	2028	34,133,103	15,087,221	8,988,794	5,996,017	4,051,071
1955–56	2028	33,150,809	14,108,961	9,080,002	5,692,479	4,269,367
1956–57	2028	32,744,405	13,803,037	8,718,162	5,622,189	4,601,017
1957–58	2028	33,562,208	14,468,652	8,663,712	6,097,183	4,332,661

Season	Matches	Total	Div. 1	Div. 2	Div. 3	Div. 4
1958–59	2028	33,610,985	14,727,691	8,641,997	5,946,600	4,276,697
1959–60	2028	32,538,611	14,391,227	8,399,627	5,739,707	4,008,050
1960–61	2028	28,619,754	12,926,948	7,033,936	4,784,256	3,874,614
1961–62	2015	27,979,902	12,061,194	7,453,089	5,199,106	3,266,513
1962–63	2028	28,885,852	12,490,239	7,792,770	5,341,362	3,261,481
1963–64	2028	28,535,022	12,486,626	7,594,158	5,419,157	3,035,081
1964–65	2028	27,641,168	12,708,752	6,984,104	4,436,245	3,512,067
1965–66	2028	27,206,980	12,480,644	6,914,757	4,779,150	3,032,429
1966–67	2028	28,902,596	14,242,957	7,253,819	4,421,172	2,984,648
1967–68	2028	30,107,298	15,289,410	7,450,410	4,013,087	3,354,391
1968–69	2028	29,382,172	14,584,851	7,382,390	4,339,656	3,075,275
1969–70	2028	29,600,972	14,868,754	7,581,728	4,223,761	2,926,729
1970–71	2028	28,194,146	13,954,337	7,098,265	4,377,213	2,764,331
1971–72	2028	28,700,729	14,484,603	6,769,308	4,697,392	2,749,426
1972–73	2028	25,448,642	13,998,154	5,631,730	3,737,252	2,081,506
1973–74	2027	24,982,203	13,070,991	6,326,108	3,421,624	2,163,480
1974–75	2028	25,577,977	12,613,178	6,955,970	4,086,145	1,992,684
1975–76	2028	24,896,053	13,089,861	5,798,405	3,948,449	2,059,338
1976–77	2028	26,182,800	13,647,585	6,250,597	4,152,218	2,132,400
1977–78	2028	25,392,872	13,255,677	6,474,763	3,332,042	2,330,390
1978–79	2028	24,540,627	12,704,549	6,153,223	3,374,558	2,308,297
1979–80	2028	24,623,975	12,163,002	6,112,025	3,999,328	2,349,620
1980–81	2028	21,907,569	11,392,894	5,175,442	3,637,854	1,701,379
1981–82	2028	20,006,961	10,420,793	4,750,463	2,836,915	1,998,790
1982–83	2028	18,766,158	9,295,613	4,974,937	2,943,568	1,552,040
1983–84	2028	18,358,631	8,711,448	5,359,757	2,729,942	1,557,484
1984–85	2028	17,849,835	9,761,404	4,030,823	2,667,008	1,390,600
1985–86	2028	16,488,577	9,037,854	3,551,968	2,490,481	1,408,274
1986–87	2028	17,379,218	9,144,676	4,168,131	2,350,970	1,715,441
1987–88	2030	17,959,732	8,094,571	5,341,599	2,751,275	1,772,287
1988–89	2036	18,464,192	7,809,993	5,887,805	3,035,327	1,791,067
1989–90	2036	19,445,442	7,883,039	6,867,674	2,803,551	1,891,178
1990–91	2036	19,508,202	8,618,709	6,285,068	2,835,759	1,768,666
1991–92	2064*	20,487,273	9,989,160	5,809,787	2,993,352	1,694,974

Season	Matches	Total	FA Premier	Div. 1	Div. 2	Div. 3
1992–93	2028	20,657,327	9,759,809	5,874,017	3,483,073	1,540,428
1993–94	2028	21,683,381	10,644,551	6,487,104	2,972,702	1,579,024
1994–95	2028	21,856,020	11,213,168	6,044,293	3,037,752	1,560,807
1995–96	2036	21,844,416	10,469,107	6,566,349	2,843,652	1,965,308
1996–97	2036	22,783,163	10,804,762	6,931,539	3,195,223	1,851,639
1997–98	2036	24,692,608	11,092,106	8,330,018	3,503,264	1,767,220
1998–99	2036	25,435,542	11,620,326	7,543,369	4,169,697	2,102,150
1999–2000	2036	25,341,090	11,668,497	7,810,208	3,700,433	2,161,952
2000–01	2036	26,030,167	12,472,094	7,909,512	3,488,166	2,160,395
2001–02	2036	27,756,977	13,043,118	8,352,128	3,963,153	2,398,578
2002–03	2036	28,343,386	13,468,965	8,521,017	3,892,469	2,460,935
2003–04	2036	29,197,510	13,303,136	8,772,780	4,146,495	2,975,099

Season	Matches	Total	FA Premier	Championship	Championship 1	Championship 2
2004–05	2036	29,245,870	12,878,791	9,612,761	4,270,674	2,483,644
2005–06	2036	29,089,084	12,871,643	9,719,204	4,183,011	2,315,226
2006–07	2036	29,541,949	13,058,115	10,057,813	4,135,599	2,290,422
2007–08	2036	29,914,212	13,708,875	9,397,036	4,412,023	2,396,278
2008–09	2036	29,881,966	13,527,815	9,877,552	4,171,834	2,304,765
2009–10	2036	30,057,892	12,977,251	9,909,882	5,043,099	2,127,660
2010–11	2036	29,459,105	13,406,990	9,595,236	4,150,547	2,306,332

*Figures include matches played by Aldershot.
Football League official total for their three divisions in 2001–02 was 14,716,162.

ENGLISH LEAGUE ATTENDANCES 2010–11

FA BARCLAYCARD PREMIERSHIP ATTENDANCES

	Average Gate			Season 2010–11	
	2009–10	2010–11	+/–%	Highest	Lowest
Arsenal	59,927	60,025	+0.16	60,112	59,552
Aston Villa	38,573	37,193	–3.58	42,785	32,627
Birmingham City	25,246	25,461	+0.85	28,270	21,394
Blackburn Rovers	25,428	24,999	–1.69	29,867	21,848
Blackpool	8,611	15,779	+83.24	16,116	14,550
Bolton Wanderers	21,880	22,869	+4.52	26,881	18,139
Chelsea	41,422	41,435	+0.03	41,829	40,734
Everton	36,725	36,038	–1.87	39,673	31,808
Fulham	23,909	25,042	+4.74	25,694	23,222
Liverpool	42,863	42,820	–0.10	44,923	35,400
Manchester City	45,512	45,880	+0.81	47,393	43,077
Manchester United	74,864	75,109	+0.33	75,486	73,401
Newcastle United	43,387	47,717	+9.98	51,988	41,053
Stoke City	27,162	26,858	–1.12	27,566	25,019
Sunderland	40,355	40,011	–0.85	47,864	35,101
Tottenham Hotspur	35,794	35,703	–0.25	36,197	32,702
West Bromwich Albion	22,199	24,682	+11.19	26,196	22,846
West Ham United	33,683	33,492	–0.57	34,941	31,194
Wigan Athletic	18,006	16,812	–6.63	22,043	14,042
Wolverhampton Wanderers	28,365	27,695	–2.36	29,086	25,112

TOTAL ATTENDANCES: 13,406,990 (380 games)
Average 35,282 (+3.31%)
HIGHEST: 75,486 Manchester United v Bolton Wanderers
LOWEST: 14,042 Wigan Ath v Wolverhampton Wanderers
HIGHEST AVERAGE: 75,109 Manchester United
LOWEST AVERAGE: 15,779 Blackpool

FOOTBALL LEAGUE: CHAMPIONSHIP ATTENDANCES

	Average Gate			Season 2010–11	
	2009–10	2010–11	+/–%	Highest	Lowest
Barnsley	12,964	11,855	–8.55	20,309	10,250
Bristol City	14,600	14,604	+0.03	18,308	13,376
Burnley	20,653	14,930	–27.71	20,453	13,655
Cardiff City	20,717	23,193	+11.95	26,058	20,573
Coventry City	17,305	16,309	–5.76	28,184	12,292
Crystal Palace	14,770	15,390	+4.20	20,142	12,353
Derby County	29,230	25,892	–11.42	33,010	23,159
Doncaster Rovers	10,991	10,258	–6.67	14,312	7,921
Hull City	24,389	21,168	–13.21	24,110	19,714
Ipswich Town	20,840	19,614	–5.88	29,258	16,728
Leeds United	24,817	27,299	+10.00	33,622	20,747
Leicester City	23,942	23,666	–1.15	30,919	19,611
Middlesbrough	19,948	16,268	–18.45	23,550	13,712
Millwall	10,834	12,438	+14.81	16,724	8,937
Norwich City	24,671	25,386	+2.90	26,532	23,852
Nottingham Forest	23,831	23,274	–2.34	29,490	19,411
Portsmouth	18,249	15,707	–13.93	20,040	13,132
Preston North End	12,934	11,767	–9.02	18,417	8,994
Queens Park Rangers	13,348	15,635	+17.13	18,234	12,046
Reading	17,495	17,681	+1.06	23,677	14,029
Scunthorpe United	6,463	5,547	–14.17	8,122	4,190
Sheffield United	25,120	20,632	–17.87	23,728	17,496
Swansea City	15,407	15,507	+0.65	19,309	12,411
Watford	14,344	13,151	–8.32	15,538	10,620

TOTAL ATTENDANCES: 9,595,236 (552 games)
Average 17,383 (–3.17%)
HIGHEST: 33,622 Leeds United v Sheffield United
LOWEST: 4,190 Scunthorpe United v Preston North End
HIGHEST AVERAGE: 27,299 Leeds United
LOWEST AVERAGE: 5,547 Scunthorpe U

Premiership and Football League attendance averages and highest crowd figures for 2010–11 are unofficial.

FOOTBALL LEAGUE: DIVISION 1 ATTENDANCES

	Average Gate			Season 2010–11	
	2009–10	2010–11	+/–%	Highest	Lowest
AFC Bournemouth	5,719	7,103	+24.2	10,008	5,501
Brentford	6,017	5,172	–14.04	7,015	3,795
Brighton & Hove Albion	6,466	7,351	+13.69	8,416	6,474
Bristol Rovers	7,042	6,253	–11.2	8,340	4,829
Carlisle United	5,210	5,207	–0.06	7,412	3,354
Charlton Athletic	17,407	15,582	–10.48	24,767	12,797
Colchester United	5,529	4,246	–23.20	6,523	2,892
Dagenham & Redbridge	2,097	2,769	+32.05	4,446	1,907
Exeter City	5,832	5,393	–7.53	7,869	3,456
Hartlepool United	3,443	2,933	–14.81	4,084	2,289
Huddersfield Town	14,381	13,733	–4.51	17,024	11,462
Leyton Orient	4,937	4,581	–7.21	7,714	2,963
Milton Keynes Dons FC	10,289	8,512	–17.27	11,857	6,469
Notts County	7,352	6,586	–10.42	11,355	4,041
Oldham Athletic	4,630	4,392	–5.14	8,564	3,056
Peterborough United	8,913	6,449	–27.65	10,116	4,233
Plymouth Argyle	10,316	8,613	–16.51	14,347	4,960
Rochdale	3,443	3,537	+2.73	6,483	2,019
Sheffield Wednesday	23,179	17,817	–23.13	23,081	14,797
Southampton	20,982	22,160	+5.61	31,653	17,857
Swindon Town	8,389	8,457	+0.81	11,087	6,912
Tranmere Rovers	5,670	5,467	–3.58	12,249	4,110
Walsall	4,028	3,845	–4.54	6,015	2,072
Yeovil Town	4,664	4,291	–8.00	6,281	3,331

TOTAL ATTENDANCES: 4,150,547 (552 games)
Average 7,519 (–17.70%)
HIGHEST: 31,653 Southampton v Walsall
LOWEST: 1,907 Dagenham & Redbridge v Brentford
HIGHEST AVERAGE: 22,160 Southampton
LOWEST AVERAGE: 2,769 Dagenham & Redbridge

FOOTBALL LEAGUE: DIVISION 2 ATTENDANCES

	Average Gate			Season 2010–11	
	2009–10	2010–11	+/–%	Highest	Lowest
Accrington Stanley	1,980	1,867	–5.71	2,815	1,356
Aldershot Town	3,085	2,487	–19.38	3,722	1,847
Barnet	2,059	2,249	+9.23	4,478	1,520
Bradford City	11,422	11,127	–2.58	15,332	10,392
Burton Albion	3,195	2,947	–7.76	4,321	1,904
Bury	3,028	3,313	+9.41	6,238	2,080
Cheltenham Town	3,185	2,980	–6.44	4,349	2,191
Chesterfield	3,849	6,972	+81.14	10,089	4,801
Crewe Alexandra	4,075	4,119	+1.08	7,183	3,171
Gillingham	6,335	5,230	–17.44	6,841	4,076
Hereford United	2,138	2,516	+17.68	3,942	1,444
Lincoln City	3,670	3,508	–4.41	7,932	2,261
Macclesfield Town	1,928	1,816	–5.81	3,915	1,067
Morecambe	2,262	2,647	+17.02	10,691	1,612
Northampton Town	4,375	4,604	+5.23	6,257	3,423
Oxford United	6,003	7,277	+21.22	9,440	6,004
Port Vale	5,079	5,532	+8.92	8,607	4,112
Rotherham United	3,817	3,667	–3.93	5,365	2,490
Shrewsbury Town	5,481	5,875	+7.19	8,817	4,343
Southend United	7,718	5,344	–30.76	6,622	4,499
Stevenage	2,589	2,899	+11.97	5,016	1,549
Stockport County	4,420	4,163	–5.81	5,470	3,335
Torquay United	2,855	2,630	–7.88	5,002	1,514
Wycombe Wanderers	5,544	4,495	–18.92	8,567	2,273

TOTAL ATTENDANCES: 2,306,332 (552 games)
Average 4,178 (+8.41%)
HIGHEST: 15,332 Bradford City v Stockport County
LOWEST: 1,067 Macclesfield Town v Lincoln City
HIGHEST AVERAGE: 11,127 Bradford City
LOWEST AVERAGE: 1,816 Macclesfield Town

LEAGUE CUP FINALISTS 1961–2011

Played as a two-leg final until 1966. All subsequent finals at Wembley until 2000, then at Millennium Stadium, Cardiff.

Year	Winners	Runners-up	Score
1961	Aston Villa	Rotherham U	0-2, 3-0 (aet)
1962	Norwich C	Rochdale	3-0, 1-0
1963	Birmingham C	Aston Villa	3-1, 0-0
1964	Leicester C	Stoke C	1-1, 3-2
1965	Chelsea	Leicester C	3-2, 0-0
1966	WBA	West Ham U	1-2, 4-1
1967	QPR	WBA	3-2
1968	Leeds U	Arsenal	1-0
1969	Swindon T	Arsenal	3-1 (aet)
1970	Manchester C	WBA	2-1 (aet)
1971	Tottenham H	Aston Villa	2-0
1972	Stoke C	Chelsea	2-1
1973	Tottenham H	Norwich C	1-0
1974	Wolverhampton W	Manchester C	2-1
1975	Aston Villa	Norwich C	1-0
1976	Manchester C	Newcastle U	2-1
1977	Aston Villa	Everton	0-0, 1-1 (aet), 3-2 (aet)
1978	Nottingham F	Liverpool	0-0 (aet), 1-0
1979	Nottingham F	Southampton	3-2
1980	Wolverhampton W	Nottingham F	1-0
1981	Liverpool	West Ham U	1-1 (aet), 2-1

MILK CUP

Year	Winners	Runners-up	Score
1982	Liverpool	Tottenham H	3-1 (aet)
1983	Liverpool	Manchester U	2-1 (aet)
1984	Liverpool	Everton	0-0 (aet), 1-0
1985	Norwich C	Sunderland	1-0
1986	Oxford U	QPR	3-0

LITTLEWOODS CUP

Year	Winners	Runners-up	Score
1987	Arsenal	Liverpool	2-1
1988	Luton T	Arsenal	3-2
1989	Nottingham F	Luton T	3-1
1990	Nottingham F	Oldham Ath	1-0

RUMBELOWS LEAGUE CUP

Year	Winners	Runners-up	Score
1991	Sheffield W	Manchester U	1-0
1992	Manchester U	Nottingham F	1-0

COCA-COLA CUP

Year	Winners	Runners-up	Score
1993	Arsenal	Sheffield W	2-1
1994	Aston Villa	Manchester U	3-1
1995	Liverpool	Bolton W	2-1
1996	Aston Villa	Leeds U	3-0
1997	Leicester C	Middlesbrough	1-1 (aet), 1-0 (aet)
1998	Chelsea	Middlesbrough	2-0 (aet)

WORTHINGTON CUP

Year	Winners	Runners-up	Score
1999	Tottenham H	Leicester C	1-0
2000	Leicester C	Tranmere R	2-1
2001	Liverpool	Birmingham C	1-1 (aet)
Liverpool won 5-4 on penalties			
2002	Blackburn R	Tottenham H	2-1
2003	Liverpool	Manchester U	2-0

CARLING CUP

Year	Winners	Runners-up	Score
2004	Middlesbrough	Bolton W	2-1
2005	Chelsea	Liverpool	3-2 (aet)
2006	Manchester U	Wigan Ath	4-0
2007	Chelsea	Arsenal	2-1
2008	Tottenham H	Chelsea	2-1 (aet)
2009	Manchester U	Tottenham H	0-0 (aet)
Manchester U won 4-1 on penalties			
2010	Manchester U	Aston Villa	2-1
2011	Birmingham C	Arsenal	2-1

LEAGUE CUP WINS
Liverpool 7, Aston Villa 5, Chelsea 4, Manchester U 4, Nottingham F 4, Tottenham H 4, Leicester C 3, Arsenal 2, Birmingham C 2, Manchester C 2, Norwich C 2, Wolverhampton W 2, Blackburn R 1, Leeds U 1, Luton T 1, Middlesbrough 1, Oxford U 1, QPR 1, Sheffield W 1, Stoke C 1, Swindon T 1, WBA 1.

APPEARANCES IN FINALS
Liverpool 10, Aston Villa 8, Manchester U 8, Arsenal 7, Tottenham H 7, Chelsea 6, Nottingham F 6, Leicester C 5, Norwich C 4, Birmingham C 3, Manchester C 3, Middlesbrough 3, WBA 3, Bolton W 2, Everton 2, Leeds U 2, Luton T 2, QPR 2, Sheffield W 2, Stoke C 2, West Ham U 2, Wolverhampton W 2, Newcastle U 1, Oldham Ath 1, Oxford U 1, Rochdale 1, Rotherham U 1, Southampton 1, Sunderland 1, Swindon T 1, Tranmere R 1, Wigan Ath 1.

APPEARANCES IN SEMI-FINALS
Arsenal 14, Aston Villa 13, Liverpool 13, Tottenham H 13, Manchester U 12, Chelsea 10, West Ham U 8, Blackburn R 6, Manchester C 6, Nottingham F 6, Birmingham C 5, Leeds U 5, Leicester C 5, Middlesbrough 5, Norwich C 5, Bolton W 4, Burnley 4, Everton 4, Ipswich T 4, Sheffield W 4, WBA 4, Crystal Palace 3, QPR 3, Sunderland 3, Swindon T 3, Wolverhampton W 3, Bristol C 2, Coventry C 2, Derby Co 2, Luton T 2, Oxford U 2, Plymouth Arg 2, Southampton 2, Stoke C 2, Tranmere R 2, Watford 2, Wimbledon 2, Blackpool 1, Bury 1, Cardiff C 1, Carlisle U 1, Chester C 1, Huddersfield T 1, Newcastle U 1, Oldham Ath 1, Peterborough U 1, Rochdale 1, Rotherham U 1, Sheffield U 1, Shrewsbury T 1, Stockport Co 1, Walsall 1, Wigan Ath 1, Wycombe W 1.

HISTORY OF THE ENGLISH LEAGUE CUP

Though the League Cup was inaugurated in 1960, the idea springing from the brain of Football League secretary Alan Hardaker, it was not the first knock-out competition organised by the Football League. That was instituted during the war as a temporary replacement for the FA Cup which was mothballed during hostilities. The League War Cup was started towards the end of 1939–40 and carried on in varying forms until the FA Cup returned for the transitional 1945–46 campaign.

Yet when the 1960–61 League Cup was announced it was something of a strange affair. Hardaker's idea was for matches to be decided over two legs to give every club a home tie, unlike the pot luck provided by the FA Cup.

With most Football League clubs having had floodlights installed during the latter stages of the 1950s, the concept was for the competition to be held midweek evenings. Clubs were not forced to enter. Many First Division clubs declined, one even was rumoured not wanting to participate for fear of being eliminated by a lower division team. Arsenal, Sheffield Wednesday, Tottenham Hotspur, West Bromwich Albion and Wolverhampton Wanderers were the absentees. No fewer than 41 clubs were given byes in the first round! Forty-six teams played in the first round.

Even fewer clubs signed up for the second tournament in 1961–62. Ten declined: Arsenal, Burnley, Chelsea, Everton, Liverpool, Manchester United, Sheffield Wednesday, Tottenham Hotspur, West Bromwich Albion and Wolverhampton Wanderers.

Though there were just two byes in the first round, bizarrely there was even one in the third round and five in the fourth! Little wonder the media had its doubts about the longevity of the new competition.

The 1962–63 campaign was mercifully spared further such nonsense, doubtless aided by the fact that absentees totalled a dozen: Arsenal, Burnley, Chelsea, Everton, Ipswich Town, Liverpool, Manchester United, Nottingham Forest, Sheffield Wednesday, Tottenham Hotspur, West Bromwich Albion and Wolverhampton Wanderers.

Chelsea and Ipswich joined up in 1963–64 while in 1964–65 Cardiff City and West Ham United also participated in Europe as well as the League Cup. Burnley entered the fold in 1965–66 but Chelsea declined because of European commitments. However for 1966–67 only two stayed out: Everton in the Cup-Winners' Cup and neighbours Liverpool competing in the European Cup.

For 1967–68 Tottenham Hotspur and Manchester United opted out for exactly the same involvement in Europe. But in 1968–69 just United defending their European Cup title were absent and from 1969–70 everyone signed up.

Yet such was the indifference to the League Cup in its early stages that even the official Football League Jubilee Book made only scant written reference to the newcomer apart from listing the results of the first three tournaments. Clearly there had to be a decision taken to either insist on full membership or risk scrapping the project completely.

However, once entry to the UEFA Cup was guaranteed for the winners, there was an entirely different approach to it by Football League clubs.

Sponsorship has played its part in more recent years. The Milk Marketing Board took first sip in 1982 as the Milk Cup followed by Littlewoods in 1987, Rumbelows from 1991 and Worthington Cup in 1999. Since 2004 Carling has maintained the flow of successive sponsors.

Even though they were one of the clubs who needed time to consider entry to the League Cup, Liverpool have been the most successful club winning seven times and appearing in ten finals.

Needless to say that the growth of European cup competitions has squeezed the ideals initially put forward for the League Cup and two-legged ties and even replays have gone by the board.

First Leg: Millmoor, 22 August 1961   12,226

Rotherham United (0) 2 *(Webster, Kirkman)*

Aston Villa (0) 0

Rotherham United: Ironside; Perry, Morgan, Lambert, Madden, Waterhouse, Webster, Weston, Houghton, Kirkman, Bambridge.
Aston Villa: Sims; Lynn, Lee, Crowe, Dugdale, Deakin, MacEwan, Thomson, Brown, Wylie, McParland.

Second Leg: Villa Park, 5 September 1961   31,202

Aston Villa (0) 3 *(O'Neill, Burrows, McParland)*

Rotherham United (0) 0

Aston Villa: Sidebottom; Neal, Lee, Crowe, Dugdale, Deakin, MacEwan, O'Neill, McParland, Thomson, Burrows.
Rotherham United: Ironside; Perry, Morgan, Lambert, Madden, Waterhouse, Webster, Weston, Houghton, Kirkman, Bambridge.
aet.
Twenty-nine goal Villa played 12 games and defended title eight days after winning it!

First Leg: Spotland, 26 April 1962   11,123

Rochdale (0) 0

Norwich City (2) 3 *(Lythgoe 2, Punton)*

Rochdale: Burgin; Milburn, Winton, Bodell, Aspden, Thompson, Wragg, Hepton, Bimpson, Cairns, Whitaker.
Norwich City: Kennon; McCrohan, Ashman, Burton, Butler, Mullett, Mannion, Lythgoe, Scott, Hill, Punton.

Second Leg: Carrow Road, 1 May 1962   19,708

Norwich City (0) 1 *(Hill)*

Rochdale (0) 0

Norwich City: Kennon; McCrohan, Ashman, Burton, Butler, Mullett, Mannion, Lythgoe, Scott, Hill, Punton.
Rochdale: Burgin; Milburn, Winton, Bodell, Aspden, Thompson, Whyke, Richardson, Bimson, Cairns, Whittaker.
First big trophy for Norwich City; Rochdale from Division Four was lowest ranking finalist.

First Leg: St Andrew's, 23 May 1963 31,850
Birmingham City (1) 3 *(Leek 2, Bloomfield)*
Aston Villa (1) 1 *(Thomson)*
Birmingham City: Scofield; Lynn, Green, Hennessey, Smith, Beard, Hellawell, Bloomfield, Harris, Leek, Auld.
Aston Villa: Sims; Frazer, Aitken, Crowe, Sleeuwenhoek, Lee, Baker, Graham, Thomson, Wylie, Burrows.

Second Leg: Villa Park, 27 May 1963 37,921
Aston Villa (0) 0
Birmingham City (0) 0
Aston Villa: Sims; Frazer, Aitken, Crowe, Chatterley, Lee, Baker, Graham, Thomson, Wylie, Burrows.
Birmingham City: Scofield; Lynn, Green, Hennessey, Smith, Beard, Hellawell, Bloomfield, Harris, Leek, Auld.
Another initial such triumph for Birmingham City and Ken Leek who scored eight goals in eight games.

First Leg: Victoria Ground, 15 April 1964 22,309
Stoke City (0) 1 *(Bebbington)*
Leicester City (0) 1 *(Gibson)*
Stoke City: Leslie; Asprey, Allen, Palmer, Kinnell, Skeels, Dobing, Viollet, Ritchie, McIlroy, Bebbington.
Leicester City: Banks; Sjoberg, Appleton, Dugan, King, Cross, Riley, Heath, Keyworth, Gibson, Stringfellow.

Second Leg: Filbert Street, 22 April 1964 25,372
Leicester City (1) 3 *(Stringfellow, Gibson, Riley)*
Stoke City (0) 2 *(Viollet, Kinnell)*
Leicester City: Banks; Sjoberg, Norman, Cross, King, Appleton, Riley, Gibson, Keyworth, Sweenie, Stringfellow.
Stoke City: Irvine; Asprey, Allen, Palmer, Kinnell, Skeels, Dobing, Viollet, Ritchie, McIlroy, Bebbington.
Leicester City succeeded in keeping John Ritchie – ten goals in ten matches – quiet.

First Leg: Stamford Bridge, 15 March 1965 20,690
Chelsea (1) 3 *(Tambling, Venables (pen), McCreadie)*
Leicester City (0) 2 *(Appleton, Goodfellow)*
Chelsea: Bonetti; Hinton, Harris R, Hollins, Young, Boyle, Murray, Graham, McCreadie, Venables, Tambling.
Leicester City: Banks; Sjoberg, Norman, Chalmers, King, Appleton, Hodgson, Cross, Goodfellow, Gibson, Sweenie.

Second Leg: Filbert Street, 5 April 1965 26,958
Leicester City (0) 0
Chelsea (0) 0
Leicester City: Banks; Walker, Norman, Roberts, Sjoberg, Appleton, Hodgson, Cross, Goodfellow, Gibson, Stringfellow.
Chelsea: Bonetti; Hinton, McCreadie, Harris R, Mortimore, Upton, Murray, Boyle, Bridges, Venables, Tambling.
Holders beaten and tie remembered for fine Eddie McCreadie goal after 60-yard run.

First Leg: Upton Park, 9 March 1966 28,341
West Ham United (0) 2 *(Moore, Byrne)*
West Bromwich Albion (0) 1 *(Astle)*
West Ham United: Standen; Burnett, Burkett, Peters, Brown, Moore, Brabrook, Boyce, Byrne, Hurst, Dear.
West Bromwich Albion: Potter; Cram, Fairfax, Frazer, Campbell, Williams, Brown, Astle, Kaye, Lovett, Clark.

Second Leg: The Hawthorns, 23 March 1966 31,925
West Bromwich Albion (4) 4 *(Kay, Brown, Clark, Williams)*
West Ham United (0) 1 *(Peters)*
West Bromwich Albion: Potter; Cramb, Fairfax, Frazer, Campbell, Williams, Brown, Astle, Kay, Hope, Clark.

West Ham United: Standen; Burnett, Peters, Bovington, Brown, Moore, Brabrook, Boyce, Byrne, Hurst, Sissons.
Outstanding Baggies come back against Bobby Moore, Geoff Hurst and Martin Peters.

Final: Wembley, 4 March 1967 97,952
Queens Park Rangers (0) 3 *(Morgan R, Marsh, Lazarus)*
West Bromwich Albion (2) 2 *(Clark 2)*
Queens Park Rangers: Springett; Hazell, Langley, Sibley, Hunt, Keen, Lazarus, Sanderson, Allen, Marsh, Morgan R.
West Bromwich Albion: Sheppard; Cramb, Williams, Collard, Clarke, Frazer, Brown, Astle, Kay, Hope, Clark.
Rodney Marsh solo for fight-back Rangers denied Fairs Cup entry as a Third Division team.

Wembley, 2 March 1968 97,887
Leeds United (1) 1 *(Cooper)*
Arsenal (0) 0
Leeds United: Sprake; Reaney, Cooper, Bremner, Charlton, Hunter, Greenhoff, Lorimer, Madeley, Giles, Gray E (Belfitt).
Arsenal: Furnell; Storey, McNab, McLintock, Simpson, Ure, Radford, Jenkins (Neill), Graham, Sammels, Armstrong.
First trophy for Don Revie at Leeds as United conceded only three goals in seven games.

Wembley, 15 March 1969 98,189
Swindon Town (1) 3 *(Smart, Rogers 2)*
Arsenal (0) 1 *(Gould)*
Swindon Town: Downsborough; Thomas, Trollope, Butler, Burrows, Harland, Heath, Smart, Smith, Noble (Penman), Rogers.
Arsenal: Wilson; Storey, McNab, McLintock, Ure, Simpson (Graham), Radford, Sammels, Court, Gould, Armstrong.
aet.
Third Division Swindon triumphed on pitch recently used for Horse of the Year Show.

Wembley, 7 March 1970 97,963
Manchester City (0) 2 *(Doyle, Pardew)*
West Bromwich Albion (1) 1 *(Astle)*
Manchester City: Corrigan; Book, Mann, Doyle, Booth, Oakes, Heslop, Bell, Summerbee (Bowyer), Lee, Pardew.
West Bromwich Albion: Osborne; Frazer, Wilson, Brown, Talbut, Kaye, Cantello, Suggett, Astle, Hartford (Krzywicki), Hope.
aet.
Jeff Astle was first to score in League and FA Cup finals plus another muddy surface.

Wembley, 27 February 1971 100,000
Tottenham Hotspur (0) 2 *(Chivers 2)*
Aston Villa (0) 0
Tottenham Hotspur: Jennings; Kinnear, Knowles, Mullery, Collins, Beal, Gilzean, Perryman, Chivers, Peters, Neighbour.
Aston Villa: Dunn; Bradley, Aitken, Godfrey, Turnbull, Tiler, McMahon, Rioch, Lochhead, Hamilton, Anderson.
Third Division Villa outplayed Spurs for long periods and should have taken the lead.

Wembley, 4 March 1972 100,000
Stoke City (1) 2 *(Conroy, Eastham)*
Chelsea (1) 1 *(Osgood)*
Stoke City: Banks; Marsh, Pejic, Bernard, Smith, Bloor, Conroy, Greenhough (Mahoney), Ritchie, Dobing, Eastham.
Chelsea: Bonetti; Mulligan (Baldwin), Harris R, Hollins, Dempsey, Webb, Cooke, Garland, Osgood, Hudson, Houseman.
First major trophy for Stoke City; veteran George Eastham, 35, scored the winner.

Wembley, 3 March 1973 100,000
Tottenham Hotspur (0) 1 *(Coates)*
Norwich City (0) 0
Tottenham Hotspur: Jennings; Kinnear, Knowles, Pratt (Coates), England, Beall, Gilzean, Perryman, Chivers, Peters, Pearce.
Norwich City: Keelan; Payne, Butler, Stringer, Forbes, Briggs, Livermore, Blair (Howard), Cross, Paddon, Anderson.
Two previous winners and Ralph Coates scored the 72nd minute winner for Tottenham.

Wembley, 2 March 1974 100,000
Wolverhampton Wanderers (1) 2 *(Hibbitt, Richards)*
Manchester City (0) 1 *(Bell)*
Wolverhampton Wanderers: Pierce; Palmer, Parkin, Bailey, Munro, McAlle, Sunderland, Hibbitt, Richards, Dougan, Wagstaffe (Powell).
Manchester City: MacRae; Pardoe, Donachie, Doyle, Booth, Towers, Summerbee, Bell, Lee, Law, Marsh.
Brilliant display by Gary Pierce in the Wolves goal as Wolves won first trophy since 1960.

Wembley, 1 March 1975 100,000
Aston Villa (0) 1 *(Graydon)*
Norwich City (0) 0
Aston Villa: Cumbes; Robson, Aitken, Ross, Nicholl, McDonald, Graydon, Little, Leonard, Hamilton, Carrodus.
Norwich City: Keelan; Machin, Sullivan, Morris, Forbes, Stringer, Miller, MacDougall, Boyer, Suggett, Powell.
Villa boss Ron Saunders led third different team in three finals – Norwich and Man City!

Wembley, 28 February 1976 100,000
Manchester City (1) 2 *(Barnes, Tueart)*
Newcastle United (1) 1 *(Gowling)*
Manchester City: Corrigan; Keegan, Donachie, Doyle, Watson, Oakes, Barnes, Booth, Royle, Hartford, Tueart.
Newcastle United: Mahoney; Nattrass, Kennedy, Barrowclough, Keeley, Howard, Burns, Cassidy, Macdonald, Gowling, Craig.
Overhead kick by Dennis Tueart won it and Joe Royle had a goal disallowed as well.

Wembley, 12 March 1977 100,000
Aston Villa (0) 0
Everton (0) 0
Aston Villa: Burridge; Gidman, Robson, Phillips, Nicholl, Mortimer, Deehan, Little, Gray, Cropley, Carrodus.
Everton: Lawson; Jones, Darracott, Lyons, McNaught, King, Hamilton, Dobson, Latchford, McKenzie, Goodlass.

Replay: Hillsborough, 16 March 1977 55,000
Aston Villa (0) 1 *(Kenyon (og))*
Everton (0) 1 *(Latchford)*
Aston Villa: Burridge; Gidman, Robson, Phillips, Nicholl, Mortimer, Deehan, Little, Gray, Cowans, Carradus.
Everton: Lawson; Bernard, Darracott, Lyons, McNaught, King, Hamilton (Pearson), Kenyon, Latchford, McKenzie, Goodlass.
aet.

Second Replay: Old Trafford, 13 April 1977 54,749
Aston Villa (0) 3 *(Little 2, Nicholl)*
Everton (1) 2 *(Latchford, Lyons)*
Aston Villa: Burridge; Gidman (Smith), Robson, Phillips, Nicholl, Mortimer, Graydon, Little, Deehan, Cropley, Cowans.
Everton: Lawson; Robinson, Darracott, Lyons, McNaught, King, Hamilton, Dobson, Latchford, Pearson (Seargeant), Goodlass.
aet.
Chris Nicholl 40-yard goal and two-goal Brian Little scoring the winner in the last seconds.

Wembley, 18 March 1978 100,000
Nottingham Forest (0) 0
Liverpool (0) 0
Nottingham Forest: Woods; Anderson, Clark, McGovern (O'Hare), Lloyd, Burns, O'Neill, Bowyer, Withe, Woodcock, Robertson.
Liverpool: Clemence; Neal, Kennedy (Fairclough), Smith, Thompson, Hughes, Dalglish, Case, Heighway, McDermott, Callaghan.
aet.

Replay: Old Trafford, 22 March 1978 54,375
Nottingham Forest (0) 1 *(Robertson (pen))*
Liverpool (0) 0
Nottingham Forest: Woods; Anderson, Clark, O'Hare, Lloyd, Burns, O'Neill, Bowyer, Withe, Woodcock, Robertson.
Liverpool: Clemence; Neal, Kennedy, Smith, Thompson, Hughes, Dalglish, Case (Fairclough), Heighway, McDermott, Callaghan.
Forest in another first: League and League Cup double but penalty awarded outside area.

Wembley, 17 March 1979 100,000
Nottingham Forest (0) 3 *(Birtles 2, Woodcock)*
Southampton (1) 2 *(Peach, Holmes)*
Nottingham Forest: Shilton; Barrett, Clark, McGovern, Lloyd, Needham, O'Neill, Gemmell, Birtles, Woodcock, Robertson.
Southampton: Gennoe; Golac, Peach, Williams, Nicholl, Waldron, Ball, Boyer, Hayes (Sealy), Holmes, Curran.
First Division title winners again but Forest had to come back to overturn the Saints.

Wembley, 15 March 1980 100,000
Wolverhampton Wanderers (0) 1 *(Gray)*
Nottingham Forest (0) 0
Wolverhampton Wanderers: Bradshaw; Palmer, Parkin, Daniel, Berry, Hughes, Carr, Hibbitt, Gray, Richards, Eaves.
Nottingham Forest: Shilton; Anderson, Gray, McGovern, Needham, Burns, O'Neill, Bowyer, Birtles, Francis, Robertson.
Defensive error cost Forest's cup run and Emlyn Hughes achieved every major honour.

Wembley, 14 March 1981 100,000
Liverpool (0) 1 *(Kennedy A)*
West Ham United (0) 1 *(Stewart (pen))*
Liverpool: Clemence; Neal, Kennedy A, Irwin, Kennedy R, Hansen, Dalglish, Lee, Heighway (Case), McDermott, Souness.
West Ham United: Parkes; Stewart, Lampard, Bonds, Martin, Devonshire, Neighbour, Goddard (Pearson), Cross, Brooking, Pike.
aet.

Replay: Villa Park, 1 April 1981 36,693
Liverpool (2) 2 *(Dalglish, Hansen)*
West Ham United (1) 1 *(Goddard)*
Liverpool: Clemence; Neal, Kennedy A, Thompson, Kennedy R, Hansen, Dalglish, Lee, Rush, McDermott, Case.
West Ham United: Parkes; Stewart, Lampard, Bonds, Martin, Devonshire, Neighbour, Goddard, Cross, Brooking, Pike (Pearson).
Rare goal indeed from Alan Hansen as Liverpool were forced to overhaul Hammers lead.

Wembley, 13 March 1982   100,000

Liverpool (0) 3 *(Whelan 2, Rush)*

Tottenham Hotspur (1) 1 *(Archibald)*

Liverpool: Grobbelaar; Neal, Kennedy A, Thompson, Whelan, Lawrenson, Dalglish, Lee, Rush, McDermott (Johnson), Souness.
Tottenham Hotspur: Clemence; Hughton, Miller, Price, Hazard (Villa), Perryman, Ardiles, Archibald, Galvin, Hoddle, Crooks.
aet.
Liverpool hit 25 goals in the run compared with Spurs scoring just eight in eight matches.

Wembley, 26 March 1983   100,000

Liverpool (0) 2 *(Kennedy A, Whelan)*

Manchester United (1) 1 *(Whiteside)*

Liverpool: Grobbelaar; Neal, Kennedy A, Lawrenson, Whelan, Hansen, Dalglish, Lee, Rush, Johnston (Fairclough), Souness.
Manchester United: Bailey; Duxbury, Albiston, Moses, Moran (Macari), McQueen, Wilkins, Muhren, Stapleton, Whiteside, Coppell.
aet.
Bob Paisley's last major honour with Liverpool and United led them for over an hour.

Wembley, 25 March 1984   100,000

Liverpool (0) 0

Everton (0) 0

Liverpool: Grobbelaar; Neal, Kennedy A, Lawrenson, Whelan, Hansen, Dalglish, Lee, Rush, Johnston (Robinson), Souness.
Everton: Southall; Stevens, Bailey, Ratcliffe, Mountfield, Reid, Irvine, Heath, Sharp, Richardson, Sheedy (Harper).
aet.

Replay: Maine Road, 28 March 1984   52,089

Liverpool (1) 1 *(Souness)*

Everton (0) 0

Liverpool: Grobbelaar; Neal, Kennedy A, Lawrenson, Whelan, Hansen, Dalglish, Lee, Rush, Johnston, Souness.
Everton: Southall; Stevens, Bailey, Ratcliffe, Mountfield, Reid, Irvine (King), Heath, Sharp, Richardson, Harper.
Four in a row for the Anfield team which had lost only one leg of a tie throughout the sequence.

Wembley, 24 March 1985   100,000

Norwich City (0) 1 *(Chisholm (og))*

Sunderland (0) 0

Norwich City: Woods; Haylock, Van Wyk, Bruce, Mendham, Watson, Barham, Channon, Deehan, Hartford, Donowa.
Sunderland: Turner; Venison, Pickering, Bennett, Chisholm, Corner (Gayle), Daniel, Wallace, Hodgson, Berry, Walker.
Deflected shot by Asa Hartford, Clive Walker missed a penalty and both teams relegated.

Wembley, 20 April 1986   90,396

Oxford United (1) 3 *(Hebberd, Houghton, Charles)*

Queens Park Rangers (0) 0

Oxford United: Judge; Langan, Trewick, Phillips, Briggs, Shotton, Houghton, Aldridge, Charles, Hebberd, Brock.
Queens Park Rangers: Barron; McDonald, Dawes, Neill, Wicks, Fenwick, Allen (Rosenior), James, Bannister, Byrne, Robinson.
One-sided final and the first big prize for Oxford United during a good run in the League.

Wembley, 5 April 1987   96,000

Arsenal (1) 2 *(Nicholas 2)*

Liverpool (1) 1 *(Rush)*

Arsenal: Lukic; Anderson, Sansom, Williams, O'Leary, Adams, Rocastle, Davis, Quinn (Groves), Nicholas, Hayes (Thomas).
Liverpool: Grobbelaar; Gillespie, Venison, Spackman, Whelan, Hansen, Walsh (Dalglish), Johnston, Rush, Molby, McMahon (Wark).
Firsts: Arsenal's such cup; Liverpool loss when talisman goal scorer Ian Rush had scored.

Wembley, 24 April 1988   95,732

Luton Town (1) 3 *(Stein B 2, Wilson)*

Arsenal (0) 2 *(Hayes, Smith)*

Luton Town: Dibble; Breacker, Johnson, Hill, Foster, Donaghy, Wilson, Black, Stein B, Harford (Stein M), Preece (Grimes).
Arsenal: Lukic; Winterburn, Sansom, Thomas, Caeser, Adams, Rocastle, Davis, Smith, Groves (Hayes), Richardson.
Andy Dibble saved penalty when Arsenal and Luton hit two goals in last seven minutes.

Wembley, 9 April 1989   76,130

Nottingham Forest (0) 3 *(Clough 2 (1 pen), Webb)*

Luton Town (1) 1 *(Harford)*

Nottingham Forest: Sutton; Laws, Pearce, Walker, Wilson, Hodge, Gaynor, Webb, Clough, Chapman, Parker.
Luton Town: Sealey; Breacker, Grimes (McDonough), Preece, Foster, Beaumont, Wilson, Wegerle, Harford, Hill, Black.
Giant-killers beaten and Forest had a goal disallowed and had also won the Simod Cup.

Wembley, 29 April 1990   74,343

Nottingham Forest (0) 1 *(Jemson)*

Oldham Athletic (0) 0

Nottingham Forest: Sutton; Laws, Pearce, Walker, Chettle, Hodge, Crosby, Parker, Clough, Jemson, Carr.
Oldham Athletic: Rhodes; Irwin, Barlow, Henry, Barrett, Warhurst, Adams, Ritchie, Bunn (Palmer), Milligan, Holden R.
Forest equalled the then Liverpool record of four wins against Second Division Oldham.

Wembley, 21 April 1991   80,000

Sheffield Wednesday (1) 1 *(Sheridan)*

Manchester United (0) 0

Sheffield Wednesday: Turner; Nilsson, King, Harkes (Madden), Shirtliff, Pearson, Wilson, Sheridan, Hirst, Williams, Worthington.
Manchester United: Sealey; Irwin, Blackmore, Bruce, Webb (Phelan), Pallister, Robson, Ince, McClair, Hughes, Sharpe.
Impressive Wednesday coupled this cup success with promotion to First Division.

Wembley, 12 April 1992   76,810

Manchester United (1) 1 *(McClair)*

Nottingham Forest (0) 0

Manchester United: Schmeichel; Parker, Irwin, Bruce, Phelan, Pallister, Kanchelskis (Sharpe), Ince, McClair, Hughes, Giggs.
Nottingham Forest: Marriott; Charles (Laws), Williams, Walker, Wassall, Keane, Crosby, Gemmill, Clough, Sheringham, Black.
United became the first losing team to win the next time; Brian Clough's last big trophy.

Wembley, 18 April 1993   74,007

Arsenal (1) 2 *(Merson, Morrow)*

Sheffield Wednesday (1) 1 *(Parkes)*

Arsenal: Seaman; O'Leary, Winterburn, Parlour, Adams, Linighan, Morrow, Merson, Wright, Campbell, Davis.
Sheffield Wednesday: Woods; Nilsson, King (Hyde), Palmer, Anderson, Parkes, Wilson (Hirst), Waddle, Warhurst, Bright, Sheridan.
First of three Wembley finals for these teams; squad numbering also made its appearance.

Wembley, 27 March 1994   77,231

Aston Villa (1) 3 *(Atkinson, Saunders 2 (1 pen))*

Manchester United (0) 1 *(Hughes)*

Aston Villa: Bosnich; Barrett, Staunton (Cox), Teale, McGrath, Richardson, Daley, Townsend, Saunders, Atkinson, Fenton.
Manchester United: Sealey; Parker, Irwin, Bruce (McClair), Kanchelskis, Pallister, Cantona, Ince, Keane, Hughes, Giggs (Sharpe).
Villa denied United of a treble after League and FA Cup; Andrei Kanchelskis was sent off.

Wembley, 2 April 1995   75,595

Liverpool (1) 2 *(McManaman 2)*

Bolton Wanderers (0) 1 *(Thompson)*

Liverpool: James; Jones, Bjornebye, Scales, Babb, Ruddock, McManaman, Redknapp, Rush, Barnes, Fowler.
Bolton Wanderers: Branagan; Green (Bergsson), Phillips, McAteer, Seagraves, Stubbs, Lee, Sneekes, Paatelainen, McGinlay, Thompson.
Steve McManaman was rightly awarded Man of the Match accolade for his two fine goals.

Wembley, 24 March 1996   77,056

Aston Villa (1) 3 *(Milosevic, Taylor, Yorke)*

Leeds United (0) 0

Aston Villa: Bosnich; Charles, Wright, Southgate, McGrath, Ehiogu, Taylor, Draper, Milosevic, Townsend, Yorke.
Leeds United: Lukic; Kelly, Radebe (Brolin), Parker, Wetherall, Pemberton, Gray, Ford (Deane), Yeboah, McAllister, Speed.
An emphatic victory for Villa levelled the Liverpool achievement of five such cup victories.

Wembley, 6 April 1997   76,757

Leicester City (0) 1 *(Heskey)*

Middlesbrough (0) 1 *(Ravanelli)*

Leicester City: Keller; Grayson, Whitlow (Robins), Kamark, Walsh, Prior, Lennon, Parker, Claridge, Izzet (Taylor), Heskey.
Middlesbrough: Schwarzer; Cox, Fleming, Mustoe, Pearson, Festa, Emerson, Hignett, Beck, Juninho, Ravanelli.
aet.

Replay: Hillsborough, 16 April 1997   39,428

Leicester City (0) 1 *(Claridge)*

Middlesbrough (0) 0

Leicester City: Keller; Grayson, Whitlow (Lawrence), Kamark, Walsh, Prior, Lennon, Parker, Claridge (Robins), Izzet, Heskey.
Middlesbrough: Roberts; Cox (Moore), Kinder, Festa (Vickers), Pearson, Blackmore, Emerson, Mustoe, Ravanelli, Juninho, Hignett (Beck).
aet.
The last final decided by a replay; Emile Heskey had equalised two minutes from time.

Wembley, 29 March 1998   77,698

Chelsea (0) 2 *(Sinclair, Di Matteo)*

Middlesbrough (0) 0

Chelsea: De Goey; Petrescu (Clarke), Le Saux, Sinclair, Leboeuf, Duberry, Newton, Di Matteo, Zola, Hughes M (Flo), Wise.
Middlesbrough: Schwarzer; Festa, Kinder, Vickers, Pearson, Mustoe, Ricard (Gascoigne), Townsend, Branca, Merson, Maddison (Beck).
aet.
Boro beaten again and Chelsea also went on to win the European Cup-Winners' Cup.

Wembley, 21 March 1999   77,892

Leicester C (0) 0

Tottenham H (0) 1 *(Nielsen 90)*

Leicester C: Keller; Ullathorne, Guppy, Elliott, Walsh, Taggart, Lennon, Izzet, Cottee, Savage (Zagorakis), Heskey (Marshall).
Tottenham H: Walker; Carr, Edinburgh, Freund, Vega, Campbell, Anderton, Nielsen, Iversen, Ferdinand, Ginola (Sinton).
Referee: T. Heilbron (Newton Aycliffe).
Last minute diving header by Allan Nielsen but Spurs had Justin Edinburgh sent off.

Wembley, 27 February 2000   74,313

Leicester C (1) 2 *(Elliott 29, 81)*

Tranmere R (0) 1 *(Kelly 77)*

Leicester C: Flowers; Savage, Guppy, Elliott, Taggart, Sinclair, Lennon, Izzet, Cottee (Marshall), Oakes (Impey), Heskey.
Tranmere R: Murphy; Hazell, Roberts, Henry, Hill, Challinor, Mahon, Parkinson (Yates), Jones G, Kelly, Taylor S.
Referee: A. Wilkie (Chester-le-Street).
(P. Richards (Preston) (substitute 57 minutes)).
Clint Hill had two yellow cards but Tranmere kept plugging away against Leicester City.

Millennium Stadium, 25 February 2001   73,500

Birmingham C (0) 1 *(Purse 90 (pen))*

Liverpool (1) 1 *(Fowler 30)*

Birmingham C: Bennett; Eaden, Grainger, Sonner (Hughes), Purse, Johnson M, McCarthy, O'Connor, Horsfield (Marcelo), Adebola (Johnson A), Lazaridis.
Liverpool: Westerveld; Babbel, Carragher, Hamann, Henchoz, Hyypia, Gerrard (McAllister), Smicer (Barmby), Heskey, Fowler, Biscan (Ziege).
aet; Liverpool won 5-4 on penalties.
Referee: D. Elleray (Harrow).
Birmingham also had penalty appeal turned down in extra time in first shoot-out final.
Penalties: McAllister scored; Grainger missed; Barmby scored; Purse scored; Ziege scored; Marcelo scored; Hamann missed; Lazaridis scored; Fowler scored, Hughes scored; Carragher scored; sub Johnson missed.

Millennium Stadium, 24 February 2002   72,500

Blackburn R (1) 2 *(Jansen 25, Cole 69)*

Tottenham H (1) 1 *(Ziege 33)*

Blackburn R: Friedel; Taylor, Bjornebye, Dunn, Berg, Johansson, Gillespie (Hignett), Jansen (Yordi), Cole, Hughes, Duff.
Tottenham H: Sullivan; Taricco (Davies), Ziege, Thatcher, Perry, King, Anderton, Sherwood, Ferdinand, Sheringham, Poyet (Iversen).
Referee: G. Poll.
Teddy Sheringham was denied a penalty in the last minute; Blackburn's first such cup win.

Millennium Stadium, 2 March 2003 74,500
Liverpool (1) 2 *(Gerrard 38, Owen 86)*
Manchester U (0) 0
Liverpool: Dudek; Carragher, Riise, Hamann, Henchoz, Hyypia, Gerrard, Diouf (Biscan), Heskey (Baros) (Smicer), Owen, Murphy.
Manchester U: Barthez; Neville G, Silvestre, Brown (Solskjaer), Keane, Ferdinand, Beckham, Veron, Van Nistelrooy, Scholes, Giggs.
Referee: P. Durkin (Portland).
Steven Gerrard's goal was a deflection off David Beckham; Michael Owen soloed the second.

Millennium Stadium, 29 February 2004 72,634
Middlesbrough (2) 2 *(Job 2, Zenden 7 (pen))*
Bolton W (1) 1 *(Davies 21)*
Middlesbrough: Schwarzer; Mills, Queudrue, Southgate, Ehiogu, Doriva, Mendieta, Boateng, Job (Ricketts), Juninho, Zenden.
Bolton W: Jaaskelainen; Hunt (Giannakopoulos), Charlton, Campo, N'Gotty, Emerson, Nolan (Javi Moreno), Frandsen (Pedersen), Davies, Djorkaeff, Okocha.
Referee: M. Riley (W. Yorkshire).
Fastest final goal and Boudewijn Zenden slipped taking the penalty as Boro finally won.

Millennium Stadium, 27 February 2005 78,000
Liverpool (1) 2 *(Riise 1, Nunez 113)*
Chelsea (0) 3 *(Gerrard 79 (og), Drogba 107, Kezman 112)*
Liverpool: Dudek; Finnan, Traore (Biscan), Hamann, Carragher, Hyypia, Kewell (Nunez), Gerrard, Luis Garcia, Morientes (Baros), Riise.
Chelsea: Cech; Paulo Ferreira, Gallas (Kezman), Makelele, Terry, Ricardo Carvalho, Jarosik (Gudjohnsen), Lampard, Drogba, Cole (Johnson), Duff.
aet.
Referee: S. Bennett (Orpington).
Even faster goal and the own goal came from a Paulo Ferreira free kick for Chelsea leveller.

Millennium Stadium, 26 February 2006 66,866
Manchester U (1) 4 *(Rooney 33, 61, Saha 55, Ronaldo 59)*
Wigan Ath (0) 0
Manchester U: Van der Sar; Neville, Silvestre (Evra), Park, Brown (Vidic), Ferdinand, Ronaldo (Richardson), O'Shea, Saha, Rooney, Giggs.
Wigan Ath: Pollitt (Filan); Chimbonda, Baines, Kavanagh (Ziegler), Henchoz (McCulloch), De Zeeuw, Teale, Bullard, Camara, Roberts, Scharner.
Referee: A. Wiley (Staffordshire).
Easy success for United whose ex-goalkeeper Mike Pollitt was injured after 14 minutes play.

Millennium Stadium, 25 February 2007 70,073
Chelsea (1) 2 *(Drogba 20, 84)*
Arsenal (1) 1 *(Walcott 12)*
Chelsea: Cech; Diarra, Bridge, Makelele (Robben), Terry (Mikel■), Ricardo Carvalho, Essien, Lampard, Drogba, Shevchenko (Kalou), Ballack.
Arsenal: Almunia; Hoyte, Traore (Eboue), Denilson, Toure■, Senderos, Walcott, Fabregas, Aliadiere (Adebayor■), Julio Baptista, Diaby (Hleb).
Referee: H. Webb (South Yorkshire).
First all-London final and first to have three players sent off in the dying minutes of the game.

Wembley, 24 February 2008 87,660
Tottenham H (0) 2 *(Berbatov 70 (pen), Woodgate 94)*
Chelsea (1) 1 *(Drogba 39)*
Tottenham H: Robinson; Hutton, Chimbonda (Huddlestone), Zokora, Woodgate, King, Chimbonda, Berbatov, Keane (Kaboul), Malbranque (Tainio).
Chelsea: Cech; Belletti, Bridge, Mikel (Cole J), Terry, Ricardo Carvalho, Essien (Ballack), Lampard, Drogba, Anelka, Wright-Phillips (Kalou).
aet.
Referee: M. Halsey (Lancashire).
Didier Drogba was the first to score in three League Cup finals; Wayne Bridge hands for penalty.

Wembley, 1 March 2009 88,217
Manchester U (0) 0
Tottenham H (0) 0
Manchester U: Foster; O'Shea (Vidic), Evra, Gibson (Giggs), Ferdinand, Evans, Ronaldo, Scholes, Welbeck (Anderson), Tevez, Nani.
Tottenham H: Gomes; Corluka, Assou-Ekotto, Zokora, Dawson, King, Lennon (Bentley), Jenas (Bale), Pavlyuchenko (O'Hara), Bent, Modric.
aet; Manchester U won 4-1 on penalties: Giggs scored; O'Hara saved; Tevez scored; Corluka scored; Ronaldo scored; Bentley missed; Anderson scored.
Referee: C. Foy (Merseyside).
Penalties – though Carlos Tevez and Roman Pavlyuchenko had each scored six goals en route.

Wembley, 28 February 2010 88,596
Aston Villa (1) 1 *(Milner 5 (pen))*
Manchester U (1) 2 *(Owen 12, Rooney 74)*
Aston Villa: Friedel; Cuellar (Carew), Warnock, Collins JM, Dunne, Downing, Milner, Petrov, Agbonlahor, Heskey, Young A.
Manchester U: Kuszczak; Rafael (Neville), Evra, Carrick, Evans J, Vidic, Valencia, Fletcher, Berbatov, Owen (Rooney), Park (Gibson).
Referee: P. Dowd (Staffordshire).
Evenly contested final, fourth win for United and their third in five years after Villa lead early.

Wembley, Sunday, 27 February 2011 88,851
Birmingham C (1) 2 *(Zigic 28, Martins 89)*
Arsenal (1) 1 *(Van Persie 39)*
Arsenal: Szczesny; Sagna, Clichy, Song Billong, Djourou, Koscielny, Rosicky, Wilshere, Van Persie (Bendtner), Arshavin (Chamakh), Nasri.
Birmingham C: Foster; Carr, Ridgewell, Bowyer, Jiranek, Johnson, Larsson, Ferguson, Zigic (Jerome), Gardner (Beausejour), Fahey (Martins).
Referee: M. Dean (Wirral).
Birmingham upset form, win place in Europa League but find themselves relegated later on.

CARLING CUP 2010–11

■ *Denotes player sent off.*

FIRST ROUND

Monday, 9 August 2010
Stevenage (1) 1 *(Murphy 19)*
Portsmouth (2) 2 *(Ciftci 8, Brown 36)*   4236
Stevenage: Day; Henry, Laird, Murphy (Long), Roberts, Bostwick, Sinclair (Winn), Byrom, Griffin, Beardsley, Odubade (Boylan).
Portsmouth: Ashdown; Ward, Wilson, Mullins (Gregory), Sonko, Ritchie, Hughes, Ciftci, Utaka, Nugent, Brown.

Tuesday, 10 August 2010
Aldershot T (0) 0
Watford (2) 3 *(Graham 14, 48, Sordell 45)*   3292
Aldershot T: Young; Herd, Vincent, Panther (McGlashan), Fortune, Charles, Guttridge (Small), Harding, Morgan (Spencer), Hylton, Straker.
Watford: Gilmartin; Hodson, Doyley, Eustace (Jenkins), Taylor M, Mariappa, Cowie, McGinn, Sordell, Graham (Deeney), Buckley (Bryan).

Barnsley (0) 0
Rochdale (0) 1 *(Elding 56)*   4107
Barnsley: Steele; Trippier, McEveley, Shackell, Foster (Hassell), Doyle, Butterfield (Devaney), Colace, Lovre (Hume), Dickinson, Hammill.
Rochdale: Lillis; Wiseman, Widdowson, Jones, Holness, Dawson, Kennedy J, Barry-Murphy, O'Grady, Akpa Akpro (Elding), Joe Thompson (Done).

Bradford C (0) 2 *(Syers 57, Hanson 100)*
Nottingham F (1) 1 *(Thornhill 35)*   5175
Bradford C: McLaughlin; Rehman, O'Brien L, Bullock (Ramsden), Williams, Duff, Daley (Hanson), Doherty, Moult, Speight, Neilson (Syers).
Nottingham F: Camp; Lynch (McKenna), Cohen, Chambers, Morgan, Moussi, Anderson (Adebola), McGugan (Blackstock), Tyson, Thornhill, McCleary.
aet.

Brentford (2) 2 *(Simpson 31, Woodman 35)*
Cheltenham T (0) 1 *(Jeffers 61)*   2049
Brentford: Moore; Osborne, Woodman, Bean, Legge, Balkestein, Simpson, O'Connor, Alexander, Forster (MacDonald), Wood.
Cheltenham T: Brown; Lowe, Andrew, Pook, Elliott, Riley, Low (Melligan), Artus, Jeffers, Goulding (Shroot), Smikle.

Carlisle U (0) 0
Huddersfield T (0) 1 *(Rhodes 89)*   3475
Carlisle U: Collin; Simek, McDaid, Thirlwell (Bridge-Wilkinson), Chester, Harte, Taiwo, Berrett, Zoko (Robson), Curran, Madine.
Huddersfield T: Smithies; Peltier, Naysmith, Gudjonsson, Clarke P, McCombe, Pilkington, Arfield (Johnson), Rhodes, Garner (Novak), Roberts (Carey).

Chesterfield (0) 1 *(Mattis 68)*
Middlesbrough (2) 2 *(McDonald 8, Arca 33)*   6509
Chesterfield: Lee; Hunt, Griffiths, Mattis, Breckin, Ford, Talbot, Allott, Page (Niven), Lester, Whitaker.
Middlesbrough: Steele; Hoyte, Bennett, Bailey, Wheater, Grounds (Hines), Williams L (Miller), Walker, Lita, McDonald, Arca.

Crewe Alex (1) 1 *(Barker 45 (og))*
Derby Co (0) 0   3778
Crewe Alex: Taylor; Tootle, Blanchett, Murphy, Artell, Ada, Ashley R Westwood, Bell, Zola, Miller (Moore), Donaldson.
Derby Co: Bywater; Brayford, Moxey, Bailey, Barker (Roberts), Leacock, Pringle (Doyle), Savage, Porter (Hulse), Commons, Cywka.

Doncaster R (0) 1 *(Payne 47)*
Accrington S (0) 2 *(Turner 83, Lindfield 93)*   4603
Doncaster R: Sullivan; Dumbuya, Friend, O'Connor, Lockwood, Hird, Clarke, Payne (Martis), Fairhurst, Brooker (Hayter) (Grayson), Shiels.
Accrington S: Cisak; Bateson (Turner), Winnard, Hessey, Edwards, Procter, Ryan, Joyce (Parkinson), McConville, Lindfield, Putterill (Murphy).
aet.

Exeter C (0) 2 *(Harley 54, 81)*
Ipswich T (0) 3 *(Murray 63, Norris 73, 99)*   4520
Exeter C: Jones P; Jones B, Tully, Noble (Dunne), Duffy (Stewart), Taylor, Sercombe, Harley, O'Flynn (Logan), Nardiello, Golbourne.
Ipswich T: Murphy; Ainsley (Peters), O'Connor, Brown (Smith), Eastman, Leadbitter, Hyam, Lambe (Murray), Stead, Healy, Norris.
aet.

Hereford U (0) 0
Colchester U (2) 3 *(Mooney 40, 44, Henderson I 65)* 1996
Hereford U: Bartlett; Green, Valentine, Kovacs, Townsend, Lunt, Thompson (Stratford), McQuilkin, Manset (Canham), Fleetwood, Colbeck (Malsom).
Colchester U: Cousins; Wilson, Tierney, Perkins, Reid, Okuonghae, Bond (James), Izzet, Mooney (Odejayi), Wordsworth (Vincent), Henderson I.

Leeds U (3) 4 *(Howson 2, Becchio 7, Sam 30, Kilkenny 71 (pen))*
Lincoln C (0) 0   12,602
Leeds U: Schmeichel; Connolly, Bessone, Howson (Hughes), Collins, Bruce, Johnson (Grella), Kilkenny, Sam, Becchio (White), Watt.
Lincoln C: Anyon, Green, Anderson (Clapham), Watts, Swaibu, Kerr (Hutchinson A), Carayol, O'Keefe, Hughton, McCallum (Facey), Jarrett.

Leicester C (1) 4 *(Neilson 35, Fryatt 47, 51, Wellens 70)*
Macclesfield T (1) 3 *(Brown 15, Mukendi 64, Daniel 83)*   6142
Leicester C: Logan; Neilson, Kennedy, Wellens, Moreno (Verma), Hobbs, N'Guessan, Oakley (Morrison), Howard, Fryatt, Gallagher (Campbell).
Macclesfield T: Veiga; Brisley, Tremarco, Bencherif, Brown, Bolland (Chalmers), Hamshaw (Wedgbury), Butcher, Sinclair (Mukendi), Barnett, Daniel.

Milton Keynes D (0) 2 *(Ibehre 56, 79)*
Dagenham & R (1) 1 *(McCrory 13)*   3502
Milton Keynes D: Martin D; Howell (Baldock S), Lewington, Leven, Pele (Chicksen), Woodards, Guy (Chadwick), Carrington, Easter, Ibehre, Balanta.
Dagenham & R: Roberts; Ogogo, McCrory, Arber, Doe, Vincelot, Lewis, Nurse, Benson (Scannell), Scott (Walsh), Currie (Gain).

Morecambe (1) 2 *(Fleming 45, 61)*
Coventry C (0) 0   4002
Morecambe: Roche; Moss, Wilson, Scott, McCready, Parrish, Fleming (Hunter), Stanley, Shuker, Jevons (Mullin), Rundle (Duffy).
Coventry C: Doyle C; Clarke, Grandison, Hussey (Christie), Wood, McPake, Bell (Clarke-Harris), Baker, Platt, O'Donovan, McIndoe.

Northampton T (2) 2 *(Jacobs 13, McKay 18)*
Brighton & HA (0) 0   2431
Northampton T: Jansson; Johnson, Hall, Wedderburn, Jacobs, Beckwith, Gilligan (Thornton), Osman, Guinan (Purcell), McKay (Herbert), Holt.
Brighton & HA: Poke; Whing, Painter, Dicker, Elphick, El-Abd, Hart, Sparrow■, Holroyd (Bennett), Baz (Navarro) (Smith), Battipiedi.

Norwich C (2) 4 *(Martin C 26, 90, Holt 32, 55)*
Gillingham (1) 1 *(Palmer 12)*   13,068
Norwich C: Ruddy; Martin R, Drury, Smith K, Nelson, Ward, Hoolahan (McNamee), Fox (Gill), Martin C, Holt (Johnson), Lappin.
Gillingham: Julian; Sinclair, Nutter, Payne J (Maher), Bentley, Gowling, Rooney (Payne S), Palmer, Barcham, Akinfenwa (White), Spiller.

Oxford U (4) 6 *(Heslop 18, 90, Green 23, Constable 27, 52, Midson 29)*
Bristol R (1) 1 *(Lines 24)*   5008
Oxford U: Clarke; Batt, Tonkin, Bulman, Worley, Wright, Hall (Clist), Heslop, Constable (Deering), Midson, Green (Potter).
Bristol R: Green; Regan, Sawyer, Campbell, Anthony, Tunniclife, Blizzard (Reece), Lines, Hoskins, Osei-Kuffour, Hughes (Swallow).

Peterborough U (2) 4 *(Bennett 34, Boyd 39, McLean 60, Mackail-Smith 85)*
Rotherham U (1) 1 *(Marshall 9)*   4145
Peterborough U: Lewis; Little, Ofori-Twumasi (Rowe), Lee, Bennett, Langmead, Wesolowski, Mendez-Laing (Hibbert), Mackail-Smith, McLean (Tomlin), Boyd.
Rotherham U: Warrington; Brogan, Newey, Harrison, Cresswell, Ashworth, Law, Taylor J (Warne), Marshall, Le Fondre, Ellison.

Plymouth Arg (0) 0
Notts Co (0) 1 *(Spicer 52)*   5454
Plymouth Arg: Larrieu; Duguid, Molyneux (Paterson), Clark, Johnson R, Arnason, Noone, Peterlin (Nelson), Fallon (MacLean), Wright-Phillips, Bhasera.
Notts Co: Nelson; Pearce, Harley, Ravenhill, Chilvers, Edwards, Westcarr, Bishop, Davies (Hunt), Burgess (Jervis), Spicer (Smith).

QPR (0) 1 *(German 62)*
Port Vale (2) 3 *(Richards J 30, 48, Rigg 36)*   6619
QPR: Kenny; Orr, Borrowdale, Derry (Oastler), Hall, Connolly, Ephraim, Mackie, Clarke (German), Parker (Rose), Leigertwood.
Port Vale: Tomlinson; Yates, Collins, Griffith, McCombe, Owen, Rigg (Taylor K), Roberts (Fraser), Richards M, Richards J (Dodds), Loft.

Scunthorpe U (0) 2 *(Forte 65, Woolford 83)*
Oldham Ath (1) 1 *(Bembo-Leta 23)*   2602
Scunthorpe U: Slocombe; Byrne, McNulty, Wright J (Togwell*), Raynes, Jones, Thompson, O'Connor (Collins), Dagnall (Grant), Forte, Woolford.
Oldham Ath: Brill; Black, Lee, Furman, Mvoto, Jarrett, Jones, Stephens, Bembo-Leta, Kelly (Taylor), Alessandra (Crompton).

Sheffield W (0) 1 *(Coke 60)*
Bury (0) 0   7390
Sheffield W: Weaver; Jones D (Coke), Spurr, Potter, Beevers, Purse, Otsemobor, Palmer (O'Connor), Heffernan (Morrison C), Mellor, Teale.
Bury: Belford; Picken, Lees, Jones M, Sodje, Sweeney (Worrall), Haworth, Schumacher, Lowe (Carlton), Bishop (John-Lewis), Skarz.

Shrewsbury T (2) 4 *(Robinson 36, Mambo 42 (og), O'Donnell 61, Harrold 76)*
Charlton Ath (3) 3 *(Abbott 25, 28, Martin 32)*   3700
Shrewsbury T: Smith; Raven, Sadler, O'Donnell, Sharps, McAllister, Wright, Disley, Harrold, Robinson (Van den Broek), Ainsworth.
Charlton Ath: Worner; Francis, Mambo (Doherty), Racon, Llera, Solly, Wagstaff, Stavrinou (Sodje), Abbott, Martin, Smart (Reid).

Southampton (0) 2 *(Lallana 63, Oxlade-Chamberlain 86)*
Bournemouth (0) 0   17,135
Southampton: Davis; Butterfield, Dickson (Harding), Wotton, Seaborne, Fonte, Puncheon, Hammond, Barnard (Lambert), Lallana (Holmes), Oxlade-Chamberlain.

Bournemouth: Jalal; Purches, Wiggins, Garry (Bradbury), Pearce, Bartley (Symes), Pugh, Robinson, Pitman, Cooper (Hollands), Feeney.

Southend U (1) 3 *(Paterson 31 (pen), 104, Corr 88)*
Bristol C (1) 2 *(McAllister 2, Sproule 82)*   2940
Southend U: Morris; Simpson, Barker, Easton, Coughlan, Prosser, Grant, Zaaboub (Corr), Sturrock (Hall), Paterson, Soares (Spencer).
Bristol C: Gerken; Hunt, McAllister, Fontaine, Skuse (Elliott), Johnson, Williams G, Sproule, Clarkson, Adomah (Jackson), Campbell-Ryce (Akinde).
aet.

Stockport Co (0) 0
Preston NE (1) 5 *(Davidson 45 (pen), James 58, Hayes 67 (pen), 73, King 89)*   3724
Stockport Co: fon Williams; Halls, Lynch, Turnbull, Swailes, Assoumani, Poole, Tansey, Conlon (Partridge), Donnelly (Fisher), Rowe (Pilkington).
Preston NE: Lonergan; Gray, Davidson, Wright, Jones, James, Mayor, Coutts (Barton), Brown C (King), Hayes (Middleton), Parry.

Swansea C (1) 3 *(Van der Gun 24, Pratley 72, Kuqi 88)*
Barnet (0) 0   6644
Swansea C: De Vries; Serran, Tate, Allen (Gower), Monk, Donnelly (Pratley), Orlandi, Morgan (Dyer), Walsh, Kuqi, Van der Gun.
Barnet: Cole; Cox (Parkes), Leach, Southam, Dennehy, Uddin, Marshall (Hart), Byrne, Holmes, Poole, Hughes (Kelly).

Swindon T (1) 1 *(McGovern 35)*
Leyton Orient (0) 2 *(Jarvis 67, Revell 72)*   4450
Swindon T: Smith P; Caddis, Rose (Ferry), Douglas, Cuthbert, Lescinel, McGovern, Ball (Dossevi), O'Brien (Amankwaah), Austin, Prutton.
Leyton Orient: Jones; Omozusi, Cestor, Smith, Chorley, Forbes, Dawson, Spring, Jarvis (Tehoue), Revell (McGleish), Cox (Chambers).

Walsall (0) 0
Tranmere R (1) 1 *(Goodison 40)*   2253
Walsall: Brain; Westlake (McDonald), Lescott, Taundry (Marshall), Lancashire, Smith, Jones, Richards, Byfield, Nicholls (Grigg), Gray.
Tranmere R: Collister; Darville, Cresswell, Wood, Goodison, McLaren, Welsh, Labadie, Thomas-Moore, Showunmi, Gornell.

Wycombe W (0) 1 *(Strevens 76)*
Millwall (1) 2 *(Harris 26, Dunne 105)*   3028
Wycombe W: Bull; Foster (Sandell), McCoy, Montrose, Bennett, Johnson, Phillips, Murtagh (Bloomfield), Rendell (Strevens), Pittman, Betsy.
Millwall: Forde; Smith, Barron, Laird (Dunne), Robinson P, Ward, Henry (Hackett), Mkandawire, Harris, Lisbie (Marquis), Schofield.
aet.

Yeovil T (0) 0
Crystal Palace (0) 1 *(Lee 90)*   3720
Yeovil T: Sullivan; Alcock, Jones, Ayling, Huntington, Virgo, Williams A, Kalala, Williams S, Bowditch, Freeman (Smith).
Crystal Palace: Speroni; Clyne, Bennett, Cadogan, McCarthy, Barrett, Ambrose, Pinney (Zaha), Lee, Andrew (Djilali), Dorman.

Wednesday, 11 August 2010
Cardiff C (1) 4 *(Bothroyd 17, McCormack 107, 110, Chopra 118)*
Burton Alb (1) 1 *(Harrad 19)*   6080
Cardiff C: Heaton; Matthews (Quinn), John, Rae (Koumas), Gerrard, Gyepes, Whittingham, Drinkwater, Bothroyd (McCormack), Chopra, Burke.
Burton Alb: Legzdins; Boertien, Webster (Phillips), Stanton, James, McGrath, Young (Preen), Penn, Harrad (Ellison), Pearson, Bolder.
aet.

Hartlepool U (1) 2 *(Brown 6, Boyd 61 (pen))*
Sheffield U (0) 0 2520
Hartlepool U: Flinders; Haslam, Horwood, Gamble, Collins, Liddle, Sweeney, Murray (Fredriksen), Brown (McSweeney), Boyd (Behan), Monkhouse.
Sheffield U: Simonsen; Kozluk, Taylor, Montgomery, Morgan, Ertl, Yeates (Quinn), Britton, Chapell, Cresswell (Bartley), James (Ward).

Torquay U (0) 0
Reading (0) 1 *(Rasiak 120)* 2832
Torquay U: Bevan; Robertson, Nicholson, Ellis, Branston, Mansell, Stevens (Lathrope), Wroe, Benyon, Kee (O'Kane), Zebroski.
Reading: Hamer; Griffin, Williams, Gunnarsson, Pearce, Howard, Kebe, Antonio (Obita), Bignall (Karacan), Rasiak, Tabb.
aet.

SECOND ROUND

Tuesday, 24 August 2010

Blackburn R (1) 3 *(Biram Diouf 29, 80, 84)*
Norwich C (0) 1 *(Berthel Askou 90)* 9235
Blackburn R: Bunn; Jacobsen, Chimbonda, Linganzi, Givet (Olsson), Samba (Nzonzi), Emerton, Grella (Jones P), Hoilett, Biram Diouf, Pedersen.
Norwich C: Rudd; Martin R (Hughes), Francomb, Gill, Berthel Askou, Ward, Hoolahan (McNamee), Fox, Jackson, Holt (Johnson), Lappin.

Bradford C (0) 1 *(Speight 83)*
Preston NE (1) 2 *(Coutts 45, Treacy 109)* 4221
Bradford C: McLaughlin; Rehman, O'Brien L, Syers, Williams, Oliver, Doherty (Hanson), Adeyemi, Evans (Chilaka), Moult, Daley (Speight).
Preston NE: Lonergan; Morgan, Davidson, Gray, St Ledger-Hall (Wright), James, Mayor (Russell), Coutts, King, Hayes (Brown C), Treacy.
aet.

Brentford (1) 2 *(Simpson 20, Bean 88)*
Hull C (1) 1 *(Cullen 6)* 3335
Brentford: Lee; O'Connor, Woodman, Bean, Osborne, Legge, Simpson, Diagouraga, Alexander, MacDonald, Weston.
Hull C: Duke; Solano, Kilbane, Devitt, McShane (Gardner), Cooper, Koren, Cairney, Simpson (Barmby), Cullen, Garcia.

Crewe Alex (0) 0
Ipswich T (0) 1 *(Norris 101)* 3309
Crewe Alex: Taylor; Tootle (Connerton), Blanchett, Ashley R Westwood, Artell, Ada, Bell, Murphy, Miller (Moore), Donaldson, Grant (Shelley).
Ipswich T: Murphy; O'Connor, Smith, Brown, McAuley, O'Dea (Peters), Edwards (Murray), Hyam (Scotland), Priskin, Norris, Leadbitter.
aet.

Hartlepool U (0) 0
Wigan Ath (1) 3 *(Collins 3 (og), Gomez 76, Moses 86)* 3196
Hartlepool U: Flinders; Haslam, Horwood, Sweeney, Collins, Liddle, Murray (McSweeney), Gamble, Boyd (Behan), Brown (Larkin), Monkhouse.
Wigan Ath: Al Habsi; Boyce, Figueroa, McArthur (McCarthy), Caldwell S, Alcaraz, Gomez, Thomas, Boselli (N'Zogbia), Rodallega (Moses), Watson.

Leeds U (1) 1 *(Somma 32)*
Leicester C (0) 2 *(Wellens 66, Howard 89 (pen))* 16,509
Leeds U: Higgs; Connolly, Bessone, Howson (Watt), Collins, Bruce, Gradel, Kilkenny, Somma, Becchio (Hughes), Johnson.
Leicester C: Logan; Lamey (Neilson), Berner, Moreno (King A), Morrison, Hobbs, Moussa (Kennedy), Wellens, Gallagher, Howard, N'Guessan.

Leyton Orient (0) 0
WBA (1) 2 *(Pablo 29, Wood 90)* 2349
Leyton Orient: Jones; Omozusi (Cox), Cestor (Spring), Chambers, Chorley, Forbes, Dawson, Smith, McGleish, Tehoue (Revell), Daniels.
WBA: Myhill; Zuiverloon, Shorey, Mantom, Pablo, Barnett, Barnes (Cech) (Jara), Reid, Bednar (Wood), Cox, Moore.

Millwall (2) 2 *(Morison 29 (pen), Trotter 39)*
Middlesbrough (0) 1 *(McDonald 89)* 6704
Millwall: Forde; Dunne, Barron, Trotter, Robinson P, Ward, Henry, Abdou, Morison, Harris (Lisbie), Schofield (Carter).
Middlesbrough: Steele; Hoyte, Kilgallon (Halliday), Bailey, Wheater, McManus, Robson, Arca, Lita (Boyd), McDonald, Kink.

Milton Keynes D (1) 4 *(Baldock S 1, Easter 55, 57, Guy 110)*
Blackpool (0) 3 *(Ormerod 52, Sylvestre 58, Adam 82 (pen))* 7458
Milton Keynes D: Martin D; Woodards, Lewington, Doumbe, O'Hanlon, Leven, Chadwick, Hamann (Guy), Easter, Baldock S (Ibehre), Balanta (Carrington).
Blackpool: Halstead; Eardley, Coid, Husband (Adam), Keinan, Edwards, Basham, Demontagnac, Barkhuizen (Taylor-Fletcher), Ormerod, Sylvestre (Grandin).
aet.

Morecambe (1) 1 *(Jevons 12)*
Burnley (1) 3 *(Eagles 30, Thompson 61 (pen), McDonald 83)* 5003
Morecambe: Roche; Moss (Mullin), Parrish, Scott, McCready, Wilson, Fleming (Hunter), Stanley (Drummond), Shuker, Duffy, Jevons.
Burnley: Grant; Eckersley (McDonald), Easton, Cork, Cort, Carlisle, Eagles (King), Edgar, Thompson, Rodriguez (Fletcher), Elliott.

Peterborough U (0) 2 *(Mackail-Smith 74, Boyd 88)*
Cardiff C (1) 1 *(Bothroyd 31)* 3806
Peterborough U: Lewis; Rowe, Ofori-Twumasi, McCann, Bennett, Langmead, Wesolowski, Davies (Lee), Mackail-Smith, McLean, Boyd.
Cardiff C: Heaton; Matthews, Naylor (Quinn), Olofinjana (McPhail) (Wildig), Hudson, Gerrard, Whittingham, Drinkwater, Bothroyd, Koumas, Burke.

Portsmouth (0) 1 *(Nugent 57)*
Crystal Palace (0) 1 *(Sonko 81 (og))* 8412
Portsmouth: Ashdown; Mullins (Pack), Dickinson, Mokoena, Sonko, Brown, Hughes, Ritchie (Ward), Smith, Nugent (Ciftci), Wilson.
Crystal Palace: Speroni; Clyne, Marrow, Garvan, McCarthy, Barrett, Djilali, Davids (Parsons), Counago (Cadogan), Zaha[*], Dorman (Obika).
aet; Portsmouth won 4-3 on penalties.

Reading (1) 3 *(Mills 16, 113, Robson-Kanu 62)*
Northampton T (1) 3 *(Holt 20, Thornton 64, Mills 120 (og))* 6986
Reading: Hamer; Kelly (Taylor), Williams, Karacan, Mills, Pearce, Antonio (Kebe), Howard, Church, Hunt (Long), Robson-Kanu.
Northampton T: Jansson; Rodgers, Holt, Thornton, Hall, Beckwith, Herbert (Jacobs), Osman, Purcell (Konstantinou), McKay (Guinan), Wedderburn.
aet; Northampton T won 4-2 on penalties.

Scunthorpe U (1) 4 *(Collins 45, Dagnall 49, 82, O'Connor 68 (pen))*
Sheffield W (2) 2 *(Tudgay 74 (pen), Mellor 83)* 4680
Scunthorpe U: Murphy; Byrne, Nolan, Togwell, Raynes, Canavan, Wright J, O'Connor (Wright A), Dagnall (Boyes), Forte (Grant), Collins.
Sheffield W: Weaver; Otsemobor, Jones D, Potter, Hinds[*], Beevers, Sedgwick (Tudgay), O'Connor, Morrison C, Heffernan (Mellor), Teale (Miller).

Southampton (0) 0
Bolton W (1) 1 *(Klasnic 31)* 10,251
Southampton: Davis; Butterfield (Mills), Harding, Schneiderlin (Oxlade-Chamberlain), Martin, Fonte, Puncheon, Hammond, Barnard, Lambert (Connolly), Lallana.
Bolton W: Bogdan; Ricketts, Alonzo, Davies M, O'Brien A, Knight, Taylor, Blake, Klasnic (Elmander), Davies K, Gardner (Holden).

Stoke C (2) 2 *(Walters 26, Tuncay 37)*
Shrewsbury T (0) 1 *(Leslie 79)* 11,995
Stoke C: Nash; Wilkinson, Higginbotham, Whelan, Huth, Shawcross, Tonge (Delap), Pugh, Walters, Tuncay (Fuller), Etherington (Whitehead).
Shrewsbury T: Neal C; Raven, Sadler, McAllister, Sharps, Cansdell-Sherriff, Wright, Disley, Leslie, Van den Broek (Bradshaw), McIntyre (Neal L).

Sunderland (2) 2 *(Bent 19, 37)*
Colchester U (0) 0 13,532
Sunderland: Mignolet; Bardsley, Ferdinand, Turner, Bramble, Cattermole, Zenden (Waghorn), Welbeck (Reid), Campbell, Bent (Colback), Richardson.
Colchester U: Cousins; Wilson, White, Perkins (Vincent), Baldwin, Okuonghae, James, Izzet (Beevers), Odejayi, Wordsworth, Henderson I (Elito).

Tranmere R (1) 1 *(Showunmi 22)*
Swansea C (0) 3 *(Van der Gun 73, Sinclair 74, Kuqi 90)* 2450
Tranmere R: Collister; Darville, Cresswell, Blanchard, Goodison, McLaren (McGurk), Welsh, Labadie, Thomas-Moore, Showunmi, Gornell (Akins).
Swansea C: De Vries; Serran, Taylor (Tate), Allen, Monk, Williams, Orlandi, Van der Gun, Thomas (Sinclair), Kuqi, Lopez (Dobbie).

Watford (0) 1 *(Deeney 78)*
Notts Co (0) 2 *(Davies 46, Smith 67)* 6434
Watford: Gilmartin; Thompson (Oshodi), Doyley, Jenkins, Bennett, Mariappa, Cowie, McGinn, Sordell, Deeney, Buckley (Graham) (Bryan).
Notts Co: Nelson; Pearce, Thompson, Ravenhill, Hunt, Chilvers, Smith (Lee), Bishop, Hubbins (Westcarr), Jarvis (Harley), Davies.

West Ham U (0) 1 *(Parker 90)*
Oxford U (0) 0 20,902
West Ham U: Stech; Faubert, Spector, Parker, Ben-Haim, Tomkins, Barrera, Noble, Sears (McCarthy), Piquionne, Stanislas (Cole).
Oxford U: Clarke; Purkiss, Tonkin, Bulman (Baker), Worley, Wright, Hall, Heslop, Constable, Cole (Clist), Potter (Green).

Wolverhampton W (1) 2 *(Milijas 27 (pen), Stearman 120)*
Southend U (0) 1 *(Easton 80)* 10,284
Wolverhampton W: Hennessey; Zubar, Elokobi, Edwards (Foley), Stearman, Batth, Halford, Guedioura, Hemmings (Ebanks-Blake), Winnall (Doyle), Milijas.
Southend U: Morris; Clohessy, Gilbert, Simpson, Barker, Mohsni, Grant, Easton, Sturrock (Paterson), Corr (Soares), Zaaboub (Hall).
aet.

Wednesday, 25 August 2010

Accrington S (1) 2 *(Putterill 45, Hessey 90)*
Newcastle U (1) 3 *(Taylor R 36, Ameobi 48, Lovenkrands 67)* 4098
Accrington S: Dunbavin; Bateson (Turner), Winnard, Hessey, Edwards, Procter, Ryan, Barnett, McConville, Parkinson, Putterill.
Newcastle U: Krul; Taylor R, Ferguson, Donaldson, Kadar, Tavernier, Ranger, Vuckic (Nolan), Ameobi, Lovenkrands, LuaLua.

Everton (2) 5 *(Fellaini 7, Rodwell 14, Beckford 50 (pen), Saha 77, Osman 85)*
Huddersfield T (1) 1 *(Heitinga 40 (og))* 28,901
Everton: Mucha; Coleman, Baines (Hibbert), Rodwell, Heitinga, Distin, Pienaar (Saha), Osman, Beckford, Gueye (Bilyaletdinov), Fellaini.
Huddersfield T: Smithies (Bennett); Peltier[■], Naysmith (Kay), Gudjonsson, Clarke P, McCombe, Croft, Johnson, Robinson (Novak), Arfield, Roberts.

Fulham (4) 6 *(Gera 10, 45, Dembele 26, Zamora 36, 66, Dempsey 70)*
Port Vale (0) 0 9031
Fulham: Stockdale; Pantsil, Briggs (Kelly), Murphy, Hughes, Hangeland, Duff, Etuhu (Greening), Dembele (Dempsey), Zamora, Gera.
Port Vale: Tomlinson; Yates (Taylor R), Collins, Griffith (Fraser), McCombe, Owen, Rigg, Roberts (Bell-Baggie), Richards M, Richards J, Dodds.

Thursday, 26 August 2010

Birmingham C (1) 3 *(McFadden 28 (pen), Murphy 48, Derbyshire 53)*
Rochdale (1) 2 *(Jones 26, 76)* 6431
Birmingham C: Taylor; Fahey, Murphy, Bowyer, Dann, Johnson, Valles (Redmond), Michel, Derbyshire (Zigic), O'Connor, McFadden (Larsson).
Rochdale: Lillis; Wiseman, Widdowson, Jones, Holness (Done), Dawson, Kennedy J, Barry-Murphy, O'Grady, Elding (Akpa Akpro), Tutte (Josh Thompson).

THIRD ROUND

Tuesday, 21 September 2010

Birmingham C (3) 3 *(Hleb 24, Zigic 26, Gardner 28)*
Milton Keynes D (0) 1 *(Wilbraham 80)* 9450
Birmingham C: Taylor; Parnaby, Murphy, Michel (Gardner), Jiranek, Johnson, Fahey, Beausejour (Valles), Zigic, Derbyshire, Hleb (Phillips).
Milton Keynes D: Martin D; Woodards, Lewington, Leven, O'Hanlon (MacKenzie), Doumbe, Guy, Carrington, Easter (Wilbraham), Chadwick, Balanta (Ibehre).

Brentford (1) 1 *(Alexander 41)*
Everton (1) 1 *(Coleman 6)* 8960
Brentford: Lee; Spillane, Woodman, Diagouraga, Osborne, Balkestein, Adams (Saunders), O'Connor (Bean), Alexander (Forster), MacDonald, Weston.
Everton: Mucha; Coleman, Baines, Neville, Distin, Jagielka, Bilyaletdinov (Arteta), Osman, Yakubu (Beckford), Fellaini, Gueye (Pienaar).
aet; Brentford won 4-3 on penalties.

Burnley (1) 1 *(Elliott 45)*
Bolton W (0) 0 17,602
Burnley: Grant; Mears, Fox, Carlisle, Bikey, Cork, Elliott, Alexander, Iwelumo (Thompson), Rodriguez (Marney), Eagles (Paterson).
Bolton W: Bogdan; Steinsson, Alonso, Davies M, Knight, Ricketts, Taylor, Blake, Klasnic (Elmander), Moreno (Lee), Cohen.

Millwall (0) 1 *(Morison 62)*
Ipswich T (2) 2 *(Priskin 23, McAuley 45)* 5070
Millwall: Forde; Dunne, Craig, Trotter, Robinson P, Mkandawire, Hackett, Henry (Harris), Morison, Barron, Schofield (Ward).
Ipswich T: Murphy; Eastman, Kennedy, Peters, McAuley, Delaney, Healy (Scotland), Hyam, Priskin (Wickham), Lambe, Townsend (Leadbitter).

Peterborough U (1) 1 *(Mackail-Smith 7)*
Swansea C (2) 3 *(Sinclair 5, 41, 78)* 4164
Peterborough U: Lewis; Ofori-Twumasi (Davies), Rowe, Lee, Zakuani, Langmead, Whelpdale (Tomlin), Mendez-Laing (Hibbert), Mackail-Smith, McLean, Boyd.
Swansea C: Ma-Kalambay; Richards, Tate, Lopez (Gower), Serran, Williams, Cotterill, Pratley, Dobbie, Van der Gun (Allen), Sinclair (Dyer).

Portsmouth (0) 1 *(Lawrence 82)*
Leicester C (2) 2 *(Morrison 3, Dyer 43)*   8327
Portsmouth: Ashdown; Ward, Dickinson, Mokoena, Sonko, Mullins, Lawrence, Hughes[■], Kanu (Brown), Nugent (Utaka), Ritchie (Kitson).
Leicester C: Logan; Lamey, Kennedy, King A (N'Guessan), Miguel Vitor, Morrison, Abe, Moreno, Gallagher (Wellens), Howard, Dyer (Moussa).

Stoke C (1) 2 *(Higginbotham 23, Jones 79)*
Fulham (0) 0   12,778
Stoke C: Begovic; Wilkinson, Higginbotham, Whelan, Huth, Shawcross, Diao (Delap), Tuncay (Pugh), Jones, Fuller (Walters), Etherington.
Fulham: Schwarzer; Kelly, Salcido, Murphy, Hughes, Hangeland, Gera, Etuhu, Dembele (Greening), Dempsey, Davies (Johnson E).

Sunderland (1) 1 *(Gyan 41)*
West Ham U (1) 2 *(Piquionne 35, Obinna 59)*   21,907
Sunderland: Mignolet; Bardsley, Richardson, Riveros, Onuoha, Ferdinand (Da Silva), Elmohamady, Henderson (Zenden), Gyan (Malbranque), Bent, Welbeck.
West Ham U: Stech; Faubert, Da Costa, Parker, Ben-Haim, Tomkins, Obinna (Dyer), Kovac, Barrera (Noble), Piquionne (Cole), Boa Morte.

Tottenham H (0) 1 *(Keane 49)*
Arsenal (1) 4 *(Lansbury 15, Nasri 92 (pen), 96 (pen), Arshavin 105)*   35,883
Tottenham H: Pletikosa; Naughton, Assou-Ekotto, Palacios, Bassong, Caulker, Bentley, Livermore (Lennon), Pavlyuchenko, Giovani (Keane), Sandro (Kranjcar).
Arsenal: Fabianski; Eboue, Gibbs (Clichy), Denilson, Djourou, Koscielny, Lansbury, Wilshere, Vela (Chamakh), Rosicky (Arshavin), Nasri.
aet.

Wolverhampton W (0) 4 *(Milijas 83 (pen), Fletcher 92, Doyle 105, 119)*
Notts Co (0) 2 *(Hughes 57, Smith 114)*   11,516
Wolverhampton W: Hennessey; Stearman, Elokobi, Guedioura, Berra, Mouyokolo (Bia), Foley, Halford, Ebanks-Blake (Doyle), Bent (Fletcher), Milijas.
Notts Co: Burch; Thompson (Edwards), Harley, Judge, Chilvers[■], Pearce, Spicer (Smith), Bishop, Hughes (Jervis), Westcarr, Davies.
aet.

Wednesday, 22 September 2010
Aston Villa (0) 3 *(Heskey 59, Young A 75, 77)*
Blackburn R (1) 1 *(Givet 34)*   18,753
Aston Villa: Guzan; Lichaj, Warnock, Sidwell, Cuellar, Clark (Davies), Young A, Reo-Coker, Agbonlahor (Delfouneso), Carew (Heskey), Bannan.
Blackburn R: Bunn; Chimbonda, Olsson, Jones P, Nelsen (Samba), Givet, Emerton, N'Zonzi, Mwaruwari (Biram Diouf), Hoilett (Kalinic), Pedersen.

Chelsea (1) 3 *(Van Aanholt 6, Anelka 70, 87 (pen))*
Newcastle U (2) 4 *(Ranger 27, Taylor R 32, Ameobi 49, 90)*   41,511
Chelsea: Turnbull; Paulo Ferreira, Van Aanholt, Ramires, Terry (Kalou) (McEachran), Bruma, Benayoun, Sturridge, Anelka, Kakuta (Alex), Zhirkov.
Newcastle U: Krul; Taylor R (Tiote), Ferguson (Barton), Vuckic, Coloccini (Williamson), Campbell, Ranger, Smith, Ameobi, Lovenkrands, Gutierrez.

Liverpool (1) 2 *(Jovanovic 9, N'Gog 116)*
Northampton T (0) 2 *(McKay 56, Jacobs 98)*   22,577
Liverpool: Jones; Kelly, Wilson, Lucas, Kyrgiakos, Agger, Pacheco (Ince), Spearing, N'Gog, Jovanovic (Eccleston), Babel (Shelvey).
Northampton T: Dunn; Johnson (Wedderburn), Davis, Thornton, Holt, Tozer, Rodgers (Herbert), Osman, McKay (Guinan), Jacobs, Gilligan.
aet; Northampton T won 4-2 on penalties.

Scunthorpe U (1) 2 *(Wright J 19, Woolford 90)*
Manchester U (2) 5 *(Gibson 23, Smalling 36, Owen 49, 71, Park 54)*   9077
Scunthorpe U: Murphy; Nolan, Byrne, Togwell (Collins), Mirfin, Canovan, Wright J, O'Connor (Grant), Dagnall (Godden), Forte, Woolford.
Manchester U: Kuszczak; Brown, Rafael, Anderson, Ferdinand, Smalling, Park (Bebe), Gibson, Owen, Macheda, Hernandez (Obertan).

WBA (0) 2 *(Zuiverloon 55, Cox 57)*
Manchester C (1) 1 *(Jo 19)*   10,418
WBA: Myhill; Zuiverloon, Shorey (Jara), Tchoyi, Pablo, Meite, Reid, Barnes, Bednar (Fortune), Cox, Dorrans.
Manchester C: Given; Vidal (Zabaleta), Cunningham, Vieira, Boyata, Mee, Ibrahim (Milner), Guidetti, Santa Cruz (Silva), Jo, Johnson A.

Wigan Ath (0) 2 *(Gomez 87, N'Zogbia 90)*
Preston NE (1) 1 *(Treacy 23)*   6987
Wigan Ath: Al Habsi; Stam, Figueroa, Thomas (McCarthy), Caldwell S, Alcaraz, Gomez, Watson, Boselli, Di Santo, McArthur (N'Zogbia).
Preston NE: Lonergan; Gray, Jones, Russell, Brown W, St Ledger Hall, Mayor, Coutts, Brown C (Parkin), Barton, Treacy (Parry).

FOURTH ROUND

Tuesday, 26 October 2010
Birmingham C (0) 1 *(Phillips 90)*
Brentford (0) 1 *(Wood 68)*   15,166
Birmingham C: Taylor; Carr, Parnaby, Bowyer, Dann, Ridgewell, Gardner, Michel (Ferguson), Phillips, O'Connor (Redmond), Derbyshire (Zigic).
Brentford: Lee; Spillane, Woodman, Bean, Osborne, Legge, Wood, O'Connor, Alexander (Grabban), MacDonald (Hunt), Weston (Simpson).
aet; Birmingham C won 4-3 on penalties.

Ipswich T (2) 3 *(Edwards 26, Delaney 44, Priskin 88)*
Northampton T (1) 1 *(Davis 16)*   12,929
Ipswich T: Murphy; Eastman, Smith, Delaney, McAuley, Leadbitter, Edwards (Griffiths), Norris, Priskin, Scotland (Murray), Townsend (Peters).
Northampton T: Dunn; Rodgers, Davis, Thornton (Holt), Hinton, Hall, Gilligan, Osman, Jacobs, McKay, Wedderburn.

Leicester C (0) 1 *(Shorey 53 (og))*
WBA (1) 4 *(Cox 21, 90, Tchoyi 62, Reid 79)*   16,957
Leicester C: Logan; Neilson (Lamey), Berner, King A (Fryatt), Miguel Vitor, Morrison, Abe, Gallagher, Moussa, Howard, Dyer (Wellens).
WBA: Myhill; Zuiverloon, Pablo, Tchoyi, Cech (Shorey), Meite (Mantom), Reid, Barnes, Bednar (Miller), Cox, Dorrans.

Manchester U (0) 3 *(Bebe 56, Park 70, Hernandez 90)*
Wolverhampton W (0) 2 *(Elokobi 60, Foley 76)*   46,083
Manchester U: Amos; Brown, Fabio (Neville), Carrick, Evans J, Smalling, Obertan, Gibson, Macheda, Bebe (Hernandez), Park (Morrison).
Wolverhampton W: Hennessey; Foley, Elokobi, Mancienne, Berra, Mouyokolo, Hunt, Jones, Ebanks-Blake (Bent), Fletcher, Jarvis (Doyle).

Wigan Ath (0) 2 *(Boselli 51, Watson 90 (pen))*
Swansea C (0) 0   11,705
Wigan Ath: Al Habsi; Stam, Figueroa, Thomas, Caldwell G, Alcaraz, Moses, Watson, Boselli (Di Santo), Gomez (N'Zogbia), Diame.
Swansea C: Ma-Kalambay; Rangel, Taylor, Pratley, Tate, Serran (Monk), Cotterill, Agustien (Orlandi), Beattie (Dobbie), Emnes, Van der Gun.

Wednesday, 27 October 2010
Aston Villa (0) 2 *(Heskey 86, Downing 96)*
Burnley (0) 1 *(Carlisle 89)* 34,618
Aston Villa: Friedel; Lichaj, Beye, Sidwell (Collins JM), Cuellar, Clark, Albrighton■, Reo-Coker, Young A, Bannan (Downing), Ireland (Heskey).
Burnley: Grant; Mears, Fox, Duff, Carlisle, Marney (Elliott), Alexander, Cork (Thompson), Rodriguez, Paterson (Iwelumo), Wallace.
aet.

Newcastle U (0) 0
Arsenal (1) 4 *(Krul 45 (og), Walcott 53, 88, Bendtner 83)*
33,157
Newcastle U: Krul; Perch, Taylor R, Guthrie, Kadar, Williamson, Routledge (Gutierrez), Smith (Barton), Ranger, Lovenkrands (Carroll), Vuckic.
Arsenal: Szczesny; Eboue, Gibbs (Sagna), Denilson, Djourou, Koscielny, Walcott, Eastmond, Vela (Fabregas), Bendtner (Emmanuel-Thomas), Rosicky.

West Ham U (0) 3 *(Parker 84, Da Costa 96, Obinna 118)*
Stoke C (1) 1 *(Jones 6)* 25,304
West Ham U: Stech; Faubert, Ben-Haim, Parker, Da Costa, Tomkins, Barrera, Kovac (Obinna), Cole, McCarthy (Noble), Boa Morte (Behrami).
Stoke C: Begovic; Wilkinson, Higginbotham, Whelan, Huth, Shawcross, Pennant (Pugh), Whitehead, Jones (Gudjohnsen), Walters, Tuncay (Delap).
aet.

QUARTER-FINALS

Tuesday, 30 November 2010
Arsenal (1) 2 *(Alcaraz 42 (og), Bendtner 67)*
Wigan Ath (0) 0 59,525
Arsenal: Szczesny; Eboue, Gibbs, Denilson, Djourou, Koscielny, Walcott, Wilshere (Nasri), Bendtner (Emmanuel-Thomas), Van Persie (Eastmond), Vela.
Wigan Ath: Al Habsi; Gohouri, Stam (McManaman), Thomas, Caldwell S, Alcaraz, McArthur, Watson, Boselli (Gomez), Moses (N'Zogbia), Figueroa.

West Ham U (2) 4 *(Spector 22, 37, Cole 56, 66)*
Manchester U (0) 0 33,551
West Ham U: Green; Faubert, Ben-Haim, Spector, Tomkins (Reid), Upson, Barrera (Hines), Kovac, Cole (Stanislas), Obinna, Boa Morte.
Manchester U: Kuszczak; O'Shea, Fabio (Rafael), Fletcher, Smalling, Evans J (Brown), Obertan, Anderson, Bebe (Macheda), Hernandez, Giggs.

Wednesday, 1 December 2010
Birmingham C (1) 2 *(Larsson 12 (pen), Zigic 84)*
Aston Villa (1) 1 *(Agbonlahor 30)* 27,679
Birmingham C: Foster; Carr, Ridgewell, Bowyer (Gardner), Dann, Johnson, Larsson (Murphy), Ferguson, Jerome, Zigic (Derbyshire), Fahey.
Aston Villa: Friedel; Young L, Warnock (Pires), Clark, Dunne, Collins JM, Hogg (Delfouneso), Bannan (Ireland), Young A, Agbonlahor, Downing.

Ipswich T (0) 1 *(Leadbitter 69 (pen))*
WBA (0) 0 11,363
Ipswich T: Murphy; Peters, O'Dea, Smith, Brown, Leadbitter, Lambe (Edwards), Norris, Priskin, Scotland (Healy), Townsend (O'Connor).
WBA: Myhill; Hurst, Cech, Tchoyi, Meite, Pablo, Reid, Barnes, Fortune (Miller), Cox, Dorrans.

SEMI-FINALS FIRST LEG

Tuesday, 11 January 2011
West Ham U (1) 2 *(Noble 13, Cole 78)*
Birmingham C (0) 1 *(Ridgewell 56)* 34,754
West Ham U: Green; Faubert, Reid, Noble (Kovac), Tomkins, Upson, Sears (Hines), Parker, Obinna■, Piquionne (Cole), Spector.
Birmingham C: Foster; Carr, Ridgewell, Ferguson, Dann (Murphy), Johnson, Larsson (Zigic), Gardner, Jerome, Fahey, Hleb (Beausejour).

Birmingham City's Nikola Zigic (19) scores the opening goal in the Carling Cup Final at Wembley. Although Robin van Persie equalised just before half-time, a defensive mix-up allowed Obafemi Martins to score the winning goal for the Blues in the last minute. (PA Photos)

Wednesday, 12 January 2011
Ipswich T (0) 1 *(Priskin 78)*
Arsenal (0) 0   29,146

Ipswich T: Fulop; Peters, Kennedy, Delaney, O'Dea, Edwards, Norris, Priskin (Murray), Wickham, Healy.

Arsenal: Szczesny; Eboue, Gibbs, Denilson, Djourou, Koscielny, Walcott, Fabregas, Wilshere (Song Billong), Arshavin (Vela), Bendtner (Chamakh).

SEMI-FINALS SECOND LEG

Tuesday, 25 January 2011
Arsenal (0) 3 *(Bendtner 61, Koscielny 64, Fabregas 77)*
Ipswich T (0) 0   59,387

Arsenal: Szczesny; Sagna (Eboue), Clichy, Djourou, Koscielny, Wilshere, Fabregas, Van Persie (Walcott), Arshavin (Nasri), Bendtner.

Ipswich T: Fulop; Kennedy, O'Dea, McAuley, Delaney, Leadbitter, Edwards, Norris, Priskin (Scotland), Wickham, Healy (O'Connor).

Wednesday, 26 January 2011
Birmingham C (0) 3 *(Bowyer 59, Johnson 79, Gardner 94)*
West Ham U (1) 1 *(Cole 31)*   27,519

Birmingham C: Foster; Carr, Ridgewell, Bowyer, Johnson, Jiranek, Larsson (Murphy), Ferguson, Jerome, Derbyshire (Zigic), Gardner (Beausejour).

West Ham U: Green; Faubert, Bridge, Parker, Tomkins, Upson, Spector (McCarthy), Noble, Cole, Boa Morte (O'Neil), Hines (Dyer).

aet.

CARLING CUP FINAL

Sunday, 27 February 2011

Birmingham C (1) 2   Arsenal (1) 1

(at Wembley Stadium, attendance 88,851)

Arsenal: Szczesny; Sagna, Clichy, Song Billong, Djourou, Koscielny, Rosicky, Wilshere, Van Persie (Bendtner), Arshavin (Chamakh), Nasri.
Scorer: Van Persie 39.

Birmingham C: Foster; Carr, Ridgewell, Bowyer, Jiranek, Johnson, Larsson, Ferguson, Zigic (Jerome), Gardner (Beausejour), Fahey (Martins).
Scorers: Zigic 28, Martins 89.

Referee: M. Dean (Wirral).

Birmingham City's Nikola Zigic leads his teammates in their post-match celebrations after beating Arsenal 2-1 in the Carling Cup Final at Wembley. (Action Images/Lee Smith)

JOHNSTONE'S PAINT TROPHY 2010–11

■ *Denotes player sent off.*

NORTHERN SECTION FIRST ROUND

Tuesday, 31 August 2010

Hartlepool U (0) 4 *(Horwood 66, Sweeney 69, Monkhouse 71, Behan 75)*
Northampton T (0) 0   1359
Hartlepool U: Flinders; Haslam, Horwood, Gamble, Collins, Liddle, Brown (Behan), Murray (Humphreys), Boyd (Yantorno), Sweeney, Monkhouse.
Northampton T: Dunn; Rodgers, Jacobs, Thornton (McKay), Hall (Beckwith), Holt, Harris, Osman, Guinan, Herbert (Davis), Wedderburn.

Macclesfield T (1) 1 *(Mukendi 42)*
Morecambe (0) 0   720
Macclesfield T: Veiga; Reid, Tremarco, Bencherif, Brown, Morgan, Wedgbury, Chalmers (Bolland), Barnett, Mukendi (Brisley), Daniel.
Morecambe: Roche (Walker); Moss, Wilson, Drummond, Parrish (Bentley), Haining, Duffy, Shuker, Spencer (Hendrie), Mullin, Hunter.

Oldham Ath (0) 0
Shrewsbury T (0) 1 *(Leslie 83)*   2703
Oldham Ath: Brill; Lee, Black, Furman, Mvoto, Hazell (McDonald), Smalley (Dikaba), Stephens, Kelly (Tounkara), Bembo-Leta, Taylor.
Shrewsbury T: Neal C; Raven, Sadler, McAllister (Disley), Sharps, Cansdell-Sherriff, Neal L, McIntyre, Harrold (Bright), Robinson (Van den Broek), Leslie.

Port Vale (1) 2 *(Richards M 27, Richards J 70)*
Rochdale (0) 1 *(Done 79)*   2442
Port Vale: Martin; Yates, Collins, Griffith (Taylor K), Sutton, Owen, Bell-Baggie, Fraser, Richards M (Rigg), Richards J (Dodds), Roberts.
Rochdale: Lillis; Wiseman, Goodall, Redshaw (Tutte), Holness (Widdowson), Josh Thompson, Joe Thompson, Barry-Murphy (Andre), Akpa Akpro, Elding, Done.

Rotherham U (0) 1 *(Le Fondre 47)*
Lincoln C (0) 0   1677
Rotherham U: Annerson; Mullins, Newey, Harrison, Cresswell, Geohaghon (Ashworth), Law, Taylor J, Ani (Warne), Le Fondre (Green), Ellison.
Lincoln C: Anyon; Green (Facey), Anderson, Watts, Swaibu, Kerr, Hughton, Keltie (Adams), Hutchinson B, Hutchinson A, O'Keefe.

Tranmere R (0) 1 *(Showunmi 79)*
Accrington S (0) 1 *(Putterill 55)*   2020
Tranmere R: Collister; Darville, Cresswell, Blanchard (Goodison), Grandison, Fraughan, Akins, Welsh (Mendy), McGurk, Showunmi, Brown (Morrow).
Accrington S: Cisak; Bateson (Smyth), Winnard, Murphy, Edwards, Owens, Ryan, Joyce, Boulding (Richardson), Parkinson, Putterill (Turner).
Accrington S won 5-3 on penalties but then withdrew from competition.

Walsall (1) 1 *(Reid 19)*
Chesterfield (2) 2 *(Bowery 13, Morgan 33)*   1793
Walsall: Brain; Westlake, Lescott, Taundry (Paterson), Lancashire (McDonald), Smith, Marshall, Richards, Reid, Macken, Gray.
Chesterfield: Lee; Hunt, Griffiths, Niven, Mattis, Ford, Talbot, Allott, Davies, Morgan (Boden), Bowery (Whitaker).

Wednesday, 1 September 2010

Sheffield W (2) 2 *(O'Connor 2, 14)*
Notts Co (1) 1 *(Davies 23)*   10,551
Sheffield W: Weaver; Otsemobor, Jones D, Potter, Beevers, Purse, Sedgwick (Miller), O'Connor, Morrison C (Mellor), Tudgay, Teale.
Notts Co: Burch; Thompson, Harley, Ravenhill, Edwards, Chilvers, Spicer, Hubbins (Westcarr), Jervis (Hawley), Smith (Pearce), Davies.

SOUTHERN SECTION FIRST ROUND

Tuesday, 31 August 2010

Aldershot T (1) 2 *(Hylton 17, Spencer 58)*
Oxford U (0) 0   1607
Aldershot T: Young; Herd, Fortune, Guttridge, Jones, Charles, Hylton, Halls (Harding), Spencer, Small, Straker (McGlashan).
Oxford U: Clarke; Purkiss, Tonkin, Baker, Creighton, Wright, Potter, Payne (Bulman), Green (Midson), Cole (Deering), Clist.

Bournemouth (0) 0
Torquay U (0) 0   3140
Bournemouth: Jalal; Purches (Bradbury), Cummings, Hollands, Pearce, Garry, Pugh, Bartley, Stockley (Taylor), Arter, Feeney (Robinson).
Torquay U: Bevan; Robertson, Nicholson, Mansell, Branston, Ellis, Stevens (Kee), Wroe, Benyon (Gritton), Zebroski, O'Kane (Lathrope).
Torquay U won 3-0 on penalties.

Charlton Ath (0) 1 *(Racon 57)*
Dagenham & R (0) 0   4630
Charlton Ath: Worner; Francis, Fry, Racon, Dailly, Llera, Wagstaff, Semedo (McCormack), Benson, Sodje (Abbott), Martin (Reid).
Dagenham & R: Lewington; Ogogo, Gwillim, Arber, Antwi, Vincelot, Danny Green (Currie), Gain, Nurse, Scott, Scannell (Montgomery).

Southampton (0) 0
Swindon T (1) 3 *(Pericard 29, 90, Austin 63)*   8333
Southampton: Davis; Butterfield (Dickson), Harding, Schneiderlin, Jaidi, Fonte, Puncheon (Oxlade-Chamberlain), Hammond, Lambert, Connolly, Do Prado (Barnard■).
Swindon T: Lucas; Amankwaah, Kennedy, Douglas (Evans), Cuthbert, Morrison, McGovern, Ferry, Pericard, Austin (O'Brien), Timlin.

Southend U (0) 0
Gillingham (0) 0   3073
Southend U: Evans; Simpson, Gilbert, Bouzid (Zaaboub), Barker, Mohsni, Grant, Easton, Sturrock, Corr (Paterson), Hall (Soares).
Gillingham: Cronin; Fuller, Nutter, Maher, Gowling, Sinclair, Spiller, Payne J, McCammon, McDonald (Payne S), Rooney (Barcham).
Southend U won 4-3 on penalties.

Stevenage (0) 0
Brentford (1) 1 *(Simpson 29)*   1916
Stevenage: Day; Henry, Laird, Bostwick, Roberts (Bridges), Ashton, Byrom (Sinclair), Mousinho, Beardsley (Sills), Odubade, Winn.
Brentford: Lee; Spillane, Woodman, O'Connor, Osborne, Balkestein, Adams (Cort), Diagouraga, Simpson, Forster (Wood), Weston.

Yeovil T (0) 1 *(Welsh 76)*
Exeter C (1) 3 *(Cureton 10, 78, Harley 90)*   2954
Yeovil T: Sullivan; Alcock, Smith, Tudor Jones, Huntington, Virgo, Stewart (Freeman), Kalala (Ayling), Williams S■, Bowditch, Welsh.
Exeter C: Jones P; Duffy, Tully, Sercombe, Archibald-Henville (Edwards), Jones B (Thomson), Dunne, Harley, Logan, Cureton, Golbourne.

Wednesday, 1 September 2010

Brighton & HA (0) 0
Leyton Orient (1) 1 *(Cox 21)*   3124
Brighton & HA: Ankergren; Calderon, Painter, Bridcutt, Elphick, El-Abd (Baz), Sparrow, Dicker, Barnes (Hart), Murray (Smith), Bennett.
Leyton Orient: Jones; Omozusi, Dawson, Chambers (Chorley), Brown A, Forbes, Cox (Cestor), Spring, Tehoue (Revell), Jarvis, Smith.

NORTHERN SECTION SECOND ROUND

Tuesday, 5 October 2010

Bury (0) 0
Shrewsbury T (0) 0   1944

Bury: Belford; Picken, Skarz, Lees, Futcher, Mozika, Bennett, Sweeney, Ajose, John-Lewis (Lowe), Haworth (Worrall).
Shrewsbury T: Smith; Raven, Sadler, McIntyre, Sharps, O'Donnell, Leslie, Disley (McAllister), Harrold, Bradshaw, Neal L.
Bury won 6-5 on penalties.

Carlisle U (0) 2 *(Chester 76, Price 81)*
Port Vale (1) 2 *(Norwood 42 (og), Richards M 64)*   2273

Carlisle U: Collin; Simek, McDaid, Murphy, Chester, Taiwo, Norwood (Hurst), Marshall (Robson), Curran, Madine (Price), Berrett.
Port Vale: Martin; Yates, Taylor K, Loft (Roberts), Sutton, Collins, Johnson (Richards J), Taylor R, Richards M, Rigg (Fraser), Dodds.
Carlisle U won 4-3 on penalties.

Hartlepool U (0) 1 *(McSweeney 69)*
Bradford C (0) 0   1728

Hartlepool U: Kean; Austin, Horwood, Hartley, Haslam, Liddle, Bjornsson, Yantorno (Gamble), Behan (Monkhouse), Boyd (Larkin), McSweeney.
Bradford C: McLaughlin; Rehman, O'Brien L, Gill, Oliver, Williams, Hendrie, Adeyemi, Bullock, Moult (Speight), Daley (Flynn).

Huddersfield T (3) 3 *(Carey 6, Pilkington 12, 24)*
Peterborough U (0) 2 *(McLean 51, Little 87)*   2904

Huddersfield T: Bennett; Peltier, Ridehalgh, Gudjonsson, Clarke P, Kay, Pilkington, Carey (Croft), Lee (Rhodes), Novak, Johnson.
Peterborough U: Lewis; Little, Ofori-Twumasi, Lee, Zakuani (Davies), Langmead, Mendez-Laing (McLean), Frecklington, Mackail-Smith, Hibbert (Tomlin), Boyd.

Macclesfield T (2) 2 *(Ada 13 (og), 30 (og))*
Crewe Alex (2) 4 *(Daniel 4 (og), Bell 29 (pen), Artell 48, Grant 59)*   1103

Macclesfield T: Veiga; Chalmers, Beardsley, Bencherif (Butcher), Brown, Morgan, Hamshaw, Bolland (Wedgbury), Sinclair, Mukendi (Barnett), Daniel.
Crewe Alex: Taylor; Tootle, Blanchett, Murphy, Artell, Ada, Ashley R Westwood, Bell (Mitchel-King), Moore, Donaldson, Grant (Zola).

Wednesday, 6 October 2010

Burton Alb (0) 1 *(Walker 83)*
Rotherham U (0) 2 *(Bradley 65, Ellison 79 (pen))*   1360

Burton Alb: Poole; Corbett, Boertien, Bolder, Austin, Stanton, Preen (Gilroy), Penn (Dyer), Phillips, Pearson, Young (Walker).
Rotherham U: Annerson; Holden, Green, Bradley, Fenton, Geohaghon, Law, Taylor J, Pope, Elliott (Warne), Ellison.

Sheffield W (1) 2 *(Mellor 12, Tudgay 90)*
Chesterfield (1) 2 *(Morgan 10, Davies 84)*   15,003

Sheffield W: Weaver; Buxton, Jones D, Potter, Beevers (Otsemobor), Purse, Sedgwick, Coke, Morrison C (Tudgay), Mellor (Heffernan), Teale.
Chesterfield: Lee; Hunt, Griffiths, Niven, Mattis, Ford, Talbot, Whitaker, Davies, Bowery (Lester), Morgan (Clay).
Sheffield W won 8-7 on penalties.

Tuesday, 26 October 2010

Tranmere R (0) 0
Stockport Co (0) 0   2223

Tranmere R: Gulacsi; Darville (Fraughan), Bakayogo, Blanchard, Goodison, Wootton, Welsh, Labadie, Thomas-Moore, Jennings, Morrow.
Stockport Co: Glennon; Lynch, Williams R, Turnbull, Rose, Assoumani, Simpson (Rowe), Pulis (Tansey), Fletcher (Darkwah), Donnelly, Griffin.
Tranmere R won 4-3 on penalties.

SOUTHERN SECTION SECOND ROUND

Tuesday, 5 October 2010

Barnet (0) 1 *(Marshall 79)*
Southend U (1) 3 *(Paterson 22, 55, Soares 85)*   1356

Barnet: Cole; Devera (Cox), Basey, Kamdjo, Parkes, Taylor (Vilhete), Jarvis, Byrne, Walsh, Holmes, Marshall.
Southend U: Evans; Clohessy, Gilbert, Simpson, Barker, Mohsni[a], Grant, Soares, Crawford (Coughlan), Paterson (Jarvis), Hall (Zaaboub).

Bristol R (0) 1 *(Hoskins 90)*
Aldershot T (0) 0   4050

Bristol R: Andersen; Regan, Sawyer, Campbell, Coles, Anthony, Blizzard (Brown), Akinde (Richards), Hoskins, Osei-Kuffour (Reece), Hughes.
Aldershot T: Young; Halls, Straker, Panther (Harding), Morris, Fortune, McGlashan, Guttridge, Hylton, Spencer, Small.

Cheltenham T (0) 0
Plymouth Arg (1) 2 *(MacLean 10, Noone 46)*   1597

Cheltenham T: Brown; Lowe (Lewis), Andrew, Pook, Elliott, Gallinagh, Low (Shroot), Bird, Jeffers, Goulding (Pack), Smikle.
Plymouth Arg: Larrieu; N'Gala, Molyneux, Fletcher (Clark), Johnson R, Seip, Stephens, Parrett, MacLean, Bolasie (Wright-Phillips), Noone.

Colchester U (0) 0
Wycombe W (0) 2 *(Betsy 75, Davies 82)*   2379

Colchester U: Williams B; James, White, Izzet (Bender), Okuonghae, Heath, Henderson I, Henderson L, Mooney (Odejayi), Wordsworth, Vincent (Gillespie).
Wycombe W: Bull; McCoy, Sandell, Montrose, Winfield, Johnson (Westwood), Strevens, Davies, Beavon (McClure), Rendell (Murtagh), Betsy.

Hereford U (0) 0
Exeter C (1) 3 *(Nardiello 12 (pen), O'Flynn 53, Duffy 90)*
                                                           1286

Hereford U: Bartlett; Green, Valentine, James, Townsend, Rose (Evans), Werling (Gwynne), McQuilkin, Bauza (Lunt), Canham, Colbeck.
Exeter C: Krysiak; Duffy, Heath, Noble, Jones B (Edwards), Archibald-Henville (Shephard), Cozic, Dunne, O'Flynn (Stewart), Nardiello, Thomson.

Leyton Orient (0) 0
Brentford (0) 0   1152

Leyton Orient: Butcher; Omozusi, Dawson, Forbes, Chorley, Brown A, Smith (Cox), Spring, Walker, Jarvis (Tehoue), M'Poku (Daniels).
Brentford: Lee; Legge, Woodman, Diagouraga (Saunders), McCracken, Balkestein, Adams (Hunt), Bean (Hudson), Alexander, Forster, Wood.
Brentford won 5-4 on penalties.

Milton Keynes D (1) 1 *(Chadwick 2)*
Charlton Ath (0) 2 *(Abbott 53, Wagstaff 85)*   3773

Milton Keynes D: Martin; Woodards, Lewington, Leven, Howell (O'Hanlon), Doumbe, Chadwick, Carrington, Balanta (Easter), Wilbraham (Ibehre), Guy.
Charlton Ath: Elliot; Francis, Jackson, Racon, Doherty (Fortune), Dailly, Wagstaff, Semedo, Abbott, Martin (Benson), Reid.

Swindon T (2) 2 *(Ball 10, Pericard 45)*
Torquay U (0) 0   3625

Swindon T: Lucas; Amankwaah, Rose, Douglas, Cuthbert (Thompson), Morrison, McGovern, Ferry, Ball (O'Brien), Pericard, Ritchie.
Torquay U: Potter; Senda (Carlisle), Charnock, Mansell, Robertson (Macklin), Ellis, Rowe-Turner, O'Kane, Benyon, Kee, Wroe (Gritton).

NORTHERN SECTION QUARTER-FINALS

Tuesday, 9 November 2010

Bury (0) 0

Tranmere R (1) 1 *(Thomas-Moore 8)*   1961

Bury: Branagan; Picken, Skarz, Lees, Futcher, Sweeney, Bennett, Schumacher, John-Lewis (Carlton), Ajose, Haworth.
Tranmere R: Gulacsi; Cathalina, Cresswell, Broomes, Grandison, Akins, Welsh, Labadie, Thomas-Moore, Showunmi (Morrow), Bakayogo.

Carlisle U (1) 3 *(Donaldson 14 (og), Murphy 72, 85)*

Crewe Alex (0) 1 *(Donaldson 76)*   2142

Carlisle U: Collin; Simek, Cruise, Murphy, Michalik (Chester), Taiwo, Marshall, Berrett, Grella (Zoko), Madine (Curran), Robson.
Crewe Alex: Taylor; Tootle, Blanchett, Ashley R Westwood, Dugdale, Ada, Powell (Bell), Murphy, Moore, Donaldson, Leitch-Smith.

Rotherham U (1) 2 *(Taylor R 11, Cresswell 90)*

Huddersfield T (3) 5 *(Rhodes 1, 23, Afobe 28, 72, Arfield 52)*   2185

Rotherham U: Annerson; Mullins (Ashworth), Green, Brogan, Cresswell, Fenton, Law, Taylor J (Bradley), Pope, Taylor R (Warne), Marshall.
Huddersfield T: Bennett; Peltier, Ridehalgh, Gudjonsson (Croft), McCombe, Kay, Arfield, Carey (Roberts), Rhodes (Garner), Afobe, Johnson.

Wednesday, 10 November 2010

Sheffield W (2) 4 *(Mellor 9, 29, 48 (pen), Teule 55)*

Hartlepool U (1) 1 *(Yantorno 43)*   10,909

Sheffield W: Weaver; Otsemobor (Beevers), Spurr, Miller, Buxton, Purse (Sedgwick), Coke, O'Connor, Morrison C, Mellor (Tudgay), Teale.
Hartlepool U: Kenn; Austin, Horwood, Sweeney, Collins, Murray (Hartley), Liddle, Gamble, Bjornsson (MacSweeney), Yantorno (Poole), Monkhouse.

SOUTHERN SECTION QUARTER-FINALS

Tuesday, 9 November 2010

Plymouth Arg (0) 1 *(Clark 52)*

Exeter C (1) 2 *(Harley 2, Nardiello 90)*   9431

Plymouth Arg: Larrieu; Duguid, Bhasera, Clifford, Nelson (Seip), N'Gala, Noone, Clark, Fallon (Mason), Wright-Phillips, Bolasie.
Exeter C: Krysiak; Duffy, Tully, Sercombe, Jones B, Archibald-Henville, Dunne, Harley, Logan, Cureton (Nardiello), Golbourne.

Southend U (0) 0

Charlton Ath (1) 1 *(Racon 28)*   4373

Southend U: Evans; Clohessy, Gilbert, Simpson, Prosser, Mohsni, Grant, Easton (Soares), Sturrock (German), Corr, Hall (Zaaboub).
Charlton Ath: Elliot; Francis, Jackson, Racon, Doherty (Dailly), Fortune, McCormack, Semedo (Wagstaff), Abbott, Reid (Fry), Martin.

Swindon T (1) 1 *(Austin 12)*

Brentford (1) 1 *(Simpson 38)*   3469

Swindon T: Smith P; Cuthbert, Rose, Ritchie (Caddis), Lescinel, Morrison, McGovern (O'Brien), Timlin, Pericard (Ball), Austin, Prutton.
Brentford: Lee; Spillane, Woodman, Diagouraga, Legge, Balkestein, Saunders (MacDonald), O'Connor, Forster (Weston), Simpson, Wood.
Brentford won 4-2 on penalties.

Wycombe W (0) 3 *(Rendell 58, 83 (pen), 89)*

Bristol R (2) 6 *(Osei-Kuffour 22, 40, 59, Lines 62, Hughes 77 (pen), Swallow 90)*   1591

Wycombe W: Bull; McCoy, Johnson, Murtagh, Foster, Bennett, Strevens (McClure), Bloomfield, Beavon (Harris), Rendell, Betsy.

Bristol R: Andersen; Regan, Sawyer, Campbell, Coles (Tunnicliffe), Anthony, Brown (Swallow), Lines, Akinde (Richards), Osei-Kuffour, Hughes.

NORTHERN SECTION SEMI-FINALS

Tuesday, 30 November 2010

Carlisle U (1) 3 *(Zoko 30, Michalik 61, Marshall 69)*

Sheffield W (0) 1 *(Purse 85)*   3149

Carlisle U: Collin; Simek, Cruise, Thirlwell, Chester, Michalik, Berrett (Robson), Taiwo, Zoko, Madine, Marshall (Hurst).
Sheffield W: Weaver; Jones D, Spurr, Potter, Beevers, Purse, Sedgwick (Heffernan), Miller, Morrison C, Mellor (Coke), Johnson J (O'Connor).

Tuesday, 14 December 2010

Tranmere R (0) 0

Huddersfield T (1) 2 *(Rhodes 18, 67)*   2598

Tranmere R: Nielsen; Wootton, Bakayogo, Welsh, Goodison, Grandison, Elford-Alliyu (Cresswell), Taylor, Akins, Showunmi, Jennings (McGurk).
Huddersfield T: Smithies; Peltier, Ridehalgh, Gudjonsson, McCombe, Kay, Pilkington, Arfield, Rhodes (Garner), Lee (Novak), Roberts.

SOUTHERN SECTION SEMI-FINALS

Tuesday, 14 December 2010

Brentford (0) 0

Charlton Ath (0) 0   2783

Brentford: Lee; Wright, Woodman, O'Connor, Legge, Osborne, Simpson (Spillane), Bean (Wood), Alexander, MacDonald, Diagouraga.
Charlton Ath: Elliot; Fry, Jenkinson, Racon, Doherty, Dailly, McCormack (Jackson), Semedo, Abbott (Benson), Martin (Anyinsah), Reid.
Brentford won 3-1 on penalties.

Bristol R (1) 2 *(Hoskins 20, Swallow 78)*

Exeter C (0) 2 *(Anthony 65 (og), Harley 89)*   3881

Bristol R: Andersen; Regan, Sawyer, Campbell, Coles, Anthony, Lines, Reece, Hoskins, Akinde (Richards), Swallow.
Exeter C: Krysiak; Tully, Duffy, Dunne (Noble), Archibald-Henville (Jones B), Taylor, Harley, Sercombe, Logan, Cureton, Golbourne (Nardiello).
Exeter C won 5-4 on penalties.

NORTHERN SECTION FINAL FIRST LEG

Tuesday, 18 January 2011

Carlisle U (2) 4 *(Marshall 19, Taiwo 23, Murphy 62, Michalik 65)*

Huddersfield T (0) 0   3706

Carlisle U: Collin; Simek, Murphy, Noble, Cooper (Livesey), Michalik, Marshall, Berrett, Zoko, Curran, Taiwo.
Huddersfield T: Bennett; Peltier (Gudjonsson), Clarke T, Kay, Clarke P, McCombe, Pilkington, Kilbane, Rhodes, Novak (Lee), Arfield (Roberts).

NORTHERN SECTION FINAL SECOND LEG

Tuesday, 8 February 2011

Huddersfield T (1) 3 *(Pilkington 30, Lee 70, 81)*

Carlisle U (0) 0   6528

Huddersfield T: Colgan; Peltier, Kilbane, Gudjonsson, Clarke P, McCombe, Kay (Cadamarteri), Arfield, Lee, Pilkington, Roberts.
Carlisle U: Collin; Simek, Borrowdale, Noble, Michalik, Murphy, Marshall, Berrett, Curran, Loy (Robson), Zoko (Taiwo).

SOUTHERN SECTION FINAL FIRST LEG

Monday, 17 January 2011
Brentford (0) 1 *(Alexander 64)*
Exeter C (1) 1 *(Cureton 39)*   3093

Brentford: Lee; Laird, Woodman, Bean (Diagouraga), Legge, Balkestein, Spillane, O'Connor, Alexander, Forster, Weston.
Exeter C: Jones P; Tully, Duffy, Noble (Archibald-Henville), Sercombe, Taylor, Dunne, Nardiello (Jones B), Logan (O'Flynn), Cureton, Golbourne.

SOUTHERN SECTION FINAL SECOND LEG

Monday, 7 February 2011
Exeter C (0) 1 *(Nardiello 90)*
Brentford (2) 2 *(Saunders 20, Alexander 26)*   5322

Exeter C: Hamer; Duffy, Jones B (Golbourne), Noble, Archibald-Henville, Taylor, Dunne (Nardiello), Harley, O'Flynn (Logan), Cureton, Sercombe.
Brentford: Lee; O'Connor, Woodman, Bean, Osborne, Legge, Saunders (Grabban), Diagouraga, Alexander (Simpson), MacDonald (Bignall), Weston.

JOHNSTONE'S PAINT TROPHY FINAL

Sunday, 3 April 2011

(at Wembley Stadium, attendance 40,476)

Brentford (0) 0   Carlisle U (1) 1

Brentford: Moore; Neilson, Woodman (O'Connor), Diagouraga■, Osborne, Legge, Saunders, Reed (Bean), Alexander, Schlupp, Weston (Grabban).

Carlisle U: Collin; Simek, Robson, Thirlwell, Michalik, Murphy, Marshall (Noble), Berrett, Curran, Zoko (Madden), Taiwo (Loy).
Scorer: Murphy 12.

Referee: G. Salisbury (Lancs).

FOOTBALL LEAGUE COMPETITION ATTENDANCES

LEAGUE CUP ATTENDANCES

Season	Attendances	Games	Average
1960–61	1,204,580	112	10,755
1961–62	1,030,534	104	9,909
1962–63	1,029,893	102	10,097
1963–64	945,265	104	9,089
1964–65	962,802	98	9,825
1965–66	1,205,876	106	11,376
1966–67	1,394,553	118	11,818
1967–68	1,671,326	110	15,194
1968–69	2,064,647	118	17,497
1969–70	2,299,819	122	18,851
1970–71	2,035,315	116	17,546
1971–72	2,397,154	123	19,489
1972–73	1,935,474	120	16,129
1973–74	1,722,629	132	13,050
1974–75	1,901,094	127	14,969
1975–76	1,841,735	140	13,155
1976–77	2,236,636	147	15,215
1977–78	2,038,295	148	13,772
1978–79	1,825,643	139	13,134
1979–80	2,322,866	169	13,745
1980–81	2,051,576	161	12,743
1981–82	1,880,682	161	11,681
1982–83	1,679,756	160	10,498
1983–84	1,900,491	168	11,312
1984–85	1,876,429	167	11,236
1985–86	1,579,916	163	9,693
1986–87	1,531,498	157	9,755
1987–88	1,539,253	158	9,742
1988–89	1,552,780	162	9,585
1989–90	1,836,916	168	10,934
1990–91	1,675,496	159	10,538
1991–92	1,622,337	164	9,892
1992–93	1,558,031	161	9,677
1993–94	1,744,120	163	10,700
1994–95	1,530,478	157	9,748
1995–96	1,776,060	162	10,963
1996–97	1,529,321	163	9,382
1997–98	1,484,297	153	9,701
1998–99	1,555,856	153	10,169
1999–2000	1,354,233	153	8,851
2000–01	1,501,304	154	9,749
2001–02	1,076,390	93	11,574
2002–03	1,242,478	92	13,505
2003–04	1,267,729	93	13,631
2004–05	1,313,693	93	14,216
2005–06	1,072,362	93	11,531
2006–07	1,098,403	93	11,811
2007–08	1,332,841	94	14,179
2008–09	1,329,753	93	14,298
2009–10	1,376,405	93	14,800
2010–11	1,197,917	93	12,881

CARLING CUP 2010–11

Round	Aggregate	Games	Average
One	175,731	35	5,021
Two	209,512	25	8,380
Three	244,980	16	15,311
Four	195,919	8	24,490
Quarter-finals	132,118	4	33,030
Semi-finals	150,806	4	37,702
Final	88,851	1	88,851
Total	1,197,917	93	12,881

JOHNSTONE'S PAINT TROPHY 2010–11

Round	Aggregate	Games	Average
One	52,042	16	3,253
Two	47,756	16	2,985
Area Quarter-finals	36,061	8	4,508
Area Semi-finals	12,411	4	3,103
Area finals	18,649	4	4,662
Final	40,476	1	40,476
Total	207,395	49	4,233

FA CUP FINALS 1872–2011

1872 and 1874–92	Kennington Oval	1911	Replay at Old Trafford
1873	Lillie Bridge	1912	Replay at Bramall Lane
1886	Replay at Derby (Racecourse Ground)	1915	Old Trafford, Manchester
1893	Fallowfield, Manchester	1920–22	Stamford Bridge
1894	Everton	1923–2000	Wembley
1895–1914	Crystal Palace	1970	Replay at Old Trafford
1901	Replay at Bolton	2001–2006	Millennium Stadium, Cardiff
1910	Replay at Everton	2007 to date	Wembley

Year	Winners	Runners-up	Score
1872	Wanderers	Royal Engineers	1-0
1873	Wanderers	Oxford University	2-0
1874	Oxford University	Royal Engineers	2-0
1875	Royal Engineers	Old Etonians	2-0 (after 1-1 draw aet)
1876	Wanderers	Old Etonians	3-0 (after 1-1 draw aet)
1877	Wanderers	Oxford University	2-1 (aet)
1878	Wanderers*	Royal Engineers	3-1
1879	Old Etonians	Clapham R	1-0
1880	Clapham R	Oxford University	1-0
1881	Old Carthusians	Old Etonians	3-0
1882	Old Etonians	Blackburn R	1-0
1883	Blackburn Olympic	Old Etonians	2-1 (aet)
1884	Blackburn R	Queen's Park, Glasgow	2-1
1885	Blackburn R	Queen's Park, Glasgow	2-0
1886	Blackburn R†	WBA	2-0 (after 0-0 draw)
1887	Aston Villa	WBA	2-0
1888	WBA	Preston NE	2-1
1889	Preston NE	Wolverhampton W	3-0
1890	Blackburn R	The Wednesday	6-1
1891	Blackburn R	Notts Co	3-1
1892	WBA	Aston Villa	3-0
1893	Wolverhampton W	Everton	1-0
1894	Notts Co	Bolton W	4-1
1895	Aston Villa	WBA	1-0
1896	The Wednesday	Wolverhampton W	2-1
1897	Aston Villa	Everton	3-2
1898	Nottingham F	Derby Co	3-1
1899	Sheffield U	Derby Co	4-1
1900	Bury	Southampton	4-0
1901	Tottenham H	Sheffield U	3-1 (after 2-2 draw)
1902	Sheffield U	Southampton	2-1 (after 1-1 draw)
1903	Bury	Derby Co	6-0
1904	Manchester C	Bolton W	1-0
1905	Aston Villa	Newcastle U	2-0
1906	Everton	Newcastle U	1-0
1907	The Wednesday	Everton	2-1
1908	Wolverhampton W	Newcastle U	3-1
1909	Manchester U	Bristol C	1-0
1910	Newcastle U	Barnsley	2-0 (after 1-1 draw)
1911	Bradford C	Newcastle U	1-0 (after 0-0 draw)
1912	Barnsley	WBA	1-0 (aet, after 0-0 draw)
1913	Aston Villa	Sunderland	1-0
1914	Burnley	Liverpool	1-0
1915	Sheffield U	Chelsea	3-0
1920	Aston Villa	Huddersfield T	1-0 (aet)
1921	Tottenham H	Wolverhampton W	1-0
1922	Huddersfield T	Preston NE	1-0
1923	Bolton W	West Ham U	2-0
1924	Newcastle U	Aston Villa	2-0
1925	Sheffield U	Cardiff C	1-0
1926	Bolton W	Manchester C	1-0
1927	Cardiff C	Arsenal	1-0
1928	Blackburn R	Huddersfield T	3-1
1929	Bolton W	Portsmouth	2-0
1930	Arsenal	Huddersfield T	2-0
1931	WBA	Birmingham	2-1
1932	Newcastle U	Arsenal	2-1
1933	Everton	Manchester C	3-0
1934	Manchester C	Portsmouth	2-1
1935	Sheffield W	WBA	4-2

Year	Winners	Runners-up	Score
1936	Arsenal	Sheffield U	1-0
1937	Sunderland	Preston NE	3-1
1938	Preston NE	Huddersfield T	1-0 (aet)
1939	Portsmouth	Wolverhampton W	4-1
1946	Derby Co	Charlton Ath	4-1 (aet)
1947	Charlton Ath	Burnley	1-0 (aet)
1948	Manchester U	Blackpool	4-2
1949	Wolverhampton W	Leicester C	3-1
1950	Arsenal	Liverpool	2-0
1951	Newcastle U	Blackpool	2-0
1952	Newcastle U	Arsenal	1-0
1953	Blackpool	Bolton W	4-3
1954	WBA	Preston NE	3-2
1955	Newcastle U	Manchester C	3-1
1956	Manchester C	Birmingham C	3-1
1957	Aston Villa	Manchester U	2-1
1958	Bolton W	Manchester U	2-0
1959	Nottingham F	Luton T	2-1
1960	Wolverhampton W	Blackburn R	3-0
1961	Tottenham H	Leicester C	2-0
1962	Tottenham H	Burnley	3-1
1963	Manchester U	Leicester C	3-1
1964	West Ham U	Preston NE	3-2
1965	Liverpool	Leeds U	2-1 (aet)
1966	Everton	Sheffield W	3-2
1967	Tottenham H	Chelsea	2-1
1968	WBA	Everton	1-0 (aet)
1969	Manchester C	Leicester C	1-0
1970	Chelsea	Leeds U	2-1 (aet)
	(after 2-2 draw, after extra time)		
1971	Arsenal	Liverpool	2-1 (aet)
1972	Leeds U	Arsenal	1-0
1973	Sunderland	Leeds U	1-0
1974	Liverpool	Newcastle U	3-0
1975	West Ham U	Fulham	2-0
1976	Southampton	Manchester U	1-0
1977	Manchester U	Liverpool	2-1
1978	Ipswich T	Arsenal	1-0
1979	Arsenal	Manchester U	3-2
1980	West Ham U	Arsenal	1-0
1981	Tottenham H	Manchester C	3-2
	(after 1-1 draw, after extra time)		
1982	Tottenham H	QPR	1-0
	(after 1-1 draw, after extra time)		
1983	Manchester U	Brighton & HA	4-0
	(after 2-2 draw, after extra time)		
1984	Everton	Watford	2-0
1985	Manchester U	Everton	1-0 (aet)
1986	Liverpool	Everton	3-1
1987	Coventry C	Tottenham H	3-2 (aet)
1988	Wimbledon	Liverpool	1-0
1989	Liverpool	Everton	3-2 (aet)
1990	Manchester U	Crystal Palace	1-0
	(after 3-3 draw, after extra time)		
1991	Tottenham H	Nottingham F	2-1 (aet)
1992	Liverpool	Sunderland	2-0
1993	Arsenal	Sheffield W	2-1 (aet)
	(after 1-1 draw, after extra time)		
1994	Manchester U	Chelsea	4-0
1995	Everton	Manchester U	1-0
1996	Manchester U	Liverpool	1-0
1997	Chelsea	Middlesbrough	2-0
1998	Arsenal	Newcastle U	2-0
1999	Manchester U	Newcastle U	2-0
2000	Chelsea	Aston Villa	1-0
2001	Liverpool	Arsenal	2-1
2002	Arsenal	Chelsea	2-0
2003	Arsenal	Southampton	1-0
2004	Manchester U	Millwall	3-0
2005	Arsenal	Manchester U	0-0 (aet)
	(Arsenal won 5-4 on penalties)		
2006	Liverpool	West Ham U	3-3 (aet)
	(Liverpool won 3-1 on penalties)		
2007	Chelsea	Manchester U	1-0 (aet)
2008	Portsmouth	Cardiff C	1-0
2009	Chelsea	Everton	2-1
2010	Chelsea	Portsmouth	1-0
2011	Manchester C	Stoke C	1-0

* *Won outright, but restored to the Football Association.* † *A special trophy was awarded for third consecutive win.*

FA CUP WINS

Manchester U 11, Arsenal 10, Tottenham H 8, Aston Villa 7, Liverpool 7, Chelsea 6, Blackburn R 6, Newcastle U 6, Everton 5, Manchester C 5, The Wanderers 5, WBA 5, Bolton W 4, Sheffield U 4, Wolverhampton W 4, Sheffield W 3, West Ham U 3, Bury 2, Nottingham F 2, Old Etonians 2, Portsmouth 2, Preston NE 2, Sunderland 2, Barnsley 1, Blackburn Olympic 1, Blackpool 1, Bradford C 1, Burnley 1, Cardiff C 1, Charlton Ath 1, Clapham R 1, Coventry C 1, Derby Co 1, Huddersfield T 1, Ipswich T 1, Leeds U 1, Notts Co 1, Old Carthusians 1, Oxford University 1, Royal Engineers 1, Southampton 1, Wimbledon 1.

APPEARANCES IN FINALS

Manchester U 18, Arsenal 17, Everton 13, Liverpool 13, Newcastle U 13, Aston Villa 10, Chelsea 10, WBA 10, Manchester C 9, Tottenham H 9, Blackburn R 8, Wolverhampton W 8, Bolton W 7, Preston NE 7, Old Etonians 6, Sheffield U 6, Sheffield W 6, Huddersfield T 5, Portsmouth 5, *The Wanderers 5, West Ham U 5, Derby Co 4, Leeds U 4, Leicester C 4, Oxford University 4, Royal Engineers 4, Southampton 4, Sunderland 4, Blackpool 3, Burnley 3, Cardiff C 3, Nottingham F 3, Barnsley 2, Birmingham C 2, *Bury 2, Charlton Ath 2, Clapham R 2, Notts Co 2, Queen's Park (Glasgow) 2, *Blackburn Olympic 1, *Bradford C 1, Brighton & HA 1, Bristol C 1, *Coventry C 1, Crystal Palace 1, Fulham 1, *Ipswich T 1, Luton T 1, Middlesbrough 1, Millwall 1, *Old Carthusians 1, QPR 1, Stoke C 1, Watford 1, *Wimbledon 1.
* Denotes undefeated.

APPEARANCES IN SEMI-FINALS

Manchester U 27, Arsenal 26, Everton 24, Liverpool 22, Aston Villa 20, WBA 20, Chelsea 19, Blackburn R 18, Tottenham H 18, Newcastle U 17, Sheffield W 16, Bolton W 14, Wolverhampton W 14, Derby Co 13, Sheffield U 13, Nottingham F 12, Sunderland 12, Manchester C 11, Southampton 11, Preston NE 10, Birmingham C 9, Burnley 8, Leeds U 8, Leicester C 8, Huddersfield T 7, Portsmouth 7, West Ham U 7, Old Etonians 6, Fulham 6, Oxford University 6, Notts Co 5, The Wanderers 5, Watford 5, Cardiff C 4, Luton T 4, Millwall 4, Queen's Park (Glasgow) 4, Royal Engineers 4, Stoke C 4, Barnsley 3, Blackpool 3, Clapham R 3, Crystal Palace (professional club) 3, Ipswich T 3, Middlesbrough 3, Norwich C 3, Old Carthusians 3, Oldham Ath 3, The Swifts 3, Blackburn Olympic 2, Bristol C 2, Bury 2, Charlton Ath 2, Grimsby T 2, Swansea T 2, Swindon T 2, Wimbledon 2, Bradford C 1, Brighton & HA 1, Cambridge University 1, Chesterfield 1, Coventry C 1, Crewe Alex 1, Crystal Palace (amateur club) 1, Darwen 1, Derby Junction 1, Glasgow R 1, Hull C 1, Marlow 1, Old Harrovians 1, Orient 1, Plymouth Arg 1, Port Vale 1, QPR 1, Reading 1, Shropshire W 1, Wycombe W 1, York C 1.

FA CUP ATTENDANCES 1969–2011

	1st Round	2nd Round	3rd Round	4th Round	5th Round	6th Round	Semi-finals & Final	Total	No. of matches	Average per match
2010–11	169,259	101,291	637,202	390,524	284,311	164,092	250,256	1,996,935	150	13,313
2009–10	147,078	100,476	613,113	335,426	288,604	144,918	254,806	1,884,421	151	12,480
2008–09	161,526	96,923	631,070	529,585	297,364	149,566	264,635	2,131,669	163	13,078
2007–08	175,195	99,528	704,300	356,404	276,903	142,780	256,210	2,011,320	152	13,232
2006–07	168,884	113,924	708,628	478,924	340,612	230,064	177,810	2,218,846	158	14,043
2005–06	188,876	107,456	654,570	388,339	286,225	163,449	177,723	1,966,638	160	12,291
2004–05	161,197	98,702	602,152	477,472	339,082	127,914	193,233	1,999,752	146	13,697
2003–04	162,738	117,967	624,732	347,964	292,521	156,780	167,401	1,870,103	149	12,551
2002–03	189,905	104,103	577,494	404,599	242,483	156,244	175,498	1,850,326	150	12,336
2001–02	198,369	119,781	566,284	330,434	249,190	173,757	171,278	1,809,093	148	12,224
2000–01	171,689	122,061	577,204	398,241	256,899	100,663	177,778	1,804,535	151	11,951
1999–2000	181,485	127,728	514,030	374,793	182,511	105,443	214,921	1,700,913	158	10,765
1998–99	191,954	132,341	609,486	431,613	359,398	181,005	202,150	2,107,947	155	13,599
1997–98	204,803	130,261	629,127	455,557	341,290	192,651	172,007	2,125,696	165	12,883
1996–97	209,521	122,324	651,139	402,293	199,873	67,035	191,813	1,843,998	151	12,211
1995–96	185,538	115,669	748,997	391,218	274,055	174,142	156,500	2,046,199	167	12,252
1994–95	219,511	125,629	640,017	438,596	257,650	159,787	174,059	2,015,249	161	12,517
1993–94	190,683	118,031	691,064	430,234	172,196	134,705	228,233	1,965,146	159	12,359
1992–93	241,968	174,702	612,494	377,211	198,379	149,675	293,241	2,047,670	161	12,718
1991–92	231,940	117,078	586,014	372,576	270,537	155,603	201,592	1,935,340	160	12,095
1990–91	194,195	121,450	594,592	530,279	276,112	124,826	196,434	2,038,518	162	12,583
1989–90	209,542	133,483	683,047	412,483	351,423	123,065	277,420	2,190,463	170	12,885
1988–89	212,775	121,326	690,199	421,255	206,781	176,629	167,353	1,966,318	164	12,173
1987–88	204,411	104,561	720,121	443,133	281,461	119,313	177,585	2,050,585	155	13,229
1986–87	209,290	146,761	593,520	349,342	263,550	119,396	195,533	1,877,400	165	11,378
1985–86	171,142	130,034	486,838	495,526	311,833	184,262	192,316	1,971,951	168	11,738
1984–85	174,604	137,078	616,229	320,772	269,232	148,690	242,754	1,909,359	157	12,162
1983–84	192,276	151,647	625,965	417,298	181,832	185,382	187,000	1,941,400	166	11,695
1982–83	191,312	150,046	670,503	452,688	260,069	193,845	291,162	2,209,625	154	14,348
1981–82	236,220	127,300	513,185	356,987	203,334	124,308	279,621	1,840,955	160	11,506
1980–81	246,824	194,502	832,578	534,402	320,530	288,714	339,250	2,756,800	169	16,312
1979–80	267,121	204,759	804,701	507,725	364,039	157,530	355,541	2,661,416	163	16,328
1978–79	243,773	185,343	880,345	537,748	243,683	263,213	249,897	2,604,002	166	15,687
1977–78	258,248	178,930	881,406	540,164	400,751	137,059	198,020	2,594,578	160	16,216
1976–77	379,230	192,159	942,523	631,265	373,330	205,379	258,216	2,982,102	174	17,139
1975–76	255,533	178,099	867,880	573,843	471,925	206,851	205,810	2,759,941	161	17,142
1974–75	283,956	170,466	914,994	646,434	393,323	268,361	291,369	2,968,903	172	17,261
1973–74	214,236	125,295	840,142	747,909	346,012	233,307	273,051	2,779,952	167	16,646
1972–73	259,432	169,114	938,741	735,825	357,386	241,934	226,543	2,928,975	160	18,306
1971–72	277,726	236,127	986,094	711,399	486,378	230,292	248,546	3,158,562	160	19,741
1970–71	329,687	230,942	956,683	757,852	360,687	304,937	279,644	3,220,432	162	19,879
1969–70	345,229	195,102	925,930	651,374	319,893	198,537	390,700	3,026,765	170	17,805

THE E.ON FA CUP 2010–11
PRELIMINARY AND QUALIFYING ROUNDS

EXTRA PRELIMINARY ROUND

Pickering T v South Shields	1-4
Bishop Auckland v Consett	3-3, 3-2
Hallam v Atherton Coll	2-3
Causeway U v Ellesmere R	2-1
Biddulph Vic v Wellington	1-1, 1-1
Biddulph Vic won 4-3 on penalties.	
Kentish T v Stansted	1-0
Sidley U v Lancing	0-3
Greenwich Bor v South Park	1-2
Littlehampton T v Beckenham T	1-1, 0-3
Lingfield v Sevenoaks T	1-0
Highworth T v Melksham T	2-1
St Francis R v Banstead Ath	1-3
Hadley v Barking	0-0, 0-1
Lymington T v Moneyfields	1-3
Nelson removed v Atherton LR w.o.	
Nostell MW v St Helens T	1-1, 2-2
St Helens T won 5-4 on penalties.	
Hemsworth MW v AFC Liverpool	4-1
Ledbury T removed v Castle Vale JKS w.o.	
Norton U v Hinckley Downes	1-0
Heanor T v Borrowash Vic	0-0, 1-2
Diss T v Daventry U	1-2
Alton T v Chichester City U	4-1
Erith T v Colliers Wood U	2-1
VCD Ath v AFC Uckfield	3-1
Amesbury T v Almondsbury UWE	0-5
Sherborne T v Portishead T	2-1
Keynsham T v Tavistock	0-2
Ryton v Scarborough Ath	0-1
Liversedge v Whitley Bay	0-3
Brandon U v Chester-Le-Street T	1-2
Shildon v Sunderland RCA	4-3
Ashington v Billingham T	4-1
Tow Law T v Jarrow Roofing Boldon CA	0-2
West Auckland T v Whickham	2-1
West Allotment C v Tadcaster Alb	1-2
Norton & Stockton Ancients v Penrith	2-1
Guisborough T v Armthorpe Wel	0-3
Brighouse T v Dunston UTS	1-2
Hebburn T v Marske U	1-1, 0-2
Whitehaven v Team Northumbria	4-1
Esh Winning v Northallerton T	0-4
Pontefract Coll v Selby T	0-2
Silsden v Crook T	2-2, 0-1
Hall Road R v Newcastle Benfield	2-2, 1-3
Bridlington T v Horden CW	5-1
Stokesley SC v Thackley	1-1, 1-2
Leeds Carnegie v Billingham Syn	0-0, 1-3
Spennymoor T v Bedlington Terr	1-0
Seaham Red Star v North Shields	0-1
Irlam v Chadderton	1-2
Rossendale U v Formby	3-1
Ashton Ath v Parkgate	0-2
Ramsbottom U v Winsford U	4-1
Leek CSOB v Bootle	1-1, 0-6
New Mills v Alsager T	10-2
Holker OB v Abbey Hey	1-1, 1-0
Daisy Hill v Congleton T	0-8
Glossop NE v Wigan Robin Park	2-2, 1-0
Runcorn Linnets v Maine Road	1-1, 4-3
Staveley MW v Padiham	5-0
Flixton v Bacup Bor	0-3
Colne v Ashton T	2-0
Cheadle T v Squires Gate	3-0
Willenhall T v Bartley Green	0-6
Coalville T v Stone Dominoes	1-1, 3-0
Loughborough Univ v Stratford T	1-4
Boldmere St M v Westfields	0-1
Coventry Sphinx v Castle Vale	3-0
Pegasus Juniors v Heather St Johns	1-1, 1-5
Rocester v Pilkington XXX	1-2
Eccleshall v Southam U	3-0
Cradley T v Malvern T	3-4
Shifnal T v Dudley T	1-1, 0-2
Kirby Muxloe v Walsall Wood	4-2
Alvechurch v Tipton T	0-5
Bardon Hill Sp v Bewdley T	2-5

Tividale v Oadby T	1-2
Pelsall Villa v Dosthill Colts	0-2
Bridgnorth T v Highgate U	4-0
AFC Wulfrunians v Heath Hayes	1-3
Brocton v Coleshill T	4-4, 1-2
Nuneaton Griff v Studley	2-1
Wednesfield v Bolehall Swifts	2-0
Gedling T v Boston T	2-4
Blackstones v Maltby Main	1-1, 0-0
Maltby Main won 4-3 on penalties.	
Long Eaton U v Barton T OB	1-1, 0-1
Holbeach U v Radcliffe Olympic	0-1
Wisbech T v St Andrews	5-0
Rossington Main v Shirebrook T	0-3
Greenwood Meadows v Winterton R	3-4
Teversal v Bottesford T	0-0, 1-3
Barrow T v Arnold T	2-1
Dunkirk v Dinnington T	4-3
Gedling MW v Holwell Sp	2-2, 4-3
Holbrook Sp v Sleaford T	4-0
Lincoln Moorlands Railway v Friar Lane & Epworth	3-1
Deeping R v Gresley	0-2
Haverhill R v Hadleigh U	2-1
Brantham Ath v Woodbridge T	4-2
St Neots T v Dereham T	2-0
Newmarket T v Yaxley	3-0
Whitton U v Thetford T	1-1, 2-0
Northampton Spencer v Leiston	0-2
Wellingborough T v Kirkley & Pakefield	3-0
Walsham Le Willows v Long Buckby	1-4
Team Bury v Ampthill T	2-1
Ely C v Raunds T	4-0
Wroxham v Rothwell Cor	5-1
Felixstowe & Walton U v Mildenhall T	4-1
Great Yarmouth T v Norwich U	0-4
March T U v Gorleston	1-0
St Ives T v Cogenhoe U	2-3
Rothwell T v Desborough T	3-4
Godmanchester R v AFC Kempston R	1-1, 0-4
St Margaretsbury v Welwyn Garden C	2-1
Biggleswade U v Newport Pagnell T	1-4
Saffron Walden T v Mauritius Sp Ass	3-2
Chalfont St Peter v Stotfold	1-0
Clapton v Stanway R	0-4
Burnham Ramblers v Hoddesdon T	2-1
Oxhey Jets v Hatfield T	3-2
Bethnal Green U v Basildon U	4-0
Bowers & Pitsea v Dunstable T	4-1
Takeley v Hertford T	0-4
Cockfosters v Hullbridge Sp	2-1
Kingsbury London Tigers v FC Clacton	1-2
Witham T v Wembley	3-0
Colney Heath v Broxbourne Bor V&E	3-0
Langford v Aylesbury U	1-3
Tring Ath v Enfield 1893	2-0
Leverstock Green v Harefield U	1-2
Haringey Bor v Hillingdon Bor	3-0
London APSA v Halstead T	3-3, 0-2
Hanwell T v London Colney	1-3
Royston T v Crawley Green	1-2
Eton Manor v Bedford	3-0
Barkingside v Southend Manor	0-2
Cobham v Wick	2-0
Hassocks v Eastbourne U	7-1
Farnham T v Badshot Lea	2-1
Molesey v Hartley Wintney	0-2
Croydon v Crowborough Ath	5-2
Chessington & Hook U v Raynes Park Vale	1-2
Alresford T v Herne Bay	5-2
Binfield v Crawley Down	3-2
Horley T v Ash U	4-1
East Grinstead T v Holyport	2-0
Camberley T v Petersfield T	2-1
Cove v Three Bridges	1-1, 1-4
Arundel v Hailsham T	4-1
Epsom & Ewell v Shoreham	3-0
Holmesdale v Erith & Belvedere	0-2
Mile Oak v Tunbridge Wells	0-1
Egham T v Guildford C	1-3

Hythe T v Bookham	4-0
Selsey v Worthing U	1-4
Lordswood v Pagham	1-5
Norton Sp v Redhill	2-0
Flackwell Heath v Oakwood	2-1
Deal T v Sandhurst T	3-0
Frimley Green v Peacehaven & Telscombe	0-4
Dorking v Bracknell T	0-5
East Preston v Ringmer	1-4
Brading T v Romsey T	1-1, 4-0
Bradford T v Wootton Bassett T	1-1, 3-3
Wootton Bassett T won 4-3 on penalties.	
Fairford T v Lydney T	0-0, 1-3
Christchurch v Hamble ASSC	0-1
Thame U v Shrivenham	3-0
Hayling U v Blackfield & Langley	1-2
Bournemouth v Abingdon T	1-0
Wantage T v Shortwood U	2-3
Downton v Bitton	0-2
Hallen v Winchester C	4-1
Milton U v Witney U	0-2
Bristol Manor Farm v Ardley U	5-3
Calne T v Corsham T	2-1
Calne T removed; tie awarded to Corsham T.	
Newport (IW) v Kidlington	1-0
New Milton T v Longwell Green Sp	1-1, 2-3
Bicester T v Westbury U	0-2
Warminster T v Reading U	1-2
Fareham T v Clanfield 85	3-1
Hook Norton v Laverstock & Ford	1-6
Brockenhurst v Old Woodstock T	0-1
Larkhall Ath v Gillingham T	5-1
Bridport v Welton R	3-0
Launceston v Bodmin T	0-3
Willand R v Merthyr T	2-0
Elmore v Hamworthy U	1-5
St Blazey v Torpoint Ath	1-1, 1-5
Odd Down v Verwood T	1-1, 4-1
Street v Barnstaple T	4-1
Buckland Ath v Radstock T	4-4, 2-3
Brislington v Wellington	0 1
Saltash U v Bishop Sutton	1-1, 4-4
Bishop Sutton won 4-3 on penalties.	
Poole T v Dawlish T	3-0
Ilfracombe T v Falmouth T	4-4, 2-1
Potton U v Stewarts & Lloyds	1-2
Mole Valley SCR v Chertsey T	0-5
Totton & Eling v Bemerton Heath Harle	2-0
Ringwood T v Cowes Sp	5-0

PRELIMINARY ROUND

Spennymoor T v Crook T	2-0
Selby T v Ossett Alb	0-4
Chester-Le-Street T v Scarborough Ath	2-1
South Shields v Dunston UTS	1-1, 0-3
Newcastle Benfield v North Shields	3-3, 1-0
Armthorpe Wel v Marske U	2-4
Wakefield v Ashington	2-3
Garforth T v Tadcaster Alb	0-1
Jarrow Roofing Boldon CA v Durham C	1-2
Thackley v Harrogate Railway Ath	5-0
Billingham Syn v West Auckland T	0-3
Shildon v Bridlington T	1-0
Whitehaven v Norton & Stockton Ancients	1-5
Bishop Auckland v Whitley Bay	2-2, 1-3
Radcliffe Bor v Lancaster C	2-1
Holker OB v Trafford	0-2
Curzon Ashton v Congleton T	0-0, 2-1
Cheadle T v Ramsbottom U	1-3
Skelmersdale U v AFC Fylde	3-1
New Mills v Chadderton	3-1
Bacup Bor v Clitheroe	5-3
Staveley MW v Parkgate	1-3
Bootle v Warrington T	1-2
Atherton Coll v Prescot Cables	2-2, 0-2
St Helens T v Glossop NE	1-1, 1-3
Sheffield v Colne	3-1
Leigh Genesis v Runcorn Linnets	1-0
Salford C v Chorley	2-1
Atherton LR v Woodley Sp	0-0, 0-3
Rossendale U v Cammell Laird	5-2
Mossley v Witton Alb	2-0
Rugby T v Atherstone T	1-1, 3-0
Pilkington XXX w.o. v Bromsgrove R removed	

Leek T v Eccleshall	0-1
Bridnorth T v Coventry Sphinx	1-1, 0-1
Kidsgrove Ath v Biddulph Vic	0-0, 4-0
Causeway U v Bartley Green	2-2, 2-4
Bewdley T v Sutton Coldfield T	2-3
Tipton T v Stratford T	3-1
Heather St Johns v Coleshill T	2-3
Westfields v Market Drayton T	0-2
Oadby T v Malvern T	2-0
Stourport Swifts v Dosthill Colts	3-3, 0-1
Bedworth U v Dudley T	6-1
Rushall Olympic v Romulus	0-0, 2-4
Kirby Muxloe v Norton U	1-3
Coalville T v Heath Hayes	5-1
Newcastle T v Nuneaton Griff	5-0
Lincoln U v Boston T	2-2, 4-2
Bottesford T v Barrow T	2-1
Loughborough Dyn v Shepshed Dyn	1-1, 3-2
Gresley v Quorn	4-0
Barton T OB v Shirebrook T	1-4
Dunkirk v Grantham T	2-2, 3-2
Spalding U v Goole	1-0
Maltby Main v Winterton R	0-1
Gedling MW v Barwell	0-1
Radcliffe Olympic v Wisbech T	1-0
Belper T v Holbrook Sp	1-3
Norwich U v AFC Kempston R	2-2, 2-3
Wellingborough T v Haverhill R	1-1, 3-1
Daventry T v Needham Market	2-3
Whitton U v Woodford U	0-3
Stewarts & Lloyds v Soham T R	2-1
AFC Sudbury v Stamford	2-2, 1-2
March T U v Desborough T	1-2
Felixstowe & Walton U v Team Bury	2-1
Wroxham v Ely C	2-2, 1-1
Ely City won 4-3 on penalties.	
Cogenhoe U v Leiston	0-3
Newmarket T v Biggleswade T	1-5
Brantham Ath v St Neots T	1-2
North Greenford U v Bowers & Pitsea	4-3
Arlesey T v Aylesbury	1-1, 2-1
Witham T v Ilford	0-0, 0-0
Ilford won 3-2 on penalties.	
Crawley Green v Harefield U	2-0
Barking v Redbridge	0-1
Waltham Forest v Enfield T	0-3
Hitchin T v Ware	2-1
Halstead T v Stanway R	1-2
Burnham Ramblers v Haringey Bor	5-1
Oxhey Jets v St Margaretsbury	4-1
Burnham v Chalfont St Peter	2-1
Marlow v London Colney	1-2
Uxbridge v Tilbury	0-1
Tring Ath v AFC Hayes	3-2
Southend Manor v Brentwood T	0-4
Newport Pagnell T v Potters Bar T	3-2
Colney Heath v FC Clacton	0-0, 5-1
Harlow T v Barton R	1-0
Maldon & Tiptree v Hertford T	4-2
Leighton T v Heybridge Swifts	2-2, 1-0
East Thurrock U v Waltham Abbey	3-0
Cheshunt v Cockfosters	2-2, 2-1
Saffron Walden T v Great Wakering R	1-1, 1-3
Wingate & Finchley v Northwood	0-0, 1-3
Thamesmead T v Beckenham T	2-3
Binfield v Camberley T	5-1
AFC Totton v Sholing	1-2
Norton Sp v Banstead Ath	2-0
Hartley Wintney v Whitehawk	2-2, 0-4
Fleet T v Bedfont U	4-0
Lingfield v Corinthian Casuals	0-2
Epsom & Ewell v Flackwell Heath	3-2
Deal T v Hythe T	2-4
Whitstable T v Croydon	3-0
Cobham v Alresford T	2-2, 4-0
Leatherhead v Burgess Hill T	0-2
Peacehaven & Telscombe v Ashford T (Middx)	1-2
Chipstead v Whyteleafe	4-3
Guildford C v Three Bridges	2-1
Ramsgate v Godalming T	1-1, 0-3
Walton & Hersham v Bracknell T	3-0
Ashford T removed v Erith T w.o.	
Faversham T v Pagham	2-0
Chertsey T v Chatham T	2-1
Alton T v Merstham	2-1

Raynes Park Vale v East Grinstead T	1-4
VCD Ath v Eastbourne T	1-1, 1-2
Horley T v Met Police	0-6
Sittingbourne v Andover	0-1
Tunbridge Wells v Dulwich Hamlet	3-3, 1-0
Lancing v Slough T	1-4
Hassocks v Farnham T	3-2
Bognor Regis T v Ringmer	1-0
South Park v Horsham YMCA	4-0
Gosport Bor v Erith & Belvedere	0-0, 1-2
Old Woodstock T v Laverstock & Ford	6-3
Bitton v Fareham T	2-0
Reading T v Newport (IW)	1-4
Almondsbury UWE v Wootton Bassett T	0-1
Blackfield & Langley v Almondsbury T	0-2
Bournemouth v Highworth T	0-2
Cinderford T v North Leigh	2-1
Hallen v Bristol Manor Farm	3-4
Hungerford T v Moneyfields	2-1
Corsham T v Brading T	0-1
Bishop's Cleeve v Westbury U	4-0
Thatcham T v Witney U	2-2, 4-2
Thame U v Lydney T	2-1
Ringwood T v Yate T	4-1
Mangotsfield U v Abingdon U	5-0
Longwell Green Sp v Hamble ASSC	0-3
Bridgwater T v Street	1-0
Frome T v Ilfracombe T	1-0
Bideford v Wimborne T	1-2
Willand R v Radstock T	1-0
Paulton R v Larkhall Ath	4-1
Bridport v Clevedon T	0-6
Torpoint Ath v Odd Down	1-1, 1-0
Poole T v Bishop Sutton	3-0
Hamworthy U v Sherborne T	2-2, 0-3
Tavistock v Taunton T	1-2
Hemsworth MW v Bamber Bridge	0-0, 1-4
Castle Vale JKS v Wednesfield	3-3, 0-6
Brigg T v Rainworth MW	6-2
Carlton T v Borrowash Vic	2-1
Long Buckby v Daventry U	4-1
Walton Casuals v Worthing U	3-0
Worthing v Arundel	6-0
AFC Emley v Northallerton T	0-1
Glapwell v Lincoln Moorlands Railway	0-6
Kentish v Bethnal Green U	1-3
Romford v Beaconsfield SYCOB	3-1
Aylesbury U v Eton Manor	3-2
Wellington v Bodmin T	0-3
Totton & Eling v Shortwood U	0-0, 3-1

FIRST QUALIFYING ROUND

Tadcaster Alb v Shildon	1-1, 2-4
Ossett Alb v Whitley Bay	1-2
North Ferriby U v Ossett T	2-1
Ashington v Northallerton T	3-1
Norton & Stockton Ancients v Chester-Le-Street T	2-1
West Auckland T v Bradford PA	3-1
Newcastle Benfield v Spennymoor T	1-0
Thackley v Marske U	3-1
FC Halifax T v Whitby T	2-0
FC United of Manchester v Radcliffe Bor	3-0
Parkgate v Warrington T	1-3
Nantwich T v Burscough	4-0
Salford C v Northwich Vic	0-1
Curzon Ashton v New Mills	1-1, 2-3
Prescot Cables v Ashton U	2-2, 0-4
Frickley Ath v Kendal T	3-2
Marine v Colwyn Bay	1-1, 0-2
Bamber Bridge v Bacup Bor	2-0
Rossendale U v Leigh Genesis	3-4
Stocksbridge PS v Trafford	4-2
Glossop NE v Mossley	0-4
Ramsbottom U v Skelmersdale U	0-2
Wednesfield v Rugby T	5-1
Stourbridge v Romulus	2-0
Evesham U v Coleshill T	1-3
Leamington v Brackley T	2-2, 0-2
Pilkington XXX v Market Drayton T	0-2
Oadby T v Dosthill Colts	2-1
Coventry Sphinx v Sutton Coldfield T	1-0
Tipton T v Romulus	1-0
Kidsgrove Ath v Chasetown	3-0
Coalville T v Eccleshall	5-0
Bartley Green v Bedworth U	1-1, 0-4

Hednesford T v Newcastle T	1-2
Winterton R v Radcliffe Olympic	2-2, 0-2
Bottesford T v Buxton	0-3
Lincoln Moorlands Railway v Gresley	2-2, 2-1
Matlock T v Worksop T	3-1
Spalding U v Brigg T	2-2, 0-4
Holbeach Sp v Loughborough Dyn	1-3
Barwell v Hucknall T	2-0
Shirebrook T v Lincoln U	1-3
Carlton T v Dunkirk	1-1, 2-1
Retford U v Mickleover Sp	0-5
Cambridge C v Long Buckby	3-0
Lowestoft T v Desborough T	7-1
Ely C v Stewarts & Lloyds	0-1
Woodford U v Bury T	1-3
Felixstowe & Walton U v Wellingborough T	2-1
Needham Market v AFC Kempston R	6-1
Leiston v St Neots T	3-2
Biggleswade T v Stamford	3-3, 0-3
Great Wakering R v Harrow Bor	2-4
Brentwood T v Aylesbury U	4-0
Wealdstone v Tring Ath	7-0
Hemel Hempstead T v Concord R	1-2
Burnham v Colney Heath	2-1
Romford v Crawley Green	1-1, 2-1
North Greenford U v Northwood	2-1
Ilford v Maldon & Tiptree	0-1
AFC Hornchurch v Oxhey Jets	8-2
Canvey Island v Newport Pagnell T	4-1
Redbridge v London Colney	2-0
Stanway R v Bedford T	1-1, 0-2
Arlesey T v Enfield T	0-2
Billericay T v Tilbury	1-0
East Thurrock U v Leighton T	2-1
Hitchin T v Aveley	2-1
Harlow T v Bethnal Green U	1-1, 4-0
Burnham Ramblers v Chesham U	0-3
Hythe T v Epsom & Ewell	2-0
Sholing v Hassocks	5-0
Corinthian Casuals v Erith & Belvedere	1-2
Cobham v Chipstead	0-1
Sutton U v Alton T	1-2
Carshalton Ath v Tunbridge Wells	2-1
Tonbridge Angels v Guildford C	0-1
Tooting & Mitcham U v Walton Casuals	4-1
Godalming T v Met Police	1-2
Erith T v Slough T	1-0
Beckenham T v Norton Sp	3-2
Burgess Hill T v Eastbourne T	3-2
Fleet T v Faversham T	3-1
Folkestone Invicta v Horsham	4-2
Whitstable T v East Grinstead T	1-0
Ashford T (Middlesex) v Worthing	1-1, 1-5
Whitehawk v Maidstone U	3-1
Binfield v Margate	0-3
Bognor Regis T v Hastings U	3-2
Walton & Hersham v Bashley	1-4
Andover v Chertsey T	0-4
Bitton v Old Woodstock T	2-3
Oxford C v Mangotsfield U	0-1
Swindon Supermarine v Brading T	4-0
Banbury U v Chippenham T	1-2
Newport (IW) v Bishop's Cleeve	0-3
Thatcham T v Thame U	0-1
Almondsbury T v Bristol Manor Farm	1-1, 2-2
Bristol Manor Farm won 3-1 on penalties.	
Hungerford T v Totton & Eling	6-2
Highworth T v Salisbury C	1-1, 0-5
Hamble ASSC v Wootton Bassett T	1-1, 2-0
Cinderford T v Ringwood T	5-0
Cirencester T v Didcot T	0-0, 1-3
Tiverton T v Paulton R	1-1, 0-2
Truro C v Bridgwater T	8-2
Torpoint Ath v Clevedon T	2-4
Wimborne T v Sherborne T	1-3
Bodmin T v Poole T	1-4
Taunton T v Weymouth	1-2
Frome T v Willand R	1-0
Durham C v Dunston UTS	1-3
Grays Ath v Windsor & Eton	1-0
Hendon v Cheshunt	4-1
Cray W v South Park	1-0
Woodley Sp v Sheffield	2-2, 1-3
Kingstonian w.o. v Croydon Ath withdrew	

SECOND QUALIFYING ROUND

Frickley Ath v Newcastle Benfield	2-1
Bamber Bridge v Warrington T	1-1, 2-4
Norton & Stockton Ancients v Leigh Genesis	2-1
New Mills v Harrogate T	0-2
Vauxhall Motors v Blyth Spartans	5-1
North Ferriby U v Stocksbridge PS	5-2
Dunston UTS v Mossley	1-2
Ashington v Thackley	1-0
Colwyn Bay v Guiseley	1-1, 0-3
Nantwich T v Whitley Bay	2-3
FC United of Manchester v Gainsborough T	2-1
Hyde v Droylsden	0-0, 1-3
Ashton U v FC Halifax T	1-2
Stalybridge C v Alfreton T	1-1, 2-1
Shildon v Skelmersdale U	2-0
Sheffield v Northwich Vic	2-2, 2-1
Workington v West Auckland T	2-1
Boston U v Worcester C	2-3
Ilkeston T removed v Lincoln Moorlands Railway w.o.	
Tipton T v Market Drayton T	2-0
Eastwood T v Stafford R	1-1, 3-1
Brigg T v Nuneaton T	3-3, 0-2
Coleshill T v Lincoln U	5-1
Hinckley U v Coventry Sphinx	2-0
Oadby T v Radcliffe Olympic	1-3
Barwell v Coalville T	3-2
Loughborough Dyn v Redditch U	0-2
Stewarts & Lloyds v Mickleover Sp	2-2, 2-3
Brackley T v Buxton	1-3
Carlton T v Matlock T	0-1
Bedworth U v Corby T	0-1
Newcastle T v Wednesfield	5-3
Solihull Moors v Kidsgrove Ath	2-0
AFC Telford U v Stourbridge	5-2
Hythe T v Erith & Belvedere	4-1
Erith T v Dover Ath	1-5
Bury T v Grays Ath	2-2, 4-1
Chesham U v Wealdstone	2-2, 1-4
Braintree T v Welling U	2-0
Tooting & Mitcham U v Staines T	1-4
Bishop's Stortford v Bromley	2-2, 1-2
Cambridge C v Hitchin T	2-2, 2-0
Billericay T v Concord R	1-1, 0-1
Folkestone Invicta v Leiston	1-1, 1-2
Lewes v Harlow T	2-0
AFC Hornchurch v Brentwood T	0-0, 0-1
East Thurrock U v Carshalton Ath	1-1, 2-1
Hendon v Maldon & Tiptree	2-1
Enfield T v Worthing	1-0
North Greenford U v Felixstowe & Walton U	1-1, 3-0
Needham Market v Chipstead	0-0, 2-0
Romford v Hampton & Richmond Bor	0-4
Canvey Island v Whitstable T	1-0
Redbridge v Harrow Bor	1-2
Burnham v Whitehawk	2-6
Bedford T v Boreham Wood	0-2
Thurrock v Stamford	3-1
Cray W v Ebbsfleet U	2-2, 2-4
St Albans C v Beckenham T	3-1
Met Police v Burgess Hill T	2-1
Margate v Kingstonian	1-1, 1-1
Kingstonian won 3-2 on penalties.	
Dartford v Lowestoft T	2-1
Chelmsford C v Chertsey T	7-0
Hamble ASSC v Old Woodstock T	2-1
Eastleigh v Bognor Regis T	2-0
Sholing v Salisbury C	2-2, 1-5
Chippenham T v Farnborough	0-1
Havant & Waterlooville v Frome T	1-0
Mangotsfield U v Dorchester T	1-4
Paulton R v Didcot T	0-1
Bristol Manor Farm v Basingstoke T	2-2, 0-1
Sherborne T v Hungerford T	1-2
Bashley v Fleet T	2-2, 2-0
Poole T v Thame U	1-1, 1-0
Guildford C v Clevedon T	1-2
Bishop's Cleeve v Woking	1-2
Gloucester C v Weston-Super-Mare	0-2
Swindon Supermarine v Weymouth	3-0
Maidenhead U v Truro C	1-0
Alton T v Cinderford T	2-2, 1-2

THIRD QUALIFYING ROUND

FC Halifax T v Harrogate T	4-0
Sheffield v Frickley Ath	1-1, 2-1
Guiseley v Whitley Bay	3-0
Norton & Stockton Ancients v FC United of Manchester	
	2-5
Workington v Shildon	2-1
North Ferriby U v Vauxhall Motors	2-2, 1-1
Vauxhall Motors won 4-3 on penalties.	
Warrington T v Stalybridge Celtic	1-3
Lincoln Moorlands Railway v Mossley	1-1, 1-4
Ashington v Droylsden	1-4
Solihull Moors v Barwell	1-1, 1-3
Mickleover Sp v Newcastle T	1-2
Buxton v AFC Telford U	1-1, 2-2
Buxton won 5-4 on penalties.	
Redditch U v Hinckley U	1-0
Corby T v Worcester C	2-1
Matlock T v Eastwood T	0-3
Nuneaton T v Coleshill T	6-0
Radcliffe Olympic v Tipton T	3-3, 0-2
Chelmsford C v Bromley	2-2, 3-0
Leiston v North Greenford U	5-0
Brentwood T v Woking	1-1, 0-1
Harrow Bor v Hampton & Richmond Bor	2-1
St Albans C v Kingstonian	0-0, 2-1
Met Police v Wealdstone	1-1, 2-1
Lewes v Thurrock	2-1
Needham Market v Ebbsfleet U	0-1
Whitehawk v Hendon	1-2
Boreham Wood v Enfield T	3-1
Carshalton Ath v Braintree T	4-1
Concord R v Hythe T	0-1
Dover Ath v Cambridge C	3-1
Bury T v Staines T	2-2, 0-2
Canvey Island v Dartford	2-2, 3-3
Dartford won 9-8 on penalties.	
Swindon Supermarine v Hungerford T	4-0
Salisbury C v Weston-Super-Mare	1-0
Didcot T v Basingstoke T	0-4
Havant & Waterlooville v Dorchester T	4-1
Farnborough v Hamble ASSC	2-0
Poole T v Bashley	1-0
Clevedon T v Eastleigh	0-5
Cinderford T v Maidenhead U	0-4

FOURTH QUALIFYING ROUND

Mossley v Darlington	2-6
Sheffield v Tipton T	2-2, 0-2
Guiseley v Redditch U	2-1
Fleetwood T v Buxton	2-1
Altrincham v Gateshead	0-2
Vauxhall Motors v Newcastle T	1-0
FC United of Manchester v Barrow	1-0
Workington v Nuneaton T	1-1, 0-1
Tamworth v Grimsby T	1-1, 1-0
Kidderminster H v York C	0-2
FC Halifax T v Mansfield T	0-1
Wrexham v Southport	1-2
Stalybridge C v Eastwood T	1-2
Droylsden v Barwell	3-0
Woking v Eastleigh	3-2
Hythe T v Staines T	2-0
Eastbourne Bor v Harrow Bor	2-4
Cambridge U v Lewes	3-0
Corby T v Salisbury C	3-0
Newport Co v Crawley T	0-1
Luton T v St Albans C	4-0
Farnborough v Dover Ath	1-1, 0-5
Kettering T v Rushden & D	1-2
Carshalton Ath v Chelmsford C	1-1, 2-3
Hendon v Met Police	0-0, 2-0
Leiston v Dartford	0-0, 2-3
Basingstoke T v AFC Wimbledon	0-1
Swindon Supermarine v Bath C	0-0, 4-3
Havant & Waterlooville v Histon	2-0
Forest Green R v Maidenhead U	1-0
Poole T v Hayes & Yeading U	1-3
Ebbsfleet U v Boreham Wood	3-0

THE E.ON FA CUP 2010–11
COMPETITION PROPER

Denotes player sent off.

FIRST ROUND

Friday, 5 November 2010
Rochdale (0) 2 *(Elding 53, Dawson 78)*
FC United of Manchester (1) 3 *(Platt 42, Cotterill 49, Norton 90)*   7048
Rochdale: Lillis; Wiseman, Widdowson, Jones, Holness, Dawson, Kennedy J, Barry-Murphy, O'Grady, Elding, Adams (Akpa Akpro).
FC United of Manchester: Ashton; Jacobs, Battersby (Holden), Platt, Munroe, McManus, Roca (Ovington), Cotterill, Norton, Wright, Deegan (Carden).

Saturday, 6 November 2010
Accrington S (2) 3 *(Putterill 8, 52, Ryan 36)*
Oldham Ath (0) 2 *(Feeney 69, Stephens 75 (pen))*   2275
Accrington S: Dunbavin; Long, Winnard, Hessey, Edwards, Procter, Joyce, Ryan, McConville, Gornell, Putterill.
Oldham Ath: Brill; Winchester, Black, Jarrett (Dikaba), Mvoto, Hazell, Evina, Stephens, Tounkara (Feeney), Jones (Alessandra), Taylor.

AFC Wimbledon (0) 0
Ebbsfleet U (0) 0   3219
AFC Wimbledon: Brown; Hatton, Blackman, Gregory, Yakubu, Harris, Jackson (Moore S), Yussuff, Kedwell, Jolley■, Moore L (Nwokeji).
Ebbsfleet U: Edwards; Stone, Duncan, Carew■, Easton, Lorraine, West (Williams), Marwa (Howe), Willock, Shakes, Phipp.

Barnet (0) 0
Charlton Ath (0) 0   2684
Barnet: Cole; Devera, Parkes, Southam, Basey, Uddin, Francomb, Marshall, Kabba (Vilhete), Gallen (Holmes), Byrne.
Charlton Ath: Elliot; Francis, Fry, Racon, Doherty, Dailly, Wagstaff, Semedo, Anyinsah (Abbott), Benson, Jackson (Reid).

Bournemouth (3) 5 *(McQuoid 1, 4, 57, Pugh 7, Feeney 61)*
Tranmere R (2) 3 *(Cresswell 27, Goodison 42, Thomas-Moore 53)*   3951
Bournemouth: Jalal; Smith, Cummings, Hollands, Pearce, Bartley (Wiggins), Pugh, Robinson, McQuoid (Purches), Fletcher (Arter), Feeney.
Tranmere R: Collister; Cathalina, Cresswell, Broomes, Goodison, Blanchard (Akins), Welsh, Labadie, Thomas-Moore (Morrow), Showunmi, Jennings (Fraughan).

Brentford (1) 1 *(MacDonald 20)*
Aldershot T (1) 1 *(Small 13)*   4090
Brentford: Lee; Wright, Woodman, Bean, Osborne, Balkestein, Simpson (Hudson), Diagouraga (O'Connor), Forster, MacDonald, Weston.
Aldershot T: Young; Herd, Vincent, Morris, Jones, Charles, McGlashan, Harding, Small (Hylton), Guttridge, Straker.

Brighton & HA (0) 0
Woking (0) 0   5868
Brighton & HA: Brezovan; Calderon, Painter (Smith), Bridcutt, Elphick, Dunk, Sparrow, Dicker, Barnes, Murray (Battipiedi), Baz (Hart).
Woking: Little; Anane, Aswad, Maledon, McNerney, Doyle, Ademola, Faulconbridge, Hammond (Sagbanmu), Quarm (Turnbull), Federico (Watkins).

Bury (1) 2 *(Sodje 28, Lees 53)*
Exeter C (0) 0   2359
Bury: fon Williams; Picken, Skarz, Lees, Sodje, Mozika, Haworth (Worrall), Schumacher, Lowe (John-Lewis), Ajose, Jones M (Bennett).
Exeter C: Krysiak; Duffy, Tully, Noble (Harley), Jones B, Archibald-Henville, Dunne, Sercombe, Logan (Cureton), Nardiello (Stewart), Golbourne.

Cambridge U (0) 0
Huddersfield T (0) 0   3127
Cambridge U: Naisbitt; Roberts, Jennings, McAuley, Partridge, Coulson, Russell, Carden, Wright, Gray, Willmott.
Huddersfield T: Bennett; Peltier, Ridehalgh, Gudjonsson, Clarke P, Kay, Pilkington, Carey (Arfield), Rhodes (McCombe), Afobe, Johnson.

Carlisle U (5) 6 *(Zoko 5, 19, Madine 9, 12, 41, 82)*
Tipton T (0) 0   4241
Carlisle U: Collin; Simek, Cruise, Murphy, Chester, Taiwo (Hurst), Marshall, Berrett, Zoko (McKenna), Madine, Robson (Curran).
Tipton T: Sargeant; Hill, Brown, Bate, Parker, Palmer (Mosedale), Bowen, Bragholi, Jackson (Jones), Barker, Campbell (Jakab).

Chelmsford C (2) 3 *(Higgins 8, Bricknell 28, Cook 68)*
Hendon (1) 2 *(Busby 43 (pen), 80)*   1685
Chelmsford C: Pullen■; Nunn, Coker, Haines, El-Abd, Lock, Modeste, Martin (Reed), Higgins (Harrison), Cook, Bricknell (Ake).
Hendon: Laurencin; Coke, Cousins, Vargas (Peacock), Parker, MacLaren K (Wishaft), Guentchev, O'Leary, Morgan (Haule), MacLaren C, Busby.

Cheltenham T (0) 1 *(Thomas 80)*
Morecambe (0) 0   2066
Cheltenham T: Brown; Lowe, Low, Bird, Gallinagh, Riley, Melligan (Thomas), Pack, Shroot (Elliott), Goulding, Smikle.
Morecambe: Roche; Hunter, Wilson, Stanley, McCready, Parrish, Duffy, Drummond, Jevons, Mullin (Spencer), Brown (Wainwright).

Colchester U (2) 4 *(Bond 7, Mooney 20, 64 (pen), Wilson 54)*
Bradford C (2) 3 *(Hanson 8, 79, Syers 32)*   2736
Colchester U: Williams B; Wilson, Williams T (Tierney), Perkins, Heath, Reid, Bond, Izzet (Wordsworth), Mooney (Henderson L), Odejayi, Vincent.
Bradford C: Pidgeley; Rehman, O'Brien L, Doherty (Evans), Williams, Oliver, Syers, Adeyemi, Hendrie (Chilaka), Hanson, Moult (Price).

Corby T (1) 1 *(Mackey 14)*
Luton T (0) 1 *(Barnes-Homer 83)*   2000
Corby T: MacKenzie; Pitham, Charlton, Hope, Gulliver, Lavery, Hall, Towers, Jarman (Diggin), Mackey (Webster), Walker.
Luton T: Tyler; Gleeson, Murray F, Keane, Asafu-Adjaye, Pilkington G, Walker D (Poku), Howells, Barnes-Homer, Atieno, Gnakpa.

Dagenham & R (1) 1 *(Danny Green 45)*
Leyton Orient (1) 1 *(Revell 45)*   3378
Dagenham & R: Lewington; Ogogo, McCrory, Arber, Antwi, Vincelot, Danny Green, Palsson, Nurse, Savage, Taiwo.
Leyton Orient: Butcher; Omozusi, Smith, Chorley, Forbes, Dawson, Cox, Spring, Tehoue (McGleish), Revell, Daniels.

Darlington (1) 2 *(Brough 14, Smith G 57)*
Bristol R (1) 1 *(Hoskins 17)* 1602
Darlington: Russell; Miller, Brown, Brough, Hone, Moore, Bridge-Wilkinson, Hatch, Wright (Main), Senior (Gray), Smith G.
Bristol R: Green; Regan, Sawyer, Lines, Coles, Anthony, Reece (Swallow), Brown (Richards), Hoskins (Akinde), Osei-Kuffour, Hughes.

Dartford (1) 1 *(Bradbrook 39)*
Port Vale (0) 1 *(McCombe 84)* 3679
Dartford: Young; Burgess, Bonner, Champion, Goodacre, Shinn, Hayes, Harris, Rook (Sheringham), Burns, Bradbrook.
Port Vale: Tomlinson; Yates, Collins (Taylor K), Griffith, McCombe, Owen, Loft, Roberts (Haldane), Dodds, Richards J (Rigg), Fraser.

Fleetwood T (0) 1 *(Mullan 50)*
Walsall (1) 1 *(Richards 4)* 2319
Fleetwood T: Davies; Beeley, Cavanagh, Barry (Horne), McNulty, Gregan, Pond, Craney (Thorpe), Warlow, Seddon, Miles (Mullan).
Walsall: Walker; Westlake, McGivern[■], Taundry, McDonald (Lancashire), Smith, Devaney (Reid), Richards, Dickinson, Macken, Jones (Lescott).

Forest Green R (0) 0
Northampton T (2) 3 *(Johnson 30, Guinan 40, Jacobs 76)* 1479
Forest Green R: Bittner; Hodgkiss, Armstrong, Fowler M (Head), Jones, Quinn, Dyer, Klukowski, Styche, Enver-Marum (Kamara), Turk.
Northampton T: Dunn; Johnson, Davis, Osman, Tozer, Beckwith, Rodgers (Jacobs), Guinan, McKay (Thornton), Holt, Wedderburn.

Gillingham (0) 0
Dover Ath (2) 2 *(Birchall 18, L'Anson 28)* 7475
Gillingham: Julian; Fuller, Nutter[■], Payne J, Lawrence (Payne S), Sinclair, Southall, Palmer (Inkango), Oli (Akinfenwa), McDonald, Spiller.
Dover Ath: Flitney; Fish, Wynter, Tabiri, Schulz (Aisien), Gillman, Baker, L'Anson, Charles (Hunt), Birchall, Long (Wallis).

Guiseley (0) 0
Crawley T (2) 5 *(Tubbs 15, Neilson 36, Hall 56, Brodie 72, Torres 75)* 1609
Guiseley: Drench; Toulson, Merris, Peyton, Ellis, Ainge, Rothery (James), Sharry (Boshell), O'Neill (Stamp), Walshaw, Needham.
Crawley T: Kuipers; Hall, Rents, Bulman, McFadzean, Mills, Neilson, Masterton, McAllister (Cook), Tubbs (Brodie), Howell (Torres).

Harrow Bor (0) 0
Chesterfield (0) 2 *(Boden 74, Davies 90)* 2500
Harrow Bor: Jupp; Frempong, Watts, Walters, Leech, Ijaha, Clarke, McGonigle, Baptiste, Hewitt, Nakashima (Delgardo).
Chesterfield: Lee; Lomax, Robertson, Whitaker, Griffiths, Mattis, Talbot, Allott, Bowery (Davies), Boden (Morgan), Morris (Niven).

Hartlepool U (0) 0
Vauxhall Motors (0) 0 2381
Hartlepool U: Kean; Austin, Horwood, Sweeney, Collins, Hartley, Liddle, Gamble (Bjornsson), McSweeney (Humphreys[■]), Larkin (Poole), Monkhouse.
Vauxhall Motors: Tynan (Ritchie); Noone, Dames, Taylor, Nicholas, Mannix, Mahon (Hannigan), Prince, Anorou, Wilson, Brown.

Havant & Waterlooville (0) 0
Droylsden (0) 2 *(Hardiker 57, Kilheeney 89)* 1102
Havant & Waterlooville: Howe; Hinshelwood (Woodford), McDonald, Selley, Pearce (Sewell), Simpemba, Fogden, Hopkinson, Williams, Tiryaki, Igoe (Sole).
Droylsden: Phillips; Roche, Brownhill, Kerr, Hardiker, Brown, Killeen, Connors (Gardner), Kilheeney, Banim (Rouse), McNiven (Smith).

Hayes & Yeading U (0) 1 *(Holmes 70)*
Wycombe W (0) 2 *(Beavon 61, Ainsworth 90)* 1426
Hayes & Yeading U: Harrison (Bulmer); Cadmore, Brown, Holmes, Bygrave, Webb (Buchanan), Pritchard, Hand, Hyde, Malcolm, Yiadom (Deen).
Wycombe W: Bull; Foster, Sandell, Westwood, Winfield, Montrose, Ainsworth, Davies, Beavon, Strevens (Rendell), Betsy.

Hereford U (4) 5 *(Rose 8, Purdie 21, Manset 39, 44, Fleetwood 90)*
Hythe T (1) 1 *(Micklesborough 26)* 2217
Hereford U: Bartlett; Weir, Werling, Rose, Green, Townsend, Fleetwood, McQuilkin (Featherstone), Manset (Canham), Purdie (Thomas), Colbeck.
Hythe T: Mann; Smith, Walker (Bond), Kingwell, Shearer, Dolan, Cook, Linfield, Byrne (Thompson), Cass, Micklesborough (Conlen).

Lincoln C (0) 1 *(Jarrett 90)*
Nuneaton T (0) 0 3084
Lincoln C: Anyon; Hoyte, Clapham, Watts, Gowling, Howell, Jarrett, Keltie[■], Hutchinson B (Facey), Grimes (Kerr), Carayol (Anderson).
Nuneaton T: Alcock; Armson, Nisevic (Forsdick), Noon, Denn, Pierpoint, Marsden, Walker, Dillon (Spencer), Moore, Hadland (Simmonds).

Macclesfield T (1) 2 *(Daniel 8, Brown 47)*
Southend U (1) 2 *(German 33 (pen), Corr 76)* 1582
Macclesfield T: Veiga; Nsiala, Tremarco, Bolland, Brown (Mukendi), Morgan, Chalmers, Draper, Barnett, Daniel, Bencherif.
Southend U: Morris; Clohessey, Prosser, Simpson, Coughlan, Mohsni, Grant, Easton, German (Hall), Midson, Zaaboub (Corr).

Mansfield T (0) 0
Torquay U (0) 1 *(Benyon 87)* 2179
Mansfield T: Pilkington; Silk (Foster), Stonehouse, Murray, Grand, Cook, Briscoe, Nix (Thompson), Parker, Vincenti (Duffy), Smith A.
Torquay U: Bevan; Robertson, Nicholson, Ellis, Charnock (O'Kane), Wroe, Oastler (Stevens), Mansell, Benyon, Zebroski, Rose (Kee).

Notts Co (1) 2 *(Davies 22 (pen), Rodgers 83)*
Gateshead (0) 0 3235
Notts Co: Burch; Darby, Hunt, Ravenhill, Edwards (Sodje), Chilvers, Spicer (Bishop), Ince (Rodgers), Hughes, Hawley, Davies.
Gateshead: Deasy; Baxter (Fisher), Kay, Gate, Curtis, Clark, Brittain (Marwood), Ferrell (Winn), Mulligan, Shaw, Nelthorpe.

Plymouth Arg (0) 0
Swindon T (2) 4 *(Morrison 23, Austin 41, Pericard 52, Ritchie 69)* 5226
Plymouth Arg: Larrieu; Duguid, Bhasera (Molyneux), Peterlin, Nelson, Seip, Noone, Parrett[■], Fallon (Clark), Wright-Phillips (Mason), Bolasie.
Swindon T: Smith P; Cuthbert, Rose, Ritchie, Lescinel (O'Brien), Morrison, McGovern (Caddis), Timlin, Pericard (Dossevi), Austin, Prutton.

Rotherham U (0) 0
York C (0) 0 3227
Rotherham U: Warrington; Mullins, Newey, Harrison, Cresswell, Fenton, Law, Taylor J, Taylor R, Le Fondre, Marshall.
York C: Ingham; Parslow, Meredith, Smith J, McGurk, Smith C, Lawless, Till (Racchi), Sangare, Rankine, McDermott (Fyfield).

Rushden & D (0) 0
Yeovil T (0) 1 *(Williams A 83)* 1666
Rushden & D: Joe Day; Osano, Jamie Day, Porter, Huke (Miller), Corcoran, Power, O'Connor, Howe, Charles (Farrell), Spence (Robinson).
Yeovil T: Sullivan; Kalala, Jones, Tudor Jones, Huntington, Virgo, Williams A, MacDonald, Williams S, Bowditch, Welsh.

Southampton (0) 2 *(Connolly 89, Lallana 90)*
Shrewsbury T (0) 0 10,410
Southampton: Davis; Richardson, Harding, Chaplow, Jaidi, Seaborne, Oxlade-Chamberlain (Lambert), Hammond, Do Prado (Holmes), Barnard (Connolly), Lallana.
Shrewsbury T: Neal C; Holden, Sadler, McAllister, Geohaghon, Cansdell-Sherriff, Obadeyi (Ainsworth), Disley, Wright, Robinson (Harrold), McIntyre.

Stevenage (0) 0
Milton Keynes D (0) 0 2956
Stevenage: Day; Henry, Laird, Bostwick, Roberts, Ashton, Wilson (Sinclair), Mousinho, Long (Odubade), May (Dixon), O'Shea.
Milton Keynes D: Martin D; Gleeson, Lewington, Carrington, Woodards, Doumbe, Chadwick, Leven, Guy (Johnson), Baldock S, Balanta.

Stockport Co (1) 1 *(Griffin 20)*
Peterborough U (1) 1 *(McLean 28)* 2001
Stockport Co: Glennon; Lynch, Williams R, Turnbull, Rose, Assoumani, Poole (Darkwah), Pulis, Fletcher (Conlon), Donnelly, Griffin.
Peterborough U: Lewis; Little, Ofori-Twumasi, McCann (Mendez-Laing), Bennett, Langmead, Wesolowski, Davies, Mackail-Smith, McLean (Hibbert), Tomlin.

Swindon Supermarine (2) 2 *(Holgate 16, Wells 27)*
Eastwood T (0) 1 *(Stevenson 47)* 2603
Swindon Supermarine: Scott; Lapham, Robinson, Allen C, Henry, Bampton (Horgan), Wells, Gosling (Allen D), Holgate, Taylor, Stanley.
Eastwood T: Danby; Markell Bailey (Mat Bailey), Riley (Todd), Simpson, Haggerty, Cooke, D'Laryea (Rhead), Stevenson, Muller, Meikle, Duncum.

Tamworth (1) 2 *(Rodman 15, Thomas 55)*
Crewe Alex (0) 1 *(Ashley R Westwood 88)* 1776
Tamworth: Severn; Tait, Barrow, Oakes (Wilkinson), Wylde, Mitchell, Bradley D, MacKenzie, Perry (Lake-Gaskin), Rodman (Marshall), Thomas.
Crewe Alex: Taylor; Tootle, Mitchel-King (Blanchett), Ashley R Westwood, Artell, Ada, Bell, Murphy, Moore (Powell), Donaldson, Grant (Leitch-Smith).

Sunday, 7 November 2010
Burton Alb (0) 1 *(Webster 85)*
Oxford U (0) 0 2483
Burton Alb: Legzdins; Austin, Malone, Stanton, James, McGrath (Webster), Penn, Bolder, Harrad, Collins (Gilroy), Maghoma.
Oxford U: Clarke; Purkiss (Hall), Kinniburgh (Potter), Payne, Worley, Creighton, Batt, Clist (Deering), Green, Craddock, Tonkin.

Southport (0) 2 *(Barratt 52, McGinn 58)*
Sheffield W (1) 5 *(Teale 11, Mellor 54, Morrison C 61, 62, Spurr 64)* 4490
Southport: Dickinson; Williams, Lever, Flynn, Davis, Lee (Powell), Barratt, Moogan, McNeil, Simm (Gray T), Blakeman (McGinn).
Sheffield W: Weaver; Otsemobor, Spurr, Miller (Tudgay), Beevers, Purse, O'Connor, Coke, Morrison C (Heffernan), Mellor (Sedgwick), Teale.

FIRST ROUND REPLAYS

Tuesday, 16 November 2010
Aldershot T (1) 1 *(Small 8)*
Brentford (0) 0 3627
Aldershot T: Young; Herd, Vincent, Guttridge, Jones, Morris, McGlashan, Straker, Small (Hylton), Little (Harding), Morgan.
Brentford: Lee; Wright, Woodman, O'Connor, Legge, Spillane, Saunders (Forster), Diagouraga, Simpson, MacDonald, Wood (Weston).

Charlton Ath (1) 1 *(Reid 18)*
Barnet (0) 0 4803
Charlton Ath: Elliot; Francis, Fry, Racon, Fortune (Doherty), Dailly, Wagstaff (Benson), McCormack, Abbott (Sodje), Reid, Jackson.
Barnet: Cole; Devera, Basey, Southam, Uddin, Hughes, Francomb, Marshall, Kabba (Stimson), Gallen (McLeod), Jarvis (Holmes).

Huddersfield T (0) 2 *(Peltier 89, Roberts 90)*
Cambridge U (0) 1 *(McAuley 53)* 3766
Huddersfield T: Bennett; Peltier, Ridehalgh, Carey (Gudjonsson), Clarke P, Kay (McCombe), Johnson, Arfield, Lee (Rhodes), Afobe, Roberts.
Cambridge U: Naisbitt; Roberts, Jennings, McAuley, Partridge, Coulson, Russell, Carden, Wright, Gray, Willmott.

Leyton Orient (2) 3 *(McGleish 2, 76, Revell 24)*
Dagenham & R (0) 2 *(Danny Green 67 (pen), Taiwo 68)* 2901
Leyton Orient: Butcher; Omozusi, Daniels, Smith, Chorley, Forbes, M'Poku (Walker), Spring, McGleish, Revell (Tehoue), Cox.
Dagenham & R: Lewington; Ogogo, McCrory (Currie), Arber, Antwi, Vincelot, Danny Green, Taiwo, Nurse (Tomlin), Savage, Gain (Scannell).

Milton Keynes D (0) 1 *(Guy 49)*
Stevenage (0) 1 *(Charles 90)* 3977
Milton Keynes D: Martin; Woodards (O'Hanlon), Lewington, Carrington, MacKenzie, Doumbe, Gleeson, Leven, Guy (Chadwick), Baldock S, Johnson (Powell).
Stevenage: Day; Wilson, Laird, Bostwick, Roberts, Ashton, Long, Mousinho, May (Griffin), Beardsley (Charles), Bridges (Odubade).
aet; Stevenage won 7-6 on penalties.

Peterborough U (1) 4 *(Langmead 24, Mackail-Smith 47, Tomlin 56, McLean 90)*
Stockport Co (0) 1 *(Tansey 72)* 2312
Peterborough U: Lewis; Little, Bennett, McCann, Zakuani, Langmead, Davies, Tomlin (Mendez-Laing), Mackail-Smith (Hibbert) (Wesolowski), McLean, Boyd.
Stockport Co: Glennon; Lynch, Williams R, Turnbull, Rose, Assoumani, Poole, Pulis (Tansey), Fletcher (Salem), Donnelly, Griffin (Simpson).

Port Vale (2) 4 *(Richards M 17 (pen), 26, Richards J 72, Rigg 57)*
Dartford (0) 0 3590
Port Vale: Tomlinson; Yates, Taylor K, Roberts (Fraser), McCombe, Owen, Rigg (Dodds), Taylor R (Haldane), Richards M, Richards J, Loft.
Dartford: Young; Bruce, Bonner, Champion, Goodacre, Shinn, Hayes (Noble), Harris (White), Rook (Sheringham), Burns, Bradbrook.

Southend U (0) 2 *(Simpson 87, Corr 105)*
Macclesfield T (0) 2 *(Sinclair 61, Nsiala 99)* 2194
Southend U: Morris; Clohessy, Gilbert, Simpson, Prosser (German), Mohsni, Grant, Easton, Corr, Midson (Sturrock), Zaaboub (Hall).
Macclesfield T: Veiga; Nsiala, Reid, Bolland (Draper), Brown, Morgan, Chalmers, Daniel, Sinclair (Mukendi), Barnett, Bencherif.
aet; Macclesfield T won 5-3 on penalties.

Vauxhall Motors (0) 0
Hartlepool U (0) 1 *(Brown 70)* 2406
Vauxhall Motors: Ritchie; Noone, Dames, Taylor, Nicholas, Mannix, Mahon (Grice), Prince (Hannigan), Anorou, Wilson, Brown.
Hartlepool U: Kean; Austin, Horwood, Sweeney, Collins, Hartley, Poole (Brown), Liddle, McSweeney, Bjornsson (Gamble), Monkhouse.

Walsall (0) 2 *(Reid 58, 90)*
Fleetwood T (0) 0 2056
Walsall: Walker; Westlake, Lescott, Taundry,'Lancashire, Smith, Marshall, Richards, Reid, Dickinson, Nicholls.
Fleetwood T: Davies; Beeley, Cavanagh, Barry, McNulty, Linwood, McGuire, Clancy (Mullan), Thorpe, Seddon, Miles.

Woking (0) 2 *(Greer 72 (og), Sagbanmu 103)*
Brighton & HA (0) 2 *(Sparrow 57, Bennett 105)* 4193
Woking: Little; Anane, Aswad, Ricketts, McNerney, Doyle, Ademola (Faulconbridge), Maledon, Hammond, Quarm (Turnbull), Federico (Sagbanmu).
Brighton & HA: Brezovan; Calderon, Taricco■, Kishishev (Battipiedi), Elphick, Greer, Sparrow, Dicker, Barnes (Murray), Hart (Baz), Bennett.
aet; Brighton & HA won 3-0 on penalties.

Wednesday, 17 November 2010

Luton T (2) 4 *(Barnes-Homer 5, Atieno 29, 62, Gnakpa 81)*
Corby T (0) 2 *(Walker 84, Hope 86)* 3050
Luton T: Tyler; Gleeson, Murray F (O'Donnell), Keane, Asafu-Adjaye, Pilkington G, Drury (Poku), Howells, Barnes-Homer (Walker D), Atieno, Gnakpa.
Corby T: MacKenzie; Pitham, Charlton (Dolman), Hope, Gulliver, Lavery (Green), Hall (Diggin), Towers, Jarman■, Mackey, Walker.

York C (0) 3 *(Smith C 66, Rankine 71 (pen), 79)*
Rotherham U (0) 0 2644
York C: Ingham; Parslow, Meredith, Smith J (Mackin), McGurk, Smith C, McDermott (Barrett), Sangare, Racchi, Rankine, Carruthers (Fyfield).
Rotherham U: Annerson; Mullins, Newey, Bradley, Ashworth, Fenton, Law, Marshall, Taylor R, Le Fondre, Brogan (Ellison).

Thursday, 18 November 2010

Ebbsfleet U (2) 2 *(Carew 12 (pen), 18)*
AFC Wimbledon (1) 3 *(Nwokeji 9, Moore S 90, 120)* 2306
Ebbsfleet U: Edwards; Stone, Duncan, Carew (Howe), Easton, Lorraine, West (Williams), Marwa, Willock, Shakes (Ginty), Phipp.
AFC Wimbledon: Brown; Jackson, Blackman (Wellard), Gregory, Yakubu, Franks (Johnson), Moore S, Yussuff, Kedwell, Nwokeji (Moore L), Hatton.
aet.

SECOND ROUND

Friday, 26 November 2010

Crawley T (0) 1 *(Tubbs 76)*
Swindon T (0) 1 *(Austin 66)* 3895
Crawley T: Kuipers; Wilson, Howell, Masterton (Smith B), McFadzean, Mills, Neilson (Bell-Baggie), Bulman, Tubbs, Brodie (McAllister), Torres.

Swindon T: Smith P; Caddis, Rose (Sheehan), Ritchie, Cuthbert, Morrison, McGovern (Ferry), Timlin, Pericard (Dossevi), Austin, Prutton.

Port Vale (1) 1 *(Richards J 24)*
Accrington S (0) 0 4016
Port Vale: Tomlinson; Yates, Taylor K, Roberts, McCombe, Owen, Rigg (Haldane), Taylor R (Dodds), Richards M, Richards J (Fraser), Loft.
Accrington S: Dunbavin; Edwards, Winnard, Hessey (Richardson), Long, Procter, Parkinson (Turner), Barnett, Jacobson, Gornell, Putterill (Boulding).

Saturday, 27 November 2010

AFC Wimbledon (0) 0
Stevenage (1) 2 *(Walker 24, Odubade 81)* 3633
AFC Wimbledon: Brown; Hatton, Bush, Gregory, Yakubu, Harris■, Moore S, Wellard (Main), Kedwell, Jolley (Yussuff), Moore L.
Stevenage: Day; Wilson, Laird, Roberts, Henry, Ashton (Odubade), Bostwick, Mousinho, Beardsley (Dixon), O'Shea (Bridges), Walker.

Brighton & HA (0) 1 *(Taricco 83)*
FC United of Manchester (1) 1 *(Platt 40)* 5362
Brighton & HA: Brezovan; Taricco, Painter, Kishishev (Battipedi), Bridcutt, Elphick, Dunk, Baz (Hart), Barnes, Murray (Sandaza), Bennett.
FC United of Manchester: Ashton; Jacobs (Holden), Ovington (Wolfenden), Platt, Munroe, McManus■, Roca, Cotterill, Norton, Wright, Deegan (Parker).

Burton Alb (2) 3 *(Webster 12, Maghoma 22, Collins 90)*
Chesterfield (0) 1 *(Bowery 90)* 3881
Burton Alb: Legzdins; Corbett, Malone, Stanton, Moore, McGrath, Penn, Bolder, Webster, Collins, Maghoma (Phillips).
Chesterfield: Lee; Gray (Breckin), Robertson, Smalley (Darikwa), Ford, Mattis, Talbot, Allott, Davies (Bowery), Lester, Whitaker.

Bury (0) 1 *(Lowe 51)*
Peterborough U (2) 2 *(Tomlin 13, Mackail-Smith 38)* 2514
Bury: fon Williams; Picken (Worrall), Skarz, Lees, Sodje, Sweeney (John Lewis), Jones M, Wallace, Lowe, Ajose, Haworth (Carlton).
Peterborough U: Lewis; Bennett, Rowe, McCann (Davies), Zakuani, Langmead, Wesolowski, Tomlin, Mackail-Smith, McLean (Little), Boyd.

Carlisle U (0) 3 *(Madine 50, Zoko 86, Chester 90)*
Tamworth (1) 2 *(Marshall 30, Thomas 75)* 3599
Carlisle U: Collin; Simek, Comminges (Thirlwell), Eastham, Chester, Taiwo (Curran), Marshall, Berrett, Zoko, Madine, Robson (Cruise).
Tamworth: Atkins; Tait (Bojang), Marshall, Oakes (Lake-Gaskin), Wylde, Barrow, Smith, Bradley D, Perry, Rodman (Sheridan), Thomas.

Charlton Ath (2) 2 *(Anyinsah 6, Jackson 34)*
Luton T (1) 2 *(Drury 30, 83)* 8682
Charlton Ath: Elliot; Francis, Jackson, Racon, Llera, Fortune, Wagstaff, McCormack, Anyinsah (Sodje), Benson, Reid.
Luton T: Tyler; Gleeson, Howells, Keane, Kroca, Pilkington G, Drury, Morgan-Smith (Walker D), Barnes-Homer, Crowe (Atieno), Gnakpa.

Colchester U (1) 1 *(Mooney 21)*
Swindon Supermarine (0) 0 3047
Colchester U: Williams B; Wilson, Williams T, Perkins, Baldwin, Reid, Mooney, Izzet, Odejayi (Henderson L), Henderson I (Wordsworth), Vincent.
Swindon Supermarine: Puddy; Lapham, Robinson, Allen C (Hopper), Henry, Bampton, Wells (Morris), Gosling (Cook), Holgate, Taylor, Stanley.

Darlington (0) 0
York C (1) 2 *(Sangare 44, Chambers 90)*   2500
Darlington: Russell; Miller, Brown, Brough, Hone, Hatch, Verma, Bridge-Wilkinson, Wright (Arnison), Senior, Gillespie (Moore).
York C: Ingham; Smith J (Barrett), Meredith, Smith C, McGurk, Sangare, Racchi, Till (Fyfield), Rankine (Constantine), Chambers, Weir.

Dover Ath (0) 2 *(Birchall 54, 90 (pen))*
Aldershot T (0) 0   4123
Dover Ath: Flitney; Fish, Wynter, Wallis (Long), Schulz, Gillman, Baker, L'Anson, Hunt (Tabiri), Birchall, Cogan.
Aldershot T: Young; Herd, Vincent (McGlashan), Panther, Jones, Fortune, Little (Ngo Baheng), Guttridge, Small, Straker, Morgan (Hylton).

Hereford U (1) 2 *(Purdie 23, Manset 86 (pen))*
Lincoln C (2) 2 *(Grimes 19, Carayol 27)*   1803
Hereford U: Bartlett; Purdie, Heath, Lunt (Bauza), Townsend, Rose, Gwynne, Featherstone, Fleetwood, Canham (Manset), Colbeck (Lund).
Lincoln C: Anyon; Hoyte, Anderson, Watts, Gowling, O'Keefe, Carayol, Jarrett, Hutchinson B, Grimes (Broughton), Kerr.

Huddersfield T (3) 6 *(Rhodes 19, Pilkington 35, Afobe 45, McCombe 49, Kay 53, Roberts 73)*
Macclesfield T (0) 0   4924
Huddersfield T: Smithies; Peltier, Carey, McCombe, Clarke P, Kay, Pilkington (Arfield), Johnson (Atkinson), Rhodes (Lee), Afobe, Roberts.
Macclesfield T: Veiga; Reid (Hamshaw), Nsiala, Bolland, Brown, Morgan, Chalmers, Draper, Sinclair, Barnett (Tremarco), Daniel (Mukendi).

Sheffield W (2) 3 *(Beevers 6, Miller 37 (pen), 89 (pen))*
Northampton T (0) 2 *(McKay 56, Thornton 90)*   8932
Sheffield W: Weaver; Jones D, Spurr, Potter, Beevers, Purse, Sedgwick (Johnson J), Miller, Morrison C, Mellor, Teale (Coke).
Northampton T: Dunn; Rodgers, Davis, Wedderburn (Thornton), Tozer, Beckwith, Gilligan (Jacobs), Osman, King, McKay (Jarvis), Holt.

Southampton (1) 3 *(Lallana 8, Do Prado 50, Gobern 87)*
Cheltenham T (0) 0   9276
Southampton: Bialkowski; Richardson (Butterfield), Dickson, Gobern, Jaidi, Fonte, Holmes (Oxlade-Chamberlain), Hammond, Do Prado, Lambert (Harding), Lallana.
Cheltenham T: Brown; Lowe, Andrew, Bird (Pook), Gallinagh, Riley, Low, Pack, Shroot (Thomas), Goulding (Jeffers), Smikle.

Torquay U (1) 1 *(Kee 41 (pen))*
Walsall (0) 0   2334
Torquay U: Bevan; Mansell, Nicholson, Ellis, Branston, Wroe, Oastler, O'Kane (Robertson), Kee (Gritton), Hemmings (Stevens), Zebroski.
Walsall: Walker; Westlake, Lescott, Taundry, Lancashire, Butler, Marshall (Gray), Richards, Dickinson (Jones), Grigg, Nicholls.

Wycombe W (1) 3 *(Rendell 22, 73, Beavon 84)*
Chelmsford C (0) 1 *(Higgins 59)*   3205
Wycombe W: Bull; Westwood, Sandell, Lewis (Montrose), Winfield, Johnson, Ainsworth (Strevens), Bloomfield, Beavon, Rendell (Harris), Betsy.
Chelmsford C: Pullen; Nunn, Coker, Haines, El-Abd, Rainford, Lock (Bricknell), Martin (Mulley), Higgins (Green), Cook, Modeste.

Monday, 29 November 2010
Droylsden (1) 1 *(Kilheeney 24)*
Leyton Orient (0) 1 *(McGleish 73)*   1762
Droylsden: Phillips; Roche, Brownhill, Kerr, Hardiker, Brown (Gardner), Killeen, Connors, Kilheeney, Banim (McNiven), Holden (Rouse).
Leyton Orient: Brown J; Brown A, Daniels, Smith, Chorley, Forbes, M'Poku (Dawson), Spring, McGleish, Revell (Tehoue), Cox.

Tuesday, 14 December 2010
Hartlepool U (2) 4 *(Sweeney 35, 40, 59, Humphreys 49)*
Yeovil T (2) 2 *(Williams A 18, Upson 31)*   1914
Hartlepool U: Kean; Austin, Horwood, Liddle, Collins, Hartley, Gamble (Haslam), Sweeney, McSweeney (Yantorno), Humphreys (Boyd), Monkhouse.
Yeovil T: Sullivan; Alcock, Jones, MacDonald (Calver), Parkes, Upson, Williams A, Kalala, Bowditch (Gibson), Ayling, Welsh (Williams S).

Notts Co (3) 3 *(Pearce 18, Hughes 35, Cummings 45 (og))*
Bournemouth (0) 1 *(Fletcher 84)*   2881
Notts Co: Burch; Darby, Harley, Ravenhill (Woods), Edwards, Pearce, Westcarr, Bishop, Hughes (Miller), Ince (Hunt), Davies.
Bournemouth: Stewart; Purches (Smith), Wiggins, Cummings (Bradbury), Pearce, Bartley, Hollands, Robinson, Taylor, Pugh (Fletcher), Feeney.

SECOND ROUND REPLAYS

Tuesday, 7 December 2010
Leyton Orient (0) 8 *(Chorley 77 (pen), Tehoue 89, 99, 107, M'Poku 93, McGleish 97, 108, 119)*
Droylsden (1) 2 *(Kilheeney 6, Brown 54)*   1345
Leyton Orient: Brown J; Omozusi, Daniels, Dawson, Chorley■, Forbes■, Smith (Tehoue), Spring, McGleish, Revell (Brown A), M'Poku (Walker).
Droylsden: Phillips; Roche■, Brownhill, Kerr■, Hardiker, Brown (Byron), Killeen (Cryan), Gardner, Kilheeney, Banim, McNiven (Rouse).
aet.

Swindon T (2) 2 *(McGovern 18, Austin 41)*
Crawley T (1) 3 *(Smith B 16, 118, Smith P 69 (og))*   2955
Swindon T: Smith P; Amankwaah, Rose, Douglas■, Cuthbert, Morrison, McGovern, Ritchie (Sheehan), Pericard (Timlin), Austin (Dossevi), Prutton.
Crawley T: Kuipers; Wilson, Howell, Bulman, McFadzean, Mills, Neilson (Cook), Smith B, McAllister (Brodie), Tubbs, Torres.
aet.

Wednesday, 8 December 2010
FC United of Manchester (0) 0
Brighton & HA (2) 4 *(Sandaza 25, Calderon 45, Bennett 86, Sparrow 90)*   7000
FC United of Manchester: Ashton; Jacobs (Battersby), Quistin (Carden), Platt, Munroe, Parker, Roca, Cotterill, Norton, Ovington (Wolfenden), Deegan.
Brighton & HA: Brezovan; Calderon, Painter, Kishishev (Smith), Greer, El-Abd, Sparrow, Bridcutt, Sandaza, Murray (Hart), Bennett (Baz).
Played at Bury.

Thursday, 9 December 2010
Luton T (1) 1 *(Kroca 38)*
Charlton Ath (1) 3 *(Wagstaff 44, Anyinsah 66, Jackson 80)*   5914
Luton T: Tyler; Gleeson, Howells, Keane, Kroca, Pilkington G, Drury, Morgan-Smith (Poku), Barnes-Homer, Crow (Atieno), Gnakpa.
Charlton Ath: Elliot; Francis, Fry, Racon (McCormack), Doherty, Fortune, Wagstaff, Semedo, Anyinsah (Sodje), Benson (Abbott), Jackson.

Saturday, 8 January 2011
Lincoln C (2) 3 *(Clapham 6, Facey 24, Grimes 48)*
Hereford U (3) 4 *(Manset 4, 72, Fleetwood 36, 43)* 1794
Lincoln C: Anyon; Hughton, Clapham, Green, Swaibu, Howell, Jarrett, Hoyte (Kerr), Facey, Grimes, Carayol (Hutchinson B).
Hereford U: Bartlett; Green■, Heath, Kovacs, Townsend, Rose, Fleetwood, McQuilken, Manset (Bauza), Lunt, Featherstone.

THIRD ROUND

Saturday, 8 January 2011
Arsenal (0) 1 *(Fabregas 90 (pen))*
Leeds U (0) 1 *(Snodgrass 54 (pen))* 59,520
Arsenal: Szczesny; Eboue, Gibbs, Denilson, Squillaci, Djourou, Song Billong (Fabregas), Bendtner, Chamakh (Walcott), Arshavin, Rosicky (Vela).
Leeds U: Schmeichel; Connolly, Parker, Howson, Bruce, O'Brien, Johnson, Watt (Bromby), Gradel (Hughes), Becchio (Somma), Snodgrass.

Blackburn R (0) 1 *(Hoilett 77)*
QPR (0) 0 10,284
Blackburn R: Bunn; Salgado (Linganzi), Givet (Morris), Lowe, Nelsen, Hanley, Biram Diouf, Hoilett, Mwaruwari (Roberts), E-H Diouf, Pedersen.
QPR: Kenny; Orr, Borrowdale, Derry, Hill, Gorkss, Clarke, Mackie (Andrade), Hulse (Doughty), Vaagan Moen, Faurlin (Cook).

Bolton W (0) 2 *(Davies K 83, Elmander 89)*
York C (0) 0 13,120
Bolton W: Bogdan; Ricketts, Alonso, Davies M, Knight, Cahill, Moreno, Cohen (Taylor), Klasnic (Davies K), Blake (Elmander), Petrov.
York C: Ingham; Parslow, Meredith (Racchi), Smith J, McGurk, Smith C, Weir, Barrett (Reed), Rankine, Chambers (Till), Carruthers.

Brighton & HA (2) 3 *(Wood 26, Barnes 45 (pen), Sandaza 90)*
Portsmouth (0) 1 *(Kilbey 88)* 7792
Brighton & HA: Brezovan; Taricco (Bridcutt), Painter, Kishishev, Elphick, El-Abd, Sparrow, Barnes, Wood (Sandaza), Murray (Holroyd), Bennett.
Portsmouth: Ashdown; Ward, Dickinson, Mokoena, Sonko, Mullins, Lawrence (Kilbey), Utaka, Kitson■, Nugent (Ciftci), Kanu (Hreidarsson).

Bristol C (0) 0
Sheffield W (0) 3 *(Teale 49, Mellor 55, Morrison C 65)* 11,378
Bristol C: James; Skuse, Nyatanga, Cisse, Caulker (Fontaine), Johnson (Ribeiro) (Clarkson), Elliott, Adomah, Pitman, Stead, Campbell-Ryce.
Sheffield W: Weaver; Johnson R, Jones D, Miller, Morrison M, Purse, Sedgwick, O'Connor, Morrison C, Mellor, Teale.

Burnley (2) 4 *(Carlisle 4, Mears 21, Eagles 50, Alexander 76 (pen))*
Port Vale (1) 2 *(Taylor R 15, 82)* 9442
Burnley: Grant; Mears, Fox, Carlisle, Duff (Bikey), Cork, Elliott (Marney), Alexander, Iwelumo (Thompson), Rodriguez, Eagles.
Port Vale: Tomlinson; Yates, Collins, Griffith, McCombe, Owen, Dodds (Morsy), Roberts, Haldane (Rigg), Richards J (Fraser), Taylor R.

Burton Alb (0) 2 *(Harrad 82, 90)*
Middlesbrough (0) 1 *(O'Neil 58)* 5236
Burton Alb: Legzdins; Austin, Malone, Stanton (James), Moore (Phillips), McGrath (Pearson), Penn, Bolder, Webster, Harrad, Maghoma.
Middlesbrough: Coyne; McMahon, Bennett, Bailey, Bates, Hines, Hoyte, O'Neil, Lita, Boyd (Franks), Arca.

Coventry C (2) 2 *(Eastwood 15, Baker 17)*
Crystal Palace (0) 1 *(Danns 81)* 8162
Coventry C: Westwood; Keogh, O'Halloran, Doyle M, Cranie, Wood, Baker, Gunnarsson, Jutkiewicz (Platt), Eastwood (O'Donovan), McSheffrey (Thomas).
Crystal Palace: Speroni; Clyne, Wright, Gardner, McCarthy, Garvan, Danns, Cadogan (Zaha), Iversen, N'Diaye (Counago), Dorman (Andrew).

Doncaster R (2) 2 *(Sharp 41, Hayter 43)*
Wolverhampton W (1) 2 *(Milijas 38, Hunt 58 (pen))* 8616
Doncaster R: Sullivan; Chambers (Friend), Mills, O'Connor, Lockwood, Hird, Coppinger, Wilson, Hayter (Brooker), Sharp, Oster.
Wolverhampton W: Hahnemann; Doherty, Elokobi■, Edwards (Jones), Berra, Stearman, Jarvis, Milijas, Fletcher (Doyle), Hunt, Ward.

Fulham (2) 6 *(Kamara 32, 59, 76, Etuhu 45, Gera 66, Greening 89)*
Peterborough U (0) 2 *(Tomlin 71, McCann 86 (pen))* 15,936
Fulham: Stockdale; Pantsil, Baird, Murphy, Hughes, Hangeland (Halliche), Duff, Etuhu, Dempsey (Greening), Kamara, Davies (Gera).
Peterborough U: Lewis; Little, Rowe, McCann, Zakuani, Langmead, Whelpdale (Mendez-Laing), Clayton (Agard), Mackail-Smith, Tomlin, Davies (Obika).

Huddersfield T (2) 2 *(Arfield 7, Roberts 8)*
Dover Ath (0) 0 7894
Huddersfield T: Smithies; Peltier, Ridehalgh, Arfield (Clarke T), Clarke P, Kay, Pilkington, Kilbane, Rhodes (Lee), Novak, Roberts (Carey).
Dover Ath: Flitney; Fish, Wynter, Cutler (Wallis), Schulz, Gillman, Baker, L'Anson, Hunt, Birchall, Cogan (Long).

Hull C (0) 2 *(Barmby 74, 89)*
Wigan Ath (1) 3 *(Diame 21, 77, McManaman 56)* 10,433
Hull C: Duke; Solano, Dawson, Ashbee, Gerrard, Zayatte, Bullard (Barmby), Harper, Simpson (Koren), Fryatt, Stewart (Devitt).
Wigan Ath: Al Habsi; Lopez (Robinson), De Ridder, Diame, Caldwell S, Boyce, McArthur (Redmond), Thomas, McManaman, Gomez, Figueroa (Mustoe).

Millwall (0) 1 *(Schofield 90)*
Birmingham C (3) 4 *(Derbyshire 17, 45, Murphy 27, Jerome 72)* 9841
Millwall: Forde; Smith, Craig (Schofield), Mkandawire, Robinson P, Shittu (Ward), Henry, Abdou, Morison, Harris (Lisbie), Barron.
Birmingham C: Taylor; Parnaby, Murphy, Mutch, Dann, Jiranek, Hleb (Fahey), Gardner, Derbyshire (Phillips), Zigic (Jerome), Beausejour.

Norwich C (0) 0
Leyton Orient (1) 1 *(Smith 20)* 18,087
Norwich C: Rudd; Martin R, Drury (Holt), Smith K, Barnett, Whitbread, McNamee, Fox, Martin C (Jackson), Wilbraham (Lappin), Hoolahan.
Leyton Orient: Jones; Omozusi (Whing), Daniels, Chorley, Forbes, Dawson, Smith, Spring, Tehoue (McGleish), Revell, Cox (M'Poku).

Preston NE (1) 1 *(Carter 35)*
Nottingham F (0) 2 *(Anderson 50, Chambers 89)* 9636
Preston NE: Lonergan; McLaughlin, Jones, Nicholson (Douglas), Morgan, St Ledger-Hall, Mayor, Russell, Brown C (Hayes), Carter, Treacy (Coutts).
Nottingham F: Camp; Gunter, Lynch, Moussi, Morgan, Chambers, Anderson (McCleary), McGugan, Earnshaw (Tyson), McGoldrick (Adebola), Cohen.

Reading (1) 1 *(Long 41)*
WBA (0) 0 13,005
Reading: Federici; Cummings, Harte, Karacan, Mills, Pearce, Kebe, Leigertwood, Long (Church), Hunt (Robson-Kanu), McAnuff.
WBA: Myhill; Hurst, Cech, Jara, Zuiverloon, Scharner (Olsson■), Barnes (Thomas), Morrison, Miller (Bednar), Brunt, Dorrans.

Scunthorpe U (0) 1 *(Collins 46)*
Everton (2) 5 *(Saha 4, Beckford 33, Coleman 58,*
Fellaini 73, Baines 83) 7028
Scunthorpe U: Murphy; Wright A, Nolan, O'Connor,
Mirfin, Jones (Raynes), Wright J (Togwell), Collins,
Dagnall (Godden), Forte, Woolford.
Everton: Howard; Hibbert, Baines, Osman, Distin,
Heitinga, Coleman (Gueye), Fellaini (Rodwell), Saha
(Anichebe), Beckford, Bilyaletdinov.

Sheffield U (0) 1 *(Ward 48 (pen))*
Aston Villa (2) 3 *(Walker 9, Albrighton 33, Petrov 90)*
16,888
Sheffield U: Simonsen; Parrino (Slew), Kozluk,
Montgomery, Bartley, Ertl, Williamson (McAllister),
Britton, Evans, Bogdanovic, Ward.
Aston Villa: Friedel; Walker, Clark, Cuellar, Dunne,
Reo-Coker (Collins JM), Albrighton, Pires (Downing),
Agbonlahor, Young A[■], Bannan (Petrov).

Southampton (0) 2 *(Barnard 53, Do Prado 88)*
Blackpool (0) 0 21,464
Southampton: Bialkowski; Richardson, Harding,
Schneiderlin, Martin, Seaborne, Lallana (Do Prado),
Hammond (Dickson), Barnard (Oxlade-Chamberlain),
Lambert, Puncheon.
Blackpool: Rachubka; Eardley (Francis-Reynolds), John
Baptiste, Southern, Edwards, Keinan, Tomsett
(Barkhuizen), Sylvestre, Ormerod (Roberts), Euell,
Phillips.

Stevenage (0) 3 *(Williamson 50 (og), Bostwick 55,*
Winn 90)
Newcastle U (0) 1 *(Barton 90)* 6644
Stevenage: Day; Henry (Bridges), Laird, Roberts,
Ashton, Bostwick, Long, Mousinho, Wilson, Beardsley,
Winn (Odubade).
Newcastle U: Krul; Perch, Simpson, Nolan, Coloccini,
Williamson, Barton, Smlth (Tiote[■]), Best (Ranger),
Lovenkrands (Airey), Routledge.

Stoke C (1) 1 *(Tuncay 45)*
Cardiff C (1) 1 *(Chopra 8)* 18,629
Stoke C: Sorensen; Shotton, Higginbotham (Delap),
Whelan, Shawcross, Huth, Pennant (Etherington),
Wilson, Fuller, Walters (Jones), Tuncay.
Cardiff C: Marshall; McNaughton, Naylor, Rae, Hudson,
Quinn, Whittingham, McPhail, Keogh (Blake), Chopra,
Burke (Matthews).

Sunderland (0) 1 *(Bent 81 (pen))*
Notts Co (1) 2 *(Westcarr 5, Hughes 75)* 17,582
Sunderland: Mignolet; Angeleri (Bardsley), Richardson,
Riveros (Elmohamady), Da Silva, Ferdinand,
Malbranque, Reid, Gyan, Bent, Colback (Henderson).
Notts Co: Nelson; Thompson, Harley, Ravenhill,
Edwards, Pearce, Judge (Hunt), Bishop, Hughes
(Woods), Westcarr (Hawley), Davies.

Swansea C (2) 4 *(Monk 25, Pratley 35, Van der Gun 68,*
Sinclair 82)
Colchester U (0) 0 7005
Swansea C: Ma-Kalambay; Alfei, Richards, Allen, Monk
(Serran), Williams, Gower (Agustien), Pratley, Moore
(Easter), Van der Gun, Sinclair.
Colchester U: Williams B; Beevers, Heath, Perkins,
White, Reid, Bond (Hackney), Izzet (Odejayi), Mooney,
Wordsworth, Henderson I (James).

Torquay U (1) 1 *(O'Kane 6)*
Carlisle U (0) 0 3005
Torquay U: Bevan; Robertson, Nicholson, Ellis,
Branston, Wroe, Mansell, O'Kane (Oastler), Benyon
(Kee), Zebroski, Stevens (Hemmings).
Carlisle U: Collin; Simek, Robson (Hurst), Thirlwell,
Cruise (Gbarssin), Murphy, Taiwo (Curran), Berrett,
Zoko, Madine, Marshall.

Watford (0) 4 *(Mingoia 66, Sordell 68, 82, Graham 90)*
Hartlepool U (1) 1 *(Sweeney 45)* 8950
Watford: Gilmartin; Mariappa, Doyley, Whichelow,
Taylor M, Bennett, Deeney (Graham), Mingoia, Sordell
(Massey), Jenkins, Buckley (McGinn).
Hartlepool U: Kean; Austin, Horwood, Gamble, Liddle,
Hartley, Sweeney, Murray (Yantorno), McSweeney
(Larkin), Humphreys (Brown), Monkhouse.

West Ham U (1) 2 *(Spector 29, Piquionne 90)*
Barnsley (0) 0 32,159
West Ham U: Green; Faubert, Reid, Noble, Tomkins,
Spector, Barrera, Hines (Edgar), Nouble (Piquionne),
Obinna (Parker), Boa Morte.
Barnsley: Steele; Hassell, Hill, Shackell, Foster, Doyle,
Trippier (O'Brien), Arismendi (Colace), Lovre
(Butterfield), O'Connor, Hammill.

Sunday, 9 January 2011

Chelsea (3) 7 *(Kalou 32, Sturridge 33, 52, Edwards 41 (og),*
Anelka 49, Lampard 78, 79)
Ipswich T (0) 0 41,654
Chelsea: Cech; Bosingwa, Van Aanholt (Bruma),
McEachran, Terry, Ivanovic, Ramires, Lampard, Anelka,
Sturridge, Kalou (Kakuta).
Ipswich T: Fulop; Brown, Kennedy, Peters, McAuley,
O'Dea, Edwards, Norris, Wickham (Priskin), Scotland
(Murray), Healy.

Leicester C (1) 2 *(Bamba 1, King A 64)*
Manchester C (2) 2 *(Milner 23, Tevez 45)* 31,200
Leicester C: Weale; Naughton, Berner (Neilson), King A,
Bamba, Hobbs, Abe, Wellens, Gallagher, Vassell
(Howard), Dyer (Waghorn).
Manchester C: Hart; Boateng, Kolarov, Vieira, Toure K,
Lescott, Wright-Phillips (De Jong), Milner, Jo
(Zabaleta), Tevez, Johnson A.

Manchester U (1) 1 *(Giggs 5 (pen))*
Liverpool (0) 0 74,727
Manchester U: Kuszczak; Rafael, Evra, Carrick,
Ferdinand, Evans J (Smalling), Nani, Fletcher
(Anderson), Berbatov, Hernandez (Owen), Giggs.
Liverpool: Reina; Kelly, Fabio Aurelio, Raul Meireles
(Babel), Agger, Skrtel, Kuyt, Lucas, Torres (N'Gog),
Gerrard[■], Rodriguez (Shelvey).

Tottenham H (0) 3 *(Townsend 49, Defoe 58, 60)*
Charlton Ath (0) 0 35,698
Tottenham H: Cudicini; Corluka, Assou-Ekotto, Palacios
(Modric), Bassong, Dawson, Kranjcar, Sandro,
Pavlyuchenko, Defoe, Townsend.
Charlton Ath: Elliot; Francis, Jackson, Racon, Doherty,
Dailly, Wagstaff, McCormack (Reid), Anyinsah (Sodje),
Semedo, Fry.

Monday, 10 January 2011

Crawley T (1) 2 *(McAllister 30, Torres 90)*
Derby Co (0) 1 *(Addison 63)* 4145
Crawley T: Kuipers; Wilson, Howell, Bulman,
McFadzean, Mills, Neilson (Hunt), Torres, McAllister
(Brodie), Tubbs, Smith B (Cook).
Derby Co: Bywater; Brayford, Roberts (Davies S),
Addison, Barker, Green, Bailey, Savage (Moxey), Porter,
Commons, Pringle (Cywka).

Tuesday, 11 January 2011

Wycombe W (0) 0
Hereford U (1) 1 *(Manset 32)* 2353
Wycombe W: Bull; McCoy, Sandell, Lewis, Westwood,
Bennett, Ainsworth (Rendell), Donnelly (Strevens),
Beavon, Bloomfield, Betsy (McClure).
Hereford U: Bartlett; Rose, Heath (Bauza), Lunt,
Kovacs, Townsend, Featherstone, McQuilkin, Manset
(Canham), Fleetwood, Colbeck.

Sergio Torres (left) with the injury-time winner for Crawley Town in their famous FA Cup Third Round 2-1 victory over Derby County at Broadfield Stadium. (Action Images/Paul Childs)

THIRD ROUND REPLAYS

Tuesday, 18 January 2011

Cardiff C (0) 0

Stoke C (0) 2 *(Walters 92, 115)*   13,671

Cardiff C: Heaton; Blake, Naylor, Rae, Hudson, Gyepes, Drinkwater (Matthews), McPhail (Wildig), Parkin (Chopra), Keogh, Burke.
Stoke C: Sorensen; Shotton, Higginbotham (Tonge), Whelan, Collins, Diagne Faye, Pennant (Soares), Pugh, Fuller, Walters, Diao (Wilson).
aet.

Manchester C (3) 4 *(Tevez 15, Vieira 37, Johnson A 38, Kolarov 90)*

Leicester C (1) 2 *(Gallagher 19 (pen), Dyer 83)*   27,755

Manchester C: Hart; Zabaleta, Kolarov, Vieira, Lescott, Kompany, Milner, Toure Y (Jo), Silva (Barry), Tevez, Johnson A.
Leicester C: Weale; Naughton, Berner, King A, Bamba, Hobbs, Abe, Wellens (Oakley), Gallagher (Moussa), Howard (Waghorn), Dyer.

Wolverhampton W (1) 5 *(Fletcher 5, Bia 61, Doyle 66, Jarvis 74, Jones 90)*

Doncaster R (0) 0   10,031

Wolverhampton W: Hahnemann; Zubar, Mouyokolo, Jones, Craddock, Stearman, Bia, Henry, Doyle (Vokes), Fletcher (Ward), Hunt (Jarvis).
Doncaster R: Sullivan; O'Connor, Chambers (Friend), Wilson, Lockwood, Hird, Coppinger (Souza), Shiels, Hayter, Sharp (Brooker), Oster.

Wednesday, 19 January 2011

Leeds U (1) 1 *(Johnson 37)*

Arsenal (2) 3 *(Nasri 5, Sagna 35, Van Persie 76)*   38,232

Leeds U: Schmeichel; Connolly, Parker, Howson, Bruce, O'Brien (Bromby), Johnson, Watt (Sam), Gradel, Paynter (Somma), Snodgrass.
Arsenal: Szczesny; Sagna, Gibbs, Denilson, Djourou, Koscielny, Song Billong, Bendtner, Chamakh (Van Persie), Arshavin (Fabregas), Nasri (Clichy).

FOURTH ROUND

Saturday, 29 January 2011

Aston Villa (3) 3 *(Clark 11, Pires 35, Delfouneso 42)*

Blackburn R (1) 1 *(Kalinic 18)*   26,067

Aston Villa: Friedel; Walker, Baker■, Reo-Coker, Cuellar, Clark, Pires (Collins JM), Bannan, Agbonlahor (Downing), Heskey, Delfouneso (Albrighton).
Blackburn R: Robinson; Salgado, Olsson, Andrews (Grella), Samba, Hanley, Nzonzi, Hoilett, Santa Cruz (Kalinic), Roberts (Mwaruwari), Pedersen.

Birmingham C (1) 3 *(Bentley 35, Parnaby 67, Phillips 73)*

Coventry C (2) 2 *(Wood 26, King 11)*   16,669

Birmingham C: Doyle; Parnaby, Murphy, Fahey, Jiranek, Ridgewell, Bentley, Beausejour (Gardner), Phillips, Zigic (Jerome), Hleb.
Coventry C: Westwood; Keogh, O'Halloran, Gunnarsson, Cranie, Wood, Baker, Thomas (Cameron), Platt (Eastwood), King, McSheffrey.

Bolton W (0) 0

Wigan Ath (0) 0   14,950

Bolton W: Jaaskelainen; Ricketts, Robinson, Muamba (Holden), Knight, Wheater, Petrov (Blake), Davies M, Elmander, Davies K, Taylor (Moreno).
Wigan Ath: Pollitt; Boyce, Figueroa, Diame, Caldwell G, Lopez, McArthur (McCarthy), Watson, Moses (Di Santo), Gomez, McManaman.

Burnley (1) 3 *(Eagles 29, 70, Paterson 90)*

Burton Alb (0) 1 *(Zola 80)*   11,664

Burnley: Grant; Mears, Fox, Duff, Carlisle, Marney, Elliott (Paterson), Cork, Thompson (Iwelumo), Rodriguez (Wallace), Eagles.
Burton Alb: Legzdins; Corbett (Austin), Webster (Young), Stanton, Moore, McGrath (Pearson), Penn, Bolder, Malone, Zola, Maghoma.

Everton (0) 1 *(Saha 62)*
Chelsea (0) 1 *(Kalou 75)* 28,376
Everton: Howard; Neville, Baines, Rodwell (Beckford), Distin, Heitinga, Coleman, Fellaini, Saha, Bilyaletdinov, Arteta.
Chelsea: Cech; Bosingwa, Cole, Essien, Terry, Ivanovic, Ramires, Lampard (Mikel), Anelka, Drogba, Malouda (Kalou).

Sheffield W (1) 4 *(Potter 15, Morrison C 69 (pen), 79 (pen), Johnson J 77)*
Hereford U (1) 1 *(Fleetwood 9)* 16,578
Sheffield W: Weaver; Jones D, Spurr, Potter (O'Connor), Morrison M, Johnson R, Teale, Coke (Sedgwick), Morrison C, Heffernan, Johnson J.
Hereford U: Bartlett; Heath[*], Rose, Kovacs, Townsend, Lunt (Purdie), Featherstone, McQuilkin (Thomas), Fleetwood, Jervis, Colbeck (Green).

Southampton (1) 1 *(Chaplow 45)*
Manchester U (0) 2 *(Owen 65, Hernandez 75)* 28,792
Southampton: Bialkowski; Butterfield, Harding, Chaplow (Gobern), Seaborne, Fonte, Do Prado (N'Guessan), Schneiderlin, Barnard (Dickson), Lambert, Oxlade-Chamberlain.
Manchester U: Lindegaard; O'Shea, Fabio (Brown), Anderson (Nani), Smalling, Evans J, Gibson (Giggs), Scholes, Owen, Hernandez, Obertan.

Stevenage (0) 1 *(Charles 72)*
Reading (1) 2 *(Leigertwood 23, Long 87)* 6614
Stevenage: Day; Henry, Laird, Roberts, Ashton, Bostwick, Charles (Odubade), Bridges (Sinclair), Winn (Long), Beardsley, Wilson.
Reading: Federici; Griffin, Harte, Karacan, Mills, Ingimarsson, Robson-Kanu (Antonio), Leigertwood, Long, Church, McAnuff.

Swansea C (1) 1 *(Van der Gun 45)*
Leyton Orient (1) 2 *(Smith 35, Tate 88 (og))* 6281
Swansea C: Ma-Kalambay, Alfei, Agustien (Dobbie), Allen, Tate, Williams, Orlandi (Rangel), Pratley, Moore, Van der Gun (Dyer), Sinclair.
Leyton Orient: Jones; Whing, Daniels, Dawson (Chambers), Chorley, Forbes, Smith, Spring, McGleish (Tehoue), Revell (M'Poku), Cox.

Torquay U (0) 0
Crawley T (1) 1 *(Tubbs 39)* 5065
Torquay U: Bevan; Robertson (Lathrope), Nicholson, Ellis, Branston, Wroe (Kee), Mansell, O'Kane, Benyon, Zebroski[*], Stevens (Halpin).
Crawley T: Kuipers; Wilson, Howell[*], Bulman, McFadzean, Mills, Smith B (Hunt), Torres, McAllister, Tubbs (Brodie), Cook (Rents).

Watford (0) 0
Brighton & HA (1) 1 *(Barnes 16)* 14,519
Watford: Gilmartin; Hodson, Doyley, McGinn, Taylor M, Mariappa, Deeney (Whichelow), Mingoia (Kiernan), Sordell, Graham, Buckley (Weimann).
Brighton & HA: Brezovan; Calderon, Painter, Bridcutt, Greer, Elphick, Sparrow (Dunk), Dicker, Wood, Murray, Barnes.

Sunday, 30 January 2011
Arsenal (1) 2 *(Clarke P 22 (og), Fabregas 86 (pen))*
Huddersfield T (0) 1 *(Lee 66)* 59,375
Arsenal: Almunia; Eboue, Gibbs, Denilson, Squillaci[*], Koscielny, Diaby (Fabregas), Bendtner, Chamakh (Song Billong), Arshavin, Nasri (Rosicky).
Huddersfield T: Bennett; Peltier, Kilbane, Gudjonsson, Clarke P, McCombe, Hunt, Clarke T (Arfield), Lee, Pilkington, Roberts.

Fulham (4) 4 *(Murphy 11 (pen), 14 (pen), Hangeland 23, Dembele 45)*
Tottenham H (0) 0 21,829
Fulham: Stockdale; Pantsil, Salcido, Murphy (Greening), Hughes, Hangeland, Duff, Sidwell, Johnson A (Gera), Dembele (Davies), Dempsey.

Tottenham H: Gomes; Hutton, Assou-Ekotto, Sandro (Gallas), Bassong, Dawson[*], Lennon, Modric, Van der Vaart (Jenas), Defoe (Crouch), Pienaar.

Notts Co (0) 1 *(Bishop 59)*
Manchester C (0) 1 *(Dzeko 80)* 16,587
Notts Co: Nelson; Darby, Harley, Ravenhill, Edwards, Pearce, Westcarr, Bishop, Hughes, Gow (Hawley), Martin.
Manchester C: Hart; Richards (Kompany), Zabaleta (Kolarov), Vieira, Lescott, Boateng, Milner, Toure Y, Jo (Silva), Dzeko, Barry.

West Ham U (2) 3 *(Obinna 4, 42, 52 (pen))*
Nottingham F (2) 2 *(Adebola 18, McGoldrick 40)* 29,287
West Ham U: Green; Jacobsen, Ilunga, Noble (Boa Morte), Reid, Gabbidon, Barrera (Hines), Kovac, Sears, Piquionne (Nouble), Obinna.
Nottingham F: Camp; Gunter, Lynch, Chambers, Morgan, Majewski (Tyson), McKenna (McCleary), McGugan, McGoldrick, Adebola (Earnshaw), Cohen.

Wolverhampton W (0) 0
Stoke C (0) 1 *(Huth 81)* 11,967
Wolverhampton W: Hahnemann; Zubar, Elokobi, Milijas, Berra, Stearman, Jarvis, Henry, Fletcher (Ebanks-Blake), Hunt (Edwards), Ward (Vokes).
Stoke C: Sorensen; Wilkinson (Wilson), Pugh, Diao (Whelan), Huth, Diagne Faye, Walters, Delap, Jones (Fuller), Carew, Etherington.

FOURTH ROUND REPLAYS

Wednesday, 16 February 2011
Wigan Ath (0) 0
Bolton W (0) 1 *(Klasnic 66)* 7515
Wigan Ath: Pollitt; Stam, Lopez, Diame, Caldwell G, Caldwell S, McArthur, Thomas, Di Santo, Gomez, McManaman (Moses).
Bolton W: Bogdan; Ricketts (Alonso), Robinson, Muamba (Cohen), Wheater, Cahill, Lee, Davies M, Elmander, Klasnic (Davies K), Petrov.

Saturday, 19 February 2011
Chelsea (0) 1 *(Lampard 104)*
Everton (0) 1 *(Baines 119)* 41,113
Chelsea: Cech; Paulo Ferreira, Cole, Mikel (Essien), Terry, Ivanovic, Ramires, Lampard, Kalou (Zhirkov), Drogba, Malouda (Anelka).
Everton: Howard; Neville, Baines, Osman (Heitinga), Distin, Jagielka, Coleman, Fellaini, Beckford (Anichebe), Cahill (Bilyaletdinov), Arteta.
aet; Everton won 4-3 on penalties.

Sunday, 20 February 2011
Manchester C (1) 5 *(Vieira 37, 58, Tevez 84, Dzeko 78, Richards 90)*
Notts Co (0) 0 27,276
Manchester C: Hart; Richards, Kolarov, Vieira, Toure K, Lescott, Balotelli (Tevez), Toure Y (Barry), Silva (Jo), Dzeko, Zabaleta.
Notts Co: Nelson; Darby (Thompson), Harley, Ravenhill, Edwards, Pearce (Chilvers), Westcarr, Bishop, Hughes (Gobern), Hawley, Gow.

FIFTH ROUND

Saturday, 19 February 2011
Birmingham C (2) 3 *(Beausejour 6, Martins 17, Murphy 53)*
Sheffield W (0) 0 14,607
Birmingham C: Doyle; Carr, Parnaby, Bowyer, Murphy, Johnson (Mutch), Fahey, Beausejour, Jerome (Phillips), Martins, Hleb (Bentley).
Sheffield W: Weaver; Reynolds (Hinds), Spurr, Osbourne, Morrison M (Beevers), Johnson R, Jones D, O'Connor (Palmer), Morrison C, Mellor, Teale.

Manchester U (1) 1 *(Brown 28)*
Crawley T (0) 0 74,778
Manchester U: Lindegaard; Rafael (Smalling), Fabio (Fletcher), Carrick, Brown, O'Shea, Gibson, Anderson (Rooney), Obertan, Hernandez, Bebe.
Crawley T: Kuipers; Hunt, Howell, Bulman, McFadzean, Mills, Gibson (Cook), Torres, McAllister (Brodie), Tubbs, Smith B (Rusk).

Stoke C (3) 3 *(Carew 14, Walters 22, Shawcross 43)*
Brighton & HA (0) 0 21,312
Stoke C: Sorensen; Wilson, Pugh, Whelan, Shawcross, Huth, Pennant (Whitehead), Delap, Walters, Carew (Jones), Etherington (Fuller).
Brighton & HA: Brezovan; Calderon, Painter, Bridcutt, Greer, Elphick, Battipiedi (Caskey), Dicker, Barnes (Baz), Murray (Sandaza), Bennett.

Sunday, 20 February 2011
Fulham (0) 0
Bolton W (1) 1 *(Klasnic 19)* 19,571
Fulham: Schwarzer; Baird, Salcido, Murphy, Hughes, Hangeland, Gera (Zamora), Sidwell, Johnson A, Dembele, Dempsey.
Bolton W: Bogdan; Alonso, Robinson, Muamba, Cahill, Wheater, Lee, Holden, Klasnic (Elmander), Davies K, Petrov.

Leyton Orient (0) 1 *(Tehoue 89)*
Arsenal (0) 1 *(Rosicky 53)* 9136
Leyton Orient: Jones; Whing, Daniels, Dawson, Chorley, Forbes, Smith, Crowe (Carroll), McGleish (Tehoue), Revell (M'Poku), Cox.
Arsenal: Almunia; Sagna, Gibbs, Denilson, Squillaci, Miquel, Song Billong, Bendtner, Chamakh, Arshavin, Rosicky.

Monday, 21 February 2011
West Ham U (1) 5 *(Hitzlsperger 23, Cole 48, 50, Reid 59, Sears 90)*
Burnley (0) 1 *(Rodriguez 71)* 30,000
West Ham U: Green; Reid, Bridge, Noble, Tomkins, Jacobsen, Sears, Parker, Cole (Spector), Ba (Piquionne), Hitzlsperger (Barrera).

Burnley: Grant; Mears, Fox, Duff, Carlisle, Marney (Alexander), Elliott, Cork, Eagles (Thompson), Rodriguez, Wallace (Iwelumo).

Tuesday, 1 March 2011
Everton (0) 0
Reading (1) 1 *(Mills 26)* 29,976
Everton: Howard; Neville (Baxter), Baines, Rodwell, Distin, Jagielka, Coleman (Beckford), Osman, Saha, Bilyaletdinov (Anichebe), Arteta.
Reading: McCarthy; Gunnarsson, Harte, Leigertwood, Mills, Khizanishvili, Kebe, McAnuff (Robson-Kanu), Long, Hunt (Church), Tabb.

Wednesday, 2 March 2011
Manchester C (2) 3 *(Toure Y 5, Balotelli 25, Silva 70)*
Aston Villa (0) 0 25,570
Manchester C: Hart; Richards (Boyata), Zabaleta, Vieira, Lescott, Boateng, Barry, Toure Y (Jo), Silva, Balotelli (Tevez), Kolarov.
Aston Villa: Friedel; Herd, Delph, Clark, Dunne (Walker), Petrov, Agbonlahor, Bradley (Downing), Delfouneso (Young A), Heskey, Bannan.

FIFTH ROUND REPLAY

Wednesday, 2 March 2011
Arsenal (3) 5 *(Chamakh 7, Bendtner 30, 43, 62 (pen), Clichy 75)*
Leyton Orient (0) 0 59,361
Arsenal: Almunia; Eboue, Gibbs, Denilson, Squillaci, Miquel, Diaby (Wilshere), Henderson, Chamakh, Bendtner (Clichy), Rosicky (Nasri).
Leyton Orient: Jones; Whing, Daniels, Dawson, Chorley, Forbes, Carroll, Crowe (Spring), McGleish (Tehoue), Revell (M'Poku), Cox.

Manchester City's Carlos Tevez (right) is challenged by Ryan Shawcross of Stoke City in the FA Cup Final at Wembley. Yaya Toure scored the only goal of the match after 75 minutes, giving City their first FA Cup trophy in 42 years. (Action Images/Carl Recine)

SIXTH ROUND

Saturday, 12 March 2011

Birmingham C (1) 2 *(Jerome 38, Phillips 80)*
Bolton W (1) 3 *(Elmander 21, Davies K 66 (pen), Lee 90)*
                                                          23,699
Birmingham C: Foster; Parnaby, Murphy (Derbyshire), Ferguson (Redmond), Davies, Jiranek (Ridgewell), Larsson, Mutch, Jerome, Phillips, Beausejour.
Bolton W: Jaaskelainen; Steinsson, Robinson, Muamba (Davies M), Cahill, Wheater, Elmander, Holden, Klasnik (Lee), Davies K, Petrov (Taylor).

Manchester U (1) 2 *(Fabio 28, Rooney 49)*
Arsenal (0) 0   74,693
Manchester U: Van der Sar; Brown, Evra (Scholes), O'Shea, Smalling, Vidic, Rafael (Giggs), Gibson, Hernandez, Rooney, Fabio (Valencia).
Arsenal: Almunia; Sagna, Gibbs, Denilson (Chamakh), Djourou, Koscielny, Diaby (Ramsey), Wilshere, Arshavin (Rosicky), Van Persie, Nasri.

Sunday, 13 March 2011

Manchester C (0) 1 *(Richards 74)*
Reading (0) 0   41,150
Manchester C: Hart; Richards, Kolarov, Vieira (Balotelli), Lescott, Kompany, De Jong (Barry), Toure Y, Silva, Tevez, Wright-Phillips (Boyata).
Reading: McCarthy; Tabb (Howard), Harte, Karacan, Khizanishvili, Gunnarsson, Kebe, Leigertwood, Long, Hunt (Church), McAnuff (Robson-Kanu).

Stoke C (1) 2 *(Huth 12, Higginbotham 63)*
West Ham U (1) 1 *(Piquionne 30)*   24,550
Stoke C: Sorensen; Wilson, Higginbotham, Huth, Shawcross, Whelan, Pennant (Whitehead), Delap, Jones (Fuller), Walters, Etherington (Collins).
West Ham U: Green; Da Costa, Bridge, Noble (Hines), Tomkins, Upson, Piquionne (Spector), Parker, Cole, Obinna (Keane), Hitzlsperger.

SEMI-FINALS (at Wembley)

Saturday, 16 April 2011

Manchester C (0) 1 *(Toure Y 52)*
Manchester U (0) 0   86,549
Manchester C: Hart; Zabaleta, Kolarov, De Jong, Lescott, Kompany, Barry, Toure Y, Balotelli, Silva (Vieira), Johnson A (Wright-Phillips).
Manchester U: Van der Sar; O'Shea (Fabio 84), Evra, Carrick, Ferdinand, Vidic, Valencia (Hernandez), Scholes[■], Berbatov (Anderson), Nani, Park.

Sunday, 17 April 2011

Bolton W (0) 0
Stoke C (3) 5 *(Etherington 11, Huth 17, Jones 30, Walters 68, 81)*   75,064
Bolton W: Jaaskelainen; Steinsson, Robinson, Muamba (Moreno), Cahill, Knight, Elmander, Lee, Klasnik (Davies M), Davies K, Petrov (Taylor).
Stoke C: Sorensen; Wilkinson, Wilson, Huth, Shawcross, Whelan, Pennant (Whitehead), Delap, Jones (Fuller), Walters, Etherington (Pugh).

THE FA CUP FINAL

(Saturday, 14 May 2011 at Wembley Stadium, attendance 88,643)

Manchester C (0) 1   Stoke C (0) 0

Manchester C: Hart; Richards, Kolarov, De Jong, Lescott, Kompany, Barry (Johnson A), Toure Y, Balotelli, Tevez (Zabaleta), Silva (Vieira).
Scorer: (Toure Y 74)

Stoke C: Sorensen; Wilkinson, Wilson, Huth, Shawcross, Whelan (Pugh), Pennant, Delap (Carew), Jones, Walters, Etherington (Whitehead).

Referee: M. Atkinson (West Yorkshire).

Manchester City's Carlos Tevez, lifts the FA Cup for Manchester City after their final win over Stoke City at Wembley. (PA Photos)

BLUE SQUARE PREMIER 2010–11

Once it was Aldershot Town setting the record, then Stevenage Borough came close – then came 2010–11 and Crawley Town, who shredded previous Conference statistics. With considerable finance in place and a more than useful FA Cup run that ended with another pot of gold at Old Trafford, it became just a matter of how many points.

Crawley's last defeat in the Blue Square Premier was at home to Newport County on 16 October. It was one of only three such. Thereafter it was 30 games undefeated and 105 points. Crawley lost just once away at AFC Wimbledon, while Grimsby Town on the opening day of the season were the other winners at Crawley.

AFC Dons stuck gamely to the task of wading in the wake of this and deservedly joined Crawley in League Two, a return to their roots. But Luton Town were difficult play-off opponents and it was only a penalty shoot-out that pushed AFC Wimbledon through. A strong finish of seven matches undefeated adjusted their worst run of three successive losses.

Luton looked the part in mid-season. In ten games they scored goals for fun and conceded just three, but it faded. Wrexham at the time of Crawley's last reverse embarked on a splendid run of 14 without loss, then stayed stuck fourth and defeat by Luton in the play-offs. Newcomers Fleetwood Town acquitted themselves well, ten without losing at one stage and just one loss in the last eight. But AFC Dons provided the knock-out in the play-offs.

Kidderminster Harriers without a five-point deduction would not have gained a play-off spot, but they went 15 games without defeat to mid-April. Darlington had too many draws in a starting run but another run of eight games undefeated to March. The Quakers' prize was winning the FA Trophy at Mansfield's expense.

York City shaped up after a poor first half term and had two runs of seven without loss. Return team Newport County were riding high but at the turn of the year suffered a dozen games without a win. Another of the golden oldies Bath City took time to adjust but showed a vast improvement from November.

Grimsby Town who had been relegated from League Two were still fourth in September, but never achieved more than two wins on the spin thereafter. Rushden & Diamonds needed a push in the last third of the season but won only two of their last fourteen. Worse for them they were thrown out of the Conference over their financial situation.

Mansfield Town even led the table late August before a slow drift to half-way ruined their prospects. Kettering Town, never better than tenth all season, had their best run from late September with seven unbeaten. Gateshead enjoyed a purple patch in February with five wins and seventeen goals but then tailed off.

Hayes & Yeading United's concerns were removed with improved goal scoring from March that lifted them from the danger zone. Cambridge United disappointed again and never succeeded in putting together more than two wins at any time.

For Barrow four successive wins in March had an immediate effect and helped towards avoiding the drop. Tamworth fell away after a useful start and had no wins in eleven to late November and another similar eight lacking victory to early April, but survived by four points.

Those escape artists Forest Green Rovers pulled it off once more despite just once managing two wins in succession and a disastrous spell of twelve without one. Yet goal difference of just two kept them up at the expense of Southport.

The Sandgrounders hit the skids with one win in seventeen after a reasonable opening. A reprieve came when Rushden collapsed. Altrincham did go down, their problems began initially with one point taken out of the first nine matches! Eastbourne Borough topped that with nineteen without a win including eleven defeats in a row. Histon were the first casualties on 9 April having never been out of the bottom four after November.

BLUE SQUARE PREMIER ATTENDANCES BY CLUB 2010–11

	Aggregate 2010–11	Average 2010–11	Highest Attendance 2010–11
Luton Town	143,562	6,242	7,283 v AFC Wimbledon
AFC Wimbledon	77,979	3,390	4,287 v Luton Town
Grimsby Town	70,672	3,073	5,037 v York City
Wrexham	70,398	3,061	4,630 v Crawley Town
Crawley Town	58,297	2,535	4,054 v AFC Wimbledon
Cambridge United	57,822	2,514	3,225 v Histon
York City	57,166	2,485	3,176 v Darlington
Mansfield Town	48,825	2,123	3,266 v Wrexham
Newport County	48,078	2,090	3,462 v AFC Wimbledon
Darlington	43,384	1,886	2,966 v York City
Fleetwood Town	40,295	1,752	2,831 v Luton Town
Kidderminster Harriers	37,504	1,631	3,028 v Wrexham
Kettering Town	31,535	1,371	2,906 v Luton Town
Rushden & Diamonds	28,856	1,255	2,459 v Luton Town
Barrow	27,925	1,214	1,718 v Darlington
Southport	26,541	1,154	1,866 v Darlington
Eastbourne Borough	25,406	1,105	2,518 v Luton Town
Tamworth	25,077	1,090	1,717 v Forest Green Rovers
Bath City	24,606	1,070	2,301 v Luton Town
Altrincham	23,919	1,040	1,982 v Wrexham
Forest Green Rovers	21,845	950	1,824 v AFC Wimbledon
Gateshead	17,318	753	1,231 v York City
Histon	14,176	616	1,903 v Cambridge United
Hayes & Yeading United	8,877	386	801 v Luton Town

BLUE SQUARE PREMIER 2010–11

(P) *Promoted into division at end of 2009–10 season.*　　(R) *Relegated into division at end of 2009–10 season.*

			Total				Home					Away					
		P	W	D	L	F	A	W	D	L	F	A	W	D	L	F	A	GD	Pts
1	Crawley T	46	31	12	3	93	30	18	3	2	57	19	13	9	1	36	11	63	105
2	AFC Wimbledon¶	46	27	9	10	83	47	17	3	3	46	15	10	6	7	37	32	36	90
3	Luton T	46	23	15	8	85	37	14	7	2	57	17	9	8	6	28	20	48	84
4	Wrexham	46	22	15	9	66	49	13	7	3	36	24	9	8	6	30	25	17	81
5	Fleetwood T (P)	46	22	12	12	68	42	12	8	3	35	19	10	4	9	33	23	26	78
6	Kidderminster H	46	20	17	9	74	60	13	6	4	40	27	7	11	5	34	33	14	72
7	Darlington (R)	46	18	17	11	61	42	13	6	4	37	14	5	11	7	24	28	19	71
8	York C	46	19	14	13	55	50	14	6	3	31	13	5	8	10	24	37	5	71
9	Newport Co (P)	46	18	15	13	78	60	11	7	5	44	29	7	8	8	34	31	18	69
10	Bath C (P)	46	16	15	15	64	68	10	10	3	38	27	6	5	12	26	41	−4	63
11	Grimsby T (R)	46	15	17	14	72	62	7	12	4	37	28	8	5	10	35	34	10	62
12	Rushden & D*	46	16	14	16	65	62	10	6	7	37	27	6	8	9	28	35	3	62
13	Mansfield T	46	17	10	19	73	75	9	6	8	40	37	8	4	11	33	38	−2	61
14	Kettering T	46	15	13	18	64	75	8	8	7	33	32	7	5	11	31	43	−11	58
15	Gateshead	46	14	15	17	65	68	8	9	6	28	28	6	6	11	37	40	−3	57
16	Hayes & Yeading U	46	15	6	25	57	81	10	2	11	34	38	5	4	14	23	43	−24	51
17	Cambridge U	46	11	17	18	53	61	7	7	9	32	28	4	10	9	21	33	−8	50
18	Barrow	46	12	14	20	52	67	9	6	8	31	22	3	8	12	21	45	−15	50
19	Tamworth	46	12	13	21	62	83	6	8	9	34	41	6	5	12	28	42	−21	49
20	Forest Green R	46	10	16	20	53	72	7	10	6	28	25	3	6	14	25	47	−19	46
21	Southport (P)†	46	11	13	22	56	77	9	6	8	39	33	2	7	14	17	44	−21	46
22	Altrincham	46	11	11	24	47	87	6	8	9	29	38	5	3	15	18	49	−40	44
23	Eastbourne B	46	10	9	27	62	104	6	5	12	36	46	4	4	15	26	58	−42	39
24	Histon	46	8	9	29	41	90	4	3	16	18	45	4	6	13	23	45	−49	28

Kidderminster H deducted 5 points. Histon deducted 5 points. ¶AFC Wimbledon promoted via play-offs.
*Rushden & D expelled from Blue Square Premier. †Southport reprieved from relegation.
Altrincham and Histon relegated to Blue Square North, Eastbourne B relegated to Blue Square South.

BLUE SQUARE PREMIER LEADING GOALSCORERS 2010–11

	Club	League	Play-Offs	FA Cup	Total
Matt Tubbs	(Crawley T)	37	0	3	40
Alan Connell	(Grimsby T)	25	0	1	26
Danny Kedwell	(AFC Wimbledon)	23	1	0	24
Magno Vieira	(Fleetwood T)	22	0	0	22
Jean-Paul Marna	(Kettering T)	19	0	0	19
Craig Reid	(Newport Co)	18	0	0	18
Kyle Perry	(Tamworth)	17	0	1	18
Chris McPhee	(Kidderminster H)	17	0	0	17
Jon Shaw	(Gateshead)	17	0	0	17
Matthew Barnes-Homer	(Luton T)	16	0	2	18

BLUE SQUARE PREMIER LEAGUE PLAY-OFFS

■ *Denotes player sent off.*

SEMI-FINALS FIRST LEG

Thursday, 5 May 2011

Wrexham (0) 0　　　　　　　　　　7211
Luton T (3) 3 *(Lawless 16, Gnakpa 28, Asafu-Adjaye 35)*
Wrexham: Maxwell; Obeng, Ashton, Sinclair, Creighton, Blackburn (Fowler), Harris, Keates, Mangan, Taylor (Tolley), Knight-Percival (Anoruo).
Luton T: Tyler; Gleeson, Asafu-Adjaye, Keane, Kroca, Pilkington G, Lawless, Howells, Walker J, Gnakpa (Barnes-Homer), Willmott.

Friday, 6 May 2011

Fleetwood T (0) 0
AFC Wimbledon (1) 2 *(Moore L 38, Mohamed 50)*　　4112
Fleetwood T: Hurst (Davies); Clancy (Parker), Beeley, Barry, McNulty, Gregan, Mullan (Harvey), McGuire, Seddon, Vieira, Brown.
AFC Wimbledon: Brown; Hatton, Gwillim (Yakubu), Gregory, Stuart, Johnson, Yussuff (Minshull), Wellard, Kedwell, Mohamed, Moore L (Jolley).

SEMI-FINALS SECOND LEG

Tuesday, 10 May 2011

Luton T (1) 2 *(Kroca 29, Walker J 81)*
Wrexham (1) 1 *(Mangan 8)*　　　　　　　9078
Luton T: Tyler; Gleeson, Asafu-Adjaye, Keane (Newton), Kroca, Pilkington G, Lawless, Howells, Walker J, Gnakpa (Barnes-Homer), Willmott.

Wrexham: Maxwell; Obeng, Ashton, Keates, Creighton, Sinclair (Andrews), Fowler, Harris (Anoruo), Mangan, Taylor (Tolley), Cieslewicz.

Wednesday, 11 May 2011

AFC Wimbledon (3) 6 *(Mohamed 1, 35, 63, Kedwell 28, Jolley 67, Mulley 80)*
Fleetwood T (0) 1 *(Seddon 47)*　　　　　　4538
AFC Wimbledon: Brown; Hatton, Gwillim (Yakubu), Gregory, Stuart, Johnson, Moore L (Jolley), Wellard, Kedwell (Mulley), Mohamed, Yussuff.
Fleetwood T: Hurst; Cavanagh, Brown, Barry, McNulty, Gregan (Linwood), McGuire, Harvey, Donnelly, Vieira (Clancy), Seddon.

FINAL (at Eastlands)

Saturday, 21 May 2011

AFC Wimbledon (0) 0
Luton T (0) 0　　　　　　　　　　18,195
AFC Wimbledon: Brown; Hatton, Gwillim (Yakubu), Gregory (Minshull), Stuart, Johnson, Yussuff, Wellard (Mulley), Kedwell, Mohamed, Moore L.
Luton T: Tyler; Gleeson, Asafu-Adjaye, Keane, Kroca, Pilkington G, Lawless, Howells, Walker J, Gnakpa (Newton), Willmott (Barnes-Homer).
aet; AFC Wimbledon won 4-3 on penalties.

BLUE SQUARE NORTH & SOUTH 2010–11

(P) *Promoted into division at end of 2009–10 season.*   (R) *Relegated into division at end of 2009–10 season.*

BLUE SQUARE NORTH 2010–11

		P	W	D	L	F	A	W	D	L	F	A	W	D	L	F	A	GD	Pts
						Total				Home					Away				
1	Alfreton T	40	29	5	6	97	33	16	3	1	55	11	13	2	5	42	22	64	92
2	AFC Telford U¶	40	23	13	4	71	29	12	6	2	42	17	11	7	2	29	12	42	82
3	Boston U (P)	40	23	10	7	72	33	13	4	3	34	14	10	6	4	38	19	39	79
4	Eastwood T	40	22	7	11	82	50	13	2	5	40	23	9	5	6	42	27	32	73
5	Guiseley (P)	40	20	13	7	56	41	9	6	5	29	21	11	7	2	27	20	15	73
6	Nuneaton T (P)	40	21	9	10	66	44	10	5	5	30	21	11	4	5	36	23	22	72
7	Solihull Moors	40	18	10	12	66	49	11	4	5	36	24	7	6	7	30	25	17	64
8	Droylsden	40	17	9	14	69	67	11	2	7	41	36	6	7	7	28	31	2	60
9	Blyth Spartans	40	16	10	14	61	54	9	5	6	30	22	7	5	8	31	32	7	58
10	Stalybridge Celtic	40	16	9	15	64	55	8	6	6	28	23	8	3	9	36	32	9	57
11	Workington	40	16	6	18	52	60	10	3	7	32	28	6	3	11	20	32	-8	54
12	Harrogate T	40	13	11	16	53	66	9	7	4	34	24	4	4	12	19	42	-13	50
13	Corby T	40	13	10	17	58	80	7	5	8	28	33	6	5	9	30	47	-22	49
14	Gloucester C	40	14	5	21	49	63	7	3	10	26	31	7	2	11	23	32	-14	47
15	Hinckley U	40	13	7	20	76	76	9	4	7	47	29	4	3	13	29	47	0	46
16	Worcester C (S)	40	12	10	18	49	55	7	4	9	29	29	5	6	9	20	26	-6	46
17	Vauxhall Motors	40	12	9	19	52	71	7	5	8	28	34	5	4	11	24	37	-19	45
18	Gainsborough Trinity	40	12	5	23	50	74	4	4	12	20	40	8	1	11	30	34	-24	41
19	Hyde U	40	10	6	24	44	73	4	3	13	18	38	6	3	11	26	35	-29	36
20	Stafford Rangers	40	8	8	24	39	78	5	3	12	20	43	3	5	12	19	35	-39	32
21	Redditch U	40	2	8	30	30	105	1	6	13	16	52	1	2	17	14	53	-75	9

Redditch U deducted 5 points. ¶AFC Telford U promoted via play-offs.

BLUE SQUARE SOUTH 2010–11

		P	W	D	L	F	A	W	D	L	F	A	W	D	L	F	A	GD	Pts
						Total				Home					Away				
1	Braintree T	42	27	8	7	78	33	15	4	2	45	17	12	4	5	33	16	45	89
2	Farnborough (P)	42	25	7	10	83	47	12	5	4	37	22	13	2	6	46	25	36	82
3	Ebbsfleet U¶ (R)	42	22	12	8	75	51	9	7	5	34	26	13	5	3	41	25	24	78
4	Chelmsford C	42	23	8	11	82	50	14	3	4	48	16	9	5	7	34	34	32	77
5	Woking	42	22	10	10	62	42	13	5	3	35	17	9	5	7	27	25	20	76
6	Welling U	42	24	8	10	81	47	14	3	4	44	20	10	5	6	37	27	34	75
7	Dover Ath	42	22	8	12	80	51	9	5	7	36	26	13	3	5	44	25	29	74
8	Eastleigh	42	22	6	14	74	53	12	1	8	39	30	10	5	6	35	23	21	72
9	Havant & Waterlooville	42	16	10	16	56	51	8	5	8	31	27	8	5	8	25	24	5	58
10	Dartford (P)	42	15	12	15	60	60	9	7	5	37	28	6	5	10	23	32	0	57
11	Bromley	42	15	12	15	49	61	7	6	8	24	30	8	6	7	25	31	-12	57
12	Weston Super Mare	42	15	8	19	56	67	12	3	6	34	24	3	5	13	22	43	-11	53
13	Basingstoke T	42	13	10	19	50	63	8	4	9	34	32	5	6	10	16	31	-13	49
14	Boreham Wood (P)	42	12	11	19	56	67	8	5	8	35	33	4	6	11	21	34	-11	47
15	Staines T	42	11	14	17	48	63	7	5	9	25	30	4	9	8	23	33	-15	47
16	Bishop's Stortford	42	13	6	23	48	79	6	3	12	19	38	7	3	11	29	41	-31	45
17	Dorchester T	42	13	6	23	48	59	5	9	7	23	28	5	5	11	26	31	-10	44
18	Hampton & Richmond B	42	9	15	18	43	60	3	8	10	19	30	6	7	8	24	30	-17	42
19	Maidenhead U	42	10	10	22	43	70	3	6	12	16	34	7	4	10	27	36	-27	40
20	Thurrock	42	8	13	21	50	77	5	7	9	28	40	3	6	12	22	37	-27	37
21	Lewes	42	9	9	24	34	70	5	5	11	19	38	4	4	13	15	32	-36	36
22	St Albans C	42	7	13	22	39	75	3	6	12	15	33	4	7	10	24	42	-36	24

Welling U deducted 5 points. St Albans City deducted 10 points. ¶Ebbsfleet U promoted via play-offs.

BLUE SQUARE NORTH & SOUTH PLAY-OFFS

BLUE SQUARE NORTH

SEMI-FINALS FIRST LEG

Nuneaton T 1 *(Storer 74)*
AFC Telford U 1 *(Trainer 90)*   2089

Guiseley 1 *(Peyton 75)*
Boston U 0   1022

SEMI-FINALS SECOND LEG

AFC Telford U 2 *(Adams 16, Newton 44 (pen))*
Nuneaton T 1 *(Spencer 56)*   3442

Boston U 3 *(Pearson 19, Church 79, Davidson 113)*
Guiseley 2 *(Rothery 60, Stamp 108)*   2640
aet.

FINAL

AFC Telford U 3 *(Newton 9 (pen), Murray 79, Trainer 90)*
Guiseley 2 *(Walshaw 44 (pen), Stamp 45)*   5436

BLUE SQUARE SOUTH

SEMI-FINALS FIRST LEG

Chelmsford C 1 *(Modeste 45)*
Ebbsfleet U 4 *(West 22, 26, Shakes 78, 88)*   1701

Woking 0
Farnborough T 1 *(Holloway 71)*   2726

SEMI-FINALS SECOND LEG

Ebbsfleet U 2 *(West 27, 35)*
Chelmsford C 1 *(Gray 62)*   1538

Farnborough T 1 *(McDonald 111)*
Woking 1 *(Hammond 45)*   2137
aet.

FINAL

Farnborough T 2 *(McMahon 88, Booth 90)*
Ebbsfleet U 4 *(West 29, 74, Shakes 53, Willock 90)*   4267

AFC WIMBLEDON FL Championship 2

Ground: The Cherry Red Records Fans' Stadium, Kingsmeadow, Jack Goodchild Way, 422a Kingston Road,
Kingston-Upon-Thames, Surrey KT1 3PB.   *Tel:* (0208) 547 3528. *Fax:* (0808) 2800 816.   *Year Formed:* 2002.
Record Gate: 4722 (2009 v St Albans City).   *Nickname:* The Dons.   *Manager:* Terry Brown.
Secretary: David Charles.   *Colours:* All blue with gold shirt trimmings.

AFC WIMBLEDON 2010–11 LEAGUE RECORD

Match No.	Date	Venue	Opponents	Result	H/T Score	Lg Pos.	Goalscorers	Attendance
1	Aug 14	A	Southport	W 1-0	0-0	—	Jolley [72]	1802
2	17	H	Histon	W 2-0	0-0	—	Kedwell (pen) [89], Wellard [90]	3126
3	21	H	Tamworth	W 3-0	1-0	2	Moore, S [37], Kedwell 2 [60, 79]	3144
4	24	A	Rushden & D	L 0-1	0-0	—		1365
5	28	A	Eastbourne Bor	W 3-2	1-0	1	Kedwell 2 [31, 90], Minshull [55]	2485
6	30	H	Newport Co	D 2-2	1-1	2	Kedwell (pen) [16], Jolley [56]	3828
7	Sept 4	A	Kettering T	W 2-1	1-1	1	Hatton [14], Kedwell [57]	1727
8	11	H	Bath C	W 4-0	2-0	1	Moore, S [18], Yakubu [36], Jolley [65], Kedwell [68]	2300
9	17	A	Luton T	L 0-3	0-2	—		7283
10	23	H	Crawley T	W 2-1	0-1	—	Hatton [77], Kedwell [80]	4018
11	26	A	Kidderminster H	L 0-2	0-1	3		1565
12	29	H	Cambridge U	W 3-0	0-0	—	Franks 2 [69, 90], Jolley [75]	3119
13	Oct 2	H	Forest Green R	D 1-1	0-1	2	Jolley [68]	3204
14	5	A	Mansfield T	W 5-2	3-1	—	Moore, S 2 [1, 74], Jolley [9], Kedwell [43], Jackson [60]	2699
15	9	A	Wrexham	W 2-1	0-1	2	Jolley [47], Yussuff [84]	3277
16	16	H	Gateshead	W 1-0	0-0	1	Yakubu [72]	3330
17	30	H	Darlington	L 0-2	0-1	2		3952
18	Nov 9	A	Altrincham	W 2-0	2-0	—	Kedwell 2 [1, 44]	901
19	13	A	Barrow	L 0-2	0-1	1		1375
20	21	H	Kettering T	W 3-2	3-0	1	Moore, L 2 (1 pen) [11, 18 (p)], Jolley [35]	3114
21	Dec 28	H	Eastbourne Bor	W 3-0	1-0	—	Nwokeji [45], Wellard [80], Yussuff [89]	3364
22	Jan 1	H	Hayes & Y	W 3-1	0-0	1	Jackson [49], Mulley [51], Moore, L [83]	3176
23	3	A	Newport Co	D 3-3	1-3	2	Mulley [28], Hatton [47], Yussuff [82]	3402
24	8	A	Darlington	D 0-0	0-0	1		2046
25	12	H	Luton T	D 0-0	0-0	—		4287
26	18	A	Fleetwood T	D 1-1	1-1	—	Kedwell [16]	1808
27	22	H	Southport	W 5-0	1-0	1	Mulley 2 [20, 90], Moore, L [50], Moore, S [56], Hatton (pen) [87]	3408
28	25	A	Bath C	D 2-2	2-0	—	Kedwell (pen) [32], Hudson [45]	1135
29	28	A	Gateshead	W 2-0	0-0	—	Jolley [48], Kedwell [78]	922
30	Feb 1	A	York C	L 1-4	0-2	—	Jolley [63]	2438
31	5	H	Fleetwood T	W 1-0	0-0	—	Jolley [84]	3298
32	12	H	York C	W 1-0	1-0	1	Hatton [20]	3532
33	19	A	Tamworth	W 5-2	1-0	1	Mulley [18], Kedwell 2 (1 pen) [50, 89 (p)], Broughton [75], Yussuff [90]	1496
34	22	H	Wrexham	L 0-1	0-0	—		3486
35	26	H	Altrincham	W 4-1	2-0	1	Kedwell 3 [37, 45, 60], Broughton [81]	3078
36	Mar 1	A	Hayes & Y	D 0-0	0-0	—		708
37	5	A	Grimsby T	L 1-2	1-1	1	Yussuff [24]	3182
38	12	H	Kidderminster H	L 1-2	0-1	2	Minshull [82]	3517
39	18	H	Crawley T	L 1-3	1-2	—	Johnson [39]	4054
40	26	H	Rushden & D	W 1-0	1-0	2	Kedwell (pen) [29]	3069
41	Apr 2	H	Barrow	W 2-0	1-0	2	Johnson [32], Yussuff [83]	3264
42	9	A	Cambridge U	W 2-1	0-0	2	Johnson [11], Mohamed [32]	2907
43	16	A	Histon	W 4-0	1-0	2	Kedwell 2 [13, 67], Moore, L 2 [63, 64]	750
44	22	H	Mansfield T	W 2-1	0-1	—	Stuart [68], Jolley [86]	3613
45	25	A	Forest Green R	D 0-0	0-0	2		1824
46	30	H	Grimsby T	W 2-1	1-1	2	Moore, L [7], Johnson [51]	3752

Final League Position: 2

GOALSCORERS

League (83): Kedwell 23 (5 pens), Jolley 12, Moore, L 7 (1 pen), Yussuff 6, Hatton 5 (1 pen), Moore, S 5, Mulley 5, Johnson 4, Broughton 2, Franks 2, Jackson 2, Minshull 2, Wellard 2, Yakubu 2, Hudson 1, Mohamed 1, Nwokeji 1, Stuart 1.
FA Cup (4): Moore, S 2, Harris 1, Nwokeji 1.

Brown 45	Hatton 40	Blackman 12+1	Gregory 41+1	Yakubu 26+1	Johnson 21+2	Moore S 27+1	Wellard 22+3	Kedwell 43+2	Main 7+9	Moore L 19+14	Jolley 22+10	Jackson 23+14	Minshull 9+10	Yussuff 21+17	Jones 1+2	Harris 15+1	Franks 15+9	Nwokeji 6+12	Bush 12+1	Mulley 19+3	Hudson 11+3	Stuart 18+3	Gwillim 20	Broughton 3+5	Kiernan 1+1	Mohamed 6+1	Turner 1	Match No.
1	2	3	4	5	6	7	8³	9	10²	11¹	12	13	14⁴															1
1	2	3	4	5	6	7³	8	9	10²	11¹	12	13		14														2
1	2	3	4	5	6	7²	8³	9	10¹	11	12		14	13														3
1	2¹	3	4	5³	6	7		9	10²	11	13	12			8	14												4
1	2	3¹	4	5	6	7²		9		11	10	12			8	13												5
1	2	3	4	5	6¹	7	8²	9	10³	14	11				12	13												6
1	2	3	4¹	5		7	12	9		14	11			8³	10	6²	13											7
1	2³	3¹	4	5		7²		9			12	10	11	8	13	6	14											8
1	2	3	4	5		7³	13	9	14	10²	11			8¹	12	6												9
1	2		4			7	8¹	9	10²					12		6	5	13	3									10
1	2	12	4			7	14	9		11¹		13	3			6	8	10¹	5²									11
1	2	3³	4	5¹		7	8²	9			13	10	11			6	12	14										12
1	2	3	4¹			7	8³	9	13	12	10	11²	14			6	5											13
1	2		4	5²		7	8	9³	14	12	10¹	11				6	13	3										14
1	2		4	5		7¹	8²	9	10	11	12	13				6	3											15
1	2		4¹	5		7	8²	9	10	11³	12	13	14			6	3											16
1	2		4	5		7¹		9	10	11²	12	13		8		6	3											17
1	2	3	4²				8	9	10¹			7³	14	13	11	6	5	12										18
1	2		14	5		7	8²	9		12		11¹	13	6³		4	10	3										19
1	2¹		5			7	8	14		11	9	12²	4			6	13	10³	3									20
1	2		4¹				8	9	13		11²	5	7	12		6	10	3										21
1				5		7¹	8	9	13		11	4²	12		6	10³	3	2	14									22
1	2		4					9		10²	12	11¹	13	6³		5	14	3	8	7								23
1	2		4			7		9	12	10²	11¹					6	13	3	8		5							24
1	2		4²	5		7¹		9		11	12	14	13			3				8	10³	6						25
1	2		4	5		7³		9²	12	11¹	14					13				8	10	6	3					26
1	2		4			7¹		9³	11²	13	12					6	14			8	10	5	3					27
1	2		4			7²		9	11³	12	13					6	14			8	10¹	5	3					28
1	2		4	0				9³	11¹	10	12	7²				13	14			8		5	3					29
1	2		4	13			8²	9	10	11¹						6	12			7		5	3					30
1	2		4¹	6	7			9	10	11	12									8		5	3					31
1	2		4	6				9	11¹	10	12	7²				13				8		5	3					32
1	2		4	6				9	10¹	11						13				8	7²	5	3	12				33
1	2		4	6				9	10¹	12	11		14							8²	7³	5	3	13				34
1	2³		4¹	13	6			9	10	11			14							8	7	5²	3	12				35
1			4	6				9	13	11	12					2				8	7¹	5	3			10²		36
1			4	6	14		8¹	9		11	12	13				2					7³	5	3			10²		37
1			4	6	2²			9	10¹	11	12	13								8	7³	5	3	14				38
1	8		4					9²		11	12				2	6³				7⁴	14	5	3	10¹	13			39
1	2		4	5	6		8	9²		11¹	12		14								7³		3	13		10		40
1	2		4³	5	6		8¹	9		11	12	13									7	14	3			10²		41
1	2		4	5	6	7³	8¹	9²		11	12	13										14	3			10		42
1	2		4	5	6	7²	8¹	9		11³	12	13	14										3			10		43
	2		4		6			9		11²	12	14					13			8³	7¹	5	3			10	1	44
1				5	14		8		12	11				3	2	6		10¹			7	9²		4³	13			45
1	2			5	6		8³	9	12		10²		4				13				7	14	3	11¹				46

FA Cup
Fourth Qualifying Round

	Basingstoke T	(a)	1-0
First Round	Ebbsfleet U	(h)	0-0
		(a)	3-2
Second Round	Stevenage	(h)	0-1

ALTRINCHAM Blue Square North

Ground: Moss Lane, Altrincham WA15 8AP. *Tel:* (0161) 928 1045. *Fax:* (0161) 926 9934. *Year Formed:* 1903.
Record Gate: 10,275 (1991 Altrincham Boys v Sunderland Boys, ESFA Shield). *Nickname:* The Robins.
Manager: Lee Sinnott. *Secretary:* Derek Wilshaw. *Colours:* Red and white striped shirts, black shorts, red stockings.

ALTRINCHAM 2010–11 LEAGUE RECORD

Match No.	Date	Venue	Opponents	Result	H/T Score	Lg Pos.	Goalscorers	Attendance
1	Aug 14	A	Luton T	L 1-2	0-1	—	Reeves [70]	6665
2	17	H	Darlington	D 2-2	0-0	—	Denham [51], Johnson [78]	1099
3	21	H	Crawley T	L 0-1	0-0	23		776
4	24	A	Southport	L 0-1	0-0	—		1088
5	28	A	York C	L 0-3	0-0	24		2095
6	30	H	Mansfield T	L 0-4	0-2	24		1261
7	Sept 4	H	Kidderminster H	L 1-2	0-0	24	Reeves [75]	929
8	11	A	Gateshead	L 0-2	0-1	24		539
9	18	A	Eastbourne Bor	L 0-5	0-3	24		1117
10	21	H	Barrow	W 2-0	0-0	—	Densmore (pen) [55], Reeves [74]	1042
11	25	H	Grimsby T	D 2-2	0-1	24	Denham [53], Densmore [90]	1364
12	28	A	Kettering T	D 3-3	2-2	—	Denham [19], Reeves [30], Hewson [81]	1194
13	Oct 2	H	Rushden & D	D 2-2	1-1	24	Reeves [8], Williams [89]	897
14	9	A	Histon	L 0-3	0-1	24		655
15	16	H	Fleetwood T	W 1-0	0-0	24	Twiss [60]	1106
16	30	A	Hayes & Y	W 1-0	0-0	24	Densmore (pen) [81]	274
17	Nov 6	A	Bath C	D 2-2	1-0	—	Clee [38], Twiss [47]	794
18	9	H	AFC Wimbledon	L 0-2	0-2	—		901
19	13	A	Luton T	L 0-1	0-0	24		1416
20	20	A	Crawley T	L 0-7	0-4	24		1331
21	27	A	Cambridge U	L 0-4	0-2	—		2123
22	Jan 1	H	Wrexham	D 0-0	0-0	24		1982
23	3	A	Mansfield T	W 1-0	0-0	24	Reeves [59]	2229
24	8	A	Rushden & D	W 2-1	1-1	23	Reeves [40], Milne [55]	1024
25	18	A	Tamworth	D 1-1	1-0	—	Reeves [7]	795
26	22	H	Bath C	L 0-3	0-1	23		831
27	25	H	Hayes & Y	W 4-2	1-1	—	Wedgbury [45], Clee [53], Reeves [72], Twiss [79]	558
28	Feb 1	A	Wrexham	L 1-2	0-1	—	Clee [87]	3300
29	12	A	Kidderminster H	L 1-2	1-2	22	Baynes [43]	2930
30	15	H	Histon	L 0-3	0-0	—		621
31	19	H	Kettering T	W 3-2	1-2	22	Reeves (pen) [22], Baynes [64], Young [88]	752
32	22	H	York C	D 0-0	0-0	—		1143
33	26	A	AFC Wimbledon	L 1-4	0-2	22	Joseph [69]	3078
34	Mar 5	H	Gateshead	D 1-1	0-0	22	Joseph [88]	765
35	8	A	Barrow	L 0-1	0-0	—		953
36	12	A	Newport Co	L 1-2	1-1	22	Reeves [1]	1201
37	15	H	Forest Green R	W 2-1	0-1	—	Joseph [57], Twiss [59]	598
38	19	H	Tamworth	W 2-0	1-0	22	Reeves [36], Johnson [60]	895
39	26	A	Darlington	W 1-0	0-0	21	Reeves [86]	1967
40	29	H	Southport	D 1-1	1-0	—	Reeves (pen) [20]	1210
41	Apr 2	A	Cambridge U	D 2-2	2-1	22	Lawton [27], Reeves (pen) [34]	1161
42	9	A	Forest Green R	L 0-1	0-0	22		937
43	16	A	Fleetwood T	L 1-3	0-2	—	Johnson [90]	1966
44	23	H	Newport Co	L 1-3	0-2	22	Johnson [90]	963
45	25	A	Grimsby T	W 1-0	0-0	22	Joseph [52]	4311
46	30	H	Eastbourne Bor	L 3-4	0-3	22	Beesley 2 [60, 82], Clee [76]	1649

Final League Position: 22

GOALSCORERS

League (47): Reeves 15 (3 pens), Clee 4, Johnson 4, Joseph 4, Twiss 4, Denham 3, Densmore 3 (2 pens), Baynes 2, Beesley 2, Hewson 1, Lawton 1, Milne 1, Wedgbury 1, Williams 1, Young 1.
FA Cup (0).

Coburn 25	Smith 32	Brown 24+9	Joseph 38+1	Williams 44+1	Densmore 32	Lawton 37+2	Reeves 33+10	Johnson 7+6	Danylyk 15+13	Clee 33+5	Denham 11+5	Holmes 2+3	Welch 8+3	Holsgrove 4+9	McCready —+2	Crowell 7+2	Twiss 16+16	McCarthy 5+3	Coates 9	Hewson 10+8	Jones 1	Milne 9	Somner 9	Baynes 20+6	Beesley 8+10	Piergianni 21	Wedgbury 6	Foster —+1	Dootson 12	Young 11	Connors 11	Bateson 6+3	Match No.
1	2	3	4	5	6	7	8	9^1	10^2	11^3	12	13	14																				1
1	2	3	4	5	6	7^3	8^2	12	10	11^1	9	14		13																			2
1	2	3^1	4	5	8			9^2	13	7^3	11	10	14	6	12																		3
1	2	3	4	5			12		9^2		11	10^1	7	6		8	13																4
1	2	3	4	5	6		8^1	12	11^3				7^2	9	14	10	13																5
1	2	3	4	5	6			9			14	11^2	8^3	10^1		7	13	12															6
	2	3		5	6	7^1	12	11		9				4		10		8	1														7
	2	3		5	6	7^3	12	14		11^2				4		10	13	9^1	1	8													8
	2	3	4^1	5	6	7	8			11^2		12	14	10		9^3			1	13													9
	2	3	4	5	6	7	12	11		10^2		8	13			9^1			1														10
	2	3^2	4	5	6	7	14	11		10		8^1		13		9^3			1	12													11
	2		4	5	6	7^2	8^3	10	11	9		13	12			1	14	3^1															12
	2		4	5	6	7	8^3	10	11	9^1		12	3^2	14		1	13																13
	2	3		5	6	7	8^2	11^1	14	9		4^3	13	10	12	1																	14
1	2	14	4	5	6	12		11		9^1						10^2	13	8^3				3	7										15
1		3	4	5^2	6	12	14			13	11					9^3			2^1			10		8	7								16
1		3	4	5	6	7	13	12	11^1							9^1						2		8	10								17
1		3	4^1	5	6	7^2			11	13						9		12				2		8	10								18
1	2	3		5	6		12			4^2	11^1	13				9						7		8	10								19
1		3	4	5	6	7^3	12				13	10				9^2		14				2		8	11^1								20
1	2	3	4	5	6					11	12		14			9^2							7^1	8	10^3	13							21
1	2^1		4	5	6					13		7				10		9^2				12		8	11	3							22
1		3	4	5	6	7		9			13	11^1				12		8^2				2			10^3	14							23
1		3	4	5	6	7^3		9^2					14			13		12				2		8	11	10^1							24
	2	12	4^4	5	6	7	8^3				13	14				9^1		1	11						10	3^2							25
1	2			5	6	7^1	8			12	13					9^2		4						10^4	11	3							26
1	2	14		5	6	7	8^2			11^3						12		4						9^1		3			10	13			27
1	2			5	6	7	8			11						12		4						9^1		3			10				28
	2^3	12		5	6	7^1	9^1			11	13													10^4	14	4^2	8		1	3			29
		12	4	5		7	8			11						9			2^1					10^2	13	6			1	3			30
			4^1	5		7	8	14		11		13				12		9^2						10		3			1	2		6^3	31
	2		4	5		7^1	10	14		11	12	13						9^2						8		3			1			6	32
	2		4	5^1		7		9^2		11	12	10	14					13^3						8		3			1			6^4	33
	13		4	5^1		7		9		11^3	12		14					8^2		10						3			1	2	6		34
	14		4	5^1		7^2		9		11	12	13								10						3			1	2	6^3	8	35
		8^1	4	5		7		9		11	12									10						3			1	2	6		36
1	2	13	4	5		7		9		11	12					8^1								10^2		3					6		37
1	2	8^2	4	5		7		9		11^1	12	14												10		3					6^3	13	38
1	2		4	5^3		7		9		12	11^2	13				10^1										3				6	8	14	39
1	2^1		4			7	8^4	9^2	10	11														13		3				5	6	12	40
1			4	5^3		7		9^1	10^2	11	12		14											13		3				6	8^4	2	41
1			4	5^1		7	8	9		11	12	13												10		3^2				6		2	42
	2	13	4	14^1	6	7		9		11	12									10						3^2				1	5	8^3	43
		12	4	5	6		2	9^3	10	11			14											8^1	13	3				1	7^2		44
	2	8	4	5	6	7		9^1	10^2	11^3			13											12	14	3				1			45
	2	8^1	4	5	6	7		9	10	11															12	3				1			46

FA Cup
Fourth Qualifying Round
Gateshead   (h)   0-2

BARROW   Blue Square Premier

Ground: Holker Street, Wilkie Road, Barrow-in-Furness LA14 5UH. *Tel:* (01229) 828 227.   *Year Formed:* 1901.
Record Gate: 16,854 (1954 v Swansea T, FA Cup 3rd rd).   *Nickname:* Bluebirds.   *Managers:* Dave Bayliss and
Darren Sheridan.   *Colours:* White shirts, blue shorts, white stockings.

BARROW 2010–11 LEAGUE RECORD

Match No.	Date	Venue	Opponents	Result	H/T Score	Lg Pos.	Goalscorers	Attendance
1	Aug 14	A	Histon	L	1-3	1-2	—	Clerima (og) [12]	533
2	17	H	Gateshead	L	1-3	1-1	—	Boyd [30]	1440
3	21	H	Rushden & D	W	2-0	0-0	17	Walker 2 (1 pen) [69, 76 (p)]	1145
4	24	A	York C	D	0-0	0-0	—		2212
5	28	A	Wrexham	D	1-1	1-0	18	Walker [23]	2525
6	30	H	Darlington	D	1-1	0-0	19	Walker (pen) [73]	1718
7	Sept 4	A	Bath C	D	1-1	1-0	19	Pearson, M [32]	875
8	11	H	Eastbourne Bor	W	4-0	1-0	14	Walker 3 (1 pen) [41, 61, 73 (p)], Forrest [70]	1092
9	18	H	Forest Green R	W	3-0	2-0	9	Walker [11], Wiles 2 [22, 48]	1246
10	21	A	Altrincham	L	0-2	0-0	—		1042
11	25	A	Hayes & Y	L	0-2	0-1	17		340
12	28	H	Fleetwood T	L	0-2	0-2	—		1634
13	Oct 2	H	Luton T	L	0-1	0-1	20		1416
14	5	A	Tamworth	D	2-2	1-1	—	Wylde (og) [13], Walker (pen) [75]	779
15	9	H	Crawley T	D	1-1	0-1	19	Walker (pen) [59]	1155
16	16	A	Cambridge U	L	1-3	0-2	22	Owen [79]	2726
17	30	A	Rushden & D	L	0-5	0-3	22		1107
18	Nov 6	H	Newport Co	W	2-1	0-1	—	Walker [55], Chadwick [69]	1089
19	13	H	AFC Wimbledon	W	2-0	1-0	17	Owen [43], Goodfellow [77]	1375
20	20	A	Grimsby T	D	1-1	0-0	18	Chadwick [61]	3225
21	Jan 1	H	Southport	D	1-1	0-0	18	Spender (pen) [84]	1339
22	3	A	Darlington	L	1-3	0-2	18	Almond [59]	1407
23	8	H	Cambridge U	L	1-2	0-1	20	Almond [90]	1015
24	15	A	Kidderminster H	W	2-1	1-0	—	Almond 2 [17, 54]	906
25	18	A	Gateshead	L	0-3	0-1	—		518
26	22	A	Kidderminster H	L	0-2	0-1	18		1232
27	25	H	Histon	D	1-1	0-1	—	Rutherford [75]	883
28	Feb 5	H	Wrexham	L	0-1	0-0	—		1318
29	12	A	Kettering T	D	1-1	1-0	20	Chadwick [18]	1410
30	19	H	Mansfield T	D	2-2	1-0	21	Rutherford [30], Connor (og) [54]	1130
31	22	H	Tamworth	L	0-2	0-1	—		874
32	26	A	Crawley T	L	2-3	2-2	21	Cook [19], Rutherford [42]	3941
33	Mar 5	A	York C	D	0-0	0-0	21		1342
34	8	H	Altrincham	W	1-0	0-0	—	Rutherford [46]	953
35	12	A	Forest Green R	W	3-2	1-1	19	Pearson, M [2], Baker [48], Curtis [83]	757
36	15	A	Southport	W	4-2	1-0	—	Baker [17], Ferrell [68], Almond 2 (1 pen) [84, 90 (p)]	889
37	19	A	Eastbourne Bor	W	2-0	0-0	17	Baker [49], Ferrell [87]	1041
38	26	H	Bath C	L	0-1	0-1	17		1121
39	29	A	Luton T	D	0-0	0-0	—		5528
40	Apr 2	A	AFC Wimbledon	L	0-2	0-1	17		3264
41	9	H	Kettering T	W	5-0	0-0	16	Rutherford 3 [54, 85, 90], Smith 2 [59, 66]	1015
42	12	A	Mansfield T	D	1-1	0-0	—	Forrest [78]	1253
43	16	A	Newport Co	L	0-5	0-4	17		1331
44	23	H	Grimsby T	L	0-2	0-0	18		1274
45	25	A	Fleetwood T	L	0-1	0-1	18		2788
46	30	H	Hayes & Y	W	2-0	0-0	18	Baker 2 [52, 61]	1445

Final League Position: 18

GOALSCORERS

League (52): Walker 11 (5 pens), Rutherford 7, Almond 6 (1 pen), Baker 5, Chadwick 3, Ferrell 2, Forrest 2, Owen 2, Pearson, M 2, Smith 2, Wiles 2, Boyd 1, Cook 1, Curtis 1, Goodfellow 1, Spender 1 (1 pen), own goals 3.
FA Cup (0).

Martin 14	Spender 45 + 1	Nicholas 3 + 7	Milne 2	Bolland 40	Owen 30 + 2	Wiles 8 + 2	Boyd 11 + 2	Walker 18	Blundell 7 + 2	Goodfellow 9 + 10	Cook 7 + 26	Pearson M 40 + 4	Forrest 10 + 4	Rutherford 41 + 1	Edwards 43	Jones 14 + 2	Sheridan 23 + 1	Hulbert 17 + 3	Pearson S 6 + 1	Donnelly 6 + 10	Wainwright 6	Chadwick 10 + 5	Clay 1	Darwikwa 1	Masters 25	Halstead 1	Grant 3 + 2	Almond 17 + 3	Smith 13	Curtis 15	Baker 12 + 2	Ferrell 8	Match No.
1	2	3³	4	5	6	7	8	9	10¹	11²	12	13	14																				1
1	2	3	4	5	6	7	8	9		10		12	11¹																				2
1	2			5	6	12	8¹	9²		11³	13		14	7	3	4	10																3
1	2			5	6	12	8	9		11²			13	7¹	3	4	10																4
1	2			5	6	7²	8	9			13		11		3	4	12	10¹															5
1	2			5	6	7	8²	9			12	13	10¹	3	4⁸		11																6
	2			5	6	7	8	9¹			12	4		3		10	1	11															7
1	2			5	14	7	8³	9²		13		4	10	11¹	3		6	12															8
1	2			5		7	8	9³	14		13	4	10²	11¹	3		6	12															9
1	2³			5		7¹	8	9	14		13	4	10²	11	3		6	12															10
1	2			5⁸	6		8²	9	10¹		12	3		7	11		4	13															11
1	2				6			9		12		3	10¹	7	5	4		8		11													12
1	2				6			9	10¹		3	12	7	5	4		8		11														13
	2				6			9				3		7	5	4	10	8	1	12	11¹												14
	2				6	13		9				5		7	3	4	8²	10¹	1	12	11												15
	2				6			9				5		7	3	4	10¹		1	8	11	12											16
	2			5	6			9	14			3		12		4			1	10	11³	13	7²	8¹									17
	2			5	6			9		11		4		7	3		8				10		1										18
	2			5	6				10¹	11		4		7	3		8		12		9		1										19
	2			5	6			13	10³	11		3		7¹	4	8²		12		9		1		14									20
1	2			5	6				10	11¹		4		7	3		8⁸								9	12							21
1	2			5	6				10¹	12		4		7	3		8⁸							9	11								22
	2²			5	6				10¹	12		4		7	3	13		8					1		9	11							23
	2			5	6			11¹	13			4		7	3			12		10²			1		9	8							24
	2			5	6			11¹	12			4		7	3			13		10³			1		14	9	8²						25
	2			5	6				12			4		7	3	15	11			10⁶			1⁸		9	8¹							26
	2			5	6				13	12		4		7	3			1	11	10¹					9	8²							27
	2				8					11¹		4		7	3	5		6		12			1		9	10⁸							28
	2			5					12	3		7		11	4		8			10			1		9¹	6							29
	2			5					12	13	3			7	11	4	6¹			10			1		9²		8						30
12	7			5					13		3			8	6	4²	11¹			10			1		9	2							31
	2			5					12	11	3			7	6	8				1			9¹	10	4								32
	2			5					10¹	6		7	3	11					1				12		9	4	8						33
	2			5					10¹	6		7	3	8					1				12		9	4	11						34
	2	13		5					12	6		7	3	8					1				10¹		9²	4	11						35
	2	13		5					12	6		7	3	8					1				10¹		9²	4	11						36
	2	12		5					13	14	6			7³	3	8			1				10¹		9²	4	11						37
	2			5		13			12	6²		7	3	4¹					1				10		9	11⁸	8						38
	2	12		5					6			7	3	4					1				10¹	11	9		8						39
	2	14		5					12	13	6			7	3	11³			1				10¹	4²	9		8						40
	2	14		5	8¹				13	6	10	7	3²	4	12								11	9³									41
	2			5	7²				14	6	11	10	3	4¹	13				1				8	9¹	12								42
	2			5	11²				13	6	8	7	3	4¹	12				1				10	9³	14								43
	2			5	14				13	12	6	7¹	10	3	4²				1				11³	9	8								44
	2	13		5	11¹				9	6	10	3		4	12				1				7²	8									45
	2			5²	11				12	6	7³	3	13	4	14				1				10	9¹	8								46

FA Cup
Fourth Qualifying Round
    FC United of Manchester (a)   0-1

BATH CITY

Blue Square Premier

Ground: Twerton Park, Twerton, Bath BA2 1DB. *Tel:* (01225) 423 087. *Fax:* (01225) 481 391. *Year Formed:* 1889.
Record Gate: 18,020 (1960 v Brighton & HA). *Nickname:* The Romans. *Manager:* Adie Britton.
Secretary: Quentin Edwards. *Colours:* Black and white stripes.

BATH CITY 2010–11 LEAGUE RECORD

Match No.	Date	Venue	Opponents	Result	H/T Score	Lg Pos.	Goalscorers	Atten- dance
1	Aug 14	A	Hayes & Y	L 1-2	0-0	—	Jones [90]	328
2	17	H	Rushden & D	W 2-1	0-1	—	Connolly [46], Edwards, D [58]	876
3	21	H	York C	D 2-2	1-1	9	Harris [38], Phillips [66]	1066
4	24	A	Crawley T	L 1-2	0-2	—	Webb [75]	1252
5	28	A	Forest Green R	D 0-0	0-0	17		1464
6	30	H	Wrexham	L 0-2	0-1	21		1262
7	Sept 4	H	Barrow	D 1-1	0-1	22	Edwards, D [77]	875
8	11	A	AFC Wimbledon	L 0-4	0-2	23		2300
9	18	H	Darlington	D 2-2	0-1	22	Hogg [89], Mackie [90]	951
10	21	A	Tamworth	D 2-2	2-1	—	Mohamed [19], Connolly [33]	920
11	25	A	Fleetwood T	L 1-2	0-1	22	Mohamed (pen) [87]	1481
12	28	H	Kidderminster H	W 2-0	2-0	—	Mohamed (pen) [16], Russell [45]	742
13	Oct 2	A	Cambridge U	W 2-1	1-1	18	Canham [28], Mohamed [90]	2670
14	9	H	Eastbourne Bor	D 1-1	1-0	20	Mohamed [27]	1074
15	16	A	York C	D 1-1	0-1	21	Russell [63]	2331
16	30	A	Luton T	L 1-3	0-3	21	Phillips [65]	7003
17	Nov 6	H	Altrincham	D 2-2	0-1	—	Phillips 2 [63, 74]	794
18	9	H	Hayes & Y	W 3-1	1-0	—	Mohamed [20], Jones [87], Phillips [90]	532
19	13	A	Southport	W 3-2	0-2	14	Mohamed [49], Webb [78], Phillips [85]	947
20	20	H	Fleetwood T	D 1-1	1-0	14	Canham [16]	905
21	25	A	Histon	W 2-1	1-0	—	Jombati [45], Phillips [55]	470
22	Dec 28	H	Forest Green R	L 2-4	1-3	—	Mohamed (pen) [26], Phillips [68]	1222
23	Jan 1	A	Newport Co	W 2-1	0-0	11	Mohamed [57], Jones [90]	2903
24	3	A	Wrexham	L 0-2	0-1	13		2602
25	8	H	Luton T	D 0-0	0-0	13		2301
26	18	H	Crawley T	L 0-2	0-1	—		836
27	22	A	Altrincham	W 3-0	1-0	13	Phillips 2 [36, 88], Mohamed [81]	831
28	25	H	AFC Wimbledon	D 2-2	0-2	—	Canham [52], Murray [85]	1135
29	29	H	Cambridge U	W 4-0	0-0	—	Canham [47], Mohamed 2 (2 pens) [78, 88], Murray [83]	1338
30	Feb 5	A	Kidderminster H	L 0-1	0-1	—		1500
31	12	H	Tamworth	W 2-0	0-0	11	Watson [80], Murray [90]	899
32	15	A	Kettering T	L 1-2	1-1	—	Jombati [31]	796
33	22	H	Newport Co	D 2-2	2-2	—	Murray [9], Phillips [23]	1551
34	26	H	Southport	W 2-1	1-1	12	Lever (og) [33], Phillips [53]	792
35	Mar 1	A	Rushden & D	L 1-5	1-4	—	Murray (pen) [15]	804
36	5	H	Kettering T	D 1-1	0-1	14	Mohamed [90]	890
37	19	H	Grimsby T	W 2-1	1-0	12	Watkins [32], Mackie [85]	1808
38	26	A	Barrow	W 1-0	1-0	11	Phillips [6]	1121
39	Apr 2	H	Gateshead	W 1-0	0-0	10	Phillips [47]	952
40	4	A	Gateshead	D 1-1	0-1	—	Clough [88]	522
41	9	A	Darlington	L 1-3	0-3	11	Phillips [75]	1752
42	14	A	Mansfield T	L 0-2	0-0	—		2026
43	16	A	Grimsby T	D 2-2	0-2	13	Murray [80], Clough [90]	2389
44	23	H	Histon	W 2-1	1-0	11	Watkins [8], Hogg [74]	754
45	25	A	Eastbourne Bor	L 0-2	0-0	13		1014
46	30	H	Mansfield T	W 2-0	0-0	10	Watkins [52], Murray [75]	1051

Final League Position: 10

GOALSCORERS
League (64): Phillips 15, Mohamed 13 (5 pens), Murray 7 (1 pen), Canham 4, Jones 3, Watkins 3, Clough 2, Connolly 2, Edwards, D 2, Hogg 2, Jombati 2, Mackie 2, Russell 2, Webb 2, Harris 1, Watson 1, own goal 1.
FA Cup (3): Connolly 1, Jombati 1, Mackie 1.

Robinson 31	Simpson 35 + 1	Ruddick 9	Webb 27 + 2	Jones 36 + 3	Harris 17 + 8	Murray 13 + 20	Connolly 43 + 2	Phillips 41 + 2	Canham 44 + 1	Hogg 10 + 10	Rollo 26 + 12	Mohamed 28 + 6	Mackie 3 + 16	Jombati 43	Edwards D 5 + 8	Reid — + 4	Borhy 2	Coupe 1	Badman — + 1	Edwards J 8 + 2	Watkins 20 + 2	Hart 1 + 2	Russell 12	Burnell 21 + 4	Pentney 13	Jeanne — + 3	Watson 5 + 2	Brown — + 2	Henry 3 + 1	Clough 9 + 2	Lennox — + 3	Egan — + 1	Match No.
1	2	3^1	4	5	6^3	7^2	8	9	10	11	12	13	14																				1
1	2		4	5	6		8	9^2	10	11	13			3	7^1	12																	2
1	2		4	5	6		8	9^2	10	11^3	13	12	14	3	7^1																		3
	2		4	5	6^3		8	9^2	12	11		10	14	7	13			1		3^1													4
1	2		4	5	6		8	9^2	10	11		7¹	13	3	12																		5
1	2		4	5	6		8	9	10	11^2	13			3	7^1	12																	6
1	2		4	5	6^2		8	14	10	3	11	7^1		9^3	12						13												7
1	2		4	5	6^3		8	9	10	12	14	13	11^1	7						3^2													8
1	2		4	5^2			8	9^3	10	11	13	7	12	3	14					6^1													9
1	2		4	13			8	9^1	10	11	5	7^2		3	12					6													10
1	2^2		4		6^1		8^3	9	10		5	11		3	13					7	12	14											11
1	12		4		14		8	9^2	10		5	11		3	13					2	6^1		7^3										12
1	2		4		6			9^1	10		5	11	13	3	12						7		8^2										13
1	2		4		6	14	13	9^1	10		5	11		3	12						7^3		8^2										14
1	2^1			5		13	8	9^3	10		4	11^2		3	14					12	7		6										15
1			4	5^2		14	8	12	10		6	11^3		3						2	9^1		7	13									16
			4				12	8	9	10		5	11	3							2		7	6^1	1								17
			4	12	13	8^1	6	9	10		5	11		3						14			7^3	2^1	1								18
			4	5	6	14	12	9	10		6^1	11		3						2			7	12	1								19
			4	5	6	14	12	9	10		2^2	11^3		3								13	7^1	8	1								20
	11^1	4	2	13	14	8	9	10		12	7^3			3									6^7	5	1								21
	2^1	$3^■$	4	5			12	8^3	9	10^2	11		7										6	13	1	14							22
	2	13	5	6	12	8	9^3		11			7^2		3									10^1	4	1	14							23
	2^1		5	6^2	12	8	9	10	13	3^9	7		11											4	1	14							24
7			12	5	6	13	8	9^2	10		3	11		2										4^1	1								25
		3	4	5	6^2	12	8		10	13	2^1	9		7											1				11				26
		3	4	5	13	12	8	9	10		2^2	7		6											1				11^1				27
		3	4	14	6^1	12	8	9^3	10	13	5	7		2											1				11^2				28
	3	6^1	12		13	8	9	10	14	2	7												5^3	1					11^2				29
1	2			5	11^2	8	9^3	10	14	6^1	7			3						12			4				13						30
1	2			5	12	8	9	10	13	3^2	7^3		11							6^1			4				14						31
1	2	3^2		5	12	8		10	13	9		11								6^1			4				7						32
1	2	3		5	7^1	8	9	10	12	6			11							4^2									13				33
1	2			5	7^2	4	9^3	10			3	13	11							8	6^1									14	12		34
1	2			5	7^1	8	9^2	10		3	12	13	11							4									6				35
1	2^1			5	7	4		10		12	11	13	3							8			6^2						9				36
1	2			5	7^1	8	9	10		13		12	3							11^2			4						6				37
1	2			5	7^2	8	9	10		14		13	3							11^1			4^3						6	12			38
1	2			5	7^1	8	9	10^2		13		14	3							11			4^3						6	12			39
1	2			5	13	8	9	10^3		6^2		14	3							11			4						7^1	12			40
1	2				12	8	9	10		5			3							7			4						11^1	6			41
1	2			5	14	12	8	9	10^3			7^1	3							11			4						6	13			42
1	2			5	7	8^1	9	10	12			13	3							11^2			4						6				43
1	2			5	7^3	8^2	9	10	12			14	3							11^1			4						6		13		44
	2	6	5			8	9	10^3	11	4		13	3^2	1							14						7^1	12				45
1	2^1	6	5^2	14		7	8^3	9	10	13	12		3							11			4										46

FA Cup
Fourth Qualifying Round

Swindon Supermarine	(a)	0-0
	(h)	3-4

CAMBRIDGE UNITED — Blue Square Premier

Ground: R Costings Abbey Stadium, Newmarket Road, Cambridge CB5 8LN. *Tel:* (01223) 566 500.
Fax: (01223) 729 220. *Year Formed:* 1912. *Record Gate:* 14,000 (1970 v Chelsea, Friendly). *Nickname:* The U's.
Manager: Jez George. *Secretary:* Claire Osbourn. *Colours:* Navy and sky blue shirts, sky blue shorts, sky blue stockings.

CAMBRIDGE UNITED 2010–11 LEAGUE RECORD

Match No.	Date	Venue	Opponents	Result	H/T Score	Lg Pos.	Goalscorers	Attendance
1	Aug 14	A	Wrexham	L 0-1	0-1	—		4040
2	17	H	Crawley T	D 2-2	2-2	—	Russell [18], Saah [29]	2558
3	21	H	Southport	D 0-0	0-0	21		2506
4	24	A	Tamworth	D 1-1	0-0	—	Wright [54]	863
5	28	A	Mansfield T	L 0-1	0-0	23		2257
6	30	H	Eastbourne Bor	W 2-0	2-0	17	Coulson [7], Jennings [43]	2465
7	Sept 4	H	Gateshead	W 5-0	1-0	11	Wright [29], Clare [53], Russell [74], Saah [76], Gray [82]	2637
8	11	A	Luton T	L 0-2	0-2	17		6691
9	18	A	Kidderminster H	D 0-0	0-0	18		1291
10	21	H	Kettering T	W 3-0	0-0	—	Gray [71], Willmott [80], Wright [82]	2646
11	25	H	Newport Co	L 0-1	0-1	16		2648
12	29	A	AFC Wimbledon	L 0-3	0-0	—		3119
13	Oct 2	H	Bath C	L 1-2	1-1	19	Russell [5]	2670
14	5	A	Hayes & Y	L 0-2	0-1	—		362
15	10	A	Fleetwood T	D 2-2	1-1	22	Willmott 2 (1 pen) [8, 81 (p)]	2360
16	16	H	Barrow	W 3-1	2-0	18	Russell [14], Pearson, M (og) [45], Coulson [89]	2726
17	30	A	Gateshead	W 3-2	3-1	14	Coulson [28], Gray [31], Russell [45]	1083
18	Nov 9	H	Grimsby T	D 1-1	1-1	—	Wright [22]	2303
19	13	A	Kettering T	D 2-2	2-0	15	Willmott 2 [38, 45]	1959
20	20	H	Tamworth	D 3-3	0-2	15	Willmott (pen) [68], Patrick [75], Marriott [77]	2809
21	27	H	Altrincham	W 4-0	2-0	—	Wright 2 [15, 65], Gray 2 [23, 56]	2123
22	Dec 28	H	Mansfield T	L 1-5	0-2	—	Willmott [66]	2505
23	Jan 1	H	Histon	D 0-0	0-0	14		3225
24	3	A	Eastbourne Bor	W 2-0	2-0	12	Willmott [3], Gray [32]	983
25	8	A	Barrow	W 2-1	1-0	10	Willmott [18], Gray [54]	1015
26	22	H	Wrexham	L 1-3	0-3	14	Willmott [59]	2469
27	25	A	Crawley T	L 0-3	0-0	—		3241
28	29	A	Bath C	L 0-4	0-0	—		1338
29	Feb 1	A	Rushden & D	L 1-2	1-0	—	Wright [3]	1279
30	5	H	Rushden & D	L 0-2	0-2	—		2366
31	12	A	Grimsby T	D 1-1	0-1	17	Coulson [61]	3142
32	15	H	Darlington	L 0-1	0-0	—		1635
33	18	H	Kidderminster H	L 1-2	0-1	—	Marriott [89]	1869
34	22	A	Histon	W 2-0	1-0	—	Wright [44], Marriott [50]	1903
35	Mar 1	A	Newport Co	D 1-1	1-0	—	Russell [9]	1360
36	5	A	Darlington	L 0-1	0-0	17		2080
37	12	A	Southport	D 1-1	0-0	17	Berry [90]	1107
38	15	H	Luton T	D 0-0	0-0	—		2831
39	19	H	York C	W 2-1	1-1	16	Hughes [19], Wright [78]	2474
40	26	H	Forest Green R	D 1-1	1-0	16	Bentley [43]	2086
41	Apr 2	A	Altrincham	D 2-2	1-2	16	Hughes [39], Saah [59]	1161
42	9	H	AFC Wimbledon	L 1-2	0-2	17	Wright [82]	2907
43	16	A	Forest Green R	D 1-1	1-1	18	Sinclair [45]	1092
44	23	H	Hayes & Y	W 1-0	0-0	17	Patrick [76]	2619
45	25	A	York C	D 0-0	0-0	17		2939
46	30	H	Fleetwood T	L 0-1	0-0	17		2745

Final League Position: 17

GOALSCORERS
League (53): Willmott 10 (2 pens), Wright 10, Gray 7, Russell 6, Coulson 4, Marriott 3, Saah 3, Hughes 2, Patrick 2, Bentley 1, Berry 1, Clare 1, Jennings 1, Sinclair 1, own goal 1.
FA Cup (4): Gray 1, McAuley 1, Russell 1, Wright 1.

Brown 32	Roberts 37+1	Jennings 38	Carden 24	Saah 36+2	Partridge 27+2	Russell 31	Miller 5	Wright 45	Platt 19+9	Willmott 26+1	Coulson 35+3	Marriott 9+24	Gray 14+9	Ives 4+11	Clare 10+10	Coakley 3+2	McAuley 28+7	Thorpe 2+3	Stavrinou 7	Patrick 14+12	Naisbitt 14	Hughes 10+8	Berry 12+2	Wellard 9	Brighton —+1	Walker 4+2	Jeffers —+2	Bentley 6	Hudson —+2	Sinclair 5+1	Herbert —+1	Eades —+1	Match No.
1	2	3	4	5	6^1	7	8	9^3	10^2	11	12	13	14																				1
1	2	3	4	5		7	8	9	10^1	11	6	12																					2
1	2	3	4^1	5		7		9^3	10	11	6	8^2	14	12	13																		3
1	2		4	5	6	7	8	9^2	10^1	11	3	13																					4
1	2^1	3*	4	5		7	8	9	10^2	11^3	6			12	14	13																	5
1		3	4	5		7	8^1	9^2		11^3	12	6	14	13	10		2																6
1		3	4	5		7	8^2	9^3		11	6	12	14	13	10^1		2																7
1		3^3	4	5		7	8^1	9		11	6	14	13	12	10^2		2																8
1		3^3	4	5		7	8	9^2		11	6	13	12	14	10^1		2																9
1	2		4^2	5		7	8	9		11^3	6	14	12	13	10^1		3																10
1	2		4	5	3	7		9^1		11	6	13			10	12	8^2																11
1	2		4	5	6	7		9^1		11	3	13			10	12	8^2																12
1	2	3	4	5^3	14	7		9^1		11	6	12	13		10^2		8																13
1		3		5	12^2	7		9^3		11	4^1	10^2	14	6	13		8	2															14
1		3	4	5		7^2		9		11	6				10^1	12	2			8	13												15
	12	3	4	5		7		9	13	11^2	6				10^1		2			8	1												16
	2	3		5		7		9^1	12	11	6	8	4		10						1												17
	2	3				7	8^1	9		11	6				10^2		5			4	1	12	13										18
	2	3		5		7		9^2		11	6				10	4	8^1			12	1	13											19
	2	3^2		5		7		9		11	4	13			10	6	8^1			12	1												20
	2^1	3	4		6	7		9^2	14	11^3	5	13			10	12	8				1												21
	2^1	3^2	14		6	7		9		11	5	13			10	4	8^3			12	1												22
	2	3	4		6	7		9^2		11	5	14			10^3	13	8^1			12	1												23
	2	3	4	5	6	7		9		11		8			10^1		12				1												24
	2	3*	4	5	6	7		9^1		11		8			10^2		12				1	13											25
		3	4	0*	6	7^2			12	11	5	13			10^3		9^1	2			1		14										26
1	2	3	8		6^1	7		9^3	12	11	5	13			10^2		4					14											27
1	5	3	8			7^3		9		11^1	6	13			10	4	2*			12^2		14											28
1	6	3^1	8			7^2		9	10		5	4	12				2			11		14	13										29
1	8	6	3					9		11^1	5	13	12		10^2		2			7		4											30
1	2		12	5^1				9			6				13	3	4			7^3		10	11^2			8	14						31
1	2			5				9	13		6	12				3	4^1			7		10	11^2	8									32
1	2	3		5				9^3	11^1		6	10					12			14		4	8			7^2	13						33
1	2	3		5				9				10					13			12		4	8			7^1							34
1	2	3		5	6	7		9				10^2					12			13		4	8				11^1						35
1	2	3		5	6			9		11^3		10^2					12			14		4	8			7^1	13						36
1	2	3		5	6^2			9		11		14			10							4	8^1			12		7^3	13				37
1	2	3		5	6			9	12						10							11^2	4	8^1				7	13				38
1	2	3		5	6			9^2	13			14			11^3		10			4^1		8				12		7					39
1	2	3		5	6			9	10^1					13			4	12		7^2		11					8						40
1	2	3		5	6			9	11			14					13			7^1		10^3					8			4^2	12		41
1	2	3		5	6^3			9	11^2	14	13									7		10	12				8			4^1			42
1	2	3		5	6			9	13		14	10^2					4			7^3		11	8^1					12					43
	2	3*		5				9^2	11		6	14					12			7^1	1	10	4					8^3					44
	2	3		5				9	11^1		6	13	12				4			7	1	10^2						8					45
	2			5				9^2	11		6	10	12				3	4		7^3	1	13						8^1				14	46

FA Cup
Fourth Qualifying Round
	Lewes	(h)	3-0
First Round	Huddersfield T	(h)	0-0
		(a)	1-2

CRAWLEY TOWN FL Championship 2

Ground: Broadfield Stadium, Winfield Way, Crawley, West Sussex RH11 9RX. *Tel:* (01293) 410 000.
Fax: (01293) 410 002. *Year Formed:* 1896. *Record Gate:* 4,522 (2004 v Weymouth, Dr Martens League).
Nickname: The Reds. *Manager:* Steve Evans. *Secretary:* Barry Munn. *Colours:* All red.

CRAWLEY TOWN 2010–11 LEAGUE RECORD

Match No.	Date	Venue	Opponents	Result	H/T Score	Lg Pos.	Goalscorers	Attendance
1	Aug 14	H	Grimsby T	L	0-1	0-1	—	2428
2	17	A	Cambridge U	D	2-2	2-2	—	Tubbs 2 [5, 8]	2558
3	21	A	Altrincham	W	1-0	0-0	13	Masterton [62]	776
4	24	H	Bath C	W	2-1	2-0	—	Tubbs [20], McAllister (pen) [42]	1252
5	28	A	Hayes & Y	W	3-0	2-0	3	McAllister 2 [17, 26], Torres [71]	320
6	30	H	Forest Green R	W	1-0	0-0	3	Tubbs (pen) [74]	1458
7	Sept 4	H	Fleetwood T	D	1-1	1-1	2	McAllister [8]	1637
8	11	A	Histon	W	2-0	2-0	2	McFadzean [20], Brodie [39]	497
9	18	H	Gateshead	W	2-1	0-0	1	Tubbs 2 (1 pen) [47 (p), 90]	1412
10	23	A	AFC Wimbledon	L	1-2	1-0	2	Tubbs [43]	4018
11	26	A	Rushden & D	W	1-0	1-0	1	Tubbs [45]	1162
12	29	H	Tamworth	W	3-1	1-1	—	Tubbs 2 [41, 76], Smith [47]	1355
13	Oct 2	H	Kidderminster H	W	2-0	0-0	1	Neilson [68], McAllister [76]	1483
14	5	A	Luton T	W	2-1	0-0	—	Brodie [80], McAllister [90]	6895
15	9	A	Barrow	D	1-1	1-0	1	Tubbs [42]	1155
16	16	H	Newport Co	L	2-3	2-2	2	Brodie [32], Neilson [38]	2566
17	30	A	Mansfield T	W	4-1	1-1	1	Bulman [21], McAllister 2 [70, 90], Tubbs [87]	2615
18	Nov 13	A	Darlington	D	1-1	1-1	2	Neilson [37]	2012
19	20	H	Altrincham	W	7-0	4-0	2	Tubbs 3 (2 pens) [2 (p), 35, 38 (p)], Neilson [8], Torres [87], Brodie 2 [89, 90]	1331
20	Jan 1	H	Eastbourne Bor	W	3-1	2-0	2	Smith [13], Tubbs 2 (1 pen) [28, 61 (p)]	1894
21	3	A	Forest Green R	W	3-0	1-0	2	McAllister [4], Tubbs 2 [63, 66]	1027
22	15	A	Kettering T	W	2-1	0-1	—	Brodie [60], Tubbs (pen) [62]	1812
23	18	A	Bath C	W	2-0	1-0	—	Tubbs 2 [10, 83]	836
24	22	A	Grimsby T	D	0-0	0-0	2		3382
25	25	H	Cambridge U	W	3-0	0-0	—	McAllister 2 [61, 85], Cook [69]	3241
26	Feb 3	A	Kettering T	D	0-0	0-0	—		1216
27	12	H	Wrexham	W	3-2	0-2	2	Tubbs 3 (1 pen) [50, 82, 86 (p)]	3331
28	15	A	Wrexham	D	0-0	0-0	—		4630
29	22	H	Southport	W	1-0	0-0	—	Mills [75]	3765
30	26	A	Barrow	W	3-2	2-2	2	McAllister [5], Brodie (pen) [28], Mills [86]	3941
31	Mar 5	H	Histon	W	5-0	2-0	2	Tubbs (pen) [21], Smith [45], Simpson [77], Hunt [82], Gibson [89]	3031
32	8	A	Kidderminster H	D	0-0	0-0	—		1816
33	12	A	Fleetwood T	W	2-1	1-0	1	Tubbs (pen) [32], Brodie [49]	2027
34	15	H	Hayes & Y	W	5-2	2-2	—	Dempster [25], Simpson [38], Tubbs 2 [58, 75], Mills [90]	2236
35	18	H	AFC Wimbledon	W	3-1	2-1	—	Tubbs [5], McFadzean [9], Dance [53]	4054
36	22	A	Eastbourne Bor	W	2-1	1-0	—	Wassmer [25], Torres [57]	2054
37	26	A	Gateshead	D	0-0	0-0	1		751
38	29	H	Mansfield T	W	2-0	1-0	—	McFadzean [13], Tubbs [82]	3162
39	Apr 2	H	Darlington	W	1-0	0-0	1	Smith [67]	3554
40	5	A	York C	D	1-1	0-1	—	Torres [49]	3060
41	9	A	Tamworth	W	3-0	1-0	1	Tubbs 2 (1 pen) [26, 59 (p)], Wassmer [84]	1569
42	12	H	Luton T	D	1-1	1-1	—	Brodie [2]	3326
43	16	A	Southport	W	4-0	0-0	1	Brodie 2 [7, 20], Neilson [57], Simpson [76]	1011
44	22	H	Rushden & D	W	4-0	1-0	—	Tubbs 3 [34, 68, 82], Cook [90]	3083
45	25	A	Newport Co	W	1-0	0-0	1	Howell [68]	2026
46	30	H	York C	D	1-1	0-1	1	Tubbs (pen) [68]	2945

Final League Position: 1

GOALSCORERS

League (93): Tubbs 37 (11 pens), McAllister 12 (1 pen), Brodie 11 (1 pen), Neilson 5, Smith 4, Torres 4, McFadzean 3, Mills 3, Simpson 3, Cook 2, Wassmer 2, Bulman 1, Dance 1, Dempster 1, Gibson 1, Howell 1, Hunt 1, Masterton 1.
FA Cup (13): Tubbs 3, McAllister 2, Smith 2, Torres 2, Brodie 1, Hall 1, Neilson 1, own goal 1.

Kuipers 26	Rusk 9 + 7	Mills 32	Wilson 32 + 7	Quinn 11	Hall 9 + 5	Masterton 12 + 1	Torres 34 + 5	McAllister 27 + 14	Tubbs 38 + 3	Cogan 2 + 1	Enver-Marum 1 + 2	Malcolm — + 3	Jordan 5 + 2	Neilson 23 + 4	McFadzean 34 + 3	Reason — + 4	Flood — + 3	Hutchinson — + 1	Wright — + 9	Brodie 25 + 13	Smith 22 + 7	Howell 35	Bulman 31	Rents 4 + 1	Cook 6 + 15	Hunt 22 + 3	Simpson 20 + 6	Dance 2 + 5	Dempster 8 + 2	Gibson 11 + 3	Shearer 15 + 1	Wassmer 10 + 2	Match No.
1^1	2^2	3	4	5	6	7	8	9^9	10	11^1	12	13	15																				1
	2	3	4	5	6	7	8^2	9^1	10^3	13	12	14	1	11																			2
1	2	3	4	5	6	7^3	8^2	12	10				9^1	11	13	14																	3
1	2	3	4	5	6	7^1	8^2	9	10^3			14		11	12	13																	4
1	2	3^3	4	5	6	7^1	8	9	10^2					11	14	12	13																5
1^1	2	3	4	5	6		8	9^6	10^2				15	11^1	7^8				12	13													6
	2	3	4	5	6	7^1	8	9^1	10				1	11^2	12				14	13													7
	2	3	4	5		7	8^3	12	10^1				1	11	6	14			13	9^2													8
	2^1	3	4	5		7^2	8	14	10^3	11			1	12	6				9	13													9
		3	4	5		7	8	13	10				1	2^2	6				9	12	11^1												10
1		3	4			14	8	12	10^2					2	5						13	9^1	7^3	6	11								11
1		3	4			12	8	13	10^3					2	5^1						14	9^2	6	11	7								12
1		3^1	4			14	8	9^1	10^2					11	5						12	13	6		7	2							13
1		3	4			14	8^1	12	10^3					2^2	5						13	9	6	11	7								14
1		3	4					12	9	10				2^1	5						13	11^2	8	6	7								15
1			4	2^2		14	8	12	10					11	5						13	9^1	7^3	3	6								16
1		3	4^1			12	7^3	14	9	13				11	5						10^2		6	8	2								17
1		3			6		8^1	12	9					7	5	14					10^2		11^3	4	2	13							18
1		3	4		6	7	8	14	10^1					2^3							12	3	11		13	9^2							19
1		3	4				8^1	9	10^2					2	5						13	11^3	6	7	12	14							20
1		3	14				8	9	10^7					7^1	5						12		6	4^5	13	2	11						21
1		6	2					12	10					11^1	5					9^2		3			7	4	8	13					22
1		6					8^2	9^3	10					12	5					11^1	7	3	4			2		13	14				23
1		6	2				8	9	10^1						5						12	14	13		7^1	11^2							24
1		6					8	9							5^3					11	7^2	3	4		12	2	13	10^1	14				25
1		6						14	9	13					5					10^2	7	4	3		11^1	2	8^3		12				26
1		6					8^2	9	10						5					14	7^1	3	4		12	13		2	11^3				27
	2							12	14	10					5					9^2		3	4		13	7^1	8^3			6	11	1	28
1	14	6						12	10						5					9^1	7^2	3	4		11^3	2	8		13				29
		6	2				8^1	9	13						5					10^2	7	3			12	4					11	1	30
1			12				8	9^1	10						5					13	7^2	3	4		2	14				6^1	11		31
1	14		12				8		10						5					13		3	4		9^2	2	7		11^3	6^1			32
1^6	13	6	12				8		10						5					9		3	4		2^1	7				11^2	15		33
		6	2				8^2		10^1											9	13	3	4		12		7	14	5	11^3		1	34
		6					8		10^2					5						9^1	11	3	4^4		13	2^3	7	12			1	14	35
	14	6	4				8	9^1	10^2					5						11^1		3			13	2	7	12			1	5	36
	13	6^1	2				8	9	10^3					5						11^2		3	4		14	7		12			1	5	37
	14		4				8	9^2	10^1						5					13	11	3			12	2	7^3				1	6	38
	14						8	9^1	10^3						5					12	11^2	3	4		13	2	7				1	6	39
	14		2				8	9							5					10^2	7^1	3	4		13		12			11^3	1	6	40
	13						8	9^1	10						5					12	14	3	4		2^1	7				11^3	1	6	41
	14							9^2					7^3	5						10	11^1	3	4		13	2	8		12		1	6	42
	2												12	5						10	13	3^2	4		9	8	7			6	11^1	1	43
								9	10^3				11	5^1						14	7^2	3	4		13	2	8			6	1	12	44
	2							13	10^2				12							9	11^1	3	4		8	7				6	1	5	45
	2							12	10				7^2							9^1	14	3	4^3		13	8			5	11	1	6	46

FA Cup

Fourth Qualifying Round   Newport Co   (a) 1-0
First Round   Guiseley   (a) 5-0
Second Round   Swindon T   (h) 1-1   (a) 3-2
Third Round   Derby Co   (h) 2-1
Fourth Round   Torquay U   (a) 1-0
Fifth Round   Manchester U   (a) 0-1

DARLINGTON
Blue Square Premier

Ground: The Northern Echo Arena, Neasham Road, Darlington DL2 1DL. *Tel:* (01325) 387 000.
Year Formed: 1883. *Record Gate:* 21,023 (1960 v Bolton W, League Cup 3rd rd, 14 November, at Feethams).
Nickname: The Quakers. *Manager:* Mark Cooper. *Secretary:* Colin Galloway. *Colours:* White with black trim.

DARLINGTON 2010–11 LEAGUE RECORD

Match No.	Date	Venue	Opponents	Result	H/T Score	Lg Pos.	Goalscorers	Attendance
1	Aug 14	H	Newport Co	W 1-0	1-0	—	Hatch [4]	2597
2	17	A	Altrincham	D 2-2	0-0	—	Coburn (og) [82], Wright [90]	1099
3	21	A	Kettering T	D 0-0	0-0	7		1350
4	24	H	Grimsby T	L 0-1	0-0	—		1993
5	28	H	Gateshead	W 2-0	1-0	7	Terry [45], Clarke [54]	2233
6	30	A	Barrow	D 1-1	0-0	9	Terry [62]	1718
7	Sept 4	A	Eastbourne Bor	D 1-1	1-0	9	Senior [43]	1464
8	11	H	Forest Green R	W 3-0	2-0	7	Senior [3], Caines (og) [10], Chandler [83]	1520
9	18	A	Bath C	D 2-2	1-0	7	Senior [25], Hatch [69]	951
10	21	H	Luton T	D 2-2	1-1	—	Hatch [26], Brown [73]	1665
11	25	H	Southport	W 1-0	0-0	13	McReady [90]	1633
12	27	A	York C	D 0-0	0-0	—		3176
13	Oct 2	H	Wrexham	L 0-1	0-0	9		1690
14	5	A	Rushden & D	L 1-2	1-0	—	Powell [14]	1034
15	9	H	Hayes & Y	L 0-1	0-0	14		1536
16	16	A	Mansfield T	D 1-1	0-1	13	Wright [90]	2234
17	30	A	AFC Wimbledon	W 2-0	1-0	12	Senior [14], Bridge-Wilkinson [62]	3952
18	Nov 9	H	Tamworth	W 1-0	1-0	—	Hone [35]	2625
19	13	H	Crawley T	D 1-1	1-1	11	Bridge-Wilkinson [21]	2012
20	20	A	Wrexham	L 1-2	0-1	11	Hatch [58]	2619
21	Jan 1	A	Fleetwood T	L 0-1	0-1	13		1432
22	3	H	Barrow	W 3-1	2-0	11	Smith, M [12], Bridge-Wilkinson [33], Brown [61]	1407
23	8	H	AFC Wimbledon	D 0-0	0-0	12		2046
24	11	H	Histon	W 3-1	1-0	—	Verma [42], Arnison [52], Hatch [86]	1489
25	22	A	Tamworth	D 1-1	0-0	12	Hatch [64]	1034
26	25	H	Mansfield T	D 0-0	0-0	—		1614
27	Feb 1	A	Luton T	L 0-4	0-0	—		5770
28	12	H	Eastbourne Bor	W 6-1	5-0	13	Bridge-Wilkinson 3 (2 pens) [19, 29 (p), 33 (p)], Hatch [34], Campbell [37], Verma [58]	1660
29	15	A	Cambridge U	W 1-0	0-0	—	Smith, G [50]	1635
30	19	A	Forest Green R	D 1-1	0-0	10	Smith, M [66]	851
31	22	H	Kidderminster H	D 1-1	0-1	—	Smith, M [63]	1615
32	Mar 1	H	Fleetwood T	W 4-0	2-0	—	Miller [2], Bridge-Wilkinson 2 (1 pen) [14 (p), 49], Smith, M [83]	1446
33	5	H	Cambridge U	W 1-0	0-0	8	Hatch [67]	2080
34	8	A	Gateshead	D 2-2	2-0	—	Miller [44], Bridge-Wilkinson [45]	1204
35	22	A	Kettering T	D 1-1	1-1	—	Smith, M [2]	1829
36	26	H	Altrincham	L 0-1	0-0	10		1967
37	29	H	Grimsby T	W 1-0	1-0	—	Hatch [21]	2642
38	Apr 2	A	Crawley T	L 0-1	0-0	9		3554
39	5	A	Newport Co	L 1-2	0-2	—	Verma [68]	1300
40	9	H	Bath C	W 3-1	3-0	9	Hatch 2 [1, 16], Campbell [36]	1752
41	12	A	Histon	W 1-0	0-0	—	Campbell [81]	277
42	16	A	Hayes & Y	L 2-3	0-2	—	Bygrave (og) [66], Miller [69]	432
43	19	A	Kidderminster H	W 2-1	0-1	—	Chandler [66], Moore [76]	1626
44	23	H	York C	W 2-1	0-0	8	Wright [54], Miller [56]	2966
45	25	A	Southport	D 1-1	0-1	8	Verma [72]	1866
46	30	H	Rushden & D	W 2-0	0-0	7	Wright [64], Campbell [86]	2009

Final League Position: 7

GOALSCORERS

League (61): Hatch 11, Bridge-Wilkinson 9 (3 pens), Smith, M 5, Campbell 4, Miller 4, Senior 4, Verma 4, Wright 4, Brown 2, Chandler 2, Terry 2, Arnison 1, Clarke 1, Hone 1, McReady 1, Moore 1, Powell 1, Smith, G 1, own goals 3.
FA Cup (8): Smith, G 2, Senior 2, Austin 1, Bridge-Wilkinson 1, Brough 1, Wright 1 (pen).

Russell 43	Arnison 34 + 3	Austin 13	Chandler 23 + 5	Hone 21	Miller 37	Terry 20 + 4	Senior 16 + 13	Hatch 37	Offiong 3 + 3	Smith G 37	Moore 9 + 5	Wright 9 + 13	Smith M 20 + 9	Gray J 3 + 10	Clarke 7 + 3	Brown 40	McReady 8 + 7	Main 5 + 11	Powell 3 + 2	Waite 1 + 4	Louis 4 + 2	Bridge-Wilkinson 27	Brough 5	Verma 25 + 1	Gillespie 1	Burn 9 + 1	Quinn 14	Taylor 14 + 2	Modest 6 + 7	Campbell 7 + 5	St Louis-Hamilton 3	Gray P 2 + 3	Match No.
1	2	3	4	5	6	7	8²	9³	10¹	11	12	13	14																				1
1	2	3¹	4	5	6	7	8²	9	10³	11		14		13	12																		2
1	2		4¹	5	6	7	14	9	13	11				10³	8²	3	12																3
1	2			5	6	7	14	9	10¹	11³			12	8²	13	3	4																4
1	2		4¹	5	6		13	9³		11²		10	7	14	8	3						12											5
1	2		4		5	7	8²	12		11		9¹	10	13	6	3																	6
1	2	3	4¹		5		7	8	9²	13	11³			10	12	6	14																7
1	2	3	12	5			7³	8²	9	11			10			4¹	6	14	13														8
1	2	6		4	5		7	8	9²	11			10¹	12		3		13															9
1	2	4	12	5			7	8²	9	11¹			10	13	6	3																	10
1	2	6			5		7	8	9	11			10¹			4²	3	13	12														11
1	2ᵇ	6	14	5			7	8	9¹	11³			12			4²	3	13	10														12
1		4	13	5	6¹	7	8	9²		11³			14			12	3	2		10													13
1	2	11	4¹	5	6	7	8²					13	9			3			10	12													14
1	2	4²		5	6	7¹	14			11		13				3	8	10³	12	9													15
1		2¹			5	6	13	9		11³	8		12			3		14	7	10²	4												16
1					5	6	10²	7		11	8	9¹				3		13	14	12	4	2³											17
1	14				5	2	10²	7³		11	6	9¹				3		12			13	8	4										18
1					5	2	10¹	4		11³	7			13		3ᵇ		12		14	9²	8	6										19
1		3			5	2		6		7	12			13		10¹				11²	4	8	9										20
1					5	2		6		11¹	7³	14		13		3		12		9	8	4²	10										21
1	2		4		5			6²		11		12	9¹			3	10					8		7			13						22
1	2		4		5			7		11		12				3	10¹					8		9			6						23
1	2		4		5			10		11		13	9¹			3	12					8					6	7²					24
1	2³		4		5			7		11²		12ᵇ				3	14					8		6			13	9¹					25
1			4		5			6¹		11³		14	12			3	13					8		10			2	7	9²				26
1	2		4¹		5					11			12			3						8		7			6	9²	13	10			27
1	7		9²		6			14		5³			11			10						8		7			3	13	12	4¹			28
1	2				5			9		11			12			3						8		7			6	4	10¹				29
1	2	12			5			13		11			9³			3	14					8		7			6	4¹	10²				30
1	2				5					11			12	9		3	10¹					8		7			6						31
1	2		4		6			13	10¹				12	9		3	11					8²		7		5							32
1	2		4		6			12	9				11	10¹		3						8		7		5							33
1	2		4		6				10				11	9		3						8		7		5							34
1	2				6			12	10				11	9²		3	4¹					8		7		5			13				35
1	2	4²			6	12	13	10		11			9³			3						8¹		7		5			14				36
1					6	12		10		11						3	8							7¹		5	4	2	13	9²			37
1	2				6	4²		10		11³			13			3	14					8				5	7	12	9¹				38
1					6	13	10			11²			9¹			3						8		7		5	4	2	12				39
1	2				6	4²	12	10								3	13					8		7		5	11		9¹				40
	12				6		14	10¹		11ᵇ							4							7		5	2	8²	13		1	3	41
1	2				6	11	10¹									3ᵇ						8		7		5	4	14	9³		13		42
	2		4		6	11						13	12	10		3						8³		7¹			5		9²	1	14	43
1	2		4		6	7¹		10³				11	9²	13		3						8		12			5					14	44
	12							11	8	13	9²	6					2¹							7		5	4	10³	14	1	3	45
1	2		4		6	12		5		11	10	9³				3						8²		7¹			14	13				46

FA Cup
Fourth Qualifying Round

	Mossley	(a)	6-2
First Round	Bristol R	(h)	2-1
Second Round	York C	(h)	0-2

EASTBOURNE BOROUGH Blue Square South

Ground: Langney Sports Club, Priory Lane, Eastbourne, Sussex BN23 7QH. *Tel:* (01323) 766 265.
Year Formed: 1964. *Record Gate:* 3,770 (2005 v Oxford U, FA Cup 1st rd). *Nickname:* The Sports.
Manager: Garry Wilson. *Secretary:* Myra Stephens. *Colours:* Red shirts, black shorts, red stockings.

EASTBOURNE BOROUGH 2010–11 LEAGUE RECORD

Match No.	Date		Venue	Opponents	Result		H/T Score	Lg Pos.	Goalscorers	Attendance
1	Aug	14	A	Tamworth	L	2-4	0-3	—	Pacquette [49], Elphick [83]	723
2		17	H	Hayes & Y	W	5-0	2-0	—	Elphick [31], Pacquette 2 [45, 90], Crabb, M [71], Taylor [73]	902
3		21	H	Wrexham	W	4-3	2-2	3	Pacquette [10], Elphick [44], Weatherstone 2 (2 pens) [52, 90]	1055
4		24	A	Histon	D	1-1	1-0	—	Treleavan [14]	421
5		28	H	AFC Wimbledon	L	2-3	0-1	9	Weatherstone [69], Atkin [78]	2485
6		30	A	Cambridge U	L	0-2	0-2	14		2465
7	Sept	4	H	Darlington	D	1-1	0-1	16	Taylor [69]	1464
8		11	A	Barrow	L	0-4	0-1	19		1092
9		18	H	Altrincham	W	5-0	3-0	14	Treleavan 2 [2, 13], Pacquette [38], Austin [65], Weatherstone (pen) [75]	1117
10		21	A	Forest Green R	W	4-3	3-3	—	Taylor 2 [32, 44], Pacquette [45], Crabb, M [90]	709
11		25	A	Mansfield T	L	0-4	0-2	15		2312
12		29	H	Rushden & D	L	0-2	0-2	—		802
13	Oct	2	H	York C	W	2-1	1-0	14	Taylor [44], Johnson [59]	1104
14		5	A	Newport Co	D	3-3	1-2	—	Weatherstone (pen) [9], Crabb, M [47], Langston [90]	2403
15		9	A	Bath C	D	1-1	0-1	15	Langston [82]	1074
16		16	H	Luton T	L	2-4	1-1	15	Cook [35], Johnson [67]	2518
17		30	A	Grimsby T	D	2-2	0-1	15	Rooney [50], Taylor [67]	2894
18	Nov	9	H	Forest Green R	D	0-0	0-0	—		722
19		13	H	Newport Co	D	0-0	0-0	16		1065
20		20	A	Kidderminster H	L	1-2	0-1	17	Pacquette [71]	1271
21	Dec	7	A	Hayes & Y	L	1-2	0-2	—	Crabb, N [86]	190
22		28	A	AFC Wimbledon	L	0-3	0-1	—		3364
23	Jan	1	A	Crawley T	L	1-3	0-2	20	Walker [85]	1894
24		3	H	Cambridge U	L	0-2	0-2	21		983
25		8	H	Mansfield T	L	1-3	0-1	22	Taylor [54]	903
26		22	A	Kettering T	L	0-3	0-1	22		1146
27		25	H	Tamworth	L	1-4	0-1	—	Taylor [69]	551
28		29	H	Grimsby T	L	2-3	1-1	—	Taylor [30], Walker [62]	1002
29	Feb	1	H	Gateshead	L	0-3	0-2	—		612
30		12	A	Darlington	L	1-6	0-5	24	Smart [85]	1660
31		19	H	Histon	D	2-2	0-1	24	Baker [47], Elphick [57]	783
32		22	A	Rushden & D	L	0-2	0-1	—		905
33		26	A	Fleetwood T	W	1-0	0-0	24	Smart [83]	1222
34	Mar	5	H	Southport	W	4-1	2-1	23	Elphick [36], Purcell [37], Crabb, M [79], Taylor [88]	1004
35		8	A	Wrexham	L	1-2	1-2	—	Taylor [8]	2410
36		12	A	York C	L	0-1	0-1	23		2357
37		19	H	Barrow	L	0-2	0-0	23		1041
38		22	H	Crawley T	L	1-2	0-1	—	Purcell [71]	2054
39		26	H	Kettering T	L	1-3	0-1	23	Taylor [90]	673
40	Apr	2	A	Southport	W	3-1	3-0	23	Smart [17], Pacquette [27], Ledsham (og) [43]	923
41		9	H	Fleetwood T	L	0-6	0-2	23		864
42		12	A	Gateshead	L	0-3	0-0	—		617
43		16	H	Kidderminster H	D	1-1	1-0	23	Pacquette [28]	688
44		23	A	Luton T	L	0-3	0-1	23		6171
45		25	H	Bath C	W	2-0	0-0	23	Pacquette [46], Taylor [83]	1014
46		30	A	Altrincham	W	4-3	3-0	23	Taylor 2 [17, 21], Brinkhurst [44], Purcell [90]	1649

Final League Position: 23

GOALSCORERS
League (62): Taylor 15, Pacquette 10, Elphick 5, Weatherstone 5 (4 pens), Crabb, M 4, Purcell 3, Smart 3, Treleavan 3, Johnson 2, Langston 2, Walker 2, Atkin 1, Austin 1, Baker 1, Brinkhurst 1, Cook 1, Crabb, N 1, Rooney 1, own goal 1.
FA Cup (2): Taylor 2.

Banks 41	Austin 40 + 1	Jenkins 35 + 2	Weatherstone 25 + 8	Elphick 21 + 2	Langston 18	Brown 7 + 4	Johnson 26 + 9	Treleaven 9	Pacquette 29 + 4	Crabb M 37 + 3	Taylor 42 + 3	Brinkhurst 19 + 18	Smart 22 + 11	Baker 27 + 6	Atkin 5 + 6	Strevett 8 + 12	Wills 1	Crabb N 2 + 16	Cook 7	Mambo 3 + 2	Nelson 8	Rooney 4	Partington 4	Jenkinson 3 + 1	Walker 6 + 1	Norwood 3 + 1	Masterton 4 + 1	Hutchinson 17 + 1	Spencer 1	Demetriou 5 + 5	Forecast 5	Purcell 10 + 7	Kelly 12	Match No.
1	2	3	4^3	5	6	7^2	8	9^1	10	11	12	13	14																					1
1	2	3	4^1	5	6	12	8^3	9^2	10	11	7	13	14																					2
1	2	3	4	5^3	6		8^1	9	10	11	7^2	13	12	14																				3
1	2	3	4^2	5	6	13		9	10	11	7^1	12	8																					4
1	2	3	4	5	6			9	10^1	11	7^2	13	8	12																				5
1		4	5	6	3		7			14	10	13		2	9^3	8^2	11^1	12																6
1^*	2	3^*	4^3	5	6	14	12	9^2	11	7	13	8	10^1																					7
1	2		4^1	5	6^3	3	12	7	11	9	13	8	10^2																					8
1	5^2		4^3		3	8	9^1		10	11	7	12	14	2					6	13														9
1		4		3	8		10	11	9^2	7^1	2	13	12						5	6														10
1		4^3		3	8		10^2	11	9	7^1	14	2	13	12					5	6														11
1	13	3	4^3		8		10^2	11	9	14	2^1	12	7						5	6														12
1	2	3	4	6	14	12	10^2	11	9^3	7	8^1	13	5																					13
1	2	3	4	6	7^1	8	11	9	10^3	14	13	12	5^2																					14
1	5	3	4	14	6	8	11	9	10^3	2^2	12	7^1	13																					15
1	2	3	4	6	8		10^2	11	9	7^1	12	13	5																					16
1	2	3	4	6	8	12	9^1	10	14	13	5					7^3	11^2																	17
1	2	3	4	6	8^2	10	13	9		14	13					5^1	11	7	12															18
1	5	3	4	6	8		10^1	9	12	13						11^2	7^8	2																19
1	5	3	4^2	6	8	12	11	9	14	2^3	13					10^1	7																	20
1	5	3	4^3	6^1			10^2	11	9	7	12		14	13			8^2																	21
1	2	3^3	12	6^1		8	10^8	11	9	4	14	7^2	13	5																				22
1	2	3	5		8^1		11^3	9^2	13	4		12	14										6		7	10								23
1		3	5				11		12	4	6	9^2	8	13						2					10	7^1								24
1	6	3	5^1				11	9		4	12	13^3	14							2					7	10^2	8							25
1	2	3^1			12		11	9³	7^2	8^8	5	10	13							4						14	6							26
1	2	13	5^1		8^3		11^2	9		3	14	4											10	12	7	6								27
1	2	3^3	4	5	9			6	12	7	14	11													8^1	10^2	13							28
	2	3	4	5			12	9		6		10^2	8^3			7												14			1	11^1		29
	3	4^2	5		8				12	11^3	9^1	10	7	2		13												6		1		14		30
	2	3	4	5			12	10		11^3	9^2	8	7^1	6		14													1		13			31
	2	3					8^2	10	13	12		6^1	11	5		7												4		1		9		32
	2	3	13	5			10^1	11^2	9	4		6	12			7												1		8			33
1	5	3^2		6			10^1	11^3	9	14	4	2	12	7														13				8	34
1	5	3	13			14	10	11^1	9	12	4^3	2	8															7^2					6	35
1	5	3	13			12	10^3	9	7^2	4	2	11^1	8															14					6	36
1	5	3	13	6^2		12	10	9		4	2	11																				8^1	7	37
1	5	3				8	11	9		12	4^1	2	7															10					6	38
1	5	3	13			8^1	12	11	9	14	4^2	2	7																			10^3	6	39
1	5	3	13				10^3	11	9	14	4^2	2	6															12				8^1	7	40
1	5	3^1	14				10	11	9	13	4	2																8^3		12		7^2	6	41
1	5	12				8	10^1	11^3	9^2	7	2	14																4		3		13	6	42
1	5					8	10^1	11	9^2	7	2	13																4		3		12	6	43
1	5	12				8	10^2	11	9	7	14	2^8																4^3		3^1		13	6	44
1	2	14	5			8	10^1	11^3	9^2	7	13																	4		3		12	6	45
1	5		6			8	10^2	11	9^1	7	12																	4		3		13	2	46

FA Cup
Fourth Qualifying Round
Harrow Bor   (h)   2-4

FLEETWOOD TOWN   Blue Square Premier

Ground: Highbury Stadium, Fleetwood, Lancashire FY7 6TX.   *Tel:* (01253) 770 702.   *Fax:* (0871) 770 702.
Year Formed: 1908.   *Record Gate:* 6,150 (1965 v Rochdale).   *Nickname:* The Trawlermen or The Cod Army.
Manager: Micky Mellon.   *Secretary:* Steve Edwards.   *Colours:* All white with red trim.

FLEETWOOD TOWN 2010–11 LEAGUE RECORD

Match No.	Date	Venue	Opponents	Result	H/T Score	Lg Pos.	Goalscorers	Attendance
1	Aug 14	A	Rushden & D	D	1-1	1-0	—	Vieira [23]	1248
2	17	H	Mansfield T	W	3-0	3-0	—	Curtis [6], Vieira 2 [19, 34]	1849
3	21	H	Luton T	L	0-3	0-2	11		2831
4	24	A	Gateshead	W	2-0	2-0	—	Vieira [35], McGuire [44]	623
5	28	A	Southport	L	0-1	0-1	11		1546
6	30	H	York C	W	2-1	1-0	5	Seddon [7], Vieira [83]	2020
7	Sept 4	A	Crawley T	D	1-1	1-1	7	Vieira [25]	1637
8	11	H	Kettering T	W	4-1	1-1	5	Craney 2 [45, 58], Vieira 2 [48, 81]	1602
9	18	A	Grimsby T	W	2-1	1-0	5	Seddon [44], Pond [59]	3099
10	21	H	Kidderminster H	D	1-1	1-0	—	Craney [20]	1411
11	25	H	Bath C	W	2-1	1-0	4	Vieira [31], Wright [58]	1481
12	28	A	Barrow	W	2-0	2-0	—	Curtis 2 [19, 22]	1634
13	Oct 2	H	Histon	D	1-1	0-0	3	Vieira [63]	1458
14	5	A	Wrexham	D	0-0	0-0	—		2689
15	10	H	Cambridge U	D	2-2	1-1	4	Vieira [7], McNulty [54]	2360
16	16	A	Altrincham	L	0-1	0-0	5		1106
17	30	A	Tamworth	W	2-0	1-0	6	Beeley [21], Vieira [51]	946
18	Nov 9	H	Gateshead	D	0-0	0-0	—		1011
19	13	H	Rushden & D	D	1-1	1-0	4	Barry [8]	1429
20	20	A	Bath C	D	1-1	0-1	5	Rogan [65]	905
21	Dec 18	H	Newport Co	D	1-1	1-0	—	Vieira [21]	1142
22	28	H	Southport	W	2-0	1-0	—	Marsh-Evans (og) [27], Beeley [77]	2051
23	Jan 1	H	Darlington	W	1-0	1-0	5	Seddon [20]	1432
24	8	A	Forest Green R	L	0-1	0-0	6		762
25	11	A	Mansfield T	W	5-2	1-1	—	Vieira 3 [45, 57, 59], Seddon [48], McGuire [62]	1725
26	18	H	AFC Wimbledon	D	1-1	1-1	—	Vieira [45]	1808
27	22	H	Hayes & Y	D	1-1	1-1	5	McGuire [30]	1281
28	25	A	Kettering T	L	1-2	0-0	—	McGuire [90]	798
29	29	H	Forest Green R	W	2-0	0-0	—	Brown [56], Clancy [80]	1335
30	Feb 1	A	Histon	L	0-1	0-1	—		255
31	5	A	AFC Wimbledon	L	0-1	0-0	—		3298
32	12	A	Luton T	W	3-1	1-1	5	Seddon 2 [9, 55], Barry [53]	6227
33	15	H	York C	L	0-1	0-0	—		2220
34	19	H	Grimsby T	W	3-0	1-0	5	Vieira [43], Seddon [78], Parker [90]	2004
35	26	H	Eastbourne Bor	L	0-1	0-0	6		1222
36	Mar 1	A	Darlington	L	0-4	0-2	—		1446
37	5	A	Newport Co	W	3-1	1-0	6	Seddon 2 (1 pen) [34 (p), 84], Donnelly [90]	1716
38	12	H	Crawley T	L	1-2	0-1	6	Donnelly [63]	2027
39	19	H	Wrexham	W	1-0	0-0	6	Clancy [48]	2207
40	26	A	Hayes & Y	W	2-1	2-0	6	Pond [12], Brown [45]	303
41	Apr 2	H	Tamworth	W	2-1	1-0	5	McGuire [34], Vieira (pen) [87]	1580
42	9	A	Eastbourne Bor	W	6-0	2-0	5	Parker [35], Vieira 2 (1 pen) [45 (p), 53], McGuire [57], Jenkins (og) [59], Donnelly [73]	864
43	16	H	Altrincham	W	3-1	2-0	5	Clancy [37], Seddon [44], Donnelly [90]	1966
44	22	A	Kidderminster H	L	1-2	1-0	—	Mullan [39]	2738
45	25	H	Barrow	W	1-0	1-0	5	Vieira [45]	2788
46	30	A	Cambridge U	W	1-0	0-0	5	Harvey [77]	2745

Final League Position: 5

GOALSCORERS
League (68): Vieira 22 (2 pens), Seddon 10 (1 pen), McGuire 6, Donnelly 4, Clancy 3, Craney 3, Curtis 3, Barry 2, Beeley 2, Brown 2, Parker 2, Pond 2, Harvey 1, McNulty 1, Mullan 1, Rogan 1, Wright 1, own goals 2.
FA Cup (3): Mullan 1, Seddon 1, Warlow 1.

Hurst 16	Beeley 38	McNulty 38	Barry 44	Grand 4	Linwood 18	McGuire 30+7	Craney 19	Curtis 18+2	Vieira 38+2	Pond 16+7	Beesley 1+4	Miles 6+2	Thorpe 4+14	Seddon 29+5	Cavanagh 15+1	Connors 2+6	Mullan 14+14	Brown 20+1	Davies 30+1	Clancy 20+11	Wright 15+3	Rogan 1+2	Gregan 26	Warlow 1+2	Horne 1	Worthington 3	Milligan 8+4	Donnelly 13+7	Rowe 2+3	Haining 7	Parker 7+6	Harvey 1+3	Camozzi 1	Match No.
1	2	3	4	5	6	7	8	9	10^1	11	12																							1
1	2	3	4	5	6		8	9^1	10^2	11				7	12	13																		2
1	2	3	4	5	6^8	12	8	9^2	10	7						11^1	13																	3
1	2	3	4			7	8	9^2	10		11^1			5	13	6	12																	4
1	2	3			6	13	8	9^1	10	4	14			11^3	12	5	7^2																	5
1	2	3	4		6	7	8^2	9	10					11	5^1	12	13																	6
1^6	2	3	4		6	7	8^1	9^2	10	12	13			11				5		15														7
	2	3	4		6	7^4	8	9	10	13				11				5^1	1	12														8
	2	3	4		6^3		8	9^1	10				14	11	12		7	5^2	1	13														9
	2	3	4	5			8^3	9	10^1	7	14			11^2		13			1	12														10
	2	3	4		6	14	8^2	9	10	7^3				11^1			13		1	12	5													11
	2	3	4		6	12	8	9	10	7^1				11^2					1	13	5													12
	2	3	4		6	12^4	8	9^2	10	7^1				11					1	13	5													13
	2	3	4		6		8	9^1	10	7	12			11					1		5													14
	2	3	4		6	13	8^1	9^2	10	7				11					1	12	5													15
	2	3	4		6		8^2	9	10	7^4				13				5	1	12	11^1													16
	2	3	4			7^1	8	9	10^2					11					1		5		6	13										17
	2	5	4			7	8	9^1	10^3				14	11^2			13		1	12			6			3								18
		3	4			7		9^2	10^3				14	11			12	2	1	8^1	5		6	13										19
	2	3	4			7		9^3	10^1				14	11			13	5	1	8^2	12		6											20
	2	3^4	4					9	10								13		1	12			6^1			11	5	7	8					21
	2		4^1		6	12		9^1	10				14	11			13		1	8^3	5					3	7							22
	2		4^2		6	13	8	9^1	10				14	11^1	12				1		5					3		7						23
	2		4		6	7	8^2	9^1	10				14				13		1	3^3	12		5				11							24
	2	5	4			7		9	10^2								12		1	11^1	3		6				8	13						25
	2	5	4				8	9	10								12		1	7^1	3		6					11						26
	2^1	5	4			7^3		9	10	14^4							13		1	11^2	3		6				12	8						27
	2	5	4			7		9	10										1	11^1	3		6				12	8						28
	2^1	5	4			7			10^3					11			13		1	12	3		6				9^2	8	14					29
	2	5	4			12	8		10								13		1	7^2	3		6				9^1	11^3	14					30
	2		4				8	9	10	7^1				11			12		1		3^4		6								5			31
	2		4			7^1		9^2	10					11			12		1	8	3		6								13	5		32
	2		4^3			7			10					11^1			12		1	8^2	3		6				13	9	14		5			33
	2		4			7		9^2	10								13		1	8^1	3		6				11^2		14		5	12		34
	2		4				8	9^1	10					11^2					1		3		6				13	7^3	14		12	5		35
	2	5	4				8^1	9	10^2								12		1		3		6				13	7	14		11^3			36
1	2		4		6^2				10^1	11				9^3			13	5		8	3		7						14		12			37
1	2	5	4				8	9^1	10					11^2						7^3	3		6				13		14		12			38
1	2	5	4				8		10^1					11			7				3		6				12	9						39
1	2	5	4^1		11		8		10								7^2				3		6					9			13	12		40
1	2	5	4^2				8		10^1					11^3			12				3		6				13	7			9	14		41
1	2	5^1	4				8	9^2	10								12			7^3	3		6				13				11	14		42
1	2	5	4				8	9^2	10								12			7	3		6				13				11^1			43
1	2	5	4				8	9^2						11			13			7^1	3		6					10^4			12			44
1	2	5	4				8	9	10^1					11						7^2	3		6				13				12			45
					6				10^1					5				4	1	12	3							9		11	7	8	2	46

FA Cup
Fourth Qualifying Round

	Buxton	(h)	2-1
First Round	Walsall	(h)	1-1
	Walsall	(a)	0-2

FOREST GREEN ROVERS Blue Square Premier

Ground: The New Lawn, Smiths Way, Nailsworth, Gloucestershire GL6 0FG. *Tel:* (01453) 834 860.
Fax: (01453) 835 291. *Year Formed:* 1890. *Record Gate:* 4,836 (2009 v Derby Co, FA Cup 3rd rd)
Nickname: Rovers. *Manager:* David Hockaday. *Secretary:* Philip Catherall. *Colours:* Black and white striped shirts,
black shorts, red stockings.

FOREST GREEN ROVERS 2010–11 LEAGUE RECORD

Match No.	Date	Venue	Opponents	Result	H/T Score	Lg Pos.	Goalscorers	Atten- dance
1	Aug 14	A	Mansfield T	L 1-3	0-0	—	Caines 52	2474
2	17	H	Wrexham	W 3-0	1-0	—	Styche 20, Jones 75, Klukowski 80	1216
3	21	H	Gateshead	D 1-1	1-0	8	Styche 10	882
4	24	A	Hayes & Y	W 4-3	1-1	—	Styche 28, Harrison (og) 47, McDonald 63, Else 90	286
5	28	A	Bath C	D 0-0	0-0	6		1464
6	30	A	Crawley T	L 0-1	0-0	11		1458
7	Sept 4	H	Southport	D 0-0	0-0	13		1064
8	11	A	Darlington	L 0-3	0-2	18		1520
9	18	A	Barrow	L 0-3	0-2	19		1246
10	21	H	Eastbourne Bor	L 3-4	3-3	—	Klukowski 35, Norwood 38, Herring (pen) 45	709
11	25	H	Kettering T	L 0-2	0-1	21		779
12	28	A	Newport Co	L 1-3	1-2	—	Klukowski 15	2677
13	Oct 2	A	AFC Wimbledon	D 1-1	1-1	22	Watson 5	3204
14	7	H	Grimsby T	D 3-3	2-1	—	Styche 12, Norwood 18, Klukowski 52	1007
15	16	H	Histon	L 0-1	0-0	23		741
16	19	A	Luton T	L 1-6	1-3	—	Styche 39	5704
17	30	H	York C	W 2-1	1-0	23	Caines 4, Styche 58	792
18	Nov 9	A	Eastbourne Bor	D 0-0	0-0	—		722
19	13	H	Mansfield T	W 2-1	1-0	22	Klukowski (pen) 9, Styche 49	767
20	20	A	Gateshead	D 1-1	0-1	20	Styche 69	601
21	27	H	Rushden & D	D 2-2	2-0	—	McDonald 2 20, 25	642
22	Dec 28	A	Bath C	W 4-2	3-1	—	Quinn 3, Jones 37, Styche 45, Dyer 77	1222
23	Jan 1	A	Kidderminster H	L 0-1	0-0	19		1370
24	3	H	Crawley T	L 0-3	0-1	19		1027
25	8	H	Fleetwood T	W 1-0	0-0	18	Guinan 77	762
26	22	A	York C	L 1-2	0-0	19	Styche (pen) 76	2468
27	25	H	Kidderminster H	D 1-1	1-0	—	Guinan 20	687
28	29	A	Fleetwood T	L 0-2	0-0	—		1335
29	Feb 5	H	Hayes & Y	W 1-0	0-0	—	Klukowski (pen) 47	787
30	12	A	Southport	L 0-4	0-3	19		1006
31	19	H	Darlington	D 1-1	0-0	19	Guinan 90	851
32	22	A	Grimsby T	D 1-1	1-1	—	Styche 36	2401
33	26	H	Tamworth	W 4-0	1-0	18	Guinan 25, Dyer 2 54, 89, Styche 78	681
34	Mar 1	H	Luton T	L 0-1	0-1	—		1015
35	5	A	Wrexham	L 1-2	0-2	19	Dyer 66	3386
36	8	A	Rushden & D	D 2-2	0-1	—	Styche 79, Davies 88	759
37	12	H	Barrow	L 2-3	1-1	20	Caines 34, Klukowski 63	757
38	15	A	Altrincham	L 1-2	1-0	—	Styche 27	598
39	19	H	Newport Co	D 0-0	0-0	21		1362
40	26	A	Cambridge U	D 1-1	0-1	22	Forbes 81	2086
41	Apr 2	A	Histon	W 3-0	1-0	21	Guinan 20, Dyer 80, Styche 86	426
42	9	H	Altrincham	W 1-0	0-0	19	McDonald 71	937
43	16	H	Cambridge U	D 1-1	1-1	20	Matthews 45	1092
44	23	A	Kettering T	L 1-2	0-0	20	Forbes 61	891
45	25	H	AFC Wimbledon	D 0-0	0-0	19		1824
46	30	A	Tamworth	L 1-2	0-1	20	Somner 52	1717

Final League Position: 20

GOALSCORERS

League (53): Styche 15 (1 pen), Klukowski 7 (2 pens), Dyer 5, Guinan 5, McDonald 4, Caines 3, Forbes 2, Jones 2, Norwood 2, Davies 1, Else 1, Herring 1 (1 pen), Matthews 1, Quinn 1, Somner 1, Watson 1, own goal 1.
FA Cup (1): Styche 1.

Bittner 46	Jones 45	Armstrong 24	Baldwin 1+3	Caines 36+7	Grimes 4+1	Smith 6+4	Klukowski 30+7	Styche 41+2	Norwood 11	Imudia 2+1	Fowler L11	Fowler M 18+2	Matthews 4+3	Else 5+12	Cleaver —+1	Herring 10+3	Davies 1+9	McDonald 22+1	Bartlett 6+4	Gill 2+1	Dyer 26+5	Watson 6+1	Hodgkiss 21+2	Flood 5	Head —+4	Mills 1+1	Enver-Marum 7+11	Kamara 1+1	Turk 23+2	Quinn 6	Guinan 10+8	Gray 4+9	Forbes 23+2	Allen 3+2	Hall 16+1	Somner 14+2	Stokes 14	Henry —+1	Young 1	Match No.
1	2	3³	4²	5	6	7	8	9¹	10	11	12	13	14																											1
1	2	3		5		7	8	9²	10¹	11		4		12		6	13																							2
1	6	3		5		7¹	8	9	10	11		4		12		2																								3
1	6	3	14	5		7²	8³	9	10¹	11				12		2	13	4																						4
1	5	13	6				8¹	10²	9			11	4	7		2	12	3																						5
1	6	3³	5■	14			10	9		8	7¹	11²		4	13	12		2■																						6
1	5		6	12		10	9		7		8¹	11²		2	13	3		4																						7
1	4		5	13		8	9	3■	6	11¹		2		7	14	10³	12²																							8
1	5	11	6	7¹	8			10²			4	13		2	12	3				9																				9
1	5¹		6	12		8	9	10■			7			2		3	4			11																				10
1	5		6	14		8	9		7	11²		2		3	4¹	13			10³	12																				11
1	5	13	6			8²	9	10	11	4			3			12	2	7¹																						12
1	5	14	6			9³	10	11²	4	13		12	3				8	2	7¹																					13
1	5		6			12	9	10	11	4	14		13	3				8³	2²	7¹																				14
1	5		6			8	9	10²		4	12		13	3				11	2¹	7³	14																			15
1	5		6			8	9²	10¹	13					3				2	7	14	4	11³	12																	16
1	5	3	6			8	9³		11²									12		2	14	13	10	7¹	4															17
1	5	3	14			8	9¹			4³	13					11²				10	2		12			7	6													18
1	5	3	14			8	9¹			4³	13					11²				10	2		12			7	6													19
1	5	3	12			8	9²			4¹						11				10	2	13				7	6													20
1	5	3	13			8				4²						11				10	2		9¹			7	6	12											21
1	5	3	4			8	9¹				13									10	2					7	6		11²	12									22
1	5	3	4			8	9¹													10	2					7	6	12	11²	13									23
1	5	3	6			8¹	9³				14							12		2						7		10²	13	11	4								24
1	5	3	6			12	9¹											13		2						7		10	11²	8³	14	4							25
1	5	3	6			8¹	12											10²		2		13				7		9		11	4								26
1	5	3	13			8	9											11		2		12				7²		10¹		4	6								27
1	5	3	6¹			8²	9											11³		2		13				7		12	14	10	4								28
1	5	3				8	9³											12		2		13				7¹		10²	14	11	4	6							29
1	5	3²	13															12■		10	2¹		11			7		9	14	8³	4	6							30
1	5		6			8²	9					13						11				10¹				12		7	14	2³	4	3							31
1	5		6			8¹	9											10				11²	13			12		7		2	4	3							32
1	5		6			12	9³											7				11¹	13			10²	14	8		2	4	3							33
1	5		6			8¹	9											10				13	7²			12		11		2	4	3							34
1	5		6			12	9¹						10					10				14	7	11■			8		2²	4³	3	13							35
1	5		6			8¹	9							12		13	10				14	7³					11		2²	4	3								36
1	5		6			12²	9							7		2³	10				13						11		14	4	3		8¹						37
1	5	3²	6			9						12		13		2¹	11				7						11		4	8								38
1	3		6			9						12				11				7			10		8¹		2	4	5									39
1	5		6	14		9¹			10			3³		7						12	13	8			2²	4	11												40
1	5		6	14		13			10²			11³		8						7	9¹	12	4		2		3												41
1	5		6			9			13			4		10				7			11²	8¹		2	12	3													42
1	5		6			9	2		10			8¹		11				7			12	4				3													43
1	5		6			9¹	2³		10²			8		11	14			12	7			4			13	3■												44
1	5	3	6			9¹			12			11²		10		2						13	4	7		8													45
1	5	3²	6			9¹			12			10		11		2						13	4	7		8													46

FA Cup
Fourth Qualifying Round   Maidenhead U   (h)   1-0
First Round   Northampton T   (h)   0-3

GATESHEAD
Blue Square Premier

Ground: Gateshead International Stadium, Neilson Road, Gateshead NE10 0EF. *Tel:* (0191) 478 3883.
Fax: (0191) 440 0404. *Year Formed:* 1889 (Reformed 1977). *Record Gate:* 24,348 (1927 v Swansea T, FA Cup
Quarter-Final). *Nickname:* The Tynesiders, The Heed. *Manager:* Ian Bogie. *Secretary:* Mike Coulson. *Colours:*
White shirts, black shorts and stockings.

GATESHEAD 2010–11 LEAGUE RECORD

Match No.	Date	Venue	Opponents	Result	H/T Score	Lg Pos.	Goalscorers	Attendance
1	Aug 14	H	Kettering T	D	0-0	0-0	—	639
2	17	A	Barrow	W	3-1	1-1	—	Brittain 2 (1 pen) [34, 83 (p)], Turnbull [70]	1440
3	21	A	Forest Green R	D	1-1	0-1	6	Mulligan [66]	882
4	24	H	Fleetwood T	L	0-2	0-2	—		623
5	28	A	Darlington	L	0-2	0-1	19		2233
6	Sept 4	A	Cambridge U	L	0-5	0-1	23		2637
7	7	H	Southport	W	1-0	0-0	—	Nelthorpe [90]	471
8	11	H	Altrincham	W	2-0	1-0	12	Gate [38], Shaw [82]	539
9	18	A	Crawley T	L	1-2	0-0	17	Shaw [51]	1412
10	21	H	Grimsby T	D	0-0	0-0	—		863
11	25	H	Luton T	W	1-0	1-0	13	Shaw [7]	1075
12	28	A	Histon	W	3-1	2-0	—	Mulligan [7], Nelthorpe 2 [35, 89]	285
13	Oct 2	H	Mansfield T	D	1-1	0-1	11	Kay [80]	1046
14	5	A	Kidderminster H	L	1-2	1-0	—	Brittain (pen) [8]	937
15	9	H	Tamworth	W	3-1	2-1	9	Shaw [38], Gate [39], Ferrell [90]	807
16	16	A	AFC Wimbledon	L	0-1	0-0	11		3330
17	30	H	Cambridge U	L	2-3	1-3	13	Shaw 2 [29, 54]	1083
18	Nov 9	A	Fleetwood T	D	0-0	0-0	—		1011
19	13	A	Tamworth	D	1-1	0-1	13	Mulligan [63]	802
20	20	H	Forest Green R	D	1-1	1-0	12	Mulligan [28]	601
21	Jan 1	H	York C	L	0-3	0-0	17		1231
22	3	A	Southport	L	1-5	1-0	17	Brittain [45]	904
23	8	H	Kidderminster H	D	2-2	1-2	17	Liddle [16], Shaw [73]	508
24	18	H	Barrow	W	3-0	1-0	—	Shaw [22], Brittain (pen) [75], Fisher [90]	518
25	22	A	Luton T	D	2-2	2-2	17	Gate [10], Howells (og) [16]	5958
26	28	H	AFC Wimbledon	L	0-2	0-0	—		922
27	Feb 1	A	Eastbourne Bor	W	3-0	2-0	—	Brittain 2 [15, 17], Fisher [82]	612
28	12	A	Rushden & D	W	2-0	1-0	14	Prosser (og) [30], Shaw [87]	874
29	15	H	Hayes & Y	W	1-0	1-0	—	Fisher [31]	463
30	19	A	Wrexham	W	7-2	5-1	13	Shaw 3 [1, 72, 77], Fisher 2 [14, 33], Brittain (pen) [18], Nelthorpe [43]	3078
31	22	A	Kettering T	W	4-1	2-1	—	Turnbull [44], Shaw 2 [45, 53], Clark [77]	812
32	Mar 1	A	York C	L	1-2	0-1	—	Curtis [50]	2290
33	5	A	Altrincham	D	1-1	0-0	13	Winn [57]	765
34	8	H	Darlington	D	2-2	0-2	—	Brittain (pen) [71], Clark [90]	1204
35	22	A	Grimsby T	D	2-2	0-2	—	Offiong [86], Fisher [90]	2517
36	26	H	Crawley T	D	0-0	0-0	15		751
37	29	A	Newport Co	L	1-2	0-1	—	Fisher [69]	1027
38	Apr 2	A	Bath C	L	0-1	0-0	15		952
39	4	H	Bath C	D	1-1	1-0	—	Fisher [14]	522
40	9	H	Histon	W	2-0	1-0	13	Gillies [2], Shaw [73]	567
41	12	H	Eastbourne Bor	W	3-0	0-0	—	Shaw [51], Ferrell 2 [59, 90]	617
42	16	A	Rushden & D	D	2-2	2-1	12	Fisher [33], Shaw [42]	701
43	19	A	Hayes & Y	L	1-3	0-1	—	Winn [50]	502
44	23	H	Wrexham	L	0-1	0-0	14		743
45	25	A	Mansfield T	L	2-3	2-0	14	Mulligan 2 [19, 40]	1749
46	30	H	Newport Co	L	1-7	1-2	15	Mulligan [24]	824

Final League Position: 15

GOALSCORERS

League (65): Shaw 17, Brittain 9 (5 pens), Fisher 9, Mulligan 7, Nelthorpe 4, Ferrell 3, Gate 3, Clark 2, Turnbull 2, Winn 2, Curtis 1, Gillies 1, Kay 1, Liddle 1, Offiong 1, own goals 2.
FA Cup (2): Fisher 1, Turnbull 1.

Deasy 41	Baxter 24 + 4	Heckingbottom 21	Gate 34	Jones 14 + 5	Clark 43	Brittain 39 + 2	Turnbull 46	Mulligan 24 + 7	Marwood 10 + 11	Ferrell 13 + 7	Neilthorpe 24 + 10	Fisher 19 + 21	Allan — + 3	Francis 1	Wake — + 12	Curtis 35	Shaw 36 + 1	Gillies 4 + 14	Kay 8	Clarke 1 + 1	Winn 8 + 5	Farman 5 + 1	White 3	Tavernier 13	Liddle 23	Edmundsson 5	Rundle 7	Offiong 5 + 6	Baptist — + 2	Match No.
1	2	3	4	5	6	7	8	9	10^1	11^2	12	13																		1
1	2	3	4	5	6	7^3	8	9	10^1	11^2	12	13	14																	2
1	2	3	4	5	6	7^1	8	9	10	11^2	13	12																		3
1	2	3	4	5	6	12	8	9	10		11^2	13		7^1																4
1	2	3	4	5	6	7^2	8	9^1	11	13	14	10^3			12															5
1	2	3	4		6	7^2	8		10^1	11	12				14	5	9^3	13												6
1	13	3	4	2	6	7^3	8		11	10^1					12	5	9	14												7
1		3	4^2	2	6	7^3	8	10^1	13	11	12					5	9	14												8
1		3	4^2	2	6	7^1	8	9	13	11	12					5	10^3	14												9
1		3	4	2	6	7^1	8	9	12	11	13					5	10^2													10
1	12	3	4	2^1	6	7	8	9^2		14	11^3				13	5	10													11
1	2	3	4		6	7	8	9		11	12					5	10^1													12
1		3	4		6	7	8	9		11						5	10		2											13
1		3	4		6	7^2	8	9^1	13	14	11^3	12				5	10		2											14
1		3	4		6	7	8		12	9	11^1					5	10		2											15
1		3	4		6	7^1	8		10^2	11^3	12					5	9	14	2	13										16
1	2^2		4		6	7	8	9	12	11^1	13					5	10		3											17
1^5	2		4		6	7	8		12	11^2	13					5	10^1	3		9	15									18
	2		4	13	6	7	8		12	11^3			14			5^2	10	3		9^1	1									19
	2		4		6	12	8	9		11					10			3		7^1	1	5								20
	2	3			8	7^1	8	9^0	12	11^0	14	13			10					4^0	1	5								21
	2		4^1	3	6	7^3	8	9^2	11	12		13	14			5	10			1										22
1			4		6	7^1	8	13	12							5	10				11^2	2	3		9					23
1			4		6	7	8	9^2			13					5	10	12			3	2	11^1							24
1	12		4		3^2	7	8	9^3			14					5	10^2				2	6	11^1							25
1		4	6			7	8	9^2			13	12				5	10				2	3	11^1							26
1			4		6	7	8	9^2			13	12				5	10				2	3	11^1							27
1		4	13	6	7	8			11^2	9^1		14				5	10^3	12			2	3								28
1		4		6	7	8			11^1	9		13				5	10^2	12			2	3								29
1		4^2		6	7^3	8			11	9		12				5	10^1	14		13	2	3								30
1	13	4		3	7	8			11^1	9		14				5	10^3	12			2	6^2								31
1		4^4		6		8			9^2	7^1		13				5	10			12	2	3		11						32
1				6	7	8			14	12						5	10^1	13		4	2	3		11^3	9^2					33
1			5	6	7	8	12			9										4^1	2	3		11^2	10	13				34
1		4^3		6	7^2	8	14		12	9						5	10				2	3		11^1	13					35
1	2		4	13		7	8	14	11			9^1				5^2	10^3		6			3		11^2	10					36
1	2		4	5	6		8	9	7^3		12	13				14					3^1			11^2	10					37
1	2	3			6	7^2	8		4			9				10	11^1				5				12	13				38
1	2	3			6	7	4		12	11^1		9				10	13				5				8^2					39
1	2				6	7^2	8^1		13	4		9				5	10	11^3		12					3			14		40
1	2				6		8	12	7^2	4		9				5	10^1	11		13					3					41
1	2				6	7^1	8	13		4		9				5	10			12					3			11^2		42
1	2^3				6		8	13	12	4^2		9				5	10	14		7					3			11^1		43
1	2				6		8	10	12		11^2	9				5				4					3		7^1	13		44
	2	3	12	6	7	8	10^2		4	11	9^3					5^1		14				1						13		45
1^4	2	6	13		7	8	10^3		4	12	9	14				5		11^1						3^2						46

FA Cup
Fourth Qualifying Round

	Altrincham	(a)	2-0
First Round	Notts Co	(a)	0-2

GRIMSBY TOWN

Blue Square Premier

Ground: Blundell Park, Cleethorpes, NE Lincolnshire DN35 7PY. *Tel:* (01472) 605 050. *Fax:* (01472) 693 665.
Year Formed: 1878. *Record Gate:* 31,657 (1937 v Wolverhampton W). *Nickname:* Mariners.
Team Managers: Rob Scott & Paul Hurst. *Secretary:* Ian Fleming. *Colours:* Black and white stripes.

GRIMSBY TOWN 2010–11 LEAGUE RECORD

Match No.	Date	Venue	Opponents	Result	H/T Score	Lg Pos.	Goalscorers	Attendance
1	Aug 14	A	Crawley T	W 1-0	1-0	—	Peacock [39]	2428
2	17	H	York C	D 0-0	0-0	—		5037
3	21	H	Hayes & Y	L 1-2	0-1	14	Connell [90]	3405
4	24	A	Darlington	W 1-0	0-0	—	Watt [48]	1993
5	28	A	Rushden & D	L 1-4	0-1	12	Hudson [47]	1575
6	30	H	Histon	W 2-1	1-1	8	Connell 2 (1 pen) [39 (p), 85]	2925
7	Sept 4	H	Luton T	W 2-0	1-0	4	Connell (pen) [30], Cummins [71]	3822
8	11	A	Tamworth	L 1-2	0-2	8	Connell [69]	1616
9	18	H	Fleetwood T	L 1-2	0-1	11	Connell [67]	3099
10	21	A	Gateshead	D 0-0	0-0	—		863
11	25	A	Altrincham	D 2-2	1-0	12	Bore [28], Connell [77]	1364
12	28	H	Wrexham	W 2-1	1-0	—	Watt [17], Connell [65]	2532
13	Oct 2	H	Newport Co	W 2-0	1-0	7	Connell 2 [30, 50]	3246
14	7	A	Forest Green R	D 3-3	1-2	—	Eagle 2 [20, 68], Wright [65]	1007
15	10	A	Kidderminster H	L 2-3	1-3	8	Eagle [31], Connell [70]	1587
16	16	H	Southport	D 1-1	0-1	9	Connell [73]	3101
17	30	H	Eastbourne Bor	D 2-2	1-0	9	Coulson [40], Connell (pen) [78]	2894
18	Nov 9	A	Cambridge U	D 1-1	1-1	—	Eagle [41]	2303
19	13	A	Hayes & Y	W 3-0	2-0	9	Hudson [14], Eagle [44], Connell (pen) [90]	551
20	20	H	Barrow	D 1-1	0-0	10	Atkinson [66]	3225
21	Jan 1	H	Mansfield T	W 7-2	2-1	9	Bore 3 [5, 51, 89], Coulson [7], Connell 2 [56, 81], Kempson [69]	3654
22	3	A	Histon	W 6-1	1-0	8	Ademeno 2 [21, 49], Sinclair [65], Hudson [80], Peacock [84], Eagle [90]	1122
23	8	A	Wrexham	L 0-2	0-0	9		3013
24	11	A	York C	L 0-1	0-1	—		3028
25	18	H	Kettering T	W 2-1	1-1	—	Atkinson [45], Eagle [65]	2291
26	22	H	Crawley T	D 0-0	0-0	9		3382
27	25	A	Luton T	L 0-1	0-1	—		5609
28	29	A	Eastbourne Bor	W 3-2	1-1	—	Duffy [1], Connell 2 [75, 84]	1002
29	Feb 1	A	Southport	D 2-2	0-2	—	Duffy [74], Atkinson [84]	853
30	12	H	Cambridge U	D 1-1	1-0	7	Sinclair [8]	3142
31	19	A	Fleetwood T	L 0-3	0-1	8		2004
32	22	H	Forest Green R	D 1-1	1-1	—	Coulson [8]	2401
33	Mar 5	A	AFC Wimbledon	W 2-1	1-1	10	Coulson 2 [37, 53]	3182
34	12	A	Kettering T	W 2-1	0-1	10	Connell [80], Sinclair [82]	1403
35	19	A	Bath C	L 1-2	0-1	10	Coulson [60]	1808
36	22	H	Gateshead	D 2-2	2-0	—	Connell [10], Eagle [34]	2517
37	26	H	Tamworth	D 2-2	1-0	8	Eagle [15], Hudson [48]	3002
38	29	H	Darlington	L 0-1	0-1	—		2642
39	Apr 2	A	Newport Co	L 1-2	0-0	11	Coulson [52]	1506
40	9	H	Kidderminster H	D 3-3	1-2	12	Hudson [24], Connell [56], Peacock [63]	2402
41	13	H	Rushden & D	D 1-1	1-1	—	Atkinson [28]	2071
42	16	H	Bath C	D 2-2	2-0	14	Connell 2 [12, 23]	2389
43	19	A	Mansfield T	W 2-0	1-0	—	Coulson [43], L'Anson [83]	1787
44	23	A	Barrow	W 2-0	0-0	10	Connell [55], Leary [73]	1274
45	25	H	Altrincham	L 0-1	0-0	10		4311
46	30	A	AFC Wimbledon	L 1-2	1-1	11	Connell [39]	3752

Final League Position: 11

GOALSCORERS

League (72): Connell 25 (4 pens), Eagle 9, Coulson 8, Hudson 5, Atkinson 4, Bore 4, Peacock 3, Sinclair 3, Ademeno 2, Duffy 2, Watt 2, Cummins 1, Kempson 1, L'Anson 1, Leary 1, Wright 1.
FA Cup (1): Connell 1.

Arthur 28	Watt 21 + 4	Ridley 30	Hudson 24 + 16	Kempson 24	Leary 13 + 7	Bore 34 + 3	Wood 36 + 7	Connell 46	Peacock 15 + 21	Coulson 29	Eagle 29 + 10	Dixon — + 2	Samuels 9 + 2	Ademeno 6 + 6	Cummins 32 + 4	Corner 2 + 9	Gobern 7 + 2	Croudson 8	O'Donnell 10	Garner 13 + 4	Carlton 6	Wright 9	Atkinson 24 + 1	Sinclair 10 + 2	Stockdale 1	Makofo 4 + 6	Duffy 14 + 3	Hughes 3	Thanoj 4 + 3	L'Anson 4	Southwell — + 3	Mulreade 1 + 1	Match No.
1	2	3	4	5	6	7	8¹	9²	10	11	12	13																					1
1	2	3	4	5	6	7		9	10	11	8																						2
1	2	3	4	5	6²	7		9		11¹	10		8³	12	13	14																	3
1	2	3¹	4	5		7	12	9	14		11³			13	8	10²	6																4
1	2		4	5			8	9	10		11¹		3	12	7	13	6²																5
6		4	5				3	9	10		12		2	11¹	8	13	7²	1															6
6	3	4	5			2	11¹	9	10		13			8	12	7²		1															7
6	3	4	5■			2	8²	9	10³		13			11	12	7¹		1	14														8
1	5	3	4			2	14	9	13	11¹	7²			8	10³	12	6																9
2	3	12	5		6¹	7	8²	9	10		13			11		4		1															10
2	3	4	5			7	8	9	12		11			6¹				1	10														11
2¹	3	14	5			7	8	9	12	11²	13					6	1	12	10²	4³													12
	3	13	5			7³	2	9	12		11		14		4²			1	6	10¹	8												13
2	3¹		5			7	4	9	13		11		12		6			1		10²	8												14
2¹		13	5	14		7	8	9			11³		3		6²			1	12	10	4												15
	3	12	5			7	8	9	13				2¹		11			1		10²	6	4											16
	3	13				2³	14	9	10		11¹	7			12	8²			1	6	4	5											17
	3	4	5				12	9			11³	7			10²		13	14	1	2¹	8	6											18
	3	2	5	14			8	9			11³	10²			7¹	12	13	1			4	6											19
1		3	4	5		12	2	9			11	7²			10¹	13					8	6											20
1		3	14	5		7	2	9	12		11²	13			10¹	4							6	8³									21
1		3	12	5		7	2	9³	14	11²	13				10	4							6	8¹									22
1		3	12	5		7	2²	9³	10	11	13	14			4								6	8¹									23
1		3	13	5		7	2¹	9	12	11	10				4								6	8²									24
1	12		14	5	13	7	3	9	10■		11				4²								6	8³	2¹								25
1	2¹		12	5	13	7	3	9			11				4²								6	8		10							26
1	2²		13	5	4¹	7	3	9			11				8³					14			6	12		10							27
1	11²		13	5		2	3	9							4	14							6	8²		7¹	10³						28
1	2		14	5¹		7	3	9	13		11²				4■								6			12	10	8³					29
1		3	4	5			2	9	13	11		7¹											6	8		12	10²						30
1	13	3³	4²	5	14		2		10	12	11				8■								6			7¹	9						31
1	6	3¹	4³	5	13	12	2	9			11	7												8²		14	10						32
14	3	4■	5		8	2	13	9	12	11³	7¹					1							6	13		14	10³						33
	3		5	4	2	8¹	9	12	11	7²						1							6	13		14	10³						34
3	2		4		8	9	12	11	7						1							6	5		10¹								35
1	5	3		14	2	13	9	12	11²	7		8						6							10¹		4³						36
1	5¹	3³	4		2	12	9²	14	11	7	13	8						6							10								37
1		4			3	9²		11	7¹	2	13	8³						6				5	12	10		14							38
1		4			3	9	12	11	7²	2								6				5	13	10¹	8								39
1		4	5	8	12	3	9	10	11³	14	2¹	13						6								7²							40
	4	5¹	7³	2	3	9	10²	11		8		1	6										12			14	13						41
	3¹	4		2	8	9	10³	11	7²	12		1	6										5			14	13						42
1			7	2	4	9	10	11¹		8			6															3	5	12			43
1	13		7²	2	3	9¹	12	11		8			6										10¹			4		5	14			44
1	4¹		7³		3	9	10²	11	12	2	8			6								13					5		14			45
1				2	3	9	12	11		8			6									10²				4	5	13	7¹			46

FA Cup

Fourth Qualifying Round

Tamworth	(a)	1-1
	(h)	0-1

HAYES & YEADING UNITED
Blue Square Premier

Ground: All fixtures for 2011–12 will be played at Woking FC ground, Kingfield Stadium, Kingfield Road, Woking GU22 9AA. *Tel:* (0208) 573 2075. *Fax:* (0208) 573 0933. *Year Formed:* 2007. *Record Gate:* 1,234 (2009 v Histon, Blue Square Premier). *Nickname:* United. *Manager:* Nas Bashir. *Secretary:* John Bond Jr. *Colours:* Red shirts, black shorts, black stockings.

HAYES & YEADING UNITED 2010–11 LEAGUE RECORD

Match No.	Date	Venue	Opponents	Result	H/T Score	Lg Pos.	Goalscorers	Attendance
1	Aug 14	H	Bath C	W 2-1	0-0	—	Wright 2 [47, 83]	328
2	17	A	Eastbourne Bor	L 0-5	0-2	—		902
3	21	A	Grimsby T	W 2-1	1-0	5	Hand [19], Pritchard [69]	3405
4	24	H	Forest Green R	L 3-4	1-1	—	Wright 3 (1 pen) [39 (p), 55, 69]	286
5	28	H	Crawley T	L 0-3	0-2	16		320
6	30	A	Luton T	D 1-1	0-0	15	Pritchard [54]	6354
7	Sept 4	H	Histon	L 1-2	1-1	20	Buchanan [15]	359
8	11	A	Kidderminster H	L 1-3	1-1	21	Patulea [28]	1102
9	18	A	York C	L 0-2	0-0	23		2252
10	21	H	Newport Co	L 1-2	1-0	—	Malcolm [39]	478
11	25	H	Barrow	W 2-0	1-0	20	Enver-Marum [45], Pritchard [64]	340
12	28	A	Southport	D 0-0	0-0	—		753
13	Oct 2	A	Kettering T	L 1-2	1-1	21	Holmes [45]	1391
14	5	H	Cambridge U	W 2-0	1-0	—	Malcolm [11], Pritchard [71]	362
15	9	A	Darlington	W 1-0	0-0	17	Patulea [49]	1536
16	16	H	Wrexham	L 0-3	0-0	20		417
17	30	H	Altrincham	L 0-1	0-0	20		274
18	Nov 9	A	Bath C	L 1-3	0-1	—	Deen [82]	532
19	13	H	Grimsby T	L 0-3	0-2	23		551
20	20	A	Mansfield T	L 2-3	2-1	23	Hyde [2], Ferrell [28]	2019
21	27	A	Newport Co	L 1-2	0-1	—	Pritchard [00]	1001
22	Dec 7	A	Eastbourne Bor	W 2-1	2-0	—	Patulea (pen) [17], Cadmore [23]	190
23	Jan 1	A	AFC Wimbledon	L 1-3	0-0	22	Hyde [73]	3176
24	4	H	Luton T	L 0-1	0-0	—		801
25	8	H	Tamworth	W 2-1	1-0	21	Buchanan 2 [39, 58]	249
26	18	H	Rushden & D	D 3-3	2-0	—	Buchanan 3 [5, 43, 58]	307
27	22	A	Fleetwood T	D 1-1	1-1	21	Pritchard [4]	1281
28	25	A	Altrincham	L 2-4	1-1	—	Louis [12], Pritchard [90]	558
29	29	H	Kidderminster H	L 0-4	0-1	—		288
30	Feb 5	A	Forest Green R	L 0-1	0-0	—		787
31	12	A	Histon	W 1-0	1-0	21	Holmes [40]	463
32	15	A	Gateshead	L 0-1	0-1	—		463
33	19	H	Southport	W 1-0	1-0	20	Pritchard [34]	303
34	26	H	York C	L 1-2	0-1	20	Holmes [75]	458
35	Mar 1	A	AFC Wimbledon	D 0-0	0-0	—		708
36	5	A	Rushden & D	D 1-1	1-1	20	Yiadom [36]	1129
37	12	A	Tamworth	W 3-2	1-1	21	Pritchard [14], Brown (pen) [52], Buchanan [76]	1171
38	15	A	Crawley T	L 2-5	2-2	—	Buchanan [2], Pritchard [45]	2236
39	19	H	Kettering T	W 3-2	2-1	19	Cadmore [17], Brown (pen) [25], Buchanan [73]	305
40	26	H	Fleetwood T	L 1-2	0-2	20	Masterton [50]	303
41	Apr 2	A	Wrexham	W 2-0	2-0	19	Hand [7], Pritchard [30]	3207
42	9	H	Mansfield T	W 4-0	3-0	18	Pritchard [12], Buchanan 2 [20, 25], Thompson (og) [81]	316
43	16	H	Darlington	W 3-2	2-0	16	Pritchard [10], Buchanan [28], Rents [53]	432
44	19	H	Gateshead	W 3-1	1-0	—	Pritchard [10], Wright [71], Brown (pen) [90]	502
45	23	A	Cambridge U	L 0-1	0-0	16		2619
46	30	A	Barrow	L 0-2	0-0	16		1445

Final League Position: 16

GOALSCORERS

League (57): Pritchard 14, Buchanan 12, Wright 6 (1 pen), Brown 3 (3 pens), Holmes 3, Patulea 3 (1 pen), Cadmore 2, Hand 2, Hyde 2, Malcolm 2, Deen 1, Enver-Marum 1, Ferrell 1, Louis 1, Masterton 1, Rents 1, Yiadom 1, own goal 1.
FA Cup (4): Brown 3 (1 pen), Holmes 1.

Harrison 25+1	Ferrell 32+2	Green 23+1	Cadmore 40	Bygrave 44	Holmes 44	Mulley 10+3	Pritchard 46	Wright 15+7	Buchanan 21+14	Deen 8+6	Yiadom 16+20	McLean —+5	Wassmer 17+2	Hand 40	Wishart —+13	Lennie 7+2	Webb 11+5	Malcolm 15+1	Brown 28	Patulea 8+1	Enver-Marum 3+5	Appiah 3+17	Hyde 7+2	Bulmer 5	Montgomery 3	Louis 10	Preddie 8	Joseph-Dubois —+4	Rents 8	Masterton 8	McWeeney 1	Match No.
1	2	3	4	5	6	7	8	9	10[1]	11	12																					1
1	2	3	4[3]	5	6	7	8	9	10[1]	11[2]	13	12	14																			2
1	2	3		5	6	7[1]	8	9[2]	13	11	12			4	10																	3
1	2	3		5	6	14	8	9	10[1]	11[2]	13			4[3]		7	12															4
	2[2]	3	4	5	6	7	8[3]		10[1]	11	13			9	12	1	14															5
1[6]	2	3	4	5	6	7	8	12	10[1]	11					15		9															6
	2	3	4	5	6	7[1]	8	10	12	11	13					1	9[2]															7
	2		4	5	6[1]	12	8		14	11[2]			7	13	1				9[8]	3		10[3]										8
1	2[2]		4	5	6	13	8		14	11	9[1]		7	12						3		10[3]										9
1	2		4		6	7[2]	8	12		11[1]			5	13					9	3		10										10
1	2		4	5	6	7[2]	8	12						13	11				9	3		10[1]										11
1[6]	2		4	5	6	7[2]	8							13	11	15			9	3		10[1]										12
	2		4	5	6	7[1]	8							13	11	1			9	3		10[2]	12									13
	2		4	5	6		8							7	11	1			9	3		10[1]	12									14
	2[2]		4	5	6		8						7	13	11	1			9	3		10[1]	12									15
	2		4	5	6		8							13	11[3]	7[2]	1		9	3		10[1]	12	14								16
1	2		4	5	6		8						7[1]	12	11				9	3		10										17
		3	4	5	6[2]	7		13	12	11[1]	14			8					2	10		9[3]		1								18
		3		5	6		8	14	13			4[2]	7[3]	2	11[8]				9	10[1]		12		1								19
	2[2]	3	4	5	6[1]		8	13	12	11			7						9					1		10						20
	2	3	4	5	6[1]		8								11[2]				10			12	13	1	7	9						21
		3	4		6		8[8]	12		11			5[1]		14				2			10[2]	13	1		9[3]	7					22
1	2	3[2]	4	5	6		8		10	11[1]	12								7[8]		14	13				9[3]						23
1	2[3]	3	4	5	6		8		10		7[2]				14				11			12	13			9[1]						24
1	12	3	4	5	6[2]		8	9	10						11				7		2[1]		13									25
1	2	3	4	5	6[1]		8	9	10[2]						11				7				12		13							26
1	2	3	4	5			8	9	12						11				8	13			7[1]			10						27
	2[2]	3	4[8]	5			8	9[3]	12						11				6	13	14		7[1]			10	1					28
1			4	5	6		8	9	12				7[1]		11				2	3						10						29
1		3[2]	4	5	6	7		12	9[1]					8	11				2	13						10						30
1			4	5	6		8	9					7		11[1]				2	3		12				10						31
		3	4	5	6		8[2]	9[1]	12				7[3]	13					2		14	11				10	1					32
			4	5	6		8	9[1]	12				7	13	11				2	3						10[2]	1					33
			4	5	6		8	11	13	10[1]	12		7						2[3]	3	14					9[2]	1					34
		3[2]	4	5		7	8	12	13						11				2		10					9[1]	1					35
12	11[2]	5[1]	4		6	7[3]	8		13						10				2	3	14					9	1					36
		3	4	5	6		8[2]	9[1]	12				7		11[3]				10	2	14	13					1					37
15			4	5	6	7	8	10	9					13					2[2]	3		11[1]			16	12	1					38
1	6		4	5			8	11	10						9[1]				2			12	13						3	7[2]		39
1	2[2]		4	5	6	7		9[1]	10					13						3		13						12	11	8		40
1	2	14	4	5	6	7		9[1]	10											3		13						12	11[3]	8[2]		41
1	2		4	5	6		8[2]	9[1]	14	10[3]										3		13						12	11	7	1	42
1	2[2]		4	5	6[1]		8	10	13					9[3]						3	14	12							11	7		43
1	2[2]		4	5	6	7		10	13					9[3]						3	14	12							11	8[1]		44
1	2[1]		4	5	6[3]	7		12	13					9						3	14	10							11	8[2]		45
1	2		4	5	6[1]	7		14	10[2]					9[3]						3	13	12							11	8		46

FA Cup
Fourth Qualifying Round

	Poole T	(a)	3-1
First Round	Wycombe W	(h)	1-2

HISTON

Blue Square North

Ground: Glassworld Stadium, Bridge Road, Impington, Cambridge CB24 9PH. *Tel:* (01223) 237 373.
Year Formed: 1904. *Record Gate:* 4,500 (2008 v Leeds U, FA Cup 2nd rd). *Nickname:* The Stutes.
Player-Manager: David Livermore. *Secretary:* Lisa Baldwin. *Colours:* Red shirts, black shorts, black stockings.

HISTON 2010–11 LEAGUE RECORD

Match No.	Date	Venue	Opponents	Result	H/T Score	Lg Pos.	Goalscorers	Attendance
1	Aug 14	H	Barrow	W 3-1	2-1	—	McCrae [29], Attwood 2 [45, 70]	533
2	17	A	AFC Wimbledon	L 0-2	0-0	—		3126
3	21	A	Newport Co	D 2-2	1-2	10	McCrae [29], Okay [64]	1927
4	24	H	Eastbourne Bor	D 1-1	0-1	—	Oyebanjo [87]	421
5	28	H	Kettering T	L 0-3	0-1	21		681
6	30	A	Grimsby T	L 1-2	1-1	22	Wootton [23]	2925
7	Sept 4	A	Hayes & Y	W 2-1	1-1	17	Murray [34], Riza (pen) [50]	359
8	11	H	Crawley T	L 0-2	0-2	20		497
9	18	H	Tamworth	L 1-2	1-0	20	Riza [41]	653
10	21	A	Rushden & D	L 0-2	0-0	—		926
11	25	A	Wrexham	L 0-4	0-3	23		2376
12	28	H	Gateshead	L 1-3	0-2	—	Riza (pen) [90]	285
13	Oct 2	A	Fleetwood T	D 1-1	0-0	23	Murray [67]	1458
14	5	H	Southport	W 2-1	2-1	—	Clerima [9], Murray [19]	368
15	9	H	Altrincham	W 3-0	1-0	21	Oyebanjo (pen) [15], Murray [74], Mills, D [90]	655
16	16	A	Forest Green R	W 1-0	0-0	17	Sparkes [46]	741
17	30	H	Wrexham	D 1-1	0-0	17	Murray [90]	914
18	Nov 13	H	Kidderminster H	L 0-1	0-1	20		571
19	20	A	Luton T	L 1-5	1-3	21	Murray [43]	5963
20	25	H	Bath C	L 1-2	0-1	—	Sparkes [77]	470
21	Jan 1	A	Cambridge U	D 0-0	0-0	21		3225
22	3	H	Grimsby T	L 1-6	0-1	22	Riza [83]	1122
23	11	A	Darlington	L 1-3	0-1	—	Murray [60]	1489
24	15	A	York C	L 1-2	1-0	—	Stevenson [40]	578
25	22	A	Mansfield T	L 0-1	0-0	24		1880
26	25	A	Barrow	D 1-1	1-0	—	Clerima [2]	883
27	29	H	Newport Co	D 0-0	0-0	—		452
28	Feb 1	H	Fleetwood T	W 1-0	1-0	—	Riza [13]	255
29	5	A	Tamworth	W 1-0	1-0	—	Riza (pen) [38]	885
30	12	H	Hayes & Y	L 0-1	0-1	23		463
31	15	A	Altrincham	W 3-0	0-0	—	Attwood [47], Riza [72], Clerima [86]	621
32	19	A	Eastbourne Bor	D 2-2	1-0	23	Riza [39], Clerima [49]	783
33	22	H	Cambridge U	L 0-2	0-1	—		1903
34	Mar 1	A	Southport	L 1-3	0-0	—	Riza (pen) [90]	652
35	5	A	Crawley T	L 0-5	0-2	24		3031
36	15	H	Kettering T	L 3-4	3-1	—	Riza [16], Clerima [31], Murray [38]	782
37	22	H	Mansfield T	L 2-3	2-0	—	Riza (pen) [41], Stevenson [45]	380
38	26	A	York C	L 0-1	0-0	24		2364
39	Apr 2	H	Forest Green R	L 0-3	0-1	24		426
40	5	H	Rushden & D	L 0-2	0-0	—		363
41	9	A	Gateshead	L 0-2	0-1	24		567
42	12	H	Darlington	L 0-1	0-0	—		277
43	16	H	AFC Wimbledon	L 0-4	0-1	24		750
44	23	A	Bath C	L 1-2	0-1	24	Sparkes [62]	754
45	25	H	Luton T	L 0-4	0-2	24		1159
46	30	A	Kidderminster H	D 2-2	1-0	24	Riza [40], Murray [77]	1496

Final League Position: 24

GOALSCORERS

League (41): Riza 12 (5 pens), Murray 9, Clerima 5, Attwood 3, Sparkes 3, McCrae 2, Oyebanjo 2 (1 pen), Stevenson 2, Mills, D 1, Okay 1, Wootton 1.
FA Cup (0).

Welch 36	Oyebanjo 38	Okay 37 + 2	Mills Z 38 + 1	Clerima 43	Ilesanmi 15 + 1	McCrae 17 + 1	Wootton 31 + 1	Mills D 13 + 5	Attwood 16 + 10	Sparkes 27 + 6	Adjei 2 + 8	Stewart 8 + 2	Sagna — + 1	Stevenson 21 + 8	Pavett 3 + 1	Diarra 1 + 1	Taaffe 10 + 15	Murray 35 + 1	Riza 34 + 1	Smith 32 + 6	Clarke 2 + 2	Fitzsimons 6	Livermore 11 + 3	Ainsley 2	Lawton 1 + 2	York — + 2	Okojie 5 + 6	Dowie 3 + 3	Foderingham 9	Asafu-Adjaye 5	Cox 2 + 3	Day 1 + 2	Sessions — + 1	Hawkins 2 + 2	Asensi — + 1	Match No.
1	2	3	4	5	6	7	8^8	9	10	11^1	12																									1
1	2	4	8	5	6^8	7		9	10	11^1				3^3	12^2	13	14																			2
1	2	3	4	5^2		7	8	9	10		12			6		11^1	13																			3
1	2	3	4	5	14	7	8	9	10^1					6^3			11^2	12	13																	4
1	2	3^3	4	5	6	7	8	9			12			14				13	10^2	11^1																5
1	2	3^2	12	5	6	7	8	9^3			14	4^1						13	10	11																6
1		3	2	5	6	7	8	9	12			4^1						13	10	11^2																7
1		3	2	5	6	7	8	9	10^1	11^2								4	12	13																8
1		2	3	5	6	7	8^8	9^1	10^2	11								4	12	13																9
1		3	4	5	6	7		9^1	10^2	11	13			14			8		12	2^3																10
1		3		5	6	7^1		9		11	13	12							10^2	4	8	2														11
1		2		5	6	7^1	8	9		11	12								10	4		3														12
1	2	3		5	6	7^1	8			12		11						9	10	4																13
1	2	3		5	6	7	8			12		11						9^1	10	4																14
1	2	3		5	6	7^2	8	14	12	11		11						9	13^3	10	4															15
1	2	3		5	6	7	8					11						9	10	4																16
1	2	3	4^2	5	6		8			12	13	11						10^1	9	7																17
1	2	3	4	5			8	9^3	13	11	14	12						10		7^2			6^1													18
1^6		4	6	5			8			11		3						10^2	13	9			7^1	2	15											19
1	2			5		7	8	12		11		3						10^1	9	6			4													20
1	2	3^8	4	5			8	12		11^2		13						9	10^1	7			6													21
1	2	4		5			8			11		7^2		12				9	10	3			6^1					13								22
1	2	3	4	5			8			11^1				12^2	13		14	9	10	7^3			6^8													23
1	2	3	6	5			8			11^2		7		12				9	10				4^1					13								24
1	2	3	6	5			8			11^1		12						4	9	10			7													25
1	2	3	6	5			8			11		13		12				9^2	10^1	7			4^8													26
1	2	3	4	5			8	12		11^1		7		13				9	10^2				6													27
1	2	3	4	5			8	12		11^1		7		13				9	10^3				8													28
1	2		4	5			8	12		11^1		7						9	10^2				6			13		3								29
1	2	3	4	5			8	13		11^1		6^3		12				9	10	7^2								14								30
1	2	12	3	5			8^3			11		4						7^1	9	10^2			13				6	14								31
1	2	12	4	5			8^1			11		7		6^2				9	10	13			3													32
1	2		4	5			8^2		13	11		7^1						9	10	12			6					3								33
1	2	3^2	6	5	12		8^8		13	11^1								9	10	7			4													34
1^8	2	3^1	6	5			8^8		13	11^6	12							9	10^2	7			4							15						35
	2	3	4	5			8			11								9	10	7			6						1							36
1	2	3^8	6	5			8^2			11^1	12	7^3						9	10				4				13	14								37
		3		5			8		13	11		4		12				9^2	10				6						1		2			7^1		38
		3	6	5			8	9^1		11		4							10							12	7^2		1		2	13				39
		3	6	5	12		8			11^3		4							10							13	7^2		1		2	9^1		14		40
	2	3	4						8^2	11^1		7^3					14	9	10				6				13		1	5	12					41
	2		6	5			8			11^2		4		12				9	10								7^1		1		13	3				42
	2	3^1	6				8			11		4^3						9	10								13	14	1	5	7^2			12		43
	2	3^3	6	5			8			11		4						9	10^1								7^2		1		13			14	12	44
	2	3	6	5			8			11^2		4		12				9	10^1								7		1		13					45
		3	4	5			8			11				12				9	10				6				7^1		1		2					46

FA Cup
Fourth Qualifying Round

Havant & W'ville (a) 0-2

KETTERING TOWN

Blue Square Premier

Ground: Rockingham Road, Kettering, Northants NN16 9AW.   *Tel:* (01536) 483 028.   *Year Formed:* 1872.
Record Gate: 11,536 v Peterborough U.   *Nickname:* Poppies.   *Manager:* Morell Maison.   *Colours:* Red shirts, black and white trim, red shorts, black stockings.

KETTERING TOWN 2010–11 LEAGUE RECORD

Match No.	Date	Venue	Opponents	Result	H/T Score	Lg Pos.	Goalscorers	Attendance
1	Aug 14	A	Gateshead	D	0-0	0-0	—	639
2	17	H	Luton T	L	1-3	1-1	—	Christie [32]	2906
3	21	H	Darlington	D	0-0	0-0	22		1350
4	24	A	Mansfield T	D	1-1	0-1	—	Ashikodi [87]	2089
5	28	A	Histon	W	3-0	1-0	15	Marna (pen) [4], Makofo [54], Kelly [87]	681
6	30	H	Rushden & D	L	0-1	0-1	18		2313
7	Sept 4	H	AFC Wimbledon	L	1-2	1-1	21	Marna [19]	1727
8	11	A	Fleetwood T	L	1-4	1-1	22	Christie [43]	1602
9	18	H	Wrexham	D	1-1	0-1	21	Marna (pen) [85]	1533
10	21	A	Cambridge U	L	0-3	0-0	—		2646
11	25	A	Forest Green R	W	2-0	1-0	19	Marna (pen) [45], Christie [69]	779
12	28	H	Altrincham	D	3-3	2-2	—	Marna 3 [12, 20, 71]	1194
13	Oct 2	H	Hayes & Y	W	2-1	1-1	17	Makofo [5], Dance [49]	1391
14	5	A	York C	W	1-0	0-0	—	Dempster [51]	1978
15	9	A	Southport	W	2-1	2-0	12	Dance [39], Marna [45]	1117
16	16	H	Kidderminster H	D	1-1	1-0	12	Solkhon [4]	1650
17	30	A	Newport Co	W	2-1	1-1	10	Dance 2 [11, 70]	2230
18	Nov 9	H	Mansfield T	L	0-2	0-0	—		1270
19	13	H	Cambridge U	D	2-2	0-2	12	Green [66], Furlong [70]	1959
20	21	A	AFC Wimbledon	L	2-3	0-3	12	Solkhon [53], Furlong [80]	3114
21	Jan 1	H	Tamworth	L	0-1	0-0	15		1164
22	3	A	Rushden & D	W	2-1	1-0	15	Christie 2 [7, 79]	2216
23	11	A	Kidderminster H	L	1-4	0-1	—	Solkhon [59]	1036
24	15	A	Crawley T	L	1-2	1-0	—	Marna (pen) [15]	1812
25	18	A	Grimsby T	L	1-2	1-1	—	Flanagan [3]	2291
26	22	H	Eastbourne Bor	W	3-0	1-0	16	Furlong 2 [17, 86], Solkhon [61]	1146
27	25	H	Fleetwood T	W	2-1	0-0	—	Solkhon [54], Christie [90]	798
28	Feb 3	H	Crawley T	D	0-0	0-0	—		1216
29	12	H	Barrow	D	1-1	0-1	15	O'Neill [64]	1410
30	15	H	Bath C	W	2-1	1-1	—	Marna (pen) [12], Mills [89]	796
31	19	A	Altrincham	L	2-3	2-1	15	Marna 2 [41, 44]	752
32	22	H	Gateshead	L	1-4	1-2	—	Marna [28]	812
33	26	H	Newport Co	W	2-0	2-0	15	Marna [8], Warren (og) [10]	1056
34	Mar 2	A	Tamworth	L	1-3	0-3	—	Mills [83]	609
35	5	A	Bath C	D	1-1	1-0	15	Marna [29]	890
36	12	H	Grimsby T	L	1-2	1-0	15	Marna [19]	1403
37	15	H	Histon	W	4-3	1-3	—	Mills 2 [19, 90], McKoy [78], Wilson [85]	782
38	19	A	Hayes & Y	L	2-3	1-2	15	McKoy [3], Marna [81]	305
39	22	A	Darlington	D	1-1	1-1	—	Marna [7]	1829
40	26	A	Eastbourne Bor	W	3-1	1-0	13	Solkhon [7], McKoy [70], Kelly [74]	673
41	Apr 2	H	York C	D	1-1	0-1	14	St Aimie [73]	1365
42	5	A	Luton T	D	2-2	0-1	—	Solkhon [49], Mills [90]	5715
43	9	A	Barrow	L	0-5	0-0	15		1015
44	16	A	Wrexham	L	0-2	0-0	15		3662
45	23	H	Forest Green R	W	2-1	0-0	15	Marna (pen) [48], Mills [55]	891
46	30	H	Southport	W	3-1	1-0	14	Cunnington [25], O'Neill [87], Challinor [90]	1403

Final League Position: 14

GOALSCORERS

League (64): Marna 19 (6 pens), Solkhon 7, Christie 6, Mills 6, Dance 4, Furlong 4, McKoy 3, Kelly 2, Makofo 2, O'Neill 2, Ashikodi 1, Challinor 1, Cunnington 1, Dempster 1, Flanagan 1, Green 1, St Aimie 1, Wilson 1, own goal 1.
FA Cup (1): Furlong 1.

Harper 1	Graham 22 + 3	Davis 16 + 6	Westwood 12	Cunnington 11 + 3	Dempster 17 + 1	Boucaud 19 + 1	Raynor 1 + 1	O'Leary 1	Taylor 13	Furlong 10 + 17	Dance 21 + 1	Christie 12 + 7	Marna 43 + 3	Noubissie 30 + 3	Roper 24 + 7	Abbey 11	Makofo 17 + 6	Solkhon 34 + 9	Smith — + 1	Ashikodi 2 + 4	St Aimie 3 + 3	Kelly 28 + 12	Jaszczun 1	Jack 9	McKoy 25 + 5	Green 5	Towers — + 1	Bussey 7	Flanagan 22	McDonald 14 + 5	Collins 3 + 2	Wilson 16 + 1	Halstead 3	Harding — + 1	Challinor 4 + 9	Gueret 14	O'Neill 18 + 1	John 3	Mills 11 + 6	McCrae 3 + 5	Match No.
1	2	3	4	5^5	6^2	7			8^1	9	10	11^3	12	13	14																										1
	2	3	4		6^2				12	10	11^8	9^1	7	5^8	1	8	13																									2
	2		4	5	6^3	8			9^2	10^1	11	3			1	7	14	12	13																						3
	2		4	5	6	8			9	10	11	3^2			1	7^1	13					12																			4
	2		4	5	6^3	8			13	10	7^2	3			1	11	14					9^1	12																		5
	2		4	5	6^3	7			10	13	11	3			1	8^1	14					9^2	12																		6
	2		4	5^3	6	8			10^2	9	11	3			1	12	13					14	7^1																		7
5	3^1	4	12	6		8			10	9	11^3	2^2			1	14					13	7																			8
14			4	5	6^3				13	10	9	11		2	1	12	8					7^1	3^2																		9
	2		4^8	5	6				13	10^1	9^2	11	7	3	1	12	8																								10
	2	3^1		5	6					10	9	11	4	12	1	8^2	7					13																			11
	2			5	6	8^2				10	9	11	3	13	1	7^1	4					12																			12
	2			5	6	4				10	9	11^1	3		7	8						12	1																		13
	2			5	6	4			9^1	10	11	3		7^2	8							13	1	12																	14
	2	4^8		6		8			14	10	11^3	3	5	9^1	7^2							13	1	12																	15
	2			5	6	8				10	11	3	9	4^1								12	1	7																	16
	2	3		5	6	8^8	9^1		10	11^2	4	13	12	7^3		14						1																			17
	2^1	3		5	14				12	10	11	8^3	6	13	4						7^2	1			9																18
	2	3		5	6^1				12	10	11^2	4^3	9	13	8					7	1	14		7																	19
	2	3^1		5	6^3				9	10	13	4		8	12	11^2				7	1	14																			20
	2		4						9	10^3	13	12	3	8^1	6	11				7	1			5^2	14																21
	14									9^1	10^2	2	5	11^1	8		3			7	4				1				6	12	13										22
	12	13								9^2	10	2	5	11^3	8		3			4^1				1				6	7	14										23
	13									14	10	2^5	5	7	3		11			8^3				1				6	12	9^1	4									24
										14	13	10	2^3	5	7		3			4				6	9^2	11	8^1	1	12										25
	2									12	9^2	10		5	7		3			4				6	8	11^1		1	13										26
	2									9	13	10^2		5	7		3			4				6	11^1	8		1	12										27
										9^1	12^2	10	13	5	8		3			7				6	11	4		1	2										28
	13									12	10	14	5	8	3		4^3			7^2				11				1	2				9^1						29
	12									9^2	10		5	8	3		4			7^1				6				1	2	11^3	13	14							30
	3									14	10	6	5^2	8	11		4			13				7				1	2^1					9^1	12				31
	3									14	10	8^1	5	4	6		13			7				12				1	2^2	11^3	9								32
		9^1			15					10^6	5	7	3	4	6		8			11^2				12	1^2	2	13												33
	12	9^3			1^8				14	10	5	7	3	4	6		8			11^8				2^2	13														34
	13	11			10					12	5	3	4^1	1	6		14		7						2										9^2	8^3			35
		11^1			12					10	14	5^1	3	4	6		13		7^2					1	2										9	8			36
	12	14			10					13	5	3	4	6^3	11		7^1						1	2										9	8^2			37
	2	8^2			13					10	5	6	3	4	11		7^3						1	12										9^1	14			38
	3	11^2			13					10	8	5	12	4	6		9^1			7^3				1	2										14				39
	3	9^2			13					10	5	8^3	11^1	4	6		7			14				1	2										12				40
	3	9^3			10					4	13	11^1	5	6		8^2	7							1	2										12				41
	3^1	13			10					5	8	11	12	4	6		7^2							1	2										9				42
	14	9^2			10					4	11	3	5^1	6	8		12							1	2^3									7	13				43
	3^2	12			10					7^3	5	8	11^1	13	4		6			14				1	2										9				44
		11			10^3	7				5	4^2	12	3	1	6		8			13				2											9^1	14			45
		11			10^2	7				5	8^1	13	3	12	1		6			4				14	2										9^3				46

FA Cup
Fourth Qualifying Round
Rushden & D   (h)   1-2

KIDDERMINSTER HARRIERS Blue Square Premier

Ground: Aggborough Stadium, Hoo Road, Kidderminster DY10 1NB.   *Tel:* (01562) 823 931.   *Fax:* (01562) 827 329.
Year Formed: 1886.   *Record Gate:* 9,155 (1948 v Hereford U).   *Nickname:* Harriers.   *Manager:* Steve Burr.
Secretary: David Colwell.   *Colours:* Red shirts, white shorts, red stockings.

KIDDERMINSTER HARRIERS 2010–11 LEAGUE RECORD

Match No.	Date	Venue	Opponents	Result	H/T Score	Lg Pos.	Goalscorers	Atten- dance
1	Aug 14	A	York C	W 2-1	1-0	—	Gittings [10], Shaw (pen) [89]	2682
2	17	H	Southport	L 3-4	1-1	—	Briscoe [5], Wright [58], Williams, Marc [88]	1417
3	21	H	Mansfield T	L 1-3	1-0	16	Shaw (pen) [8]	1487
4	24	A	Wrexham	D 2-2	1-2	—	Wright 2 [45, 52]	2477
5	28	A	Newport Co	L 0-3	0-2	22		2026
6	30	H	Tamworth	D 2-2	1-1	23	Briggs [43], Byrne [90]	1271
7	Sept 4	A	Altrincham	W 2-1	0-0	18	Gittings [72], McPhee (pen) [80]	929
8	11	H	Hayes & Y	W 3-1	1-1	11	Wright [15], McPhee [72], Gittings [90]	1102
9	18	H	Cambridge U	D 0-0	0-0	13		1291
10	21	A	Fleetwood T	D 1-1	0-1	—	Byrne [79]	1411
11	26	H	AFC Wimbledon	W 2-0	1-0	11	McPhee [44], Williams, Marc [83]	1565
12	28	A	Bath C	L 0-2	0-2	—		742
13	Oct 2	A	Crawley T	L 0-2	0-0	16		1483
14	5	H	Gateshead	W 2-1	0-1	—	Byrne [53], Blair [75]	937
15	10	H	Grimsby T	W 3-2	3-1	10	McPhee [5], Blair 2 [11, 35]	1587
16	16	A	Kettering T	D 1-1	0-1	10	McPhee [84]	1650
17	29	A	Southport	D 2-2	0-2	—	Morris [52], McPhee (pen) [58]	1447
18	Nov 9	H	Rushden & D	W 1-0	1-0	—	McPhee (pen) [16]	1225
19	13	A	Histon	W 1-0	1-0	7	McPhee [34]	571
20	20	H	Eastbourne Bor	W 2-1	1-0	6	Morris [9], Williams, Marc [67]	1271
21	30	H	York C	D 0-0	0-0	—		1066
22	Dec 28	H	Newport Co	L 2-3	0-2	—	Blair [61], Matt [64]	1757
23	Jan 1	H	Forest Green R	W 1-0	0-0	6	McPhee (pen) [90]	1370
24	3	A	Tamworth	D 2-2	2-2	6	Wright [3], Blair [25]	1183
25	8	A	Gateshead	D 2-2	2-1	7	Blair [22], Wright [24]	508
26	11	H	Kettering T	W 4-1	1-0	—	Morris [11], Blair [50], Briggs [66], Gittings [90]	1036
27	15	A	Barrow	L 1-2	0-1	—	Wright [79]	906
28	22	H	Barrow	W 2-0	1-0	8	Morris [40], McPhee (pen) [85]	1232
29	25	A	Forest Green R	D 1-1	0-1	—	McPhee [82]	687
30	29	A	Hayes & Y	W 4-0	1-0	—	Shaw [32], McPhee 2 [65, 78], Byrne [87]	288
31	Feb 5	H	Bath C	W 1-0	1-0	—	Shaw [34]	1500
32	12	H	Altrincham	W 2-1	2-1	6	Byrne [24], Wright [37]	2930
33	18	A	Cambridge U	W 2-1	1-0	—	Canham [43], Matt [90]	1869
34	22	H	Darlington	D 1-1	1-0	—	Briggs [14]	1615
35	26	H	Wrexham	W 1-0	1-0	5	McPhee (pen) [37]	3028
36	Mar 5	A	Luton T	D 1-1	0-1	5	Shaw [52]	6108
37	8	H	Crawley T	D 0-0	0-0	—		1816
38	12	A	AFC Wimbledon	W 2-1	1-0	5	Canham [42], Matt [74]	3517
39	26	A	Mansfield T	W 2-1	1-0	5	McPhee [15], Briggs [63]	2079
40	Apr 2	H	Luton T	D 3-3	1-0	6	McPhee (pen) [25], Morris [86], Williams, Mike [90]	2756
41	9	A	Grimsby T	D 3-3	2-1	6	Blair 3 [33, 44, 83]	2402
42	16	A	Eastbourne Bor	D 1-1	0-1	6	Shaw [76]	688
43	19	H	Darlington	L 1-2	1-0	6	Briggs [30]	1626
44	22	H	Fleetwood T	W 2-1	0-1	—	Byrne 2 [53, 57]	2738
45	25	A	Rushden & D	L 1-2	0-0	6	McPhee [85]	1569
46	30	H	Histon	D 2-2	0-1	6	Blair [79], Briggs [80]	1496

Final League Position: 6

GOALSCORERS

League (74): McPhee 17 (7 pens), Blair 11, Wright 8, Byrne 7, Briggs 6, Shaw 6 (2 pens), Morris 5, Gittings 4, Matt 3, Williams, Marc 3, Canham 2, Briscoe 1, Williams, Mike 1.
FA Cup (0).

Lewis 46	Shaw 26 + 16	Williams Mike 41 + 1	Briggs 43	Briscoe 43 + 2	Albrighton 28 + 2	Hankin 17 + 10	Gittings 25 + 19	Morris 23 + 5	McPhee 43 + 2	Byrne 32 + 5	Wright 24 + 15	Blair 30 + 12	Griffiths 2 + 3	Williams Marc 7 + 10	Sharpe 14	Hadley — + 1	Vaughan 33 + 1	Verma 1	Thorne 9	Matt 8 + 14	Lindfield — + 1	McPike — + 2	Canham 10 + 2	Lowe 1	Thompson-Brown — + 1	Match No.
1	2	3	4	5	6	7^3	8^2	9^1	10	11	12	13	14													1
1	2	3	4	5	6	7^1	8^2		10	11	9	13		12												2
1	2	3	4	5	6	7	8^1		10^2	11	9	13		12												3
1	2	3	4			7^2	8^1	9	12	11	10	13			6					14						4
1	11^2	3	4	5		7		14	12	13	9			10	6^1		2		8^3							5
1	7	3	4	13	6^8	14		9	5	11	8^3	12		10^1			2									6
1	6^1	3	4	5		13	12	9^2	10	11	8						2		7							7
1		3	4	5^3	14	7^2	8		10	11^1	9	13		12			2		6							8
1	14	3	4	5			8^2	9^1	10	11	7^3	13		12			2		6							9
1	14	3	4	5		7^1	8^3	9^2	10	11		13		12			2		6							10
1	14	3	4	5		7^1	8^3	9^2	10	11	12	13					2		6							11
1	14	3	4	5		7^1	8^2	9^3	10	11	12	13					2		6							12
1	14	3	4	5			8^3	9^1	10	11	13	7^2		12			2		6							13
1	14	3	4	5	12		8^3		10	11	13	7		9^2			2		6^1							14
1	12	3	4	5	6		8^1	9^3	10	11^2	13	7	14				2									15
1	12		4^2	5	6	13		9^3	10	11	8^1	7	3^8	14			2									16
1	2^2	3		5	6	12	8	13	10	11^8	7^1			9			4									17
1	12	3	4^3	5		7^1	14	9^2	8		13	11		10	6		2									18
1	13	3	4	5		7^3	14	9^2	8		11			10^1	6		2						12			19
1	14	3	4	5		7^3	12	9	8		11^1			10^2	6		2						13			20
1			4	5		7^1	12	9^1	10	11		8^2		3	6		2					13	14			21
1	2		4	5			8^1	9		11^2	13	7			6				3	10		12				22
1	3		4	5	6	7^2	13		10	11	12	8					2			9^1						23
1	3	12	4	5	6^8	13	7^3		10	11	9	8^2	14				2^1									24
1	2	3	4	5		13	7		10	11	9^1	8^2			6							12				25
1	2	3	4			13	12	9^1	10	11	6^2	8^3	14	5					7							26
1	2	3	4	12	6	14		9	10	11^3	13	8		5^1						7^2						27
1	14	3	4	5	6	13	12	10^1	10	11	7^1	8^2					2									28
1		3	4	5	6	7	8^1	9^3	10	12	14	13					2						11^2			29
1	11	3	4^2	5	6	7^3	12		10	13	9	8^1					2						14			30
1	7	3	4	5	6		8		10	11	9^1						2						12			31
1	7^1	3	4	5	6	13			10	11	9^3	12					2			14			8^2			32
1	7	3	4^1	5	6	13			10	11	8^2	12					2			14			9^3			33
1	13	3	4^2	5	6	12			10	11^8	7^1	8					2			14			9^3			34
1	2	3	4	5	6	14	12		10	11^1	8^2				7					13			9^3			35
1	7	3	4^1	5	6		8	12	10	11							2			13			9^2			36
1	7	3		5	6	14	8	9^3	10		13	4		2^1		12				11^2						37
1	7	3	4	5	6	13	8	9^2		11							2			12			10^1			38
1	11^1	3	4	5	6		12	13	10		7^2	8					2						9			39
1		3	4	5	6		8^2	13	10	12	11^1	7					2			14			9^3			40
1	7^2	3		5	6	13			10	11		8	4				2			12			9^1			41
1	14	3	8^3	5	6	13		7	10	11^2		4					2			12			9^1			42
1	7^3	3	4	5	6		11^2	14	10		13	8					2			9^1			12			43
1	12	3	4^1	5	6		8	9^2	10	11	13	7					2									44
1	14	3	4^3	5	6		8^1	9^2	10	11^8	12	7					2						13			45
1	11^3	3	4	5	6	7^2	13		10^1		12	8								9				2	14	46

FA Cup
Fourth Qualifying Round
York C (h) 0-2

LUTON TOWN
Blue Square Premier

Ground: Kenilworth Stadium, 1 Maple Road, Luton LU4 8AW.   *Tel:* (01582) 411 622.   *Year Formed:* 1885.
Record Gate: 30, 869 (1959 v Blackpool, FA Cup 6th rd replay).   *Nickname:* The Hatters.   *Manager:* Gary Brabin.
Secretary: Adam Cockfield.   *Colours:* Orange shirts, white shorts, orange stockings.

LUTON TOWN 2010–11 LEAGUE RECORD

Match No.	Date	Venue	Opponents	Result	H/T Score	Lg Pos.	Goalscorers	Attendance
1	Aug 14	H	Altrincham	W 2-1	1-0	—	Kroca [22], Barnes-Homer [88]	6665
2	17	A	Kettering T	W 3-1	1-1	—	Barnes-Homer 3 (2 pens) [25 (p), 73, 84 (p)]	2906
3	21	A	Fleetwood T	W 3-0	2-0	1	Barnes-Homer [14], Gnakpa [22], Craddock [88]	2831
4	24	H	Newport Co	D 1-1	1-1	—	Kroca [31]	6945
5	28	A	Tamworth	L 1-3	0-1	2	Craddock [48]	1694
6	30	H	Hayes & Y	D 1-1	0-0	4	Drury [60]	6354
7	Sept 4	A	Grimsby T	L 0-2	0-1	6		3822
8	11	H	Cambridge U	W 2-0	2-0	6	Drury [34], Pilkington, G [45]	6691
9	17	H	AFC Wimbledon	W 3-0	2-0	—	Pilkington, G [23], Kroca [38], Barnes-Homer [49]	7283
10	21	A	Darlington	D 2-2	1-1	—	Gnakpa [14], Howells [80]	1665
11	25	A	Gateshead	L 0-1	0-1	7		1075
12	28	H	Mansfield T	W 2-0	0-0	—	Crow [51], Morgan-Smith [54]	6024
13	Oct 2	A	Barrow	W 1-0	1-0	4	Barnes-Homer [37]	1416
14	5	H	Crawley T	L 1-2	0-0	—	Drury (pen) [65]	6895
15	16	A	Eastbourne Bor	W 4-2	1-1	4	Pilkington, G [18], Barnes-Homer [63], Crow 2 (1 pen) [72, 76 (p)]	2518
16	19	H	Forest Green R	W 6-1	3-1	—	Drury [6], Morgan-Smith [14], Crow 2 [34, 49], Barnes-Homer [81], Walker, D [90]	5704
17	30	H	Bath C	W 3-1	3-0	3	Crow [16], Pilkington, G [28], Atieno [34]	7003
18	Nov 11	A	Wrexham	L 0-1	0-1	—		2733
19	13	A	Altrincham	W 1-0	0-0	3	Lawless [47]	1416
20	20	H	Histon	W 5-1	3-1	3	Gnakpa [7], Howells [19], Walker, J [39], Drury (pen) [69], Atieno [78]85963
21	Jan 1	H	Rushden & D	W 3-0	1-0	3	Barnes-Homer 2 [44, 51], Gnakpa [75]	6928
22	4	A	Hayes & Y	W 1-0	0-0	—	Gnakpa [75]	801
23	8	A	Bath C	D 0-0	0-0	3		2301
24	12	A	AFC Wimbledon	D 0-0	0-0	—		4287
25	18	H	York C	W 5-0	4-0	—	Drury [18], Gnakpa [31], Owusu [36], Kroca [45], Atieno [66]	5997
26	22	H	Gateshead	D 2-2	2-2	3	Crow [27], Gnakpa [37]	5958
27	25	H	Grimsby T	W 1-0	1-0	—	Gnakpa [25]	5609
28	Feb 1	H	Darlington	W 4-0	0-0	—	Gnakpa [68], Owusu 2 [74, 82], Lawless [90]	5770
29	12	H	Fleetwood T	L 1-3	1-1	3	Owusu [7]	6227
30	18	A	Newport Co	D 1-1	0-0	—	Willmott [18]	2834
31	Mar 1	A	Forest Green R	W 1-0	1-0	—	Owusu [38]	1015
32	5	H	Kidderminster H	D 1-1	1-0	3	Barnes-Homer [27]	6108
33	8	H	Tamworth	W 2-0	1-0	—	Owusu [38], Barnes-Homer [60]	5737
34	15	A	Cambridge U	D 0-0	0-0	—		2831
35	22	A	Rushden & D	W 1-0	0-0	3	Willmott [11]	2459
36	26	A	Southport	L 1-2	0-0	3	Barnes-Homer [74]	1695
37	29	H	Barrow	D 0-0	0-0	—		5528
38	Apr 2	A	Kidderminster H	D 3-3	0-1	3	Willmott [57], Gnakpa [80], Walker, J [89]	2756
39	5	H	Kettering T	D 2-2	1-0	—	Howells [40], Morgan-Smith [54]	5715
40	9	H	Southport	W 6-0	2-0	3	Morgan-Smith [22], Willmott [39], Murray, F [84], Walker, J [88], Kroca [89], Gnakpa [90]	5844
41	12	A	Crawley T	D 1-1	1-1	—	Lawless [29]	3326
42	16	A	Mansfield T	D 0-0	0-0	3		2203
43	19	A	York C	L 0-1	0-0	—		2955
44	23	H	Eastbourne Bor	W 3-0	1-0	3	Willmott 2 [18, 77], Gnakpa [65]	6171
45	25	A	Histon	W 4-0	2-0	3	Morgan-Smith [12], Barnes-Homer 2 [34, 90], Gnakpa [47]	1159
46	30	H	Wrexham	D 1-1	0-1	3	Walker, J (pen) [88]	6443

Final League Position: 3

GOALSCORERS
League (85): Barnes-Homer 16 (2 pens), Gnakpa 13, Crow 7 (1 pen), Drury 6 (2 pens), Owusu 6, Willmott 6, Kroca 5, Morgan-Smith 5, Pilkington, G 4, Walker, J 4 (1 pen), Atieno 3, Howells 3, Lawless 3, Craddock 2, Murray, F 1, Walker, D 1.
FA Cup (12): Morgan-Smith 3, Atieno 2, Barnes-Homer 2, Drury 2, Crow 1, Gnakpa 1, Kroca 1.
Play-Offs (5): Asafu-Adjaye 1, Gnakpa 1, Kroca 1, Lawless 1, Walker, J 1.

Tyler 43	Gleeson 33 + 1	Murray F 28	Keane 39	Kroca 45	Pilkington G 45	Drury 23	Barnes-Homer 39 + 5	Gallen 4 + 2	Howells 34 + 8	Crow 17 + 11	Gnakpa 33 + 9	Craddock 1 + 3	Pilkington K 3	Besta 3 + 3	Newton 14 + 5	Blackett 7 + 1	Atieno 6 + 7	Walker D 1 + 11	Morgan-Smith 15 + 5	Poku 2 + 7	Lawless 15 + 5	Walker J 8 + 12	Asafu-Adjaye 3 + 2	Owusu 13	Watkins — + 3	Willmott 12 + 3	Graham 6 + 4	Carden 8 + 2	Lacey — + 1	Match No.
1	2	3	4	5	6	7	8	9^3	10^1	11^2	12	13	14																	1
	2	3	4	5	6	7	8^3	9	10^1	13	12	11^2		1	14															2
1	2	3	4	5	6	7		9		12	10^2	11^1	13		8															3
1	2	3	4^1	5	6	7		9^3	10^2	12	13	11^1	14		8															4
	2	3		5	6	7	8	9^2	13	12		11^1	10	1	4^3	14														5
1	2		4	5	6	7^8	8	9^1	12	11^2	10	13			3															6
1	2		4^1	5	6		8	9	10^2		13	11^3			12	7	3	14												7
1	2^1	3		5	6		8	9		13	14	11^3			12	4	10^2													8
1		3		5	6	7		9^1	8		11				2	4	10	12												9
1	12	3		5	6	7		9		4	13	11			2	8^2	10^1													10
1	2	3	4	5^1	6		9^1	12	13	11^2					7	8	10^8	14												11
1	2	3	4	5	6	12	9^1	7	10^3	11					13		14		8^2											12
1	2	3	4	5	6	7	9^3	8	10^1	11^2					14				12	13										13
1	2	3	4	5	6	7	9		12	11							8		10^1											14
1	2	3	4	5	6	7^2	9	11	10								13		8^1	12										15
1	2	3	4	5	6	7^1	9	11^2	10^3	12					14				8	13										16
1	2	3	4	5	6	7	9	11	10^2	12					8^1				13											17
1	2	3	4	5	6	7	9	8^2	11^1						12	13		10												18
1	2	3	4	5	6	7	9	12	10^2	11^1					13			8												19
1	3^1		4	5	6	7	9^2	8	11						12	13			2^3	10	14									20
1	2		4	5	6	7	9	3	10^1	11^2									8^1	14	13	12								21
1	2		4	5	6	7	9^2	3	10^1	11									8		13	12								22
1	2		4	5	6	7	9^1	3	10	11^2									8		13	12								23
1	2		4	5	6	7	9	3	10^2	11									8^1		12	13								24
1	2		4	5	6	7^2	9^3	3	14	11					12				8			10^1	13							25
1			4	5	6		9^2	3	10	11					13				12		7	2^1	8^1	14						26
1	2		4	5	6	8	9^1	3	11												7	12	10							27
1	2		4	5	6		9^1	3	11										8^2	7	12	10^3	13	14						28
1	2		4	5	6		9	3^2	11^3										8^1	13	7	14	10	12						29
1	2^1	3	4	5	6						13	11									9^2		10		7	12	8			30
1		3	4	5	6		9^2	8	13	7													10		11^1	2	12			31
1	2	3	4	5	6		9	7^1	11										12		7	13	10^2				8			32
1	2	3	4	5	6		9	8	11^1										12		7	13	10^2							33
1			4	5	6	14	8	10^3	13						3^1				12		9			11	2	7^2				34
1			4	5	6		9	11	10^2						2				8^1	13	12			3		7				35
1			4	5	6		9	3	12	11^2					7				14	13		10^3			2^1	8				36
1			4	5	6		9	7	10	12					2							11	8^1							37
1	2	3^1	4	5	6		9^2	8	10^3	12					14						7	13			11					38
1			4	5	6	12	3	10^2							2^3				8^1		7	9			11	13	14			39
1		3	4	5	6	13	10	12							2				8^2		7	9			11^1					40
1		3	4	5	6	13	4	10							2				12		7	9^1			11		8^2			41
1	2	3	4	5	6	12	11	10^2							8^1				7		9				13					42
1	2	3^1	4		6		9^2	11	12						7			14	8^3		10				13	5				43
1	2	4^1	5	6		3	8^2								12		14				7	9	13	10	11^3					44
	2			5			9		12				1		7		13	10^2	8^1	14	3			11^1	6	4			45
1				5	6^2		9						7		4			8		14	2	10^3	12	11^1	3			13		46

FA Cup

Fourth Qualifying Round	St Albans C	(h)	4-0
First Round	Corby T	(a)	1-1
		(h)	4-2
Second Round	Charlton Ath	(a)	2-2
		(h)	1-3

Play-Offs

Semi-Final	Wrexham	(a)	3-0
		(h)	2-1
Final	AFC Wimbledon		0-0
(at Old Trafford).			

MANSFIELD TOWN — Blue Square Premier

Ground: Field Mill Ground, Quarry Lane, Mansfield, Notts NG18 5DA. *Tel:* (01623) 482 482. *Fax:* (01623) 482 495.
Year Formed: 1897. *Record Gate:* 24,467 (1953 v Nottingham F, FA Cup 3rd rd). *Nickname:* The Stags.
Manager: Paul Cox. *Secretary:* Catherine Hannant. *Colours:* Yellow shirts, blue shorts, blue stockings.

MANSFIELD TOWN 2010–11 LEAGUE RECORD

Match No.	Date		Venue	Opponents	Result	H/T Score	Lg Pos.	Goalscorers	Atten- dance
1	Aug	14	H	Forest Green R	W 3-1	0-0	—	Connor 2 [47, 72], Mills [57]	2474
2		17	A	Fleetwood T	L 0-3	0-3	—		1849
3		21	A	Kidderminster H	W 3-1	0-1	4	Medley [54], Connor [57], Duffy [90]	1487
4		24	H	Kettering T	D 1-1	1-0	—	Sandwith [20]	2089
5		28	H	Cambridge U	W 1-0	0-0	4	Parker (pen) [62]	2257
6		30	A	Altrincham	W 4-0	2-0	1	Connor [11], Smith, A [18], Parker 2 (1 pen) [81, 90 (p)]	1261
7	Sept	4	H	Tamworth	L 0-1	0-1	3		2516
8		11	A	Southport	W 2-1	2-0	3	Istead [18], Gregory [40]	1289
9		18	A	Newport Co	L 0-1	0-0	6		2713
10		21	H	York C	W 5-0	1-0	—	Smith, A [22], Duffy [55], Connor [64], Nix [69], Medley [90]	2202
11		25	H	Eastbourne Bor	W 4-0	2-0	2	Smith, C [43], Duffy (pen) [45], Medley 2 [74, 79]	2312
12		28	A	Luton T	L 0-2	0-0	—		6024
13	Oct	2	A	Gateshead	D 1-1	1-0	5	Connor [29]	1046
14		5	H	AFC Wimbledon	L 2-5	1-3	—	Connor [34], Briscoe [83]	2699
15		9	A	Rushden & D	L 0-1	0-1	7		1480
16		16	H	Darlington	D 1-1	1-0	7	Connor [9]	2234
17		30	H	Crawley T	L 1-4	1-1	8	Parker (pen) [42]	2615
18	Nov	9	A	Kettering T	W 2-0	0-0	—	Jack (og) [59], Briscoe [90]	1270
19		13	A	Forest Green R	L 1-2	0-1	10	Mitchley [74]	767
20		20	H	Hayes & Y	W 3-2	1-2	9	Smith, A [3], Connor [78], Medley [82]	2019
21		27	A	Wrexham	D 1-1	1-1	—	Connor [19]	2505
22	Dec	28	A	Cambridge U	W 5-1	2-0	—	Murray [33], Smith, A [37], Duffy [73], Coulson (og) [89], Mitchley [90]	2505
23	Jan	1	A	Grimsby T	L 2-7	1-2	8	Duffy [44], Briscoe [57]	3054
24		3	A	Altrincham	L 0-1	0-0	9		2229
25		8	A	Eastbourne Bor	W 3-1	1-0	8	Nix [22], Murray [76], Parker [90]	903
26		11	H	Fleetwood T	L 2-5	1-1	—	Murray [38], Foster [73]	1725
27		22	H	Histon	W 1-0	0-0	7	Connor [90]	1880
28		25	A	Darlington	D 0-0	0-0	—		1614
29		29	H	Wrexham	L 2-3	2-1	—	Briscoe [39], Thompson [45]	3266
30	Feb	12	H	Newport Co	D 3-3	3-3	10	Moult 2 [31, 45], Briscoe (pen) [35]	1986
31		19	A	Barrow	D 2-2	0-1	11	Smith, A 2 [73, 86]	1130
32	Mar	5	A	Tamworth	W 2-0	0-0	12	Cain [65], Briscoe [69]	1162
33		15	A	York C	L 1-2	1-0	—	Naylor [28]	2261
34		22	A	Histon	W 3-2	0-2	—	Briscoe 3 [49, 68, 80]	380
35		26	H	Kidderminster H	L 1-2	0-1	14	Murray [79]	2079
36		29	A	Crawley T	L 0-2	0-1	—		3162
37	Apr	2	H	Rushden & D	W 2-1	1-1	13	Medley [29], Briscoe [90]	1758
38		5	H	Southport	D 2-2	2-0	—	Higginson [30], Briscoe [44]	1467
39		9	A	Hayes & Y	L 0-4	0-3	14		316
40		12	H	Barrow	D 1-1	0-0	—	Briscoe [63]	1253
41		14	H	Bath C	W 2-0	0-0	—	Higginson [62], Nix [74]	2026
42		16	H	Luton T	D 0-0	0-0	11		2203
43		19	H	Grimsby T	L 0-2	0-1	—		1787
44		22	A	AFC Wimbledon	L 1-2	1-0	—	Thompson [14]	3613
45		25	H	Gateshead	W 3-2	0-2	12	Murray 2 [75, 89], Briscoe [90]	1749
46		30	A	Bath C	L 0-2	0-0	13		1051

Final League Position: 13

GOALSCORERS

League (73): Briscoe 13 (1 pen), Connor 11, Medley 6, Murray 6, Smith, A 6, Duffy 5 (1 pen), Parker 5 (3 pens), Nix 3, Higginson 2, Mitchley 2, Moult 2, Thompson 2, Cain 1, Foster 1, Gregory 1, Istead 1, Mills 1, Naylor 1, Sandwith 1, Smith, C 1, own goals 2.
FA Cup (1): Briscoe 1.

Marriott 17	Silk 33 + 1	Stonehouse 20 + 3	Mills 15 + 3	Foster 33	Smith C 15	Briscoe 36 + 6	Thompson 26 + 1	Connor 34 + 6	Parker 13 + 7	Smith A 27 + 4	Medley 11 + 20	Cain 17 + 3	Istead 18 + 11	Duffy 8 + 11	Sandwith 32 + 1	Nix 15 + 10	Gregory 2	Naylor 16 + 1	Murray 32	Aksalu 2	Day 8	Pilkington 10	Cook 8	Vincenti 3	Grand 6	Mitchley 8 + 9	Williams 2	Collett 5	Moult 3	Grof 12 + 1	Spence 6	O'Rafferty 4 + 3	Higginson 5 + 3	Hall — + 3	Preece 4 + 1	Match No.
1	2	3	4	5	6	7	8	9[3]	10[1]	11[2]	12	13	14																							1
1	2	3	4	5	6	7	8	9[2]	10	11[1]	13		12																							2
1	2	3	4	5	6	7	8	9[2]	10[1]	11[3]	12			13	14																					3
1	2		4	5	6	7	8	9[3]	12	11[2]	10[1]		14		3	13																				4
1	2		4	5	6	7[1]	8	9	10[2]	11[3]	13		14		3	12																				5
1	2		4	5	6	7[1]	8	9	10	11[2]	12		14		3	13																				6
1	2		4	5	6	7[1]	8[2]	9	10[3]	11	12		14		3	13																				7
1	2		4	5	6			9		11[2]	12	7	13		3	8		10[1]																		8
1	2		4	5	6	13		9	12[4]	11[2]		7[3]	14		3	8		10[1]																		9
1	2	14	4	5	6	12		9[3]		11	13	7[1]	10[2]		3	8																				10
1	2	12	4	5	6	14		9[2]		11	13	7[3]	10[1]		3	8																				11
1	2		4	5[4]	6	14		9		11[1]	13	7[3]	10[2]		3	8	12																			12
1	2	12	4		6	7[2]		9[3]		11[4]	14	13			3	8[1]		10	5																	13
1	2		4	5	6	7		9[2]		12	11	13			3	8[1]		10																		14
	2		4	5	6	7[3]		9[2]	12	10	11[1]	14	13		3	8				1																15
	2	3		5		7	8	9[3]	14	12	10[1]	13	11[2]		6				4	1																16
13	3			5		7	8	9[1]	12	11			14					10	4[4]	1		2[2]	6[3]													17
				5		7	8	9[2]	12	11[3]			14		3				4		1	2	10[1]	6	13											18
				5[4]		7	8	9[2]	12	11[3]			14		3				4		1	2	10[1]	6	13											19
						7[2]	8[1]	9		11	13				3			10	4		5	1	2		6	12										20
						7		9[2]		11[1]	13	6	12		3	8			4		5	1	2			10										21
		13				7				12	10[1]	11[2]			3	8[2]		9[3]	4		5	1	2		6	14										22
						7				12	10[1]	11[2]			3	8		9	4		5	1	2		6	13										23
	2	14				7[2]				10	13	11	12		3	8[3]		9[1]	4		5	1	6													24
	2	14	5					13	10	12	7				3	8[3]			4		6										9[2]	3[3]	11[1]			25
	2		5					13	10[1]	12	7	14			3	8[3]			4		6					11[2]										26
	2	6	5			7	8	9	10[1]		11				3	13			4[2]							12	1									27
	2	6	5			7	0	9		13	11	14			3	12[3]			4[1]							10[2]	1									28
	2	6	5			7	8	9	12		11				3				4							10[1]	1									29
	2					7	8	9[1]	12		11				3			6	4	5								1	10							30
	2	3[3]				7	8	9		12	11[1]				5	14		6	4							13				10[2]	1					31
	2					7	8	9			11				5			6	4							12				10[1]	1	3				32
		3		5		13		12		11		7[2]	8			14		6	4							10[3]				1	2	9[1]				33
		3				7	8	9		11					5			6	4							10[1]				1	2	12				34
	2	3				7	8	9		11[2]			13		5	12		6	4											1		10[1]				35
	2	3				7	8	9		10			11		5			6	4											1						36
1[0]		3		5		7	8	9		10			11					6	4							15				1	12	2[1]				37
		3		5		7[1]	8	9		10			2					6	4							1				12	11[2]	13				38
				5		7[3]	8	9[4]		13	10[2]		2		3	12		6	4							14				1		11[1]				39
	2	3				7				10	11				5	8		6	4							9[1]				1		12				40
	2	3		5		7				10[1]	11				8			6	4							9				1		12				41
	2	3		5		7				13		11	4		8			6[1]								9[2]				1		10		12	42
	2	3		5		7		9		11	12				8				4											1		10[1]		6	43
	2			5		13	8	9[1]		11	10[3]	7	14						4								1			3		12[2]		6	44
1	2			5		7	8			11[2]	12	10							4											3	9[1]		13	6	45
1		3		5			12			11	10[2]	7	8[8]		4															2	9[1]		13	6	46

FA Cup
Fourth Qualifying Round   FC Halifax T   (a)   1-0
First Round   Torquay U   (h)   0-1

NEWPORT COUNTY   Blue Square Premier

Ground: Newport Stadium, Stadium Way, Newport International Sports Village, Newport NP19 4PT.
Tel: (01633) 662 262.   *Fax:* (01633) 666 107.   *Year Formed:* 1912.   *Record Gate:* 4,616 (at Newport Stadium 2006 v
Swansea C).   *Nickname:* The Ironsides.   *Manager:* Anthony Hudson.   *Secretary:* Mike Everett.   *Colours:* Red shirts,
black shorts.

NEWPORT COUNTY 2010–11 LEAGUE RECORD

Match No.	Date	Venue	Opponents	Result	H/T Score	Lg Pos.	Goalscorers	Attendance
1	Aug 14	A	Darlington	L	0-1	0-1	—	2597
2	17	H	Tamworth	D	1-1	0-1	— Reid (pen) [71]	2217
3	21	H	Histon	D	2-2	2-1	19	Rose [6], Matthews [18]	1927
4	24	A	Luton T	D	1-1	1-1	—	Henry [26]	6945
5	28	H	Kidderminster H	W	3-0	2-0	13	Matthews [35], Reid 2 (2 pens) [44, 53]	2026
6	30	A	AFC Wimbledon	D	2-2	1-1	13	Reid 2 (1 pen) [25 (p), 79]	3828
7	Sept 5	H	Wrexham	D	1-1	0-1	15	Knights [89]	3206
8	11	A	Rushden & D	W	1-0	1-0	9	Reid [33]	1351
9	18	H	Mansfield T	W	1-0	0-0	8	Rose [60]	2713
10	21	A	Hayes & Y	W	2-1	0-1	—	Reid [47], Warren [55]	478
11	25	A	Cambridge U	W	1-0	1-0	5	Collins [3]	2648
12	28	H	Forest Green R	W	3-1	2-1	—	Foley [18], Reid 2 [34, 74]	2677
13	Oct 2	A	Grimsby T	L	0-2	0-1	6		3246
14	5	H	Eastbourne Bor	D	3-3	2-1	—	Matthews [3], Collins [18], Rogers [80]	2403
15	9	H	York C	W	4-0	2-0	3	Foley 2 [6, 27], Reid 2 [62, 70]	2802
16	16	A	Crawley T	W	3-2	2-2	3	Rose [25], Reid [42], Knights [47]	2566
17	30	H	Kettering T	L	1-2	1-1	4	Henry [4]	2230
18	Nov 6	A	Barrow	L	1-2	1-0	—	Warren [42]	1089
19	13	A	Eastbourne Bor	D	0-0	0-0	5		1065
20	20	H	Southport	W	2-0	0-0	4	Wright [53], Reid [56]	1867
21	27	H	Hayes & Y	W	2-1	1-0	—	Knights [5], Reid (pen) [67]	1601
22	Dec 18	A	Fleetwood T	D	1-1	0-1	—	Matthews [76]	1142
23	28	A	Kidderminster H	W	3-2	2-0	—	Reid [29], Shaw (og) [37], Bignot [82]	1757
24	Jan 1	H	Bath C	L	1-2	0-0	4	Reid [83]	2903
25	3	H	AFC Wimbledon	D	3-3	3-1	4	Todd [10], Collins 2 [18, 36]	3462
26	8	A	Southport	L	1-2	1-0	4	Todd [43]	1032
27	11	A	Tamworth	L	2-3	1-0	—	Reid 2 [10, 66]	803
28	22	H	Rushden & D	L	1-3	1-2	6	Rose [26]	1743
29	29	H	Histon	D	0-0	0-0	—		452
30	Feb 12	A	Mansfield T	D	3-3	3-3	8	Matthews [1], Griffin [2], Rose [28]	1986
31	18	H	Luton T	D	1-1	0-1	—	Collins (pen) [90]	2834
32	22	A	Bath C	D	2-2	2-2	—	Odubade [14], Hatswell [21]	1551
33	26	A	Kettering T	L	0-2	0-2	8		1056
34	Mar 1	H	Cambridge U	D	1-1	0-1	—	Collins (pen) [52]	1360
35	5	H	Fleetwood T	L	1-3	0-1	11	Warren [74]	1716
36	12	H	Altrincham	W	2-1	1-1	11	Piergianni (og) [6], Warren [70]	1201
37	19	A	Forest Green R	D	0-0	0-0	11		1362
38	27	A	Wrexham	L	0-1	0-0	12		3685
39	29	H	Gateshead	W	2-1	1-0	—	Todd [8], Hughes [58]	1027
40	Apr 2	H	Grimsby T	W	2-1	0-0	8	Knights [59], Todd [72]	1506
41	5	H	Darlington	W	2-1	2-0	—	Griffin [20], Knights [37]	1300
42	9	A	York C	L	1-2	0-0	8	Collins [90]	2565
43	16	A	Barrow	W	5-0	4-0	8	Warren [8], Knights 2 [15, 31], Foley [24], Morgan [56]	1331
44	23	A	Altrincham	W	3-1	2-0	9	Warren [7], Collins [32], Foley [60]	963
45	25	H	Crawley T	L	0-1	0-0	9		2026
46	30	A	Gateshead	W	7-1	2-1	9	Collins 2 (1 pen) [35 (p), 45], Todd [61], Miller [72], Rose [73], Baker [87], Griffin [88]	824

Final League Position: 9

GOALSCORERS

League (78): Reid 18 (5 pens), Collins 10 (3 pens), Knights 7, Rose 6, Warren 6, Foley 5, Matthews 5, Todd 5, Griffin 3,
Henry 2, Baker 1, Bignot 1, Hatswell 1, Hughes 1, Miller 1, Morgan 1, Odubade 1, Rogers 1, Wright 1, own goals 2.
FA Cup (0).

Thompson 39	Bignot 41	Collins 44+1	Odhiambo 26+8	Warren 39+2	Todd 40+1	Rose 46	Rogers 10+10	Matthews 19+16	Henry 16+3	Foley 22+18	Sole 1+1	Knights 27+14	Morgan 15+18	Taggart —+3	John 9	Garner 7+1	Clough —+2	Challinor —+3	Goodall 8	Wright 3+2	Deering 3	Smith —+1	Montgomery 5+3	McDonald 2+2	Fowler 1+2	Hughes 10	Burns 1	Miller 9+4	Hatswell 11	Griffin 13+2	Odubade 4+7	Lennon 6+3	Baker —+1	Match No.
1	2^3	3	4	5	6	7	8^1	9	10^2	11	12	13	14																					1
1	2	4	3	5	6	7	13	9	12	11^2	10	8^1																						2
1	2	3	4^1	5	6	7	8	9	10^2	11^3	14	13	12																					3
1	2	3	4	5	6	7	14	9^3	10	11^2	12	13	8^1																					4
1	2	3	4	5	6	7	13	9^3	10^3	11	14	8^1	12																					5
1	2	3	4	5	6	7	14	9^3	10	11^2		13	8^1	12																				6
1	2	3	4	5	6	7		9	10^3	11^2	12	14	8^1	13																				7
1	2	3	4	5	6	7		9	10^1	11^2	12	13			8																			8
1	2^a	3	14	5	6	7		9^3	12	11	10^2	13	8^1		4																			9
1		3	4	5	6	7	13	9	10^1	11^2	8^3	12	14		2																			10
1	2	3	4	5		7	13	9^1	10	11^3	12	8^2	14		6																			11
1^6	2	3	4	5	12	7^2		9	10^1	11	8	13			6	15																		12
	2	3^3	4	5	6	7		9	12	11^2	10^1	13			8	1	14																	13
		3	4	5^a	6	7	12	9^2	10	14	8^3	11^1			2	1	13																	14
	2	3	4		6	7	14	9^3	10	12	8^1	11^2	13		5	1																		15
	2	3	4	5	6	7		9	10	12	8	11				1																		16
1	2	3	4	5	6	7		9	14	11	10^2	13			8^1			12^3																17
1	2	4		5	6	7		9	10^2	11^3	12	8^1	14						3	13														18
1	2	5	4		6	7		9		11^1	13	12	8^3						14	3	10^2													19
1	2	3	4	14	6	7		9	13		12	8^1	10^3							11	5^2													20
1	2	5	4	13	6	7		9	12			8^3								3	11^1		10^2	14										21
1	2	8	4	5	6	7		9^2	12			11									13	3	10^1											22
1	2	8	4	5	6	11	9^3	14	12			7^2	13									3	10^1											23
1	2	0	4^2	5	8^3	7		9	13		10^1	11										3	14		12									24
1	2	4	12	5	6	7		9	10^3	13		11^1											3			8^2	14							25
1	2	4	13	5^1	6	7		9				10	11													8^3	3	12						26
1	2	3^a		5^a	6	7	14	9	12	10^2		11^3														8^1	4	13						27
1	2	3	12		6	7		9	10			8	11^3	13												14		4^2	5^1					28
	2	12			6	7		9	14	10^3		11^2	13			1										8		3^1	4	5				29
	2	3	4		6^a	7				10^1		13	11^2	12		1										8		5		9^3	14			30
1	2	3		5		7				10^1		11^2	14										13			8		4^3	6	9	12			31
1	2	3		5		7				13		11	14										8^1					4	12	6	9^2	10^3		32
1	2	3		5		14		8				11^1	13												4^2			12	6^3	9	10			33
1	2	3		5	6	7		8		12		11^2													13			4		9^1	10			34
1	2	3	4	5	6	7^2		9^1	10			13	11													8^a		12						35
1	2	3	9^3	5	6	7	8	12	10^1			13	11^2																4	14				36
1	2	3		5	6	7	8	13	10^1	14		11^3																	4	12	9^2			37
1	2	3		5	6	7	8		14			12	10^3													4				9^2	13	11^1		38
1	2	3		5	6	7	8	14				11	10																	9^1	12	4^2		39
1	2	3	13	5	6	7		14				11	10^1															4		12	9^2	8^3		40
1	2	3^3	13	5	6	7	12					11	10^2															4		14	9	8^1		41
1	2	3		5	6	7		13				11^1	8^2															4		9	12	10		42
1	2^1	12		5	6^3	7	8	10			11	14																4	3	9^2	13			43
1		4	12	5		7	8	10				11^3	14															3	2^1	6	9^2	13		44
1		3		5	6	7	8	12				11	13													10			4^3	9^1	14		2^2	45
		4	2	5	6	7	8					11^3	12	10^2	1													9		3^1	14		13	46

FA Cup
Fourth Qualifying Round
         Crawley T   (h)   0-1

RUSHDEN & DIAMONDS

TBC

Ground: Nene Park, Irthlingborough, Northants NN9 5QF.   *Tel:* (01933) 652 000.   *Year Formed:* 1992.
Record Gate: 6,431 (1999 v Leeds U, FA Cup 3rd rd).   *Nickname:* The Diamonds.   *Manager:* Justin Edinburgh.
Secretary: Matt Wild.   *Colours:* White shirts, white shorts, white stockings.

RUSHDEN & DIAMONDS 2010–11 LEAGUE RECORD

Match No.	Date	Venue	Opponents	Result	H/T Score	Lg Pos.	Goalscorers	Atten- dance
1	Aug 14	H	Fleetwood T	D 1-1	0-1	—	Corcoran [90]	1248
2	17	A	Bath C	L 1-2	1-0	—	Porter [6]	876
3	21	A	Barrow	L 0-2	0-0	24		1145
4	24	H	AFC Wimbledon	W 1-0	0-0	—	Howe [64]	1365
5	28	H	Grimsby T	W 4-1	1-0	10	Miller [41], Charles [59], Howe [60], Porter [66]	1575
6	30	A	Kettering T	W 1-0	1-0	6	Westwood (og) [32]	2313
7	Sept 4	A	York C	L 0-2	0-0	10		2306
8	11	H	Newport Co	L 0-1	0-1	16		1351
9	18	A	Southport	D 2-2	0-1	16	O'Connor [57], Johnson [86]	876
10	21	H	Histon	W 2-0	0-0	—	Miller [50], O'Connor [67]	926
11	26	H	Crawley T	L 0-1	0-1	14		1162
12	29	A	Eastbourne Bor	W 2-0	2-0	—	Howe [27], Miller [36]	802
13	Oct 2	A	Altrincham	D 2-2	1-1	12	Howe (pen) [15], O'Connor [73]	897
14	5	H	Darlington	W 2-1	0-1	—	Howe [65], O'Connor [71]	1034
15	9	H	Mansfield T	W 1-0	1-0	6	Sills [8]	1480
16	16	A	Tamworth	W 2-1	1-1	6	Howe [10], Power [90]	1002
17	30	H	Barrow	W 5-0	3-0	5	Charles 2 [8, 45], O'Connor [23], Porter [58], Corcoran [65]	1107
18	Nov 9	A	Kidderminster H	L 0-1	0-1	—		1225
19	13	A	Fleetwood T	D 1-1	0-1	6	O'Connor [73]	1429
20	20	A	York C	L 0-4	0-3	8		1132
21	27	A	Forest Green R	D 2-2	0-2	—	Power (pen) [51], O'Connor [90]	642
22	Jan 1	A	Luton T	L 0-3	0-1	10		6928
23	3	H	Kettering T	L 1-2	0-1	10	Stuart [66]	2216
24	8	H	Altrincham	L 1-2	1-1	11	O'Connor [22]	1024
25	18	A	Hayes & Y	D 3-3	0-2	—	Smith 2 [68, 78], Prosser [85]	307
26	22	A	Newport Co	W 3-1	2-1	11	Gash [19], O'Connor [40], Johnson [89]	1743
27	29	H	Tamworth	D 1-1	0-0	—	Power [68]	1216
28	Feb 1	H	Cambridge U	W 2-1	0-1	—	Smith [74], Farrell [89]	1279
29	5	A	Cambridge U	W 2-0	2-0	—	O'Connor [14], Day, Jamie [21]	2366
30	12	H	Gateshead	L 0-2	0-1	9		874
31	22	H	Eastbourne Bor	W 2-0	1-0	—	Cowan-Hall [22], Oshodi [90]	905
32	Mar 1	H	Bath C	W 5-1	4-1	—	Gash 4 [9, 26, 44, 73], Charles [40]	804
33	5	H	Hayes & Y	D 1-1	1-1	9	Gash [45]	1129
34	8	H	Forest Green R	D 2-2	1-0	—	Charles 2 [31, 51]	759
35	12	A	Wrexham	D 1-1	0-1	8	Huke [52]	3187
36	19	H	Southport	D 2-2	1-1	8	Johnson [28], Porter [77]	1061
37	22	H	Luton T	L 0-1	0-1	—		2459
38	26	A	AFC Wimbledon	L 0-1	0-1	9		3069
39	Apr 2	A	Mansfield T	L 1-2	1-1	12	O'Connor [15]	1758
40	5	A	Histon	W 2-0	0-0	—	O'Connor (pen) [59], Huke [83]	363
41	9	H	Wrexham	D 2-2	0-1	10	Shariff [79], O'Connor [90]	1181
42	13	A	Grimsby T	D 1-1	1-1	—	Shariff [38]	2071
43	16	A	Gateshead	D 2-2	1-2	10	Shariff 2 [18, 55]	701
44	22	A	Crawley T	L 0-4	0-1	—		3083
45	25	H	Kidderminster H	W 2-1	0-0	11	O'Connor (pen) [49], Charles [90]	1569
46	30	A	Darlington	L 0-2	0-0	12		2009

Final League Position: 12

GOALSCORERS

League (65): O'Connor 14 (2 pens), Charles 7, Gash 6, Howe 6 (1 pen), Porter 4, Shariff 4, Johnson 3, Miller 3, Power 3 (1 pen), Smith 3, Corcoran 2, Huke 2, Cowan-Hall 1, Day, Jamie 1, Farrell 1, Oshodi 1, Prosser 1, Sills 1, Stuart 1, own goal 1.
FA Cup (2): Howe 1 (pen), Spence 1.

Roberts 8	Miller 27 + 5	Corcoran 22 + 5	Porter 43	Stuart 21	Osano 39 + 1	Power 40 + 1	Spence 5 + 10	Farrell 11 + 16	Howe 18 + 1	Simmonds 1 + 1	Charles 22 + 17	Huke 29 + 2	Johnson 22 + 22	Green 7 + 2	Robinson 6 + 6	Koranteng — + 4	Day Jamie 34 + 4	O'Connor 35 + 1	Day Joe 32	Sills 9 + 2	Keehan 3 + 3	Smith 3 + 4	Gash 18	King — + 1	Prosser 6	Thorne 2	Mills 19 + 1	Oshodi 11 + 1	Shariff 5 + 6	Cowan-Hall 2 + 1	Woolley — + 1	Evans 6	Cousins — + 6	Match No.
1	2	3	4²	5	6	7	8³	9	10	11¹	12	13	14																					1
1	2³	3	4	5	6	7	8¹	9²	10		12	13	11	14																				2
1		2	4	5ᵃ	6	7¹	12		10	14	9³	13	8	11²	3																			3
1	14	2³	4		6	7	12		9	11²	5	8	10¹	3	13																			4
1	2		4	5	6	7	12		10		9²	8¹	11³	3	13	14																		5
1	2ᵃ		4	5	6	7¹	12		10³		9	8	11²	3	14	13																		6
1		2		5	6	7	8		10		9		4²	11¹	3³	14	12	13																7
1	2		4³	5	6	7	12	13	10		8		14	11²	3			9¹																8
	2²		4	5	6	7		9	10¹		12	11	13				3	8	1															9
	2		4	5	6	7¹		9	11³	8	12	13	14				3²	10	1															10
	2		4	5	6	7¹		10	14	8²	12	13					3	9	1	11³														11
	2		4	5	6	13		10	14	8	7²	12					3¹	9³	1	11														12
	2		4	5	6	13		10		12	8	7					3	9²	1	11¹														13
	2¹		4	5	6			10		13	8	7	12				3	9	1	11²														14
			4	5	6	7³	14	10		13	2	8	12				3¹	9	1	11²														15
	14		4	5	2	7	12	10³	13		6	11¹					3	9	1	8²														16
13	3		4	6²	7	14		11	5	8¹	12						2	9³	1	10														17
	6		4	5	2	7¹	11³	13		9	12	14					3	10	1	8²														18
	6		4	5	2	7³	14		9	12	8						3	10²	1	13	11¹													19
	8¹		4	5	2	7	14	9²	11³	6	12						3*	10	1	13														20
2			4	6		7	0⁷	9	13	0¹	12			3			11	1	10⁴		14													21
2	13			5	6	7			12		4		3²	8³				10	1		11¹				9		14							22
6	7		4	5	2	8			12		11¹						3	10	1						9									23
14	7		4³		2	8			11		12		13				3	10²	1						9¹	5	6							24
11	4				2	7³			8¹		14						3	10	1			12	9	5	6²	13								25
	6		4		2	8²		14			11¹		13				3	10³	1			12	9	5		7								26
	3		4³		2	8					11²		14				6	10	1			13	9	5¹		7	12							27
13	5		4		2	8		14			12						3	10	1			11³	9¹			7	6²							28
	6		4		2	8³		13			12		14				3	10	1			11¹	9	5		7								29
	6		4³		2	8		11¹			12²		14				3	10	1				9	5		7	13							30
	4				2	8¹		13					6	12			3	10	1				9²			7	5	11						31
2			4		3	8³		12			11¹	6	13					10	1				9²			7	5	14						32
2	13				3	8		12			11¹	6	4					10	1				9			7	5	5²						33
2			4		3¹	14		13		11		6	8³			12	10²	1					9			7	5							34
2			4			8		12			10¹	6	13				3		1				9			7	5	11²						35
2	12		4			8		10²				6	11				3		1				9			7¹	5	13						36
	2		4			8				10		6	7¹				3		1				9			11	5	12						37
12	2		4			8³		13		10	6	11²					3		1			14	9			7	5¹							38
	2³	5	4					13	8		14	11	6²	12			3	10¹	1							7								39
	2	5	4					8³	9			6	11²				3	10¹	1		14					7		12		13				40
	2		4		5	8		9²				6	11³				3	10		12						7¹		13			1	14	41
	2		4		5			9¹				6	13				3	10				8²				7		11			1	12	42
2	13		4		5					9¹		6	12				3	10				8²				7		11³			1	14	43
	2		4ᵃ		6		8					5	10²				3	9								7ᵇ		11¹	13		1	12	44
2	3				5		7				12	6	8				11	9²									4	10¹			1	13	45
3	7		4		2		8			14		6	12				11¹	9									5²	10³			1	13	46

FA Cup
Fourth Qualifying Round

	Kettering T	(a)	2-1
First Round	Yeovil T	(h)	0-1

SOUTHPORT

Blue Square Premier

Ground: Haig Avenue, Southport PR8 6JZ. *Tel:* (01704) 533 422. *Year Formed:* 1881.
Record Gate: 20,010 (1932 v Newcastle U). *Nickname:* The Sandgrounders. *Manager:* Liam Watson.
Secretary: Ken Hilton. *Colours:* Yellow and black shirts, black shorts.

SOUTHPORT 2010–11 LEAGUE RECORD

Match No.	Date	Venue	Opponents	Result	H/T Score	Lg Pos.	Goalscorers	Atten- dance
1	Aug 14	H	AFC Wimbledon	L 0-1	0-0	—		1802
2	17	A	Kidderminster H	W 4-3	1-1	—	McNeil 2 [34, 48], McGinn 2 (1 pen) [74, 85 (p)]	1417
3	21	A	Cambridge U	D 0-0	0-0	12		2506
4	24	H	Altrincham	W 1-0	0-0	—	Gray, T [82]	1088
5	28	H	Fleetwood T	W 1-0	1-0	5	Davis [31]	1546
6	Sept 4	A	Forest Green R	D 0-0	0-0	8		1064
7	7	A	Gateshead	L 0-1	0-0	—		471
8	11	H	Mansfield T	L 1-2	0-2	10	Daly [80]	1289
9	18	H	Rushden & D	D 2-2	1-0	12	McGinn (pen) [6], Blakeman [67]	876
10	21	A	Wrexham	L 1-2	0-2	—	Daly [63]	2221
11	25	A	Darlington	L 0-1	0-0	18		1633
12	28	H	Hayes & Y	D 0-0	0-0	—		753
13	Oct 2	H	Tamworth	W 2-1	2-1	15	McNeil [30], Daly [36]	966
14	5	A	Histon	L 1-2	1-2	—	Gray, T [34]	368
15	9	H	Kettering T	L 1-2	0-2	18	Barratt [83]	1117
16	16	A	Grimsby T	D 1-1	1-0	19	Blakeman [25]	3101
17	29	H	Kidderminster H	D 2-2	2-0	—	Simm [17], Marsh-Evans [40]	1447
18	Nov 13	H	Bath C	L 2-3	2-0	21	Barratt [17], Powell [25]	947
19	20	A	Newport Co	L 0-2	0-0	22		1867
20	23	A	York C	L 0-2	0-0	—		2104
21	Dec 28	A	Fleetwood T	L 0-2	0-1	—		2051
22	Jan 1	A	Barrow	D 1-1	0-0	23	McNeil [81]	1339
23	3	H	Gateshead	W 5-1	0-1	20	Barratt [50], Ledsham [58], Kissock [67], McNeil [87], Powell [90]	904
24	8	H	Newport Co	W 2-1	0-1	19	Lee [87], Gray, T (pen) [90]	1032
25	18	H	Wrexham	L 0-1	0-1	—		1464
26	22	A	AFC Wimbledon	L 0-5	0-1	20		3408
27	29	H	York C	W 4-0	3-0	—	Lever (pen) [3], Whalley 2 [4, 51], Lee [21]	1308
28	Feb 1	H	Grimsby T	D 2-2	2-0	—	Whalley [8], Davis [29]	853
29	12	A	Forest Green R	W 4-0	3-0	18	Ledsham 2 [7, 23], Marsh-Evans [18], Lee [53]	1006
30	19	A	Hayes & Y	L 0-1	0-1	18		303
31	22	A	Crawley T	L 0-1	0-0	—		3765
32	26	A	Bath C	L 1-2	1-1	19	Lee [44]	792
33	Mar 1	H	Histon	W 3-1	0-0	—	Whalley [47], Ledsham [52], Gray, T [80]	652
34	5	A	Eastbourne Bor	L 1-4	1-2	18	Whalley (pen) [33]	1004
35	12	H	Cambridge U	D 1-1	0-0	18	Kissock [55]	1107
36	15	H	Barrow	L 2-4	0-1	—	Marsh-Evans [57], Whalley [86]	889
37	19	A	Rushden & D	D 2-2	1-1	20	McGinn (pen) [37], Whalley [55]	1061
38	26	H	Luton T	W 2-1	0-0	19	Moogan [82], Lee [88]	1695
39	29	A	Altrincham	D 1-1	0-1	—	Daly [61]	1210
40	Apr 2	H	Eastbourne Bor	L 1-3	0-3	20	Daly [90]	923
41	5	A	Mansfield T	D 2-2	0-2	—	Turner [57], McGinn (pen) [83]	1467
42	9	A	Luton T	L 0-6	0-2	21		5844
43	16	A	Crawley T	L 0-4	0-2	21		1011
44	23	A	Tamworth	W 1-0	0-0	21	Daly [63]	944
45	25	H	Darlington	D 1-1	1-0	20	Kissock [13]	1866
46	30	A	Kettering T	L 1-3	0-1	21	Whalley [63]	1403

Final League Position: 21

GOALSCORERS

League (56): Whalley 8 (1 pen), Daly 6, Lee 5, McGinn 5 (4 pens), McNeil 5, Gray, T 4 (1 pen), Ledsham 4, Barratt 3, Kissock 3, Marsh-Evans 3, Blakeman 2, Davis 2, Powell 2, Lever 1 (1 pen), Moogan 1, Simm 1, Turner 1.
FA Cup (4): Barratt 1, McGinn 1, own goals 2.

McMillan 45	Williams 29+4	Lever 27+3	Flynn 23+5	Davis 39+3	Powell 14+13	Winn 13+1	Moogan 40+1	McNeil 31+4	Gray T 20+18	McGinn 28+5	Collins —+6	Barratt 17+21	Blakeman 16+6	Lee 33+1	Daly 17+13	Simm 7+1	Morley —+1	Gray S 3	Marsh-Evans 26+2	Dickinson 1+1	Lloyd-McGoldrick —+4	Kissock 22+2	Ledsham 21+3	Whalley 15+2	Turner 19	Match No.
1	2	3	4	5	6^2	7	8	9	10^1	11^3	12	13	14													1
1	4	3		5	6^2	7	8	9^3	10^1	11		12	13	2	14											2
1	4	3	14	5	6^1	7^3	8	9	10^2	11		12	13	2												3
1	2	3^2	13	5		7	8	9^3	10	11		12	6^1	4	14											4
1	2		4	5	6	7	8	9	10^1	11^2			13		3	12										5
1	3		4	5	12	7	8			11	13	6^1	10^2	2				9^3	14							6
1	3		4	5	6	7	8			11	12	13	9^1	2				10^2								7
1	13	3^1	4^2	5		7	8	9	12	11		14	6^3	2	10											8
1	3		4	5		7	8	9^3	10^1	11	14	12	6^2	2	13											9
1	2		4	5	6^1	7	8		10^3			14	12	3^2	13	9			11							10
1	2		4	5	6	7	13		10^1	12		11^2			8	9		3								11
1	2		4	5	12	7	8		10^1	11			3		6	9										12
1	2	3	4	5	14	12	8	9	13	11^3		7	6^3	10^2												13
1	2	3		5	6	7	8	9^2	10	12		13		11				4^1								14
1		3	4	5	12		8		10^2	11	13	7	6^1	2	9											15
1	2	3	4		13		8^3	9	14	12		7	11^2	6		10^1			5							16
1*		3	4	5	6		9		12	11		7	8		10			2^1	15							17
1		3^2	4	5	6		9		11			7	12	8	13	10^1		2								18
1	2			5	6		8	9^1	12	11		7^3		3	10^2	13		4	14							19
		3^1	12	5			8		10		11	7^2	2	9	6			4	1	13						20
1	14			4	12	6^2	8	9	10^3	11	13			2					5			3	7^1			21
1	2	3^2	4	5	6		8	12	10^1	13^3			11		9			14				7				22
1	2	3	4	12	13			9	14			8	10^2	6					5^1			11^3	7			23
1	2^2		4	5	14		8	9	12			6^1	11^3	3		13						10	7			24
1	2		4	5	12		8	9	13	14		6^1	10^2			3						7	11^3			25
1	2	13		5	12		8^1	9		11^2		14	3^3	4					6			10	7			26
1	12	3	4^1		13		8^2	9	14			6	2						5			10	11	7^3		27
1	2	3		5	12		8		10^2			4	13									9	11^1	7^4	6	28
1		3		5^1			8	9^2	10			12		2	13				4		14	7^3	11		6	29
1		3		5			8	9^3	10^2			12		2	14				6		13	11^1	7		4	30
1		3		5	13		8		10			12		2	9^1				6			11^2	7		4	31
1		3^1	4	5	14			9^2				12		2	13				6			11	7	10	8^3	32
1	14			5			8	9^2	13			3		2	12				6			11^1	7	10^3	4	33
1		3^1	4		12		8	9^3	14			10		2	13				5			11^2	7		6	34
1		3		5			8^2	9	12					2					6			10	11	7^1	4	35
		2^1		5			8		13	11		3			9				6			10^2	7	12	4	36
1	2	3		5			8	12	10^2	11^3					9^1				6			14	13	7	4	37
1				5			8	10	12	3		13		2					6			9^2	7	11	4	38
1	12	3		5			8	14	10^3	11					2^1	9			6			13	7		4^2	39
1	2^1			5			8	10^2	14	3		13							6			11	7	9^2	4	40
1	2	13	5^2				8	10		3					9				6			11	7^1	12	4	41
1		3	13	5			8	12	14	11				2^1				9^3	6^2			7	10		4	42
1		5	12				8^2	10		3		13		2^1	14				6			7	11	9^3	4	43
1		5	2				8	9	12	3			14	13					6			11^1	7	10^3	4	44
1	6	2		5			8^2	9	12	3			14	13								11^1	7	10^3	4	45
1	6	3		5			8	9		11				2^1	10							13	12	7	4^2	46

FA Cup

Fourth Qualifying Round

	Wrexham	(a)	2-1
First Round	Sheffield W	(h)	2-5

TAMWORTH

Blue Square Premier

Ground: The Lamb Ground, Kettlebrook, Tamworth B77 1AA. *Tel:* (01827) 65798. *Fax:* (01827) 62236.
Year Formed: 1933. *Record Gate:* 4,920 (1948 v Atherstone T). *Nickname:* The Lambs. *Manager:* Marcus Law.
Secretary: Rod Hadley. *Colours:* Red shirts with white trim, white shorts, red stockings.

TAMWORTH 2010–11 LEAGUE RECORD

Match No.	Date	Venue	Opponents	Result	H/T Score	Lg Pos.	Goalscorers	Atten- dance
1	Aug 14	H	Eastbourne Bor	W 4-2	3-0	—	Perry [11], Marshall [19], Thomas [30], Rodman [67]	723
2	17	A	Newport Co	D 1-1	1-0	—	Wylde [3]	2217
3	21	A	AFC Wimbledon	L 0-3	0-1	15		3144
4	24	H	Cambridge U	D 1-1	0-0	—	Bradley, D [82]	863
5	28	H	Luton T	W 3-1	1-0	8	Perry [11], Thomas [78], Bradley, D [90]	1694
6	30	A	Kidderminster H	D 2-2	1-1	10	Perry 2 [45, 79]	1271
7	Sept 4	A	Mansfield T	W 1-0	1-0	5	Wilkinson [30]	2516
8	11	H	Grimsby T	W 2-1	2-0	4	Rodman [14], Perry [38]	1616
9	18	A	Histon	W 2-1	0-1	3	Perry (pen) [66], Barrow [89]	653
10	21	A	Bath C	D 2-2	1-2	—	Rodman [38], Smith [68]	920
11	25	H	York C	L 1-3	0-1	6	Barrow [81]	1282
12	29	A	Crawley T	L 1-3	1-1	—	Wylde [40]	1355
13	Oct 2	A	Southport	L 1-2	1-2	10	Lake-Gaskin [45]	966
14	5	H	Barrow	D 2-2	1-1	—	Rodman 2 (1 pen) [19, 90 (p)]	779
15	9	A	Gateshead	L 1-3	1-2	13	Rodman [17]	807
16	16	H	Rushden & D	L 1-2	1-1	14	Perry [11]	1002
17	30	H	Fleetwood T	L 0-2	0-1	16		946
18	Nov 9	A	Darlington	L 0-1	0-1	—		2625
19	13	H	Gateshead	D 1-1	1-0	18	Smith [44]	802
20	20	A	Cambridge U	D 3-3	2-0	19	Thomas 2 [20, 58], Perry [32]	2809
21	Jan 1	A	Kettering T	W 1-0	0-0	16	Furlong (og) [57]	1164
22	3	H	Kidderminster H	D 2-2	2-2	16	Vaughan (og) [12], Yussuf [17]	1183
23	8	A	Hayes & Y	L 1-2	0-1	16	Marshall [90]	249
24	11	H	Newport Co	W 3-2	0-1	—	Rodman 3 (1 pen) [47, 76, 90 (p)]	803
25	18	H	Altrincham	D 1-1	0-1	—	Perry [79]	795
26	22	H	Darlington	D 1-1	0-0	15	Wylde [90]	1034
27	25	A	Eastbourne Bor	W 4-1	1-0	—	Thomas [36], Bradley, J [62], Perry (pen) [68], Yussuf [89]	551
28	29	A	Rushden & D	D 1-1	0-0	—	MacKenzie [75]	1216
29	Feb 5	H	Histon	L 0-1	0-1	—		885
30	12	A	Bath C	L 0-2	0-0	16		899
31	19	H	AFC Wimbledon	L 2-5	0-1	16	Wylde [51], Bradley, D [65]	1496
32	22	A	Barrow	W 2-0	1-0	—	Thomas [42], Perry [54]	874
33	26	A	Forest Green R	L 0-4	0-1	16		681
34	Mar 2	H	Kettering T	W 3-1	3-0	—	Tait [3], Bradley, D [16], Perry [43]	609
35	5	H	Mansfield T	L 0-2	0-0	16		1162
36	8	H	Luton T	L 0-2	0-1	—		5737
37	12	H	Hayes & Y	L 2-3	1-1	16	Perry 2 [34, 90]	1171
38	19	A	Altrincham	L 0-2	0-1	18		895
39	26	A	Grimsby T	D 2-2	0-1	18	Perry [71], Marshall [80]	3002
40	29	H	Wrexham	D 1-1	0-0	—	Bradley, J [69]	1082
41	Apr 2	A	Fleetwood T	L 1-2	0-1	18	Thomas [66]	1580
42	9	H	Crawley T	L 0-3	0-1	20		1569
43	16	A	York C	W 2-1	1-0	19	Wilkinson [26], Perry [74]	2484
44	23	H	Southport	L 0-1	0-0	19		944
45	25	A	Wrexham	L 2-4	0-1	21	Barrow [57], Perry [81]	4330
46	30	H	Forest Green R	W 2-1	1-0	19	Smith [3], Sheridan [77]	1717

Final League Position: 19

GOALSCORERS

League (62): Perry 17 (2 pens), Rodman 9 (2 pens), Thomas 7, Bradley, D 4, Wylde 4, Barrow 3, Marshall 3, Smith 3, Bradley, J 2, Wilkinson 2, Yussuf 2, Lake-Gaskin 1, MacKenzie 1, Sheridan 1, Tait 1, own goals 2.
FA Cup (6): Thomas 2, McKenzie 1, Marshall 1, Perry 1, Rodman 1.

Atkins 29	Tait 41	Barrow 41+1	Rodman 25	Wylde 38+2	Marshall 37+2	Smith 35+1	MacKenzie 16+10	Perry 35+5	Thomas 44+1	Bradley D 37+6	Oakes 3+7	Sheridan 22+12	Farrell 4+7	Mitchell A 11+6	Lake-Gaskin 13+12	Wilkinson 22+6	Lyttle 2+1	Severn 3	Bojang —+2	Yussuf 6+4	Bradley J 9+9	Kamara —+8	Christie —+2	Courtney 17+1	Mitchell L 11	Ward 1	Hendrie 2+2	Connor 2	Belford —+1	Match No.
1	2	3	4[2]	5	6	7[1]	8	9[3]	10	11	12	13	14																	1
1	2	3[2]	4	5	6	7	8[1]	9	10	11	12	13																		2
1	2		4	5	6	7	8[1]	9[3]	10	11[2]	13		14	3	12															3
1	2	3	4	5	6	7[2]	8[1]	9	10	11	13	12																		4
1	2	3	4	5	6	7		9[1]	10	11		12				8														5
1	2[3]	3	4	5	6	7	12	9	10[2]	11[1]	13			8	14															6
1	2	3	4	5	6	7		9	10	11						8														7
1	2	3	4	5	6	7	12	9	10			8		11[1]																8
1	2	3	4	5	6	7		9	10	12				8[2]	13	11[1]														9
1	2	3	4	5	6	7		9	10	11[1]		12				8														10
1	2	3	4	5	6[3]	7		9	10		13		14	8[1]	12	11[2]														11
1	2	8	4	5	6	7		9[3]	10	11[2]			14	3[1]	13	12														12
1	2	11	4	5	6	7		9[2]	10[1]			12		3	13	8														13
1	2	3	4	5	6	7[2]		9[1]	10		14	13		11	12	8[3]														14
1	2	3	10	5	6	7[3]	12	9[2]		4		13	14	11		8[1]														15
	2[2]	3	4[1]	5	6	7	13	9	10	11		12				8		1												16
	2	3	4	5	14	7[2]	8	9	10[3]	12		13		6		11[1]		1												17
		3	10	5		7	8[3]	9[1]	11	4	2[2]	13		6	12	14		1												18
1	2	3	4[1]	5		7	8		10	11		9		6	12															19
1	2	3		5		7	8[1]	9[2]	10	11	4	6		12	13															20
1	2	3[1]	0		6	7	13	8	10	11[2]		5		4					12											21
1	2	3	10		6	7[1]	12	9[3]				8		5	14	4			13		11[2]									22
1	2	3	10[1]		6		9	7				8		5	12	4[2]					11									23
1	2	7	10		6		8	12	9			3		4[1]	5	13					11[2]									24
1	2	3	10[3]	5	6		8	9	7					4[1]							11[2]	13	14							25
1	2	3[2]	10	5	6		8	9		11[1]	7								12		4	13								26
1	2[3]	3		5	6		8	9[1]	10	11			4						12	7[2]	13									27
1	2	4	5	3	7			9[1]	11[2]	6	8[4]								12	7[2]	13									28
1	2	3		5	6		8[3]	9[2]	11	4	7[1]	10							13		12	14								29
1	2[3]	3		5	6	13	8[2]	9	10	7		14		11[1]						12		4								30
1	2	3		5	6		8[1]	9	10	7		13	12	4							11[2]									31
1		3		5	6	7		9[1]	10	11				8					12	2										32
		3		5	6	7		9	10[2]	11	8								12	13				2[1]	1					33
	2	3		5		7[1]	12	9[2]	10	11	8[3]	14	6						13					4	1					34
	2	3		5		7		9	10	11	6[2]			8[1]					12	13				4	1					35
	2	3		5	15	7[2]		9[1]	10	8	6	13	11						12					4	1[6]					36
	2	3		5		7		9	10[2]	8	6[1]			12					13					4	1	1	11			37
	2[3]	3		5		6		9	10[2]	7	13	14		8					12					4	1		11[1]			38
	2	3[1]		5	6	11		13	12	8		9		7					10[2]					4	1					39
	2			5	6		12	10	8		13	9[1]		7	3[2]				11					4	1					40
	2			5	6	7[2]		10	8		12	9[1]		3[3]	13				11					4	1		14			41
	2	14		5	6	7		10		12		9[2]		3[3]	8[1]				11					4	1		13			42
	2	3[3]	12	5	6			9[2]	11[1]		7	14		10	8				13					4	1					43
	2	3[3]	14	5		7[2]		9	10	13		6		11[1]	8				12					4	1[8]					44
		3		5		12		9	10[2]	7		6	13	2[4]		8			11					4[1]	1[6]				15	45
		3		5	8	13		9		2		7	12	11[1]		6			10[2]					4	1					46

FA Cup
Fourth Qualifying Round

	Grimsby T	(h)	1-1
		(a)	1-0
First Round	Crewe Alex	(h)	2-1
Second Round	Carlisle U	(a)	2-3

WREXHAM

Blue Square Premier

Ground: Racecourse Ground, Mold Road, Wrexham LL11 2AH. *Tel:* (01978) 262 129. *Fax:* (01978) 357 821.
Year Formed: 1872. *Record Gate:* 34,445 (1957 v Manchester U, FA Cup 4th rd). *Nickname:* Red Dragons.
Manager: Dean Saunders. *Secretary:* Geraint Parry. *Colours:* Red shirts, white shorts, red stockings.

WREXHAM 2010–11 LEAGUE RECORD

Match No.	Date	Venue	Opponents	Result		H/T Score	Lg Pos.	Goalscorers	Attendance
1	Aug 14	H	Cambridge U	W	1-0	1-0	—	Morrell [25]	4040
2	17	A	Forest Green R	L	0-3	0-1	—		1216
3	21	A	Eastbourne Bor	L	3-4	2-2	18	Smith 2 [15, 76], Andrews [20]	1055
4	24	H	Kidderminster H	D	2-2	2-1	—	Brown [4], Keates [6]	2477
5	28	H	Barrow	D	1-1	0-1	20	Pearson, M (og) [90]	2525
6	30	A	Bath C	W	2-0	1-0	12	Morrell [28], Smith [58]	1262
7	Sept 5	A	Newport Co	D	1-1	1-0	14	Morrell [23]	3206
8	11	H	York C	D	1-1	1-1	15	Morrell [8]	2446
9	18	A	Kettering T	D	1-1	1-0	15	Keates [43]	1533
10	21	H	Southport	W	2-1	2-0	—	Taylor [27], Harris [41]	2221
11	25	H	Histon	W	4-0	3-0	9	Tolley [11], Keates [18], Taylor [38], Knight-Percival [79]	2376
12	28	A	Grimsby T	L	1-2	0-1	—	Knight-Percival [90]	2532
13	Oct 2	A	Darlington	W	1-0	0-0	8	Knight-Percival [87]	1690
14	5	H	Fleetwood T	D	0-0	0-0	—		2689
15	9	H	AFC Wimbledon	L	1-2	1-0	11	Mangan [27]	3277
16	16	A	Hayes & Y	W	3-0	0-0	8	Harris [61], Cieslewicz [85], Taylor [90]	417
17	30	A	Histon	D	1-1	0-0	7	Taylor [89]	914
18	Nov 11	H	Luton T	W	1-0	1-0	—	Mangan [5]	2733
19	14	A	York C	D	1-1	1-0	8	Tolley [13]	2601
20	20	H	Darlington	W	2-1	1-0	7	Mangan 2 [10, 90]	2619
21	27	H	Mansfield T	D	1-1	1-1	—	Andrews [37]	2505
22	Jan 1	A	Altrincham	D	0-0	0-0	7		1982
23	3	H	Bath C	W	2-0	1-0	7	Taylor (pen) [34], Pogba [86]	2602
24	8	H	Grimsby T	W	2-0	0-0	5	Harris [70], Morrell [76]	3013
25	18	A	Southport	W	1-0	1-0	—	Morrell [25]	1464
26	22	A	Cambridge U	W	3-1	3-0	4	Mangan [2], Pogba [14], Blackburn [20]	2469
27	29	A	Mansfield T	W	3-2	1-2	—	Pogba [8], Morrell [72], Harris [90]	3266
28	Feb 1	H	Altrincham	W	2-1	1-0	—	Morrell [43], Cieslewicz [85]	3300
29	5	A	Barrow	W	1-0	0-0	—	Mangan (pen) [83]	1318
30	12	A	Crawley T	L	2-3	2-0	4	Mangan 2 [8, 31]	3331
31	15	H	Crawley T	D	0-0	0-0	—		4630
32	19	H	Gateshead	L	2-7	1-5	4	Morrell [12], Tolley [64]	3078
33	22	A	AFC Wimbledon	W	1-0	0-0	—	Pogba [78]	3486
34	26	A	Kidderminster H	L	0-1	0-1	3		3028
35	Mar 5	H	Forest Green R	W	2-1	2-0	4	Mangan [5], Morrell [36]	3386
36	8	H	Eastbourne Bor	W	2-1	2-1	—	Fowler [27], Tolley [44]	2410
37	12	H	Rushden & D	D	1-1	1-0	3	Mangan [14]	3187
38	19	A	Fleetwood T	L	0-1	0-0	4		2207
39	27	H	Newport Co	W	1-0	0-0	4	Mangan [74]	3685
40	29	A	Tamworth	D	1-1	0-0	—	Keates [82]	1082
41	Apr 2	H	Hayes & Y	L	0-2	0-2	4		3207
42	9	A	Rushden & D	D	2-2	1-0	4	Mangan 2 [30, 52]	1181
43	16	A	Kettering T	W	2-0	0-0	4	Mangan [56], Keates [88]	3662
44	23	A	Gateshead	W	1-0	0-0	4	Keates [48]	743
45	25	H	Tamworth	W	4-2	1-0	4	Obeng [10], Knight-Percival [53], Mangan [68], Taylor [79]	4330
46	30	A	Luton T	D	1-1	1-0	4	Moss [12]	6443

Final League Position: 4

GOALSCORERS

League (66): Mangan 15 (1 pen), Morrell 10, Keates 6, Taylor 6 (1 pen), Harris 4, Knight-Percival 4, Pogba 4, Tolley 4, Smith 3, Andrews 2, Cieslewicz 2, Blackburn 1, Brown 1, Fowler 1, Moss 1, Obeng 1, own goal 1.
FA Cup (1): Tolley 1.

Shearer 9	Walker 5+1	Ashton 41	Sinclair 37+2	Blackburn 43	Harris 38+2	Brown 6+3	Keates 40	Mangan 40+2	Morrell 40+1	Knight-Percival 11+21	Tolley 15+9	Gall 3+2	Taylor 20+13	Andrews 20+9	Smith 5+1	Cieslewicz 3+17	Obeng 32+2	Hunt 2+1	Maxwell 36	Pogba 19+10	Creighton 27	Williams 1+3	McMillan 4+1	Fowler 7+5	Mayebi 1	Moss 1	Tomassen —+1	Stevens —+1	Salathiel —+1	Match No.
1	2	3	4	5	6	7^1	8	9	10^2	11	12	13																		1
1	2	3	4	5	6^2	7^1	8	9	10	11	13		12																	2
1	12	3	4^1	2	6^2	14	8	9	10	11^3			13	5	7															3
1	2	3		5	12	7^1	8	9	10^3	11^2			14	4	6	13														4
1	2	3		5	6	7^2	8	9^1	10	11			12	13	4															5
1		3		5			8	4	10	11	14	9^1	13	6^3	7	12^2	2													6
1	3^8	4	5	6			8	12	10^1	11			9		7^2		2													7
1			4	5	6		8	12	10	11^3	13		9^1	14	7^2		2	3												8
1		3	4	5	6^2		8	9	10	12			7^3	11^1	2	13	14													9
		3	4	5	6		8	9^1	10				7	11	2		12		1											10
		3	4	2	6	14	8^3	9	10^1	13			7	11^2	5		12		1											11
		3^3	4	5	6^1		8	9	10^2	12			7	11	2		13	14	1											12
		3	4	5			8	9^1		11			7	10	6	2	12		1											13
		3	4	5	12		8	9		11			7^1	10	6	2^2			1	13										14
		3	4	5^1	6^2		8	9	10	13				11	7	2			1	12										15
		3	4	5	6		8	9^2	10^1	12				11	7	13	2		1											16
		3	4	5	6	14	8	9^1	10^2	13	11^3		7	2					1	12										17
		3		5	6		8	9^1	10^2	12	7			11	4	2			1	13										18
				5	6		8	9^2	13	11	7^1			10	3	12	2		1			4								19
				5	6		8	9	10^2	13	7^3			11^3	3	14	2		1	12		4								20
		3		5			8	9^8	10	13	7^2			11^1	4	2			1	12	6									21
		3	14	2	6	7	8		10^1					9^2	4^3		11		1	12	5	13								22
		3	4		6	7	8		10^1	12				9			11^2	2	1	13	5									23
		3	4		6	7	8	9^2	10^3	14	13							2	1	11^1	5	12								24
		3	4		6	7	8	9^1	10	12								2	1	11	5									25
		3	4		6	7	8	9	10^1	12								2	1	11	5									26
		3	4		6	7	8	9^2	10	12				13				2	1	11^1	5									27
		3	4		6	7	8	9^3	10^1	13				14			17	7	1	11^2	5									28
		3^1	4^2		6	7	8	9	10					14		12	13	2	1	11	5									29
		3	4		6^1	7^8	8	9	10^3	12				14	13		2^2		1	11	5									30
		3	4		6		8	9	10^2	14	7^3			12			13		1	11^1	5		2							31
		3	12		6^1	7	8	9	10	13				14	4				1	11^2	5		2^3							32
		3	4		6	7		9^3		12			10^1	14		13	2		1	11^2	5			8						33
		3	4		6^3	7		9^1	10	14	13			11			2		1	12	5			8^2						34
		3	4		6	7		9	10^1					13		12	2		1	11^2	5			8						35
		3	4		6			9^1	10^2	12	7			13		14	2		1	11^3	5			8						36
		3	4					9	10		7						2		1	11	5		6	8						37
		3	4		6^3	7		9	10^2					14		13	2		1	11^1	5	12		8						38
		3	4		6	7	8	9^3	10^2					14		12	2		1	11^1	5		13							39
		3	4		6^1	7	8	9	10					12			2		1	11^1	5		13							40
		3	4		6	7	8	9	10^2					14		13	2^1		1	11^3	5		12							41
		3	4		6	7	8	9	10^2	12				14			2^3		1	11^1	5		13							42
		3	4		6	7	8	9	10				11				2		1		5									43
		3	4		6	7^2	8	9	10^1				11				2		1	12	5		13							44
		3	4^2		6	7	8	9			12		10	13			2		1	11^1	5^3		14							45
		2			6							7		8			11		5	10^2	4	3^1	1	9^3			12	13	14	46

FA Cup
Fourth Qualifying Round
          Southport   (h)   1-2

YORK CITY   Blue Square Premier

Ground: Bootham Cresent, York YO30 7AQ.   *Tel:* (01904) 624 447.   *Fax:* (01904) 631 457.   *Year Formed:* 1922.
Record Gate: 28,123 (1938 v Huddersfield T, FA Cup 6th rd).   *Nickname:* Minster Men.
Manager: Gary Mills.   *Secretary:* Lisa Charlton.   *Colours:* Red shirts, navy shorts, navy stockings.

YORK CITY 2010–11 LEAGUE RECORD

Match No.	Date	Venue	Opponents	Result		H/T Score	Lg Pos.	Goalscorers	Atten- dance
1	Aug 14	H	Kidderminster H	L	1-2	0-1	—	Rankine (pen) 86	2682
2	17	A	Grimsby T	D	0-0	0-0	—		5037
3	21	A	Bath C	D	2-2	1-1	20	Gash 43, Till 81	1066
4	24	H	Barrow	D	0-0	0-0	—		2212
5	28	H	Altrincham	W	3-0	0-0	14	Rankine 2 70, 90, Brodie (pen) 75	2095
6	30	A	Fleetwood T	L	1-2	0-1	16	Young 87	2020
7	Sept 4	H	Rushden & D	W	2-0	0-0	12	Till 76, Constantine 78	2306
8	11	A	Wrexham	D	1-1	1-1	13	Till 19	2446
9	18	H	Hayes & Y	W	2-0	0-0	10	Rankine 56, Constantine 73	2252
10	21	A	Mansfield T	L	0-5	0-1	—		2202
11	25	A	Tamworth	W	3-1	1-0	10	Rankine (pen) 27, Lawless 58, Fyfield 72	1282
12	27	H	Darlington	D	0-0	0-0	—		3176
13	Oct 2	A	Eastbourne Bor	L	1-2	0-1	13	Lawless 68	1104
14	5	H	Kettering T	L	0-1	0-0	—		1978
15	9	A	Newport Co	L	0-4	0-2	16		2802
16	16	H	Bath C	D	1-1	1-0	16	Rankine (pen) 30	2331
17	30	A	Forest Green R	L	1-2	0-1	19	Lawless 72	792
18	Nov 14	H	Wrexham	D	1-1	0-1	19	Rankine (pen) 79	2601
19	20	A	Rushden & D	W	4-0	3-0	16	Racchi 8, Rankine 24, Chambers 36, Barrett 86	1132
20	23	H	Southport	W	2-0	0-0	—	Constantine (pen) 88, McDermott 90	2104
21	30	A	Kidderminster H	D	0-0	0-0	—		1066
22	Jan 1	A	Gateshead	W	3-0	0-0	12	Smith, J 61, Barrett 66, Constantine 89	1231
23	11	H	Grimsby T	W	1-0	1-0	—	Constantine 19	3028
24	15	A	Histon	W	2-1	0-1	—	Constantine 76, Till 86	578
25	18	A	Luton T	L	0-5	0-4	—		5997
26	22	H	Forest Green R	W	2-1	0-0	10	Reed 56, Mackin 85	2468
27	29	A	Southport	L	0-4	0-3	—		1308
28	Feb 1	H	AFC Wimbledon	W	4-1	2-0	—	Parslow 16, Meredith 45, Rankine 70, Chambers 84	2438
29	12	A	AFC Wimbledon	L	0-1	0-1	12		3532
30	15	H	Fleetwood T	W	1-0	0-0	—	Reed 48	2220
31	22	A	Altrincham	D	0-0	0-0	—		1143
32	26	A	Hayes & Y	W	2-1	1-0	7	Smith, J 23, Rankine 80	458
33	Mar 1	H	Gateshead	W	2-1	1-0	—	Smith, J 8, Constantine (pen) 63	2290
34	5	A	Barrow	D	0-0	0-0	7		1342
35	12	H	Eastbourne Bor	W	1-0	1-0	7	Rankine 16	2357
36	15	H	Mansfield T	W	2-1	0-1	—	Reed 2 59, 69	2261
37	19	A	Cambridge U	L	1-2	1-1	7	Reed 24	2474
38	26	H	Histon	W	1-0	0-0	7	Reed 48	2364
39	Apr 2	A	Kettering T	D	1-1	1-0	7	Reed 8	1365
40	5	H	Crawley T	D	1-1	1-0	—	Smith, J 14	3060
41	9	H	Newport Co	W	2-1	0-0	7	Rankine (pen) 50, Reed 70	2565
42	16	A	Tamworth	L	1-2	0-1	7	Constantine 89	2484
43	19	A	Luton T	W	1-0	0-0	—	Reed 65	2955
44	23	A	Darlington	L	1-2	0-0	7	Carruthers 87	2966
45	25	H	Cambridge U	D	0-0	0-0	7		2939
46	30	A	Crawley T	D	1-1	1-0	8	Hunt (og) 5	2945

Final League Position: 8

GOALSCORERS

League (55): Rankine 12 (5 pens), Reed 9, Constantine 8 (2 pens), Smith, J 4, Till 4, Lawless 3, Barrett 2, Chambers 2, Brodie 1 (1 pen), Carruthers 1, Fyfield 1, Gash 1, Mackin 1, McDermott 1, Meredith 1, Parslow 1, Racchi 1, Young 1, own goal 1.
FA Cup (7): Rankine 2 (1 pen), Chambers 1, Racchi 1, Sangare 1, Smith, C 1, Smith, J 1.

Ingham 45	Parslow 41+1	Meredith 43+2	Smith J 30+8	McGurk 34	Sangare 9+1	Lawless 16	Mackin 6+6	Gash 12+5	Brodie 6	Carruthers 14+12	Till 29+12	Rankine 34+8	Courtney 4+3	Barrett 19+3	Purcell —+1	McDermott 8+9	Young 9+3	Constantine 13+13	Racchi 15+2	Fyfield 9+2	Dowson —+5	Beesley 2+1	Smith C 24	Chambers 22+4	Weir 5	Boucaud 10+9	Reed 12+11	Knight 1	Hatfield 1+3	Darville 17	Kerr 16	Match No.
1	2	3	4	5	6³	7	8¹	9	10	11²	12	13	14																			1
1	2	3	13	5	6	7		9	10	11				8¹		4²	12															2
1	2	3	13	5	6	7		9	10	11³	12			8²		4¹	14															3
1	2	3	4²	5	6	7		9	10³	11¹	13	12		8		14																4
1	2	3	13	5	6	7		9	10	11¹	8²	12		4																		5
1	2	3	4	5³	14	7		9	10²	12	11			8¹		13	6															6
1	2	3	4	5	6¹	7		9²		11	10	12		8		13																7
1	6	3	4	5		7		9¹		11	10²	2		8		13	12															8
1	6	3	13	5		7					12			8	9	2	4		10²	11¹												9
1	6	3	4⁸	5		7					13			8²	9	2		11	12	10¹												10
1	6	3		5		7		9			10²	12		4		11¹		8	2	13												11
1	6	3	12	5		7		9		7³	10²	4¹		11		13		8	2	14												12
1	2	3		5		7		9²		8	10¹			4		6	12	11	13													13
1	2	3	14	5		7					12			8		4³	6	10¹	11	13	9²											14
1	2	3		5		7					12	13		8		6	10¹	4	11²	14	9³											15
1	6	3	4³	5		7		9¹						8²		10	2	13	11	14	12											16
1	2	3	4	5		7				13	12			9³		14	8	10¹	11²							6						17
1	2	3		5	6					13	12			9		8²	4			7¹						10	11					18
1	2	3		5	6¹					13		9³		12		4²	14	8		7						10	11					19
1	2	3	4¹	5	6					8²	9³			12		14	7	13		6						10	11					20
1	2	3		5	6					12	9	13		8		4²	7¹									10	11³		14			21
1	2	3³	4¹	5						11		9²	6	14		13										8	10		7		12	22
1	2	13	4¹	5						12		11	7	14		10³	6							3		8	9²					23
1	2		4							3	7	13				6	10	11¹					5	12		8	9²					24
1¹	2	13	11⁸	5³						10²	3	8¹	9	12		14		4	7		6											25
	2	3		5						13	14	8	9	7¹			4²					6	10	11³	12	1						26
1	2	3¹		5⁸				8		11	7	9³				12		4	10					6²	14	13						27
1	5	3	4			7¹		12		8	9²			13									6	10³			14			2	11	28
1	2	3	7²	5				8		9³		4¹		14									6	10			13	12			11	29
1		3	4²	5				11¹		8	9³			14									6	10			13	12		2	7	30
1	14	3	13	5³				8		9	7¹							6						10		4²	12			2	11	31
1	6	3	4							13	12			10									5	8²		14	9¹	7³		2	11	32
1	6	3	4							12	8	9¹		10									5	7³		13	14			2	11¹²	33
1	6	3	4								8	9²		10		12							5	7¹		13				2	11	34
1	6	3	4							8¹	9			10³									5	7²		14	12		13	2	11	35
1	6	3	4							8³	9			10²		7¹							5			14	12		13	2	11	36
1	6	3	4²	5						12	8	9		7		13										10¹				2	11	37
1	6	3	4	5						12	8	9²				10¹										13				2	11	38
1	2	3	4	5				8		11²	12	13				6		10¹								7	9			2	11	39
1	6	3	4	5						12	8¹	9²		14												7	13		10³	2	11	40
1	6	3	4²	5						13	12	8¹		9												7	14		10³	2	11	41
1	6	3	4²							14	8	9¹		13									5	7		12			10³	2	11	42
1	6¹	3	4							14	12	13		8²									10³	5		7	9			2	11¹	43
1		5	4¹					14		3	12	13		8					10²	6				7		11³	9			2		44
1		5	4¹					14		3	12	13		8³					10	6				7		11	9²			2		45
1		3	13							4²	10	14		9¹					5³	6				8		7	12			2	11	46

FA Cup
Fourth Qualifying Round

	Kidderminster H	(a)	2-0
First Round	Rotherham U	(a)	0-0
		(h)	3-0
Second Round	Darlington	(a)	2-0
Third Round	Bolton W	(a)	0-2

REVIEW OF THE SCOTTISH SEASON 2010–11

Scottish Premier League seasons have invariably settled around the exploits of Rangers and Celtic both on and off the field, but only rarely have sectarian issues been raised to the alarming levels of 2010–11. Once politicians get involved there are serious problems with which to deal. For the predominantly non-fanatical sectarian supporters it is a tragedy. But when the manager of Celtic Neil Lennon receives death threats, bullets and parcel bombs in the post plus being attacked at Tynecastle by a spectator, one wonders where it will end.

Rangers and Celtic are destined to play each other on a regular basis. Last season they met seven times; four games in the SPL, twice in the Active Nation Scottish Cup and once in the CIS Insurance Cup. Naturally each was heavily concerned in the outcome of the championship. When was it any different? This is another concern as the perpetually restless attitude to the structure of football in Scotland is likely to take another lurch.

It will either be ten clubs or fourteen for the SPL. The bigger clubs favour ten; the alternative would result in far-reaching complications, though this is the option apparently favoured more by the fans. Changes are afoot at the Scottish FA, too.

As to the actual football in the Premier League it went close to the wire again, even Rangers ensuring success for the third year in a row on the last day to give Walter Smith a fine retirement present. But Celtic needed a win and their rivals to lose to overturn the situation. Curious how certain events might have changed the course of the season such as Celtic's match at Inverness on 2 April being called off because of a waterlogged pitch. When it was replayed a month later, Celtic suffered what proved to be a devastating defeat.

There were few consolations for the Parkhead faithful, Rangers even beat them in the CIS final. Both teams scored freely, each hoisting over a century in all competitions. Rangers used 27 different players in the league, Celtic two more than their rivals. Rangers had the better start, unbeaten in the first eleven Premier matches including the scalp of Celtic, yet at the same juncture their rivals had smitten Aberdeen for their heaviest defeat scoring nine without reply.

A better season for Hearts yet they still finished in third place, a massive 30 points adrift of the title. This again illustrates the overall problem. Dundee United – despite six wins in a row – dropped a place to fourth but Kilmarnock, despite a vast improvement on 2009–10, started and ended the season in disappointing fashion, after manager Mixu Paatelainen accepted an offer to coach the Finland national team.Two wins in a row was the best at any time for Motherwell, but they made the cut and finished runners-up in the Scottish Cup.

Inverness Caley came good at the close as did St Johnstone after a run of eleven without a win. Aberdeen had trouble finding goals as well as conceding them as witness the Celtic debacle but a dire time for Hibernian who rarely looked capable of finishing in the top six and without five wins in succession from February it might have been far worse. St Mirren just avoided relegation but Hamilton Accies' inability to win at home until the second-last fixture virtually cost them their place in the Premier League.

In the Champions League, Rangers held Manchester United scoreless at Old Trafford and made it to the Europa League before eventually failing at home to PSV Eindhoven in the last sixteen. Celtic followed a similar dual trail (see European Review).

With the second stage of the qualifying competition to Euro 2012 in view, Craig Levein's preparations for Scotland included appearing in the Carling Nations Cup. This came after some indifferent displays in both friendly and European games. The best showing was the spirited encounter with Spain that tested the World Cup holders in several areas before the Scots were just edged to defeat. To further underline the experiments, no fewer than 48 different players were used in full international fixtures.

As to the Scottish League, but for the last day when Dundee lost and Dunfermline Athletic – pushed all season by Raith Rovers – won, the embarrassment of the Division One champions was spared as the Tayside Dees' savage 25-point deduction – clearly designed to relegate – prevented them topping the table! Despite the handicap Dundee had a club record run of 23 League games without defeat.

Stirling Albion were the first to suffer the drop. Cowdenbeath hung on hoping for Ross County to slip up, but were forced into the play-offs before joining them. Ross had the added lift of winning the Alba Challenge Cup against Queen of the South.

Livingston, consistent after Brechin City's early effort faded, won promotion from Division 2 and were joined by Ayr United who came through their play-off test. Alloa Athletic were not as fortunate at this stage after a bright start and went down to Division 3. Stranraer for long leaders slipped slowly out of contention replaced by a Queen's Park team fresh from twelve without loss. But Arbroath finishing strongly were clear winners, thus gaining promotion to Division 2. Albion Rovers joined them.

SCOTTISH LEAGUE TABLES 2010–11

(P) Promoted into division at end of 2009–10 season.   (R) Relegated into division at end of 2009–10 season.

CLYDESDALE BANK SCOTTISH PREMIER LEAGUE 2010–11

		P	W	D	L	F	A	Total W	D	L	F	A	Home W	D	L	F	A	GD	Pts
1	Rangers	38	30	3	5	88	29	14	2	3	43	14	16	1	2	45	15	59	93
2	Celtic	38	29	5	4	85	22	15	3	1	51	11	14	2	3	34	11	63	92
3	Hearts	38	18	9	11	53	45	9	5	5	27	21	9	4	6	26	24	8	63
4	Dundee U	38	17	10	11	55	50	13	1	5	34	22	4	9	6	21	28	5	61
5	Kilmarnock	38	13	10	15	53	55	6	4	9	26	31	7	6	6	27	24	-2	49
6	Motherwell	38	13	7	18	40	60	8	3	8	24	24	5	4	10	16	36	-20	46
7	Inverness CT (P)	38	14	11	13	52	44	7	4	8	25	24	7	7	5	27	20	8	53
8	St Johnstone	38	11	11	16	23	43	6	5	8	10	19	5	6	8	13	24	-20	44
9	Aberdeen	38	11	5	22	39	59	6	2	11	22	21	5	3	11	17	38	-20	38
10	Hibernian	38	10	7	21	39	61	5	6	8	21	29	5	1	13	18	32	-22	37
11	St Mirren	38	8	9	21	33	57	4	6	9	20	27	4	3	12	13	30	-24	33
12	Hamilton A	38	5	11	22	24	59	1	8	10	12	26	4	3	12	12	33	-35	26

Top 6 teams split after 33 games.

IRN-BRU SCOTTISH FOOTBALL LEAGUE FIRST DIVISION 2010–11

		P	W	D	L	F	A	Total W	D	L	F	A	Home W	D	L	F	A	GD	Pts
1	Dunfermline Ath	36	20	10	6	66	31	11	6	1	39	14	9	4	5	27	17	35	70
2	Raith R	36	17	9	10	47	35	9	3	6	25	20	8	6	4	22	15	12	60
3	Falkirk (R)	36	17	7	12	57	41	9	3	6	32	22	8	4	6	25	19	16	58
4	Queen of the S	36	14	7	15	54	53	7	3	8	31	30	7	4	7	23	23	1	49
5	Partick Th	36	12	11	13	44	39	8	6	4	23	11	4	5	9	21	28	5	47
6	Dundee	36	19	12	5	54	34	11	7	0	29	13	8	5	5	25	21	20	44
7	Morton	36	11	10	15	39	43	7	5	6	18	17	4	5	9	21	26	-4	43
8	Ross Co	36	9	14	13	30	34	4	7	7	15	17	5	7	6	15	17	-4	41
9	Cowdenbeath (P)	36	9	8	19	41	72	5	4	9	21	31	4	4	10	20	41	-31	35
10	Stirling Alb (P)	36	4	8	24	32	82	2	4	12	17	39	2	4	12	15	43	-50	20

Dundee deducted 25 points.

IRN-BRU SCOTTISH FOOTBALL LEAGUE SECOND DIVISION 2010–11

		P	W	D	L	F	A	Total W	D	L	F	A	Home W	D	L	F	A	GD	Pts
1	Livingston (P)	36	25	4	7	79	33	13	5	0	41	14	12	2	4	38	19	46	82
2	Ayr U¶ (R)	36	18	5	13	62	55	11	3	4	28	21	7	2	9	34	34	7	59
3	Forfar Ath (P)	36	17	8	11	50	48	10	5	3	32	22	7	3	8	18	26	2	59
4	Brechin C	36	15	12	9	63	45	9	3	6	35	26	6	9	3	28	19	18	57
5	East Fife	36	14	10	12	77	60	8	3	7	42	30	6	7	5	35	30	17	52
6	Airdrie U (R)	36	13	9	14	52	60	5	7	6	24	29	8	2	8	28	31	-8	48
7	Dumbarton	36	11	7	18	52	70	7	3	8	33	29	4	4	10	19	41	-18	40
8	Stenhousemuir	36	10	8	18	46	59	7	3	8	28	26	3	5	10	18	33	-13	38
9	Alloa Ath	36	9	9	18	49	71	5	6	7	27	31	4	3	11	22	40	-22	36
10	Peterhead	36	5	11	20	47	76	5	5	8	27	32	0	6	12	20	44	-29	26

¶Ayr U promoted via play-offs.

IRN-BRU SCOTTISH FOOTBALL LEAGUE THIRD DIVISION 2010–11

		P	W	D	L	F	A	Total W	D	L	F	A	Home W	D	L	F	A	GD	Pts
1	Arbroath (R)	36	20	6	10	80	61	11	4	3	39	24	9	2	7	41	37	19	66
2	Albion R¶	36	17	10	9	56	40	9	4	5	25	16	8	6	4	31	24	16	61
3	Queen's Park	36	18	5	13	57	43	10	3	5	31	17	8	2	8	26	26	14	59
4	Annan Ath	36	16	11	9	58	45	8	5	5	32	25	8	6	4	26	20	13	59
5	Stranraer	36	15	12	9	72	57	10	4	4	39	25	5	8	5	33	32	15	57
6	Berwick R	36	12	13	11	62	56	7	7	4	38	31	5	6	7	24	25	6	49
7	Elgin City	36	13	6	17	53	63	8	2	8	30	29	5	4	9	23	34	-10	45
8	Montrose	36	10	7	19	47	61	6	4	8	28	27	4	3	11	19	34	-14	37
9	East Stirling	36	10	4	22	33	62	6	3	9	18	27	4	1	13	15	35	-29	34
10	Clyde (R)	36	8	8	20	37	67	4	5	9	23	31	4	3	11	14	36	-30	32

¶Albion R promoted via play-offs.

ABERDEEN   Premier League

Year Formed: 1903. *Ground & Address:* Pittodrie Stadium, Pittodrie St, Aberdeen AB24 5QH. *Telephone:* 01224 650400. *Fax:* 01224 644173. *E-mail:* feedback@afc.co.uk *Website:* www.afc.co.uk
Ground Capacity: all seated: 21,421. *Size of Pitch:* 115yd × 72yd.
Chairman: Stewart Milne. *Secretary:* David Johnston.
Manager: Craig Brown. *Assistant Manager:* Archie Knox. *U-19 Coach:* Neil Cooper.
Club Nicknames: The Dons, The Reds, The Dandies.
Previous Grounds: None.
Record Attendance: 45,061 v Hearts, Scottish Cup 4th rd, 13 Mar 1954.
Record Transfer Fee received: £1.75 million for Eoin Jess to Coventry City (February 1996).
Record Transfer Fee paid: £1m+ for Paul Bernard from Oldham Athletic (September 1995).
Record Victory: 13-0 v Peterhead, Scottish Cup, 9 Feb 1923.
Record Defeat: 0-9 v Celtic, Premier League, 6 Nov 2010.
Most Capped Player: Alex McLeish, 77 (Scotland).
Most League Appearances: 556: Willie Miller, 1973-90.
Most League Goals in Season (Individual): 38: Benny Yorston, Division I, 1929-30.
Most Goals Overall (Individual): 199: Joe Harper, 1969-72; 1976-81.

ABERDEEN 2010–11 LEAGUE RECORD

Match No.	Date		Venue	Opponents	Result	Score	H/T Score	Lg Pos.	Goalscorers	Atten-dance
1	Aug	14	H	Hamilton A	W	4-0	2-0	—	Hartley 3 (3 pens) [19, 40, 66], Diamond [51]	12,005
2		21	A	St Johnstone	W	1-0	0-0	1	Mackie [86]	6523
3		28	H	Kilmarnock	L	0-1	0-0	3		11,287
4	Sept	11	A	Dundee U	L	1-3	1-3	3	Vernon [26]	9793
5		18	A	Motherwell	D	1-1	0-1	4	Vernon [56]	5251
6		26	H	Rangers	L	2-3	2-1	6	Vernon [19], Maguire [30]	15,307
7	Oct	2	A	Inverness CT	L	0-2	0-1	7		6144
8		16	H	Hearts	L	0-1	0-0	9		8999
9		23	H	Hibernian	W	4-2	2-0	8	Maguire [18], Vernon 2 [32, 50], Hartley (pen) [61]	7587
10		30	A	St Mirren	L	1-2	0-1	8	McArdle [57]	4589
11	Nov	6	A	Celtic	L	0-9	0-4	9		48,754
12		9	H	Inverness CT	L	1-2	0-1	—	Velicka [49]	5917
13		13	A	Rangers	L	0-2	0-2	11		44,919
14		20	H	St Johnstone	L	0-1	0-0	11		7841
15		27	A	Kilmarnock	L	0-2	0-1	11		5013
16	Dec	11	A	Hearts	L	0-5	0-2	—		13,434
17		26	A	Hibernian	W	2-1	1-1	—	Folly [36], Vernon [62]	10,115
18		29	H	Hamilton A	W	1-0	0-0	11	Vernon [90]	2968
19	Jan	1	H	Dundee U	D	1-1	1-0	9	Maguire [36]	12,487
20		15	H	St Mirren	W	2-0	0-0	9	Vernon 2 [50, 67]	9740
21		22	A	Celtic	L	0-1	0-1	9		48,717
22		26	A	Inverness CT	W	2-0	1-0	—	Jack [44], Blackman [49]	4468
23	Feb	1	H	Celtic	L	0-3	0-1	—		12,901
24		15	H	Motherwell	L	1-2	1-1	—	Aluko [3]	6882
25		19	H	Kilmarnock	W	5-0	2-0	9	Vernon [14], Aluko [25], Maguire (pen) [59], McArdle [70], Magennis [82]	7371
26		22	H	Hamilton A	W	1-0	1-0	—	Maguire (pen) [30]	7019
27		26	H	Hearts	D	0-0	0-0	8		9100
28	Mar	2	A	St Johnstone	D	0-0	0-0	—		2909
29		7	A	Dundee U	L	1-3	0-2	—	Magennis [51]	7416
30	Apr	2	A	Motherwell	L	1-2	0-1	10	Vujadinovic [90]	4458
31		6	A	St Mirren	L	2-3	0-1	—	Murray (og) [47], Milsom [90]	3489
32		9	H	Hibernian	L	0-1	0-1	10		7400
33		13	H	Rangers	L	0-1	0-1	—		11,925
34		25	A	Hamilton A	D	1-1	0-0	—	Blackman [74]	2140
35		30	H	Inverness CT	W	1-0	0-0	10	Pawlett [75]	6280
36	May	7	A	St Johnstone	L	0-2	0-1	10		6361
37		10	H	St Mirren	L	0-1	0-0	—		5955
38		14	A	Hibernian	W	3-1	0-1	9	Magennis [48], Maguire 2 [75, 77]	11,767

Final League Position: 9

Honours

League Champions: Division I 1954-55. Premier Division 1979-80, 1983-84, 1984-85; *Runners-up:* Division I 1910-11, 1936-37, 1955-56, 1970-71, 1971-72. Premier Division 1977-78, 1980-81, 1981-82, 1988-89, 1989-90, 1990-91, 1992-93, 1993-94.
Scottish Cup Winners: 1947, 1970, 1982, 1983, 1984, 1986, 1990; *Runners-up:* 1937, 1953, 1954, 1959, 1967, 1978, 1993, 2000.
League Cup Winners: 1955-56, 1976-77, 1985-86, 1989-90, 1995-96; *Runners-up:* 1946-47, 1978-79, 1979-80, 1987-88, 1988-89, 1992-93, 1999-2000.
Drybrough Cup Winners: 1971, 1980.

European: *European Cup:* 12 matches (1980-81, 1984-85, 1985-86); *Cup Winners' Cup:* 39 matches (1967-68, 1970-71, 1978-79, 1982-83 winners, 1983-84 semi-finals, 1986-87, 1990-91, 1993-94); *UEFA Cup:* 56 matches (*Fairs Cup:* 1968-69. *UEFA Cup:* 1971-72, 1972-73, 1973-74, 1977-78, 1979-80, 1981-82, 1987-88, 1988-89, 1989-90, 1991-92, 1994-95, 1996-97, 2000-01, 2002-03, 2007-08). *Europa League:* 2 matches (2009–10).

Club colours: All red.

Goalscorers: *League (39):* Vernon 10, Maguire 7 (2 pens), Hartley 4 (4 pens), Magennis 3, Aluko 2, Blackman 2, McArdle 2, Diamond 1, Folly 1, Jack 1, Mackie 1, Milsom 1, Pawlett 1, Velicka 1, Vujadinovic 1, own goal 1.
Scottish Cup (10): Maguire 4, Vernon 3, McArdle 1, Magennis 1, own goal 1.
CIS Cup (9): Hartley 4 (3 pens), Vernon 3, McArdle 1, Maguire 1.

Howard M 8+1	McArdle R 27+1	Considine A 26+1	Folly Y 18	Diamond Z 32	Ifil J 13+4	Pawlett P 6+7	Hartley P 23+1	Magennis J 10+19	Maguire C 35	Aluko S 27+1	Fyvie F 1+4	Mackie D 7+4	Young D 20+9	Vernon S 29+4	Megginson M 1+5	Foster R —+1	Vujadinovic N 13+5	Langfield J 30+1	Jack R 26+4	Paton M 4+6	Jarvis D —+1	Velicka A 1+5	Fraser R —+2	Robertson C 7+6	Hansson H —+1	McNamee D 9+1	Milsom R 18	Blackman N 10+5	Smith S 15+1	Anderson M —+1	Low N —+1	Grimmer J 1+1	Shaughnessy J 1	Match No.
1	2	3	4	5	6	7¹	8³	9	10	11²	12	13	14																					1
1	2	3	4	5	6	7³	8	9¹	10²	11	14	12		13																				2
1	2	3	4	5	6	7	8	9¹	10¹			11³				12	13	14																3
1	2	3	4	5	6¹	7²	8	14	11	13		9		10³		12																		4
	2	3	4	5		7	8		10¹	11		9		12			8	1																5
	2	6²	8	5	4	13	7	10	11³	9				12			3¹	1	14															6
1	2	3	4	5	6		9²	10	11¹	8				13³			7	12	14															7
1	2	3	4	5			8	10²		12			/			15	6	9¹	13															8
1	2	4²	5¹	6			8	10	11³	9				12			7	3	13	14														9
1	2	4	5	6²			8	10³	11¹	7		9					3	12	14	13														10
	2	4	5				8	13	10	11¹		7		12			9²	1	6	3														11
6		4	5				13	10	11	8¹		2		9			1	7²	12	3														12
	2	4⁶	5	6			8	13	10¹	11		12		9			1	7	3															13
2		3		5	6		8	10	11	9				1			4	12	7¹															14
	3	4²	5	6			8	10	11	9				1			7	13	2¹	12														15
	3	4¹	5	6	12		8	10²	11	7		9		14			1	13	2³															16
2	3	4	5²	13	14		8	12	10³	11¹		7		9			6	1																17
2	3	4	5	12			8	9³	10	14		7²		11			6¹	1	13															18
2	6	4¹	5	14			8	13	10	11		12		9			1	7²	3³															19
4	3		5		13		10²	8				7		9	14		12	1	6³					2¹		11								20
2	6		5		14		4	13	10			7²		9³			1	12						11		8¹								21
2³	6		5				8	12	10²			13		9¹	3		1	4						14	7	11								22
4	3⁸		5		14		6	7				12		9			1	8¹						2²	11	10³	13							23
			5				6⁸	13	7	11¹				9			4	1	8	12				2		10²	3							24
4			5				13	10	11³			8¹		9			1	7						2	6²		3	14						25
4²	13		5				12	14	10	11		8¹		9²			1	7						2	6		3							26
4	5						8	14	10	11³		12		9²			1	7						2¹	6	13	3							27
4¹	5						8	14		11		13		9	12		1	7²						2	6	10³	3							28
12	6		5¹				8	13		11²		10		9			1	7						2³	4	14	3							29
2	6						12	13	10	11²		7		9³			1	14						4	8	3¹								30
2¹	6		5²		11			9³	10			8	14	13			1	12	7					4		3								31
	6					7³		14	10	11		2²	12	5			1	8						13		4	9¹	3						32
	6		5					10²	7	11		2	9				1	8	12							4	13	3¹						33
15	6		5				12	10	11	2		9²		1⁶			7¹	8								4	13	3						34
			5		12			13	10	11³		2	6				1	8	7¹					14		4	9²	3						35
			5¹					10³	8	11	13			2	3		1	7						12		4	9²	6			14			36
					12			10	11	13		5	3				1	7²	8¹	2						4	14	6			9³			37
								9	10	11²	8	6		1			2	13		4				7¹		3					12	5	38

AIRDRIE UNITED

Second Division

Year Formed: 1965. *Ground & Address:* Shyberry Excelsior Stadium, Broomfield Park, Craigneuk Avenue, Airdrie ML6 8QZ. *Telephone:* (Stadium) 01236 622000. *Fax:* 01236 626002. *Postal Address:* 60 St Enoch Square, Glasgow G1 4AG.
E-mail: annmarie@airdrieunitedfc.com *Website:* www.airdrieunited.com
Ground Capacity: all seated: 10,171. *Size of Pitch:* 105m × 67m.
Chairman: Jim Ballantyne. *Secretary:* Ann Marie Ballantyne.
Manager: Jimmy Boyle. *First Team Coaches:* Paul Jack and Alan Lawrence.
Club Nickname: The Diamonds.
Record Attendance: 5924 v Motherwell, Scottish Cup 3rd rd, 6 Jan 2007.
Record Victory: 7-0 v Dundee, First Division, 11 March 2006.
Record Defeat: 1-6 v Morton, Second Division, 1 Nov 2003.
Most League Appearances: 197, Paul Lovering 2004-11.
Most League Goals in Season (Individual): 19: Alan Russell, 2007-08.
Most Goals Overall (Individual): 33: Stephen McKeown, 2002-08.

AIRDRIE UNITED 2010–11 LEAGUE RECORD

Match No.	Date	Venue	Opponents	Result	H/T Score	Lg Pos.	Goalscorers	Atten- dance
1	Aug 7	A	East Fife	D 3-3	0-1	—	Gemmill [50], Grant [64], Watt [70]	810
2	14	H	Ayr U	D 2-2	0-1	6	Wallace (pen) [81], Donnelly [85]	1127
3	21	A	Livingston	L 1-2	1-1	8	Gemmill [5]	1863
4	28	A	Stenhousemuir	W 3-1	1-0	6	McCord [38], Lovering (pen) [46], Gemmill [90]	820
5	Sept 11	H	Brechin C	D 1-1	0-1	6	Gibson [53]	946
6	18	H	Peterhead	D 2-2	1-1	7	Stevenson [19], Gemmill [81]	846
7	25	A	Forfar Ath	W 2-1	0-1	5	McCord [58], Wallace [75]	677
8	Oct 2	A	Dumbarton	W 3-1	0-0	5	McCord [52], Wallace [62], Gemmill [74]	812
9	16	H	Alloa Ath	L 0-1	0-1	5		1030
10	23	A	Brechin C	L 1-3	1-1	6	Watt [26]	564
11	30	H	Stenhousemuir	W 1-0	0-0	6	Bain [73]	848
12	Nov 6	A	Ayr U	L 0-1	0-0	6		1439
13	13	H	Livingston	L 0-1	0-0	6		1013
14	Dec 14	A	Peterhead	L 1-5	0-3	—	Gemmill [51]	312
15	18	A	Alloa Ath	W 3-2	1-0	—	Ferguson [6], Stevenson [89], Watt [90]	502
16	Jan 15	H	Brechin C	D 2-2	0-0	6	Ferguson [48], Forrest [55]	806
17	22	A	Stenhousemuir	L 0-1	0-0	—		819
18	Feb 1	H	Dumbarton	L 1-2	0-1	—	McCord (pen) [84]	591
19	5	A	Peterhead	W 1-0	1-0	6	Craig [30]	660
20	12	A	Dumbarton	D 1-1	0-1	6	Morton [90]	723
21	15	A	Livingston	L 0-2	0-1	—		890
22	19	H	Alloa Ath	L 0-2	0-1	7		731
23	22	H	Forfar Ath	W 2-0	0-0	—	Donnelly [49], Gemmill [71]	437
24	26	A	East Fife	W 1-0	1-0	5	Gemmill [40]	664
25	Mar 5	H	Ayr U	L 0-5	0-0	6		966
26	8	H	East Fife	D 1-1	1-1	—	Johnston [12]	447
27	19	A	Stenhousemuir	D 2-2	1-2	7	Owens 2 [16, 81]	642
28	26	H	Forfar Ath	W 3-1	3-1	5	Gallacher (og) [22], McCord (pen) [40], Donnelly [43]	594
29	29	A	Forfar Ath	W 2-1	1-1	—	Owens [4], Morton [90]	419
30	Apr 2	A	Peterhead	W 4-2	4-1	5	McVitie (og) [6], Johnston [29], Bain [32], Gemmill [42]	831
31	5	A	Brechin C	W 2-1	1-0	—	McLauchlan (og) [32], Donnelly [56]	438
32	9	A	Alloa Ath	L 0-1	0-1	5		688
33	16	H	Dumbarton	W 2-1	0-1	5	Sally [76], Morton [81]	773
34	23	H	Livingston	L 2-4	1-2	6	Lovering [32], Owens [55]	872
35	30	A	Ayr U	L 1-3	0-0	6	Morton [46]	1402
36	May 7	H	East Fife	D 2-2	1-1	6	McCord [41], Sally [83]	861

Final League Position: 6

Honours
League Champions: Second Division 2003-04; *Runners-up:* Second Division 2007-08.
League Challenge Cup Winners: 2008-09; *Runners-up:* 2003-04.

Club colours: Shirt: White with red trim. Shorts: White. Stockings: White.

Goalscorers: *League (52):* Gemmill 9, McCord 6 (2 pens), Donnelly 4, Morton 4, Owens 4, Wallace 3 (1 pen), Watt 3, Bain 2, Ferguson 2, Johnston 2, Lovering 2 (1 pen), Sally 2, Stevenson 2, Craig 1, Forrest 1, Gibson 1, Grant 1, own goals 3.
Scottish Cup (10): Gemmill 2, Mackay-Steven 2, Stevenson 2, Bain 1, Lovering 1, McCord 1, Sally 1.
CIS Cup (3): Gemmill 1, Grant 1, McCord 1.
Alba Challenge Cup (1): Muir 1 (pen).

Ridgers M 34	Bain J 32	Grant E 19 + 1	Gibson S 13	Lovering P 23 + 4	Stallard K 28	Keast F 3 + 2	Devlin R 30	McCord R 32	Muir G 4 + 9	Gemmill S 30	Wallace R 2 + 6	Watt A 12 + 3	Johnston P 26 + 2	McGregor H 1 + 3	Donnelly R 10 + 7	Sally S 1 + 2	Szpilcynski A 2	Craig C 4 + 7	Malone A — + 1	Stevenson J 20 + 7	Forrest E 9	Macfarlane N 1	Ferguson A 3 + 3	Goodall G 3 + 1	Mackay-Steven G 15 + 4	Fisher J — + 1	Hill C 5	McKeown S 5	Gray D 4 + 2	Fairweather A 2 + 3	Morton S 3 + 6	Blockley M 11 + 5	Owens G 11 + 1	Smith G 7 + 1	Match No.
1	2	3	4	5¹	6	7²	8	9	10	11	12	13																							1
1	2²	5	4		3	6¹	8	7		11	13³	10²	9³	12	14																				2
1		3	4		2	6¹	7	8		10	12	11³	5	9²	13	14																			3
1	2	3	4	5	6		8	9¹		10		11²	7	12	13																				4
	2	6	3ᵃ	5¹	4		8	7		10²			11	9³		13	1	12	14																5
1	2	4		3	5		6	7	13	9		10¹	11²					12		8															6
1	2	3ᵃ	4	5			8	6		10	12	11²	9¹	14	13					7³															7
1	2		5	3	4		8	7		10³	12	11²	9¹	13		14				8															8
1	2		5	3	4ᵃ		6ᵃ	7		9	12	10²	11¹		14			13		8³															9
1	2		5	4			6	11³	10²	12	9	13		7²		14				8	3														10
1	2		5	3				11³		9	10¹	7²		14		12		13		8	4	6													11
1	2	3ᵃ	5	12	6		8	13		7ᵃ	10³			14		11²		9	4																12
1	2		4	5	6	14	8		9¹			10³	7²		13			12		11	3														13
1	2	3	5ᵃ	6		8	7	13	11³	10⁷				14				12		9	4¹														14
1	2¹	5	4		3		7	8		10		13	6		9²					14			11³	12											15
1	2	4					6	10	13	9		7¹						8		5		12	3	11²											16
1	2	4					6	8	13	9¹								12		7²	5		10³	3	11	14									17
1		5		4	6			9		11²								13		7¹	3³		14		8		2	10	12						18
1	2			5	4		7ᵃ	8	12				9¹					13		11³							3	10²	6	14					19
1	2			5	4		7						13	12				10					11¹		8²		3	9³	6		14				20
1	2¹	11		3	4		6	8										9		13					12		5	10³	7²		14				21
1		5			4			8	13	10										7	3				9³		2¹	11ᵃ	6²	12	14				22
1		3		5	2			8		11¹			6²	10	12			9					13						4		7				23
1	5	4		2	3		8			11			9	10²	12			7					6¹					13							24
1	2	4ᵃ		3³			6	8		11			7²	9¹				10		12			13				5			14					25
1	2			5	8			11²		7		13			14			6					10¹			12					9³	4			26
1	2		3³	4			6	9	13	10			7²	12									11							8	5				27
1	2	14			3		8	7		11¹			6	10									9³						12	13	4²	5			28
1	2	3					8	7		11²			6	5						12			9¹					13	10	4				29
1	2			3			7	8		11			6	10²						12			9¹					13	14	4³	5			30
1	2		14	3			4	8		11³			6	10						13			9²						12	7¹	5			31
1	2		13	3			4	7		11			6³		9¹	14				12			10²							8	5ᵃ			32
1	2		3	4			5	8		9¹			7					12		13			11³						10	14	6²			33
1	2		3	4			5	8		10¹			7					12		9									11		6			34
1	3³			2	4		5	8ᵃ	14	11			7¹							9					12				10			6	13	35
	2			14	3	12	5	8		11²						10	1			6					4	9³						13	7¹		36

ALBION ROVERS   Second Division

Year Formed: 1882. *Ground & Address:* Cliftonhill Stadium, Main St, Coatbridge ML5 3RB. *Telephone/Fax:* 01236 606334.
E-mail: info@albionrovers.co.uk *Website:* albionroversfc.com
Ground capacity: 1249 (seated 489). *Size of Pitch:* 110yd × 72yd.
Chairman and Secretary: Frank Meade ACMA.
Manager: Paul Martin. *Assistant Manager:* Todd Lumsden. *Physio:* John McMenamy.
Club Nickname: The Wee Rovers.
Previous Grounds: Cowheath Park, Meadow Park, Whifflet.
Record Attendance: 27,381 v Rangers, Scottish Cup 2nd rd, 8 Feb 1936.
Record Transfer Fee received: £40,000 from Motherwell for Bruce Cleland.
Record Transfer Fee paid: £7000 for Gerry McTeague to Stirling Albion, September 1989.
Record Victory: 12-0 v Airdriehill, Scottish Cup, 3 Sept 1887.
Record Defeat: 1-11 v Partick Th, League Cup, 11 Aug 1993.
Most Capped Player: Jock White, 1 (2), Scotland.
Most League Appearances: 399: Murdy Walls, 1921-36.
Most League Goals in Season (Individual): 41: Jim Renwick, Division II, 1932-33.
Most Goals Overall (Individual): 105: Bunty Weir, 1928-31.

ALBION ROVERS 2010–11 LEAGUE RECORD

Match No.	Date		Venue	Opponents	Result	H/T Score	Lg Pos.	Goalscorers	Atten-dance
1	Aug	7	H	Berwick R	D 2-2	1-1	—	McLeod [29], Smith, I [79]	369
2		14	A	Stranraer	L 2-3	1-0	8	McLeod [45], Smith, I [77]	312
3		21	H	Queen's Park	W 2-1	1-0	5	Hamilton, C 2 [32, 72]	497
4		28	A	Clyde	W 2-1	1-1	4	Stevenson (pen) [18], Love [90]	1014
5	Sept	11	H	Montrose	W 3-1	2-0	3	Stevenson (pen) [17], Love [23], Gemmell [81]	337
6		18	A	Arbroath	D 1-1	0-0	4	Love [70]	408
7		25	H	Elgin C	W 3-1	1-1	4	Stevenson (pen) [7], McLeod [71], Gemmell [81]	353
8	Oct	2	H	East Stirling	W 1-0	1-0	1	McGowan [28]	367
9		16	A	Annan Ath	L 1-4	0-1	4	Canning [67]	517
10		30	H	Clyde	W 3-1	3-0	2	Boyle [17], Donnelly [20], Hamilton, C [39]	473
11	Nov	6	A	Montrose	W 2-0	2-0	2	Gemmell [32], Love [37]	401
12		13	A	Queen's Park	W 1-0	0-0	2	Hamilton, C [71]	529
13	Dec	14	A	Elgin C	D 2-2	2-2	—	Hamilton, C [11], Love [13]	426
14	Jan	15	H	Montrose	L 0-2	0-1	3		312
15		18	H	Queen's Park	L 1-2	1-0	—	Boyle [17]	402
16		25	H	Annan Ath	D 0-0	0-0	—		323
17		29	H	Elgin C	W 2-0	1-0	3	Chaplain [11], Gemmell [81]	323
18	Feb	5	A	Arbroath	L 0-3	0-1	3		612
19		12	H	East Stirling	W 2-0	1-0	2	Love [21], Canning [90]	346
20		15	H	Stranraer	L 1-2	0-1	—	Innes [72]	326
21		19	A	Annan Ath	D 2-2	1-0	3	Lawless [14], Boyle [90]	467
22		22	A	Clyde	W 1-0	1-0	—	Boyle [19]	507
23		26	H	Berwick R	L 0-1	0-1	3		373
24	Mar	2	A	East Stirling	D 0-0	0-0	—		226
25		5	A	Stranraer	W 3-1	0-1	3	Love [63], Donnelly [67], Smith, I [88]	390
26		8	H	Arbroath	L 0-2	0-1	—		352
27		12	A	Montrose	W 2-0	1-0	3	Gemmell [7], Chaplain [76]	235
28		15	A	Berwick R	W 6-1	3-1	—	Gemmell [30], Lumsden [42], Chaplain 3 [45, 50, 85], Hamilton, C [71]	258
29		19	H	Clyde	D 1-1	1-1	2	Chaplain [22]	523
30		26	A	Elgin C	D 1-1	1-0	3	Love [19]	574
31	Apr	2	H	Arbroath	W 3-0	3-0	3	Chaplain (pen) [5], Benton [38], Love [41]	412
32		9	H	Annan Ath	D 0-0	0-0	3		396
33		16	A	East Stirling	W 2-1	0-0	2	Lawless [55], McGowan [62]	323
34		23	A	Queen's Park	L 1-2	1-1	2	Lawless [15]	715
35		30	H	Stranraer	W 1-0	0-0	2	Chaplain [58]	421
36	May	7	A	Berwick R	D 2-2	1-1	2	Love [5], Gilmartin [88]	436

Final League Position: 2

Honours
League Champions: Division II 1933-34, Second Division 1988-89; *Runners-up:* Division II 1913-14, 1937-38, 1947-48. *Promoted to Second Division:* 2010-11 (play-offs).
Scottish Cup Runners-up: 1920.

Club colours: Shirt: Yellow with black trim. Shorts: Blue. Stockings: Blue.

Goalscorers: *League (56):* Love 10, Chaplain 8 (1 pen), Gemmell 6, Hamilton C 6, Boyle 4, Lawless 3, McLeod 3, Smith I 3, Stevenson 3 (3 pens), Canning 2, Donnelly 2, McGowan 2, Benton 1, Gilmartin 1, Innes 1, Lumsden 1.
Scottish Cup (0).
CIS Cup (0).
Alba Challenge Cup (1): Donnelly 1.
Play-Offs (7): Love 3, Gemmell 2, Chaplain 1, Donnelly 1.

Gaston D 25+1	Benton A 24+2	Lumsden T 20	McGowan M 36	Reid A 33	Donnelly C 35	Canning S 31+1	Gilmartin J 1+10	Hamilton C 17+10	McLeod P 9+6	Love R 36	Stevenson A 21+11	Smith I 3+15	Kerr H 2+1	Boyle C 18+1	Gemmell J 22+7	Ferry D 5+7	Lawless S 11+14	Innes P 19+4	Meechan S 1+1	Chaplain S 16+1	Barnes D —+1	Flynn T 11	Smith D —+1	McCluskey S —+1	Match No.
1	2	3	4	5	6	7	8¹	9	10	11²	12	13													1
1	3	4	5	2	9		13	8	10	11¹	6	12	7²												2
1	5	4	3	8	7			11	9³	10²	2	14	12	6¹	13										3
1	5		3	2	4	10		11³	9²	7	8	13	6¹		12	14									4
1	5	4	3	8	6	7		11¹	9³	10		7²		14		12	13								5
1	3	4	2	7	8	6		10	11¹	9²	5	13		12											6
1	2	4	3	6	7	8		9³	11	10²	5¹		13		14	12									7
1	4		2		7	8		9²	11³	3	13		10	14	12	5¹	6								8
1	2	3¹	5	6	7			10²	11	4	13		8	14	9		12³								9
1	2		3	5	6	7		9²	14	11³	13		8¹	10		12	4								10
1	3		2	5	6	7		13		9³	12	14	8¹	11²		10	4								11
1	2		3	5	6	7		12	14	11	13		0¹	10		9³	4²								12
1	2		3	5	0	7¹		9¹	14	10	12		8²	11		13	4								13
1	2		3	6	7	8		9	13	11²	5		10			12	4¹								14
1	3		2	5	6	7		11³	13	10²	14		8¹	9		12	4								15
	2	3	5	6	7			9²		10		14		8¹	11³		12	4		13					16
	6	5	2	4	7			14		8¹	12	13		9²			11	3		10³					17
1*		4	3	5	6	7¹		12		9⁶				8	11		2			10	15				18
	4	3	5	6	7			9²	13	14				8¹	10³		12	2		11		1			19
1	4	2	5	6	7			8²	13	12				9¹			11	3*		10					20
	2	3	5	6	7		13	9²	4	12				8	11¹		10					1			21
	2	3²	4	5	6		8	11		14				7¹	10³		12	13		9		1			22
	2	3	5	6	7		9³	10	14	12				8²	11¹		13	4				1			23
	2		3	5	6	7		9¹	8	4	10				11							1	1	12	24
3	5	2		4	7	13	9¹	10	6²	11				12			8			1					25
2	3	4		6	7	12		10	13	11¹				9³	5²		8			1			14		26
4		2	5	6	7	12	13	10	3					11¹	8²			9		1					27
12	2	3	5	6¹	8	14	13	11	4					10³	7²			9		1					28
15		4	5	2	3			11²	8		12	10	9		6		7	1⁸							29
1	14	3	4	6	7	8⁴	12		11²	2				9¹	13	5	10³								30
1	4		2	5	6		13		7¹	8				11³	9²	14	12	3		10					31
1	3		4	6	7	12	14	9²	5³					8	10¹		13	2		11					32
1	3		4	5	6	12	14	8²	2					7	10³	13	9¹			11					33
1	2		3	5	6	7		13		9	4			8¹	12	14	11²			10³					34
	2	3	5	6	7		13			9¹	4			8	12		10²	14		11³					35
	2		3	5	6	7	12	10		11				9		8¹	4					1			36

ALLOA ATHLETIC
Third Division

Year Formed: 1878. *Ground & Address:* Recreation Park, Clackmannan Rd, Alloa FK10 1RY. *Telephone:* 01259
722695. *Fax:* 01259 210886. *E-mail:* fcadmin@alloaatheltic.co.uk *Website:* www.alloaathletic.co.uk
Ground Capacity: total: 3100, seated: 400. *Size of Pitch:* 101m × 69m.
Honorary President: George Ormiston. *Chairman:* Mike Mulraney. *Secretary:* Ewen G. Cameron.
Player-Manager: Paul Hartley. *Assistant Manager:* Paddy Connolly. *Coach:* Ronnie Scott. *Physio:* Jim Law.
Club Nicknames: The Wasps, The Hornets.
Previous Grounds: West End Public Park, Gabberston Park, Belleview Park.
Record Attendance: 13,000 v Dunfermline Athletic, Scottish Cup 3rd rd replay, 26 Feb 1939.
Record Transfer Fee received: £100,000 for Martin Cameron to Bristol Rovers.
Record Transfer Fee paid: £26,000 for Ross Hamilton from Stenhousemuir.
Record Victory: 9-0 v Selkirk, Scottish Cup First Round, 28 November 2005.
Record Defeat: 0-10 v Dundee, Division II, 8 Mar 1947 v Third Lanark, League Cup, 8 Aug 1953.
Most Capped Player: Jock Hepburn, 1, Scotland.
Most League Goals in Season (Individual): 49: 'Wee' Willie Crilley, Division II, 1921-22.

ALLOA ATHLETIC 2010–11 LEAGUE RECORD

Match No.	Date		Venue	Opponents	Result	H/T Score	Lg Pos.	Goalscorers	Attendance
1	Aug	7	A	Livingston	D	3-3	0-2	—	Smith [53], Prunty [57], Scott [90]	1389
2		14	H	East Fife	W	3-2	0-0	4	Prunty [51], McDonald [68], Lister [77]	688
3		21	A	Stenhousemuir	W	1-0	1-0	1	Prunty [13]	619
4		28	A	Brechin C	L	1-3	1-2	5	Gormley [29]	418
5	Sept	11	H	Ayr U	W	4-1	2-1	2	Lister [16], Prunty [45], McDonald 2 (2 pens) [53, 64]	641
6		18	H	Dumbarton	D	0-0	0-0	2		559
7		25	A	Peterhead	L	0-1	0-0	3		534
8	Oct	2	H	Forfar Ath	W	3-2	3-1	3	McDonald 2 [6, 17], Gibson [29]	436
9		16	A	Airdrie U	W	1-0	1-0	3	Prunty [34]	1030
10		23	A	Ayr U	L	1-2	0-1	3	McDonald (pen) [75]	1176
11		30	H	Brechin C	D	2-2	1-1	5	Dunlop [36], Prunty [55]	513
12	Nov	6	A	East Fife	L	1-4	0-1	5	Walker [50]	435
13		13	H	Stenhousemuir	W	1-0	0-0	5	Prunty [55]	455
14	Dec	4	H	Peterhead	D	2-2	1-2	—	Noble [35], McDonald (pen) [90]	601
15		18	H	Airdrie U	L	2-3	0-1	—	Noble [60], Lister [70]	502
16		26	H	Livingston	D	2-2	2-0	—	Noble [28], Dunlop [45]	566
17	Jan	2	A	Stenhousemuir	W	3-2	2-0	—	Noble [12], McGowan [15], Gormley [72]	459
18		15	H	Ayr U	L	0-1	0-0	4		527
19		18	A	Dumbarton	L	1-4	0-2	—	Gibson [56]	350
20		29	A	Peterhead	L	1-4	1-2	4	Noble [13]	469
21	Feb	5	H	Dumbarton	L	2-3	0-1	5	Motion [64], Prunty [70]	483
22		12	H	Forfar Ath	L	0-3	0-0	5		414
23		15	A	Forfar Ath	D	1-1	0-0	—	Lister [81]	390
24		19	A	Airdrie U	W	2-0	1-0	5	Noble [28], McGowan [72]	731
25		26	A	Livingston	L	0-4	0-0	6		1377
26	Mar	5	H	East Fife	L	1-3	0-3	7	McGowan (pen) [66]	579
27		12	A	Ayr U	L	0-1	0-1	—		1049
28		19	H	Brechin C	D	2-2	1-1	8	Walker [22], Lister [48]	375
29		26	H	Peterhead	D	0-0	0-0	8		406
30		29	A	Brechin C	L	2-3	1-2	—	Lister [40], McGowan (pen) [90]	411
31	Apr	2	A	Dumbarton	D	2-2	0-1	8	McGowan 2 [48, 78]	640
32		9	H	Airdrie U	W	1-0	1-0	8	McGowan [18]	688
33		16	A	Forfar Ath	L	1-3	0-1	8	Lister [56]	458
34		23	H	Stenhousemuir	L	1-2	1-0	8	Walker [20]	584
35		30	A	East Fife	L	1-3	0-1	8	Motion [61]	846
36	May	7	H	Livingston	L	1-3	0-1	9	Dunlop [53]	647

Final League Position: 9

Honours

League Champions: Division II 1921-22; Third Division 1997-98. *Runners-up:* Division II 1938-39. Second Division 1976-77, 1981-82, 1984-85, 1988-89, 1999-2000, 2001-02.
League Challenge Cup Winners: 1999-2000; *Runners-up:* 2001-02.

Club colours: Shirt: Black with gold hoops on front. Shorts: Black. Stockings: Black.

Goalscorers: *League (49):* Prunty 8, Lister 7, McDonald 7 (4 pens), McGowan 7 (2 pens), Noble 6, Dunlop 3, Walker 3, Gibson 2, Gormley 2, Motion 2, Scott 1, Smith 1.
Scottish Cup (4): McDonald 3, Noble 1.
CIS Cup (2): Prunty 1, Tully 1.
Alba Challenge Cup (1): Walker 1.
Play-Offs (1): Scott 1.

Robertson S 16	McClune D 22+4	Walker S 31+1	McAvoy D 1+2	Brown M 19+2	Gibson W 32	Grant J 11+5	McDonald K 24+3	Smith D 27+3	Prunty B 26+4	Noble S 17+7	Lister J 19+15	Scott A 16+13	Gormley D 10+5	Dunlop M 33	Wilson D 1+4	Hay J 5+12	Ewings J 20	Thomson J —+4	McGowan M 20+2	Bloom J 10+1	Motion K 10+3	Taggart N 2+5	Philp R 6	Forrest F 3	Duffin R 1	Ferguson B 7	Pitman S —+1	Byrne K 6	O'Brien K 1	Match No.
1	2	3	4	5	6	7³	8¹	9	10	11²	12	13	14																	1
1	2	3		5	6		7	9	10³	11²	13		8¹	14		4	12													2
1	2	3		4		7	8	6	10¹	11²		13	12	9³	5		14													3
1	2²	3		5	6	7¹	8³	9	10		12	13	11	4		14														4
1	14		4	13	2	5³	7¹	6	11	9		10²		8	3		12													5
1		4		2	5	7	8	11	9		10		8¹	3	12															6
1	2	3		5	6	7		9	10		11¹		8	4	12															7
1		3		2	5	7	6	9²	10		11¹	12	8	4		13														8
1	14	4		3	5	6	7³	11	9¹		10	12	8²	2	13															9
1			4	13	2	5	6³	7	11²	9		8	10¹	3	14	12														10
1	4	3		5	6	12	7¹	9	10		11⁷	8¹	13	2		14														11
	2	4²		5	6	12	7	9	10	11³	8¹	14		3		13	1													12
2¹	4⁸	3			6	7	9	11²	10³	13	12	8	5					1	14											13
	2	7		5	8	9¹	10	11	12	13	6²	4		14	1				3³											14
2	4	3			14	8	9	11²	12	13		5	6³			1		7¹												15
2	4			5	14	7²	11	9¹	10	12	8		3			6³		1	13											16
1	2	3			7	12	6²		10	9³	14	8¹	13	4	5				11											17
1	2	3			5		7	10²	11		12	9¹		4		6		13	8											18
1	2	5		12	4	8³	11		9²	7	13			3		6¹		14	10											19
1	2	4²		7	3	12	9		11	10	13			5		8¹		6												20
1	2			5	6		9¹	13	11	10				3		14		12	4	7³	8²									21
	2	14		3	6	7¹	9	11²	10	12				4			1		5³	8										22
		4			8	7		10¹	11²	12				3			1	13	5	2	9		6							23
		2			7		8	14	10³	11	13			3			1		4²	5	9		13	6						24
		3			8			6²	12	10³	11	13	14	2			1		7	4¹	9		5							25
					5			7³	9	10	11²	13	14	2		12	1		6	3¹	8		4							26
13								9	10¹	12	11	8³		2		14	1		6				5	3	4	7²				27
12	3							9²	10³	14	11	8		4			1		6				13	5	2	7¹				28
2	4		14	7			13		11	10	9²			5			1		6		12				3³	8¹				29
2¹	5		4	8			13		11	10³	7			3			1		6	9²	12							14		30
	2				5		7¹		12	11	9			3			1		6	4	8²	13						10		31
2	3				5			9²	12	10	8						1		7	4	6	13						11¹		32
2	3				6			11		13	9	5²					1		7	4	12					8		10¹		33
2	3				5		9¹	13		10	8			4			1		6		12		7					11²		34
2	3				5		10¹	14	12		13			4			1		6		8	9²				7³		11		35
	3				5			14	13	9	11³			2			1		7	12	6					4		10²	8¹	36

ANNAN ATHLETIC Third Division

Year Formed: 1942. *Ground & Address:* Galabank, North Street, Annan DG12 5DQ. *Telephone:* 01461 204108.
E-mail: annanathleticfc@aol.com *Website:* www.annanathleticfc.com
Ground capacity: 3000 (426 seated). *Size of Pitch:* 100m × 69m.
Chairman: Henry McLelland.
Secretary: Alan Irving.
Manager: Harry Cairney.
Assistant Manager: Derek Townsley.
Coaches: George Paterson and Pietro Baldotto.
Club Nicknames: Galabankies, Black and Golds.
Most League Appearances: 63: Kevin Neilson, 2008-10.
Most League Goals in Season (Individual): 15: Mike Jack, 2008-09.
Most Goals Overall (Individual): 18: Mike Jack, 2008-10.

ANNAN ATHLETIC 2010–11 LEAGUE RECORD

Match No.	Date	Venue	Opponents	Result	H/T Score	Lg Pos.	Goalscorers	Attendance
1	Aug 7	H	East Stirling	W 3-1	3-1	—	Jack [16], Halsman [18], Sloan, S [20]	539
2	14	A	Arbroath	W 2-0	2-0	1	Cox [38], Neilson [40]	506
3	21	H	Stranraer	D 2-2	1-2	2	Harty [13], Halsman [67]	671
4	28	A	Montrose	D 1-1	0-1	2	Gilfillan [66]	332
5	Sept 11	H	Elgin C	L 0-1	0-1	5		505
6	18	A	Clyde	W 2-0	1-0	3	Gilfillan [6], Felvus [72]	1043
7	25	H	Queen's Park	W 2 1	1-0	3	Harty [33], Cox [83]	546
8	Oct 2	A	Berwick R	D 2-2	1-2	3	Sloan, S [25], Steele [90]	440
9	16	H	Albion R	W 4-1	1-0	2	Halsman 2 [42, 56], Gilfillan [70], Jardine [80]	517
10	Nov 6	A	Elgin C	L 0-2	0-2	4		507
11	9	H	Montrose	D 2-2	2-1	—	Cox [25], Muirhead [43]	377
12	13	A	Stranraer	D 2-2	1-0	5	O'Connor [45], Harty [48]	463
13	Jan 15	H	Elgin C	D 2-2	1-2	6	Gilfillan [6], Macfarlane [90]	311
14	22	A	Montrose	W 1-0	0-0	—	Neilson [90]	335
15	25	A	Albion R	D 0-0	0-0	—		323
16	Feb 1	H	Queen's Park	L 1-2	0-0	—	Sloan, S [55]	293
17	5	A	Clyde	W 2-0	1-0	5	O'Connor [21], Harty [74]	568
18	12	A	Berwick R	W 3-2	1-2	5	Harty 2 (1 pen) [27, 78 (p)], Muirhead [57]	311
19	15	H	Arbroath	L 1-2	0-0	—	Griffin (og) [81]	304
20	19	H	Albion R	D 2-2	0-1	4	Harty 2 [57, 77]	467
21	22	A	Queen's Park	L 0-3	0-1	—		327
22	26	H	East Stirling	W 2-1	0-0	5	Gilfillan [67], Neilson [76]	402
23	Mar 1	H	Berwick R	D 1-1	1-0	—	Neilson [35]	309
24	5	A	Arbroath	L 1-2	0-1	5	Gilfillan [53]	575
25	8	H	Stranraer	W 2-1	2-1	—	O'Connor [26], Harty [41]	307
26	12	A	Elgin C	W 3-2	2-0	5	O'Connor [12], Neilson [39], Dempsie (og) [84]	511
27	15	A	East Stirling	W 5-1	3-0	—	Harty [2], Cox [15], O'Connor [29], Docherty [48], Bell [90]	178
28	19	H	Montrose	W 2-1	0-1	3	Harty 2 (1 pen) [46, 52 (p)]	473
29	26	A	Queen's Park	W 1-0	1-0	2	Sloan, S [16]	561
30	29	H	Clyde	L 0-2	0-1	—		465
31	Apr 2	H	Clyde	W 1-0	1-0	2	Harty [36]	585
32	9	A	Albion R	D 0-0	0-0	2		396
33	16	H	Berwick R	L 2-3	0-2	3	Gilfillan [64], O'Connor [80]	515
34	23	A	Stranraer	D 1-1	0-1	3	Harty [59]	493
35	30	H	Arbroath	W 3-0	1-0	3	O'Connor 2 [23, 66], Sloan, S [72]	651
36	May 7	A	East Stirling	L 0-2	0-1	4		322

Final League Position: 4

Honours
East of Scotland Premier League: Winners (4).
East of Scotland League Cup: Winners (1).
East of Scotland Div 1: Winners (1).
South of Scotland League: Winners (2).
South of Scotland League Cup: Winners (4).
Scottish Challenge Cup South: Winners (1).
Scottish Qualifying Cup South: Winners (1).

Club colours: Shirt: Black and gold stripes. Shorts: Black. Stockings: Black.

Goalscorers: *League (58):* Harty 14 (2 pens), O'Connor 8, Gilfillan 7, Neilson 5, Sloan S 5, Cox 4, Halsman 4, Muirhead 2, Bell 1, Docherty 1, Felvus 1, Jack 1, Jardine 1, Macfarlane 1, Steele 1, own goals 2.
Scottish Cup (9): Gilfillan 2, Harty 2, Aitken 1, Amaya 1, Halsman 1, MacBeth 1, Muirhead 1.
CIS Cup (0).
Alba Challenge Cup (2): Halsman 1, Muirhead 1.
Play-Offs (5): Gilfillan 2, Harty 1, Muirhead 1, Steele 1.

Summersgill C 27	Muirhead A 28+3	Neilson K 34+1	Aitken A 29+1	Gilfillan B 30+2	MacBeth J 23+2	Halsman J 13	Sloan S 31+5	Jack M 4+1	Cox D 31+1	Harty I 30+1	Walker P 1+6	Felvus B 2+13	Jardine C 21+5	Steele J 15+12	Sloan L 1+4	Jamieson J 8	Amaya J —+2	Connolly A —+2	O'Connor S 22	Bell G 2+12	Macfarlane N 10+5	Watson P 18+1	Docherty M 15+3	Mitchell A 1	Atkinson J —+1	Slattery P —+1	Watson J —+1	Match No.
1	2	3	4	5	6	7	8	9^1	10	11^2	12	13																1
1	2	3	4	5	6	7	8	9^1	10^2	11^3	13	14	12															2
1	2	4	3	5	6	7^1	8	9^2	10	11	12		13															3
1	2	4	5	7	3	6^2	8	9^1	11	10	13			12														4
1	2	3	4	7	5	8^1	9^2	12	11	10^3			14	6	13													5
	2	4	3	7	5	8	9		11	10^1	12			6		1												6
	2	3	4	7	5	8^1	9^2		11	10^3	14	13	12	6		1												7
	2	3	4	8	5^1	9^2	6		11	10^3	14	12	7	13		1												8
	2	3	4	6^2	7	11	8	9	10^2	5^1	12		14	13		1												9
	3	14	4	6	5^1	7	8	11	10	9^2			2^3			1	12	13										10
	2	3	4	5^1	6	7	9	10	8	11^2	12					1		13										11
	2	3	4	7	12	5	6	9	10^2	8^1	13					1	11											12
1	2	3	4	6	7^1	6	8		10	9^8	14		11	12					11	12	13							13
1		4		5	3	7			10^1		8	9							11	12	2	6						14
1	12	3	13	5	4^2	8		10		9	6								11^3	14	2^1	7						15
	12	3		4	5	7		10	13		2^1		1						11^3	14	8^2	6	9					16
1	2	4	5	6	3	14		10^3	9	8^2									11^1	12	13		7					17
1	2	3	4		5	7^1		9	10	6									11	12		8						18
1	2	3	4		5^5	6^2		11	9	7	13								10	12			8^1					19
1	2	3	4^8	12		7	9^2	10	6^3	14									11^1	8		5	13					20
1	2	3		5	4	7^3	13	11	8^1										10^2	9	14	6	12					21
1	4^8	2	3	5	6	13	11^3	10^2		9^1	14									12	8	7						22
1		2	3	4	5	8	11		9^1										10	12		7	6					23
1		3	4	5	2	7	11^2		8										10	13	9^1	6	12					24
1	4	2	3	5	6	12	11^1	10	13	8									9^2			7						25
1		2	3^8	4		7	9^1	10	13	8	12								11^2			5	6					26
1	3	2		4		7^2	11	9^3	12	8	13								10^1	14		5	6					27
1	2	3		4		6^1	9	10	13	7									11^{12}	12		5	8					28
1	4^3	2	3	5	13	9	10	11	14	8^2	12											6^1	7					29
1	12	2	3	4^2		7^1	9	10	8^3	13									11	14		5	6					30
1	4	2	3	12		13	11^2	10	5										9			7^1	6	8				31
1	4	2	3		8^2	10	13	12	5^1										11			7	6	9				32
1	2^1	3		5	13	9	10^3	14	12	4									11			7	6	8^2				33
1	6	3	4	5	8	9	10		2	5									11			7						34
1	2	3^2	4	6^1	8	9^3		10	13	5									11			12	14	7				35
		3		4	9^3		10^1	11^2	7	2									8	5	6				1	12	13 14	36

Match No.

ARBROATH   Second Division

Year Formed: 1878. *Ground & Address:* Gayfield Park, Arbroath DD11 1QB. *Telephone:* 01241 872157. *Fax:* 01241 431125. *E-mail:* afc@gayfield.fsnet.co.uk *Website:* www.arbroathfc.co.uk
Ground Capacity: 4165 (seated 860; standing 3305). *Size of Pitch:* 115yd × 71yd.
Chairman: John D. Christison. *Secretary:* Dr Gary Callon. *Administrator:* Mike Cargill.
Manager: Paul Sheerin. *Assistant Manager:* Stewart Petrie. *Physio:* Frank Kenny.
Club Nicknames: The Red Lichties, The Smokies.
Previous Grounds: None.
Record Attendance: 13,510 v Rangers, Scottish Cup 3rd rd, 23 Feb 1952.
Record Transfer Fee received: £120,000 for Paul Tosh to Dundee (Aug 1993).
Record Transfer Fee paid: £20,000 for Douglas Robb from Montrose (1981).
Record Victory: 36-0 v Bon Accord, Scottish Cup 1st rd, 12 Sept 1885.
Record Defeat: 1-9 v Celtic, League Cup 3rd rd, 25 Aug 1993.
Most Capped Player: Ned Doig, 2 (5), Scotland.
Most League Appearances: 445: Tom Cargill, 1966-81.
Most League Goals in Season (Individual): 45: Dave Easson, Division II, 1958-59.
Most Goals Overall (Individual): 120: Jimmy Jack, 1966-71.

ARBROATH 2010–11 LEAGUE RECORD

Match No.	Date	Venue	Opponents	Result	H/T Score	Lg Pos.	Goalscorers	Atten- dance
1	Aug 7	A	Elgin C	W 5-3	1-0	—	Gibson 2 [16, 58], McGowan [53], Falkingham 2 [71, 83]	518
2	14	H	Annan Ath	L 0-2	0-2	5		506
3	21	A	Montrose	L 0-3	0-3	9		565
4	28	H	East Stirling	W 2-0	1-0	5	Swankie [27], McGowan [81]	499
5	Sept 4	H	Queen's Park	W 1-0	0-0	—	Swankie [77]	515
6	11	A	Berwick R	L 1-4	0-3	4	McAnespie [90]	441
7	18	H	Albion R	D 1-1	0-0	5	Doris [78]	408
8	25	A	Stranraer	L 1-4	0-1	5	Doris [71]	379
9	Oct 2	A	Queen's Park	L 2-5	1-2	6	Swankie [12], Doris (pen) [49]	433
10	16	H	Clyde	W 3-2	0-0	6	Swankie 2 [58, 88], Malcolm [80]	481
11	Nov 6	H	Berwick R	W 3-2	2-1	6	Durnan [27], Doris [31], McGowan [82]	402
12	10	A	East Stirling	W 3-1	1-1	—	Gibson [15], Falkingham [46], McGowan [82]	238
13	10	H	Montrose	W 4-0	1-0	3	Doris 3 (1 pen) [21 (p), 62, 66], Sheerin, P [71]	738
14	Dec 15	H	Stranraer	D 0-0	0-0	—		302
15	Jan 2	A	Montrose	W 5-0	2-0	—	Falkingham 2 [34, 51], Swankie 2 [40, 66], Doris (pen) [90]	1034
16	15	A	Berwick R	W 4-0	0-0	2	Swankie 2 [68, 70], Chisholm [78], Gibson [88]	369
17	25	H	East Stirling	L 3-5	2-2	—	McAnespie [23], Rattray [42], Doris (pen) [67]	436
18	29	A	Stranraer	W 4-3	2-1	1	Swankie 3 [26, 56, 65], Falkingham [38]	441
19	Feb 5	H	Albion R	W 3-0	1-0	1	Swankie 2 [7, 85], Sheerin, P (pen) [69]	612
20	12	A	Queen's Park	D 1-1	1-1	1	Malcolm [4]	467
21	15	A	Annan Ath	W 2-1	0-0	—	McGowan [49], Wedderburn [53]	304
22	23	H	Elgin C	W 2-0	2-0	—	Swankie [3], Sheerin, P [20]	403
23	26	A	Elgin C	L 2-3	0-0	1	Gibson [52], Strachan [84]	629
24	Mar 5	H	Annan Ath	W 2-1	1-0	1	Doris [25], Swankie [49]	575
25	8	A	Albion R	W 2-0	1-0	—	Doris 2 [19, 54]	352
26	12	H	Berwick R	W 2-1	1-0	1	Gibson [22], Doris [52]	491
27	19	A	East Stirling	W 5-2	1-1	1	Chisholm [43], Doris [58], Swankie 3 [63, 79, 90]	349
28	22	A	Clyde	D 1-1	0-0	—	Falkingham [60]	532
29	26	H	Stranraer	D 2-2	0-0	1	Gallacher (og) [67], Swankie [82]	701
30	Apr 2	A	Albion R	L 0-3	0-3	1		412
31	9	A	Clyde	W 3-0	2-0	1	Gibson [19], Strachan [22], McGowan [71]	725
32	13	H	Clyde	W 2-0	2-0	—	Doris [25], Swankie [43]	604
33	16	H	Queen's Park	D 2-2	1-1	1	Gibson [39], Wedderburn [49]	912
34	23	H	Montrose	W 4-1	2-0	1	Doris (pen) [5], Falkingham [44], Sheerin, P [61], Strachan [90]	1243
35	30	A	Annan Ath	L 0-3	0-1	1		651
36	May 7	H	Elgin C	L 3-5	1-2	1	Sheerin, P [29], Swankie [50], Falkingham [72]	1125

Final League Position: 1

Honours
League Champions: Third Division 2010-11. *League Runners-up:* Division II 1934-35, 1958-59, 1967-68, 1971-72; Second Division 2000-01; Third Division 1997-98, 2007-08. *Promoted to Second Division:* 2007-08 (play-offs). *Scottish Cup:* Quarter-finals 1993.

Club colours: All maroon.

Goalscorers: *League (80):* Swankie 22, Doris 16 (5 pens), Falkingham 9, Gibson 8, McGowan 6, Sheerin P 5 (1 pen), Strachan 3, Chisholm 2, Malcolm 2, McAnespie 2, Wedderburn 2, Durnan 1, Rattray 1, own goal 1.
Scottish Cup (3): Rattray 2, Doris 1.
CIS Cup (2): Sheerin P 1, Swankie 1.
Alba Challenge Cup (0).

Hill D 35	McMullan K 30+1	Malcolm S 24	Griffin D 14+4	Falkingham J 33+2	McCulloch M 8+1	Swankie G 35+1	Gibson K 26+1	Sheerin P 30+5	McGowan D 8+24	Hamilton J 4+3	Sheerin J 2+12	Thomson D 5+1	Nimmo I —+2	Dimita D 7+11	Ross R 1+4	Shields J 2+2	McAnespie K 27	Durnan M 9	Doris S 25+5	Rattray A 9	McIlravey M —+1	Chisholm R 20+1	Deane P 1+4	Wedderburn C 12+4	Strachan A 12+4	Sibanda L 5+6	McManus A 11	Burns D 1+1	Match No.
1	2	3	4	5	6	7^3	8^2	9	10	11^1	12	13	14																1
1	2	3	4	5	6	7	8^1	9^3	11					10^2		14	12	13											2
1	2	3	4	7	5^1	11	8^3	10^2	9			6					12	13	14										3
1	2	4	14	7^3	8	6^1		12	11	10^2				9	13				3	5									4
1	2	3^1	12	7	8^2	6		13	11	10				9					5	4									5
1	2^1	3	5	7^2	8	10		8		11^3					14	13	9	4	12										6
1	2		3	7	14	10		8		13					9^1	11^{12}	5^3	6	4	12									7
1	5^1		4	8	9	10		14	13						12		7^1	6^3	3	11^3	2								8
1	2^1		4	7	8	11		9		12						6^2		5	10^4	3	13								9
1		5		4		10	9^1	12	14	13		3			6^3			8		2		7^4	11^2						10
1		3		5		9	8^1	10	12			7					4	6	11^2	2		13							11
1	14	4		6		10^3	7	8	13						9		6	11^3	2^1		3	12							12
1	2	3		7		10^3	8^1	9	13			12					6	4	11^4		5	14							13
1	2	5		7^1		10^3	8	9	13			12			6			11^2	3		4	14							14
1	2^2	3	13	8^3		11	7	9^1	14			12			6			10	4		5								15
1	2	4		7		10	8	9^3	12	14		13			6			11^1	3		5^2								16
1	2	3		7		10	8^3	9^2	14	13					6			11	4^1		5	12							17
1	2	3		7^4		10^2	8	9	12	13					6			11^1			5^4	4							18
1	2	3	5^2			10	7^3	9	12	13					6			11^1				4	8	14					19
1	2	4		7		10	8	9	12	14					6^1			5			11^2	3							20
1	2	3^4	12	9^3		7^1	8	11	10^2	14					6			13			5	4^4							21
1	2		5	7		11	8^3	9^2	10^1			3			12			6				13	14	4					22
1	2^3	3	4	7^1		10	8	9	13						6			11^2			5		14	12					23
1	2		13			10^3	8^2	9	12	14	3				11^1			6			5	7		4					24
1	2	4		10		12	13	8	14			5			11^3			6^2			9	7^1	3						25
1	2	3^1		6		10	8	9	13	14		5^2			11^3			12	7			4							26
1	2		7^2			10	8^1	12		14	5				11^3			6			4	9	13	3					27
1	2		7^3			10	8^1	9	13		5^4				11^2			6			3	14	12	4					28
1^4	2		4	6		10		9	13		5				11^2			3			8	12^6	7^1	15					29
	2	5^1		7		10	8	11	14		3				9^3			4			12	13		6^2	1				30
1			4	7^3		10^2	8	9	12	13				14	5			11^1			3	6	2						31
1			4	8		11^3	7	9	12	14				13	5			10^1			3	6^2	2						32
1			3	7		9	8	12						6				11^1			4	5	10	2					33
1	2			6		9^3	8^1	10	13	14					5			11^2			12	3	7	4					34
1	2	3		12		8^3		11	10^2	14					13			6			5^1	9	7	4					35
1	2	4		7		9		10	13					6^1				11			3	8^2	12	5					36

AYR UNITED　　　　　　　　　　First Division

Year Formed: 1910. *Ground & Address:* Somerset Park, Tryfield Place, Ayr KA8 9NB. *Telephone:* 01292 263435.
Fax: 01292 281314. *E-mail:* info@ayrunitedfc.co.uk *Website:* ayrunitedfc.co.uk
Ground Capacity: 10,185, seated: 1597. *Size of Pitch:* 101m × 66m.
Chairman and Managing Director: Lachlan Cameron.
Manager: Brian Reid. *Assistant Manager:* Scott MacKenzie. *Physio:* Kevin MacLellan.
Club Nickname: The Honest Men.
Previous Grounds: None.
Record Attendance: 25,225 v Rangers, Division I, 13 Sept 1969.
Record Transfer Fee received: £300,000 for Steven Nicol to Liverpool (Oct 1981).
Record Transfer Fee paid: £90,000 for Mark Campbell from Stranraer (March 1999).
Record Victory: 11-1 v Dumbarton, League Cup, 13 Aug 1952.
Record Defeat: 0-9 in Division I v Rangers (1929); v Hearts (1931); B Division v Third Lanark (1954).
Most Capped Player: Jim Nisbet, 3, Scotland.
Most League Appearances: 459: John Murphy, 1963-78.
Most League League and Cup Goals in Season (Individual): 66: Jimmy Smith, 1927-28.
Most League and Cup Goals Overall (Individual): 213: Peter Price, 1955-61.

AYR UNITED 2010–11 LEAGUE RECORD

Match No.	Date	Venue	Opponents	Result	H/T Score	Lg Pos.	Goalscorers	Attendance
1	Aug 7	H	Brechin C	L 0-2	0-1	—		1212
2	14	A	Airdrie U	D 2-2	1-0	8	Roberts 2 [5, 73]	1127
3	21	H	Dumbarton	W 1-0	1-0	7	Maxwell (og) [35]	1242
4	28	H	Peterhead	D 1-1	0-1	7	Roberts (pen) [90]	1099
5	Sept 11	A	Alloa Ath	L 1-4	1-2	7	Smith [27]	641
6	18	A	East Fife	W 3-2	2-2	5	Roberts 3 (3 pens) [13, 45, 90]	664
7	25	H	Stenhousemuir	W 2-0	1-0	4	McCann [45], McKay [87]	1065
8	Oct 2	H	Livingston	W 3-1	0-1	4	Malone [75], Roberts 2 [80, 82]	1270
9	16	A	Forfar Ath	L 1-4	0-1	4	Easton [89]	544
10	23	H	Alloa Ath	W 2-1	1-0	4	Roberts [36], Grant (og) [83]	1176
11	30	A	Peterhead	W 4-2	2-1	3	Roberts (pen) [33], Trouten [38], McCann [67], McKay [82]	560
12	Nov 6	H	Airdrie U	W 1-0	0-0	3	McLaughlin [90]	1439
13	13	A	Dumbarton	L 2-3	0-1	3	Roberts [66], Rodgers [90]	811
14	Jan 2	H	Dumbarton	W 2-0	1-0	—	Roberts (pen) [11], McKay [78]	1224
15	15	A	Alloa Ath	W 1-0	0-0	1	Easton [64]	527
16	22	H	Peterhead	D 2-2	2-0	—	Roberts 2 (2 pens) [12, 29]	1226
17	29	H	Stenhousemuir	W 4-3	1-1	2	Roberts 2 (1 pen) [6 ipi, 63], Lauchlan [51], Robertson [54]	1181
18	Feb 12	H	Livingston	L 0-3	0-0	3		1614
19	23	H	East Fife	L 0-4	0-2	—		789
20	26	H	Brechin C	W 2-0	1-0	3	Bannigan [45], McLaughlin [63]	1092
21	Mar 1	A	Stenhousemuir	L 1-3	1-1	—	Bannigan [5]	484
22	5	A	Airdrie U	W 5-0	0-0	3	Willis [50], Roberts [62], Moffat [69], McLaughlin [82], Rodgers (pen) [87]	966
23	12	H	Alloa Ath	W 1-0	1-0	—	McCann [45]	1049
24	19	A	Peterhead	W 2-1	1-0	2	Trouten [24], Moffat [68]	536
25	23	H	Forfar Ath	L 0-1	0-0	—		909
26	26	A	Stenhousemuir	L 1-2	0-1	3	Roberts [90]	568
27	29	A	East Fife	L 2-3	1-2	—	Moffat 2 [39, 89]	350
28	Apr 2	H	East Fife	D 1-1	1-1	3	Trouten [16]	976
29	5	A	Forfar Ath	L 2-3	1-0	—	Trouten [37], McLaughlin [71]	341
30	9	H	Forfar Ath	W 3-1	2-0	3	Bannigan 2 [8, 82], Roberts [13]	851
31	12	A	Brechin C	W 3-0	2-0	—	Moffat [33], Roberts (pen) [35], Crawford II [85]	394
32	16	A	Livingston	D 0-0	0-0	2		1492
33	19	A	Livingston	L 2-3	1-1	—	Roberts (pen) [40], Robertson [90]	904
34	23	A	Dumbarton	W 2-1	2-0	2	Trouten [10], Moffat [16]	830
35	30	H	Airdrie U	W 3-1	0-0	2	Rodgers 2 (1 pen) [48, 60 ipi], Moffat [65]	1402
36	May 7	A	Brechin C	L 0-1	0-1	2		577

Final League Position: 2

Honours
League Champions: Division II 1911-12, 1912-13, 1927-28, 1936-37, 1958-59, 1965-66. Second Division 1987-88, 1996-97;
Runners-up: Division II 1910-11, 1955-56, 1968-69. Second Divison 2008-09. *Promoted to First Division:* 2008-09
(play-offs). *Promoted to First Division:* 2010-11 (play-offs).
Scottish Cup: Semi-finals 2002.
League Cup: Runners-up: 2001-02.
B&Q Cup Runners-up: 1990-91, 1991-92.

Club colours: Shirt: White with thin black hoops. Shorts: Black with white trim. Stockings: White.

Goalscorers: *League (62):* Roberts 21 (11 pens), Moffat 7, Trouten 5, Bannigan 4, McLaughlin 4, Rodgers 4 (2 pens),
McCann 3, McKay 3, Easton 2, Robertson 2, Crawford II 1, Lauchlan 1, Malone 1, Smith 1, Willis 1, own goals 2.
Scottish Cup (7): Roberts 4 (3 pens), Rodgers 2, Bannigan 1.
CIS Cup (2): Connelly 1, McKeown 1.
Alba Challenge Cup (5): Rodgers 2, Campbell 1, Roberts 1, Trouten 1.
Play-Offs (10): Moffat 4, McCann 1, McLaughlin 1, Roberts 1, Rodgers 1, Trouten 1 (pen), own goal 1.

Crawford D 18	Robertson R 8+13	Smith C 29+1	Campbell M 29	McLaughlin S 33	Tiffoney J 24+5	Keenan D 7+1	Trouten A 31+1	McKeown S 4	Reynolds S 4+3	Arbuckle G 1	Connolly A —+2	Paterson R —+3	Easton W 18+9	Roberts M 30+2	McWilliams R —+2	Main A 3	McKay D 9+3	Rodgers A 16+15	Taggart S 2+4	Woodburn A —+4	Malone E 28	McCann R 21+2	Bannigan S 15+2	Moffat M 20+2	Aitken C 1	Lauchlan J 16	Willis P 6	McLean D —+1	Martin A 15	Donnelly R 6+1	Crawford II D 2+5	Shankland M —+1	Armstrong G —+1	Match No.
1	2	3	4	5	6	7	8	9	10²	11¹	12	13																						1
1	14	3	2	7	4	5	6	9	11²			12		8¹			10³	13																2
13	5	4	8	2	3	6	7	9¹						11		1	10²	12																3
13	3	2	7	4	6²	10³	14							8	12	1	9¹	11	5															4
13	2³	3	7	12		6		9						5¹	11	1	8²	10	4	14														5
1	12	2¹	6	4²	7		8		13					5			10²	11			3	9												6
1	3¹	9	4	6	7									5	13		8	11			12²	2	10	3	9									7
1	13	3	8	4	7	5								11	6		10¹	12				2	9²											8
1	4¹	3	9	5¹	8²	7	14							6	11²		10³	13	12			2												9
1		2	4	7		5	6²							8	11		12	10¹			13	3	9											10
1	14	3	2³	7	4	12	6							8¹	11²		9	13				5	10											11
1		2	4¹	7	5		6							9²	11		8	13	12			3	10											12
1		4	3	7	5³		6							11			9¹	12			2	10	8											13
1	14	4	3	7		5¹								8	11²		12	10			13	2	9	6³										14
1	14	4	3	7	5									8³	11²		13	10				2	9	6¹	12									15
1		2	3	7		4								11			10¹				5	9	6	12	8									16
1	12	13	3	7	5²		6							8¹	11²		4	9				10	2											17
1	6	5					8	2¹						12	11			13			3	7	9²	10	4									18
1		5	8¹	2²										11	10			13	3		6	9		4	7	12								19
1		3	5	8	12	6								10²			13				4	9	11	2	7¹									20
1	14	5	4	7	13	8								10³			12				2	9	11	3	6²									21
		3	5	7			8							11¹			12	4	9		10	2	6			1								22
		3	5	7	12		8¹							11²			14	4	9	13	10	2	6³			1								23
		5	4	7		6								12	11²		13	3			8	10	2	9¹		1								24
		5	4	7	12	6								9¹	11²		13	3			8	10	2			1								25
		4	3¹	7	5	6								12	13		10				9	8²	11	2		1								26
		3		6	4	5								12	11		9¹				8	7	10			1	2							27
		3¹		7			6							8	11²		13	4	10		9		5			1	2	12						28
		5		8			7¹							11²	10		3	6	13	9		2				1	4	12						29
	5	2		6		8								13	11¹		10				3	9	7			1	4²	12						30
	4	3		5³		7								12	11²		10				6	14	8	9		1	2¹	13						31
	6¹	3	5	2		8								12	10		9²				4	13	11	7³		1		14						32
	13	3	8²	2		7	14							10³			12				5	6	11⁸	9¹	4	1								33
	13	3	5	8		7¹	6							12	10³		14				4	11¹²	9	2		1								34
	6	4	5	8³			12					13	9¹				11²	3					10			2			1	14	7			35
	7	5		9			6					14	4				10						11³			2			1	3²	8¹	12	13	36

BERWICK RANGERS

Third Division

Year Formed: 1881. *Ground & Address:* Shielfield Park, Tweedmouth, Berwick-upon-Tweed TD15 2EF. *Telephone:* 01289 307424. *Fax:* 01289 309424. *Email:* club@berwickrangers.net *Website:* berwickrangers.net
Ground Capacity: 4131, seated: 1366. *Size of Pitch:* 110yd × 70yd.
Chairman: Brian Porteous. *Vice-Chairman:* Moray McLaren. *Football Secretary:* Dennis McCleary.
Manager: Jimmy Crease. *Assistant Player-Manager:* Ian Little. *Physio:* Jamie Dougal. *Ground/Kit:* Ian Oliver.
Club Nicknames: The Borderers, Black and Gold, The Dream Team.
Previous Grounds: Bull Stob Close, Pier Field, Meadow Field, Union Park, Old Shielfield.
Record Attendance: 13,283 v Rangers, Scottish Cup 1st rd, 28 Jan 1967.
Record Victory: 8-1 v Forfar Ath, Division II, 25 Dec 1965; v Vale of Leithen, Scottish Cup, Dec 1966.
Record Defeat: 1-9 v Hamilton A, First Division, 9 Aug 1980.
Most League Appearances: 435: Eric Tait, 1970-87.
Most League Goals in Season (Individual): 33: Ken Bowron, Division II, 1963-64.
Most Goals Overall (Individual): 115: Eric Tait, 1970-87.

BERWICK RANGERS 2010–11 LEAGUE RECORD

Match No.	Date	Venue	Opponents	Result	H/T Score	Lg Pos.	Goalscorers	Attendance
1	Aug 7	A	Albion R	D 2-2	1-1	—	Gordon [32], Currie, P [85]	369
2	14	H	Elgin C	W 6-2	4-0	2	McLeod [4], Gribben 3 [11, 34, 50], O'Reilly [39], Currie, P [52]	409
3	21	A	Clyde	W 4-1	1-0	1	Notman [8], Currie, P 2 [64, 84], O'Reilly [70]	772
4	28	A	Queen's Park	W 2-0	1-0	1	Gribben (pen) [29], O'Reilly [52]	479
5	Sept 11	H	Arbroath	W 4-1	3-0	1	O'Reilly [21], Gribben 3 [24, 28, 51]	441
6	18	H	Stranraer	D 2-2	1-0	1	Gribben [28], Brazil [88]	489
7	25	A	East Stirling	D 0-0	0-0	1		383
8	Oct 2	H	Annan Ath	D 2-2	2-1	2	Gribben 2 [1, 30]	448
9	16	A	Montrose	D 1-1	1-0	3	Gribben [25]	376
10	30	H	Queen's Park	D 1-1	0-0	3	Gribben [76]	520
11	Nov 6	A	Arbroath	L 2-3	1-2	3	Brazil [19], McLeod [52]	402
12	13	H	Clyde	W 2-1	0-0	4	Little [79], Currie, P (pen) [81]	432
13	Dec 11	A	Stranraer	D 1-1	1-0	—	Brazil [2]	267
14	Jan 15	H	Arbroath	L 0-4	0-0	5		369
15	22	A	Queen's Park	L 0-1	0-0	—		485
16	29	A	East Stirling	L 0-1	0-1	6		341
17	Feb 12	A	Annan Ath	L 2-3	2-1	7	Gray [25], Little [43]	311
18	15	A	Clyde	L 0-2	0-1	—		385
19	19	A	Montrose	D 1-1	0-0	7	O'Reilly [69]	301
20	22	H	Montrose	W 1-0	0-0	—	Currie, P [89]	285
21	26	A	Albion R	W 1-0	1-0	7	O'Reilly [20]	373
22	Mar 1	A	Annan Ath	D 1-1	0-1	—	Gribben [74]	309
23	5	H	Elgin C	W 4-0	3-0	7	Gray 3 [25, 35, 76], Gribben [33]	305
24	8	H	East Stirling	W 3-0	1-0	—	Gribben 2 [12, 79], McLean [46]	266
25	12	A	Arbroath	L 1-2	0-1	6	Hill (og) [90]	491
26	15	H	Albion R	L 1-6	1-3	6	Gray [8]	258
27	19	H	Queen's Park	W 3-1	2-0	6	Currie, P (pen) [37], Greenhill D 2 [45, 74]	398
28	22	A	Elgin C	W 2-1	0-0	—	Currie, P 2 [53, 83]	412
29	26	H	East Stirling	D 1-1	0-1	5	Brazil [90]	367
30	29	H	Stranraer	D 3-3	2-2	—	McLeod [9], Gribben [40], Gray [77]	297
31	Apr 2	A	Stranraer	L 1-3	0-1	6	Currie, P [56]	331
32	9	H	Montrose	L 0-1	0-0	6		353
33	16	A	Annan Ath	W 3-2	2-0	6	Gray 2 [17, 44], Currie, P [53]	515
34	23	H	Clyde	D 1-1	0-0	6	Currie, L [59]	427
35	30	A	Elgin C	L 2-3	2-1	6	Currie, P 2 [13, 20]	496
36	May 7	H	Albion R	D 2-2	1-1	6	Brazil [42], Ponton [49]	436

Final League Position: 6

Honours
League Champions: Second Division 1978-79. Third Division 2006-07; *Runners-up:* Second Division 1993-94. Third Division 1999-2000, 2005-06 (not promoted).
Scottish Cup: Quarter-finals 1953-54, 1979-80.
League Cup: Semi-finals 1963-64.
League Challenge Cup: Quarter-finals 2004-05.

Club colours: Shirt: Black with gold vertical stripes. Shorts: Black. Stockings: Gold.

Goalscorers: *League (62):* Gribben 17 (1 pen), Currie P 13 (2 pens), Gray 8, O'Reilly 6, Brazil 5, McLeod 3, Greenhill D 2, Little 2, Currie L 1, Gordon 1, McLean 1, Notman 1, Ponton 1, own goal 1.
Scottish Cup (5): McMullan 2, Brazil 1, Currie P 1, Greenhill D 1.
CIS Cup (0).
Alba Challenge Cup (1): McLean 1.

McCaldon I 15+1	McLeod C 26+1	Smith E 16+2	McMullan P 12+1	O'Reilly C 15+6	Notman S 29	Greenhill D 26+4	McLaren F 11+5	Currie P 29+1	McLean A 36	Gordon K 16+14	Ewart J 19+6	Brazil A 15+18	Gribben D 28+3	Peat M 21	Holms R —+1	Malone E 1	O'Connor G —+1	Ponton A 2+6	Little I 10+9	Kerr G —+1	Thomson S 5	Grant J 16+2	Motion K —+1	Callaghan S 20	Gray D 11+6	Roseburgh S 1	Currie L 16	Neill K —+2	Match No.
1	2	3	4^1	5	6	7	8^3	9	10	11^2	12	13	14																1
	4	5	9^1	10	2	8	6^3	7	3	12		14	11^2	1	13														2
1	2	3	4	5	6	10	8^1	9	7	13	12		11^2																3
	2	3	4	10^1	5	8	7	6	9	12			11	1															4
	2	13	3	4^1	5^2	9	14	8	6	10	12		11^3	1		7													5
	4	5	3^3	2^2	6^8	9	12	8	7	10^1	13	14	11	1															6
15	7	3^0	4	5	9	12	8	6	10	2			11^1	1^8															7
1^6	4	5	9	10^1	2	8^4	6	7	3	12		13	11^2				15												8
	4	2		5^2	7		8	6	10	3	13		11^3	1				9^1	12	14									9
	2		4^2	10^1	5	9	7^3	8	6	14	12		11	1					13		3								10
	4	2	5	9^2	7	8		6	12	10			11^1	1					13		3								11
	3	2	5	12	8	9^3	7	6		10^1			11^2	1					14		13	4							12
	5	2	4^2	17	7	6	9	8	11				10^1	1					13		3								13
	3	2		14	6	8		7	5	12	13		10^3	11	1				9^1		4^2								14
	4	5	13	12	2	8		7	3	6^2			10	11^1	1				9										15
1	2	3		10^1	4	6^2	14	7	5	9^2	13	11										8	12						16
1	2		14	3	12	6^2	7^1	4	13			11^3										9		8	5		10		17
5^2			2	14	7^1	8	4		13	12^8	9	1										6		3	10		11^3		18
	3	4			7^1	9	5		2	10	11	1										8		6	12				19
	3^3	4	9		8	5	14	2	11^2	12			10^1									7		6	13				20
	4^1	5			8	6	12	2	11				10^2									9		7	13		3		21
	4^1	5			6	11	2		10^2	13		1	9									8		7	12		3		22
3		14	6^1	4	12	2	9^2	11	1	13		8^3												5	10	7			23
3		7^1	8	5	9^2	2	14	10^3	11	1	12	13										6		11	4				24
3	13		8	7	5^2	12	2	11	1	14	10^3		9^1									6		6	4				25
	2		14	7^3	4	6	3^1		10	1			9^2									12		5	11		8		26
1	2^1		4	8	9	5	13		14	10^3									12^2			7		6	11		3		27
1			4	7	8	5		2	13	10^1									12			9		6	11^2		3		28
1	13		4	7^2	8	5	14	2	12	10									9^3			6		6	11^1		3		29
1	3			5	7		8		2	11^1	10								9			6		6	12		4		30
1			4	8	12	5		2	13	10							7^1		9			6		6	11^2		3		31
1	2			5	8^2	9	6	11^1	3	13	10											7		12			4		32
1	9		4	7		8^1	5	13	2	14	10^2								12			6		11^3			3		33
1	3			8		9	6	13	2	12	10								5^2			7		11^1			4		34
1	3^2			12		7^1	5	9^3	2	11	10		13						8			6					4	14	35
1				7	14		5	9^2	2	11^3	10^1		8	12					4			6					3	13	36

BRECHIN CITY   Second Division

Year Formed: 1906. *Ground & Address:* Glebe Park, Trinity Rd, Brechin, Angus DD9 6BJ. *Telephone:* 01356 622856.
Fax: 01382 206331. *E-mail:* secretary@brechincityfc.com *Website:* www.brechincity.com
Ground Capacity: total: 3960, seated: 1519. *Size of Pitch:* 110yd × 67yd.
Chairman: Kenneth Ferguson. *Vice-Chairman:* Martin Smith. *Secretary:* Gus Fairlie.
Manager: Jim Weir. *Assistant Manager:* Kevin McGowne. *Physio:* Tom Gilmartin.
Club Nicknames: The City, The Hedgemen.
Previous Grounds: Nursery Park.
Record Attendance: 8122 v Aberdeen, Scottish Cup 3rd rd, 3 Feb 1973.
Record Transfer Fee received: £100,000 for Scott Thomson to Aberdeen (1991) and Chris Templeman to Morton (2004).
Record Transfer Fee paid: £16,000 for Sandy Ross from Berwick Rangers (1991).
Record Victory: 12-1 v Thornhill, Scottish Cup 1st rd, 28 Jan 1926.
Record Defeat: 0-10 v Airdrieonians, Albion R and Cowdenbeath, all in Division II, 1937-38.
Most League Appearances: 459: David Watt, 1975-89.
Most League Goals in Season (Individual): 26: Ronald McIntosh, Division II, 1959-60.
Most Goals Overall (Individual): 131: Ian Campbell, 1977-85.

BRECHIN CITY 2010–11 LEAGUE RECORD

Match No.	Date	Venue	Opponents	Result	H/T Score	Lg Pos.	Goalscorers	Atten- dance
1	Aug 7	A	Ayr U	W 2-0	1-0	—	McLauchlan [7], Molloy [85]	1212
2	14	H	Stenhousemuir	D 0-0	0-0	3		404
3	21	A	Forfar Ath	D 1-1	0-0	4	King [77]	782
4	28	H	Alloa Ath	W 3-1	2-1	2	Booth [20], McAllister 2 [21, 81]	418
5	Sept11	A	Airdrie U	D 1-1	1-0	4	Byers [23]	946
6	18	H	Livingston	L 1-3	0-2	4	Moyes [90]	526
7	25	A	Dumbarton	W 3-1	2-0	2	Booth [36], McKenna [40], McAllister [88]	626
8	Oct 2	H	Peterhead	W 4-2	2-1	1	Molloy [2], McAllister 3 [39, 58, 66]	473
9	16	A	East Fife	W 3-1	1-1	1	Molloy [42], McKenna 2 [56, 63]	336
10	23	H	Airdrie U	W 3-1	1-1	1	Janczyk [20], McAllister [53], Molloy [90]	564
11	30	A	Alloa Ath	D 2-2	1-1	1	Byers [22], Bolger [69]	513
12	Nov 6	A	Stenhousemuir	D 0-0	0-0	2		491
13	13	H	Forfar Ath	D 0-0	0-0	2		786
14	Dec 11	A	Peterhead	W 5-0	2-0	—	McAllister 4 (1 pen) [6, 34 (p), 58, 79], Archdeacon [90]	466
15	Jan 15	A	Airdrie U	D 2-2	0-0	2	Janczyk [49], McLean [87]	806
16	29	A	Dumbarton	W 2-1	1-0	3	Hill [22], Molloy [72]	565
17	Feb 1	A	Livingston	L 0-2	0-1	—		847
18	12	H	Peterhead	W 3-1	0-1	2	McKenna 2 [52, 70], Redman [88]	503
19	19	A	East Fife	D 0-0	0-0	2		526
20	22	H	Livingston	W 1-0	0-0	—	Molloy [87]	565
21	26	A	Ayr U	L 0-2	0-1	2		1092
22	Mar 1	H	Dumbarton	D 3-3	1-1	—	Byers 2 [9, 64], McAllister [69]	411
23	5	H	Stenhousemuir	W 3-1	1-1	2	McAllister [43], Redman [55], Janczyk [82]	503
24	8	A	Forfar Ath	L 1-2	0-0	—	Moyes [65]	604
25	19	A	Alloa Ath	D 2-2	1-1	3	McKenna [9], Moyes [68]	375
26	26	H	Dumbarton	W 6-0	1-0	2	McKenna 3 [7, 79, 85], Redman [46], McAllister [52], Megginson [83]	514
27	29	H	Alloa Ath	W 3-2	2-1	—	McAllister [4], Molloy [14], Janczyk [78]	411
28	Apr 2	A	Livingston	D 0-0	0-0	2		1553
29	5	H	Airdrie U	L 1-2	0-1	—	McKenna [46]	438
30	9	H	East Fife	L 1-3	0-1	2	Moyes [61]	504
31	12	H	Ayr U	L 0-3	0-2	—		394
32	16	A	Peterhead	D 1-1	1-1	4	Megginson [39]	498
33	19	H	East Fife	L 2-3	0-0	—	Redman [54], Molloy (pen) [58]	441
34	23	H	Forfar Ath	L 0-1	0-0	4		825
35	30	A	Stenhousemuir	W 3-1	2-1	4	McAllister 3 (2 pens) [5 (p), 45, 90 (p)]	672
36	May 7	H	Ayr U	W 1-0	1-0	4	McAllister [19]	577

Final League Position: 4

Honours
League Champions: C Division 1953-54. Second Division 1982-83, 1989-90, 2004-05. Third Division 2001-02. *Runners-up:* Second Division 1992-93, 2002-03. Third Division 1995-96.
League Challenge Cup: Runners-up 2002-03. Semi-finals 2001-02.

Club colours: Shirt: White with red broad stripe. Shorts: Red. Stockings: Red.

Goalscorers: *League (63):* McAllister 19 (3 pens), McKenna 10, Molloy 8 (1 pen), Byers 4, Janczyk 4, Moyes 4, Redman 4, Booth 2, Megginson 2, Archdeacon 1, Bolger 1, Hill 1, King 1, McLauchlan 1, McLean 1.
Scottish Cup (13): McAllister 6 (1 pen), McKenna 4, Byers 2, Molloy 1.
CIS Cup (5): McAllister 3, McLauchlan 1, Molloy 1.
Alba Challenge Cup (3): Janczyk 1, McAllister 1, Moyes 1.
Play-Offs (6): Janczyk 1, Kirkpatrick 1, Megginson 1, Molloy 1, Redman 1, own goal 1.

Scott D 3	McLean P 25+2	Cook A 34+2	McLauchlan G 29	Moyes E 33	Smith B 5+3	Docherty M 4+6	Molloy C 34	Janczyk N 31+2	McKenna D 27+7	McAllister R 29	King C 4+4	Byers K 19+6	Gray C —+1	Fusco G 17+11	Nelson C 33	Booth C 11	Redman J 19+6	White D 9+2	Bolger A —+3	Mulrooney P —+2	Archdeacon M 1+8	Hill D 4	Kirkpatrick J 3+11	McKay D 2+14	Megginson M 9+5	McBain R 11	Match No.
1	2	3	4	5	6	7^3	8	9^2	10^1	11	12	13	14														1
1	2	3	4	5	12	6	7	8^2	10^1	11	9			13													2
	2	3	4	5	6^2	8^1	7	9	10	11	13	12			1												3
	2	5	3	4	6	14	9	13	12	10	11^2	8^1			1		7^3										4
	2	5	3	4	6^7		9	13	10^8	11		8^1			1		7	12									5
13	2^2		4	5	6^3	14	7	9^1	11	10	12				1	3	8										6
13	5	3	4	14		7	8^3	10^1	11	12					1	6	9	2^2									7
	2	3	4	5	13	6^3	7^2	10^1	11	12	14				1	9	8										8
	2	5	3	4	14	8^3	7^2	10^1	11	12				13	1	6	9										9
	2	3	5	4	13	9	8^1	11^2	10	12					1	6	7										10
	2	3	4	5		9	7^1	11					10^2		1	6	8^3			13	14						11
	2	3	4	5	13	9	7^2	11^3		10^1			8		1	6			12	14							12
	2	5	3			9		11^1	10	13		8			1	6^2	7^3	4	12	14							13
	2	5	3	4	13	9^2	8	10	11^1	7^3		14			1	6			12								14
	2	3		5		9^2	8	6^3	11	10		7^1		12	1	13	4		14								15
	2	6	3	4		9	8	11^1	10^2	13					1	7			12	5							16
	2	6^1	3^*	4		9	8^2	11^3	10^4	13					1	7			14	5	12						17
2^*	14		5			9	7^2	11^3		8		10			1	12	4		6^1	3	13						18
	2	3	4			8	7^2	11^1	10	9				6	1	13				5^4	12						19
	2	5	3	4		8		13	11	6				7	1	12					10	9^2					20
	2	3	4	5		8	6^3	13	11	10				7^1	1	12					14	9^2					21
	2	3	4	5		8	12	11^2	10	9				7^1	1	6						13					22
	2	3	4	5			6	11^1	10	9^2				8	1	7					13	12					23
	2	3	4	5		7	6^3	14	10^1	9^2		8			1						12	13	11				24
	2	5		4		7	9^3	10^1	11			8			1	6				14	12	13	3^2				25
		2	3	4		7	8^2	11	10^3	9^1					1	6					12	14	13	5			26
		2	4	5		7	8^3	11^2	10	9^1		14			1	6						13	12	3			27
		2	4	5		8	6	13	9					7^1	1						11^2	12	10^1	3			28
		2	3	4		7	6	11	10	8^1					1	6^2					13	12	9^2	5			29
		2	4	5		7^*	8^3	11	10	9^1		14			1	6^2					12	13	3				30
		2		4			7	11	10	6^2		8			1			3			13	9^1	14	12^3	5		31
	2	5		4		7	8							9	1	10^2	3				13		12	11	6^1		32
	2	4^3				8	9	11^2		12				6	1		7^3				14	13	10	5^1			33
	2	13				8	6^2	11^8		9^1		5		1		7^4					14	12	10^2	3			34
1		2	3^2	4		7	8		10	6						9	13				12		11^1	5			35
		3	4^1	5		6	8	13	10^3					7	1						14		11^2	2			36

CELTIC Premier League

Year Formed: 1888. *Ground & Address:* Celtic Park, Glasgow G40 3RE. *Telephone:* 0871 226 1888. *Fax:* 0141 551 4223.
E-mail: customerservices@celticfc.co.uk *Website:* www.celticfc.net
Ground Capacity: all seated: 60,355. *Size of Pitch:* 105m × 68m.
Chairman: John Reid. *Chief Executive:* Peter Lawwell. *Secretary:* Robert Howat.
Manager: Neil Lennon. *Assistant Manager:* Johan Mjallby. *First Team Coaches:* Alan Thompson and Garry Parker.
Physio: Graham Parsons.
Club Nicknames: The Bhoys, The Hoops, The Celts. *Previous Grounds:* None.
Record Attendance: 92,000 v Rangers, Division I, 1 Jan 1938.
Record Transfer Fee received: £6,500,000 for Stilian Petrov to Aston Villa (August 2007).
Record Transfer Fee paid: £6,000,000 for Chris Sutton from Chelsea (July 2000).
Record Victory: 11-0 Dundee, Division I, 26 Oct 1895.
Record Defeat: 0-8 v Motherwell, Division I, 30 Apr 1937.
Most Capped Player: Pat Bonner 80, Republic of Ireland.
Most League Appearances: 486: Billy McNeill, 1957-75.
Most League Goals in Season (Individual): 50: James McGrory, Division I, 1935-36.
Most Goals Overall (Individual): 397: James McGrory, 1922-39.

Honours
League Champions: (42 times) Division I 1892-93, 1893-94, 1895-96, 1897-98, 1904-05, 1905-06, 1906-07, 1907-08, 1908-09, 1909-10, 1913-14, 1914-15, 1915-16, 1916-17, 1918-19, 1921-22, 1925-26, 1935-36, 1937-38, 1953-54, 1965-66, 1966-67, 1967-68, 1968-69, 1969-70, 1970-71, 1971-72, 1972-73, 1973-74. Premier Division 1976-77, 1978-79, 1980-81, 1981-82, 1985-86, 1987-88, 1997-98, 2000-01, 2001-02, 2003-04, 2005-06, 2006-07, 2007-08. *Runners-up:* 31 times.
Scottish Cup Winners: (35 times) 1892, 1899, 1900, 1904, 1907, 1908, 1911, 1912, 1914, 1923, 1925, 1927, 1931, 1933, 1937, 1951, 1954, 1965, 1967, 1969, 1971, 1972, 1974, 1975, 1977, 1980, 1985, 1988, 1989, 1995, 2001, 2004, 2005, 2007, 2011. *Runners-up:* 18 times.

CELTIC 2010–11 LEAGUE RECORD

Match No.	Date	Venue	Opponents	Result	H/T Score	Lg Pos.	Goalscorers	Attendance
1	Aug 14	A	Inverness CT	W 1-0	0-0	—	McCourt [56]	7547
2	22	H	St Mirren	W 4-0	2-0	2	Ledley [5], Maloney [23], Forrest [69], Ki [81]	46,812
3	29	A	Motherwell	W 1-0	0-0	1	Murphy (pen) [73]	9207
4	Sept 11	H	Hearts	W 3-0	2-0	1	Forrest [28], Maloney [44], McCourt [90]	49,023
5	19	A	Kilmarnock	W 2-1	1-1	2	Murphy (pen) [41], Stokes [52]	8645
6	25	H	Hibernian	W 2-1	1-0	2	Brown [5], Loovens [51]	48,625
7	Oct 2	H	Hamilton A	W 3-1	1-1	1	Maloney 2 [25, 64], Hooper [71]	47,446
8	17	A	Dundee U	W 2-1	1-1	2	Hooper 2 [13, 89]	11,790
9	24	H	Rangers	L 1-3	1-0	2	Hooper [45]	58,874
10	30	A	St Johnstone	W 3-0	2-0	2	McGinn 2 [2, 89], Izaguirre [41]	6866
11	Nov 6	H	Aberdeen	W 9-0	4-0	2	Stokes 3 (2 pens) [26 (p), 45 (p), 74], Hooper 3 [28, 33, 63], Magennis (og) [61], Ledley [71], McCourt (pen) [85]	48,754
12	10	A	Hearts	L 0-2	0-1	—		15,632
13	14	A	St Mirren	W 1-0	0-0	2	Hooper [90]	6073
14	20	H	Dundee U	D 1-1	1-0	2	Hooper [23]	47,523
15	27	H	Inverness CT	D 2-2	1-0	2	Ki [38], McCourt [65]	46,096
16	Dec 21	H	Kilmarnock	D 1-1	0-0	—	Rogne [84]	44,522
17	26	H	St Johnstone	W 2-0	0-0	2	Cha [89], Ki [90]	41,522
18	29	H	Motherwell	W 1-0	1-0	1	McCourt [27]	40,750
19	Jan 2	A	Rangers	W 2-0	0-0	1	Samaras 2 (1 pen) [62, 70 (p)]	50,222
20	12	A	Hamilton A	D 1-1	0-1	—	Stokes (pen) [90]	5163
21	15	A	Hibernian	W 3-0	1-0	1	Hooper [44], Stokes 2 (1 pen) [50 (p), 65]	13,649
22	22	H	Aberdeen	W 1-0	1-0	1	Stokes [27]	48,717
23	26	H	Hearts	W 4-0	2-0	—	Forrest [7], Stokes 3 [45, 53, 71]	49,460
24	Feb 1	A	Aberdeen	W 3-0	1-0	—	Hooper [12], Wilson [75], Stokes [78]	12,901
25	13	A	Dundee U	W 3-1	2-0	1	Stokes [16], Wilson [36], Majstorovic [78]	11,414
26	20	H	Rangers	W 3-0	2-0	1	Hooper 2 [17, 28], Commons [70]	58,748
27	27	A	Motherwell	L 0-2	0-1	1		9716
28	Mar 5	H	Hamilton A	W 2-0	1-0	1	Commons 2 [42, 52]	51,811
29	Apr 1	H	Hibernian	W 3-1	3-0	—	Stokes [4], Hooper 2 (1 pen) [20 (p), 39]	47,809
30	9	H	St Mirren	W 1-0	0-0	1	Commons [78]	50,318
31	12	A	St Johnstone	W 1-0	1-0	—	Kayal [45]	6338
32	20	A	Kilmarnock	W 4-0	3-0	—	Commons 2 [4, 34], Hooper [41], Stokes [58]	9117
33	24	A	Rangers	D 0-0	0-0	2		50,248
34	May 1	H	Dundee U	W 4-1	1-0	2	Hooper [23], Kayal [54], Commons [85], Murphy [90]	48,599
35	4	A	Inverness CT	L 2-3	1-1	—	Commons 2 (1 pen) [9, 90 (p)]	6702
36	8	A	Kilmarnock	W 2-0	1-0	2	Brown [45], Commons [68]	9720
37	11	A	Hearts	W 3-0	1-0	—	Hooper 2 [12, 49], Commons [78]	16,681
38	15	H	Motherwell	W 4-0	2-0	2	Hooper [29], Samaras [40], Maloney [53], McCourt [71]	57,294

Final League Position: 2

League Cup Winners: (14 times) 1956-57, 1957-58, 1965-66, 1966-67, 1967-68, 1968-69, 1969-70, 1974-75, 1982-83, 1997-98, 1999-2000, 2000-01, 2005-06, 2008-09; *Runners-up:* 15 times.

European: *European Cup:* 140 matches (1966-67 winners, 1967-68, 1968-69, 1969-70 runners-up, 1970-71, 1971-72, 1972-73, 1973-74 semi-finals, 1974-75, 1977-78, 1979-80, 1981-82, 1982-83, 1986-87, 1988-89, 1998-99, 2001-02, 2002-03, 2003-04, 2004-05, 2005-06, 2006-07, 2007-08, 2008-09, 2009-10, 2010-11). *Cup Winners' Cup:* 28 matches (1963-64 semi-finals, 1965-66 semi-finals, 1975-76, 1980-81, 1984-85, 1985-86, 1989-90, 1995-96). *UEFA Cup:* 75 matches (*Fairs Cup:* 1962-63, 1964-65. *UEFA Cup:* 1976-77, 1983-84, 1987-88, 1991-92, 1992-93, 1993-94, 1996-97, 1997-98, 1998-99, 1999-2000, 2000-01, 2001-02, 2002-03 runners-up, 2003-04 quarter-finals). *Europa League:* 8 matches (2009-10, 2010-11).

Club colours: Shirt: Emerald green and white hoops. Shorts: White with emerald green trim. Stockings: White with emerald green trim.

Goalscorers: *League (85):* Hooper 20 (1 pen), Stokes 15 (4 pens), Commons 11 (1 pen), McCourt 6 (1 pen), Maloney 5, Forrest 3, Ki 3, Murphy 3 (2 pens), Samaras 3 (1 pen), Brown 2, Kayal 2, Ledley 2, McGinn 2, Wilson 2, Cha 1, Izaguirre 1, Loovens 1, Majstorovic 1, Rogne 1, own goal 1.
Scottish Cup (14): Ledley 3, Brown 2, Commons 2 (1 pen), Mulgrew 2, Ki 1, Majstorovic 1, Maloney 1, Wilson 1, own goal 1.
CIS Cup (14): Stokes 5 (2 pens), Samaras 3, Commons 1, Hooper 1, Ledley 1, McGinn 1, Mulgrew 1, Rogne 1.
Champions League (2): Hooper 1, Juarez 1.
Europa League (2): Juarez 1, Samaras 1.

Zaluska L 2	Cha D 14+2	Mulgrew C 20+3	Brown S 26+2	Loovens G 13	Hooiveld J 4+1	McCourt P 8+17	Ledley J 26+3	Samaras G 16+6	Maloney S 15+6	Fortune M 2	Forrest J 15+4	Juarez E 5+8	Kayal B 18+3	Majstorovic D 32	Ki S 18+8	Murphy D 9+9	Forster F 36	Izaguirre E 33	Stokes A 22+7	Hooper G 26	Crosas M —+1	Wilson M 25	Rogne T 14+2	McGinn N 6+5	Towell R —+1	Kapo O 1+1	Ljungberg F 1+6	Commons K 11+3	Toshney L —+1	Match No.
1	2	3	4	5	6	7¹	8	9	10	11²	12	13																		1
1			4		6	12	8	9¹	10	11³	7	2	3²	5	13	14														2
	2		4		6	12	8	9	10		7			5	11		1	3	9³											3
	2		4¹		6	14	8	13	11		7	12		5	10²		1	3	9³											4
	2		4⁷	5		7¹	8		10			13	11³		14	9	1	3	12											5
	2	3¹	4	6			8	13	11		7			5	12		1	3	9	10²										6
	2		4	5			8	9¹	11		3¹		6	7	13		1	3	14	10²	12									7
			5			12	8	9	7¹		6			4			1	3	11	10		2								8
			5			13	8	9	11¹		12		6	4			1	3	7²	10		2								9
	2					8	9						5	4			1	3	10		11	6	7							10
	2		12	13	8		11				14		5	4³			1	3	9	10²		6⁸		7¹						11
	12		6		8⁸	7	11						5	4			1	3	9²	10		2¹		13						12
	7²				14		11				4²		5	8	13		1	3	9¹	10		2	6	12						13
	2				13	8	12	11			14		5	7	9²		1	3		10³		2	6	4¹						14
	2	3	6²	12	8		11¹						5	7	9³		1	3	14	10		4		13						15
	2		13		14	8²		11					5	4	9		1	3	12	10¹		6	7²							16
	2		4		11³	10¹					14		5	7	9²		1	3	12			6	8		13					17
		4⁸			7	8		11³				13	5	12²		1	3	9				2	6	14	10¹					18
	11				9	8	10				7¹		4	5			1	3				2	6	12						19
	11	12			10	8³					7⁸	4¹	5				1	3	9			2²	6	13			14			20
	14	8			11³	12					7	4¹	5				1	3	9	10²		2	6				13			21
	12	4			11²	14					8³	5¹					1	3	9	10		2	6	7			13			22
	5	4			12	11					7¹	13	8²				1	3	9	10³		2	6							23
	5	4³			12	8					6	7¹			13		1	3	9²	10²	2						11	14		24
	6	7³			8	13					4	5	12				1	3	9²	10	2						14	11¹		25
	6	8			7	9		13			4¹	5	12				1	3	14	10³	2						11²			26
	6	8			7	13		14	12		5	4³					1	3	9²	10	2¹						11			27
	6	7		14		9		13			8	5¹	4				1	3	10²		2	12					11³			28
	6	7	5¹		8			11²			4³						1	3	9	10	2	12		14	13				29
	2	6		5		13		12		11		4	8²				1	3	9	10¹	2						7³	14		30
	6	7	5		13	8	9²	12			4			10			1	3			2						11¹			31
	6	8			14	7		4¹	5	12					1	3³		9	10	2		13		11²						32
	6	8			11¹	9		4	5	7					1	3	13	10²	2		12									33
	6	8³			13			7¹			4	5	12	14	1	3	9	10²	2		11									34
	6	8			13			7			4³	5	14	12	1	3	9¹	10²	2		11									35
	13	8			14			12			7¹	5	4	9	1	3²	10³	2	6		11									36
13	6	8	4			9²	12				3¹		5	7	14	1	10	2²	11⁸											37
	6	8	4		13		9³	12			11²	14	5	7	1	3¹		10	2											38

CLYDE   Third Division

Year Formed: 1877. *Ground & Address:* Broadwood Stadium, Cumbernauld, G68 9NE. *Telephone:* 01236 451511.
Fax: 01236 733490. *E-mail:* info@clydefc.co.uk *Website:* www.clydefc.co.uk
Ground Capacity: all seated: 8006. *Size of Pitch:* 112yd × 76yd.
Chairman: John Alexander. *Secretary:* John D. Taylor. *Director of Football:* Neill Watt.
Manager: Jim Duffy. *Assistant Manager:* Chic Charnley. *Physio:* Iain McKinlay.
Club Nickname: The Bully Wee.
Previous Grounds: Barrowfield Park 1877-97, Shawfield Stadium 1897-1986, Firhill Stadium 1986-91, Douglas Park 1991-94.
Record Attendance: 52,000 v Rangers, Division I, 21 Nov 1908.
Record Transfer Fee received: £200,000 from Blackburn R for Gordon Greer (May 2001).
Record Transfer Fee paid: £14,000 for Harry Hood from Sunderland (1966).
Record Victory: 11-1 v Cowdenbeath, Division II, 6 Oct 1951.
Record Defeat: 0-11 v Dumbarton, Scottish Cup 4th rd, 22 Nov, 1879; v Rangers, Scottish Cup 4th rd, 13 Nov 1880.
Most Capped Player: Tommy Ring, 12, Scotland.
Most League Appearances: 420: Brian Ahern, 1971-81; 1987-88.
Most League Goals in Season (Individual): 32: Bill Boyd, 1932-33.

CLYDE 2010–11 LEAGUE RECORD

Match No.	Date		Venue	Opponents		Result	H/T Score	Lg Pos.	Goalscorers	Atten- dance
1	Aug	7	H	Stranraer	D	2-2	2-1	—	McCusker 2 [10, 25]	827
2		14	A	Queen's Park	W	1-0	0-0	4	McCusker [50]	849
3		21	H	Berwick R	L	1-4	0-1	6	McCusker [59]	772
4		28	H	Albion R	L	1-2	1-1	8	Dingwall [37]	1014
5	Sept	11	A	East Stirling	D	0-0	0-0	7		532
6		18	H	Annan Ath	L	0-2	0-1	9		1043
7		25	A	Montrose	L	1-8	0-2	10	Lithgow [80]	424
8	Oct	2	H	Elgin C	D	1-1	0-0	7	Strachan (pen) [76]	881
9		16	A	Arbroath	L	2-3	0-0	10	Paterson [48], Lithgow [83]	481
10		30	A	Albion R	L	1-3	0-3	10	Mills [80]	473
11	Nov	6	H	East Stirling	L	1-2	1-2	10	Mills [21]	652
12		13	A	Berwick R	L	1-2	0-0	10	Lithgow [63]	432
13	Jan	15	A	East Stirling	L	0-2	0-0	10		467
14		29	A	Montrose	L	1-3	1-0	10	McCusker [45]	422
15	Feb	5	H	Annan Ath	L	0-2	0-1	10		568
16		12	H	Elgin C	D	3-3	2-1	10	Stewart [4], McCusker (pen) [41], Paterson [68]	600
17		15	H	Berwick R	W	2-0	1-0	—	Stewart [13], Finlayson [88]	385
18		22	H	Albion R	L	0-1	0-1	—		507
19		26	H	Stranraer	W	4-2	1-1	10	McCusker 2 (1 pen) [11, 55 (p)], Scullion [67], Waddell [83]	703
20	Mar	1	A	Stranraer	L	1-3	0-1	—	Stewart [49]	307
21		5	A	Queen's Park	L	0-4	0-3	10		1148
22		8	H	Queen's Park	L	2-3	1-2	—	McCusker [25], Paterson [57]	502
23		19	A	Albion R	D	1-1	1-1	10	McCusker [14]	523
24		22	H	Arbroath	D	1-1	0-0	—	Sawyers [70]	532
25		26	H	Montrose	W	2-0	1-0	10	Stewart [20], Sawyers [81]	725
26		29	A	Annan Ath	W	2-0	1-0	—	McCluskey [18], Scullion [65]	465
27	Apr	2	A	Annan Ath	L	0-1	0-1	10		585
28		5	H	Montrose	D	1-1	0-0	—	Scullion [85]	516
29		9	H	Arbroath	L	0-3	0-2	10		725
30		13	A	Arbroath	L	0-2	0-2	—		604
31		16	A	Elgin C	W	1-0	1-0	10	McCusker [4]	621
32		19	H	East Stirling	W	2-0	0-0	—	Stewart 2 (1 pen) [53 (p), 75]	591
33		23	A	Berwick R	D	1-1	0-0	10	Stewart (pen) [62]	427
34		26	A	Elgin C	W	1-0	0-0	—	Stewart [83]	272
35		30	H	Queen's Park	L	0-2	0-1	9		1021
36	May	7	A	Stranraer	L	0-3	0-1	10		439

Final League Position: 10

Honours
League Champions: Division II 1904-05, 1951-52, 1956-57, 1961-62, 1972-73. Second Division 1977-78, 1981-82, 1992-93, 1999-2000.
Runners-up: Division II 1903-04, 1905-06, 1925-26, 1963-64. First Division 2002-03, 2003-04.
Scottish Cup Winners: 1939, 1955, 1958; *Runners-up:* 1910, 1912, 1949.
League Challenge Cup Runners-up: 2006-07.

Club colours: Shirt: White with red trim. Shorts: Black. Stockings: Red.

Goalscorers: *League (37):* McCusker 11 (2 pens), Stewart 8 (2 pens), Lithgow 3, Paterson 3, Scullion 3, Mills 2, Sawyers 2, Dingwall 1, Finlayson 1, McCluskey 1, Strachan 1 (1 pen), Waddell 1.
Scottish Cup (1): Finlayson 1.
CIS Cup (4): McCusker 3, Strachan 1.
Alba Challenge Cup (1): Strachan 1.

Hutchison J 15	Park A 21+2	McMillan R 30	Henderson M 5+2	McGowan N 22+5	Finlayson K 29+2	Stevenson C 6+12	Sweeney J 25+5	Strachan A 13	McCusker M 21	Dingwall B 6+3	Stewart J 19+11	Lithgow A 20+2	Sawyers W 10+10	Girvan G 10+4	Connolly K 1	Mills S 4+7	Waddell R 26+5	Paterson N 15+1	Allan J 6	Gray I 11+1	Anson S 2	Cochrane H 2+7	Brown G 14+1	McMullan P 1	Halliwell B 15	MacBeth R 5	Scullion J 18+1	Mulrooney P 3+3	Thomson D 1+4	Miller C 4+1	Gramoviti A 7+2	McCluskey J 9	Match No.
1	2	3	4	5	6	7	8	9	10	11^1	12																						1
1	2	3		5	6	7	8	9	10^2	11^1	13	4		12																			2
1	2	3		5^1	6	7	8	9	10	11^2		4	13	12																			3
1	2		4		3	7			10	11	8^1	9^1	13	5		6^2	12																4
1	2	3		5		7	12	9^1	8		11	13	4	10^2		6																	5
1	2		4	5		7^2	9	12	8^1	10^3	13	3	14			11	6																6
1	2	7^4	4		12		10	9		11^2	13	3	8^4			5	6^1																7
	2		4	12	6^1	13	8	9		14	11^3	3	10^2			5	7		1														8
	2	4^1	12	3^8	6^2		13	11		14	10	5	8			9^3	7		1														9
	3		7^4	13	9^1	10		11^1	4		12	6^2	8			1	2	5	14														10
	4		3		14	9	10^2		13^4	5		11	7^3	8		1	2	6^1	12														11
1	2^1	3	13	5	6		8^3	9	10		4^4	11^2		12		14	7																12
	2^1	3	4	6^2	14	5	8	10		12		11	13	7		9^3	1																13
1	14		5					10	13	4	11^2	3		9		7	8					12	2^3	6^1									14
1	12	4		3	7		9		11^3	13	5		6	14	8							10^2	2^1										15
	2	4		3	7	13	12		11^8		10	5^1				9^2	8								1		6						16
	2	5		3	12	13			11^3							9	8						6^2		1		7		4	10^1	14		17
	3	4		5	9		13^8		11							6^3	7^1					14	2		1		8		10^2	12			18
1	4			3	7				10^2		11					12	13		5			2^3				8	6	14		9^1			19
1	4			3^2	7	14			11							12	10^3	8	6			2					5	13	9^1				20
	3	4		5	8				9							11		12				2^1			1		6	7^2	13	14	10^3		21
	5			3	8		2				13	6				12	9^1								1		7^3	4	11	14	10^2		22
	3			5^1	9	8		11	10							12	6								1		4		7				23
	4				7		10	11^1		12	2					5	6						13		1		3			8	9^2		24
	4				7	12	11	10^2		13						6		5							1		3			8^1	9		25
	3			6	7	10		11								5		2							1		4			8	9		26
4^3	3	14	8	7^2		10^1	11	12								5		2							1		6			13	9		27
	5			7	6	10^3	14	13	11^1		3					2^8		1									4	12	8^2	9			28
2	3^1		9	13	8	10	11^3	12	14		4							1									5	7^2	6				29
	3		14	6	10	5	11	12	7^2		9	13	2^1	1		4		8^3															30
1	5	4	13	7	9	11		12	2		6						8^1					3									10^2		31
6^3	5		3	8	9^2	7	11	12	4		13		2										1		14						10^1		32
1		3		13		12	7	10	4	11		9		6		5^1					2									8^2			33
		5		7	8^1	9		11^3	4	14	12	10^2		1	6	13^2				3													34
	5		3	8	13	7		11	4	12	6^2	10^3		2	14		1													9^1			35
1	3^1		12	8	9		10	4	11	14	7^2		6		5^3		2						13										36

COWDENBEATH Second Division

Year Formed: 1881. *Ground & Address:* Central Park, Cowdenbeath KY4 9QQ. *Telephone:* 01383 610166. *Fax:* 01383 512132.
E-mail: bluebrazil@cowdenbeathfc.com *Website:* www.cowdenbeathfc.com
Ground Capacity: total: 4370, seated: 1431. *Size of Pitch:* 98m × 59m.
Chairman: Donald Findlay QC. *Secretary:* Alex Anderson.
Club Nicknames: The Blue Brazil, Cowden, The Miners.
Manager: Colin Cameron. *Assistant Manager:* Lee Makel. *Physio:* Ian McIvor.
Previous Grounds: North End Park, Cowdenbeath.
Record Attendance: 25,586 v Rangers, League Cup quarter-final, 21 Sept 1949.
Record Transfer Fee received: £30,000 for Nicky Henderson to Falkirk (March 1994).
Record Victory: 12-0 v Johnstone, Scottish Cup 1st rd, 21 Jan 1928.
Record Defeat: 1-11 v Clyde, Division II, 6 Oct 1951.
Most Capped Player: Jim Paterson, 3, Scotland.
Most League and Cup Appearances: 491 Ray Allan 1972-75, 1979-89.
Most League Goals in Season (Individual): 54, Rab Walls, Division II, 1938-39.
Most Goals Overall (Individual): 127, Willie Devlin, 1922-26, 1929-30.

COWDENBEATH 2010–11 LEAGUE RECORD

Match No.	Date	Venue	Opponents	Result	H/T Score	Lg Pos.	Goalscorers	Attendance
1	Aug 7	H	Ross Co	L 0-2	0-0	—		481
2	14	A	Stirling A	W 3-1	0-1	4	Sibanda [61], Brett [70], Dempster [77]	820
3	22	H	Queen of the S	L 1-3	0-1	8	McKenzie [65]	672
4	28	H	Partick Th	W 2-1	1-1	6	Fairbairn [18], Dempster [54]	881
5	Sept 11	A	Morton	W 2-1	0-0	4	Ramsay [52], Dempster [72]	1839
6	18	A	Dunfermline Ath	L 1-2	1-0	5	Dempster [7]	4316
7	25	H	Dundee	W 2-1	2-0	4	Ramsay [12], Fairbairn [44]	1154
8	Oct 2	A	Falkirk	L 1-5	0-3	5	Ramsay (pen) [83]	3764
9	16	H	Raith R	L 1-2	0-0	6	Cameron [79]	1508
10	23	H	Morton	D 2-2	2-2	6	McKenzie [16], Cameron [24]	582
11	30	A	Partick Th	L 0-1	0-0	6		1841
12	Nov 6	H	Stirling A	W 5-1	2-1	6	Allison (og) [19], Stewart [27], Ramsay [53], Fairbairn [73], Miller [82]	507
13	13	A	Queen of the S	L 0-3	0-2	6		1782
14	Dec 14	A	Dundee	L 0-3	0-1	—		3503
15	29	A	Dunfermline Ath	L 0-5	0-1	—		2942
16	Jan 15	A	Morton	L 0-3	0-1	7		1375
17	Feb 5	A	Ross Co	D 1-1	0-1	7	Fitzpatrick (og) [52]	2020
18	12	A	Dunfermline Ath	L 0-4	0-0	9		2192
19	15	H	Partick Th	D 1-1	1-0	—	Campbell (pen) [8]	411
20	19	H	Raith R	L 0-3	0-3	8		1413
21	26	A	Falkirk	L 0-2	0-1	9		3581
22	Mar 1	H	Queen of the S	D 2-2	1-1	—	Campbell (pen) [36], Stewart [90]	670
23	5	A	Stirling A	W 4-3	0-1	9	Ramsay 2 (1 pen) [77, 82 (p)], Campbell [89], Stewart [90]	735
24	8	H	Dundee	L 1-3	0-1	—	Stewart [55]	977
25	15	A	Raith R	L 1-2	0-1	—	Stewart [51]	1495
26	19	H	Partick Th	W 1-0	0-0	8	Stewart [50]	1754
27	22	H	Morton	L 0-2	0-1	—		359
28	26	A	Dundee	D 2-2	1-1	9	Crawford [9], Linton [57]	4311
29	29	H	Falkirk	D 0-0	0-0	—		803
30	Apr 2	H	Dunfermline Ath	L 0-1	0-0	9		2104
31	5	H	Ross Co	W 2-1	2-0	—	Ramsay [6], Linton [21]	296
32	9	A	Raith R	D 2-2	0-0	—	Stewart 2 [55, 70]	2284
33	16	H	Falkirk	L 1-2	1-0	9	Stewart [32]	636
34	23	A	Queen of the S	D 2-2	2-2	9	Campbell 2 (1 pen) [2, 31 (p)]	1102
35	30	H	Stirling A	W 1-0	0-0	9	Crawford [79]	415
36	May 7	A	Ross Co	L 0-3	0-1	9		2886

Final League Position: 9

Honours
League Champions: Division II 1913-14, 1914-15, 1938-39; *Champions:* Third Division 2005-06. *Runners-up:* Division II 1921-22, 1923-24, 1969-70. Second Division 1991-92. *Runners-up:* Third Division 2000-01, 2008-09. *Promoted to First Division:* 2009-10 (play-offs).
Scottish Cup: Quarter-finals 1931.
League Cup: Semi-finals 1959-60, 1970-71.

Club colours: Shirt: Royal blue with white sleeves. Shorts: White. Stockings: Royal blue.

Goalscorers: *League (41):* Stewart 9, Ramsay 7 (2 pens), Campbell 5 (3 pens), Dempster 4, Fairbairn 3, Cameron 2, Crawford 2, Linton 2, McKenzie 2, Brett 1, Miller 1, Sibanda 1, own goals 2.
Scottish Cup (0).
CIS Cup (1): Ramsay 1.
Alba Challenge Cup (1): Armstrong 1.
Play-Offs (2): Coult 1, Linton 1.

Hay D 30	Baxter M 26	Armstrong J 21	Linton S 28+5	O'Brien T 10+3	McKenzie M 16+14	Winter C 30	Cameron C 25+1	Ramsay M 32+3	Dempster J 17+1	Fairbairn B 7+6	Brett D 3+2	Stewart G 16+16	Adamson K 26	Sibanda L 4+7	Robertson J 17+5	Mbu J 8+1	Ferguson J 4+3	Smith M 3+2	Old S 4	Vauls R 6+2	Wilson L —+1	Roy L 6	Miller K 7+2	Byran P 2	Coult L 9+8	Crawford S 15+3	Makel L 9+1	Campbell A 13+4	Malcolm R 2	Milne L —+1	Match No.
1	2	3	4	5¹	6	7	8	9	10²	11	12	13																			1
1	2¹	3	5	13	6²	8	7	10	11	14	12			4	9³																2
1		2	4¹		6	7	8³	10	11	13	5	14	3	9²	12																3
1	2	3	5		7	6	9	8¹	10²	11		13	4	12																	4
1	2	4¹	5	8²	9	7	10	6	11¹		14	3	13	12																	5
1	2	3	6		10	8²	9	7	11¹³	12		13	5	14		4															6
1	2	3²	5	13	9¹	6	8	7	11³	10		14	4				12														7
1		8		4	6	7	10²	9¹	3	13	2	14	5³		11	12															8
1	2		3		9	5	7	6	11¹	10²		12		13	4		8														9
1*	2	4	10	6	8		11²		13				9	7			3⁶	5¹	12	15											10
	2	4	10	6	8	9	11	12	13				7²				3¹	5		1											11
1	2¹	6		8	9³	7	10	13	11			14	12	3	5²		4														12
1		4	12	5	7	9³	10²	6	2	11		14		13	3			8¹													13
1	2	4	3		6	7	8	11	10³	12		13		9²	14	5¹															14
1	2	3	4		12	7	6	5²	11³	8¹		14	13		9							10									15
1	2	4	3		12	5	8	14	13	11¹		14		7³		10		6					9²								16
1		2	5		9¹	7	8	12	10³				4	13								14	3	6²11							17
1		4			3	7	12	10³		14	8		2				5¹						13	11	9²	6						18
1	2				6		9			11²	4		12	3¹				7				13	5	8	10						19
1	2	13		14	6	8	7			11²	4			3							9¹	12	5³		10						20
1	2	3	12			10	8			14	5¹			4					13			6²	7³	9	11						21
1	2	3	6		12		10	8					13	5²			4						7		9¹	11					22
1	2	3	13		14		8³	10		12			5				4¹					6²	7		11	9					23
1	6	3	4		12		7	8					11	5								13	2¹		10	9²					24
1	6	2²12		13	3	7³	9			8	5		14	4¹									11		10						25
1	2				12	5	8			10²	3		9				4				6		13	7¹11						26
1	2	5			12	6	8			10	3		7				4³				13		14	9²	11¹					27
1	2		6	12	8	7			10				11²	3			9				4¹			13	5					28
1	2	4	7	8	6		9						11²	3			10						12	5¹	13					29
1	2	4	10	8¹	7		6						3	9									12	5	11					30
1	2	5	9³14		8		7						11	3			10			13			4²	6¹	12					31
	2	5	9		8		7						11²	3			10			1			4	6¹12	13					32
	2²	5	8	14	7	13	9						11	3			10			1			4³	6¹	12					33
		4	7	13	6	8⁸	9						11¹	2⁸			5			1			3²12	10						34
		3	5	6	12		7						11			8						1	10¹	2	4	9				35
		2	12	8¹	6		7²						3	4		11					1	10	9		5			13		36

DUMBARTON

Second Division

Year Formed: 1872. *Ground:* Strathclyde Homes Stadium, Castle Road, Dumbarton G82 1JJ. *Telephone:* 01389 762569.
Fax: 01389 762629. *E-mail:* david_prophet58@hotmail.com *Website:* www.dumbartonfootballclub.com
Ground Capacity: total: 2025. *Size of Pitch:* 110yd × 75yd.
Joint Chairmen: Colin Hosie and Alan Jardine. *Club Secretary:* David Prophet. *Chief Executive Officer:* Gilbert Lawrie.
Manager: Alan Adamson. *Assistant Manager:* Peter Allan. *Physio:* Beth Sleith.
Club Nickname: The Sons.
Previous Grounds: Broadmeadow, Ropework Lane, Townend Ground, Boghead Park, Cliftonhill Stadium.
Record Attendance: 18,000 v Raith Rovers, Scottish Cup, 2 Mar 1957.
Record Transfer Fee received: £125,000 for Graeme Sharp to Everton (March 1982).
Record Transfer Fee paid: £50,000 for Charlie Gibson from Stirling Albion (1989).
Record Victory: 13-1 v Kirkintilloch Central. 1st rd, 1 Sept 1888.
Record Defeat: 1-11 v Albion Rovers, Division II; 30 Jan, 1926: v Ayr United, League Cup, 13 Aug 1952.
Most Capped Player: James McAulay, 9, Scotland.
Most League Appearances: 297: Andy Jardine, 1957-67.
Most Goals in Season (Individual): 38: Kenny Wilson, Division II, 1971-72. *(League and Cup):* 46 Hughie Gallacher, 1955-56.
Most Goals Overall (Individual): 169: Hughie Gallacher, 1954-62 (including C Division 1954-55). *(League and Cup):* 202 Hughie Gallacher, 1954-62

DUMBARTON 2010–11 LEAGUE RECORD

Match No.	Date		Venue	Opponents	Result		H/T Score	Lg Pos.	Goalscorers	Attendance
1	Aug	7	A	Forfar Ath	L	1-4	1-1	—	Chaplain (pen) [5]	510
2		14	H	Livingston	L	1-2	0-1	10	Chaplain (pen) [70]	643
3		21	A	Ayr U	L	0-1	0-1	10		1242
4		28	A	East Fife	L	0-6	0-3	6		687
5	Sept	11	H	Stenhousemuir	W	1-0	0-0	9	Carcary [77]	600
6		18	A	Alloa Ath	D	0-0	0-0	9		559
7		25	H	Brechin C	L	1-3	0-2	10	Carcary [73]	626
8	Oct	2	H	Airdrie U	L	1-3	0-0	10	Maxwell [67]	812
9		16	A	Peterhead	L	0-1	0-0	10		496
10		23	A	Stenhousemuir	L	0-4	0-3	10		392
11		30	H	East Fife	W	4-1	1-1	10	McShane [31], Durie (og) [46], Gilhaney 2 [89, 90]	585
12	Nov	6	A	Livingston	L	0-2	0-1	10		1417
13		13	H	Ayr U	W	3-2	1-0	10	Cook (pen) [29], Walker [54], Campbell [84]	811
14	Jan	2	A	Ayr U	L	0-2	0-1	—		1224
15		15	H	Stenhousemuir	L	0-1	0-0	10		490
16		18	H	Alloa Ath	W	4-1	2-0	—	McNiff [14], Walker [41], Carcary [53], Geggan [80]	350
17		25	H	Forfar Ath	L	1-2	1-0	—	Walker [26]	404
18		29	H	Brechin C	L	1-2	0-1	10	Gilhaney [86]	565
19	Feb	1	A	Airdrie U	W	2-1	1-0	—	Gilhaney [21], Walker [48]	591
20		5	A	Alloa Ath	W	3-2	1-0	8	Walker [35], McShane [57], McStay [74]	483
21		12	H	Airdrie U	D	1-1	1-0	9	McShane [4]	723
22		15	A	East Fife	W	3-1	2-1	—	Walker [17], Gilhaney [23], Geggan [55]	392
23		19	A	Peterhead	W	2-1	1-0	6	McStay [25], McShane [78]	388
24		22	H	Peterhead	W	3-0	1-0	—	Gilhaney 2 [32, 54], McShane [60]	376
25		26	A	Forfar Ath	L	1-2	1-1	7	McShane [36]	487
26	Mar	1	A	Brechin C	D	3-3	1-1	—	McShane 2 [11, 85], Walker [65]	411
27		5	H	Livingston	L	0-3	0-2	8		853
28		19	H	East Fife	W	4-2	1-1	6	Geggan [39], McShane 2 [51, 77], Gilhaney [68]	615
29		26	A	Brechin C	L	0-6	0-1	7		514
30		29	A	Stenhousemuir	D	2-2	0-0	—	McShane 2 [50, 68]	398
31	Apr	2	H	Alloa Ath	D	2-2	1-0	7	McLeish [36], Geggan [49]	640
32		9	H	Peterhead	W	5-2	2-0	7	McShane [28], Walker [40], Halsman [64], Gilhaney (pen) [73], McLeish [82]	526
33		16	A	Airdrie U	L	1-2	1-0	7	Halsman [16]	773
34		23	H	Ayr U	L	1-2	0-2	7	Malone (og) [63]	830
35		30	A	Livingston	D	1-1	1-0	7	Walker [42]	1549
36	May	7	H	Forfar Ath	D	0-0	0-0	7		787

Final League Position: 7

Honours
League Champions: Division I 1890-91 (shared with Rangers), 1891-92. Division II 1910-11, 1971-72. Second Division 1991-92. Third Division 2008-09; *Runners-up:* First Division 1983-84. Division II 1907-08. Second Division 1994-95. Third Division 2001-02.
Scottish Cup Winners: 1883; *Runners-up:* 1881, 1882, 1887, 1891, 1897.

Club colours: Amber with black trim and white flashes.

Goalscorers: *League (52):* McShane 13, Gilhaney 9 (1 pen), Walker 9, Geggan 4, Carcary 3, Chaplain 2 (2 pens), Halsman 2, McLeish 2, McStay 2, Campbell 1, Cook 1 (1 pen), Maxwell 1, McNiff 1, own goals 2.
Scottish Cup (1): Geggan 1.
CIS Cup (1): Carcary 1.
Alba Challenge Cup (0).

Grindley S 30	Nugent P 32	McManus A 8	Gordon B 32	Chisholm I 11+5	McNiff M 24+3	Geggan A 33+1	McStay R 25+5	Maxwell P 5+4	Campbell R 8+9	Carcary D 8+14	Cook A 4+5	McShane J 25+4	Wilson G 3+1	Creaney J 25	Gilhaney M 24+5	Smith G 1+3	White M 6	Smith S 6	Wallace T 3+1	Brannan K 5+8	Hunter R 1	Metcalf R 1+3	Devlin N 21	McGowan M 1	McLeish C 7+3	Walker P 24	Linsay J 2	Devlin J 2	Halsman J 13+1	White J 1+7	Match No.
1	2	3	4	5	6	7	8¹	9²	10³	11	12	13	14																		1
1	2³	3	4	13	5	6	7²	12	10	11¹	9	14	8																		2
1	2	3	4	10	7	6	8¹	9²		12		13	11³	5	14																3
1	2	3	4		6	7¹	12		10		11	8²	5	9	13																4
	2⁴	4	3	6	13	8²	9	11³		12	10¹		14	1	5	7															5
	4	5	2	9	7	6¹	10²	11³	12	13		1	3	8	14																6
	3²	4	2	6	7	8	12	14	11	13	10¹	1	5		9³																7
1		4	5	2	6	7²	8	12	10	11³	9	14	3¹	13																	8
1	3		4	2³	6	7	8¹	13	11	12		5	9²	10	14																9
1	3		4		7	6		8	10²		12	13	9	14	5¹								2		11³						10
1	5		4	14	8	7		10²		12	9¹	3	13		11					6³	2										11
1	5		4		7	6²	13		11		9	3	10¹		12					2	8										12
1	3		13	6	7		12	5	11	4	9				2²	8	10¹														13
1	3		7	8	14	13	12	5	4¹				10²	2	9³	11	6														14
1	3		6	7	13	14	10³	5		12				9¹	2	8²	11	4													15
1	5		4	10	8	13	12	6		9¹	3	7		2	11²																16
1	5		4	7	6	13	10¹	8		3	9	12		11	2²																17
1	3		4	2	7⁸	6	8¹	10	9²	12	13	5	11																		18
1	4		3	7	6		12		10					5	9¹								2		11				8		19
1	3		4	7	8		12		11					5	9										10¹	2	6				20
1	4		3	8	7		12	13	10²					5	9								2		11¹		6				21
1	5		4	13	7	8¹	12		10					3	9								2		11²		6				22
1	4		3	7	6		12		10					5	9								2		11¹		8				23
1	4		3	14	7	8	13	12	11					5	9								2³		10²		6¹				24
1	5		4	14	7	8³	13	12	11					3	9								2		10²		6¹				25
1	4		3	6	7	8	12	11						5¹	9								2		10						26
1			4	6	7	8	10		3					9								2		13	11¹			5²	12	27
1	4		3	2	6	7	8	13	10²					5	9										11¹			12		28
1	4		3	2	6	8	7	13	10					5¹	9³										11²		14	12		29
1	4		3	6	7									10	5	9							2		8	11					30
	3		4	13	6	7³	10							5	9	1				14			2		8²	11¹			12		31
	3		4	14	7	8³	10¹							5	9	1				2			13		11	6²			12		32
	5		4	7	8²	12	3	9								1				2			13		11	6			10¹		33
1	5		4	8	7	12	3	9						14						2					11³	6¹			13		34
1	5		4	2	8	7	10²	3	9¹					13						11					6				12		35
1	3		4	8	7	10	5	11	12	13				2	9²					6¹											36

DUNDEE

First Division

Year Formed: 1893. *Ground & Address:* Dens Park Stadium, Sandeman St, Dundee DD3 7JY. *Telephone:* 01382 889966.
Fax: 01382 832284. *E-mail:* laura@dundeefc.co.uk *Website:* www.thedees.co.uk
Ground Capacity: all seated: 11,760. *Size of Pitch:* 101m × 66m.
Operations/Company Secretary: Jim Thomson. *Club Secretary:* Laura Hayes (tel: 01382 826104; mob: 07855 410 929).
Email: laura@dundeefc.co.uk
Manager: Barry Smith. *Player-Assistant Managers:* Matthew Lockwood and Robert Douglas. *Youth Development Coach:* Gordon Wallace. *Physio:* Karen Gibson.
Club Nicknames: The Dark Blues or The Dee.
Previous Grounds: Carolina Port 1893-98.
Record Attendance: 43,024 v Rangers, Scottish Cup, 1953.
Record Transfer Fee received: £1,200,000 for Robert Douglas to Celtic (2000).
Record Transfer Fee paid: £600,000 for Fabian Caballero (2000).
Record Victory: 10-0 Division II v Alloa, 9 Mar 1947 and v Dunfermline Ath, 22 Mar 1947.
Record Defeat: 0-11 v Celtic, Division I, 26 Oct 1895.
Most Capped Player: Alex Hamilton, 24, Scotland.
Most League Appearances: 400: Barry Smith, 1995-2006.
Most League Goals in Season (Individual): 52: Alan Gilzean, 1960-64.
Most Goals Overall (Individual): 113: Alan Gilzean 1960-64.

DUNDEE 2010–11 LEAGUE RECORD

Match No.	Date		Venue	Opponents	Result		H/T Score	Lg Pos.	Goalscorers	Atten- dance
1	Aug	7	H	Queen of the S	W	1-0	1-0	—	Harkins [23]	4644
2		14	A	Partick Th	L	0-1	0-0	5		2801
3		21	H	Ross Co	D	0-0	0-0	6		3946
4		28	H	Falkirk	W	2-0	2-0	3	O'Donnell [43], Riley [45]	4557
5	Sept	11	A	Dunfermline Ath	L	1-3	0-2	5	Harkins [51]	4037
6		18	H	Raith R	D	0-0	0-0	7		4532
7		25	A	Cowdenbeath	L	1-2	0-2	7	Griffiths [82]	1154
8	Oct	2	H	Morton	W	2-1	1-1	6	Lockwood (pen) [25], McMenamin [57]	4068
9		16	A	Stirling A	D	1-1	0-0	5	Griffiths [56]	1578
10		23	H	Dunfermline Ath	D	2-2	0-2	4	Griffiths [48], Higgins [81]	5636
11		30	A	Falkirk	D	3-3	2-0	4	Griffiths [2], Higgins [7], Witteveen [84]	4667
12	Nov	6	H	Partick Th	W	2-1	1-0	4	Griffiths [14], Adams [86]	6022
13		13	A	Ross Co	W	3-0	1-0	4	Griffiths 2 [18, 75], Riley [51]	2331
14	Dec	11	A	Morton	W	1-0	0-0	—	Lockwood (pen) [62]	1568
15		14	H	Cowdenbeath	W	3-0	1-0	—	Forsyth [37], Riley [66], McKeown [68]	3503
16		18	H	Stirling A	W	2-0	1-0	—	O'Donnell [36], Griffiths [46]	3842
17	Jan	2	H	Ross Co	W	2-0	1-0	—	Lockwood (pen) [28], Harkins [83]	4725
18		15	A	Dunfermline Ath	D	0-0	0-0	10		3385
19		22	H	Falkirk	W	1-0	1-0	—	Forsyth [8]	4763
20	Feb	5	A	Queen of the S	W	2-1	1-0	9	Forsyth [35], Higgins [77]	2006
21		12	H	Raith R	W	2-1	0-0	7	Harkins [84], McCann [90]	5105
22		19	A	Stirling A	W	1-0	1-0	7	Higgins [35]	1990
23		22	A	Raith R	W	2-1	1-0	—	Higgins 2 [34, 54]	2716
24		26	H	Morton	D	1-1	1-0	7	Higgins [26]	4769
25	Mar	5	A	Partick Th	D	0-0	0-0	7		2671
26		8	A	Cowdenbeath	W	3-1	1-0	—	Higgins [23], Lockwood (pen) [48], Forsyth [85]	977
27		12	H	Queen of the S	W	2-1	0-1	6	Higgins [65], Forsyth [87]	4242
28		19	A	Falkirk	D	2-2	0-1	6	Irvine [65], Forsyth [81]	4099
29		22	H	Dunfermline Ath	D	1-1	0-1	—	Hyde [71]	4507
30		26	H	Cowdenbeath	D	2-2	1-1	7	Hyde 2 [24, 73]	4311
31	Apr	2	A	Raith R	L	1-2	0-1	7	O'Donnell [71]	3143
32		10	H	Stirling A	D	1-1	0-1	—	McIntosh [50]	4177
33		16	A	Morton	W	3-1	2-0	7	McIntosh 2 [6, 75], Harkins [42]	2069
34		23	A	Ross Co	W	1-0	0-0	7	McIntosh [65]	3205
35		30	H	Partick Th	W	3-2	0-0	5	Forsyth 2 [59, 62], Lockwood (pen) [71]	7746
36	May	7	A	Queen of the S	L	0-3	0-2	6		2590

Final League Position: 6

Honours
League Champions: Division I 1961-62. First Division 1978-79, 1991-92, 1997-98. Division II 1946-47; *Runners-up:* Division I 1902-03, 1906-07, 1908-09, 1948-49. First Division 1980-81, 2007-08, 2009-10.
Scottish Cup Winners: 1910; *Runners-up:* 1925, 1952, 1964, 2003.
League Cup Winners: 1951-52, 1952-53, 1973-74; *Runners-up:* 1967-68, 1980-81, 1995-96.
League Challenge Cup Winners: 2009-10.
B&Q (Centenary) Cup Winners: 1990-91; *Runners-up:* 1994-95.

European: *European Cup:* 8 matches (1962-63 semi-finals). *Cup Winners' Cup:* 2 matches: (1964-65).
UEFA Cup: 22 matches: (*Fairs Cup:* 1967-68 semi-finals. *UEFA Cup:* 1971-72, 1973-74, 1974-75, 2003-04).

Club colours: Shirt: Navy blue. Shorts: White. Stockings: Navy blue.

Goalscorers: *League (54):* Higgins 9, Forsyth 8, Griffiths 8, Harkins 5, Lockwood 5 (5 pens), McIntosh 4, Hyde 3, O'Donnell 3, Riley 3, Adams 1, Irvine 1, McCann 1, McKeown 1, McMenamin 1, Witteveen 1.
Scottish Cup (0).
CIS Cup (5): Griffiths 3 (1 pen), Riley 2.
Alba Challenge Cup (3): Griffiths 1, Higgins 1, McMenamin 1.

Douglas R 34	Irvine G 31	McKeown C 34	Weston R 29+1	Sansara N 1	Forsyth C 26+7	McHale P 1+1	Riley N 32+1	McMenamin C 3+5	Griffiths L 18	O'Donnell S 31+2	Higgins S 19+7	Paton E 3+1	Shimmin D 1	Adams J 11	Grant C 2	Lockwood M 33	Witteveen D 2+3	Fox S 1+1	Kuqi N 3	Misun M 2	Kerr B 2	McIntosh L 7+5	Stewart J 4+6	Robb S 1	Benedictis K 10	Brighton T 3	Greacen —+1	McCann N 2+1	Robertson C 2+1	Bayne G 1+1	Rennie C 4+2	Hyde J 2	Bartlett G 2	Webster G 2+1	Tulleth A —+3	Gibson J 1	Match No.
1	2	3	4	5¹	6	7¹	8³	9⁴	10	11²	12	13	14																								1
1	2	3			5	12	9		10	11	6²	13		4	7	8¹																					2
1	2	4	12		7		8	6	11²	10		13		9¹	3	5																					3
1¹		3	4		9¹	6	12	11⁶	8	13	2			7		5	10²	15																			4
		3	4		12		9	6¹	14	11	8	13	2		7³	5	1	10²																		5
1		3	13		9	6³	12	11	8²	14	2			7		5	10¹	4																		6
1	2	3			8	14	13	11	12	9³				6		5	10²	4¹	7																	7
1	2	4	13		9	5	12	11³	7²	14				6	3	10¹	8																			8
1	2	3	4		12		9	6	10	8	11¹			7		5																				9
1	2	3	4		12		9	6¹	10	7	11			8		5																				10
1	2	3	4		13		9²	6	10	7	11¹			8		5	12																			11
1	2	3	4		12		9	6¹	10²	7	11			8		5	13																			12
1	2	4	5		7		9	6	10¹	8	11				3	12																				13
1	2	3	4		7		8	6	11	9	10¹					5						12														14
1	2	4	5		9		8	6	10²	7	11¹					3						13	12													15
1	2	3	4		7		9	6¹	10²	8	11					5						13	12													16
1	2	3	4		6¹		8		10	9	11					5						12	7													17
1	2	3	4		9		8	6	7	11						5						13	12		5¹	10²										18
1	2	3	4		9		8	6	10	7						5						12							11¹							19
1	2	4	5		7		8	3			11					6							9¹					10	12							20
1	2	4	5		9		8	7	6		11					3						10¹								12						21
1	2⁸	3	4		7		9	6	8		11					5						12							10¹							22
1		2	3		6		8	5	9	10						4						7							11							23
1	2	3	4		7		8	6	9	10						5													11							24
1	2	3	4		7		10	6	8		11					5							9¹								12					25
1	2		4		9		7	6	8	10¹						5						12	3						11							26
1	2	3	4		9		8	6	7	10						5												11								27
1	2	3	4		7		10	6	9							5						11¹	8								12					28
1	2		5		6¹		8		9	7						3						10	4						12	11						29
1	2	3	4		7		9	6	8							5						10							11							30
1	6	3¹	4		9		8									5						11	2								7	10				31
1					5		8	4		9						2						10	3					6					7	11¹	12		32
1	5	2	6		8		9	4		10						3						11	7¹								12					33
1	2	4	6		8		9	7		10						3						11¹	5								12					34
1	2	3	4		8		11	6¹		9						5						7										10			12	35
	2	3			6		8	5		9						4						7										10¹		11	12	1	36

DUNDEE UNITED Premier League

Year Formed: 1909 (1923). *Ground & Address:* Tannadice Park, Tannadice St, Dundee DD3 7JW. *Telephone:* 01382 833166. *Fax:* 01382 889398. *E-mail:* enquiries@dundeeunited.co.uk *Website:* www.dundeeunitedfc.co.uk
Ground Capacity: total: 14,223 all seated: stands: east 2868, west 2096, south 2201, Fair Play 1601, George Fox 5151, executive boxes 292. *Size of Pitch:* 110yd × 72yd.
Chairman: Stephen Thompson, OBE. *Vice-Chairman:* Cath Thompson. *Secretary:* Spence Anderson.
Manager: Peter Houston. *First Team Coaches:* Paul Hegarty and Gary Kirk. *Physio:* Jeff Clarke.
Club Nickname: The Terrors.
Previous Grounds: None.
Record Attendance: 28,000 v Barcelona, Fairs Cup, 16 Nov 1966.
Record Transfer Fee received: £4,000,000 for Duncan Ferguson from Rangers (July 1993).
Record Transfer Fee paid: £750,000 for Steven Pressley from Coventry C (July 1995).
Record Victory: 14-0 v Nithsdale Wanderers, Scottish Cup 1st rd, 17 Jan 1931.
Record Defeat: 1-12 v Motherwell, Division II, 23 Jan 1954.
Most Capped Player: Maurice Malpas, 55, Scotland.
Most League Appearances: 618, Maurice Malpas, 1980-2000.
Most Appearances in European Matches: 76, Dave Narey (record for Scottish player).
Most League Goals in Season (Individual): 41: John Coyle, Division II, 1955-56.
Most Goals Overall (Individual): 158: Peter McKay, 1947-54.

DUNDEE UNITED 2010–11 LEAGUE RECORD

Match No.	Date	Venue	Opponents	Result	H/T Score	Lg Pos.	Goalscorers	Atten-dance
1	Aug 14	A	St Mirren	D 1-1	0-0	—	Daly [89]	5618
2	22	H	Inverness CT	L 0-4	0-1	9		6575
3	29	A	Hearts	D 1-1	0-1	11	Gomis [85]	12,898
4	Sept 11	H	Aberdeen	W 3-1	3-1	7	Daly [3], Howard (og) [6], Goodwillie (pen) [9]	9793
5	18	A	Rangers	L 0-4	0-1	8		44,786
6	25	H	St Johnstone	W 1-0	0-0	5	Goodwillie [61]	7397
7	Oct 2	A	Kilmarnock	W 2-1	1-0	4	Goodwillie [15], Daly [69]	4633
8	17	H	Celtic	L 1-2	1-1	6	Goodwillie [38]	11,790
9	23	A	Motherwell	L 1-2	0-1	7	Goodwillie (pen) [50]	4635
10	30	H	Hibernian	W 1-0	0-0	6	Goodwillie [87]	7377
11	Nov 6	A	Hamilton A	W 1-0	0-0	10	Goodwillie [76]	2456
12	10	H	St Mirren	L 1-2	0-1	—	Buaben [86]	5548
13	13	H	Kilmarnock	D 1-1	1-1	6	Russell [23]	6597
14	20	A	Celtic	D 1-1	0-1	6	Dillon [90]	47,523
15	Dec 29	A	Hibernian	D 2-2	2-1	7	Goodwillie 2 [2, 35]	10,252
16	Jan 1	A	Aberdeen	D 1-1	0-1	7	Goodwillie [90]	12,487
17	12	H	Motherwell	W 2-0	0-0	—	Russell [53], Goodwillie [90]	4918
18	22	A	Kilmarnock	D 1-1	0-1	7	Kenneth [90]	5120
19	26	A	St Mirren	D 1-1	0-1	—	Robertson, D [88]	3095
20	30	H	Hibernian	W 3-0	1-0	—	Daly [13], Conway [48], Russell [81]	6215
21	Feb 13	H	Celtic	L 1-3	0-2	6	Goodwillie [64]	11,414
22	19	A	Hearts	L 1-2	1-1	7	Douglas [6]	15,473
23	22	A	St Johnstone	D 0-0	0-0	—		3507
24	26	A	Hamilton A	D 1-1	0-1	7	Shala [63]	2011
25	Mar 1	A	Inverness CT	W 2-0	0-0	—	Buaben [75], Robertson, D [90]	3392
26	7	H	Aberdeen	W 3-1	2-0	—	Douglas [29], Conway [33], Swanson [60]	7416
27	10	H	Hamilton A	W 2-1	1-1	—	Goodwillie [42], Daly [90]	5766
28	16	H	Hearts	W 2-0	0-0	—	Russell 2 [83, 90]	6718
29	19	H	Inverness CT	W 1-0	1-0	4	Swanson [43]	6548
30	Apr 2	A	Rangers	W 3-2	1-1	4	Robertson, D [45], Russell [77], Goodwillie [89]	46,697
31	6	A	Motherwell	L 1-2	0-2	—	Russell [79]	3435
32	9	H	St Johnstone	W 2-0	1-0	4	Russell [45], Robertson, D [85]	6398
33	19	H	Rangers	L 0-4	0-1	—		11,626
34	23	H	Kilmarnock	W 4-2	2-0	4	Severin [25], Goodwillie 2 [38, 47], Conway [49]	5225
35	May 1	A	Celtic	L 1-4	0-1	4	Russell [90]	48,599
36	7	H	Motherwell	W 4-0	2-0	4	Daly 3 [36, 43, 49], Watson [88]	5951
37	10	A	Rangers	L 0-2	0-2	—		49,267
38	15	H	Hearts	W 2-1	1-1	4	Goodwillie [22], Daly [71]	7119

Final League Position: 4

Honours
League Champions: Premier Division 1982-83. Division II 1924-25, 1928-29; *Runners-up:* Division II 1930-31, 1959-60. First Division Runners-up 1995-96.
Scottish Cup Winners: 1994, 2010; *Runners-up:* 1974, 1981, 1985, 1987, 1988, 1991, 2005.
League Cup Winners: 1979-80, 1980-81; *Runners-up:* 1981-82, 1984-85, 1997-98, 2007-08.
League Challenge Cup Runners-up: 1995-96.
Summer Cup Runners-up: 1964-65. *Scottish War Cup Runners-up:* 1939-40.

European: *European Cup:* 8 matches (1983-84, semi-finals). *Cup Winners' Cup:* 10 matches (1974-75, 1988-89, 1994-95). *UEFA Cup:* 86 matches (*Fairs Cup:* 1966-67, 1969-70, 1970-71). *UEFA Cup:* 1975-76, 1977-78, 1978-79, 1979-80, 1980-81, 1981-82, 1982-83, 1984-85, 1985-86, 1986-87 runners-up, 1987-88, 1989-90, 1990-91, 1993-94, 1997-98, 2005-06). *Europa League:* 2 matches (2010-11).

Club colours: Shirt: Tangerine with black trim. Shorts: Black. Stockings: Tangerine with black hoop.

Goalscorers: *League (55):* Goodwillie 17 (2 pens), Daly 9, Russell 9, Robertson D 4, Conway 3, Buaben 2, Douglas 2, Swanson 2, Dillon 1, Gomis 1, Kenneth 1, Severin 1, Shala 1, Watson 1, own goal 1.
Scottish Cup (5): Daly 2, Buaben 1, Dixon 1, Goodwillie 1.
CIS Cup (2): Goodwillie 1 (pen), own goal 1.
Europa League (1): Daly 1.

Pernis D 38	Dillon S 34	Dixon P 28 + 2	Buaben P 29 + 6	Dods D 3	Kenneth G 26 + 2	Robertson S 29 + 5	Gomis M 32 + 2	Goodwillie D 37 + 1	Daly J 18 + 11	Conway C 21 + 2	Myrie-Williams J — + 1	Cadamarteri D 2 + 8	Watson K 27 + 2	Douglas B 19 + 4	Swanson D 9 + 12	Robertson D 22 + 8	Shala A 1 + 9	Severin S 14 + 1	Russell J 21 + 9	Armstrong S 2 + 10	Dow R — + 1	Van der Meulen T 4 + 3	Kovacevic M 2	Match No.
1	2	3	4	5	6	7¹	8	9	10	11²	12	13												1
1	2	3¹	4		5	7	8	9	10	11²	12	6	13											2
1	2		4		5	7³	13	9	10	11		6²	3	8¹	12	14								3
1	2	13	4		3	12	8	9	10	11¹				5		7²		6						4
1	2	3	4		6¹	7	8	9⁸			12	5²		14	11	13								5
1	2	3	4	5	6²	12	8¹	9	10							11	13	7						6
1	2	3²	4³	5¹	6	12	8	9	10			14	13			11		7						7
1	2	3	4	5		8	9	10³	11¹	12			13			7²		6	14					8
1	2	3	4	5		8	9	10	11¹			12				7²		6	13					9
1	2	13	4¹		6	7	8	9	10³			14	3	5	12²	11								10
1	2	3	4	5	7³	8	12	13		10²	6		11					9¹	14					11
1	2	3	4	5	7	8³	9	13		10²	6		11¹			14		12						12
1	2	3	4	5	7¹	8	9	14		6	11³	13				10	12²							13
1	2	3	4	5	7²	8	9	12		6	11	13				10¹								14
1	2	3	4		7²	8	9	10	13	5	6	12				11¹								15
1	2	3	10	5	7²	8¹	9	12		6	11³		13			4		14						16
1	2	3	6¹	5	12	8	9	10³	13	4			7²			11		14						17
1	2	6	13	7	8	9	5	11¹	12	4	3					10²		14						18
1	2	6	5		8	9	11³	13	4	7		12	14			10²	3¹							19
1	2	6³	5	7		9¹	10	3²	4	8	13	11				12	14							20
1	2	3	6²	5	7	8¹	9		11	4		12	10			13								21
1	2	3	6	5¹	8³	9		4	11	13	7	14				10²		12						22
1	2	3	6²		7	13	9	11¹	4		12	8				10		5						23
1	2	3	6²		7		9	11	4		12	8¹	14			10	13	5¹						24
1	2	3	12		7	8	9	11	6	5	10²	13					4¹							25
1	2	6		7	8	9³		11¹	4	3	10²	13	12			10		5						26
1	2	12		7³	11²	9	14		4	3	13	8	6¹			10		5						27
1	2	3		7	8	9	5		6	4¹	12	11				10								28
1		3		8	4	9	5		2	6	11	7				10¹	12							29
1	2	3	14	7²	6	9	13		5	4¹	11³	8	12	10										30
1	2	3	12	7	6	9	14	11³	5¹		13	8²	4	10										31
1	2	3	6	5	12	8³	9	13	11²	7¹	14		4	10										32
1	3	14		5	8	6	9²	12	7³	11¹			4	10								13	2	33
1		6		5	8		9	14	11³	2	3	10¹	7²			4	12	13						34
1	2	3	6²	5	7	8	9	12	11			10¹				4	13							35
1		3	13		5	7¹	6	9	10³	11	2		12	14		4	8²							36
1		3	13		5	7²	6	9	12	11	2		8³			4	10¹	14						37
1	2	11	6			8	9³	5	7		14	12	4	10¹		13	3²							38

DUNFERMLINE ATHLETIC   Premier League

Year Formed: 1885. *Ground & Address:* East End Park, Halbeath Rd, Dunfermline KY12 7RB.
Telephone: 01383 724295. *Fax:* 01383 745 949. *E-mail:* enquiries@dafc.co.uk
Website: www.dafc.co.uk
Ground Capacity: all seated: 12,509. *Size of Pitch:* 115yd × 71yd.
Chairman: John Yorkston. *Chief Executive:* Bill Hodgins.
Player-Manager: Jim McIntyre. *Assistant Manager:* Gerry McCabe. *Physio:* Gerry Docherty. *Head of Youth Development:* Steven Wright.
Club Nickname: The Pars.
Previous Grounds: None.
Record Attendance: 27,816 v Celtic, Division I, 30 Apr 1968.
Record Transfer Fee received: £650,000 for Jackie McNamara to Celtic (Oct 1995).
Record Transfer Fee paid: £540,000 for Istvan Kozma from Bordeaux (Sept 1989).
Record Victory: 11-2 v Stenhousemuir, Division II, 27 Sept 1930.
Record Defeat: 1-11 v Hibernian, Scottish Cup, 3rd rd replay, 26 Oct 1889.
Most Capped Player: Colin Miller 16 (61), Canada.
Most League Appearances: 497: Norrie McCathie, 1981-96.
Most League Goals in Season (Individual): 53: Bobby Skinner, Division II, 1925-26.
Most Goals Overall (Individual): 154: Charles Dickson, 1954-64.

DUNFERMLINE ATHLETIC 2010–11 LEAGUE RECORD

Match No.	Date		Venue	Opponents	Result		H/T Score	Lg Pos.	Goalscorers	Attendance
1	Aug	7	A	Falkirk	W	1-0	1-0	—	Clarke [16]	6947
2		14	H	Morton	W	2-0	0-0	2	Kirk 2 [77, 83]	3113
3		21	A	Raith R	L	0-2	0-0	3		6169
4		28	A	Stirling A	W	5-1	2-1	2	Bell [13], McDougall [15], Cardle [78], Kirk 2 [88, 90]	1370
5	Sept	11	H	Dundee	W	3-1	2-0	2	Gibson (pen) [20], Bell [42], Clarke [78]	4037
6		18	H	Cowdenbeath	W	2-1	0-1	1	Bell [64], Cardle [77]	4316
7		25	A	Partick Th	W	2-0	1-0	1	Clarke [29], Kirk [70]	2188
8	Oct	2	A	Queen of the S	L	0-2	0-0	1		2139
9		16	H	Ross Co	W	3-2	2-1	1	Gibson [28], Clarke [44], McDougall [90]	2803
10		23	A	Dundee	D	2-2	2-0	2	Gibson 2 (2 pens) [30, 33]	5636
11		30	H	Stirling A	W	3-0	2-0	2	Gibson [18], Kirk [30], Woods [80]	3025
12	Nov	6	A	Morton	L	1-2	0-2	2	Gibson [83]	1813
13		13	H	Raith R	D	2-2	2-0	2	Clarke [19], Woods [31]	7158
14	Dec	11	H	Queen of the S	W	1-0	0-0	—	Cardle [86]	2062
15		14	H	Partick Th	D	0-0	0-0	—		1743
16		29	H	Cowdenbeath	W	5-0	1-0	—	Kirk [29], Clarke 2 [63, 86], Phinn [68], Linton (og) [89]	2942
17	Jan	2	A	Raith R	L	1-2	0-0	—	Phinn [54]	6534
18		15	H	Dundee	D	0-0	0-0	2		3385
19		29	A	Partick Th	L	0-2	0-2	—		2720
20	Feb	12	A	Cowdenbeath	W	4-0	0-0	2	Graham, D 2 [46, 75], Buchanan [69], Kirk [84]	2192
21		15	H	Falkirk	D	1-1	0-0	—	Kirk [85]	5082
22		22	A	Ross Co	D	0-0	0-0	—		2198
23		26	A	Queen of the S	W	3-1	0-0	2	Buchanan [51], Harris (og) [55], Cardle [88]	2052
24	Mar	5	H	Morton	L	1-3	0-1	2	Buchanan [77]	2867
25		8	H	Ross Co	D	1-1	0-0	—	Kirk (pen) [81]	1699
26		12	A	Falkirk	W	2-1	2-0	2	Woods [28], Hardie [44]	5121
27		15	A	Stirling A	D	1-1	1-1	—	Kirk [5]	944
28		19	H	Stirling A	W	4-1	2-0	2	Hardie 3 (2 pens) [31 (pl), 45 (pl), 90], Buchanan [55]	2553
29		22	A	Dundee	D	1-1	1-0	—	Burke [32]	4507
30		26	H	Partick Th	D	0-0	0-0	2		3019
31		29	A	Ross Co	W	1-0	0-0	—	Hardie [90]	2059
32	Apr	2	A	Cowdenbeath	W	1-0	0-0	1	Buchanan [60]	2104
33		16	H	Queen of the S	W	6-1	1-0	1	Hardie [32], Graham, D 2 [51, 69], Higgins [65], Kirk [76], Clarke [82]	3255
34		23	H	Raith R	W	2-1	0-1	1	Hardie 2 [55, 78]	11,052
35		30	A	Morton	W	2-0	1-0	1	McDougall [8], Graham, D [51]	4626
36	May	7	H	Falkirk	W	3-0	1-0	1	Phinn 2 [21, 53], Clarke [87]	7826

Final League Position: 1

Honours
League Champions: First Division 1988-89, 1995-96, 2010-11. Division II 1925-26. Second Division 1985-86; *Runners-up:* First Division 1986-87, 1993-94, 1994-95, 1999-2000. Division II 1912-13, 1933-34, 1954-55, 1957-58, 1972-73. Second Division 1978-79.
Scottish Cup Winners: 1961, 1968; *Runners-up:* 1965, 2004, 2007.
League Cup Runners-up: 1949-50, 1991-92, 2005-06.
League Challenge Cup Runners-up: 2007-08.

European: *Cup Winners' Cup:* 14 matches (1961-62, 1968-69 semi-finals). *UEFA Cup:* 32 matches (*Fairs Cup:* 1962-63, 1964-65, 1965-66, 1966-67, 1969-70. *UEFA Cup:* 2004-05, 2007-08).

Club colours: Shirt: White and black stripes. Shorts: White. Stockings: White.

Goalscorers: *League (66):* Kirk 12 (1 pen), Clarke 9, Hardie 8 (2 pens), Gibson 6 (3 pens), Buchanan 5, Graham D 5, Cardle 4, Phinn 4, Bell 3, McDougall 3, Woods 3, Burke 1, Higgins 1, own goals 2.
Scottish Cup (7): Graham 2, Kirk 2, Clarke 1, Gibson 1 (pen), McDougall 1.
CIS Cup (10): Kirk 4, McDougall 2, Cardle 1, Willis 1, Woods 1, own goal 1.
Alba Challenge Cup (2): Kirk 2.

Smith C 36	Woods C 32	Dowie A 24+2	Higgins C 17+4	McCann A 35	Willis P 5+3	Phinn N 11+6	Mason G 34	Cardle J 23+9	Clarke P 14+17	Kirk A 29+2	Graham D 24+6	Gibson W 12+3	McDougall S 16+19	McGregor N 3+2	Bell S 10	Keddie A 25	Allison K —+1	Thomson R 2+7	Buchanan L 13+4	Rutkiewicz K 12	Hardie M 12+2	Burke A 5+3	Bayne G 1+1	Hyde J 1+1	Graham L —+1	Match No.
1	2	3	4	5	6^1	7	8	9^2	10	11^3	12	13	14													1
1	2	3	4	5	7^1	6	8^3	10^2	11	9	12	13		14												2
1	2	3	4	5		10	7	9	13	11^2				6^1	12	8										3
1	2	3	4^1	5	14	12	7^3	9	13	11				6	10^2	8										4
1	2	3	4	5		13	8^1	9	12	11				6	10^1		7									5
1	2	3	4	5		13	7^2	9	12	11				6	10^1	8										6
1	2	3	4	5	6^2	13	7	9	11^1	10		12				8										7
1	2	3	4	5	12	13	7^2	9	10^3	11				6^1	14	8										8
1	2	3		5		8	9^1	10	11^2	13				6	12	7	4									9
1	2	3	4	5		7	9^2	10	11^1	13				6	12	8										10
1^6	2	3	4	5		7	13	10^1	11	9^2	6	12				8		15								11
1	2	3	4	5		7	13	10^3	11	9^2	6	14				8^1			12							12
1	2	3	14	5		8	12	10	11^2	9^1	7^3		6^4			4			13							13
1	2	3		5		8	7	13	10^1	11^2	9		6^4		12	4										14
1	2	3		5	12	7	6	8^1	13	11^2	9		10			4										15
1	2	3		5	6^2	8^3	7	14	12	11^1	9		10			4		13								16
1	2	3		5	6^2	7	8	13	11^1	12	9		10			4										17
1	2		14	5	6^1		7^3		10^2	11	9	12	13	3		4		8								18
1	2	4	12	3		8^1	7		14	10	9^3	6	13			5			11^2							19
1	2			5		8^2	7^3	9^1		11	6		12			4			10	3	13	14				20
1	2			5		7^2	6	8^1		11	9		12			4			10	3	13					21
1	2			3			7		9^2	10	11		13	14		4		6^1	12	5^3	8					22
1	2		3	5			8	12		11^2	6		9			4		13	10^1		7					23
1	2		4^3	5			6	12	11^2	13	9		8^1	3				14	10		7					24
1	2			5			6	8	12	11	9^2		13			4			10^1	3	7					25
1	2		3	5			7	8		11	14		10^3			4		12			6^1	9^2	13			26
1	2		3	5			6	7	12	11	8		9^2			4			13				10^1			27
1	2^3			5			6^4	8^2	12	9			11^1			4		13	10	3	7	14				28
1	2	4	14	3				12	13	11			8^1			6			10	5	7^3	9^2				29
1	2		3				6		12		10^1	8				4			13	7	9					30
1	2		3				6	8	14		12		9^1			5			11^3	4	7	10^2	13			31
1	5	2		6				8^2	12		13	14				4			10^3	3	7	9	11^1			32
1		12	5				6	8^2	14	11^3	9		13	2		3			10^1		4^8	7				33
1	2	14	3	5			6	8^2		11^3	9	12				4			11		7			13		34
1	2^2	6		5		13	7	8^3	12	11	9		10^1			3			14	4						35
1	2			5		7^3	6	8^1	13	11^2	9		10			4			12	3		14				36

EAST FIFE

Second Division

Year Formed: 1903. *Ground & Address:* Bayview Stadium, Harbour View, Methil, Fife KY8 3RW. *Telephone:* 01333 426323. *Fax:* 01333 426376. *E-mail:* office@eastfife.org. *Website:* www.eastfife.org
Ground Capacity: 1992. *Size of Pitch:* 105m × 65m.
Chairman: Sid Columbine. *Secretary:* John Sharp.
Manager: Stevie Crawford. *Assistant Manager:* Jason Dair. *Physio:* Brian McNeill.
Club Nickname: The Fifers.
Previous Ground: Bayview Park.
Record Attendance: 22,515 v Raith Rovers, Division I, 2 Jan 1950.
Record Transfer Fee received: £150,000 for Paul Hunter from Hull C (March 1990).
Record Transfer Fee paid: £70,000 for John Sludden from Kilmarnock (July 1991).
Record Victory: 13-2 v Edinburgh City, Division II, 11 Dec 1937.
Record Defeat: 0-9 v Hearts, Division I, 5 Oct 1957.
Most Capped Player: George Aitken, 5 (8), Scotland.
Most League Appearances: 517: David Clarke, 1968-86.
Most League Goals in Season (Individual): 41: Jock Wood, Division II; 1926-27 and Henry Morris, Division II, 1947-48.
Most Goals Overall (Individual): 225: Phil Weir, 1922-35.

EAST FIFE 2010–11 LEAGUE RECORD

Match No.	Date		Venue	Opponents	Result	H/T Score	Lg Pos.	Goalscorers	Atten- dance
1	Aug	7	H	Airdrie U	D 3-3	1-0	—	Hislop [30], Young [52], Linn [59]	810
2		14	A	Alloa Ath	L 2-3	0-0	7	Johnstone [54], Smart [65]	688
3		21	H	Peterhead	W 2-1	0-1	6	Johnstone [76], Sloan [82]	565
4		28	H	Dumbarton	W 6-0	3-0	3	Young [15], Byrne 3 [35, 44, 71], Linn [59], Sloan [83]	687
5	Sept	11	A	Forfar Ath	L 2-3	1-0	5	Johnstone [13], Ovenstone [86]	590
6		18	H	Ayr U	L 2-3	2-2	6	Sloan (pen) [28], Byrne [34]	664
7		25	A	Livingston	D 1-1	0-0	7	Byrne [69]	1669
8	Oct	2	A	Stenhousemuir	D 1-1	0-0	7	Ovenstone [51]	679
9		16	H	Brechin C	L 1-3	1-1	7	Linn [14]	336
10		23	H	Forfar Ath	L 1-3	0-1	8	Linn [53]	524
11		30	A	Dumbarton	L 1-4	1-1	8	Byrne [39]	585
12	Nov	6	H	Alloa Ath	W 4-1	1-0	7	Linn [16], Hislop [55], Sloan 2 (1 pen) [61 (p), 82]	435
13		13	A	Peterhead	D 2-2	0-0	7	Byrne [46], Johnstone [60]	594
14	Dec	11	H	Stenhousemuir	W 6-0	4-0	—	Muir [19], Crawford 2 [32, 68], Johnstone [33], Sloan (pen) [45], Linn [61]	472
15	Jan	18	H	Livingston	L 2-4	1-0	—	Crawford [19], Sloan (pen) [61]	548
16		29	A	Livingston	L 3-4	1-2	9	Linn [28], Crawford [72], Muir [75]	1340
17	Feb	1	A	Forfar Ath	D 0-0	0-0	—		438
18		12	A	Stenhousemuir	W 2-0	1-0	8	Young [45], Linn [48]	590
19		15	H	Dumbarton	L 1-3	1-2	—	Park [44]	392
20		19	H	Brechin C	D 0-0	0-0	9		526
21		23	A	Ayr U	W 4-0	2-0	—	Hamilton [31], Wallace 2 [34, 66], Park [49]	789
22		26	H	Airdrie U	L 0-1	0-1	8		664
23	Mar	1	H	Peterhead	W 3-1	2-0	—	Hislop [22], Linn 2 [32, 54]	314
24		5	A	Alloa Ath	W 3-1	3-0	5	Johnstone 2 [34, 45], Philp (og) [44]	579
25		8	A	Airdrie U	D 1-1	1-1	—	Smart [22]	447
26		12	H	Forfar Ath	W 3-0	1-0	—	Hislop [33], Smart [74], Linn [88]	469
27		19	A	Dumbarton	L 2-4	1-1	5	Linn [27], Johnstone [61]	615
28		26	H	Livingston	L 1-3	0-1	6	Wallace [60]	707
29		29	H	Ayr U	W 3-2	2-1	—	Wallace [15], Durie [32], Linn [46]	350
30	Apr	2	A	Ayr U	D 1-1	1-1	6	Park [8]	976
31		9	A	Brechin C	W 3-1	1-0	6	McCulloch [27], Cook (og) [52], Wallace [71]	504
32		16	H	Stenhousemuir	D 1-1	0-0	6	Durie [96]	562
33		19	A	Brechin C	W 3-2	0-0	—	McGowan [52], Wallace 2 (1 pen) [62 (p), 83]	441
34		23	A	Peterhead	W 2-0	1-0	5	Johnstone [28], Muir [54]	473
35		30	H	Alloa Ath	W 3-1	1-0	5	Wallace [16], Park [54], Durie [87]	846
36	May	7	A	Airdrie U	D 2-2	1-1	5	Muir [33], Hislop [64]	861

Final League Position: 5

Honours
League Champions: Division II 1947-48. Third Division 2007-08. *Runners-up:* Division II 1929-30, 1970-71. Second Division 1983-84, 1995-96. Third Division 2002-03.
Scottish Cup Winners: 1938; *Runners-up:* 1927, 1950.
League Cup Winners: 1947-48, 1949-50, 1953-54.

Club colours: Shirt: Gold with black stripes. Shorts: Black. Stockings: Gold.

Goalscorers: *League (77):* Linn 13, Johnstone 9, Wallace 8 (1 pen), Byrne 7, Sloan 7 (4 pens), Hislop 5, Crawford 4, Muir 4, Park 4, Durie 3, Smart 3, Young 3, Ovenstone 2, Hamilton 1, McCulloch 1, McGowan 1, own goals 2.
Scottish Cup (3): Hislop 1, Johnstone 1, Sloan 1 (pen).
CIS Cup (1): Linn 1.
Alba Challenge Cup (7): Byrne 1, Cargill 1, Crawford 1, Durie 1, Johnstone 1, Linn 1, Sloan 1 (pen).

Baillie S 3	Durie S 29+1	Muir D 33+2	Smart J 18+8	Deland M 4+1	Murdoch S 10	Sloan R 17+2	Young L 27+7	Linn R 34+1	Byrne K 13+1	Hislop S 31+5	Ovenstone J 29+3	Tansey P —+7	Johnstone C 27+4	Campbell S 9+4	Brown M 29+1	Crawford S 3+7	Cargill S —+6	McGowan D 23	Weir S —+1	Hamilton J 7+2	Fagan S —+8	McCulloch M 18	Park M 18+1	Wallace R 10+3	Newbigging K —+1	Brown R 4+1	Devlin J —+1	Match No.
1	2	3⁴	4	5³	6	7¹	8	9	10	11	12²	13	14															1
1	2	3	4	5	6		8	9	11	10¹			12	7²	13													2
	2	5	3	4²		7	13	6	9	11¹	10	14		8³		1	12											3
	5	2	4		6	3	7	9	11²	10			8¹			1	13	12										4
	3	2	4		5¹	7	6	9	10	11³	12	13	8²	14		1												5
1ᵇ	4	2	12	13	5	8	7	11ᵇ	9³	10¹			6²	3			14											6
	4	2			6	7¹	9		10	11³	5	13	8²	3		1	14	12										7
	3	2			6	7¹	8	12	10²	11	5		9	4		1	13											8
	2	12	13		5	7²	8	6	10	11	4¹	14	9	3³		1												9
	2	6	4	5³		12	7²	9	10	13		14	8¹	3		1	11											10
1ᵇ	2²	13	5		6ᵇ	7	12	9	10¹	11	3		8⁶	4	15													11
	2	6	4		7	12	9¹	10	11³	5	13		8²	3		1	14											12
	2	6	4			9	11¹	10	5			8	3		1	12												13
13	8	4			7	14	6³	12	11	5		9	3²	1	10¹		2											14
	2	6	5		7	12	9		11²	3		8¹		1	10³		4	13	14									15
	2	6	5³		10	12	7	9²	3	11¹		1	13	4		8	14											16
	2	5			8	12	7	11	3	9¹		1	4	10		6												17
	2	5			7	12	9	10¹	3	8²		1	4	11		6	13											18
	2	7		5¹	9	8	14	4	13		1	6	10²	12	3	11³												19
	2	5			7	10	9¹	4	8	1		3	11		6	12												20
	2	6³	14		10	7¹	13	4	11	1		5	9²	12	3	8												21
		4			8	9	12	2	6	1		3	11²	13	7	5	10¹											22
	3	2			7¹	10	11	4	9	1	12	5			8	6												23
	5	2			7	11	10¹	4	9	1		3		12	8	6												24
	5	2			8	11	10¹	3	9	1		4	12²	13	6	7												25
	5	4			7¹	11	10	3	9	1		2		6	8	12												26
	5	2			8	9	10¹	3	11	1		4		6	7	12												27
	2	5			9²	11	10	3	6¹	1		4	14	8³	7	12	13											28
	2	5			7	9	10¹	3		12	4		8	6	11	1												29
	2	3			7	9	10¹	4		1	12	5		8	6	11												30
	2	5	12		7	10	11¹	3		4		8	6	9	1													31
	2	5	13		8	9	11²	4	12	1		3	7	6	10¹													32
	2	5	6³		8²	10¹	14	3	12	13	1	4	9	7	11													33
	2	5	12		10	9²	3	8¹	13	1	4		7	6	11													34
	2	5	12		7	9	10¹	4		3		8	6	11²	1	13												35
	2	5¹	13		8	9	10²	3		4		12	7	6	11	1												36

EAST STIRLINGSHIRE   Third Division

Year Formed: 1880. *Ground & Address:* Ochilview Park, Gladstone Road, Stenhousemuir FK5 4QL. *Postal Address:* 202 Stirling Road, Larbert, Falkirk FK5 3NJ. *Telephone:* 01324 557 862. *Fax:* 01324 557 862.
E-mail: fceaststirlingshire@gmail.com *Website:* www.eaststirlingfc.com
Ground Capacity: 3776 (626 seated). *Size of Pitch:* 110yd × 72yd.
Chairman/Chief Executive/Secretary: Les Thomson. *Vice-Chairman:* Andy Miller.
Head Coach: John Coughlin. *Assistant Coaches:* David Nicholls and John O'Neill. *Physio:* Steve O'Neill.
Club Nickname: The Shire.
Previous Grounds: Burnhouse, Randyford Park, Merchiston Park, New Kilbowie Park, Firs Park.
Record Attendance: 12,000 v Partick Th, *Scottish Cup* 3rd rd, 21 Feb 1921.
Record Transfer Fee received: £35,000 for Jim Docherty to Chelsea (1978).
Record Transfer Fee paid: £6,000 for Colin McKinnon from Falkirk (March 1991).
Record Victory: 11-2 v Vale of Bannock, *Scottish Cup* 2nd rd, 22 Sept 1888.
Record Defeat: 1-12 v Dundee United, Division II, 13 Apr 1936.
Most Capped Player: Humphrey Jones, 5 (14), Wales.
Most League Appearances: 415: Gordon Russell, 1983-2001.
Most League Goals in Season (Individual): 36: Malcolm Morrison, Division II, 1938-39.

EAST STIRLINGSHIRE 2010–11 LEAGUE RECORD

Match No.	Date		Venue	Opponents	Result		H/T Score	Lg Pos.	Goalscorers	Attendance
1	Aug	7	A	Annan Ath	L	1-3	1-3	—	Summersgill (og) [38]	539
2		14	H	Montrose	W	2-1	0-1	7	Maguire (pen) [76], Stevenson [88]	332
3		21	A	Elgin C	W	2-0	0-0	3	Dunn (pen) [78], Stevenson [89]	602
4		28	A	Arbroath	L	0-2	0-1	6		499
5	Sept	11	H	Clyde	D	0-0	0-0	6		532
6		18	A	Queen's Park	L	0-2	0-2	6		460
7		25	H	Berwick R	D	0-0	0-0	6		383
8	Oct	2	A	Albion R	L	0-1	0-1	8		367
9		9	A	Elgin C	L	0-2	0-1	—		475
10		16	H	Stranraer	L	0-1	0-1	9		317
11	Nov	6	A	Clyde	W	2-1	2-1	8	Dunn [9], Cawley [36]	652
12		10	H	Arbroath	L	1-3	1-1	—	Cawley [5]	238
13		13	H	Elgin C	L	0-2	0-1	8		243
14	Jan	15	H	Clyde	W	2-0	0-0	8	Walker [57], Maguire [74]	467
15		25	A	Arbroath	W	5-3	2-2	—	Johnston [28], Dunn 2 [38, 64], Maguire [46], Beveridge [82]	436
16		29	H	Berwick R	W	1-0	1-0	7	McLeod (og) [31]	341
17	Feb	5	A	Queen's Park	L	0-2	0-2	8		504
18		12	A	Albion R	L	0-2	0-1	9		346
19		16	H	Queen's Park	L	0-1	0-0	—		293
20		19	H	Stranraer	L	0-2	0-1	9		294
21		23	A	Stranraer	L	1-4	1-3	—	Maguire [15]	269
22		26	A	Annan Ath	L	1-2	0-0	9	Cawley [59]	402
23	Mar	2	H	Albion R	D	0-0	0-0	—		226
24		5	H	Montrose	L	1-2	1-0	9	Weaver [8]	306
25		8	A	Berwick R	L	0-3	0-1	—		266
26		15	H	Annan Ath	L	1-5	0-3	—	Johnston [64]	178
27		19	H	Arbroath	L	2-5	1-1	9	Cawley [27], Scott [82]	349
28		22	A	Montrose	W	2-0	1-0	—	Neil [44], Team [90]	259
29		26	A	Berwick R	D	1-1	1-0	8	Neil [5]	367
30	Apr	2	H	Queen's Park	W	3-2	2-1	8	Johnston [29], Cawley 2 [41, 90]	391
31		9	A	Stranraer	L	0-2	0-1	9		373
32		16	H	Albion R	L	1-2	0-0	9	Kelly [65]	323
33		19	A	Clyde	L	0-2	0-0	—		591
34		23	H	Elgin C	W	2-1	1-1	9	Maguire [27], Dunn [85]	215
35		30	A	Montrose	L	0-3	0-3	10		361
36	May	7	H	Annan Ath	W	2-0	1-0	9	Cawley 2 [42, 90]	322

Final League Position: 9

Honours
League Champions: Division II 1931-32; C Division 1947-48. *Runners-up:* Division II 1962-63. Second Division 1979-80. Division Three 1923-24.

Club colours: Shirt: Black and white hoops. Shorts: Black. Stockings: Black and white hoops.

Goalscorers: *League (33):* Cawley 8, Dunn 5 (1 pen), Maguire 5 (1 pen), Johnston 3, Neil 2, Stevenson 2, Beveridge 1, Kelly 1, Scott 1, Team 1, Walker 1, Weaver 1, own goals 2.
Scottish Cup (7): Cawley 4, Dunn 2, Weaver 1.
CIS Cup (1): Cawley 1.
Alba Challenge Cup (3): Cawley 1, Maguire 1 (pen), Richardson 1.

Andrews M 36	Neil J 27 + 6	Tully C 14 + 2	Richardson D 25 + 3	Hay P 36	Donaldson C 23	Weaver P 23 + 2	Dunn D 28 + 4	Johnston S 32 + 4	Cawley K 34 + 1	Maguire S 25 + 5	Walker A 16 + 2	Ure D 18 + 12	Stevenson J 2 + 2	Kelly D 12 + 6	Anderson S — + 4	Team F — + 21	Watts K 4 + 4	Beveridge S 17 + 5	Grant C 11 + 2	Wilkie R 2 + 5	Scott C 3 + 7	Kennedy R 1	Jackson S 7	Glasgow J — + 2	Gibson A — + 1	Match No.
1	2	3¹	4	5	6	7	8²	9³	10	11	12	13	14													1
1	3²	2	4	7	8	6¹	13	9³	10	5	12	11	14													2
1		3¹	2	5	4	7⁸	8	14	10	11³	6	9²	13	12												3
1	8	5²	6	4	2		10³	12	11	9		3¹	7	13	14											4
1	2		3	4	8	7	6	10¹	9²	11³	5	13				12		14								5
1	2		3	4	7	6³	8	11	10²		5	12		9¹		14		13								6
1	6	2	4	3		7⁸	10²	8		5¹	9			13		14		11³	12							7
1	6		2	5	4⁸	7		11	8¹		10	12				13		9²	3							8
1	3		4	5	7		11	8	9	6¹		13				12		10²	2							9
1	8¹		2	4	6	7		11	10⁷		5	9			14	13	12	3¹								10
1	2³	12	3	5			8	11	9	10²	6¹					13	14	4	7							11
1	2⁵	5	3	7			6³	11	10	9¹				13		14	12	4	8							12
1		2	6	3¹	5		9³	14	10	13	4			8		12	11²	7								13
1	13	2²	3	5	4	6	8³	10¹	9	11		7⁸	14			12										14
1	13		3	2	5	4	7	8¹	10³	9	11²					14		6								15
1	13		3¹	5	4	6	7	8	11	9²	10³	12				14		2								16
1	13		2²	3¹	5	4	6	8	11	9³	10					14		7								17
1	8		3¹	4	5	7	9	11²	14⁸	13	6	10³				12		2								18
1	8¹	2	3	5	4	7	9	10²		11		12			6	13										19
1		5¹	3	2	6	8	11	9	10²		13				7³	12		4			14					20
1	13		5	3	8	4²	9	11	10	6³	12				7¹			2	14							21
1	6		2¹	5	3	7	12	9	10	11	4²					13		8³	14							22
1	6		3	2	5	14	9³	8	10²	4¹	7					12		11	13							23
1	3		2²	4	7	12	10	8	11	5³						13	14	9	6¹							24
1	2	3	5¹	4	7	6³	9	10²		14						13	12	8								25
1	6	2	4²	3	7³	12	11	8	9	5¹	13					14	10									26
1	12	13	3²	5		7	9	11	10		4³					2	8	6¹	14							27
1	8	3		5		9	11³	6²	12	10				13		4	7			14	2¹					28
1	6	3³	12	4		8	11	10²	13	5¹	9					2	7			14						29
1	11		4		14	6²	10	8	9³	7				5¹		3	12			2						30
1	6	3²	2			7¹	11	10	9	8						5	13	12		4						31
1	10²	3¹	5	12		11	7	8³	9	4						2	14	13	6							32
1	9	2¹	4		5³	11	7	8²	10	3		12				14	13	6								33
1	10	12	4		5	9²	8¹	7	6	3						13	11				2		14			34
1	11	3²	5		6³	9	8¹	12	10	4						13	7				2	14				35
1	10	13	3		9¹	11	7	8³	5	2						12²	6				4		14			36

ELGIN CITY
Third Division

Year Formed: 1893. *Ground and Address:* Borough Briggs, Borough Briggs Road, Elgin IV30 1AP.
Telephone: 01343 551114. *Fax:* 01343 547921. *E-mail:* elgincityfc@ukonline.co.uk *Website:* www.elgincity.com
Ground Capacity: 3927, seated 478, standing 3449. *Size of pitch:* 111yd × 72yd.
Chairman: Graham Tatters. *Secretary:* Ian A. Allan.
Manager: Ross Jack. *Assistant Manager:* Barry Wilson. *Physios:* Lynda Anderson and Eilidh Paterson.
Previous names: 1893-1900 Elgin City, 1900–03 Elgin City United, 1903– Elgin City.
Club Nicknames: City or Black & Whites.
Previous Grounds: Association Park 1893-95; Milnfield Park 1895-1909; Station Park 1909-19; Cooper Park 1919-21.
Record Attendance: 12,608 v Arbroath, Scottish Cup, 17 Feb 1968.
Record Transfer Fee received: £32,000 for Michael Teasdale to Dundee (Jan 1994).
Record Transfer Fee paid: £10,000 to Fraserburgh for Russell McBride (July 2001).
Record Victory: 18-1 v Brora Rangers, North of Scotland Cup, 6 Feb 1960.
Record Defeat: 1-14 v Hearts, Scottish Cup, 4 Feb 1939.
Most League Appearances: 224: David Hind, 2001-09.
Most League Goals in Season (Individual): 20: Martin Johnston, 2005-06.
Most Goals Overall (Individual): 39: Martin Johnston, 2005-07.

ELGIN CITY 2010–11 LEAGUE RECORD

Match No.	Date	Venue	Opponents	Result	H/T Score	Lg Pos.	Goalscorers	Attendance
1	Aug 7	H	Arbroath	L 3-5	0-1	—	Millar 2 [52, 79], Cameron [74]	518
2	14	A	Berwick R	L 2-6	0-4	10	Gunn (pen) [57], MacLeod [80]	409
3	21	H	East Stirling	L 0-2	0-0	10		602
4	28	H	Stranraer	L 1-2	0-1	10	Millar [90]	370
5	Sept 11	A	Annan Ath	W 1-0	1-0	10	Nicolson [9]	505
6	18	H	Montrose	W 3-2	1-1	8	Wilson [33], Gunn [52], Crooks [73]	386
7	25	A	Albion R	L 1-3	1-1	9	Frizzel [20]	353
8	Oct 2	A	Clyde	D 1-1	0-0	9	Wilson (pen) [61]	881
9	9	H	East Stirling	W 2-0	1-0	—	Gunn [2], Wilson (pen) [90]	475
10	16	H	Queen's Park	W 4-2	2-0	5	Crooks [2], O'Donoghue 2 (2 pens) [27, 68], Niven [79]	517
11	30	A	Stranraer	L 1-2	1-1	5	Crooks (pen) [7]	367
12	Nov 6	H	Annan Ath	W 2-0	2-0	5	Cameron [5], Crooks [11]	507
13	13	A	East Stirling	W 2-0	1-0	6	Inglis, J [34], Frizzel [81]	243
14	Dec 11	A	Montrose	W 1-0	0-0	—	Gunn [53]	307
15	14	H	Albion R	D 2-2	2-2	—	Gunn [24], Crooks (pen) [38]	426
16	18	A	Queen's Park	D 1-1	0-0	—	Crooks [71]	452
17	Jan 15	A	Annan Ath	D 2-2	2-1	4	Crooks 2 [3, 11]	311
18	22	H	Stranraer	W 2-1	0-1	—	Gallagher (og) [52], Gunn [64]	714
19	29	A	Albion R	L 0-2	0-1	4		323
20	Feb 5	H	Montrose	W 1-0	1-0	4	Frizzel [24]	633
21	12	A	Clyde	D 3-3	1-2	4	Crooks (pen) [22], Gormley [76], Frizzel [85]	600
22	19	H	Queen's Park	L 0-1	0-1	5		725
23	23	A	Arbroath	L 0-2	0-2	—		403
24	26	H	Arbroath	W 3-2	0-0	6	Crooks [61], Nicolson [74], O'Donoghue [76]	629
25	Mar 5	A	Berwick R	L 0-4	0-3	6		305
26	12	H	Annan Ath	L 2-3	0-2	7	Gormley [66], Gunn [69]	511
27	19	A	Stranraer	W 2-1	1-0	7	Duff [21], Gormley [64]	339
28	22	H	Berwick R	L 1-2	0-0	—	Gunn [71]	412
29	26	H	Albion R	D 1-1	0-1	7	Gunn [63]	574
30	Apr 2	A	Montrose	L 0-1	0-1	7		256
31	9	A	Queen's Park	L 0-1	0-0	7		436
32	16	H	Clyde	L 0-1	0-1	7		621
33	23	A	East Stirling	L 1-2	1-1	7	Crooks [39]	215
34	26	H	Clyde	L 0-1	0-0	—		272
35	30	H	Berwick R	W 3-2	1-2	7	Crooks (pen) [37], MacDonald [56], Kaczan [79]	496
36	May 7	A	Arbroath	W 5-3	2-1	7	Gormley 3 [40, 45, 62], Gunn [55], Crooks (pen) [79]	1125

Final League Position: 7

Honours
Scottish Cup: Quarter-finals 1968.
Highland League Champions: winners 15 times.
Scottish Qualifying Cup (North): winners 7 times.
North of Scotland Cup: winners 17 times.
Highland League Cup: winners 5 times.
Inverness Cup: winners twice.

Club colours: Shirt: Black and white stripes. Shorts: Black. Stockings: Red.

Goalscorers: *League (53):* Crooks 13 (5 pens), Gunn 10 (1 pen), Gormley 6, Frizzel 4, Millar 3, O'Donoghue 3 (2 pens), Wilson 3 (2 pens), Cameron 2, Nicolson 2, Duff 1, Inglis J 1, Kaczan 1, MacDonald 1, MacLeod 1, Niven 1, own goal 1.
Scottish Cup (7): Gunn 3, Crooks 2, Millar 1, Wilson 1 (pen).
CIS Cup (3): Gunn 2 (1 pen), Millar 1.
Alba Challenge Cup (1): Gunn 1.

Dunn S 2	Niven D 28	Kaczan P 24+1	Dempsie A 30	Inglis J 32	MacDonald N 10+11	Wilson B 15+10	O'Donoghue R 35	Millar P 5+13	Crooks J 27+9	Gunn C 27+8	Cameron B 28+7	Frizzel C 26+7	MacLeod D —+1	Bain S 11	Edwards S 10+7	Duff J 24	Nicolson M 27	Donnelly P 20	Gormley D 10+6	Lawrie B 2+11	Jack A —+1	Calder J 3	Forbes F —+2	Black S —+1	Match No.
1	2	3	4	5	6[1]	7	8	9	10	11	12														1
1	2		4	5	6	3	8[3]	9	7[1]	12	11	13	10[2]	14											2
		4[1]	3	5[3]	7	6	8	9	13	11[2]	10	14	12	1	2										3
			3	5	6	9[2]	8	12	14	10[1]	13	11[3]		1	2	4	7								4
			3	2	6		14	7	8[2]	12	13	10	11[1]	1	5[4]	4	9■								5
			3	4	5		6	7	8[1]	12	11	9	10	1	2										6
		3[1]	2	6		12	7	8[2]	14	13	10[3]	11		1	5	4	9								7
2		5	3		8[1]	6	13	12	10	11[2]	9			1		4	7								8
2		4	5	13	7	8		14	10[3]	11	9[2]			1	12	3[1]	6								9
4		2	5	13		7	12	8	10[1]	11	9[2]			1	14	3[3]	6								10
3■	12	2[1]	5		14	7	13	10[2]	11	8[3]	9			1		4	6								11
		4	7[1]	5		13	7	14	10	11[3]	8	9[2]		1	12	3	6								12
2	5		4	13		6[2]	14	8	9[3]	11	10			1	12	3[1]	7								13
4[2]	3	2	5		7[1]	6		10	9	11	12	13				8	1								14
4		2	5	13	8[1]	7		10	11	9[2]	12					3	6	1							15
7	4	2	5	13	14	8[2]	12	11		10[1]	9[3]					3	6	1							16
4	3	2[2]	5	12		7	14	10[3]	11[1]	8	9			13			6	1							17
4	3	2	5[1]	12		7		10	11	8	9						6	1							18
4	3	2[2]	5	12	14	7	13	6	9[3]	10[1]	11					8		1							19
5	3	2	7	6[2]		8		10	11[1]	13	9					4		1	12						20
3	4	2	7	6[1]		8		9[2]	10[3]	13	11					5		1	12	14					21
5	3	2	7[3]	6■		8		10	12	9[2]	11[1]					4		1	13	14					22
3	4■	2			7	12	9	10[2]	13					6	5[1]	8	1		11[3]	14					23
5		4	6	13		8		10	12	9[2]		2[3]	3	7	1	11[1]	14								24
		4	5		7	13	10[3]	12	8	9[1]		2	3	6	1	11[2]			14						25
		4			13	7		10	11	8	9[2]	2[1]	5		1	5	12								26
3	4■	2			6		8	10[2]	11[3]	12	13	5	7	1		9[1]	14								27
2	4[3]	5		14	7		9[2]	10	8	12		3	6	1	11[1]	13									28
2	3	5	6[2]		14	8		10[3]	11	9[1]	12	4	7	1			13								29
	2	3	13	14	6		8	10		9[3]		4[2]	5	7		11[1]	12		1						30
4		2	5	13	6[2]	7		12	9[3]	10[1]	11	3				14	8		1						31
4			5	2	6	8		12	11[2]	10	9[3]	3				13	7[1]			1	14				32
2	3	4	5[5]		6		9	8[2]	11	10		7				1	13	12							33
3	2		4[1]	5	7		11	12	8	9[2]		6				1	10	13							34
3	2		4[1]	5[3]	7	14	10	12	8	9[2]		6				1	11					13			35
4	3		5	2[1]	6	7		9	13	11[2]	12	8				1	16	10						15	36

FALKIRK   First Division

Year Formed: 1876. *Ground & Address:* The Falkirk Stadium, Westfield, Falkirk FK2 9DX. *Telephone:* 01324 624121.
Fax: 01324 612418. *Email:* post@falkirkfc.co.uk *Website:* www.falkirkfc.co.uk
Ground Capacity: seated: 8000. *Size of Pitch:* 105m × 68m.
Chairman: Martin Ritchie. *Managing Director:* George Craig. *Secretary:* Alex Blackwood.
Manager: Steven Pressley.
Club Nickname: The Bairns.
Previous Grounds: Randyford 1876-81; Blinkbonny Grounds 1881-83; Brockville Park 1883-2003.
Record Attendance: 23,100 v Celtic, Scottish Cup 3rd rd, 21 Feb 1953.
Record Transfer Fee received: £380,000 for John Hughes to Celtic (Aug 1995).
Record Transfer Fee paid: £225,000 to Chelsea for Kevin McAllister (Aug 1991).
Record Victory: 12-1 v Laurieston, Scottish Cup 2nd rd, 23 Sept 1893.
Record Defeat: 1-11 v Airdrieonians, Division I, 28 Apr 1951.
Most Capped Player: Alex Parker, 14 (15), Scotland and Russell Latapy, Trinidad & Tobago.
Most League Appearances: 450: Tom Ferguson, 1919-32.
Most League Goals in Season (Individual): 43: Evelyn Morrison, Division I, 1928-29.
Most Goals Overall (Individual): 86: Dougie Moran, 1957-61 and 1964-67.

FALKIRK 2010–11 LEAGUE RECORD

Match No.	Date		Venue	Opponents	Result	H/T Score	Lg Pos.	Goalscorers	Atten- dance
1	Aug	7	H	Dunfermline Ath	L 0-1	0-1	—		6947
2		14	A	Ross Co	W 1-0	1-0	6	Flynn [36]	2837
3		21	H	Stirling A	W 3-0	0-0	2	Twaddle [60], Stewart [70], Compton [79]	4196
4		28	A	Dundee	L 0-2	0-2	5		4557
5	Sept	11	H	Queen of the S	W 3-1	1-0	3	McManus 2 [15, 71], Deuchar [84]	4064
6		18	H	Morton	W 2-1	1-0	3	Smyth (og) [45], Flynn [84]	3988
7		25	A	Raith R	L 1-2	1-1	3	Flynn [7]	3438
8	Oct	2	H	Cowdenbeath	W 5-1	3-0	3	Compton [11], Stewart [22], Millar 2 (1 pen) [34, 79 (p)], Finnigan [69]	3764
9		16	A	Partick Th	L 0-1	0-1	3		2783
10		23	A	Queen of the S	W 5-1	1-0	3	Finnigan 2 [4, 74], Marr [52], Deuchar [84], Twaddle [89]	2254
11		30	H	Dundee	D 3-3	0-2	3	Stewart 2 [72, 75], Millar (pen) [88]	4667
12	Nov	6	H	Ross Co	L 0-1	0-1	3		4512
13		13	A	Stirling A	W 5-0	2-0	3	Flynn [6], Stewart 2 [15, 57], Deuchar [71], Finnigan [79]	2168
14	Dec	29	A	Raith R	D 0-0	0-0	—		4037
15	Jan	2	H	Stirling A	W 4-2	3-1	3	Higginbotham 2 [5, 32], Allison (og) [20], McLean [60]	3722
16		15	H	Queen of the S	L 0-3	0-3	3		3376
17		22	A	Dundee	L 0-1	0-1	—		4763
18		29	A	Raith R	W 2-1	2-1	—	Compton [38], Stewart [42]	2829
19	Feb	12	H	Morton	W 1-0	0-0	3	Stewart [81]	3636
20		15	A	Dunfermline Ath	D 1-1	0-0	—	Scobbie [79]	5082
21		26	H	Cowdenbeath	W 2-0	1-0	3	Murdoch [20], Flynn [55]	3581
22	Mar	1	A	Morton	D 0-0	0-0	—		1343
23		5	A	Ross Co	L 1-2	1-1	3	Stewart [37]	2676
24		12	H	Dunfermline Ath	L 1-2	0-2	3	Millar (pen) [58]	5121
25		19	H	Dundee	D 2-2	1-0	3	McManus [27], Stewart [64]	4099
26		22	A	Queen of the S	W 1-0	1-0	—	McManus [25]	1270
27		26	H	Raith R	W 2-1	1-0	3	Stewart 2 [38, 79]	5008
28		29	A	Cowdenbeath	D 0-0	0-0	—		803
29	Apr	2	A	Morton	D 2-2	0-1	3	Stewart [61], Duffie [87]	1965
30		9	H	Partick Th	L 2-3	0-2	3	McManus [66], Finnigan [85]	3735
31		12	A	Partick Th	W 2-1	0-0	—	Alston [64], Finnigan [67]	1142
32		16	A	Cowdenbeath	W 2-1	0-1	3	Stewart [65], McLean [69]	636
33		19	H	Partick Th	W 2-0	1-0	—	McManus [45], Stewart [90]	3439
34		23	A	Stirling A	W 2-1	2-0	3	Millar (pen) [37], McManus [41]	1288
35		30	H	Ross Co	L 0-1	0-0	3		4143
36	May	7	A	Dunfermline Ath	L 0-3	0-1	13	7826	

Final League Position: 3

Honours
League Champions: Division II 1935-36, 1969-70, 1974-75. First Division 1990-91, 1993-94, 2002-03, 2004-05. Second Division 1979-80; *Runners-up:* Division I 1907-08, 1909-10. First Division 1985-86, 1988-89, 1997-98, 1998-99. Division II 1904-05, 1951-52, 1960-61.
Scottish Cup Winners: 1913, 1957; *Runners-up:* 1997, 2009. *League Cup Runners-up:* 1947-48. *B&Q Cup Winners:* 1993-94. *League Challenge Cup Winners:* 1997-98, 2004-05.

European: *Europa League:* 2 matches (2009-10).

Club colours: Shirt: Navy blue with white seams. Shorts: White. Stockings: White.

Goalscorers: *League (57):* Stewart 15, McManus 7, Finnigan 6, Flynn 5, Millar 5 (4 pens), Compton 3, Deuchar 3, Higginbotham 2, McLean 2, Twaddle 2, Alston 1, Duffie 1, Marr 1, Murdoch 1, Scobbie 1, own goals 2.
Scottish Cup (2): Compton 1, Millar 1.
CIS Cup (6): Flynn 2, Stewart 2, Finnigan 1, Khalis 1.
Alba Challenge Cup (0).

Olejnik R 36	Marr J 12+2	McLean B 31	Khalis M 6+1	Scobbie T 32+1	Flynn R 31+2	O'Brien B 31	Millar M 28+2	Compton J 15+9	Higginbotham K 19+11	Stewart M 31+4	Duffie K 19+4	Finnigan C 23+6	Deuchar K 4+11	Twaddle M 31	Mitchell C 6+11	McManus T 12+4	Alston B 3+4	Murdoch S 10+3	Moutinho P 6+4	Perry R 9+3	Fulton J —+2	Kingsley S 1+2	Match No.
1	2^1	3	4^3	5	6	7	8^8	9^2	10	11	12	13	14										1
1	2	3		4	7	6		12	10	9		8^1	11	5									2
1	2	4	3	8	6	7		12^2	9	10^1	11			5	13								3
1	2	4	3	8	6	7	11^1	12	9^2	13	10			5									4
1	2	3	4	9	8	7^1	11^2		13	10		14		5	12	6^1							5
1	2	3		4	7	6	8^3	11	13	10^1	12		14	5		9^2							6
1	2	3	4		6	7	12	9^2	8^1	10	11			5	13								7
1	2	4	3	7	6^2		12	10^1	9	8^3	11	13		5				14					8
1	2	3	4	9	8		10	11^1	6^2	12	7			5	13								9
1	2	4	3	8	6	7		9^1	11^2	10	12	5	13										10
1	2^1	3^2	4	13	6	7	8		9	11		10	12	5									11
1	2^2		3	4	6	8	7		9^1	10	13	11	12	5									12
1	12	3^1		4	8^2	9	7^3		13	11	2	10	14	6	5								13
1		3		4	9	8	7	13	12	10^1	2		11	6	5^2								14
1	14	3		4	8	7	9	13	11	10^1	2^3		12	6	5^2								15
1		3	13	4^2	9	6	8	11^1	14	2	10^3	12	5	7									16
1		3	4		11	7	8^3	13	14	6	12	10^4	2	5	2^1				9^2				17
1	4^8		3	7	9	8	10^3	13	5^2	2		6						12	14	11^1			18
1				4	6	7	8^8	9^2	14	12	2^1	11		5	13				10^3	3			19
1		3		4	8	7		10^1	12	9^2	2	11		5				6	13				20
1		3		4	8^2	7		13	9	12	5	10^3			14			6	11^1	2			21
1		3		4	9	6		12	7^3	11	2			5	13	14		8^2	10^1				22
1	3^2			4	8	7	6^1		9	10^3	2	11		5	12				14	13			23
1		3		4		7	8	13	9^3	10		11^2		5		12		6^1	14	2			24
1		4	3		6	7	10^1		8		11			5		9		12		2			25
1		3		4		6	7	9		8		10^2		5		11^1		13	12	2			26
1		3		4	13	6	7	9^1	14	8	2^1	11		5		10^2				12			27
1		3		4	12	7	6	9^1	13	8		10		5		11^2				2			28
1		3		4^1	8	6	7	13		9	12			5		11			10^2	2			29
1		3^1			8	6	7		12	10	2	13		5		11			9^2	4			30
1			3	8^1		7		9^2	10	2	11		5			6	4					12	13	31
1		3		4	6		7		11	9	2	10				12	8	5^1					32
1	5	3		6		8^1		11	9	2			13	10^3	7^2	4				12	14		33
1	3^3	4		8		6		10	9	2^2	13		5	12	11			7^1				14^8	34
1	4^3	3		9^2		7		11	6	2	12			5	14	10	13	8^1					35
1				4	7	6		9	10	8	2	12				11^1				3		5	36

FORFAR ATHLETIC   Second Division

Year Formed: 1885. *Ground & Address:* Station Park, Carseview Road, Forfar DD8 3BT. *Telephone:* 01307 463576.
Fax: 01307 466956. *E-mail:* pat@ramsayladders.co.uk *Website:* www.forfarathletic.co.uk
Ground Capacity: 5177 (739 seated). *Size of Pitch:* 103m × 64m.
Chairman: Neill Wilson. *Vice Chairman:* Jim Farquhar. *Secretary:* David McGregor.
Manager: Dick Campbell. *Assistant Manager:* Ian Campbell. *Physio:* Cillian Rodgers.
Club Nicknames: Loons, The Sky Blues.
Previous Grounds: None.
Record Attendance: 10,780 v Rangers, Scottish Cup 2nd rd, 2 Feb 1970.
Record Transfer Fee received: £65,000 for David Bingham to Dunfermline Ath (September 1995).
Record Transfer Fee paid: £50,000 for Ian McPhee from Airdrieonians (1991).
Record Victory: 14-1 v Lindertis, Scottish Cup 1st rd, 1 Sept 1988.
Record Defeat: 2-12 v King's Park, Division II, 2 Jan 1930.
Most League Appearances: 484: Ian McPhee, 1978-88 and 1991-98.
Most League Goals in Season (Individual): 45: Dave Kilgour, Division II, 1929-30.
Most Goals Overall: 124: John Clark, 1978-91.

FORFAR ATHLETIC 2010–11 LEAGUE RECORD

Match No.	Date		Venue	Opponents	Result	H/T Score	Lg Pos.	Goalscorers	Atten- dance
1	Aug	7	H	Dumbarton	W 4-1	1-1	—	Campbell, R [2], Hilson [51], Templeman 2 (1 pen) [59, 77 (p)]	510
2		14	A	Peterhead	W 2-1	2-0	1	Gibson [18], Hilson [27]	371
3		21	H	Brechin C	D 1-1	0-0	1	Templeman [59]	782
4		28	A	Livingston	L 0-2	0-1	4		1553
5	Sept	11	H	East Fife	W 3-2	0-1	3	Templeman 3 [54, 77, 90]	590
6		18	A	Stenhousemuir	L 0-3	0-1	3		522
7		25	H	Airdrie U	L 1-2	1-0	6	Bolocheweckyj [25]	577
8	Oct	2	A	Alloa Ath	L 2-3	1-3	6	Todd [44], Deasley [78]	436
9		16	H	Ayr U	W 4-1	1-0	6	Campbell, R (pen) [12], Templeman [59], Fotheringham, M (pen) [81], Gibson [90]	544
10		23	A	East Fife	W 3-1	1-0	5	Campbell, R 2 [44, 70], Fotheringham, M [60]	524
11		30	H	Livingston	W 1-0	0-0	4	Allan [72]	612
12	Nov	6	H	Peterhead	D 1-1	0-0	4	Fotheringham, M [88]	497
13		13	A	Brechin C	D 0-0	0-0	4		786
14	Jan	25	A	Dumbarton	W 2-1	0-1	—	Fotheringham, M [71], Deasley [72]	404
15	Feb	1	H	East Fife	D 0-0	0-0	—		438
16		5	A	Stenhousemuir	W 1-0	1-0	4	Bolocheweckyj [14]	504
17		12	A	Alloa Ath	W 3-0	0-0	4	Campbell, R 2 [61, 80], Smith, C [90]	414
18		15	H	Alloa Ath	D 1-1	0-0	—	Campbell, R (pen) [71]	390
19		22	A	Airdrie U	L 0-2	0-0	—		437
20		26	H	Dumbarton	W 2-1	1-1	4	Brady [5], Campbell, R [78]	487
21	Mar	1	A	Livingston	L 0-3	0-1	—		724
22		5	A	Peterhead	D 1-1	0-1	4	Campbell, R [90]	479
23		8	H	Brechin C	W 2-1	0-0	—	Templeman [86], Campbell, R [90]	604
24		12	A	East Fife	L 0-3	0-1	—		469
25		19	H	Livingston	L 0-4	0-2	4		552
26		23	A	Ayr U	W 1-0	0-0	—	Deasley [86]	909
27		26	A	Airdrie U	L 1-3	1-3	4	McQuade [31]	594
28		29	H	Airdrie U	L 1-2	1-1	—	Bolocheweckyj [42]	419
29	Apr	2	H	Stenhousemuir	D 1-1	1-0	4	Dow [16]	416
30		5	H	Ayr U	W 3-2	0-1	—	Campbell, R [51], Fotheringham, M 2 [75, 84]	341
31		9	A	Ayr U	L 1-3	0-2	4	Bolocheweckyj [75]	851
32		12	H	Stenhousemuir	W 2-0	2-0	—	Templeman [37], Dow [45]	347
33		16	A	Alloa Ath	W 3-1	1-0	3	Fotheringham, M [23], Templeman [60], Dow [62]	458
34		23	A	Brechin C	W 1-0	0-0	3	Hilson [58]	825
35		30	H	Peterhead	W 2-1	1-0	3	Smith, C [35], Sellars [66]	448
36	May	7	A	Dumbarton	D 0-0	0-0	3		787

Final League Position: 3

Honours
League Champions: Second Division 1983-84. Third Division 1994-95; *Runners-up:* 1996-97. C Division 1948-49. *Third Division* 2009-10. *Promoted to Second Division:* 2009-10 (play-offs).
Scottish Cup: Semi-finals 1982.
League Cup: Semi-finals 1977-78.
League Challenge Cup: Semi-finals 2004-05.

Club colours: Shirt: Sky and navy blue hoops. Shorts: Navy blue. Stockings: Sky blue.

Goalscorers: *League (50):* Campbell R 11 (2 pens), Templeman 10 (1 pen), Fotheringham M 7 (1 pen), Bolocheweckyj 4, Deasley 3, Dow 3, Hilson 3, Gibson 2, Smith C 2, Allan 1, Brady 1, McQuade 1, Sellars 1, Todd 1.
Scottish Cup (1): Tod 1.
CIS Cup (3): Campbell I 1, Campbell R 1, Templeman 1.
Alba Challenge Cup (3): Deasley 1, Sellars 1, Templeman 1.
Play-Offs (4): Campbell R 1 (pen), Hilson 1, Sellars 1, Templeman 1.

Gallacher S 29	Bishop J 27	Todd A 11	Mowat D 22 + 3	Lunan P 7 + 2	Fotheringham M 19 + 8	Sellars B 18 + 9	Gibson G 16 + 16	Hilson D 27 + 2	Campbell R 24 + 9	Templeman C 29 + 5	Watson P — + 6	Deasley B 19 + 15	Smith C 3 + 10	McLean E 2 + 1	McCulloch M 32 + 1	Campbell I 27 + 1	Tulloch S 4	Bolocheweckyj M 26 + 1	Allan S 4	Brady D 9 + 6	Ross G 23	Dow R 8 + 3	McQuade P 5	Duffy N 5 + 2	Match No.
1	2	3	4	5	6³	7	8	9²	10¹	11	12	13	14												1
1ᵃ	3	4	8	2	6¹	7	9	11²	12	10⁹		13		15	5										2
	3	2	4	6	13	8²	9³	11	12	10		14			1	7	5								3
		4	6	13	12	7	11³	9	14	10²					1	8	2	3¹	5						4
1	2	3	4	6	8		9	12	10	11¹					7	5									5
1	3	2	4ᵃ	6	8	12	9²	14	13	10³		11			7	5									6
1	4¹	3³	8		9	12	6²		13	10		11	14	2	7	5									7
1	2²	5		7¹	12			11	10³	9		14			6	4		3	8	13					8
1		4	5	12		13	8¹	11	10²	9					6	2		3	7³	14					9
1	3¹	5		12		13	8	11	10²	9³	14				6	4		2	7						10
1			3			12	10	8	9	11¹²	13				5	2		4	7	6¹					11
1	3³	5	12	14		13	11	8ᵃ	10	9ᵇ					6	2ᵃ		1	7¹						12
1	2	4	5	7		12	8¹	11	10	9					6	3									13
1	5			8³	7	12		10¹	11¹²	14	13				6	3	4		9	2					14
1	4			12	7	14	13	10³	11¹²	9					6	5		3	8¹	2					15
1	4		14		7ᵃ	13	12	10	8¹	9²	11				6	5³		3		2					16
1	3		5		7	12	8	11	10²	9¹	13				6	4				2					17
1	4			7	12	10³	8	11²	14	9¹	13				6	5		3		2					18
1	4		5¹	7		8	13	11	10²	9					6	12		3³	14	2					19
1	4		6	7	12	13		10¹	14	9³	11²				5	3		8		2					20
1	4		7	6	9²	10		13	14	11¹	12				5	3		8		2					21
1	3		6	7	11²	9	10	13		12					5	4	14	8³		2					22
1	7	9¹		8²	13	14	11	6	10³	12					4	3		5		2					23
1	3ᵃ	12		8³	7		11	9	10²	14		13			6	5¹		4		2					24
1		12			6	13	9³	8	10²	14					4	3¹		5		7	2	11			25
1	4	5			7	11¹²	9	8³	12	13	14				6	3				2	10¹				26
1		5			7³	12	10²	8	14	13					6	4	3			2	9¹	11			27
1	3	4		12			8	11³	14	9²		7	5¹		6			2		13	10				28
1ᵇ	4				12	8²	10	7	13	6		3	5		2			9	11¹	15					29
1	5			13	14	7²	9	8	12	3		6³	4		2			11¹	10						30
1ᵇ	4	6		8	13	9²	10	12	7	3		5			2¹			11	15						31
	8		7		11²	6¹	13	10	12	4		5	3		14	2		9³						1	32
	4	3	7³		9²	8¹	13	10	12	6		5			14	2		11						1	33
	3		6³	12	9	7	10	8¹	13	4		5			14	2		11²						1	34
	4			6	2	11¹	7		9	10		5			8	3		12						1	35
	5	6		13	7	10²	9	11³	8¹			14	2		4	3		12						1	36

HAMILTON ACADEMICAL · First Division

Year Formed: 1874. *Ground:* New Douglas Park, Cadzow Avenue, Hamilton ML3 0FT. *Telephone:* 01698 368650.
Fax: 01698 285422. *E-mail:* scott@acciesfc.co.uk *Website:* www.acciesfc.co.uk
Ground Capacity: 6078. *Size of Pitch:* 115yd × 75yd.
Chairman: Ronnie MacDonald. *Vice-Chairman:* Les Gray. *Secretary:* Scott A. Struthers BA.
Manager: Billy Reid. *Sports Therapist:* Avril Downs.
Club Nickname: The Accies.
Previous Grounds: Bent Farm, South Avenue, South Haugh, Douglas Park, Cliftonhill Stadium, Firhill Stadium.
Record Attendance: 28,690 v Hearts, Scottish Cup 3rd rd, 3 Mar 1937 (at Douglas Park); 5,895 v Rangers, 28 February 2009 (at New Douglas Park).
Record Transfer Fee received: £1,200,000 from Wigan Ath for James McCarthy (July 2009).
Record Transfer Fee paid: £180,000 for Tomas Cerny from Sigma Olomouc (July 2009).
Record Victory: 11-1 v Chryston, Lanarkshire Cup, 28 Nov 1885.
Record Defeat: 1-11 v Hibernian, Division I, 6 Nov 1965.
Most Capped Player: Colin Miller, 29 (61), Canada, 1988-94.
Most League Appearances: 452: Rikki Ferguson, 1974-88.
Most League Goals in Season (Individual): 35: David Wilson, Division I; 1936-37.
Most Goals Overall (Individual): 246: David Wilson, 1928-39.

HAMILTON ACADEMICAL 2010–11 LEAGUE RECORD

Match No.	Date	Venue	Opponents	Result		H/T Score	Lg Pos.	Goalscorers	Atten- dance
1	Aug 14	A	Aberdeen	L	0-4	0-2	—		12,005
2	21	H	Hearts	L	0-4	0-2	12		2899
3	28	A	Inverness CT	W	1-0	1-0	10	Imrie [1]	3851
4	Sept 11	H	Rangers	L	1-2	0-1	11	Bougherra (og) [56]	5356
5	18	A	Hibernian	D	1-1	1-1	12	Paixao, M [22]	11,294
6	25	H	Kilmarnock	D	2-2	2-0	10	Paixao, F [15], Hasselbaink [38]	3033
7	Oct 2	A	Celtic	L	1-3	1-1	11	McLaughlin [3]	47,446
8	16	A	St Mirren	D	2-2	1-0	11	Routledge [39], Imrie [47]	3577
9	23	H	St Johnstone	L	1-2	0-1	11	Mensing (pen) [68]	2431
10	30	A	Motherwell	W	1-0	1-0	10	Hasselbaink [15]	4865
11	Nov 6	H	Dundee U	L	0-1	0-0	10		2456
12	10	A	Kilmarnock	L	0-3	0-1	—		4214
13	13	H	Inverness CT	L	1-3	1-0	12	Imrie [29]	2019
14	20	A	Hearts	L	0-2	0-1	12		12,620
15	27	H	St Mirren	D	0-0	0-0	12		2280
16	Dec 29	H	Aberdeen	L	0-1	0-0	12		2968
17	Jan 1	H	Motherwell	D	0-0	0-0	12		3171
18	12	H	Celtic	D	1-1	1-0	—	Mensing [28]	5163
19	15	A	Rangers	L	0-4	0-3	12		44,639
20	22	A	Inverness CT	D	1-1	1-1	12	Antoine-Curier (pen) [45]	3241
21	29	H	Kilmarnock	D	1-1	0-1	—	Antoine-Curier [79]	2680
22	Feb 1	A	St Johnstone	L	0-2	0-1	—		2631
23	12	H	Hearts	L	0-2	0-1	12		2876
24	19	A	Motherwell	L	0-1	0-1	12		4407
25	22	A	Aberdeen	L	0-1	0-1	—		7019
26	26	H	Dundee U	D	1-1	1-0	12	Antoine-Curier (pen) [33]	2011
27	Mar 1	H	Hibernian	L	1-2	0-1	—	Paixao, F [90]	2619
28	5	A	Celtic	L	0-2	0-1	12		51,811
29	10	A	Dundee U	L	1-2	1-1	—	Paixao, F [26]	5766
30	19	H	St Johnstone	D	0-0	0-0	12		2111
31	Apr 2	A	St Mirren	L	1-3	1-0	12	Buchanan [43]	4985
32	10	H	Rangers	L	0-1	0-1	12		4526
33	17	A	Hibernian	W	2-1	2-0	—	Chambers [9], Miller (og) [34]	8173
34	25	H	Aberdeen	D	1-1	0-0	—	Imrie [64]	2140
35	May 2	A	St Mirren	W	1-0	0-0	—	Antoine-Curier [74]	5037
36	7	H	Hibernian	W	1-0	1-0	12	Hasselbaink [38]	2300
37	10	A	St Johnstone	L	0-1	0-1	—		2253
38	14	H	Inverness CT	L	1-2	0-1	12	Mensing [50]	2017

Final League Position: 12

Honours
League Champions: Division II 1903-04. First Division 1985-86, 1987-88, 2007-08; Third Division 2000-01. *Runners-up:* Division II 1952-53, 1964-65; Second Division 1996-97, 2003-04.
Scottish Cup Runners-up: 1911, 1935. *League Cup:* Semi-finalists three times. *League Challenge Cup*: Runners-up 2006. *B&Q Cup Winners:* 1991-92, 1992-93.

Club colours: Shirt: Red and white hoops. Shorts: White. Stockings: White.

Goalscorers: *League (24):* Antoine-Curier 4 (2 pens), Imrie 4, Hasselbaink 3, Mensing 3 (1 pen), Paixao F 3, Buchanan 1, Chambers 1, McLaughlin 1, Paixao M 1, Routledge 1, own goals 2.
Scottish Cup (3): Antoine-Curier 1, Flavo Paixao 1, Hasselbaink 1.
CIS Cup (0).

Cerny T 37	Ross J 2	Skelton G 14+2	Canning M 23	Mensing S 30	McDonald G 22+3	Imrie D 35	Wilkie K 3+3	Paixao F 26+4	Paixao M 9+9	Buchanan D 27+1	Thomas J 1+2	Kirkpatrick J 2+3	Routledge J 22+2	McQueen B 1	McAlister J 15+4	Gillespie G 8+9	Graham A 10+5	Hasselbaink N 21+6	Lyle D 1+3	Goodwin J 14	Casalinuovo D 6+13	Elebert D 16+3	McLaughlin M 21	Neil A 8+2	Hopkirk D 2+3	Devlin M 1	Kilday L 4+1	Antoine-Curier M 10+3	Crawford A 9+5	Wildig A 2+1	Gordon Z 2	Chambers J 6+3	Carrington M 6+6	Elliot T 1+6	Murdoch S 1	Millar K —+1	McGlinchey C —+1	Match No.
1	2	3	4	5	6³	7	8¹	9	10	11²	12	13	14																									1
1	2¹	3	4⁴	5	13	7		8	9	10			11		6²	12																						2
1	13			5		7		8²	9	10¹	3	14			4			2	6	11³	12																	3
1			4	5		7		9	10	6			11				3	8¹		2	12																	4
1			4	5		7	13	9	10				11			14	8²	2³	12	3¹	6																	5
1			4	5		7		9	10	2			11			14	8²	3³	13	12	6¹																	6
1			4	5		7	13	9	14	3			11		8¹		10³	7²	12	6																	7
1			4	5	6²	7		9		2			11			12	10³	8¹	14	13	3																	8
1			4	5	6¹	7		9	12	3			11			10²	14	2	13	8³																	9
1			4	5			8³	9	13	11			7			10²		6¹	14	2	3	12																10
1			4	5		7		9	10	3			11		13		12	8¹	14	2³	6²																	11
1		4	8	14		7		0⁷	13	3			11		5¹	10¹		2	12	6																		12
1			5			7		12	13	3			8¹	11³		6		14	4	9	2		10²															13
1	3	4	8	6¹		7		12	13	10²				14	5³		11	9	2			10²																14
1	3	4	5	6		7		9²	10³	13	14				2		12	8	11¹																			15
1	11	4	5			7		12	13	3				8				9²	2	10¹																		16
1	11	4	5	6			8	9		3					10¹	7²	12	13		2																		17
1	11	4		6⁴			8	14	9				3		12²	7³	5	10²			13		2¹															18
1	11					7		9	10²				13		4	2	14			3								5	6¹			8³	12					19
1	3	4	5	6³		7		9	14	11					12	2	10²			13												8¹						20
1	11¹	4		6		7		9		3					14	2	10²			13		5³						12		8								21
1		4				7				3			13	2	5			9²		10			12	6	8¹	11³	14											22
1	11	4			7³			13	14	2²					8	9				5	3		10			6¹		12										23
1	3	4	12					9³		7					11		14			2	5¹		10	13				6	8²									24
1	11	4	6	8				9¹		7					3		13			2	5²		10						12									25
1	3	2	4²	8				9¹		7					11	13		14		5			10⁵					12										26
1	3	4				7		9		2					13			11¹	5²	6			10	12					8									27
1	3	4	11					9²		7			6	14	10¹			2	5	12			13						8³									28
1	13	3	4	8				9		7			11			5		12	14	10²	2³								6¹									29
1	8¹	4						9		3			7	3¹		2	6	5²		10	11		13	12														30
1		4⁴		8				9		3			11	12		10¹		5	7				6									2						31
1		6	4	11				3					14	2³	9			5¹	10			7	8²					13	12									32
1		5	8	7				3					11	12	9³			6		2	10¹		4²	13	14	1												33
1		8	10					3					11	13	9			6²	5	4¹	2		12	7³		14												34
1		4	6	11				5³					3		9²			2	10⁴			12	8	13	7¹	14												35
1		5	8	10				3					2	7³	9¹			6			13	12	11	4²	14													36
1		5	6	10				3¹					7³	4	14	9		12	2⁸	8			11²	13														37
1		5	7²	10				3					2			9¹			8	12		6	11³	4											13	14	38

HEART OF MIDLOTHIAN   Premier League

Year Formed: 1874. *Ground & Address:* Tynecastle Stadium, McLeod Street, Edinburgh EH11 2NL. *Telephone:* 0871 663 1874. *Fax:* 0131 200 7222. *E-mail:* hearts@homplc.co.uk *Website:* www.heartsfc.co.uk
Ground Capacity: 17,402. *Size of Pitch:* 100m × 64m.
Chairman: Roman Romanov. *Non-Executive Directors:* Sergejus Fedotovas, Julija Goncaruk, Vitalijus Vasiliauskas.
Manager: Jim Jefferies. *Assistant Manager:* Billy Brown. *First Team Coach:* Gary Locke. *Physio:* Rob Marshall.
Club Nicknames: Hearts, Jambos.
Previous Grounds: The Meadows 1874, Powderhall 1878, Old Tynecastle 1881, (Tynecastle Park, 1886).
Record Attendance: 53,396 v Rangers, Scottish Cup 3rd rd, 13 Feb 1932 (57,857 v Barcelona, 28 July 2007 at Murrayfield).
Record Transfer Fee received: £9,000,000 for Craig Gordon to Sunderland (August 2008).
Record of Transfer paid: £850,000 for Mirsad Beslija to Genk (January 2006).
Record Victory: 21-0 v Anchor, EFA Cup, 30 Oct 1880.
Record Defeat: 1-8 v Vale of Leven, Scottish Cup, 1888.
Most Capped Player: Steven Pressley, 32, Scotland.
Most League Appearances: 515: Gary Mackay, 1980-97.
Most League Goals in Season (Individual): 44: Barney Battles, 1930-31.
Most Goals Overall (Individual): 214: John Robertson, 1983-98.

HEART OF MIDLOTHIAN 2010–11 LEAGUE RECORD

Match No.	Date	Venue	Opponents	Result	H/T Score	Lg Pos.	Goalscorers	Attendance
1	Aug 14	H	St Johnstone	D 1-1	1-1	—	Elliot [44]	14,562
2	21	A	Hamilton A	W 4-0	2-0	4	Elliot 2 [6, 81], Templeton [24], Kyle (pen) [76]	2899
3	29	H	Dundee U	D 1-1	1-0	4	Templeton [30]	12,898
4	Sept 11	A	Celtic	L 0-3	0-2	6		49,023
5	18	A	Inverness CT	W 3-1	1-1	3	Innes (og) [45], Stevenson [55], Elliot [69]	4515
6	25	H	Motherwell	L 0-2	0-0	4		13,749
7	Oct 2	H	Rangers	L 1-2	1-0	6	Skacel [12]	15,637
8	16	A	Aberdeen	W 1-0	0-0	5	Kyle [46]	8999
9	23	H	St Mirren	W 3-0	2-0	4	Skacel 3 [2, 24, 90]	12,009
10	31	H	Kilmarnock	L 0-3	0-1	5		13,056
11	Nov 7	A	Hibernian	W 2-0	1-0	4	Templeton [19], Elliott [67]	17,767
12	10	H	Celtic	W 2-0	1-0	—	Black [29], Templeton [58]	15,632
13	13	A	St Johnstone	W 2-0	0-0	3	Kyle (pen) [64], Stevenson [90]	4156
14	20	H	Hamilton A	W 2-0	1-0	3	Skacel [32], Templeton [52]	12,620
15	Dec 11	H	Aberdeen	W 5-0	2-0	—	Templeton [5], Skacel 2 [9, 58], Elliott [51], Novikovas [78]	13,434
16	14	A	Motherwell	W 2-1	1-1	—	Reynolds (og) [44], Kyle (pen) [60]	3324
17	18	H	Inverness CT	D 1-1	1-1	—	Kyle (pen) [25]	12,994
18	29	A	St Mirren	W 2-0	0-0	3	Templeton [63], Kyle (pen) [82]	4599
19	Jan 1	H	Hibernian	W 1-0	0-0	3	Kyle [86]	17,156
20	18	A	Kilmarnock	W 2-1	0-1	—	Elliott 2 [73, 86]	4996
21	22	H	Rangers	W 1-0	0-0	3	Stevenson [77]	16,737
22	26	A	Celtic	L 0-4	0-2	—		49,460
23	29	H	St Johnstone	W 1-0	1-0	—	Skacel [3]	13,430
24	Feb 2	A	Rangers	L 0-1	0-1	—		44,823
25	12	A	Hamilton A	W 2-0	1-0	3	Elliott 2 [22, 47]	2876
26	19	H	Dundee U	W 2-1	1-1	3	Skacel [45], Zaliukas [88]	15,473
27	26	A	Aberdeen	D 0-0	0-0	3		9100
28	Mar 5	H	Kilmarnock	L 0-2	0-0	3		13,836
29	16	A	Dundee U	L 0-2	0-0	—		6718
30	19	H	St Mirren	W 3-2	0-1	3	Skacel 2 [55, 90], Stevenson [82]	12,763
31	Apr 3	A	Hibernian	D 2-2	1-1	3	Stevenson [24], Elliott [83]	17,793
32	9	H	Motherwell	D 0-0	0-0	3		13,800
33	16	A	Inverness CT	D 1-1	0-1	—	Elliott [53]	4336
34	23	H	Motherwell	D 3-3	2-0	3	Thomson, C (pen) [26], Skacel [36], Stevenson [52]	13,039
35	30	A	Kilmarnock	D 2-2	0-0	3	Skacel [67], Pascali (og) [76]	5006
36	May 7	A	Rangers	L 0-4	0-3	3		46,178
37	11	H	Celtic	L 0-3	0-1	—		16,681
38	15	A	Dundee U	L 1-2	1-1	3	Glen [31]	7119

Final League Position: 3

Honours
League Champions: Division I 1894-95, 1896-97, 1957-58, 1959-60. First Division 1979-80; *Runners-up:* Division I 1893-94, 1898-99, 1903-04, 1905-06, 1914-15, 1937-38, 1953-54, 1956-57, 1958-59, 1964-65. Premier Division 1985-86, 1987-88, 1991-92; *Runners-up:* 2005-06. First Division 1977-78, 1982-83.
Scottish Cup Winners: 1891, 1896, 1901, 1906, 1956, 1998, 2006; *Runners-up:* 1903, 1907, 1968, 1976, 1986, 1996.
League Cup Winners: 1954-55, 1958-59, 1959-60, 1962-63; *Runners-up:* 1961-62, 1996-97.

European: *European Cup:* 8 matches (1958-59, 1960-61, 2006-07). *Cup Winners' Cup:* 10 matches (1976-77, 1996-97, 1998-99). *UEFA Cup:* 47 matches (*Fairs Cup:* 1961-62, 1963-64, 1965-66. *UEFA Cup:* 1984-85, 1986-87, 1988-89, 1990-91, 1992-93, 1993-94, 2000-01, 2003-04, 2004-05, 2006-07). *Europa League:* 2 matches (2009-10).

Club colours: Shirt: White with maroon sleeves and side panels. Shorts: White with maroon side panels. Stockings: Maroon with white tops.

Goalscorers: *League (53):* Skacel 13, Elliott 8, Kyle 7 (5 pens), Templeton 7, Stevenson 6, Elliot 4, Black 1, Glen 1, Novikovas 1, Thomson C 1 (1 pen), Zaliukas 1, own goals 3.
Scottish Cup (0).
CIS Cup (7): Kyle 3 (1 pen), Jonsson 1, Novikovas 1, Robinson 1, Santana 1.

Kello M 31	Thomson J 3+3	Wallace L 9	Zaliukas M 28	Barr D 11+2	Palazuelos R 31+2	Thomson C 20+7	Black I 29+3	Templeton D 27+6	Santana S 16+3	Kyle K 16+3	Elliott C 11+8	Elliot S 21+9	Novikovas A 1+5	Bouzid I 31+1	Mrowiec A 26+4	McGowan R 3+5	Jonsson E 29	Stevenson R 18+13	Obua D 7+6	Skacel R 27+2	MacDonald J 7	Glen G 2+9	Driver A 4+10	Webster A 9	Robinson S 1+3	Smith G —+1	Holt J —+1	Match No.
1	2	3	4	5	6	7	8	9¹	10²	11³	12	13	14															1
1		3	4	5	6⁴	7		8³	9¹	10	11²	13		2	12	14												2
1				5		2	8	9²		7¹	10		13	6	4		3	11	12									3
1				5	6		8²	7	13	11		9¹			4	10	2	3³	12									4
1				2	6²	4	8¹	9	10	7³	12		13	5		14	3	11										5
1	2				6			14	10²	7¹	11		9	12	5	4	3	8³	13									6
1	13			5	12	7	8³		10			9		2	4		3	14		11¹	6²							7
1			4	5	6			10	11¹	9	12	7		8	2		13	3²										8
1			4	5	6		13	14	10¹	11³	9	12		2	7²		3	8										9
1			4	5¹	6	13		14	10²	7	9	12		2	8³		3	11										10
1			4		6		8	10¹	13	9		7²		5	2		3		12	11								11
1			4		6	13	8¹		10	7¹	0	14		5	2		3		12	11¹								12
1			4		6	14	8	10²	13	9		7³		5	2		3		12	11¹								13
1			4		6	13	8¹		10²	9		7	14	5	2		3		12	11²								14
1			4		6		8²	10³	12	9		7¹	14	5	2		3	13		11								15
1			4	5	6	12	8²	10¹	13	9		7			2		3			11								16
1			4		6		8	10²	13	9		7		5¹	2		3		12	11								17
			4		6		8	10²	13	9		7¹		5	2		3	11		12	1							18
			4		6		8	10²	13	9		7¹		5	2		3	14		11³	1	12						19
1	3		4		6		8³		10¹	9	12			5	7		2	14		11²		13						20
1	3		4		6	13	14	9¹	10					5	7		2	8³		11²		12						21
1	3		4	12		6³		9²	13	10				5	7		2	8		14		11¹						22
1	3		4	12	6	2	8		7²	12				5	14			9		11³		10¹	13					23
1			4		6	2	8¹		9²	10				5	7		3	12		11³			14	13				24
1	3		4		6	2²	8³		12	7¹	10		14		9					11			13	5				25
1	3¹		4	6⁴		12	8	13	7²	10				2	9²					11			14	5				26
1					6	2		7	13	9³	12	8			3		4	10		14		11²		5¹				27
1			4			2	8	10²	9	12				5	7		3	6¹		11		13						28
1	3		4			2	8³	9	10²	5¹	7				11	14				13	12	6						29
1			4		6	2	8	9³	10	7²					14		3¹	11		12		5	13					30
12			4⁴		6	3	8³	7¹	10					2	13		9	14	1	11²		5						31
	2				6	3	8²	7¹	12		9³			5	10			11	1	13	4	14						32
					6	3	4	13	7	9				5	12		8	10¹	1	11²	2							33
1					6	2	8	13	7²	10				5	12		3	9		13³		14	4¹					34
		5			6	2	8	9¹	10³			7		13			3	4		11²	1	14	12					35
					6	2	8	9¹		12		7³		5		3⁴		10		11²	1	13						36
1					6	13	8		10¹			2		5	4		3	9³		7⁸	11²	14	12					37
1	12				6	2	8	7				3		5	4					9²	11¹	10³			13	14		38

HIBERNIAN

Premier League

Year Formed: 1875. *Ground & Address:* Easter Road Stadium, 12 Albion Place, Edinburgh EH7 5QG. *Telephone:* 0131 661 2159. *Fax:* 0131 659 6488. *E-mail:* club@hibernianfc.co.uk *Website:* www.hibernianfc.co.uk
Ground Capacity: total: 17,400. *Size of Pitch:* 112yd × 74yd.
Chairman: Rod Petrie. *Chief Executive:* Scott Lindsay. *Club Secretary:* Garry O'Hagan.
Manager: Colin Calderwood. *Physio:* Colin McLelland.
Club Nickname: Hibees.
Previous Grounds: Meadows 1875-78, Powderhall 1878-79, Mayfield 1879-80, First Easter Road 1880-92, Second Easter Road 1892-.
Record Attendance: 65,860 v Hearts, Division I, 2 Jan 1950.
Record Transfer Fee received: £4,400,000 for Scott Brown from Celtic (2007).
Record of Transfer paid: £700,000 to LDU Quito for Ulises de la Cruz (2001).
Record Victory: 22-1 v 42nd Highlanders, 3 Sept 1881.
Record Defeat: 0-10 v Rangers, 24 Dec 1898.
Most Capped Player: Lawrie Reilly, 38, Scotland.
Most League Appearances: 446: Arthur Duncan.
Most League Goals in Season (Individual): 42: Joe Baker, 1959-60.
Most Goals Overall (Individual): 364: Gordon Smith, 1941-1959.

HIBERNIAN 2010–11 LEAGUE RECORD

Match No.	Date	Venue	Opponents	Result	H/T Score	Lg Pos.	Goalscorers	Atten-dance
1	Aug 15	A	Motherwell	W 3-2	1-1	—	Stokes [45], Hanlon [64], Miller [73]	5172
2	22	H	Rangers	L 0-3	0-0	7		17,145
3	29	A	St Mirren	L 0-1	0-0	9		4480
4	Sept 11	H	Inverness CT	D 1-1	1-0	8	Riordan [8]	10,358
5	18	H	Hamilton A	D 1-1	1-1	7	Riordan [9]	11,294
6	25	A	Celtic	L 1-2	0-1	9	Riordan [54]	48,625
7	Oct 2	A	St Johnstone	L 0-2	0-0	10		3819
8	16	H	Kilmarnock	W 2-1	2-1	8	Hogg 2 [38, 45]	11,256
9	23	A	Aberdeen	L 2-4	0-2	9	Nish [63], Bamba [90]	7587
10	30	A	Dundee U	L 0-1	0-0	11		7377
11	Nov 7	H	Hearts	L 0-2	0-1	11		17,767
12	10	A	Rangers	W 3-0	2-0	—	Miller [6], Rankin [19], Dickoh [76]	41,514
13	13	H	Motherwell	W 2-1	2-1	8	Riordan 2 [14, 27]	11,178
14	20	A	Inverness CT	L 2-4	0-1	8	Riordan [66], Miller (pen) [78]	4217
15	27	H	St Johnstone	D 0-0	0-0	8		10,248
16	Dec 18	A	Kilmarnock	L 1-2	0-2	—	Riordan [55]	4216
17	26	H	Aberdeen	L 1-2	1-1	—	Riordan [45]	10,115
18	29	H	Dundee U	D 2-2	1-2	9	Bamba [44], Hanlon [89]	10,252
19	Jan 1	A	Hearts	L 0-1	0-0	10		17,156
20	15	H	Celtic	L 0-3	0-1	10		13,649
21	22	A	Motherwell	L 0-2	0-2	11		4202
22	26	H	Rangers	L 0-2	0-2	—		11,696
23	30	A	Dundee U	L 0-3	0-1	—		6215
24	Feb 2	H	St Mirren	W 2-0	0-0	—	Riordan [63], Wotherspoon [90]	9436
25	12	H	Kilmarnock	W 2-1	0-0	10	Sodje [52], Palsson (pen) [70]	11,082
26	20	A	St Mirren	W 1-0	0-0	10	Dickoh [87]	3505
27	26	H	Inverness CT	W 2-0	0-0	10	Booth [58], Stevenson [89]	13,841
28	Mar 1	A	Hamilton A	W 2-1	1-0	—	Sodje [37], Riordan [75]	2619
29	5	A	St Johnstone	D 1-1	0-0	8	Wotherspoon [80]	4446
30	Apr 3	H	Hearts	D 2-2	1-1	9	Miller (pen) [35], Vas Te [80]	17,793
31	6	A	Celtic	L 1-3	0-3	—	Miller (pen) [67]	47,809
32	9	A	Aberdeen	W 1-0	1-0	8	Sodje [15]	7400
33	17	H	Hamilton A	L 1-2	0-2	—	Sodje [66]	8173
34	24	H	St Mirren	D 1-1	1-1	8	Sodje [26]	7238
35	30	H	St Johnstone	L 1-2	1-0	8	Sodje [23]	7492
36	May 7	A	Hamilton A	L 0-1	0-1	9		2300
37	11	A	Inverness CT	L 0-2	0-1	—		3344
38	14	H	Aberdeen	L 1-3	1-0	10	Riordan [21]	11,767

Final League Position: 10

Honours
League Champions: Division I 1902-03, 1947-48, 1950-51, 1951-52. First Division 1980-81, 1998-99. Division II 1893-94, 1894-95, 1932-33; *Runners-up:* Division I 1896-97, 1946-47, 1949-50, 1952-53, 1973-74, 1974-75.
Scottish Cup Winners: 1887, 1902; *Runners-up:* 1896, 1914, 1923, 1924, 1947, 1958, 1972, 1979, 2001.
League Cup Winners: 1972-73, 1991-92, 2006-07; *Runners-up:* 1950-51, 1968-69, 1974-75, 1993-94, 2003-04.

European: *European Cup:* 6 matches (1955-56 semi-finals). *Cup Winners' Cup:* 6 matches (1972-73). *UEFA Cup:* 63 matches (*Fairs Cup:* 1960-61 semi-finals, 1961-62, 1962-63, 1965-66, 1967-68, 1968-69, 1970-71. *UEFA Cup:* 64 matches (1973-74, 1974-75, 1975-76, 1976-77, 1978-79, 1989-90, 1992-93, 2001-02, 2005-06). *Europa League:* 2 matches (2010-11).

Club colours: Shirt: Green with white sleeves. Shorts: White. Stockings: Green.

Goalscorers: *League (39):* Riordan 11, Sodje 6, Miller 5 (3 pens), Bamba 2, Dickoh 2, Hanlon 2, Hogg 2, Wotherspoon 2, Booth 1, Nish 1, Palsson 1 (1 pen), Rankin 1, Stevenson 1, Stokes 1, Vas Te 1.
Scottish Cup (0).
CIS Cup (1): Grounds 1.
Europa League (2): De Graaf 2.

Stack G 6	Hart M 16+2	Hanlon P 30+3	Miller L 30+3	Hogg C 6+1	Bamba S 16	De Graaf E 16+2	McBride K 10+1	Nish C 11+9	Stokes A 3	Riordan D 28+5	Wotherspoon D 26+9	Stephens D 6+4	Brown M 26	Galbraith D 8+14	Rankin J 14+3	Thicot S 4+3	Murray I 14+6	Grounds J 13	Dickoh F 27+1	Trakys V 4+5	Stevenson L 11+8	Zemmama M 3+1	Duffy D 2+5	Byrne K —+3	Smith G 3+1	Booth C 17	Towell R 15+1	Scott M 8+3	Palsson V 15+1	Thornhill M 5+3	Sodje A 13+2	Vas Te R 7+3	Divis J 3	Taggart S 2+1	Horner L —+1	Handling D —+1	Match No.
1	2	3	4	5	6	7¹	8	9²	10	11	12	13																									1
	2³	3²	4	5	6	11	8⁸	13	10	9¹	7				1	12	14																				2
		3¹	4	5	6	8		9	10	11³	7				1	12	14	2²	13																		3
	2¹		4		6	8²	11	9		10	7				1	13		12		3	5																4
	2	14	4		6	7	8	9³		10	11¹				1	12			3²	5	13																5
	2²	3	4			7¹	8			10	11	12			1	13	9³		5	6	14																6
	2		4		6			8	9	10	11				1		7		3	5																	7
12	3	4	5¹	6	14	8	9³			10	2²				1	13	11		7																		8
	3	4	5	6		8²	9³	13	7¹						1	12	10			2	14	11															9
	2	3	4		6	7				10					1	8¹	9		5		12	11															10
	2	3	4		6	7				10⁸	13				1	8²	9¹	14	5		12	11¹³															11
	2		4	14	6	7					11¹²				1	13	10	12	5¹	3	8	9³															12
	2	13	4³		6	7¹				10					1		11	14	8	3	5⁷	9	12														13
	2¹	12⁸	4		8	7⁸		9		10	14				1	13	11		8³	3	5																14
	2		4³		6	7		9²			12	13			1	8	10		11¹	3	5	14															15
	2		4⁸		6²	11		12		10	7				1	13	9¹		8	3	5																16
	2	5	4¹	6				13		10	7				1	12	9		8	3		11²															17
	2	3	14		6	7				10	11¹				1	9			4²		5		8³	12	13												18
		3	4			7		12		11	13				1	14		6	8³	2	5	9¹			10²												19
		3			6¹	13				10	2²				1	7		4	8		5		11	9³	12	14											20
		3				8	12			13					9	11¹²	2	4			5		6³	10¹	14	1	7										21
		3				12	7¹	9		13	14				10	11		4³			5		8³			1	6	2									22
		3	8					9³			11				10²				5		12	13	1	6	2¹	4	7	14									23
1		3	12					13		10¹	7				14				4		5			6	2		11	8¹	9²								24
1	14	3	13							10¹	7								4		5⁸			6	2	12	8	11¹³	9²								25
1		3	4					13		10³	11				14				5		12			6	2	7	8	9²									26
1		3	4¹					14		10³	7²								5		12			6	2	11	8	13	9								27
1⁶		3	4¹							10	7				12				5			13		15	6	2	11	8		9²							28
		3								10¹	7	1				4			5		14	13			6²	2		8	11¹³	9	12						29
		3	8³							10	13	1				14			5						6	2	11¹	7²	4	9	12						30
	2	3	4							10¹	7	5	1			13			6							8¹	11	14	12	9¹							31
		6	4								12				13	5	1		14		11³				3	2		7	8	10¹	9²						32
		3	4							11	7	14	1						5		13				6	2²	12	8¹		10	9²						33
		6	4³							10	7²		1				12		5		14				3	2	8	11¹		9	13						34
		3								14	12	4		13					5		11				6³	2	7²	8		10¹	9	1					35
		3	8							14	2	4		1					5⁸		11¹²				6	12		7¹		10	9³	1	13				36
		5	4²								7	6							11³						3	2	14	8		12	9	1	10¹	13			37
		5	8							11¹³	7	6	1						12		3				4		13			10	9¹		2²		14		38

INVERNESS CALEDONIAN THISTLE
Premier League

Year Formed: 1994. *Ground & Address:* Tulloch Caledonian Stadium, Stadium Road, Inverness IV1 1FF. *Telephone:* 01463 222880. *Fax:* 01463 227479. *E-mail:* jim.falconer@ictfc.co.uk *Website:* www.ictfc.co.uk
Ground Capacity (seated): 7780. *Size of Pitch:* 115yd × 75yd.
Chairman: George Fraser. *Company Secretary:* Ian MacDonald. *Director of Football:* Graeme Bennett.
Club Nicknames: Caley Thistle, ICT.
Manager: Terry Butcher. *Assistant Manager:* Maurice Malpas.
Record Attendance: 7753 v Rangers, SPL, 20 January 2008.
Record Victory: 8-1, v Annan Ath, Scottish Cup 3rd rd, 24 January 1998.
Record Defeats: 0-5, v Celtic, Premier League, 15 September 2007 and 0-5, v Rangers, Premier League, 1 November 2008.
Most League Appearances: 476: Ross Tokely, 1995-2009.
Most League Goals in Season: 27: Iain Stewart, 1996-97; Denis Wyness, 2002-03.
Most Goals Overall (Individual): 118: Denis Wyness, 2000-03, 2005-08.

INVERNESS CALEDONIAN TH 2010–11 LEAGUE RECORD

Match No.	Date		Venue	Opponents	Result		H/T Score	Lg Pos.	Goalscorers	Atten- dance
1	Aug	14	H	Celtic	L	0-1	-0-0	—		7547
2		22	A	Dundee U	W	4-0	1-0	5	McCann [34], Rooney 2 (1 pen) [51, 82 (p)], Duncan [53]	6575
3		28	H	Hamilton A	L	0-1	0-1	6		3851
4	Sept	11	A	Hibernian	D	1-1	0-1	8	Rooney (pen) [82]	10,358
5		18	H	Hearts	L	1-3	1-1	9	Odhiambo [37]	4515
6		25	A	St Mirren	W	2-1	1-0	7	Odhiambo 2 [45, 50]	3954
7	Oct	2	H	Aberdeen	W	2-0	1-0	5	Hayes [19], Rooney [61]	6144
8		16	H	St Johnstone	D	1-1	0-1	4	Hayes [71]	4883
9		23	A	Kilmarnock	W	2-1	1-0	5	Rooney (pen) [42], Hayes [66]	4508
10		30	A	Rangers	D	1-1	0-1	4	Odhiambo [81]	43,697
11	Nov	6	H	Motherwell	L	1-2	0-2	6	Duff [75]	4054
12		9	A	Aberdeen	W	2-1	1-0	—	Rooney (pen) [34], Munro [81]	5917
13		13	A	Hamilton A	W	3-1	0-1	5	Rooney 2 [49, 59], Hayes [52]	2019
14		20	H	Hibernian	W	4-2	1-0	4	Foran [7], Rooney 3 (1 pen) [51 (p), 70, 80]	4217
15		27	A	Celtic	D	2-2	0-1	4	Foran [70], Munro [83]	46,096
16	Dec	11	H	Rangers	D	1-1	1-0	—	Hayes [31]	6799
17		18	A	Hearts	D	1-1	1-1	—	Munro [17]	12,994
18		26	H	St Mirren	L	1-2	1-1	—	Cox [8]	3819
19		29	H	Kilmarnock	L	1-3	0-1	5	Foran [71]	3735
20	Jan	2	A	St Johnstone	L	0-1	0-0	5		3126
21		15	A	Motherwell	D	0-0	0-0	5		3728
22		18	A	Rangers	L	0-1	0-1	—		41,623
23		22	H	Hamilton A	D	1-1	1-1	5	Sanchez [18]	3241
24		26	H	Aberdeen	L	0-2	0-1	—		4468
25	Feb	12	A	St Mirren	D	3-3	2-2	5	Rooney 2 [6, 61], Doran [33]	3203
26		19	H	St Johnstone	W	2-0	1-0	6	Tokely [28], Duncan [62]	3942
27		26	A	Hibernian	L	0-2	0-0	6		13,841
28	Mar	1	H	Dundee U	L	0-2	0-0	—		3392
29		5	H	Motherwell	W	3-0	1-0	6	Sutherland [18], Foran [64], MacDonald [72]	3563
30		19	A	Dundee U	L	0-1	0-1	7		6548
31	Apr	9	A	Kilmarnock	D	1-1	1-1	7	Hayes [10]	4518
32		16	H	Hearts	D	1-1	1-0	—	Doran [6]	4336
33		25	A	St Johnstone	W	3-0	1-0	—	Innes [36], Doran [57], Foran [70]	2395
34		30	A	Aberdeen	L	0-1	0-0	7		6280
35	May	4	H	Celtic	W	3-2	1-1	—	Mulgrew (og) [7], Munro [53], Sutherland [62]	6702
36		7	H	St Mirren	W	1-0	0-0	7	Rooney [85]	3446
37		11	H	Hibernian	W	2-0	1-0	—	Foran [42], Ross [51]	3344
38		14	A	Hamilton A	W	2-1	1-0	7	Foran [44], Rooney [57]	2017

Final League Position: 7

Honours
Scottish Cup: Semi-finals 2003, 2004; Quarter-finals 1996.
League Champions: First Division 2003-04, 2009-10. Third Division 1996-97; *Runners-up:* Second Division 1998-99.
League Challenge Cup Winners: 2003-04. *Runners-up:* 1999-2000, 2009-10.

Club colours: Shirt: Blue with red stripes. Shorts: Blue. Stockings: Blue with red tops.

Goalscorers: *League (52):* Rooney 15 (5 pens), Foran 7, Hayes 6, Munro 4, Odhiambo 4, Doran 3, Duncan 2, Sutherland 2, Cox 1, Duff 1, Innes 1, MacDonald 1, McCann 1, Ross 1, Sanchez 1, Tokely 1, own goal 1.
Scottish Cup (8): Rooney 4 (1 pen), Foran 2, Hogg 1, Sanchez 1.
CIS Cup (6): Rooney 2 (1 pen), Cox 1, Munro 1, Odihambo 1, Tokely 1.

Esson R 35	McCann K 8	Gillet K 12+1	Munro G 34+1	Tokely R 34+1	Cox L 25+2	Ross N 30+4	Duncan R 20+4	Odhiambo E 18+14	Rooney A 37+1	Hayes J 23+1	Blumenstein G 1+4	Proctor D 7+3	Sutherland S 9+20	Sanchez D 3+6	Duff S 34	Innes C 10+3	Golabek S —+2	Foran R 30+2	Shinnie G 19	Morrison G 3+7	McBain R —+2	Doran A 11+3	Hogg C 10	MacDonald A 2+8	Tuffey J 3	Polworth L —+1	Match No.
1	2	3	4	5	6	7^1	8	9	10	11^3	12^2	13	14														1
1	2	3	4		6	7	8	9^2	10	11^1			5	12	13												2
1	2^1	3	4	12	6	7^2	8	9	10	11			5		13												3
1		3^1	4	5	6	7^2		9^3	10	11			2	14	13	8	12										4
1			4	5	6	7^4		9^2	10	11			2	14		8	3^1	12	13								5
1			4	5		12	8	9^2	10	11^3	14	2^1			3			7	6	13							6
1			4	5		7	8^2	9^3	10	11^1		12			3			6	2	14	13						7
1	2^1		4	5		7	12	9^2	10	11		13		6				8	3								8
1			4	5		7	8	9	10^2	11		13		6				3	12								9
1	2		4	5		7^1	8	12	10^2	11		13		6				9	3								10
1	2		4	5		7		9	10	11		13		6				8^2	3	17							11
1	2		4	5		7^1		12	10	11				6				0	3	0							12
1	2		4	5	12	7		13	10	11				6				9^2	3	8^1							13
1			4	5	6	7^3	8	13	10	11^2			12	14	2			9^1	3								14
1			4	5	6	7	8	12	10	11					2			9^1	3								15
1			4	5	6		8	9^1	10	11			13		2			7^2	3		12						16
1			4	5	6	7^3	8	13	10	11^2			12		2	14		9^1	3								17
1			4	5	6^2	7	8	12	10		13		11		2			9^1	3								18
1			4	5	6	7	8	9	10		13		12		2			11^2	3								19
1			4	5	6^2	7		9	10	8^1		13		2	3			12	11								20
1			4	5		7	8^1	13	10^2			11	12	2	6			9	3								21
1			4	5		7		9	10^2		13	12	11^1	2	6			8	3								22
1			4	5		7	12	9^1	10^2	14		13	11^3	2	6			8	3								23
1		4^8	5		7			13	10	11^2	12		9^1	2^3	6			8	3		14						24
1			6			8	12	10	11^1	2			3	5	9					4	7						25
1		5	6		8		10^3	2^1	7	4	12	14	9^2						11	3	13						26
1		4	5	6	12	8^2	9^1	10^3	14	2		7						11	3	13							27
1		4	5	6	12		10^3	11^2	14	2	8	9						7^1	3	13							28
1		4	5	6	7^2	8	13	10^1	11	2		9^3	14						3	12							29
1	13	3	5	6^2	8	7^3	10^1	11	2		9							14	4	12							30
1	11		5	6^2	4		7	3	2		9	12						10^1	8	13							31
1	2	14	5^8	6	7		10^1	11^2	13	3		8						9^3	4	12							32
1	3	2		6	8	13	10^1	11		5		9^2						7	4	12							33
1	3	4	5	6	7	13	12	10	11^2	2								8	9^1								34
1	3	4	5	8	7		12	10^2	11^1	2	6							13	9								35
	3	6	5	14	13	8^8	7^3	12		2								9	4^2	10		11^1	1				36
	3	6	5	8	7^2		10^3		11^1	12^2	2							9		13	4		1	14			37
	3	4^1	5	6	7	12		10		11^2 13^2	2							9		8			1				38

KILMARNOCK
Premier League

Year Formed: 1869. *Ground & Address:* Rugby Park, Kilmarnock KA1 2DP. *Telephone:* 01563 545300. *Fax:* 01563 522181. *Email:* kirstencallaghan@kilmarnockfc.co.uk *Website:* www.kilmarnockfc.co.uk
Ground Capacity: all seated: 18,128. *Size of Pitch:* 115yd × 74yd.
Chairman: Michael Johnston. *Secretary:* Kirsten Callaghan.
Manager: Kenny Shiels. *Assistant Manager:* Jimmy Nicholl.
Club Nickname: Killie.
Previous Grounds: Rugby Park (Dundonald Road); The Grange; Holm Quarry; Present ground since 1899.
Record Attendance: 35,995 v Rangers, Scottish Cup, 10 Mar 1962.
Record Transfer Fee received: £2,000,000 for Stephen Naismith to Rangers (2007).
Record Transfer Fee paid: £300,000 for Paul Wright from St Johnstone (1995).
Record Victory: 11-1 v Paisley Academical, Scottish Cup, 18 Jan 1930 (15-0 v Lanemark, Ayrshire Cup, 15 Nov 1890).
Record Defeat: 1-9 v Celtic, Division I, 13 Aug 1938.
Most Capped Player: Joe Nibloe, 11, Scotland.
Most League Appearances: 481: Alan Robertson, 1972-88.
Most League Goals in Season (Individual): 34: Harry 'Peerie' Cunningham 1927-28; Andy Kerr 1960-61.
Most Goals Overall (Individual): 148: Willy Culley, 1912-23.

KILMARNOCK 2010–11 LEAGUE RECORD

Match No.	Date	Venue	Opponents	Result	H/T Score	Lg Pos.	Goalscorers	Attendance
1	Aug 14	A	Rangers	L	1-2	0-1	—	Hamill (pen) [60]	45,739
2	22	H	Motherwell	L	0-1	0-1	11		5399
3	28	A	Aberdeen	W	1-0	0-0	8	Hamill [90]	11,287
4	Sept 11	H	St Mirren	W	2-1	1-0	5	Dayton [29], Eremenko [56]	6064
5	19	H	Celtic	L	1-2	1-1	6	Sammon [7]	8645
6	25	A	Hamilton A	D	2-2	0-2	8	Hamill (pen) [83], Sammon [89]	3033
7	Oct 2	H	Dundee U	L	1-2	0-1	8	Sammon [90]	4633
8	16	A	Hibernian	L	1-2	1-2	10	Silva [2]	11,256
9	23	H	Inverness CT	L	1-2	0-1	10	Rui Miguel [74]	4508
10	31	A	Hearts	W	3-0	1-0	9	Wright [45], Sammon [80], Eremenko [82]	13,056
11	Nov 6	A	St Johnstone	W	3-0	1-0	7	Duberry (og) [37], Sammon [83], Kelly [90]	3230
12	10	H	Hamilton A	W	3-0	1-0	—	Gordon [34], Sammon 2 [46, 52]	4214
13	13	A	Dundee U	D	1-1	1-1	7	Sammon [22]	6597
14	20	H	Rangers	L	2-3	1-1	7	Sammon 2 [21, 59]	10,177
15	27	H	Aberdeen	W	2-0	1-0	6	Sammon [18], Hamill (pen) [51]	5013
16	Dec 18	H	Hibernian	W	2-1	2-0	—	Kelly 2 [9, 43]	4216
17	21	A	Celtic	D	1-1	0-0	—	Sammon [53]	44,522
18	29	A	Inverness CT	W	3-1	1-0	4	Bryson [26], Kelly [68], Hamill [78]	3735
19	Jan 3	A	St Mirren	W	2-0	0-0	—	Kelly [64], Bryson [79]	6118
20	15	H	St Johnstone	D	1-1	1-0	4	Sammon [16]	4885
21	18	H	Hearts	L	1-2	1-0	—	Rui Miguel [19]	4996
22	22	H	Dundee U	D	1-1	1-0	4	Sammon [41]	5120
23	29	A	Hamilton A	D	1-1	1-0	—	Sammon [15]	2680
24	Feb 2	A	Motherwell	W	1-0	0-0	—	Silva [81]	3640
25	12	A	Hibernian	L	1-2	0-0	4	Hamill (pen) [74]	11,082
26	19	A	Aberdeen	L	0-5	0-2	4		7371
27	26	H	St Mirren	W	2-0	2-0	4	Gros [13], Eremenko [29]	5243
28	Mar 5	A	Hearts	W	2-0	0-0	4	Silva [50], Eremenko [56]	13,836
29	13	A	Rangers	L	1-2	0-1	—	Hamill (pen) [61]	42,417
30	19	H	Motherwell	W	3-1	2-1	5	Pascali [24], Hamill (pen) [44], Kelly [51]	4259
31	Apr 2	A	St Johnstone	D	0-0	0-0	5		3083
32	9	H	Inverness CT	D	1-1	1-1	5	Kelly [13]	4518
33	20	H	Celtic	L	0-4	0-3	—		9117
34	23	A	Dundee U	L	2-4	0-2	5	Silva [70], Pascali [87]	5225
35	30	H	Hearts	D	2-2	0-0	5	Fowler [55], Agard [86]	5006
36	May 8	H	Celtic	L	0-2	0-1	5		9720
37	11	A	Motherwell	D	1-1	0-1	—	Aubameyang [49]	4101
38	15	H	Rangers	L	1-5	0-3	5	Dayton [65]	16,173

Final League Position: 5

Honours
League Champions: Division I 1964-65. Division II 1897-98, 1898-99; *Runners-up:* Division I 1959-60, 1960-61, 1962-63, 1963-64. First Division 1975-76, 1978-79, 1981-82, 1992-93. Division II 1953-54, 1973-74. Second Division 1989-90.
Scottish Cup Winners: 1920, 1929, 1997; *Runners-up:* 1898, 1932, 1938, 1957, 1960.
League Cup Runners-up: 1952-53, 1960-61, 1962-63, 2000-01, 2006-07.

European: *European Cup:* 4 matches (1965-66). *Cup Winners' Cup:* 4 matches (1997-98). *UEFA Cup:* 32 matches (*Fairs Cup:* 1964-65, 1966-67, 1969-70, 1970-71. *UEFA Cup:* 1998-99, 1999-2000, 2001-02).

Club colours: Shirts: Blue and white vertical stripes. Shorts: Blue with white trim. Stockings: Blue with white tops.

Goalscorers: *League (53):* Sammon 15, Hamill 8 (6 pens), Kelly 7, Eremenko 4, Silva 4, Bryson 2, Dayton 2, Pascali 2, Rui Miguel 2, Agard 1, Aubameyang 1, Fowler 1, Gordon 1, Gros 1, Wright 1, own goal 1.
Scottish Cup (0).
CIS Cup (9): Sammon 3, Hamill 2 (1 pen), Kelly 1, Silva 1, Sissoko 1, Wright 1.

Bell C 31	Hamill J 31+1	Gordon B 18	Fowler J 21+5	Wright F 27	Pascali M 34+1	Silva D 17+12	Bryson C 33	Invincibile D 3+4	Dayton J 7+3	Kelly L 30+2	Hay G 17+5	Sammon C 19+4	Sissoko M 26+1	Eremenko A 31	Forrester H 3+4	Clancy T 19+2	Rui Miguel M 8+13	Taouil M 18+6	Berntsson B —+4	Aubameyang W 4+2	Agard K 3+5	Jaakkola A 7+1	Gros W 8+3	Fisher G —+3	O'Leary R 3	McKenzie R —+1	Pursehouse A —+1	Match No.
1	2	3	4	5	6	7¹	8	9²	10	11	12	13																1
1	2	3	4¹	5	6	7	8²	9	10	13				12	11													2
1	2	3	4	5	11	7	8		10					9	6													3
1	2	3	13	5	4	7¹	8		10²					11	6	9	12											4
1	4	3		5	6		8	12			14	11¹²	10		7	9¹	2³	13										5
1	2	3		5	6	7²	8	12				10	4	11	9¹		13											6
1	2			5	6	7	8	9¹				3²	10	4	11		12	13										7
1	2	3			6	7²	8	13		11			10	5	9	4¹	12											8
1	2	3		5	6	7	8²			11³		10¹	4	9	12		13	14										9
1	2	3		5	6		8			11³	13	12	4	9		14	10¹	7²										10
1	2²	3		5	6		8	12		11		10³	4	9		13	14	7¹										11
1	2	3	12	5¹	6		8			11		10	4	9²	14	13	7¹											12
1	2	3		5	6	12	8			11		10	4	9			7¹											13
1	2	3		5	6		8			11²		10	4⁸	9	12		13	7¹										14
1	2	3	4	5	6	12	8			11		10		9			7¹											15
1	2	3	4	5	6	12	8			11		10		9			7¹											16
1	2	3	4	5	6		8			11		10		9			7											17
1	2	3	4	5	6	12	8			11		10²		9			13	7¹										18
1	2	3¹	4	5		14	8			11	12	10³	6	9			13	7²										19
1			4	5	8					11	3	10	6	9		2		7¹ 12										20
1		4³	5	7	14					11	3	13	6	9		2	10²	8¹ 12										21
1	2			5	6					11	3	10	4	9⁸		7	8¹ 12											22
1	2⁸		13	5	6²	14				11	3	10	4			7	9¹	8³	12									23
1	12		5¹	6	13					11	3⁸		4	9		2	10	7³ 14	8²									24
1⁶	2	.	13		4	12	8			11²	3		5			6	9¹	7			10	15						25
1	12		5	13		8³				11²	3		4	7		2	9¹	6			10		14					26
	2	4	5	6	13	8				3	11	10		12		7¹	1	9²										27
	2	4	5	6	7²	8				11	13		9⁸			3	12	1	10¹									28
	3	4		6	10	8				7	11		5²			2	12	13	1	9¹								29
	3	4		6	9	8				11			5	7		2		12	1	10¹								30
11		4	5³	7¹	8					3		6	9		2	12		13	1	10² 14								31
	6	4³		14	8	13	11	3				7		2	9²			1	10¹	5	12							32
	3	4		6	10	8		11¹	12			7	2²		13		14	1	9³	5								33
1	3	4		10	13	8²	12	11	6				5	9	2					9³	5¹							34
·1	6	3²		4	11	8		13	7			5	9	2			10¹	12										35
1				10	9²	8		4³	11	3		6¹	7	2		13		5			14		12					36
1	4			5	7	8		6¹	11	3			9	2		12	10²		13									37
1	4			5	9¹	8		6³	11	3		12		2		7	10²			13 14								38

LIVINGSTON First Division

Year Formed: 1974. *Ground:* The Braidwood Motor Company Stadium, Almondvale Stadium Road, Livingston EH54 7DN. *Telephone:* 01506 417000. *Fax:* 01506 418888. *Email:* info@livingstonfc.co.uk *Website:* www.livingstonfc.co.uk
Ground Capacity: 10,005 (all seated). *Size of Pitch:* 107yd × 75yd.
Chairman: Gordon McDougall. *Vice Chairman:* Albert Tait.
Manager: Gary Bollan. *Assistant Manager:* Scott Paterson. *Physio:* TJ Johansen.
Club Nickname: Livi Lions.
Previous Grounds: Meadowbank Stadium (as Meadowbank Thistle).
Record Attendance: 10,024 v Celtic, Premier League, 18 Aug 2001.
Record Transfer Fee received: £1,000,000 for David Fernandez to Celtic (June 2002).
Record Transfer Fee paid: £120,000 for Wes Hoolahan from Shelbourne (December 2005).
Record Victory: 7-0 v Queen of the South, Scottish Cup, 29 Jan 2000.
Record Defeat: 0-8 v Hamilton A. Division II, 14 Dec 1974.
Most Capped Player (under 18): I. Little.
Most League Appearances: 446: Walter Boyd, 1979-89.
Most League Goals in Season (Individual): 22: Leigh Griffiths, 2008-09; Iain Russell, 2010-11.
Most Goals Overall (Individual): 64: David Roseburgh, 1986-93.

LIVINGSTON 2010–11 LEAGUE RECORD

Match No.	Date	Venue	Opponents	Result	H/T Score	Lg Pos.	Goalscorers	Atten- dance
1	Aug 7	H	Alloa Ath	D 3-3	2-0	—	Jacobs, Kyle [2], Russell [21], McAvoy (og) [64]	1389
2	14	A	Dumbarton	W 2-1	1-0	5	Winters (pen) [25], Russell [77]	643
3	21	H	Airdrie U	W 2-1	1-1	3	Russell [24], De Vita [73]	1863
4	28	H	Forfar Ath	W 2-0	1-0	1	Winters [24], Jacobs, Keaghan [68]	1553
5	Sept 11	A	Peterhead	D 0-0	0-0	1		431
6	18	A	Brechin C	W 3-1	2-0	1	Russell [43], Barr, C [45], De Vita [74]	526
7	25	H	East Fife	D 1-1	0-0	1	De Vita [53]	1669
8	Oct 2	A	Ayr U	L 1-3	1-0	2	Fox [33]	1270
9	16	H	Stenhousemuir	W 4-1	4-1	2	Winters [14], Scullion (og) [23], Conway [24], Russell [40]	1606
10	23	H	Peterhead	W 1-0	0-0	2	Winters [62]	1295
11	30	A	Forfar Ath	L 0-1	0-0	2		612
12	Nov 6	H	Dumbarton	W 2-0	1-0	1	Watson [19], Russell [87]	1417
13	13	A	Airdrie U	W 1-0	0-0	1	Russell [64]	1013
14	Dec 26	A	Alloa Ath	D 2-2	0-2	—	Sinclair [59], De Vita [71]	566
15	Jan 15	A	Peterhead	L 0-3	0-1	3		585
16	18	A	East Fife	W 4-2	0-1	—	Deuchar 3 [57, 65, 87], Russell [82]	548
17	29	H	East Fife	W 4-3	2-1	1	Jacobs, Keaghan 2 [1, 89], Fox [12], Barr, R [82]	1340
18	Feb 1	A	Brechin C	W 2-0	1-0	—	Russell [25], Winters [89]	847
19	12	A	Ayr U	W 3-0	0-0	1	Barr, R [61], Deuchar [73], Fox [84]	1614
20	15	A	Airdrie U	W 2-0	1-0	—	Russell 2 (1 pen) [34, 70 (p)]	890
21	19	H	Stenhousemuir	W 2-1	2-0	1	Russell [34], Barr, R [40]	1246
22	22	A	Brechin C	L 0-1	0-0	—		565
23	26	A	Alloa Ath	W 4-0	0-0	1	Russell (pen) [55], De Vita 2 [56, 77], Barr, R [90]	1377
24	Mar 1	H	Forfar Ath	W 3-0	1-0	—	Russell (pen) [5], De Vita [61], Winters [88]	724
25	5	A	Dumbarton	W 3-0	2-0	1	Jacobs, Keaghan [5], Russell [7], Fox [70]	853
26	8	A	Stenhousemuir	W 2-1	2-0	1	Russell [3], De Vita [31]	431
27	19	A	Forfar Ath	W 4-0	2-0	1	Deuchar 2 [23, 57], Fox [45], Russell [60]	552
28	26	A	East Fife	W 3-1	1-0	1	Deuchar 2 [27, 70], Jacobs, Kyle [88]	707
29	29	H	Peterhead	W 5-1	0-1	—	Hamill [51], Russell 2 [62, 83], De Vita [74], Fox [89]	754
30	Apr 2	H	Brechin C	D 0-0	0-0	1		1553
31	9	A	Stenhousemuir	W 3-0	1-0	1	Jacobs, Kyle [35], Fox [59], Sinclair [90]	837
32	16	H	Ayr U	D 0-0	0-0	1		1492
33	19	H	Ayr U	W 3-2	1-1	—	Barr, C [31], Sinclair [66], De Vita [68]	904
34	23	A	Airdrie U	W 4-2	2-1	1	Russell 2 [5, 7], De Vita [61], McNulty [80]	872
35	30	A	Dumbarton	D 1-1	0-1	1	Winters [80]	1549
36	May 7	H	Alloa Ath	W 3-1	1-0	1	Jacobs, Keaghan [43], De Vita [77], Russell [87]	647

Final League Position: 1

Honours

League Champions: First Division 2000-01. Second Division 1986-87, 1998-99, 2010-11. Third Division 1995-96, 2009-10; *Runners-up:* Second Division 1982-83. First Division 1987-88.
Scottish Cup: Semi-finals 2001, 2004.
League Cup Winners: 2003-04. Semi-finals 1984-85. *B&Q Cup:* Semi-finals 1992-93, 1993-94, 2001.
League Challenge Cup Runners-up: 2000-01.

European: *UEFA Cup:* 4 matches (2002-03).

Club colours: Shirt: Yellow. Shorts: Black. Stockings: Yellow.

Goalscorers: *League (79):* Russell 22 (3 pens), De Vita 12, Deuchar 8, Fox 7, Winters 7 (1 pen), Jacobs, Keaghan 5, Barr R 4, Jacobs, Kyle 3, Sinclair 3, Barr C 2, Conway 1, Hamill 1, McNulty 1, Watson 1, own goals 2.
Scottish Cup (1): Russell 1.
CIS Cup (1): Russell 1.
Alba Challenge Cup (2): MacDonald 1, Sinclair 1.

Bullock T 34	Barr C 33	O'Byrne M 12	MacDonald C 4+2	Talbot J 24+1	Fox L 30+2	Jacobs Kyle 25+6	Jacobs Keaghan 25+2	Barr R 20+5	Russell I 31+3	Winters R 15+15	Sinclair D 16+10	De Vita R 15+16	Conway A 6+7	Watson P 33	Malone C 10+4	Hastings N 1	McNulty M —+5	Scougall S —+2	Jacobs D 11+1	Hamill J 22	Deuchar K 15+4	Cowan D 8+1	McDowall C 1	Fordyce C 3	Jamieson D 1	Docherty R 1	Gray R —+1	Match No.
1	2	3	4^3	5	6	7	8^1	9	10^2	11	12	13	14															1
1	2^1	3^4		4	8	7	12	9	10	11^3	6	14		5	13													2
1	2			5	6	3	7	11	9^2	10^1	8	12					4	13										3
1	2	4		3	8			7	9	10^{11}	6	12		5														4
1	3	4		6	8	13	7	9	10^{11}	11	2^2	12		5														5
1	2	5		3	7^3	14	8^2	12	9	10	4	11^{11}	13	6														6
1	2	3		4	8		7^2	12	10	11^1	6	9	13	5														7
1	2	3		8	12	7^1		9	10^2	13	4	11		5	6													8
1	2	4		8^3	14		7	10	11^2	3		9^1		5	6		13	12										9
1	2	4^2	13		6	14		9	11	10^3	3	12	8^1	7	5													10
1	2	4			7	8		9	10	11^1	3^2	12	13	5	6													11
1	2		3		7	6		0	13	11^7	12	10	0^1	4	5													12
1	2		3		8	6		9	12	11	5	10^1		4	7													13
1	2^1		12^2		7	6	8	9^9	10	11	13	14		4	5				3									14
1		4	13	7	8	6		11^2	10^8	14	12			3	5					2^1	9^2							15
1	2	4^4		3	7		8		12			10^1	11^2	5	13						6	9						16
1	2	4^2		3	7		8	12	10	14			11^1	5	13						6	9^3						17
1	2			4			7	8	9	11	12			5							3	6	10^1					18
1	2			5	12	6^3	8	9^2	10	13				7						4	3	11^1	14					19
1				5			8	7	9	11^2	12		13	3						2	6	10^1	4					20
1	4			5^3	7	6		9	11^2	12			3	13						2	8	10^1						21
1	3				7	6		9	11^2	12			13		5					2	8	10^1	4					22
1	2			5	8	6		12	11^2	13	14	9		4							7^3	10^1	3					23
1	4			3	6	14	10^2	9	11^3	12		8^1		5							7	13	2					24
1	2			3	12	7	8	9^1	11^3	14		13		5							6	10^2	4					25
1	4			3	7	9	8^1		11^3	13	12	10^1	14	5							6		2					26
1	2			3	6	9	8		11^3	13	12	14		5							7	10^2	4^1					27
1	2			3	6	9			11^2		5	13	10^1	4						12	8	7						28
1	4			3	8	9	2		11		6	12		5							7	10^1						29
1	4			3	7	8	9		11			12		5						2	6	10^1						30
1	2			4	7	8^1	9		10^2	13	12	11^3		5							6	14	3					31
1	5			3	7	9^1	8		11^8		12	10^2	14	4^3						2	6	13						32
1	4			3	8		9^2		12	6	10^3	14	5				13			2	7	11^1						33
	2				8	12		11^3	9^2	6	10^1		5		13					3	7	14	1	4				34
1	3				7^3	9^2	8	13		12	14	11		4	5						6	10^1		2				35
					8	7		9^1	11		5^2	10^3		4			13	12			6			3	1	2	14	36

MONTROSE   Third Division

Year Formed: 1879. *Ground & Address:* Links Park, Wellington St, Montrose DD10 8QD. *Telephone:* 01674 673200.
Fax: 01674 677311. *E-mail:* montrosefootballclub@tesco.net *Website:* www.montrosefc.co.uk
Ground Capacity: total: 3292, seated: 1338. *Size of Pitch:* 113yd × 70yd.
Chairman: Derek Sim. *Vice-Chairman:* John Crawford. *Secretary:* Malcolm J. Watters.
Player Manager: Steven Tweed. *Assistant Manager:* Ray Farningham. *Physio:* Craig Smith.
Club Nickname: The Gable Endies.
Previous Grounds: None.
Record Attendance: 8983 v Dundee, Scottish Cup 3rd rd, 17 Mar 1973.
Record Transfer Fee received: £50,000 for Gary Murray to Hibernian (Dec 1980).
Record Transfer Fee paid: £17,500 for Jim Smith from Airdrieonians (Feb 1992).
Record Victory: 12-0 v Vale of Leithen, Scottish Cup 2nd rd, 4 Jan 1975.
Record Defeat: 0-13 v Aberdeen, 17 Mar 1951.
Most Capped Player: Alexander Keillor, 2 (6), Scotland.
Most League Appearances: 432: David Larter, 1987-98.
Most League Goals in Season (Individual): 28: Brian Third, Division II, 1972-73.

MONTROSE 2010–11 LEAGUE RECORD

Match No.	Date	Venue	Opponents	Result	H/T Score	Lg Pos.	Goalscorers	Attendance
1	Aug 7	H	Queen's Park	L 1-2	0-1	—	Sinclair [75]	415
2	14	A	East Stirling	L 1-2	1-0	9	Tosh (pen) [25]	332
3	21	H	Arbroath	W 3-0	3-0	7	Campbell [8], Hegarty [22], Tosh [32]	565
4	28	H	Annan Ath	D 1-1	1-0	7	Tosh (pen) [16]	332
5	Sept 11	A	Albion R	L 1-3	0-2	8	Sinclair [88]	337
6	18	A	Elgin C	L 2-3	1-1	10	McCord [6], Sinclair [76]	386
7	25	H	Clyde	W 8-1	2-0	7	Tosh 3 (1 pen) [30 (p), 61, 63], McCord 2 [39, 72], Thompson [56], Boyle [70], Watson [82]	424
8	Oct 2	A	Stranraer	W 2-1	2-1	5	Thompson 2 [16, 25]	352
9	9	H	Stranraer	D 3-3	0-2	—	Tosh [52], McCord [65], McNalley [76]	335
10	16	H	Berwick R	D 1-1	0-1	7	Tosh (pen) [80]	376
11	Nov 6	H	Albion R	L 0-2	0-2	7		401
12	9	A	Annan Ath	D 2-2	1-2	—	Campbell [41], Tosh [60]	377
13	13	A	Arbroath	L 0-4	0-1	7		738
14	Dec 11	H	Elgin C	L 0-1	0-0	—		307
15	Jan 2	H	Arbroath	L 0-5	0-2	—		1034
16	15	A	Albion R	W 2-0	1-0	7	Smith [34], Cameron [54]	312
17	22	H	Annan Ath	L 0-1	0-0	—		335
18	29	H	Clyde	W 3-1	0-1	8	Tosh (pen) [46], Crighton [56], Boyle [81]	422
19	Feb 5	A	Elgin C	L 0-1	0-1	9		633
20	12	A	Stranraer	D 2-2	1-1	8	Thompson [7], Nicol [71]	320
21	19	H	Berwick R	D 1-1	0-0	8	Tosh (pen) [62]	301
22	22	A	Berwick R	L 0-1	0-0	—		285
23	26	H	Queen's Park	L 0-2	0-1	8		414
24	Mar 5	A	East Stirling	W 2-1	0-1	8	Boyle [46], Smith [59]	306
25	12	H	Albion R	L 0-2	0-1	8		235
26	19	A	Annan Ath	L 1-2	1-0	8	Tosh [21]	473
27	22	H	East Stirling	L 0-2	0-1	—		259
28	26	A	Clyde	L 0-2	0-1	9		725
29	29	A	Queen's Park	L 0-1	0-0	—		325
30	Apr 2	H	Elgin C	W 1-0	1-0	9	Crawford [12]	256
31	5	A	Clyde	D 1-1	0-0	—	Thompson [86]	516
32	9	A	Berwick R	W 1-0	0-0	8	Masson [80]	353
33	16	H	Stranraer	W 3-2	2-0	8	Nicol 2 (1 pen) [12 (p), 64], Cameron [14]	316
34	23	A	Arbroath	L 1-4	0-2	8	Masson [70]	1243
35	30	H	East Stirling	W 3-0	3-0	8	Tierce 2 [8, 17], Nicol (pen) [11]	361
36	May 7	A	Queen's Park	L 1-4	0-1	8	Masson [86]	767

Final League Position: 8

Honours
League Champions: Second Division 1984-85; *Runners-up:* Second Division 1990-91. Third Division 1994-95.
Scottish Cup: Quarter-finals 1973, 1976.
League Cup: Semi-finals 1975-76.
B&Q Cup: Semi-finals 1992-93.
League Challenge Cup: Semi-finals 1996-97.

Club colours: All royal blue.

Goalscorers: *League (47):* Tosh 12 (6 pens), Thompson 5, McCord 4, Nicol 4 (2 pens), Boyle 3, Masson 3, Sinclair 3, Cameron 2, Campbell 2, Smith 2, Tierce 2, Crawford 1, Crighton 1, Hegarty 1, McNalley 1, Watson 1.
Scottish Cup (12): Tosh 6 (3 pens), Boyle 1, Hegarty 1, McCord 1, Pope 1, Sinclair 1, own goal 1.
CIS Cup (0).
Alba Challenge Cup (0).

Wood S 10	McNalley S 30+1	Sinclair A 31+4	Campbell A 31	Crighton S 31+2	Milligan F 6+6	Davidson H 18+3	Smith N 6+8	McCord R 28+5	Nicol D 9+14	Tosh P 26+2	Thompson C 24+7	Hegarty C 18+6	Bennett S 8	Fleming S —+2	Collier J —+1	Pope G 21+1	Fraser M 1	Watson P 2+6	Crawford J 18+1	Tweed S 6	Boyle M 9+14	Giordano D 3	Cameron D 26	Masson T 13+2	Stuart D —+1	Benedictus K 5	Gonzalez R 14	Tierce S 2+5	Murray S —+1	Match No.
1	2	3	4	5	6^1	7	8	9	10	11^2	12	13																		1
	2	3	4	5		8	7^3	9^2	11^4	10^1	12	6	1	13	14															2
	2^1	10	3	4	6	8	12	13		11	9^2	7	1			5														3
	2^3	7	4	5	6	9^1	12	14	13	10	11^2	8	1			3														4
	2	8	3	5^1	4^2		13	14	11	10	9					6	1	7^3	12											5
6	14	3						8	12	10	11^1	9^3	1	13		5		7^2	2	4										6
7	9	3	4					6	14	10^2	11	2	1			5^1		12	8^3	13										7
4	5^1	2	3					8	14	11	9^2	7	1			6		12	10^3	13										8
7	9		5					6		10^2	11	2	1			3		12	8	4^1	13									9
5	6	3	4				13^3	9		11	10^1	7^2	1			2		14	8	12										10
	6	3	4	5^1	13			8		10	11^2	7				2			12		1	9								11
5	6^1	3	7	13				17		8	14	10	11^3	7		4^2					1	9								12
1	5	4^1	2	3	14		7			9	10	11^2	6^3						13				8							13
	5	2	3				8^2	13	7		10^3	11^1	6			4		14			12	1	9							14
1	5	12	3	4			13	10^2	8		14	6^4				2^4					11^3	9	7^1							15
1	2	6	5	3					9^1	7^2		10		13					4	12	11	8								16
1	2	9	4	5	12	8					11					3^2				10	6	7^1	13							17
1	2	10	4	5			9		6^2	13	11								12		3	7^1	8							18
1	4	6	5	3			10		12	14	11	7^2							13		9^3	8^1	2							19
1	2	6^1	4					9	14		12	10^3	11	13					5		3	8^2	7							20
1	5	14	2	12				6		9^3	13	10	11						3^1		8	7^2	4							21
1	6	7	4	3				8			12	10^2	11			5			13		9^1	2								22
6	7^1	4	2					9^2	13	10	11^3	14				5		8	12	3							1			23
2		4	3	12				9^3	8	14	11^2	10^1				7		6	13	5							1			24
6	12	4	2					9^1		10	11^2	8				5		7	13	3							1			25
2	6	4^1	14					13	12	10^3		7^2				5		8	3^1	11	9						1			26
5	6		2					9	14	10^2	13	7^3				3^1		8	11	4	12						1			27
2	7	4	3	13				8		6^2	12	10^1						9	11	5							1			28
2	5	4	3				12	6^2		10^1	11	13				7		9	8								1			29
2	3	4	5	7				8^2		11		6^1				10		9	12				1				13			30
2	3	5	4			12		9	11^3	13						7		10^2	6^1	8							1	14		31
	5	3^1	2			7	10^2			11	12					4		6			9	8					1	13		32
	5		3	7			9	10^1		11	2					4					8	6					1	12		33
12	2	3	14	8^3			9	10	11^2							4		5^1			6	7					1	13		34
2	5	4^1	3			8		6^2	11	13					12			9	7								1	10		35
2	5			8^1		7^3		13	12			4				3					10^2	9	6				1	11	14	36

MORTON   First Division

Year Formed: 1874. *Ground & Address:* Cappielow Park, Sinclair St, Greenock PA15 2TY. *Telephone:* 01475 723571.
Fax: 01475 781084. *E-mail:* info@gmfc.net *Website:* www.gmfc.net
Ground Capacity: total: 11,612, seated: 6062. *Size of Pitch:* 110yd × 71yd.
Chairman: Douglas Rae. *Chief Executive:* Gillian Donaldson. *Company Secretary:* Mary Davidson.
Manager: Allan Moore. *Assistant Manager:* Mark McNally. *Physios:* Paul Kelly and John Tierney.
Club Nickname: The Ton.
Previous Grounds: Grant Street 1874, Garvel Park 1875, Cappielow Park 1879, Ladyburn Park 1882, (Cappielow Park 1883).
Record Attendance: 23,500 v Celtic, 29 April 1922.
Record Transfer Fee received: £350,000 for Neil Orr to West Ham U.
Record Transfer Fee paid: £150,000 for Alan Mahood from Nottingham Forest (August 1998).
Record Victory: 11-0 v Carfin Shamrock, Scottish Cup 1st rd, 13 Nov 1886.
Record Defeat: 1-10 v Port Glasgow Ath, Division II, 5 May, 1894 and v St Bernards, Division II, 14 Oct 1933.
Most Capped Player: Jimmy Cowan, 25, Scotland.
Most League Appearances: 534: Derek Collins, 1987-98, 2001-05.
Most League Goals in Season (Individual): 58: Allan McGraw, Division II, 1963-64.
Most Goals Overall (Individual): 117: Allan McGraw, 1961-66.

MORTON 2010–11 LEAGUE RECORD

Match No.	Date	Venue	Opponents	Result		H/T Score	Lg Pos.	Goalscorers	Attendance
1	Aug 7	H	Stirling A	D	0-0	0-0	—		2375
2	14	A	Dunfermline Ath	L	0-2	0-0	9		3113
3	21	H	Partick Th	W	2-0	1-0	5	Kean [18], Tidser [88]	2706
4	28	A	Raith R	L	0-1	0-0	7		2344
5	Sept 11	H	Cowdenbeath	L	1-2	0-0	8	Kean [59]	1839
6	18	A	Falkirk	L	1-2	0-1	8	Kean [79]	3988
7	25	H	Ross Co	D	0-0	0-0	8		1632
8	Oct 2	A	Dundee	L	1-2	1-1	10	Weatherson [41]	4068
9	16	H	Queen of the S	W	2-0	0-0	10	Weatherson 2 (1 pen) [50 (p), 73]	1777
10	23	A	Cowdenbeath	D	2-2	2-2	8	Graham [10], Jenkins [45]	582
11	30	H	Raith R	L	0-1	0-0	10		1858
12	Nov 6	H	Dunfermline Ath	W	2-1	2-0	8	Graham [24], Monti (pen) [36]	1813
13	13	A	Partick Th	D	0-0	0-0	7		2436
14	Dec 11	A	Dundee	L	0-1	0-0	—		1568
15	14	A	Ross Co	D	2-2	2-1	—	Graham [26], Jenkins [31]	1759
16	Jan 15	H	Cowdenbeath	W	3-0	1-0	6	O'Brien [33], Jenkins [54], Graham [57]	1375
17	22	A	Raith R	D	2-2	0-2	—	Lyle [53], Weatherson [89]	2220
18	29	H	Ross Co	W	2-1	0-1	—	Lyle [59], Jenkins [82]	1675
19	Feb 12	A	Falkirk	L	0-1	0-0	6		3636
20	15	A	Stirling A	W	1-0	0-0	—	Graham [84]	626
21	19	H	Queen of the S	L	0-4	0-2	6		1754
22	22	H	Partick Th	W	1-0	1-0	—	Lyle (pen) [15]	1267
23	26	A	Dundee	D	1-1	0-1	5	Jenkins [76]	4769
24	Mar 1	H	Falkirk	D	0-0	0-0	—		1343
25	5	A	Dunfermline Ath	W	3-1	1-0	4	Lyle [1], O'Brien [48], Weatherson [88]	2867
26	16	A	Queen of the S	L	0-2	0-2	—		956
27	19	H	Raith R	D	0-0	0-0	5		1809
28	22	A	Cowdenbeath	W	2-0	1-0	—	Monti (pen) [2], Jenkins [60]	359
29	26	A	Ross Co	L	0-2	0-0	6		2379
30	Apr 2	H	Falkirk	D	2-2	1-0	7	O'Brien [9], Graham [78]	1965
31	5	H	Stirling A	W	2-0	2-0	—	Forsyth (og) [9], O'Brien [36]	980
32	13	A	Queen of the S	W	4-1	2-0	—	Weatherson [3], Jenkins 2 [29, 90], Graham [62]	966
33	16	H	Dundee	L	1-3	0-2	4	O'Brien [66]	2069
34	23	A	Partick Th	L	0-2	0-0	5		2060
35	30	H	Dunfermline Ath	L	0-2	0-1	7		4626
36	May 7	A	Stirling A	L	2-3	1-2	7	Monti (pen) [28], McCaffrey [90]	701

Final League Position: 7

Honours
League Champions: First Division 1977-78, 1983-84, 1986-87. Division II 1949-50, 1963-64, 1966-67. Second Division 1994-95, 2006-07. Third Division 2002-03. *Runners-up:* Division 1 1916-17, Division II 1899-1900, 1928-29, 1936-37.
Scottish Cup Winners: 1922; *Runners-up:* 1948. *League Cup Runners-up:* 1963-64.
B&Q Cup Runners-up: 1992-93.

European: *UEFA Cup:* 2 matches (*Fairs Cup*): 1968-69).

Club colours: Shirt: Blue and white hoops. Shorts: Blue. Stockings: Blue.

Goalscorers: *League (39):* Jenkins 8, Graham 7, Weatherson 6 (1 pen), O'Brien 5, Lyle 4 (1 pen), Kean 3, Monti 3 (3 pens), McCaffrey 1, Tidser 1, own goal 1.
Scottish Cup (10): Graham 4, Jenkins 2, Kean 1, Lyle 1, Monti 1 (pen), O'Brien 1.
CIS Cup (7): Kean 2, Weatherson 2, Holmes 1, Kelbie 1, Monti 1.
Alba Challenge Cup (1): Kelbie 1.

Stewart C 27+1	MacGregor D 13	Evans G 28	Smyth M 32+1	McKinlay K 23+2	Holmes G 14+11	Bachirou F 16+3	Tidser M 33+1	O'Brien D 24+6	Weatherson P 19+12	Kean S 18+10	McCarthy S 1+1	Monti C 16+10	Jenkins A 31+4	McCaffrey S 34	Kelbie K 1+7	Shepherd N —+1	Kane R —+2	Malone E 1	Graham B 16+12	Fitzharris S 9+6	Cregg P 1	Toto J 3+1	Greacen S 2+1	Cuthbert K 9+1	Young D 9+4	Lyle D 16+4	Match No.
1	2¹	3	4	5³	6	7	8	9²	10	11	12	13	14														1
1		2	3	5	6		8		10	12		9	7	4	11¹												2
1		2	4	5¹		7	8		10³	11		6²	9	3	14	12	13										3
1		2	3			7	8	12	10²	11		9¹	6	4	13				5³	14							4
1		2	3		8	5¹	6	7	10²	11		12	4	13					14	9³							5
1		2	3	5	7¹	12	6	8	14	10		9²	4	13	11³												6
1		2	3	5		6¹	8³	9		11		14	4	13	12	7	10²										7
1	2¹	3	5³			6	8²	10	11			7	4	14	9		12	13									8
1	2	13	5		7	8	10	11		6²	3	12³	14	9¹	4												9
1	2		5		6²	8¹	11	9	12	7	4	14	10			3³		13									10
1	5	2	4	14		8	9²	10¹		13	6	3	11			12		7³									11
1	2		3	5	13	8	14	12		9¹	6²	4	10			11¹		7									12
1	2		3	5	13	8	14		12	9⁴	6²	4	10			11¹		7									13
1	2		4	5		7	9²		11³	13	6¹	3	14	10	12		8										14
1	3	2	4		12	6	9³		11	14	7	5	13	10²			8¹										15
1		2	4	3¹	8	14	6³	11		13	12	7	5	10²				9									16
1		2		5²	7¹		8	9²	12	6	13	4	3	14	11			10									17
1	2		3	5	14		8	9²	12	6	13	7	4	11¹				10³									18
1	2³		3	5	12	8⁸		11¹		9⁸	6	4	13	14				7²	10								19
1		2	3	5	14		8	11²	12		7	4	13	9¹				6	10³								20
1	2		3	5¹		12	13	14	9	8²	6	4	11					7	10³								21
	2		3	5	13	9¹	8		12	11		6	4	14		1	7²	10¹									22
	5	2	3	9¹	8²	7		12	14	11³		6	4	13		1		10									23
	2	3	5		7	8	9	11¹		10	4	12	6²		1		13										24
	2	3	5		8	6	9	12	13		7	4	10²		1		11¹										25
	2³	3	5		6¹	7	8²	12		14	9	4	13	10⁸		1		11									26
	2	3		7	8		12	11¹		5	6	4	10		1	9											27
	2	3	13	6²	8		10¹	14		5	7	4	11³	12		1		9									28
	2	3	7¹	8	6	12	13	14		5	9	4	11²		1		10³										29
15	2	3	6	7	8	9	11²			5	4	13	10¹	1⁶	12												30
1	2	3	14	6²	7	8	11	10¹		5³	13	4	12		9												31
1	2	4	6¹		8	9	10		5	7	3	11²	12	13													32
1	2	4	7²	12	6	9	11³	14	3¹	5	8	10		13													33
1	2³	3	14		7	8	9¹	12	11	5	6³	4	13	10													34
1	2	3	5¹	14	7	8	9	11²	13	12	6	4	10³														35
1	2³	3	13	7³	8	10	11¹	12	5	6	4	9	14														36

MOTHERWELL   Premier League

Year Formed: 1886. *Ground & Address:* Fir Park Stadium, Motherwell ML1 2QN. *Telephone:* 01698 333333. *Fax:* 01698 338001.
E-mail: mfc@motherwellfc.co.uk *Website:* www.motherwellfc.co.uk
Ground Capacity: all seated: 13,742. *Size of Pitch:* 110yd × 75yd.
Secretary: TBC.
Manager: Stuart McCall. *Assistant Manager:* Kenny Black. *Physio:* John Porteous.
Club Nicknames: The Well, The Steelmen.
Previous Grounds: Roman Road, Dalziel Park.
Record Attendance: 35,632 v Rangers, Scottish Cup 4th rd replay, 12 Mar 1952.
Record Transfer Fee received: £1,750,000 for Phil O'Donnell to Celtic (September 1994).
Record Transfer Fee paid: £500,000 for John Spencer from Everton (Jan 1999).
Record Victory: 12-1 v Dundee U, Division II, 23 Jan 1954.
Record Defeat: 0-8 v Aberdeen, Premier Division, 26 Mar 1979.
Most Capped Player: Tommy Coyne, 13, Republic of Ireland.
Most League Appearances: 626: Bobby Ferrier, 1918-37.
Most League Goals in Season (Individual): 52: Willie McFadyen, Division I, 1931-32.
Most Goals Overall (Individual): 283: Hugh Ferguson, 1916-25.

MOTHERWELL 2010–11 LEAGUE RECORD

Match No.	Date	Venue	Opponents	Result	H/T Score	Lg Pos.	Goalscorers	Atten- dance
1	Aug 15	H	Hibernian	L 2-3	1-1	—	Sutton [13], Murphy (pen) [75]	5172
2	22	A	Kilmarnock	W 1-0	1-0	6	Blackman [37]	5399
3	29	H	Celtic	L 0-1	0-0	7		9207
4	Sept11	A	St Johnstone	W 2-0	2-0	4	Blackman [3], Rutkiewicz (og) [39]	3254
5	18	H	Aberdeen	D 1-1	1-0	5	Murphy [35]	5251
6	25	A	Hearts	W 2-0	0-0	3	Blackman [58], Sutton [70]	13,749
7	Oct 2	H	St Mirren	W 3-1	1-0	3	Humphrey [3], Hateley (pen) [87], Murphy [88]	4384
8	16	A	Rangers	L 1-4	1-0	3	Blackman [44]	44,609
9	23	H	Dundee U	W 2-1	1-0	3	Severin (og) [1], Dillon (og) [75]	4635
10	30	H	Hamilton A	L 0-1	0-1	3		4865
11	Nov 6	A	Inverness CT	W 2-1	2-0	3	Gow [33], Blackman [43]	4054
12	10	H	St Johnstone	W 4-0	3-0	—	Blackman 3 [12, 24, 45], Sutton [88]	3361
13	13	A	Hibernian	L 1-2	1-2	4	Blackman (pen) [10]	11,178
14	20	A	St Mirren	D 1-1	0-1	5	Blackman [74]	4213
15	Dec 14	H	Hearts	L 1-2	1-1	—	Lasley [45]	3324
16	26	H	Rangers	L 1-4	0-2	—	Sutton [46]	9371
17	29	A	Celtic	L 0-1	0-1	6		40,750
18	Jan 1	A	Hamilton A	D 0-0	0-0	6		3171
19	12	A	Dundee U	L 0-2	0-0	—		4918
20	15	H	Inverness CT	D 0-0	0-0	6		3728
21	22	H	Hibernian	W 2-0	2-0	6	Murphy [20], Saunders [24]	4202
22	26	A	St Johnstone	L 0-1	0-0	—		2268
23	Feb 2	H	Kilmarnock	L 0-1	0-0	—		3640
24	12	A	Rangers	L 0-6	0-3	8		43,789
25	15	A	Aberdeen	W 2-1	1-1	—	Jeffers [14], Murphy [71]	6882
26	19	H	Hamilton A	W 1-0	1-0	5	Sutton (pen) [36]	4407
27	23	H	St Mirren	L 0-1	0-0	—		3613
28	27	H	Celtic	W 2-0	1-0	5	Sutton 2 (1 pen) [2, 49 (p)]	9716
29	Mar 5	A	Inverness CT	L 0-3	0-1	5		3563
30	19	A	Kilmarnock	L 1-3	1-2	6	Sutton [15]	4259
31	Apr 2	H	Aberdeen	W 2-1	1-0	6	Humphrey [15], Hutchinson [88]	4458
32	6	H	Dundee U	W 2-1	2-0	—	Murphy [26], Humphrey [41]	3435
33	9	A	Hearts	D 0-0	0-0	6		13,800
34	23	A	Hearts	D 3-3	0-2	6	Sutton 2 [55, 88], Hateley [59]	13,039
35	30	H	Rangers	L 0-5	0-1	6		8968
36	May 7	A	Dundee U	L 0-4	0-2	6		5951
37	11	H	Kilmarnock	D 1-1	1-0	—	Jones [8]	4101
38	15	A	Celtic	L 0-4	0-2	6		57,294

Final League Position: 6

Honours
League Champions: Division I 1931-32. First Division 1981-82, 1984-85. Division II 1953-54, 1968-69; *Runners-up:* Premier Division 1994-95. Division I 1926-27, 1929-30, 1932-33, 1933-34. Division II 1894-95, 1902-03. *Scottish Cup:* 1952, 1991; *Runners-up:* 1931, 1933, 1939, 1951, 2011. *League Cup Winners:* 1950-51; *Runners-up:* 1954-55, 2004-05. *Scottish Summer Cup:* 1944, 1965.

European: *Cup Winners' Cup:* 2 matches (1991-92). *UEFA Cup:* 8 matches (1994-95, 1995-96, 2008-09). *Europa League:* 12 matches (2009-10, 2010-11).

Club colours: Shirt: Amber with claret hoop and trimmings. Shorts: Maroon. Stockings: Amber.

Goalscorers: *League (40):* Blackman 10 (1 pen), Sutton 10 (2 pens), Murphy 6 (1 pen), Humphrey 3, Hateley 2 (1 pen), Gow 1, Hutchinson 1, Jeffers 1, Jones 1, Lasley 1, Saunders 1, own goals 3.
Scottish Cup (14): Sutton 6, Murphy 3, Craigan 1, Humphrey 1, Jeffers 1, Jennings 1, Jones 1.
CIS Cup (4): Page 2, Gow 1, Lasley 1.
Europa League (7): Murphy 3, Forbes 1, Hateley 1, Page 1, Sutton 1.

Randolph D 37	Saunders S 22+3	Hammell S 26+5	Reynolds M 19	Craigan S 32+3	Hateley T 36+2	Humphrey C 33+3	Jennings S 30	Murphy J 31+4	Casagolda E 3+10	Lasley K 26	Blackman N 15+3	Page J 3+6	Fitzpatrick M 3+2	McHugh R —+11	Forbes R 11+12	Gow A 9+6	Pollock J —+3	Hutchinson S 18+1	Meechan S —+2	Jones S 10+2	Gunning G 12+2	Jeffers F 8+2	Ross M 5+1	Carswell S 3+1	Smith G —+1	Hollis L 1	Match No.
1	2	3	4	5	6	7²	8	9¹	10	13	11	12															1
1	2	3	4	13	6	7³	8		14	10¹		9	5²	11	12												2
1	2■	3¹	4	5	6	7³	8²	9	10	11	13	12		14													3
1		3	4	5	6	2	8¹	7	10²	11	9³		13	12	14												4
1	2		4	5	6	7	8	9¹	11	3	10¹		13	14	12												5
1	2		4	5	6	7²	8¹	9	10	11	3³		13	12	14												6
1	2¹	12	4	5	6	7³	8	9²	10	11	3			13	14												7
1		3³	4	5	6	7	8	9¹	11	2	10²	14		12	13												8
1	12	3	4	5	6	7³	8	13	11	2¹	9			14	10²												9
1	2¹	3	4	5	6	7	8	12			9		13	11	10²												10
1	2	3	4	5	6	7	8	9²	12		11¹		13		14	10³											11
1		3³	4	5	6	7²	8	9	11	12	10¹		14	2	13												12
1	2	3	4	5	6	7	8	12	11¹	14	9²		13		10³												13
1	2²	3	4	5	6	7	8	12	11¹		9		13		10												14
1		3	4	5	2	7¹	6⁸	12	9		8	11		13	10²												15
1	2	3	4	5	6¹	7		12	9³		8	11²	13	14	10												16
1	2	3	4	5	6	7		13	9¹		8	12	11²		10												17
1	2²	3	4	5	6	7		12	9	14	8	11³	13		10¹												18
1		3	4	5	6	7	8	9	10	13	2²				11¹		12										19
1		3		5	6	7	8	9	10	13	11¹				4²				2	12							20
1	2	3		5	6¹	7	8	9	10		13				4				12	11²							21
1	2	3		5	6²	7	8	9	10¹	12			13		4				11								22
1	2	3³		5	13	7	8	12	9	10¹	6²				4				11	14							23
1				5	6	7	8	9³	13		11		2¹		12		4		10²	3	14						24
1	13			5	6	12	8	9	10		11²				2		4		3	7¹							25
1	12			5	6	13	8	9	11		2				7¹		4		3	10²							26
1	12			5	6	7	8	9	11	13	2¹						4		3	10²							27
1	3			5		7	8	9	10		6				11¹	12	4		2								28
1	13	3			5²	12	8	9	11		7				6¹		4		2	10							29
1	2¹			5	6	7	8	9	10	13		11³			12²		4		14	3							30
1	14	3		13	6	7		9	10²	8			12				4		11¹	5⁴		2					31
1	2			5	6	7		9	10	8		12			11¹		4					3					32
1	2¹	12		5	6	7³	13	14	10²						11		4		9			3	8				33
1	2¹			5	6			9	11	8					4				7	3	10	12					34
1	3¹			5	14		8	9	11	4³		13			12		7		6	10²	2						35
1		13	2	7³	8		9								11¹		4		14	5	10	3²	6	12			36
1	2	3²		5	6	7	8	10			11³						4		9¹	13	12		14				37
	2	3		6	7²			14			12		13	11			4¹		9	8	10³		5		1	38

PARTICK THISTLE First Division

Year Formed: 1876. *Ground & Address:* Firhill Stadium, 80 Firhill Rd, Glasgow G20 7AL. *Telephone:* 0141 579 1971. *Fax:* 0141 945 1525. *E-mail:* mail@ptfc.co.uk *Website:* www.ptfc.co.uk
Ground Capacity: total: 13,141, seated: 10,921. *Size of Pitch:* 105yd × 68yd.
Acting Chairman: David Beattie. *Secretary:* Antonia Kerr.
Manager: Jackie McNamara. *Assistant Manager:* Simon Donnelly. *Coach:* Ian Cameron. *Head of Youth Development:* Gerry Britton. *Physio:* Kenny Crichton.
Club Nickname: The Jags.
Previous Grounds: Jordanvale Park; Muirpark; Inchview; Meadowside Park.
Record Attendance: 49,838 v Rangers, Division I, 18 Feb 1922. *Ground Record:* 54,728, Scotland v Ireland, 25 Feb 1928.
Record Transfer Fee received: £200,000 for Mo Johnston to Watford.
Record Transfer Fee paid: £85,000 for Andy Murdoch from Celtic (Feb 1991).
Record Victory: 16-0 v Royal Albert, Scottish Cup 1st rd, 17 Jan 1931.
Record Defeat: 0-10 v Queen's Park, Scottish Cup, 3 Dec 1881.
Most Capped Player: Alan Rough, 51 (53), Scotland.
Most League Appearances: 410: Alan Rough, 1969-82.
Most League Goals in Season (Individual): 41: Alex Hair, Division I, 1926-27.

PARTICK THISTLE 2010–11 LEAGUE RECORD

Match No.	Date	Venue	Opponents	Result	H/T Score	Lg Pos.	Goalscorers	Attendance
1	Aug 7	A	Raith R	L	0-4	0-3	—		2238
2	14	H	Dundee	W	1-0	0-0	7	Boyle 71	2801
3	21	A	Morton	L	0-2	0-1	9		2706
4	28	A	Cowdenbeath	L	1-2	1-1	9	Doolan 18	881
5	Sept 11	H	Stirling A	L	1-2	0-0	10	Doolan 50	1994
6	18	A	Queen of the S	I	1-2	1-0	10	Flannigan 34	2013
7	25	H	Dunfermline Ath	L	0-2	0-1	10		2100
8	Oct 2	A	Ross Co	W	2-0	1-0	9	Boyle 14, Erskine 84	2263
9	16	H	Falkirk	W	1-0	1-0	8	Paton 17	2783
10	23	A	Stirling A	L	2-4	1-3	10	Doolan 2 15, 79	1386
11	30	H	Cowdenbeath	W	1-0	0-0	7	Buchanan 53	1841
12	Nov 6	A	Dundee	L	1-2	0-1	9	Hodge 57	6022
13	13	H	Morton	D	0-0	0-0	9		2436
14	Dec 11	H	Ross Co	D	1-1	1-1	—	Erskine 41	1509
15	14	A	Dunfermline Ath	D	0-0	0-0	—		1743
16	26	H	Raith R	D	0-0	0-0	—		2036
17	Jan 15	H	Stirling A	W	6-1	2-0	5	Doolan 23, Flannigan 34, Buchanan 2 (1 pen) 51 (p), 67, Fraser 74, Campbell 82	1689
18	29	H	Dunfermline Ath	W	2-0	2-0	—	Erskine 14, Doolan 41	2720
19	Feb 12	A	Queen of the S	D	3-3	2-1	5	Grehan 33, Doolan 40, Flannigan 83	1860
20	15	A	Cowdenbeath	D	1-1	0-1	—	Flannigan 85	411
21	22	A	Morton	L	0-1	0-1	—		1267
22	26	A	Ross Co	D	0-0	0-0	6		2316
23	Mar 5	H	Dundee	D	0-0	0-0	6		2671
24	8	H	Queen of the S	W	3-1	1-0	—	Doolan 34, Erskine 84, Fraser 87	1001
25	12	A	Raith R	W	2-0	0-0	4	Doolan 49, Boyle 90	2065
26	19	H	Cowdenbeath	L	0-1	0-0	7		1754
27	22	A	Stirling A	W	3-0	2-0	—	Doolan 2 (1 pen) 27, 73 (p), Balatoni 36	651
28	26	A	Dunfermline Ath	D	0-0	0-0	5		3019
29	Apr 2	H	Queen of the S	D	0-0	0-0	5		1806
30	9	A	Falkirk	W	3-2	2-0	—	Erskine 2 8, 24, Doolan 62	3735
31	12	H	Falkirk	L	1-2	0-0	—	Kinniburgh, W 90	1142
32	16	H	Ross Co	D	1-1	1-1	6	Doolan (pen) 4	1714
33	19	A	Falkirk	L	0-2	0-1	—		3439
34	23	H	Morton	W	2-0	0-0	4	Erskine 60, Boyle 72	2060
35	30	A	Dundee	L	2-3	0-0	6	Stewart 68, Doolan 90	7746
36	May 7	H	Raith R	W	3-0	0-0	5	Stewart 50, Doolan (pen) 78, Rowson 90	2279

Final League Position: 5

Honours
League Champions: First Division 1975-76, 2001-02; *Runners-up:* 2008-09. Division II 1896-97, 1899-1900, 1970-71; Second Division 2000-01; *Runners-up:* First Division 1991-92. Division II 1901-02. *Promoted to First Division:* 2005-06 (play-offs).
Scottish Cup Winners: 1921; *Runners-up:* 1930; *Semi-finals:* 2002.
League Cup Winners: 1971-72; *Runners-up:* 1953-54, 1956-57, 1958-59.
League Challenge Cup: Quarter-finals 2004-05.

European: *Fairs Cup:* 4 matches (1963-64). *UEFA Cup:* 2 matches (1972-73). *Intertoto Cup:* 4 matches 1995-96.

Club colours: Shirt: Yellow with red design hoops. Shorts: Red. Stockings: Black.

Goalscorers: *League (44):* Doolan 15 (3 pens), Erskine 7, Boyle 4, Flannigan 4, Buchanan 3 (1 pen), Fraser 2, Stewart 2, Balatoni 1, Campbell 1, Grehan 1, Hodge 1, Kinniburgh, W 1, Paton 1, Rowson 1.
Scottish Cup (6): Buchanan 1, Cairney 1, Donnelly 1, Doolan 1, Erskine 1, Grehan 1.
CIS Cup (1): Donnelly 1.
Alba Challenge Cup (8): Doolan 2, Boyle 1, Buchanan 1, Cairney 1, Kinniburgh 1, MacBeth 1, Rowson 1.

Halliwell B 10	Robertson J 20	Kinniburgh W 4	Boyle P 35	Paton P 25 + 1	Cairney P 24 + 5	Flannigan I 22 + 7	Rowson D 28 + 1	Hodge B 13 + 3	Buchanan L 12 + 5	Donnelly S 7 + 7	Balatoni C 16 + 6	Erskine C 21 + 13	MacBeth R — + 1	Maxwell I 4	Grehan M 18 + 8	Doolan K 29 + 4	McNamara J 15	Bannigan S 1 + 1	Archibald A 27	Kinniburgh W 19	Hardie M 4	Fox S 24	Fraser S — + 14	Campbell J 6 + 6	Shepherd G 1	McGowan R 6 + 1	Burns K 1 + 1	McGeough R — + 2	Stewart T 3 + 2	McGrotty J — + 1	Lochhead K — + 3	Scully R 1	Match No.
1	2	3[4]	4	5	6[1]	7	8	9	10[3]	11[2]	12	13	14																				1
1	3		4	6	7	9	8		10[1]			5			2	11	12																2
1	3		5	6	7	9	8		10[3]	12	2[1]	13			4	11[2]	14																3
1		2	4	5	6	9	8		10	7[1]	13	12			3[2]	14	11[3]																4
1			4	6	7		8		9[2]	12	3[1]	13			5	14	11[3]	2	10														5
1		2	5	6	12	7	8	9	10			11	3						4[1]														6
1	3	5	6	2		7	8[1]	12	10[2]	9[3]		13			14	11	4																7
1	6		4	7	8	9		12		13		10[2]	11[1]	5	2	3																	8
1	2		6	7	8	10[3]		12		14		13	11[1]	5	4	3	9[2]																9
1	5		4	7	8[3]	9		12		13	14		11	3	2[1]	6[2]	10																10
	2		4	5	6	7		10		3		9[2]			12	11[1]	13					8	1										11
	2		4	7	12	8			13	10		6[1]	14			11[3]	5					3	9[2]	1									12
	9		5	6	8	14	7[1]	10[2]	13		12				11[3]				4	3	2	1											13
	4		5	6	14	7	8	10[1]	11[2]	12	9[3]		13						3[4]	2		1											14
	4		6	7	13	8	10	12	11[3]	5[2]	9[1]		14	2					3			1											15
	5		6	7[2]	14	8	9	13	10	12	11[3]			3					4	2[1]		1											16
3		2	5	12	6[3]	8	7[1]	10[2]		9					11				4			1	13	14									17
	2		5	6	10[1]	7	8		9[3]		12	11[2]			4	3			1	13	14												18
	2		5	13	6[2]	12	7	8		14		9[1]			11	10[3]			4	3			1										19
	2		4	6	12	9	7	8[1]		14		13			10[2]	11			3			1		5[3]									20
	3		5	7[1]	10	8	6[3]		14		9[2]				12	11			4	2		1		13									21
			6	13	10	8	7	9[3]		12		14		11	5[2]				4	3[1]		1											22
	3		5	2	10[1]	13	8	12				9			11[3]				4			1	14					7[2]	6				23
	3		5	2		9[3]	7	8[1]		14	12				11[2]	10			4			1	13					6					24
	2		4	7			8					9			11	10[1]	6		3			1	12					5					25
	2		4	7			8					9[3]			11[1]	10	6[2]		3			1	14	13				5					26
	2[3]		5			7	8					3	9[2]		11[1]	10	6		4			1	12	13			14						27
	2		5			7	8			12	3	9[2]			11[1]	10			4	3		1	13	12	6								28
	2		5			7	8					6	9[1]		11	10[2]			4	3		1	13	12									29
			5		7		8					3	9[1]		10	11			4	2		1	12	6									30
			6		7		8					3	9[1]		11	10[3]	5[2]		4	2		1	14					13	12				31
			5		7		8					3	9		10[1]	11			4	2		1	12	6									32
			5		6	8[4]						3	11		9[1]	10			4	2		1	7			12							33
			5		6[2]							3	8		11[3]	10			4	2		1	14	7				9[1]	12	13			34
			5		7	12						3	9		10[1]	11			4	2[4]		1	13	6[2]				8[3]	14				35
			4		8[1]	10	7					2	6[2]		11				3			14	5			13		9[3]	12	1			36

PETERHEAD

Third Division

Year Formed: 1891. *Ground and Address:* Balmoor Stadium, Balmoor Terrace, Peterhead AB42 1EU.
Telephone: 01779 478256. *Fax:* 01779 490682. *E-mail:* office@peterheadfc.co.uk *Website:* www.peterheadfc.co.uk
Ground Capacity: 3250, seated 1000.
Chairman: Rodger Morrison. *Vice-Chairman:* Ian Grant. *Secretary:* Brian McCombie.
Manager: John Sheran. *Physio:* Greg Smith.
Club Nickname: Blue Toon.
Previous Ground: Recreation Park.
Record Attendance: 6310 friendly v Celtic, 1948.
Record Victory: 17-0 v Fort William, 1998-99 (in Highland League).
Record Defeat: 0-13 v Aberdeen, Scottish Cup, 1923-24.
Most League Appearances: 239: Martin Bavidge, 2003-11.
Most League Goals in Season (Individual): 21: Iain Stewart, 2002-03; 21, Scott Michie, 2004-05.
Most Goals Overall (Individual): 86 Martin Bavidge, 2003-11.

PETERHEAD 2010–11 LEAGUE RECORD

Match No.	Date		Venue	Opponents	Result		H/T Score	Lg Pos.	Goalscorers	Atten-dance
1	Aug	7	A	Stenhousemuir	L	1-3	1-1	—	Donald 37	423
2		14	H	Forfar Ath	L	1-2	0-2	9	Gethans 77	371
3		21	A	East Fife	L	1-2	1-0	9	Bavidge 43	565
4		28	A	Ayr U	D	1-1	1-0	—	Emslie 11	1099
5	Sept	11	H	Livingston	D	0-0	0-0	10		431
6		18	A	Airdrie U	D	2-2	1-1	10	Gethans 20, Bavidge 72	046
7		25	H	Alloa Ath	W	1-0	0-0	9	Anderson 86	534
8	Oct	2	A	Brechin C	L	2-4	1-2	9	Wyness (pen) 11, Bavidge 90	473
9		16	H	Dumbarton	W	1-0	0-0	8	Ross, D 49	496
10		23	A	Livingston	L	0-1	0-0	9		1295
11		30	H	Ayr U	L	2-4	1-2	9	Smith, Stuart 18, Robertson (og) 87	560
12	Nov	6	A	Forfar Ath	D	1-1	0-0	9	Clark 79	497
13		13	H	East Fife	D	2-2	0-0	9	Bavidge 87, Anderson 89	594
14	Dec	4	A	Alloa Ath	D	2-2	2-1	—	Strachan (pen) 22, Clark 44	601
15		11	H	Brechin C	L	0-5	0-2	—		466
16		14	H	Airdrie U	W	5-1	3-0	—	Sharp 3, Clark 39, Ross, D 2 44, 79, McCord (og) 90	312
17	Jan	15	H	Livingston	W	3-0	1-0	7	Ross, D 26, Strachan 2 (1 pen) 50 (p), 71	585
18		22	A	Ayr U	D	2-2	0-2	—	Sharp 54, Ross, D 65	1226
19		29	A	Alloa Ath	W	4-1	2-1	6	Wyness 2 22, 70, Bavidge 27, Gethans 90	469
20	Feb	5	A	Airdrie U	L	0-1	0-1	7		660
21		12	A	Brechin C	L	1-3	1-0	7	Strachan 32	503
22		19	H	Dumbarton	L	1-2	0-1	8	Smith, Stuart 49	388
23		22	A	Dumbarton	L	0-3	0-1	—		376
24		26	A	Stenhousemuir	L	2-4	2-3	9	Emslie 35, MacDonald 38	363
25	Mar	1	A	East Fife	L	1-3	0-2	—	Bavidge 73	314
26		5	H	Forfar Ath	D	1-1	1-0	10	Gethans 34	479
27		19	H	Ayr U	L	1-2	0-1	10	Wyness (pen) 81	536
28		22	H	Stenhousemuir	D	2-2	1-2	—	Wyness 2 (1 pen) 41, 61 (p)	384
29		26	A	Alloa Ath	D	0-0	0-0	10		406
30		29	A	Livingston	L	1-5	1-0	—	Bavidge 28	754
31	Apr	2	H	Airdrie U	L	2-4	1-4	10	Tosh 2 22, 61	831
32		9	A	Dumbarton	L	2-5	0-2	10	Wyness 60, Ross, D 81	526
33		16	H	Brechin C	D	1-1	1-1	10	Clark 42	498
34		23	H	East Fife	L	0-2	0-1	10		473
35		30	A	Forfar Ath	L	1-2	0-1	10	Wyness 64	448
36	May	7	H	Stenhousemuir	L	0-3	0-1	10		405

Final League Position: 10

Honours
Third Division Runners up: 2004-05.
Scottish Cup: Quarter-finals 2001.
Highland League Champions: winners 5 times.
Scottish Qualifying Cup (North): winners 6 times.
North of Scotland Cup: winners 5 times.
Aberdeenshire Cup: winners: 20 times.

Club colours: Shirt: Navy blue with royal blue sleeves. Shorts: Navy blue. Stockings: Navy blue.

Goalscorers: *League (47):* Wyness 8 (3 pens), Bavidge 7, Ross D 6, Clark 4, Gethans 4, Strachan 4 (2 pens), Anderson 2, Emslie 2, Sharp 2, Smith, Stuart 2, Tosh 2, Donald 1, MacDonald 1, own goals 2.
Scottish Cup (3): McVitie 1, Sharp 1, Strachan 1.
CIS Cup (1): Wyness 1.
Alba Challenge Cup (15): Wyness 4, Bavidge 3, Gethans 2, MacDonald 2, Emslie 1, Stuart Smith 1, own goals 2.

Jarvie P 15+1	Donald D 33	Mann R 9	MacDonald C 30+3	Smith Stuart 34	Sharp G 25+6	McVitie N 28+2	Emslie P 23+4	Moore D 11+5	Bavidge M 30	Wyness D 21+7	Gethans C 11+15	Anderson S 13+1	Strachan R 23+6	Bateman J 21+2	Ross S 17+3	Ross D 19+7	Clark N 14+10	Campbell P —+2	Smith Stirling 13+1	Tosh P 4+2	Stephens B 2+4	Robertson S —+1	Maclachlan J —+1	Match No.
1	2	3^3	4	5	6	7^2	8	9^1	10	11	12	13	14											1
1	2	3	4	12	6	8	5	9	10	11			7^1											2
1	2	4	3	9	6	7	5	11	10	12			8^1											3
1^6	2	4	3	6^1	7	9^4	5	11	10	12			8	15										4
		4	5	6	12	8	7^2	10	11	2	9^1	3				1	13							5
	2		5	3	12	7	8	11	10	6^1	9	4				1								6
	2	3	5	12	6	8	9	10	11^1	7		4				1								7
	2	5	3	7^2	6^1	8	13	11	10	9		4				1	12							8
	2	3	4	9	6	8	5	10^2	11^1	7	13					1	12							9
	2	3	4	7	8^1	10	6		5	9						1	11	12						10
15	2	3	4	9	7^6	6^2	10	11^1	13	8	5	1^8					12							11
1	2	4^2	5	3	7	8	9		10		8^1	13				11	12							12
	2	3	4	5		7^1	9^4		11		6^2	10	13	1	6	13	9^2	8	12					13
	2		3	5	8^1	4		11		12	10	7	1	6	13	9^2								14
	2	3	4	5	8		11	12		7^8	6	1		10^1	9									15
	2	3^3	14	5	8	7		11^1	12	6	1	4	10	9^2	13									16
	2		3	5	8	7^1	12		9	14	6	1	4^2	11^3	10	13								17
	2		4	8	7		10	12		6	1	5	11	9^1	3									18
	2	12	4	9	7		6	10^2	13	8	1	3^1	11	5										19
	2		3	8	7	13		11^1	10^3	12	6^2	1	4	9	14	5								20
	2	13	4	8	7		9^2		11^1	12	6	1	5	10	3									21
	2		4	8	7^1	12	13	10	11^3	6	1	3	9	14	5^2									22
	2^8	4	3	9	13	8^3		11^1	12^2	7	6	1	10	14	5									23
		5	3^1	7		6	12	9		13	2	1	4	8^2	10	11								24
1	2	5			8	13	9	11^2	12	6		4	10^1	7	3									25
1^6		3	4		8^1	9	10	11		6	2^2	15	13	12	7	5								26
1	2	4	5	3	12	7	9	13	11	14	10^3				8^1		6^2							27
	2		4	5	6^3	7	8	9^1	10	11^2	13		1	3	14	12								28
1	2^8	3	5	6^1	7	8		9	10^2	13	12		4	11^3	14									29
1		3	4	5		13	8		9^1	10	12		7	2^2	11^3	14	6							30
1	2	3^1	4	5	9	7^2	8^3		11		6		12		13				10	14				31
1	2^1		3	5	10^3		9		13	6^2				4	12	8		7	11	14				32
1	2		4	5^1			7		10	13			12		3	9^3	8	6^1	11^2	14				33
1	2		3	5^1	12		8		10	14			6^1		4	9^2	7		11^3	13				34
1	2		5	3	7^1	8^3	14		11		4		6^8		10^2	12			13	9				35
	2		4	5	9^1	7		11		3	1		10^3	8		12	6^2	13	14					36

QUEEN OF THE SOUTH   First Division

Year Formed: 1919. *Ground & Address:* Palmerston Park, Dumfries DG2 9BA. *Telephone:* 01387 254853.
Fax: 01387 240470. *E-mail:* admin@qosfc.com *Website:* www.qosfc.com
Ground Capacity: 6412 *Size of Pitch:* 112yd × 73yd.
Chairman: David Rae. *Vice-Chairman:* Craig Paterson. *Club Secretary:* Eric Moffat.
Manager: Gus MacPherson. *Assistant Manager:* Andy Millen. *Physio:* John Kerr.
Club Nickname: The Doonhamers.
Previous Grounds: None.
Record Attendance: 26,552 v Hearts, Scottish Cup 3rd rd, 23 Feb 1952.
Record Transfer Fee received: £250,000 for Andy Thomson to Southend U (1994).
Record Transfer Fee paid: £30,000 for Jim Butter from Alloa Athletic (1995).
Record Victory: 11-1 v Stranraer, Scottish Cup 1st rd, 16 Jan 1932.
Record Defeat: 2-10 v Dundee, Division I, 1 Dec 1962.
Most Capped Player: Billy Houliston, 3, Scotland.
Most League Appearances: 731: Allan Ball, 1963-82.
Most League Goals in Season (Individual): 37: Jimmy Gray, Division II, 1927-28.
Most Goals in Season: 41: Jimmy Rutherford, 1931-32.
Most Goals Overall (Individual): 250: Jim Patterson, 1949-63.

QUEEN OF THE SOUTH 2010–11 LEAGUE RECORD

Match No.	Date	Venue	Opponents	Result	H/T Score	Lg Pos.	Goalscorers	Atten- dance
1	Aug 7	A	Dundee	L	0-1	0-1	—	4644
2	14	H	Raith R	L	1-3	0-2	10	Carmichael [46]	1961
3	22	A	Cowdenbeath	W	3-1	1-0	7	Burns [3], Holmes [54], McGuffie [86]	672
4	28	H	Ross Co	W	3-0	2-0	4	Quinn [2], Conroy [22], McLaren [89]	1644
5	Sept 11	A	Falkirk	L	1-3	0-1	6	Burns [66]	4064
6	18	H	Partick Th	W	2-1	0-1	4	Johnston [76], Quinn [87]	2013
7	25	A	Stirling A	D	0-0	0-0	5		945
8	Oct 2	H	Dunfermline Ath	W	2-0	0-0	4	Dowie (og) [53], McLaren [62]	2139
9	16	A	Morton	L	0-2	0-0	4		1777
10	23	H	Falkirk	L	1-5	0-1	5	Burns [49]	2254
11	30	A	Ross Co	D	1-1	1-0	5	McMenamin [18]	2186
12	Nov 6	A	Raith R	W	1-0	0-0	5	Conroy [75]	2108
13	13	H	Cowdenbeath	W	3-0	2-0	5	Burns [20], Conroy [34], McLaren [80]	1782
14	Dec 11	A	Dunfermline Ath	L	0-1	0-0	—		2062
15	Jan 15	A	Falkirk	W	3-0	3-0	4	Johnston 2 [27, 44], McMenamin [39]	3376
16	Feb 5	H	Dundee	L	1-2	0-1	4	McGuffie [60]	2006
17	12	H	Partick Th	D	3-3	1-2	4	McLaren 2 [43, 87], Johnston [90]	1860
18	19	A	Morton	W	4-0	2-0	4	McLaren (pen) [2], Weatherston 3 [32, 64, 76]	1754
19	22	H	Stirling A	D	2-2	0-1	—	McMenamin [50], McGuffie [69]	1185
20	26	H	Dunfermline Ath	L	1-3	0-0	4	McMenamin [68]	2052
21	Mar 1	A	Cowdenbeath	D	2-2	1-1	—	Weatherston [17], McMenamin [84]	670
22	5	H	Raith R	L	0-2	0-1	5		1754
23	8	A	Partick Th	L	1-3	0-1	—	Carmichael [86]	1001
24	12	A	Dundee	L	1-2	1-0	7	McMenamin [34]	4242
25	16	H	Morton	W	2-0	2-0	—	McMenamin [16], McLaren [26]	956
26	19	A	Ross Co	W	2-1	2-1	4	Harris (pen) [26], Weatherston [44]	2181
27	22	H	Falkirk	L	0-1	0-1	—		1270
28	26	H	Stirling A	W	4-1	2-1	4	McLaren 2 (1 pen) [23 (p), 36], McMenamin 2 [54, 76]	1392
29	29	A	Stirling A	W	2-0	2-0	—	Orsi [4], Lilley [45]	444
30	Apr 2	A	Partick Th	D	0-0	0-0	4		1806
31	13	H	Morton	L	1-4	0-2	—	Degnan [71]	966
32	16	A	Dunfermline Ath	L	1-6	0-1	5	Harris [62]	3255
33	23	H	Cowdenbeath	D	2-2	2-2	6	Carmichael [17], Holmes [45]	1102
34	26	H	Ross Co	L	0-1	0-1	—		266
35	30	A	Raith R	W	1-0	0-0	4	McMenamin [90]	2001
36	May 7	H	Dundee	W	3-0	2-0	4	Johnston [18], McMenamin [24], Burns [61]	2590

Final League Position: 4

Scottish League Clubs – Queen of the South

Honours
League Champions: Division II 1950-51. Second Division 2001-02. *Runners-up:* Division II 1932-33, 1961-62, 1974-75. Second Division 1980-81, 1985-86.
Scottish Cup Runners-up: 2007-08.
League Cup: semi-finals 1950-51, 1960-61.
B&Q Cup: semi-finals 1991-92. *League Challenge Cup Winners:* 2002-03; *Runners-up:* 1997-98, 2010-11.

European: *UEFA Cup:* 2 matches (2008-09).

Club colours: Shirt: Royal blue. Shorts: White. Stockings: Royal blue.

Goalscorers: *League (54):* McMenamin 11, McLaren 9 (2 pens), Burns 5, Johnston 5, Weatherston 5, Carmichael 3, Conroy 3, McGuffie 3, Harris 2 (1 pen), Holmes 2, Quinn 2, Degnan 1, Lilley 1, Orsi 1, own goal 1.
Scottish Cup (1): McMenamin 1.
CIS Cup (9): Holmes 2 (1 pen), Carmichael 1, Harris 1 (pen), Johnston 1, McLaren 1, Quinn 1, Riley 1, Weatherston 1.
Alba Challenge Cup (10): Burns 4, Harris 1, Holmes 1, McGuffie 1, Reid 1, Weatherston 1, own goal 1.

Robinson L 2	Reid C 32	McGuffie R 32+2	Harris R 30+1	McKenna S 29	Burns P 26	Quinn R 16+2	Young D 2	Carmichael D 15+13	Holmes D 29+1	Weatherston D 18+11	Reilly G —+1	Lilley D 30+1	Hutton D 25	Johnston A 25+1	McLaren W 28+4	Scally N —+4	Conroy R 11	McMenamin C 26	McShane I 3+10	Orsi D 4+3	O'Hear K —+1	Smylie R —+5	McKenzie R 9	Black S 1+3	Degnan S 1+4	McGowan J 2+1	Match No.
1	2	3	4	5	6	7	8	9¹	10	11	12																1
1	2⁸	5	4	7	9	6	8¹	12	10	11		3															2
	2	4	6	7	8			12	10	11¹		3⁸	1		5			9²	13								3
	2²	4	7	6	8¹			12	10	11		3	1		5			9	13								4
	2	6	9⁸	3¹	7			12	10	13		4	1	11²				9		8							5
	2	4	8	6	7			12	10¹	11		3	1		5			9									6
	2	5	4	8		7		13	10	11		3	1	6¹				9²	12								7
	2	6	4	7¹	8⁸			13	12	11		3	1	9	5³			10²	14								8
	2	3	5	7	8			13	12	11¹		4	1	6²				9	10								9
	2²	13	4	6	7	8		14	12	11¹		3	1	10	5²			9									10
	2	12	5	4	7¹	8		13	10	11³		3	1	6				9²	14								11
	2	4	5	7	6				10	11		3	1		8			9									12
	2²	6	4	5	7			14	10³	13		3	1	12	8		11¹	9									13
	2	8	4	7²	6			12	10¹	11		3	1		5			9	13								14
	2	3	4	7	6			12	10	13			1	5²	8²		11	9¹	14								15
	2	4	6	5	7			12	10			3	1		8		11	9¹									16
	2	3	5	6	7			12	10			4	1		8		11	9¹									17
	2	3	5	6	8³	7		12	10¹	11²		4	1				14	9	13								18
	2	6	4	8	5	7			10	11		3	1					9									19
	2	3	5	4	8¹	7		12	10	11			1	6				9									20
	2²	3	6	4	8¹	7		12	10	11			1		5			9	13								21
	2	3	5	8		7¹		12	10	11		4	1	6				9									22
	2	4	5	7				12	10	11²		3	1	6	8			9¹	13								23
	2	3	5	8		7		12	10	11		4	1	6				9¹									24
	2	3	5	8		7		14	10³	11		4	1	6¹	12			9²	13								25
	2¹	3	4	6	8	7		12	10	11				5				9					1				26
	2²	5	4	7	6			12	10	11¹		3			8			9	13				1				27
	2	4	6	5¹		7		12	10	11²		3¹			8			9	14				1	13			28
	2	4	13	5	6	7		12	10³	11²		3			8¹			9	14				1				29
	2	5	4	7	6			12	10¹	11²		3	1		8			9	13								30
	2	4	5		6	7		12	10²	11¹		3			8			9	13				1				31
	2	4	5	6	8	7			10	11		3						9⁸					1				32
	2⁸	4	5	6¹		7		12	10	11		3			8			9²					1		13		33
	2	5	4¹	6		7		12	10	11		3			8			9²	13				1				34
	2	4	5		8	7		12	10	11³		3		6¹				9²	14				1		13		35
	2		5	4	8	7		12	10¹	11³		3²	1	6				9	14						13		36

QUEEN'S PARK   Third Division

Year Formed: 1867. *Ground & Address:* Hampden Park, Mount Florida, Glasgow G42 9BA. *Telephone:* 0141 632 1275.
Fax: 0141 636 1612. *E-mail:* secretary@queensparkfc.co.uk *Website:* queensparkfc.co.uk
Ground Capacity: all seated: 52,000. *Size of Pitch:* 115yd × 75yd.
President: Alan Hutchison. *Secretary:* Alistair MacKay. *Treasurer:* David Gordon.
Head Coach: Gardner Spiers. *Physios:* R. C. Findlay and A. Myles.
Club Nickname: The Spiders.
Previous Grounds: 1st Hampden (Recreation Ground); (Titwood Park was used as an interim measure between 1st &
2nd Hampdens); 2nd Hampden (Cathkin); 3rd Hampden.
Record Attendance: 95,772 v Rangers, Scottish Cup, 18 Jan 1930.
Record for Ground: 149,547 Scotland v England, 1937.
Record Transfer Fee received: Not applicable due to amateur status.
Record Transfer Fee paid: Not applicable due to amateur status.
Record Victory: 16-0 v St. Peters, Scottish Cup 1st rd, 29 Aug 1885.
Record Defeat: 0-9 v Motherwell, Division I, 26 Apr 1930.
Most Capped Player: Walter Arnott, 14, Scotland.
Most League Appearances: 532: Ross Caven, 1982-2002.
Most League Goals in Season (Individual): 30: William Martin, Division I, 1937-38.
Most Goals Overall (Individual): 163: James B. McAlpine, 1919-33.

QUEEN'S PARK 2010–11 LEAGUE RECORD

Match No.	Date	Venue	Opponents	Result	H/T Score	Lg Pos.	Goalscorers	Attendance
1	Aug 7	A	Montrose	W 2-1	1-0	—	Smith [12], McBride, M [90]	415
2	14	H	Clyde	L 0-1	0-0	6		849
3	21	A	Albion R	L 1-2	0-1	8	McBride, M (pen) [90]	497
4	28	H	Berwick R	L 0-2	0-1	9		479
5	Sept 4	A	Arbroath	L 0-1	0-0	—		515
6	11	A	Stranraer	L 0-1	0-0	9		408
7	18	H	East Stirling	W 2-0	2-0	7	Longworth [18], Smith [26]	460
8	25	A	Annan Ath	L 1-2	0-1	8	Smith [62]	546
9	Oct 2	H	Arbroath	W 5-2	2-1	7	Brough 2 [15, 66], Watt [45], Smith [71], Daly [90]	433
10	16	A	Elgin C	L 2-4	0-2	8	Nicolson (og) [77], O'Hara [90]	517
11	30	A	Berwick R	D 1-1	0-0	8	McBride, M [68]	520
12	Nov 6	H	Stranraer	L 1-3	1-0	9	Harkins [18]	636
13	13	H	Albion R	L 0-1	0-0	9		529
14	Dec 18	H	Elgin C	D 1-1	0-0	—	Quinn, T [66]	452
15	Jan 15	A	Stranraer	L 1-2	0-1	9	Gallagher [70]	341
16	18	A	Albion R	W 2-1	0-1	—	Quinn, T 2 [87, 89]	402
17	22	H	Berwick R	W 1-0	0-0	—	McBride, M [72]	485
18	Feb 1	A	Annan Ath	W 2-1	0-0	—	Daly [67], Murray [69]	293
19	5	H	East Stirling	W 2-0	2-0	6	Murray [32], Daly [37]	504
20	12	H	Arbroath	D 1-1	1-1	6	McBride, M (pen) [45]	467
21	16	A	East Stirling	W 1-0	0-0	—	Daly [46]	293
22	19	A	Elgin C	W 1-0	1-0	6	McBride, M (pen) [19]	725
23	22	H	Annan Ath	W 3-0	1-0	—	Daly [27], Longworth [59], Smith [85]	327
24	26	A	Montrose	W 2-0	1-0	4	Meggatt [36], McGinn [86]	414
25	Mar 5	H	Clyde	W 4-0	3-0	4	Murray 2 [14, 16], Watt [41], Longworth [51]	1148
26	8	A	Clyde	W 3-2	2-1	—	Longworth 2 [36, 41], Daly [71]	502
27	12	H	Stranraer	D 3-3	1-1	4	McBride, M [41], Little [81], Longworth [88]	607
28	19	A	Berwick R	L 1-3	0-2	5	Quinn, T [66]	398
29	26	H	Annan Ath	L 0-1	0-1	6		561
30	29	H	Montrose	W 1-0	0-0	—	Lauchlan [80]	325
31	Apr 2	A	East Stirling	L 2-3	1-2	5	Capuano [9], Beveridge (og) [55]	391
32	9	H	Elgin C	W 1-0	0-0	5	Longworth [50]	436
33	16	A	Arbroath	D 2-2	1-1	5	Smith [25], Longworth [80]	912
34	23	H	Albion R	W 2-1	1-1	5	Meggatt [30], Watt [90]	715
35	30	A	Clyde	W 2-0	1-0	4	Longworth [14], McBride [64]	1021
36	May 7	H	Montrose	W 4-1	1-0	3	Longworth 3 [27, 59, 83], Watt [77]	767

Final League Position: 3

Honours
League Champions: Division II 1922-23. B Division 1955-56. Second Division 1980-81. Third Division 1999-2000.
Promoted to Second Division: 2006-07 (play-offs).
Scottish Cup Winners: 1874, 1875, 1876, 1880, 1881, 1882, 1884, 1886, 1890, 1893; *Runners-up:* 1892, 1900.
FA Cup runners-up: 1884, 1885.

Club colours: Shirt: White with thin black hoops. Shorts: White. Stockings: White.

Goalscorers: *League (57):* Longworth 12, McBride, M 8 (3 pens), Daly 6, Smith 6, Murray 4, Quinn, T 4, Watt 4, Brough 2, Meggatt 2, Capuano 1, Gallagher 1, Harkins 1, Lauchlan 1, Little 1, McGinn 1, O'Hara 1, own goals 2.
Scottish Cup (1): Brough 1.
CIS Cup (0).
Alba Challenge Cup (5): Eagleshan 3 (1 pen), McBride, M 1, Watt 1.
Play-Offs (1): Smith 1.

Hamilton P 1	Little R 35	Burns P 2+1	Gallagher P 19+2	Sinclair R 3	McBride M 30+3	Anderson D 32+1	Watt J 27+5	O'Hara M 4+5	Eagleshan G 9+4	Smith C 11+13	Longworth J 16+11	Murray D 17+8	Quinn T 13+9	Strain A 32	Harkins P 8+5	Meggatt D 30	Henry J 1+2	Brough J 11	Daly M 17+12	Capuano G 26+1	McPherson G 3+1	McGinn P 26	Lauchlan G 4+6	Milne A 1	Baillie S —+1	Millen A 18	Match No.
1	2	3	4	5	6	7	8²	9	10¹	11³	12	13	14														1
	2	5	4	3	6²	7	14	9	10³	11¹	12			8	1	13											2
	2	5	4		6		10	9²		11¹			13	7	1	8	3	12									3
	2		4		6	8¹	9	13	14	11²	10	7³		1		12		5	3								4
	2		3		7¹	8	12	8		11²		14	13	1		9		5	4	10³							5
	2		4			7		9⁸	11¹		12	10		1		13		5	3	8²		6					6
	2		4	12	8³		10	11²	9			14		1		5		7¹	3	13		6					7
	2		3	13	8	7		11	10¹			9		1		5		4	12			6²					8
	2		3		8		11	9	10²		12	7¹		1⁶		5		4	13			6	15				9
	2		3	14	7³	12	9		11		10²	8		1		5		4	13			6¹					10
	2	5			7	13	11²	12				8	9¹	4		3		10		1		6					11
	3				6⁸	7	10¹		12		13	8		9²		5		4⁸	11			1	2				12
	2		3		7	11³	14	12	13		8	1		9		4		10²				5	6¹				13
	3		4	6	8	11²	13	14	9³		1	10¹	5			12		7	2								14
	3		4		6	8²	10¹		11	9		1	13	2		12		5	7								15
	3			6	12	8¹	11	14		13	9	1	10³	2		4		5²	7								16
	2			6	8	11	13	9¹		1	10²	4	3			12		5	7								17
	2		5	8		13	11	10²	1	9¹		6						7							3	12	18
	2		6	8		10³	12	11	1	13	4					9¹	5²	7	14							3	19
	2		6	8		10	12	11	1		4					9¹	5	7								3	20
	2			5	8	11¹	12	10	1		4⁸					9²	6	7	13							3	21
	4	2		5	8	10¹	12	13	11		1					9²	6	7								3	22
	2			5	8³	9¹	12	13	11	1		4				10²	6	7	14							3	23
	3	12		6	8	9²	13	10³	11	14	1					2¹	5	7								4	24
	2	3		5	8	9³	13	10¹	11²	1		12					6	7	14							4	25
	4	3		7	8	9²	13	10¹	11³	1		12					6	2	14							5	26
	2	3		5	8	11³	9¹	12	10	14	1	13					6²	7								4	27
	2			5	8	9¹	12	10	11³	13	1		4			14	6²	7								3	28
	2			5	8	10²	12	11	1		4					9	6¹	7	13							3	29
	3			6	8	10²	13	11	12	1		5				9¹	2	7								4	30
	2			5	8	13	11¹	10	12	1		4	14			6³	7	9²								3	31
	3	7		6	8	11²	12	10	1		5	13	14			2	9¹		4³								32
	4			6	8	12	11	10²	13	1		3				9¹	2	7								5	33
	2	13		5	8	12	10¹	11	1		4					9	6²	7								3	34
	3			6	8	12	11¹	10	1		2					9	5	7								4	35
	2	13		5	8	12	11¹	10³	14	1		4				9	6	7								3²	36

RAITH ROVERS

First Division

Year Formed: 1883. *Ground & Address:* Stark's Park, Pratt St, Kirkcaldy KY1 1SA. *Telephone:* 01592 263514. *Fax:* 01592 642833. *E-mail:* office@raithroversfc.com *Website:* www.raithroversfc.com
Ground Capacity: all seated: 10,104. *Size of Pitch:* 113yd × 70yd.
Chairman: David Somerville. *General Manager & Secretary:* Bob Mullen.
Manager: John McGlynn. *Assistant Manager:* Paul Smith.
Club Nickname: Rovers.
Previous Grounds: Robbie's Park.
Record Attendance: 31,306 v Hearts, Scottish Cup 2nd rd, 7 Feb 1953.
Record Transfer Fee received: £900,000 for Steve McAnespie to Bolton Wanderers (Sept 1995).
Record Transfer Fee paid: £225,000 for Paul Harvey from Airdrieonians (1996).
Record Victory: 10-1 v Coldstream, Scottish Cup 2nd rd, 13 Feb 1954.
Record Defeat: 2-11 v Morton, Division II, 18 Mar 1936.
Most Capped Player: David Morris, 6, Scotland.
Most League Appearances: 430: Willie McNaught, 1946-51.
Most League Goals in Season (Individual): 38: Norman Haywood, Division II, 1937-38.
Most Goals Overall (Individual): 154: Gordon Dalziel (League), 1987-94.

RAITH ROVERS 2010–11 LEAGUE RECORD

Match No.	Date	Venue	Opponents	Result	H/T Score	Lg Pos.	Goalscorers	Attendance
1	Aug 7	H	Partick Th	W 4-0	3-0	—	Ferry [7], Baird 3 (1 pen) [31, 42 (p), 82]	2238
2	14	A	Queen of the S	W 3-1	2-0	1	Ferry [7], Baird [13], Mole [90]	1961
3	21	H	Dunfermline Ath	W 2-0	0-0	1	Davidson [73], Ellis [79]	6169
4	28	H	Morton	W 1-0	0-0	1	Tade [84]	2344
5	Sept 11	A	Ross Co	D 0-0	0-0	1		2500
6	18	A	Dundee	D 0-0	0-0	2		4532
7	25	H	Falkirk	W 2-1	1-1	2	Tade [37], Dyer [78]	3438
8	Oct 2	H	Stirling A	L 0-2	0-1	2		2010
9	16	A	Cowdenbeath	W 2-1	0-0	2	Baird [88], Simmons [90]	1508
10	23	H	Ross Co	W 1-0	0-0	1	Mole [90]	1776
11	30	A	Morton	W 1-0	0-0	1	Walker [61]	1858
12	Nov 6	H	Queen of the S	L 0-1	0-0	1		2108
13	13	A	Dunfermline Ath	D 2-2	0-2	1	Williamson [84], Walker [90]	7158
14	Dec 26	A	Partick Th	D 0-0	0-0	—		2036
15	29	A	Falkirk	D 0-0	0-0	—		4037
16	Jan 2	H	Dunfermline Ath	W 2-1	0-0	—	Campbell [51], Tade [70]	6534
17	15	A	Ross Co	W 1-0	0-0	1	Ellis [65]	2408
18	22	H	Morton	D 2-2	2-0	1	Baird [16], Walker [31]	2220
19	29	H	Falkirk	L 1-2	1-2	—	Ellis [10]	2829
20	Feb 5	A	Stirling A	W 3-1	1-1	1	Tade 2 [16, 53], Walker [66]	1193
21	12	A	Dundee	L 1-2	0-0	1	Murray [51]	5105
22	19	A	Cowdenbeath	W 3-0	0-0	1	Baird [18], Simmons [24], Campbell [31]	1413
23	22	H	Dundee	L 1-2	0-1	—	Walker [50]	2716
24	26	H	Stirling A	W 2-1	1-0	1	Murray [35], Baird [63]	1918
25	Mar 5	A	Queen of the S	W 2-0	1-0	1	Baird [24], Campbell [59]	1754
26	12	H	Partick Th	L 0-2	0-0	1		2065
27	15	H	Cowdenbeath	W 2-1	1-0	—	Tade [45], Baird [85]	1495
28	19	A	Morton	D 0-0	0-0	1		1809
29	22	H	Ross Co	D 1-1	0-0	—	Tade [55]	1639
30	26	A	Falkirk	L 1-2	0-1	1	Baird [74]	5008
31	Apr 2	H	Dundee	W 2-1	1-0	2	Tade [43], Walker [90]	3143
32	9	H	Cowdenbeath	D 2-2	0-0	—	Murray [60], Campbell [89]	2284
33	16	A	Stirling A	W 2-1	1-0	2	Walker [15], Baird [80]	1162
34	23	A	Dunfermline Ath	L 1-2	1-0	2	Baird [41]	11,052
35	30	H	Queen of the S	L 0-1	0-0	2		2001
36	May 7	A	Partick Th	L 0-3	0-0	2		2279

Final League Position: 2

Honours

League Champions: First Division: 1992-93, 1994-95. Second Division: 2008-09. Division II 1907-08, 1909-10 (shared), 1937-38, 1948-49; *Runners-up:* Division II 1908-09, 1926-27, 1966-67. Second Division 1975-76, 1977-78, 1986-87. *Scottish Cup Runners-up:* 1913. *League Cup Winners:* 1994-95. *Runners-up:* 1948-49.

European: *UEFA Cup:* 6 matches (1995-96).

Club colours: Shirt: Navy blue with red flashings. Shorts: Navy blue with red side flashings. Stockings: Navy blue with red flashings.

Goalscorers: *League (47):* Baird 13 (1 pen), Tade 8, Walker 7, Campbell 4, Ellis 3, Murray 3, Ferry 2, Mole 2, Simmons 2, Davidson 1, Dyer 1, Williamson 1.
Scottish Cup (2): Baird 1, Murray 1.
CIS Cup (7): Tade 3, Mole 2, Baird 1, Ferry 1.
Alba Challenge Cup (0).

McGurn D 21+1	Wilson C 26+4	Murray G 36	Ellis L 29	Dyer W 26+4	Walker A 34	Williamson I 12+10	Simmons S 26+3	Ferry M 13+9	Tade G 34+2	Baird J 34+2	Mole J 5+6	McBride S 18+4	Weir G 1+24	Davidson I 29+2	McNeil A 15+1	Campbell M 22+2	Wales G —+7	Hill D 8	McKechnie J —+1	McBride K 7	Callachan R —+1	Donaldson R —+1	Match No.
1	2	3	4	5	6	7³	8		9²	10¹	11	12	13	14									1
1	2	3	4	5	7	6³	8	9	11¹	10²	12	14	13										2
1	2	3	4	5	6	7¹	8	9	10³	11²	13	14	12										3
1	2	3	4	5	7²	13	8	9	10	11¹	12			6									4
1	2	3	4	5	7	13	8²	9	10³	11¹	14		12	6									5
1	2	3	4	5	7		8	9	10	11¹	12			6									6
1	2	3	4	5	6	13	8	9	11¹	10²	12	7³	14										7
1	2	3	4	5	7		8	9¹	10⁷	11¹	13	14		6	12								8
1	2	3	4	5	7	9¹	8		10²	12	11		13	6									9
1	2	3	4	5	7	9¹	8³	12	13	11²	10		14	6									10
1	2	3	4	5	8	9¹		12	7²	11	10³	14	13	6									11
1	2	3	4	5	7²	12	8		9	11¹	10		13	8									12
1	2	3	4	5	8	10		7	9¹	11¹	10³	14		6									13
1		2	4	5	8	7	12		9¹	11²		10	13	6		3							14
1		2	3	5	8	7¹	12	13	9	11		10²		4		6							15
1		2	4	5	8	7¹	12	13	9	11³		10²	14	6		3							16
1	14	2³	3	5	7		8	12	9²	10		11¹	13	4		6							17
1		2	4	5	7		8		9	11		10		6		3							18
1	13	2²	4	5	7	12	8		9	11		10¹		6		3							19
12	2	5	3	7	14		8		9³	10²		11	13	6	1	4¹							20
	2	6	4	5	7	13	8		11	10¹		9²	12	3	1								21
	2	4	5	7	12		8		9²	11³		10	14	6¹	1	3	13						22
	2	4	5	7	12		8¹		9	11³		10²	14	6	1	3	13						23
5	2	4		7	9¹	8			10	11		12			1	3	6						24
	2	6		5	7	8¹	9³	11	10²	12					1	3	13	4	14				25
	2	6		5	7	8	9¹	10²	11³	13		12			1	3	14	4					26
	2	4	5¹	12	6		7	9	11	10²				8	1	3	13						27
	2	4		12	7		8		9	11	10			6	1	3		5¹					28
	2	4		13	7		8¹	12	9	11³	10			6	1	3	14	5²					29
	2	4			7				9	11	10¹			3	1	6	12	5		8			30
15	2	4			7			12	9	11		10²	13	6¹	1⁶	3		5		8			31
	2	4		5	7				9	11		10¹	12	6	1	3				8			32
	2²	4	5		6		8	12	11	10		9¹	13		1	3				7			33
	2¹	4	5		7		9		10	11	12			6	1	3				8			34
1	12	2	5			7¹		14	13	10		9³	11²	6		3		4		8			35
1	2²	3	5	14		7¹			9	10	11			6²		4				8	12	13	36

RANGERS   Premier League

Year Formed: 1873. *Ground & Address:* Ibrox Stadium, 150 Edmiston Drive, Glasgow G51 2XD.
Telephone: 0871 702 1972. *Fax:* 0870 600 1978. *Website:* www.rangers.co.uk
Ground Capacity: all seated: 51,082. *Size of Pitch:* 105m × 68m.
Executive Director: Craig Whyte. *Chief Executive:* Martin Bain.
Manager: Ally McCoist. *Assistant Manager:* Kenny McDowall. *Physio:* Pip Yeates. *Head of Football Administration:* Andrew Dickson.
Club Nickname: The Gers.
Previous Grounds: Flesher's Haugh, Burnbank, Kinning Park, Old Ibrox.
Record Attendance: 118,567 v Celtic, Division I, 2 Jan 1939.
Record Transfer Fee received: £9,000,000 for Alan Hutton to Tottenham H (January 2008).
Record Transfer Fee paid: £12,000,000 for Tore Andre Flo from Chelsea (November 2000).
Record Victory: 14-2 v Blairgowrie, Scottish Cup 1st rd, 20 Jan, 1934. *Record Defeat:* 2-10 v Airdrieonians; 1886.
Most Capped Player: Ally McCoist, 60, Scotland.
Most League Appearances: 496: John Greig, 1962-78.
Most League Goals in Season (Individual): 44: Sam English, Division I, 1931-32.
Most Goals Overall (Individual): 355: Ally McCoist; 1985-98.

Honours
League Champions: (54 times) Division I 1890-91 (shared), 1898-99, 1899-1900, 1900-01, 1901-02, 1910-11, 1911-12, 1912-13, 1917-18, 1919-20, 1920-21, 1922-23, 1923-24, 1924-25, 1926-27, 1927-28, 1928-29, 1929-30, 1930-31, 1932-33, 1933-34, 1934-35, 1936-37, 1938-39, 1946-47, 1948-49, 1949-50, 1952-53, 1955-56, 1956-57, 1958-59, 1960-61, 1962-63, 1963-64, 1974-75. Premier Division: 1975-76, 1977-78, 1986-87, 1988-89, 1989-90, 1990-91, 1991-92, 1992-93, 1993-94, 1994-95, 1995-96, 1996-97, 1998-99, 1999-2000, 2002-03, 2004-05, 2008-09, 2009-10, 2010-11; *Runners-up:* 29 times.

RANGERS 2010–11 LEAGUE RECORD

Match No.	Date	Venue	Opponents	Result	H/T Score	Lg Pos.	Goalscorers	Atten-dance
1	Aug 14	H	Kilmarnock	W 2-1	1-0	—	Miller [16], Naismith [57]	45,739
2	22	A	Hibernian	W 3-0	0-0	3	Miller 3 [64, 70, 90]	17,145
3	28	H	St Johnstone	W 2-1	1-1	2	Papac [33], Miller [79]	46,109
4	Sept 11	A	Hamilton A	W 2-1	1-0	2	Jelavic [6], Miller [90]	5356
5	18	H	Dundee U	W 4-0	1-0	1	Dillon (og) [9], Miller 2 [69, 82], Naismith [77]	44,786
6	26	A	Aberdeen	W 3-2	1-2	1	Miller 2 (1 pen) [34 (p), 52], Jelavic [67]	15,307
7	Oct 2	A	Hearts	W 2-1	0-1	2	Lafferty [80], Naismith [90]	15,637
8	16	H	Motherwell	W 4-1	0-1	1	Naismith [47], Davis [62], Miller [65], Weiss [67]	44,609
9	24	A	Celtic	W 3-1	0-1	1	Loovens (og) [49], Miller 2 (1 pen) [55, 67 (p)]	58,874
10	30	H	Inverness CT	D 1-1	1-0	1	Edu [11]	43,697
11	Nov 7	A	St Mirren	W 3-1	0-0	1	McAusland (og) [48], Naismith [58], Miller [68]	5674
12	10	H	Hibernian	L 0-3	0-2	—		41,514
13	13	H	Aberdeen	W 2-0	2-0	1	Miller [21], Weiss [32]	44,919
14	20	A	Kilmarnock	W 3-2	1-1	1	Miller 3 (2 pens) [42 (p), 55 (p), 64]	10,177
15	Dec 11	A	Inverness CT	D 1-1	0-1	—	Miller [57]	6799
16	26	A	Motherwell	W 4-1	2-0	—	Miller 2 [26, 61], Saunders (og) [34], Weiss [51]	9371
17	Jan 2	H	Celtic	L 0-2	0-0	2		50,222
18	15	H	Hamilton A	W 4-0	3-0	2	Weiss 2 [25, 45], Whittaker (pen) [28], Edu [82]	44,639
19	18	H	Inverness CT	W 1-0	1-0	—	Davis [45]	41,623
20	22	A	Hearts	L 0-1	0-0	2		16,737
21	26	A	Hibernian	W 2-0	2-0	—	Bougherra [26], Jelavic [35]	11,696
22	Feb 2	H	Hearts	W 1-0	1-0	—	Lafferty [4]	44,823
23	12	A	Motherwell	W 6-0	3-0	2	Naismith [5], Jelavic 3 [34, 37, 79], Hutchinson (og) [76], Healy [83]	43,789
24	20	A	Celtic	L 0-3	0-2	2		58,748
25	27	H	St Johnstone	W 4-0	2-0	2	Jelavic 2 [5, 90], Lafferty [41], Papac [81]	43,125
26	Mar 6	A	St Mirren	W 1-0	1-0	2	Bartley [24]	5405
27	13	H	Kilmarnock	W 2-1	1-0	—	Diouf [38], Clancy (og) [87]	42,417
28	Apr 2	H	Dundee U	L 2-3	1-1	2	Jelavic [19], Naismith [52]	46,697
29	5	A	St Johnstone	W 2-0	1-0	—	Lafferty [20], Naismith [83]	5820
30	10	A	Hamilton A	W 1-0	1-0	2	Jelavic [44]	4526
31	13	A	Aberdeen	W 1-0	1-0	—	Jelavic [22]	11,925
32	16	H	St Mirren	W 2-1	1-1	—	Papac [33], Whittaker (pen) [52]	46,392
33	19	A	Dundee U	W 4-0	1-0	—	Whittaker 2 (2 pens) [22, 60], Jelavic [72], Lafferty [83]	11,626
34	24	H	Celtic	D 0-0	0-0	1		50,248
35	30	A	Motherwell	W 5-0	1-0	1	Lafferty [18], Davis [51], Jelavic [64], Naismith 2 [76, 90]	8968
36	May 7	H	Hearts	W 4-0	3-0	1	Jelavic [23], Lafferty [40], Davis [44], Stevenson (og) [84]	46,178
37	10	H	Dundee U	W 2-0	2-0	—	Jelavic [21], Lafferty [25]	49,267
38	15	A	Kilmarnock	W 5-1	3-0	1	Lafferty 3 [1, 7, 53], Naismith [5], Jelavic [49]	16,173

Final League Position: 1

Scottish Cup Winners: (33 times) 1894, 1897, 1898, 1903, 1928, 1930, 1932, 1934, 1935, 1936, 1948, 1949, 1950, 1953, 1960, 1962, 1963, 1964, 1966, 1973, 1976, 1978, 1979, 1981, 1992, 1993, 1996, 1999, 2000, 2002, 2003, 2008, 2009; *Runners-up:* 17 times.

League Cup Winners: (27 times) 1946-47, 1948-49, 1960-61, 1961-62, 1963-64, 1964-65, 1970-71, 1975-76, 1977-78, 1978-79, 1981-82, 1983-84, 1984-85, 1986-87, 1987-88, 1988-89, 1990-91, 1992-93, 1993-94, 1996-97, 1998-99, 2001-02, 2002-03, 2004-05, 2007-08, 2009-10, 2010-11; *Runners-up:* 7 times.

European: *European Cup:* 159 matches (1956-57, 1957-58, 1959-60 semi-finals, 1961-62, 1963-64, 1964-65, 1975-76, 1976-77, 1978-79, 1987-88, 1989-90, 1990-91, 1991-92, 1992-93 final pool, 1993-94, 1994-95, 1995-96; 1996-97, 1997-98, 1999-2000, 2000-01, 2001-02, 2003-04, 2004-05, 2005-06, 2007-08, 2008-09, 2009-10, 2010-11).

Cup Winners' Cup: 54 matches (1960-61, 1962-63, 1966-67 runners-up, 1969-70, 1971-72 winners, 1973-74, 1977-78, 1979-80, 1981-82, 1983-84).

UEFA Cup: 88 matches (*Fairs Cup:* 1967-68, 1968-69 semi-finals, 1970-71. *UEFA Cup:* 1982-83, 1984-85, 1985-86, 1986-87, 1988-89, 1997-98, 1998-99, 1999-2000, 2000-01, 2001-02, 2002-03, 2004-05, 2006-07, 2007-08 runners-up). *Europa League:* 4 matches (2010-11).

Club colours: Shirt: Royal blue with red and white trim. Shorts: White. Stockings: Black with red tops.

Goalscorers: *League (88):* Miller 21 (4 pens), Jelavic 16, Lafferty 11, Naismith 11, Weiss 5, Davis 4, Whittaker 4 (4 pens), Papac 3, Edu 2, Bartley 1, Bougherra 1, Diouf 1, Healy 1, own goals 7.
Scottish Cup (5): Whittaker 2 (2 pens), Lafferty 1, McCulloch 1, Ness 1.
CIS Cup (13): Jelavic 3, Lafferty 3, Naismith 3, Bougherra 1, Davis 1, Edu 1, Little 1.
Champions League (5): Jelavic 2, Edu 1, Miller 1, Naismith 1. *Europa League (3):* Diouf 1, Edu 1, Whittaker 1.

McGregor A 37	Broadfoot K 5+3	Papac S 34	Edu M 27+6	Weir D 37	Bougherra M 31	Whittaker S 36	Naismith S 28+3	Beattie J 5+2	Miller K 17+1	Lafferty K 23+8	Hutton K 1+6	Davis S 37	Weiss V 17+6	McCulloch L 17+4	Jelavic N 20+3	Foster R 11+4	Alexander N 1	Loy R —+1	Wylde G 9+6	Fleck J 3+10	Ness J 8+3	Webster A 1	Diouf E 6+9	Bartley K 5	Healy D 2+6	Kerkar S —+1	Match No.
1	2	3	4	5	6	7	8	9^1	10	11	12																1
1		3	4	5	6	7	8	9^1	10	11^8		7	12														2
1		3	12	5	6	2	11	9^1	10			8	7^2	4	13												3
1	2^1	3	4	5	6		8	9^2	14	11^3		7	13	10	12												4
1		3	4^1	5	6	2	12		10	13		7	11^f	8	9												5
1	12	3	13	5	6	2^1	7		10	14		8^2	11^3	4	9												6
1		3	4	5	6	2	7		10	12		8	11		9^1												7
1		3	4^3	5	6	2	8		10^1	9	14	7	11^2				1	12	13								8
1	12	3^1	4	5	6	2	8	14	10^2	9^3		7	13	11													9
1	2	3	4^1	5	6		13		10	9		7	11^2	8					12								10
1		3	4	5	6	2	9		10	12		7	11^1	8													11
1	13	3^2	4^1	5	6	2	11		10	9		7	12	8													12
1		3		5	6	2	9		10			8	11^1	4					12	7							13
1	6	5			3		9		10	11		7	12	4		2			8^1								14
1		3		5	6	2	9	12	10			8	11^1	4		7^2			13								15
1		3		5	6	2	9^1		10			8	11^2	4		7			12	13							16
1		3		5	6	9			10	12	13	8	11	4		2^1				7^2							17
1		3^3	13	5	6	2			10	9		7^2	11^1	4	14				12	8							18
1	14	5		2				9^2	10			7	11^1	4	13	3			12	8^3	6						19
1		3	8^2	5	6	2	10	9^1				7	14	4					12		13	11^3					20
1		3	12	5	6	2	10	13				7	11^1	4	9^2				8								21
1		3	8	5	6	2	13	9				7	11^2	4^1					10		12						22
1		3	14	5	6	2	8^1					7	11	9							12		10^2	4^3	13		23
1		3	8	5	6	2	11^1	12				7	9										10^2	4	13		24
1		3	4		6	2			10^3			7	11^1	9	14						12		13	5	8^2		25
1			4		6	7						13	8			2			12	9^1	10		3		11^2		26
1	11	8		5	6	2				12		7	13	9		3^2							10^1		4		27
1		3	4	5	6	7						8	9	2					11				10				28
1		3	4	5	6	7			10^2			8	9	2					11^1	12	13						29
1		3	4^2	5	6	7			10^3			8	9	2					11^1	14			13				30
1		3	4	5	6	7			10	13		8		9^3		2^1			11^2		12		14				31
1		3	4	5	6				11	12		8	9	2						7^1			10				32
1		3	4	5	6	2			10^2	11		7^1	8	9^3						13			12	14			33
1			4^2	5	6	2			10			7	8	9		11^1							12	13			34
1		3	4	5	6	2	7		10^1			8	9	11^2									12	13			35
1		3	4^2	5	6	2	7		10^3			8	13	9^1		11							12	14			36
1		3	4	5	6	2	7		10^3			8	12	9^2	14	11^1							13				37
1		3	4	5	6	2	7		10^3			8	12	9^2		11^1							13	14			38

ROSS COUNTY   First Division

Year Formed: 1929. *Ground & Address:* Victoria Park Stadium, Jubilee Road, Dingwall IV15 9QZ. *Telephone:* 01349 860860. *Fax:* 01349 866277. *E-mail:* donnie.macbean@rosscountyfootballclub.co.uk
Website: www.rosscountyfootballclub.co.uk
Ground Capacity: 6700. *Size of Ground:* 105×68m.
Chairman: Rory MacGregor. *Secretary:* Donnie MacBean.
Manager: Derek Adams. *Assistant Manager:* Stuart Balmer. *Director of Football:* George Adams. *Physio:* Douglas Sim.
Club Nickname: The Staggies.
Record Attendance: 6600, benefit match v Celtic, 31 August 1970.
Record Transfer Fee Received: £200,000 for Neil Tarrant to Aston Villa (April 1999).
Record Transfer Fee Paid: £50,000 for Derek Holmes from Hearts (1999).
Record Victory: 11-0 v St Cuthbert Wanderers, Scottish Cup, 11 Dec 1993.
Record Defeat: 1-10 v Inverness Thistle, Highland League.
Most League Appearances: 230: Mark McCulloch, 2002-2009.
Most League Goals in Season: 24: Andrew Barrowman, 2007-08.
Most League Goals (Overall): 47: Sean Higgins, 2002-09.

ROSS COUNTY 2010–11 LEAGUE RECORD

Match No.	Date	Venue	Opponents	Result	H/T Score	Lg Pos.	Goalscorers	Atten- dance
1	Aug 7	A	Cowdenbeath	W 2-0	0-0	—	Gardyne [52], Di Giacomo [82]	481
2	14	H	Falkirk	L 0-1	0-1	3		2837
3	21	A	Dundee	D 0-0	0-0	4		3946
4	28	A	Queen of the S	L 0-3	0-2	8		1644
5	Sept 11	H	Raith R	D 0-0	0-0	7		2500
6	18	H	Stirling A	W 3-1	2-1	6	Wood 2 [22, 50], Morrison [38]	2125
7	25	A	Morton	D 0-0	0-0	6		1632
8	Oct 2	H	Partick Th	L 0-2	0-1	7		2263
9	16	A	Dunfermline Ath	L 2-3	1-2	7	Boyd [25], Craig [48]	2803
10	23	A	Raith R	L 0-1	0-0	9		1776
11	30	H	Queen of the S	D 1-1	0-1	9	Vigurs [81]	2186
12	Nov 6	A	Falkirk	W 1-0	1-0	7	Barrowman [27]	4512
13	13	H	Dundee	L 0-3	0-1	8		2331
14	Dec 11	A	Partick Th	D 1-1	1-1	—	Brittain (pen) [19]	1509
15	14	H	Morton	D 2-2	1-2	—	Barrowman [23], Boyd [90]	1759
16	Jan 2	A	Dundee	L 0-2	0-1	—		4725
17	15	H	Raith R	L 0-1	0-0	8		2408
18	29	A	Morton	L 1-2	1-0	—	Craig [38]	1675
19	Feb 5	H	Cowdenbeath	D 1-1	1-0	8	Marr [30]	2020
20	12	H	Stirling A	D 0-0	0-0	8		2114
21	22	H	Dunfermline Ath	D 0-0	0-0	—		2198
22	26	H	Partick Th	D 0-0	0-0	8		2316
23	Mar 1	A	Stirling A	D 0-0	0-0	—		514
24	5	H	Falkirk	W 2-1	1-1	8	Brittain [24], Barrowman [87]	2676
25	8	A	Dunfermline Ath	D 1-1	0-0	—	Barrowman [67]	1699
26	19	A	Queen of the S	L 1-2	1-2	9	Barrowman [21]	2181
27	22	A	Raith R	D 1-1	0-0	—	Flynn [49]	1639
28	26	H	Morton	W 2-0	0-0	8	Gardyne [46], Milne [86]	2379
29	29	H	Dunfermline Ath	L 0-1	0-0	—		2059
30	Apr 2	A	Stirling A	W 2-0	1-0	8	Vigurs [44], Flynn [67]	461
31	5	A	Cowdenbeath	L 1-2	0-2	—	Brittain (pen) [87]	296
32	16	A	Partick Th	D 1-1	1-1	8	Lawson [37]	1714
33	23	H	Dundee	L 0-1	0-0	8		3205
34	26	A	Queen of the S	W 1-0	1-0	—	Gardyne [29]	266
35	30	A	Falkirk	W 1-0	0-0	8	Flynn [90]	4143
36	May 7	H	Cowdenbeath	W 3-0	1-0	8	Morrison [32], Boyd [83], Corcoran [89]	2886

Final League Position: 8

Honours
League Champions: Second Division 2007-08. Third Division 1998-99.
Scottish Cup Runners-up: 2009-10.
League Challenge Cup Winners: 2006-07, 2010-11; *Runners-up:* 2004-05, 2008-09.

Club colours: Shirt: Navy blue with white sleeves. Shorts: Navy blue with white flashes. Stockings: Navy blue.

Goalscorers: *League (30):* Barrowman 5, Boyd 3, Brittain 3 (2 pens), Flynn 3, Gardyne 3, Craig 2, Morrison 2, Vigurs 2, Wood 2, Corcoran 1, Di Giacomo 1, Lawson 1, Marr 1, Milne 1.
Scottish Cup (4): Barrowman 2, Craig 1, Miller 1.
CIS Cup (6): Barrowman 1, Brittain 1, Craig 1, Di Giacomo 1, Gardyne 1, Vigurs 1.
Alba Challenge Cup (11): Lawson 3, Barrowman 2, Scott 2, Gardyne 1, Morrison 1, Vigurs 1, own goal 1.

McGovern M 36	Miller G 29+2	Boyd S 33	McCormack D 15+1	Morrison S 21+3	Brittain R 32+2	Scott M 15+1	Corcoran M 12+8	Di Giacomo P 8+6	Gardyne R 25+5	Barrowman A 22+6	Wood G 11+15	Craig S 11+7	Lawson P 25	Vigurs J 20+11	Malin J —+1	Smith D 2+5	Kettlewell S 18+6	Flynn J 22+1	Marr J 9+4	Gartland G 3	Fitzpatrick M 16+1	Milne S 11+2	Match No.
1	2	3	4	5	6	7	8	9	10¹	11²	12	13											1
1		2	3	4	6	7	8¹	11	10		9³	13	5	12									2
1	2	4	3	5	10	7	8¹	13	11³		9²	14	6	12									3
1	2	4	5	7	6¹		9²	13	10³	12	11	8	14										4
1	2	3	5	4	10		8	11		9¹		7¹	6	12	13								5
1	2	3	4	5	12	6³	14	11¹	10		9		7²	8			13						6
1	2		4	5	12	7	8¹	14	11		9²			13		10³	6	3					7
1	2	3	4	5¹	6¹	12	9²	11	10		13		7	8			14						8
1	2	3¹	5	4	8	7	9¹		10	12	13	11²					6	14					9
1	2	3	4	13	9	7		10	12		11²	6					8¹	5					10
1	2	3¹	4	12	8	7²		13	10		11	6	9				5						11
1	2		5	4	7	8		12	11		10	6	9¹				3						12
1	2		5	3	8	7³		13	10	14	11²	6	9			12	4¹						13
1	2	3	4	5	6	9¹		11	12	10	8	7											14
1	2	4	5	3	8²	7³	12	10	11	14	13	6	9¹										15
1	2¹	4	12²	3	8	6		10	11		14	7	9³			13⁸	5						16
1	12	3		5	9	8	13		11	14	10³		7²			2¹	4	6					17
1		3		5	6		9	12		10	11¹			13	7²		2	4	8				18
1		3			8		9³	11²	12	13	7¹		14		6		2	4	5	10			19
1		3			8		9¹	12	11³	14	7²		13		6	4	2		5	10			20
1	2	3		5	6		13	10¹	11³	14		9²		7	4			8	12				21
1	2	4		3	9	12	11¹		13	8²	6³			7	5	14			10				22
1	2	3		10		8²		12	9¹	5³	13		7	4⁸	14		6	11					23
1	2	3		6			9	11		7	12	13	8²		4		5	10¹					24
1	2²	3		8			10	11		5	13		7	4	12		6	9¹					25
1	2²	3		8			10¹	9	12	7	13		4	5		6	11						26
1		3		8		12	10¹	11		5	7		4	2		6	9						27
1	12	3		8		14	11³	10		6	7²		13	4	2¹		5	9					28
1	2	3		8			11²	10	13	6	7¹		12	4			5	9					29
1	2	3		8			10¹	11	12	13	5³	9²		14	7	4		6					30
1	2	3		9		14	13	11	10²	8	12		7¹	4³	5		6						31
1	2	3					11	10	13	9²	7	8¹		6	4	12		5					32
1	2	4	14				8	10	12	9²		7	13	5	3		6³	11¹					33
1	2	3	5	7		9¹	6	11	12		10		4	8									34
1	2	4	5	11			6	10		3¹	9		7	8				12					35
1	2	3	5	6	14	10²	11³	12		8	9¹	7	4		13								36

ST JOHNSTONE   Premier League

Year Formed: 1884. *Ground & Address:* McDiarmid Park, Crieff Road, Perth PH1 2SJ. *Telephone:* 01738 459090. *Fax:* 01738 625 771. *Email:* karin@perthsaints.co.uk *Website:* www.perthstjohnstonefc.co.uk
Ground Capacity: all seated: 10,673. *Size of Pitch:* 115yd × 75yd.
Chairman: Geoff Brown.
Manager: Derek McInnes. *Assistant Manager:* Tony Docherty. *Youth Coach:* Tommy Campbell. *Physio:* Frank Kenny.
Club Nickname: Saints.
Previous Grounds: Recreation Grounds, Muirton Park.
Record Attendance: (McDiarmid Park): 10,545 v Dundee, Premier Division, 23 May 1999.
Record Transfer Fee received: £1,750,000 for Calum Davidson to Blackburn R (March 1998).
Record Transfer Fee paid: £400,000 for Billy Dodds from Dundee (1994).
Record Victory: 9-0 v Albion R, League Cup, 9 Mar 1946.
Record Defeat: 1-10 v Third Lanark, Scottish Cup, 24 Jan 1903.
Most Capped Player: Nick Dasovic, 26, Canada.
Most League Appearances: 298: Drew Rutherford, 1976-85.
Most League Goals in Season (Individual): 36: Jimmy Benson, Division II, 1931-32.
Most Goals Overall (Individual): 140: John Brogan, 1977-83.

ST JOHNSTONE 2010–11 LEAGUE RECORD

Match No.	Date	Venue	Opponents	Result		H/T Score	Lg Pos.	Goalscorers	Atten- dance
1	Aug 14	A	Hearts	D	1-1	1-1	—	Parkin [45]	14,562
2	21	H	Aberdeen	L	0-1	0-0	8		6523
3	28	A	Rangers	L	1-2	1-1	12	Grainger [25]	46,109
4	Sept 11	H	Motherwell	L	0-2	0-2	12		3254
5	18	H	St Mirren	W	2-1	2-1	10	Jackson [3], Parkin [33]	3349
6	25	A	Dundee U	L	0-1	0-0	11		7397
7	Oct 2	H	Hibernian	W	2-0	0-0	9	Craig [76], Haber [90]	3819
8	16	A	Inverness CT	D	1-1	1-0	7	Samuel [8]	4883
9	23	A	Hamilton A	W	2-1	1-0	6	Parkin [19], Grainger [86]	2431
10	30	H	Celtic	L	0-3	0-2	7		6866
11	Nov 6	H	Kilmarnock	L	0-3	0-1	8		3230
12	10	A	Motherwell	L	0-4	0-3	—		3361
13	13	H	Hearts	L	0-2	0-0	10		4156
14	20	A	Aberdeen	W	1-0	0-0	9	Diamond (og) [83]	7841
15	27	A	Hibernian	D	0-0	0-0	9		10,248
16	Dec 11	A	St Mirren	W	2-1	0-0	—	Parkin [53], Craig [90]	2701
17	26	A	Celtic	L	0-2	0-0	—		41,522
18	Jan 2	H	Inverness CT	W	1-0	0-0	8	Samuel [85]	3126
19	15	A	Kilmarnock	D	1-1	0-1	8	Taylor [86]	4885
20	22	H	St Mirren	D	0-0	0-0	8		3009
21	26	H	Motherwell	W	1-0	0-0	—	Craig (pen) [62]	2268
22	29	A	Hearts	L	0-1	0-1	—		13,430
23	Feb 1	H	Hamilton A	W	2-0	1-0	—	May 2 [4, 46]	2631
24	19	A	Inverness CT	L	0-2	0-1	8		3942
25	22	H	Dundee U	D	0-0	0-0	—		3507
26	27	A	Rangers	L	0-4	0-2	9		43,125
27	Mar 2	A	Aberdeen	D	0-0	0-0	—		2909
28	5	H	Hibernian	D	1-1	0-0	9	Towell (og) [46]	4446
29	19	A	Hamilton A	D	0-0	0-0	8		2111
30	Apr 2	H	Kilmarnock	D	0-0	0-0	8		3083
31	5	H	Rangers	L	0-2	0-1	—		5820
32	9	A	Dundee U	L	0-2	0-1	9		6398
33	12	H	Celtic	L	0-1	0-1	—		6338
34	25	H	Inverness CT	L	0-3	0-1	—		2395
35	30	A	Hibernian	W	2-1	0-1	9	Craig [74], Moon [90]	7492
36	May 7	A	Aberdeen	W	2-0	1-0	8	Smith (og) [8], Adams [60]	6361
37	10	H	Hamilton A	W	1-0	1-0	—	Craig (pen) [29]	2253
38	14	A	St Mirren	D	0-0	0-0	8		4230

Final League Position: 8

Honours
League Champions: First Division 1982-83, 1989-90, 1996-97, 2008-09. Division II 1923-24, 1959-60, 1962-63; *Runners-up:* Division II 1931-32. First Division 2005-06, 2006-07. Second Division 1987-88.
Scottish Cup: Semi-finals 1934, 1968, 1989, 1991, 2007, 2008.
League Cup Runners-up: 1969-70, 1998-99.
League Challenge Cup Winners: 2007-08; *Runners-up:* 1996-97.

European: *UEFA Cup:* 10 matches (1971-72, 1999-2000).

Club colours: All royal blue with white trim.

Goalscorers: *League (23):* Craig 5 (2 pens), Parkin 4, Grainger 2, May 2, Samuel 2, Adams 1, Haber 1, Jackson 1, Moon 1, Taylor 1, own goals 3.
Scottish Cup (6): Craig 1, Davidson 1, Invincibile 1, MacDonald 1, Millar 1, Samuel 1.
CIS Cup (7): Davidson 2, Dobie 1, Haber 1, Millar 1, Morris 1 (pen), Parkin 1.

Enckelman P 29	MacKay D 32	Grainger D 31+2	Morris J 23	Anderson S 24+1	Duberry M 32+1	Davidson M 33+1	Millar C 29+1	Parkin S 17+4	Haber M 5+6	Craig L 29+5	Taylor C 11+10	Rutkiewicz K 4+6	Samuel C 20+8	Maybury A 23+7	Dobie S 1+3	Smith G 9	Caddis L 1+2	Milne S 1+1	Jackson A 10+7	Myrie-Williams J 4+2	MacDonald P 14+10	Adams J 9+2	May S 8+11	Novikovas A 1+5	Invincibile D 8+2	Gartland G 4+3	Reynolds S —+5	Robertson J 2+4	Moon K 4+2	Match No.
1	2²	3¹	4	5¹	6	7	8	9	10³	11	12	13	14																	1
1		12	4		6	7	8	9	10³	11¹	3²	5	13	2	14															2
		3	4	11³	6	7¹	8		10		13	5	9²	2	14	1	12													3
	2³	3			6	7	8	9	10²		11	5		12	1	4¹	13	14												4
1	5	3	4		6	8		9²	13	11		12	2				10¹	7												5
1	5	3	4	12	6	7³	8	9	13	14			2¹				10²	11												6
1	5	3	4		6	7	8	9³	14	13			10¹	2			12	11²												7
	5	3¹	4		6		8	9¹	12	11		14	10²	2	1		7	13												8
	2	3			6	7	8	9³	12	11		14	10²	4		1	13	5¹												9
	5	3¹			6		8	12	4	11		14	13	2		1	9¹		7²	10²										10
	2		4		6	7¹	8	9³	14	11	12	5		3²	13	1	10													11
1	5³	3	4	8	6		9²		11	7	14	13	2	10¹					12											12
1		3	4	5	6	8		13	11¹	7		10²	2						12	9³	14									13
1		3	4	5	6	7		12		11	14	10³	2					13		9²	8¹									14
1		3	4	5	6	7³	8	9		12	11¹	10²	2					13			14									15
1	2	3	4	5	6	7¹	8	9³		11	12	13	14							10²										16
1	5	3		4	6		8	9		11³	7¹	10²	2					14	13		12									17
1	2	3	4	5²	6	12	8	9		11	7¹	14	13					10³												18
1	2	3³	4	5	6	7	8	13		11¹	12	10²					9	14												19
1	2	3²	4	5	6	7	8	9¹		12	13	11³					10	14												20
1	2	3	4	5	6	7	8		11³	12		10²	14				13	9¹												21
1	3		4	5	6	7	8	9¹		11	12	10³	2²				14	13												22
1	2		4³	5	6	7	8		11	14		10²	12				13	9	3¹											23
1	2	3	4	5	6	7	8¹	9²	11								13	14		10³	12									24
1	2	3	4	5	6	8		11	9¹	10³							14	13	7²	12										25
1	2	3	4	5	6¹	8		11	7²	10	12							9³	14	13										26
1	2	3	4²	5		8		11		10³							7	13	14		9¹	6	12							27
1	2	3		5		8		11		10¹							12	9	4²	13		7	6							28
1	5	3		6		4	7	11³	13	10²	2						12		8¹		9	14								29
1	5	3		6	4	8		11³		9²	2						10¹			14	7			12	13					30
1	5	3¹		6	4	7		11			2						13		14	12	9			10³	8²					31
	3		5¹	6	4	7			10	2	1						11¹				9²	12		13	8					32
	5²	3³		13	4¹	12		11	7		2	1							8	9	14		6		10					33
	5	3		4	8			11²			2	1		10					9¹		7³	6	14	12	13					34
1	5	3			4²	7		12			2			10			11³	6			9¹	13		14	8					35
1	2			5	6	4¹	7	11			12			9²			10³	3	14				13		8					36
1	2			5	6	4	7	11			3¹			9²			10	8³	13		12		14							37
1	2	12		5	6	4	7							9			10²	8³	11¹				13							38

ST MIRREN

Premier League

Year Formed: 1877. *Ground & Address:* St Mirren Park, Greenhill Road, Paisley PA3 1RU. *Telephone:* 0141 889 2558.
Fax: 0141 848 6444. *E-mail:* info@saintmirren.net *Website:* www.saintmirren.net
Ground Capacity: 10,476 (all seated). *Size of Pitch:* 105yd × 68yd.
Chairman: Stewart Gilmour. *Vice-Chairman:* George Campbell. *Secretary:* Chris Stewart.
Manager: Danny Lennon. *Assistant Manager:* Iain Jenkins. *Youth Development Officer:* David Longwell. *Physio:* Gerry Docherty.
Club Nickname: The Buddies.
Previous Grounds: Short Roods 1877-79, Thistle Park Greenhill 1879-83, Westmarch 1883-94, Love Street 1894-2009.
Record Attendance: 47,438 v Celtic, League Cup, 20 Aug 1949.
Record Transfer Fee received: £850,000 for Ian Ferguson to Rangers (1988).
Record Transfer Fee paid: £400,000 for Thomas Stickroth from Bayer Uerdingen (1990).
Record Victory: 15-0 v Glasgow University, Scottish Cup 1st rd, 30 Jan 1960.
Record Defeat: 0-9 v Rangers, Division I, 4 Dec 1897.
Most Capped Player: Godmundor Torfason, 29, Iceland.
Most League Appearances: 371: Hugh Murray, 1997-2010.
Most League Goals in Season (Individual): 45: Dunky Walker, Division I, 1921-22.
Most Goals Overall (Individual): 221: David McCrae, 1923-34.

ST MIRREN 2010–11 LEAGUE RECORD

Match No.	Date	Venue	Opponents	Result		H/T Score	Lg Pos.	Goalscorers	Atten- dance
1	Aug 14	H	Dundee U	D	1-1	0-0	—	Lynch [73]	5618
2	22	A	Celtic	L	0-4	0-2	10		46,812
3	29	H	Hibernian	W	1-0	0-0	5	Dargo [58]	4480
4	Sept 11	A	Kilmarnock	L	1-2	0-1	10	Thomson [48]	6064
5	18	A	St Johnstone	L	1-2	1-2	11	Lynch [37]	3349
6	25	H	Inverness CT	L	1-2	0-1	12	McGowan [77]	3954
7	Oct 2	A	Motherwell	L	1-3	0-1	12	Wardlaw [64]	4384
8	16	H	Hamilton A	D	2-2	0-1	12	Higdon 2 [60, 73]	3577
9	23	A	Hearts	L	0-3	0-2	12		12,009
10	30	H	Aberdeen	W	2-1	1-0	12	McAusland [28], Travner [90]	4589
11	Nov 7	H	Rangers	L	1-3	0-0	12	Higdon (pen) [76]	5674
12	10	A	Dundee U	W	2-1	1-0	—	Higdon 2 [41, 65]	5548
13	14	H	Celtic	L	0-1	0-0	9		6073
14	20	H	Motherwell	D	1-1	1-0	10	Wardlaw [37]	4213
15	27	A	Hamilton A	D	0-0	0-0	10		2280
16	Dec 11	H	St Johnstone	L	1-2	0-0	—	Higdon [62]	2701
17	26	A	Inverness CT	W	2-1	1-1	—	Thomson 2 [44, 85]	3819
18	29	H	Hearts	L	0-2	0-0	10		4599
19	Jan 3	H	Kilmarnock	L	0-2	0-0	—		6118
20	15	A	Aberdeen	L	0-2	0-0	11		9740
21	22	A	St Johnstone	D	0-0	0-0	10		3009
22	26	H	Dundee U	D	1-1	1-0	—	McGregor [38]	3095
23	Feb 2	A	Hibernian	L	0-2	0-0	—		9436
24	12	H	Inverness CT	D	3-3	2-2	11	Higdon (pen) [28], Thomson [29], McGregor [74]	3203
25	20	H	Hibernian	L	0-1	0-0	11		3505
26	23	A	Motherwell	W	1-0	0-0	—	Higdon [82]	3613
27	26	A	Kilmarnock	L	0-2	0-2	11		5243
28	Mar 6	H	Rangers	L	0-1	0-1	11		5405
29	19	A	Hearts	L	2-3	1-0	11	Higdon 2 [15, 69]	12,763
30	Apr 2	H	Hamilton A	W	3-1	0-1	11	Higdon 3 (1 pen) [61, 64 (p), 71]	4985
31	6	H	Aberdeen	W	3-2	1-0	—	Higdon [6], Dargo [57], Thomson [68]	50,318
32	9	A	Celtic	L	0-1	0-0	11		50,318
33	16	A	Rangers	L	1-2	1-1	—	McGregor [38]	46,392
34	24	A	Hibernian	D	1-1	1-1	11	Dargo (pen) [39]	7238
35	May 2	H	Hamilton A	L	0-1	0-0	11		5037
36	7	A	Inverness CT	L	0-1	0-0	11		3446
37	10	A	Aberdeen	W	1-0	0-0	—	Wardlaw [65]	5955
38	14	H	St Johnstone	D	0-0	0-0	11		4230

Final League Position: 11

Honours
League Champions: First Division 1976-77, 1999-2000, 2005-06; *Runners-up:* 2004-05. Division II 1967-68; *Runners-up:* 1935-36.
Scottish Cup Winners: 1926, 1959, 1987; *Runners-up:* 1908, 1934, 1962.
League Cup Runners-up: 1955-56, 2009-10.
League Challenge Cup Winners: 2005-06.
B&Q Cup Runners-up: 1993-94. *Anglo-Scottish Cup:* 1979-80.

European: *Cup Winners' Cup:* 4 matches (1987-88). *UEFA Cup:* 10 matches (1980-81, 1983-84, 1985-86).

Club colours: Shirt: Black and white vertical stripes. Shorts: Black. Stockings: White.

Goalscorers: *League (33):* Higdon 14 (3 pens), Thomson 5, Dargo 3 (1 pen), McGregor 3, Wardlaw 3, Lynch 2, McAusland 1, McGowan 1, Travner 1.
Scottish Cup (10): McGowan 4, Dargo 2, McQuade 2, Mooy 1, own goal 1.
CIS Cup (3): Higdon 1, McGowan 1, McGregor 1.

Gallacher P 27	Van Zanten D 25+3	Travner J 35+2	Lynch S 8+6	McGregor D 36	Potter J 32+2	Murray H 21+3	Thomson S 25+2	Wardlaw G 16+7	McGowan P 33	Robb S 3	Mair L 22+2	Love A —+1	Dargo C 14+8	Brady G 3+2	McAusland M 24+1	McLennan M —+1	Ramage G —+1	Hegarty N 2+1	McQuade P —+5	McCluskey J —+3	Samson C 11	Cregg P 18+4	Higdon M 26+2	McLean K 10+9	Mooy A 7+6	Barron D 4+5	Goodwin J 16+1	Lamont M —+1	McKernon J —+1	Match No.
1	2	3	4	5	6	7	8	9¹	10	11²	12	13																		1
1	2¹	3	4	5	6	7			11³	8			9		10²	12	13	14												2
1	13	3	12	8	6	7		11	10		5				9¹	4	2²													3
1		11	12	4	6	7	8¹	9	10⁸		5				2²	3					13									4
1	2	3	4	5	6	7	0		11¹	8			12²				10													5
1	2	3	4²	5	6	7		9	10		8							11¹	12	13										6
	2	3		5	6	7		9	10			4									1	8	11							7
	2	3	4	5	6		8	9			7										1	11¹	10	12						8
		3		5	6	7²		9	10				13		4			14			1	11	8³	2¹	12					9
	2	3	4	5	12			9	11						6						1	7	10	8¹						10
	2	3	4	5	6			9²	10				7							13	1	11	12	8¹						11
	2	3	12	4	6	7¹		9¹	11				5								1	8	10	13						12
	2	3	4¹	5	6		12	9²					7								1	11	10	8	13					13
	2¹	3		5	6		12	9	11				4								1	7	10⁸	8						14
	2²	3	12	5	6		8³	9	10				4							14	1	7		11¹	13					15
	2	3		5	6		8	9²	11				4							13	1	7	10	12						16
1	13	3	12	5	6		8		11				9¹		4							7	10			2²				17
1	2	3	4	5	6⁸		8	9¹			12		7²									11³	10	13	14					18
1	2	3	4	5			12	11				6	9²	7¹								8	10	13						19
1	2	3	4¹	7	6		8		10		5		9²					12				7	10	13			11			20
1		3		5	6		8	9					2	12	4¹							7	10				11			21
1		3		5	6	12	8²	9					2		4				13			7¹	10				11			22
1		3		5	6	12	8³	9					2		4²					14	13	7¹	10				11			23
1	2	12	13	3	6	7²	8		11		5¹		9		4								10							24
1		3		5	6	7	8		11				9		2							12	10				4¹			25
1	2	3		5	6	7²	8		10				9¹		2							12		13			11			26
1	2	3		5	6	7	8						9²		4							10	12				11¹	13		27
1	2	3			6	7	8	9				5	12									10	4²	13			11¹			28
1		3			6	13	4		12			5	7		2							10	9²	8¹			11			29
1	2	3			6	7	8					5	12		4							13	10²	9³	14		11¹			30
1	2	3		5	6	7			13				11		4							9²	10	12			8¹			31
1	12			5	6	7²			13				2³		4		3					8	10	9¹		14	11			32
1	2	3		5¹	6			14	10				12	9³	4							7		13	8		11²			33
1	2	3		5	6	7²	8		12					9³	4					14		10		13			11¹			34
1	2	3⁸		6	13	7¹	8	14			5		9²		4							10	12				11³			35
1					6				7				8	5	9			2				12	10	4²	13	3	11¹			36
1	13	3		5	6		8¹		10						4			2				12	9	7²			11			37
	11			6³	7²			9			5		12		2						1		10	4¹	8	3	14		13	38

STENHOUSEMUIR

Second Division

Year Formed: 1884. *Ground & Address:* Ochilview Park, Gladstone Rd, Stenhousemuir FK5 4QL. *Telephone:* 01324 562992. *Fax:* 01324 562980. *E-mail:* info@stenhousemuirfc.com *Website:* www.stenhousemuirfc.com
Ground Capacity: 3776 (626 seated). *Size of Pitch:* 110yd × 72yd.
Chairman: Martin McNairney. *Vice Chairman:* Bill Darroch. *Secretary/General Manager:* Margaret Kilpatrick.
Manager: Dave Irons. *Assistant Manager:* Kevin McGoldrick. *Physio:* Laura Chimimba.
Club Nickname: The Warriors.
Previous Grounds: Tryst Ground 1884-86, Goschen Park 1886-90.
Record Attendance: 12,500 v East Fife, Scottish Cup 4th rd, 11 Mar 1950.
Record Transfer Fee received: £70,000 for Euan Donaldson to St Johnstone (May 1995).
Record Transfer Fee paid: £20,000 to Livingston for Ian Little (June 1995); £20,000 to East Fife for Paul Hunter (September 1995).
Record Victory: 9-2 v Dundee U, Division II, 16 Apr 1937.
Record Defeat: 2-11 v Dunfermline Ath, Division II, 27 Sept 1930.
Most League Appearances: 434: Jimmy Richardson, 1957-73.
Most League Goals in Season (Individual): 32: Robert Taylor, Division II, 1925-26.

STENHOUSEMUIR 2010–11 LEAGUE RECORD

Match No.	Date	Venue	Opponents	Result	H/T Score	Lg Pos.	Goalscorers	Attendance
1	Aug 7	H	Peterhead	W 3-1	1-1	—	Clark 2 [17, 68], Williams [50]	423
2	14	A	Brechin C	D 0-0	0-0	2		404
3	21	H	Alloa Ath	L 0-1	0-1	5		619
4	28	H	Airdrie U	L 1-3	0-1	8	Williams [69]	820
5	Sept 11	A	Dumbarton	L 0-1	0-0	8		600
6	18	II	Forfar Ath	W 3-0	1-0	8	Quinn 2 [4, 69], Scullion [72]	522
7	25	A	Ayr U	L 0-2	0-1	8		1065
8	Oct 2	H	East Fife	D 1-1	0-0	8	Murray [66]	679
9	16	A	Livingston	L 1-4	1-4	9	Lyle [28]	1606
10	23	H	Dumbarton	W 4-0	3-0	7	Quinn [3], Clark 2 (1 pen) [22 (p), 43], Plenderleith [89]	392
11	30	A	Airdrie U	L 0-1	0-0	7		848
12	Nov 6	H	Brechin C	D 0-0	0-0	8		491
13	13	A	Alloa Ath	L 0-1	0-0	8		455
14	Dec 11	A	East Fife	L 0-6	0-4	—		472
15	Jan 2	H	Alloa Ath	L 2-3	0-2	—	Anderson [89], Thom [90]	459
16	15	A	Dumbarton	W 1-0	0-0	9	Dalziel [90]	490
17	22	H	Airdrie U	W 1-0	0-0	—	Murray [84]	819
18	29	A	Ayr U	L 3-4	1-1	8	Clark (pen) [33], Lynch [77], Smith [87]	1181
19	Feb 5	H	Forfar Ath	L 0-1	0-1	9		504
20	12	H	East Fife	L 0-2	0-1	10		590
21	19	A	Livingston	L 1-2	0-2	10	Williams [64]	1246
22	26	H	Peterhead	W 4-2	3-2	10	Williams [29], Dalziel [40], Anderson [45], Lynch [88]	363
23	Mar 1	A	Ayr U	W 3-1	1-1	—	Dalziel [36], Smith [53], Williams (pen) [64]	484
24	5	A	Brechin C	L 1-3	1-1	9	Dalziel [8]	503
25	8	H	Livingston	L 1-2	0-2	—	Williams [76]	431
26	19	A	Airdrie U	D 2-2	2-1	9	Devlin [14], Lynch [42]	642
27	22	A	Peterhead	D 2-2	2-1	—	Anderson 2 [35, 39]	384
28	26	H	Ayr U	W 2-1	1-0	9	Lynch [3], Devlin [90]	568
29	29	H	Dumbarton	D 2-2	0-0	—	Paton (pen) [80], Hunter [83]	398
30	Apr 2	A	Forfar Ath	D 1-1	0-1	9	Anderson [78]	416
31	9	H	Livingston	L 0-3	0-1	9		837
32	12	A	Forfar Ath	L 0-2	0-2	—		347
33	16	A	East Fife	D 1-1	0-0	9	Murray [90]	562
34	23	A	Alloa Ath	W 2-1	0-1	9	Anderson [57], Paton [61]	584
35	30	H	Brechin C	L 1-3	1-2	9	Devlin [27]	672
36	May 7	A	Peterhead	W 3-0	1-0	8	Anderson [42], Paton [68], Dalziel [75]	405

Final League Position: 8

Honours
League Champions: Third Division runners-up: 1998-99. *Promoted to Second Division:* 2008-09 (play-offs).
Scottish Cup: Semi-finals 1902-03. Quarter-finals 1948-49, 1949-50, 1994-95.
League Cup: Quarter-finals 1947-48, 1960-61, 1975-76.
League Challenge Cup Winners: 1995-96.

Club colours: All maroon.

Goalscorers: *League (46):* Anderson 7, Williams 6 (1 pen), Clark 5 (2 pens), Dalziel 5, Lynch 4, Devlin 3, Murray 3, Paton 3 (1 pen), Quinn 3, Smith 2, Hunter 1, Lyle 1, Plenderleith 1, Scullion 1, Thom 1.
Scottish Cup (10): Clark 3 (1 pen), Williams 3, Dalziel 1, Smith 1, Stirling 1, own goal 1.
CIS Cup (1): Anderson 1.
Alba Challenge Cup (8): Williams 3, Anderson 1, Dalziel 1, Motion 1, Quinn 1, own goal 1.

McCluskey C 12+1	Lyle W 35	Gibb S 21+1	Smith J 23	Thomson S 5	Anderson G 30+2	Clark R 11+4	Murray S 32	Williams A 12+5	Connachan K 1	Quinn P 15+8	Dalziel S 17+6	Stirling A 10+10	Thom G 23+3	Thomson I 31	Motion K 8+3	Fusco S 5+2	Brown A 24+1	Scullion P 5+3	Archdeacon M —+1	McLennan J 2+1	Plenderleith G —+10	Love A 4+2	Dickson S 21+2	Paton E 18	Strachan A 1	Lynch S 11+6	Sloan L 2+7	Devlin M 10	Gilmuir B 7+2	Hunter M —+7	Match No.
1	2	3	4	5	6¹	7	8	9	10	11²	12	13																			1
1	2	4	5¹	3			8	11³		10²	14	13	6	7	9	12															2
	2	4		5¹			13	9	11	14	10³	6	3	7²	8	12	1														3
	2		3			7	8	11³		14	10	4¹	12	6	5²	9³	1	13													4
	2	4	5			7	8¹	10		12	11		6	3	9		1														5
	2	5	4		6¹	12				10	11²		3	8	9		1					7	13								6
	4	2	3			7				11	10	13	5	6	9¹		1						8²	12							7
	2	4	5			7		10		11			3	6	9		1						8								8
1	2	4	5			7	12	9¹			10³	14	3	8	6		11²				13										9
1	2	3	4			7	9	10		11		6¹	5	8							12										10
1	2	4	5			7	8³	11		9¹	10		3	6²	13					14		17									11
	2	4	5			8¹		10²		11		13	3				1					12	7								12
	2¹	3	4			10		9		12		11²		14	7	8	13		1			6	5³								13
	2	5³	3			7		10		12		11²		6	4	8¹			1		9		13	14							14
	2		4		6	7¹		10		11²			3	8	9		1				12	13	5								15
1	2		4		6²	7	9	10¹		13	11		3	8								12	5								16
1	2		4		8²	9³	10	12		11¹			3	7	14							13	6	5							17
1	2		4		6¹	8²	9			11			3	7								12	5			10	13				18
	2	3	4		14	8¹	9	13		11²				7³			1						6	5		10	12				19
	2	3	4	5	12			9⁸		10		13		7³			1						14	8		11²	6¹				20
	2	5	3¹		10			12		11			4		9	7	1							8		6					21
	2		4			7²	13	9¹		8	11³			6	5		1						3	10		12	14				22
	2	3¹	4				9	11		10³	5	12	8				1							7		6	13				23
	2	3				7¹	8	11²		10	12			6		9	1						5	4		13					24
	2	3²					8	10		11			5¹	4	7		1						6	9		12	13				25
	2					7¹		11	10			13	12	4	6		1						3	9³		8²	14	5			26
	2						6	9	10¹				14	3⁸			1						12	5		11³	7²	4	8	13	27
	2						6²	8					14	11		9	1						5	4		10¹	12	3	7³	13	28
	2						9	7					12	10¹			1	5⁸					6	4		11²	13	3	8³	14	29
15	2						6	9		11²			13	4			1⁶						7	3		10¹	5⁸	8	12		30
1	2	4				7	9³	10		11¹	12			5									6	3²		14	13	8			31
	2	3					6	9					14	8			1					13	5	7		11²		4¹	10³	12	32
1	2	3				7	9						12	8			1					10	6	4		11		5¹			33
1	2					7²	9						12	3	8		1					10¹	6	5		11³		4	13	14	34
1⁸	2					7²	9			13	11			3				15				8⁶	4			10		5	8¹	12	35
	2	14				7	9			11²	10¹			3³	8		1					12	6	5		4			13		36

STIRLING ALBION   Second Division

Year Formed: 1945. *Ground & Address:* The Doubletree, Dunblane Stadium, Springkerse, Stirling FK7 7UJ. *Telephone:*
01786 450399. *Fax:* 01786 448592. *Email:* stirlingalbion@btconnect.com *Website:* www.stirlingalbionfc.co.uk
Ground Capacity: 3808, seated: 2508. *Size of Pitch:* 110yd × 74yd.
Chairman: TBC.
Manager: Jocky Scott. *Assistant Manager:* John Blackley.
Club Nickname: The Binos.
Previous Grounds: Annfield 1945-92.
Record Attendance: 26,400 (at Annfield) v Celtic, Scottish Cup 4th rd, 14 Mar 1959; 3808 v Aberdeen, Scottish Cup
4th rd, 15 February 1996 (Forthbank).
Record Transfer Fee received: £90,000 for Stephen Nicholas to Motherwell (Mar 1999).
Record Transfer Fee paid: £25,000 for Craig Taggart from Falkirk (Aug 1994).
Record Victory: 20-0 v Selkirk, Scottish Cup 1st rd, 8 Dec 1984.
Record Defeat: 0-9 v Dundee U, Division I, 30 Dec 1967; 0-9 v Ross Co Scottish Cup 5th rd, 6 Feb 2010.
Most League Appearances: 504: Matt McPhee, 1967-81.
Most League Goals in Season (Individual): 27: Joe Hughes, Division II, 1969-70.
Most Goals Overall (Individual): 129: Billy Steele, 1971-83.

STIRLING ALBION 2010–11 LEAGUE RECORD

Match No.	Date	Venue	Opponents	Result	H/T Score	Lg Pos.	Goalscorers	Atten-dance
1	Aug 7	A	Morton	D	0-0	0-0	—		2375
2	14	H	Cowdenbeath	L	1-3	1-0	8	Robertson [34]	820
3	21	A	Falkirk	L	0-3	0-0	10		4196
4	28	H	Dunfermline Ath	L	1-5	1-2	10	Smith [34]	1370
5	Sept 11	A	Partick Th	W	2-1	0-0	9	Gibson [54], Smith [75]	1994
6	18	A	Ross Co	L	1-3	1-2	9	Smith [41]	2125
7	25	H	Queen of the S	D	0-0	0-0	9		945
8	Oct 2	A	Raith R	W	2-0	1-0	8	Aitken (pen) [45], Smith [90]	2010
9	16	H	Dundee	D	1-1	0-0	9	Forsyth [70]	1578
10	23	H	Partick Th	W	4-2	3-1	7	Smith 2 [2, 27], Aitken 2 (1 pen) [29 (p), 66]	1386
11	30	A	Dunfermline Ath	L	0-3	0-2	8		3025
12	Nov 6	A	Cowdenbeath	L	1-5	1-2	10	Smith [9]	507
13	13	H	Falkirk	L	0-5	0-2	10		2168
14	Dec 18	A	Dundee	L	0-2	0-1	—		3842
15	Jan 2	A	Falkirk	L	2-4	1-3	—	Witteveen [25], McHale [88]	3722
16	15	H	Partick Th	L	1-6	0-2	9	Aitken (pen) [90]	1689
17	Feb 5	H	Raith R	L	1-3	1-1	10	Borris [39]	1193
18	12	A	Ross Co	D	0-0	0-0	10		2114
19	15	H	Morton	L	0-1	0-0	—		626
20	19	H	Dundee	L	0-1	0-1	10		1990
21	22	A	Queen of the S	D	2-2	1-0	—	Aitken [17], Smith [87]	1185
22	26	A	Raith R	L	1-2	0-1	10	Smith [53]	1918
23	Mar 1	H	Ross Co	D	0-0	0-0	—		514
24	5	H	Cowdenbeath	L	3-4	1-0	10	Welsh [40], Mullen 2 [58, 67]	735
25	15	H	Dunfermline Ath	D	1-1	1-1	—	Borris [32]	944
26	19	A	Dunfermline Ath	L	1-4	0-2	10	Kane [75]	2553
27	22	H	Partick Th	L	0-3	0-2	—		651
28	26	A	Queen of the S	L	1-4	1-2	10	Smith (pen) [32]	1392
29	29	H	Queen of the S	L	0-2	0-2	—		444
30	Apr 2	H	Ross Co	L	0-2	0-1	10		461
31	5	A	Morton	L	0-2	0-2	—		980
32	10	A	Dundee	D	1-1	1-0	—	Mullen [23]	4177
33	16	H	Raith R	L	1-2	0-1	10	Flood [63]	1162
34	23	A	Falkirk	L	1-2	0-2	10	Smith [53]	1288
35	30	A	Cowdenbeath	L	0-1	0-0	10		415
36	May 7	H	Morton	W	3-2	2-1	10	Stirling 2 (1 pen) [42, 45 (p)], Mullen [89]	701

Final League Position: 10

Honours
League Champions: Division II 1952-53, 1957-58, 1960-61, 1964-65. Second Division 1976-77, 1990-91, 1995-96, 2009-10; *Runners-up:* Division II 1948-49, 1950-51. Second Division 2006-07. Third Division 2003-04. *Promoted to First Division:* 2006-07 (play-offs).
League Cup: Semi-finals 1961-62.

Club colours: All red with white trim.

Goalscorers: *League (32):* Smith 11 (1 pen), Aitken 5 (3 pens), Mullen 4, Borris 2, Stirling 2 (1 pen), Flood 1, Forsyth 1, Gibson 1, Kane 1, McHale 1, Robertson 1, Welsh 1, Witteveen 1.
Scottish Cup (1): Smith 1.
CIS Cup (1): Taggart 1.
Alba Challenge Cup (1): Devine 1.

Christie S 20+2	Corrigan M 20+2	McDonald G 7+1	Buist S 26	Forsyth R 25+1	Kane J 15+11	Gibson A 11+8	Aitken C 24+3	Robertson S 30+2	Taggart N 5+6	Colquhoun D 1+3	Mullen M 13+12	Borris R 22+5	Gilhaney M —+1	Smith G 31+3	Kirwan R —+1	Brown J 18	Heeking J 14	Yohan M —+1	Reidford C 16	Conwallus S 1+5	Allison B 23+2	McHale P 22+1	Flood J 4+1	Hamill J —+1	Currie L 2	Doyle M 17+2	Witteveen D 2	Ashe D —+1	Stirling S 2+8	Welsh S 15+2	Brighton T 10+3	Brass G —+1	Match No.
1	2	3	4	5	6	7^2	8	9	10^3	11^1	12	13	14																				1
1	2	3^2	4	5	8^1	6^3	9^a	7	10	12	14			11	13																		2
1	2	3	4			8	6^1		10	9^2	12			11		5	7	13															3
1	2	3^1	4	6	9^3		12	7	13	14	10			11		5^2	8																4
		3	4	5	13	6	7	8	12		14	8^1		11^a		2	10^1		1														5
		3	4	5		6^1	9	7	12		13	10^2		11		2	8		1														6
		3	4	5		6^1	8	7	12		13	10^2		11		2	9		1														7
		3	4	5	12		7	8	6^2			10^2		11		2	9^1		1	13	14												8
		3	4	5			8	9	6			10^1		11^2		2^a	7		1	12	13												9
		4	3	5^1	12	7	6	9			14	10^2		11^3			8		1	13	2												10
		3	4		8^1	6^2	9					10		11		5	7		1	12	2	13											11
15	3	13	4		5^1	7^7	0	6				10^3		11			9		1^6	12	2^a												12
1	4	3	2^a		5		8	9	13					11			7					6^2	10^1	12									13
1	2	4			5	6		7	12					10		3	8				11^1	9											14
		3		5								13	9^1	11		7^2			1		2	8	12		4	6	10^3	14					15
		4				12	8	7				13	9	11		6^2			1		3				2	5^1	10^3		14				16
15			13	6^2	12	8	7					10^1	9	11		2			1^6		3	5			4								17
1		3	2		12	9	8					10^1		11		5					4	7			6								18
1		3	2	13		8	9^1					10^3	14	11		5^2					4	7			6					12			19
1		2^1	3	5		14	8^3					10^2	9	11							4	7			6					13	12		20
1			3^1	5	12		7							9		11					4	8			2					6	10		21
1			4			7^1	12							9		11			2		3	8			5					6	10		22
1			3			8	9^2					12	13	11		2					4	6			5					7	10^1		23
1	4		2^a	14	13	8^3		11	12		10			5^1							3	9^2			6					7			24
1	2			14		7^1	8					11^3	9	13							3	6			4^a				12	5	10^2		25
1	2^a	3	5	14	13		10^2					12	9								4	7^a							8^3	6	11^1		26
1	5	2	4	13	14		8					11	9	12							3^2				6					7^3	10^1		27
1	3	2	4	7	9^2							13	11								8				5				10^1	6	12		28
1	12		2^1	3	5	14		8				13	9	11							4	6								7^3	10^2		29
			4	9	14	8^3	12					11			13	2		1			3^1	7			5					6	10^2		30
			2	8		13^a	5					11	7		10^1	3		1				9^2			6					4	12		31
	13		2	7^3			6					11	9^1		10	4		1			3^2	8			5			14	12				32
		5			7	8						13	9		10	1					4^3	3	6^1		14			12	2	11^2			33
			12		7	8						9^1	11			1					2	6	5^3		4			14	3	10^2	13		34
1		3	4		7	6						11		10							2	5	8^1							9	12		35
1	3		4	9	14	7^2	8					11		10							2^3	6			12				13	5^1			36

STRANRAER Third Division

Year Formed: 1870. *Ground & Address:* Stair Park, London Rd, Stranraer DG9 8BS. *Telephone and Fax:* 01776 703271.
E-mail: secretary@stranraerfc.org *Website:* www.stranraerfc.org
Ground Capacity: 5600, seated: 1830. *Size of Pitch:* 110yd × 70yd.
Chairman: Alex Connor. *Vice Chairman:* Robert Rice. *Secretary:* Hilde Law.
Manager: Keith Knox. *Assistant Manager:* Stephen Aitken. *Physio:* Walter Cannon.
Club Nicknames: The Blues, The Clayholers.
Previous Grounds: None.
Record Attendance: 6500 v Rangers, Scottish Cup 1st rd, 24 Jan 1948.
Record Transfer Fee received: £90,000 for Mark Campbell to Ayr U (1999).
Record Transfer Fee paid: £15,000 for Colin Harkness from Kilmarnock (Aug 1989).
Record Victory: 9-0 v St Cuthbert Wanderers, Scottish Cup 2nd rd, 23 Oct 2010.
Record Defeat: 1-11 v Queen of the South, Scottish Cup 1st rd, 16 Jan 1932.
Most League Appearances: 301: Keith Knox, 1986-90; 1999-2001.
Most League Goals in Season (Individual): 59: Tommy Sloan.

STRANRAER 2010–11 LEAGUE RECORD

Match No.	Date	Venue	Opponents	Result	H/T Score	Lg Pos.	Goalscorers	Attendance
1	Aug 7	A	Clyde	D 2-2	1-2	—	Malcolm [43], Winter [64]	827
2	14	H	Albion R	W 3-2	0-1	3	Agnew [71], Malcolm [84], One [87]	312
3	21	A	Annan Ath	D 2-2	2-1	4	Malcolm [3], Bouadji [7]	671
4	28	A	Elgin C	W 2-1	1-0	3	Bouadji [23], Malcolm [70]	370
5	Sept 11	H	Queen's Park	W 1-0	0-0	2	Malcolm [90]	408
6	18	A	Berwick R	D 2-2	0-1	2	Agnew (pen) [56], Winter [65]	489
7	25	H	Arbroath	W 4-1	1-0	2	Agnew 2 [15, 59], Winter [75], One [89]	379
8	Oct 2	H	Montrose	L 1-2	1-2	4	One [44]	352
9	9	A	Montrose	D 3-3	2-0	—	Winter [8], Malcolm 2 [33, 49]	335
10	16	A	East Stirling	W 1-0	1-0	1	One [1]	317
11	30	H	Elgin C	W 2-1	1-1	1	One [33], Agnew (pen) [82]	367
12	Nov 6	A	Queen's Park	W 3-1	0-1	1	One [74], Moore [77], Gallacher [83]	636
13	13	H	Annan Ath	D 2-2	0-1	1	Winter [76], Moore [82]	463
14	Dec 11	H	Berwick R	D 1-1	0-1	—	Malcolm [86]	267
15	15	A	Arbroath	D 0-0	0-0	—		302
16	Jan 15	H	Queen's Park	W 2-1	1-0	1	Agnew [27], Malcolm [81]	341
17	22	A	Elgin C	L 1-2	1-0	—	Moore [19]	714
18	29	H	Arbroath	L 3-4	1-2	2	Agnew [14], One [50], Mitchell, G [90]	441
19	Feb 12	H	Montrose	D 2-2	1-1	3	Malcolm [12], Winter [74]	320
20	15	A	Albion R	W 2-1	1-0	—	Malcolm [28], One [90]	326
21	19	A	East Stirling	W 2-0	1-0	2	Agnew [42], One [81]	294
22	23	H	East Stirling	W 4-1	3-1	—	Agnew [6], One 3 [34, 37, 67]	269
23	26	A	Clyde	L 2-4	1-1	2	Malcolm [6], One [64]	703
24	Mar 1	H	Clyde	W 3-1	1-0	—	One 2 [43, 81], Malcolm [66]	307
25	5	H	Albion R	L 1-3	1-0	2	Agnew [11]	390
26	8	A	Annan Ath	L 1-2	1-2	—	Murphy [25]	307
27	12	A	Queen's Park	D 3-3	1-1	2	Nicoll [13], Malcolm [46], One [58]	607
28	19	H	Elgin C	L 1-2	0-1	4	Murphy [86]	339
29	26	A	Arbroath	D 2-2	0-0	4	Agnew [71], One [72]	701
30	29	A	Berwick R	D 3-3	2-2	4	Murphy [4], Agnew 2 (1 pen) [45 (pl, 90]	297
31	Apr 2	H	Berwick R	W 3-1	1-0	4	McColm 2 [40, 67], Gallacher [52]	331
32	9	H	East Stirling	W 2-0	1-0	4	Kennedy [35], Winter [50]	373
33	16	A	Montrose	L 2-3	0-2	4	McColm [54], Gallacher [73]	316
34	23	H	Annan Ath	D 1-1	1-0	4	Winter [7]	493
35	30	A	Albion R	L 0-1	0-0	5		421
36	May 7	H	Clyde	W 3-0	1-0	5	Malcolm [17], Noble [72], McColm [87]	439

Final League Position: 5

Honours
League Champions: Second Division 1993-94, 1997-98; *Runners-up:* 2004-05, 2007-08. Third Division 2003-04.
Qualifying Cup Winners: 1937.
Scottish Cup: Quarter-finals 2003
League Challenge Cup Winners: 1996-97.

Club colours: Shirt: Royal blue. Shorts: White. Stockings: Royal blue.

Goalscorers: *League (72):* One 17, Malcolm 15, Agnew 13 (3 pens), Winter 8, McColm 4, Gallacher 3, Moore 3, Murphy 3, Bouadji 2, Kennedy 1, Mitchell G 1, Nicoll 1, Noble 1.
Scottish Cup (17): Malcolm 6, One 5, Agnew 2 (1 pen), Gallacher 1, Moore 1, Murphy 1, Winter 1.
CIS Cup (1): McColm 1.
Alba Challenge Cup (1): Malcolm 1.

Mitchell David 32	Gallacher G 35	Mitchell G 4+7	Nicoll K 20+5	Sharp L 20+5	Mitchell Danny 24+8	Agnew S 36	Noble S 19+5	Moore M 11+17	Malcolm C 34	McColm S 18+17	One A 24+11	Murphy P 30+1	Bouadji R 4	McAuliffe D 5+1	McInnes P —+1	Gallacher D 26	Cochrane A 2+5	Kurakins A 18+1	Aitken S —+1	Marshall R 4	Kennedy R 7	Match No.
1	2	3	4	5	6	7	8	9¹	10²	11	12	13										1
1	2³	4	3	5	6	8¹	7	9²	10	11	13	12	14									2
1	2		3	5	6	12	8	9³	10²	11	14	13	7¹	4								3
1	2		4	5	6	14	8	9²	10¹	11	13	12	7	3³								4
1	2	14	4■	5	6	12	7		10²	9	11³	13	8	3¹								5
1	5	3¹		6	11	8	9³		13	10	12	4²	2		7	14						6
1	2	13	5	12	8	7	6		14	11³	9	10	4¹		3²							7
1	6	2	4	13		8	7		12	11	9	10	3¹		5²							8
1	2		5	4	10	8	6	12	13	9	11¹	7		3²								9
1	2	14	4	5	7	6	8	12	13	11²	9¹	10³	3									10
1	2	14		5	6	7	8	12	13	11²	9¹	10²	3			4						11
1	?		6	7	8	5	12	11³	9¹	10¹	3	13				4	14					12
1	2		5¹	8	7	6	12	13	11	9²	10	3				4						13
1	2		7¹	8²	6	5	9	12	11	13	10	3				4						14
1	2		5		6	7	8	12	11	9	10¹		4			3						15
1	2	14	13	4	7³		8	6	12	11		10¹	9		3²	5						16
1	2		5	6¹	7		8	9	11	10²	12	13	3			4						17
1	2	14	5²	6¹		8	7	9	11³	12	10					3	13	4				18
1	2		6	13	8	7	9		11	12	10¹	4²				5		3				19
1	2		12		13	7	6	8²		10	11¹	9	4			5		3				20
1	2	10	12			7	6		9	11¹	8²	3				4	13	5				21
1	2		13	12	7	6		11	9¹	10²	4					5	8³	3	14			22
1	2		13		7	6		12	11	9²	8	4■				5	10¹	3				23
	2	5	6	13	8¹	7		14	11	9²	10³	4				4	12	3	1			24
1	2²		7	9	8¹		6		13	11	12	10	4			5		3				25
1	2		6	9¹		8	7²	10■	11	13	12	3				4		5				26
1	2		6¹		7	8	9		11	13	10³	3				4	12	5				27
	2	4		9	8³	7	14	12	11■	13	10²	5				6		3¹	1			28
	2	5³	6	13	8	7	9	11¹		10²	12	3				4		14	1			29
	2			7²	6	9	12	11	13	10	8					4		5	1	3¹		30
1	5	14		7³	12	8	9	11²		10	13	6¹				3		4		2		31
1	5¹	14		8	12	6	9		11	10²	13	7				4³		2		3		32
1		5		6	13	8	9²		11	12	10¹	7				3		4		2		33
1	2	14		8³		6	9²	12	11	13	10¹	7				5		3		4		34
1	2			11¹	12	5		10²	6	9	13	7				4		3		8		35
1	5		13	9²		12	6	7	10³	11	14		8¹			4		2		3		36

SCOTTISH LEAGUE PLAY-OFFS 2010–11

* *Denotes player sent off.*

DIVISION 1 SEMI-FINALS FIRST LEG

Wednesday, 11 May 2011

Brechin C (0) 2 *(Kirkpatrick 45, Megginson 51)*
Cowdenbeath (2) 2 *(Linton 4, Coult 26)*   596
Brechin C: Nelson; Cook, McBain, McLauchlan, Moyes, Janczyk (Kirkpatrick), Fusco (McKenna), Molloy, Redman, McAllister, Megginson (Byers).
Cowdenbeath: Roy (Hay); Baxter, Adamson, Crawford, Armstrong, Linton, Coult, O'Brien, Ramsay, Robertson, Stewart.

Forfar Ath (1) 1 *(Templeman 10)*
Ayr U (2) 4 *(Moffat 2, Bishop 35 (og), McCann 52, Rodgers 87)*   924
Forfar Ath: Duffy; Ross G, Bishop (Sellars), Bolocheweckyi, Campbell I (Mowat), McCulloch, Fotheringham, Campbell R (Deasley), Hilson, Templeman, Gibson.
Ayr U: Martin; Lauchlan, Malone, Campbell, Smith, Trouten, Tiffoney (Bannigan), McLaughlin, McCann, Moffat, Roberts (Rodgers).

DIVISION 1 SEMI-FINALS SECOND LEG

Saturday, 14 May 2011

Ayr U (1) 3 *(Moffat 12, McLaughlin 48, Trouten 90 (pen))*
Forfar Ath (1) 3 *(Hilson 31, Sellars 56, Campbell R 90 (pen))*   1198
Ayr U: Martin; Lauchlan, Smith, Malone, Campbell, McLaughlin, Trouten, Bannigan (Easton), McCann (Tiffoney), Moffat, Roberts (Robertson).
Forfar Ath: Duffy; Ross G, Campbell I, Tulloch, McCulloch, Brady (Campbell R), Fotheringham (Gibson), Sellars, Templeman, Hilson (Deasley), Dow.

Cowdenbeath (0) 0
Brechin C (0) 2 *(Redman 78, Molloy 84)*   645
Cowdenbeath: Hay; Baxter (Coult) (McKenzie), Armstrong, O'Brien, Linton, Robertson, Ramsay, Cameron, Makel, Crawford, Stewart.
Brechin C: Nelson; Cook, McLauchlan (White D), Moyes, McBain, McKenna, Molloy, Redman, Kirkpatrick (Janczyk), McAllister, Megginson (Fusco).

DIVISION 1 FINAL FIRST LEG

Wednesday, 18 May 2011

Ayr U (1) 1 *(Moffat 31)*
Brechin C (0) 1 *(Janczyk 86)*   2020
Ayr U: Martin; Lauchlan, Smith, Malone, Campbell, Bannigan (Easton), McLaughlin, Trouten, Moffat, Roberts (Rodgers), McCann (Tiffoney).
Brechin C: Nelson; Cook, McLean, McLauchlan, Moyes, Redman, Molloy, McKenna (Byers), McAllister, Megginson (Janczyk), Kirkpatrick (Fusco).

DIVISION 1 FINAL SECOND LEG

Sunday, 22 May 2011

Brechin C (1) 1 *(Tiffoney 44 (og))*
Ayr U (0) 2 *(Roberts 77, Moffat 88)*   2404
Brechin C: Nelson; Cook, McBain, McLauchlan, Moyes, Janczyk (Kirkpatrick), Fusco (McLean), Molloy, Redman, McAllister, McKenna (Megginson).
Ayr U: Martin; Lauchlan (Tiffoney), Smith, Malone, Campbell, McLaughlin, Trouten, Bannigan (Rodgers), McCann (Robertson), Moffat, Roberts.

DIVISION 2 SEMI-FINALS FIRST LEG

Wednesday, 11 May 2011

Annan Ath (1) 2 *(Muirhead 14, Steele 60)*
Alloa Ath (0) 1 *(Scott 65)*   621
Annan Ath: Summersgill; Watson, Neilson (MacBeth), Aitken, Muirhead, Gilfillan (Macfarlane), Steele, Docherty, Sloan S, Harty, O'Connor.
Alloa Ath: Ewings; McClune, Walker, Dunlop, Gibson, McGowan, Motion, Ferguson (McDonald), Scott (Smith), Lister, Noble (Prunty).

Queen's Park (1) 1 *(Smith 11)*
Albion R (0) 1 *(Chaplain 80)*   789
Queen's Park: Strain; McGinn, Little, Millen, Meggatt, McBride M, Capuano, Anderson, Daly, Longworth (Burns), Smith (Watt).
Albion R: Gaston; Reid, Donnelly, Lumsden, McGowan, Love (Boyle), Stevenson, Canning, Hamilton, Gemmell, Chaplain (Innes).

DIVISION 2 SEMI-FINALS SECOND LEG

Saturday, 14 May 2011

Albion R (0) 2 *(Gemmell 67, 89)*
Queen's Park (0) 0   859
Albion R: Gaston; McGowan, Stevenson, Lumsden, Reid, Donnelly, Canning, Boyle (Hamilton), Love (Ferry), Gemmell, Chaplain (Innes).
Queen's Park: Strain; Meggatt, Little, Millen, Capuano (Quinn A), McBride M, McGinn, Anderson, Daly (Burns), Longworth, Smith (Watt).

Alloa Ath (0) 0
Annan Ath (0) 0   622
Alloa Ath: Ewings; Walker, Dunlop, McDonald, Gibson, McGowan, Motion, Scott (Prunty), Smith (O'Brien), Lister, Noble.
Annan Ath: Summersgill; Steele (Gilfillan), Neilson, Aitken (MacBeth), Muirhead, Docherty, Macfarlane, Sloan S, Watson, Harty, O'Connor (Felvus).

DIVISION 2 FINAL FIRST LEG

Wednesday, 18 May 2011

Albion R (1) 3 *(Love 14, 67, 76)*
Annan Ath (1) 1 *(Harty 42)*   1014
Albion R: Gaston; Lumsden, McGowan, Stevenson, Reid, Donnelly, Canning, Chaplain, Love (Innes), Gemmell, Lawless (Ferry).
Annan Ath: Summersgill; Neilson, Aitken, Muirhead (Felvus), Steele, Watson, Docherty, Macfarlane (Gilfillan), Sloan S, Harty, O'Connor.

DIVISION 2 FINAL SECOND LEG

Sunday, 22 May 2011

Annan Ath (0) 2 *(Gilfillan 51, 65)*
Albion R (1) 1 *(Donnelly 24)*   1165
Annan Ath: Summersgill; Muirhead, Neilson, Aitken, Steele (MacBeth), Gilfillan*****, Docherty (Watson), Sloan S, Macfarlane, Harty, O'Connor (Felvus).
Albion R: Gaston; Lumsden, McGowan, Stevenson, Reid, Donnelly, Canning, Love, Lawless (Boyle), Gemmell, Chaplain.

SCOTTISH LEAGUE HONOURS 1890 to 2011

*On goal average (ratio)/difference.   †Held jointly after indecisive play-off.   ‡Won on deciding match.
††Held jointly.   ¶Two points deducted for fielding ineligible player.
Competition suspended 1940–45 during war; Regional Leagues operating.   ‡‡Two points deducted for registration
irregularities.   §Not promoted after play-offs.

PREMIER LEAGUE
Maximum points: 108

	First	Pts	Second	Pts	Third	Pts
1998–99	Rangers	77	Celtic	71	St Johnstone	57
1999–2000	Rangers	90	Celtic	69	Hearts	54

Maximum points: 114

	First	Pts	Second	Pts	Third	Pts
2000–01	Celtic	97	Rangers	82	Hibernian	66
2001–02	Celtic	103	Rangers	85	Livingston	58
2002–03	Rangers*	97	Celtic	97	Hearts	63
2003–04	Celtic	98	Rangers	81	Hearts	68
2004–05	Rangers	93	Celtic	92	Hibernian*	61
2005–06	Celtic	91	Hearts	74	Rangers	73
2006–07	Celtic	84	Rangers	72	Aberdeen	65
2007–08	Celtic	89	Rangers	86	Motherwell	60
2008–09	Rangers	86	Celtic	82	Hearts	59
2009–10	Rangers	87	Celtic	81	Dundee U	63
2010–11	Rangers	93	Celtic	92	Hearts	63

PREMIER DIVISION
Maximum points: 72

	First	Pts	Second	Pts	Third	Pts
1975–76	Rangers	54	Celtic	48	Hibernian	43
1976–77	Celtic	55	Rangers	46	Aberdeen	43
1977–78	Rangers	55	Aberdeen	53	Dundee U	40
1978–79	Celtic	48	Rangers	45	Dundee U	44
1979–80	Aberdeen	48	Celtic	47	St Mirren	42
1980–81	Celtic	56	Aberdeen	49	Rangers*	44
1981–82	Celtic	55	Aberdeen	53	Rangers	43
1982–83	Dundee U	56	Celtic*	55	Aberdeen	55
1983–84	Aberdeen	57	Celtic	50	Dundee U	47
1984–85	Aberdeen	59	Celtic	52	Dundee U	47
1985–86	Celtic*	50	Hearts	50	Dundee U	47

Maximum points: 88

	First	Pts	Second	Pts	Third	Pts
1986–87	Rangers	69	Celtic	63	Dundee U	60
1987–88	Celtic	72	Hearts	62	Rangers	60

Maximum points: 72

	First	Pts	Second	Pts	Third	Pts
1988–89	Rangers	56	Aberdeen	50	Celtic	46
1989–90	Rangers	51	Aberdeen*	44	Hearts	44
1990–91	Rangers	55	Aberdeen	53	Celtic*	41

Maximum points: 88

	First	Pts	Second	Pts	Third	Pts
1991–92	Rangers	72	Hearts	63	Celtic	62
1992–93	Rangers	73	Aberdeen	64	Celtic	60
1993–94	Rangers	58	Aberdeen	55	Motherwell	54

Maximum points: 108

	First	Pts	Second	Pts	Third	Pts
1994–95	Rangers	69	Motherwell	54	Hibernian	53
1995–96	Rangers	87	Celtic	83	Aberdeen*	55
1996–97	Rangers	80	Celtic	75	Dundee U	60
1997–98	Celtic	74	Rangers	72	Hearts	67

FIRST DIVISION
Maximum points: 52

	First	Pts	Second	Pts	Third	Pts
1975–76	Partick Th	41	Kilmarnock	35	Montrose	30

Maximum points: 78

	First	Pts	Second	Pts	Third	Pts
1976–77	St Mirren	62	Clydebank	58	Dundee	51
1977–78	Morton*	58	Hearts	58	Dundee	57
1978–79	Dundee	55	Kilmarnock*	54	Clydebank	54
1979–80	Hearts	53	Airdrieonians	51	Ayr U*	44
1980–81	Hibernian	57	Dundee	52	St Johnstone	51
1981–82	Motherwell	61	Kilmarnock	51	Hearts	50
1982–83	St Johnstone	55	Hearts	54	Clydebank	50
1983–84	Morton	54	Dumbarton	51	Partick Th	46
1984–85	Motherwell	50	Clydebank	48	Falkirk	45
1985–86	Hamilton A	56	Falkirk	45	Kilmarnock	44

Maximum points: 88

	First	Pts	Second	Pts	Third	Pts
1986–87	Morton	57	Dunfermline Ath	56	Dumbarton	53
1987–88	Hamilton A	56	Meadowbank Th	52	Clydebank	49

	First	Pts	Second	Pts	Third	Pts
			Maximum points: 78			
1988–89	Dunfermline Ath	54	Falkirk	52	Clydebank	48
1989–90	St Johnstone	58	Airdrieonians	54	Clydebank	44
1990–91	Falkirk	54	Airdrieonians	53	Dundee	52
			Maximum points: 88			
1991–92	Dundee	58	Partick Th*	57	Hamilton A	57
1992–93	Raith R	65	Kilmarnock	54	Dunfermline Ath	52
1993–94	Falkirk	66	Dunfermline Ath	65	Airdrieonians	54
			Maximum points: 108			
1994–95	Raith R	69	Dunfermline Ath*	68	Dundee	68
1995–96	Dunfermline Ath	71	Dundee U*	67	Morton	67
1996–97	St Johnstone	80	Airdieonians	60	Dundee*	58
1997–98	Dundee	70	Falkirk	65	Raith R*	60
1998–99	Hibernian	89	Falkirk	66	Ayr U	62
1999–2000	St Mirren	76	Dunfermline Ath	71	Falkirk	68
2000–01	Livingston	76	Ayr U	69	Falkirk	56
2001–02	Partick Th	66	Airdrieonians	56	Ayr U	52
2002–03	Falkirk	81	Clyde	72	St Johnstone	67
2003–04	Inverness CT	70	Clyde	69	St Johnstone	57
2004–05	Falkirk	75	St Mirren*	60	Clyde	60
2005–06	St Mirren	76	St Johnstone	66	Hamilton A	59
2006–07	Gretna	66	St Johnstone	65	Dundee*	53
2007–08	Hamilton A	76	Dundee	69	St Johnstone	58
2008–09	St Johnstone	65	Partick Th	55	Dunfermline Ath	51
2009–10	Inverness CT	73	Dundee	61	Dunfermline Ath	58
2010–11	Dunfermline Ath	70	Raith R	60	Falkirk	58

SECOND DIVISION

	First	Pts	Second	Pts	Third	Pts
			Maximum points: 52			
1975–76	Clydebank*	40	Raith R	40	Alloa Ath	35
			Maximum points: 78			
1976–77	Stirling Alb	55	Alloa Ath	51	Dunfermline Ath	50
1977–78	Clyde*	53	Raith R	53	Dunfermline Ath	48
1978–79	Berwick R	54	Dunfermline Ath	52	Falkirk	50
1979–80	Falkirk	50	East Stirling	49	Forfar Ath	46
1980–81	Queen's Park	50	Queen of the S	46	Cowdenbeath	45
1981–82	Clyde	59	Alloa Ath*	50	Arbroath	50
1982–83	Brechin C	55	Meadowbank Th	54	Arbroath	49
1983–84	Forfar Ath	63	East Fife	47	Berwick R	43
1984–85	Montrose	53	Alloa Ath	50	Dunfermline Ath	49
1985–86	Dunfermline Ath	57	Queen of the S	55	Meadowbank Th	49
1986–87	Meadowbank Th	55	Raith R*	52	Stirling Alb*	52
1987–88	Ayr U	61	St Johnstone	59	Queen's Park	51
1988–89	Albion R	50	Alloa Ath	45	Brechin C	43
1989–90	Brechin C	49	Kilmarnock	48	Stirling Alb	47
1990–91	Stirling Alb	54	Montrose	46	Cowdenbeath	45
1991–92	Dumbarton	52	Cowdenbeath	51	Alloa Ath	50
1992–93	Clyde	54	Brechin C*	53	Stranraer	53
1993–94	Stranraer	56	Berwick R	48	Stenhousemuir*	47
			Maximum points: 108			
1994–95	Morton	64	Dumbarton	60	Stirling Alb	58
1995–96	Stirling Alb	81	East Fife	67	Berwick R	60
1996–97	Ayr U	77	Hamilton A	74	Livingston	64
1997–98	Stranraer	61	Clydebank	60	Livingston	59
1998–99	Livingston	77	Inverness CT	72	Clyde	53
1999–2000	Clyde	65	Alloa Ath	64	Ross Co	62
2000–01	Partick Th	75	Arbroath	58	Berwick R*	54
2001–02	Queen of the S	67	Alloa Ath	59	Forfar Ath	53
2002–03	Raith R	59	Brechin C	55	Airdrie U	54
2003–04	Airdrie U	70	Hamilton A	62	Dumbarton	60
2004–05	Brechin C	72	Stranraer	63	Morton	62
2005–06	Gretna	88	Morton§	70	Peterhead*§	57
2006–07	Morton	77	Stirling Alb	69	Raith R§	62
2007–08	Ross Co	73	Airdrie U	66	Raith R§	60
2008–09	Raith R	76	Ayr U	74	Brechin C§	62
2009–10	Stirling Alb*	65	Alloa Ath§	65	Cowdenbeath	54
2010–11	Livingston	82	Ayr U*	59	Forfar Ath§	59

THIRD DIVISION

	First	Pts	Second	Pts	Third	Pts
			Maximum points: 108			
1994–95	Forfar Ath	80	Montrose	67	Ross Co	60
1995–96	Livingston	72	Brechin C	63	Inverness CT	57
1996–97	Inverness CT	76	Forfar Ath*	67	Ross Co	67
1997–98	Alloa Ath	76	Arbroath	68	Ross Co*	67

	First	Pts	Second	Pts	Third	Pts
1998–99	Ross Co	77	Stenhousemuir	64	Brechin C	59
1999–2000	Queen's Park	69	Berwick R	66	Forfar Ath	61
2000–01	Hamilton A*	76	Cowdenbeath	76	Brechin C	72
2001–02	Brechin C	73	Dumbarton	61	Albion R	59
2002–03	Morton	72	East Fife	71	Albion R	70
2003–04	Stranraer	79	Stirling Alb	77	Gretna	68
2004–05	Gretna	98	Peterhead	78	Cowdenbeath	51
2005–06	Cowdenbeath*	76	Berwick R§	76	Stenhousemuir§	73
2006–07	Berwick R	75	Arbroath§	70	Queen's Park	68
2007–08	East Fife	88	Stranraer	65	Montrose§	59
2008–09	Dumbarton	67	Cowdenbeath§	63	East Stirling§	61
2009–10	Livingston	78	Forfar Ath	63	East Stirling§	61
2010–11	Arbroath	66	Albion R	61	Queen's Park*§	59

DIVISION 1 to 1974–75

Maximum points: a 36; b 44; c 40; d 52; e 60; f 68; g 76; h 84.

	First	Pts	Second	Pts	Third	Pts
1890–91a	Dumbarton††	29	Rangers††	29	Celtic	21
1891–92b	Dumbarton	37	Celtic	35	Hearts	34
1892–93a	Celtic	29	Rangers	28	St Mirren	20
1893–94a	Celtic	29	Hearts	26	St Bernard's	23
1894–95a	Hearts	31	Celtic	26	Rangers	22
1895–96a	Celtic	30	Rangers	26	Hibernian	24
1896–97a	Hearts	28	Hibernian	26	Rangers	25
1897–98a	Celtic	33	Rangers	29	Hibernian	22
1898–99a	Rangers	36	Hearts	26	Celtic	24
1899–1900a	Rangers	32	Celtic	25	Hibernian	24
1900–01c	Rangers	35	Celtic	29	Hibernian	25
1901–02a	Rangers	28	Celtic	26	Hearts	22
1902–03b	Hibernian	37	Dundee	31	Rangers	29
1903–04d	Third Lanark	43	Hearts	39	Celtic*	38
1904–05d	Celtic‡	41	Rangers	41	Third Lanark	35
1905–06e	Celtic	49	Hearts	43	Airdrieonians	38
1906–07f	Celtic	55	Dundee	48	Rangers	45
1907–08f	Celtic	55	Falkirk	51	Rangers	50
1908–09f	Celtic	51	Dundee	50	Clyde	48
1909–10f	Celtic	54	Falkirk	52	Rangers	46
1910–11f	Rangers	52	Aberdeen	48	Falkirk	44
1911–12f	Rangers	51	Celtic	45	Clyde	42
1912–13f	Rangers	53	Celtic	49	Hearts*	41
1913–14g	Celtic	65	Rangers	59	Hearts*	54
1914–15g	Celtic	65	Hearts	61	Rangers	50
1915–16g	Celtic	67	Rangers	56	Morton	51
1916–17g	Celtic	64	Morton	54	Rangers	53
1917–18f	Rangers	56	Celtic	55	Kilmarnock*	43
1918–19f	Celtic	58	Rangers	57	Morton	47
1919–20h	Rangers	71	Celtic	68	Motherwell	57
1920–21h	Rangers	76	Celtic	66	Hearts	50
1921–22h	Celtic	67	Rangers	66	Raith R	51
1922–23g	Rangers	55	Airdrieonians	50	Celtic	46
1923–24g	Rangers	59	Airdrieonians	50	Celtic	46
1924–25g	Rangers	60	Airdrieonians	57	Hibernian	52
1925–26g	Celtic	58	Airdrieonians*	50	Hearts	50
1926–27g	Rangers	56	Motherwell	51	Celtic	49
1927–28g	Rangers	60	Celtic*	55	Motherwell	55
1928–29g	Rangers	67	Celtic	51	Motherwell	50
1929–30g	Rangers	60	Motherwell	55	Aberdeen	53
1930–31g	Rangers	60	Celtic	58	Motherwell	56
1931–32g	Motherwell	66	Rangers	61	Celtic	48
1932–33g	Rangers	62	Motherwell	59	Hearts	50
1933–34g	Rangers	66	Motherwell	62	Celtic	47
1934–35g	Rangers	55	Celtic	52	Hearts	50
1935–36g	Celtic	66	Rangers*	61	Aberdeen	61
1936–37g	Rangers	61	Aberdeen	54	Celtic	52
1937–38g	Celtic	61	Hearts	58	Rangers	49
1938–39g	Rangers	59	Celtic	48	Aberdeen	46
1946–47e	Rangers	46	Hibernian	44	Aberdeen	39
1947–48e	Hibernian	48	Rangers	46	Partick Th	36
1948–49e	Rangers	46	Dundee	45	Hibernian	39
1949–50e	Rangers	50	Hibernian	49	Hearts	43
1950–51e	Hibernian	48	Rangers*	38	Dundee	38
1951–52e	Hibernian	45	Rangers	41	East Fife	37
1952–53e	Rangers*	43	Hibernian	43	East Fife	39
1953–54e	Celtic	43	Hearts	38	Partick Th	35
1954–55e	Aberdeen	49	Celtic	46	Rangers	41

	First	Pts	Second	Pts	Third	Pts
1955–56f	Rangers	52	Aberdeen	46	Hearts*	45
1956–57f	Rangers	55	Hearts	53	Kilmarnock	42
1957–58f	Hearts	62	Rangers	49	Celtic	46
1958–59f	Rangers	50	Hearts	48	Motherwell	44
1959–60f	Hearts	54	Kilmarnock	50	Rangers*	42
1960–61f	Rangers	51	Kilmarnock	50	Third Lanark	42
1961–62f	Dundee	54	Rangers	51	Celtic	46
1962–63f	Rangers	57	Kilmarnock	48	Partick Th	46
1963–64f	Rangers	55	Kilmarnock	49	Celtic*	47
1964–65f	Kilmarnock*	50	Hearts	50	Dunfermline Ath	49
1965–66f	Celtic	57	Rangers	55	Kilmarnock	45
1966–67f	Celtic	58	Rangers	55	Clyde	46
1967–68f	Celtic	63	Rangers	61	Hibernian	45
1968–69f	Celtic	54	Rangers	49	Dunfermline Ath	45
1969–70f	Celtic	57	Rangers	45	Hibernian	44
1970–71f	Celtic	56	Aberdeen	54	St Johnstone	44
1971–72f	Celtic	60	Aberdeen	50	Rangers	44
1972–73f	Celtic	57	Rangers	56	Hibernian	45
1973–74f	Celtic	53	Hibernian	49	Rangers	48
1974–75f	Rangers	56	Hibernian	49	Celtic	45

DIVISION 2 to 1974–75

Maximum points: a 76; b 72; c 68; d 52; e 60; f 36; g 44.

	First	Pts	Second	Pts	Third	Pts
1893–94f	Hibernian	29	Cowlairs	27	Clyde	24
1894–95f	Hibernian	30	Motherwell	22	Port Glasgow	20
1895–96f	Abercorn	27	Leith Ath	23	Renton	21
1896–97f	Partick Th	31	Leith Ath	27	Kilmarnock*	21
1897–98f	Kilmarnock	29	Port Glasgow	25	Morton	22
1898–99f	Kilmarnock	32	Leith Ath	27	Port Glasgow	25
1899–1900f	Partick Th	29	Morton	28	Port Glasgow	20
1900–01f	St Bernard's	25	Airdrieonians	23	Abercorn	21
1901–02g	Port Glasgow	32	Partick Th	31	Motherwell	26
1902–03g	Airdrieonians	35	Motherwell	28	Ayr U*	27
1903–04g	Hamilton A	37	Clyde	29	Ayr U	28
1904–05g	Clyde	32	Falkirk	28	Hamilton A	27
1905–06g	Leith Ath	34	Clyde	31	Albion R	27
1906–07g	St Bernard's	32	Vale of Leven*	27	Arthurlie	27
1907–08g	Raith R	30	Dumbarton*‡‡	27	Ayr U	27
1908–09g	Abercorn	31	Raith R*	28	Vale of Leven	28
1909–10g	Leith Ath‡	33	Raith R	33	St Bernard's	27
1910–11g	Dumbarton	31	Ayr U	27	Albion R	25
1911–12g	Ayr U	35	Abercorn	30	Dumbarton	27
1912–13d	Ayr U	34	Dunfermline Ath	33	East Stirling	32
1913–14g	Cowdenbeath	31	Albion R	27	Dunfermline Ath*	26
1914–15d	Cowdenbeath*	37	St Bernard's*	37	Leith Ath	37
1921–22a	Alloa Ath	60	Cowdenbeath	47	Armadale	45
1922–23a	Queen's Park	57	Clydebank¶	50	St Johnstone¶	45
1923–24a	St Johnstone	56	Cowdenbeath	55	Bathgate	44
1924–25a	Dundee U	50	Clydebank	48	Clyde	47
1925–26a	Dunfermline Ath	59	Clyde	53	Ayr U	52
1926–27a	Bo'ness	56	Raith R	49	Clydebank	45
1927–28a	Ayr U	54	Third Lanark	45	King's Park	44
1928–29b	Dundee U	51	Morton	50	Arbroath	47
1929–30a	Leith Ath*	57	East Fife	57	Albion R	54
1930–31a	Third Lanark	61	Dundee U	50	Dunfermline Ath	47
1931–32a	East Stirling*	55	St Johnstone	55	Raith R*	46
1932–33c	Hibernian	54	Queen of the S	49	Dunfermline Ath	47
1933–34c	Albion R	45	Dunfermline Ath*	44	Arbroath	44
1934–35c	Third Lanark	52	Arbroath	50	St Bernard's	47
1935–36c	Falkirk	59	St Mirren	52	Morton	48
1936–37c	Ayr U	54	Morton	51	St Bernard's	48
1937–38c	Raith R	59	Albion R	48	Airdrieonians	47
1938–39c	Cowdenbeath	60	Alloa Ath*	48	East Fife	48
1946–47d	Dundee	45	Airdrieonians	42	East Fife	31
1947–48e	East Fife	53	Albion R	42	Hamilton A	40
1948–49e	Raith R*	42	Stirling Alb	42	Airdrieonians*	41
1949–50e	Morton	47	Airdrieonians	44	Dunfermline Ath*	36
1950–51e	Queen of the S*	45	Stirling Alb	45	Ayr U*	36
1951–52e	Clyde	44	Falkirk	43	Ayr U	39
1952–53e	Stirling Alb	44	Hamilton A	43	Queen's Park	37
1953–54e	Motherwell	45	Kilmarnock	42	Third Lanark*	36
1954–55e	Airdrieonians	46	Dunfermline Ath	42	Hamilton A	39
1955–56b	Queen's Park	54	Ayr U	51	St Johnstone	49
1956–57b	Clyde	64	Third Lanark	51	Cowdenbeath	45

	First	Pts		Second	Pts		Third	Pts
1957–58b	Stirling Alb	55		Dunfermline Ath	53		Arbroath	47
1958–59b	Ayr U	60		Arbroath	51		Stenhousemuir	46
1959–60b	St Johnstone	53		Dundee U	50		Queen of the S	49
1960–61b	Stirling Alb	55		Falkirk	54		Stenhousemuir	50
1961–62b	Clyde	54		Queen of the S	53		Morton	44
1962–63b	St Johnstone	55		East Stirling	49		Morton	48
1963–64b	Morton	67		Clyde	53		Arbroath	46
1964–65b	Stirling Alb	59		Hamilton A	50		Queen of the S	45
1965–66b	Ayr U	53		Airdrieonians	50		Queen of the S	47
1966–67a	Morton	69		Raith R	58		Arbroath	57
1967–68b	St Mirren	62		Arbroath	53		East Fife	49
1968–69b	Motherwell	64		Ayr U	53		East Fife*	48
1969–70b	Falkirk	56		Cowdenbeath	55		Queen of the S	50
1970–71b	Partick Th	56		East Fife	51		Arbroath	46
1971–72b	Dumbarton*	52		Arbroath	52		Stirling Alb	50
1972–73b	Clyde	56		Dunfermline Ath	52		Raith R*	47
1973–74b	Airdrieonians	60		Kilmarnock	58		Hamilton A	55
1974–75a	Falkirk	54		Queen of the S*	53		Montrose	53

Elected to First Division: 1894 Clyde; 1895 Hibernian; 1896 Abercorn; 1897 Partick Th; 1899 Kilmarnock; 1900 Morton and Partick Th; 1902 Port Glasgow and Partick Th; 1903 Airdrieonians and Motherwell; 1905 Falkirk and Aberdeen; 1906 Clyde and Hamilton A; 1910 Raith R; 1913 Ayr U and Dumbarton.

RELEGATED FROM PREMIER LEAGUE

1998–99 Dunfermline Ath
1999–2000 *No relegation due to League reorganization*
2000–01 St Mirren
2001–02 St Johnstone
2002–03 *No relegated team*
2003–04 Partick Th
2004–05 Dundee

2005–06 Livingston
2006–07 Dunfermline Ath
2007–08 Gretna
2008–09 Inverness CT
2009–10 Falkirk
2010–11 Hamilton A

RELEGATED FROM PREMIER DIVISION

1974–75 *No relegation due to League reorganization*
1975–76 Dundee, St Johnstone
1976–77 Hearts, Kilmarnock
1977–78 Ayr U, Clydebank
1978–79 Hearts, Motherwell
1979–80 Dundee, Hibernian
1980–81 Kilmarnock, Hearts
1981–82 Partick Th, Airdrieonians
1982–83 Morton, Kilmarnock
1983–84 St Johnstone, Motherwell
1984–85 Dumbarton, Morton
1985–86 *No relegation due to League reorganization*

1986–87 Clydebank, Hamilton A
1987–88 Falkirk, Dunfermline Ath, Morton
1988–89 Hamilton A
1989–90 Dundee
1990–91 *None*
1991–92 St Mirren, Dunfermline Ath
1992–93 Falkirk, Airdrieonians
1993–94 *See footnote*
1994–95 Dundee U
1995–96 Partick Th, Falkirk
1996–97 Raith R
1997–98 Hibernian

RELEGATED FROM DIVISION 1

1975–76 Dunfermline Ath, Clyde
1976–77 Raith R, Falkirk
1977–78 Alloa Ath, East Fife
1981–82 East Stirling, Queen of the S
1982–83 Dunfermline Ath, Queen's Park
1983–84 Raith R, Alloa Ath
1984–85 Meadowbank Th, St Johnstone
1985–86 Ayr U, Alloa Ath
1986–87 Brechin C, Montrose
1987–88 East Fife, Dumbarton
1988–89 Kilmarnock, Queen of the S
1989–90 Albion R, Alloa Ath
1990–91 Clyde, Brechin C
1992–93 Meadowbank Th, Cowdenbeath
1993–94 *See footnote*
1994–95 Ayr U, Stranraer
1995–96 Hamilton A, Dumbarton
1978–79 Montrose, Queen of the S

1979–80 Arbroath, Clyde
1980–81 Stirling Alb, Berwick R
1996–97 Clydebank, East Fife
1997–98 Partick Th, Stirling Alb
1998–99 Hamilton A, Stranraer
1999–2000 Clydebank
2000–01 Morton, Alloa Ath
2001–02 Raith R
2002–03 Alloa Ath, Arbroath
2003–04 Ayr U, Brechin C
2004–05 Partick Th, Raith R
2005–06 Stranraer, Brechin C
2006–07 Airdrie U, Ross Co
2007–08 Stirling Alb
2008–09 Clyde
2009–10 Airdrie U, Ayr U
2010–11 Cowdenbeath, Stirling Alb

RELEGATED FROM DIVISION 2

1994–95 Meadowbank Th, Brechin C
1995–96 Forfar Ath, Montrose
1996–97 Dumbarton, Berwick R
1997–98 Stenhousemuir, Brechin C
1998–99 East Fife, Forfar Ath
1999–2000 Hamilton A**
2000–01 Queen's Park, Stirling Alb
2001–02 Morton
2002–03 Stranraer, Cowdenbeath

2003–04 East Fife, Stenhousemuir
2004–05 Arbroath, Berwick R
2005–06 Dumbarton
2006–07 Stranraer, Forfar Ath
2007–08 Cowdenbeath, Berwick R
2008–09 Stranraer, Queen's Park
2009–10 Arbroath, Clyde
2010–11 Alloa Ath, Peterhead

RELEGATED FROM DIVISION 1 (TO 1973–74)

1921–22 *Queen's Park, Dumbarton, Clydebank	1951–52 Morton, Stirling Alb
1922–23 Albion R, Alloa Ath	1952–53 Motherwell, Third Lanark
1923–24 Clyde, Clydebank	1953–54 Airdrieonians, Hamilton A
1924–25 Third Lanark, Ayr U	1954–55 *No clubs relegated*
1925–26 Raith R, Clydebank	1955–56 Stirling Alb, Clyde
1926–27 Morton, Dundee U	1956–57 Dunfermline Ath, Ayr U
1927–28 Dunfermline Ath, Bo'ness	1957–58 East Fife, Queen's Park
1928–29 Third Lanark, Raith R	1958–59 Queen of the S, Falkirk
1929–30 St Johnstone, Dundee U	1959–60 Arbroath, Stirling Alb
1930–31 Hibernian, East Fife	1960–61 Ayr U, Clyde
1931–32 Dundee U, Leith Ath	1961–62 St Johnstone, Stirling Alb
1932–33 Morton, East Stirling	1962–63 Clyde, Raith R
1933–34 Third Lanark, Cowdenbeath	1963–64 Queen of the S, East Stirling
1934–35 St Mirren, Falkirk	1964–65 Airdrieonians, Third Lanark
1935–36 Airdrieonians, Ayr U	1965–66 Morton, Hamilton A
1936–37 Dunfermline Ath, Albion R	1966–67 St Mirren, Ayr U
1937–38 Dundee, Morton	1967–68 Motherwell, Stirling Alb
1938–39 Queen's Park, Raith R	1968–69 Falkirk, Arbroath
1946–47 Kilmarnock, Hamilton A	1969–70 Raith R, Partick Th
1947–48 Airdrieonians, Queen's Park	1970–71 St Mirren, Cowdenbeath
1948–49 Morton, Albion R	1971–72 Clyde, Dunfermline Ath
1949–50 Queen of the S, Stirling Alb	1972–73 Kilmarnock, Airdrieonians
1950–51 Clyde, Falkirk	1973–74 East Fife, Falkirk

*Season 1921–22 – only 1 club promoted, 3 clubs relegated. **15pts deducted for failing to field a team.

Scottish League Championship wins: Rangers 54, Celtic 42, Aberdeen 4, Hearts 4, Hibernian 4, Dumbarton 2, Dundee 1, Dundee U 1, Kilmarnock 1, Motherwell 1, Third Lanark 1.

At the end of the 1993–94 season four divisions were created assisted by the admission of two new clubs Ross County and Caledonian Thistle. Only one club was promoted from Division 1 and Division 2. The three relegated from the Premier joined with teams finishing second to seventh in Division 1 to form the new Division 1. Five relegated from Division 1 combined with those who finished second to sixth to form a new Division 2 and the bottom eight in Division 2 linked with the two newcomers to form a new Division 3. At the end of the 1997–98 season the nine clubs remaining in the Premier Division plus the promoted team from Division 1 formed a breakaway Premier League. At the end of the 1999–2000 season two teams were added to the Scottish League. There was no relegation from the Premier League but two promoted from the First Division and three from each of the Second and Third Divisions. One team was relegated from the First Division and one from the Second Division, leaving 12 teams in each division. In season 2002–03, Falkirk were not promoted to the Premier League due to the failure of their ground to meet League rules. Inverness CT were promoted after a previous refusal in 2003–04 because of ground sharing. At the end of 2005–06 the Scottish League introduced play-offs for the team finishing second from the bottom of Division 1 against the winners of the second, third and fourth finishing teams in Division 2 and with a similar procedure for Division 2 and Division 3.

From 1946–47 to 1955–56 the two divisions were known as A and B. A division 3 had existed for three years from 1923–24 and was revived for three more seasons from 1946–47 as Division C when it included reserve teams.

SCOTTISH LEAGUE ATTENDANCES 2010–11

PREMIER LEAGUE

	Average	Highest	Lowest
Aberdeen	9,071	15,307	5,917
Celtic	49,089	58,874	40,750
Dundee U	7,389	11,790	4,918
Hamilton A	2,897	5,356	2,011
Hearts	14,184	17,156	12,009
Hibernian	11,672	17,793	7,238
Inverness CT	4,526	7,547	3,241
Kilmarnock	6,416	16,173	4,214
Motherwell	5,254	9,716	3,324
Rangers	45,304	50,248	41,514
St Johnstone	3,841	6,866	2,253
St Mirren	4,449	6,118	2,701

SECOND DIVISION

	Average	Highest	Lowest
Airdrie U	788	1,127	437
Alloa Ath	536	688	375
Ayr U	1,156	1,614	789
Brechin C	514	825	394
Dumbarton	624	853	350
East Fife	548	846	314
Forfar Ath	500	782	341
Livingston	1,303	1,863	724
Peterhead	489	831	312
Stenhousemuir	559	837	363

FIRST DIVISION

	Average	Highest	Lowest
Cowdenbeath	892	2,192	296
Dundee	4,727	7,746	3,503
Dunfermline Ath	3,996	11,052	1,699
Falkirk	4,224	6,947	3,376
Morton	1,912	4,626	980
Partick Th	2,023	2,801	1,001
Queen of the S	1,621	2,590	266
Raith R	2,718	6,534	1,495
Ross Co	2,357	3,205	1,759
Stirling Alb	1,054	2,168	444

THIRD DIVISION

	Average	Highest	Lowest
Albion R	383	523	312
Annan Ath	457	671	293
Arbroath	608	1,243	302
Berwick R	378	520	258
Clyde	698	1,043	385
East Stirling	319	532	178
Elgin C	521	725	272
Montrose	393	1,034	235
Queen's Park	565	1,148	325
Stranraer	366	493	267

SCOTTISH LEAGUE CUP FINALS 1946–2011

Season	Winners	Runners-up	Score
1946–47	Rangers	Aberdeen	4-0
1947–48	East Fife	Falkirk	4-1 after 0-0 draw (*aet.*)
1948–49	Rangers	Raith R	2-0
1949–50	East Fife	Dunfermline Ath	3-0
1950–51	Motherwell	Hibernian	3-0
1951–52	Dundee	Rangers	3-2
1952–53	Dundee	Kilmarnock	2-0
1953–54	East Fife	Partick Th	3-2
1954–55	Hearts	Motherwell	4-2
1955–56	Aberdeen	St Mirren	2-1
1956–57	Celtic	Partick Th	3-0 after 0-0 draw
1957–58	Celtic	Rangers	7-1
1958–59	Hearts	Partick Th	5-1
1959–60	Hearts	Third Lanark	2-1
1960–61	Rangers	Kilmarnock	2-0
1961–62	Rangers	Hearts	3-1 after 1-1 draw
1962–63	Hearts	Kilmarnock	1-0
1963–64	Rangers	Morton	5-0
1964–65	Rangers	Celtic	2-1
1965–66	Celtic	Rangers	2-1
1966–67	Celtic	Rangers	1-0
1967–68	Celtic	Dundee	5-3
1968–69	Celtic	Hibernian	6-2
1969–70	Celtic	St Johnstone	1-0
1970–71	Rangers	Celtic	1-0
1971–72	Partick Th	Celtic	4-1
1972–73	Hibernian	Celtic	2-1
1973–74	Dundee	Celtic	1-0
1974–75	Celtic	Hibernian	6-3
1975–76	Rangers	Celtic	1-0
1976–77	Aberdeen	Celtic	2-1
1977–78	Rangers	Celtic	2-1 (*aet.*)
1978–79	Rangers	Aberdeen	2-1
1979–80	Dundee U	Aberdeen	3-0 after 0-0 draw (*aet.*)
1980–81	Dundee U	Dundee	3-0
1981–82	Rangers	Dundee U	2-1
1982–83	Celtic	Rangers	2-1
1983–84	Rangers	Celtic	3-2
1984–85	Rangers	Dundee U	1-0
1985–86	Aberdeen	Hibernian	3-0
1986–87	Rangers	Celtic	2-1
1987–88	Rangers	Aberdeen	3-3
		(aet; Rangers won 5-3 on penalties)	
1988–89	Rangers	Aberdeen	3-2 (*aet.*)
1989–90	Aberdeen	Rangers	2-1
1990–91	Rangers	Celtic	2-1
1991–92	Hibernian	Dunfermline Ath	2-0
1992–93	Rangers	Aberdeen	2-1 (*aet.*)
1993–94	Rangers	Hibernian	2-1
1994–95	Raith R	Celtic	2-2
		(aet; Raith R won 6-5 on penalties)	
1995–96	Aberdeen	Dundee	2-0
1996–97	Rangers	Hearts	4-3
1997–98	Celtic	Dundee U	3-0
1998–99	Rangers	St Johnstone	2-1
1999–2000	Celtic	Aberdeen	2-0
2000–01	Celtic	Kilmarnock	3-0
2001–02	Rangers	Ayr U	4-0
2002–03	Rangers	Celtic	2-1
2003–04	Livingston	Hibernian	2-0
2004–05	Rangers	Motherwell	5-1
2005–06	Celtic	Dunfermline Ath	3-0
2006–07	Hibernian	Kilmarnock	5-1
2007–08	Rangers	Dundee U	2-2
		(aet; Rangers won 3-2 on penalties)	
2008–09	Celtic	Rangers	2-0 (*aet.*)
2009–10	Rangers	St Mirren	1-0
2010–11	Rangers	Celtic	2-1 (*aet.*)

SCOTTISH LEAGUE CUP WINS

Rangers 27, Celtic 14, Aberdeen 5, Hearts 4, Dundee 3, East Fife 3, Hibernian 3, Dundee U 2, Livingston 1, Motherwell 1, Partick Th 1, Raith R 1.

APPEARANCES IN FINALS

Rangers 34, Celtic 28, Aberdeen 12, Hibernian 9, Dundee 6, Dundee U 6, Hearts 6, Kilmarnock 5, Partick Th 4, Dunfermline Ath 3, East Fife 3, Motherwell 3, Raith R 2, St Johnstone 2, St Mirren 2, Ayr U 1, Falkirk 1, Livingston 1, Morton 1, Third Lanark 1.

CIS SCOTTISH LEAGUE CUP 2010–11

■ *Denotes player sent off.*

FIRST ROUND

Saturday, 31 July 2010

Albion R (0) 0

Airdrie U (0) 1 *(Gemmill 67)* 1200

Albion R: Gaston; McGowan, Gilmartin (Stevenson), Benton, Lumsden, Reid, Canning■, Donnelly, Hamilton C, Gemmell (Dalrymple), Love (McLeod).
Airdrie U: Ridgers; Bain, Lovering, Gibson, Stallard, Grant, Devlin, McCord (McGregor), Muir■, Gemmill, Watt (Wallace).

Annan Ath (0) 0

Partick Th (0) 1 *(Donnelly 84)* 1025

Annan Ath: Summersgill; Muirhead, Aitken, Neilson (Lawless), Gilfillan, MacBeth, Halsman (Cox), Sloan S, Jardine (Jack), Walker, Harty.
Partick Th: Halliwell; Robertson, Kinniburgh, Boyle, Paton, MacBeth (Cairney), Rowson, Flannigan, Hodge (Erskine), Buchanan, Donnelly.

Clyde (0) 2 *(McCusker 58, 67)*

Cowdenbeath (0) 1 *(Ramsay 78)* 667

Clyde: Hutchison; Park, Henderson, McGowan, McMillan, Finlayson, Stevenson, Sweeney, Strachan, McCusker, Dingwall (Stewart).
Cowdenbeath: Hay; Baxter, Armstrong, Linton, Adamson, O'Brien, Fairbairn (Brett), Cameron, Ramsay, McKenzie, Dempster (Stewart).

Dundee (1) 3 *(Riley 33, 79, Griffiths 70 (pen))*

Montrose (0) 0 2111

Dundee: Douglas; Irvine, Forsyth, Weston, McKeown (McHale), Adams, O'Donnell (Paton), Harkins, Riley, Griffiths, McMenamin (Higgins).
Montrose: Wood; McNalley, Crighton, Tweed (Milligan), Campbell, Sinclair (Fleming), Masson (McCord), Davidson, Smith, Nicol, Tosh.

Dunfermline Ath (1) 5 *(Kirk 14, 76, Willis 74, McDougall 82, Malcolm 90 (og))*

Arbroath (1) 2 *(Sheerin P 12, Swankie 88)* 1283

Dunfermline Ath: Smith; Woods, Dowie, Keddie, McCann, Willis, Mason, Phinn, Cardle, Clarke (McDougall), Kirk.
Arbroath: Hill; Malcolm, Griffin, Shields, McAnespie (Suttie), Swankie, McCulloch, Falkingham, Sheerin P, Hamilton J (McGowan), Sheerin J (Ross).

Elgin C (1) 3 *(Gunn 43 (pen), 69, Millar 120)*

Ayr U (1) 2 *(McKeown 17, Connolly 77)* 594

Elgin C: Dunn S; Inglis J, Kaczan, Niven, Dempsie, Wilson (Cameron), O'Donoghue, Nicolson, Crooks (Millar), Gunn, Frizzel.
Ayr U: Crawford; Campbell, Smith, Tiffoney■, Easton, Trouten, McLaughlin, McKeown, Reynolds (Connolly), Roberts, Rodgers (Taggart) (Robertson).
aet.

Inverness CT (1) 3 *(Cox 22, Odihambo 55, Tokely 57)*

Queen's Park (0) 0 1099

Inverness CT: Esson; Tokely, Golabek, Munro (Innes) (McBain), McCann, Cox, Duncan, Blumenshtein (Odihambo), Ross, Rooney, Sanchez.
Queen's Park: Hamilton P; Little, Burns, Gallagher, Brough, McBride M, Anderson, Eagleshan (Quinn T), O'Hara (Harkins), Watt, Murray (Smith).

Peterhead (0) 1 *(Wyness 82)*

Berwick R (0) 0 399

Peterhead: Jarvie; Donald, Mann, MacDonald, Stuart Smith, Sharp (Gethans), McVitie, Emslie, Moore, Wyness, Bavidge.
Berwick R: McCaldon; McLeod, Smith E, McMullan, Notman, McLean, McLaren (Gribben), Currie P, Greenhill D, Gordon (Brazil), Riley (Holmes).

Queen of the S (2) 5 *(Holmes 18, 28 (pen), Johnston 56, Quinn 78, Riley 89)*

Dumbarton (0) 1 *(Carcary 58)* 1329

Queen of the S: Robinson; McGuffie, Reid, Harris, McKenna, Burns, Johnston (Scally), Quinn, Carmichael, Holmes (Reilly), Weatherston (McLaren).
Dumbarton: Grindley; McManus, Gordon, Geggan, McStay (McShane), Wallace, Chaplain, McNiff, Campbell (Brannan), Carcary, Maxwell.

Raith R (3) 4 *(Tade 6, 10, Baird 29, Mole 73)*

East Fife (0) 1 *(Linn 49)* 2187

Raith R: McGurn; Wilson, Murray, Ellis, Dyer, Davidson (Williamson), Walker, Simmons, Ferry (McBride S), Tade (Mole), Baird.
East Fife: Brown M; Muir, Ovenstone, Deland, Durie, Murdoch, Sloan, Tansey (Young), Linn, Johnstone (Smart), Crawford (Byrne).

Ross Co (1) 2 *(Di Giacomo 37, Barrowman 69)*

Livingston (0) 1 *(Russell 48)* 1215

Ross Co: McGovern; Miller, Boyd, McCormack, Morrison, Scott, Lawson, Vigurs■, Brittain, Corcoran (Barrowman), Di Giacomo (Craig).
Livingston: Bullock; Barr C (McNulty), O'Byrne, MacDonald, Talbot, Sinclair (Kyle Jacobs), Fox, Keaghan Jacobs, Barr R, Russell (Da Vita), Winters.

Stenhousemuir (1) 1 *(Anderson 8)*

Brechin C (2) 3 *(McLauchlan 18, Molloy 29, McAllister 53)* 384

Stenhousemuir: McCluskey; Gibb, Thom, Thomson S (Thomson I), Anderson, Motion, Clark (Dalziel), Murray, Williams, Fusco, Quinn (Stirling).
Brechin C: Scott; McLean, McLauchlan, Moyes, Booth, Smith, Molloy, Docherty, Janczyk, McKenna (Byers), McAllister.

Stirling Alb (0) 1 *(Taggart 65)*

Forfar Ath (1) 2 *(Campbell I 16, Campbell R 51)* 599

Stirling Alb: Christie; Corrigan, Allison, Buist, Kane (Robertson), Gibson, Devine (McDonald), Aitken, Taggart, Colquhoun (Borris), Mullen.
Forfar Ath: Gallacher; Mowat, Bishop, Campbell I, Lunan, McCulloch, Bolocheweckyj, Gibson, Campbell R, Hilson (Smith C), Templeman.

Stranraer (0) 1 *(McColm 55)*

Morton (2) 7 *(Kean 27, 50, Holmes 31, Monti 54, Weatherson 71, 76, Kelbie 83)* 470

Stranraer: Marshall; Gallagher, Sharp, Murphy, Bouadji (McAuliffe), Winter (Mitchell G), McColm (Nicoll), Danny Mitchell, Agnew, One, Moore.
Morton: Stewart; MacGregor, Smyth, Evans, McKinlay, Monti, Jenkins (Bachirou), Holmes (O'Brien), Tidser, Weatherson, Kean (Kelbie).

Sunday, 1 August 2010

East Stirling (1) 1 *(Cawley 17)*

Alloa Ath (1) 2 *(Prunty 45, Tully 60)* 543

East Stirling: Andrews; Tully (Ure), Neil, Richardson, Donaldson, Hay, Weaver, Dunn, Cawley (Kelly), Johnston (Team), Maguire.
Alloa Ath: Robertson; Brown, Walker, Dunlop, Gibson, McDonald (McClune), Grant, Smith (McAvoy), Scott, Prunty, Noble (Lister).

SECOND ROUND

Tuesday, 24 August 2010

Alloa Ath (0) 0

Aberdeen (2) 3 *(Hartley 18 (pen), McArdle 38, Maguire 60)* 1649

Alloa Ath: Robertson■; McClune, Walker, Dunlop, Brown, Gibson, Grant, McDonald (Flynn), Smith (Noble), Lister, Prunty (Gormley).

Aberdeen: Howard; McArdle, Ifil, Diamond, Considine, Folly, Hartley (Vernon), Fyvie (Young), Maguire, Magennis (Megginson), Mackie.

Brechin C (0) 2 *(McAllister 63, 64)*
Dundee (0) 2 *(Griffiths 71, 74)* 1090
Brechin C: Nelson; McLean■, Cook, McLauchlan, Moyes, Smith, Molloy, Janczyk (Booth), King (Byers), McAllister, McKenna (Doherty).
Dundee: Douglas; Irvine (Riley), Lockwood, McKeown, Weston, Forsyth■, Adams (Paton), Grant (O'Donnell), Harkins, McMenamin, Griffiths.
aet; Brechin C won 3-1 on penalties.

Dunfermline Ath (1) 3 *(Kirk 44, 86, McDougall 67)*
Clyde (2) 2 *(Strachan 2, McCusker 45)* 1107
Dunfermline Ath: Smith; Woods, Dowie, Keddie, McCann, Gibson, Bell, Cardle (Phinn), Burke (Willis), Kirk, Clarke (McDougall).
Clyde: Hutchison; Park, McMillan, Lithgow, Gray, Henderson, Finlayson, Strachan, Sweeney, McCusker (Sawyers), Mills (Stevenson).

Hearts (2) 4 *(Jonsson 11, Kyle 33, Novikovas 59, Robinson 84)*
Elgin C (0) 0 4922
Hearts: Balogh; Thomson C, Bouzid, Wallace (Santana), Jonsson, Templeton (Robinson), Black (Mrowiec), Palazuelos, Stevenson, Novikovas, Kyle.
Elgin C: Dunn S; Dempsie, Edwards, Kaczan, MacDonald (Frizzel), Inglis J, O'Donoghue, Nicolson, Wilson (Millar), Crooks (Cameron), Gunn.

Partick Th (0) 0
Falkirk (0) 1 *(Flynn 58)* 1619
Partick Th: Halliwell; Kinniburgh, Robertson, Balatoni, Boyle, Paton, Cairney (Flannigan), Rowson, Hodge (Erskine), Donnelly, Doolan (Buchanan).
Falkirk: Olejnik; Marr, McLean, Scobbie, Twaddle, O'Brien, Millar, Flynn, Compton (Alston), Deuchar, Stewart.

Raith R (0) 1 *(Ferry 68)*
Hamilton A (0) 0 1674
Raith R: McGurn; Wilson, Murray, Ellis, Dyer, Davidson, Walker (Hill), Simmons, Ferry, Tade, Baird (Mole).
Hamilton A: Cerny; Canning, Mensing, McQueen, McDonald (Routledge), Skelton (Lyle), McAlister, Imrie, Flavio Paixao, Marco Paixao, Thomas (Gillespie).

St Johnstone (1) 2 *(Dobie 22, Davidson 80)*
Morton (0) 0 1530
St Johnstone: Smith; Maybury, Rutkiewicz, Duberry, Grainger, Millar, Davidson, Taylor, Samuel (Caddis), Parkin (Haber), Dobie (Jackson).
Morton: Cuthbert; Evans, Greacen, McCarthy, Shepherd, Kane (Kelbie), Holmes (Weatherson), Jenkins, Monti, Tidser, Kean.

Wednesday, 25 August 2010

Inverness CT (2) 3 *(Rooney 32 (pen), 49, Munro 38)*
Peterhead (0) 0 1001
Inverness CT: Tuffey; Proctor (Golabek), McBain, Munro, Gillet (Shinnie), Cox, Duncan (Morrison), Ross, Hayes, Odhiambo, Rooney.
Peterhead: Jarvie; Donald, Stuart Smith, MacDonald (Ross S), Gethans, McVitie (Clark), Moore, Sharp, Emslie, Anderson (Strachan), Wyness.

Kilmarnock (3) 6 *(Sammon 4, 5, 90, Wright 32, Kelly 64, Sissoko 77)*
Airdrie U (1) 2 *(McCord 17, Grant 87)* 3066
Kilmarnock: Bell; Clancy, Wright, Sissoko, Gordon, Hay, Kelly, Pascali (Taouil), Dayton (Fowler), Silva (Invincibile), Sammon.
Airdrie U: Ridgers; Bain, Grant, Gibson, Stallard, McGregor (Sally), McCord, Devlin, Johnston, Gemmill, Watt.

Queen of the S (2) 4 *(McLaren 16, Harris 22 (pen), Weatherston 63, Carmichael 76)*
Forfar Ath (0) 1 *(Templeman 57)* 981
Queen of the S: Robinson; McGuffie (Carmichael), Lilley, Reid, Johnston (Scally), Harris, Burns, McKenna, Quinn (Weatherston), McLaren, Holmes.
Forfar Ath: McLean; Tod, Bolocheweckyj, Campbell I, Lunan (Watson), McCulloch, Sellars, Fotheringham M, Campbell R (Gibson), Templeman (Hilson), Deasley.

Ross Co (0) 3 *(Gardyne 69, Brittain 78, Craig 95)*
St Mirren (1) 3 *(McGregor 44, Higdon 79, McGowan 91)* 1239
Ross Co: McGovern; Miller, Boyd, McCormack, Morrison, Brittain, Lawson, Scott (Vigurs), Corcoran, Gardyne, Wood (Craig).
St Mirren: Gallacher; McAusland, Mair, Potter, Travner, McGregor, Murray, McGowan, Lynch (Robb), Dargo (Van Zanten), Higdon.
aet; Ross Co won 4-3 on penalties.

THIRD ROUND

Tuesday, 21 September 2010

Brechin C (0) 0
Motherwell (1) 2 *(Page 16, 59)* 903
Brechin C: Nelson; White (Fusco), Cook, McLauchlan, Moyes, Molloy, Byers (McKenna), Janczyk (King), McAllister, Redman, Booth.
Motherwell: Randolph; Saunders, Page, Reynolds, Craigan, Hateley, Humphrey (McHugh), Lasley (Jennings), Gow (Sutton), Blackman, Forbes.

Falkirk (2) 4 *(Stewart 13, 90, Finnigan 41, Flynn 80)*
Hearts (0) 3 *(Kyle 67 (pen), 78, Santana 74)* 4216
Falkirk: Olejnik; Marr (Duffie), Twaddle, McLean, Scobbie, O'Brien, Flynn, Higginbotham (Millar), Finnigan, McManus (Stewart), Compton.
Hearts: Kello; Thomson C■, Jonsson, Bouzid, Barr, Palazuelos, Santana, Templeton, Kyle, Elliot (Mrowiec), Stevenson.

Rangers (3) 7 *(Jelavic 21, 59, Lafferty 23, 47, 71, Bougherra 38, Naismith 77)*
Dunfermline Ath (1) 2 *(Woods 41, Cardle 46)* 23,120
Rangers: Alexander; Little, Broadfoot, Hutton, Bougherra, Webster (McCulloch), Naismith, Davis, Jelavic (Wylde), Lafferty, Weiss.
Dunfermline Ath: Smith; Woods, McCann, Burke, Dowie, Higgins, Gibson, Bell, Phinn (McDougall), Kirk (Clarke), Cardle (Willis).

St Johnstone (0) 3 *(Morris 68 (pen), Haber 72, Millar 74)*
Queen of the S (0) 0 1624
St Johnstone: Enckelman; Maybury, Grainger, Morris, MacKay, Duberry, Myrie-Williams, Davidson (Anderson), Parkin, Samuel (Haber), Craig (Millar).
Queen of the S: Robinson; Reid, Harris, McKenna (McGuffie), Lilley, Conroy, Burns, Quinn, Holmes (Weatherston), Johnston (Carmichael), McLaren.

Wednesday, 22 September 2010

Aberdeen (1) 3 *(Hartley 10 (pen), Vernon 56, 78)*
Raith R (2) 2 *(Mole 24, Tade 38)* 5936
Aberdeen: Langfield; McArdle, Considine (Vujadinovic), Folly, Diamond, Ifil, Young, Hartley (Jack), Vernon, Maguire, Megginson (Mackie).
Raith R: McGurn; Wilson, Dyer, Murray, Ellis, Davidson, Walker, Simmons, Mole (Baird), Tade, Ferry (Williamson).

Celtic (3) 6 *(Samaras 17, 37, 57, Hooper 21, Stokes 74 (pen), 81)*
Inverness CT (0) 0 17,429
Celtic: Forster; Wilson, Izaguirre (Mulgrew), Ki, Majstorovic, Loovens, Juarez, Ledley (Crosas), Stokes, Hooper, Samaras (Maloney).
Inverness CT: Tuffey; Proctor, Golabek (Foran), Duncan, Tokely, Munro, Shinnie, Cox (McBain), Sutherland, Ross, Hayes.

Kilmarnock (1) 3 *(Hamill 29, 71 (pen), Silva 74)*
Hibernian (1) 1 *(Grounds 8)*   4074
Kilmarnock: Bell; Sissoko (Kelly), Gordon, Hamill, Wright, Pascali, Forrester, Bryson, Silva (Invincibile), Sammon, Eremenko (Clancy).
Hibernian: Brown; Hart, Grounds, Miller, Dickoh, Bamba (Hanlon), Rankin (Galbraith), De Graaf (Wotherspoon), Nish, Riordan, McBride.

Ross Co (0) 1 *(Vigurs 87)*
Dundee U (0) 2 *(Goodwillie 61 (pen), Boyd 101 (og))*
                                                     2269
Ross Co: McGovern; Miller, Morrison (Gregersen), Scott (Smith D), Boyd, McCormack, Brittain, Lawson, Corcoran (Di Giacomo), Vigurs, Wood.
Dundee U: Pernis; Dillon, Dixon, Severin, Dods, Buaben, Robertson D, Gomis (Cadamarteri), Goodwillie (Russell), Daly (Shala), Robertson S.
aet.

QUARTER-FINALS

Tuesday, 26 October 2010
Aberdeen (0) 2 *(Hartley 64, 90 (pen))*
Falkirk (1) 1 *(Khalis 33)*   6710
Aberdeen: Howard; Ifil, Robertson, McArdle, Diamond, Hartley, Jack, Mackie, Vernon, Maguire, Aluko.
Falkirk: Olejnik; Marr, Twaddle, McLean, Khalis, O'Brien, Higginbotham, Millar, Finnigan, Flynn, Stewart.

Motherwell (0) 1 *(Gow 86)*
Dundee U (0) 0   4838
Motherwell: Randolph; Saunders, Hammell, Reynolds, Craigan, Hateley, Humphrey, Jennings (Forbes), Murphy (Sutton), Gow (Page), Blackman.
Dundee U: Pernis; Dillon, Dixon (Douglas), Buaben, Kenneth, Watson, Robertson D (Shala), Gomis, Goodwillie, Daly (Cadamarteri), Robertson S.

Wednesday, 27 October 2010
Kilmarnock (0) 0
Rangers (1) 2 *(Little 25, Naismith 61)*   7561
Kilmarnock: Bell; Hamill, Gordon, Pascali (Rui Miguel), Wright, Sissoko, Kelly (Clancy), Bryson, Eremenko, Sammon, Taouil (Silva).
Rangers: Alexander; Broadfoot, Whittaker, Edu, Weir, Bougherra, Wylde, McCulloch, Naismith (Hutton), Little (Miller), Weiss.

St Johnstone (1) 2 *(Parkin 31, Davidson 54)*
Celtic (3) 3 *(Stokes 8, 13, McGinn 12)*   5151
St Johnstone: Smith; Anderson (Myrie-Williams), Maybury, Davidson, Mackay, Duberry, Grainger, Millar, Parkin, Samuel (Haber), Craig (MacDonald).
Celtic: Forster; Cha, Izaguirre (Mulgrew), Ki, Loovens, Majstorovic, McGinn, Ledley, Samaras, Hooper, Stokes.

SEMI-FINAL

Saturday, 29 January 2011
Aberdeen (0) 1 *(Vernon 61)*
Celtic (4) 4 *(Commons 6, Mulgrew 10, Rogne 21, Stokes 34 (pen))*   38,085
Aberdeen: Langfield; McArdle, Vujadinovic (Jack), Milsom, Diamond, Considine, McNamee (Magennis), Young (Pawlett), Vernon, Maguire, Hartley.
Celtic: Forster; Wilson, Izaguirre, Kayal (McCourt), Rogne (Juarez), Mulgrew, Ledley, Brown, Stokes (Murphy), Hooper, Commons.

Sunday, 30 January 2011
Rangers (1) 2 *(Edu 20, Naismith 75)*
Motherwell (0) 1 *(Lasley 66)*   23,432
Rangers: Alexander; Whittaker, Papac, McCulloch, Weir, Bougherra, Davis, Edu, Jelavic (Weiss), Lafferty (Fleck), Naismith.
Motherwell: Randolph; Saunders, Hammell, Hutchinson, Craigan, Hateley (Jones), Humphrey, Lasley, Sutton, Murphy, Jennings.

FINAL (at Hampden Park)

Sunday, 20 March 2011
Celtic (1) 1 *(Ledley 31)*
Rangers (1) 2 *(Davis 24, Jelavic 98)*   51,181
Celtic: Forster; Wilson, Izaguirre*, Kayal, Rogne (Loovens), Mulgrew, Ledley, Brown (Ki), Samaras, Hooper, Commons (McCourt).
Rangers: Alexander; Whittaker, Papac, Edu, Weir, Bougherra (Hutton), Wylde, Davis, Jelavic (Diouf), Lafferty (Weiss), Naismith.
Referee: C. Thomson.
aet.

LEAGUE CHALLENGE FINALS 1991–2011

Year	Winners	Runners-up	Score	Year	Winners	Runners-up	Score
1990–91	Dundee	Ayr U	3-2	2001–02	Airdrieonians	Alloa Ath	2-1
1991–92	Hamilton A	Ayr U	1-0	2002–03	Queen of the S	Brechin C	2-0
1992–93	Hamilton A	Morton	3-2	2003–04	Inverness CT	Airdrie U	2-0
1993–94	Falkirk	St Mirren	3-0	2004–05	Falkirk	Ross Co	2-1
1994–95	Airdrieonians	Dundee	3-2	2005–06	St Mirren	Hamilton A	2-1
1995–96	Stenhousemuir	Dundee U	0-0	2006–07	Ross Co	Clyde	1-1
	(aet; Stenhousemuir won 5-4 on penalties)				*(aet; Ross Co won 5-4 on penalties)*		
1996–97	Stranraer	St Johnstone	1-0	2007–08	St Johnstone	Dunfermline Ath	3-2
1997–98	Falkirk	Queen of the S	1-0	2008–09	Airdrie U	Ross Co	2-2
1998–99	no competition				*(aet; Airdrie U won 3-2 on penalties)*		
1999–2000	Alloa Ath	Inverness CT	4-4	2009–10	Dundee	Inverness CT	3-2
	(aet; Alloa Ath won 5-4 on penalties)			2010–11	Ross Co	Queen of the S	2-0
2000–01	Airdrieonians	Livingston	2-2				
	(aet; Airdrieonians won 3-2 on penalties)						

ALBA LEAGUE CHALLENGE CUP 2010–11

▪ *Denotes player sent off.*

FIRST ROUND NORTH EAST

Saturday, 24 July 2010
Dundee (0) 2 *(McMenamin 86, Higgins 90)*
Alloa Ath (0) 1 *(Walker 74)* 1522
Dundee: Fox; Irvine, McKeown, Benedictis, Forsyth, Riley (McMenamin), Kerr (McHale), Harkins, O'Donnell, Antoine-Curier (Higgins), Griffiths.
Alloa Ath: Robertson; Gibson, Dunlop, Walker, Brown, Scott (McAvoy), Grant, McDonald, Smith, Prunty (Gormley), Noble (Lister).

Dunfermline Ath (0) 1 *(Kirk 64)*
Arbroath (0) 0 976
Dunfermline Ath: Smith; Woods, Dowie, Keddie, McCann, Willis (Cardle), Bell (Phinn), Mason, Graham, Clarke, Kirk (McDougall).
Arbroath: Hill; Shields, Malcolm, Griffith, McAnespie, Dimilta, McCulloch, Gibson (Swankie), Falkingham, Sheerin P, McGowan (Scott) (Nimmo).

East Fife (0) 4 *(Floan 56 (pen), Crawford 88, Durie 93, Linn 119)*
Brechin C (1) 3 *(McAllister 27, Janczyk 90, Moyes 101)* 497
East Fife: Brown M; Durie, Muir, Ovenstone, Delane, Linn, Murdoch, Floan, Pansey (Cargill), Johnstone (Bryce▪), Crawford.
Brechin C: Nelson▪; McLean, McLauchlan, Moyes, Booth, Molloy, Smith (Docherty), Fusco (Byers), Janczyk, King (Scott), McAllister.
aet.

Elgin C (0) 1 *(Gunn 82)*
Ross Co (0) 2 *(Scott 55, Lawson 62)* 855
Elgin C: Dunn S; Niven, Dempsie, Kaczan, MacDonald (Millar), Inglis J (Edwards), O'Donoghue, Nicolson, Crooks, Gunn, Frizzel (Cameron).
Ross Co: McGovern; Miller, Boyd, McCormack, Morrison, Scott, Lawson (Smith D), Vigurs, Brittain, Corcoran (Barrowman), Di Giacomo (Wood).

Peterhead (1) 5 *(Wyness 7, 56, McNalley 50 (og), Emslie 66, Bavidge 76)*
Montrose (0) 0 357
Peterhead: Jarvie; Donald, Mann, MacDonald (Strachan), Stuart Smith, Sharp (Gethans), McVitie, Emslie, Moore, Wyness, Bavidge (Bruce).
Montrose: Bennett; McNalley, Campbell, Crighton, Pope, Smith, Hegarty (Collier), Davidson, Fleming, Tosh, Nicol.

Raith R (0) 0
Cowdenbeath (0) 1 *(Armstrong 58)* 1564
Raith R: McGurn; Wilson, Murray, Ellis, Dyer, Williamson (Walker), Davidson, Simmons, McBride S (Mole), Weir (Baird), Tade.
Cowdenbeath: Hay; Baxter, Ramsay, Armstrong, Adamson, Fairbairn, Winter, Cameron, Linton, Dempster (Stewart), McKenzie.

Stirling Alb (0) 0
Falkirk (0) 0 1542
Stirling Alb: Christie; Corrigan, Allison, Buist, Forsyth, Gibson, Aitken (Devine), Kane, Robertson, Taggart (Colquhoun), Mullen (Borris).
Falkirk: Marr; Marr, Scobbie, McLean, Twaddle, Millar, O'Brien, Higginbotham (Khalis), Flynn (McLeish), Compton (Finnigan), Stewart.
aet; Stirling Alb won 3-1 on penalties.

FIRST ROUND SOUTH WEST

Saturday, 24 July 2010
Airdrie U (0) 1 *(Muir 51 (pen))*
Ayr U (0) 2 *(Trouten 83, Rodgers 87)* 624
Airdrie U: Ridgers; Bain, Gibson, Grant, Lovering, Muir, Stallard, Devlin, Burns (Morgan), Wallace, Watt (McCabe).
Ayr U: Crawford; Tiffoney, Smith, Donnelly (Connolly 46), Campbell, McLaughlin, Trouten, Woodburn (Robertson), Rodgers, Roberts (Paterson), Easton.

Partick Th (1) 2 *(Buchanan 12, MacBeth 71)*
Clyde (1) 1 *(Strachan 31)* 1759
Partick Th: Halliwell; Paton, Kinniburgh (Bannigan), Robertson, Boyle, MacBeth, Rowson, Hodge, Doolan (Grehan), Donnelly, Buchanan (Burns).
Clyde: Hutchison; Girvan (Mills), McMillan, Park (Gray), McGowan, Finlayson, Stevenson, Sweeney, Strachan, McCusker, Dingwall (Stewart).

Queen of the S (1) 2 *(McGuffie 18, Burns 73)*
Albion R (0) 1 *(Donnelly 48)* 1115
Queen of the S: Robinson; McGuffie, Reid, Harris, McKenna, Burns, Johnston, Quinn, MacLaren, Holmes, Weatherston (Carmichael).
Albion R: Gaston; Reid, Benton, Lumsden, McGowan, Love, Canning, Donnelly, Hamilton C, McLeod (Watt), Dalrymple (Gilmartin) (Ferry).

Queen's Park (1) 3 *(Eagleshan 40, 96, 103 (pen))*
Livingston (1) 2 *(MacDonald 25, Sinclair 119)* 605
Queen's Park: Hamilton P; Little, Burns, Gallagher, Brough, McBride M, Anderson, Eagleshan (Quinn T), O'Hara (Harkins), Smith (Murray).
Livingston: Bullock▪; MacDonald, Malone, Sinclair, O'Byrne, Watson (Kyle Jacobs), Barr R, Keaghan Jacobs, De Vita, Winters (McNulty), Hamill (McDowall).
aet.

Stenhousemuir (3) 3 *(Watson 29 (og), Williams 43, 45)*
Annan Ath (0) 2 *(Halsman 89, Muirhead 90)* 223
Stenhousemuir: McCluskey; Lyle, Gibb, Smith, Thomson S, Anderson, Clark (Thomson I), Motion, Murray, Williams (Dalziel), Quinn (Scullion).
Annan Ath: Summersgill; Muirhead, Watson, Aitken, MacBeth, Sloan S, Jardine (Lawless), Gilfillan, Sloan L (Jamieson), Harty (Halsman), Walker.

Stranraer (0) 1 *(Malcolm 78)*
East Stirling (0) 2 *(Cawley 51, Richardson 117)* 269
Stranraer: David Mitchell; Murphy, Bouadji (McColm), McAuliffe (Moore), Sharp, Danny Mitchell, Nicoll, Agnew, Gallagher, One, Malcolm (Mitchell G).
East Stirling: Andrews; Duigan, Hay, Tully, Weaver, Donaldson (Ure), Richardson, Cawley, Dunn, Maguire (Team), Johnston (Kelly).
aet.

Sunday, 25 July 2010
Dumbarton (0) 0
Morton (0) 0 1301
Dumbarton: Grindley; Nugent, McManus, Gordon, NcNiff, McStay, Geggan, Carcary (Cook), Chaplain (Maxwell), Wilson (Brannan), Campbell.
Morton: Stewart; MacGregor, Smyth, Evans, McKinlay, Holmes, Jenkins (Bachirou), Tidser, Monti (O'Brien), Weatherson (Kelbie), Kean.
aet; Morton won 4-3 on penalties.

SECOND ROUND

Tuesday, 10 August 2010
Ayr U (0) 2 *(Campbell 63, Roberts 73)*
Cowdenbeath (0) 0   556
Ayr U: McWilliams; Smith, Campbell (Robertson), Tiffoney, Keenan, Trouten (Woodburn), McLaughlin, Easton, McKeown, Reynolds (Connolly), Roberts.
Cowdenbeath: Hay; Baxter, Linton (Stewart), Armstrong (Fairbairn), Adamson, Winter, Ramsay, Cameron, O'Brien (Sibanda), Dempster, McKenzie.

Dunfermline Ath (0) 1 *(Kirk 82)*
Queen of the S (0) 1 *(Weatherston 53)*   1160
Dunfermline Ath: Smith; Woods, Dowie, Keddie, Higgins, Gibson (Cardle), Phinn, Mason, Graham, Clarke (Kirk), McDougall (Willis).
Queen of the S: Robinson; McGuffie, Reid, Harris, Weatherston (Reilly), McKenna, Burns, Quinn, McLaren, Carmichael, Holmes (Scally).
aet; Queen of the S won 6-5 on penalties.

East Fife (1) 3 *(Byrne 3, Johnstone 50, Cargill 90)*
Stirling Alb (1) 1 *(Devine 29)*   512
East Fife: Baillie; Eurie, Smart, Deland, Muir, Murdoch, Young, Johnstone (Tansey), Linn (Sloan), Crawford (Cargill), Byrne.
Stirling Alb: Christie; Corrigan, McDonald, Buist (Kirwan), Forsyth, Kane, Gibson (Colquhoun), Devine (Robertson), Taggart, Mullen, Borris.

Partick Th (1) 2 *(Cairney 40, Rowson 80)*
Berwick R (1) 1 *(McLean 28)*   931
Partick Th: Halliwell; Robertson, Balatoni, Boyle, Grehan, Paton, Cairney, Rowson, Flannigan, Donnelly (Erskine), Buchanan (Doolan).
Berwick R: McCaldon; Smith E, McLeod, McMullan, McLean, Greenhill D, McLaren, Currie P, Gordon (Holms), Brazil (O'Reilly), Gribben.

Peterhead (1) 6 *(Stuart Smith 14, Hay 54 (og), Bavidge 66, MacDonald 71, 74, Gethans 84)*
East Stirling (1) 1 *(Maguire 38 (pen))*   368
Peterhead: Jarvie; Donald, MacDonald, Stuart Smith, Gethans, Moore, Anderson (Strachan), McVitie (Young), Emslie, Wyness, Bavidge.
East Stirling: Andrews; Neil, Tully, Richardson (Johnston), Hay, Donaldson, Walker, Weaver, Dunn, Maguire (Kelly), Stevenson (Cawley).

Queen's Park (1) 2 *(Watt 31, McBride M 70)*
Forfar Ath (0) 3 *(Templeman 74, Deasley 76, Sellars 94)*   404
Queen's Park: Strain; Little, Gallagher, Brough, Burns, McBride M, Anderson (Longworth), Quinn T, Watt, Eagleshan, Smith (Murray).
Forfar Ath: McLean; Bolocheweckyj, Bishop, Tod, Campbell I[■], Lunan, Fotheringham M (Mowat), Sellars, Watson (Hilson), Templeman, Gibson (Deasley).

Ross Co (1) 3 *(McKinlay 37 (og), Gardyne 58, Scott 90)*
Morton (1) 1 *(Kelbie 16)*   856
Ross Co: McGovern; Miller (Lawson), Boyd, Morrison, McCormack, Scott, Corcoran, Brittain, Gardyne, Barrowman (Wood), Di Giacomo.
Morton: Cuthbert; Evans, Smyth, McCaffrey, McKinlay, Jenkins (Monti), Tidser (Weatherson), Holmes, Bachirou, Kean, Kelbie.

Stenhousemuir (2) 4 *(Williams 9, Anderson 16, Quinn 63, Motion 83)*
Dundee (0) 1 *(Griffiths 74)*   665
Stenhousemuir: McCluskey; Lyle, Thom, Thomson S, Clark (Motion), Anderson (Scullion), Thomson I, Murray, Fusco, Williams (Quinn), Dalziel.
Dundee: Fox; Irvine, McKeown, Weston (Paton), Sansara, Forsyth, McHale (O'Donnell), Harkins, Riley (McMenamin), Higgins, Griffiths.

QUARTER-FINALS

Saturday, 4 September 2010
Forfar Ath (0) 0
Ross Co (1) 2 *(Lawson 11, 70)*   552
Forfar Ath: McLean; Bishop, Tod, Bolochewekyj[■], McCulloch, Lunan, Sellars (Deasley), Fotheringham M, Gibson, Templeman (Smith C), Campbell R (Hilson).
Ross Co: McGovern; Miller, McCormack, Boyd, Morrison, Scott[■], Lawson, Brittain, Wood (Di Giacomo), Vigurs (Kettlewell), Gardyne (Corcoran).

Partick Th (2) 2 *(Doolan 3, 33)*
Ayr U (1) 1 *(Rodgers 36)*   1831
Partick Th: Halliwell; Robertson (Erskine), McNamara, Balatoni, Boyle, Paton, Bannigan (Flannigan), Rowson, Hodge, Buchanan (Donnelly), Doolan.
Ayr U: Crawford; Campbell, Smith, Tiffoney (McKay), Taggart, Trouten, Keenan (Reynolds), McLaughlin, Easton, Rodgers, Roberts.

Queen of the S (1) 5 *(Burns 32, 46, 79, Ovenstone 64 (og), Harris 90)*
East Fife (0) 0   1751
Queen of the S: Robinson; Reid, Lilley, Harris, Johnston (Carmichael), Burns, McKenna (McShane), Conroy, McLaren, Weatherston (Scally), Holmes.
East Fife: Brown; Muir, Smart, Murdock, Durie, Sloan (Cargill), Johnstone (Ovenstone), Young, Linn, Byrne, Hislop (Crawford).

Sunday, 5 September 2010
Peterhead (2) 3 *(Wyness 9, 50, Gethans 43)*
Stenhousemuir (0) 1 *(Dalziel 76)*   442
Peterhead: Bateman; Donald, MacDonald, Stuart Smith, Gethans, Moore, McVitie (Strachan), Anderson, Emslie (Clark), Bavidge, Wyness.
Stenhousemuir: Brown; Lyle, Fusco, Smith, Thomson S, Anderson (Scullion), Thomson I, Clark (Stirling), Murray, Dalziel, Williams.

SEMI-FINALS

Saturday, 9 October 2010
Peterhead (0) 1 *(Bavidge 78)*
Queen of the S (0) 2 *(Reid 66, Holmes 69)*   1003
Peterhead: Bateman; Donald, MacDonald, Stuart Smith, Moore, McVitie (Strachan), Anderson, Emslie, Sharp, Bavidge, Wyness (Ross D).
Queen of the S: Robinson; McGuffie, Lilley, Harris, Reid, Johnston, Burns, Quinn (Scally), Conroy, McLaren, Holmes (Weatherston).

Sunday, 10 October 2010
Ross Co (0) 2 *(Morrison 54, Barrowman 88)*
Partick Th (1) 2 *(Kinniburgh 8, Boyle 64)*   1307
Ross Co: McGovern; Miller, Boyd, McCormack, Morrison, Brittain, Vigurs (Lawson), Scott, Wood (Barrowman), Craig, Gardyne.
Partick Th: Halliwell; Boyle, McNamara, Archibald, Kinniburgh (Hodge), Robertson, Paton, Flannigan, Cairney, Doolan (Buchanan), Grehan (Erskine).
aet; Ross Co won 4-3 on penalties.

FINAL (at Perth)

Sunday, 10 April 2011
Queen of the S (0) 0
Ross Co (2) 2 *(Barrowman 9, Vigurs 39)*   5124
Queen of the S: Hutton; Reid, Lilley, McGuffie, Harris, Johnston, Burns, McKenna, McLaren, Holmes, Carmichael (Degnan).
Ross Co: McGovern; Miller, Flynn, Boyd, Fitzpatrick, Brittain, Kettlewell, Lawson (Morrison), Vigurs, Gardyne (Milne), Barrowman (Wood).
Referee: E. Norris.

SCOTTISH CUP FINALS 1874–2011

Year	Winners	Runners-up	Score
1874	Queen's Park	Clydesdale	2-0
1875	Queen's Park	Renton	3-0
1876	Queen's Park	Third Lanark	2-0 after 1-1 draw
1877	Vale of Leven	Rangers	3-2 after 0-0 and 1-1 draws
1878	Vale of Leven	Third Lanark	1-0
1879	Vale of Leven*	Rangers	
1880	Queen's Park	Thornlibank	3-0
1881	Queen's Park†	Dumbarton	3-1
1882	Queen's Park	Dumbarton	4-1 after 2-2 draw
1883	Dumbarton	Vale of Leven	2-1 after 2-2 draw
1884	Queen's Park‡	Vale of Leven	
1885	Renton	Vale of Leven	3-1 after 0-0 draw
1886	Queen's Park	Renton	3-1
1887	Hibernian	Dumbarton	2-1
1888	Renton	Cambuslang	6-1
1889	Third Lanark§	Celtic	2-1
1890	Queen's Park	Vale of Leven	2-1 after 1-1 draw
1891	Hearts	Dumbarton	1-0
1892	Celtic¶	Queen's Park	5-1
1893	Queen's Park	Celtic	2-1
1894	Rangers	Celtic	3-1
1895	St Bernard's	Renton	2-1
1896	Hearts	Hibernian	3-1
1897	Rangers	Dumbarton	5-1
1898	Rangers	Kilmarnock	2-0
1899	Celtic	Rangers	2-0
1900	Celtic	Queen's Park	4-3
1901	Hearts	Celtic	4-3
1902	Hibernian	Celtic	1-0
1903	Rangers	Hearts	2-0 after 1-1 and 0-0 draws
1904	Celtic	Rangers	3-2
1905	Third Lanark	Rangers	3-1 after 0-0 draw
1906	Hearts	Third Lanark	1-0
1907	Celtic	Hearts	3-0
1908	Celtic	St Mirren	5-1
1909	••		
1910	Dundee	Clyde	2-1 after 2-2 and 0-0 draws
1911	Celtic	Hamilton A	2-0 after 0-0 draw
1912	Celtic	Clyde	2-0
1913	Falkirk	Raith R	2-0
1914	Celtic	Hibernian	4-1 after 0-0 draw
1920	Kilmarnock	Albion R	3-2
1921	Partick Th	Rangers	1-0
1922	Morton	Rangers	1-0
1923	Celtic	Hibernian	1-0
1924	Airdrieonians	Hibernian	2-0
1925	Celtic	Dundee	2-1
1926	St Mirren	Celtic	2-0
1927	Celtic	East Fife	3-1
1928	Rangers	Celtic	4-0
1929	Kilmarnock	Rangers	2-0
1930	Rangers	Partick Th	2-1 after 0-0 draw
1931	Celtic	Motherwell	4-2 after 2-2 draw
1932	Rangers	Kilmarnock	3-0 after 1-1 draw
1933	Celtic	Motherwell	1-0
1934	Rangers	St Mirren	5-0
1935	Rangers	Hamilton A	2-1
1936	Rangers	Third Lanark	1-0
1937	Celtic	Aberdeen	2-1
1938	East Fife	Kilmarnock	4-2 after 1-1 draw
1939	Clyde	Motherwell	4-0
1947	Aberdeen	Hibernian	2-1
1948	Rangers	Morton	1-0 after 1-1 draw
1949	Rangers	Clyde	4-1
1950	Rangers	East Fife	3-0
1951	Celtic	Motherwell	1-0
1952	Motherwell	Dundee	4-0
1953	Rangers	Aberdeen	1-0 after 1-1 draw
1954	Celtic	Aberdeen	2-1
1955	Clyde	Celtic	1-0 after 1-1 draw
1956	Hearts	Celtic	3-1
1957	Falkirk	Kilmarnock	2-1 after 1-1 draw
1958	Clyde	Hibernian	1-0
1959	St Mirren	Aberdeen	3-1
1960	Rangers	Kilmarnock	2-0
1961	Dunfermline Ath	Celtic	2-0 after 0-0 draw
1962	Rangers	St Mirren	2-0
1963	Rangers	Celtic	3-0 after 1-1 draw

Year	Winners	Runners-up	Score
1964	Rangers	Dundee	3-1
1965	Celtic	Dunfermline Ath	3-2
1966	Rangers	Celtic	1-0 after 0-0 draw
1967	Celtic	Aberdeen	2-0
1968	Dunfermline Ath	Hearts	3-1
1969	Celtic	Rangers	4-0
1970	Aberdeen	Celtic	3-1
1971	Celtic	Rangers	2-1 after 1-1 draw
1972	Celtic	Hibernian	6-1
1973	Rangers	Celtic	3-2
1974	Celtic	Dundee U	3-0
1975	Celtic	Airdrieonians	3-1
1976	Rangers	Hearts	3-1
1977	Celtic	Rangers	1-0
1978	Rangers	Aberdeen	2-1
1979	Rangers	Hibernian	3-2 after 0-0 and 0-0 draws
1980	Celtic	Rangers	1-0
1981	Rangers	Dundee U	4-1 after 0-0 draw
1982	Aberdeen	Rangers	4-1 (aet)
1983	Aberdeen	Rangers	1-0 (aet)
1984	Aberdeen	Celtic	2-1 (aet)
1985	Celtic	Dundee U	2-1
1986	Aberdeen	Hearts	3-0
1987	St Mirren	Dundee U	1-0 (aet)
1988	Celtic	Dundee U	2-1
1989	Celtic	Rangers	1-0
1990	Aberdeen	Celtic	0-0 (aet)
		(Aberdeen won 9-8 on penalties)	
1991	Motherwell	Dundee U	4-3 (aet)
1992	Rangers	Airdrieonians	2-1
1993	Rangers	Aberdeen	2-1
1994	Dundee U	Rangers	1-0
1995	Celtic	Airdrieonians	1-0
1996	Rangers	Hearts	5-1
1997	Kilmarnock	Falkirk	1-0
1998	Hearts	Rangers	2-1
1999	Rangers	Celtic	1-0
2000	Rangers	Aberdeen	4-0
2001	Celtic	Hibernian	3-0
2002	Rangers	Celtic	3-2
2003	Rangers	Dundee	1-0
2004	Celtic	Dunfermline Ath	3-1
2005	Celtic	Dundee U	1-0
2006	Hearts	Gretna	1-1 (aet)
		(Hearts won 4-2 on penalties)	
2007	Celtic	Dunfermline Ath	1-0
2008	Rangers	Queen of the S	3-2
2009	Rangers	Falkirk	1-0
2010	Dundee U	Ross Co	3-0
2011	Celtic	Motherwell	3-0

*Vale of Leven awarded cup, Rangers failing to appear for replay after 1-1 draw.
†After Dumbarton protested the first game, which Queen's Park won 2-1.
‡Queen's Park awarded cup, Vale of Leven failing to appear.
§Replay by order of Scottish FA because of playing conditions in first match, won 3-0 by Third Lanark.
¶After mutually protested game which Celtic won 1-0.
**Owing to riot, the cup was withheld after two drawn games – between Celtic and Rangers 2-2 and 1-1.

SCOTTISH CUP WINS

Celtic 35, Rangers 33, Queen's Park 10, Aberdeen 7, Hearts 7, Clyde 3, Kilmarnock 3, St Mirren 3, Vale of Leven 3, Dundee U 2, Dunfermline Ath 2, Falkirk 2, Hibernian 2, Motherwell 2, Renton 2, Third Lanark 2, Airdrieonians 1, Dumbarton 1, Dundee 1, East Fife 1, Morton 1, Partick Th 1, St Bernard's 1.

APPEARANCES IN FINAL

Celtic 54, Rangers 50, Aberdeen 15, Hearts 13, Queen's Park 12, Hibernian 11, Dundee U 9, Kilmarnock 8, Motherwell 7, Vale of Leven 7, Clyde 6, Dumbarton 6, St Mirren 6, Third Lanark 6, Dundee 5, Dunfermline Ath 5, Renton 5, Airdrieonians 4, Falkirk 4, East Fife 3, Hamilton A 2, Morton 2, Partick Th 2, Albion R 1, Cambuslang 1, Clydesdale 1, Gretna 1, Queen of the S 1, Raith R 1, Ross Co 1, St Bernard's 1, Thornlibank 1.

ACTIVE NATION SCOTTISH CUP 2010–11

■ *Denotes player sent off.*

FIRST ROUND

Beith v Linlithgow Rose	2-0
Civil Service Strollers v Wigtown & Bladnoch	1-2
Coldstream v Forres Mechanics	1-3
Deveronvale v Inverurie Loco Works	0-0, 5-0
Edinburgh City v Clachnacuddin	1-0
Edinburgh Univ v Brora R	2-2, 1-2
Fraserburgh v St Cuthbert W	3-3, 1-3
Gala Fairydean v Sunnybank	1-6
Glasgow Univ v Burntisland	1-0
Golspie Sutherland v Fort William	2-2, 3-2
Hawick Royal Albert v Dalbeattie Star	0-3
Huntly v Girvan	2-2, 1-2
Lossiemouth v Whitehill Welfare	0-2
Newton Stewart v Preston Athletic	1-1, 0-3
Rothes v Nairn Co	2-2, 1-4
Selkirk v Bo'ness	1-6
Vale of Leithen v Keith	1-3

SECOND ROUND

Deveronvale v Dalbeattie Star	1-0
Forres Mechanics v East Stirling	0-0, 0-4
Preston Ath v Annan Ath	0-0, 0-5
Clyde v Berwick R	1-2
Wigtown & Bladnoch v Buckie Th	1-7
Beith v Glasgow Univ	8-1
Nairn Co v Cove R	0-1
Keith v Spartans	0-3
Stranraer v St Cuthbert W	9-0
Bo'ness v Queen's Park	2-1
Golspie Sutherland v Girvan	2-2, 0-4
Montrose v Arbroath	1-1, 3-2
Edinburgh C v Threave R	2-4
Albion R v Sunnybank	0-1
Elgin C v Brora R	5-3
Whitehill Welfare v Wick Academy	4-3

THIRD ROUND

Saturday, 20 November 2010

Airdrie U (0) 2 *(Lovering 79, Bain 90)*
Beith (1) 2 *(McKeown 32, McLean 63)*   1412
Airdrie U: Ridgers; Bain, Forrest, Gibson, Lovering,
Johnston (Sally), Devlin, Stevenson, Muir (Watt),
Wallace, Craig (Donnelly).
Beith: Robertson; McShane■, McCulloch, Sheridan,
Staunton, McKeown, Bradley, McGarvey (Spence),
Stewart (O'Keane), Reid (Carrouth), McLean.

Alloa Ath (2) 4 *(McDonald 41, 42, 66, Noble 48)*
Raith R (1) 2 *(Baird 27, Murray 86)*   1039
Alloa Ath: Ewings; Grant, Gibson, Walker, Dunlop,
Gormley (Hay), McDonald (Scott), McGowan, Smith,
Prunty, Noble (Lister).
Raith R: McGurn; Wilson, Murray, Ellis, Dyer■,
Williamson (Ferry), Walker, Davidson, McBride S
(Tade), Baird, Weir (Nanetti).

Ayr U (2) 5 *(Bannigan 44, Roberts 45 (pen), 74 (pen),
Rodgers 86, 90)*
Sunnybank (0) 0   1069
Ayr U: Crawford; Malone, Smith, Tiffoney, Easton,
McLaughlin (Kelly), Trouten (Woodburn), Bannigan,
Rodgers, Roberts, McCann (Robertson).
Sunnybank: Sweeney L; Thompson, Steel W■, Clark
(Bartlett M■), Douglas, Adams, Greig, Fettes (Shand),
Bartlett S, Gordon (Steel C), McAlister.

Bo'ness (0) 0
Buckie Th (1) 2 *(Charlesworth 5, 57)*   1301
Bo'ness: McGurk; Snowdon, Duffin, McQueen, Fleming
(Crawford), Ballantine (Mcfadyen), Fraser, Shirra,
Donnelly, Shields (Anson), Walker.
Buckie Th: Main; Angus, MacKinnon, Morrison, Munro
H, Napier (MacRae), Stewart, Brown (Shewan),
Davidson, Sutherland, Charlesworth (Gardiner).

Brechin C (1) 2 *(McKenna 32, 57)*
Annan Ath (0) 2 *(Muirhead 52, Gilfillan 68)*   402
Brechin C: Nelson; McLean, Cook, McLauchlan, White
D, Fusco, Mulrooney (Redman), Molloy, Janczyk
(Doherty), McAllister, McKenna (Byers).
Annan Ath: Jamieson; Muirhead (Steele), MacBeth,
Nielson, Aitken, Gilfillan, Sloan S, Jardine, Halsman,
Harty, Cox.

Cove R (0) 0
Berwick R (2) 3 *(Brazil 26, Greenhill 30, McMullan 67)*
                                                            250
Cove R: McKenzie; Redford, Lawrie, Watson E, Jaffrey,
McCulloch (Tosh), Johnston, Livingstone (Webster),
Black, Watson C (Park), Milne.
Berwick R: Peat; Smith E, Thomson, McLeod, McLean,
Notman (Little), McMullan, Currie P, Greenhill D,
Brazil, Gordon.

Dumbarton (1) 1 *(Geggan 11)*
Morton (1) 2 *(Graham 42, 49)*   905
Dumbarton: Grindley; Devlin N, Nugent, McNiff,
Creaney (Chisholm), Brannan, Geggan, McLeish
(McStay), Cook, McShane, Campbell (Smith G 60).
Morton: Stewart; MacGregor■, Smyth, McCaffrey,
McKinlay, Holmes (O'Brien), Young (Bachirou), Tidser,
Monti (Weatherson), Kean, Graham.

East Fife (2) 3 *(Sloan 24 (pen), Johnstone 45, Hislop 47)*
Forfar Ath (0) 1 *(Tod 81)*   695
East Fife: Brown M; Durie (McGowan), Campbell,
Smart, Ovenstone, Linn, Muir, Sloan, Johnstone, Hislop,
Crawford (Young).
Forfar Ath: Gallacher; Divine (Sellars), Tod, Tulloch,
Campbell I, Gibson, Mowat, Campbell R (Brady),
Deasley (Smith C), Templeman, Hilson.

Elgin C (2) 2 *(Gunn 61, Crooks 78)*
Livingston (0) 1 *(Russell 74)*   802
Elgin C: Donnelly; Dempsie, Duff, Nicolson, Kaczan,
Cameron, O'Donoghue (Niven), Inglis J, Wilson
(Millar), Crooks, Gunn (MacDonald).
Livingston: Bullock; Barr C, MacDonald, Watson,
Malone, Kyle Jacobs (De Vita), Fox, Sinclair, Barr R,
Russell, Winters (Scougall).

Montrose (2) 3 *(Tosh 21 (pen), 40 (pen), Pope 75)*
Whitehill Welfare (1) 1 *(Hall 7)*   435
Montrose: Giordano (Wood); Hegarty, Cameron, Pope,
Crighton, McCord, McNalley, Davidson (Watson),
Sinclair, Tosh, Boyle (Thompson).
Whitehill Welfare: Benjaoui; Cornett■, Morrison, Kidd W,
Adamson (Caddow), Hall (Taylor), McGlashan, Kidd A,
Devlin, Allum (Beattie), Gormley.

Peterhead (1) 2 *(Strachan 42, McVitie 50)*
Cowdenbeath (0) 0   510
Peterhead: Bateman; Donald, Mann, MacDonald, Stuart
Smith, Strachan, Anderson, Clark, Bavidge, Wyness
(McVitie), Sharp.
Cowdenbeath: Hay; Baxter, Mbu, Armstrong (Ramsay),
Linton, Fairbairn (Ferguson), Cameron, Winter, Sibanda,
Dempster, Stewart (McKenzie).

Ross Co (2) 4 *(Miller 29, Barrowman 45, 90, Craig 62)*
Deveronvale (0) 1 *(McKenzie 80 (pen))*   1170
Ross Co: McGovern; Miller (Kettlewell), Lawson[■], Flynn, Morrison, Gardyne, McCormack, Brittain, Craig (Wood), Barrowman, Vigurs (Scott).
Deveronvale: Blanchard; Rennie (Carstairs), Chisholm, Henry, Dlugonski, Blackhall (McKenzie), Smith D (Gauld), Smith M, McGown, Lombardi, Rodger.

Spartans (0) 1 *(McLeod 54)*
East Stirling (1) 2 *(Weaver 42, Dunn 69)*   601
Spartans: Flockhart; Archibald, Townsley, Sidwright, Fowlie (O'Donnell), Malin, King, Manson, Besley (Kader), Henretty, McLeod.
East Stirling: Andrews; Tully (Maguire), Hay, Walker, Richardson, Weaver, Cawley (Watts), Beveridge (Kelly), Dunn, Johnston, Neil.

Stenhousemuir (0) 2 *(Stirling 67, Williams 90)*
Threave R (1) 2 *(Middlemass P 31, Warren 56)*   429
Stenhousemuir: Brown; Lyle, Love (Quinn), Gibb (Murray), Smith, Thom, Anderson (Stirling), Thomson I, Plenderleith, Dickson, Williams.
Threave R: Parker; Wilby, Kerr, Patterson, Fingland, Irons (Milligan), Baty, Middlemass P (Cook), Struthers, Donley (Middlemass G), Warren.

Stirling Alb (0) 1 *(Smith 73)*
Partick Th (0) 3 *(Cairney 59, Donnelly 86, Grehan 90)* 1146
Stirling Alb: Christie; Corrigan, Buist, Allison, Kane (McHale), Gibson (Comvalius), Heeking, Aitken, Robertson, Borris (Flood), Smith.
Partick Th: Fox; Paton, Kinniburgh, Archibald, Boyle, Cairney, Hodge, Rowson, Erskine (Campbell), Doolan (Donnelly), Buchanan (Grehan).

Stranraer (2) 4 *(Agnew 34 (pen), Malcolm 42, 80, Gallacher 48)*
Girvan (1) 2 *(Moffat 6, Connell 55)*   840
Stranraer: David Mitchell; Gallagher, Murphy, Gallacher (Sharp), Noble, Agnew, Danny Mitchell, Winter, One (McColm), Moore, Malcolm.
Girvan: Leavy; McGilp, Cunningham, Peacock (Shankland), McCrae, Love, Connell (Murphy), Biggart, Gilmour (Harvey), Wallace, Moffat.

THIRD ROUND REPLAYS

Tuesday, 4 January 2011

Annan Ath (1) 2 *(Gilfillan 6, Aitken 55)*
Brechin C (4) 5 *(McAllister 2, 82, Molloy 23, McKenna 38, Byers 41)*   512
Annan Ath: Jamieson; Aitken, Neilson, MacBeth (Steele), Muirhead, Halsman, Sloan S (Felvus), Jardine (Sloan L), Gilfillan, Cox, Harty.
Brechin C: Nelson; White D, Cook, McLean, Moyes, Molloy, Docherty, Byers (Redman), Janczyk (Fusco), McAllister, McKenna (Archdeacon).

Beith (0) 3 *(O'Keane 62, Craig 65, Fraser 79)*
Airdrie U (3) 4 *(Gemmill 7, 42, Stevenson 12, McCord 48)*   1809
Beith: Robertson; Staunton, McCulloch, Sheridan, Carruth (O'Keane), Bradley, Stewart (Fraser), McKeown[■], McGarvey, Reid (Craig), McLean.
Airdrie U: Ridgers; Forrest, Grant, Gibson, McCord (Donnelly), Stevenson, Fisher, Bain, Devlin, Johnston, Gemmill (Muir).

Wednesday, 12 January 2011

Threave R (0) 1 *(Donley 48)*
Stenhousemuir (2) 5 *(Clarke 15, 25, Williams 57, 67, Smith 81)*   240
Threave R: Parker; Wilby, Kerr, Patterson, Fingland, Middlemass P (Cook), Dunglinson, Baty (Middlemass G), Donley (Milligan), Struthers, Warren.
Stenhousemuir: McCluskey; Lyle, Dickson, Thom, Smith, Thomson I, Anderson, Clarke (Motion), Williams (Quinn), Dalziel, Murray.

FOURTH ROUND

Saturday, 8 January 2011

Aberdeen (4) 6 *(Maguire 13, 24, 42, Vernon 30, 81, Magennis 90)*
East Fife (0) 0   6918
Aberdeen: Langfield; McNamee (Vujadinovic), Considine, McArdle, Diamond, Hartley, Young (Magennis), Jack, Vernon, Maguire, Aluko (Pawlett).
East Fife: Brown M; McGowan, Ovenstone, Campbell (Durie), Smart, Muir, Linn, Crawford (Weir), Hislop, Sloan, Johnstone (Young).

Dundee U (0) 0
Ross Co (0) 0   4041
Dundee U: Pernis; Dillon, Dixon, Watson, Kenneth, Buaben, Robertson S, Gomis, Daly (Cadamarteri), Russell (Shala), Douglas.
Ross Co: McGovern; Marr, Morrison, Kettlewell, Boyd, Flynn, Gardyne (Scott), Craig, Barrowman, Brittain, Vigurs (Wood).

Hamilton A (1) 2 *(Hasselbaink 33, Flavio Paixao 90)*
Alloa Ath (0) 0   1054
Hamilton A: Cerny; Graham, Buchanan, Canning, Mensing, McLaughlin (Skelton), Gillespie, Imrie, Flavio Paixao, Marco Paixao (McAlister), Hasselbaink (Casalinuovo).
Alloa Ath: Robertson[■]; McClune, Dunlop, Gibson, Walker, Hay (Lister), Scott (Gormley), McDonald, Prunty, McGowan (Grant), Noble.

Hibernian (0) 0
Ayr U (0) 0   6056
Hibernian: Brown; Hanlon, Grounds, Miller, Dickoh, Thicot, Zemmama (Trakys), Murray (McBride), Duffy (Wotherspoon), Riordan, Galbraith.
Ayr U: Crawford; Tiffoney, Smith, Malone, Campbell, McCann (Robertson), Trouten, McLaughlin, Bannigan, Roberts (Rodgers), Easton (Woodburn).

Inverness CT (0) 2 *(Sanchez 89, Rooney 90)*
Elgin C (0) 0   2808
Inverness CT: Tuffley; Duff, Shinnie, Innes, Tokely, Cox, Odhiambo (Sutherland), Munro, Foran (Sanchez), Rooney, Ross.
Elgin C: Donnelly; Dempsie (Niven), Inglis J, Kaczan, Duff, Crooks (Millar), Gunn, O'Donoghue, Cameron, Nicolson, Frizzel.

Montrose (1) 2 *(Tosh 26, 90)*
Dunfermline Ath (0) 2 *(Clarke 73, Kirk 81)*   1030
Montrose: Wood; McNalley, Pope, Campbell, Tweed, Cameron, McCord (Crighton), Masson (Davidson), Tosh, Smith (Boyle), Sinclair.
Dunfermline Ath: Smith; Woods, McCann, Mason, McGregor, Keddie, Willis, Phinn, McDougall (Clarke), Kirk, Graham D.

St Mirren (0) 0
Peterhead (0) 0   2312
St Mirren: Gallacher; McAusland (Van Zanten), Travner, Goodwin, McGregor, Potter, Cregg, Thomson, Higdon (Wardlaw), Dargo, McGowan (Mooy).
Peterhead: Bateman; Donald, Stuart Smith, Mann (MacDonald), Ross S (Emslie), McVitie, Sharp, Clark (Gethans), Bavidge, Strachan, Ross D.

Sunday, 9 January 2011

Berwick R (0) 0
Celtic (1) 2 *(Majstorovic 17, Brown 82)*   3877
Berwick R: Peat; Smith E, Thomson, McLean, McLeod, Greenhill D, McLaren, Currie P, Gribben (Brazil), Notman, Little (McMullan).
Celtic: Zaluska; Wilson, Mulgrew, Kayal (Crosas), Majstorovic, Rogne, Forrest, Ledley, Samaras (Stokes), McCourt, Ljungberg (Brown).

Dundee (0) 0
Motherwell (1) 4 *(Sutton 3, 47, Jennings 81, Murphy 87)*
4285
Dundee: Douglas; Irvine, Lockwood, O'Donnell, McKeown, Weston, Stewart (Benedictis), Harkins, Griffiths■, Higgins, Forsyth.
Motherwell: Randolph; Fitzpatrick, Hammell, Reynolds, Craigan, Hateley, Humphrey, Jennings, Sutton, Murphy (McHugh), Lasley (Forbes).

Monday, 10 January 2011
Rangers (2) 3 *(McCulloch 20, Lafferty 37, Whittaker 71 (pen))*
Kilmarnock (0) 0
13,215
Rangers: McGregor; Whittaker, Papac, McCulloch, Weir, Bougherra, Davis, Ness (Edu), Beattie (Weiss), Lafferty, Naismith (Foster).
Kilmarnock: Bell; Hamill (Clancy), Hay, Pascali (Rui Miguel), Wright, Sissoko, Taouil, Bryson (Silva), Eremenko, Sammon, Kelly.

Tuesday, 11 January 2011
Falkirk (1) 2 *(Millar 37, Compton 72)*
Partick Th (1) 2 *(Buchanan 8, Doolan 86)*
2039
Falkirk: Olejnik; Duffy, Scobbie, McLean, Mitchell (Compton), Twaddle, O'Brien, Millar, Higginbotham (Finnigan), Flynn, Stewart.
Partick Th: Fox; Paton, Boyle, McNamara (Erskene), Kinniburgh, Archibald, Cairney, Rowson, Buchanan (Fraser), Donnelly, Hodge (Doolan).

Hearts (0) 0
St Johnstone (0) 1 *(MacDonald 86)*
6261
Hearts: MacDonald; Mrowiec, Jonsson, Zaliukas, Bouzid, Palazuelos, Stevenson, Black (Templeton), Kyle (Obua), Elliott, Novikas (Elliot).
St Johnstone: Enckelman; MacKay, Grainger, Morris, Anderson, Duberry, Davidson, Millar, Parkin (MacDonald), Samuel (May), Craig (Maybury).

Queen of the S (0) 1 *(McMenamin 66)*
Brechin C (2) 2 *(Byers 17, McAllister 35)*
1169
Queen of the S: Robinson; Reid, Harris, McKenna, Lilley (Johnston), McGuffie, Burns, Quinn (Carmichael), Holmes, McMenamin, McLaren (Weatherston).
Brechin C: Nelson; McLean, Cook, White D, Moyes, Janczyk, Byers (Fusco), Molloy, McAllister, McKenna (Redman), Docherty (Scott).

Tuesday, 18 January 2011
Morton (0) 2 *(Graham 52, Kean 64)*
Airdrie U (1) 2 *(Mackay-Steven 23, Stevenson 47)* 1339
Morton: Stewart; Evans, McKinlay, Smyth■, McCaffrey, Tidser, Jenkins, Holmes (Bachirou), Kean, Graham (Weatherson), O'Brien.
Airdrie U: Ridgers; Bain (Muir), Goodall (Lovering), Grant, Forrest, Devlin, Stevenson, McCord, Gemmill, Ferguson (Craig), Mackay-Steven.

Stenhousemuir (0) 0
Stranraer (0) 0
405
Stenhousemuir: McCluskey; Lyle, Dickson, Thom, Smith, Thomson I, Anderson, Clark (Motion), Williams (Plenderleith), Dalziel (Quinn), Murphy.
Stranraer: David Mitchell; Gallagher, Sharp, Murphy, McAuliffe (McColm), Agnew, One (Moore), Danny Mitchell, Malcolm, Winter, Noble.

Wednesday, 19 January 2011
East Stirling (0) 1 *(Cawley 88)*
Buckie Th (0) 0
630
East Stirling: Andrews; Donaldson, Richardson (Neil), Hay, Tully, Walker, Cawley, Weaver, McGuire (Ure), Dunn, Johnstone (Team).

Buckie Th: Main; Munro H, Angus, Stewart, Small, Morrison, Murray■, Brown (MacRae), Low, Charlesworth (Gardiner), Sutherland (Davidson).
East Stirling fielded an ineligible player; Buckie Th awarded the tie.

FOURTH ROUND REPLAYS
Tuesday, 18 January 2011
Ayr U (1) 1 *(Roberts 19)*
Hibernian (0) 0
3826
Ayr U: Crawford; Tiffoney, Smith, Malone, Campbell, McCann, Bannigan, McLaughlin, Rodgers, Roberts (Robertson), Easton.
Hibernian: Smith; Hart (Wotherspoon), Hanlon (Booth), Miller, Dickoh, Murray, Rankin, McBride, Nish, Riordan, Duffy (Zemmama).

Dunfermline Ath (2) 5 *(Kirk 11, McDougall 40, Graham D 48, 52, Gibson 61 (pen))*
Montrose (0) 3 *(Woods 47 (og), Tosh 72, 88 (pen))* 1541
Dunfermline Ath: Smith■; Woods, McCann, Mason (Phinn), McGregor, Keddie, Gibson (Willis), Thomson, McDougall, Kirk (Clarke), Graham D.
Montrose: Wood; McNalley, Pope, Campbell, Tweed (Crighton), Cameron, McCord (Hegarty), Masson, Tosh, Smith (Boyle), Sinclair.

Partick Th (1) 1 *(Erskine 6)*
Falkirk (0) 0
2024
Partick Th: Fox; Paton, Boyle, Hodge, Kinniburgh, Archibald, Cairney (Robertson), Rowson, Buchanan, Doolan (Flannigan), Erskine (Fraser).
Falkirk: Olejnik; Mitchell, Twaddle, McLean, Khalis, O'Brien, Murdoch, Millar, Finnigan, Flynn, Compton (Higginbotham).

Peterhead (0) 1 *(Sharp 89)*
St Mirren (4) 6 *(McGowan 22, 33, 46, Mooy 31, McQuade 45, 56)*
1610
Peterhead: Bateman; Donald, Stuart Smith, Ross S, MacDonald, McVitic (Emslie); Sharp, Ross D, Wyness (Clark), Strachan, Anderson (Gethans).
St Mirren: Gallacher, Van Zanten, Travner, McGregor (McLean), Mair, Potter, Thomson (Cregg), Goodwin, McGowan (Dargo), McQuade, Mooy.

Ross Co (0) 0
Dundee U (0) 0
2430
Ross Co: McGovern; Marr (Miller), Morrison, Kettlewell, Boyd, Flynn, Scott, Craig (Wood), Barrowman, Brittain, Corcoran (Vigurs).
Dundee U: Banks; Dillon, Dixon (Douglas), Watson, Kenneth (Conway), Buaben, Robertson D, Gomis (Robertson S), Goodwillie, Daly, Russell.
Dundee U won 4-3 on penalties.

Tuesday, 25 January 2011
Airdrie U (0) 2 *(Mackay-Steven 77, Sally 80)*
Morton (1) 5 *(O'Brien 14, Jenkins 61, 71, Graham 68, Monti 84 (pen))*
1033
Airdrie U: Ridgers; Bain, Grant, Forrest■, Goodall (Ferguson), Muir, Devlin (Sally), Fisher (Donnelly), Mackay-Steven, Johnston, McCord.
Morton: Stewart; MacGregor, Evans, McCarthy (Monti) McKinlay, Kean (Bachirou), Jenkins, Tidser, O'Brien, Kelbie (Weatherson), Graham.

Stranraer (2) 4 *(One 19, 74, Malcolm 44, Murphy 49)*
Stenhousemuir (2) 3 *(Dalziel 17, Gallagher 45 (og), Clark 90 (pen))*
521
Stranraer: David Mitchell; Gallagher, Murphy (Mitchell G), Gallacher, Noble, Agnew, Danny Mitchell, Winter (McColm), Nicoll, Malcolm, Moore (One).
Stenhousemuir: McCluskey; Lyle, Thom, Smith, Dickson, Anderson (Quinn), Hunter, Clark, Murray, Williams (Plenderleith), Dalziel.

FIFTH ROUND

Saturday, 5 February 2011
Ayr U (0) 1 *(Roberts 58 (pen))*
St Mirren (2) 2 *(Dargo 7, 45)*   5997
Ayr U: Crawford; Tiffoney, Malone, Lauchlan, Campbell, McCann, Robertson, McLaughlin, Bannigan, Roberts, Smith.
St Mirren: Gallacher; Van Zanten, McGregor, McAusland, Mair, Potter, McGowan (Murray), Thomson, Dargo (McLean), Higdon (Mooy), Goodwin.

Buckie Th (0) 0
Brechin C (2) 2 *(McKenna 18, McAllister 30)*   1482
Buckie Th: Main; Munro H, Duncan (Angus), Small, Morrison, Brown (Napier), Sutherland, MacRae, Charlesworth (Bruce), Low, Davidson.
Brechin C: Nelson; McLean, Hill, McLaughlan, Moyes, Janczyk, Byers, Molloy, McAllister (Archdeacon), McKenna (Redman), Fusco.

Hamilton A (0) 1 *(Antoine-Curier 46)*
Dundee U (2) 3 *(Daly 20, Dixon 39, Buaben 59)*   2577
Hamilton A: Cerny; Canning, Kilday, McLaughlin, Graham (Casalinuovo), Routledge, Carrington, Buchanan, Marco Paixao (McAlister), Antoine-Curier, Imrie (Wildig).
Dundee U: Pernis; Dillon, Dixon, Watson, Kenneth, Buaben, Robertson D, Robertson S (Gomis), Goodwillie, Daly, Conway.

Inverness CT (2) 5 *(Foran 19, 86, Rooney 38, 66, Hogg 62)*
Morton (0) 1 *(Lyle 83)*   1893
Inverness CT: Tuffey; Duff, Cox, Doran, Tokely, Hogg, Odhiambo (Sanchez) (Proctor), Duncan, Foran, Rooney (MacDonald), Shinnie.
Morton: Stewart; MacGregor, McKinlay, Smyth, McCaffrey, Tidser, Kean (Bachirou), Jenkins, Lyle, Graham (Monti), O'Brien (Weatherson).

Stranraer (0) 0
Motherwell (1) 2 *(Jones 45, Sutton 82)*   2042
Stranraer: David Mitchell; Gallagher, Kurakins, Murphy, Gallacher, Agnew, One (Cochrane), Danny Mitchell, Malcolm, Nicoll (McColm), Noble.
Motherwell: Randolph; Saunders (Page), Gunning, Hutchinson, Craigan, Hateley, Humphrey, Jennings, Sutton (Casagolda), Jones, Lasley (Murphy).

Sunday, 6 February 2011
Aberdeen (0) 1 *(McGregor 90 (og))*
Dunfermline Ath (0) 0   5636
Aberdeen: Langfield; McArdle, Smith, Vujadinovic, Diamond, Hartley, Maguire, Jack (Magennis), Vernon, Blackman (Pawlett), Milsom (Young).
Dunfermline Ath: Allison; Woods, McCann, Mason, Rutkiewicz (McGregor), Keddie, Graham D, Burke (Phinn), Clarke, Kirk, Cardle (Thomson).

Rangers (2) 2 *(Ness 3, Whittaker 41 (pen))*
Celtic (1) 2 *(Commons 16, Brown 65)*   50,230
Rangers: McGregor; Whittaker, Papac, Edu, Weir, Bougherra, Davis, Ness, Jelavic (Lafferty), Diouf (Weiss), Naismith■.
Celtic: Forster■; Wilson, Izaguirre, Kayal (Samaras), Majstorovic, Mulgrew, Ki, Brown, Hooper, Commons (Zaluska), Ledley.

Wednesday, 9 February 2011
St Johnstone (1) 2 *(Davidson 42, Craig 57)*
Partick Th (0) 0   2441
St Johnstone: Enckelman; MacKay, Grainger, Morris, Anderson, Duberry, Millar, Davidson, May (Parkin), Samuel (MacDonald), Taylor (Craig).
Partick Th: Fox; Paton, Boyle, Hodge, Kinniburgh, Archibald, Cairney (Donnelly), Rowson, Grehan (Fraser), Flannigan, Erskene (Campbell).

FIFTH ROUND REPLAY

Wednesday, 2 March 2011
Celtic (0) 1 *(Wilson 48)*
Rangers (0) 0   57,847
Celtic: Zaluska; Wilson, Izaguirre, Ki, Majstorovic, Mulgrew, Brown, Kayal, Samaras, Hooper, Commons.
Rangers: McGregor; Foster, Papac (Wylde), Bartley, Weir, Bougherra■, Whittaker■, Edu, Fleck (Hutton), Diouf■, Davis.

QUARTER-FINALS

Saturday, 12 March 2011
Brechin C (1) 2 *(McAllister 42 (pen), 78)*
St Johnstone (0) 2 *(Millar 48, Invincibile 62)*   3472
Brechin C: Nelson; McLean, Cook, McLauchlan, Moyes, Janczyk, Redman, Molloy, Byers (Fusco), McAllister, McKenna (McKay).
St Johnstone: Enckelman; MacKay, Grainger, Adams (Millar), Anderson, Gartland, Davidson, Craig, Invincibile, Samuel (Reynolds), MacDonald.

St Mirren (0) 1 *(McGowan 77)*
Aberdeen (0) 1 *(McArdle 90)*   4120
St Mirren: Gallacher; Van Zanten, McGregor, Thomson, Mair, Potter (Higdon), Murray, Goodwin (McLean), Dargo (Mooy), McGowan, Travner.
Aberdeen: Langfield; McNamee (McArdle), Vujadinovic, Milsom, Diamond, Considine, Magennis, Hartley, Vernon (Blackman), Maguire, Smith (Aluko).

Sunday, 13 March 2011
Dundee U (1) 2 *(Goodwillie 40, Daly 73)*
Motherwell (1) 2 *(Sutton 1, 72)*   7358
Dundee U: Pernis; Dillon, Dixon, Gomis, Watson, Buaben, Swanson (Robertson D), Robertson S, Goodwillie, Douglas, Conway (Daly).
Motherwell: Randolph; Saunders, Gunning, Hutchinson, Craigan, Hateley, Murphy (Humphrey), Lasley (Forbes), Sutton, Jeffers, Hammell.

Wednesday, 16 March 2011
Inverness CT (1) 1 *(Rooney 44 (pen))*
Celtic (1) 2 *(Ledley 45, 68)*   6064
Inverness CT: Esson; Duff, Munro, Duncan, Tokely, Hogg, Ross (Doran), Cox, Foran, Rooney, Sutherland (Hayes).
Celtic: Forster; Juarez, Izaguirre, Ki, Loovens, Mulgrew, Kayal, Ledley, Samaras, Hooper, Commons (Forrest).

QUARTER-FINAL REPLAYS

Wednesday, 16 March 2011
Aberdeen (2) 2 *(Maguire 4, Vernon 44)*
St Mirren (0) 1 *(Vujadinovic 87 (og))*   7330
Aberdeen: Langfield; McArdle, Smith, Milsom, Diamond, Considine, Jack (Magennis), Hartley (Young), Vernon, Maguire, Aluko (Vujadinovic).
St Mirren: Gallacher; Van Zanten (Mooy), McGregor, Thomson (Goodwin), Mair, Potter, Murray, McGowan, Dargo, Higdon, Travner (McLean).

Tuesday, 22 March 2011
St Johnstone (1) 1 *(Samuel 37)*
Brechin C (0) 0   3891
St Johnstone: Enckelman; Maybury, Grainger, Davidson, MacKay, Anderson, Millar, MacDonald (Moon), Invincibile, Samuel, Craig.
Brechin C: Nelson; McLean (White), Cook, McLauchlan, Moyes, Janczyk, Fusco (Archdeacon), Molloy, McAllister, McKenna, Byers (McKay).

Wednesday, 30 March 2011
Motherwell (2) 3 *(Murphy 8, Humphrey 36, Jeffers 63)*
Dundee U (0) 0   8337
Motherwell: Randolph; Gunning, Hammell (Craigan), Jennings, Hutchinson, Hateley, Humphrey (Jones), Lasley, Sutton, Jeffers (Forbes), Murphy.
Dundee U: Pernis; Dillon, Dixon, Watson, Daly, Buaben (Shala), Robertson S, Robertson D (Douglas), Goodwillie, Swanson, Conway (Russell).

SEMI-FINALS (at Hampden Park)

Saturday, 16 April 2011
Motherwell (3) 3 *(Craigan 5, Murphy 14, Sutton 39)*
St Johnstone (0) 0   11,920
Motherwell: Randolph; Hateley, Hammell, Hutchinson, Craigan, Lasley, Humphrey (Jones), Jennings (Ross), Sutton, Jeffers (McHugh), Murphy.
St Johnstone: Enckelman; MacKay, Grainger, Morris, Anderson, Duberry, Moon (May), Davidson, Invincibile, Samuel (Robertson), Craig.

Sunday, 17 April 2011
Aberdeen (0) 0
Celtic (0) 4 *(Mulgrew 49, Ledley 57, Commons 63 (pen), Maloney 84)*   30,381
Aberdeen: Langfield; Young (Vujadinovic), Smith, Milsom, Diamond, Considine■, Jack, Magennis (Blackman), Vernon (Paton), Maguire, Aluko.
Celtic: Forster; Wilson, Izaguirre, Kayal (McCourt), Rogne, Mulgrew, Ledley (Maloney), Brown, Stokes, Hooper (Majstorovic), Commons.

ACTIVE NATION SCOTTISH CUP FINAL

Saturday, 21 May 2011

Motherwell (0) 0   Celtic (1) 3

(at Hampden Park, attendance 49,618)

Motherwell: Randolph; Hateley, Hammell (Jeffers), Hutchinson, Craigan, Lasley, Humphrey, Jennings, Sutton, Murphy (Jones), Gunning.

Celtic: Forster; Wilson, Izaguirre, Loovens, Majstorovic, Mulgrew, Ki, Brown, Samaras (Stokes), Hooper (McCourt), Commons (Forrest).
Scorers: Ki 32, Craigan 76 (og), Mulgrew 88.

Referee: C. Murray.

Georgios Samaras and Scott Brown of Celtic celebrate victory after the 3-0 defeat of Motherwell in the Scottish FA Cup Final at Hampden Park. (Action Images/Craig Brough)

WELSH FOOTBALL 2010–11

A pivotal match, a 4-2 result and a hat-trick – including a pair of penalties – by the club's leading goalscorer. Sound familiar? For the dilapidated Vetch Field read the reinvigorated Wembley; for James Thomas read Scott Sinclair. Eight years after retaining their Football League status by beating Hull, Swansea City became the first Welsh team to reach the Premier League at the glorious climax to an encouraging season for the club game in Wales. Their sometimes breathtaking brand of football – based on manager Brendan Rodgers' twin mantras of "style and steel" and "penetration with possession" – swept the Swans to victory over Reading in an exhilarating play-off final. There were near-misses for Cardiff and Wrexham, Newport County made a promising return to non-league's premier division while Colwyn Bay – for the second year running – and Merthyr both won promotion.

It was another frustrating international season as manager John Toshack's six-year reign ended. They say pride comes before a fall and Toshack has always been a proud and principled man. A little like Marmite, his contribution has polarised opinion. He was criticised for poor results, falling attendances, the early retirement of too many senior players and for being out of touch with modern-day footballers. But he rebuilt an ageing and unsuccessful team and bequeathed a squad of very talented youngsters to his successor. While Toshack had a 41 per cent wins-per-games ratio – the best of any Welsh manager – his team fell from 68th to 84th in the world rankings. After defeat in Montenegro in the first Euro 2012 qualifier, Wales lost to Bulgaria and Switzerland under caretaker Brian Flynn before Gary Speed was belatedly appointed. Like Toshack's predecessor, Mark Hughes, Speed has little managerial experience – a mere four months at Sheffield United – but his standing in the game is good. He chose another rookie in Aaron Ramsey as his captain, Wales were completely outclassed by England at the Millennium Stadium in their next qualifier and it wasn't until his fourth game – in the inaugural Carling Nations Cup against Northern Ireland – that his first victory arrived.

Thirty years ago, Swansea City rose from the bottom to the top in four seasons under Toshack. The journey took twice as long this time but the achievement arguably surpasses that of the 1981 side. Credit must go to the board and previous managers Flynn, Kenny Jackett, Roberto Martinez and Paulo Sousa. Rodgers managed to marry Martinez's attacking flair with Sousa's more defensive approach as Swansea overcame Nottingham Forest and then Reading, Rodgers' former club, in the play-offs.

After a play-off near-miss and defeat in last year's final, Cardiff City's automatic promotion challenge again petered out and they finished fourth. A goalless draw at Reading was followed by some woeful defending and a 3-0 defeat in the semi-final's second leg – leading to Dave Jones being sacked after six years in charge. He may have been the club's most successful manager but he became a victim, not so much of circumstance as of expectation.

Wrexham came close both to returning to the Football League and going out of business. Against a backdrop of near-financial meltdown, manager Dean Saunders consistently employed an adventurous 4-3-3 formation to secure fourth place but a bad night against Luton in the first leg of the semi-final at The Racecourse scuppered any chance of reaching the Blue Square Premier play-off final. Potential owners – including the Wrexham Supporters Trust – came and went during the season.

Newport County marked their return to English football's "Fifth Division" with a creditable ninth-placed finish and, under new manager Anthony Hudson, the Exiles have now gone full-time. The rise and rise of Colwyn Bay continued as, in manager Dave Challinor's debut season, they reached the Blue Square North by beating FC United in the Northern Premier League's top divisional play-off final. A year after dropping two divisions to secure their future, reborn Merthyr Town won the Toolstation Western League First Division and will now return to Penydarren Park after a season at Taffs Well.

European football proved a slightly happier hunting ground than usual for some Welsh Premier League clubs. By beating Bohemians from Ireland 4-1 on aggregate in the second round of the Champions League, The New Saints advanced in Europe for the first time in 12 attempts. They then lost 6-1 to Anderlecht before dropping into the Europa League and going out 5-2 to CSKA Sofia. Llanelli were beaten 5-4 by Lithuania's FK Tauras, European debutants Port Talbot Town lost 7-1 to TPS Turku of Finland while the third Europa League team, Bangor City, beat Finland's FC Honka 3-2 thanks to an away draw and home win at Wrexham before being beaten 10-3 by Portuguese League side Maritimo from Madeira.

A new-look "Super 12" Welsh Premier League – aimed at improving standards by increasing competition – led to a top-six championship conference and a bottom-six play-off conference. Bangor won the title, The New Saints finished second, third-placed Neath beat Prestatyn 3-2 in the play-off final while Llanelli became the third team to qualify for the Europa League by lifting the Welsh Cup for the first time after beating Bangor 4-1. Reaction to the revamped format was largely positive and attendances rose by nearly 25 per cent.

With the Speed era now underway, "fire up your voice" is the Welsh FA's current rallying cry to long-suffering supporters. Most will be happy to oblige but I'm not sure how many will share the optimism of Speed's assistant, Raymond Verheijen, who maintains Wales have more talent than the two Irish sides or skipper Ramsey's belief that they will qualify for Brazil 2014. Let's hope, at least, that some of Swansea City's stardust will fall on the national team.

GRAHAME LLOYD

PRINCIPALITY BUILDING SOCIETY WELSH PREMIER LEAGUE 2010–11

					Total			*Home*					*Away*						
		P	W	D	L	F	A	W	D	L	F	A	W	D	L	F	A	GD	Pts
1	Bangor C	32	22	4	6	80	44	12	1	3	51	21	10	3	3	29	23	36	70
2	The New Saints	32	20	8	4	87	34	13	2	1	57	15	7	6	3	30	19	53	68
3	Neath Ath	32	16	10	6	62	41	7	6	3	27	18	9	4	3	35	23	21	58
4	Llanelli	32	15	8	9	58	41	8	3	5	32	25	7	5	4	26	16	17	53
5	Prestatyn T	32	10	10	12	44	46	6	7	3	22	14	4	3	9	22	32	–2	40
6	Port Talbot T	32	8	12	12	37	48	4	5	7	18	19	4	7	5	19	29	–11	36
7	Aberystwyth T	32	11	9	12	42	54	6	5	5	21	23	5	4	7	21	31	–12	42
8	Airbus UK Broughton	32	11	8	13	53	52	5	6	5	33	26	6	2	8	20	26	1	41
9	Newtown	32	8	11	13	40	55	4	7	5	18	21	4	4	8	22	34	–15	35
10	Carmarthen T	32	10	5	17	39	64	5	2	9	22	30	5	3	8	17	34	–25	35
11	Bala T	32	10	3	19	41	57	6	1	9	24	25	4	2	10	17	32	–16	33
12	Haverfordwest Co	32	5	4	23	30	77	3	1	12	17	34	2	3	11	13	43	–47	19

Top 6 teams split after 22 games.

PREVIOUS WELSH LEAGUE WINNERS

1993	Cwmbran Town	1998	Barry Town	2003	Barry Town	2008	Llanelli
1994	Bangor City	1999	Barry Town	2004	Rhyl	2009	Rhyl
1995	Bangor City	2000	TNS	2005	TNS	2010	The New Saints
1996	Barry Town	2001	Barry Town	2006	TNS	2011	Bangor C
1997	Barry Town	2002	Barry Town	2007	TNS		

MACWHIRTER WELSH LEAGUE 2010–11

		P	W	D	L	F	A	GD	Pts
1	Bryntirion Ath	30	23	1	6	76	27	49	70
2	Afan Lido	30	20	5	5	63	28	35	65
3	Cambrian & Clydach	30	17	6	7	68	37	31	57
4	Pontardawe T	30	15	6	9	54	44	10	51
5	Caerau (Ely)	30	15	4	11	66	52	14	49
6	Bridgend T	30	14	5	11	60	47	13	47
7	West End	30	13	6	11	57	47	10	45
8	Cardiff Corinthians	30	12	4	14	58	52	6	40
9	Taffs Well	30	12	3	15	47	57	–10	39
10	Aberaman Ath	30	12	3	15	58	74	–16	39
11	Goytre U	30	10	8	12	47	53	–6	38
12	Cwmbran Celtic	30	10	7	13	45	50	–5	37
13	Barry T	30	9	8	13	39	55	–16	35
14	Caldicot T	30	8	3	19	37	48	–11	27
15	Garden Village	30	6	7	17	41	75	–34	25
16	Penrhiwceiber Rangers	30	4	4	22	27	97	–70	16

HUWS GRAY-FITLOCK CYMRU ALLIANCE LEAGUE 2010–11

				Total				*Home*			*Away*				
		P	W	D	L	F	A	W	D	L	W	D	L	GD	Pts
1	Gap Connahs Quay	30	23	2	5	89	33	11	1	3	12	1	2	56	71
2	Rhyl	30	19	5	6	73	32	10	2	3	9	3	3	41	62
3	Cefn Druids	30	18	6	6	60	29	11	3	1	7	3	5	31	60
4	Rhos Aelwyd	30	15	6	9	68	64	8	3	4	7	3	5	4	51
5	Caersws	30	15	5	10	59	49	4	1	5	5	1	9	10	50
6	Llandudno	30	13	10	7	50	35	9	3	3	4	7	4	15	49
7	Flint Town U	30	13	7	10	64	55	8	4	3	5	3	7	9	46
8	Porthmadog	30	14	4	12	59	53	6	2	7	8	2	5	6	46
9	Buckley T	30	13	6	11	46	48	7	2	6	6	4	5	–2	45
10	Llangefni T	30	11	4	15	67	64	4	2	9	7	2	6	3	37
11	Penrhyncoch	30	9	10	11	49	56	5	7	3	4	3	8	–7	37
12	Ruthin T	30	11	4	15	39	58	7	2	6	4	2	9	–19	37
13	Guilsfield	30	8	6	16	43	56	3	2	10	5	4	6	–13	30
14	Rhydymwyn	30	4	6	20	27	82	4	3	8	0	3	12	–55	18
15	Rhayader T	30	4	3	23	34	76	4	2	9	0	1	14	–42	15
16	Technogroup Welshpool	30	5	6	19	39	76	3	3	9	2	3	10	–37	3

Technogroup Welshpool deducted 18 points for breach of rules and failing to fulfill fixtures.

WELSH CUP 2010–11

QUALIFYING ROUND ONE NORTH

Aberaeron v Bodedern Ath	0-7
Caernarfon W v Bro Goronwy	2-7
Connah's Quay T v Llanfair U	10-3
CPD Bethel v FC Nomads of Connah's Quay	0-2
Greenfield v Machynlleth	5-3
Halkyn U v Amlwch T	2-3
Llandymog U v CPD Llanystumdwy	1-1
Landymog U won 4-2 on penalties.	
Llanllyfni v Borras Park Alb	3-3
Borras Park Alb won 4-2 on penalties.	
Meifod v Gaerwen	1-2
Penmaenmawr Phoenix v Glantraeth	4-1
Trearddur Bay U v Brynford U	1-0
Tregaron Turfs v Montgomery T	2-3
Y Felinheli v Blaenau Ffestiniog	2-1

QUALIFYING ROUND ONE SOUTH

Brecon Cor v Monmouth T	0-5
Cardiff Hibs v Cwmbran T	3-4
Corus Steel v Cwmamman U	1-0
Ferndale & District v Bridgend Street	0-3
Fochrhiw v Baglan Dragons	2-1
Llanwern v Tredegar T	2-1
Newport Civil Service v Goytre	2-3
Penclawdd withdrew v Seven Sisters w.o.	
Penrhiwceiber Con Ath v RTB Ebbw Vale	1-1
RTB Ebbw Vale won 4-3 on penalties.	
Pontyclun v Rhydyfelin	3-1
Risca U v Pontypridd T	0-1
South Gower v Cadoxton Barry	2-0
STM Sp v Llantwit Fadre	3-0
Talgarth T v Fleur de Lys	0-5
Treowen Stars v Cornelly U	6-0
Trethomas B'birds v Llandrindod Wells	2-1
Troedyrhiw v Nelson Cavaliers	3-3
Nelson Cavaliers won 4-3 on penalties.	

ROUND TWO NORTH

Amlwch T v Coedpoeth U	1-3
Barmouth & Dyffryn U v Hawarden R	3-2
Borras Park Alb v Glan Conwy	7-3
Bro Goronwy v Connah's Quay T	2-4
Brymbo v Waterloo R	0-4
Caernarfon T v Holywell T	5-1
Carno v Chirk AAA	4-3
Conwy U v Denbigh T	2-1
Corwen v Dolgellau Ath Amat	0-1
CPD Dyffryn Nantlle v Llanrhaedr ym Mochnant	0-1
CPD Gwalchmai v CPD Dyffryn Banw	4-0
CPD Llanberis v Brickfield R	0-4
Gaerwen v Greenfield	1-3
Lex XI v FC Nomads of Connah's Quay	3-2
Llandudno Junction v Holyhead Hotspurs	2-4
Llandyrnog U v Llangollen T	4-2
Llanidloes T v Llansantffraid Vil	2-1
Llay Wel v Bow Street	2-4
Montgomery T v Penmaenmawr Phoenix	1-2
Nefyn U v Llanrwst U	2-1
Overton Rec v Llanfairpwll	1-3
Penparcau v Gresford Ath	4-0
Penycae v Llanrug U	3-1
Pwllheli v Bodedern Ath	5-1
Trearddur Bay U v Mold Alex	3-0
Tywyn Bryncrug v Berriew	3-2
Venture Community v Johnstown Youth	2-3
Y Felinheli v Bethesda Ath	3-5

ROUND TWO SOUTH

Abertillery B'birds v Pontyclun	1-2
Ammanford v Presteigne St And	3-0
Bridgend Street v Fochrhiw	11-1
Briton Ferry Llan v Pontypridd T	1-2
Caerau v Newport YMCA	4-1
Cardiff Grange Harle v Llanwern	3-2
Corus Steel v AFC Llwydcoed	3-2
Cwmaman Inst v Aberbargoed Buds	1-0
Ely R v Caerleon	3-2
Goytre v Llangeinor	5-4
Hay St Mary v AFC Porth	1-5
Nelson Cavaliers v Monmouth T	2-4
Newbridge on Wye v South Gower	3-5
Newcastle Emlyn v Dinas Powys	2-1
RTB Ebbw Vale v Fleur de Lys	1-4

Seven Sisters v Croesyceilog	0-1
SMT Sp v Trethomas B'birds	4-3
Ton Pentre v Bettws	0-1
Treowen Stars v Treharris Ath West	2-3
UWIC v Cwmbran T	2-1

FIRST ROUND NORTH

Borras Park Alb v Rhos Alewyd	0-8
Bow Street v Lex XI	2-1
Brickfield R v Bethesda Ath	3-4
Caersws v Rhayader T	4-0
Carno v CPD Porthmadog	1-5
Cefn Druids v Penycae	6-4
Coedpoeth U v Greenfield	4-3
Connah's Quay T v Johnstown Youth	6-1
Conwy U v Waterloo R	4-1
CPD Gwalchmai v Barmouth & Dyffryn U	4-0
Dolgellau Ath Amat v Llandudno T	1-2
Holyhead Hotspurs v Tec Welshpool	4-0
Llandyrnog U v Flint T U	1-5
Llangefni T v Llanfairpwll	3-2
Llanidloes T v Ruthin T	1-0
Llanrhaedr ym Mochnant v Rhyl	0-5
Nefyn U v Tywyn Bryncrug	3-2
Penmaenmawr Phoenix v Caernarfon T	3-5
Penrhyncoch v Guilsfield	2-2
Guilsfield won 6-4 on penalties.	
Pwllheli v Gap Connah's Quay	1-6
Rhydymwyn v Buckley T	1-4
Trearddur Bay U v Penparcau	7-3

FIRST ROUND SOUTH

Barry T v STM Sp	3-0
Bettws v Aberaman Ath	0-3
Bridgend T v Monmouth T	5-3
Bryntirion Ath v Cwmbran Celtic	0-0
Bryntirion Ath won 4-2 on penalties.	
Caerau v Afan Lido	1-3
Cardiff Grange Harl v Bridgend Street	4-2
Corus Steel v Cardiff Cor	5-2
Croesyceilog v Garden Vil	0-2
Cwmaman Inst v Taffs Wells	1-2
Fleur de Lys v Ely R	1-0
Goytre v Caerau Ely	3-1
Goytre U v Ammanford	5-3
Newcastle Emlyn v South Gower	4-0
Penrhiwceiber R v Cambrian & Clydach V	0-2
Pontypridd T v Pontardawe T	2-0
Treharris Ath West v Pontyclun	2-1
UWIC v Caldicot T	2-0
West End v AFC Porth	1-2

SECOND ROUND NORTH

Caernarfon T v Guilsfield	1-2
Connah's Quay T v Bow Street	1-2
Conwy U v CPD Porthmadog	1-4
CPD Gwalchmai v Buckley T	2-2
CPD Gwalchmai won 4-2 on penalties.	
Flint T U v Llanidloes T	3-4
Gap Connah's Quay v Bethesda Ath	6-1
Holyhead Hotspurs v Llangefni T	1-0
Nefyn U v Caersws	1-3
Rhos Aelwyd v Coedpoeth U	2-1
Rhyl v Llandudno T	2-1
Trearddur Bay U v Cefn Druids	0-7

SECOND ROUND SOUTH

Afan Lido v Cambrian & Clydach V	1-2
AFC Porth v Goytre	2-0
Barry T v Corus Steel	1-2
Garden Vil v Aberaman Ath	1-6
Goytre U v Fleur de Lys	3-1
Cardiff Grange Harl v Treharris Ath West	3-0
Newcastle Emlyn v UWIC	1-4
Pontypridd T v Bryntirion Ath	1-2
Taffs Wells v Bridgend T	2-4

THIRD ROUND

Aberaman Ath v Cefn Druids	0-4
Airbus UK v The New Saints	2-3
Bangor C v Bryntirion Ath	2-1
Bow Street v UWIC	2-2
UWIC won 6-5 on penalties.	
Caersws v Llanidloes T	4-2

Cambrian & Clydach V v Prestatyn T		2-3
Corus Steel v Cardiff Grange Harl		0-2
CPD Gwalchmai v Port Talbot T		1-4
CPD Porthmadog v Bala T		0-1
Gap Connah's Quay v AFC Porth		5-3
Goytre U v Carmarthen T		2-3
Guilsfield v Rhos Aelwyd		1-2
Haverfordwest Co v Holyhead Hotspurs		3-2
Llanelli v Aberysthwyth T		1-0
Neath v Rhyl		1-1
Rhyl won 7-6 on penalties.		
Newtown v Bridgend T		1-2

FOURTH ROUND

Bangor C v Haverfordwest Co		5-3
Cardiff Grange Harl v Bridgend T		1-0
Carmarthen T v Gap Connah's Quay		2-3
Cefn Druids v Llanelli		1-4
Port Talbot T v Caersws		3-0
Rhos Aelwyd v Prestatyn T		1-6
Rhyl v The New Saints		1-2
UWIC v Bala T		4-1

QUARTER-FINALS

Gap Connah's Quay v UWIC	4-0
Llanelli v Prestatyn T	1-0
Port Talbot T v Bangor C	0-3
The New Saints v Cardiff Grange Harl	2-0

SEMI-FINALS

Bangor C v Gap Connah's Quay	1-0
Llanelli v The New Saints	1-0

FINAL (at Llanelli)

8 May 2011

Bangor C (0) 1, Llanelli (2) 4
Bangor C: Smith; Hoy, Roberts, Johnston, Moss, Morley, Williams (Smyth 62), Ward, Jones C (Edwards 75), Davies, Bull (Jebb 75).
Scorer: Bull 51.
Llanelli: Morris; Thomas K, Venables, Jones S, Thomas W, Bowen (Follows 74), Corbisiero, Griffiths, Moses, Evans.
Scorers: Griffiths 15, 60, Moses 20, Venables 64.
Attendance: 1719
Referee: M. Petch (Deganwy).

PREVIOUS WELSH CUP WINNERS

1878	Wrexham Town	1909	Wrexham	1950	Swansea Town	1981	Swansea City
1879	White Star Newtown	1910	Wrexham	1951	Merthyr Tydfil	1982	Swansea City
1880	Druids	1911	Wrexham	1952	Rhyl	1983	Swansea City
1881	Druids	1912	Cardiff City	1953	Rhyl	1984	Shrewsbury Town
1882	Druids	1913	Swansea Town	1954	Flint Town United	1985	Shrewsbury Town
1883	Wrexham	1914	Wrexham	1955	Barry Town	1986	Wrexham
1884	Oswestry United	1915	Wrexham	1956	Cardiff City	1987	Merthyr Tydfil
1885	Druids	1920	Cardiff City	1957	Wrexham	1988	Cardiff City
1886	Druids	1921	Wrexham	1958	Wrexham	1989	Swansea City
1887	Chirk	1922	Cardiff City	1959	Cardiff City	1990	Hereford United
1888	Chirk	1923	Cardiff City	1960	Wrexham	1991	Swansea City
1889	Bangor	1924	Wrexham	1961	Swansea Town	1992	Cardiff City
1890	Druids	1925	Wrexham	1962	Bangor City	1993	Cardiff City
1891	Shrewsbury Town	1926	Ebbw Vale	1963	Borough United	1994	Barry Town
1892	Chirk	1927	Cardiff City	1964	Cardiff City	1995	Wrexham
1893	Wrexham	1928	Cardiff City	1965	Cardiff City	1996	TNS
1894	Chirk	1929	Connah's Quay	1966	Swansea Town	1997	Barry Town
1895	Newtown	1930	Cardiff City	1967	Cardiff City	1998	Bangor City
1896	Bangor	1931	Wrexham	1968	Cardiff City	1999	Inter Cable-Tel
1897	Wrexham	1932	Swansea Town	1969	Cardiff City	2000	Bangor City
1898	Druids	1933	Chester	1970	Cardiff City	2001	Barry Town
1899	Druids	1934	Bristol City	1971	Cardiff City	2002	Barry Town
1900	Aberystwyth	1935	Tranmere Rovers	1972	Wrexham	2003	Barry Town
1901	Oswestry United	1936	Crewe Alexandra	1973	Cardiff City	2004	Rhyl
1902	Wellington Town	1937	Crewe Alexandra	1974	Cardiff City	2005	TNS
1903	Wrexham	1938	Shrewsbury Town	1975	Wrexham	2006	Rhyl
1904	Druids	1939	South Liverpool	1976	Cardiff City	2007	Carmarthen Town
1905	Wrexham	1940	Wellington Town	1977	Shrewsbury Town	2008	Bangor C
1906	Wellington Town	1947	Chester	1978	Wrexham	2009	Bangor C
1907	Oswestry United	1948	Lovell's Athletic	1979	Shrewsbury Town	2010	Bangor C
1908	Chester	1949	Merthyr Tydfil	1980	Newport County	2011	Llanelli

THE LOOSEMORES OF CARDIFF CHALLENGE CUP 2010–11

FIRST ROUND FIRST LEG

Airbus UK v Newtown	4-2
Bala T v Prestatyn T	2-2
Carmarthen T v Aberysthwyth T	0-0
Haverfordwest Co v Neath	2-1

FIRST ROUND SECOND LEG

Newtown v Airbus UK	1-0
Prestatyn T v Bala T	2-0
Aberysthwyth T v Carmarthen T	3-0
Neath v Haverfordwest Co	2-2

SECOND ROUND FIRST LEG

Prestatyn T v Bangor C	3-2
The New Saints v Airbus UK	2-0
Haverfordwest Co v Aberysthwyth T	1-1
Llanelli v Port Talbot T	1-2

SECOND ROUND SECOND LEG

Bangor C v Prestatyn T	2-1
Airbus UK v The New Saints	2-2
Aberysthwyth T v Haverfordwest Co	3-0
Port Talbot T v Llanelli	0-2

SEMI-FINAL FIRST LEG

Aberysthwyth T v Llanelli	0-1
The New Saints v Bangor C	9-0

SEMI-FINAL SECOND LEG

Llanelli v Aberysthwyth T	3-1
Bangor C v The New Saints	1-3

FINAL (at Aberysthwyth)

2 May 2011

Llanelli (0) 3 *(Holloway 76, Moses 87, Follows 90)*
The New Saints (1) 4 *(Edwards 43, Sharp 73, 89, Ruscoe 120)* 310
Llanelli: Morris; Thomas K, Jones S, Thomas W, Bowen, Corbisiero, Holloway, Moses, Follows, Batley, Legg (Orme 82).
The New Saints: Harrison; Holmes D (Marriott C 91), Hogan, Rawlinson, Giglio, Seargeant (Ruscoe 82), Wood, Edwards, Darlington, Sharp, Berkeley (Jones C 75).
aet.
Referee: B. James.

NORTHERN IRISH FOOTBALL 2010–11

Light can be seen at the end of the tunnel for Northern Ireland football with the government announcing a £60m cash input into the Irish FA for stadia improvements, including a massive and much-needed refurbishment of Windsor Park, Northern Ireland's home international venue. Priority at last is being given to upgrading a stadium with a unique heritage, tradition and atmosphere – a shrine to Linfield fans and Northern Ireland's Green and White Army.

For more than a decade controversy has enveloped the stadium issue, particularly when the site of the former Maze Prison was rejected and the Irish FA opted for Windsor Park, Gaelic football for a rebuilt Casement Park and Rugby Union for Ravenhill.

A new lease agreement by the owners, Linfield, and the Irish FA has been given the green light by the club members pending top legal discussions on a package of other issues, ensuring that Linfield has always an administrative presence in the ground. The name Windsor Park must be retained – that is sacrosanct – with Linfield playing all their games there and the second eleven, too. In a nutshell, a separate company will operate the stadium for the Irish FA and be responsible for its maintenance over a 40 year period. It will be the headquarters of the Irish FA and Linfield – a similar arrangement to that at Hampden between the Scottish FA and Queen's Park.

It has been a long haul but don't expect any magical overnight appearance of a new structure. It will take three years from building commencement to completion under the phased financial arrangements in the current economic climate but, thankfully, everybody seems to be singing from the same hymn sheet. With all-round-co-operation the Grand Old Lady, which in the sixties housed 58,000 crowds for internationals, will become pristine again.

In many ways, it has been a dramatic year for Linfield who won their fifth League and Cup double in six years – an appropriate way to celebrate the club's 125th anniversary highlighted by an August visit from Rangers, a club with whom they have traditional affiliations, and an historic banquet in the majestic setting of Belfast City Hall. David Jeffrey, known to the fans as "The Special One", was named Manager of the Year – a reward for his dedication and success at a club where victory is constantly demanded and failure not included in the vocabulary.

Linfield set the standard, despite a couple of hiccups along the way, chased by Crusaders, who finished runners-up and also beaten Cup finalists, and Glentoran, whose manager Scott Young performed miracles operating on a severely restricted budget. Now he is involved in rebuilding for a new season but again, it appears a difficult job in the circumstances. Nobody deserved success more than the Glaswegian with such passionate fervour for football.

A wage cap has been imposed by the Irish FA on clubs paying astronomical wages for part-time professionals. Everybody attempted to keep up with the Joneses. Now they can only use 60 per cent of their allowable income on salaries and for Linfield that doesn't include the £200,000 per annum obtained for international use of Windsor Park.

"The cap won't worry us," said Jeffrey. "We have always operated within our budget and never touched that pot." Jeffrey, like all managers, reckons strict policing of the new scheme is essential and any breach of the regulations should be severely punished. The days of the little brown envelopes are over!

Internationally, it has been a mixed bag with the main disappointment a 1-1 away draw with the Faeroe Islands in the European Championship Group Three. There is still a possibility, perhaps a little remote, of Northern Ireland finishing second and obtaining a play-off place. Manager Nigel Worthington, whose contract expires in December, has been meticulous in his approach at all levels, giving Irish League players their chance when merited. Participation in the Carling Nations Cup at the Aviva Stadium, Dublin, proved a headache with virtually the entire first team panel unavailable due primarily to pre-planned family vacations, players' delayed surgery, marriages and fatigue after an arduous season. Not surprisingly, Northern Ireland collected the wooden spoon while the Republic took top prize in the tournament's inaugural season.

Sponsorship still remained difficult to obtain but, all things considered, the Irish FA did exceptionally well thanks to the Sky TV cash. Now UEFA are taking over TV negotiations which means the amount of revenue should not diminish but increase.

DR MALCOLM BRODIE MBE

CARLING PREMIERSHIP 2010–11

SECTION A

	P	W	D	L	F	A	GD	Pts
Linfield	38	26	7	5	80	29	51	85
Crusaders	38	23	5	10	78	59	19	74
Glentoran	38	20	6	12	63	41	22	66
Cliftonville	38	17	7	14	60	56	4	58
Portadown	38	15	5	18	49	58	–9	50
Lisburn Distillery	38	14	6	18	50	66	–16	48

SECTION B

Coleraine	38	17	5	16	51	50	1	56
Dungannon Swifts	38	14	9	15	50	53	–3	51
Ballymena United	38	12	13	13	48	56	–8	49
Glenavon	38	12	9	17	60	59	1	45
Donegal Celtic	38	8	8	22	55	89	–34	32
Newry City	38	6	8	24	37	65	–28	26

Newry City relegated.

IFA RESERVE LEAGUE 2010–11

	P	W	D	L	F	A	GD	Pts
Linfield Swifts	33	26	3	4	130	44	86	81
Crusaders Res	33	20	7	6	92	35	57	67
Glentoran II	33	20	5	8	84	33	51	65
Glenavon Res	33	18	6	9	57	55	2	60
Cliftonville Olympic	33	17	6	10	71	55	16	57
Donegal Celtic Res	33	13	5	15	66	76	–10	44
Dungannon Swifts Res	33	10	8	15	59	76	–17	38
Coleraine Res	33	10	6	17	41	66	–25	36
Lisburn Distillery II	33	9	5	19	56	72	–16	32
Ballymena U Res	33	10	2	21	62	100	–38	32
Portadown Res	33	9	4	20	47	93	–46	31
Newry City Res	33	7	1	25	36	96	–60	22

LADBROKES.COM CHAMPIONSHIP

DIVISION ONE

	P	W	D	L	F	A	GD	Pts
Carrick Rangers	26	18	4	4	57	27	30	58
Limavady U	26	15	6	5	53	27	26	51
Dergview	26	15	3	8	51	32	19	48
Bangor	26	11	8	7	45	38	7	41
Ballinamallard U	26	11	6	9	45	38	7	39
HW Welders	26	11	6	9	45	38	7	39
Ards	26	9	7	10	37	42	–5	34
Institute	26	10	4	12	28	43	–15	34
Larne	26	8	6	12	38	41	–3	30
Loughgall	26	8	6	12	37	48	–11	30
Banbridge T	26	7	7	12	31	39	–8	28
Glebe Rangers	26	7	7	12	36	46	–10	28
Ballymoney U	26	5	8	13	31	48	–17	23
Ballyclare Comrades	26	5	6	15	28	55	–27	21

Carrick Rangers promoted; Ballymoney U and Ballyclare Comrades relegated.

DIVISION TWO

	P	W	D	L	F	A	GD	Pts
Warrenpoint T	30	22	7	1	84	26	58	73
Tobermore U	30	20	4	6	67	36	31	64
Knockbreda	30	19	5	6	59	32	27	62
Dundela	30	16	9	5	74	41	33	57
Queen's University	30	17	4	9	61	35	26	55
Coagh U	30	16	6	8	66	48	18	54
Wakehurst	30	13	7	10	62	54	8	46
Sport & Leisure Swifts	30	12	6	12	52	58	–6	42
Portstewart	30	12	2	16	51	52	–1	38
PSNI	30	11	4	15	56	58	–2	37
Lurgan Celtic	30	9	6	15	48	62	–14	33
Armagh C	30	8	9	13	43	60	–17	33
Annagh U	30	7	5	18	34	66	–32	26
Killymoon Rangers	30	5	9	16	37	64	–27	24
Moyola Park	30	6	5	19	31	67	–36	23
Chimney Corner	30	1	4	25	35	101	–66	7

Warrenpoint T and Tobermore U promoted.

IRISH LEAGUE CHAMPIONSHIP WINNERS

1891	Linfield	1913	Glentoran	1940	Belfast Celtic	1970	Glentoran
1892	Linfield	1914	Linfield	1948	Belfast Celtic	1971	Linfield
1893	Linfield	1915	Belfast Celtic	1949	Linfield	1972	Glentoran
1894	Glentoran	1920	Belfast Celtic	1950	Linfield	1973	Crusaders
1895	Linfield	1921	Glentoran	1951	Glentoran	1974	Coleraine
1896	Distillery	1922	Linfield	1952	Glenavon	1975	Linfield
1897	Glentoran	1923	Linfield	1953	Glentoran	1976	Crusaders
1898	Linfield	1924	Queen's Island	1954	Linfield	1977	Glentoran
1899	Distillery	1925	Glentoran	1955	Linfield	1978	Linfield
1900	Belfast Celtic	1926	Belfast Celtic	1956	Linfield	1979	Linfield
1901	Distillery	1927	Belfast Celtic	1957	Glentoran	1980	Linfield
1902	Linfield	1928	Belfast Celtic	1958	Ards	1981	Glentoran
1903	Distillery	1929	Belfast Celtic	1959	Linfield	1982	Linfield
1904	Linfield	1930	Linfield	1960	Glenavon	1983	Linfield
1905	Glentoran	1931	Glentoran	1961	Linfield	1984	Linfield
1906	Cliftonville	1932	Linfield	1962	Linfield	1985	Linfield
	Distillery	1933	Belfast Celtic	1963	Distillery	1986	Linfield
1907	Linfield	1934	Linfield	1964	Glentoran	1987	Linfield
1908	Linfield	1935	Linfield	1965	Derry City	1988	Glentoran
1909	Linfield	1936	Belfast Celtic	1966	Linfield	1989	Linfield
1910	Cliftonville	1937	Belfast Celtic	1967	Glentoran	1990	Portadown
1911	Linfield	1938	Belfast Celtic	1968	Glentoran	1991	Portadown
1912	Glentoran	1939	Belfast Celtic	1969	Linfield	1992	Glentoran

1993	Linfield
1994	Linfield
1995	Crusaders
1996	Portadown
1997	Crusaders
1998	Cliftonville
1999	Glentoran
2000	Linfield
2001	Linfield
2002	Portadown
2003	Glentoran
2004	Linfield
2005	Glentoran
2006	Linfield
2007	Linfield
2008	Linfield
2009	Glentoran
2010	Linfield
2011	Linfield

LADBROKES.COM CHAMPIONSHIP (Previously First Division)

1996	Coleraine	2002	Lisburn Distillery	2008	Loughgall
1997	Ballymena United	2003	Dungannon Swifts	2009	Portadown
1998	Newry Town	2004	Loughgall	2010	Loughgall
1999	Distillery	2005	Armagh City	2011	Carrick Rangers
2000	Omagh Town	2006	Crusaders		
2001	Ards	2007	Institute		

IFA YOUTH LEAGUE 2010–11

SECTION A	P	W	D	L	F	A	GD	Pts
Glentoran Colts	22	14	6	2	64	32	48	
Linfield Rangers	22	14	5	3	80	30	50	47
Cliftonville Strollers	22	13	7	2	50	25	25	46
Ballinamallard U III	22	9	5	8	46	42	4	32
Lisburn Distillery III	22	9	5	8	38	35	3	32
Glenavon III	22	8	7	7	48	41	7	31
Carrick Rangers Colts	22	8	5	9	63	61	2	29
Dungannon Swifts Youth	22	7	5	10	33	45	−12	26
Newington YC	22	6	5	11	49	63	−14	23
Donegal Celtic Youth	22	5	7	10	35	66	−31	22
Ballymena U III	22	5	4	13	37	66	−29	15
Newry C Wanderers	22	4	3	15	30	67	−37	15

SECTION A	P	W	D	L	F	A	GD	Pts
Crusaders Colts	18	17	0	1	114	17	97	51
Institute Colts	18	11	3	4	61	39	22	36
Portadown III	18	11	3	4	45	29	16	36
Larne FC	18	9	2	7	36	48	−12	29
Ballymoney United Colts	18	7	6	5	50	43	7	27
Loughgall Youth	18	7	4	7	51	35	16	25
Cookstown Youth	18	8	1	9	50	54	−4	25
Coleraine Colts	18	5	2	11	38	60	−22	17
Ballyclare Comrades Colts	17	1	1	13	19	51	−32	10
Crewe United Youth	17	0	0	17	16	104	−88	0

SETANTA SPORTS CUP 2010–11

FIRST ROUND FIRST LEG

Linfield v Dundalk	3-5
UCD v Lisburn Distillery	0-0
Cliftonville v St Patrick's Ath	3-0
Bohemians v Portadown	1-2

FIRST ROUND SECOND LEG

Dundalk v Linfield	1-1
Lisburn Distillery v UCD	2-0
St Patrick's Ath v Cliftonville	2-0
Portadown v Bohemians	2-0

QUARTER-FINALS FIRST LEG

Glentoran v Dundalk	0-1
Cliftonville v Crusaders	4-2
Lisburn Distillery v Shamrock Rovers	0-3
Sligo Rovers v Portadown	3-0

QUARTER-FINALS SECOND LEG

Dundalk v Glentoran	1-1
Crusaders v Cliftonville	4-6
Shamrock Rovers v Lisburn Distillery	4-2
Portadown v Sligo Rovers	0-2

SEMI-FINALS FIRST LEG

Cliftonville v Dundalk	1-3
Sligo Rovers v Shamrock Rovers	0-2

SEMI-FINALS SECOND LEG

Dundalk v Cliftonville	2-1
Shamrock Rovers v Sligo Rovers	2-1

FINAL

14 May 2011, 4789
(at Tallaght Stadium, Dublin).

Dundalk (0) 0

Shamrock Rovers (0) 2 *(O'Neill 65, Dennehy 90)*

Dundalk: Cherrie; Hawkins, Madden, Murphy N, Hector, Bolger, McDonnell (Bennett 9), Kearns, Quigley, Byrne (Ward 59), Gaynor (Breen 85).
Shamrock Rovers: Mannus; Murray, Oman, Sullivan, Stevens, Rice (Twigg 64), Finn, McCormack, Dennehy, O'Neill, Sheppard (McCabe 79).
Referee: A. Kelly.

SETANTA SPORTS CUP WINNERS

2004–05 Linfield	2006–07 Drogheda United	2009–10 Bohemians
2005–06 Drogheda United	2007–08 Cork City	2010–11 Shamrock Rovers

CO-OPERATIVE INSURANCE CUP 2010–11

FINAL *(at Mourneview Park, Lurgan)*

Lisburn Distillery 2 *(Davidson 61, Cushley 87)*

Portadown 1 *(Tipton 44)*

Lisburn Distillery: Brennan; Callaghan, Hunter, Simpson, McShane, Thompson (Davidson 45), Kilmartin, Cooling, Browne (Cushley 45), Liggett, Ferguson.

Portadown: Miskelly; O'Hara, Gartland, Breen, Redman, Mouncey, Clarke (Craig 88), McCabe, Baker (Boyle 75), Tipton (Lecky 81), Braniff.
This was Glenn Ferguson's 30th trophy triumph after a distinguished career and heralded his retirement from football. His 563 goals gained him second place in the Northern Ireland's Scorer List behind Jimmy Jones (Belfast Celtic) 646 goals.

JJB SPORTS IRISH CUP 2010–11

FIFTH ROUND

Albert Foundry v Nortel	0-2
Annagh United v Glenavon	2-6
Ballinamallard United v Larne	3-1
Ballymena United v Glentoran	1-1, 2-3
Carrick Rangers v Shankill United	3-3, 6-1
Crusaders v Newry City	3-2
Dundela v Lisburn Distillery	1-4
Dungannon v Ballymoney United	5-1
Linfield v Institute	5-1
Dunmurry Rec v Kilmore Rec	2-2, 5-0
Loughgall v Sport and Leisure	3-1
Portadown v Donegal Celtic	4-3
Queen's University v Crumlin Utd	1-0
Warrenpoint Town v Cliftonville	1-1, 0-0
Warrenpoint Town won 3-1 on penalties.	
Ards v H&W Welders	2-2, 0-1
Limavady United v Coleraine	1-2

SIXTH ROUND

Carrick Rangers v Coleraine	1-3
Crusaders v Nortel	2-1
Dungannon v Warrenpoint Town	4-2
Glenavon v Queen's University	2-0
Glentoran v Loughgall	3-1
H&W Welders v Portadown	1-1, 0-1
Linfield v Dunmurry Rec	1-1, 3-0
Lisburn Distillery v Ballinamallard United	2-2, 2-4

QUARTER-FINALS

Ballinamallard United v Crusaders	0-5
Dungannon v Linfield	0-2
Glentoran v Coleraine	1-1, 3-3
Glentoran won 3-2 on penalties.	
Portadown v Glenavon	3-3, 3-0

SEMI-FINALS

Crusaders v Portadown	3-1
(at Mourneview Park).	
Glentoran v Linfield	0-2
(at Windsor Park).	

FINAL

(at Windsor Park, 7 May 2011)

Linfield 2 *(Thompson 78, McAllister 88)*

Crusaders 1 *(Caddell 54)* 9000

Linfield: Blayney; Douglas, Gault, Curran, Lowry (Mulgrew 63), Thompson, Carvill, Garrett, Ervin (Tomelty 75), McAllister, Casement.
Crusaders: Keenan; McKeown, McBride, Magowan, Coates, Dallas, Halliday (Rainey 80), Morrow (McMaster 83), Caddell, Owens, Watson.
Referee: M. Courtney.
Man of the Match: Jamie Mulgrew (Linfield).

IRISH CUP FINALS (from 1946–47)

1946–47 Belfast Celtic 1, Glentoran 0	
1947–48 Linfield 3, Coleraine 0	
1948–49 Derry City 3, Glentoran 1	
1949–50 Linfield 2, Distillery 1	
1950–51 Glentoran 3, Ballymena U 1	
1951–52 Ards 1, Glentoran 0	
1952–53 Linfield 5, Coleraine 0	
1953–54 Derry City 1, Glentoran 0	
1954–55 Dundela 3, Glenavon 0	
1955–56 Distillery 1, Glentoran 0	
1956–57 Glenavon 2, Derry City 0	
1957–58 Ballymena U 2, Linfield 0	
1958–59 Glenavon 2, Ballymena U 0	
1959–60 Linfield 5, Ards 1	
1960–61 Glenavon 5, Linfield 1	
1961–62 Linfield 4, Portadown 0	
1962–63 Linfield 2, Distillery 1	
1963–64 Derry City 2, Glentoran 0	
1964–65 Coleraine 2, Glenavon 1	
1965–66 Glentoran 2, Linfield 0	
1966–67 Crusaders 3, Glentoran 1	
1967–68 Crusaders 2, Linfield 0	
1968–69 Ards 4, Distillery 2	
1969–70 Linfield 2, Ballymena U 1	
1970–71 Distillery 3, Derry City	
1971–72 Coleraine 2, Portadown 1	
1972–73 Glentoran 3, Linfield 2	
1973–74 Ards 2, Ballymena U 1	
1974–75 Coleraine 1:0:1, Linfield 1:0:0	
1975–76 Carrick Rangers 2, Linfield 1	
1976–77 Coleraine 4, Linfield 1	
1977–78 Linfield 3, Ballymena U 1	
1978–79 Cliftonville 3, Portadown 2	
1979–80 Linfield 2, Crusaders 0	
1980–81 Ballymena U 1, Glenavon 0	

1981–82 Linfield 2, Coleraine 1	
1982–83 Glentoran 1:2, Linfield 1:1	
1983–84 Ballymena U 4, Carrick Rangers 1	
1984–85 Glentoran 1:1, Linfield 1:0	
1985–86 Glentoran 2, Coleraine 1	
1986–87 Glentoran 1, Larne 0	
1987–88 Glentoran 1, Glenavon 0	
1988–89 Ballymena U 1, Larne 0	
1989–90 Glentoran 3, Portadown 0	
1990–91 Portadown 2, Glenavon 1	
1991–92 Glenavon 2, Linfield 1	
1992–93 Bangor 1:1:1, Ards 1:1:0	
1993–94 Linfield 2, Bangor 0	
1994–95 Linfield 3, Carrick Rangers 1	
1995–96 Glentoran 1, Glenavon 0	
1996–97 Glenavon 1, Cliftonville 0	
1997–98 Glentoran 1, Glenavon 0	
1998–99 *Portadown awarded trophy after Cliftonville were eliminated for using an ineligible player in semi-final.*	
1999–2000 Glentoran 1, Portadown 0	
2000–01 Glentoran 1, Linfield 0	
2001–02 Linfield 2, Portadown 1	
2002–03 Coleraine 1, Glentoran 0	
2003–04 Glentoran 1, Coleraine 0	
2004–05 Portadown 5, Larne 1	
2005–06 Linfield 2, Glentoran 1	
2006–07 Linfield 2, Dungannon Swifts 2	
(aet; Linfield won 3-2 on penalties).	
2007–08 Linfield 2, Coleraine 1	
2008–09 Crusaders 1, Cliftonville 0	
2009–10 Linfield 2, Portadown 1	
2010–11 Linfield 2, Crusaders 1	

ULSTER CUP WINNERS

1949 Linfield	1962 Linfield	1975 Coleraine	1988 Glentoran	2001 *No competition*	
1950 Larne	1963 Crusaders	1976 Glentoran	1989 Glentoran	2002 *No competition*	
1951 Glentoran	1964 Linfield	1977 Linfield	1990 Portadown	2003 Dungannon Swifts	
1952 *No competition*	1965 Coleraine	1978 Linfield	1991 Bangor	*(Confined to*	
1953 Glentoran	1966 Glentoran	1979 Linfield	1992 Linfield	*First Division clubs)*	
1954 Crusaders	1967 Linfield	1980 Ballymena U	1993 Crusaders	2004 *No competition*	
1955 Glenavon	1968 Coleraine	1981 Glentoran	1994 Bangor	2005 *No competition*	
1956 Linfield	1969 Coleraine	1982 Glentoran	1995 Portadown	2006 *No competition*	
1957 Linfield	1970 Linfield	1983 Glentoran	1996 Portadown	2007 *No competition*	
1958 Distillery	1971 Linfield	1984 Linfield	1997 Coleraine	2008 *No competition*	
1959 Glenavon	1972 Coleraine	1985 Coleraine	1998 Ballyclare Comrades	2009 *No competition*	
1960 Linfield	1973 Ards	1986 Coleraine	1999 Distillery	2010 *No competition*	
1961 Ballymena U	1974 Linfield	1987 Larne	2000 *No competition*	2011 *No competition*	

ROLL OF HONOUR SEASON 2010-11

Competition	Winner	Runner-up
Carling Irish Premiership	Linfield	Crusaders
JJB Sports Irish Cup	Linfield	Crusaders
Ladbroke.Com First Division	Carrick Rangers	Limavady United
Ladbroke.Com Second Division	Warrenpoint Town	Tobermore United
Co-Operative Insurance Cup	Lisburn Distillery	Portadown
County Antrim Shield	Glentoran	Linfield
Steel & Sons Cup	H&W Welders	Knockbreda
Co Antrim Junior Shield	Kelvin Old Boys	St Patrick's YM
Coca-Cola Irish Junior Cup	Woodvale	Bessbrook United
WKD Intermediate Cup	Carrick Rangers	H&W Welders
Mid Ulster Cup	Glenavon	Dungannon Swifts
Harry Cavan Youth Cup	Glenavon III	Ballinamallard Youth
George Wilson Mem Cup	Linfield Swifts	Lisburn Distillery II
Irish FA League Youth Cup	Glentoran Colts	Glenavon III
North West Senior Cup	Institute	Coleraine
NW Craig Cup	Limavady United	Tobermore United
NW Morrison Cup	Newtowne FC	Liverpool Supporters FC
Mid Ulster FA Kennedy Cup	Bessbrook	St Marys
Belfast Telegraph Marshall Shield	Celtic Club No.1 Lurgan	
Belfast Telegraph Radcliffe Cup (Intermediate)	Banbridge Town	Rathfriland Rangers
BT Mid Ulster Cup (Senior)	Glenavon	Dungannon Swifts
Newcastle & District League Premier	Castlewellan	Ballyvance
Fermanagh & Western FA Intermediate Cup	Ballinamallard United	Mountjoy United
Mulhern Cup	Ballinamallard United Res	Tummery Ath Res

AWARDS

ULSTER FOOTBALLER OF THE YEAR
(Castlereagh Glentoran Club)
Alan Blayney *(Linfield)*.

NORTHERN IRELAND PLAYER OF THE YEAR
(Northern Ireland Football Writers' Association)
Stuart Dallas *(Crusaders)*.

YOUNG PLAYER OF THE YEAR
Stuart Dallas *(Crusaders)*.

MANAGER OF THE YEAR
David Jeffrey *(Linfield)*.

OUTSTANDING NON SENIOR TEAM
Carrick Rangers

INTERNATIONAL PERSONALITY
Gareth McAuley *(WBA)*.

CARLING LEADING SCORER
Premier Division
Peter Thompson *(Linfield)* 41

CARLING TEAM OF THE YEAR (NIFWA)
Alan Blayney *(Linfield)*
Michael Smith *(Ballymena U)*
Colin Coates *(Crusaders)*
Colin Nixon *(Glentoran)*
Ross Redman *(Portadown)*
Michael Gault *(Linfield)*
Robert Farrett *(Linfield)*
Stuart Dallas *(Crusaders)*
Chris Morrow *(Crusaders)*
Jordan Owens *(Crusaders)*
Peter Thompson *(Linfield)*

TOP GOALSCORERS 2010-11

All competitions					
Peter Thompson (Linfield)	32	Stuart Dallas (Crusaders)	17	George McMullan (Cliftonville)	15
Jordan Owens (Crusaders)	24	Leon Knight (Coleraine)	17	Michael Ward (Dungannon Swifts)	15
Paul McVeigh (Donegal Celtic)	23	Richard Lecky (Portadown)	17	Glenn Ferguson (Lisburn Distillery)	14
Matthew Burrows (Glentoran)	22	Gary Ligget (Lisburn Distillery)	17	Trevor Molloy (Glenavon)	14
Daryl Fordyce (Glentoran)	22	Andy Waterworth (Glentoran)	16	Timmy Adamson	
Gary Hamilton (Glenavon)	20	Kevin Braniff (Portadown)	15	(Dungannon Swifts)	13
(1 for Glentoran)		Michael Halliday (Crusaders)	15	Curtis Allen (Linfield)	13
Gary Browne (Lisburn Distillery)	19	Ryan Henderson (Donegal Celtic)	15	Philip Lowry (Linfield)	13
		Gary McCutcheon (Ballymena U)	15	Mark McAllister (Linfield)	13

CARLING PLAYER OF THE MONTH

Month	Player	Team
August	Daryl Fordyce	Glentoran
September	Alan Blayney	Linfield
October	Robert Garrett	Linfield
November	Gary Hamilton	Glenavon
December	Stephen Garrett	Cliftonville
January	Sean Mackle	Portadown
February	Stuart Dallas	Crusaders
March	Matty Burrows	Glentoran
April	Aidan Watson	Crusaders

CARLING MANAGER OF THE MONTH

Month	Manager	Team
August	Scott Young	Glentoran
September	David Platt	Coleraine
October	David Jeffery	Linfield
November	Marty Quinn	Glenavon
December	Eddie Patterson	Cliftonville
January	David Jeffery	Linfield
February	Stephen Baxter	Crusaders
March	Stephen Baxter	Crusaders
April	David Jeffery	Linfield

CHAMPIONSHIP PLAYER OF THE MONTH

Month	Player	Team
August	Dean Smith	Loughgall
September	Paul Heatley	Carrick Rangers
October	Marty Verner	H&W Welders
November	Adam Dick	Larne
December	n/a	
January	Anthony Lagan	Carrick Rangers
February	Andy Crawford	Ballinamallard U
March	Tony Anderson	Carrick Rangers
April	David McAlinden	Carrick Rangers

GOALS OF THE MONTH

Month	Player	Team
August	M. Donnelly	Crusaders v Lisburn Dist
September	D. Murray	Newry City v Glenavon
October	M. Burrows	Glentoran v Portadown
November	A. Watson	Ballymena U v Glenavon
December	N Henderson	Dungannon S v Ballymena U
January	S. Mackle	Portadown v Coleraine
February	G. Browne	Lisburn Dist v Dungannon S
March	J. Owens	3rd for Crusaders v Cliftonville
April	G. McCutcheon	Ballymena U v Donegal Celtic

EUROPEAN FOOTBALL REVIEW 2010–11

One can only marvel at the majestic performance of Barcelona in the Champions League final at Wembley. Manchester United played their part in the classic but were outclassed on the occasion. Superlatives apart, there were many facts worth noting.

As to the run of play, United's game plan was to prevent the Catalans from settling into their all-action passing game. It had success for ten to fifteen minutes before Barcelona readjusted their strategy and virtually assumed control. Chances arrived and were either snuffed out or stifled before too much danger.

But in the 27th minute Pedro drilled the opening goal and one expected serious problems for United. Incredibly it was Barcelona's 150th goal in all competitions during the season. Amazingly seven minutes later Wayne Rooney – easily United's best player – exchanged passes with Ryan Giggs and curled in a fine equaliser, totally against the run of play at the time. For Rooney it was his first ever goal against Spanish opposition and his 24th in the Champions League levelling with Paul Scholes.

Still anything Rooney could do, Lionel Messi could at least equal. His left foot snap shot just outside the area was his first on English soil, his twelfth in the competition in 2010–11 and took his total of goals in the season to 53. David Villa with a delightful long-range chip then finally pinned the emblem on the trophy in the 69th minute.

Accusations that Sir Alex Ferguson's game plan did not work, his tactics after the initial stages were wrong as was his team selection, only serve to belittle Barcelona's extraordinary performance. But there was scarcely a weak link in the Catalan chain mail of intricate passing, masterminded by the midfield maestro Xavi, statistics for whom claimed over 95 per cent accuracy. Meanwhile Messi lived up to his reputation as the best player on the planet, perhaps in a team appearing to come from another civilisation.

While this was a splendid finale to the season there needs to be reference to other British teams in this competition and the Europa League. Chelsea reached the quarter-finals before succumbing to Manchester United home and away. Tottenham Hotspur also reached this stage and recaptured some of their glory days of the 1960s with victories over AC Milan and Internazionale, before they came up against the reality of Madrid.

In the last sixteen Arsenal had actually taken a 2-1 lead over Barcelona at The Emirates before losing the tie at the Nou Camp. At the same stage of the Europa League Manchester City were narrowly beaten by Dynamo Kiev and Glasgow Rangers conceded at home to PSV Eindhoven having finished third in their Champions League group earlier on. Liverpool lost out, too, but they had struggled throughout uncharacteristically finding goal scoring difficult.

At the respective group stages of the two tournaments, Spurs, Chelsea and Manchester United had headed affairs, Arsenal finishing second and Rangers third as stated. For the Europa League, Liverpool and Manchester City had led the way, too.

The play-off stages of the Europa saw the end for Aston Villa, Dundee United, Motherwell and The New Saints, the latter three above expectations. The cull at the third qualifying round accounted for Bangor City, Shamrock Rovers, Cliftonville plus Hibernian.

At the Europa League start Port Talbot Town and Llanelli from Wales, Portadown and Glentoran from Northern Ireland plus Dundalk from the Republic had not been disgraced in the first qualifying round of the Europa. Indeed Portadown and Dundalk moved on, joined by Bangor, Motherwell, Cliftonville, Shamrock Rovers and Sporting Fingal.

In the Champions League The New Saints knocked-out Bohemians in the second qualifying round, Linfield were eliminated by Rosenborg. Celtic just defeated Braga in their home leg of the third qualifying round but the three-goal deficit away had been too great.

Braga of course continued in the Europa League reaching the final where they were beaten by Porto. Clearly Iberia rules in Europe.

Manchester United's Javier Hernandez (left) is tackled strongly by Chelsea's Ashley Cole during the UEFA Champions League Quarter-final Second Leg at Old Trafford. The 2-1 win by United saw them through to the semi-final 3-1 on aggregate. (Action Images/Jason Cairnduff)

EUROPEAN CUP FINALS

EUROPEAN CUP FINALS 1956–1992

Year	Winners		Runners-up		Venue	Attendance	Referee
1956	Real Madrid	4	Reims	3	Paris	38,000	Ellis (E)
1957	Real Madrid	2	Fiorentina	0	Madrid	124,000	Horn (Ho)
1958	Real Madrid	3	AC Milan	2 (aet)	Brussels	67,000	Alsteen (Bel)
1959	Real Madrid	2	Reims	0	Stuttgart	80,000	Dutsch (WG)
1960	Real Madrid	7	Eintracht Frankfurt	3	Glasgow	135,000	Mowat (S)
1961	Benfica	3	Barcelona	2	Berne	28,000	Dienst (Sw)
1962	Benfica	5	Real Madrid	3	Amsterdam	65,000	Horn (Ho)
1963	AC Milan	2	Benfica	1	Wembley	45,000	Holland (E)
1964	Internazionale	3	Real Madrid	1	Vienna	74,000	Stoll (A)
1965	Internazionale	1	Benfica	0	Milan	80,000	Dienst (Sw)
1966	Real Madrid	2	Partizan Belgrade	1	Brussels	55,000	Kreitlein (WG)
1967	Celtic	2	Internazionale	1	Lisbon	56,000	Tschenscher (WG)
1968	Manchester U	4	Benfica	1 (aet)	Wembley	100,000	Lo Bello (I)
1969	AC Milan	4	Ajax	1	Madrid	50,000	Ortiz (Sp)
1970	Feyenoord	2	Celtic	1 (aet)	Milan	50,000	Lo Bello (I)
1971	Ajax	2	Panathinaikos	0	Wembley	90,000	Taylor (E)
1972	Ajax	2	Internazionale	0	Rotterdam	67,000	Helies (F)
1973	Ajax	1	Juventus	0	Belgrade	93,500	Guglovic (Y)
1974	Bayern Munich	1	Atletico Madrid	1	Brussels	49,000	Loraux (Bel)
Replay	Bayern Munich	4	Atletico Madrid	0	Brussels	23,000	Delcourt (Bel)
1975	Bayern Munich	2	Leeds U	0	Paris	50,000	Kitabdjian (F)
1976	Bayern Munich	1	St Etienne	0	Glasgow	54,864	Palotai (H)
1977	Liverpool	3	Moenchengladbach	1	Rome	57,000	Wurtz (F)
1978	Liverpool	1	FC Brugge	0	Wembley	92,000	Corver (Ho)
1979	Nottingham F	1	Malmo	0	Munich	57,500	Linemayr (A)
1980	Nottingham F	1	Hamburg	0	Madrid	50,000	Garrido (P)
1981	Liverpool	1	Real Madrid	0	Paris	48,360	Palotai (H)
1982	Aston Villa	1	Bayern Munich	0	Rotterdam	46,000	Konrath (F)
1983	Hamburg	1	Juventus	0	Athens	80,000	Rainea (R)
1984	Liverpool	1	Roma	1	Rome	69,693	Fredriksson (Se)
	(aet; Liverpool won 4-2 on penalties)						
1985	Juventus	1	Liverpool	0	Brussels	58,000	Daina (Sw)
1986	Steaua Bucharest	0	Barcelona	0	Seville	70,000	Vautrot (F)
	(aet; Steaua won 2-0 on penalties)						
1987	Porto	2	Bayern Munich	1	Vienna	59,000	Ponnet (Bel)
1988	PSV Eindhoven	0	Benfica	0	Stuttgart	70,000	Agnolin (I)
	(aet; PSV won 6-5 on penalties)						
1989	AC Milan	4	Steaua Bucharest	0	Barcelona	97,000	Tritschler (WG)
1990	AC Milan	1	Benfica	0	Vienna	57,500	Kohl (A)
1991	Red Star Belgrade	0	Marseille	0	Bari	56,000	Lanese (I)
	(aet; Red Star won 5-3 on penalties)						
1992	Barcelona	1	Sampdoria	0 (aet)	Wembley	70,827	Schmidhuber (G)

UEFA CHAMPIONS LEAGUE FINALS 1993–2011

1993	Marseille*	1	AC Milan	0	Munich	64,400	Rothlisberger (Sw)
1994	AC Milan	4	Barcelona	0	Athens	70,000	Don (E)
1995	Ajax	1	AC Milan	0	Vienna	49,730	Craciunescu (R)
1996	Juventus	1	Ajax	1	Rome	67,000	Vega (Sp)
	(aet; Juventus won 4-2 on penalties)						
1997	Borussia Dortmund	3	Juventus	1	Munich	59,000	Puhl (H)
1998	Real Madrid	1	Juventus	0	Amsterdam	47,500	Krug (G)
1999	Manchester U	2	Bayern Munich	1	Barcelona	90,000	Collina (I)
2000	Real Madrid	3	Valencia	0	Paris	78,759	Braschi (I)
2001	Bayern Munich	1	Valencia	1	Milan	71,500	Jol (Ho)
	(aet; Bayern Munich won 5-4 on penalties)						
2002	Real Madrid	2	Leverkusen	1	Glasgow	52,000	Meier (Sw)
2003	AC Milan	0	Juventus	0	Manchester	63,215	Merk (G)
	(aet; AC Milan won 3-2 on penalties)						
2004	Porto	3	Monaco	0	Gelsenkirchen	52,000	Nielsen (D)
2005	Liverpool	3	AC Milan	3	Istanbul	65,000	González (Sp)
	(aet; Liverpool won 3-2 on penalties)						
2006	Barcelona	2	Arsenal	1	Paris	79,500	Hauge (N)
2007	AC Milan	2	Liverpool	1	Athens	74,000	Fandel (G)
2008	Manchester U	1	Chelsea	1	Moscow	69,552	Michel (Slo)
	(aet; Manchester U won 6-5 on penalties)						
2009	Barcelona	2	Manchester U	0	Rome	62,467	Busacca (Sw)
2010	Internazionale	2	Bayern Munich	0	Madrid	74,954	Webb (E)
2011	Barcelona	3	Manchester U	1	Wembley	87,695	Kassai (H)

Subsequently stripped of title.

UEFA CHAMPIONS LEAGUE 2010–11

* Denotes player sent off.

FIRST QUALIFYING ROUND FIRST LEG

Tuesday, 29 June 2010
Santa Coloma (0) 0
Birkirkara (0) 0
Match forfeited, result given as 0-3 by UEFA.

Wednesday, 30 June 2010
Tre Fiori (0) 0
Rudar (2) 3 *(Useni 31, Vlahovic 40, Jovanovic I 90)*   681
Tre Fiori: Micheletti; Andreini, Macerata, Benedettini, Nardone, Tarini (Amici 73), Martini, Vannoni (Menin 56), Canarezza, Lisi, Aruta (Grana 89).
Rudar: Radanovic; Bojic, Igumanovic, Bojovic, Ivanovic, Vlahovic, Brnovic (Minic 75), Sekulic (Micic 60), Tomic (Jovanovic I 68), Useni, Randelovic.

FIRST QUALIFYING ROUND SECOND LEG

Tuesday, 6 July 2010
Birkirkara (4) 4 *(Galea 10, 31, Cilia 35, 45)*
Santa Coloma (2) 3 *(Urbani N 21, Jimenez 44, Urbani M 84)*   878
Birkirkara: Lovizon; Paris, Zerafa (Pulo 67), Nisevic, Vukanac, Bajada (Tabone 75), Fenech, De Cesare, Galea, Cilia (Buhagiar 82), Muscat.
Santa Coloma: Fernandez; Gil, Javi Sanchez, Alfonso Sanchez, Ribolleda (Txema 46), Ayala, Garcia (Bodjo 54), Urbani M, Sonejee (Gilbert Sanchez 77), Jimenez, Urbani N.

Wednesday, 7 July 2010
Rudar (1) 4 *(Randelovic 7, 67, Vlahovic 83, Jovanovic M 85)*
Tre Fiori (1) 1 *(Vannoni 29)*   400
Rudar: Radanovic; Bojic, Igumanovic, Bojovic, Ivanovic, Vlahovic, Brnovic, Sekulic (Micic 78), Tomic (Jovanovic M 46), Useni (Jovanovic I 61), Randelovic.
Tre Fiori: Micheletti; Andreini, Macerata, Benedettini, Nardone, Tarini (Berardi 87), Vannoni, Canarezza, Lisi, Macina (Manzari 80), Menin (Amici 52).

SECOND QUALIFYING ROUND FIRST LEG

Tuesday, 13 July 2010
AIK Stockholm (0) 1 *(Englom 57)*
Jeunesse Esch (0) 0   11,515
AIK Stockholm: Turina; Karlsson, Johansson, Atta, Tjernstrom, Pavey, Johnson (Gustavsson 85), Danielsson, Ljubojevic (Catovic 54), Antonio Flavio, Engblom.
Jeunesse Esch: Oberweis; Hoffmann, Collette, Portier, Servais, Leweck C, Fullenwarth (De Sousa 82), Martin, Peters, Piron (Pupovac 46), Rodriguez (Cantonnet 87).

Birkirkara (1) 1 *(Vukanac 1)*
Zilina (0) 0   688
Birkirkara: Lovizon; Zerafa, Buhagiar, Nisevic, Vukanac (Borg 72), Bajada, Fenech, De Cesare (Scicluna R 85), Pulo (Scicluna A 81), Galea, Tabone.
Zilina: Dubravka; Sourek, Angelovic, Piacek, Jez, Zosak (Leitner 80), Mraz, Rilke (Poliacek 60), Oravec, Majtan (Fotyik 68), Bello.

Bohemians (0) 1 *(Brennan 66)*
The New Saints (0) 0   2314
Bohemians: Murphy B; Heary, Powell, Oman, Higgins, Brennan, Shelley, Cretaro (Byrne 75), Keegan, Quigley, Madden.
The New Saints: Harrison; Evans, Baker, Holmes D, Marriott, Jones C, Hogan, Ruscoe, Berkeley (Wood 77), Williams M (Darlington 83), Sharp.

Dinamo Zagreb (2) 5 *(Mandzukic 30, 63, Slepicka 38, Sammir 77, Etto 80)*
Koper (1) 1 *(Bubanja 11)*   7116
Dinamo Zagreb: Butina; Etto, Biscan, Ibanez (Barbaric 85), Mesaric, Chago, Sammir, Morales (Sivonjic 60), Badelj (Calello 76), Slepicka, Mandzukic.
Koper: Hasic; Handanagic, Andraz Struna (Aljaz Struna 56), Polovanec, Karic, Kovacevic, Pavlin M (Guberac 84), Marceta, Sesar, Brulc (Jelenic 79), Bubanja.

Hapoel Tel Aviv (5) 5 *(Al Lala 10, 31, 38, Shivon 12, Beslija 28 (og))*
Zeljeznicar (0) 0   10,931
Hapoel Tel Aviv: Ben Senan; Kende, Ben Dayan, Douglas (Fransman 65), Vermouth, Badir, Shivhon (Maree 74), Yadin, Zahavi, Al Lala (Rocchi 56), Shechter.
Zeljeznicar: Sehic; Mesic, Bogicevic, Radovanovic, Savic, Visca, Beslija M, Zeba (Gancev 46), Culum (Svraka 46), Popovic (Rovcanin 88), Stanic.

Inter Baku (0) 0
Lech (0) 1 *(Wichniarek 47)*   7000
Inter Baku: Lomaia; Zhelev, Kruglov (Hajiyev 52), Mzhavanadze, Kandelaki, Levin, Chertoganov, Chervenka, Zlatinov, Odikadze (Dashdemirov 82), Poskus (Karlsons 83).
Lech: Kotorowski; Bosacki, Gancarczyk, Wojtkowiak, Bandrowski, Injac, Peszko (Wilk 90), Krivets, Kikut, Stilic (Kielb 63), Wichniarek (Mikolajczak 71).

Levadia (0) 1 *(Neemelo 59)*
Debrecen (0) 1 *(Rezes 90)*   1800
Levadia: Kaalma; Kalimullin, Morozov, Teniste, Podholjuzin, Malov, Leitan, Nahk, Felipe Nunes, Ivanov, Neemelo (Dmitrijev 76).
Debrecen: Malinauskas; Mijadinoski, Fodor, Komlosi, Nagy, Czvitkovics, Kiss (Dombi 78), Szakaly, Bodi (Yannick 61), Kabat (Rezes 69), Coulibaly.

Litex (1) 1 *(Popov 8)*
Rudar (0) 0   6900
Litex: Galatto; Nikolov, Bodurov, Barthe, Zanev, Jelenkovic, Popov (Yanev 61), Sandrinho, Wellington (Bratu 69), Doka Madureira (Tsvetanov 78), Niflore.
Rudar: Radanovic; Bojic, Igumanovic, Bojovic*, Ivanovic, Vlahovic, Brnovic (Sekulic 79), Micic, Useni (Adzic 89), Randelovic, Jovanovic M (Jovanovic I 56).

Metalurgs Liepaya (0) 0
Sparta Prague (1) 3 *(Kadlec 37, Wilfried 51, 58)*   3330
Metalurgs Liepaya: Spole; Puljiz, Surnins, Klava, Kirhners (Aleksejevs 54), Kavaliauskas, Rafalskis (Golovins 70), Tamasauskas, Grebis, Kalns, Rakels.
Sparta Prague: Blazek; Hoheneder, Brabec, Repka, Sionko, Matejovsky, Kladrubsky, Zofcak (Vacek 65), Kucka (Jeslinek 78), Wilfried (Lacny 83), Kadlec.

Omonia (2) 3 *(Konstantinou 7 (pen), 62, Davidson Morais 28)*
Renova (0) 0   13,400
Omonia: Georgallides; Wenzel, Karipidis, Leandro, Spungin (Efrem 46), Aloneftis (Victor 80), Grammozis (Panagi 83), Davidson Morais, Makridis, Kaseke, Konstantinou.
Renova: Elezi; Ignjatovski*, Stojanov, Stepanovski M, Statovci, Gashi, Bajrami (Fetai 62), Memedi, Emini (Gafuri 81), Nuhiu, Ali (Janchevski 90).

Salzburg (2) 5 *(Zurate 21, Jantscher 43, Ulmer 46, Wallner 63, Hierlander 82)*
HB Torshavn (0) 0   9100
Salzburg: Tremmel; Schiemer, Ulmer, Sekagya, Schwegler, Mendes da Silva (Pokrivac 60), Svento (Cziommer 60), Jantscher, Leitgeb, Wallner (Hierlander 75), Zarate.

HB Torshavn: Dawid; Mortensen, Jorgensen, Lag (Holm 77), Benjaminsen, Hreidarsson, Kuljic (Hanssen 59), Poulsen R, Samuelsen, Flotum (Akselsen 75), Rubeksen.

Wednesday, 14 July 2010

Aktobe (1) 2 *(Smakov 40 (pen), 53)*

Olimpi (0) 0 10,000

Aktobe: Sidelnikov; Ba, Bono, Badlo, Smakov, Karpovich, Golovskoy (Tleshev 71), Khayrullin, Essomba, Peric (Khokhlov 88), Averchenko (Darabaev 82).

Olimpi: Bediashvili; Kvakhadze, Gongadze, Rekhviashvili, Kemoklidze, Chelidze (Dolidze 86), Razmadze, Bolkvadze (Khidesheli 75), Getsadze, Modebadze, Chedia (Dobrovolski 56).

BATE Borisov (0) 5 *(Nekhajchik 48, 85, 88, Renan 58, Rodionov 90)*

Hafnarfjordur (0) 1 *(Bjornsson 89)* 5200

BATE Borisov: Veremko; Radkov, Yurevich, Bordachev, Shitov, Likhtarovich (Olekhnovich 63), Nekhajchik, Renan (Volodko A 68), Pavlov, Rodionov, Kontsevoy (Skavysh 78).

Hafnarfjordur: Gunnleifsson; Fredsgaard-Nielsen (Motland 67), Saevarsson, Vidarsson, Valgardsson, Sverrisson, Thrastarson (Bjarnason 59), Bjornsson, Snorrason, Gudnason, Vilhjalmsson.

Ekranas (1) 1 *(Radavicius 3)*

HJK Helsinki (0) 0 2500

Ekranas: Cerniauskas; Gleveckas, Matovic, Arlauskas, Tomkevicius, Radavicius, Kucys (Banys 85), Ademolu (Markevicius 90), Sidlauskas, Pogreban (Varnas 65), Rimkus.

HJK Helsinki: Wallen; Kansikas, Ojala, Magnusson, Rafinha, Medo, Zeneli (Parikka 62), Sorsa (Westo 83), Riihilahti (Fowler 76), Bah, Hoesen.

Linfield (0) 0

Rosenborg (0) 0 1715

Linfield: Blayncy; Bailie, Lindsay, Burns B (Ervin 76), Burns A, Garrett, Mulgrew, Curran, Lowry (McAllister 70), McCaul (Carvill 61), Thompson.

Rosenborg: Orlund; Dorsin, Stadsgaard, Lustig, Demidov, Annan, Traore (Strand 46), Winsnes, Henriksen, Iversen, Moldskred (Olsen 87).

Partizan Belgrade (2) 3 *(Tomic 29, Almami Moreira 45, Cleo 59)*

Pyunik (1) 1 *(Yedigarian 30)* 11,134

Partizan Belgrade: Ilic R; Krstajic, Jovanovic M, Lazevski, Stevanovic, Ilic S, Almami Moreira (Davidov 75), Petrovic (Jovanovic B 85), Tomic, Cleo, Scepovic (Bogunovic 55).

Pyunik: Lesko; Hovsepian, Minasian, Adedeji, Mkrtchian, Pizzelli, Yedigarian (Barseghian 90), Manoian, Ghazarian, Yuspashian, Goharian (Manasian 66).

Serif (1) 3 *(Volkov 9, Nikolic 62, Jose Nadson 70)*

Dinamo Tirana (1) 1 *(Malacarne 12)* 6951

Serif: Stoyanov; Adamovic, Jose Nadson, Tarkhnishvili, Brankovic, Volkov, Vranjes, Bulat (Erokhin 46), Fred (Haceaturov 90), Nikolic (Gheorghiev 76), Jymmy Franca.

Dinamo Tirana: Hidi; Pisha, Xhafa, Putincanin, Garcia (Sosa 79), Vila, Malacarne, Diop, Martinena, Muzaka (Allmuca 72), Elis Bakaj■.

SECOND QUALIFYING ROUND SECOND LEG

Tuesday, 20 July 2010

Dinamo Tirana (1) 1 *(Vila 18)*

Serif (0) 0 3000

Dinamo Tirana: Hidi; Pisha, Xhafa (Peqini 72), Mallota (Garcia 65), Putincanin, Vila, Malacarne, Sosa, Martinena, Sefa, Muzaka (Daja 88).

Serif: Stoyanov; Adamovic (Samardzic 80), Jose Nadson, Tarkhnishvili, Brankovic, Volkov, Vranjes, Bulat (Fred 57), Erokhin, Nikolic (Diedhiou 46), Jymmy Franca.

HB Torshavn (0) 1 *(Samuelsen 73)*

Salzburg (0) 0 250

HB Torshavn: Thomsen; Mortensen, Jorgensen, Benjaminsen, Hreidarsson, Holm, Hanssen, Poulsen R, Samuelsen, Flotum (Mouritsen 89), Rubeksen.

Salzburg: Walke; Dudic, Schiemer, Ulmer, Sekagya, Cziommer (Svento 46), Mendes da Silva (Pokrivac 34), Jantscher (Ngwat-Mahop 71), Leitgeb, Hierlander, Zarate.

Koper (1) 3 *(Handanagic 11, Guberac 54, Brulc 78 (pen))*

Dinamo Zagreb (0) 0 720

Koper: Hasic; Handanagic, Andraz Struna, Polovanec, Karic (Maric 60), Aljaz Struna, Kovacevic (Guberac 46), Marceta, Sesar (Bozicic 68), Brulc, Jelenic.

Dinamo Zagreb: Butina; Etto, Biscan■, Ibanez (Mesaric 57), Barbaric, Calello, Chago, Sammir, Slepicka (Morales 46), Sivonjic (Simic 78), Dodo.

Renova (0) 0

Omonia (2) 2 *(Aloneftis 15, Leandro 24)* 600

Renova: Elezi; Stojanov, Stepanovski M, Statovci (Bajrami 61), Gashi (Mickov 52), Memedi, Emini (Fetai 83), Nuhiu, Gafuri, Janchevski, Ali.

Omonia: Georgallides; Iago Bouzon, Charalambous, Karipidis, Leandro, Aloneftis (Rueda 74), Davidson Morais, Makridis (Rengifo 46), Kaseke, Efrem, Konstantinou (Lua Lua 63).

Rudar (0) 0

Litex (2) 4 *(Niflore 28, Jelenkovic 39, Bratu 74, 90)* 2137

Rudar: Radanovic; Bojic, Igumanovic, Adzic, Ivanovic, Vlahovic (Idrizovic 46), Brnovic (Jovanovic M 58), Micic (Sekulic 78), Useni, Randelovic, Jovanovic I.

Litex: Galatto; Nikolov, Bodurov, Barthe, Zanev, Petkov, Jelenkovic, Popov (Milanov 63), Sandrinho (Yanev 76), Wellington, Niflore (Bratu 72).

The New Saints (3) 4 *(Jones C 6, Williams M 14, 73, Sharp 20)*

Bohemians (0) 0 1056

The New Saints: Harrison; Evans, Baker, Holmes D, Marriott, Jones C, Hogan, Ruscoe, Berkeley (Wood 89), Williams M, Sharp.

Bohemians: Murphy B; Heary, Powell (McGuinness 46), Oman, Higgins (Cronin 46), Brennan, Shelley, Keegan, Quigley, Byrne (Greene 67), Madden.

Wednesday, 21 July 2010

Debrecen (2) 3 *(Coulibaly 24, Yannick 32, Szakaly 55)*

Levadia (1) 2 *(Nahk 3, Leitan 53)* 7500

Debrecen: Malinauskas; Mijadinoski, Fodor, Komlosi, Nagy, Kulcsar (Rezes 46), Czvitkovics, Kiss, Szakaly (Varga 73), Yannick (Dombi 85), Coulibaly.

Levadia: Kaalma; Kalimullin, Morozov, Teniste, Podholjuzin, Malov■, Leitan, Nahk, Felipe Nunes (Subbotin 80), Ivanov, Neemelo.

Hafnarfjordur (0) 0

BATE Borisov (1) 1 *(Rodionov 15)* 522

Hafnarfjordur: Gunnleifsson; Fredsgaard-Nielsen (Bjarnason 78), Vidarsson, Valgardsson (Gunnlaugsson 43), Jonsson, Sverrisson, Thrastarson, Motland, Bjornsson (Gudnason 64), Snorrason, Vilhjalmsson.

BATE Borisov: Veremko; Sosnovski, Bordachev, Shitov, Likhtarovich, Baga, Renan, Volodko A (Yurevich 77), Olekhnovich (Pavlov 58), Rodionov (Patotskiy 71), Skavysh.

HJK Helsinki (0) 2 *(Ojala 77, Sidlauskas 119 (og))*

Ekranas (0) 0 6030

HJK Helsinki: Wallen; Karkkainen, Kansikas, Ojala, Rafinha, Medo, Sorsa, Riihilahti (Fowler 100), Bah■, Makela (Zeneli 72), Parikka (Pelvas 63).

Ekranas: Kauneckas; Gleveckas, Matovic, Arlauskas (Skinderis 90), Galkevicius (Pogreban 58), Tomkevicius■, Radavicius, Kucys, Ademolu, Sidlauskas, Rimkus (Varnas 68).

aet.

Jeunesse Esch (0) 0

AIK Stockholm (0) 0   1568

Jeunesse Esch: Oberweis; Hoffmann, Collette, Portier, Servais, Leweck C, Fullenwarth (Cantonnet 21), Martin, Peters, Pupovac (Piron 59), Rodriguez (Goncalves 68).
AIK Stockholm: Turina; Karlsson, Johansson, Atta, Backman, Tjernstrom, Pavey, Johnson, Danielsson, Antonio Flavio (Lundberg 77), Engblom (Ljubojevic 69).

Lech (0) 0

Inter Baku (0) 1 *(Karlsons 84)*   13,700

Lech: Kotorowski; Bosacki, Gancarczyk, Wojtkowiak, Arboleda, Djurdjevic (Wilk 98), Injac, Peszko, Krivets, Stilic, Wichniarek (Kielb 78).
Inter Baku: Lomaia; Mzhavanadze (Dashdemirov 71), Kandelaki, Levin, Accioly, Chertoganov, Chervenka, Zlatinov, Odikadze, Hajiyev (Kruglov 46), Poskus (Karlsons 84).
aet; Lech won 9-8 on penalties.

Olimpi (1) 1 *(Rekhviashvili 30)*

Aktobe (0) 1 *(Tleshev 90)*   4200

Olimpi: Bediashvili (Batiashvili 79); Kvakhadze, Gongadze, Rekhviashvili, Kemoklidze, Chelidze (Dolidze 68), Razmadze, Dobrovolski, Bolkvadze, Getsadze (Chedia 53), Modebadze.
Aktobe: Sidelnikov; Ba, Bono (Badlo 90), Kenzhisariev, Smakov, Karpovich, Golovskoy (Khokhlov 86), Khayrullin, Essomba, Peric (Tleshev 46), Averchenko.

Pyunik (0) 0

Partizan Belgrade (1) 1 *(Cleo 45)*   4500

Pyunik: Lesko; Hovsepian, Haroian, Adedeji, Mkrtchian, Pizzelli, Yedigarian (Manucharian 49), Manoian, Ghazarian, Yuspashian, Goharian (Malakian 61).
Partizan Belgrade: Ilic R; Krstajic (Stankovic 36); Kizito, Jovanovic M, Stevanovic, Ilic S, Almami Moreira, Petrovic (Jovanovic B 83), Tomic, Cleo, Scepovic (Davidov 66).

Rosenborg (1) 2 *(Prica 32, Henriksen 87)*

Linfield (0) 0   6645

Rosenborg: Orlund; Dorsin, Stadsgaard, Lustig, Demidov, Annan, Skjelbred (Strand 82), Henriksen, Iversen, Moldskred (Winsnes 74), Prica (Olsen 74).
Linfield: Blayney; Bailie, Lindsay, Burns B, Burns A (Munster 81), Garrett, Mulgrew, Curran, Lowry (Carvill 68), McCaul (Allen 63), Thompson.

Sparta Prague (2) 2 *(Matejovsky 12, Zeman 43)*

Metalurgs Liepaya (0) 0   8025

Sparta Prague: Blazek; Brabec, Repka, Pamic, Vacek, Matejovsky (Zofcak 56), Kladrubsky, Kucka (Hoheneder 46), Jeslinek, Lacny (Zeman 41), Kadlec.
Metalurgs Liepaya: Spole (Steinbors 46); Puljiz (Kirhners 64), Surnins, Jemelins (Aleksejevs 69), Klava, Akahoshi, Kavaliauskas, Rafalskis, Tamasauskas, Kalns, Rakels.

Zeljeznicar (0) 0

Hapoel Tel Aviv (0) 1 *(Douglas 76)*   4500

Zeljeznicar: Sehic; Mesic, Bogicevic, Radovanovic, Gancev (Stanic 46), Savic (Culum 76), Visca, Beslija M (Sphic 78), Zeba, Svraka, Rovcanin.
Hapoel Tel Aviv: Ben Senan; Kende, Ben Dayan, Douglas, Vermouth, Badir, Shivhon (Maree 60), Yadin, Zahavi (Shaish 71), Al Lala (Rocchi 46), Shechter.

Zilina (1) 3 *(Piacek 21, Lietava 77, Oravec 90)*

Birkirkara (0) 0   5511

Zilina: Dubravka; Sourek, Angelovic, Piacek, Jez, Mraz, Rilke (Poliacek 71), Lietava, Oravec, Majtan (Zosak 59), Bello (Guldan 90).
Birkirkara: Lovizon; Borg, Zerafa, Buhagiar, Nisevic (Scicluna R 87), Vukanac, Bajada, Fenech, Galea, Tabone (Pulo 66), Muscat (Paris 75).

THIRD QUALIFYING ROUND FIRST LEG

Tuesday, 27 July 2010

Dynamo Kiev (1) 3 *(Yarmolenko 19, Shevchenko 80, Zozulya 90)*

Gent (0) 0   15,000

Dynamo Kiev: Boyko; Betao, Mikhalik, Danilo Silva, Eremenko (Zozulya 76), Vukojevic, Gerson Magrao, Garmash, Milevskiy (Bertoglio 50) (Leandro Almeida 90), Shevchenko, Yarmolenko.
Gent: Jorgacevic; Hanstveit, Wils, Adriano, Myrie (Smolders 73), Thijs, Grondin, Lepoint, De Smet (Coulibaly 83), Leye (Arbeitman 59), El Ghanassy.

Litex (0) 1 *(Wellington 79)*

Zilina (0) 1 *(Majtan 65)*   6000

Litex: Galatto; Nikolov, Bodurov, Barthe, Zanev, Petkov, Jelenkovic (Yanev 85), Popov, Sandrinho (Bratu 73), Wellington (Milanov 89), Niflore.
Zilina: Dubravka; Sourek, Guldan, Leitner, Piacek, Jez, Rilke (Zosak 78), Oravec (Chupac 87), Ceesay (Lietava 69), Majtan, Bello.

Omonia (0) 1 *(Lua Lua 90 (pen))*

Salzburg (1) 1 *(Zarate 8)*   20,000

Omonia: Jevric; Iago Bouzon, Charalambous, Karipidis, Leandro, Aloneftis (Lua Lua 46), Davidson Morais, Makridis, Kaseke (Avraam 64), Efrem, Konstantinou (Rengifo 82).
Salzburg: Tremmel; Afolabi, Schiemer (Dudic 86), Ulmer, Sekagya, Schwegler, Mendes da Silva, Svento (Jantscher 82), Leitgeb, Wallner (Tchoyi 71), Zarate.

Sparta Prague (0) 1 *(Brabec 76)*

Lech (0) 0   14,588

Sparta Prague: Blazek; Hoheneder, Brabec, Repka, Pamic, Sionko, Matejovsky (Hejda 90), Kladrubsky, Kucka, Wilfried (Tresnak 86), Kadlec (Jeslinek 73).
Lech: Kotorowski; Bosacki, Gancarczyk, Wojtkowiak, Arboleda, Injac, Peszko, Krivets (Mikolajczak 85), Stilic (Wilk 87), Drygas, Wichniarek (Tshibamba 78).

The New Saints (0) 1 *(Jones C 52)*

Anderlecht (2) 3 *(Kljestan 7, Legear 18, Suarez 73)*   2486

The New Saints: Harrison; Evans, Baker, Holmes D, Marriott (Holmes T 21), Jones C (Holmes T 21), Berkeley (Seargeant 78), Williams M, Sharp (Darlington 84).
Anderlecht: Proto; Juhasz, Deschacht, Mazuch (Lecjaks 83), Biglia, Kljestan (Kanu 87), Boussoufa, Gillet, Legear, Kouyate, Suarez (De Sutter 76).

Unirea (0) 0

Zenit (0) 0   12,000

Unirea: Arlauskis; Marin, Maftei, Galamaz, Bordeanu, Paraschiv, Paduretu R■, Frunza (Onofras 72), Marinescu, Neaga (Rusescu 86), Bilasco (Dale 89).
Zenit: Malafeev; Fernando Meira, Anyukov, Lombaerts, Hubocan, Bystrov (Kanunnikov 80), Danny, Shirokov (Faizulin 70), Zyrianov (Rosina 59), Denisov, Kerzhakov.

Wednesday, 28 July 2010

AIK Stockholm (0) 0

Rosenborg (1) 1 *(Henriksen 33)*   16,768

AIK Stockholm: Turina; Karlsson, Johansson, Backman, Tjernstrom, Pavey, Johnson, Persson, Danielsson (Lundberg 75), Ljubojevic (Engblom 81), Bangura.
Rosenborg: Orlund; Dorsin, Stadsgaard, Lustig, Demidov, Annan, Skjelbred, Henriksen, Iversen, Moldskred (Olsen 78), Prica (Winsnes 72).

Ajax (1) 1 *(Suarez 13)*

PAOK Salonika (0) 1 *(Ivic 72)*   24,151

Ajax: Stekelenburg; Vertonghen, Van der Wiel, Anita, Alderweireld, Emanuelson (Sarpong 79), Lindgren (De Zeeuw 62), De Jong, Enoh, Suarez, Sulejmani (Eriksen 67).
PAOK Salonika: Chalkias (Kresic 15); Cirillo, Sznaucer, Malezas, Boussaidi, Sorlin, Vitolo, Pablo Garcia, Vieirinha, Ivic (Fotakis 75), Salpingidis (Papazoglou 90).

Aktobe (0) 1 *(Smakov 67 (pen))*
Hapoel Tel Aviv (0) 0   12,100
Aktobe: Sidelnikov; Ba, Bono, Badlo, Kenzhisariev, Smakov, Karpovich, Khayrullin (Khokhlov 80), Essomba, Peric (Tleshev 46), Averchenko (Darabaev 55).
Hapoel Tel Aviv: Enyeama; Kende, Ben Dayan, Douglas, Vermouth, Badir, Rocchi (Shivhon 68), Yadin, Zahavi, Al Lala (Sahar 57), Shechter.

BATE Borisov (0) 0
FC Copenhagen (0) 0   5300
BATE Borisov: Veremko; Radkov, Yurevich, Bordachev, Shitov, Likhtarovich (Skavysh 77), Nekhajchik, Pavlov, Olekhnovich, Rodionov (Baga 85), Kontsevoy (Renan 65).
FC Copenhagen: Wiland; Wendt, Ottesen, Antonsson, Kvist Jorgensen, Pospech, Norregaard, Vingaard, Claudemir, Cesar Santin (Gronkjaer 82), N'Doye.

Braga (1) 3 *(Alan 26 (pen), Elderson 76, Matheus 88)*
Celtic (0) 0   12,295
Braga: Mario Felgueiras; Rodriguez, Miguel Garcia, Elderson, Andres Madrid, Vandinho, Moises, Salino, Alan (Helder Barbosa 90), Lima (Matheus 66), Paulo Cesar.
Celtic: Zaluska; Cha, Hooiveld, Mulgrew, Loovens, Juarez (Forrest 79), Brown, Ki, Ledley, Maloney (Murphy 71), Samaras.

Debrecen (0) 0
Basle (1) 2 *(Stocker 34, Xhaka 90)*   6500
Debrecen: Verpecz; Mijadinoski, Bernath, Fodor, Komlosi, Czvitkovics, Kiss, Rezes (Farkas 55), Varga, Yannick (Dombi 75), Coulibaly.
Basle: Costanzo; Safari, Abraham, Cagdas, Inkoom, Huggel, Stocker (Xhaka 89), Shaqiri (Tembo 62), Cabral, Frei, Zoua (Almerares 76).

Partizan Belgrade (2) 3 *(Iliev 8, Ilic S 42, Cleo 90)*
HJK Helsinki (0) 0   14,300
Partizan Belgrade: Ilic R; Krstajic (Stankovic 72), Jovanovic M, Lazevski, Stevanovic, Ilic S (Jovanovic B 69), Almami Moreira (Davidov 46), Petrovic, Tomic, Iliev, Cleo.
HJK Helsinki: Wallen; Karkkainen, Kansikas, Ojala, Rafinha, Fowler (Parikka 46), Medo, Zeneli (Westo 27), Sorsa, Riihilahti, Makela (Pelvas 73).

Serif (1) 1 *(Erokhin 35)*
Dinamo Zagreb (1) 1 *(Sammir 3)*   9150
Serif: Stoyanov; Adamovic, Samardzic, Jose Nadson (Fred 32), Tarkhnishvili, Brankovic, Volkov (Gheorghiev 88), Vranjes, Erokhin, Diedhiou (Nikolic 66), Jymmy Franca.
Dinamo Zagreb: Butina; Cufre, Etto, Ibanez, Barbaric*, Mesaric, Calello, Chago, Sammir (Sivonjic 85), Badelj (Dodo 70), Slepicka (Simic 64).

Young Boys (1) 2 *(Dudar 18, Costanzo 89 (pen))*
Fenerbahce (2) 2 *(Emre B 5, Stoch 42)*   19,091
Young Boys: Burki; Spycher, Sutter, Dudar, El Jemal, Affolter, Degen, Doubai T (Mayuka 83), Lulic (Regazzoni 65), Costanzo, N' Tsama (Schneuwly M 58).
Fenerbahce: Volkan; Onder, Andre Santos, Bilica, Bekir, Emre B (Deivid de Souza 65), Kazim-Richards, Alex (Semih 80), Cristian Baroni, Stoch, Gokhan U (Selcuk 72).

THIRD QUALIFYING ROUND SECOND LEG

Tuesday, 3 August 2010
Anderlecht (1) 3 *(De Sutter 17, Lukaku 69, 74)*
The New Saints (0) 0   19,338
Anderlecht: Proto; Juhasz, Lecjaks, Bernardez, Rnic, Kljestan (Gillet 73), Chatelle, Marecek, De Sutter (Lukaku 59), Suarez (Diandy 46), Chavarria.

The New Saints: Harrison; Evans (Edwards 74), Baker, Holmes T, Holmes D, Jones C, Hogan, Ruscoe, Wood (Seargeant 87), Williams M, Sharp (Darlington 83).

Hapoel Tel Aviv (3) 3 *(Zahavi 16, Sahar 31, Ba 35 (og))*
Aktobe (0) 1 *(Tleshev 90)*   12,000
Hapoel Tel Aviv: Enyeama; Shaish, Kende, Douglas, Vermouth, Badeer, Shivhon (Rocchi 64), Yadin, Sahar (Al Lala 54), Zahavi (Abutbul 70), Shechter.
Aktobe: Sidelnikov; Ba, Bono, Badlo, Kenzhisariev, Smakov, Khayrullin, Khokhlov (Chichulin 56), Essomba, Peric, Averchenko (Tleshev 46).

Wednesday, 4 August 2010
Basle (1) 3 *(Cagdas 26, Chipperfield 59, Shaqiri 64)*
Debrecen (0) 1 *(Coulibaly 74)*   17,376
Basle: Costanzo; Safari, Abraham, Cagdas, Inkoom, Yapi-Yapo (Cabral 77), Chipperfield (Almerares 67), Huggel (Xhaka 87), Shaqiri, Tembo, Zoua.
Debrecen: Verpecz; Mijadinoski, Laczko, Bernath, Komlosi, Kulcsar (Kabat 67), Czvitkovics (Farkas 81), Kiss, Varga, Yannick (Bodi 67), Coulibaly.

Celtic (0) 2 *(Hooper 52, Juarez 79)*
Braga (1) 1 *(Paulo Cesar 20)*   53,592
Celtic: Zaluska; Cha, Hooiveld, Mulgrew (Fortune 47), Loovens, Juarez, Brown (McCourt 88), Ledley, Maloney (Murphy 64), Samaras, Hooper.
Braga: Mario Felgueiras; Rodriguez, Miguel Garcia, Elderson, Andres Madrid (Paulao 86), Vandinho, Moises, Salino (Meyong 90), Alan, Paulo Cesar, Matheus (Lima 67).

Dinamo Zagreb (0) 1 *(Sammir 55 (pen))*
Serif (1) 1 *(Volkov 16)*   7811
Dinamo Zagreb: Loncaric; Cufre, Etto, Biscan, Mesaric (Ibanez 46), Sammir, Ademi (Calello 76), Badelj, Vrsaljko, Slepicka, Rukavina (Dodo 88).
Serif: Stoyanov; Adamovic, Samardzic, Jose Nadson (Scripcenco 95), Brankovic, Volkov, Vranjes, Erokhin, Fred (Haceaturov 79), Diedhiou (Nikolic 72), Jymmy Franca.
aet; Serif won 6-5 on penalties.

FC Copenhagen (2) 3 *(Cesar Santin 2, Kvist Jorgensen 27, N'Doye 60)*
BATE Borisov (2) 2 *(Kontsevoy 40, Nekhajchik 44)*   15,533
FC Copenhagen: Wiland; Wendt, Ottesen, Antonsson, Kvist Jorgensen, Pospech, Norregaard (Gronkjaer 55), Vingaard, Claudemir (Zanka Jorgensen 88), Cesar Santin (Kristensen 80), N'Doye.
BATE Borisov: Veremko; Radkov, Yurevich, Sosnovski*, Bordachev (Baga 82), Likhtarovich (Olekhnovich 61), Nekhajchik, Renan, Pavlov (Skavysh 68), Rodionov, Kontsevoy.

Fenerbahce (0) 0
Young Boys (1) 1 *(N'Tsama 40)*   35,260
Fenerbahce: Volkan; Andre Santos, Bilica, Ilhan, Bekir (Selcuk 46), Emre B, Alex (Gokhan G 46), Cristian Baroni, Stoch*, Dia (Semih 81), Gokhan U.
Young Boys: Wolffi; Spycher, Sutter, Dudar, El Jemal, Affolter, Degen, Doubai T (Raimondi 70), Lulic (Schneuwly C 78), Costanzo (Hochstrasser 62), N' Tsama.

Gent (0) 1 *(Coulibaly 85)*
Dynamo Kiev (1) 3 *(Garmash 32, Milevskiy 55, Gusev 90)*   6049
Gent: Jorgacevic; Thompson, Adriano (Ljubijankic 47), Suler, Myrie, Thijs, Grondin, Lepoint (Smolders 69), Custovic (Arbeitman 46), Coulibaly, El Ghanassy.
Dynamo Kiev: Boyko; Betao, Mikhalik, Danilo Silva, Eremenko (Zozulya 68), Vukojevic, Gerson Magrao (El Kaddouri 43), Garmash, Milevskiy, Shevchenko, Yarmolenko (Gusev 77).

HJK Helsinki (1) 1 *(Medo 39)*
Partizan Belgrade (1) 2 *(Cleo 9, 90)*   4230
HJK Helsinki: Wallen; Kansikas, Ojala, Magnusson, Rafinha, Medo, Sorsa, Riihilahti (Fowler 33), Bah, Parikka (Westo 75), Pelvas (Makela 62).
Partizan Belgrade: Ilic R; Krstajic (Stankovic 82), Jovanovic M, Lazevski, Stevanovic, Ilic S, Smiljanic, Petrovic (Jovanovic B 70), Tomic, Iliev (Davidov 62), Cleo.

Lech (0) 0
Sparta Prague (0) 1 *(Kladrubsky 50 (pen))*   13,200
Lech: Kotorowski; Bosacki■, Gancarczyk, Wojtkowiak (Kielb 86), Arboleda, Injac, Wilk (Tshibamba 53), Peszko, Krivets, Drygas (Stilic 57), Wichniarek.
Sparta Prague: Blazek; Hoheneder, Brabec, Repka, Pamic, Sionko■, Matejovsky■, Kladrubsky, Kucka (Hejda 75), Wilfried (Lacny 90), Kadlec (Zofcak 67).

PAOK Salonika (1) 3 *(Vieirinha 16, Salpingidis 56, Ivic 90)*
Ajax (0) 3 *(Suarez 48, De Jong 50, Lindgren 55)*   24,109
PAOK Salonika: Kresic; Cirillo, Contreras, Sznaucer (Filomeno 83), Boussaidi, Sorlin, Vitolo (Muslimovic 64), Pablo Garcia, Vieirinha, Ivic, Salpingidis.
Ajax: Stekelenburg; Vertonghen, Van der Wiel, Anita, Alderweireld, Emanuelson, De Zeeuw, Lindgren, De Jong, Suarez (Oleguer 90), Sulejmani (Eriksen 78).

Rosenborg (0) 3 *(Prica 55, Demidov 64, Lustig 76)*
AIK Stockholm (0) 0   14,709
Rosenborg: Orlund; Dorsin, Stadsgaard, Lustig, Demidov, Annan, Skjelbred, Henriksen, Iversen (Strand 74), Moldskred (Olsen 56), Prica (Bakenga 82).
AIK Stockholm: Turina; Karlsson, Johansson, Atta, Tjernstrom, Pavey, Johnson, Persson (Lundberg 69), Danielsson, Ljubojevic (Antonio Flavio 59), Bangura.

Salzburg (3) 4 *(Svento 21, Schiemer 37, 40, Boghossian 58)*
Omonia (0) 1 *(Rengifo 90)*   14,400
Salzburg: Tremmel; Afolabi, Schiemer (Augustinussen 70), Sekagya, Schwegler, Mendes da Silva (Hierlander 84), Svento, Jantscher, Leitgeb (Ngwat-Mahop 86), Zarate, Boghossian.
Omonia: Georgallides; Iago Bouzon, Charalambous, Karipidis, Leandro, Aloneftis, Davidson Morais, Makridis, Kaseke (Avraam 68), Lua Lua (Efrem 66), Konstantinou (Rengifo 72).

Zenit (1) 1 *(Danny 33)*
Unirea (0) 0   21,100
Zenit: Malafeev; Fernando Meira, Anyukov, Lombaerts, Hubocan, Bystrov (Rosina 46), Danny, Shirokov (Faizulin 64), Zyrianov, Denisov, Kerzhakov (Kanunnikov 76).
Unirea: Arlauskis; Maftei, Galamaz, Nicu, Bordeanu, Frunza (Onofras 88), Brandan, Marinescu, Semedo (Dale 53), Bilasco, Rusescu (Neaga 58).

Zilina (0) 3 *(Rilke 52, Oravec 70, Ceesay 84)*
Litex (0) 1 *(Sandrinho 50)*   8123
Zilina: Dubravka; Sourek, Guldan, Pecalka, Jez, Mraz, Rilke (Poliacek 81), Oravec, Ceesay (Fotyik 90), Majtan (Zosak 63), Bello.
Litex: Galatto; Berberovic, Nikolov, Bodurov, Zanev, Jelenkovic, Yanev (Wellington 61), Popov■, Sandrinho, Milanov, Niflore (Bratu 66).

PLAY-OFF ROUND FIRST LEG

Tuesday, 17 August 2010
Dynamo Kiev (0) 1 *(Gusev 66)*
Ajax (0) 1 *(Vertonghen 58)*   16,500
Dynamo Kiev: Koval; Leandro Almeida, Betao, Popov, Mikhalik, Gusev (Danilo Silva 82), Eremenko, Vukojevic, Garmash■, Shevchenko (El Kaddouri 76), Yarmolenko (Andre 70).

Ajax: Stekelenburg; Vertonghen, Oleguer, Van der Wiel, Anita (Sulejmani 61), Emanuelson, De Zeeuw, De Jong, Enoh (Eriksen 69), El Hamdaoui, Suarez.

Rosenborg (1) 2 *(Iversen 23, Henriksen 57)*
FC Copenhagen (0) 1 *(Gronkjaer 84)*   18,822
Rosenborg: Orlund; Dorsin, Stadsgaard, Lustig, Demidov, Annan, Skjelbred, Henriksen, Iversen (Winsnes 85), Prica, Olsen (Bakenga 65).
FC Copenhagen: Wiland; Wendt, Antonsson, Kvist Jorgensen, Pospech, Zanka Jorgensen, Gronkjaer, Kristensen (Norregaard 67), Vingaard (Bergvold 68), Claudemir, N'Doye.

Sparta Prague (0) 0
Zilina (0) 2 *(Ceesay 51, Oravec 73)*   18,744
Sparta Prague: Blazek; Hoheneder, Brabec, Repka, Pamic, Bondoa, Vachousek (Jeslinek 90), Zofcak (Zeman 77), Kucka, Lacny (Tresnak 68), Kweuke.
Zilina: Dubravka; Guldan, Pecalka, Piacek, Jez, Mraz, Rilke (Zosak 79), Oravec, Ceesay (Sourek 90), Majtan (Poliacek 87), Bello.

Young Boys (3) 3 *(Lulic 4, N'Tsama 13, Hochstrasser 28)*
Tottenham H (1) 2 *(Bassong 42, Pavlyuchenko 83)* 30,166
Young Boys: Wolfli; Spycher, Sutter, El Jemal, Affolter, Degen (Raimondi 90), Hochstrasser, Doubai, Lulic, Costanzo (Schneuwly C 65), N'Tsama.
Tottenham H: Gomes; Corluka, Assou-Ekotto (Huddlestone 36), Palacios, Dawson, Bassong, Giovani, Modric (Kranjcar 46), Pavlyuchenko, Defoe (Keane 66), Bale.

Zenit (1) 1 *(Kerzhakov 3)*
Auxerre (0) 0   21,405
Zenit: Malafeev; Bruno Alves, Anyukov, Lombaerts, Hubocan, Semak (Zyryanov 90), Danny, Shirokov, Denisov, Lazovic (Huszti 60), Kerzhakov (Bukharov 78).
Auxerre: Sorin; Grichting, Mignot, Coulibaly, Hengbart, Pedretti, Ndinga, Birsa (Contout 70), Oliech (Quercia 90), Jelen, Le Tallec.

Wednesday, 18 August 2010
Basle (0) 1 *(Stocker 54)*
Serif (0) 0   13,460
Basle: Costanzo; Safari, Abraham, Cagdas, Inkoom, Yapi Yapo, Huggel, Stocker, Shaqiri (Tembo 71), Frei (Chipperfield 88), Zoua (Almerares 80).
Serif: Stoyanov; Adamovic (Haceaturov 79), Samardzic, Jose Nadson, Brankovic, Volkov (Gheorghiev 90), Vranjes, Erokhin■, Rouamba, Balima, Diedhiou (Durovic 57).

Braga (0) 1 *(Matheus 62)*
Sevilla (0) 0   16,646
Braga: Felipe; Rodriguez, Miguel Garcia (Silvio 46), Elderson, Vandinho, Moises, Aguiar (Lima 57), Leandro Salino, Alan, Paulo Cesar, Matheus (Elton 75).
Sevilla: Palop; Dabo, Escude, Fernando Navarro, Fazio, Zokora, Renato, Jesus Navas, Diego Capel (Perotti 70), Kanoute (Negredo 79), Luis Fabiano.

Partizan Belgrade (0) 2 *(Cleo 58, Lecjaks 64 (og))*
Anderlecht (0) 2 *(Gillet 54, Juhasz 66)*   28,565
Partizan Belgrade: Ilic R; Krstajic, Jovanovic M, Lazevski, Stevanovic, Ilic S, Moreira (Smiljanic 53), Petrovic, Tomic (Davidov 74), Iliev (Bogunovic 87), Cleo.
Anderlecht: Proto; Polak (Badibanga 90), Juhasz, Deschacht, Mazuch, Lecjaks, Boussoufa (Marecek 84), Gillet, Kouyate, Suarez, Lukaku (Kanu 61).

Salzburg (1) 2 *(Pokrivac 28, Wallner 67 (pen))*
Hapoel Tel Aviv (2) 3 *(Enyeama 3 (pen), Sahar 44, Shechter 53)*   18,900
Salzburg: Tremmel; Afolabi, Schiemer (Alan 67), Sekagya, Schwegler, Svento, Pokrivac, Jantscher, Leitgeb, Zarate (Ngwat-Mahop 78), Boghossian (Wallner 59).

Hapoel Tel Aviv: Enyeama; Kende, Ben Dayan, Douglas, Vermouth (Fransman 90), Badir, Shivhon (Rocchi 72), Yadin, Sahar (Maree 78), Zahavi, Shechter.

Werder Bremen (0) 3 *(Fritz 51, Frings 67 (pen), Pizarro 69)*

Sampdoria (0) 1 *(Pazzini 90)*   25,276

Werder Bremen: Wiese; Mertesacker, Pasanen (Boenisch 77), Fritz, Prodl, Borowski, Frings, Bargfrede, Hunt (Marin 85), Hugo Almeida (Arnautovic 88), Pizarro.
Sampdoria: Curci; Ziegler, Gastaldello, Lucchini■, Volta, Palombo, Semioli (Stankevicius 68), Tissone (Poli 59), Mannini (Guberti 65), Cassano, Pazzini.

PLAY-OFF ROUND SECOND LEG

Tuesday, 24 August 2010
Anderlecht (0) 2 *(Lukaku 64, Gillet 71)*
Partizan Belgrade (1) 2 *(Cleo 15, 53)*   19,551
Anderlecht: Proto; Polak, Juhasz, Deschacht, Mazuch, Biglia, Boussoufa, Gillet, Kouyate (Legear 60), Suarez, Lukaku.
Partizan Belgrade: Ilic R; Krstajic, Jovanovic M, Lazevski, Stevanovic, Ilic S (Davidov 19), Smiljanic, Petrovic, Tomic (Stankovic 82), Iliev (Bogunovic 101), Cleo.
aet; Partizan Belgrade won 3-2 on penalties.

Hapoel Tel Aviv (0) 1 *(Zahavi 90)*
Salzburg (1) 1 *(Douglas 42 (og))*   13,348
Hapoel Tel Aviv: Enyeama; Kende, Ben Dayan, Douglas, Vermouth, Badir, Rocchi (Abutbul 74), Sahar (Shaish 90), Zahavi, Shechter, Maree (Fransman 65).
Salzburg: Tremmel, Afolabi, Sekagya, Schwegler, Mendes da Silva, Svento, Pokrivac, Leitgeb, Wallner (Boghossian 74), Zarate, Ngwat-Mahop (Alan 65).

Sampdoria (2) 3 *(Pazzini 8, 10, Cassano 85)*
Werder Bremen (0) 2 *(Rosenberg 90, Pizarro 100)* 27,574
Sampdoria: Curci; Ziegler, Gastaldello, Volta, Stankevicius, Palombo, Semioli, Dessena, Guberti (Tissone 66) (Mannini 73), Cassano (Pozzi 88), Pazzini.
Werder Bremen: Wiese; Mertesacker, Pasanen (Boenisch 80), Fritz, Prodl, Borowski (Arnautovic 63), Frings, Marin, Bargfrede, Pizarro, Wagner (Rosenberg 72).
aet.

Serif (0) 0
Basle (0) 3 *(Streller 74, Frei 80, 87)*   12,300
Serif: Stoyanov; Adamovic, Jose Nadson, Tarkhnishvili■, Volkov, Vranjes, Rouamba, Fred (Durovic 76), Balima, Diedhiou (Nikolic 66), Jymmy Franca (Haceaturov 79).
Basle: Costanzo; Safari, Abraham, Cagdas, Inkoom, Yapi Yapo (Ferati 87), Huggel, Stocker (Shaqiri 85), Frei, Streller (Chipperfield 78), Zoua.

Sevilla (0) 3 *(Luis Fabiano 60, Jesus Navas 84, Kanoute 90)*
Braga (1) 4 *(Matheus 31, Lima 58, 85, 89)*   31,350
Sevilla: Palop; Dabo (Negredo 77), Escude, Konko (Renato 61), Fazio, Zokora, Cigarini (Jose Carlos 61), Jesus Navas, Perotti, Kanoute, Luis Fabiano.
Braga: Felipe; Rodriguez, Elderson, Silvio, Vandinho, Moises, Aguiar (Lima 55), Leandro Salino, Alan, Paulo Cesar (Paulao 68), Matheus (Elton 80).

Wednesday, 25 August 2010
Ajax (1) 2 *(Suarez 43, El Hamdaoui 75)*
Dynamo Kiev (0) 1 *(Shevchenko 84 (pen))*   50,249
Ajax: Stekelenburg; Vertonghen, Van der Wiel, Alderweireld, Emanuelson, De Zeeuw, De Jong, Enoh, Eriksen (Sulejmani 73), El Hamdaoui (Ooijer 85), Suarez.
Dynamo Kiev: Koval; Popov, Mikhalik, Danilo Silva, Khacheridi, Gusev (Ninkovic 76), Eremenko, Vukojevic (Andre 88), Milevskiy (Guilherme 86), Shevchenko, Yarmolenko.

Auxerre (1) 2 *(Hengbart 9, Jelen 53)*
Zenit (0) 0   15,277
Auxerre: Sorin; Grichting, Mignot, Coulibaly, Hengbart, Pedretti, Contout, Ndinga, Oliech (Chafni 86), Jelen, Le Tallec (Birsa 63).
Zenit: Malafeev■; Fernando Meira (Bukharov 79), Bruno Alves, Anyukov, Hubocan■, Bystrov (Zhevnov 66), Semak, Danny, Shirokov, Zyryanov (Lazovic 55), Kerzhakov.

FC Copenhagen (1) 1 *(Ottesen 33)*
Rosenborg (0) 0   31,180
FC Copenhagen: Wiland; Wendt, Ottesen, Antonsson, Kvist Jorgensen, Pospech, Gronkjaer (Zanka Jorgensen 90), Vingaard (Larsson 90), Claudemir, Cesar Santin (Norregaard 67), N'Doye.
Rosenborg: Orlund; Dorsin, Stadsgaard, Lustig, Demidov, Wangberg (Strand 46), Skjelhred (Winsnes 63), Henriksen, Iversen, Prica, Olsen (Moldskred 77).

Tottenham H (2) 4 *(Crouch 5, 61, 78 (pen), Defoe 32)*
Young Boys (0) 0   34,709
Tottenham H: Gomes (Cudicini 46); Corluka, Assou-Ekotto, Palacios, Dawson, King, Lennon, Huddlestone, Crouch, Defoe (Pavlyuchenko 62), Bale (Kranjcar 82).
Young Boys: Wolfli; Spycher, Sutter (Schneuwly M 62), El Jemal, Affolter, Degen, Hochstrasser, Doubai (Schneuwly C 82), Lulic■, Costanzo (Regazzoni 62), N'Tsama.

Zilina (1) 1 *(Ceesay 18)*
Sparta Prague (0) 0   10,892
Zilina: Dubravka; Guldan, Pecalka, Piacek, Jez, Mraz, Rilke (Zosak 90), Oravec, Ceesay (Vittor 80), Majtan (Poliacek 74), Bello.
Sparta Prague: Blazek; Hoheneder, Pamic (Tresnak 85), Bondoa (Kweuke 46), Hejda, Sionko (Kaderabek 61), Vachousek, Kladrubsky, Kucka, Krejci, Wilfried.

GROUP STAGE

GROUP A

Tuesday, 14 September 2010

Twente (2) 2 *(Janssen 20, Milito 30 (og))*
Internazionale (2) 2 *(Sneijder 14, Eto'o 41)*   23,800
Twente: Mihaylov; Wisgerhof, Tiendalli, Rosales, Douglas, Janssen, Brama, Chadli (Landzaat 88), Ruiz, Janko (Bajrami 78), De Jong.
Internazionale: Julio Cesar; Lucio, Zanetti, Maicon, Samuel, Sneijder, Cambiasso, Mariga, Eto'o, Milito (Muntari 87), Pandev (Philippe Coutinho 61).

Werder Bremen (1) 2 *(Hugo Almeida 43, Marin 47)*
Tottenham H (2) 2 *(Pasanen 12 (og), Crouch 18)*   30,344
Werder Bremen: Wiese; Silvestre, Pasanen, Fritz, Prodl, Frings, Marin, Bargfrede (Hunt 37), Wesley (Borowski 67), Hugo Almeida (Wagner 79), Arnautovic.
Tottenham H: Cudicini; Corluka, Assou-Ekotto, Huddlestone, Kaboul, King, Lennon (Palacios 76), Jenas, Crouch, Van der Vaart (Keane 49), Bale.

Wednesday, 29 September 2010

Internazionale (3) 4 *(Eto'o 21, 27, 81, Sneijder 34)*
Werder Bremen (0) 0   48,126
Internazionale: Julio Cesar (Castellazzi 46); Lucio (Santon 62), Cordoba, Maicon, Chivu, Sneijder, Cambiasso, Stankovic (Obi 80), Philippe Coutinho, Eto'o, Biabiany.
Werder Bremen: Wiese; Mertesacker, Silvestre, Prodl, Borowski (Pasanen 46), Jensen, Marin (Hunt 63), Bargfrede, Wesley, Hugo Almeida (Wagner 78), Arnautovic.

Tottenham H (0) 4 *(Van der Vaart 48, Pavlyuchenko 51 (pen), 65 (pen), Bale 85)*
Twente (0) 1 *(Chadli 57)*   32,518
Tottenham H: Gomes; Hutton, Assou-Ekotto, Huddlestone, Bassong, King, Van der Vaart[■], Modric (Lennon 82), Crouch (Jenas 66), Pavlyuchenko (Keane 89), Bale.
Twente: Mihaylov; Wisgerhof, Rosales, Douglas, Kuiper, Landzaat (De Jong 69), Janssen, Brama, Bajrami (Chadli 28), Ruiz, Janko.

Wednesday, 20 October 2010

Internazionale (4) 4 *(Zanetti 2, Eto'o 11, 35, Stankovic 14)*
Tottenham H (0) 3 *(Bale 52, 89, 90)*   49,551
Internazionale: Julio Cesar; Lucio, Zanetti, Maicon, Samuel, Chivu (Pandev 61), Sneijder, Stankovic (Santon 50), Philippe Coutinho, Eto'o, Biabiany (Cordoba 75).
Tottenham H: Gomes[■]; Hutton, Assou-Ekotto, Huddlestone (Palacios 80), Bassong, Gallas, Lennon, Jenas, Crouch (Keane 67), Modric (Cudicini 10), Bale.

Twente (0) 1 *(Janssen 75)*
Werder Bremen (0) 1 *(Arnautovic 80)*   23,248
Twente: Mihaylov; Wisgerhof (Bengtsson 24), Tiendalli, Rosales, Douglas, Landzaat (De Jong 86), Janssen, Brama, Chadli, Ruiz, Janko.
Werder Bremen: Wiese (Mielitz 37); Mertesacker, Pasanen, Fritz, Prodl, Frings, Bargfrede (Marin 77), Wesley, Hunt, Hugo Almeida (Arnautovic 59), Pizarro.

Tuesday, 2 November 2010

Tottenham H (1) 3 *(Van der Vaart 18, Crouch 61, Pavlyuchenko 89)*
Internazionale (0) 1 *(Eto'o 80)*   34,103
Tottenham H: Cudicini; Hutton, Assou-Ekotto, Huddlestone, Gallas, Kaboul, Lennon (Palacios 84), Modric, Crouch (Pavlyuchenko 76), Van der Vaart (Jenas 46), Bale.
Internazionale: Castellazzi; Lucio, Zanetti, Maicon, Samuel, Chivu, Sneijder, Muntari (Nwankwo 53), Eto'o, Pandev (Milito 71), Biabiany (Philippe Coutinho 64).

Werder Bremen (0) 0
Twente (0) 2 *(Chadli 81, De Jong 84)*   30,200
Werder Bremen: Mielitz; Mertesacker, Prodl, Frings[■], Jensen, Marin, Bargfrede (Arnautovic 59), Wesley, Hunt, Hugo Almeida, Pizarro.
Twente: Mihaylov; Wisgerhof, Bengtsson (Schimpelsberger 76), Rosales, Douglas, Landzaat, Chadli (Vujicevic 85), Leugers, Ruiz, Janko, De Jong (Stockentree 90).

Wednesday, 24 November 2010

Internazionale (0) 1 *(Cambiasso 55)*
Twente (0) 0   29,466
Internazionale: Castellazzi; Materazzi, Lucio, Cordoba, Zanetti, Sneijder (Nwankwo 87), Cambiasso, Stankovic, Eto'o, Pandev (Biraghi 90), Biabiany (Santon 80).
Twente: Mihaylov; Wisgerhof, Rosales, Douglas, Janssen, Brama, Chadli, Leugers (Buysse 80), Ruiz, Janko (Landzaat 70), De Jong.

Tottenham H (2) 3 *(Kaboul 6, Modric 45, Crouch 79)*
Werder Bremen (0) 0   33,546
Tottenham H: Gomes; Hutton, Assou-Ekotto, Modric, Gallas, Kaboul, Lennon, Jenas (Palacios 76), Crouch, Pavlyuchenko (Defoe 57), Bale (Kranjcar 81).
Werder Bremen: Wiese; Mertesacker, Fritz, Prodl, Schmidt, Jensen (Pasanen 86), Marin, Bargfrede, Hunt (Thy 80), Wagner, Kroos (Ayik 55).

Tuesday, 7 December 2010

Twente (1) 3 *(Landzaat 22 (pen), Rosales 56, Chadli 64)*
Tottenham H (1) 3 *(Wisgerhof 12 (og), Defoe 47, 59)*   24,000
Twente: Boschker; Wisgerhof, Tiendalli, Rosales, Douglas, Landzaat, Janssen, Brama, Chadli, Janko (Vujicevic 73), De Jong.
Tottenham H: Gomes; Corluka, Assou-Ekotto, Palacios, Gallas, Bassong, Kranjcar (Crouch 86), Jenas (Lennon 34), Pavlyuchenko (Keane 73), Defoe, Bale.

Werder Bremen (1) 3 *(Prodl 39, Arnautovic 49, Pizarro 88)*
Internazionale (0) 0   30,400
Werder Bremen: Wiese; Mertesacker, Pasanen (Silvestre 83), Fritz, Prodl, Schmidt, Frings (Bargfrede 78), Marin, Hunt, Hugo Almeida (Pizarro 76), Arnautovic.
Internazionale: Orlandoni; Cordoba, Zanetti (Natalino 54), Santon (Biabiany 50), Cambiasso, Muntari, Thiago Motta (Mariga 76), Nwankwo, Biraghi, Eto'o, Pandev.

Group A Table	P	W	D	L	F	A	Pts
Tottenham H	6	3	2	1	18	11	11
Internazionale	6	3	1	2	12	11	10
Twente	6	1	3	2	9	11	6
Werder Bremen	6	1	2	3	6	12	5

GROUP B

Tuesday, 14 September 2010

Benfica (1) 2 *(Luisao 21, Cardozo 68)*
Hapoel Tel Aviv (0) 0   31,512
Benfica: Roberto; Luisao, Fabio Coentrao, David Luiz, Aimar (Airton 71), Javi Garcia, Ruben Amorim, Gaitan (Maxi Pereira 57), Carlos Martins, Saviola (Cesar Peixoto 87), Cardozo.
Hapoel Tel Aviv: Enyeama; Bondarv, Fransman (Badir 74), Ben Dayan, Douglas, Vermouth, Rocchi (Shivhon 61), Zahavi, Yadin, Sahar (Tamuz 58), Schechter.

Lyon (1) 1 *(Michel Bastos 21)*
Schalke (0) 0   35,552
Lyon: Lloris; Diakathe, Reveillere, Lovren, Kolodziejczak, Toulalan, Michel Bastos (Pied 71), Gourcuff (Makoun 86), Pjanic, Briand (Kallstrom 90), Lisandro Lopez.
Schalke: Neuer; Sarpei (Schmitz 75), Plestan, Howedes[■], Jones (Kluge 70), Rakitic, Deac (Matip 46), Moritz, Raul, Huntelaar, Farfan.

Gareth Bale of Tottenham Hotspur strides past Maicon of Inter Milan (left) during the UEFA Champions League Group A match at White Hart Lane. Spurs won the match 3-1 on their way to heading Group A and a memorable Champions League run which ended in defeat to Real Madrid in the quarter-final. (Action Images/John Sibley)

Wednesday, 29 September 2010

Hapoel Tel Aviv (0) 1 *(Enyeama 79 (pen))*
Lyon (2) 3 *(Michel Bastos 7 (pen), 36, Pjanic 90)*   12,226
Hapoel Tel Aviv: Enyeama; Bondarv, Ben Dayan, Douglas, Vermouth, Badir, Rocchi (Abutbul 59), Zahavi (Shivhon 59), Yadin, Sahar (Tamuz 76), Shechter.
Lyon: Lloris; Diakathe, Reveillere, Cissokho, Lovren, Kallstrom, Toulalan, Michel Bastos (Gonalons 89), Gourcuff (Pjanic 77), Gomis (Pied 63), Briand.

Schalke (0) 2 *(Farfan 73, Huntelaar 85)*
Benfica (0) 0   50,436
Schalke: Neuer; Metzelder, Uchida (Sarpei 58), Papadopoulos, Jurado (Kluge 78), Rakitic (Jones 65), Schmitz, Matip, Raul, Huntelaar, Farfan.
Benfica: Roberto; Luisao, Cesar Peixoto, Maxi Pereira, Fabio Coentrao, David Luiz, Javi Garcia, Gaitan (Salvio 46), Carlos Martins, Saviola (Aimar 62), Cardozo (Kardec 71).

Wednesday, 20 October 2010

Lyon (1) 2 *(Briand 21, Lisandro Lopez 51)*
Benfica (0) 0   36,816
Lyon: Lloris; Cris, Diakathe, Reveillere, Cissokho, Michel Bastos (Pied 64), Gourcuff (Kallstrom 71), Pjanic, Gonalons, Briand, Lisandro Lopez (Gomis 83).
Benfica: Roberto; Luisao, Maxi Pereira, Fabio Coentrao, David Luiz, Aimar (Jara 71), Javi Garcia, Gaitan⁸, Carlos Martins (Salvio 77), Saviola (Cesar Peixoto 57), Kardec.

Schalke (1) 3 *(Raul 3, 58, Jurado 68)*
Hapoel Tel Aviv (0) 1 *(Shechter 90)*   50,900
Schalke: Neuer; Metzelder, Uchida, Howedes, Jones (Matip 75), Jurado, Schmitz, Moritz (Rakitic 53), Raul, Huntelaar, Farfan (Hao Junmin 67).
Hapoel Tel Aviv: Enyeama; Shaish, Kende, Douglas, Vermouth, Badir, Abutbul (Tuama 58), Zahavi, Yadin (Fransman 73), Tamuz (Sahar 58), Shechter.

Tuesday, 2 November 2010

Benfica (3) 4 *(Kardec 20, Fabio Coentrao 32, 67, Javi Garcia 42)*
Lyon (0) 3 *(Gourcuff 75, Gomis 85, Lovren 90)*   37,394
Benfica: Roberto; Luisao, Cesar Peixoto, Maxi Pereira, Fabio Coentrao, David Luiz, Javi Garcia, Carlos Martins (Felipe Menezes 75), Salvio, Saviola (Jara 70), Kardec (Weldon 71).
Lyon: Lloris; Cris, Diakathe (Gomis 59), Reveillere, Lovren, Michel Bastos, Gourcuff, Pjanic (Makoun 70), Pied (Lacazette 71), Gonalons, Briand.

Hapoel Tel Aviv (0) 0
Schalke (0) 0   12,132
Hapoel Tel Aviv: Enyeama; Bondarv, Ben Dayan, Douglas (Fransman 42), Tuama (Shivhon 60), Vermouth, Badir, Abutbul, Zahavi, Sahar (Maree 70), Tamuz.
Schalke: Neuer; Metzelder, Uchida, Howedes, Sergio, Kluge (Moritz 46), Jurado, Rakitic (Edu 74), Raul, Huntelaar, Farfan (Deac 81).

Wednesday, 24 November 2010

Hapoel Tel Aviv (1) 3 *(Zahavi 24, 90, Douglas 74)*
Benfica (0) 0   11,668
Hapoel Tel Aviv: Enyeama; Bondarv, Fransman, Ben Dayan, Douglas, Vermouth, Abutbul (Badir 78), Zahavi, Yadin, Tamuz (Sahar 66), Shechter (Shivhon 58).
Benfica: Roberto; Luisao, Maxi Pereira, Fabio Coentrao, David Luiz, Aimar, Javi Garcia (Jara 79), Gaitan, Salvio (Carlos Martins 65), Saviola (Cardozo 46), Kardec.

Schalke (2) 3 *(Farfan 13, Huntelaar 20, 89)*
Lyon (0) 0   51,132
Schalke: Neuer; Metzelder, Uchida, Howedes, Jones (Matip 70), Kluge, Jurado (Deac 85), Schmitz, Raul, Huntelaar, Farfan (Edu 65).
Lyon: Lloris; Diakathe, Reveillere, Cissokho (Gomis 46), Lovren, Kallstrom, Toulalan, Michel Bastos, Gourcuff (Pjanic 61), Briand, Lisandro Lopez (Pied 74).

Tuesday, 7 December 2010

Benfica (0) 1 *(Luisao 87)*

Schalke (1) 2 *(Jurado 20, Howedes 81)* 23,348

Benfica: Roberto; Luisao, Cesar Peixoto (Gaitan 46), Maxi Pereira (Aimar 46), Fabio Coentrao, David Luiz, Javi Garcia, Ruben Amorim, Carlos Martins (Salvio 79), Saviola, Cardozo.
Schalke: Neuer; Metzelder, Uchida, Howedes, Papadopoulos, Kluge (Matip 82), Jurado (Jendrisek 88), Rakitic, Schmitz, Raul, Huntelaar (Edu 85).

Lyon (0) 2 *(Lisandro Lopez 62, Lacazette 88)*

Hapoel Tel Aviv (0) 2 *(Sahar 63, Zahavi 69)* 32,245

Lyon: Lloris; Cris, Diakathe, Reveillere, Cissokho (Pied 78), Makoun, Pjanic (Lacazette 68), Gonalons, Gomis (Michel Bastos 60), Briand, Lisandro Lopez.
Hapoel Tel Aviv: Enyeama; Shaish, Bondarv, Fransman, Douglas, Vermouth, Abutbul (Badir 80), Zahavi, Yadin, Tamuz (Tuama 62), Shechter (Sahar 25).

Group B Table	P	W	D	L	F	A	Pts
Schalke	6	4	1	1	10	3	13
Lyon	6	3	1	2	11	10	10
Benfica	6	2	0	4	7	12	6
Hapoel Tel Aviv	6	1	2	3	7	10	5

GROUP C

Tuesday, 14 September 2010

Bursa (0) 0

Valencia (2) 4 *(Tino Costa 16, Aduriz 41, Pablo Hernandez 68, Soldado 76)* 22,055

Bursa: Ivankov; Ali, Stepanov, Omer, Vederson, Ergic (Svensson 77), Insua, Volkan, Ozan, Huseyin (Sercan 61), Nunez (Turgay 59).
Valencia: Cesar; Ricardo Costa, Mathieu, David Navarro, Bruno, Joaquin, Mehmet Topal, Tino Costa (Manuel Fernandes 81), Pablo Hernandez, Aduriz (Soldado 72), Chori Domingez (Mata 77).

Manchester U (0) 0

Rangers (0) 0 74,408

Manchester U: Kuszczak; Fabio (Evans J 75), Smalling, Fletcher, Brown, Ferdinand, Valencia (Giggs 63), Gibson, Hernandez, Rooney, Park (Owen 75).
Rangers: McGregor; Whittaker, Papac, Broadfoot, Weir, Bougherra, Davis, Edu, Naismith, Miller (Lafferty 81), McCulloch.

Wednesday, 29 September 2010

Rangers (1) 1 *(Naismith 18)*

Bursa (0) 0 41,905

Rangers: McGregor; Whittaker, Papac, McCulloch, Weir, Bougherra, Broadfoot, Davis, Naismith, Miller (Lafferty 87), Edu.
Bursa: Ivankov; Ali, Stepanov, Omer, Vederson, Ergic (Insua 39), Svensson, Batalla (Nunez 71), Volkan, Ozan, Sercan (Turgay 72).

Valencia (0) 0

Manchester U (0) 1 *(Hernandez 85)* 34,946

Valencia: Cesar; Maduro, Miguel, Mathieu, David Navarro, Albelda (Mehmet Topal 88), Tino Costa (Manuel Fernandes 74), Pablo Hernandez, Soldado, Chori Dominguez (Aduriz 59), Mata.
Manchester U: Van der Sar; Rafael (O'Shea 90), Evra, Carrick, Ferdinand, Vidic, Nani, Fletcher, Berbatov (Macheda 85), Anderson (Hernandez 77), Park.

Wednesday, 20 October 2010

Manchester U (1) 1 *(Nani 7)*

Bursa (0) 0 72,610

Manchester U: Kuszczak; Rafael, Evra, Carrick, Smalling, Vidic, Park (Obertan 71), Fletcher, Macheda, Anderson (Hernandez 78), Nani.
Bursa: Ivankov; Ali (Mustafa 71), Stepanov (Turgay 46), Omer, Vederson, Ergic, Insua, Svensson, Volkan, Ozan, Sercan (Ibrahim 46).

Rangers (1) 1 *(Edu 34)*

Valencia (0) 1 *(Edu 46 (og))* 45,153

Rangers: McGregor; Whittaker, Papac, Foster, Weir, Bougherra, Davis, Edu, Naismith, Miller, Weiss (Lafferty 88).
Valencia: Cesar; Ricardo Costa, Mathieu, David Navarro, Bruno, Mehmet Topal, Tino Costa (Manuel Fernandes 76), Pablo Hernandez, Aduriz, Chori Dominguez (Soldado 46), Mata (Vicente 85).

Tuesday, 2 November 2010

Bursa (0) 0

Manchester U (0) 3 *(Fletcher 48, Obertan 73, Ali 77 (og))* 19,050

Bursa: Ivankov; Ali, Omer, Ibrahim, Vederson, Ergic, Insua (Nunez 75), Svensson, Volkan (Ismail 82), Turgay, Sercan (Ozan 75).
Manchester U: Van der Sar; Rafael, Evra (Fabio 81), Carrick, Smalling, Vidic, Fletcher (Bebe 62), Scholes, Berbatov, Obertan, Nani (Park 29).

Valencia (1) 3 *(Soldado 33, 71, Tino Costa 90)*

Rangers (0) 0 26,821

Valencia: Cesar; Ricardo Costa, Miguel, Mathieu, David Navarro, Albelda, Joaquin (Pablo Hernandez 85), Banega (Tino Costa 70), Aduriz, Soldado (Manuel Fernandes 77), Mata.
Rangers: McGregor; Whittaker, Papac, Broadfoot, Weir, Bougherra, Davis, Edu (Lafferty 83), Naismith, Miller, McCulloch.

Wednesday, 24 November 2010

Rangers (0) 0

Manchester U (0) 1 *(Rooney 87 (pen))* 49,764

Rangers: McGregor; Hutton (Beattie 88), Whittaker, Foster, Weir, Broadfoot, Davis, McCulloch, Naismith, Miller, Weiss (Fleck 79).
Manchester U: Van der Sar; Fabio, O'Shea, Carrick, Smalling, Evans J, Nani (Obertan 77), Scholes (Anderson 67), Berbatov (Hernandez 76), Rooney, Giggs.

Valencia (4) 6 *(Mata 17 (pen), Soldado 21, 55, Aduriz 30, Joaquin 37, Chori Dominguez 78)*

Bursa (0) 1 *(Batalla 69)* 31,225

Valencia: Moya (Guaita 23); Maduro, Ricardo Costa, Bruno, Albelda, Joaquin, Tino Costa, Jordi Alba, Aduriz (Chori Domingez 61), Soldado (Isco 71), Mata.
Bursa: Ivankov; Mustafa, Omer, Ibrahim, Vederson (Serdar 46), Ergic (Batalla 59), Insua, Svensson, Volkan, Turgay, Sercan (Ismail 84).

Tuesday, 7 December 2010

Bursa (0) 1 *(Sercan 79)*

Rangers (1) 1 *(Miller 20)* 9673

Bursa: Yavuz; Mustafa, Stepanov, Serdar (Omer 46), Vederson, Insua, Bekir, Ozan, Huseyin (Batalla 46), Nunez (Turgay 62), Sercan.
Rangers: McGregor; Whittaker, Foster, McCulloch, Weir, Bougherra, Davis, Hutton, Naismith (Weiss 71), Miller (Beattie 63), Cole (McMillan 82).

Manchester U (0) 1 *(Anderson 62)*

Valencia (1) 1 *(Pablo Hernandez 32)* 74,513

Manchester U: Amos; Rafael, Fabio, Carrick, Ferdinand (Smalling 50), Vidic, Nani (Giggs 81), Anderson (Fletcher 90), Berbatov, Rooney, Park.
Valencia: Guaita; Ricardo Costa, Miguel, Mathieu, Dealbert, Albelda, Banega, Pablo Hernandez (Sofiane 81), Jordi Alba (Mata 68), Aduriz, Chori Dominguez (Isco 90).

Group C Table	P	W	D	L	F	A	Pts
Manchester U	6	4	2	0	7	1	14
Valencia	6	3	2	1	15	4	11
Rangers	6	1	3	2	3	6	6
Bursa	6	0	1	5	2	16	1

GROUP D

Tuesday, 14 September 2010

Barcelona (3) 5 *(Messi 22, 44, David Villa 33, Pedro 78, Dani Alves 90)*

Panathinaikos (1) 1 *(Govou 20)*   69,738

Barcelona: Valdes; Puyol, Abidal, Dani Alves, Pique (Gabi Milito 76), Iniesta, Xavi (Mascherano 79), Sergio Busquets, Messi, David Villa (Bojan 70), Pedro.
Panathinaikos: Tzorvas; Boumsong, Kante, Vyntra, Marinos, Gilberto Silva, Katsouranis (Karagounis 64), Simao, Leto (Ninis 81), Govou (Luis Garcia 71), Cisse.

FC Copenhagen (0) 1 *(N'Doye 87)*

Rubin (0) 0   29,661

FC Copenhagen: Wiland; Wendt, Ottesen, Antonsson, Kvist Jorgensen, Pospech, Gronkjaer, Vingaard (Norregaard 90), Claudemir (Zanka Jorgensen 90), Cesar Santin (Bolanos 75), N'Doye.
Rubin: Ryzhikov; Bocchetti (Kuzmin 66), Orekhov, Kaleshin, Salukvadze, Ansaldi, Noboa, Carlos Eduardo (Gokdeniz 77), Murawski, Martins (Kasaev 58), Kornilenko.

Wednesday, 29 September 2010

Panathinaikos (0) 0

FC Copenhagen (2) 2 *(N'Doye 28, Vingaard 37)*   43,607

Panathinaikos: Tzorvas; Sarriegi, Vyntra, Marinos, Gilberto Silva, Katsouranis (Spiropoulos 46), Simao, Ninis (Plessis 58), Leto, Luis Garcia (Karagounis 46), Cisse.
FC Copenhagen: Wiland; Wendt, Antonsson, Kvist Jorgensen, Pospech, Zanka Jorgensen, Gronkjaer, Vingaard, Claudemir (Delaney 79), N'Doye (Cesar Santin 76), Bolanos (Norregaard 58).

Rubin (1) 1 *(Noboa 30 (pen))*

Barcelona (0) 1 *(David Villa 60)*   23,950

Rubin: Ryzhikov; Bocchetti, Cesar Navas, Kaleshin, Salukvadze, Ansaldi, Gokdeniz (Martins 65), Ryazantsev, Noboa (Natcho 88), Murawski, Kornilenko (Sibaya 61).
Barcelona: Valdes; Puyol, Dani Alves, Maxwell, Pique, Mascherano (Messi 61), Iniesta, Xavi, Sergio Busquets, David Villa (Bojan 86), Pedro.

Wednesday, 20 October 2010

Barcelona (1) 2 *(Messi 19, 90)*

FC Copenhagen (0) 0   75,852

Barcelona: Pinto; Puyol, Abidal, Dani Alves, Maxwell (Pedro 73), Pique, Mascherano, Iniesta (Keita 90), Sergio Busquets, Messi, David Villa (Xavi 73).
FC Copenhagen: Wiland; Wendt (Larsson 89), Antonsson, Kvist Jorgensen, Pospech, Zanka Jorgensen, Gronkjaer, Vingaard (Bolanos 62), Claudemir, Cesar Santin (Zohore 74), N'Doye.

Panathinaikos (0) 0

Rubin (0) 0   36,748

Panathinaikos: Tzorvas; Boumsong, Sarriegi, Vyntra, Marinos (Mavrias 78), Spiropoulos, Karagounis (Plessis 61), Katsouranis (Christodoulopoulos 61), Simao, Luis Garcia, Cisse.
Rubin: Ryzhikov; Bocchetti, Cesar Navas, Kaleshin, Ansaldi, Gokdeniz (Martins 66), Ryazantsev, Noboa, Natcho, Kasaev (Bystrov 86), Kornilenko (Sibaya 90).

Tuesday, 2 November 2010

FC Copenhagen (1) 1 *(Claudemir 33)*

Barcelona (1) 1 *(Messi 31)*   37,049

FC Copenhagen: Wiland; Wendt, Antonsson, Kvist Jorgensen, Pospech, Zanka Jorgensen, Gronkjaer, Vingaard (Ottesen 89), Claudemir, N'Doye, Bolanos (Delaney 90).
Barcelona: Valdes; Puyol, Abidal, Dani Alves, Pique, Iniesta, Xavi, Keita, Sergio Busquets, Messi, David Villa (Pedro 80).

Rubin (0) 0

Panathinaikos (0) 0   16,400

Rubin: Ryzhikov; Bocchetti, Cesar Navas, Kaleshin, Ansaldi, Ryazantsev, Noboa, Carlos Eduardo (Martins 73), Natcho, Kasaev (Gokdeniz 73), Kornilenko (Medvedev 85).
Panathinaikos: Tzorvas; Boumsong (Marinos 58), Kante, Vyntra, Spiropoulos, Gilberto Silva, Karagounis (Christodoulopoulos 81), Katsouranis, Simao, Luis Garcia (Govou 69), Cisse.

Wednesday, 24 November 2010

Panathinaikos (0) 0

Barcelona (1) 3 *(Pedro 27, 69, Messi 62)*   58,466

Panathinaikos: Tzorvas; Boumsong, Kante, Vyntra, Marinos (Dimoutsos 46), Spiropoulos, Gilberto Silva, Katsouranis (Plessis 67), Christodoulopoulos, Luis Garcia (Petropoulos 64), Cisse.
Barcelona: Valdes; Puyol, Dani Alves, Adriano (Maxwell 76), Pique (Abidal 72), Mascherano, Iniesta, Xavi (Keita 71), Messi, David Villa, Pedro.

Rubin (1) 1 *(Noboa 45 (pen))*

FC Copenhagen (0) 0   18,720

Rubin: Ryzhikov; Bocchetti, Cesar Navas, Kaleshin (Salukvadze 85), Ansaldi, Gokdeniz, Ryazantsev, Noboa, Natcho, Kasaev (Bystrov 69), Kornilenko (Medvedev 81).
FC Copenhagen: Wiland; Wendt, Antonsson, Kvist Jorgensen, Pospech, Zanka Jorgensen, Gronkjaer, Vingaard (Zohore 73), Claudemir, N'Doye, Bolanos.

Tuesday, 7 December 2010

Barcelona (0) 2 *(Andreu Fontas 51, Victor Vazquez 82)*

Rubin (0) 0   50,436

Barcelona: Pinto; Maxwell, Adriano, Pique, Andreu Fontas, Mascherano, Sergio Busquets, Jeffren (Victor Vazquez 13), Thiago, Jonathan Dos Santos (Messi 63), Bojan (Marc Bartra 35).
Rubin: Ryzhikov; Bocchetti, Cesar Navas, Kuzmin, Kaleshin, Ansaldi, Gokdeniz (Bystrov 75), Ryazantsev (Kasaev 62), Noboa, Murawski, Martins (Medvedev 66).

FC Copenhagen (1) 3 *(Vingaard 26, Gronkjaer 50 (pen), Cisse 73 (og))*

Panathinaikos (0) 1 *(Kante 90)*   36,797

FC Copenhagen: Wiland; Wendt, Antonsson (Ottesen 77), Kvist Jorgensen, Pospech, Zanka Jorgensen, Gronkjaer (Zohore 86), Vingaard, Claudemir, N'Doye (Cesar Santin 80), Bolanos.
Panathinaikos: Tzorvas; Boumsong, Kante, Vyntra, Marinos, Spiropoulos, Gilbert Silva (Ninis 46), Christodoulopoulos (Leto 46), Simao, Luis Garcia (Petropoulos 75), Cisse.

Group D Table	P	W	D	L	F	A	Pts
Barcelona	6	4	2	0	14	3	14
FC Copenhagen	6	3	1	2	7	5	10
Rubin	6	1	3	2	2	4	6
Panathinaikos	6	0	2	4	2	13	2

GROUP E

Wednesday, 15 September 2010

Bayern Munich (0) 2 *(Muller 78, Klose 83)*

Roma (0) 0   66,000

Bayern Munich: Butt; Lahm, Van Buyten, Badstuber, Contento, Schweinsteiger, Van Bommel, Hamit Altintop (Klose 67), Kroos, Olic (Gomez 67), Muller (Pranjic 82).
Roma: Julio Sergio; Burdisso N, Juan, Rosi, Cassetti, De Rossi, Perrotta, Pizarro, Brighi, Totti (Menez 80), Borriello.

Cluj (2) 2 *(Rada 9, Traore 13)*

Basle (1) 1 *(Stocker 44)*   9593

Cluj: Nuno Claro; Rada, Panin, Ricardo Cadu, Hugo Alcantara, Dica, Muresan, Culio, Hora (Kone 54), Rafael Bastos (De Zerbi 53), Traore (Sforzini 79).
Basle: Costanzo; Safari (Tembo 73), Abraham, Cagdas, Inkoom, Yapi-Yapo, Huggel, Stocker (Chipperfield 73), Shaqiri, Frei, Streller.

Tuesday, 28 September 2010

Basle (1) 1 *(Frei 18)*

Bayern Munich (0) 2 *(Schweinsteiger 56 (pen), 89)* 37,500

Basle: Costanzo; Safari, Abraham, Ferati, Inkoom, Yapi-Yapo (Almerares 90), Huggel (Cabral 87), Stocker, Shaqiri (Chipperfield 80), Frei, Streller.
Bayern Munich: Butt; Lahm, Van Buyten, Badstuber, Schweinsteiger, Van Bommel, Hamit Altintop (Gomez 46), Pranjic, Kroos (Olic 57), Klose (Tymoschuk 77), Muller.

Roma (0) 2 *(Mexes 69, Borriello 71)*

Cluj (0) 1 *(Rada 78)* 30,252

Roma: Lobont; Burdisso N, Cicinho (Borriello 64), Mexes, Castellini, De Rossi, Perrotta, Pizarro, Totti, Menez (Adriano 46), Vucinic (Cassetti 64).
Cluj: Nuno Claro; Rada, Panin, Ricardo Cadu, Hugo Alcantara, Edimar Fraga (Kone 69), Kivuvu, Dica, Culio, Hora (De Zerbi 76), Traore (Bjelanovic 82).

Tuesday, 19 October 2010

Bayern Munich (2) 3 *(Ricardo Cadu 32 (og), Panin 38 (og), Gomez 77)*

Cluj (1) 2 *(Ricardo Cadu 28, Culio 86)* 64,000

Bayern Munich: Butt; Lahm, Badstuber, Schweinsteiger (Braafheid 80), Tymoschuk, Hamit Altintop, Ottl, Pranjic, Kroos, Gomez, Muller.
Cluj: Stancioiu; Rada, Panin, Ricardo Cadu, Piccolo, Kivuvu, Dica, Culio, Rafael Bastos (Hora 56), De Zerbi, Traore (Bjelanovic 76).

Roma (1) 1 *(Borriello 27)*

Basle (2) 3 *(Frei 12, Inkoom 44, Cabral 90)* 22,365

Roma: Lobont; Burdisso N, Riise (Castellini 60), Mexes, Cassetti, Perrotta (Julio Baptista 74), Pizarro, Taddei, Brighi, Totti, Borriello.
Basle: Costanzo; Safari, Abraham, Ferati, Inkoom, Yapi-Yapo, Huggel, Stocker (Chipperfield 70), Shaqiri, Frei (Almerares 90), Streller (Cabral 81).

Wednesday, 3 November 2010

Basle (0) 2 *(Frei 69, Shaqiri 83)*

Roma (2) 3 *(Menez 17, Totti 26 (pen), Greco 76)* 36,375

Basle: Costanzo; Safari, Abraham, Ferati (Chipperfield 88), Inkoom, Yapi-Yapo, Huggel, Stocker*, Shaqiri, Frei, Streller.
Roma: Julio Sergio; Burdisso N (Burdisso G 81), Juan, Riise, Cassetti, De Rossi, Perrotta, Fabio Simplicio, Totti, Menez (Greco 74), Vucinic (Borriello 70).

Cluj (0) 0

Bayern Munich (2) 4 *(Gomez 12, 24, 71, Muller 90)* 14,097

Cluj: Stancioiu; Rada, Panin, Ricardo Cadu (Tony 78), Piccolo, Dica (Hora 46), Culio, Costa, Rafael Bastos (Edimar Fraga 46), De Zerbi, Traore.
Bayern Munich: Butt; Lahm, Van Buyten, Demichelis, Schweinsteiger (Muller 75), Tymoschuk, Hamit Altintop, Ottl, Pranjic, Kroos, Gomez.

Tuesday, 23 November 2010

Basle (1) 1 *(Almerares 15)*

Cluj (0) 0 34,239

Basle: Costanzo; Safari, Abraham, Ferati, Inkoom, Yapi-Yapo, Tembo (Zanni 89), Shaqiri (Xhaka 87), Cabral, Frei (Cagdas 90), Almerares.
Cluj: Nuno Claro; Rada, Ricardo Cadu, Tony, Piccolo*, Leonardo Veloso (Kone 58), Kivuvu, Culio (Sforzini 74), Costa, Rafael Bastos, Traore (Bjelanovic 46).

Roma (0) 3 *(Borriello 49, Di Rossi 81, Totti 84 (pen))*

Bayern Munich (2) 2 *(Gomez 33, 39)* 42,789

Roma: Julio Sergio; Burdisso N, Riise, Mexes, Cassetti, Di Rossi, Brighi (Totti 75), Greco (Fabio Simplicio 46), Menez, Borriello, Vucinic (Pizarro 62).
Bayern Munich: Kraft; Lahm, Van Buyten, Demichelis, Ribery (Hamit Altintop 77), Tymoschuk, Ottl, Pranjic, Kroos, Gomez, Muller (Contento 72).

Wednesday, 8 December 2010

Bayern Munich (2) 3 *(Ribery 35, 50, Tymoschuk 37)*

Basle (0) 0 64,000

Bayern Munich: Kraft; Lahm, Breno, Contento, Schweinsteiger, Van Bommel, Ribery, Tymoschuk, Kroos (Hamit Altintop 68), Gomez, Muller.
Basle: Costanzo; Safari, Abraham, Ferati, Inkoom, Yapi-Yapo, Stocker, Shaqiri (Tembo 75), Cabral (Almerares 55), Frei, Streller (Xhaka 46).

Cluj (0) 1 *(Traore 88)*

Roma (1) 1 *(Borriello 21)* 12,800

Cluj: Stancioiu; Rada, Panin, Ricardo Cadu, Edimar Fraga (Bjelanovic 63), Kivuvu, Dica (Leonardo Veloso 46), Culio, Kone, De Zerbi (Rafael Bastos 78), Traore.
Roma: Lobont; Burdisso N, Mexes, Cassetti (Cicinho 64), Castellini, Di Rossi, Fabio Simplicio, Brighi, Totti, Menez (Greco 46), Borriello.

Group E Table	P	W	D	L	F	A	Pts
Bayern Munich	6	5	0	1	16	6	15
Roma	6	3	1	2	10	11	10
Basle	6	2	0	4	8	11	6
Cluj	6	1	1	4	6	12	4

GROUP F

Wednesday, 15 September 2010

Marseille (0) 0

Spartak Moscow (0) 1 *(Azpilicueta 82 (og))* 45,729

Marseille: Mandanda; Heinze, Hilton, Taiwo, Azpilicueta, Gonzalez (Ayew J 83), Cheyrou, Valbuena, Cisse, Brandao (Gignac 62), Ayew A.
Spartak Moscow: Dikan; Pareja, Parshivlyuk, Suchy, Sheshukov (Ari 88), Makeev, McGeady (Sabitov 83), Ibson, Kombarov D, Alex (Stranzl 90), Welliton.

Zilina (0) 1 *(Oravec 55)*

Chelsea (3) 4 *(Essien 13, Anelka 24, 28, Sturridge 48)* 10,829

Zilina: Dubravka; Guldan (Angelovic 79), Pecalka, Piacek, Jez, Vladavic, Mraz, Rilke (Poliacek 57), Oravec, Ceesay (Majtan 62), Bello.
Chelsea: Cech; Ivanovic, Zhirkov, Mikel, Terry, Alex, Benayoun (McEachran 79), Essien, Anelka, Sturridge (Kakuta 62), Malouda (Van Aanholt 88).

Tuesday, 28 September 2010

Chelsea (2) 2 *(Terry 7, Anelka 28 (pen))*

Marseille (0) 0 40,675

Chelsea: Cech; Ivanovic, Cole, Mikel (McEachran 88), Terry, Alex, Malouda, Essien, Anelka, Kakuta (Ramires 61), Zhirkov (Sturridge 73).
Marseille: Mandanda; Heinze, Diawara, Gonzalez, Cheyrou (Valbuena 59), M'Bia, Cisse, Kabore, Gignac (Ayew A 59), Remy, Brandao.

Spartak Moscow (1) 3 *(Ari 34, 61, Ibson 89)*

Zilina (0) 0 37,000

Spartak Moscow: Dikan; Pareja, Parshivlyuk, Suchy, Sheshukov (Sabitov 90), Makeev, McGeady, Kombarov D (Maidana 83), Alex, Ari, Welliton (Ibson 68).
Zilina: Dubravka; Sourek, Guldan, Pecalka (Ceesay 46), Piacek, Jez, Mraz, Vittor, Rilke (Vladavic 65), Oravec, Majtan (Angelovic 81).

Tuesday, 19 October 2010

Marseille (0) 1 *(Diawara 48)*

Zilina (0) 0 49,250

Marseille: Mandanda; Heinze, Diawara, Taiwo, Azpilicueta, Gonzalez (Abriel 74), M'Bia, Valbuena, Gignac (Cisse 82), Brandao (Remy 66), Ayew A.
Zilina: Dubravka; Sourek, Guldan, Leitner, Angelovic, Piacek, Jez, Zosak (Vladavic 79), Gergel (Rilke 63), Ceesay, Majtan (Oravec 68).

Spartak Moscow (0) 0
Chelsea (2) 2 *(Zhirkov 23, Anelka 43)* 75,000
Spartak Moscow: Dikan; Pareja, Parshivlyuk, Suchy, Sheshukov, Makeev, McGeady, Ibson, Kombarov D, Ari (Ananidze 85), Welliton.
Chelsea: Cech; Paulo Ferreira, Cole (Van Aanholt 87), Mikel, Terry, Ivanovic, Malouda (Kakuta 82), Essien, Anelka, Kalou (McEachran 74), Zhirkov.

Wednesday, 3 November 2010
Chelsea (0) 4 *(Anelka 49, Drogba 62 (pen), Ivanovic 66, 90)*
Spartak Moscow (0) 1 *(Bazhenov 86)* 40,477
Chelsea: Cech; Paulo Ferreira, Cole, Mikel (McEachran 69), Ivanovic, Alex, Ramires, Kalou, Anelka (Sturridge 76), Drogba (Kakuta 76), Zhirkov.
Spartak Moscow: Dikan; Pareja, Suchy, Ivanov, Sheshukov (Drincic 68), Makeev, McGeady (Bazhenov 80), Ibson, Kombarov D, Alex (Kozlov 69), Welliton.

Zilina (0) 0
Marseille (4) 7 *(Gignac 12, 21, 54, Heinze 24, Remy 36, Gonzalez 52, 63)* 9664
Zilina: Dubravka; Sourek, Leitner, Pecalka, Angelovic, Jez, Vladavic (Gergel 60), Vittor (Zosak 33), Bello, Oravec, Ceesay (Majtan 78).
Marseille: Mandanda; Heinze (Taiwo 62), Diawara, Azpilicueta, Gonzalez, Cheyrou, M'Bia, Valbuena (Ayew A 62), Kabore, Gignac (Brandao 71), Remy.

Tuesday, 23 November 2010
Chelsea (0) 2 *(Sturridge 51, Malouda 86)*
Zilina (1) 1 *(Bello 19)* 40,266
Chelsea: Turnbull; Paulo Ferreira, Van Aanholt, McEachran (Mellis 90), Ivanovic, Bruma, Ramires, Kakuta (Kalou 46), Sturridge (Anelka 74), Drogba, Malouda.
Zilina: Dubravka; Guldan, Pecalka, Angelovic, Piacek, Jez, Vladavic (Rilke 90), Gergel, Bello, Oravec (Ceesay 64), Majtan (Poliacek 85).

Spartak Moscow (0) 0
Marseille (1) 3 *(Valbuena 18, Remy 54, Brandao 68)* 43,217
Spartak Moscow: Dikan; Pareja, Stranzl, Suchy, Sheshukov (Drincic 75), Makeev, McGeady, Ibson (Ananidze 76), Kombarov D, Ari, Welliton[*].
Marseille: Mandanda; Heinze, Diawara, Azpilicueta, Gonzalez (Abriel 76), M'Bia, Valbuena (Cheyrou 69), Cisse, Remy (Kabore 82), Brandao, Ayew A.

Wednesday, 8 December 2010
Marseille (0) 1 *(Brandao 81)*
Chelsea (0) 0 50,604
Marseille: Mandanda; Heinze, Diawara, Taiwo, Abriel (Ayew A 63), Cheyrou, Valbuena (Gonzalez 62), N'Diaye (Ayew J 85), Kabore, Remy, Brandao.
Chelsea: Cech; Bosingwa (Van Aanholt 79), Paulo Ferreira, McEachran, Terry (Bruma 72), Ivanovic, Essien, Ramires, Kalou, Drogba (Sturridge 62), Malouda.

Zilina (0) 1 *(Majtan 48)*
Spartak Moscow (0) 2 *(Alex 54, Ibson 61)* 7208
Zilina: Dubravka; Guldan, Pecalka, Angelovic, Piacek, Jez (Ceesay 69), Poliacek (Rilke 56), Gergel, Bello, Oravec, Majtan (Mraz 85).
Spartak Moscow: Dikan; Stranzl, Suchy, Sheshukov, Makeev (Ozobic 56), McGeady, Ibson[*], Kombarov K (Ivanov 83), Kombarov D, Alex, Kozlov (Drincic 46).

Group F Table

	P	W	D	L	F	A	Pts
Chelsea	6	5	0	1	14	4	15
Marseille	6	4	0	2	12	3	12
Spartak Moscow	6	3	0	3	7	10	9
Zilina	6	0	0	6	3	19	0

GROUP G

Wednesday, 15 September 2010
AC Milan (0) 2 *(Ibrahimovic 66, 69)*
Auxerre (0) 0 69,317
AC Milan: Abbiati; Nesta, Zambrotta, Bonera, Antonini (Abate 72), Pirlo, Seedorf, Ambrosini (Boateng 15), Ronaldinho, Ibrahimovic, Alexandre Pato (Robinho 55).
Auxerre: Sorin; Grichting, Mignot, Coulibaly, Hengbart, Pedretti, Langil (Chafni 80), Ndinga, Birsa (Le Tallec 73), Oliech, Jelen.

Real Madrid (1) 2 *(Anita 31 (og), Higuain 73)*
Ajax (0) 0 69,639
Real Madrid: Casillas; Ricardo Carvalho, Pepe, Arbeloa, Marcelo, Xabi Alonso (Diarra L 83), Ozil (Canales 88), Khedira, Di Maria (Pedro Leon 80), Cristiano Ronaldo, Higuain.
Ajax: Stekelenburg; Ooijer, Van der Wiel, Anita, Alderweireld, Emanuelson, De Zeeuw (Tainio 69), De Jong, Enoh, El Hamdaoui, Sulejmani (Eriksen 85).

Tuesday, 28 September 2010
Ajax (1) 1 *(El Hamadaoui 23)*
AC Milan (1) 1 *(Ibrahimovic 37)* 51,276
Ajax: Stekelenburg; Vertonghen, Van der Wiel, Anita (Sulejmani 38), Alderweireld, Emanuelson, De Zeeuw (Lindgren 79), De Jong, Enoh, El Hamdaoui, Suarez.
AC Milan: Abbiati; Nesta, Zambrotta, Antonini, Thiago Silva, Gattuso, Pirlo, Flamini (Boateng 52), Seedorf (Abate 85), Robinho (Inzaghi 85), Ibrahimovic.

Auxerre (0) 0
Real Madrid (0) 1 *(Di Maria 81)* 19,525
Auxerre: Sorin; Grichting, Coulibaly, Hengbart, Dudka, Pedretti, Chafni (Quercia 88), Langil (Traore 77), Ndinga, Oliech, Contout (Jelen 46).
Real Madrid: Casillas; Sergio Ramos, Pepe, Arbeloa, Marcelo, Xabi Alonso, Diarra L (Di Maria 73), Khedira, Cristiano Ronaldo, Benzema (Ozil 58), Higuain (Diarra M 86).

Tuesday, 19 October 2010
Ajax (2) 2 *(De Zeeuw 7, Suarez 41)*
Auxerre (0) 1 *(Birsa 56)* 51,383
Ajax: Stekelenburg; Ooijer[*], Vertonghen, Van der Wiel, Emanuelson, De Zeeuw, Lindgren, Enoh, El Hamdaoui, Suarez, Sulejmani (Oleguer 60).
Auxerre: Sorin; Grichting, Coulibaly, Hengbart, Dudka, Pedretti, Chafni (Quercia 65), Ndinga, Birsa, Oliech[*], Contout (Bourgeois 79).
Unused substitute Mignot also sent off.

Real Madrid (2) 2 *(Cristiano Ronaldo 13, Ozil 14)*
AC Milan (0) 0 71,657
Real Madrid: Casillas; Ricardo Carvalho, Pepe, Arbeloa, Marcelo, Xabi Alonso, Ozil (Diarra L 83), Khedira, Di Maria (Granero 87), Cristiano Ronaldo, Higuain (Benzema 89).
AC Milan: Amelia; Nesta, Zambrotta, Bonera, Antonini, Gattuso (Boateng 59), Pirlo, Seedorf, Ronaldinho (Robinho 71), Ibrahimovic, Alexandre Pato (Inzaghi 78).

Wednesday, 3 November 2010
AC Milan (0) 2 *(Inzaghi 68, 78)*
Read Madrid (1) 2 *(Higuain 43, Pedro Leon 90)* 76,357
AC Milan: Abbiati; Nesta, Zambrotta, Thiago Silva, Gattuso (Seedorf 85), Pirlo, Boateng, Abate, Ronaldinho (Inzaghi 59), Ibrahimovic, Alexandre Pato (Ambrosini 73).
Read Madrid: Casillas; Sergio Ramos, Ricardo Carvalho, Pepe (Pedro Leon 80), Marcelo, Xabi Alonso, Ozil (Albiol 90), Khedira, Di Maria, Cristiano Ronaldo, Higuain (Benzema 73).

Auxerre (1) 2 *(Sammaritano 9, Langil 84)*
Ajax (0) 1 *(Alderweireld 79)* 18,727
Auxerre: Sorin; Grichting, Coulibaly, Hengbart, Dudka, Pedretti, Ndinga, Sammaritano (Berthod 86), Birsa, Quercia (Langil 62), Contout (Chafni 81).
Ajax: Stekelenburg; Vertonghen, Van der Wiel, Anita (Sulejmani 59), Alderweireld, Emanuelson, De Zeeuw (Eriksen 83), Lindgren, Enoh (De Jong 46), El Hamdaoui, Suarez.

Tuesday, 23 November 2010
Ajax (0) 0
Real Madrid (2) 4 *(Benzema 36, Arbeloa 44,*
Cristiano Ronaldo 70, 81 (pen)) 48,491
Ajax: Stekelenburg; Vertonghen, Van der Wiel, Anita, Alderweireld, Emanuelson, De Jong (Lindgren 76), Enoh, El Hamdaoui (De Zeeuw 46), Suarez, Sulejmani (Eriksen 88).
Real Madrid: Casillas; Sergio Ramos■, Albiol, Arbeloa, Marcelo, Xabi Alonso■, Özil, Diarra L (Mateos 82), Pedro Leon (Di Maria 65), Cristiano Ronaldo, Benzema (Canales 82).

Auxerre (0) 0
AC Milan (0) 2 *(Ibrahimovic 64, Ronaldinho 90)* 19,244
Auxerre: Sorin; Grichting, Coulibaly, Hengbart (Chafni 59), Dudka, Pedretti, Ndinga, Sammaritano (Quercia 66), Birsa, Oliech, Contout (Traore 82).
AC Milan: Abbiati; Nesta, Zambrotta, Thiago Silva, Gattuso (Strasser 90), Flamini, Seedorf (Boateng 76), Ambrosini, Abate, Robinho, Ibrahimovic (Ronaldinho 85).

Wednesday, 8 December 2010
AC Milan (0) 0
Ajax (0) 2 *(De Zeeuw 57, Alderweireld 66)* 72,960
AC Milan: Amelia; Yepes, Bonera, Antonini, Thiago Silva, Pirlo, Flamini (Boateng 26), Seedorf, Ambrosini (Ibrahimovic 63), Ronaldinho, Robinho (Merkel 76).
Ajax: Stekelenburg; Vertonghen, Van der Wiel, Alderweireld, Emanuelson, De Zeeuw (Lindgren 82), De Jong (El Hamdaoui 84), Enoh, Eriksen, Suarez (Tainio 90), Sulejmani.

Real Madrid (1) 4 *(Benzema 12, 72, 88,*
Cristiano Ronaldo 49)
Auxerre (0) 0 54,917
Real Madrid: Dudek (Adan 45); Ricardo Carvalho, Albiol, Arbeloa, Marcelo (Garay 76), Diarra M, Diarra L, Granero, Pedro Leon, Cristiano Ronaldo (Pablo Sarabia 72), Benzema.
Auxerre: Sorin; Grichting, Mignot, Coulibaly, Dudka, Pedretti (Sammaritano 62), Chafni, Traore, Birsa (Langil 90), Oliech, Contout (Quercia 73).

Group G Table	P	W	D	L	F	A	Pts
Real Madrid	6	5	1	0	15	2	16
AC Milan	6	2	2	2	7	7	8
Ajax	6	2	1	3	6	10	7
Auxerre	6	1	0	5	3	12	3

GROUP H

Wednesday, 15 September 2010
Arsenal (3) 6 *(Fabregas 9 (pen), 53, Arshavin 30,*
Chamakh 34, Vela 68, 84)
Braga (0) 0 59,333
Arsenal: Almunia; Sagna, Clichy, Song Billong (Vela 63), Squillaci, Koscielny, Wilshere, Fabregas, Chamakh (Denilson 63), Arshavin (Eboue 70), Nasri.
Braga: Felipe; Rodriguez, Miguel Garcia, Silvio, Hugo Viana (Marcio Mossoro 55), Vandinho, Moises, Aguiar, Alan, Paulo Cesar (Helder Barbosa 70), Matheus (Lima 60).

Shakhter Donetsk (0) 1 *(Srna 71)*
Partizan Belgrade (0) 0 48,512
Shakhter Donetsk: Pyatov; Srna, Kucher, Rat, Hubschman, Rakitskiy, Willian, Jadson (Alex Teixeira 58), Douglas Costa, Gai, Luiz Adriano (Vitsenets 83).
Partizan Belgrade: Stojkovic; Krstajic (Stankovic 90), Lazevski, Miljkovic, Savic, Ilic S, Kamara, Smiljanic, Tomic, Iliev (Boya 58), Cleo.

Tuesday, 28 September 2010
Braga (0) 0
Shakhter Donetsk (0) 3 *(Luiz Adriano 56, 77,*
Douglas Costa 90 (pen)) 12,083
Braga: Felipe; Rodriguez (Paulao 36), Miguel Garcia, Silvio, Vandinho (Marcio Mossoro 74), Moises, Aguiar, Salino (Lima 56), Alan, Paulo Cesar, Matheus.

Shakhter Donetsk: Pyatov; Srna, Kucher, Rat, Hubschman (Vitsenets 79), Rakitskiy, Willian, Mkhitaryan, Douglas Costa, Gai (Jadson 66), Luiz Adriano (Eduardo Da Silva 74).

Partizan Belgrade (1) 1 *(Cleo 33 (pen))*
Arsenal (1) 3 *(Arshavin 15, Chamakh 71, Squillaci 82)* 29,348
Partizan Belgrade: Stojkovic; Krstajic, Jovanovic M■, Lazevski, Stevanovic, Ilic S, Kamara, Petrovic (Smiljanic 69), Tomic (Savic 60), Boya (Iliev 83), Cleo.
Arsenal: Fabianski; Sagna, Gibbs, Denilson, Squillaci, Djourou, Song Billong, Wilshere (Nasri 74), Chamakh (Vela 75), Arshavin (Clichy 85), Rosicky.

Tuesday, 19 October 2010
Arsenal (2) 5 *(Song Billong 19, Nasri 42,*
Fabregas 59 (pen), Wilshere 66, Chamakh 69)
Shakhter Donetsk (0) 1 *(Eduardo Da Silva 82)* 60,016
Arsenal: Fabianski; Djourou, Squillaci, Clichy, Rosicky, Eboue, Fabregas (Denilson 63), Song Billong, Wilshere, Chamakh (Walcott 72), Nasri (Arshavin 72).
Shakhter Donetsk: Pyatov; Srna, Kucher, Rat, Hubschman, Rakitskiy, Willian (Douglas Costa 46), Alex Teixeira, Mkhitaryan, Gai (Jadson 68), Luiz Adriano (Eduardo Da Silva 63).

Braga (1) 2 *(Lima 35, Matheus 90)*
Partizan Belgrade (0) 0 11,454
Braga: Felipe; Paulao, Elderson, Silvio, Andres Madrid (Aguiar 73), Vandinho, Moises, Alan, Lima (Marcio Mossoro 87), Paulo Cesar (Salino 69), Matheus.
Partizan Belgrade: Stojkovic; Krstajic, Lazevski, Miljkovic, Savic, Ilic S, Smiljanic, Almami Moreira (Kamara 46), Tomic (Babovic 88), Cleo, Scepovic (Boya 54).

Wednesday, 3 November 2010
Partizan Belgrade (0) 0
Braga (1) 1 *(Moises 36)* 28,295
Partizan Belgrade: Stojkovic; Krstajic, Jovanovic M, Lazevski, Miljkovic, Ilic S, Almami Moreira, Petrovic, Iliev (Scepovic 78), Boya (Babovic 58), Cleo.
Braga: Felipe; Rodriguez, Elderson, Silvio, Marcio Mossoro (Salino 50), Vandinho, Moises, Aguiar, Alan (Andres Madrid 68), Paulo Cesar, Matheus (Lima 88).

Shakhter Donetsk (2) 2 *(Chygrynskiy 28,*
Eduardo Da Silva 45)
Arsenal (1) 1 *(Walcott 10)* 51,153
Shakhter Donetsk: Pyatov; Srna, Chygrynskiy, Rat, Hubschman, Rakitskiy, Willian, Jadson (Douglas Costa 74), Gai (Alex Teixeira 62), Luiz Adriano (Moreno 88), Eduardo Da Silva.
Arsenal: Fabianski; Eboue, Clichy, Eastmond (Vela 59), Squillaci, Djourou, Walcott (Emmanuel-Thomas 82), Wilshere, Bendtner (Chamakh 73), Rosicky, Nasri.

Tuesday, 23 November 2010
Braga (0) 2 *(Matheus 83, 90)*
Arsenal (0) 0 14,809
Braga: Felipe; Rodriguez, Miguel Garcia, Elderson, Vandinho (Hugo Viana 89), Moises, Aguiar (Andres Madrid 80), Salino, Alan, Lima (Elton 81), Matheus.
Arsenal: Fabianski; Eboue, Gibbs, Denilson, Squillaci, Djourou, Walcott (Vela 77), Fabregas (Nasri 69), Bendtner (Chamakh 74), Wilshere, Rosicky.

Partizan Belgrade (0) 0
Shakhter Donetsk (0) 3 *(Stepanenko 52, Jadson 59,*
Eduardo Da Silva 68) 17,473
Partizan Belgrade: Stojkovic; Krstajic, Jovanovic M, Lazevski, Stevanovic, Ilic S (Iliev 84), Smiljanic, Babovic, Almami Moreira (Davidov 73), Petrovic (Kamara 64), Cleo.
Shakhter Donetsk: Pyatov; Srna, Chygrynskiy, Rat, Rakitskiy, Willian, Jadson (Alex Teixeira 75), Stepanenko, Douglas Costa (Eduardo Da Silva 62), Gai (Vitsenets 74), Luiz Adriano.

Wednesday, 8 December 2010
Arsenal (1) 3 *(Van Persie 30 (pen), Walcott 73, Nasri 77)*
Partizan Belgrade (0) 1 *(Cleo 52)* 58,845
Arsenal: Fabianski; Sagna■, Gibbs (Eboue 24), Denilson, Squillaci, Koscielny, Song Billong, Van Persie, Chamakh (Bendtner 76), Arshavin (Walcott 67), Nasri.
Partizan Belgrade: Stojkovic; Krstajic, Jovanovic M, Lazevski, Savic, Ilic S, Kamara, Babovic (Davidov 81), Almami Moreira (Brasanac 90), Petrovic, Cleo.

Shakhtar Donetsk (0) 2 *(Rat 78, Luiz Adriano 83)*
Braga (0) 0 47,627
Shakhtar Donetsk: Pyatov; Srna, Chygrynskiy, Rat, Rakitskiy, Willian, Jadson (Mkhitaryan 72), Stepanenko, Douglas Costa (Alex Teixeira 62), Gai (Kobin 85), Luiz Adriano.

Braga: Artur Moraes; Rodriguez, Miguel Garcia, Anibal, Silvio, Vandinho, Aguiar (Hugo Viana 72), Salino (Helder Barbosa 81), Alan (Lima 68), Paulo Cesar, Matheus.

Group H Table

	P	W	D	L	F	A	Pts
Shakhtar Donetsk	6	5	0	1	12	6	15
Arsenal	6	4	0	2	18	7	12
Braga	6	3	0	3	5	11	9
Partizan Belgrade	6	0	0	6	2	13	0

KNOCK-OUT STAGE

KNOCK-OUT ROUND FIRST LEG

Tuesday, 15 February 2011
AC Milan (0) 0
Tottenham H (0) 1 *(Crouch 80)* 75,652
AC Milan: Abbiati (Amelia 18); Nesta, Yepes, Antonini, Thiago Silva, Gattuso, Flamini, Seedorf (Alexandre Pato 46), Abate, Robinho, Ibrahimovic.
Tottenham H: Gomes; Corluka (Woodgate 59), Assou-Ekotto, Palacios, Gallas, Dawson, Lennon, Pienaar (Kranjcar 76), Crouch, Sandro, Van der Vaart (Modric 62).

Valencia (1) 1 *(Soldado 17)*
Schalke (0) 1 *(Raul 64)* 42,703
Valencia: Guaita; Ricardo Costa, Miguel, Mathieu (Jordi Alba 79), David Navarro, Mehmet Topal, Banega (Joaquin 68), Tino Costa, Aduriz, Soldado, Chori Dominguez (Vicente 68).
Schalke: Neuer; Metzelder, Uchida, Howedes, Kluge, Jurado (Edu 83), Schmitz■, Matip, Raul, Huntelaar (Hao Junmin 90), Farfan (Draxler 79).

Wednesday, 16 February 2011
Arsenal (0) 2 *(Van Persie 78, Arshavin 83)*
Barcelona (1) 1 *(David Villa 26)* 59,927
Arsenal: Sczcesny; Eboue, Clichy, Song Billong (Arshavin 69), Djourou, Koscielny, Walcott (Bendtner 77), Fabregas, Van Persie, Wilshere, Nasri.
Barcelona: Valdes; Abidal, Dani Alves, Maxwell, Pique, Iniesta (Adriano 89), Xavi, Sergio Busquets, Messi, David Villa (Keita 68), Pedro.

Roma (1) 2 *(Perrotta 28, Menez 61)*
Shakhtar Donetsk (3) 3 *(Jadson 29, Douglas Costa 36, Luiz Adriano 42)* 35,873
Roma: Doni; Burdisso N, Riise (Castellini 46), Mexes, Cassetti, De Rossi, Perrotta, Taddei, Totti, Menez, Vucinic (Borriello 68).
Shakhtar Donetsk: Pyatov; Srna, Chygrynskiy, Rat, Hubschman, Rakitskiy, Willian, Jadson (Alex Teixeira 85), Mkhitaryan (Vitsenets 78), Douglas Costa (Eduardo Da Silva 66), Luiz Adriano.

Tuesday, 22 February 2011
FC Copenhagen (0) 0
Chelsea (1) 2 *(Anelka 17, 54)* 36,713
FC Copenhagen: Wiland; Wendt (Bengtsson 75), Antonsson, Kvist Jorgensen, Pospech, Zanka Jorgensen, Gronkjaer (Zohore 87), Claudemir, Cesar Santin (Vingaard 46), N'Doye, Bolanos.
Chelsea: Cech; Bosingwa, Cole, Ramires, Terry, Ivanovic, Essien, Lampard, Torres (Kalou 90), Anelka (Drogba 73), Malouda (Zhirkov 85).

Lyon (0) 1 *(Gomis 83)*
Real Madrid (0) 1 *(Benzema 65)* 40,299
Lyon: Lloris; Cris, Reveillere, Cissokho, Lovren, Kallstrom (Pjanic 77), Toulalan, Michel Bastos (Briand 70), Gourcuff, Gomis, Delgado (Pied 69).

Real Madrid: Casillas; Sergio Ramos, Ricardo Carvalho, Pepe, Arbeloa, Xabi Alonso, Ozil (Marcelo 75), Khedira (Diarra L 68), Di Maria, Cristiano Ronaldo, Adebayor (Benzema 64).

Wednesday, 23 February 2011
Internazionale (0) 0
Bayern Munich (0) 1 *(Gomez 90)* 75,925
Internazionale: Julio Cesar; Lucio, Zanetti, Maicon, Chivu, Ranocchia (Kharja 73), Sneijder, Cambiasso, Stankovic, Thiago Motta, Eto'o.
Bayern Munich: Kraft; Lahm, Badstuber, Robben, Schweinsteiger, Ribery, Tymoschuk, Pranjic (Breno 38), Luiz Gustavo, Gomez, Muller.

Marseille (0) 0
Manchester U (0) 0 57,957
Marseille: Mandanda; Heinze, Fanni, Diawara, Gonzalez, M'Bia, Cisse (Cheyrou 70), Kabore, Remy (Valbuena 79), Brandao, Ayew A.
Manchester U: Van der Sar; O'Shea, Evra, Carrick, Smalling, Vidic, Gibson (Scholes 73), Fletcher, Berbatov, Rooney, Nani.

KNOCK-OUT ROUND SECOND LEG

Tuesday, 8 March 2011
Barcelona (1) 3 *(Messi 45, 71 (pen), Xavi 69)*
Arsenal (0) 1 *(Sergio Busquets 53 (og))* 95,486
Barcelona: Valdes; Abidal, Dani Alves, Adriano (Maxwell 90), Mascherano (Keita 89), Iniesta, Xavi, Sergio Busquets, Messi, David Villa (Afellay 82), Pedro.
Arsenal: Sczcesny (Almunia 19); Sagna, Clichy, Diaby, Djourou, Koscielny, Wilshere, Fabregas (Bendtner 78), Van Persie■, Rosicky (Arshavin 74), Nasri.

Shakhtar Donetsk (1) 3 *(Hubschman 18, Willian 58, Eduardo Da Silva 87)*
Roma (0) 0 46,543
Shakhtar Donetsk: Pyatov; Srna, Chygrynskiy, Rat, Hubschman, Rakitskiy, Willian, Jadson, Mkhitaryan (Alex Teixeira 67), Douglas Costa (Eduardo Da Silva 60), Luiz Adriano (Moreno 75).
Roma: Doni; Burdisso N, Juan, Riise, Mexes■, De Rossi, Perrotta (Caprari 86), Pizarro, Taddei (Rosi 46), Borriello, Vucinic (Brighi 66).

Wednesday, 9 March 2011
Schalke (1) 3 *(Farfan 40, 90, Gavranovic 52)*
Valencia (1) 1 *(Ricardo Costa 17)* 53,517
Schalke: Neuer; Metzelder, Uchida, Howedes, Sergio, Kluge (Sarpei 82), Jurado (Draxler 76), Matip (Papadopoulos 60), Raul, Farfan, Gavranovic.
Valencia: Guaita; Ricardo Costa, Mathieu, David Navarro, Bruno, Joaquin, Mehmet Topal, Banega (Tino Costa 70), Pablo Hernandez (Soldado 54), Aduriz (Jonas 74), Mata.

Tottenham H (0) 0
AC Milan (0) 0   34,320
Tottenham H: Gomes; Corluka, Assou-Ekotto, Modric, Gallas, Dawson, Lennon, Sandro, Crouch (Pavlyuchenko 83), Van der Vaart (Bale 66), Pienaar (Jenas 71).
AC Milan: Abbiati; Nesta, Jankulovski (Antonini 70), Thiago Silva, Boateng (Merkel 76), Flamini (Strasser 87), Seedorf, Abate, Robinho, Ibrahimovic, Alexandre Pato.

Tuesday, 15 March 2011
Bayern Munich (2) 2 *(Gomez 21, Muller 31)*
Internazionale (1) 3 *(Eto'o 4, Sneijder 63, Pandev 88)*
                                                      66,000
Bayern Munich: Kraft; Lahm, Van Buyten (Badstuber 70), Breno (Kroos 90), Robben (Hamit Altintop 68), Schweinsteiger, Ribery, Pranjic, Luiz Gustavo, Gomez, Muller.
Internazionale: Julio Cesar; Lucio, Maicon, Chivu (Nagatomo 87), Ranocchia, Sneijder, Cambiasso, Stankovic (Philippe Coutinho 51), Thiago Motta, Eto'o, Pandev (Kharja 90).

Manchester U (1) 2 *(Hernandez 5, 75)*
Marseille (0) 1 *(Brown 81 (og))*   73,996
Manchester U: Van der Sar; O'Shea (Rafael 37) (Fabio 70), Evra, Carrick, Brown, Smalling, Nani (Valencia 62), Scholes, Hernandez, Rooney, Giggs.
Marseille: Mandanda; Heinze, Fanni, Diawara, Taiwo, Gonzalez, Cheyrou, M'Bia (Ayew J 80), Gignac (Valbuena 69), Remy, Ayew A.

Wednesday, 16 March 2011
Chelsea (0) 0
FC Copenhagen (0) 0   36,454
Chelsea: Cech; Bosingwa, Cole, Mikel (Essien 83), Terry, Ivanovic, Ramires, Lampard, Anelka (Torres 68), Drogba, Zhirkov (Malouda 75).
FC Copenhagen: Wiland; Wendt, Bengtsson (Zohore 61), Antonsson, Kvist Jorgensen, Zanka Jorgensen, Gronkjaer, Vingaard (Cesar Santin 74), Claudemir, N'Doye, Bolanos (Kristensen 90).

Real Madrid (1) 3 *(Marcelo 37, Benzema 66, Di Maria 76)*
Lyon (0) 0   70,034
Real Madrid: Casillas; Sergio Ramos, Ricardo Carvalho, Pepe, Marcelo, Xabi Alonso, Ozil, Khedira, Di Maria (Granero 79), Cristiano Ronaldo (Adebayor 74), Benzema (Diarra L 84).
Lyon: Lloris; Cris, Reveillere, Cissokho, Lovren, Kallstrom, Toulalan, Gourcuff (Pied 69), Briand (Gomis 46), Lisandro Lopez, Delgado (Pjanic 80).

QUARTER-FINALS FIRST LEG
Tuesday, 5 April 2011
Internazionale (2) 2 *(Stankovic 1, Milito 34)*
Schalke (2) 5 *(Matip 17, Edu 40, 75, Raul 53, Ranocchia 57 (og))*   72,770
Internazionale: Julio Cesar; Zanetti, Maicon, Chivu■, Ranocchia, Sneijder, Cambiasso, Stankovic (Kharja 24), Thiago Motta (Nagatomo 76), Eto'o, Milito.
Schalke: Neuer; Sarpei, Uchida, Howedes, Papadopoulos, Baumjohann (Schmitz 76), Jurado (Draxler 83), Matip, Raul (Karimi 87), Edu, Farfan.

Real Madrid (1) 4 *(Adebayor 5, 57, Di Maria 72, Cristiano Ronaldo 87)*
Tottenham H (0) 0   71,657
Real Madrid: Casillas; Sergio Ramos, Ricardo Carvalho, Pepe, Marcelo, Xabi Alonso, Ozil, Khedira (Diarra L 61), Di Maria (Kaka 77), Cristiano Ronaldo, Adebayor (Higuain 75).
Tottenham H: Gomes; Corluka (Bassong 79), Assou-Ekotto, Modric, Gallas, Dawson, Van der Vaart (Defoe 46), Jenas, Crouch■, Sandro, Bale.

Wednesday, 6 April 2011
Barcelona (2) 5 *(Iniesta 2, Dani Alves 34, Pique 53, Keita 61, Xavi 86)*
Shakhtar Donetsk (0) 1 *(Rakitskiy 60)*   71,657
Barcelona: Valdes; Dani Alves, Adriano (Maxwell 77), Pique, Mascherano, Iniesta (Afellay 90), Xavi, Keita, Sergio Busquets, Messi, David Villa (Pedro 71).
Shakhtar Donetsk: Pyatov; Srna, Rat, Hubschman (Eduardo Da Silva 83), Ishchenko, Rakitskiy, Willian (Alex Teixeira 75), Jadson (Fernandinho 70), Mkhitarian, Douglas Costa, Luiz Adriano.

Chelsea (0) 0
Manchester U (1) 1 *(Rooney 24)*   37,915
Chelsea: Cech; Bosingwa (Mikel 78), Cole, Essien, Terry, Ivanovic, Ramires, Lampard, Torres, Drogba (Anelka 71), Zhirkov (Malouda 70).
Manchester U: Van der Sar; Rafael (Nani 51), Evra, Carrick, Ferdinand, Vidic, Valencia, Park (Smalling 90), Hernandez (Berbatov 78), Rooney, Giggs.

QUARTER-FINALS SECOND LEG
Tuesday, 12 April 2011
Manchester U (1) 2 *(Hernandez 43, Park 77)*
Chelsea (0) 1 *(Drogba 76)*   74,672
Manchester U: Van der Sar; O'Shea, Evra, Carrick, Ferdinand, Vidic, Park, Giggs, Hernandez, Rooney, Nani (Valencia 75).
Chelsea: Cech; Ivanovic, Cole, Essien, Terry, Alex (Paulo Ferreira 82), Ramires■, Lampard, Torres (Drogba 46), Anelka (Kalou 60), Malouda.

Shakhtar Donetsk (0) 0
Barcelona (1) 1 *(Messi 43)*   51,759
Shakhtar Donetsk: Pyatov; Hubschman (Fernandinho 75), Shevchuk, Ishchenko, Rakitskiy, Willian, Jadson, Kobin, Mkhitarian, Douglas Costa (Eduardo Da Silva 58), Luiz Adriano (Moreno 67).
Barcelona: Valdes; Dani Alves, Adriano, Pique (Gabi Milito 70), Mascherano, Xavi (Pedro 66), Keita, Afellay, Sergio Busquets, Messi, David Villa (Jeffren 75).

Wednesday, 13 April 2011
Schalke (1) 2 *(Raul 45, Howedes 81)*
Internazionale (0) 1 *(Thiago Motta 50)*   54,142
Schalke: Neuer; Metzelder, Sarpei, Uchida, Howedes, Papadopoulos, Baumjohann (Draxler 73), Jurado (Schmitz 86), Matip, Raul, Edu (Charisteas 77).
Internazionale: Julio Cesar; Lucio, Zanetti, Maicon, Nagatomo, Ranocchia, Sneijder (Philippe Coutinho 80), Stankovic (Pandev 46), Thiago Motta, Eto'o, Milito.

Tottenham H (0) 0
Real Madrid (0) 1 *(Cristiano Ronaldo 50)*   34,311
Tottenham H: Gomes; Corluka, Assou-Ekotto, Huddlestone (Sandro 71), Gallas, Dawson, Lennon (Defoe 61), Modric (Kranjcar 83), Pavlyuchenko, Van der Vaart, Bale.
Real Madrid: Casillas; Sergio Ramos (Granero 57), Ricardo Carvalho, Albiol, Arbeloa, Marcelo, Xabi Alonso (Benzema 75), Ozil, Khedira, Cristiano Ronaldo (Kaka 65), Adebayor.

SEMI-FINALS FIRST LEG
Tuesday, 26 April 2011
Schalke (0) 0
Manchester U (0) 2 *(Giggs 67, Rooney 69)*   54,142
Schalke: Neuer; Metzelder, Sarpei (Sergio 72), Uchida, Papadopoulos, Baumjohann (Kluge 53), Jurado (Draxler 83), Matip, Raul, Edu, Farfan.
Manchester U: Van der Sar; Fabio, Evra, Carrick, Ferdinand, Vidic, Valencia, Park (Anderson 73), Hernandez (Scholes 73), Rooney (Nani 83), Giggs.

Wednesday, 27 April 2011
Real Madrid (0) 0
Barcelona (0) 2 *(Messi 76, 87)*   71,567
Real Madrid: Casillas; Sergio Ramos, Albiol, Pepe▪, Arbeloa, Marcelo, Xabi Alonso, Ozil (Adebayor 46), Diarra L, Di Maria, Cristiano Ronaldo.
Barcelona: Valdes; Puyol, Dani Alves, Pique, Mascherano, Xavi, Keita, Sergio Busquets, Messi, David Villa (Sergi Roberto 90), Pedro (Afellay 71).

SEMI-FINALS SECOND LEG

Tuesday, 3 May 2011
Barcelona (0) 1 *(Pedro 54)*
Real Madrid (0) 1 *(Marcelo 64)*   95,701
Barcelona: Valdes (Abidal 90), Dani Alves, Pique, Mascherano, Iniesta, Xavi, Sergio Busquets, Messi, David Villa (Keita 74), Pedro (Afellay 90).
Real Madrid: Casillas; Ricardo Carvalho, Albiol, Arbeloa, Marcelo, Kaka (Ozil 60), Xabi Alonso, Diarra L, Di Maria, Cristiano Ronaldo, Higuain (Adebayor 55).

Wednesday, 4 May 2011
Manchester U (2) 4 *(Valencia 26, Gibson 31, Anderson 72, 76)*
Schalke (1) 1 *(Jurado 35)*   74,687
Manchester U: Van der Sar; O'Shea, Rafael (Evra 60), Anderson, Smalling, Evans J, Valencia, Scholes (Fletcher 73), Berbatov (Owen 77), Gibson, Nani.
Schalke: Neuer; Metzelder, Uchida, Howedes (Huntelaar 70), Papadopoulos, Sergio, Baumjohann (Edu 46), Jurado, Draxler, Raul, Farfan (Matip 75).

UEFA CHAMPIONS LEAGUE FINAL

Saturday, 28 May 2011

(at Wembley, 87,695)

Barcelona (1) 3 *(Pedro 27, Messi 54, David Villa 70)*   **Manchester U (1) 1** *(Rooney 34)*

Barcelona: Valdes; Abidal, Dani Alves (Puyol 88), Pique, Mascherano, Iniesta, Xavi, Sergio Busquets, Messi, David Villa (Afellay 90).

Manchester U: Van der Sar; Fabio (Nani 69), Evra, Carrick (Scholes 77), Ferdinand, Vidic, Valencia, Giggs, Hernandez, Rooney, Park.

Referee: V. Kassai (Hungary).

Barcelona's Lionel Messi (left) scores their second goal past Manchester United's Patrice Evra in the UEFA Champions League Final at Wembley. Although Rooney equalised Pedro's opener for Barcelona, the Catalans ran out comfortable 3-1 winners with this goal from Messi and a third added by David Villa. (PA Photos)

EUROPEAN CUP-WINNERS' CUP
FINALS 1961–99

Year	Winners		Runners-up		Venue	Attendance	Referee
1961	Fiorentina	2	Rangers	0 *(1st Leg)*	Glasgow	80,000	Steiner (A)
	Fiorentina	2	Rangers	1 *(2nd Leg)*	Florence	50,000	Hernadi (H)
1962	Atletico Madrid	1	Fiorentina	1	Glasgow	27,389	Wharton (S)
Replay	Atletico Madrid	3	Fiorentina	0	Stuttgart	38,000	Tschenscher (WG)
1963	Tottenham Hotspur	5	Atletico Madrid	1	Rotterdam	49,000	Van Leuwen (Ho)
1964	Sporting Lisbon	3	MTK Budapest	3 *(aet)*	Brussels	3000	Van Nuffel (Bel)
Replay	Sporting Lisbon	1	MTK Budapest	0	Antwerp	19,000	Versyp (Bel)
1965	West Ham U	2	Munich 1860	0	Wembley	100,000	Szolt (H)
1966	Borussia Dortmund	2	Liverpool	1 *(aet)*	Glasgow	41,657	Schwinte (F)
1967	Bayern Munich	1	Rangers	0 *(aet)*	Nuremberg	69,480	Lo Bello (I)
1968	AC Milan	2	Hamburg	0	Rotterdam	53,000	Ortiz (Sp)
1969	Slovan Bratislava	3	Barcelona	2	Basle	19,000	Van Ravens (Ho)
1970	Manchester C	2	Gornik Zabrze	1	Vienna	8,000	Schiller (A)
1971	Chelsea	1	Real Madrid	1 *(aet)*	Athens	42,000	Scheurer (Sw)
Replay	Chelsea	2	Real Madrid	1 *(aet)*	Athens	35,000	Bucheli (Sw)
1972	Rangers	3	Moscow Dynamo	2	Barcelona	24,000	Ortiz (Sp)
1973	AC Milan	1	Leeds U	0	Salonika	45,000	Mihas (Gr)
1974	Magdeburg	2	AC Milan	0	Rotterdam	4000	Van Gemert (Ho)
1975	Dynamo Kiev	3	Ferencvaros	0	Basle	13,000	Davidson (S)
1976	Anderlecht	4	West Ham U	2	Brussels	58,000	Wurtz (F)
1977	Hamburg	2	Anderlecht	0	Amsterdam	65,000	Partridge (E)
1978	Anderlecht	4	Austria/WAC	0	Paris	48,679	Adlinger (WG)
1979	Barcelona	4	Fortuna Dusseldorf	3 *(aet)*	Basle	58,000	Palotai (H)
1980	Valencia	0	Arsenal	0	Brussels	36,000	Christov (Cz)
	(aet; Valencia won 5-4 on penalties)						
1981	Dynamo Tbilisi	2	Carl Zeiss Jena	1	Dusseldorf	9000	Lattanzi (I)
1982	Barcelona	2	Standard Liege	1	Barcelona	100,000	Eschweiler (WG)
1983	Aberdeen	2	Real Madrid	1 *(aet)*	Gothenburg	17,804	Menegali (I)
1984	Juventus	2	Porto	1	Basle	60,000	Prokop (EG)
1985	Everton	3	Rapid Vienna	1	Rotterdam	50,000	Casarin (I)
1986	Dynamo Kiev	3	Atletico Madrid	0	Lyon	39,300	Wohrer (A)
1987	Ajax	1	Lokomotiv Leipzig	0	Athens	35,000	Agnolin (I)
1988	Mechelen	1	Ajax	0	Strasbourg	39,446	Pauly (WG)
1989	Barcelona	2	Sampdoria	0	Berne	45,000	Courtney (E)
1990	Sampdoria	2	Anderlecht	0	Gothenburg	20,103	Galler (Sw)
1991	Manchester U	2	Barcelona	1	Rotterdam	42,000	Karlsson (Se)
1992	Werder Bremen	2	Monaco	0	Lisbon	16,000	D'Elia (I)
1993	Parma	3	Antwerp	1	Wembley	37,393	Assenmacher (G)
1994	Arsenal	1	Parma	0	Copenhagen	33,765	Krondl (CzR)
1995	Zaragoza	2	Arsenal	1	Paris	42,424	Ceccarini (I)
1996	Paris St Germain	1	Rapid Vienna	0	Brussels	37,500	Pairetto (I)
1997	Barcelona	1	Paris St Germain	0	Rotterdam	45,000	Merk (G)
1998	Chelsea	1	Stuttgart	0	Stockholm	30,216	Braschi (I)
1999	Lazio	2	Mallorca	1	Villa Park	33,021	Benko (A)

INTER-CITIES FAIRS CUP FINALS 1958–71

(Winners in italics)

Year	First Leg	Attendance	Second Leg	Attendance
1958	London 2 Barcelona 2	45,466	*Barcelona* 6 London 0	62,000
1960	Birmingham C 0 Barcelona 0	40,500	*Barcelona* 4 Birmingham C 1	70,000
1961	Birmingham C 2 Roma 2	21,005	*Roma* 2 Birmingham C 0	60,000
1962	Valencia 6 Barcelona 2	65,000	Barcelona 1 *Valencia* 1	60,000
1963	Dynamo Zagreb 1 Valencia 2	40,000	*Valencia* 2 Dynamo Zagreb 0	55,000
1964	*Zaragoza* 2 Valencia 1	50,000	(in Barcelona)	
1965	*Ferencvaros* 1 Juventus 0	25,000	(in Turin)	
1966	Barcelona 0 Zaragoza 1	70,000	Zaragoza 2 *Barcelona* 4	70,000
1967	Dynamo Zagreb 2 Leeds U 0	40,000	Leeds U 0 *Dynamo Zagreb* 0	35,604
1968	Leeds U 1 Ferencvaros 0	25,368	Ferencvaros 0 *Leeds U* 0	70,000
1969	Newcastle U 3 Ujpest Dozsa 0	60,000	Ujpest Dozsa 2 *Newcastle U* 3	37,000
1970	Anderlecht 3 Arsenal 1	37,000	*Arsenal* 3 Anderlecht 0	51,612
1971	Juventus 0 Leeds U 0 *(abandoned 51 minutes)*	42,000		
	Juventus 2 Leeds U 2	42,000	*Leeds U* 1* Juventus 1	42,483

UEFA CUP FINALS 1972–97

(Winners in italics)

Year	First Leg	Attendance	Second Leg	Attendance
1972	Wolverhampton W 1 Tottenham H 2	45,000	*Tottenham H* 1 Wolverhampton W 1	48,000
1973	Liverpool 0 Moenchengladbach 0			
	(abandoned 27 minutes)	44,967		
	Liverpool 3 Moenchengladbach 0	41,169	Moenchengladbach 2 *Liverpool* 0	35,000
1974	Tottenham H 2 Feyenoord 2	46,281	*Feyenoord* 2 Tottenham H 0	68,000
1975	Moenchengladbach 0 Twente 0	45,000	Twente 1 *Moenchengladbach* 5	24,500
1976	Liverpool 3 FC Brugge 2	56,000	FC Brugge 1 *Liverpool* 1	32,000
1977	Juventus 1 Athletic Bilbao 0	75,000	Athletic Bilbao 2 *Juventus* 1*	43,000
1978	Bastia 0 PSV Eindhoven 0	15,000	*PSV Eindhoven* 3 Bastia 0	27,000
1979	Red Star Belgrade 1 Moenchengladbach 1	87,500	*Moenchengladbach* 1 Red Star Belgrade 0	45,000
1980	Moenchengladbach 3 Eintracht Frankfurt 2	25,000	*Eintracht Frankfurt* 1* Moenchengladbach 0	60,000
1981	Ipswich T 3 AZ 67 Alkmaar 0	27,532	AZ 67 Alkmaar 4 *Ipswich T* 2	28,500
1982	Gothenburg 1 Hamburg 0	42,548	Hamburg 0 *Gothenburg* 3	60,000
1983	Anderlecht 1 Benfica 0	45,000	Benfica 1 *Anderlecht* 1	80,000
1984	Anderlecht 1 Tottenham H 1	40,000	*Tottenham H* 1[1] Anderlecht 1	46,258
1985	Videoton 0 Real Madrid 3	30,000	*Real Madrid* 0 Videoton 1	98,300
1986	Real Madrid 5 Cologne 1	80,000	Cologne 2 *Real Madrid* 0	15,000
1987	Gothenburg 1 Dundee U 0	50,023	Dundee U 1 *Gothenburg* 1	20,911
1988	Espanol 3 Bayer Leverkusen 0	42,000	*Bayer Leverkusen* 3[2] Espanol 0	22,000
1989	Napoli 2 Stuttgart 1	83,000	Stuttgart 3 *Napoli* 3	67,000
1990	Juventus 3 Fiorentina 1	45,000	Fiorentina 0 *Juventus* 0	32,000
1991	Internazionale 2 Roma 0	68,887	Roma 1 *Internazionale* 0	70,901
1992	Torino 2 Ajax 2	65,377	*Ajax* 0* Torino 0	40,000
1993	Borussia Dortmund 1 Juventus 3	37,000	*Juventus* 3 Borussia Dortmund 0	62,781
1994	Salzburg 0 Internazionale 1	47,500	*Internazionale* 1 Salzburg 0	80,326
1995	Parma 1 Juventus 0	23,000	Juventus 1 *Parma* 1	80,750
1996	Bayern Munich 2 Bordeaux 0	62,000	Bordeaux 1 *Bayern Munich* 3	36,000
1997	Schalke 1 Internazionale 0	56,824	Internazionale 1 *Schalke* 0[3]	81,670

*won on away goals   [1]aet; Tottenham H won 4-3 on penalties   [2]aet; Bayer Leverkusen won 3-2 on penalties
[3]aet; Schalke won 4-1 on penalties

UEFA CUP FINALS 1998–2009

Year	Winners		Runners-up		Venue	Attendance	Referee
1998	Internazionale	3	Lazio	0	Paris	42,938	Nieto (Sp)
1999	Parma	3	Marseille	0	Moscow	61,000	Dallas (S)
2000	Galatasaray	0	Arsenal	0	Copenhagen	38,919	Nieto (Sp)
	(aet; Galatasaray won 4-1 on penalties)						
2001	Liverpool	5	Alaves	4	Dortmund	65,000	Veissiere (F)
	(aet; Liverpool won on sudden death)						
2002	Feyenoord	3	Borussia Dortmund	2	Rotterdam	45,000	Pereira (P)
2003	Porto	3	Celtic	2	Seville	52,972	Michel (Slo)
	(aet)						
2004	Valencia	2	Marseille	0	Gothenburg	40,000	Collina (I)
2005	CSKA Moscow	3	Sporting Lisbon	1	Lisbon	48,000	Poll (E)
2006	Sevilla	4	Middlesbrough	0	Eindhoven	36,500	Fandel (G)
2007	Sevilla	2	Espanyol	2	Glasgow	50,670	Busacca (Sw)
	(aet; Sevilla won 3-1 on penalties)						
2008	Zenit St Petersburg	2	Rangers	0	Manchester	43,878	Fröjdfeldt (Se)
2009	Shakhtar Donetsk	2	Werder Bremen	1	Istanbul	40,000	Chantalejo (Sp)

UEFA EUROPA LEAGUE FINALS 2010–2011

Year	Winners		Runners-up		Venue	Attendance	Referee
2010	Atletico Madrid	2	Fulham	1	Hamburg	49,000	Rizzoli (I)
	(aet)						
2011	Porto	1	Braga	0	Dublin	45,391	Carballo (Sp)

UEFA EUROPA LEAGUE 2010–11

■ *Denotes player sent off.*

FIRST QUALIFYING ROUND FIRST LEG

Thursday, 1 July 2010

Anorthosis (2) 3 *(Katsavakis 23, Okkas 30, Cafu 64)*
Banants (0) 0 7300
Anorthosis: Kozacik; Leiwakabessy (Vidovic 74), Janicio, Georgiou, Katsavakis, Skopelitis, Laban, Marangos, Okkas (Tofas 81), Cafu, Christovao (Miguel Pedro 71).
Banants: Ghazaryan; Nikolov, Daghbashyan, Hambardzumyan, Ararat Arakelyan, Melkonyan (Kasule 40), Karapetyan, Voskaniyan A (Balabekyan 74), Beto, Poghosyan V, Ortega.

Dinamo Tbilisi (1) 2 *(Kakhelishvili 22, Khmaladze 63 (pen))*
Flora (1) 1 *(Dupikov 9)* 2,500
Dinamo Tbilisi: Loria; Tomashvili, Kakubava, Chaduneli, Khmaladze, Ednilson, Kakhelishvili, Koshkadze, Tekturmanidze (Pirtskhalava 76), Vatsadze (Metreveli 86), Djousse (Lekvtadze 86).
Flora: Pedok; Allas, Palatu, Kams, Jurgenson, Minkenen, Kasimir, Mosnikov (Post 83), Konsa, Luts (Masitsev 86), Dupikov (Alliku 73).

Grevenmacher (0) 3 *(Heinz 63, Gaspar 73, Almeida 76)*
Dundalk (1) 3 *(Kudozovic 26, Hatswell 51, Benichou 80 (og))* 731
Grevenmacher: Pleimling; Heinz, Mendes (Almeida 67), Furst, Louadj, Hartung, Benichou, Baur (Stojadinovic 90), Gaspar, Hoffmann, Muller (Braun 83).
Dundalk: Gregg; Hatswell, Kelly, Breen G, Murphy N (McGuigan 62), Cawley, Maher, Miller, Fenn, Kudozovic, Gaynor (McGowan 79).

Kalmar (0) 1 *(Ricardo Santos 79)*
EB/Streymur (0) 0 1082
Kalmar: Wasta; Carlsson (Alander 53), Larsson, Lindberg, Johansson, Rydstrom, Sobralense, Eriksson (Daniel Mendes 77), Israelsson (Marcel Sacramento 78), Ricardo Santos, Dauda.
EB/Streymur: Torgard; Bo, Hansen G, Djurhuus, Davidsen, Nielsen, Jorgensen (Amar Dam 65), Jacobsen (Brian Olsen 76), Udsen, Anghel, Hansen A.

Karabakh (2) 4 *(Rashad F Sadygov 26 (pen), Ismayilov 45, Imamaliyev 84, Adamia 89)*
Metalurg (0) 1 *(Simonovski 90)* 6000
Karabakh: Veliyev; Rashad F Sadygov, Teli■, Gashimov, Agolli, Rashad A Sadygov, Mammadov E (Abbasov 55), Kerimov (Yusifov 65), Ismayilov (Imamaliyev 76), Adamia, Aliyev.
Metalurg: Georgievski; Kralevski, Vajs, Petkovski (Simonovski 77), Ilievski (Bogdanovic 64), Mihajlovic (Kostencoski 72), Demiri, Tenekedzhiev, Djuric, Krstev, Kostovski.

KR Reykjavik (2) 3 *(Gunnarsson 12, Finnbogason 32, Takefusa 62)*
Glentoran (0) 0 813
KR Reykjavik: Moldskred; Fridgeirsson, Gunnarsson, Sigurdarson, Rutgers, Amarsson, Gudjonsson, Sigurdsson B, Hauksson (Kristjansson 84), Takefusa (Baldvinsson 81), Finnbogason (Jonsson G 88).
Glentoran: Morris; Hill, Ward, McGovern, Johnny Taylor, Fordyce, Gawley (Southam 66), McCabe (Gardiner 46), Clarke, Hamilton, Waterworth (Black 66).

Laci (1) 1 *(Marashi 45)*
Dnepr Mogilev (0) 1 *(Turlin 90)* 2000
Laci: Llani; Kaja, Cela, Brahja, Kastrati, Vucaj, Gega (Jushi 87), Nina, Shazivari (Marashi 26), Veliaj, Nimani.
Dnepr Mogilev: Kopantsov; Raspopov, Shuneiko, Gonchar, Kapov, Poryvaev, Tereshchenko (Lyasyuk 57), Bychenok, Tupchiy (Karpovich 87), Yurchanka, Turlin.

Llanelli (1) 2 *(Thomas D 17, Jones S 47)*
Tauras (2) 2 *(Kizys 9, 20)* 556
Llanelli: Morris; Jones S, Thomas D, Giles, Thomas C, Llewellyn (Legg 77), Corbisiero, Holloway■, Venables, Follows (Griffiths 62), Moses.
Tauras: Kilijonas; Regelskis, Vaitkus, Mockus, Kizys, Jasaitis, Maciulis, Buitkus, Savastas (Gedgaudas 66), Lekis, Daunoravicius (Jose Vide 46).

Nitra (1) 2 *(Toth 13, Sloboda 80)*
Gyor (1) 2 *(Kink 38, 58)* 2560
Nitra: Hrosso; Toth, Lesko, Glenda, Kasprak, Stetina, Kolmokov M, Hodur, Balis (Sloboda 70), Simonek (Mikus 46), Valenta (Kolar 56).
Gyor: Santa; Djordjevic, Feher, Szabo (Volgyi 74), Stanisic, Pilibaitis (Copa 32), Kink, Koltai (Cetkovic 62), Tokody, Aleksidze, Nicorec.

NSI (0) 0
Gefle (1) 2 *(Gerndt 34, 60)* 370
NSI: Gango; Hansen E, Davidsen, Joensen J, Petersen J, Lakjuni H (Potemkin 61), Hansen J, Mortensen (Danielsen E 79), Frederiksberg J, Olsen K (Danielsen D 79), Jacobsen C.
Gefle: Hugosson; Bernhardsson, Theorin, Portin, Senatore, Jawo (Frempong 81), Lantto, Hansson, Gerndt (Westlin 65), Dahlberg, Orlov.

Olimpia (0) 0
Xazar (0) 0 5800
Olimpia: Pascenco; Orlovschi, Cheltuiala (Kourouma 90), Ogada, Valuta, Tcaciuc, Adaramola (Somide 79), Kamara, Jerome, Khorolskyy (Paseciniuc 65), Ovsianicov.
Xazar: Agayev; Allahverdiyev, Beqiri, Ayhan, Imedashvili, Amirguliyev, Gurbanov (Ramazanov 86), Todorov, Mario Sergio, Opara (Huseynov 90), Lalin (Mammedov K 89).

Olimpija (0) 0
Siroki (1) 2 *(Wagner 45, Renato 68)* 1700
Olimpija: Botonjic; Salkic, Cvijanovic, Kasnik, Vuckic, Lovrecic, Gabriel (Jovic 62), Skerjanc, Bozic, Prasnikar (Rujovic 53), Cimirotic (Rakovic 46).
Siroki: Bandovic; Topic, Renato, Barisic, Kozul (Markic 79), Wagner, Silic, Ljubic (Roskam 50), Diogo (Coric 68), Ivankovic, Varea.

Portadown (1) 1 *(Lecky 38)*
Skonto Riga (0) 1 *(Laizans 90)* 571
Portadown: Armstrong; Kelly, O'Hara, Redman, Ramsey■, McCafferty (Mackle 73), Mouncey, Boyle, Clarke, Lecky, Teggart (Haire 83).
Skonto Riga: Ikstens (Malins 46); Smirnovs, Rode, Laizans, Tarasovs, Fertovs, Dubra, Sinelnikovs (Petersons 16), Maksimenko, Karasausks, Nathan Junior.

Rabotnicki (2) 5 *(Ze Carlos 24, Wandeir 35, Fabio 55, 57, Muarem 60)*
Lusitanos (0) 0 800
Rabotnicki: Naumovski; Dimovski, Sekulovski, Bojovic, Fernando, Gligorov, Muarem, Ze Carlos (Petkovski 65), Tuneski, Wandeir (Sinkovic 73), Fabio (Marcio 59).
Lusitanos: Benitez; Leonel Antunes, Abidan (Meza 53), Hugo Veloso (Francisco Hernandez 64), Bruno Silva, Joao Cunha, Filipe Barros, Luis Filipe Pinto, Franklin Soares, Pedro Miguel Reis (Juan Raya 50), Luis Miguel dos Reis.

Randers (3) 6 *(Sane 16, Movsisyan 17, 90, Olsen 33, Pedersen 47 (pen), Brock-Madsen 88)*
F91 Dudelange (0) 1 *(Benzouien 49 (pen))* 3068
Randers: Ousted; Fischer, Pedersen, Egholm, Fenger, Lorentzen (Cramer 67), Karlsen, Sane (Brock-Madsen 87), Olsen (Sorensen 84), Movsisyan, Berg.

F91 Dudelange: Joubert; Caillet, Wiggers, Mouny, Rentmeister, Benzouien, Payal (Bensi 84), Remy, Da Mota, Abdullei (Gruszczynski 55), Melisse (Hareau 46).

Shakhter Karagandy (1) 1 *(Dzidic 7)*
Ruch (1) 2 *(Janoszka 45, Grzyb 48 (pen))*   10,000
Shakhter Karagandy: Sarana; Dordevic, Danaev, Tarasov, Dzidic, Suchkov (Skorykh 61), Vicius, Bogdanov, Borantaev (Borovskiy 72), Kislitsyn, Finonchenko.
Ruch: Pilarz; Nykiel (Malinowski 70), Jakubowski, Grzyb, Stawarczyk, Grodzicki, Pulkowski, Straka, Janoszka (Swierblewski 84), Sobiech, Olszar (Zajac 52).

Sibenik (0) 0
Sliema Wanderers (0) 0   2000
Sibenik: Blazevic; Ceric, Medvid, Spahija, Gusic, Alispahic, Bloudek (Bozic 63), Bacelic-Grgic (Elez 63), Husmani, Jakolis, Fustar.
Sliema Wanderers: Szentpeteri; Azzopardi, Baldacchino, Muscat G, Tidane, Scerri, Woods, Mintoff (Failla 57), Andre Portulez, Triganza (Turner 90), Lattes.

SK Tirana (0) 0
Zalaegerszegi (0) 0   1854
SK Tirana: Lika I; Lila, Sina, Osmani, Pashaj, Karabeci, Ahmataj, Hajdari (Malindi 56), Lilaj, Plaku, Pejic (Bici 86).
Zalaegerszegi: Vlaszak; Kocsardi (Kovacs 61), Miljatovic, Bogunovic, Mate (Magasfoldi 46), Kamber, Panikvar, Illes (Horvath 78), Rajcomar, Pavicevic, Szalai.

Tobol (1) 1 *(Zhumaskaliev 13)*
Zrinjski (0) 2 *(Dragicevic 53, 82)*   6500
Tobol: Petukhov; Turtenwald, Irismetov, Mukanov, Abdulin, Sabirov (Suyumagambetov 59), Kharaboro (Travin 81), Nurgaliyev, Yurin (Kuantayev 73), Zhumaskaliev, Bakayev.
Zrinjski: Melher; Dzidic, Ivankovic, Sunjic, Rizvanovic, Zizovic, Zadro, Susic, Stjepanovic, Dragicevic (Pehar 90), Selimovic (Zovko 90).

Torpedo Zhodino (0) 3 *(Krivobok 52, Ogar 59, Kontsevoy 66)*
Fylkir (0) 0   2500
Torpedo Zhodino: Bushma; Ostroukh, Kontsevoy, Karshakevich, Kozlov, Levitski, Ogar, Brusnikin (Solovey 65), Kazarin, Krivobok, Karolik (Aleksievich 73).
Fylkir: Thorgeirsson; Johannesson, Gislason, Valdimarsson, Hannesson, Stigsson (Faye 60), Oskarsson (Thorsteinsson 79), Petursson, Ingason (Thrainsson 86), Breiddal, Asgeirsson.

TPS Turku (3) 3 *(Riku Riski 24, 35, Wusu 30)*
Port Talbot Town (0) 1 *(Rose 70)*   1405
TPS Turku: Moisander; Rahmonen, Jovanovic, Nyberg, Manninen, Riku Riski (Virtanen 75), Cleaver, Kolehmainen, Johansson, Aaritalo (Roope Riski 78), Wusu.
Port Talbot Town: Kendall; De Vulgt (Holland 46), Surman, Rees, Barrow, Phillips, Lewis, Grist, John (Bowen 87), McCreesh, Rose (Fahiya 87).

Trans (0) 0
MyPa (0) 2 *(Votinov 47, Gorskov 53 (og))*   150
Trans: Stonys; Starovoitov (Mandinho 63), Kitto, Rimas, Mitin, Gorskov, Kazakov (Lepik 38), Bezykornovas, Bazjukin (Saulenas 71), Abramenko, Felipe Rodrigues.
MyPa: Kuismala; Aho, Timoska, Oksanen, Tuunainen (Uimaniemi 3), Hietanen, Aijala, Okkonen, Saxman (Felipe Benevides 76), Votinov, Ricketts (Koljonen 90).

UE Santa Coloma (0) 0
Mogren (1) 3 *(Grbic 14, Culafic 83, Cetkovic 90)*   450
UE Santa Coloma: Rivas; Rubio, Codina (Orosa 71), Pedescoll, Martinez, Prat, Sirvan, Aloy (Ribera 87), Lafoz, Miguel, Bernat.

Mogren: Janjusevic; Janicic, Pejovic, Simovic, Kapisoda, Nuhi (Neric 62), Jovanovic, Cetkovic, Grbic (Culafic 77), Mirkovic, Gluscevic (Bozovic B 46).

Ulisses (0) 0
Bnei Yehuda (0) 0   2000
Ulisses: Malkov; Aleksanyan (Ugrekhelidze 32), Andrikyan, Hakhnazaryan, Grigoryan D, Tibilashvili (Sahakyan 46), Krasovski, Grigoryan N, Grigoryan AG, Adamyan, Jikia (Ledenev 61).
Bnei Yehuda: Aiyenugba; Azoz, Hadad, Mori, Linic, Edri, Rali, Zairi, Menashe (Baldut 65), Levi (Afek 46), Biton.

Zestafoni (3) 5 *(Gelashvili 20 (pen), 23, Dvali 22, 64, Gorgiashvili 90)*
Faetano (0) 0   3900
Zestafoni: Kvashkhvadze; Oniani (Kobakhidze 77), Eliava, Khidesheli, Benashvili, Daushvili, Dzaria (Pipia 65), Babunashvili (Gorgiashvili 55), Grigalashvili, Gelashvili, Dvali.
Faetano: Dimetto; Della Valle, Pellegrino (Giardi 40), Valentini, Borroni, Rinaldi M, Raggini (Mariani 89), Bucci, Moroni, Ricci (Rinaldi G 75), Viroli.

Zeta (0) 1 *(Pelicic 78 (pen))*
Dacia (1) 1 *(Orbu 39)*   1500
Zeta: Ivanovic; Petrovic, Kaluderovic, Radulovic MM, Zlaticanin, Boljevic, Burzanovic (Krkotic 46), Kojasevic, Duretic (Pelicic 46), Simovic, Jugovic (Lambulic 72).
Dacia: Matiughin; Gamezardashvili[■], Lomidze, Popovici, Grosev, Cojocari, Bulat (Negrescu 77), Gorceac (Dragovozov 65), Korgalidze, Orbu, Sischin (Bursuc 58).

FIRST QUALIFYING ROUND SECOND LEG

Thursday, 8 July 2010

Banants (0) 0
Anorthosis (1) 1 *(Laban 36)*   3000
Banants: Ghazaryan; Nikolov, Daghbashyan, Hambardzumyan, Ararat Arakelyan, Melkonyan (Poghosyan V 46), Karapetyan, Kasule, Beto (Voskaniyan A 84), Balabekyan (Avetisyan 90), Ortega.
Anorthosis: Kozacik; Leiwakabessy, Janicio, Georgiou, Katsavakis, Skopelitis, Laban (Mintikkis 62), Marangos (Papathanasiou 71), Okkas, Cafu, Christovao (Constantinou A 77).

Bnei Yehuda (1) 1 *(Menashe 45)*
Ulisses (0) 0   1313
Bnei Yehuda: Aiyenugba; Azoz, Hadad, Mori (Garrido 46), Linic, Edri, Baldut, Rali (Zairi 58), Menashe, Afek (Levi 73), Biton.
Ulisses: Malkov; Andrikyan (Davtyan 46), Ugrekhelidze, Hakhnazaryan, Grigoryan D, Tibilashvili (Sahakyan 67), Krasovski, Grigoryan N, Grigoryan AG, Adamyan, Ledenev (Jikia 72).

Dacia (0) 0
Zeta (0) 0   6200
Dacia: Matiughin; Lomidze, Popovici, Negrescu, Grosev, Bursuc, Cojocari, Bulat[■], Korgalidze (Gorceac 85), Orbu (Guchashvili 90), Sischin (Dragovozov 58).
Zeta: Ivanovic; Petrovic, Kaluderovic, Radulovic MM, Zlaticanin, Boljevic, Krkotic (Ladic 61), Pelicic, Kojasevic, Simovic (Burzanovic 76), Jugovic (Lambulic 70).

Dnepr Mogilev (3) 7 *(Bychenok 10, 80, Yurchanka 17 (pen), 56, 81, Zenkovich 42, Cernych 87)*
Laci (0) 1 *(Nimani 60)*   3500
Dnepr Mogilev: Kopantsov; Shuneiko, Karpovich (Raspopov 61), Gonchar, Kapov, Obrazov, Poryvaev (Kozlov 46), Bychenok, Yurchanka, Zenkovich (Cernych 67), Turlin.
Laci: Llani; Kaja (Shazivari 46), Cela, Brahja[■], Kastrati, Vucaj, Tafaj, Gega (Marashi 30), Nina, Veliaj, Nimani.

Dundalk (2) 2 *(Fenn 5 (pen), Kudozovic 16)*
Grevenmacher (0) 1 *(Muller 90)* 2000
Dundalk: Gregg; Hatswell, Kelly, Breen G, Cawley, Maher (McDonnell 77), Miller, Fenn, Kudozovic (Breen J 90), Mulvenna (McGowan 71), Gaynor.
Grevenmacher: Pleimling; Heinz, Mendes (Almeida 61), Furst, Louadj, Hartung, Benichou (Lorig 46), Baur, Gaspar (Brzyski 72), Hoffmann, Muller.

EB/Streymur (0) 0
Kalmar (1) 3 *(Israelsson 9, Eriksson 47, Ricardo Santos 50)* 607
EB/Streymur: Torgard; Bo, Hansen G, Djurhuus, Davidsen, Nielsen (Niclasen 61), Jorgensen (Samuelsen 70), Jacobsen, Udsen, Anghel (Jakobsen 80), Hansen A.
Kalmar: Wasta; Larsson, Lindberg, Nouri, Arajuuri, Rydstrom, Sobralense (Johansson 88), Eriksson, Israelsson, Daniel Mendes (Bertilsson 70), Ricardo Santos (Marcel Sacramento 70).

F91 Dudelange (1) 2 *(Caillet 37, Gruszczynski 67)*
Randers (1) 1 *(Lorentzen 17)* 636
F91 Dudelange: Joubert; Caillet, Wiggers, Nicolle, Guthleber, Rentmeister, Benzouien, Remy (Karaca 87), Gruszczynski, Bensi, Melisse.
Randers: Ousted; Ahmed (Fenger* 58), Fischer, Pedersen, Arzumanyan, Egholm, Jensen (Hastrup 46), Lorentzen, Olsen, Movsisyan (Karlsen 27), Berg.

Faetano (0) 0
Zestafoni (0) 0 500
Faetano: Gozzi; Della Valle, Giardi, Pellegrino, Valentini, Borroni, Rinaldi M, Raggini (Ugolini 90), Bucci, Moroni, Ricci (Viroli 68).
Zestafoni: Mamaladze; Eliava, Khidesheli, Kobakhidze, Benashvili, Gorgiashvili, Dzaria (Grigalashvili 70), Babunashvili, Lomia (Gelashvili 64), Pipia, Mikaberidze (Dvali 64).

Flora (0) 0
Dinamo Tbilisi (0) 0 632
Flora: Meerits; Allas, Palatu, Kams, Jurgenson, Jahhimovits, Minkenen (Alliku 74), Kasimir, Konsa, Luts, Dupikov (Post 46).
Dinamo Tbilisi: Loria; Tomashvili, Kakubava, Khmaladze, Ednilson, Kakhelishvili, Koshkadze, Tekturmanidze (Gvelesiani 90), Vatsadze (Metreveli 72), Djousse, Robertinho (Lekvtadze 85).

Fylkir (1) 1 *(Faye 32 (pen))*
Torpedo Zhodino (1) 3 *(Ostroukh 41, Krivobok 86 (pen), 88)* 658
Fylkir: Bazi; Valdimarsson, Hannesson, Arnthorsson (Hermannsson 84), Johannesson, Ingason (Thrainsson 70), Thorhallsson, Breiddal (Thorsteinsson 70), Faye, Asgeirsson, Jonsson A.
Torpedo Zhodino: Bushma; Ostroukh, Kontsevoy, Karshakevich, Kozlov, Levitski, Martynets, Brusnikin (Solovey 74), Kazarin (Gintov 82), Krivobok, Karolik (Aleksievich 68).

Gefle (1) 2 *(Bernhardsson 22, Berggren 63)*
NSI (0) 1 *(Potemkin 90)* 380
Gefle: Hugosson; Bernhardsson, Theorin, Senatore, Jawo, Lantto, Hansson (Dahlberg 53), Ohagen (Larsson 70), Chibsah, Gerndt, Orlov (Berggren 60).
NSI: Gango; Hansen E (Potemkin 35), Danielsen E (Frederiksberg A 85), Davidsen, Joensen J, Petersen J, Lakjuni H, Hansen J, Mortensen, Frederiksberg J, Olsen K (Danielsen D 71).

Glentoran (1) 2 *(Callachar 22, Hamilton 56 (pen))*
KR Reykjavik (1) 2 *(Finnbogason 45, Black 54 (og))* 771
Glentoran: Morris; Nixon, Ward, McGovern, Black, Gawley, Clarke, Gardiner (Martyn 56), Callachar (Fordyce 75), Hamilton, Waterworth.
KR Reykjavik: Moldskred; Fridgeirsson*, Gunnarsson (Jonsson G 80), Sigurdarson, Rutgers, Amarsson (Eggert Einarsson 56), Gudjonsson, Sigurdsson B, Hauksson, Takefusa (Jordao Diogo 66), Finnbogason.

Gyor (1) 3 *(Aleksidze 22, Nicorec 60, Kink 90)*
Nitra (1) 1 *(Hodur 10)* 4200
Gyor: Santa; Djordjevic, Feher, Szabo, Kiss (Babic 46), Pilibaitis, Kink, Koltai (Nicolas 57), Tokody, Aleksidze (Copa 75), Nicorec.
Nitra: Hrosso; Toth, Lesko, Glenda, Kasprak, Stetina, Hodur, Balis (Kolar 46), Simoncic, Sloboda (Valenta 61), Mikus (Rak 51).

Lusitanos (0) 0
Rabotnicki (3) 6 *(Wandeir 25, 68, Fabio 33, 42, 54, Gligorov 71)* 450
Lusitanos: Benitez; Leonel Antunes, Bruno Silva, Victor Manuel Pereira, Daniel Laguna (Hugo Veloso 43), Filipe Barros, Luis Filipe Pinto, Franklin Soares, Francisco Hernandez (Rebelo Leitao 83), Pedro Miguel Reis (Luis Miguel dos Reis 46), Juan Raya.
Rabotnicki: Bogatinov; Dimovski (Todorovski 59), Sekulovski (Adem 46), Bojovic, Fernando, Gligorov, Muarem, Ze Carlos, Tuneski, Wandeir, Fabio (Petkovski 69).

Metalurg (0) 1 *(Krstev 78)*
Karabakh (0) 1 *(Imamaliyev 69)* 860
Metalurg: Nikov; Kralevski, Vajs, Petkovski, Dameski, Demiri, Mitrev (Tenekedzhiev 46), Kostencoski, Djuric (Mihajlovic 84), Krstev, Kostovski (Simonovski 72).
Karabakh: Veliyev; Rashad F Sadygov, Abbasov, Medvedev, Gashimov, Garayev, Rashad A Sadygov, Yusifov (Kerimov 89), Imamaliyev, Ismayilov (Mammadov E 85), Adamia (Nadirov 83).

Mogren (2) 2 *(Culafic 18, Gluscevic 20)*
UE Santa Coloma (0) 0 200
Mogren: Janjusevic; Janicic, Pejovic, Simovic, Kapisoda, Jovanovic (Martinovic 68), Culafic (Jovovic 58), Cetkovic (Markovic 77), Bozovic B, Mirkovic, Gluscevic.
UE Santa Coloma: Rivas; Rubio, Codina, Orosa, Pedescoll (Prat 22), Martinez, Sirvan, Aloy, Lafoz (Blazquez 46), Miguel (Garcia 89), Bernat.

MyPa (0) 5 *(Ricketts 62, Aijala 67, 74, Koljonen 77, Felipe Benevides 80)*
Trans (0) 0 1127
MyPa: Kuismala; Aho, Timoska, Oksanen, Uimaniemi, Hietanen, Aijala, Okkonen (Felipe Benevides 70), Saxman (Rautiainen 81), Votinov, Ricketts (Koljonen 72).
Trans: Stonys; Lepik, Kitto, Rimas, Mitin, Gorskov, Bezykornovas, Bazjukin (Saulenas 65), Leontovits (Mandinho 73), Abramenko, Felipe Rodrigues(Kazakov 46).

Port Talbot Town (0) 0
TPS Turku (2) 4 *(Wusu 26, Kolehmainen 32, Riku Riski 69, Roope Riski 90)* 676
Port Talbot Town: Kendall; Holland (Brooks 46), Surman, Palmer (Thomas D 67), Rees, Barrow, Lewis, Grist, John, McCreesh (Bowen 76), Rose.
TPS Turku: Moisander; Rahmonen, Heinikangas (Jovanovic 63), Nyberg, Manninen (Milsom 46), Riku Riski, Cleaver, Kolehmainen, Johansson, Aaritalo, Wusu (Roope Riski 55).

Ruch (0) 1 *(Sobiech 59)*
Shakhter Karagandy (0) 0 6000
Ruch: Pilarz; Nykiel, Jakubowski, Grzyb, Grodzicki, Zajac (Malinowski 63), Pulkowski (Piech 76), Sadlok, Straka, Janoszka, Sobiech (Stawarczyk 90).
Shakhter Karagandy: Sarana; Kozyulin, Danaev, Tarasov, Dzidic, Suchkov (Borovskiy 70), Skorykh, Vicius, Bogdanov, Kislitsyn, Finonchenko.

Siroki (0) 3 *(Roskam 81, Weitzer 83, Misic 90)*
Olimpija (0) 0 3000
Siroki: Bandovic; Topic, Renato, Barisic, Kozul (Weitzer 61), Wagner (Glavina 86), Silic, Diogo, Ivankovic, Varea (Misic 77), Roskam.
Olimpija: Botonjic; Salkic, Cvijanovic*, Kasnik, Vuckic, Lovrecic, Rujovic (Prasnikar 88), Skerjanc, Jovic*, Rakovic (Stojanovic 85), Cimirotic (Bozic 84).

Skonto Riga (0) 0
Portadown (1) 1 *(Lecky 29)* 6000
Skonto Riga: Ikstens; Smirnovs, Rode, Laizans, Tarasovs (Petersons 33), Fertovs, Dubra, Maksimenko (Astafjevs 59), Pereplotkins, Karasausks (Turkovs 46), Nathan Junior.
Portadown: Miskelly; Kelly, O'Hara, Redman, Mackle, Mouncey, Boyle, Clarke (McCafferty 85), Braniff, Lecky, Teggart (Haire 79).

Sliema Wanderers (0) 0
Sibenik (0) 3 *(Medvid 64, Jakolis 73, Bulat 89)* 480
Sliema Wanderers: Szentpeteri; Azzopardi█, Baldacchino, Muscat G, Tidane, Failla, Scerri, Woods, Mintoff, Triganza (Mercieca 90), Lattes (Andre Portulez 79).
Sibenik: Blazevic; Ceric, Medvid, Bulat, Jurcevic, Alispahic, Bloudek (Bakovic 81), Bacelic-Grgic (Elez 84), Husmani, Jakolis (Subic 87), Fustar.

Tauras (2) 3 *(Irkha 17, 31, Regelskis 104)*
Llanelli (2) 2 *(Llewellyn 19, Bowen 36)* 350
Tauras: Kilijonas; Regelskis, Vaitkus, Mockus, Kizys, Jasaitis (Jose Vide 69), Maciulis, Savastas, Lekis█, Daunoravicius (Gedgaudas 38), Irkha.
Llanelli: Morris; Jones S (Follows 114), Thomas D, Giles, Thomas C, Bowen, Llewellyn (Legg 106), Corbisiero, Venables, Griffiths█, Moses█.
aet.

Xazar (0) 1 *(Lalin 78)*
Olimpia (1) 1 *(Jerome 14)* 11,250
Xazar: Agayev; Allahverdiyev, Beqiri, Ayhan (Gurbanov 58), Imedashvili, Amirguliyev, Todorov, Mario Sergio, Opara (Mammedov K 67), Ramazanov (Huseynov 64), Lalin.
Olimpia: Pascenco; Orlovschi, Cheltuiala, Ogada, Valuta, Tcaciuc (Kourouma 90), Adaramola, Kamara (Somide 85), Pasecniuc, Jerome (Khorolskyy 75), Ovsianicov.

Zalaegerszegi (0) 0
SK Tirana (0) 1 *(Karabeci 107)* 4000
Zalaegerszegi: Vlaszak; Kocsardi, Milijatovic, Bogunovic, Mate, Kamber, Panikvar, Illes (Horvath 91), Rudnevs, Magasfoldi (Balazs 46), Pavicevic (Rajcomar 106).
SK Tirana: Lika I; Lila, Sina, Osmani, Pashaj, Karabeci, Hajdari (Malindi 61), Metani, Lilaj, Plaku (Sorra 120), Pejic.
aet.

Zrinjski (1) 2 *(Dzidic 10, Pehur 72)*
Tobol (0) 1 *(Zhumaskaliev 57)* 5000
Zrinjski: Melher; Dzidic, Ivankovic, Sunjic, Rizvanovic, Zizovic, Zadro, Susic (Pehar 69), Stjepanovic, Dragicevic, Selimovic.
Tobol: Petukhov; Turtenwald, Irismetov, Lotov, Abdulin, Sabirov, Nurgaliyev (Malyshev 81), Yurin, Zhumaskaliev, Kuantayev, Bakayev.

SECOND QUALIFYING ROUND FIRST LEG

Thursday, 15 July 2010

Anorthosis (0) 0
Sibenik (1) 2 *(Bloudek 10, Bacelic-Grgic 61 (pen))* 7500
Anorthosis: Kozacik; Leiwakabessy, Janicio, Katsavakis, Constantinou A, Skopelitis, Laban (Papathanasiou 72), Marangos (Miguel Pedro 65), Okkas, Cafu, Christovao (Carlos Coto 51).
Sibenik: Blazevic; Ceric, Medvid, Bulat, Elez, Jurcevic, Bloudek (Gusic 83), Bacelic-Grgic, Jakolis, Bozic (Jordan 76), Fustar (Bakovic 90).

Atyrau (0) 0
Gyor (1) 2 *(Pilibaitis 26, Bouguerra 88)* 6400
Atyrau: Shabanov; Crnogorac, Alyev, Zhumabaev, Vorotnikov, Mamonov, Peikrishvili (Chureev 84), Kostrub, Shakin, Sakhalbaev (Larin 76), Frunza (Khizhnichenko 59).
Gyor: Stevanovic; Djordjevic, Feher, Babic, Szabo, Stanisic, Pilibaitis, Kink (Bouguerra 65), Koltai (Nicolas 46), Copa, Aleksidze (Trajkovic 46).

Baku (0) 2 *(Kajkut 77, Jaba 90)*
Buducnost (1) 1 *(Beciraj 38)* 15,000
Baku: Sissokho; Nibombe, Kargbo, Savinov, Boret, Kajkut, Ramim, Skulic, Solic (Angulo 55), Jaba, Epalle.
Buducnost: Dragojevic; Mazic, Dikanovic, Golubovic (Boskovic 81), Adamovic, Dokaj, Jovan Nikolic (Vukcevic P 83), Ajkovic, Brnovic, Beciraj, Vukovic.

Besa (0) 0
Olympiakos (2) 5 *(Oscar Gonzalez 19, 31, Dudu Cearense 47, Diogo 70, 83)* 5000
Besa: Shehi; Lazarevski, Ferizovic, Aliju, Jakupi, Poci, Mihani (Hoxha 71), Osmani M (Shtini 81), Dhembi, Cikalleshi (Semir Hadzibulic 65), Dos Santos.
Olympiakos: Nikopolidis; Modesto, Bravo, Holebas, Galitsios, Maresca, Dudu Cearense (Katsikogiannis 84), Zairi (Fetfatzidis 75), Oscar Gonzalez (Mitroglou 66), Mirallas, Diogo.

Besiktas (1) 3 *(Nihat 19, 65, Mert Nobre 90)*
Vikingur (0) 0 16,803
Besiktas: Hakan; Ibrahim T, Ibrahim U, Erhan (Dag 73), Sivok, Ernst, Quaresma, Delgado (Mert Nobre 83), Rodrigo Tabata, Nihat (Necip 83), Bobo.
Vikingur: Tamas; Niclasen, Jacobsen H, Hansen B, Stankovic, Sam Jacobsen, Djurhuus (Bartalsstovu 46), Jacobsen E, Vatnhamar (Petersen A 89), Justinussen, Klettskard (Martin Olsen 76).

Brondby (0) 3 *(Nilsson 51, Jallow 80, 85)*
Vaduz (0) 0 7966
Brondby: Andersen; Bischoff, Rasmussen, Von Schlebrugge (Van der Schaaf 43), Wass, Kristiansen (Madsen 76), Krohn-Dehli, Holmen, Nilsson, Bernburg (Larsen 66), Jallow.
Vaduz: Faivre; Schwegler, Denicola, Bader, Bellon, Sara, Burgmeier (Christen 64), Ciccone (Sabia 79), Sturm, Leocadio (Hasler 90), Merenda.

Cliftonville (0) 1 *(Caldwell 82)*
Cibalia (0) 0 775
Cliftonville: Connolly; Scannell R, Donaghy, Holland B, Catney, McMullan, Caldwell, Holland M, Scannell C (O'Connor 83), Garrett, Boyce (Patterson 90).
Cibalia: Matkovic; Parmakovic, Bozic, Lucic, Tomic, Radotic (Prgomet 86), Juric, Grgic (Kvesic 89), Mazalovic, Baraban (Simunac 81), Kresinger.

CS Brugge (0) 0
TPS Turku (1) 1 *(Aaritalo 32)* 2754
CS Brugge: Verbist; Portier, Viane, Evens, Cornelis, Vidarsson (Serebrennikov 62), Boi, Nyoni, Van Eenoo (Renato Neto 46), Reynaldo, Foley (Yang Wang 73).
TPS Turku: Moisander; Rahmonen, Heinikangas, Nyberg, Milsom, Manninen, Riku Riski, Cleaver, Kolehmainen, Johansson, Aaritalo (Roope Riski 87).

Differdange (2) 3 *(Veselinov 6 (og), Bettmer 11, Piskor 73)*
Spartak Subotica (2) 3 *(Ubiparip 14, Torbica 28 (pen), Siebenaler 89 (og))* 805
Differdange: Hym; Bukvic, Kintziger, Andre Filipe, Janisch (Franzoni 77), Lebresne (Diop 57), Soraire (Kettenmeyer 70), Bettmer, Siebenaler, Albanese, Piskor.
Spartak Subotica: Jorgic; Sarac, Bratic, Puskaric (Stevanovic 61), Torbica, Veselinov (Adamovic 72), Milankovic, Oletu (Noskovic 85), Simovic, Ubiparip, Miric.

Dynamo Minsk (2) 5 *(Saszankov 12, 33, Putsila 60, Rekish 87, Chukhley 90)*
Sillamae (0) 1 *(Koyaev 79)* 1850
Dynamo Minsk: Gorbunov; Veretilo, Martynovich, Kondratyev, Putsila, Marakhovskiy, Strakhanovich (Kugan 81), Dragun, Rekish, Buloychik (Chukhley 46), Sazankov (Matveenko 61).
Sillamae: Starodubtsev; Gorbunov, Kulik, Naumov, Vihrov, Tarassenkov, Zubavicius (Dudarev 46), Stankevicius (Gornev 69), Aleksejev (Kabayev 71), Vasiliauskas, Kolyaev.

Elfsborg (0) 2 *(Keene 56, Ericsson 79 (pen))*
Iskra-Stal (0) 1 *(Tofan 87)* 3270
Elfsborg: Christiansen; Floren, Wikstrom, Karlsson, Andersson M, Svensson, Mobaeck, Ericsson, Nordmark (Hult 64), Larsson (Ishizaki 71), Keene (Jawo 81).
Iskra-Stal: Gaiducevici; Gafina, Feshchenko, Novicov, Casian, Rudac, Burcovschi, Mihaliov (Tofan 68), Taranu (Chiriliuc 79), Popovici, Kilikevich (Porfireanu 74).

FK Austria (0) 2 *(Linz 50, Schumacher 57)*
Siroki (1) 2 *(Wagner 25, Topic 54)*
FK Austria: Lindner; Ortlechner, Suttner, Dragovic, Klein (Margreitter 83), Vorisek (Schumacher 46), Junuzovic, Baumgartlinger (Hlinka 72), Liendl, Stankovic, Linz.
Siroki: Bandovic; Topic, Renato, Barisic, Kozul (Weitzer 70), Wagner (Brekalo 90), Silic, Diogo, Ivankovic, Varea (Pinjuh A 62), Roskam.
Behind closed doors.

Gefle (0) 1 *(Berggren 51 (pen))*
Dinamo Tbilisi (1) 2 *(Vatsadze 11, Khmaladze 87 (pen))* 500
Gefle: Hugosson; Bernhardsson, Theorin, Senatore, Jawo, Lantto, Hansson (Gerndt 46), Chibsah, Dahlberg, Berggren, Orlov.
Dinamo Tbilisi: Loria; Tomashvili, Kakubava, Khmaladze, Ednilson, Kakhelishvili, Koshkadze (Pirtskhalava 76), Tektumanidze, Vatsadze (Metreveli 82), Djousse, Robertinho (Lekvtadze 34).

Gorica (0) 0
Randers (0) 3 *(Lorentzen 51, Cramer 55, 71)* 567
Gorica: Simcic; Balazic, Zarifovic, Mevlja M (Martinovic 60), Komel, Krsic, Demirovic, Rakuscek, Stojanovic (Arcon 75), Sirok, Velikonja (Volaric 90).
Randers: Ousted; Ahmed, Pedersen, Egholm (Arzumanian 81), Jensen, Cramer, Lorentzen, Karlsen (Brock-Madsen 79), Beckmann, Olsen (Fischer 72), Berg.

Honka (1) 1 *(Savage 43)*
Bangor City (0) 1 *(Jones C 58)* 1279
Honka: Peltonen; Koskinen, Heikkila, Aalto (Otaru 79), Koskimaa, Lepola, Paatelainen (Vasara 65), Schuller, Vuorinen (Rasimus 71), Puustinen, Savage.
Bangor City: Smith; Morley, Roberts, Brewerton (Edwards 52), Hoy, Johnston, Garside, Davies (Williams 79), Ward, Jebb (Bull 61), Jones C.

Kalmar (0) 0
Dacia (0) 0 1976
Kalmar: Wasta; Carlsson, Larsson, Johansson, Nouri, Rydstrom, Sobralense (Marcel Sacramento 82), Eriksson, Israelsson (Bertilsson 46), Daniel Mendes (Dauda 67), Ricardo Santos.
Dacia: Matiughin; Gamezardashvili, Lomidze, Popovici, Grosev, Bursuc, Cojocari, Korgalidze, Sischin (Gorceac 50), Guchashvili (Kum Maka 57) (Orbu 80), Dragovozov.

KR Reykjavik (0) 0
Karpaty (0) 3 *(Guruli 46, Tkachuk 51, Batista 57)* 848
KR Reykjavik: Moldskred; Eggert Einarsson, Gunnarsson (Jordao Diogo 60), Sigurdarson, Rutgers, Arnarsson (Jonsson G 60), Gudjonsson, Sigurdsson B, Hauksson, Takefusa (Kristjansson 70), Finnbogason.
Karpaty: Tlumak; Tubic, Petrivskiy, Milosevic, Goodwin (Gabovda 80), Khudobyak, Tkachuk, Kozhanov (Zenjov 61), Danilo Avelar, Batista (Genison 65), Guruli.

Lausanne (1) 1 *(Silvio 19)*
Borac (0) 0 3800
Lausanne: Favre; Sonnerat, Meoli, Katz, Celestini, Marazzi, Abdul Carrupt (Stadelmann 90), Steuble (Mayila 90), Nelson Borges, Roux (Helin 74), Silvio.
Borac: Avdukic; Trivunovic, Stancheski (Jandric 85), Benovic, Petric, Stupar (Zaric 46), Muminovic, Mikic, Raspudic, Nikolic (Sakan 58), Vukelja.

Levski (3) 6 *(Yovov 12, Mladenov 14, 46, Dembele 42, Isa 86, 90)*
Dundalk (0) 0 8655
Levski: Petkov; Minev, Stanchev, Miliev, Ivanov, Gadzhev, Joazinho, Tasevski (Aleksandrov 64), Yovov (Baltanov 52), Dembele (Isa 77), Mladenov.
Dundalk: Cherrie; Hatswell, Kelly, Breen G, McGuigan, Cawley, Maher, Miller, Fenn (Lennon 60), Kudozovic (McGowan 80), Gaynor.

Maccabi Tel Aviv (0) 2 *(Ziv 49, Medunjanin 52)*
Mogren (0) 0 11,178
Maccabi Tel Aviv: Strauber; Nivaldo, Ziv, Strul, Saban, Baning, Medunjanin (Sidibe 66), Yeini (Avidor 46), Colautti, Itzhaki, Buzaglo (Malul 76).
Mogren: Janjusevic; Janicic, Pejovic, Simovic, Kapisoda (Jovovic 82), Nuhi, Jovanovic, Bozovic B (Culafic 60), Grbic (Cetkovic 65), Mirkovic, Gluscevic.

Maritimo (0) 3 *(Ricardo Esteves 78, Cherrad 85, Tcho 90)*
Sporting Fingal (1) 2 *(Crowe 33, Fitzgerald 87)* 1961
Maritimo: Pecanha; Robson, Alonso, Joao Guilherme, Roberto De Sousa, Ricardo Esteves, Tcho, Kanu (Danilo Dias 46), Djalma Campos (Luciano Amaral 74), Baba, Marquinho (Cherrad 46).
Sporting Fingal: Clarke; Browne, O'Brien, Hawkins (Maher 73), Fitzgerald, Kirby, McFaul, Byrne (Cahill 88), Finn, Williams, Crowe (Zayed 64).

Molde (0) 1 *(Fall 90)*
Jelgava (0) 0 2343
Molde: Lillebakk; Johansson (Thioune 60), Simonsen, Rindaroy, Andreasson (Gjerde 84), Forren, Holm, Berg Hestad, Mostrom (Skjolsvik 79), Hoseth, Fall.
Jelgava: Bogdanovs; Bogdaskins, Gubins, Savcenkovs, Redjko, Lapkovskis V, Lazdins, Lapkovskis I, Bormakovs (Petkevics 87), Malasenoks (Medeckis 90), Kozlovs (Hohlovs 75).

Motherwell (0) 1 *(Forbes 63)*
Breidablik (0) 0 5990
Motherwell: Randolph; Craigan, Reynolds, Hammell, Lasley, Forbes (Saunders 72), Humphrey (Smith 59), Jennings, Hateley, Sutton, Murphy.
Breidablik: Kale; Adalsteinsson, Jonsson, Helgason, Arsaelsson, Kristjansson, Elisabetarson, Steindorsson (Sigurgeirsson 73), Margeirsson, Petursson, Finnbogason.

MyPa (1) 3 *(Ricketts 43, Aijala 56, 65 (pen))*
Sant Julia (0) 0 1167
MyPa: Kuismala; Aho, Oksanen (Alonen 85), Lindberg, Uimaniemi, Hietanen, Aijala, Okkonen, Saxman, Koljonen (Kurittu 65), Ricketts (Felipe Benevides 73).
Sant Julia: Burgos; Wagner, Varela, Miguel Ruiz, Josep (Fernandez 61), Yael Fontan, Xinos (Leonardo Leites 84), Peppe, Gomes, Besora, Gomez (Iguacel 87).

OFK Belgrade (1) 2 *(Zeravica 45, Injac 90)*
Torpedo Zhodino (1) 2 *(Krivobok 14, Brusnikin 89)* 500
OFK Belgrade: Saranov; Mijatovic, Nikolic, Rodic■, Planic, Trivunovic, Simic, Zeravica (Beljic 65), Sasa Markovic, Krstic (Kecojevic 46), Milic (Injac 55).
Torpedo Zhodino: Bushma; Ostroukh, Papush (Solovey 57), Kontsevoy, Karshakevich, Kozlov, Levitski, Martynets, Aleksievich (Brusnikin 71), Kazarin, Krivobok (Karolik 46).

Olimpia (0) 0
Dinamo Bucharest (1) 2 *(Pulhac 41, Ganea 83)* 6300
Olimpia: Pascenco; Orlovschi, Cheltuiala■, Ogada, Valuta, Tcaciuc (Somide 60), Adaramola, Kamara, Paseciniuc (Khorolskiyy 81), Jerome (Repinetchi 68), Ovsianicov.
Dinamo Bucharest: Curca; Pulhac, Moti, Scarlatache, Homei, Margaritescu, Adrian Cristea (Munteanu C 65), N'Doye, Kone (Torje 65), Andrei Cristea (Ganea 82), Niculae■.

Portadown (1) 1 *(Lecky 29)*
Karabakh (0) 2 *(Ismayilov 67, 86)* 765
Portadown: Miskelly; Kelly, O'Hara, Redman, Ramsey, McCafferty, Mouncey, Boyle, Braniff (Haire 80), Lecky, Teggart.
Karabakh: Veliyev; Rashad F Sadygov, Abbasov, Medvedev, Gashimov, Garayev, Rashad A Sadygov, Imamaliyev (Aliyev 46), Mammadov E (Kerimov 76), Ismayilov, Adamia (Nadirov 82).

Rabotnicki (0) 1 *(Wandeir 87)*
Mika (0) 0 1000
Rabotnicki: Bogatinov; Dimovski, Sekulovski, Adem, Fernando■, Gligorov, Muarem (Sinkovic 74), Ze Carlos (Todorovski 64), Tuneski, Wandeir, Fabio (Belica 41).
Mika: Klevinskas; Alex Henrique, Tadevosian, Mkoian, Mkrtchian, Petrosian, Ulisses (Aram Voskanian 26), Pedro Lopez, Ferreira Edney, Edilson (Beglarian 84), Demel (Grigalevicius 75).

Shamrock Rovers (0) 1 *(Bayly 90)*
Bnei Yehuda (1) 1 *(Afek 26)* 4850
Shamrock Rovers: Mannus; Murray, Price (Dennehy W 64), Sives, Stevens, Rice, Turner (Bayly 71), Kavanagh, Chambers, Stewart, Twigg.
Bnei Yehuda: Aiyenugba; Garrido, Azoz, Hadad, Linic, Edri, Baldut, Zairi, Menashe (Abu Zaid 73), Biton (Afek 19), Yavruyan (Rali 57).

Siauliai (0) 0
Wilsa (0) 2 *(Pawel Brozek 78, Piotr Brozek 80)* 2428
Siauliai: Kosov; Kancelskis, Lunskis, Pilypas, Kolic, Janusauskas (Lapeikis 61), Kuklys, Silenas, Kozlovs, Jasaitis (Burksaitis 83), Viktoravicius (Raskov 46).
Wilsa: Jovanic; Cleber, Piotr Brozek, Diaz, Kowalski, Cikos, Sobolewski, Malecki (Zurawski 64), Gargula (Jirsak 71), Pawel Brozek, Boguski.

Stabaek (1) 2 *(Skjelvik 22, Gunnarsson 53)*
Dnepr Mogliev (2) 2 *(Turlin 14, Kozlov 23)* 1134
Stabaek: Austbo; Hoiland, Onstad, Eiriksson, Hedenstad (Stenvoll 67), Hauger, Hoff (Diogo 63), Diskerud, Skjelvik, Gunnarsson, Tommernes (Hulsker 87).
Dnepr Mogliev: Kopantsov; Shuneiko, Karpovich, Gonchar, Kapov, Obrazov, Kozlov (Raspopov 59), Tereshchenko (Cernych 68), Bychenok, Zenkovich, Turlin (Poryvaev 90).

Suduva (0) 0
Rapid Vienna (1) 2 *(Hofmann 12, Trimmel 81)* 1900
Suduva: Valincius; Skroblas, Leimonas, Valaitis, Slavickas, Kozyuberda, Gogberashvili, Grande, Liu Chao (Urbsys 88), Beniusis (Luksys 70), Esau (Grigaitis 46).
Rapid Vienna: Hedl; Katzer, Patocka, Sonnleitner, Hofmann, Kavlak (Drazan 68), Heikkinen, Kayhan, Salihi (Hinum 46), Jelavic, Trimmel (Dober 85).

Tauras (0) 0
Apoel (0) 3 *(Charalambidis 50, Helio Pinto 80, Gustavo Manduca 83)* 500
Tauras: Kilijonas; Vaitkus, Mockus, Jasaitis (Bielskis 53), Gedgaudas, Maciulis, Buitkus, Jose Vide (Auryla 72), Kuznecovs, Daunoravicius (Martisauskas 62), Irkha.
Apoel: Chiotis; Broerse, Paulo Jorge, Grncharov, William, Nuno Morais (Satsias 13), Marcinho (Helio Pinto 72), Charalambidis, Solomou, Solari (Trichkovski 69), Gustavo Manduca.

Utrecht (3) 4 *(Van Wolfswinkel 8, Pashaj 27 (og), Asare 30, Mertens 75)*
SK Tirana (0) 0 9900
Utrecht: Sinouh; Wuytens, Schut (Van der Maarel 77), Corneilsse, Nesu, Lensky, Asare, Mertens (Oar 89), Maguire, Mulenga (Loval Landre 80), Van Wolfswinkel.
SK Tirana: Lika I■; Lila, Sina, Osmani, Pashaj, Karabeci (Nallbani 87), Ahmataj, Hysa (Malindi 69), Lilaj, Plaku, Pejic.

Valletta (0) 1 *(Scerri 77)*
Ruch (1) 1 *(Grzyb 18 (pen))* 1149
Valletta: Hogg; Caruana, Bezzina (Pace 80), Ramon, Borg, Denni, Briffa, Temile, Falzon (Sammut 56), Agius, Zammit (Scerri 66).
Ruch: Pilarz; Nykiel, Jakubowski, Grzyb, Grodzicki, Zajac (Piech 59), Pulkowski, Sadlok, Straka (Malinowski 74), Janoszka, Olszar (Flis 77).

Ventspils (0) 0
Teteks (0) 0 2500
Ventspils: Kolinko; Gabovs (Shpakov 36), Krjauklis, Bespalovs, Postnikov, Visnakovs A, Zjuzins (Kosmacovs 73), Tukura, Solovjovs, Dedov, Visnakovs E (Zigajevs 49).
Teteks: Marko Jovanovski; Jovanovski D, Mishkovski, Naumovski, Ristevski (Radonic 87), Ristov, Zaharievski, Peev (Belchev 90), Iseni, Gligorovski (Miroslav Jovanovski 59), Stojanovski.

Videoton (0) 1 *(Horvath 79)*
Maribor (1) 1 *(Mezga 30)* 3850
Videoton: Bozovic; Andic, Horvath, Liptak, Sandor, Farkas, Polonkai (Lencse 46), Elek, Andre Alves, Vujovic (Djordjic 46), Gosztonyi (Nikolic 83).
Maribor: Pridigar; Rajcevic, Viler, Andelkovic (Dzinic 80), Cvijanovic (Jelic 90), Mejac, Mezga (Ilicic 71), Bacinovic, Mertelj, Marcos Tavares, Volas.

WIT Georgia (0) 0
Banik Ostrava (1) 6 *(Nando 33, 56 (pen), 64 (pen), Pilik 61, Neuwirth 70, Husbauer 78)* 1500
WIT Georgia: Mikaberidze; Adamadze, Lomaia, Bechvaia, Klimiashvili, Maisashvili (Kasradze 82), Vasadze (Chimakadze 67), Guram Gureshidze, Chankvetadze, Lipartia (Janclidze 71), Kvaratskhelia.
Banik Ostrava: Danek; Bolf, Neuwirth, Reznik, Nando, Lukes, Marek (Husbauer 68), Gregus, Varadi, Senkerik (Frejlach 65), Pilik (Smejkal 74).

Zestafoni (1) 3 *(Dvali 24, 65, Dzaria 48)*
Bystrica (0) 0 3200
Zestafoni: Kvaskhvadze; Oniani, Eliava, Khidesheli, Benashvili, Daushvili, Dzaria, Babunashvili (Aptsiauri 30), Grigalashvili (Pipia 79), Gelashvili, Dvali (Aladashvili 79).
Bystrica: Boros; Adamik, Pleva, Poljovka, Pancik, Savie, Hucko (Pich 66), Gajdos (Durica 77), Brasen, Povazanec, Duris.

Zrinjski (4) 4 *(Ivankovic 1, 21 (pen), Susic 33, Zadro 38)*
Tre Penne (1) 1 *(Dzidic 35 (og))* 3150
Zrinjski: Melher; Dzidic, Ivankovic, Sunjic, Rizvanovic, Zizovic, Zadro, Susic (Pehar 88), Stjepanovic, Dragicevic, Selimovic.
Tre Penne: Valentini F; Franchini, Palazzi, Valentini S, Zavoli, Raggini, Cibelli, Chiaruzzi, Lisi (Francini 56), Protti (Rossi 63), Pignieri (Di Giuli 72).

SECOND QUALIFYING ROUND SECOND LEG

Thursday, 22 July 2010

Apoel (1) 3 *(Solari 18, 86 (pen), Trichkovski 80)*
Tauras (0) 1 *(Irkha 48)* 9632
Apoel: Chiotis; Grncharov, William, Kontis, Marcinho (Trichkovski 64), Poursaitidis, Satsias (Michael 75), Solomou, Solari, Alexandrou (Broerse 88), Helio Pinto.
Tauras: Kilijonas; Regelskis, Vaitkus (Mockus 46), Jasaitis (Martisauskas 67), Gedgaudas (Jose Vide 61), Maciulis, Buitkus, Savastas, Kuznecovs■, Daunoravicius, Irkha.

Bangor City (0) 2 *(Morley 84, Jones C 90)*
Honka (1) 1 *(Koskinen 21)* 954
Bangor City: Smith; Morley, Roberts, Brewerton, Hoy, Johnston, Edwards, Davies, Ward, Jebb (Bull 62), Jones C.
Honka: Peltonen; Koskinen, Heilala, Koskimaa, Otaru, Lepola, Paatelainen (Vasara 70), Schuller, Vuorinen, Puustinen, Savage.
At Wrexham.

Banik Ostrava (0) 0
WIT Georgia (0) 0   3405
Banik Ostrava: Baranek; Koukal, Reznik, Frydrych, Nando, Lukes, Wojnar (Husbauer 72), Gregus, Senkerik (Pilik 57), Fantis (Zeher 46), Vrt'o.
WIT Georgia: Mikaberidze; Adamadze, Lomaia, Bechvaia, Klimiashvili, Maisahvili (Guram Gureshidze 80), Janelidze (Zakradze 75), Vasadze, Chankvetadze, Lipartia, Kvaratskhelia (Chimakadze 63).

Bnei Yehuda (0) 0
Shamrock Rovers (0) 1 *(Stewart 70)*   1784
Bnei Yehuda: Aiyenugba; Garrido, Azoz (Baldut 79), Hadad, Linic (Menashe 74), Edri, Rali, Zairi, Afek, Abu Zaid (Levi 90), Yavruyan.
Shamrock Rovers: Mannus; Murray, Price, Sives, Stevens, Rice, Turner (Bradley 84), Chambers (Dennehy W 64), Bayly (Kavanagh 58), Stewart, Twigg.

Borac (0) 1 *(Vukelja 70)*
Lausanne (0) 1 *(Roux 65)*   9000
Borac: Avdukic; Trivunovic, Stancheski, Benovic, Zaric, Sakan (Sreco 73), Muminovic, Jandric (Nikolic 52), Mikic, Raspudic, Vukelja.
Lausanne: Favre; Sonnerat, Meoli, Katz (Buntschu 74), Nelson Borges (Stadelmann 46), Celestini, Marazzi, Abdul Carrupt (Avanzini 64), Steuble, Roux, Silvio.

Breidablik (0) 0
Motherwell (1) 1 *(Murphy 42)*   1700
Breidablik: Kale; Adalsteinsson, Jonsson (Gunnarsson 78), Helgason, Arsaelsson, Kristjansson, Elisabetarson, Steindorsson, Margeirsson (Baldvinsson 72), Petursson (Yeoman 61), Finnbogason.
Motherwell: Randolph; Craigan, Reynolds, Hammell, Saunders, Lasley, Forbes (Humphrey 74), Jennings, Hateley, Sutton (Pollock 83), Murphy (McHugh 87).

Buducnost (0) 1 *(Brnovic 64)*
Baku (2) 2 *(Solic 28, Jaba 42)*   3200
Buducnost: Dragojevic; Mazic, Dikanovic, Adamovic, Dokaj, Jovan Nikolic (Brnovic 46), Vukcevic P, Ajkovic, Kudemor, Beciraj, Vukovic (Boskovic 86).
Baku: Sissokho; Nibombe, Kargbo, Savinov, Boret (Angulo 84), Kajkut, Ramim (Gurbanov 62), Maharramov, Skulic (Sofroni 75), Solic, Jaba.
Baku given two match suspension for fielding an ineligible player; tie awarded to Buducnost.

Bystrica (1) 1 *(Duris 28)*
Zestafoni (0) 0   2880
Bystrica: Boros; Adamik, Poljovka, Pancik, Savic, Hucko, Gajdos (Durica 75), Brasen (Pich 65), Vajda (Pleva 68), Seye, Duris.
Zestafoni: Kvaskhvadze; Oniani, Eliava, Khidesheli, Benashvili (Aladashvili 56), Gorgiashvili (Babunashvili 57), Dzaria, Grigalashvili, Aptsiauri (Pipia 83), Gelashvili, Dvali.

Cibalia (0) 0
Cliftonville (0) 0   5200
Cibalia: Matkovic; Parmakovic, Bozic (Culjak 68), Lucic, Tomic, Radotic, Juric, Mazalovic (Grgic 46), Baraban, Malcic (Prgomet 46), Kresinger.
Cliftonville: Connolly; Scannell R, Donaghy, Holland B, Catney, McMullan, Caldwell (Smyth 85), Holland M (O'Hara 40), Scannell C (Patterson 81), Garrett, Boyce.

Dacia (0) 0
Kalmar (1) 2 *(Israelsson 12, Sobralense 88)*   6000
Dacia: Matiughin; Gamezardashvili, Lomidze, Caraulan, Grosev (Sischin 71), Bursuc (Gorceac 76), Cojocari, Korgalidze, Orbu, Molla, Dragovozov (Glega 63).
Kalmar: Wasta; Carlsson, Larsson, Johansson (Bertilsson 46), Nouri, Rydstrom, Sobralense, Eriksson, Israelsson (Alander 89), Daniel Mendes (Augustsson 46), Ricardo Santos.

Dinamo Bucharest (3) 5 *(Andrei Cristea 3, Adrian Cristea 32, N'Doye 45, Munteanu C 59, Torje 62 (pen))*
Olimpia (0) 1 *(Adaramola 90)*   4367
Dinamo Bucharest: Curca; Munteanu C, Pulhac, Moti, Scarlatache (Garat 46), Homei, Margaritescu, Adrian Cristea (Ganea 60), Torje, N'Doye (Paun 68), Andrei Cristea.
Olimpia: Paius; Orlovschi, Ogada, Verbetchi, Valuta (Gusacov 60), Tcaciuc, Adaramola, Kamara, Paseciniuc (Khorolskyy 46), Jerome (Somide 70), Ovsianicov.

Dinamo Tbilisi (0) 2 *(Vatsadze 68, Pirtskhalava 82)*
Gefle (0) 1 *(Orlov 90)*   2500
Dinamo Tbilisi: Loria; Tomashvili, Kakubava, Khmaladze, Ednilson, Kakhelishvili, Koshkadze, Tektumanidze (Gvelesiani 85), Vatsadze (Metreveli 82), Djousse, Robertinho (Pirtskhalava 67).
Gefle: Hugosson; Bernhardsson, Portin, Senatore, Lantto, Hansson, Ohagen (Larsson 73), Chibsah, Dahlberg (Nystrom 84), Westlin (Gram 55), Orlov.

Dnepr Mogilev (0) 1 *(Yurchanka 85)*
Stabaek (1) 1 *(Gunnarsson 37)*   4500
Dnepr Mogilev: Kopantsov; Shuneiko, Karpovich, Kapov, Obrazov, Zhevnerov, Kozlov (Zenkovich 46), Tereshchenko, Bychenok (Cernych 73), Yurchanka, Turlin (Raspopov 89).
Stabaek: Knudsen; Hoiland, Stenvoll (Farnerud 59), Eiriksson, Hedenstad, Hauger, Diskerud (Palmason 79), Skjelvik, Diogo, Gunnarsson, Tommernes (Hulsker 87).

Dundalk (0) 0
Levski (2) 2 *(Dembele 4, 33)*   1000
Dundalk: Cherrie; Hatswell, Kelly, Breen G, McGuigan, Maher, Lennon (Mulvenna 59), Miller, McDonnell, Kudozovic, Gaynor.
Levski: Petkov; Mulder, Minev, Miliev, Ivanov, Gadzhev (Ognyanov 61), Baltanov, Joaozinho (Kirov 71), Tasevski, Dembele (Isa 56), Mladenov.

Gyor (0) 2 *(Aleksidze 47, Nicorec 52)*
Atyrau (0) 0   3300
Gyor: Stevanovic; Djordjevic, Babic, Szabo, Stanisic, Pilibaitis, Kink, Dinjar (Copa 59), Koltai (Sharashenidze 67), Aleksidze (Bouguerra 77), Nicorec.
Atyrau: Shabanov; Alyev, Chureev, Zhumabaev, Vorotnikov, Croitoru, Peikrishvili (Larin 70), Kostrub, Shakin (Khizhnichenko 62), Sakhalbaev (Mamonov 75), Frunza.

Iskra-Stal (0) 0
Elfsborg (0) 1 *(Ishizaki 60)*   2905
Iskra-Stal: Gaiducevici; Gafina, Feshchenko, Novicov, Casian, Rudac (Tofan 52), Porfireanu, Burcovschi, Mihaliov (Kilikevich 62), Taranu (Gorodetchi 78), Popovici.
Elfsborg: Covic; Floren, Andersson M, Jonsson, Klarstrom, Svensson, Mobaeck, Ishizaki (Hult 82), Larsson (Nordmark 78), Keene, Jawo.

Jelgava (2) 2 *(Bormakovs 30, Bogdaskins 45)*
Molde (1) 1 *(Fall 14)*   2000
Jelgava: Bogdanovs; Bogdaskins, Gubins, Savcenkovs, Kazura (Lapkovskis V 46), Redjko, Lazdins, Lapkovskis I (Hohlovs 74), Bormakovs (Petkevics 70), Malasenoks, Kozlovs.
Molde: Lillebakk; Johansson, Simonen, Rindaroy, Gjerde (Andreasson 66), Forren, Holm (Thioune 55), Berg Hestad, Mostrom (Skjolsvik 77), Hoseth, Fall.

Karabakh (0) 1 *(Ismayilov 83)*
Portadown (0) 1 *(Braniff 71)*   20,000
Karabakh: Veliyev; Rashad F Sadygov, Abbasov, Teli, Medvedev, Agolli, Rashad A Sadygov, Mammadov E (Nadirov 63), Ismayilov, Adamia, Aliyev (Kerimov 76).
Portadown: Miskelly; O'Hara, Redman, Ramsey, McCafferty, Mackle (Coleman 90), Mouncey, Boyle, Clarke (McCullough 85), Braniff, Teggart (Haire 70).

Karpaty (2) 3 *(Zenjov 2, Fedetskiy 25, Baranets B 69)*
KR Reykjavik (0) 2 *(Finnbogason 61, 65)*   13,200
Karpaty: Rudenko; Oshchipko (Martynyuk 67), Milosevic, Tarasenko, Kopolovets, Baranets B, Fedetskiy, Genison, Danilo Avelar, Baranets G (Tkachuk 81), Zenjov (Gabovda 46).
KR Reykjavik: Molskred; Fridgeirsson, Sigurdarson, Rutgers, Gudjonsson, Sigurdsson B, Hauksson, Kristjansson (Finnbogason 23), Jordao Diogo, Jonsson G(Arnarsson 60), Baldvinsson (Takefusa 69).

Maribor (1) 2 *(Volas 39, 80)*
Videoton (0) 0   6700
Maribor: Pridigar; Rajcevic, Viler, Andelkovic, Mejac, Mezga (Pavlicic 89), Bacinovic, Mertelj, Ilicic (Cvijanovic 78), Marcos Tavares, Volas (Jelic 90).
Videoton: Bozovic; Horvath, Lazar, Liptak, Sandor, Farkas, Polonkai (Djordic 27), Elek, Andre Alves, Lencse (Nikolic 62), Gosztonyi.

Mika (0) 0
Rabotnicki (0) 0   5000
Mika: Klevinskas; Alex Henrique, Tadevosian, Mkoian, Mkrtchian, Petrosian (Hakobian 63), Pedro Lopez, Edilson, Beglarian (Grigalevicius 66), Demel, Aram Voskanian (Ferreira Edney 75).
Rabotnicki: Bogatinov; Dimovski, Sekulovski, Adem, Belica, Gligorov, Todorovski, Muarem (Marcio 78), Ze Carlos (Fabio 64), Tuneski, Wandeir (Carlos Roberto 73).

Mogren (0) 2 *(Gluscevic 58 (pen), 80)*
Maccabi Tel Aviv (1) 1 *(Medunjanin 7)*   700
Mogren: Janjusevic; Janicic, Pejovic, Simovic, Kapisoda (Bozovic B 46), Nuhi, Jovanovic, Culafic, Cetkovic (Grbic 46), Mirkovic (Bozovic D 70), Gluscevic.
Maccabi Tel Aviv: Strauber; Nivaldo, Ziv, Strul, Saban, Baning, Medunjanin, Yeini (Avidor 61), Colautti (Kahlon 77), Itzhaki, Buzaglo (Sidibe 61).

Olympiakos (0) 6 *(Dudu Cearense 46, 78, Derbyshire 53, Maresca 75, 90, Fetfatzidis 89)*
Besa (0) 1 *(Lazarevski 48)*   25,000
Olympiakos: Urko, Mellberg, Bravo, Holebas, Galitsios, Maresca, Dudu Cearense, Zairi (Derbyshire 46), Oscar Gonzalez (Mitroglou 46), Mirallas, Diogo (Fetfatzidis 70).
Besa: Edvan Bakaj; Lazarevski, Ferizovic, Aliju, Jakupi (Hoxha 76), Poci, Osmani M, Dhembi (Shtini 72), Semir Hadzibulic, Cikalleshi (Tragaj 85), Dos Santos.

Randers (1) 1 *(Cramer 42)*
Gorica (0) 1 *(Zigon 79)*   2171
Randers: Ousted; Pedersen, Egholm, Jensen, Fenger, Cramer, Lorentzen, Karlsen (Sane 70), Olsen (Sorensen 57), Movsisyan (Brock-Madsen 66), Berg.
Gorica: Simcic; Balazic, Zarifovic, Gregoric (Sirok 57), Mevlja M■, Komel, Krsic (Zigon 78), Demirovic, Rakuscek, Stojanovic (Arcon 63), Velikonja.

Rapid Vienna (1) 4 *(Jelavic 20, 90, Gartler 86, 89)*
Suduva (0) 2 *(Grigaitis 70, Beniusis 85)*   11,800
Rapid Vienna: Hedl; Eder, Katzer, Patocka, Kavlak (Saurer 9), Heikkinen, Drazan (Gartler 82), Kayhan, Pehlivan (Hinum 60), Jelavic, Trimmel.
Suduva: Valincius; Skroblas■, Radzius, Leimonas, Valaitis, Slavickas (Liu Chao 65), Kozyuberda, Urbsys (Luksys 55), Gogberashvili, Grande, Grigaitis (Beniusis 73).

Ruch (0) 0
Valletta (0) 0   6500
Ruch: Perdijic; Nykiel, Jakubowski, Grzyb, Grodzicki, Pulkowski, Sadlok, Straka, Janoszka (Bronowicki 78), Sobiech (Malinowski 89), Olszar (Piech 60).

Valletta: Hogg; Caruana, Ramon (Bezzina 71), Borg, Denni, Sammut (Falzon 64), Briffa, Temile (Zammit 80), Scerri, Agius, Pace.

Sibenik (0) 0
Anorthosis (2) 3 *(Laban 16, Christovao 25, Okkas 96)*   2850
Sibenik: Blazevic; Ceric, Medvid, Bulat (Gusic 54), Elez, Alispahic, Bloudek (Males 99), Bacelic-Grgic, Jakolis, Bozic, Fustar (Bakovic 46).
Anorthosis: Arguello; Leiwakabessy, Janicio, Georgiou, Katsavakis, Laban, Garcia (Constantinou A 90), Marangos (Vidovic 102), Okkas, Cafu, Christovao (Carlos Coto 86).
aet.

Sillamae (0) 0
Dynamo Minsk (3) 5 *(Dragun 2, Sazankov 17, Chukhley 19, 65, Rekish 46)*   264
Sillamae: Starodubtsev; Gorbunov, Kulik, Naumov, Jadal (Dudarev 24), Dubokin, Zubavicius (Vihrov 81), Stankevicius, Aleksejev, Kabayev (Nikulin 58), Kolyaev.
Dynamo Minsk: Gorbunov; Veretilo, Montaroup, Kondratyev, Marakhovskiy (Kruk 78), Strakhanovich, Dragun (Kugan 72), Chukhley, Rekish, Buloychik, Sazankov (Leonardo 46).

Siroki (0) 0
FK Austria (0) 1 *(Junuzovic 80)*   4000
Siroki: Bandovic; Topic, Renato, Barisic, Kozul (Weitzer 83), Silic, Ljubic (Misic 33) (Pinjuh A 55), Diogo, Ivankovic, Varea, Roskam.
FK Austria: Lindner; Ortlechner, Suttner (Leovac 75), Dragovic, Klein, Hlinka (Baumgartlinger■ 68), Junuzovic, Liendl, Stankovic (Schumacher 61), Jun, Linz.

SK Tirana (1) 1 *(Lila 10)*
Utrecht (1) 1 *(Van Wolfswinkel 3)*   3000
SK Tirana: Nallbani; Lila, Sina, Osmani, Pashaj (Metani 69), Karabeci, Ahmataj, Hysa (Malindi 63), Lilaj (Hajdari 83), Plaku, Pejic.
Utrecht: Sinouh; Schut, Cornelisse, Nesu, Vostermans, Lensky (Nijholt 79), Asare, Mertens (Sarota 71), Maguire, Mulenga (Loval Landre 60), Van Wolfswinkel.

Spartak Subotica (1) 2 *(Ubiparip 25, Adamovic 88)*
Differdange (0) 0   1500
Spartak Subotica: Labus; Sarac, Bratic, Stevanovic, Puskaric (Adamovic 55), Torbica, Antonic, Veselinov (Cheng Mouyi 85), Milankovic, Simovic, Ubiparip (Noskovic 70).
Differdange: Weber; Bukvic, Kintziger, Andre Filipe, Janisch (Alunni 77), Kettenmeyer (Diop 46), Lebresne, Bettmer, Siebenaler, Albanese (Franzoni 54), Piskor.

Sporting Fingal (0) 2 *(Zayed 81, 90)*
Maritimo (1) 3 *(Alonso 20 (pen), Marquinho 67, Kanu 87)*   2150
Sporting Fingal: Clarke; Browne, O'Brien, Maher, Fitzgerald, Kirby, McFaul (Zayed 64), Byrne, Finn, Williams, Crowe.
Maritimo: Pecanha; Robson, Alonso, Joao Guilherme, Roberto De Sousa, Ricardo Esteves, Tcho (Kanu 81), Cherrad (Fidelis 90), Baba, Marquinho (Luciano Amaral 72), Danilo Dias.

Teteks (2) 3 *(Postnikov 15 (og), Ristevski 34, Gligorovski 54)*
Ventspils (0) 1 *(Bespalovs 81)*   2000
Teteks: Marko Jovanovski; Jovanovski D, Mishkovski (Belchev 49), Naumovski, Ristevski, Ristov, Zaharievski, Peev (Miroslav Jovanovski71), Iseni (Radonic 82), Gligorovski, Stojanovski.
Ventspils: Kolinko; Bespalovs, Kryuchkov, Postnikov, Kosmacovs, Visnakovs A (Visnakovs E 56), Chirkin■, Solovjovs, Rugins (Zigajevs 53), Dedov (Mishchenko 71), Shumilin.

Torpedo Zhodino (0) 0
OFK Belgrade (0) 1 *(Kecojevic 67)*   3100
Torpedo Zhodino: Bushma; Ostroukh, Papush, Kontsevoy, Karshakevich, Kozlov (Gintov 62), Levitski, Martynets, Aleksievich, Kazarin (Brusnikin 58), Krivobok (Karolik 72).
OFK Belgrade: Saranov; Mijatovic, Nikolic, Planic (Petkovic 46), Kecojevic, Trivunovic, Simic, Zeravica, Injac (Aleksic 35), Milic, Milunovic (Krstic 60).

TPS Turku (1) 1 *(Johansson 30 (pen))*
CS Brugge (0) 2 *(Reynaldo 51, Van Eenoo 86)*   4020
TPS Turku: Moisander; Rahmonen, Heinikangas, Nyberg (Ferati 89), Milsom, Manninen (Roope Riski 80), Riku Riski, Cleaver, Kolehmainen, Johansson, Aaritalo (Jovanovic 66).
CS Brugge: Verbist; Viane (Portier 46), Evens, Cornelis, Kehlar, Vidarsson, Boi (D'Haene 78), Van Eenoo, Reynaldo (Nyoni 86), Renato Neto, Foley.

Tre Penne (1) 2 *(Palazzi 28, 81)*
Zrinjski (4) 9 *(Selimovic 3, 27, Susic 7, Zizovic 10, 55 (pen), Zadro 53, 65, Pehar 69, Sunjic 87)*   571
Tre Penne: Valentini F; Franchini, Palazzi, Zavoli, Raggini, Cibelli, Simoncini (Valentini S 56), Chiaruzzi (Rossi 39), Mikhaylovskiy, Protti, Pignieri (Valli 80).
Zrinjski: Melher; Ivankovic (Bartulica 46), Sunjic, Anicic J, Rizvanovic, Zizovic, Zadro, Susic, Stjepanovic (Milicevic 42), Dragicevic (Pehar 61), Selimovic.

Vaduz (0) 0
Brondby (0) 0   1984
Vaduz: Faivre; Schwegler, Denicola (Rechsteiner 43), Bader■, Oehri (Christen 58), Bellon, Sara, Burgmeier, Sturm, Leocadio, Merenda (Ciccone 78).
Brondby: Andersen; Bischoff, Rasmussen, Wass, Kristiansen (Bernburg 62), Van der Schaaf, Krohn-Dehli (Larsen 57), Jensen, Nilsson, Farnerud, Jallow (Madsen 72).

Vikingur (0) 0
Besiktas (4) 4 *(Dag 4, Nihat 10, Bobo 32, 44)*   651
Vikingur: Tamas; Niclasen, Jacobsen H, Hansen B, Stankovic, Sam Jacobsen, Djurhuus (Bartalsstovu 53), Jacobsen E, Vatnhamar (Hansen H 87), Justinussen, Klettskard (Sverri Jacobsen 76).
Besiktas: Hakan; Erhan, Zapotocny, Sivok (Ugur 46), Ismail, Ernst (Ferrari 46), Quaresma, Delgado, Dag (Onur 57), Nihat, Bobo.

Wisla (1) 5 *(Piotr Brozek 23, Zurawski 48, Diaz 62, Pawel Brozek 66, Boguski 90)*
Siauliai (0) 0   5500
Wisla: Jovanic; Cleber, Piotr Brozek (Kirm 77), Diaz, Kowalski, Cikos, Sobolewski, Gargula (Jirsak 63), Pawel Brozek (Malecki 71), Zurawski, Boguski.
Siauliai: Kosov; Kancelskis■, Lunskis, Pilypas, Kolic, Kuklys, Silenas, Kozlovs (Janusauskas 46), Jasaitis, Lapeikis, Raskov (Viktoravicius 67).

Friday, 23 July 2010
Sant Julia (0) 0
MyPa (2) 5 *(Votinov 7, 14, 64, Kurittu 49, Okkonen 61)*   1050
Sant Julia: Goldswill; Varela (Goncalves 46), Xavier Moreno, Miguel Ruiz, Leonardo Leites (Nastri 62), Yael Fontan, Xinos, Peppe, Fernandez (Gomes 56), Besora, Gomez.
MyPa: Johansson; Aho, Timoska (Rautianen 69), Oksanen, Uimaniemi, Hietanen, Aijala, Okkonen (Lindberg 65), Saxman, Kurittu (Koljonen 57), Votinov.
Original match on 22 July suspended at 0-1 due to thunderstorms.

THIRD QUALIFYING ROUND FIRST LEG
Tuesday, 27 July 2010
CSKA Sofia (1) 3 *(Vidanov 9, Marquinhos 72, Trifonov 74)*
Cliftonville (0) 0   2500
CSKA Sofia: Karadzhov; Minev, Trifonov, Vidanov, Aquaro, Stoyanov K, Marquinhos, Yanchev, Galchev (Yanev 86), Tonev (Kostadinov 70), Rui Miguel (Iliev 59).
Cliftonville: Connolly; Hutton, Scannell R, Donaghy, Holland B, Catney, McMullan, Caldwell, Scanell C (O'Connor 78), Garrett■, Boyce.

Thursday, 29 July 2010
Aalesund (0) 1 *(Mathisen 90 (pen))*
Motherwell (0) 1 *(Murphy 48)*   8450
Aalesund: Lindegaard; Arnefjord, Jaager, Jalasto, Arneng, Larsen (Fredriksen 56), Herrera (Mathisen 57), Phillips, Aaroy, Parr, Olsen (Carlsen 70).
Motherwell: Randolph; Craigan, Reynolds, Hammell, Saunders, Lasley, Forbes (Humphrey 46), Jennings, Hateley, Sutton (McHugh 46), Murphy.

Apoel (0) 1 *(Solari 55)*
Jablonec (0) 0   13,978
Apoel: Chiotis; Broerse (Trichkovski 77), Paulo Jorge, Grncharov, William, Marcinho, Charalambidis (Satsias 77), Solomou, Solari (Alexandrou 90), Gustavo Manduca, Helio Pinto.
Jablonec: Spit; Drsek (Huber 47), Pavlik, Krajcik, Jablonsky, Jarolim, Loucka, Elias, Kovarik (Pitak 82), Lafata, Vosahlik (Haurdic 65).

AZ (0) 2 *(Klavan 52, Gudmundsson 55)*
IFK Gotheburg (0) 0   11,563
AZ: Didulica; Jaliens, Klavan, Marcellis (Swerts 65), Moisander, Viergever (Ortiz 71), Martens, Wernbloom, Falkenburg, Gudmundsson, Benschop (Van der Velden 46).
IFK Gotheburg: Sandberg; Johansson A, Jonsson, Sigurdsson, Lund, Svensson, Olsson (Bjarnason 60), Johansson J, Selakovic (Soder 78), Hysen, Stiller (Ericsson 84).

Beroe (0) 0 *(Zlatinov 85)*
Rapid Vienna (1) 1 *(Hofmann 45 (pen))*   5000
Beroe: Ilchev; Penev, Iliev, Kovachev, Bachev, Kostadinov (Zlatinov 70), Stankov (Hristov 57), Dimitrov (Mladenov 78), Zhekov, Velev, Yordanov.
Rapid Vienna: Hedl; Dober, Katzer, Patocka, Sonnleitner, Saurer (Trimmel 58), Hofmann, Heikkinen, Hinum (Kulovits 90), Jelavic, Gartler (Salihi 65).

Buducnost (0) 1 *(Beciraj 90)*
Brondby (0) 2 *(Adamovic 73 (og), Jensen 87)*   4345
Buducnost: Dragojevic; Mazic, Dikanovic, Adamovic, Vukcevic P, Ajkovic, Brnovic, Kudemor (Tiodorovic 81), Beciraj, Vukovic, Boskovic (Golubovic 68).
Brondby: Andersen; Bischoff, Rasmussen, Wass, Kristiansen (Bernburg 60), Van der Schaaf, Krohn-Dehli (Madsen 85), Jensen, Nilsson, Larsen, Jallow (Farnerud 60).

CS Brugge (0) 1 *(Foley 68)*
Anorthosis (0) 0   4672
CS Brugge: Verbist; Portier, Evens, Cornelis, Kelhar, D'Haene (Reynaldo 61), Boi (Vidarsson 85), Sererennikov, Van Eenoo (Nyoni 74), Renato Neto, Foley.
Anorthosis: Arguello; Leiwakabessy, Janicio, Georgiou, Katsavakis, Skopelitis, Laban (Miguel Pedro 88), Marangos (Carlos Coto 71), Okkas, Cafu, Christovao (Papathanasiou 79).

Dinamo Bucharest (2) 3 *(Andrei Cristea 6 (pen), Garat 40, Kone 70)*
Hajduk Split (0) 1 *(Tomasov 64)*   12,000
Dinamo Bucharest: Curca; Garat, Pulhac, Scarlatache, Homei, Adrian Cristea, Torje (Munteanu C 54), N'Doye, Kone, Ganea, Andrei Cristea (Paun 77).
Hajduk Split: Subasic; Vejic, Buljat, Maloca, Strinic, Rezic, Anas Sharbini, Andric, Ljubicic (Brkljaca 44), Ibricic, Oremus (Tomasov 46).

Dnepr Mogliev (0) 1 *(Zenkovich 63)*
Banik Ostrava (0) 0   6000
Dnepr Mogliev: Kopantsov; Karpovich, Gonchar, Kapov, Obrazov, Zhevnerov, Tereshchenko (Cermych 78), Bychenok (Raspopov 89), Yurchanka, Zenkovich, Turlin (Kozlov 71).
Banik Ostrava: Danek; Bolf, Neuwirth, Reznik, Nando, Lukes, Frejlach (Husbauer 75), Marek, Zeher (Smejkal 69), Varadi, Pilik (Senkerik 46).

Elfsborg (1) 5 *(Ishizaki 29, Svensson 50, Avdic 57, Nordmark 66, Keene 77)*
Teteks (0) 0   2470
Elfsborg: Covic; Floren, Andersson M, Jonsson, Klarstrom, Svensson, Mabaeck, Ishizaki (Nordmark 65), Ericsson (Keene 62), Larsson, Avdic (Hult 81).
Teteks: Marko Jovanovski; Jovanovski D, Belchev, Mishkovski, Naumovski, Ristevski, Peev, Miroslav Jovanovski (Aliji 65), Urosevic (Simovski 49), Iseni (Ristovski 79), Stojanovski.

Galatasaray (1) 2 *(Arda 26, 76)*
OFK Belgrade (0) 2 *(Krstic 80, Injac 86)*   20,000
Galatasaray: Aykut; Neill, Servet, Sabri, Arda, Ayhan, Serdar (Pino 59), Mustafa, Hakan Balta, Ozbek (Cana 83), Mehmet (Kewell 68).
OFK Belgrade: Saranov; Mijatovic (Filipovic 46), Nikolic, Rodic, Kecojevic, Petkovic, Trivunovic, Simic, Zeravica (Krstic 67), Sasa Markovic, Milic (Injac 78).

Gyor (0) 0
Montpellier (1) 1 *(Giroud 32)*   7000
Gyor: Stevanovic; Djordjevic, Babic, Szabo, Stanisic, Pilibaitis, Dinjar, Koltai (Sharashenidze 66), Aleksidze (Bouguerra 58), Nicolas, Nicorec (Copa 52).
Montpellier: Jourdren; Jeunechamp, Spahic, Yangumbiwa, El Kaoutari, Pitau, Estrada (Saihi 90), Belhanda (Marveaux 71), Camara, Hasan Kabze (Ait Fana 64), Giroud.

Inter Turku (0) 1 *(Grot 53)*
Genk (2) 5 *(De Bruyne 17, Ogunjimi 44, Barda 61, Vossen 77, 85)*   3247
Inter Turku: Reponen; Sanevuori, Aho, Nikkari, Lehtonen, Nyman, Makitalo (Furuholm 74), Kauko, Nwanganga (Egwin 84), Antunez, Grot (Paajanen 80).
Genk: Courtois; Matoukou, Joao Carlos, Ngcongca, Durwael, Tozser, Hubert, De Bruyne (Camus 79), Buffel (Ndabashinze 83), Barda (Vossen 69), Ogunjimi.

Jagiellonia (1) 1 *(Grzyb 24)*
Aris Salonika (2) 2 *(Calvo 4 (pen), 7)*   5100
Jagiellonia: Sandomierski; Skerla, Norambuena, Lewczuk (Hermes 23), Thiago Rangel, Lato (Burkhardt 60), Grosicki, Grzyb, Kascelan, Kupisz, Frankowski (Makuszewski 82).
Aris Salonika: Sifakis; Michel, Neto, Ronaldo, Lazaridis, Nafti (Prittas 79), Toja, Calvo (Cesnauskis 64), Koke (Kaznaferis 70), Javito, Cesarec.

Kalmar (0) 1 *(Dauda 84)*
Levski (1) 1 *(Joaozinho 28)*   2489
Kalmar: Wasta; Carlsson, Larsson, Johansson, Rydstrom, Augustsson, Eriksson, Israelsson (Marcel Sacramento 77), Daniel Mendes (Bertilsson 78), Ricardo Santos, Douglas (Dauda 77).
Levski: Mitrev; Mulder, Minev, Miliev, Ivanov, Gadzhev (Baltanov 86), Joaozinho, Tasevski (Telkiyski 78), Yovovo, Dembele, Mladenov (Aleksandrov 69).

Karpaty (1) 1 *(Khudobyak 6)*
Zestafoni (0) 0   12,100
Karpaty: Tlumak; Tubic, Oshchipko, Milosevic, Goodwin (Baranets G 77), Khudobyak, Tkachuk, Kozhanov (Baranets B 85), Fedetskiy, Batista, Zenjov (Guruli 53).
Zestafoni: Kvaskhvadze; Oniani, Eliava, Khidesheli, Aladashvili, Daushvili, Dzaria (Pipia 80), Babunashvili (Aptsiauri 58), Grigalashvili, Gelashvili (Mamaladze 90), Dvali.

Maccabi Haifa (1) 1 *(Dvalishvili 30)*
Dynamo Minsk (0) 0   9000
Maccabi Haifa: Edri; Masilela, Osman, Maimon, Gustavo Boccoli, Refaelov (Hemed 70), Culma, Canuto, Dvalishvili, Katan (Adrien Silva 89), Ghadir (Golasa 55).
Dynamo Minsk: Gorbunov; Veretilo, Montaroup, Kondratyev, Putsila, Marakhovskiy, Strakhanovich, Dragun, Chukhley (Leonardo 80), Rekish (Buloychik 74), Sazankov (Shkabara 58).

Maribor (1) 3 *(Ilicic 31, 52, Marcos Tavares 60)*
Hibernian (0) 0   9200
Maribor: Pridigar; Rajcevic, Viler, Andelkovic, Mejac, Mezga (Cvijanovic 71), Bacinovic, Mertelj, Ilicic (Pavlicic 79), Marcos Tavares, Volas (Plut 90).
Hibernian: Stack; Murray, Hogg, Hart, Hanlon, McBride (Stokes 68), Rankin, De Graaf, Miller, Wotherspoon (Galbraith 77), Nish (Riordan 68).

Maritimo (2) 8 *(Tcho 33, 79, Danilo Dias 38, 75, Baba 51, 78, Kanu 80, Fidelis 89)*
Bangor City (0) 2 *(Ward 73, Jebb 90)*   2000
Maritimo: Marcelo Boeck; Robson, Alonso, Joao Guilherme, Roberto De Sousa, Ricardo Esteves, Tcho (Fidelis 83), Cherrad (Rafael Miranda 70), Baba, Marquinho (Kanu 64), Danilo Dias.
Bangor City: Smith; Morley, Roberts, Brewerton[*], Hoy, Johnston, Williams (Jebb 66), Bull, Edwards, Davies (Ward 46), Jones C (Hurdman 81).

Molde (0) 2 *(Mostrom 65, Hoseth 76)*
Stuttgart (1) 3 *(Rudy 27, Kuzamnovic 74, Harnik 82)* 3270
Molde: Lillebakk; Simonsen, Rindaroy, Andreasson, Forren, Holm, Berg Hestad (Skjolsvik 79), Mostrom (Runstrom 87), Hoseth, Thioune (Johansson 66), Fall.
Stuttgart: Ulreich; Molinaro, Niedermeier, Trasch (Funk 79), Celozzi, Gentner, Gebhart, Kuzmanovic, Rudy (Didavi 72), Marica, Pogrebnyak (Harnik 79).

MyPa (0) 1 *(Ricketts 50)*
Timisoara (1) 2 *(Tames 34, Axente 74)*   2500
MyPa: Kuismala; Timoska, Oksanen (Felipe Benevides 87), Lindberg, Uimaniemi, Hietanen, Aijala, Okkonen, Saxman, Votinov (Kurittu 82), Ricketts (Koljonen 60).
Timisoara: Pantilimon; Scutaru, Luchin, Cisovsky, Mera, Chiacu (Contra 46), Alexa, Goga, Tames (Bourceanu 84), Curtean (Axente 46), Magera.

Nordsjaelland (0) 0
Sporting Lisbon (1) 1 *(Vukcevic 24)*   5000
Nordsjaelland: Hansen; Bengtsson, Parkhurst, Kildentoft, Jensen D, Stokholm, Laudrup (Granskov 84), Adu, Matti Nielsen (Bernier 66), Fetai (Mikkelsen 72), Bille Nielsen.
Sporting Lisbon: Rui Patricio; Polga, Joao Pereira, Daniel Carrico, Evaldo, Maniche, Pedro Mendes (Miguel Veloso 46), Vukcevic (Valdes 71), Helder Postiga, Yannick Djalo (Liedson 81), Saleiro.

Odense (4) 5 *(Gislason 16, Absalonsen 23, Utaka 31, 60, Andreasen 37)*
Zrinjski (1) 3 *(Zadro 15, 71, Zizovic 65 (pen))*   4302
Odense: Carroll; Haland (Helveg 46), Ruud, Moller Christensen, Sorensen, Gislason (Hansen H 46), Andreasen, Traore (Caca 71), Absalonsen, Toft, Utaka.
Zrinjski: Melher; Sunjic, Anicic M, Anicic J, Rizvanovic (Pehar 63), Zizovic, Zadro, Susic (Puljic 63), Stjepanovic, Dragicevic, Selimovic.

Olympiakos (0) 2 *(Zairi 67, Rommedahl 73)*
Maccabi Tel Aviv (1) 1 *(Medunjanin 18)*
Olympiakos: Nikopolidis; Mellberg, Modesto, Holebas, Galitsios, Maresca, Dudu Cearense, Mirallas (Zairi 52), Derbyshire (Mitroglou 58), Rommedahl (Ibagaza 82), Diogo.
Maccabi Tel Aviv: Strauber; Nivaldo, Ziv, Strul, Gafni, Saban, Baning[*], Medunjanin (Buzaglo 82), Sidibe, Colautti (Yeini 62), Itzhaki (Avidor 72).
Behind closed doors.

Rabotnicki (0) 0
Liverpool (1) 2 *(N'Gog 17, 59)*   23,000
Rabotnicki: Bogatinov; Dimovski, Sekulovski (Adem 44), Fernando, Belica, Gligorov, Todorovski, Ze Carlos (Mojsov 57), Tuneski (Petkovski 78), Wandeir, Fabio.
Liverpool: Cavalieri; Kyrgiakos, Agger (Darby 72), Skrtel, Kelly, Aquilani (Dalla Valle 83), Lucas, Spearing, N'Gog, Jovanovic, Amoo (Eccleston 84).

Randers (1) 2 *(Movsisyan 7, 81)*
Lausanne (1) 3 *(Steuble 41, Silvio 62 (pen), 84)*   2751
Randers: Ousted; Fischer, Egholm (Ahmed 46), Jensen, Fenger, Cramer (Olsen 75), Lorentzen (Sane 90), Karlsen, Beckmann, Movsisyan, Berg.
Lausanne: Favre; Sonnerat, Meoli (Buntschu 46), Katz, Nelson Borges, Celestini, Marazzi, Steuble, Avanzini (Stadelmann 87), Roux (Rodrigo 64), Silvio.

Red Star Belgrade (0) 1 *(Trifunovic 63)*
Slovan Bratislava (1) 2 *(Ivana 43, Salata 68)*   40,826
Red Star Belgrade: Stamenkovic; Tosic, Dordevic, Ninkov, Vilotic, Bogdanovic (Vesovic 78), Cadu, Milovanovic, Koroman (Jeremic 82), Jevtic (Trifunovic 62), Perovic.
Slovan Bratislava: Putnocky; Had, Dosoudil, Salata, Janosik, Bagayoko (Kolcak 90), Guede, Bozic, Grendel (Kiss 82), Ivana, Sylvestr (Kuzma 75).

Ruch (1) 1 *(Pulkowski 4)*
FK Austria (2) 3 *(Linz 7, Hlinka 43, Jun 73)*   7000
Ruch: Pilarz; Nykiel, Jakubowski, Grzyb, Grodzicki, Malinowski (Stawarczyk 79), Pulkowski, Sadlok, Janoszka (Zajac 46), Sobiech, Olszar (Flis 69).
FK Austria: Lindner; Ortlechner, Suttner, Dragovic, Klein, Hlinka, Vorisek, Junuzovic, Liendl (Leovac 80), Jun (Salomon 86), Linz (Schumacher 76).

Shamrock Rovers (0) 0
Juventus (1) 2 *(Amauri 3, 75)*   5800
Shamrock Rovers: Mannus; Murray, Price, Sives, Stevens, Rice (Dennehy W 66), Turner, Chambers (Kavanagh 78), Bayly (Bradley 90), Stewart, Twigg.
Juventus: Storari; Bonucci, Motta, Chiellini, De Ceglie, Diego (Del Piero 82), Sissoko, Pepe, Marchisio (Ekdal 89), Amauri, Lanzafame (Martinez 52).

Sibir (0) 1 *(Medvedev 74)*
Apollon (0) 0   10,277
Sibir: Kowalewski; Filipenko, Molosh, Vychodil, Valentic, Makarenko (Belyaev 46), Cizek (Aravin 64), Astafyev, Nagibin, Antipenko (Shevchenko 41), Medvedev.
Apollon: Chvalovsky; Morris, Martorell, Raul, Kosowski (Adorno 68), Quinteros, Kolar, Bangura, Oseni, Mrdakovic (Jose Semedo 55), Antonio Nunez (Ogbuke 79)

Spartak Subotica (1) 2 *(Torbica 16 (pen), 90 (pen))*
Dnepr (1) 1 *(Kravchenko 23)*   1500
Spartak Subotica: Labus; Sarac, Cheng Mouyi (Puskaric 46), Bratic, Torbica, Antonic, Veselinov (Miric 46), Milankovic, Simovic, Adamovic, Ubiparip (Noskovic 75).
Dnepr: Kanibolotskiy; Rusol, Denisov, Cheberyachko, Pashaev, Kalinichenko (Nazarenko 59), Ferreyra, Kravchenko, Gomenyuk, Seleznev (Fedorchuk 59), Konoplyanka.

Sturm Graz (0) 2 *(Feldhofer 49, Kienast 59)*
Dinamo Tbilisi (0) 0   4657
Sturm Graz: Gratzei; Standfest, Feldhofer, Schildenfeld, Purcher, Kienzl, Bukva (Haas 81), Holzl (Ehrenreich 88), Weber, Szabics, Kienast (Muratovic 77).
Dinamo Tbilisi: Loria; Tomashvili, Kakubava, Khmaladze, Pirtskhalava (Robertinho 60), Ednilson, Kakhelishvili, Koshkadze, Tektumanidze, Djousse, Metreveli (Sikharulidze 86).

Utrecht (1) 1 *(Mertens 35)*
Lucerne (0) 0   12,100
Utrecht: Sinouh; Wuytens, Schut, Cornelisse, Nesu, Silberbauer (Maguire 82), Lensky (Nijholt 73), Asare, Mulenga, Mertens, Van Wolfswinkel (Oar 68).
Lucerne: Zibung; Kibebe, Lustenberger, Veskovac, Adekunle (Fanger 63), Yakin, Nelson Ferreira (Zverotic 58), Renggli, Kukeli, Gygax (Prager 81), Ianu.

Viktoria Plzen (1) 1 *(Limbersky 28)*
Besiktas (1) 1 *(Delgado 45 (pen))*   5875
Viktoria Plzen: Krbecek; Bystron, Rada, Navratil, Limbersky, Rajtoral, Petrzela (Hajovsky 90), Kolar (Strihavka 68), Horvath, Jiracek (Hruska 86), Rezek.
Besiktas: Hakan; Ibrahim T, Ibrahim U, Erhan, Sivok, Hilbert (Rodrigo Tabata 67), Ernst, Quaresma, Delgado, Nihat (Necip 47), Mert Nobre (Bobo 77).

Wisla (0) 0
Karabakh (0) 1 *(Nadirov 69)*   4200
Wisla: Jovanic; Piotr Brozek, Kowalski, Cikos, Sobolewski, Jirsak, Paljic (Kirm 67), Pawel Brozek (Lobodzinski 75), Zurawski, Boguski (Malecki 46), Bunoza[*].
Karabakh: Veliyev; Rashad F Sadygov, Abbasov, Teli, Medvedev, Agolli, Rubins (Imamaliyev 41), Rashad A Sadygov, Ismayilov, Adamia (Kerimov 90), Aliyev (Nadirov 69).

THIRD QUALIFYING ROUND SECOND LEG

Tuesday, 3 August 2010
Rapid Vienna (1) 3 *(Jelavic 5, 60, Katzer 71)*
Beroe (0) 0   11,700
Rapid Vienna: Hedl; Katzer, Patocka, Sonnleitner, Saurer (Kavlak 62), Hofmann, Kulovits, Heikkinen, Kayhan, Salihi (Gartler 79), Jelavic (Nuhiu 85).
Beroe: Ilchev; Penev, Iliev, Kovachev (Tomash 32), Bachev, Kostadinov (Genchev 58), Dimitrov, Zhekov (Yordanov 62), Velev, Hristov, Zlatinov.

Thursday, 5 August 2010
Anorthosis (1) 3 *(Cafu 45, 60, 87)*
CS Brugge (0) 1 *(Acheampong 78)*   8500
Anorthosis: Arguello; Leiwakabessy, Janicio, Georgiou, Katsavakis, Skopelitis (Miguel Pedro 81), Laban, Garcia, Okkas (Marangos 68), Cafu, Christovao (Fotheringham 74).
CS Brugge: Verbist; Portier (Viane 81), Evens, Cornelis, Kelhar, D'Haene (Van Eenoo 62), Vidarsson, Boi, Serebrennikov (Renato Neto 58), Reynaldo, Acheampong.

Apollon (1) 2 *(Jose Semedo 12, Antonio Nunez 71)*
Sibir (0) 1 *(Shevchenko 63)*   6000
Apollon: Chvalovsky; Neva, Morris, Raul, Kosowski[*], Quinteros, Kolar, Jose Semedo (Toni 78), Oseni (Bangura 85), Adorno, Antonio Nunez (Ogbuke 81).
Sibir: Solosin; Bukhryakov, Klimavicius, Vychodil, Valentic, Cisek (Degtyarev 46), Astafyev, Shulenin (Makarenko 46), Nagibin, Shevchenko (Filipenko 88), Medvedev.

Aris Salonika (1) 2 *(Cesarec 19, 75 (pen))*
Jagiellonia (1) 2 *(Burkhardt 25, 66)*   15,139
Aris Salonika: Sifakis; Michel, Neto (Koulocheris 84), Ronaldo, Lazaridis, Nafti (Prittas 78), Toja, Calvo (Cesnauskis 69), Koke, Javito, Cesarec.
Jagiellonia: Sandomierski; Skerla, Norambuena, Sidqy (Kascelan 46), Kijanskas, Hermes, Burkhardt (Lato 83), Grosicki, Grzyb, Makuszewski (Frankowski 50), Kupisz.

Bangor City (1) 1 *(Bull 9)*
Maritimo (0) 2 *(Adilson 48, Marquinho 58)*   556
Bangor City: Smith; Morley, Roberts, Hoy, Johnston, Bull, Garside (Hurdman 67), Edwards (Williams 77), Ward, Jebb (Davies 66), Jones C.

Maritimo: Marcelo Boeck; Briguel, Luciano Amaral, Robson, Joao Guilherme, Rafael Miranda, Tcho, Baba, Marquinho (Dylan 80), Danilo Dias (Luis Olim 63), Adilson (Fidelis 72).
At Wrexham.

Banik Ostrava (1) 1 *(Reznik 26)*
Dnepr Mogilev (1) 2 *(Yurchanka 24 (pen), Zenkovich 70)*
                                     4800

Banik Ostrava: Danek; Bolf (Gregus 83), Neuwirth, Reznik, Nando, Lukes, Frejlach, Marek, Smejkal (Senkerik 56), Husbauer (Pilik 67), Varadi.
Dnepr Mogilev: Kopantsov; Shuneiko (Raspopov 89), Karpovich, Gonchar, Kapov, Obrazov, Zhevnerov, Tereshchenko (Cernych 84), Bychenok (Turlin 81), Yurchanka, Zenkovich.

Besiktas (1) 3 *(Quaresma 39, Delgado 57, Holosko 70)*
Viktoria Plzen (0) 0   25,975
Besiktas: Hakan; Ibrahim T (Ferrari 46), Ibrahim U, Erhan, Zapotocny, Ernst, Quaresma, Delgado (Rodrigo Tabata 60), Necip, Bobo (Nihat 68), Holosko.
Viktoria Plzen: Krbecek; Bystron, Rada, Navratil[■], Limbersky[■], Rajtoral, Petrzela (Hajovsky 75), Kolar (Hruska 75), Horvath (Rydel 84), Jiracek, Rezek.

Brondby (1) 1 *(Jallow 11)*
Buducnost (0) 0   7003
Brondby: Andersen; Frederiksen, Von Schlebrugge, Wass, Kristiansen, Van der Schaaf, Jensen, Nilsson (Randrup 78), Farnerud (Madsen 80), Larsen, Jallow (Bruno Batata 64).
Buducnost: Dragojevic; Mazic, Dikanovic, Golubovic (Nikac 61), Adamovic, Jovan Nikolic, Vukcevic P (Milan Radulovic 46), Brnovic (Mugosa 84), Kudemor, Beciraj, Boskovic.

Cliftonville (1) 1 *(Boyce 42)*
CSKA Sofia (0) 2 *(Kostadinov 85, Marquinhos 88)*   776
Cliftonville: Connolly; Hutton, Scannell R, Donaghy[■], Holland B, Catney (Patterson 80), McMullan, O'Connor (Smyth 74), Caldwell, Scannell C, Boyce.
CSKA Sofia: Karadzhov; Popov, Trifonov, Vidanov, Aquaro, Grandin, Yanev, Marquinhos, Yanchev (Galchev 67), Iliev (Rui Miguel 58), Delev (Kostadinov 81).

Dinamo Tbilisi (1) 1 *(Robertinho 11)*
Sturm Graz (1) 1 *(Muratovic 40 (pen))*   5000
Dinamo Tbilisi: Loria; Tomashvili, Kakubava, Khmaladze[■], Ednilson, Kakhelishvili[■], Koshkadze, Tektumanidze (Mamuchishvili 77), Vatsadze, Djousse (Gvelesiani 69), Robertinho (Getiashvili 83).
Sturm Graz: Gratzei; Standfest, Feldhofer, Schildenfeld, Purcher, Kienzl (Foda 46), Bukva, Holzl, Muratovic, Weber (Haas 66), Szabics (Kienast 80).

Dnepr (1) 2 *(Seleznev 45, Holek 48)*
Spartak Subotica (0) 0   24,428
Dnepr: Kanibolotskiy; Rusol, Denisov, Cheberyachko, Lobzhanidze, Kalinichenko (Nazarenko 75), Ferreyra, Holek, Kravchenko (Rotan 30), Seleznev (Gomenyuk 71), Konoplyanka.
Spartak Subotica: Labus; Sarac, Bratic, Stevanovic, Puskaric, Torbica, Antonic, Veselinov (Noskovic 80), Simovic, Adamovic, Ubiparip (Miric 46).

Dynamo Minsk (1) 3 *(Strakhanovic 35, Putsila 54, 90)*
Maccabi Haifa (1) 1 *(Dvalishvili 27)*   5000
Dynamo Minsk: Gorbunov; Veretilo, Montaroup, Kondratyev, Putsila, Marakhovskiy, Strakhanovic, Kislyak (Buloychik 81), Dragun, Chukhley (Shkabara 90), Sazankov (Rekish 70).
Maccabi Haifa: Edri; Masilela, Maimon, Meshumar, Gustavo Boccoli, Refaelov (Osman 54), Culma, Golasa (Adrien Silva 52), Canuto, Dvalishvili (Hemed 74), Katan.

FK Austria (3) 3 *(Klein 4 (pen), Baumgartlinger 10, 21)*
Ruch (0) 0   10,000
FK Austria: Lindner; Ortlechner, Suttner, Dragovic (Margreitter 71), Klein, Hlinka, Vorisek (Salomon 62), Baumgartlinger, Liendl, Jun (Tiffner 46), Linz.
Ruch: Pilarz; Nykiel, Jakubowski, Grzyb, Stawarczyk, Grodzicki[■], Zajac (Jankowski 80), Pulkowski (Lisowski 69), Sadlok, Straka, Olszar (Bronowicki 62).

Genk (1) 3 *(Ogunjimi 24, Tozser 80 (pen), Huysegems 85)*
Inter Turku (1) 2 *(Antunez 35, 90)*   15,407
Genk: Courtois; Joneleit, Joao Carlos, Daeseleire, Ngcongca (Durwael 82), Camus, Hubert (Tozser 79), Ndabashinze, Huysegems, Ogunjimi (Koita 79), Yeboah.
Inter Turku: Monsalve; Aho, Nikkari (Makitalo 68), Lehtonen (Almeida 46), Nyman, Rancan[■], Paajanen, Ojala, Kauko, Antunez, Egwin (Kauppi 86).

Hajduk Split (3) 3 *(Vukusic 12, Brkljaca 23, Tomasov 38)*
Dinamo Bucharest (0) 0   25,000
Hajduk Split: Subasic; Buljat, Maloca, Strinic, Anas Sharbini, Andric, Tomasov (Rezic 78), Brkljaca (Trebotic 70), Ibricic, Oremus, Vukusic (Vejic 89).
Dinamo Bucharest: Curca; Garat (Homei 28), Pulhac, Moti, Scarlatache, Adrian Cristea, Torje (Munteanu C 70), N'Doye, Kone, Ganea, Niculae (Andrei Cristea 61).

Hibernian (0) 2 *(De Graaf 54, 89)*
Maribor (1) 3 *(Marcos Tavares 20, 73, Mezga 67 (pen))*
                        13,500
Hibernian: Smith; Murray (Wotherspoon 70), Hogg, Hart (Galbraith 70), Bamba, McBride, De Graaf, Miller, Riodan, Nish, Stokes.
Maribor: Pridigar; Rajcevic, Viler, Andelkovic, Mejac, Mezga (Cvijanovic 90), Bacinovic, Mertelj, Ilicic, Marcos Tavares, Volas (Plut 90).

IFK Gothenburg (0) 1 *(Selakovic 67)*
AZ (0) 0   10,115
IFK Gothenburg: Sandberg; Johansson A, Jonsson, Sigurdsson, Lund (Barkroth 82), Svensson, Johansson J (Soder 62), Selakovic, Bjarnason, Hysen, Stiller.
AZ: Didulica; Jaliens, Klavan, Marcellis, Moisander, Martens, Van der Velden (Holman 66), Wernbloom, Falkenburg (Sigthorsson 75), Gudmundsson, Ortiz.

Jablonec (1) 1 *(Pavlik 33)*
Apoel (3) 3 *(Paulo Jorge 24, Charalambidis 27, Solari 37)*
                        3622
Jablonec: Spit; Drsek, Pavlik, Zabojnik, Krajcik, Jarolim, Loucka (Pitak 46), Elias (Vosahlik 46), Kovarik, Pekhart, Lafata (Haurdic 80).
Apoel: Chiotis; Broerse, Paulo Jorge, Grncharov, William, Marcinho (Ailton Almeida 66), Charalambidis, Solomou, Solari (Kontis 88), Gustavo Manduca (Michael 83), Helio Pinto.

Juventus (0) 1 *(Del Piero 74)*
Shamrock Rovers (0) 0   17,579
Juventus: Storari; Bonucci, Motta, Chiellini, De Ceglie, Diego (Del Piero 46), Sissoko, Pepe, Marchisio, Amauri (Trezeguet 81), Lanzafame.
Shamrock Rovers: Mannus; Flynn, Murray, Price, Murphy, Rice (Bayly 59), Bradley, Kavanagh (Stewart 46), Chambers (Turner 46), Dennehy W, Twigg.

Karabakh (3) 3 *(Ismayilov 28, Aliyev 33, Rashad A Sadygov 35)*
Wisla (0) 2 *(Pawel Brozek 56, Boguski 88)*   29,500
Karabakh: Veliyev; Rashad F Sadygov, Abbasov, Teli, Medvedev, Agolli, Rubins (Imamaliyev 86), Rashad A Sadygov, Ismayilov, Adamia (Kerimov 81), Aliyev (Nadirov 61).
Wisla: Jovanic; Piotr Brozek, Diaz, Kowalski, Cikos, Sobolewski, Jirsak (Wilk 46), Malecki (Lobodzinski 79), Paljic (Pawel Brozek 46), Zurawski, Boguski.

Lausanne (0) 1 _(Rodrigo 68)_
Randers (0) 1 _(Movsisyan 49)_ 8150
Lausanne: Favre; Sonnerat, Meoli, Katz■, Buntschu, Celestini, Marazzi, Steuble, Avanzini (Abdul Carrupt 90), Roux (Rodrigo 57), Silvio (Stadelmann 82).
Randers: Ousted; Pedersen, Egholm (Ahmed 82), Jensen, Fenger, Cramer (Fischer 63), Lorentzen, Beckmann, Sane (Olsen 75), Movsisyan, Berg.

Levski (2) 5 _(Dembele 12, 70, Mladenov 33, Isa 89, 90)_
Kalmar (0) 2 _(Eriksson 82, Daniel Mendes 84)_ 9470
Levski: Petkov; Mulder, Minev, Miliev, Ivanov, Gadzhev, Joaozinho, Tasevski (Ognyanov 69), Yovov (Baltanov 24), Dembele (Isa 73), Mladenov.
Kalmar: Wasta; Lantz (Bertilsson 49), Carlsson, Larsson, Johansson, Rydstrom, Augustsson, Eriksson, Israelsson, Dauda (Daniel Mendes 47), Douglas.

Liverpool (2) 2 _(N'Gog 22, Gerrard 40 (pen))_
Rabotnicki (0) 0 31,202
Liverpool: Cavalieri; Carragher, Johnson, Skrtel, Kelly, Cole, Gerrard (Aquilani 62), Lucas (Spearing 73), N'Gog, Jovanovic (Rodriguez 67), Pacheco.
Rabotnicki: Bogatinov; Dimovski, Adem, Fernando, Belica, Gligorov, Todorovski (Petkovski 88), Ze Carlos (Mojsov 62), Tuneski, Wandeir, Fabio (Marcio 81).

Lucerne (0) 1 _(Pacar 54)_
Utrecht (3) 3 _(Asare 13, Van Wolfswinkel 22,
Silberbauer 28)_ 7100
Lucerne: Zibung; Lustenberger, Veskovac, Yakin (Pacar 46), Nelson Ferreira, Renggli, Wiss, Kukeli (Prager 46), Zverotic, Gygax, Ianu (Joao Paiva 59).
Utrecht: Vorm; Wuytens, Schut, Cornelisse, Nesu, Silberbauer, Lensky (Nijholt 77), Asare (Maguire 46), Mulenga, Mertens, Van Wolfswinkel (Loval Landre 72).

Maccabi Tel Aviv (1) 1 _(Colautti 42)_
Olympiakos (0) 0 12,421
Maccabi Tel Aviv: Strauber; Nivaldo, Ziv (Malul 86), Strul, Gafni, Saban, Medunjanin, Sidibe, Yeini, Colautti (Buzaglo 69), Itzhaki (Avidor 80).
Olympiakos: Nikopolidis; Mellberg, Modesto (Torosidis 46), Holebas, Papadopoulos, Maresca (Mitroglou 71), Dudu Cearense, Zairi (Ibagaza 58), Oscar Gonzalez, Rommedahl, Diogo■.

Montpellier (0) 0
Gyor (1) 1 _(Babic 40)_ 9918
Montpellier: Jourdren; Spahic, Yangambiwa, Collin (Armand 94), Stambouli, Estrada, Saihi, Marveaux (Camara 63), Hasan Kabze, Ait Fana, Giroud.
Gyor: Stevanovic; Djordjevic, Babic, Szabo, Stanisic■, Pilibaitis, Koltai (Cetkovic 78), Tokody, Aleksidze, Nicolas (Copa 66), Nicorec (Feher 46).
aet; Gyor won 4-3 on penalties.

Motherwell (2) 3 _(Murphy 4, Sutton 13, Page 89)_
Aalesund (0) 0 7721
Motherwell: Randolph; Craigan, Reynolds, Hammell, Saunders, Lasley (Fitzpatrick 74), Humphrey, Jennings (Forbes 90), Hateley, Sutton (Page 86), Murphy.
Aalesund: Lindegaard; Jalasto, Tollas, Arneng, Fredriksen, Mathisen (Flotre 65), Larsen (Karlsen 70), Herrera, Aaroy, Parr, Olsen.

OFK Belgrade (1) 1 _(Nikolic 32)_
Galatasaray (2) 5 _(Mustafa 12, Kewell 22, 57 (pen),
Arda 71, Mehmet 81)_ 6000
OFK Belgrade: Saranov; Nikolic■, Rodic, Kecojevic, Petkovic, Trivunovic, Simic, Zeravica (Filipovic 74), Sasa Markovic, Krstic (Sindic 59), Milic (Injac 75).
Galatasaray: Aykut; Neill, Servet, Kewell (Mehmet 72), Cana, Sabri, Arda (Ali 82), Ayhan, Serdar (Pino 61), Mustafa, Hakan Balta.

Slovan Bratislava (1) 1 _(Dordevic 2 (og))_
Red Star Belgrade (0) 1 _(Cadu 73)_ 9250
Slovan Bratislava: Putnocky; Had, Dosoudil■, Salata, Janosik, Bagayoko, Guede, Bozic (Kolcak 89), Grendel (Kiss 68), Ivana (Kuzma 76), Sylvestr.

Red Star Belgrade: Stamenkovic; Tosic, Dordevic■, Ninkov, Vilotic, Cadu, Milovanovic (Subasic 81), Issah, Vesovic (Jeremic 62), Koroman (Jevtic 88), Trifunovic.

Sporting Lisbon (1) 2 _(Helder Postiga 24, Maniche 90)_
Nordsjaelland (0) 1 _(Lawan 79)_ 27,152
Sporting Lisbon: Rui Patricio; Polga, Joao Pereira, Evaldo, Daniel Carrico, Maniche, Vukcevic (Yannick Djalo 62), Andre Santos, Helder Postiga (Pongolle 78), Liedson, Valdes (Matias Fernandez 71).
Nordsjaelland: Hansen; Bengtsson, Parkhurst, Kildentoft, Jensen D, Stokholm, Bernier (Matti Nielsen 67), Laudrup (Lawan 63), Adu, Mikkelsen (Granskov 84), Bille Nielsen.

Stuttgart (0) 2 _(Pogrebnyak 55, Gebhart 90)_
Molde (1) 2 _(Johansson 41, Rindaroy 49)_ 11,500
Stuttgart: Ulreich; Molinaro, Niedermeier, Trasch, Gentner, Gebhart, Kuzmanovic, Funk (Boulahrouz 61), Rudy (Didavi 71), Marica (Harnik 86), Pogrebnyak.
Molde: Lillebakk; Johansson (Diouf 86), Simonsen, Rindaroy, Andreasson, Forren, Berg Hestad, Mostrom (Skjolsvik 89), Hoseth, Thioune (Holm 79), Fall.

Teteks (1) 1 _(Stojanovski 31)_
Elfsborg (1) 2 _(Kurbegovic 43, Jawo 56)_ 700
Teteks: Marko Jovanovski; Jovanovski D, Belchev, Naumovski, Ristevski (Aliji 71), Ristov, Zaharievski, Miroslav Jovanovski (Simovski 61), Iseni (Ristovski 46), Gligorovski, Stojanovski.
Elfsborg: Covic; Lucic, Floren (Klarstrom 61), Wikstrom, Karlsson, Mobaeck (Avdic 46), Ishizaki (Ericsson 46), Kurbegovic, Nordmark, Keene, Jawo.

Timisoara (0) 3 _(Axente 53, Zicu 80, Cisovsky 90)_
MyPa (3) 3 _(Aijala 18, Ricketts 20, 25)_ 8000
Timisoara: Taborda; Sepsi, Cisovsky, Dukic (Bourceanu 46), Mera, Contra, Alexa, Goga, Tames (Zicu 57), Magera (Gueye 72), Axente.
MyPa: Kuismala; Aho (Lindberg 57), Timoska, Oksanen (Felipe Benevides 73), Uimaniemi, Hietanen, Aijala, Okkonen, Saxman, Votinov, Ricketts (Kurittu 89).

Zestafoni (0) 0
Karpaty (0) 1 _(Kozhanov 90)_ 4558
Zestafoni: Kvaskhvadze; Oniani, Eliava, Khidesheli, Aladashvili, Daushvili (Benashvili 80), Dzaria (Babunashvili 60), Grigalashvili, Aptsiauri, Gelashvili, Dvali (Tsinamdzgvrishvili 67).
Karpaty: Tlumak; Tupic, Oshchipko (Danilo Avelar 32), Milosevic, Goodwin, Khudobyak, Tkachuk, Kozhanov (Baranets G 90), Fedetskiy, Batista, Zenjov (Guruli 46).

Zrinjski (0) 0
Odense (0) 0 10,250
Zrinjski: Melher; Dzidic, Ivankovic, Sunjic, Anicic M, Zizovic, Zadro, Susic (Pehar 81), Stjepanovic, Dragicevic, Selimovic.
Odense: Carroll; Helveg, Haland, Ruud, Moller Christensen, Sorensen, Gislason, Djemba-Djemba (Demba-Nyren 90), Andreasen, Traore, Utaka (Hansen H 90).

PLAY-OFF ROUND FIRST LEG

Tuesday, 17 August 2010

Aris Salonika (0) 1 _(Ruiz 90)_
FK Austria (0) 0 20,000
Aris Salonika: Sifakis; Oriol, Michel, Neto, Ronaldo, Nafti, Cesnauskis (Mendrinos 60), Toja (Prittas 78), Koke, Javito, Cesarec (Ruiz 63).
FK Austria: Lindner; Margreitter, Suttner, Dragovic, Klein, Hlinka, Vorisek, Baumgartlinger, Liendl (Leovac 71), Jun (Stankovic 80), Linz (Schumacher 89).

Besiktas (1) 2 _(Hilbert 35, Quaresma 66)_
HJK Helsinki (0) 0 19,040
Besiktas: Cenk; Ferrari, Zapotocny, Ismail, Hilbert, Ernst, Guti, Quaresma (Nihat 88), Dag, Rodrigo Tabata (Necip 70), Bobo (Holosko 83).

HJK Helsinki: Wallen; Kansikas, Ojala, Magnusson, Rafinha, Fowler, Sorsa, Bah, Dema (Karkkainen 75), Pelvas (Makela 46), Westo (Parikka 69).

Thursday, 19 August 2010

AIK Stockholm (0) 0

Levski (0) 0 8212

AIK Stockholm: Turina; Karlsson, Johansson, Backman, Lorentzson (Lundberg 70), Tjernstrom, Pavey, Persson, Danielsson, Jagne (Antonio Flavio 60), Bangura.
Levski: Mitrev; Mulder, Minev, Miliev, Ivanov, Greene, Gadzhev (Benzoukane 85), Joaozinho, Tasevski (Aleksandrov 69), Dembele, Mladenov (Kirov 75).

AZ (2) 2 *(Holman 20, Wernbloom 27)*

Aktobe (0) 0 10,385

AZ: Didulica; Klavan, Marcellis, Moreno, Moisander, Martens (Ortiz 85), Schaars, Holman (Van der Velden 77), Wernbloom, Falkenburg (Sigthorsson 74), Gudmundsson.
Aktobe: Sidelnikov; Badlo, Kenzhisariev, Smakov, Karpovich, Khokhlov, Semenov, Chichulin, Darabaev, Essomba, Averchenko (Lisenkov 87).

BATE Borisov (0) 3 *(Olekhnovich 56, Renan 60, Pavlov 70)*

Maritimo (0) 0 5230

BATE Borisov: Veremko; Radkov, Yurevich, Bordachev, Shitov, Nekhajchik, Renan (Skavysh 85), Pavlov (Baga 81), Olekhnovich, Rodionov, Kontsevoy (Patotski 90).
Maritimo: Marcelo Boeck; Robson, Alonso, Joao Guilherme, Roberto De Sousa, Ricardo Esteves, Rafael Miranda, Tcho (Djalma Campos 62), Baba, Marquinho (Cherrad 69), Danilo Dias (Luciano Amaral 85).

Borussia Dortmund (4) 4 *(Kagawa 13, 41, Barrios 21, 29)*

Karabakh (0) 0 47,800

Borussia Dortmund: Weidenfeller, Hummels, Subotic, Schmelzer, Kehl (Bender 66), Nuri, Piszczek, Blaszczykowski (Gotze 49), Kagawa (Lewandowski 70), Barrios, Grosskreutz.
Karabakh: Veliyev; Rashad F Sadygov, Abbasov, Teli (Gashimov 70), Medvedev, Agolli, Rubins, Rashad A Sadygov, Amamaliyev (Yusifov 46), Adamia, Aliyev (Nadirov 46).

Celtic (2) 2 *(Juarez 19, Samaras 34)*

Utrecht (0) 0 35,755

Celtic: Zaluska; Cha, Juarez, Brown, Majstorovic, Loovens, Kayal (Forrest 69), Ledley, Samaras, Maloney, Fortune.
Utrecht: Vorm; Wuytens, Schut, Cornelisse, Nesu, Silberbauer, Lensky (Nijholt 82), Asare, Mulenga (Duplan 17), Mertens, Van Wolfswinkel.

Club Brugge (0) 2 *(Hoefkens 71 (pen), Blondel 84)*

Dynamo Minsk (1) 1 *(Dragun 6)* 24,587

Club Brugge: Stijnen; Van der Heyden, Donk, Camozzato, Hoefkens, Blondel, Odjidja-Ofoe, Perisic, Vargas (Dirar 46), Dalmat (Lestienne 79), Kouemaha (Akpala 66).
Dynamo Minsk: Gorbunov; Veretilo, Montaroup, Kondratyev, Putsila, Marakhovskiy, Strakhanovic, Kislyak (Shkabara 86), Dragun, Chukhley (Rekish 63), Sazankov (Leonardo 77).

CSKA Moscow (2) 4 *(Doumbia 13, 20, Tosic 47, 74)*

Anorthosis (0) 0 6000

CSKA Moscow: Akinfeev; Berezutski V, Ignashevich, Nababkin, Schennikov, Semberas, Mamaev, Oliseh (Gonzalez 74), Tosic, Vagner Love (Necid 81), Doumbia (Dzagoev 69).
Anorthosis: Arguello[■]; Leiwakabessy, Janicio, Katsavakis, Frontini, Laban, Garcia, Marangos (Laborde 51), Okkas, Cafu (Kozacik 78), Christovao (Carlos Coto 60).

CSKA Sofia (0) 3 *(Aquaro 81, Nelson 82, Delev 90)*

The New Saints (0) 0 2950

CSKA Sofia: Karadzhov; Trifonov, Vidanov, Aquaro, Marquinhos, Yanchev, Galchev, Tonev (Kostadinov 71), Iliev (Sheridan 46), Delev, Saidhodzha (Nelson 64).

The New Saints: Harrison; Evans, Baker, Holmes T, Holmes D, Jones C(Wood 78), Hogan, Ruscoe, Seargeant, Williams M (Darlington 87), Sharp (Berkeley 76).

Debrecen (2) 2 *(Coulibaly 22, Laczko 33)*

Litex (0) 0 8125

Debrecen: Malinauskas; Mijadinoski, Laczko, Bernath, Komlosi, Czvitkovics, Kiss, Szakaly (Dombi 76), Varga, Kabat (Farkas 81), Coulibaly (Mbengono 86).
Litex: Golubovic; Berberovic, Venkov, Barthe[■], Petkov, Jelenkovic, Sandrinho (Todorov 66), Wellington (Tsvetanov 78), Milanov G, Tsvetkov, Niflore (Yanev 71).

Dnepr (0) 0

Lech (1) 1 *(Arboleda 5)* 21,420

Dnepr: Kanibolotskiy; Rusol, Denisov, Cheberyachko, Pashaev (Gomenyuk 58), Lobzhanidze, Kalinichenko, Ferreyra (Kravchenko 46), Holek, Gladkiy (Shakhov 66), Seleznev.
Lech: Buric; Henriquez, Arboleda, Djurdjevic, Bandrowski, Injac, Krivets, Kikut, Stilic (Mozdzen 89), Kielb (Wilk 72), Tshibamba (Zapotoka 86).

Dundee U (0) 0

AEK Athens (1) 1 *(Djebbour 11)* 12,116

Dundee U: Pernis; Dillon, Dixon, Buaben, Kenneth, Watson, Robertson S (Cadamarteri 81), Gomis, Daly, Goodwillie, Conway.
AEK Athens: Saja; Dallas, Jahic, Manolas, Makos, Leonardo (Burns 71), Kafes, Lagos, Liberopoulos (Eder 89), Nacho Scocco, Djebbour (Bouba Diop 82).

Feyenoord (0) 1 *(Fer 78)*

Gent (0) 0 22,500

Feyenoord: Mulder; De Cler, Vlaar, De Vrij, Martins Indi, Bruins, El Ahmadi, Wijnaldum, Fer, Smolov (Castaignos 76), Schaken.
Gent: Jorgacevic; Hanstveit, Wils, Skarabot, Myrie, Thijs, Grondin, Azofeifa (De Smet 68), Soumahoro (Ljubijankic 69), Coulibaly, El Ghanassy (Smolders 83).

Galatasaray (0) 2 *(Baros 59, 86)*

Karpaty (2) 2 *(Kuznetsov 34, Zenjov 41)* 15,182

Galatasaray: Aykut; Neill, Hakan Balta (Serkan 79), Servet, Ali, Kewell, Arda, Ayhan, Serdar (Ozbek 54), Mustafa, Mehmet (Baros 36).
Karpaty: Tlumak; Milosevic, Checher, Goodwin, Khudobyak, Kozhanov (Gudyma 65), Golodyuk, Fedetskiy, Danilo Avelar, Kuznetsov (Batista 72), Zenjov (Kopolovets 85).

Genk (0) 0

Porto (1) 3 *(Falcao 29 (pen), Souza 82, Belluschi 90)* 13,711

Genk: Courtois; Matoukou[■], Joneleit, Ngcongca, Tozser, Hubert, Pudil, De Bruyne (Camus 86), Buffel (Ndabashinze 82), Vossen (Ogunjimi 46), Barda.
Porto: Helton; Sapunaru, Rolando, Maicon, Belluschi, Joao Moutinho, Alvaro Pereira, Fernando, Silvestre Varela (Souza 60), Falcao (Walter 82), Ukra (Ruben Micael 74).

Getafe (1) 1 *(Parejo 43)*

Apoel (0) 0 4235

Getafe: Ustari; Miguel Torres, Cata Diaz, Mane, Rafa, Boateng, Borja (Manu Del Moral 46), Gavilan, Parejo, Arizmendi (Albin 46), Adrian Colunga (Miku 67).
Apoel: Chiotis; Paulo Jorge, Grncharov, William, Nuno Morais, Marcinho, Charalambidis (Poursaitidis 90), Solomou, Solari (Trichkovski 87), Gustavo Manduca (Ailton Almeida 66), Helio Pinto.

Gyor (0) 0

Dinamo Zagreb (2) 2 *(Rukavina 19, 28)* 8500

Gyor: Stevanovic; Djordjevic, Szabo, Feher, Pilibaitis (Trajkovic 78), Dinjar (Ji Parana 34), Koltai, Tokody, Copa (Bogunare 53), Aleksidze, Nicolas.
Dinamo Zagreb: Loncaric; Cufre, Etto (Ademi 87), Biscan, Ibanez, Calello, Sammir, Morales (Mesaric 56), Badelj, Vrsaljko, Rukavina (Sivonjic 76).

Hajduk Split (1) 4 *(Ibricic 39, 66, Brkljaca 78, Cop 85)*
Unirea (1) 1 *(Frunza 34)* 35,000
Hajduk Split: Radosevic; Buljat, Maloca (Vejic 87), Strinic, Anas Sharbini, Andric, Tomasov, Ibricic, Oremus, Trebotic (Brkljaca 74), Vukusic (Cop 66).
Unirea: Grigore; Maftei, Galamaz, Nicu, Bordeanu, Frunza, Brandan, Marinescu (Paraschiv 47), Onofras (Neaga 61), Bilasco, Rusescu (Dale 74).

Lausanne (1) 1 *(Traore 28)*
Lokomotiv Moscow (0) 1 *(Sychev 65)* 11,200
Lausanne: Favre; Sonnerat, Meoli, Buntschu, Celestini, Marazzi, Abdul Carrupt (Stadelmann 81), Avanzini (Kilinc 85), Traore, Munsy, Silvio (Roux 72).
Lokomotiv Moscow: Guilherme; Shishkin, Rodolfo, Yanbayev, Burlak, Tarasov, Aliyev, Torbinski (Gatagov 70), Glushakov (Loskov 56), Sychev, Maicon (Traore 46).

Leverkusen (1) 3 *(Kadlec 1, 83, Ballack 90 (pen))*
Tavriya (0) 0 13,000
Leverkusen: Adler; Friedrich, Kadlec, Schwaab, Vidal, Reinartz, Renato Augusto, Sam (Barnetta 46), Bender (Ballack 46), Kiessling, Helmes (Derdiyok 66).
Tavriya: Postransky; Gumenyuk, Markovic, Monakhov, Messias, Galyuza, Ljubenovic, Matyazh (Lutsenko 71), Shynder (Golaydo 46), Kovpak, Idahor (Gigiadze 82).

Liverpool (1) 1 *(Babel 45)*
Trabzonspor (0) 0 40,941
Liverpool: Reina; Kelly, Kyrgiakos, Poulsen, Carragher, Fabio Aurelio, Lucas, Rodriguez (N'Gog 73), Jovanovic, Cole, Babel (Torres 46).
Trabzonspor: Onur; Egemen, Glowacki, Cale, Serkan, Burak (Alanzinho 56), Selcuk, Colman (Remzi 77), Ceyhun, Umut (Yattara 86), Gutierrez.

Napoli (1) 1 *(Lavezzi 45)*
Elfsborg (0) 0 33,534
Napoli: De Sanctis; Dossena (Zuniga 83), Maggio, Aronica, Grava, Cannavaro, Pazienza (Cavani 62), Gargano, Hamsik (Blasi 77), Quagliarella, Lavezzi.
Elfsborg: Christiansen; Lucic, Floren, Jonsson, Klarstrom, Svensson, Mobaeck, Ishizaki (Ericsson 44), Larsson (Jawo 70), Avdic, Keene (Karlsson 87).

Odense (1) 2 *(Sorensen 31, Utaka 78)*
Motherwell (0) 1 *(Hateley 90)* 5127
Odense: Carroll; Haland, Ruud, Moller Christensen, Sorensen, Gislason (Johansson 74), Djemba-Djemba, Caca (Hansen H 46), Andreasen, Absalonsen, Utaka.
Motherwell: Randolph; Saunders, Hammell, Reynolds, Craigan, Hateley, Humphrey, Jennings■, Sutton (McHugh 85), Murphy (Blackman 73), Lasley (Forbes 72).

Omonia (0) 0
Metalist Kharkiv (1) 1 *(Devic 24)* 10,179
Omonia: Georgallides; Iago Bouzon, Charalambous I, Wenzel, Leandro, Aloneftis (Efrem 56), Davidson Morais, Makridis, Kaseke (Jose Manuel Rueda 66), Avraam (Rengifo 74), Konstantinou.
Metalist Kharkiv: Startsev; Fininho, Villagra, Obradovic, Romanchuk, Berezovchuk, Shelayev, Cleiton Xavier (Bordian 73), Valyaev (Gueye 87), Edmar, Devic (Vorobei 81).

Palermo (2) 3 *(Maccarone 37 (pen), Hernandez 39, Pastore 77)*
Maribor (0) 0 28,400
Palermo: Sirigu; Cassani, Bovo, Balzaretti, Glik, Liverani, Migliaccio, Nocerino, Pastore, Maccarone (Pinilla 70), Hernandez (Kasami 78).
Maribor: Pridigar■; Rajcevic, Viler, Andelkovic, Mejac, Mezga (Radan 36), Bacinovic (Dodlek 87), Mertelj, Ilicic, Marcos Tavares, Volas (Cvijanovic 46).

PAOK Salonika (1) 1 *(Vieirinha 19)*
Fenerbahce (0) 0 23,353
PAOK Salonika: Kresic; Contreras, Malezas, Boussaidi, Vitolo■, Garcia, Lino, Vieirinha, Ivic (Filomeno 77), Muslimovic (Sorlin 60), Salpingidis (Papazoglou 86).

Fenerbahce: Volkan; Lugano, Andre Santos, Ilhan, Gokhan G, Alex, Selcuk (Gokhan U 80), Mehmet Topuz, Caner (Ozer 70), Cristian Baroni, Semih (Niang 46).

Paris St Germain (1) 2 *(Luyindula 3, Hoarau 60)*
Maccabi Tel Aviv (0) 0 8500
Paris St Germain: Edel; Armand, Ceara, Sakho, Makonda (Jallet 76), Clement, Chantome, Luyindula, Giuly, Hoarau (Mevlut 74), Maurice (Sessegnon 83).
Maccabi Tel Aviv: Strauber; Pavicevic, Ziv, Strul, Gafni (Buzaglo 64), Saban, Baning (Yeini 73), Medunjanin, Sidibe, Itzhaki, Atar (Avidor 65).

Rapid Vienna (1) 1 *(Nuhiu 33)*
Aston Villa (1) 1 *(Bannan 12)* 17,500
Rapid Vienna: Hedl; Soma, Katzer, Sonnleitner, Hofmann, Kavlak, Heikkinen, Hinum (Drazan 86), Kayhan, Salihi (Gartler 73), Nuhiu.
Aston Villa: Guzan; Beye, Warnock, Reo-Coker, Davies, Lichaj, Albrighton (Weimann 79) (Osbourne 86), Bannan (Delfouneso 74), Hogg, Heskey, Downing.

Sibir (0) 1 *(Degtyarev 90)*
PSV Eindhoven (0) 0 11,500
Sibir: Solosin; Bukhryakov, Vychodil, Joseph-Reinette, Shumulikoski, Astafyev, Aravin (Molosh 90), Zinovyev (Degtyarev 64), Canas, Shevchenko■, Belyaev (Cizek 71).
PSV Eindhoven: Isaksson; Rodriguez■, Pieters, Vukovic, Manolev, Engelaar, Hutchinson (Ojo 81), Lens, Berg (Marcelo 63), Toivonen, Amrabat.

Slovan Bratislava (0) 0
Stuttgart (0) 1 *(Harnik 88)* 8120
Slovan Bratislava: Putnocky; Had, Salata, Janosik, Dobrotka, Bagayoko, Guede, Grendel (Kuzma 82), Kiss, Ivana (Breznanik 61), Sylvestr (Slovak 67).
Stuttgart: Ulreich; Boulahrouz, Degen, Molinaro, Niedermeier, Trasch (Audel 61), Gentner, Gebhart, Kuzmanovic, Cacau (Marica 85), Pogrebnyak (Harnik 67).

Sporting Lisbon (0) 0
Brondby (1) 2 *(Kristiansen 43, Jallow 52)* 20,057
Sporting Lisbon: Rui Patricio; Joao Pereira, Evaldo, Daniel Carrico, Nuno Andre Coelho, Maniche, Matias Fernandez (Vukcevic 56), Andre Santos, Helder Postiga (Yannick Djalo 62), Liedson, Valdes (Saleiro 76).
Brondby: Andersen; Bischoff, Rasmussen, Von Schlebrugge, Wass, Kristiansen (Farnerud 89), Krohn-Dehli, Jensen, Nilsson (Randrup 53), Larsen, Jallow (Madsen 73).

Steaua (0) 1 *(Stancu 71)*
Grasshoppers (0) 0 17,000
Steaua: Tatarusanu; Emeghara, Abrudan, Latovlevici, Geraldo Alves, Nicolita (Radut 67), Bicfalvi, Stoica, Tanase, Kapetanos (Surdu 59), Stancu (Angelov 86).
Grasshoppers: Konig; Paulo, Smiljanic, Voser, Colina (Abrashi 46), Guillermo Vallori, Cabanas, Salatic, Lang (Emeghara 90), Rennella, Zuber (Adili 69).

Sturm Graz (0) 1 *(Schildenfeld 82)*
Juventus (1) 2 *(Bonucci 15, Amauri 90)* 15,322
Sturm Graz: Gratzei; Standfest, Feldhofer, Schildenfeld, Purcher, Kienzl (Muratovic 82), Bukva, Weber, Kainz (Klem 72), Szabics, Kienast (Haas 75).
Juventus: Storari; Bonucci, Motta, Chiellini, De Ceglie, Diego (Del Piero 74), Sissoko, Pepe, Marchisio (Felipe Melo 70), Amauri, Lanzafame (Martinez 55).

Timisoara (0) 0
Manchester C (0) 1 *(Balotelli 72)* 24,695
Timisoara: Pantilimo; Sepsi, Scutaru (Zicu 71), Luchin, Cisovsky, Contra (Mera 80), Alexa, Curtean, Bourceanu, Magera (Goga 83), Axente.
Manchester C: Hart; Toure K, Lescott, De Jong, Zabaleta, Kompany, Toure Y, Barry (Balotelli 57), Silva (Johnson A 66), Adebayor, Tevez (Jo 77).

Vaslui (0) 0

Lille (0) 0   3821

Vaslui: Kuciak; David Rivas, Milanov, Gladstone (Genchev 35), Hugo Luz, Papp, Sanmartean, Pavlovic, Costin (Bello 79), Wesley, Pouga.
Lille: Landreau; Emerson, Beria, Chedjou, Mavuba, Cabaye, Debuchy, Dumont, Obraniak (De Melo 35), Sow (Hazard 77), Frau (Gervinho 67).

Villarreal (4) 5 *(Marchena 10, Cazorla 17, Borja Valero 35, Cani 45, Nilmar 75)*

Dnepr Mogilev (0) 0   7913

Villarreal: Diego Lopez; Marchena, Angel, Musacchio, Capdevila, Senna, Cani, Cazorla (Jefferson Montero 58), Borja Valero (Nilmar 46), Bruno, Rossi (Altidore 74).
Dnepr Mogilev: Kopantsov; Shuneiko (Tupchiy 76), Karpovich, Gonchar (Raspopov 40), Kapov, Obrazov, Zhevnerov, Tereshchenko, Yurchanka, Zenkovich (Cernych 64), Turlin.

PLAY-OFF ROUND SECOND LEG

Tuesday, 24 August 2010

Anorthosis (0) 1 *(Cafu 76)*

CSKA Moscow (0) 2 *(Doumbia 85, Gonzalez 89)*   4000

Anorthosis: Kozacik; Georgiou, Frontini, Sielis (Vidovic 60), Alvaro Brachi, Garcia, Marangos, Okkas, Cafu, Christovao (Chatzigeorgiou 70), Laborde (Concistre 19).
CSKA Moscow: Akinfeev; Berezutski V, Ignashevich, Berezutski A, Schennikov, Semberas, Mamaev (Honda 63), Dzagoev (Rahimic 80), Oliseh, Tosic (Gonzalez 68), Doumbia.

Thursday, 26 August 2010

AEK Athens (1) 1 *(Bouba Diop 23)*

Dundee U (0) 1 *(Daly 78)*   700

AEK Athens: Saja; Georgeas (Gentzoglou 46), Jahic, Manolas, Bouba Diop, Makos, Leonardo (Karabelas 89), Kafes, Lagos, Nacho Scocco, Djebbour (Blanco 58).
Dundee U: Pernis; Dillon, Dixon, Buaben, Kenneth, Watson, Robertson D, Gomis (Daly 63), Robertson S (Swanson 59), Cadamarteri (Goodwillie 49), Conway.

Aktobe (0) 2 *(Tleshev 67, 88)*

AZ (1) 1 *(Wernbloom 10)*   12,600

Aktobe: Sidelnikov; Ba, Bono, Kenzhisariev, Smakov, Karpovich, Khayrullin (Peric 59), Chichulin, Essomba, Tleshev, Averchenko (Darabaev 70).
AZ: Didulica; Klavan, Marcellis, Moreno, Moisander, Martens, Schaars, Holman (Ortiz 87), Wernbloom, Falkenburg (Jonathas 61), Gudmundsson (Sigthorsson 68).

Apoel (1) 1 *(Ailton Almeida 41)*

Getafe (0) 1 *(Miguel Torres 99)*   18,643

Apoel: Chiotis; Paulo Jorge, Grncharov, William (Poursaitidis 90), Nuno Morais, Charalambidis, Solomou, Solari (Broerse**#** 74), Gustavo Manduca (Trichkovski 74), Ailton Almeida, Helio Pinto.
Getafe: Ustari; Miguel Torres, Cata Diaz, Rafa, Marcano, Boateng, Parejo, Pedro Rios (Arizmendi 46), Manu Del Moral, Albin (Mosquera 91), Adrian Colunga (Miku 75).
aet.

Aston Villa (1) 2 *(Agbonlahor 22, Heskey 77)*

Rapid Vienna (0) 3 *(Nuhiu 52, Sonnleitner 78, Gartler 81)*   29,980

Aston Villa: Guzan; Beye, Collins JM, Petrov, Cuellar, Davies, Ireland, Reo-Coker (Delfouneso 82), Agbonlahor (Albrighton 40), Heskey, Young A.
Rapid Vienna: Hedl; Soma, Dober, Katzer, Sonnleitner, Saurer (Trimmel 73), Hofmann (Patocka 90), Kavlak, Heikkinen, Pehlivan (Gartler 78), Nuhiu.

Brondby (0) 0

Sporting Lisbon (1) 3 *(Evaldo 45, Nuno Andre Coelho 75, Yannick Djalo 90)*   20,389

Brondby: Andersen; Bischoff, Rasmussen, Von Schlebrugge, Wass, Kristiansen, Jensen, Nilsson, Larsen, Krohn-Dehli, Jallow (Bruno Batata 77).
Sporting Lisbon: Rui Patricio; Abel, Evaldo, Daniel Carrico, Nuno Andre Coelho, Maniche, Vukcevic (Valdes 84), Andre Santos, Helder Postiga (Matias Fernandez 67), Liedson (Saleiro 90), Yannick Djalo.

Dinamo Zagreb (1) 2 *(Sammir 45 (pen), 84 (pen))*

Gyor (1) 1 *(Nicolas 17)*   5538

Dinamo Zagreb: Loncaric; Cufre, Biscan, Mesaric (Etto 33), Sammir, Ademi, Morales (Dodo 66), Badelj, Vrsaljko, Rukavina, Kramaric (Chago 79).
Gyor: Stevanovic; Djordjevic, Babic, Stanisic (Szabo 33), Feher, Pilibaitis, Koltai (Dinjar 56), Tokody, Volgyi, Aleksidze (Bouguerra 66), Nicolas.

Dnepr Mogilev (1) 1 *(Yurchanka 19)*

Villarreal (2) 2 *(Nilmar 45, Marco Ruben 90)*   6542

Dnepr Mogilev: Kopantsov; Shuneiko, Gonchar, Kapov (Karpovich 90), Obrazov, Zhevnerov, Tereshchenko, Bychenok, Yurchanka, Zenkovich, Turlin (Bulochyk 84).
Villarreal: Juan Carlos; Musacchio (Marchena 56), Catala, Joan Oriol, Kikos, Mario Gaspar, Cristobal**#**, Matilla, Altidore (Cani 72), Nilmar (Marco Ruben 61), Jefferson Montero.

Dynamo Minsk (0) 2 *(Chukhley 47, Dragun 90)*

Club Brugge (3) 3 *(Hoefkens 5 (pen), 32 (pen), Dalmat 26)*   7125

Dynamo Minsk: Gorbunov; Veretilo, Montaroup, Kondratyev, Tsyenchen, Putsila, Kislyak (Buloychik 84), Dragun, Chukhley, Rekish (Lucas Sotero 46), Sazankov (Bruno Furlan 68).
Club Brugge: Stijnen; Van der Heyden, Donk, Camozzato, Hoefkens, Blondel, Dirar (Scepovic 73), Odjidja-Ofoe, Perisic, Dalmat (Geraerts 65), Akpala (Kouemaha 13).

Elfsborg (0) 0

Napoli (2) 2 *(Cavani 29, 38)*   10,621

Elfsborg: Covic; Lucic, Floren, Andersson M (Wikstrom 66), Klarstrom (Karlsson 70), Svensson, Mobaeck, Ericsson, Larsson, Avdic, Keene (Jawo 76).
Napoli: De Sanctis; Dossena, Aronica, Grava, Cannavaro, Pazienza, Maggio (Zuniga 55), Gargano, Hamsik (Blasi 64), Cavani, Lavezzi (Campagnaro 73).

Fenerbahce (0) 1 *(Emre B 51)*

PAOK Salonika (0) 1 *(Muslimovic 102)*   39,863

Fenerbahce: Volkan; Lugano, Andre Santos, Bilica, Gokhan G, Emre B (Selcuk 76), Alex, Mehmet Topuz (Ozer 91), Cristian Baroni (Gokhan U 106), Stoch, Niang.
PAOK Salonika: Kresic; Contreras, Malezas, Boussaidi (Sznaucer 75), Fotakis (Koutsianikoulis 91), Sorlin, Garcia, Lino, Vieirinha, Filomeno (Muslimovic 83), Salpingidis.
aet.

FK Austria (0) 1 *(Linz 56)*

Aris Salonika (1) 1 *(Ruiz 42)*   11,000

FK Austria: Lindner; Troyansky (Stankovic 62), Margreitter, Suttner (Leovac 74), Dragovic, Klein, Hlinka, Baumgartlinger, Liendl (Schumacher 46), Jun, Linz.
Aris Salonika: Sifakis; Michel, Neto, Ronaldo, Lazaridis, Nafti, Toja (Prittas 55), Calvo (Cesnauskis 57), Koke, Ruiz (Cesarec 74), Javito.

Gent (1) 2 *(Soumahoro 34, Coulibaly 61)*

Feyenoord (0) 0   8787

Gent: Jorgacevic; Hanstveit, Thompson, Wils, Myrie (Adriano 83), Thijs (Ljubijankic 65), Grondin, Azofeifa (Smolders 68), Soumahoro, Coulibaly, El Ghanassy.
Feyenoord: Mulder; De Cler (Cabral 81), Vlaar, Leerdam, De Vrij, Martins Indi, Bruins, Wijnaldum, Fer, Cisse (Smolov 59), Schaken (Castaignos 75).

Grasshoppers (0) 1 *(Salatic 77)*

Steaua (0) 0   5200

Grasshoppers: Benito; Paulo, Smiljanic, Voser, Guillermo Vallori, Cabanas (Abrashi 82), Salatic, Toko, Lang (Hajrovic 46), Zuber (Adili 72), Emeghara.
Steaua: Tatarusanu; Emeghara, Abrudan, Latovlevici, Geraldo Alves, Bicfalvi, Stoica (Angelov 55), Tanase, Radut (Matei 83), Surdu, Stancu.
aet; Steaua won 4-3 on penalties.

HJK Helsinki (0) 0
Besiktas (1) 4 *(Quaresma 15, Guti 67, Necip 77,*
Holosko 90)   9054
HJK Helsinki: Wallen; Sumusalo, Ojala, Magnusson, Rafinha (Parikka 77), Fowler, Bah, Dema (Ring 71), Makela, Pelvas (Sorsa 46), Westo.
Besiktas: Cenk; Ferrari, Zapotocny, Ismail, Hilbert, Ernst, Guti (Nihat 74), Quaresma (Holosko 68), Dag, Necip, Bobo (Mert Nobre 81).

Juventus (0) 1 *(Del Piero 53)*
Sturm Graz (0) 0   15,585
Juventus: Storari; Bonucci, Motta, Chiellini, De Ceglie, Sissoko, Felipe Melo (Giandonato 85), Pepe, Martinez, Amauri (Lanzafame 43), Del Piero.
Sturm Graz: Gratzei; Standfest, Burgstaller, Schildenfeld, Ehrenreich (Kainz 62), Purcher, Kienzl, Bukva (Klem 71), Weber, Szabics (Haas 61), Kienast.

Karabakh (0) 0
Borussia Dortmund (0) 1 *(Barrios 90)*   17,000
Karabakh: Veliyev; Rashad F Sadygov, Abbasov (Kerimov 87), Teli, Medvedev, Agolli, Rubins (Karimov 68), Rashad A Sadygov, Adamia (Mammadov E 68), Nadirov, Aliyev.
Borussia Dortmund: Weidenfeller; Owomoyela, Hummels, Subotic, Schmelzer, Kehl, Nuri, Piszczek (Rangelov 76), Kagawa (Lewandowski 61), Barrios, Grosskreutz (Gotze 61).

Karpaty (0) 1 *(Fedetskiy 90)*
Galatasaray (0) 1 *(Aydin 89)*   25,000
Karpaty: Tlumak; Tubic, Milosevic, Khudobyak, Tkachuk, Kozhanov (Kopolovets 79), Golodyuk (Guruli 41), Fedetskiy■, Danilo Avelar, Kuznetsov■, Zenjov (Batista 89).
Galatasaray: Ufuk; Neill, Hakan Balta, Servet, Ali (Emre C 81), Arda, Ayhan, Serdar (Cana 49), Mustafa (Aydin 74), Ozbek, Baros.

Lech (0) 0
Dnepr (0) 0   14,000
Lech: Buric; Henriquez, Wojtkowiak, Arboleda, Djurdjevic, Bandrowski, Krivets (Zapotoka 90), Kikut, Stilic (Drygas 84), Kielb, Tshibamba (Wichniarek 68).
Dnepr: Kanibolotskiy; Rusol, Denisov, Mandzyuk, Cheberyachko, Kalinichenko (Gomenyuk 55), Rotan, Holek, Kravchenko, Seleznev (Gladkiy 61), Konoplyanka.

Levski (0) 2 *(Mladenov 49, Dembele 51)*
AIK Stockholm (1) 1 *(Bangura 11)*   18,300
Levski: Mitrev; Mulder, Minev, Miliev, Ivanov, Gadzhev, Joaozinho, Tasevski (Aleksandrov 66), Yovov (Greene 76), Dembele, Mladenov (Kirov 81).
AIK Stockholm: Turina; Karlsson, Johansson, Backman, Tjernstrom, Pavey, Persson, Danielsson (Ljubojevic 86), Lundberg (Lorentzson 75), Engblom (Antonio Flavio 46), Bangura.

Lille (0) 2 *(Cabaye 69 (pen), Chedjou 80)*
Vaslui (0) 0   16,876
Lille: Landreau; Debuchy, Beria (Emerson 10), Rami, Chedjou, Balmont, Mavuba, Cabaye (Frau 85), Hazard, Sow, Gervinho (Wade 89).
Vaslui: Kuciak■; Milanov, Farkas, Hugo Luz, Papp, Sanmartean, Gheorghiu (Puia 69), Pavlovic (Costin 52), Genchev, Wesley (Pancu 81), Pouga.

Litex (0) 1 *(Niflore 68)*
Debrecen (0) 2 *(Mbengono 53, Czvitkovics 81)*   2500
Litex: Vinicius; Nikolov, Bodurov, Zanev, Petkov, Jelenkovic (Tsvetko 84), Yanev, Sandrinho, Wellington (Bratu 61), Milanov G (Doka Madureira 61), Niflore.
Debrecen: Malinauskas; Mijadinoski, Laczko, Bernath, Komlosi, Czvitkovics, Kiss, Szakaly (Dombi 74), Varga (Mate 90), Kabat (Mbengono 50), Coulibaly.

Lokomotiv Moscow (0) 1 *(Aliyev 85)*
Lausanne (1) 1 *(Silvio 17)*   11,053
Lokomotiv Moscow: Guilherme; Basa, Shishkin, Rodolfo (Loskov 68), Yanbayev, Asatiani (Tarasov 46), Aliyev, Torbinski (Maicon 77), Gatagov, Traore, Sychev.
Lausanne: Favre (Castejon 90); Sonnerat, Meoli, Katz, Celestini, Marazzi, Abdul Carrupt, Avanzini (Kilinc 78), Traore, Munsy (Rodrigo 51), Silvio.
aet; Lausanne won 4-3 on penalties.

Maccabi Tel Aviv (0) 4 *(Atar 48, 90, Avidor 68,*
Medunjanin 83 (pen))
Paris St Germain (1) 3 *(Hoarau 40 (pen), Giuly 64,*
Nene 89 (pen))   8674
Maccabi Tel Aviv: Strauber; Pavicevic, Ziv, Strul, Saban, Medunjanin, Sidibc, Ycini (Malul 65), Colautti (Avidor 46), Atar, Buzaglo (Kahlon 79).
Paris St Germain: Edel; Jallet, Armand, Sakho (Camara 78), Makonda, Clement, Nene, Chantome, Luyindula, Giuly, Hoarau (Maurice 67).

Manchester C (1) 2 *(Wright-Phillips 43, Boyata 59)*
Timisoara (0) 0   23,542
Manchester C: Hart; Richards, Zabaleta, De Jong (Cunningham 64), Boyata, Kompany, Wright-Phillips, Vieira, Adebayor, Jo, Silva.
Timisoara: Pantilimon; Sepsi, Burca, Luchin, Mera, Contra, Alexa (Chiacu 82), Curtean (Goga 57), Bourceanu, Magera (Zicu 46), Axente.

Maribor (1) 3 *(Marcos Tavares 14, Ilicic 58, Andelkovic 89)*
Palermo (0) 2 *(Hernandez 62, 68)*   12,200
Maribor: Randan; Rajcevic, Viler, Andelkovic, Cvijanovic (Beric 72), Mezga, Bacinovic, Mertelj, Ilicic (Jelic 79), Marcos Tavares, Volas (Plut 72).
Palermo: Sirigu; Cassani, Bovo, Balzaretti, Munoz, Liverani (Rigoni 70), Migliaccio, Nocerino, Pastore, Maccarone (Kasami 57), Hernandez (Pinilla 76).

Maritimo (0) 1 *(Kanu 89)*
BATE Borisov (0) 2 *(Pavlov 52, Skavysh 90)*   2073
Maritimo: Marcelo Boeck; Briguel, Luciano Amaral, Robson, Joao Guilherme, Roberto De Sousa, Rafael Miranda (Adilson 60), Djalma Campos (Kanu 64), Cherrad (Marquinho 46), Baba, Danilo Dias.
BATE Borisov: Gutor; Radkov, Yurevich, Bordachev, Shitov, Likhtarovich (Skavysh 70), Renan (Baga 66), Pavlov, Olekhnovich, Rodionov, Kontsevoy (Patotski 85).

Metalist Kharkiv (0) 2 *(Devic 67, Cleiton Xavier 71)*
Omonia (0) 2 *(Leandro 59, Rengifo 63)*   30,360
Metalist Kharkiv: Startsev; Fininho, Villagra, Obradovic, Romanchuk, Berezovchuk (Bordian 87), Shelayev (Oleynik 67), Cleiton Xavier (Pshenichnikh 89), Valyaev, Edmar, Devic.
Omonia: Georgallides; Iago Bouzon, Charalambous I (Victor 86), Wenzel, Leandro, Davidson Morais, Makridis (Aloneftis 76), Kaseke (Jose Manuel Rueda 80), Efrem, Avraam, Rengifo.

Motherwell (0) 0
Odense (0) 1 *(Utaka 28)*   9105
Motherwell: Randolph; Saunders, Hammell, Reynolds, Craigan, Hateley, Humphrey, Lasley, Sutton, Murphy, Blackman.
Odense: Carroll; Haland (Johansson 53), Ruud■, Moller Christensen■, Sorensen, Gislason, Djemba-Djemba, Andreasen, Traore, Toft (Demba-Nyren 66), Utaka (Kadrii 88).

Porto (1) 4 *(Hulk 36, 59 (pen), 63, Fernando 53)*
Genk (0) 2 *(Vossen 22, 56)*   33,512
Porto: Beto; Sapunaru, Rolando, Maicon, Joao Moutinho (Belluschi 62), Souza, Alvaro Pereira, Fernando, Ruben Micael (Castro 73), Falcao (Silvestre Varela 56), Hulk.
Genk: Koteles; Daeseleire, Ngcongca, Durwael, Tozser, Camus, Pudil, Ndabashinze, Huysegems (De Bruyne 81), Vossen (Ogunjimi 63), Yeboah (Aquino 74).

PSV Eindhoven (1) 5 *(Berg 38, Engelaar 56,*
Toivonen 64, Dzsudzsak 73, 90 (pen))
Sibir (0) 0 20,900
PSV Eindhoven: Isaksson; Pieters, Marcelo, Vukovic,
Manolev, Engelaar, Hutchinson, Lens (Amrabat 86), Berg
(Koevermans 71), Toivonen (Bakkal 80), Dzsudzsak.
Sibir: Solosin; Bukhryakov, Vychodil, Joseph-Reinette,
Shumulikoski (Klimavicius 71), Astafyev, Degtyarev,
Aravin, Zinovyev (Cisek 73), Canas, Belyaev (Vasilyev 66).

Stuttgart (0) 2 *(Gebhart 56, Gentner 64)*
Slovan Bratislava (1) 2 *(Dobrotka 9, Sylvestr 53)* 12,100
Stuttgart: Ulreich; Boulahrouz, Molinaro, Niedermeier,
Trasch, Gentner, Gebhart (Funk 89), Kuzmanovic,
Didavi (Audel 68), Cacau, Marica (Harnik 46).
Slovan Bratislava: Putnocky; Salata, Janosik (Slovak 75),
Dobrotka, Bagayoko, Guede, Bozic, Grendel
(Stepanovsky 88), Breznanik■, Ivana (Kiss 75), Sylvestr.

Tavirya (1) 1 *(Idahor 5 (pen))*
Leverkusen (0) 3 *(Vidal 50 (pen), Golaydo 74 (og),*
Castro 90) 10,700
Tavirya: Postransky; Markovic, Monakhov, Kornev,
Lutsenko (Platon 57), Galyuza, Ljubenovic, Golaydo,
Mukhovykov (Messias 34), Kovpak, Idahor (Feshchuk
80).
Leverkusen: Adler; Friedrich, Schwaab, Vidal, Reinartz,
Castro, Barnetta (Kadlec 77), Balitsch, Bender, Kaplan
(Renato Augusto 46), Derdiyok (Jorgensen 79).

The New Saints (1) 2 *(Williams M 14, Evans 61)*
CSKA Sofia (1) 2 *(Aquaro 11, Tiboni 79)* 843
The New Saints: Harrison; Evans, Baker, Holmes T,
Holmes D, Jones C (Wood 83), Hogan, Ruscoe,
Seargeant, Williams M■, Sharp (Berkeley 85).

CSKA Sofia: Karadzhov; Trifonov, Vidanov, Aquaro,
Yanev, Yanchev, Tonev (Delev 77), Tiboni, Nelson
(Kostadinov 86), Iliev (Marquinhos 58), Sheridan.
at Wrexham.

Trabzonspor (1) 1 *(Gutierrez 4)*
Liverpool (0) 2 *(Remzi Giray 83 (og), Kuyt 88)* 18,630
Trabzonspor: Onur; Egemen, Remzi, Cale (Jaja Coelho
87), Serkan, Burak, Yattara (Alanzinho 46), Selcuk,
Colman, Ceyhun (Baris 65), Gutierrez.
Liverpool: Reina; Johnson, Kyrgiakos, Fabio Aurelio
(Pacheco 77), Carragher, Kelly, Poulsen (Skrtel 90),
Lucas, N'Gog (Babel 86), Kuyt, Cole.

Unirea (1) 1 *(Bilasco 2)*
Hajduk Split (0) 1 *(Vukusic 88)* 918
Unirea: Grigore; Maftei■, Mehmedovic, Galamaz, Nicu,
Bordeanu, Brandan, Neaga (Dale 78), Onofras, Bilasco,
Rusescu (Frunza 64).
Hajduk Split: Subasic; Jozinovic, Buljat, Maloca, Anas
Sharbini (Jonjic 76), Andric, Tomasov (Vejic 46),
Brkljaca■, Ibricic, Oremus, Vukusic (Cop 89).

Utrecht (2) 4 *(Van Wolfswinkel 11 (pen), 18 (pen), 46,*
Maguire 62)
Celtic (0) 0 18,000
Utrecht: Vorm; Wuytens, Schut, Cornelisse, Nesu,
Silberbauer, Lensky, Asare (Maguire 53), Duplan,
Mertens (Nijholt 75), Van Wolfswinkel (Oar 90).
Celtic: Zaluska; Cha, Juarez (Ki 65), Brown (Maloney
51), Majstorovic, Hooiveld, Kayal, Ledley, Samaras
(McCourt 72), Fortune, Forrest.

GROUP STAGE

GROUP A

Thursday, 16 September 2010

Juventus (1) 3 *(Chiellini 44, 50, Del Piero 68)*
Lech (2) 3 *(Rudnevs 14 (pen), 30, 90)* 10,837
Juventus: Manninger; Grygera, Chiellini, Legrottaglie, De
Ceglie (Motta 44), Sissoko, Felipe Melo, Krasic,
Lazafame (Pepe 55), Iaquinta (Marchisio 79), Del Piero.
Lech: Kotorowski; Henriquez, Wojtkowiak, Arboleda,
Djurdjevic, Injac, Peszko (Wichniarek 73), Krivets, Kikut
(Wilk 81), Stilic (Tshibamba 80), Rudnevs.

Salzburg (0) 0
Manchester C (1) 2 *(Silva 8, Jo 63)* 25,100
Salzburg: Tremmel; Afolabi, Schiemer, Sekagya,
Schwegler, Mendes da Silva (Augustinussen 74), Svento,
Pokrivac (Jantscher 55), Leitgeb, Zarate, Boghossian
(Wallner 54).
Manchester C: Hart; Zabaleta, Bridge (Boyata 68), De
Jong, Toure K, Kompany, Silva (Wright-Phillips 84),
Toure Y, Jo, Tevez (Vieira 79), Barry.

Thursday, 30 September 2010

Lech (0) 2 *(Arboleda 47, Peszko 80)*
Salzburg (0) 0 42,000
Lech: Buric; Bosacki, Henriquez, Wojtkowiak (Kielb 53),
Arboleda, Injac (Drygas 86), Peszko, Krivets, Kikut,
Stilic, Rudnevs (Wichniarek 82).
Salzburg: Tremmel; Afolabi, Schiemer, Sekagya,
Schwegler, Cziommer (Wallner 77), Mendes da Silva,
Svento, Leitgeb (Boghossian 77), Zarate (Jantscher 57),
Alan.

Manchester C (1) 1 *(Johnson A 37)*
Juventus (1) 1 *(Iaquinta 11)* 35,212
Manchester C: Hart; Boateng (Milner 84), Zabaleta
(Boyata 46), Vieira, Toure K, Kompany, Barry, Toure Y,
Adebayor (Silva 74), Tevez, Johnson A.
Juventus: Manninger; Grygera, Bonucci, Chiellini, De
Ceglie (Motta 72), Sissoko, Krasic (Felipe Melo 75),
Martinez (Pepe 54), Marchisio, Iaquinta, Del Piero.

Thursday, 21 October 2010

Manchester C (2) 3 *(Adebayor 13, 25, 73)*
Lech (0) 1 *(Tshibamba 50)* 33,388
Manchester C: Hart; Richards, Zabaleta (Bridge 85), De
Jong, Boyata, Lescott, Wright-Phillips (Jo 77), Vieira,
Adebayor, Silva (Toure Y 74), Johnson A
Lech: Buric; Bosacki, Henriquez, Arboleda (Djurdjevic
70), Injac, Wilk (Stilic 56), Peszko, Krivets, Kikut, Drygas
(Rudnevs 55), Tshibamba.

Salzburg (1) 1 *(Svento 36)*
Juventus (0) 1 *(Krasic 48)* 19,200
Salzburg: Tremmel; Afolabi, Schiemer, Sekagya,
Schwegler, Hinteregger, Mendes da Silva (Leitgeb 52),
Svento, Pokrivac, Wallner, Zarate (Jantscher 82).
Juventus: Manninger; Grygera (Motta 80), Bonucci,
Chiellini, De Ceglie, Sissoko, Pepe (Krasic 46), Martinez
(Felipe Melo 64), Marchisio, Del Piero, Amauri.

Thursday, 4 November 2010

Juventus (0) 0
Salzburg (0) 0 14,000
Juventus: Storari; Bonucci, Motta, Legrottaglie, Sissoko,
Pepe (Giannetti 83), Krasic (Buchel 62), Marchisio,
Giandonato (Liviero 51), Amauri, Del Piero.
Salzburg: Tremmel; Afolabi, Schiemer, Sekagya,
Schwegler, Hinteregger, Mendes da Silva (Augustinussen
80), Pokrivac (Leitgeb 65), Jantscher, Wallner (Alan 74),
Zarate.

Lech (2) 3 *(Injac 30, Arboleda 36, Mozdzen 90)*
Manchester C (0) 1 *(Adebayor 51)* 43,000
Lech: Buric; Bosacki, Henriquez, Arboleda, Djurdjevic,
Injac (Kielb 52), Peszko (Wilk 73), Krivets, Kikut, Stilic
(Mozdzen 62), Rudnevs.
Manchester C: Given; Richards, Bridge (Kolarov 70),
Vieira, Lescott, Zabaleta, Wright-Phillips (Silva 46),
Boyata, Milner (Kompany 78), Adebayor, Johnson A.

Wednesday, 1 December 2010
Lech (1) 1 *(Rudnevs 12)*
Juventus (0) 1 *(Iaquinta 84)* 42,590
Lech: Kotorowski; Bozacki, Henriquez, Wojtkowiak, Arboleda, Djurdjevic, Injac, Peszko, Krivets (Kikut 54), Stilic (Kaminski 83), Rudnevs (Mozdzen 61).
Juventus: Manninger; Bonucci, Traore (Libertazzi 80), Chiellini, Camilleri, Sissoko (Felipe Melo 75), Pepe (Lanzafame 67), Krasic, Marchisio, Iaquinta, Del Piero.

Manchester C (1) 3 *(Balotelli 18, 65, Johnson 78)*
Salzburg (0) 0 37,552
Manchester C: Given; Zabaleta, Boateng, Vieira, Toure K (Richards 81), Lescott, Wright-Phillips, Milner, Balotelli (Adebayor 71), Jo, Johnson.
Salzburg: Tremmel; Afolabi, Schiemer, Sekagya, Hinteregger (Svento 46), Cziommer (Alan 57), Mendes da Silva (Augustinussen 67), Jantscher, Leitgeb, Hierlander, Boghossian.

Thursday, 16 December 2010
Juventus (1) 1 *(Giannetti 43)*
Manchester C (0) 1 *(Jo 77)* 6992
Juventus: Manninger; Grygera, Traore (Boniperti 67), Chiellini, Legrottaglie, Sissoko, Felipe Melo, Pepe, Krasic (Camilleri 57), Del Piero, Giannetti (Buchel 79).
Manchester C: Given; Boateng, Bridge, Vieira, Richards, Boyata, Wright-Phillips (Chantler 90), Milner, Jo, Tchuimeni-Nimely (Zabaleta 61), Johnson A.

Salzburg (0) 0
Lech (1) 1 *(Stilic 30)* 5300
Salzburg: Walke; Afolabi, Schiemer, Sekagya, Hinteregger, Cziommer, Mendes da Silva, Jantscher (Hierlander 68), Offenbacher (Alan 58), Zarate, Boghossian (Wallner 74).
Lech: Kotorowski; Bosacki, Henriquez (Wilk 36), Arboleda, Djurdjevic (Wojtkowiak 46), Injac, Peszko, Krivets, Kikut, Stilic (Bandrowski 76), Rudnevs.

Group A Table	P	W	D	L	F	A	Pts
Manchester C	6	3	2	1	11	6	11
Lech	6	3	2	1	11	8	11
Juventus	6	0	6	0	7	7	6
Salzburg	6	0	2	4	1	9	2

GROUP B

Thursday, 16 September 2010
Aris Salonika (0) 1 *(Javito 59)*
Atletico Madrid (0) 0 23,225
Aris Salonika: Sifakis; Michel, Ronaldo, Vangjeli, Lazaridis, Faty, Prittas, Mendrinos, Koke, Ruiz (Kaznaferis 90), Javito.
Atletico Madrid: De Gea; Antonio Lopez, Valera, Godin, Alvaro Dominguez, Simao, Tiago, Raul Garcia (Diego Costa 46), Fran Merida (Reyes 60), Camacho (Mario Suarez 77), Forlan.

Leverkusen (2) 4 *(Helmes 4, 58, 61, Reinartz 38)*
Rosenborg (0) 0 13,065
Leverkusen: Adler; Friedrich, Hyypia, Schwaab, Reinartz, Castro (Vida 78), Sam, Bender (Balitsch 67), Derdiyok (Barnetta 78), Helmes, Jorgensen.
Rosenborg: Orlund; Bjarsmyr, Dorsin, Lustig, Demidov, Annan, Strand (Sare 56), Skjelbred, Henriksen (Jamtfall 72), Iversen (Olsen 79), Prica.

Thursday, 30 September 2010
Atletico Madrid (0) 1 *(Simao 51)*
Leverkusen (1) 1 *(Derdiyok 39)* 28,052
Atletico Madrid: De Gea; Ujfalusi, Perea, Filipe Luis, Alvaro Dominguez, Reyes, Simao, Raul Garcia (Tiago 46), Assuncao, Forlan (Fran Merida 46), Diego Costa.
Leverkusen: Adler; Friedrich, Hyypia, Kadlec, Schwaab, Reinartz, Barnetta, Balitsch (Rolfes 61), Vidal (Bender 62), Sam, Derdiyok (Helmes 68).

Rosenborg (1) 2 *(Moldskred 37, Prica 68)*
Aris (1) 1 *(Ruiz 43)* 11,016
Rosenborg: Orlund; Bjarsmyr, Dorsin, Lustig, Demidov, Annan, Skjelbred, Henriksen, Iversen, Moldskred (Olsen 90), Prica (Jamtfall 86).
Aris: Sifakis; Michel, Ronaldo, Vangjeli, Lazaridis, Faty (Toja 70), Prittas, Calvo (Cesnauskis 82), Koke, Ruiz (Cesarec 63), Javito.

Thursday, 21 October 2010
Aris Salonika (0) 0
Leverkusen (0) 0 16,372
Aris Salonika: Sifakis; Michel, Ronaldo, Vangjeli, Lazaridis, Faty, Toja, Calvo, Koke (Mendrinos 70), Ruiz, Javito.
Leverkusen: Adler; Friedrich, Kadlec, Vida, Reinartz, Balitsch (Vidal 61), Rolfes (Derdiyok 76), Bender, Kaplan, Helmes, Jorgensen (Barnetta 60).

Atletico Madrid (1) 3 *(Godin 17, Aguero 66, Diego Costa 78)*
Rosenborg (0) 0 28,472
Atletico Madrid: Joel; Ujfalusi, Valera (Perea 21), Filipe Luis, Godin, Reyes, Simao, Tiago (Raul Garcia 71), Assuncao, Forlan (Aguero 65), Diego Costa.
Rosenborg: Orlund; Bjarsmyr, Dorsin, Lustig, Demidov, Annan, Skjelbred (Sare 69), Henriksen, Iversen (Jamtfall 82), Moldskred, Prica.

Thursday, 4 November 2010
Leverkusen (0) 1 *(Vidal 90)*
Aris Salonika (0) 0 18,265
Leverkusen: Adler; Friedrich, Kadlec, Reinartz, Balitsch, Vidal, Sam, Bender (Derdiyok 46), Kaplan (Barnetta 63), Helmes, Jorgensen (Rolfes 46).
Aris Salonika: Sifakis; Michel, Ronaldo, Vangjeli, Lazaridis, Faty, Toja, Calvo (Kaznaferis 79), Koke (Prittas 90), Ruiz (Cesnauskis 57), Javito.

Rosenborg (0) 1 *(Henriksen 52)*
Atletico Madrid (1) 2 *(Aguero 4, Tiago 84)* 14,250
Rosenborg: Orlund; Bjarsmyr, Dorsin, Lustig, Demidov, Annan (Sare 61), Skjelbred, Henriksen, Iversen, Moldskred, Prica.
Atletico Madrid: De Gea; Ujfalusi, Antonio Lopez, Perea, Alvaro Dominguez, Simao, Tiago, Raul Garcia, Assuncao (Mario Suarez 71), Aguero (Forlan 61), Diego Costa (Camacho 90).

Wednesday, 1 December 2010
Atletico Madrid (2) 2 *(Forlan 11, Aguero 16)*
Aris Salonika (1) 3 *(Koke 2, 51 (pen), Lazaridis 81)* 21,154
Atletico Madrid: De Gea; Ujfalusi, Antonio Lopez (Raul Garcia 86), Godin, Alvaro Dominguez, Reyes, Simao (Diego Costa 74), Tiago (Fran Merida 86), Mario Suarez, Aguero, Forlan.
Aris Salonika: Sifakis; Oriol, Michel, Vangjeli, Lazaridis, Faty, Toja, Mendrinos (Kaznaferis 71), Koke (Prittas 77), Javito, Cesarec (Ruiz 83).

Rosenborg (0) 0
Leverkusen (1) 1 *(Sam 35)* 11,096
Rosenborg: Orlund; Bjarsmyr, Dorsin, Lustig, Demidov, Annan, Skjelbred, Henriksen, Iversen, Moldskred, Prica.
Leverkusen: Giefer; Friedrich, Hyypia, Kadlec, Vida, Reinartz, Balitsch, Sam (Kaplan 68), Bender, Helmes (Castro 85), Jorgensen (Derdiyok 76).

Thursday, 16 December 2010
Aris Salonika (1) 2 *(Cesarec 45, Faty 90)*
Rosenborg (0) 0 17,283
Aris Salonika: Sifakis; Michel, Koulocheris, Vangjeli, Lazaridis, Toja, Prittas, Mendrinos (Kaznaferis 83), Koke (Faty 87), Javito, Cesarec (Ruiz 78).
Rosenborg: Orlund; Bjarsmyr, Dorsin, Lustig, Demidov, Annan, Skjelbred, Jamtfall (Iversen 66), Henriksen, Moldskred, Prica.

Leverkusen (0) 1 *(Helmes 69)*
Atletico Madrid (0) 1 *(Fran Merida 72)*   18,903
Leverkusen: Giefer; Hyypia, Schwaab, Vida, Castro (Da Costa 46), Balitsch, Renato Augusto (Kiessling 46), Bender (Vidal 88), Kaplan, Helmes, Jorgensen.
Atletico Madrid: De Gea; Perea, Valera, Filipe Luis, Alvaro Dominguez, Simao (Fran Merida 71), Mario Suarez (Tiago 85), Raul Garcia, Assuncao, Aguero, Forlan (Diego Costa 67).

Group B Table	P	W	D	L	F	A	Pts
Leverkusen	6	3	3	0	8	2	12
Aris Salonika	6	3	1	2	7	5	10
Atletico Madrid	6	2	2	2	9	7	8
Rosenborg	6	1	0	5	3	13	3

GROUP C

Thursday, 16 September 2010
Levski (1) 3 *(Joaozinho 43, Dembele 60, Greene 84)*
Gent (1) 2 *(Azofeifa 24, Suler 49)*   22,240
Levski: Petkov; Mulder, Benzokane, Minev, Ivanov, Greene, Aleksandrov (Ognyanov 76), Joaozinho, Tasevski (Isa 69), Dembele, Mladenov (Kirov 90).
Gent: Jorgacevic; Wils, Suler, Wallace, Baric, Thijs, Grondin (Smolders 78), Azofeifa, Soumahoro (El Ghanassy 66), De Smet (Arbeitman 68), Ljubijankic.

Lille (0) 1 *(Frau 57)*
Sporting Lisbon (2) 2 *(Vukcevic 11, Helder Postiga 34)*   16,350
Lille: Landreau; Rozehnal, Debuchy, Rami, Vandam (Emerson 39), Balmont, Mavuba (Cabaye 73), Dumont (Hazard 39), Obraniak, Frau, Gervinho.
Sporting Lisbon: Tiago; Polga, Torsiglieri, Abel, Daniel Carrico, Zapater, Vukcevic (Joao Pereira 73), Andre Santos, Helder Postiga, Saleiro (Nuno Andre Coelho 90), Diogo Salomao (Evaldo 82).

Thursday, 30 September 2010
Gent (1) 1 *(De Smet 5)*
Lille (1) 1 *(Frau 21)*   7843
Gent: Jorgacevic; Wils, Suler, Conte (Ljubijankic 65), Skarabot, Baric, Smolders, Azofeifa, De Smet (Arbeitman 84), Coulibaly, El Ghanassy.
Lille: Landreau; Rozehnal, Debuchy, Emerson, Chedjou, Balmont, Cabaye (Sow 84), Obraniak, Hazard, Gueye (Rami 78), Frau (Gervinho 69).

Sporting Lisbon (2) 5 *(Daniel Carrico 30, Maniche 43, Diogo Salomao 53, Helder Postiga 61, Matias Fernandez 79)*
Levski (0) 0   15,801
Sporting Lisbon: Rui Patricio; Polga, Joao Pereira, Evaldo, Daniel Carrico, Maniche (Andre Santos 70), Zapater, Vukcevic (Abel 77), Matias Fernandez, Helder Postiga (Saleiro 64), Diogo Salomao.
Levski: Petkov; Mulder, Minev, Miliev, Ivanov, Greene, Joaozinho (Kirov 79), Tasevski, Yovov (Ognyanov 67), Dembele, Mladenov (Slory 56).

Thursday, 21 October 2010
Lille (0) 1 *(Chedjou 50)*
Levski (0) 0   14,646
Lille: Landreau; Rozehnal, Beria, Chedjou, Vandam, Balmont (Mavuba 80), Dumont, Obraniak, Hazard (Gervinho 71), Gueye, Frau (Sow 55).
Levski: Mitrev; Mulder, Minev, Miliev, Ivanov, Greene, Gadzhev, Joaozinho, Ognyanov (Isa 63), Dembele, Mladenov (Slory 72).

Sporting Lisbon (4) 5 *(Diogo Salomao 6, Liedson 13, 27, Maniche 37, Helder Postiga 60)*
Gent (1) 1 *(Wils 15)*   15,008
Sporting Lisbon: Hildebrand; Polga (Torsiglieri 44), Abel, Joao Pereira, Evaldo, Daniel Carrico, Maniche (Zapater 63), Andre Santos, Helder Postiga, Liedson (Vukcevic 73), Diogo Salomao.
Gent: Jorgacevic; Hanstveit, Wils, Conte, Skarabot, Baric (Grondin 46), Thijs, Smolders (Coulibaly 46), Azofeifa, Ljubijankic, El Ghanassy (Soumahoro 67).

Thursday, 4 November 2010
Gent (1) 3 *(Smolders 7 (pen), Conte 79, Arbeitman 82)*
Sporting Lisbon (1) 1 *(Saleiro 39)*   8795
Gent: Jorgacevic; Wils (Hanstveit 28), Suler, Wallace, Baric, Thijs, Smolders, De Smet (Conte 73), Ljubijankic, Coulibaly (Arbeitman 66), El Ghanassy.
Sporting Lisbon: Hildebrand; Torsiglieri, Abel*, Evaldo, Nuno Andre Coelho, Cedric (Helder Postiga 59), Zapater, Andre Santos, Yannick Djalo, Saleiro (Valdes 68), Diogo Salomao (Joao Pereira 79).

Levski (1) 2 *(Dembele 11, Gadzhev 82)*
Lille (1) 2 *(De Melo 35, Ivanov 88 (og))*   21,000
Levski: Akalski; Mulder, Minev, Miliev, Greene, Gadzhev, Joaozinho, Tasevski (Ivanov 87), Yovov (Ognyanov 60), Slory (Mladenov 58), Dembele.
Lille: Landreau; Rozehnal, Beria, Chedjou, Souare, Mavuba (Cabaye 56), Dumont, Obraniak, Gueye, De Melo (Hazard 76), Gervinho (Sow 57).

Wednesday, 1 December 2010
Gent (0) 1 *(Wallace 77)*
Levski (0) 0   8662
Gent: Jorgacevic; Wils, Suler, Wallace, Baric, Thijs, Smolders, Azofeifa (Lepoint 90), Ljubijankic, Arbeitman, El Ghanassy.
Levski: Mitrev; Mulder (Stanchev 46), Minev, Miliev, Greene, Gadzhev, Baltanov (Ognyanov 53), Joaozinho, Yovov, Dembele, Mladenov (Isa 77).

Sporting Lisbon (1) 1 *(Polga 28)*
Lille (0) 0   16,569
Sporting Lisbon: Rui Patricio; Polga, Joao Pereira, Evaldo, Daniel Carrico, Maniche (Zapater 90), Pedro Mendes, Andre Santos, Helder Postiga (Vukcevic 80), Liedson, Yannick Djalo (Valdes 62).
Lille: Landreau; Rozehnal, Emerson, Beria, Chedjou, Balmont (Cabaye 78), Mavuba, Obraniak, Hazard (Sow 72), Gueye (Frau 62), De Melo.

Thursday, 16 December 2010
Levski (1) 1 *(Mladenov 45)*
Sporting Lisbon (0) 0   5000
Levski: Mitrev; Mulder, Miliev, Ivanov, Shtarkov, Greene, Gadzhev (Baltanov 90), Joaozinho, Tasevski (Ognyanov 77), Dembele, Mladenov (Kirov 89).
Sporting Lisbon: Tiago; Torsiglieri, Abel, Evaldo, Nuno Andre Coelho (Cedric 76), Maniche, Zapater (Diogo Salomao 46), Andre Santos, Helder Postiga, Yannick Djalo, Valdes (Saleiro 70).

Lille (1) 3 *(Obraniak 30, Frau 56, Sow 89)*
Gent (0) 0   15,285
Lille: Landreau; Rozehnal, Debuchy, Emerson, Rami, Balmont (Beria 85), Cabaye, Obraniak, Hazard (Sow 61), Frau (Mavuba 72), De Melo.
Gent: Jorgacevic; Wils, Suler, Wallace, Thijs, Smolders, Azofeifa (Conte 46), Lepoint, Ljubijankic, Coulibaly (Arbeitman 63), El Ghanassy (Soumahoro 63).

Group C Table	P	W	D	L	F	A	Pts
Sporting Lisbon	6	4	0	2	14	6	12
Lille	6	2	2	2	8	6	8
Gent	6	2	1	3	8	13	7
Levski	6	2	1	3	6	11	7

GROUP D

Thursday, 16 September 2010
Club Brugge (0) 1 *(Kouemaha 61)*
PAOK Salonika (0) 1 *(Malezas 78)*   17,525
Club Brugge: Stijnen; Donk, Vermeulen (Simaeys 24), Hoefkens, Diaz, Dirar, Geraerts, Odjidja-Ofoe, Perisic, Dalmat (Vargas 80), Kouemaha.
PAOK Salonika: Kresic; Contreras, Sznaucer, Malezas, Vitolo, Garcia, Lino, Vierinha, Ivic (Fotakis 88), Papazoglou (El Zhar 74), Salpingidis (Filomeno 90).

Dinamo Zagreb (1) 2 *(Rukavina 18, Sammir 80)*
Villarreal (0) 0   22,000
Dinamo Zagreb: Kelava; Cufre, Tonel, Biscan, Sammir (Beciraj 87), Ademi, Morales (Chago 56), Tomecak, Badelj, Vrsaljko, Rukavina (Ibanez 72).
Villarreal: Diego Lopez; Gonzalo, Musacchio, Capdevila, Mario Gaspar, Senna■, Cani (Cazorla 63), Bruno (Rossi 47), Altidore, Marco Ruben (Borja Valero 47), Jefferson Montero.

Thursday, 30 September 2010
PAOK Salonika (0) 1 *(Ivic 56)*
Dinamo Zagreb (0) 0   17,927
PAOK Salonika: Kresic; Cirillo (Zuela 62), Contreras, Sznaucer, Boussaidi (Sakellariou 15), Vitolo, Garcia, Vieirinha, Ivic, Muslimovic, El Zhar (Salpingidis 80).
Dinamo Zagreb: Kelava; Cufre, Tonel, Etto (Tomecak 71), Biscan, Ibanez (Morales 77), Chago, Sammir, Badelj, Vrsaljko, Rukavina (Beciraj 83).

Villarreal (1) 2 *(Rossi 41, Gonzalo 56)*
Club Brugge (1) 1 *(Donk 45)*   14,900
Villarreal: Diego Lopez; Marchena, Gonzalo, Angel, Capdevila, Cani (Jefferson Montero 34), Cazorla, Borja Valero, Bruno, Rossi (Matilla 75), Altidore (Marco Ruben 86).
Club Brugge: De Vlieger (Coosemans 60); Donk, Simaeys, Camozzato, Hoefkens, Diaz, Blondel (Van Gijseghem 86), Geraerts, Odjidja-Ofoe (Dirar 77), Perisic, Vargas■.

Thursday, 21 October 2010
Dinamo Zagreb (0) 0
Club Brugge (0) 0   17,270
Dinamo Zagreb: Kelava; Cufre, Tonel, Biscan, Chago, Sammir, Ademi (Tomecak 69), Morales (Ibanez 87), Badelj, Vrsaljko, Rukavina (Beciraj 79).
Club Brugge: De Vlieger; Simaeys, Camozzato, Hoefkens, Diaz, Dirar, Geraerts, Odjidja-Ofoe, Perisic, Dalmat, Kouemaha.

Villarreal (1) 1 *(Marco Ruben 38)*
PAOK Salonika (0) 0   14,760
Villarreal: Diego Lopez; Gonzalo, Angel, Musacchio, Capdevila, Cani, Cazorla (Jefferson Montero 77), Borja Valero, Bruno, Rossi (Nilmar 70), Marco Ruben (Altidore 82).
PAOK Salonika: Kresic; Cirillo, Contreras, Sznaucer, Boussaidi, Fotakis, Vitolo, Vieirinha, Ivic, Muslimovic (Athanasiadis 80), El Zhar (Koutsianikoulis 85).

Thursday, 4 November 2010
Club Brugge (0) 0
Dinamo Zagreb (0) 2 *(Sammir 55, Biscan 59)*   17,751
Club Brugge: De Vlieger; Donk, Simaeys, Camozzato (Scepovic 74), Hoefkens, Diaz (Van der Heyden 53), Blondel, Geraerts, Perisic, Dalmat (Lestienne 46), Kouemaha.
Dinamo Zagreb: Kelava; Cufre, Tonel, Biscan, Ibanez, Calello (Barbaric 80), Chago, Sammir, Badelj, Vrsaljko (Etto 72), Beciraj (Ademi 90).

PAOK Salonika (0) 1 *(Vierinha 70)*
Villarreal (0) 0   26,000
PAOK Salonika: Kresic; Cirillo, Contreras, Boussaidi, Sakellariou, Fotakis (Filomeno 90), Vitolo, Garcia, Vieirinha, Ivic (El Zhar 40), Salpingidis (Muslimovic 65).
Villarreal: Diego Lopez; Marchena, Gonzalo, Angel, Musacchio (Jefferson Montero 72), Capdevila, Cani (Cazorla 68), Borja Valero, Bruno, Altidore (Rossi 63), Nilmar.

Wednesday, 1 December 2010
PAOK Salonika (1) 1 *(Vierinha 25)*
Club Brugge (0) 1 *(Scepovic 89)*   19,424
PAOK Salonika: Kresic; Cirillo, Contreras, Sakellariou, Fotakis, Vitolo, Garcia, Vierinha, Ivic (El Zhar 72), Zuela, Salpingidis (Athanasidis 82).
Club Brugge: Stijnen; Van der Heyden, Donk, Simaeys, Vermeulen (Odjidja-Ofoe 71), Van Gijseghem, Blondel,

Geraerts, Perisic (Dalmat 62), Akpala (Dirar 62), Scepovic.

Villarreal (1) 3 *(Rossi 25 (pen), 80, Marco Ruben 62)*
Dinamo Zagreb (0) 0   11,911
Villarreal: Diego Lopez; Marchena, Angel, Musacchio, Catala, Cani, Cazorla, Borja Valero (Nilmar 79), Bruno, Rossi (Jefferson Montero 82), Marco Ruben (Senna 63).
Dinamo Zagreb: Kelava; Cufre, Tonel, Biscan■, Ibanez, Calello, Sammir (Rukavina 71), Ademi (Morales 79), Badelj, Vrsaljko, Beciraj (Barbaric 89).

Wednesday, 15 December 2010
Club Brugge (1) 1 *(Kouemaha 28)*
Villarreal (2) 2 *(Rossi 30, 34 (pen))*   16,265
Club Brugge: De Vlieger; Donk, Simaeys, Van Gijseghem, Camozzato, Blondel, Odjidja-Ofoe (Van der Heyden 73), Perisic (Lestienne 65), Vargas (Dirar 66), Dalmat, Kouemaha.
Villarreal: Diego Lopez; Gonzalo, Musacchio, Capdevila, Senna, Cani (Borja Valero 60), Cazorla (Angel 82),Bruno, Marcos Gullon, Rossi, Marco Ruben (Altidore 78).

Dinamo Zagreb (0) 0
PAOK Salonika (0) 1 *(Salpingidis 60)*   29,226
Dinamo Zagreb: Kelava; Cufre, Tonel, Etto (Kramaric 75), Barbaric, Calello (Rukavina 59), Sammir, Ademi (Slepicka 67), Tomecak, Badelj, Beciraj.
PAOK Salonika: Chalkias; Cirillo, Contreras, Sznaucer, Boussaidi, Fotakis (Balafas 90), Vitolo, Garcia, Vieirinha, Salpingidis (El Zhar 68), Athanasiadis (Filomeno 82).

Group D Table

	P	W	D	L	F	A	Pts
Villarreal	6	4	0	2	8	5	12
PAOK Salonika	6	3	2	1	5	3	11
Dinamo Zagreb	6	2	1	3	4	5	7
Club Brugge	6	0	3	3	4	8	3

GROUP E

Thursday, 16 September 2010
AZ (1) 2 *(Gudmundsson 14, Jaliens 83)*
Serif (0) 1 *(Moreno 68 (og))*   10,624
AZ: Didulica; Jaliens, Klavan (Poulsen 46), Marcellis, Moreno, Martens, Schaars, Wernbloom, Elm, Falkenburg (Jonathas 60), Gudmundsson (Sigthorsson 77).
Serif: Stoyanov; Adamovic (Gauracs 88), Samardzic, Jose Nadson, Brankovic, Erokhin (Fred 62), Rouamba, Nikolic, Balima, Diedhiou, Jymmy Franca (Durovic 69).

Dynamo Kiev (2) 2 *(Milevskiy 34, Eremenko 44)*
BATE Borisov (1) 2 *(Rodionov 3, Nekhajchik 54)* 11,080
Dynamo Kiev: Koval; Leandro Almeida (Andre 74), Betao, Mikhalik, Khacheridi, Gusev (Garmash 57), Eremenko, Ninkovic, Gerson Magrao (El Kaddouri 79), Milevskiy, Yarmolenko.
BATE Borisov: Veremko; Radkov, Yurevich, Bordachev, Shitov, Likhtarovich (Baga 38), Nekhajchik, Renan (Volodko M 76), Pavlov (Skavysh 63), Olekhnovich, Rodionov.

Thursday, 30 September 2010
BATE Borisov (1) 4 *(Rodionov 5, Kontsevoy 49, Renan 77 (pen), Olekhnovich 83)*
AZ (0) 1 *(Sigthorsson 89)*   12,100
BATE Borisov: Veremko; Yurevich, Sosnovski (Radkov 48), Bordachev, Shitov, Nekhajchik, Renan (Skavysh 84), Volodko A, Olekhnovich, Rodionov, Kontsevoy (Baga 79).
AZ: Romero; Klavan, Marcellis, Moreno, Moisander (Jaliens 83), Schaars, Wernbloom (Van der Velden 78), Elm, Gudmundsson (Holman 68), Sigthorsson, Jonathas.

Serif (2) 2 *(Erokhin 8, Jymmy Franca 37 (pen))*
Dynamo Kiev (0) 0   12,600
Serif: Stoyanov; Adamovic (Samardzic 78), Jose Nadson, Tarkhnishvili, Volkov, Vranjes, Erokhin, Rouamba,

Balima, Diedhiou (Brankovic 46), Jymmy Franca (Gauracs 63).
Dynamo Kiev: Boyko; El Kaddouri (Popov 46), Khacheridi, Gusev, Yussuf, Eremenko, Ninkovic (Garmash 71), Vukojevic, Milevskiy, Shevchenko, Yarmolenko.

Thursday, 21 October 2010

AZ (1) 1 *(Falkenburg 35)*

Dynamo Kiev (2) 2 *(Milevsky 16, Khacheridi 39)* 12,338

AZ: Romero; Marcellis, Moreno, Moisander[■], Viergever, Martens (Gudmundsson 77), Schaars, Holman (Sigthorsson 68), Wernbloom, Falkenburg (Van der Velden 81), Jonathas.
Dynamo Kiev: Koval; El Kaddouri, Leandro Almeida, Betao, Mikhalik, Khacheridi, Gusev (Yarmolenko 76), Eremenko, Vukojevic, Milevskiy (Zozulya 89), Shevchenko (Danilo Silva 58).

Serif (0) 0

BATE Borisov (1) 1 *(Sosnovski 9)* 7000

Serif: Stoyanov; Adamovic, Jose Nadson, Tarkhnishvili, Brankovic, Vranjes, Erokhin, Rouamba, Gauracs (Jymmy Franca 64), Balima (Gheorghiev 82), Diedhiou (Volkov 64).
BATE Borisov: Veremko; Yurevich, Sosnovski, Bordachev, Shitov, Nekhajchik, Renan (Baga 68), Volodko A, Olekhnovich (Likhtarovich 74), Rodionov, Kontsevoy (Skavysh 83).

Thursday, 4 November 2010

BATE Borisov (1) 3 *(Rodionov 16, Pavlov 70, Renan 75)*

Serif (1) 1 *(Erokhin 32)* 16,500

BATE Borisov: Veremko; Yurevich, Sosnovski, Bordachev, Shitov, Likhtarovich (Skavysh 66), Vaga, Renan (Radkov 82), Pavlov (Volodko A 72), Olekhnovich, Rodionov.
Serif: Stoyanov (Stajila 58); Adamovic (Haccaturov 75), Jose Nadson, Tarkhnishvili, Brankovic, Volkov (Gauracs 71), Vranjes, Erokhin, Rouamba, Balima, Diedhiou.

Dynamo Kiev (0) 2 *(Milevsky 47, 61)*

AZ (0) 0 17,500

Dynamo Kiev: Koval; El Kaddouri, Leandro Almeida, Betao, Mikhalik (Yussuf 51), Khacheridi, Gusev, Eremenko, Vukojevic, Milevskiy (Zozulya 90), Yarmolenko (Ninkovic 58).
AZ: Romero; Jaliens, Klavan, Marcellis, Moreno, Martens (Sigthorsson 72), Schaars, Holman, Wernbloom, Elm (Gudmundsson 72), Jonathas (Falkenburg 72).

Wednesday, 1 December 2010

BATE Borisov (0) 1 *(Nekhajchik 84)*

Dynamo Kiev (2) 4 *(Vukojevic 16, Yarmolenko 43, Gusev 50 (pen), Milevskiy 68)* 10,620

BATE Borisov: Gutor; Radkov, Yurevich, Sosnovski (Renan 46), Bordachev, Shitov, Likhtarovich, Nekhajchik, Baga (Skavysh 70), Volodko A (Olekhnovich 79), Rodionov.
Dynamo Kiev: Shovkovskiy, El Kaddouri (Garmash 85), Leandro Almeida, Betao, Popov, Mikhalik, Gusev, Eremenko (Zozulya 80), Vukojevic, Milevskiy (Kravets 90), Yarmolenko.

Serif (0) 1 *(Rouamba 54)*

AZ (1) 1 *(Holman 17)* 3500

Serif: Stajila; Adamovic (Fred 73), Samardzic, Jose Nadson, Brankovic, Volkov (Diedhiou 62), Vranjes, Erokhin, Rouamba, Balima (Gheorghiev 77), Jymmy Franca.
AZ: Romero; Klavan, Marcellis, Moreno (Jaliens 70), Moisander, Martens (Ortiz 64), Schaars, Holman, Wernbloom, Elm (Falkenburg 75), Sigthorsson.

Wednesday, 15 December 2010

AZ (1) 3 *(Sigthorsson 7, 84, Maher 86)*

BATE Borisov (0) 0 13,852

AZ: Romero; Jaliens, Moreno, Moisander, Viergever (Poulsen 61), Martens (Gudmundsson 46), Schaars, Holman, Wernbloom (Maher 71), Falkenburg, Sigthorsson.

BATE Borisov: Veremko; Radkov, Yurevich, Sosnovski (Olekhnovich 56), Shitov, Likhtarovich (Volodko A 85), Nekhajcik, Baga, Renan, Pavlov (Skavysh 62), Rodionov.

Dynamo Kiev (0) 0

Serif (0) 0 10,800

Dynamo Kiev: Shovkovskiy; Leandro Almeida, Betao (Nesmachny 57), Popov, Mikhalik, Khacheridi, Eremenko, Vukojevic, Milevskiy (Zozulya 88), Shevchenko, Yarmolenko.
Serif: Stajila; Adamovic, Samardzic, Jose Nadson, Brankovic, Volkov (Gauracs 90), Erokhin, Fred (Gheorghiev 76), Balima, Diedhiou (Nikolic 80), Jymmy Franca.

Group E Table	P	W	D	L	F	A	Pts
Dynamo Kiev	6	3	2	1	10	6	11
BATE Borisov	6	3	1	2	11	11	10
AZ	6	2	1	3	8	10	7
Serif	6	1	2	3	5	7	5

GROUP F

Thursday, 16 September 2010

Lausanne (0) 0

CSKA Moscow (1) 3 *(Vagner Love 22, 81 (pen), Ignashevich 68)* 11,500

Lausanne: Favre; Sonnerat, Katz, Getaz, Celestini, Marazzi, Avanzini (Abdul Carrupt 84), Traore (Basha 64), Rodrigo, Roux (Munsy 73), Silvio.
CSKA Moscow: Akinfeev; Berezutski V, Ignashevich, Berezutski A, Schennikov, Gonzalez (Oliseh 64), Semberas, Mamaev, Dzagoev (Honda 72), Tosic (Necid 84), Vagner Love.

Sparta Prague (1) 3 *(Wilfried 17, Kladrubsky 68, Kadlec 75)*

Palermo (1) 2 *(Maccarone 38, Hernandez 83)* 13,766

Sparta Prague: Blazek; Hoheneder, Brabec, Repka, Pamic, Bondoa, Sionko (Kaderabek 90), Kladrubsky, Podany, Wilfried (Kweuke 90), Kadlec (Trcsnak 82).
Palermo: Sirigu; Bovo, Darmian, Balzaretti, Glik, Liverani, Migliaccio (Kasami 58), Pastore, Rigoni (Joao Pedro 78), Maccarone, Hernandez.

Thursday, 30 September 2010

CSKA Moscow (0) 3 *(Doumbia 72, 86, Gonzalez 84 (pen))*

Sparta Prague (0) 0 12,900

CSKA Moscow: Akinfeev; Berezutski V, Ignashevich, Berezutski A, Nababkin, Gonzalez, Semberas, Honda (Tosic 87), Mamaev, Vagner Love (Dzagoev 76), Doumbia (Necid 87).
Sparta Prague: Blazek; Brabec, Repka, Pamic, Bondoa, Vacek, Kladrubsky (Kweuke 81), Kucka, Podany (Zeman 82), Wilfried (Matejovsky 90), Kadlec.

Palermo (0) 1 *(Maccarone 79)*

Lausanne (0) 0 9772

Palermo: Benussi; Cassani, Bovo, Munoz, Garcia (Balzaretti 60), Migliaccio, Nocerino, Pastore, Kasami, Maccarone (Darmian 86), Miccoli (Pinilla 43).
Lausanne: Favre; Sonnerat, Rochat, Meoli, Katz, Celestini, Marazzi, Avanzini (Pasche 82), Rodrigo (Steuble 80), Roux (Munsy 83), Silvio.

Thursday, 21 October 2010

Palermo (0) 0

CSKA Moscow (1) 3 *(Doumbia 34, 59, Necid 82)* 17,548

Palermo: Benussi; Cassani, Bovo, Goian, Darmian (Kasami 56), Balzaretti, Migliaccio, Nocerino, Pastore[■], Maccarone (Pinilla 64), Hernandez (Joao Pedro 76).
CSKA Moscow: Akinfeev; Berezutski V, Ignashevich, Nababkin, Schennikov, Gonzalez (Tosic 65), Honda, Mamaev, Oliseh, Vagner Love (Dzagoev 75), Doumbia (Necid 60).

Sparta Prague (3) 3 *(Wilfried 10, 23, Kucka 21)*

Lausanne (1) 3 *(Meoli 6, Steuble 75, Silvio 90)* 12,430

Sparta Prague: Blazek; Brabec, Kusnir, Repka, Pamic, Sionko, Vacek, Kucka, Podany (Kladrubsky 80), Wilfried (Kweuke 76), Kadlec (Matejovsky 90).

Lausanne: Favre; Sonnerat, Rochat, Meoli, Katz (Roux 82), Celestini, Marazzi, Pasche (Rodrigo 68), Steuble, Munsy (Avanzini 74), Silvio.

Thursday, 4 November 2010
CSKA Moscow (0) 3 *(Honda 47, Necid 50, 54)*
Palermo (1) 1 *(Maccarone 10)* 12,000
CSKA Moscow: Akinfeev; Berezutski V, Nababkin, Schennikov, Gonzalez (Oliseh 68), Semberas, Honda (Dzagoev 70), Mamaev (Aldonin 71), Tosic, Vagner Love, Necid.
Palermo: Benussi; Bovo, Goian, Darmian, Glik (Cassani 55), Garcia (Balzaretti 65), Nocerino■, Rigoni, Kasami, Maccarone, Miccoli (Pinilla 60).

Lausanne (1) 1 *(Katz 6)*
Sparta Prague (1) 3 *(Wilfried 45, 90, Kweuke 75)* 8000
Lausanne: Favre; Sonnerat, Rochat, Meoli, Katz (Roux 83), Celestini, Marazzi, Pasche, Steuble (Avanzini 62), Rodrigo (Munsy 70), Silvio.
Sparta Prague: Blazek; Brabec, Repka, Pamic, Bondoa (Matejovsky 70), Vacek (Hoheneder 90), Kladrubsky, Kucka, Podany, Kweuke, Wilfried.

Wednesday, 1 December 2010
CSKA Moscow (3) 5 *(Necid 18, 82, Oliseh 22, Tosic 40, Dzagoev 71)*
Lausanne (0) 1 *(Abdul Carrupt 90)* 4500
CSKA Moscow: Akinfeev; Berezutski V, Ignashevich, Schennikov, Semberas, Rahimic, Honda (Gonzalez 61), Dzagoev, Oliseh (Aldonin 61), Tosic (Vasilyev 75), Necid.
Lausanne: Castejon; Sonnerat, Rochat, Meoli, Katz, Celestini, Marazzi, Steuble (Roux 77), Avanzini (Pasche 58), Rodrigo, Silvio (Abdul Carrupt 52).
Played in Khimki.

Palermo (1) 2 *(Rigoni 23, Pinilla 59 (pen))*
Sparta Prague (0) 2 *(Kladrubsky 51 (pen), Kucka 62)* 8623
Palermo: Benussi; Cassani, Goian■, Balzaretti, Munoz, Liverani (Kasami 69), Migliaccio, Pastore■, Rigoni, Maccarone (Bovo 53), Pinilla (Miccoli 76).
Sparta Prague: Blazek; Brabec, Kusnir (Kadlec 69), Repka, Pamic, Vacek, Kladrubsky, Kucka, Podany (Zeman 83), Kweuke (Hoheneder 90), Wilfried.

Wednesday, 15 December 2010
Lausanne (0) 0
Palermo (0) 1 *(Munoz 84)* 7150
Lausanne: Favre; Sonnerat, Rochat, Meoli, Katz, Celestini (Roux 87), Abdul Carrupt (Munsy 83), Steuble, Avanzini (Pasche 77), Rodrigo, Silvio.
Palermo: Benussi; Cassani (Munoz 57), Glik, Garcia, Prestia, Liverani, Nocerino (Ardizzone 65), Rigoni, Kasami, Joao Pedro, Maccarone (Zerbo 90).

Sparta Prague (1) 1 *(Kadlec 44)*
CSKA Moscow (1) 1 *(Dzagoev 15)* 12,707
Sparta Prague: Zitka; Brabec, Pamic, Bondoa, Hejda, Sionko (Zeman 77), Vacek, Kucka (Matejovsky 83), Podany (Kweuke 68), Wilfried, Kadlec.
CSKA Moscow: Chepchugov; Berezutski A, Schennikov, Fedotov, Semberas, Rahimic, Aldonin, Dzagoev, Oliseh, Tosic, Necid.

Group F Table	P	W	D	L	F	A	Pts
CSKA Moscow	6	5	1	0	18	3	16
Sparta Prague	6	2	3	1	12	12	9
Palermo	6	2	1	3	7	11	7
Lausanne	6	0	1	5	5	16	1

GROUP G

Thursday, 16 September 2010
AEK Athens (1) 3 *(Djebbour 12, Liberopoulos 65, Nacho Scocco 89)*
Hajduk Split (1) 1 *(Ibricic 29 (pen))* 25,000
AEK Athens: Arabatzis; Dellas, Jahic, Manolas, Bouba Diop, Kafes (Leonardo 74), Lagos, Liberopoulos (Blanco 90), Nacho Scocco, Burns (Patsatzoglou 70), Djebbour.

Hajduk Split: Subasic; Vejic, Bujat, Maloca, Strinic, Anas Sharbini (Cop 61), Ljubicic, Bulku (Trebotic 81), Tomasov (Oremus 67), Ibricic, Vukusic.

Anderlecht (0) 1 *(Juhasz 66)*
Zenit (3) 3 *(Kerzhakov 8, 33, 44)* 13,386
Anderlecht: Proto; Juhasz, Deschacht, Bernardez, Rnic (Legear 46), Polak, Biglia, Boussoufa, Gillet, Suarez, Lukaku.
Zenit: Zhevnov; Lukovic, Bruno Alves, Lombaerts, Semak, Danny (Krizanac 90), Shirokov (Faizulin 36), Zyryanov, Denisov, Lazovic, Kerzhakov (Ionov 79).

Thursday, 30 September 2010
Hajduk Split (0) 1 *(Vukusic 90)*
Anderlecht (0) 0 33,000
Hajduk Split: Subasic; Vejic, Buljat, Maloca, Strinic, Anas Sharbini (Cop 64), Ljubicic, Tomasov (Bulku 53), Brkljaca (Trebotic 77), Bricicic, Vukusic.
Anderlecht: Proto; Juhasz, Deschacht, Mazuch, Polak, Biglia, Boussoufa, Gillet, Marecek (Legear 66), Kouyate, Suarez (Lukaku 79).

Zenit (3) 4 *(Hubocan 1, Bruno Alves 13, Lazovic 43 (pen), 58)*
AEK Athens (1) 2 *(Liberopoulos 37, Kafes 83 (pen))* 19,000
Zenit: Malafeev; Lukovic, Bruno Alves, Krizanac, Hubocan, Bystrov (Kanunnikov 74), Danny (Rosina 66), Zyryanov, Denisov (Shirokov 66), Lazovic, Bukharov.
AEK Athens: Arabatzis; Dellas, Nasuti■, Makos, Patsatzoglou, Kafes, Lagos, Gentzoglou, Liberopoulos (Jahic 46), Nacho Scocco (Blanco 82), Djebbour (Bouba Diop 59).

Thursday, 21 October 2010
Anderlecht (1) 3 *(Boussoufa 31, Lukaku 72, Juhasz 75)*
AEK Athens (0) 0 14,508
Anderlecht: Proto; Juhasz, Deschacht, Mazuch, Polak, Biglia, Kljestan, Boussoufa, Gillet, Kanu (Suarez 66), Lukaku (Chavarria 79).
AEK Athens: Saja; Dellas, Argiriou, Bouba Diop, Makos (Djebbour 46), Kafes, Lagos, Gentzoglou, Nacho Scocco (Burns 22), Blanco, Eder (Leonardo 64).

Zenit (1) 2 *(Bukharov 24, Danny 68)*
Hajduk Split (0) 0 19,500
Zenit: Zhevnov; Lukovic, Krizanac, Anyukov, Lombaerts, Semak, Danny (Kanunnikov 77), Faizulin (Zyrianov 64), Denisov, Lazovic (Ionov 71), Bukharov.
Hajduk Split: Subasic; Buljat, Maloca, Strinic, Anas Sharbini (Cop 46), Ljubicic, Bulku (Jozinovic 80), Brkljaca (Trebotic 87), Ibricic, Oremus, Vukusic.

Thursday, 4 November 2010
AEK Athens (0) 1 *(Blanco 49 (pen))*
Anderlecht (0) 1 *(Polak 55)* 11,113
AEK Athens: Saja; Patsatzoglou, Dadomo, Nasuti, Manolas, Leonardo (Eder 65), Kafes, Lagos (Froxilias 72), Gentzoglou (Makos 86), Djebbour, Blanco.
Anderlecht: Proto; Juhasz, Mazuch, Lecjaks, Polak (Suarez 77), Kljestan, Boussoufa (Kanu 67), Gillet, Legear (Badibanga 90), Kouyate, Lukaku.

Hajduk Split (0) 2 *(Ljubicic 68, Vukusic 82)*
Zenit (1) 3 *(Ionov 32, Huszti 47 (pen), Rosina 51)* 30,000
Hajduk Split: Subasic; Vejic, Buljat, Maloca, Strinic, Anas Sharbini, Ljubicic, Bulku, Tomasov (Oremus 61), Ibricic, Vukusic.
Zenit: Malafeev; Fernando Meira, Lukovic, Krizanac (Kanunnikov 56), Anyukov, Huszti, Rosina (Lazovic 72), Faizulin, Denisov (Semak 65), Ionov, Bukharov.

Wednesday, 1 December 2010
Hajduk Split (0) 1 *(Buljat 90)*
AEK Athens (0) 3 *(Nacho Scocco 50 (pen), Manolas 61, Blanco 84)* 13,726
Hajduk Split: Radosevic; Jozinovic, Buljat, Maloca, Strinic, Anas Sharbini, Ljubicic (Cop 53), Tomasov (Andric 53), Ibricic, Oremus, Vukusic.

AEK Athens: Saja; Dellas, Karabelas, Jahic, Manolas, Bouba Diop, Makos, Gentzoglou, Liberopoulos (Blanco 80), Nacho Scocco (Leonardo 77), Burns (Lagos 70).

Zenit (1) 3 *(Ionov 12, Bukharov 65, Huszti 88)*
Anderlecht (0) 1 *(Kanu 87)*   13,900
Zenit: Malafeev; Fernando Meira, Lukovic (Hubocan 80), Krizanac, Lombaerts, Rosina (Huszti 73), Danny, Shirokov, Zyryanov, Ionov, Bukharov (Kanunnikov 65).
Anderlecht: Proto; Juhasz, Mazuch, Lecjaks, Polak, Kljestan, Gillet, Legear (Suarez 46), Marecek (Badibanga 68), Kanu, Lukaku (De Sutter 77).

Thursday, 16 December 2010
AEK Athens (0) 0
Zenit (1) 3 *(Bukharov 44, Rosina 67, Denisov 88)*   13,605
AEK Athens: Saja; Dellas (Bouba Diop 74), Karabelas, Jahic, Manolas, Makos (Leonardo 80), Kafes, Gentzoglou (Burns 54), Liberopoulos, Nacho Scocco, Blanco.
Zenit: Malafeev; Lukovic, Bruno Alves, Lombaerts, Hubocan, Rosina, Shirokov, Zyrianov (Ionov 77), Denisov, Lazovic (Huszti 74), Bukharov (Kanunnikov 83).

Anderlecht (2) 2 *(De Sutter 12, Suarez 41)*
Hajduk Split (0) 0   14,979
Anderlecht: Proto; Juhasz, Mazuch, Lecjaks, Polak, Kljestan, Boussoufa, Gillet, Legear (Marecek 78), De Sutter (Lukaku 86), Suarez.
Hajduk Split: Radosevic; Vejic, Jozinovic (Ljubicic 60), Buljat, Strinic, Jonjic, Andric, Ibricic (Tomasov 60), Oremus, Trebotic (Andrijasevic 80), Vukusic.

Group G Table	P	W	D	L	F	A	Pts
Zenit	6	6	0	0	18	6	18
Anderlecht	6	2	1	3	8	8	7
AEK Athens	6	2	1	3	9	13	7
Hajduk Split	6	1	0	5	5	13	3

GROUP H

Thursday, 16 September 2010
Getafe (0) 2 *(Arizmendi 51, Pedro Rios 81)*
Odense (1) 1 *(Andreasen 44)*   1650
Getafe: Codina; Cata Diaz, Mane, Marcano, Sanchez, Boateng, Borja (Casquero 47), Gavilan (Miku 6), Parejo (Pedro Rios 73), Arizmendi, Adrian Colunga.
Odense: Carroll; Troest, Helveg (Caca 48), Haland, Sorensen, Johansson (Toft 78), Gislason, Andreasen, Traore, Utaka, Kadri (Feldballe 86).

Stuttgart (1) 3 *(Claudemir da Silva 23 (pen), Gentner 59, Tasci 90)*
Young Boys (0) 0   15,000
Stuttgart: Ulreich; Tasci, Boka, Niedermeier, Camoranesi (Marica 80), Gentner, Kuzmanovic, Trasch, Didavi (Molinaro 84), Claudemir da Silva (Harnik 68), Pogrebnyak.
Young Boys: Wolfli; Spycher, Sutter (Regazzoni 62), Nef, El Jemal, Affolter, Hochstrasser (Mayuka 62), Doubai T, Costanzo, Schneuwly M (Schneuwly C 74), N'Tsama.

Thursday, 30 September 2010
Odense (0) 1 *(Johansson 78)*
Stuttgart (0) 2 *(Kuzmanovic 72, Harnik 86)*   8854
Odense: Carroll; Troest, Haland, Ruud, Sorensen, Johansson (Demba-Nyren 80), Gislason (Kadri 70), Djemba-Djemba, Andreasen, Traore (Feldballe 90), Utaka.
Stuttgart: Ulreich; Delpierre, Tasci, Molinaro (Boka 60), Celozzi, Camoranesi, Gentner, Bah, Kuzmanovic, Claudemir da Silva (Harnik 73), Marica.

Young Boys (1) 2 *(Degen 10, 64)*
Getafe (0) 0   12,830
Young Boys: Wolfli; Spycher, Sutter, Nef, El Jemal, Affolter, Degen, Doubai T, Lulic (Regazzoni 79), Costanzo (Hochstrasser 90), Mayuka (N' Tsama 72).

Getafe: Ustari; Mario, Miguel Torres (Adrian Sardinero 69), Mane, Marcano, Sanchez, Borja, Mosquera (Parejo 62), Albin, Adrian Colunga (Pedro Rios 74), Miku.

Thursday, 21 October 2010
Stuttgart (1) 1 *(Marica 29)*
Getafe (0) 0   17,400
Stuttgart: Ulreich; Boulahrouz (Bah 75), Boka, Niedermeier, Celozzi, Camoranesi, Gentner, Kuzmanovic, Trasch (Funk 64), Claudemir da Silva, Marica (Pogrebnyak 65).
Getafe: Ustari; Cata Diaz, Rafa, Marcano, Sanchez (Casquero 46), Pintos, Borja, Arizmendi (Gavilan 46), Manu Del Moral, Albin (Adrian Colunga 72), Miku.

Young Boys (2) 4 *(N'Tsama 25, Sutter 34, Degen 61, Lulic 74)*
Odense (0) 2 *(Utaka 48, Sorensen 84 (pen))*   12,511
Young Boys: Wolfli; Spycher, Nef, Affolter, Degen, Hochstrasser (El Jemal 68), Sutter, Doubai T, Lulic, Costanzo (Regazzoni 79), N'Tsama (Raimondi 87).
Odense: Lund-Hansen; Haland, Ruud, Moller Christensen, Sorensen, Johansson, Gislason (Helveg 72), Djemba-Djemba, Traore, Utaka (Demba-Nyren 77), Kadrii (Absalonsen 86).

Thursday, 4 November 2010
Getafe (0) 0
Stuttgart (1) 3 *(Marica 26, Gebhart 64, Harnik 76)*   4000
Getafe: Ustari; Ibrahim (Miku 65), Cata Diaz, Mane, Sanchez, Boateng (Casquero 46), Borja, Arizmendi, Albin, Adrian Colunga, Adrian Sardinero (Manu Del Moral 58).
Stuttgart: Ulreich; Delpierre (Niedermeier 46), Tasci (Gebhart 58), Molinaro, Boka, Camoranesi (Gentner 71), Bah, Kuzmanovic, Funk, Harnik, Marica■.

Odense (1) 2 *(Andreasen 12, 60)*
Young Boys (0) 0   5334
Odense: Carroll; Haland, Ruud, Moller Christensen, Sorensen, Johansson, Djemba-Djemba, Andreasen, Traore (Gislason 81), Absalonsen (Kadrii 82), Utaka (Toft 87).
Young Boys: Burki; Spycher, Nef, El Jemal (Mayuka 68), Affolter, Sutter, Doubai T (Hochstrasser 46), Lulic, Costanzo, Regazzoni (Degen 67), N'Tsama.

Wednesday, 1 December 2010
Odense (0) 1 *(Andreasen 90)*
Getafe (1) 1 *(Pedro Rios 17)*   5599
Odense: Carroll; Haland, Ruud, Moller Christensen, Sorensen, Djemba-Djemba, Andreasen, Traore (Johansson 72), Toft, Utaka, Kadrii (Feldballe 66).
Getafe: Ustari; Miguel Torres, Cata Diaz, Mane, Marcano, Boateng, Parejo (Borja 80), Pedro Rios, Manu Del Moral, Sanchez 68), Albin (Mosquera 86), Miku.

Young Boys (1) 4 *(Degen 39, Sutter 78, Mayuka 82, 87)*
Stuttgart (0) 2 *(Pogrebnyak 48, Schipplock 68)*   18,627
Young Boys: Wolfli; Spycher, Nef, El Jemal, Affolter, Degen, Sutter, Doubai T (Schneuwly M 67), Lulic (Regazzoni 74), Costanzo (Schneuwly C 56), Mayuka.
Stuttgart: Ziegler; Degen (Funk 69), Molinaro, Niedermeier, Bicakcic, Camoranesi, Elson, Bah, Kuzmanovic, Harnik (Didavi 74), Pogrebnyak (Schipplock 66).

Thursday, 16 December 2010
Getafe (1) 1 *(Adrian Sardinero 15)*
Young Boys (0) 0   1631
Getafe: Ustari; Ibrahim (Miguel Torres 72), Cata Diaz (Alex 41), Pintos, Casquero, Mosquera, Canas, Arizmendi (Escasi 57), Albin, Adrian Colunga, Adrian Sardinero.
Young Boys: Wolfli; Spycher (Schneuwly C 57), Nef, Affolter, Degen (Schneuwly M 73), Hochstrasser (Raimondi 57), Sutter, Doubai T, Lulic, Costanzo, Mayuka.

Stuttgart (1) 5 *(Gebhart 20, Hoegh 48 (og), Gentner 65, Pogrebnyak 70, Marica 90)*
Odense (0) 1 *(Utaka 72)* 14,000

Stuttgart: Ulreich; Degen, Molinaro, Boka, Niedermeier, Bicakcic, Bah (Gentner 59), Gebhart (Camoranesi 60), Kuzmanovic, Marica, Pogrebnyak (Claudemir da Silva 71).
Odense: Ousager; Helveg, Ruud, Moller Christensen, Sorensen, Hoegh, Djemba-Djemba, Andreasen, Traore (Feldballe 78), Toft (Johansson 76), Utaka (Jensen 88).

Group H Table	P	W	D	L	F	A	Pts
Stuttgart	6	5	0	1	16	6	15
Young Boys	6	3	0	3	10	10	9
Getafe	6	2	1	3	4	8	7
Odense	6	1	1	4	8	14	4

GROUP I

Thursday, 16 September 2010

Debrecen (0) 0
Metalist Kharkiv (2) 5 *(Edmar 24, 74, Cleiton Xavier 34, Fininho 77, Valyaev 89)* 6500

Debrecen: Malinauskas; Mijadinoski, Laczko, Komlosi, Nagy, Czvitkovics, Kiss (Ramos 46), Szakaly (Rezes 66), Varga, Mbengono (Coulibaly 46), Kabat■.
Metalist Kharkiv: Disljenkovic; Fininho, Villagra, Obradovic, Gueye (Bordian 81), Pshenichnikh, Cleiton Xavier, Valyaev, Edmar, Vorobei (Oleynik 55), Taison (Kaita 77).

PSV Eindhoven (0) 1 *(Dzsudzsak 90)*
Sampdoria (1) 1 *(Cacciatore 25)* 15,500

PSV Eindhoven: Isaksson; Pieters, Bouma, Marcelo, Afellay, Engelaar, Hutchinson, Dzsudzsak, Lens (Amrabat 80), Berg (Koevermans 75), Toivonen (Reis 84).
Sampdoria: Curci; Ziegler, Gastaldello, Volta, Cacciatore, Palombo, Semioli (Padalino 68), Koman (Dessena 81), Mannini, Cassano, Marilungo (Guberti 87).

Thursday, 30 September 2010

Metalist Kharkiv (0) 0
PSV Eindhoven (2) 2 *(Dzsudzsak 27 (pen), Engelaar 30)* 37,800

Metalist Kharkiv: Disljenkovic; Fininho, Villagra■, Obradovic, Gueye, Romanchuk, Shelayev, Valyaev (Kaita 46), Edmar, Vorobei (Oleynik 31) (Postupalenko 82), Taison.
PSV Eindhoven: Isaksson; Pieters, Bouma (Rodriguez 65), Marcelo, Afellay (Bakkal 83), Engelaar, Hutchinson, Dzsudzsak (Amrabat 75), Lens, Berg, Toivonen.

Sampdoria (1) 1 *(Pazzini 18 (pen))*
Debrecen (0) 0 12,159

Sampdoria: Curci; Accardi, Lucchini, Volta, Cacciatore (Zauri 73), Palombo, Dessena, Koman (Marilungo 80), Mannini (Guberti 58), Cassano, Pazzini.
Debrecen: Malinauskas; Mijadinoski, Simac, Laczko, Nagy, Czvitkovics, Kiss, Szakaly (Kulcsar 46), Varga, Mbengono (Bodi 87), Coulibaly.

Thursday, 21 October 2010

Debrecen (1) 1 *(Mijadinoski 35)*
PSV Eindhoven (1) 2 *(Engelaar 40, Reis 66)* 18,000

Debrecen: Malinauskas; Mijadinoski, Simac, Fodor, Nagy, Czvitkovics, Kiss, Szakaly (Rezes 80), Varga, Mbengono (Bodi 66), Coulibaly.
PSV Eindhoven: Isaksson; Pieters, Bouma, Marcelo, Afellay, Engelaar, Hutchinson, Dzsudzsak, Lens (Reis 46), Berg, Toivonen (Bakkal 84).

Metalist Kharkiv (1) 2 *(Taison 38, Cleiton Xavier 73)*
Sampdoria (1) 1 *(Koman 32)* 34,580

Metalist Kharkiv: Disljenkovic; Fininho (Oleynik 63), Obradovic, Gueye, Pshenichnikh, Cleiton Xavier (Vorobei 88), Valyaev, Edmar, Bordian, Devic (Shelayev 84), Taison■.
Sampdoria: Curci; Ziegler, Gastaldello, Volta, Cacciatore, Dessena (Guberti 82), Poli (Mannini 65), Koman (Tissone 74), Cassano, Pozzi, Marilungo.

Thursday, 4 November 2010

PSV Eindhoven (2) 3 *(Afellay 22, Reis 44, Wuytens 88)*
Debrecen (0) 0 17,000

PSV Eindhoven: Isaksson; Pieters (Wuytens 78), Bouma (Rodriguez 47), Marcelo, Afellay, Engelaar, Hutchinson, Dzsudzsak, Lens (Bakkal 64), Toivonen, Reis.
Debrecen: Malinauskas; Mijadinoski, Simac, Laczko, Nagy, Czvitkovics, Kiss, Szakaly, Varga, Bodi (Dombi 73), Coulibaly.

Sampdoria (0) 0
Metalist Kharkiv (0) 0 20,000

Sampdoria: Junior Costa; Ziegler, Gastaldello, Volta, Cacciatore, Palombo, Dessena, Guberti (Koman 72), Poli (Mannini 63), Pozzi, Marilungo (Pazzini 63).
Metalist Kharkiv: Disljenkovic; Fininho, Villagra (Shelayev 74), Obradovic, Gueye, Cleiton Xavier, Valyaev, Edmar, Bordian, Oleynik (Vorobei 88), Devic (Romanchuk 64).

Wednesday, 1 December 2010

Metalist Kharkiv (0) 2 *(Bodi 52 (og), Oleynik 88)*
Debrecen (0) 1 *(Czvitkovics 48)* 31,200

Metalist Kharkiv: Startsev; Villagra, Obradovic, Gueye, Pshenichnikh, Cleiton Xavier, Valyaev, Edmar, Bordian (Lysenko 46) (Shelayev 90), Oleynik, Devic (Vorobei 73).
Debrecen: Malinauskas; Mijadinoski, Simac, Laczko, Bernath, Czvitkovics, Kiss, Szakaly (Ramos 80), Varga, Bodi (Mbengono 55), Kabat (Coulibaly 64).

Sampdoria (1) 1 *(Pazzini 45)*
PSV Eindhoven (0) 2 *(Toivonen 51, 90)* 12,131

Sampdoria: Curci; Ziegler, Gastaldello, Lucchini (Volta 31), Cacciatore, Palombo, Dessena, Poli (Mannini 77), Koman (Guberti 69), Pazzini, Marilungo■.
PSV Eindhoven: Isaksson; Pieters, Bouma, Marcelo, Manolev, Afellay, Engelaar, Hutchinson, Dzsudzsak, Toivonen, Reis (Berg 84).

Thursday, 16 December 2010

Debrecen (0) 2 *(Kabat 48, 86)*
Sampdoria (0) 0 5500

Debrecen: Verpecz; Mijadinoski, Simac, Laczko, Bernath, Czvitkovics, Szakaly (Fodor 90), Varga, Mbengono (Kiss 65), Bodi (Dombi 89), Kabat.
Sampdoria: Junior Costa; Rossini, Volta, Grieco, Messina, Sammarco, Dessena, Poli (Mannini 80), Koman, Krsticic (Lamorte 88), Pedro Obiang (Guberti 72).

PSV Eindhoven (0) 0
Metalist Kharkiv (0) 0 15,300

PSV Eindhoven: Cassio; Rodriguez, Pieters (Vukovic 46), Marcelo, Afellay (Dzsudzsak 90), Bakkal, Wuytens, Tamata, Lens, Berg, Amrabat (Toivonen 68).
Metalist Kharkiv: Startsev; Villagra, Obradovic, Gueye, Pshenichnikh, Shelayev, Cleiton Xavier, Edmar (Lysenko 81), Bordian (Vorobei 61), Oleynik, Taison.

Group I Table	P	W	D	L	F	A	Pts
PSV Eindhoven	6	4	2	0	10	3	14
Metalist Kharkiv	6	3	2	1	9	4	11
Sampdoria	6	1	2	3	4	7	5
Debrecen	6	1	0	5	4	13	3

GROUP J

Thursday, 16 September 2010

Karpaty (1) 3 *(Golodyuk 44, Kopolovets 52, Kozhanov 79)*
Borussia Dortmund (2) 4 *(Nuri 12 (pen), Gotze 27, 90, Barrios 87)* 28,045

Karpaty: Tlumak; Tubic, Petrivskiy, Milosevic, Goodwin, Khudobyak, Kozhanov (Checher 90), Golodyuk, Danilo Avelar, Batista (Kopolovets 15), Zenjov.
Borussia Dortmund: Weidenfeller; Owomoyela, Hummels, Subotic, Schmelzer, Nuri, Bender (Antonio Da Silva 80), Gotze, Barrios, Kagawa (Lewandowski 64), Grosskreutz (Kuba 64).

Sevilla (0) 0
Paris St Germain (0) 1 *(Nene 76)* 45,000
Sevilla: Palop; Dabo, Alexis, Konko, Caceres, Zokora, Cigarini (Guarente 46), Jesus Navas, Diego Capel (Perotti 62), Jose Carlos (Kanoute 46), Luis Fabiano.
Paris St Germain: Edel; Jallet, Camara, Tiene (Sakho 90), Armand, Clement, Nene (Hoarau 77), Chantome, Luyindula, Mevlut (Makelele 66), Maurice.

Thursday, 30 September 2010
Borussia Dortmund (0) 0
Sevilla (1) 1 *(Cigarini 45)* 49,100
Borussia Dortmund: Weidenfeller; Hummels, Piszczek, Subotic, Schmelzer■, Nuri, Blaszczykowski (Owomoyela 76), Bender (Lewandowski 76), Grosskreutz (Antonio Da Silva 86), Barrios, Kagawa.
Sevilla: Palop; Dabo (Escude 66), Fernando Navarro, Alexis, Caceres, Zokora, Cigarini (Kanoute 53), Jesus Navas, Guarente, Perotti, Luis Fabiano (Negredo 82).

Paris St Germain (2) 2 *(Jallet 4, Nene 20)*
Karpaty (0) 0 9117
Paris St Germain: Edel; Jallet, Camara, Tiene, Sakho, Clement, Sessegnon (Makonda 90), Nene (Hoarau 76), Chantome, Luyindula, Mevlut (Kezman 69).
Karpaty: Tlumak; Tubic, Checher, Goodwin, Khudobyak, Kozhanov (Gudyma 71), Fedetskiy, Danilo Avelar, Kuznetsov, Zenjov (Kopolovets 57), Guruli (Golodyuk 57).

Thursday, 21 October 2010
Borussia Dortmund (0) 1 *(Nuri 50 (pen))*
Paris St Germain (0) 1 *(Chantome 87)* 50,200
Borussia Dortmund: Weidenfeller; Dede, Hummels, Piszczek, Subotic, Nuri, Blaszczykowski (Feulner 82), Bender (Gotze 46), Grosskreutz, Barrios, Kagawa (Lewandowski 65).
Paris St Germain: Edel; Jallet, Camara, Tiene, Sakho, Makelele, Sessegnon, Bodmer (Clement 68), Nene (Chantome 82), Luyindula, Mevlut (Hoarau 72).

Karpaty (0) 0
Sevilla (1) 1 *(Kanoute 34)* 27,925
Karpaty: Rudenko; Tubic, Checher■, Khudobyak, Kopolovets (Gabovda 56), Tkachuk, Kozhanov (Gudyma 76), Golodyuk, Fedetskiy, Danilo Avelar, Zenjov (Kuznetsov 46).
Sevilla: Palop; Dabo, Escude, Fernando Navarro, Konko, Caceres, Zokora, Guarente (Jose Carlos 81), Perotti, Kanoute (Romaric 68), Negredo (Luis Fabiano 74).

Thursday, 4 November 2010
Paris St Germain (0) 0
Borussia Dortmund (0) 0 16,000
Paris St Germain: Edel; Camara, Tiene, Ceara, Sakho, Clement, Sessegnon, Bodmer (Hoarau 81), Nene (Jallet 66), Luyindula, Mevlut (Chantome 75).
Borussia Dortmund: Weidenfeller; Hummels, Piszczek (Blaszczykowski 46), Subotic, Schmelzer, Nuri, Bender, Grosskreutz, Gotze (Feulner 87), Barrios (Lewandowski 68), Kagawa.

Sevilla (3) 4 *(Alfaro 9, 42, Cigarini 31, Negredo 51)*
Karpaty (0) 0 25,000
Sevilla: Javi Varas; Escude, Fernando Navarro (Dabo 46), Konko, Caceres, Zokora, Cigarini (Romaric 75), Diego Capel (Perotti 60), Jose Carlos, Alfaro, Negredo.
Karpaty: Tlumak; Tubic, Milosevic, Goodwin, Khudobyak, Kozhanov (Kopolovets 69), Golodyuk, Fedetskiy, Danilo Avelar, Kuznetsov (Zenjov 62), Guruli (Tkachuk 40).

Wednesday, 1 December 2010
Borussia Dortmund (1) 3 *(Kagawa 5, Hummels 49, Lewandowski 89)*
Karpaty (0) 0 40,100
Borussia Dortmund: Weidenfeller; Hummels, Piszczek, Subotic, Schmelzer, Nuri, Blaszczykowski, Bender (Antonio Da Silva 67), Grosskreutz (Le Tallec 80), Kagawa (Zidan 67), Lewandowski.

Karpaty: Rudenko; Tubic, Checher, Goodwin (Baranets G 77), Khudobyak, Kopolovets (Guruli 63), Tkachuk, Kozhanov (Baranets B 86), Fedetskiy, Danilo Avelar, Kuznetsov.

Paris St Germain (3) 4 *(Bodmer 17, Hoarau 20, 47, Nene 45)*
Sevilla (2) 2 *(Kanoute 32, 36)* 18,783
Paris St Germain: Edel; Camara, Tiene, Ceara, Zakho, Clement, Sessegnon, Bodmer (Jallet 79), Nene (Luyindula 66), Chantome, Hoarau (Giuly 70).
Sevilla: Palop; Dabo, Escude, Fernando Navarro, Caceres, Romaric (Cigarini 78), Zokora (Negredo 46), Renato, Diego Capel (Alfaro 65), Perotti, Kanoute.

Wednesday, 15 December 2010
Karpaty (1) 1 *(Fedetskiy 45)*
Paris St Germain (1) 1 *(Luyindula 39)* 14,000
Karpaty: Tlumak; Tubic, Milosevic, Khudobyak, Tkachuk, Martynyuk, Baranets G (Gabovda 62), Kozhanov (Guruli 68), Fedetskiy, Danilo Avelar, Kuznetsov (Gudyma 81).
Paris St Germain: Coupet; Camara, Tiene, Traore, Ceara, Makonda (Maurice 69), Clement, Sessegnon, Bodmer (Qasmi 78), Luyindula, Mevlut (Makhedjouf 90).

Sevilla (2) 2 *(Romaric 31, Kanoute 35)*
Borussia Dortmund (1) 2 *(Kagawa 4, Subotic 49)* 27,062
Sevilla: Palop; Dabo, Escude, Alexis, Konko, Romaric (Fazio 86), Zokora, Diego Capel, Perotti (Caceres 60), Kanoute (Renato 41), Luis Fabiano.
Borussia Dortmund: Weidenfeller; Hummels, Piszczek, Subotic, Schmelzer (Le Tallec 87), Nuri, Blaszczykowski (Lewandowski 67), Bender (Antonio Da Silva 78), Gotze, Barrios, Kagawa.

Group J Table	P	W	D	L	F	A	Pts
Paris St Germain	6	3	3	0	9	4	12
Sevilla	6	3	1	2	10	7	10
Borussia Dortmund	6	2	3	1	10	7	9
Karpaty	6	0	1	5	4	15	1

GROUP K

Thursday, 16 September 2010
Liverpool (1) 4 *(Cole 1, N'Gog 55 (pen), 90, Lucas 81)*
Steaua (1) 1 *(Tanase 13)* 25,605
Liverpool: Reina; Kyrgiakos, Konchesky, Raul Meireles, Agger, Kelly, Rodriguez (Pacheco 85), Spearing, N'Gog, Cole (Eccleston 88), Babel (Lucas 79).
Steaua: Tatarusanu; Emeghara (Nicolita 20), Abrudan, Latovlevici, Geraldo Alves, Angelov (Eder Bonfim 52), Bicfalvi, Tanase, Radut (Surdu 73), Kapetanos, Stancu.

Napoli (0) 0
Utrecht (0) 0 35,210
Napoli: De Sanctis; Dossena (Maggio 69), Aronica, Zuniga, Cannavaro, Santacroce, Yebda (Lucarelli 76), Gargano, Sosa (Hamsik 56), Cavani, Lavezzi.
Utrecht: Vorm; Wuytens, Schut, Cornelisse, Nesu, Silberbauer, Lensky, Demouge, Duplan (Maguire 84), Mertens (Danso 89), Van Wolfswinkel.

Thursday, 30 September 2010
Steaua (3) 3 *(Emilson Cribari 2 (og), Tanase 11, Kapetanos 16)*
Napoli (1) 3 *(Vitale 44, Hamsik 73, Cavani 90)* 10,203
Steaua: Tatarusanu; Latovlevici, Geraldo Alves, Eder Bonfim, Gardos, Nicolita, Ricardo, Apostol (Angelov 79), Tanase (Radut 75), Kapetanos■, Stancu (Surdu 90).
Napoli: De Sanctis; Emilson Cribari, Zuniga (Hamsik 58), Grava, Santacroce (Lavezzi 46), Vitale, Yebda (Dumitru 86), Maggio, Gargano, Sosa, Cavani.

Utrecht (0) 0
Liverpool (0) 0 23,662
Utrecht: Vorm; Wuytens, Schut, Cornelisse, Nesu, Silberbauer, Lensky (Nijholt 82), Duplan (Maguire 69), Mulenga, Mertens, Van Wolfswinkel.
Liverpool: Reina; Johnson, Kelly, Raul Meireles, Carragher, Skrtel, Lucas, Poulsen, Torres, Kuyt, Cole (Rodriguez 81).

Thursday, 21 October 2010
Napoli (0) 0
Liverpool (0) 0 52,910
Napoli: De Sanctis; Dossena, Aronica, Cannavaro, Campagnaro, Pazienza, Maggio (Zuniga 75), Gargano (Yebda 83), Hansik (Sosa 85), Cavani, Lavezzi.
Liverpool: Reina; Kelly, Konchesky (Fabio Aurelio 65), Poulsen, Carragher (Kyrgiakos 46), Skrtel, Spearing, Shelvey, N'Gog, Jovanovic, Babel (Cole 77).

Utrecht (0) 1 *(Duplan 60)*
Steaua (0) 1 *(Schut 75 (og))* 24,000
Utrecht: Vorm; Wuytens, Schut, Cornelisse, Nesu, Silberbauer, Nijholt (Vostermans 80), Duplan, Mulenga, Mertens, Van Wolfswinkel.
Steaua: Tatarusanu; Latovlevici, Geraldo Alves, Eder Bonfim, Gardos, Nicolita, Angelov (Radut 66), Ricardo, Tanase, Surdu (Szekely 77), Stancu.

Thursday, 4 November 2010
Liverpool (0) 3 *(Gerrard 76, 88 (pen), 89)*
Napoli (1) 1 *(Lavezzi 28)* 33,895
Liverpool: Reina; Johnson, Konchesky, Raul Meireles, Carragher, Kyrgiakos, Spearing, Poulsen (Eccleston 65), N'Gog (Lucas 82), Jovanovic (Gerrard 46), Shelvey.
Napoli: De Sanctis; Dossena, Aronica, Cannavaro, Campagnaro, Pazienza, Maggio, Gargano, Hamsik (Yebda 84), Cavani, Lavezzi.

Steaua (1) 3 *(Gardos 29, Stancu 52, 53)*
Utrecht (1) 1 *(Mertens 33)* 9000
Steaua: Tatarusanu; Latovlevici, Geraldo Alves, Martinovic, Gardos, Nicolita, Ricardo, Apostol (Bicfalvi 46), Tanase (Szekely 83), Surdu (Angelov 87), Stancu.
Utrecht: Vorm; Wuytens, Schut, Cornelisse, Nesu, Silberbauer, Lensky, Demouge (De Kogel 82), Duplan (Danso 76), Mertens, Van Wolfswinkel.

Wednesday, 1 December 2010
Steaua (0) 1 *(Eder Bonfim 61)*
Liverpool (1) 1 *(Jovanovic 19)* 13,639
Steaua: Tatarusanu; Latovlevici, Geraldo Alves, Eder Bonfim, Gardos, Nicolita, Bicfalvi (Angelov 46), Ricardo, Tanase, Surdu (Szekely 80), Stancu.
Liverpool: Reina; Kelly, Fabio Aurelio, Poulsen, Kyrgiakos, Wilson, Shelvey, Cole (N'Gog 75), Jovanovic (Eccleston 79), Pacheco (Lucas 89), Babel.

Utrecht (3) 3 *(Van Wolfswinkel 6, 28 (pen), Demouge 35)*
Napoli (2) 3 *(Cavani 5, 42, 70 (pen))* 22,500
Utrecht: Vorm; Wuytens, Schut, Cornelisse, Nesu, Silberbauer (Nijholt 64), Lensky (Maguire 53), Demouge, Duplan (De Kogel 84), Mertens, Van Wolfswinkel.
Napoli: De Sanctis; Emilson Cribari, Zuniga (Dumitru 87), Grava (Maggio 63), Campagnaro (Cannavaro 84), Vitale, Yebda, Gargano, Hamsik, Cavani, Lavezzi.

Wednesday, 15 December 2010
Liverpool (0) 0
Utrecht (0) 0 37,800
Liverpool: Jones; Kelly, Fabio Aurelio, Poulsen, Skrtel (Kyrgiakos 46), Wilson, Shelvey, Eccleston (Pacheco 56), Jovanovic (Kuyt 73), Cole, Babel.
Utrecht: Vorm; Wuytens, Cornelisse, Keller, Nesu, Silberbauer, Nijholt, Maguire (Sarota 84), Duplan (Oar 71), Mertens, Van Wolfswinkel (De Kogel 46).

Napoli (0) 1 *(Cavani 90)*
Steaua (0) 0 40,631
Napoli: De Sanctis; Aronica, Zuniga, Cannavaro[*], Campagnaro (Sosa 52), Vitale (Dossena 79), Yebda (Dumitru 68), Pazienza, Maggio, Hamsik, Cavani.
Steaua: Tatarusanu; Latovlevici, Geraldo Alves, Eder Bonfim, Martinovic, Gardos (Bicfalvi 65), Angelov (Radut 89), Szekely (Matei 90), Ricardo, Surdu, Stancu.

Group K Table	P	W	D	L	F	A	Pts
Liverpool	6	2	4	0	8	3	10
Napoli	6	1	4	1	8	9	7
Steaua	6	1	3	2	9	11	6
Utrecht	6	0	5	1	5	7	5

GROUP L

Thursday, 16 September 2010
Besiktas (0) 1 *(Ernst 90)*
CSKA Sofia (0) 0 28,000
Besiktas: Hakan; Ferrari (Ibrahim T 37), Ibrahim U, Zapotocny, Hilbert, Ernst, Guti, Dag, Rodrigo Tabata (Bobo 72), Mert Nobre, Holosko (Quaresma 59).
CSKA Sofia: M'Bolhi; Trifonov, Vidanov, Aquaro, Stoyanov K, Tiero (Galchev 46), Marquinhos, Yanchev, Tonev (Trecarichi 58), Nelson (Saidhodzha 79), Sheridan.

Porto (1) 3 *(Rolando 26, Falcao 65, Ruben Micael 77)*
Rapid Vienna (0) 0 30,014
Porto: Helton; Fucile, Rolando, Maicon, Cristian Rodriguez, Joao Moutinho, Alvaro Pereira, Fernando, Ruben Micael (Castro 83), Falcao (Walter 79), Hulk (Belluschi 68).
Rapid Vienna: Hedl; Soma, Dober (Patocka 80), Sonnleitner, Kayhan, Saurer (Drazan 62), Hofmann (Trimmel 73), Kavlak, Kulovits, Hinum, Nuhiu.

Thursday, 30 September 2010
CSKA Sofia (0) 0
Porto (1) 1 *(Falcao 16)* 10,600
CSKA Sofia: M'Bolhi; Trifonov, Vidanov, Aquaro, Dechev, Grillo (Delev 67), Tiero (Trecarichi 58), Marquinhos, Yanchev, Michel (Galchev 79), Sheridan.
Porto: Helton; Sapunaru, Otamendi, Maicon, Cristian Rodriguez, Belluschi (Guarin 75), Joao Moutinho, Souza, Alvaro Pereira, Falcao (Walter 72), Hulk (Silvestre Varela 65).

Rapid Vienna (0) 1 *(Kavlak 51)*
Besiktas (0) 2 *(Holosko 55, Bobo 64)* 50,000
Rapid Vienna: Hedl; Soma, Patocka, Sonnleitner, Kayhan, Hofmann, Kavlak, Kulovits, Pehlivan (Salihi 80), Nuhiu, Trimmel (Vennegoor of Hesselink 67).
Besiktas: Hakan; Ferrari, Ibrahim T, Ibrahim U, Hilbert, Ernst, Guti (Necip 87), Quaresma (Holosko 32), Mehmet Aurelio, Rodrigo Tabata, Bobo (Mert Nobre 76).

Thursday, 21 October 2010
Besiktas (0) 1 *(Bobo 90)*
Porto (1) 3 *(Falcao 26, Hulk 59, 78)* 21,722
Besiktas: Hakan; Ibrahim T, Ibrahim U (Ismail 78), Zapotocny (Ali 71), Hilbert, Ernst, Rodrigo Tabata, Necip, Nihat, Mert Nobre (Ersan 83), Bobo.
Porto: Helton; Sapunaru, Rolando, Maicon[*], Cristian Rodriguez (Silvestre Varela 75), Belluschi, Joao Moutinho (Guarin 81), Alvaro Pereira, Fernando[*], Falcao (Otamendi 46), Hulk.

CSKA Sofia (0) 0
Rapid Vienna (2) 2 *(Vennegoor of Hesselink 28, Hofmann 32)* 7996
CSKA Sofia: M'Bolhi; Minev (Tiboni 46), Trifonov, Vidanov, Aquero, Stoyanov K (Dechev 72), Marquinhos, Yanchev, Nelson (Tonev 57), Delev, Sheridan.
Rapid Vienna: Hedl; Soma, Katzer, Sonnleitner, Kayhan, Saurer (Drazan 64), Hofmann (Trimmel 84), Kavlak, Heikkinen, Pehlivan, Vennegoor of Hesselink (Nuhiu 77).

Thursday, 4 November 2010
Porto (1) 1 *(Falcao 36 (pen))*
Besiktas (0) 1 *(Nihat 62)* 24,139
Porto: Helton; Fucile, Rolando, Otamendi, Cristian Rodriguez[*], Belluschi (Souza 73), Alvaro Pereira, Guarin, Ruben Micael, Falcao (Walter 79), Hulk (Joao Moutinho 63).
Besiktas: Hakan; Ibrahim T[*], Ibrahim U, Hilbert, Ernst, Guti, Mehmet Aurelio, Ersan, Rodrigo Tabata (Holosko 46), Nihat (Erhan 90), Bobo (Necip 84).

Rapid Vienna (0) 1 *(Salihi 56 (pen))*
CSKA Sofia (0) 2 *(Yanchev 50, Marquinhos 65)*   48,500
Rapid Vienna: Hedl; Soma, Katzer (Trimmel 68), Sonnleitner, Kayhan, Kavlak, Heikkinen, Drazan, Pehlivan (Dober 83), Salihi, Nuhiu (Gartler 68).
CSKA Sofia: M'Bolhi; Minev, Trifonov (Grillo 88), Aquaro, Stoyanov K, Marquinhos, Yanchev, Galchev, Tonev (Yanev 90), Nelson (Delev 82), Michel.

Wednesday, 1 December 2010
CSKA Sofia (0) 1 *(Sheridan 79)*
Besiktas (0) 2 *(Zapotocny 59, Holosko 64)*   9100
CSKA Sofia: M'Bohli; Minev, Vidanov, Stoyanov K, Grillo, Marquinhos, Yanchev, Galchev (Yanev 74), Tonev (Sheridan 75), Michel, Delev.
Besiktas: Cenk (Hakan 46); Zapotocny, Ismail, Hilbert, Ernst, Guti, Mehmet Aurelio, Ersan, Rodrigo Tabata (Necip 75), Mert Nobre (Ali 46), Holosko.

Rapid Vienna (1) 1 *(Trimmel 39)*
Porto (1) 3 *(Falcao 42, 86, 88)*   47,200
Rapid Vienna: Hedl; Soma, Patocka, Sonnleitner, Kayhan, Saurer, Kulovits, Heikkinen, Drazan (Salihi 63), Gartler (Nuhiu 77), Trimmel (Dober 83).
Porto: Helton; Fucile, Sapunaru, Rolando, Otamendi, Joao Moutinho, Fernando (Guarin 16), Ruben Micael (Belluschi 71), Silvestre Varela (Ukra 46), Falcao, Hulk.

Wednesday, 15 December 2010
Besiktas (2) 2 *(Quaresma 32, Ernst 45)*
Rapid Vienna (0) 0   16,686
Besiktas: Cenk; Ferrari, Zapotocny (Ersan 24), Ismail, Ali, Hilbert (Erhan 82), Ernst, Guti, Quaresma (Mert Nobre 68), Mehmet Aurelio, Rodrigo Tabata.
Rapid Vienna: Payer; Soma, Katzer, Sonnleitner, Kayhan (Patocka 67), Kavlak, Kulovits (Saurer 46), Drazan, Pehlivan, Gartler, Trimmel (Dober 46).

Porto (1) 3 *(Otamendi 22, Ruben Micael 54, James Rodriguez 90)*
CSKA Sofia (0) 1 *(Delev 48)*   22,930
Porto: Helton; Fucile, Otamendi, Maicon, Belluschi, Souza (Guarin 80), Alvaro Pereira, Ruben Micael (Joao Moutinho 71), James Rodriguez, Falcao (Hulk 60), Walter.
CSKA Sofia: M'Bolhi; Vidanov, Aquaro, Stoyanov K, Grillo (Dechev 63), Yanev, Marquinhos, Yanchev (Galchev 88), Tonev (Sheridan 77), Michel, Delev.

Group L Table	P	W	D	L	F	A	Pts
Porto	6	5	1	0	14	4	16
Besiktas	6	4	1	1	9	6	13
Rapid Vienna	6	1	0	5	5	12	3
CSKA Sofia	6	1	0	5	4	10	3

KNOCK-OUT STAGE

SECOND ROUND FIRST LEG

Tuesday, 15 February 2011
Aris Salonika (0) 0
Manchester C (0) 0   21,000
Aris Salonika: Sifakis; Michel, Neto (Castillo 88), Ronaldo, Vangjeli, Lagaridis, Faty, Toja, Prittas, Sukutu, Bobadilla (Cesarec 72).
Manchester C: Hart; Boateng, Kolarov, Barry, Toure K, Richards, Silva, Toure Y, Dzeko (Zabaleta 84), Tevez, Wright-Phillips (Balotelli 77).

Thursday, 17 February 2011
Anderlecht (0) 0
Ajax (1) 3 *(Alderweireld 32, Eriksen 59, El Hamdaoui 68)*   21,195
Anderlecht: Proto; Juhasz, Wasilewski, Mazuch, Lecjaks, Biglia, Boussoufa, Gillet (Kouyate 81), Suarez, Kanu, Lukaku (De Sutter 68).
Ajax: Stekelenburg; Vertonghen, Van der Wiel, Blind (Anita 77), Alderweireld, De Jong, Enoh, Eriksen, El Hamdaoui, Sulejmani (Oleguer 81), Ebicilio.

Basle (2) 2 *(Frei 36, Streller 41)*
Spartak Moscow (0) 3 *(Kombarov D 61, Dzyuba 70, Ananidze 90)*   13,073
Basle: Costanzo; Safari, Abraham, Kusunga, Yapi-Yapo (Cabral 88), Steinhofer, Stocker (Zoua 87), Shaqiri■, Xhaka, Frei (Tembo 80), Streller.
Spartak Moscow: Dikan; Suchy, Rojo, Sheshukov (Ananidze 46), Makeev (Yakovlev 85), McGeady, Kombarov K, Kombarov D, Alex, Rafael Carioca, Dzyuba.

BATE Borisov (1) 2 *(Renan 16, Gordeychuk 81)*
Paris St Germain (1) 2 *(Mevlut 30, Luyindula 89)*   6080
BATE Borisov: Gutor; Yurevich, Bordachev, Shitov, Simic, Nekhajchik, Renan (Gordeychuk 75), Volodko A, Rudik (Likhtarovich 66), Olekhnovich, Rodionov (Skavysh 83).
Paris St Germain: Edel; Jallet, Camara, Ceara, Sakho, Clement, Nene (Maurice 63), Chantome, Luyindula, Giuly (Bodmer 68), Mevlut (Makonda 83).

Benfica (0) 2 *(Cardozo 70, Jara 82)*
Stuttgart (1) 1 *(Harnik 21)*   44,852
Benfica: Roberto; Luisao, Sidnei, Maxi Pereira, Fabio Coentrao, Aimar (Carlos Martins 75), Javi Garcia, Gaitan, Salvio (Kardec 74), Cardozo, Jara (Felipe Menezes 87).
Stuttgart: Ulreich; Boulahrouz, Delpierre, Tasci, Molinaro, Hajnal (Elson 63), Kuzmanovic (Niedermeier 76), Trasch, Harnik, Claudir da Silva, Okazaki.

Besiktas (1) 1 *(Quaresma 37)*
Dynamo Kiev (1) 4 *(Vukojevic 27, Shevchenko 50, Yussuf 56, Gusev 90 (pen))*   21,809
Besiktas: Hakan; Ferrari, Sivok, Ismail, Hilbert, Ernst (Erhan 56), Guti, Quaresma■, Mehmet Aurelio (Necip 80), Mert Nobre (Hugo Almeida 69), Bobo.
Dynamo Kiev: Shovkovskiy; Leandro Almeida, Mikhalik (Popov 73), Danilo Silva, Gusev, Yussuf, Eremenko, Vukojevic, Milevskiy, Shevchenko (Kravets 84), Yarmolenko (Garmash 88).

Lech (0) 1 *(Rudnevs 72)*
Braga (0) 0   29,133
Lech: Kotorowski; Bosacki, Gancarczyk, Arboleda, Djurdjevic, Wilk (Kielb 53), Krivets, Kikut, Stilic, Slusarski (Mozdzen 46), Rudnevs (Ubiparip 84).
Braga: Artur Moraes; Rodriguez, Kaka, Miguel Garcia, Silvio, Hugo Viana, Helder Barbosa (Alan 68), Custodio,Salino, Meyong (Marcio Mossoro 86), Lima.

Lille (2) 2 *(Gueye 6, De Melo 31)*
PSV Eindhoven (0) 2 *(Bouma 83, Toivonen 84)*   16,951
Lille: Landreau; Rozehnal, Debuchy (Beria 75), Emerson, Chedjou, Vandam (Cabaye 70), Dumont, Obraniak, Gueye, Frau (Gervinho 83), De Melo.
PSV Eindhoven: Isaksson; Rodriguez, Pieters, Bouma (Marcelo 85), Manolev, Engelaar (Wuytens 68), Hutchinson, Dzsudzsak, Lens (Bakkal 67), Berg, Toivonen.

Metalist Kharkiv (0) 0
Leverkusen (1) 4 *(Derdiyok 23, Castro 72, Sam 89, 90)*   35,150
Metalist Kharkiv: Disljenkovic; Fininho, Villagra, Obradovic, Pshenichnikh (Berezovchuk 15), Cleiton Xavier, Blanco, Valyaev, Oleynik, Cristaldo (Lysenko 68), Taison.
Leverkusen: Adler; Friedrich, Kadlec, Vida, Reinartz, Balitsch (Castro 46), Renato Augusto (Rolfes 74), Vidal, Sam, Bender, Derdiyok (Kiessling 79).

Napoli (0) 0
Villarreal (0) 0   47,529
Napoli: De Sanctis; Emilson Cribari, Dossena, Aronica■, Campagnaro, Yebda (Pazienza 68), Maggio, Gargano (Sosa 78), Mascara (Hamsik 61), Cavani, Lavezzi.
Villarreal: Diego Lopez; Gonzalo, Musacchio, Capdevila, Mario Gaspar, Senna (Marchena 61), Cazorla (Catala 87), Borja Valero, Bruno, Rossi (Marco Ruben 77), Nilmar.

PAOK Salonika (0) 0
CSKA Moscow (1) 1 *(Necid 29)*   22,245
PAOK Salonika: Chalkias (Kresic 46); Cirillo, Contreras, Sznaucer, Vitolo (El Zhar 57), Garcia, Lino, Vieirinha, Ivic (Athanasiadis 70), Tsoukalas, Salpingidis.
CSKA Moscow: Akinfeev; Berezutski V, Ignashevich, Nababkin, Schennikov, Semberas, Mamaev, Cauna (Aldonin 66), Tosic (Berezutski A 90), Doumbia (Dzagoev 85), Necid.

Rangers (0) 1 *(Whittaker 66)*
Sporting (0) 1 *(Fernandez 89)*   34,095
Rangers: McGregor; Whittaker, Papac, Foster, Weir, Bougherra, Davis, Edu, Lafferty, Diouf, Weiss.
Sporting: Rui Patricio; Anderson Polga, Joao Pereira, Evaldo, Daniel Carrico, Maniche (Fernandez 77), Pedro Mendes, Alberto Zapater, Cristiano (Carlos Saleiro 74), Helder Postiga (Diogo Salomao 85), Yannick Djalo.

Rubin (0) 0
Twente (0) 2 *(De Jong 77, Wisgerhof 88)*   657
Rubin: Arlauskis; Bocchetti, Cesar Navas, Kuzmin, Ansaldi, Gokdeniz (Kasaev 73), Noboa, Natcho, Bystrov, Lebedenko (Medvedev 87), Dyadyun.
Twente: Mihaylov; Onyewu, Wisgerhof, Rosales, Douglas, Landzaat, Janssen, Brama, Chadli, Ruiz (Bajrami 86), De Jong.

Sevilla (0) 1 *(Kanoute 66)*
Porto (0) 2 *(Rolando 58, Guarin 85)*   21,555
Sevilla: Palop; Fernando Navarro, Fazio, Sergio Sanchez, Caceres, Jesus Navas, Rakitic (Romaric 78), Medel, Perotti (Diego Capel 86), Kanoute, Luis Fabiano (Negredo 74).
Porto: Helton; Fucile, Sapunaru, Rolando, Otamendi, Belluschi (Alvaro Pereira 86), Joao Moutinho, Fernando, James Rodriguez (Cristian Rodriguez 59), Silvestre Varela (Guarin 69), Hulk.

Sparta Prague (0) 0
Liverpool (0) 0   17,569
Sparta Prague: Blazek; Brabec, Kusnir, Repka, Pamic, Vacek, Matejovsky (Pekhart 90), Abena, Keric (Sionko 73), Kweuke, Kadlec (Zeman 89).
Liverpool: Reina; Johnson, Wilson, Raul Meireles, Carragher, Kyrgiakos, Rodriguez, Lucas, N'Gog (Skrtel 83), Kuyt, Fabio Aurelio (Cole 37).

Young Boys (0) 2 *(Lulic 46, Mayuka 90)*
Zenit (1) 1 *(Lombaerts 20)*   15,026
Young Boys: Wolfli; Nef, Dudar (Raimondi 59), El Jemal, Affolter, Degen, Sutter, Doubai T, Lulic, Costanzo (Mayuka 83), N'Tsama.
Zenit: Malafeev; Bruno Alves, Anyukov, Lombaerts (Fernando Meira 54), Hubocan, Danny, Shirokov (Semak 79), Denisov, Ionov, Lazovic (Bystrov* 44), Kerzhakov.

SECOND ROUND SECOND LEG

Tuesday, 22 February 2011
CSKA Moscow (0) 1 *(Ignashevich 80)*
PAOK Salonika (0) 1 *(Muslimovic 67)*   10,000
CSKA Moscow: Akinfeev (Chepchugov 66); Berezutski V, Ignashevich, Nababkin, Schennikov, Semberas, Mamaev, Cauna (Aldonin 62), Tosic, Vagner Love (Berezutski A 90), Necid.
PAOK Salonika: Kresic; Cirillo, Contreras, Sznaucer, Garcia, Lino, Vierinha, Ivic (Athanasiadis 87), Tsoukalas, Muslimovic, Salpingidis.
Played in Khimki.

Wednesday, 23 February 2011
Porto (0) 0
Sevilla (0) 1 *(Luis Fabiano 71)*   35,609
Porto: Helton; Fucile, Rolando, Otamendi, Belluschi, Joao Moutinho (Guarin 74), Alvaro Pereira*, Fernando, Silvestre Varela (Maicon 86), Falcao (Sapunaru 74), Hulk.

Sevilla: Javi Varas; Fernando Navarro, Alexis*, Fazio, Sergio Sanchez (Luis Fabiano 55), Zokora (Medel 46), Jesus Navas, Rakitic, Perotti (Rodri 86), Kanoute, Negredo.

Thursday, 24 February 2011
Ajax (2) 2 *(Sulejmani 11, 17)*
Anderlecht (0) 0   42,591
Ajax: Stekelenburg (Verhoeven 46); Vertonghen, Van der Wiel, Blind, Alderweireld, De Jong, Enoh (Lindgren 16), Eriksen, El Hamdaoui, Sulejmani, Ebecilio (De Zeeuw 71).
Anderlecht: Proto; Juhasz, Wasilewski (De Sutter 72), Mazuch, Lecjaks, Biglia, Gillet, Kouyate, Suarez, Kanu (Marecek 77), Lukaku.

Braga (2) 2 *(Alan 8, Lima 36)*
Lech (0) 0   12,000
Braga: Artur Moraes; Rodriguez, Kaka, Miguel Garcia, Silvio, Hugo Viana, Marcio Mossoro (Salino 69), Helder Barbosa (Paulo Cesar 68), Custodio, Alan (Elderson 82), Lima.
Lech: Kotorowski; Bosacki, Gancarczyk, Arboleda, Djurdjevic, Wolakiewicz (Kielb 61), Injac (Wilk 46), Krivets, Kikut*, Stilic (Ubiparip 71), Rudnevs.

Dynamo Kiev (1) 4 *(Vukojevic 3, Yarmolenko 55, Gusev 64, Shevchenko 74)*
Besiktas (0) 0   15,000
Dynamo Kiev: Shovkovskiy; Leandro Almeida, Popov, Danilo Silva, Gusev, Yussuf, Eremenko, Vukojevic, Milevskiy (Kravets 69), Shevchenko (Zozulya 77), Yarmolenko (Ninkovic 62).
Besiktas: Rustu; Ferrari (Ibrahim T 59), Sivok, Ismail, Hilbert, Ernst, Guti (Onur 72), Mehmet Aurelio, Necip, Hugo Almeida (Mert Nobre 58), Bobo.

Leverkusen (0) 2 *(Rolfes 47, Ballack 70)*
Metalist Kharkiv (0) 0   16,212
Leverkusen: Adler; Friedrich, Schwaab, Vida, Castro, Ballack, Rolfes (Da Costa 64), Renato Augusto (Kampl 64), Bender (Vidal 46), Kiessling, Jorgensen.
Metalist Kharkiv: Disljenkovic; Fininho, Obradovic, Gueye, Romanchuk, Shelayev, Cleiton Xavier (Vorobei 76), Blanco, Oleynik, Devic (Valyaev 57), Taison (Cristaldo 57).

Liverpool (0) 1 *(Kuyt 86)*
Sparta Prague (0) 0   42,949
Liverpool: Reina; Wilson, Kelly (Carragher 46), Raul Meireles, Kyrgiakos, Agger (Skrtel 85), Poulsen (Spearing 65), Lucas, N'Gog, Kuyt, Cole.
Sparta Prague: Blazek; Brabec, Kusnir, Repka, Pamic (Keric 90), Sionko (Podany 74), Vacek, Matejovsky, Abena (Pekhart 78), Kweuke, Kadlec.

Manchester C (2) 3 *(Dzeko 7, 12, Toure Y 75)*
Aris Salonika (0) 0   36,748
Manchester C: Hart; Boateng, Kolarov, Barry, Lescott, Kompany (Zabaleta 35), Balotelli, Toure Y, Dzeko, Tevez (Vieira 79), Silva (Wright-Phillips 80).
Aris Salonika: Sifakis; Michel, Neto (Kaznaferis 80), Ronaldo, Vangjeli, Lazaridis, Faty, Toja, Prittas, Sakata (Mendrinos 46), Bobadilla (Koke 61).

Paris St Germain (0) 0
BATE Borisov (0) 0   5000
Paris St Germain: Edel; Camara, Tiene, Armand, Ceara, Clement, Bodmer (Kebano 73), Chantome, Luyindula, Mevlut (Hoarau 67), Maurice (Makonda 83).
BATE Borisov: Gutor; Yurevich, Bordachev, Shitov, Simic, Likhtarovich (Gordeychuk 61), Nekhajchik, Renan (Skavysh 77), Volodko A, Rudik (Olekhnovich 66), Rodionov.

PSV Eindhoven (0) 3 *(Dzsudsak 55, Lens 67, Marcelo 73)*
Lille (1) 1 *(Frau 23)*   28,500
PSV Eindhoven: Isaksson; Pieters, Bouma, Marcelo, Manolev, Engelaar (Wuytens 81), Hutchinson, Dzsudsak (Bakkal 87), Lens, Berg, Toivonen.

Lille: Mouko; Rozehnal, Emerson, Rami (Chedjou 77), Vandam, Mavuba (Hazard 65), Dumont, Obraniak, Gueye, Frau■, De Melo (Sow 69).

Spartak Moscow (0) 1 *(McGeady 90)*
Basle (1) 1 *(Chipperfield 15)*   12,000
Spartak Moscow: Dikan; Suchy, Rojo, Sheshukov, Makeev (Yakovlev 79), McGeady, Kombarov K, Kombarov D, Alex, Ananidze, Dzyuba.
Basle: Costanzo; Safari, Steinhofer, Abraham, Kusunga, Chipperfield, Cabral, Stocker, Tembo (Frei 66), Xhaka (Yapi-Yapo 76), Zoua.

Sporting (1) 2 *(Pedro Mendes 42, Yannick Djalo 83)*
Rangers (1) 2 *(Diouf 20, Edu 90)*   15,375
Sporting: Rui Patricio; Anderson Polga, Torsiglieri, Abel, Joao Pereira, Evaldo, Pedro Mendes (Carlos Saleiro 81), Alberto Zapater, Fernandez (Nuno Coelho 90), Helder Postiga (Andre Santos 87), Yannick Djalo.
Rangers: McGregor; Whittaker, Papac, Foster, Weir (Lafferty 71), Bougherra, Davis, Edu, Fleck (Weiss 72), Diouf (Healy 82), Bartley.

Stuttgart (0) 0
Benfica (1) 2 *(Salvio 30, Cardozo 78)*   25,800
Stuttgart: Ziegler (Ulreich 52); Boulahrouz (Gebhart 61), Delpierre, Molinaro, Niedermeier, Hajnal (Elson 79), Kuzmanovic■, Trasch, Harnik, Okazaki, Schipplock.
Benfica: Roberto; Luisao, Sidnei, Maxi Pereira, Fabio Coentrao, Aimar (Carlos Martins 73), Gaitan, Airton, Salvio, Cardozo (Felipe Menezes 88), Jara (Kardec 90).

Twente (1) 2 *(Janssen 45, Douglas 47)*
Rubin (2) 2 *(Ansaldi 22, Noboa 24)*   23,000
Twente: Mihaylov; Onyewu, Wisgerhof, Rosales, Douglas, Landzaat, Janssen, Brama, Chadli (Janko 86), Ruiz (Bajrami 73), De Jong (Buysse 90).
Rubin: Ryzhikov; Bocchetti, Cesar Navas, Kaleshin, Ansaldi (Kuzmin 80), Gokdeniz (Kasaev 75), Ryazantsev, Noboa, Bystrov (Natcho 69), Lebedenko, Dyadyun.

Villarreal (2) 2 *(Nilmar 43, Rossi 45)*
Napoli (1) 1 *(Hamsik 17)*   25,000
Villarreal: Diego Lopez; Gonzalo, Musacchio, Capdevila, Mario Gaspar, Cani (Marcos Gullon 80), Cazorla (Catala 78), Borja Valero, Bruno, Rossi (Marco Ruben 89), Nilmar.
Napoli: Di Sanctis; Emilson Cribari (Mascara 82), Dossena, Zuniga, Campagnaro, Victor Ruiz, Yebda (Pazienza 64), Gargano, Sosa (Cavani 53), Hamsik, Lavezzi.

Zenit (1) 3 *(Lazovic 41, Semak 52, Shirokov 76)*
Young Boys (1) 1 *(El Jemal 21)*   17,500
Zenit: Malafeev; Fernando Meira, Lukovic, Bruno Alves, Anyukov, Semak, Danny, Shirokov (Huszti 84), Zyryanov (Ionov 72), Denisov, Lazovic (Faizulin 90).
Young Boys: Wolfli; Spycher, Dudar, El Jemal, Affolter, Degen (Mayuka 80), Raimondi (Schneuwly C 79), Sutter, Doubai T, Lulic (Schneuwly M 85), N'Tsama.

THIRD ROUND FIRST LEG

Thursday, 10 March 2011

Ajax (0) 0
Spartak Moscow (0) 1 *(Alex 57)*   32,841
Ajax: Stekelenburg; Vertonghen, Van der Wiel, Anita, Blind, Alderweireld, De Zeeuw (Enoh 74), De Jong, Eriksen, Sulejmani, Ebecilio (Ozbiliz 85).
Spartak Moscow: Dikan; Suchy, Rojo, Makeev, McGeady (Yakovlev 90), Ibson (Welliton 57), Kombarov K, Kombarov D, Alex, Rafael Carioca (Sheshukov 84), Dzyuba.

Benfica (1) 2 *(Pereira 42, Jara 82)*
Paris St Germain (1) 1 *(Luyindula 15)*   33,928
Benfica: Roberto; Luisao, Sidnei, Maxi Pereira, Fabio Coentrao, Javi Garcia, Gaitan (Aimar 71), Carlos Martins (Cesar Peixoto 85), Salvio (Jara 66), Saviola, Cardozo.
Paris St Germain: Edel; Camara, Traore, Armand, Ceara, Makonda (Makhedjouf 75), Bodmer (Kebano 70), Nene, Chantome, Luyindula (Maurice 44), Mevlut.

Braga (1) 1 *(Alan 18 (pen))*
Liverpool (0) 0   12,991
Braga: Artur Moraes; Rodriguez, Kaka, Miguel Garcia, Silvio, Hugo Viana, Marcio Mossoro (Paulao 69), Salino, Alan, Lima (Meyong 77), Paulo Cesar (Helder Barbosa 90).
Liverpool: Reina; Johnson, Kyrgiakos, Raul Meireles, Carragher, Skrtel, Lucas, Poulsen (Carroll 57), Spearing, Kuyt, Cole.

CSKA Moscow (0) 0
Porto (0) 1 *(Guarin 70)*   20,000
CSKA Moscow: Akinfeev; Berezutski V, Ignashevich, Nababkin, Schennikov, Semberas, Honda (Tosic 75), Mamaev, Dzagoev, Vagner Love, Doumbia (Necid 79).
Porto: Helton; Fucile, Sapunaru, Rolando, Otamendi, Joao Moutinho, Guarin (Souza 81), Fernando, James Rodriguez (Silvestre Varela 58), Falcao, Hulk (Cristian Rodriguez 73).

Dynamo Kiev (1) 2 *(Shevchenko 25, Gusev 77)*
Manchester C (0) 0   16,315
Dynamo Kiev: Shovkovskiy; Popov, Danilo Silva, Khacheridi, Gusev, Yussuf, Eremenko, Vukojevic, Milevskiy, Shevchenko (Ninkovic 88), Yarmolenko.
Manchester C: Hart; Richards, Kolarov (Wright Phillips 82), Barry, Lescott, Kompany, Silva, Toure Y, Balotelli (Tevez 57), Dzeko, Zabaleta.

Leverkusen (1) 2 *(Kadlec 33, Castro 72)*
Villarreal (1) 3 *(Rossi 42, Nilmar 70, 90)*   20,126
Leverkusen: Adler; Kadlec, Schwaab, Vida, Reinartz, Castro, Rolfes (Bender 88), Renato Augusto, Vidal, Sam (Jorgensen 76), Derdiyok (Kiessling 46).
Villarreal: Diego Lopez; Marchena, Gonzalo, Musacchio, Catala, Mario Gaspar, Borja Valero, Bruno, Mubarak (Cazorla 61), Rossi (Nilmar 69), Marco Ruben (Joan Oriol 84).

PSV Eindhoven (0) 0
Rangers (0) 0   26,000
PSV Eindhoven: Isaksson; Pieters, Bouma, Marcelo, Manolev, Engelaar, Hutchinson, Dzsudzsak, Lens, Berg (Koevermans 70), Toivonen (Bakkal 84).
Rangers: Alexander; Whittaker, Foster, Bartley, Weir, Bougherra, Davis, Edu, Lafferty (Wylde 80), Diouf (Weiss 64), Hutton.

Twente (1) 3 *(De Jong 25, 90, Landzaat 56)*
Zenit (0) 0   20,750
Twente: Mihaylov; Wisgerhof, Buysse, Rosales, Douglas, Landzaat, Janssen, Brama, Bajrami (John 76), Chadli, De Jong.
Zenit: Malafeev; Fernando Meira, Lukovic, Bruno Alves, Anyukov, Danny, Shirokov (Huszti 69), Zyryanov (Faizulin 69), Denisov, Ionov (Kerzhakov 86), Lazovic.

THIRD ROUND SECOND LEG

Thursday, 17 March 2011

Liverpool (0) 0
Braga (0) 0   37,494
Liverpool: Reina; Johnson, Wilson, Raul Meiereles, Carragher, Skrtel, Rodriguez (N'Gog 75), Cole (Spearing 75), Carroll, Kuyt, Lucas.
Braga: Artur Moraes; Rodriguez, Paulao, Miguel Garcia, Silvio, Hugo Viana, Vandinho (Kaka 74), Salino (Marcio Mossoro 89), Alan, Lima (Meyong 85), Paulo Cesar.

Manchester C (1) 1 *(Kolarov 39)*
Dynamo Kiev (0) 0 27,816
Manchester C: Hart; Richards, Kolarov (Milner 88), Barry (Johnson A 71), Lescott, Kompany, De Jong, Silva (Dzeko 76), Balotelli**, Tevez, Toure Y.
Dynamo Kiev: Shovkovskiy; Leandro Almeida, Popov, Danilo Silva, Gusev, Yussuf, Eremenko, Ninkovic (Zozulya 46), Vukojevic, Shevchenko (Garmash 62), Yarmolenko (Betao 90).

Paris St Germain (1) 1 *(Bodmer 35)*
Benfica (1) 1 *(Gaitan 27)* 40,193
Paris St Germain: Edel; Jallet, Tiene, Armand, Ceara (Maurice 78), Sakho, Makelele, Bodmer (Hoarau 68), Nene, Chantome, Mevlut (Giuly 68).
Benfica: Roberto; Luisao, Sidnei, Maxi Pereira, Fabio Coentrao, Aimar (Cesar Peixoto 80), Javi Garcia, Gaitan (Jardel 90), Salvio, Saviola (Carlos Martins 64), Cardozo.

Porto (2) 2 *(Hulk 1, Guarin 24)*
CSKA Moscow (1) 1 *(Tosic 29)* 32,712
Porto: Helton; Fucile, Sapunaru, Rolando, Otamendi, Joao Moutinho, Guarin, Fernando, James Rodriguez (Belluschi 52), Falcao (Silvestre Varela 77), Hulk (Cristian Rodriguez 87).
CSKA Moscow: Akinfeev; Berezutski V, Ignashevich, Nababkin, Schennikov, Honda, Aldonin, Dzagoev (Gonzalez 74), Tosic (Oliseh 72), Vagner Love, Doumbia (Necid 65).

Rangers (0) 0
PSV Eindhoven (1) 1 *(Lens 14)* 35,373
Rangers: Alexander; Whittaker, Papac, Foster (Healy 86), Weir (Naismith 46), Bougherra, Davis, Edu, Lafferty (Diouf 66), Bartley, Wylde.
PSV Eindhoven: Isaksson; Pieters, Bouma, Marcelo, Engelaar, Hutchinson, Dzsudzsak, Tamata, Lens, Berg (Bakkal 66), Toivonen.

Spartak Moscow (2) 3 *(Kombarov D 21, Welliton 30, Alex 54)*
Ajax (0) 0 33,631
Spartak Moscow: Dikan; Rojo, Sheshukov, Makeev, McGeady (Ari 67), Ibson, Kombarov K, Kombarov D, Alex (Dzyuba 84), Rafael Carioca, Welliton.
Ajax: Verhoeven; Vertonghen, Van der Wiel, Anita, Blind (Ozbiliz 46), Alderweireld, De Zeeuw, De Jong, Eriksen (Cvitanich 63), Sulejmani (Enoh 46), Ebecilio.

Villarreal (1) 2 *(Cazorla 33, Rossi 61)*
Leverkusen (0) 1 *(Derdiyok 82)* 19,779
Villarreal: Diego Lopez; Marchena, Gonzalo, Musacchio, Catala, Mario Gaspar, Cazorla (Cani 80), Borja Valero (Capdevila 74), Bruno, Rossi (Nilmar 69), Marco Ruben.
Leverkusen: Adler; Hyypia, Kadlec, Vida (Schwaab 62), Reinartz, Castro (Sam 43), Rolfes, Renato Augusto, Bender, Kiessling (Ballack 53), Derdiyok.

Zenit (2) 2 *(Shirokov 16, Kerzhakov 37)*
Twente (0) 0 18,000
Zenit: Zhevnov; Fernando Meira (Huszti 46), Lukovic, Bruno Alves, Anyukov, Danny, Shirokov, Denisov, Ionov, Lazovic (Bukharov 64), Kerzhakov (Zyryanov 70).
Twente: Mihaylov; Onyewu, Wisgerhof, Buysse, Rosales, Landzaat, Janssen, Brama, Bajrami (John 72), Chadli, De Jong.

QUARTER-FINALS FIRST LEG
Thursday, 7 April 2011
Benfica (2) 4 *(Aimar 37, Salvio 45, 52, Saviola 90)*
PSV Eindhoven (0) 1 *(Labyad 80)* 60,026
Benfica: Roberto; Luisao, Maxi Pereira, Fabio Coentrao, Jardel, Aimar (Jara 78), Javi Garcia, Gaitan (Cesar Peixoto 78), Salvio, Saviola, Cardozo (Felipe Menezes 90).

PSV Eindhoven: Isaksson; Pieters (Wuytens 72), Bouma, Marcelo, Manolev, Bakkal, Engelaar, Hutchinson, Dzsudzsak, Lens, Berg (Labyad 79).

Dynamo Kiev (1) 1 *(Yarmolenko 6)*
Braga (1) 1 *(Gusev 13 (og))* 16,150
Dynamo Kiev: Shovkovskiy; Popov, Danilo Silva, Khacheridi, Gusev, Yussuf, Eremenko, Vukojevic, Milevskiy, Kravets (Shevchenko** 46), Yarmolenko.
Braga: Artur Moraes; Paulao (Custodio 46), Kaka, Miguel Garcia, Silvio, Hugo Viana, Vandinho, Salino (Marcio Mossoro 74), Alan, Lima (Meyong 82), Paulo Cesar.

Porto (1) 5 *(Falcao 38, 84, 90, Silvestre Varela 65, Maicon 70)*
Spartak Moscow (0) 1 *(Kombarov K 71)* 38,209
Porto: Helton; Fucile, Rolando, Maicon, Joao Moutinho, Silvestre Varela (James Rodriguez 72), Alvaro Pereira, Guarin (Belluschi 69), Fernando, Falcao, Hulk (Cristian Rodriguez 80).
Spartak Moscow: Dikan; Suchy, Rojo, Makeev (Yakovlev 86), McGeady (Dzyuba 68), Ibson, Kombarov K, Kombarov D, Alex, Rafael Carioca, Welliton.

Villarreal (3) 5 *(Marchena 22, Borja Valero 43, Nilmar 45, 80, Rossi 55)*
Twente (0) 1 *(Janko 90)* 19,094
Villarreal: Diego Lopez; Marchena, Gonzalo (Capdevila 71), Musacchio, Catala (Kiko 82), Mario Gaspar, Cazorla, Borja Valero (Cani 79), Bruno, Rossi, Nilmar.
Twente: Mihaylov; Onyewu, Wisgerhof, Tiendalli, Rosales, Douglas, Janssen, Brama (Landzaat 77), Bajrami, Ruiz (Chadli 60), De Jong (Janko 32).

QUARTER-FINALS SECOND LEG
Thursday, 14 April 2011
Braga (0) 0
Dynamo Kiev (0) 0 18,000
Braga: Artur Moraes; Paulao, Silvio, Hugo Viana, Vandinho, Custodio, Salino, Meyong (Marcio Mossoro 70), Alan, Lima (Helder Barbosa 90), Paulo Cesar**.
Dynamo Kiev: Shovkovskiy; Popov**, Danilo Silva, Khacheridi (Leandro Almeida 46), Gusev, Yussuf, Eremenko, Vukojevic, Milevskiy, Kravets (Garmash 65), Yarmolenko.

PSV Eindhoven (2) 2 *(Dzsudzsak 17, Lens 25)*
Benfica (1) 2 *(Luisao 45, Gardozo 63 (pen))* 30,000
PSV Eindhoven: Isaksson; Rodriguez, Marcelo (Berg 72), Manolev (Nijland 85), Bakkal, Hutchinson, Dzsudzsak, Wuytens, Labyad, Tamata (Vukovic 72), Lens.
Benfica: Roberto; Luisao, Cesar Peixoto, Maxi Pereira, Fabio Coentrao, Jardel, Javi Garcia, Gaitan (Airton 79), Salvio (Aimar 67), Saviola (Carlos Martins 20), Cardozo.

Spartak Moscow (0) 2 *(Dzuba 52, Ari 72)*
Porto (2) 5 *(Hulk 28, Cristian Rodriguez 45, Guarin 47, Falcao 54, Ruben Micael 89)* 38,209
Spartak Moscow: Dikan; Suchy, Sheshukov, Makeev, McGeady, Kombarov K (Kombarov D 46), Alex, Rafael Carioca (Ibson 69), Welliton (Ari 46), Dzuba, Yakovlev.
Porto: Helton; Fucile (Sapunaru 28), Rolando, Otamendi, Cristian Rodriguez, Joao Moutinho (Ruben Micael 46), Alvaro Pereira, Guarin, Fernando, Falcao (James Rodriguez 72), Hulk.

Twente (1) 1 *(Bajrami 32)*
Villarreal (0) 3 *(Rossi 60 (pen), Marco Ruben 83 (pen), Cani 89)* 23,500
Twente: Boschker; Onyewu, Tiendalli**, Buysse, Douglas, Janssen, Brama (Landzaat 61), Bajrami, Leugers, Ruiz (Bannink 78), Janko (John 71).
Villarreal: Diego Lopez; Marchena (Joan Oriol 76), Musacchio, Catala, Mario Gaspar, Borja Valero (Cani 62), Bruno, Mubarak, Matilla, Rossi (Perez 73), Marco Ruben.

SEMI-FINALS FIRST LEG

Thursday, 28 April 2011

Benfica (0) 2 *(Jardel 50, Cardozo 59)*

Braga (0) 1 *(Vandinho 53)*   67,778

Benfica: Roberto; Luisao, Cesar Peixoto (Gaitan 65), Maxi Pereira, Fabio Coentrao, Jardel, Aimar, Javi Garcia, Carlos Martins (Jara 65), Saviola (Airton 86), Cardozo.
Braga: Artur Moraes; Rodriguez, Paulao, Miguel Garcia, Silvio, Hugo Viana (Marcio Mossoro 62), Vandinho, Salino, Meyong (Custodio 55), Alan, Lima (Kaka 84).

Porto (0) 5 *(Falcao 49 (pen), 67, 75, 90, Guarin 61)*

Villarreal (1) 1 *(Cani 45)*   44,719

Porto: Helton; Sapunaru, Rolando, Otamendi, Cristian Rodriguez (Silvestre Varela 72), Joao Moutinho, Alvaro Pereira, Guarin (Souza 79), Fernando, Falcao, Hulk (James Rodriguez 84).
Villarreal: Diego Lopez; Marchena, Musacchio, Catala, Mario Gaspar, Cani (Matilla 71), Cazorla, Borja Valero (Mubarak 67), Bruno, Rossi, Nilmar (Marco Ruben 72).

SEMI-FINALS SECOND LEG

Thursday, 5 May 2011

Braga (1) 1 *(Custodio 19)*

Benfica (0) 0   25,384

Braga: Artur Moraes; Rodriguez, Paulao, Miguel Garcia, Silvio, Hugo Viana, Marcio Mossoro (Kaka 80), Custodio, Meyong (Helder Barbosa 87), Alan, Lima (Salino 73).
Benfica: Roberto; Luisao, Cesar Peixoto (Jara 58), Maxi Pereira, Fabio Coentrao, Jardel, Javi Garcia, Gaitan, Carlos Martins (Kardec 81), Saviola (Felipe Menezes 87), Cardozo.

Villarreal (1) 3 *(Cani 17, Capdevila 75, Rossi 80 (pen))*

Porto (1) 2 *(Hulk 39, Falcao 48)*   21,500

Villarreal: Diego Lopez; Musacchio, Capdevila, Mario Gaspar, Cani, Cazorla (Marchena 57), Bruno, Matilla (Mubarak 57), Rossi, Nilmar (Senna 67), Marco Ruben.
Porto: Helton; Sapunaru, Rolando, Otamendi, Cristian Rodriguez (James Rodriguez 32), Joao Moutinho (Souza 52), Alvaro Pereira, Guarin, Fernando (Ruben Micael 61), Falcao, Hulk.

UEFA EUROPA LEAGUE FINAL

Wednesday, 18 May 2011

(in Dublin, 45,391)

Porto (1) 1 *(Falcao 44)*   **Braga (0) 0**

Porto: Helton; Sapunaru, Rolando, Otamendi, Joao Moutinho, Silvestre Varela (James Rodriguez 79), Pereira, Guarin (Belluschi 73), Fernando, Falcao, Hulk.

Braga: Artur; Rodriguez (Kaka 46), Paulao, Miguel Garcia, Silvio, Hugo Viana (Marcio Mossoro 46), Vandinho, Custodio, Alan, Lima (Meyong 66), Paulo Cesar.

Referee: Velasco (Spain).

Cristian Sapunaru (left) of FC Porto moves to close down Silvio of Sporting Braga during the 2011 UEFA Europa League Final at Aviva Stadium, Dublin. Porto won the match with a goal from Falcao just before half-time.
(Action Images/Jason Cairnduff)

UEFA CHAMPIONS LEAGUE 2011–12

PARTICIPATING CLUBS
This list is provisional and subject to final confirmation from UEFA.

UEFA CHAMPIONS LEAGUE GROUP STAGE
FC Barcelona (ESP) – holders
Manchester United FC (ENG)
Chelsea FC (ENG)
Real Madrid CF (ESP)
FC Porto (POR)
FC Internazionale Milano (ITA)
AC Milan (ITA)
FC Shakhtar Donetsk (UKR)
Valencia CF (ESP)
PFC CSKA Moskva (RUS)
Olympique de Marseille (FRA)
FC Zenit St Petersburg (RUS)
AFC Ajax (NED)
Bayer 04 Leverkusen (GER)
Olympiacos FC (GRE)
Fenerbahçe SK (TUR)
Manchester City FC (ENG)
LOSC Lille Métropole (FRA)
FC Basel 1893 (SUI)
Borussia Dortmund (GER)
SSC Napoli (ITA)
FC Oţelul Galaţi (ROU)

UEFA CHAMPIONS LEAGUE PLAY-OFF – LEAGUE ROUTE
FC Bayern München (GER)
Arsenal FC (ENG)
Olympique Lyonnais (FRA)
Villarreal CF (ESP)
Udinese Calcio (ITA)

UEFA CHAMPIONS LEAGUE THIRD QUALIFYING ROUND – LEAGUE ROUTE
SL Benfica (POR)
FC Dynamo Kyiv (UKR)
Panathinaikos FC (GRE)
FC Twente (NED)
R. Standard de Liège (BEL)
FC Rubin Kazan (RUS)
FC Zürich (SUI)
Odense BK (DEN)
Trabzonspor AŞ (TUR)
FC Vaslui (ROU)

UEFA CHAMPIONS LEAGUE THIRD QUALIFYING ROUND – CHAMPIONS ROUTE
Rangers FC (SCO)
FC København (DEN)
KRC Genk (BEL)

UEFA CHAMPIONS LEAGUE SECOND QUALIFYING ROUND
FC BATE Borisov (BLR)
Macabi Haifa FC (ISR)
NK Dinamo Zagreb (CRO)
Rosenborg BK (NOR)
FK Partizan (SRB)
APOEL FC (CYP)
Wisła Kraków (POL)
SK Sturm Graz (AUT)
PFC Litex Lovech (BUL)
ŠK Slovan Bratislava (SVK)
FC Viktoria Plzeň (CZE)
NK Maribor (SVN)
HJK Helsinki (FIN)
FK Ekranas (LTU)
FC Zestafoni (GEO)
Malmö FF (SWE)
Shamrock Rovers FC (IRL)
FC Dacia Chisinau (MDA)
FC Pyunik (ARM)
FK Borac Banja Luka (BIH)
FK Mogren (MNE)
Skonto FC (LVA)
Videoton FC (HUN)
Bangor City FC (WAL)
HB Tórshavn (FRO)
Linfield FC (NIR)
FC Tobol Kostanay (KAZ)
FC Flora Tallinn (EST)
Breidablik (ISL)
Neftçi PFK (AZE)
FK Skendija 79 (MKD)
KS Skënderbeu (ALB)

UEFA CHAMPIONS LEAGUE FIRST QUALIFYING ROUND
F91 Dudelange (LUX)
Valletta FC (MLT)
FC Santa Coloma (AND)
SP Tre Fiori (SMR)

UEFA EUROPA LEAGUE 2011–12

PARTICIPATING CLUBS
This list is provisional and subject to final confirmation from UEFA.

UEFA EUROPA LEAGUE PLAY-OFFS
Sevilla FC (ESP)
AS Roma (ITA)
Tottenham Hotspur FC (ENG)
PSV Eindhoven (NED)
Sporting Clube de Portugal (POR)
SC Braga(POR)
FC Schalke 04 (GER)*
FC Spartak Moskva (RUS)
Paris Saint-Germain FC (FRA)
RSC Anderlecht (BEL)
Celtic FC (SCO)*
Beşiktaş JK (TUR)*
FC Metalist Kharkiv (UKR)
AEK Athens FC (GRE)*
FC Steaua Bucureşti (ROU)*
Athletic Club (ESP)
S.S. Lazio (ITA)
FC Lokomotiv Moskva (RUS)
Birmingham City FC (ENG)
FC Rapid Bucureşti (ROU)
Hannover 96 (GER)
FC Sochaux-Montbéliard (FRA)
FC Dnipro Dnipropetrovsk (UKR)
PFC CSKA Sofia (BUL)*

FC Sion (SUI)*
FC Nordsjælland (DEN)*

UEFA EUROPA LEAGUE THIRD QUALIFYING ROUND

Club Atlético de Madrid (ESP)
AZ Alkmaar (NED)
Hapoel Tel-Aviv FC (ISR)*
Club Brugge KV (BEL)
AC Sparta Praha (CZE)
US Città di Palermo (ITA)†
FC Dinamo Bucureşti (ROU)
PAOK FC (GRE)
Stoke City FC (ENG)†
Stade Rennais FC (FRA)
BSC Young Boys (SUI)
PFC Levski Sofia (BUL)
1. FSV Mainz 05 (GER)
FK Mladá Boleslav (CZE)*
Bursaspor (TUR)
Vitória SC (POR)
Helsingborgs IF (SWE)*
FC Karpaty Lviv (UKR)
Brøndby IF (DEN)
FK Crvena zvezda (SRB)
FC Alania Vladikavkaz (RUS)†
Heart of Midlothian FC (SCO)
HNK Hajduk Split (CRO)
AC Omonia (CYP)*
Legia Warszawa (POL)*
SV Ried (AUT)
FC Gomel (BLR)*
FK Senica (SVK)
Strømsgodset IF (NOR)*
Sligo Rovers FC (IRL)*

UEFA EUROPA LEAGUE SECOND QUALIFYING ROUND

FC Salzburg (AUT)
FK Austria Wien (AUT)
Anorthosis Famagusta FC (CYP)
MŠK Žilina (SVK)
CD Nacional (POR)
FC Vorskla Poltava (UKR)
FC Sheriff (MDA)
ADO Den Haag (NED)
PFC Lokomotiv Sofia (BUL)
Gaziantepspor (TUR)
Olympiacos Volou FC (GRE)
Dundee United FC (SCO)
Bnei Yehuda Tel-Aviv FC (ISR)
FC Midtjylland (DEN)
Maccabi Tel-Aviv FC (ISR)
KVC Westerlo (BEL)†
FK Jablonec (CZE)
AS Gaz Metan Mediaş (ROU)
FK Ventspils (LVA)*
FC Thun (SUI)
Vålerenga Fotball (NOR)
FC Aktobe (KAZ)
FK Vojvodina (SRB)
Bohemian FC (IRL)
AEK Larnaca FC (CYP)
FK Sarajevo (BIH)
FC Levadia Tallinn (EST)
RNK Split (CRO)
FC Shakhtyor Soligorsk (BLR)
WKS Śląsk Wrocław (POL)
FH Hafnarfjördur (ISL)*
SK Liepājas Metalurgs (LVA)
Örebro SK (SWE)
FK Željezničar (BIH)*

FC Iskra-Stal (MDA)*
FK Sūduva (LTU)
FC Vaduz (LIE)*
TPS Turku (FIN)*
KF Tirana (ALB)*
FK Tauras (LTU)
KuPS Kuopio (FIN)
FK Rudar Pljevlja (MNE)*
Kecskeméti TE (HUN)*
UE Sant Julià (AND)*
EB/Streymur (FRO)*
Xäzär Länkäran FK (AZE)*
FC Gagra (GEO)*
FC Metalurg Skopje (MKD)*
FC Differdange 03 (LUX)*
FC Mika (ARM)*
NK Domžale (SVN)
Llanelli AFC (WAL)*
Crusaders FC (NIR)
AC Juvenese-Dogana (SMR)*
Floriana FC (MLT)*

UEFA EUROPA LEAGUE FIRST QUALIFYING ROUND

Fulham FC (ENG)¶
IL Elfsborg (SWE)
Tromsø IL (NOR)
Saint Patrick's Athletic FC (IRL)
Qarabağ FK (AZE)
Jagiellonia Białystok (POL)
FK Rabotnicki (MKD)
Aalesunds FK (NOR)¶
FC Spartak Trnava (SVK)
FC Dinamo Tbilisi (GEO)
FC Honka Espoo (FIN)
NK Varaždin (CRO)†
FC Minsk (BLR)
Metalurgi Rustavi (GEO)
FK Rad (SRB)
BK Häcken (SWE)¶
NK Široki Brijeg (BIH)
FK Budućnost Podgorica (MNE)
KR Reykjavík (ISL)
The New Saints FC (WAL)
FK Renova (MKD)
FC Koper (SVN)
Birkirkara FC (MLT)
Ferencvárosi TC (HUN)
Paksi SE (HUN)
Glentoran FC (NIR)
FC Milsami Orhei (MDA)
FK Banga (LTU)†
FC Daugava Daugavpils (LVA)
NK Olimpija Ljubljana (SVN)
Cliftonville FC (NIR)
KS Flaumurtari (ALB)
KS Vllaznia (ALB)
JK Trans Narva (EST)
Olimpik-Şüvälan PFK (AZE)
FC Irtysh Pavlodar (KAZ)
FC Shakhter Karagandy (KAZ)†
FK Zeta (MNE)
FC Banants (ARM)
JK Nõmme Kalju (EST)
ÍBV Vestmannaeyjar (ISL)
NSÍ Runavík (FRO)
Ulisses FC (ARM)
SP Tre Penne (SMR)
Neath FC (WAL)
UN Käerjéng 97 (LUX)
FC Lusitans (AND)
UE Santa Coloma (AND)
ÍF Fuglafjørdur (FRO)
CS Fola Esch (LUX)

* – cup winners; † – losing cup finalists; ¶ – Fair Play winners.

SUMMARY OF APPEARANCES

EUROPEAN CUP AND CHAMPIONS LEAGUE (1955–2011)

ENGLISH CLUBS
23 Manchester U
20 Liverpool
15 Arsenal
9 Chelsea
4 Leeds U
3 Everton, Newcastle U, Nottingham F
2 Aston Villa, Derby Co, Tottenham H, Wolverhampton W
1 Blackburn R, Burnley, Ipswich T, Manchester C

SCOTTISH CLUBS
29 Rangers
26 Celtic
3 Aberdeen, Hearts
1 Dundee, Dundee U, Hibernian, Kilmarnock

WELSH CLUBS
6 Barry T
5 The New Saints
2 Rhyl
1 Cwmbran T, Llanelli

NORTHERN IRELAND CLUBS
25 Linfield
12 Glentoran
3 Crusaders, Portadown
2 Glenavon
1 Ards, Cliftonville, Coleraine, Derry C, Distillery

REPUBLIC OF IRELAND CLUBS
7 Dundalk, Shamrock R
6 Bohemians, Shelbourne, Waterford
3 Derry C*, Drumcondra, St Patrick's Ath
2 Athlone T, Cork City, Limerick
1 Celtic, Cork Hibs, Cork Drogheda U, Sligo R

Winners: Celtic 1966–67; Manchester U 1967–68, 1998–99, 2007–08; Liverpool 1976–77, 1977–78, 1980–81, 1983–84, 2004–05; Nottingham F 1978–79, 1979–80; Aston Villa 1981–82

Finalists: Celtic 1969–70; Leeds U 1974–75; Liverpool 1984–85, 2006–07; Arsenal 2005–06; Chelsea 2007–08; Manchester U 2008–09, 2010–11

UEFA EUROPA LEAGUE 2010–11

ENGLISH CLUBS
2 Aston Villa, Liverpool
1 Everton, Fulham, Manchester C

SCOTTISH CLUBS
2 Celtic, Motherwell
1 Aberdeen, Dundee U, Falkirk, Hearts, Hibernian, Rangers

WELSH CLUBS
2 Bangor C, Llanelli
1 Port Talbot T, The New Saints

NORTHERN IRELAND CLUBS
1 Cliftonville, Crusaders, Glentoran, Linfield, Lisburn Distillery, Portadown

REPUBLIC OF IRELAND CLUBS
1 Derry C*, Dundalk, Shamrock R, Sligo R, Sporting Fingal, St Patrick's Ath

Finalists: Fulham 2009–10

EUROPEAN CUP-WINNERS' CUP (1960–99)

ENGLISH CLUBS
6 Tottenham H   5 Chelsea, Liverpool, Manchester U
4 West Ham U   3 Arsenal, Everton   2 Manchester C
1 Ipswich T, Leeds U, Leicester C, Newcastle U, Southampton, Sunderland, WBA, Wolverhampton W

SCOTTISH CLUBS
10 Rangers   8 Aberdeen, Celtic   3 Dundee U, Hearts
2 Dunfermline Ath   1 Airdrieonians, Dundee, Hibernian, Kilmarnock, Motherwell, St Mirren

WELSH CLUBS
14 Cardiff C   8 Wrexham   7 Swansea C   3 Bangor C
1 Barry T, Borough U, Cwmbran T, Llansantfraid, Merthyr Tydfil, Newport Co

NORTHERN IRELAND CLUBS
9 Glentoran   5 Glenavon   4 Ballymena U, Coleraine
3 Crusaders, Linfield   2 Ards, Bangor   1 Derry C, Distillery, Carrick Rangers, Cliftonville, Portadown

REPUBLIC OF IRELAND CLUBS
6 Shamrock R   4 Shelbourne   3 Bohemians, Dundalk, Limerick, Waterford   2 Cork City, Cork Hibs, Derry C*, Galway U, Sligo R   1 Bray W, Cork Celtic, Finn Harps, Home Farm, St Patrick's Ath, University College Dublin

Winners: Tottenham H 1962–63; West Ham U 1964–65; Manchester C 1969–70; Chelsea 1970–71, 1997–98; Rangers 1971–72; Aberdeen 1982–83; Everton 1984–85; Manchester U 1990–91; Arsenal 1993–94

Finalists: Rangers 1960–61, 1966–67; Liverpool 1965–66; Leeds U 1972–73; West Ham U 1975–76; Arsenal 1979–80, 1994–95

EUROPEAN FAIRS CUP & UEFA CUP (1955–2009)

ENGLISH CLUBS
13 Leeds U, Liverpool   11 Aston Villa   10 Ipswich T, Newcastle U   9 Arsenal, Everton, Tottenham H
7 Manchester U   6 Blackburn R, Chelsea, Manchester C, Southampton   5 Nottingham F   4 Birmingham C, WBA, Wolverhampton W   3 Sheffield W   2 Bolton W, Derby Co, Leicester C, Middlesbrough, QPR, Stoke C, West Ham U   1 Burnley, Coventry C, Fulham, London Rep XI, Millwall, Norwich C, Portsmouth, Watford

SCOTTISH CLUBS
19 Dundee U   17 Rangers   16 Aberdeen, Celtic, Hibernian   13 Hearts   7 Dunfermline Ath, Kilmarnock   5 Dundee   3 Motherwell, St Mirren   2 Partick T, St Johnstone   1 Gretna, Livingston, Morton, Queen of the S, Raith R

WELSH CLUBS
5 Bangor C, TNS   3 Cwmbran T, Inter Cardiff (formerly Inter Cable-Tel), Rhyl   2 Barry T, Carmarthen T, Newtown   1 Afan Lido, Llanelli, Haverfordwest

NORTHERN IRELAND CLUBS
18 Glentoran   9 Coleraine   8 Linfield, Portadown
5 Glenavon   3 Crusaders   1 Ards, Ballymena U, Bangor, Cliftonville, Dungannon Swifts

REPUBLIC OF IRELAND CLUBS
11 Bohemians   7 Shelbourne   6 Dundalk, St Patrick's Ath   5 Cork City, Shamrock R   4 Derry C*
3 Drogheda U, Finn Harps, Longford T   2 Drumcondra
1 Athlone T, Bray Wanderers, Cork Hibs, Galway U, Limerick

Winners: Leeds U 1967–68, 1970–71; Newcastle U 1968–69; Arsenal 1969–70, 1999–2000; Tottenham H 1971–72, 1983–84; Liverpool 1972–73, 1975–76, 2000–01; Ipswich T 1980–81

Finalists: London 1955–58, Birmingham C 1958–60, 1960–61; Leeds U 1966–67; Wolverhampton W 1971–72; Tottenham H 1973–74; Dundee U 1986–87; Celtic 2002–03; Middlesbrough 2005–06; Rangers 2007–08

Now play in League of Ireland

FIFA CLUB WORLD CUP 2010

Formerly known as the FIFA Club World Championship, this tournament is played annually between the champion clubs from all 6 continental confederations, although since 2007 the champions of Oceania must play a qualifying play-off against the champion club of the host country.

FIFA CLUB WORLD CUP 2010

(Finals in UAE)

QUARTER-FINAL PLAY-OFF

8 December 2010

Al-Wahda SC (2) 3 *(Hugo 40, Fernando Baiano 44, Abdulraheem Jumaa 71)*

Hekari U (0) 0 23,895

Al-Wahda SC: Adel Al Hosani; Magrao, Fernando Baiano (Diarra 72), Ismaeil Matar (Bazuhair 83), Fahed Masoud (Abdulraheem Jumaa 63), Basheer Saeed, Ali, Al Hammadi, Eisa Ahmed, Al Kamali, Hugo.
Hekari U: Tamanisau; Omokirio, Iniga (Hans 79), Vakatalesau, Muta, Bolatoga, Jack, Upaiga, Tiwa, Singh, Faarodo.

QUARTER-FINALS

10 December 2010

TP Mazembe Englebert (1) 1 *(Bedi 21)*

CF Pachuca (0) 0 17,960

TP Mazembe Englebert: Kidiaba; Kimwaki, Kasusula, Nkulukuta, Singuluma, Kabangu (Tshani 85), Bedi, Kalyuitaka (Kanda 91), Sunzu■, Mihayo, Ekanga (Kasongo 46).
CF Pachuca: Calero; Lopez, Luna (Gomez 74), Torres (Brambila 73), Cvitanich, Manso, Aguilar, Martinez, Arizala, Munoz, Pena (Benitez 58).

11 December 2010

Al-Wahda SC (1) 1 *(Fernando Baiano 27)*

Seongnam Llhwa Chunma (2) 4 *(Molina 4, Ognenovski 30, Choi 71, Cho DG 81)* 30,625

Al-Wahda SC: Adel Al Hosani; Magrao (Khalid Jalal 90), Fernando Baiano, Ismaeil Matar, Fahed Masoud (Al Kathiri 64), Basheer Saeed, Ali (Al Shehhi 54), Al Hammadi, Eisa Ahmed, Al Kamali, Hugo.
Seongnam Llhwa Chunma: Jung; Ko, Ognenovski, Cho BK, Cheon (In 46), Choi, Cho DG, Radoncic (Song 69), Molina (Kim JR 84), Kim SH, Hong.

SEMI-FINALS

14 December 2010

TP Mazembe Englebert (0) 2 *(Kabangu 53, Kalyuitaka 85)*

SC Internacional (0) 0 22,131

TP Mazembe Englebert: Kidiaba; Kimwaki, Kasusula, Nkulukuta, Singuluma, Kabangu (Kanda 85), Bedi, Kalyuitaka, Mihayo, Ekanga, Kasongo.

SC Internacional: Renan; Bolivar, Indio, Nei, Guinazu, Kleber, Tinga (Giuliano 63), Alecsandro (Leandro Damiao 63), Alessandro, Rafael Sobis (Oscar 76), Wilson Matias.

15 December 2010

Seongnam Llhwa Chunma (0) 0

Internazionale (2) 3 *(Stankovic 3, Zanetti 32, Milito 73)* 35,995

Seongnam Llhwa Chunma: Jung; Ko, Ognenovski, Cho BK, Choi (Song 67), Cho DG, Radoncic (Kim JR 87), Molina, Kim SH, Hong, Jo (Cheon 68).
Internazionale: Julio Cesar; Cordoba, Zanetti, Stankovic, Lucio, Eto'o, Sneijder (Thiago Motta 4), Cambiasso, Milito (Muntari 77), Chievu (Santon 79), Pandev.

MATCH FOR FIFTH AND SIXTH PLACE

15 December 2010

CF Pachuca (0) 2 *(Cvitanich 82, 89)*

Al-Wahda SC (1) 2 *(Ismaeil Matar 44, Al Hammadi 77)* 10,908

CF Pachuca: Calero; Lopez, Gomez (Rojas 62), Luna, Montes, Torres, Manso, Aguilar (Benitez 62), Martinez (Cvitanich 77), Arizala, Munoz.
Al-Wahda SC: Adel Al Hosani; Yaqoub Al Hosani, Ismaeil Matar (Ahmed 75), Al Kathiri (Diarra 46), Fahed Masoud (Al Shehhi 64), Basheer Saeed, Abdulraheem Jumaa, Al Hammadi, Eisa Ahmed, Al Kamali, Hugo.
aet; CF Pachuca won 4-2 on penalties.

MATCH FOR THIRD AND FOURTH PLACE

18 December 2010

SC Internacional (2) 4 *(Tinga 15, Alecsandro 27, 71, Alessandro 52)*

Seongnam Llhwa Chunma (0) 2 *(Molina 84, 90)* 16,563

SC Internacional: Renan (Abbondanzieri 74); Bolivar, Indio, Nei, Guinazu, Kleber, Tinga, Alecsandro, Alessandro, Rafael Sobis (Giuliano 62), Wilson Matias (Andrezinho 81).
Seongnam Llhwa Chunma: Jung; Ko, Yun, Choi, Cho DG, Molina, Song (Radoncic 28) (Kim JR 43) (Cheon 78), Kim SH, Hong, Jang■, Jo.

FINAL 2010

18 December 2010 (attendance 42,174)

TP Mazembe Englebert (0) 0

Internazionale (2) 3 *(Pandev 13, Eto'o 17, Biabiany 85)*

TP Mazembe Englebert: Kidiaba; Kimwaki, Kasusula, Nkulukuta, Singuluma, Kabangu, Bedi, Kaluyituka (Ndonga 90), Mihayo, Ekanga, Kasongo (Kanda 46).

Internazionale: Julio Cesar; Cordoba, Zanetti, Lucio, Thiago Motta (Mariga 87), Eto'o, Maicon, Cambiasso, Milito (Biabiany 70), Chievu (Stankovic 54), Pandev.

PREVIOUS FINALS

2000 Corinthians beat Vaso de Gama 4-3 on penalties after 0-0 draw
2005 Sao Paulo beat Liverpool 1-0
2006 Internacional beat Barcelona 1-0

2007 AC Milan beat Boca Juniors 4-2
2008 Manchester U beat Liga De Quito 1-0
2009 Barcelona beat Estudiantes 2-1

■ *Denotes player sent off.*

WORLD CLUB CHAMPIONSHIP

Played annually up to 1974 and intermittently since then between the winners of the European Cup and the winners of the South American Champions Cup — known as the Copa Libertadores. In 1980 the winners were decided by one match arranged in Tokyo in February 1981 which remained the venue until 2004, when the match was superseded by the FIFA Club World Championship. AC Milan replaced Marseille who had been stripped of their European Cup title in 1993.

1960 Real Madrid beat Penarol 0-0, 5-1	1985 Juventus beat Argentinos Juniors 4-2 on penalties
1961 Penarol beat Benfica 0-1, 5-0, 2-1	after a 2-2 draw
1962 Santos beat Benfica 3-2, 5-2	1986 River Plate beat Steaua Bucharest 1-0
1963 Santos beat AC Milan 2-4, 4-2, 1-0	1987 FC Porto beat Penarol 2-1 after extra time
1964 Inter-Milan beat Independiente 0-1, 2-0, 1-0	1988 Nacional (Uru) beat PSV Eindhoven 7-6 on
1965 Inter-Milan beat Independiente 3-0, 0-0	penalties after 1-1 draw
1966 Penarol beat Real Madrid 2-0, 2-0	1989 AC Milan beat Atletico Nacional (Col) 1-0 after
1967 Racing Club beat Celtic 0-1, 2-1, 1-0	extra time
1968 Estudiantes beat Manchester United 1-0, 1-1	1990 AC Milan beat Olimpia 3-0
1969 AC Milan beat Estudiantes 3-0, 1-2	1991 Red Star Belgrade beat Colo Colo 3-0
1970 Feyenoord beat Estudiantes 2-2, 1-0	1992 Sao Paulo beat Barcelona 2-1
1971 Nacional beat Panathinaikos* 1-1, 2-1	1993 Sao Paulo beat AC Milan 3-2
1972 Ajax beat Independiente 1-1, 3-0	1994 Velez Sarsfield beat AC Milan 2-0
1973 Independiente beat Juventus* 1-0	1995 Ajax beat Gremio Porto Alegre 4-3 on penalties
1974 Atlético Madrid* beat Independiente 0-1, 2-0	after 0-0 draw
1975 Independiente and Bayern Munich could not agree	1996 Juventus beat River Plate 1-0
dates; no matches.	1997 Borussia Dortmund beat Cruzeiro 2-0
1976 Bayern Munich beat Cruzeiro 2-0, 0-0	1998 Real Madrid beat Vasco da Gama 2-1
1977 Boca Juniors beat Borussia Moenchengladbach*	1999 Manchester U beat Palmeiras 1-0
2-2, 3-0	2000 Boca Juniors beat Real Madrid 2-1
1978 Not contested	2001 Bayern Munich beat Boca Juniors 1-0 after extra
1979 Olimpia beat Malmö* 1-0, 2-1	time
1980 Nacional beat Nottingham Forest 1-0	2002 Real Madrid beat Olimpia 2-0
1981 Flamengo beat Liverpool 3-0	2003 Boca Juniors beat AC Milan 3-1 on penalties after
1982 Penarol beat Aston Villa 2-0	1-1 draw
1983 Gremio Porto Alegre beat SV Hamburg 2-1	2004 Porto beat Once Caldas 8-7 on penalties after 0-0
1984 Independiente beat Liverpool 1-0	draw

*European Cup runners-up; winners declined to take part.

EUROPEAN SUPER CUP 2010

Played annually between the winners of the European Champions' Cup and the European Cup-Winners' Cup (UEFA Cup from 2000; UEFA Europa League from 2010). AC Milan replaced Marseille in 1993–94.

EUROPEAN SUPER CUP 2010
27 August 2010, Monaco (attendance 17,265)

Internazionale (0) 0   **Atletico Madrid (0) 2** *(Reyes 62, Aguero 83)*

Internazionale: Julio Cesar; Maicon, Samuel, Lucio, Chivu, Stankovic (Pandev 68), Zanetti, Cambiasso, Sneijder (Coutinho 79), Eto'o, Milito.

Atletico Madrid: De Gea; Ujfalusi, Perea, Godin, Alvaro Dominguez, Paulo Assuncao, Reyes (Merida 69), Garcia, Simao (Camacho 90), Aguero, Forlan (Jurado 82).

Referee: M. Busacca (Switzerland).

PREVIOUS MATCHES

1972 Ajax beat Rangers 3-1, 3-2	1991 Manchester U beat Red Star Belgrade 1-0
1973 Ajax beat AC Milan 0-1, 6-0	1992 Barcelona beat Werder Bremen 1-1, 2-1
1974 Not contested	1993 Parma beat AC Milan 0-1, 2-0
1975 Dynamo Kiev beat Bayern Munich 1-0, 2-0	1994 AC Milan beat Arsenal 0-0, 2-0
1976 Anderlecht beat Bayern Munich 4-1, 1-2	1995 Ajax beat Zaragoza 1-1, 4-0
1977 Liverpool beat Hamburg 1-1, 6-0	1996 Juventus beat Paris St Germain 6-1, 3-1
1978 Anderlecht beat Liverpool 3-1, 1-2	1997 Barcelona beat Borussia Dortmund 2-0, 1-1
1979 Nottingham F beat Barcelona 1-0, 1-1	1998 Chelsea beat Real Madrid 1-0
1980 Valencia beat Nottingham F 1-0, 1-2	1999 Lazio beat Manchester U 1-0
1981 Not contested	2000 Galatasaray beat Real Madrid 2-1
1982 Aston Villa beat Barcelona 0-1, 3-0	2001 Liverpool beat Bayern Munich 3-2
1983 Aberdeen beat Hamburg 0-0, 2-0	2002 Real Madrid beat Feyenoord 3-1
1984 Juventus beat Liverpool 2-0	2003 AC Milan beat Porto 1-0
1985 Juventus v Everton not contested due to UEFA ban	2004 Valencia beat Porto 2-1
on English clubs	2005 Liverpool beat CSKA Moscow 3-1
1986 Steaua Bucharest beat Dynamo Kiev 1-0	2006 Sevilla beat Barcelona 3-0
1987 FC Porto beat Ajax 1-0, 1-0	2007 AC Milan beat Sevilla 3-1
1988 KV Mechelen beat PSV Eindhoven 3-0, 0-1	2008 Zenit beat Manchester U 2-1
1989 AC Milan beat Barcelona 1-1, 1-0	2009 Barcelona beat Shakhtar Donetsk 1-0
1990 AC Milan beat Sampdoria 1-1, 2-0	2010 Atletico Madrid beat Internazionale 2-0

INTERNATIONAL DIRECTORY

The latest available information has been given regarding numbers of clubs and players registered with FIFA, the world governing body. Where known, official colours are listed. With European countries, League tables show a number of signs. * indicates relegated teams, + play-offs, *+ relegated after play-offs, ++ promoted.

There are 207 member associations. The four home countries, England, Scotland, Northern Ireland and Wales, are dealt with elsewhere in the Yearbook; but basic details appear in this directory. The following countries are not members of FIFA: Gibraltar, Kosovo, and Northern Cyprus.

EUROPE

ALBANIA

The Football Association of Albania, Rruga Labinoti, Pallati Perballe Shkolles 'Gjuhet e Huaja'.
Founded: 1930; *National Colours:* Red shirts, black shorts, red stockings.

International matches 2010
Northern Ireland (h) 1-0, Montenegro (a) 1-0, Andorra (h) 1-0, Uzbekistan (h) 1-0, Romania (a) 1-1, Luxembourg (h) 1-0, Bosnia (h) 1-1, Belarus (a) 0-2, Macedonia (h) 0-0.

League Championship wins (1930–37; 1945–2011)
SK Tirana 24 (including 17 Nentori 8); Dinamo Tirana 18; Partizani Tirana 15; Vllaznia 9; Elbasan 2 (including Labinoti 1); Skenderbeu 2; Flamurtari 1; Teuta 1.

Cup wins (1948–2011)
Partizani Tirana 15; SK Tirana 14 (including 17 Nentori 8); Dinamo Tirana 13; Vllaznia 6; Teuta 3; Flamurtari 3; Elbasan 2 (including Labinoti 1); Besa 2; Apolonia 1.

Final League Table 2010–11

	P	W	D	L	F	A	Pts
Skenderbeu	33	23	4	6	52	23	73
Flamurtari	33	22	3	8	62	27	66
Vllaznia	33	17	8	8	41	27	59
Laci	33	14	5	14	44	44	47
SK Tirana	33	11	11	11	42	31	44
Bylis	33	13	4	16	44	48	43
Teuta	33	11	9	13	38	40	42
Kastrioti	33	11	9	13	40	47	42
Shkumbini+	33	12	6	15	43	54	42
Dinamo Tirana+	33	10	9	14	46	50	39
Besa*	33	10	9	14	35	47	39
Elbasani*	33	4	3	26	30	79	12

Elbasani and Flamurtari deducted 3 points.
Top scorer: Xhafaj (Flamurtari) 19.
Cup Final: SK Tirana 1, Dinamo Tirana 1.
SK Tirana won 4-3 on penalties.

ANDORRA

Federacio Andorrana de Futbol, Avinguda Carlemany 67, 3er Pis, Apartado postal 65, Escaldes-Engordany, Principat D'Andorra.
Founded: 1994; *National Colours:* Yellow shirts, red shorts, blue stockings.

International matches 2010
Iceland (a) 0-4, Albania (a) 0-1, Cyprus (a) 0-1, Russia (h) 0-2, Republic of Ireland (a) 1-3, Macedonia (h) 0-2, Armenia (a) 0-4.

League Championship wins (1996–2011)
FC Santa Coloma 6; Principat 3; Encamp 2; Ranger's 2; St Julia 2; Constelacio 1.

Cup wins (1991–2011)
FC Santa Coloma 8; Principat 6; St Julia 3; Constelacio 1; Lusitanos 1.

Qualifying League Table 2010–11

	P	W	D	L	F	A	Pts
St Julia	14	10	4	0	39	4	34
FC Santa Coloma	14	10	3	1	63	7	33
Lusitanos	14	10	2	2	34	12	32
UE Santa Coloma	14	9	0	5	51	16	27
Inter Club	14	4	1	9	17	46	13
Principat	14	3	3	8	19	32	12
Casa Benfica	14	1	2	11	10	67	5
Encamp	14	1	1	12	14	63	4

Championship Play-Offs

	P	W	D	L	F	A	Pts
FC Santa Coloma	6	4	2	0	71	11	47
St Julia	6	2	3	1	47	9	43
Lusitanos	6	1	3	2	43	20	38
UE Santa Coloma	6	1	0	5	54	27	30

Relegation Play-Offs

	P	W	D	L	F	A	Pts
Principat	6	5	1	0	49	34	28
Inter Club	6	2	2	2	28	54	21
Encamp+	6	3	0	3	24	79	13
Casa Benfica*+	6	0	1	5	15	97	6

Top scorer: Cuadros (UE Santa Coloma) 16.
Cup Final: UE Santa Coloma 1, St Julia 3.

ARMENIA

Football Federation of Armenia, Saryan 38, Yerevan, 375 010, Armenia.
Founded: 1992; *National Colours:* Red shirts, blue shorts, orange stockings.

International matches 2010
Belarus (h) 1-3, Uzbekistan (h) 3-1, Iran (h) 1-3, Republic of Ireland (h) 0-1, Macedonia (a) 2-2, Slovakia (h) 3-1, Andorra (h) 4-0.

League Championship wins (1992–2010)
Pyunik 13 (including Homenetmen 3); Shirak Gyumri 4*; Ararat Yerevan 3*; Araks 2 (including Tsement); FC Yerevan 1.
*Includes one unofficial title.

Cup wins (1992–2011)
Mika 6; Ararat Yerevan 5; Pyunik 4; Tsement 2; Banants 2; Pyunik (including Homenetmen) 1.

Final League Table 2010

	P	W	D	L	F	A	Pts
Pyunik	28	20	5	3	73	22	65
Banants	28	20	4	4	58	24	64
Ulysses	28	17	4	7	44	23	55
Mika	28	14	4	10	47	31	46
Impuls	28	10	7	11	29	43	37
Gandzasar	28	8	3	17	24	45	27
Kilikia	28	4	3	21	19	60	15
Shirak*	28	2	4	22	22	68	10

Top scorers: Pizzelli (Pyunik) 16, Ghazarian (Pyunik) 16.
Cup Final: Shirak 1, Mika 4.

AUSTRIA

Oesterreichischer Fussball-Bund, Ernst-Happel Stadion – Sektor A/F, Postfach 340, Meierestrasse 7, Wien 1021.
Founded: 1904; *National Colours:* White shirts, black shorts, white stockings.

International matches 2010
Denmark (h) 2-1, Croatia (h) 0-1, Switzerland (h) 0-1, Kazakhstan (h) 2-0, Azerbaijan (h) 3-0, Belgium (a) 4-4, Greece (h) 1-2.

League Championship wins (1912–2011)
Rapid Vienna 32; FK Austria (formerly Amateure) 23; Tirol-Svarowski-Innsbruck 10; Admira-Energie-Wacker 8; First Vienna 6; Austria Salzburg 6; Wiener Sportklub 3; Sturm Graz 3; WAC 1; FAC 1; Hakoah 1; Linz ASK 1; WAF 1; Voest Linz 1; Graz 1; WAC 1; Wacker 1.

Cup wins (1919–2011)
FK Austria (formerly Amateure) 27; Rapid Vienna 14; TS Innsbruck (formerly Wacker Innsbruck) 7; Admira-Energie-Wacker (formerly Sportklub Admira & Admira-Energie) 5; Graz 4; Sturm Graz 4; First Vienna 3; WAC 3; Ried 2; Linz ASK 1; Wacker Vienna 1; WAF 1; Wiener Sportklub 1; Kremser 1; Stockerau 1; Karnten 1; WAC 1; Kremser 1, Horn 1.

Final League Table 2010–11

	P	W	D	L	F	A	Pts
Sturm Graz	36	19	9	8	66	33	66
Salzburg	36	17	12	7	53	31	63
FK Austria	36	17	10	9	65	37	61
Ried	36	16	10	10	51	38	58
Rapid Vienna	36	14	11	11	52	42	53
Wacker Innsbruck	36	13	11	12	43	42	50
Neustadt	36	14	8	14	44	52	50
Kapfenberger	36	9	11	16	42	61	38
Mattersburg	36	7	10	19	29	56	31
LASK Linz*	36	3	10	23	22	75	19

Top scorer: Linz (FK Austria) 21.
Cup Final: Ried 2, Lustenau 0.

AZERBAIJAN

Association of Football Federations of Azerbaijan, 42 Gussi Gadjiev Street, Baku 370 009.
Founded: 1992; *National Colours:* White shirts, blue shorts, white stockings.

International matches 2010
Jordan (a) 2-0, Luxembourg (a) 2-1, Moldova (a) 1-1, Macedonia (h) 1-3, Honduras (h) 0-0, Kuwait (h) 1-1, Germany (a) 1-6, Austria (a) 0-3, Turkey (h) 1-0, Montenegro (a) 0-2.

League Championship wins (1992–2011)
Neftchi 6; Kapaz 3; Shamkir 3; Baku 2; Inter 2; Karabakh 1; Turan 1; Xazar 1.
Includes one unofficial title for Shamkir in 2002.

Cup wins (1992–2011)
Neftchi 5; Kapaz 4; Karabakh 3; Xazar 3; Baku 2; Inshatchi 1; Shafa 1.

Qualifying League Table 2010–11

	P	W	D	L	F	A	Pts
Neftchi	22	14	6	2	40	9	48
Xazar	22	14	5	3	28	12	47
Karabakh	22	13	3	6	30	14	42
Inter	22	12	4	6	24	16	40
AZAL	22	9	9	4	27	16	36
Baku	22	9	6	7	28	21	33
Kabala	22	8	7	7	19	14	31
Mugan	22	7	6	9	14	23	27
Ganja	22	5	9	8	23	27	24
Turan	22	3	6	13	17	35	15
Simurq	22	2	6	14	12	34	12
MOIK	22	1	3	18	6	47	6

Final League Table 2010–11

	P	W	D	L	F	A	Pts
Neftchi	10	5	4	1	53	17	67
Xazar	10	2	7	1	38	18	60
Karabakh	10	4	4	2	41	22	58
AZAL	10	4	1	5	36	28	49
Inter	10	1	6	3	29	24	49
Baku	10	1	4	5	33	32	40

Relegation Table 2010–11

	P	W	D	L	F	A	Pts
Kabala	10	5	5	0	31	18	51
Mugan	10	6	2	2	29	31	47
Ganja	10	3	3	4	33	37	36
Turan	10	4	0	6	24	47	27
Simurq*	10	2	1	7	20	52	19
MOIK*	10	3	3	4	14	55	18

AZAL formerly named Olimpik.
Top scorer: Adamia (Karabakh) 18.
Cup Final: Inter 1, Xazar 1.
Xazar won 4-2 on penalties.

BELARUS

Belarus Football Federation, Kirova Street 8/2, Minsk 220 600, Belarus.
Founded: 1992; *National Colours:* Red shirts, green shorts, red stockings.

International matches 2010
Armenia (a) 3-1, Honduras (h) 2-2, South Korea (h) 1-0, Sweden (h) 0-1, Lithuania (a) 2-0, France (a) 1-0, Romania (h) 0-0, Luxembourg (a) 0-0, Albania (h) 2-0, Oman (a) 4-0.

League Championship wins (1992–2010)
Dynamo Minsk 7; BATE Borisov 7; Slavia Mozyr (formerly MPKC Mozyr) 2; Dnepr Mogilev 1; Belshina 1; Gomel 1; Shakhtyor 1.

Cup wins (1992–2011)
Belshina 3; Dynamo Minsk 3; Slavia Mozyr (formerly MPKC Mozyr) 2; MTZ-RIPO 2; BATE Borisov 2; Gomel 2; Neman 1; Dynamo 93 Minsk 1; Lokomotiv 96 1; Shakhtyor 1; Dynamo Brest 1; Naftan 1.

Final League Table 2010

	P	W	D	L	F	A	Pts
BATE Borisov	33	21	9	3	64	18	72
Shakhtyor	33	19	9	5	51	23	66
Minsk	33	18	6	9	59	32	60
Dynamo Minsk	33	17	5	11	49	34	56
Dynamo Brest	33	12	10	11	48	40	46
Belshina	33	12	9	12	31	42	45
Naftan	33	11	11	11	41	34	44
Dnepr	33	11	7	15	40	53	40
FK Vitebsk	33	7	11	15	31	52	32
Neman	33	7	10	16	27	42	31
Torpedo Zhodino+	33	7	7	19	33	58	28
Partizan*	33	5	8	20	24	70	23

Partizan formerly named MTZ-RIPO.
Top scorer: Bressan (BATE Borisov) 15.
Cup Final: Neman 0, Gomel 2.

BELGIUM

Union Royale Belge Des Societes De Football Association, 145 Avenue Houba de Strooper, B-1020 Bruxelles.
Founded: 1895; *National Colours:* All red.

International matches 2010
Bulgaria (h) 2-1, Finland (a) 0-1, Germany (h) 0-1, Turkey (a) 2-3, Kazakhstan (a) 2-0, Austria (h) 4-4, Russia (a) 2-0.

League Championship wins (1896–2011)
Anderlecht 30; Club Brugge 13; Union St Gilloise 11; Standard Liege 9; Beerschot 7; RC Brussels 6; FC Liege 5; Daring Brussels 5; Antwerp 4; Mechelen 4; Lierse SK 4; Cercle Brugge 3; Genk 4; Beveren 2; RWD Molenbeek 1.

Cup wins (1912–14; 1927; 1935; 1954–2011)
Club Brugge 10; Anderlecht 8; Standard Liege 7; Racing Genk 3; Gent 3; Beerschot (became Germinal) 2; Waterschei (became Racing Genk) 2; Beveren 2; Antwerp 2; Lierse SK 2; Union St Gilloise 2; Cercle Brugge 2; Mechelen 1; FC Liege 1; Ekeren (became Germinal) 1; Westerlo 1; La Louviere 1; Zulte-Waregem 1; Daring 1; Germinal 1; Tournai 1; Racing 1; Waregem 1.

Qualifying League Table 2010–11

	P	W	D	L	F	A	Pts
Anderlecht	30	19	8	3	58	20	65
Genk	30	19	7	4	64	27	64
Gent	30	17	6	7	59	42	57
Club Brugge	30	16	5	9	60	35	53
Lokeren	30	13	11	6	43	36	50
Standard Liege	30	15	4	11	50	38	49
Mechelen	30	13	9	8	34	30	48
Westerlo	30	11	8	11	41	40	41
Cercle Brugge	30	11	6	13	33	34	39
Kortrijk	30	11	5	14	36	39	38
Waregem	30	7	12	11	39	41	33
Beerschot	30	5	11	14	24	40	26
Lierse	30	4	12	14	26	58	24
Eupen+	30	5	8	17	28	50	23
Charleroi+	30	4	7	19	20	54	19

Championship Play-Off

	P	W	D	L	F	A	Pts
Genk	10	6	1	3	16	12	51
Standard Liege	10	8	2	0	18	6	51
Anderlecht	10	3	2	5	14	16	44
Club Brugge	10	4	4	2	13	6	43
Gent	10	0	4	6	9	22	33
Lokeren	10	1	3	6	9	17	31

Genk became champions as their half of the qualifying points was greater than Standard Liege.

Europa League Qualifying Table A

	P	W	D	L	F	A	Pts
Cercle Brugge	6	2	3	1	5	5	9
Lierse	6	2	2	2	10	8	8
Mechelen	6	2	2	2	9	10	8
St Truiden	6	1	3	2	6	7	6

Europa League Qualifying Table B

	P	W	D	L	F	A	Pts
Westerlo	6	3	3	0	16	6	12
Waregem	6	3	1	2	6	10	10
Beerschot	6	1	3	2	6	6	6
Kortrijk	6	0	3	3	2	8	3

Relegation Table

	P	W	D	L	F	A	Pts
Eupen*+	4	2	1	1	9	8	10
Charleroi*	4	1	1	2	8	9	4

Top scorer: Perisic (Club Brugge) 22.
Cup Final: Standard Liege 2, Westerlo 0.

BOSNIA-HERZEGOVINA

Football Federation of Bosnia & Herzegovina, Ferhadija 30, Sarajevo 71000.
Founded: 1992; *National Colours:* White shirts, blue shorts, white stockings.

International matches 2010
Ghana (h) 2-1, Sweden (a) 2-4, Germany (a) 1-3, Qatar (h) 1-1, Luxembourg (a) 3-0, France (h) 0-2, Albania (a) 1-1, Slovakia (a) 3 2, Poland (a) 2-2.

League Championship wins (1998–2011)
Zeljeznicar 4 Siroki 2; Sarajevo 2; Zrinjski 2; Brotnjo 1; Leotar 1; Modrica 1; Borac 1.

Cup wins (1998–2011)
Sarajevo 3; Zeljeznicar 4; Modrica 1; Orasje 1; Siroki 1; Zrinjski 1; Slavija 1; Borac 1.

Final League Table 2010–11

	P	W	D	L	F	A	Pts
Borac	30	19	7	4	37	15	64
Sarajevo	30	17	6	7	51	26	57
Zeljeznicar	30	17	4	9	50	25	55
Siroki	30	16	2	12	59	45	50
Olimpik	30	14	6	10	35	33	48
Sloboda	30	14	4	12	28	29	46
Zrinjski	30	13	3	14	41	39	42
Zvijezda	30	11	9	10	40	38	42
Rudar	30	11	8	11	37	41	41
Celik	30	11	7	12	30	30	40
Slavija	30	11	5	14	44	46	38
Travnik	30	11	4	15	44	43	37
Velez	30	11	3	16	31	43	36
Leotar	30	10	5	15	29	49	35
Buducnost*	30	6	7	17	25	44	25
Drina*	30	7	2	21	18	53	23

Top scorer: Lendric (Zrinjski) 16.
Cup Final: Zeljeznicar 1, 3, Celik 0, 0.

BULGARIA

Bulgarian Football Union, Karnigradska Street 19, BG-1000 Sofia.
Founded: 1923; *National Colours:* White shirts, green shorts, white stockings.

International matches 2010
Poland (a) 0-2, Belgium (a) 1-2, South Africa (a) 1-1, Russia (a) 0-1, England (a) 0-4, Montenegro (h) 0-1, Wales (a) 1-0, Saudi Arabia (a) 2-0, Serbia (h) 0-1.

League Championship wins (1925–2011)
CSKA Sofia 31; Levski Sofia 26; Slavia Sofia 7; Litex 4; Vladislav Varna 3; Lokomotiv Sofia 3; Botev Plovdiv (includes Trakija) 2; AC 23 Sofia 1; SC Sofia 1; Sokol Varna 1; Spartak Plovdiv 1; Tichka Varna 1; JSZ Sofia 1; Botev Stara Zagora 1; Etur 1; Lokomotiv Plovdiv 1.

Cup wins (1946–2011)
Levski Sofia 24; CSKA Sofia 19; Slavia Sofia 7; Lokomotiv Sofia 4; Litex 4; Botev Plovdiv (includes Trakija) 2; Spartak Plovdiv 1; Septemvri Sofia 1; Marek Dupnica 1; Spartak Varna 1; Sliven 1; Beroe 1.

Final League Table 2010–11

	P	W	D	L	F	A	Pts
Litex	30	23	6	1	56	13	75
Levski Sofia	30	23	3	4	67	24	72
CSKA Sofia	30	18	7	5	53	26	61
Lokomotiv Plovdiv	30	14	10	6	54	28	52
Lokomotiv Sofia	30	16	4	10	47	33	52
Cherno More	30	15	6	9	36	28	51
Beroe	30	13	7	10	33	34	46
Chernomorets	30	9	10	11	19	28	37
Minjor	30	10	6	14	33	45	36
Slavia Sofia	30	9	5	16	34	38	32
Montana	30	8	8	14	30	46	32
Kaliakara	30	8	6	16	19	40	30
Pirin	30	6	9	15	32	39	27
Rakovski+	30	6	7	17	26	52	25
Akademik*	30	5	5	20	16	51	20
Sliven*	30	4	7	19	22	52	19

Top scorer: Dembele (Levski Sofia) 26.
Cup Final: CSKA Sofia 1, Slavia Sofia 0.

CHANNEL ISLANDS

Guernsey

League Championship wins (1894–2011)
Northerners AC 29; Rangers 17; Vale Recreation 15; St Martin's AC 13; Sylvans 10; Belgrave Wanderers 6; 2nd Batt Manchesters 3; 2nd Batt Royal Irish Regt 2; 2nd Batt Wiltshires 2; 10th Comp W Div Royal Artillery 1; 2nd Batt Leicesters 1; 2nd Batt PA Somerset Light Infantry 1; 2nd Middlesex Regt 1; Athletics 1; Band Comp 2nd Batt Royal Fusiliers 1; G&H Comp Royal Fusiliers 1; Grange 1; Yorkshire Regt (Green Howards) 1.

Final League Table 2010–11

	P	W	D	L	F	A	Pts
St Martin's AC	18	16	1	1	77	17	49
Belgrave Wanderers	18	10	3	5	38	27	33
North	18	9	2	7	46	35	29
Vale Recreation	18	7	4	7	23	34	25
Rangers	18	6	2	10	47	56	20
Rovers AC	18	6	1	11	30	47	19
Sylvans S&FC	18	2	1	15	21	66	7

Jersey

League Championship wins (1905–2011)
Jersey Wanderers 20; First Tower United 19; St Paul's 14; Jersey Scottish 9; Beeches Old Boys 5; Magpies 4; 2nd Batt King's Own Regt 3; Oaklands 3; St Peter 3; 1st Batt Devon Regt 2; 1st Batt East Surrey Regt 2; Georgetown 2; Mechanics 2; YMCA 2; 2nd Batt East Surrey Regt 1; 20th Comp Royal Garrison Artillery 1; National Rovers 1; Sporting Academics 1; Trinity 1.

Final League Table 2010–11

	P	W	D	L	F	A	Pts
St Paul's	16	14	2	0	56	7	44
Jersey Wanderers	16	9	2	5	41	28	29
Grouville	16	6	4	6	29	29	22
St Peter	16	6	4	6	24	24	22
Trinity	16	7	1	8	28	40	22
Jersey Scottish	16	6	3	7	29	27	21
St Ouen	16	6	1	9	28	33	19
Portuguese Club	16	5	4	7	20	31	19
St Clement	16	2	1	13	20	56	7

Upton Park Trophy (For Guernsey & Jersey Winners)
Northerners AC 16; First Tower United 12; Jersey Wanderers 11; St Martin's AC 11; St Paul's 6; Rangers 5; Jersey Scottish 5; Vale Recreation 4; Belgrave Wanderers 4; Sylvans 3; Beeches Old Boys 3; Old St Paul's 3; Magpies 3; St Peter 2; Jersey Mechanics 1; Jersey YMCA 1; National Rovers 1; Sporting Academics 1; Trinity 1. 2011 St Martin's 2, St Paul's 1.

CROATIA

Croatian Football Federation, Rusanova 13, Zagreb, 10 3000, Croatia.
Founded: 1912; *National Colours:* Red & white shirts, white shorts, blue stockings.

International matches 2010
Austria (a) 1-0, Wales (h) 2-0, Estonia (a) 0-0, Slovakia (a) 1-1, Latvia (a) 3-0, Greece (h) 0-0, Israel (a) 2-1, Norway (h) 2-1, Malta (h) 3-0.

League Championship wins (1941–46; 1992–2011)
Dinamo Zagreb (formerly Croatia Zagreb) 13; Hajduk Split 8; Gradjanski 1; Concordia 1; Zagreb 1.

Cup wins (1992–2011)
Dinamo Zagreb (formerly Croatia Zagreb) 11; Hajduk Split 5; Rijeka 2, Inker Zapresic 1; Osijek 1.

Final League Table 2010–11

	P	W	D	L	F	A	Pts
Dinamo Zagreb	30	22	6	2	52	12	72
Hajduk Split	30	16	7	7	54	32	55
Split	30	16	5	9	38	22	53
Cibalia	30	12	8	10	33	24	44
Inter	30	12	6	12	31	35	42
Karlovac	30	11	8	11	25	27	41
Slaven	30	10	10	10	34	30	40
Osijek	30	9	12	9	31	29	39
Rijeka	30	9	12	9	29	35	39
Zadar	30	11	5	14	31	34	38
Varazdin	30	9	9	12	32	38	36
Zagreb	30	9	8	13	32	39	35
Sibenik	30	8	11	11	37	38	35
Lokomotiva*	30	8	9	13	24	37	33
Istra*	30	9	4	17	24	44	31
Hrvatski*	30	5	8	17	24	55	23

Top scorer: Krstanovic (Zagreb) 19.
Cup Final: Dinamo Zagreb 5, 3, Varazdin 1, 1.

CYPRUS

Cyprus Football Association, 1 Stasinos Str., Engomi, P.O. Box 25071, Nicosia 2404.
Founded: 1934; *National Colours:* Blue shirts, white shorts, blue stockings.

International matches 2010
Iceland (h) 0-0, Andorra (h) 1-0, Portugal (a) 4-4, Norway (h) 1-2, Denmark (a) 0-2, Jordan (a) 0-0.

League Championship wins (1935–2011)
Apoel 21; Omonia 20; Anorthosis 13; AEL 5; EPA 3; Olympiakos 3; Apollon 3; Pezoporikos 2; Cetinkaya 1; Trast 1.

Cup wins (1935–2011)
Apoel 19; Omonia 13; Anorthosis 10; AEL 6; Apollon 6; EPA 5; Trast 3; Cetinkaya 2; Olympiakos 1; Pezoporikos 1; Salamina 1; AEK 1; APOP 1.

Qualifying League Table 2010–11

	P	W	D	L	F	A	Pts
Apoel	26	20	2	4	55	19	62
Omonia	26	14	8	4	38	16	50
Anorthosis	26	13	6	7	46	31	45
AEK	26	12	6	8	36	30	42
Apollon	26	11	5	10	40	37	38
Olympiakos	26	9	9	8	41	41	36
Enosis	26	10	6	10	26	25	36
AEL	26	8	9	9	28	35	33
Ethnikos Achnas	26	8	9	9	25	27	33
Ermis	26	7	9	10	31	38	30
Alki	26	8	5	13	30	40	29
Paphos*	26	6	8	12	33	37	26
Doxa*	26	5	5	16	25	55	20
APOP*	26	4	7	15	24	47	19

Play-Offs League Table 2010-11

Group A	P	W	D	L	F	A	Pts
Apoel	6	4	0	2	63	22	74
Omonia	6	4	1	1	45	19	63
Anorthosis	6	3	1	2	51	34	55
AEK	6	0	0	6	37	42	42

Group B	P	W	D	L	F	A	Pts
Apollon	6	3	2	1	55	44	49
Enosis	6	2	2	2	33	34	44
AEL	6	2	2	2	37	45	41
Olympiakos	6	1	2	3	48	53	41

Relegation Table 2010-11

Group C	P	W	D	L	F	A	Pts
Alki	6	3	1	2	40	48	39
Ethnikos Achnas	6	2	0	4	29	37	39
Ermis	6	2	2	2	38	45	38
Paphos*	6	2	3	1	44	44	35

Top scorer: Mrdakovic (Apollon) 21.
Cup Final: Apollon 1, Omonia 1.
Omonia won 4-3 on penalties.

CZECH REPUBLIC

Football Association of Czech Republic, Diskarska 100, Prague 6 16017 – Strahov, Czech Republic.
Founded: 1901; *National Colours:* Red shirts, white shorts, blue stockings.

International matches 2010
Scotland (a) 0-1, Turkey (a) 1-2, USA (a) 4-2, Latvia (h) 4-1, Lithuania (h) 0-1, Scotland (h) 1-0, Liechtenstein (a) 2-0, Denmark (a) 0-0.

League Championship wins (1925–93)
Sparta Prague 19; Dukla Prague (prev. UDA, now Marila Pribram) 11; Slavia Prague 9; Slovan Bratislava (formerly NV Bratislava) 8; Spartak Trnava 5; Banik Ostrava 3; Inter-Bratislava 1; Spartak Hradec Kralove 1; Viktoria Zizkov 1; Zbrojovka Brno 1; Bohemians 1; Vitkovice 1.

Cup wins (1961–93)
Dukla Prague 8; Sparta Prague 8; Slovan Bratislava 5; Spartak Trnava 4; Banik Ostrava 3; Lokomotiva Kosice 2; TJ Gottwaldov 1; Dunajska Streda 1; Kosice 1.
From 1993–94, there were two separate countries; the Czech Republic and Slovakia.

League Championship wins (1994–2011)
Sparta Prague 11; Slavia Prague 3; Slovan Liberec 2; Banik Ostrava 1; Viktoria Plzen 1.

Cup wins (1994–2011)
Sparta Prague 4; Slavia Prague 4; Viktoria Zizkov 2; Teplice 2; Spartak Hradec Kralove 1; Jablonec 1; Slovan Liberec 1; Banik Osrava 1; Viktoria Plzen 1; Mlada 1.

Final League Table 2010–11

	P	W	D	L	F	A	Pts
Viktoria Plzen	30	21	6	3	70	28	69
Sparta Prague	30	22	2	6	54	21	68
Jablonec	30	17	7	6	65	34	58
Sigma Olomouc	30	14	5	11	47	29	47
Mlada	30	13	7	10	49	40	46
Bohemians 1905	30	12	7	11	33	33	43
Slovan Liberec	30	12	7	11	45	36	43
Hradec Kralove	30	11	8	11	26	36	41
Slavia Prague	30	9	13	8	41	36	40
Teplice	30	10	9	11	39	46	39
Ceske	30	7	12	11	30	48	33
Slovacko	30	8	7	15	27	43	31
Pribram	30	8	7	15	22	36	31
Banik Ostrava	30	7	9	14	31	46	30
Brno*	30	7	3	20	33	55	24
Usti nad Labem*	30	4	7	19	22	67	19

Top scorer: Lafata (Jablonec) 19.
Cup Final: Mlada 1, Sigma Olomouc 1
Mlada won 4-3 on penalties.

DENMARK

Danish Football Association, Idraettens Hus, Brondby Stadion 20, DK-2605, Brondby.
Founded: 1889; *National Colours:* Red shirts, white shorts, red stockings.

International matches 2010

Poland (a) 3-1, Singapore (h) 5-1, Thailand (a) 3-0, Austria (a) 1-2, Senegal (h) 2-0, Australia (a) 0-1, South Africa (a) 0-1, Holland (n) 0-2, Cameroon (n) 2-1, Japan (n) 1-3, Germany (h) 2-2, Iceland (h) 1-0, Portugal (a) 1-3, Cyprus (h) 2-0, Czech Republic (h) 0-0.

League Championship wins (1913–2011)

KB Copenhagen 15; Brondby 10; B 93 Copenhagen 9; AB (Akademisk) 9; FC Copenhagen 9; B 1903 Copenhagen 7; Frem 6; Esbjerg BK 5; Vejle BK 5; AGF Aarhus 5; Hvidovre 3; OB Odense 3; AaB Aalborg 3; B 1909 Odense 2; Koge BK 2; Lyngby 2; Silkeborg 1; Herfolge 1.

Cup wins (1955–2011)

AGF Aarhus 9; Vejle BK 6; Brondby 6; OB Odense 5; Randers Freja 4; FC Copenhagen 4; Lyngby 3; B 1909 Odense 2; Aab Aalborg 2; Esbjerg BK 2; Frem 2; B 1903 Copenhagen 2; Nordsjaelland 2; B 93 Copenhagen 1; KB Copenhagen 1; Vanlose 1; Hvidovre 1; B1913 Odense 1; AB (Akademisk) 1, Viborg 1; Silkeborg 1.

Final League Table 2010–11

	P	W	D	L	F	A	Pts
FC Copenhagen	33	25	6	2	77	29	81
Odense	33	16	7	10	55	41	55
Brondby	33	13	12	8	52	39	51
Midtjylland	33	13	10	10	50	42	49
Silkeborg	33	10	13	10	43	49	43
Nordsjaelland	33	10	9	14	38	50	39
Sonderjyske	33	11	6	16	32	46	39
Lyngby	33	10	8	15	42	52	38
Horsens	33	9	10	14	29	40	37
Aalborg	33	8	11	14	38	48	35
Randers*	33	6	16	11	41	48	34
Esbjerg*	33	7	12	14	36	49	33

Top scorer: N'Doye (FC Copenhagen) 25.
Cup Final: Nordsjaelland 3, Midtjylland 2.

ENGLAND

The Football Association, 25 Soho Square, London W1D 4FA.
Founded: 1863; *National Colours:* White shirts with navy blue collar, navy shorts, white stockings.

ESTONIA

Estonian Football Association, Rapia 8/10, Tallinn 11312.
Founded: 1921; *National Colours:* Blue shirts, black shorts, white stockings.

International matches 2010

Georgia (a) 3-2, Finland (h) 2-0, Croatia (h) 0-0, Latvia (h) 0-0, Lithuania (a) 0-2, Faeroes (h) 2-1, Italy (h) 1-2, Uzbekistan (h) 3-3, Serbia (a) 3-1, Slovenia (h) 0-1, Liechtenstein (h) 1-1, China (a) 0-3, Qatar (a) 0-2.

League Championship wins (1921–40; 1992–2010)

Sport 9; Levadia Tallinn (includes Levadia Maardu) 8; Flora Tallinn 8; Estonia 5; Tallinn JK 2; Norma 2; Lantana (formerly Nikol) 2; Kalev 2; Olimpia 1; VMK Tallinn 1.

Cup wins (1993–2011)

Levadia Tallinn (includes Levadia Maardu) 6; Flora Tallinn 5; Sadam 2; VMV Tallinn 2; Lantana (formerly Nikol) 1; Trans 1; Levadia Tallinn (pre-2004) 1; Norma 1.

Final League Table 2010

	P	W	D	L	F	A	Pts
Flora	36	29	4	3	104	32	91
Levadia Tallinn	36	26	8	2	100	16	86
Trans	36	23	7	6	67	31	76
Kalju	36	18	8	10	59	42	62
Kalev Sillamae	36	18	5	13	79	52	59
Tammeka	36	11	7	18	50	66	40
Tulevik	36	8	5	23	33	62	29
Paide	36	6	7	23	30	79	25
Kuressaare+	36	7	3	26	32	93	24
Lootus*	36	6	2	28	22	103	20

Top scorer: Post (Flora) 24.
Cup Final: Flora 2, Trans 0.

FAEROE ISLANDS

Fotboltssamband Foroya, The Faeroes' Football Assn., Gundalur, P.O. Box 3028, FR-110, Torshavn.
Founded: 1979; *National Colours:* White shirts, blue shorts, white stockings.

International matches 2010

Iceland (a) 0-2, Luxembourg (a) 0-0, Estonia (a) 1-2, Serbia (h) 0-3, Italy (a) 0-5, Slovenia (a) 1-5, Northern Ireland (h) 1-1, Scotland (a) 0-3.

League Championship wins (1942–2010)

HB Torshavn 21; KI Klaksvik 17; B36 Torshavn 8; TB Tvoroyri 8; GI Gotu 6; B68 Toftir 3; SI Sorvag 1; IF Fuglafjordur 1; B71 Sandur 1; VB Vagur 1; NSI Runavik 1; EB/Streymur 1.

Cup wins (1955–2010)

HB Torshavn 26; GI Gotu 6; KI Klaksvik 5; TB Tvoroyri 5; B36 Torshavn 5; EB/Streymur 3; NSI Runavik 2; VB Vagur 1; B71 Sandur 1; Vikingur 1.

Final League Table 2010

	P	W	D	L	F	A	Pts
HB	27	16	6	5	49	32	54
EB/Streymur	27	14	9	4	65	30	51
NSI	27	14	6	7	60	33	48
IF	27	12	7	8	50	41	43
Vikingur	27	12	7	8	44	35	43
B36	27	11	7	9	44	36	40
B68	27	8	7	12	42	47	31
B71	27	5	8	14	24	65	23
FC Suduroy*	27	5	7	15	33	54	22
AB*	27	2	8	17	27	65	14

FC Suduroy formerly VB/Sumba.
Top scorers: Hansen (EB/Streymur) 22, Jacobsen (NSI) 22.
Cup Final: EB/Streymur 1, IF 0.

FINLAND

Suomen Palloliitto Finlands Bollfoerbund, Urheilukatu 5, P.O. Box 191, Helsinki 00251.
Founded: 1907; *National Colours:* White shirts, blue shorts, white stockings.

International matches 2010

South Korea (h) 0-2, Malta (a) 2-1, Estonia (a) 0-2, Poland (a) 0-0, Belgium (h) 1-0, Moldova (a) 0-2, Holland (a) 1-2, Hungary (h) 1-2, San Marino (h) 8-0.

League Championship wins (1908–2010)

HJK Helsinki 23; Haka Valkeakoski 9; HPS Helsinki 9; TPS Turku 8; HIFK Helsinki 7; Tampere United (includes IKIssat and Ilves) 5; KuPS Kuopio 5; Kuusysi Lahti 5; KIF Helsinki 4; AIFK Turku 3; Reipas Lahti 3; VIFK Vaasa 3; Jazz Pori 2; KTP Kotka 2; OPS Oulu 2; VPS Vaasa 2; Unitas Helsinki 1; PUS Helsinki 1; Sudet Viipuri 1; HT Helsinki 1; Pyrkiva Turku 1; KPV Kokkola 1; TPV Tampere 1; MyPa Anjalankoski 1; Inter 1.

Cup wins (1955–2010)

Haka Valkeakoski 12; HJK Helsinki 10; Reipas Lahti 7; KTP Kotka 4; MyPa Anjalankoski 3; Tampere United (includes Ilves) 3; TPS Turku 3; KuPS Kuopio 2; Kuusysi Lahti 2; Mikkeli 2; PPojat 1; Drott (renamed Jaro) 1; HPS Helsinki 1; AIFK Turku 1; RoPS Rovaniemi 1; Jokerit (formerly PK-35) 1; Allianssi (formerly Atlantis) 1; Inter 1.

Final League Table 2010

	P	W	D	L	F	A	Pts
HJK Helsinki	26	15	7	4	43	19	52
KuPS	26	15	3	8	45	36	48
TPS Turku	26	13	6	7	46	30	45
Honka	26	12	5	9	42	34	41
Jaro	26	11	5	10	42	34	38
Inter	26	10	7	9	34	32	37
Tampere U	26	10	4	12	37	46	34
Haka	26	9	6	11	30	38	33
MyPa	26	7	11	8	36	39	32
VPS	26	8	7	11	29	40	31
Oulu	26	8	6	12	31	44	30
Mariehamn	26	7	7	12	38	43	28
Jyvaskyla+	26	8	3	15	34	41	27
Lahti*	26	5	11	10	26	37	26

Top scorer: Makela (HJK Helsinki) 16.
Cup Final: TPS Turku 2, HJK Helsinki 0.

FRANCE

Federation Francaise De Football, 60 Bis Avenue d'Iena, Paris 75116.
Founded: 1919; *National Colours:* Blue shirts, white shorts, red stockings.

International matches 2010

Spain (h) 0-2, Costa Rica (h) 2-1, Tunisia (a) 1-1, China (h) 0-1, Uruguay (n) 0-0, Mexico (n) 0-2, South Africa (n) 1-2, Norway (a) 1-2, Belarus (h) 0-1, Bosnia (a) 2-0, Romania (h) 2-0, Luxembourg (h) 2-0, England (a) 2-1.

League Championship wins (1933–2011)

Saint Etienne 10; Olympique Marseille 9; Nantes 8; AS Monaco 7; Lyon 7; Stade de Reims 6; Girondins de Bordeaux 6; OGC Nice 4; Lille OSC (includes Olympique Lillois) 4; Paris St Germain 2; FC Sete 2; Sochaux 2; Racing Club Paris 1; Roubaix-Tourcoing 1; Strasbourg 1; Auxerre 1; Lens 1.

Cup wins (1918–2011)

Olympique Marseille 10; Paris St Germain 8; Saint Etienne 6; Lille OSC 6; AS Monaco 5; Racing Club Paris 5; Red Star 5; Auxerre 4; Lyon 4; Girondins de Bordeaux 3; OGC Nice 3; Nantes 3; Strasbourg 3; CAS Genereaux 2; Nancy 2; Sedan 2; FC Sete 2; Stade de Reims 2; SO Montpellier 2; Stade Rennes 2; Metz 2; Sochaux 2; AS Cannes 1; Club Français 1; Excelsior Roubaix 1; Le Havre 1; Olympique de Pantin 1; CA Paris 1; Toulouse 1; Bastia 1; Lorient 1; Guingamp 1.

Final League Table 2010–11

	P	W	D	L	F	A	Pts
Lille	38	21	13	4	68	36	76
Marseille	38	18	14	6	62	39	68
Lyon	38	17	13	8	61	40	64
Paris St Germain	38	15	15	8	56	41	60
Sochaux	38	17	7	14	60	43	58
Rennes	38	15	11	12	38	35	56
Bordeaux	38	12	15	11	43	42	51
Toulouse	38	14	8	16	38	36	50
Auxerre	38	10	19	9	45	41	49
St Etienne	38	12	13	13	46	47	49
Lorient	38	12	13	13	46	48	49
Valenciennes	38	10	18	10	45	41	48
Nancy	38	13	9	16	43	48	48
Montpellier	38	12	11	15	32	43	47
Caen	38	11	13	14	46	51	46
Brest	38	11	13	14	36	43	46
Nice	38	11	13	14	33	48	46
Monaco*	38	9	17	12	36	40	44
Lens*	38	7	14	17	35	58	35
Arles*	38	3	11	24	21	70	20

Top scorer: Sow (Lille) 25.
Cup Final: Paris St Germain 0, Lille 1.

GEORGIA

Georgian Football Federation, 76a Tchavtchavadze Avenue, Tbilisi 380062.
Founded: 1990; *National Colours:* All white.

International matches 2010

Estonia (h) 2-1, Cameroon (h) 0-0, Moldova (a) 0-0, Greece (a) 1-1, Israel (h) 0-0, Malta (h) 1-0, Latvia (a) 1-1, Slovenia (a) 2-1.

League Championship wins (1990–2011)

Dinamo Tbilisi 13; Torpedo Kutaisi 3; WIT Georgia 2; Olimpi 2; Sioni 1; Zestafoni 3.

Cup wins (1990–2011)

Dinamo Tbilisi 9; Lokomotivi 3; Torpedo Kutaisi 2; Ameri 2; Dynamo Batumi 1; Guria 1; Zestafoni 1; WIT 1; Gagra 1.

Final League Table 2010–11

	P	W	D	L	F	A	Pts
Zestafoni	36	24	6	6	72	19	78
Dinamo Tbilisi	36	21	9	6	55	22	72
Olimpi	36	20	6	10	52	31	66
Torpedo Kutaisi	36	14	13	9	31	22	55
WIT	36	14	6	16	35	41	48
Baia	36	13	5	18	36	51	44
Kolkheti	36	10	10	16	25	47	40
Sioni	36	10	9	17	27	45	39
Spartaki+	36	7	11	18	32	42	32
Samtredia*+	36	6	7	23	27	72	25

Top scorer: Gelashvili (Zestafoni) 18.
Cup Final: Gagra 1, Torpedo Kutaisi 0.

GERMANY

Deutscher Fussball-Bund, Otto-Fleck-Schneise 6, Postfach 710265, Frankfurt Am Main 60492.
Founded: 1900; *National Colours:* White shirts, black shorts, white stockings.

International matches 2010

Argentina (h) 0-1, Malta (h) 3-0, Hungary (a) 3-0, Bosnia (h) 3-1, Australia (n) 4-0, Serbia (n) 0-1, Ghana (n) 1-0, England (n) 4-1, Argentina (n) 4-0, Spain (n) 0-1, Uruguay (n) 3-2, Denmark (a) 2-2, Belgium (a) 1-0, Azerbaijan (h) 6-1, Turkey (h) 3-0, Kazakhstan (a) 3-0, Sweden (a) 0-0.

League Championship wins (1903–2011)

Bayern Munich 22; 1.FC Nuremberg 9; Schalke 04 7; Borussia Dortmund 7; SV Hamburg 6; Borussia Moenchengladbach 5; VfB Stuttgart 5; 1.FC Kaiserslautern 4; Werder Bremen 4; VfB Leipzig 3; SpVgg Furth 3; 1.FC Cologne 3; Viktoria Berlin 2; Hertha Berlin 2; Hannover 96 2; Dresden SC 2; Munich 1860 1; Union Berlin 1; FC Freiburg 1; Phoenix Karlsruhe 1; Karlsruher FV 1; Holstein Kiel 1; Fortuna Dusseldorf 1; Rapid Vienna 1; VfR Mannheim 1; Rot-Weiss Essen 1; Eintracht Frankfurt 1; Eintracht Brunswick 1;Wolfsburg 1.

Cup wins (1935–2011)

Bayern Munich 15; Werder Bremen 6; 1.FC Cologne 4; Eintracht Frankfurt 4; Schalke 04 5; 1.FC Nuremberg 4; SV Hamburg 3; Moenchengladbach 3; VfB Stuttgart 3; Dresden SC 2; Fortuna Dusseldorf 2; Karlsruhe SC 2; Munich 1860 2; Borussia Dortmund 2; 1.FC Kaiserslautern 2; First Vienna 1; VfB Leipzig 1; Kickers Offenbach 1; Rapid Vienna 1; Rot-Weiss Essen 1; SW Essen 1; Bayer Uerdingen 1; Hannover 96 1; Leverkusen 1.

Final League Table 2010–11

	P	W	D	L	F	A	Pts
Borussia Dortmund	34	23	6	5	67	22	75
Leverkusen	34	20	8	6	64	44	68
Bayern Munich	34	19	8	7	81	40	65
Hannover	34	19	3	12	49	45	60
Mainz	34	18	4	12	52	39	58
Nuremberg	34	13	8	13	47	45	47
Kaiserslautern	34	13	7	14	48	51	46
Hamburg	34	12	9	13	46	52	45
Feiburg	34	13	5	16	41	50	44
Cologne	34	13	5	16	47	62	44
Hoffenheim	34	11	10	13	50	50	43
Stuttgart	34	12	6	16	60	59	42
Werder Bremen	34	10	11	13	47	61	41
Schalke	34	11	7	16	38	44	40
Wolfsburg	34	9	11	14	43	48	38
Moenchengladbach+	34	10	6	18	48	65	36
Eintracht Frankfurt*	34	9	7	18	31	49	34
St Pauli*	34	8	5	21	35	68	29

Top scorer: Gomez (Bayern Munich) 28.
Cup Final: Duisburg 0, Schalke 5.

GIBRALTAR

Gibraltar Football Association, 32a Rosia Road, Gibraltar.
Founded: 1905. *National Colours:* Red shirts, white shorts, white stockings.

League Championship wins (1896–2011)
Prince of Wales 19; Glacis United 17; Britannia 14; Gibraltar United 11; Lincoln 11; Manchester United 7; Europa 6; Newcastle (formerly Lincoln) 5; St Theresas 3; Chief Construction 2; Exiles 2; Gibraltar FC 2; Jubilee 2; South United 2; Albion 1; Athletic 1; Commander of the Yard 1; Royal Soverign 1; St Joseph's 1.

Cup wins (1896–2011)
Lincoln 8; St Joseph's 7; Europa 5; Glacis United 5; Newcastle (formerly Lincoln) 4; Britannia 3; Gibraltar United 3; Manchester United 3; AARA 1; Gibraltar FC 1; HMS Hood 1; Lincoln ABG 1; Lincoln Reliance 1; Manchester United Reserves 1; Prince of Wales 1; St Theresas 1; 2nd Battalion RGS 1; 2nd Battalion The King's Regiment 1; 4th Battalion Royal Scots 1; RAF Gibraltar 1; RAF New Camp 1.

Final League Table 2010–11

	P	W	D	L	F	A	Pts
Lincoln	20	16	4	0	72	22	52
Glacis U	20	10	6	4	36	32	36
Manchester U	20	8	3	9	34	31	27
Gibraltar U	20	7	2	11	31	40	23
St Joseph's	20	6	4	10	27	43	22
Lynx	20	3	1	16	18	50	10

Cup Final: Lincoln 2, Glacis U 1.
2010 Cup Final: Lincoln 5, Gibraltar U 1.

GOZO

Gozo Football Association.
Founded: 1936.

League Championship wins (1938-2011)

Victoria Hotspurs 11; Nadur Youngsters 10; Sannat Lions 10; Ghajnsielem 6; Salesian Youths 6; Victoria Athletics 4; Xaghra United 4; Xewkija Tigers 4; Calypcians 1; Kercem Ajax 1; Victoria City 1; Victoria Stars 1; Victoria United 1; Xaghra Blue Stars 1; Xaghra Young Stars 1; Zebbug Rovers 1.

Cup wins (1972–2011)
Sannat Lions 9; Xewkija Tigers 7; Nadur Youngsters 7; Ghajnsielem 5; Xaghra United 4; S.K. Calyptians 1; Calypsians Bosco Youths 1; Victoria Hotspurs 1; Kercem Ajax 1; Quala St. Joseph 1.

Final League Table 2010-11

	P	W	D	L	F	A	Pts
Sannat Lions	18	12	4	2	46	14	40
Ghajnsielem	18	11	4	3	28	18	37
Nadur Youngsters	18	10	2	6	38	25	32
Victoria Hotspurs	18	6	4	8	33	37	22
Victoria Wanderers	18	5	5	8	23	32	20
Xewkija Tigers	18	4	2	12	18	33	14
St Lawrence Spurs	18	4	1	13	19	45	13

Cup Final: Sannat Lions 0, Nadur Youngsters 1.

GREECE

Hellenic Football Federation, Singrou Avenue 137, Nea Smirni, 17121 Athens.
Founded: 1926; *National Colours:* Blue shirts, white shorts, blue stockings.

International matches 2010
Senegal (h) 0-2, North Korea (h) 2-2, Paraguay (h) 0-2, South Korea (n) 0-2, Nigeria (n) 2-1, Argentina (n) 0-2, Serbia (a) 1-0, Georgia (h) 1-1, Croatia (a) 0-0, Latvia (h) 1-0, Israel (h) 2-1, Austria (h) 2-1.

League Championship wins (1928–2011)
Olympiakos 38; Panathinaikos 20; AEK Athens 11; Aris Salonika 3; PAOK Salonika 2; Larisa 1.

Cup wins (1932–2011)
Olympiakos 24; Panathinaikos 17; AEK Athens 14; PAOK Salonika 4; Panionios 2; Larisa 2; Aris Salonika 1; Ethnikos 1; Iraklis 1; Kastoria 1; OFI Crete 1.

Final League Table 2010-11

	P	W	D	L	F	A	Pts
Olympiakos	30	24	1	5	65	18	73
Panathinaikos	30	18	6	6	47	26	60
AEK Athens	30	15	5	10	46	37	50
PAOK Salonika	30	14	6	10	32	29	48
Volos	30	12	11	7	40	28	47
Aris Salonika	30	13	6	11	29	29	25
Kavala	30	10	10	10	29	27	40
Ergotelis	30	11	6	13	32	38	39
Xanthi	30	9	9	12	29	35	36
Panionios	30	8	11	11	25	35	35
Iraklis	30	7	14	9	22	28	35
Atromitos	30	7	13	10	30	34	34
Kerkyra	30	9	6	15	30	40	33
Asteras*	30	7	10	13	21	29	31
Larissa*	30	5	10	15	29	47	25
Panserraikos*	30	6	6	18	22	48	24

Top scorer: Cisse (Pnathinaikos) 20.
Cup Final: Atromitos 0, AEK Athens 3.

HOLLAND

Koninklijke Nederlandsche Voetbalbond, Wouden-bergseweg 56–58, Postbus 515, NL-3700 AM, Zeist.
Founded: 1889; *National Colours:* Orange shirts, black shorts, orange stockings.

International matches 2010
USA (h) 2-1, Mexico (h) 2-1, Ghana (h) 4-1, Hungary (h) 6-1, Denmark (n) 2-0, Japan (n) 1-0, Cameroon (n) 2-1, Slovakia (n) 2-1, Brazil (n) 2-1, Uruguay (n) 3-2, Spain (n) 0-1, Ukraine (a) 1-1, San Marino (a) 5-0, Finland (h) 2-1, Moldova (a) 1-0, Sweden (h) 4-1, Turkey (h) 1-0.

League Championship wins (1898–2011)
Ajax Amsterdam 30; PSV Eindhoven 21; Feyenoord 14; HVV The Hague 8; Sparta Rotterdam 6; Go Ahead Deventer 4; HBS The Hague 3; Willem II Tilburg 3; RAP Amsterdam 2; RCH Heemstede 2; Heracles 2; ADO The Hague 2; AZ 67 Alkmaar 2; Quick The Hague 1; BVV Den Bosch 1; NAC Breda 1; Eindhoven 1; Enschede 1; Volewijckers Amsterdam 1; Limburgia 1; Rapid JC Den Heerlen 1; DOS Utrecht 1; DWS Amsterdam 1; Haarlem 1; SVV Schiedam 1; Be Quick Groningen 1; Twente 1.

Cup wins (1899–2011)
Ajax Amsterdam 18; Feyenoord 11; PSV Eindhoven 8; Quick The Hague 4; AZ Alkmaar 3; Sparta Rotterdam 3; Utrecht 3; HFC Haarlem 3; Twente Enschede 3; DFC 2; Fortuna Geleen 2; Haarlem 2; HBS The Hague 2; RCH Haarlem 2; Roda JC 2; VOC 2; Wageningen 2; Willem II Tilburg 2; FC Den Haag (includes ADO) 2; Concordia Delft 1; CVV 1; Eindhoven 1; HVV The Hague 1; Longa 1; Quick Nijmegen 1; RAP Amsterdam 1; Roermond 1; Schoten 1; Velocitas Breda 1; Velocitas Groningen 1; VSV 1; VUC 1; VVV Groningen 1; ZFC Zaandam 1; NAC Breda 1; Heerenveen 1.

Final League Table 2010–11

	P	W	D	L	F	A	Pts
Ajax	34	22	7	5	72	30	73
Twente	34	21	8	5	65	34	71
PSV Eindhoven	34	20	9	5	79	34	69
AZ	34	17	8	9	55	44	59
Groningen	34	17	6	11	65	52	57
Roda JC	34	14	13	7	65	50	55
Den Haag	34	16	6	12	63	55	54
Heracles	34	14	7	13	65	56	49
Utrecht	34	13	8	13	55	51	47
Feyenoord	34	12	8	14	53	54	44
NEC Nijmegen	34	10	13	11	57	56	43
Heerenveen	34	10	11	13	60	54	41
NAC Breda	34	12	5	17	44	60	40
De Graafschap	34	9	11	14	31	56	38
Vitesse	34	9	8	17	42	61	35
Excelsior+	34	10	5	19	45	66	35
VVV+	34	6	3	25	34	76	21
Willem II*	34	3	6	25	37	98	15

NAC Breda deducted 1 point.
Top scorer: Vleminckx (NEC Nijmegen) 23.
Cup Final: Twente 3, Ajax 2.

HUNGARY

Hungarian Football Federation, Robert Karoly krt 61-65, Robert Haz Budapest 1134.
Founded: 1901; *National Colours:* Red shirts, white shorts, green stockings.

International matches 2010
Russia (h) 1-1, Germany (h) 0-3, Holland (a) 1-6, England (a) 1-2, Sweden (a) 0-2, Moldova (h) 2-1, San Marino (h) 8-0, Finland (a) 2-1, Lithuania (h) 2-0.

League Championship wins (1901–2011)
Ferencvaros 28; MTK-Hungaria Budapest 23; Ujpest 20; Kispest Honved 13; Vasas Budapest 6; Debrecen 5; Csepel 4; Raba Gyor 3; BTC 2; Nagyvarad 1; Vac 1; Dunaferr 1; Zalaegerszeg 1; Videoton 1.

Cup wins (1910–2011)
Ferencvaros 20; MTK-Hungaria Budapest 12; Ujpest 8; Kispest Honved 7; Raba Gyor 4; Vasas Budapest 4; Debrecen 4; Diösgyör 2; Bocskai 1; III Ker 1; Soroksar 1; Szolnoki MAV 1; Siofok Banyasz 1; Bekescsaba 1; Pecsi 1; Matav 1; Fehervar (now Videoton) 1; Kecskemeti 1.
Cup not regularly held until 1964.

Final League Table 2010–11

	P	W	D	L	F	A	Pts
Videoton	30	18	7	5	59	29	61
Paksi	30	17	5	8	54	38	56
Ferencvaros	30	15	5	10	50	43	50
Zalaegerszeg	30	14	6	10	51	47	48
Debrecen	30	12	10	8	53	43	46
Ujpest	30	13	6	11	50	38	45
Kaposvari	30	13	4	13	41	42	43
Szombathelyi Haladas	30	11	8	11	42	36	41
Gyor	30	10	11	9	40	35	41
Honved	30	11	7	12	36	39	40
Vasas	30	11	7	12	34	46	40
Kecskemeti	30	11	3	16	51	56	36
Papa	30	10	5	15	39	52	35
Siofok	30	8	10	12	29	41	34
MTK*	30	8	6	16	35	49	30
Szolnoki*	30	5	6	19	26	56	21

Top scorer: Andre Alves (Videoton) 24.
Cup Final: Kecskemeti 3, Videoton 2.

ICELAND

Knattspyrnusamband Island, Laugardal, 104 Reykjavik.
Founded: 1929; *National Colours;* All blue.

International matches 2010
Cyprus (a) 0-0, Faeroes (h) 2-0, Mexico (a) 0-0, Andorra (h) 4-0, Liechtenstein (h) 1-1, Norway (h) 1-2, Denmark (a) 0-1, Portugal (h) 1-3, Israel (a) 2-3.

League Championship wins (1912–2010)
KR 24; Valur 20; Fram 18; IA Akranes 18; Vikingur 5; FH Hafnarfjordur 5; IBK Keflavik 4; IBV Vestmannaeyjar 3; KA Akureyri 1; Breidablik 1.

Cup wins (1960–2010)
KR 11; Valur 9; IA Akranes 9; Fram 7; IBV Vestmannaeyjar 4; IBK Keflavik 4; Fylkir 2; FH Hafnarfjordur 2; IBA Akureyri 1; Vikingur 1; Breidablik 1.

Final League Table 2010

	P	W	D	L	F	A	Pts
Breidablik	22	13	5	4	47	23	44
FH	22	13	5	4	48	31	44
IBV	22	13	3	6	36	27	42
KR	22	11	5	6	45	31	38
Fram	22	9	5	8	35	35	32
Keflavik	22	8	6	8	30	32	30
Valur	22	7	7	8	34	41	28
Stjarnan	22	6	7	9	39	42	25
Fylkir	22	7	3	12	36	42	24
Grindavik	22	5	6	11	28	39	21
Haukar*	22	4	8	10	29	45	20
Selfoss*	22	5	2	15	32	51	17

Top scorers: Finnbogason (Breidablik) 14, Bjornsson (FH) 14, Mbang Ondo (Grindavik) 14.
Cup Final: FH 4, KR 0.

REPUBLIC OF IRELAND

The Football Association of Ireland (Cumann Peile Na H-Eireann), 80 Merrion Square, South Dublin 2.
Founded: 1921; *National Colours:* Green shirts, white shorts, green and white stockings.

League Championship wins (1922–2010)
Shamrock Rovers 16; Shelbourne 13; Bohemians 11; Dundalk 9; Cork Athletic (formerly Cork United) 7; St Patrick's Athletic 7; Waterford 6; Drumcondra 5; St James's Gate 2; Sligo Rovers 2; Limerick 2; Athlone Town 2; Derry City 2; Cork City 2; Dolphin 1; Cork Hibernians 1; Cork Celtic 1; Drogheda United 1.

Cup wins (1922–2010)
Shamrock Rovers 24; Dundalk 9; Bohemians 7; Shelbourne 7; Drumcondra 5; Cork Athletic (formerly Cork United) 4; Derry City 4; Sligo Rovers 3; Cork City 2; St James's Gate 2; St Patrick's Athletic 2; Cork Hibernians 2; Limerick 2; Waterford 2; Bray Wanderers 2; Longford Town 2; Alton United 1; Athlone Town 1; Fordsons 1; Cork 1; Transport 1; Finn Harps 1; Home Farm 1; UCD 1; Galway United 1; Drogheda United 1; Sporting Fingal 1.

Final League Table 2010

	P	W	D	L	F	A	Pts
Shamrock Rovers	36	19	10	7	57	34	67
Bohemians	36	19	10	7	50	29	67
Sligo Rovers	36	17	12	7	61	36	63
Sporting Fingal	36	16	14	6	60	38	62
St Patrick's Ath	36	16	9	11	55	33	57
Dundalk	36	14	6	16	46	50	48
UCD	36	11	8	17	47	54	41
Galway United+	36	9	11	16	38	59	38
Bray Wanderers+	36	6	9	21	35	72	27
Drogheda United*	36	4	9	23	30	74	21

Top scorer: Twigg (Shamrock Rovers) 21.
Cup Final: Shamrock Rovers 0, Sligo Rovers 0.
Sligo Rovers won 2-0 on penalties.

ISRAEL

Israel Football Association, Ramat-Gan Stadium, 299 Aba Hilell Street, Ramat-Gan 52134.
Founded· 1948; *National Colours:* Blue shirts, white shorts, blue stockings.

International matches 2010
Uruguay (a) 1-4, Chile (a) 0-3, Malta (h) 3-1, Georgia (a) 0-0, Croatia (h) 1-2, Greece (a) 1-2, Iceland (h) 3-2.

League Championship wins (1932–2011)
Maccabi Tel Aviv 18; Maccabi Haifa 12; Hapoel Tel Aviv 11; Hapoel Petah Tikva 6; Beitar Jerusalem 6; Maccabi Netanya 5; Hakoah Ramat Gan 2; Hapoel Beersheba 2; Bnei Yehouda 1; British Police 1; Hapoel Kfar Saba 1; Hapoel Ramat Gan 1; Hapoel Haifa 1.

Cup wins (1928–2011)
Maccabi Tel Aviv 22; Hapoel Tel Aviv 15; Beitar Jerusalem 7; Maccabi Haifa 5; Hapoel Haifa 3; Hapoel Kfar Saba 3; Beitar Tel Aviv 2; Bnei Yehouda 2; Hakoah Ramat Gan 2; Hapoel Petah Tikva 2; Maccabi Petah Tikva 2; Maccabi Hashmonai Jerusalem 1; British Police 1; Gunners 1; Hapoel Jerusalem 1; Hapoel Yehud 1; Hapoel Lod 1; Maccabi Netanya 1; Hapoel Beersheba 1; Hapoel Ramat Gan 1; Hapoel Bnei Sakhnin 1.

Qualifying League Table 2010–11

	P	W	D	L	F	A	Pts
Maccabi Haifa	30	21	7	2	55	25	70
Hapoel Tel Aviv	30	20	5	5	65	27	65
Maccabi Tel Aviv	30	15	5	10	41	33	50
Ironi Kiryat	30	13	9	8	50	34	48
Bnei Yehouda	30	13	9	8	33	27	48
Maccabi Netanya	30	11	11	8	39	33	44
Hapoel Haifa	30	12	8	10	38	37	44
Maccabi Petah Tikva	30	11	9	10	50	39	42
Hapoel Acre	30	10	11	9	43	38	41
Hapoel Beersheba	30	10	8	12	36	38	38
Beitar Jerusalem	30	10	8	12	30	32	38
Hapoel Petah Tikva	30	9	6	15	36	51	33
Ashdod	30	8	9	13	36	52	33
Hapoel Ashkelon	30	7	5	18	29	56	26
Bnei Sakhnin	30	6	7	17	19	40	25
Hapoel Ramat Gan	30	1	9	20	18	56	8

Hapoel Ramat Gan deducted 4 points.

Championship Play-Off Table 2010–11

	P	W	D	L	F	A	Pts
Maccabi Haifa	5	3	1	1	63	28	45
Hapoel Tel Aviv	5	1	2	2	72	36	38
Maccabi Tel Aviv	5	3	1	1	53	40	35
Bnei Yehouda	5	2	1	2	42	34	31
Ironi Kiryat	5	1	1	3	57	45	28
Maccabi Netanya	5	1	2	2	47	47	27

Middle Play-Off Table 2010–11

	P	W	D	L	F	A	Pts
Maccabi Petah Tikva	3	2	1	0	57	41	28
Hapoel Acre	3	2	0	1	49	45	27
Hapoel Beersheba	3	1	1	1	41	43	23
Hapoel Haifa	3	0	0	3	40	43	22

Relegation Table 2010–11

	P	W	D	L	F	A	Pts
Beitar Jerusalem	5	2	1	2	38	35	26
Ashdod	5	2	2	1	42	55	25
Bnei Sakhnin	5	3	1	1	25	44	23
Hapoel Petah Tikva+	5	1	2	2	42	58	22
Hapoel Ashkelon*	5	2	0	3	33	66	19
Hapoel Ramat Gan*	5	2	0	3	24	65	10

Top scorer: Tamuz (Hapoel Tel Aviv) 21.
Cup Final: Hapoel Tel Aviv 1, Maccabi Haifa 0.

ITALY

Federazione Italiana Giuoco Calcio, Via Gregorio Allegri 14, Roma 00198.
Founded: 1898; *National Colours:* Blue shirts, white shorts, blue stockings.

International matches 2010

Cameroon (h) 0-0, Mexico (h) 1-2, Switzerland (a) 1-1, Paraguay (n) 1-1, New Zealand (n) 1-1, Slovakia (n) 2-3, Ivory Coast (h) 0-1, Estonia (a) 2-1, Faeroes (h) 5-0, Northern Ireland (a) 0-0, Serbia (h) 3-0 (score awarded), Romania (a) 1-1.

League Championship wins (1898–2011)

Juventus 27 (excludes two titles revoked); Internazionale 18 (includes one title awarded); AC Milan 18; Genoa 9; Torino 7 (excludes one title revoked); Pro Vercelli 7; Bologna 7; AS Roma 3; Fiorentina 2; Lazio 2; Napoli 2; Casale 1; Novese 1; Cagliari 1; Verona 1; Sampdoria 1.

Cup wins (1928–2011)

AS Roma 9; Juventus 9; Internazionale 7; Fiorentina 6; AC Milan 5; Torino 5; Lazio 5; Sampdoria 4; Napoli 3; Parma 3; Bologna 2; Atalanta 1; Genoa 1; Vado 1; Venezia 1; Vicenza 1.

Final League Table 2010–11

	P	W	D	L	F	A	Pts
AC Milan	38	24	10	4	65	24	82
Internazionale	38	23	7	8	69	42	76
Napoli	38	21	7	10	59	39	70
Udinese	38	20	6	12	65	43	66
Lazio	38	20	6	12	55	39	66
Roma	38	18	9	11	59	52	63
Juventus	38	15	13	10	57	47	58
Palermo	38	17	5	16	58	63	56
Fiorentina	38	12	15	11	49	44	51
Genoa	38	14	9	15	45	47	51
Chievo	38	11	13	14	38	40	46
Parma	38	11	13	14	39	47	46
Catania	38	12	10	16	40	52	46
Cagliari	38	12	9	17	44	51	45
Cesena	38	11	10	17	38	50	43
Bologna	38	11	12	15	35	52	42
Lecce	38	11	8	19	46	66	41
Sampdoria*	38	8	12	18	33	49	36
Brescia*	38	7	11	20	34	52	32
Bari*	38	5	9	24	27	56	24

Bologna deducted 3 points.
Top scorer: Di Natale (Udinese) 28.
Cup Final: Internazionale 3, Palermo 1.

KAZAKHSTAN

The Football Union of Kazakhstan, Satpayev Street, 29/3 Almaty 480 072, Kazakhstan.
Founded: 1914; *National Colours:* Blue shirts, blue shorts, yellow stockings.

International matches 2010

Moldova (h) 0-1, Oman (h) 3-1, Turkey (h) 0-3, Austria (a) 0-2, Belgium (h) 0-2, Germany (h) 0-3.

League Championship wins (1992–2010)

Irtysh (includes Ansat) 5; Aqtobe 4; Yelimai 3; Astana (includes Zhenis) 3; Kairat 2; Taraz 1; Tobol 1.

Cup wins (1992–2010)

Kairat 5; Astana (includes Zhenis) 3; Dostyk 1; Vostok 1; Yelimai 1; Irtysh 1; Kaisar 1; Taraz 1; Almaty 1; Tobol 1; Aqtobe 1; Atirau 1; Lokomotiv Astana 1.

Qualifying League Table 2010

	P	W	D	L	F	A	Pts
Tobol	22	14	5	3	37	15	47
Yertis	22	12	7	3	30	16	43
Aqtobe	22	11	4	7	32	22	37
Shakhtyor	22	11	4	7	28	19	37
Lokomotiv Astana	22	11	3	8	33	21	36
Atirau	22	11	3	8	29	26	36
Zhetysu	22	9	7	6	22	16	34
Odabasy	22	8	6	8	20	20	30
Kairat	22	4	8	10	11	22	20
Taraz	22	4	6	12	21	33	18
Akzhayik	22	3	5	14	19	43	14
Oqjetpes	22	3	4	15	16	45	13

Championship Play-Off 2010

	P	W	D	L	F	A	Pts
Tobol	10	5	2	3	53	25	64
Aqtobe	10	8	2	0	56	30	63
Yertis	10	4	1	5	39	30	56
Lokomotiv Astana	10	3	5	2	41	28	50
Atirau	10	2	2	6	36	44	44
Shakhtyor	10	0	4	6	32	30	41

Relegation Play-Off 2010

	P	W	D	L	F	A	Pts
Zhetysu	10	4	3	3	36	26	49
Odabasy	10	4	3	3	37	34	45
Taraz	10	5	4	1	36	40	37
Kairat	10	2	3	5	17	38	29
Akzhayik*	10	4	0	6	33	58	26
Oqjeteps*	10	3	3	4	24	57	25

Top scorer: Bakaev (Tobol) 16.
Cup Final: Lokomotiv Astana 1, Shakhtyor 0.

KOSOVO

Football Federation Kosova, Agim Ramadani 45, Prishtina, Kosovo 10000.
Founded: 1946; *National Colours:* Blue shirts, white shorts, blue stockings.

League Championship wins (1945–2011)

Prishtina 12; Vellaznimi 9; Trepca 7; Liria 5; Buduqnosti 4; Red Star 3; Rudari 3; Besa 3; Fushe-Kosova 2; Jedinstvo 2; Kosova Prishtina 2; Obiliqi 2; Slloga 2; Besiana 1; Drita 1; Dukagjini 1; KNI Ramiz Sadiku 1; KXEK Kosova 1; Proletari 1; Rudniku 1; Hysi 1.

Cup wins (1992–2008)

Liria 3; Besa 2; Flamurtari 2; Prishtina 2; Besiana 1; Drita 1; Gjilani 1; KEK-u 1; Kosova Prishtina 1; Trepca 1; Vellaznimi 1.

Final League Table 2010–11

	P	W	D	L	Pts
Hysi	32	23	3	6	72
Prishtina	32	21	5	6	68
Liria	33	13	8	12	47
Drenica	33	13	5	15	44
Besa	33	12	7	14	43
KEK-u	33	12	7	14	43
Trepca 89	33	12	7	14	43
Trepca	33	11	9	13	42
Vellaznimi	33	12	5	16	41
Ballkani+	33	11	8	14	41
Flamurtari*	33	11	6	16	39
Ferizaj*	33	7	8	18	29

Cup Final: Besa 2, Prishtina 1.

LATVIA

Latvian Football Federation, Augsiela 1, LV-1009, Riga.
Founded: 1921; *National Colours:* Carmine red shirts, white shorts, carmine red stockings.

International matches 2010
South Korea (h) 0-1, Ghana (a) 0-1, Lithuania (a) 0-0, Estonia (a) 0-0, Czech Republic (a) 1-4, Croatia (h) 0-3, Malta (a) 2-0, Greece (a) 0-1, Georgia (h) 1-1, China (a) 0-1.

League Championship wins (1922–2010)
Skonto Riga 15; ASK Riga 9; RFK Riga 8; Sarkanais Metalurgs Liepaya 8; Olympija Liepaya 7; VEF Riga 6; Energija Riga 4; Elektrons Riga 3; Torpedo Riga 3; FK Ventspils 3; Daugava Liepaya 2; ODO Riga 2; Khimikis Daugavpils 2; RAF Yelgava 2; Keisermezhs Riga 2; Dinamo Riga 1; Zhmilyeva Team 1; Darba Rezervi 1; RER Riga 1; Starts Brotseni 1; Venta Ventspils 1; Yurnieks Riga 1; Alta Riga 1; Gauja Valmiera 1; Metalurgs Liepaya 1.

Cup wins (1937–2011)
Elektrons Riga 7; Skonto Riga 7; Sarkanais Metalurgs Liepaya 5; FK Ventspils 5; ODO Riga 3; VEF Riga 3; ASK Riga 3; Tseltnieks Riga 3; RAF Yelgava 3; RFK Riga 2; Daugava Liepaya 2; Starts Brotseni 2; Selmash Liepaya 2; Yurnieks Riga 2; Khimikis Daugavpils 2; Rigas Vilki 1; Dinamo Liepaya 1; Dinamo Riga 1; RER Riga 1; Voulkan Kouldiga 1; Baltika Liepaya 1; Venta Ventspils 1; Pilots Riga 1; Lielupe Yurmala 1; Energija Riga 1; Torpedo Riga 1; Daugava SKIF Riga 1; Tseltnieks Daugavpils 1; Olympija Riga 1; FK Riga 1; Metalurgs Liepaya 1; Daugava Daugavpils 1; Jelgava 1.

Final League Table 2010

	P	W	D	L	F	A	Pts
Skonto Riga	27	22	3	2	86	16	69
FK Ventspils	27	20	3	4	68	18	63
Metalurgs Liepaya	27	19	4	4	70	20	61
Daugava Daugavpils	27	16	8	3	35	16	56
Jurmala	27	8	4	15	30	45	28
Jelgava	27	6	7	14	36	45	25
Blazna	27	7	3	17	27	57	24
RFS/Olimps	27	5	6	16	31	63	21
Tranzits*	27	5	4	18	17	56	19
Jauniba*	27	4	4	19	60	80	16

Top scorers: Rakels (Metalurgs Liepaya) 18, Nathan Junior (Skonto Riga) 18.
Cup Final: FK Ventspils 3, Metalurgs Liepaya 1.

LIECHTENSTEIN

Liechtensteiner Fussball-Verband, Malbuner Huus Altenbach 11, Postfach 165, 9490 Vaduz.
Founded: 1934; *National Colours:* Blue shirts, red shorts, blue stockings.

International matches 2010
Iceland (a) 1-1, Spain (h) 0-4, Scotland (a) 1-2, Czech Republic (h) 0-2, Estonia (a) 1-1.
Liechtenstein has no national league. Teams compete in Swiss regional leagues.

Cup wins (1937–2011)
Vaduz 40; Balzers 11; Triesen 8; Eschen/Mauren 4; Schaan 3.
Cup Final: Vaduz 5, Eschen 0.

LITHUANIA

Lithuanian Football Federation, Seimyniskiu str. 15, 2005 Vilnius.
Founded: 1922; *National Colours:* Yellow shirts, green shorts, yellow stockings.

International matches 2010
Ukraine (a) 0-4, Latvia (h) 0-0, Estonia (h) 2-0, Belarus (h) 0-2, Scotland (h) 0-0, Czech Republic (a) 1-0, Spain (a) 1-3, Hungary (a) 0-2.

League Championship wins (1990–2010)
FBK Kaunas 8 (including Zalgiris Kaunas 1); Ekranas Panevezys 5; Zalgiris Vilnius 3; Kareda 2; Inkaras Kaunas 2; Sirijus Klaipeda 1; ROMAR Mazeikiai 1.

Cup wins (1990–2011)
Zalgiris Vilnius 5; FBK Kaunas 4; Ekranas Panevezys 4; Kareda 2; Atlantas 2; Suduva 2; Sirijus Klaipeda 1; Lietuvos Makabi Vilnius 1; Inkaras Kaunas 1.

Final League Table 2010

	P	W	D	L	F	A	Pts
Ekranas	27	20	3	4	64	19	63
Suduva	27	16	8	3	56	16	56
Zalgiris	27	16	8	3	47	16	56
Tauras	27	14	5	8	41	27	47
Siauliai	27	11	8	8	37	28	41
Banga	27	10	9	8	34	30	39
Kruoja	27	8	11	8	41	45	35
Klaipeda	27	3	6	18	19	74	15
Mazeikiai	27	2	6	19	17	59	12
Atletas	27	0	6	21	14	56	0

Vetra expelled for financial irregularities.
Atletas deducted 6 points due to licensing irregularities.
Top scorer: Luksys (Suduva) 16.
Cup Final: Ekranas 4, Banga 2.

LUXEMBOURG

Federation Luxembourgeoise De Football (F.L.F.), 68 Rue De Gasperich, Luxembourg 1617.
Founded: 1908; *National Colours:* All red.

International matches 2010
Azerbaijan (h) 1-2, Faeroes (h) 0-0, Wales (a) 1-5, Bosnia (h) 0-3, Albania (a) 0-1, Belarus (h) 0-0, France (a) 0-2, Algeria (h) 0-0.

League Championship wins (1910–2011)
Jeunesse Esch 28; Spora Luxembourg 11; Stade Dudelange 10; F91 Dudelange 9; Red Boys Differdange 6; Union Luxembourg 6; Avenir Beggen 6; US Hollerich-Bonnevoie 5; Fola Esch 5; Aris Bonnevoie 3; Progres Niedercorn 3; Sporting Club 2; Racing Club 1; National Schifflange 1; Grevenmacher 1.

Cup wins (1922–2011)
Red Boys Differdange 16 (now Differdange 03); Jeunesse Esch 12; Union Luxembourg 10; Spora Luxembourg 8; Avenir Beggen 7; Stade Dudelange 4; Progres Niedercorn 4; Grevenmacher 4; F91 Dudelange 4; Fola Esch 3; Alliance Dudelange 1; US Rumelange 2; Aris Bonnevoie 1; US Dudelange 1; Jeunesse Hautcharage 1; National Schifflange 1; Racing Club 1; SC Tetange 1; Swift Hesperange 1; Etzella Ettelbruck 1; CS Petange 1; FC Differdange 1.

Final League Table 2010–11

	P	W	D	L	F	A	Pts
F91 Dudelange	26	19	2	5	75	24	59
Fola Esch	26	14	5	7	48	28	47
Kaerjeng	26	13	5	8	54	34	44
Differdange	26	12	7	7	51	37	43
Progres	26	12	5	9	43	43	41
Grevenmacher	26	11	6	9	43	39	39
Petange	26	10	8	8	37	36	38
Jeunesse Esch	26	10	7	9	40	37	37
Hamm Benfica	26	11	3	12	47	46	36
Hesperange	26	9	4	13	38	49	41
Racing	26	8	5	13	38	38	29
Wiltz*+	26	8	2	16	38	78	26
Etzella*	26	5	6	15	31	60	21
Jeunesse Canach*	26	5	5	16	28	62	20

Top scorer: Ibrahimovic (Wiltz) 18.
Cup Final: Differdange 1, F91 Dudelange 0.

MACEDONIA

Football Association of Macedonia, VIII-ma Udarna Brigada 31-A, Skopje 1000.
Founded: 1948; *National Colours:* All red.

International matches 2010
Azerbaijan (a) 3-1, Romania (a) 1-0, Malta (a) 1-1, Slovakia (a) 0-1, Armenia (h) 2-2, Andorra (a) 2-0, Russia (h) 0-1, Albania (a) 0-0, China (a) 0-0.

League Championship wins (1993–2011)
Vardar 5; Sileks 3; Sloga Jugomagnat 3; Rabotnicki 3; Pobeda 2; Makedonija 1; Renova 1; Skendija 79 1.

Cup wins (1993–2011)
Vardar 5; Sloga Jugomagnat 3; Sileks 2; Rabotnicki 2; Pelister 1; Pobeda 1; Cement 1; Baskimi 1; Makedonija 1; Teteks 1; Metalurg 1.

Final League Table 2010–11

	P	W	D	L	F	A	Pts
Skendija 79	33	21	9	3	65	23	72
Metalurg	33	17	10	6	48	24	61
Renova	33	17	9	7	54	31	60
Rabotnicki	33	15	10	8	53	31	55
Sileks	33	13	8	12	39	38	47
Turnovo	33	13	6	14	35	35	45
Teteks	33	12	8	13	38	36	44
Bregalnica	33	12	5	16	33	49	41
Skopje*+	33	9	10	14	36	39	37
Napredok+	33	10	7	16	30	48	37
Vardar*	33	9	5	19	24	44	29
Pelister*	33	5	3	25	25	82	18

Vardar deducted 3 points.
Top scorer: Kirovski (Skopje) 20.
Cup Final: Metalurg 2, Teteks 0.

MALTA

Malta Football Association, 280 St Paul Street, Valletta VLT07.
Founded: 1900; *National Colours:* Red shirts, white shorts, red stockings.

International matches 2010
Finland (h) 1-2, Germany (a) 0-3, Macedonia (h) 1-1, Israel (a) 1-3, Latvia (h) 0-2, Georgia (a) 0-1, Croatia (a) 0-3.

League Championship wins (1910–2011)
Sliema Wanderers 26; Floriana 25; Valletta 20; Hibernians 10; Hamrun Spartans 7; Birkirkara 3; Rabat Ajax 2; St George's 1; KOMR 1; Marsaxlokk 1.

Cup wins (1935–2011)
Sliema Wanderers 20; Floriana 19; Valletta 12; Hibernians 8; Hamrun Spartans 6; Birkirkara 4; Gzira United 1; Melita 1; Zurrieq 1; Rabat Ajax 1.

Qualifying League Table 2010–11

	P	W	D	L	F	A	Pts
Valletta	18	13	5	0	42	11	44
Tarxien Rainbows	18	8	5	5	25	22	29
Floriana	18	8	3	7	25	20	27
Birkirkara	18	7	6	5	23	23	27
Marsaxlokk	18	5	9	4	25	25	24
Hamrun Spartans	18	7	2	9	31	36	23
Sliema Wanderers	18	5	7	6	22	26	22
Qormi	18	5	6	7	22	26	21
Hibernians	18	3	6	9	23	33	15
Vittoriosa Stars	18	2	5	11	30	36	11

Championship Table 2010–11

	P	W	D	L	F	A	Pts
Valletta	10	5	5	0	59	17	42
Floriana	10	6	2	2	46	32	34
Birkirkara	10	4	3	3	42	40	29
Marsaxlokk	10	4	2	4	45	43	26
Tarxien Rainbows	10	2	2	6	41	45	23
Hamrun Spartans	10	0	4	6	44	66	16

Relegation Table 2010–11

	P	W	D	L	F	A	Pts
Sliema Wanderers	6	5	0	1	37	31	26
Qormi	6	2	1	3	37	43	18
Hibernians	6	3	0	3	34	46	17
Vittoriosa Stars*	6	1	1	4	26	48	10

Top scorer: Effiong (Marsaxlokk) 17.
Cup Final: Valletta 0, Floriana 1.

MOLDOVA

Football Association of Moldova, 39 Tricolorului Str, 2012, Chisinau.
Founded: 1990; *National Colours:* Red shirts, blue shorts, red stockings.

International matches 2010
Kazakhstan (a) 1-0, Azerbaijan (h) 1-1, UAE (a) 2-3, Georgia (h) 0-0, Finland (h) 2-0, Hungary (a) 1-2, Holland (h) 0-1, San Marino (a) 2-0.

League Championship wins (1992–2011)
Sheriff 10; Zimbru Chisinau 8; Constructorul 1; Dacia 1.

Cup wins (1992–2011)
Sheriff 7; Zimbru Chisinau 5; Tiligul 3; Constructorul 2; Comrat 1; Nistru Otaci 1; Iskra-Stal 1.

Final League Table 2010–11

	P	W	D	L	F	A	Pts
Dacia	39	27	11	1	66	16	92
Sheriff	39	24	11	4	81	16	83
Milsami Orhei	39	23	9	7	71	23	78
Zimbru Chisinau	39	22	10	7	56	20	76
Iskra-Stal	39	21	11	7	62	26	74
Olimpia	39	21	11	7	59	31	74
Tiraspol	39	17	6	16	57	45	57
Rapid Ghidighici	39	15	10	14	39	37	55
Acaemia	39	14	10	15	44	37	52
Costuleni	39	7	6	26	23	68	27
Nistru	39	7	4	28	33	75	25
Sfintul	39	6	7	26	30	83	25
Gagauziya*	39	7	2	30	38	89	23
Dinamo*	39	6	4	29	25	118	22

Top scorer: Boghiu (Milsami Orhei) 26.
Cup Final: Iskra-Stal 2, Olimpia 1.

MONTENEGRO

Football Association of Montenegro.
Founded: 1931.

International matches 2010
Albania (h) 0-1, Norway (a) 1-2, Northern Ireland (h) 2-0, Wales (h) 1-0, Bulgaria (a) 1-0, Switzerland (h) 1-0, England (a) 0-0, Azerbaijan (h) 2-0.

League Championship wins (2006–11)
Mogren 2; Buducnost 1; Zeta 1; Rudar 1.

Cup wins (2006–11)
Rudar 3; Mogren 1; Petrovac 1.

Final League Table 2010–11

	P	W	D	L	F	A	Pts
Mogren	33	22	7	4	60	24	73
Buducnost	33	22	7	4	58	29	73
Rudar	33	16	7	10	44	29	55
Zeta	33	12	13	8	36	29	49
Mladost	33	10	11	12	36	35	41
Decic	33	10	9	14	24	33	39
Grbalj	33	10	8	15	30	35	38
Lovcen	33	9	10	14	29	36	37
Petrovac	33	8	11	14	26	38	35
Mornar*+	33	9	7	17	25	45	34
Sutjeska+	33	9	7	17	32	54	34
Bar*	33	7	11	15	30	43	32

Top scorer: Vukovic (Buducnost) 20.
Cup Final: Mogren 2, Rudar 2
Rudar won 5-4 on penalties.

NORTHERN CYPRUS

Turkish Republic of Northern Cyprus.
Founded: 1955; *National Colours:* All red with white trim.
League Championship wins (1956–63; 1969–74; 1976–2011)
Cetinkaya 12; Gonyeli 9; Magusa 7; Dogan 7; Yenicami 5; BAF Ulku 4; Kucuk 4; Akincilar 1; Binatli 1; Kaymaki 1.

Cup wins (1956-2011)
Cetinkaya 17; Gonyeli 8; Kucuk 6; Magusa 5; Yenicami 5; Turk Ocagi 4; Binatli 1; Dogan 1; Genclik 1; Lefke 1; Yalova 1.

Final League Table 2010–11

	P	W	D	L	F	A	Pts
Kucuk	26	21	2	3	84	22	65
Bagcil	26	19	2	5	66	31	59
Dogan Turk	26	12	5	9	55	36	41
Cetinkaya	26	12	5	9	55	36	41
Letinkaya	26	11	8	7	43	31	12
Lapta	26	12	4	10	22	46	40
Lefke	26	10	9	7	43	36	39
Cihangir	26	9	8	9	45	51	35
Tatlisu	26	9	7	10	57	60	34

Magusa	26	8	7	11	49	55	31
Duzkaya	26	6	9	11	43	56	27
Gonyeli	26	6	7	13	31	48	25
Yesilova	26	5	8	13	37	65	23
Turkmenkoy	26	5	7	14	30	51	22
Ozankoy	26	5	5	16	39	66	20

Cup Final: Cetinkaya 3, Lefke 0.

NORTHERN IRELAND

Irish Football Association Ltd, 20 Windsor Avenue, Belfast BT9 6EE.
Founded: 1880; *National Colours:* Green shirts, white shorts, green stockings.

NORWAY

Norges Fotballforbund, Ullevaal Stadion, Sognsveien 75J, Serviceboks 1, Oslo 0855.
Founded: 1902; *National Colours:* Red shirts, white shorts, blue stockings.

International matches 2010
Slovakia (a) 1-0, Montenegro (h) 2-1, Ukraine (h) 0-1, France (h) 2-1, Iceland (a) 2-1, Portugal (h) 1-0, Cyprus (a) 2-1, Croatia (a) 1-2, Republic of Ireland (a) 2-1.

League Championship wins (1938–2010)
Rosenborg Trondheim 22; Fredrikstad 9; Viking Stavanger 8; Lillestrom 5; Valerenga 5; Larvik Turn 3; Brann Bergen 3; Lyn Oslo 2; IK Start 2; Freidig 1; Fram 1; Skeid Oslo 1; Strömsgodset Drammen 1; Moss 1; Stabaek 1.

Cup wins (1902–2010)
Odd Grenland 12; Fredrikstad 11; Rosenborg Trondheim 9; Lyn Oslo 8; Skeid Oslo 8; Rosenborg Trondheim 8; Sarpsborg 6; Brann Bergen 6; Viking Stavanger 5; Lillestrom 5; Orn Horten 4; Strömsgodset Drammen 5; Valerenga 4; Frigg 3; Mjondalen 3; Bodo/Glimt 2; Mercantile 2; Tromso 2; Molde 2; Grane Nordstrand 1; Kvik Halden 1; Sparta 1; Gjovik/Lyn 1; Moss 1; Bryne 1; Stabaek 1; Aalesund 1.
(Known as the Norwegian Championship for HM The King's Trophy).

Final League Table 2010
	P	W	D	L	F	A	Pts
Rosenborg	30	19	11	0	58	24	68
Valerenga	30	19	4	7	69	36	61
Tromso	30	14	8	8	36	30	50
Aalesunds	30	14	5	11	46	37	47
Odd	30	12	10	8	48	41	46
Haugesund	30	12	9	9	51	39	45
Stromsgodset	30	13	4	13	51	59	43
Start	30	11	9	10	57	60	42
Viking	30	10	11	9	48	41	41
Lillestrom	30	9	13	8	51	44	40
Molde	30	10	10	10	42	45	40
Stabaek	30	11	6	13	46	47	39
Brann	30	8	10	12	48	50	34
Honefoss*+	30	7	6	17	28	62	27
Kongsvinger*	30	4	8	18	27	58	20
Sandefjord*	30	2	6	22	25	58	12

Top scorer: Fall (Molde) 16.
Cup Final: Stromsgodset 2, Follow 0.

POLAND

Polish Football Association, Polski Zwiazek Pilki Noznej, Miodowa 1, Warsaw 00-080.
Founded: 1919; *National Colours:* White shirts, red shorts, white stockings.

International matches 2010
Denmark (h) 1-3, Thailand (a) 3-1, Singapore (h) 6-1, Bulgaria (h) 2-0, Finland (h) 0-0, Serbia (a) 0-0, Spain (a) 0-6, Cameroon (h) 0-3, Australia (h) 1-1, USA (a) 2-2, Ecuador (a) 2-2, Ivory Coast (h) 3-1, Bosnia (h) 2-2.

League Championship wins (1921–2011)
Gornik Zabrze 14; Ruch Chorzow 14; Wisla Krakow 14; Legia Warsaw 8; Lech Poznan 6; Cracovia 5; Pogon Lwow 4; Widzew Lodz 4; Warta Poznan 2; Polonia Bytom 2; Stal Mielec 2; LKS Lodz 2; Polonia Warsaw 2; Zaglebie Lubin 2; Garbarnia Krakow 1; Slask Wroclaw 1; Szombierki Bytom 1.

Cup wins (1951–2011)
Legia Warsaw 14; Gornik Zabrze 6; Lech Poznan 5; Zaglebie Sosnowiec 4; GKS Katowice 3; Ruch Chorzow 3; Amica Wronki 3; Wisla Krakow 3; Slask Wroclaw 2; Polonia Warsaw 2; Groclin 2; Gwardia Warsaw 1; LKS Lodz 1; Stal Rzeszow 1; Arka Gdynia 1; Lechia Gdansk 1; Widzew Lodz 1; Miedz Legnica 1; Wisla Plock 1; Jagiellonia 1.

Final League Table 2010–11
	P	W	D	L	F	A	Pts
Wisla	30	17	5	8	44	29	56
Slask	30	13	10	7	46	34	49
Legia	30	15	4	11	45	38	49
Jagiellonia	30	14	6	10	38	32	48
Lech	30	13	6	11	37	23	45
Gornik Zabrze	30	13	6	11	36	40	45
Polonia W	30	12	8	10	41	26	44
Lechia	30	12	7	11	37	36	43
Widzew	30	11	10	9	41	34	43
GKS Belchatow	30	10	10	10	31	33	40
Zaglebie	30	10	9	11	31	38	39
Ruch	30	10	8	12	29	32	38
Korona	30	10	7	13	34	48	37
Cracovia	30	8	5	17	37	47	29
Arka*	30	6	10	14	22	43	28
Polonia B*	30	6	9	15	29	45	27

Top scorer: Frankowski (Jagiellonia) 14.
Cup Final: Lech 1, Legia 1.
Legia on 5-4 on penalties.

PORTUGAL

Federacao Portuguesa De Futebol, Praca De Alegria N.25, Apartado 21.100, P-1127, Lisboa 1250-004.
Founded: 1914; *National Colours:* Red shirts, green shorts, red stockings.

International matches 2010
Cape Verde Islands (h) 0-0, Cameroon (h) 3-1, Mozambique (h) 3-0, Ivory Coast (n) 0-0, North Korea (n) 7-0, Brazil (n) 0-0, Spain (n) 0-1, Cyprus (h) 4-4, Norway (a) 0-1, Denmark (h) 3-1, Iceland (a) 3-1, Spain (h) 4-0.

League Championship wins (1935–2011)
Benfica 32; Porto 25; Sporting Lisbon 18; Belenenses 1; Boavista 1.

Cup wins (1939–2011)
Benfica 24; Porto 16; Sporting Lisbon 15; Boavista 5; Belenenses 3; Vitoria Setubal 3; Academica Coimbra 1; Leixoes 1; Sporting Braga 1; Estrela Amadora 1; Beira Mar 1.

Final League Table 2010–11
	P	W	D	L	F	A	Pts
Porto	30	27	3	0	73	16	84
Benfica	30	20	3	7	61	31	63
Sporting Lisbon	30	13	9	8	41	31	48
Braga	30	13	7	10	45	33	46
Guimaraes	30	12	7	11	36	37	43
Nacional	30	11	9	10	28	31	42
Pacos de Ferreira	30	10	11	9	35	42	41
Rio Ave	30	10	8	12	35	33	38
Maritimo	30	9	8	13	33	32	35
Uniao Leiria	30	9	8	13	25	38	35
Olhanense	30	7	13	10	24	34	34
Setubal	30	8	10	12	29	42	34
Beira-Mar	30	7	12	11	32	36	33
Academica	30	7	9	14	32	48	30
Portimonense*	30	6	7	17	29	49	25
Naval*	30	5	8	17	26	51	23

Top scorer: Hulk (Porto) 23.
Cup Final: Guimaraes 2, Porto 6.

ROMANIA

Federatia Romana De Fotbal, House of Football, Str. Serg. Serbanica Vasile 12, Bucharest 73412.
Founded: 1909; *National Colours:* All yellow.

International matches 2010
Ukraine (a) 2-3, Macedonia (h) 0-1, Honduras (h) 3-0, Turkey (a) 0-2, Albania (h) 1-1, Belarus (a) 0-0, France (a) 0-2, Italy (h) 1-1.

League Championship wins (1910–2011)
Steaua Bucharest 23; Dinamo Bucharest 18; Venus Bucharest 8; Chinezul Timisoara 6; UT Arad 6; Ripensia Timisoara 4; Uni Craiova 4; Petrolul Ploiesti 3; Rapid Bucharest 3; Olimpia Bucharest 2; Colentina Bucharest 2; Arges Pitesti 2; Cluj 2; ICO Oradea 1; Romano-Americana Bucharest 1; Prahova Ploiesti 1; Coltea Brasov 1; Juventus Bucharest 1; Metalochimia Resita 1; United Ploiesti 1; Unirea Tricolor 1; Unirea 1; Otelul 1.

Cup wins (1934–2011)
Steaua Bucharest 22; Rapid Bucharest 13; Dinamo Bucharest 12; Uni Craiova 6; Cluj 3; UT Arad 2; Ripensia Timisoara 2; Politehnica Timisoara 2; Petrolul Ploiesti 2; Metalochimia Resita 1; Universitata Cluj (includes Stiinta) 1; CFR Turnu Severin 1; Chimia Ramnicu Vilcea 1; Jiul Petrosani 1; Progresul Bucharest 1; Progresul Oradea (formerly ICO) 1; Ariesul Turda 1; Gloria Bistrita 1.

Final League Table 2010–11

	P	W	D	L	F	A	Pts
Otelul	34	21	7	6	46	25	70
Timisoara*	34	17	15	2	63	38	66
Vaslui	34	18	11	5	51	28	65
Rapid Bucharest	34	16	11	7	43	22	59
Steaua	34	16	9	9	44	27	57
Dinamo Bucharest	34	16	8	10	68	52	56
Gaz Metan	34	14	13	7	41	32	55
Univ Cluj	34	13	8	13	48	54	47
Targu	34	12	9	13	34	41	45
Cluj	34	11	12	11	50	45	45
Astra	34	10	15	9	36	30	45
Brasov	34	10	13	11	34	40	43
Pandurii	34	9	10	15	36	46	37
Gloria*	34	8	11	15	34	49	35
Univcrsitatca*	34	7	9	18	35	48	30
Victoria*	34	5	10	19	35	61	25
Unirea*	34	6	7	21	23	63	25
Sportul	34	7	2	25	38	58	23

Timisoara and Gloria relegated to third level for financial irregularities. Sportul exempted from relegation.
Top scorer: Zicu (Timisoara) 18.
Cup Final: Dinamo Bucharest 1, Steaua 2.

RUSSIA

Football Union of Russia; Luzhnetskaya Naberezyhnaja 8, Moscow 119 992.
Founded: 1912; *National Colours:* All white.

International matches 2010
Hungary (a) 1-1, Bulgaria (h) 1-0, Andorra (a) 2-0, Slovakia (h) 0-1, Republic of Ireland (a) 3-2, Macedonia (a) 1-0, Belgium (h) 0-2.

League Championship wins (1936–2010)
Spartak Moscow 21; Dynamo Kiev 13; Dynamo Moscow 11; CSKA Moscow 10; Torpedo Moscow 3; Zenit St Petersburg (formerly Zenit Leningrad) 3; Dinamo Tbilisi 2; Dnepr Dnepropetrovsk 2; Lokomotiv Moscow 2; Rubin 2; Saria Voroshilovgrad 1; Ararat Erevan 1; Dynamo Minsk 1; Spartak Vladikavkaz 1.

Cup wins (1936–2011)
Spartak Moscow 13; CSKA Moscow 11; Dynamo Kiev 9; Torpedo Moscow 7; Dynamo Moscow 7; Lokomotiv Moscow 7; Shakhtar Donetsk 4; Zenit St Petersburg (formerly Zenit Leningrad) 3; Dinamo Tbilisi 2; Ararat Erevan 2; Karpaty Lvov 1; SKA Rostov 1; Metalist Kharkov 1; Dnepr 1; Terek Groznyi 1.

Final League Table 2010

	P	W	D	L	F	A	Pts
Zenit	30	20	8	2	61	21	68
CSKA Moscow	30	18	8	4	51	22	62
Rubin	30	15	13	2	37	16	58
Spartak Moscow	30	13	10	7	43	33	49
Lokomotiv Moscow	30	13	9	8	34	29	48
Spartak Nalchik	30	12	8	10	40	37	44
Dynamo Moscow	30	9	13	8	38	31	40
Tomsk	30	10	7	13	35	43	37
Saturn	30	8	10	12	27	38	34
FK Rostov	30	10	4	16	27	44	34
Terek	30	8	9	13	28	34	33
Anzhi	30	9	6	15	29	39	33
Krylia Sovekov	30	7	10	13	28	40	31
Amkar	30	8	6	16	24	35	30
Alaniya*	30	7	9	14	25	41	30
Sibir*	30	4	8	18	34	58	20

Saturn disbanded for financial reasons.
Top scorer: Welliton (Spartak Moscow) 19.
Cup Final: CSKA Moscow 2, Alaniya 1.

SAN MARINO

Federazione Sammarinese Giuoco Calcio, Viale Campo dei Giudei, 14; Rep. San Marino 47890.
Founded: 1931; *National Colours:* All light blue.

International matches 2010
Holland (h) 0-5, Sweden (a) 0-6, Hungary (a) 0-8, Moldova (h) 0-2, Finland (a) 0-8.

League Championship wins (1986–2011)
Tre Fiori 7; Domagnano 4; Faetano 3; Folgore Falciano 3; Murata 3; La Fiorita 2; Montevito 1; Libertas 1; Cosmos 1; Pennarossa 1.

Cup wins (1937–2011)
Libertas 10; Domagnono 8; Tre Fiore 6; Juvenes 5; Tre Penne 5; Cosmos 4; Caetano 3; Murata 3; Dogana 2; Pennarossa 2; Juvenes/Dogana 2; La Fiorita 1.

Qualifying League Table 2010–11

Group A	P	W	D	L	F	A	Pts
Pennarossa	20	13	3	4	31	15	42
La Fiorita	20	10	6	4	44	28	36
Cosmos	20	11	3	6	22	22	36
Juvenes/Dogana	20	8	5	7	37	31	29
Faetano	20	7	3	10	30	33	24
Fiorentino	20	5	4	11	22	37	19
Cailungo	20	2	4	14	17	40	10

Group B	P	W	D	L	F	A	Pts
Tre Fiore	21	11	6	4	41	26	39
Libertas	21	10	7	4	26	13	37
Tre Penne	21	10	6	5	32	19	36
Murata	21	9	8	4	34	19	35
Virtus	21	8	6	7	32	32	30
San Giovanni	21	9	2	10	29	34	29
Folgore/Falciano	21	3	4	14	21	44	13
Domagnano	21	0	9	12	17	42	9

Play-Offs: Libertas 0, Cosmos 2; La Fiorita 3, Tre Penne 1; Libertas 1, Tre Penne 4; Cosmos 4, La Fiorita 2; Pennarossa 1, Tre Fiore 2; Tre Penne 2, La Fiorita 0; Tre Penne 3, Pennarossa 1; Tre Fiore 2, Cosmos 0; Tre Penne 2, Cosmos 1; Tre Fiore 1, Tre Penne 0.
Top scorers: Fantini (Juvenes/Dogana), Hirsh (Virtus), Giunta (Tre Fiore), Viroli (Faetano), Gatti (Murata) all 12.
Cup Final: Juvenes/Dogana 4, Virtus 1.

SCOTLAND

The Scottish Football Association Ltd, Hampden Park, Glasgow G42 9AY.
Founded: 1873; *National Colours:* Dark blue shirts, white shorts, dark blue stockings.

SERBIA

Football Association of Serbia, Terazije 35, P.O. Box 263, 11000 Beograd.
Founded: 1919; *National Colours:* Blue shirts, white shorts, red stockings.

International matches 2010
Japan (a) 3-0, New Zealand (a) 0-1, Poland (h) 0-0, Cameroon (h) 4-3, Ghana (h) 0-1, Germany (n) 1-0, Australia (n) 1-2, Greece (h) 0-1, Faeroes (a) 3-0, Slovenia (h) 1-1, Estonia (h) 1-3, Italy (a) 0-3 (score awarded), Bulgaria (a) 1-0.

League Championship wins (1923–2011)
Red Star Belgrade 25; Partizan Belgrade 23; Hajduk Split 9; Gradjanski Zagreb 5; BSK Belgrade 5; Dinamo Zagreb 4; Jugoslavija Belgrade 2; Concordia Zagreb 2; FC Sarajevo 2; Vojvodina Novi Sad 2; HASK Zagreb 1; Zeljeznicar 1; Obilic 1.

Cup wins (1947–2011)
Red Star Belgrade 23; Partizan Belgrade 12; Hajduk Split 9; Dinamo Zagreb 8; BSK Belgrade (includes OFK) 2; Rijeka 2; Velez Mostar 2; Vardar Skopje 1; Borac Banjaluka 1; Sartid 1; Zeleznik 1.

Final League Table 2010–11

	P	W	D	L	F	A	Pts
Partizan Belgrade	30	24	4	2	75	21	76
Red Star Belgrade	30	22	4	4	52	18	70
Vojvodina	30	20	7	3	44	14	67
Rad	30	14	10	6	38	21	52
Spartak	30	11	10	9	34	27	43
Sevojno	30	12	7	11	34	35	43
OFK Belgrade	30	12	6	12	27	26	42
Javor	30	10	11	9	21	24	41
Borac	30	8	12	10	22	31	36
Smederevo	30	8	11	11	24	31	35
Borca	30	8	9	13	23	37	33
Jagodina	30	8	8	14	26	33	32
Hajduk Kula	30	7	8	15	25	37	29
Metalac	30	8	5	17	21	38	29
Indija*	30	7	5	18	29	47	26
Cukaricki*	30	0	5	25	10	65	5

Top scorers: Kaluderovic (Red Star Belgrade) 13, Iliev (Partizan Belgrade) 13.
Cup Final: Partizan Belgrade 3, Vojvodina 0.

SLOVAKIA

Slovak Football Association, Junacka 6, 83280 Bratislava, Slovakia.
Founded: 1993; *National Colours:* All blue and white.

International matches 2010
Norway (h) 0-1, Cameroon (h) 1-1, Costa Rica (h) 3-0, New Zealand (n) 1-1, Paraguay (n) 0-2, Italy (n) 3-2, Holland (n) 1-2, Croatia (h) 1-1, Macedonia (h) 1-0, Russia (a) 1-0, Armenia (a) 1-3, Republic of Ireland (h) 1-1, Bosnia (h) 2-3.

League Championship wins (1939–44; 1994–2011)
Slovan Bratislava 10; Zilina 5; Kosice 2; Inter Bratislava 2; Artmedia Petrzalka 2; Bystrica 1; OAP Bratislava 1; Ruzomberok 1.

Cup wins (1994–2011)
Slovan Bratislava 5; Inter Bratislava 3; Artmedia Petrzalka 2; Humenne 1; Spartak Trnava 1; Koba Senec 1; Matador Puchov 1; Bystrica 1; Ruzomberok 1; ViOn Zlate 1; Kosice 1.

Final League Table 2010–11

	P	W	D	L	F	A	Pts
Slovan Bratislava	33	20	8	5	63	22	68
Senica	33	18	7	8	54	30	61
Zilina	33	14	12	7	47	28	54
Spartak Trnava	33	13	10	10	40	30	49
Dukla	33	13	9	11	39	32	48
Zlate	33	12	10	11	35	31	46
Ruzomberok	33	10	11	12	23	33	41
Nitra	33	11	7	15	30	51	40
DAC	33	9	9	15	24	39	36
Kosice	33	8	9	16	28	44	33
Tatran	33	9	6	18	30	49	33
Dubnica*	33	7	10	16	23	47	31

Top scorer: Sebo (Slovan Bratislava) 22.
Cup Final: Slovan Bratislava 3, Zilina 3
Slovan Bratislava won 5-4 on penalties.

SLOVENIA

Football Association of Slovenia, Nogometna zveza Slovenije, Cerinova 4, P.P. 3986, 1001 Ljubljana, Slovenia.
Founded: 1920; *National Colours:* White shirts with green sleeves, white shorts, white stockings.

International matches 2010
Qatar (h) 4-1, New Zealand (h) 3-1, Algeria (n) 1-0, USA (n) 2-2, England (n) 0-1, Australia (h) 2-0, Northern Ireland (h) 0-1, Serbia (a) 1-1, Faeroes (h) 5-1, Estonia (a) 1-0, Georgia (h) 1-2.

League Championship wins (1992–2011)
Maribor 9; SCT Olimpija 4; Gorica 4; Domzale 2; Koper 1.

Cup wins (1992–2011)
Maribor 6; SCT Olimpija 4; Gorica 2; Koper 2; Interblock 2; Mura 1; Rudar 1; Publikum 1; Domzale 1.

Final League Table 2010–11

	P	W	D	L	F	A	Pts
Maribor	36	21	12	3	65	25	75
Domzale	36	20	7	9	57	35	67
Koper	36	17	9	10	57	43	60
Olimpija	36	15	10	11	59	43	55
Gorica	36	13	9	14	42	53	48
Rudar	36	12	10	14	58	50	46
Triglav	36	10	9	17	38	59	39
Celje	36	9	10	17	41	55	37
Nafta+	36	10	7	19	47	67	37
Primorje*	36	8	7	21	40	74	31

Top scorer: Marcos Tavares (Maribor) 16.
Cup Final: Domzale 4, Maribor 3.

SPAIN

Real Federacion Espanola De Futbol, Ramon y Cajal, s/n, Apartado Postale 385, Madrid 28230.
Founded: 1913; *National Colours:* Red shirts, blue shorts, blue stockings with red, blue and yellow border.

International matches 2010
France (a) 2-0, Saudi Arabia (h) 3-2, South Korea (h) 1-0, Poland (h) 6-0, Switzerland (n) 0-1, Honduras (n) 2-0, Chile (n) 2-1, Portugal (n) 1-0, Paraguay (n) 1-0, Germany (n) 1-0, Holland (n) 1-0, Mexico (a) 1-1, Argentina (a) 1-4, Liechtenstein (a) 4-0, Lithuania (h) 3-1, Scotland (a) 3-2, Portugal (a) 0-4.

League Championship wins (1929–36; 1940–2011)
Real Madrid 31; Barcelona 21; Atletico Madrid 9; Athletic Bilbao 8; Valencia 6; Real Sociedad 2; Real Betis 1; Sevilla 1; La Coruna 1.

Cup wins (1994–2011)
Barcelona 25; Athletic Bilbao 23; Real Madrid 18; Atletico Madrid 9; Valencia 7; Real Zaragoza 6; Sevilla 5; Espanyol 4; Real Union de Irun 3; La Coruna 2; Real Sociedad (includes Ciclista) 2; Real Betis 2; Arenas 1; Racing de Irun 1; Vizcaya Bilbao 1; Real Sociedad 1; Mallorca 1.

Final League Table 2010–11

	P	W	D	L	F	A	Pts
Barcelona	38	30	6	2	95	21	96
Real Madrid	38	29	5	4	102	33	92
Valencia	38	21	8	9	64	44	71
Villarreal	38	18	8	12	54	44	62
Sevilla	38	17	7	14	62	61	58
Athletic Bilbao	38	18	4	16	59	55	58
Atletico Madrid	38	17	7	14	62	53	58
Espanyol	38	15	4	19	46	55	49
Osasuna	38	13	8	17	45	46	47
Gijon	38	11	14	13	35	42	47
Malaga	38	13	7	18	54	68	46
Santander	38	12	10	16	41	56	46
Real Zaragoza	38	12	9	17	40	53	45
Levante	38	12	9	17	41	52	45
Real Sociedad	38	14	3	21	49	66	45
Getafe	38	12	8	18	49	60	44
Mallorca	38	12	8	18	41	56	44
La Coruna*	38	10	13	15	31	47	43
Hercules*	38	9	8	21	36	60	35
Almeria*	38	6	12	20	36	70	30

Top scorer: Cristiano Ronaldo (Real Madrid) 40.
Cup Final: Barcelona 0, Real Madrid 1.

SWEDEN

Svenska Fotbollfoerbundet, Box 1216, S-17123 Solna.
Founded: 1904; *National Colours:* Yellow shirts, blue shorts, yellow stockings.

International matches 2010
Oman (a) 1-0, Syria (h) 1-1, Wales (a) 1-0, Bosnia (h) 4-2, Belarus (a) 1-0, Scotland (h) 3-0, Hungary (h) 2-0, San Marino (h) 6-0, Holland (a) 1-4, Germany (h) 0-0.

League Championship wins (1896–2010)

IFK Gothenburg 19; Malmo FF 16; Orgryte 14; IFK Norrköping 12; Djurgaarden 11; AIK Stockholm 11; GAIS Gothenburg 6; IF Helsingborg 6; IF Elfsborg 5; Oster Vaxjo 4; Halmstad 4; Atvidaberg 2; IFK Eskilstuna 1; IF Gavic Brynas 1; IF Gothenburg 1; Fassbergs 1; IK Sleipner 1; Hammarby 1; Kalmar 1.

Cup wins (1941–2010)

Malmo FF 14; AIK Stockholm 8; IFK Norrköping 6; IFK Gothenburg 5; Djurgaarden 4; Helsingborg 4; Kalmar 3; Atvidaberg 2; IF Elfsborg 2; GAIS Gothenburg 1; IF Raa 1; Landskrona 1; Oster Vaxjo 1; Degerfors 1; Halmstad 1; Orgryte 1.

Final League Table 2010

	P	W	D	L	F	A	Pts
Malmo	30	21	4	5	59	24	67
Helsingborg	30	20	5	5	49	26	65
Orebro	30	16	4	10	40	30	52
Elfsborg	30	12	11	7	55	40	47
Trelleborg	30	13	5	12	39	42	44
Mjallby	30	11	10	9	36	29	43
IFK Gothenburg	30	10	10	10	42	29	40
Hacken	30	11	7	12	40	42	40
Kalmar	30	10	10	10	36	38	40
Djurgaarden	30	11	7	12	35	42	40
AIK	30	10	5	15	29	36	35
Halmstad	30	10	5	15	31	42	35
GAIS Gothenburg	30	8	8	14	24	35	32
Gefle+	30	7	8	15	33	46	29
Atvidaberg*	30	7	8	15	32	51	29
Brommapojkarna*	30	6	7	17	20	48	25

Top scorer: Gerndt (Helsingborg) 20.
Cup Final: Hammarby 0, Helsingborg 1.

SWITZERLAND

Schweizerisher Fussballverband, Postfach 3000, Berne 15.
Founded: 1895; *National Colours:* Red shirts, white shorts, red stockings.

International matches 2010

Uruguay (h) 1-3, Costa Rica (h) 0-1, Italy (h) 1-1, Spain (n) 1-0, Chile (n) 0-1, Honduras (n) 0-0, Australia (h) 0-0, Austria (a) 1-0, England (h) 1-3, Montenegro (a) 0-1, Wales (h) 4-1, Ukraine (h) 2-2.

League Championship wins (1898–2011)

Grasshoppers 26; Servette 17; FC Basle 14; FC Zurich 12; Young Boys Berne 11; Lausanne 7; La Chaux-de-Fonds 3; FC Lugano 3; Winterthur 3; FC Aarau 3; Neuchatel Xamax 2; Sion 2; St Gallen 2; FC Anglo-American Club 1; FC Brühl 1; Cantonal-Neuchatel 1; Biel-Bienne 1; Bellinzona 1; FC Etoile La Chaux-de-Fonds 1; Lucerne 1.

Cup wins (1926–2011)

Grasshoppers 18; FC Sion 12; FC Basle 10; Lausanne 9; Servette 7; FC Zurich 7; La Chaux-de-Fonds 6; Young Boys Berne 6; FC Lugano 3; Lucerne 2; FC Grenchen 1; St Gallen 1; Urania Geneva 1; Young Fellows Zurich 1; FC Aarau 1; Wil 1.

Final League Table 2010–11

	P	W	D	L	F	A	Pts
Basle	36	21	10	5	76	44	73
Zurich	36	21	9	6	74	44	72
Young Boys	36	15	12	9	65	50	57
Sion	36	15	9	12	47	36	54
Thun	36	11	16	9	48	43	49
Lucerne	36	13	9	14	62	57	48
Grasshoppers	36	10	11	15	45	54	41
Neuchatel Xamax	36	8	8	20	44	67	32
Bellinzona*+	36	7	11	18	42	75	32
St Gallen*	36	8	7	21	34	67	31

Top scorer: Frei (Basle) 27.
Cup Final: Neuchatel Xamax 0, Sion 2.

TURKEY

Turkiye Futbol Federasyonu, Konaklar Mah. Ihlamurlu Sok. 9, 4 Levent, Istanbul 80620.
Founded: 1923; *National Colours:* All white.

International matches 2010

Honduras (h) 2-0, Czech Republic (h) 2-1, Northern Ireland (a) 2-0, USA (a) 1-2, Romania (h) 2-0, Kazakhstan (a) 3-0, Belgium (h) 3-2, Germany (a) 0-3, Azerbaijan (a) 0-1, Holland (a) 0-1.

League Championship wins (1959–2011)

Fenerbahce 18; Galatasaray 17; Besiktas 11; Trabzonspor 6; Bursa 1.

Cup wins (1963–2011)

Galatasaray 14; Besiktas 9; Trabzonspor 8; Fenerbahce 4; Goztepe Izmir 2; Altay Izmir 2; Ankaragucu 2; Genclerbirligi 2; Kocaelispor 2; Eskisehirspor 1; Bursapor 1; Sakaryaspor 1; Kayseri 1.

Final League Table 2010–11

	P	W	D	L	F	A	Pts
Fenerbahce	34	26	4	4	84	34	82
Trabzonspor	34	25	7	2	69	23	82
Bursa	34	17	10	7	50	29	61
Gaziantep	34	17	8	9	44	33	59
Besiktas	34	15	9	10	53	36	54
Kayseri	34	14	9	11	46	44	51
Eskisehir	34	12	11	11	41	40	47
Galatasaray	34	14	4	16	41	46	46
Karabuk	34	12	8	14	46	53	44
Manisa	34	13	4	17	49	52	43
Antalya	34	10	12	12	41	48	42
Istanbul	34	12	6	16	40	45	42
Ankaragucu	34	10	11	13	52	62	41
Genclerbirligi	34	10	10	14	43	51	40
Sivas	34	8	11	15	43	57	35
Buca*	34	6	8	20	37	65	26
Konya*	34	4	12	18	28	49	24
Kasimpasa*	34	5	8	21	31	71	23

Top scorer: Alex (Fenerbahce) 28.
Cup Final: Besiktas 2, Istanbul 2
Besiktas won 4-3 on penalties.

UKRAINE

Football Federation of Ukraine, Laboratorna Str. 1, P.O. Box 293, Kiev 03150.
Founded: 1991; *National Colours:* All yellow and blue.

International matches 2010

Lithuania (h) 4-0, Romania (h) 3-2, Norway (a) 1-0, Holland (h) 1-1, Poland (a) 1 1, Chile (h) 2-1, Canada (h) 2-2, Brazil (a) 0-2, Switzerland (a) 2-2.

League Championship wins (1992–2011)

Dynamo Kiev 13; Shakhtar Donetsk 6; Tavriya Simferopol 1.

Cup wins (1992–2011)

Dynamo Kiev 9; Shakhtar Donetsk 7; Chernomorets Odessa 2; Vorskla 1; Tavriya Simferopol 1.

Final League Table 2010–11

	P	W	D	L	F	A	Pts
Shakhtar Donetsk	30	23	3	4	53	16	72
Dynamo Kiev	30	20	5	5	60	24	65
Metalist	30	18	6	6	58	26	60
Dnepr	30	16	9	5	46	20	57
Karpaty	30	13	9	8	41	34	48
Vorskla	30	10	9	11	37	32	39
Tavriya	30	10	9	11	44	46	39
Metalurg Donetsk	30	11	5	14	36	45	38
Arsenal Kiev	30	10	7	13	36	38	37
Obolon	30	9	7	14	26	38	34
Volyn	30	9	7	14	27	49	34
Zorya	30	7	9	14	28	40	30
Krivbas	30	6	11	13	27	45	29
Illichivets	30	7	8	15	45	67	29
Sevastopol*	30	7	6	17	26	48	27
Metalurg Zapor*	30	6	6	18	18	40	24

Top scorer: Seleznyov (Dnepr) 17.
Cup Final: Dynamo Kiev 0, Shakhtar Donetsk 2.

WALES

The Football Association of Wales Limited, Plymouth Chambers, 3 Westgate Street, Cardiff, CF10 1DP.
Founded: 1876; *National Colours:* All red.

SOUTH AMERICA

ARGENTINA

Asociacion Del Futbol Argentina, Viamonte 1366/76, 1053 Buenos Aires.
Founded: 1893; *National Colours:* Light blue and white vertical striped shirts, dark blue shorts, white stockings.
International matches 2010
Costa Rica (h) 3-2, Jamaica (h) 2-1, Germany (a) 1-0, Haiti (h) 4-0, Canada (h) 5-0, Nigeria (n) 1-0, South Korea (n) 4-1, Greece (n) 2-0, Mexico (n) 3-1, Germany (n) 0-4, Republic of Ireland (a) 1-0, Spain (h) 4-1, Japan (a) 0-1, Brazil (h) 1-0.

BOLIVIA

Federacion Boliviana De Futbol, Av. Libertador Bolivar No. 1168, Casilla de Correo 484, Cochabamba, Bolivia.
Founded: 1925; *National Colours:* Green shirts, white shorts, green stockings.
International matches 2010
Mexico (a) 0-5, Colombia (h) 1-1, Venezuela (h) 1-3.

BRAZIL

Confederacao Brasileira De Futebol, Rua Victor Civita 66, Bloco 1-Edificio 5-5 Andar, Barra da Tijuca, Rio De Janeiro 22775-040.
Founded: 1914; *National Colours:* Yellow shirts with green collar and cuffs, blue shorts, white stockings with green and yellow border.
International matches 2010
Republic of Ireland (a) 2-0, Zimbabwe (a) 3-0, Tanzania (a) 5-1, North Korea (n) 2-1, Ivory Coast (n) 3-1, Portugal (n) 0-0, Chile (n) 3-0, Holland (n) 1-2, USA (a) 2-0, Iran (a) 3-0, Ukraine (h) 2-0, Brazil (h) 0-1.

CHILE

Federacion De Futbol De Chile, Avda: Quillin No. 5635, Casilla postal 3733, Correo Central, Santiago de Chile.
Founded: 1895; *National Colours:* Red shirts with blue collar and cuffs, blue shorts, white stockings.
International matches 2010
Panama (h) 2-1, Venezuela (h) 0-0, Trinidad & Tobago (h) 2-0, Mexico (a) 0-1, Zambia (h) 3-0, Northern Ireland (h) 1-0, Israel (h) 3-0, Honduras (n) 1-0, Switzerland (n) 1-0, Spain (n) 1-2, Brazil (n) 0-3, Ukraine (a) 1-2, UAE (a) 2-0, Oman (a) 1-0, Uruguay (h) 2-0.

COLOMBIA

Federacion Colombiana De Futbol, Avenida 32, No. 16–22 piso 4o. Apartado Aereo 17602, Santafe de Bogota.
Founded: 1924; *National Colours:* Yellow shirts, blue shorts, red stockings.
International matches 2010
South Africa (a) 1-2, Nigeria (a) 1-1, Bolivia (a) 1-1, Venezuela (a) 2-0, Mexico (a) 0-1, Ecuador (h) 1-0, USA (a) 0-0, Peru (h) 1-1.

ECUADOR

Federacion Ecuatoriana del Futbol, km 4 1/2 via a la Costa (Avda. del Bombero), PO Box 09-01-7447 Guayaquil.
Founded: 1925; *National Colours:* Yellow shirts, blue shorts, red stockings.
International matches 2010
Mexico (a) 0-0, South Korea (a) 0-2, Mexico (a) 2-1, Venezuela (a) 0-1, Colombia (h) 0-1, Poland (h) 2-2, Venezuela (h) 4-1.

PARAGUAY

Asociacion Paraguaya de Futbol, Estadio De Los Defensores del Chaco, Calles Mayor Martinez 1393, Asuncion.
Founded: 1906; *National Colours:* Red and white shirts, blue shorts, blue stockings.

International matches 2010
South Africa (h) 1-1, North Korea (h) 1-0, Republic of Ireland (a) 1-2, Ivory Coast (h) 2-2, Greece (h) 2-0, Italy (n) 1-1, Slovakia (n) 2-0, New Zealand (n) 0-0, Japan (n) 0-0, Spain (n) 0-1, Costa Rica (h) 2-0, Japan (a) 0-1, China (a) 1-1, Australia (a) 0-1, New Zealand (a) 2-0, Hong Kong (a) 7-0.

PERU

Federacion Peruana De Futbol, Av. Aviacion 2085, San Luis, Lima 30.
Founded: 1922; *National Colours:* White shirts with red stripe, white shorts with red lines, white stockings with red line.
International matches 2010
Canada (a) 2-0, Jamaica (h) 2-1, Costa Rica (h) 2-0, Panama (a) 0-1, Colombia (a) 1-1.

URUGUAY

Asociacion Uruguaya De Futbol, Guayabo 1531, 11200 Montevideo.
Founded: 1900; *National Colours:* Sky blue shirts with white collar/cuffs, black shorts and stockings with sky blue borders.
International matches 2010
Switzerland (a) 3-1, Israel (h) 4-1, France (n) 0-0, South Africa (n) 3-0, Mexico (n) 1-0, South Korea (n) 2-1, Ghana (n) 1-1, Holland (n) 2-3, Germany (n) 2-3, Algeria (h) 2-0, Indonesia (a) 7-1, China (a) 4-0, Chile (a) 0-2.

VENEZUELA

Federacion Venezolana De Futbol, Avda. Santos Erminy Ira, Calle las Delicias Torre Mega II, P.H. Sabana Grande, Caracas 1050.
Founded: 1926; *National Colours:* Burgundy shirts, white shorts and stockings.
International matches 2010
Japan (a) 0-0, Panama (h) 1-2, North Korea (h) 2-1, Chile (a) 0-0, Honduras (a) 1-0, Aruba (a) 3-0, Canada (h) 1-1, Panama (a) 1-3, Colombia (h) 0-2, Ecuador (h) 1-0, Bolivia (a) 3-1, Mexico (a) 2-2, Ecuador (a) 1-4.

ASIA

AFGHANISTAN

Afghanistan Football Federation, PO Box 5099, Kabul.
Founded: 1933; *National Colours*: All white with red lines.
International matches 2010
Tajikistan (a) 0-1.

AUSTRALIA

Soccer Australia Ltd, Level 3, East Stand, Stadium Australia, Edwin Flack Avenue, Homebush, NSW 2127.
Founded: 1961; *National Colours:* All green with gold trim.
International matches 2010
Kuwait (a) 2-2, Indonesia (h) 1-0, New Zealand (h) 2-1, Denmark (h) 1-0, USA (a) 1-3, Germany (n) 0-4, Ghana (n) 1-1, Serbia (n) 2-1, Slovenia (a) 0-2, Switzerland (a) 0-0, Poland (a) 2-1, Paraguay (h) 1-0, Egypt (a) 0-3.

BAHRAIN

Bahrain Football Association, P.O. Box 5464, Manama.
Founded: 1957; *National Colours:* All red.
International matches 2010
Hong Kong (h) 4-0, Yemen (a) 0-3, Kuwait (a) 1-4, Japan (a) 0-2, China (a) 1-1, Qatar (a) 1-1, Jordan (a) 0-2, Iran (a) 0-3, Oman (h) 2-0, Kuwait (a) 3-1, Uzbekistan (h) 2-4, Uganda (h) 0-0, Syria (h) 0-2, Oman (a) 1-1, Iraq (h) 2-3, UAE (a) 1-3.

BANGLADESH

Bangladesh Football Federation, Bangabandhu National Stadium-1, Dhaka 1000.
Founded: 1972; *National Colours:* Orange shirts, white shorts, green stockings.
International matches 2010
Tajikistan (a) 2-1, Burma (a) 1-2, Sri Lanka (a) 0-3.

BHUTAN

Bhutan Football Federation, P.O. Box 365, Thimphu.
National Colours: All yellow and red.

BRUNEI DARUSSALAM

The Football Association of Brunei Darussalam, P.O. Box 2010, 1920 Bandar Seri Begawan BS 8674.
Founded: 1959; *Number of Clubs:* 22; *Number of Players:* 830; *National Colours:* Yellow shirts, black shorts, black and white stockings.
Telephone: 00673-2/382 761; *Fax:* 00673-2/382 760.

BURMA

Myanmar Football Federation, Youth Training Centre, Thingankyun Township, Yangon.
Founded: 1947; *National Colours:* Red shirts, white shorts, red stockings.
International matches 2010
Sri Lanka (a) 4-0, Bangladesh (a) 2-1, Tajikistan (a) 0-3, North Korea (a) 0-5, Tajikistan (a) 0-1, Vietnam (a) 1-7, Singapore (a) 1-2, Philippines (h) 0-0.

CAMBODIA

Cambodian Football Federation, Chaeng Maeng Village, Rd. Kah Srov, Sangkat Samrong Krom, Khan Dangkor, Phnom-Penh .
Founded: 1933; *National Colours:* All blue.
International matches 2010
Laos (a) 0-0, Timor-Leste (h) 4-2, Philippines (a) 0-0.

CHINA PR

Football Association of The People's Republic of China, 9 Tiyuguan Road, Beijing 100763.
Founded: 1924; *National Colours:* All white.
International matches 2010
Syria (h) 0-0, Vietnam (a) 2-1, Japan (a) 0-0, South Korea (h) 3-0, Hong Kong (h) 2-0, France (a) 1-0, Tajikistan (h) 4-0, Bahrain (h) 1-1, Iran (h) 0-2, Paraguay (h) 1-1, Syria (h) 2-1, Uruguay (h) 0-4, Latvia (h) 1-0, Estonia (h) 3-0, Macedonia (h) 1-0.

CHINESE TAIPEI

Chinese Taipei Football Association, 2F No. Yu Men St., Taipei, Taiwan 104.
Founded: 1936; *National Colours:* Blue shirts and shorts, white stockings.
International matches 2010
Philippines (h) 0-0, Macao (h) 7-1, Philippines (h) 1-1, Hong Kong (h) 1-1, Indonesia (a) 0-2.

GUAM

Guam Football Association, P.O.Box 5093, Agana, Guam 96932.
Founded: 1975; *National Colours:* Blue shirts, white shorts, blue stockings.

HONG KONG

The Hong Kong Football Association Ltd, 55 Fat Kwong Street, Homantin, Kowloon, Hong Kong.
Founded: 1914; *National Colours:* All red.
International matches 2010
Bahrain (a) 0-4, South Korea (a) 0-5, Japan (a) 0-3, China (a) 0-2, Yemen (h) 0-0, India (a) 1-0, Philippines (h) 4-2, Macao (h) 4-0, Taiwan (a) 1-1, Paraguay (h) 0-7.

INDIA

All India Football Federation, Nehru Stadium (West Stand), Fatorda Margao-Goa 403 602.
Founded: 1937; *National Colours:* Sky blue shirts, navy blue shorts, sky and navy blue stockings.
International matches 2010
Thailand (a) 0-1, Thailand (h) 1-2, Namibia (h) 2-0, Hong Kong (h) 0-1, Vietnam (h) 3-1, Yemen (h) 3-6, Iraq (a) 0-2, Kuwait (h) 1-9, UAE (a) 0-5.

INDONESIA

Football Association of Indonesia, Gelora Bung Karno, Pintu X-XI, Jakarta 10270.
Founded: 1930; *National Colours:* Red shirts, white shorts, red stockings.
International matches 2010
Oman (h) 1-2, Australia (a) 0-1, Uruguay (h) 1-7, Maldives (h) 3-0, Timor-Leste (h) 6-0, Taiwan (h) 2-0, Malaysia (h) 5-1, Laos (h) 6-0, Thailand (h) 2-1, Philippines (h) 1-0, Philippines (h) 1-0, Malaysia (a) 0-3.

IRAN

IR Iran Football Federation, No. 16-4th deadend, Pakistan Street, PO Box 15316-6967 Shahid Beheshti Avenue, Tehran 15316.
Founded: 1920; *National Colours:* All white.
International matches 2010
North Korea (h) 1-0, Singapore (a) 3-1, Thailand (h) 1-0, Armenia (a) 3-1, China (a) 2-0, South Korea (a) 1-0, Bahrain (h) 3-0, Oman (a) 2-2, Iraq (h) 2-1, Kuwait (h) 1-2, Brazil (h) 0-3.

IRAQ

Iraqi Football Association, Olympic Committee Building, Palestine Street, PO Box 484, Baghdad.
Founded: 1948; *National Colours:* All black.
International matches 2010
Jordan (a) 1-4, Oman (h) 3-2, Yemen (h) 2-1, Palestine (h) 3-0, Iran (a) 1-2, Qatar (a) 2-1, India (h) 2-0, Kuwait (h) 1-1, UAE (h) 0-0, Bahrain (a) 3-2, Oman (a) 0-0, Kuwait (a) 2-2, Syria (h) 0-1, Syria (a) 1-0.

JAPAN

Japan Football Association, JFA House, 3-10-15, Hongo, Bunkyo-ku, Tokyo 113-0033.
Founded: 1921; *National Colours:* Blue shirts, white shorts, blue stockings.
International matches 2010
Yemen (a) 3-2, Venezuela (h) 0-0, China (h) 0-0, Hong Kong (h) 3-0, South Korea (h) 1-3, Bahrain (h) 2-0, Serbia (h) 0-3, South Korea (h) 0-2, England (h) 1-2, Ivory Coast (h) 0-2, Cameroon (n) 1-0, Holland (n) 0-1, Denmark (n) 3-1, Paraguay (n) 0-0, Paraguay (h) 1-0, Guatemala (h) 2-1, Argentina (h) 1-0, South Korea (a) 0-0 .

JORDAN

Jordan Football Association, P.O. Box 962024 Al Hussein Sports City, 11196 Amman.
Founded: 1949; *National Colours:* All white and red.
International matches 2010
Thailand (a) 0-0, Azerbaijan (h) 0-2, Singapore (h) 2-1, Iraq (h) 4-1, Bahrain (h) 2-0, Syria (h) 1-1, Kuwait (a) 2-2, Cyprus (h) 0-0.

KOREA, NORTH

Football Association of The Democratic People's Rep. of Korea, Kumsong-dong, Kwangbok Street, Mangyongdae Distr, PO Box 56, Pyongyang FNJ-PRK.
Founded: 1945; *National Colours:* All white.
International matches 2010
Iran (a) 0-1, Turkmenistan (h) 1-1, Kyrgyzstan (h) 4-0, Burma (h) 5-0, Turkmenistan (h) 1-1, Venezuela (a) 1-2, Mexico (a) 1-2, South Africa (a) 0-0, Paraguay (a) 0-1,

Greece (a) 2-2, Nigeria (a) 1-3, Brazil (n) 1-2, Portugal (n) 0-7, Ivory Coast (n) 0-3, Vietnam (a) 0-0, Singapore (a) 2-1, Vietnam (a) 2-0, Yemen (a) 1-1, Kuwait (a) 1-2.

KOREA, SOUTH

Korea Football Association, 1-131 Sinmunno, 2-ga, Jongno-Gu, Seoul 110-062.
Founded: 1928; *National Colours:* Red shirts, blue shorts, red stockings.
International matches 2010
Zambia (a) 2-4, Finland (a) 2-0, Latvia (a) 1-0, Hong Kong (h) 5-0, China (a) 0-3, Japan (a) 3-1, Ivory Coast (a) 2-0, Ecuador (h) 2-0, Japan (a) 2-0, Belarus (a) 0-1, Spain (a) 0-1, Greece (n) 2-0, Argentina (n) 1-4, Nigeria (n) 2-2, Uruguay (n) 1-2, Nigeria (h) 2-1, Iran (h) 0-1, Japan (h) 0-0.

KUWAIT

Kuwait Football Association, P.O. Box 2029, Udiliya, Block 4 Al-Ittihad Street, Safat 13021.
Founded: 1952; *National Colours:* All blue.
International matches 2010
Australia (h) 2-2, Syria (h) 1-1, Bahrain (h) 4-1, Oman (a) 0-0, Azerbaijan (a) 1-1, Syria (h) 3-0, UAE (a) 0-3, Syria (h) 2-1, Jordan (h) 2-2, Yemen (h) 1-1, Iran (a) 2-1, Bahrain (h) 1-3, Vietnam (h) 3-1, India (a) 9-1, Iraq (a) 1-1, Qatar (h) 1-0, Saudi Arabia (a) 0-0, Yemen (a) 3-0, Iraq (h) 2-2, Saudi Arabia (h) 1-0, North Korea (h) 2-1; Zambia (h) 4-0.

KYRGYZSTAN

Football Federation of Kyrgyz Republic, PO Box 1484, Kurenkeeva Street 195, Bishkek 720040, Kyrgyzstan.
Founded: 1992; *National Colours:* Red shirts, white shorts, red stockings.
International matches 2010
North Korea (h) 0-4, Turkmenistan (a) 0-1.

LAOS

Federation Lao de Football, National Stadium, Kounboulo Street, PO Box 3777, Vientiane 856-21, Laos.
Founded: 1951; *National Colours:* All red.
International matches 2010
Cambodia (h) 0-0, Philippines (h) 2-2, Timor-Leste (h) 6-1, Thailand (a) 2-2, Indonesia (a) 0-6, Malaysia (a) 1-5.

LEBANON

Federation Libanaise De Football-Association, P.O. Box 4732, Verdun Street, Bristol, Radwan Centre Building, Beirut.
Founded: 1933; *National Colours:* Red shirts, white shorts, red stockings.
International matches 2010
Vietnam (h) 1-1, Syria (a) 0-4.

MACAO

Associacao De Futebol De Macau (AFM), Ave. da Amizade 405, Seng Vo Kok, 13 Andar "A", Macau.
Founded: 1939; *National Colours:* All green.
International matches 2010
Taiwan (a) 1-7, Hong Kong (a) 0-4, Philippines (a) 0-5.

MALAYSIA

Football Association of Malaysia, 3rd Floor, Wisma Fam, Jalan, SSA/9, Kelana Jaya Selangor Darul Ehsan 47301.
Founded: 1933; *National Colours:* All yellow and black.
International matches 2010
UAE (a) 0-1, Yemen (h) 1-0, Oman (a) 0-3, Indonesia (a) 1-5, Thailand (a) 0-0, Laos (h) 5-1, Vietnam (h) 2-0, Vietnam (a) 0-0, Indonesia (h) 3-0.

MALDIVES REPUBLIC

Football Association of Maldives, National Stadium G. Banafsaa Magu 20-04, Male.
Founded: 1982; *National Colours:* Red shirts, Green shorts, white stockings.
International matches 2010
Indonesia (a) 0-3.

MONGOLIA

Mongolia Football Federation, PO Box 259 Ulaan-Baatar 210646.
National Colours: White shirts, red shorts, white stockings.

NEPAL

All-Nepal Football Association, AMFA House, Ward No. 4, Bishalnagar, PO Box 12582, Kathmandu.
Founded: 1951; *National Colours:* All red.

OMAN

Oman Football Association, P.O. Box 3462, Ruwi Postal Code 112.
Founded: 1978; *National Colours:* All white.
International matches 2010
Indonesia (a) 2-1, Sweden (h) 0-1, Kuwait (h) 0-0, Yemen (a) 1-0, Kazakhstan (a) 1-3, Malaysia (h) 3-0, Qatar (a) 1-1, Iraq (a) 2-3, Bahrain (a) 0-2, Iran (h) 2-2, Gabon (h) 1-0, Chile (h) 0-1, Belarus (h) 0-4, Bahrain (h) 1-1, UAE (h) 0-0, Iraq (h) 0-0.

PAKISTAN

Pakistan Football Federation, 6 National Hockey Stadium, Feroze Pure Road, Lahore, Pakistan.
Founded: 1948; *National Colours:* All green and white.

PALESTINE

Palestinian Football Federation, Al-Yarmouk, Gaza.
Founded: 1928; *National Colours:* White shirts, black shorts, white stockings.
International matches 2010
Sudan (a) 1-1, Mauritania (a) 0-0, Yemen (h) 1-3, Iraq (h) 0-3.

PHILIPPINES

Philippine Football Federation, Room 405, Building V, Philsports Complex, Meralco Avenue, Pasig City, Metro Manila.
Founded: 1907; *National Colours:* All blue.
International matches 2010
Taiwan (a) 0-0, Hong Kong (a) 2-4, Taiwan (a) 1-1, Macao (h) 5-0, Timor-Leste (h) 5-0, Laos (h) 2-2, Cambodia (h) 0-0, Singapore (a) 1-1, Vietnam (a) 2-0, Burma (a) 0-0, Indonesia (a) 0-1, Indonesia (a) 0-1.

QATAR

Qatar Football Association, 7th Floor, QNOC Building, Cornich, P.O. Box 5333, Doha.
Founded: 1960; *National Colours:* All white.
International matches 2010
Mali (h) 0-0, Slovenia (a) 1-4, Bosnia (a) 1-1, Bahrain (h) 1-1, Oman (h) 1-1, Iraq (h) 1-2, Haiti (h) 0-1, Kuwait (a) 0-1, Yemen (a) 2-1, Saudi Arabia (h) 1-1, Egypt (h) 2-1, Estonia (h) 2-0.

SAUDI ARABIA

Saudi Arabian Football Federation, Al Mather Quarter (Olympic Complex), Prince Faisal Bin Fahad Street, P.O. Box 5844, Riyadh 11432.
Founded: 1959; *National Colours:* White shirts, green shorts, white stockings.
International matches 2010
DR Congo (a) 2-0, Nigeria (a) 0-0, Spain (a) 2-3, Togo (h) 1-0, Uzbekistan (h) 4-0, Bulgaria (h) 0-2, Gabon (h) 1-0, Uganda (h) 0-0, Ghana (h) 0-0, Yemen (a) 4-0, Kuwait (h) 0-0, Qatar (a) 1-1, UAE (a) 1-0, Kuwait (a) 0-1.

SINGAPORE

Football Association of Singapore, Jalan Besar Stadium, 100 Tyrwhitt Road, Singapore 207542.
Founded: 1892; *National Colours:* All red.
International matches 2010
Iran (h) 1-3, Thailand (a) 0-1, Denmark (a) 1-5, Poland (a) 1-6, Jordan (a) 1-2, Thailand (a) 0-1, North Korea (h) 1-2, Vietnam (a) 1-1, Philippines (h) 1-1, Burma (h) 2-1, Vietnam (a) 0-1.

SRI LANKA

Football Federation of Sri Lanka, 100/9, Independence Avenue, Colombo 07.
Founded: 1939; *National Colours:* All white.
International matches 2010
Burma (h) 0-4, Tajikistan (h) 1-3, Bangladesh (h) 3-0.

SYRIA

Syrian Football Federation, PO Box 421, Maysaloon Street, Damascus.
Founded: 1936; *National Colours:* All red.
International matches 2010
China (a) 0-0, Sweden (h) 1-1, Kuwait (a) 1-1, Lebanon (h) 4-0, Kuwait (a) 0-3, Yemen (a) 1-2, Jordan (a) 1-1, Kuwait (h) 1-2, China (a) 1-2, Bahrain (a) 2-0, Iraq (a) 1-0, Iraq (h) 0-1.

TAJIKISTAN

Tajikistan Football Federation, 22 Shotemur Ave., Dushanbe 734 025.
Founded: 1991; *National Colours:* All white.
International matches 2010
Yemen (a) 1-0, Bangladesh (h) 1-2, Sri Lanka (h) 3-1, Burma (h) 3-0, Turkmenistan (h) 0-2, Burma (h) 1-0, China (a) 0-4, Afganistan (h) 1-0.

THAILAND

The Football Association of Thailand, Gate 3, Rama I Road, Patumwan, Bangkok 10330.
Founded: 1916; *National Colours:* All red.
International matches 2010
Jordan (h) 0-0, Singapore (h) 1-0, Poland (h) 1-3, Denmark (h) 0-3, Iran (a) 0-1, South Africa (a) 0-4, Singapore (h) 1-0, India (h) 1-0, India (a) 2-1, Laos (h) 2-2, Malaysia (h) 0-0, Indonesia (a) 1-2.

TIMOR-LESTE

Federacao Futebol Timor-Leste, Rua 12 de Novembro Str., Cruz, Dili.
Founded: 2002; *National Colours:* Red shirts, black shorts, red stockings.
International matches 2010
Philippines (a) 0-5, Cambodia (a) 2-4, Laos (a) 1-6, Indonesia (a) 0-6

TURKMENISTAN

Football Association of Turkmenistan, 32 Belinskiy Street, Stadium Kopetdag, Ashgabat 744 001.
Founded: 1992; *National Colours:* Green shirts, white shorts, green stockings.
International matches 2010
North Korea (h) 1-1, Kyrgyzstan (h) 1-0, Tajikistan (h) 2-0, North Korea (a) 1-1.

UNITED ARAB EMIRATES

United Arab Emirates Football Association, P.O. Box 916, Abu Dhabi.
Founded: 1971; *National Colours:* All white.
International matches 2010
Malaysia (h) 1-0, Uzbekistan (a) 1-0, Moldova (h) 3-2, Algeria (a) 0-1, Kuwait (h) 3-0, Chile (h) 0-2, Angola (h) 0-2, India (h) 5-0, Iraq (a) 0-0, Oman (a) 0-0, Bahrain (h) 3-1, Saudi Arabia (a) 0-1.

UZBEKISTAN

Uzbekistan Football Federation, Massiv Almazar Furkat Street 15/1, 700003 Tashkent, Uzbekistan.
Founded: 1946; *National Colours:* All white.
International matches 2010
UAE (h) 0-1, Armenia (a) 1-3, Albania (a) 0-1, Estonia (a) 3-3, Saudi Arabia (a) 0-4, Bahrain (a) 4-2.

VIETNAM

Vietnam Football Federation, 18 Ly van Phuc, Dong Da District, Hanoi 844.
Founded: 1962; *National Colours:* All red.

International matches 2010
Lebanon (a) 1-1, China (h) 1-2, North Korea (h) 0-0, India (a) 1-3, Kuwait (a) 1-3, Singapore (h) 1-1, North Korea (h) 0-2, Burma (h) 7-1, Philippines (h) 0-2, Singapore (h) 1-0, Malaysia (a) 0-2, Malaysia (h) 0-0.

YEMEN

Yemen Football Association, Quarter of Sport – Al Jeraf, Behind the Stadium of Ali Mushsen, Al Moreissy in the Sport, Al-Thawra City.
Founded: 1962; *National Colours:* All green.
International matches 2010
Tajikistan (h) 0-1, Japan (h) 2-3, Kenya (h) 3-1, Bahrain (h) 3-0, Malaysia (a) 0-1, Hong Kong (a) 0-0, Malawi (h) 1-0, Oman (h) 0-1, Syria (h) 2-1, Zambia (h) 0-1, Iraq (a) 1-2, Palestine (h) 3-1, Kuwait (a) 1-1, India (a) 6-3, Uganda (h) 2-2, North Korea (h) 1-1, Saudi Arabia (h) 0-4, Qatar (h) 1-2, Kuwait (h) 0-3.

CONCACAF

ANGUILLA

Anguilla Football Association, P.O. Box 1318, The Valley, Anguilla, BWI.
National Colours: Turquoise, white, orange and blue shirts and shorts, turquoise and orange stockings.
International matches 2010
British Virgin Islands (h) 1-2, Puerto Rico (a) 1-3, Cayman Islands (h) 1-4, St Martin (h) 2-1.

ANTIGUA & BARBUDA

The Antigua/Barbuda Football Association, Newgate Street, P.O. Box 773, St John's.
Founded: 1928; *National Colours:* Red, black, yellow and blue shirts, black shorts and stockings.
International matches 2010
Trinidad & Tobago (a) 1-4, St Kitts & Nevis (a) 1-1, Trinidad & Tobago (h) 0-0, St Lucia (h) 5-0, Surinam (h) 2-1, Dominica (h) 0-0, Cuba (h) 0-0, Jamaica (h) 1-3, Guyana (h) 1-0, Guadeloupe (h) 0-1.

ARUBA

Arubaanse Voetbal Bond, Ferguson Street, Z/N P.O. Box 376, Oranjestad, Aruba.
Founded: 1932; *National Colours:* Yellow shirts, blue shorts, yellow and blue stockings.
International matches 2010
Venezuela (h) 0-3, Netherlands Antilles (a) 0-3.

BAHAMAS

Bahamas Football Association, Plaza on the Way, West Bay Street, P.O. Box N 8434, Nassau, NP.
Founded: 1967; *National Colours:* Yellow shirts, black shorts, yellow stockings.

BARBADOS

Barbados Football Association, Hildor No. 4, 10th Avenue, P.O. Box 1362, Belleville-St. Michael, Barbados.
Founded: 1910; *National Colours:* Royal blue and gold shirts, gold shorts, white, gold and blue stockings.
International matches 2010
Dominica (h) 0-2, Dominica (h) 1-3, St Kitts & Nevis (h) 1-1, Montserrat (h) 5-0, St Vincent & The Grenadines (h) 0-0.

BELIZE

Belize National Football Association, 26 Hummingbird Highway, Belmopan, P.O. Box 1742, Belize City.
Founded: 1980; *National Colours:* Red, white and black shirts, black shorts, red and black stockings.
International matches 2010
Trinidad & Tobago (h) 0-0, Guatemala (a) 2-4.

BERMUDA

The Bermuda Football Association, 48 Cedar Avenue, Hamilton HM12.
Founded: 1928; *National Colours:* All blue.

BRITISH VIRGIN ISLANDS

British Virgin Islands Football Association, P.O. Box 29, Road Town, Tortola, BVI.
National Colours: Gold and green shirts, green shorts, and stockings.
International matches 2010
Anguilla (h) 2-1, Dominican Republic (a) 0-17, Dominica (h) 0-10.

US VIRGIN ISLANDS

USVI Soccer Federation Inc., 54, Castle Coakley, PO Box 2346, Kingshill, St Croix 00851.
National Colours: Royal blue and gold shirts, royal blue shorts and stockings.

CANADA

The Canadian Soccer Association, Place Soccer Canada, 237 Metcalfe Street, Ottawa, ONT K2P 1R2.
Founded: 1912; *National Colours:* All red.
International matches 2010
Jamaica (a) 0-1, Argentina (a) 0-5, Venezuela (a) 1-1, Peru (h) 0-2, Honduras (h) 2-1, Ukraine (a) 0-2.

CAYMAN ISLANDS

Cayman Islands Football Association, PO Box 178 GT, Truman Bodden Sports Complex, Olympic Way Off Walkers Rd, George Town, Grand Cayman, Cayman Islands WI.
Founded: 1966; *National Colours:* Red and white shirts, blue and white shorts, white and red stockings.
International matches 2010
St Martin (a) 1-1, Anguilla (h) 4-1, Puerto Rico (a) 0-2.

COSTA RICA

Federacion Costarricense De Futbol, Costado Norte Estatua Leon Cortes, San Jose 670-1000.
Founded: 1921; *National Colours:* Red shirts, blue shorts, white stockings.
International matches 2010
Argentina (a) 2-3, France (a) 1-2, Switzerland (a) 1-0, Slovakia (a) 0-3, Paraguay (a) 0-2, Panama (a) 2-2, Jamaica (a) 0-1, Peru (a) 0-2, El Salvador (h) 2-1, Jamaica (a) 0-0 .

CUBA

Asociacion de Futbol de Cuba, Calle 13 No. 661, Esq. C. Vedado, ZP 4, La Habana.
Founded: 1924; *National Colours:* All red, white and blue.
International matches 2010
Panama (a) 3-0, Dominica (h) 4-2, Surinam (a) 3-3, Antigua & Barbuda (a) 0-0, Trinidad & Tobago (a) 2-0, Martinique (a) 1-0, Grenada (h) 0-0, Guadeloupe (h) 1-2, Grenada (h) 1-0.

DOMINICA

Dominica Football Association, 33 Great Marlborough Street, Roseau.
Founded: 1970; *National Colours:* Emerald green shirts, black shorts, green stockings.
International matches 2010
Barbados (a) 2-0, Barbados (a) 3-1, British Virgin Islands (a) 10-0, Dominican Republic (a) 1-0, Cuba (a) 2-4, Antigua & Barbuda (a) 0-0, Surinam (a) 0-5.

DOMINICAN REPUBLIC

Federacion Dominicana De Futbol, Centro Olimpico Juan Pablo Duarte, Ensanche Miraflores, Apartado De Correos No. 1953, Santo Domingo.
Founded: 1953; *National Colours:* Navy blue shirts, white shorts, red stockings.

International matches 2010
British Virgin Islands (h) 17-0, Dominica (h) 0-1.

EL SALVADOR

Federacion Salvadorena De Futbol, Primera Calle Poniente No. 2025, San Salvador CA1029.
Founded: 1935; *National Colours:* All blue.
International matches 2010
USA (a) 1-2, Guatemala (h) 1-2, Honduras (h) 2-2, Panama (a) 0-1, Costa Rica (a) 1-2.

GRENADA

Grenada Football Association, P.O. Box 326, National Stadium, Queens Park, St George's, Grenada, W.I.
Founded: 1924; *National Colours:* Green and yellow striped shirts, red shorts, yellow stockings.
International matches 2010
St Vincent & The Grenadines (a) 1-0, St Vincent & The Grenadines (a) 0-0, Puerto Rico (a) 3-1, St Kitts & Nevis (h) 2-0, Guadeloupe (h) 0-3, Martinique (a) 1-1, Trinidad & Tobago (h) 1-0, Cuba (h) 0-0, Jamaica (h) 1-2, Cuba (h) 0-1.

GUADELOUPE

Ligue Guadeloupeenne de Football, Rue de la Ville D'Orly, Bergevin, 97110, Pointe-a-Pitre.
Not affiliated to FIFA.
International matches 2010
New Caledonia (h) 1-1, Tahiti (h) 1-1, Martinique (h) 2-0, St Kitts & Nevis (h) 2-1, Puerto Rico (h) 3-2, Grenada (a) 3-0, Guyana (h) 1-1, Jamaica (h) 0-2, Antigua & Barbuda (h) 1-0, Cuba (h) 2-1, Jamaica (h) 1-1.

GUATEMALA

Federacion Nacional de Futbol de Guatemala, 2a Calle 15-57, Zona 15, Boulevard Vista Hermosa, Guatemala City 01009.
Founded: 1946; *National Colours:* Blue shirts, white shorts, blue stockings.
International matches 2010
El Salvador (a) 2-1, South Africa (a) 0-5, Nicaragua (h) 5-0, Japan (a) 1-2, Belize (h) 4-2, Honduras (a) 0-2, Guyana (a) 3-0.

GUYANA

Guyana Football Federation, 159 Rupununi Street, Bel Air Park, P.O. Box 10727, Georgetown.
Founded: 1902; *National Colours:* Green shirts and shorts, yellow stockings.
International matches 2010
Trinidad & Tobago (h) 1-1, St Lucia (h) 1-0, Netherlands Antilles (a) 3-2, Surinam (a) 2-0, Haiti (a) 0-0, Trinidad & Tobago (a) 1-2, St Vincent & The Grenadines (h) 2-0, Guatemala (h) 0-3, Guadeloupe (h) 1-1, Antigua & Barbuda (a) 0-1, Jamaica (h) 0-4.

GUYANE

International matches 2010
Reunion (h) 0-1.

HAITI

Federation Haitienne De Football, 128 Avenue Christiophe, P.O. Box 2258, Port-Au-Prince.
Founded: 1904; *National Colours:* Blue shirts, red shorts, blue stockings.
International matches 2010
Martinique (a) 0-0, Argentina (a) 0-4, Guyana (h) 0-0, St Vincent & The Grenadines (a) 3-1, Trinidad & Tobago (a) 0-4, Qatar (a) 1-0.

HONDURAS

Federacion Nacional Autonoma De Futbol De Honduras, Colonia Florencia Norte, Ave Roble, Edificio Plaza America, Ave. Roble 1 y 2 Nivel, Tegucigalpa, D.C.
Founded: 1951; *National Colours:* All white.

International matches 2010
USA (a) 3-1, Turkey (a) 0-2, Venezuela (h) 0-1, Belarus (a) 2-2, Azerbaijan (a) 0-0, Romania (a) 0-3, Chile (n) 0-1, Spain (n) 0-2, Switzerland (n) 0-0, El Salvador (a) 2-2, Canada (a) 1-2, New Zealand (a) 1-1, Guatemala (h) 2-0, Panama (a) 0-2, Panama (h) 2-1.

JAMAICA

Jamaica Football Federation Ltd, 20 St Lucia Crescent, Kingston 5.
Founded: 1910; *National Colours:* Gold shirts, black shorts, gold stockings.
International matches 2010
Canada (h) 1-0, Argentina (a) 1-2, South Africa (a) 0-2, Trinidad & Tobago (a) 3-1, Costa Rica (h) 1-0, Peru (h) 1-2, Trinidad & Tobago (h) 1-0, Costa Rica (h) 0-0, Antigua & Barbuda (h) 3-1, Guadeloupe (h) 2-0, Guyana (h) 4-0, Grenada (h) 2-1, Guadeloupe (h) 1-1.

MARTINIQUE

2, Rue Saint John Perse, Nome Tartenson, BP 307, 97203 Fort de France.
Not affiliated to FIFA.
International matches 2010
Haiti (h) 0-0, Tahiti (h) 4-1, New Caledonia (h) 4-0, Guadeloupe (h) 0-2, Reunion (h) 0-0, Grenada (h) 1-1, Cuba (h) 0-1, Trinidad & Tobago (h) 0-1.

MEXICO

Federacion Mexicana De Futbol Asociacion, A.C., Colima No. 373, Colonia Roma Mexico DF 06700.
Founded: 1927; *National Colours:* Green shirts with white collar, white shorts, red stockings.
International matches 2010
Bolivia (h) 5 0, New Zealand (h) 2-0, North Korea (h) 2-1, Iceland (h) 0-0, Ecuador (h) 0-0, Senegal (h) 1-0, Angola (h) 1-0, Chile (h) 1-0, England (a) 1-3, Holland (a) 1-2, Gambia (h) 5-1, Italy (a) 2-1, South Africa (n) 1-1, France (n) 2-0, Uruguay (n) 0-1, Argentina (n) 1-3, Spain (h) 1-1, Ecuador (h) 1-2, Colombia (h) 1-0, Venezuela (h) 2-2.

MONSERRAT

Monserrat Football Association Inc., P.O. Box 505, Woodlands, Monserrat.
National Colours: Green shirts with black and white stripes, green shorts with white stripes, green stockings with black and white stripes.
International matches 2010
St Vincent & The Grenadines (a) 0-7, Barbados (h) 0-5, St Kitts & Nevis (h) 0-4.

NETHERLANDS ANTILLES

Nederlands Antiliaanse Voetbal Unie, Bonamweg 49, Curacao, NA.
Founded: 1921; *National Colours:* White shirts with red and blue stripes, red shorts with blue and white stripes, white stockings with red stripes.
International matches 2010
Surinam (a) 1-2, Guyana (h) 2-3, St Lucia (a) 2-2, Aruba (h) 3-0, Surinam (h) 2-2.

NICARAGUA

Federacion Nicaraguense De Futbol, Hospital Pautista 1, Cuadra avajo, 1 cuada al Sur y 1/2, Cuadra Abajo, Managua 976.
Founded: 1931; *National Colours:* Blue shirts, white shorts, blue stockings.
International matches 2010
Guatemala (h) 0-5.

PANAMA

Federacion Panamena De Futbol, Estadio Rommel Fernandez, Puerta 24, Ave. Jose Aeustin Araneo, Apartado Postal 8-391, Zona 8, Panama.

Founded: 1937; *National Colours:* All red.
International matches 2010
Chile (a) 1-2, Venezuela (a) 2-1, Venezuela (h) 3-1, Costa Rica (h) 2-2, Trinidad & Tobago (h) 3-0, El Salvador (h) 1-0, Peru (h) 1-0, Cuba (h) 0-3, Honduras (h) 2-0, Honduras (a) 1-2.

PUERTO RICO

Federacion Puertorriquena De Futbol, P.O. Box 193590 San Juan 00919.
Founded: 1940; *National Colours:* Red, blue and white shirts and shorts, red and blue stockings.
International matches 2010
Anguilla (h) 3-1, St Martin (h) 2-0, Cayman Islands (h) 2-0, Grenada (a) 1-3, St Kitts & Nevis (h) 0-1, Guadeloupe (a) 2-3.

ST KITTS & NEVIS

St Kitts & Nevis Football Association, P.O. Box 465, Warner Park, Basseterre, St Kitts, W.I.
Founded: 1932; *National Colours:* Green and yellow shirts, red shorts, yellow stockings.
International matches 2010
Antigua & Barbuda (h) 1-1, Barbados (h) 1-1, St Vincent & The Grenadines (a) 1-1, Monserrat (h) 4-0, Guadeloupe (h) 1-2, Grenada (a) 0-2, Puerto Rico (h) 1-0.

ST LUCIA

St Lucia National Football Association, PO Box 255, Sans Souci, Castries, St Lucia.
Founded: 1979; *National Colours:* White shirts and shorts with yellow, blue and black stripes, white, blue and yellow stockings.
International matches 2010
St Vincent & The Grenadines (h) 1-5, Trinidad & Tobago (a) 0-3, Antigua & Barbuda (a) 0-5, Guyana (h) 0-1, Surinam (a) 1-2, Netherlands Antilles (h) 2-2.

ST MARTIN

Comite de Football des Iles du Nord, PO Box 811, S-M 97059.
Not affiliated to FIFA.
International matches 2010
Cayman Islands (h) 1-1, Puerto Rico (a) 0-2, Anguilla (h) 1-2.

ST VINCENT & THE GRENADINES

St Vincent & The Grenadines Football Federation, Sharpe Street, PO Box 1278, Saint George.
Founded: 1979; *National Colours:* Green shirts with yellow border, blue shorts, yellow stockings.
International matches 2010
St Lucia (a) 5-1, Grenada (h) 0-1, Grenada (h) 0-0, Monserrat (h) 7-0, St Kitts & Nevis (h) 1-1, Barbados (h) 0-0, Trinidad & Tobago (a) 2-6, Haiti (h) 1-3, Guyana (h) 0-2.

SURINAM

Surinaamse Voetbal Bond, Letitia Vriesde Laan 7, P.O. Box 1223, Paramaribo.
Founded: 1920; *National Colours:* White, green and red shirts, green and white shirts and stockings.
International matches 2010
Netherlands Antilles (h) 2-1, St Lucia (h) 2-1, Guyana (h) 0-2, Netherlands Antilles (a) 2-2, Antigua & Barbuda (a) 1-2, Cuba (h) 3-3, Dominica (h) 5-0.

TRINIDAD & TOBAGO

Trinidad & Tobago Football Federation, 24–26 Dundonald Street, PO Box 400, Port of Spain.
Founded: 1908; *National Colours:* Red shirts, black shorts, white stockings.

International matches 2010
Chile (a) 0-2, Antigua & Barbuda (h) 4-3, Jamaica (h) 1-3, Panama (a) 0-3, Belize (a) 0-0, Antigua & Barbuda (a) 1-0, St Lucia (h) 3-0, Guyana (a) 1-1, Jamaica (a) 0-1, St Vincent & The Grenadines (h) 6-2, Guyana (h) 2-1, Haiti (h) 4-0, Cuba (h) 0-2, Grenada (h) 0-1, Martinique (a) 1-0.

TURKS & CAICOS

Turks & Caicos Islands Football Association, P.O. Box 626, Tropicana Plaza, Leeward Highway, Providenciales.
National Colours: All white.

USA

US Soccer Federation, US Soccer House, 1801–1811 S. Prairie Avenue, Chicago, Illinois 60616.
Founded: 1913; *National Colours:* White shirts, blue shorts, white stockings.
International matches 2010
Honduras (h) 1-3, El Salvador (h) 2-1, Holland (a) 1-2, Czech Republic (h) 2-4, Turkey (h) 2-1, Australia (h) 3-1, England (n) 1-1, Slovenia (n) 2-2, Algeria (n) 1-0, Ghana (n) 1-2, Brazil (h) 0-2, Poland (h) 2-2, Colombia (h) 0-0, South Africa (a) 1-0.

OCEANIA

AMERICAN SAMOA

American Samoa Football Association, P.O. Box 282, Pago Pago AS 96799.
National Colours: Navy blue shirts, white shorts, red stockings.

COOK ISLANDS

Cook Islands Football Association, Victoria Road, Tupapa, P.O. Box 29, Avarua, Rarotonga, Cook Islands.
Founded: 1971; *National Colours:* Green shirts with white sleeves, green shorts, white stockings.

FIJI

Fiji Football Association, PO Box 2514, Government Buildings, Suva.
Founded: 1938; *National Colours:* White shirts, blue shorts and stockings.

NEW CALEDONIA

Federation Caledonienne de Football, 7 bis, Rue Suffren Quartien latin, BP 560, 99845 Noumea, New Caledonia.
Founded: 1928; *National Colours:* Grey shirts, red shorts, grey stockings.
International matches 2010
Tahiti (a) 1-1.

NEW ZEALAND

New Zealand Soccer Inc., PO Box 301 043, Albany, Auckland, New Zealand.
Founded: 1891; *National Colours:* All white.
International matches 2010
Mexico (h) 0-2, Australia (a) 1-2, Serbia (h) 1-0, Slovenia (a) 1-3, Slovakia (n) 1-1, Italy (n) 1-1, Paraguay (n) 0-0, Honduras (h) 1-1, Paraguay (h) 0-2.

PAPUA NEW GUINEA

Papua New Guinea Football Association, PO Box 957, Room II Level I, Haus Tisa, Lae.
Founded: 1962; *National Colours:* Red and yellow shirts, black shorts, yellow stockings.

SAMOA

The Samoa Football Soccer Federation, P.O. Box 960, Apia.
Founded: 1968; *National Colours:* Blue, white and red shirts, blue and white shorts, red and blue stockings.

SOLOMON ISLANDS

Solomon Islands Football Federation, PO Box 854, Honiara, Solomon Islands.
Founded: 1978; *National Colours:* Gold and blue shirts, blue and white shorts, white and blue stockings.

TAHITI

Federation Tahitienne de Football, Rue Coppenrath Stade de Fautana, PO Box 50858 Pirae 98716.
Founded: 1989; *National Colours:* Red shirts, white shorts, red stockings.
International matches 2010
New Caledonia (h) 1-1.

TONGA

Tonga Football Association, Tungi Arcade, Taufa'Ahau Road, P.O. Box 852, Nuku'Alofa, Tonga.
Founded: 1965; *National Colours:* Red shirts, white shorts, red stockings.

TUVALU

Not affiliated to FIFA.

VANUATU

Vanuatu Football Federation, P.O. Box 266, Port Vila, Vanuatu.
Founded: 1934; *National Colours:* Gold and black shirts, black shorts, gold and black stockings.

AFRICA

ALGERIA

Federation Algerienne De Foot-ball, Chemin Ahmed Ouaked, Boite Postale No. 39, Dely-Ibrahim-Alger.
Founded: 1962; *National Colours:* Green shirts, white shorts, green stockings.
International matches 2010
Malawi (a) 0-3, Mali (a) 1-0, Angola (a) 0-0, Ivory Coast (a) 3-2, Egypt (h) 0-4, Nigeria (a) 0-1, Republic of Ireland (a) 0-3, UAE (h) 1-0, Slovenia (n) 0-1, England (n) 0-0, USA (n) 0-1, Gabon (h) 1-2, Tanzania (h) 1-1, Central African Republic (a) 0-2, Luxembourg (a) 0-0.

ANGOLA

Federation Angolaise De Football, Compl. da Cidadela Desportiva, B.P. 3449, Luanda.
Founded: 1979; *National Colours:* Red shirts, black shorts, red stockings.
International matches 2010
Gambia (h) 1-1, Mali (h) 4-4, Malawi (h) 2-0, Algeria (h) 0-0, Ghana (h) 0-1, Mexico (a) 0-1, Uruguay (h) 0-2, Uganda (a) 0-3, Guinea-Bissau (h) 1-0, UAE (a) 2-0.

BENIN

Federation Beninoise De Football, Stade Rene Pleven d'Akpakpa, B.P. 965, Cotonou 01.
Founded: 1962; *National Colours:* Green shirts, Yellow shorts, red stockings.
International matches 2010
Libya (h) 1-0, Mozambique (a) 2-2, Nigeria (a) 0-1, Egypt (a) 0-2, Niger (h) 0-0, Burundi (h) 1-1, Rwanda (a) 3-0.

BOTSWANA

Botswana Football Association, P.O. Box 1396, Gabarone.
Founded: 1970; *National Colours:* Blue, white and black striped shirts, blue, white and black shorts and stockings.
International matches 2010
Mozambique (a) 1-0, Namibia (a) 0-0, Tunisia (a) 1-0, Chad (h) 1-0, Zimbabwe (h) 2-0, Malawi (a) 1-1, Togo (h) 2-1, Guinea Equatorial (a) 2-0, Swaziland (h) 2-0, Tunisia (h) 1-0.

BURKINA FASO

Federation Burkinabe De Foot-Ball, 01 B.P. 57, Ouagadougou 01.
Founded: 1960; *National Colours:* All green, red and white.
International matches 2010
Ivory Coast (a) 0-0, Ghana (h) 0-1, Congo (h) 3-0, Gabon (h) 1-1, Gambia (h) 3-1, Guinea (a) 2-1.

BURUNDI

Federation De Football Du Burundi, Bulding Nyogozi, Boulevard de l'Uprona, B.P. 3426, Bujumbura.
Founded: 1948; *National Colours:* Red and white shirts, white and red shorts, green stockings.
International matches 2010
Benin (a) 1-1, Ivory Coast (h) 0-1, Somalia (h) 2-0, Zambia (a) 0-0, Tanzania (a) 0-2.

CAMEROON

Federation Camerounaise De Football, B.P. 1116, Yaounde.
Founded: 1959; *National Colours:* Green shirts, red shorts, yellow stockings.
International matches 2010
Kenya (a) 3-1, Gabon (h) 0-1, Zambia (h) 3-2, Tunisia (h) 2-2, Egypt (a) 1-3, Italy (a) 0-0, Georgia (a) 0-0, Slovakia (a) 1-1, Portugal (a) 1-3, Serbia (a) 3-4, Japan (n) 0-1, Denmark (n) 1-2, Holland (n) 1-2, Poland (a) 3-0, Mauritius (a) 3-1, DR Congo (h) 1-1.

CAPE VERDE ISLANDS

Federacao Cabo-Verdiana De Futebol, Praia Cabo Verde, FCF CX, P.O. Box 234, Praia.
Founded: 1982; *National Colours:* Blue and white shirts and shorts, blue and red stockings.
International matches 2010
Portugal (a) 0-0, Senegal (a) 0-1, Mali (h) 1-0, Zimbabwe (a) 0-0, Guinea-Bissau (h) 2-1.

CENTRAL AFRICAN REPUBLIC

Federation Centrafricaine De Football, Immeuble Soca Constructa, B.P. 344, Bangui.
Founded: 1937; *National Colours:* Blue and white shirts, white shorts, blue stockings.
International matches 2010
Morocco (a) 0-0, Algeria (h) 2-0.

CHAD

Federation Tchadienne de Football, B.P. 886, N'Djamena.
Founded: 1962; *National Colours:* Blue shirts, yellow shorts, red stockings.
International matches 2010
Niger (a) 1-1, Togo (h) 2-2, Botswana (a) 0-1, Tunisia (h) 1-3, Ethiopia (a) 0-1, Malawi (a) 2-6, Togo (a) 0-0.

COMOROS

Comoros FA, BP 798, Moroni.
Founded: 1979.
International matches 2010
Madagascar (a) 0-1, Zambia (a) 0-4, Mozambique (h) 0-1.

CONGO

Federation Congolaise De Football, 80 Rue Eugene-Etienne, Centre Ville, PO Box 11, Brazzaville.
Founded: 1962; *National Colours:* Green shirts, yellow shorts, red stockings.
International matches 2010
Burkina Faso (a) 0-3, Sudan (a) 0-2, Swaziland (h) 3-1.

CONGO DR

Federation Congolaise De Football-Association, Av. de l'Enseignemt 210, C/Kasa-Vubu, Kinshasa 1.
Founded: 1919; *National Colours:* Blue and yellow shirts, yellow and blue shorts, white and blue stockings.

International matches 2010
Nigeria (a) 2-5, Saudi Arabia (h) 0-2, Egypt (a) 3-6, Senegal (h) 2-4, Cameroon (a) 1-1, Mali (a) 1-3.

DJIBOUTI

Federation Djiboutienne de Football, Stade el Haoj Hassan Gouled, B.P. 2694, Djibouti.
Founded: 1977; *National Colours:* Green shirts, white shorts, blue stockings.

EGYPT

Egyptian Football Association, 5 Gabalaya Street, Guezira, El Borg Post Office, Cairo.
Founded: 1921; *National Colours:* Red shirts, white shorts, black stockings.
International matches 2010
Mali (h) 1-0, Nigeria (h) 3-1, Mozambique (h) 2-0, Benin (h) 2-0, Cameroon (h) 3-1, Algeria (a) 4-0, Ghana (a) 1-0, England (a) 1-3, DR Congo (h) 6-3, Sierra Leone (h) 1-1, Niger (a) 0-1, Australia (h) 3-0, Qatar (a) 1-2.

ERITREA

The Eritrean National Football Federation, Sematat Avenue 29–31, P.O. Box 3665, Asmara.
National Colours: Blue shirts, red shorts, green stockings.

ETHIOPIA

Ethiopia Football Federation, Addis Ababa Stadium, P.O. Box 1080, Addis Ababa.
Founded: 1943; *National Colours:* Green shirts, yellow shorts, red stockings.
International matches 2010
Kenya (h) 0-3, Chad (h) 1-0, Guinea (h) 1-4, Madagascar (a) 1-0, Uganda (a) 1-2, Kenya (h) 2-1, Malawi (a) 1-1, Zambia (a) 2-1, Ivory Coast (h) 0-1, Uganda (h) 3-4.

GABON

Federation Gabonaise De Football, B.P. 181, Libreville.
Founded: 1962; *National Colours:* Green, yellow and blue shirts, blue and yellow shorts, white stockings with tri-colour trims.
International matches 2010
Cameroon (a) 1-0, Tunisia (h) 1-0, Zambia (h) 1-2, Togo (h) 3-0, Algeria (a) 2-1, Burkina Faso (a) 1-1, Senegal (a) 1-2.

GAMBIA

Gambia Football Association, Independence Stadium, Bakau, P.O. Box 523, Banjul.
Founded: 1952; *National Colours:* All red, blue and white.
International matches 2010
Angola (a) 1-1, Tunisia (a) 2-1, Mexico (a) 1-5, Namibia (h) 3-1, Burkina Faso (a) 1-3.

GHANA

Ghana Football Association, National Sports Council, P.O. Box 1272, Accra.
Founded: 1957; *National Colours:* All yellow.
International matches 2010
Malawi (h) 0-0, Ivory Coast (a) 1-3, Burkina Faso (a) 1-0, Angola (a) 1-0, Nigeria (h) 1-0, Egypt (h) 0-1, Bosnia (a) 1-2, Holland (a) 1-4, Latvia (h) 1-0, Serbia (n) 1-0, Australia (n) 1-1, Germany (n) 0-1, USA (n) 2-1, Uruguay (n) 1-1, South Africa (a) 0-1, Swaziland (a) 3-0, Sudan (h) 0-0, Saudi Arabia (a) 0-0.

GUINEA

Federation Guineenne De Football, P.O. Box 3645, Conakry.
Founded: 1959; *National Colours:* Red shirts, yellow shorts, green stockings.
International matches 2010
Mali (a) 2-0, Ethiopia (a) 4-1, Nigeria (h) 1-0, Burkina Faso (h) 1-2.

GUINEA-BISSAU

Federacao De Football Da Guinea-Bissau, Alto Bandim (Nova Sede), PO Box 375 Bissau 1035.
Founded: 1974; *National Colours:* Red, green and yellow shirts, green and yellow shorts, red, green and yellow stockings.
International matches 2010
Kenya (h) 1-0, Angola (a) 0-1, Cape Verde Islands (a) 1-2.

GUINEA, EQUATORIAL

Federacion Ecuatoguineana De Futbol, c/P Patricio Lumumba (Estadio La Paz), Malabo 1071.
Founded: 1986; *National Colours:* All red.
International matches 2010
Morocco (a) 1-2, Botswana (h) 0-2.

IVORY COAST

Federation Ivoirienne De Football, 01 PO Box 1202, Abidjan 01.
Founded: 1960; *National Colours:* Orange shirts, black shorts, green stockings.
International matches 2010
Tanzania (a) 1-0, Rwanda (a) 2-0, Burkina Faso (h) 0-0, Ghana (h) 3-1, Algeria (h) 2-3, South Korea (h) 0-2, Paraguay (a) 2-2, Japan (a) 2-0, Portugal (n) 0-0, Brazil (n) 1-3, North Korea (n) 3-0, Italy (a) 1-0, Rwanda (h) 3-0, Burundi (a) 1-0, Poland (a) 1-3.

KENYA

Kenya Football Federation, Nyayo National Stadium, P.O. Box 40234, Nairobi.
Founded: 1960; *National Colours:* All red.
International matches 2010
Cameroon (h) 1-3, Yemen (a) 1-3, Tanzania (a) 1-1, Ethiopia (a) 3-0, Guinea Bissau (a) 0-1, Uganda (h) 0-0, Malawi (a) 2-3, Ethiopia (a) 1-2, Uganda (a) 0-2.

LESOTHO

Lesotho Football Association, P.O. Box 1879, Maseru-100, Lesotho.
Founded: 1932; *National Colours:* Blue shirts, green shorts, white stockings.

LIBERIA

Liberia Football Association, Broad and Center Streets, PO Box 10-1066, Monrovia 1000.
Founded: 1936; *National Colours:* Blue shirts, white shorts, red stockings.
International matches 2010
Zimbabwe (h) 1-1, Mali (a) 1-2.

LIBYA

Libyan Football Federation, Asayadi Street, Near Janat Al-Areet, P.O. Box 5137, Tripoli.
Founded: 1963; *National Colours:* Green and black shirts, black shorts and stockings.
International matches 2010
Benin (a) 0-1, Mali (h) 2-1, Niger (h) 1-1, Mozambique (a) 0-0, Zambia (h) 1-0.

MADAGASCAR

Federation Malagasy de Football, Immeuble Preservatrice Vie-Lot IBF-9B, Rue Rabearivelo-Antsahavola, PO Box 4409, Antananarivo 101.
Founded: 1961; *National Colours:* Red and green shirts, white and green shorts, green and white stockings.
International matches 2010
Comores (h) 1-0, Nigeria (a) 0-2, Ethiopia (h) 0-1.

MALAWI

Football Association of Malawi, Mpira House, Old Chileka Road, P.O. Box 865, Blantyre.
Founded: 1966; *National Colours:* Red shirts, white shorts, red and black stockings.

International matches 2010
Ghana (a) 0-0, Algeria (h) 3-0, Angola (a) 0-2, Mali (a) 1-3, Zimbabwe (a) 1-2, Yemen (a) 0-1, Togo (a) 1-1, Botswana (h) 1-1, Tunisia (a) 2-2, Chad (h) 6-2, Rwanda (h) 2-1, Kenya (h) 3-2, Uganda (h) 1-1, Ethiopia (h) 1-1.

MALI

Federation Malienne De Football, Avenue du Mali, Hamdallaye ACI 2000, PO Box 1020, Bamako 12582.
Founded: 1960; *National Colours:* Green shirts, yellow shorts, red stockings.
International matches 2010
Qatar (a) 0-0, Egypt (a) 0-1, Angola (a) 4-4, Algeria (h) 0-1, Malawi (h) 3-1, Libya (a) 1-2, Guinea (h) 0-2, Cape Verde Islands (a) 0-1, Liberia (h) 2-1, DR Congo (h) 3-1.

MAURITANIA

Federation De Foot-Ball De La Rep. Islamique. De Mauritanie, B.P. 566, Nouakchott.
Founded: 1961; *National Colours:* Green and yellow shirts, yellow shorts, green stockings.
International matches 2010
Palestine (h) 0-0.

MAURITIUS

Mauritius Football Association, Chancery House, 2nd Floor Nos. 303–305, 14 Lislet Geoffroy Street, Port Louis.
Founded: 1952; *National Colours:* All red.
International matches 2010
Cameroon (h) 1-3, Senegal (a) 0-7.

MOROCCO

Federation Royale Marocaine De Football, 51 Bis Av. Ibn Sina, PO Box 51, Agdal, Rabat 10 000.
Founded: 1955; *National Colours:* All green white and red.
International matches 2010
Guinea Equatorial (h) 2-1, Central African Republic (h) 0-0, Tanzania (a) 1-0, Northern Ireland (a) 1-1.

MOZAMBIQUE

Federacao Mocambicana De Futebol, Av. Samora Machel 11-2, Caixa Postal 1467, Maputo.
Founded: 1978; *National Colours:* Red shirts, black shorts, red and black stockings.
International matches 2010
Gabon (a) 0-2, Benin (h) 2-2, Egypt (a) 0-2, Nigeria (a) 0-3, Botswana (h) 0-1, Portugal (a) 0-3, Swaziland (h) 2-1, Libya (h) 0-0, Comores (a) 1-0.

NAMIBIA

Namibia Football Association, Abraham Mashego Street 8521, Katurua Council of Churches in Namibia, P.O. Box 1345, Windhoek 9000, Namibia.
Founded: 1990; *National Colours:* All red.
International matches 2010
South Africa (a) 1-1, Botswana (h) 0-0, Gambia (a) 1-3, India (a) 0-2.

NIGER

Federation Nigerienne De Football, Rue de la Tapoa, PO Box 10299, Niamey.
Founded: 1967; *National Colours:* Orange shirts, white shorts, green stockings.
International matches 2010
Chad (h) 1-1, Benin (a) 0-0, South Africa (a) 0-2, Egypt (h) 1-0, Libya (a) 1-1.

NIGERIA

Nigeria Football Association, Plot 2033, Olusegun, Obasanjo Way, Zone 7, Wuse Abuja, PO Box 5101 Garki, Abuja, Nigeria.
Founded: 1945; *National Colours:* All green and white.
International matches 2010
Egypt (a) 1-3, Benin (h) 1-0, Mozambique (h) 3-0,

Zambia (a) 0-0, Ghana (a) 0-1, Algeria (h) 1-0, DR Congo (h) 5-2, Saudi Arabia (h) 0-0, Colombia (h) 1-1, North Korea (h) 3-1, Argentina (n) 0-1, Greece (n) 1-2, South Korea (n) 2-2, South Korea (a) 1-2, Madagascar (h) 2-0, Guinea (a) 0-1.

RWANDA

Federation Rwandaise De Football Amateur, B.P. 2000, Kigali.
Founded: 1972; *National Colours:* Red, green and yellow shirts, green shorts, red stockings.
International matches 2010
Ivory Coast (h) 0-2, Ivory Coast (a) 0-1, Benin (h) 0-3, Sudan (a) 0-0, Tanzania (a) 0-1, Malawi (a) 1-2.

SENEGAL

Federation Senegalaise De Football, Stade Leopold Sedar Senghor, Route De L'Aeroport De Yoff, B.P. 130 21, Dakar.
Founded: 1960; *National Colours:* All white and green.
International matches 2010
Greece (a) 2-0, Mexico (a) 0-1, Denmark (a) 0-2, Cape Verde Islands (h) 1-0, DR Congo (a) 4-2, Mauritius (h) 7-0, Gabon (h) 2-1.

SEYCHELLES

Seychelles Football Federation, P.O. Box 843, People's Stadium, Victoria-Mahe, Seychelles.
Founded: 1979; *National Colours:* Red and green shirts and shorts, red stockings.

ST THOMAS AND PRINCIPE

Federation Santomense De Futebol, Rua Ex-Joao de Deus No. QXXIII-426/26, PO Box 440, Sao Tome.
Founded: 1975; *National Colours:* Green and red shirts, yellow shorts, green stockings.

SIERRA LEONE

Sierra Leone Football Association, 21 Battery Street, Kingtorn, P.O. Box 672, National Stadium, Brookfields, Freetown.
Founded: 1967; *National Colours:* Green and blue shirts, green, blue and white shorts and stockings.
International matches 2010
Egypt (a) 1-1, South Africa (h) 0-0.

SOMALIA

Somali Football Federation, PO Box 222, Mogadishu BN 03040.
Founded: 1951; *National Colours:* Sky blue and white shirts and shorts, white and sky blue stockings.
International matches 2010
Burundi (a) 0-2, Tanzania (a) 0-3, Zambia (a) 0-6.

SOUTH AFRICA

South African Football Association, First National Bank Stadium, PO Box 910, Johannesburg 2000, South Africa.
Founded: 1991; *National Colours:* White shirts with yellow striped sleeves, white shorts with yellow stripes, white stockings.
International matches 2010
Zimbabwe (h) 3-0, Namibia (h) 1-1, Paraguay (a) 1-1, North Korea (h) 0-0, Jamaica (h) 2-0, Thailand (h) 4-0, Bulgaria (h) 1-1, Colombia (h) 2-1, Guatemala (h) 5-0, Denmark (h) 1-0, Mexico (n) 1-1, Uruguay (n) 0-3, France (n) 2-1, Ghana (h) 1-0, Niger (h) 2-0, Sierra Leone (a) 0-0, USA (h) 0-1.

SUDAN

Sudan Football Association, Bladia Street, Khartoum.
Founded: 1936; *National Colours:* Red shirts, white shorts, black stockings.
International matches 2010
Palestine (h) 1-1, Tunisia (h) 2-6, Congo (h) 2-0, Ghana (a) 0-0, Rwanda (h) 0-0.

SWAZILAND

National Football Association of Swaziland, Sigwaca House, Plot 582, Sheffield Road, PO Box 641, Mbabane H100.
Founded: 1968; *National Colours:* Blue shirts, gold shorts, red stockings.
International matches 2010
Mozambique (a) 1-2, Ghana (h) 0-3, Congo (a) 1-3, Botswana (a) 0-2.

TANZANIA

Football Association of Tanzania, Uhuru/Shaurimoyo Road, Karume Memorial Stadium, P.O. Box 1574, Ilala/Dar Es Salaam.
Founded: 1930; *National Colours:* Green, yellow and blue shirts, black shorts, green stockings with horizontal stripe.
International matches 2010
Ivory Coast (h) 0-1, Uganda (h) 2-3, Brazil (h) 1-5, Kenya (h) 1-1, Algeria (a) 1-1, Morocco (h) 0-1, Zambia (h) 0-1, Kenya (h) 1-0, Somalia (h) 3-0, Burundi (h) 2-0, Rwanda (h) 1-0, Uganda (h) 0-0.

TOGO

Federation Togolaise De Football, C.P. 5, Lome.
Founded: 1960; *National Colours:* White shirts, green shorts, red stockings with yellow and green stripes.
International matches 2010
Gabon (a) 0-3, Chad (a) 2-2, Malawi (h) 1-1, Saudi Arabia (a) 0-1, Botswana (a) 1-2, Tunisia (h) 1-2, Chad (h) 0-0.

TUNISIA

Federation Tunisienne De Football, Maison des Federations Sportives, Cite Olympique, Tunis 1003.
Founded: 1956; *National Colours:* Red shirts, white shorts, red stockings.
International matches 2010
Gambia (h) 1-2, Zambia (a) 1-1, Gabon (a) 0-0, Cameroon (a) 2-2, France (h) 1-1, Sudan (a) 6-2, Botswana (h) 0-1, Chad (a) 3-1, Malawi (h) 2-2, Togo (a) 2-1, Botswana (a) 0-1.

UGANDA

Federation of Uganda Football Associations, Plot No. 879, Kyadondo Block 8, Mengo Wakaliga Road, P.O. Box 22518, Kampala.
Founded: 1924; *National Colours:* All yellow, red and white.
International matches 2010
Tanzania (a) 3-2, Zambia (h) 1-1, Angola (h) 3-0, Kenya (a) 0-0, Yemen (a) 2-2, Bahrain (a) 0-0, Saudi Arabia (a) 0-0, Ethiopia (h) 2-1, Malawi (a) 1-1, Kenya (h) 2-0, Tanzania (a) 0-0, Ethiopia (a) 4-3.

ZAMBIA

Football Association of Zambia, Football House, Alick Nkhata Road, P.O. Box 34751, Lusaka.
Founded: 1929; *National Colours:* White and green shirts, green and white shorts, white and green stockings.
International matches 2010
South Korea (h) 4-2, Tunisia (h) 1-1, Cameroon (a) 2-3, Gabon (a) 2-1, Nigeria (h) 0-0, Chile (a) 0-3, Uganda (a) 1-1, Comores (h) 4-0, Yemen (a) 1-0, Libya (a) 0-1, Tanzania (a) 1-0, Burundi (h) 0-0, Somalia (h) 6-0, Ethiopia (h) 1-2, Kuwait (a) 0-4.

ZIMBABWE

Zimbabwe Football Association, P.O. Box CY 114, Causeway, Harare.
Founded: 1965; *National Colours:* All green and gold.
International matches 2010
South Africa (a) 0-3, Malawi (h) 2-1, Brazil (h) 0-3, Botswana (a) 0-2, Liberia (a) 1-1, Cape Verde Islands (h) 0-0.

THE WORLD CUP 1930–2010

Year	Winners		Runners-up		Venue	Attendance	Referee
1930	Uruguay	4	Argentina	2	Montevideo	90,000	Langenus (B)
1934	Italy*	2	Czechoslovakia	1	Rome	50,000	Eklind (Se)
1938	Italy	4	Hungary	2	Paris	45,000	Capdeville (F)
1950	Uruguay	2	Brazil	1	Rio de Janeiro	199,854	Reader (E)
1954	West Germany	3	Hungary	2	Berne	60,000	Ling (E)
1958	Brazi	5	Sweden	2	Stockholm	49,737	Guigue (F)
1962	Brazil	3	Czechoslovakia	1	Santiago	68,679	Latychev (USSR)
1966	England*	4	West Germany	2	Wembley	93,802	Dienst (Sw)
1970	Brazil	4	Italy	1	Mexico City	107,412	Glockner (EG)
1974	West Germany	2	Holland	1	Munich	77,833	Taylor (E)
1978	Argentina*	3	Holland	1	Buenos Aires	77,000	Gonella (I)
1982	Italy	3	West Germany	1	Madrid	90,080	Coelho (Br)
1986	Argentina	3	West Germany	2	Mexico City	114,580	Filho (Br)
1990	West Germany	1	Argentina	0	Rome	73,603	Mendez (Mex)
1994	Brazil*	0	Italy	0	Los Angeles	94,194	Puhl (H)
	(Brazil won 3-2 on penalties)						
1998	France	3	Brazil	0	St-Denis	75,000	Belqola (Mor)
2002	Brazil	2	Germany	0	Yokohama	69,029	Collina (I)
2006	Italy*	1	France	1	Berlin	69,000	Elizondo (Arg)
	(Italy won 5-3 on penalties)						
2010	Spain	1	Holland	0	Johannesburg	84,490	Webb (E)

(*After extra time)

GOALSCORING AND ATTENDANCES IN WORLD CUP FINAL ROUNDS

Venue		Matches	Goals (av)	Attendance (av)
1930	Uruguay	18	70 (3.9)	434,500 (24,138)
1934	Italy	17	70 (4.1)	395,000 (23,235)
1938	France	18	84 (4.6)	483,000 (26,833)
1950	Brazil	22	88 (4.0)	1,337,000 (60,772)
1954	Switzerland	26	140 (5.4)	943,000 (36,270)
1958	Sweden	35	126 (3.6)	868,000 (24,800)
1962	Chile	32	89 (2.8)	776,000 (24,250)
1966	England	32	89 (2.8)	1,614,677 (50,458)
1970	Mexico	32	95 (2.9)	1,673,975 (52,311)
1974	West Germany	38	97 (2.5)	1,774,022 (46,684)
1978	Argentina	38	102 (2.7)	1,610,215 (42,374)
1982	Spain	52	146 (2.8)	2,064,364 (38,816)
1986	Mexico	52	132 (2.5)	2,441,731 (46,956)
1990	Italy	52	115 (2.2)	2,515,168 (48,368)
1994	USA	52	141 (2.7)	3,567,415 (68,604)
1998	France	64	171 (2.6)	2,775,400 (43,366)
2002	Japan/S. Korea	64	161 (2.5)	2,705,566 (42,274)
2006	Germany	64	147 (2.3)	3,354,646 (52,416)
2010	South Africa	64	145 (2.3)	3,178,856 (49,670)

LEADING GOALSCORERS

Year	Player	Goals
1930	Guillermo Stabile (Argentina)	8
1934	Angelo Schiavio (Italy), Oldrich Nejedly (Czechoslovakia), Edmund Conen (Germany)	4
1938	Leonidas da Silva (Brazil)	8
1950	Ademir (Brazil)	9
1954	Sandor Kocsis (Hungary)	11
1958	Just Fontaine (France)	13
1962	Valentin Ivanov (USSR), Leonel Sanchez (Chile), Garrincha, Vava (both Brazil), Florian Albert (Hungary), Drazen Jerkovic (Yugoslavia)	4
1966	Eusebio (Portugal)	9
1970	Gerd Muller (West Germany)	10
1974	Grzegorz Lato (Poland)	7
1978	Mario Kempes (Argentina)	6
1982	Paolo Rossi (Italy)	6
1986	Gary Lineker (England)	6
1990	Salvatore Schillaci (Italy)	6
1994	Oleg Salenko (Russia), Hristo Stoichkov (Bulgaria)	6
1998	Davor Suker (Croatia)	6
2002	Ronaldo (Brazil)	8
2006	Miroslav Klose (Germany)	5
2010	Thomas Muller (Germany), David Villa (Spain), Wesley Sneijder (Holland), Diego Forlan (Uruguay)	5

EUROPEAN FOOTBALL CHAMPIONSHIP
(formerly EUROPEAN NATIONS' CUP)

Year	Winners		Runners-up		Venue	Attendance
1960	USSR	2	Yugoslavia	1	Paris	17,966
1964	Spain	2	USSR	1	Madrid	120,000
1968	Italy	2	Yugoslavia	0	Rome	60,000
	After 1-1 draw					75,000
1972	West Germany	3	USSR	0	Brussels	43,437
1976	Czechoslovakia	2	West Germany	2	Belgrade	45,000
	(Czechoslovakia won on penalties)					
1980	West Germany	2	Belgium	1	Rome	47,864
1984	France	2	Spain	0	Paris	48,000
1988	Holland	2	USSR	0	Munich	72,308
1992	Denmark	2	Germany	0	Gothenburg	37,800
1996	Germany	2	Czech Republic	1	Wembley	73,611
	(Germany won on sudden death)					
2000	France	2	Italy	1	Rotterdam	50,000
	(France won on sudden death)					
2004	Greece	1	Portugal	0	Lisbon	62,865
2008	Spain	1	Germany	0	Vienna	51,428

EURO 2012 REVIEW

There seemed to have been little changed from the last World Cup when the opening stages of the qualifying competition for Euro 2012 swung into action. Spain, the 2010 winners in South Africa, knocked off their first five fixtures and the runners-up Holland did even better with six wins in a row.

As far as the home countries were concerned, England began the most confident of the quartet easily beating Bulgaria 4-0 at Wembley. This was followed with a 3-1 win in Switzerland that on the potential strength of five-team Group G augured well for the campaign as a whole.

The initial surprise came when Montenegro made it a first opposition at this level for England. A goalless draw was reminiscent of days when eastern Europeans came to the old Wembley and invariably managed a draw. This was no exception. However, there was an improvement when Wales were defeated, which left the home match with the Swiss.

Again there was frustration for a tired looking England side as defensive errors put the visitors 2-0 ahead before a Frank Lampard penalty quickly reduced arrears and substitute Ashley Young levelled matters just after half-time. But two home ties in succession with only two points to show for the effort was a worrying fact and trips to Montenegro and Bulgaria to follow.

Fortunately on the same day of the Swiss draw, Montenegro also dropped points to Bulgaria but remained level on points with England albeit with an inferior goal difference.

Perhaps some warning might have been issued when the tournament began with Wales losing in Montenegro. The Welsh then lost at home to Bulgaria and more heavily 4-1 in Switzerland, before the fourth defeat against England. Four games, no points and qualification almost certainly beyond them with less than half of the fixtures still to come.

Northern Ireland, albeit in a tough section, did slightly better than Scotland in their respective groups, though the Irish in Group C made a fine start winning away to Slovenia and holding Italy at Windsor Park. Even so, victory in the Faeroes would have really set things up, yet they had to be satisfied with a draw.

Then the promise faded a little when Serbia won their home match against Northern Ireland who then only drew at home with Slovenia, to leave them in fifth. The Italians had dropped just those two points against the boys in green and headed the table.

The Scots for their part had a goalless draw in Lithuania and only just edged Lichtenstein at home, though not quite the pushovers of old. Indeed victory over Lithuania underlined the improvement made by the minnows.

A 1-0 defeat in the Czech Republic was followed by the best performance even though it ended in another defeat. At least this was against the might of Spain and there were definite signs of a fight and spirit keeping the outcome uncertain until the end. Scotland will almost certainly have to beat the Czechs at Hampden Park in September before further ambition.

The situation in Group B after five matches was fascinating. Slovakia, Russia and the Republic were separated only by goal difference, each with ten points. Slovakia had won their away fixture with the Russians who in turn had succeeded in Dublin while Armenia had surprisingly defeated the Slovaks.

Match six left it much the same except for the positioning. Slovakia with only a single goal win over Andorra dropped to third, with the Republic's 2-0 win in Macedonia swapping places to lead the group. This one will definitely go to the wire.

France, after their World Cup disaster, had problems with Belarus who won in Paris and held the French in Minsk. However in Groups A and E with the seven in succession winning Germans and Dutch looking as though accidents would be unlikely events, the runners-up spot appears the more interesting aspect of each one. In Group A, Belgium have a point more than Turkey, but they have a game in hand. In Group E, Sweden will be expected to hold off the challenge of Hungary.

In Group F, Croatia's lead was overtaken when unbeaten Greece won their game in hand against Malta leaving the Croats and Israel on the same number of points. Greece have already held Croatia to a goalless draw away.

However in the five-team Group H there is another rather more open competition ensuing and another three-way split. Portugal have already been held at home in a goals share of eight with Cyprus and beaten in Norway, but won this return game for the Norwegians' only defeat. Denmark's sole reverse was in Portugal. So there are three on ten points.

It is worth noting that the finals are to be jointly held by Poland and The Ukraine. Both nations have automatic qualification. All group winners, nine in total, plus the best placed runner-up – the tie-breaker being the second placed team with the most points taken from the teams below it in the group – move on. The remaining eight in second places are paired off and the four winners also reach the final stages.

Footnote: Bosnia's suspension from 1st April was lifted on 26th May in time for a return to Euro 2012 qualifying matches.

England's Jermain Defoe scores his second goal of his hat-trick against Bulgaria in the UEFA Euro 2012 Group G match at Wembley. (PA Photos)

EURO 2012 QUALIFYING COMPETITION

GROUP A

Brussels, 3 September 2010, 41,126

Belgium (0) 0

Germany (0) 1 *(Klose 51)*

Belgium: Bailly; Kompany, Van Buyten, Vermaelen, Vertonghen, Alderweireld, Simons (Vossen 83), Fellaini, Hazard (Benteke 73), Dembele, Lukaku (Defour 73).
Germany: Neuer; Jansen (Westermann 46), Lahm, Mertesacker, Badstuber, Schweinsteiger, Ozil (Cacau 88), Khedira, Klose, Podolski (Kroos 70), Muller.
Referee: Hauge (Norway).

Astana, 3 September 2010, 15,800

Kazakhstan (0) 0

Turkey (2) 3 *(Arda 24, Hamit Altintop 26, Nihat 75)*

Kazakhstan: Sidelnikov; Popov, Kirov, Abdulin, Karpovich (Rodionov 64), Schmidtgal, Nurgaliev, Zhumaskaliev, Kislitsyn (Rozhkov 85), Ostapenko (Maltsev 72), Azovskiy.
Turkey: Onur; Sabri, Omer, Hakan Balta, Servet, Hamit Altintop, Emre B, Arda, Mehmet Aurelio (Kazim-Richards 89), Nihat (Selcuk I 82), Tuncay (Halil Altintop 80).
Referee: Vad II (Hungary).

Wals-Siezenheim, 7 September 2010, 22,500

Austria (0) 2 *(Linz R 89, Hoffer 90)*

Kazakhstan (0) 0

Austria: Macho; Pogatetz, Schiemer, Prodl, Fuchs, Dag, Kavlak, Jantscher (Alaba 66), Harnik (Hoffer 66), Janko (Maierhofer 78), Linz.
Kazakhstan: Sidelnikov; Popov, Kirov, Abdulin, Karpovich, Geteriev, Nurgaliev (Azovskly 59), Zhumaskaliev, Kislitsyn (Rozhkov 75), Maltsev (Khizhnichenko 46), Averchenko.
Referee: Strahonja (Croatia).

Cologne, 7 September 2010, 43,751

Germany (3) 6 *(Westermann 28, Podolski 44, Klose 45, 90, Rashad F Sadygov 53 (og), Badstuber 86)*

Azerbaijan (0) 1 *(Javadov 57)*

Germany: Neuer; Lahm, Mertesacker (Westermann 11), Badstuber, Schweinsteiger (Cacau 78), Ozil, Khedira, Riether, Klose, Podolski, Muller (Marin 62).
Azerbaijan: Agayev K; Melikov, Allahverdiyev, Rashad F Sadygov, Abbasov, Shukurov, Yunisoglu (Huseynov V 56), Medvedev, Chertoganov (Rashad A Sadygov 64), Nadirov (Abdullayev 85), Javadov.
Referee: Strombergsson (Sweden).

Istanbul, 7 September 2010, 43,538

Turkey (0) 3 *(Hamit Altintop 48, Semih 66, Arda 78)*

Belgium (1) 2 *(Van Buyten 28, 69)*

Turkey: Onur; Sabri (Gokhan G 73), Omer, Servet, Ismail, Hamit Altintop, Emre B, Arda, Mehmet Aurelio, Selcuk I (Semih 47), Tuncay (Selcuk S 82).
Belgium: Bailly; Kompany■, Van Buyten, Vermaelen, Vertonghen, Alderweireld, Simons, Gillet (Hazard 82), Fellaini, Dembele (Mirallas 63), Lukaku (Witsel 76).
Referee: Skomina (Slovenia).

Vienna, 8 October 2010, 26,500

Austria (1) 3 *(Prodl 3, Arnautovic 53, 90)*

Azerbaijan (0) 0

Austria: Macho; Scharner, Schiemer, Prodl, Fuchs, Klein, Junuzovic (Baumgartlinger 78), Harnik (Kavlak 55), Maierhofer, Linz (Hoffer 59), Arnautovic.
Azerbaijan: Agayev K; Melikov, Allahverdiyev, Rashad F Sadygov, Abbasov, Shukurov, Yunisoglu, Mammadov E (Nadirov 59), Amirguliyev, Javadov (Rashad A Sadygov 74), Aliyev.
Referee: Vollquartz (Denmark).

Berlin, 8 October 2010, 74,244

Germany (1) 3 *(Klose 42, 87, Ozil 79)*

Turkey (0) 0

Germany: Neuer; Lahm, Mertesacker, Westermann, Badstuber, Ozil (Marin 90), Khedira, Kroos, Klose (Cacau 90), Podolski (Trasch 86), Muller.
Turkey: Volkan; Sabri, Omer, Gokhan G, Servet, Nuri (Sercan 78), Hamit Altintop, Emre B, Mehmet Aurelio (Tuncay 24), Ozer, Halil Altintop (Semih 68).
Referee: Webb (England).

Astana, 8 October 2010, 8500

Kazakhstan (0) 0

Belgium (0) 2 *(Ogunjimi 53, 70)*

Kazakhstan: Sidelnikov; Popov, Kirov, Abdulin, Karpovich, Geteriev, Schmidtgal, Nurgaliev (Rozhkov 74), Zhumaskaliev (Averchenko 87), Kislitsyn■, Khizhnichenko.
Belgium: Bailly; Van Buyten, Van Damme (Legear 79), Deschacht, Lombaerts, Alderweireld, Simons, Fellaini, Witsel, Vossen, Lukaku (Ogunjimi 46).
Referee: Borski (Poland).

Baku, 12 October 2010, 29,500

Azerbaijan (1) 1 *(Rashad F Sadygov 39)*

Turkey (0) 0

Azerbaijan: Agayev K; Melikov (Chertoganov 45), Allahverdiyev, Rashad F Sadygov, Abishov, Shukurov, Yunisoglu, Amirguliyev, Nadirov, Javadov (Huseynov V 85), Guliyev (Aliyev 72).
Turkey: Volkan; Ibrahim T, Hakan Balta, Gokhan G, Servet, Hamit Altintop, Emre B, Ozer (Nihat 46), Selcuk I (Halil Altintop 82), Tuncay (Sercan 62), Semih.
Referee: Deaconu (Romania).

Brussels, 12 October 2010, 25,000

Belgium (1) 4 *(Vossen 11, Fellaini 47, Ogunjimi 87, Lombaerts 90)*

Austria (2) 4 *(Schiemer 14, 62, Arnautovic 29, Harnik 90)*

Belgium: Bailly; Kompany, Vertonghen, Lombaerts, Alderweireld (Boyata 46), Simons (Lukaku 73), Fellaini (Hazard 81), Witsel, Legear, Vossen, Ogunjimi.
Austria: Macho; Scharner■, Schiemer, Prodl, Fuchs, Klein, Kavlak (Hoffer 57), Junuzovic (Pehlivan 73), Baumgartlinger, Maierhofer, Arnautovic (Harnik 88).
Referee: Dean (England).

Astana, 12 October 2010, 20,000

Kazakhstan (0) 0

Germany (0) 3 *(Klose 48, Gomez 76, Podolski 86)*

Kazakhstan: Sidelnikov; Popov, Irismetov (Rozhkov 68), Kirov, Abdulin, Geteriev, Schmidtgal, Nurgaliev (Averchenko 63), Zhumaskaliev, Azovskiy, Khizhnichenko (Finonchenko 79).
Germany: Neuer; Lahm, Mertesacker, Westermann, Badstuber, Ozil (Cacau 79), Khedira, Kroos, Klose (Gomez 56), Podolski, Muller (Marin 71).
Referee: Tudor (Romania).

Vienna, 25 March 2011, 45,000

Austria (0) 0

Belgium (1) 2 *(Witsel 6, 50)*

Austria: Macho; Pogatetz, Fuchs, Dragovic, Dag, Junuzovic (Korkmaz 68), Baumgartlinger, Alaba (Maierhofer 54), Harnik, Janko (Pehlivan 54), Arnautovic.
Belgium: Mignolet; Kompany, Van Buyten, Vertonghen, Ciman, Simons, Defour, Witsel, Chadli, Dembele, Ogunjimi (Mirallas 80).
Referee: Bezborodov (Russia).

Kaiserslautern, 26 March 2011, 47,849

Germany (3) 4 *(Klose 4, 88, Muller 25, 44)*

Kazakhstan (0) 0

Germany: Neuer; Lahm, Mertesacker, Aogo, Badstuber, Schweinsteiger (Kroos 77), Ozil, Khedira, Klose, Podolski (Gomez 65), Muller (Gotze 78).

Kazakhstan: Loria; Irismetov, Nurdauletov, Chichulin, Abdulin, Chernyshov, Geteriev (Ostapenko 81), Nurgaliev (Kukeev 60), Zhumaskaliev (Baizhanov 46), Konysbaev, Khizhnichenko.
Referee: Stavrev (Macedonia).

Brussels, 29 March 2011, 34,985

Belgium (3) 4 *(Vertonghen 12, Simons 32 (pen), Chadli 45, Vossen 74)*

Azerbaijan (1) 1 *(Abishov 16)*

Belgium: Mignolet; Van Buyten (Van Damme 80), Vertonghen, Lombaerts, Ciman, Simons, Defour (Odjidja-Ofoe 90), Witsel, Chadli, Dembele (Hazard 64), Vossen.
Azerbaijan: Agayev K; Rashad F Sadykov, Melikov, Abishov, Levin, Shukurov, Chertoganov, Mammadov E (Huseynov J 78), Amirguliyev, Javadov (Nadirov 76), Aliyev.
Referee: Stalhammar (Sweden).

Istanbul, 29 March 2011, 40,420

Turkey (1) 2 *(Arda 28, Gokhan G 78)*

Austria (0) 0

Turkey: Volkan; Hakan Balta, Gokhan G, Servet, Serdar, Nuri, Hamit Altintop, Arda (Mehmet Topal 87), Burak (Semih 72), Selcuk I, Mehmet E (Mehmet Topuz 63).
Austria: Macho; Scharner, Pogatetz, Fuchs, Dragovic, Dag, Baumgartlinger (Hoffer 46), Alaba, Pehlivan (Korkmaz 57), Harnik (Arnautovic 69), Maierhofer.
Referee: Kralovec (Czech Republic).

Vienna, 3 June 2011, 47,500

Austria (0) 1 *(Friedrich 50 (og))*

Germany (1) 2 *(Gomez 44, 90)*

Austria: Gratzei; Scharner, Pogatetz, Fuchs, Dag (Junuzovic 66), Klein, Kulovits, Baumgartlinger, Alaba, Harnik (Royer 81), Hoffer (Janko 88).
Germany: Neuer; Friedrich, Lahm, Hummels, Schmelzer, Ozil, Khedira (Badstuber 69), Kroos (Aogo 90), Gomez, Podolski (Schurrle 68), Muller.
Referee: Busacca (Switzerland).

Brussels, 3 June 2011, 44,185

Belgium (1) 1 *(Ogunjimi 4)*

Turkey (1) 1 *(Burak 22)*

Belgium: Mignolet; Kompany, Vertonghen (Vermaelen 46), Lombaerts, Alderweireld, Simons, Defour (Vossen 88), Witsel, Hazard (Mertens 60), Chadli, Ogunjimi.
Turkey: Volkan; Sabri, Caglar, Servet, Kazim-Richards, Servet, Emre B, Arda (Semih 85), Selcuk S, Burak (Mehmet E 76), Selcuk I (Mehmet Topal 78).
Referee: Rizzoli (Italy).

Astana, 3 June 2011, 3000

Kazakhstan (0) 2 *(Gridin 57, 68)*

Azerbaijan (0) 1 *(Nadirov 63)*

Kazakhstan: Nesterenko; Smakov, Nurdauletov, Mukhtarov, Geteriev, Schmidtgal, Khayrullin (Kirov 82), Logvinenko (Rozhkov 65), Konysbaev, Ostapenko (Khizhnichenko 79), Gridin.
Azerbaijan: Agayev K; Rashad F Sadygov, Melikov, Abishov, Levin, Medvedev, Rashad A Sadygov, Huseynov J (Nadirov 61), Ismayilov, Javadov, Aliyev (Huseynov M 79).
Referee: Norris (Scotland).

Baku, 7 June 2011, 25,000

Azerbaijan (0) 1 *(Huseynov M 89)*

Germany (2) 3 *(Ozil 30, Gomez 41, Schurrle 90)*

Azerbaijan: Agayev K; Rashad F Sadygov, Melikov, Allahverdiyev, Abishov, Huseynov V, Chertoganov (Rashad A Sadygov 86), Amirguliyev, Ismayilov (Isayev 58), Nadirov, Javadov (Huseynov M 72).
Germany: Neuer; Lahm, Howedes, Aogo, Hummels, Badstuber, Ozil, Kroos (Gotze 81), Gomez, Podolski (Schurrle 78), Muller (Holtby 88).
Referee: Koukoulakis (Greece).

Group A	P	W	D	L	F	A	Pts
Germany	7	7	0	0	22	3	21
Belgium	7	3	2	2	15	10	11
Turkey	6	3	1	2	9	7	10

	P	W	D	L	F	A	Pts
Austria	6	2	1	3	10	10	7
Azerbaijan	6	1	0	5	5	18	3
Kazakhstan	6	1	0	5	2	15	3

GROUP B

Andorra la Vella, 3 September 2010, 1100

Andorra (0) 0

Russia (1) 2 *(Pogrebnyak 14, 64 (pen))*

Andorra: Gomes; Lima I, Jordi Rubio (Lorenzo 58), Marc Bernaus, Martinez, Josep Ayala, Vieira, Moreno (Manolo Jimenez 76), Pujol (Mejias 89), Silva, Gomez.
Russia: Akinfeev; Berezutski V, Ignashevich, Anyukov, Bystrov (Dzagoev 61), Semshov, Bilyaletdinov, Shirokov, Zyryanov, Arshavin, Pogrebnyak (Pavlyuchenko 86).
Referee: Borg (Malta).

Erevan, 3 September 2010, 8600

Armenia (0) 0

Republic of Ireland (0) 1 *(Fahey 76)*

Armenia: Berezovskiy; Arzumanian, Arakelian, Hovespian, Artur Yedigarian (Manoian 68), Artak Yedigarian (Hambardzumian 71), Pachajian, Mkhitarian, Malakian (Manucharian 78), Mkrtchian K, Movsisian.
Republic of Ireland: Given; Dunne, Kilbane, Whelan, St Ledger-Hall, O'Shea, Lawrence, Green, Keane (Keogh 85), Doyle, McGeady (Fahey 68).
Referee: Szabo (Hungary).

Bratislava, 3 September 2010, 5980

Slovakia (0) 1 *(Holosko 90)*

Macedonia (0) 0

Slovakia: Mucha; Skrtel, Hubocan, Pekarik (Sylvestr 90), Salata (Kucka 76), Sapara, Hamsik, Strba, Stoch, Weiss (Jendrisek 61), Holosko.
Macedonia: Nuredinoski; Mitreski, Noveski, Shikov, Popov, Shumulikoski, Georgievski, Despotovski (Lazevski 73), Pandev, Naumoski (Ristic 61), Trichkovski (Grncharov 80).
Referee: Circhetta (Switzerland).

Skopje, 7 September 2010, 9000

Macedonia (1) 2 *(Durovski 42, Naumoski 89 (pen))*

Armenia (1) 2 *(Movsisian 40, Manucharian 90)*

Macedonia: Nuredinoski; Mitreski, Noveski, Popov, Todorovski, Shumulikoski, Georgievski (Despotovski 67), Durovski (Ilijoski 75), Pandev, Ristic (Naumoski 62), Trichkovski.
Armenia: Berezovskiy; Arzumanian, Arakelian, Hovsepian, Artak Yedigarian, Pachajian (Artur Yedigarian 70), Mkhitarian, Malakian (Manucharian 58), Mkrtchian K (Mkoian 90), Manoian, Movsisian.
Referee: Berntsen (Norway).

Dublin, 7 September 2010, 40,283

Republic of Ireland (2) 3 *(Kilbane 15, Doyle 41, Keane 54)*

Andorra (1) 1 *(Martinez 45)*

Republic of Ireland: Given; Dunne, Kilbane, Whelan (Gibson 61), St Ledger-Hall, O'Shea (Kelly 75), Lawrence, Green, Keane, Doyle (Keogh 82), McGeady.
Andorra: Gomes; Lima I, Escura, Marc Bernaus, Martinez, Josep Ayala (Andorra 71), Vieira, Moreno (Manolo Jimenez 59), Pujol (Oscar Sonejee 86), Silva, Gomez.
Referee: Trattou (Cyprus).

Moscow, 7 September 2010, 27,052

Russia (0) 0

Slovakia (1) 1 *(Stoch 27)*

Russia: Akinfeev; Berezutski V, Ignashevich (Bilyaletdinov 81), Anyukov, Zhirkov, Semshov (Bystrov 61), Shirokov, Zyryanov, Arshavin, Dzagoev, Pogrebnyak (Pavlyuchenko 71).
Slovakia: Mucha; Skrtel, Zabavnik, Hubocan, Salata, Karhan (Sapara 73), Hamsik, Strba, Kucka (Jendrisek 58), Stoch (Pecalka 90), Holosko.
Referee: De Bleeckere (Belgium).

Andorra la Vella, 8 October 2010, 550

Andorra (0) 0

Macedonia (1) 2 *(Naumoski 42, Shikov 60)*

Andorra: Gomes; Escura, Marc Bernaus, Martinez (Manolo Jimenez 74), Josep Ayala (Bousenine 86), Vieira, Vales, Meijas (Lorenzo 62), Moreno, Silva, Gomez.
Macedonia: Nuredinoski; Mitreski, Noveski, Lazarevski, Shikov, Shumulikoski (Grncharov 83), Georgievski (Durovski 34), Despotovski, Naumoski (Ibraimi 73), Ristic, Trichkovski.
Referee: Mazelka (Lithuania).

Erevan, 8 October 2010, 8500

Armenia (1) 3 *(Movsisian 23, Ghazarian 50, Mkhitarian 89)*

Slovakia (1) 1 *(Weiss 37)*

Armenia: Berezovskiy; Arzumanian (Arakelian 79), Hovsepian, Mkoian, Artak Yedigarian, Pachajian (Manucharian 46), Mkhitarian, Mkrtchian K, Pizzelli (Artur Yedigarian 72), Movsisian, Ghazarian.
Slovakia: Mucha; Skrtel, Zabavnik (Sebo 81), Pekarik, Salata, Karhan, Hamsik, Kopunek (Holosko 57), Stoch (Kucka 57), Weiss, Sestak.
Referee: Orsato (Italy).

Dublin, 8 October 2010, 50,411

Republic of Ireland (0) 2 *(Keane 72 (pen), Long 78)*

Russia (2) 3 *(Kerzhakov 10, Dzagoev 28, Shirokov 51)*

Republic of Ireland: Given; O'Shea, Kilbane, Whelan (Gibson 66), Dunne, St Ledger-Hall, Lawrence (Long 62), Green, Doyle (Fahey 71), Keane, McGeady.
Russia: Akinfeev; Berezutski V, Ignashevich, Anyukov, Zhirkov, Shirokov, Zyryanov (Semshov 68), Denisov, Dzagoev (Berezutski A 85), Kerzhakov (Pogrebnyak 80), Arshavin.
Referee: Blom (Holland).

Erevan, 12 October 2010, 12,000

Armenia (3) 4 *(Ghazarian 4, Mkhitarian 16, Movsisian 33, Pizzelli 52)*

Andorra (0) 0

Armenia: Berezovskiy; Arzumanian, Hovsepian, Artur Yedigarian, Mkoian, Artak Yedigarian, Mkhitarian, Pizzelli (Yuspashian 82), Manucharian, Movsisian (Goharian 54), Ghazarian (Malakian 67).
Andorra: Gomes; Lima I, Escura, Marc Bernaus, Martinez (Jordi Rubio 87), Josep Ayala, Vieira, Vales (Andorra 64), Moreno (Manolo Jimenez 53), Silva, Gomez.
Referee: Mikulski (Poland).

Skopje, 12 October 2010, 10,500

Macedonia (0) 0

Russia (1) 1 *(Kerzhakov 8)*

Macedonia: Nuredinoski; Mitreski, Noveski, Shikov, Lazevski, Shumulikoski, Despotovski (Georgievski 77), Durovski (Alimi 80), Naumoski, Ibraimi (Ristic 49), Trichkovski.
Russia: Akinfeev; Berezutski V, Ignashevich, Anyukov, Zhirkov, Shirokov, Zyryanov, Denisov, Dzagoev (Berezutski A 62), Kerzhakov (Pogrebnyak 79), Arshavin (Bystrov 81).
Referee: Johannesson (Sweden).

Zilina, 12 October 2010, 10,892

Slovakia (1) 1 *(Durica 36)*

Republic of Ireland (1) 1 *(St Ledger-Hall 16)*

Slovakia: Mucha; Zabavnik, Hubocan, Salata, Durica, Karhan, Hamsik, Kucka, Weiss (Holosko 70), Jendrisek (Oravec 84), Sestak (Stoch 70).
Republic of Ireland: Given; O'Shea, Kilbane, Whelan, Dunne, St Ledger-Hall, Green (Gibson 41), Fahey (Keogh 71), Long, Keane, McGeady.
Referee: Mallenco (Spain).

Andorra la Vella, 26 March 2011, 850

Andorra (0) 0

Slovakia (1) 1 *(Sebo 21)*

Andorra: Gomis; Lima I, Jordi Rubio, Marc Bernaus, Garcia, Martinez, Josep Ayala (Juli Sanchez 81), Manolo Jimenez (Oscar Sonejee 87), Vales, Moreno, Gomez (Vieira 72).
Slovakia: Mucha; Skrtel, Pekarik, Durica, Kona, Hamsik, Luksik, Stoch (Salata 90), Vittek (Piroska 78), Jendrisek (Holosko 87), Sebo.
Referee: Masiah (Israel).

Erevan, 26 March 2011, 14,800

Armenia (0) 0

Russia (0) 0

Armenia: Berezovskiy; Arzumanian, Hovsepian, Mkoian, Mkhitarian, Malakian (Manucharian 49), Mkrtchian K, Hayrapetian (Artak Yedigarian 67), Pizzelli (Artur Yedigarian 57), Movsisian, Ghazarian.
Russia: Akinfeev; Berezutski V, Shishkin, Ignashevich, Zhirkov, Shirokov, Zyryanov, Denisov, Dzagoev, Kerzhakov (Pogrebnyak 78), Arshavin (Bilyaletdinov 90).
Referee: Thomson (Scotland).

Dublin, 26 March 2011, 33,200

Republic of Ireland (2) 2 *(McGeady 2, Keane 21)*

Macedonia (1) 1 *(Trichkovski 45)*

Republic of Ireland: Westwood; Dunne, O'Dea, Foley, Whelan, McGeady, Kilbane, Gibson (Fahey 77), Doyle (Long 20), Keane (McCarthy 87), Duff.
Macedonia: Nuredinoski; Novevski, Grncharov, Shikov, Popov, Shumulikoski, Demiri (Georgievski 84), Tasevski (Durovski 61), Pandev, Naumoski (Ristic 68), Trichkovski.
Referee: Vad II (Hungary).

Skopje, 4 June 2011, 29,500

Macedonia (0) 0

Republic of Ireland (2) 2 *(Keane 8, 36)*

Macedonia: Bogatinov; Noveski, Grncharov, Shikov, Popov, Shumulikoski, Despotovski (Durovski 57), Demiri (Savic 72), Pandev, Naumoski (Hasani 10), Trichkovski.
Republic of Ireland: Given; O'Dea, O'Shea, Kelly, McGeady, Hunt, Kilbane, Whelan, Andrews, Keane, Cox (Long 64).
Referee: Meyer (Germany).

St Petersburg, 4 June 2011, 18,000

Russia (1) 3 *(Pavlyuchenko 26, 59, 73 (pen))*

Armenia (1) 1 *(Pizzelli 25)*

Russia: Akinfeev; Berezutski V, Ignashevich, Anyukov (Yanbayev 74), Zhirkov, Semshov (Glushakov 69), Zyryanov (Dzagoev 82), Denisov, Torbinski, Pavlyuchenko, Arshavin.
Armenia: Berezovskiy; Arzumanian, Hovsepian, Mkoian, Pachajian (Manucharian 57), Mkhitarian K, Mkrtchian (Artak Yedigarian 89), Hayrapetian, Pizzelli (Artur Yedigarian 67), Movsisian, Ghazarian.
Referee: Lannoy (France).

Bratislava, 4 June 2011, 4300

Slovakia (0) 1 *(Karhan 63)*

Andorra (0) 0

Slovakia: Kello; Cech (Salata 83), Hubocan, Durica, Karhan, Hamsik, Jez, Kucka (Sestak 46), Vittek, Sebo, Holosko (Zofcak 74).
Andorra: Gomes; Lima I, Jordi Rubio, Marc Bernaus, Garcia, Martinez, Josep Ayala (Andorra 16), Manolo Jimenez (Salvat 86), Vieira, Vales, Silva (Gomez 64).
Referee: Jemini (Albania).

Group B	P	W	D	L	F	A	Pts
Republic of Ireland	6	4	1	1	11	6	13
Russia	6	4	1	1	9	4	13
Slovakia	6	4	1	1	6	4	13
Armenia	6	2	2	2	10	7	8
Macedonia	6	1	1	4	5	8	4
Andorra	6	0	0	6	1	13	0

GROUP C

Tallinn, 11 August 2010, 5470

Estonia (0) 2 *(Saag 89, Piiroja 90)*

Faeroes (1) 1 *(Edmundsson 28)*

Estonia: Pareiko; Klavan, Piiroja, Jaager, Barengrub, Kruglov (Post 70), Dmitrijev, Puri (Purje 77), Vassiljev, Oper (Saag 62), Kink.
Faeroes: Nielsen; Borg (Poulsen 67), Benjaminsen, Gregersen, Davidsen, Naes, Samuelsen (Hansen J 74), Petersen J (Lokin 85), Holst, Edmundsson, Rubeksen.
Referee: Vucemilovic (Croatia).

Tallinn, 3 September 2010, 8600

Estonia (1) 1 *(Zenjov 31)*

Italy (0) 2 *(Cassano 60, Bonucci 63)*

Estonia: Pareiko; Klavan, Piiroja, Jaager, Rahn, Kruglov (Kink 82), Dmitrijev, Puri (Purje 77), Vunk, Vassiljev, Zenjov (Saag 64).
Italy: Sirigu; Bonucci, Cassani, Molinaro, Chiellini, De Rossi, Pirlo, Montolivo (Palombo 75), Pepe (Quagliarella 61), Cassano (Antonelli 80), Pazzini.
Referee: Velasco (Spain).

Torshavn, 3 September 2010, 1847

Faeroes (0) 0

Serbia (2) 3 *(Lazovic 14, Stankovic 18, Zigic 90)*

Faeroes: Nielsen; Rubeksen, Gregersen, Davidsen, Naes, Samuelsen, Petersen J (Hansen J 73), Benjaminsen, Udsen (Mouritsen 46), Holst (Hansen A 79), Edmundsson.
Serbia: Duricic; Vidic, Subotic, Rukavina, Obradovic (Lukovic 46), Stankovic (Petrovic 58), Krasic, Kuzmanovic, Zigic, Lazovic (Ninkovic 83), Jovanovic.
Referee: Toussaint (Luxembourg).

Maribor, 3 September 2010, 12,000

Slovenia (0) 0

Northern Ireland (0) 1 *(Evans C 70)*

Slovenia: Handanovic; Cesar, Jokic, Brecko, Mavric, Koren, Kirm (Dedic 74), Radosavljevic, Birsa, Novakovic (Ilicic 74), Ljubijankic (Matavz 88).
Northern Ireland: Taylor; Baird, McAuley, McCann (Lafferty 67), Hughes, Craigan, Cathcart, Davis, Healy (Evans C 67), Feeney, Brunt (Gorman 89).
Referee: Balaj (Romania).

Florence, 7 September 2010, 19,266

Italy (3) 5 *(Gilardino 11, De Rossi 22, Cassano 27, Quagliarella 81, Pirlo 90)*

Faeroes (0) 0

Italy: Viviano; Bonucci, De Silvestri, Chiellini, De Rossi (Palombo 76), Pirlo, Montolivio, Antonelli, Gilardino (Pazzini 59), Rossi (Quagliarella 58), Cassano.
Faeroes: Nielsen; Bo, Rubeksen, Gregersen, Davidsen, Samuelsen, Petersen J, Benjaminsen, Lokin (Naes 74), Edmundsson (Udsen 89), Mouritsen (Holst 75).
Referee: Kulbakov (Belarus).

Belgrade, 7 September 2010, 24,028

Serbia (0) 1 *(Zigic 86)*

Slovenia (0) 1 *(Novakovic 63)*

Serbia: Duricic; Vidic, Lukovic, Subotic, Rukavina, Stankovic (Kacar 71), Kuzmanovic, Tosic (Krasic 46), Zigic, Lazovic, Jovanovic (Ninkovic 64).
Slovenia: Handanovic; Cesar, Jokic, Brecko, Mavric, Koren, Kirm (Stevanovic 89), Radosavljevic, Birsa (Ljubijankic 77), Dedic (Ilic 77), Novakovic.
Referee: Olegario Benquerenca (Portugal).

Belfast, 8 October 2010, 15,200

Northern Ireland (0) 0

Italy (0) 0

Northern Ireland: Taylor; Baird, McAuley, Craigan, Hughes, Evans J, Davis, McCann (Evans C 80), Healy (Lafferty 66), Brunt (McGinn 71), Feeney.
Italy: Viviano; Bonucci, Cassani, Chiellini, Criscito, De Rossi, Pirlo, Mauri (Marchisio 79), Pepe (Rossi 84), Cassano, Borriello (Pazzini 74).
Referee: Chapron (France).

Belgrade, 8 October 2010, 12,000

Serbia (0) 1 *(Kuzmanovic 60)*

Estonia (0) 3 *(Kink 63, Vassiljev 73, Lukovic 90 (og))*

Serbia: Stojkovic; Vidic, Lukovic, Ivanovic, Lomic, Stankovic, Krasic, Kuzmanovic (Lazovic 79), Kacar (Tosic 46), Zigic, Jovanovic (Ninkovic 46).
Estonia: Pareiko; Klavan, Piiroja, Jaager, Rahn, Kruglove, Dmitrijev, Puri (Purje 70), Vassiljev, Kink (Saag 64), Zenjov (Vunk 88).
Referee: Layushkin (Russia).

Ljubljana, 8 October 2010, 15,750

Slovenia (2) 5 *(Matavz 25, 36, 66, Novakovic 72 (pen), Dedic 84)*

Faeroes (0) 1 *(Mouritsen 90)*

Slovenia: Handanovic; Cesar, Jokic, Brecko, Suler, Koren, Radosavljevic (Bacinovic 59), Ilicic, Birsa (Kirm 51), Novakovic (Dedic 73), Matavz.
Faeroes: Mikkelsen; Bo, Rubeksen, Gregersen, Naes, Benjaminsen, Hansen J, Lokin (Elttor 41), Udsen (Mouritsen 81), Holst (Petersen J 81), Edmundsson.
Referee: Todorov (Bulgaria).

Tallinn, 12 October 2010, 5722

Estonia (0) 0

Slovenia (0) 1 *(Sidorenkov 66 (og))*

Estonia: Pareiko; Klavan, Jaager, Sidorenkov, Rahn (Palatu 55), Kruglov, Dmitrijev, Puri (Purje 69), Vassalijev, Kink (Zenjov 59), Saag.
Slovenia: Handanovic; Cesar, Jokic, Brecko, Suler, Koren, Radosavljevic, Ilicic (Kirm 67), Birsa (Ljubijankic 90), Novakovic, Matavz (Dedic 53).
Referee: Skjerven (Norway).

Toftir, 12 October 2010, 1921

Faeroes (0) 1 *(Holst 60)*

Northern Ireland (0) 1 *(Lafferty 76)*

Faeroes: Mikkelsen; Gregersen, Davidsen, Naes, Samuelsen (Hansen A 78), Benjaminsen, Jacobsen, Udsen (Petersen J 68), Holst (Hansen J 85), Edmundsson, Elttor.
Northern Ireland: Taylor; Baird, McAuley, Craigan, Hughes, Evans J, Davis, McGinn (Evans C 83), Lafferty, Feeney (Healy 50), Brunt.
Referee: Zimmermann (Switzerland).

Genoa, 12 October 2010

Italy (0) 0

Serbia (0) 0

Referee: Thomson (Scotland).
Abandoned 7 minutes; crowd trouble. Italy awarded the match 3-0.

Belgrade, 25 March 2011, 350

Serbia (0) 2 *(Pantelic 65, Tosic 74)*

Northern Ireland (1) 1 *(McAuley 40)*

Serbia: Brkic; Ivanovic, Bisevac, Subotic, Kolarov, Stankovic, Krasic (Petrovic 86), Milijas (Jovanovic 47), Tosic, Ljajic (Ninkovic 47), Pantelic.
Northern Ireland: Camp; Baird, Cathcart, McAuley, Hughes, Evans J (McCourt 86), Evans C, Clingan, Lafferty (Healy 46), Gorman (Feeney 78), Brunt.
Referee: Gumienny (Belgium).

Ljubljana, 25 March 2011, 15,790

Slovenia (0) 0

Italy (0) 1 *(Thiago Motta 73)*

Slovenia: Handanovic; Cesar, Jokic, Brecko (Andelkovic 70), Suler, Koren, Kirm, Radosavljevic, Birsa (Ilicic 74), Dedic (Ljubijankic 56), Novakovic.
Italy: Buffon; Bonucci, Chiellini, Balzaretti, Thiago Motta, Aquilani, Montolivo (Marchisio 87), Mauri (Nocerino 63), Maggio, Cassano (Rossi 74), Pazzini.
Referee: Brych (Germany).

Tallinn, 29 March 2011, 5185

Estonia (0) 1 *(Vassiljev 84)*

Serbia (1) 1 *(Pantelic 38)*

Estonia: Pareiko; Klavan, Piiroja, Jaager, Rahn, Kruglov, Dmitrijev, Puri (Purje 29), Vassiljev, Ahjupera (Oper 55), Saag (Kink 66).
Serbia: Brkic; Vidic, Ivanovic, Bisevac, Kolarov, Ninkovic (Trivunovic 14), Milijas, Tosic, Petrovic, Pantelic, Jovanovic (Zigic 74).
Referee: Nijhuis (Holland).

Belfast, 29 March 2011, 14,200

Northern Ireland (0) 0

Slovenia (0) 0

Northern Ireland: Camp; Baird, Cathcart, Craigan, McAuley, Evans J, Evans C (Boyce 90), McCann (McQuoid 72), Brunt, Feeney (McCourt 82), Clingan.
Slovenia: Handanovic; Jokic, Brecko, Mavric, Suler, Koren, Kirm, Bacinovic (Sukalo 90), Ilicic (Ljubijankic 29), Birsa, Novakovic (Dedic 84).
Referee: Kuipers (Holland).

Toftir, 3 June 2011, 974

Faeroes (0) 0

Slovenia (1) 2 *(Matavz 29, Baldvinsson 47 (og))*

Faeroes: Mikkelsen; Hansen E, Justinussen, Davidsen, Naes (Olsen S 81), Benjaminsen, Udsen (Danielsen 46), Baldvinsson, Holst (Mouritsen 75), Edmundsson, Elttor.
Slovenia: Handanovic; Cesar, Jokic, Brecko, Suler[*], Koren, Bacinovic, Ilicic, Birsa (Mavric 47), Novakovic (Ljubijankic 55), Matavz (Kirm 76).
Referee: Drachta (Austria).

Modena, 3 June 2011, 19,434

Italy (2) 3 *(Rossi 21, Cassano 39, Pazzini 68)*

Estonia (0) 0

Italy: Buffon; Chiellini, Balzaretti, Ranocchia, Pirlo, Aquilani (Nocerino 24), Montolivo, Maggio, Marchisio, Rossi (Giovinco 79), Cassano (Pazzini 65).
Estonia: Pareiko; Klavan, Piiroja, Jaager, Teniste (Saag 59), Rahn, Kruglov, Puri, Vunk, Kink (Kams 78), Zenjov (Ahjupera 58).
Referee: Tudor (Romania).

Toftir, 7 June 2011, 1715

Faeroes (1) 2 *(Benjaminsen 43 (pen), Hansen A 47)*

Estonia (0) 0

Faeroes: Mikkelsen; Hansen E, Justinussen[*], Gregersen, Danielsen, Naes, Benjaminsen, Baldvinsson, Holst (Mouritsen 85), Hansen A (Samuelsen 69), Elttor (Olsen S 90).
Estonia: Pareiko; Piiroja, Jaager, Rahn, Kruglov, Puri[*], Vassiljev, Ahjupera (Kams 67), Kink, Saag (Mosnikov 83), Zenjov.
Referee: Munukka (Finland).

Group C	P	W	D	L	F	A	Pts
Italy	6	5	1	0	14	1	16
Slovenia	7	3	2	2	9	4	11
Serbia	6	2	2	2	8	9	8
Estonia	7	2	1	4	7	11	7
Northern Ireland	5	1	3	1	3	3	6
Faeroes	7	1	1	5	5	18	4

GROUP D

Paris, 3 September 2010, 76,395

France (0) 0

Belarus (0) 1 *(Kislyak 86)*

France: Lloris; Sagna, Clichy, Mexes, Rami, Malouda, Diaby, M'Vila, Menez (Saha 69) (Gameiro 80), Remy (Valbuena 34), Hoarau.
Belarus: Zhevnov; Omelyanchuk, Tigorev, Yurevich, Shitov, Martynovich, Hleb A, Kulchiy, Kutuzov (Kislyak 74), Rodionov (Kornilenko 85), Hleb V (Putsila 89).
Referee: Collum (Scotland).

Luxembourg, 3 September 2010, 7327

Luxembourg (0) 0

Bosnia (3) 3 *(Ibricic 6, Pjanic 12, Dzeko 16)*

Luxembourg: Joubert; Hoffmann, Schnell, Kintziger, Mutsch, Gerson, Janisch, Peters, Bettmer (Laterza 86), Collette (Da Mota 76), Bensi (Kitenge 46).
Bosnia: Hasagic; Spahic, Nadarevic, Mujdza, Misimovic, Rahimic (Jahic 67), Pjanic (Zec 78), Lulic, Ibricic (Medunjanin 72), Ibisevic, Dzeko.
Referee: Banari (Moldova).

Piatra Neamt, 3 September 2010, 13,400

Romania (0) 1 *(Stancu 80)*

Albania (0) 1 *(Muzaka 88)*

Romania: Lobont; Tamas, Rat, Contra (Muresan 57), Radoi, Cocis (Herea 78), Torje, Deac, Florescu, Niculae (Stancu 64), Marica.
Albania: Beqaj; Vangjeli, Lila, Dallku, Curri, Cana, Skela (Lika 79), Agolli, Bulku, Duro (Muzaka 82), Bogdani (Salihi 57).
Referee: Schorgenhofer (Austria).

Tirana, 7 September 2010, 10,000

Albania (1) 1 *(Salihi 37)*

Luxembourg (0) 0

Albania: Beqaj; Dallku, Curri, Cana, Skela, Agolli, Bulku, Duro (Lila 90), Bogdani, Salihi, Muzaka (Hyka 80).
Luxembourg: Joubert; Hoffmann, Schnell, Kintziger, Blaise, Mutsch[*], Payal, Peters, Bettmer (Collette 90), Laterza (Martino 82), Da Mota.
Referee: Trutz (Slovakia).

Minsk, 7 September 2010, 26,354

Belarus (0) 0

Romania (0) 0

Belarus: Zhevnov; Omelyanchuk, Yurevich, Shitov, Martynovich, Hleb A (Putsila 73), Kulchiy, Kislyak, Kutuzov (Krivets 87), Kornilenko (Rodionov 76), Hleb V.
Romania: Pantilimon; Chivu, Tamas, Rat, Maftei, Radoi, Torje (Cocis 46), Deac (Marica 83), Florescu, Stancu (Niculae 73), Bilasco.
Referee: Kralovec (Czech Republic).

Sarajevo, 7 September 2010, 28,000

Bosnia (0) 0

France (0) 2 *(Benzema 72, Malouda 78)*

Bosnia: Hasagic; Spahic, Nadarevic, Mujdza, Misimovic, Rahimic (Zec 74), Pjanic, Lulic, Ibricic, Ibisevic (Jahic 75), Dzeko.
France: Lloris; Sagna, Clichy, Mexes, Rami, Diarra A, Malouda (Matuidi 80), Valbuena, Diaby, M'Vila, Benzema.
Referee: Brych (Germany).

Tirana, 8 October 2010, 14,220

Albania (1) 1 *(Duro 45)*

Bosnia (1) 1 *(Ibisevic 21)*

Albania: Beqaj; Vangjeli, Lila, Dallku, Cana, Agolli, Bulku, Duro, Muzaka (Lika 65), Bogdani (Skela 46), Salihi (Hyka 85).
Bosnia: Hasagic (Begovic 46); Spahic, Mravac (Pandza 46), Mujdza, Misimovic, Medunjanin, Rahimic, Pjanic, Lulic, Ibisevic, Dzeko (Ibricic 89).
Referee: Jakobsson (Iceland).

Luxembourg, 8 October 2010, 1857

Luxembourg (0) 0

Belarus (0) 0

Luxembourg: Joubert; Hoffmann, Schnell, Kintziger, Blaise, Leweck, Payal (Kettenmeyer 77), Peters, Bettmer (Gerson 62), Laterza, Joachim (Da Mota 66).
Belarus: Zhevnov; Omelyanchuk, Tigorev (Rodionov 67), Yurevich (Molosh 87), Shitov, Martynovich, Kulchiy, Kalachev, Kislyak, Kornilenko[*], Hleb V (Putsila 67).
Referee: Stavrev (Macedonia).

Paris, 9 October 2010, 79,299

France (0) 2 *(Remy 83, Gourcuff 90)*

Romania (0) 0

France: Lloris; Reveillere, Clichy, Mexes, Rami, Diarra A, Malouda, Valbuena (Remy 68), Nasri (Gourcuff 74), M'Vila, Benzema (Payet 86).
Romania: Pantilimon; Chivu, Tamas, Rat, Sapunaru, Radoi, Cocis (Roman 87), Florescu, Niculae (Marica 63), Zicu (Deac 46), Stancu.
Referee: Proenca (Portugal).

Mogilev, 12 October 2010, 7000

Belarus (1) 2 *(Rodionov 10, Krivets 77)*

Albania (0) 0

Belarus: Zhevnov; Omelyanchuk, Molosh (Yurevich 86), Tigorev, Shitov, Martynovich, Kulchiy (Krivets 75), Putsila (Hleb V 82), Kalachev, Kislyak, Rodionov.
Albania: Beqaj; Vangjeli, Lila, Dallku■, Teli, Skela (Kapllani 81), Agolli, Bulku (Muzaka 59), Duro, Lika (Bakaj 76), Salihi.
Referee: Rasmussen (Denmark).

Longeville-les-Metz, 12 October 2010, 24,710

France (1) 2 *(Benzema 22, Gourcuff 76)*

Luxembourg (0) 0

France: Lloris; Reveillere, Clichy, Mexes, Rami, Diarra A, Malouda (Payet 63), Diaby, Gourcuff, Benzema (Nasri 63), Hoarau (Remy 73).
Luxembourg: Joubert; Hoffmann, Schnell, Blaise, Mutsch, Leweck, Payal, Peters■, Bettmer (Da Mota 84), Laterza (Strasser 70), Joachim (Kitenge 53).
Referee: Jug (Slovenia).

Luxembourg, 25 March 2011, 8052

Luxembourg (0) 0

France (1) 2 *(Mexes 28, Gourcuff 72)*

Luxembourg: Joubert; Hoffmann, Schnell, Blaise, Mutsch, Gerson (Da Mota 71), Leweck (Plein 90), Payal, Bettmer, Laterza (Martino 54), Joachim.
France: Lloris; Sagna, Evra, Mexes, Rami, Malouda, Ribery, Nasri, Gourcuff, M'Vila, Benzema.
Referee: Hagen (Norway).

Tirana, 26 March 2011, 13,020

Albania (0) 1 *(Salihi 62)*

Belarus (0) 0

Albania: Ujkani; Vangjeli, Lila, Teli, Cana, Lala, Skela (Duro 80), Agolli, Bulku, Bogdani (Bakaj 75), Salihi (Muzaka 90).
Belarus: Veremko; Omelyanchuk, Molosh, Tigorev, Shitov, Martynovich, Kulchiy (Bychenok 62), Putsila (Sitko 82), Krivets (Kovel 46), Kislyak, Hleb V.
Referee: Strombergsson (Sweden).

Zenica, 26 March 2011, 13,000

Bosnia (0) 2 *(Ibisevic 63, Dzeko 83)*

Romania (1) 1 *(Marica 29)*

Bosnia: Hasagic; Spahic, Mravac, Mujdza, Misimovic (Ibricic 81), Medunjanin (Maletic 71), Rahimic, Pjanic, Lulic, Ibisevic (Muslimovic 76), Dzeko.
Romania: Pantilimon; Goian, Tamas, Rat, Rapa, Alexa, Torje (Cocis 71), Deac (Zicu 87), Florescu (Ropotan 76), Mutu, Marica.
Referee: Teixeira (Spain).

Ceahlaul, 29 March 2011, 13,500

Romania (1) 3 *(Mutu 24, 68, Zicu 78)*

Luxembourg (1) 1 *(Gerson 22)*

Romania: Tatarusanu; Tamas (Goian 65), Rat, Sapunaru, Gardos, Ropotan, Muresan, Mutu (Alexe 84), Marica, Zicu, Stancu (Torje 46).
Luxembourg: Joubert; Hoffmann, Schnell (Martino 90), Blaise, Mutsch, Gerson (Da Mota 58), Leweck, Payal, Peters, Bettmer (Laterza 81), Joachim.
Referee: Huseyin (Turkey).

Minsk, 3 June 2011, 26,500

Belarus (1) 1 *(Abidal 20 (og))*

France (1) 1 *(Malouda 22)*

Belarus: Veremko; Omelyanchuk, Tigorev, Bordachev, Shitov, Verkhovtsov, Martynovich, Trubila, Putsila (Kislyak 86), Kalachev (Hleb V 90), Varankov.
France: Lloris; Abidal, Sagna, Sakho, Rami, Diarra A, Malouda, Ribery, Nasri, Diaby (Remy 73), Benzema.
Referee: Fernandez (Spain).

Bucharest, 3 June 2011, 8200

Romania (2) 3 *(Mutu 37, Marica 41, 55)*

Bosnia (0) 0

Romania: Tatarusanu; Tamas, Rat, Sapunaru, Papp, Sanmartean (Tanase 63), Muresan, Torje, Bourceanu, Mutu (Surdu 83), Marica (Alexe 87).
Bosnia: Hasagic; Spahic, Mravac, Mujdza, Misimovic, Medunjanin (Ibisevic 46), Rahimic, Pjanic, Lulic, Ibricic (Muslimovic 64), Dzeko (Stilic 64).
Referee: Eriksson (Sweden).

Minsk, 7 June 2011, 8000

Belarus (0) 2 *(Kornilenko 48 (pen), Putsila 73)*

Luxembourg (0) 0

Belarus: Zhevnov; Omelyanchuk, Tigorev, Bordachev, Shitov, Verkhovtsov, Kulchiy (Kislyak 87), Trubila (Hleb V 62), Putsila, Kalachev, Varankov (Kornilenko 46).
Luxembourg: Joubert; Hoffmann, Martino, Schnell, Blaise, Malget (Kitenge 61), Gerson, Leweck (Collette 84), Payal, Peters, Da Mota (Laterza 77).
Referee: Salmanov (Azerbaijan).

Zenica, 7 June 2011, 10,000

Bosnia (0) 2 *(Medunjanin 67, Maletic 90)*

Albania (0) 0

Bosnia: Hasagic; Spahic, Pandza, Mujdza (Maletic 73), Misimovic, Medunjanin, Rahimic, Pjanic (Besic 77), Lulic, Ibisevic (Muslimovic 61), Dzeko.
Albania: Ujkani; Vangjeli, Dallku, Curri, Cana, Lala (Muzaka 72), Skela, Agolli (Lila■ 60), Bulku, Bogdani (Duro 46), Salihi.
Referee: Blom (Holland).

Group D	P	W	D	L	F	A	Pts
France	6	4	1	1	9	2	13
Belarus	7	3	3	1	6	2	12
Bosnia	6	3	1	2	8	7	10
Romania	6	2	2	2	8	6	8
Albania	6	2	2	2	4	6	8
Luxembourg	7	0	1	6	1	13	1

GROUP E

Chisinau, 3 September 2010, 10,300

Moldova (0) 2 *(Suvorov 69, Doros 73)*

Finland (0) 0

Moldova: Namasco; Epureanu, Bulgaru, Savinov, Cebotaru, Boret, Bordian, Josan (Suvorov 58), Frunza, Tigirlas (Bugaev 69), Doros (Andronic 75).
Finland: Fredrikson; Pasanen, Hyypia■, Heikkinen, Moisander, Eremenko R, Sparv, Eremenko A Jr (Forssell 81), Porokara (Vayrynen 75), Litmanen (Hamalainen 46), Johansson.
Referee: Malek (Poland).

Serravalle, 3 September 2010, 4127

San Marino (0) 0

Holland (2) 5 *(Kuyt 16 (pen), Huntelaar 38, 48, 67, Van Nistelrooy 90)*

San Marino: Simoncini A; Vitaioli F, Alessandro Della Valle (Bacciocchi 61), Simoncini D, Valentini C, Berretti, Vannucci, Mazza, Manuel Marani (Gasperoni A 76), Selva A, Vitaioli M (Ciacci 83).
Holland: Stekelenburg; Mathijsen, Maduro, Pieters, Van der Wiel, Sneijder, Van Bommel, De Jong (Van der Vaart 46), Kuyt (Van Nistelrooy 68), Elia (Afellay 59), Huntelaar.
Referee: Lee (Wales).

Stockholm, 3 September 2010, 32,304
Sweden (0) 2 *(Wernbloom 51, 73)*
Hungary (0) 0
Sweden: Isaksson (Wiland 46); Mellberg, Safari, Majstorovic, Lustig, Svensson (Kallstrom 33), Bajrami, Wernbloom, Ibrahimovic, Elmander (Larsson S 49), Toivonen.
Hungary: Kiraly; Juhasz, Laczko, Lazar, Liptak, Vadocz, Gera, Koman, Dzsudzsak (Huszti 46), Elek (Priskin 59), Rudolf (Hajnal 82).
Referee: Atkinson (England).

Rotterdam, 7 September 2010, 25,000
Holland (2) 2 *(Huntelaar 7, 16 (pen))*
Finland (1) 1 *(Forssell 18)*
Holland: Stekelenburg; Heitinga, Mathijsen, Van der Wiel, Anita, Sneijder, Van Bommel, Van der Vaart (Elia 64), De Jong, Afellay (Lens 74), Huntelaar (Van Nistelrooy 82).
Finland: Fredrikson; Pasanen, Heikkinen, Lampi, Moisander, Vayrynen, Eremenko R, Sparv, Hamalainen (Porokara 46), Forssell (Eremenko A Jr 81), Sjolund (Johansson 68).
Referee: Nikolaev (Russia).

Budapest, 7 September 2010, 9209
Hungary (0) 2 *(Rudolf 50, Koman 66)*
Moldova (0) 1 *(Suvorov 79)*
Hungary: Kiraly; Juhasz, Laczko, Lazar, Liptak, Gera, Koman (Vadocz 88), Dzsudzsak, Czvitkovics (Szalai 46), Elek, Rudolf (Vanczak 64).
Moldova: Namasco; Epureanu, Racu, Bulgaru, Bolohan, Cebotaru (Cojocari 71), Suvorov, Bordian, Josan (Doros 59), Frunza (Bugaev 84), Tigirlas.
Referee: Kovarik (Czech Republic).

Malmo, 7 September 2010, 21,083
Sweden (3) 6 *(Ibrahimovic 7, 77, Simoncini D 12 (og), Simoncini A 26 (og), Granqvist 51, Berg 90)*
San Marino (0) 0
Sweden: Wiland; Mellberg■, Safari, Majstorovic, Lustig, Kallstrom, Bajrami, Wernbloom (Elmander 69), Larsson S, Ibrahimovic (Berg 82), Toivonen (Granqvist 47).
San Marino: Simoncini A; Vitaioli F, Alesssandro Della Valle, Simoncini D, Bacciocchi (Valentini C 79), Vannucci, Chiaruzzi (Gasperoni A 72), Mazza, Manuel Marani (Berretti 56), Selva A, Vitaioli M.
Referee: McKeon (Republic of Ireland).

Budapest, 8 October 2010, 10,596
Hungary (4) 8 *(Rudolf 11, 25, Szalai 18, 27, 49, Koman 61, Dzsudzsak 89, Gera 90 (pen))*
San Marino (0) 0
Hungary: Kiraly; Juhasz, Vanczak, Laczko, Vermes, Gera, Koman (Czvitkovics 79), Dzsudzsak, Elek (Vadocz 64), Rudolf, Szalai (Priskin 64).
San Marino: Simoncini A; Vitaioli F, Alessandro Della Valle, Bacciocchi (Nicola Albani 53), Bollini (Cervellini 84), Valentini C, Berretti, Vannucci, Manuel Marani, Vitaioli M (Bugli 77), Montagna.
Referee: Kaasik (Estonia).

Chisinau, 8 October 2010, 10,500
Moldova (0) 0
Holland (1) 1 *(Huntelaar 37)*
Moldova: Namasco; Epureanu, Golovatenco, Racu, Bulgaru, Bolohan, Cebotaru (Andronic 69), Suvorov, Bordian, Frunza (Bugaev 46), Doros (Josan 78).
Holland: Stekelenburg; Heitinga, Mathijsen, Pieters, Van der Wiel, Sneijder, Van Bommel, Van der Vaart, Afellay (Emanuelson 90), Kuyt, Huntelaar.
Referee: Meyer (Germany).

Helsinki, 12 October 2010, 18,532
Finland (0) 1 *(Forssell 86)*
Hungary (0) 2 *(Szalai 50, Dzsudzsak 90)*
Finland: Jaaskelainen; Pasanen, Hyypia, Moisander, Vayrynen, Eremenko R, Sparv (Litmanen 72), Porokara (Eremenko A Jr 71), Heikkinen, Forssell, Sjolund (Kuqi 81).

Hungary: Kiraly; Juhasz, Laczko (Vanczak 86), Vermes, Liptak, Vadocz (Pinter 75), Gera, Dzsudzsak, Elek, Rudolf (Koman 46), Szalai.
Referee: Kelly (Republic of Ireland).

Amsterdam, 12 October 2010, 46,000
Holland (2) 4 *(Huntelaar 4, 55, Afellay 37, 59)*
Sweden (0) 1 *(Granqvist 69)*
Holland: Stekelenburg; Heitinga, Mathijsen, Pieters, Van der Wiel, Sneijder, Van Bommel (Brama 72), Van der Vaart, Afellay, Kuyt (Lens 29), Huntelaar (Van Nistelrooy 84).
Sweden: Isaksson; Granqvist, Safari (Wendt 46), Majstorovic, Lustig, Svensson, Wernbloom (Kallstrom 54), Larsson S, Ibrahimovic, Elmander, Toivonen (Berg 79).
Referee: Lannoy (France).

Serravalle, 12 October 2010, 714
San Marino (0) 0
Moldova (1) 2 *(Josan 20, Doros 86 (pen))*
San Marino: Simoncini A; Vitaioli F, Simoncini D, Bacciocchi, Cervellini (Berretti 60), Bollini (Ciacci 67), Vannucci, Mazza, Manuel Marani, Vitaioli M, Montagna (Coppini 82).
Moldova: Namasco; Epureanu, Golovatenco, Suvorov, Boret, Bordian, Cojocari (Savinov 82), Josan (Zmeu 69), Andronic, Frunza, Bugaev (Doros 62).
Referee: Courtney (Northern Ireland).

Helsinki, 17 November 2010, 8192
Finland (1) 8 *(Vayrynen 39, Hamalainen 49, 67, Forssell 51, 59, 78, Litmanen 71 (pen), Porokara 73)*
San Marino (0) 0
Finland: Fredrikson; Pasanen, Lampi, Moisander, Vayrynen, Eremenko R, Eremenko A Jr (Kuqi 80), Hamalainen (Porokara 70), Heikkinen, Forssell, Sjolund (Litmanen 46).
San Marino: Simoncini A; Vitaioli F (Vannucci 72), Alessandro Della Valle, Cervellini, Berretti (Alex Della Valle 67), Bugli, Coppini, Nicola Albani, Selva A, Vitaioli M, Montagna (Manuel Marani 79).
Referee: Matejek (Czech Republic).

Budapest, 25 March 2011, 23,817
Hungary (0) 0
Holland (2) 4 *(Van der Vaart 8, Afellay 45, Kuyt 54, Van Persie 62)*
Hungary: Kiraly; Juhasz, Vanczak, Laczko, Liptak, Gera, Koman (Vadocz 46), Dzsudzsak, Varga (Czvitkovics 46), Elek (Priskin 80), Rudolf.
Holland: Vorm; Heitinga, Mathijsen, Pieters, Van der Wiel, Sneijder, Van der Vaart (Van Nistelrooy 82), De Jong, Afellay (Elia 63), Kuyt (Strootman 82), Van Persie.
Referee: Velasco (Spain).

Amsterdam, 29 March 2011, 51,700
Holland (1) 5 *(Van Persie 13, Sneijder 61, Van Nistelrooy 73, Kuyt 78, 81)*
Hungary (0) 3 *(Rudolf 47, Gera 50, 75)*
Holland: Vorm; Heitinga, Mathijsen, Pieters (Emanuelson 64), Van der Wiel, Sneijder, Van der Vaart, De Jong, Afellay, Kuyt (Elia 90), Van Persie (Van Nistelrooy 46).
Hungary: Fulop; Juhasz, Vanczak, Laczko, Pinter (Koman 46), Lazar, Vadocz (Czvitkovics 90), Gera, Dzsudzsak, Rudolf, Priskin (Tokoli 73).
Referee: Moen (Norway).

Stockholm, 29 March 2011, 25,544
Sweden (2) 2 *(Lustig 30, Larsson S 32)*
Moldova (0) 1 *(Suvorov 90)*
Sweden: Isaksson; Wendt, Granqvist, Antonsson, Lustig, Kallstrom, Bajrami (Olsson 73), Wernbloom (Elm R 65), Larsson S, Ibrahimovic, Elmander (Gerndt 89).
Moldova: Namasco; Golovatenco, Racu, Armas, Bolohan, Cebotaru, Suvorov, Boret, Gatcan (Andronic 83), Frunza (Bugaev 46), Doros (Cheptine 72).
Referee: Kircher (Germany).

Chisinau, 3 June 2011, 10,500
Moldova (0) 1 *(Bugaev 61)*
Sweden (2) 4 *(Toivonen 11, Elmander 30, 58, Gerndt 88)*
Moldova: Namasco; Golovatenco, Racu, Armas, Bolohan, Ivanov, Cebotaru (Patras 78), Suvorov, Gatcan (Tigirlas 46), Bugaev, Doros (Boghiu 63).
Sweden: Isaksson; Mellberg, Wendt, Majstorovic, Lustig, Kallstrom, Svensson, Larsson S, Elmander (Gerndt 75), Toivonen (Wilhelmsson 68), Hysen (Wernbloom 40).
Referee: Marriner (England).

Serravalle, 3 June 2011, 1218
San Marino (0) 0
Finland (1) 1 *(Forssell 41)*
San Marino: Simoncini A; Vitaioli F (Bacciocchi 88), Alessandro Della Valle, Simoncici D, Cervellini, Bollini, Vannucci, Mazza (Berretti 77), Manuel Marani, Selva A, Vitaioli M (Montagna 80).
Finland: Hradecky; Pasanen, Raitala, Lampi, Moisander, Vayrynen, Eremenko A Jr (Riski 68), Hamalainen, Heikkinen, Hetemaj (Sjolund 84), Forssell (Sadik 90).
Referee: Sipailo (Latvia).

Serravalle, 7 June 2011, 1900
San Marino (0) 0
Hungary (1) 3 *(Liptak 41, Szabics 49, Koman 83)*
San Marino: Simoncini A; Vitaioli F (Alex Della Valle 46), Alessandro Della Valle, Benedettini, Cervellini, Bollini (Bacciocchi 80), Vannucci, Mazza, Manuel Marani (Berretti 64), Selva A, Vitaioli M.
Hungary: Kiraly; Juhasz, Vanczak, Laczko, Liptak (Pinter 87), Hajnal (Czvitkovics 71), Koman, Dzsudzsak, Elek, Szabics (Koltai 84), Nemeth.
Referee: Radovanovic (Montenegro).

Stockholm, 7 June 2011, 32,128
Sweden (3) 5 *(Kallstrom 11, Ibrahimovic 31, 35, 53, Bujruml 74)*
Finland (0) 0
Sweden: Isaksson; Mellberg, Wendt, Majstorovic, Lustig, Kallstrom, Svensson, Bajrami, Larsson S (Wilhelmsson 89), Elmander (Wernbloom 81), Toivonen (Ibrahimovic 25).
Finland: Jaakkola; Pasanen, Moisander, Toivio, Vayrynen, Eremenko R, Eremenko A Jr (Ring 79), Hamalainen (Halsti 46), Heikkinen (Aaritalo 46), Hetemaj, Forssell.
Referee: Gautier (France).

Group E	P	W	D	L	F	A	Pts
Holland	6	6	0	0	21	5	18
Sweden	6	5	0	1	20	6	15
Hungary	7	4	0	3	18	13	12
Finland	6	2	0	4	11	11	6
Moldova	6	2	0	4	7	9	6
San Marino	7	0	0	7	0	33	0

GROUP F

Tel Aviv, 2 September 2010, 17,365
Israel (1) 3 *(Benayoun 7, 64 (pen), 75)*
Malta (1) 1 *(Pace 38)*
Israel: Awat; Ben Haim T, Bondarv, Ben Dayan, Benayoun, Cohen T, Zahavi (Vermouth 51), Refaelov, Almog Cohen, Kayal (Golasa 86), Sahar (Arbeitman 73).
Malta: Hogg; Caruana, Mamo, Agius, Sciberras, Bajada, Briffa (Failla 82), Mifsud, Pace, Bogdanovic (Cohen 57), Herrera (Muscat 80).

Piraeus, 3 September 2010, 14,794
Greece (0) 1 *(Spiropoulos 72)*
Georgia (1) 1 *(Iashvili 3)*
Greece: Sifakis; Seitaridis (Mitroglou 71), Papadopoulos, Torosidis, Papastathopoulos, Spiropoulos, Karagounis, Katsouranis, Samaras (Ninis 59), Gekas, Salpingidis.
Georgia: Revishvili; Kobiashvili, Khizanishvili, Kaladze, Amisulashvili, Asatiani, Kvirkvelia, Lobzhanidze, Gogua (Merebashvili 87), Iashvili (Ananidze 54), Dvalishvili (Gelashvili 60).
Referee: Gomez (Spain).

Riga, 3 September 2010, 7600
Latvia (0) 0
Croatia (1) 3 *(Petric 43, Olic 51, Srna 82)*
Latvia: Vanins; Gorkss, Mihadjuks, Ivanovs, Klava, Laizans (Astafjevs 87), Rafalskis, Rubins (Zigajevs 85), Cauna, Verpakovskis, Karlsons (Rudnevs 63).
Croatia: Runje; Simunic, Srna, Corluka, Strinic, Kranjcar, Rakitic, Vukojevic (Pranjic 70), Olic, Eduardo Da Silva (Jelavic 62), Petric (Mandzukic 84).
Referee: Kuipers (Holland).

Zagreb, 7 September 2010, 24,399
Croatia (0) 0
Greece (0) 0
Croatia: Runje; Simunic, Srna, Corluka, Strinic, Kranjcar, Modric, Pranjic, Vukojevic (Rakitic 57), Olic (Eduardo Da Silva 73), Petric (Jelavic 46).
Greece: Sifakis; Papadopoulos, Torosidis (Seitaridis 90), Vyntra, Papastathopoulos, Tzvelas, Karagounis (Ninis 70), Katsouranis, Tziolis, Samaras, Salpingidis (Gekas 59).
Referee: Larsen (Denmark).

Tbilisi, 7 September 2010, 45,000
Georgia (0) 0
Israel (0) 0
Georgia: Revishvili; Kobiashvili, Khizanishvili, Kaladze, Amisulashvili, Asatiani, Lobzhanidze, Gogua (Aptsiauri 75), Ananidze, Iashvili (Siradze 46), Dvalishvili (Merebashvili 63).
Israel: Awat; Ben Haim T, Bondarv, Keinan, Ben Dayan, Benayoun, Cohen T (Zahavi 61), Refaelov (Vermouth 75), Almog Cohen, Kayal, Sahar (Arbeitman 53).
Referee: Kever (Switzerland).

Ta'Qali, 7 September 2010, 6255
Malta (0) 0
Latvia (1) 2 *(Gorkss 42, Verpakovskis 85)*
Malta: Hogg; Caruana, Mamo (Fenech R 77), Muscat (Bogdanovic 59), Agius, Sciberras (Failla 77), Bajada, Briffa, Mifsud, Cohen, Pace.
Latvia: Vanins; Gorkss, Mihadjuks, Ivanovs, Klava, Laizans, Rafalskis (Astafjevs 82), Rubins, Cauna, Verpakovskis (Pereplotkins 90), Rudnevs (Karlsons 70).
Referee: Asumaa (Finland).

Tbilisi, 8 October 2010, 38,000
Georgia (0) 1 *(Siradze 90)*
Malta (0) 0
Georgia: Revishvili; Khizanishvili, Kaladze, Amisulashvili, Asatiani, Salukvadze, Kobiashvili, Gogua, Merebashvili (Siradze 46), Ananidze (Daushvili 73), Dvalishvili (Iashvili 46).
Malta: Haber; Caruana, Mamo, Agius, Schembri (Fenech P 80), Sciberras (Fenech R 69), Bajada, Briffa, Mifsud, Cohen (Grima 90), Pace.
Referee: Black (Northern Ireland).

Piraeus, 8 October 2010, 13,520
Greece (0) 1 *(Torosidis 58)*
Latvia (0) 0
Greece: Sifakis; Papadopoulos, Torosidis, Papastathopoulos, Tzvelas, Karagounis (Kafes 89), Katsouranis, Tziolis, Ninis (Fetfatzidis 83), Samaras, Mitroglou (Salpingidis 78).
Latvia: Vanins; Gorkss, Ivanovs, Zirnis, Klava, Laizans (Pereplotkins 82), Rubins (Zigajevs 66), Astafjevs, Cauna, Verpakovskis, Rudnevs (Karlsons 74).
Referee: Damato (Italy).

Tel Aviv, 9 October 2010, 33,421
Israel (0) 1 *(Shechter 81)*
Croatia (2) 2 *(Kranjcar 36 (pen), 41)*
Israel: Awat; Ben Haim T, Ziv, Keinan, Vermouth, Natcho, Cohen T (Colautti 51), Almog Cohen, Barda (Refaelov 56), Shechter, Alroey Cohen (Golasa 69).
Croatia: Runje; Simunic, Corluka, Schildenfeld, Strinic, Kranjcar, Modric, Pranjic, Rakitic (Vukojevic 77), Olic (Bilic 72), Eduardo Da Silva (Mandzukic 57).
Referee: Stark (Germany).

Piraeus, 12 October 2010, 16,935

Greece (1) 2 *(Salpingidis 22, Karagounis 63 (pen))*

Israel (0) 1 *(Spiropoulos 59 (og))*

Greece: Sifakis; Papadopoulos, Vyntra, Papastathopoulos, Spiropoulos, Karagounis, Katsouranis, Ninis (Fetfatzidis 15), Kafes, Samaras (Mitroglou 81), Salpingidis (Maniatis 87).
Israel: Awat; Bondarv, Keinan, Gershon, Natcho (Vermouth 65), Cohen T (Alroey Cohen 69), Refaelov, Golasa, Almog Cohen, Colautti (Barda 75), Shechter.
Referee: Hansson (Sweden).

Riga, 12 October 2010, 4330

Latvia (0) 1 *(Cauna 90)*

Georgia (0) 1 *(Siradze 74)*

Latvia: Vanins; Gorkss, Ivanovs, Zirnis, Klava, Laizans (Grebis 82), Zigajevs (Pereplotkins 86), Rubins, Astafjevs, Cauna, Rudnevs.
Georgia: Revishvili; Kaladze, Amisulashvili, Asatiani, Kvirkvelia (Gogua 69), Lobzhanidze, Kobiashvili, Daushvili, Ananidze (Salukvadze 79), Iashvili (Koshkadze 87), Siradze.
Referee: De Sousa (Portugal).

Zagreb, 17 November 2010, 10,000

Croatia (2) 3 *(Kranjcar 19, 42, Kalinic 81)*

Malta (0) 0

Croatia: Runje; Srna, Corluka, Schildenfeld, Kranjcar, Modric, Pranjic, Rakitic (Ilicevic 69), Dujmovic, Eduardo Da Silva (Mandzukic 78), Petric (Kalinic 60).
Malta: Hogg; Caruana, Grima, Hutchinson, Schembri (Fenech R 70), Sciberras (Fenech P 88), Bajada, Briffa, Mifsud, Pace, Bogdanovic (Sammut 83).
Referee: Duarte (Portugal).

Tbilisi, 26 March 2011, 55,000

Georgia (0) 1 *(Kobiashvili 90)*

Croatia (0) 0

Georgia: Revishvili; Khizanishvili, Kaladze, Amisulashvili, Salukvadze, Khubutia, Kobiashvili, Kankava, Daushvili (Siradze 46), Iashvili (Martsvaladze 62), Dvalishvili (Gogua 73).
Croatia: Runje; Srna, Corluka, Strinic, Lovren, Kranjcar (Jelavic 70), Modric, Rakitic (Perisic 61), Dujmovic, Petric (Pranjic 84), Kalinic.
Referee: Tagliavento (Italy).

Tel Aviv, 26 March 2011, 10,801

Israel (1) 2 *(Barda 16, Kayal 81)*

Latvia (0) 1 *(Gorkss 62)*

Israel: Awat; Ben Haim T, Ziv (Sahar 66), Cohen T, Tawatha, Gershon, Natcho, Refaelov (Vermouth 85), Kayal, Barda (Buzaglo 69), Damari.
Latvia: Vanins; Gorkss, Krjauklis, Kacanovs, Ivanovs, Rafalskis (Zigajevs 58), Lazdins, Rubins (Pereplotkins 58), Verpakovskis (Turkovs 73), Rudnevs, Lukjanovs.
Referee: Mazic (Serbia).

Ta'Qali, 26 March 2011, 10,605

Malta (0) 0

Greece (0) 1 *(Torosidis 90)*

Malta: Haber; Caruana (Pace 46), Mamo, Agius, Hutchinson, Schembri (Cohen 90), Sciberras, Bajada (Fenech R 78), Briffa, Mifsud, Bogdanovic.
Greece: Tzorvas; Papadopoulos, Torosidis, Papastathopoulos■, Tzavelas, Karagounis, Katsouranis, Ninis (Kone 81), Samaras, Liberopoulos (Mitroglou 70), Salpingidis (Fetfatzidis 61).
Referee: Weiner (Germany).

Tel Aviv, 29 March 2011, 13,716

Israel (0) 1 *(Ben Haim T II 59)*

Georgia (0) 0

Israel: Awat; Ben Haim T, Bondarv, Keinan, Gershon, Natcho (Ben Haim T II 52), Refaelov (Vermouth 63), Almog Cohen, Buzaglo, Kayal, Barda (Benayoun 71).
Georgia: Revishvili; Khizanishvili, Kaladze, Amisulashvili, Salukvadze, Khubutia, Kobiashvili, Kankava, Daushvili (Kvirkvelia 46), Iashvili (Dvalishvili 63), Martsvaladze (Siradze 73).
Referee: Fautrel (France).

Split, 3 June 2011, 28,000

Croatia (0) 2 *(Mandzukic 76, Kalinic 78)*

Georgia (1) 1 *(Kankava 16)*

Croatia: Runje; Simunic, Srna, Corluka, Modric, Pranjic, Perisic (Dujmovic 70), Vukojevic (Klasnic 70), Eduardo Da Silva, Jelavic (Kalinic 46), Mandzukic.
Georgia: Loria; Khizanishvili, Kaladze, Salukvadze, Kvirkvelia, Grigalava, Khubutia, Kashia (Ananidze 80), Kankava, Iashvili (Daushvili 62), Siradze (Dvalishvili 56).
Referee: Johannesson (Sweden).

Piraeus, 4 June 2011, 14,746

Greece (2) 3 *(Fetfatzidis 8, 64, Papadopoulos 26)*

Malta (0) 1 *(Mifsud 54)*

Greece: Konstantopoulos; Torosidis, Papadopoulos, Moras, Spiropoulos, Karagounis (Kafes 70), Katsouranis, Tziolis, Ninis (Christodoulopoulos 79), Fetfatzidis, Salpingidis (Mitroglou 90).
Malta: Hogg; Caruana, Agius, Hutchinson (Fenech P 87), Schembri, Sciberras, Bajada (Failla 80), Briffa, Fenech R, Mifsud, Bogdanovic (Cohen 59).
Referee: Gil (Poland).

Riga, 4 June 2011, 6147

Latvia (0) 1 *(Cauna 62 (pen))*

Israel (2) 2 *(Benayoun 20, Ben Haim T 43 (pen))*

Latvia: Vanins; Gorkss, Krjauklis, Ivanovs, Klava, Rafalskis (Zigajevs 28), Lazdins, Cauna, Visnakovs (Rugins 71), Rudnevs, Pereplotkins (Cauna 60).
Israel: Awat; Ben Haim T, Keinan, Shpungin, Gershon, Benayoun, Zahavi (Golasa 89), Refaelov (Ben Haim T II 79), Almog Cohen, Buzaglo (Natcho 69), Hemed.
Referee: Kelly (Republic of Ireland).

Group F	P	W	D	L	F	A	Pts
Greece	6	4	2	0	8	3	14
Croatia	6	4	1	1	10	3	13
Israel	7	4	1	2	10	7	13
Georgia	7	2	3	2	5	5	9
Latvia	6	1	1	4	5	9	4
Malta	6	0	0	6	2	13	0

GROUP G

Wembley, 3 September 2010, 73,426

England (1) 4 *(Defoe 3, 61, 86, Johnson A 83)*

Bulgaria (0) 0

England: Hart; Johnson G, Cole, Barry, Dawson (Cahill 56), Jagielka, Walcott (Johnson A 74), Gerrard, Defoe (Young A 87), Rooney, Milner.
Bulgaria: Mihaylov; Milanov, Stoyanov, Ivanov, Manolev (Minev 66), Petrov S, Yankov, Petrov M, Angelov, Popov (Peev 79), Bozhinov (Rangelov 63).
Referee: Kassai (Hungary).

Podgorica, 3 September 2010, 7442

Montenegro (1) 1 *(Vucinic 30)*

Wales (0) 0

Montenegro: Bozovic M; Basa, Dzudovic, Jovanovic, Zverotic, Pavicevic, Boskovic B (Bozovic V 74), Pekovic, Vukcevic (Beciraj 87), Vucinic, Dalovic (Novakovic 83).
Wales: Hennessey; Gunter, Bale, Collins J (Morgan C 75), Williams A, Ricketts, Edwards D (Earnshaw 68), Ledley, Morison (Church 78), Bellamy, Vaughan.
Referee: Kakos (Greece).

Sofia, 7 September 2010, 9470

Bulgaria (0) 0

Montenegro (1) 1 *(Zverotic 35)*

Bulgaria: Mihaylov; Milanov (Genchev 47), Stoyanov, Minev, Ivanov, Petrov S, Petrov M, Angelov, Peev (Domovchiyski 67), Popov, Rangelov (Bozhinov 47).
Montenegro: Bozovic M; Basa, Dzudovic, Jovanovic, Zverotic (Novakovic 68), Pavicevic, Boskovic B (Bozovic V 64), Pekovic, Vukcevic, Vucinic, Dalovic (Kascelan 77).
Referee: Bezborodov (Russia).

Basle, 7 September 2010, 37,500

Switzerland (0) 1 *(Shaqiri 71)*

England (1) 3 *(Rooney 10, Johnson A 69, Bent 88)*

Switzerland: Benaglio; Grichting, Lichtsteiner[■], Ziegler, Von Bergen, Degen (Streller 64), Schwegler (Costanzo 83), Inler, Margairaz (Shaqiri 46), Frei, Derdiyok.
England: Hart; Johnson G, Cole, Barry, Lescott, Jagielka, Walcott (Johnson A 13), Gerrard, Defoe (Bent 70), Rooney (Wright-Phillips 79), Milner.
Referee: Rizzoli (Italy).

Podgorica, 8 October 2010, 10,750

Montenegro (0) 1 *(Vucinic 67)*

Switzerland (0) 0

Montenegro: Bozovic M; Basa, Dzudovic, Jovanovic, Savic, Boskovic B (Kascelan 46), Vukcevic (Beciraj 86), Zverotic, Novakovic, Vucinic, Balovic (Batak 90).
Switzerland: Wolfli; Grichting, Ziegler, Von Bergen, Schwegler, Inler, Sutter, Stocker (Yakin 76), Shaqiri (Barnetta 67), Frei, Streller (Derdiyok 67).
Referee: Gonzalez (Spain).

Cardiff, 8 October 2010, 14,061

Wales (0) 0

Bulgaria (0) 1 *(Popov 48)*

Wales: Hennessey; Gunter[■], Bale, Collins D, Williams A, Collins J, Ricketts, Edwards D (Church 69), Morison (Robson-Kanu 82), Ledley (King 59), Vaughan.
Bulgaria: Mihaylov; Iliev (Vidanov 37), Ivanov, Dimov, Zanev, Petrov S, Petrov M, Peev (Rangelov 72), Georgiev, Popov, Makriev (Yankov 87).
Referee: Eriksson (Sweden).

Wembley, 12 October 2010, 73,451

England (0) 0

Montenegro (0) 0

England: Hart; Johnson G, Cole, Barry, Ferdinand, Lescott, Young A (Wright-Phillips 74), Gerrard, Crouch (Davies 70), Rooney, Johnson A.
Montenegro: Bozovic M; Basa, Dzudovic, Jovanovic, Savic, Boskovic B (Beciraj 82), Pekovic, Vukcevic, Zverotic, Novakovic (Kascelan 62), Dalovic (Delibasic 77).
Referee: Grafe (Germany).

Basle, 12 October 2010, 26,000

Switzerland (2) 4 *(Stocker 9, 89, Streller 22, Inler 82 (pen))*

Wales (1) 1 *(Bale 13)*

Switzerland: Benaglio (Wolfli 8); Grichting, Lichtsteiner, Ziegler, Von Bergen, Barnetta, Schwegler (Gelson 90), Inler, Stocker, Frei (Derdiyok 79), Streller.
Wales: Hennessey; Blake (Ribeiro 54), Bale, Collins J, Williams A, Collins D, Edwards D (Morison 77), King, Church, Crofts, Vaughan (MacDonald 89).
Referee: Hamer (Luxembourg).

Sofia, 26 March 2011, 9600

Bulgaria (0) 0

Switzerland (0) 0

Bulgaria: Mihaylov; Ivanov, Manolev, Bandalovski, Zanev, Stoyanov, Petrov S, Georgiev, Popov (Angelov 85), Stoyanov, Petrov S, Georgiev, Popov (Angelov 85).
Switzerland: Wolfli; Grichting, Lichtsteiner, Ziegler, Von Bergen, Behrami (Gelson 17), Dzemaili, Inler, Stocker (Derdiyok 67), Frei, Streller (Gavranovic 77).
Referee: Collum (Scotland).

Cardiff, 26 March 2011, 68,959

Wales (0) 0

England (2) 2 *(Lampard 7 (pen), Bent 15)*

Wales: Hennessey; Gunter, Collins D, King (Vaughan 65), Collins J, Williams A, Crofts, Ramsey, Morison (Evans C 65), Bellamy, Ledley.
England: Hart; Johnson G, Cole, Parker (Jagielka 88), Terry, Dawson, Young A, Lampard, Bent, Rooney (Milner 70), Wilshere (Downing 82).
Referee: Benquerenca (Portugal).

Wembley, 4 June 2011, 84,459

England (1) 2 *(Lampard 37 (pen), Young A 51)*

Switzerland (2) 2 *(Barnetta 32, 35)*

England: Hart; Johnson G, Cole (Baines 30), Parker, Terry, Ferdinand, Walcott (Downing 77), Wilshere, Bent, Lampard (Young A 46), Milner.
Switzerland: Benaglio; Djourou, Senderos, Lichtsteiner, Ziegler, Barnetta (Emeghara 90), Behrami (Dzemaili 58), Inler, Shaqiri, Xhaka, Derdiyok (Mehmedi 74).
Referee: Skomina (Slovenia).

England's Leighton Baines hurdles a challenge from Switzerland's Stephan Lichtsteiner (left) in the UEFA Euro 2012 Group C game at Wembley. England were 2-0 down before a Frank Lampard penalty and a terrific strike from substitute Ashley Young saved their blushes. (PA Photos)

Podgorica, 4 June 2011, 11,500
Montenegro (0) 1 *(Dalovic 53)*
Bulgaria (0) 1 *(Popov 66)*
Montenegro: Bozovic M (Fatic 76); Basa, Zverotic (Jovetic 72), Pavicevic (Kascelan 82), Pejovic, Savic, Pekovic, Drincic, Bozovic V, Vucinic, Dalovic.
Bulgaria: Mihaylov; Ivanov, Manolev, Bodurov, Bandalovski, Zanev, Petrov S (Yankov 46), Petrov M (Delev 88), Yanev (Genkov 84), Marquinhos, Popov.
Referee: Yefet (Israel).

Group G	P	W	D	L	F	A	Pts
England	5	3	2	0	11	3	11
Montenegro	5	3	2	0	4	1	11
Switzerland	5	1	2	2	7	7	5
Bulgaria	5	1	2	2	2	6	5
Wales	4	0	0	4	1	8	0

GROUP H

Reykjavik, 3 September 2010, 6137
Iceland (1) 1 *(Helguson 38)*
Norway (0) 2 *(Hangeland 59, Abdellaoue 75)*
Iceland: Gunnleifsson; Steinsson (Adalsteinsson 76), Ottesen, Sigurdsson K, Sigurdsson I, Jonsson, Gunnarsson A, Sigurdsson G, Gudmundsson J (Gislason 87), Helguson, Gunnarsson V (Bjarnason 76).
Norway: Knudsen; Riise J, Hangeland, Waehler, Hogli, Pedersen M, Hauger, Riise B (Iversen 57), Grindheim, Huseklepp (Ruud 76), Abdellaoue (Solli 88).
Referee: Banti (Italy).

Guimaraes, 3 September 2010, 9100
Portugal (2) 4 *(Hugo Almeida 8, Raul Meireles 29, Danny 50, Manuel Fernandes 60)*
Cyprus (2) 4 *(Aloneftis 3, Konstantinou 11, Okkas 57, Avraam 89)*
Portugal: Eduardo; Ricardo Carvalho, Miguel, Bruno Alves, Fabio Coentrao, Raul Meireles, Quaresma, Nani, Manuel Fernandes (Joao Moutinho 79), Danny (Liedson 61), Hugo Almeida (Yannick Djalo 84).
Cyprus: Georgallides; Charalambous, Ilia (Poursaitidis 66), Merkis, Aloneftis (Okkas 56), Charalambidis (Nikolaou 76), Makridis, Dobrasinovic, Satsias, Avraam, Konstantinou.
Referee: Clattenburg (England).

Copenhagen, 7 September 2010, 18,908
Denmark (0) 1 *(Kahlenberg 90)*
Iceland (0) 0
Denmark: Lindegaard; Agger, Kjaer, Jessen, Jacobsen, Kahlenberg, Poulsen C, Eriksen (Junker 56), Krohn-Dehli (Vingaard 77), Rommedahl, Pedersen (Skoubo 71).
Iceland: Gunnleifsson; Ottesen, Sigurdsson K, Sigurdsson I, Saevarsson, Gislason, Jonsson, Gunnarsson A, Sigurdsson G, Gudmundsson J (Bjarnason 90), Helguson (Sigurdsson R 77).
Referee: McDonald (Scotland).

Oslo, 7 September 2010, 24,535
Norway (1) 1 *(Huseklepp 21)*
Portugal (0) 0
Norway: Knudsen; Hangeland, Ruud, Waehler (Demidov 28), Hogli, Pedersen M, Hauger, Riise B, Grindheim (Jenssen 86), Carew (Abdellaoue 38), Huseklepp.
Portugal: Eduardo; Ricardo Carvalho, Bruno Alves, Silvio, Tiago (Danny 72), Raul Meireles, Quaresma (Liedson 84), Nani, Manuel Fernandes, Miguel Veloso, Hugo Almeida.
Referee: Duhamel (France).

Larnaca, 8 October 2010, 7648
Cyprus (0) 1 *(Okkas 58)*
Norway (2) 2 *(Riise J 2, Carew 42)*
Cyprus: Georgallides; Charalambous (Efrem 86), Poursaitidis, Merkis (Christofi 81), Aloneftis, Charalambidis (Satsias 46), Makridis, Dobrasinovic, Avraam, Okkas, Konstantinou.
Norway: Knudsen; Riise J, Hangeland, Waehler, Hogli, Pedersen, Hauger, Riise B (Moen 74), Grindheim, Carew (Abdellaoue 83), Huseklepp (Ruud 80).
Referee: Gumienny (Belgium).

Oporto, 8 October 2010, 27,117
Portugal (2) 3 *(Nani 29, 31, Cristiano Ronaldo 85)*
Denmark (0) 1 *(Ricardo Carvalho 79 (og))*
Portugal: Eduardo; Ricardo Carvalho, Pepe, Fabio Coentrao, Joao Pereira, Raul Meireles, Nani (Silvestre Varela 86), Joao Moutinho, Carlos Martins (Tiago 75), Cristiano Ronaldo, Hugo Almeida (Helder Postiga 69).
Denmark: Sorensen (Lindegaard 32), Kroldrup, Kvist (Lovenkrands 72), Kjaer, Jacobsen, Jensen (Eriksen 58), Poulsen C, Silberbauer, Vingaard, Rommedahl, Pedersen.
Referee: Braamhaar (Holland).

Copenhagen, 12 October 2010, 15,544
Denmark (0) 2 *(Rasmussen 48, Lorentzen 81)*
Cyprus (0) 0
Denmark: Lindegaard; Agger (Kroldrup 39), Kjaer, Jessen, Jacobsen, Poulsen C, Junker (Rasmussen 46), Krohn-Dehli (Eriksen 65), Rommedahl, Lorentzen, Pedersen.
Cyprus: Georgallides; Charalambous (Christou 28), Merkis, Satsias, Poursaitidis, Makrides, Dobrasinovic, Okkas, Konstantinou, Avraam (Garpozis 64), Aloneftis (Charalambides 54).
Referee: Fernandez (Spain).

Reykjavik, 12 October 2010, 9767
Iceland (1) 1 *(Helguson 17)*
Portugal (2) 3 *(Cristiano Ronaldo 3, Raul Meireles 27, Helder Postiga 72)*
Iceland: Gunnleifsson; Steinsson, Sigurdsson R, Sigurdsson K, Sigurdsson I (Adalsteinsson 86), Saevarsson (Gunnarsson V 85), Skulason, Danielsson, Bjarnason (Thorvaldsson 68), Helguson, Gudjohnsen.
Portugal: Eduardo; Ricardo Carvalho, Pepe, Fabio Coentrao, Joao Pereira, Raul Meireles, Nani (Danny 88), Joao Moutinho, Carlos Martins (Tiago 77), Cristiano Ronaldo, Hugo Almeida (Helder Postiga 66).
Referee: Einwaller (Austria).

Strovolos, 26 March 2011, 2088
Cyprus (0) 0
Iceland (0) 0
Cyprus: Georgallides; Poursaitidis (Ilia 61), Merkis, Sielis (Demetriou 46), Aloneftis, Charalambidis, Makridis, Dobrasinovic, Michael, Avraam, Christofi (Alexandrou 73).
Iceland: Magnusson; Hreidarsson, Sigurdsson K, Sigurdsson I, Saevarsson, Gislason (Finnbogason 63), Jonsson, Gunnarsson A, Gudmundsson J (Smarason 59), Sigurdsson G (Bjarnason 90), Helguson.
Referee: Ceferin (Slovenia).

Oslo, 26 March 2011, 24,828
Norway (0) 1 *(Huseklepp 81)*
Denmark (1) 1 *(Rommedahl 28)*
Norway: Jarstein; Riise J, Hangeland, Ruud (Braaten 78), Waehler, Pedersen, Hauger, Riise B, Grindheim, Huseklepp (Iversen 89), Abdellaoue.
Denmark: Sorensen; Agger, Kvist, Jacobsen, Jorgensen, Poulsen C (Poulsen J 70), Silberbauer, Eriksen, Krohn-Dehli (Enevoldsen 82), Rommedahl (Wass 90), Bendtner.
Referee: Rocchi (Italy).

Reykjavik, 4 June 2011, 7629
Iceland (0) 0
Denmark (0) 2 *(Schone 60, Eriksen 75)*
Iceland: Magnusson; Hreidarsson, Sigurdsson K, Saevarsson, Eiriksson, Skulason (Finnbogason 67), Gunnarsson A, Sigurdsson G, Helguson (Gudmundsson J 77), Gudjohnsen, Sigthorsson.
Denmark: Sorensen; Svensson, Kvist (Poulsen C 62), Kjaer, Jacobsen, Zimling, Poulsen S, Eriksen, Krohn-Dehli (Schone 46), Rommedahl, Bendtner.
Referee: Firat (Turkey).

Lisbon, 4 June 2011, 47,829
Portugal (0) 1 *(Helder Postiga 53)*
Norway (0) 0
Portugal: Eduardo; Pepe, Bruno Alves, Fabio Coentrao, Joao Pereira (Silvio 73), Raul Meireles, Nani (Silvestre Varela 86), Joao Moutinho, Carlos Martins (Ruben 69), Cristiano Ronaldo, Helder Postiga.

Norway: Jarstein; Riise J, Hangeland, Hogli, Demidov, Pedersen, Hauger, Riise B, Grindheim (Henriksen 83), Carew (Abdellaoue 60), Huseklepp (Braaten 75).
Referee: Cuneyt (Turkey).

Group H	P	W	D	L	F	A	Pts
Portugal	5	3	1	1	11	7	10
Denmark	5	3	1	1	7	4	10
Norway	5	3	1	1	6	4	10
Cyprus	4	0	2	2	5	8	2
Iceland	5	0	1	4	2	8	1

GROUP I

Vaduz, 3 September 2010, 6100

Liechtenstein (0) 0

Spain (2) 4 *(Torres 18, 54, David Villa 26, David Silva 62)*

Liechtenstein: Jehle; Martin Stocklasa, Oehri (Vogt 46), Michael Stocklasa, Eberle (Rechsteiner 46), Burgmeier, Polverino, Wieser (Buchel R 82), Frick M, Erne, Hasler D.
Spain: Casillas; Marchena, Sergio Ramos, Pique, Capdevila, Iniesta (Pedro 65), Xabi Alonso, Xavi (Fabregas 46), Sergio Busquets, Torres (David Silva 58), David Villa.
Referee: Bulent (Turkey).

Kaunas, 3 September 2010, 5248

Lithuania (0) 0

Scotland (0) 0

Lithuania: Karcemarskas; Stankevicius, Skerla, Kijanskas, Mikoliunas (Poskus 71), Semberas, Cesnauskis E, Panka, Sernas (Luksa 80), Radavicius, Danilevicius (Ivaskevicius 90).
Scotland: McGregor; Hutton, Whittaker (Berra 90), McCulloch, Weir, McManus, Robson (McFadden 69), Brown (Morrison 76), Fletcher D, Miller, Naismith.
Referee: Cuneyt (Turkey).

Olomouc, 7 September 2010, 12,038

Czech Republic (0) 0

Lithuania (1) 1 *(Sernas 26)*

Czech Republic: Cech; Hubschman, Hubnik, Pospech, Kadlec M, Plasil, Polak (Stajner 75), Rosicky, Pudil (Bednar 83), Baros, Fenin (Necid 63).
Lithuania: Karcemarskas; Stankevicius, Skerla, Kijanskas, Mikoliunas (Luksa 76), Semberas, Cesnauskis E, Panka, Sernas (Poskus 65), Radavicius, Danilevicius (Ivaskevicius 90).
Referee: Yefet (Israel).

Hampden Park, 7 September 2010, 37,050

Scotland (0) 2 *(Miller 62, McManus 90)*

Liechtenstein (0) 1 *(Frick M 46)*

Scotland: McGregor; Hutton, Wallace L (Robson 54), McCulloch, Weir, McManus, Fletcher D, Brown, Boyd (Naismith 66), Miller, McFadden (Morrison 46).
Liechtenstein: Jehle; Martin Stocklasa, Oehri, Michael Stocklasa, Rechsteiner, Burgmeier, Polverino, Wieser (Buchel R 71), Frick M (D'Elia 79), Erne, Hasler D (Hasler N 90).
Referee: Shvetsov (Ukraine).

Prague, 8 October 2010, 14,922

Czech Republic (0) 1 *(Hubnik 69)*

Scotland (0) 0

Czech Republic: Cech; Hubschman, Hubnik, Suchy, Pospech, Kadlec M, Plasil (Rajnoch 90), Polak, Rosicky, Necid (Holek 84), Magera (Bednar 59).
Scotland: McGregor; Hutton, Whittaker, Morrison (Robson 84), Caldwell G (Iwelumo 76), Weir, McManus, Fletcher D, Mackie (Miller 78), Naismith, Dorrans.
Referee: Bebek (Croatia).

Salamanca, 8 October 2010, 16,800

Spain (0) 3 *(Llorente 47, 56, David Silva 79)*

Lithuania (0) 1 *(Sernas 54)*

Spain: Casillas; Puyol, Sergio Ramos (Arbeloa 83), Pique, Capdevila, Iniesta, David Silva, Cazorla, Sergio Busquets, David Villa (Pablo Hernandez 76), Llorente (Aduriz 77).

Lithuania: Karcemarskas; Stankevicius, Skerla, Kijanskas, Mikoliunas (Cesnauskis D 59), Semberas, Cesnauskis E (Poskus 84), Panka, Sernas, Radavicius, Danilevicius (Ivaskevicius 82).
Referee: Rocchi (Italy).

Vaduz, 12 October 2010, 2555

Liechtenstein (0) 0

Czech Republic (2) 2 *(Necid 12, Kadlec V 28)*

Liechtenstein: Jehle; Martin Stocklasa, Oehri, Michael Stocklasa, Rechsteiner, Burgmeier, Polverino, Wieser (Buchel R 84), Frick M, Beck T (Hasler N 67), Erne (Hanselmann 78).
Czech Republic: Cech; Hubschman, Hubnik, Suchy, Pospech, Kadlec M, Plasil, Polak (Stajner 59), Rosicky, Necid (Petrzela 89), Kadlec V (Bednar 64).
Referee: Sukhina (Russia).

Glasgow, 12 October 2010, 51,322

Scotland (0) 2 *(Naismith 58, Pique 66 (og))*

Spain (1) 3 *(David Villa 44 (pen), Iniesta 56, Llorente 79)*

Scotland: McGregor; Whittaker[■], Bardsley, McCulloch (Adam 46), Weir, McManus, Morrison (Maloney 88), Fletcher D, Naismith, Miller, Dorrans (Mackie 80).
Spain: Casillas; Puyol, Sergio Ramos, Pique, Capdevila, Iniesta, Xabi Alonso, David Silva (Llorente 76), Cazorla (Pablo Hernandez 70), Sergio Busquets (Marchena 90), David Villa.
Referee: Busacca (Switzerland).

Grenada, 25 March 2011, 16,301

Spain (0) 2 *(David Villa 69, 72 (pen))*

Czech Republic (1) 1 *(Plasil 29)*

Spain: Casillas; Sergio Ramos, Arbeloa, Pique, Capdevila (Cazorla 58), Iniesta, Xabi Alonso (Torres 46), Xavi, Jesus Navas (Marchena 87), Sergio Busquets, David Villa.
Czech Republic: Cech; Hubschman, Hubnik, Sivok, Pospech, Kadlec M, Plasil, Rosicky, Pudil (Hlousek 78), Baros, Rezek (Necid 84).
Referee: Kassai (Hungary).

Budejovice, 29 March 2011, 6600

Czech Republic (1) 2 *(Baros 3, Kadlec M 70)*

Liechtenstein (0) 0

Czech Republic: Cech; Hubschman, Hubnik, Sivok, Pospech, Kadlec M, Plasil, Rosicky (Polak 84), Moravek (Hlousek 56), Baros, Lafata (Necid 59).
Liechtenstein: Jehle; Martin Stocklasa, Michael Stocklasa, Rechsteiner, Burgmeier, Buchel M (Kieber 10) (Christen A 81), Hasler N, Frick M, Beck T, Erne, Hasler D.
Referee: Hategan (Romania).

Kaunas, 29 March 2011, 9180

Lithuania (0) 1 *(Stankevicius 57)*

Spain (1) 3 *(Xavi 19, Kijanskas 70 (og), Mata 83)*

Lithuania: Karcemarskas; Zaliukas, Stankevicius, Skerla, Kijanskas, Mikoliunas (Radavicius 71), Semberas, Cesnauskis E, Panka, Sernas (Labukas 74), Danilevicius (Galkevicius 85).
Spain: Casillas; Albiol, Arbeloa, Pique (Sergio Ramos 89), Andoni Iraola, Xabi Alonso, Xavi, Javi Martinez, Cazorla (Mata 67), David Villa (David Silva 54), Llorente.
Referee: Duhamel (France).

Vaduz, 3 June 2011, 1886

Liechtenstein (2) 2 *(Erne 6, Polverino 36)*

Lithuania (0) 0

Liechtenstein: Buchel B; Ritzberger, Martin Stocklasa, Kaufmann, Burgmeier, Buchel M, Polverino, Hasler N, Fischer (Christen M 72), Beck T (Christen A 84), Erne (Hanselmann 87).
Lithuania: Setkus; Stankevicius (Labukas 46), Skerla, Kijanskas, Mikoliunas, Semberas, Cesnauskis E (Savenas 68), Panka, Sernas, Radavicius, Danilevicius (Cesnauskis D 46).
Referee: Kuchin (Kazakhstan).

Group I	P	W	D	L	F	A	Pts
Spain	5	5	0	0	15	5	15
Czech Republic	5	3	0	2	6	3	9
Scotland	4	1	1	2	4	5	4
Lithuania	5	1	1	3	3	8	4
Liechtenstein	5	1	0	4	3	10	3

EURO 2012 REMAINING FIXTURES

10 AUGUST 2011
Group C   Northern Ireland v Faeroe Islands

02 SEPTEMBER 2011
Group A   Germany v Austria
Group A   Turkey v Kazakhstan
Group A   Azerbaijan v Belgium
Group B   Russia v FYR Macedonia
Group B   Republic of Ireland v Slovakia
Group B   Andorra v Armenia
Group C   Northern Ireland v Serbia
Group C   Slovenia v Estonia
Group C   Faeroe Islands v Italy
Group D   Belarus v Bosnia-Herzegovina
Group D   Albania v France
Group D   Luxembourg v Romania
Group E   Netherlands v San Marino
Group E   Finland v Moldova
Group E   Hungary v Sweden
Group F   Israel v Greece
Group F   Georgia v Latvia
Group F   Malta v Croatia
Group G   Bulgaria v England
Group G   Wales v Montenegro
Group H   Norway v Iceland
Group H   Cyprus v Portugal
Group I   Lithuania v Liechtenstein

03 SEPTEMBER 2011
Group I   Scotland v Czech Republic

06 SEPTEMBER 2011
Group A   Austria v Turkey
Group A   Azerbaijan v Kazakhstan
Group B   Russia v Republic of Ireland
Group B   Slovakia v Armenia
Group B   FYR Macedonia v Andorra
Group C   Italy v Slovenia
Group C   Serbia v Faeroe Islands
Group C   Estonia v Northern Ireland
Group D   Romania v France
Group D   Bosnia-Herzegovina v Belarus
Group D   Luxembourg v Albania
Group E   Finland v Netherlands
Group E   Moldova v Hungary
Group E   San Marino v Sweden
Group F   Croatia v Israel
Group F   Latvia v Greece
Group F   Malta v Georgia
Group G   England v Wales
Group G   Switzerland v Bulgaria
Group H   Denmark v Norway

Group H   Iceland v Cyprus
Group I   Spain v Liechtenstein
Group I   Scotland v Lithuania

07 OCTOBER 2011
Group A   Turkey v Germany
Group A   Belgium v Kazakhstan
Group A   Azerbaijan v Austria
Group E   Netherlands v Moldova
Group E   Finland v Sweden
Group B   Slovakia v Russia
Group B   Armenia v FYR Macedonia
Group B   Andorra v Republic of Ireland
Group C   Serbia v Italy
Group C   Northern Ireland v Estonia
Group D   France v Albania
Group D   Romania v Belarus
Group D   Bosnia-Herzegovina v Luxembourg
Group F   Greece v Croatia
Group F   Latvia v Malta
Group G   Wales v Switzerland
Group G   Montenegro v England
Group H   Portugal v Iceland
Group H   Cyprus v Denmark
Group I   Czech Republic v Spain

08 OCTOBER 2011
Group I   Liechtenstein v Scotland

11 OCTOBER 2011
Group A   Germany v Belgium
Group A   Turkey v Azerbaijan
Group A   Kazakhstan v Austria
Group B   Russia v Andorra
Group B   Republic of Ireland v Armenia
Group B   FYR Macedonia v Slovakia
Group C   Italy v Northern Ireland
Group C   Slovenia v Serbia
Group D   France v Bosnia-Herzegovina
Group D   Albania v Romania
Group E   Sweden v Netherlands
Group E   Hungary v Finland
Group E   Moldova v San Marino
Group F   Croatia v Latvia
Group F   Georgia v Greece
Group F   Malta v Israel
Group G   Switzerland v Montenegro
Group G   Bulgaria v Wales
Group H   Denmark v Portugal
Group H   Norway v Cyprus
Group I   Spain v Scotland
Group I   Lithuania v Czech Republic

BRITISH AND IRISH INTERNATIONAL RESULTS 1872–2011

Note: In the results that follow, wc=World Cup, ec=European Championship, ui=Umbro International Trophy. tf = Tournoi de France. nc = Nations Cup. For Ireland, read Northern Ireland from 1921. *After extra time.

ENGLAND v SCOTLAND

Played: 110; England won 45, Scotland won 41, Drawn 24. Goals: England 192, Scotland 169.

Year	Date	Venue	E	S
1872	30 Nov	Glasgow	0	0
1873	8 Mar	Kennington Oval	4	2
1874	7 Mar	Glasgow	1	2
1875	6 Mar	Kennington Oval	2	2
1876	4 Mar	Glasgow	0	3
1877	3 Mar	Kennington Oval	1	3
1878	2 Mar	Glasgow	2	7
1879	5 Apr	Kennington Oval	5	4
1880	13 Mar	Glasgow	4	5
1881	12 Mar	Kennington Oval	1	6
1882	11 Mar	Glasgow	1	5
1883	10 Mar	Sheffield	2	3
1884	15 Mar	Glasgow	0	1
1885	21 Mar	Kennington Oval	1	1
1886	31 Mar	Glasgow	1	1
1887	19 Mar	Blackburn	2	3
1888	17 Mar	Glasgow	5	0
1889	13 Apr	Kennington Oval	2	3
1890	5 Apr	Glasgow	1	1
1891	6 Apr	Blackburn	2	1
1892	2 Apr	Glasgow	4	1
1893	1 Apr	Richmond	5	2
1894	7 Apr	Glasgow	2	2
1895	6 Apr	Everton	3	0
1896	4 Apr	Glasgow	1	2
1897	3 Apr	Crystal Palace	1	2
1898	2 Apr	Glasgow	3	1
1899	8 Apr	Birmingham	2	1
1900	7 Apr	Glasgow	1	4
1901	30 Mar	Crystal Palace	2	2
1902	3 Mar	Birmingham	2	2
1903	4 Apr	Sheffield	1	2
1904	9 Apr	Glasgow	1	0
1905	1 Apr	Crystal Palace	1	0
1906	7 Apr	Glasgow	1	2
1907	6 Apr	Newcastle	1	1
1908	4 Apr	Glasgow	1	1
1909	3 Apr	Crystal Palace	2	0
1910	2 Apr	Glasgow	0	2
1911	1 Apr	Everton	1	1
1912	23 Mar	Glasgow	1	1
1913	5 Apr	Chelsea	1	0
1914	14 Apr	Glasgow	1	3
1920	10 Apr	Sheffield	5	4
1921	9 Apr	Glasgow	0	3
1922	8 Apr	Aston Villa	0	1
1923	14 Apr	Glasgow	2	2
1924	12 Apr	Wembley	1	1
1925	4 Apr	Glasgow	0	2
1926	17 Apr	Manchester	0	1
1927	2 Apr	Glasgow	2	1
1928	31 Mar	Wembley	1	5
1929	13 Apr	Glasgow	0	1
1930	5 Apr	Wembley	5	2
1931	28 Mar	Glasgow	0	2
1932	9 Apr	Wembley	3	0
1933	1 Apr	Glasgow	1	2
1934	14 Apr	Wembley	3	0
1935	6 Apr	Glasgow	0	2
1936	4 Apr	Wembley	1	1
1937	17 Apr	Glasgow	1	3
1938	9 Apr	Wembley	0	1
1939	15 Apr	Glasgow	2	1
1947	12 Apr	Wembley	1	1
1948	10 Apr	Glasgow	2	0
1949	9 Apr	Wembley	1	3
wc1950	15 Apr	Glasgow	1	0
1951	14 Apr	Wembley	2	3
1952	5 Apr	Glasgow	2	1
1953	18 Apr	Wembley	2	2
wc1954	3 Apr	Glasgow	4	2
1955	2 Apr	Wembley	7	2
1956	14 Apr	Glasgow	1	1
1957	6 Apr	Wembley	2	1
1958	19 Apr	Glasgow	4	0
1959	11 Apr	Wembley	1	0
1960	9 Apr	Glasgow	1	1
1961	15 Apr	Wembley	9	3
1962	14 Apr	Glasgow	0	2
1963	6 Apr	Wembley	1	2
1964	11 Apr	Glasgow	0	1
1965	10 Apr	Wembley	2	2
1966	2 Apr	Glasgow	4	3
EC1967	15 Apr	Wembley	2	3
EC1968	24 Jan	Glasgow	1	1
1969	10 May	Wembley	4	1
1970	25 Apr	Glasgow	0	0
1971	22 May	Wembley	3	1
1972	27 May	Glasgow	1	0
1973	14 Feb	Glasgow	5	0
1973	19 May	Wembley	1	0
1974	18 May	Glasgow	0	2
1975	24 May	Wembley	5	1
1976	15 May	Glasgow	1	2
1977	4 June	Wembley	1	2
1978	20 May	Glasgow	1	0
1979	26 May	Wembley	3	1
1980	24 May	Glasgow	2	0
1981	23 May	Wembley	0	1
1982	29 May	Glasgow	1	0
1983	1 June	Wembley	2	0
1984	26 May	Glasgow	1	1
1985	25 May	Glasgow	0	1
1986	23 Apr	Wembley	2	1
1987	23 May	Glasgow	0	0
1988	21 May	Wembley	1	0
1989	27 May	Glasgow	2	0
EC1996	15 June	Wembley	2	0
EC1999	13 Nov	Glasgow	2	0
EC1999	17 Nov	Wembley	0	1

ENGLAND v WALES

Played: 100; England won 65, Wales won 14, Drawn 21. Goals: England 244, Wales 90.

Year	Date	Venue	E	W
1879	18 Jan	Kennington Oval	2	1
1880	15 Mar	Wrexham	3	2
1881	26 Feb	Blackburn	0	1
1882	13 Mar	Wrexham	3	5
1883	3 Feb	Kennington Oval	5	0
1884	17 Mar	Wrexham	4	0

			E	W
1885	14 Mar	Blackburn	1	1
1886	29 Mar	Wrexham	3	1
1887	26 Feb	Kennington Oval	4	0
1888	4 Feb	Crewe	5	1
1889	23 Feb	Stoke	4	1
1890	15 Mar	Wrexham	3	1
1891	7 May	Sunderland	4	1
1892	5 Mar	Wrexham	2	0
1893	13 Mar	Stoke	6	0
1894	12 Mar	Wrexham	5	1
1895	18 Mar	Queen's Club, Kensington	1	1
1896	16 Mar	Cardiff	9	1
1897	29 Mar	Sheffield	4	0
1898	28 Mar	Wrexham	3	0
1899	20 Mar	Bristol	4	0
1900	26 Mar	Cardiff	1	1
1901	18 Mar	Newcastle	6	0
1902	3 Mar	Wrexham	0	0
1903	2 Mar	Portsmouth	2	1
1904	29 Feb	Wrexham	2	2
1905	27 Mar	Liverpool	3	1
1906	19 Mar	Cardiff	1	0
1907	18 Mar	Fulham	1	1
1908	16 Mar	Wrexham	7	1
1909	15 Mar	Nottingham	2	0
1910	14 Mar	Cardiff	1	0
1911	13 Mar	Millwall	3	0
1912	11 Mar	Wrexham	2	0
1913	17 Mar	Bristol	4	3
1914	16 Mar	Cardiff	2	0
1920	15 Mar	Highbury	1	2
1921	14 Mar	Cardiff	0	0
1922	13 Mar	Liverpool	1	0
1923	5 Mar	Cardiff	2	2
1924	3 Mar	Blackburn	1	2
1925	28 Feb	Swansea	2	1
1926	1 Mar	Crystal Palace	1	3
1927	12 Feb	Wrexham	3	3
1927	28 Nov	Burnley	1	2
1928	17 Nov	Swansea	3	2
1929	20 Nov	Chelsea	6	0
1930	22 Nov	Wrexham	4	0
1931	18 Nov	Liverpool	3	1
1932	16 Nov	Wrexham	0	0
1933	15 Nov	Newcastle	1	2
1934	29 Sept	Cardiff	4	0
1936	5 Feb	Wolverhampton	1	2
1936	17 Oct	Cardiff	1	2
1937	17 Nov	Middlesbrough	2	1
1938	22 Oct	Cardiff	2	4
1946	13 Nov	Manchester	3	0
1947	18 Oct	Cardiff	3	0
1948	10 Nov	Aston Villa	1	0
wc1949	15 Oct	Cardiff	4	1
1950	15 Nov	Sunderland	4	2
1951	20 Oct	Cardiff	1	1
1952	12 Nov	Wembley	5	2
wc1953	10 Oct	Cardiff	4	1
1954	10 Nov	Wembley	3	2
1955	27 Oct	Cardiff	1	2
1956	14 Nov	Wembley	3	1
1957	19 Oct	Cardiff	4	0
1958	26 Nov	Aston Villa	2	2
1959	17 Oct	Cardiff	1	1
1960	23 Nov	Wembley	5	1
1961	14 Oct	Cardiff	1	1
1962	21 Oct	Wembley	4	0
1963	12 Oct	Cardiff	4	0
1964	18 Nov	Wembley	2	1
1965	2 Oct	Cardiff	0	0
EC1966	16 Nov	Wembley	5	1
EC1967	21 Oct	Cardiff	3	0
1969	7 May	Wembley	2	1
1970	18 Apr	Cardiff	1	1
1971	19 May	Wembley	0	0
1972	20 May	Cardiff	3	0
wc1972	15 Nov	Cardiff	1	0
wc1973	24 Jan	Wembley	1	1
1973	15 May	Wembley	3	0
1974	11 May	Cardiff	2	0
1975	21 May	Wembley	2	2
1976	24 Mar	Wrexham	2	1
1976	8 May	Cardiff	1	0
1977	31 May	Wembley	0	1
1978	3 May	Cardiff	3	1
1979	23 May	Wembley	0	0
1980	17 May	Wrexham	1	4
1981	20 May	Wembley	0	0
1982	27 Apr	Cardiff	1	0
1983	23 Feb	Wembley	2	1
1984	2 May	Wrexham	0	1
wc2004	9 Oct	Old Trafford	2	0
wc2005	3 Sept	Cardiff	1	0
EC2011	26 Mar	Cardiff	2	0

ENGLAND v IRELAND

Played: 98; England won 75, Ireland won 7, Drawn 16. Goals: England 323, Ireland 81.

			E	I
1882	18 Feb	Belfast	13	0
1883	24 Feb	Liverpool	7	0
1884	23 Feb	Belfast	8	1
1885	28 Feb	Manchester	4	0
1886	13 Mar	Belfast	6	1
1887	5 Feb	Sheffield	7	0
1888	31 Mar	Belfast	5	1
1889	2 Mar	Everton	6	1
1890	15 Mar	Belfast	9	1
1891	7 Mar	Wolverhampton	6	1
1892	5 Mar	Belfast	2	0
1893	25 Feb	Birmingham	6	1
1894	3 Mar	Belfast	2	2
1895	9 Mar	Derby	9	0
1896	7 Mar	Belfast	2	0
1897	20 Feb	Nottingham	6	0
1898	5 Mar	Belfast	3	2
1899	18 Feb	Sunderland	13	2
1900	17 Mar	Dublin	2	0
1901	9 Mar	Southampton	3	0
1902	22 Mar	Belfast	1	0
1903	14 Feb	Wolverhampton	4	0
1904	12 Mar	Belfast	3	1
1905	25 Feb	Middlesbrough	1	1
1906	17 Feb	Belfast	5	0
1907	16 Feb	Everton	1	0
1908	15 Feb	Belfast	3	1
1909	13 Feb	Bradford	4	0
1910	12 Feb	Belfast	1	1
1911	11 Feb	Derby	2	1
1912	10 Feb	Dublin	6	1
1913	15 Feb	Belfast	1	2
1914	14 Feb	Middlesbrough	0	3
1919	25 Oct	Belfast	1	1
1920	23 Oct	Sunderland	2	0
1921	22 Oct	Belfast	1	1
1922	21 Oct	West Bromwich	2	0
1923	20 Oct	Belfast	1	2
1924	22 Oct	Everton	3	1
1925	24 Oct	Belfast	0	0
1926	20 Oct	Liverpool	3	3
1927	22 Oct	Belfast	0	2

Year	Date	Venue	E	I
1928	22 Oct	Everton	2	1
1929	19 Oct	Belfast	3	0
1930	20 Oct	Sheffield	5	1
1931	17 Oct	Belfast	6	2
1932	17 Oct	Blackpool	1	0
1933	14 Oct	Belfast	3	0
1935	6 Feb	Everton	2	1
1935	19 Oct	Belfast	3	1
1936	18 Nov	Stoke	3	1
1937	23 Oct	Belfast	5	1
1938	16 Nov	Manchester	7	0
1946	28 Sept	Belfast	7	2
1947	5 Nov	Everton	2	2
1948	9 Oct	Belfast	6	2
wc1949	16 Nov	Manchester	9	2
1950	7 Oct	Belfast	4	1
1951	14 Nov	Aston Villa	2	0
1952	4 Oct	Belfast	2	2
wc1953	11 Nov	Everton	3	1
1954	2 Oct	Belfast	2	0
1955	2 Nov	Wembley	3	0
1956	10 Oct	Belfast	1	1
1957	6 Nov	Wembley	2	3
1958	4 Oct	Belfast	3	3
1959	18 Nov	Wembley	2	1
1960	8 Oct	Belfast	5	2
1961	22 Nov	Wembley	1	1
1962	20 Oct	Belfast	3	1
1963	20 Nov	Wembley	8	3
1964	3 Oct	Belfast	4	3
1965	10 Nov	Wembley	2	1
EC1966	20 Oct	Belfast	2	0
EC1967	22 Nov	Wembley	2	0
1969	3 May	Belfast	3	1
1970	21 Apr	Wembley	3	1
1971	15 May	Belfast	1	0
1972	23 May	Wembley	0	1
1973	12 May	Everton	2	1
1974	15 May	Wembley	1	0
1975	17 May	Belfast	0	0
1976	11 May	Wembley	4	0
1977	28 May	Belfast	2	1
1978	16 May	Wembley	1	0
EC1979	7 Feb	Wembley	4	0
1979	19 May	Belfast	2	0
EC1979	17 Oct	Belfast	5	1
1980	20 May	Wembley	1	1
1982	23 Feb	Wembley	4	0
1983	28 May	Belfast	0	0
1984	24 Apr	Wembley	1	0
wc1985	27 Feb	Belfast	1	0
wc1985	13 Nov	Wembley	0	0
EC1986	15 Oct	Wembley	3	0
EC1987	1 Apr	Belfast	2	0
wc2005	26 Mar	Old Trafford	4	0
wc2005	7 Sept	Belfast	0	1

SCOTLAND v WALES

Played: 105; Scotland won 61, Wales won 21, Drawn 23. Goals: Scotland 241, Wales 120.

Year	Date	Venue	S	W
1876	25 Mar	Glasgow	4	0
1877	5 Mar	Wrexham	2	0
1878	23 Mar	Glasgow	9	0
1879	7 Apr	Wrexham	3	0
1880	3 Apr	Glasgow	5	1
1881	14 Mar	Wrexham	5	1
1882	25 Mar	Glasgow	5	0
1883	12 Mar	Wrexham	3	0
1884	29 Mar	Glasgow	4	1
1885	23 Mar	Wrexham	8	1
1886	10 Apr	Glasgow	4	1
1887	21 Mar	Wrexham	2	0
1888	10 Mar	Edinburgh	5	1
1889	15 Apr	Wrexham	0	0
1890	22 Mar	Paisley	5	0
1891	21 Mar	Wrexham	4	3
1892	26 Mar	Edinburgh	6	1
1893	18 Mar	Wrexham	8	0
1894	24 Mar	Kilmarnock	5	2
1895	23 Mar	Wrexham	2	2
1896	21 Mar	Dundee	4	0
1897	20 Mar	Wrexham	2	2
1898	19 Mar	Motherwell	5	2
1899	18 Mar	Wrexham	6	0
1900	3 Feb	Aberdeen	5	2
1901	2 Mar	Wrexham	1	1
1902	15 Mar	Greenock	5	1
1903	9 Mar	Cardiff	1	0
1904	12 Mar	Dundee	1	1
1905	6 Mar	Wrexham	1	3
1906	3 Mar	Edinburgh	0	2
1907	4 Mar	Wrexham	0	1
1908	7 Mar	Dundee	2	1
1909	1 Mar	Wrexham	2	3
1910	5 Mar	Kilmarnock	1	0
1911	6 Mar	Cardiff	2	2
1912	2 Mar	Tynecastle	1	0
1913	3 Mar	Wrexham	0	0
1914	28 Feb	Glasgow	0	0
1920	26 Feb	Cardiff	1	1
1921	12 Feb	Aberdeen	2	1
1922	4 Feb	Wrexham	1	2
1923	17 Mar	Paisley	2	0
1924	16 Feb	Cardiff	0	2
1925	14 Feb	Tynecastle	3	1
1925	31 Oct	Cardiff	3	0
1926	30 Oct	Glasgow	3	0
1927	29 Oct	Wrexham	2	2
1928	27 Oct	Glasgow	4	2
1929	26 Oct	Cardiff	4	2
1930	25 Oct	Glasgow	1	1
1931	31 Oct	Wrexham	3	2
1932	26 Oct	Edinburgh	2	5
1933	4 Oct	Cardiff	2	3
1934	21 Nov	Aberdeen	3	2
1935	5 Oct	Cardiff	1	1
1936	2 Dec	Dundee	1	2
1937	30 Oct	Cardiff	1	2
1938	9 Nov	Edinburgh	3	2
1946	19 Oct	Wrexham	1	3
1947	12 Nov	Glasgow	1	2
wc1948	23 Oct	Cardiff	3	1
1949	9 Nov	Glasgow	2	0
1950	21 Oct	Cardiff	3	1
1951	14 Nov	Glasgow	0	1
wc1952	18 Oct	Cardiff	2	1
1953	4 Nov	Glasgow	3	3
1954	16 Oct	Cardiff	1	0
1955	9 Nov	Glasgow	2	0
1956	20 Oct	Cardiff	2	2
1957	13 Nov	Glasgow	1	1
1958	18 Oct	Cardiff	3	0
1959	4 Nov	Glasgow	1	1
1960	20 Oct	Cardiff	0	2
1961	8 Nov	Glasgow	2	0
1962	20 Oct	Cardiff	3	2
1963	20 Nov	Glasgow	2	1
1964	3 Oct	Cardiff	2	3
EC1965	24 Nov	Glasgow	4	1
EC1966	22 Oct	Cardiff	1	1
1967	22 Nov	Glasgow	3	2
1969	3 May	Wrexham	5	3

			S	W				S	W
1970	22 Apr	Glasgow	0	0	1980	21 May	Glasgow	1	0
1971	15 May	Cardiff	0	0	1981	16 May	Swansea	0	2
1972	24 May	Glasgow	1	0	1982	24 May	Glasgow	1	0
1973	12 May	Wrexham	2	0	1983	28 May	Cardiff	2	0
1974	14 May	Glasgow	2	0	1984	28 Feb	Glasgow	2	1
1975	17 May	Cardiff	2	2	wc1985	27 Mar	Glasgow	0	1
1976	6 May	Glasgow	3	1	wc1985	10 Sept	Cardiff	1	1
wc1976	17 Nov	Glasgow	1	0	1997	27 May	Kilmarnock	0	1
1977	28 May	Wrexham	0	0	2004	18 Feb	Cardiff	0	4
wc1977	12 Oct	Liverpool	2	0	2009	14 Nov	Cardiff	0	3
1978	17 May	Glasgow	1	1	nc2011	25 May	Dublin	3	1
1979	19 May	Cardiff	0	3					

SCOTLAND v IRELAND

Played: 95; Scotland won 63, Ireland won 15, Drawn 17. Goals: Scotland 260, Ireland 81.

			S	I				S	I
1884	26 Jan	Belfast	5	0	1934	20 Oct	Belfast	1	2
1885	14 Mar	Glasgow	8	2	1935	13 Nov	Edinburgh	2	1
1886	20 Mar	Belfast	7	2	1936	31 Oct	Belfast	3	1
1887	19 Feb	Glasgow	4	1	1937	10 Nov	Aberdeen	1	1
1888	24 Mar	Belfast	10	2	1938	8 Oct	Belfast	2	0
1889	9 Mar	Glasgow	7	0	1946	27 Nov	Glasgow	0	0
1890	29 Mar	Belfast	4	1	1947	4 Oct	Belfast	0	2
1891	28 Mar	Glasgow	2	1	1948	17 Nov	Glasgow	3	2
1892	19 Mar	Belfast	3	2	1949	1 Oct	Belfast	8	2
1893	25 Mar	Glasgow	6	1	1950	1 Nov	Glasgow	6	1
1894	31 Mar	Belfast	2	1	1951	6 Oct	Belfast	3	0
1895	30 Mar	Glasgow	3	1	1952	5 Nov	Glasgow	1	1
1896	28 Mar	Belfast	3	3	1953	3 Oct	Belfast	3	1
1897	27 Mar	Glasgow	5	1	1954	3 Nov	Glasgow	2	2
1898	26 Mar	Belfast	3	0	1955	8 Oct	Belfast	1	2
1899	25 Mar	Glasgow	9	1	1956	7 Nov	Glasgow	1	0
1900	3 Mar	Belfast	3	0	1957	5 Oct	Belfast	1	1
1901	23 Feb	Glasgow	11	0	1958	5 Nov	Glasgow	2	2
1902	1 Mar	Belfast	5	1	1959	3 Oct	Belfast	4	0
1902	9 Aug	Belfast	3	0	1960	9 Nov	Glasgow	5	2
1903	21 Mar	Glasgow	0	2	1961	7 Oct	Belfast	6	1
1904	26 Mar	Dublin	1	1	1962	7 Nov	Glasgow	5	1
1905	18 Mar	Glasgow	4	0	1963	12 Oct	Belfast	1	2
1906	17 Mar	Dublin	1	0	1964	25 Nov	Glasgow	3	2
1907	16 Mar	Glasgow	3	0	1965	2 Oct	Belfast	2	3
1908	14 Mar	Dublin	5	0	1966	16 Nov	Glasgow	2	1
1909	15 Mar	Glasgow	5	0	1967	21 Oct	Belfast	0	1
1910	19 Mar	Belfast	0	1	1969	6 May	Glasgow	1	1
1911	18 Mar	Glasgow	2	0	1970	18 Apr	Belfast	1	0
1912	16 Mar	Belfast	4	1	1971	18 May	Glasgow	0	1
1913	15 Mar	Dublin	2	1	1972	20 May	Glasgow	2	0
1914	14 Mar	Belfast	1	1	1973	16 May	Glasgow	1	2
1920	13 Mar	Glasgow	3	0	1974	11 May	Glasgow	0	1
1921	26 Feb	Belfast	2	0	1975	20 May	Glasgow	3	0
1922	4 Mar	Glasgow	2	1	1976	8 May	Glasgow	3	0
1923	3 Mar	Belfast	1	0	1977	1 June	Glasgow	3	0
1924	1 Mar	Glasgow	2	0	1978	13 May	Glasgow	1	1
1925	28 Feb	Belfast	3	0	1979	22 May	Glasgow	1	0
1926	27 Feb	Glasgow	4	0	1980	17 May	Belfast	0	1
1927	26 Feb	Belfast	2	0	wc1981	25 Mar	Glasgow	1	1
1928	25 Feb	Glasgow	0	1	1981	19 May	Glasgow	2	0
1929	23 Feb	Belfast	7	3	wc1981	14 Oct	Belfast	0	0
1930	22 Feb	Glasgow	3	1	1982	28 Apr	Belfast	1	1
1931	21 Feb	Belfast	0	0	1983	24 May	Glasgow	0	0
1931	19 Sept	Glasgow	3	1	1983	13 Dec	Belfast	0	2
1932	12 Sept	Belfast	4	0	1992	19 Feb	Glasgow	1	0
1933	16 Sept	Glasgow	1	2	2008	20 Aug	Glasgow	0	0
					nc2011	9 Feb	Dublin	3	0

WALES v IRELAND

Played: 94; Wales won 44, Ireland won 27, Drawn 23. Goals: Wales 189, Ireland 131.

			W	I				W	I
1882	25 Feb	Wrexham	7	1	1886	27 Feb	Wrexham	5	0
1883	17 Mar	Belfast	1	1	1887	12 Mar	Belfast	1	4
1884	9 Feb	Wrexham	6	0	1888	3 Mar	Wrexham	11	0
1885	11 Apr	Belfast	8	2	1889	27 Apr	Belfast	3	1

			W	I				W	I
1890	8 Feb	Shrewsbury	5	2	1938	16 Mar	Belfast	0	1
1891	7 Feb	Belfast	2	7	1939	15 Mar	Wrexham	3	1
1892	27 Feb	Bangor	1	1	1947	16 Apr	Belfast	1	2
1893	8 Apr	Belfast	3	4	1948	10 Mar	Wrexham	2	0
1894	24 Feb	Swansea	4	1	1949	9 Mar	Belfast	2	0
1895	16 Mar	Belfast	2	2	wc1950	8 Mar	Wrexham	0	0
1896	29 Feb	Wrexham	6	1	1951	7 Mar	Belfast	2	1
1897	6 Mar	Belfast	3	4	1952	19 Mar	Swansea	3	0
1898	19 Feb	Llandudno	0	1	1953	15 Apr	Belfast	3	2
1899	4 Mar	Belfast	0	1	wc1954	31 Mar	Wrexham	1	2
1900	24 Feb	Llandudno	2	0	1955	20 Apr	Belfast	3	2
1901	23 Mar	Belfast	1	0	1956	11 Apr	Cardiff	1	1
1902	22 Mar	Cardiff	0	3	1957	10 Apr	Belfast	0	0
1903	28 Mar	Belfast	0	2	1958	16 Apr	Cardiff	1	1
1904	21 Mar	Bangor	0	1	1959	22 Apr	Belfast	1	4
1905	18 Apr	Belfast	2	2	1960	6 Apr	Wrexham	3	2
1906	2 Apr	Wrexham	4	4	1961	12 Apr	Belfast	5	1
1907	23 Feb	Belfast	3	2	1962	11 Apr	Cardiff	4	0
1908	11 Apr	Aberdare	0	1	1963	3 Apr	Belfast	4	1
1909	20 Mar	Belfast	3	2	1964	15 Apr	Swansea	2	3
1910	11 Apr	Wrexham	4	1	1965	31 Mar	Belfast	5	0
1911	28 Jan	Belfast	2	1	1966	30 Mar	Cardiff	1	4
1912	13 Apr	Cardiff	2	3	EC1967	12 Apr	Belfast	0	0
1913	18 Jan	Belfast	1	0	EC1968	28 Feb	Wrexham	2	0
1914	19 Jan	Wrexham	1	2	1969	10 May	Belfast	0	0
1920	14 Feb	Belfast	2	2	1970	25 Apr	Swansea	1	0
1921	9 Apr	Swansea	2	1	1971	22 May	Belfast	0	1
1922	4 Apr	Belfast	1	1	1972	27 May	Wrexham	0	0
1923	14 Apr	Wrexham	0	3	1973	19 May	Everton	0	1
1924	15 Mar	Belfast	1	0	1974	18 May	Wrexham	1	0
1925	18 Apr	Wrexham	0	0	1975	23 May	Belfast	0	1
1926	13 Feb	Belfast	0	3	1976	14 May	Swansea	1	0
1927	9 Apr	Cardiff	2	2	1977	3 June	Belfast	1	1
1928	4 Feb	Belfast	2	1	1978	19 May	Wrexham	1	0
1929	2 Feb	Wrexham	2	2	1979	25 May	Belfast	1	1
1930	1 Feb	Belfast	0	7	1980	23 May	Cardiff	0	1
1931	22 Apr	Wrexham	3	2	1982	27 May	Wrexham	3	0
1931	5 Dec	Belfast	0	4	1983	31 May	Belfast	1	0
1932	7 Dec	Wrexham	4	1	1984	22 May	Swansea	1	1
1933	4 Nov	Belfast	1	1	wc2004	8 Sept	Cardiff	2	2
1935	27 Mar	Wrexham	3	1	wc2005	8 Oct	Belfast	3	2
1936	11 Mar	Belfast	2	3	2007	6 Feb	Belfast	0	0
1937	17 Mar	Wrexham	4	1	NC2011	27 May	Dublin	2	0

OTHER BRITISH INTERNATIONAL RESULTS 1908–2010

ENGLAND

		v ALBANIA	E	A			v AUSTRALIA	E	A
wc1989	8 Mar	Tirana	2	0	1980	31 May	Sydney	2	1
wc1989	26 Apr	Wembley	5	0	1983	11 June	Sydney	0	0
wc2001	28 Mar	Tirana	3	1	1983	15 June	Brisbane	1	0
wc2001	5 Sept	Newcastle	2	0	1983	18 June	Melbourne	1	1
					1991	1 June	Sydney	1	0
		v ALGERIA	E	A	2003	12 Feb	West Ham	1	3
wc2010	18 June	Cape Town	0	0					
							v AUSTRIA	E	A
		v ANDORRA	E	A	1908	6 June	Vienna	6	1
EC2006	2 Sept	Old Trafford	5	0	1908	8 June	Vienna	11	1
EC2007	28 Mar	Barcelona	3	0	1909	1 June	Vienna	8	1
wc2008	6 Sept	Barcelona	2	0	1930	14 May	Vienna	0	0
wc2009	10 June	Wembley	6	0	1932	7 Dec	Chelsea	4	3
					1936	6 May	Vienna	1	2
		v ARGENTINA	E	A	1951	28 Nov	Wembley	2	2
1951	9 May	Wembley	2	1	1952	25 May	Vienna	3	2
1953	17 May	Buenos Aires	0	0	wc1958	15 June	Boras	2	2
(abandoned after 21 mins)					1961	27 May	Vienna	1	3
wc1962	2 June	Rancagua	3	1	1962	4 Apr	Wembley	3	1
1964	6 June	Rio de Janeiro	0	1	1965	20 Oct	Wembley	2	3
wc1966	23 July	Wembley	1	0	1967	27 May	Vienna	1	0
1974	22 May	Wembley	2	2	1973	26 Sept	Wembley	7	0
1977	12 June	Buenos Aires	1	1	1979	13 June	Vienna	3	4
1980	13 May	Wembley	3	1	wc2004	4 Sept	Vienna	2	2
wc1986	22 June	Mexico City	1	2	wc2005	8 Oct	Old Trafford	1	0
1991	25 May	Wembley	2	2	2007	16 Nov	Vienna	1	0
wc1998	30 June	St Etienne	2	2					
2000	23 Feb	Wembley	0	0			v AZERBAIJAN	E	A
wc2002	7 June	Sapporo	1	0	wc2004	13 Oct	Baku	1	0
2005	12 Nov	Geneva	3	2	wc2005	30 Mar	Newcastle	2	0

v BELARUS		E	B
wc2008	15 Oct Minsk	3	1
wc2009	14 Oct Wembley	3	0

v BELGIUM		E	B
1921	21 May Brussels	2	0
1923	19 Mar Highbury	6	1
1923	1 Nov Antwerp	2	2
1924	8 Dec West Bromwich	4	0
1926	24 May Antwerp	5	3
1927	11 May Brussels	9	1
1928	19 May Antwerp	3	1
1929	11 May Brussels	5	1
1931	16 May Brussels	4	1
1936	9 May Brussels	2	3
1947	21 Sept Brussels	5	2
1950	18 May Brussels	4	1
1952	26 Nov Wembley	5	0
wc1954	17 June Basle	4	4*
1964	21 Oct Wembley	2	2
1970	25 Feb Brussels	3	1
EC1980	12 June Turin	1	1
wc1990	27 June Bologna	1	0*
1998	29 May Casablanca	0	0
1999	10 Oct Sunderland	2	1

v BOHEMIA		E	B
1908	13 June Prague	4	0

v BRAZIL		E	B
1956	9 May Wembley	4	2
wc1958	11 June Gothenburg	0	0
1959	13 May Rio de Janeiro	0	2
wc1962	10 June Vina del Mar	1	3
1963	8 May Wembley	1	1
1964	30 May Rio de Janeiro	1	5
1969	12 June Rio de Janeiro	1	2
wc1970	7 June Guadalajara	0	1
1976	23 May Los Angeles	0	1
1977	8 June Rio de Janeiro	0	0
1978	19 Apr Wembley	1	1
1981	12 May Wembley	0	1
1984	10 June Rio de Janeiro	2	0
1987	19 May Wembley	1	1
1990	28 Mar Wembley	1	0
1992	17 May Wembley	1	1
1993	13 June Washington	1	1
UI1995	11 June Wembley	1	3
TF1997	10 June Paris	0	1
2000	27 May Wembley	1	1
wc2002	21 June Shizuoka	1	2
2007	1 June Wembley	1	1
2009	14 Nov Doha	0	1

v BULGARIA		E	B
wc1962	7 June Rancagua	0	0
1968	11 Dec Wembley	1	1
1974	1 June Sofia	1	0
EC1979	6 June Sofia	3	0
EC1979	22 Nov Wembley	2	0
1996	27 Mar Wembley	1	0
EC1998	10 Oct Wembley	0	0
EC1999	9 June Sofia	1	1
EC2010	3 Sept Wembley	4	0

v CAMEROON		E	C
wc1990	1 July Naples	3	2*
1991	6 Feb Wembley	2	0
1997	15 Nov Wembley	2	0
2002	26 May Kobe	2	2

v CANADA		E	C
1986	24 May Burnaby	1	0

v CHILE		E	C
wc1950	25 June Rio de Janeiro	2	0
1953	24 May Santiago	2	1
1984	17 June Santiago	0	0
1989	23 May Wembley	0	0
1998	11 Feb Wembley	0	2

v CHINA		E	C
1996	23 May Beijing	3	0

v CIS		E	C
1992	29 Apr Moscow	2	2

v COLOMBIA		E	C
1970	20 May Bogota	4	0
1988	24 May Wembley	1	1
1995	6 Sept Wembley	0	0
wc1998	26 June Lens	2	0
2005	31 May New Jersey	3	2

v CROATIA		E	C
1996	24 Apr Wembley	0	0
2003	20 Aug Ipswich	3	1
EC2004	21 June Lisbon	4	2
EC2006	11 Oct Zagreb	0	2
EC2007	21 Nov Wembley	2	3
wc2008	10 Sept Zagreb	4	1
wc2009	9 Sept Wembley	5	1

v CYPRUS		E	C
EC1975	16 Apr Wembley	5	0
EC1975	11 May Limassol	1	0

v CZECHOSLOVAKIA		E	C
1934	16 May Prague	1	2
1937	1 Dec Tottenham	5	4
1963	29 May Bratislava	4	2
1966	2 Nov Wembley	0	0
wc1970	11 June Guadalajara	1	0
1973	27 May Prague	1	1
EC1974	30 Oct Wembley	3	0
EC1975	30 Oct Bratislava	1	2
1978	29 Nov Wembley	1	0
wc1982	20 June Bilbao	2	0
1990	25 Apr Wembley	4	2
1992	25 Mar Prague	2	2

v CZECH REPUBLIC		E	C
1998	18 Nov Wembley	2	0
2008	20 Aug Wembley	2	2

v DENMARK		E	D
1948	26 Sept Copenhagen	0	0
1955	2 Oct Copenhagen	5	1
wc1956	5 Dec Wolverhampton	5	2
wc1957	15 May Copenhagen	4	1
1966	3 July Copenhagen	2	0
EC1978	20 Sept Copenhagen	4	3
EC1979	12 Sept Wembley	1	0
EC1982	22 Sept Copenhagen	2	2
EC1983	21 Sept Wembley	0	1
1988	14 Sept Wembley	1	0
1989	7 June Copenhagen	1	1
1990	15 May Wembley	1	0
EC1992	11 June Malmo	0	0
1994	9 Mar Wembley	1	0
wc2002	15 June Niigata	3	0
2003	16 Nov Old Trafford	2	3
2005	17 Aug Copenhagen	1	4
2011	9 Feb Copenhagen	2	1

v ECUADOR		E	Ec
1970	24 May Quito	2	0
wc2006	25 June Stuttgart	1	0

v EGYPT		E	Eg
1986	29 Jan Cairo	4	0
wc1990	21 June Cagliari	1	0
2010	3 Mar Wembley	3	1

v ESTONIA		E	Es
EC2007	6 June Tallinn	3	0
EC2007	13 Oct Wembley	3	0

v FIFA		E	FIFA
1938	26 Oct Highbury	3	0
1953	21 Oct Wembley	4	4
1963	23 Oct Wembley	2	1

v FINLAND		E	F
1937	20 May Helsinki	8	0
1956	20 May Helsinki	5	1
1966	26 June Helsinki	3	0
wc1976	13 June Helsinki	4	1

			E	F
wc1976	13 Oct	Wembley	2	1
1982	3 June	Helsinki	4	1
wc1984	17 Oct	Wembley	5	0
wc1985	22 May	Helsinki	1	1
1992	3 June	Helsinki	2	1
wc2000	11 Oct	Helsinki	0	0
wc2001	24 Mar	Liverpool	2	1

v FRANCE			E	F
1923	10 May	Paris	4	1
1924	17 May	Paris	3	1
1925	21 May	Paris	3	2
1927	26 May	Paris	6	0
1928	17 May	Paris	5	1
1929	9 May	Paris	4	1
1931	14 May	Paris	2	5
1933	6 Dec	Tottenham	4	1
1938	26 May	Paris	4	2
1947	3 May	Highbury	3	0
1949	22 May	Paris	3	1
1951	3 Oct	Highbury	2	2
1955	15 May	Paris	0	1
1957	27 Nov	Wembley	4	0
EC1962	3 Oct	Sheffield	1	1
EC1963	27 Feb	Paris	2	5
wc1966	20 July	Wembley	2	0
1969	12 Mar	Wembley	5	0
wc1982	16 June	Bilbao	3	1
1984	29 Feb	Paris	0	2
1992	19 Feb	Wembley	2	0
EC1992	14 June	Malmo	0	0
TF1997	7 June	Montpellier	1	0
1999	10 Feb	Wembley	0	2
2000	2 Sept	Paris	1	1
EC2004	13 June	Lisbon	1	2
2008	26 Mar	Paris	0	1
2010	17 Nov	Wembley	1	2

v GEORGIA			E	G
wc1996	9 Nov	Tbilisi	2	0
wc1997	30 Apr	Wembley	2	0

v GERMANY			E	G
1930	10 May	Berlin	3	3
1935	4 Dec	Tottenham	3	0
1938	14 May	Berlin	6	3
1991	11 Sept	Wembley	0	1
1993	19 June	Detroit	1	2
EC1996	26 June	Wembley	1	1*
EC2000	17 June	Charleroi	1	0
wc2000	7 Oct	Wembley	0	1
wc2001	1 Sept	Munich	5	1
2007	22 Aug	Wembley	1	2
2008	19 Nov	Berlin	2	1
wc2010	27 June	Bloemfontein	1	4

v EAST GERMANY			E	EG
1963	2 June	Leipzig	2	1
1970	25 Nov	Wembley	3	1
1974	29 May	Leipzig	1	1
1984	12 Sept	Wembley	1	0

v WEST GERMANY			E	WG
1954	1 Dec	Wembley	3	1
1956	26 May	Berlin	3	1
1965	12 May	Nuremberg	1	0
1966	23 Feb	Wembley	1	0
wc1966	30 July	Wembley	4	2*
1968	1 June	Hanover	0	1
wc1970	14 June	Leon	2	3*
EC1972	29 Apr	Wembley	1	3
EC1972	13 May	Berlin	0	0
1975	12 Mar	Wembley	2	0
1978	22 Feb	Munich	1	2
wc1982	29 June	Madrid	0	0
1982	13 Oct	Wembley	1	2
1985	12 June	Mexico City	3	0
1987	9 Sept	Dusseldorf	1	3
wc1990	4 July	Turin	1	1*

v GHANA			E	G
2011	29 Mar	Wembley	1	1

v GREECE			E	G
EC1971	21 Apr	Wembley	3	0
EC1971	1 Dec	Piraeus	2	0
EC1982	17 Nov	Salonika	3	0
EC1983	30 Mar	Wembley	0	0
1989	8 Feb	Athens	2	1
1994	17 May	Wembley	5	0
wc2001	6 June	Athens	2	0
wc2001	6 Oct	Old Trafford	2	2
2006	16 Aug	Old Trafford	4	0

v HOLLAND			E	H
1935	18 May	Amsterdam	1	0
1946	27 Nov	Huddersfield	8	2
1964	9 Dec	Amsterdam	1	1
1969	5 Nov	Amsterdam	1	0
1970	14 Jun	Wembley	0	0
1977	9 Feb	Wembley	0	2
1982	25 May	Wembley	2	0
1988	23 Mar	Wembley	2	2
EC1988	15 June	Dusseldorf	1	3
wc1990	16 June	Cagliari	0	0
2005	9 Feb	Villa Park	0	0
wc1993	28 Apr	Wembley	2	2
wc1993	13 Oct	Rotterdam	0	2
EC1996	18 June	Wembley	4	1
2001	15 Aug	Tottenham	0	2
2002	13 Feb	Amsterdam	1	1
2006	15 Nov	Amsterdam	1	1
2009	12 Aug	Amsterdam	2	2

v HUNGARY			E	H
1908	10 June	Budapest	7	0
1909	29 May	Budapest	4	2
1909	31 May	Budapest	8	2
1934	10 May	Budapest	1	2
1936	2 Dec	Highbury	6	2
1953	25 Nov	Wembley	3	6
1954	23 May	Budapest	1	7
1960	22 May	Budapest	0	2
wc1962	31 May	Rancagua	1	2
1965	5 May	Wembley	1	0
1978	24 May	Wembley	4	1
wc1981	6 June	Budapest	3	1
wc1982	18 Nov	Wembley	1	0
EC1983	27 Apr	Wembley	2	0
EC1983	12 Oct	Budapest	3	0
1988	27 Apr	Budapest	0	0
1990	12 Sept	Wembley	1	0
1992	12 May	Budapest	1	0
1996	18 May	Wembley	3	0
1999	28 Apr	Budapest	1	1
2006	30 May	Old Trafford	3	1
2010	11 Aug	Wembley	2	1

v ICELAND			E	I
1982	2 June	Reykjavik	1	1
2004	5 June	City of Manchester	6	1
EC2007	24 Mar	Tel Aviv	0	0

v REPUBLIC OF IRELAND			E	RI
1946	30 Sept	Dublin	1	0
1949	21 Sept	Everton	0	2
wc1957	8 May	Wembley	5	1
wc1957	19 May	Dublin	1	1
1964	24 May	Dublin	3	1
1976	8 Sept	Wembley	1	1
EC1978	25 Oct	Dublin	1	1
EC1980	6 Feb	Wembley	2	0
1985	26 Mar	Wembley	2	1
EC1988	12 June	Stuttgart	0	1
wc1990	11 June	Cagliari	1	1
EC1990	14 Nov	Dublin	1	1
EC1991	27 Mar	Wembley	1	1
1995	15 Feb	Dublin	0	1
(abandoned after 27 mins)				

v ISRAEL			E	I
1986	26 Feb	Ramat Gan	2	1
1988	17 Feb	Tel Aviv	0	0
EC2007	24 Mar	Tel Aviv	0	0
EC2007	8 Sept	Wembley	3	0

v ITALY			E	I
1933	13 May	Rome	1	1
1934	14 Nov	Highbury	3	2

			E	I
1939	13 May	Milan	2	2
1948	16 May	Turin	4	0
1949	30 Nov	Tottenham	2	0
1952	18 May	Florence	1	1
1959	6 May	Wembley	2	2
1961	24 May	Rome	3	2
1973	14 June	Turin	0	2
1973	14 Nov	Wembley	0	1
1976	28 May	New York	3	2
wc1976	17 Nov	Rome	0	2
wc1977	16 Nov	Wembley	2	0
EC1980	15 June	Turin	0	1
1985	6 June	Mexico City	1	2
1989	15 Nov	Wembley	0	0
wc1990	7 July	Bari	1	2
wc1997	12 Feb	Wembley	0	1
TF1997	4 June	Nantes	2	0
wc1997	11 Oct	Rome	0	0
2000	15 Nov	Turin	0	1
2002	27 Mar	Leeds	1	2

		v JAMAICA	E	J
2006	3 June	Old Trafford	6	0

		v JAPAN	E	J
UI1995	3 June	Wembley	2	1
2004	1 June	City of Manchester	1	1
2010	30 May	Graz	2	1

		v KAZAKHSTAN	E	K
wc2008	11 Oct	Wembley	5	1
wc2009	6 June	Almaty	4	0

		v KUWAIT	E	K
wc1982	25 June	Bilbao	1	0

		v LIECHTENSTEIN	E	L
EC2003	29 Mar	Vaduz	2	0
EC2003	10 Sept	Old Trafford	2	0

		v LUXEMBOURG	E	L
1927	21 May	Esch-sur-Alzette	5	2
wc1960	19 Oct	Luxembourg	9	0
wc1961	28 Sept	Highbury	4	1
wc1977	30 Mar	Wembley	5	0
wc1977	12 Oct	Luxembourg	2	0
EC1982	15 Dec	Wembley	9	0
EC1983	16 Nov	Luxembourg	4	0
EC1998	14 Oct	Luxembourg	3	0
EC1999	4 Sept	Wembley	6	0

		v MACEDONIA	E	M
EC2002	16 Oct	Southampton	2	2
EC2003	6 Sept	Skopje	2	1
EC2006	6 Sept	Skopje	1	0
EC2006	7 Oct	Old Trafford	0	0

		v MALAYSIA	E	M
1991	12 June	Kuala Lumpur	4	2

		v MALTA	E	M
EC1971	3 Feb	Valletta	1	0
EC1971	12 May	Wembley	5	0
2000	3 June	Valletta	2	1

		v MEXICO	E	M
1959	24 May	Mexico City	1	2
1961	10 May	Wembley	8	0
wc1966	16 July	Wembley	2	0
1969	1 June	Mexico City	0	0
1985	9 June	Mexico City	0	1
1986	17 May	Los Angeles	3	0
1997	29 Mar	Wembley	2	0
2001	25 May	Derby	4	0
2010	24 May	Wembley	3	1

		v MOLDOVA	E	M
wc1996	1 Sept	Chisinau	3	0
wc1997	10 Sept	Wembley	4	0

		v MONTENEGRO	E	M
EC1989	8 Mar	Tirana	2	0
2010	12 Oct	Wembley	0	0

		v MOROCCO	E	M
wc1986	6 June	Monterrey	0	0
1998	27 May	Casablanca	1	0

		v NEW ZEALAND	E	NZ
1991	3 June	Auckland	1	0
1991	8 June	Wellington	2	0

		v NIGERIA	E	N
1994	16 Nov	Wembley	1	0
wc2002	12 June	Osaka	0	0

		v NORWAY	E	N
1937	14 May	Oslo	6	0
1938	9 Nov	Newcastle	4	0
1949	18 May	Oslo	4	1
1966	29 June	Oslo	6	1
wc1980	10 Sept	Wembley	4	0
wc1981	9 Sept	Oslo	1	2
wc1992	14 Oct	Wembley	1	1
wc1993	2 June	Oslo	0	2
1994	22 May	Wembley	0	0
1995	11 Oct	Oslo	0	0

		v PARAGUAY	E	P
wc1986	18 June	Mexico City	3	0
2002	17 Apr	Liverpool	4	0
wc2006	10 June	Frankfurt	1	0

		v PERU	E	P
1959	17 May	Lima	1	4
1962	20 May	Lima	4	0

		v POLAND	E	P
1966	5 Jan	Everton	1	1
1966	5 July	Chorzow	1	0
wc1973	6 June	Chorzow	0	2
wc1973	17 Oct	Wembley	1	1
wc1986	11 June	Monterrey	3	0
wc1989	3 June	Wembley	3	0
wc1989	11 Oct	Katowice	0	0
EC1990	17 Oct	Wembley	2	0
EC1991	13 Nov	Poznan	1	1
wc1993	29 May	Katowice	1	1
wc1993	8 Sept	Wembley	3	0
wc1996	9 Oct	Wembley	2	1
wc1997	31 May	Katowice	2	0
EC1999	27 Mar	Wembley	3	1
EC1999	8 Sept	Warsaw	0	0
wc2004	8 Sept	Katowice	2	1
wc2005	12 Oct	Old Trafford	2	1

		v PORTUGAL	E	P
1947	25 May	Lisbon	10	0
1950	14 May	Lisbon	5	3
1951	19 May	Everton	5	2
1955	22 May	Oporto	1	3
1958	7 May	Wembley	2	1
wc1961	21 May	Lisbon	1	1
wc1961	25 Oct	Wembley	2	0
1964	17 May	Lisbon	4	3
1964	4 June	São Paulo	1	1
wc1966	26 July	Wembley	2	1
1969	10 Dec	Wembley	1	0
1974	3 Apr	Lisbon	0	0
EC1974	20 Nov	Wembley	0	0
EC1975	19 Nov	Lisbon	1	1
wc1986	3 June	Monterrey	0	1
1995	12 Dec	Wembley	1	1
1998	22 Apr	Wembley	3	0
EC2000	12 June	Eindhoven	2	3
2002	7 Sept	Villa Park	1	1
2004	18 Feb	Faro	1	1
EC2004	24 June	Lisbon	2	2*
wc2006	1 July	Gelsenkirchen	0	0

		v ROMANIA	E	R
1939	24 May	Bucharest	2	0
1968	6 Nov	Bucharest	0	0
1969	15 Jan	Wembley	1	1
wc1970	2 June	Guadalajara	1	0
wc1980	15 Oct	Bucharest	1	2
wc1981	29 April	Wembley	0	0
wc1985	1 May	Bucharest	0	0
wc1985	11 Sept	Wembley	1	1
1994	12 Oct	Wembley	1	1
wc1998	22 June	Toulouse	1	2
EC2000	20 June	Charleroi	2	3

		v RUSSIA	E	R
EC2007	12 Sept	Wembley	3	0
EC2007	17 Oct	Moscow	1	2

		v SAN MARINO	E	SM
wc1992	17 Feb	Wembley	6	0
wc1993	17 Nov	Bologna	7	1

v SAUDI ARABIA

			E	SA
1988	16 Nov	Riyadh	1	1
1998	23 May	Wembley	0	0

v SERBIA-MONTENEGRO

			E	S-M
2003	3 June	Leicester	2	1

v SLOVAKIA

			E	S
EC2002	12 Oct	Bratislava	2	1
EC2003	11 June	Middlesbrough	2	1
2009	28 Mar	Wembley	4	0

v SLOVENIA

			E	S
2009	5 Sept	Wembley	2	1
wc2010	23 June	Port Elizabeth	1	0

v SOUTH AFRICA

			E	SA
1997	24 May	Old Trafford	2	1
2003	22 May	Durban	2	1

v SOUTH KOREA

			E	SK
2002	21 May	Seoguipo	1	1

v SPAIN

			E	S
1929	15 May	Madrid	3	4
1931	9 Dec	Highbury	7	1
wc1950	2 July	Rio de Janeiro	0	1
1955	18 May	Madrid	1	1
1955	30 Nov	Wembley	4	1
1960	15 May	Madrid	0	3
1960	26 Oct	Wembley	4	2
1965	8 Dec	Madrid	2	0
1967	24 May	Wembley	2	0
EC1968	3 Apr	Wembley	1	0
EC1968	8 May	Madrid	2	1
1980	26 Mar	Barcelona	2	0
EC1980	18 June	Naples	2	1
1981	25 Mar	Wembley	1	2
wc1982	5 July	Madrid	0	0
1987	18 Feb	Madrid	4	2
1992	9 Sept	Santander	0	1
FC 1996	22 June	Wembley	0	0
2001	28 Feb	Villa Park	3	0
2004	17 Nov	Madrid	0	1
2007	7 Feb	Old Trafford	0	1
2009	11 Feb	Seville	0	2

v SWEDEN

			E	S
1923	21 May	Stockholm	4	2
1923	24 May	Stockholm	3	1
1937	17 May	Stockholm	4	0
1947	19 Nov	Highbury	4	2
1949	13 May	Stockholm	1	3
1956	16 May	Stockholm	0	0
1959	28 Oct	Wembley	2	3
1965	16 May	Gothenburg	2	1
1968	22 May	Wembley	3	1
1979	10 June	Stockholm	0	0
1986	10 Sept	Stockholm	0	1
wc1988	19 Oct	Wembley	0	0
wc1989	6 Sept	Stockholm	0	0
EC1992	17 June	Stockholm	1	2
UI1995	8 June	Leeds	3	3
EC1998	5 Sept	Stockholm	1	2
EC1999	5 June	Wembley	0	0
2001	10 Nov	Old Trafford	1	1
wc2002	2 June	Saitama	1	1
2004	31 Mar	Gothenburg	0	1
wc2006	20 June	Cologne	2	2

v SWITZERLAND

			E	S
1933	20 May	Berne	4	0
1938	21 May	Zurich	1	2
1947	18 May	Zurich	0	1
1948	2 Dec	Highbury	6	0
1952	28 May	Zurich	3	0
wc1954	20 June	Berne	2	0
1962	9 May	Wembley	3	1
1963	5 June	Basle	8	1
EC1971	13 Oct	Basle	3	2
EC1971	10 Nov	Wembley	1	1
1975	3 Sept	Basle	2	1
1977	7 Sept	Wembley	0	0
wc1980	19 Nov	Wembley	2	1
wc1981	30 May	Basle	1	2
1988	28 May	Lausanne	1	0
1995	15 Nov	Wembley	3	1
EC1996	8 June	Wembley	1	1

			E	S
1998	25 Mar	Berne	1	1
EC2004	17 June	Coimbra	3	0
2008	6 Feb	Wembley	2	1
EC1989	8 Mar	Tirana	2	0
EC2010	7 Sept	Basle	3	1
EC2011	4 June	Wembley	2	2

v TRINIDAD & TOBAGO

			E	Tr
wc2006	15 June	Nuremberg	2	0
2008	2 June	Port of Spain	3	0

v TUNISIA

			E	T
1990	2 June	Tunis	1	1
wc1998	15 June	Marseilles	2	0

v TURKEY

			E	T
wc1984	14 Nov	Istanbul	8	0
wc1985	16 Oct	Wembley	5	0
EC1987	29 Apr	Izmir	0	0
EC1987	14 Oct	Wembley	8	0
EC1991	1 May	Izmir	1	0
EC1991	16 Oct	Wembley	1	0
wc1992	18 Nov	Wembley	4	0
wc1993	31 Mar	Izmir	2	0
EC2003	2 Apr	Sunderland	2	0
EC2003	11 Oct	Istanbul	0	0

v UKRAINE

			E	U
2000	31 May	Wembley	2	0
2004	18 Aug	Newcastle	3	0
wc2009	1 Apr	Wembley	2	1
wc2009	10 Oct	Dnepr	0	1

v URUGUAY

			E	U
1953	31 May	Montevideo	1	2
wc1954	26 June	Basle	2	4
1964	6 May	Wembley	2	1
wc1966	11 July	Wembley	0	0
1969	8 June	Montevideo	2	1
1977	15 June	Montevideo	0	0
1984	13 June	Montevideo	0	2
1990	22 May	Wembley	1	2
1995	29 Mar	Wembley	0	0
2006	1 Mar	Liverpool	2	1

v USA

			E	USA
wc1950	29 June	Belo Horizonte	0	1
1953	8 June	New York	6	3
1959	28 May	Los Angeles	8	1
1964	27 May	New York	10	0
1985	16 June	Los Angeles	5	0
1993	9 June	Foxboro	0	2
1994	7 Sept	Wembley	2	0
2005	28 May	Chicago	2	1
2008	28 May	Wembley	2	0
wc2010	12 June	Rustenburg	1	1

v USSR

			E	USSR
1958	18 May	Moscow	1	1
wc1958	8 June	Gothenburg	2	2
wc1958	17 June	Gothenburg	0	1
1958	22 Oct	Wembley	5	0
1967	6 Dec	Wembley	2	2
EC1968	8 June	Rome	2	0
1973	10 June	Moscow	2	1
1984	2 June	Wembley	0	2
1986	26 Mar	Tbilisi	1	0
EC1988	18 June	Frankfurt	1	3
1991	21 May	Wembley	3	1

v YUGOSLAVIA

			E	Y
1939	18 May	Belgrade	1	2
1950	22 Nov	Highbury	2	2
1954	16 May	Belgrade	0	1
1956	28 Nov	Wembley	3	0
1958	11 May	Belgrade	0	5
1960	11 May	Wembley	3	3
1965	9 May	Belgrade	1	1
1966	4 May	Wembley	2	0
EC1968	5 June	Florence	0	1
1972	11 Oct	Wembley	1	1
1974	5 June	Belgrade	2	2
EC1986	12 Nov	Wembley	2	0
EC1987	11 Nov	Belgrade	4	1
1989	13 Dec	Wembley	2	1

SCOTLAND

v ARGENTINA			S	A
1977	18 June	Buenos Aires	1	1
1979	2 June	Glasgow	1	3
1990	28 Mar	Glasgow	1	0
2008	19 Nov	Glasgow	0	1

v AUSTRALIA			S	A
wc1985	20 Nov	Glasgow	2	0
wc1985	4 Dec	Melbourne	0	0
1996	27 Mar	Glasgow	1	0
2000	15 Nov	Glasgow	0	2

v AUSTRIA			S	A
1931	16 May	Vienna	0	5
1933	29 Nov	Glasgow	2	2
1937	9 May	Vienna	1	1
1950	13 Dec	Glasgow	0	1
1951	27 May	Vienna	0	4
wc1954	16 June	Zurich	0	1
1955	19 May	Vienna	4	1
1956	2 May	Glasgow	1	1
1960	29 May	Vienna	1	4
1963	8 May	Glasgow	4	1
(abandoned after 79 mins)				
wc1968	6 Nov	Glasgow	2	1
wc1969	5 Nov	Vienna	0	2
EC1978	20 Sept	Vienna	2	3
EC1979	17 Oct	Glasgow	1	1
1994	20 Apr	Vienna	2	1
wc1996	31 Aug	Vienna	0	0
wc1997	2 Apr	Celtic Park	2	0
2003	30 Apr	Glasgow	0	2
2005	17 Aug	Graz	2	2
2007	30 May	Vienna	1	0

v BELARUS			S	B
wc1997	8 June	Minsk	1	0
wc1997	7 Sept	Aberdeen	4	1
wc2005	8 June	Minsk	0	0
wc2005	8 Oct	Glasgow	0	1

v BELGIUM			S	B
1947	18 May	Brussels	1	2
1948	28 Apr	Glasgow	2	0
1951	20 May	Brussels	5	0
EC1971	3 Feb	Liège	0	3
EC1971	10 Nov	Aberdeen	1	0
1974	2 June	Brussels	1	2
EC1979	21 Nov	Brussels	0	2
EC1979	19 Dec	Glasgow	1	3
EC1982	15 Dec	Brussels	2	3
EC1983	12 Oct	Glasgow	1	1
EC1987	1 Apr	Brussels	1	4
EC1987	14 Oct	Glasgow	2	0
wc2001	24 Mar	Glasgow	2	2
wc2001	5 Sept	Brussels	0	2

v BOSNIA			S	B
EC1999	4 Sept	Sarajevo	2	1
EC1999	5 Oct	Glasgow	1	0

v BRAZIL			S	B
1966	25 June	Glasgow	1	1
1972	5 July	Rio de Janeiro	0	1
1973	30 June	Glasgow	0	1
wc1974	18 June	Frankfurt	0	0
1977	23 June	Rio de Janeiro	0	2
wc1982	18 June	Seville	1	4
1987	26 May	Glasgow	0	2
wc1990	20 June	Turin	0	1
wc1998	10 June	Saint-Denis	1	2
2011	27 Mar	Emirates	0	2

v BULGARIA			S	B
1978	22 Feb	Glasgow	2	1
EC1986	10 Sept	Glasgow	0	0
EC1987	11 Nov	Sofia	1	0
EC1990	14 Nov	Sofia	1	1
EC1991	27 Mar	Glasgow	1	1
2006	11 May	Kobe	5	1

v CANADA			S	C
1983	12 June	Vancouver	2	0
1983	16 June	Edmonton	3	0
1983	20 June	Toronto	2	0
1992	21 May	Toronto	3	1
2002	15 Oct	Easter Road	3	1

v CHILE			S	C
1977	15 June	Santiago	4	2
1989	30 May	Glasgow	2	0

v CIS			S	C
EC1992	18 June	Norrkoping	3	0

v COLOMBIA			S	C
1988	17 May	Glasgow	0	0
1996	30 May	Miami	0	1
1998	23 May	New York	2	2

v COSTA RICA			S	CR
wc1990	11 June	Genoa	0	1

v CROATIA			S	C
wc2000	11 Oct	Zagreb	1	1
wc2001	1 Sept	Glasgow	0	0
2008	26 Mar	Glasgow	1	1

v CYPRUS			S	C
wc1968	17 Dec	Nicosia	5	0
wc1969	11 May	Glasgow	8	0
wc1989	8 Feb	Limassol	3	2
wc1989	26 Apr	Glasgow	2	1

v CZECHOSLOVAKIA			S	C
1937	22 May	Prague	3	1
1937	8 Dec	Glasgow	5	0
wc1961	14 May	Bratislava	0	4
wc1961	26 Sept	Glasgow	3	2
wc1961	29 Nov	Brussels	2	4*
1972	2 July	Porto Alegre	0	0
wc1973	26 Sept	Glasgow	2	1
wc1973	17 Oct	Prague	0	1
wc1976	13 Oct	Prague	0	2
wc1977	21 Sept	Glasgow	3	1

v CZECH REPUBLIC			S	C
EC1999	31 Mar	Glasgow	1	2
EC1999	9 June	Prague	2	3
2008	30 May	Prague	1	3
2010	3 Mar	Glasgow	1	0
EC2010	8 Oct	Prague	0	1

v DENMARK			S	D
1951	12 May	Glasgow	3	1
1952	25 May	Copenhagen	2	1
1968	16 Oct	Copenhagen	1	0
EC1970	11 Nov	Glasgow	1	0
EC1971	9 June	Copenhagen	0	1
wc1972	18 Oct	Copenhagen	4	1
wc1972	15 Nov	Glasgow	2	0
EC1975	3 Sept	Copenhagen	1	0
EC1975	29 Oct	Glasgow	3	1
wc1986	4 June	Nezahualcayotl	0	1
1996	24 Apr	Copenhagen	0	2
1998	25 Mar	Glasgow	0	1
2002	21 Aug	Glasgow	0	1
2004	28 Apr	Copenhagen	0	1

v ECUADOR			S	E
1995	24 May	Toyama	2	1

v EGYPT			S	E
1990	16 May	Aberdeen	1	3

v ESTONIA			S	E
wc1993	19 May	Tallinn	3	0
wc1993	2 June	Aberdeen	3	1
wc1997	11 Feb	Monaco	0	0
wc1997	29 Mar	Kilmarnock	2	0
EC1998	10 Oct	Edinburgh	3	2
EC1999	8 Sept	Tallinn	0	0
2004	27 May	Tallinn	1	0

v FAEROES		S	F
EC1994	12 Oct	Glasgow	5	1
EC1995	7 June	Toftir	2	0
EC1998	14 Oct	Aberdeen	2	1
EC1999	5 June	Toftir	1	1
EC2002	7 Sept	Toftir	2	2
EC2003	6 Sept	Glasgow	3	1
EC2006	2 Sept	Celtic Park	6	0
EC2007	6 June	Toftir	2	0
2010	16 Nov	Aberdeen	3	0

v FINLAND		S	F
1954	25 May	Helsinki	2	1
wc1964	21 Oct	Glasgow	3	1
wc1965	27 May	Helsinki	2	1
1976	8 Sept	Glasgow	6	0
1992	25 Mar	Glasgow	1	1
EC1994	7 Sept	Helsinki	2	0
EC1995	6 Sept	Glasgow	1	0
1998	22 Apr	Edinburgh	1	1

v FRANCE		S	F
1930	18 May	Paris	2	0
1932	8 May	Paris	3	1
1948	23 May	Paris	0	3
1949	27 Apr	Glasgow	2	0
1950	27 May	Paris	1	0
1951	16 May	Glasgow	1	0
wc1958	15 June	Orebro	1	2
1984	1 June	Marseilles	0	2
wc1989	8 Mar	Glasgow	2	0
wc1989	11 Oct	Paris	0	3
1997	12 Nov	St Etienne	1	2
2000	29 Mar	Glasgow	0	2
2002	27 Mar	Paris	0	5
EC2006	7 Oct	Glasgow	1	0
EC2007	12 Sept	Paris	1	0

v GEORGIA		S	G
EC2007	24 Mar	Glasgow	2	1
EC2007	17 Oct	Tblisi	0	2

v GERMANY		S	G
1929	1 June	Berlin	1	1
1936	14 Oct	Glasgow	2	0
EC1992	15 June	Norrkoping	0	2
1993	24 Mar	Glasgow	0	1
1998	28 Apr	Bremen	1	0
EC2003	7 June	Glasgow	1	1
EC2003	10 Sept	Dortmund	1	2

v EAST GERMANY		S	EG
1974	30 Oct	Glasgow	3	0
1977	7 Sept	East Berlin	0	1
EC1982	13 Oct	Glasgow	2	0
EC1983	16 Nov	Halle	1	2
1985	16 Oct	Glasgow	0	0
1990	25 Apr	Glasgow	0	1

v WEST GERMANY		S	WG
1957	22 May	Stuttgart	3	1
1959	6 May	Glasgow	3	2
1964	12 May	Hanover	2	2
wc1969	16 Apr	Glasgow	1	1
wc1969	22 Oct	Hamburg	2	3
1973	14 Nov	Glasgow	1	1
1974	27 Mar	Frankfurt	1	2
wc1986	8 June	Queretaro	1	2

v GREECE		S	G
EC1994	18 Dec	Athens	0	1
EC1995	16 Aug	Glasgow	1	0

v HOLLAND		S	H
1929	4 June	Amsterdam	2	0
1938	21 May	Amsterdam	3	1
1959	27 May	Amsterdam	2	1
1966	11 May	Glasgow	0	3
1968	30 May	Amsterdam	0	0
1971	1 Dec	Rotterdam	1	2
wc1978	11 June	Mendoza	3	2
1982	23 Mar	Glasgow	2	1
1986	29 Apr	Eindhoven	0	0
EC1992	12 June	Gothenburg	0	1
1994	23 Mar	Glasgow	0	1
1994	27 May	Utrecht	1	3
EC1996	10 June	Birmingham	0	0
2000	26 Apr	Arnhem	0	0
EC2003	15 Nov	Glasgow	1	0
EC2003	19 Nov	Amsterdam	0	6
wc2009	28 Mar	Amsterdam	0	3
wc2009	9 Sept	Glasgow	0	1

v HONG KONG XI		S	HK
†2002	23 May	Hong Kong	4	0

†match not recognised by FIFA

v HUNGARY		S	H
1938	7 Dec	Glasgow	3	1
1954	8 Dec	Glasgow	2	4
1955	29 May	Budapest	1	3
1958	7 May	Glasgow	1	1
1960	5 June	Budapest	3	3
1980	31 May	Budapest	1	3
1987	9 Sept	Glasgow	2	0
2004	18 Aug	Glasgow	0	3

v ICELAND		S	I
wc1984	17 Oct	Glasgow	3	0
wc1985	28 May	Reykjavik	1	0
EC2002	12 Oct	Reykjavik	2	0
EC2003	29 Mar	Glasgow	2	1
wc2008	10 Sept	Reykjavik	2	1
wc2009	1 Apr	Glasgow	2	1

v IRAN		S	I
wc1978	7 June	Cordoba	1	1

v REPUBLIC OF IRELAND		S	RI
wc1961	3 May	Glasgow	4	1
wc1961	7 May	Dublin	3	0
1963	9 June	Dublin	0	1
1969	21 Sept	Dublin	1	1
EC1986	15 Oct	Dublin	0	0
EC1987	18 Feb	Glasgow	0	1
2000	30 May	Dublin	2	1
2003	12 Feb	Glasgow	0	2
NC2011	29 May	Dublin	0	1

v ISRAEL		S	I
wc1981	25 Feb	Tel Aviv	1	0
wc1981	28 Apr	Glasgow	3	1
1986	28 Jan	Tel Aviv	1	0

v ITALY		S	I
1931	20 May	Rome	0	3
wc1965	9 Nov	Glasgow	1	0
wc1965	7 Dec	Naples	0	3
1988	22 Dec	Perugia	0	2
wc1992	18 Nov	Glasgow	0	0
wc1993	13 Oct	Rome	1	3
wc2005	26 Mar	Milan	0	2
wc2005	3 Sept	Glasgow	1	1
EC2007	28 Mar	Bari	0	2
EC2007	17 Nov	Glasgow	3	1

v JAPAN		S	J
1995	21 May	Hiroshima	0	0
2006	13 May	Saitama	0	0
2009	10 Oct	Yokohama	0	2

v LATVIA		S	L
wc1996	5 Oct	Riga	2	0
wc1997	11 Oct	Glasgow	2	0
wc2000	2 Sept	Riga	1	0
wc2001	6 Oct	Glasgow	2	1

v LIECHTENSTEIN		S	L
EC2010	7 Sept	Glasgow	2	1

v LITHUANIA		S	L
EC1998	5 Sept	Vilnius	0	0
EC1999	9 Oct	Glasgow	3	0
EC2003	2 Apr	Kaunas	0	1
EC2003	11 Oct	Glasgow	1	0
EC2006	6 Sept	Kaunas	2	1
EC2007	8 Sept	Glasgow	3	1
EC2010	3 Sept	Kaunas	0	0

v LUXEMBOURG — S / L

			S	L
1947	24 May	Luxembourg	6	0
EC1986	12 Nov	Glasgow	3	0
EC1987	2 Dec	Esch	0	0

v MACEDONIA — S / M

			S	M
wc2008	6 Sept	Skopje	0	1
wc2009	5 Sept	Glasgow	2	0

v MALTA — S / M

			S	M
1988	22 Mar	Valletta	1	1
1990	28 May	Valletta	2	1
wc1993	17 Feb	Glasgow	3	0
wc1993	17 Nov	Valletta	2	0
1997	1 June	Valletta	3	2

v MOLDOVA — S / M

			S	M
EC2004	13 Oct	Chisinau	1	1
EC2005	4 June	Glasgow	2	0

v MOROCCO — S / M

			S	M
wc1998	23 June	St Etienne	0	3

v NEW ZEALAND — S / NZ

			S	NZ
wc1982	15 June	Malaga	5	2
2003	27 May	Tynecastle	1	1

v NIGERIA — S / N

			S	N
2002	17 Apr	Aberdeen	1	2

v NORWAY — S / N

			S	N
1929	28 May	Oslo	7	3
1954	5 May	Glasgow	1	0
1954	19 May	Oslo	1	1
1963	4 June	Bergen	3	4
1963	7 Nov	Glasgow	6	1
1974	6 June	Oslo	2	1
EC1978	25 Oct	Glasgow	3	2
EC1979	7 June	Oslo	4	0
wc1988	14 Sept	Oslo	2	1
wc1989	15 Nov	Glasgow	1	1
1992	3 June	Oslo	0	0
wc1998	16 June	Bordeaux	1	1
2003	20 Aug	Oslo	0	0
wc2004	9 Oct	Glasgow	0	1
wc2005	7 Sept	Oslo	2	1
wc2008	11 Oct	Glasgow	0	0
wc2009	12 Aug	Oslo	0	4

v PARAGUAY — S / P

			S	P
wc1958	11 June	Norrkoping	2	3

v PERU — S / P

			S	P
1972	26 Apr	Glasgow	2	0
wc1978	3 June	Cordoba	1	3
1979	12 Sept	Edinburgh	1	1

v POLAND — S / P

			S	P
1958	1 June	Warsaw	2	1
1960	4 June	Glasgow	2	3
wc1965	23 May	Chorzow	1	1
wc1965	13 Oct	Glasgow	1	2
1980	28 May	Poznan	0	1
1990	19 May	Glasgow	1	1
2001	25 Apr	Bydgoszcz	1	1

v PORTUGAL — S / P

			S	P
1950	21 May	Lisbon	2	2
1955	4 May	Glasgow	3	0
1959	3 June	Lisbon	0	1
1966	18 June	Glasgow	0	1
EC1971	21 Apr	Lisbon	0	2
EC1971	13 Oct	Glasgow	2	1
1975	13 May	Glasgow	1	0
EC1978	29 Nov	Lisbon	0	1
EC1980	26 Mar	Glasgow	4	1
wc1980	15 Oct	Glasgow	0	0
wc1981	18 Nov	Lisbon	1	2
wc1992	14 Oct	Glasgow	0	0
wc1993	28 Apr	Lisbon	0	5
2002	20 Nov	Braga	0	2

v ROMANIA — S / R

			S	R
EC1975	1 June	Bucharest	1	1
EC1975	17 Dec	Glasgow	1	1
1986	26 Mar	Glasgow	3	0
EC1990	12 Sept	Glasgow	2	1
EC1991	16 Oct	Bucharest	0	1
2004	31 Mar	Glasgow	1	2

v RUSSIA — S / R

			S	R
EC1994	16 Nov	Glasgow	1	1
EC1995	29 Mar	Moscow	0	0

v SAN MARINO — S / SM

			S	SM
EC1991	1 May	Serravalle	2	0
EC1991	13 Nov	Glasgow	4	0
EC1995	26 Apr	Serravalle	2	0
EC1995	15 Nov	Glasgow	5	0
wc2000	7 Oct	Serravalle	2	0
wc2001	28 Mar	Glasgow	4	0

v SAUDI ARABIA — S / SA

			S	SA
1988	17 Feb	Riyadh	2	2

v SLOVENIA — S / Sl

			S	Sl
wc2004	8 Sept	Glasgow	0	0
wc2005	12 Oct	Celje	3	0

v SOUTH AFRICA — S / SA

			S	SA
2002	20 May	Hong Kong	0	2
2007	22 Aug	Aberdeen	1	0

v SOUTH KOREA — S / SK

			S	SK
2002	16 May	Busan	1	4

v SPAIN — S / Sp

			S	Sp
wc1957	8 May	Glasgow	4	2
wc1957	26 May	Madrid	1	4
1963	13 June	Madrid	6	2
1965	8 May	Glasgow	0	0
EC1974	20 Nov	Glasgow	1	2
EC1975	5 Feb	Valencia	1	1
1982	24 Feb	Valencia	0	3
wc1984	14 Nov	Glasgow	3	1
wc1985	27 Feb	Seville	0	1
1988	27 Apr	Madrid	0	0
2004	3 Sept	Valencia	1	1

Match abandoned afer 60 minutes; floodlight failure.

			S	Sp
EC2010	12 Oct	Glasgow	2	3

v SWEDEN — S / Sw

			S	Sw
1952	30 May	Stockholm	1	3
1953	6 May	Glasgow	1	2
1975	16 Apr	Gothenburg	1	1
1977	27 Apr	Glasgow	3	1
wc1980	10 Sept	Stockholm	1	0
wc1981	9 Sept	Glasgow	2	0
wc1990	16 June	Genoa	2	1
1995	11 Oct	Stockholm	0	2
wc1996	10 Nov	Glasgow	1	0
wc1997	30 Apr	Gothenburg	1	2
2004	17 Nov	Edinburgh	1	4
2010	11 Aug	Stockholm	0	3

v SWITZERLAND — S / Sw

			S	Sw
1931	24 May	Geneva	3	2
1948	17 May	Berne	1	2
1950	26 Apr	Glasgow	3	1
wc1957	19 May	Basle	2	1
wc1957	6 Nov	Glasgow	3	2
1973	22 June	Berne	0	1
1976	7 Apr	Glasgow	1	0
EC1982	17 Nov	Berne	0	2
EC1983	30 May	Glasgow	2	2
EC1990	17 Oct	Glasgow	2	1
EC1991	11 Sept	Berne	2	2
wc1992	9 Sept	Berne	1	3
wc1993	8 Sept	Aberdeen	1	1
wc1996	18 June	Birmingham	1	0
2006	1 Mar	Glasgow	1	3

v TRINIDAD & TOBAGO — S / TT

			S	TT
2004	30 May	Edinburgh	4	1

v TURKEY — S / T

			S	T
1960	8 June	Ankara	2	4

v UKRAINE — S / U

			S	U
EC2006	11 Oct	Kiev	0	2
EC2007	13 Oct	Glasgow	3	1

v URUGUAY — S / U

			S	U
wc1954	19 June	Basle	0	7
1962	2 May	Glasgow	2	3

			S	U
1983	21 Sept	Glasgow	2	0
wc1986	13 June	Nezahualcoyotl	0	0

v USA			S	USA
1952	30 Apr	Glasgow	6	0
1992	17 May	Denver	1	0
1996	26 May	New Britain	1	2
1998	30 May	Washington	0	0
2005	11 Nov	Glasgow	1	1

v USSR			S	USSR
1967	10 May	Glasgow	0	2
1971	14 June	Moscow	0	1
wc1982	22 June	Malaga	2	2
1991	6 Feb	Glasgow	0	1

v YUGOSLAVIA			S	Y
1955	15 May	Belgrade	2	2
1956	21 Nov	Glasgow	2	0
wc1958	8 June	Vasteras	1	1
1972	29 June	Belo Horizonte	2	2
wc1974	22 June	Frankfurt	1	1
1984	12 Sept	Glasgow	6	1
wc1988	19 Oct	Glasgow	1	1
wc1989	6 Sept	Zagreb	1	3

v ZAIRE			S	Z
wc1974	14 June	Dortmund	2	0

WALES

v ALBANIA			W	A
EC1994	7 Sept	Cardiff	2	0
EC1995	15 Nov	Tirana	1	1

v ARGENTINA			W	A
1992	3 June	Tokyo	0	1
2002	13 Feb	Cardiff	1	1

v ARMENIA			W	A
wc2001	24 Mar	Erevan	2	2
wc2001	1 Sept	Cardiff	0	0

v AUSTRIA			W	A
1954	9 May	Vienna	0	2
EC1955	23 Nov	Wrexham	1	2
rc1974	4 Sept	Vienna	1	2
1975	19 Nov	Wrexham	1	0
1992	29 Apr	Vienna	1	1
EC2005	26 Mar	Cardiff	0	2
EC2005	30 Mar	Vienna	0	1

v AZERBAIJAN			W	A
EC2002	20 Nov	Baku	2	0
EC2003	29 Mar	Cardiff	4	0
wc2004	4 Sept	Baku	1	1
wc2005	12 Oct	Cardiff	2	0
wc2008	6 Sept	Cardiff	1	0
wc2009	6 June	Baku	1	0

v BELARUS			W	B
EC1998	14 Oct	Cardiff	3	2
EC1999	4 Sept	Minsk	2	1
wc2000	2 Sept	Minsk	1	2
wc2001	6 Oct	Cardiff	1	0

v BELGIUM			W	B
1949	22 May	Liège	1	3
1949	23 Nov	Cardiff	5	1
EC1990	17 Oct	Cardiff	3	1
EC1991	27 Mar	Brussels	1	1
wc1992	18 Nov	Brussels	0	2
wc1993	31 Mar	Cardiff	2	0
wc1997	29 Mar	Cardiff	1	2
wc1997	11 Oct	Brussels	2	3

v BOSNIA			W	B
2003	12 Feb	Cardiff	2	2

v BRAZIL			W	B
wc1958	19 June	Gothenburg	0	1
1962	12 May	Rio de Janeiro	1	3
1962	16 May	São Paulo	1	3
1966	14 May	Rio de Janeiro	1	3
1966	18 May	Belo Horizonte	0	1
1983	12 June	Cardiff	1	1
1991	11 Sept	Cardiff	1	0
1997	12 Nov	Brasilia	0	3
2000	23 May	Cardiff	0	3
2006	5 Sept	Cardiff	0	2

v BULGARIA			W	B
EC1983	27 Apr	Wrexham	1	0
EC1983	16 Nov	Sofia	0	1
EC1994	14 Dec	Cardiff	0	3
EC1995	29 Mar	Sofia	1	3
2006	15 Aug	Swansea	0	0
2007	22 Aug	Burgas	1	0
EC2010	8 Oct	Cardiff	0	1

v CANADA			W	C
1986	10 May	Toronto	0	2
1986	20 May	Vancouver	3	0
2004	30 May	Wrexham	1	0

v CHILE			W	C
1966	22 May	Santiago	0	2

v COSTA RICA			W	CR
1990	20 May	Cardiff	1	0

v CROATIA			W	C
2002	21 Aug	Varazdin	1	1
2010	23 May	Osijek	0	2

v CYPRUS			W	C
wc1992	14 Oct	Limassol	1	0
wc1993	13 Oct	Cardiff	2	0
2005	16 Nov	Limassol	0	1
EC2006	11 Oct	Cardiff	3	1
EC2007	13 Oct	Nicosia	1	3

v CZECHOSLOVAKIA			W	C
wc1957	1 May	Cardiff	1	0
wc1957	26 May	Prague	0	2
EC1971	21 Apr	Swansea	1	3
EC1971	27 Oct	Prague	0	1
wc1977	30 Mar	Wrexham	3	0
wc1977	16 Nov	Prague	0	1
wc1980	19 Nov	Cardiff	1	0
wc1981	9 Sept	Prague	0	2
EC1987	29 Apr	Wrexham	1	1
EC1987	11 Nov	Prague	0	2
wc1993	28 Apr	Ostrava†	1	1
wc1993	8 Sept	Cardiff†	2	2

†*Czechoslovakia played as RCS (Republic of Czechs and Slovaks).*

v CZECH REPUBLIC			W	CR
2002	27 Mar	Cardiff	0	0
EC2006	2 Sept	Teplice	1	2
EC2007	2 June	Cardiff	0	0

v DENMARK			W	D
wc1964	21 Oct	Copenhagen	0	1
wc1965	1 Dec	Wrexham	4	2
EC1987	9 Sept	Cardiff	1	0
EC1987	14 Oct	Copenhagen	0	1
1990	11 Sept	Copenhagen	0	1
EC1998	10 Oct	Copenhagen	2	1
EC1999	9 June	Liverpool	0	2
2008	19 Nov	Brondby	1	0

v ESTONIA		W	E
1994	23 May	Tallinn	2	1
2009	29 May	Llanelli	1	0

v FINLAND		W	F
EC1971	26 May	Helsinki	1	0
EC1971	13 Oct	Swansea	3	0
EC1987	10 Sept	Helsinki	1	1
EC1987	1 Apr	Wrexham	4	0
wc1988	19 Oct	Swansea	2	2
wc1989	6 Sept	Helsinki	0	1
2000	29 Mar	Cardiff	1	2
EC2002	7 Sept	Helsinki	2	0
EC2003	10 Sept	Cardiff	1	1
wc2009	28 Mar	Cardiff	0	2
wc2009	10 Oct	Helsinki	1	2

v FAEROES		W	F
wc1992	9 Sept	Cardiff	6	0
wc1993	6 June	Toftir	3	0

v FRANCE		W	F
1933	25 May	Paris	1	1
1939	20 May	Paris	1	2
1953	14 May	Paris	1	6
1982	2 June	Toulouse	1	0

v GEORGIA		W	G
EC1994	16 Nov	Tbilisi	0	5
EC1995	7 June	Cardiff	0	1
2008	20 Aug	Swansea	1	2

v GERMANY		W	G
EC1995	26 Apr	Dusseldorf	1	1
EC1995	11 Oct	Cardiff	1	2
2002	14 May	Cardiff	1	0
EC2007	8 Sept	Cardiff	0	2
EC2007	21 Nov	Frankfurt	0	0
wc2008	15 Oct	Moenchengladbach	0	1
wc2009	1 Apr	Cardiff	0	2

v EAST GERMANY		W	EG
wc1957	19 May	Leipzig	1	2
wc1957	25 Sept	Cardiff	4	1
wc1969	16 Apr	Dresden	1	2
wc1969	22 Oct	Cardiff	1	3

v WEST GERMANY		W	WG
1968	8 May	Cardiff	1	1
1969	26 Mar	Frankfurt	1	1
1976	6 Oct	Cardiff	0	2
1977	14 Dec	Dortmund	1	1
EC1979	2 May	Wrexham	0	2
EC1979	17 Oct	Cologne	1	5
wc1989	31 May	Cardiff	0	0
wc1989	15 Nov	Cologne	1	2
EC1991	5 June	Cardiff	1	0
EC1991	16 Oct	Nuremberg	1	4

v GREECE		W	G
wc1964	9 Dec	Athens	0	2
wc1965	17 Mar	Cardiff	4	1

v HOLLAND		W	H
wc1988	14 Sept	Amsterdam	0	1
wc1989	11 Oct	Wrexham	1	2
1992	30 May	Utrecht	0	4
wc1996	5 Oct	Cardiff	1	3
wc1996	9 Nov	Eindhoven	1	7
2008	1 June	Rotterdam	0	2

v HUNGARY		W	H
wc1958	8 June	Sanviken	1	1
wc1958	17 June	Stockholm	2	1
1961	28 May	Budapest	2	3
EC1962	7 Nov	Budapest	1	3
EC1963	20 Mar	Cardiff	1	1
EC1974	30 Oct	Cardiff	2	0
EC1975	16 Apr	Budapest	2	1
1985	16 Oct	Cardiff	0	3
2004	31 Mar	Budapest	2	1
2005	9 Feb	Cardiff	2	0

v ICELAND		W	I
wc1980	2 June	Reykjavik	4	0
wc1981	14 Oct	Swansea	2	2
wc1984	12 Sept	Reykjavik	0	1
wc1984	14 Nov	Cardiff	2	1
1991	1 May	Cardiff	1	0
2008	28 May	Reykjavik	1	0

v IRAN		W	I
1978	18 Apr	Teheran	1	0

v REPUBLIC OF IRELAND		W	RI
1960	28 Sept	Dublin	3	2
1979	11 Sept	Swansea	2	1
1981	24 Feb	Dublin	3	1
1986	26 Mar	Dublin	1	0
1990	28 Mar	Dublin	0	1
1991	6 Feb	Wrexham	0	3
1992	19 Feb	Dublin	1	0
1993	17 Feb	Dublin	1	2
1997	11 Feb	Cardiff	0	0
EC2007	24 Mar	Dublin	0	1
EC2007	17 Nov	Cardiff	2	2
NC2011	8 Feb	Dublin	0	3

v ISRAEL		W	I
wc1958	15 Jan	Tel Aviv	2	0
wc1958	5 Feb	Cardiff	2	0
1984	10 June	Tel Aviv	0	0
1989	8 Feb	Tel Aviv	3	3

v ITALY		W	I
1965	1 May	Florence	1	4
wc1968	23 Oct	Cardiff	0	1
wc1969	4 Nov	Rome	1	4
1988	4 June	Brescia	1	0
1996	24 Jan	Terni	0	3
EC1998	5 Sept	Liverpool	0	2
EC1999	5 June	Bologna	0	4
EC2002	16 Oct	Cardiff	2	1
EC2003	6 Sept	Milan	0	4

v JAMAICA		W	J
1998	25 Mar	Cardiff	0	0

v JAPAN		W	J
1992	7 June	Matsuyama	1	0

v KUWAIT		W	K
1977	6 Sept	Wrexham	0	0
1977	20 Sept	Kuwait	0	0

v LATVIA		W	L
2004	18 Aug	Riga	2	0

v LIECHTENSTEIN		W	L
2006	14 Nov	Swansea	4	0
wc2008	11 Oct	Cardiff	2	0
wc2009	14 Oct	Vaduz	2	0

v LUXEMBOURG		W	L
EC1974	20 Nov	Swansea	5	0
EC1975	1 May	Luxembourg	3	1
EC1990	14 Nov	Luxembourg	1	0
EC1991	13 Nov	Cardiff	1	0
2008	26 Mar	Luxembourg	2	0
2010	11 Aug	Llanelli	5	1

v MALTA		W	M
EC1978	25 Oct	Wrexham	7	0
EC1979	2 June	Valletta	2	0
1988	1 June	Valletta	3	2
1998	3 June	Valletta	3	0

v MEXICO		W	M
wc1958	11 June	Stockholm	1	1
1962	22 May	Mexico City	1	2

v MOLDOVA		W	M
EC1994	12 Oct	Kishinev	2	3
EC1995	6 Sept	Cardiff	1	0

v MONTENEGRO		W	M
2009	12 Aug	Podgorica	1	2
EC2010	3 Sept	Podgorica	0	1

v NEW ZEALAND		W	NZ
2007	26 May	Wrexham	2	2

v NORWAY			W	N
EC1982	22 Sept	Swansea	1	0
EC1983	21 Sept	Oslo	0	0
1984	6 June	Trondheim	0	1
1985	26 Feb	Wrexham	1	1
1985	5 June	Bergen	2	4
1994	9 Mar	Cardiff	1	3
wc2000	7 Oct	Cardiff	1	1
wc2001	5 Sept	Oslo	2	3
2004	27 May	Oslo	0	0
2008	6 Feb	Wrexham	3	0

v PARAGUAY			W	P
2006	1 Mar	Cardiff	0	0

v POLAND			W	P
wc1973	28 Mar	Cardiff	2	0
wc1973	26 Sept	Katowice	0	3
1991	29 May	Radom	0	0
wc2000	11 Oct	Warsaw	0	0
wc2001	2 June	Cardiff	1	2
wc2004	13 Oct	Cardiff	2	3
wc2005	7 Sept	Warsaw	0	1
2009	11 Feb	Vila Real	0	1

v PORTUGAL			W	P
1949	15 May	Lisbon	2	3
1951	12 May	Cardiff	2	1
2000	2 June	Chaves	0	3

v QATAR			W	Q
2000	23 Feb	Doha	1	0

v ROMANIA			W	R
EC1970	11 Nov	Cardiff	0	0
EC1971	24 Nov	Bucharest	0	2
1983	12 Oct	Wrexham	5	0
wc1992	20 May	Bucharest	1	5
wc1993	17 Nov	Cardiff	1	2

v RUSSIA			W	R
EC2003	15 Nov	Moscow	0	0
EC2003	19 Nov	Cardiff	0	1
wc2008	10 Sept	Moscow	1	2
wc2009	9 Sept	Cardiff	1	3

v SAN MARINO			W	SM
wc1996	2 June	Serravalle	5	0
wc1996	31 Aug	Cardiff	6	0
EC2007	28 Mar	Cardiff	3	0
EC2007	17 Oct	Serravalle	2	1

v SAUDI ARABIA			W	SA
1986	25 Feb	Dahran	2	1

v SERBIA-MONTENEGRO			W	SM
EC2003	20 Aug	Belgrade	0	1
EC2003	11 Oct	Cardiff	2	3

v SLOVAKIA			W	S
EC2006	7 Oct	Cardiff	1	5
EC2007	12 Sept	Trnava	5	2

v SLOVENIA			W	Sl
2005	17 Aug	Swansea	0	0

v SPAIN			W	S
wc1961	19 Apr	Cardiff	1	2
wc1961	18 May	Madrid	1	1
1982	24 Mar	Valencia	1	1
wc1984	17 Oct	Seville	0	3
wc1985	30 Apr	Wrexham	3	0

v SWEDEN			W	S
wc1958	15 June	Stockholm	0	0
1988	27 Apr	Stockholm	1	4
1989	26 Apr	Wrexham	0	2
1990	25 Apr	Stockholm	2	4
1994	20 Apr	Wrexham	0	2
2010	3 Mar	Swansea	0	1

v SWITZERLAND			W	S
1949	26 May	Berne	0	4
1951	16 May	Wrexham	3	2
1996	24 Apr	Lugano	0	2
EC1999	31 Mar	Zurich	0	2
EC1999	9 Oct	Wrexham	0	2
EC2010	12 Oct	Basle	1	4

v TRINIDAD & TOBAGO			W	TT
2006	27 May	Graz	2	1

v TUNISIA			W	T
1998	6 June	Tunis	0	4

v TURKEY			W	T
EC1978	29 Nov	Wrexham	1	0
EC1979	21 Nov	Izmir	0	1
wc1980	15 Oct	Cardiff	4	0
wc1981	25 Mar	Ankara	1	0
wc1996	14 Dec	Cardiff	0	0
wc1997	20 Aug	Istanbul	4	6

v REST OF UNITED KINGDOM			W	UK
1951	5 Dec	Cardiff	3	2
1969	28 July	Cardiff	0	1

v UKRAINE			W	U
wc2001	28 Mar	Cardiff	1	1
wc2001	6 June	Kiev	1	1

v USA			W	USA
2003	27 May	San Jose	0	2

v URUGUAY			W	U
1986	21 Apr	Wrexham	0	0

v USSR			W	USSR
wc1965	30 May	Moscow	1	2
wc1965	27 Oct	Cardiff	2	1
wc1981	30 May	Wrexham	0	0
wc1981	18 Nov	Tbilisi	0	3
1987	18 Feb	Swansea	0	0

v YUGOSLAVIA			W	Y
1953	21 May	Belgrade	2	5
1954	22 Nov	Cardiff	1	3
EC1976	24 Apr	Zagreb	0	2
EC1976	22 May	Cardiff	1	1
EC1982	15 Dec	Titograd	4	4
EC1983	14 Dec	Cardiff	1	1
1988	23 Mar	Swansea	1	2

NORTHERN IRELAND

v ALBANIA			NI	A
wc1965	7 May	Belfast	4	1
wc1965	24 Nov	Tirana	1	1
EC1982	15 Dec	Tirana	0	0
EC1983	27 Apr	Belfast	1	0
wc1992	9 Sept	Belfast	3	0
wc1993	17 Feb	Tirana	2	1
wc1996	14 Dec	Belfast	2	0
wc1997	10 Sept	Zurich	0	1
2010	3 Mar	Tirana	0	1

v ALGERIA			NI	A
wc1986	3 June	Guadalajara	1	1

v ARGENTINA			NI	A
wc1958	11 June	Halmstad	1	3

v ARMENIA			NI	A
wc1996	5 Oct	Belfast	1	1
wc1997	30 Apr	Erevan	0	0
EC2003	29 Mar	Erevan	0	1
EC2003	10 Sept	Belfast	0	1

v AUSTRALIA			NI	A
1980	11 June	Sydney	2	1
1980	15 June	Melbourne	1	1
1980	18 June	Adelaide	2	1

v AUSTRIA			NI	A
wc1982	1 July	Madrid	2	2
EC1982	13 Oct	Vienna	0	2
EC1983	21 Sept	Belfast	3	1
EC1990	14 Nov	Vienna	0	0

			NI	A
EC1991	16 Oct	Belfast	2	1
EC1994	12 Oct	Vienna	2	1
EC1995	15 Nov	Belfast	5	3
wc2004	13 Oct	Belfast	3	3
wc2005	12 Oct	Vienna	0	2

v AZERBAIJAN			NI	A
wc2004	9 Oct	Baku	0	0
wc2005	3 Sept	Belfast	2	0

v BARBADOS			NI	B
2004	30 May	Waterford	1	1

v BELGIUM			NI	B
wc1976	10 Nov	Liège	0	2
wc1977	16 Nov	Belfast	3	0
1997	11 Feb	Belfast	3	0

v BRAZIL			NI	B
wc1986	12 June	Guadalajara	0	3

v BULGARIA			NI	B
wc1972	18 Oct	Sofia	0	3
wc1973	26 Sept	Sheffield	0	0
EC1978	29 Nov	Sofia	2	0
EC1979	2 May	Belfast	2	0
wc2001	28 Mar	Sofia	3	4
wc2001	2 June	Belfast	0	1
2008	6 Feb	Belfast	0	1

v CANADA			NI	C
1995	22 May	Edmonton	0	2
1999	27 Apr	Belfast	1	1
2005	9 Feb	Belfast	0	1

v CHILE			NI	C
1989	26 May	Belfast	0	1
1995	25 May	Edmonton	1	2
2010	30 May	Chillan	0	1

v COLOMBIA			NI	C
1994	4 June	Boston	0	2

v CYPRUS			NI	C
EC1971	3 Feb	Nicosia	3	0
EC1971	21 Apr	Belfast	5	0
wc1973	14 Feb	Nicosia	0	1
wc1973	8 May	London	3	0
2002	21 Aug	Belfast	0	0

v CZECHOSLOVAKIA			NI	C
wc1958	8 June	Halmstad	1	0
wc1958	17 June	Malmo	2	1*

*After extra time

v CZECH REPUBLIC			NI	C
wc2001	24 Mar	Belfast	0	1
wc2001	6 June	Teplice	1	3
wc2008	10 Sept	Belfast	0	0
wc2009	14 Oct	Prague	0	0

v DENMARK			NI	D
EC1978	25 Oct	Belfast	2	1
EC1979	6 June	Copenhagen	0	4
1986	26 Mar	Belfast	1	1
EC1990	17 Oct	Belfast	1	1
EC1991	13 Nov	Odense	1	2
wc1992	18 Nov	Belfast	0	1
wc1993	13 Oct	Copenhagen	0	1
wc2000	7 Oct	Belfast	1	1
wc2001	1 Sept	Copenhagen	1	1
EC2006	7 Oct	Copenhagen	0	0
EC2007	17 Nov	Belfast	2	1

v ESTONIA			NI	E
2004	31 Mar	Tallinn	1	0
2006	1 Mar	Belfast	1	0

v FAEROES			NI	F
EC1991	1 May	Belfast	1	1
EC1991	11 Sept	Landskrona	5	0
EC2010	12 Oct	Toftir	1	1

v FINLAND			NI	F
wc1984	27 May	Pori	0	1
wc1984	14 Nov	Belfast	2	1

			NI	F
EC1998	10 Oct	Belfast	1	0
EC1998	9 Oct	Helsinki	1	4
2003	12 Feb	Belfast	0	1
2006	16 Aug	Helsinki	2	1

v FRANCE			NI	F
1928	21 Feb	Paris	0	4
1951	12 May	Belfast	2	2
1952	11 Nov	Paris	1	3
wc1958	19 June	Norrkoping	0	4
1982	24 Mar	Paris	0	4
wc1982	4 July	Madrid	1	4
1986	26 Feb	Paris	0	0
1988	27 Apr	Belfast	0	0
1999	18 Aug	Belfast	0	1

v GEORGIA			NI	G
2008	26 Mar	Belfast	4	1

v GERMANY			NI	G
1992	2 June	Bremen	1	1
1996	29 May	Belfast	1	1
wc1996	9 Nov	Nuremberg	1	1
wc1997	20 Aug	Belfast	1	3
EC1999	27 Mar	Belfast	0	3
EC1999	8 Sept	Dortmund	0	4
2005	4 June	Belfast	1	4

v WEST GERMANY			NI	WG
wc1958	15 June	Malmo	2	2
wc1960	26 Oct	Belfast	3	4
wc1961	10 May	Hamburg	1	2
1966	7 May	Belfast	0	2
1977	27 Apr	Cologne	0	5
EC1982	17 Nov	Belfast	1	0
EC1983	16 Nov	Hamburg	1	0

v GREECE			NI	G
wc1961	3 May	Athens	1	2
wc1961	17 Oct	Belfast	2	0
1988	17 Feb	Athens	2	3
EC2003	2 Apr	Belfast	0	2
EC2003	11 Oct	Athens	0	1

v HOLLAND			NI	H
1962	9 May	Rotterdam	0	4
wc1965	17 Mar	Belfast	2	1
wc1965	7 Apr	Rotterdam	0	0
wc1976	13 Oct	Rotterdam	2	2
wc1977	12 Oct	Belfast	0	1

v HONDURAS			NI	H
wc1982	21 June	Zaragoza	1	1

v HUNGARY			NI	H
wc1988	19 Oct	Budapest	0	1
wc1989	6 Sept	Belfast	1	2
2000	26 Apr	Belfast	0	1
2008	19 Nov	Belfast	0	2

v ICELAND			NI	I
wc1977	11 June	Reykjavik	0	1
wc1977	21 Sept	Belfast	2	0
wc2000	11 Oct	Reykjavik	0	1
wc2001	5 Sept	Belfast	3	0
EC2006	2 Sept	Belfast	0	3
EC2007	12 Sept	Reykjavik	1	2

v REPUBLIC OF IRELAND			NI	RI
EC1978	20 Sept	Dublin	0	0
EC1979	21 Nov	Belfast	1	0
wc1988	14 Sept	Belfast	0	0
wc1989	11 Oct	Dublin	0	3
wc1993	31 Mar	Dublin	0	3
wc1993	17 Nov	Belfast	1	1
EC1994	16 Nov	Belfast	0	4
EC1995	29 Mar	Dublin	1	1
1999	29 May	Dublin	1	0
NC2011	24 May	Dublin	0	5

v ISRAEL			NI	I
1968	10 Sept	Jaffa	3	2
1976	3 Mar	Tel Aviv	1	1
wc1980	26 Mar	Tel Aviv	0	0
wc1981	18 Nov	Belfast	1	0

			NI	I
1984	16 Oct	Belfast	3	0
1987	18 Feb	Tel Aviv	1	1
2009	12 Aug	Belfast	1	1

		v ITALY	`NI	I
wc1957	25 Apr	Rome	0	1
1957	4 Dec	Belfast	2	2
wc1958	15 Jan	Belfast	2	1
1961	25 Apr	Bologna	2	3
1997	22 Jan	Palermo	0	2
2003	3 June	Campobasso	0	2
2009	6 June	Pisa	0	3
EC2010	8 Oct	Belfast	0	0

		v LATVIA	NI	L
wc1993	2 June	Riga	2	1
wc1993	8 Sept	Belfast	2	0
EC1995	26 Apr	Riga	1	0
EC1995	7 June	Belfast	1	2
EC2006	11 Oct	Belfast	1	0
EC2007	8 Sept	Riga	0	1

		v LIECHTENSTEIN	NI	L
EC1994	20 Apr	Belfast	4	1
EC1995	11 Oct	Eschen	4	0
2002	27 Mar	Vaduz	0	0
EC2007	24 Mar	Vaduz	4	1
EC2007	22 Aug	Belfast	3	1

		v LITHUANIA	NI	L
wc1992	28 Apr	Belfast	2	2
wc1993	25 May	Vilnius	1	0

		v LUXEMBOURG	NI	L
2000	23 Feb	Luxembourg	3	1

		v MALTA	NI	M
wc1988	21 May	Belfast	3	0
wc1989	26 Apr	Valletta	2	0
2000	28 Mar	Valletta	3	0
wc2000	2 Sept	Belfast	1	0
wc2001	6 Oct	Valletta	1	0
2005	17 Aug	Ta'Qali	1	1

		v MEXICO	NI	M
1966	22 June	Belfast	4	1
1994	11 June	Miami	0	3

		v MOLDOVA	NI	M
EC1998	18 Nov	Belfast	2	2
EC1999	31 Mar	Chisinau	0	0

		v MONTENEGRO	NI	M
2010	11 Aug	Podgorica	0	2

		v MOROCCO	NI	M
1986	23 Apr	Belfast	2	1
2010	17 Nov	Belfast	1	1

		v NORWAY	NI	N
1922	25 May	Bergen	1	2
EC1974	4 Sept	Oslo	1	2
EC1975	29 Oct	Belfast	3	0
1990	27 Mar	Belfast	2	3
1996	27 Mar	Belfast	0	2
2001	28 Feb	Belfast	0	4
2004	18 Feb	Belfast	1	4

		v POLAND	NI	P
EC1962	10 Oct	Katowice	2	0
EC1962	28 Nov	Belfast	2	0
1988	23 Mar	Belfast	1	1
1991	5 Feb	Belfast	3	1
2002	13 Feb	Limassol	1	4
EC2004	4 Sept	Belfast	0	3
EC2005	30 Mar	Warsaw	0	1
wc2009	28 Mar	Belfast	3	2
wc2009	5 Sept	Chorzow	1	1

		v PORTUGAL	NI	P
wc1957	16 Jan	Lisbon	1	1
wc1957	1 May	Belfast	3	0
wc1973	28 Mar	Coventry	1	1
wc1973	14 Nov	Lisbon	1	1
wc1980	19 Nov	Lisbon	0	1
wc1981	29 Apr	Belfast	1	0
EC1994	7 Sept	Belfast	1	2
EC1995	3 Sept	Lisbon	1	1

			NI	P
wc1997	29 Mar	Belfast	0	0
wc1997	11 Oct	Lisbon	0	1
2005	15 Nov	Belfast	1	1

		v ROMANIA	NI	R
wc1984	12 Sept	Belfast	3	2
wc1985	16 Oct	Bucharest	1	0
1994	23 Mar	Belfast	2	0
2006	27 May	Chicago	0	2

		v SAN MARINO	NI	SM
wc2008	15 Oct	Belfast	4	0
wc2009	11 Feb	Serravalle	3	0

		v ST KITTS & NEVIS	NI	SK
2004	2 June	Basseterre	2	0

		v SERBIA	NI	S
2009	14 Nov	Belfast	0	1
EC2011	25 Mar	Belgrade	1	2

		v SERBIA-MONTENEGRO	NI	SM
2004	28 Apr	Belfast	1	1

		v SLOVAKIA	NI	S
1998	25 Mar	Belfast	1	0
wc2008	6 Sept	Bratislava	1	2
wc2009	9 Sept	Belfast	0	2

		v SLOVENIA	NI	S
wc2008	11 Oct	Maribor	0	2
wc2009	1 Apr	Belfast	1	0
EC2010	3 Sept	Maribor	1	0
EC2011	29 Mar	Belfast	0	0

		v SOUTH AFRICA	NI	SA
1924	24 Sept	Belfast	1	1

		v SPAIN	NI	S
1958	15 Oct	Madrid	2	6
1963	30 May	Bilbao	1	1
1963	30 Oct	Belfast	0	1
EC1970	11 Nov	Seville	0	3
EC1972	16 Feb	Hull	1	1
wc1982	25 June	Valencia	1	0
1985	27 Mar	Palma	0	0
wc1986	7 June	Guadalajara	1	2
wc1988	21 Dec	Seville	0	4
wc1989	8 Feb	Belfast	0	2
wc1992	14 Oct	Belfast	0	0
wc1993	28 Apr	Seville	1	3
1998	2 June	Santander	1	4
2002	17 Apr	Belfast	0	5
EC2002	12 Oct	Albacete	0	3
EC2003	11 June	Belfast	0	0
EC2006	6 Sept	Belfast	3	2
EC2007	21 Nov	Las Palmas	0	1

		v SWEDEN	NI	S
EC1974	30 Oct	Solna	2	0
EC1975	3 Sept	Belfast	1	2
wc1980	15 Oct	Belfast	3	0
wc1981	3 June	Solna	0	1
1996	24 Apr	Belfast	1	2
EC2007	28 Mar	Belfast	2	1
EC2007	17 Oct	Stockholm	1	1

		v SWITZERLAND	NI	S
wc1964	14 Oct	Belfast	1	0
wc1964	14 Nov	Lausanne	1	2
1998	22 Apr	Belfast	1	0
2004	18 Aug	Zurich	0	0

		v THAILAND	NI	T
1997	21 May	Bangkok	0	0

		v TRINIDAD & TOBAGO	NI	TT
2004	6 June	Bacolet	3	0

		v TURKEY	NI	T
wc1968	23 Oct	Belfast	4	1
wc1968	11 Dec	Istanbul	3	0
EC1983	30 Mar	Belfast	2	1
EC1983	12 Oct	Ankara	0	1

			NI	T
wc1985	1 May	Belfast	2	0
wc1985	11 Sept	Izmir	0	0
EC1986	12 Nov	Izmir	0	0
EC1987	11 Nov	Belfast	1	0
EC1998	5 Sept	Istanbul	0	3
EC1999	4 Sept	Belfast	0	3
2010	26 May	New Britain	0	2

v UKRAINE			NI	U
wc1996	31 Aug	Belfast	0	1
wc1997	2 Apr	Kiev	1	2
EC2002	16 Oct	Belfast	0	0
EC2003	6 Sept	Donetsk	0	0

v URUGUAY			NI	U
1964	29 Apr	Belfast	3	0
1990	18 May	Belfast	1	0
2006	21 May	New Jersey	0	1

v USSR			NI	USSR
wc1969	19 Sept	Belfast	0	0
wc1969	22 Oct	Moscow	0	2
EC1971	22 Sept	Moscow	0	1
EC1971	13 Oct	Belfast	1	1

v YUGOSLAVIA			NI	Y
EC1975	16 Mar	Belfast	1	0
EC1975	19 Nov	Belgrade	0	1
wc1982	17 June	Zaragoza	0	0
EC1987	29 Apr	Belfast	1	2
EC1987	14 Oct	Sarajevo	0	3
EC1990	12 Sept	Belfast	0	2
EC1991	27 Mar	Belgrade	1	4
2000	16 Aug	Belfast	1	2

REPUBLIC OF IRELAND

v ALBANIA			RI	A
wc1992	26 May	Dublin	2	0
wc1993	26 May	Tirana	2	1
EC2003	2 Apr	Tirana	0	0
EC2003	7 June	Dublin	2	1

v ALGERIA			RI	A
1982	28 Apr	Algiers	0	2
2010	28 May	Dublin	3	0

v ANDORRA			RI	A
wc2001	28 Mar	Barcelona	3	0
wc2001	25 Apr	Dublin	3	1
EC2010	7 Sept	Dublin	3	1

v ARGENTINA			RI	A
1951	13 May	Dublin	0	1
†1979	29 May	Dublin	0	0
1980	16 May	Dublin	0	1
1998	22 Apr	Dublin	0	2
2010	11 Aug	Dublin	0	1

†Not considered a full international.

v ARMENIA			RI	A
EC2010	3 Sept	Erevan	1	0

v AUSTRALIA			RI	A
2003	19 Aug	Dublin	2	1
2009	12 Aug	Limerick	0	3

v AUSTRIA			RI	A
1952	7 May	Vienna	0	6
1953	25 Mar	Dublin	4	0
1958	14 Mar	Vienna	1	3
1962	8 Apr	Dublin	2	3
EC1963	25 Sept	Vienna	0	0
EC1963	13 Oct	Dublin	3	2
1966	22 May	Vienna	0	1
1968	10 Nov	Dublin	2	2
EC1971	30 May	Dublin	1	4
EC1971	10 Oct	Linz	0	6
EC1995	11 June	Dublin	1	3
EC1995	6 Sept	Vienna	1	3

v BELGIUM			RI	B
1928	12 Feb	Liège	4	2
1929	30 Apr	Dublin	4	0
1930	11 May	Brussels	3	1
wc1934	25 Feb	Dublin	4	4
1949	24 Apr	Dublin	0	2
1950	10 May	Brussels	1	5
1965	24 Mar	Dublin	0	2
1966	25 May	Liège	3	2
wc1980	15 Oct	Dublin	1	1
wc1981	25 Mar	Brussels	0	1
EC1986	10 Sept	Brussels	2	2
EC1987	29 Apr	Dublin	0	0
wc1997	29 Oct	Dublin	1	1
wc1997	16 Nov	Brussels	1	2

v BOLIVIA			RI	B
1994	24 May	Dublin	1	0
1996	15 June	New Jersey	3	0
2007	26 May	Boston	1	1

v BRAZIL			RI	B
1974	5 May	Rio de Janeiro	1	2
1982	27 May	Uberlandia	0	7
1987	23 May	Dublin	1	0
2004	18 Feb	Dublin	0	0
2008	6 Feb	Dublin	0	1
2010	2 Mar	Emirates	0	2

v BULGARIA			RI	B
wc1977	1 June	Sofia	1	2
wc1977	12 Oct	Dublin	0	0
EC1979	19 May	Sofia	0	1
EC1979	17 Oct	Dublin	3	0
wc1987	1 Apr	Sofia	1	2
wc1987	14 Oct	Dublin	2	0
2004	18 Aug	Dublin	1	1
wc2009	28 Mar	Dublin	1	1
wc2009	6 June	Sofia	1	1

v CAMEROON			RI	C
wc2002	1 June	Niigata	1	1

v CANADA			RI	C
2003	18 Nov	Dublin	3	0

v CHILE			RI	C
1960	30 Mar	Dublin	2	0
1972	21 June	Recife	1	2
1974	12 May	Santiago	2	1
1982	22 May	Santiago	0	1
1991	22 May	Dublin	1	1
2006	24 May	Dublin	0	1

v CHINA			RI	C
1984	3 June	Sapporo	1	0
2005	29 Mar	Dublin	1	0

v COLOMBIA			RI	C
2008	29 May	Fulham	1	0

v CROATIA			RI	C
1996	2 June	Dublin	2	2
EC1998	5 Sept	Dublin	2	0
EC1999	4 Sept	Zagreb	0	1
2001	15 Aug	Dublin	2	2
2004	16 Nov	Dublin	1	0

v CYPRUS			RI	C
wc1980	26 Mar	Nicosia	3	2
wc1980	19 Nov	Dublin	6	0
wc2001	24 Mar	Nicosia	4	0
wc2001	6 Oct	Dublin	4	0
wc2004	4 Sept	Dublin	3	0
wc2005	8 Oct	Nicosia	1	0
EC2006	7 Oct	Nicosia	2	5
EC2007	17 Oct	Dublin	1	1
2008	15 Oct	Dublin	1	0
wc2009	5 Sept	Nicosia	2	1

v CZECHOSLOVAKIA

			RI	C
1938	18 May	Prague	2	2
EC1959	5 Apr	Dublin	2	0
EC1959	10 May	Bratislava	0	4
wc1961	8 Oct	Dublin	1	3
wc1961	29 Oct	Prague	1	7
EC1967	21 May	Dublin	0	2
EC1967	22 Nov	Prague	2	1
wc1969	4 May	Dublin	1	2
wc1969	7 Oct	Prague	0	3
1979	26 Sept	Prague	1	4
1981	29 Apr	Dublin	3	1
1986	27 May	Reykjavik	1	0

v CZECH REPUBLIC

			RI	C
1994	5 June	Dublin	1	3
1996	24 Apr	Prague	0	2
1998	25 Mar	Olomouc	1	2
2000	23 Feb	Dublin	3	2
2004	31 Mar	Dublin	2	1
EC2006	11 Oct	Dublin	1	1
EC2007	12 Sept	Prague	0	1

v DENMARK

			RI	D
wc1956	3 Oct	Dublin	2	1
wc1957	2 Oct	Copenhagen	2	0
wc1968	4 Dec	Dublin	1	1
(abandoned after 51 mins)				
wc1969	27 May	Copenhagen	0	2
wc1969	15 Oct	Dublin	1	1
EC1978	24 May	Copenhagen	3	3
EC1979	2 May	Dublin	2	0
wc1984	14 Nov	Copenhagen	0	3
wc1985	13 Nov	Dublin	1	4
wc1992	14 Oct	Copenhagen	0	0
wc1993	28 Apr	Dublin	1	1
2002	27 Mar	Dublin	3	0
2007	22 Aug	Copenhagen	4	0

v ECUADOR

			RI	E
1972	19 June	Natal	3	2
2007	23 May	New Jersey	1	1

v EGYPT

			RI	E
wc1990	17 June	Palermo	0	0

v ENGLAND

			RI	E
1946	30 Sept	Dublin	0	1
1949	21 Sept	Everton	2	0
wc1957	8 May	Wembley	1	5
wc1957	19 May	Dublin	1	1
1964	24 May	Dublin	1	3
1976	8 Sept	Wembley	1	1
EC1978	25 Oct	Dublin	1	1
EC1980	6 Feb	Wembley	0	2
1985	26 Mar	Wembley	1	2
EC1988	12 June	Stuttgart	1	0
wc1990	11 June	Cagliari	1	1
EC1990	14 Nov	Dublin	1	1
EC1991	27 Mar	Wembley	1	1
1995	15 Feb	Dublin	1	0
(abandoned after 27 mins)				

v ESTONIA

			RI	E
wc2000	11 Oct	Dublin	2	0
wc2001	6 June	Tallinn	2	0

v FAEROES

			RI	F
EC2004	13 Oct	Dublin	2	0
EC2005	8 June	Toftir	2	0

v FINLAND

			RI	F
wc1949	8 Sept	Dublin	3	0
wc1949	9 Oct	Helsinki	1	1
1990	16 May	Dublin	1	1
2000	15 Nov	Dublin	3	0
2002	21 Aug	Helsinki	3	0

v FRANCE

			RI	F
1937	23 May	Paris	2	0
1952	16 Nov	Dublin	1	1
wc1953	4 Oct	Dublin	3	5
wc1953	25 Nov	Paris	0	1
wc1972	15 Nov	Dublin	2	1
wc1973	19 May	Paris	1	1
wc1976	17 Nov	Paris	0	2
wc1977	30 Mar	Dublin	1	0
wc1980	28 Oct	Paris	0	2
wc1981	14 Oct	Dublin	3	2
1989	7 Feb	Dublin	0	0
wc2004	9 Oct	Paris	0	0
wc2005	7 Sept	Dublin	0	1
wc2009	14 Nov	Dublin	0	1
wc2009	18 Nov	Paris	1	1

v GEORGIA

			RI	G
EC2003	29 Mar	Tbilisi	2	1
EC2003	11 June	Dublin	2	0
wc2008	6 Sept	Mainz	2	1
wc2009	11 Feb	Dublin	2	1

v GERMANY

			RI	G
1935	8 May	Dortmund	1	3
1936	17 Oct	Dublin	5	2
1939	23 May	Bremen	1	1
1994	29 May	Hanover	2	0
wc2002	5 June	Ibaraki	1	1
EC2006	2 Sept	Stuttgart	0	1
EC2007	13 Oct	Dublin	0	0

v WEST GERMANY

			RI	WG
1951	17 Oct	Dublin	3	2
1952	4 May	Cologne	0	3
1955	28 May	Hamburg	1	2
1956	25 Nov	Dublin	3	0
1960	11 May	Dusseldorf	1	0
1966	4 May	Dublin	0	4
1970	9 May	Berlin	1	2
1975	1 Mar	Dublin	1	0†
1979	22 May	Dublin	1	3
1981	21 May	Bremen	0	3†
1989	6 Sept	Dublin	1	1

†v West Germany 'B'

v GREECE

			RI	G
2000	26 Apr	Dublin	0	1
2002	20 Nov	Athens	0	0

v HOLLAND

			RI	N
1932	8 May	Amsterdam	2	0
1934	8 Apr	Amsterdam	2	5
1935	8 Dec	Dublin	3	5
1955	1 May	Dublin	1	0
1956	10 May	Rotterdam	4	1
wc1980	10 Sept	Dublin	2	1
wc1981	9 Sept	Rotterdam	2	2
EC1982	22 Sept	Rotterdam	1	2
EC1983	12 Oct	Dublin	2	3
EC1988	18 June	Gelsenkirchen	0	1
wc1990	21 June	Palermo	1	1
1994	20 Apr	Tilburg	1	0
wc1994	4 July	Orlando	0	2
EC1995	13 Dec	Liverpool	0	2
1996	4 June	Rotterdam	1	3
wc2000	2 Sept	Amsterdam	2	2
wc2001	1 Sept	Dublin	1	0
2004	5 June	Amsterdam	1	0
2006	16 Aug	Dublin	0	4

v HUNGARY

			RI	H
1934	15 Dec	Dublin	2	4
1936	3 May	Budapest	3	3
1936	6 Dec	Dublin	2	3
1939	19 Mar	Cork	2	2
1939	18 May	Budapest	2	2
wc1969	8 June	Dublin	1	2
wc1969	5 Nov	Budapest	0	4
wc1989	8 Mar	Budapest	0	0
wc1989	4 June	Dublin	2	0
1991	11 Sept	Gyor	2	1

v ICELAND

			RI	I
EC1962	12 Aug	Dublin	4	2
EC1962	2 Sept	Reykjavik	1	1
EC1982	13 Oct	Dublin	2	0
EC1983	21 Sept	Reykjavik	3	0
1986	25 May	Reykjavik	2	1
wc1996	10 Nov	Dublin	0	0
wc1997	6 Sept	Reykjavik	4	2

v IRAN

			RI	I
1972	18 June	Recife	2	1
wc2001	10 Nov	Dublin	2	0
wc2001	15 Nov	Tehran	0	1

		v N. IRELAND	RI	NI
EC1978	20 Sept	Dublin	0	0
EC1979	21 Nov	Belfast	0	1
wc1988	14 Sept	Belfast	0	0
wc1989	11 Oct	Dublin	3	0
wc1993	31 Mar	Dublin	3	0
wc1993	17 Nov	Belfast	1	1
EC1994	16 Nov	Belfast	4	0
EC1995	29 Mar	Dublin	1	1
1999	29 May	Dublin	0	1
NC2011	24 May	Dublin	5	0

		v ISRAEL	RI	I
1984	4 Apr	Tel Aviv	0	3
1985	27 May	Tel Aviv	0	0
1987	10 Nov	Dublin	5	0
EC2005	26 Mar	Tel Aviv	1	1
EC2005	4 June	Dublin	2	2

		v ITALY	RI	I
1926	21 Mar	Turin	0	3
1927	23 Apr	Dublin	1	2
EC1970	8 Dec	Rome	0	3
EC1971	10 May	Dublin	1	2
1985	5 Feb	Dublin	1	2
wc1990	30 June	Rome	0	1
1992	4 June	Foxboro	0	2
wc1994	18 June	New York	1	0
2005	17 Aug	Dublin	1	2
wc2009	1 Apr	Bari	1	1
wc2009	10 Oct	Dublin	2	2
2011	7 June	Liege	2	0

		v JAMAICA	RI	J
2004	2 June	Charlton	1	0

		v LATVIA	RI	L
wc1992	9 Sept	Dublin	4	0
wc1993	2 June	Riga	2	1
EC1994	7 Sept	Riga	3	0
EC1995	11 Oct	Dublin	2	1

		v LIECHTENSTEIN	RI	L
EC1994	12 Oct	Dublin	4	0
EC1995	3 June	Eschen	0	0
wc1996	31 Aug	Eschen	5	0
wc1997	21 May	Dublin	5	0

		v LITHUANIA	RI	L
wc1993	16 June	Vilnius	1	0
wc1993	8 Sept	Dublin	2	0
wc1997	20 Aug	Dublin	0	0
wc1997	10 Sept	Vilnius	2	1

		v LUXEMBOURG	RI	L
1936	9 May	Luxembourg	5	1
wc1953	28 Oct	Dublin	4	0
wc1954	7 Mar	Luxembourg	1	0
EC1987	28 May	Luxembourg	2	0
EC1987	9 Sept	Dublin	2	1

		v MACEDONIA	RI	M
wc1996	9 Oct	Dublin	3	0
wc1997	2 Apr	Skopje	2	3
EC1999	9 June	Dublin	1	0
EC1999	9 Oct	Skopje	1	1
EC2011	26 Mar	Dublin	2	1
EC2011	4 June	Podgorica	2	0

		v MALTA	RI	M
EC1983	30 Mar	Valletta	1	0
EC1983	16 Nov	Dublin	8	0
wc1989	28 May	Dublin	2	0
wc1989	15 Nov	Valletta	2	0
1990	2 June	Valletta	3	0
EC1998	14 Oct	Dublin	5	0
EC1999	8 Sept	Valletta	3	2

		v MEXICO	RI	M
1984	8 Aug	Dublin	0	0
wc1994	24 June	Orlando	1	2
1996	13 June	New Jersey	2	2
1998	23 May	Dublin	0	0
2000	4 June	Chicago	2	2

		v MONTENEGRO	RI	M
wc2008	10 Sept	Podgorica	0	0
wc2009	14 Oct	Dublin	0	0

		v MOROCCO	RI	M
1990	12 Sept	Dublin	1	0

		v NIGERIA	RI	N
2002	16 May	Dublin	1	2
2004	29 May	Charlton	0	3
2009	29 May	Fulham	1	1

		v NORWAY	RI	N
wc1937	10 Oct	Oslo	2	3
wc1937	7 Nov	Dublin	3	3
1950	26 Nov	Dublin	2	2
1951	30 May	Oslo	3	2
1954	8 Nov	Dublin	2	1
1955	25 May	Oslo	3	1
1960	6 Nov	Dublin	3	1
1964	13 May	Oslo	4	1
1973	6 June	Oslo	1	1
1976	24 Mar	Dublin	3	0
1978	21 May	Oslo	0	0
wc1984	17 Oct	Oslo	0	1
wc1985	1 May	Dublin	0	0
1988	1 June	Oslo	0	0
wc1994	28 June	New York	0	0
2003	30 Apr	Dublin	1	0
2008	20 Aug	Oslo	1	1
2010	17 Nov	Dublin	1	2

		v PARAGUAY	RI	P
1999	10 Feb	Dublin	2	0
2010	25 May	Dublin	2	1

		v POLAND	RI	P
1938	22 May	Warsaw	0	6
1938	13 Nov	Dublin	3	2
1958	11 May	Katowice	2	2
1958	5 Oct	Dublin	2	2
1964	10 May	Kracow	1	3
1964	25 Oct	Dublin	3	2
1968	15 May	Dublin	2	2
1968	30 Oct	Katowice	0	1
1970	6 May	Dublin	1	2
1970	23 Sept	Dublin	0	2
1973	16 May	Wroclaw	0	2
1973	21 May	Dublin	1	0
1976	26 May	Poznan	2	0
1977	24 Apr	Dublin	0	0
1978	12 Apr	Lodz	0	3
1981	23 May	Bydgoszcz	0	3
1984	23 May	Dublin	0	0
1986	12 Nov	Warsaw	0	1
1988	22 May	Dublin	3	1
EC1991	1 May	Dublin	0	0
EC1991	16 Oct	Poznan	3	3
2004	28 Apr	Bydgoszcz	0	0
2008	19 Nov	Dublin	2	3

		v PORTUGAL	RI	P
1946	16 June	Lisbon	1	3
1947	4 May	Dublin	0	2
1948	23 May	Lisbon	0	2
1949	22 May	Dublin	1	0
1972	25 June	Recife	1	2
1992	7 June	Boston	2	0
EC1995	26 Apr	Dublin	1	0
EC1995	15 Nov	Lisbon	0	3
1996	29 May	Dublin	0	1
wc2000	7 Oct	Lisbon	1	1
wc2001	2 June	Dublin	1	1
2005	9 Feb	Dublin	1	0

		v ROMANIA	RI	R
1988	23 Mar	Dublin	2	0
wc1990	25 June	Genoa	0	0*
wc1997	30 Apr	Bucharest	0	1
wc1997	11 Oct	Dublin	1	1
2004	27 May	Dublin	1	0

		v RUSSIA	RI	R
1994	23 Mar	Dublin	0	0
1996	27 Mar	Dublin	0	2
2002	13 Feb	Dublin	2	0
EC2002	7 Sept	Moscow	2	4

			RI	R
EC2003	6 Sept	Dublin	1	1
EC2010	8 Oct	Dublin	2	3

v SAN MARINO			RI	SM
EC2006	15 Nov	Dublin	5	0
EC2007	7 Feb	Serravalle	2	1

v SAUDI ARABIA			RI	SA
wc2002	11 June	Yokohama	3	0

v SERBIA			RI	S
2008	24 May	Dublin	1	1

v SCOTLAND			RI	S
wc1961	3 May	Glasgow	1	4
wc1961	7 May	Dublin	0	3
1963	9 June	Dublin	1	0
1969	21 Sept	Dublin	1	1
EC1986	15 Oct	Dublin	0	0
EC1987	18 Feb	Glasgow	1	0
2000	30 May	Dublin	1	2
2003	12 Feb	Glasgow	2	0
NC2011	29 May	Dublin	1	0

v SLOVAKIA			RI	S
EC2007	28 Mar	Dublin	1	0
EC2007	8 Sept	Bratislava	2	2
EC2010	12 Oct	Zilina	1	1

v SOUTH AFRICA			RI	SA
2000	11 June	New Jersey	2	1
2009	8 Sept	Limerick	1	0

v SPAIN			RI	S
1931	26 Apr	Barcelona	1	1
1931	13 Dec	Dublin	0	5
1946	23 June	Madrid	1	0
1947	2 Mar	Dublin	3	2
1948	30 May	Barcelona	1	2
1949	12 June	Dublin	1	4
1952	1 June	Madrid	0	6
1955	27 Nov	Dublin	2	2
EC1964	11 Mar	Seville	1	5
EC1964	8 Apr	Dublin	0	2
wc1965	5 May	Dublin	1	0
wc1965	27 Oct	Seville	1	4
wc1965	10 Nov	Paris	0	1
EC1966	23 Oct	Dublin	0	0
EC1966	7 Dec	Valencia	0	2
1977	9 Feb	Dublin	0	1
FC1982	17 Nov	Dublin	3	3
EC1983	27 Apr	Zaragoza	0	2
1985	26 May	Cork	0	0
wc1988	16 Nov	Seville	0	2
wc1989	26 Apr	Dublin	1	0
wc1992	18 Nov	Seville	0	0
wc1993	13 Oct	Dublin	1	3
wc2002	16 June	Suwon	1	1

v SWEDEN			RI	S
wc1949	2 June	Stockholm	1	3
wc1949	13 Nov	Dublin	1	3
1959	1 Nov	Dublin	3	2
1960	18 May	Malmo	1	4
EC1970	14 Oct	Dublin	1	1
EC1970	28 Oct	Malmo	0	1
1999	28 Apr	Dublin	2	0
2006	1 Mar	Dublin	3	0

v SWITZERLAND			RI	S
1935	5 May	Basle	0	1
1936	17 Mar	Dublin	1	0
1937	17 May	Berne	1	0
1938	18 Sept	Dublin	4	0
1948	5 Dec	Dublin	0	1

			RI	S
EC1975	11 May	Dublin	2	1
EC1975	21 May	Berne	0	1
1980	30 Apr	Dublin	2	0
wc1985	2 June	Dublin	3	0
wc1985	11 Sept	Berne	0	0
1992	25 Mar	Dublin	2	1
EC2002	16 Oct	Dublin	1	2
EC2003	11 Oct	Basle	0	2
wc2004	8 Sept	Basle	1	1
wc2005	12 Oct	Dublin	0	0

v TRINIDAD & TOBAGO			RI	TT
1982	30 May	Port of Spain	1	2

v TUNISIA			RI	T
1988	19 Oct	Dublin	4	0

v TURKEY			RI	T
EC1966	16 Nov	Dublin	2	1
EC1967	22 Feb	Ankara	1	2
EC1974	20 Nov	Izmir	1	1
EC1975	29 Oct	Dublin	4	0
1976	13 Oct	Ankara	3	3
1978	5 Apr	Dublin	4	2
1990	26 May	Izmir	0	0
EC1990	17 Oct	Dublin	5	0
EC1991	13 Nov	Istanbul	3	1
EC2000	13 Nov	Dublin	1	1
EC2000	17 Nov	Bursa	0	0
2003	9 Sept	Dublin	2	2

v URUGUAY			RI	U
1974	8 May	Montevideo	0	2
1986	23 Apr	Dublin	1	1
2011	29 Mar	Dublin	2	3

v USA			RI	USA
1979	29 Oct	Dublin	3	2
1991	1 June	Boston	1	1
1992	29 Apr	Dublin	4	1
1992	30 May	Washington	1	3
1996	9 June	Boston	1	2
2000	6 June	Boston	1	1
2002	17 Apr	Dublin	2	1

v USSR			RI	USSR
wc1972	18 Oct	Dublin	1	2
wc1973	13 May	Moscow	0	1
EC1974	30 Oct	Dublin	3	0
EC1975	18 May	Kiev	1	2
wc1984	12 Sept	Dublin	1	0
wc1985	16 Oct	Moscow	0	2
EC1988	15 June	Hanover	1	1
1990	25 Apr	Dublin	1	0

v WALES			RI	W
1960	28 Sept	Dublin	2	3
1979	11 Sept	Swansea	1	2
1981	24 Feb	Dublin	1	3
1986	26 Mar	Dublin	0	1
1990	28 Mar	Dublin	1	0
1991	6 Feb	Wrexham	3	0
1992	19 Feb	Dublin	0	1
1993	17 Feb	Dublin	2	1
1997	11 Feb	Cardiff	0	0
EC2007	24 Mar	Dublin	1	0
EC2007	17 Nov	Cardiff	2	2
NC2011	8 Feb	Dublin	3	0

v YUGOSLAVIA			RI	Y
1955	19 Sept	Dublin	1	4
1988	27 Apr	Dublin	2	0
EC1998	18 Nov	Belgrade	0	1
EC1999	1 Sept	Dublin	2	1

OTHER BRITISH AND IRISH INTERNATIONAL MATCHES 2010–11

FRIENDLIES

■ *Denotes player sent off.*

Wembley, 11 August 2010, 72,024

England (0) 2 *(Gerrard 69, 73)*

Hungary (0) 1 *(Jagielka 63 (og))*

England: Hart; Johnson G, Cole A (Gibbs 46), Barry, Terry (Dawson 46), Jagielka, Walcott (Young A 46), Lampard (Zamora 46), Rooney (Milner 66), Gerrard (Wilshere 82), Johnson A.

Hungary: Kiraly; Liptak (Komlosi 55), Vanczak (Laczko 46), Juhasz, Szelesi, Vadocz, Dzsudzsak (Koman 46), Rudolf (Priskin 83), Elek (Toth 59), Gera, Huszti (Hajnal 46).

Referee: S. Lannoy (France).

Wembley, 17 November 2010, 85,495

England (0) 1 *(Crouch 86)*

France (1) 2 *(Benzema 16, Valbuena 55)*

England: Foster; Jagielka, Gibbs (Warnock 72), Gerrard (Crouch 84), Ferdinand (Richards 46), Lescott, Walcott (Johnson A 46), Henderson, Carroll (Bothroyd 72), Barry (Young A 46), Milner.

France: Lloris; Sagna (Reveillere 86), Abidal, Rami, Mexes (Sakho 46), Gourcuff (Hoarau 85), Malouda (Payet 77), M'Vila, Valbuena (Diarra 68), Benzema (Remy 67), Nasri.

Referee: Bo Larsen (Denmark).

Copenhagen, 9 February 2011, 21,523

Denmark(1) 1 *(Agger 7)*

England (1) 2 *(Bent 10, Young A 68)*

Denmark: Sorensen; Poulsen C, Jorgensen (Kjaer 46), Agger, Poulsen S (Wass 46), Jacobsen (Silberbauer 60), Kvist (Vingaard 90), Eriksen, Krohn-Delhi (Pedersen 70), Rommedahl (Enevoldsen 82), Bendtner.

England: Hart; Johnson G, Cole A (Baines 81), Wilshere (Parker 46), Terry, Dawson (Cahill 60), Walcott (Downing 67), Lampard (Barry 46), Rooney (Young A 46), Bent, Milner.

Referee: J. Eriksson (Sweden).

Wembley, 29 March 2011, 80,102

England (1) 1 *(Carroll 43)*

Ghana (0) 1 *(Gyan 90)*

England: Hart; Johnson G, Baines, Barry, Cahill, Jagielka (Lescott 46), Milner, Wilshere (Jarvis 69), Carroll (Defoe 59), Young A (Welbeck 81), Downing.

Ghana: Kingson; Pantsil, Addy (Jonathan Mensah 46), Vorsah (Boateng 46), John Mensah, Annan (Opare 46), Agyemang-Badu, Adiyiah (Tagoe 69), Gyan, Muntari (Ayew-Dede 59), Asamoah (Inkoom 84).

Referee: C. Cuneyt (Turkey).

Stockholm, 11 August 2010, 25,249

Sweden (2) 3 *(Ibrahimovic 4, Bajrami 39, Toivonen 56)*

Scotland (0) 0

Sweden: Isaksson; Lustig (Larsson 46), Mellberg, Majstorovic, Safari, Svensson (Wendt 73), Wernbloom (Kallstrom 46), Elmander (Berg 78), Toivonen, Bajrami (Wilhelmsson 64), Ibrahimovic (Hysen 59).

Scotland: McGregor; Broadfoot (Whittaker 74), Kenneth, Berra, Wallace L, Robson (Iwelumo 78), Fletcher D, Thomson (Robertson S 54), Adam (Morrison 64), McFadden, Fletcher S (Boyd 64).

Referee: G. Rocchi (Italy).

Aberdeen, 16 November 2010, 25,064

Scotland (3) 3 *(Wilson 24, Commons 31, Mackie 45)*

Faeroes (0) 0

Scotland: Gordon (Bell 68); Bardsley (Saunders 71), Caldwell S, Wilson (Kenneth 60), Crainey, Commons (Goodwillie 76), Bannan, Fletcher D (Bryson 68), Adam (McArthur 55), Maloney, Mackie.

Faeroes: Nielsen; Naes, Davidsen, Gregersen, Jacobsen, Udsen (Juspinusen 86), Petersen (Mouritsen 60), Lokin, Elttor, Holst (Poulsen 56), Edmundsson.

Referee: P. van Boekel (Holland)

Emirates Stadium, 27 March 2011, 53,087

Scotland (0) 0

Brazil (1) 2 *(Neymar 42, 77 (pen))*

Scotland: McGregor; Hutton, Crainey, Brown, Caldwell G, Berra (Wilson D 73), Morrison (Cowie 90), Adam (Snodgrass 78), Miller K (Mackail-Smith 87), McArthur (Bannan 56), Whittaker (Commons 64).

Brazil: Julio Cesar; Dani Alves, Lucio, Thiago Silva, Andre Santos, Lucas (Sandro 86), Elano (Elias 82), Ramires, Jadson (Lucas Rodriguez 72), Neymar (Renato Augusto 89), Leandro Damiao (Oliveira 78).

Referee: H. Webb (England).

Llanelli, 11 August 2010, 10,000

Wales (1) 5 *(Cotterill 35, Ledley 48 (pen), King 55, Williams A 78, Bellamy 82)*

Luxembourg (1) 1 *(Kitenge 44)*

Wales: Hennessey (Myhill 46); Ricketts, Morgan, Williams A (Eardley 85), Gunter, Ledley, Cotterill (Crofts 81), Stock (King 46), Bellamy, Morison, Earnshaw (Vaughan 46).

Luxembourg: Joubert; Mutsch■, Janisch (Collette 79), Kintziger, Hoffmann, Schnell, Peters, Krogh Gerson (Pedro 60), Bettmer (Bernard 86), Da Mota (Laterza 68), Kitenge.

Referee: M. Gestranius (Finland).

Podgorica, 11 August 2010, 5000

Montenegro (1) 2 *(Djalovic 43, 59)*

Northern Ireland (0) 0

Montenegro: Bozovic M; Pavicevic (Bozovic D 52), Djudovic, Jovanovic (Savic 75), Pekovic M (Novakovic 62), Vukcevic, Pejovic (Tomasevic 56), Zverotic (Beciraj 83), Bozovic V, Vucinic, Djalovic (Delibasic 77).

Northern Ireland: Taylor; Little, McGivern (Healy 68), Evans J, Craigan, Baird (Feeney 46), Davis, Clingan (Norwood 64), Paterson (Evans C 46), Lafferty (Gorman 58), Brunt (McCann 46).

Referee: B. Jovanetic (Serbia).

Belfast, 17 November 2010, 15,000

Northern Ireland (0) 1 *(Patterson 86 (pen))*

Morocco (0) 1 *(Chamakh 55)*

Northern Ireland: Tuffey (Blayney 46); Hodson, McGivern (Coates 62), Barton, Evans J, Hughes (McArdle 46), McCourt (O'Connor 46), McGinn (Magennis 69), Patterson, Gorman, Brunt (McQuoid 47).

Morocco: Lamyaghri; Soulaimani, El Kaddouri, Kantari, Mehdi Benatia (Mohamed Berrabeh 78), Hermach (El Ahmadi 89), Belhanda (Benzoukane 75), Kharja, Hadji (El Zhar 80), Chadli, Chamakh (El Arabi 71).

Referee: T. Hagen (Norway).

Dublin, 11 August 2010, 49,500

Republic of Ireland (0) 0

Argentina (1) 1 *(Di Maria 20)*

Republic of Ireland: Given; McShane, Dunne, O'Shea, Kilbane (Cunningham 57), Fahey (Treacy 77), Andrews (Gibson 67), Green, Duff, Keane, Sheridan (Keogh 56).

Argentina: Romero; Demichelis, Burdisso (Zabaleta 46), Samuel (Coloccini 83), Heinze (Insua 72), Mascherano, Gago, Banega, Messi (Lavezzi 58), Di Maria (Gutierrez 75), Higuain (Milito 46).

Referee: P. Rasmussen (Denmark).

Dublin, 17 November 2010, 25,000
Republic of Ireland (1) 1 *(Long 5 (pen))*
Norway (1) 2 *(Pedersen 34, Huseklepp 86)*

Republic of Ireland: Given; Kelly, Cunningham, O'Shea, O'Dea (Foley 67), Whelan, Lawrence (Walters 46), Fahey, Long, Doyle (McGeady 46), Duff (Hunt S 74).
Norway: Knudsen (Pettersen 46); Hogli, Waehler, Hangeland, Riise J, Hauger, Pedersen, Grindheim (Yettergard Jenssen 55), Moen (Haestad 78), Helstad (Riise B 46), Huseklepp (Moldskred 90).
Referee: K. Jakobsson (Iceland).

Dublin, 29 March 2011, 25,611
Republic of Ireland (1) 2 *(Long 15, Fahey 48 (pen))*
Uruguay (3) 3 *(Lugano 12, Cavani 22, Hernandez 39)*

Republic of Ireland: Westwood; Kelly, O'Dea, Kelly, Clark (Delaney 75), Lawrence (McGeady 78), Green, Fahey (Gibson 66), Keogh (Stokes 85), McCarthy (Treacy 66), Long.
Uruguay: Muslera; Lugano, Godin, Caceres, Maxi Pereira, Arevalo Rios (Gargano 64), Perez (Scotti 90), Pereira, Hernandez (Eguren 84), Forlan, Cavani.
Referee: S. Ennjimi (France).

Liege, 7 June 2011, 21,516
Italy (0) 0
Republic of Ireland (1) 2 *(Andrews 36, Cox 90)*

Italy: Viviano; Cassani, Gamberini, Criscito (Balzaretti 66), Chiellini, Marchisio, Pirlo (Palombo 46), Nocerino (Giovinco 59), Montolivo, Rossi (Matri 46), Pazzini (Gilardino 59).
Republic of Ireland: Forde; McShane, Ward (Delaney 90), St Ledger-Hall, O'Dea (Kelly 83), Foley (Whelan 60), Coleman, Andrews, Hunt, Long (Cox 60), Keogh (Treacy 74).
Referee: S. Gumienny (Belgium).

CARLING NATIONS CUP

Dublin, 8 February 2011, 19,783
Republic of Ireland (0) 3 *(Gibson 60, Duff 67, Fahey 83)*
Wales (0) 0

Republic of Ireland: Given; O'Shea (O'Dea 85), St Ledger-Hall, Dunne, Clark, Coleman (Fahey 58), Whelan (Green 76), Gibson (Wilson 81), Duff (Keogh 71), Walters, Doyle (Long 46).
Wales: Hennessey; Eardley (Gunter 46), Collins D, Collins JM, Ricketts (Nyatanga 83), Crofts, Vaughan (Ledley 61), King, Robson-Kanu (Eastwood 68), Church, Earnshaw (Easter 80).
Referee: M. Courtney (N. Ireland).

Dublin, 9 February 2011, 18,742
Northern Ireland (0) 0
Scotland (2) 3 *(Miller K 19, McArthur 32, Commons 51)*

Northern Ireland: Tuffey; McArdle (Hodson 46), Baird, McAuley, Craigan (Thompson 66), McCourt, Evans J, Davis (Norwood 58), McCann (Healy 46), McGinn (Boyce 72), Patterson.
Scotland: McGregor; Hutton, Caldwell S, Berra, Bardsley (Wilson M 57), Morrison (Maguire 79), Adam (Bannan 57), Commons (Conway 72), McArthur, Naismith (Snodgrass 58), Miller K (Wilson D 90).
Referee: T. Connolly (Republic of Ireland).

Dublin, 24 May 2011, 12,083
Republic of Ireland (3) 5 *(Ward 24, Keane 37, 54 (pen), Cathcart 45 (og), Cox 80)*
Northern Ireland (0) 0

Republic of Ireland: Given (Forde 72); McShane, Ward, Kelly, Delaney, Coleman (Lawrence 55), Andrews, Foley (Hunt 70), Treacy, Keane (Keogh 62), Cox.
Northern Ireland: Blayney; Thompson■, Cathcart, McAuley, Hodson, Carson (McGinn 73), Clingan, Davis (Garrett 76), Gorman (Coates 55), Feeney (Boyce 73), McQuoid (Norwood 46).
Referee: C. Thomson (Scotland).

Dublin, 25 May 2011, 6036
Wales (1) 1 *(Earnshaw 36)*
Scotland (0) 3 *(Morrison 55, Miller K 64, Berra 70)*

Wales: Myhill; Eardley (Matthews 61), Morgan, Blake, Taylor (Gunter 46), Tudur Jones (Vaughan 72), Dorman (Cotterill 60), King (Ramsey 61), Vokes (Morison 72), Earnshaw, Easter.
Scotland: McGregor; Whittaker (Bardsley 81), Caldwell G (Hanley 84), Berra, Crainey (Martin 81), Naismith, Brown, Adam (McArthur 88), Morrison (Robson 74), McCormack (Bannan 73), Miller, K.
Referee: R. Crangle (Northern Ireland).

Dublin, 27 May 2011, 529
Wales (1) 2 *(Ramsey 35, Earnshaw 68)*
Northern Ireland (0) 0

Wales: Hennessey (Price 74); Gunter (Matthews 72), Taylor, Collison (Tudur Jones 61), Collins D, Gabbidon, Cotterill, Bellamy (Earnshaw 61), Morison (Vokes 80), Ramsey (Dorman 89), Vaughan.
Northern Ireland: Tuffey; Hodson, Coates, Cathcart (Dallas 61), McAuley, Norwood, Curson, Garrett (Winchester 75), McGinn (Owens 80), Feeney (Boyce 72), Gorman.
Referee: A. Kelly (Republic of Ireland).

Dublin, 29 May 2011, 17,694
Repbulic of Ireland (1) 1 *(Keane 23)*
Scotland (0) 0

Republic of Ireland: Given; McShane, O'Dea (Foley 66), Kelly, Ward, Lawrence (Coleman 62), Andrews, Fahey, Hunt, Keane (Treacy 83), Cox.
Scotland: McGregor; Whittaker, Hanley, Berra, Bardsley, Forrest (McCormack 85), Brown, Adam (Bannan 63), Robson (Maguire 75), Naismith, Miller K.
Referee: M. Whitby (Wales).

	P	W	D	L	F	A	Pts
Republic of Ireland	3	3	0	0	9	0	9
Scotland	3	2	0	1	6	2	6
Wales	3	1	0	2	3	6	3
Northern Ireland	3	0	0	3	0	10	0

INTERNATIONAL APPEARANCES 1872–2011

This is a list of full international appearances by Englishmen, Irishmen, Scotsmen and Welshmen in matches against the Home Countries and against foreign nations. It does not include unofficial matches against Commonwealth and Empire countries. The year indicated refers to the player's international debut season; i.e. 2005 is the 2004–05 season. **Bold type** indicates players who have made an international appearance in season 2010–11.

As at July 2011.

ENGLAND

Abbott, W. 1902 (Everton)	1	Barham, M. 1983 (Norwich C)	2
A'Court, A. 1958 (Liverpool)	5	Barkas, S. 1936 (Manchester C)	5
Adams, T. A. 1987 (Arsenal)	66	Barker, J. 1935 (Derby Co)	11
Adcock, H. 1929 (Leicester C)	5	Barker, R. 1872 (Herts Rangers)	1
Agbonlahor, G. 2009 (Aston Villa)	3	Barker, R. R. 1895 (Casuals)	1
Alcock, C. W. 1875 (Wanderers)	1	Barlow, R. J. 1955 (WBA)	1
Alderson, J. T. 1923 (C Palace)	1	Barmby, N. J. 1995 (Tottenham H, Middlesbrough,	
Aldridge, A. 1888 (WBA, Walsall Town Swifts)	2	Everton, Liverpool)	23
Allen, A. 1888 (Aston Villa)	1	Barnes, J. 1983 (Watford, Liverpool)	79
Allen, A. 1960 (Stoke C)	3	Barnes, P. S. 1978 (Manchester C, WBA, Leeds U)	22
Allen, C. 1984 (QPR, Tottenham H)	5	Barnet, H. H. 1882 (Royal Engineers)	1
Allen, H. 1888 (Wolverhampton W)	5	Barrass, M. W. 1952 (Bolton W)	3
Allen, J. P. 1934 (Portsmouth)	2	Barrett, A. F. 1930 (Fulham)	1
Allen, R. 1952 (WBA)	5	Barrett, E. D. 1991 (Oldham Ath, Aston Villa)	3
Alsford, W. J. 1935 (Tottenham H)	1	Barrett, J. W. 1929 (West Ham U)	1
Amos, A. 1885 (Old Carthusians)	2	**Barry, G. 2000 (Aston Villa, Manchester C)**	**46**
Anderson, R. D. 1879 (Old Etonians)	1	Barry, L. 1928 (Leicester C)	5
Anderson, S. 1962 (Sunderland)	2	Barson, F. 1920 (Aston Villa)	1
Anderson, V. A. 1979 (Nottingham F, Arsenal,		Barton, J. 1890 (Blackburn R)	1
Manchester U)	30	Barton, J. 2007 (Manchester C)	1
Anderton, D. R. 1994 (Tottenham H)	30	Barton, P. H. 1921 (Birmingham)	7
Angus, J. 1961 (Burnley)	1	Barton, W. D. 1995 (Wimbledon, Newcastle U)	3
Armfield, J. C. 1959 (Blackpool)	43	Bassett, W. I. 1888 (WBA)	16
Armitage, G. H. 1926 (Charlton Ath)	1	Bastard, S. R. 1880 (Upton Park)	1
Armstrong, D. 1980 (Middlesbrough, Southampton)	3	Bastin, C. S. 1932 (Arsenal)	21
Armstrong, K. 1955 (Chelsea)	1	Batty, D. 1991 (Leeds U, Blackburn R, Newcastle U,	
Arnold, J. 1933 (Fulham)	1	Leeds U)	42
Arthur, J. W. H. 1885 (Blackburn R)	7	Daugh, R. 1886 (Stafford Road, Wolverhampton W)	2
Ashcroft, J. 1906 (Woolwich Arsenal)	3	Bayliss, A. E. J. M. 1891 (WBA)	1
Ashmore, G. S. 1926 (WBA)	1	Baynham, R. L. 1956 (Luton T)	3
Ashton, C. T. 1926 (Corinthians)	1	Beardsley, P. A. 1986 (Newcastle U, Liverpool,	
Ashton, D. 2008 (West Ham U)	1	Newcastle U)	59
Ashurst, W. 1923 (Notts Co)	5	Beasant, D. J. 1990 (Chelsea)	2
Astall, G. 1956 (Birmingham C)	2	Beasley, A. 1939 (Huddersfield T)	1
Astle, J. 1969 (WBA)	5	Beats, W. E. 1901 (Wolverhampton W)	2
Aston, J. 1949 (Manchester U)	17	Beattie, J. S. 2003 (Southampton)	5
Athersmith, W. C. 1892 (Aston Villa)	12	Beattie, T. K. 1975 (Ipswich T)	9
Atyeo, P. J. W. 1956 (Bristol C)	6	Beckham, D. R. J. 1997 (Manchester U, Real Madrid,	
Austin, S. W. 1926 (Manchester C)	1	LA Galaxy)	115
		Becton, F. 1895 (Preston NE, Liverpool)	2
Bach, P. 1899 (Sunderland)	1	Bedford, H. 1923 (Blackpool)	2
Bache, J. W. 1903 (Aston Villa)	7	Bell, C. 1968 (Manchester C)	48
Baddeley, T. 1903 (Wolverhampton W)	5	Bennett, W. 1901 (Sheffield U)	2
Bagshaw, J. J. 1920 (Derby Co)	1	Benson, R. W. 1913 (Sheffield U)	1
Bailey, G. R. 1985 (Manchester U)	2	**Bent, D. A. 2006 (Charlton Ath, Tottenham H,**	
Bailey, H. P. 1908 (Leicester Fosse)	5	**Sunderland, Aston Villa)**	**10**
Bailey, M. A. 1964 (Charlton Ath)	2	Bentley, D. M. 2008 (Blackburn R, Tottenham H)	7
Bailey, N. C. 1878 (Clapham Rovers)	19	Bentley, R. T. F. 1949 (Chelsea)	12
Baily, E. F. 1950 (Tottenham H)	9	Beresford, J. 1934 (Aston Villa)	1
Bain, J. 1877 (Oxford University)	1	Berry, A. 1909 (Oxford University)	1
Baines, L. J. 2010 (Everton)	**5**	Berry, J. J. 1953 (Manchester U)	4
Baker, A. 1928 (Arsenal)	1	Bestall, J. G. 1935 (Grimsby T)	1
Baker, B. H. 1921 (Everton, Chelsea)	2	Betmead, H. A. 1937 (Grimsby T)	1
Baker, J. H. 1960 (Hibernian, Arsenal)	8	Betts, M. P. 1877 (Old Harrovians)	1
Ball, A. J. 1965 (Blackpool, Everton, Arsenal)	72	Betts, W. 1889 (Sheffield W)	1
Ball, J. 1928 (Bury)	1	Beverley, J. 1884 (Blackburn R)	3
Ball, M. J. 2001 (Everton)	1	Birkett, R. H. 1879 (Clapham Rovers)	1
Balmer, W. 1905 (Everton)	1	Birkett, R. J. E. 1936 (Middlesbrough)	1
Bamber, J. 1921 (Liverpool)	1	Birley, F. H. 1874 (Oxford University, Wanderers)	2
Bambridge, A. L. 1881 (Swifts)	3	Birtles, G. 1980 (Nottingham F)	3
Bambridge, E. C. 1879 (Swifts)	18	Bishop, S. M. 1927 (Leicester C)	4
Bambridge, E. H. 1876 (Swifts)	1	Blackburn, F. 1901 (Blackburn R)	3
Banks, G. 1963 (Leicester C, Stoke C)	73	Blackburn, G. F. 1924 (Aston Villa)	1
Banks, H. E. 1901 (Millwall)	1	Blenkinsop, E. 1928 (Sheffield W)	26
Banks, T. 1958 (Bolton W)	6	Bliss, H. 1921 (Tottenham H)	1
Bannister, W. 1901 (Burnley, Bolton W)	2	Blissett, L. L. 1983 (Watford, AC Milan)	14
Barclay, R. 1932 (Sheffield U)	3	Blockley, J. P. 1973 (Arsenal)	1
Bardsley, D. J. 1993 (QPR)	2	Bloomer, S. 1895 (Derby Co, Middlesbrough)	23

Blunstone, F. 1955 (Chelsea)	5
Bond, R. 1905 (Preston NE, Bradford C)	8
Bonetti, P. P. 1966 (Chelsea)	7
Bonsor, A. G. 1873 (Wanderers)	2
Booth, F. 1905 (Manchester C)	1
Booth, T. 1898 (Blackburn R, Everton)	2
Bothroyd, J. 2011 (Cardiff C)	**1**
Bould, S. A. 1994 (Arsenal)	2
Bowden, E. R. 1935 (Arsenal)	6
Bower, A. G. 1924 (Corinthians)	5
Bowers, J. W. 1934 (Derby Co)	3
Bowles, S. 1974 (QPR)	5
Bowser, S. 1920 (WBA)	1
Bowyer, L. D. 2003 (Leeds U)	1
Boyer, P. J. 1976 (Norwich C)	1
Boyes, W. 1935 (WBA, Everton)	3
Boyle, T. W. 1913 (Burnley)	1
Brabrook, P. 1958 (Chelsea)	3
Bracewell, P. W. 1985 (Everton)	3
Bradford, G. R. W. 1956 (Bristol R)	1
Bradford, J. 1924 (Birmingham)	12
Bradley, W. 1959 (Manchester U)	3
Bradshaw, F. 1908 (Sheffield W)	1
Bradshaw, T. H. 1897 (Liverpool)	1
Bradshaw, W. 1910 (Blackburn R)	4
Brann, G. 1886 (Swifts)	3
Brawn, W. F. 1904 (Aston Villa)	2
Bray, J. 1935 (Manchester C)	6
Brayshaw, E. 1887 (Sheffield W)	1
Bridge W. M. 2002 (Southampton, Chelsea, Manchester C)	36
Bridges, B. J. 1965 (Chelsea)	4
Bridgett, A. 1905 (Sunderland)	11
Brindle, T. 1880 (Darwen)	2
Brittleton, J. T. 1912 (Sheffield W)	5
Britton, C. S. 1935 (Everton)	9
Broadbent, P. F. 1958 (Wolverhampton W)	7
Broadis, I. A. 1952 (Manchester C, Newcastle U)	14
Brockbank, J. 1872 (Cambridge University)	1
Brodie, J. B. 1889 (Wolverhampton W)	3
Bromilow, T. G. 1921 (Liverpool)	5
Bromley-Davenport, W. E. 1884 (Oxford University)	2
Brook, E. F. 1930 (Manchester C)	18
Brooking, T. D. 1974 (West Ham U)	47
Brooks, J. 1957 (Tottenham H)	3
Broome, F. H. 1938 (Aston Villa)	7
Brown, A. 1882 (Aston Villa)	3
Brown, A. 1971 (WBA)	1
Brown, A. S. 1904 (Sheffield U)	2
Brown, G. 1927 (Huddersfield T, Aston Villa)	9
Brown, J. 1881 (Blackburn R)	5
Brown, J. H. 1927 (Sheffield W)	6
Brown, K. 1960 (West Ham U)	1
Brown, W. 1924 (West Ham U)	1
Brown, W. M. 1999 (Manchester U)	23
Bruton, J. 1928 (Burnley)	3
Bryant, W. I. 1925 (Clapton)	1
Buchan, C. M. 1913 (Sunderland)	6
Buchanan, W. S. 1876 (Clapham R)	1
Buckley, F. C. 1914 (Derby Co)	1
Bull, S. G. 1989 (Wolverhampton W)	13
Bullock, F. E. 1921 (Huddersfield T)	1
Bullock, N. 1923 (Bury)	3
Burgess, H. 1904 (Manchester C)	4
Burgess, H. 1931 (Sheffield W)	4
Burnup, C. J. 1896 (Cambridge University)	1
Burrows, H. 1934 (Sheffield W)	3
Burton, F. E. 1889 (Nottingham F)	1
Bury, L. 1877 (Cambridge University, Old Etonians)	2
Butcher, T. 1980 (Ipswich T, Rangers)	77
Butler, J. D. 1925 (Arsenal)	1
Butler, W. 1924 (Bolton W)	1
Butt, N. 1997 (Manchester U, Newcastle U)	39
Byrne, G. 1963 (Liverpool)	2
Byrne, J. J. 1962 (C Palace, West Ham U)	11
Byrne, R. W. 1954 (Manchester U)	33
Cahill, G. J. 2011 (Bolton W)	**3**
Callaghan, I. R. 1966 (Liverpool)	4

Calvey, J. 1902 (Nottingham F)	1
Campbell, A. F. 1929 (Blackburn R, Huddersfield T)	8
Campbell, S. 1996 (Tottenham H, Arsenal, Portsmouth)	73
Camsell, G. H. 1929 (Middlesbrough)	9
Capes, A. J. 1903 (Stoke)	1
Carr, J. 1905 (Newcastle U)	2
Carr, J. 1920 (Middlesbrough)	2
Carr, W. H. 1875 (Owlerton, Sheffield)	1
Carragher, J. L. 1999 (Liverpool)	38
Carrick, M. 2001 (West Ham U, Tottenham H, Manchester U)	22
Carroll, A. T. 2011 (Newcastle U, Liverpool)	**2**
Carson, S. P. 2008 (Liverpool, WBA)	3
Carter, H. S. 1934 (Sunderland, Derby Co)	13
Carter, J. H. 1926 (WBA)	3
Catlin, A. E. 1937 (Sheffield W)	5
Chadwick, A. 1900 (Southampton)	2
Chadwick, E. 1891 (Everton)	7
Chamberlain, M. 1983 (Stoke C)	8
Chambers, H. 1921 (Liverpool)	8
Channon, M. R. 1973 (Southampton, Manchester C)	46
Charles, G. A. 1991 (Nottingham F)	2
Charlton, J. 1965 (Leeds U)	35
Charlton, R. 1958 (Manchester U)	106
Charnley, R. O. 1963 (Blackpool)	1
Charsley, C. C. 1893 (Small Heath)	1
Chedgzoy, S. 1920 (Everton)	8
Chenery, C. J. 1872 (C Palace)	3
Cherry, T. J. 1976 (Leeds U)	27
Chilton, A. 1951 (Manchester U)	2
Chippendale, H. 1894 (Blackburn R)	1
Chivers, M. 1971 (Tottenham H)	24
Christian, E. 1879 (Old Etonians)	1
Clamp, E. 1958 (Wolverhampton W)	4
Clapton, D. R. 1959 (Arsenal)	1
Clare, T. 1889 (Stoke)	4
Clarke, A. J. 1970 (Leeds U)	19
Clarke, H. A. 1954 (Tottenham H)	1
Clay, T. 1920 (Tottenham H)	4
Clayton, R. 1956 (Blackburn R)	35
Clegg, J. C. 1872 (Sheffield W)	1
Clegg, W. E. 1873 (Sheffield W, Sheffield Albion)	2
Clemence, R. N. 1973 (Liverpool, Tottenham H)	61
Clement, D. T. 1976 (QPR)	5
Clough, B. H. 1960 (Middlesbrough)	2
Clough, N. H. 1989 (Nottingham F)	14
Coates, R. 1970 (Burnley, Tottenham H)	4
Cobbold, W. N. 1883 (Cambridge University, Old Carthusians)	9
Cock, J. G. 1920 (Huddersfield T, Chelsea)	2
Cockburn, H. 1947 (Manchester U)	13
Cohen, G. R. 1964 (Fulham)	37
Cole, A. 2001 (Arsenal, Chelsea)	**89**
Cole, A. A. 1995 (Manchester U)	15
Cole, C. 2009 (West Ham U)	7
Cole, J. J. 2001 (West Ham U, Chelsea)	56
Colclough, H. 1914 (C Palace)	1
Coleman, E. H. 1921 (Dulwich Hamlet)	1
Coleman, J. 1907 (Woolwich Arsenal)	1
Collymore, S. V. 1995 (Nottingham F, Aston Villa)	3
Common, A. 1904 (Sheffield U, Middlesbrough)	3
Compton, L. H. 1951 (Arsenal)	2
Conlin, J. 1906 (Bradford C)	1
Connelly, J. M. 1960 (Burnley, Manchester U)	20
Cook, T. E. R. 1925 (Brighton)	1
Cooper, C. T. 1995 (Nottingham F)	2
Cooper, N. C. 1893 (Cambridge University)	1
Cooper, T. 1928 (Derby Co)	15
Cooper, T. 1969 (Leeds U)	20
Coppell, S. J. 1978 (Manchester U)	42
Copping, W. 1933 (Leeds U, Arsenal, Leeds U)	20
Corbett, B. O. 1901 (Corinthians)	1
Corbett, R. 1903 (Old Malvernians)	1
Corbett, W. S. 1908 (Birmingham)	3
Corrigan, J. T. 1976 (Manchester C)	9
Cottee, A. R. 1987 (West Ham U, Everton)	7
Cotterill, G. H. 1891 (Cambridge University, Old Brightonians)	4

Cottle, J. R. 1909 (Bristol C) — 1
Cowan, S. 1926 (Manchester C) — 3
Cowans, G. S. 1983 (Aston Villa, Bari, Aston Villa) — 10
Cowell, A. 1910 (Blackburn R) — 1
Cox, J. 1901 (Liverpool) — 3
Cox, J. D. 1892 (Derby Co) — 1
Crabtree, J. W. 1894 (Burnley, Aston Villa) — 14
Crawford, J. F. 1931 (Chelsea) — 1
Crawford, R. 1962 (Ipswich T) — 2
Crawshaw, T. H. 1895 (Sheffield W) — 10
Crayston, W. J. 1936 (Arsenal) — 8
Creek, F. N. S. 1923 (Corinthians) — 1
Cresswell, W. 1921 (South Shields, Sunderland, Everton) — 7
Crompton, R. 1902 (Blackburn R) — 41
Crooks, S. D. 1930 (Derby Co) — 26
Crouch, P. J. 2005 (Southampton, Liverpool, Portsmouth, Tottenham H) — **42**
Crowe, C. 1963 (Wolverhampton W) — 1
Cuggy, F. 1913 (Sunderland) — 2
Cullis, S. 1938 (Wolverhampton W) — 12
Cunliffe, A. 1933 (Blackburn R) — 2
Cunliffe, D. 1900 (Portsmouth) — 1
Cunliffe, J. N. 1936 (Everton) — 1
Cunningham, L. 1979 (WBA, Real Madrid) — 6
Curle, K. 1992 (Manchester C) — 3
Currey, E. S. 1890 (Oxford University) — 2
Currie, A. W. 1972 (Sheffield U, Leeds U) — 17
Cursham, A. W. 1876 (Notts Co) — 6
Cursham, H. A. 1880 (Notts Co) — 8

Daft, H. B. 1889 (Notts Co) — 5
Daley, A. M. 1992 (Aston Villa) — 7
Danks, T. 1885 (Nottingham F) — 1
Davenport, P. 1985 (Nottingham F) — 1
Davenport, J. K. 1885 (Bolton W) — 2
Davies, K. C. 2011 (Bolton W) — **1**
Davis, G 1904 (Derby Co) — 2
Davis, H. 1903 (Sheffield W) — 3
Davison, J. E. 1922 (Sheffield W) — 1
Dawson, J. 1922 (Burnley) — 2
Dawson, M. R. 2011 (Tottenham H) — **4**
Day, S. H. 1906 (Old Malvernians) — 3
Dean, W. R. 1927 (Everton) — 16
Deane, B. C. 1991 (Sheffield U) — 3
Deeley, N. V. 1959 (Wolverhampton W) — 2
Defoe, J. C. 2004 (Tottenham H, Portsmouth, Tottenham H) — **46**
Devey, J. H. G. 1892 (Aston Villa) — 2
Devonshire, A. 1980 (West Ham U) — 8
Dewhurst, F. 1886 (Preston NE) — 9
Dewhurst, G. P. 1895 (Liverpool Ramblers) — 1
Dickinson, J. W. 1949 (Portsmouth) — 48
Dimmock, J. H. 1921 (Tottenham H) — 3
Ditchburn, E. G. 1949 (Tottenham H) — 6
Dix, R. W. 1939 (Derby Co) — 1
Dixon, J. A. 1885 (Notts Co) — 1
Dixon, K. M. 1985 (Chelsea) — 8
Dixon, L. M. 1990 (Arsenal) — 22
Dobson, A. T. C. 1882 (Notts Co) — 4
Dobson, C. F. 1886 (Notts Co) — 1
Dobson, J. M. 1974 (Burnley, Everton) — 5
Doggart, A. G. 1924 (Corinthians) — 1
Dorigo, A. R. 1990 (Chelsea, Leeds U) — 15
Dorrell, A. R. 1925 (Aston Villa) — 4
Douglas, B. 1958 (Blackburn R) — 36
Downing, S. 2005 (Middlesbrough, Aston Villa) — **27**
Downs, R. W. 1921 (Everton) — 1
Doyle, M. 1976 (Manchester C) — 5
Drake, E. J. 1935 (Arsenal) — 5
Dublin, D. 1998 (Coventry C, Aston Villa) — 4
Ducat, A. 1910 (Woolwich Arsenal, Aston Villa) — 6
Dunn, A. T. B. 1883 (Cambridge University, Old Etonians) — 4
Dunn, D. J. I. 2003 (Blackburn R) — 1
Duxbury, M. 1984 (Manchester U) — 10
Dyer, K. C. 2000 (Newcastle U, West Ham U) — 33

Earle, S. G. J. 1924 (Clapton, West Ham U) — 2

Eastham, G. 1963 (Arsenal) — 19
Eastham, G. R. 1935 (Bolton W) — 1
Eckersley, W. 1950 (Blackburn R) — 17
Edwards, D. 1955 (Manchester U) — 18
Edwards, J. H. 1874 (Shropshire Wanderers) — 1
Edwards, W. 1926 (Leeds U) — 16
Ehiogu, U. 1996 (Aston Villa, Middlesbrough) — 4
Ellerington, W. 1949 (Southampton) — 2
Elliott, G. W. 1913 (Middlesbrough) — 3
Elliott, W. H. 1952 (Burnley) — 5
Evans, R. E. 1911 (Sheffield U) — 4
Ewer, F. H. 1924 (Casuals) — 2

Fairclough, P. 1878 (Old Foresters) — 1
Fairhurst, D. 1934 (Newcastle U) — 1
Fantham, J. 1962 (Sheffield W) — 1
Fashanu, J. 1989 (Wimbledon) — 2
Felton, W. 1925 (Sheffield W) — 1
Fenton, W. 1938 (Middlesbrough) — 1
Fenwick, T. W. 1984 (QPR, Tottenham H) — 20
Ferdinand, L. 1993 (QPR, Newcastle U, Tottenham H) 17
Ferdinand, R. G. 1998 (West Ham U, Leeds U, Manchester U) — **81**
Field, E. 1876 (Clapham Rovers) — 2
Finney, T. 1947 (Preston NE) — 76
Fleming, H. J. 1909 (Swindon T) — 11
Fletcher, A. 1889 (Wolverhampton W) — 2
Flowers, R. 1955 (Wolverhampton W) — 49
Flowers, T. D. 1993 (Southampton, Blackburn R) — 11
Forman, Frank 1898 (Nottingham F) — 9
Forman, F. R. 1899 (Nottingham F) — 3
Forrest, J. H. 1884 (Blackburn R) — 11
Fort, J. 1921 (Millwall) — 1
Foster, B. 2007 (Manchester U, Birmingham C) — **5**
Foster, R. E. 1900 (Oxford University, Corinthians) — 5
Foster, S. 1982 (Brighton & HA) — 3
Foulke, W. J. 1897 (Sheffield U) — 1
Foulkes, W. A. 1955 (Manchester U) — 1
Fowler, R. B. 1996 (Liverpool, Leeds U) — 26
Fox, F. S. 1925 (Millwall) — 1
Francis, G. C. J. 1975 (QPR) — 12
Francis, T. 1977 (Birmingham C, Nottingham F, Manchester C, Sampdoria) — 52
Franklin, C. F. 1947 (Stoke C) — 27
Freeman, B. C. 1909 (Everton, Burnley) — 5
Froggatt, J. 1950 (Portsmouth) — 13
Froggatt, R. 1953 (Sheffield W) — 4
Fry, C. B. 1901 (Corinthians) — 1
Furness, W. I. 1933 (Leeds U) — 1

Galley, T. 1937 (Wolverhampton W) — 2
Gardner, A. 2004 (Tottenham H) — 1
Gardner, T. 1934 (Aston Villa) — 2
Garfield, B. 1898 (WBA) — 1
Garraty, W. 1903 (Aston Villa) — 1
Garrett, T. 1952 (Blackpool) — 3
Gascoigne, P. J. 1989 (Tottenham H, Lazio, Rangers, Middlesbrough) — 57
Gates, E. 1981 (Ipswich T) — 2
Gay, L. H. 1893 (Cambridge University, Old Brightonians) — 3
Geary, F. 1890 (Everton) — 2
Geaves, R. L. 1875 (Clapham Rovers) — 1
Gee, C. W. 1932 (Everton) — 3
Geldard, A. 1933 (Everton) — 4
George, C. 1977 (Derby Co) — 1
George, W. 1902 (Aston Villa) — 3
Gerrard, S. G. 2000 (Liverpool) — **89**
Gibbins, W. V. T. 1924 (Clapton) — 2
Gibbs, K. J. R. 2011 (Arsenal) — **2**
Gidman, J. 1977 (Aston Villa) — 1
Gillard, I. T. 1975 (QPR) — 3
Gilliat, W. E. 1893 (Old Carthusians) — 1
Goddard, P. 1982 (West Ham U) — 1
Goodall, F. R. 1926 (Huddersfield T) — 25
Goodall, J. 1888 (Preston NE, Derby Co) — 14
Goodhart, H. C. 1883 (Old Etonians) — 3
Goodwyn, A. G. 1873 (Royal Engineers) — 1
Goodyer, A. C. 1879 (Nottingham F) — 1

Gosling, R. C. 1892 (Old Etonians) 5
Gosnell, A. A. 1906 (Newcastle U) 1
Gough, H. C. 1921 (Sheffield U) 1
Goulden, L. A. 1937 (West Ham U) 14
Graham, L. 1925 (Millwall) 2
Graham, T. 1931 (Nottingham F) 2
Grainger, C. 1956 (Sheffield U, Sunderland) 7
Gray, A. A. 1992 (C Palace) 1
Gray, M. 1999 (Sunderland) 3
Greaves, J. 1959 (Chelsea, Tottenham H) 57
Green, F. T. 1876 (Wanderers) 1
Green, G. H. 1925 (Sheffield U) 8
Green, R. P. 2005 (Norwich C, West Ham U) 11
Greenhalgh, E. H. 1872 (Notts Co) 2
Greenhoff, B. 1976 (Manchester U, Leeds U) 18
Greenwood, D. H. 1882 (Blackburn R) 2
Gregory, J. 1983 (QPR) 6
Grimsdell, A. 1920 (Tottenham H) 6
Grosvenor, A. T. 1934 (Birmingham) 3
Gunn, W. 1884 (Notts Co) 2
Guppy, S. 2000 (Leicester C) 1
Gurney, R. 1935 (Sunderland) 1

Hacking, J. 1929 (Oldham Ath) 3
Hadley, H. 1903 (WBA) 1
Hagan, J. 1949 (Sheffield U) 1
Haines, J. T. W. 1949 (WBA) 1
Hall, A. E. 1910 (Aston Villa) 1
Hall, G. W. 1934 (Tottenham H) 10
Hall, J. 1956 (Birmingham C) 17
Halse, H. J. 1909 (Manchester U) 1
Hammond, H. E. D. 1889 (Oxford University) 1
Hampson, J. 1931 (Blackpool) 3
Hampton, H. 1913 (Aston Villa) 4
Hancocks, J. 1949 (Wolverhampton W) 3
Hapgood, E. 1933 (Arsenal) 30
Hardinge, H. T. W. 1910 (Sheffield U) 1
Hardman, H. P. 1905 (Everton) 4
Hardwick, G. F. M. 1947 (Middlesbrough) 13
Hardy, H. 1925 (Stockport Co) 1
Hardy, S. 1907 (Liverpool, Aston Villa) 21
Harford, M. G. 1988 (Luton T) 2
Hargreaves, F. W. 1880 (Blackburn R) 3
Hargreaves, J. 1881 (Blackburn R) 2

Hargreaves, O. 2002 (Bayern Munich, Manchester U) 42
Harper, E. C. 1926 (Blackburn R) 1
Harris, G. 1966 (Burnley) 1
Harris, P. P. 1950 (Portsmouth) 2
Harris, S. S. 1904 (Cambridge University, Old Westminsters) 6
Harrison, A. H. 1893 (Old Westminsters) 2
Harrison, G. 1921 (Everton) 2
Harrow, J. H. 1923 (Chelsea) 2
Hart, C. 2008 (Manchester C) **11**
Hart, E. 1929 (Leeds U) 8
Hartley, F. 1923 (Oxford C) 1
Harvey, A. 1881 (Wednesbury Strollers) 1
Harvey, J. C. 1971 (Everton) 1
Hassall, H. W. 1951 (Huddersfield T, Bolton W) 5
Hateley, M. 1984 (Portsmouth, AC Milan, Monaco, Rangers) 32
Hawkes, R. M. 1907 (Luton T) 5
Haworth, G. 1887 (Accrington) 5
Hawtrey, J. P. 1881 (Old Etonians) 2
Haygarth, E. B. 1875 (Swifts) 1
Haynes, J. N. 1955 (Fulham) 56
Healless, H. 1925 (Blackburn R) 2
Hector, K. J. 1974 (Derby Co) 2
Hedley, G. A. 1901 (Sheffield U) 1
Hegan, K. E. 1923 (Corinthians) 4
Hellawell, M. S. 1963 (Birmingham C) 2
Henderson, J. B. 2011 (Sunderland) **1**
Hendrie, L. A. 1999 (Aston Villa) 1
Henfrey, A. G. 1891 (Cambridge University, Corinthians) 5
Henry, R. P. 1963 (Tottenham H) 1
Heron, F. 1876 (Wanderers) 1
Heron, G. H. H. 1873 (Uxbridge, Wanderers) 5
Heskey, E. W. I. 1999 (Leicester C, Liverpool, Birmingham C, Wigan Ath, Aston Villa) 62
Hibbert, W. 1910 (Bury) 1
Hibbs, H. E. 1930 (Birmingham) 25
Hill, F. 1963 (Bolton W) 2
Hill, G. A. 1976 (Manchester U) 6
Hill, J. H. 1925 (Burnley, Newcastle U) 11
Hill, R. 1983 (Luton T) 3
Hill, R. H. 1926 (Millwall) 1
Hillman, J. 1899 (Burnley) 1

England manager Fabio Capello. (PA Photos)

Luntley, E. 1880 (Nottingham F)	2
Lyttelton, Hon. A. 1877 (Cambridge University)	1
Lyttelton, Hon. E. 1878 (Cambridge University)	1
Mabbutt, G. 1983 (Tottenham H)	16
Macaulay, R. H. 1881 (Cambridge University)	1
McCall, J. 1913 (Preston NE)	5
McCann, G. P. 2001 (Sunderland)	1
McDermott, T. 1978 (Liverpool)	25
McDonald, C. A. 1958 (Burnley)	8
Macdonald, M. 1972 (Newcastle U)	14
McFarland, R. L. 1971 (Derby Co)	28
McGarry, W. H. 1954 (Huddersfield T)	4
McGuinness, W. 1959 (Manchester U)	2
McInroy, A. 1927 (Sunderland)	1
McMahon, S. 1988 (Liverpool)	17
McManaman, S. 1995 (Liverpool, Real Madrid)	37
McNab, R. 1969 (Arsenal)	4
McNeal, R. 1914 (WBA)	2
McNeil, M. 1961 (Middlesbrough)	9
Macrae, S. 1883 (Notts Co)	5
Maddison, F. B. 1872 (Oxford University)	1
Madeley, P. E. 1971 (Leeds U)	24
Magee, T. P. 1923 (WBA)	5
Makepeace, H. 1906 (Everton)	4
Male, C. G. 1935 (Arsenal)	19
Mannion, W. J. 1947 (Middlesbrough)	26
Mariner, P. 1977 (Ipswich T, Arsenal)	35
Marsden, J. T. 1891 (Darwen)	1
Marsden, W. 1930 (Sheffield W)	3
Marsh, R. W. 1972 (QPR, Manchester C)	9
Marshall, T. 1880 (Darwen)	2
Martin, A. 1981 (West Ham U)	17
Martin, H. 1914 (Sunderland)	1
Martyn, A. N. 1992 (C Palace, Leeds U)	23
Marwood, B. 1989 (Arsenal)	1
Maskrey, H. M. 1908 (Derby Co)	1
Mason, C. 1887 (Wolverhampton W)	3
Matthews, R. D. 1956 (Coventry C)	5
Matthews, S. 1935 (Stoke C, Blackpool)	54
Matthews, V. 1928 (Sheffield U)	2
Maynard, W. J. 1872 (1st Surrey Rifles)	2
Meadows, J. 1955 (Manchester C)	1
Medley, L. D. 1951 (Tottenham H)	6
Meehan, T. 1924 (Chelsea)	1
Melia, J. 1963 (Liverpool)	2
Mercer, D. W. 1923 (Sheffield U)	2
Mercer, J. 1939 (Everton)	5
Merrick, G. H. 1952 (Birmingham C)	23
Merson, P. C. 1992 (Arsenal, Middlesbrough, Aston Villa)	21
Metcalfe, V. 1951 (Huddersfield T)	2
Mew, J. W. 1921 (Manchester U)	1
Middleditch, B. 1897 (Corinthians)	1
Milburn, J. E. T. 1949 (Newcastle U)	13
Miller, B. G. 1961 (Burnley)	1
Miller, H. S. 1923 (Charlton Ath)	1
Mills, D. J. 2001 (Leeds U)	19
Mills, G. R. 1938 (Chelsea)	3
Mills, M. D. 1973 (Ipswich T)	42
Milne, G. 1963 (Liverpool)	14
Milner, J. P. 2010 (Aston Villa, Manchester C)	**19**
Milton, C. A. 1952 (Arsenal)	1
Milward, A. 1891 (Everton)	4
Mitchell, C. 1880 (Upton Park)	5
Mitchell, J. F. 1925 (Manchester C)	1
Moffat, H. 1913 (Oldham Ath)	1
Molyneux, G. 1902 (Southampton)	4
Moon, W. R. 1888 (Old Westminsters)	7
Moore, H. T. 1883 (Notts Co)	2
Moore, J. 1923 (Derby Co)	1
Moore, R. F. 1962 (West Ham U)	108
Moore, W. G. B. 1923 (West Ham U)	1
Mordue, J. 1912 (Sunderland)	2
Morice, C. J. 1872 (Barnes)	1
Morley, A. 1982 (Aston Villa)	6
Morley, H. 1910 (Notts Co)	1
Morren, T. 1898 (Sheffield U)	1
Morris, F. 1920 (WBA)	2

Morris, J. 1949 (Derby Co)	3
Morris, W. W. 1939 (Wolverhampton W)	3
Morse, H. 1879 (Notts Co)	1
Mort, T. 1924 (Aston Villa)	3
Morten, A. 1873 (C Palace)	1
Mortensen, S. H. 1947 (Blackpool)	25
Morton, J. R. 1938 (West Ham U)	1
Mosforth, W. 1877 (Sheffield W, Sheffield Albion, Sheffield W)	9
Moss, F. 1922 (Aston Villa)	5
Moss, F. 1934 (Arsenal)	4
Mosscrop, E. 1914 (Burnley)	2
Mozley, B. 1950 (Derby Co)	3
Mullen, J. 1947 (Wolverhampton W)	12
Mullery, A. P. 1965 (Tottenham H)	35
Murphy, D. B. 2002 (Liverpool)	9
Neal, P. G. 1976 (Liverpool)	50
Needham, E. 1894 (Sheffield U)	16
Neville, G. A. 1995 (Manchester U)	85
Neville, P. J. 1996 (Manchester U, Everton)	59
Newton, K. R. 1966 (Blackburn R, Everton)	27
Nicholls, J. 1954 (WBA)	2
Nicholson, W. E. 1951 (Tottenham H)	1
Nish, D. J. 1973 (Derby Co)	5
Norman, M. 1962 (Tottenham H)	23
Nugent, D. J. 2007 (Preston NE)	1
Nuttall, H. 1928 (Bolton W)	3
Oakley, W. J. 1895 (Oxford University, Corinthians)	16
O'Dowd, J. P. 1932 (Chelsea)	3
O'Grady, M. 1963 (Huddersfield T, Leeds U)	2
Ogilvie, R. A. M. M. 1874 (Clapham R)	1
Oliver, L. F. 1929 (Fulham)	1
Olney, B. A. 1928 (Aston Villa)	2
Osborne, F. R. 1923 (Fulham, Tottenham H)	4
Osborne, R. 1928 (Leicester C)	1
Osgood, P. L. 1970 (Chelsea)	4
Osman, R. 1980 (Ipswich T)	11
Ottaway, C. J. 1872 (Oxford University)	2
Owen, J. R. B. 1874 (Sheffield)	1
Owen, M. J. 1998 (Liverpool, Real Madrid, Newcastle U)	89
Owen, S. W. 1954 (Luton T)	3
Page, L. A. 1927 (Burnley)	7
Paine, T. L. 1963 (Southampton)	19
Pallister, G. A. 1988 (Middlesbrough, Manchester U)	22
Palmer, C. L. 1992 (Sheffield W)	18
Pantling, H. H. 1924 (Sheffield U)	1
Paravicini, P. J. de 1883 (Cambridge University)	3
Parker, P. A. 1989 (QPR, Manchester U)	19
Parker, S. M. 2004 (Charlton Ath, Chelsea, Newcastle U, West Ham U)	**6**
Parker, T. R. 1925 (Southampton)	1
Parkes, P. B. 1974 (QPR)	1
Parkinson, J. 1910 (Liverpool)	2
Parlour, R. 1999 (Arsenal)	10
Parr, P. C. 1882 (Oxford University)	1
Parry, E. H. 1879 (Old Carthusians)	3
Parry, R. A. 1960 (Bolton W)	2
Patchitt, B. C. A. 1923 (Corinthians)	2
Pawson, F. W. 1883 (Cambridge University, Swifts)	2
Payne, J. 1937 (Luton T)	1
Peacock, A. 1962 (Middlesbrough, Leeds U)	6
Peacock, J. 1929 (Middlesbrough)	3
Pearce, S. 1987 (Nottingham F, West Ham U)	78
Pearson, H. F. 1932 (WBA)	1
Pearson, J. H. 1892 (Crewe Alex)	1
Pearson, J. S. 1976 (Manchester U)	15
Pearson, S. C. 1948 (Manchester U)	8
Pease, W. H. 1927 (Middlesbrough)	1
Pegg, D. 1957 (Manchester U)	1
Pejic, M. 1974 (Stoke C)	4
Pelly, F. R. 1893 (Old Foresters)	3
Pennington, J. 1907 (WBA)	25
Pentland, F. B. 1909 (Middlesbrough)	5
Perry, C. 1890 (WBA)	3
Perry, T. 1898 (WBA)	1

Perry, W. 1956 (Blackpool) 3
Perryman, S. 1982 (Tottenham H) 1
Peters, M. 1966 (West Ham U, Tottenham H) 67
Phelan, M. C. 1990 (Manchester U) 1
Phillips, K. 1999 (Sunderland) 8
Phillips, L. H. 1952 (Portsmouth) 3
Pickering, F. 1964 (Everton) 3
Pickering, J. 1933 (Sheffield U) 1
Pickering, N. 1983 (Sunderland) 1
Pike, T. M. 1886 (Cambridge University) 1
Pilkington, B. 1955 (Burnley) 1
Plant, J. 1900 (Bury) 1
Platt, D. 1990 (Aston Villa, Bari, Juventus, Sampdoria, Arsenal) 62
Plum, S. L. 1923 (Charlton Ath) 1
Pointer, R. 1962 (Burnley) 3
Porteous, T. S. 1891 (Sunderland) 1
Powell, C. G. 2001 (Charlton Ath) 5
Priest, A. E. 1900 (Sheffield U) 1
Prinsep, J. F. M. 1879 (Clapham Rovers) 1
Puddefoot, S. C. 1926 (Blackburn R) 2
Pye, J. 1950 (Wolverhampton W) 1
Pym, R. H. 1925 (Bolton W) 3

Quantrill, A. 1920 (Derby Co) 4
Quixall, A. 1954 (Sheffield W) 5

Radford, J. 1969 (Arsenal) 2
Raikes, G. B. 1895 (Oxford University) 4
Ramsey, A. E. 1949 (Southampton, Tottenham H) 32
Rawlings, A. 1921 (Preston NE) 1
Rawlings, W. E. 1922 (Southampton) 2
Rawlinson, J. F. P. 1882 (Cambridge University) 1
Rawson, H. E. 1875 (Royal Engineers) 1
Rawson, W. S. 1875 (Oxford University) 2
Read, A. 1921 (Tufnell Park) 1
Reader, J. 1894 (WBA) 1
Reaney, P. 1969 (Leeds U) 3
Redknapp, J. F. 1996 (Liverpool) 17
Reeves, K. P. 1980 (Norwich C, Manchester C) 2
Regis, C. 1982 (WBA, Coventry C) 5
Reid, P. 1985 (Everton) 13
Revie, D. G. 1955 (Manchester C) 6
Reynolds, J. 1892 (WBA, Aston Villa) 8
Richards, C. H. 1898 (Nottingham F) 1
Richards, G. H. 1909 (Derby Co) 1
Richards, J. P. 1973 (Wolverhampton W) 1
Richards, M. 2007 (Manchester C) **12**
Richardson, J. R. 1933 (Newcastle U) 2
Richardson, K. 1994 (Aston Villa) 1
Richardson, K. E. 2005 (Manchester U) 8
Richardson, W. G. 1935 (WBA) 1
Rickaby, S. 1954 (WBA) 1
Ricketts, M. B. 2002 (Bolton W) 1
Rigby, A. 1927 (Blackburn R) 5
Rimmer, E. J. 1930 (Sheffield W) 4
Rimmer, J. J. 1976 (Arsenal) 1
Ripley, S. E. 1994 (Blackburn R) 2
Rix, G. 1981 (Arsenal) 17
Robb, G. 1954 (Tottenham H) 1
Roberts, C. 1905 (Manchester U) 3
Roberts, F. 1925 (Manchester C) 4
Roberts, G. 1983 (Tottenham H) 6
Roberts, H. 1931 (Arsenal) 1
Roberts, H. 1931 (Millwall) 1
Roberts, R. 1887 (WBA) 3
Roberts, W. T. 1924 (Preston NE) 2
Robinson, J. 1937 (Sheffield W) 4
Robinson, J. W. 1897 (Derby Co, New Brighton Tower, Southampton) 11
Robinson, P. W. 2003 (Leeds U, Tottenham H, Blackburn R) 41
Robson, B. 1980 (WBA, Manchester U) 90
Robson, R. 1958 (WBA) 20
Rocastle, D. 1989 (Arsenal) 14
Rooney, W. 2003 (Everton, Manchester U) **70**
Rose, W. C. 1884 (Swifts, Preston NE, Wolverhampton W) 5
Rostron, T. 1881 (Darwen) 2

Rowe, A. 1934 (Tottenham H) 1
Rowley, J. F. 1949 (Manchester U) 6
Rowley, W. 1889 (Stoke) 2
Royle, J. 1971 (Everton, Manchester C) 6
Ruddlesdin, H. 1904 (Sheffield W) 3
Ruddock, N. 1995 (Liverpool) 1
Ruffell, J. W. 1926 (West Ham U) 6
Russell, B. B. 1883 (Royal Engineers) 1
Rutherford, J. 1904 (Newcastle U) 11

Sadler, D. 1968 (Manchester U) 4
Sagar, C. 1900 (Bury) 2
Sagar, E. 1936 (Everton) 4
Salako, J. A. 1991 (C Palace) 5
Sandford, E. A. 1933 (WBA) 1
Sandilands, R. R. 1892 (Old Westminsters) 5
Sands, J. 1880 (Nottingham F) 1
Sansom, K. G. 1979 (C Palace, Arsenal) 86
Saunders, F. E. 1888 (Swifts) 1
Savage, A. H. 1876 (C Palace) 1
Sayer, J. 1887 (Stoke) 1
Scales, J. R. 1995 (Liverpool) 3
Scattergood, E. 1913 (Derby Co) 1
Schofield, J. 1892 (Stoke) 3
Scholes, P. 1997 (Manchester U) 66
Scott, L. 1947 (Arsenal) 17
Scott, W. R. 1937 (Brentford) 1
Seaman, D. A. 1989 (QPR, Arsenal) 75
Seddon, J. 1923 (Bolton W) 6
Seed, J. M. 1921 (Tottenham H) 5
Settle, J. 1899 (Bury, Everton) 6
Sewell, J. 1952 (Sheffield W) 6
Sewell, W. R. 1924 (Blackburn R) 1
Shackleton, L. F. 1949 (Sunderland) 5
Sharp, J. 1903 (Everton) 2
Sharpe, L. S. 1991 (Manchester U) 8
Shaw, G. E. 1932 (WBA) 1
Shaw, G. L. 1959 (Sheffield U) 5
Shea, D. 1914 (Blackburn R) 2
Shearer, A. 1992 (Southampton, Blackburn R, Newcastle U) 63
Shellito, K. J. 1963 (Chelsea) 1
Shelton, A. 1889 (Notts Co) 6
Shelton, C. 1888 (Notts Rangers) 1
Shepherd, A. 1906 (Bolton W, Newcastle U) 2
Sheringham, E. P. 1993 (Tottenham H, Manchester U, Tottenham H) 51
Sherwood, T. A. 1999 (Tottenham H) 3
Shilton, P. L. 1971 (Leicester C, Stoke C, Nottingham F, Southampton, Derby Co) 125
Shimwell, E. 1949 (Blackpool) 1
Shorey, N. 2007 (Reading) 2
Shutt, G. 1886 (Stoke) 1
Silcock, J. 1921 (Manchester U) 3
Sillett, R. P. 1955 (Chelsea) 3
Simms, E. 1922 (Luton T) 1
Simpson, J. 1911 (Blackburn R) 8
Sinclair, T. 2002 (West Ham U, Manchester C) 12
Sinton, A. 1992 (QPR, Sheffield W) 12
Slater, W. J. 1955 (Wolverhampton W) 12
Smalley, T. 1937 (Wolverhampton W) 1
Smart, T. 1921 (Aston Villa) 5
Smith, A. 1891 (Nottingham F) 3
Smith, A. 2001 (Leeds U, Manchester U, Newcastle U) 19
Smith, A. K. 1872 (Oxford University) 1
Smith, A. M. 1989 (Arsenal) 13
Smith, B. 1921 (Tottenham H) 2
Smith, C. E. 1876 (C Palace) 1
Smith, G. O. 1893 (Oxford University, Old Carthusians, Corinthians) 20
Smith, H. 1905 (Reading) 4
Smith, J. 1920 (WBA) 2
Smith, Joe 1913 (Bolton W) 5
Smith, J. C. R. 1939 (Millwall) 2
Smith, J. W. 1932 (Portsmouth) 3
Smith, Leslie 1939 (Brentford) 1
Smith, Lionel 1951 (Arsenal) 6
Smith, R. A. 1961 (Tottenham H) 15
Smith, S. 1895 (Aston Villa) 1

Smith, S. C. 1936 (Leicester C) 1
Smith, T. 1960 (Birmingham C) 2
Smith, T. 1971 (Liverpool) 1
Smith, W. H. 1922 (Huddersfield T) 3
Sorby, T. H. 1879 (Thursday Wanderers, Sheffield) 1
Southgate, G. 1996 (Aston Villa, Middlesbrough) 57
Southworth, J. 1889 (Blackburn R) 3
Sparks, F. J. 1879 (Herts Rangers, Clapham Rovers) 3
Spence, J. W. 1926 (Manchester U) 2
Spence, R. 1936 (Chelsea) 2
Spencer, C. W. 1924 (Newcastle U) 2
Spencer, H. 1897 (Aston Villa) 6
Spiksley, F. 1893 (Sheffield W) 7
Spilsbury, B. W. 1885 (Cambridge University) 3
Spink, N. 1983 (Aston Villa) 1
Spouncer, W. A. 1900 (Nottingham F) 1
Springett, R. D. G. 1960 (Sheffield W) 33
Sproston, B. 1937 (Leeds U, Tottenham H,
 Manchester C) 11
Squire, R. T. 1886 (Cambridge University) 3
Stanbrough, M. H. 1895 (Old Carthusians) 1
Staniforth, R. 1954 (Huddersfield T) 8
Starling, R. W. 1933 (Sheffield W, Aston Villa) 2
Statham, D. J. 1983 (WBA) 3
Steele, F. C. 1937 (Stoke C) 6
Stein, B. 1984 (Luton T) 1
Stephenson, C. 1924 (Huddersfield T) 1
Stephenson, G. T. 1928 (Derby Co, Sheffield W) 3
Stephenson, J. E. 1938 (Leeds U) 2
Stepney, A. C. 1968 (Manchester U) 1
Sterland, M. 1989 (Sheffield W) 1
Steven, T. M. 1985 (Everton, Rangers, Marseille) 36
Stevens, G. A. 1985 (Tottenham H) 7
Stevens, M. G. 1985 (Everton, Rangers) 46
Stewart, J. 1907 (Sheffield W, Newcastle U) 3
Stewart, P. A. 1992 (Tottenham H) 3
Stiles, N. P. 1965 (Manchester U) 28
Stoker, J. 1933 (Birmingham) 3
Stone, S. B. 1996 (Nottingham F) 9
Storer, H. 1924 (Derby Co) 2
Storey, P. E. 1971 (Arsenal) 19
Storey-Moore, I. 1970 (Nottingham F) 1
Strange, A. H. 1930 (Sheffield W) 20
Stratford, A. H. 1874 (Wanderers) 1
Streten, B. 1950 (Luton T) 1
Sturgess, A. 1911 (Sheffield U) 2
Summerbee, M. G. 1968 (Manchester C) 8
Sunderland, A. 1980 (Arsenal) 1
Sutcliffe, J. W. 1893 (Bolton W, Millwall) 5
Sutton, C. R. 1998 (Blackburn R) 1
Swan, P. 1960 (Sheffield W) 19
Swepstone, H. A. 1880 (Pilgrims) 6
Swift, F. V. 1947 (Manchester C) 19

Tait, G. 1881 (Birmingham Excelsior) 1
Talbot, B. 1977 (Ipswich T, Arsenal) 6
Tambling, R. V. 1963 (Chelsea) 3
Tate, J. T. 1931 (Aston Villa) 3
Taylor, E. 1954 (Blackpool) 1
Taylor, E. H. 1923 (Huddersfield T) 8
Taylor, J. G. 1951 (Fulham) 2
Taylor, P. H. 1948 (Liverpool) 3
Taylor, P. J. 1976 (C Palace) 4
Taylor, T. 1953 (Manchester U) 19
Temple, D. W. 1965 (Everton) 1
Terry, J. G. 2003 (Chelsea) 68
Thickett, H. 1899 (Sheffield U) 2
Thomas, D. 1975 (QPR) 8
Thomas, D. 1983 (Coventry C) 2
Thomas, G. R. 1991 (C Palace) 9
Thomas, M. L. 1989 (Arsenal) 2
Thompson, A. 2004 (Celtic) 1
Thompson, P. 1964 (Liverpool) 16
Thompson, P. B. 1976 (Liverpool) 42
Thompson T. 1952 (Aston Villa, Preston NE) 2
Thomson, R. A. 1964 (Wolverhampton W) 8
Thornewell, G. 1923 (Derby Co) 4
Thornley, I. 1907 (Manchester C) 1
Tilson, S. F. 1934 (Manchester C) 4

Titmuss, F. 1922 (Southampton) 2
Todd, C. 1972 (Derby Co) 27
Toone, G. 1892 (Notts Co) 2
Topham, A. G. 1894 (Casuals) 1
Topham, R. 1893 (Wolverhampton W, Casuals) 2
Towers, M. A. 1976 (Sunderland) 3
Townley, W. J. 1889 (Blackburn R) 2
Townrow, J. E. 1925 (Clapton Orient) 2
Tremelling, D. R. 1928 (Birmingham) 1
Tresadern, J. 1923 (West Ham U) 2
Tueart, D. 1975 (Manchester C) 6
Tunstall, F. E. 1923 (Sheffield U) 7
Turnbull, R. J. 1920 (Bradford) 1
Turner, A. 1900 (Southampton) 2
Turner, H. 1931 (Huddersfield T) 2
Turner, J. A. 1893 (Bolton W, Stoke, Derby Co) 3
Tweedy, G. J. 1937 (Grimsby T) 1

Ufton, D. G. 1954 (Charlton Ath) 1
Underwood, A. 1891 (Stoke C) 2
Unsworth, D. G. 1995 (Everton) 1
Upson, M. J. 2003 (Birmingham C, West Ham U) 21
Urwin, T. 1923 (Middlesbrough, Newcastle U) 4
Utley, G. 1913 (Barnsley) 1

Vassell, D. 2002 (Aston Villa) 22
Vaughton, O. H. 1882 (Aston Villa) 5
Veitch, C. C. M. 1906 (Newcastle U) 6
Veitch, J. G. 1894 (Old Westminsters) 1
Venables, T. F. 1965 (Chelsea) 2
Venison, B. 1995 (Newcastle U) 2
Vidal, R. W. S. 1873 (Oxford University) 1
Viljoen, C. 1975 (Ipswich T) 2
Viollet, D. S. 1960 (Manchester U) 2
Von Donop 1873 (Royal Engineers) 2

Wace, H. 1878 (Wanderers) 3
Waddle, C. R. 1985 (Newcastle U, Tottenham H,
 Marseille) 62
Wadsworth, S. J. 1922 (Huddersfield T) 9
Wainscoat, W. R. 1929 (Leeds U) 1
Waiters, A. K. 1964 (Blackpool) 5
Walcott, T. J. 2006 (Arsenal) 17
Walden, F. I. 1914 (Tottenham H) 2
Walker, D. S. 1989 (Nottingham F, Sampdoria,
 Sheffield W) 59
Walker, I. M. 1996 (Tottenham H, Leicester C) 4
Walker, W. H. 1921 (Aston Villa) 18
Wall, G. 1907 (Manchester U) 7
Wallace, C. W. 1913 (Aston Villa) 3
Wallace, D. L. 1986 (Southampton) 1
Walsh, P. A. 1983 (Luton T) 5
Walters, A. M. 1885 (Cambridge University,
 Old Carthusians) 9
Walters, K. M. 1991 (Rangers) 1
Walters, P. M. 1885 (Oxford University,
 Old Carthusians) 13
Walton, N. 1890 (Blackburn R) 1
Ward, J. T. 1885 (Blackburn Olympic) 1
Ward, P. 1980 (Brighton & HA) 1
Ward, T. V. 1948 (Derby Co) 2
Waring, T. 1931 (Aston Villa) 5
Warner, C. 1878 (Upton Park) 1
Warnock, S. 2008 (Blackburn R, Aston Villa) 2
Warren, B. 1906 (Derby Co, Chelsea) 22
Waterfield, G. S. 1927 (Burnley) 1
Watson, D. 1984 (Norwich C, Everton) 12
Watson, D. V. 1974 (Sunderland, Manchester C,
 Werder Bremen, Southampton, Stoke C) 65
Watson, V. M. 1923 (West Ham U) 5
Watson, W. 1913 (Burnley) 3
Watson, W. 1950 (Sunderland) 4
Weaver, S. 1932 (Newcastle U) 3
Webb, G. W. 1911 (West Ham U) 2
Webb, N. J. 1988 (Nottingham F, Manchester U) 26
Webster, M. 1930 (Middlesbrough) 3
Wedlock, W. J. 1907 (Bristol C) 26
Weir, D. 1889 (Bolton W) 2
Welbeck, D. 2011 (Manchester U) 1

Welch, R. de C. 1872 (Wanderers, Harrow Chequers) 2
Weller, K. 1974 (Leicester C) 4
Welsh, D. 1938 (Charlton Ath) 3
West, G. 1969 (Everton) 3
Westwood, R. W. 1935 (Bolton W) 6
Whateley, O. 1883 (Aston Villa) 2
Wheeler, J. E. 1955 (Bolton W) 1
Wheldon, G. F. 1897 (Aston Villa) 4
White, D. 1993 (Manchester C) 1
White, T. A. 1933 (Everton) 1
Whitehead, J. 1893 (Accrington, Blackburn R) 2
Whitfeld, H. 1879 (Old Etonians) 1
Whitham, M. 1892 (Sheffield U) 1
Whitworth, S. 1975 (Leicester C) 7
Whymark, T. J. 1978 (Ipswich T) 1
Widdowson, S. W. 1880 (Nottingham F) 1
Wignall, F. 1965 (Nottingham F) 2
Wilcox, J. M. 1996 (Blackburn R, Leeds U) 3
Wilkes, A. 1901 (Aston Villa) 5
Wilkins, R. C. 1976 (Chelsea, Manchester U, AC Milan) 84
Wilkinson, B. 1904 (Sheffield U) 1
Wilkinson, L. R. 1891 (Oxford University) 1
Williams, B. F. 1949 (Wolverhampton W) 24
Williams, O. 1923 (Clapton Orient) 2
Williams, S. 1983 (Southampton) 6
Williams, W. 1897 (WBA) 6
Williamson, E. C. 1923 (Arsenal) 2
Williamson, R. G. 1905 (Middlesbrough) 7
Willingham, C. K. 1937 (Huddersfield T) 12
Willis, A. 1952 (Tottenham H) 1
Wilshaw, D. J. 1954 (Wolverhampton W) 12
Wilshere, J. A. 2011 (Arsenal) **5**
Wilson, C. P. 1884 (Hendon) 2
Wilson, C. W. 1879 (Oxford University) 2
Wilson, G. 1921 (Sheffield W) 12
Wilson, G. P. 1900 (Corinthians) 2
Wilson, R. 1960 (Huddersfield T, Everton) 63
Wilson, T. 1928 (Huddersfield T) 1
Winckworth, W. N. 1892 (Old Westminsters) 2
Windridge, J. E. 1908 (Chelsea) 8
Wingfield-Stratford, C. V. 1877 (Royal Engineers) 1

Winterburn, N. 1990 (Arsenal) 2
Wise, D. F. 1991 (Chelsea) 21
Withe, P. 1981 (Aston Villa) 11
Wollaston, C. H. R. 1874 (Wanderers) 4
Wolstenholme, S. 1904 (Everton, Blackburn R) 3
Wood, H. 1890 (Wolverhampton W) 3
Wood, R. E. 1955 (Manchester U) 3
Woodcock, A. S. 1978 (Nottingham F, Cologne, Arsenal) 42
Woodgate, J. S. 1999 (Leeds U, Newcastle U, Real Madrid, Tottenham H) 8
Woodger, G. 1911 (Oldham Ath) 1
Woodhall, G. 1888 (WBA) 2
Woodley, V. R. 1937 (Chelsea) 19
Woods, C. C. E. 1985 (Norwich C, Rangers, Sheffield W) 43
Woodward, V. J. 1903 (Tottenham H, Chelsea) 23
Woosnam, M. 1922 (Manchester C) 1
Worrall, F. 1935 (Portsmouth) 2
Worthington, F. S. 1974 (Leicester C) 8
Wreford-Brown, C. 1889 (Oxford University, Old Carthusians) 4
Wright, E. G. D. 1906 (Cambridge University) 1
Wright, I. E. 1991 (C Palace, Arsenal, West Ham U) 33
Wright, J. D. 1939 (Newcastle U) 1
Wright, M. 1984 (Southampton, Derby Co, Liverpool) 45
Wright, R. I. 2000 (Ipswich T, Arsenal) 2
Wright, T. J. 1968 (Everton) 11
Wright, W. A. 1947 (Wolverhampton W) 105
Wright-Phillips, S. C. 2005 (Manchester C, Chelsea, Manchester C) **36**
Wylie, J. G. 1878 (Wanderers) 1

Yates, J. 1889 (Burnley) 1
York, R. E. 1922 (Aston Villa) 2
Young, A. 1933 (Huddersfield T) 9
Young, A. S. 2008 (Aston Villa) **15**
Young, G. M. 1965 (Sheffield W) 1
Young, L. P. 2005 (Charlton Ath) 7

Zamora, R. L. 2011 (Fulham) **1**

NORTHERN IRELAND

Addis, D. J. 1922 (Cliftonville) 1
Aherne, T. 1947 (Belfast C, Luton T) 4
Alexander, T. E. 1895 (Cliftonville) 1
Allan, C. 1936 (Cliftonville) 1
Allen, J. 1887 (Limavady) 1
Anderson, J. 1925 (Distillery) 1
Anderson, T. 1973 (Manchester U, Swindon T, Peterborough U) 22
Anderson, W. 1898 (Linfield, Cliftonville) 4
Andrews, W. 1908 (Glentoran, Grimsby T) 3
Armstrong, G. J. 1977 (Tottenham H, Watford, Real Mallorca, WBA, Chesterfield) 63

Baird, C. P. 2003 (Southampton, Fulham) **51**
Baird, G. 1896 (Distillery) 3
Baird, H. C. 1939 (Huddersfield T) 1
Balfe, J. 1909 (Shelbourne) 2
Bambrick, J. 1929 (Linfield, Chelsea) 11
Banks, S. J. 1937 (Cliftonville) 1
Barr, H. H. 1962 (Linfield, Coventry C) 3
Barron, J. H. 1894 (Cliftonville) 7
Barry, J. 1888 (Cliftonville) 3
Barry, J. 1900 (Bohemians) 1
Barton, A. J. 2011 (Preston NE) **1**
Baxter, R. A. 1887 (Distillery) 1
Baxter, S. N. 1887 (Cliftonville) 1
Bennett, L. V. 1889 (Dublin University) 1
Best, G. 1964 (Manchester U, Fulham) 37
Bingham, W. L. 1951 (Sunderland, Luton T, Everton, Port Vale) 56
Black, K. T. 1988 (Luton T, Nottingham F) 30
Black, T. 1901 (Glentoran) 1
Blair, H. 1928 (Portadown, Swansea T) 4

Blair, J. 1907 (Cliftonville) 5
Blair, R. V. 1975 (Oldham Ath) 5
Blanchflower, J. 1954 (Manchester U) 12
Blanchflower, R. D. 1950 (Barnsley, Aston Villa, Tottenham H) 56
Blayney, A. 2006 (Doncaster R, Linfield) **5**
Bookman, L. J. O. 1914 (Bradford C, Luton T) 4
Bothwell, A. W. 1926 (Ards) 5
Bowler, G. C. 1950 (Hull C) 3
Boyce, L. 2011 (Werder Bremen) **4**
Boyle, P. 1901 (Sheffield U) 5
Braithwaite, R. M. 1962 (Linfield, Middlesbrough) 10
Braniff, K. R. 2010 (Portadown) 2
Breen, T. 1935 (Belfast C, Manchester U) 9
Brennan, B. 1912 (Bohemians) 1
Brennan, R. A. 1949 (Luton T, Birmingham C, Fulham) 5
Briggs, W. R. 1962 (Manchester U, Swansea T) 2
Brisby, D. 1891 (Distillery) 1
Brolly, T. H. 1937 (Millwall) 4
Brookes, E. A. 1920 (Shelbourne) 1
Brotherston, N. 1980 (Blackburn R) 27
Brown, J. 1921 (Glenavon, Tranmere R) 3
Brown, J. 1935 (Wolverhampton W, Coventry C, Birmingham C) 10
Brown, N. M. 1887 (Limavady) 1
Brown, W. G. 1926 (Glenavon) 1
Browne, F. 1887 (Cliftonville) 5
Browne, R. J. 1936 (Leeds U) 6
Bruce, A. 1925 (Belfast C) 1
Bruce, W. 1961 (Glentoran) 2
Brunt, C. 2005 (Sheffield W, WBA) **33**
Bryan, M. A. 2010 (Watford) 2
Buckle, H. R. 1903 (Cliftonville, Sunderland, Bristol R) 3

Buckle, J. 1882 (Cliftonville) 1
Burnett, J. 1894 (Distillery, Glentoran) 5
Burnison, J. 1901 (Distillery) 2
Burnison, S. 1908 (Distillery, Bradford, Distillery) 8
Burns, J. 1923 (Glenavon) 1
Burns, W. 1925 (Glentoran) 1
Butler, M. P. 1939 (Blackpool) 1

Camp, L. M. J. 2011 (Nottingham F) **2**
Campbell, A. C. 1963 (Crusaders) 2
Campbell, D. A. 1986 (Nottingham F, Charlton Ath) 10
Campbell, James 1897 (Cliftonville) 14
Campbell, John 1896 (Cliftonville) 1
Campbell, J. P. 1951 (Fulham) 2
Campbell, R. M. 1982 (Bradford C) 2
Campbell, W. G. 1968 (Dundee) 6
Capaldi, A. C. 2004 (Plymouth Arg, Cardiff C) 22
Carey, J. J. 1947 (Manchester U) 7
Carroll, E. 1925 (Glenavon) 1
Carroll, R. E. 1997 (Wigan Ath, Manchester U,
    West Ham U) 19
Carson, J. G. 2011 (Ipswich T) **2**
Carson, S. 2009 (Coleraine) 1
Casement, C. 2009 (Ipswich T) 1
Casey, T. 1955 (Newcastle U, Portsmouth) 12
Caskey, W. 1979 (Derby Co, Tulsa R) 8
Cassidy, T. 1971 (Newcastle U, Burnley) 24
Cathcart, C. G. 2011 (Blackpool) **5**
Caughey, M. 1986 (Linfield) 2
Chambers, J. R. 1921 (Distillery, Bury, Nottingham F) 12
Chatton, H. A. 1925 (Partick Th) 3
Christian, J. 1889 (Linfield) 1
Clarke, C. J. 1986 (Bournemouth, Southampton, QPR,
    Portsmouth) 38
Clarke, R. 1901 (Belfast C) 2
Cleary, J. 1982 (Glentoran) 5
Clements, D. 1965 (Coventry C, Sheffield W, Everton,
    New York Cosmos) 48
**Clingan, S. G. 2006 (Nottingham F, Norwich C,
    Coventry C)** **28**
Clugston, J. 1888 (Cliftonville) 14
Clyde, M. G. 2005 (Wolverhampton W) 3
Coates, C. 2009 (Crusaders) **6**
Cochrane, D. 1939 (Leeds U) 12
Cochrane, G. 1903 (Cliftonville) 1
Cochrane, G. T. 1976 (Coleraine, Burnley,
    Middlesbrough, Gillingham) 26
Cochrane, M. 1898 (Distillery, Leicester Fosse) 8
Collins, F. 1922 (Celtic) 1
Collins, R. 1922 (Cliftonville) 1
Condy, J. 1882 (Distillery) 3
Connell, T. E. 1978 (Coleraine) 1
Connor, J. 1901 (Glentoran, Belfast C) 13
Connor, M. J. 1903 (Brentford, Fulham) 3
Cook, W. 1933 (Celtic, Everton) 15
Cooke, S. 1889 (Belfast YMCA, Cliftonville) 3
Coote, A. 1999 (Norwich C) 6
Coulter, J. 1934 (Belfast C, Everton, Grimsby T,
    Chelmsford C) 11
Cowan, J. 1970 (Newcastle U) 1
Cowan, T. S. 1925 (Queen's Island) 4
Coyle, F. 1956 (Coleraine, Nottingham F) 4
Coyle, L. 1989 (Derry C) 1
Coyle, R. I. 1973 (Sheffield W) 5
Craig, A. B. 1908 (Rangers, Morton) 9
Craig, D. J. 1967 (Newcastle U) 25
Craigan, S. J. 2003 (Partick Th, Motherwell) **54**
Crawford, A. 1889 (Distillery, Cliftonville) 7
Croft, T. 1922 (Queen's Island) 3
Crone, R. 1889 (Distillery) 4
Crone, W. 1882 (Distillery) 12
Crooks, W. J. 1922 (Manchester U) 1
Crossan, E. 1950 (Blackburn R) 3
Crossan, J. A. 1960 (Sparta-Rotterdam, Sunderland,
    Manchester C, Middlesbrough) 24
Crothers, C. 1907 (Distillery) 1
Cumming, L. 1929 (Huddersfield T, Oldham Ath) 3
Cunningham, W. 1892 (Ulster) 1

Cunningham, W. E. 1951 (St Mirren, Leicester C,
    Dunfermline Ath) 30
Curran, S. 1926 (Belfast C) 4
Curran, J. J. 1922 (Glenavon, Pontypridd, Glenavon) 5
Cush, W. W. 1951 (Glenavon, Leeds U, Portadown) 26

Dallas, S. 2011 (Crusaders) **1**
Dalrymple, J. 1922 (Distillery) 1
Dalton, W. 1888 (YMCA, Linfield) 11
D'Arcy, S. D. 1952 (Chelsea, Brentford) 5
Darling, J. 1897 (Linfield) 22
Davey, H. H. 1926 (Reading, Portsmouth) 5
Davis, S. 2005 (Aston Villa, Fulham, Rangers) **46**
Davis, T. L. 1937 (Oldham Ath) 1
Davison, A. J. 1996 (Bolton W, Bradford C, Grimsby T) 3
Davison, J. R. 1882 (Cliftonville) 8
Dennison, R. 1988 (Wolverhampton W) 18
Devine, A. O. 1886 (Limavady) 4
Devine, J. 1990 (Glentoran) 1
Dickson, D. 1970 (Coleraine) 4
Dickson, T. A. 1957 (Linfield) 1
Dickson, W. 1951 (Chelsea, Arsenal) 12
Diffin, W. J. 1931 (Belfast C) 1
Dill, A. H. 1882 (Knock, Down Ath, Cliftonville) 9
Doherty, I. 1901 (Belfast C) 1
Doherty, J. 1928 (Portadown) 1
Doherty, J. 1933 (Cliftonville) 2
Doherty, L. 1985 (Linfield) 2
Doherty, M. 1938 (Derry C) 1
Doherty, P. D. 1935 (Blackpool, Manchester C, Derby
    Co, Huddersfield T, Doncaster R) 16
Doherty, T. E. 2003 (Bristol C) 9
Donaghey, B. 1903 (Belfast C) 1
Donaghy, M. M. 1980 (Luton T, Manchester U, Chelsea)
    91
Donnelly, L. 1913 (Distillery) 1
Donnelly, M. 2009 (Crusaders) 1
Doran, J. F. 1921 (Brighton) 3
Dougan, A. D. 1958 (Portsmouth, Blackburn R,
    Aston Villa, Leicester C, Wolverhampton W) 43
Douglas, J. P. 1947 (Belfast C) 1
Dowd, H. O. 1974 (Glenavon, Sheffield W) 3
Dowie, I. 1990 (Luton T, West Ham U, Southampton,
    C Palace, West Ham U, QPR) 59
Duff, M. J. 2002 (Cheltenham T, Burnley) 22
Duggan, H. A. 1930 (Leeds U) 8
Dunlop, G. 1985 (Linfield) 4
Dunne, J. 1928 (Sheffield U) 7

Eames, W. L. E. 1885 (Dublin U) 3
Eglington, T. J. 1947 (Everton) 6
Elder, A. R. 1960 (Burnley, Stoke C) 40
Elleman, A. R. 1889 (Cliftonville) 2
Elliott, S. 2001 (Motherwell, Hull C) 39
Elwood, J. H. 1929 (Bradford) 1
Emerson, W. 1920 (Glentoran, Burnley) 11
English, S. 1933 (Rangers) 2
Enright, J. 1912 (Leeds C) 1
Evans, C. J. 2009 (Manchester U) **11**
Evans, J. G. 2007 (Manchester U) **26**

Falloon, E. 1931 (Aberdeen) 2
Farquharson, T. G. 1923 (Cardiff C) 7
Farrell, P. 1901 (Distillery) 2
Farrell, P. 1938 (Hibernian) 1
Farrell, P. D. 1947 (Everton) 7
Feeney, J. M. 1947 (Linfield, Swansea T) 2
Feeney, W. 1976 (Glentoran) 1
**Feeney, W. J. 2002 (Bournemouth, Luton T, Cardiff C,
    Oldham Ath)** **42**
Ferguson, G. 1999 (Linfield) 5
Ferguson, S. 2009 (Newcastle U) 1
Ferguson, W. 1966 (Linfield) 2
Ferris, J. 1920 (Belfast C, Chelsea, Belfast C) 6
Ferris, R. O. 1950 (Birmingham C) 3
Fettis, A. W. 1992 (Hull C, Nottingham F, Blackburn R)
    25
Finney, T. 1975 (Sunderland, Cambridge U) 14
Fitzpatrick, J. C. 1896 (Bohemians) 2

Flack, H. 1929 (Burnley) 1
Fleming, J. G. 1987 (Nottingham F, Manchester C,
Barnsley) 31
Forbes, G. 1888 (Limavady, Distillery) 3
Forde, J. T. 1959 (Ards) 4
Foreman, T. A. 1899 (Cliftonville) 1
Forsythe, J. 1888 (YMCA) 2
Fox, W. T. 1887 (Ulster) 2
Frame, T. 1925 (Linfield) 1
Fulton, R. P. 1928 (Larne, Belfast C) 21

Gaffikin, G. 1890 (Linfield Ath) 15
Galbraith, W. 1890 (Distillery) 1
Gallagher, P. 1920 (Celtic, Falkirk) 11
Gallogly, C. 1951 (Huddersfield T) 2
Gara, A. 1902 (Preston NE) 3
Gardiner, A. 1930 (Cliftonville) 5
Garrett, J. 1925 (Distillery) 1
Garrett, R. 2009 (Linfield) **5**
Gaston, R. 1969 (Oxford U) 1
Gaukrodger, G. 1895 (Linfield) 1
Gault, M. 2008 (Linfield) 1
Gaussen, A. D. 1884 (Moyola Park, Magherafelt) 6
Geary, J. 1931 (Glentoran) 2
Gibb, J. T. 1884 (Wellington Park, Cliftonville) 10
Gibb, T. J. 1936 (Cliftonville) 1
Gibson W. K. 1894 (Cliftonville) 14
Gillespie, K. R. 1995 (Manchester U, Newcastle U,
Blackburn R, Leicester C, Sheffield U) 86
Gillespie, S. 1886 (Hertford) 6
Gillespie, W. 1889 (West Down) 1
Gillespie, W. 1913 (Sheffield U) 25
Goodall, A. L. 1899 (Derby Co, Glossop) 10
Goodbody, M. F. 1889 (Dublin University) 2
Gordon, H. 1895 (Linfield) 3
Gordon R. W. 1891 (Linfield) 7
Gordon, T. 1894 (Linfield) 2
Gorman, R. J. 2010 (Wolverhampton W) **8**
Gorman, W. C. 1947 (Brentford) 4
Gough, J. 1925 (Queen's Island) 1
Gowdy, J. 1920 (Glentoran, Queen's Island, Falkirk) 6
Gowdy, W. A. 1932 (Hull C, Sheffield W, Linfield,
Hibernian) 6
Graham, W. G. L. 1951 (Doncaster R) 14
Gray, P. 1993 (Luton T, Sunderland, Nancy, Luton T,
Burnley, Oxford U) 26
Greer, W. 1909 (QPR) 3
Gregg, H. 1954 (Doncaster R, Manchester U) 25
Griffin, D. J. 1996 (St Johnstone, Dundee U,
Stockport Co) 29

Hall, G. 1897 (Distillery) 1
Halligan, W. 1911 (Derby Co, Wolverhampton W) 2
Hamill, M. 1912 (Manchester U, Belfast C,
Manchester C) 7
Hamill, R. 1999 (Glentoran) 1
Hamilton, B. 1969 (Linfield, Ipswich T, Everton,
Millwall, Swindon T) 50
Hamilton, G. 2003 (Portadown) 5
Hamilton, J. 1882 (Knock) 2
Hamilton, R. 1928 (Rangers) 5
Hamilton, W. D. 1885 (Dublin Association) 1
Hamilton, W. J. 1885 (Dublin Association) 1
Hamilton, W. J. 1908 (Distillery) 1
Hamilton, W. R. 1978 (QPR, Burnley, Oxford U) 41
Hampton, H. 1911 (Bradford C) 9
Hanna, J. 1912 (Nottingham F) 1
Hanna, J. D. 1899 (Royal Artillery, Portsmouth) 1
Hannon, D. J. 1908 (Bohemians) 6
Harkin, J. T. 1968 (Southport, Shrewsbury T) 5
Harland, A. I. 1922 (Linfield) 2
Harris, J. 1921 (Cliftonville, Glenavon) 2
Harris, V. 1906 (Shelbourne, Everton) 20
Harvey, M. 1961 (Sunderland) 34
Hastings, J. 1882 (Knock, Ulster) 7
Hatton, S. 1963 (Linfield) 2
Hayes, W. E. 1938 (Huddersfield T) 4
**Healy, D. J. 2000 (Manchester U, Preston NE, Leeds U,
Fulham, Sunderland, Rangers)** **86**

Healy, P. J. 1982 (Coleraine, Glentoran) 4
Hegan, D. 1970 (WBA, Wolverhampton W) 7
Henderson, J. 1885 (Ulster) 3
Hewison, G. 1885 (Moyola Park) 2
Hill, C. F. 1990 (Sheffield U, Leicester C, Trelleborg,
Northampton T) 27
Hill, M. J. 1959 (Norwich C, Everton) 7
Hinton, E. 1947 (Fulham, Millwall) 7
Hodson, L. J. S. 2011 (Watford) **4**
Holmes, S. P. 2002 (Wrexham) 1
Hopkins, J. 1926 (Brighton) 1
Horlock, K. 1995 (Swindon T, Manchester C) 32
Houston, J. 1912 (Linfield, Everton) 6
Houston, W. 1933 (Linfield) 1
Houston, W. J. 1885 (Moyola Park) 1
Hughes, A. W. 1998 (Newcastle U, Aston Villa, Fulham)
76
Hughes, J. 2006 (Lincoln C) 2
Hughes, M.A. 2006 (Oldham Ath) 2
Hughes, M. E. 1992 (Manchester C, Strasbourg,
West Ham U, Wimbledon, C Palace) 71
Hughes, P. A. 1987 (Bury) 3
Hughes, W. 1951 (Bolton W) 1
Humphries, W. M. 1962 (Ards, Coventry C, Swansea T)
14
Hunter, A. 1905 (Distillery, Belfast C) 8
Hunter, A. 1970 (Blackburn R, Ipswich T) 53
Hunter, B. V. 1995 (Wrexham, Reading) 15
Hunter, R. J. 1884 (Cliftonville) 3
Hunter, V. 1962 (Coleraine) 2

Ingham, M. G. 2005 (Sunderland, Wrexham) 3
Irvine, R. J. 1962 (Linfield, Stoke C) 8
Irvine, R. W. 1922 (Everton, Portsmouth,
Connah's Quay, Derry C) 15
Irvine, W. J. 1963 (Burnley, Preston NE,
Brighton & HA) 23
Irving, S. J. 1923 (Dundee, Cardiff C, Chelsea) 18

Jackson, T. A. 1969 (Everton, Nottingham F,
Manchester U) 35
Jamison, J. 1976 (Glentoran) 1
Jenkins, I. 1997 (Chester C, Dundee U) 6
Jennings, P. A. 1964 (Watford, Tottenham H, Arsenal,
Tottenham H) 119
Johnson, D. M. 1999 (Blackburn R, Birmingham C) 56
Johnston, H. 1927 (Portadown) 1
Johnston, R. S. 1882 (Distillery) 5
Johnston, R. S. 1905 (Distillery) 1
Johnston, S. 1890 (Linfield) 4
Johnston, W. 1885 (Oldpark) 2
Johnston, W. C. 1962 (Glenavon, Oldham Ath) 2
Jones, J. 1930 (Linfield, Hibernian, Glenavon) 23
Jones, J. 1956 (Glenavon) 3
Jones, S. 1934 (Distillery, Blackpool) 2
Jones, S. G. 2003 (Crewe Alex, Burnley) 29
Jordan, T. 1895 (Linfield) 2

Kavanagh, P. J. 1930 (Celtic) 1
Keane, T. R. 1949 (Swansea T) 1
Kearns, A. 1900 (Distillery) 6
Kee, P. V. 1990 (Oxford U, Ards) 9
Keith, R. M. 1958 (Newcastle U) 23
Kelly, H. R. 1950 (Fulham, Southampton) 4
Kelly, J. 1896 (Glentoran) 1
Kelly, J. 1932 (Derry C) 11
Kelly, P. J. 1921 (Manchester C) 1
Kelly, P. M. 1950 (Barnsley) 1
Kennedy, A. L. 1923 (Arsenal) 2
Kennedy, P. H. 1999 (Watford, Wigan Ath) 20
Kernaghan, N. 1936 (Belfast C) 3
Kirk, A. R. 2000 (Hearts, Boston U, Northampton T,
Dunfermline Ath) 11
Kirkwood, H. 1904 (Cliftonville) 1
Kirwan, J. 1900 (Tottenham H, Chelsea, Clyde) 17

Lacey, W. 1909 (Everton, Liverpool, New Brighton) 23
Lafferty, K. 2006 (Burnley, Rangers) **29**
Lawrie, J. 2009 (Port Vale) 3

Lawther, R. 1888 (Glentoran) 2
Lawther, W. I. 1960 (Sunderland, Blackburn R) 4
Leatham, J. 1939 (Belfast C) 1
Ledwidge, J. J. 1906 (Shelbourne) 2
Lemon, J. 1886 (Glentoran, Belfast YMCA) 3
Lennon, N. F. 1994 (Crewe Alex, Leicester C, Celtic) 40
Leslie, W. 1887 (YMCA) 1
Lewis, J. 1899 (Glentoran, Distillery) 4
Little, A. 2009 (Rangers) 6
Lockhart, H. 1884 (Rossall School) 1
Lockhart, N. H. 1947 (Linfield, Coventry C, Aston Villa) 8
Lomas, S. M. 1994 (Manchester C, West Ham U) 45
Loyal, J. 1891 (Clarence) 1
Lutton, R. J. 1970 (Wolverhampton W, West Ham U) 6
Lynas, R. 1925 (Cliftonville) 1
Lyner, D. R. 1920 (Glentoran, Manchester U, Kilmarnock) 6
Lytle, J. 1898 (Glentoran) 1

McAdams, W. J. 1954 (Manchester C, Bolton W, Leeds U) 15
McAlery, J. M. 1882 (Cliftonville) 2
McAlinden, J. 1938 (Belfast C, Portsmouth, Southend U) 4
McAllen, J. 1898 (Linfield) 9
McAlpine, S. 1901 (Cliftonville) 1
McArdle, R. A. 2010 (Rochdale, Aberdeen) 4
McArthur, A. 1886 (Distillery) 1
McAuley, G. 2005 (Lincoln C, Leicester C, Ipswich T) 30
McAuley, J. L. 1911 (Huddersfield T) 6
McAuley, P. 1900 (Belfast C) 1
McBride, S. D. 1991 (Glenavon) 4
McCabe, J. J. 1949 (Leeds U) 6
McCabe, W. 1891 (Ulster) 1
McCambridge, J. 1930 (Ballymena, Cardiff C) 4
McCandless, J. 1912 (Bradford) 5
McCandless, W. 1920 (Linfield, Rangers) 9
McCann, G. S. 2002 (West Ham U, Cheltenham T, Barnsley, Scunthorpe U, Peterborough U) 33
McCann, P. 1910 (Belfast C, Glentoran) 7
McCarthy, J. D. 1996 (Port Vale, Birmingham C) 18
McCartney, A. 1903 (Ulster, Linfield, Everton, Belfast C, Glentoran) 15
McCartney, G. 2002 (Sunderland, West Ham U, Sunderland) 34
McCashin, J. W. 1896 (Cliftonville) 5
McCavana, W. T. 1955 (Coleraine) 3
McCaw, J. H. 1927 (Linfield) 6
McClatchey, J. 1886 (Distillery) 3
McClatchey, T. 1895 (Distillery) 1
McCleary, J. W. 1955 (Cliftonville) 1
McCleery, W. 1922 (Cliftonville, Linfield) 10
McClelland, J. 1980 (Mansfield T, Rangers, Watford, Leeds U) 53
McClelland, J. T. 1961 (Arsenal, Fulham) 6
McCluggage, A. 1922 (Cliftonville, Bradford, Burnley) 13
McClure, G. 1907 (Cliftonville, Distillery) 4
McConnell, E. 1904 (Cliftonville, Glentoran, Sunderland, Sheffield W) 12
McConnell, P. 1928 (Doncaster R, Southport) 2
McConnell, W. G. 1912 (Bohemians) 6
McConnell, W. H. 1925 (Reading) 8
McCourt, F. J. 1952 (Manchester C) 6
McCourt, P. J. 2002 (Rochdale, Celtic) 7
McCoy, R. K. 1987 (Coleraine) 1
McCoy, S. 1896 (Distillery) 1
McCracken, E. 1928 (Barking) 1
McCracken, R. 1921 (C Palace) 4
McCracken, R. 1922 (Linfield) 3
McCracken, W. R. 1902 (Distillery, Newcastle U, Hull C) 16
McCreery, D. 1976 (Manchester U, QPR, Tulsa R, Newcastle U, Hearts) 67
McCrory, S. 1958 (Southend U) 1
McCullough, K. 1935 (Belfast C, Manchester C) 5
McCullough, W. J. 1961 (Arsenal, Millwall) 10
McCurdy, C. 1980 (Linfield) 1
McDonald, A. 1986 (QPR) 52

McDonald, R. 1930 (Rangers) 2
McDonnell, J. 1911 (Bohemians) 4
McElhinney, G. M. A. 1984 (Bolton W) 6
McEvilly, L. R. 2002 (Rochdale) 1
McFaul, W. S. 1967 (Linfield, Newcastle U) 6
McGarry, J. K. 1951 (Cliftonville) 3
McGaughey, M. 1985 (Linfield) 1
McGibbon, P. C. G. 1995 (Manchester U, Wigan Ath) 7
McGinn, N. 2009 (Celtic) 13
McGivern, R. 2009 (Manchester C) 13
McGovern, M. 2010 (Ross Co) 1
McGrath, R. C. 1974 (Tottenham H, Manchester U) 21
McGregor, S. 1921 (Glentoran) 1
McGrillen, J. 1924 (Clyde, Belfast C) 2
McGuire, E. 1907 (Distillery) 1
McGuire, J. 1928 (Linfield) 1
McIlroy, H. 1906 (Cliftonville) 1
McIlroy, J. 1952 (Burnley, Stoke C) 55
McIlroy, S. B. 1972 (Manchester U, Stoke C, Manchester C) 88
McIlvenny, P. 1924 (Distillery) 1
McIlvenny, H. 1890 (Distillery, Ulster) 2
McKeag, W. 1968 (Glentoran) 2
McKeague, T. 1925 (Glentoran) 1
McKee, F. W. 1906 (Cliftonville, Belfast C) 5
McKelvey, H. 1901 (Glentoran) 2
McKenna, J. 1950 (Huddersfield T) 7
McKenzie, H. 1922 (Distillery) 1
McKenzie, R. 1967 (Airdrieonians) 1
McKeown, N. 1892 (Linfield) 7
McKie, H. 1895 (Cliftonville) 3
Mackie, J. A. 1923 (Arsenal, Portsmouth) 3
McKinney, D. 1921 (Hull C, Bradford C) 2
McKinney, V. J. 1966 (Falkirk) 1
McKnight, A. D. 1988 (Celtic, West Ham U) 10
McKnight, J. 1912 (Preston NE, Glentoran) 2
McLaughlin, J. C. 1962 (Shrewsbury T, Swansea T) 12
McLean, B. S. 2006 (Rangers) 1
McLean, T. 1885 (Limavady) 1
McMahon, G. J. 1995 (Tottenham H, Stoke C) 17
McMahon, J. 1934 (Bohemians) 1
McMaster, G. 1897 (Glentoran) 3
McMichael, A. 1950 (Newcastle U) 40
McMillan, G. 1903 (Distillery) 2
McMillan, S. T. 1963 (Manchester U) 2
McMillen, W. S. 1934 (Manchester U, Chesterfield) 7
McMordie, A. S. 1969 (Middlesbrough) 21
McMorran, E. J. 1947 (Belfast C, Barnsley, Doncaster R) 15
McMullan, D. 1926 (Liverpool) 3
McNally, B. A. 1986 (Shrewsbury T) 5
McNinch, J. 1931 (Ballymena) 3
McParland, P. J. 1954 (Aston Villa, Wolverhampton W) 34
McQuoid, J. J. 2011 (Millwall) 3
McShane, J. 1899 (Cliftonville) 4
McVeigh, P. M. 1999 (Tottenham H, Norwich C) 20
McVicker, J. 1888 (Linfield, Glentoran) 2
McWha, W. B. R. 1882 (Knock, Cliftonville) 7
Madden, O. 1938 (Norwich C) 1
Magee, G. 1885 (Wellington Park) 3
Magennis, J. B. D. 2010 (Cardiff C, Aberdeen) 3
Magill, E. J. 1962 (Arsenal, Brighton & HA) 26
Magilton, J. 1991 (Oxford U, Southampton, Sheffield W, Ipswich T) 52
Maginnis, H. 1900 (Linfield) 8
Mahood, J. 1926 (Belfast C, Ballymena) 9
Mannus, A. 2004 (Linfield) 4
Manderson, R. 1920 (Rangers) 5
Mansfield, J. 1901 (Dublin Freebooters) 1
Martin, C. 1882 (Cliftonville) 3
Martin, C. 1925 (Bo'ness) 1
Martin, C. J. 1947 (Glentoran, Leeds U, Aston Villa) 6
Martin, D. K. 1934 (Belfast C, Wolverhampton W, Nottingham F) 10
Mathieson, A. 1921 (Luton T) 2
Maxwell, J. 1902 (Linfield, Glentoran, Belfast C) 7
Meek, H. L. 1925 (Glentoran) 1
Mehaffy, J. A. C. 1922 (Queen's Island) 1

Sloan, H. A. de B. 1903 (Bohemians) 8
Sloan, J. W. 1947 (Arsenal) 1
Sloan, T. 1926 (Cardiff C, Linfield) 11
Sloan, T. 1979 (Manchester U) 3
Small, J. M. 1887 (Clarence, Cliftonville) 4
Smith, A. W. 2003 (Glentoran, Preston NE) 18
Smith, E. E. 1921 (Cardiff C) 4
Smith, J. E. 1901 (Distillery) 2
Smyth, R. H. 1886 (Dublin University) 1
Smyth, S. 1948 (Wolverhampton W, Stoke C) 9
Smyth, W. 1949 (Distillery) 4
Snape, A. 1920 (Airdrieonians) 1
Sonner, D. J. 1998 (Ipswich T, Sheffield W,
　Birmingham C, Nottingham F, Peterborough U) 13
Spence, D. W. 1975 (Bury, Blackpool, Southend U) 29
Spencer, S. 1890 (Distillery) 6
Spiller, E. A. 1883 (Cliftonville) 5
Sproule, I. 2006 (Hibernian, Bristol C) 11
Stanfield, O. M. 1887 (Distillery) 30
Steele, A. 1926 (Charlton Ath, Fulham) 4
Stevenson, A. E. 1934 (Rangers, Everton) 17
Stewart, A. 1967 (Glentoran, Derby Co) 7
Stewart, D. C. 1978 (Hull C) 1
Stewart, I. 1982 (QPR, Newcastle U) 31
Stewart, R. K. 1890 (St Columb's Court, Cliftonville) 11
Stewart, T. C. 1961 (Linfield) 1
Swan, S. 1899 (Linfield) 1

Taggart, G. P. 1990 (Barnsley, Bolton W, Leicester C) 51
Taggart, J. 1899 (Walsall) 1
Taylor, M. S. 1999 (Fulham, Birmingham C) 87
Thompson, A. L. 2011 (Watford) 2
Thompson, F. W. 1910 (Cliftonville, Linfield, Bradford C,
　Clyde) 12
Thompson, J. 1897 (Distillery) 1
Thompson, P. 2006 (Linfield, Stockport Co) 8
Thompson, R. 1928 (Queen's Island) 1
Thompson, W. 1889 (Belfast Ath) 1
Thunder, P. J. 1911 (Bohemians) 1
Todd, S. J. 1966 (Burnley, Sheffield W) 11
Toner, C. 2003 (Leyton Orient) 2
Toner, J. 1922 (Arsenal, St Johnstone) 8
Torrans, R. 1893 (Linfield) 1
Torrans, S. 1889 (Linfield) 26
Trainor, D. 1967 (Crusaders) 1
Tuffey, J. 2009 (Partick T, Inverness CT) 8
Tully, C. P. 1949 (Celtic) 10
Turner, A. 1896 (Cliftonville) 1
Turner, E. 1896 (Cliftonville) 1
Turner, W. 1886 (Cliftonville) 3
Twomey, J. F. 1938 (Leeds U) 2

Uprichard, W. N. M. C. 1952 (Swindon T, Portsmouth) 18

Vernon, J. 1947 (Belfast C, WBA) 17

Waddell, T. M. R. 1906 (Cliftonville) 1
Walker, J. 1955 (Doncaster R) 1
Walker, T. 1911 (Bury) 1
Walsh, D. J. 1947 (WBA) 9
Walsh, W. 1948 (Manchester C) 5
Waring, J. 1899 (Cliftonville) 1
Warren, P. 1913 (Shelbourne) 2
Watson, J. 1883 (Ulster) 9
Watson, P. 1971 (Distillery) 1
Watson, T. 1926 (Cardiff C) 1
Wattie, J. 1899 (Distillery) 1
Webb, C. G. 1909 (Brighton & HA) 3
Webb, S. M. 2006 (Ross Co) 4
Weir, E. 1939 (Clyde) 1
Welsh, E. 1966 (Carlisle U) 4
Whiteside, N. 1982 (Manchester U, Everton) 38
Whiteside, T. 1891 (Distillery) 1
Whitfield, E. R. 1886 (Dublin University) 1
Whitley, Jeff 1997 (Manchester C, Sunderland, Cardiff C) 20
Whitley, Jim 1998 (Manchester C) 3
Williams, J. R. 1886 (Ulster) 2
Williams, M. S. 1999 (Chesterfield, Watford, Wimbledon,
　Stoke C, Wimbledon, Milton Keynes D) 36
Williams, P. A. 1991 (WBA) 1
Williamson, J. 1890 (Cliftonville) 3
Willighan, T. 1933 (Burnley) 2
Willis, G. 1906 (Linfield) 4
Wilson, D. J. 1987 (Brighton & HA, Luton T,
　Sheffield W) 24
Wilson, H. 1925 (Linfield) 2
Wilson, K. J. 1987 (Ipswich T, Chelsea, Notts Co,
　Walsall) 42
Wilson, M. 1884 (Distillery) 3
Wilson, R. 1888 (Cliftonville) 1
Wilson, S. J. 1962 (Glenavon, Falkirk, Dundee) 12
Wilton, J. M. 1888 (St Columb's Court, Cliftonville, St
　Columb's Court) 7
Winchester, C. 2011 (Oldham Ath) 1
Wood, T. J. 1996 (Walsall) 1
Worthington, N. 1984 (Sheffield W, Leeds U, Stoke C) 66
Wright, J. 1906 (Cliftonville) 6
Wright, T. J. 1989 (Newcastle U, Nottingham F,
　Manchester C) 31

Young, S. 1907 (Linfield, Airdrieonians, Linfield) 9

SCOTLAND

Adam, C. G. 2007 (Rangers, Blackpool) 11
Adams, J. 1889 (Hearts) 3
Agnew, W. B. 1907 (Kilmarnock) 3
Aird, J. 1954 (Burnley) 4
Aitken, A. 1901 (Newcastle U, Middlesbrough,
　Leicester Fosse) 14
Aitken, G. G. 1949 (East Fife, Sunderland) 8
Aitken, R. 1886 (Dumbarton) 2
Aitken, R. 1980 (Celtic, Newcastle U, St Mirren) 57
Aitkenhead, W. A. C. 1912 (Blackburn R) 1
Albiston, A. 1982 (Manchester U) 14
Alexander, D. 1894 (East Stirlingshire) 2
Alexander, G. 2002 (Preston NE, Burnley) 40
Alexander, N. 2006 (Cardiff C) 3
Allan, D. S. 1885 (Queen's Park) 3
Allan, G. 1897 (Liverpool) 1
Allan, H. 1902 (Hearts) 1
Allan, J. 1887 (Queen's Park) 1
Allan, T. 1974 (Dundee) 2
Ancell, R. F. D. 1937 (Newcastle U) 2
Anderson, A. 1933 (Hearts) 23
Anderson, F. 1874 (Clydesdale) 1
Anderson, G. 1901 (Kilmarnock) 1
Anderson, H. A. 1914 (Raith R) 1
Anderson, J. 1954 (Leicester C) 1

Anderson, K. 1896 (Queen's Park) 3
Anderson, R. 2003 (Aberdeen, Sunderland) 11
Anderson, W. 1882 (Queen's Park) 6
Andrews, P. 1875 (Eastern) 1
Archibald, A. 1921 (Rangers) 8
Archibald, S. 1980 (Aberdeen, Tottenham H, Barcelona) 27
Armstrong, M. W. 1936 (Aberdeen) 3
Arnott, W. 1883 (Queen's Park) 14
Auld, J. R. 1887 (Third Lanark) 3
Auld, R. 1959 (Celtic) 3

Baird, A. 1892 (Queen's Park) 2
Baird, D. 1890 (Hearts) 3
Baird, H. 1956 (Airdrieonians) 1
Baird, J. C. 1876 (Vale of Leven) 3
Baird, S. 1957 (Rangers) 7
Baird, W. U. 1897 (St Bernard) 1
Bannan, B. 2011 (Aston Villa) 5
Bannon, E. J. 1980 (Dundee U) 11
Barbour, A. 1885 (Renton) 1
Bardsley, P. A. 2011 (Sunderland) 5
Barker, J. B. 1893 (Rangers) 2
Barr, D. 2009 (Falkirk) 1
Barrett, F. 1894 (Dundee) 2

Battles, B. 1901 (Celtic) 3
Battles, B. jun. 1931 (Hearts) 1
Bauld, W. 1950 (Hearts) 3
Baxter, J. C. 1961 (Rangers, Sunderland) 34
Baxter, R. D. 1939 (Middlesbrough) 3
Beattie, A. 1937 (Preston NE) 7
Beattie, C. 2006 (Celtic, WBA) 7
Beattie, R. 1939 (Preston NE) 1
Begbie, I. 1890 (Hearts) 4
Bell, A. 1912 (Manchester U) 1
Bell, C. 2011 (Kilmarnock) **1**
Bell, J. 1890 (Dumbarton, Everton, Celtic) 10
Bell, M. 1901 (Hearts) 1
Bell, W. J. 1966 (Leeds U) 2
Bennett, A. 1904 (Celtic, Rangers) 11
Bennie, R. 1925 (Airdrieonians) 3
Bernard, P. R. J. 1995 (Oldham Ath) 2
Berra, C. 2008 (Hearts, Wolverhampton W) **13**
Berry, D. 1894 (Queen's Park) 3
Berry, W. H. 1888 (Queen's Park) 4
Bett, J. 1982 (Rangers, Lokeren, Aberdeen) 25
Beveridge, W. W. 1879 (Glasgow University) 3
Black, A. 1938 (Hearts) 3
Black, D. 1889 (Hurlford) 1
Black, E. 1988 (Metz) 2
Black, I. H. 1948 (Southampton) 1
Blackburn, J. E. 1873 (Royal Engineers) 1
Blacklaw, A. S. 1963 (Burnley) 3
Blackley, J. 1974 (Hibernian) 7
Blair, D. 1929 (Clyde, Aston Villa) 8
Blair, J. 1920 (Sheffield W, Cardiff C) 8
Blair, J. 1934 (Motherwell) 1
Blair, J. A. 1947 (Blackpool) 1
Blair, W. 1896 (Third Lanark) 1
Blessington, J. 1894 (Celtic) 4
Blyth, J. A. 1978 (Coventry C) 2
Bone, J. 1972 (Norwich C) 2
Booth, S. 1993 (Aberdeen, Borussia Dortmund, Twente) 21
Bowie, J. 1920 (Rangers) 2
Bowie, W. 1891 (Linthouse) 1
Bowman, D. 1992 (Dundee U) 6
Bowman, G. A. 1892 (Montrose) 1
Boyd, J. M. 1934 (Newcastle U) 1
Boyd, K. 2006 (Rangers, Middlesbrough) **18**
Boyd, R. 1889 (Mossend Swifts) 2
Boyd, T. 1991 (Motherwell, Chelsea, Celtic) 72
Boyd, W. G. 1931 (Clyde) 2
Bradshaw, T. 1928 (Bury) 1
Brand, R. 1961 (Rangers) 8
Brandon, T. 1896 (Blackburn R) 1
Brazil, A. 1980 (Ipswich T, Tottenham H) 13
Breckenridge, T. 1888 (Hearts) 1
Bremner, D. 1976 (Hibernian) 1
Bremner, W. J. 1965 (Leeds U) 54
Brennan, F. 1947 (Newcastle U) 7
Breslin, B. 1897 (Hibernian) 1
Brewster, G. 1921 (Everton) 1
Broadfoot, K. 2009 (Rangers) **4**
Brogan, J. 1971 (Celtic) 4
Brown, A. 1890 (St Mirren) 2
Brown, A. 1904 (Middlesbrough) 1
Brown, A. D. 1950 (East Fife, Blackpool) 14
Brown, G. C. P. 1931 (Rangers) 19
Brown, H. 1947 (Partick Th) 3
Brown, J. B. 1939 (Clyde) 1
Brown, J. G. 1975 (Sheffield U) 1
Brown, R. 1884 (Dumbarton) 2
Brown, R. 1890 (Cambuslang) 1
Brown, R. 1947 (Rangers) 3
Brown, R. jun. 1885 (Dumbarton) 1
Brown, S. 2006 (Hibernian, Celtic) **25**
Brown, W. D. F. 1958 (Dundee, Tottenham H) 28
Browning, J. 1914 (Celtic) 1
Brownlie, J. 1909 (Third Lanark) 16
Brownlie, J. 1971 (Hibernian) 7
Bruce, D. 1890 (Vale of Leven) 1
Bruce, R. F. 1934 (Middlesbrough) 1
Bryson, C. 2011 (Kilmarnock) **1**

Buchan, M. M. 1972 (Aberdeen, Manchester U) 34
Buchanan, J. 1889 (Cambuslang) 1
Buchanan, J. 1929 (Rangers) 2
Buchanan, P. S. 1938 (Chelsea) 1
Buchanan, R. 1891 (Abercorn) 1
Buckley, P. 1954 (Aberdeen) 3
Buick, A. 1902 (Hearts) 2
Burchill, M. J. 2000 (Celtic) 6
Burke, C. 2006 (Rangers) 2
Burley, C. W. 1995 (Chelsea, Celtic, Derby Co) 46
Burley, G. E. 1979 (Ipswich T) 11
Burns, F. 1970 (Manchester U) 1
Burns, K. 1974 (Birmingham C, Nottingham F) 20
Burns, T. 1981 (Celtic) 8
Busby, M. W. 1934 (Manchester C) 1

Cairns, T. 1920 (Rangers) 8
Calderhead, D. 1889 (Q of S Wanderers) 1
Calderwood, C. 1995 (Tottenham H) 36
Calderwood, R. 1885 (Cartvale) 3
Caldow, E. 1957 (Rangers) 40
Caldwell, G. 2002 (Newcastle U, Hibernian, Celtic, Wigan Ath) **40**
Caldwell, S. 2001 (Newcastle U, Sunderland, Burnley,Wigan Ath) **12**
Callaghan, P. 1900 (Hibernian) 1
Callaghan, W. 1970 (Dunfermline Ath) 2
Cameron, C. 1999 (Hearts, Wolverhampton W) 28
Cameron, J. 1886 (Rangers) 1
Cameron, J. 1896 (Queen's Park) 1
Cameron, J. 1904 (St Mirren, Chelsea) 2
Campbell, C. 1874 (Queen's Park) 13
Campbell, H. 1889 (Renton) 1
Campbell, Jas 1913 (Sheffield W) 1
Campbell, J. 1880 (South Western) 1
Campbell, J. 1891 (Kilmarnock) 2
Campbell, John 1893 (Celtic) 12
Campbell, John 1899 (Rangers) 4
Campbell, K. 1920 (Liverpool, Partick Th) 8
Campbell, P. 1878 (Rangers) 2
Campbell, P. 1898 (Morton) 1
Campbell, R. 1947 (Falkirk, Chelsea) 5
Campbell, W. 1947 (Morton) 5
Canero, P. 2004 (Leicester C) 1
Carabine, J. 1938 (Third Lanark) 3
Carr, W. M. 1970 (Coventry C) 6
Cassidy, J. 1921 (Celtic) 4
Chalmers, S. 1965 (Celtic) 5
Chalmers, W. 1885 (Rangers) 1
Chalmers, W. S. 1929 (Queen's Park) 1
Chambers, T. 1894 (Hearts) 1
Chaplin, G. D. 1908 (Dundee) 1
Cheyne, A. G. 1929 (Aberdeen) 5
Christie, A. J. 1898 (Queen's Park) 3
Christie, R. M. 1884 (Queen's Park) 1
Clark, J. 1966 (Celtic) 4
Clark, R. B. 1968 (Aberdeen) 17
Clarke, S. 1988 (Chelsea) 6
Clarkson, D. 2008 (Motherwell) 2
Cleland, J. 1891 (Royal Albert) 1
Clements, R. 1891 (Leith Ath) 1
Clunas, W. L. 1924 (Sunderland) 2
Collier, W. 1922 (Raith R) 1
Collins, J. 1988 (Hibernian, Celtic, Monaco, Everton) 58
Collins, R. Y. 1951 (Celtic, Everton, Leeds U) 31
Collins, T. 1909 (Hearts) 1
Colman, D. 1911 (Aberdeen) 4
Colquhoun, E. P. 1972 (Sheffield U) 9
Colquhoun, J. 1988 (Hearts) 2
Combe, J. R. 1948 (Hibernian) 3
Commons, K. 2009 (Derby Co, Celtic) **9**
Conn, A. 1956 (Hearts) 1
Conn, A. 1975 (Tottenham H) 2
Connachan, E. D. 1962 (Dunfermline Ath) 2
Connelly, G. 1974 (Celtic) 2
Connolly, J. 1973 (Everton) 1
Connor, J. 1886 (Airdrieonians) 1
Connor, J. 1930 (Sunderland) 4
Connor, R. 1986 (Dundee, Aberdeen) 4

Jackson, D. 1995 (Hibernian, Celtic)	28
Jackson, J. 1931 (Partick Th, Chelsea)	8
Jackson, T. A. 1904 (St Mirren)	6
James, A. W. 1926 (Preston NE, Arsenal)	8
Jardine, A. 1971 (Rangers)	38
Jarvie, A. 1971 (Airdrieonians)	3
Jenkinson, T. 1887 (Hearts)	1
Jess, E. 1993 (Aberdeen, Coventry C, Aberdeen)	18
Johnston, A. 1999 (Sunderland, Rangers, Middlesbrough)	18
Johnston, L. H. 1948 (Clyde)	2
Johnston, M. 1984 (Watford, Celtic, Nantes, Rangers)	38
Johnston, R. 1938 (Sunderland)	1
Johnston, W. 1966 (Rangers, WBA)	22
Johnstone, D. 1973 (Rangers)	14
Johnstone, J. 1888 (Abercorn)	1
Johnstone, J. 1965 (Celtic)	23
Johnstone, Jas 1894 (Kilmarnock)	1
Johnstone, J. A. 1930 (Hearts)	3
Johnstone, R. 1951 (Hibernian, Manchester C)	17
Johnstone, W. 1887 (Third Lanark)	3
Jordan, J. 1973 (Leeds U, Manchester U, AC Milan)	52
Kay, J. L. 1880 (Queen's Park)	6
Keillor, A. 1891 (Montrose, Dundee)	6
Keir, L. 1885 (Dumbarton)	5
Kelly, H. T. 1952 (Blackpool)	1
Kelly, J. 1888 (Renton, Celtic)	8
Kelly, J. C. 1949 (Barnsley)	2
Kelso, R. 1885 (Renton, Dundee)	7
Kelso, T. 1914 (Dundee)	1
Kennaway, J. 1934 (Celtic)	1
Kennedy, A. 1875 (Eastern, Third Lanark)	6
Kennedy, J. 1897 (Hibernian)	1
Kennedy, J. 1964 (Celtic)	6
Kennedy, J. 2004 (Celtic)	1
Kennedy, S. 1905 (Partick Th)	1
Kennedy, S. 1975 (Rangers)	5
Kennedy, S. 1978 (Aberdeen)	8
Kenneth, G. 2011 (Dundee U)	**2**
Ker, G. 1880 (Queen's Park)	5
Ker, W. 1872 (Queen's Park)	2
Kerr, A. 1955 (Partick Th)	2
Kerr, B. 2003 (Newcastle U)	3
Kerr, P. 1924 (Hibernian)	1
Key, G. 1902 (Hearts)	1
Key, W. 1907 (Queen's Park)	1
King, A. 1896 (Hearts, Celtic)	6
King, J. 1933 (Hamilton A)	2
King, W. S. 1929 (Queen's Park)	1
Kinloch, J. D. 1922 (Partick Th)	1
Kinnaird, A. F. 1873 (Wanderers)	1
Kinnear, D. 1938 (Rangers)	1
Kyle, K. 2002 (Sunderland, Kilmarnock)	10
Lambert, P. 1995 (Motherwell, Borussia Dortmund, Celtic)	40
Lambie, J. A. 1886 (Queen's Park)	3
Lambie, W. A. 1892 (Queen's Park)	9
Lamont, W. 1885 (Pilgrims)	1
Lang, A. 1880 (Dumbarton)	1
Lang, J. J. 1876 (Clydesdale, Third Lanark)	2
Latta, A. 1888 (Dumbarton)	2
Law, D. 1959 (Huddersfield T, Manchester C, Torino, Manchester U, Manchester C)	55
Law, G. 1910 (Rangers)	3
Law, T. 1928 (Chelsea)	2
Lawrence, J. 1911 (Newcastle U)	1
Lawrence, T. 1963 (Liverpool)	3
Lawson, D. 1923 (St Mirren)	1
Leckie, R. 1872 (Queen's Park)	1
Leggat, G. 1956 (Aberdeen, Fulham)	18
Leighton, J. 1983 (Aberdeen, Manchester U, Hibernian, Aberdeen)	91
Lennie, W. 1908 (Aberdeen)	2
Lennox, R. 1967 (Celtic)	10
Leslie, L. G. 1961 (Airdrieonians)	5
Levein, C. 1990 (Hearts)	16
Liddell, W. 1947 (Liverpool)	28

Liddle, D. 1931 (East Fife)	3
Lindsay, D. 1903 (St Mirren)	1
Lindsay, J. 1880 (Dumbarton)	8
Lindsay, J. 1888 (Renton)	3
Linwood, A. B. 1950 (Clyde)	1
Little, R. J. 1953 (Rangers)	1
Livingstone, G. T. 1906 (Manchester C, Rangers)	2
Lochhead, A. 1889 (Third Lanark)	1
Logan, J. 1891 (Ayr)	1
Logan, T. 1913 (Falkirk)	1
Logie, J. T. 1953 (Arsenal)	1
Loney, W. 1910 (Celtic)	2
Long, H. 1947 (Clyde)	1
Longair, W. 1894 (Dundee)	1
Lorimer, P. 1970 (Leeds U)	21
Love, A. 1931 (Aberdeen)	3
Low, A. 1934 (Falkirk)	1
Low, J. 1891 (Cambuslang)	1
Low, T. P. 1897 (Rangers)	1
Low, W. L. 1911 (Newcastle U)	5
Lowe, J. 1887 (St Bernards)	1
Lundie, J. 1886 (Hibernian)	1
Lyall, J. 1905 (Sheffield W)	1
McAdam, J. 1880 (Third Lanark)	1
McAllister, B. 1997 (Wimbledon)	3
McAllister, G. 1990 (Leicester C, Leeds U, Coventry C)	57
McAllister, J. R. 2004 (Livingston)	1
Macari, L. 1972 (Celtic, Manchester U)	24
McArthur, D. 1895 (Celtic)	3
McArthur, J. 2011 (Wigan Ath)	**4**
McAtee, A. 1913 (Celtic)	1
McAulay, J. 1884 (Arthurlie)	1
McAulay, J. D. 1882 (Dumbarton)	9
McAulay, R. 1932 (Rangers)	2
Macauley, A. R. 1947 (Brentford, Arsenal)	7
McAvennie, F. 1986 (West Ham U, Celtic)	5
McBain, E. 1894 (St Mirren)	1
McBain, N. 1922 (Manchester U, Everton)	3
McBride, J. 1967 (Celtic)	2
McBride, P. 1904 (Preston NE)	6
McCall, A. 1888 (Renton)	1
McCall, A. S. M. 1990 (Everton, Rangers)	40
McCall, J. 1886 (Renton)	5
McCalliog, J. 1967 (Sheffield W, Wolverhampton W)	5
McCallum, N. 1888 (Renton)	1
McCann, N. 1999 (Hearts, Rangers, Southampton)	26
McCann, R. J. 1959 (Motherwell)	5
McCartney, W. 1902 (Hibernian)	1
McClair, B. 1987 (Celtic, Manchester U)	30
McClory, A. 1927 (Motherwell)	3
McCloy, P. 1924 (Ayr U)	2
McCloy, P. 1973 (Rangers)	4
McCoist, A. 1986 (Rangers, Kilmarnock)	61
McColl, I. M. 1950 (Rangers)	14
McColl, R. S. 1896 (Queen's Park, Newcastle U, Queen's Park)	13
McColl, W. 1895 (Renton)	1
McCombie, A. 1903 (Sunderland, Newcastle U)	4
McCorkindale, J. 1891 (Partick Th)	1
McCormack, R. 2008 (Motherwell, Cardiff C, Leeds U)	**7**
McCormick, R. 1886 (Abercorn)	1
McCrae, D. 1929 (St Mirren)	2
McCreadie, A. 1893 (Rangers)	2
McCreadie, E. G. 1965 (Chelsea)	23
McCulloch, D. 1935 (Hearts, Brentford, Derby Co)	7
McCulloch, L. 2005 (Wigan Ath, Rangers)	**18**
MacDonald, A. 1976 (Rangers)	1
McDonald, J. 1886 (Edinburgh University)	1
McDonald, J. 1956 (Sunderland)	2
MacDougall, E. J. 1975 (Norwich C)	7
McDougall, J. 1887 (Vale of Leven)	5
McDougall, J. 1926 (Airdrieonians)	1
McDougall, J. 1931 (Liverpool)	2
McEveley, J. 2008 (Derby Co)	3
McFadden, J. 2002 (Motherwell, Everton, Birmingham C)	**48**
McFadyen, W. 1934 (Motherwell)	2

Macfarlane, A. 1904 (Dundee)	5
Macfarlane, W. 1947 (Hearts)	1
McFarlane, R. 1896 (Greenock Morton)	1
McGarr, E. 1970 (Aberdeen)	2
McGarvey, F. P. 1979 (Liverpool, Celtic)	7
McGeoch, A. 1876 (Dumbreck)	4
McGhee, J. 1886 (Hibernian)	1
McGhee, M. 1983 (Aberdeen)	4
McGinlay, J. 1994 (Bolton W)	13
McGonagle, W. 1933 (Celtic)	6
McGrain, D. 1973 (Celtic)	62
McGregor, A. 2007 (Rangers)	**13**
McGregor, J. C. 1877 (Vale of Leven)	1
McGrory, J. 1928 (Celtic)	7
McGrory, J. E. 1965 (Kilmarnock)	3
McGuire, W. 1881 (Beith)	2
McGurk, F. 1934 (Birmingham)	1
McHardy, H. 1885 (Rangers)	1
McInally, A. 1989 (Aston Villa, Bayern Munich)	8
McInally, J. 1987 (Dundee U)	10
McInally, T. B. 1926 (Celtic)	2
McInnes, D. 2003 (WBA)	2
McInnes, T. 1889 (Cowlairs)	1
McIntosh, W. 1905 (Third Lanark)	1
McIntyre, A. 1878 (Vale of Leven)	2
McIntyre, H. 1880 (Rangers)	1
McIntyre, J. 1884 (Rangers)	1
MacKay, D. 1959 (Celtic)	14
Mackay, D. C. 1957 (Hearts, Tottenham H)	22
Mackay, G. 1988 (Hearts)	4
Mackay, M. 2004 (Norwich C)	5
McKay, J. 1924 (Blackburn R)	1
McKay, R. 1928 (Newcastle U)	1
McKean, R. 1976 (Rangers)	1
McKenzie, D. 1938 (Brentford)	1
Mackenzie, J. A. 1954 (Partick Th)	9
McKeown, M. 1889 (Celtic)	2
McKie, J. 1898 (East Stirling)	1
McKillop, T. R. 1938 (Rangers)	1
McKimmie, S. 1989 (Aberdeen)	40
McKinlay, D. 1922 (Liverpool)	2
McKinlay, T. 1996 (Celtic)	22
McKinlay, W. 1994 (Dundee U, Blackburn R)	29
McKinnon, A. 1874 (Queen's Park)	1
McKinnon, R. 1966 (Rangers)	28
McKinnon, R. 1994 (Motherwell)	3
MacKinnon, W. 1883 (Dumbarton)	4
MacKinnon, W. W. 1872 (Queen's Park)	9
McLaren, A. 1929 (St Johnstone)	5
McLaren, A. 1947 (Preston NE)	4
McLaren, A. 1992 (Hearts, Rangers)	24
McLaren, A. 2001 (Kilmarnock)	1
McLaren, J. 1888 (Hibernian, Celtic)	3
McLean, A. 1926 (Celtic)	4
McLean, D. 1896 (St Bernards)	1
McLean, D. 1912 (Sheffield W)	1
McLean, G. 1968 (Dundee)	1
McLean, T. 1969 (Kilmarnock)	6
McLeish, A. 1980 (Aberdeen)	77
McLeod, D. 1905 (Celtic)	4
McLeod, J. 1888 (Dumbarton)	5
MacLeod, J. M. 1961 (Hibernian)	4
MacLeod, M. 1985 (Celtic, Borussia Dortmund, Hibernian)	20
McLeod, W. 1886 (Cowlairs)	1
McLintock, A. 1875 (Vale of Leven)	3
McLintock, F. 1963 (Leicester C, Arsenal)	9
McLuckie, J. S. 1934 (Manchester C)	1
McMahon, A. 1892 (Celtic)	6
McManus, S. 2007 (Celtic, Middlesbrough)	**26**
McMenemy, J. 1905 (Celtic)	12
McMenemy, J. 1934 (Motherwell)	1
McMillan, I. L. 1952 (Airdrieonians, Rangers)	6
McMillan, J. 1897 (St Bernards)	1
McMillan, T. 1887 (Dumbarton)	1
McMullan, J. 1920 (Partick Th, Manchester C)	16
McNab, A. 1921 (Morton)	2
McNab, A. 1937 (Sunderland, WBA)	2
McNab, C. D. 1931 (Dundee)	6

McNab, J. S. 1923 (Liverpool)	1
McNair, A. 1906 (Celtic)	15
McNamara, J. 1997 (Celtic, Wolverhampton W)	33
McNamee, D. 2004 (Livingston)	4
McNaught, W. 1951 (Raith R)	5
McNaughton, K. 2002 (Aberdeen, Cardiff C)	4
McNeill, W. 1961 (Celtic)	29
McNiel, H. 1874 (Queen's Park)	10
McNiel, M. 1876 (Rangers)	2
McPhail, J. 1950 (Celtic)	5
McPhail, R. 1927 (Airdrieonians, Rangers)	17
McPherson, D. 1892 (Kilmarnock)	1
McPherson, D. 1989 (Hearts, Rangers)	27
McPherson, J. 1875 (Clydesdale)	1
McPherson, J. 1879 (Vale of Leven)	8
McPherson, J. 1888 (Kilmarnock, Cowlairs, Rangers)	9
McPherson, J. 1891 (Hearts)	1
McPherson, R. 1882 (Arthurlie)	1
McQueen, G. 1974 (Leeds U, Manchester U)	30
McQueen, M. 1890 (Leith Ath)	2
McRorie, D. M. 1931 (Morton)	1
McSpadyen, A. 1939 (Partick Th)	2
McStay, P. 1984 (Celtic)	76
McStay, W. 1921 (Celtic)	13
McSwegan, G. 2000 (Hearts)	2
McTavish, J. 1910 (Falkirk)	1
McWattie, G. C. 1901 (Queen's Park)	2
McWilliam, P. 1905 (Newcastle U)	8
Mackail-Smith, C. 2011 (Peterborough U)	**1**
Mackie, J. C. 2011 (QPR)	**3**
Madden, J. 1893 (Celtic)	2
Maguire, C. 2011 (Aberdeen)	**2**
Main, F. R. 1938 (Rangers)	1
Main, J. 1909 (Hibernian)	1
Maley, W. 1893 (Celtic)	2
Maloney, S. R. 2006 (Celtic, Aston Villa, Celtic)	**19**
Malpas, M. 1984 (Dundee U)	55
Marshall, D. J. 2005 (Celtic, Cardiff C)	5
Marshall, G. 1992 (Celtic)	1
Marshall, H. 1899 (Celtic)	2
Marshall, J. 1885 (Third Lanark)	4
Marshall, J. 1921 (Middlesbrough, Llanelly)	7
Marshall, J. 1932 (Rangers)	3
Marshall, R. W. 1892 (Rangers)	2
Martin, B. 1995 (Motherwell)	2
Martin, F. 1954 (Aberdeen)	6
Martin, N. 1965 (Hibernian, Sunderland)	3
Martin, R. K. A. 2011 (Norwich C)	**1**
Martis, J. 1961 (Motherwell)	1
Mason, J. 1949 (Third Lanark)	7
Massie, A. 1932 (Hearts, Aston Villa)	18
Masson, D. S. 1976 (QPR, Derby Co)	17
Mathers, D. 1954 (Partick Th)	1
Matteo, D. 2001 (Leeds U)	6
Maxwell, W. S. 1898 (Stoke C)	1
May, J. 1906 (Rangers)	5
Meechan, P. 1896 (Celtic)	1
Meiklejohn, D. D. 1922 (Rangers)	15
Menzies, A. 1906 (Hearts)	1
Mercer, R. 1912 (Hearts)	2
Middleton, R. 1930 (Cowdenbeath)	1
Millar, J. 1897 (Rangers)	3
Millar, J. 1963 (Rangers)	2
Miller, A. 1939 (Hearts)	1
Miller, C. 2001 (Dundee U)	1
Miller, J. 1931 (St Mirren)	5
Miller, K. 2001 (Rangers, Wolverhampton W, Celtic, Derby Co, Rangers, Bursa)	**55**
Miller, L. 2006 (Dundee U, Aberdeen)	3
Miller, P. 1882 (Dumbarton)	3
Miller, T. 1920 (Liverpool, Manchester U)	3
Miller, W. 1876 (Third Lanark)	1
Miller, W. 1947 (Celtic)	6
Miller, W. 1975 (Aberdeen)	65
Mills, W. 1936 (Aberdeen)	3
Milne, J. V. 1938 (Middlesbrough)	2
Mitchell, D. 1890 (Rangers)	5
Mitchell, J. 1908 (Kilmarnock)	3
Mitchell, R. C. 1951 (Newcastle U)	2

Whittaker, S. G. 2010 (Rangers) — 12
Whyte, D. 1988 (Celtic, Middlesbrough, Aberdeen) — 12
Wilkie, L. 2002 (Dundee) — 11
Williams, G. 2002 (Nottingham F) — 5
Wilson, A. 1907 (Sheffield W) — 6
Wilson, A. 1954 (Portsmouth) — 1
Wilson, A. N. 1920 (Dunfermline, Middlesbrough) — 12
Wilson, D. 1900 (Queen's Park) — 1
Wilson, D. 1913 (Oldham Ath) — 1
Wilson, D. 1961 (Rangers) — 22
Wilson, D. 2011 (Liverpool) — **3**
Wilson, G. W. 1904 (Hearts, Everton, Newcastle U) — 6
Wilson, Hugh 1890 (Newmilns, Sunderland, Third Lanark) — 4
Wilson, I. A. 1987 (Leicester C, Everton) — 5
Wilson, J. 1888 (Vale of Leven) — 4
Wilson, M. 2011 (Celtic) — **1**
Wilson, P. 1926 (Celtic) — 4
Wilson, P. 1975 (Celtic) — 1

Wilson, R. P. 1972 (Arsenal) — 2
Winters, R. 1999 (Aberdeen) — 1
Wiseman, W. 1927 (Queen's Park) — 2
Wood, G. 1979 (Everton, Arsenal) — 4
Woodburn, W. A. 1947 (Rangers) — 24
Wotherspoon, D. N. 1872 (Queen's Park) — 2
Wright, K. 1992 (Hibernian) — 1
Wright, S. 1993 (Aberdeen) — 2
Wright, T. 1953 (Sunderland) — 3
Wylie, T. G. 1890 (Rangers) — 1

Yeats, R. 1965 (Liverpool) — 2
Yorston, B. C. 1931 (Aberdeen) — 1
Yorston, H. 1955 (Aberdeen) — 1
Young, A. 1905 (Everton) — 2
Young, A. 1960 (Hearts, Everton) — 8
Young, G. L. 1947 (Rangers) — 53
Young, J. 1906 (Celtic) — 1
Younger, T. 1955 (Hibernian, Liverpool) — 24

WALES

Adams, H. 1882 (Berwyn R, Druids) — 4
Aizlewood, M. 1986 (Charlton Ath, Leeds U, Bradford C, Bristol C, Cardiff C) — 39
Allchurch, I. J. 1951 (Swansea T, Newcastle U, Cardiff C, Swansea T) — 68
Allchurch, L. 1955 (Swansea T, Sheffield U) — 11
Allen, B. W. 1951 (Coventry C) — 2
Allen, J. M. 2009 (Swansea C) — 2
Allen, M. 1986 (Watford, Norwich C, Millwall, Newcastle U) — 14
Arridge, S. 1892 (Bootle, Everton, New Brighton Tower) — 8
Astley, D. J. 1931 (Charlton Ath, Aston Villa, Derby Co, Blackpool) — 13
Atherton, R. W. 1899 (Hibernian, Middlesbrough) — 9

Bailiff, W. E. 1913 (Llanelly) — 4
Baker, C. W. 1958 (Cardiff C) — 7
Baker, W. G. 1948 (Cardiff C) — 1
Bale, G. 2006 (Southampton, Tottenham H) — **27**
Bamford, T. 1931 (Wrexham) — 5
Barnard, D. S. 1998 (Barnsley, Grimsby T) — 22
Barnes, A. 1948 (Arsenal) — 22
Bartley, T. 1898 (Glossop NE) — 1
Bastock, A. M. 1892 (Shrewsbury T) — 1
Beadles, G. H. 1925 (Cardiff C) — 2
Bell, W. S. 1881 (Shrewsbury Engineers, Crewe Alex) — 5
Bellamy, C. D. 1998 (Norwich C, Coventry C, Newcastle U, Blackburn R, Liverpool, West Ham U, Manchester C) — **62**
Bennion, S. R. 1926 (Manchester U) — 10
Berry, G. F. 1979 (Wolverhampton W, Stoke C) — 5
Blackmore, C. G. 1985 (Manchester U, Middlesbrough) — 39
Blake, D. J. 2011 (Cardiff C) — **2**
Blake, N. A. 1994 (Sheffield U, Bolton W, Blackburn R, Wolverhampton W) — 29
Blew, H. 1899 (Wrexham) — 22
Boden, T. 1880 (Wrexham) — 1
Bodin, P. J. 1990 (Swindon T, C Palace, Swindon T) — 23
Boulter, L. M. 1939 (Brentford) — 1
Bowdler, H. E. 1893 (Shrewsbury T) — 1
Bowdler, J. C. H. 1890 (Shrewsbury T, Wolverhampton W, Shrewsbury T) — 4
Bowen, D. L. 1955 (Arsenal) — 19
Bowen, E. 1880 (Druids) — 2
Bowen, J. P. 1994 (Swansea C, Birmingham C) — 2
Bowen, M. R. 1986 (Tottenham H, Norwich C, West Ham U) — 41
Bowsher, S. J. 1929 (Burnley) — 1
Boyle, T. 1981 (C Palace) — 2
Bradley, M. S. 2010 (Walsall) — 1
Britten, T. J. 1878 (Parkgrove, Presteigne) — 2
Brookes, S. J. 1900 (Llandudno) — 2
Brown, A. I. 1926 (Aberdare Ath) — 1
Brown, J. R. 2006 (Gillingham, Blackburn R) — 2

Browning, M. T. 1996 (Bristol R, Huddersfield T) — 5
Bryan, T. 1886 (Oswestry) — 2
Buckland, T. 1899 (Bangor) — 1
Burgess, W. A. R. 1947 (Tottenham H) — 32
Burke, T. 1883 (Wrexham, Newton Heath) — 8
Burnett, T. B. 1877 (Ruabon) — 1
Burton, A. D. 1963 (Norwich C, Newcastle U) — 9
Butler, J. 1893 (Chirk) — 3
Butler, W. T. 1900 (Druids) — 2

Cartwright, L. 1974 (Coventry C, Wrexham) — 7
Carty, T. See McCarthy (Wrexham).
Challen, J. B. 1887 (Corinthians, Wellingborough GS) — 4
Chapman, T. 1894 (Newtown, Manchester C, Grimsby T) — 7
Charles, J. M. 1981 (Swansea C, QPR, Oxford U) — 19
Charles, M. 1955 (Swansea T, Arsenal, Cardiff C) — 31
Charles, W. J. 1950 (Leeds U, Juventus, Leeds U, Cardiff C) — 38
Church, S. R. 2009 (Reading) — **12**
Clarke, R. J. 1949 (Manchester C) — 22
Coleman, C. 1992 (C Palace, Blackburn R, Fulham) — 32
Collier, D. J. 1921 (Grimsby T) — 1
Collins, D. L. 2005 (Sunderland, Stoke C) — **12**
Collins, J. M. 2004 (Cardiff C, West Ham U, Aston Villa) — **39**
Collins, W. S. 1931 (Llanelly) — 1
Collison, J. D. 2008 (West Ham U) — **8**
Conde, C. 1884 (Chirk) — 3
Cook, F. C. 1925 (Newport Co, Portsmouth) — 8
Cornforth, J. M. 1995 (Swansea C) — 2
Cotterill, D. R. G. B. 2006 (Bristol C, Wigan Ath, Sheffield U, Swansea C) — **19**
Coyne, D. 1996 (Tranmere R, Grimsby T, Leicester C, Burnley, Tranmere R) — 16
Crofts, A. L. 2006 (Gillingham, Brighton & HA, Norwich C) — **17**
Crompton, W. 1931 (Wrexham) — 3
Cross, E. A. 1876 (Wrexham) — 2
Crosse, K. 1879 (Druids) — 3
Crossley, M. G. 1997 (Nottingham F, Middlesbrough, Fulham) — 8
Crowe, V. H. 1959 (Aston Villa) — 16
Cumner, R. H. 1939 (Arsenal) — 3
Curtis, A. T. 1976 (Swansea C, Leeds U, Swansea C, Southampton, Cardiff C) — 35
Curtis, E. R. 1928 (Cardiff C, Birmingham) — 3

Daniel, R. W. 1951 (Arsenal, Sunderland) — 21
Darvell, S. 1897 (Oxford University) — 2
Davies, A. 1876 (Wrexham) — 2
Davies, A. 1904 (Druids, Middlesbrough) — 2
Davies, A. 1983 (Manchester U, Newcastle U, Swansea C, Bradford C) — 13
Davies, A. O. 1885 (Barmouth, Swifts, Wrexham, Crewe Alex) — 9

Davies, A. R. 2006 (Yeovil T) 1
Davies, A. T. 1891 (Shrewsbury T) 1
Davies, C. 1972 (Charlton Ath) 1
Davies, C. M. 2006 (Oxford U, Verona, Oldham Ath) 5
Davies, D. 1904 (Bolton W) 3
Davies, D. C. 1899 (Brecon, Hereford) 2
Davies, D. W. 1912 (Treharris, Oldham Ath) 2
Davies, E. Lloyd 1904 (Stoke, Northampton T) 16
Davies, E. R. 1953 (Newcastle U) 6
Davies, G. 1980 (Fulham, Manchester C) 16
Davies, Rev. H. 1928 (Wrexham) 1
Davies, Idwal 1923 (Liverpool Marine) 1
Davies, J. E. 1885 (Oswestry) 1
Davies, Jas 1878 (Wrexham) 1
Davies, John 1879 (Wrexham) 1
Davies, Jos 1888 (Newton Heath, Wolverhampton W) 7
Davies, Jos 1889 (Everton, Chirk, Ardwick, Sheffield U,
   Manchester C, Millwall, Reading) 11
Davies, J. P. 1883 (Druids) 2
Davies, Ll. 1907 (Wrexham, Everton, Wrexham) 13
Davies, L. S. 1922 (Cardiff C) 23
Davies, O. 1890 (Wrexham) 1
Davies, R. 1883 (Wrexham) 3
Davies, R. 1885 (Druids) 1
Davies, R. O. 1892 (Wrexham) 2
Davies, R. T. 1964 (Norwich C, Southampton,
   Portsmouth) 29
Davies, R. W. 1964 (Bolton W, Newcastle U, Manchester
   C, Manchester U, Blackpool) 34
Davies, S. 2001 (Tottenham H, Everton, Fulham) 58
Davies, S. I. 1996 (Manchester U) 1
Davies, Stanley 1920 (Preston NE, Everton, WBA,
   Rotherham U) 18
Davies, T. 1886 (Oswestry) 1
Davies, T. 1903 (Druids) 4
Davies, W. 1884 (Wrexham) 1
Davies, W. 1924 (Swansea T, Cardiff C, Notts Co) 17
Davies, William 1903 (Wrexham, Blackburn R) 11
Davies, W. C. 1908 (C Palace, WBA, C Palace) 4
Davies, W. D. 1975 (Everton, Wrexham, Swansea C) 52
Davies, W. H. 1876 (Oswestry) 4
Davis, G. 1978 (Wrexham) 3
Davis, W. O. 1913 (Millwall Ath) 5
Day, A. 1934 (Tottenham H) 1
Deacy, N. 1977 (PSV Eindhoven, Beringen) 12
Dearson, D. J. 1939 (Birmingham) 3
Delaney, M. A. 2000 (Aston Villa) 36
Derrett, S. C. 1969 (Cardiff C) 4
Dewey, F. T. 1931 (Cardiff Corinthians) 2
Dibble, A. 1986 (Luton T, Manchester C) 3
Dorman, A. 2010 (St Mirren, Crystal Palace) **3**
Doughty, J. 1886 (Druids, Newton Heath) 8
Doughty, R. 1888 (Newton Heath) 2
Duffy, R. M. 2006 (Portsmouth) 13
Durban, A. 1966 (Derby Co) 27
Dwyer, P. J. 1978 (Cardiff C) 10

Eardley, N, 2008 (Oldham Ath, Blackpool) **16**
Earnshaw, R. 2002 (Cardiff C, WBA, Norwich C,
   Derby Co, Nottingham F) **54**
Easter, J. M. 2007 (Wycombe W, Plymouth Arg,
   Milton Keynes D, Crystal Palace) **10**
Eastwood, F. 2008 (Wolverhampton W, Coventry C) **11**
Edwards, C. 1878 (Wrexham) 1
Edwards, C. N. H. 1996 (Swansea C) 1
Edwards, D. 2008 (Luton T, Wolverhampton W) **22**
Edwards, G. 1947 (Birmingham C, Cardiff C) 12
Edwards, H. 1878 (Wrexham Civil Service, Wrexham) 8
Edwards, J. H. 1876 (Wanderers) 1
Edwards, J. H. 1895 (Oswestry) 3
Edwards, J. H. 1898 (Aberystwyth) 1
Edwards, L. T. 1957 (Charlton Ath) 2
Edwards, R. I. 1978 (Chester, Wrexham) 4
Edwards, R. O. 2003 (Aston Villa, Wolverhampton W) 15
Edwards, R. W. 1998 (Bristol C) 4
Edwards, T. 1932 (Linfield) 1
Egan, W. 1892 (Chirk) 1
Ellis, B. 1932 (Motherwell) 6
Ellis, E. 1931 (Nunhead, Oswestry) 3

Emanuel, W. J. 1973 (Bristol C) 2
England, H. M. 1962 (Blackburn R, Tottenham H) 44
Evans, B. C. 1972 (Swansea C, Hereford U) 7
Evans, C. M. 2008 (Manchester C, Sheffield U) **13**
Evans, D. G. 1926 (Reading, Huddersfield T) 4
Evans, H. P. 1922 (Cardiff C) 6
Evans, I. 1976 (C Palace) 13
Evans, J. 1893 (Oswestry) 3
Evans, J. 1912 (Cardiff C) 8
Evans, J. H. 1922 (Southend U) 4
Evans, Len 1927 (Aberdare Ath, Cardiff C, Birmingham)
   4
Evans, M. 1884 (Oswestry) 1
Evans, P. S. 2002 (Brentford, Bradford C) 2
Evans, R. 1902 (Clapton) 1
Evans, R. E. 1906 (Wrexham, Aston Villa, Sheffield U)10
Evans, R. O. 1902 (Wrexham, Blackburn R, Coventry C)
   10
Evans, R. S. 1964 (Swansea T) 1
Evans, S. J. 2007 (Wrexham) 7
Evans, T. J. 1927 (Clapton Orient, Newcastle U) 4
Evans, W. 1933 (Tottenham H) 6
Evans, W. A. W. 1876 (Oxford University) 2
Evans, W. G. 1890 (Bootle, Aston Villa) 3
Evelyn, E. C. 1887 (Crusaders) 1
Eyton-Jones, J. A. 1883 (Wrexham) 4

Farmer, G. 1885 (Oswestry) 2
Felgate, D. 1984 (Lincoln C) 1
Finnigan, R. J. 1930 (Wrexham) 1
Fletcher, C. N. 2004 (Bournemouth, West Ham U,
   Crystal Palace) 36
Flynn, B. 1975 (Burnley, Leeds U, Burnley) 66
Ford, T. 1947 (Swansea T, Aston Villa, Sunderland,
   Cardiff C) 38
Foulkes, H. E. 1932 (WBA) 1
Foulkes, W. I. 1952 (Newcastle U) 11
Foulkes, W. T. 1884 (Oswestry) 2
Fowler, J. 1925 (Swansea T) 6
Freestone, R. 2000 (Swansea C) 1

Gabbidon, D. L. 2002 (Cardiff C, West Ham U) **44**
Garner, G. 2006 (Leyton Orient) 1
Garner, J. 1896 (Aberystwyth) 1
Giggs, R. J. 1992 (Manchester U) 64
Giles, D. C. 1980 (Swansea C, C Palace) 12
Gillam, S. G. 1889 (Wrexham, Shrewsbury, Clapton) 5
Glascodine, G. 1879 (Wrexham) 1
Glover, E. M. 1932 (Grimsby T) 7
Godding, G. 1923 (Wrexham) 2
Godfrey, B. C. 1964 (Preston NE) 3
Goodwin, U. 1881 (Ruthin) 1
Goss, J. 1991 (Norwich C) 9
Gough, R. T. 1883 (Oswestry White Star) 1
Gray, A. 1924 (Oldham Ath, Manchester C, Manchester
   Central, Tranmere R, Chester) 24
Green, A. W. 1901 (Aston Villa, Notts Co,
   Nottingham F) 8
Green, C. R. 1965 (Birmingham C) 15
Green, G. H. 1938 (Charlton Ath) 4
Green, R. M. 1998 (Wolverhampton W) 2
Grey, Dr W. 1876 (Druids) 2
Griffiths, A. T. 1971 (Wrexham) 17
Griffiths, F. J. 1900 (Blackpool) 2
Griffiths, G. 1887 (Chirk) 1
Griffiths, J. H. 1953 (Swansea T) 1
Griffiths, L. 1902 (Wrexham) 1
Griffiths, M. W. 1947 (Leicester C) 11
Griffiths, P. 1884 (Chirk) 6
Griffiths, P. H. 1932 (Everton) 1
Griffiths, T. P. 1927 (Everton, Bolton W, Middlesbrough,
   Aston Villa) 21
Gunter, C. R. 2007 (Cardiff C, Tottenham H,
   Nottingham F) **29**

Hall, G. D. 1988 (Chelsea) 9
Hallam, J. 1889 (Oswestry) 1
Hanford, H. 1934 (Swansea T, Sheffield W) 7
Harrington, A. C. 1956 (Cardiff C) 11

Harris, C. S. 1976 (Leeds U)	24
Harris, W. C. 1954 (Middlesbrough)	6
Harrison, W. C. 1899 (Wrexham)	5
Hartson, J. 1995 (Arsenal, West Ham U, Wimbledon, Coventry C, Celtic)	51
Haworth, S. O. 1997 (Cardiff C, Coventry C)	5
Hayes, A. 1890 (Wrexham)	2
Hennessey, W. R. 2007 (Wolverhampton W)	**32**
Hennessey, W. T. 1962 (Birmingham C, Nottingham F, Derby Co)	39
Hersee, A. M. 1886 (Bangor)	2
Hersee, R. 1886 (Llandudno)	1
Hewitt, R. 1958 (Cardiff C)	5
Hewitt, T. J. 1911 (Wrexham, Chelsea, South Liverpool)	8
Heywood, D. 1879 (Druids)	1
Hibbott, H. 1880 (Newtown Excelsior, Newtown)	3
Higham, G. G. 1878 (Oswestry)	2
Hill, M. R. 1972 (Ipswich T)	2
Hockey, T. 1972 (Sheffield U, Norwich C, Aston Villa)	9
Hoddinott, T. F. 1921 (Watford)	2
Hodges, G. 1984 (Wimbledon, Newcastle U, Watford, Sheffield U)	18
Hodgkinson, A. V. 1908 (Southampton)	1
Holden, A. 1984 (Chester C)	1
Hole, B. G. 1963 (Cardiff C, Blackburn R, Aston Villa, Swansea C)	30
Hole, W. J. 1921 (Swansea T)	9
Hollins, D. M. 1962 (Newcastle U)	11
Hopkins, I. J. 1935 (Brentford)	12
Hopkins, J. 1983 (Fulham, C Palace)	16
Hopkins, M. 1956 (Tottenham H)	34
Horne, B. 1988 (Portsmouth, Southampton, Everton, Birmingham C)	59
Howell, E. G. 1888 (Builth)	3
Howells, R. G. 1954 (Cardiff C)	2
Hugh, A. R. 1930 (Newport Co)	1
Hughes, A. 1894 (Rhos)	2
Hughes, A. 1907 (Chirk)	1
Hughes, C. M. 1992 (Luton T, Wimbledon)	8
Hughes, E. 1899 (Everton, Tottenham H)	14
Hughes, E. 1906 (Wrexham, Nottingham F, Wrexham, Manchester C)	16
Hughes, F. W. 1882 (Northwich Victoria)	6
Hughes, I. 1951 (Luton T)	4
Hughes, J. 1877 (Cambridge University, Aberystwyth)	2
Hughes, J. 1905 (Liverpool)	3
Hughes, J. I. 1935 (Blackburn R)	1
Hughes, L. M. 1984 (Manchester U, Barcelona, Manchester U, Chelsea, Southampton)	72
Hughes, P. W. 1887 (Bangor)	3
Hughes, W. 1891 (Bootle)	3
Hughes, W. A. 1949 (Blackburn R)	5
Hughes, W. M. 1938 (Birmingham)	10
Humphreys, J. V. 1947 (Everton)	1
Humphreys, R. 1888 (Druids)	1
Hunter, A. H. 1887 (FA of Wales Secretary)	1
Jackett, K. 1983 (Watford)	31
Jackson, W. 1899 (St Helens Rec)	1
James, E. 1893 (Chirk)	8
James, E. G. 1966 (Blackpool)	9
James, L. 1972 (Burnley, Derby Co, QPR, Burnley, Swansea C, Sunderland)	54
James, R. M. 1979 (Swansea C, Stoke C, QPR, Leicester C, Swansea C)	47
James, W. 1931 (West Ham U)	2
Jarrett, R. H. 1889 (Ruthin)	2
Jarvis, A. L. 1967 (Hull C)	3
Jenkins, E. 1925 (Lovell's Ath)	1
Jenkins, J. 1924 (Brighton &_HA)	8
Jenkins, R. W. 1902 (Rhyl)	1
Jenkins, S. R. 1996 (Swansea C, Huddersfield T)	16
Jenkyns, C. A. L. 1892 (Small Heath, Woolwich Arsenal, Newton Heath, Walsall)	8
Jennings, W. 1914 (Bolton W)	11
John, R. F. 1923 (Arsenal)	15
John, W. R. 1931 (Walsall, Stoke C, Preston NE, Sheffield U, Swansea T)	14
Johnson, A. J. 1999 (Nottingham F, WBA)	15

Johnson, M. G. 1964 (Swansea T)	1
Jones, A. 1987 (Port Vale, Charlton Ath)	6
Jones, A. F. 1877 (Oxford University)	1
Jones, A. T. 1905 (Nottingham F, Notts Co)	2
Jones, Bryn 1935 (Wolverhampton W, Arsenal)	17
Jones, B. S. 1963 (Swansea T, Plymouth Arg, Cardiff C)	15
Jones, Charlie 1926 (Nottingham F, Arsenal)	8
Jones, Cliff 1954 (Swansea T, Tottenham H, Fulham)	59
Jones, C. W. 1935 (Birmingham)	2
Jones, D. 1888 (Chirk, Bolton W, Manchester C)	14
Jones, D. E. 1976 (Norwich C)	8
Jones, D. O. 1934 (Leicester C)	7
Jones, Evan 1910 (Chelsea, Oldham Ath, Bolton W)	7
Jones, F. R. 1885 (Bangor)	3
Jones, F. W. 1893 (Small Heath)	1
Jones, G. P. 1907 (Wrexham)	2
Jones, H. 1902 (Aberaman)	1
Jones, Humphrey 1885 (Bangor, Queen's Park, East Stirlingshire, Queen's Park)	14
Jones, Ivor 1920 (Swansea T, WBA)	10
Jones, Jeffrey 1908 (Llandrindod Wells)	3
Jones, J. 1876 (Druids)	1
Jones, J. 1883 (Berwyn Rangers)	3
Jones, J. 1925 (Wrexham)	1
Jones, J. L. 1895 (Sheffield U, Tottenham H)	21
Jones, J. Love 1906 (Stoke, Middlesbrough)	2
Jones, J. O. 1901 (Bangor)	2
Jones, J. P. 1976 (Liverpool, Wrexham, Chelsea, Huddersfield T)	72
Jones, J. T. 1912 (Stoke, C Palace)	15
Jones, K. 1950 (Aston Villa)	1
Jones, Leslie J. 1933 (Cardiff C, Coventry C, Arsenal	11
Jones, M. A. 2007 (Wrexham)	2
Jones, M. G. 2000 (Leeds U, Leicester C)	13
Jones, P. L. 1997 (Liverpool, Tranmere R)	2
Jones, P. S. 1997 (Stockport Co, Southampton, Wolverhampton W, QPR)	50
Jones, P. W. 1971 (Bristol R)	1
Jones, R. 1887 (Bangor, Crewe Alex)	3
Jones, R. 1898 (Leicester Fosse)	1
Jones, R. 1899 (Druids)	1
Jones, R. 1900 (Bangor)	2
Jones, R. 1906 (Millwall)	2
Jones, R. A. 1884 (Druids)	4
Jones, R. A. 1994 (Sheffield W)	1
Jones, R. S. 1894 (Everton)	1
Jones, S. 1887 (Wrexham, Chester)	2
Jones, S. 1893 (Wrexham, Burton Swifts, Druids)	6
Jones, T. 1926 (Manchester U)	4
Jones, T. D. 1908 (Aberdare)	1
Jones, T. G. 1938 (Everton)	17
Jones, T. J. 1932 (Sheffield W)	2
Jones, V. P. 1995 (Wimbledon)	9
Jones, W. E. A. 1947 (Swansea T, Tottenham H)	4
Jones, W. J. 1901 (Aberdare, West Ham U)	4
Jones, W. Lot 1905 (Manchester C, Southend U)	20
Jones, W. P. 1889 (Druids, Wynnstay)	4
Jones, W. R. 1897 (Aberystwyth)	1
Keenor, F. C. 1920 (Cardiff C, Crewe Alex)	32
Kelly, F. C. 1899 (Wrexham, Druids)	3
Kelsey, A. J. 1954 (Arsenal)	41
Kenrick, S. L. 1876 (Druids, Oswestry, Shropshire Wanderers)	5
Ketley, C. F. 1882 (Druids)	1
King, A. 2009 (Leicester C)	**9**
King, J. 1955 (Swansea T)	1
Kinsey, N. 1951 (Norwich C, Birmingham C)	7
Knill, A. R. 1989 (Swansea C)	1
Koumas, J. 2001 (Tranmere R, WBA, Wigan Ath)	34
Krzywicki, R. L. 1970 (WBA, Huddersfield T)	8
Lambert, R. 1947 (Liverpool)	5
Latham, G. 1905 (Liverpool, Southport Central, Cardiff C)	10
Law, B. J. 1990 (QPR)	1
Lawrence, E. 1930 (Clapton Orient, Notts Co)	2
Lawrence, S. 1932 (Swansea T)	8

Lea, A. 1889 (Wrexham) 4
Lea, C. 1965 (Ipswich T) 2
Leary, P. 1889 (Bangor) 1
Ledley, J. C. 2006 (Cardiff C, Celtic) 37
Leek, K. 1961 (Leicester C, Newcastle U, Birmingham C,
Northampton T) 13
Legg, A. 1996 (Birmingham C, Cardiff C) 6
Lever, A. R. 1953 (Leicester C) 1
Lewis, B. 1891 (Chester, Wrexham, Middlesbrough,
Wrexham) 10
Lewis, D. 1927 (Arsenal) 3
Lewis, D. 1983 (Swansea C) 1
Lewis, D. J. 1933 (Swansea T) 2
Lewis, D. M. 1890 (Bangor) 2
Lewis, J. 1906 (Bristol R) 1
Lewis, J. 1926 (Cardiff C) 1
Lewis, T. 1881 (Wrexham) 2
Lewis, W. 1885 (Bangor, Crewe Alex, Chester,
Manchester C, Chester) 27
Lewis, W. L. 1927 (Swansea T, Huddersfield T) 6
Llewellyn, C. M. 1998 (Norwich C, Wrexham) 6
Lloyd, B. W. 1976 (Wrexham) 3
Lloyd, J. W. 1879 (Wrexham, Newtown) 2
Lloyd, R. A. 1891 (Ruthin) 2
Lockley, A. 1898 (Chirk) 1
Lovell, S. 1982 (C Palace, Millwall) 6
Lowndes, S. R. 1983 (Newport Co, Millwall, Barnsley) 10
Lowrie, G. 1948 (Coventry C, Newcastle U) 4
Lucas, P. M. 1962 (Leyton Orient) 4
Lucas, W. H. 1949 (Swansea T) 7
Lumberg, A. 1929 (Wrexham, Wolverhampton W) 4

MacDonald, S. B. 2011 (Swansea C) 1
McCarthy, T. P. 1889 (Wrexham) 1
McMillan, R. 1881 (Shrewsbury Engineers) 2
Maguire, G. T. 1990 (Portsmouth) 7
Mahoney, J. F. 1968 (Stoke C, Middlesbrough,
Swansea C) 51
Mardon, P. J. 1996 (WBA) 1
Margetson, M. W. 2004 (Cardiff C) 1
Marriott, A. 1996 (Wrexham) 5
Martin, T. J. 1930 (Newport Co) 1
Marustik, C. 1982 (Swansea C) 6
Mates, J. 1891 (Chirk) 3
Matthews, A. J. 2011 (Cardiff C) 2
Matthews, R. W. 1921 (Liverpool, Bristol C, Bradford) 3
Matthews, W. 1905 (Chester) 2
Matthias, J. S. 1896 (Brymbo, Shrewsbury T,
Wolverhampton W) 5
Matthias, T. J. 1914 (Wrexham) 12
Mays, A. W. 1929 (Wrexham) 1
Medwin, T. C. 1953 (Swansea T, Tottenham H) 30
Melville, A. K. 1990 (Swansea C, Oxford U, Sunderland,
Fulham, West Ham U) 65
Meredith, S. 1900 (Chirk, Stoke, Leyton) 8
Meredith, W. H. 1895 (Manchester C, Manchester U) 48
Mielczarek, R. 1971 (Rotherham U) 1
Millership, H. 1920 (Rotherham Co) 6
Millington, A. H. 1963 (WBA, C Palace,
Peterborough U, Swansea C) 21
Mills, T. J. 1934 (Clapton Orient, Leicester C) 4
Mills-Roberts, R. H. 1885 (St Thomas' Hospital,
Preston NE, Llanberis) 8
Moore, G. 1960 (Cardiff C, Chelsea, Manchester U,
Northampton T, Charlton Ath) 21
**Morgan, C. 2007 (Milton Keynes D, Peterborough U,
Preston NE)** 23
Morgan, J. R. 1877 (Cambridge University,
Derby School Staff) 10
Morgan, J. T. 1905 (Wrexham) 1
Morgan-Owen, H. 1902 (Oxford University, Corinthians)
4
Morgan-Owen, M. M. 1897 (Oxford University,
Corinthians) 13
Morison, S. W. 2011 (Millwall) 7
Morley, E. J. 1925 (Swansea T, Clapton Orient) 4
Morris, A. G. 1896 (Aberystwyth, Swindon T,
Nottingham F) 21
Morris, C. 1900 (Chirk, Derby Co, Huddersfield T) 27

Morris, E. 1893 (Chirk) 3
Morris, H. 1894 (Sheffield U, Manchester C, Grimsby T)
3
Morris, J. 1887 (Oswestry) 1
Morris, J. 1898 (Chirk) 1
Morris, R. 1900 (Chirk, Shrewsbury T) 6
Morris, R. 1902 (Newtown, Druids, Liverpool, Leeds C,
Grimsby T, Plymouth Arg) 11
Morris, S. 1937 (Birmingham) 5
Morris, W. 1947 (Burnley) 5
Moulsdale, J. R. B. 1925 (Corinthians) 1
Murphy, J. P. 1933 (WBA) 15
Myhill, G. O. 2008 (Hull C, WBA) 10

Nardiello, D. 1978 (Coventry C) 2
Nardiello, D. A. 2007 (Barnsley, QPR) 3
Neal, J. E. 1931 (Colwyn Bay) 2
Neilson, A. B. 1992 (Newcastle U, Southampton) 5
Newnes, J. 1926 (Nelson) 1
Newton, L. F. 1912 (Cardiff Corinthians) 1
Nicholas, D. S. 1923 (Stoke, Swansea T) 3
Nicholas, P. 1979 (C Palace, Arsenal, C Palace, Luton T,
Aberdeen, Chelsea, Watford) 73
Nicholls, J. 1924 (Newport Co, Cardiff C) 4
Niedzwiecki, E. A. 1985 (Chelsea) 2
Nock, W. 1897 (Newtown) 1
Nogan, L. M. 1992 (Watford, Reading) 2
Norman, A. J. 1986 (Hull C) 5
Nurse, M. T. G. 1960 (Swansea T, Middlesbrough) 12
Nyatanga, L. J. 2006 (Derby Co, Bristol C) 34

O'Callaghan, E. 1929 (Tottenham H) 11
Oliver, A. 1905 (Bangor, Blackburn R) 2
Oster, J. M. 1998 (Everton, Sunderland) 13
O'Sullivan, P. A. 1973 (Brighton & HA) 3
Owen, D. 1879 (Oswestry) 1
Owen, E. 1884 (Ruthin Grammar School) 3
Owen, G. 1888 (Chirk, Newton Heath, Chirk) 4
Owen, J. 1892 (Newton Heath) 1
Owen, T. 1879 (Oswestry) 1
Owen, Trevor 1899 (Crewe Alex) 2
Owen, W. 1884 (Chirk) 16
Owen, W. P. 1880 (Ruthin) 12
Owens, J. 1902 (Wrexham) 1

Page, M. E. 1971 (Birmingham C) 28
Page, R. J. 1997 (Watford, Sheffield U, Cardiff C,
Coventry C) 41
Palmer, D. 1957 (Swansea T) 3
Parris, J. E. 1932 (Bradford) 1
Parry, B. J. 1951 (Swansea T) 1
Parry, C. 1891 (Everton, Newtown) 13
Parry, E. 1922 (Liverpool) 5
Parry, M. 1901 (Liverpool) 16
Parry, P. I. 2004 (Cardiff C) 12
Parry, T. D. 1900 (Oswestry) 7
Parry, W. 1895 (Newtown) 1
Partridge, D. W. 2005 (Motherwell, Bristol C) 7
Pascoe, C. 1984 (Swansea C, Sunderland) 10
Paul, R. 1949 (Swansea T, Manchester C) 33
Peake, E. 1908 (Aberystwyth, Liverpool) 11
Peers, E. J. 1914 (Wolverhampton W, Port Vale) 12
Pembridge, M. A. 1992 (Luton T, Derby Co, Sheffield W,
Benfica, Everton, Fulham) 54
Perry, E. 1938 (Doncaster R) 3
Perry, J. 1994 (Cardiff C) 1
Phennah, E. 1878 (Civil Service) 1
Phillips, C. 1931 (Wolverhampton W, Aston Villa) 13
Phillips, D. 1984 (Plymouth Arg, Manchester C,
Coventry C, Norwich C, Nottingham F) 62
Phillips, L. 1971 (Cardiff C, Aston Villa, Swansea C,
Charlton Ath) 58
Phillips, T. J. S. 1973 (Chelsea) 4
Phoenix, H. 1882 (Wrexham) 1
Pipe, D. R. 2003 (Coventry C) 1
Poland, G. 1939 (Wrexham) 2
Pontin, K. 1980 (Cardiff C) 2
Powell, A. 1947 (Leeds U, Everton, Birmingham C) 8
Powell, D. 1968 (Wrexham, Sheffield U) 11

Walsh, I. P. 1980 (C Palace, Swansea C) — 18
Ward, D. 1959 (Bristol R, Cardiff C) — 2
Ward, D. 2000 (Notts Co, Nottingham F) — 5
Warner, J. 1937 (Swansea T, Manchester U) — 2
Warren, F. W. 1929 (Cardiff C, Middlesbrough, Hearts) 6
Watkins, A. E. 1898 (Leicester Fosse, Aston Villa, Millwall) — 5
Watkins, W. M. 1902 (Stoke, Aston Villa, Sunderland, Stoke) — 10
Webster, C. 1957 (Manchester U) — 4
Weston, R. D. 2000 (Arsenal, Cardiff C) — 7
Whatley, W. J. 1939 (Tottenham H) — 2
White, P. F. 1896 (London Welsh) — 1
Wilcock, A. R. 1890 (Oswestry) — 1
Wilding, J. 1885 (Wrexham Olympians, Bootle, Wrexham) — 9
Williams, A. 1994 (Reading, Wolverhampton W, Reading) — 13
Williams, A. E. 2008 (Stockport Co, Swansea C) — **25**
Williams, A. L. 1931 (Wrexham) — 1
Williams, A. P. 1998 (Southampton) — 2
Williams, B. 1930 (Bristol C) — 1
Williams, B. D. 1928 (Swansea T, Everton) — 10
Williams, D. G. 1988 (Derby Co, Ipswich T) — 13
Williams, D. M. 1986 (Norwich C) — 5
Williams, D. R. 1921 (Merthyr T, Sheffield W, Manchester U) — 8
Williams, E. 1893 (Crewe Alex) — 2
Williams, E. 1901 (Druids) — 5

Williams, G. 1893 (Chirk) — 6
Williams, G. E. 1960 (WBA) — 26
Williams, G. G. 1961 (Swansea T) — 5
Williams, G. J. 2006 (West Ham U, Ipswich T) — 2
Williams, G. J. J. 1951 (Cardiff C) — 1
Williams, G. O. 1907 (Wrexham) — 1
Williams, H. J. 1965 (Swansea T) — 3
Williams, H. T. 1949 (Newport Co, Leeds U) — 4
Williams, J. H. 1884 (Oswestry) — 1
Williams, J. J. 1939 (Wrexham) — 1
Williams, J. T. 1925 (Middlesbrough) — 1
Williams, J. W. 1912 (C Palace) — 2
Williams, R. 1935 (Newcastle U) — 2
Williams, R. P. 1886 (Caernarvon) — 1
Williams, S. G. 1954 (WBA, Southampton) — 43
Williams, W. 1876 (Druids, Oswestry, Druids) — 11
Williams, W. 1925 (Northampton T) — 1
Witcomb, D. F. 1947 (WBA, Sheffield W) — 3
Woosnam, A. P. 1959 (Leyton Orient, West Ham U, Aston Villa) — 17
Woosnam, G. 1879 (Newtown Excelsior) — 1
Worthington, T. 1894 (Newtown) — 1
Wynn, G. A. 1909 (Wrexham, Manchester C) — 11
Wynn, W. 1903 (Chirk) — 1

Yorath, T. C. 1970 (Leeds U, Coventry C, Tottenham H, Vancouver W) — 59
Young, E. 1990 (Wimbledon, C Palace, Wolverhampton W) — 21

REPUBLIC OF IRELAND

Aherne, T. 1946 (Belfast C, Luton T) — 16
Aldridge, J. W. 1986 (Oxford U, Liverpool, Real Sociedad, Tranmere R) — 69
Ambrose, P. 1955 (Shamrock R) — 5
Anderson, J. 1980 (Preston NE, Newcastle U) — 16
Andrews, K. J. 2009 (Blackburn R) — **20**
Andrews, P. 1936 (Bohemians) — 1
Arrigan, T. 1938 (Waterford) — 1

Babb, P. A. 1994 (Coventry C, Liverpool, Sunderland) 35
Bailham, E. 1964 (Shamrock R) — 1
Barber, E. 1966 (Shelbourne, Birmingham C) — 2
Barrett, G. 2003 (Arsenal, Coventry C) — 6
Barry, P. 1928 (Fordsons) — 2
Beglin, J. 1984 (Liverpool) — 15
Bennett, A. J. 2007 (Reading) — 2
Bermingham, J. 1929 (Bohemians) — 1
Bermingham, P. 1935 (St James' Gate) — 1
Best, L. J. B. 2009 (Coventry C, Newcastle U) — 7
Bonner, P. 1981 (Celtic) — 80
Braddish, S. 1978 (Dundalk) — 2
Bradshaw, P. 1939 (St James' Gate) — 5
Brady, F. 1926 (Fordsons) — 2
Brady, T. R. 1964 (QPR) — 6
Brady, W. L. 1975 (Arsenal, Juventus, Sampdoria, Internazionale, Ascoli, West Ham U) — 72
Branagan, K. G. 1997 (Bolton W) — 1
Breen, G. 1996 (Birmingham C, Coventry C, West Ham U, Sunderland) — 63
Breen, T. 1937 (Manchester U, Shamrock R) — 5
Brennan, F. 1965 (Drumcondra) — 1
Brennan, S. A. 1965 (Manchester U, Waterford) — 19
Brown, J. 1937 (Coventry C) — 3
Browne, W. 1964 (Bohemians) — 3
Bruce, A. S. 2007 (Ipswich T) — 2
Buckley, L. 1984 (Shamrock R, Waregem) — 1
Burke, F. 1952 (Cork Ath) — 1
Burke, J. 1929 (Shamrock R) — 1
Burke, J. 1934 (Cork) — 1
Butler, P. J. 2000 (Sunderland) — 1
Butler, T. 2003 (Sunderland) — 2
Byrne, A. B. 1970 (Southampton) — 14
Byrne, D. 1929 (Shelbourne, Shamrock R, Coleraine) — 3
Byrne, J. 1928 (Bray Unknowns) — 1
Byrne, J. 1985 (QPR, Le Havre, Brighton & HA, Sunderland, Millwall) — 23

Byrne, J. 2004 (Shelbourne) — 2
Byrne, P. 1931 (Dolphin, Shelbourne, Drumcondra) — 3
Byrne, P. 1984 (Shamrock R) — 8
Byrne, S. 1931 (Bohemians) — 1

Campbell, A. 1985 (Santander) — 3
Campbell, N. 1971 (St Patrick's Ath, Fortuna Cologne) 11
Cannon, H. 1926 (Bohemians) — 2
Cantwell, N. 1954 (West Ham U, Manchester U) — 36
Carey, B. P. 1992 (Manchester U, Leicester C) — 3
Carey, J. J. 1938 (Manchester U) — 29
Carolan, J. 1960 (Manchester U) — 2
Carr, S. 1999 (Tottenham H, Newcastle U) — 44
Carroll, B. 1949 (Shelbourne) — 2
Carroll, T. R. 1968 (Ipswich T, Birmingham C) — 17
Carsley, L. K. 1998 (Derby Co, Blackburn R, Coventry C, Everton) — 39
Cascarino, A. G. 1986 (Gillingham, Millwall, Aston Villa, Celtic, Chelsea, Marseille, Nancy) — 88
Chandler, J. 1980 (Leeds U) — 2
Chatton, H. A. 1931 (Shelbourne, Dumbarton, Cork) — 3
Clark, C. 2011 (Aston Villa) — **2**
Clarke, C. R. 2004 (Stoke C) — 2
Clarke, J. 1978 (Drogheda U) — 1
Clarke, K. 1948 (Drumcondra) — 2
Clarke, M. 1950 (Shamrock R) — 1
Clinton, T. J. 1951 (Everton) — 3
Coad, P. 1947 (Shamrock R) — 11
Coffey, T. 1950 (Drumcondra) — 1
Coleman, S. 2011 (Everton) — **4**
Colfer, M. D. 1950 (Shelbourne) — 2
Colgan, N. 2002 (Hibernian, Barnsley) — 9
Collins, F. 1927 (Jacobs) — 1
Conmy, O. M. 1965 (Peterborough U) — 5
Connolly, D. J. 1996 (Watford, Feyenoord, Wolverhampton W, Excelsior, Feyenoord, Wimbledon, West Ham U, Wigan Ath) — 41
Connolly, H. 1937 (Cork) — 1
Connolly, J. 1926 (Fordsons) — 1
Conroy, G. A. 1970 (Stoke C) — 27
Conway, J. P. 1967 (Fulham, Manchester C) — 20
Corr, P. J. 1949 (Everton) — 4
Courtney, E. 1946 (Cork U) — 1
Cox, S. R. 2011 (WBA) — **4**
Coyle, O. C. 1994 (Bolton W) — 1
Coyne, T. 1992 (Celtic, Tranmere R, Motherwell) — 22

Crowe, G. 2003 (Bohemians) 2
Cummins, G. P. 1954 (Luton T) 19
Cuneen, T. 1951 (Limerick) 1
Cunningham, G. R. 2010 (Manchester C) 3
Cunningham, K. 1996 (Wimbledon, Birmingham C) 72
Curtis, D. P. 1957 (Shelbourne, Bristol C, Ipswich T, Exeter C) 17
Cusack, S. 1953 (Limerick) 1

Daish, L. S. 1992 (Cambridge U, Coventry C) 5
Daly, G. A. 1973 (Manchester U, Derby Co, Coventry C, Birmingham C, Shrewsbury T) 48
Daly, J. 1932 (Shamrock R) 2
Daly, M. 1978 (Wolverhampton W) 2
Daly, P. 1950 (Shamrock R) 1
Davis, T. L. 1937 (Oldham Ath, Tranmere R) 4
Deacy, E. 1982 (Aston Villa) 4
Delaney, D. F. 2008 (QPR, Ipswich T) 5
Delap, R. J. 1998 (Derby Co, Southampton) 11
De Mange, K. J. P. P. 1987 (Liverpool, Hull C) 2
Dempsey, J. T. 1967 (Fulham, Chelsea) 19
Dennehy, J. 1972 (Cork Hibernians, Nottingham F, Walsall) 11
Desmond, P. 1950 (Middlesbrough) 4
Devine, J. 1980 (Arsenal, Norwich C) 13
Doherty, G. M. T. 2000 (Luton T, Tottenham H, Norwich C) 34
Donnelly, J. 1935 (Dundalk) 10
Donnelly, T. 1938 (Drumcondra, Shamrock R) 2
Donovan, D. C. 1955 (Everton) 5
Donovan, T. 1980 (Aston Villa) 2
Douglas, J. 2004 (Blackburn R, Leeds U) 8
Dowdall, C. 1928 (Fordsons, Barnsley, Cork) 3
Doyle, C. 1959 (Shelbourne) 1
Doyle, Colin 2007 (Birmingham C) 1
Doyle, D. 1926 (Shamrock R) 1
Doyle, K. E. 2006 (Reading, Wolverhampton W) 41
Doyle, L. 1932 (Dolphin) 1
Doyle, M. P. 2004 (Coventry C) 1
Duff, D. A. 1998 (Blackburn R, Chelsea, Newcastle U, Fulham) 87
Duffy, B. 1950 (Shamrock R) 1
Duggan, H. A. 1927 (Leeds U, Newport Co) 5
Dunne, A. P. 1962 (Manchester U, Bolton W) 33
Dunne, J. 1930 (Sheffield U, Arsenal, Southampton, Shamrock R) 15
Dunne, J. C. 1971 (Fulham) 1
Dunne, L. 1935 (Manchester C) 2
Dunne, P. A. J. 1965 (Manchester U) 5
Dunne, R. P. 2000 (Everton, Manchester C, Aston Villa) 65
Dunne, S. 1953 (Luton T) 15
Dunne, T. 1956 (St Patrick's Ath) 3
Dunning, P. 1971 (Shelbourne) 2
Dunphy, E. M. 1966 (York C, Millwall) 23
Dwyer, N. M. 1960 (West Ham U, Swansea T) 14

Eccles, P. 1986 (Shamrock R) 1
Egan, R. 1929 (Dundalk) 1
Eglington, T. J. 1946 (Shamrock R, Everton) 24
Elliott, S. W. 2005 (Sunderland) 9
Ellis, P. 1935 (Bohemians) 7
Evans, M. J. 1998 (Southampton) 1

Fagan, E. 1973 (Shamrock R) 1
Fagan, F. 1955 (Manchester C, Derby Co) 8
Fagan, J. 1926 (Shamrock R) 1
Fahey, K. D. 2010 (Birmingham C) 11
Fairclough, M. 1982 (Dundalk) 2
Fallon, S. 1951 (Celtic) 8
Fallon, W. J. 1935 (Notts Co, Sheffield W) 9
Farquharson, T. G. 1929 (Cardiff C) 4
Farrell, P. 1937 (Hibernian) 2
Farrell, P. D. 1946 (Shamrock R, Everton) 28
Farrelly, G. 1996 (Aston Villa, Everton, Bolton W) 6
Feenan, J. J. 1937 (Sunderland) 2
Finnan, S. 2000 (Fulham, Liverpool, Espanyol) 53
Finucane, A. 1967 (Limerick) 11
Fitzgerald, F. J. 1955 (Waterford) 2

Fitzgerald, P. J. 1961 (Leeds U, Chester) 5
Fitzpatrick, K. 1970 (Limerick) 1
Fitzsimons, A. G. 1950 (Middlesbrough, Lincoln C) 26
Fleming, C. 1996 (Middlesbrough) 10
Flood, J. J. 1926 (Shamrock R) 5
Fogarty, A. 1960 (Sunderland, Hartlepools U) 11
Folan, C. C. 2009 (Hull C) 7
Foley, D. J. 2000 (Watford) 6
Foley, J. 1934 (Cork, Celtic) 7
Foley, K. P. 2009 (Wolverhampton W) 8
Foley, M. 1926 (Shelbourne) 1
Foley, T. C. 1964 (Northampton T) 9
Forde, D. 2011 (Millwall) 2
Foy, T. 1938 (Shamrock R) 2
Fullam, J. 1961 (Preston NE, Shamrock R) 11
Fullam, R. 1926 (Shamrock R) 2

Gallagher, C. 1967 (Celtic) 2
Gallagher, M. 1954 (Hibernian) 1
Gallagher, P. 1932 (Falkirk) 1
Galvin, A. 1983 (Tottenham H, Sheffield W, Swindon T) 29
Gamble, J. 2007 (Cork C) 2
Gannon, E. 1949 (Notts Co, Sheffield W, Shelbourne) 14
Gannon, M. 1972 (Shelbourne) 1
Gaskins, P. 1934 (Shamrock R, St James' Gate) 7
Gavin, J. T. 1950 (Norwich C, Tottenham H, Norwich C) 7
Geoghegan, M. 1937 (St James' Gate) 1
Gibbons, A. 1952 (St Patrick's Ath) 4
Gibson, D. T. D. 2008 (Manchester U) 16
Gilbert, R. 1966 (Shamrock R) 1
Giles, C. 1951 (Doncaster R) 1
Giles, M. J. 1960 (Manchester U, Leeds U, WBA, Shamrock R) 59
Given, S. J. J. 1996 (Blackburn R, Newcastle U, Manchester C) 113
Givens, D. J. 1969 (Manchester U, Luton T, QPR, Birmingham C, Neuchatel X) 56
Gleeson, S. M. 2007 (Wolverhampton W) 2
Glen, W. 1927 (Shamrock R) 8
Glynn, D. 1952 (Drumcondra) 2
Godwin, T. F. 1949 (Shamrock R, Leicester C, Bournemouth) 13
Golding, J. 1928 (Shamrock R) 2
Goodman, J. 1997 (Wimbledon) 4
Goodwin, J. 2003 (Stockport Co) 1
Gorman, W. C. 1936 (Bury, Brentford) 13
Grace, J. 1926 (Drumcondra) 1
Grealish, A. 1976 (Orient, Luton T, Brighton & HA, WBA) 45
Green, P. J. 2010 (Derby Co) 9
Gregg, E. 1978 (Bohemians) 8
Griffith, R. 1935 (Walsall) 1
Grimes, A. A. 1978 (Manchester U, Coventry C, Luton T) 18

Hale, A. 1962 (Aston Villa, Doncaster R, Waterford) 14
Hamilton, T. 1959 (Shamrock R) 2
Hand, E. K. 1969 (Portsmouth) 20
Harrington, W. 1936 (Cork) 5
Harte, I. P. 1996 (Leeds U, Levante) 64
Hartnett, J. B. 1949 (Middlesbrough) 2
Haverty, J. 1956 (Arsenal, Blackburn R, Millwall, Celtic, Bristol R, Shelbourne) 32
Hayes, A. W. P. 1979 (Southampton) 1
Hayes, W. E. 1947 (Huddersfield T) 2
Hayes, W. J. 1949 (Limerick) 1
Healey, R. 1977 (Cardiff C) 2
Healy, C. 2002 (Celtic, Sunderland) 13
Heighway, S. D. 1971 (Liverpool, Minnesota K) 34
Henderson, B. 1948 (Drumcondra) 2
Henderson, W. C. P. 2006 (Brighton & HA, Preston NE) 6
Hennessy, J. 1965 (Shelbourne, St Patrick's Ath) 5
Herrick, J. 1972 (Cork Hibernians, Shamrock R) 3
Higgins, J. 1951 (Birmingham C) 1
Holland, M. R. 2000 (Ipswich T, Charlton Ath) 49

Murray, T. 1950 (Dundalk) 1

Newman, W. 1969 (Shelbourne) 1
Nolan. E. W. 2009 (Preston NE) 3
Nolan, R. 1957 (Shamrock R) 10

O'Brien, A. 2007 (Newcastle U) 5
O'Brien, A. J. 2001 (Newcastle U, Portsmouth) 26
O'Brien, F. 1980 (Philadelphia F) 3
O'Brien J. M. 2006 (Bolton W) 3
O'Brien, L. 1986 (Shamrock R, Manchester U, Newcastle U, Tranmere R) 16
O'Brien, M. T. 1927 (Derby Co, Walsall, Norwich C, Watford) 4
O'Brien, R. 1976 (Notts Co) 5
O'Byrne, L. B. 1949 (Shamrock R) 1
O'Callaghan, B. R. 1979 (Stoke C) 6
O'Callaghan, K. 1981 (Ipswich T, Portsmouth) 21
O'Cearuill, J. 2007 (Arsenal) 2
O'Connell, A. 1967 (Dundalk, Bohemians) 2
O'Connor, T. 1950 (Shamrock R) 4
O'Connor, T. 1968 (Fulham, Dundalk, Bohemians) 7
O'Dea, D. 2010 (Celtic, Ipswich T) **9**
O'Driscoll, J. F. 1949 (Swansea T) 3
O'Driscoll, S. 1982 (Fulham) 3
O'Farrell, F. 1952 (West Ham U, Preston NE) 9
O'Flanagan, K. P. 1938 (Bohemians, Arsenal) 10
O'Flanagan, M. 1947 (Bohemians) 1
O'Halloran, S. E. 2007 (Aston Villa) 2
O'Hanlon, K. G. 1988 (Rotherham U) 1
O'Kane, P. 1935 (Bohemians) 3
O'Keefe, E. 1981 (Everton, Port Vale) 5
O'Keefe, T. 1934 (Cork, Waterford) 3
O'Leary, D. 1977 (Arsenal) 68
O'Leary, P. 1980 (Shamrock R) 7
O'Mahoney, M. T. 1938 (Bristol R) 6
O'Neill, F. S. 1962 (Shamrock R) 20
O'Neill, J. 1952 (Everton) 17
O'Neill, J. 1961 (Preston NE) 1
O'Neill, K. P. 1996 (Norwich C, Middlesbrough) 13
O'Neill, W. 1936 (Dundalk) 11
O'Regan, K. 1984 (Brighton & HA) 4
O'Reilly, J. 1932 (Brideville, Aberdeen, Brideville, St James' Gate) 20
O'Reilly, J. 1946 (Cork U) 2
O'Shea, J. F. 2002 (Manchester U) **70**

Peyton, G. 1977 (Fulham, Bournemouth, Everton) 33
Peyton, N. 1957 (Shamrock R, Leeds U) 6
Phelan, T. 1992 (Wimbledon, Manchester C, Chelsea, Everton, Fulham) 42
Potter, D. M. 2007 (Wolverhampton W) 5

Quinn, A. 2003 (Sheffield W, Sheffield U) 8
Quinn, B. S. 2000 (Coventry C) 4
Quinn, N. J. 1986 (Arsenal, Manchester C, Sunderland) 91

Reid, A. M. 2004 (Nottingham F, Tottenham H, Charlton Ath, Sunderland) 27
Reid, C. 1931 (Brideville) 1
Reid, S. J. 2002 (Millwall, Blackburn R) 23
Richardson, D. J. 1972 (Shamrock R, Gillingham) 3
Rigby, A. 1935 (St James' Gate) 3
Ringstead, A. 1951 (Sheffield U) 20
Robinson, J. 1928 (Bohemians, Dolphin) 2
Robinson, M. 1981 (Brighton & HA, Liverpool, QPR) 24

Roche, P. J. 1972 (Shelbourne, Manchester U) 8
Rogers, E. 1968 (Blackburn R, Charlton Ath) 19
Rowlands, M. C. 2004 (QPR) 5
Ryan, G. 1978 (Derby Co, Brighton & HA) 18
Ryan, R. A. 1950 (WBA, Derby Co) 16

Sadlier, R. T. 2002 (Millwall) 1
Savage, D. P. T. 1996 (Millwall) 5
Saward, P. 1954 (Millwall, Aston Villa, Huddersfield T) 18
Scannell, T. 1954 (Southend U) 1
Scully, P. J. 1989 (Arsenal) 1
Sheedy, K. 1984 (Everton, Newcastle U) 46
Sheridan, C. 2010 (Celtic, CSKA Sofia) **3**
Sheridan, J. J. 1988 (Leeds U, Sheffield W) 34
Slaven, B. 1990 (Middlesbrough) 7
Sloan, J. W. 1946 (Arsenal) 2
Smyth, M. 1969 (Shamrock R) 1
Squires, J. 1934 (Shelbourne) 1
Stapleton, F. 1977 (Arsenal, Manchester U, Ajax, Le Havre, Blackburn R) 71
Staunton, S. 1989 (Liverpool, Aston Villa, Liverpool, Aston Villa) 102
St Ledger-Hall, S. P. 2009 (Preston NE) **18**
Stevenson, A. E. 1932 (Dolphin, Everton) 7
Stokes, A. 2007 (Sunderland, Celtic) **4**
Strahan, F. 1964 (Shelbourne) 5
Sullivan, J. 1928 (Fordsons) 1
Swan, M. M. G. 1960 (Drumcondra) 1
Synnott, N. 1978 (Shamrock R) 3

Taylor, T. 1959 (Waterford) 1
Thomas, P. 1974 (Waterford) 2
Thompson, J. 2004 (Nottingham F) 1
Townsend, A. D. 1989 (Norwich C, Chelsea, Aston Villa, Middlesbrough) 70
Traynor, T. J. 1954 (Southampton) 8
Treacy, K. 2011 (Preston NE) **5**
Treacy, R. C. P. 1966 (WBA, Charlton Ath, Swindon T, Preston NE, WBA, Shamrock R) 42
Tuohy, L. 1956 (Shamrock R, Newcastle U, Shamrock R) 8
Turner, C. J. 1936 (Southend U, West Ham U) 10
Turner, P. 1963 (Celtic) 2

Vernon, J. 1946 (Belfast C) 2

Waddock, G. 1980 (QPR, Millwall) 21
Walsh, D. J. 1946 (Linfield, WBA, Aston Villa) 20
Walsh, J. 1982 (Limerick) 1
Walsh, M. 1976 (Blackpool, Everton, QPR, Porto) 21
Walsh, M. 1982 (Everton) 4
Walsh, W. 1947 (Manchester C) 9
Walters, J. R. 2011 (Stoke C) **2**
Ward, S. R. 2011 (Wolverhampton W) **3**
Waters, J. 1977 (Grimsby T) 2
Watters, F. 1926 (Shelbourne) 1
Weir, E. 1939 (Clyde) 3
Westwood, K. 2009 (Coventry C) **7**
Whelan, G. D. 2008 (Stoke C) **29**
Whelan, R. 1964 (St Patrick's Ath) 2
Whelan, R. 1981 (Liverpool, Southend U) 53
Whelan, W. 1956 (Manchester U) 4
White, J. J. 1928 (Bohemians) 1
Whittaker, R. 1959 (Chelsea) 1
Williams, J. 1938 (Shamrock R) 1
Wilson, M. D. 2011 (Stoke C) **1**

BRITISH AND IRISH INTERNATIONAL GOALSCORERS SINCE 1872

Where two players with the same surname and initials have appeared for the same country, and one or both have scored, they have been distinguished by reference to the club which appears *first* against their name in the international appearances section.

ENGLAND

A'Court, A.	1	Buchan, C. M.	4	Forman, Fred	3	Kail, E. I. L.	2

Name	Goals	Name	Goals	Name	Goals	Name	Goals
A'Court, A.	1	Buchan, C. M.	4	Forman, Fred	3	Kail, E. I. L.	2
Adams, T. A.	5	Bull, S. G.	4	Foster, R. E.	3	Kay, A. H.	1
Adcock, H.	1	Bullock, N.	2	Fowler, R. B.	7	Keegan, J. K.	21
Alcock, C. W.	1	Burgess, H.	4	Francis, G. C. J.	3	Kelly, R.	8
Allen, A.	3	Butcher, T.	3	Francis, T.	12	Kennedy, R.	3
Allen, R.	2	Byrne, J. J.	8	Freeman, B. C.	3	Kenyon-Slaney, W. S.	2
Amos, A.	1			Froggatt, J.	2	Keown, M. R.	2
Anderson, V.	2	Campbell, S. J.	1	Froggatt, R.	2	Kevan, D. T.	8
Anderton, D. R.	7	Camsell, G. H.	18			Kidd, B.	1
Astall, G.	1	**Carroll, A. T.**	**1**	Galley, T.	1	King, L. B.	2
Athersmith, W. C.	3	Carter, H. S.	7	Gascoigne, P. J.	10	Kingsford, R. K.	1
Atyeo, P. J. W.	5	Carter, J. H.	4	Geary, F.	3	Kirchen, A. J.	2
		Chadwick, E.	3	**Gerrard, S. G.**	**19**	Kirton, W. J.	1
Bache, J. W.	4	Chamberlain, M.	1	Gibbins, W. V. T.	3		
Bailey, N. C.	2	Chambers, H.	5	Gilliatt, W. E.	3	**Lampard, F. J.**	**22**
Baily, E. F.	5	Channon, M. R.	21	Goddard, P.	1	Langton, R.	1
Baker, J. H.	3	Charlton, J.	6	Goodall, J.	12	Latchford, R. D.	5
Ball, A. J.	8	Charlton, R.	49	Goodyer, A. C.	1	Latheron, E. G.	1
Bambridge, A. L.	1	Chenery, C. J.	1	Gosling, R. C.	2	Lawler, C.	1
Bambridge, E. C.	11	Chivers, M.	13	Goulden, L. A.	4	Lawton, T.	22
Barclay, R.	2	Clarke, A. J.	10	Grainger, C.	3	Lee, F.	10
Barmby, N. J.	4	Cobbold, W. N.	6	Greaves, J.	44	Lee, J.	1
Barnes, J.	11	Cock, J. G.	2	Grovesnor, A. T.	2	Lee, R. M.	2
Barnes, P. S.	4	Cole, A.	1	Gunn, W.	1	Lee, S.	2
Barry, G.	2	Cole, J. J.	10			Le Saux, G. P.	1
Barton, J.	1	Common, A.	2	Haines, J. T. W.	2	Lindley, T.	14
Bassett, W. I.	8	Connelly, J. M.	7	Hall, G. W.	9	Lineker, G.	48
Bastin, C. S.	12	Coppell, S. J.	7	Halse, H. J.	2	Lofthouse, J. M.	3
Beardsley, P. A.	9	Cotterill, G. H.	2	Hampson, J.	5	Lofthouse, N.	30
Beasley, A.	1	Cowans, G.	2	Hampton, H.	2	Hon. A. Lyttelton	1
Beattie, T. K.	1	Crawford, R.	1	Hancocks, J.	2		
Beckham, D. R. J.	17	Crawshaw, T. H.	1	Hardman, H. P.	1	Mabbutt, G.	1
Becton, F.	2	Crayston, W. J.	1	Harris, S. S.	2	Macdonald, M.	6
Bedford, H.	1	Creek, F. N. S.	1	Hassall, H. W.	4	Mannion, W. J.	11
Bell, C.	9	Crooks, S. D.	7	Hateley, M.	9	Mariner, P.	13
Bent, D. A.	**3**	**Crouch, P. J.**	**22**	Haynes, J. N.	18	Marsh, R. W.	1
Bentley, R. T. F.	9	Currey, E. S.	2	Hegan, K. E.	4	Matthews, S.	11
Bishop, S. M.	1	Currie, A. W.	3	Henfrey, A. G.	2	Matthews, V.	1
Blackburn, F.	1	Cursham, A. W.	2	Heskey, E. W.	7	McCall, J.	1
Blissett, L.	3	Cursham, H. A.	5	Hilsdon, G. R.	14	McDermott, T.	3
Bloomer, S.	28			Hine, E. W.	4	McManaman, S.	3
Bond, R.	2	Daft, H. B.	3	Hinton, A. T.	1	Medley, L. D.	1
Bonsor, A. G.	1	Davenport, J. K.	2	Hirst, D. E.	1	Melia, J.	1
Bowden, E. R.	1	Davis, G.	1	Hitchens, G. A.	5	Mercer, D. W.	1
Bowers, J. W.	2	Davis, H.	1	Hobbis, H. H. F.	1	Merson, P. C.	3
Bowles, S.	1	Day, S. H.	2	Hoddle, G.	8	Milburn, J. E. T.	10
Bradford, G. R. W.	1	Dean, W. R.	18	Hodgetts, D.	1	Miller, H. S.	1
Bradford, J.	7	**Defoe, J. C.**	**15**	Hodgson, G.	1	Mills, G. R.	3
Bradley, W.	2	Devey, J. H. G.	1	Holley, G. H.	8	Milward, A.	3
Bradshaw, F.	3	Dewhurst, F.	11	Houghton, W. E.	5	Mitchell, C.	5
Brann, G.	1	Dix, W. R.	1	Howell, R.	1	Moore, J.	1
Bridge, W. M.	1	Dixon, K. M.	4	Hughes, E. W.	1	Moore, R. F.	2
Bridges, B. J.	1	Dixon, L. M.	1	Hulme, J. H. A.	4	Moore, W. G. B.	2
Bridgett, A.	3	Dorrell, A. R.	1	Hunt, G. S.	1	Morren, T.	1
Brindle, T.	1	Douglas, B.	11	Hunt, R.	18	Morris, F.	1
Britton, C. S.	1	Drake, E. J.	6	Hunter, N.	2	Morris, J.	3
Broadbent, P. F.	2	Ducat, A.	1	Hurst, G. C.	24	Mortensen, S. H.	23
Broadis, I. A.	8	Dunn, A. T. B.	2			Morton, J. R.	1
Brodie, J. B.	1			Ince, P. E. C.	2	Mosforth, W.	3
Bromley-Davenport, W.	2	Eastham, G.	2			Mullen, J.	6
Brook, E. F.	10	Edwards, D.	5	Jack, D. N. B.	3	Mullery, A. P.	1
Brooking, T. D.	5	Ehiogu, U.	1	Jeffers, F.	1	Murphy, D. B	1
Brooks, J.	2	Elliott, W. H.	3	Jenas, J. A.	1		
Broome, F. H.	3	Evans, R. E.	1	**Johnson, A.**	**2**	Neal, P. G.	5
Brown, A.	4			Johnson, D. E.	6	Needham, E.	3
Brown, A. S.	1	Ferdinand, L.	5	Johnson, E.	2	Nicholls, J.	1
Brown, G.	5	Ferdinand, R. G.	3	Johnson, G. M. C.	1	Nicholson, W. E.	1
Brown, J.	3	Finney, T.	30	Johnson, J. A.	2	Nugent, D. J.	1
Brown, W.	1	Fleming, H. J.	9	Johnson, T. C. F.	5		
Brown, W. M.	1	Flowers, R.	10	Johnson, W. H.	1	O'Grady, M.	3
		Forman, Frank	1			Osborne, F. R.	3

Owen, M. J.	40
Own goals	31
Page, L. A.	1
Paine, T. L.	7
Palmer, C. L.	1
Parry, E. H.	1
Parry, R. A.	1
Pawson, F. W.	1
Payne, J.	2
Peacock, A.	3
Pearce, S.	5
Pearson, J. S.	5
Pearson, S. C.	5
Perry, W.	2
Peters, M.	20
Pickering, F.	5
Platt, D.	27
Pointer, R.	2
Quantrill, A.	1
Ramsay, A. E.	3
Revie, D. G.	4
Redknapp, J. F.	1
Reynolds, J.	3
Richards, M.	1
Richardson, K. E.	2
Richardson, J. R.	2
Rigby, A.	3
Rimmer, E. J.	2
Roberts, F.	2
Roberts, H.	1
Roberts, W. T.	2
Robinson, J.	3
Robson, B.	26
Robson, R.	4
Rooney, W.	**26**
Rowley, J. F.	6
Royle, J.	2
Rutherford, J.	3
Sagar, C.	1
Sandilands, R. R.	3
Sansom, K.	1
Schofield, J.	1
Scholes, P.	14
Seed, J. M.	1
Settle, J.	6
Sewell, J.	3
Shackleton, L. F.	1
Sharp, J.	1
Shearer, A.	30
Shelton, A.	1
Shepherd, A.	2
Sheringham, E. P.	11
Simpson, J.	1
Smith, A.	1
Smith, A. M.	2
Smith, G. O.	11
Smith, Joe	1
Smith, J. R.	2
Smith, J. W.	4
Smith, R.	13
Smith, S.	1
Sorby, T. H.	1
Southgate, G.	2
Southworth, J.	3
Sparks, F. J.	3
Spence, J. W.	1
Spiksley, F.	5
Spilsbury, B. W.	5
Steele, F. C.	8
Stephenson, G. T.	2
Steven, T. M.	4
Stewart, J.	2
Stiles, N. P.	1
Storer, H.	1
Stone, S. B.	2
Summerbee, M. G.	1
Tambling, R. V.	1

Taylor, P. J.	2
Taylor, T.	16
Terry, J. G.	6
Thompson, P. B.	1
Thornewell, G.	1
Tilson, S. F.	6
Townley, W. J.	2
Tueart, D.	2
Upson, M. J.	2
Vassell, D.	6
Vaughton, O. H.	6
Veitch, J. G.	3
Viollet, D. S.	1
Waddle, C. R.	6
Walcott, T. J.	3
Walker, W. H.	9
Wall, G.	2
Wallace, D.	1
Walsh, P.	1
Waring, T.	4
Warren, B.	2
Watson, D. V.	4
Watson, V. M.	4
Webb, G. W.	1
Webb, N.	4
Wedlock, W. J.	2
Weller, K.	1
Welsh, D.	1
Whateley, O.	2
Wheldon, G. F.	6
Whitfield, H.	1
Wignall, F.	2
Wilkes, A.	1
Wilkins, R. G.	3
Willingham, C. K.	1
Wilshaw, D. J.	10
Wilson, G. P.	1
Winckworth, W. N.	1
Windridge, J. E.	7
Wise, D. F.	1
Withe, P.	1
Wollaston, C. H. R.	1
Wood, H.	1
Woodcock, T.	16
Woodhall, G.	1
Woodward, V. J.	29
Worrall, F.	2
Worthington, F. S.	2
Wright, I. E.	9
Wright, M.	1
Wright, W. A.	3
Wright-Phillips, S. C.	6
Wylie, J. G.	1
Yates, J.	3
Young, A. S.	**2**

NORTHERN IRELAND

Anderson, T.	4
Armstrong, G.	12
Bambrick, J.	12
Barr, H. H.	1
Barron, H.	3
Best, G.	9
Bingham, W. L.	10
Black, K.	1
Blanchflower, D.	2
Blanchflower, J.	1
Brennan, B.	1
Brennan, R. A.	1
Brotherston, N.	3
Brown, J.	1
Browne, F.	2
Brunt, C.	1
Campbell, J.	1
Campbell, W. G.	1
Casey, T.	2

Caskey, W.	1
Cassidy, T.	1
Chambers, J.	3
Clarke, C. J.	13
Clements, D.	2
Cochrane, T.	1
Condy, J.	1
Connor, M. J.	1
Coulter, J.	1
Croft, T.	1
Crone, W.	1
Crossan, E.	1
Crossan, J. A.	10
Curran, S.	2
Cush, W. W.	5
Dalton, W.	4
D'Arcy, S. D.	1
Darling, J.	1
Davey, H. H.	1
Davis S.	2
Davis, T. L.	1
Dill, A. H.	1
Doherty, L.	1
Doherty, P. D.	3
Dougan, A. D.	8
Dowie, I.	12
Dunne, J.	4
Elder, A. R.	1
Elliott, S.	1
Emerson, W.	1
English, S.	1
Evans, C.	**1**
Evans, J. G.	1
Feeney, W.	1
Feeney, W. J.	5
Ferguson, W.	1
Ferris, J.	1
Ferris, R. O.	1
Finney, T.	2
Gaffkin, J.	4
Gara, A.	3
Gaukrodger, G.	1
Gibb, J. T	2
Gibb, T. J	1
Gibson, W.	1
Gillespie, K. R.	2
Gillespie, W.	13
Goodall, A. L.	2
Griffin, D. J.	1
Gray, P.	6
Halligan, W.	1
Hamill, M.	1
Hamilton, B.	4
Hamilton, W. R.	5
Hannon, D. J.	1
Harkin, J. T.	2
Harvey, M.	3
Healy, D. J.	35
Hill, C. F.	1
Hughes, M. E.	5
Humphries, W.	1
Hunter, A. (*Distillery*)	1
Hunter, A. (*Blackburn R*) 1	
Hunter, B. V.	1
Irvine, R. W.	3
Irvine, W. J.	8
Johnston, H.	2
Johnston, S.	2
Johnston, W. C.	1
Jones, S.	1
Jones, S. (*Crewe Alex*)	1
Jones, J.	1
Kelly, J.	4
Kernaghan, N.	2

Kirwan, J.	2
Lacey, W.	3
Lafferty, K.	**8**
Lemon, J.	2
Lennon, N. F.	2
Lockhart, N.	3
Lomas, S. M.	3
Magilton, J.	5
Mahood, J.	2
Martin, D. K.	3
Maxwell, J.	2
McAdams, W. J.	7
McAllen, J.	1
McAuley, G.	**2**
Mcauley, J. L.	1
McCann, G. S.	4
McCartney, G.	1
McCandless, J.	2
McCandless, W.	1
McCaw, J. H.	1
McClelland, J.	1
McCluggage, A.	2
McCracken, W.	1
McCrory, S.	1
McCurdy, C.	1
McDonald, A.	3
McGarry, J. K.	1
McGrath, R. C.	4
McIlroy, J.	10
McIlroy, S. B.	5
McKenzie, H	1
McKnight, J.	2
McLaughlin, J. C.	6
McMahon, G. J.	2
McMordie, A. S.	3
McMorran, E. J.	4
McParland, P. J.	10
McWha, W. B. R.	1
Meldon, P. A.	1
Mercer, J. T.	1
Millar, W.	1
Milligan, D.	1
Milne, R. G.	2
Molyneux, T. B.	1
Moreland, V.	1
Morgan, S.	3
Morrow, S. J.	1
Morrow, W. J.	1
Mulryne, P. P.	3
Murdock, C. J.	1
Murphy, N.	1
Neill, W. J. T.	2
Nelson, S.	1
Nicholl, C. J.	3
Nicholl, J. M.	1
Nicholson, J. J.	6
O'Boyle, G.	1
O'Hagan, C.	2
O'Kane, W. J.	1
O'Neill, J.	2
O'Neill, M. A.	4
O'Neill, M. H.	8
Own goals	9
Patterson, D. J.	1
Patterson, R.	**1**
Peacock, R.	2
Peden, J.	7
Penney, S.	2
Pyper, James	2
Pyper, John	1
Quinn, J. M.	12
Quinn, S. J.	4
Reynolds, J.	1
Rowland, K.	1
Rowley, R. W. M.	2
Rushe, F.	1

Sheridan, J.	2	Brown, S.	2	Fraser, M. J. E.	3	Kay, J. L.	5
Sherrard, J.	1	Buchanan, P. S.	1	Freedman, D. A.	1	Keillor, A.	3
Sherrard, W. C.	2	Buchanan, R.	1			Kelly, J.	1
Simpson, W. J.	5	Buckley, P.	1	Gallacher, H. K.	23	Kelso, R.	1
Sloan, H. A. de B.	4	Buick, A.	2	Gallacher, K. W.	9	Ker, G.	10
Smyth, S.	5	Burke, C.	2	Gallacher, P.	1	King, A.	1
Spence, D. W.	3	Burley, C. W.	3	Galt, J. H.	1	King, J.	1
Sproule, I.	1	Burns, K.	1	Gemmell, T. (*St Mirren*)	1	Kinnear, D.	1
Stanfield, O. M.	11			Gemmell, T. (*Celtic*)	1	Kyle, K.	1
Stevenson, A. E.	5	Cairns, T.	1	Gemmill, A.	8		
Stewart, I.	2	Caldwell, G.	2	Gemmill, S.	1	Lambert, P.	1
		Calderwood, C.	1	Gibb, W.	1	Lambie, J.	1
Taggart, G. P.	7	Calderwood, R.	2	Gibson, D. W.	3	Lambie, W. A.	5
Thompson, F. W.	2	Caldow, E.	4	Gibson, J. D.	1	Lang, J. J.	2
Torrans, S.	1	Cameron, C.	2	Gibson, N.	1	Latta, A.	2
Tully, C. P.	3	Campbell, C.	1	Gillespie, Jas.	3	Law, D.	30
Turner, A.	1	Campbell, John (*Celtic*)	5	Gillick, T.	3	Leggat, G.	8
		Campbell, John (*Rangers*)	4	Gilzean, A. J.	12	Lennie, W.	1
Walker, J.	1			Gossland, J.	2	Lennox, R.	3
Walsh, D. J.	5	Campbell, J. (*South Western*)	1	Goudie, J.	1	Liddell, W.	6
Welsh, E.	1			Gough, C. R.	6	Lindsay, J.	6
Whiteside, N.	9	Campbell, P.	2	Gourlay, J.	1	Linwood, A. B.	1
Whiteside, T.	1	Campbell, R.	1	Graham, A.	2	Logan, J.	1
Whitley, Jeff	2	Cassidy, J.	1	Graham, G.	3	Lorimer, P.	4
Williams, J. R.	1	Chalmers, S.	3	Gray, A.	7	Love, A.	1
Williams, M. S.	1	Chambers, T.	1	Gray, E.	3	Low, J. (*Cambuslang*)	1
Williamson, J.	1	Cheyne, A. G.	4	Gray, F.	1	Lowe, J. (*St Bernards*)	1
Wilson, D. J.	1	Christie, A. J.	1	Greig, J.	3		
Wilson, K. J.	6	Clarkson, D.	1	Groves, W.	4	Macari, L.	5
Wilson, S. J.	7	Clunas, W. L.	1			MacDougall, E. J.	3
Wilton, J. M.	2	Collins, J.	12	Hamilton, G.	4	MacFarlane, A.	1
		Collins, R. Y.	10	Hamilton, J.		MacLeod, M.	1
Young, S.	1	Combe, J. R.	1	(*Queen's Park*)	3	Mackay, D. C.	4
N.B. In 1914 Young goal		**Commons, K.**	**2**	Hamilton, R. C.	15	Mackay, G.	1
should be credited to		Conn, A.	1	Harper, J. M.	2	MacKenzie, J. A.	1
Gillespie W v Wales		Cooper, D.	6	Hartley, P. J.	1	**Mackie, J. C.**	**1**
		Craig, J.	1	Harrower, W.	5	MacKinnon, W. W.	5
		Craig, T.	1	Hartford, R. A.	4	Madden, J.	5
SCOTLAND		Crawford, S.	4	Heggie, C. W	4	Maloney, S.	1
Aitken, R. (*Celtic*)	1	Cunningham, A. N.	5	Henderson, J. G.	1	Marshall, H.	1
Aitken, R. (*Dumbarton*)	1	Curran, H. P.	1	Henderson, W.	5	Marshall, J.	1
Aitkenhead, W. A. C.	2			Hendry, E. C. J.	3	Mason, J.	4
Alexander, D.	1	Dailly, C.	6	Herd, D. G.	3	Massie, A.	1
Allan, D. S.	4	Dalglish, K.	30	Herd, G.	1	Masson, D. S.	5
Allan, J.	2	Davidson, D.	1	Hewie, J. D.	2	McAdam, J.	1
Anderson, F.	1	Davidson, J. A.	1	Higgins, A. (*Newcastle U*)	1	McAllister, G.	5
Anderson, W.	4	Delaney, J.	3			**McArthur, J.**	**1**
Andrews, P.	1	Devine, A.	1	Higgins, A. (*Kilmarnock*)		McAulay, J. D.	1
Archibald, A.	1	Dewar, G.	1		4	McAvennie, F.	1
Archibald, S.	4	Dewar, N.	4	Highet, T. C.	1	McCall, J.	1
		Dickov, P.	1	Holt, G.J.	1	McCall, S. M.	1
Baird, D.	2	Dickson, W.	4	Holton, J. A.	2	McCalliog, J.	1
Baird, J. C.	2	Divers, J.	1	Hopkin, D.	2	McCallum, N.	1
Baird, S.	2	Dobie, R. S.	1	Houliston, W.	2	McCann, N.	3
Bannon, E.	1	Docherty, T. H.	1	Howie, H.	1	McClair, B. J.	2
Barbour, A.	1	Dodds, D.	1	Howie, J.	2	McCoist, A.	19
Barker, J. B.	4	Dodds, W.	7	Hughes, J.	1	McColl, R. S.	13
Battles, B. Jr	1	Donaldson, A.	1	Hunter, W.	1	McCormack, R.	1
Bauld, W.	2	Donnachie, J.	1	Hutchison, D.	6	McCulloch, D.	3
Baxter, J. C.	3	Dougall, J.	1	Hutchison, T.	1	McCulloch, L.	1
Beattie, C.	1	Drummond, J.	2	Hutton, J.	1	McDougall, J.	4
Bell, J.	5	Dunbar, M.	1	Hyslop, T.	1	McFadden, J.	15*
Bennett, A.	2	Duncan, D.	7			McFadyen, W.	2
Berra, C.	**1**	Duncan, D. M.	1	Imrie, W. N.	1	McGhee, M.	2
Berry, D.	1	Duncan, J.	1			McGinlay, J.	4
Bett, J.	1	Dunn, J.	2	Jackson, A.	8	McGregor, J.	1
Beveridge, W. W.	1	Durie, G. S.	7	Jackson, C.	1	McGrory, J.	6
Black, A.	3			Jackson, D.	4	McGuire, W.	1
Black, D.	1	Easson, J. F.	1	James, A. W.	4	McInally, A.	3
Bone, J.	1	Elliott, M. S.	1	Jardine, A.	1	McInnes, T.	2
Booth, S.	6	Ellis, J.	1	Jenkinson, T.	1	McKie, J.	2
Boyd, K	7			Jess, E.	2	McKimmie, S.	1
Boyd, R.	2	Ferguson, B.	3	Johnston, A.	2	McKinlay, W.	4
Boyd, T.	1	Ferguson, J.	6	Johnston, L. H.	1	McKinnon, A.	1
Boyd, W. G.	1	Fernie, W.	1	Johnston, M.	14	McKinnon, R.	1
Brackenridge, T.	1	Fitchie, T. T.	1	Johnstone, D.	2	McLaren, A.	4
Brand, R.	8	Flavell, R.	2	Johnstone, J.	4	McLaren, J.	1
Brazil, A.	1	Fleming, C.	1	Johnstone, Jas.	1	McLean, A.	1
Bremner, W. J.	3	Fleming, J. W.	3	Johnstone, R.	10	McLean, T.	1
Broadfoot, K.	1	Fletcher, D.	4	Johnstone, W.	1	McLintock, F.	1
Brown, A. D.	6	Fletcher, S.	1	Jordan, J.	11	McMahon, A.	6

* The Scottish FA officially changed Robsons's goal against Iceland on 10 September 2008 to McFadden.

McManus, S. 2
McMenemy, J. 5
McMillan, I. L. 2
McNeill, W. 3
McNiel, H. 5
McPhail, J. 3
McPhail, R. 7
McPherson, J. 5
McPherson, J. (*Vale of Leven*) 1
McPherson, R. 1
McQueen, G. 5
McStay, P. 9
McSwegan, G. 1
Meiklejohn, D. D. 3
Millar, J. 2
Miller, K. 14
Miller, T. 2
Miller, W. 1
Mitchell, R. C. 1
Morgan, W. 1
Morris, D. 1
Morris, H. 3
Morrison, J. C. 1
Morton, A. L. 5
Mudie, J. K. 9
Mulhall, G. 1
Munro, A. D. 1
Munro, N. 2
Murdoch, R. 5
Murphy, F. 1
Murray, J. 1

Napier, C. E. 3
Narey, D. 1
Naismith, S. 1
Naysmith, G. A. 1
Neil, R. G. 2
Nevin, P. K. F. 5
Nicholas, C. 5
Nisbet, J. 2

O'Connor, G. 4
O'Donnell, F. 2
O'Hare, J. 5
Ormond, W. E. 2
O'Rourke, F. 1
Orr, R. 1
Orr, T. 1
Oswald, J. 1
Own goals 17

Parlane, D. 1
Paul, H. McD. 2
Paul, W. 5
Pettigrew, W. 2
Provan, D. 1

Quashie, N. F. 1
Quinn, J. 7
Quinn, P. 1

Rankin, G. 2
Rankin, R. 2
Reid, W. 4
Reilly, L. 22
Renny-Tailyour, H. W. 1
Richmond, J. T. 1
Ring, T. 2
Rioch, B. D. 6
Ritchie, J. 1
Ritchie, P. S. 1
Robertson, A. 2
Robertson, J. 3
Robertson, J. N. 8
Robertson, J. T. 2
Robertson, T. 1
Robertson, W. 1
Russell, D. 1

Scott, A. S. 5
Sellar, W. 4
Sharp, G. 1

Shaw, F. W. 1
Shearer, D. 2
Simpson, J. 1
Smith, A. 5
Smith, G. 4
Smith, J. 1
Smith, John 13
Somerville, G. 1
Souness, G. J. 4
Speedie, F. 2
St John, I. 9
Steel, W. 12
Stein, C. 10
Stevenson, G. 4
Stewart, A. 1
Stewart, R. 1
Stewart, W. E. 1
Strachan, G. 5
Sturrock, P. 3

Taylor, J. D. 1
Templeton, R. 1
Thompson, S. 3
Thomson, A. 1
Thomson, C. 4
Thomson, R. 1
Thomson, W. 1
Thornton, W. 1

Waddell, T. S. 1
Waddell, W. 6
Walker, J. 2
Walker, R. 7
Walker, T. 9
Wallace, I. A. 1
Wark, J. 7
Watson, J. A. K. 1
Watt, F. 2
Watt, W. W. 1
Webster, A. 1
Weir, A. 1
Weir, D. 1
Weir, J. B. 2
White, J. A. 3
Wilkie, L. 1
Wilson, A. 2
Wilson, A. N. 13
Wilson, D. (*Liverpool*) 1
Wilson, D. (*Queen's Park*) 2
Wilson, D. (*Rangers*) 9
Wilson, H. 1
Wylie, T. G. 1

Young, A. 5

WALES
Allchurch, I. J. 23
Allen, M. 3
Astley, D. J. 12
Atherton, R. W. 2

Bale, G. 3
Bamford, T. 1
Barnes, W. 1
Bellamy, C. D. 18
Blackmore, C. G. 1
Blake, N. A. 4
Bodin, P. J. 3
Boulter, L. M. 1
Bowdler, J. C. H. 3
Bowen, D. L. 1
Bowen, M. 3
Boyle, T. 1
Bryan, T. 1
Burgess, W. A. R. 1
Burke, T. 1
Butler, W. T. 1

Chapman, T. 2
Charles, J. 1
Charles, M. 6

Charles, W. J. 15
Church, S. R. 1
Clarke, R. J. 5
Coleman, C. 4
Collier, D. J. 1
Collins, J. 2
Cotterill, D. 1
Crosse, K. 1
Cumner, R. H. 1
Curtis, A. 6
Curtis, E. R. 3

Davies, D. W. 1
Davies, E. Lloyd 1
Davies, G. 2
Davies, L. S. 6
Davies, R. T. 9
Davies, R. W. 6
Davies, Simon 6
Davies, Stanley 5
Davies, W. 6
Davies, W. H. 1
Davies, William 5
Davis, W. O. 1
Deacy, N. 4
Doughty, J. 6
Doughty, R. 2
Durban, A. 2
Dwyer, P. 2

Earnshaw, R. 16
Eastwood, F. 4
Edwards, D. 3
Edwards, G. 2
Edwards, R. I. 4
England, H. M. 4
Evans, C. 2
Evans, I. 1
Evans, I. 1
Evans, R. E. 2
Evans, W. 1
Eyton-Jones, J. A. 1

Fletcher, C. 1
Flynn, B. 7
Ford, T. 23
Foulkes, W. I. 1
Fowler, J. 3

Giles, D. 2
Giggs, R. J. 12
Glover, E. M. 7
Godfrey, B. C. 2
Green, A. W. 3
Griffiths, A. T. 6
Griffiths, M. W. 2
Griffiths, T. P. 3

Harris, C. S. 1
Hartson, J. 14
Hersee, R. 1
Hewitt, R. 1
Hockey, T. 1
Hodges, G. 2
Hole, W. J. 1
Hopkins, I. J. 2
Horne, B. 2
Howell, E. G. 3
Hughes, L. M. 16

James, E. 2
James, L. 10
James, R. 7
Jarrett, R. H. 3
Jenkyns, C. A. 1
Jones, A. 1
Jones, Bryn 6
Jones, B. S. 2
Jones, Cliff 16
Jones, C. W. 1
Jones, D. E. 1
Jones, Evan 1
Jones, H. 1

Jones, I. 1
Jones, J. L. 1
Jones, J. O. 1
Jones, J. P. 1
Jones, Leslie J. 1
Jones, R. A. 2
Jones, W. L. 6

Keenor, F. C. 2
King, A. 1
Koumas, J. 10
Krzywicki, R. L. 1

Ledley, J. 3
Leek, K. 5
Lewis, B. 4
Lewis, D. M. 2
Lewis, W. 8
Lewis, W. L. 3
Llewelyn, C. M 1
Lovell, S. 1
Lowrie, G. 2

Mahoney, J. F. 1
Mays, A. W. 1
Medwin, T. C. 6
Melville, A. K 3
Meredith, W. H. 11
Mills, T. J. 1
Moore, G. 1
Morgan, J. R. 2
Morgan-Owen, H. 1
Morgan-Owen, M. M. 2
Morris, A. G. 9
Morris, H. 2
Morris, R. 1
Morris, S. 1

Nicholas, P. 2

O'Callaghan, E. 3
O'Sullivan, P. A. 1
Owen, G. 2
Owen, W. 4
Owen, W. P. 6
Own goals 14

Palmer, D. 3
Parry, P. I. 1
Parry, T. D. 3
Paul, R. 1
Peake, E. 1
Pembridge, M. 6
Perry, E. 1
Phillips, C. 5
Phillips, D. 2
Powell, A. 1
Powell, D. 1
Price, J. 4
Price, P. 1
Pryce-Jones, W. E. 3
Pugh, D. H. 2

Ramsay, A. 3
Reece, G. I. 2
Rees, R. R. 3
Richards, R. W. 1
Roach, J. 2
Robbins, W. W. 4
Roberts, J. (*Corwen*) 1
Roberts, Jas. 1
Roberts, P. S. 1
Roberts, R. (*Druids*) 1
Roberts, W. (*Llangollen*) 1
Roberts, W. (*Wrexham*) 1
Roberts, W. H. 1
Robinson, C. P. 1
Robinson, J. R. C. 3
Rush, I. 28
Russell, M. R. 1

Sabine, H. W. 1

Saunders, D.	22	Carey, J.	3	Green, P. J.	1	Moran, K.	6
Savage, R. W.	2	Carroll, T.	1	Grimes, A. A.	1	Morrison, C. H.	9
Shaw, E. G.	2	Cascarino, A.	19			Moroney, T.	1
Sisson, H.	4	Coad, P.	3	Hale, A.	2	Mulligan, P.	1
Slatter, N.	2	Connolly, D. J.	9	Hand, E.	2		
Smallman, D. P.	1	Conroy, T.	2	Harte, I. P.	11	O'Brien, A. J.	1
Speed, G. A.	7	Conway, J.	3	Haverty, J.	3	O'Callaghan, K.	1
Symons, C. J.	2	**Cox, S. R.**	**2**	Healy, C.	1	O'Connor, T.	2
		Coyne, T.	6	Holland, M. R.	5	O'Farrell, F.	2
Tapscott, D. R.	4	Cummins, G.	5	Holmes, J.	1	O'Flanagan, K.	3
Taylor, G. K.	1	Curtis, D.	8	Horlacher, A.	2	O'Keefe, E.	1
Thomas, M.	4			Houghton, R.	6	O'Leary, D. A.	1
Thomas, T.	1	Daly, G.	13	Hughton, C.	1	O'Neill, F.	1
Toshack, J. B.	12	Davis, T.	4	Hunt, S. P.	1	O'Neill, K. P.	4
Trainer, H.	2	Dempsey, J.	1	Hurley, C.	2	O'Reilly, J. (*Brideville*)	2
		Dennehy, M.	2			O'Reilly, J. (*Cork*)	1
Vaughan, D. O.	1	Doherty, G. M. T.	4	Ireland, S. J.	4	O'Shea, J. F.	1
Vaughan, John	2	Donnelly, J.	4	Irwin, D.	4	**Own goals**	**11**
Vernon, T. R.	8	Donnelly, T.	1				
Vizard, E. T.	1	**Doyle, K. E.**	**9**	Jordan, D.	1	Quinn, N.	21
Vokes, S. M.	2	**Duff, D. A.**	**8**				
		Duffy, B.	1	Kavanagh, G. A.	1	Reid, A. M.	4
Walsh, I.	7	Duggan, H.	1	**Keane, R. D.**	**51**	Reid, S. J.	2
Warren, F. W.	3	Dunne, J.	13	Keane, R. M.	9	Ringstead, A.	7
Watkins, W. M.	4	Dunne, L.	1	Kelly, D.	9	Robinson, M.	4
Wilding, J.	4	Dunne, R. P.	7	Kelly, G.	2	Rogers, E.	5
Williams, A.	**2**			Kelly, J.	2	Ryan, G.	1
Williams, D. R.	2	Eglington, T.	2	Kennedy, M.	4	Ryan, R.	3
Williams, G. E.	1	Elliott, S. W.	1	Keogh, A.	1		
Williams, G. G.	1	Ellis, P.	1	Kernaghan, A. N.	1	**St Ledger-Hall, S.**	**2**
Williams, W.	1			**Kilbane, K. D.**	**8**	Sheedy, K.	9
Woosnam, A. P.	3	Fagan, F.	5	Kinsella, M. A.	3	Sheridan, J.	5
Wynn, G. A.	1	**Fahey, K.**	**3**			Slaven, B.	1
		Fallon, S.	2	Lacey, W.	1	Sloan, J.	1
Yorath, T. C.	2	Fallon, W.	2	Lawrence, L.	1	Squires, J.	1
Young, E.	1	Farrell, P.	3	Lawrenson, M.	5	Stapleton, F.	20
		Finnan, S.	2	Leech, M.	2	Staunton, S.	7
		Fitzgerald, P.	2	**Long, S. P.**	**6**	Strahan, J.	1
REPUBLIC OF IRELAND		Fitzgerald, J.	1			Sullivan, J.	1
Aldridge, J.	19	Fitzsimons, A.	7	McAteer, J. W.	3		
Ambrose, P.	1	Flood, J. J.	4	McCann, J.	1	Townsend, A. D.	7
Anderson, J.	1	Fogarty, A.	3	McCarthy, M.	2	Treacy, R.	5
Andrews, K.	**2**	Foley, D.	2	McEvoy, A.	6	Touhy, L.	4
		Fullam, J.	1	**McGeady, A.**	**1**		
Barrett, G.	2	Fullam, R.	1	McGee, P.	4	Waddock, G.	3
Bermingham, P.	1			McGrath, P.	8	Walsh, D.	5
Bradshaw, P.	4	Galvin, A.	1	McLoughlin, A. F.	2	Walsh, M.	3
Brady, L.	9	Gavin, J.	2	McPhail, S. J. P.	1	**Ward, S.**	**1**
Breen, G.	7	Geoghegan, M.	2	Mancini, T.	1	Waters, J.	1
Brown, J.	1	**Gibson, D.**	**1**	Martin, C.	6	White, J. J.	2
Byrne, D.	1	Giles, J.	5	Martin, M.	4	Whelan, G. D.	2
Byrne, J.	4	Givens, D.	19	Miller, L. W. P.	1	Whelan, R.	3
		Glynn, D.	1	Mooney, J.	1		
Cantwell, J.	14	Grealish, T.	8	Moore, P.	7		

BRITISH & IRISH INTERNATIONAL MANAGERS

England
Walter Winterbottom 1946–1962 (after period as coach); Alf Ramsey 1963–1974; Joe Mercer (caretaker) 1974; Don Revie 1974–1977; Ron Greenwood 1977–1982; Bobby Robson 1982–1990; Graham Taylor 1990–1993; Terry Venables (coach) 1994–1996; Glenn Hoddle 1996–1999; Kevin Keegan 1999–2000; Sven-Goran Eriksson 2001–2006; Steve McClaren 2006–07; Fabio Capello from January 2008.

Northern Ireland
Peter Doherty 1951–1952; Bertie Peacock 1962–1967; Billy Bingham 1967–1971; Terry Neill 1971–1975; Dave Clements (player-manager) 1975–1976; Danny Blanchflower 1976–1979; Billy Bingham 1980–1994; Bryan Hamilton 1994–1998; Lawrie McMenemy 1998–1999; Sammy McIlroy 2000–2003; Lawrie Sanchez 2004–2007; Nigel Worthington from June 2007.

Scotland (since 1967)
Bobby Brown 1967–1971; Tommy Docherty 1971–1972; Willie Ormond 1973–1977; Ally MacLeod 1977–1978; Jock Stein 1978–1985; Alex Ferguson (caretaker) 1985–1986 Andy Roxburgh (coach) 1986–1993; Craig Brown 1993–2001; Berti Vogts 2002–2004; Walter Smith 2004–2007; Alex McLeish 2007; George Burley 2008–2009; Craig Levein from December 2009.

Wales (since 1974)
Mike Smith 1974–1979; Mike England 1980–1988; David Williams (caretaker) 1988; Terry Yorath 1988–1993; John Toshack 1994 for one match; Mike Smith 1994–1995; Bobby Gould 1995–1999; Mark Hughes 1999–2004; John Toshack 2004–2010; Gary Speed from December 2010.

Republic of Ireland
Liam Tuohy 1971–1972; Johnny Giles 1973–1980 (after period as player-manager); Eoin Hand 1980–1985; Jack Charlton 1986–1996; Mick McCarthy 1996–2002; Brian Kerr 2003–2006; Steve Staunton 2006–07; Giovanni Trapattoni from February 2008.

SOUTH AMERICA

COPA SUDAMERICANA 2010

FIRST ROUND FIRST LEG
Defensor 2, Olimpia 0
Dep Quito 3, Univ San Martin 2
Atletico Huila 4, Trujillanos 1
Univ Cesar Vallejo 1, Barcelona 2
Universitario 2, Colo Colo 0
Dep Lara 2, Santa Fe 0
Guarani 2, River Plate (Uru) 0
Univ de Chile 2, Oriente Petrolero 2

FIRST ROUND SECOND LEG
Olimpia 1, Defensor 1
Univ San Martin 2, Dep Quito 1
Trujillanos 1, Atletico Huila 1
Barcelona 3, Univ Cesar Vallejo 1
Colo Colo 3, Universitario 1
Santa Fe 4, Dep Lara 0
River Plate (Uru) 4, Guarani 2
Oriente Petrolero 1, Univ de Chile 0

SECOND ROUND FIRST LEG
Gremio Prudente 0, Atletico Mineiro 0
Goias 1, Gremio 1
Vitoria 2, Palmeiras 0
Santos 1, Avai 3
Independiente 1, Argentinos Juniors 0
Barcelona 0, Penarol 1
Velez Sarsfield 0, Banfield 1
Guarani 1, Union San Felipe 1
Atletico Huila 1, San Jose 1
Universitario 1, Cerro Porteno 0
Oriente Petrolero 1, Dep Tolima 0
Univ San Martin 2, Emelec 1
Newells Old Boys 1, Estudiantes 0
Santa Fe 2, Caracas 1
Defensor 9, Sport Huancayo 0

SECOND ROUND SECOND LEG
Atletico Mineiro 1, Gremio Prudente 0
Gremio 0, Goias 2
Palmeiras 3, Vitoria 0
Avai 0, Santos 1
Argentinos Juniors 1, Independiente 1
Penarol 2, Barcelona 1
Banfield 1, Velez Sarsfield 1
Union San Felipe 1, Guarani 1
Union San Felipe won 8-7 on penalties.
San Jose 4, Atletico Huila 0
Cerro Porteno 2, Universitario 2
Dep Tolima 2, Oriente Petrolero 0
Emelec 5, Univ San Martin 0

SEMI-FINALS FIRST LEG
Univ de Chile 1, Guadalajara 1
Sao Paulo 0, Internacional 1

SEMI FINALS SECOND LEG
Guadalajara 2, Univ de Chile 0
Internacional 1, Sao Paulo 2

Estudiantes 1, Newells Old Boys 1
Caracas 0, Sante Fe 0
Sport Huancayo 2, Defensor 0

THIRD ROUND FIRST LEG
Defensor 1, Independiente 0
Banfield 2, Dep Tolima 0
Newells Old Boys 6, San Jose 0
Union San Felipe 4, LDU Quito 2
Goias 1, Penarol 0
Atletico Mineiro 2, Santa Fe 0
Emelec 2, Avai 1
Universitario 0, Palmeiras 1

THIRD ROUND SECOND LEG
Independiente 4, Defensor 2
Dep Tolima 3, Banfield 0
San Jose 2, Newells Old Boys 0
LDU Quito 6, Union San Felipe 1
Penarol 3, Goias 2
Santa Fe 1, Atletico Mineiro 0
Avai 3, Emelec 1
Palmeiras 3, Universitario 1

QUARTER-FINALS FIRST LEG
Atletico Mineiro 1, Palmeiras 1
Goias 2, Avai 2
Newells Old Boys 0, LDU Quito 0
Dep Tolima 2, Independiente 2

QUARTER-FINALS SECOND LEG
Palmeiras 2, Atletico Mineiro 0
Avai 0, Goias 1
LDU Quito 1, Newells Old Boys 0
Independiente 0, Dep Tolima 0

SEMI-FINALS FIRST LEG
Goias 0, Palmeiras 1
LDU Quito 3, Independiente 2

SEMI-FINALS SECOND LEG
Palmeiras 1, Goias 2
Independiente 2, LDU Quito 1

FINAL FIRST LEG
Goias 2, Independiente 0

FINAL SECOND LEG
Independiente 3, Goias 1
Independendiente won 5-3 on penalties.

COPA LIBERTADORES 2010

FINAL FIRST LEG
Guadalajara 1, Internacional 2

FINAL SECOND LEG
Internacional 3, Guadalajara 2

COPA SANTANDER LIBERTADORES 2011

FIRST STAGE FIRST LEG
Dep Tolima 0, Corinthians 0
Jaguares 2, Alianza 0
Dep Petare 0, Cerro Porteno 1
Union Espanola 1, Bolivar 0
Dep Quito 0, Independiente 2
Gremio 2, Liverpool (Uru) 2

FIRST STAGE SECOND LEG
Corinthians 0, Dep Tolima 2
Alianza 0, Jaguares 2
Cerro Porteno 1, Dep Petare 1
Bolivar 0, Union Espanola 0
Independiente 0, Dep Quito 1
Liverpool (Uru) 1, Gremio 3

GROUP 1	P	W	D	L	F	A	Pts
Libertad	6	4	2	0	13	5	14
Once Caldas	6	1	4	1	7	8	7
Univ San Martin	6	2	0	4	7	11	6
San Luis	6	1	2	3	6	9	5

GROUP 2	P	W	D	L	F	A	Pts
Junior	6	4	1	1	9	7	13
Gremio	6	3	1	2	9	6	10
Oriente Petrolero	6	2	0	4	7	8	6
Leon	6	1	2	3	4	8	5

GROUP 3	P	W	D	L	F	A	Pts
America	6	3	1	2	8	7	10
Fluminense	6	2	2	2	9	9	8
Nacional (Uru)	6	2	2	2	3	3	8
Argentinos Juniors	6	2	1	3	9	10	7

GROUP 4	P	W	D	L	F	A	Pts
Univ Catolica	6	3	2	1	11	9	11
Velez Sarsfield	6	3	1	2	12	7	10
Caracas	6	3	0	3	7	10	9
Union Espanola	6	1	1	4	7	11	4

GROUP 5	P	W	D	L	F	A	Pts
Cerro Porteno	6	3	2	1	13	8	11
Santos	6	3	2	1	11	8	11
Colo Colo	6	3	0	3	15	16	9
Dep Tachira	6	0	2	4	5	12	2

GROUP 6	P	W	D	L	F	A	Pts
Internacional	6	4	1	1	14	3	13
Jaguares	6	3	0	3	6	8	9
Emelec	6	2	2	2	4	5	8
Jorge Wilstermann	6	1	1	4	3	11	4

GROUP 7	P	W	D	L	F	A	Pts
Cruzeiro	6	5	1	0	20	1	16
Estudiantes	6	3	1	2	9	11	10
Dep Tolima	6	2	2	2	5	8	8
Guarani	6	0	0	6	2	16	0

GROUP 8	P	W	D	L	F	A	Pts
LDU Quito	6	3	1	2	12	4	10
Penarol	6	3	0	3	6	11	9
Independiente	6	2	2	2	7	8	8
Godoy Cruz	6	2	1	3	8	10	7

FIRST ROUND FIRST LEG
Cruzeiro 2, Once Caldas 1
America 0, Santos 1
Junior 1, Jaguares 1
Cerro Porteno 0, Estudiantes 0
Libertad 1, Fluminense 3
LDU Quito 0, Velez Sarsfield 3
Internacional 1, Penarol 1
Univ Catolica 2, Gremio 1

FIRST ROUND SECOND LEG
Once Caldas 2, Cruzeiro 0
Santos 0, America 0
Jaguares 3, Junior 3
Estudiantes 0, Cerro Porteno 0
Cerro Porteno won 5-3 on penalties.
Fluminense 0, Libertad 3
Velez Sarsfield 2, LDU Quito 0
Penarol 2, Internacional 1
Gremio 0, Univ Catolica 1

QUARTER-FINALS FIRST LEG
Once Caldas 0, Santos 1
Jaguares 1, Cerro Porteno 1
Libertad 0, Velez Sarsfield 3
Penarol 2, Univ Catolica 0

QUARTER-FINALS SECOND LEG
Santos 1, Once Caldas 1
Cerro Porteno 1, Jaguares 0
Velez Sarsfield 4, Libertad 2
Univ Catolica 2, Penarol 1

SEMI-FINALS FIRST LEG
Santos 1, Cerro Porteno 0
Penarol 1, Velez Sarsfield 0

SEMI-FINALS SECOND LEG
Cerro Porteno 3, Santos 3
Velez Sarsfield 2, Penarol 1

FINAL FIRST LEG
Penarol 0, Santos 0

FINAL SECOND LEG
Santos 2, Penarol 1

CONCACAF

GOLD CUP

GROUP 4	P	W	D	L	F	A	Pts
Mexico	3	3	0	0	14	1	9
Costa Rica	3	1	1	1	7	5	4
El Salvador	3	1	1	1	7	7	4
Cuba	3	0	0	3	1	16	0

GROUP 5	P	W	D	L	F	A	Pts
Jamaica	3	3	0	0	7	0	9
Honduras	3	1	1	1	7	2	4
Guatemala	3	1	1	1	4	2	4
Grenada	3	0	0	3	1	15	0

GROUP 6	P	W	D	L	F	A	Pts
Panama	3	2	1	0	6	4	7
USA	3	2	0	1	4	2	6
Canada	3	1	1	1	2	3	4
Guadeloupe	3	0	0	3	2	5	0

QUARTER-FINALS
Costa Rica 1, Honduras 1
Honduras won 4-2 on penalties.
Mexico 2, Guatemala 1
Jamaica 0, USA 2
Panama 1, El Salvador 1
Panama won 5-3 on penalties.

SEMI-FINALS
USA 1, Panama 0
Honduras 0, Mexico 1

FINAL
Mexico 4, USA 2

ASIA

ASIAN CUP

GROUP A	P	W	D	L	F	A	Pts
Uzbekistan	3	2	1	0	6	3	7
Qatar	3	2	0	1	5	2	6
China	3	1	1	1	4	4	4
Kuwait	3	0	0	3	1	7	0

GROUP B	P	W	D	L	F	A	Pts
Japan	3	2	1	0	8	2	7
Jordan	3	2	1	0	4	2	7
Syria	3	1	0	2	4	5	3
Saudi Arabia	3	0	0	3	1	8	6

GROUP C	P	W	D	L	F	A	Pts
Australia	3	2	1	0	6	1	7
South Korea	3	2	1	0	7	3	7
Bahrain	3	1	0	2	6	5	3
India	3	0	0	3	3	13	0

GROUP D	P	W	D	L	F	A	Pts
Iran	3	3	0	0	6	1	9
Iraq	3	2	0	1	3	2	6
North Korea	3	0	1	2	2	4	1
UAE	3	0	1	2	0	4	1

QUARTER-FINALS
Japan 3, Qatar 2
Uzbekistan 2, Jordan 1
Australia 1, Iraq 0
Iran 0, South Korea 1

SEMI-FINALS
Japan 2, South Korea 2
Japan won 3-0 on penalties.
Uzbekistan 0, Australia 6

MATCH FOR THIRD PLACE
Uzbekistan 2, South Korea 3

FINAL
Australia 0, Japan 1

GULF CUP

GROUP A	P	W	D	L	F	A	Pts
Kuwait	3	2	1	0	4	0	7
Saudi Arabia	3	1	2	0	5	1	5
Qatar	3	1	1	1	3	3	4
Yemen	3	0	0	3	1	9	0

GROUP B	P	W	D	L	F	A	Pts
UAE	3	1	2	0	3	1	5
Iraq	3	1	2	0	3	2	5
Oman	3	0	3	0	1	1	3
Bahrain	3	0	1	2	4	7	1

SEMI-FINALS
Kuwait 2, Iraq 2
Kuwait won 5-4 on penalties.
UAE 0, Saudi Arabia 1

FINAL
Kuwait 1, Saudi Arabia 0

NORTH AMERICA

MAJOR LEAGUE SOCCER 2010

EASTERN CONFERENCE

	P	W	D	L	F	A	Pts
New York Red Bulls	30	15	6	9	38	29	51
Columbus Crew	30	14	8	8	40	34	50
Sporting KC	30	11	6	13	36	35	39
Chicago Fire	30	9	9	12	37	38	36
Toronto	30	9	8	13	33	41	35
New England Rev	30	9	5	16	32	50	32
Philadelphia Union	30	8	7	15	35	49	31
DC United	30	6	4	20	21	47	22

WESTERN CONFERENCE

	P	W	D	L	F	A	Pts
Los Angeles Galaxy	30	18	5	7	44	26	59
Real Salt Lake	30	15	11	4	45	20	56
Dallas	30	12	14	4	42	28	50
Seattle Sounders	30	14	8	10	39	35	48
Colorado Rapids	30	12	10	8	44	32	46
San Jose Earthquakes	30	13	7	10	34	33	46
Houston Dynamo	30	9	6	15	40	49	33
Chivas USA	30	8	4	18	31	45	28

EASTERN SEMI-FINALS FIRST LEG
Dallas v Real Salt Lake — 2-1
Colorado Rapids v Columbus Crew — 1-0

EASTERN SEMI-FINALS SECOND LEG
Real Salt Lake v Dallas — 1-1
Columbus Crew v Colorado Rapids — 2-1
Colorado Rapids won 5-4 on penalties.

WESTERN SEMI-FINALS FIRST LEG
San Jose Earthquakes v New York Red Bulls — 0-1
Seattle Sounders v Los Angeles Galaxy — 0-1

WESTERN SEMI-FINALS SECOND LEG
New York Red Bulls v San Jose Earthquakes — 1-3
Los Angeles Galaxy v Seattle Sounders — 2-1

EASTERN FINAL
Colorado Rapids v San Jose Earthquakes — 1-0

WESTERN FINAL
Los Angeles Galaxy v Dallas — 0-3

MLS CUP 2010
Dallas v Colorado Rapids — 1-2

AFRICA

AFRICA CUP OF NATIONS

GROUP 1	P	W	D	L	F	A	Pts
Cape Verde Islands	4	2	1	1	5	3	7
Mali	4	2	0	2	4	4	6
Zimbabwe	4	1	2	1	3	3	5
Liberia	4	1	1	2	5	7	4

GROUP 2	P	W	D	L	F	A	Pts
Guinea	4	3	1	0	10	3	10
Nigeria	4	2	1	1	8	3	7
Ethiopia	4	1	1	2	4	10	4
Madagascar	4	0	1	3	2	8	1

GROUP 3	P	W	D	L	F	A	Pts
Zambia	4	3	0	1	9	1	9
Libya	4	2	2	0	5	1	8
Mozambique	4	1	1	2	1	5	4
Comoros	4	0	1	3	1	9	1

GROUP 4	P	W	D	L	F	A	Pts
Morocco	4	2	1	1	5	1	7
Central Africa	4	2	1	1	5	3	7
Tanzania	4	1	1	2	4	5	4
Algeria	4	1	1	2	2	7	4

GROUP 5	P	W	D	L	F	A	Pts
Senegal	4	3	1	0	12	2	10
DR Congo	4	2	1	1	8	6	7
Cameroon	4	1	2	1	4	3	5
Mauritius	4	0	0	4	2	15	0

GROUP 6	P	W	D	L	F	A	Pts
Burkina Faso	3	3	0	0	11	2	9
Gambia	2	1	0	1	4	4	3
Namibia	3	0	0	3	2	11	0

GROUP 7	P	W	D	L	F	A	Pts
South Africa	4	2	2	0	3	0	8
Niger	4	2	0	2	4	4	6
Sierra Leone	4	1	2	1	3	4	5
Egypt	4	0	2	2	1	3	2

GROUP 8	P	W	D	L	F	A	Pts
Ivory Coast	4	4	0	0	12	3	12
Burundi	4	1	1	2	5	6	4
Benin	4	1	1	2	7	9	4
Rwanda	4	1	0	3	4	10	3

GROUP 9	P	W	D	L	F	A	Pts
Ghana	4	3	1	0	9	1	10
Sudan	4	3	1	0	7	1	10
Congo	4	1	0	3	4	9	3
Swaziland	4	0	0	4	2	11	0

GROUP 10	P	W	D	L	F	A	Pts
Uganda	4	3	1	0	6	0	10
Angola	4	2	0	2	3	5	6
Kenya	4	1	1	2	2	3	4
Guinea-Bissau	4	1	0	3	1	4	3

GROUP 11	P	W	D	L	F	A	Pts
Botswana	7	5	2	0	7	2	17
Tunisia	6	3	1	2	12	6	10
Malawi	6	2	4	0	11	6	10
Togo	6	0	3	3	5	8	3
Chad	7	0	2	5	5	18	2

Competition still being played.

UEFA UNDER-17 CHAMPIONSHIP 2010–11

ELITE ROUND

GROUP 1
Italy 0, Scotland 0
Slovakia 0, Czech Republic 1
Italy 1, Czech Republic 2
Scotland 2, Slovakia 0
Slovakia 1, Italy 1
Czech Republic 1, Scotland 1

GROUP 2
Portugal 0, Croatia 0
Holland 2, Austria 1
Portugal 0, Austria 2
Croatia 0, Holland 0
Holland 1, Portugal 0
Austria 0, Croatia 2

GROUP 3
Greece 2, Latvia 0
Denmark 2, Republic of Ireland 2
Republic of Ireland 1, Greece 1
Denmark 1, Latvia 0
Greece 0, Denmark 1
Latvia 1, Republic of Ireland 4

GROUP 4
Germany 2, Turkey 0
Switzerland 1, Ukraine 0
Turkey 2, Switzerland 1
Germany 2, Ukraine 0
Switzerland 0, Germany 2
Ukraine 2, Turkey 2

GROUP 5
England 3, Northern Ireland 2
Spain 3, Belgium 1
Spain 5, Northern Ireland 1
Belgium 1, England 2
England 2, Spain 1
Northern Ireland 2, Belgium 1

GROUP 6
Norway 5, Belarus 1
Georgia 0, France 2
Belarus 1, Georgia 0
Norway 2, France 2
Georgia 0, Norway 5
France 9, Belarus 0

GROUP 7
Romania 0, Iceland 0
Hungary 1, Russia 2
Romania 2, Russia 1
Iceland 0, Hungary 2
Hungary 1, Romania 2
Russia 2, Iceland 0

Final tournament in Serbia

GROUP A
Serbia 2, Denmark 3
France 2, England 2
Serbia 1, France 1
Denmark 2, England 0
England 3, Serbia 0
Denmark 1, France 0

GROUP B
Germany 0, Holland 2
Czech Republic 1, Romania 1
Germany 1, Czech Republic 1
Holland 1, Romania 0
Romania 0, Germany 1
Holland 0, Czech Republic 0

SEMI-FINALS
Holland 1, England 0
Denmark 0, Germany 2

FINAL (in Novi Sad)
15 May

Germany (2) 2 *(Yesil 8, Aydin 32)*
Holland (3) 5 *(Trindade de Vilhena 23, 34, Depay 43, Kongolo 52, Ebecilio 77)*
Germany: Vlachodimos; Weiser, Rocker (Toljan 65), Gunter, Perrey (Weihrauch 73), Yalcin, Can, Yesil, Aydin, Mende (Berko 57), Schnelhardt.
Holland: De Jong; Disveld, Kongolo, Rekik, Willens, Ebecilio, Ayoub, Achahbar, Trindade de Vilhena, Depay (Gravenberch 71), De Bondt (Ake 64).

UEFA UNDER-19 CHAMPIONSHIP 2010

Final tournament in France

GROUP A
Austria v England	2-3
France v Holland	4-1
France v Austria	5-0
Holland v England	1-0
England v France	1-1
Holland v Austria	0-1

GROUP B
Croatia v Spain	1-2
Italy v Portugal	0-2
Spain v Portugal	2-1
Croatia v Italy	0-0
Portugal v Croatia	0-5
Spain v Italy	3-0

SEMI-FINALS
Spain v England	3-1
France v Croatia	2-1

FINAL (in Caen)
30 July

France (0) 2 *(Sunu 49, Lacazette 85)*
Spain (1) 1 *(Rodrigo 18)*   20,188
France: Diallo; Nego, Mavinga, Faure, Kakuta, Fofana, Sunu (Lacazette 69), Griezmann (Tafer 46), Coquelin, Kolodziejczak, Bakambu.
Spain: Alex; Montoya, Planas, Bartra, Pulido (Calvente 87), Romeu, Keko (Muniain 64), Thiago Alcantara, Rodrigo (Rochina 73), Canales, Pacheco.
Referee: S. Studer (Switzerland).

FIFA UNDER-17 WORLD CUP 2011

Finals in Mexico

GROUP A
Congo 1, Holland 0
Mexico 3, South Korea 1
South Korea 1, Holland 1
Mexico 2, Congo 1
South Korea 1, Congo 1
Mexico 3, Holland 2

GROUP B
France 3, Argentina 0
Japan 1, Jamaica 0
Japan 1, France 1
Jamaica 1, Argentina 2
Japan 3, Argentina 1
Jamaica 1, France 1

GROUP C
Rwanda 0, England 2
Uruguay 3, Canada 0
Uruguay 1, Rwanda 0
Canada 2, England 2
Uruguay 0, England 2
Canada 0, Rwanda 0

GROUP D
Uzbekistan 1, New Zealand 4
USA 3, Czech Republic 0
USA 1, Uzbekistan 2
Czech Republic 1, New Zealand 0
USA 0, New Zealand 0
Czech Republic 1, Uzbekistan 2

GROUP E
Germany 6, Ecuador 1
Burkina Faso 0, Panama 1
Burkina Faso 0, Germany 3
Panama 1, Ecuador 2
Burkina Faso 0, Ecuador 2
Panama 0, Germany 2

GROUP F
Brazil 3, Denmark 0
Australia 2, Ivory Coast 1
Australia 0, Brazil 1
Ivory Coast 4, Denmark 2
Australia 1, Denmark 1
Ivory Coast 3, Brazil 3

FIRST ROUND
Congo 1, Uruguay 2
Uzbekistan 4, Australia 0
Japan 6, New Zealand 0
Brazil 2, Ecuador 0
Germany 4, USA 0
England 1, Argentina 1
England won 4-2 on penalties.
France 3, Ivory Coast 2
Mexico 2, Panama 0

QUARTER-FINALS
Uruguay 2, Uzbekistan 0
Japan 2, Brazil 3
Germany 3, England 2
France 1, Mexico 2

SEMI-FINALS
Uruguay 3, Brazil 0
Germany 2, Mexico 3

MATCH FOR THIRD PLACE
Brazil 3, Germany 4

FINAL
Uruguay 0, Mexico 2

UEFA REGIONS' CUP

GROUP A
Braga 3, Zlin 1
Yednyst Plysky 0, Wurttemberg 2
Braga 2, Yednyst Plysky 1
Zlin 1, Wurttemberg 0
Wurttenberg 1, Braga 3
Zlin 2, Yednyst Plysky 1

GROUP B
Ankara 0, Leinster & Munster 0
South Region Russia 2, Belgrade 3

South Region Russia 1, Ankara 2
Belgrade 0, Leinster & Munster 1
Leinster & Munster 2, South Region Russia 1
Belgrade 2, Ankara 0
The two group winners advanced to the Final; the runners-up receiving medals.

FINAL
Braga 2, Leinster & Munster 1

ENGLAND UNDER-21 RESULTS 1976–2011

EC *UEFA Competition for Under-21 Teams*

Year	Date		Venue	Eng	Opp
			v ALBANIA	Eng	Alb
EC1989	Mar	7	Shkroda	2	1
EC1989	April	25	Ipswich	2	0
EC2001	Mar	27	Tirana	1	0
EC2001	Sept	4	Middlesbrough	5	0
			v ANGOLA	Eng	Ang
1995	June	10	Toulon	1	0
1996	May	28	Toulon	0	2
			v ARGENTINA	Eng	Arg
1998	May	18	Toulon	0	2
2000	Feb	22	Fulham	1	0
			v AUSTRIA	Eng	Aus
1994	Oct	11	Kapfenberg	3	1
1995	Nov	14	Middlesbrough	2	1
EC2004	Sept	3	Krems	2	0
EC2005	Oct	7	Leeds	1	2
			v AZERBAIJAN	Eng	Az
EC2004	Oct	12	Baku	0	0
EC2005	Mar	29	Middlesbrough	2	0
2009	June	8	Milton Keynes	7	0
			v BELGIUM	Eng	Bel
1994	June	5	Marseille	2	1
1996	May	24	Toulon	1	0
			v BRAZIL	Eng	B
1993	June	11	Toulon	0	0
1995	June	6	Toulon	0	2
1996	June	1	Toulon	1	2
			v BULGARIA	Eng	Bul
EC1979	June	5	Pernik	3	1
EC1979	Nov	20	Leicester	5	0
1989	June	5	Toulon	2	3
EC1998	Oct	9	West Ham	1	0
EC1999	June	8	Vratsa	1	0
EC2007	Sept	11	Sofia	2	0
EC2007	Nov	16	Milton Keynes	2	0
			v CROATIA	Eng	Cro
1996	Apr	23	Sunderland	0	1
2003	Aug	19	West Ham	0	3
			v CZECHOSLOVAKIA	Eng	Cz
1990	May	28	Toulon	2	1
1992	May	26	Toulon	1	2
1993	June	9	Toulon	1	1
			v CZECH REPUBLIC	Eng	CzR
1998	Nov	17	Ipswich	0	1
EC2007	June	11	Arnhem	0	0
2008	Nov	18	Bramall Lane	2	0
EC2011	June	19	Viborg	1	2
			v DENMARK	Eng	Den
EC1978	Sept	19	Hvidovre	2	1
EC1979	Sept	11	Watford	1	0
EC1982	Sept	21	Hvidovre	4	1
EC1983	Sept	20	Norwich	4	1
EC1986	Mar	12	Copenhagen	1	0
EC1986	Mar	26	Manchester	1	1
1988	Sept	13	Watford	0	0
1994	Mar	8	Brentford	1	0
1999	Oct	8	Bradford	4	1
2005	Aug	16	Herning	1	0
2011	Mar	24	Viborg	4	0
			v EQUADOR	Eng	E
2009	Feb	10	Malaga	2	3
			v FINLAND	Eng	Fin
EC1977	May	26	Helsinki	1	0
EC1977	Oct	12	Hull	8	1
EC1984	Oct	16	Southampton	2	0
EC1985	May	21	Mikkeli	1	3
EC2000	Oct	10	Valkeakoski	2	2
EC2001	Mar	23	Barnsley	4	0
EC2009	June	15	Halmstad	2	1
			v FRANCE	Eng	Fra
EC1984	Feb	28	Sheffield	6	1
EC1984	Mar	28	Rouen	1	0
1987	June	11	Toulon	0	2
EC1988	April	13	Besancon	2	4
EC1988	April	27	Highbury	2	2
1988	June	12	Toulon	2	4
1990	May	23	Toulon	7	3
1991	June	3	Toulon	1	0
1992	May	28	Toulon	0	0
1993	June	15	Toulon	1	0
1994	May	31	Aubagne	0	3
1995	June	10	Toulon	0	2
1998	May	14	Toulon	1	1
1999	Feb	9	Derby	2	1
EC2005	Nov	11	Tottenham	1	1
EC2005	Nov	15	Nancy	1	2
2009	Mar	31	Nottingham	0	2
			v GEORGIA	Eng	Geo
EC1996	Nov	8	Batumi	1	0
EC1997	April	29	Charlton	0	0
2000	Aug	31	Middlesbrough	6	1
			v GERMANY	Eng	Ger
1991	Sept	10	Scunthorpe	2	1
EC2000	Oct	6	Derby	1	1
EC2001	Aug	31	Frieburg	2	1
2005	Mar	25	Hull	2	2
2005	Sept	6	Mainz	1	1
EC2006	Oct	6	Coventry	1	0
EC2006	Oct	10	Leverkusen	2	0
EC2009	June	22	Halmstad	1	1
EC2009	June	29	Malmo	0	4
2010	Nov	16	Wiesbaden	0	2
			v EAST GERMANY	Eng	EG
EC1980	April	16	Sheffield	1	2
EC1980	April	23	Jena	0	1
			v WEST GERMANY	Eng	WG
EC1982	Sept	21	Sheffield	3	1
EC1982	Oct	12	Bremen	2	3
1987	Sept	8	Ludenscheid	0	2
			v GREECE	Eng	Gre
EC1982	Nov	16	Piraeus	0	1
EC1983	Mar	29	Portsmouth	2	1
1989	Feb	7	Patras	0	1
EC1997	Nov	13	Heraklion	0	2
EC1997	Dec	17	Norwich	4	2
EC2001	June	5	Athens	1	3
EC2001	Oct	5	Ewood Park	2	1
EC2009	Sept	8	Tripoli	1	1
EC2010	Mar	3	Doncaster	1	2
			v HOLLAND	Eng	H
EC1993	April	27	Portsmouth	3	0
EC1993	Oct	12	Utrecht	1	1
2001	Aug	14	Reading	4	0
EC2001	Nov	9	Utrecht	2	2
EC2001	Nov	13	Derby	1	0
2004	Feb	17	Hull	3	2
2005	Feb	8	Derby	1	2
2006	Nov	14	Alkmaar	1	0
EC2007	June	20	Heerenveen	1	1
2009	Aug	11	Groningen	0	0

v HUNGARY

				Eng	Hun
EC1981	June	5	Keszthely	2	1
EC1981	Nov	17	Nottingham	2	0
EC1983	April	26	Newcastle	1	0
EC1983	Oct	11	Nyiregyhaza	2	0
1990	Sept	11	Southampton	3	1
1992	May	12	Budapest	2	2
1999	April	27	Budapest	2	2

v ICELAND

				Eng	Ice
2011	Mar	28	Preston	1	2

v REPUBLIC OF IRELAND

				Eng	RoI
1981	Feb	25	Liverpool	1	0
1985	Mar	25	Portsmouth	3	2
1989	June	9	Toulon	0	0
EC1990	Nov	13	Cork	3	0
EC1991	Mar	26	Brentford	3	0
1994	Nov	15	Newcastle	1	0
1995	Mar	27	Dublin	2	0
EC2007	Oct	16	Cork	3	0
EC2008	Feb	5	Southampton	3	0

v ITALY

				Eng	Italy
EC1978	Mar	8	Manchester	2	1
EC1978	April	5	Rome	0	0
EC1984	April	18	Manchester	3	1
EC1984	May	2	Florence	0	1
EC1986	April	9	Pisa	0	2
EC1986	April	23	Swindon	1	1
EC1997	Feb	12	Bristol	1	0
EC1997	Oct	10	Rieti	1	0
EC2000	May	27	Bratislava	0	2
2000	Nov	14	Monza*	0	0
2002	Mar	26	Valley Parade	1	1
EC2002	May	20	Basle	1	2
2003	Feb	11	Pisa	0	1
2007	Mar	24	Wembley	3	3
EC2007	June	14	Arnhem	2	2
2011	Feb	8	Empoli	0	1

Abandoned 11 mins; fog.

v ISRAEL

				Eng	Isr
1985	Feb	27	Tel Aviv	2	1

v LATVIA

				Eng	Lat
1995	April	25	Riga	1	0
1995	June	7	Burnley	4	0

v LITHUANIA

				Eng	Lith
EC2009	Nov	17	Vilnius	0	0
EC2010	Sept	7	Colchester	3	0

v LUXEMBOURG

				Eng	Lux
EC1998	Oct	13	Greven Macher	5	0
EC1999	Sept	3	Reading	5	0

v MACEDONIA

				Eng	M
EC2002	Oct	15	Reading	3	1
EC2003	Sept	5	Skopje	1	1
EC2009	Sept	4	Prilep	2	1
EC2009	Oct	9	Coventry	6	3

v MALAYSIA

				Eng	Mal
1995	June	8	Toulon	2	0

v MEXICO

				Eng	Mex
1988	June	5	Toulon	2	1
1991	May	29	Toulon	6	0
1992	May	25	Toulon	1	1
2001	May	24	Leicester	3	0

v MOLDOVA

				Eng	Mol
EC1996	Aug	31	Chisinau	2	0
EC1997	Sept	9	Wycombe	1	0
EC2006	Aug	15	Ipswich	2	2

v MONTENEGRO

				Eng	M
EC2007	Sept	7	Podgorica	3	0
EC2007	Oct	12	Leicester	1	0

v MOROCCO

				Eng	Mor
1987	June	7	Toulon	2	0
1988	June	9	Toulon	1	0

v NORWAY

				Eng	Nor
EC1977	June	1	Bergen	2	1
EC1977	Sept	6	Brighton	6	0
1980	Sept	9	Southampton	3	0
1981	Sept	8	Drammen	0	0
EC1992	Oct	13	Peterborough	0	2
EC1993	June	1	Stavanger	1	1
1995	Oct	10	Stavanger	2	2
2006	Feb	28	Reading	3	1
2009	Mar	27	Sandefjord	5	0
2011	June	5	Southampton	2	0

v POLAND

				Eng	Pol
EC1982	Mar	17	Warsaw	2	1
EC1982	April	7	West Ham	2	2
EC1989	June	2	Plymouth	2	1
EC1989	Oct	10	Jastrzebie	3	1
EC1990	Oct	16	Tottenham	0	1
EC1991	Nov	12	Pila	1	2
EC1993	May	28	Zdroj	4	1
EC1993	Sept	7	Millwall	1	2
EC1996	Oct	8	Wolverhampton	0	0
EC1997	May	30	Katowice	1	1
EC1999	Mar	26	Southampton	5	0
EC1999	Sept	7	Plock	1	3
EC2004	Sept	7	Rybnik	3	1
EC2005	Oct	11	Hillsborough	4	1
2008	Mar	25	Wolverhampton	0	0

v PORTUGAL

				Eng	Por
1987	June	13	Toulon	0	0
1990	May	21	Toulon	0	1
1993	June	7	Toulon	2	0
1994	June	7	Toulon	2	0
EC1994	Sept	6	Leicester	0	0
1995	Sept	2	Lisbon	0	2
1996	May	30	Toulon	1	3
2000	Apr	16	Stoke	0	1
EC2002	May	22	Zurich	1	3
EC2003	Mar	28	Rio Major	2	4
EC2003	Sept	9	Everton	1	2
EC2008	Nov	20	Agueda	1	1
2008	Sept	5	Wembley	2	0
EC2009	Nov	14	Wembley	1	0
EC2010	Sept	3	Barcelos	1	0

v ROMANIA

				Eng	Rom
EC1980	Oct	14	Ploesti	0	4
EC1981	April	28	Swindon	3	0
EC1985	April	30	Brasov	0	0
EC1985	Sept	10	Ipswich	3	0
2007	Aug	21	Bristol	1	1
EC2010	Oct	8	Norwich	2	1
EC2010	Oct	12	Botosani	0	0

v RUSSIA

				Eng	Rus
1994	May	30	Bandol	2	0

v SAN MARINO

				Eng	SM
EC1993	Feb	16	Luton	6	0
EC1993	Nov	17	San Marino	4	0

v SENEGAL

				Eng	Sen
1989	June	7	Toulon	6	1
1991	May	27	Toulon	2	1

v SERBIA

				Eng	Ser
EC2007	June	17	Nijmegen	2	0

v SERBIA-MONTENEGRO

				Eng	S-M
2003	June	2	Hull	3	2

v SCOTLAND

				Eng	Sco
1977	April	27	Sheffield	1	0
EC1980	Feb	12	Coventry	2	1
EC1980	Mar	4	Aberdeen	0	0
EC1982	April	19	Glasgow	1	0
EC1982	April	28	Manchester	1	1

				Eng	Sco
EC1988	Feb	16	Aberdeen	1	0
EC1988	Mar	22	Nottingham	1	0
1993	June	13	Toulon	1	0

			v SLOVAKIA	Eng	Slo
EC2002	June	1	Bratislava	0	2
EC2002	Oct	11	Trnava	4	0
EC2003	June	10	Sunderland	2	0
2007	June	5	Norwich	5	0

			v SLOVENIA	Eng	Slo
2000	Feb	12	Nova Gorica	1	0
2008	Aug	19	Hull	2	1

			v SOUTH AFRICA	Eng	SA
1998	May	16	Toulon	3	1

			v SPAIN	Eng	Spa
EC1984	May	17	Seville	1	0
EC1984	May	24	Sheffield	2	0
1987	Feb	18	Burgos	2	1
1992	Sept	8	Burgos	1	0
2001	Feb	27	Birmingham	0	4
2004	Nov	16	Alcala	0	1
2007	Feb	6	Derby	2	2
EC2009	June	18	Gothenburg	2	0
EC2011	June	12	Herning	1	1

			v SWEDEN	Eng	Swe
1979	June	9	Vasteras	2	1
1986	Sept	9	Ostersund	1	1
EC1988	Oct	18	Coventry	1	1
EC1989	Sept	5	Uppsala	0	1
EC1998	Sept	4	Sundvall	2	0
EC1999	June	4	Huddersfield	3	0
2004	Mar	30	Kristiansund	2	2
EC2009	June	26	Gothenburg	3	3

			v SWITZERLAND	Eng	Swit
EC1980	Nov	18	Ipswich	5	0
EC1981	May	31	Neuenburg	0	0
1988	May	28	Lausanne	1	1
1996	April	1	Swindon	0	0
1998	Mar	24	Brugglifeld	0	2
EC2002	May	17	Zurich	2	1
EC2006	Sept	6	Lucerne	3	2

			v TURKEY	Eng	Tur
EC1984	Nov	13	Bursa	0	0
EC1985	Oct	15	Bristol	3	0
EC1987	April	28	Izmir	0	0
EC1987	Oct	13	Sheffield	1	1
EC1991	April	30	Izmir	2	2
1991	Oct	15	Reading	2	0
EC1992	Nov	17	Orient	0	1
EC1993	Mar	30	Izmir	0	0
EC2000	May	29	Bratislava	6	0
EC2003	April	1	Newcastle	1	1
EC2003	Oct	10	Istanbul	0	1

			v UKRAINE	Eng	Uk
2004	Aug	17	Middlesbrough	3	1
EC2011	June	15	Herning	0	0

			v USA	Eng	USA
1989	June	11	Toulon	0	2
1994	June	2	Toulon	3	0

			v UZBEKISTAN	Eng	Uzb
2010	Aug	10	Bristol	2	0

			v USSR	Eng	USSR
1987	June	9	Toulon	0	0
1988	June	7	Toulon	1	0
1990	May	25	Toulon	2	1
1991	May	31	Toulon	2	1

			v WALES	Eng	Wales
1976	Dec	15	Wolverhampton	0	0
1979	Feb	6	Swansea	1	0
1990	Dec	5	Tranmere	0	0
EC2004	Oct	8	Blackburn	2	0
EC2005	Sept	2	Wrexham	4	0
2008	May	5	Wrexham	2	0
EC2008	Oct	10	Cardiff	3	2
EC2008	Oct	14	Villa Park	2	2

			v YUGOSLAVIA	Eng	Yugo
EC1978	April	19	Novi Sad	1	2
EC1978	May	2	Manchester	1	1
EC1986	Nov	11	Peterborough	1	1
EC1987	Nov	10	Zemun	5	1
EC2000	Mar	29	Barcelona	3	0
2002	Sept	6	Bolton	1	1

ENGLAND C 2010–11

14 Sept

Wales Under-23 2 *(Moses 78, Jones 82)*

England C 2 *(McFadzean 2, Rodman 45)*

(in Newtown).
Wales: Cann (Idzi 46); Pearson, McDonald, Johnston (Surman 65), Mike Williams, Williams A, Reed (Christopher 55), Jones (Moses 55), Sherbon (Williams R 76), Darlington (Marc Williams 55), Barrow.
England: Roberts (Brown 46); Hatton, Taylor, Flint (Saah 46), Gregory (Rose 46), McFadzean, Henry, Porter, Barnes-Homer (Gash 32), Howells, Rodman (Wright 46).

FA XI

20 Oct

Hallam 1 *(Preece 87 (pen))*

FA XI 6 *(Taylor 17 (og), Walshaw 28, Mooney 33, Duncum 45, Waterfall 62, Mills 90)*

(in Hallam).
FA XI: Evans; Law, Brownhill, Murphy, Storer (Church 46), Waterfall, Duncum, Dillon (Thorley 46), Walshaw (Mills 46), Mooney (Marsden 46), Holden.

INTERNATIONAL CHALLENGE TROPHY

12 Oct

Estonia Under-23 0

England 1 *(Votti 52 (og))*

(in Tallinn).
England: Brown; Hatton, Newton, Flint, Gregory, Wylde, Henry, Porter, Barnes-Homer (Wright), Howells, Rodman (Nix).

9 Feb

England 1 *(Barnes-Homer 7)*

Belgium 0　　　　　　　　　　　　2315

(at Luton).
England: Brown; Hatton (Bignot 70), Day, Atkinson, Gregory, Wylde, Morgan-Smith (Mangan 74), Simpson, Barnes-Homer, Porter, Howells.

18 May

England 0

Portugal 1 *(Tavares 63)*　　　　　1517

(at Northampton).
England: Edwards; Vaughan, Franklin (Blair 65), Atkinson, Porter, Wylde (Coulson 73), Mangan, Rose (Byrne 81), Donnelly, Simpson (Styche 71), Clancy.

BRITISH AND IRISH UNDER-21 TEAMS 2010–11

■ *Denotes player sent off.*

ENGLAND

Bristol, 10 August 2010, 9821
England (0) 2 *(Rose 64, Kelly 78)*
Uzbekistan (0) 0
England: Fielding (McCarthy 77); Walker, Smalling, Jones (Kelly 46), Mancienne, Henderson (Cork 46), Rodwell (Lansbury 61), Rose, Cleverley, Sturridge (Albrighton 71), Moses (Welbeck 46).

Colchester, 7 September 2010, 7240
England (0) 3 *(Welbeck 51, 90, Albrighton 79)*
Lithuania (0) 0
England: Fielding; Bertrand, Mancienne, Smalling, Walker (Wilshere 46), Cleverley (Albrighton 64), Sturridge (Cork 78), Welbeck, Jones, Henderson, Rose.

Barcelos, 3 September 2010, 6821
Portugal (0) 0
England (1) 1 *(Sturridge 32)*
England: Fielding; Bertrand (Cork 84), Mancienne (Muamba 74), Smalling, Walker, Cleverley, Sturridge (Delfounesco 90), Welbeck, Jones, Henderson, Rose.

Norwich, 8 October 2010, 25,794
England (0) 2 *(Henderson 63, Smalling 83)*
Romania (0) 1 *(Bertrand 71 (og))*
England: Fielding; Jones, Bertrand, Muamba, Mancienne, Smalling, Cleverley (Albrighton 75), Wilshere (Cork 90), Welbeck (Sturridge 81), Henderson, Rose.

Botosani, 12 October 2010, 6400
Romania (0) 0
England (0) 0
England: Fielding; Mancienne, Bertrand, Smalling, Jones, Muamba, Henderson, Welbeck (Delfouneso 90), Sturridge (Lansbury 62), Rose (Cork 82), Cleverley.

Wiesbaden, 16 November 2010, 5600
Germany (1) 2 *(Rausch 37, Tosun 59 (pen))*
England (0) 0
England: Loach (Steele■ 46); Trippier, Bertrand, Rodwell (Mee 66), Mancienne, Cork, Kelly (Caulker 77), Lansbury, Delfouneso (McEachran 87), Sinclair (Wickham 66), Rose.

Empoli, 8 February 2011, 3700
Italy (0) 1 *(Macheda 88 (pen))*
England (0) 0
England: Fielding; Naughton, Bennett, Rodwell (Cork 12), Mee■, Muamba, Albrighton (Sinclair 73), Lansbury (Oxlade-Chamberlain 60), McEachran (Trippier 83), Vaughan (Rodriguez 60), Delfouneso (Howson 60).

Viborg, 24 March 2011
Denmark (0) 0
England (1) 4 *(Welbeck 23, Sinclair 58, Sturridge 62, Henderson 72)*
England: McCarthy; Naughton, Bertrand, Muamba (Albrighton 87), Richards (Tomkins 5), Smalling, Cleverley (Delfouneso 79), Henderson (Cork 79), Sturridge (Wickham 87), Welbeck (McEachran 67), Sinclair (Rose 67).

Preston, 28 March 2011, 14,622
England (1) 1 *(Delfouneso 13)*
Iceland (1) 2 *(Smarason 41, Eyjolfsson 67)*
England: McCarthy (Loach 46); Naughton (Spence 73), Bertrand (Bennett 74), Tomkins, Albrighton (Sinclair 83), McEachran (Mutch 83), Rose, Cork (Cleverley 46), Wickham, Delfouneso (Hammill 74), Baker.

Southampton, 5 June 2011, 17,996
England (2) 2 *(Sturridge 9, Rose 40)*
Norway (0) 0
England: Fielding; Mancienne, Bertrand (Cleverley 46), Muamba (Gibbs 46), Smalling, Jones P (Tomkins 83), Sturridge (Delfouneso 65), Henderson (Cork 46), Welbeck (Albrighton 46), Rodwell, Rose (Lansbury 46).

Herning, 12 June 2011, 8046
Spain (1) 1 *(Herrera 14)*
England (0) 1 *(Welbeck 88)*
England: Fielding; Mancienne (Lansbury 67), Bertrand, Smalling, Jones P, Henderson, Welbeck, Sturridge, Walker, Cleverley (Sinclair 81), Rose (Rodwell 67).

Herning, 15 June 2011, 3495
Ukraine (0) 0
England (0) 0
England: Fielding; Mancienne (Muamba 89), Bertrand, Smalling, Jones P, Henderson, Welbeck, Sturridge, Walker, Rodwell (Lansbury 57), Rose (Sinclair 58).

Viborg, 19 June 2011, 5262
Czech Republic (0) 2 *(Chramosta 89, Pekhart 90)*
England (0) 1 *(Welbeck 76)*
England: Fielding; Bertrand, Muamba, Smalling, Jones P, Henderson (Lansburg 64), Welbeck, Sturridge, Sinclair (Rose 87), Walker, Cleverley (Albrighton 77).

WALES

Ta'Qali, 10 August 2010
Malta (1) 1 *(Vella 31)*
Wales (0) 1 *(Robson-Kanu 82)*
Wales: Bond (Cornell 46); Richards (Alfei 46), Taylor N, Bradley (Lucas 46), Stephens (Bender 54), Morris, Bodin, Partington (Williams J 62), Robson-Kanu, Taylor J (Chamberlain 46), MacDonald.

Szekesfehervar, 4 September 2010, 7000
Hungary (0) 0
Wales (0) 1 *(Robson-Kanu 68)*
Wales: Maxwell; Matthews (Richards 16), Taylor N, Doble, Stephens, Morris, Allen, Bradley, Robson-Kanu, Marc Williams (Partington 60), MacDonald.

Pescara, 7 September 2010, 8650
Italy (1) 1 *(Mustacchio 14)*
Wales (0) 0
Wales: Maxwell; Matthews (Richards 34), Taylor N, King, Eardley, Morris, Allen (Marc Williams 80), Bradley (Doble 56), Robson-Kanu, Church, MacDonald.

Newport, 17 November 2010, 1041
Wales (0) 1 *(Chamberlain 74)*
Austria (0) 0
Wales: Taylor R (Cornell 46); Richards, Bloom (Dummett 46), Lucas (Brown 56), Stephens (Bender 79), Alfei, Partington, Bodin (Thomas 73), Ogleby (Chamberlain 70), Doble, Craig (Williams J 46).

Wrexham, 9 February 2011, 700
Wales (1) 2 *(Alfei 41, Ogleby 77)*
Northern Ireland (0) 0
Wales: Taylor R; Richards, Dummett (Bender 56), Lucas, Alfei, Brown, Taylor J (Matthews 80), Jones (Partington 46), Doble, Chamberlain (Ogleby 75), Williams J (Bodin 56).
Northern Ireland: Devlin; Clucas, Blake (Millar 61), McLaughlin P, Hegarty (Devine 46), McGivern, Lawrie (Mitchell 75), Lund (Winchester 75), Grigg (Gray 83), Carson (Magennis 46), Ferguson.

Andorra la Vella, 29 March 2011, 200
Andorra (0) 0
Wales (1) 1 *(Fajardo 21 (og))*
Wales: Taylor R; Brown, Matthews, Alfei, Partington, Richards, Doble, Taylor J, Lucas (Bodin 60), Williams J (Ogleby 83), Chamberlain (Cassidy 69).

SCOTLAND

Paisley, 11 August 2010, 2726
Scotland (0) 1 *(Wotherspoon 90)*
Sweden (1) 1 *(Avdic 16)*
Scotland: Martin (Gallacher 46); Marr, Perry, Wilson, Hanlon (Scobbie 46), Bannan (Easton 72), Shinnie (Saunders 64), Davidson (Cairney 64), Wotherspoon, Maguire, Murphy (Inman 46).

Borisov City, 3 September 2010, 4500
Belarus (1) 1 *(Nekhaychik 36)*
Scotland (0) 1 *(Maguire 64 (pen))*
Scotland: Martin; Caddis, Scobbie, Wilson, Hanlon, Arfield, Wotherspoon, Coutts (McGinn 84), Maguire, Murphy (Forrest 62), Bannan (Goodwillie 62).

Aberdeen, 7 September 2010, 2064
Scotland (1) 2 *(Bannan 29, Maguire 89)*
Austria (1) 1 *(Arnautovic 10)*
Scotland: Martin; Caddis, Scobbie, Wilson, Hanlon, Arfield, Wotherspoon (Forrest 71), Coutts, Maguire, Goodwillie (Murphy 77), Bannan (McGinn 90).

Reykjavik, 7 October 2010, 7255
Iceland (0) 2 *(Gudmundsson 34, Ormarsson 78)*
Scotland (1) 1 *(Murphy 19)*
Scotland: Martin, Hanlon, Caddis, Wilson, Scobbie, McGinn, Arfield, Bannan, Wotherspoon (Goodwillie 55), Maguire, Murphy (Templeton 85).

Edinburgh, 11 October 2010, 12,320
Scotland (0) 1 *(Maguire 75)*
Iceland (0) 2 *(Sigurdsson 74, 80)*
Scotland: Martin; Caddis, Wilson, Hanlon, Scobbie (Griffiths 83), Wotherspoon, Coutts, McGinn (Goodwillie 81), Bannan, Murphy (Templeton 86), Maguire.

Firhill, 17 November 2010,1764
Scotland (1) 3 *(Griffiths 12, Hanlon 64, Ross 90)*
Northern Ireland (1) 1 *(O'Kane 31)*
Scotland: Barclay; Thomson, Hanlon (Booth 66), Perry, Hanley, Hutton (Duffie 75), Armstrong (Ross 86), Inman (Palmer 46), Griffiths (MacDonald 46), Russell (Wylde 66), Fleck (Ness 75).
Northern Ireland: Drummond; McLaughlin C, Ferguson, Breeze (Clucas), McCaskin, Devine (Bagnall), Bryan (Lavery), McLaughlin P, Kee (Boyce), Grigg, O'Kane (Carson).

Deinze, 24 March 2011, 650
Belgium (1) 1 *(El Ghanassy 44)*
Scotland (0) 0
Scotland: Adam (Andrews 86); Thomson (Cole 79), Booth, Perry, Palmer, Hanlon, Wotherspoon (Armstrong 70), Cairney (McLean 79), Griffiths (Russell 58), Rhodes (MacDonald 58), Forrest.

NORTHERN IRELAND

Coleraine, 3 September 2010, 84
Northern Ireland (2) 4 *(Little 4, 85 (pen),*
McGivern 15 (pen), Grigg 90)
San Marino (0) 0 Della Valle■
Northern Ireland: Drummond; McGivern, Hodson, McLaughlin C (Blake 86), Thompson, Weir, Ferguson, Norwood, Little, Boyce (Millar 55), Magennis (Grigg 71).

Ingolstadt, 7 September 2010, 2021
Germany (1) 3 *(Holtby 42, 60, Herrmann 67)*
Northern Ireland (0) 0
Northern Ireland: Devlin; McGivern, Hodson, Flynn, Thompson (Grigg 72), Weir, Ferguson, Norwood (McLaughlin 44), Little, Boyce, McKay (Magennis 64).

Torshavn, 31 May 2011
Faeroes (0) 0
Northern Ireland (0) 0
Northern Ireland: Devlin; Hanley, Ramsey, Hegarty, Lund, Norwood, Carson, Clucas (Winchester 82), Grigg (Ball 71), Boyce, Magennis (Bryan 46).

REPUBLIC OF IRELAND

Dublin, 10 August 2010, 3010
Republic of Ireland (2) 5 *(Stokes 15, 30 (pen), McCarthy 62, Hourihane 86, Garvan 90)*
Estonia (0) 0
Republic of Ireland: Henderson; Coleman (Oyebanjo 87), Gunning, Kiernan, Nolan, McCarthy (Hourihane 82), Gleeson, Garvan, Sheridan (Judge 77), Clifford, Stokes.

Lugano, 3 September 2010, 2254
Switzerland (0) 1 *(Frei 48)*   **Republic of Ireland (0) 0**
Republic of Ireland: Henderson, Coleman, Nolan, Gunning, Towell, Judge, Hourihane, Kiernan, Clifford (Mason 81), Brady, Stokes (Rooney 76).

Izmet, 7 September 2010, 354
Turkey (0) 1 *(Tevfik 81)*   **Republic of Ireland (0) 0**
Republic of Ireland: Henderson; Coleman, Moloney, Towell, Hourihane, Kiernan (McEleney 58), Conneely, Carey, Clifford (Mason 79), Brady (Kearns 35), Rooney.

Larnaca, 9 February 2011, 100
Cyprus (0) 0
Republic of Ireland (0) 0
Republic of Ireland: Branagan (McLoughlin 46); Towell (Stevens 72), Duffy, Kiernan, Dunleavy, Connolly, Clifford, Hourihane (Devitt 46), Doran (Doyle C 46), Scannell (Gibbons 80), Collins JS (Collins M 75).

Agueda, 25 March 2011, 3000
Portugal (0) 2 *(Josue 89, Abel Camara 90)*
Republic of Ireland (0) 0
Republic of Ireland: McLoughlin (Quirke 46); Connolly (Oyebanjo 46), Gunning (Dunleavy 67), Kiernan, Canavan (Duffy 46), Towell, Barton, Clifford, Henderson (Madden 55), O'Connor (Hourihane 46), Doran (Murray 76).

BRITISH UNDER-21 APPEARANCES 1976–2011

Bold type indicates players who made an international appearance in season 2010–11.

ENGLAND

Ablett, G. 1988 (Liverpool)	1
Adams, N. 1987 (Everton)	1
Adams, T. A. 1985 (Arsenal)	5
Addison, M. 2010 (Derby Co)	1
Agbonlahor, G. 2007 (Aston Villa)	16
Albrighton, M. K. 2011 (Aston Villa)	**8**
Allen, B. 1992 (QPR)	8
Allen, C. 1980 (QPR, C Palace)	3
Allen, C. A. 1995 (Oxford U)	2
Allen, M. 1987 (QPR)	2
Allen, P. 1985 (West Ham U, Tottenham H)	3
Allen, R. W. 1998 (Tottenham H)	3
Alnwick, B. R. 2008 (Tottenham H)	1
Ambrose, D. P. F. 2003 (Ipswich T, Newcastle U, Charlton Ath)	10
Ameobi, F. 2001 (Newcastle U)	19
Anderson, V. A. 1978 (Nottingham F)	1
Anderton, D. R. 1993 (Tottenham H)	12
Andrews, I. 1987 (Leicester C)	1
Ardley, N. C. 1993 (Wimbledon)	10
Ashcroft, L. 1992 (Preston NE)	1
Ashton, D. 2004 (Crewe Alex, Norwich C)	9
Atherton, P. 1992 (Coventry C)	1
Atkinson, B. 1991 (Sunderland)	6
Awford, A. T. 1993 (Portsmouth)	9
Bailey, G. R. 1979 (Manchester U)	14
Baines, L. J. 2005 (Wigan Ath)	16
Baker, G. E. 1981 (Southampton)	2
Baker, N. L. 2011 (Aston Villa)	**1**
Ball, M. J. 1999 (Everton)	7
Barker, S. 1985 (Blackburn R)	4
Barmby, N. J. 1994 (Tottenham H, Everton)	4
Bannister, G. 1982 (Sheffield W)	1
Barnes, J. 1983 (Watford)	1
Barnes, P. S. 1977 (Manchester C)	9
Barrett, E. D. 1990 (Oldham Ath)	4
Barry, G. 1999 (Aston Villa)	27
Barton, J. 2004 (Manchester C)	2
Bart-Williams, C. G. 1993 (Sheffield W)	16
Batty, D. 1988 (Leeds U)	7
Bazeley, D. S. 1992 (Watford)	1
Beagrie, P. 1988 (Sheffield U)	2
Beardsmore, R. 1989 (Manchester U)	5
Beattie, J. S. 1999 (Southampton)	5
Beckham, D. R. J. 1995 (Manchester U)	9
Bennett, J. 2011 (Middlesbrough)	**2**
Bent, D. A. 2003 (Ipswich T, Charlton Ath)	14
Bent, M. N. 1998 (C Palace)	8
Bentley, D. M. 2004 (Arsenal, Blackburn R)	8
Beeston, C 1988 (Stoke C)	1
Benjamin, T. J. 2001 (Leicester C)	1
Bertrand, R. 2009 (Chelsea)	**16**
Bertschin, K. E. 1977 (Birmingham C)	3
Birtles, G. 1980 (Nottingham F)	2
Blackstock, D. A. 2008 (QPR)	2
Blackwell, D. R. 1991 (Wimbledon)	6
Blake, M. A. 1990 (Aston Villa)	2
Blissett, L. L. 1979 (Watford)	4
Booth, A. D. 1995 (Huddersfield T)	3
Bothroyd, J. 2001 (Coventry C)	1
Bowyer, L. D. 1996 (Charlton Ath, Leeds U)	13
Bracewell, P. 1983 (Stoke C)	13
Bradbury, L. M. 1997 (Portsmouth, Manchester C)	3
Bramble, T. M. 2001 (Ipswich T, Newcastle U)	10
Branch, P. M. 1997 (Everton)	1
Bradshaw, P. W. 1977 (Wolverhampton W)	4
Breacker, T. 1986 (Luton T)	2
Brennan, M. 1987 (Ipswich T)	1
Bridge, W. M. 1999 (Southampton)	8
Bridges, M. 1997 (Sunderland, Leeds U)	3

Brightwell, I. 1989 (Manchester C)	4
Briscoe, L. S. 1996 (Sheffield W)	5
Brock, K. 1984 (Oxford U)	4
Broomes, M. C. 1997 (Blackburn R)	2
Brown, M. R. 1996 (Manchester C)	4
Brown, W. M. 1999 (Manchester U)	8
Bull, S. G. 1989 (Wolverhampton W)	5
Bullock, M. J. 1998 (Barnsley)	1
Burrows, D. 1989 (WBA, Liverpool)	7
Butcher, T. I. 1979 (Ipswich T)	7
Butt, N. 1995 (Manchester U)	7
Butters, G. 1989 (Tottenham H)	3
Butterworth, I. 1985 (Coventry C, Nottingham F)	8
Bywater, S. 2001 (West Ham U)	6
Cadamarteri, D. L. 1999 (Everton)	3
Caesar, G. 1987 (Arsenal)	3
Cahill, G. J. 2007 (Aston Villa)	3
Callaghan, N. 1983 (Watford)	9
Camp, L. M. J. 2005 (Derby Co)	5
Campbell, A. P. 2000 (Middlesbrough)	4
Campbell, F. L. 2008 (Manchester U)	14
Campbell, K. J. 1991 (Arsenal)	4
Campbell, S. 1994 (Tottenham)	11
Carbon, M. P. 1996 (Derby Co)	4
Carr, C. 1985 (Fulham)	1
Carr, F. 1987 (Nottingham F)	9
Carragher, J. L. 1997 (Liverpool)	27
Carroll, A. T. 2010 (Newcastle U)	5
Carlisle, C. J. 2001 (QPR)	3
Carrick, M. 2001 (West Ham U)	14
Carson, S. P. 2004 (Leeds U, Liverpool)	29
Casper, C. M. 1995 (Manchester U)	1
Caton, T. 1982 (Manchester C)	14
Cattermole, L. B. 2008 (Middlesbrough, Wigan Ath, Sunderland)	16
Caulker, S. R. 2011 (Tottenham H)	**1**
Chadwick, L. H. 2000 (Manchester U)	13
Challis, T. M. 1996 (QPR)	2
Chamberlain, M. 1983 (Stoke C)	4
Chaplow, R. D. 2004 (Burnley)	1
Chapman, L. 1981 (Stoke C)	1
Charles, G. A. 1991 (Nottingham F)	4
Chettle, S. 1988 (Nottingham F)	12
Chopra, R. M. 2004 (Newcastle U)	1
Clark, L. R. 1992 (Newcastle U)	11
Clarke, P. M. 2003 (Everton)	8
Christie, M. N. 2001 (Derby Co)	11
Clegg, M. J. 1998 (Manchester U)	2
Clemence, S. N. 1999 (Tottenham H)	1
Cleverley, T. W. 2010 (Manchester U)	**16**
Clough, N. H. 1986 (Nottingham F)	15
Cole, A. 2001 (Arsenal)	4
Cole, A. A. 1992 (Arsenal, Bristol C, Newcastle U)	8
Cole, C. 2003 (Chelsea)	19
Cole, J. J. 2000 (West Ham U)	8
Coney, D. 1985 (Fulham)	4
Connor, T. 1987 (Brighton & HA)	1
Cooke, R. 1986 (Tottenham H)	1
Cooke, T. J. 1996 (Manchester U)	4
Cooper, C. T. 1988 (Middlesbrough)	8
Cork, J. F. P. 2009 (Chelsea)	**13**
Corrigan, J. T. 1978 (Manchester C)	3
Cort, C. E. R. 1999 (Wimbledon)	12
Cottee, A. R. 1985 (West Ham U)	8
Couzens, A. J. 1995 (Leeds U)	3
Cowans, G. S. 1979 (Aston Villa)	5
Cox, N. J. 1993 (Aston Villa)	6
Cranie, M. J. 2008 (Portsmouth)	16
Cranson, I. 1985 (Ipswich T)	5
Cresswell, R. P. W. 1999 (York C, Sheffield W)	4

Croft, G. 1995 (Grimsby T)	4
Crooks, G. 1980 (Stoke C)	4
Crossley, M. G. 1990 (Nottingham F)	3
Crouch, P. J. 2002 (Portsmouth, Aston Villa)	5
Cundy, J. V. 1991 (Chelsea)	3
Cunningham, L. 1977 (WBA)	6
Curbishley, L. C. 1981 (Birmingham C)	1
Curtis, J. C. K. 1998 (Manchester U)	16
Daniel, P. W. 1977 (Hull C)	7
Dann, S. 2008 (Coventry C)	2
Davenport, C. R. P. 2005 (Tottenham H)	8
Davies, A. J. 2004 (Middlesbrough)	1
Davies, C. E. 2006 (WBA)	3
Davies, K. C. 1998 (Southampton, Blackburn R, Southampton)	3
Davis, K. G. 1995 (Luton T)	3
Davis, P. 1982 (Arsenal)	11
Davis, S. 2001 (Fulham)	11
Dawson, M. R. 2003 (Nottingham F, Tottenham H)	13
Day, C. N. 1996 (Tottenham H, C Palace)	6
D'Avray, M. 1984 (Ipswich T)	2
Deehan, J. M. 1977 (Aston Villa)	7
Defoe, J. C. 2001 (West Ham U)	23
Delfouneso, N. 2010 (Aston Villa)	**8**
Delph, F. 2009 (Leeds U, Aston Villa)	4
Dennis, M. E. 1980 (Birmingham C)	3
Derbyshire, M. A. 2007 (Blackburn R)	14
Dichio, D. S. E. 1996 (QPR)	1
Dickens, A. 1985 (West Ham U)	1
Dicks, J. 1988 (West Ham U)	4
Digby, F. 1987 (Swindon T)	5
Dillon, K. P. 1981 (Birmingham C)	1
Dixon, K. M. 1985 (Chelsea)	1
Dobson, A. 1989 (Coventry C)	4
Dodd, J. R. 1991 (Southampton)	8
Donowa, L. 1985 (Norwich C)	3
Dorigo, A. R. 1987 (Aston Villa)	11
Downing, S. 2004 (Middlesbrough)	8
Dozzell, J. 1987 (Ipswich T)	9
Draper, M. A. 1991 (Notts Co)	3
Driver, A. 2009 (Hearts)	1
Duberry, M. W. 1997 (Chelsea)	5
Dunn, D. J. I. 1999 (Blackburn R)	20
Duxbury, M. 1981 (Manchester U)	7
Dyer, B. A. 1994 (C Palace)	10
Dyer, K. C. 1998 (Ipswich T, Newcastle U)	11
Dyson, P. I. 1981 (Coventry C)	4
Eadie, D. M. 1994 (Norwich C)	7
Ebanks-Blake, S. 2009 (Wolverhampton W)	1
Ebbrell, J. 1989 (Everton)	14
Edghill, R. A. 1994 (Manchester C)	3
Ehiogu, U. 1992 (Aston Villa)	15
Elliott, P. 1985 (Luton T)	3
Elliott, R. J. 1996 (Newcastle U)	2
Elliott, S. W. 1998 (Derby Co)	3
Etherington, N. 2002 (Tottenham H)	3
Euell, J. J. 1998 (Wimbledon)	6
Evans, R. 2003 (Chelsea)	2
Fairclough, C. 1985 (Nottingham F, Tottenham H)	7
Fairclough, D. 1977 (Liverpool)	1
Fashanu, J. 1980 (Norwich C, Nottingham F)	11
Fear, P. 1994 (Wimbledon)	3
Fenton, G. A. 1995 (Aston Villa)	1
Fenwick, T. W. 1981 (C Palace, QPR)	11
Ferdinand, A. J. 2005 (West Ham U)	17
Ferdinand, R. G. 1997 (West Ham U)	5
Fereday, W. 1985 (QPR)	5
Fielding, F. D. 2009 (Blackburn R)	**12**
Flitcroft, G. W. 1993 (Manchester C)	10
Flowers, T. D. 1987 (Southampton)	3
Ford, M. 1996 (Leeds U)	2
Forster, N. M. 1995 (Brentford)	4
Forsyth, M. 1988 (Derby Co)	1
Foster, S. 1980 (Brighton & HA)	1
Fowler, R. B. 1994 (Liverpool)	8

Fox, D. J. 2008 (Coventry C)	1
Froggatt, S. J. 1993 (Aston Villa)	2
Futcher, P. 1977 (Luton T, Manchester C)	11
Gabbiadini, M. 1989 (Sunderland)	2
Gale, A. 1982 (Fulham)	1
Gallen, K. A. 1995 (QPR)	4
Gardner, A. 2002 (Tottenham H)	1
Gardner, C. 2008 (Aston Villa)	14
Gascoigne, P. J. 1987 (Newcastle U)	13
Gayle, H. 1984 (Birmingham C)	3
Gernon, T. 1983 (Ipswich T)	1
Gerrard, P. W. 1993 (Oldham Ath)	18
Gerrard, S. G. 2000 (Liverpool)	4
Gibbs, K. J. R. 2009 (Arsenal)	**15**
Gibbs, N. 1987 (Watford)	5
Gibson, C. 1982 (Aston Villa)	1
Gilbert, W. A. 1979 (C Palace)	11
Goddard, P. 1981 (West Ham U)	8
Gordon, D. 1987 (Norwich C)	4
Gordon, D. D. 1994 (C Palace)	13
Gosling, D. 2010 (Everton)	2
Grant, A. J. 1996 (Everton)	1
Grant, L. A. 2003 (Derby Co)	4
Granville, D. P. 1997 (Chelsea)	3
Gray, A. 1988 (Aston Villa)	2
Greening, J. 1999 (Manchester U, Middlesbrough)	18
Griffin, A. 1999 (Newcastle U)	3
Guppy, S. A. 1998 (Leicester C)	1
Haigh, P. 1977 (Hull C)	1
Hall, M. T. J. 1997 (Coventry C)	8
Hall, R. A. 1992 (Southampton)	11
Hamilton, D. V. 1997 (Newcastle U)	1
Hammill, A. 2010 (Wolverhampton W)	**1**
Harding, D. A. 2005 (Brighton & HA)	4
Hardyman, P. 1985 (Portsmouth)	2
Hargreaves, O. 2001 (Bayern Munich)	3
Harley, J. 2000 (Chelsea)	3
Hart, C. 2007 (Manchester C)	21
Hateley, M. 1982 (Coventry C, Portsmouth)	10
Hayes, M. 1987 (Arsenal)	3
Hazell, R. J. 1979 (Wolverhampton W)	1
Heaney, N. A. 1992 (Arsenal)	6
Heath, A. 1981 (Stoke C, Everton)	8
Heaton, T. D. 2008 (Manchester U)	3
Henderson, J. B. 2011 (Sunderland)	**10**
Hendon, I. M. 1992 (Tottenham H)	7
Hendrie, L. A. 1996 (Aston Villa)	13
Hesford, I. 1981 (Blackpool)	7
Heskey, E. W. I. 1997 (Leicester C, Liverpool)	16
Hilaire, V. 1980 (C Palace)	9
Hill, D. R. L. 1995 (Tottenham H)	4
Hillier, D. 1991 (Arsenal)	1
Hinchcliffe, A. 1989 (Manchester C)	1
Hines, Z. 2010 (West Ham U)	2
Hinshelwood, P. A. 1978 (C Palace)	2
Hirst, D. E. 1988 (Sheffield W)	7
Hislop, N. S. 1998 (Newcastle U)	1
Hoddle, G. 1977 (Tottenham H)	12
Hodge, S. B. 1983 (Nottingham F, Aston Villa)	8
Hodgson, D. J. 1981 (Middlesbrough)	6
Holdsworth, D. 1989 (Watford)	1
Holland, C. J. 1995 (Newcastle U)	10
Holland, P. 1995 (Mansfield T)	4
Holloway, D. 1998 (Sunderland)	1
Horne, B. 1989 (Millwall)	5
Howe, E. J. F. 1998 (Bournemouth)	2
Howson, J. M. 2011 (Leeds U)	**1**
Hoyte, J. R. 2004 (Arsenal)	18
Hucker, P. 1984 (QPR)	2
Huckerby, D. 1997 (Coventry C)	4
Huddlestone, T. A. 2005 (Derby Co, Tottenham H)	33
Hughes, S. J. 1997 (Arsenal)	8
Humphreys, R. J. 1997 (Sheffield W)	3
Hunt, N. B. 2004 (Bolton W)	10
Impey, A. R. 1993 (QPR)	1
Ince, P. E. C. 1989 (West Ham U)	2

Jackson, M. A. 1992 (Everton)	10
Jagielka, P. N. 2003 (Sheffield U)	6
James, D. B. 1991 (Watford)	10
James, J. C. 1990 (Luton T)	2
Jansen, M. B. 1999 (C Palace, Blackburn R)	6
Jeffers, F. 2000 (Everton, Arsenal)	16
Jemson, N. B. 1991 (Nottingham F)	1
Jenas, J. A. 2002 (Newcastle U)	9
Jerome, C. 2006 (Cardiff C, Birmingham C)	10
Joachim, J. K. 1994 (Leicester C)	9
Johnson, A. 2008 (Middlesbrough)	19
Johnson, G. M. C. 2003 (West Ham U, Chelsea)	14
Johnson, M. 2008 (Manchester C)	2
Johnson, S. A. M. 1999 (Crewe Alex, Derby Co, Leeds U)	15
Johnson, T. 1991 (Notts Co, Derby Co)	7
Johnston, C. P. 1981 (Middlesbrough)	2
Jones, D. R. 1977 (Everton)	1
Jones, C. H. 1978 (Tottenham H)	1
Jones, D. F. L. 2004 (Manchester U)	1
Jones, P. A. 2011 (Blackburn R)	**9**
Jones, R. 1993 (Liverpool)	2
Keegan, G. A. 1977 (Manchester C)	1
Kelly, M. R. 2011 (Liverpool)	**2**
Kenny, W. 1993 (Everton)	1
Keown, M. R. 1987 (Aston Villa)	8
Kerslake, D. 1986 (QPR)	1
Kightly, M. J. 2008 (Wolverhampton W)	7
Kilcline, B. 1983 (Notts C)	2
Kilgallon, M. 2004 (Leeds U)	5
King, A. E. 1977 (Everton)	2
King, L. B. 2000 (Tottenham H)	12
Kirkland, C. E. 2001 (Coventry C, Liverpool)	8
Kitson, P. 1991 (Leicester C, Derby Co)	7
Knight, A. 1983 (Portsmouth)	2
Knight, I. 1987 (Sheffield W)	2
Knight, Z. 2002 (Fulham)	4
Konchesky, P. M. 2002 (Charlton Ath)	15
Kozluk, R. 1998 (Derby Co)	2
Lake, P. 1989 (Manchester C)	5
Lallana, A. D. 2009 (Southampton)	1
Lampard, F. J. 1998 (West Ham U)	19
Langley, T. W. 1978 (Chelsea)	1
Lansbury, H. G. 2010 (Arsenal)	**9**
Leadbitter, G. 2008 (Sunderland)	4
Lee, D. J. 1990 (Chelsea)	10
Lee, R. M. 1986 (Charlton Ath)	2
Lee, S. 1981 (Liverpool)	6
Lennon, A. J. 2006 (Tottenham H)	6
Le Saux, G. P. 1990 (Chelsea)	4
Lescott, J. P. 2003 (Wolverhampton W)	2
Lewis, J. P. 2008 (Peterborough U)	5
Lita, L. H. 2005 (Bristol C, Reading)	9
Loach, S. J. 2009 (Watford)	**14**
Lowe, D. 1988 (Ipswich T)	2
Lukic, J. 1981 (Leeds U)	7
Lund, G. 1985 (Grimsby T)	3
McCall, S. H. 1981 (Ipswich T)	6
McCarthy, A. S. 2011 (Reading)	**3**
McDonald, N. 1987 (Newcastle U)	5
McEachran, J. 2011 (Chelsea)	**4**
McEveley, J. 2003 (Blackburn R)	1
McGrath, L. 1986 (Coventry C)	1
MacKenzie, S. 1982 (WBA)	3
McLeary, A. 1988 (Millwall)	1
McLeod, I. M. 2006 (Milton Keynes D)	1
McMahon, S. 1981 (Everton, Aston Villa)	6
McManaman, S. 1991 (Liverpool)	7
Mabbutt, G. 1982 (Bristol R, Tottenham H)	7
Makin, C. 1994 (Oldham Ath)	5
Mancienne, M. I. 2008 (Chelsea)	**30**
Marney, D. E. 2005 (Tottenham H)	1
Marriott, A. 1992 (Nottingham F)	1
Marsh, S. T. 1998 (Oxford U)	1
Marshall, A. J. 1995 (Norwich C)	4

Marshall, L. K. 1999 (Norwich C)	1
Martin, L. 1989 (Manchester U)	2
Martyn, A. N. 1988 (Bristol R)	11
Matteo, D. 1994 (Liverpool)	4
Mattock, J. W. 2008 (Leicester C)	5
Matthew, D. 1990 (Chelsea)	9
May, A. 1986 (Manchester C)	1
Mee, B. 2011 (Manchester C)	**2**
Merson, P. C. 1989 (Arsenal)	4
Middleton, J. 1977 (Nottingham F, Derby Co)	3
Miller, A. 1988 (Arsenal)	4
Mills, D. J. 1999 (Charlton Ath, Leeds U)	14
Mills, G. R. 1981 (Nottingham F)	2
Milner, J. P. 2004 (Leeds U, Newcastle U, Aston Villa)	46
Mimms, R. 1985 (Rotherham U, Everton)	3
Minto, S. C. 1991 (Charlton Ath)	6
Moore, I. 1996 (Tranmere R, Nottingham F)	7
Moore, L. I. 2006 (Aston Villa)	5
Moran, S. 1982 (Southampton)	2
Morgan, S. 1987 (Leicester C)	2
Morris, J. 1997 (Chelsea)	7
Mortimer, P. 1989 (Charlton Ath)	2
Moses, A. P. 1997 (Barnsley)	2
Moses, R. M. 1981 (WBA, Manchester U)	8
Moses, V. 2011 (Wigan Ath)	**1**
Mountfield, D. 1984 (Everton)	1
Muamba, F. N. 2008 (Birmingham C, Bolton W)	**33**
Muggleton, C. D. 1990 (Leicester C)	1
Mullins, H. I. 1999 (C Palace)	3
Murphy, D. B. 1998 (Liverpool)	4
Murray, P. 1997 (QPR)	4
Murray, M. W. 2003 (Wolverhampton W)	5
Mutch, A. 1989 (Wolverhampton W)	1
Mutch, J. J. E. S. 2011 (Birmingham C)	**1**
Myers. A. 1995 (Chelsea)	4
Naughton, K. 2009 (Sheffield U, Tottenham H)	**9**
Naylor, M. 2000 (Wolverhampton W)	3
Nethercott, S. H. 1994 (Tottenham H)	8
Neville, P. J. 1995 (Manchester U)	7
Newell, M. 1986 (Luton T)	4
Newton, A. L. 2001 (West Ham U)	1
Newton, E. J. I. 1993 (Chelsea)	2
Newton, S. O. 1997 (Charlton Ath)	3
Nicholls, A. 1994 (Plymouth Arg)	1
Noble, M. J. 2007 (West Ham U)	20
Nolan, K. A. J. 2003 (Bolton W)	1
Nugent, D. J. 2006 (Preston NE)	14
Oakes, M. C. 1994 (Aston Villa)	6
Oakes, S. J. 1993 (Luton T)	1
Oakley, M. 1997 (Southampton)	4
O'Brien, A. J. 1999 (Bradford C)	1
O'Connor, J. 1996 (Everton)	3
O'Hara, J. D. 2008 (Tottenham H)	6
Oldfield, D. 1989 (Luton T)	1
Olney, I. A. 1990 (Aston Villa)	10
O'Neil, G. P. 2005 (Portsmouth)	9
Onuoha, C. 2006 (Manchester C)	21
Ord, R. J. 1991 (Sunderland)	3
Osman, R. C. 1979 (Ipswich T)	7
Owen, G. A. 1977 (Manchester C, WBA)	22
Owen, M. J. 1998 (Liverpool)	1
Oxlade-Chamberlain, A. M. D. 2011 (Southampton)	**1**
Painter, I. 1986 (Stoke C)	1
Palmer, C. L. 1989 (Sheffield W)	4
Parker, G. 1986 (Hull C, Nottingham F)	6
Parker, P. A. 1985 (Fulham)	8
Parker, S. M. 2001 (Charlton Ath)	12
Parkes, P. B. F. 1979 (QPR)	1
Parkin, S. 1987 (Stoke C)	5
Parlour, R. 1992 (Arsenal)	12
Parnaby, S. 2003 (Middlesbrough)	1
Peach, D. S. 1977 (Southampton)	6
Peake, A. 1982 (Leicester C)	1
Pearce, I. A. 1995 (Blackburn R)	3
Pearce, S. 1987 (Nottingham F)	1

Pennant, J. 2001 (Arsenal) 24
Pickering N. 1983 (Sunderland, Coventry C) 15
Platt, D. 1988 (Aston Villa) 3
Plummer, C. S. 1996 (QPR) 5
Pollock, J. 1995 (Middlesbrough) 3
Porter, G. 1987 (Watford) 12
Potter, G. S. 1997 (Southampton) 1
Pressman, K. 1989 (Sheffield W) 1
Proctor, M. 1981 (Middlesbrough, Nottingham F) 4
Prutton, D. T. 2001 (Nottingham F, Southampton) 25
Purse, D. J. 1998 (Birmingham C) 2

Quashie, N. F. 1997 (QPR) 4
Quinn, W. R. 1998 (Sheffield U) 2

Ramage, C. D. 1991 (Derby Co) 3
Ranson, R. 1980 (Manchester C) 10
Redknapp, J. F. 1993 (Liverpool) 19
Redmond, S. 1988 (Manchester C) 14
Reeves, K. P. 1978 (Norwich C, Manchester C) 10
Regis, C. 1979 (WBA) 6
Reid, N. S. 1981 (Manchester C) 6
Reid, P. 1977 (Bolton W) 6
Reo-Coker, N. S. A. 2004 (Wimbledon, West Ham U) 23
Richards, D. I. 1995 (Wolverhampton W) 4
Richards, J. P. 1977 (Wolverhampton W) 2
Richards, M. 2007 (Manchester C) **15**
Richards, M. L. 2005 (Ipswich T) 1
Richardson, K. E. 2005 (Manchester U)
Rideout, P. 1985 (Aston Villa, Bari) 5
Ridgewell, L. M. 2004 (Aston Villa) 8
Riggott, C. M. 2001 (Derby Co) 8
Ripley, S. E. 1988 (Middlesbrough) 8
Ritchie, A. 1982 (Brighton & HA) 1
Rix, G. 1978 (Arsenal) 7
Roberts, A. J. 1995 (Millwall, C Palace) 5
Roberts, B. J. 1997 (Middlesbrough) 1
Robins, M. G. 1990 (Manchester U) 6
Robinson, P. P. 1999 (Watford) 3
Robinson, P. W. 2000 (Leeds U) 11
Robson, B. 1979 (WBA) 7
Robson, S. 1984 (Arsenal, West Ham U) 8
Rocastle, D. 1987 (Arsenal) 14
Roche, L. P. 2001 (Manchester U) 1
Rodger, G. 1987 (Coventry C) 4
Rodriguez, J. E. 2011 (Burnley) **1**
Rodwell, J. 2009 (Everton) **17**
Rogers, A. 1998 (Nottingham F) 3
Rosario, R. 1987 (Norwich C) 4
Rose, D. L. 2009 (Tottenham H) **20**
Rose, M. 1997 (Arsenal) 2
Rosenior, L. J. 2005 (Fulham) 7
Routledge, W. 2005 (C Palace, Tottenham H) 12
Rowell, G. 1977 (Sunderland) 1
Ruddock, N. 1989 (Southampton) 4
Rufus, R. R. 1996 (Charlton Ath) 6
Ryan, J. 1983 (Oldham Ath) 1
Ryder, S. H. 1995 (Walsall) 3

Samuel, J. 2002 (Aston Villa) 7
Samways, V. 1988 (Tottenham H) 5
Sansom, K. G. 1979 (C Palace) 8
Scimeca, R. 1996 (Aston Villa) 9
Scowcroft, J. B. 1997 (Ipswich T) 5
Seaman, D. A. 1985 (Birmingham C) 10
Sears, F. D. 2010 (West Ham U) 3
Sedgley, S. 1987 (Coventry C, Tottenham H) 11
Sellars, S. 1988 (Blackburn R) 3
Selley, I. 1994 (Arsenal) 3
Serrant, C. 1998 (Oldham Ath) 2
Sharpe, L. S. 1989 (Manchester U) 8
Shaw, G. R. 1981 (Aston Villa) 7
Shawcross, R. J. 2008 (Stoke C) 2
Shearer, A. 1991 (Southampton) 11
Shelton, G. 1985 (Sheffield W) 1
Sheringham, E. P. 1988 (Millwall) 1
Sheron, M. N. 1992 (Manchester C) 16
Sherwood, T. A. 1990 (Norwich C) 4

Shipperley, N. J. 1994 (Chelsea, Southampton) 7
Sidwell, S. J. 2003 (Reading) 5
Simonsen, S. P. A. 1998 (Tranmere R, Everton) 4
Simpson, P. 1986 (Manchester C) 5
Sims, S. 1977 (Leicester C) 10
Sinclair, S. A. 2011 (Swansea C) **7**
Sinclair, T. 1994 (QPR, West Ham U) 5
Sinnott, L. 1985 (Watford) 1
Slade, S. A. 1996 (Tottenham H) 4
Slater, S. I. 1990 (West Ham U) 3
Small, B. 1993 (Aston Villa) 12
Smalling, C. L. 2010 (Fulham, Manchester U) **14**
Smith, A. 2000 (Leeds U) 10
Smith, D. 1988 (Coventry C) 10
Smith, M. 1981 (Sheffield W) 5
Smith, M. 1995 (Sunderland) 1
Smith, T. W. 2001 (Watford) 1
Snodin, I. 1985 (Doncaster R) 4
Soares, T. J. 2006 (C Palace) 4
Spence, J. 2011 (West Ham U) **1**
Stanislaus, F. J. 2010 (West Ham U) 2
Statham, B. 1988 (Tottenham H) 3
Statham, D. J. 1978 (WBA) 6
Stead, J. G. 2004 (Blackburn R, Sunderland) 11
Stearman, R. J. 2009 (Wolverhampton W) 4
Steele, J. 2011 (Middlesbrough) **1**
Stein, B. 1984 (Luton T) 3
Sterland, M. 1984 (Sheffield W) 7
Steven, T. M. 1985 (Everton) 2
Stevens, G. A. 1983 (Brighton & HA, Tottenham H) 8
Stewart, J. 2003 (Leicester C) 1
Stewart, P. 1988 (Manchester C) 1
Stockdale, R. K. 2001 (Middlesbrough) 5
Stuart, G. C. 1990 (Chelsea) 5
Stuart, J. C. 1996 (Charlton Ath) 4
Sturridge, D. A. 2010 (Chelsea) **15**
Suckling, P. 1986 (Coventry C, Manchester C, C Palace) 10
Summerbee, N. J. 1993 (Swindon T) 3
Sunderland, A. 1977 (Wolverhampton W) 1
Surman, A. R. E. 2008 (Southampton) 4
Sutch, D. 1992 (Norwich C) 4
Sutton, C. R. 1993 (Norwich C) 13
Swindlehurst, D. 1977 (C Palace) 1

Talbot, B. 1977 (Ipswich T) 1
Taylor, A. D. 2007 (Middlesbrough) 13
Taylor, M. 2001 (Blackburn R) 1
Taylor, M. S. 2003 (Portsmouth) 3
Taylor, R. A. 2006 (Wigan Ath) 4
Taylor, S. J. 2002 (Arsenal) 3
Taylor, S. V. 2004 (Newcastle U) 29
Terry, J. G. 2001 (Chelsea) 9
Thatcher, B. D. 1996 (Millwall, Wimbledon) 4
Thelwell, A. A. 2001 (Tottenham H) 1
Thirlwell, P. 2001 (Sunderland) 1
Thomas, D. 1981 (Coventry C, Tottenham H) 7
Thomas, J. W. 2006 (Charlton Ath) 2
Thomas, M. 1986 (Luton T) 3
Thomas, M. L. 1988 (Arsenal) 12
Thomas, R. E. 1990 (Watford) 1
Thompson, A. 1995 (Bolton W) 2
Thompson, D. A. 1997 (Liverpool) 7
Thompson, G. L. 1981 (Coventry C) 6
Thorn, A. 1988 (Wimbledon) 5
Thornley, B. L. 1996 (Manchester U) 4
Tiler, C. 1990 (Barnsley, Nottingham F) 13
Tomkins, J. O. C. 2009 (West Ham U) **10**
Tonge, M. W. E. 2004 (Sheffield U) 2
Trippier, K. J. 2011 (Manchester C) **2**

Unsworth, D. G. 1995 (Everton) 6
Upson, M. J. 1999 (Arsenal) 11

Vassell, D. 1999 (Aston Villa) 11
Vaughan, J. O. 2007 (Everton) **4**
Venison, B. 1983 (Sunderland) 10
Vernazza, P. A. P. 2001 (Arsenal, Watford) 2

Vinnicombe, C. 1991 (Rangers) 12

Waddle, C. R. 1985 (Newcastle U) 1
Walcott, T. J. 2007 (Arsenal) 21
Wallace, D. L. 1983 (Southampton) 14
Wallace, Ray 1989 (Southampton) 4
Wallace, Rod 1989 (Southampton) 11
Walker, D. 1985 (Nottingham F) 7
Walker, I. M. 1991 (Tottenham H) 9
Walker, K. 2010 (Tottenham H) 7
Walsh, G. 1988 (Manchester U) 1
Walsh, P. A. 1983 (Luton T) 4
Walters, K. 1984 (Aston Villa) 9
Ward, P. 1978 (Brighton & HA) 2
Warhurst, P. 1991 (Oldham Ath, Sheffield W) 8
Watson, B. 2007 (C Palace) 1
Watson, D. 1984 (Norwich C) 7
Watson, D. N. 1994 (Barnsley) 5
Watson, G. 1991 (Sheffield W) 2
Watson, S. C. 1993 (Newcastle U) 12
Weaver, N. J. 2000 (Manchester C) 10
Webb, N. J. 1985 (Portsmouth, Nottingham F) 3
Welbeck, D. 2009 (Manchester U) 14
Welsh, J. J. 2004 (Liverpool, Hull C) 8
Wheater, D. J. 2008 (Middlesbrough) 11
Whelan, P. J. 1993 (Ipswich T) 3
Whelan, N. 1995 (Leeds U) 2
Whittingham, P. 2004 (Aston Villa, Cardiff C) 17
White, D. 1988 (Manchester C) 6

Whyte, C. 1982 (Arsenal) 4
Wickham, C. N. R. 2011 (Ipswich T) 3
Wicks, S. 1982 (QPR) 1
Wilkins, R. C. 1977 (Chelsea) 1
Wilkinson, P. 1985 (Grimsby T, Everton) 4
Williams, D. 1998 (Sunderland) 2
Williams, P. 1989 (Charlton Ath) 4
Williams, P. D. 1991 (Derby Co) 6
Williams, S. C. 1977 (Southampton) 14
Wilshere, J. A. 2010 (Arsenal) 7
Wilson, M. A. 2001 (Manchester U, Middlesbrough) 6
Winterburn, N. 1986 (Wimbledon) 1
Wise, D. F. 1988 (Wimbledon) 1
Woodcook, A. S. 1978 (Nottingham F) 2
Woodgate, J. S. 2000 (Leeds U) 1
Woodhouse, C. 1999 (Sheffield U) 4
Woods, C. C. E. 1979 (Nottingham F, QPR, Norwich C) 6
Wright, A. G. 1993 (Blackburn R) 2
Wright, M. 1983 (Southampton) 4
Wright, R. I. 1997 (Ipswich T) 15
Wright, S. J. 2001 (Liverpool) 10
Wright, W. 1979 (Everton) 6
Wright-Phillips, S. C. 2002 (Manchester C) 6

Yates, D. 1989 (Notts Co) 5
Young, A. S. 2007 (Watford, Aston Villa) 10
Young, L. P. 1999 (Tottenham H, Charlton Ath) 12

Zamora, R. L. 2002 (Brighton & HA) 6

NORTHERN IRELAND

Allen, C. 2009 (Lisburn Distillery) 1
Armstrong, D. T. 2007 (Hearts) 1

Bagnall, L. 2011 (Sunderland) 1
Bailie, N. 1990 (Linfield) 2
Baird, C. P. 2002 (Southampton) 6
Ball, M. 2011 (Norwich C) 1
Beatty, S. 1990 (Chelsea, Linfield) 2
Black, J. 2003 (Tottenham H) 1
Black, K. T. 1990 (Luton T) 1
Black, R. Z. 2002 (Morecambe) 1
Blackledge, G. 1978 (Portadown) 1
Blake, R. G. 2011 (Brentford) 2
Blayney, A. 2003 (Southampton) 4
Boyce, L. 2010 (Cliftonville, Werder Bremen) 5
Boyle, W. S. 1998 (Leeds U) 7
Braniff, K. R. 2002 (Millwall) 11
Breeze, J. 2011 (Wigan Ath) 1
Brotherston, N. 1978 (Blackburn R) 1
Browne, G. 2003 (Manchester C) 5
Brunt, C. 2005 (Sheffield W) 1
Bryan, M. A. 2010 (Watford) 4
Buchanan, D. T. H. 2006 (Bury) 15
Buchanan, W. B. 2002 (Bolton W, Lisburn Distillery) 5
Burns, L. 1998 (Port Vale) 13

Callaghan, A. 2006 (Limavady U, Ballymena U,
   Derry C) 15
Campbell, S. 2003 (Ballymena U) 1
Capaldi, A. C. 2002 (Birmingham C, Plymouth Arg) 14
Carlisle, W. T. 2000 (C Palace) 9
Carroll, R. E. 1998 (Wigan Ath) 11
Carson, J. G. 2011 (Ipswich T) 3
Carson, S. 2000 (Rangers, Dundee U) 2
Carson, T. 2007 (Sunderland) 15
Carvill, M. D. 2008 (Wrexham, Linfield) 8
Casement, C. 2007 (Ipswich T, Dundee) 18
Cathcart, C. 2007 (Manchester U) 15
Catney, R. 2007 (Lisburn Distillery) 1
Chapman, A. 2008 (Sheffield U, Oxford U) 7
Clarke, L. 2003 (Peterborough U) 4
Clarke, R. 2006 (Newry C) 7
Clarke, R. D. J. 1999 (Portadown) 5
Clingan, S. G. 2003 (Wolverhampton W, Nottingham F) 11
Close, B. 2002 (Middlesbrough) 10

Clucas, M. S. 2011 (Preston NE) 3
Clyde, M. G. 2002 (Wolverhampton W) 5
Colligan, L. 2009 (Ballymena U) 1
Connell, T. F. 1978 (Coleraine) 1
Coote, A. 1998 (Norwich C) 12
Convery, J. 2000 (Celtic) 4

Davey, H. 2004 (UCD) 3
Davis, S. 2004 (Aston Villa) 3
Devine, D. 1994 (Omagh T) 1
Devine, D. G. 2011 (Preston NE) 2
Devine, J. 1990 (Glentoran) 1
Devlin, C. 2011 (Manchester U) 3
Dickson, H. 2002 (Wigan Ath) 1
Doherty, M. 2007 (Hearts) 1
Dolan, J. 2000 (Millwall) 6
Donaghy, M. M. 1978 (Larne) 1
Donnelly, M. 2007 (Sheffield U, Crusaders) 5
Dowie, I. 1990 (Luton T) 1
Drummond, W. 2011 (Rangers) 2
Dudgeon, J. P. 2010 (Manchester U) 2
Duff, S. 2003 (Cheltenham T) 1
Duffy, S. P. M. 2010 (Everton) 3

Elliott, S. 1999 (Glentoran) 3
Ervin, J. 2005 (Linfield) 2
Evans, C. J. 2009 (Manchester U) 10
Evans, J. 2006 (Manchester U) 3

Feeney, L. 1998 (Linfield, Rangers) 8
Feeney, W. 2002 (Bournemouth) 8
Ferguson, M. 2000 (Glentoran) 2
Ferguson, S. 2009 (Newcastle U) 7
Fitzgerald, D. 1998 (Rangers) 4
Flynn, J. J. 2009 (Blackburn R, Ross Co) 11
Fordyce, D. T. 2007 (Portsmouth, Glentoran) 12
Friars, E. C. 2005 (Notts Co) 7
Friars, S. M. 1998 (Liverpool, Ipswich T) 21

Garrett, R. 2007 (Stoke C, Linfield) 14
Gault, M. 2005 (Linfield) 2
Gibb, S. 2009 (Falkirk, Drogheda U) 2
Gilfillan, B. J. 2005 (Gretna, Peterhead) 9
Gillespie, K. R. 1994 (Manchester U) 1
Glendinning, M. 1994 (Bangor) 1
Graham, G. L. 1999 (C Palace) 5

Graham, R. S. 1999 (QPR)	15	McGovern, M. 2005 (Celtic)	10
Gray, P. 1990 (Luton T)	1	McGowan, M. V. 2006 (Clyde)	2
Griffin, D. J. 1998 (St Johnstone)	10	McGurk, A. 2010 (Aston Villa)	1
Grigg, W. D. 2011 (Walsall)	**5**	McIlroy, T. 1994 (Linfield)	1
		McKay, W. 2009 (Leicester C, Northampton T)	**7**
Hamilton, G. 2000 (Blackburn R, Portadown)	12	McKenna, K. 2007 (Tottenham H)	6
Hamilton, W. R. 1978 (Linfield)	1	McKnight, P. 1998 (Rangers)	3
Hanley, N. 2011 (Linfield)	**1**	**McLaughlin, C. G. 2010 (Preston NE)**	**2**
Harkin, M. P. 2000 (Wycombe W)	9	**McLaughlin, P. 2010 (Newcastle U)**	**5**
Harvey, J. 1978 (Arsenal)	1	McLean, B. S. 2006 (Rangers)	1
Hawe, S. 2001 (Blackburn R)	2	McLean, J. 2009 (Derry C)	4
Hayes, T. 1978 (Luton T)	1	McMahon, G. J. 2002 (Tottenham H)	1
Hazley, M. 2007 (Stoke C)	3	McMenamin, L. A. 2009 (Sheffield W)	4
Healy, D. J. 1999 (Manchester U)	8	McQuilken, J. 2009 (Tescoma Zlin)	1
Hegarty, C. 2011 (Rangers)	**2**	McQuoid, J. J. B. 2009 (Bournemouth)	8
Herron, C. J. 2003 (QPR)	2	McVeigh, A. 2002 (Ayr U)	1
Higgins, R. 2006 (Derry C)	1	McVeigh, P. M. 1998 (Tottenham H)	11
Hodson, L. J. S. 2010 (Watford)	**7**	McVey, K. 2006 (Coleraine)	8
Holmes, S. 2000 (Manchester C, Wrexham)	13	Meenan, D. 2007 (Finn Harps, Monaghan U)	3
Howland, D. 2007 (Birmingham C)	4	Melaugh, G. M. 2002 (Aston Villa, Glentoran)	11
Hughes, J. 2006 (Lincoln C)	7	**Millar, K. S. 2011 (Lincoln Ath)**	**2**
Hughes, M. A. 2003 (Tottenham H, Oldham Ath)	12	Millar, W. P. 1990 (Port Vale)	1
Hughes, M. E. 1990 (Manchester C)	1	Miskelly, D. T. 2000 (Oldham Ath)	10
Hunter, M. 2002 (Glentoran)	1	Moreland, V. 1978 (Glentoran)	1
		Morgan, M. P. T. 1999 (Preston NE)	1
Ingham, M. G. 2001 (Sunderland)	4	Morris, E. J. 2002 (WBA, Glentoran)	8
		Morrison, O. 2001 (Sheffield W, Sheffield U)	7
Jarvis, D. 2010 (Aberdeen)	2	Morrow, A. 2001 (Northampton T)	1
Johnson, D. M. 1998 (Blackburn R)	11	Morrow, S. 2005 (Hibernian)	4
Johnston, B. 1978 (Cliftonville)	1	Mulgrew, J. 2007 (Linfield)	10
Julian, A. A. 2005 (Brentford)	1	Mulryne, P. P. 1999 (Manchester U, Norwich C)	5
		Murray, W. 1978 (Linfield)	1
Kane, A. M. 2008 (Blackburn R)	5	Murtagh, C. 2005 (Hearts)	1
Kee, B. R. 2010 (Leicester C, Torquay U)	**6**		
Kee, P. V. 1990 (Oxford U)	1	Nicholl, J. M. 1978 (Manchester U)	1
Kelly, D. 2000 (Derry C)	11	Nixon, C. 2000 (Glentoran)	1
Kelly, N. 1990 (Oldham Ath)	1	**Norwood, O. J. 2010 (Manchester U)**	**7**
Kirk, A. R. 1999 (Hearts)	9		
		O'Connor, M. J. 2008 (Crewe Alex)	3
Lafferty, D. 2009 (Celtic)	6	O'Hara, G. 1994 (Leeds U)	1
Lafferty, K. 2006 (Burnley)	2	**O'Kane, E. 2009 (Everton, Torquay U)**	**4**
Lavery, C. 2011 (Ipswich T)	**1**	O'Neill, J. P. 1978 (Leicester C)	1
Lawrie, J. 2009 (Port Vale, AFC Telford U)	**9**	O'Neill, M. A. M. 1994 (Hibernian)	1
Lennon, N. F. 1990 (Manchester C, Crewe Alex)	2	O'Neill, S. 2009 (Ballymena U)	4
Lindsay, K. 2006 (Larne)	1		
Little, A. 2009 (Rangers)	**6**	Paterson, M. A. 2007 (Stoke C)	2
Lowry, P. 2009 (Institute, Linfield)	6	Patterson, D. J. 1994 (C Palace)	1
Lund, M. 2011 (Stoke C)	**2**		
Lyttle, G. 1998 (Celtic, Peterborough U)	8	Quinn, S. J. 1994 (Blackpool)	1
Magee, J. 1994 (Bangor)	1	**Ramsey, C. 2011 (Portadown)**	**1**
Magee, J. 2009 (Lisburn Distillery)	1	Ramsey, K. 2006 (Institute)	1
Magennis, J. B. D. 2010 (Cardiff C, Aberdeen)	**9**	Robinson, S. 1994 (Tottenham H)	1
Magilton, J. 1990 (Liverpool)	1		
Magnay, C. 2010 (Chelsea)	1	Scullion, D. 2006 (Dungannon Swifts)	8
Matthews, N. P. 1990 (Blackpool)	1	Shiels, D. 2005 (Hibernian)	6
McAllister, M. 2007 (Dungannon Swifts)	4	Shroot, R. 2009 (Harrow B, Birmingham C)	4
McArdle, R. A. 2006 (Sheffield W, Rochdale)	19	Simms, G. 2001 (Hartlepool U)	14
McAreavey, P. 2000 (Swindon T)	7	Skates, G. 2000 (Blackburn R)	4
McBride, J. 1994 (Glentoran)	1	Sloan, T. 1978 (Ballymena U)	1
McCaffrey, D. 2006 (Hibernian)	8	Smylie, D. 2006 (Newcastle U, Livingston)	6
McCallion, E. 1998 (Coleraine)	1	Stewart, S. 2009 (Aberdeen)	1
McCann, G. S. 2000 (West Ham U)	11	Stewart, T. 2006 (Wolverhampton W, Linfield)	19
McCann, P. 2003 (Portadown)	1		
McCann, R. 2002 (Rangers, Linfield)	2	Taylor, J. 2007 (Hearts, Glentoran)	10
McCartney, G. 2001 (Sunderland)	5	Taylor, M. S. 1998 (Fulham)	1
McCashin, S. 2011 (Jerez Industrial)	**1**	Teggart, N. 2005 (Sunderland)	2
McChrystal, M. 2005 (Derry C)	1	**Thompson, A. L. 2011 (Watford)**	**2**
McClean, J. 2010 (Derry C)	3	Thompson, P. 2006 (Linfield)	4
McCourt, P. J. 2002 (Rochdale, Derry C)	8	Toner, C. 2000 (Tottenham H, Leyton Orient)	17
McCoy, R. K. 1990 (Coleraine)	1	Tuffey, J. 2007 (Partick T)	13
McCreery, D. 1978 (Manchester U)	1	Turner, C. 2007 (Sligo R, Bohemians)	12
McEvilly, L. R. 2003 (Rochdale)	9		
McFlynn, T. M. 2000 (QPR, Woking, Margate)	19	Ward, J. J. 2006 (Aston Villa, Chesterfield)	7
McGibbon, P. C. G. 1994 (Manchester U)	1	Ward, M. 2006 (Dungannon Swifts)	1
McGivern, R. 2010 (Manchester C)	**5**	Ward, S. 2005 (Glentoran)	10
McGlinchey, B. 1998 (Manchester C, Port Vale, Gillingham)	14	Waterman, D. G. 1998 (Portsmouth)	14
		Waterworth, A. 2008 (Lisburn Distillery, Hamilton A)	7

Webb, S. M. 2004 (Ross Co, St Johnstone, Ross Co)   6
Weir, R. J. 2009 (Sunderland)   8
Wells, D. P. 1999 (Barry T)   1

Whitley, J. 1998 (Manchester C)   17
Willis, P. 2006 (Liverpool)   1
Winchester, C. 2011 (Oldham Ath)   2

SCOTLAND

Adam, C. G. 2006 (Rangers)   5
Adam, G. 2011 (Rangers)   1
Adams, J. 2007 (Kilmarnock)   1
Aitken, R. 1977 (Celtic)   16
Albiston, A. 1977 (Manchester U)   5
Alexander, N. 1997 (Stenhousemuir, Livingston)   10
Anderson, I. 1997 (Dundee, Toulouse)   15
Anderson, R. 1997 (Aberdeen)   15
Andrews, M. 2011 (East Stirling)   1
Anthony, M. 1997 (Celtic)   3
Archdeacon, O. 1987 (Celtic)   1
Archibald, A. 1998 (Partick Th)   5
Archibald, S. 1980 (Aberdeen, Tottenham H)   5
Arfield, S. 2008 (Falkirk, Huddersfield T)   17
Armstrong, S. 2011 (Dundee U)   2

Bagen, D. 1997 (Kilmarnock)   4
Bain, K. 1993 (Dundee)   4
Baker, M. 1993 (St Mirren)   10
Baltacha, S. S. 2000 (St Mirren)   3
Bannan, B. 2009 (Aston Villa)   10
Bannon, E. J. 1979 (Hearts, Chelsea, Dundee U)   7
Barclay, J. 2011 (Falkirk)   1
Beattie, C. 2004 (Celtic)   7
Beattie, J. 1992 (St Mirren)   4
Beaumont, D. 1985 (Dundee U)   1
Bell, D. 1981 (Aberdeen)   2
Bernard, P. R. J. 1992 (Oldham Ath)   15
Berra, C. 2005 (Hearts)   6
Bett, J. 1981 (Rangers)   7
Black, E. 1983 (Aberdeen)   8
Blair, A. 1980 (Coventry C, Aston Villa)   5
Bollan, G. 1992 (Dundee U, Rangers)   17
Bonar, P. 1997 (Raith R)   4
Booth, C. 2011 (Hibernian)   2
Booth, S. 1991 (Aberdeen)   14
Bowes, M. J. 1992 (Dunfermline Ath)   1
Bowman, D. 1985 (Hearts)   1
Boyack, S. 1997 (Rangers)   1
Boyd, K. 2003 (Kilmarnock)   8
Boyd, T. 1987 (Motherwell)   5
Brazil, A. 1978 (Hibernian)   1
Brazil, A. 1979 (Ipswich T)   5
Brebner, G. I. 1997 (Manchester U, Reading, Hibernian)   18
Brighton, T. 2005 (Rangers, Clyde)   7
Broadfoot, K. 2005 (St Mirren)   5
Brough, J. 1981 (Hearts)   1
Brown, A. H. 2004 (Hibernian)   1
Brown, S. 2005 (Hibernian)   10
Browne, P. 1997 (Raith R)   1
Bryson, C. 2006 (Clyde)   1
Buchan, J. 1997 (Aberdeen)   13
Burchill, M. J. 1998 (Celtic)   15
Burke, A. 1997 (Kilmarnock)   4
Burke, C. 2004 (Rangers)   3
Burley, C. W. 1992 (Chelsea)   7
Burley, G. E. 1977 (Ipswich T)   5
Burns, H. 1985 (Rangers)   2
Burns, T. 1977 (Celtic)   5

Caddis, P. 2008 (Celtic, Dundee U, Celtic, Swindon T)   13
Cairney, T. 2011 (Hull C)   2
Caldwell, G. 2000 (Newcastle U)   19
Caldwell, S. 2001 (Newcastle U)   4
Cameron, G. 2008 (Dundee U)   3
Campbell, R. 2008 (Hibernian)   6
Campbell, S. 1989 (Dundee)   3
Campbell, S. P. 1998 (Leicester C)   15
Canero, P. 2000 (Kilmarnock)   17
Carey, L. A. 1998 (Bristol C)   1
Casey, J. 1978 (Celtic)   1

Christie, M. 1992 (Dundee)   3
Clark, R. B. 1977 (Aberdeen)   3
Clarke, S. 1984 (St Mirren)   8
Clarkson, D. 2004 (Motherwell)   13
Cleland, A. 1990 (Dundee U)   11
Cole, D. 2011 (Rangers)   1
Collins, J. 1988 (Hibernian)   8
Collins, N. 2005 (Sunderland)   7
Connolly, P. 1991 (Dundee U)   3
Connor, R. 1981 (Ayr U)   2
Conroy, R. 2007 (Celtic)   4
Considine, A. 2007 (Aberdeen)   5
Cooper, D. 1977 (Clydebank, Rangers)   6
Cooper, N. 1982 (Aberdeen)   13
Coutts, P. A. 2009 (Peterborough U, Preston NE)   7
Crabbe, S. 1990 (Hearts)   2
Craig, M. 1998 (Aberdeen)   2
Craig, T. 1977 (Newcastle U)   1
Crainey, S. D. 2000 (Celtic)   7
Crainie, D. 1983 (Celtic)   1
Crawford, S. 1994 (Raith R)   19
Creaney, G. 1991 (Celtic)   11
Cummings, W. 2000 (Chelsea)   8
Cuthbert, S. 2007 (Celtic, St Mirren)   13

Dailly, C. 1991 (Dundee U)   34
Dalglish, P. 1999 (Newcastle U, Norwich C)   6
Dargo, C. 1998 (Raith R)   10
Davidson, C. I. 1997 (St Johnstone)   2
Davidson, H. N. 2000 (Dundee U)   3
Davidson, M. 2011 (St Johnstone)   1
Dawson, A. 1979 (Rangers)   8
Deas, P. A. 1992 (St Johnstone)   2
Dempster, J. 2004 (Rushden & D)   1
Dennis, S. 1992 (Raith R)   1
Diamond, A. 2004 (Aberdeen)   12
Dickov, P. 1992 (Arsenal)   4
Dixon, P. 2008 (Dundee)   2
Dodds, D. 1978 (Dundee U)   1
Dods, D. 1997 (Hibernian)   5
Doig, C. R. 2000 (Nottingham F)   13
Donald, G. S. 1992 (Hibernian)   3
Donnelly, S. 1994 (Celtic)   11
Dorrans, G. 2007 (Livingston)   6
Dow, A. 1993 (Dundee, Chelsea)   3
Dowie, A. J. 2003 (Rangers, Partick Th)   14
Duff, J. 2009 (Inverness CT)   1
Duff, S. 2003 (Dundee U)   9
Duffie, K. 2011 (Falkirk)   1
Duffy, D. A. 2005 (Falkirk, Hull C)   8
Duffy, J. 1987 (Dundee)   1
Durie, G. S. 1987 (Chelsea)   4
Durrant, I. 1987 (Rangers)   4
Doyle, J. 1981 (Partick Th)   2

Easton, B. 2009 (Hamilton A)   3
Easton, C. 1997 (Dundee U)   21
Elliot, B. 1998 (Celtic)   2
Elliot, C. 2006 (Hearts)   9
Esson, R. 2000 (Aberdeen)   7

Fagan, S. M. 2005 (Motherwell)   1
Ferguson, B. 1997 (Rangers)   12
Ferguson, D. 1987 (Rangers)   5
Ferguson, D. 1992 (Dundee U)   7
Ferguson, D. 1992 (Manchester U)   5
Ferguson, I. 1983 (Dundee)   4
Ferguson, I. 1989 (Clyde, St Mirren, Rangers)   6
Ferguson, R. 1977 (Hamilton A)   1
Findlay, W. 1991 (Hibernian)   5
Fitzpatrick, A. 1977 (St Mirren)   5
Fitzpatrick, M. 2007 (Motherwell)   4

Flannigan, C. 1993 (Clydebank)	1
Fleck, J. 2009 (Rangers)	**4**
Fleck, R. 1987 (Rangers, Norwich C)	6
Fleming, G. 2008 (Gretna)	1
Fletcher, D. B. 2003 (Manchester U)	2
Fletcher, S. 2007 (Hibernian)	7
Forrest, J. 2011 (Celtic)	**3**
Foster, R. M. 2005 (Aberdeen)	5
Fotheringham, M. M. 2004 (Dundee)	3
Fowler, J. 2002 (Kilmarnock)	3
Foy, R. A. 2004 (Liverpool)	5
Fraser, S. T. 2000 (Luton T)	4
Freedman, D. A. 1995 (Barnet, C Palace)	8
Fridge, L. 1989 (St Mirren)	2
Fullarton, J. 1993 (St Mirren)	17
Fulton, M. 1980 (St Mirren)	5
Fulton, S. 1991 (Celtic)	7
Gallacher, K. W. 1987 (Dundee U)	7
Gallacher, P. 1999 (Dundee U)	7
Gallacher, S. 2009 (Rangers)	**2**
Gallagher, P. 2003 (Blackburn R)	11
Galloway, M. 1989 (Hearts, Celtic)	2
Gardiner, J. 1993 (Hibernian)	1
Geddes, R. 1982 (Dundee)	5
Gemmill, S. 1992 (Nottingham F)	4
Germaine, G. 1997 (WBA)	1
Gilles, R. 1997 (St Mirren)	7
Gillespie, G. T. 1979 (Coventry C)	8
Glass, S. 1995 (Aberdeen)	11
Glover, L. 1988 (Nottingham F)	3
Goodwillie, D. 2009 (Dundee U)	**9**
Goram, A. L. 1987 (Oldham Ath)	1
Gordon, C. S. 2003 (Hearts)	5
Gough, C. R. 1983 (Dundee U)	5
Graham, D. 1998 (Rangers)	8
Grant, P. 1985 (Celtic)	10
Gray, D. P. 2009 (Manchester U)	2
Gray, S. 1987 (Aberdeen)	1
Gray S. 1995 (Celtic)	7
Griffiths, L. 2010 (Dundee, Wolverhampton W)	**5**
Gunn, B. 1984 (Aberdeen)	9
Hagen, D. 1992 (Rangers)	8
Hamill, J. 2008 (Kilmarnock)	11
Hamilton, B. 1989 (St Mirren)	4
Hamilton, J. 1995 (Dundee, Hearts)	14
Hammell, S. 2001 (Motherwell)	11
Handyside, P. 1993 (Grimsby T)	7
Hanley, G. 2011 (Blackburn R)	**1**
Hanlon, P. 2009 (Hibernian)	**12**
Hannah, D. 1993 (Dundee U)	16
Harper, K. 1995 (Hibernian)	7
Hartford, R. A. 1977 (Manchester C)	1
Hartley, P. J. 1997 (Millwall)	1
Hegarty, P. 1987 (Dundee U)	6
Hendry, J. 1992 (Tottenham H)	1
Hetherston, B. 1997 (St Mirren)	1
Hewitt, J. 1982 (Aberdeen)	6
Hogg, G. 1984 (Manchester U)	4
Hood, G. 1993 (Ayr U)	3
Horn, R. 1997 (Hearts)	6
Howie, S. 1993 (Cowdenbeath)	5
Hughes, R. D. 1999 (Bournemouth)	9
Hughes, S. 2002 (Rangers)	12
Hunter, G. 1987 (Hibernian)	3
Hunter, P. 1989 (East Fife)	3
Hutton, A. 2004 (Rangers)	7
Hutton, K. 2011 (Rangers)	**1**
Inman, B. 2011 (Newcastle U)	**2**
Irvine, G. 2006 (Celtic)	2
James, K. F. 1997 (Falkirk)	1
Jardine, I. 1979 (Kilmarnock)	1
Jess, E. 1990 (Aberdeen)	14
Johnson, G. I. 1992 (Dundee U)	6
Johnston, A. 1994 (Hearts)	3

Johnston, F. 1993 (Falkirk)	1
Johnston, M. 1984 (Partick Th, Watford)	3
Jordan, A. J. 2000 (Bristol C)	3
Jupp, D. A. 1995 (Fulham)	9
Kennedy, J. 2003 (Celtic)	15
Kenneth, G. 2008 (Dundee U)	8
Kerr, B. 2003 (Newcastle U)	14
Kerr, M. 2001 (Kilmarnock)	1
Kerr, S. 1993 (Celtic)	10
Kinniburgh, W. D. 2004 (Motherwell)	3
Kirkwood, D. 1990 (Hearts)	1
Kyle, K. 2001 (Sunderland)	12
Lambert, P. 1991 (St Mirren)	11
Langfield, J. 2000 (Dundee)	2
Lappin, S. 2004 (St Mirren)	10
Lauchlan, J. 1998 (Kilmarnock)	11
Lavety, B. 1993 (St Mirren)	9
Lavin, G. 1993 (Watford)	7
Lawson, P. 2004 (Celtic)	10
Leighton, J. 1982 (Aberdeen)	1
Lennon, S. 2008 (Rangers)	6
Levein, C. 1985 (Hearts)	2
Leven, P. 2005 (Kilmarnock)	2
Liddell, A. M. 1994 (Barnsley)	12
Lindsey, J. 1979 (Motherwell)	1
Locke, G. 1994 (Hearts)	10
Love, G. 1995 (Hibernian)	1
Loy, R. 2009 (Dunfermline Ath, Rangers)	5
Lynch, S. 2003 (Celtic, Preston NE)	13
McAllister, G. 1990 (Leicester C)	1
McAllister, R. 2008 (Inverness CT)	2
McAlpine, H. 1983 (Dundee U)	5
McAnespie, K. 1998 (St Johnstone)	4
McArthur, J. 2008 (Hamilton A)	2
McAuley, S. 1993 (St Johnstone)	1
McAvennie, F. 1982 (St Mirren)	5
McBride, J. 1981 (Everton)	1
McBride, J. P. 1998 (Celtic)	2
McCall, A. S. M. 1988 (Bradford C, Everton)	2
McCann, K. 2008 (Hibernian)	4
McCann, N. 1994 (Dundee)	9
McClair, B. 1984 (Celtic)	8
McCluskey, G. 1979 (Celtic)	6
McCluskey, S. 1997 (St Johnstone)	2
McCoist, A. 1984 (Rangers)	1
McConnell, I. 1997 (Clyde)	1
McCormack, D. 2008 (Hibernian)	1
McCormack, R. 2006 (Rangers, Motherwell, Cardiff C)	13
McCracken, D. 2002 (Dundee U)	5
McCulloch, A. 1981 (Kilmarnock)	1
McCulloch, I. 1982 (Notts Co)	2
McCulloch, L. 1997 (Motherwell)	14
McCunnie, J. 2001 (Dundee U, Ross Co, Dunfermline Ath)	20
MacDonald, A. 2011 (Burnley)	**2**
MacDonald, J. 1980 (Rangers)	8
MacDonald, J. 2007 (Hearts)	11
McDonald, C. 1995 (Falkirk)	5
McDonald, K. 2008 (Dundee, Burnley)	14
McEwan, C. 1997 (Clyde, Raith R)	17
McEwan, D. 2003 (Livingston)	2
McFadden, J. 2003 (Motherwell)	7
McFarlane, D. 1997 (Hamilton A)	3
McGarry, S. 1997 (St Mirren)	3
McGarvey, F. P. 1977 (St Mirren, Celtic)	3
McGarvey, S. 1982 (Manchester U)	4
McGhee, M. 1981 (Aberdeen)	1
McGinn, S. 2009 (St Mirren, Watford)	**8**
McGinnis, G. 1985 (Dundee U)	1
McGlinchey, M. R. 2007 (Celtic)	1
McGregor, A. 2003 (Rangers)	6
McGrillen, P. 1994 (Motherwell)	2
McGuire, D. 2002 (Aberdeen)	2
McInally, J. 1989 (Dundee U)	1
McKean, K. 2011 (St Mirren)	**1**

McKenzie, R. 1997 (Hearts)	2
McKimmie, S. 1985 (Aberdeen)	3
McKinlay, T. 1984 (Dundee)	6
McKinlay, W. 1989 (Dundee U)	6
McKinnon, R. 1991 (Dundee U)	6
McLaren, A, 1989 (Hearts)	11
McLaren, A. 1993 (Dundee U)	4
McLaughlin, B. 1995 (Celtic)	8
McLaughlin, J. 1981 (Morton)	10
McLean, E. 2008 (Dundee U, St Johnstone)	2
McLean, S. 2003 (Rangers)	4
McLeish, A. 1978 (Aberdeen)	6
MacLeod, A. 1979 (Hibernian)	3
McLeod, J. 1989 (Dundee U)	2
MacLeod, M. 1979 (Dumbarton, Celtic)	5
McManus, T. 2001 (Hibernian)	14
McMillan, S. 1997 (Motherwell)	4
McNab, N. 1978 (Tottenham H)	1
McNally, M. 1991 (Celtic)	2
McNamara, J. 1994 (Dunfermline Ath, Celtic)	12
McNaughton, K. 2002 (Aberdeen)	1
McNeil, A. 2007 (Hibernian)	1
McNichol, J. 1979 (Brentford)	7
McNiven, D. 1977 (Leeds U)	3
McNiven, S. A. 1996 (Oldham Ath)	1
McParland, A. 2003 (Celtic)	1
McPhee, S. 2002 (Port Vale)	1
McPherson, D. 1984 (Rangers, Hearts)	4
McQuilken, J. 1993 (Celtic)	2
McStay, P. 1983 (Celtic)	5
McWhirter, N. 1991 (St Mirren)	1
Maguire, C. 2009 (Aberdeen)	**12**
Main, A. 1988 (Dundee U)	3
Malcolm, R. 2001 (Rangers)	1
Maloney, S. 2002 (Celtic)	21
Malpas, M. 1983 (Dundee U)	8
Marr, B. 2011 (Ross Co)	**1**
Marshall, D. J. 2004 (Celtic)	10
Marshall, S. R. 1995 (Arsenal)	5
Martin, A. 2009 (Leeds U, Ayr U)	**12**
Mason, G. R. 1999 (Manchester C, Dunfermline Ath)	2
Mathieson, D. 1997 (Queen of the South)	3
May, E. 1989 (Hibernian)	2
Meldrum, C. 1996 (Kilmarnock)	6
Melrose, J, 1977 (Partick Th)	8
Millar, M, 2009 (Celtic)	1
Miller, C. 1995 (Rangers)	8
Miller, J. 1987 (Aberdeen, Celtic)	7
Miller, K. 2000 (Hibernian, Rangers)	7
Miller, W. 1978 (Aberdeen)	2
Miller, W. 1991 (Hibernian)	7
Milne, K. 2000 (Hearts)	1
Milne, R. 1982 (Dundee U)	3
Mitchell, C. 2008 (Falkirk)	7
Money, I. C. 1987 (St Mirren)	3
Montgomery, N. A. 2003 (Sheffield U)	7
Morrison, S. A. 2004 (Aberdeen, Dunfermline Ath)	12
Muir, L. 1977 (Hibernian)	1
Mulgrew, C. P. 2006 (Celtic, Wolverhampton W, Aberdeen)	14
Murphy J. 2009 (Motherwell)	**13**
Murray, H. 2000 (St Mirren)	3
Murray, I. 2001 (Hibernian)	15
Murray, N. 1993 (Rangers)	16
Murray, R. 1993 (Bournemouth)	1
Murray, S. 2004 (Kilmarnock)	2
Narey, D. 1977 (Dundee U)	4
Naismith, S. J. 2006 (Kilmarnock, Rangers)	15
Naysmith, G. A. 1997 (Hearts)	22
Neilson, R. 2000 (Hearts)	1
Ness, J, 2011 (Rangers)	**1**
Nevin, P. 1985 (Chelsea)	5
Nicholas, C. 1981 (Celtic, Arsenal)	6
Nicholson, B. 1999 (Rangers)	7
Nicol, S. 1981 (Ayr U, Liverpool)	14
Nisbet, S. 1989 (Rangers)	5
Noble, D. J. 2003 (West Ham U)	2

Notman, A. M. 1999 (Manchester U)	10
O'Brien, B. 1999 (Blackburn R, Livingston)	6
O'Connor, G. 2003 (Hibernian)	8
O'Donnell, P. 1992 (Motherwell)	8
O'Leary, R. 2008 (Kilmarnock)	2
O'Neil, B. 1992 (Celtic)	7
O'Neil, J. 1991 (Dundee U)	1
O'Neill, M. 1995 (Clyde)	6
Orr, N. 1978 (Morton)	7
Palmer, L. J. 2011 (Sheffield W)	**2**
Parker, K. 2001 (St Johnstone)	1
Parlane, D. 1977 (Rangers)	1
Paterson, C. 1981 (Hibernian)	2
Paterson, J. 1997 (Dundee U)	9
Payne, G. 1978 (Dundee U)	3
Peacock, L. A. 1997 (Carlisle U)	1
Pearce, A. J. 2008 (Reading)	2
Pearson, S. P. 2003 (Motherwell)	8
Perry, R. 2010 (Rangers, Falkirk)	**6**
Pressley, S. J. 1993 (Rangers, Coventry C, Dundee U)	26
Provan, D. 1977 (Kilmarnock)	1
Prunty, B. 2004 (Aberdeen)	6
Quinn, P. C. 2004 (Motherwell)	3
Quinn, R. 2006 (Celtic)	9
Rae, A. 1991 (Millwall)	8
Rae, G. 1999 (Dundee)	6
Redford, I. 1981 (Rangers)	6
Reid, B. 1991 (Rangers)	4
Reid, C. 1993 (Hibernian)	3
Reid, M. 1982 (Celtic)	2
Reid, R. 1977 (St Mirren)	3
Reilly, A. 2004 (Wycombe W)	1
Renicks, S. 1997 (Hamilton A)	1
Reynolds, M. 2007 (Motherwell)	9
Rhodes, J. L. 2011 (Huddersfield T)	**1**
Rice, B. 1985 (Hibernian)	1
Richardson, L. 1980 (St Mirren)	2
Riordan, D. G. 2004 (Hibernian)	5
Ritchie, A. 1980 (Morton)	1
Ritchie, P. S. 1996 (Hearts)	7
Robertson, A. 1991 (Rangers)	1
Robertson, C. 1977 (Rangers)	1
Robertson, D. 1987 (Aberdeen)	7
Robertson, D. 2007 (Dundee U)	4
Robertson, G. A. 2004 (Nottingham F, Rotherham U)	15
Robertson, H. 1994 (Aberdeen)	2
Robertson, J. 1985 (Hearts)	2
Robertson, L. 1993 (Rangers)	3
Robertson, S. 1998 (St Johnstone)	2
Roddie, A. 1992 (Aberdeen)	5
Ross, G. 2007 (Dunfermline Ath)	1
Ross, N. 2011 (Inverness CT)	**1**
Ross, T. W. 1977 (Arsenal)	1
Rowson, D. 1997 (Aberdeen)	5
Russell, H. 2011 (Dundee U)	**2**
Russell, R. 1978 (Rangers)	3
Salton, D. B. 1992 (Luton T)	6
Samson, C. I. 2004 (Kilmarnock)	6
Saunders, S. 2011 (Motherwell)	**1**
Scobbie, T. 2008 (Falkirk)	**12**
Scott, M. 2006 (Livingston)	1
Scott, P. 1994 (St Johnstone)	4
Scrimgour, D. 1997 (St Mirren)	3
Seaton, A. 1998 (Falkirk)	1
Severin, S. D. 2000 (Hearts)	10
Shannon, R. 1987 (Dundee)	7
Sharp, G. M. 1982 (Everton)	1
Sharp, R. 1990 (Dunfermline Ath)	4
Sheerin, P. 1996 (Southampton)	1
Shields, G. 1997 (Rangers)	2
Shinnie, A. 2009 (Dundee, Rangers)	**3**
Simmons, S. 2003 (Hearts)	1
Simpson, N. 1982 (Aberdeen)	11

Sinclair, G. 1977 (Dumbarton) 1
Skilling, M. 1993 (Kilmarnock) 2
Smith, B. M. 1992 (Celtic) 5
Smith, C. 2008 (St Mirren) 2
Smith, D. L. 2006 (Motherwell) 2
Smith, G. 1978 (Rangers) 1
Smith, G. 2004 (Rangers) 8
Smith, H. G. 1987 (Hearts) 2
Smith, S. 2007 (Rangers) 1
Sneddon, A. 1979 (Celtic) 1
Snodgrass, R. 2008 (Livingston) 2
Soutar, D. 2003 (Dundee) 11
Speedie, D. R. 1985 (Chelsea) 1
Spencer, J. 1991 (Rangers) 3
Stanton, P. 1977 (Hibernian) 1
Stark, W. 1985 (Aberdeen) 1
Stephen, R. 1983 (Dundee) 1
Stevens, G. 1977 (Motherwell) 1
Stevenson, L. 2008 (Hibernian) 8
Stewart, C. 2002 (Kilmarnock) 1
Stewart, J. 1978 (Kilmarnock, Middlesbrough) 3
Stewart, M. J. 2000 (Manchester U) 17
Stewart, R. 1979 (Dundee U, West Ham U) 12
Stillie, D. 1995 (Aberdeen) 14
Strachan, G. D. 1980 (Aberdeen) 1
Strachan, G. D. 1998 (Coventry C) 7
Sturrock, P. 1977 (Dundee U) 9
Sweeney, P. H. 2004 (Millwall) 8
Sweeney, S. 1991 (Clydebank) 1

Tarrant, N. K. 1999 (Aston Villa) 5
Teale, G. 1997 (Clydebank, Ayr U) 6
Telfer, P. N. 1993 (Luton T) 3
Templeton, D. 2011 (Hearts) **2**
Thomas, K. 1993 (Hearts) 8
Thompson, S. 1997 (Dundee U) 12
Thomson, C. 2011 (Hearts) **2**
Thomson, K. 2005 (Hibernian) 6
Thomson, W. 1977 (Partick Th, St Mirren) 10

Tolmie, J. 1980 (Morton) 1
Tortolano, J. 1987 (Hibernian) 2
Turner, I. 2005 (Everton) 6
Tweed, S. 1993 (Hibernian) 3

Wales, G. 2000 (Hearts) 1
Walker, A. 1988 (Celtic) 1
Wallace, I. A. 1978 (Coventry C) 1
Wallace, L. 2007 (Hearts) 10
Wallace, R. 2004 (Celtic, Sunderland) 4
Walsh, C. 1984 (Nottingham F) 5
Wark, J. 1977 (Ipswich T) 8
Watson, A. 1981 (Aberdeen) 4
Watson, K. 1977 (Rangers) 2
Watt, M. 1991 (Aberdeen) 12
Watt. S. M. 2005 (Chelsea) 5
Webster, A. 2003 (Hearts) 2
Whiteford, A. 1997 (St Johnstone) 1
Whittaker, S. G. 2005 (Hibernian) 18
Whyte, D. 1987 (Celtic) 9
Wilkie, L. 2000 (Dundee) 6
Will, J. A. 1992 (Arsenal) 9
Williams, G. 2002 (Nottingham F) 9
Wilson, D. 2011 (Liverpool) **5**
Wilson, M. 2004 (Dundee U, Celtic) 19
Wilson, S. 1999 (Rangers) 7
Wilson, T. 1983 (St Mirren) 1
Wilson, T. 1988 (Nottingham F) 4
Winnie, D. 1988 (St Mirren) 1
Woods, M. 2006 (Sunderland) 1
Wotherspoon, D. 2011 (Hibernian) **6**
Wright, P. 1989 (Aberdeen, QPR) 3
Wright, S. 1991 (Aberdeen) 14
Wright, T. 1987 (Oldham Ath) 1
Wylde, G. 2011 (Rangers) **1**

Young, Darren 1997 (Aberdeen) 8
Young, Derek 2000 (Aberdeen) 5

WALES

Adams, N. W. 2008 (Bury, Leicester C) 5
Alfei, D. M. 2010 (Swansea C) **5**
Aizlewood, M. 1979 (Luton T) 2
Allen, J. M. 2008 (Swansea C) **13**
Anthony, B. 2005 (Cardiff C) 8

Baddeley, L. M. 1996 (Cardiff C) 2
Balcombe, M. 1982 (Leeds U) 1
Bale, G. 2006 (Southampton, Tottenham H) 4
Barnhouse, D. J. 1995 (Swansea C) 3
Basey, G. W. 2009 (Charlton Ath) 1
Bater, P. T. 1977 (Bristol R) 2
Beevers, L. J. 2005 (Boston U, Lincoln C) 7
Bellamy, C. D. 1996 (Norwich C) 8
Bender, T. J. 2011 (Colchester U) **3**
Birchall, A. S. 2003 (Arsenal, Mansfield T) 12
Bird, A. 1993 (Cardiff C) 6
Blackmore, C. 1984 (Manchester U) 3
Blake, D. J. 2007 (Cardiff C) 14
Blake, N. A. 1991 (Cardiff C) 5
Blaney, S. D. 1997 (West Ham U) 3
Bloom, J. 2011 (Falkirk) **1**
Bodin, B. P. 2010 (Swindon T) **6**
Bodin, P. J. 1983 (Cardiff C) 1
Bond, J. H. 2011 (Watford) **1**
Bowen, J. P. 1993 (Swansea C) 5
Bowen, M. R. 1983 (Tottenham H) 3
Boyle, T. 1982 (C Palace) 1
Brace, D. P. 1995 (Wrexham) 6
Bradley, M. S. 2007 (Walsall) **17**
Brough, M. 2003 (Notts Co) 3
Brown, J. D. 2008 (Cardiff C) 6
Brown, J. R. 2003 (Gillingham) 7
Brown, T. A. F. 2011 (Ipswich T) **3**
Byrne, M. T. 2003 (Bolton W) 1

Calliste, R. T. 2005 (Manchester U, Liverpool) 15
Carpenter, R. E. 2005 (Burnley) 1
Cassidy, J. A. 2011 (Wolverhampton W) **1**
Cegielski, W. 1977 (Wrexham) 2
Chamberlain, E. C. 2010 (Leicester C) **6**
Chapple, S. R. 1992 (Swansea C) 8
Charles, J. M. 1979 (Swansea C) 2
Church, S. R. 2008 (Reading) **15**
Clark, J. 1978 (Manchester U, Derby Co) 2
Coates, J. S. 1996 (Swansea C) 5
Coleman, C. 1990 (Swansea C) 3
Collins, J. M. 2003 (Cardiff C) 7
Collins, M. J. 2007 (Fulham, Swansea C) 2
Collison, J. D. 2008 (West Ham U) 7
Cornell, D. J. 2010 (Swansea C) **3**
Cotterill, D. R. G. B. 2005 (Bristol C, Wigan Ath) 11
Coyne, D. 1992 (Tranmere R) 7
Craig, N. L. 2009 (Everton) **4**
Critchell, K. A. R. 2005 (Southampton) 3
Crofts, A. L. 2005 (Gillingham) 10
Crowell, M. T. 2004 (Wrexham) 7
Curtis, A. T. 1977 (Swansea C) 1

Davies, A. 1982 (Manchester U) 6
Davies, A. G. 2006 (Cambridge U) 6
Davies, A. R. 2005 (Southampton, Yeovil T) 14
Davies, C. M. 2005 (Oxford U, Verona, Oldham Ath) 9
Davies, D. 1999 (Barry T) 1
Davies, G. M. 1993 (Hereford U, C Palace) 7
Davies, I. C. 1978 (Norwich C) 1
Davies, L. 2005 (Bangor C) 1
Davies, R. J. 2006 (WBA) 4
Davies, S. 1999 (Peterborough U, Tottenham H) 10
Day, R. 2000 (Manchester C, Mansfield T) 11
Deacy, N. 1977 (PSV Eindhoven) 1
De-Vulgt, L. S. 2002 (Swansea C) 2

Dibble, A. 1983 (Cardiff C)	3
Doble, R. A. 2010 (Southampton)	**6**
Doyle, S. C. 1979 (Preston NE, Huddersfield T)	2
Duffy, R. M. 2005 (Portsmouth)	7
Dummett, P. 2011 (Newcastle U)	**2**
Dwyer, P. J. 1979 (Cardiff C)	1
Eardley, N. 2007 (Oldham Ath, Blackpool)	**11**
Earnshaw, R. 1999 (Cardiff C)	10
Easter, D. J. 2006 (Cardiff C)	1
Ebdon, M. 1990 (Everton)	2
Edwards, C. N. H. 1996 (Swansea C)	7
Edwards, D. A. 2006 (Shrewsbury T, Luton T, Wolverhampton W)	9
Edwards, R. I. 1977 (Chester)	2
Edwards, R. W. 1991 (Bristol C)	13
Evans, A. 1977 (Bristol R)	1
Evans, C. 2007 (Manchester C, Sheffield U)	13
Evans, K. 1999 (Leeds U, Cardiff C)	4
Evans, P. S. 1996 (Shrewsbury T)	1
Evans, S. J. 2001 (C Palace)	2
Evans, T. 1995 (Cardiff C)	3
Fish, N. 2005 (Cardiff C)	2
Fleetwood, S. 2005 (Cardiff C)	5
Flynn, C. P. 2007 (Crewe Alex)	1
Folland, R. W. 2000 (Oxford U)	1
Foster, M. G. 1993 (Tranmere R)	1
Fowler, L. A. 2003 (Coventry C, Huddersfield T)	9
Freestone, R. 1990 (Chelsea)	1
Gabbidon, D. L. 1999 (WBA, Cardiff C)	17
Gale, D. 1983 (Swansea C)	2
Gall, K. A. 2002 (Bristol R, Yeovil T)	8
Gibson, N. D. 1999 (Tranmere R, Sheffield W)	11
Giggs, R. J. 1991 (Manchester U)	1
Gilbert, P. 2005 (Plymouth Arg)	12
Giles, D. C. 1977 (Cardiff C, Swansea C, C Palace)	4
Giles, P. 1982 (Cardiff C)	3
Graham, D. 1991 (Manchester U)	1
Green, R. M. 1998 (Wolverhampton W)	16
Griffith, C. 1990 (Cardiff C)	1
Griffiths, C. 1991 (Shrewsbury T)	1
Grubb, D. 2007 (Bristol C)	1
Gunter, C. 2006 (Cardiff C, Tottenham H)	8
Haldane, L. O. 2007 (Bristol R)	1
Hall, G. D. 1990 (Chelsea)	1
Hartson, J. 1994 (Luton T, Arsenal)	9
Haworth, S. O. 1997 (Cardiff C, Coventry C, Wigan Ath)	12
Hennessey, W. R. 2006 (Wolverhampton W)	6
Hillier, I. M. 2001 (Tottenham H, Luton T)	5
Hodges, G. 1983 (Wimbledon)	5
Holden, A. 1984 (Chester C)	1
Holloway, C. D. 1999 (Exeter C)	2
Hopkins, J. 1982 (Fulham)	5
Hopkins, S. A. 1999 (Wrexham)	1
Huggins, D. S. 1996 (Bristol C)	1
Hughes, D. 2005 (Kaiserslautern, Regensburg)	2
Hughes, D. R. 1994 (Southampton)	1
Hughes, I. 1992 (Bury)	11
Hughes, L. M. 1983 (Manchester U)	5
Hughes, R. D. 1996 (Aston Villa, Shrewsbury T)	13
Hughes, W. 1977 (WBA)	3
Jackett, K. 1981 (Watford)	2
Jacobson, J. M. 2006 (Cardiff C, Bristol R)	15
James, L. R. S. 2006 (Southampton)	10
James, R. M. 1977 (Swansea C)	3
Jarman, L. 1996 (Cardiff C)	10
Jeanne, L. C. 1999 (QPR)	8
Jelleyman, G. A. 1999 (Peterborough U)	1
Jenkins, L. D. 1998 (Swansea C)	9
Jenkins, S. R. 1993 (Swansea C)	2
Jones, C. T. 2007 (Swansea C)	1
Jones, E. P. 2000 (Blackpool)	1
Jones, F. 1981 (Wrexham)	1

Jones, J. A. 2001 (Swansea C)	3
Jones, L. 1982 (Cardiff C)	3
Jones, M. A. 2004 (Wrexham)	4
Jones, M. G. 1998 (Leeds U)	7
Jones, P. L. 1992 (Liverpool)	12
Jones, R. 2011 (AFC Wimbledon)	**1**
Jones, R. A. 1994 (Sheffield W)	3
Jones, S. J. 2005 (Swansea C)	1
Jones, V. 1979 (Bristol R)	2
Kendall, L. M. 2001 (C Palace)	2
Kendall, M. 1978 (Tottenham H)	1
Kenworthy, J. R. 1994 (Tranmere R)	3
King, A. 2008 (Leicester C)	**11**
Knott, G. R. 1996 (Tottenham H)	1
Law, B. J. 1990 (QPR)	2
Lawless, A. 2006 (Torquay U)	1
Ledley, J. C. 2005 (Cardiff C)	5
Letheran, G. 1977 (Leeds U)	2
Letheran, K. C. 2006 (Swansea C)	1
Lewis, D. 1982 (Swansea C)	9
Lewis, J. 1983 (Cardiff C)	1
Llewellyn, C. M. 1998 (Norwich C)	14
Loveridge, J. 1982 (Swansea C)	3
Low, J. D. 1999 (Bristol R, Cardiff C)	1
Lowndes, S. R. 1979 (Newport Co, Millwall)	4
Lucas, L. P. 2011 (Swansea C)	**4**
MacDonald, S. B. 2006 (Swansea C)	**25**
McCarthy, A. J. 1994 (QPR)	3
McDonald, C. 2006 (Cardiff C)	3
Mackin, L. 2006 (Wrexham)	1
Maddy, P. 1982 (Cardiff C)	2
Margetson, M. W. 1992 (Manchester C)	7
Martin, A. P. 1999 (C Palace)	1
Martin, D. A. 2006 (Notts Co)	1
Marustik, C. 1982 (Swansea C)	7
Matthews, A. J. 2010 (Cardiff C)	**5**
Maxwell, C. 2009 (Wrexham)	**9**
Maxwell, L. J. 1999 (Liverpool, Cardiff C)	14
Meaker, M. J. 1994 (QPR)	2
Melville, A. K. 1990 (Swansea C, Oxford U)	2
Micallef, C. 1982 (Cardiff C)	3
Morgan, A. M. 1995 (Tranmere R)	4
Morgan, C. 2004 (Wrexham, Milton Keynes D)	12
Morris, A. J. 2009 (Cardiff C, Aldershot T)	**8**
Moss, D. M. 2003 (Shrewsbury T)	6
Mountain, P. D. 1997 (Cardiff C)	2
Mumford, A. O. 2003 (Swansea C)	4
Nardiello, D. 1978 (Coventry C)	1
Neilson, A. B. 1993 (Newcastle U)	7
Nicholas, P. 1978 (C Palace, Arsenal)	3
Nogan, K. 1990 (Luton T)	2
Nogan, L. M. 1991 (Oxford U)	1
Nyatanga, L. J. 2005 (Derby Co)	10
Ogleby, R. 2011 (Hearts)	**3**
Oster, J. M. 1997 (Grimsby T, Everton)	9
Owen, G. 1991 (Wrexham)	8
Page, R. J. 1995 (Watford)	4
Parslow, D. 2005 (Cardiff C)	4
Partington, J. M. 2009 (Bournemouth)	**8**
Partridge, D. W. 1997 (West Ham U)	1
Pascoe, C. 1983 (Swansea C)	4
Pearce, S. 2006 (Bristol C)	3
Pejic, S. M. 2003 (Wrexham)	6
Pembridge, M. A. 1991 (Luton T)	1
Perry, J. 1990 (Cardiff C)	3
Peters, M. 1992 (Manchester C, Norwich C)	3
Phillips, D. 1984 (Plymouth Arg)	3
Phillips, G. R. 2001 (Swansea C)	3
Phillips, L. 1979 (Swansea C, Charlton Ath)	2
Pipe, D. R. 2003 (Coventry C, Notts Co)	12
Pontin, K. 1978 (Cardiff C)	1
Powell, L. 1991 (Southampton)	4

Powell, L. 2004 (Leicester C)	3
Powell, R. 2006 (Bolton W)	1
Price, J. J. 1998 (Swansea C)	7
Price, L. P. 2005 (Ipswich T)	10
Price, M. D. 2001 (Everton, Hull C, Scarborough)	13
Price, P. 1981 (Luton T)	1
Pritchard, M. O. 2006 (Swansea C)	4
Pugh, D. 1982 (Doncaster R)	2
Pugh, S. 1993 (Wrexham)	2
Pulis, A. J. 2006 (Stoke C)	5
Ramasut, M. W. T. 1997 (Bristol R)	4
Ramsey, A. J. 2008, (Cardiff C, Arsenal)	12
Ratcliffe, K. 1981 (Everton)	2
Ready, K. 1992 (QPR)	5
Rees, A. 1984 (Birmingham C)	1
Rees, J. M. 1990 (Luton T)	3
Rees, M. R. 2003 (Millwall)	4
Ribeiro, C. M. 2008 (Bristol C)	8
Richards, A. D. J. 2010 (Swansea C)	**10**
Roberts, A. M. 1991 (QPR)	2
Roberts, C. J. 1999 (Cardiff C)	1
Roberts, G. 1983 (Hull C)	1
Roberts, G. W. 1997 (Liverpool, Panionios, Tranmere R) 11	
Roberts, J. G. 1977 (Wrexham)	1
Roberts, N. W. 1999 (Wrexham)	3
Roberts, P. 1997 (Porthmadog)	1
Roberts, S. I. 1999 (Swansea C)	13
Roberts, S. W. 2000 (Wrexham)	3
Robinson, C. P. 1996 (Wolverhampton W)	6
Robinson, J. R. C. 1992 (Brighton & HA, Charlton Ath)	5
Robson-Kanu, K. H. 2010 (Reading)	**4**
Rowlands, A. J. R. 1996 (Manchester C)	5
Rush, I. 1981 (Liverpool)	2
Savage, R. W. 1995 (Crewe Alex)	3
Sayer, P. A. 1977 (Cardiff C)	2
Searle, D. 1991 (Cardiff C)	6
Slatter, D. 2000 (Chelsea)	6
Slatter, N. 1983 (Bristol R)	6
Somner, M. J. 2004 (Brentford)	2
Speed, G. A. 1990 (Leeds U)	3
Spencer, S. 2005 (Wrexham)	6
Stephens, D. 2011 (Hibernian)	**3**
Stevenson, N. 1982 (Swansea C)	2
Stevenson, W. B. 1977 (Leeds U)	3
Stock, B. B. 2003 (Bournemouth)	4
Symons, C. J. 1991 (Portsmouth)	2
Taylor, G. K. 1995 (Bristol R)	4

Taylor, J. W. T. 2010 (Reading)	**4**
Taylor, N. J. 2008 (Wrexham, Swansea C)	**13**
Taylor, R. F. 2008 (Chelsea)	**4**
Thomas, C. E. 2010 (Swansea C)	**2**
Thomas, D. G. 1977 (Leeds U)	3
Thomas, D. J. 1998 (Watford)	2
Thomas, J. A. 1996 (Blackburn R)	21
Thomas, Martin R. 1979 (Bristol R)	2
Thomas, Mickey R. 1977 (Wrexham)	2
Thomas, S. 2001 (Wrexham)	5
Tibbott, L. 1977 (Ipswich T)	2
Tipton, M. J. 1998 (Oldham Ath)	6
Tolley, J. C. 2001 (Shrewsbury T)	12
Tudur-Jones, O. 2006 (Swansea C)	3
Twiddy, C. 1995 (Plymouth Arg)	3
Valentine, R. D. 2001 (Everton, Darlington)	8
Vaughan, D. O. 2003 (Crewe Alex)	8
Vaughan, N. 1982 (Newport Co)	2
Vokes, S. M. 2007 (Bournemouth, Wolverhampton W)	14
Walsh, D. 2000 (Wrexham)	8
Walsh, I. P. 1979 (C Palace, Swansea C)	2
Walton, M. 1991 (Norwich C.)	1
Ward, D. 1996 (Notts Co)	2
Warlow, O. J. 2007 (Lincoln C)	2
Weston, R. D. 2001 (Arsenal, Cardiff C)	4
Whitfield, P. M. 2003 (Wrexham)	1
Wiggins, R. 2006 (C Palace)	9
Williams, A. P. 1998 (Southampton)	9
Williams, A. S. 1996 (Blackburn R)	16
Williams, D. 1983 (Bristol R)	1
Williams, D. I. L. 1998 (Liverpool, Wrexham)	9
Williams, D. T. 2006 (Yeovil T)	1
Williams, E. 1997 (Caernarfon T)	2
Williams, G. 1983 (Bristol R)	2
Williams, G. A. 2003 (C Palace)	5
Williams, J. P. 2011 (C Palace)	**4**
Williams, M. 2001 (Manchester U)	10
Williams, M. P. 2006 (Wrexham)	14
Williams, M. R. 2006 (Wrexham)	**6**
Williams, O. fon 2007 (Crewe Alex, Stockport Co)	11
Williams, R. 2007 (Middlesbrough)	10
Williams, S. J. 1995 (Wrexham)	4
Wilmot, R. 1982 (Arsenal)	6
Wilson, J. S. 2009 (Bristol C)	3
Worgan, L. J. 2005 (Milton Keynes D, Rushden & D)	5
Wright, A. A. 1998 (Oxford U)	3
Young, S. 1996 (Cardiff C)	5

UEFA UNDER-21 CHAMPIONSHIP 2009–11

QUALIFYING ROUND

GROUP 1
Romania 2, Andorra 0
Russia 4, Andorra 0
Latvia 4, Andorra 0
Faeroes 0, Romania 4
Faeroes 1, Russia 0
Andorra 0, Romania 2
Moldova 1, Latvia 0
Faeroes 1, Moldova 1
Latvia 0, Russia 4
Andorra 0, Russia 4
Romania 3, Moldova 0
Faeroes 1, Latvia 3
Latvia 5, Romania 1
Russia 2, Faeroes 0

Moldova 1, Andorra 0
Romania 3, Faeroes 0
Russia 3, Moldova 1
Romania 4, Latvia 1
Moldova 0, Russia 3
Latvia 0, Faeroes 1
Andorra 1, Faeroes 1
Andorra 1, Moldova 3
Russia 2, Latvia 1
Moldova 0, Romania 1
Faeroes 3, Andorra 1
Romania 3, Russia 0
Andorra 0, Latvia 1
Moldova 1, Faeroes 0
Latvia 1, Moldova 1
Russia 0, Romania 0

GROUP 2
Republic of Ireland 0, Turkey 3
Switzerland 2, Armenia 1
Armenia 2, Turkey 5
Switzerland 0, Estonia 1
Armenia 1, Switzerland 3
Estonia 2, Georgia 0
Georgia 4, Turkey 0
Estonia 1, Republic of Ireland 1
Estonia 1, Switzerland 4
Republic of Ireland 1, Georgia 1
Turkey 1, Armenia 0
Republic of Ireland 1, Switzerland 1
Georgia 1, Republic of Ireland 1
Armenia 1, Estonia 1
Turkey 1, Switzerland 3
Armenia 4, Republic of Ireland 1

Turkey 0, Estonia 0
Switzerland 1, Georgia 0
Georgia 2, Estonia 0
Republic of Ireland 1, Armenia 2
Estonia 2, Armenia 3
Estonia 1, Turkey 0
Switzerland 0, Turkey 2
Georgia 0, Switzerland 0
Republic of Ireland 5, Estonia 0
Armenia 2, Georgia 3
Switzerland 1, Republic of Ireland 0
Turkey 0, Georgia 1
Turkey 1, Republic of Ireland 0
Georgia 0, Armenia 2

GROUP 3
Luxembourg 0, Wales 0
Wales 4, Luxembourg 1
Hungary 3, Luxembourg 0
Luxembourg 0, Hungary 1
Wales 4, Hungary 1
Bosnia 0, Luxembourg 1
Wales 2, Italy 1
Italy 2, Luxembourg 0
Wales 2, Bosnia 0
Italy 1, Bosnia 1
Hungary 2, Italy 0
Luxembourg 0, Italy 4
Bosnia 2, Wales 1
Luxembourg 0, Bosnia 1
Italy 2, Hungary 0
Bosnia 0, Hungary 2
Bosnia 0, Italy 1
Hungary 0, Wales 1
Italy 1, Wales 0
Hungary 0, Bosnia 0

GROUP 4
Poland 2, Liechtenstein 0
Spain 2, Poland 0
Holland 2, Finland 0
Liechtenstein 0, Spain 4
Poland 2, Finland 1
Liechtenstein 0, Poland 5
Finland 0, Holland 1
Poland 0, Holland 4
Liechtenstein 0, Finland 4
Spain 1, Finland 0
Holland 3, Liechtenstein 0
Holland 2, Spain 1
Spain 3, Liechtenstein 1
Holland 3, Poland 2
Liechtenstein 0, Holland 3
Finland 1, Spain 1
Spain 2, Holland 1
Finland 2, Poland 0
Finland 3, Liechtenstein 0
Poland 0, Spain 1

GROUP 5
San Marino 0, Czech Republic 8
Iceland 0, Czech Republic 2
Germany 6, San Marino 0
Czech Republic 2, Northern Ireland 0
Germany 1, Czech Republic 2
Northern Ireland 2, Iceland 6
Iceland 8, San Marino 0
Iceland 2, Northern Ireland 1
San Marino 0, Iceland 6
Northern Ireland 1, Germany 1
San Marino 0, Germany 11
Northern Ireland 1, Czech Republic 2
Germany 2, Iceland 2
San Marino 0, Northern Ireland 3
Czech Republic 5, San Marino 0
Iceland 4, Germany 1
Czech Republic 1, Germany 1
Northern Ireland 4, San Marino 0
Germany 3, Northern Ireland 0
Czech Republic 3, Iceland 1

GROUP 6
Israel 1, Kazakhstan 1
Kazakhstan 2, Bulgaria 0
Kazakhstan 0, Montenegro 2
Bulgaria 3, Israel 4

Bulgaria 3, Kazakhstan 0
Montenegro 0, Sweden 2
Kazakhstan 1, Israel 2
Sweden 2, Bulgaria 1
Bulgaria 1, Montenegro 1
Kazakhstan 1, Sweden 1
Montenegro 3, Kazakhstan 1
Montenegro 1, Israel 0
Sweden 5, Kazakhstan 1
Israel 4, Bulgaria 0
Montenegro 2, Bulgaria 0
Israel 0, Sweden 1
Sweden 2, Montenegro 0
Sweden 1, Israel 2
Bulgaria 0, Sweden 1
Israel 5, Montenegro 0

GROUP 7
Croatia 0, Cyprus 2
Norway 2, Slovakia 2
Cyprus 1, Norway 3
Serbia 1, Slovakia 2
Norway 1, Croatia 3
Slovakia 1, Cyprus 0
Norway 0, Serbia 1
Serbia 2, Cyprus 0
Croatia 3, Serbia 1
Cyprus 0, Slovakia 1
Cyprus 1, Croatia 2
Serbia 3, Norway 2
Slovakia 1, Croatia 2
Croatia 1, Slovakia 1
Slovakia 2, Serbia 1
Croatia 4, Norway 1
Norway 1, Cyprus 3
Serbia 2, Croatia 2
Cyrpus 1, Serbia 3
Slovakia 1, Norway 4

GROUP 8
Malta 0, Slovenia 2
Ukraine 1, Malta 0
Malta 0, Belgium 1
Slovenia 1, France 3
Belgium 2, Slovenia 0
France 2, Ukraine 2
Ukraine 1, Belgium 1
Malta 0, France 2
Belgium 0, France 0
Slovenia 1, Ukraine 2
Slovenia 1, Malta 0
Belgium 0, Ukraine 2
France 1, Slovenia 0
Belgium 1, Malta 0
Malta 0, Ukraine 3
France 0, Belgium 1
Slovenia 2, Belgium 2
Ukraine 2, France 2
France 2, Malta 0
Ukraine 0, Slovenia 0

GROUP 9
Greece 3, Macedonia 1
Lithuania 0, Greece 1
Macedonia 1, England 2
Portugal 4, Lithuania 1
Greece 1, England 1
Macedonia 1, Lithuania 1
Greece 2, Portugal 1
England 6, Macedonia 3
Macedonia 1, Portugal 1
Greece 1, Lithuania 0
Lithuania 1, Macedonia 0
England 1, Portugal 0
Lithuania 0, England 0
Portugal 2, Greece 1
England 1, Greece 2
Lithuania 0, Portugal 1
Portugal 0, England 1
Macedonia 1, Greece 2
England 3, Lithuania 2
Portugal 3, Macedonia 1

GROUP 10
Albania 0, Scotland 1
Scotland 5, Albania 2

Belarus 2, Austria 1
Albania 1, Azerbaijan 0
Austria 1, Scotland 0
Azerbaijan 2, Belarus 3
Austria 3, Albania 1
Azerbaijan 1, Austria 2
Scotland 1, Belarus 0
Belarus 4, Albania 2
Albania 2, Austria 2
Azerbaijan 0, Scotland 4
Albania 1, Belarus 2
Austria 4, Azerbaijan 0
Scotland 2, Azerbaijan 2
Austria 3, Belarus 3
Belarus 1, Scotland 1
Azerbaijan 3, Albania 2
Belarus 1, Azerbaijan 0
Scotland 2, Austria 1

PLAY-OFFS FIRST LEG
Switzerland 4, Sweden 1
Iceland 2, Scotland 1
Czech Republic 3, Greece 0
Italy 2, Belarus 0
England 2, Romania 1
Holland 1, Ukraine 3
Spain 2, Croatia 1

PLAY-OFFS SECOND LEG
Sweden 1, Switzerland 1
Scotland 1, Iceland 2
Greece 0, Czech Republic 2
Belarus 3, Italy 0
Romania 0, England 0
Ukraine 0, Holland 2
Croatia 0, Spain 3

FINALS (in Denmark)

GROUP A
Belarus 2, Iceland 0
Denmark 0, Switzerland 1
Switzerland 2, Iccland 0
Denmark 2, Belarus 1
Iceland 3, Denmark 1
Switzerland 3, Belarus 0

GROUP B
Czech Republic 2, Ukraine 1
Spain 1, England 1
Czech Republic 0, Spain 2
Ukraine 0, England 0
England 1, Czech Republic 2
Ukraine 0, Spain 3

SEMI-FINALS
Spain 3, Belarus 1
Switzerland 1, Czech Republic 0

MATCH FOR THIRD PLACE
Czech Republic 0, Belarus 1

FINAL
Spain (1) 2 *(Herrera 41, Alcantara 81)*
Switzerland (0) 0

Spain: De Gea; Alvaro Dominguez, Javi Martinez, Adrian Lopez (Suarez 80), Mata, Montoya, Vila, Herrera (Capel 90), Alcantara, Botia, Muniain (Parejo 85).
Switzerland: Sommer; Koch, Rossini, Lustenberger, Emeghara (Gavranovic 53), Frei (Abrashi 54), Shaqiri, Mehmedi, Xhaka (Kasami 67), Klose, Berardi.
Referee: Tagliavento (Italy).

FA SCHOOLS & YOUTH GAMES 2010–11

ENGLAND UNDER-16

FRIENDLY

15 February *(in Koper)*.

Slovenia 0   England 0

England: Gunn (Fry 41); Inniss (Rothwell 63); Clark (Shaw 41), Akpom, Chambers (Webb 15), Gordon, Mitchell, Poyet, Jebb (Houghton 63), Lipman (Moli 58), Wallace (McQueen 58).

VICTORY SHIELD

15 October *(at Haverfordwest)*.

Wales 4 *(O'Sullivan 7, John 21 (pen), 28 (pen), James 31)*

England 0

Wales: Stephens; Watkins (Miles 46), Strong (Barrow 41), Dalley, Yorwerth, Weeks, Holden (Williams L 66), Jones G, James (Reid 41), O'Sullivan (Bowen 53), John.
England: Rose; Facey, Johns (Clark 41), Graham, Hayden (Swift 41), Houghton, Poyet, Ward (Woodland 69), Long (Lipman 41), Moli (Mitchell 71), Chambers.

23 March *(in Ballymena)*.

Northern Ireland 0

England 3 *(Cole 39, Jebb 55, Rothwell 71)*

England: Gunn; Rothwell, Jebb (Glendon 70), Houghton, Campbell (Lewis 41), Cole (Mitchell 65), Dabo, Gorman (Akpom 41), Hayden, Wilson, Ormonde-Ottewill (Johns 68).

30 March *(at Morecambe)*.

England 2 *(Moli 7, Inniss 30)* **Scotland 1** *(Kirwan 71)* 2352

England: Willis; Chambers, Facey (Pearson 48), Graham (Long 62), Inniss, Lipman (Gordon 41), Moli (Thomas 62), Poyet (Robinson 41), Shaw, Wallace, Rothwell.
Scotland: Crump; Ramsay, Madden (Lunday 38), Turnbull, Findlay, Lindsay, Storie (Murdoch 64), Munn (Kirwan 28), Johnstone (Sibbald 73), Kidd, Smith (Finnie 40).

	P	W	D	L	F	A	Pts
England	3	2	0	1	5	5	6
Wales	3	1	1	1	5	2	4
Scotland	3	1	1	1	5	3	4
Northern Ireland	3	1	0	2	1	6	3

ENGLAND UNDER-17

Ansah (Arsenal); Redmond (Birmingham C); Cotton (Blackburn R); Caskey (Brighton & HA); Cousins (Charlton Ath); Chalobah (Chelsea); Clayton, Garratt, Powell (Crewe Alex); Browning, Hope, Johns, Lundstram (Everton); Belford, Dunn, Morgan, Regan, Smith, Sterling (Liverpool); Woodrow (Luton T); Evans, Henshall, Hutton, Walters, Plummer (Manchester C); Blackett, Hendrie (Manchester U); Jackson (Middlesbrough); Magri (Portsmouth); Willis (Sheffield U); Ward-Prowse (Southampton); Pickford (Sunderland); Lewis, Nabi (WBA); Fanimo, Turgott (West Ham U).

NORDIC TOURNAMENT

3 August *(in Vaasa)*.

Finland 0

England 5 *(Morgan 18, 78, Caskey 40, Nabi 66, 67)*

England: Willis; Henshall (Fanimo 71), Hutton, Jackson, Johns, Lundstram, Plummer (Walters 74), Browning, Caskey (Ward-Prowse 66), Morgan, Nabi (Redmond 71).

4 August *(in Kauhava)*.

England 2 *(Redmond 69, Clayton 73)*

Denmark 0

England: Lewis; Lundstram (Browning 66), Plummer, Redmond (Nabi 74), Caskey (Hutton 41), Fanimo, Clayton, Morgan (Henshall 41), Ward-Prowse, Magri, Walters.

6 August *(in Vaasa)*.

Iceland 0

England 2 *(Clayton 49, Sveinsson 83 (og))*

England: Willis; Browning, Johns, Jackson (Caskey 60), Redmond, Fanimo (Morgan 65), Clayton, Hutton, Ward-Prowse (Magri 60), Nabi, Walters.

8 August *(in Vaasa)*.

England 2 *(Clayton 5, Morgan 47)*

Sweden 1 *(Soderstrom 43)*

England: Lewis; Browning, Magri, Walters, Plummer (Johns 41), Lundstram, Caskey (Hutton 67), Clayton (Ward-Prowse 77), Fanimo (Nabi 72), Morgan, Henshall (Redmond 67).

FRIENDLY TOURNAMENTS

25 August *(at Lincoln)*.

England 2 *(Hope 45 (pen), Regan 48)*

Turkey 2 *(Ibrahim 17, 34)*

England: Pickford; Clayton (Caskey 64), Henshall (Hendrie 41), Plummer (Chalobah 72), Magri, Regan, Powell, Cotton (Fanimo 41), Sterling (Walters 72), Hope (Morgan 65), Cousins.

27 August *(at Grimsby)*.

England 4 *(Fanimo 34, Walters 37, Sterling 44, Powell 80)*

Australia 0 2040

England: Garratt; Henshall, Magri, Chalobah (Clayton 41), Regan (Plummer 56), Cousins (Powell 41), Hendrie, Caskey, Fanimo (Sterling 41), Walters, Morgan (Hope 64).

29 August *(at Scunthorpe)*.

England 3 *(Hope 21, 26, Powell 45)*

Portugal 1 *(Cancelo 51)* 804

England: Pickford; Cousins, Magri (Regan 50), Walters (Hendrie 41) (Caskey 62), Plummer, Clayton, Cotton, Chalobah, Powell (Henshall 50), Sterling, Hope (Morgan 65).

EUROPEAN CHAMPIONSHIP

18 October *(in Tbilisi)*.

Sweden 0   England 3 *(Hope 8, 42, Magri 23)*

England: Pickford; Chalobah, Regan, Powell (Turgott 65), Sterling (Fanimo 56), Hope, Magri (Walters 41), Cousins, Redmond, Jackson.

20 October *(in Tbilisi)*.

Georgia 1 *(Arabuli 63)*   **England 1** *(Hope 9)*

England: Pickford; Chalobah (Hendrie 54), Regan, Powell, Sterling, Fanimo (Morgan 70), Hope, Walters, Jackson, Caskey (Turgott 54), Cousins.

23 October *(in Tbilisi)*.

Poland 0   England 1 *(Turgott 61)*

England: Pickford; Chalobah, Regan, Powell, Cotton (Hendrie 70), Sterling (Fanimo 73), Hope (Morgan 61), Cousins, Redmond, Jackson, Turgott.

26 March *(in Geel)*.

Northern Ireland 2 *(McCartan 35, 65 (pen))*

England 3 *(Turgott 40, Hope 42 (pen), Powell 49)*

Northern Ireland: Brennan; McLaughlin, Jones, McNair, Barton, Wilson, McCarten, McElroy, Healey (McKinney 73), Rogan (McAloon 41), McGeehan (Ball 33).
England: Pickford; Chalobah, Cousins, Turgott (Clayton 66), Henshall, Lundstram, Redmond, Hope (Morgan 53), Powell (Caskey 57), Smith, Magri.

28 March *(in Geel)*.

Belgium 1 *(Cabumi 37)*

England 2 *(Powell 40, Turgott 66)*

England: Pickford; Cousins, Lundstram, Clayton (Turgott 53), Redmond, Morgan (Hope 61), Chalobah, Sterling (Jackson 74), Magri, Powell, Smith.

31 March *(in Mol)*.

Spain 1 *(Iniguez 80)* **England 2** *(Redmond 55, Jackson 62)*

England: Pickford; Cousins, Jackson, Lundstram, Redmond, Chalobah, Hope, Sterling, Powell (Caskey 74), Magri, Smith.

EUROPEAN CHAMPIONSHIP FINALS

3 May *(in Indjija)*.

France 2 *(Haller 16, 65)* **England 2** *(Hope 8, Powell 28)*

England: Pickford; Cousins, Smith, Lundstram, Jackson, Powell (Morgan 71), Hope, Magri, Henshall (Clayton 71), Redmond, Turgott.

6 May *(in Novi Sad)*.

Denmark 2 *(Fischer 13, Zohore 21)* **England 0** 1082

England: Pickford; Cousins, Smith, Lundstram, Chalobah, Sterling (Clayton 38), Powell, Hope (Morgan 66), Magri, Redmond (Henshall 55), Turgott.

9 May *(in Indjija)*.

Serbia 0 **England 3** *(Smith 7, Hope 9, 18)* 3950

England: Pickford; Cousins, Smith, Lundstram, Chalobah, Powell (Clayton 40), Hope (Morgan 65), Caskey, Magri, Henshall, Turgott (Redmond 74).

12 May *(in Novi Sad)*.

Holland 1 *(Ebecilio 26)* **England 0**

England: Pickford; Cousins, Smith, Lundstram, Jackson (Morgan 50), Chalobah, Hope, Caskey (Clayton 66), Magri, Henshall (Redmond 50), Turgott.

ALGARVE TOURNAMENT

24 February *(in Lagos)*.

Romania 1 *(Iancu 25)* **England 1** *(Woodrow 44)*

England: Garratt; Walters (Regan 65), Jackson, Turgott, Evans (Henshall 74), Blackett, Dunn (Nabi 65), Woodrow (Clayton 65), Redmond (Ansah 65), Ward-Prowse (Lundstram 41).

25 February *(in Algarve)*.

Germany 3 *(Berko 12, Ayhan 53, Yesil 62)* **England 1** *(Ansah 56)*

England: Belford; Regan, Cousins, Walters (Ward-Prowse 41), Turgott, Nabi (Evans 64), Henshall, Lundstram (Redmond 64), Clayton (Jackson 70), Magri (Dunn 70), Ansah (Woodrow 70).

27 February *(in Lagos)*.

Portugal 2 *(Teixeira 52 (pen), Medeiros 80)* **England 2** *(Henshall 16, Jackson 18)*

England: Garratt (Belford 41); Regan, Cousins (Walters 46), Jackson (Magri 21), Nabi (Turgott 41), Henshall (Blackett 76), Evans, Lundstram (Ward-Prowse 32), Clayton (Woodrow 56), Ansah, Redmond (Dunn! 41).

FIFA WORLD CUP

19 June *(in Pachuca)*.

Rwanda 0

England 2 *(Hope 68, Sterling 86)* 12,600

England: Pickford; Cousins, Smith (Regan 73), Lundstram, Chalobah, Sterling, Powell, Hope (Morgan 85), Caskey (Clayton 77), Magri, Turgott.

23 June *(in Pachuca)*.

Canada 2 *(Jalali 50, Roberts 88)*

England 2 *(Morgan 46, Turgott 76)* 17,882

England: Pickford; Cousins, Lundstram (Turgott 69), Chalobah, Sterling, Powell (Clayton 59), Caskey, Morgan, Magri, Redmond (Dunn 82), Regan.

25 June *(in Torreon)*.

Uruguay 0

England 2 *(Chalobah 45, Clayton 58)*

England: Pickford; Cousins, Smith, Chalobah, Powell (Dunn 71), Hope, Clayton, Caskey (Evans 53), Magri (Jackson 54), Henshall, Turgott.

30 June *(in Pachuca)*.

Argentina 1 *(Padilla 12)*

England 1 *(Sterling 40)*

England won 4-2 on penalties.
England: Pickford; Cousins, Smith, Chalobah, Sterling (Morgan 81), Powell (Lundstram 65), Hope, Clayton, Caskey, Magri, Turgott (Redmond 71).

4 July *(in Morelia)*.

Germany (2) 3 *(Yesil 7, 54, Ayhan 24)*

England (0) 2 *(Magri 67 (pen), Hope 83)* 16,020

England: Pickford; Cousins, Smith, Lundstram (Dunn 68), Chalobah, Sterling, Hope, Clayton, Caskey (Redmond 79), Magri, Henshall (Powell 46).

ENGLAND UNDER-18

Aneke (Arsenal); Thomas (Coventry C); Bidwell (Everton); Hopper (Leicester C); Fowler, Gibson (Middlesbrough); Alnwick (Newcastle U); Bamford (Nottingham F); Nelson (Plymouth Arg); Long (Sheffield U); Laing (Sunderland); Hall, Moncur (West Ham U).

16 November *(at Wycombe)*.

England 3 *(Taft 44, Berahino 51, Obita 80)*

Poland 0 2250

England: Alnwick (Pickford 83); Ramm, Garbutt (Pearson 69), Thorpe, Taft (Robinson 46), Berahino (Bamford 68), Coady, Yennaris, Aneke (Moncur 69), Morrison (Fowler 81), Oxlade-Chamberlain (Obita 46).

12 April *(in Carpi)*.

Italy 1 *(Beltrame 62)*

England 1 *(Berahino 44)*

England: Alnwick (Long 82); Pilatos, Gibson, Coady, Laing, Lascelles (Bamford 46), Thorne (Bidwell 46), Moncur (Nelson 72), Berahino (Fowler 65), Thomas, Hall (Hopper 65).

CENTENARY SHIELD

4 March *(at Telford)*.

England 0

Northern Ireland 2 *(McGuigan 40, Winchester 82)* 781

25 Mar *(at Yeovil)*.

England 1 *(Aryis 52)*

Wales 0 6197

21 April *(at Inverness)*.

Scotland 1 *(Love)*

England 0

28 April *(in Dublin)*.

Republic of Ireland 2

England 3 *(De Abreu 38, 82, Wood 52)* 1000

Northern Ireland 2, Scotland 2
Republic of Ireland 2, Wales 2
Northern Ireland 2, Republic of Ireland 0
Wales 0, Scotland 2
Scotland 1, Republic of Ireland 1
Wales 0, Northern Ireland 0

	P	W	D	L	F	A	Pts
Northern Ireland	4	2	2	0	6	2	8
Scotland	4	2	2	0	6	3	8
England	4	2	0	2	4	5	6
Republic of Ireland	4	0	2	2	5	8	2
Wales	4	0	2	2	2	5	2

ENGLAND UNDER-19

Afobe, Yennaris (Arsenal); Gardner (Aston Villa); Butland (Birmingham C); Dean-Conteh, McEachran (Chelsea); Jeffers (Coventry C); Zara (Crystal Palace); Barkley, Garbutt (Everton); Wickham (Ipswich T); Taft (Leicester C); Coady, Flanagan, Ince, Ngoo, Robinson, Shelvey, Wisdom (Liverpool); Kennedy (Manchester C); Fryers, Johnstone, Keane W, Thorpe (Manchester U); Pilatos, Williams L (Middlesbrough); Steer (Norwich C); Lascelles (Nottingham F); MacDonald, Mills, Obita (Reading); Slew (Sheffield U); Oxlade-Chamberlain (Southampton); Laing (Sunderland); Bostock, Carroll Fredericks, Kane, Nicholson (Tottenham H); Berahino, Hurst, Thorne (WBA); Nicholls (Wigan Ath).

UEFA QUALIFYING CHAMPIONSHIP

18 July *(in Flers).*

Austria 2 *(Alaba 52, Trauner 73)*

England 3 *(Nouble 13, 29, Cruise 55)*   2111

England: Rudd; Caulker (Thompson 87), Briggs (Clyne 56), Brown, Cruise, Bostock (Mellis 78), Delfouncso, Parrett, James, Baker, Nouble.

21 July *(in Bayeux).*

Holland 1 *(Berghuis 6)*

England 0   2113

England: Rudd; Caulker, Clyne, Brown, Mellis (Donaldson 83), Delfouneso, Parrett, Phillips (Noble 72), James, Baker, Nouble.

24 July *(in St-Lo).*

England 1 *(Phillips 90)*

France 1 *(Tafer 56)*   4620

England: Rudd; Caulker, Cruise, Mellis (Bostock 78), Clyne, Delfouneso, Donaldson (Phillips 76), Parrett (Noble 74), Thompson, James, Nouble.

27 July *(in St-Lo).*

Spain 3 *(Pacheco 12, Gallardo 34, Canales 56)*

England 1 *(Bostock 37)*   3538

England: Rudd; Baker (Bostock 18), Caulker, Cruise, Clyne, Mellis (Noble 59), Thompson, James, Delfouneso, Donaldson (Phillips 71), Nouble.

8 October *(in Vise).*

England 6 *(McEachran 17, Kane 18, 71, Wickham 45, Shelvey 88 (pen), Afobe 88)*

Albania 1 *(Shkurtaj 73 (pen))*   100

England: Johnstone; Fryers, McEachran (Williams L 46), Mills, Shelvey, Wisdom, MacDonald (Thorne 62), Barkley, Bostock, Wickham (Afobe 70), Kane.

10 October *(in Malmedy).*

Cyprus 0

England 4 *(Afobe 4, 33, 74, Shelvey 54)*   150

England: Steer; Conteh, Ngoo, Pilatos, Williams L, Wisdom, MacDonald, Bostock (McEachran 56), Shelvey (Barkley 61), Thorne, Afobe (Wickham 76).

13 October *(in Vise).*

Belgium 2 *(Mpoku 45, Van Der Bruggen 88)*

England 1 *(Ngoo 86)*

England: Johnstone; Conteh, Fryers, McEachran (Kane 61), Barkley (Pilatos 45), Thorne, Wisdom (MacDonald 45), Shelvey, Wickham, Afobe, Ngoo.

31 May *(in Yverdon).*

England 1 *(Kane 51)*

Montenegro 0

England: Johnstone; Hurst, Robinson, Wisdom, Taft, Thorne, Oxlade-Chamberlain (Ngoo 60), Coady, Kane (Williams L 72), McEachran, Ince (Obita 87).

2 June *(in Nyon).*

Switzerland 2 *(Kamber 14, Seferovic 89)*

England 3 *(Williams L 20, Ngoo 44, Thorne 90)*

England: Butland; Hurst, Robinson, Wisdom, Taft, Coady, Ngoo, McEachran (Kennedy 46), Thorne, Williams L (Oxlade-Chamberlain 62), Obita (Lascelles 76).

5 June *(in Nyon).*

England 1 *(Kane 45)*

Spain 1 *(Isco 26)*

England: Butland; Hurst, Robinson, Wisdom, Taft (Lascelles 37), Oxlade-Chamberlain, Coady, Ngoo (Berahino 60), Ince, Kane, Obita (Kennedy 71).

FRIENDLIES

2 September *(at Crewe).*

England 2 *(Ngoo 16, Shelvey 72)*

Slovakia 0   3013

England: Butland (Johnstone 46); Conteh (Jeffers 69), Fryers, McEachran (Keane 61), Mills, Ngoo (Afobe 61), Pilatos (Laing 61), Shelvey (Williams L 76), Wisdom, MacDonald, Barkley (Yennaris 46).

8 February *(at Chesterfield).*

England 0

Germany 1 *(Thomalla 42)*   9141

England: Nicholls; Robinson (Garbutt 75), Thorpe, Taft, Coady, Keane (Obita 46), Zaha (Berahino 60), Thorne (Nicholson 74), Ince (Kennedy 80), Wickham (Slew 60).

29 March *(at Putten).*

Holland 3 *(Castaignos 20, 57, John 79)*

England 0

England: Steer (Butland 61); Hurst (Fredericks 46), Garbutt (Thorne 81), Wisdom, Thorpe (Lascelles 46), Taft, Carroll (Jeffers 72), Gardner, Zaha (Obita 61), Kane (Slew 72), Ince.

ENGLAND UNDER-20

Mutch (Birmingham C); Kean, Lowe, Morris (Blackburn R); Phillips (Blackpool); Cameron, Clarke (Coventry C); Severn (Derby Co); Wallace (Everton); Stewart (Hull C); Wabara (Manchester C); Brown (Manchester U); Mason, Parrett, Smith (Tottenham H); Sordell (Watford).

FRIENDLY

9 February *(at Shrewsbury).*

England 1 *(Sordell 11)*

France 2 *(Grenier 38, Lacazette 64)*   5581

England: Kean (Severn 82); Brown, Clarke, Mutch (Wallace 82), Wabara, Cameron, Phillips, Parrett, Sordell (Smith A 62), Stewart (Lowe 46), Morris (Mason 70).

SCHOOLS FOOTBALL 2010–11

BOODLES INDEPENDENT SCHOOLS FA CUP 2010–11

FIRST ROUND
Alleyn's 7 Ewell Castle 1
Ardingly 1 Eton 2 *aet*
Birkdale 3 Aldenham 2
Cheadle Hulme 2 RGS Newcastle 2
  (aet; Cheadle Hulme won 5-4 on penalties)
Dover College 0 Brentwood 6
Dulwich College 1 St Bede's College, Manchester 0
Forest 1 QEGS Blackburn 1
  (aet; Forest won 5-4 on penalties)
Frensham Heights 1 Colfe's 3
Hampton 6 St Mary's College, Crosby 0
Ibstock Place 1 KES Witley 3
Latymer Upper 3 Bradfield 4
Licensed Victuallers 1 John Lyon 3
Malvern 1 City of London 2
Millfield 6 King's School, Chester 0
Norwich 2 Chigwell 3
Oldham Hulme GS 0 Lancing 5
Royal Russell 1 Manchester GS 6
St Bede's School, Hailsham 4 St Edmund's Cantab 0
St Columba's College 0 Bury GS 5
Westminster 0 Repton 3
Winchester 1 Grammar School at Leeds 2

SECOND ROUND
Alleyn's 5 Colfe's 1
Birkdale 1 Millfield 3
Bolton 0 City of London 3
Bradfield 4 Forest 0
Chigwell 1 Tonbridge 1
  (aet; Tonbridge won 3-1 on penalties)
Dulwich College 1 Kimbolton 4
Eton 7 Bristol GS 0
Haileybury 1 Charterhouse 6
Highgate 0 Grammar School at Leeds 1
John Lyon 4 Bedford Modern 4
  (aet; John Lyon won 5-4 on penalties)
Lancing 2 Brentwood 1
Manchester GS 1 Bury GS 1
  (aet; Bury won 4-3 on penalties)
Repton 4 QEH Bristol 0
Shrewsbury 1 Hampton 1
  (aet; Shrewsbury won 3-1 on penalties)
St Bede's School, Hailsham 1 Cheadle Hulme 1
  (aet: Cheadle Hulme won 4-2 on penalties)
Wolverhampton GS 2 KES Witley 3

THIRD ROUND
Alleyn's 2 Cheadle Hulme 1
Bradfield 2 Eton 3
City of London 0 Charterhouse 4
John Lyon 2 Bury GS 4
KES Witley 2 Kimbolton 2
  (aet; KES won 3-0 on penalties)
Millfield 5 Tonbridge 0
Repton 5 Lancing 2
Shrewsbury 1 Grammar School at Leeds 2

FOURTH ROUND
Bury GS 7 Alleyn's 1
Charterhouse 2 Repton 1 *aet*
KES Witley 2 Eton 5
Millfield 5 Grammar School at Leeds 0

SEMI-FINALS
Charterhouse 3 Millfield 2
Eton 2 Bury GS 0

FINAL (at Milton Keynes Dons FC)

Charterhouse 2 *(Lineker, Ryder-Smith)*

Eton 0

Charterhouse: O. Plummer, N. Orr, E. Strang, A. McClean, R. Carnegie-Brown, C. Kimmins (D. Bolt), T. Downes, J. Ryder-Smith, T. Gilbey (F. Payne), H. Lineker, E. Mole (F. Hamer).
Eton: T. Shaw; T. Spooner, H. Lighton, F. Shah (C. Gayner), J. Morris, H. Lloyd, R. Rogan, J. Lighton (J. Cardona), V. Ratib (B. Collins), H. Ashe-Taylor, M. Haldane.
Referee: Mr M. Atkinson (Yorkshire).

RENSBURG SHEPPARDS ISFA U15 CUP FINAL
Whitgift 4 Bolton 0
(at Burton Albion FC)

RENSBURG SHEPPARDS ISFA U13 CUP FINAL
Whitgift 2 Hampton 1
(at Burton Albion FC)

UNIVERSITY FOOTBALL 2011

127th UNIVERSITY MATCH

(Friday 6 May, at Kassam Stadium, Oxford)

Oxford 3   Cambridge 1

Oxford: Whylly, Adebasi, Squires, Ward, Beddows, Thomas (c), Quigley, Rubenstein, Healy, Wright (O'Brien), Zagajewski (Frost).
Substitutes: Haigh, Castro, Fellows.
Scorers: Ward (2), Thomas.

Cambridge: Ferguson, Peacock, Hakimi (Totten), Day (c), Revell, Broadway, Rutt (Sellman), Hartley (Baxter), Sherif, McCrickerd, Griffiths.
Substitutes: Gillingham, Hill.
Scorer: Griffiths.

Oxford have won 51 games, Cambridge 48 and 28 drawn.   *Oxford have scored 201 goals, Cambridge 199 goals.*

WOMEN'S FOOTBALL 2010–11

There have been two items in the Women's game of significant importance. The first is the creation of the long promised Super League and the other is England's senior women's team reaching and taking part in the Women's World Cup in Germany during June/July 2011.

So far as the Women's Super League is concerned, this is under the aegis of the Football Association who indicated that their intention in developing such a League was to ensure that the Country's talented players could play semi-professional football in "a top flight domestic league", which would hopefully help produce more players for international competition. In order to help foster interest and allow for more spectators, media coverage and sponsorship the League, which started on the 13th of April 2011, is a summer League. This year it has broken midway through, to enable England's women's team to take part in the aforementioned World Cup, the break being for 9 weeks and in 2012 the Olympic year the break will be shorter. So that the Super League could get a good launch the FA invested over 3 million pounds of new money in to it and looks to build the league over the forthcoming two years. A broadcast partnership was set up with ESPN to televise a number of matches and the opening period has gone well so far as attendances at matches are concerned. Another of the stated and indeed desired aims of the WSL is to encourage more women and girls to enter the game ostensibly as players and participants but also to progress in other related fields such as refereeing, coaching or becoming physiotherapists or administrators. The main differences between the WSL and the existing structure comprising the FA Women's Premier League and its pyramid leagues below are that as stated the WSL is a summer league which is semi-professional as opposed to an amateur winter league and runs from a yearly basis rather than a season's basis, whilst entry to the WSL is also on a very strict financial footing. The initial and now existing eight clubs were required to go through a stringent process and several well known women's clubs failed to make the cut. Another differentiating rule is that WSL clubs can only register 20 players although there are special provisions to cover for injuries. The clubs who have achieved 2 year licences for years 2011 and 2012 are in alphabetical order – Arsenal Ladies, Birmingham City Ladies; Bristol Academy Women; Chelsea Ladies; Doncaster Rovers Belles Ladies; Everton Ladies; Lincoln Ladies; Liverpool Ladies. As the WSL players are paid according to their contracts (although no more than 4 players a club can be paid more than £20,000 a year) there is no restriction on registering foreign international players from the EU, or elsewhere if granted a work permit. At the halfway stage in May when they broke to support the Women's World Cup squad Birmingham City Ladies led the League with 17 points from 7 games with Arsenal Ladies second with 13 points from 6 matches. The unfortunate side propping up the others was Liverpool Ladies with 3 points from 7 games. The League was due to restart on the 22nd July 2011.

Notwithstanding the creation of an older sister league, the Women's Premier League still had plenty to commend it last season, even though shorn of those sides who had upgraded to the WSL. In the National Division of the League Sunderland WFC were Champions with 30 points from their 14 games which was 7 points clear of the runners-up Nottingham Forest LFC. The relegated clubs were Blackburn Rovers LFC and Millwall Lionesses LFC who finished bottom. The Northern Division saw Aston Villa LFC take top spot with 42 points from 18 games but runners-up Coventry City LFC were only a point behind in a close-run finish. Relegated were Newcastle United WFC and bottom side Curzon Ashton. In the Southern Division the Champions were Charlton Athletic WFC making a long awaited comeback. They topped only on goal difference from Cardiff City LFC. Both sides had identical wins, draws and losses but with a goal difference of 18 to Cardiff's 7 the Robins took the laurels over the Bluebirds. The two at the bottom were Gillingham LFC in ninth spot and Yeovil Town LFC in tenth. There is also a healthy Reserve section to the League so in Mid/North Division One Everton LFC not surprisingly were top with 40 points from their 18 matches ten clear of another strong club Doncaster Rovers Belles LFC. Both of these Clubs were fielding their first teams in the WSL. In the Mid/North Division Two, Birmingham City LFC, a further side with a first team in the WSL were top with 35 points from 18 games and were another side who won on goal difference from Coventry City LFC. Again there were matching results but the goal difference was only two. The Southern Division One section was a triumph for Chelsea LFC who won it by two points over 14 games from Arsenal LFC; and finally the Southern Division Two was won by Gillingham LFC who were 9 points clear of Brighton & Hove Albion WFC notching 34 points to the Seagulls' 25 again over 14 matches.

In the Premier League Reserve Cup Final Bristol Academy, one of the most up and coming clubs, defeated Millwall Lionesses by two goals to one.

In the main FA Women's Premier League Cup Final it was perhaps the surprise team of the year Barnet Ladies who were triumphant. Not only did they finish 5th in the Premier League but they defeated Nottingham Forest Ladies (who as we have seen were runners up in the Premier League) by 4-3 on penalties after extra time. The match played on the 24th of March at Adams Park, the home of Wycombe Wanderers, saw both sides reach their first Premier Final in this competition. The teams were well matched and although Barnet had a player sent off, both at full time and after 30 minutes extra time neither side could be separated and neither had found the net. Finally in the penalty shoot-out Sally Wade netted what proved to be the winning penalty kick to give Barnet (formerly known as Wembley some years back) their crown,

Arsenal Ladies as has been their custom over many years, despite now being out of the Premier League loop, again managed to win a trophy when on the 21st of May they beat a fellow WSL team Bristol Academy Women by 2-0 to win the Women's FA Cup.

Although the women's game aspires to have its Finals at Wembley just like their counterparts in the men's game, at present their Finals have a nomadic nature. This one was played at Coventry City's Ricoh Arena, after both teams had raced to the Final with vibrant victories in their semi-finals – Bristol Academy by 3-0 against Liverpool and Arsenal 5-0 against Barnet. It was Bristol's debut final having been thwarted 3 times in semi-finals against Arsenal. Unfortunately for the Academy side, who had drawn once and lost once, to Arsenal in their two recent games in the WSL, they were destined to lose again as the Gunners triumphed by two goals to nil. Arsenal attacked from the start and almost scored in the early minutes before they did find the net in the 19th minute when Kim Little started on a mazy run which she ended with a clever curling shot into the corner of the goal. The Gunners doubled that lead in the 32nd minute when Niamh Fahey crossed perfectly from the left flank for Julie Fleeting to rise above the Bristol defence to head home. The crowd figure was 13,885 and it was Arsenal's 5th Cup win in this competition in the last 6 years.

Arsenal Ladies along with Everton Ladies were involved with the UEFA Women's Champions League for season 2010–11 and whilst Everton went out earlier Arsenal battled their way to the semi-finals. Unfortunately they went down 5-2 on aggregate over the two legs to the eventual winners. They were Olympique Lyonnais who returned to London to play FFC Turbine Potsdam at Fulham's Craven Cottage. The French side, as they had

against Arsenal, proved too strong for the German team and defeated them by 2-0, the goals coming from Wendie Renard on 27 minutes and Lara Dickenmann shortly before the final whistle. Owing to the fact that the WSL will not finish before completion of the entry period for this season's competition the two teams competing in the last Women's FA Cup namely Arsenal Ladies and Bristol Academy Women will be England's representatives for the forthcoming season.

England Women's Head Coach Hope Powell now both an OBE and CBE together with her very able second in command Brent Hills lead England's Women's senior side into the Finals of the Women's World Cup in Germany during June and July 2011. They have been drawn in a Group which also contains Mexico, Japan and New Zealand. The side has progressed over the past few years so that they were quarter finalists in the last World Cup and runners- up in the European Championship. They qualified for the current Finals not only topping their Group but remaining undefeated and have recently beaten both Sweden and the USA in friendly matches, the latter being currently rated number one in World rankings. Unfortunately this Yearbook goes to press before the details of the tournament including England's participation are known.

The Football Association are happy to report that Soccer remains the nation's number one female team sport and 1.38 million girls and women are now playing the game on a regular basis. Not only in the realms of playing but also in other fields relating to the game are numbers rising. Indeed over 200 females have obtained a coaching qualification of some kind and full time Women's Development Officers are employed across the country in the various County FAs who support female football. The FA has also been active in refereeing matters having launched a "Female Referees Strategy" and the number of women referees has increased by 21 per cent. For season 2010–11 there were three women referees on the National List of Assistant Referees. Currently there are 49 Licensed FA Centres of Excellence in England, who provide coaching and a programme for talented girls between the ages of eight and sixteen. One recent initiative was to promote the game in London for girls who had never played the game to see if they would like to give it a try, which involved the FA, the London FA, Arsenal, Tottenham Hotspur, the AFA and the National Playing Fields Association who combined to put on a "come and play" morning at Regents Park. The morning was well attended and it is hoped to make it a regular feature.

KEN GOLDMAN

FA WOMEN'S PREMIER LEAGUE 2010–11

NATIONAL DIVISION

		P	W	D	L	GD	Pts
1	Sunderland WFC	14	9	3	2	14	30
2	Nottingham F LFC	14	6	5	3	3	23
3	Reading FC Women	14	6	2	6	3	20
4	Leeds U LFC	14	5	3	6	0	18
5	Barnet FC Ladies	14	4	4	6	-2	16
6	Watford LFC	14	3	7	4	-5	16
7	Blackburn R LFC	14	4	4	6	-6	16
8	Millwall Lionesses LFC	14	3	4	7	-7	13

NORTHERN DIVISION

		P	W	D	L	GD	Pts
1	Aston Villa LFC	18	14	0	4	22	42
2	Coventry C LFC	18	13	2	3	23	41
3	Leicester C WFC	18	12	1	5	39	37
4	Manchester C LFC	18	12	1	5	19	37
5	Derby Co LFC	18	8	3	7	-1	27
6	Leeds City Vixens LFC	18	5	2	11	-15	17
7	Rochdale AFC Ladies	18	5	1	12	-21	16
8	Preston NE WFC	18	4	3	11	-24	15
9	Newcastle U WFC	18	4	3	11	-26	15
10	Curzon Ashton LFC	18	3	4	11	-16	13

SOUTHERN DIVISION

		P	W	D	L	GD	Pts
1	Charlton Ath WFC	18	11	3	4	18	36
2	Cardiff C LFC	18	11	3	4	7	36
3	West Ham U LFC	18	10	3	5	12	33
4	Portsmouth FC Ladies	18	10	1	7	3	31
5	Keynsham T LFC	18	9	3	6	4	30
6	Colchester U FC	18	6	3	9	-1	21
7	Brighton & HA WFC	18	5	4	9	-10	19
8	QPR LFC	18	5	3	10	-10	18
9	Gillingham LFC	18	5	2	11	-10	17
10	Yeovil T LFC	18	3	5	10	-13	14

FA WOMEN'S PREMIER RESERVE LEAGUES 2010–11

SOUTHERN DIVISION ONE (RESERVES)

		P	W	D	L	GD	Pts
1	Chelsea LFC	14	10	2	2	20	32
2	Arsenal LFC	14	9	3	2	33	30
3	Charlton Ath WFC	14	7	2	5	0	23
4	Bristol Academy WFC	14	5	6	3	5	21
5	Watford LFC	14	5	1	8	-6	16
6	West Ham U LFC	14	4	4	6	-8	16
7	Cardiff C LFC	14	3	2	9	-19	11
8	Reading FC Women*	14	3	0	11	-25	7

adjustment made

SOUTHERN DIVISION TWO (RESERVES)

		P	W	D	L	GD	Pts
1	Gillingham LFC	14	11	1	2	28	34
2	Brighton & HA WFC	14	8	1	5	0	25
3	Colchester U LFC	14	7	2	5	10	23
4	Barnet FC Ladies	14	5	4	5	-2	19
5	Millwall Lionesses LFC	14	4	6	4	-6	18
6	Yeovil T LFC	14	4	6	4	-6	18
7	QPR LFC	14	2	4	8	-23	10
8	Portsmouth FC Ladies*	14	2	2	10	-12	6

adjustment made

MID/NORTH DIVISION ONE (RESERVES)

		P	W	D	L	GD	Pts
1	Everton LFC	18	13	1	4	34	40
2	Doncaster R Belles LFC	18	10	0	8	2	30
3	Liverpool LFC	18	9	2	7	11	29
4	Manchester C LFC	18	9	2	7	4	29
5	Blackburn R LFC	18	9	0	9	21	27
6	Sunderland WFC	18	6	1	11	-22	19
7	Leicester C WFC	18	4	0	14	-50	12

MID/NORTH DIVISION TWO (RESERVES)

		P	W	D	L	GD	Pts
1	Birmingham C LFC	18	11	2	5	17	35
2	Coventry C LFC	18	11	2	5	15	35
3	Lincoln LFC	18	9	3	6	10	30
4	Nottingham F LFC	18	8	5	5	7	29
5	Preston NE WFC	18	6	3	9	-3	21
6	Derby Co LFC	18	5	3	10	-19	18
7	Newcastle U WFC	18	3	2	13	-27	11

PREMIER RESERVE LEAGUE CUP FINAL

Bristol Academy 2, Millwall Lionesses 1

THE FA TESCO WOMEN'S PREMIER LEAGUE CUP 2010–11

FINAL (at Wycombe)

24 March 2011
Barnet 0
Nottingham F 0   1281
aet; Barnet won 4-3 on penalties.
Barnet: Rowlands; Dempster, Wade, Prosser, Reidy (O'Leary 120), Rudman, Murphy, Sowden, Trimnell, Boardman, Pond (Lance 77).
Nottingham F: Wallhead; Gilliatt, Tomkins, Bailey, Bell, Connor-Iommi, Lawson, Clarke, Davies (Hinton 116), Stainthorpe (Howard 83), Murray (Waddell 61).

THE FA WOMEN'S CUP 2010–11
SPONSORED BY E.ON

FIRST QUALIFYING ROUND

Rutherford Ravens v Gateshead Cl'd Hall	2-5
Seaton Carew v Forest Hall WYPC	0-1
California Ladies v Ashington CFC Ladies	2-1
Prudhoe YC v Percy Main AFC L	1-6
North Shields Ladies v York C	0-11
Lumley Ladies w.o. v Walker Central removed	
Norton v Stockton Ancients v Birtley T Ladies	2-1
St Francis 2000 Ladies v Tynedale Ladies	2-2
Tynedale Ladies won 5-4 on penalties.	
Accrington G & L v Chester C	1-3
Kendal T v Morecambe Ladies	1-9
Middleton Ath v Crown Newlaithes	9-0
Abbeytown Womens v Dalton G & L	1-3
Kirklees v Bradford PA	6-1
Hemsworth MW v Steel C W	0-3
Asfordby Amat Ladies v Friar Lane & Epworth	0-5
Market Warsop v Retford U	3-0
Huntingdon T Ladies v Mansfield T	0-4
Tipton T Ladies v Rugby T	1-1
Rugby T won 4-1 on penalties.	
Crusaders Ladies v AFC Telford U Ladies	5-0
Redditch U Women's v Silverdale	4-5
Rothwell T v Leighton U Vixens	2-0
AFC Trinity Ladies v Brackley Sp	6-3
Thorplands U v Brandon Ladies	2-7
Stevenage Bor v Whitwell Ladies	4-0
Leverstock Green v Hemel Hempstead T	1-2
C&K Basildon v Colchester T	1-2
Runwell Hosp v Barking	0-4
Tring Ath v Brentwood T	0-1
Billericay T v Hoddesdon Owls	2-0
Hannakins Ladies v St Albans City Ladies	3-2
Hampstead v Leyton Ladies	5-1
Wandgas v Haringey Bor	3-3
Haringey Bor won 4-2 on penalties.	
AFC Wimbledon Ladies v Victoire Ladies	8-0
Seahaven Harriers L&G v Rottingdean Village	3-2
Christchurch v New Forest Ladies	2-4
Univ Portsmouth v Crawley Wasps	5-2
Boscombe Alb v Andover New Street	0-11
Henley T v Maidenhead U Ladies	0-2
Bitton Ladies w.o. v Reading Girls removed	
Marlow Ladies v Reading T	0-7
Forest of Dean v Stony Stratford T	1-2
Swindon Spitfires v Swindon Superm Ladies	2-2
Swindon Spitfires won 5-4 on penalties.	
Ilminster T v Launceston	2-1
Exeter C v Keynsham T Dev	1-2
Weymouth Ladies w.o. v Winscombe removed	
Purbeck Ladies v Marine Acad (Plymouth)	2-6
Stalham T Ladies v Bungay T	0-5

SECOND QUALIFYING ROUND

Peterlee T v Brandon U	5-1
Lumley Ladies v Redcar Ath	5-1
Percy Main AFC L v Forest Hall WYPC	4-2
Teesside Sp v Gateshead Cl'd Hall	4-2
Norton & Stockton Ancients v Tynedale Ladies	2-1
York C v Whitley Bay Women	2-6
Durham C v California Ladies	6-2
Whitehaven Ladies v Birkenhead Ladies	2-4
Dalton G & L v Middleton Ath	3-5
Warrington T v Blackpool Wren R	1-4
Morecambe Ladies v Bolton W	8-0

Crewe Alex v Chester C	1-0
Penrith AFC Ladies v Blackpool G & L	3-2
Huddersfield T v Hull C	5-4
Barnsley v Steel C W	2-0
Sheffield U Community v Kirklees	6-0
Guiseley Ladies v Ossett Alb	2-1
Oadby & Wigston G&L withdrew v Sandiacre T w.o.	
Long Eaton U v Mansfield T	1-1
Mansfield T won 5-4 on penalties.	
Peterborough w.o. v Hucknall T withdrew	
Market Warsop v West Bridgford	2-1
Peterborough Azure failed to fulfil fixture v Friar Lane & Epworth w.o.	
Loughborough Foxes v Shepshed Dyn	1-0
Hereford Pegasus v Cottage Farm Rangers	0-2
Bedworth U v Silverdale	4-3
Southam U v Stafford T Ladies	1-3
Crusaders Ladies v Walsall	2-3
Solihull Ladies v Rugby T	11-0
Stratford T v Lichfield Diamonds	2-0
Hethersedd Ath v Cambridge Univ	4-4
Cambridge Univ won 4-3 on penalties.	
Fakenham T v Arlesey T Ladies	1-2
Thorpe U v Bungay T	5-1
Haverhill R v Woodbridge T	1-5
Daventry T v Brandon Ladies	8-2
Corby S&L v AFC Trinity Ladies	4-2
Kingsthorpe L&G v Rothwell T	1-8
Raunds T v Kettering T	1-8
Hutton Ladies v Brentwood T	2-3
Barking v Colchester T	3-2
Hannakins Ladies v Sawbridgeworth T	2-1
Hemel Hempstead T v Boreham Wood Ladies	2-1
Billericay T v Stevenage B	1-1
Billericay T won 3-1 on penalties.	
Chelmsford C w.o. v Royston T failed to fulfil fixture.	
Panthers v AFC Wimbledon Ladies	6-1
MSA Ladies v Haringey Bor	2-0
Denham U v Hampstead	5-0
Westfield Ladies v Dorking	9-1
Ramsgate v London Cor	1-4
Milton & Fulston U v Maidstone T	1-5
Bexhill U v Seahaven Harriers L&G	1-4
Eastbourne Bor v Eastbourne T	1-7
Shanklin v Andover New Street	1-3
Aldershot T v Univ Portsmouth	1-1
Aldershot T won 3-1 on penalties.	
Chichester C v New Forest Ladies	3-0
East Preston & Little'n Ladies v Haywards Heath T	5-2
Banbury U v Cheltenham T Ladies	0-4
Beaconsfield SYCOB v Launton	3-4
Stony Stratford T withdrew v Bitton Ladies w.o.	
Oxford U v Maidenhead U Ladies	1-2
Bracknell T v Newbury Ladies	5-0
Swindon Spitfires v Salisbury C	3-4
Stoke Lane Ath v Reading T	5-0
Keynsham T Dev v Falmouth T Ladies	5-1
Ilminster T v Poole T	3-1
Marjon Old Su'ns v Marine Acad (Plymouth)	0-2
Larkhall Ath v Taunton T	5-1
Frome T v Weymouth Ladies	1-3

THIRD QUALIFYING ROUND

Birkenhead Ladies v Salford Ladies	1-2

Middleton Ath v Teesside Sp	3-1
Blackpool Wren R v Durham C	4-1
South Durham Rail Ath v Crewe Alex	2-2
South Durham Rail Ath won 4-3 on penalties.	
Percy Main AFC L v Liverpool Feds	0-7
Middlesbrough v Lumley Ladies	5-1
Whitley Bay Women v Tranmere R	2-1
Stockport Co v Norton & Stockton Ancients	4-0
Mossley Hill v Peterlee T	4-3
Morecambe Ladies v Penrith AFC Ladies	4-3
Sheffield Ladies v Bradford C	2-0
Rotherham U v Wakefield Ladies	3-1
Guiseley Ladies v Sheffield U Community	1-3
Barnsley v Scunthorpe U	3-2
Huddersfield T v Sheffield W Women	1-5
Sporting Club Alb v Market Warsop	12-0
Loughborough Foxes v Leafield Ath	2-4
Solihull Ladies v Walsall	6-1
MK Dons Ladies v Wolverhampton W	2-2
Wolverhampton W won 5-3 on penalties.	
Stratford T v Sandiacre T	6-3
Leicester C Ladies v TNS Ladies	5-0
Stafford T Ladies v Stoke C	1-8
Radcliffe Olym v Mansfield T	2-1
Peterborough v Bedworth U	3-1
Cottage Farm Rangers v Copsewood (Coventry)	0-8
Friar Lane & Epworth v Loughborough Students	1-7
Cambridge Women's v Braintree T	4-0
Luton T Ladies v Rothwell T	7-0
Thorpe U v Cambridge Univ	0-3
Kettering T v Woodbridge T	0-1
Daventry T v Corby S&L	3-2
Northampton T v Ipswich T	3-3
Ipswich T won 5-4 on penalties.	
Norwich C Ladies v Arlesey T Ladies	5-1
Chelmsford C v Barking	2-2
Chelmsford C won 6-5 on penalties.	
Brentwood T v Tottenham H	1-4
Billericay T v Enfield T	1-5
Panthers v MSA Ladics	5-1
Hannakins Ladies v Denham U	0-4
Old Actonians v Hemel Hempstead T	1-2
East Preston & Little'n Ladies v Westfield Ladies	2-1
Seahaven Harriers L&G v Ebbsfleet U	1-4
London Cor v Crystal Palace	0-1
Lewes v Chichester C	5-1
Aldershot T v Havant & Waterlooville	0-8
Maidstone T v Eastbourne T	3-1
Bracknell T v Cheltenham T Ladies	2-0
Forest Green R v Swindon T	7-2
Salisbury C v Andover New Street	3-5
Maidenhead U Ladies v Oxford C	3-4
Chesham U v Launton	8-0
Southampton Saints v Gloucester C	3-1
Plymouth Arg v Bitton Ladies	6-0
Cullompton Rangers v Marine Acad (Plymouth)	4-1
Newquay Ladies w.o. v Ilminster T failed to fulfil fixture.	
Stoke Lane Ath v Weymouth Ladies	0-1
Keynsham T Dev v Larkhall Ath	1-2

FIRST ROUND

Blackpool Wren R v Salford Ladies	2-1
Middleton Ath v Whitley Bay Women	1-2
Middlesbrough v Stockport Co	2-0
Mossley Hill v South Durham Rail Ath	2-0
Liverpool Feds v Morecambe Ladies	4-3
Loughborough Students v Leafield Ath	5-2
Barnsley v Sheffield Ladies	0-2
Sheffield U Community v Stoke C	3-4
Wolverhampton W v Solihull Ladies	4-0
Stratford T v Sheffield W Women	1-2
Radcliffe Olym v Sporting Club Alb	0-3
Daventry T v Rotherham U	1-11
Copsewood (Coventry) v Leicester C Ladies	0-2
Ipswich T v Cambridge Women's	1-2
Peterborough v Hemel Hempstead T	2-3
Norwich C Ladies v Cambridge Univ	6-1
Tottenham H v Chelmsford C	5-0
Luton T Ladies v Woodbridge T	4-1
Crystal Palace v Panthers	6-0
Ebbsfleet U v Maidstone T	3-0
Enfield T v Lewes	2-1
Chesham U v Denham U	1-2
East Preston & Little'n Ladies v Havant & W'ville	0-5
Newquay Ladies v Weymouth Ladies	4-2
Oxford C v Plymouth Arg	1-3

Forest Green R v Andover New Street	5-5
Andover New Street won 3-2 on penalties.	
Larkhall Ath v Southampton Saints	1-3
Cullompton Rangers v Bracknell T	4-2

SECOND ROUND

Blackpool Wren R v Sheffield W Women	0-6
Manchester C v Mossley Hill	2-3
Rochdale Ladies v Preston NE	3-1
Newcastle U v Liverpool Feds	2-0
Whitley Bay Women v Leeds C Vixens	1-2
Curzon Ashton v Middlesbrough	4-1
Stoke C v Cambridge Women's	3-3
Cambridge Women's won 4-3 on penalties.	
Derby Co v Rotherham U	4-2
Sheffield Ladies v Loughborough Students	1-2
Leicester C v Leicester C Ladies	5-1
Wolverhampton W v Coventry C	2-3
Aston Villa v Sporting Club Alb	0-2
Tottenham H v Colchester U	1-2
Ebbsfleet U v Gillingham	0-6
Havant & Waterlooville v Enfield T	1-2
Portsmouth v Crystal Palace	6-1
West Ham U v Norwich C Ladies	4-1
Hemel Hempstead T v Brighton & HA	3-3
Brighton & HA won 3-1 on penalties.	
Denham U v Charlton Ath	0-8
Luton T Ladies v QPR	2-1
Southampton Saints v Keynsham T	1-0
Yeovil T v Cardiff C	0-1
Newquay Ladies v Plymouth Arg	2-1
Collompton Rangers v Andover New Street	1-6

THIRD ROUND

Sunderland v Portsmouth	7-2
Mossley Hill v Luton T Ladies	3-2
Sporting Club Alb v Millwall Lionesses	0-4
Coventry C v Rochdale Ladies	1-2
Nottingham F v Leicester C	4-2
Curzon Ashton v Charlton Ath	1-3
Gillingham v Reading Women	3-5
Derby Co v Plymouth Arg	2-0
Leeds U Ladies v Blackburn R	0-0
Blackburn R won 5-4 on penalties.	
Colchester U v Newcastle U	2-1
Andover New Street v Watford	2-3
Cardiff C v Sheffield W Women	1-2
Loughborough Students v Barnet Ladies	0-4
West Ham U v Brighton & HA	1-0
Cambridge Women's v Leeds C Vixens	2-3
Southampton Saints v Enfield T	0-1

FOURTH ROUND

Enfield T v Mossley Hill	4-2
Blackburn R v Millwall Lionesses	0-3
Derby Co v Sunderland	0-0
Sunderland won 4-2 on penalties.	
Reading Women v Charlton Ath	2-2
Charlton Ath won 5-4 on penalties.	
Leeds C Vixens v Barnet Ladies	0-1
Nottingham F v Watford	3-3
Watford won 4-3 on penalties.	
West Ham U v Colchester U	4-2
Rochdale Ladies v Sheffield W Women	1-3

FIFTH ROUND

Enfield T v West Ham U	0-1
Sheffield W Women v Bristol Acad	0-8
Liverpool v Charlton Ath	5-0
Birmingham C v Barnet Ladies	1-2
Everton v Arsenal	0-2
Chelsea v Doncaster R Belles	0-1
Sunderland v Lincoln Ladies	1-0
Millwall Lionesses v Watford	5-0

SIXTH ROUND

Sunderland v Arsenal	2-3
Millwall Lionesses v Bristol Acad	1-2
Liverpool v Doncaster R Belles	3-0
Barnet v West Ham U	3-2

SEMI-FINALS

Liverpool v Bristol Acad	0-3
Barnet v Arsenal	0-5

WOMEN'S FA CUP FINAL

Saturday, 21 May 2011

Arsenal (2) 2   Bristol Acad (0) 0

(at Coventry, attendance 13,885)

Arsenal: Byrne; Houghton, Grant, Flaherty, Fahey, Nobbs, Chapman, White, Little, Yankey (Carter 90), Fleeting (Beattie 80).
Scorers: Little 19, Fleeting 32

Bristol Acad: Chamberlain; McCatty, Rose, Yorston, Culvin (Clark 68), Hoogendijk, Daley, Dykes, Fishlock (Billson 46), Bleazard, Heatherson.

Referee: S. Massey (West Midlands).

Arsenal's Julie Fleeting (left), challenged by Bristol Academy's Alex Culvin, scores the decisive second goal in the Women's FA Cup Final at the Ricoh Arena, Coventry. The Gunners won 2-0 to bring the trophy back to north London for a record 11th time in 12 showpiece appearances. (PA Photos)

FIFA WOMEN'S WORLD CUP 2011

FINALS IN GERMANY

GROUP A
Nigeria 0, France 1
Germany 2, Canada 1
Canada 0, France 4
Germany 1, Nigeria 0
France 2, Germany 4
Canada 0, Nigeria 1

GROUP B
Japan 2, New Zealand 1
Mexico 1, England 1
Japan 4, Mexico 0
New Zealand 1, England 2

England 2, Japan 0
New Zealand 2, Mexico 2

GROUP C
Colombia 0, Sweden 1
USA 2, North Korea 0
North Korea 0, Sweden 1
USA 3, Colombia 0
Sweden 2, USA 1
North Korea 0, Colombia 0

GROUP D
Norway 1, Equatorial Guinea 0

Brazil 1, Australia 0
Australia 3, Equatorial Guinea 2
Brazil 3, Norway 0
Equatorial Guinea 0, Brazil 3
Australia 2, Norway 1

QUARTER-FINALS
Germany 0, Japan 1
England 1, France 1
France won 4-3 on penalties.
Sweden v Australia
Brazil v USA

UEFA WOMEN'S CHAMPIONS LEAGUE 2010–11

QUALIFYING ROUND
GROUP 1
NSA Sofia 7, Gazi Univ 0
Brondby 6, Roma Calfa 0
Brondby 12, Gazi Univ 0
Roma Calfa 0, NSA Sofia 4
NSA Sofia 0, Brondby 3
Gazi Univ 3, Roma Calfa 3

GROUP 2
Everton 6, Klaksvik 0
Gintra 4, Borec 0
Everton 10, Borec 0
Klaksvik 0, Gintra 0
Gintra 0, Everton 7
Borec 0, Klaksvik 2

GROUP 3
Umea 3, Tel Aviv 0
Sarajevo 1, Apollon 6
Umea 1, Apollon 4
Tel Aviv 3, Sarajevo 1
Sarajevo 0, Umea 1
Apollon 3, Tel Aviv 0

GROUP 4
Juvisy Essonne 5, Targu Mures 1
Breidablik 8, Levadia 1
Juvisy Essonne 12, Levadia 0
Targu Mures 0, Breidablik 7
Breidablik 3, Juvisy Essonne 3
Levadia 1, Targu Mures 2

GROUP 5
Bardolino 7, Swansea 0
Bardolino 3, Baia Zugdidi 0
Swansea 0, Krka 4
Krka 4, Baia Zugdidi 0
Krka 1, Bardolino 4
Baia Zugdidi 1, Swansea 2

GROUP 6
Rossiyanka 5, Osijek 0
1st Dezembro 1, St Francis 4
Rossiyanka 9, St Francis 0
Osijek 1, 1st Dezembro 4

1st Dezembro 1, Rossiyanka 4
St Francis 5, Osijek 3

GROUP 7
Duisburg 3, Slovan Bratislava 0
Glasgow 8, Newtonabbey 0
Slovan Bratislava 0, Glasgow 4
Duisburg 6, Newtonabbey 1
Glasgow 0, Duisburg 4
Newtonabbey 0, Slovan Bratislava 1

FIRST ROUND FIRST LEG
Zorka-BDU 1, Roa 2
Masinac 1, Arsenal 3
Apollon 1, Zvezda-2005 2
Umea 1, Brondby 2
Legenda Chernigiv 1, Rossiyanka 3
Krka 0, Linkoping 7
PAOK 1, Neulengbach 0
Aland United 0, Potsdam 9
AZ 1, Lyon 2
Fortuna 8, Bardolino 0
Zurich 2, Torres 3
CSHVSM 0, Duisburg 5
Breidablik 0, Juvisy Essonne 3
MTK 0, Everton 0
Rayo 3, Valur 0
St Truiden 0, Sparta Prague 3

FIRST ROUND SECOND LEG
Duisburg 6, CSHVSM 0
Roa 0, Zorka-BDU 0
Zvezda-2005 2, Apollon 1
Torres 4, Zurich 1
Potsdam 6, Aland United 0
Valur 1, Rayo 1
Neulengbach 3, PAOK 0
Brondby 0, Umea 1
Bardolino 1, Fortuna 6
Rossiyanka 4, Legenda Chernigiv 0
Arsenal 9, Masinac 0
Sparta Prague 7, St Truiden 0
Lyon 8, AZ 0
Linkoping 5, Krka 0
Juvisy Essonne 6, Breidablik 0
Everton 7, MTK 1

SECOND ROUND FIRST LEG
Linkoping 2, Sparta Prague 0
Potsdam 7, Neulengbach 0
Duisburg 4, Fortuna 0
Roa 1, Zvezda-2005 1
Brondby 1, Everton 4
Torres 1, Juvisy Essonne 2
Rossiyanka 1, Lyon 6
Rayo 2, Arsenal 0

SECOND ROUND SECOND LEG
Sparta Prague 0, Linkoping 1
Zvezda-2005 4, Roa 0
Lyon 5, Rossiyanka 0
Fortuna 0, Duisburg 3
Neulengbach 0, Potsdam 9
Juvisy Essonne 2, Torres 2
Arsenal 4, Rayo 1
Everton 1, Brondby 1

QUARTER-FINALS FIRST LEG
Juvisy Essonne 0, Potsdam 3
Zvezda-2005 0, Lyon 0
Arsenal 1, Linkoping 1
Everton 1, Duisburg 3

QUARTER-FINALS SECOND LEG
Duisburg 2, Everton 0
Lyon 1, Zvezda-2005 0
Linkoping 2, Arsenal 2
Potsdam 6, Juvisy Essonne 2

SEMI-FINALS FIRST LEG
Duisburg 2, Potsdam 2
Lyon 2, Arsenal 0

SEMI-FINALS SECOND LEG
Arsenal 2, Lyon 3
Potsdam 1, Duisburg 0

FINAL
Lyon 2, Potsdam 0

ENGLAND WOMEN'S INTERNATIONALS 2010–11

FRIENDLIES

2 Apr
England 2 *(Clarke 8, Yankey 26)*
USA 1 *(Rapinoe 39)*
(at Leyton Orient).
England: Bardsley; Scott A, Stoney, Unitt, White F (Bradley 68), Scott J, Williams F, Yankey (Carney 75), Clarke, White E, Smith K.

17 May
England 2 *(Scott J 46, Carney 70 (pen))*
Sweden 0   5167
(at Oxford).
England: Bardsley (Chamberlain 78); Scott A, Unitt (Aluko 46), Asante (Carney 46), Bradley, Stoney (Whelan 87), Clarke, Scott J, White E (Houghton 46), Smith K (Rafferty 46), Yankey.

CYPRUS CUP

2 Mar
Italy 0
England 2 *(White E 3, Smith K 38 (pen))*
(in Larnaca).
England: Bardsley; Susi (Smith S 80), Unitt, White F, Yankey, Clarke (Scott A 66), White E, Stoney, Smith K, Houghton, Asante.

7 Mar
Canada 2 *(Sinclair 45, Timko 55)*
England 0
(in Nicosia).
England: Bardsley; Scott A, Susi, White F, Williams F, Yankey, White E, Bradley (Stoney 73), Smith K, Houghton, Asante.

4 Mar
Scotland 2 *(Little 26, Beattie 52)*
England 0
(in Nicosia).
England: Chamberlain; Johnson, Scott A, Stoney, Unitt, Scott J, Williams F, Clarke (Susi 68), Aluko, Bassett, Smith S.

9 Mar
England 2 *(Smith S 16, 80)*
South Korea 0
(in Larnaca).
England: Bardsley (Chamberlain 46); Johnson, Stoney, Susi (Scott A 46), Unitt (Houghton 58), Scott J, Clarke (White E 62), Aluko, Smith K, Bassett, Smith S.

THE PEACE CUP

19 Oct
South Korea 0
England 0
(in South Korea).
England: Brown; Scott A, Stoney, Scott J, Williams F, Yankey, Clarke (Aluko 74), Bradley, Houghton, Smith K (White E 60), Rafferty.

21 Oct
England 0
New Zealand 0
(in South Korea).
England: Bardsley; Johnson, Scott A, Susi (White E 75), Unitt, White F, Clarke, Aluko (Yankey 86), Smith K (Williams F 84), Bassett, Asante.

FIFA 2011 WOMEN'S WORLD CUP – QUALIFYING COMPETITION

29 July
England 3 *(Yankey 22, White E 58, Clarke 76)*
Turkey 0
(at Walsall).
England: Brown; Scott A, Stoney, Unitt, White F, Chapman, Scott J, Williams F (Bassett 77), Yankey, Clarke (Susi 77), Aluko (White E 46).

21 Aug
Austria 0
England 4 *(Scott A 40, Smith K 7, 30, White E 80)*
(in Krems).
England: Brown; Scott A, Stoney, Unitt, White F (White E 46), Chapman (Houghton 60), Scott J, Williams F, Yankey, Smith K (Bradley 46), Carney.

12 Sept
England 2 *(Williams F 44, Smith K 45)*
Switzerland 0   4119
(at Shrewsbury).
England: Brown; Scott A, Stoney, Unitt, White F, Chapman, Scott J, Williams F, Yankey (Clarke 89), Aluko, Smith K.

16 Sept
Switzerland 2 *(Bachmann 41, Zumbuhl 65)*   1800
England 3 *(Smith K 32, Aluko 34, Williams F 50 (pen))*
(in Wahlen).
England: Brown!; Scott A, Stoney, Unitt, White F, Chapman, Scott J, Williams F, Yankey (Clarke 78), Aluko (Chamberlain 42), Smith K (White E 88).

FIFA WOMEN'S WORLD CUP FINALS GERMANY 2011

27 June
Mexico 1 *(Ocampo 34)*
England 1 *(Williams F 21)*   18,702
(in Wolfsburg).
England: Bardsley; Scott A, Unitt, Scott J, White F (Bradley 83), Stoney, Williams F, Smith K, Yankey, Carney (White E 72), Aluko.

1 July
New Zealand 1 *(Gregorius 18)*
England 2 *(Scott J 63, Clarke 81)*   19,110
(in Dresden).
England: Bardsley; Scott A, Unitt, Scott J, White F (Bradley 86), Stoney, Williams F, White E, Smith K, Yankey (Clarke 66), Aluko (Carney 46).

5 July
England 2 *(White E 15, Yankey 66)*
Japan 0   20,777
(in Augsburg).
England: Bardsley; Scott A, Unitt, Scott J, Stoney, Clarke (Yankey 46), White E (Bassett 90), Smith K (Aluko 63), Carney, Bradley, Asante.

QUARTER-FINALS

9 July
France 1 *(Bussaglia 88)*
England 1 *(Scott J 59)*   26,395
(in Leverkusen).
France won 4-3 on penalties.
France: Deville; Georges, Soubeyrand (Thomis 67), Bompastor, Abily, Lepailleur, Necib (Bretigny 79) (Le Sommer 106), Bussaglia, Thiney, Delie, Viguier.
England: Bardsley; Scott A (Houghton 81), Unitt (Rafferty 81), Scott J, White F, Stoney, Williams F, White E, Smith K, Yankey (Asante 84), Carney.
Penalties: Abily (saved); Smith K (scored); Bussaglia (scored); Carney (scored); Thiney (scored); Stoney (scored); Bompastor (scored); Rafferty (missed); Le Sommer (scored); White F (hit bar).

WOMEN'S EUROPEAN UNDER-19 CHAMPIONSHIP 2010–11

Final tournament in Italy

GROUP A
Italy 2, Russia 1
Switzerland 4, Belgium 1
Italy 1, Switzerland 0
Russia 3, Belgium 1
Belgium 1, Italy 3
Russia 0, Switzerland 0

GROUP B
Germany 3, Norway 1
Spain 1, Holland 1
Germany 1, Spain 0
Norway 3, Holland 0
Holland 1, Germany 2
Norway 5, Spain 1

SEMI-FINALS
Italy 2, Norway 3
Germany 3, Switzerland 1

FINAL
Norway 1 *(Bjanesoy 72)*
Germany 8 *(Wensing 29, Schmid 50, 79, Lotzen 55, 60, Petzelberger 58, Rudelic 70, Hegenauer 88)*
Norway: Fimreite; Sonstevold (Aardalen 74), Sondena, Knudsen, Thorisdottir, Andrine Hegerberg, Skaug, Bjanesoy, Hegland, Dekkerhus (Reiten 70), Ada Hegerberg (Hansen 46).
Germany: Schmitz; Maier, Simon (Pyko 58), Elsig, Wensing, Hendrich (Hegenauer 64), Beckmann (Rudelic 63), Schmid, Petzelberger, Lotzen, Cramer.
Referee: S. Bastos (Portugal).

NON-LEAGUE TABLES 2010–11

EVO-STIK NORTHERN PREMIER LEAGUE PREMIER DIVISION 2010–11

		P	W	D	L	F	A	W	D	L	F	A	W	D	L	F	A	GD	Pts
				Total					Home					Away					
1	FC Halifax T	42	30	8	4	108	36	15	5	1	54	18	15	3	3	54	18	72	98
2	Colwyn Bay¶	42	24	7	11	67	56	12	2	7	33	30	12	5	4	34	26	11	79
3	Bradford Park Avenue	42	23	8	11	84	55	14	2	5	50	24	9	6	6	34	31	29	77
4	FC United	42	24	4	14	76	53	14	1	6	44	25	10	3	8	32	28	23	76
5	North Ferriby U	42	22	7	13	78	51	12	1	8	45	24	10	6	5	33	27	27	73
6	Buxton	42	20	10	12	71	52	10	7	4	38	20	10	3	8	33	32	19	70
7	Kendal T	42	21	5	16	80	77	12	3	6	42	34	9	2	10	38	43	3	68
8	Marine	42	20	7	15	74	64	9	4	8	41	43	11	3	7	33	21	10	67
9	Worksop T	42	21	6	15	72	54	11	5	5	38	20	10	1	10	34	34	18	66
10	Chasetown	42	20	6	16	76	59	11	4	6	40	24	9	2	10	36	35	17	66
11	Matlock T	42	20	6	16	74	59	10	3	8	35	28	10	3	8	39	31	15	66
12	Northwich Victoria	42	18	9	15	66	55	11	3	7	35	27	7	6	8	31	28	11	63
13	Stocksbridge PS	42	17	6	19	75	75	10	2	9	40	34	7	4	10	35	41	0	57
14	Ashton U	42	16	5	21	57	62	11	0	10	36	34	5	5	11	21	28	−5	53
15	Mickleover Sports	42	15	7	20	70	76	7	3	11	41	42	8	4	9	29	34	−6	52
16	Whitby T	42	14	9	19	58	77	8	5	8	31	34	6	4	11	27	43	−19	51
17	Nantwich T	42	13	7	22	68	90	10	3	8	34	41	3	4	14	34	49	−22	46
18	Frickley Ath	42	11	11	20	43	68	6	7	8	18	19	5	4	12	25	49	−25	44
19	Burscough†	42	12	7	23	56	73	7	3	11	28	32	5	4	12	28	41	−17	43
20	Hucknall T	42	11	10	21	57	80	6	7	8	35	37	5	3	13	22	43	−23	43
21	Ossett T	42	9	5	28	45	103	1	4	16	15	56	8	1	12	30	47	−58	32
22	Retford U	42	5	2	35	31	111	2	2	17	14	53	3	0	18	17	58	−80	17

Worksop T deducted 3 points. ¶Colwyn Bay promoted via play-offs. †Burscough not relegated.

ZAMARETTO SOUTHERN LEAGUE PREMIER DIVISION 2010–11

		P	W	D	L	F	A	W	D	L	F	A	W	D	L	F	A	GD	Pts
				Total					Home					Away					
1	Truro C	40	27	6	7	91	35	16	2	2	48	15	11	4	5	43	20	56	87
2	Hednesford T	40	26	5	9	82	38	14	3	3	43	17	12	2	6	39	21	44	83
3	Salisbury C¶	40	23	10	7	82	45	15	2	3	52	26	8	8	4	30	19	37	79
4	Cambridge C	40	24	7	9	74	40	12	4	4	46	21	12	3	6	28	19	34	79
5	Learnington	40	24	6	10	68	39	16	1	3	42	19	8	5	7	26	20	29	78
6	Chesham U	40	20	11	9	64	35	14	5	1	38	10	6	6	8	26	25	29	71
7	Chippenham T	40	18	14	8	54	41	12	5	3	31	13	6	9	5	23	28	13	68
8	Stourbridge	40	18	8	14	72	61	12	4	4	46	27	6	4	10	26	34	11	62
9	Brackley T	40	16	10	14	67	47	10	7	3	38	19	6	3	11	29	28	20	58
10	Swindon Supermarine	40	17	7	16	56	58	10	3	7	29	23	7	4	9	27	35	−2	58
11	Bashley	40	14	10	16	55	63	8	5	7	24	31	6	5	9	31	32	−8	52
12	Evesham U	40	14	9	17	54	49	8	6	6	32	24	6	3	11	22	25	5	51
13	Cirencester T	40	13	8	19	59	67	8	3	9	31	29	5	5	10	28	38	−8	47
14	Oxford C	40	11	12	17	48	54	4	9	7	26	27	7	3	10	22	27	−6	45
15	Hemel Hempstead T	40	13	6	21	50	59	6	3	11	16	26	7	3	10	34	33	−9	45
16	Banbury U	40	11	8	21	44	67	6	5	9	21	30	5	3	12	23	37	−23	40
17	Bedford T	40	10	7	23	41	76	6	4	10	20	33	4	3	13	21	43	−35	37
18	Weymouth	40	12	8	20	55	85	8	5	7	33	33	4	3	13	22	52	−30	34
19	Didcot T	40	7	11	22	39	69	3	5	12	16	36	4	6	10	23	33	−30	32
20	Tiverton T	40	7	8	25	33	77	5	6	9	21	31	2	2	16	12	46	−44	29
21	Halesowen T	40	5	9	26	24	107	3	3	14	14	55	2	6	12	10	52	−83	24

Banbury U deducted 1 point. Weymouth deducted 10 points. ¶Salisbury C promoted via play-offs.
Windsor & Eton record expunged following Winding Up Order on 2 February 2011.

RYMAN ISTHMIAN LEAGUE PREMIER DIVISION 2010–11

		P	W	D	L	F	A	W	D	L	F	A	W	D	L	F	A	GD	Pts
				Total					Home					Away					
1	Sutton U	42	26	9	7	76	33	17	4	0	48	16	9	5	7	28	17	43	87
2	Tonbridge Angels¶	42	22	10	10	71	45	12	5	4	41	24	10	5	6	30	21	26	76
3	Bury T	42	22	10	10	67	49	11	5	5	33	25	11	5	5	34	24	18	76
4	Lowestoft T	42	20	15	7	68	30	9	10	2	37	12	11	5	5	31	18	38	75
5	Harrow Borough	42	22	7	13	77	51	12	5	4	40	18	10	2	9	37	33	26	73
6	Canvey Island	42	21	10	11	69	51	13	4	4	39	24	8	6	7	30	27	18	73
7	Kingstonian	42	21	9	12	66	50	13	2	6	36	25	8	7	6	30	25	16	72
8	Concord Rangers	42	21	8	13	72	55	11	5	5	33	25	10	3	8	39	30	17	71
9	Cray Wanderers	42	20	9	13	72	46	12	2	7	35	20	8	7	6	37	26	26	69
10	AFC Hornchurch	42	19	12	11	58	46	12	6	3	32	16	7	6	8	26	30	12	69
11	Billericay T	42	20	9	13	56	45	14	2	5	31	17	6	7	8	25	28	11	69
12	Wealdstone	42	16	10	16	58	54	9	6	6	27	25	7	4	10	31	29	4	58
13	Carshalton Ath	42	14	10	18	49	57	7	6	8	24	28	7	4	10	25	29	−8	52
14	Tooting & Mitcham	42	13	10	19	63	85	9	4	8	36	43	4	6	11	27	42	−22	49
15	Hendon	42	12	10	20	61	81	7	5	9	32	35	5	5	11	29	46	−20	46
16	Margate	42	11	12	19	52	64	6	6	9	31	33	5	6	10	21	31	−12	45
17	Horsham	42	11	11	20	43	77	4	8	9	21	37	7	3	11	22	40	−34	44
18	Hastings U	42	9	11	22	50	65	6	4	11	27	30	3	7	11	23	35	−15	38
19	Aveley	42	10	8	24	35	62	4	5	12	17	34	6	3	12	18	28	−27	38
20	Maidstone U	42	9	10	23	43	75	2	5	14	17	37	7	5	9	26	38	−32	37
21	Croydon Ath	42	10	4	28	44	95	5	2	14	24	49	5	2	14	20	46	−51	31
22	Folkestone Invicta	42	5	12	25	34	68	3	7	11	19	31	2	5	14	15	37	−34	27

Croydon Ath deducted 3 points. ¶Tonbridge Angels promoted via play-offs.

THE FA TROPHY 2010–11
IN PARTNERSHIP WITH CARLSBERG

PRELIMINARY ROUND

Newcastle T v Goole	2-2, 2-1
Loughborough Dyn v Romulus	2-4
Shepshed Dyn v Warrington T	2-1
Woodley Sp v Lancaster C	1-1, 1-7
Atherstone T v Stamford	2-4
Witton Alb v Sutton Coldfield T	1-0
Brigg T v Bedworth U	1-3
Leigh Genesis v Garforth T	0-5
AFC Fylde v Market Drayton T	1-2
Lincoln U v Barwell	3-2
Ossett Alb v Salford C	4-1
Skelmersdale U v Wakefield	5-1
Clitheroe v Leek T	5-0
Glapwell v Spalding U	3-0
Belper T v Harrogate Rail Ath	0-1
Rainworth MW v Sheffield	1-1, 1-3
Grantham T v Carlton T	0-2
Mossley v Kidsgrove Ath	1-1, 4-1
Rushall Olympic v Trafford	1-0
Brentwood T v East Thurrock U	4-3
Barton R v Maldon & Tiptree	3-1
Waltham Abbey v Soham T R	0-2
Eastbourne T v Walton Cas	1-2
Needham Market v Hitchin T	4-2
Ilford v Whitstable T	2-0
Ware v Whitehawk	1-2
Fleet T v Tilbury	3-1
Wingate & Finchley v Horsham YMCA	4-1
Thamesmead T v Heybridge Swifts	0-0, 2-1
Chipstead v Godalming T	1-2
Walton & Hersham v Faversham T	1-2
Ashford T withdrew v Ramsgate w.o	
Merstham v AFC Sudbury	4-6
Corinthian Cas v Potters Bar T	0-3
Leatherhead v Enfield T	1-3
Arlesey T v Sittingbourne	2-0
Met Police v Biggleswade T	1-1, 0-2
Bognor Regis T v Whyteleafe	0-0, 6-1
Cheshunt v Great Wakering R	0-2
Redbridge v Chatham T	2-1
Burnham v Northwood	1-1, 2-1
Andover v Bideford	2-3
Slough T v Marlow	2-2, 3-0
Leighton T v Rugby T	0-1
Bromsgrove R withdrew v Frome T w.o	
Wimborne T v Gosport Bor	2-1
AFC Totton v Yate T	3-0
Cinderford T v Mangotsfield U	1-1, 2-1
Bedfont T v Uxbridge	0-2
Clevedon T v Bishop's Cleeve	0-1
North Greenford U v Thatcham T	2-1
Stourport Swifts v Bridgwater T	0-1
North Leigh v Sholing	3-2
Taunton T v Hungerford T	2-2, 0-1

Kendal T v Frickley Ath	3-0
Northwich Vic v Lincoln U	0-0, 3-2
Durham C v FC Halifax T	0-2
Market Drayton T v Worksop T	1-1, 0-1
Wealdstone v Potters Bar T	2-2, 3-1
Bury T v Barton R	2-0
Bognor Regis T v Croydon Ath	1-0
Harrow Bor v Hendon	0-1
Canvey Island v AFC Sudbury	1-2
Arlesey T v Ramsgate	0-0, 3-2
Enfield T v Walton Cas	2-1
Great Wakering R v Thamesmead T	1-2
Dulwich Hamlet v Hastings U	2-2, 2-1
Sutton U v Tooting & Mitcham U	3-1
Cray W v Wingate & Finchley	2-1
Maidstone U v Burgess Hill T	2-0
Soham T R v Grays Ath	1-2
Needham Market v Lowestoft T	2-2, 2-6
Waltham Forest v Romford	0-2
Tonbridge Angels v Concord R	3-2
Cambridge C v Aveley	1-0
Faversham T v Kingstonian	1-2
Fleet T v Godalming T	0-2
AFC Hornchurch v Brentwood T	2-1
Harlow T v Bedford T	3-2
Carshalton Ath v Ilford	2-0
Margate v Whitehawk	5-1
Biggleswade T v Billericay T	0-1
Folkestone Invicta v Worthing	4-2
Horsham v Redbridge	3-0
Swindon Supermarine v Beaconsfield SYCOB	4-2
Uxbridge v Abingdon U	4-1
Truro C v Bishop's Cleeve	1-0
Woodford U v Leamington	1-3
Windsor & Eton v Aylesbury U	1-1, 2-1
Almondsbury T v Didcot T	1-0
Weymouth v Bashley	2-0
Cinderford T v Hungerford T	2-2, 2-1
Bridgwater T v Stourbridge	1-3
Ashford T (Mddx) v North Greenford U	6-2
Burnham v Brackley T	0-0, 0-4
Banbury U v Wimborne T	1-1, 3-1
Slough T v Chippenham T	1-1, 1-4
Cirencester T v Halesowen T	3-0
Evesham U v Frome T	1-0
Paulton R v North Leigh	3-3, 2-1
Bideford v Tiverton T	4-2
Chesham U v Salisbury C	1-1, 1-2
Hemel Hempstead T v Rugby T	2-3
AFC Totton v AFC Hayes	5-0
Oxford C v Daventry T	1-4

SECOND QUALIFYING ROUND

Curzon Ashton v FC Halifax T	2-1
Leamington v Bamber Bridge	3-0
Romulus v Harrogate Railway Ath	1-2
Kendal T v Matlock T	1-1, 2-1
Worksop T v Lancaster C	2-1
Rushall Olympic v Stourbridge	0-1
Mossley v Nantwich T	2-3
Mickleover Sp v Chasetown	2-5
FC United of Manchester v Colwyn Bay	2-1
Radcliffe Bor v Witton Alb	1-1, 1-3
Chorley v Marine	3-1
Whitby T v Clitheroe	3-1
Northwich Vic v Glapwell	4-0
Stocksbridge PS v Rugby T	3-2
Kingstonian v Wealdstone	3-5
Salisbury C v Almondsbury T	2-1
Cirencester T v Weymouth	2-1
Margate v AFC Hornchurch	1-2
Tonbridge Angels v Enfield T	2-0
Billericay T v Banbury U	2-1
AFC Sudbury v Hendon	5-1
Brackley T v Windsor & Eton	4-0
Arlesey T v Uxbridge	2-2, 2-4
Daventry T v Cambridge C	1-2
Paulton R v Swindon Supermarine	4-5

FIRST QUALIFYING ROUND

Marine v Ashton U	2-2, 3-1
Matlock T v Bedworth U	10-0
Nantwich T v Prescot Cables	6-2
Hednesford T v Whitby T	1-2
Cammell Laird v Witton Alb	1-2
Lancaster C v Ossett T	4-2
North Ferriby U v Bamber Bridge	0-2
Sheffield v Chasetown	1-1, 1-2
Harrogate Railway Ath v Ossett Alb	2-1
Carlton T v Rushall Olympic	1-1, 1-4
Colwyn Bay v Bradford (PA)	2-0
Chorley v Quorn	1-0
Retford U v Romulus	2-2, 1-2
Curzon Ashton v Skelmersdale U	3-1
FC United of Manchester v Newcastle T	5-0
Burscough v Clitheroe	0-2
Buxton v Stocksbridge PS	1-2
Shepshed Dyn v Mossley	1-4
Radcliffe Bor v Garforth T	1-1, 2-1
Mickleover Sp v Hucknall T	2-1
Glapwell v Stamford	2-0

Grays Ath v Cinderford T	2-1
Truro C v Horsham	2-0
Folkestone Invicta v Thamesmead T	0-0, 3-1
Bognor Regis T v Godalming T	1-1, 5-2
Evesham U v Sutton U	0-1
Harlow T v Carshalton Ath	2-0
Ashford T (Mddx) v Bury T	2-1
Cray W v Maidstone U	1-2
Bideford v Dulwich Hamlet	1-0
Chippenham T v Lowestoft T	1-1, 1-3
AFC Totton v Romford	1-3

THIRD QUALIFYING ROUND

Alfreton T v Kendal T	4-0
Vauxhall Motors v Stalybridge C	1-3
Blyth Spartans v Stafford R	1-0
Whitby T v Northwich Vic	2-2, 0-1
AFC Telford U v Corby T	2-1
Curzon Ashton v Solihull Moors	2-1
Leamington v Hyde	1-2
FC United of Manchester v Hinckley U	1-2
Worksop T v Stocksbridge PS	4-1
Boston U v Gainsborough Tr	2-1
Droylsden v Stourbridge	3-2
Eastwood T v Cambridge C	2-0
Chorley v Guiseley	0-1
Harrogate T v Witton Alb	1-1, 2-1
Harrogate Railway Ath v Nantwich T	3-4
Workington v Chasetown	0-0, 0-4
Nuneaton T v Worcester C	1-2
Dover Ath v Woking	1-2
Braintree T v Farnborough	2-0
Lewes v Salisbury C	1-3
Maidenhead U v Uxbridge	2-4
Weston-S-M v Dorchester T	1-3
Basingstoke T v Havant & Waterlooville	2-2, 2-1
Eastleigh v Folkestone Invicta	2-1
Cirencester T v Grays Ath	2-2, 1-0
Sutton U v Billericay T	4-2
Ebbsfleet U v Bromley	4-0
Thurrock v Dartford	0-2
Boreham Wood v Romford	3-0
Welling U v Tonbridge Angels	1-0
St Albans C v Staines T	3-1
Truro C v AFC Sudbury	1-2
Bishop's Stortford v Ashford T (Mddx)	1-2
Brackley T v Wealdstone	0-1
Lowestoft T v Swindon Supermarine	2-1
Bideford v AFC Hornchurch	0-3
Harlow T v Maidstone U	3-0
Bognor Regis T v Hampton & Richmond Bor	2-2, 0-2
Gloucester C v Chelmsford C	1-0

FIRST ROUND

Wrexham v Kidderminster H	2-0
Rushden & D v Eastwood T	1-1, 3-4
Worksop T v Mansfield T	0-5
Droylsden v Hinckley U	4-3
Curzon Ashton v Altrincham	0-2
Darlington v Tamworth	3-2
Harrogate T v AFC Telford U	0-3
Chasetown v Kettering T	3-3, 2-1
Stalybridge C v Nantwich T	2-1
York C v Boston U	0-1
Blyth Spartans v Fleetwood T	2-0
Alfreton T v Hyde	3-0
Worcester C v Northwich Vic	1-0
Grimsby T v Redditch U	3-0
Barrow v Guiseley	2-3
Gateshead v Southport	2-2, 1-0
Dorchester T v St Albans C	3-0
Histon v Bath C	2-3
Luton T v Welling U	0-0, 2-1
Eastleigh v Sutton U	1-1, 4-0

Harlow T v Woking	0-2
Ashford T (Mddx) v AFC Hornchurch	1-0
Cirencester T v Gloucester C	1-1, 0-3
Eastbourne Bor v Boreham Wood	3-1
Ebbsfleet U v Hayes & Yeading U	3-1
Cambridge U v Forest Green R	2-1
Crawley T v Dartford	3-3, 0-1
AFC Sudbury v Hampton & Richmond Bor	1-4
Lowestoft T v Uxbridge	2-3
Newport Co v Wealdstone	0-0, 1-0
AFC Wimbledon v Braintree T	3-0
Basingstoke T v Salisbury C	0-2

SECOND ROUND

Gateshead v Hampton & Richmond Bor	6-0
Boston U v Gloucester C	0-1
AFC Wimbledon v Woking	2-3
Droylsden v Ebbsfleet U	1-0
Chasetown v Grimsby T	2-1
Alfreton T v Cambridge U	3-3, 6-3
Ashford T (Mddx) v Dartford	0-1
Luton T v Uxbridge	4-0
AFC Telford U v Eastwood T	1-0
Darlington v Bath C	4-1
Mansfield T v Newport Co	4-2
Blyth Spartans v Altrincham	2-1
Dorchester T v Eastbourne Bor	3-3, 0-1
Guiseley v Stalybridge C	2-1
Eastleigh v Worcester C	3-3, 4-1
Salisbury C v Wrexham	1-0

THIRD ROUND

Eastbourne Bor v Guiseley	1-1, 1-2
Mansfield T v Alfreton T	1-1, 2-1
Blyth Spartans v Droylsden	2-2, 4-0
Luton T v Gloucester C	1-0
AFC Telford U v Darlington	0-3
Woking v Salisbury C	0-2
Eastleigh v Chasetown	1-3
Gateshead v Dartford	3-0

FOURTH ROUND

Blyth Spartans v Gateshead	0-2
Guiseley v Luton T	0-1
Darlington v Salisbury C	2-1
Chasetown v Mansfield T	2-2, 1-3

SEMI-FINAL FIRST LEG

Mansfield T v Luton T	1-0
Darlington v Gateshead	3-2

SEMI-FINAL SECOND LEG

Luton T v Mansfield T	1-1
Gateshead v Darlington	0-0

FINAL (at Wembley)

Saturday, 7 May 2011

Darlington (0) 1 *(Senior 119)*

Mansfield T (0) 0   24,668

Darlington: Russell; Arnison, Brown, Chandler, Miller, Wright, Moore, Bridge-Wilkinson (Terry), Campbell (Senior), Hatch, Smith G (Verma).
Mansfield T: Marriott; Silk, Spence, Murray (Mitchley), Foster, Naylor, Briscoe, Thompson, Connor, Nix, Smith A (Cain).
aet.
Referee: S. Attwell (Warwickshire).

THE FA VASE 2010–11

IN PARTNERSHIP WITH CARLSBERG

FIRST QUALIFYING ROUND

Easington Coll v Hall Road R	5-4
Tadcaster Alb v Prudhoe T	5-0
Thornaby v Newcastle Benfield	0-3
Crook T v Team Northumbria	4-2
Darlington Railway Ath v Liversedge	2-4
Ashington v Whickham	4-0
Seaham Red Star v Scarborough Ath	0-3
Selby T v Sunderland RCA	3-2
South Shields v North Shields	2-0
Eccleshill U v Gillford Park	2-1
Willington v Bishop Auckland	0-3
Silsden v Tow Law T	1-2
West Allotment Celtic v Newton Aycliffe	5-1
Glasshoughton Wel v Brighouse T	0-2
AFC Emley v Hemsworth MW	4-2
Cheadle T v Worsborough Bridge Ath	1-2
Penrith v FC Brimington	4-1
Nelson removed v Abbey Hey w.o.	
Chadderton v Holker OB	1-2
Maltby Main v Ashton T	2-2, 1-2
Dinnington T v Wigan Robin Park	2-0
St Helens T v Brodsworth Wel	8-1
Bacup Bor v Nostell MW	3-1
Daisy Hill v Whitehaven	2-3
Parkgate v Congleton T	4-2
Hinckley v Walsall Wood	0-5
Pershore T v Leek CSOB	2-1
Ellistown v Highgate U	0-5
Bromyard T v Continental Star	2-6
Dudley T v Warstones W	4-2
Boldmere St M v Lutterworth Ath	4-1
Castle Vale JKS v Anstey Nomads	1-1, 2-3
Pelsall Villa v Bardon Hill Sp	1-0
Goodrich v Nuneaton Griff	2-0
Cradley T v Malvern T	1-3
Shifnal T v Cadbury Ath	2-0
Ellesmere R v Kirby Muxloe	2-0
Rocester v Loughborough Univ	0-1
Pilkington XXX v Coleshill T	3-1
Tividale v Oadby T	8-1
Alvechurch v Ibstock U	5-0
Shawbury U v Bridgnorth T	0-2
Dosthill Colts v Studley	1-8
Racing Club Warwick v Thurnby Nirvana	1-6
Sporting Khalsa v AFC Wulfrunians	0-3
Barrow T v Heather St Johns	1-2
Dudley Sp v Ashby Ivanhoe	3-4
Castle Vale v Stone Dominoes	0-1
Bewdley T v Wellington	2-1
Winterton R v Long Eaton U	2-0
Greenwood Meadows v Ollerton T	2-1
Forest T v Radford	7-0
Blackstones v Shirebrook T	2-0
Pinxton v Bottesford T	2-1
Sleaford T v Holbrook Sp	2-3
Newark T v Arnold T	0-1
Grimsby Bor v Radcliffe Olympic	1-0
Blackwell MW v Borrowash Vic	1-5
Teversal v Blidworth Wel	1-2
Walsham Le Willows v Cornard U	5-0
Rothwell T v Cogenhoe U	2-3
Whitton U v Rushden & Highham U	3-0
Stewarts & Lloyds v Wisbech T	0-4
Gorleston v Ely C	1-1, 1-0
Newmarket v Diss T	3-0
Huntingdon T v Mildenhall T	2-1
March T U v Daventry U	0-1
Thetford T v Rothwell Cor	2-2, 5-3
Dereham T v King's Lynn T	1-2
Brantham Ath v Stowmarket T	1-2
Hadleigh U v Yaxley	1-0
Long Melford v Fakenham T	0-0, 3-1
Haverhill R v Northampton Spencer	4-0
Codicote v Hanworth Villa	1-4
Tokyngton Manor removed v Haringey Bor w.o.	
Wodson Park v Feltham	4-1
Baldock T Letchworth v Milton U	2-1
Eton Manor v Southill Alexander	3-0
Bucks Students Union v Harefield U	2-3

Bedford v Hoddesdon T	3-1
Langford v Mountnessing	1-1, 3-2
Kingsbury London Tigers v Southend Manor	0-1
Holmer Green v Newport Pagnell T	1-1
Newport Pagnell T won 5-4 on penalties.	
Ascot U v Staines Lammas	3-0
Welwyn Garden C v Crawley Green	1-0
Sawbridgeworth T v Hatfield T	3-1
Hertford T v Mauritius Sp Ass	3-0
Shrivenham v Potton U	5-1
Basildon U v Kings Langley	5-3
AFC Kempston R v Hadley	0-1
St Margaretsbury v Oxhey Jets	1-2
Buckingham Ath v Barkingside	2-2, 0-7
Wantage T v London Colney	4-2
Bedfont Sp v AFC Dunstable	0-5
Stanway R v Broxbourne Bor V&E	2-1
Buckingham T v Saffron Walden T	0-1
Dunstable T v Hanwell T	4-2
Mile Oak v U S Portsmouth	4-2
Hayling U v Shoreham	1-3
Greenwich Bor v Newhaven	5-2
Deal T v Crawley Down	0-4
Three Bridges v Littlehampton T	5-1
Hamble ASSC v Totton & Eling	2-0
Chessington & Hook U v South Park	1-3
Selsey v Lordswood	0-1
Alresford T v Cove	0-4
Raynes Park Vale v Westfield	3-0
Horndean v Horley T	1-3
Tunbridge Wells v Hailsham T	3-0
Fleet Spurs v Petersfield T	6-1
Brockenhurst v Crowborough Ath	4-1
Winchester C v Holmesdale	1-0
Norton Sp v New Milton T	3-2
Blackfield & Langley v Hassocks	3-2
Moneyfields v Farnborough NE	5-2
Guildford C v Sevenoaks T	5-0
Newport (IW) v Whitchurch U	4-1
Lancing v AFC Uckfield	3-2
Cobham v Rye U	1-2
Andover New Street v East Cowes Vic Ath	1-3
Erith T v Badshot Lea	3-1
Hartley Wintney v Brading T	0-1
Worthing U v Lingfield	2-1
Oakwood v East Preston	3-4
Cheltenham Sar v Hallen	1-2
Devizes T v Amesbury T	2-1
Old Woodstock T v Shrewton U	3-1
Thame U v Slimbridge	2-1
Highworth T v Bradford T	1-2
Hook Norton v Laverstock & Ford	0-4
Bicester T v Cadbury Heath	1-2
Kidlington v Malmesbury Vic	5-0
Westbury U v Ardley U	0-3
Corsham T v Oxford C Nomads	1-1, 3-1
Almondsbury UWE v Pewsey Vale	4-2
Elmore v Porthleven	2-3
Odd Down v Wells C	2-0
Keynsham T v Swanage T & Herston	2-1
Larkhall Ath v Hamworthy U	0-3
Falmouth T v Saltash U	2-2, 1-3
Brislington v Witheridge	1-0
Hengrove Ath v Gillingham T	1-0
Welton R v Verwood T	0-3
St Blazey v Dartmouth	3-2
Biddulph Vic v Stafford T	2-1
Irchester U v Ipswich W	0-3
Sidley U v Corinthian	0-1
Fisher v Ringwood T	2-1
Crediton U v Cullompton R	3-3, 0-2
Molesey v Dorking	2-1
Mole Valley SCR v Banstead Ath	2-3

SECOND QUALIFYING ROUND

Erith & Belvedere v Saltdean U	2-0
Bishop Auckland v Chester-Le-Street T	1-0
AFC Emley v Rossington Main	3-0
Canning T v Wodson Park	2-3
Fisher v Norton Sp	3-0

Consett v Washington	1-3
Ryton v South Shields	0-8
Birtley T v Esh Winning	3-3, 4-3
Hebburn T v Easington Coll	3-4
Bedlington Terr v West Allotment Celtic	3-1
Northallerton T v Jarrow Roofing Boldon CA	4-3
Askern Villa v Tadcaster Alb	1-2
West Auckland T v Selby T	3-3, 3-0
Tow Law T v Pontefract Coll	3-2
Billingham Syn v Newcastle Benfield	2-1
Brandon U v Stokesley SC	1-3
Horden CW v Leeds Carnegie	0-1
Brighouse T v Yorkshire Amat	3-1
Liversedge v Eccleshill U	0-0, 1-2
Morpeth T v Ashington	0-5
Scarborough Ath v Crook T	3-2
Guisborough T v Billingham T	1-3
Formby v Alsager T	2-1
Holker OB v Colne	0-2
St Helens T v Worsborough Bridge Ath	4-0
Atherton LR v Ashton Ath	3-2
Staveley MW v Atherton Coll	4-0
Hallam v Penrith	6-2
Padiham v Bacup Bor	1-1, 1-3
Maine Road v Barnoldswick T	1-0
Runcorn Linnets v Whitehaven	1-0
Parkgate v Runcorn T	1-3
AFC Liverpool v Dinnington T	1-0
AFC Blackpool v Squires Gate	3-2
Flixton v Ashton T	2-1
Abbey Hey v Oldham Boro	0-0, 2-3
Winsford U v Irlam	1-2
Dudley T v Coventry Copsewood	2-2, 1-3
Bewdley T v Blaby & Whetstone Ath	1-3
Bustleholme v Darlaston T	5-0
Westfields v Lye T	4-0
Oldbury Ath removed v Anstey Nomads w.o.	
Boldmere St M v Norton U	3-1
Walsall Wood v Heather St Johns	0-1
Malvern T v Loughborough Univ	1-0
Ellesmere R v Pilkington XXX	1-2
Wolverhampton Cas v Pegasus Juniors	4-2
AFC Wulfrunians v Studley	2-3
Bridgnorth T v Pershore T	2-1
Goodrich v Heath Hayes	1-2
St Andrews v Shifnal T	1-2
Tividale v Highgate U	4-1
Eccleshall v Biddulph Vic	5-3
Friar Lane & Epworth v Continental Star	0-0, 1-2
Bartley Green v Bloxwich U	0-3
Holwell Sp v Alvechurch	2-1
Coventry Sphinx v Brocton	1-0
Wednesfield v Ashby Ivanhoe	5-1
Stone Dominoes v Bolehall Swifts	4-2
Heath T R w.o. v Ledbury T removed	
Gornal Ath v Pelsall Villa	7-0
Southam U v Thurnby Nirvana	1-1, 0-3
Dunkirk v Appleby Frodingham	4-1
Clipstone Wel v Kimberley T	2-1
Graham St Prims v Gedling T	1-2
Boston T v Forest T	1-3
Blackstones v Glossop NE	0-0, 1-3
Greenwood Meadows v Borrowash Vic	3-0
Heanor T v Sutton T	4-2
Grimsby Bor v Winterton T	0-3
Calverton MW v Arnold T	2-4
Barton T OB v Pinxton	3-0
Gedling MW v Holbrook Sp	0-1
Holbeach U v Blidworth Wel	3-6
Lincoln Moorlands Railway v Louth T	1-2
Ipswich W v Raunds T	4-1
Bugbrooke St M v Wellingborough T	0-1
Gorleston v Daventry U	3-2
Huntingdon T v Felixstowe & Walton U	1-3
Cogenhoe U v Long Melford	3-0
Haverhill R v Debenham LC	3-0
Godmanchester R v Eynesbury R	2-1
Woodbridge T v Whitton U	0-2
Norwich U v Desborough T	3-0
Swaffham T v Hadleigh U	0-3
Newmarket T v Wisbech T	2-3
Stowmarket T v Framlingham T	1-2
Thetford T v Walsham Le Willows	0-1
King's Lynn T v Great Yarmouth T	4-3
Harefield U v AFC Wallingford	1-2
Ampthill T v Takeley	1-2

Abingdon T v Holyport	0-1
London APSA v Sandhurst T	3-1
Wokingham & Emm'k v Langford	1-2
Bedford v Kentish T	1-3
Hanworth Villa v Stanway R	1-3
Ascot U v Hertford T	0-1
Sawbridgeworth T v Shrivenham	2-3
Hayes Gate v Hullbridge Sp	0-2
Oxhey Jets v Haringey Bor	2-5
Newport Pagnell T v Clapton	4-0
Leverstock Green v Welwyn Garden C	6-0
Basildon U v Baldock T Letchworth	1-3
Berkhamsted v Eton Manor	2-3
Biggleswade U v Barking	0-3
Colney Heath v Hadley	4-1
Binfield v Bethnal Green U	2-0
FC Clacton v Saffron Walden T	4-0
Dunstable T v Cranfield U	2-1
Cockfosters v Halstead T	4-1
Newbury v Southend Manor	3-1
Bowers & Pitsea v Wantage T	0-1
Hillingdon Bor v Wembley	1-0
Romsey T v Horley T	2-3
Blackfield & Langley v Fareham T	3-2
Moneyfields v AFC Porchester	2-1
Winchester C v Hamble ASSC	0-2
Mile Oak v St Francis R	1-2
Eastbourne U v Warlingham	1-2
South Park v Guildford C	0-1
Shoreham v East Cowes Vic Ath	7-3
Redhill v Colliers Wood U	2-5
Molesey v Brockenhurst	4-1
Worthing U v Christchurch	1-2
Croydon v Hythe & Dibden	3-1
Raynes Park Vale v Erith T	1-0
Fleet Spurs v Rye U	1-2
Lordswood v Southwick	3-0
Ash U v Corinthian	1-5
Pagham v Brading T	2-3
Banstead Ath v Lancing	2-4
Ringmer v Cove	0-2
Arundel v Three Bridges	2-5
Tunbridge Wells v East Preston	6-2
Cowes Sp v Lymington T	0-1
Alton T v Greenwich Bor	2-3
Crawley Down v Farnham T	2-0
East Grinstead T v Newport (IW)	2-3
Frimley Green v Bookham	1-2
Bradford T v Melksham T	0-1
Bitton v Thame U	3-2
Cadbury Heath v Ardley U	3-0
Kidlington v Old Woodstock T	1-0
Laverstock & Ford v Almondsbury UWE	4-0
Calne T v Longwell Green Sp	1-0
Downton v Hallen	0-0, 6-1
Clanfield 85 v Warminster T	2-1
Lydney T v Corsham T	1-0
Devizes T v Wootton Bassett T	0-4
Fairford T w.o. v Highbridge U removed	
Brislington v Shaftesbury	2-1
Tavistock v Chard T	4-3
Sherborne T v Shepton Mallet	3-0
Hamworthy U v Verwood T	2-3
Hengrove Ath v Portishead T	2-0
Porthleven v Newquay	1-4
Minehead v Keynsham T	0-1
Wadebridge T v Torpoint Ath	0-3
Street v Odd Down	0-1
Buckland Ath v Bridport	1-2
Budleigh Salterton v Liskeard Ath	3-0
Saltash U v Penzance	3-1
Barnstaple T v Radstock T	2-3
St Blazey v Cullompton R	5-2
Bodmin T v Launceston	5-2
Wellington v Merthyr T	2-1
AFC Dunstable v Barkingside	6-2
Thrapston T v Team Bury	2-1

FIRST ROUND

Bedlington Terr v Spennymoor T	0-1
Leeds Carnegie v Easington Coll	4-0
Tadcaster Alb v Tow Law T	2-0
West Auckland v Birtley T	6-0
Northallerton T v Stokesley SC	3-4
Billingham T v Ashington	3-4
Dunston UTS v Washington	2-1

Scarborough Ath v Bridlington T	2-2, 3-1
Bishop Auckland v Billingham Syn	3-4
South Shields v Thackley	0-2
Brighouse T v Eccleshill U	3-3, 1-2
AFC Liverpool v Hallam	3-0
Atherton LR v Runcorn T	2-3
Formby v Flixton	2-0
Rossendale U v Bacup Bor	0-2
Irlam v Colne	2-0
St Helens T v Oldham Boro	2-1
AFC Emley v Runcorn Linnets	3-1
Ramsbottom U v Staveley MW	0-1
Maine Road v AFC Blackpool	2-2, 1-2
Blaby & Whetstone Ath v Westfields	2-5
Coalville T v Stratford T	2-1
Coventry Sphinx v Anstey Nomads	4-3
Malvern T v Heather St Johns	2-6
Wednesfield v Studley	4-3
Holwell Sp v Tividale	4-3
Coventry Copsewood v Heath T R	2-1
Wolverhampton Cas v Bustleholme	1-3
Stone Dominoes v Heath Hayes	1-4
Willenhall T v Gornal Ath	0-2
Boldmere St M v Continental Star	1-0
Eccleshall v Bridgnorth T	2-4
Bloxwich U v Pilkington XXX	5-0
Thurnby Nirvana v Shifnal T	1-2
Gedling T v Glossop NE	2-1
Holbrook Sp v Arnold T	4-4, 3-1
Forest T v Greenwood Meadows	3-1
Dunkirk v Blidworth Wel	2-0
Louth T v Barton T OB	3-3, 0-1
Winterton R v Deeping R	3-1
Heanor T v Clipstone Wel	6-2
Wisbech T v Cogenhoe U	5-1
Gorleston v Hadleigh U	1-0
Ipswich W v Walsham Le Willows	1-2
Leiston v Haverhill R	3-2
Cambridge Reg Coll v Wellingborough T	4-0
Thrapston T v King's Lynn T	2-4
Whitton U v Norwich U	2-0
St Neots T v Felixstowe & Walton U	11-0
Godmanchester R v Framlingham T	4-0
Binfield v Hillingdon Bor	3-2
Wantage T v Shrivenham	2-1
Eton Manor v FC Clacton	4-2
Dunstable T v AFC Wallingford	5-0
Reading T v Newport Pagnell T	4-2
Chalfont St Peter v Newbury	6-0
Stansted v Takeley	2-0
Aylesbury U v Hertford T	4-3
Haringey Bor v Tring Ath	1-3
Baldock T Letchworth v Holyport	0-1
Barking v Flackwell Heath	1-2
Cockfosters v Witham T	0-3
Leverstock Green v Enfield 1893	5-4
Langford v Hullbridge Sp	1-3
Burnham Ramblers v Kentish T	2-0
AFC Dunstable v Colney Heath	3-1
Stanway R v London APSA	4-0
Bracknell T v Wodson Park	2-0
Guildford C v Horley T	3-2
Wick v VCD Ath	0-2
Corinthian v Tunbridge Wells	0-4
Fisher v Warlingham	1-3
Peacehaven & Telscombe v Hamble ASSC	1-0
Newport (IW) v Shoreham	3-0
Crawley Down v Rye U	0-1
Croydon v Beckenham T	3-7
Lancing v Christchurch	1-1, 1-0
Moneyfields v Greenwich Bor	1-0
Lymington T v Bournemouth	1-2
Raynes Park Vale v Hythe T	0-3
Colliers Wood U v Cove	5-2
Egham T v Molesey	2-0
Bookham v Herne Bay	0-4
Lordswood v Three Bridges	1-2
Camberley T v Blackfield & Langley	2-1
Brading T v St Francis R	4-2
Erith & Belvedere v Chichester C	2-1
Bemerton Heath Harle v Lydney T	5-2
Cadbury Heath v Wootton Bassett T	2-1
Calne T v Downton	1-2
Kidlington v Bitton	0-1
Clanfield 85 v Fairford T	2-1
Melksham T v Laverstock & Ford	3-1

Saltash U v Newquay	9-1
Verwood T v Budleigh Salterton	1-0
Brislington v St Blazey	0-1
Bishop Sutton v Keynsham T	2-2, 0-1
Wellington v Tavistock	5-0
Sherborne T v Bodmin T	1-1, 0-1
Odd Down v Bridport	7-0
Ilfracombe T v Hengrove Ath	1-2
Torpoint Ath v Radstock T	4-1

SECOND ROUND

Leeds Carnegie v Marske U	4-3
Billingham Syn v Stokesley SC	3-1
Eccleshill U v Runcorn T	0-2
Bootle v Shildon	1-3
Thackley v Whitley Bay	0-1
Formby v Bacup Bor	1-0
AFC Blackpool v AFC Liverpool	0-2
New Mills v Ashington	2-4
Forest T v Tadcaster Alb	0-4
Dunston UTS v AFC Emley	4-0
Winterton R v St Helens T	0-2
West Auckland T v Spennymoor T	1-3
Norton & Stockton Ancients v Irlem	4-3
Staveley MW v Pickering T	1-0
Scarborough Ath v Armthorpe Wel	1-1, 3-2
Coventry Sphinx v Dunkirk	0-3
Gresley v Heanor T	2-0
Bridgnorth T v Coalville T	2-4
Boldmere St M v Gornal Ath	1-2
Holbrook Sp v Holwell Sp	7-0
Causeway U v Gedling T	2-0
Shifnal T v Bloxwich U	0-0, 3-5
Wednesfield v Heather St Johns	1-3
Westfields v Coventry Copsewood	3-0
Bustleholme v Barton T OB	2-0
Heath Hayes v Tipton T	2-1
King's Lynn T v Gorleston	4-0
St Neots T v Burnham Ramblers	6-1
Hullbridge Sp v Leverstock Green	1-5
AFC Dunstable v Tring Ath	1-2
Dunstable T v Cambridge Regional College	2-1
Witham T v Walsham Le Willows	3-1
Stotfold v Whitton U	2-1
Kirkley & Pakefield v Long Buckby	0-1
St Ives T v Aylesbury U	2-1
Stansted v Eton Manor	3-1
Wroxham v Wisbech T	4-0
Royston T v Leiston	2-2, 0-1
Godmanchester R v Stanway R	0-1
Egham T v Newport (IW)	1-2
Chertsey T v Moneyfields	1-2
Epsom & Ewell v Bracknell T	4-0
Wantage T v Binfield	3-1
Erith & Belvedere v Lancing	0-2
VCD Ath v Hythe T	1-5
Reading T v Warlingham	1-0
Flackwell Heath v Three Bridges	1-2
Herne Bay v Camberley T	3-0
Tunbridge Wells v Holyport	8-0
Rye U v Chalfont St Peter	3-3, 2-1
Beckenham T v Peacehaven & Telscombe	2-1
Colliers Wood U v Witney U	1-0
Guildford C v Brading T	5-2
Dawlish T v Bodmin T	0-2
Clanfield 85 v Bemerton Heath Harle	0-3
Plymouth Parkway v Melksham T	6-1
St Blazey v Hengrove Ath	1-1, 2-0
Poole T v Wellington	4-3
Downton v Cadbury Heath	2-3
Bristol Manor Farm v Torpoint Ath	3-7
Bitton v Shortwood U	2-1
Verwood T v Keynsham T	2-1
Bournemouth v Odd Down	5-0
Willand R v Saltash U	2-1

THIRD ROUND

Westfields v Billingham Syn	1-2
Dunkirk v Ashington	1-2
Leeds Carnegie v Staveley MW	1-4
Shildon v Coalville T	0-2
Formby v Tadcaster Alb	2-3
Whitley Bay v AFC Liverpool	7-1
Scarborough Ath v Spennymoor T	0-3
Heath Hayes v Bloxwich U	1-3
Dunston UTS v Heather St Johns	2-0

Gresley v Bustleholme	4-2
Holbrook Sp v St Helens T	4-0
Causeway U v Norton & Stockton Ancients	0-3
Gornal Ath v Runcorn T	0-3
Tring Ath v Dunstable T	1-6
Lancing v Witham T	4-2
Wroxham v St Ives T	0-1
Stotfold v Long Buckby	0-3
Epsom & Ewell v St Neots T	1-2
Beckenham T v King's Lynn T	1-2
Leverstock Green v Tunbridge Wells	3-1
Stanway R v Stansted	0-1
Leiston v Hythe T	3-1
Three Bridges v Rye U	1-3
Herne Bay v Colliers Wood U	2-0
Cadbury Heath v Reading T	4-1
Guildford C v Moneyfields	4-3
Willand R v Bournemouth	2-1
Bitton v Newport (IW)	4-1
Poole T v Wantage T	3-2
St Blazey v Bemerton Heath Harle	1-2
Verwood T v Torpoint Ath	2-5
Plymouth Parkway v Bodmin T	1-3

FOURTH ROUND

Dunstable T v Willand R	2-0
Bloxwich U v Torpoint Ath	2-3
Leverstock Green v Bemerton Heath Harle	4-1
Gresley v St Neots T	1-3
Norton & Stockton Ancients v King's Lynn T	0-1
Holbrook Sp v Lancing	2-1
Poole T v St Ives T	3-2
Bitton v Coalville T	2-3
Bodmin T v Stansted	1-4
Long Buckby v Ashington	3-2
Herne Bay v Whitley Bay	1-2
Guildford C v Leiston	2-6
Cadbury Heath v Spennymoor T	1-5

Staveley MW v Rye U	0-3
Runcorn T v Dunston UTS	1-3
Billingham Syn v Tadcaster Alb	2-1

FIFTH ROUND

Whitley Bay v Dunstable T	5-1
Coalville T v Holbrook Sp	3-1
Torpoint Ath v Billingham Syn	1-0
Poole T v Spennymoor T	3-2
Leverstock Green v Rye U	1-2
Leiston v Long Buckby	2-1
King's Lynn T v St Neots T	2-1
Stansted v Dunston UTS	0-2

SIXTH ROUND

Poole T v Torpoint Ath	2-1
Coalville T v Leiston	1-0
King's Lynn v Rye U	3-1
Dunston UTS v Whitley Bay	1-2

SEMI-FINALS

Coalville T v King's Lynn T	3-0, 3-2
Poole T v Whitley Bay	1-2, 1-3

FINAL (at Wembley)

Sunday, 8 May 2011

Coalville T (0) 2 *(Moore 58, Goodby 80)*

Whitley Bay (1) 3 *(Chow 28, 86, Kerr 61)*   8778

Coalville T: Bowles; Brown (Gardner), Stuart, Goodby, Costello, Woodward, Miveld, Moore, Murdock, Carney (Attwood), Robbins (Wells).
Whitley Bay: Burke; McFarlane (Gibson), Anderson, Timmons, Williams (Coulson), Robson, Kerr, Chow, Robinson, Pounder (Smith), Ormston.
Referee: S. Mathieson (Cheshire).

THE FA COUNTY YOUTH CUP 2010–11

FIRST ROUND

Shropshire v Staffordshire	2-3
Nottinghamshire v Isle of Man	1-2
Northumberland v Cheshire	2-1
West Riding v North Riding	3-1
Leicestershire & Rutland v Birmingham	1-5
Herefordshire v Devon	1-1
Herefordshire won 4-2 on penalties.	
Sussex v Somerset	2-5
Essex v Huntingdonshire	3-1
Oxfordshire v Surrey	0-1
Wiltshire v Cambridgeshire	5-0
Suffolk v London	4-1
Gloucestershire v Berks & Bucks	4-6
Dorset v Norfolk	1-2

SECOND ROUND

Liverpool v Staffordshire	1-2
Lincolnshire v Manchester	1-4
Cumberland v Durham	0-4
Northumberland v Isle of Man	6-2
Westmoreland v East Riding	0-4
West Riding v Sheffield & Hallamshire	1-2
Lancashire v Birmingham	1-2
Middlesex v Suffolk	5-2
Cornwall v Northamptonshire	3-7
Kent v Berks & Bucks	0-2
Hertfordshire v Essex	1-0
Norfolk v Surrey	3-0
Guernsey v Wiltshire	2-6
Bedfordshire v Worcestershire	6-2
Herefordshire v Jersey	2 3
Amateur Football Alliance v Somerset	1-2

THIRD ROUND

Northumberland v Birmingham	1-2
Northamptonshire v Jersey	5-3

Sheffield & Hallamshire v Bedfordshire	3-1
Hertfordshire v Norfolk	0-4
Manchester v Durham	5-0
Wiltshire v East Riding	1-0
Somerset v Staffordshire	0-2
Berks & Bucks v Middlesex	1-5

FOURTH ROUND

Wiltshire v Norfolk	0-1
Sheffield & Hallamshire v Northamptonshire	2-1
Staffordshire v Manchester	2-1
Birmingham v Middlesex	0-0
Birmingham won 4-2 on penalties.	

SEMI-FINALS

Sheffield & Hallamshire v Staffordshire	0-2
Birmingham v Norfolk	0-1

FINAL (at Stoke)

Saturday, 30 April 2011

Staffordshire (1) 2 *(Timmins 6, Sherratt 81)*

Norfolk (2) 4 *(Marsden 26, Howard 45, 48, Cunningham 62 (og))*   580

Staffordshire: Wiggins; Cunningham, Burnett (Moyo), Hulin, Brown, Horton (Glover), Barnett, Southall (Kirby), Plimmer, Timmins, Sherratt.
Norfolk: Hewitt; Manning, McLiesh, Southgate (Livoti), Savory, Fryatt, Marsden (Sturman), Borrer, Butcher (George), Howard, Jones.
Referee: J. Adcock (Nottinghamshire).

THE FA YOUTH CUP 2010–11
SPONSORED BY E.ON

PRELIMINARY ROUND

Glossop NE v Oadby T	4-4
Glossop NE won 3-1 on penalties.	
Stamford v Carlton T	2-3
Bewdley T v Pegasus Juniors	6-1
Newcastle T v Romulus	1-2
Fakenham T v Brantham Ath	0-1
Walsham Le Willows v Norwich U	0-5
Histon v Hadleigh U	5-1
Diss T v Needham Market	0-6
Rushden & Higham U v Corby T	2-3
Stotfold v Raunds T	4-1
Ware v Halstead T	1-0
Hemel Hempstead T v Witham T	3-4
Hullbridge Sp v Bishop's Stortford	1-3
Ramsgate v Lewes	2-0
Crowborough Ath w.o. v Saltdean U withdrew	
Aylesbury v Marlow	2-3
Newport Pagnell T v Buckingham T	6-3
Petersfield T v Andover	1-0
Cheltenham Sar v Chard T	2-3
Tiverton T v Brislington	0-1
Chester-Le-Street T v Gateshead	4-2
Marine v Lancaster C	2-3
Nostell MW v Hallam	0-2
Mickleover Sp v Gresley	3-1
Malvern T v Wellington	3-0
Oakwood v Merstham	1-3
Lingfield v Maidstone U	0-3
Crawley Down v Carshalton Ath	0-9
South Park v Cray W	2-2
Cray W won 4-2 on penalties.	
East Grinstead T v Margate	2-0
VCD Ath v Sevenoaks T	3-1
Horsham YMCA v Whitehawk	1-3
AFC Liverpool v Wrexham	0-2
Stowmarket T v Woodbridge T	2-5
Sherborne T v Pewsey Vale	5-0
Thackley v Sheffield	0-8
Maltby Main v Pontefract Coll	4-2
Deeping R v Grimsby T	0-11
Spalding U v Blaby & Whetstone Ath	2-7
Ilkeston T v New Mills	6-3
Lincoln U v Retford U	1-0
Highgate U v Nuneaton Griff	3-0
Wolverhampton Cas v Solihull Moors	1-2
Gorleston v Ipswich W	4-0
Lowestoft T v Dereham T	3-0
Stansted v Hitchin T	3-1
Burnham Ramblers v Concord R	1-3
London Colney v Stanway R	0-1
St Albans C v Thurrock	3-4
Waltham Abbey v Romford	7-2
Uxbridge v Wealdstone	2-4
Barking v Staines T	3-2
Harefield U v Kingsbury London Tigers	4-0
Dulwich Hamlet v Croydon Ath	4-1
Redhill v Eastbourne T	1-0
Welling U v Sutton U	0-3
Folkestone Invicta v Dover Ath	1-2
Three Bridges v Whitstable T	1-0
Molesey v Kingstonian	3-2
Walton & Hersham v Worthing	2-5
Sandhurst T v Chalfont St Peter	1-3
Basingstoke T v Alton T	2-1
Bracknell T v Banbury U	2-0
Cove v Witney U	1-2
Reading T v Binfield	4-1
Eastleigh v Bournemouth	7-0
Bristol Manor Farm v Mangotsfield U	2-0
Ryton w.o. v Workington withdrew	
Congleton T v Formby	2-6
Stalybridge C v Vauxhall Motors	0-4
AFC Fylde v Altrincham	4-2
Nuneaton T v Bedworth U	0-0
Bedworth U won 6-5 on penalties.	
Brackley T v Daventry T	8-0
Chelmsford C v AFC Hornchurch	2-1
Oxhey Jets v Cheshunt	3-5
North Greenford U v Northwood	0-5
Thatcham T v AFC Wallingford	0-7
Paulton R v Bishop's Cleeve	2-4
Mile Oak v Whyteleafe	0-1
Rocester v Ellesmere R	1-4
Thrapston T v Kettering T	6-2
Tunbridge Wells v Eastbourne Bor	1-0
Dartford v Erith & Belvedere	4-1
Dorchester T v Christchurch	2-4
Bromley v Chatham T	3-0
Gloucester C v Lydney T	4-3
Worcester C v Rugby T	4-2
Bromyard T v Stone Dominoes	0-7
Stourbridge v Chasetown	3-2
AFC Telford U v Sutton Coldfield T	3-1
Thetford T v Wroxham	3-1
Wellingborough T v AFC Kempston R	2-3
Enfield T v Hampton & Richmond Bor	0-2
Hayes & Yeading U v Harrow Bor	3-2
Epsom & Ewell v Chichester C	2-1
Bitton v Portishead T	4-1
Weston-Super-Mare v Newport Co	0-0
Newport Co won 5-4 on penalties.	
York C w.o. v Sunderland RCA withdrew	
Prescot Cables v Fleetwood T	1-3
Burgess Hill T v Westfield	5-1
Cobham v Shoreham	6-2
Teversal w.o. v Barton T OB withdrew	
Bromsgrove R removed v Kidsgrove Ath w.o.	
Rothwell Cor w.o. v Dunstable T withdrew	
Leverstock Green w.o. v Harlow T withdrew	
Hanwell T w.o. v Corinthian Cas withdrew	
Dorking w.o. v Wick withdrew	
Chesham U w.o. v North Leigh withdrew	
Merthyr T v Forest Green R	1-2
Thamesmead T v Wingate & Finchley	5-2
Horsham v Chertsey T	4-1
Codicote v Grays Ath	1-2

FIRST QUALIFYING ROUND

Daisy Hill v Nantwich T	0-7
Staveley MW v North Ferriby U	2-1
Malvern T v Stratford T	0-3
Bolehall Swifts v Boldmere St Michaels	2-1
Thurrock v Ilford	3-0
Concord R v Leverstock Green	3-2
Slough T v Farnborough	1-3
Gosport Bor v Christchurch	2-0
AFC Totton v Eastleigh	2-0
Dartford v Deal T	2-0
Bromley v Dover Ath	3-1
Woking v Cobham	4-1
Yate T v Gloucester C	1-5
Harrogate Railway Ath v Yorkshire Amat	4-1
Wednesfield v Stourbridge	0-3
Highgate U v Solihull Moors	4-5
Leighton T v Bugbrooke St Michaels	6-0
Kentish T v Hampton & Richmond Bor	2-6
Tonbridge Angels v Tunbridge Wells	3-1
Pagham v Burgess Hill T	1-3
Worthing v Dorking	6-1
Epsom & Ewell v Lancing	0-5
Basingstoke T v Fleet T	5-4
Witney U v Oxford C	1-2
Marlow v AFC Wallingford	2-3
Sherborne T v Havant & Waterlooville	0-3
Newport Co v Bishop Sutton	6-0

Bath C v Elmore	4-2
Hinckley U v Blaby & Whetstone Ath	6-1
Kidsgrove Ath v Worcester C	2-5
Brackley T v Corby T	3-0
Weymouth v Ringwood T	4-1
Bishop's Cleeve v Chard T	5-2
Cirencester T v Radstock T	10-1
Dunston UTS withdrew v Darlington w.o.	
Bedlington Terr v York C	2-3
Colne withdrew v Fleetwood T w.o.	
Warrington T w.o. v Salford C withdrew	
Ilkeston T withdrew v Arnold T w.o.	
Carlton T w.o. v Mansfield T withdrew	
Braintree T withdrew v Chelmsford C w.o.	
Clapton w.o. v Tokyngton Manor withdrew	
AFC Wimbledon w.o. v Hendon withdrew	
Chipstead w.o. v Ashford T withdrew	
Poole T w.o. v Swindon Supermarine withdrew	
Moneyfields w.o. v Calne T withdrew	
Beaconsfield SYCOB v Maidenhead U	0-6
Ryton v Ashington	3-4
Luton T v Cogenhoe U	11-2
Boston U v Bottisford T	6-1
Barwell v Matlock T	5-1
Kidderminster H v Bewdley T	3-0
East Thurrock U v Bowers & Pitsea	4-0
Wealdstone v Hanwell T	4-1
Cray W v Ebbsfleet U	1-3
Burnham v Chesham U	1-5
Bristol Manor Farm v Bitton	1-5
Hallam v Stocksbridge PS	4-2
Brighouse T v Ossett T	3-4
Holwell Sp v Glossop NE	1-0
Lincoln U v Teversall	6-0
Redditch U v Coventry Sphinx	0-2
Walsall Wood v AFC Telford U	3-1
Lowestoft T v Gorleston	4-3
Great Yarmouth T v Newmarket T	1-4
Brantham Ath v Needham Market	1-5
Soham T R v Leiston	0-1
Cornard U v Cambridge U	0-4
Arlesey T v Yaxley	2-4
Cheshunt v Ware	2-2
Cheshunt won 5-4 on penalties.	
Billericay T v Aveley	2-3
Southend Manor v Bishop's Stortford	1-0
Hoddesdon T v Waltham Abbey	1-3
Royston T v Stanway R	0-1
Barking v Northwood	2-4
Harefield U v Ashford T (Middlesex)	1-0
Molesey v Carshalton Ath	0-5
Horley T v Faversham T	4-2
Leatherhead v Whitehawk	3-1
Horsham v Camberley T	1-6
Shaftesbury v Petersfield T	5-0
Almondsbury UWUE v Clevedon T	1-2
Chester-Le-Street T v Whitley Bay	0-1
East Grinstead T v Erith T	0-2
Wrexham v Ashton T	9-0
Tiverton T v Forest Green R	2-5
Southport v Vauxhall Motors	0-2
Northwich Vic v Mossley	0-2
Romulus v Stourport Swifts	3-1
St Neots T v Bedford T	2-3
St Francis R v Redhill	1-2
Whyteleafe v Tooting & Mitcham U	1-2
Flackwell Heath v Chalfont St Peter	3-2
AFC Fylde v Curzon Ashton	2-1
Bootle v Burscough	2-1
Ashton Ath v Woodley Sp	2-1
Liversedge v Maltby Main	1-3
Hemsworth MW v Sheffield	3-3
Sheffield won 5-4 on penalties.	
Goole v Wakefield	1-4
Ossett Alb v Garforth T	1-4
Loughborough Dyn v Grimsby T	0-4
Long Eaton U v Radford	2-3
Mickleover Sp v St Andrews	3-1

Ellesmere R v Eccleshall	2-2
Eccleshall won 5-4 on penalties.	
Gornal Ath v Stone Dominoes	0-4
Dosthill Colts v Bedworth U	0-2
Bury T v Thetford T	11-1
Histon v Norwich U	2-0
Woodbridge T v Felixstowe & Walton U	2-3
AFC Kempston R v Thrapston T	0-1
St Ives T v Rushden & D	0-7
Stotfold v Rothwell Cor	4-0
Witham T v Boreham Wood	0-5
Brentwood T v Stansted	1-2
Hayes & Yeading U v Thamesmead T	1-3
Met Police v Dulwich Hamlet	2-6
VCD Ath v Sutton U	1-0
Peacehaven & Telscombe v Hastings U	4-3
Ramsgate v Colliers Wood U	5-2
Merstham v Three Bridges	2-1
Crowborough Ath v Crawley T	0-2
Maidstone U v Croydon	5-1
Didcot T v Bracknell T	2-3
Abingdon U v Reading T	2-1
Newport Pagnell T v Kidlington	7-1
Sholing v Salisbury C	0-3
Lancaster C v Formby	1-0

SECOND QUALIFYING ROUND

Hallam v Maltby Main	2-1
Ossett T v Garforth T	1-2
Radford v Mickleover Sp	2-3
Bury T v Needham Market	3-2
Cambridge U v Felixstowe & Walton U	14-0
Histon v Leiston	3-0
Northwood v Clapton	1-0
Ramsgate v Redhill	2-3
Maidstone U v Ebbsfleet U	2-4
Lancing v Camberley T	2-5
AFC Totton v Salisbury C	0-3
Thamesmead T v AFC Wimbledon	0-1
Flackwell Heath v Chesham U	0-2
Shaftesbury v Havant & Waterlooville	1-3
Whitley Bay v Ashington	5-0
Ashton Ath v Nantwich T	0-2
Wakefield v Sheffield	2-0
Boston U v Arnold T	3-2
Stratford T v Stone Dominoes	2-0
Walsall Wood v Stourbridge	0-2
Bedworth U v Romulus	1-2
Lowestoft T v Newmarket T	1-4
Waltham Abbey v Southend Manor	4-0
Cheshunt v Aveley	4-2
Concord R v Stanway R	3-1
Dulwich Hamlet v Harefield U	3-1
Carshalton Ath v VCD Ath	3-1
Tooting & Mitcham U v Merstham	3-3
Tooting & Mitcham U won 5-4 on penalties.	
Farnborough v Basingstoke T	4-4
Farnborough won 3-2 on penalties.	
Bracknell T v Abingdon U	1-0
York C v Darlington	0-4
Holwell Sp v Barwell	2-2
Barwell won 6-5 on penalties.	
Solihull Moors v Kidderminster H	0-3
Rushden & D v Thrapston T	8-0
Boreham Wood v East Thurrock U	3-3
Boreham Wood won 5-4 on penalties.	
Dartford v Peacehaven & Telcombe	2-0
Chipstead v Tonbridge Angels	2-2
Tonbridge Angels won 5-4 on penalties.	
Lincoln U v Carlton	5-4
Eccleshall v Coventry Sphinx	0-5
Thurrock v Stansted	2-1
Gosport Bor v Poole T	5-1
Gloucester C v Bitton	3-2
Mossley v Lancaster C	5-1
AFC Fylde v Bootle	3-0
Harrogate Railway Ath v Staveley MW	1-2
Worcester C v Bolehall Swifts	1-2

Bedford T v Yaxley	1-2
Worthing v Leatherhead	3-3
Leatherhead won 5-3 on penalties.	
AFC Wallingford v Newport Pagnell T	3-2
Oxford C v Maidenhead U	1-4
Bath C v Newport Co	1-6
Brackley T v Luton T	1-5
Bromley v Horley T	6-0
Woking v Burgess Hill T	4-1
Weymouth v Moneyfields	1-0
Bishop's Cleeve v Cirencester T	3-5
Fleetwood T v Vauxhall Motors	6-1
Erith T v Crawley T	1-2
Forest Green R v Clevedon T	2-1
Grimsby T v Hinckley U	3-0
Wrexham v Warrington T	9-0
Hampton & Richmond Bor v Wealdstone	2-3
Stotfold v Leighton T	4-0
Chelmsford C v Grays Ath	4-2

THIRD QUALIFYING ROUND

Nantwich T v Fleetwood T	2-3
Wakefield v AFC Fylde	1-4
Whitley Bay v Staveley MW	3-0
Hallam v Wrexham	1-2
Darlington v Mossley	3-0
Barwell v Boston U	0-3
Stourbridge v Garforth T	4-2
Bolehall Swifts v Romulus	2-2
Bolehall Swifts won 5-4 on penalties.	
Grimsby T v Kidderminster H	5-1
Coventry Sphinx v Mickleover Sp	2-1
Lincoln U v Stratford T	0-1
Histon v Yaxley	2-1
Waltham Abbey v Luton T	2-3
Boreham Wood v Cambridge U	0-4
Cheshunt v Concord R	2-3
Bury T v Chelmsford C	3-2
Stotfold v Thurrock	0-3
Newmarket T v Rushden & D	1-4
Crawley T v Tooting & Mitcham U	2-1
Carshalton Ath v Chesham U	4-3
AFC Wallingford v Dulwich Hamlet	1-2
Maidenhead U v Dartford	0-1
Camberley T v Northwood	0-3
AFC Wimbledon v Wealdstone	1-0
Bromley v Tonbridge Angels	1-0
Ebbsfleet U v Redhill	5-1
Woking v Leatherhead	4-0
Havant & Waterlooville v Gosport Bor	4-1
Weymouth v Cirencester T	0-4
Forest Green R v Salisbury C	2-0
Gloucester C v Newport Co	2-4
Bracknell T v Farnborough	2-0

FIRST ROUND

Bury v Oldham Ath	2-5
Crewe Alex v AFC Fylde	4-0
Bradford C v Rochdale	4-2
Hartlepool U v Whitley Bay	3-1
Carlisle U v Wrexham	3-1
Stockport Co v Tranmere R	1-4
Macclesfield T v Fleetwood T	4-1
Accrington Stanley v Darlington	1-2
Rotherham U v Sheffield W	2-3
Huddersfield T v Morecambe	5-1
Histon v Notts Co	0-3
Bolehall Swifts v Northampton T	1-0
Chesterfield v Port Vale	1-3
Grimsby T v Stourbridge	3-0
Burton Alb v Stratford T	0-2
Lincoln C v Peterborough U	2-4
Shrewsbury T v Boston U	5-1
Milton Keynes D v Walsall	0-1
Coventry Sphinx v Hereford U	2-1
Thurrock v Leyton Orient	1-0
Barnet v Wycombe W	2-3

Northwood v Dulwich Hamlet	1-3
Brighton & HA v Ebbsfleet U	3-0
Dagenham & R v Stevenage	2-2
Dagenham & R won 3-2 on penalties.	
Colchester U v Woking	3-5
Southend U v Luton T	3-1
Charlton Ath v Crawley T	2-0
Concord R v Brentford	0-5
Rushden & D v Carshalton Ath	1-0
Gillingham v Cambridge U	1-2
Dartford v AFC Wimbledon	1-2
Newport Co v Bristol R	1-2
Forest Green R v Swindon T	1-2
Torquay U v Bracknell T	4-0
Havant & Waterlooville v Yeovil T	0-2
Cheltenham T v Oxford U	2-2
Cheltenham T won 4-1 on penalties.	
Plymouth Arg v Southampton	1-3
Cirencester T v Aldershot T	2-3
AFC Bournemouth v Exeter C	1-1
Exeter C won 3-2 on penalties.	
Bury T v Bromley	5-4

SECOND ROUND

Huddersfield T v Darlington	0-4
Peterborough U v Stratford T	5-0
Notts Co v Shrewsbury T	2-0
Port Vale v Grimsby T	1-1
Grimsby T won 5-4 on penalties.	
Carlisle U v Walsall	0-2
Bolehall Swifts v Bradford C	0-4
Oldham Ath v Sheffield W	3-2
Macclesfield T v Hartlepool U	0-2
Tranmere R v Crewe Alex	1-2
Dagenham & R v Bristol R	2-2
Bristol R won 4-2 on penalties.	
AFC Wimbledon v Aldershot T	0-3
Woking v Cheltenham T	2-4
Dulwich Hamlet v Yeovil T	3-2
Southampton v Thurrock	2-0
Brighton & HA v Torquay U	6-0
Cambridge U v Exeter C	1-2
Rushden & D v Wycombe W	1-0
Southend U v Brentford	3-0
Swindon T v Coventry Sphinx	6-1
Charlton Ath v Bury T	4-0

THIRD ROUND

West Ham U v Aldershot T	5-0
Blackburn R v Reading	3-2
Doncaster R v Middlesbrough	2-4
Dulwich Hamlet v Newcastle U	2-6
Grimsby T v Burnley	3-2
Watford v Swindon T	2-0
Leicester C v Hartlepool U	2-1
Sunderland v Chelsea	0-2
Arsenal v Darlington	6-1
Oldham Ath v Manchester C	5-6
Brighton & HA v Derby Co	0-3
Notts Co v Liverpool	0-4
Barnsley v Tottenham H	3-1
Bristol C v Birmingham C	0-2
Bristol R v Aston Villa	0-1
Wigan Ath v Stoke C	3-0
Millwall v Walsall	3-1
QPR v Nottingham F	2-2
Nottingham F won 5-3 on penalties.	
Bolton W v Crewe Alex	1-2
Fulham v WBA	6-4
Leeds U v Scunthorpe U	3-0
Norwich C v Charlton Ath	1-0
Hull C v Rushden & D	2-3
Southend U v Coventry C	3-1
Everton v Wolverhampton W	5-1
Blackpool v Exeter C	2-1
Preston NE v Swansea C	2-1
Cardiff C v Crystal Palace	0-3

Cheltenham T v Sheffield U	1-4
Bradford C v Southampton	1-1
Bradford C won 9-8 on penalties.	
Manchester U v Portsmouth	3-2
Ipswich T v Peterborough U	2-3

FOURTH ROUND
Sheffield U v Millwall	3-0
Fulham v Norwich C	3-0
Nottingham F v Manchester C	2-1
Liverpool v Crystal Palace	3-1
Crewe Alex v Leeds U	0-0
Leeds U won 3-2 on penalties.	
Watford v Wigan Ath	3-2
West Ham U v Manchester U	0-1
Blackpool v Birmingham C	4-3
Preston NE v Bradford C	1-1
Preston NE won 4-2 on penalties.	
Chelsea v Arsenal	2-1
Middlesbrough v Everton	1-0
Derby Co v Southend U	1-3
Newcastle U v Grimsby T	2-1
Leicester C v Blackburn R	3-1
Peterborough U v Aston Villa	1-3
Barnsley v Rushden & D	4-0

FIFTH ROUND
Leicester C v Preston NE	4-3
Leeds U v Aston Villa	0-2
Manchester U v Newcastle U	1-0
Fulham v Watford	0-2
Liverpool v Southend U	9-0
Sheffield U v Blackpool	3-1
Chelsea v Barnsley	2-1
Nottingham F v Middlesbrough	0-1

SIXTH ROUND
Liverpool v Manchester U	2-3
Aston Villa v Middlesbrough	3-1
Leicester C v Sheffield U	1-2
Chelsea v Watford	2-1

SEMI-FINALS (TWO LEGS)
Chelsea v Manchester U	3-2, 0-4
Aston Villa v Sheffield U	0-1, 0-2

FINAL FIRST LEG

Tuesday, 17 May 2011

Sheffield U (1) 2 *(McFadzean 45, Slew 74)*

Manchester U (1) 2 *(Lingard 14, Keane W 70)* 29,977

Sheffield U: Long; Montgomery, Maguire (Pomares 86), Kennedy, Barry, Gregory (Wilkinson 72), Harriott, Whitehouse, McFadzean, Ironside (Martin 74), Slew.

Manchester U: Johnstone; Keane M, Thorpe, Fornasier, McGinty, Lingard, Pogba, Tunnicliffe, Van Velzen (Cofie 76), Morrison, Keane W.

FINAL SECOND LEG

Monday, 23 May 2011

Manchester U (2) 4 *(Morrison 38, 70, Keane W 45, 80)*

Sheffield U (0) 1 *(Ironside 73)* 24,916

Manchester U: Johnstone; Keane M, McGinty, Thorpe, Fornasier, Lingard (Cole 78), Pogba, Tunnicliffe, Morrison (Cofie 90), Van Velzen (Blackett 84), Keane W.

Sheffield U: Long; Montgomery, Barry, Harriott, Maguire (Pomares 57), Kennedy, Gregory (Martin 68), Whitehouse, Ironside (Wilkinson 76), Slew, McFadzean.

THE NATIONAL LEAGUE SYSTEMS CUP 2010–11

PRELIMINARY ROUND
Northern Football Alliance v Lancashire & Cheshire Amateur League	2-2
Northern Football Alliance won 3-1 on penalties.	
Lancashire Amateur League v Isle of Man League	1-3
Manchester League v Wearside League	2-1
Liverpool County FA Premier League v Teesside League	2-1
Peterborough & District League v Lincolnshire League	1-2
Northamptonshire Combination v Cambridgeshire County League	1-2
Birmingham & District AFA v West Riding County Amateur League	0-2
Anglian Combination w.o. v Nottinghamshire Senior League withdrew	
Worthing & District League v Somerset County League	3-4
Gloucestershire County League v Mid Sussex League	4-0
Dorset Premier League v Hampshire Premier League	2-2
Dorset Premier League won 5-4 on penalties.	
Sussex County League (Div 3) v Brighton Hove & District League	5-0
Suffolk & Ipswich League v Bedfordshire County League	4-0
Amateur Football Combination v Surrey Elite Intermediate League	1-2
Middlesex County League v Herts Senior County League	3-3
Herts Senior County League won 5-4 on penalties.	
Reading League v Kent County League	1-1
Reading League won 6-5 on penalties.	

Competition still being played.

THE FA SUNDAY CUP 2010–11

IN PARTNERSHIP WITH CARLSBERG

PRELIMINARY ROUND

Kelloe WMC v South Bank (2006)	4-2
Sandon Dock withdrew v Oak Tree Pub w.o.	
Eagle Cons v Eden Vale	2-2
Eden Vale won 4-3 on penalties.	
Hundred Acre v Plough Barfly's	2-1

FIRST ROUND

Swanfield v Sunderland RCA Barnes	0-1
West Lee withdrew v Kelloe WMC w.o.	
AFC Blackburn Leisure v Dawdon CW	1-2
Witton Park Rose & Crown v Shankhouse U	6-1
Hartlepool Lion Hillcarter v Hessle R	5-1
Darby Lane Gym v Salford Celtic	3-1
Paddock v Ford Motors	6-1
Frizington White Star v Eden Vale	1-2
Poulton Royal v Thirly	2-0
Malt Shovel v West Bowling	1-2
Woodchurch v Oyster Martyrs	1-4
Silsden (Sunday) withdrew v Alder w.o.	
Salisbury Ath v Oak Tree Pub	4-2
Chapeltown Brazil v Mariners	0-2
Tower v Dengo U	4-2
Allerton v Lobster	2-4
Queens Park v BRNESC	2-1
Huddersfield Irish Centre v St Sebastians	3-2
Obiter v Sandstone	1-4
Nicosia withdrew v Home & Bargain w.o.	
Red Lion v Fforde Grene	2-3
St Bees Village v Brow	2-3
Towngate v JOB	1-2
Belt Road w.o. v Wisbech St Mary removed	
Loughborough Falcons v Bartley Green Sunday	4-2
Advance Couriers v Britannia Revolution	5-1
Loughborough Saints v Station Gates	10-0
Barwell Sp Bar v Hundred Acre	1-7
Warstones W (Sunday) w.o. v Birstall Stamford	
Brereton T v Clumber	0-7
The Blue Mugge v RHP Sp & Social	5-2
Kingshurst SC v Thatch	8-2
Coventry Coll v Travellers	0-8
Club Lewsey v Dee Road R	5-3
St Joseph's (Luton) v Northampton Duke of York	1-2
Britannia U v Houghton T (Sunday)	1-0
Rumours v Celtic SC (Luton)	1-1
Rumours won 5-4 on penalties.	
Wrightchoice Comm Sp Ass v Stanbridge & Tilsworth	2-0
AC Sportsman & Ravensboro v Standens Barn	2-0
Gamlinggay U Sunday v FC Houghton Centre	5-6
Wycombe T withdrew v Silsoe Park R w.o.	
AFC Donsville w.o. v Sandy (Sunday) withdrew	
St Margarets v Crawley Green (Sunday)	3-0
Comets SC v Hammer	3-3
Comets SC won 5-4 on penalties.	
Nicholas Wybacks v Bungay T	
Tie awarded to Nicholas Wybacks; Bungay T failed to fulfil fixture.	
Belstone v Gossoms End	7-2
Offley Moat v Royal Falcons	2-1
Torrun U v Nirankari Stevenage	1-3
FC Tripimeni-Aris v AFC Harrow	4-0
Broadfields U v Greengate	1-4
CB Hounslow U (Sunday) v North West Neasden	1-2
London Maccabi Lions v Enfield R	1-5
Bedfont Sunday v AFC Kumazi Strikers	3-0
Knighton Arms v Goring R	
Tie awarded to Knighton Arms; Goring R failed to fulfil fixture.	
Baldon Sp v The Lounge	2-4
Ajax LA v Golden Lion	2-6
Lebeqs Tavern Courage v Lakeside Ath	0-2
Windmill v Downend	3-0
Sporting Bristol v Wonford U	1-2
Springers v CK	4-0
Ashton v Bluebird U	3-6
Applebys v Hanham Sunday	1-11

SECOND ROUND

West Bowling v Mariners	2-5
Sunderland RCA Barnes v Derby Lane Gym	2-0
Dawdon CW v Paddock	0-3
Kelloe WMC v Oyster Martyrs	2-3
Alder v Tower	4-2

Salisbury Ath v Poulton Royal	0-0
Salisbury Ath won 4-2 on penalties.	
Huddersfield Irish Centre v Hartlepool Lion Hillcarter	4-0
Hetton Lyons CC v Brow	4-1
Witton Park Rose & Crown v Queens Park	0-2
JOB v Lobster	1-3
Fforde Grene v Sandstone	0-2
Home & Bargain v Eden Vale	2-2
Eden Vale won 4-3 on penalties.	
Hundred Acre v The Blue Mugge	6-4
Loughborough Saints v Travellers	0-3
Belt Road v Birstall Stamford	2-3
AC Sportsmen & Ravensboro v Loughborough Falcons	2-1
Clumber v Magnet Tavern	2-1
Kingshurst SC v Advance Couriers	2-0
FC Houghton Centre v Rumours	3-1
Club Lewsey v St Margarets	2-0
Silsoe Park R v Northampton Duke of York	0-4
AFC Donsville v The Lounge	2-3
Nicholas Wybacks v Golden Lion	1-3
North West Neasden v Comets SC	1-4
Greengate v Bedfont Sunday	3-4
FC Tripimeni-Aris v Enfield R	4-1
Belstone v Nirankari Stevenage	2-0
Offley Moat v Britannia U	1-4
Hanham Sunday v Lakeside Ath	4-2
Springers v Wonford U	0-3
Windmill v Knighton Arms	3-4
Bluebird U v Wrightchoice Comm Sp Ass	4-2

THIRD ROUND

Mariners v Alder	4-0
Huddersfield Irish Centre v Oyster Martyrs	3-5
Hetton Lyons CC v Paddock	2-3
Sunderland RCA Barnes v Sandstone	2-0
Eden Vale v Queens Park	2-3
Lobster v Salisbury Ath	0-4
FC Houghton Centre v Travellers	1-5
Comets SC v Clumber	4-4
Comets SC won 4-3 on penalties.	
The Lounge v Britannia U	0-3
Belstone v Birstall Stamford	2-0
Hundred Acre v Kingshurst SC	2-3
Golden Lion v Club Lewsey	2-8
Bedfont Sunday v AC Sportsmen & Ravensborough	2-0
FC Tripimeni-Aris v Northampton Duke of York	0-1
Knighton Arms v Hanham Sunday	2-1
Wonford U v Bluebird U	3-1

FOURTH ROUND

Salisbury Ath v Mariners	2-3
Oyster Martyrs v Sunderland RCA Barnes	7-1
Queens Park v Paddock	1-2
Northampton Duke of York v Travellers	2-1
Comets SC v Belstone	3-1
Club Lewsey v Kingshurst SC	3-1
Bedfont Sunday v Wonford U	2-1
Britannia U v Knighton Arms	0-4

FIFTH ROUND

Oyster Martyrs v Club Lewsey	1-0
Mariners v Northampton Duke of York	1-2
Knighton Arms v Paddock	1-4
Bedfont Sunday v Comets SC	1-2

SEMI-FINALS

Paddock v Comets SC	4-1
Northampton Duke of York v Oyster Martyrs	0-3

FINAL (at Prenton Park)

Sunday, 1 May 2011

Oyster Martyrs (0) 1 *(McGivern 76)*

Paddock (0) 0   1105

Oyster Martyrs: Eastham; Rooney I, Latham, Dames, Rendell, Smith I (Smith II), Forshaw, Lipson, Rooney II, McGivern, Rimmers.
Paddock: O'Connor; Shinks, Dolan, Marsden (Kearns), Shaw, Hussey, Brown (Riley), Wheeler, Henders, Duncan, Langley.
Referee: R. Booth (Nottinghamshire).

FA PREMIER RESERVE LEAGUES 2010–11

With the reserve teams of Premier League clubs Birmingham City, Fulham, Stoke City and Tottenham Hotspur, deciding not to enter the 2010–11 season, the organizers had to come up with an ingenious system to replace the North and South sections that had hitherto been in operation.

The 16 remaining teams were split into three sections. The North had two groups A and B consisting of five teams in each, while the South had one section of six teams. Each team in Group A played each other twice and met the five from Group B and the South section just once for a total of 19 matches. The same criteria applied to the teams in Group B and the South, though the latter played 20 games in total because of their superiority in numbers – six opposed to five in each of the Northern sections.

NORTHERN GROUP A

	P	W	D	L	GD	Pts
Manchester U	19	9	8	2	14	35
Manchester C	19	10	3	6	10	33
Wigan Ath	19	9	4	6	–1	31
Newcastle U	19	8	4	7	0	28
Bolton W	19	8	3	8	–8	27

MANCHESTER UNITED – APPEARANCES AND GOALS
Wootton 18, Vermijl 15+4, Brown R 15, Dudgeon 13, Gill 13, Norwood 13+1, Obertan 13, King 11, Bebe 10, Brady 8+3, Tunnicliffe 8+2, Devlin 8+1, Amos 7, Keane W 6+3, Morrison 6+2, Eikrem 5, Brown W 4, Johnstone 4, Stewart 4, Thorpe 3+2, Keane M 3+1, Cofie +4, Evans C 3, De Laet 3, Petrucci 2+7, Pogba 2+1, Fabio 2, Blackett 1+2, Lingard 1+2, Ajose 1+1, Anderson 1+1, Ekangamene +2, McGinty +2, Rudge +2, Cole 1, Fletcher 1, Fryers 1, James 1, O'Shea 1, Fornasier +1, Van Velzen +1.
Goals: Obertan 6, Bebe 5, Keane W 4 (1 pen), King 4, Anderson 2, Brady 2 (1 pen), Keane M 2 (1 pen), Morrison 2, Norwood 2 (1 pen), Ajose 1, Cofie 1, Eikrem 1, Fornasier 1, Stewart 1, Thorpe 1, Tunnicliffe 1, Vermijl 1, own goal 1.

Northern Group A – Leading Goalscorers
Guidetti, John Alberto	Manchester C	10
McManaman, Callum Henry	Wigan Ath	8
Obadeyi, Temitope	Bolton W	6
Obertan, Gabriel Antoine	Manchester U	6
Ranger, Nile	Newcastle U	6
Blakeman, Adam John	Bolton W	5
Eaves, Thomas James	Bolton W	5
O'Halloran, Michael Francis	Bolton W	5
Dias Correia, Tiago Manuel	Manchester U	5
Keane, William David	Manchester U	5

NORTHERN GROUP B

	P	W	D	L	GD	Pts
Blackburn R	19	7	5	7	1	26
Sunderland	19	6	6	7	2	24
Liverpool	19	5	8	6	–1	23
Everton	19	4	3	12	–11	15
Blackpool	19	4	2	13	–26	14

BLACKBURN ROVERS – APPEARANCES AND GOALS
Pearson 16+1, Morris 16, Potts 12+3, Ramm 11+4, Parry 11+1, O'Connor 10+3, Henley 9+1, Kean 9, Aley 8+2, Hitchcock 7+6, MacLaren 7+5, Evans 7+2, Knowles 7+2, Hoilett 7, Lowe 7, Bunn 6, Gunning 6, Linganzi 6, O'Connor A 5+2, O'Connor C 5+1, Hanley G 5, Goulon 4, Roberts 4, Rochina 4, Fernandez 3+2, Cogan 3, Dunn 3, Formica 3, Mwaruwari 2, Nzonzi 2, Urwin 2, Hanley R +2, Osawe 1+4, Ajagbe 1, Andrews 1, Biram Diouf 1, Chimbonda 1, Dilo 1, Emerton 1, Fielding 1, Jones P 1, Judge 1, Kalinic 1, Rigters 1, Edwards +1, O'Sullivan +1, Vastic +1, Wylie +1.
Goals: Rochina 5, Hitchcock 4, Morris 3, Pearson 3, Potts 3, Roberts 3 (1 pen), Dunn 2, Hoilett 2 (1 pen), Biram Diouf 1, Cogan 1, Goulon 1, Evans 1, Gunning 1, Kalinic 1, Knowles 1, MacLaren 1, Mwaruwari 1, Osawe 1, Rigters 1, Roberts 1, own goals 2.

Northern Group B – Leading Goalscorers
Noble, Ryan	Sunderland	7
Rochina Naixes, Ruben	Blackburn R	5
Kornilenko,		
Sergei Aleksandrovich	Blackpool	5
McAleny, Conor Michael	Everton	5
Baxter, Jose	Everton	5
Lynch, Craig Thomas	Sunderland	5

NORTHERN GROUP A AND B PLAY-OFF

Manchester U (0) 1 *(Petrucci 65 (pen))*   **Blackburn R (2) 2** *(Rochina 21, 31)*
(at Old Trafford.)
Manchester U: Amos; Vermijl, Wootton, Gill, Brady, Rafael (Petrucci), Brown R, Fletcher (Cofie), Norwood (Ajose), Obertan, King.
Blackburn R: Bunn; Henley, Morris, Lowe, Hanley G, Parry, Formica, Potts, Kalinic (Hitchcock), Rochina (Evans), Aley (Ramm).

SOUTHERN GROUP

	P	W	D	L	GD	Pts
Chelsea	20	11	3	6	3	36
Arsenal	20	10	5	5	7	35
Aston Villa	20	8	6	6	16	30
West Ham U	20	8	4	8	1	28
WBA	20	5	10	5	1	25
Wolverhampton W	20	5	2	13	–8	17

CHELSEA – APPEARANCES AND GOALS
Lalkovic 13+1, Chalobah 13, Clifford B 13, Tore 13, Djalo 11+5, Sala 11+1, Phillip 10+5, Pappoe 9, Sebek 9, Borini 8, Clifford C 8, McEachran 8, Kane 7+4, Kalas 7, Bertrand 6, Mellis 6, Walker 6, Deen-Conteh 5+6, Ince 5+1, Woods 4+4, Bruma 4, Nkumu 3+1, Van Aanholt 3, Magnay 2+1, Kakuta 2, Saville 1+6, Mitrovic 1+5, Sampayo 1+3, Philliskirk 1+2, Devyne 1+1, Affane 1, Blackman 1, Bosingwa 1, Gordon 1, Hilario 1, Mancienne 1, Turnbull 1, Davey +1, Figurira +1, Jones +1.
Goals: Borini 12 (1 pen), Phillip 8 (1 pen), Lalkovic 6, Tore 4, Chalobah 2, Clifford B 2, Kane 2, Djalo 1, Magnay 1, Mellis 1, Nkumu 1, own goal 1.

Southern Group – Leading Goalscorers
Borini, Fabio	Chelsea	12
Emmanuel-Thomas, Jay-Aston	Arsenal	10
Phillip, Adam	Chelsea	8
Delfouneso, Nathan	Aston Villa	7
Aneke, Chukwuemeka		
Ademola Amachi	Arsenal	6
Gardner, Gary	Aston Villa	6
Lalkovic, Milan	Chelsea	6
Mujangi, Bia Geoffrey	Wolverhampton W	6
Freeman, Luke Anthony	Arsenal	5
Mantom, Samuel Stephen	WBA	5
Winnall, Sam Thomas	Wolverhampton W	5

PREMIER RESERVE LEAGUE PLAY-OFF FINAL

Chelsea (0) 1 *(Kane 80)*   **Blackburn R (1) 1** *(Formica 20)*
(at Stamford Bridge, Chelsea won 5-4 on penalties, attendance 799)
Chelsea: Turnbull, Kane, Kalas, Magnay, Bertrand (Devyne), Chalobah (Deen-Conteh), Tore, Clifford C, Lalkovic, Saville (Woods), Phillip.
Substitutes not used: Walker, Gordon.
Blackburn R: Kean, Henley, Morris, Lowe, Pearson, Parry, Evans (Ramm), Potts, Hitchcock (Osawe), Formica (Knowles), Aley.
Substitutes not used: Urwin, O'Connor.

TOTESPORT.COM RESERVE LEAGUES 2010–11

TOTESPORT.COM LEAGUE

CENTRAL DIVISION	P	W	D	L	F	A	GD	Pts
Derby Co	14	11	0	3	36	16	20	33
Sheffield U	14	9	0	5	36	23	13	27
Nottingham F	14	8	1	5	28	26	2	25
Port Vale	14	7	2	5	27	27	0	23
Rotherham U	14	7	1	6	32	32	0	22
Barnsley	14	5	2	7	32	24	8	17
Bradford C	14	4	2	8	19	27	−8	14
Sheffield W	14	0	2	12	7	42	−35	2

WEST DIVISION	P	W	D	L	F	A	GD	Pts
Preston NE	18	14	1	3	53	16	37	43
Burnley	18	11	3	4	45	25	20	36
Wrexham	18	10	2	6	36	30	6	32
Oldham Ath	18	10	2	6	26	20	6	32
Morecambe	18	8	2	8	28	28	0	26
Shrewsbury T	18	5	6	7	27	32	−5	21
Tranmere R	18	5	5	8	31	36	−5	20
Macclesfield T	18	6	1	11	24	41	−17	19
Accrington S	18	5	2	11	20	38	−18	17
Bury	18	3	2	13	24	48	−24	11

EAST DIVISION	P	W	D	L	F	A	GD	Pts
Middlesbrough	14	10	1	3	35	17	18	31
Hartlepool U	14	8	4	2	26	19	7	28
Leeds U	14	7	2	5	36	23	13	23
Hull C	14	5	5	4	30	26	4	20
Lincoln C	14	6	2	6	20	18	2	20
Scunthorpe U	14	5	2	7	14	19	−5	17
Gateshead	14	3	1	10	18	38	−20	10
Grimsby T	14	1	5	8	20	39	−19	8

TOTESPORT.COM COMBINATION

CENTRAL DIVISION	P	W	D	L	GD	Pts
Brighton & HA	12	8	4	0	15	28
Leyton Orient	12	5	5	2	5	20
Wycombe W	12	4	5	3	1	17
Brentford	12	4	3	5	1	15
Gillingham	12	4	3	5	−5	15
Crawley T	11	2	2	7	−6	8
Aldershot	11	2	2	7	−11	8

EAST DIVISION	P	W	D	L	GD	Pts
Ipswich T	12	6	3	3	11	21
Oxford U	12	6	3	3	9	21
Watford	12	5	4	3	3	19
Southend U	12	4	5	3	3	17
Luton T	11	5	0	6	−1	15
Colchester U	12	3	2	7	−11	11
Stevenage	11	2	3	6	−14	9

WALES & WEST DIVISION	P	W	D	L	GD	Pts
Torquay U	12	9	2	1	16	29
Swansea C	12	5	3	4	−1	18
Exeter C	12	5	2	5	2	17
Swindon T	12	5	2	5	2	17
Forest Green R	12	4	4	4	4	16
AFC Bournemouth	12	4	2	6	−4	14
Plymouth Arg	12	2	1	9	−19	7

TOTESPORT.COM LEAGUE CUP

GROUP ONE	P	W	D	L	F	A	GD	Pts
Preston NE	3	2	0	1	3	3	0	6
Tranmere R	3	1	1	1	4	2	2	4
Carlisle U	3	1	1	1	4	3	1	4
Morecambe	3	1	0	2	3	6	−3	3

GROUP TWO	P	W	D	L	F	A	GD	Pts
Walsall	3	2	0	1	11	3	8	6
Derby Co	3	1	1	1	6	7	−1	4
Rotherham U	3	1	1	1	8	10	−2	4
Lincoln C	3	1	0	2	5	10	−5	3

GROUP THREE	P	W	D	L	F	A	GD	Pts
Sunderland	4	3	1	0	13	3	10	10
Scunthorpe U	4	2	0	2	8	12	−4	6
Gateshead	4	1	1	2	9	−1	4	
Middlesbrough	4	1	1	2	6	8	−2	4
Hartlepool U	4	1	1	2	6	9	−3	4

SEMI-FINALS
Sunderland 5, Preston NE 3
Walsall 5, Scunthorpe U 1

FINAL
Sunderland v Walsall
Match to be played in August.

FA ACADEMY UNDER 18 LEAGUE 2010–11

SOUTHERN SECTION

GROUP A	P	W	D	L	GD	Pts
Fulham	28	15	6	7	20	51
Southampton	28	15	5	8	17	50
West Ham U	27	14	1	12	8	43
Norwich C	28	12	5	11	0	41
Arsenal	28	12	3	13	−5	39
Crystal Palace	28	12	3	13	−6	39
Ipswich T	28	9	7	12	−10	34
Chelsea	25	9	5	11	−5	32
Charlton Ath	27	8	5	14	−8	29
Portsmouth	28	4	5	19	−31	17

GROUP B	P	W	D	L	GD	Pts
Aston Villa	27	17	6	4	37	57
Leicester C	28	17	5	6	28	56
Watford	27	16	5	6	16	53
Tottenham H	28	13	6	9	4	45
Reading	27	13	2	12	8	41
Birmingham C	27	11	5	11	−4	38
Bristol C	28	10	3	15	−15	33
Coventry C	28	6	12	10	−4	30
Cardiff C	28	7	6	15	−19	27
Milton Keynes D	27	2	4	21	−49	10

NORTHERN SECTION

GROUP C	P	W	D	L	GD	Pts
Everton	28	17	7	4	25	58
Liverpool	28	17	6	5	35	57
Manchester C	27	14	10	3	11	52
Bolton W	28	14	4	10	6	46
Manchester U	27	12	5	10	8	41
WBA	28	11	8	9	5	41
Wolverhampton W	28	11	5	12	1	38
Blackburn R	28	10	6	12	1	36
Crewe Alex	28	11	3	14	−5	36
Stoke C	28	5	3	20	−31	18

GROUP D	P	W	D	L	GD	Pts
Sunderland	27	15	7	5	19	52
Nottingham F	27	15	3	9	18	48
Barnsley	28	12	5	11	7	41
Newcastle U	27	11	7	9	6	40
Sheffield U	28	11	6	11	−3	39
Middlesbrough	28	11	4	13	−7	37
Leeds U	27	10	4	13	−16	34
Huddersfield T	28	7	5	16	−23	26
Derby Co	28	7	3	18	−6	24
Sheffield W	28	6	6	16	−33	24

ACADEMY PLAY-OFF SEMI-FINALS
Everton 3, Aston Villa 2
Fulham 3, Sunderland 3
Fulham won 4-1 on penalties.

ACADEMY FINAL
Fulham 1, Everton 2

IMPORTANT ADDRESSES

The Football Association: Wembley Stadium, P.O. Box 1966, London SW1P 9EQ. *0844 980 8200*

Scotland: David Taylor, Hampden Park, Glasgow G42 9AY. *0141 616 6000*

Northern Ireland (Irish FA): Chief Executive, 20 Windsor Avenue, Belfast BT9 6EE. *028 9066 9458*

Wales: 11/12 Neptune Court, Vanguard Way, Cardiff CF24 5PJ. *029 2043 5830*

Republic of Ireland National Sports Campus, Abbotstown, Dublin 15. *00 353 1 8999 500*

International Federation (FIFA): P.O. Box 85 8030 Zurich, Switzerland. *00 41 43 222 7777. Fax: 00 411 384 9696*

Union of European Football Associations: Secretary, Route de Geneve 46, Case Postale CH-1260 Nyon, Switzerland. *00 41 848 00 2727. Fax: 0041 22 994 44 88*

THE LEAGUES

The Premier League: M. Foster, 30 Gloucester Place, London W1A 8PL. *0207 864 9000*

The Football League: Andy Williamson, The Football League, Unit 5, Edward VII Quay, Navigation Way, Preston, Lancashire PR2 2YF. *0870 442 0 1888. Fax 0870 442 0 1188*

Scottish Premier League: R. Mitchell, Hampden Park, Somerville Drive, Glasgow G42 9BA. *0141 646 6962*

The Scottish League: Hampden Park, Glasgow G42 9EB. *0141 620 4160*

Football League of Ireland: D. Crowther, 80 Merrion Square, Dublin 2. *00353 16765120*

Football Conference: D. Strudwick, 3rd Floor, Wellington House, 31–34 Waterloo Street, Birmingham B2 5TJ. *0121 214 1950*

Southern League: J. Mills, Sansome Lodge, 4–6 Sansome Walk, Worcester WR1 1LH. *01905 330 444*

Northern Premier League: P. Bradley, 7 Guest Road, Prestwich, Manchester M25 7QJ. *0161 798 5198*

Isthmian League: B. Badcock, 14–15 Wisdom Facilities Centre, 42 Hollands Road, Haverhill, Suffolk CB9 8SA. *01440 768 840*

Eastern Counties League: N. Spurling, 16 Thanet Road, Ipswich, Suffolk IP4 5LB. *07952 595 290*

Essex Senior League: J. Taylor, 2 Courage Close, Hornchurch, Essex RM11 2BJ. *07739 996 861*

Hellenic League: B. King, 7 Stoneleigh Drive, Carterton, Oxon OX18 1EE. *0845 260 6644*

Kent League: A.R. Vinter, 4 Staple Court, Chilham Castle Estate, Chilham, Canterbury CT4 8DB.

Midland Alliance: J. Shaw, 176 Springthorpe Road, Erdington, Birmingham B24 0SN. *0121 350 5869*

North West Counties League: J. Deal, 24 The Pastures, Crossens, Southport PR9 8RH. *07713 622210*

Northern Counties East: B. Gould, 42 Thirlmere Drive, Dronfield, Derbyshire S18 2HW. *07773 653 238*

Northern League: T. Golightly, 85 Park Road North, Chester-le-Street, Co. Durham DH3 3SA. *0191 388 2056*

Spartan South Midlands League: M. Mitchell, 26 Leighton Court, Dunstable, Beds LU6 1EW. *07710 455 409*

Sussex County League: P. Beard, 2 Van Gogh Place, North Bersted, Bognor Regis, West Sussex PO22 9BG. *07831 497 913*

United Counties League: N. Haycox, 12 Glenfield Drive, Great Doddington, Wellingborough NN29 7TE. *07879 036235*

Wessex League: I. Craig, 7 Old River, Denmead, Hampshire PO7 6UX. *07733 212 179*

Western League: K.A. Clarke, 32 Westmead Lane, Chippenham, Wilts SN15 3HZ. *07790 002279*

Suburban League (Formerly Combined Counties): M.J. Bidmead, 55 Grange Road, Chessington, Surrey KT9 1EZ. *0208 397 4834*

Midland Combination: N. Wood, 30 Glalsdale Road, Hall Green, Birmingham B28 8PX. *07967 440007*

West Midlands League: N.R. Juggins, 14 Badger Way, Blackwell, Bromsgrove, Worcs B60 1EX. *07977 422 362*

OTHER USEFUL ADDRESSES

Amateur Football Alliance: M. Brown, Unit 3, 7 Wenlock Road, London N1 7SL. *0208 733 2613*

English Schools FA: J. Read, 4 Parker Court, Staffordshire Technology Park, Stafford ST18 0WP. *01785 785 970*

British Universities Sports Association: G. Gregory-Jones, Chief Executive: BUSA, 20–24 King's Bench Street, London SE1 0QX. *0207 633 5050*

The Football Supporters Federation: The Fans Stadium, Kingsmeadow, Jack Goodchild Way, 422a Kingston Road, Kingston-upon-Thames KT1 3PB. *0330 44 000 44*

National Playing Fields Association: 57b, 25 Ovington Square, London SW3 1LQ. *0207 584 6445*

Professional Footballers' Association: G. Taylor, 2 Oxford Court, Bishopsgate, Off Lower Moseley Street, Manchester M2 3WQ. *0161 236 0575*

Referees' Association: A. Smith, Unit 12, Ensign Business Centre, Westwood Way, Westwood Business Park, Westwood Heath, Coventry CV4 8JA. *024 7642 0360*

Women's Football Alliance: Miss K. Doyle, The Football Association, 25 Soho Square, London W1D 4FA. *020 7745 4545*

Women's Football Conference: Mike Appleby, Wembley Stadium, PO Box 1966, London SW1P 9EQ. *0844 980 8200*

League Managers Association: The Camkin Suite, 1 Pegasus House, Tachbrook Park, Warwick CV34 6LW. *01926 831 556. Fax: 01926 429 781*

Institute of Football Management and Administration: Camkin House, 8 Charles Court, Budbrooke Road, Warwick CV34 5LZ. *01926 411 884.*

World Cup (1966) Association: Hon. Secretary, David Duncan, 96 Glenlea Road, Eltham, London SE9 1DZ.

The Ninety-Two Club: Mr M. Kimberley, The Ninety-Two Club, 153 Hayes Lane, Kenley, Surrey CR8 5HP.

The Football Foundation: Whittington House, 19-30 Alfred Place, London WC1E 7EA. *08453 454 555*

Association of Provincial Football Supporters Clubs in London: Tina A. Robertson, 45 Durham Avenue, Heston, Middlesex TW5 0HG. *0208 843 9854*

World Association of Friends of English Football: Carlisle Hill, Gluck, Habichthof 2, D24939 Flensburg, Germany. *0049 461 4700222*

Football Postcard Collectors Club: PRO: Bryan Horsnell, 275 Overdown Road, Tilehurst, Reading RG31 6NX. *0118 942 4448 (and fax)*

UK Programme Collectors Club: P.O. Box 3236, Norwich NR7 7BE. *01603 449 237*

Programme Monthly & Football Collectable Magazine: P.O. Box 3236 Norwich NR7 7BE.

Scottish Football Historians Association: John Lister, 46 Milton Road, Kirkcaldy, Fife KY1 1TL. *01592 268718*

Phil Gould (Licensed Football Agent), c/o Whoppit Management Ltd, P. O. Box 27204, London N11 2WS. *07071 732 468. Fax: 07070 732 469*

The Scandinavian Union of Supporters of British Football: Postboks, 15 Stovner, N-0913 Oslo, Norway.

Football Writers' Association: 6 Chase Lane, Barkingside, Essex IG6 1BH. *0208 554 2455 (and fax)*

Programme Promotions: P.O. Box 209, Hounslow, Middlesex TW3 4DF. *01923 680 988* Web: www.footballprogrammes.com

Football Safety Officers Association: Chris Patzelt, P.O. Box 7482, Alfreton, Derbyshire. *0114 288 3366.*

Football Foundation: 30 Gloucester Place, London W1U 8FF. *0845 345 4555*

Football Licensing Authority: 27 Harcourt House, 19 Cavendish Square, London W1G 0PL. *0207 491 7191*

Sport England: 16 Upper Woburn Place, London WC1H 0QP. *0207 388 1277*

Association of Football Badge Collectors: K. Wilkinson, 18 Hinton St, Fairfield, Liverpool L6 3AR.

Soccer Nostalgia: G. Wallis, Albion Chambers, 1 Albion Road, Birchington, Kent CT7 9DN. *01303 275 432.*

Sir Norman Chester Centre for Football Research: Department of Sociology, University of Leicester LE1 7RH. *0116 252 2741/5.*

Sports Turf Research Unit: Bingley, West Yorkshire BD16 1AU. *01274 565 131*

FOOTBALL CLUB CHAPLAINCY

A sometimes voiced criticism of Football Chaplaincy runs something like this:

"Why should there be a chaplain at any club? To have religion forced upon anyone is quite wrong and goes against modern attitudes."

Of course, the criticism is misplaced. It shows no understanding of chaplaincy anywhere! A football chaplain "forces" his faith upon no-one! Neither do chaplains at a hospital, in the forces or in industry, for example.

Perhaps the experience of one chaplain helps to provide an answer – and the longer-term implications of a football chaplain's ministry!

The chaplain was always subjected to words that sought to belittle him from a former international player whenever the pair was in a dressing-room together. It was loud, disparaging and discouraging and even though some of the other players had had good reason to appreciate the chaplain's ministry, it went unchallenged, though there was a feeling of relief among everyone when the critic was transferred.

A few years later, the chaplain was surprised to receive a phone-call from his previous detractor, seeking help over a personal matter. When the pair met, all previous hostility had disappeared and in a spirit of friendship and goodwill, the chaplain offered and provided the practical support which was sought.

Today, that former critic has become one of football chaplaincy's most ardent champions!

THE REV

OFFICIAL CHAPLAINS TO FA PREMIERSHIP AND FOOTBALL LEAGUE CLUBS

Co-Chaplains Revs Mike Pusey and George Newton – Aldershot Town; Rev Ken Baker – Aston Villa; Rev Peter Amos – Barnsley; Rev Ken Howles – Blackburn R; Rev Michael Ward – Blackpool; Rev Philip Mason – Bolton W; Rev Andy Rimmer – Bournemouth; Co-Chaplains Revs Jimmy Hinton – Bradford C and Paul Deo – Bradford C Centre of Excellence; Rev Martin Batstone – Brighton & Hove Albion; Rev Derek Cleave – Bristol C; Rev Dave Jeal – Bristol R; Rev Mark Hirst – Burnley; Rev David Ottley – Bury; Rev Dr John Weaver – Cardiff C; Rev Alun Jones – Carlisle U; Rev Matt Baker – Charlton Ath/Pastoral Supp. Direc.; Rev Malcolm Allen – Cheltenham T; Rev Jim McGlade – Chesterfield; Rev Steve Clapham – Crewe Alex; Rev Chris Roe – Crystal Palace; Rev Peter Wyatt – Dagenham & Redbridge; Rev Tony Luke – Derby Co; Rev Stephen Clark – Doncaster R; Co-Chaplains Henry Corbett and Harry Ross – Everton; Rev Gary Piper – Fulham; Rev Richard Hayton – Gillingham; Rev Allen Bagshawe – Hull C; Rev Kevan McCormack – Ipswich T; Co-Chaplains Rev Paul C. Welch and Fr Steven Billington – Leeds U; Rev Richard Gamble – Leicester C; Rev Alan Comfort – Leyton Orient; Rev Canon Andrew Vaughan – Lincoln C; Rev Bill Bygroves – Liverpool; Rev Howard Stringer – Macclesfield T; Rev Chris Howitz – Manchester C; Rev John Boyers – Manchester U; Rev Canon Owen Beament – Millwall; Rev Ron Smith – Milton Keynes D; Rev Glyn Evans – Newcastle United Academy; Rev Keith Beardmore – Newport Co; Co-Chaplains Revs Arthur Bowles and Bert Cadmore – Norwich C; Rev Steve Silvester – Nottingham F; Rev Canon Mark Tanner – Notts Co; Rev John Simmons – Oldham Ath; Rev Richard Longfoot – Peterborough U; Revs Arthur Goode and John Rowlands – Plymouth Arg; Co-Chaplains Revs Jonathan Jeffrey and Mick Mellows – Portsmouth; Rev John Hibberts – Port Vale; Rev Chris Nelson – Preston NE; Co-Chaplains Revs Bob Mayo and Cameron Collington – QPR; Rev Steve Prince – Reading; Rev Alan Wright – Scunthorpe U; Rev Nigel Manges – Sheffield U; Rev Peter Allen – Sheffield W; Rev Christopher Deakin – Shrewsbury T; Rev Andy Bowerman – Southampton; Rev Bill Montgomery – Stockport Co; Rev Stephen Taylor – Sunderland; Rev Kevin Johns – Swansea C; Rev Simon Stevenette – Swindon T; Fr Gerald Courell – Tranmere R; Rev Martin Butt – Walsall; Rev Clive Ross – Watford; Co-Chaplains The Ven Elwin Cockett and Rev Alan Bolding – West Ham U; Co-Chaplains Revs David Wright and Steve Davies – Wolverhampton W; Co-Chaplains Revs John Roberts and Tim O'Brien – Wycombe W; Rev Jim Pearce – Yeovil T.

The chaplains hope that those who read this page will see the value and benefit of chaplaincy work in football and will take appropriate steps to spread the word where this is possible. They would also like to thank the editors of the Football Yearbook *for their continued support for this specialist and growing area of work.*

For further information, please contact: SCORE (Sports Chaplaincy Offering Resources and Encouragement), PO Box 123, Sale, Cheshire M33 4ZA). Telephone 0161-962-6068 or email admin@scorechaplaincy.org.uk.

OBITUARIES

Gerry Alexander (Born Kingston, Jamaica, 2 November 1928. Died Orange Grove, Jamaica, 16 April 2011.) Gerry Alexander was a defender who represented Cambridge University in the 1951–52 and 1952–53 Varsity matches. He also played for Pegasus, with whom he won an FA Amateur Cup winners' medal in 1953, when also gained England amateur caps after playing against Netherlands and Northern Ireland. Later he captained the Jamaica football team. Gerry was much better known as a cricketer, for Jamaica and the West Indies. A wicketkeeper-batsman, he played in 25 Tests and was the last white captain of the West Indies team.

Malcolm Allison (Born Dartford, Kent, 5 September 1927. Died 14 October 2010.) Malcolm Allison made just two peacetime appearances for Charlton before moving on to West Ham in February 1951. His career blossomed at Upton Park to the extent that within a year he was appointed as team captain. A stylish centre half he went on to make over 250 appearances for the Hammers before being struck down by tuberculosis. Malcolm then turned to coaching and management, and after showing early promise in charge of Plymouth Argyle he joined Manchester City as assistant to Joe Mercer. The pair took City to perhaps the greatest ever period of success in the club's history with the highlights being Football League champions (1967–68), the FA Cup (1968–69), and the Football League Cup and European Cup Winners' Cup (1969–70). Malcolm then took over as manager and went on to serve a string of clubs including Crystal Palace and Middlesbrough, his teams playing bright, attacking football.

Malcolm Allison

Charlie Atkinson (Born Hull, 17 December 1932. Died November 2010.) Charlie Atkinson developed with his hometown club, Hull City but is best known for his eight-year spell with Bradford Park Avenue, for whom he made a record total of 339 Football League appearances. Essentially a wing half or inside forward, he wound down his career with a season at local rivals Bradford City before retiring from senior football in the summer of 1965.

Eddie Baily (Born Clapton, London, 6 August 1925. Died Welwyn Garden City, 13 October 2010.) Eddie Baily joined Tottenham Hotspur in February 1940. After National Service in the Army he returned to White Hart Lane and signed as a professional. A regular in the side from November 1947, he was an important member of the team that lifted the Second Division Championship in 1949–50 and the Football League Championship 12 months later. After making more than 300 League and Cup appearances for Spurs, Eddie then had spells at Port Vale and Nottingham Forest, where he assisted in the 1956–57 promotion campaign, before concluding his playing career at Leyton Orient. He won nine caps for England and also gained representative honours for the Football League. Eddie later coached Orient for a while before returning to Tottenham where he spent 11 seasons as assistant manager to Bill Nicholson.

Cliff Baker (Born Bristol, 11 January 1924. Died Bristol, 14 December 2010.) Cliff Baker joined Bristol Rovers as an amateur in November 1946, signing professional forms the following January, by which time he had already made his League debut. However, he played just four more games for the club before moving on in the summer of 1948.

Harry Baldwin (Born Saltley, Birmingham, 17 July 1920. Died October 2010.) Goalkeeper Harry Baldwin played a handful of games for West Bromwich Albion towards the end of the 1937–38 campaign then moved on to Brighton only for his career to be placed on hold due to the war. He was the Seagulls' regular 'keeper for three seasons of peacetime football, making 183 appearances, and after a brief spell out of the League with Kettering he returned to finish his senior career with Walsall.

Ken Barnes (Born Birmingham, 16 March 1929. Died 13 July 2010.) Ken Barnes signed for Manchester City in May 1950. He established himself at right half during 1954–55 and after earning an FA Cup runners-up medal that season, went one better 12 months later, helping defeat Birmingham City as the Blues won the trophy. A superb passer of the ball, he went on to captain the team before eventually leaving in the summer of 1961. There then followed a spell as player-manager of Wrexham before he returned to Maine Road as a coach. Ken became assistant manager to Johnny Hart and thereafter he worked as the club's chief scout, assisting in the development of the team that won the FA Youth Cup in 1986.

Enzo Bearzot (Born Aiello del Fruili, Italy, 27 September 1927. Died Milan, Italy, 21 December 2010.) Enzo Bearzot enjoyed a relatively successful playing career in Italian domestic football, but it was as a coach that he excelled. After coaching at club level he took charge of the Italy U23 squad, eventually taking over the national team in 1977. He held the post until 1986 during which time he led his country to a 3-2 victory over West Germany in the 1982 World Cup final in Madrid.

John Benson (Born Arbroath, 23 December 1942. Died October 2010.) John Benson began his career with Manchester City in the summer of 1961, but it was in the lower divisions that he shone as a player, assisting Torquay United (1965–66) and Bournemouth (1970–71) to promotion from Division Four, before finishing off at Norwich. John then went on to a career in management, with spells in charge of Bournemouth, Manchester City, Burnley and Wigan Athletic. He was working on the back-room staff at Sunderland until shortly before his death.

Jim Blair (Born Calderbank, nr. Airdrie, 13 January 1947. Died Keerbergen, Belgium, 6 April 2011.) Jim Blair was an inside forward who began his career with St Mirren. He spent four years with the Paisley club separated by a season with Hibernian, helping the Buddies lift the Second Division title in 1967–68. In September 1972 he moved south, signing for Norwich City, but he was not a great success at Carrow Road and in 1974 he moved to Belgium, continuing his playing career with KV Mechelen.

Alec Boden (Born Hardgate, nr. Clydebank, 13 August 1925. Died 24 January 2011.) Alec Boden was a centre half who signed for Celtic during the war, but played his first peacetime football on loan at Cowdenbeath in the 1946–47 season. After returning to Parkhead he went on to make over 150 first-team appearances, captaining the side for a while, before finishing his career at Ayr.

Eddie Baily

Ken Boyes (Born Scarborough, 4 February 1935. Died Scarborough, 8 August 2010.) Centre half Ken Boyes spent more than a decade on the books of York City where he was mostly an understudy for Barry Jackson, making a total of 59 first-team appearances. Ken began his career as a 15-year-old with Scarborough and returned to the club after he left the Minstermen.

Terry Branston (Born Rugby, 25 July 1938. Died 22 December 2010.) Terry Branston was playing for Coventry works' team British Thomson-Houston when he was spotted by Northampton, signing for the Cobblers in October 1958. He made his debut against local rivals Peterborough United in front of a 23,000 crowd and helped Northampton rise through the divisions to the top flight. He stayed at the club until the summer of 1967 when he moved to Luton. Terry captained the Hatters to two promotions, but after losing his place at the start of the 1970–71 season he signed for Lincoln City. He narrowly lost out to Graham Taylor for the position of manager in December 1972 and soon afterwards moved into non-league football. In total he made almost 500 senior appearances during his career.

Jimmy Briggs (Born Dundee, 8 April 1937. Died Dundee, 10 April 2011.) Jimmy Briggs was a full back who signed for Dundee United in the summer of 1955, making his first-team debut shortly afterwards. Jimmy helped United gain promotion to the First Division in 1959–60 and was eventually appointed captain in the mid-1960s. A member of the team that defeated Barcelona in a Fairs Cup tie over two legs in 1966–67, he made over 400 first-team appearances during his stay at Tannadice before moving on for a short spell with Montrose.

Allan Brown (Born Kennoway, Fife, 12 October 1926. Died 19 April 2011.) Allan Brown signed for East Fife in the summer of 1944 and in the early post-war years he was a member of the Bayview club's successful team, gaining both a Scottish League Cup winners' prize and a Scottish Cup runners-up medal in 1949–50. In December 1950 he was sold to Blackpool, then one of the top English clubs, and went on to spend the next seven seasons at Bloomfield Road. He made over 150 appearances during his stay but missed out on both the 1951 and 1953 FA Cup finals due to injury. However, he featured in the 1959 final for Luton when they lost out to Nottingham Forest before ending his playing career at Portsmouth. Allan won 14 caps for Scotland, featuring for his country in the 1954 World Cup finals. He later went on to enjoy a second career in the game as a well-respected manager with Luton, Torquay, Bury, Nottingham Forest, Southport and Blackpool.

Gordon Brown (Born Church Warsop, Notts, 21 March 1929. Died Nottingham, 15 August 2010.) Gordon Brown joined Nottingham Forest as a teenager during the war, making four appearances in the emergency competitions. Although he signed professional terms at the age of 17 he failed to make the first team at the City Ground and moved on to York where his career quickly developed. An inside forward or wing half, he scored on his senior debut and went on to establish a reputation for solid, consistent play. A member of the York team that reached the FA Cup semi-finals in 1954–55, he made some 351 League and Cup appearances before leaving senior football in the summer of 1958.

Willie Brown (Died Edinburgh, 1 September 2010.) Willie Brown joined Hibs from Leith Renton in December 1941, making his debut against Queen's Park shortly afterwards. He managed a handful of North Eastern League games the following season, but made only one senior peacetime appearance at Easter Road before moving on for a more successful spell with Airdrieonians. Willie later played for Dunfermline Athletic and Cowdenbeath.

Dave Burns (Born Buckhaven, Fife, 13 March 1934. Died Linlithgow, Midlothian, 29 November 2010.) Dave Burns was a small stocky outside left who came to prominence with Petershill Juniors. Kilmarnock signed him up in the summer of 1956 and in his first season at Rugby Park he gained a Scottish Cup runners-up medal. However, a broken ankle suffered in September 1958 hampered his career and in September 1959 he signed for St Johnstone. He helped the Perth club win the Second Division title in his first season before winding down his career with spells at Arbroath and East Fife.

Richard Butcher (Born Northampton, 22 January 1981. Died Swinton, Salford, 9 January 2011.) Richard Butcher was a hard working midfield player with an eye for goal who completed over 300 senior appearances during his career and featured in two play-off finals. He began his career as a trainee with Northampton Town then had spells with Rushden & Diamonds and Kettering Town. Richard was given a second chance in the Football League when Keith Alexander took him to Lincoln City in November 2002 and he helped the Imps reach the play-offs in three consecutive seasons before moving on to Oldham. Spells with Peterborough United and Notts County followed, but he was back at Sincil Bank for the start of 2009–10. Later that season Richard joined Macclesfield on loan then signed permanently for the Silkmen in the summer of 2010. He made his final appearance for Macclesfield on 3 January in the home match against Rotherham United and tragically died suddenly at his home six days later.

John Butler (Born Birmingham, 10 March 1937. Died November 2010.) John Butler was an uncompromising defender who joined Notts County from Bestwood Colliery at the start of the 1957–58 season. He was an ever-present at right back in the Magpies team that won promotion from the old Fourth Division in 1959–60, then moved on to Chester where he switched to centre half. He enjoyed a lengthy run of consecutive appearances for the Sealand Road club taking his tally of Football League appearances beyond the 300-mark before leaving senior football.

Ian Buxton (Born Cromford, Derbys, 17 April 1938. Died Matlock, 1 October 2010.) Ian Buxton was the last all-round sportsman to combine cricket for Derbyshire and football for Derby County. A centre forward who was able to hold the ball and bring others into play, Ian scored at close on a rate of one every three games for Derby. Brian Clough sold him to Luton Town, where he gained a Division Four champions' medal, and he ended his career with brief spells at Notts County and Port Vale, where he also helped his team to promotion from the basement division. As a cricketer, Ian spent 15 years with Derbyshire, making 350 appearances and captaining the side between 1970 and 1972. He scored 11,803 runs as a middle order batsman and took 483 wickets.

Jimmy Campbell (Born Glasgow, 25 November 1918. Died 12 January 2011.) Jimmy Campbell was a winger who joined Leicester City in October 1943, playing almost 50 wartime games for the Filbert Street club. Later he spent two seasons with Walsall, making a further 14 appearances. Jimmy gained a Bachelor of Dental Surgery from Birmingham University in 1952, subsequently returning to Glasgow where he established his own dental practice.

Norman Christie (Born Kilmuir, Ross-shire, 1 September 1925. Died Forfar, 6 October 2010.) After wartime service in the RAF, Norman Christie trained as a physiotherapist in Glasgow, where he signed for Third Lanark. He went on to enjoy a successful career at centre half, helping Stirling Albion to the Division B title in 1952–53, then returning north to make over 100 appearances for Brechin and Montrose. Norman subsequently became manager of Montrose, serving from 1959 until August 1968 and later spent time on the coaching staff at Dundee United.

Brian Clark (Born Bristol, 13 January 1943. Died Cardiff, 9 August 2010.) Brian Clark was a member of the Bristol Boys team that won the English Schools Shield in 1957–58 and then signed for Bristol City. Tall and strong, he established himself in the first team in 1962–63, partnering John Atyeo up front. His goals helped City win promotion from the old Third Division in 1964–65 and he then enjoyed a spell with Huddersfield before signing for Cardiff. Brian's career took off again at Ninian Park playing alongside John Toshack. He finished leading scorer in three consecutive seasons, netting a memorable goal to defeat Real Madrid in the first leg of the European Cup Winners' Cup quarter-final in March 1971. He ended his career at Newport County.

George Clarke (Born Ipswich, 24 April 1921. Died Ipswich, 17 February 2011.) George Clarke was a defender who spent seven years on the books of Ipswich Town in the years following the war. Mostly a reserve at Portman Road, he made 34 Football League appearances before leaving senior football in 1954.

John Clarke (Born Northampton, 23 October 1946. Died 1 January 2011.) John Clarke was a defender who signed for Northampton in July 1965 when the Cobblers were about to embark on their solitary campaign of top-flight football. When he eventually established himself in the team some four years later they were on their way back to the Fourth Division. John, a right half for most of his career, went on to make over 250 League and Cup appearances during his stay at the County Ground, which was ended by injury in 1974.

Ronnie Clayton (Born Preston, 5 August 1934. Died Blackburn, 29 October 2010.) Ronnie Clayton was one of the legendary figures in the history of Blackburn Rovers, for whom he made over 650 first-team appearances. A fine defensive wing half who read the game well and was effective in the air and a powerful tackler, he captained both club and country. He joined Rovers straight from school, securing a regular place in the line-up in the 1954–55 season. An England international from November 1955, he won 35 caps for England, featuring in the squad for the 1958 World Cup finals and briefly captaining the team. Ronnie gained an FA Cup runners-up medal in 1960 when Blackburn lost to Wolves in the Wembley final and remained at Ewood Park until the end of the 1968–69 season before leaving senior football.

Jim Clyne (Born Glen Esk, Angus, 1927. Died 2011.) Centre forward Jim Clyne was a well known Junior player in the Arbroath area. He was the subject of a dispute between the Scottish FA and Scottish Junior FA after playing a few games as a triallist for Arbroath in 1951–52, but later went on to sign for the club. He also played briefly for Forfar Athletic.

Ralph Coates (Born Hetton-le-Hole, Co Durham, 26 April 1946. Died Luton, 17 December 2010.) Ralph Coates was an influential midfield player who earned four caps for England and made almost 500 Football League appearances during his career. After starting out on the Burnley groundstaff, he established himself on the left wing, and won England honours at U23 and full international level while at Turf Moor. A hard working, rather diminutive winger he was capable of powerful runs down the flank. In the summer of 1971 he was sold to Tottenham where he was a member of the team that won the UEFA Cup in 1972 and reached the final of the same competition two years later. He is best remembered at Spurs for scoring the winner in the 1973 Football League Cup final against Norwich City. Ralph concluded his senior career with Leyton Orient.

Ron Cockerill (Born Sheffield, 28 February 1935. Died 3 November 2010.) Ron Cockerill began his career as a centre half on the books of Huddersfield Town, although his career was interrupted by a two-year spell of National Service and he made just 40 appearances during his stay. In the summer of 1958 he was transferred to Grimsby Town and quickly became a key figure for the Mariners, for whom he was mostly used at left half. Ron helped Grimsby win promotion to Division Two in 1961–62 and went on to play 323 games for the club before retiring in September 1968.

Wiel Coerver (Born Kerkrade, Netherlands, 3 December 1924. Died Kerkrade, Netherlands, 22 April 2011.) Wiel Coerver was a well-respected

Ronnie Clayton

coach who is best remembered for inventing the Coerver Method of coaching. He had previously coached a number of clubs in the Netherlands, leading Feyenoord to victory over Spurs in the 1973–74 UEFA Cup final.

Avi Cohen (Born Cairo, Egypt, 14 November 1956. Died Tel Aviv, Israel, 28 December 2010.) Avi Cohen developed his career with Maccabi Tel Aviv, before becoming the first Israeli national to appear in England's top flight when he signed for Liverpool in 1979. He spent two seasons as a defender at Anfield, contributing a solitary goal in the 4-1 victory over Aston Villa which clinched the 1979–80 League title for the Reds. He also had a spell in Scotland with Rangers in the 1987–88 season. Avi won 64 caps for his country and later moved into coaching. In recent years he had been chairman of the Israel Football Players' Association.

Gerry Colgan (Born 20 June 1951. Died Glasgow, 5 February 2011.) Gerry Colgan captained the Strathclyde University team before signing for amateurs Queen's Park in June 1971. He went on to spend the next six years as a regular in the line-up for the Spiders, continuing his career with spells at Clydebank and Hamilton. He eventually left senior football in 1983, having made some 331 appearances.

Bill Collins (Born Belfast, 15 February 1920. Died 3 November 2010) Bill Collins was a wing half who developed in Irish League football before signing for Luton Town in February 1948. He made seven appearances for the Hatters then moved on to Gillingham who were at the time members of the Southern League. Bill was a regular in the line-up for the Gills' final season as a non-league club and also featured in the club's inaugural Football League campaign in 1950–51. He returned to Priestfield Stadium in 1957 in a coaching capacity and remained at the club for over 30 years, overseeing the development of young players such as Steve Bruce and Micky Adams.

Norman Corner (Born Horden, Co Durham, 16 February 1943. Died 19 February 2011.) Norman Corner was a big, powerful player who switched between the centre forward and centre half roles throughout his career. A former coal miner he joined Hull City from Horden Colliery in August 1962 but it was not until he moved on to Lincoln City some five years later that he gained regular first-team football. He became something of a cult figure at Sincil Bank and was also popular during a three-year stay at Bradford City. Norman later played for Bradford Park Avenue after they had left the League before returning to the North East.

Ronnie Coyle (Born Glasgow, 4 August 1964. Died Glasgow, 12 April 2011.) Ronnie Coyle spent his formative years with Celtic but most of his first-team football during his stay at Parkhead was played in loan spells elsewhere. He moved on to Middlesbrough and then Rochdale, but it was only after he returned to Scotland to sign for Raith Rovers in January 1988 that his career flourished. Ronnie proved to be a solid central defender. He made over 250 appearances during his stay at Stark's Park, featuring in two First Division championship sides and also experiencing European football. He concluded his career with spells at Ayr, Albion Rovers and East Fife.

Bobby Craig (Born Airdrie, 8 April 1935. Died Toronto, Canada, 1 October 2010.) Bobby Craig was a very skilful ball playing inside forward who joined Third Lanark from Blantyre Celtic shortly after the start of the 1955–56 season. He did well in four seasons at Cathkin Park, helping the club win promotion to the top flight in 1956–57, while in 1959–60 he was a member of the team defeated by Hearts in the League Cup final. He shone, too, at Sheffield Wednesday under Harry Catterick, but thereafter his career stalled somewhat and he

flitted around the clubs before eventually returning to Thirds, for whom he featured in their last-ever fixture against Dumbarton in April 1967.

Jim Cruickshank (Born Glasgow, 13 April 1941. Died Edinburgh, 18 November 2010.) Jim Cruickshank spent a season with Queen's Park before signing for Hearts in June 1960. He went on to become an iconic figure at Tynecastle, serving as Hearts' regular goalkeeper from 1963 to 1977 and making a total of 528 first-team appearances, the fourth highest in the club's history. Although on the small side for a goalkeeper he was brave and athletic. Jim won two Scottish Cup runners-up medals for Hearts and was capped at Amateur, Youth, U23 and full international levels for Scotland, also gaining honours for the Scottish League representative side.

Les Dagger (Born Lostock Hall, Lancashire, 25 April 1933. Died 9 March 2011.) Les Dagger was an out-and-out winger who was spotted playing for West Auckland while on National Service and signed for Preston North End in May 1956. He made 72 first-team appearances for North End but left when the club was relegated from the top flight at the end of 1960–61. He continued his career with spells at Carlisle and Southport, where he came known as an expert from the penalty spot. Les left senior football in the summer of 1965 after making more than 200 Football League appearances.

Frédéric Darras (Born Calais, France, 19 August 1966. Died Maligny, France, 27 October 2010.) Frédéric Darras developed at Auxerre under Guy Roux amongst a team of young talents including Eric Cantona, winning youth international honours. He made over 200 appearances in France's top flight as a solid and effective defender before spending 18 months with Swindon where he featured in both defence and midfield. On retiring as a player he moved into coaching and from January 2005 until his death he was coach of Chablis.

Eric Dobbs (Born Hingham, Norfolk, 15 October 1920. Died February 2011.) Full back Eric Dobbs spent a couple of seasons with Coventry City in the period immediately after the war, making five first-team appearances. He later moved on to Bristol Rovers, where he did not break into the senior team before switching to non-league football with Kettering Town and Lockheed Leamington.

Mike Doyle (Born Ashton-under-Lyne, 25 November 1946. Died Ashton-under-Lyne, 27 June 2011.) Mike Doyle was one of the key players in the successful Manchester City team of the late 1960s and early 1970s. A player truly committed to the City cause, Mike made 572 competitive appearances for the Blues and captained the team to victory over Newcastle in the 1976 League Cup final. A hard, uncompromising defender he helped City win a string of trophies including the Football League (1967–68), FA Cup (1979) and European Cup Winners' Cup (1970). Capped five times by England, he also played for Stoke, Bolton and Rochdale.

Ian Duthie (Born Forfar, 18 January 1930. Died Huddersfield, 27 June 2010.) Ian Duthie spent five seasons on the books of Huddersfield Town, but his time at Leeds Road was interrupted by National Service and he only was only on the fringes of the first team. He later spent two years with Bradford City, featuring fairly regularly at centre forward in the 1954–55 season prior to a move to Witton Albion.

Bill Edwards (Born Bowburn, Co Durham, 10 December 1933. Died 27 December 2010.) Bill Edwards was a centre forward who made 16 League appearances for Middlesbrough in the early 1950s, scoring on his debut at Wolves. He left the club at the end of the 1954–55 season.

Len Emmanuel (Born Treboeth, Glamorgan, 3 September 1917. Died Swansea, 24 July 2010.) Len Emmanuel was a defender who won representative honours for Wales Schoolboys before joining Swansea Town in April 1936, making his debut the following year. A full back of wing half, he served in the RAF during the war before returning to the Vetch Field for a final season. Len subsequently played for Newport County, Kidderminster Harriers and Llanelli before spending several years as player-manager of Carmarthern Town.

Brian Etheridge (Born Northampton, 4 March 1944. Died 26 March 2011.) Brian Etheridge won England Youth international honours and spent four years on the books of Northampton Town in the mid-1960s, although he was only a fringe first-team player during his time at the County Ground. He later had a short spell with Brentford before moving to Belgium where he played for Daring Brussels and Cercle Bruges before returning to the East Midlands.

Jim Farry (Born 1 July 1954. Died East Kilbride, Lanarkshire, 10 November 2010.) Jim Farry was a football administrator who joined the staff of the Scottish FA in 1972. In May 1979 he was appointed as Secretary of the Scottish League, a post he held for over a decade before being appointed as Chief Executive of the Scottish FA in 1990. He remained in post until the end of the 1990s, overseeing the redevelopment of Hampden Park Stadium during his tenure.

Jimmy Fell (Born Grimsby, 4 January 1936. Died Grimsby, 2 February 2011.) Jimmy Fell was a tall, pacy outside left who developed with Grimsby Town, for whom he made over 150 appearances before being sold to Everton for a then club record fee in March 1961. He spent 12 months at Goodison, playing regular top-flight football, then moved on to Newcastle United where he was top scorer in the 1962–63 season with 16 goals. Jimmy later played for Walsall and Lincoln City before moving into non-league football with Boston United.

Les Fell (Born Leytonstone, London, 16 December 1920. Died 9 October 2010.) Les Fell played for Arsenal nursery club Margate as a teenager, but eventually signed for Charlton Athletic at the start of the 1944–45 season. He made over 60 appearances for the Addicks during the hostilities, featuring in the side defeated by Derby County in the 1946 FA Cup final. He was then a near ever-present on the right wing during two seasons at Crystal Palace in the early 1950s before returning to play for Margate once more.

John Fraser (Born Belfast, 15 September 1938. Died Waterford, Republic of Ireland, 13 March 2011.) John Fraser was a wingman who developed in the Irish League with Distillery and Glentoran before Sunderland paid a fee for him in March 1959. Although he made 22 appearances during his stay on Wearside he never really established himself in the line-up. He later played for Portsmouth, Margate and Watford before emigrating to South Africa in the mid-1960s where he continued his career in the National Football League. He was capped once for Northern Ireland B during his time with Sunderland.

Brian Gallagher (Born Oldham, 22 July 1938. Died Fountain Valley, California, United States, 7 February 2011.) Right back Brian Gallagher joined Bury from Ashton United in October 1956 and after breaking into the first team towards the end of the 1957–58 season he went on to make over 100 appearances during his stay at Gigg Lane. Brian then played for Carlisle and Stockport County before emigrating to the United States where he played for Los Angeles Wolves in the inaugural season of the NASL.

Bill Gallier (Born Cannock, Staffs, 24 April 1932. Died 6 February 2011.) Bill Gallier was a versatile player who made 12 first-team appearances for Walsall in the 1955–56 season, playing at left half and left back. He subsequently joined Tamworth and then Hednesford Town.

Jimmy Goodfellow (Born Edinburgh, 30 July 1938. Died 1 April 2011.) Jimmy Goodfellow was a strong running winger who made his name with Third Lanark, where he made 152 senior appearances and featured in the side that finished third in the Scottish First Division in 1960–61. He moved on to Leicester, then a thriving First Division club where he played and scored in the two-legged Football League Cup final of 195 when City went down to Chelsea. Jimmy concluded his senior career at Mansfield helping the Stags in their epic run to the FA Cup quarter-finals in 1968–69.

Ian Gordon (Born Glasgow, 13 May 1929. Died 24 November 2010.) Ian Gordon was a defender in 1950s Scottish football, turning out for Hearts, Airdrieonians, Third Lanark and East Stirlingshire. Ian, who was a part-time professional throughout his career, had previously won international honours for Scotland Juniors whilst playing for Kilsyth Rangers.

Billy Gray (Born Ashington, Northumberland, 24 May 1927. Died Aspley, Nottingham, 11 April 2011.) Billy Gray was a tireless midfield worker who began his career with Leyton Orient where his performances soon attracted a transfer to Chelsea. He did well at Stamford Bridge where he was a first-team regular, making 146 Football League appearances and gaining representative honours for England B. A similarly successful spell with Burnley followed before he joined Nottingham Forest in June 1957. Billy gained an FA Cup winners' medal as a member of the team that defeated Luton in the 1959 final then moved on to Millwall where he became player-manager and oversaw the rise of the club from the Fourth Division to the Second. He also served Brentford and Notts County as manager.

Johnny Green (Born Warrington, 22 May 1939. Died 14 August 2010.) Johnny Green joined Tranmere Rovers from local football in February 1958. Once in the first team at Prenton Park he attracted the attention of bigger clubs and within a matter of months was sold to First Division Blackpool. A skilful inside forward, he later converted to right half, a role he played with craft and guile. He later had a spell in Canada with Vancouver Royals before concluding his senior career at Port Vale.

Vernon Griffiths (Born Birmingham, 14 June 1936. Died Birmingham, 27 April 2011.) Vernon Griffiths was a quick attacking wing half who spent five seasons on the books of Coventry City in the 1950s, making 15 Football League appearances, mostly in the 1957–58 season. He left Highfield Road in the summer of 1959 and signed for Rugby Town.

Terry Heath (Born Leicester, 17 November 1943. Died Rojales, Spain, 25 January 2011.) Terry Heath began his career as an apprentice with Leicester City, but although he won a professional contract he made only a few first-team appearances during his stay at Filbert Street. Ironically his final appearance for Leicester was in the first leg of the League Cup final tie at Stoke in April 1964. After a spell with Hull he enjoyed the best seasons of his career with Scunthorpe between 1968 and 1973. By now a cultured midfield schemer, Terry helped the Iron win promotion in 1971–72 before concluding his career at Lincoln City.

Ken Hencher (Born Chadwell Heath, Essex, 2 February 1928. Died Rochford, Essex, 1 August 2010.) Ken Hencher was primarily a wing half, although he could also play at centre half if required. A strong tackler, he was a part-time player throughout his career, spending two separate periods with Millwall interrupted by a two-year spell in Northern Ireland on Civil Service duties when he played for Distillery.

Ron Hewitt (Born Barrow Hill, nr. Chesterfield, 25 January 1924. Died Chesterfield, May 2011.) Ron Hewitt was a goalkeeper who made three appearances for Lincoln City in the 1948–49 season when he deputised for regular 'keeper George Moulson. Ron began his career at Sheffield United during the war and after leaving Sincil Bank played for several non-league clubs including Worksop and Grantham Town.

Mandy Hill (Born Blackpool, 15 February 1940. Died 27 November 2010.) Mandy Hill was an outside right who began his career as understudy to Stanley Matthews at Blackpool. When Matthews returned to Stoke, Mandy won a regular place in the team for a while only then to find himself back in the reserves and in September 1964 he moved on to sign for Tranmere Rovers. He spent four seasons as a regular at Prenton Park, making 130 Football League appearances and scoring 10 goals. He won caps for England U23s during his time with the Seasiders.

Bill Holden (Born Bolton, 1 April 1928. Died Morecambe, 25 January 2011.) Bill Holden was a much-travelled centre forward who first came to prominence with Burnley in the early 1950s. A regular in the Clarets' line-up for five seasons, he went on to play for Sunderland, Stockport, Bury and Halifax finishing with career totals of 161 goals from 431 Football League appearances. Bill was capped for England B against Scotland B in March 1953 when he scored both his team's goals in a 2-2 draw.

Mel Hopkins (Born Ystrad Rhondda, 7 November 1934. Died Worthing, 18 October 2010.) Mel Hopkins signed amateur forms for Tottenham Hotspur during the 1950–51 season, turning professional shortly after reaching the age of 18. He went on to become a regular at full back between 1954 and 1959, when he lost his place in the side. During this time he was also a regular for Wales and appeared in all five of their matches in the 1958 World Cup finals, when they reached the last eight of the tournament. Mel remained at White Hart Lane for several more seasons before moving to Brighton where he featured regularly in the side that won the

Division Four title in 1964–65 and also had a spell with Bradford Park Avenue towards the end of their time as League members.

Sammy Hughes (Born Ballymena, Co Antrim, circa 1925. Died 28 April 2011.) Sammy Hughes was a prolific goalscoring centre forward with Irish League club Glentoran. Sammy joined the Glens in 1949 and in a decade at the Oval he scored 297 goals in 378 appearances. Sammy was a member of the Irish League and Cup double-winning team of 1950–51, and the side that won the League in 1952–53, a season when he netted 64 goals in competitive games. He was capped five times for the Irish League representative team.

Wally Hughes (Born Liverpool, 15 March 1934. Died Auckland, New Zealand, 21 January 2011.) Wally Hughes was a winger who made a couple of appearances for Sheffield United in the 1955–56 before switching to non-league football with Wisbech. He subsequently spent time on the books of Bradford Park Avenue and Southport, adding a further 31 Football League appearances. In 1973 he emigrated to New Zealand where he became well known as a coach, leading the national team for the 1978 World Cup qualifiers.

Jeff Ireland (Born Paddington, London, 1 December 1935. Died 25 December 2010.) Jeff Ireland was an outside right who spent two seasons on the books of Tottenham Hotspur and although mostly a reserve at White Hart Lane he made three first-team appearances. Jeff moved on to Shrewsbury Town for the

Mel Hopkins

1959–60 season where he enjoyed regular first-team football and then switched to Southern League club Folkestone Town.

Tom Jarvie (Born Glasgow, 8 June 1916. Died Crawley, Sussex, 1 February 2011.) Tom Jarvie signed for Hamilton as a half back in 1935 and went on to make over 200 appearances for the Accies, including wartime games. He then had a spell with Third Lanark before moving south and later served Crawley Town as player-manager. Tom had qualified as a vet and became a prominent figure in veterinary circles in the south of England, acting as the vet for the BBC's *Blue Peter* television programme for many years.

Bill Jones (Born Whaley Bridge, Derbyshire, 13 May 1921. Died Chester, 26 December 2010.) Bill was a versatile and resolute defender who signed forms for Liverpool before the outbreak of war. He went on to play a crucial role as a member of the 1946–47 title-winning side and in all made over 250 appearances for the Reds. Bill, who also gained an FA Cup runners-up medal as a result of appearing in the 1950 final against Arsenal, won two full caps for England and won representative honours with the Football League.

Haydn Jones (Born Caernarfon, 8 May 1946. Died Bangor, 31 August 2010.) Haydn Jones spent two seasons as a professional with Wrexham making 16 senior appearances before being released in the summer of 1966 after the team had finished bottom of the Football League. Haydn then joined Rhyl and later played for a number of clubs in the area, also representing the North Wales Coast FA against Scotland Juniors.

Tony Kellow (Born Budock Water, nr. Falmouth, Cornwall, 1 May 1952. Died Truro, Cornwall, 20 February 2011.) Tony Kellow is best remembered for his exploits with Exeter City, enjoying three separate spells with the Grecians during which time he amassed an all-time club record of 129 goals from 329 appearances. A lively, wholehearted striker who could turn defences inside out and had a good eye for goal, Tony also had a decent spell with Blackpool in the late 1970s but seemed to give his best performances in the West Country.

Jack Kendall (Born Coventry, 31 March 1921. Died 7 January 2011.) Jack Kendall was a wing half who signed for Coventry City in 1944 having previously played works' football. He also featured for Leicester City in wartime games but did not make any peacetime appearances. Jack was also a talented cricketer and played a few first-class games for Warwickshire in 1948 and 1949.

Dave King (Born Hull, 24 October 1940. Died Hull, 16 July 2010.) Dave King joined Hull City as an amateur in August 1957, signing professional terms at the age of 18. He netted two on his debut against Sunderland, however he was mostly in and out of the line-up for the Tigers. After leaving Boothferry Park he played for a string of non-league clubs including King's Lynn, Goole Town and Bridlington Town and later returned to Hull as youth-team coach.

Alan Kirkman (Born Bolton, 21 June 1926. Died 14 January 2011.) Alan Kirkman was an inside forward who began his senior career with Manchester City early in 1956, but he played his best football with Rotherham between 1959 and 1963. He featured for the Millers in the first-ever League Cup final in 1960–61 and scored 58 goals during his stay. Alan went on to play for Newcastle, Scunthorpe, Torquay and Workington before switching to the non-league game.

David Knowles (Born Halifax, 11 April 1941. Died Brighouse, Yorkshire, 26 January 2011.) David Knowles was a goalkeeper who was a professional with Halifax Town between 1958 and 1963, making 72 Football League appearances. He later had spells with Bury and Bradford City before leaving the senior game at the end of the 1966–67 season.

Frank Lane (Born Wallasey, 20 July 1948. Died Wirral, 19 May 2011.) Goalkeeper Frank Lane signed for Tranmere Rovers from local club Stanley Arms in 1968 and made over 70 appearances during his stay at Prenton Park. In September 1971 he was signed by Liverpool as back-up 'keeper for Ray Clemence and he stayed at Anfield for four seasons, making just two first-team appearances. He was later with Notts County before switching to non-league football and Kettering Town.

Eddie Lewis (Born Manchester, 3 January 1935. Died Johannesburg, South Africa, 2 May 2011.) Eddie Lewis was a big, bustling centre forward who was one of the early Busby Babes at Manchester United. He was briefly a goalscoring sensation at Old Trafford but soon lost his place and moved on to Preston in 1955. Spells with West Ham and Leyton Orient followed before he eventually emigrated to South Africa. He went on to become a hugely influential figure in South African football, both as a coach and as a television analyst and commentator.

Markus Liebherr (Born Kirchdorf an der Iller, West Germany, 30 March 1948. Died Bulle, Switzerland, 10 August 2010.) Markus Liebherr was a successful businessman in Germany and Switzerland. In 2009 he purchased the holding company that owned Southampton FC and at the time of his death he was the club chairman.

Nat Lofthouse

Nat Lofthouse, OBE (Born Bolton, 27 August 1925. Died Bolton, 15 January 2011.) Nat Lofthouse was one of the iconic figures in post-war British football. A big brave centre forward he was a one-club man, who was associated with Bolton Wanderers for over 70 years in a variety of roles – player, coach, manager, scout and president. Famously known as 'The Lion of Vienna' he was the archetypal traditional English centre forward: a powerful battering ram of a man who led the line well and had a tremendous scoring record for both club and country. Nat played his first game for Wanderers as a 15-year-old during the war and his last some 24 years later. In total he scored 255 League goals for Bolton, still a club record, from 452 appearances. He won an FA Cup winners' medal in 1958, scoring both his side's goals to see off Manchester United and appeared 33 times for England, while in 1953 he was Footballer of the Year.

Johnny Love (Born Eynsham, Oxfordshire, 11 March 1937. Died 19 November 2010.) Johnny Love was a pacy outside left who joined Oxford United in their Southern League days after winning England Youth international honours. He made some 300 appearances for the U's, including 25 in the club's first two campaigns in the Football League.

Bob Lucas (Born Bethnal Green, London, 6 January 1925. Died Weymouth, 12 August 2010.) Bob Lucas was a goalkeeper who joined Crystal Palace in 1942 and made four appearances in the 1946–47 season. After a spell with Tonbridge he moved on to Weymouth, beginning a lifetime association with the South Coast club, as player, physio and president.

Doug McCracken (Born Kilwinning, Ayrshire, 21 July 1964. Died 5 May 2011.) Doug McCracken was a striker who joined Ayr United from Ardrossan Winton Rovers in November 1985 and went on to make over 100 first-team appearances during his stay. A committed, enthusiastic player he later played for Dumbarton and East Fife, switching to a defensive role towards the end of his career.

Sammy McCrory (Born Belfast, 11 October 1924. Died Donaghadee, Co. Down, 4 May 2011.) Sammy McCrory was an inside forward who developed with Linfield during the war years. Shortly after the start of the 1946–47 season he signed for Swansea Town and he went on to score at almost a goal every other game during his stay. Sammy later played for Ipswich, Plymouth and Southend, and although already into his 30s, his time with the Shrimpers saw him play some of the best football of his career. He netted 99 league and cup goals for Southend and in November 1957 won his first and only cap, scoring for Northern Ireland in a historic 3-2 win over England at Wembley.

Felix McGrogan (Born 16 October 1942. Died Glenrothes, 18 November 2010.) Felix McGrogan was a pacy winger who signed for Raith Rovers in the summer of 1962. He enjoyed regular first-team football at Stark's Park and later played for St Johnstone before moving to South Africa. He turned out for Durban City before a broken neck ended his career.

George McLuckie (Born Falkirk, 19 September 1931. Died 1 January 2011.) George McLuckie was an outside left who joined Blackburn Rovers from Lochore Welfare in August 1952. After a season at Ewood Park he moved on to Ipswich Town where he was an ever-present in the team that won the Division Three South title

in 1953–54. He made over 150 appearances for Ipswich and later spent two seasons with Reading before switching to Southern League football with Poole Town.

Reg Mansfield (Born Burton-on-Trent 1923. Died Church Gresley, 26 December 2010.) Reg Mansfield made four appearances at left half for Leicester City during the 1941–42 season. Although he later joined the professional ranks at Filbert Street when the war was over he added no further senior appearances, before moving on to join Gresley Rovers.

Svein Mathisen (Born Sauda, Norway, 30 September 1952. Died Kristiansand, Norway, 27 January 2011.) Svein Mathisen was an attacking player who spent virtually all of his career with Norwegian club Start, for whom he scored more than 100 goals in some 300 plus appearances. He also won 25 caps for Norway between 1975 and 1984. He spent a brief period in Scotland with Hibernian.

Ray Matts (Born 1941. Died 13 March 2011.) Ray Matts was a journalist who covered football for the *Express and Star* and *Birmingham Mail* before becoming the *Daily Mail*'s Midlands football correspondent in 1980. He also covered Formula One racing for the newspaper.

Shaun Mawer (Born Ulceby, Lincs, 6 August 1959. Died Hull, 17 July 2010.) Shaun Mawer was a right back who progressed through the Grimsby Town youth system and went on to spend three seasons as a professional at Blundell Park. He made a total of 60 Football League appearances before injury terminated his career.

Stan Milburn (Born Ashington, Northumberland, 27 October 1926. Died Rochdale, 30 July 2010.) Stan Milburn was a member of a famous footballing dynasty who made over 600 senior appearances in a career that spanned the period from 1947 to 1965. A solid full back, he won representative honours for England B and the Football League with Chesterfield and later helped Leicester to gain promotion to the First Division on two separate occasions. He concluded his career at Rochdale, where he was a member of the team that lost out in the 1961–62 Football League Cup final.

Norman Mitchell (Born Sunderland, 7 November 1931. Died 1 October 2010.) Norman Mitchell was a tricky, direct winger who joined Chesterfield shortly after the start of the 1951–52 campaign. He went on to make over 200 Football League appearances in a career that lasted throughout the 1950s, also turning out for Workington and Hartlepools. At Workington he played in the famous FA Cup third round tie with Manchester United in January 1958.

Tommy Moran (Born 5 February 1930. Died Edinburgh, February 2011.) Tommy Moran was a tricky winger who began his career in the lower reaches of the Scottish League with Leith Athletic. After spells with Cowdenbeath and Carlisle United, he signed for Darlington in the summer of 1956. The highlight of his career came when playing for the Quakers in an FA Cup third round tie replay against Chelsea in January 1958. Tommy scored two goals as Darlington gained an extra time victory over their First Division opponents by a 4-1 margin.

Bill Mordue (Born Sacriston, Co Durham, 23 February 1937. Died 23 September 2010.) Bill Mordue was a defender who spent four seasons as a senior player with Doncaster Rovers, making some 82 first-team appearances. A right back or centre half, he moved on to play for Scarborough for the 1961–62 season.

Johnny Morris (Born Radcliffe, Lancs, 27 September 1923. Died 6 April 2011.) Johnny Morris was an intelligent inside forward who signed for Manchester United during the war and went on to gain an FA Cup winners' medal after helping the team to a 4-2 victory over Blackpool in 1948. The following March he was sold to Derby County for what was a record British transfer fee of £24,500. The Rams finished in third place in the First Division that season, and as a result Johnny was called up to the full England squad, gaining three caps. He later spent six seasons with Leicester where he was a member of two Second Division title-winning sides.

Eddie Morrison (Born Gourock, Renfrewshire, 22 February 1948. Died 30 May 2011.) Eddie Morrison was one of the legendary figures in the post-war history of Kilmarnock. He made over 350 appearances for the Rugby Park club between 1967 and 1976, scoring 154 goals, five short of the all-time club record. An old-fashioned style centre forward whose committed displays endeared him to the Killie supporters, he later played for Morton before returning to Kilmarnock for a four-year spell as manager from 1985.

Bobby Moss (Born Chigwell, Essex, 13 February 1952. Died 1 August 2010.) Bobby Moss was a lively young striker who was an apprentice with Orient, later signing professional terms and making a handful of first-team appearances. He moved on to Colchester then enjoyed a lengthy career in non-league football, notably with Wealdstone and Chelmsford City.

Robert Muirhead (Born Dunfermline, 25 June 1964. Died Dunfermline, 19 October 2010.) Robert Muirhead was a versatile player who mostly featured at right back for East Fife during a four-year spell in the early 1980s. He made 70 first-team appearances during his stay at Bayview before leaving the senior game.

Bill Murdoch (Born 5 September 1941. Died 26 March 2011.) Bill Murdoch was a goalkeeper who played for Celtic (where he was in the reserve team) and Motherwell before becoming the regular 'keeper for Queen's Park in the 1965–66 season. In the 1980s he became a professional actor, appearing in television programmes such as *Rab C Nesbitt*, *Taggart* and *Monarch of the Glen*. He also had a role in the Martin Scorsese film *Gangs of New York*.

Doug Newlands (Born Edinburgh, 29 October 1931. Died Newlands was a flying winger who began his career with Aberdeen in 1951, however, with the exception of a loan spell at St Johnstone he saw little first-team action until moving south to join Burnley in March 1955. He eventually succeeded Billy Gray on the right flank for the Clarets and also had a spell with Stoke City before returning to Scotland. Doug amassed a total of more than 300 senior appearances, adding a second spell with St Johnstone and later playing for Airdrieonians and Forfar Athletic, where he was also manager in the 1966–67 season.

John Niven (Born Coatbridge, Lanarkshire, 15 May 1921. Died Neilston, Renfrewshire, 4 April 2011.) Goalkeeper John Niven signed for East Fife in February 1942 and almost immediately established himself as the club's first choice 'keeper. He played regularly during the club's glory days of the immediate post-war period, being a mainstay of the side that won the B Division title and the League Cup in 1947–48. He later had a short spell with Kilmarnock before leaving senior football.

Ollie Norris (Born Londonderry, 1 April 1929. Died Melbourne, Australia, 13 June 2011.) Ollie Norris was a direct forward who began his career at Middlesbrough where he spent six seasons but was mostly a fringe first-team player. After a season in the Southern League with Worcester City he joined Bournemouth in July 1955. Ollie enjoyed the best seasons of his career with the Cherries, starring in the team that defeated Wolves and Spurs to reach the sixth round of the FA Cup when they went out to the reigning League champions Manchester United. He later had spells with Northampton and Rochdale and as player-manager of Gloucester City before emigrating to Australia.

George Northcott (Born Torquay, 7 May 1935. Died Torquay, 15 November 2010.) George Northcott was a centre half who made over 150 appearances for Torquay United, where he was a member of the team that gained promotion from the old Fourth Division in 1959–60. After leaving for a season with Cheltenham he returned to the Football League with Exeter, although he was mainly a reserve for the Grecians.

Ladislaw Novak (Born Louny, Czechoslovakia, 5 December 1931. Died Ostredok, Czech Republic, 21 March 2011.) Ladislav Novak was a defender who won 75 caps for Czechoslovakia between 1952 and 1966, featuring in the 1962 World Cup final, when the Czechs went down 3-1 to Brazil. He spent most of his playing career with Dukla Prague eventually moving into coaching. He coached a number of teams in the Czech Republic and Belgium and had a brief spell in charge of the Czech national team.

Bill Ogilvie (Born Kirriemuir, Angus, 29 February 1932. Died Turriff, Aberdeenshire, 27 February 2011.) Bill Ogilvie was a centre half who joined Forfar Athletic from local juniors Forfar Celtic in May 1955. He spent five seasons with the Station Park club, where he was team captain, then a further eight seasons with Montrose, amassing some 450 senior appearances. He also spent a short period as manager of Montrose.

Ray Oliver (Born 1928. Died 27 April 2011.) Ray Oliver was a big burly centre forward who was one of the stars of amateur football in the North East during the 1950s, firstly with Whitley Bay and then with Bishop Auckland. He won two caps for England Amateurs and appeared in four consecutive FA Amateur Cup finals for Bishops, finishing on the winning side in three of them.

Willie O'Neill (Born Glasgow, 30 December 1940. Died 28 April 2011.) Willie O'Neill was a defender who spent a decade on the books of Celtic after joining from St Anthony's in October 1959. Although mostly a squad player, he made over 80 first-team appearances, seeing action in the early rounds of the club's European Cup campaign of 1966–67 and featuring at left back in the team that beat Rangers in October 1966 to take the Scottish League Cup final. Willie left Parkhead for Carlisle in the summer of 1969, but spent just one season with the Cumbrians before injury brought his career to an end.

Paddy O'Rourke (Born 1935. Died Dublin, 18 January 2011.) Paddy O'Rourke was a member of the successful St Patrick's Athletic team of the 1950s, gaining two FAI Cup winners' medals and featuring in two League of Ireland championship teams. He also made two appearances for the Republic of Ireland B team in 1958. He moved on to play for Limerick in 1963.

David Palmer (Born Bristol, 10 April 1961. Died Bristol, 2 March 2011.) David Palmer was a full back who made a solitary first-team appearance for Bristol Rovers against Wrexham in May 1979, when the Pirates fielded their youngest-ever side. He later spent many seasons with Bath City, for whom he made over 400 appearances.

Eric Parsons (Born Worthing, 9 November 1923. Died Worthing, 7 February 2011.) Eric Parsons was an outside right who signed for West Ham during the war and made over 150 appearances for the Hammers before moving on to Chelsea in December 1950. Although in and out of the side in the early years of his Stamford Bridge career he went on to become a key figure in the team that lifted the Football League title in 1954–55, when he was an ever present. Eric, who was capped for England B, concluded his senior career with Brentford before joining Dover Athletic.

Danny Paton (Born Breich, West Lothian, 27 January 1936. Died 10 March 2011.) Danny Paton was a forward who developed with Newtongrange Star before moving up to senior football with Hearts in 1956. He went on to make 70 appearances during his stay, gaining a League Cup winners' prize in 1962–63. During his spell at Tynecastle he spent a lengthy spell on loan to Southern League club Yeovil Town and he returned to the south of England in 1964 when he signed for Oxford United. He spent a season with the U's, then after playing in non-league football he moved on to the NASL where he turned out for the Washington Darts and Atlanta Chiefs.

Peter Perry (Born Treeton, Rotherham, 11 April 1936. Died April 2011.) Peter Perry was a right back who joined Rotherham United from local club Treeton Red Rose in July 1956. He went on to make over 100 first-team appearances for the Millers, featuring in the first-ever Football League Cup final in 1961. He later spent a season with York City before switching to Midland League football with Gainsborough Trinity.

Sir Daniel Pettit (Born 19 February 1915. Died July 2010.) Daniel Pettit played for Everton reserves before attending Cambridge University, where he was selected for four consecutive Varsity matches, serving as captain in 1937–38. He subsequently gained representative honours for British Universities, England Amateurs (one cap against Wales in February 1938) and for Great Britain in the 1936 Olympic Games. He went on to enjoy a successful career in industry earning him a knighthood in 1974.

Len Pickard (Born Barnstaple, 29 November 1924. Died Barnstaple, 16 March 2011.) Len Pickard was a centre forward who joined Bristol Rovers from Barnstaple Town in January 1951, but played just a few senior games before moving to local rivals Bristol City. He failed to break into the first team at Ashton Gate, but during a three-year spell with Bradford Park Avenue he was a regular, scoring 31 goals from 76 Football League games.

Ted Pole (Born Kessingland, Suffolk, 25 March 1922. Died 13 December 2010.) Ted Pole was a versatile player who spent five seasons on the books of Ipswich Town, making 40 first-team appearances both at half back and as a forward. He subsequently moved on to Leyton Orient where he stayed a further two seasons before leaving senior football.

Jan Popluhar (Born Ceklis, Czechoslovakia, 12 August 1935. Died Bernolakovo, Slovakia, 6 March 2011.) Jan Popluhar was a defensive player who won 62 caps for Czechoslovakia between 1958 and 1967 and was a member of the team defeated by Brazil in the 1962 World Cup final. He played most of his club football with Slovan Bratislava, although towards the end of his career he had a spell in France with Olympique Lyon.

Ron Rice (Born Birkenhead, 13 April 1923. Died 11 February 2011.) Ron Rice was an inside forward whose Football League career was restricted to the 1946–47 season, when he made a single appearance during a month's trial with Bradford City, then a further four during a slightly longer spell with Tranmere Rovers.

Dean Richards (Born Bradford, 9 June 1974. Died 26 February 2011.) Dean Richards was a powerful, classy central defender who made over 400 senior appearances in a career that spanned the period from 1992 to 2005. Dean joined Bradford City on leaving school, making his first-team debut at the age of 17 whilst still a trainee. In March 1995 he signed for Wolves, initially on loan before the deal was made permanent in the close season. His career continued to progress at Molineux, and in the summer of 1995 he won four caps for England U21s. Next stop in his career was Southampton, where he arrived in the summer of 1999 and immediately established himself as a player of Premier League quality with some fine performances, subsequently following Saints' manager Glenn Hoddle to Spurs in September 2001 for a reported fee of £8 million. At White Hart Lane he confirmed that he was a defender of the highest quality, commanding in the air, but he was increasingly hampered by injuries and these led to his retirement on medical advice in March 2005.

Dick Riley (Born Northampton, circa 1920. Died Northampton, 25 December 2010.) Dick Riley was a wing half or inside forward who made five wartime appearances for Leicester City. He later spent time on the books of Northampton Town without adding to his total of senior appearances.

Chic Robbie (Born Dundee, 1919. Died July 2010.) Chic Robbie joined St Johnstone from Dundee North End for the final season of pre-war football. He served in the Black Watch during the hostilities, suffering shrapnel wounds and rejoined the Perth club on his return. However, he moved on in the summer of 1947 and spent the remainder of his career in Division C with Brechin City and Forfar Athletic. A goalscoring inside forward or wing half, Chic scored over 50 senior goals before leaving the game at the end of the 1952–53 campaign.

Dale Roberts (Born Horden, Co Durham, 22 October 1986. Died Higham Ferrers, Northamptonshire, 14 December 2010.) Dale Roberts was a popular goalkeeper who represented the England C team and was playing for Conference club Rushden & Diamonds at the time of his tragic death. Dale began his career as a scholar with Middlesbrough before signing a professional contract with Nottingham Forest in 2005 and later moving on to Rushden.

Malky Robertson (Born Edinburgh, 7 July 1950. Died August 2010.) Malky Robertson was a dashing winger who joined Raith Rovers in the summer of 1971 and went on to make over 150 appearances for the club. A regular goalscorer, he later played for Ayr United and Hearts before moving to Canada where he spent a season in the NASL with Toronto Blizzard.

Idwal Robling (Born Pontypridd, Glamorgan, 1927. Died 9 June 2011.) Idwal Robling played for Lovell's Athletic, winning 13 caps for Wales Amateurs and winning selection for the Great Britain squad at the Helsinki Olympics in 1952. He later became a sports commentator for the BBC and was a member of the team covering the 1970 World Cup finals in Mexico.

Willie Rutherford (Born Lochgelly, Fife, 19 January 1945. Died Perth, Australia, 24 October 2010.) Willie Rutherford joined East Fife from Methil YC and after just over two seasons at Bayview and a brief spell at Forfar he emigrated to Australia. An explosive forward with great pace, he joined Sydney club Hakoah and featured in Australia's unsuccessful campaign to qualify for the 1970 World Cup finals, winning six caps for his adopted country.

Jack Shaw (Born Doncaster, 10 April 1924. Died Denaby Main, Yorkshire, April 2011.) Jack Shaw was a prolifically scoring centre or inside forward who netted 140 goals from 286 appearances for Rotherham United in the immediate post-war period. He was leading scorer for the Millers in 1950–51 when the Division Three North title was won, hitting a club record 46 goals in league and cup games, which included five in a 7-2 FA Cup drubbing of Darlington. He went on to spend two seasons of top-flight football with local rivals Sheffield Wednesday, later joining the coaching staff at Hillsborough.

Ron Simpson (Born Carlisle, 25 February 1934. Died Carlisle, 11 November 2010.) Ron Simpson joined the groundstaff at Huddersfield Town on leaving school. He developed into a talented left winger before moving on to Sheffield United where he helped the Blades win promotion from Division Two and reach the FA Cup semi-finals in 1960–61. Later he signed for his hometown club, Carlisle, assisting them to their first-ever Football League promotion in 1964–65.

Jackie Sinclair (Born Culross, Fife, 21 July 1943. Died 2 September 2010.) Jackie Sinclair was one of the stars of the successful Dunfermline Athletic team of the early 1960s. A skilful winger with great ball control and the ability to create chances with his crosses into the penalty area, one of his best performances came in December

1962 when he helped destroy Valencia in a Fairs Cup tie. He gained a Scottish Cup runners-up medal with the Pars in 1964–65 and then moved south to Leicester. Later at Newcastle he was a member of the team that defeated Ujpest Dozsa over two legs to win the Fairs Cup in 1968–69 then played for Sheffield Wednesday, Dunfermline (a second spell) and Stenhousemuir.

Jimmy Singer (Born Gilfach Goch, Glamorgan, 30 August 1937. Died July 2010.) Jimmy Singer was a goalscoring inside forward who progressed through local football to sign for Newport County. After two seasons of regular first-team football at Somerton Park he was sold to Birmingham City. He had mixed fortunes at St Andrews, scoring on his debut and appearing in the second leg of the Fairs Cup final with Roma in October 1961, despite struggling to establish himself in the side. He later played for Bournemouth and Newport once more, taking his total of senior appearances to close on 150, before leaving the game.

Stuart Skeet (Born Edmonton, Middlesex, 6 July 1948. Died Enfield, Middlesex, 1 February 2011.) Stuart Skeet was a young goalkeeper who graduated from the youth system for Tottenham Hotspur to become a professional in December 1965. He played reserve team football at White Hart Lane and his only senior appearance came whilst on loan at Northampton Town in April 1969.

Bobby Smith (Born Lingdale, nr. Middlesbrough, 22 February 1933. Died Enfield, 17 September 2010.) Bobby Smith joined the groundstaff at Chelsea as a 15-year-old. However, although he made his debut for the Stamford Bridge club as a teenager he never really established himself in the line-up and moved on at the end of 1955. A big, battling centre forward he proved a great success at White Hart Lane, where his goals helped the team to a League and Cup double in 1960–61, followed by the FA Cup again in 1962 and the European Cup Winners' Cup 12 months later. He also gained an Inter Cities Fairs Cup runners-up medal as a member of the London FA team that lost to Barcelona in the final of the 1955–58 competition. His final tally of 210 goals for Spurs was a club record, subsequently broken by Jimmy Greaves in 1968. Bobby concluded his career with a season at Brighton where his goals helped the Seagulls win the Division Four title in 1964–65. He also won 15 caps for England, scoring 13 goals.

David Smith, MBE (Born Barnet, 1926. Died Gloucester, 23 November 2010.) David Smith of Stonehouse, Gloucestershire, served as a referee on the Football League list from 1959 to 1974 and also on the FIFA list from 1968 to 1974. He refereed the centenary FA Cup final between Leeds and Arsenal in 1972 and his final match was the Manchester derby clash in April 1974 when Denis Law's backheeled goal for City sent United down to Division Two.

Norman Smith (Born Boldon, Co Durham, 23 November 1919. Died Coventry, 18 November 2010.) Norman Smith was a centre forward who signed for Coventry City in the summer of 1938 and made three appearances for the club before the outbreak of war. He remained at Highfield Road until December 1947, although he managed just 13 peacetime appearances, moving on to a brief spell with Millwall before returning to the Midlands to play for Bedworth Town.

Stirton Smith (Born Gorebridge, Midlothian, 28 October 1926. Died Dalkeith, Midlothian, 18 September 2010.) Winger Stirton Smith signed for Hearts from juvenile club Edinburgh Thistle during the war, but managed only one peacetime appearance. He also had a very brief spell with Third Lanark but did better at Dunfermline, where he appeared in the 1949–50 League Cup final when the Pars lost out to East Fife.

Bill Sowden (Born Manchester, 8 December 1930. Died Stockport, 13 November 2010.) Centre forward Bill Sowden spent five years on the books of Manchester City but was mostly a reserve during his time at Maine Road. In November 1954 he moved on to Chesterfield, where he scored prolifically, 62 times in 104 games, including 33 in the 1955–56 campaign. He concluded his senior career with a season at Stockport County before joining Macclesfield Town as player-coach.

Paddy Sowden (Born Bradford, 1 May 1929. Died November 2010.) Paddy Sowden was a skilful inside forward who was a young professional with Blackpool without making the grade. However, after a very brief spell with non-league Bacup Borough he rejoined the senior ranks, signing for Hull City. He made his Football League debut whilst on loan at Aldershot during a period of National Service but it was not until signing for Gillingham in the summer of 1952 that he gained regular first-team football. He later had spells with Accrington Stanley and Wrexham before turning to coaching, firstly in non-league and then with a string of clubs including Blackpool, Luton and Cambridge United.

Adam Stansfield (Born Plymouth, 10 September 1978. Died 10 August 2010.) Adam Stansfield first came to prominence with Yeovil Town, for whom he scored in the 2-0 FA Trophy final success over Stevenage Borough in 2002. He went on to make his Football League debut at the start of 2003–04 after the Glovers won promotion to the old Division Three. Adam also helped both Hereford (2005–06) and Exeter (2007–08) regain Football League status via the Conference play-offs while at St James Park he was leading scorer in 2008–09 when the club won promotion to League One. He played his last game for the Grecians in March 2010 before his tragically early death from cancer the following August.

Reg Stewart (Born Sheffield, 30 October 1925. Died 6 March 2011.) Reg Stewart signed for Sheffield Wednesday during the war, but struggled to make an impact at Hillsborough and in 1949 he moved on to then non-league club Colchester United. He helped the U's to victory in the Southern League Cup in 1949–50 and after they were elected to Division Three South he played in the club's first-ever Football League fixture. An uncompromising, no-nonsense centre half, Reg made over 250 appearances during his stay at Layer Road before moving on to play for Hastings in 1957.

Trevor Storton (Born Keighley, Yorkshire, 26 November 1949. Died 23 March 2011.) Trevor Storton was a centre half who made over 100 appearances for Tranmere Rovers before signing for Bill Shankly's Liverpool in August 1972. He was mostly a reserve in two seasons at Anfield, making just a handful of first-team appearances before joining Chester. A commanding defender he went on to make over 450 appearances during his

time at Sealand Road, playing a major role in the team that reached the semi-finals of the Football League Cup in 1974–75.

Les Stubbs (Born Great Wakering, Essex, 18 February 1929. Died Great Wakering, Essex, 1 February 2011.) Les Stubbs was a big, strong forward who joined Southend United from Great Wakering Rovers in the summer of 1948 and soon developed a reputation as a goalscorer. Sold to Chelsea in November 1952, he was an important member of the team that won the Football League championship in 1954–55 when his goals included a tremendous 40-yard effort against Portsmouth. Les returned to Southend to see out his career, finishing with a total of 77 goals from 217 League appearances.

Ronald Sword (Born Dundee, 6 May 1916. Died Worcester, 2 June 2010.) Ronald Sword was a centre half who developed in Dundee Junior football before spending the 1937–38 campaign with Dunfermline where he featured regularly in the line-up. He spent the following season at Carlisle, but made little impact before moving on to Buxton. Ronald was also a talented water polo player, representing the Scottish Midlands as a youngster.

Jeff Taylor (Born Huddersfield, 20 September 1930. Died Holmfirth, Yorkshire, 28 December 2010.) Jeff Taylor was a goalscoring inside forward who signed professional forms for Huddersfield Town in September 1947 and on breaking into the first team scored four goals in his first five appearances. In total he netted 29 goals from 71 outings for the Terriers before moving south to play for Fulham and Brentford, maintaining a respectable scoring record throughout his career. He retired from the game in 1957 and went on to achieve fame as an opera singer using the professional name Neilson Taylor. Considered a world-class performer and one of the best baritones of his generation, he later taught at the Royal Scottish Academy of Music and Drama where he was appointed Professor of Singing.

José Torres (Born Torres Novas, Portugal, 8 September 1938. Died 3 September 2010.) José Torres was a tall, powerful centre forward who was a member of the successful Benfica team of the 1960s, with whom he appeared in three European Cup finals and won nine domestic titles. He won 33 caps for Portugal in a decade from 1963, leading his country's attack in the 1966 World Cup finals when they finished in third place. José later moved into coaching and led the national side at the 1986 World Cup finals.

Jim Towers (Born Shepherds Bush, London, 15 April 1933 Died 16 September 2010.) Jim Towers was a prolific centre forward whose tally of 153 Football League goals for Brentford remains an all-time club record some 50 years after he left Griffin Park. Jim formed a deadly partnership with George Francis up front and the pair were the mainstay of the Bees' attack before being sold to local rivals Queens Park Rangers in the summer of 1961. Jim netted a total of more than 200 senior goals in his career, also playing for Millwall, Gillingham and Aldershot.

Eddie Turnbull (Born Carronshore, Falkirk, 12 April 1923. Died Edinburgh, 30 April 2011.) Eddie Turnbull was one of the all-time greats of post-war Scottish football. A member of the legendary Hibernian forward line known as 'The Famous Five', he was a lively creative inside forward with a powerful shot. Eddie arrived at Easter Road in time for the start of the 1946–47 season and stayed with the club until the end of the 1958–59 campaign, scoring 202 goals from 489 competitive first-team games. Hibs enjoyed tremendous success during this period, winning the Scottish League on three occasions. Eddie had the distinction of scoring the first-ever European Cup goal for a British club when he netted after 35 minutes of the away tie with Rot Weiss Essen in September 1955 and also won eight caps for Scotland. He subsequently became a successful manager with both Aberdeen (from 1965 to 1970) and back at Hibs (1971 to 1980).

Norman Uprichard (Born Moyraverty, Co Antrim, 20 April 1928. Died Hastings, 30 January 2011.) Goalkeeper Norman Uprichard developed with Distillery before earning a transfer to Arsenal in June 1948. However, it was not until he moved on to Swindon that he made his bow in senior football. Although on the small side for a 'keeper, he went on to make more than 250 Football league appearances for Swindon, Portsmouth and Southend. After making his debut for Northern Ireland in 1951 he went on to win 18 caps and featured for his country in the 1958 World Cup finals.

Frank Upton (Born Atherstone, Warwickshire, 18 October 1934. Died Derby, 17 May 2011.) Frank Upton was a no-nonsense defender best remembered for his two spells with Derby County (1954 to 1961 and 1965–66) during which time he made some 250 Football league appearances for the Rams. He had begun his career at Northampton and also played for Chelsea, Notts County and Workington before retiring as a player. Frank later turned to coaching, serving several English clubs as well as working in Denmark, Kuwait, Iceland, Borneo and Malaysia.

Francisco Varallo (Born La Plata, Argentina, 5 February 1910. Died La Plata, Argentina, 30 August 2010.) Francisco Varallo was the last surviving player to have appeared in the 1930 World Cup tournament. The youngest member of the Argentina team that lost 4-2 to hosts Uruguay in the inaugural final, in 1937 he featured in the side that defeated Brazil to win the Copa América. At club level Francisco won his first caps when with Gimnasia y Esgrima La Plata and went on to become a legendary goalscorer with Boca Juniors before a knee injury led to his retirement from the game in 1940.

Harry Verth (Died Edinburgh, 20 November 2010.) Harry Verth was a wing half and occasional centre forward who spent two seasons with Leith Athletic in the late 1940s, making occasional first-team appearances. He later coached Penicuick Athletic.

Ernie Walker, OBE, CBE (Born Glasgow, 7 July 1928. Died Glasgow, 14 May 2011.) Ernie Walker was a football administrator who served the Scottish FA as assistant secretary, and then as secretary from 1977 to 1990. A visionary figure who contributed to the SFA's Think Tank report of 1995, he was also chairman of the UEFA Stadia Committee for a lengthy period.

Richie Warburton (Died Belfast, 2 July 2010.) Richie Warburton was a pacy winger who played for Glentoran in the 1960s. He gained representative honours with the Irish League and also won four caps for Northern Ireland Amateurs.

Derek Warren (Born Colyton, Devon, 23 May 1923. Died 3 October 2010.) Derek Warren was a right back who joined Exeter City in January 1948 and went on to make 63 appearances while at St James Park. He later spent several seasons with Yeovil Town in the Southern League.

Norman Wilkinson (Born Alnwick, Northumberland, 16 February 1931. Died January 2011.) Norman Wilkinson was a centre forward who played a handful of games as a youngster with Hull before joining York City in July 1954. In his first season at Bootham Crescent he helped City reach the semifinals of the FA Cup and he remained with the Minstermen until the end of the 1965–66 season, scoring an all-time club record of 127 Football League goals from 354 appearances.

George Willis (Born Stanley, Co Durham, 9 November 1926. Died Exeter, 23 May 2011.) George Willis was an inside forward who was on Wolves' books as a young man. Although he did not break into the first team at Molineux, he went on to make over 100 senior appearances with Brighton, Plymouth and Exeter before injury ended his career during the 1955–56 season.

Neil Young

Alex Wilson (Born Buckie, 29 October 1933. Died 28 July 2010.) Full back Alex Wilson spent some 17 years on the books of Portsmouth after signing as a teenager. He made some 377 first-team appearances for Pompey before moving on to Chelmsford City in the summer of 1967. Alex won a single full cap for Scotland when he lined up against Finland in May 1954.

Johnny Wilson (Born Longriggend, 29 October 1916. Died Dunfermline, 2 November 2010.) Johnny Wilson was a forward who signed for Chesterfield in May 1939. He guested for a number of Scottish clubs during the war before returning to Saltergate. He also later played for Oldham and Accrington Stanley in the immediate post-war period.

Tim Womack (Born Denaby, 20 September 1934. Died Barnby Dun, Doncaster, 8 November 2010.) Tim Womack was an outside left who made two appearances for Derby before joining Southampton in May 1959. He was only a reserve with the Saints, but later added a further nine appearances for Workington before switching to Midland League football.

Norman Woof (Born Swarthmoor, Ulverston, 29 June 1924. Died Barrow-in-Furness, 14 July 2010.) Norman Woof was a centre forward who made his only appearance in senior football when he lined up for Chester against Oldham Athletic in a wartime game during December 1945.

Tommy Wright (Born Clackmannan, 20 January 1928. Died 5 May 2011.) Tommy Wright was a tricky winger who joined Partick Thistle towards the end of the war and quickly established himself in the side. In March 1959 he was sold to Sunderland for a substantial fee and he went on to score 52 goals from 170 appearances for the Wearsiders, an excellent goals ratio for a wingman. Tommy later played for East Fife and Oldham Athletic before leaving full-time football. He won three caps for Scotland, featuring in all three of the Home International fixtures in the 1952–53 season.

Neil Young (Born Manchester, 17 February 1944. Died 3 February 2011.) Neil Young joined Manchester City on leaving school, turning professional at the age of 17. Principally an inside left, he was a member of City's successful team of the late 1960s with the highlight of his career coming when he netted the winner in the 1969 FA Cup final victory over Leicester. The following year he scored in the 2-1 European Cup Winners' Cup final win against Gornik Zabrze and in total he hit 108 goals in just over 400 games for the club. Neil later had spells with Preston North End and Rochdale before retiring from the game.

Ian Nannestad
Soccer History Magazine
www.soccer-history.co.uk

LANDMARKS

Eve of season: Arsenal have 76 players on their books, 56 of them under the age of 21; Liverpool have 74 with 53 under 21.

August 28 – Manchester United achieves its 1500th point in the Premier League; the first club so to do.

September 11 – The Tottenham Hotspur v West Bromwich Albion match features players from 17 different countries.

October 7 – Manchester United announces a record operating profit of £100m.

October 8 – Manchester United announces a record loss of £83.6m.

November 3 – Filippo Inzaghi's two goals for AC Milan takes his European cups total to a record 70 overtaking Raul and Gerd Muller on 69. It also registers a club record 40th in Europe and makes him AC Milan's leading goal scorer on 125.

November 3 – Marseille 7-0 win at Zilina in the Champions League is the highest away score in the competition.

November 20 – Lionel Messi reaches 101 goals in his last 154 matches playing for Barcelona.

November 28 – The weekend's Premier League programme produced 41 goals and for the first time all teams scored at least one goal.

December 4 – Bangor City sets a British record from the start of the season with its 14th consecutive Welsh League win.

December 7 – Sir Alex Ferguson announces a change in his starting line-up for Manchester United for the 150th consecutive occasion.

December 31 – Manchester United enters the New Year unbeaten: a top flight record .

January 11 – The League Managers Association announces that 1023 managers have changed clubs since Sir Alex Ferguson was appointed at Manchester United in 1986.

January 16 – Brad Friedel the Aston Villa goalkeeper sets a Premier League record with his 250th consecutive appearance.

January 23 – Blackburn Rovers 2 West Bromwich Albion 0: 22 different nationalities represented during the match, 19 at the kick-off: Austria, Cameroon, Canada, Chile, Congo, Croatia, Czech Republic, DR Congo, England, France, Grenada, Nigeria, Northern Ireland, Norway, Paraguay, Romania, Scotland, Slovakia, Spain, Sweden, USA and Wales.

31 January – Fernando Torres breaks the record fee for a British club moving from Liverpool to Chelsea for £50m. Andy Carroll sets a British record of £35m transferring from Newcastle United to Liverpool.

31 January - £135m record for transfer fees in one day.

February 5 – 41 goals scored in eight Premier League matches including seven penalties. Wolverhampton Wanderers inflict Arsenal's first League defeat of the season. At the time Arsenal had lost just once before in the Carling Cup to West Ham United. Both defeats were sustained against the then bottom team in the Premier League. Wolves winning goal was the 700th scored in the Premier League 2010-11.

February 15 – Raul playing for Schalke scores his 69th goal in the Champions League to overhaul Gerd Muller's record in the European Cup.

March 6 – Ryan Giggs overtakes Sir Bobby Charlton's Manchester United League appearance record in his 607th match.

March 12 – Manchester United reaches the FA Cup semi-final stage for a competition record 27th occasion.

March 19 – Charlie Adam scores the 800th Premier League goal of the season for Blackpool.

March 25 – David Villa breaks Raul's Spanish international record by scoring his 46th goal in a match against the Czech Republic.

March 29 – England meets Ghana the eighth different African opposition and stays unbeaten having played a total of 17 such games previously involving Algeria, Cameroon, Egypt, Morocco, Tunisia and Morocco.

April 2 – Kevin Phillips, 37, becomes the oldest outfield player and scorer in Premier League history. Gijon ends Jose Mourinho's home record after 150 unbeaten games over nine years with four clubs: Porto, Chelsea, Internazionale and Real Madrid.

April 16 – Graham Alexander reaches his 1000th career match playing for Burnley.

April 23 – Lionel Messi scores his 50th goal in all matches in Spain during the season.

May 4 – Raul (Schalke) makes his record 144th appearance in the Champions League having already establish a record number of 71 goals in the competition initially with Real Madrid.

May 14 – DJ (Dudley) Campbell scores the 1000th Premier League goal of the season for Blackpool.

May 14 – Sir Alex Ferguson takes his managerial trophies in England and Scotland to 47 as Manchester United records its record 19th championship and 12th in the Premier League. Ryan Giggs in his 573rd Premier game collects his 12th winners' medal.

May 21 – Real Madrid's Ronaldo beats La Liga record with 39th and 40th goals. Previous joint holders Telmo Zarra (Athletic Bilbao) 1959–60 and Hugo Sanchez (Real Madrid) 1989–90 both with 38 goals.

May 22 – Premier League season ends with record 1063 goals scored.

May 23 – Manchester U win the FA Youth Cup for a record tenth time.

THE FOOTBALL RECORDS

BRITISH FOOTBALL RECORDS

ALL-TIME PREMIER LEAGUE CHAMPIONSHIP SEASONS ON POINTS AVERAGE

	Team	Season	P	W	D	L	F	A	Pts	Pts Av
1	Chelsea	2004–05	38	29	8	1	72	15	95	2.50
2	Manchester U	1999–2000	38	28	7	3	97	45	91	2.39
3	Chelsea	2005–06	38	29	4	5	72	22	91	2.39
4	Arsenal	2003–04	38	26	12	0	73	26	90	2.36
	Manchester U	2008–09	38	28	6	4	68	24	90	2.36
6	Manchester U	2006–07	38	28	5	5	83	27	89	2.34
7	Arsenal	2001–02	38	26	9	3	79	36	87	2.28
	Manchester U	2007–08	38	27	6	5	80	22	87	2.28
9	Chelsea	2009–10	38	27	5	6	103	32	86	2.26
10	Manchester U	1993–94	42	27	11	4	80	38	92	2.19
11	Manchester U	2002–03	38	25	8	5	74	34	83	2.18
12	Manchester U	1995–96	38	25	7	6	73	35	82	2.15
13	Blackburn R	1994–95	42	27	8	7	80	39	89	2.11
14	Manchester U	2000–01	38	24	8	6	79	31	80	2.10
	Manchester U	2010–11	38	23	11	4	78	37	80	2.10
15	Manchester U	1998–99	38	22	13	3	80	37	79	2.07
16	Arsenal	1997–98	38	23	9	6	68	33	78	2.05
17	Manchester U	1992–93	42	24	12	6	67	31	84	2.00
18	Manchester U	1996–97	38	21	12	5	76	44	75	1.97

PREMIER LEAGUE EVER-PRESENT CLUBS

	P	W	D	L	F	A	Pts
Manchester U	734	472	158	104	1452	628	1574
Arsenal	734	394	197	143	1271	669	1379
Chelsea	734	383	189	162	1217	695	1338
Liverpool	734	366	184	184	1189	713	1282
Aston Villa	734	276	223	235	936	870	1051
Tottenham H	734	274	195	265	1006	979	1017
Everton	734	257	207	270	924	939	978

TOP TEN PREMIERSHIP APPEARANCES

1	Giggs, Ryan	573	6	Heskey, Emile	488
2	James, David	572	7	Scholes, Paul	466
3	Speed, Gary	535	8	Carragher, Jamie	463
4	Campbell, Sol	503	9	Neville, Phil	460
5	Lampard, Frank	492	10	Shearer, Alan	441

TOP TEN PREMIERSHIP GOALSCORERS

1	Shearer, Alan	260	6	Owen, Michael	149
2	Cole, Andy	187	7	Sheringham, Teddy	146
3	Henry, Thierry	174	8	Lampard, Frank	139
4	Fowler, Robbie	163	9	Hasselbaink, Jimmy Floyd	127
5	Ferdinand, Les	149	10	Yorke, Dwight and Keane, Robbie	123

PREMIERSHIP GOAL MILESTONES

Goal	Date	Scorer	Match
1	15.8.92	Brian Deane	Sheffield U v Manchester U
100	25.8.92	Mark Walters	Liverpool v Ipswich T
1000	7.4.93	Mike Newell	Blackburn R v Nottingham F
5000	7.12.96	Andy Townsend	Aston Villa v Southampton
10,000	15.12.01	Les Ferdinand	Tottenham H v Fulham
11,000	7.12.02	Jay-Jay Okocha	Bolton W v Blackburn R
12,000	13.12.03	Alan Shearer	Newcastle U v Tottenham H
13,000	28.11.04	Frederic Kanoute	Tottenham H v Middlesbrough
14,000	26.12.05	Jermain Defoe	Tottenham H v Birmingham C
15,000	30.12.06	Moritz Volz	Fulham v Chelsea

EUROPEAN CUP AND CHAMPIONS LEAGUE RECORDS

CHAMPIONS LEAGUE ATTENDANCES AND GOALS FROM GROUP STAGES ONWARDS

Season	Attendances	Average	Goals	Games
1992–93	873,251	34,930	56	25
1993–94	1,202,289	44,529	71	27
1994–95	2,328,515	38,172	140	61
1995–96	1,874,316	30,726	159	61
1996–97	2,093,228	34,315	161	61
1997–98	2,868,271	33,744	239	85
1998–99	3,608,331	42,451	238	85
1999–2000	5,490,709	34,973	442	157
2000–01	5,773,486	36,774	449	157
2001–02	5,417,716	34,508	393	157
2002–03	6,461,112	41,154	431	157
2003–04	4,611,214	36,890	309	125
2004–05	4,946,820	39,575	331	125
2005–06	5,291,187	42,330	285	125
2006–07	5,591,463	44,732	309	125
2007–08	5,454,718	43,638	330	125
2008–09	5,003,754	40,030	329	125
2009–10	5,295,708	42,366	320	125
2010–11	5,474,654	43,797	355	125

HIGHEST AVERAGE ATTENDANCE IN ONE EUROPEAN CUP SEASON
1959–60 50,545 from a total attendance of 2,780,000.

HIGHEST SCORE IN A EUROPEAN CUP MATCH
Feyenoord (Holland) 12, KR Reykjavik (Iceland) 0 *(First Round First Leg 1969–70)*

HIGHEST AGGREGATE
Benfica (Portugal) 18, Dudelange (Luxembourg) 0 *(Preliminary Round 1965–66)*

MOST GOALS OVERALL
71 Raul (Real Madrid, Schalke) 1995–.
60 Ruud Van Nistelrooy (PSV Eindhoven, Manchester U, Real Madrid) 1997–.
58 Andriy Shevchenko (Dynamo Kiev, AC Milan, Chelsea, Dynamo Kiev) 1994–.

CHAMPIONS LEAGUE BIGGEST WINS
Liverpool 8 Besiktas 0 6.11.2007
Juventus 7, Olympiakos 0 10.12.2003
Marseille 6, CKSA Moscow 0 17.3.93

FIRST TEAM TO SCORE SEVEN GOALS
Paris St Germain 7, Rosenborg 2 24.10.2000

HIGHEST AGGREGATE OF GOALS
Monaco 8, La Coruna 3 05.11.2003

HIGHEST SCORING DRAW
Hamburg 4, Juventus 4 13.9.2000

GREATEST COMEBACKS
Werder Bremen beat Anderlecht 5-3 after being three goals down in 33 minutes on 8.12.1993. They scored five goals in 23 second-half minutes.
La Coruna beat Paris St Germain 4-3 after being three goals down in 55 minutes on 7.3.2001. They scored four goals in 27 second-half minutes.
Liverpool after being three goals down in the first half on 25.5.2005 in the Champions League Final. They scored three goals in five second-half minutes and won the penalty shoot-out after extra time 3-2.
Liverpool 3 goals down to Basle in 29 minutes on 12.11.2002. They scored three second half goals in 24 minutes to draw 3-3.

MOST GOALS IN CHAMPIONS LEAGUE MATCH
4, Marco Van Basten, AC Milan v IFK Gothenburg (33, 53 (pen), 61, 62 mins) 4-0 25.11.1992.
4, Simone Inzaghi, Lazio v Marseille (17, 37, 38, 71 mins) 5-1 14.3.2000.
4, Ruud Van Nistelrooy, Manchester U v Sparta Prague (14, 25 (pen), 60, 90 mins) 4-1 3.11.2004.
4, Dado Prso, Monaco v La Coruna (26, 30, 45, 49, 23 mins) 8-3 5.11.2003.
4, Andriy Shevchenko, AC Milan at Fenerbahce (16, 52, 70, 76 mins) 4-0 23.11.2005.

MOST WINS WITH DIFFERENT CLUBS
Clarence Seedorf (Ajax) 1995; (Real Madrid) 1998; (AC Milan) 2003, 2007.

MOST WINNERS MEDALS
6 Francisco Gento (Real Madrid) 1956, 1957, 1958, 1959, 1960, 1966.
5 Alfredo Di Stefano (Real Madrid) 1956, 1957, 1958, 1959, 1960.

5 Jose Maria Zarraga (Real Madrid) 1956, 1957, 1958, 1959, 1960.
4 Jose-Hector Rial (Real Madrid) 1956, 1957, 1958, 1959.
4 Marquitos (Real Madrid) 1956, 1957, 1959, 1960.
4 Phil Neal (Liverpool) 1977, 1978, 1981, 1984.

MOST GOALS SCORED IN FINALS
7 Alfredo Di Stefano (Real Madrid), 1956 (1), 1957 (1 pen), 1958 (1), 1959 (1), 1960 (3).
7 Ferenc Puskas (Real Madrid), 1960 (4), 1962 (3).

MOST FINAL APPEARANCES PER COUNTRY
Italy 26 (12 wins, 14 defeats).
Spain 22 (13 wins, 9 defeats)
England 18 (11 wins, 7 defeats)
Germany 14 (6 wins, 8 defeats).

MOST CLUB FINAL WINNERS
Real Madrid (Spain) 9 1956, 1957, 1958, 1959, 1960, 1966, 1998, 2000, 2002.
AC Milan (Italy) 7 1963, 1969, 1989, 1990, 1994, 2003, 2007.

MOST APPEARANCES IN FINAL
Real Madrid 12; AC Milan 11.

MOST EUROPEAN CUP APPEARANCES
Raul (Real Madrid, Schalke)

Season	European Cup A	European Cup G	CWC Cup A	CWC Cup G	Super A	Super G	WCC A	WCC G
1995–96	8	6	0	0	0	0	0	0
1997–98	11	2	0	0	0	0	0	0
1998–99	8	3	0	0	1	0	1	1
1999–2000	15	10	0	0	0	0	0	0
2000–01	12	7	4	2	1	1	1	0
2001–02	12	6	0	0	0	0	0	0
2002–03	12	9	0	0	1	0	1	0
2003–04	9	2	0	0	0	0	0	0
2004–05	10	4	0	0	0	0	0	0
2005–06	6	2	0	0	0	0	0	0
2006–07	7	5	0	0	0	0	0	0
2007–08	8	5	0	0	0	0	0	0
2008–09	7	3	0	0	0	0	0	0
2009–10	7	2	0	0	0	0	0	0
2010–11*	12	5	0	0	0	0	0	0
Total	144	71	4	2	3	1	3	1

*Schalke; A = Appearances, G = Goals

MOST SUCCESSFUL MANAGER
Bob Paisley (Liverpool) 1977, 1978, 1981.

FASTEST GOALS SCORED IN CHAMPIONS LEAGUE
10.2 sec Roy Makaay for Bayern Munich v Real Madrid 7 March 2007.
20.07 sec Gilberto Silva for Arsenal at PSV Eindhoven 25 September 2002.
20.12 sec Alessandro Del Piero for Juventus at Manchester United 1 October 1997.

YOUNGEST CHAMPIONS LEAGUE GOALSCORER
Peter Ofori-Quaye for Olympiakos v Rosenborg at 17 years 195 days in 1997–98.

FASTEST HAT-TRICK SCORED IN CHAMPIONS LEAGUE
Mike Newell, 9 mins for Blackburn R v Rosenborg (4-1) 6.12.95.

MOST SUCCESSIVE CHAMPIONS LEAGUE APPEARANCES
Manchester U (England) 15 1996–97 – 2010–11.

MOST SUCCESSIVE EUROPEAN CUP APPEARANCES
Real Madrid (Spain) 15 1955–56 – 1969–70.

MOST SUCCESSIVE WINS IN THE CHAMPIONS LEAGUE
Barcelona (Spain) 11 2002–03.

LONGEST UNBEATEN RUN IN THE CHAMPIONS LEAGUE
Manchester U (England) 25 2007–08 – 2009 (Final).

REINSTATED WINNERS EXCLUDED FROM NEXT COMPETITION
1993 Marseille originally stripped of title. This was rescinded but they were not allowed to compete the following season.

TOP TEN PREMIER LEAGUE AVERAGE ATTENDANCES 2010–11

1	Manchester U	75,109
2	Arsenal	60,025
3	Newcastle U	47,717
4	Manchester C	45,880
5	Liverpool	42,820
6	Chelsea	41,435
7	Sunderland	40,011
8	Aston Villa	37,193
9	Everton	36,038
10	Tottenham H	35,703

TOP TEN FOOTBALL LEAGUE AVERAGE ATTENDANCES 2010–11

1	Leeds U	27,299
2	Derby Co	25,892
3	Norwich C	25,386
4	Leicester C	23,666
5	Nottingham F	23,274
6	Cardiff C	23,193
7	Southampton	22,160
8	Hull C	21,168
9	Sheffield U	20,632
10	Ipswich T	19,614

TOP TEN AVERAGE ATTENDANCES

1	Manchester United	2006–07	75,826
2	Manchester United	2007–08	75,691
3	Manchester United	2008–09	75,308
4	Manchester United	2010–11	75,109
5	Manchester United	2009–10	74,863
6	Manchester United	2005–06	68,765
7	Manchester United	2004–05	67,871
8	Manchester United	2003–04	67,641
9	Manchester United	2002–03	67,630
10	Manchester United	2001–02	67,586

TOP TEN AVERAGE WORLD CUP FINAL CROWDS

1	In USA	1994	68,604
2	In Brazil	1950	60,772
3	In Germany	2006	52,416
4	In Mexico	1970	52,311
5	In England	1966	50,458
6	In South Africa	2010	49,670
7	In Italy	1990	48,368
8	In Mexico	1986	46,956
9	In West Germany	1974	46,684
10	In France	1998	43,366

TOP TEN ALL-TIME ENGLAND CAPS

1	Peter Shilton	125
2	David Beckham	115
3	Bobby Moore	108
4	Bobby Charlton	106
5	Billy Wright	105
6	Bryan Robson	90
	Andy Cole	89
7	Steven Gerrard	89
	Michael Owen	89
10	Frank Lampard	86

TOP TEN ALL-TIME ENGLAND GOALSCORERS

1	Bobby Charlton	49
2	Gary Lineker	48
3	Jimmy Greaves	44
4	Michael Owen	40
5	Tom Finney	30
6	Nat Lofthouse	30
7	Alan Shearer	30
8	Vivian Woodward	29
9	Steve Bloomer	28
10	David Platt	27

GOALKEEPING RECORDS
(without conceding a goal)

BRITISH RECORD (all competitive games)
Chris Woods, Rangers, in 1196 minutes from 26 November 1986 to 31 January 1987.

FA PREMIER LEAGUE
Edwin Van der Sar (Manchester U) in 1311 minutes during the 2008–09 season.

FOOTBALL LEAGUE
Steve Death, Reading, 1103 minutes from 24 March to 18 August 1979.

MOST CLEAN SHEETS IN A SEASON
Petr Cech (Chelsea) 24 2004–05

MOST CLEAN SHEETS OVERALL IN PREMIER LEAGUE
David James (Liverpool, Aston Villa, West Ham U, Manchester C, Portsmouth and Bristol C) 173 games.

MOST GOALS FOR IN A SEASON

FA PREMIER LEAGUE		*Goals*	*Games*
2009–10	Chelsea	103	38
FOOTBALL LEAGUE			
Division 4			
1960–61	Peterborough U	134	46
SCOTTISH PREMIER LEAGUE			
2003–04	Celtic	105	38
SCOTTISH LEAGUE			
Division 2			
1937–38	Raith R	142	34

MOST GOALS AGAINST IN A SEASON

FA PREMIER LEAGUE		*Goals*	*Games*
1993–94	Swindon T	100	42
FOOTBALL LEAGUE			
Division 2			
1898–99	Darwen	141	34
SCOTTISH PREMIER LEAGUE			
1999–2000	Aberdeen	83	36
SCOTTISH LEAGUE			
Division 2			
1931–32	Edinburgh C	146	38

MOST LEAGUE GOALS IN A SEASON

FA PREMIER LEAGUE		*Goals*	*Games*
1993–94	Andy Cole (Newcastle U)	34	40
1994–95	Alan Shearer (Blackburn R)	34	42
FOOTBALL LEAGUE			
Division 1			
1927–28	Dixie Dean (Everton)	60	39
Division 2			
1926–27	George Camsell (Middlesbrough)	59	37
Division 3(S)			
1936–37	Joe Payne (Luton T)	55	39
Division 3(N)			
1936–37	Ted Harston (Mansfield T)	55	41
Division 3			
1959–60	Derek Reeves (Southampton)	39	46
Division 4			
1960–61	Terry Bly (Peterborough U)	52	46
FA CUP			
1887–88	Jimmy Ross (Preston NE)	20	8
LEAGUE CUP			
1986–87	Clive Allen (Tottenham H)	12	9
SCOTTISH PREMIER LEAGUE			
2000–01	Henrik Larsson (Celtic)	35	37
SCOTTISH LEAGUE			
Division 1			
1931–32	William McFadyen (Motherwell)	52	34
Division 2			
1927–28	Jim Smith (Ayr U)	66	38

MOST FA CUP FINAL GOALS

Ian Rush (Liverpool) 5: 1986(2), 1989(2), 1992(1)

SCORED IN EVERY PREMIERSHIP GAME

Arsenal 2001–02 38 matches

FEWEST GOALS FOR IN A SEASON

FA PREMIER LEAGUE		*Goals*	*Games*
2007–08	Derby Co	20	38
FOOTBALL LEAGUE			
Division 2			
1899–1900	Loughborough T	18	34
SCOTTISH PREMIER LEAGUE			
2010–11	St Johnstone	23	38
SCOTTISH LEAGUE			
New Division 1			
1980–81	Stirling Alb	18	39

FEWEST GOALS AGAINST IN A SEASON

FA PREMIER LEAGUE		*Goals*	*Games*
2004–05	Chelsea	15	38
FOOTBALL LEAGUE			
Division 1			
1978–79	Liverpool	16	42
SCOTTISH PREMIER LEAGUE			
2001–02	Celtic	18	38
SCOTTISH LEAGUE			
Division 1			
1913–14	Celtic	14	38

MOST LEAGUE GOALS IN A CAREER

FOOTBALL LEAGUE			
Arthur Rowley	*Goals*	*Games*	*Season*
WBA	4	24	1946–48
Fulham	27	56	1948–50
Leicester C	251	303	1950–58
Shrewsbury T	152	236	1958–65
	434	619	

SCOTTISH LEAGUE			
Jimmy McGrory			
Celtic	1	3	1922–23
Clydebank	13	30	1923–24
Celtic	396	375	1924–38
	410	408	

MOST HAT-TRICKS

Career
34 Dixie Dean (Tranmere R, Everton, Notts Co, England)

Division 1 (one season post-war)
6 Jimmy Greaves (Chelsea), 1960–61

Three for one team one match
West, Spouncer, Hooper, Nottingham F v Leicester Fosse, Division 1, 21 April 1909
Barnes, Ambler, Davies, Wrexham v Hartlepools U, Division 4, 3 March 1962
Adcock, Stewart, White, Manchester C v Huddersfield T, Division 2, 7 Nov 1987
Loasby, Smith, Wells, Northampton T v Walsall, Division 3S, 5 Nov 1927
Bowater, Hoyland, Readman, Mansfield T v Rotherham U, Division 3N, 27 Dec 1932

MOST CUP GOALS IN A CAREER

FA CUP (Pre-Second World war)
Henry Cursham 48 (Notts Co)

FA CUP (post-war)
Ian Rush 43 (Chester, Liverpool)

LEAGUE CUP
Geoff Hurst 49 (West Ham U, Stoke C)
Ian Rush 49 (Chester, Liverpool, Newcastle U)

GOALS PER GAME (Football League to 1991–92)

Goals per game	Division 1 Games	Division 1 Goals	Division 2 Games	Division 2 Goals	Division 3 Games	Division 3 Goals	Division 4 Games	Division 4 Goals	Division 3(S) Games	Division 3(S) Goals	Division 3(N) Games	Division 3(N) Goals
0	2465	0	2665	0	1446	0	1438	0	997	0	803	0
1	5606	5606	5836	5836	3225	3225	3106	3106	2073	2073	1914	1914
2	8275	16550	8609	17218	4569	9138	4441	8882	3314	6628	2939	5878
3	7731	23193	7842	23526	3784	11352	4041	12123	2996	8988	2922	8766
4	6229	24920	5897	23588	2837	11348	2784	11136	2445	9780	2410	9640
5	3752	18755	3634	18170	1566	7830	1506	7530	1554	7770	1599	7995
6	2137	12822	2007	12042	769	4614	786	4716	870	5220	930	5580
7	1092	7644	1001	7007	357	2499	336	2352	451	3157	461	3227
8	542	4336	376	3008	135	1080	143	1144	209	1672	221	1768
9	197	1773	164	1476	64	576	35	315	76	684	102	918
10	83	830	68	680	13	130	8	80	33	330	45	450
11	37	407	19	209	2	22	7	77	15	165	15	165
12	12	144	17	204	1	12	0	0	7	84	8	96
13	4	52	4	52	0	0	0	0	2	26	4	52
14	2	28	1	14	0	0	0	0	0	0	0	0
17	0	0	0	0	0	0	0	0	0	0	1	17
	38164	117061	38140	113030	18768	51826	18631	51461	15042	46577	14374	46466

New Overall Totals (since 1992)		Totals (up to 1991–92)		Complete Overall Totals (since 1888–89)	
Games	38660	Games	143119	Games	181779
Goals	99873	Goals	426421	Goals	526294

Extensive research by statisticians has unearthed seven results from early years of the Football League which differ from the original scores. These are 26 January 1889 Wolverhampton W 5 Everton 0 (not 4-0), 16 March 1889 Notts Co 3 Derby Co 5 (not 2-5), 4 January 1896 Arsenal 5 Loughborough 0 (not 6-0), 28 November 1896 Leicester Fosse 4 Walsall 2 (not 4-1), 21 April 1900 Burslem Port Vale v Lincoln City 2-1 (not 2-0), 25 December 1902 Glossop NE 3 Stockport Co 0 (not 3-1), 26 April 1913 Hull C 2 Leicester C 0 (not 2-1).

GOALS PER GAME (from 1992–93)

Goals per game	Premier Games	Premier Goals	Championship/Div 1 Games	Championship/Div 1 Goals	League One/Div 2 Games	League One/Div 2 Goals	League Two/Div 3 Games	League Two/Div 3 Goals
0	649	0	876	0	823	0	834	0
1	1387	1387	1954	1954	1964	1964	1970	1970
2	1848	3696	2681	5362	2674	5348	2612	5224
3	1548	4644	2229	6687	2294	6882	2245	6735
4	1069	4276	1440	5760	1465	5860	1365	5460
5	526	2630	792	3960	764	3820	684	3420
6	265	1590	355	2130	313	1878	322	1932
7	109	763	117	819	133	931	124	868
8	52	416	33	264	39	312	40	320
9	10	90	5	45	16	144	14	126
10	2	20	4	40	3	30	5	50
11	1	11	2	22	0	0	3	33
	7466	19523	10488	27043	10488	27169	10218	26138

A CENTURY OF LEAGUE AND CUP GOALS IN CONSECUTIVE SEASONS

George Camsell	League	Cup	Season
Middlesbrough	59	5	1926–27
(101 goals)	33	4	1927–28

(Camsell's cup goals were all scored in the FA Cup.)

Steve Bull			
Wolverhampton W	34	18	1987–88
(102 goals)	37	13	1988–89

(Bull had 12 in the Sherpa Van Trophy, 3 Littlewoods Cup, 3 FA Cup in 1987–88; 11 Sherpa Van Trophy, 2 Littlewoods Cup in 1988–89.)

PENALTIES

Most in a Season (individual)

Division 1	Goals	Season
Francis Lee (Manchester C)	13	1971–72

Most awarded in one game

Five   Crystal Palace (4 – 1 scored, 3 missed)
        v Brighton & HA (1 scored), Div 2   1988–89

Most saved in a Season

Division 1
Paul Cooper (Ipswich T)   8 (of 10)   1979–80

MOST GOALS IN A GAME

FA PREMIER LEAGUE
19 Sept 1999 Alan Shearer (Newcastle U)
              5 goals v Sheffield W
4 Mar 1995   Andy Cole (Manchester U)
              5 goals v Ipswich T
22 Nov 2009   Jermain Defoe (Tottenham H)
              5 goals v Wigan Ath
27 Nov 2010   Dimitar Berbatov (Manchester U)
              5 goals v Blackburn R

FOOTBALL LEAGUE
Division 1
14 Dec 1935   Ted Drake (Arsenal) 7 goals v Aston V
Division 2
5 Feb 1955   Tommy Briggs (Blackburn R)
              7 goals v Bristol R
23 Feb 1957   Neville Coleman (Stoke C) 7 goals v
              Lincoln C
Division 3(S)
13 April 1936 Joe Payne (Luton T) 10 goals v Bristol R
Division 3(N)
26 Dec 1935   Bunny Bell (Tranmere R)
              9 goals v Oldham Ath
Division 3
16 Sept 1969 Steve Earle (Fulham) 5 goals v Halifax T
24 April 1965 Barrie Thomas (Scunthorpe U)
              5 goals v Luton T
20 Nov 1965   Keith East (Swindon T)
              5 goals v Mansfield T
2 Oct 1971   Alf Wood (Shrewsbury T)
              5 goals v Blackburn R
10 Sept 1983 Tony Caldwell (Bolton W)
              5 goals v Walsall
4 May 1987   Andy Jones (Port Vale)
              5 goals v Newport Co
3 April 1990 Steve Wilkinson (Mansfield T)
              5 goals v Birmingham C
5 Sept 1998   Giuliano Grazioli (Peterborough U)
              5 goals v Barnet
6 April 2002 Lee Jones (Wrexham)
              5 goals v Cambridge U
Division 4
26 Dec 1962   Bert Lister (Oldham Ath)
              6 goals v Southport
FA CUP
20 Nov 1971   Ted MacDougall (Bournemouth)
              9 goals v Margate (*1st Round*)
LEAGUE CUP
25 Oct 1989   Frankie Bunn (Oldham Ath)
              6 goals v Scarborough
SCOTTISH LEAGUE
Premier Division
17 Nov 1984   Paul Sturrock (Dundee U)
              5 goals v Morton
Premier League
23 Aug 1996   Marco Negri (Rangers) 5 goals v
              Dundee U
Division 1
14 Sept 1928 Jimmy McGrory (Celtic)
              8 goals v Dunfermline Ath
Division 2
1 Oct 1927   Owen McNally (Arthurlie)
              8 goals v Armadale
2 Jan 1930   Jim Dyet (King's Park)
              8 goals v Forfar Ath
18 April 1936 John Calder (Morton)
              8 goals v Raith R
20 Aug 1937   Norman Hayward (Raith R)
              8 goals v Brechin C
SCOTTISH CUP
12 Sept 1885 John Petrie (Arbroath)
              13 goals v Bon Accord (*1st Round*)

LONGEST SEQUENCE OF CONSECUTIVE DEFEATS

FOOTBALL LEAGUE	Team	Games
Division 2		
1898–99	Darwen	18

LONGEST UNBEATEN SEQUENCE

FA PREMIER LEAGUE	Team	Games
May 2003–October 2004	Arsenal	49
FOOTBALL LEAGUE		
Division 1		
Nov 1977–Dec 1978	Nottingham F	42

LONGEST UNBEATEN CUP SEQUENCE

Liverpool   25 rounds   League/Milk Cup   1980–84

LONGEST UNBEATEN SEQUENCE IN A SEASON

FA PREMIER LEAGUE	Team	Games
2003–04	Arsenal	38
FOOTBALL LEAGUE		
Division 1		
1920–21	Burnley	30

LONGEST UNBEATEN START TO A SEASON

FA PREMIER LEAGUE	Team	Games
2003–04	Arsenal	38
FOOTBALL LEAGUE		
Division 1		
1973–74	Leeds U	29
1987–88	Liverpool	29

LONGEST SEQUENCE WITHOUT A WIN IN A SEASON

FA PREMIER LEAGUE	Team	Games
2007–08	Derby Co	32
FOOTBALL LEAGUE	Team	Games
Division 2		
1983–84	Cambridge U	31

LONGEST SEQUENCE WITHOUT A WIN FROM SEASON'S START

FOOTBALL LEAGUE	Team	Games
Division 4		
1970–71	Newport Co	25

LONGEST SEQUENCE OF CONSECUTIVE SCORING (Individual)

FA PREMIER LEAGUE		
Ruud Van Nistelrooy		
(Manchester U)	15 in 10 games	2003–04
FOOTBALL LEAGUE RECORD		
Tom Phillipson		
(Wolverhampton W)	23 in 13 games	1926–27

LONGEST WINNING SEQUENCE

FA PREMIER LEAGUE	Team	Games
2001–02 and 2002–03	Arsenal	14
FOOTBALL LEAGUE		
Division 2		
1904–05	Manchester U	14
1905–06	Bristol C	14
1950–51	Preston NE	14
FROM SEASON'S START		
Division 3		
1985–86	Reading	13
SCOTTISH PREMIER LEAGUE		
2003–04	Celtic	25

HIGHEST WINS

Highest win in a First-Class Match
(*Scottish Cup 1st Round*)
Arbroath   36 Bon Accord   0   12 Sept 1885

Highest win in an International Match
England   13 Ireland   0   18 Feb 1882

Highest win in an FA Cup Match
Preston NE   26 Hyde U   0   15 Oct 1887
(*1st Round*)

Highest win in a League Cup Match
West Ham U   10 Bury   0   25 Oct 1983
(*2nd Round, 2nd Leg*)
Liverpool   10 Fulham   0   23 Sept 1986
(*2nd Round, 1st Leg*)

Highest win in an FA Premier League Match
Manchester U   9 Ipswich T   0   4 Mar 1995
Nottingham F   1 Manchester U   8   6 Feb 1999

Highest win in a Football League Match
Division 2 – highest home win
Newcastle U   13 Newport Co   0   5 Oct 1946
Division 3(N) – highest home win
Stockport Co   13 Halifax T   0   6 Jan 1934
Division 2 – highest away win
Burslem Port Vale 0 Sheffield U   10   10 Dec 1892

Highest wins in a Scottish League Match
Scottish Premier League – highest home win
Celtic   9 Aberdeen   0   6 Nov 2010
Scottish Division 2 – highest home win
Airdrieonians   15 Dundee Wanderers 1   1 Dec 1894
Scottish Premier League – away win
Hamilton A   0 Celtic   8   5 Nov 1988

MOST HOME WINS IN A SEASON

Brentford won all 21 games in Division 3(S), 1929–30

RECORD AWAY WINS IN A SEASON

Doncaster R won 18 of 21 games in Division 3(N), 1946–47

CONSECUTIVE AWAY WINS

FA PREMIER LEAGUE
Chelsea 9 games 2004–05

FOOTBALL LEAGUE
Division 1
Tottenham H 10 games (1959–60 (2), 1960–61 (8))

MOST WINS IN A SEASON

FA PREMIER LEAGUE		*Wins*	*Games*
2004–05	Chelsea	29	38
2005–06	Chelsea	29	38
FOOTBALL LEAGUE			
Division 3(N)			
1946–47	Doncaster R	33	42
SCOTTISH PREMIER LEAGUE			
2001–02	Celtic	33	38
SCOTTISH LEAGUE			
Division 1			
1920–21	Rangers	35	42

MOST POINTS IN A SEASON
(*under old system of two points for a win*)

FOOTBALL LEAGUE		*Points*	*Games*
Division 4			
1975–76	Lincoln C	74	46
SCOTTISH LEAGUE			
Division 1			
1920–21	Rangers	76	42

FEWEST WINS IN A SEASON

FA PREMIER LEAGUE		*Wins*	*Games*
2007–08	Derby Co	1	38
FOOTBALL LEAGUE			
Division 2			
1899–1900	Loughborough T	1	34
SCOTTISH PREMIER LEAGUE			
1998–99	Dunfermline Ath	4	36
SCOTTISH LEAGUE			
Division 1			
1891–92	Vale of Leven	0	22

UNDEFEATED AT HOME OVERALL

Liverpool 85 games (63 League, 9 League Cup, 7 European, 6 FA Cup), Jan 1978–Jan 1981

UNDEFEATED AT HOME LEAGUE

Chelsea 86 games, March 2004–October 2008

UNDEFEATED IN A SEASON

FA PREMIER LEAGUE
2003–04   Arsenal   38 games

FOOTBALL LEAGUE
1889–90   Preston NE   22 games

Division 2
1893–94   Liverpool   22 games

UNDEFEATED AWAY

Arsenal 19 games FA Premier League 2001–02 and 2003–04 (only Preston NE with 11 in 1888–89 had previously remained unbeaten away) in the top flight

HIGHEST AGGREGATE SCORES

FA PREMIER LEAGUE
Portsmouth   7 Reading   4   29 Sept 2007

Highest Aggregate Score England
Division 3(N)
Tranmere R   13 Oldham Ath   4   26 Dec 1935

Highest Aggregate Score Scotland
Division 2
Airdrieonians   15 Dundee Wanderers 1   1 Dec 1894

MOST POINTS IN A SEASON
(*three points for a win*)

FA PREMIER LEAGUE		*Points*	*Games*
2004–05	Chelsea	95	38
FOOTBALL LEAGUE			
Championship			
2005–06	Reading	106	46
SCOTTISH PREMIER LEAGUE			
2001–02	Celtic	103	38
SCOTTISH LEAGUE			
New Division 3			
2004–05	Gretna	98	36

FEWEST POINTS IN A SEASON

FA PREMIER LEAGUE		*Points*	*Games*
2007–08	Derby Co	11	38
FOOTBALL LEAGUE			
Division 2			
1904–05	Doncaster R	8	34
1899–1900	Loughborough T	8	34
SCOTTISH PREMIER LEAGUE			
2005–06	Livingston	18	38
SCOTTISH LEAGUE			
Division 1			
1954–55	Stirling Alb	6	30

ONE DEFEAT IN A SEASON

FA PREMIER LEAGUE		Defeats	Games
2004–05	Chelsea	1	38
FOOTBALL LEAGUE			
Division 1			
1990–91	Arsenal	1	38
SCOTTISH PREMIER LEAGUE			
2001–02	Celtic	1	38
SCOTTISH LEAGUE			
Premier Division			
Division 1			
1920–21	Rangers	1	42
Division 2			
1956–57	Clyde	1	36
1962–63	Morton	1	36
1967–68	St Mirren	1	36
New Division 2			
1975–76	Raith R	1	26

MOST DEFEATS IN A SEASON

FA PREMIER LEAGUE		Defeats	Games
1994–95	Ipswich T	29	42
2005–06	Sunderland	29	38
2007–08	Derby Co	29	38
FOOTBALL LEAGUE			
Division 3			
1997–98	Doncaster R	34	46
SCOTTISH PREMIER LEAGUE			
2005–06	Livingston	28	38
SCOTTISH LEAGUE			
New Division 1			
1992–93	Cowdenbeath	34	44

NO DEFEATS IN A SEASON

FA PREMIER LEAGUE		
2003–04	Arsenal	won 26, drew 12
FOOTBALL LEAGUE		
Division 1		
1888–89	Preston NE	won 18, drew 4
Division 2		
1893–94	Liverpool	won 22, drew 6
SCOTTISH LEAGUE DIVISION 1		
1898–99	Rangers	won 18

SENDINGS-OFF

SEASON
451 (League alone)   2003–04
(Before rescinded cards taken into account)

DAY
19 (League)   13 Dec 2003

FA CUP FINAL
Kevin Moran, Manchester U v Everton   1985
Jose Antonio Reyes, Arsenal v Manchester U   2005

QUICKEST
FA Premier League
Andreas Johansson Wigan Ath v Arsenal 7 May 2006
and Keith Gillespie Sheffield U v Reading 20 January
2007 both in 10 seconds
Football League
Walter Boyd, Swansea C v Darlington Div 3 as
substitute in zero seconds   23 Nov 1999

MOST IN ONE GAME
Five: Chesterfield (2) v Plymouth Arg (3) 22 Feb 1997
Five: Wigan Ath (1) v Bristol R (4)   2 Dec 1997
Five: Exeter C (3) v Cambridge U (2)   23 Nov 2002

MOST IN ONE TEAM
Wigan Ath (1) v Bristol R (4)   2 Dec 1997
Hereford U (4) v Northampton T (0)   6 Sept 1992

MOST DRAWN GAMES IN A SEASON

FA PREMIER LEAGUE		Draws	Games
1993–94	Manchester C	18	42
1993–94	Sheffield U	18	42
1994–95	Southampton	18	42
FOOTBALL LEAGUE			
Division 1			
1978–79	Norwich C	23	42
Division 3			
1997–98	Cardiff C	23	46
1997–98	Hartlepool U	23	46
Division 4			
1986–87	Exeter C	23	46
SCOTTISH PREMIER LEAGUE			
1998–99	Dunfermline Ath	16	38
SCOTTISH LEAGUE			
Premier Division			
1993–94	Aberdeen	21	44
New Division 1			
1986–87	East Fife	21	44

MOST SUCCESSFUL MANAGERS

Sir Alex Ferguson CBE
Manchester U
24 major trophies in 24 seasons:
12 Premier League, 5 FA Cup, 4 League Cup,
2 European Cup, 1 Cup-Winners' Cup.

Aberdeen
1976–86 – 9 trophies:
3 League, 4 Scottish Cup, 1 League Cup, 1 Cup-
Winners' Cup.

Bob Paisley – Liverpool
1974–83 – 13 trophies:
6 League, 3 European Cup, 3 League Cup, 1 UEFA
Cup.

Bill Struth – Rangers
1920–54 – 30 trophies:
18 League, 10 Scottish Cup, 2 League Cup

LEAGUE CHAMPIONSHIP HAT-TRICKS

Huddersfield T	1923–24 to 1925–26
Arsenal	1932–33 to 1934–35
Liverpool	1981–82 to 1983–84
Manchester U	1998–99 to 2000–01
Manchester U	2006–07 to 2008–09

MOST FA CUP MEDALS

Ashley Cole 6 (Arsenal 2002, 2003, 2005, Chelsea
2007, 2009, 2010)

MOST LEAGUE MEDALS

Ryan Giggs (Manchester U) 12: 1993, 1994, 1996, 1997,
1999, 2000, 2001, 2003, 2007, 2008, 2009 and 2011

MOST SENIOR MATCHES

1390 Peter Shilton (1005 League, 86 FA Cup, 102
League Cup, 125 Internationals, 13 Under-23, 4
Football League XI, 20 European Cup, 7 Texaco Cup,
5 Simod Cup, 4 European Super Cup, 4 UEFA Cup, 3
Screen Sport Super Cup, 3 Zenith Data Systems Cup,
2 Autoglass Trophy, 2 Charity Shield, 2 Full Members
Cup, 1 Anglo-Italian Cup, 1 Football League play-offs,
1 World Club Championship)

MOST LEAGUE APPEARANCES
(750+ matches)

1005 Peter Shilton (286 Leicester C, 110 Stoke C, 202 Nottingham F, 188 Southampton, 175 Derby Co, 34 Plymouth Arg, 1 Bolton W, 9 Leyton Orient) 1966–97

931 Tony Ford (355 Grimsby T, 9 Sunderland (loan), 112 Stoke C, 114 WBA, 68 Grimsby T, 5 Bradford C (loan), 76 Scunthorpe U, 103 Mansfield T, 89 Rochdale) 1975–2002

909 Graeme Armstrong (204 Stirling A, 83 Berwick R, 353 Meadowbank Th, 268 Stenhousemuir, 1 Alloa) 1975–2001

863 Tommy Hutchison (165 Blackpool, 314 Coventry City, 46 Manchester City, 92 Burnley, 178 Swansea City, 68 Alloa Ath) 1965–91

824 Terry Paine (713 Southampton, 111 Hereford U) 1957–77

815 Graham Alexander (Scunthorpe U, 159, Luton T 150, Preston NE 352, Burnley 154).

790 Neil Redfearn (35 Bolton W, 10 Lincoln C (loan), 90 Lincoln C, 46 Doncaster R, 57 Crystal Palace, 24 Watford, 62 Oldham Ath, 292 Barnsley, 30 Charlton Ath, 17 Bradford C, 22 Wigan Ath, 42 Halifax T, 54 Boston U, 9 Rochdale) 1982–2004

782 Robbie James (484 Swansea C, 48 Stoke C, 87 QPR, 23 Leicester C, 89 Bradford C, 51 Cardiff C) 1973–94

777 Alan Oakes (565 Manchester C, 211 Chester C, 1 Port Vale) 1959–84

774 Dave Beasant (340 Wimbledon, 20 Newcastle U, 133 Chelsea, 6 Grimsby T (loan), 4 Wolverhampton W (loan), 88 Southampton, 139 Nottingham F, 27 Portsmouth, 1 Tottenham H (loan), 16 Brighton & HA) 1979–2003

771 John Burridge (27 Workington, 134 Blackpool, 65 Aston Villa, 6 Southend U (loan), 88 Crystal Palace, 39 QPR, 74 Wolverhampton W, 6 Derby Co (loan), 109 Sheffield U, 62 Southampton, 67 Newcastle U, 65 Hibernian, 3 Scarborough, 4 Lincoln C, 3 Aberdeen, 3 Dumbarton, 3 Falkirk, 4 Manchester C, 3 Darlington, 6 Queen of the S) 1968–96

770 John Trollope (all for Swindon T) 1960–80†

764 Jimmy Dickinson (all for Portsmouth) 1946–65

763 Stuart McCall (395 Bradford C, 103 Everton, 194 Rangers, 71 Sheffield U) 1982–2004

761 Roy Sproson (all for Port Vale) 1950–72

760 Mick Tait (64 Oxford U, 106 Carlisle U, 33 Hull C, 240 Portsmouth, 99 Reading, 79 Darlington, 139 Hartlepool) 1975–97

758 Ray Clemence (48 Scunthorpe U, 470 Liverpool, 240 Tottenham H) 1966–87

758 Billy Bonds (95 Charlton Ath, 663 West Ham U) 1964–88

757 Pat Jennings (48 Watford, 472 Tottenham H, 237 Arsenal) 1963–86

757 Frank Worthington (171 Huddersfield T, 210 Leicester C, 84 Bolton W, 75 Birmingham C, 32 Leeds U, 19 Sunderland, 34 Southampton, 31 Brighton & HA, 59 Tranmere R, 23 Preston NE, 19 Stockport Co) 1966–88

752 Wayne Allison (84 Halifax T, 7 Watford, 195 Bristol C, 101 Swindon T, 74 Huddersfield T, 103 Tranmere R, 73 Sheffield U, 115 Chesterfield)

† record for one club

CONSECUTIVE
401 Harold Bell (401 Tranmere R; 459 in all games) 1946–55

YOUNGEST PLAYERS

FA Premier League appearance
Matthew Briggs, 16 years 65 days, Fulham v Middlesbrough, 13.5.2007.

FA Premier League scorer
James Vaughan, 16 years 271 days, Everton v Crystal Palace 10.4.2005

Football League appearance
Reuben Noble-Lazarus 15 years 45 days, Barnsley v Ipswich T, FL Championship 30.9.2008

Football League scorer
Ronnie Dix, 15 years 180 days, Bristol Rovers v Norwich City, Division 3S, 3.3.28.

Division 1 appearance
Derek Forster, 15 years 185 days, Sunderland v Leicester City, 22.8.64.

Division 1 scorer
Jason Dozzell, 16 years 57 days as substitute Ipswich Town v Coventry City, 4.2.84

Division 1 hat-tricks
Alan Shearer, 17 years 240 days, Southampton v Arsenal, 9.4.88
Jimmy Greaves, 17 years 10 months, Chelsea v Portsmouth, 25.12.57

FA Cup appearance (any round)
Andy Awford, 15 years 88 days as substitute Worcester City v Boreham Wood, 3rd Qual. rd, 10.10.87

FA Cup proper appearance
Luke Freeman, 15 years 273 days, Gillingham v Barnet 10.11.2007

FA Cup Final appearance
Curtis Weston, 17 years 119 days, Millwall v Manchester U, 2004

FA Cup Final scorer
Norman Whiteside, 18 years 18 days, Manchester United v Brighton & Hove Albion, 1983

FA Cup Final captain
David Nish, 21 years 212 days, Leicester City v Manchester City, 1969

League Cup appearance
Chris Coward, 16 years 30 days, Stockport Co v Sheffield W, 2005

League Cup Final scorer
Norman Whiteside, 17 years 324 days, Manchester United v Liverpool, 1983

League Cup Final captain
Barry Venison, 20 years 7 months 8 days, Sunderland v Norwich City, 1985

Scottish Premier League appearance
Scott Robinson 16 years 45 days Hearts v Inverness CT 26.4.2008

Scottish Premier League scorer
Fraser Fyvie 16 years 306 days Aberdeen v Hearts 27.1.2010.

OLDEST PLAYERS

FA Premier League appearance
John Burridge 43 years 5 months, Manchester C v QPR 14.5.1995

Football League appearance
Neil McBain, 52 years 4 months, New Brighton v Hartlepools United, Div 3N, 15.3.47 (McBain was New Brighton's manager and had to play in an emergency)

Division 1 appearance
Stanley Matthews, 50 years 5 days, Stoke City v Fulham, 6.2.65

INTERNATIONAL RECORDS

MOST GOALS IN AN INTERNATIONAL

Record/World Cup	Archie Thompson (Australia) 13 goals v American Samoa	11.4.2001
England	Malcolm Macdonald (Newcastle U) 5 goals v Cyprus, at Wembley	16.4.1975
	Willie Hall (Tottenham H) 5 goals v Ireland, at Old Trafford	16.11.1938
	Steve Bloomer (Derby Co) 5 goals v Wales, at Cardiff	16.3.1896
	Howard Vaughton (Aston Villa) 5 goals v Ireland, at Belfast	18.2.1882
Northern Ireland	Joe Bambrick (Linfield) 6 goals v Wales, at Belfast	1.2.1930
Wales	John Price (Wrexham) 4 goals v Ireland, at Wrexham	25.2.1882
	Mel Charles (Cardiff C) 4 goals v Ireland, at Cardiff	11.4.1962
	Ian Edwards (Chester) 4 goals v Malta, at Wrexham	25.10.1978

MOST GOALS IN AN INTERNATIONAL CAREER

		Goals	Games
England	Bobby Charlton (Manchester U)	49	106
Scotland	Denis Law (Huddersfield T, Manchester C, Torino, Manchester U)	30	55
	Kenny Dalglish (Celtic, Liverpool)	30	102
Northern Ireland	David Healy (Manchester U, Preston NE, Leeds U, Fulham, Sunderland)	35	86
Wales	Ian Rush (Liverpool, Juventus)	28	73
Republic of Ireland	Robbie Keane (Wolverhampton W, Coventry C, Internazionale, Leeds U, Tottenham H, Liverpool, Tottenham H)	51	108

HIGHEST SCORES

Record/World Cup Match	Australia	31	American Samoa	0	2001
European Championship	San Marino	0	Germany	13	2006
Olympic Games	Denmark	17	France	1	1908
	Germany	16	USSR	0	1912
Other International Match	Libya	21	Oman	0	1966
European Cup	Feyenoord	12	K R Reykjavik	2	1969
European Cup-Winners' Cup	Sporting Lisbon	16	Apoel Nicosia	1	1963
Fairs & UEFA Cups	Ajax	14	Red Boys	0	1984

GOALSCORING RECORDS

World Cup Final	Geoff Hurst (England) 3 goals v West Germany	1966
World Cup Final tournament	Just Fontaine (France) 13 goals	1958
Career	Artur Friedenreich (Brazil) 1329 goals	1910–30
	Pele (Brazil) 1281 goals	*1956–78
	Franz 'Bimbo' Binder (Austria, Germany) 1006 goals	1930–50
World Cup Finals fastest	Hakan Sukur (Turkey) 10.8 secs v South Korea	2002

*Pele subsequently scored two goals in Testimonial matches making his total 1283.

MOST CAPPED INTERNATIONALS IN THE BRITISH ISLES

England	Peter Shilton	125 appearances	1970–90
Northern Ireland	Pat Jennings	119 appearances	1964–86
Scotland	Kenny Dalglish	102 appearances	1971–86
Wales	Neville Southall	92 appearances	1982–97
Republic of Ireland	Shay Given	113 appearances	1996–2010

LONDON INTERNATIONAL VENUES

Eleven different venues in the London area have staged full England international games: Kennington Oval, Richmond Athletic Ground, Queen's Club, Crystal Palace, Craven Cottage, The Den, Stamford Bridge, Highbury, Wembley, Selhurst Park, White Hart Lane and Upton Park.

FOOTBALL TITLES FOR YOUR REFERENCE LIBRARY

SUNK WITHOUT TRACE: THE CHINGFORD TOWN
STORY by Jack Rollin.
An account of the brief rise and fall of the East London
club in the Southern League from 1947 to 1950.
ISBN 978-1-905891-46-7. £8.

THE MEN WHO NEVER WERE by Jack Rollin & Tony
Brown
The expunged Football League season of 1939–40.
ISBN 978-1-905891-11-5. £12.

THE FORGOTTEN CUP by Jack Rollin & Tony Brown
The FA Cup competition of 1945–46.
ISBN 978-1-899468-86-7. £10.

ASHINGTON AFC IN THE FOOTBALL LEAGUE
by Garth Dykes.
Full match details and a comprehensive Who's Who of the club's
players during their time in the League.
ISBN 978-1-905891-48-1. £10.
Also, by the same author, similar books on Nelson and Durham
City (each priced at £10).

FOOTBALL IN EUROPE 2010/11 by Graeme Riley
Now in its ninth year, the book gives results of major League and
Cup competitions for the 2010/11 season in all 53 European
countries and includes full line-ups for the Champions League,
Europa Cup and international matches.
ISBN 978-1-905891-50-4. £19.50.

FOOTBALL LEAGUE PLAYERS' RECORDS 1888–1939
by Michael Joyce.
Career details of all Football League players during this period.
ISBN 978-1-899468-67-6. £25.

THE DEFINITIVE NEWTON HEATH
by Alan Shury and Brian Landamore.
The story of the club that became Manchester United in 1902,
with contemporary press reports, results, line-ups and player
details.
ISBN 978-1-899468-16-4. £8.99.

THE FOOTBALL LEAGUE MATCH BY MATCH 1888–1970
A set of 55 volumes giving detailed results, scorers and line-up
grids for all Football League seasons from 1888/89 to 1969/70.
£12 per volume, £500 for the set.

THE SOCCERDATA REFERENCE LIBRARY
Other titles include complete results of the FA Cup and the FA
Amateur Cup (including the qualifying rounds), the FA Trophy and FA Vase.
Also, results and dates of Premiership and Football League games.
See the web site for more details.

Please send orders to Tony Brown, 4 Adrian Close, Toton, Nottingham NG9 6FL.
The web site is www.soccerdata.com. 10% of the value of your order (to a maximum of
£4) will be a welcome contribution to postage costs. Please make cheques payable to
Tony Brown.

THE FA BARCLAYS PREMIERSHIP AND COCA-COLA FOOTBALL LEAGUE FIXTURES 2011–12

*Sky Sports   All fixtures subject to change.

Friday, 5 August 2011
npower Football League
Championship
Hull C v Blackpool* (7.45)

Saturday, 6 August 2011
npower Football League
Championship
Brighton & HA v Doncaster R
Bristol C v Ipswich T
Burnley v Watford
Coventry C v Leicester C
Derby Co v Birmingham C
Middlesbrough v Portsmouth
Nottingham F v Barnsley
Peterborough U v Crystal Palace
Reading v Millwall
Southampton v Leeds U* (5.20)
West Ham U v Cardiff C

npower Football League One
Brentford v Yeovil T
Carlisle U v Notts Co
Charlton Ath v Bournemouth
Huddersfield T v Bury
Milton Keynes D v Hartlepool U
Oldham Ath v Sheffield U
Preston NE v Colchester U
Sheffield W v Rochdale
Stevenage v Exeter C
Tranmere R v Chesterfield
Walsall v Leyton Orient
Wycombe W v Scunthorpe U

npower Football League Two
AFC Wimbledon v Bristol R* (12.45)
Bradford C v Aldershot T
Gillingham v Cheltenham T
Macclesfield T v Dagenham & R
Morecambe v Barnet
Northampton T v Accrington S
Port Vale v Crawley T
Rotherham U v Oxford U
Shrewsbury T v Plymouth Arg
Southend U v Hereford U
Swindon T v Crewe Alex
Torquay U v Burton Alb

Sunday, 7 August 2011
Community Shield
Manchester C v Manchester U*
(3.00)

Saturday, 13 August 2011
Barclays Premier League
Blackburn R v Wolverhampton W
Fulham v Aston Villa
Liverpool v Sunderland

Newcastle U v Arsenal
QPR v Bolton W
Tottenham H v Everton
Wigan Ath v Norwich C

npower Football League
Championship
Barnsley v Southampton
Birmingham C v Coventry C
Blackpool v Peterborough U
Cardiff C v Bristol C
Crystal Palace v Burnley
Doncaster R v West Ham U
Ipswich T v Hull C
Leeds U v Middlesbrough
Leicester C v Reading
Millwall v Nottingham F
Portsmouth v Brighton & HA
Watford v Derby Co

npower Football League One
Bournemouth v Sheffield W
Bury v Carlisle U
Chesterfield v Stevenage
Colchester U v Wycombe W
Exeter C v Milton Keynes D
Hartlepool U v Walsall
Leyton Orient v Tranmere R
Notts Co v Charlton Ath
Rochdale v Huddersfield T
Scunthorpe U v Preston NE
Sheffield U v Brentford
Yeovil T v Oldham Ath

npower Football League Two
Accrington S v Southend U
Aldershot T v Northampton T
Barnet v Port Vale
Bristol R v Torquay U
Burton Alb v Shrewsbury T
Cheltenham T v Swindon T
Crawley T v Macclesfield T
Crewe Alex v Gillingham
Dagenham & R v AFC Wimbledon
Hereford U v Morecambe
Oxford U v Bradford C
Plymouth Arg v Rotherham U

Sunday, 14 August 2011
Barclays Premier League
Stoke C v Chelsea* (1.30)
WBA v Manchester U* (4.00)

Monday, 15 August 2011
Barclays Premier League
Manchester C v Swansea C* (8.00)

Tuesday, 16 August 2011
npower Football League
Championship
Barnsley v Middlesbrough
Birmingham C v Burnley
Blackpool v Derby Co
Cardiff C v Brighton & HA
Crystal Palace v Coventry C
Doncaster R v Nottingham F
Ipswich T v Southampton
Leeds U v Hull C
Leicester C v Bristol C
Millwall v Peterborough U
Portsmouth v Reading
Watford v West Ham U

npower Football League One
Bournemouth v Stevenage
Bury v Sheffield W
Chesterfield v Preston NE
Colchester U v Charlton Ath
Exeter C v Brentford
Hartlepool U v Huddersfield T
Leyton Orient v Wycombe W
Notts Co v Tranmere R
Rochdale v Carlisle U
Scunthorpe U v Oldham Ath
Sheffield U v Walsall
Yeovil T v Milton Keynes D

npower Football League Two
Accrington S v Bradford C
Aldershot T v Torquay U
Barnet v Gillingham
Bristol R v Northampton T
Burton Alb v Port Vale
Cheltenham T v Morecambe
Crawley T v Southend U
Crewe Alex v Rotherham U
Dagenham & R v Swindon T
Hereford U v Macclesfield T
Oxford U v Shrewsbury T
Plymouth Arg v AFC Wimbledon

Saturday, 20 August 2011
Barclays Premier League
Arsenal v Liverpool* (12.45)
Aston Villa v Blackburn R
Chelsea v WBA
Everton v QPR
Norwich C v Stoke C
Sunderland v Newcastle U (12.00)
Swansea C v Wigan Ath
Wolverhampton W v Fulham

npower Football League
Championship
Brighton & HA v Blackpool

Bristol C v Portsmouth
Burnley v Cardiff C
Coventry C v Watford
Derby Co v Doncaster R
Hull C v Crystal Palace
Middlesbrough v Birmingham C
Nottingham F v Leicester C
Peterborough U v Ipswich T* (5.20)
Reading v Barnsley
Southampton v Millwall

npower Football League One
Brentford v Leyton Orient
Carlisle U v Bournemouth
Charlton Ath v Scunthorpe U
Huddersfield T v Colchester U
Milton Keynes D v Chesterfield
Oldham Ath v Rochdale
Preston NE v Exeter C
Sheffield W v Notts Co
Stevenage v Hartlepool U
Tranmere R v Sheffield U
Walsall v Yeovil T
Wycombe W v Bury

npower Football League Two
AFC Wimbledon v Hereford U
Bradford C v Dagenham & R
Gillingham v Plymouth Arg
Macclesfield T v Bristol R
Morecambe v Aldershot T
Northampton T v Cheltenham T
Port Vale v Accrington S
Rotherham U v Barnet
Shrewsbury T v Crewe Alex
Southend U v Burton Alb
Swindon T v Oxford U
Torquay U v Crawley T

Sunday, 21 August 2011
Barclays Premier League
Bolton W v Manchester C* (4.00)

npower Football League
Championship
West Ham U v Leeds U* (1.15)

Monday, 22 August 2011
Barclays Premier League
Manchester U v Tottenham H* (8.00)

Saturday, 27 August 2011
Barclays Premier League
Aston Villa v Wolverhampton W*
　(12.05)
Blackburn R v Everton
Chelsea v Norwich C
Liverpool v Bolton W* (5.30)
Newcastle U v Fulham
Swansea C v Sunderland
Tottenham H v Manchester C
WBA v Stoke C
Wigan Ath v QPR

npower Football League
Championship
Brighton & HA v Peterborough U
Crystal Palace v Blackpool
Derby Co v Burnley
Doncaster R v Bristol C
Hull C v Reading
Ipswich T v Leeds U
Leicester C v Southampton
Middlesbrough v Coventry C

Millwall v Barnsley
Portsmouth v Cardiff C
Watford v Birmingham C

npower Football League One
Bournemouth v Walsall
Brentford v Tranmere R
Bury v Charlton Ath
Colchester U v Oldham Ath
Exeter C v Chesterfield
Huddersfield T v Wycombe W
Leyton Orient v Carlisle U
Milton Keynes D v Stevenage
Preston NE v Notts Co
Rochdale v Hartlepool U
Sheffield W v Scunthorpe U
Yeovil T v Sheffield U

npower Football League Two
Accrington S v Burton Alb
Bradford C v Barnet
Bristol R v Hereford U
Cheltenham T v Crawley T
Dagenham & R v Torquay U
Macclesfield T v AFC Wimbledon
Northampton T v Morecambe
Oxford U v Aldershot T
Plymouth Arg v Crewe Alex
Port Vale v Southend U
Rotherham U v Gillingham
Shrewsbury T v Swindon T

Sunday, 28 August 2011
Barclays Premier League
Manchester U v Arsenal* (4.00)

npower Football League
Championship
Nottingham F v West Ham U* (1.15)

Saturday, 3 September 2011
npower Football League One
Carlisle U v Milton Keynes D
Chesterfield v Leyton Orient
Hartlepool U v Exeter C
Notts Co v Bournemouth
Oldham Ath v Huddersfield T
Scunthorpe U v Colchester U
Sheffield U v Bury
Stevenage v Rochdale
Tranmere R v Yeovil T
Walsall v Brentford
Wycombe W v Preston NE

npower Football League Two
AFC Wimbledon v Port Vale
Aldershot T v Cheltenham T
Barnet v Accrington S
Burton Alb v Plymouth Arg
Crawley T v Bristol R
Crewe Alex v Oxford U
Gillingham v Shrewsbury T
Hereford U v Dagenham & R
Morecambe v Bradford C
Southend U v Northampton T
Swindon T v Rotherham R* (12.15)
Torquay U v Macclesfield T

Monday, 5 September 2011
npower Football League One
Charlton Ath v Sheffield W* (7.45)

Saturday, 10 September 2011
Barclays Premier League
Arsenal v Swansea C
Bolton W v Manchester U
Everton v Aston Villa
Manchester C v Wigan Ath
Stoke C v Liverpool
Sunderland v Chelsea
Wolverhampton W v Tottenham H

npower Football League
Championship
Barnsley v Leicester C
Birmingham C v Millwall
Blackpool v Ipswich T
Bristol C v Brighton & HA
Burnley v Middlesbrough
Cardiff C v Doncaster R
Coventry C v Derby Co* (5.20)
Leeds U v Crystal Palace
Peterborough U v Hull C
Reading v Watford
Southampton v Nottingham F
West Ham U v Portsmouth

npower Football League One
Bournemouth v Chesterfield
Bury v Rochdale
Carlisle U v Hartlepool U
Charlton Ath v Exeter C
Colchester U v Leyton Orient
Huddersfield T v Tranmere R
Notts Co v Walsall
Oldham Ath v Stevenage
Preston NE v Yeovil T
Scunthorpe U v Sheffield U
Sheffield W v Milton Keynes D
Wycombe W v Brentford

npower Football League Two
Aldershot T v AFC Wimbledon
Bradford C v Bristol R
Cheltenham T v Macclesfield T
Crewe Alex v Barnet
Gillingham v Accrington S
Morecambe v Crawley T
Northampton T v Torquay U
Oxford U v Burton Alb
Plymouth Arg v Port Vale
Rotherham U v Dagenham & R
Shrewsbury T v Hereford U
Swindon T v Southend U

Sunday, 11 September 2011
Barclays Premier League
Norwich C v WBA* (1.30)
Fulham v Blackburn R* (4.00)

Monday, 12 September 2011
Barclays Premier League
QPR v Newcastle U* (8.00)

Tuesday, 13 September 2011
npower Football League One
Brentford v Colchester U
Chesterfield v Bury
Exeter C v Notts Co
Hartlepool U v Preston NE
Leyton Orient v Bournemouth
Milton Keynes D v Charlton Ath
Rochdale v Scunthorpe U
Sheffield U v Huddersfield T
Stevenage v Sheffield W

Tranmere R v Carlisle U
Walsall v Oldham Ath
Yeovil T v Wycombe W

npower Football League Two
AFC Wimbledon v Northampton T
Accrington S v Rotherham U
Barnet v Plymouth Arg
Bristol R v Shrewsbury T
Burton Alb v Crewe Alex
Crawley T v Swindon T
Dagenham & R v Oxford U
Hereford U v Aldershot T
Macclesfield T v Morecambe
Port Vale v Bradford C
Southend U v Gillingham
Torquay U v Cheltenham T

Saturday, 17 September 2011
Barclays Premier League
Aston Villa v Newcastle U
Blackburn R v Arsenal* (12.45)
Bolton W v Norwich C
Everton v Wigan Ath
Fulham v Manchester C
Sunderland v Stoke C
Swansea C v WBA
Wolverhampton W v QPR

npower Football League
Championship
Barnsley v Watford
Blackpool v Cardiff C
Crystal Palace v Middlesbrough
Hull C v Portsmouth
Ipswich T v Coventry C
Leeds U v Bristol C
Leicester C v Brighton & HA
Millwall v West Ham U
Nottingham F v Derby Co
Peterborough U v Burnley
Reading v Doncaster R
Southampton v Birmingham C* (5.20)

npower Football League One
Brentford v Preston NE
Chesterfield v Carlisle U
Exeter C v Bournemouth
Hartlepool U v Bury
Leyton Orient v Oldham Ath
Milton Keynes D v Huddersfield T
Rochdale v Charlton Ath
Sheffield U v Colchester U
Stevenage v Notts Co
Tranmere R v Wycombe W
Walsall v Scunthorpe U
Yeovil T v Sheffield W

npower Football League Two
AFC Wimbledon v Cheltenham T
Accrington S v Crewe Alex
Barnet v Oxford U
Bristol R v Aldershot T
Burton Alb v Swindon T
Crawley T v Bradford C
Dagenham & R v Morecambe
Hereford U v Gillingham
Macclesfield T v Northampton T
Port Vale v Shrewsbury T
Southend U v Plymouth Arg
Torquay U v Rotherham U

Sunday, 18 September 2011
Barclays Premier League
Tottenham H v Liverpool* (1.30)
Manchester U v Chelsea* (4.00)

Friday, 23 September 2011
npower Football League
Championship
Brighton & HA v Leeds U* (7.45)

Saturday, 24 September 2011
Barclays Premier League
Arsenal v Bolton W
Chelsea v Swansea C
Liverpool v Wolverhampton W
Manchester C v Everton* (12.45)
Newcastle U v Blackburn R
Stoke C v Manchester U
WBA v Fulham
Wigan Ath v Tottenham H

npower Football League
Championship
Birmingham C v Barnsley
Bristol C v Hull C
Burnley v Southampton
Coventry C v Reading
Derby Co v Millwall
Doncaster R v Crystal Palace
Middlesbrough v Ipswich T
Portsmouth v Blackpool
Watford v Nottingham F
West Ham U v Peterborough U

npower Football League One
Bournemouth v Hartlepool U
Bury v Milton Keynes D
Carlisle U v Stevenage
Charlton Ath v Chesterfield
Colchester U v Walsall
Huddersfield T v Leyton Orient
Notts Co v Rochdale
Oldham Ath v Brentford
Preston NE v Tranmere R
Scunthorpe U v Yeovil T
Sheffield W v Exeter C
Wycombe W v Sheffield U

npower Football League Two
Aldershot T v Crawley T
Bradford C v AFC Wimbledon
Cheltenham T v Hereford U
Crewe Alex v Port Vale
Gillingham v Burton Alb
Morecambe v Bristol R
Northampton T v Dagenham & R
Oxford U v Accrington S
Plymouth Arg v Macclesfield T
Rotherham U v Southend U
Shrewsbury T v Torquay U
Swindon T v Barnet

Sunday, 25 September 2011
Barclays Premier League
QPR v Aston Villa* (4.00)

npower Football League
Championship
Cardiff C v Leicester C* (1.30)

Monday, 26 September 2011
Barclays Premier League
Norwich C v Sunderland* (8.00)

Tuesday, 27 September 2011
npower Football League
Championship
Birmingham C v Leeds U
Brighton & HA v Crystal Palace
Bristol C v Reading
Burnley v Nottingham F
Cardiff C v Southampton
Coventry C v Blackpool
Derby Co v Barnsley
Doncaster R v Hull C
Middlesbrough v Leicester C
Portsmouth v Peterborough U
Watford v Millwall
West Ham U v Ipswich T

Saturday, 1 October 2011
Barclays Premier League
Aston Villa v Wigan Ath
Blackburn R v Manchester C
Everton v Liverpool* (12.45)
Fulham v QPR
Manchester U v Norwich C
Sunderland v WBA
Swansea C v Stoke C
Wolverhampton W v Newcastle U

npower Football League
Championship
Barnsley v Coventry C
Blackpool v Bristol C
Crystal Palace v West Ham U
Hull C v Cardiff C
Ipswich T v Brighton & HA
Leeds U v Portsmouth
Leicester C v Derby Co
Millwall v Burnley
Nottingham F v Birmingham C*
(5.20)
Peterborough U v Doncaster R
Reading v Middlesbrough
Southampton v Watford

npower Football League One
Brentford v Huddersfield T
Chesterfield v Colchester U
Exeter C v Oldham Ath
Hartlepool U v Sheffield W
Leyton Orient v Preston NE
Milton Keynes D v Notts Co
Rochdale v Wycombe W
Sheffield U v Charlton Ath
Stevenage v Scunthorpe U
Tranmere R v Bournemouth
Walsall v Carlisle U
Yeovil T v Bury

npower Football League Two
AFC Wimbledon v Gillingham
Accrington S v Aldershot T
Barnet v Northampton T
Bristol R v Cheltenham T
Burton Alb v Bradford C
Crawley T v Plymouth Arg
Dagenham & R v Crewe Alex
Hereford U v Oxford U
Macclesfield T v Swindon T
Port Vale v Rotherham U
Southend U v Shrewsbury T
Torquay U v Morecambe

Sunday, 2 October 2011
Barclays Premier League
Bolton W v Chelsea* (1.30)
Tottenham H v Arsenal* (4.00)

Saturday, 8 October 2011
npower Football League One
Bournemouth v Rochdale
Bury v Exeter C
Carlisle U v Brentford
Charlton Ath v Tranmere R
Colchester U v Yeovil T
Huddersfield T v Stevenage
Notts Co v Hartlepool U
Oldham Ath v Milton Keynes D
Preston NE v Sheffield U
Scunthorpe U v Leyton Orient
Sheffield W v Chesterfield
Wycombe W v Walsall

npower Football League Two
Aldershot T v Macclesfield T
Bradford C v Torquay U
Cheltenham T v Dagenham & R
Crewe Alex v Southend U
Gillingham v Port Vale
Morecambe v AFC Wimbledon
Northampton T v Crawley T
Oxford U v Bristol R
Plymouth Arg v Accrington S
Rotherham U v Burton Alb
Shrewsbury T v Barnet
Swindon T v Hereford U

Friday, 14 October 2011
npower Football League Championship
Doncaster R v Leeds U* (7.45)

Saturday, 15 October 2011
Barclays Premier League
Arsenal v Sunderland
Chelsea v Everton
Liverpool v Manchester U* (12.45)
Manchester C v Aston Villa
Norwich C v Swansea C
QPR v Blackburn R
Stoke C v Fulham
WBA v Wolverhampton W (12.00)
Wigan Ath v Bolton W

npower Football League Championship
Birmingham C v Leicester C
Brighton & HA v Hull C
Bristol C v Peterborough U
Burnley v Reading
Cardiff C v Ipswich T
Coventry C v Nottingham F
Derby Co v Southampton
Middlesbrough v Millwall
Portsmouth v Barnsley* (5.20)
Watford v Crystal Palace
West Ham U v Blackpool

npower Football League One
Brentford v Scunthorpe U
Chesterfield v Notts Co
Exeter C v Huddersfield T
Hartlepool U v Wycombe W
Leyton Orient v Bury
Milton Keynes D v Bournemouth
Rochdale v Colchester U
Sheffield U v Sheffield W
Stevenage v Charlton Ath
Tranmere R v Oldham Ath
Walsall v Preston NE
Yeovil T v Carlisle U

npower Football League Two
AFC Wimbledon v Crewe Alex
Accrington S v Swindon T
Barnet v Aldershot T
Bristol R v Rotherham U
Burton Alb v Cheltenham T
Crawley T v Shrewsbury T
Dagenham & R v Plymouth Arg
Hereford U v Bradford C
Macclesfield T v Oxford U
Port Vale v Northampton T
Southend U v Morecambe
Torquay U v Gillingham

Sunday, 16 October 2011
Barclays Premier League
Manchester C v Aston Villa* (1.30)
Newcastle U v Tottenham H* (4.00)

Tuesday, 18 October 2011
npower Football League Championship
Barnsley v Burnley
Blackpool v Doncaster R
Crystal Palace v Bristol C
Hull C v Birmingham C
Ipswich T v Portsmouth
Leeds U v Coventry C
Leicester C v Watford
Millwall v Brighton & HA
Nottingham F v Middlesbrough
Peterborough U v Cardiff C
Reading v Derby Co
Southampton v West Ham U

Saturday, 22 October 2011
Barclays Premier League
Arsenal v Stoke C
Aston Villa v WBA
Blackburn R v Tottenham H
Bolton W v Sunderland
Fulham v Everton
Liverpool v Norwich C
Newcastle U v Wigan Ath
Wolverhampton W v Swansea C* (12.45)

npower Football League Championship
Blackpool v Nottingham F
Brighton & HA v West Ham U
Bristol C v Birmingham C
Cardiff C v Barnsley
Coventry C v Burnley
Hull C v Watford
Ipswich T v Crystal Palace
Leicester C v Millwall
Middlesbrough v Derby Co
Peterborough U v Leeds U
Portsmouth v Doncaster R
Reading v Southampton* (5.20)

npower Football League One
Bournemouth v Bury
Charlton Ath v Carlisle U
Chesterfield v Hartlepool U
Exeter C v Rochdale
Huddersfield T v Preston NE
Leyton Orient v Sheffield U
Milton Keynes D v Scunthorpe U
Notts Co v Brentford
Oldham Ath v Wycombe W
Sheffield W v Colchester U

Stevenage v Yeovil T
Tranmere R v Walsall

npower Football League Two
AFC Wimbledon v Crawley T
Accrington S v Cheltenham T
Bradford C v Northampton T
Burton Alb v Bristol R
Crewe Alex v Macclesfield T
Dagenham & R v Aldershot T
Gillingham v Oxford U
Hereford U v Barnet
Plymouth Arg v Swindon T
Port Vale v Morecambe
Rotherham U v Shrewsbury T
Southend U v Torquay U

Sunday, 23 October 2011
Barclays Premier League
Manchester U v Manchester C* (1.30)
QPR v Chelsea* (4.00)

Tuesday, 25 October 2011
npower Football League One
Brentford v Stevenage
Bury v Notts Co
Carlisle U v Sheffield W
Colchester U v Bournemouth
Hartlepool U v Tranmere R
Preston NE v Oldham Ath
Rochdale v Chesterfield
Scunthorpe U v Huddersfield T
Sheffield U v Milton Keynes D
Walsall v Exeter C
Wycombe W v Charlton Ath
Yeovil T v Leyton Orient

npower Football League Two
Aldershot T v Burton Alb
Barnet v Southend U
Bristol R v Port Vale
Cheltenham T v Crewe Alex
Crawley T v Dagenham & R
Macclesfield T v Bradford C
Morecambe v Rotherham U
Northampton T v Hereford U
Oxford U v Plymouth Arg
Shrewsbury T v Accrington S
Swindon T v Gillingham
Torquay U v AFC Wimbledon

Saturday, 29 October 2011
Barclays Premier League
Chelsea v Arsenal* (12.45)
Everton v Manchester U (12.00)
Manchester C v Wolverhampton W
Norwich C v Blackburn R
Sunderland v Aston Villa
Swansea C v Bolton W
WBA v Liverpool
Wigan Ath v Fulham

npower Football League Championship
Barnsley v Bristol C
Birmingham C v Brighton & HA
Burnley v Blackpool* (5.20)
Crystal Palace v Reading
Derby Co v Portsmouth
Doncaster R v Coventry C
Millwall v Ipswich T
Nottingham F v Hull C
Southampton v Middlesbrough

Watford v Peterborough U
West Ham U v Leicester C

npower Football League One
Brentford v Chesterfield
Bury v Stevenage
Carlisle U v Oldham Ath
Colchester U v Notts Co
Hartlepool U v Charlton Ath
Preston NE v Bournemouth
Rochdale v Leyton Orient
Scunthorpe U v Tranmere R
Sheffield U v Exeter C
Walsall v Milton Keynes D
Wycombe W v Sheffield W
Yeovil T v Huddersfield T

npower Football League Two
Aldershot T v Crewe Alex
Barnet v Burton Alb
Bristol R v Dagenham & R
Cheltenham T v Plymouth Arg
Crawley T v Accrington S
Macclesfield T v Southend U
Morecambe v Gillingham
Northampton T v Rotherham U
Oxford U v Port Vale
Shrewsbury T v AFC Wimbledon
Swindon T v Bradford C
Torquay U v Hereford U

Sunday, 30 October 2011
Barclays Premier League
Tottenham H v QPR* (4.00)

npower Football League
Championship
Leeds U v Cardiff C* (1.15)

Monday, 31 October 2011
Barclays Premier League
Stoke C v Newcastle U* (8.00)

Tuesday, 1 November 2011
npower Football League
Championship
Barnsley v Hull C
Birmingham C v Ipswich T
Burnley v Leicester C
Crystal Palace v Portsmouth
Derby Co v Cardiff C
Doncaster R v Middlesbrough
Leeds U v Blackpool
Millwall v Coventry C
Nottingham F v Reading
Southampton v Peterborough U
Watford v Brighton & HA
West Ham U v Bristol C

Saturday, 5 November 2011
Barclays Premier League
Arsenal v WBA
Aston Villa v Norwich C
Blackburn R v Chelsea
Bolton W v Stoke C
Liverpool v Swansea C
Manchester U v Sunderland
Newcastle U v Everton* (12.45)
QPR v Manchester C

npower Football League
Championship
Blackpool v Millwall
Brighton & HA v Barnsley

Bristol C v Burnley
Cardiff C v Crystal Palace
Coventry C v Southampton
Hull C v West Ham U
Ipswich T v Doncaster R
Leicester C v Leeds U
Middlesbrough v Watford* (1.15)
Peterborough U v Derby Co
Portsmouth v Nottingham F
Reading v Birmingham C

npower Football League One
Bournemouth v Scunthorpe U
Charlton Ath v Preston NE
Chesterfield v Yeovil T
Exeter C v Carlisle U
Huddersfield T v Walsall
Leyton Orient v Hartlepool U
Milton Keynes D v Rochdale
Notts Co v Wycombe W
Oldham Ath v Bury
Sheffield W v Brentford
Stevenage v Sheffield U
Tranmere R v Colchester U

npower Football League Two
AFC Wimbledon v Barnet
Accrington S v Bristol R
Bradford C v Cheltenham T
Burton Alb v Macclesfield T
Crewe Alex v Torquay U
Dagenham & R v Shrewsbury T
Gillingham v Northampton T
Hereford U v Crawley T
Plymouth Arg v Morecambe
Port Vale v Swindon T
Rotherham U v Aldershot T
Southend U v Oxford U

Sunday, 6 November 2011
Barclays Premier League
Wolverhampton W v Wigan Ath* (1.30)
Fulham v Tottenham H* (4.00)

Saturday, 19 November 2011
Barclays Premier League
Everton v Wolverhampton W
Manchester C v Newcastle U
Norwich C v Arsenal* (12.45)
Stoke C v QPR
Sunderland v Fulham
Swansea C v Manchester U
WBA v Bolton W
Wigan Ath v Blackburn R

npower Football League
Championship
Barnsley v Doncaster R
Birmingham C v Peterborough U
Burnley v Leeds U
Coventry C v West Ham U
Derby Co v Hull C
Leicester C v Crystal Palace
Middlesbrough v Blackpool
Millwall v Bristol C
Nottingham F v Ipswich T
Reading v Cardiff C
Southampton v Brighton & HA
Watford v Portsmouth

npower Football League One
Brentford v Charlton Ath
Colchester U v Milton Keynes D

Huddersfield T v Notts Co
Leyton Orient v Stevenage
Oldham Ath v Chesterfield
Preston NE v Rochdale
Scunthorpe U v Hartlepool U
Sheffield U v Carlisle U
Tranmere R v Sheffield W
Walsall v Bury
Wycombe W v Bournemouth
Yeovil T v Exeter C

npower Football League Two
AFC Wimbledon v Swindon T
Aldershot T v Gillingham
Bradford C v Rotherham U
Bristol R v Barnet
Cheltenham T v Port Vale
Crawley T v Oxford U
Dagenham & R v Southend U
Hereford U v Burton Alb
Macclesfield T v Accrington S
Morecambe v Crewe Alex
Northampton T v Shrewsbury T
Torquay U v Plymouth Arg

Sunday, 20 November 2011
Barclays Premier League
Chelsea v Liverpool* (4.00)

Monday, 21 November 2011
Barclays Premier League
Tottenham H v Aston Villa* (8.00)

Saturday, 26 November 2011
Barclays Premier League
Arsenal v Fulham
Bolton W v Everton
Chelsea v Wolverhampton W
Manchester U v Newcastle U
Norwich C v QPR
Sunderland v Wigan Ath
WBA v Tottenham H

npower Football League
Championship
Blackpool v Birmingham C
Brighton & HA v Coventry C
Bristol C v Southampton
Cardiff C v Nottingham F
Crystal Palace v Millwall
Doncaster R v Watford
Hull C v Burnley
Ipswich T v Reading
Leeds U v Barnsley
Peterborough U v Middlesbrough
Portsmouth v Leicester C
West Ham U v Derby Co

npower Football League One
Bournemouth v Oldham Ath
Bury v Preston NE
Carlisle U v Colchester U
Charlton Ath v Huddersfield T
Chesterfield v Sheffield U
Exeter C v Tranmere R
Hartlepool U v Yeovil T
Milton Keynes D v Wycombe W
Notts Co v Scunthorpe U
Rochdale v Brentford
Sheffield W v Leyton Orient
Stevenage v Walsall

npower Football League Two
Accrington S v Dagenham & R

Barnet v Macclesfield T
Burton Alb v AFC Wimbledon
Crewe Alex v Hereford U
Gillingham v Bradford C
Oxford U v Cheltenham T
Plymouth Arg v Northampton T
Port Vale v Torquay U
Rotherham U v Crawley T
Shrewsbury T v Morecambe
Southend U v Bristol R
Swindon T v Aldershot T

Sunday, 27 November 2011
Barclays Premier League
Swansea C v Aston Villa* (1.30)
Liverpool v Manchester C* (4.00)

Monday, 28 November 2011
Barclays Premier League
Stoke C v Blackburn R* (8.00)

Tuesday, 29 November 2011
npower Football League
Championship
Barnsley v Crystal Palace
Birmingham C v Portsmouth
Burnley v Ipswich T
Coventry C v Cardiff C
Derby Co v Brighton & HA
Leicester C v Blackpool
Middlesbrough v West Ham U
Millwall v Doncaster R
Nottingham F v Leeds U
Reading v Peterborough U
Southampton v Hull C
Watford v Bristol C

Saturday, 3 December 2011
Barclays Premier League
Aston Villa v Manchester U
Blackburn R v Swansea C
Everton v Stoke C
Fulham v Liverpool
Manchester C v Norwich C
Newcastle U v Chelsea
QPR v WBA
Tottenham H v Bolton W
Wigan Ath v Arsenal
Wolverhampton W v Sunderland

npower Football League
Championship
Blackpool v Reading
Brighton & HA v Nottingham F
Bristol C v Middlesbrough
Cardiff C v Birmingham C
Crystal Palace v Derby Co
Doncaster R v Southampton
Hull C v Leicester C
Ipswich T v Watford
Leeds U v Millwall
Peterborough U v Barnsley
Portsmouth v Coventry C
West Ham U v Burnley

Saturday, 10 December 2011
Barclays Premier League
Arsenal v Everton
Bolton W v Aston Villa
Chelsea v Manchester C
Liverpool v QPR
Manchester U v Wolverhampton W
Norwich C v Newcastle U
Stoke C v Tottenham H

Sunderland v Blackburn R
Swansea C v Fulham
WBA v Wigan Ath

npower Football League
Championship
Barnsley v Ipswich T
Birmingham C v Doncaster R
Burnley v Portsmouth
Coventry C v Hull C
Derby Co v Bristol C
Leicester C v Peterborough U
Middlesbrough v Brighton & HA
Millwall v Cardiff C
Nottingham F v Crystal Palace
Reading v West Ham U
Southampton v Blackpool
Watford v Leeds U

npower Football League One
Brentford v Hartlepool U
Colchester U v Bury
Huddersfield T v Bournemouth
Leyton Orient v Exeter C
Oldham Ath v Sheffield W
Preston NE v Stevenage
Scunthorpe U v Carlisle U
Sheffield U v Rochdale
Tranmere R v Milton Keynes D
Walsall v Charlton Ath
Wycombe W v Chesterfield
Yeovil T v Notts Co

npower Football League Two
AFC Wimbledon v Accrington S
Aldershot T v Shrewsbury T
Bradford C v Plymouth Arg
Bristol R v Swindon T
Cheltenham T v Southend U
Crawley T v Burton Alb
Dagenham & R v Port Vale
Hereford U v Rotherham U
Macclesfield T v Gillingham
Morecambe v Oxford U
Northampton T v Crewe Alex
Torquay U v Barnet

Saturday, 17 December 2011
Barclays Premier League
Aston Villa v Liverpool
Blackburn R v WBA
Everton v Norwich C
Fulham v Bolton W
Manchester C v Arsenal
Newcastle U v Swansea C
QPR v Manchester U
Tottenham H v Sunderland
Wigan Ath v Chelsea
Wolverhampton W v Stoke C

npower Football League
Championship
Blackpool v Watford
Brighton & HA v Burnley
Bristol C v Nottingham F
Cardiff C v Middlesbrough
Crystal Palace v Birmingham C
Doncaster R v Leicester C
Hull C v Millwall
Ipswich T v Derby Co
Leeds U v Reading
Peterborough U v Coventry C
Portsmouth v Southampton
West Ham U v Barnsley

npower Football League One
Bournemouth v Sheffield U
Bury v Brentford
Carlisle U v Wycombe W
Charlton Ath v Oldham Ath
Chesterfield v Walsall
Exeter C v Scunthorpe U
Hartlepool U v Colchester U
Milton Keynes D v Preston NE
Notts Co v Leyton Orient
Rochdale v Yeovil T
Sheffield W v Huddersfield T
Stevenage v Tranmere R

npower Football League Two
Accrington S v Torquay U
Barnet v Cheltenham T
Burton Alb v Dagenham & R
Crewe Alex v Crawley T
Gillingham v Bristol R
Oxford U v Northampton T
Plymouth Arg v Hereford U
Port Vale v Aldershot T
Rotherham U v AFC Wimbledon
Shrewsbury T v Macclesfield T
Southend U v Bradford C
Swindon T v Morecambe

Tuesday, 20 December 2011
Barclays Premier League
QPR v Sunderland
Tottenham H v Chelsea
Wigan Ath v Liverpool
Wolverhampton W v Norwich C

Wednesday, 21 December 2011
Barclays Premier League
Aston Villa v Arsenal
Blackburn R v Bolton W
Everton v Swansea C
Fulham v Manchester U
Manchester C v Stoke C
Newcastle U v WBA

Monday, 26 December 2011
Barclays Premier League
Arsenal v Wolverhampton W
Bolton W v Newcastle U
Chelsea v Fulham
Liverpool v Blackburn R
Manchester U v Wigan Ath
Norwich C v Tottenham H
Stoke C v Aston Villa
Sunderland v Everton
Swansea C v QPR
WBA v Manchester C

npower Football League
Championship
Barnsley v Blackpool
Birmingham C v West Ham U
Burnley v Doncaster R
Coventry C v Bristol C
Derby Co v Leeds U
Leicester C v Ipswich T
Middlesbrough v Hull C
Millwall v Portsmouth
Nottingham F v Peterborough U
Reading v Brighton & HA
Southampton v Crystal Palace
Watford v Cardiff C

npower Football League One
Brentford v Bournemouth

Colchester U v Stevenage
Huddersfield T v Chesterfield
Leyton Orient v Milton Keynes D
Oldham Ath v Hartlepool U
Preston NE v Carlisle U
Scunthorpe U v Bury
Sheffield U v Notts Co
Tranmere R v Rochdale
Walsall v Sheffield W
Wycombe W v Exeter C
Yeovil T v Charlton Ath

npower Football League Two
AFC Wimbledon v Oxford U
Aldershot T v Southend U
Bradford C v Crewe Alex
Bristol R v Plymouth Arg
Cheltenham T v Shrewsbury T
Crawley T v Gillingham
Dagenham & R v Barnet
Hereford U v Port Vale
Macclesfield T v Rotherham U
Morecambe v Accrington S
Northampton T v Burton Alb
Torquay U v Swindon T

Saturday, 31 December 2011
Barclays Premier League
Arsenal v QPR
Bolton W v Wolverhampton W
Chelsea v Aston Villa
Liverpool v Newcastle U (12.45)
Manchester U v Blackburn R
Norwich C v Fulham
Stoke C v Wigan Ath
Sunderland v Manchester C
Swansea C v Tottenham H
WBA v Everton

npower Football League Championship
Barnsley v Leeds U
Birmingham C v Blackpool
Burnley v Hull C
Coventry C v Brighton & HA
Derby Co v West Ham U
Leicester C v Portsmouth
Middlesbrough v Peterborough U
Millwall v Crystal Palace
Nottingham F v Cardiff C
Reading v Ipswich T
Southampton v Bristol C
Watford v Doncaster R

npower Football League One
Brentford v Milton Keynes D
Colchester U v Exeter C
Huddersfield T v Carlisle U
Leyton Orient v Charlton Ath
Oldham Ath v Notts Co
Preston NE v Sheffield W
Scunthorpe U v Chesterfield
Sheffield U v Hartlepool U
Tranmere R v Bury
Walsall v Rochdale
Wycombe W v Stevenage
Yeovil T v Bournemouth

npower Football League Two
AFC Wimbledon v Southend U
Aldershot T v Plymouth Arg
Bradford C v Shrewsbury T
Bristol R v Crewe Alex
Cheltenham T v Rotherham U

Crawley T v Barnet
Dagenham & R v Gillingham
Hereford U v Accrington S
Macclesfield T v Port Vale
Morecambe v Burton Alb
Northampton T v Swindon T
Torquay U v Oxford U

Monday, 2 January 2012
Barclays Premier League
Aston Villa v Swansea C
Blackburn R v Stoke C
Everton v Bolton W
Fulham v Arsenal
Manchester C v Liverpool
Newcastle U v Manchester U
QPR v Norwich C
Tottenham H v WBA
Wigan Ath v Sunderland
Wolverhampton W v Chelsea

npower Football League Championship
Blackpool v Middlesbrough
Brighton & HA v Southampton
Bristol C v Millwall
Cardiff C v Reading
Crystal Palace v Leicester C
Doncaster R v Barnsley
Hull C v Derby Co
Ipswich T v Nottingham F
Leeds U v Burnley
Peterborough U v Birmingham C
Portsmouth v Watford
West Ham U v Coventry C

npower Football League One
Bournemouth v Wycombe W
Bury v Walsall
Carlisle U v Sheffield U
Charlton Ath v Brentford
Chesterfield v Oldham Ath
Exeter C v Yeovil T
Hartlepool U v Scunthorpe U
Milton Keynes D v Colchester U
Notts Co v Huddersfield T
Rochdale v Preston NE
Sheffield W v Tranmere R
Stevenage v Leyton Orient

npower Football League Two
Accrington S v Macclesfield T
Barnet v Bristol R
Burton Alb v Hereford U
Crewe Alex v Morecambe
Gillingham v Aldershot T
Oxford U v Crawley T
Plymouth Arg v Torquay U
Port Vale v Cheltenham T
Rotherham U v Bradford C
Shrewsbury T v Northampton T
Southend U v Dagenham & R
Swindon T v AFC Wimbledon

Saturday, 7 January 2012
npower Football League One
Carlisle U v Leyton Orient
Charlton Ath v Bury
Chesterfield v Exeter C
Hartlepool U v Rochdale
Notts Co v Preston NE
Oldham Ath v Colchester U
Scunthorpe U v Sheffield W
Sheffield U v Yeovil T

Stevenage v Milton Keynes D
Tranmere R v Brentford
Walsall v Bournemouth
Wycombe W v Huddersfield T

npower Football League Two
AFC Wimbledon v Macclesfield T
Aldershot T v Oxford U
Barnet v Bradford C
Burton Alb v Accrington S
Crawley T v Cheltenham T
Crewe Alex v Plymouth Arg
Gillingham v Rotherham U
Hereford U v Bristol R
Morecambe v Northampton T
Southend U v Port Vale
Swindon T v Shrewsbury T
Torquay U v Dagenham & R

Saturday, 14 January 2012
Barclays Premier League
Aston Villa v Everton
Blackburn R v Fulham
Chelsea v Sunderland
Liverpool v Stoke C
Manchester U v Bolton W
Newcastle U v QPR
Swansea C v Arsenal
Tottenham H v Wolverhampton W
WBA v Norwich C
Wigan Ath v Manchester C

npower Football League Championship
Brighton & HA v Bristol C
Crystal Palace v Leeds U
Derby Co v Coventry C
Doncaster R v Cardiff C
Hull C v Peterborough U
Ipswich T v Blackpool
Leicester C v Barnsley
Middlesbrough v Burnley
Millwall v Birmingham C
Nottingham F v Southampton
Portsmouth v West Ham U
Watford v Reading

npower Football League One
Bournemouth v Notts Co
Brentford v Walsall
Bury v Sheffield U
Colchester U v Scunthorpe U
Exeter C v Hartlepool U
Huddersfield T v Oldham Ath
Leyton Orient v Chesterfield
Milton Keynes D v Carlisle U
Preston NE v Wycombe W
Rochdale v Stevenage
Sheffield W v Charlton Ath
Yeovil T v Tranmere R

npower Football League Two
Accrington S v Barnet
Bradford C v Morecambe
Bristol R v Crawley T
Cheltenham T v Aldershot T
Dagenham & R v Hereford U
Macclesfield T v Torquay U
Northampton T v Southend U
Oxford U v Crewe Alex
Plymouth Arg v Burton Alb
Port Vale v AFC Wimbledon
Rotherham U v Swindon T
Shrewsbury T v Gillingham

Saturday, 21 January 2012
Barclays Premier League
Arsenal v Manchester U
Bolton W v Liverpool
Everton v Blackburn R
Fulham v Newcastle U
Manchester C v Tottenham H
Norwich C v Chelsea
QPR v Wigan Ath
Stoke C v WBA
Sunderland v Swansea C
Wolverhampton W v Aston Villa

npower Football League
Championship
Barnsley v Millwall
Birmingham C v Watford
Blackpool v Crystal Palace
Bristol C v Doncaster R
Burnley v Derby Co
Cardiff C v Portsmouth
Coventry C v Middlesbrough
Leeds U v Ipswich T
Peterborough U v Brighton & HA
Reading v Hull C
Southampton v Leicester C
West Ham U v Nottingham F

npower Football League One
Bournemouth v Tranmere R
Bury v Yeovil T
Carlisle U v Walsall
Charlton Ath v Sheffield U
Colchester U v Chesterfield
Huddersfield T v Brentford
Notts Co v Milton Keynes D
Oldham Ath v Exeter C
Preston NE v Leyton Orient
Scunthorpe U v Stevenage
Sheffield W v Hartlepool U
Wycombe W v Rochdale

npower Football League Two
Aldershot T v Accrington S
Bradford C v Burton Alb
Cheltenham T v Bristol R
Crewe Alex v Dagenham & R
Gillingham v AFC Wimbledon
Morecambe v Torquay U
Northampton T v Barnet
Oxford U v Hereford U
Plymouth Arg v Crawley T
Rotherham U v Port Vale
Shrewsbury T v Southend U
Swindon T v Macclesfield T

Saturday, 28 January 2012
npower Football League One
Brentford v Wycombe W
Chesterfield v Bournemouth
Exeter C v Charlton Ath
Hartlepool U v Carlisle U
Leyton Orient v Colchester U
Milton Keynes D v Sheffield W
Rochdale v Bury
Sheffield U v Scunthorpe U
Stevenage v Oldham Ath
Tranmere R v Huddersfield T
Walsall v Notts Co
Yeovil T v Preston NE

npower Football League Two
AFC Wimbledon v Aldershot T
Accrington S v Gillingham

Barnet v Crewe Alex
Bristol R v Bradford C
Burton Alb v Oxford U
Crawley T v Morecambe
Dagenham & R v Rotherham U
Hereford U v Shrewsbury T
Macclesfield T v Cheltenham T
Port Vale v Plymouth Arg
Southend U v Swindon T
Torquay U v Northampton T

Tuesday, 31 January 2012
Barclays Premier League
Bolton W v Arsenal
Manchester U v Stoke C
Sunderland v Norwich C
Swansea C v Chelsea
Tottenham H v Wigan Ath
Wolverhampton W v Liverpool

npower Football League
Championship
Barnsley v Derby Co
Blackpool v Coventry C
Crystal Palace v Brighton & HA
Hull C v Doncaster R
Ipswich T v West Ham U
Leeds U v Birmingham C
Leicester C v Middlesbrough
Millwall v Watford
Nottingham F v Burnley
Peterborough U v Portsmouth
Reading v Bristol C
Southampton v Cardiff C

Wednesday, 1 February 2012
Barclays Premier League
Aston Villa v QPR
Blackburn R v Newcastle U
Everton v Manchester C
Fulham v WBA

Saturday, 4 February 2012
Barclays Premier League
Arsenal v Blackburn R
Chelsea v Manchester U
Liverpool v Tottenham H
Manchester C v Fulham
Newcastle U v Aston Villa
Norwich C v Bolton W
QPR v Wolverhampton W
Stoke C v Sunderland
WBA v Swansea C
Wigan Ath v Everton

npower Football League
Championship
Birmingham C v Southampton
Brighton & HA v Leicester C
Bristol C v Leeds U
Burnley v Peterborough U
Cardiff C v Blackpool
Coventry C v Ipswich T
Derby Co v Nottingham F
Doncaster R v Reading
Middlesbrough v Crystal Palace
Portsmouth v Hull C
Watford v Barnsley
West Ham U v Millwall

npower Football League One
Bournemouth v Exeter C
Bury v Hartlepool U
Carlisle U v Chesterfield

Charlton Ath v Rochdale
Colchester U v Sheffield U
Huddersfield T v Milton Keynes D
Notts Co v Stevenage
Oldham Ath v Leyton Orient
Preston NE v Brentford
Scunthorpe U v Walsall
Sheffield W v Yeovil T
Wycombe W v Tranmere R

npower Football League Two
Aldershot T v Bristol R
Bradford C v Crawley T
Cheltenham T v AFC Wimbledon
Crewe Alex v Accrington S
Gillingham v Hereford U
Morecambe v Dagenham & R
Northampton T v Macclesfield T
Oxford U v Barnet
Plymouth Arg v Southend U
Rotherham U v Torquay U
Shrewsbury T v Port Vale
Swindon T v Burton Alb

Saturday, 11 February 2012
Barclays Premier League
Aston Villa v Manchester C
Blackburn R v QPR
Bolton W v Wigan Ath
Everton v Chelsea
Fulham v Stoke C
Manchester U v Liverpool
Sunderland v Arsenal
Swansea C v Norwich C
Tottenham H v Newcastle U

npower Football League
Championship
Barnsley v Birmingham C
Blackpool v Portsmouth
Crystal Palace v Doncaster R
Hull C v Bristol C
Ipswich T v Middlesbrough
Leeds U v Brighton & HA
Leicester C v Cardiff C
Millwall v Derby Co
Nottingham F v Watford
Peterborough U v West Ham U
Reading v Coventry C
Southampton v Burnley

npower Football League One
Brentford v Oldham Ath
Chesterfield v Charlton Ath
Exeter C v Sheffield W
Hartlepool U v Bournemouth
Leyton Orient v Huddersfield T
Milton Keynes D v Bury
Rochdale v Notts Co
Sheffield U v Wycombe W
Stevenage v Carlisle U
Tranmere R v Preston NE
Walsall v Colchester U
Yeovil T v Scunthorpe U

npower Football League Two
AFC Wimbledon v Bradford C
Accrington S v Oxford U
Barnet v Swindon T
Bristol R v Morecambe
Burton Alb v Gillingham
Crawley T v Aldershot T
Dagenham & R v Northampton T
Hereford U v Cheltenham T

Macclesfield T v Plymouth Arg
Port Vale v Crewe Alex
Southend U v Rotherham U
Torquay U v Shrewsbury T

Sunday, 12 February 2012
Barclays Premier League
Wolverhampton W v WBA (12.00)

Tuesday, 14 February 2012
npower Football League
Championship
Birmingham C v Hull C
Brighton & HA v Millwall
Bristol C v Crystal Palace
Burnley v Barnsley
Cardiff C v Peterborough U
Coventry C v Leeds U
Derby Co v Reading
Doncaster R v Blackpool
Middlesbrough v Nottingham F
Portsmouth v Ipswich T
Watford v Leicester C
West Ham U v Southampton

npower Football League One
Bournemouth v Leyton Orient
Bury v Chesterfield
Carlisle U v Tranmere R
Charlton Ath v Milton Keynes D
Colchester U v Brentford
Huddersfield T v Sheffield U
Notts Co v Exeter C
Oldham Ath v Walsall
Preston NE v Hartlepool U
Scunthorpe U v Rochdale
Sheffield W v Stevenage
Wycombe W v Yeovil T

npower Football League Two
Aldershot T v Hereford U
Bradford C v Port Vale
Cheltenham T v Torquay U
Crewe Alex v Burton Alb
Gillingham v Southend U
Morecambe v Macclesfield T
Northampton T v AFC Wimbledon
Oxford U v Dagenham & R
Plymouth Arg v Barnet
Rotherham U v Accrington S
Shrewsbury T v Bristol R
Swindon T v Crawley T

Saturday, 18 February 2012
npower Football League
Championship
Barnsley v Portsmouth
Blackpool v West Ham U
Crystal Palace v Watford
Hull C v Brighton & HA
Ipswich T v Cardiff C
Leeds U v Doncaster R
Leicester C v Birmingham C
Millwall v Middlesbrough
Nottingham F v Coventry C
Peterborough U v Bristol C
Reading v Burnley
Southampton v Derby Co

npower Football League One
Brentford v Carlisle U
Chesterfield v Sheffield W
Exeter C v Bury
Hartlepool U v Notts Co

Leyton Orient v Scunthorpe U
Milton Keynes D v Oldham Ath
Rochdale v Bournemouth
Sheffield U v Preston NE
Stevenage v Huddersfield T
Tranmere R v Charlton Ath
Walsall v Wycombe W
Yeovil T v Colchester U

npower Football League Two
AFC Wimbledon v Morecambe
Accrington S v Plymouth Arg
Barnet v Shrewsbury T
Bristol R v Oxford U
Burton Alb v Rotherham U
Crawley T v Northampton T
Dagenham & R v Cheltenham T
Hereford U v Swindon T
Macclesfield T v Aldershot T
Port Vale v Gillingham
Southend U v Crewe Alex
Torquay U v Bradford C

Saturday, 25 February 2012
Barclays Premier League
Arsenal v Tottenham H
Chelsea v Bolton W
Liverpool v Everton
Manchester C v Blackburn R
Newcastle U v Wolverhampton W
Norwich C v Manchester U
QPR v Fulham
Stoke C v Swansea C
WBA v Sunderland
Wigan Ath v Aston Villa

npower Football League
Championship
Birmingham C v Nottingham F
Brighton & HA v Ipswich T
Bristol C v Blackpool
Burnley v Millwall
Cardiff C v Hull C
Coventry C v Barnsley
Derby Co v Leicester C
Doncaster R v Peterborough U
Middlesbrough v Reading
Portsmouth v Leeds U
Watford v Southampton
West Ham U v Crystal Palace

npower Football League One
Bournemouth v Milton Keynes D
Bury v Leyton Orient
Carlisle U v Yeovil T
Charlton Ath v Stevenage
Colchester U v Rochdale
Huddersfield T v Exeter C
Notts Co v Chesterfield
Oldham Ath v Tranmere R
Preston NE v Walsall
Scunthorpe U v Brentford
Sheffield W v Sheffield U
Wycombe W v Hartlepool U

npower Football League Two
Aldershot T v Barnet
Bradford C v Hereford U
Cheltenham T v Burton Alb
Crewe Alex v AFC Wimbledon
Gillingham v Torquay U
Morecambe v Southend U
Northampton T v Port Vale
Oxford U v Macclesfield T

Plymouth Arg v Dagenham & R
Rotherham U v Bristol R
Shrewsbury T v Crawley T
Swindon T v Accrington S

Saturday, 3 March 2012
Barclays Premier League
Blackburn R v Aston Villa
Fulham v Wolverhampton W
Liverpool v Arsenal
Manchester C v Bolton W
Newcastle U v Sunderland
QPR v Everton
Stoke C v Norwich C
Tottenham H v Manchester U
WBA v Chelsea
Wigan Ath v Swansea C

npower Football League
Championship
Barnsley v Nottingham F
Birmingham C v Derby Co
Blackpool v Hull C
Cardiff C v West Ham U
Crystal Palace v Peterborough U
Doncaster R v Brighton & HA
Ipswich T v Bristol C
Leeds U v Southampton
Leicester C v Coventry C
Millwall v Reading
Portsmouth v Middlesbrough
Watford v Burnley

npower Football League One
Bournemouth v Charlton Ath
Bury v Huddersfield T
Chesterfield v Tranmere R
Colchester U v Preston NE
Exeter C v Stevenage
Hartlepool U v Milton Keynes D
Leyton Orient v Walsall
Notts Co v Carlisle U
Rochdale v Sheffield W
Scunthorpe U v Wycombe W
Sheffield U v Oldham Ath
Yeovil T v Brentford

npower Football League Two
Accrington S v Port Vale
Aldershot T v Morecambe
Barnet v Rotherham U
Bristol R v Macclesfield T
Burton Alb v Southend U
Cheltenham T v Northampton T
Crawley T v Torquay U
Crewe Alex v Shrewsbury T
Dagenham & R v Bradford C
Hereford U v AFC Wimbledon
Oxford U v Swindon T
Plymouth Arg v Gillingham

Tuesday, 6 March 2012
npower Football League
Championship
Brighton & HA v Cardiff C
Bristol C v Leicester C
Burnley v Birmingham C
Coventry C v Crystal Palace
Derby Co v Blackpool
Hull C v Leeds U
Middlesbrough v Barnsley
Nottingham F v Doncaster R
Peterborough U v Millwall
Reading v Portsmouth

Southampton v Ipswich T
West Ham U v Watford

npower Football League One
Brentford v Exeter C
Carlisle U v Rochdale
Charlton Ath v Colchester U
Huddersfield T v Hartlepool U
Milton Keynes D v Yeovil T
Oldham Ath v Scunthorpe U
Preston NE v Chesterfield
Sheffield W v Bury
Stevenage v Bournemouth
Tranmere R v Notts Co
Walsall v Sheffield U
Wycombe W v Leyton Orient

npower Football League Two
AFC Wimbledon v Plymouth Arg
Bradford C v Accrington S
Gillingham v Barnet
Macclesfield T v Hereford U
Morecambe v Cheltenham T
Northampton T v Bristol R
Port Vale v Burton Alb
Rotherham U v Crewe Alex
Shrewsbury T v Oxford U
Southend U v Crawley T
Swindon T v Dagenham & R
Torquay U v Aldershot T

Saturday, 10 March 2012
Barclays Premier League
Arsenal v Newcastle U
Aston Villa v Fulham
Bolton W v QPR
Chelsea v Stoke C
Everton v Tottenham H
Manchester U v WBA
Norwich C v Wigan Ath
Sunderland v Liverpool
Swansea C v Manchester C
Wolverhampton W v Blackburn R

npower Football League Championship
Brighton & HA v Portsmouth
Bristol C v Cardiff C
Burnley v Crystal Palace
Coventry C v Birmingham C
Derby Co v Watford
Hull C v Ipswich T
Middlesbrough v Leeds U
Nottingham F v Millwall
Peterborough U v Blackpool
Reading v Leicester C
Southampton v Barnsley
West Ham U v Doncaster R

npower Football League One
Brentford v Sheffield U
Carlisle U v Bury
Charlton Ath v Notts Co
Huddersfield T v Rochdale
Milton Keynes D v Exeter C
Oldham Ath v Yeovil T
Preston NE v Scunthorpe U
Sheffield W v Bournemouth
Stevenage v Chesterfield
Tranmere R v Leyton Orient
Walsall v Hartlepool U
Wycombe W v Colchester U

npower Football League Two
AFC Wimbledon v Dagenham & R
Bradford C v Oxford U
Gillingham v Crewe Alex
Macclesfield T v Crawley T
Morecambe v Hereford U
Northampton T v Aldershot T
Port Vale v Barnet
Rotherham U v Plymouth Arg
Shrewsbury T v Burton Alb
Southend U v Accrington S
Swindon T v Cheltenham T
Torquay U v Bristol R

Saturday, 17 March 2012
Barclays Premier League
Aston Villa v Bolton W
Blackburn R v Sunderland
Everton v Arsenal
Fulham v Swansea C
Manchester C v Chelsea
Newcastle U v Norwich C
QPR v Liverpool
Tottenham H v Stoke C
Wigan Ath v WBA
Wolverhampton W v Manchester U

npower Football League Championship
Barnsley v Reading
Birmingham C v Middlesbrough
Blackpool v Brighton & HA
Cardiff C v Burnley
Crystal Palace v Hull C
Doncaster R v Derby Co
Ipswich T v Peterborough U
Leeds U v West Ham U
Leicester C v Nottingham F
Millwall v Southampton
Portsmouth v Bristol C
Watford v Coventry C

npower Football League One
Bournemouth v Carlisle U
Bury v Wycombe W
Chesterfield v Milton Keynes D
Colchester U v Huddersfield T
Exeter C v Preston NE
Hartlepool U v Stevenage
Leyton Orient v Brentford
Notts Co v Sheffield W
Rochdale v Oldham Ath
Scunthorpe U v Charlton Ath
Sheffield U v Tranmere R
Yeovil T v Walsall

npower Football League Two
Accrington S v Northampton T
Aldershot T v Bradford C
Barnet v Morecambe
Bristol R v AFC Wimbledon
Burton Alb v Torquay U
Cheltenham T v Gillingham
Crawley T v Port Vale
Crewe Alex v Swindon T
Dagenham & R v Macclesfield T
Hereford U v Southend U
Oxford U v Rotherham U
Plymouth Arg v Shrewsbury T

Tuesday, 20 March 2012
npower Football League Championship
Blackpool v Leicester C

Brighton & HA v Derby Co
Bristol C v Watford
Cardiff C v Coventry C
Crystal Palace v Barnsley
Doncaster R v Millwall
Hull C v Southampton
Ipswich T v Burnley
Leeds U v Nottingham F
Peterborough U v Reading
Portsmouth v Birmingham C
West Ham U v Middlesbrough

npower Football League One
Bournemouth v Brentford
Bury v Scunthorpe U
Carlisle U v Preston NE
Charlton Ath v Yeovil T
Chesterfield v Huddersfield T
Exeter C v Wycombe W
Hartlepool U v Oldham Ath
Milton Keynes D v Leyton Orient
Notts Co v Sheffield U
Rochdale v Tranmere R
Sheffield W v Walsall
Stevenage v Colchester U

npower Football League Two
Accrington S v Morecambe
Barnet v Dagenham & R
Burton Alb v Northampton T
Crewe Alex v Bradford C
Gillingham v Crawley T
Oxford U v AFC Wimbledon
Plymouth Arg v Bristol R
Port Vale v Hereford U
Rotherham U v Macclesfield T
Shrewsbury T v Cheltenham T
Southend U v Aldershot T
Swindon T v Torquay U

Saturday, 24 March 2012
Barclays Premier League
Arsenal v Aston Villa
Bolton W v Blackburn R
Chelsea v Tottenham H
Liverpool v Wigan Ath
Manchester U v Fulham
Norwich C v Wolverhampton W
Stoke C v Manchester C
Sunderland v QPR
Swansea C v Everton
WBA v Newcastle U

npower Football League Championship
Barnsley v Peterborough U
Birmingham C v Cardiff C
Burnley v West Ham U
Coventry C v Portsmouth
Derby Co v Crystal Palace
Leicester C v Hull C
Middlesbrough v Bristol C
Millwall v Leeds U
Nottingham F v Brighton & HA
Reading v Blackpool
Southampton v Doncaster R
Watford v Ipswich T

npower Football League One
Brentford v Rochdale
Colchester U v Carlisle U
Huddersfield T v Charlton Ath
Leyton Orient v Sheffield W
Oldham Ath v Bournemouth

Preston NE v Bury
Scunthorpe U v Notts Co
Sheffield U v Chesterfield
Tranmere R v Exeter C
Walsall v Stevenage
Wycombe W v Milton Keynes D
Yeovil T v Hartlepool U

npower Football League Two
AFC Wimbledon v Burton Alb
Aldershot T v Swindon T
Bradford C v Gillingham
Bristol R v Southend U
Cheltenham T v Oxford U
Crawley T v Rotherham U
Dagenham & R v Accrington S
Hereford U v Crewe Alex
Macclesfield T v Barnet
Morecambe v Shrewsbury T
Northampton T v Plymouth Arg
Torquay U v Port Vale

Saturday, 31 March 2012
Barclays Premier League
Aston Villa v Chelsea
Blackburn R v Manchester U
Everton v WBA
Fulham v Norwich C
Manchester C v Sunderland
Newcastle U v Liverpool
QPR v Arsenal
Tottenham H v Swansea C
Wigan Ath v Stoke C
Wolverhampton W v Bolton W

npower Football League
Championship
Blackpool v Southampton
Brighton & HA v Middlesbrough
Bristol C v Derby Co
Cardiff C v Millwall
Crystal Palace v Nottingham F
Doncaster R v Birmingham C
Hull C v Coventry C
Ipswich T v Barnsley
Leeds U v Watford
Peterborough U v Leicester C
Portsmouth v Burnley
West Ham U v Reading

npower Football League One
Bournemouth v Yeovil T
Bury v Tranmere R
Carlisle U v Huddersfield T
Charlton Ath v Leyton Orient
Chesterfield v Scunthorpe U
Exeter C v Colchester U
Hartlepool U v Sheffield U
Milton Keynes D v Brentford
Notts Co v Oldham Ath
Rochdale v Walsall
Sheffield W v Preston NE
Stevenage v Wycombe W

npower Football League Two
Accrington S v AFC Wimbledon
Barnet v Torquay U
Burton Alb v Crawley T
Crewe Alex v Northampton T
Gillingham v Macclesfield T
Oxford U v Morecambe
Plymouth Arg v Bradford C
Port Vale v Dagenham & R
Rotherham U v Hereford U

Shrewsbury T v Aldershot T
Southend U v Cheltenham T
Swindon T v Bristol R

Saturday, 7 April 2012
Barclays Premier League
Arsenal v Manchester C
Bolton W v Fulham
Chelsea v Wigan Ath
Liverpool v Aston Villa
Manchester U v QPR
Norwich C v Everton
Stoke C v Wolverhampton W
Sunderland v Tottenham H
Swansea C v Newcastle U
WBA v Blackburn R

npower Football League
Championship
Barnsley v West Ham U
Birmingham C v Crystal Palace
Burnley v Brighton & HA
Coventry C v Peterborough U
Derby Co v Ipswich T
Leicester C v Doncaster R
Middlesbrough v Cardiff C
Millwall v Hull C
Nottingham F v Bristol C
Reading v Leeds U
Southampton v Portsmouth
Watford v Blackpool

npower Football League One
Brentford v Bury
Colchester U v Hartlepool U
Huddersfield T v Sheffield W
Leyton Orient v Notts Co
Oldham Ath v Charlton Ath
Preston NE v Milton Keynes D
Scunthorpe U v Exeter C
Sheffield U v Bournemouth
Tranmere R v Stevenage
Walsall v Chesterfield
Wycombe W v Carlisle U
Yeovil T v Rochdale

npower Football League Two
AFC Wimbledon v Rotherham U
Aldershot T v Port Vale
Bradford C v Southend U
Bristol R v Gillingham
Cheltenham T v Barnet
Crawley T v Crewe Alex
Dagenham & R v Burton Alb
Hereford U v Plymouth Arg
Macclesfield T v Shrewsbury T
Morecambe v Swindon T
Northampton T v Oxford U
Torquay U v Accrington S

Monday, 9 April 2012
Barclays Premier League
Aston Villa v Stoke C
Blackburn R v Liverpool
Everton v Sunderland
Fulham v Chelsea
Manchester C v WBA
Newcastle U v Bolton W
QPR v Swansea C
Tottenham H v Norwich C
Wigan Ath v Manchester U
Wolverhampton W v Arsenal

npower Football League
Championship
Blackpool v Barnsley
Brighton & HA v Reading
Bristol C v Coventry C
Cardiff C v Watford
Crystal Palace v Southampton
Doncaster R v Burnley
Hull C v Middlesbrough
Ipswich T v Leicester C
Leeds U v Derby Co
Peterborough U v Nottingham F
Portsmouth v Millwall
West Ham U v Birmingham C

npower Football League One
Bournemouth v Huddersfield T
Bury v Colchester U
Carlisle U v Scunthorpe U
Charlton Ath v Walsall
Chesterfield v Wycombe W
Exeter C v Leyton Orient
Hartlepool U v Brentford
Milton Keynes D v Tranmere R
Notts Co v Yeovil T
Rochdale v Sheffield U
Sheffield W v Oldham Ath
Stevenage v Preston NE

npower Football League Two
Accrington S v Hereford U
Barnet v Crawley T
Burton Alb v Morecambe
Crewe Alex v Bristol R
Gillingham v Dagenham & R
Oxford U v Torquay U
Plymouth Arg v Aldershot T
Port Vale v Macclesfield T
Rotherham U v Cheltenham T
Shrewsbury T v Bradford C
Southend U v AFC Wimbledon
Swindon T v Northampton T

Saturday, 14 April 2012
Barclays Premier League
Arsenal v Wigan Ath
Bolton W v Tottenham H
Chelsea v Newcastle U
Liverpool v Fulham (12.45)
Manchester U v Aston Villa
Norwich C v Manchester C
Stoke C v Everton
Sunderland v Wolverhampton W
Swansea C v Blackburn R
WBA v QPR

npower Football League
Championship
Barnsley v Cardiff C
Birmingham C v Bristol C
Burnley v Coventry C
Crystal Palace v Ipswich T
Derby Co v Middlesbrough
Doncaster R v Portsmouth
Leeds U v Peterborough U
Millwall v Leicester C
Nottingham F v Blackpool
Southampton v Reading
Watford v Hull C
West Ham U v Brighton & HA

npower Football League One
Brentford v Notts Co
Bury v Bournemouth

Carlisle U v Charlton Ath
Colchester U v Sheffield W
Hartlepool U v Chesterfield
Preston NE v Huddersfield T
Rochdale v Exeter C
Scunthorpe U v Milton Keynes D
Sheffield U v Leyton Orient
Walsall v Tranmere R
Wycombe W v Oldham Ath
Yeovil T v Stevenage

npower Football League Two
Aldershot T v Dagenham & R
Barnet v Hereford U
Bristol R v Burton Alb
Cheltenham T v Accrington S
Crawley T v AFC Wimbledon
Macclesfield T v Crewe Alex
Morecambe v Port Vale
Northampton T v Bradford C
Oxford U v Gillingham
Shrewsbury T v Rotherham U
Swindon T v Plymouth Arg
Torquay U v Southend U

Tuesday, 17 April 2012
npower Football League
Championship
Blackpool v Leeds U
Brighton & HA v Watford
Bristol C v West Ham U
Cardiff C v Derby Co
Coventry C v Millwall
Hull C v Barnsley
Ipswich T v Birmingham C
Leicester C v Burnley
Middlesbrough v Doncaster R
Peterborough U v Southampton
Portsmouth v Crystal Palace
Reading v Nottingham F

Saturday, 21 April 2012
Barclays Premier League
Arsenal v Chelsea
Aston Villa v Sunderland
Blackburn R v Norwich C
Bolton W v Swansea C
Fulham v Wigan Ath
Liverpool v WBA
Manchester U v Everton
Newcastle U v Stoke C
QPR v Tottenham H
Wolverhampton W v Manchester C

npower Football League
Championship
Blackpool v Burnley
Brighton & HA v Birmingham C
Bristol C v Barnsley
Cardiff C v Leeds U
Coventry C v Doncaster R
Hull C v Nottingham F
Ipswich T v Millwall
Leicester C v West Ham U
Middlesbrough v Southampton
Peterborough U v Watford
Portsmouth v Derby Co
Reading v Crystal Palace

npower Football League One
Bournemouth v Colchester U
Charlton Ath v Wycombe W
Chesterfield v Rochdale
Exeter C v Walsall
Huddersfield T v Scunthorpe U
Leyton Orient v Yeovil T
Milton Keynes D v Sheffield U
Notts Co v Bury
Oldham Ath v Preston NE
Sheffield W v Carlisle U
Stevenage v Brentford
Tranmere R v Hartlepool U

npower Football League Two
AFC Wimbledon v Torquay U
Accrington S v Shrewsbury T
Bradford C v Macclesfield T
Burton Alb v Aldershot T
Crewe Alex v Cheltenham T
Dagenham & R v Crawley T
Gillingham v Swindon T
Hereford U v Northampton T
Plymouth Arg v Oxford U
Port Vale v Bristol R
Rotherham U v Morecambe
Southend U v Barnet

Saturday, 28 April 2012
Barclays Premier League
Chelsea v QPR
Everton v Fulham
Manchester C v Manchester U
Norwich C v Liverpool
Stoke C v Arsenal
Sunderland v Bolton W
Swansea C v Wolverhampton W
Tottenham H v Blackburn R
WBA v Aston Villa
Wigan Ath v Newcastle U

npower Football League
Championship
Barnsley v Brighton & HA
Birmingham C v Reading
Burnley v Bristol C
Crystal Palace v Cardiff C
Derby Co v Peterborough U
Doncaster R v Ipswich T
Leeds U v Leicester C
Millwall v Blackpool
Nottingham F v Portsmouth
Southampton v Coventry C
Watford v Middlesbrough
West Ham U v Hull C

npower Football League One
Brentford v Sheffield W
Bury v Oldham Ath
Carlisle U v Exeter C
Colchester U v Tranmere R
Hartlepool U v Leyton Orient
Preston NE v Charlton Ath
Rochdale v Milton Keynes D
Scunthorpe U v Bournemouth
Sheffield U v Stevenage
Walsall v Huddersfield T
Wycombe W v Notts Co
Yeovil T v Chesterfield

npower Football League Two
Aldershot T v Rotherham U
Barnet v AFC Wimbledon
Bristol R v Accrington S
Cheltenham T v Bradford C
Crawley T v Hereford U
Macclesfield T v Burton Alb
Morecambe v Plymouth Arg
Northampton T v Gillingham
Oxford U v Southend U
Shrewsbury T v Dagenham & R
Swindon T v Port Vale
Torquay U v Crewe Alex

Saturday, 5 May 2012
Barclays Premier League
Arsenal v Norwich C
Aston Villa v Tottenham H
Blackburn R v Wigan Ath
Bolton W v WBA
Fulham v Sunderland
Liverpool v Chelsea
Manchester U v Swansea C
Newcastle U v Manchester C
QPR v Stoke C
Wolverhampton W v Everton

npower Football League One
Bournemouth v Preston NE
Charlton Ath v Hartlepool U
Chesterfield v Brentford
Exeter C v Sheffield U
Huddersfield T v Yeovil T
Leyton Orient v Rochdale
Milton Keynes D v Walsall
Notts Co v Colchester U
Oldham Ath v Carlisle U
Sheffield W v Wycombe W
Stevenage v Bury
Tranmere R v Scunthorpe U

npower Football League Two
AFC Wimbledon v Shrewsbury T
Accrington S v Crawley T
Bradford C v Swindon T
Burton Alb v Barnet
Crewe Alex v Aldershot T
Dagenham & R v Bristol R
Gillingham v Morecambe
Hereford U v Torquay U
Plymouth Arg v Cheltenham T
Port Vale v Oxford U
Rotherham U v Northampton T
Southend U v Macclesfield T

Sunday, 13 May 2012
Barclays Premier League
Chelsea v Blackburn R
Everton v Newcastle U
Manchester C v QPR
Norwich C v Aston Villa
Stoke C v Bolton W
Sunderland v Manchester U
Swansea C v Liverpool
Tottenham H v Fulham
WBA v Arsenal
Wigan Ath v Wolverhampton W

BLUE SQUARE PREMIER FIXTURES 20011–12

Saturday, 13 August 2011
AFC Telford v Luton T
Barrow v Tamworth
Darlington v Braintree T
Ebbsfleet U v York C
Forest Green R v Stockport Co
Grimsby T v Fleetwood T
Hayes & Yeading U v Alfreton T
Kettering T v Newport Co
Kidderminster H v Gateshead
Mansfield T v Bath C
Southport v Lincoln C
Wrexham v Cambridge U

Tuesday, 16 August 2011
Alfreton T v Southport
Bath C v Wrexham
Braintree T v Grimsby T
Cambridge U v AFC Telford
Fleetwood T v Darlington
Gateshead v Mansfield T
Lincoln C v Kidderminster H
Luton T v Forest Green R
Newport Co v Hayes & Yeading U
Stockport Co v Kettering T
Tamworth v Ebbsfleet U
York C v Barrow

Saturday, 20 August 2011
Alfreton T v Forest Green R
Bath C v Barrow
Braintree T v Mansfield T
Cambridge U v Kidderminster H
Fleetwood T v Hayes & Yeading U
Gateshead v Kettering T
Lincoln C v Wrexham
Luton T v Southport
Newport Co v Grimsby T
Stockport Co v Ebbsfleet U
Tamworth v Darlington
York C v AFC Telford

Tuesday, 23 August 2011
AFC Telford v Lincoln C
Barrow v Fleetwood T
Darlington v Alfreton T
Ebbsfleet U v Newport Co
Forest Green R v Braintree T
Grimsby T v Cambridge U
Hayes & Yeading U v Bath C
Kettering T v York C
Kidderminster H v Stockport Co
Mansfield T v Luton T
Southport v Gateshead
Wrexham v Tamworth

Saturday, 27 August 2011
AFC Telford v Newport Co
Alfreton T v Wrexham
Barrow v Gateshead
Bath C v Tamworth
Cambridge U v Hayes & Yeading U
Ebbsfleet U v Forest Green R
Fleetwood T v York C
Grimsby T v Darlington
Kidderminster H v Southport
Lincoln C v Stockport Co
Luton T v Braintree T
Mansfield T v Kettering T

Monday, 29 August 2011
Braintree T v Ebbsfleet U

Darlington v Lincoln C
Forest Green R v Bath C
Gateshead v Grimsby T
Hayes & Yeading U v Luton T
Kettering T v Cambridge U
Newport Co v Kidderminster H
Southport v Barrow
Stockport Co v Mansfield T
Tamworth v AFC Telford
Wrexham v Fleetwood T
York C v Alfreton T

Saturday, 3 September 2011
Braintree T v Lincoln C
Darlington v Mansfield T
Ebbsfleet U v Barrow
Forest Green R v Grimsby T
Gateshead v Alfreton T
Hayes & Yeading U v Tamworth
Kettering T v Fleetwood T
Newport Co v Cambridge U
Southport v AFC Telford
Stockport Co v Luton T
Wrexham v Kidderminster H
York C v Bath C

Saturday, 10 September 2011
AFC Telford v Stockport Co
Alfreton T v Braintree T
Barrow v Wrexham
Bath C v Southport
Cambridge U v Forest Green R
Fleetwood T v Darlington
Grimsby T v Hayes & Yeading U
Kidderminster H v Ebbsfleet U
Lincoln C v Kettering T
Luton T v Darlington
Mansfield T v Newport Co
Tamworth v York C

Saturday, 17 September 2011
AFC Telford v Bath C
Barrow v Mansfield T
Braintree T v Newport Co
Darlington v Hayes & Yeading U
Ebbsfleet U v Fleetwood T
Forest Green R v Southport
Gateshead v Cambridge U
Kettering T v Tamworth
Kidderminster H v Alfreton T
Luton T v Lincoln C
Stockport Co v Grimsby T
Wrexham v York C

Tuesday, 20 September 2011
Alfreton T v Barrow
Bath C v Luton T
Cambridge U v Ebbsfleet U
Fleetwood T v Kidderminster H
Grimsby T v Kettering T
Hayes & Yeading U v Braintree T
Lincoln C v Gateshead
Mansfield T v AFC Telford
Newport Co v Stockport Co
Southport v Wrexham
Tamworth v Forest Green R
York C v Darlington

Saturday, 24 September 2011
Alfreton T v Ebbsfleet U
Bath C v Kettering T
Cambridge U v Darlington

Fleetwood T v AFC Telford
Grimsby T v Wrexham
Hayes & Yeading U v Gateshead
Lincoln C v Forest Green R
Mansfield T v Kidderminster H
Newport Co v Barrow
Southport v Braintree T
Tamworth v Stockport Co
York C v Luton T

Tuesday, 27 September 2011
AFC Telford v Alfreton T
Barrow v Lincoln C
Braintree T v Tamworth
Darlington v Southport
Ebbsfleet U v Bath C
Forest Green R v Newport Co
Gateshead v York C
Kettering T v Hayes & Yeading U
Kidderminster H v Grimsby T
Luton T v Cambridge U
Stockport Co v Fleetwood T
Wrexham v Mansfield T

Saturday, 1 October 2011
AFC Telford v Hayes & Yeading U
Braintree T v Fleetwood T
Darlington v Newport Co
Forest Green R v Mansfield T
Gateshead v Tamworth
Grimsby T v Alfreton T
Kettering T v Kidderminster H
Lincoln C v Bath C
Luton T v Barrow
Southport v Cambridge U
Stockport Co v York C
Wrexham v Ebbsfleet U

Saturday, 8 October 2011
Alfreton T v Kettering T
Barrow v AFC Telford
Bath C v Darlington
Cambridge U v Stockport Co
Ebbsfleet U v Gateshead
Fleetwood T v Forest Green R
Kidderminster H v Luton T
Mansfield T v Grimsby T
Newport Co v Southport
Tamworth v Lincoln C
York C v Braintree T

Sunday, 9 October 2011
Hayes & Yeading U v Wrexham

Tuesday, 11 October 2011
Alfreton T v Lincoln C
Bath C v Cambridge U
Ebbsfleet U v Luton T
Fleetwood T v Newport Co
Gateshead v Wrexham
Grimsby T v Barrow
Hayes & Yeading U v Forest Green R
Kettering T v Braintree T
Kidderminster H v AFC Telford
Southport v York C
Stockport Co v Darlington

Saturday, 15 October 2011
AFC Telford v Ebbsfleet U
Barrow v Hayes & Yeading U
Braintree T v Bath C
Cambridge U v Alfreton T

Darlington v Kidderminster H
Forest Green R v Kettering T
Lincoln C v Fleetwood T
Luton T v Gateshead
Mansfield T v Southport
Newport Co v Tamworth
Wrexham v Stockport Co
York C v Grimsby T

Tuesday, 18 October 2011
Alfreton T v Fleetwood T
Bath C v Stockport Co
Darlington v Barrow
Ebbsfleet U v Grimsby T
Forest Green R v AFC Telford
Gateshead v Southport
Kidderminster H v Braintree T
Lincoln C v Mansfield T
Luton T v Wrexham
Newport Co v Kettering T
Tamworth v Hayes & Yeading U
York C v Cambridge U

Saturday, 22 October 2011
AFC Telford v Gateshead
Barrow v Kidderminster H
Braintree T v Darlington
Cambridge U v Lincoln C
Fleetwood T v Bath C
Grimsby T v Luton T
Hayes & Yeading U v York C
Kettering T v Ebbsfleet U
Mansfield T v Alfreton T
Southport v Tamworth
Stockport Co v Forest Green R
Wrexham v Newport Co

Saturday, 5 November 2011
Bath C v Grimsby T
Darlington v AFC Telford
Forest Green R v Alfreton T
Gateshead v Braintree T
Kettering T v Southport
Kidderminster H v Tamworth
Lincoln C v Barrow
Luton T v Fleetwood T
Mansfield T v Cambridge U
Newport Co v Ebbsfleet U
Stockport Co v Hayes & Yeading U
York C v Wrexham

Saturday, 19 November 2011
AFC Telford v Mansfield T
Alfreton T v Gateshead
Barrow v York C
Braintree T v Forest Green R
Cambridge U v Luton T
Ebbsfleet U v Darlington
Fleetwood T v Stockport Co
Grimsby T v Newport Co
Hayes & Yeading U v Kidderminster H
Southport v Bath C
Tamworth v Kettering T
Wrexham v Lincoln C

Saturday, 26 November 2011
AFC Telford v Barrow
Alfreton T v Hayes & Yeading U
Bath C v Mansfield T
Braintree T v Wrexham
Darlington v Tamworth
Forest Green R v York C
Gateshead v Fleetwood T
Kettering T v Grimsby T
Kidderminster H v Cambridge U

Lincoln C v Ebbsfleet U
Newport Co v Luton T
Stockport Co v Southport

Tuesday, 29 November 2011
Barrow v Alfreton T
Cambridge U v Bath C
Ebbsfleet U v Kidderminster H
Fleetwood T v Kettering T
Grimsby T v Stockport Co
Hayes & Yeading U v Newport Co
Luton T v AFC Telford
Mansfield T v Gateshead
Southport v Forest Green R
Tamworth v Braintree T
Wrexham v Darlington
York C v Lincoln C

Saturday, 3 December 2011
Barrow v Ebbsfleet U
Bath C v AFC Telford
Cambridge U v Grimsby T
Darlington v Forest Green R
Gateshead v Kidderminster H
Luton T v Stockport Co
Mansfield T v Braintree T
Newport Co v Lincoln C
Southport v Alfreton T
Tamworth v Wrexham
York C v Kettering T

Sunday, 4 December 2011
Hayes & Yeading U v Fleetwood T

Tuesday, 6 December 2011
AFC Telford v York C
Alfreton T v Newport Co
Braintree T v Hayes & Yeading U
Ebbsfleet U v Cambridge U
Fleetwood T v Barrow
Forest Green R v Tamworth
Grimsby T v Mansfield T
Kettering T v Darlington
Kidderminster H v Bath C
Lincoln C v Luton T
Stockport Co v Gateshead
Wrexham v Southport

Saturday, 17 December 2011
Braintree T v AFC Telford
Darlington v Cambridge U
Forest Green R v Lincoln C
Grimsby T v Ebbsfleet U
Hayes & Yeading U v Barrow
Kettering T v Bath C
Newport Co v Fleetwood T
Southport v Mansfield T
Stockport Co v Alfreton T
Tamworth v Luton T
Wrexham v Gateshead
York C v Kidderminster H

Monday, 26 December 2011
AFC Telford v Wrexham
Alfreton T v Tamworth
Barrow v Stockport Co
Bath C v Newport Co
Cambridge U v Braintree T
Ebbsfleet U v Hayes & Yeading U
Fleetwood T v Southport
Gateshead v Darlington
Kidderminster H v Forest Green R
Lincoln C v Grimsby T
Luton T v Kettering T
Mansfield T v York C

Sunday, 1 January 2012
Braintree T v Cambridge U
Darlington v Gateshead
Forest Green R v Kidderminster H
Grimsby T v Lincoln C
Hayes & Yeading U v Ebbsfleet U
Kettering T v Luton T
Newport Co v Bath C
Southport v Fleetwood T
Stockport Co v Barrow
Tamworth v Alfreton T
Wrexham v AFC Telford
York C v Mansfield T

Saturday, 7 January 2012
AFC Telford v Kettering T
Alfreton T v Grimsby T
Barrow v Darlington
Bath C v Braintree T
Cambridge U v Southport
Ebbsfleet U v Wrexham
Fleetwood T v Tamworth
Gateshead v Stockport Co
Kidderminster H v Hayes & Yeading U
Lincoln C v York C
Luton T v Newport Co
Mansfield T v Forest Green R

Saturday, 21 January 2012
AFC Telford v Cambridge U
Alfreton T v Kidderminster H
Braintree T v Stockport Co
Darlington v Fleetwood T
Gateshead v Lincoln C
Grimsby T v Bath C
Mansfield T v Hayes & Yeading U
Newport Co v Forest Green R
Southport v Luton T
Tamworth v Barrow
Wrexham v Kettering T
York C v Ebbsfleet U

Tuesday, 24 January 2012
Barrow v Grimsby T
Bath C v Alfreton T
Cambridge U v Newport Co
Ebbsfleet U v Tamworth
Fleetwood T v Braintree T
Forest Green R v Wrexham
Hayes & Yeading U v Darlington
Kettering T v Gateshead
Kidderminster H v York C
Lincoln C v Southport
Luton T v Mansfield T
Stockport Co v AFC Telford

Saturday, 28 January 2012
Braintree T v Barrow
Cambridge U v Tamworth
Darlington v York C
Ebbsfleet U v Mansfield T
Forest Green R v Fleetwood T
Gateshead v Newport Co
Grimsby T v AFC Telford
Hayes & Yeading U v Southport
Kettering T v Lincoln C
Luton T v Alfreton T
Stockport Co v Kidderminster H
Wrexham v Bath C

Saturday, 4 February 2012
AFC Telford v Forest Green R
Alfreton T v Stockport Co
Barrow v Luton T
Bath C v Hayes & Yeading U

Fleetwood T v Ebbsfleet U
Kidderminster H v Wrexham
Lincoln C v Cambridge U
Mansfield T v Darlington
Newport Co v Braintree T
Southport v Kettering T
Tamworth v Grimsby T
York C v Gateshead

Tuesday, 7 February 2012
AFC Telford v Kidderminster H
Alfreton T v Mansfield T
Gateshead v Hayes & Yeading U
Kettering T v Forest Green R

Saturday, 11 February 2012
Braintree T v Southport
Cambridge U v Barrow
Darlington v Wrexham
Ebbsfleet U v Alfreton T
Forest Green R v Luton T
Gateshead v Bath C
Grimsby T v York C
Hayes & Yeading U v Lincoln C
Kettering T v AFC Telford
Mansfield T v Fleetwood T
Stockport Co v Newport Co
Tamworth v Kidderminster H

Tuesday, 14 February 2012
Lincoln C v Braintree T
Southport v Darlington

Saturday, 18 February 2012
AFC Telford v Braintree T
Alfreton T v Darlington
Barrow v Kettering T
Bath C v Ebbsfleet U
Fleetwood T v Cambridge U
Forest Green R v Gateshead
Kidderminster H v Lincoln C
Luton T v Tamworth
Newport Co v Mansfield T
Southport v Grimsby T
Wrexham v Hayes & Yeading U
York C v Stockport Co

Tuesday, 21 February 2012
Tamworth v Newport Co

Saturday, 25 February 2012
Barrow v Forest Green R
Bath C v Kidderminster H
Braintree T v Kettering T
Cambridge U v Gateshead
Darlington v Luton T
Ebbsfleet U v Southport
Fleetwood T v Alfreton T
Hayes & Yeading U v Grimsby T
Lincoln C v AFC Telford
Mansfield T v Tamworth
Newport Co v York C
Stockport Co v Wrexham

Saturday, 3 March 2012
Alfreton T v AFC Telford
Darlington v Stockport Co
Forest Green R v Cambridge U
Gateshead v Ebbsfleet U
Grimsby T v Braintree T
Kettering T v Wrexham

Kidderminster H v Barrow
Luton T v Bath C
Mansfield T v Lincoln C
Southport v Newport Co
Tamworth v Fleetwood T
York C v Hayes & Yeading U

Tuesday, 6 March 2012
Barrow v Bath C
Cambridge U v Mansfield T
Ebbsfleet U v Stockport Co
Fleetwood T v Grimsby T
Wrexham v Luton T
York C v Tamworth

Saturday, 10 March 2012
AFC Telford v Southport
Bath C v York C
Braintree T v Gateshead
Grimsby T v Forest Green R
Hayes & Yeading U v Kettering T
Kidderminster H v Fleetwood T
Lincoln C v Alfreton T
Luton T v Ebbsfleet U
Newport Co v Darlington
Stockport Co v Cambridge U
Tamworth v Mansfield T
Wrexham v Barrow

Saturday, 17 March 2012
AFC Telford v Fleetwood T
Bath C v Lincoln C
Braintree T v Kidderminster H
Cambridge U v York C
Darlington v Ebbsfleet U
Forest Green R v Hayes & Yeading U
Gateshead v Luton T
Grimsby T v Tamworth
Kettering T v Alfreton T
Mansfield T v Barrow
Newport Co v Wrexham
Southport v Stockport Co

Saturday, 24 March 2012
Alfreton T v Cambridge U
Barrow v Braintree T
Ebbsfleet U v Kettering T
Fleetwood T v Mansfield T
Hayes & Yeading U v AFC Telford
Kidderminster H v Darlington
Lincoln C v Newport Co
Luton T v Grimsby T
Stockport Co v Bath C
Tamworth v Gateshead
Wrexham v Forest Green R
York C v Southport

Saturday, 31 March 2012
AFC Telford v Darlington
Bath C v Fleetwood T
Braintree T v Alfreton T
Cambridge U v Wrexham
Forest Green R v Barrow
Grimsby T v Kidderminster H
Kettering T v Stockport Co
Lincoln C v Tamworth
Luton T v York C
Mansfield T v Ebbsfleet U
Newport Co v Gateshead
Southport v Hayes & Yeading U

Saturday, 7 April 2012
Braintree T v Luton T
Darlington v Grimsby T
Forest Green R v Ebbsfleet U
Gateshead v Barrow
Hayes & Yeading U v Cambridge U
Kettering T v Mansfield T
Newport Co v AFC Telford
Southport v Kidderminster H
Stockport Co v Lincoln C
Tamworth v Bath C
Wrexham v Alfreton T
York C v Fleetwood T

Monday, 9 April 2012
AFC Telford v Tamworth
Alfreton T v York C
Barrow v Southport
Bath C v Forest Green R
Cambridge U v Kettering T
Ebbsfleet U v Braintree T
Fleetwood T v Wrexham
Grimsby T v Gateshead
Kidderminster H v Newport Co
Lincoln C v Darlington
Luton T v Hayes & Yeading U
Mansfield T v Stockport Co

Saturday, 14 April 2012
Alfreton T v Luton T
Barrow v Cambridge U
Darlington v Bath C
Ebbsfleet U v AFC Telford
Fleetwood T v Lincoln C
Gateshead v Forest Green R
Hayes & Yeading U v Mansfield T
Kidderminster H v Kettering T
Stockport Co v Braintree T
Tamworth v Southport
Wrexham v Grimsby T
York C v Newport Co

Saturday, 21 April 2012
AFC Telford v Grimsby T
Bath C v Gateshead
Braintree T v York C
Cambridge U v Fleetwood T
Forest Green R v Darlington
Kettering T v Barrow
Lincoln C v Hayes & Yeading U
Luton T v Kidderminster H
Mansfield T v Wrexham
Newport Co v Alfreton T
Southport v Ebbsfleet U
Stockport Co v Tamworth

Saturday, 28 April 2012
Alfreton T v Bath C
Barrow v Newport Co
Darlington v Kettering T
Ebbsfleet U v Lincoln C
Fleetwood T v Luton T
Gateshead v AFC Telford
Grimsby T v Southport
Hayes & Yeading U v Stockport Co
Kidderminster H v Mansfield T
Tamworth v Cambridge U
Wrexham v Braintree T
York C v Forest Green R

THE SCOTTISH PREMIER LEAGUE AND FOOTBALL LEAGUE FIXTURES 2011–12

*Sky Sports   All fixtures subject to change.

Saturday, 23 July 2011
Clydesdale Bank Premier League
Aberdeen v St Johnstone
Hibernian v Celtic
Motherwell v Inverness CT
Rangers v Hearts* (12.30)

Monday, 25 July 2011
Clydesdale Bank Premier League
Dunfermline Ath v St Mirren* (7.45)

Sunday, 24 July 2011
Clydesdale Bank Premier League
Dundee U v Kilmarnock

Saturday, 30 July 2011
Clydesdale Bank Premier League
Celtic v Dunfermline Ath (postponed)
Inverness CT v Hibernian
Kilmarnock v Motherwell
St Johnstone v Rangers
St Mirren v Aberdeen

Sunday, 31 July 2011
Clydesdale Bank Premier League
Hearts v Dundee U

Saturday, 6 August 2011
Clydesdale Bank Premier League
Dundee U v St Mirren
Dunfermline Ath v Inverness CT
Hibernian v St Johnstone (postponed)
Rangers v Kilmarnock (postponed)

Irn-Bru First Division
Ayr U v Hamilton A
Livingston v Queen of S
Partick Th v Dundee
Raith R v Falkirk
Ross Co v Morton

Irn-Bru Second Division
Airdrie U v Dumbarton
Arbroath v Albion R
Brechin C v Stenhousemuir
Forfar Ath v Cowdenbeath
Stirling Alb v East Fife

Irn-Bru Third Division
Annan Ath v Queen's Park
Clyde v Peterhead

East Stirling v Montrose
Elgin C v Berwick R
Stranraer v Alloa Ath

Sunday, 7 August 2011
Clydesdale Bank Premier League
Aberdeen v Celtic* (12.15)
Motherwell v Hearts

Saturday, 13 August 2011
Clydesdale Bank Premier League
Celtic v Dundee U
Hearts v Aberdeen
Inverness CT v Rangers* (12.45)
Kilmarnock v Hibernian
St Johnstone v Dunfermline Ath
St Mirren v Motherwell

Irn-Bru First Division
Dundee v Ayr U
Falkirk v Partick Th
Hamilton A v Ross Co
Morton v Livingston
Queen of S v Raith R

Irn-Bru Second Division
Albion R v Forfar Ath
Cowdenbeath v Brechin C
Dumbarton v Stirling Alb
East Fife v Airdrie U
Stenhousemuir v Arbroath

Irn-Bru Third Division
Alloa Ath v Clyde
Berwick R v East Stirling
Montrose v Elgin C
Peterhead v Annan Ath
Queen's Park v Stranraer

Saturday, 20 August 2011
Clydesdale Bank Premier League
Aberdeen v Inverness CT
Dundee U v Dunfermline Ath
Hibernian v St Mirren
Kilmarnock v Hearts
Motherwell v Rangers

Irn-Bru First Division
Ayr U v Falkirk
Livingston v Dundee
Partick Th v Hamilton A

Raith R v Morton
Ross Co v Queen of S

Irn-Bru Second Division
Airdrie U v Cowdenbeath
Arbroath v East Fife
Brechin C v Dumbarton
Forfar Ath v Stenhousemuir
Stirling Alb v Albion R

Irn-Bru Third Division
Annan Ath v Alloa Ath
Clyde v Montrose
East Stirling v Peterhead
Elgin C v Queen's Park
Stranraer v Berwick R

Sunday, 21 August 2011
Clydesdale Bank Premier League
Celtic v St Johnstone

Saturday, 27 August 2011
Clydesdale Bank Premier League
Dunfermline Ath v Motherwell
Hearts v Hibernian
Inverness CT v Kilmarnock
Rangers v Aberdeen
St Johnstone v Dundee U

Irn-Bru First Division
Ayr U v Raith R
Dundee v Morton
Falkirk v Ross Co
Hamilton A v Livingston
Partick Th v Queen of S

Irn-Bru Second Division
Albion R v Brechin C
Arbroath v Stirling Alb
East Fife v Dumbarton
Forfar Ath v Airdrie U
Stenhousemuir v Cowdenbeath

Irn-Bru Third Division
Alloa Ath v Peterhead
Annan Ath v Clyde
Elgin C v East Stirling
Montrose v Stranraer
Queen's Park v Berwick R

Sunday, 28 August 2011
Clydesdale Bank Premier League
St Mirren v Celtic* (12.45)

Saturday, 10 September 2011
Clydesdale Bank Premier League
Celtic v Motherwell
Dundee U v Rangers
Inverness CT v Hearts
Kilmarnock v Dunfermline Ath
St Mirren v St Johnstone

Irn-Bru First Division
Livingston v Falkirk
Morton v Ayr U
Queen of S v Hamilton A
Raith R v Dundee
Ross Co v Partick Th

Irn-Bru Second Division
Airdrie U v Albion R
Brechin C v Forfar Ath
Cowdenbeath v East Fife
Dumbarton v Arbroath
Stirling Alb v Stenhousemuir

Irn-Bru Third Division
Berwick R v Montrose
Clyde v Queen's Park
East Stirling v Alloa Ath
Peterhead v Elgin C
Stranraer v Annan Ath

Sunday, 11 September 2011
Clydesdale Bank Premier League
Hibernian v Aberdeen

Saturday, 17 September 2011
Clydesdale Bank Premier League
Aberdeen v Kilmarnock
Dundee U v Inverness CT
Dunfermline Ath v Hibernian
Hearts v St Mirren
Motherwell v St Johnstone

Irn-Bru First Division
Falkirk v Dundee
Hamilton A v Raith R
Partick Th v Ayr U
Queen of S v Morton
Ross Co v Livingston

Irn-Bru Second Division
Albion R v Stenhousemuir
Arbroath v Airdrie U
Dumbarton v Cowdenbeath
East Fife v Brechin C
Stirling Alb v Forfar Ath

Irn-Bru Third Division
Berwick R v Peterhead
East Stirling v Stranraer
Elgin C v Clyde

Montrose v Annan Ath
Queen's Park v Alloa Ath

Sunday, 18 September 2011
Clydesdale Bank Premier League
Rangers v Celtic* (12.30)

Saturday, 24 September 2011
Clydesdale Bank Premier League
Celtic v Inverness CT
Dunfermline Ath v Rangers* (12.45)
Hibernian v Dundee U
Motherwell v Aberdeen
St Johnstone v Hearts
St Mirren v Kilmarnock

Irn-Bru First Division
Ayr U v Queen of S
Dundee v Hamilton A
Livingston v Partick Th
Morton v Falkirk
Raith R v Ross Co

Irn-Bru Second Division
Airdrie U v Stirling Alb
Brechin C v Arbroath
Cowdenbeath v Albion R
Forfar Ath v Dumbarton
Stenhousemuir v East Fife

Irn-Bru Third Division
Alloa Ath v Montrose
Annan Ath v East Stirling
Clyde v Berwick R
Peterhead v Queen's Park
Stranraer v Elgin C

Saturday, 1 October 2011
Clydesdale Bank Premier League
Aberdeen v Dunfermline Ath
Dundee U v Motherwell
Inverness CT v St Mirren
Kilmarnock v St Johnstone
Rangers v Hibernian

Irn-Bru First Division
Hamilton A v Falkirk
Livingston v Raith R
Partick Th v Morton
Queen of S v Dundee
Ross Co v Ayr U

Irn-Bru Second Division
Airdrie U v Stenhousemuir
Arbroath v Cowdenbeath
Dumbarton v Albion R
East Fife v Forfar Ath
Stirling Alb v Brechin C

Irn-Bru Third Division
Berwick R v Annan Ath
East Stirling v Queen's Park
Elgin C v Alloa Ath

Montrose v Peterhead
Stranraer v Clyde

Sunday, 2 October 2011
Clydesdale Bank Premier League
Hearts v Celtic* (12.45)

Saturday, 15 October 2011
Clydesdale Bank Premier League
Aberdeen v Dundee U
Dunfermline Ath v Hearts
Hibernian v Motherwell
Kilmarnock v Celtic
Rangers v St Mirren
St Johnstone v Inverness CT

Irn-Bru First Division
Ayr U v Livingston
Dundee v Ross Co
Falkirk v Queen of S
Morton v Hamilton A
Raith R v Partick Th

Irn-Bru Second Division
Albion R v East Fife
Brechin C v Airdrie U
Cowdenbeath v Stirling Alb
Forfar Ath v Arbroath
Stenhousemuir v Dumbarton

Irn-Bru Third Division
Alloa Ath v Berwick R
Annan Ath v Elgin C
Clyde v East Stirling
Peterhead v Stranraer
Queen's Park v Montrose

Saturday, 22 October 2011
Clydesdale Bank Premier League
Celtic v Aberdeen
Dundee U v St Johnstone
Hearts v Rangers
Inverness CT v Dunfermline Ath
Motherwell v Kilmarnock
St Mirren v Hibernian

Irn-Bru First Division
Ayr U v Dundee
Livingston v Morton
Partick Th v Falkirk
Raith R v Queen of S
Ross Co v Hamilton A

Irn-Bru Second Division
Albion R v Arbroath
Cowdenbeath v Forfar Ath
Dumbarton v Airdrie U
East Fife v Stirling Alb
Stenhousemuir v Brechin C

Saturday, 29 October 2011
Clydesdale Bank Premier League
Aberdeen v Rangers

Celtic v Hibernian
Dunfermline Ath v Dundee U
Hearts v Kilmarnock
Inverness CT v Motherwell
St Johnstone v St Mirren

Irn-Bru First Division
Dundee v Partick Th
Falkirk v Raith R
Hamilton A v Ayr U
Morton v Ross Co
Queen of S v Livingston

Irn-Bru Second Division
Airdrie U v East Fife
Arbroath v Stenhousemuir
Brechin C v Cowdenbeath
Forfar Ath v Albion R
Stirling Alb v Dumbarton

Irn-Bru Third Division
Annan Ath v Peterhead
Clyde v Alloa Ath
East Stirling v Berwick R
Elgin C v Montrose
Stranraer v Queen's Park

Saturday, 5 November 2011
Clydesdale Bank Premier League
Hibernian v Dunfermline Ath
Kilmarnock v Inverness CT
Motherwell v Celtic
Rangers v Dundee U
St Johnstone v Aberdeen
St Mirren v Hearts

Irn-Bru First Division
Ayr U v Morton
Dundee v Raith R
Falkirk v Livingston
Hamilton A v Queen of S
Partick Th v Ross Co

Irn-Bru Second Division
Albion R v Airdrie U
Arbroath v Dumbarton
East Fife v Cowdenbeath
Forfar Ath v Brechin C
Stenhousemuir v Stirling Alb

Irn-Bru Third Division
Alloa Ath v Stranraer
Berwick R v Elgin C
Montrose v East Stirling
Peterhead v Clyde
Queen's Park v Annan Ath

Saturday, 12 November 2011
Irn-Bru First Division
Livingston v Hamilton A
Morton v Dundee
Queen of S v Partick Th

Raith R v Ayr U
Ross Co v Falkirk

Irn-Bru Second Division
Airdrie U v Forfar Ath
Brechin C v Albion R
Cowdenbeath v Stenhousemuir
Dumbarton v East Fife
Stirling Alb v Arbroath

Irn-Bru Third Division
Berwick R v Queen's Park
Clyde v Annan Ath
East Stirling v Elgin C
Peterhead v Alloa Ath
Stranraer v Montrose

Saturday, 19 November 2011
Clydesdale Bank Premier League
Aberdeen v Motherwell
Dundee U v Hearts
Hibernian v Kilmarnock
Inverness CT v Celtic
Rangers v St Johnstone
St Mirren v Dunfermline Ath

Saturday, 26 November 2011
Clydesdale Bank Premier League
Celtic v St Mirren
Dunfermline Ath v Aberdeen
Hearts v Inverness CT
Kilmarnock v Rangers
Motherwell v Dundee U
St Johnstone v Hibernian

Irn-Bru First Division
Ayr U v Partick Th
Dundee v Falkirk
Livingston v Ross Co
Morton v Queen of S
Raith R v Hamilton A

Irn-Bru Second Division
Airdrie U v Arbroath
Brechin C v East Fife
Cowdenbeath v Dumbarton
Forfar Ath v Stirling Alb
Stenhousemuir v Albion R

Irn-Bru Third Division
Alloa Ath v East Stirling
Annan Ath v Stranraer
Elgin C v Peterhead
Montrose v Berwick R
Queen's Park v Clyde

Saturday, 3 December 2011
Clydesdale Bank Premier League
Dundee U v Celtic
Hearts v St Johnstone
Kilmarnock v Aberdeen
Motherwell v Hibernian

Rangers v Dunfermline Ath
St Mirren v Inverness CT

Irn-Bru First Division
Falkirk v Morton
Hamilton A v Dundee
Partick Th v Livingston
Queen of S v Ayr U
Ross Co v Raith R

Irn-Bru Second Division
Albion R v Cowdenbeath
Arbroath v Brechin C
Dumbarton v Forfar Ath
East Fife v Stenhousemuir
Stirling Alb v Airdrie U

Irn-Bru Third Division
Berwick R v Clyde
East Stirling v Annan Ath
Elgin C v Stranraer
Montrose v Alloa Ath
Queen's Park v Peterhead

Saturday, 10 December 2011
Clydesdale Bank Premier League
Aberdeen v St Mirren
Celtic v Hearts
Dunfermline Ath v Kilmarnock
Hibernian v Rangers
Inverness CT v Dundee U
St Johnstone v Motherwell

Irn-Bru First Division
Ayr U v Ross Co
Dundee v Queen of S
Falkirk v Hamilton A
Morton v Partick Th
Raith R v Livingston

Irn-Bru Second Division
Albion R v Dumbarton
Brechin C v Stirling Alb
Cowdenbeath v Arbroath
Forfar Ath v East Fife
Stenhousemuir v Airdrie U

Irn-Bru Third Division
Alloa Ath v Queen's Park
Annan Ath v Montrose
Clyde v Elgin C
Peterhead v Berwick R
Stranraer v East Stirling

Saturday, 17 December 2011
Clydesdale Bank Premier League
Aberdeen v Hibernian
Hearts v Dunfermline Ath
Kilmarnock v Dundee U
Motherwell v St Mirren
Rangers v Inverness CT
St Johnstone v Celtic

Irn-Bru First Division
Hamilton A v Morton
Livingston v Ayr U
Partick Th v Raith R
Queen of S v Falkirk
Ross Co v Dundee

Irn-Bru Second Division
Airdrie U v Brechin C
Arbroath v Forfar Ath
Dumbarton v Stenhousemuir
East Fife v Albion R
Stirling Alb v Cowdenbeath

Irn-Bru Third Division
Berwick R v Alloa Ath
East Stirling v Clyde
Elgin C v Annan Ath
Montrose v Queen's Park
Stranraer v Peterhead

Saturday, 24 December 2011
Clydesdale Bank Premier League
Celtic v Kilmarnock
Dundee U v Hibernian
Dunfermline Ath v St Johnstone
Hearts v Motherwell
Inverness CT v Aberdeen
St Mirren v Rangers

Monday, 26 December 2011
Irn-Bru First Division
Ayr U v Raith R
Dundee v Morton
Falkirk v Ross Co
Hamilton A v Livingston
Partick Th v Queen of S

Irn-Bru Second Division
Albion R v Brechin C
Arbroath v Stirling Alb
East Fife v Dumbarton
Forfar Ath v Airdrie U
Stenhousemuir v Cowdenbeath

Irn-Bru Third Division
Alloa Ath v Elgin C
Annan Ath v Berwick R
Clyde v Stranraer
Peterhead v Montrose
Queen's Park v East Stirling

Wednesday, 28 December 2011
Clydesdale Bank Premier League
Aberdeen v Hearts
Celtic v Rangers
Hibernian v Inverness CT
Motherwell v Dunfermline Ath
St Johnstone v Kilmarnock
St Mirren v Dundee U

Monday, 2 January 2012
Clydesdale Bank Premier League
Dundee U v Aberdeen
Dunfermline Ath v Celtic
Hibernian v Hearts
Inverness CT v St Johnstone
Kilmarnock v St Mirren
Rangers v Motherwell

Irn-Bru First Division
Livingston v Falkirk
Morton v Ayr U
Queen of S v Hamilton A
Raith R v Dundee
Ross Co v Partick Th

Irn-Bru Second Division
Airdrie U v Albion R
Brechin C v Forfar Ath
Cowdenbeath v East Fife
Dumbarton v Arbroath
Stirling Alb v Stenhousemuir

Irn-Bru Third Division
Berwick R v Montrose
Clyde v Queen's Park
East Stirling v Alloa Ath
Peterhead v Elgin C
Stranraer v Annan Ath

Saturday, 7 January 2012
Irn-Bru Third Division
Alloa Ath v Peterhead
Annan Ath v Clyde
Elgin C v East Stirling
Montrose v Stranraer
Queen's Park v Berwick R

Saturday, 14 January 2012
Clydesdale Bank Premier League
Aberdeen v Kilmarnock
Celtic v Dundee U
Dunfermline Ath v Hibernian
Hearts v St Mirren
Motherwell v Inverness CT
St Johnstone v Rangers

Irn-Bru First Division
Dundee v Livingston
Falkirk v Ayr U
Hamilton A v Partick Th
Morton v Raith R
Queen of S v Ross Co

Irn-Bru Second Division
Albion R v Stirling Alb
Cowdenbeath v Airdrie U
Dumbarton v Brechin C
East Fife v Arbroath
Stenhousemuir v Forfar Ath

Irn-Bru Third Division
Alloa Ath v Annan Ath

Berwick R v Stranraer
Montrose v Clyde
Peterhead v East Stirling
Queen's Park v Elgin C

Saturday, 21 January 2012
Clydesdale Bank Premier League
Dundee U v Motherwell
Hibernian v St Johnstone
Inverness CT v Hearts
Kilmarnock v Dunfermline Ath
Rangers v Aberdeen
St Mirren v Celtic

Irn-Bru First Division
Ayr U v Hamilton A
Livingston v Queen of S
Partick Th v Dundee
Raith R v Falkirk
Ross Co v Morton

Irn-Bru Second Division
Airdrie U v Dumbarton
Arbroath v Albion R
Brechin C v Stenhousemuir
Forfar Ath v Cowdenbeath
Stirling Alb v East Fife

Irn-Bru Third Division
Annan Ath v Queen's Park
Clyde v Peterhead
East Stirling v Montrose
Elgin C v Berwick R
Stranraer v Alloa Ath

Saturday, 28 January 2012
Clydesdale Bank Premier League
Aberdeen v Dunfermline Ath
Dundee U v Kilmarnock
Hearts v Celtic
Inverness CT v St Mirren
Motherwell v St Johnstone
Rangers v Hibernian

Irn-Bru First Division
Falkirk v Dundee
Hamilton A v Raith R
Partick Th v Ayr U
Queen of S v Morton
Ross Co v Livingston

Irn-Bru Second Division
Airdrie U v Stirling Alb
Brechin C v Arbroath
Cowdenbeath v Albion R
Forfar Ath v Dumbarton
Stenhousemuir v East Fife

Irn-Bru Third Division
Alloa Ath v Montrose
Annan Ath v East Stirling
Clyde v Berwick R

Peterhead v Queen's Park
Stranraer v Elgin C

Saturday, 4 February 2012
Irn-Bru Second Division
Albion R v Stenhousemuir
Arbroath v Airdrie U
Dumbarton v Cowdenbeath
East Fife v Brechin C
Stirling Alb v Forfar Ath

Irn-Bru Third Division
Berwick R v Peterhead
East Stirling v Stranraer
Elgin C v Clyde
Montrose v Annan Ath
Queen's Park v Alloa Ath

Saturday, 11 February 2012
Clydesdale Bank Premier League
Celtic v Inverness CT
Dunfermline Ath v Rangers
Hibernian v Aberdeen
Kilmarnock v Hearts
St Johnstone v Dundee U
St Mirren v Motherwell

Irn-Bru First Division
Ayr U v Queen of S
Dundee v Hamilton A
Livingston v Partick Th
Morton v Falkirk
Raith R v Ross Co

Irn-Bru Second Division
Albion R v East Fife
Brechin C v Airdrie U
Cowdenbeath v Stirling Alb
Forfar Ath v Arbroath
Stenhousemuir v Dumbarton

Irn-Bru Third Division
Alloa Ath v Berwick R
Annan Ath v Elgin C
Clyde v East Stirling
Peterhead v Stranraer
Queen's Park v Montrose

Saturday, 18 February 2012
Clydesdale Bank Premier League
Aberdeen v St Johnstone
Dundee U v St Mirren
Dunfermline Ath v Inverness CT
Hibernian v Celtic
Motherwell v Hearts
Rangers v Kilmarnock

Irn-Bru First Division
Hamilton A v Falkirk
Livingston v Raith R
Partick Th v Morton
Queen of S v Dundee
Ross Co v Ayr U

Irn-Bru Second Division
Airdrie U v Stenhousemuir
Arbroath v Cowdenbeath
Dumbarton v Albion R
East Fife v Forfar Ath
Stirling Alb v Brechin C

Irn-Bru Third Division
Berwick R v Annan Ath
East Stirling v Queen's Park
Elgin C v Alloa Ath
Montrose v Peterhead
Stranraer v Clyde

Saturday, 25 February 2012
Clydesdale Bank Premier League
Celtic v Motherwell
Hearts v Dundee U
Inverness CT v Rangers
Kilmarnock v Hibernian
St Johnstone v Dunfermline Ath
St Mirren v Aberdeen

Irn-Bru First Division
Ayr U v Livingston
Dundee v Ross Co
Falkirk v Queen of S
Morton v Hamilton A
Raith R v Partick Th

Irn-Bru Second Division
Albion R v Forfar Ath
Cowdenbeath v Brechin C
Dumbarton v Stirling Alb
East Fife v Airdrie U
Stenhousemuir v Arbroath

Irn-Bru Third Division
Alloa Ath v Clyde
Berwick R v East Stirling
Montrose v Elgin C
Peterhead v Annan Ath
Queen's Park v Stranraer

Saturday, 3 March 2012
Clydesdale Bank Premier League
Aberdeen v Celtic
Dundee U v Inverness CT
Dunfermline Ath v Motherwell
Hibernian v St Mirren
Kilmarnock v St Johnstone
Rangers v Hearts

Irn-Bru First Division
Ayr U v Falkirk
Livingston v Dundee
Partick Th v Hamilton A
Raith R v Morton
Ross Co v Queen of S

Irn-Bru Second Division
Airdrie U v Cowdenbeath
Arbroath v East Fife
Brechin C v Dumbarton

Forfar Ath v Stenhousemuir
Stirling Alb v Albion R

Irn-Bru Third Division
Annan Ath v Alloa Ath
Clyde v Montrose
East Stirling v Peterhead
Elgin C v Queen's Park
Stranraer v Berwick R

Saturday, 10 March 2012
Irn-Bru First Division
Dundee v Ayr U
Falkirk v Partick Th
Hamilton A v Ross Co
Morton v Livingston
Queen of S v Raith R

Irn-Bru Second Division
Albion R v Airdrie U
Arbroath v Dumbarton
East Fife v Cowdenbeath
Forfar Ath v Brechin C
Stenhousemuir v Stirling Alb

Irn-Bru Third Division
Alloa Ath v East Stirling
Annan Ath v Stranraer
Elgin C v Peterhead
Montrose v Berwick R

Saturday, 17 March 2012
Clydesdale Bank Premier League
Celtic v Dunfermline Ath
Dundee U v Rangers
Hearts v Hibernian
Inverness CT v Kilmarnock
Motherwell v Aberdeen
St Mirren v St Johnstone

Irn-Bru First Division
Livingston v Hamilton A
Morton v Dundee
Queen of S v Partick Th
Raith R v Ayr U
Ross Co v Falkirk

Irn-Bru Second Division
Airdrie U v Forfar Ath
Brechin C v Albion R
Cowdenbeath v Stenhousemuir
Dumbarton v East Fife
Stirling Alb v Arbroath

Irn-Bru Third Division
Berwick R v Queen's Park
Clyde v Annan Ath
East Stirling v Elgin C
Peterhead v Alloa Ath
Stranraer v Montrose

Tuesday, 20 March 2012
Irn-Bru Third Division
Queen's Park v Clyde

Saturday, 24 March 2012
Clydesdale Bank Premier League
Aberdeen v Inverness CT
Dunfermline Ath v St Mirren
Hibernian v Dundee U
Kilmarnock v Motherwell
Rangers v Celtic
St Johnstone v Hearts

Irn-Bru First Division
Ayr U v Morton
Dundee v Raith R
Falkirk v Livingston
Hamilton A v Queen of S
Partick Th v Ross Co

Irn-Bru Second Division
Airdrie U v Arbroath
Brechin C v East Fife
Cowdenbeath v Dumbarton
Forfar Ath v Stirling Alb
Stenhousemuir v Albion R

Irn-Bru Third Division
Alloa Ath v Queen's Park
Annan Ath v Montrose
Clyde v Elgin C
Peterhead v Berwick R
Stranraer v East Stirling

Saturday, 31 March 2012
Clydesdale Bank Premier League
Celtic v St Johnstone
Dundee U v Dunfermline Ath
Hearts v Aberdeen
Inverness CT v Hibernian
Motherwell v Rangers
St Mirren v Kilmarnock

Irn-Bru First Division
Falkirk v Morton
Hamilton A v Dundee
Partick Th v Livingston
Queen of S v Ayr U
Ross Co v Raith R

Irn-Bru Second Division
Albion R v Cowdenbeath
Arbroath v Brechin C
Dumbarton v Forfar Ath
East Fife v Stenhousemuir
Stirling Alb v Airdrie U

Irn-Bru Third Division
Berwick R v Clyde
East Stirling v Annan Ath
Elgin C v Stranraer
Montrose v Alloa Ath
Queen's Park v Peterhead

Saturday, 7 April 2012
Clydesdale Bank Premier League
Aberdeen v Dundee U

Dunfermline Ath v Hearts
Hibernian v Motherwell
Kilmarnock v Celtic
Rangers v St Mirren
St Johnstone v Inverness CT

Irn-Bru First Division
Ayr U v Partick Th
Dundee v Falkirk
Livingston v Ross Co
Morton v Queen of S
Raith R v Hamilton A

Irn-Bru Second Division
Albion R v Dumbarton
Brechin C v Stirling Alb
Cowdenbeath v Arbroath
Forfar Ath v East Fife
Stenhousemuir v Airdrie U

Irn-Bru Third Division
Alloa Ath v Elgin C
Annan Ath v Berwick R
Clyde v Stranraer
Peterhead v Montrose
Queen's Park v East Stirling

Tuesday, 10 April 2012
Irn-Bru First Division
Dundee v Queen of S
Falkirk v Hamilton A
Morton v Partick Th
Raith R v Livingston

Wednesday, 11 April 2012
Irn-Bru First Division
Ayr U v Ross Co

Saturday, 14 April 2012
Irn-Bru First Division
Hamilton A v Morton
Livingston v Ayr U
Partick Th v Raith R
Queen of S v Falkirk
Ross Co v Dundee

Irn-Bru Second Division
Airdrie U v Brechin C
Arbroath v Forfar Ath
Dumbarton v Stenhousemuir
East Fife v Albion R
Stirling Alb v Cowdenbeath

Irn-Bru Third Division
Berwick R v Alloa Ath
East Stirling v Clyde
Elgin C v Annan Ath
Montrose v Queen's Park
Stranraer v Peterhead

Saturday, 21 April 2012
Irn-Bru First Division
Dundee v Partick Th

Falkirk v Raith R
Hamilton A v Ayr U
Morton v Ross Co
Queen of S v Livingston

Irn-Bru Second Division
Albion R v Arbroath
Cowdenbeath v Forfar Ath
Dumbarton v Airdrie U
East Fife v Stirling Alb
Stenhousemuir v Brechin C

Irn-Bru Third Division
Alloa Ath v Stranraer
Berwick R v Elgin C
Montrose v East Stirling
Peterhead v Clyde
Queen's Park v Annan Ath

Saturday, 28 April 2012
Irn-Bru First Division
Ayr U v Dundee
Livingston v Morton
Partick Th v Falkirk
Raith R v Queen of S
Ross Co v Hamilton A

Irn-Bru Second Division
Airdrie U v East Fife
Arbroath v Stenhousemuir
Brechin C v Cowdenbeath
Forfar Ath v Albion R
Stirling Alb v Dumbarton

Irn-Bru Third Division
Annan Ath v Peterhead
Clyde v Alloa Ath
East Stirling v Berwick R
Elgin C v Montrose
Stranraer v Queen's Park

Saturday, 5 May 2012
Irn-Bru First Division
Dundee v Livingston
Falkirk v Ayr U
Hamilton A v Partick Th
Morton v Raith R
Queen of S v Ross Co

Irn-Bru Second Division
Albion R v Stirling Alb
Cowdenbeath v Airdrie U
Dumbarton v Brechin C
East Fife v Arbroath
Stenhousemuir v Forfar Ath

Irn-Bru Third Division
Alloa Ath v Annan Ath
Berwick R v Stranraer
Montrose v Clyde
Peterhead v East Stirling
Queen's Park v Elgin C

OTHER FIXTURES 2011–12

July 2011

12 Tue	UEFA CL 2 Q (1)
13 Wed	UEFA CL 2 Q (1)
14 Thu	UEFA EL Q 2 (1)
19 Tue	UEFA CL 2 Q (2)
20 Wed	UEFA CL 2 Q (2)
21 Thu	UEFA EL Q 2 (2)
26 Tue	UEFA CL 3 Q (1)
27 Wed	UEFA CL Q 3 (1)
28 Thu	UEFA EL Q 3 (1)

August 2011

02 Tue	UEFA CL 3 (2)
03 Wed	UEFA CL 3 Q (2)
04 Thu	UEFA EL Q 3 (2)
06 Sat	Football League Commences
10 Wed	ENGLAND v HOLLAND – Friendly
	FL Cup 1
13 Sat	Premier League Commences
16 Tue	UEFA CL PO (1)
17 Wed	UEFA CL PO (1)
18 Thu	UEFA EL PO (1)
20 Sat	FA Cup EP
23 Tue	UEFA CL PO (2)
24 Wed	UEFA CL PO (2)
	FL Cup 2
25 Thu	UEFA EL PO (2)
26 Fri	UEFA Super Cup
31 Wed	FL JPT 1

September 2011

02 Fri	BULGARIA v ENGLAND –
	UEFA Championship
03 Sat	FA Cup P
05 Mon	FA Youth Cup P†
06 Tue	ENGLAND v WALES –
	UEFA Championship
10 Sat	FA Vase 1Q
13 Tue	UEFA CL MD1
14 Wed	UEFA CL MD1
15 Thu	UEFA EL MD1
17 Sat	FA Cup 1Q
19 Mon	FA Youth Cup 1Q†
21 Wed	FL Cup 3
24 Sat	FA Vase 2Q
25 Sun	FA Sunday Cup P
27 Tue	UEFA CL MD2
28 Wed	UEFA CL MD2
29 Thu	UEFA EL MD

October 2011

01 Sat	FA Cup 2Q
03 Mon	FA Youth Cup 2Q†
05 Wed	FL JPT 2
06 Thu	Iceland v England –
	UEFA U21 Qualifier
07 Fri	MONTENEGRO v ENGLAND –
	UEFA Championship
08 Sat	FA Trophy P
10 Mon	Norway v England –
	UEFA U21 Qualifier
11 Tue	International Qualifier
	(England no game)
15 Sat	FA Cup 3Q
	FA County Youth 1*
16 Sun	FA Sunday Cup 1
17 Mon	FA Youth Cup 3Q†
18 Tue	UEFA CL MD3
19 Wed	UEFA CL MD3
20 Thu	UEFA EL MD3
22 Sat	FA Trophy 1Q
	FA Vase 1P
26 Wed	FL Cup 4
29 Sat	FA Cup 4Q

November 2011

01 Tue	UEFA CL MD4
02 Wed	UEFA CL MD4
03 Thu	UEFA EL MD4
05 Sat	FA Trophy 2Q
	FA Youth Cup 1P*
09 Wed	FL JPT QF
11 Fri	International Play-off/Friendly
12 Sat	FA Cup 1P
	FA County Youth 2*
14 Mon	Belgium v England –
	UEFA U21 Qualifier
15 Tue	International Play Off/Friendly
19 Sat	FA Vase 2P
	FA Youth Cup 2P*
20 Sun	FA Sunday Cup 2
22 Tue	UEFA CL MD 5
23 Wed	FA Cup 1P Replay
	UEFA CL MD 5
26 Sat	FA Trophy 3Q
30 Wed	UEFA EL MD5
	FL Cup 5

December 2011

01 Thu	UEFA EL MD5
03 Sat	FA Cup 2P
	FA Vase 3P
06 Tue	UEFA CL MD6
07 Wed	UEFA CL MD6
	FL JPT SF
10 Sat	FA Trophy 1P
11 Sun	FA Sunday Cup 3

14 Wed	UEFA EL MD6
	FA Cup 2P Replay
17 Sat	UEFA EL MD6
	FA Youth Cup 3P*
19 Sat	FA County Youth 3*
26 Mon	Bank Holiday

January 2012

07 Sat	FA Cup 3P
11 Wed	FL Cup SF1
14 Sat	FA Trophy 2P
18 Wed	FA Cup 3P Replay
	FL JPT F1
21 Sat	FA Vase 4P
	FA Youth Cup 4P*
22 Sun	FA Sunday Cup 4
25 Wed	FL Cup SF 2
28 Sat	FA Cup 4P
	FA County Youth 4*

February 2012

04 Sat	FA Trophy 3P
08 Wed	FA Cup 4P Replay
	FL JPT F2
11 Sat	FA Vase 5P
	FA Youth Cup 5P*
14 Tue	UEFA CL 16 (1)
15 Wed	UEFA CL 16 (1)
16 Thu	UEFA EL 32 (2)
18 Sat	FA Cup 5
19 Sun	FA Sunday Cup 5
21 Tue	UEFA CL 16 (1)
22 Wed	UEFA CL 16 (1)
23 Thu	UEFA EL 32 (2)
25 Sat	FA Trophy 4P
	FA Youth Cup 6P*
	FA County Youth SF*
26 Sun	FL Cup Final
29 Wed	International Friendly
	FA Cup 5P Replay

March 2012

03 Sat	FA Vase 6P
06 Tue	UEFA CL16 (2)
07 Wed	UEFA CL 16 (2)
08 Thu	UEFA EL 16 (1)

10 Sat	FA Trophy SF1
13 Tue	UEFA CL 16 (2)
14 Wed	UEFA CL 16 (2)
15 Thu	UEFA EL 16 (2)
17 Sat	FA Cup 6P
	FA Trophy SF2
	FA Youth Cup SF1*
18 Sun	FA Sunday Cup SF
24 Sat	FA Vase SF1
25 Sun	FL JPT Final
27 Tue	UEFA CL QF (1)
28 Wed	UEFA CL QF (1)
	FA Cup 6P Replay
29 Thu	UEFA EL QF (1)
31 Sat	FA Vase SF2
	FA Youth Cup SF2*

April 2012

03 Tue	UEFA CL QF (2)
04 Wed	UEFA CL QF (2)
05 Thu	UEFA EL QF (2)
14 Sat	FA Cup SF1
15 Sun	FA Cup SF1
17 Tue	UEFA CL SF (1)
18 Wed	UEFA CL SF (1)
19 Thu	UEFA EL SF (1)
21 Sat	FA Youth Cup Final 1*
24 Tue	UEFA CL SF (2)
25 Wed	UEFA CL SF (2)
26 Thu	UEFA EL SF (2)
27 Sat	FA County Youth Final (prov)
28 Sun	FA Sunday Cup Final (prov)
	FL Championship Finish

May 2012

05 Sat	FA Cup Final
	FL 1&2 Finish
	FA Youth Cup Final 2*
09 Wed	UEFA EL Cup Final
12 Sat	FA Trophy Final
13 Sun	FA Vase Final
	Premier League Finish
19 Sat	FL Championship Play-off Final
	UEFA CL Final
26 Sat	FL 1 Play-off Final
27 Sun	FL 2 Play-off Final

FA Women's Cup – dates to be confirmed.
† *Ties to be played in week commencing.*
* *Closing date of round.*

STOP PRESS

Itchy feet four: Fabregas, Modric, Nasri, Tevez ... Man C – huge sponsorship ... Copa shocks: Argentina, Brazil out ... Japs win Women's WC beating USA.

Summer transfers completed and pending:
Premier League: Arsenal: Gervinho (Lille) undisclosed. **Aston Villa:** Shay Given (Manchester C) £3,500,000. **Blackburn R:** Myles Anderson (Aberdeen) Free. **Bolton W:** Darren Pratley (Swansea C) Free. **Fulham:** John Arne Riise (Roma) £2,400,000. **Liverpool:** Charlie Adam (Blackpool) £8,500,000; Jordan Henderson (Sunderland) £20,000,000; Stewart Downing (Aston Villa) £20,000,000; Alexander Doni (Roma) Free. **Manchester C:** Stefan Savic (Partizan Belgrade) £6,000,000; Gael Clichy (Arsenal) £7,000,000. **Manchester U:** David De Gea (Atletico Madrid) £17,800,000; Ashley Young (Aston Villa) £17,000,000; Phil Jones (Blackburn R) £16,000,000. **Newcastle U:** Sylvain Marveaux (Rennes) Free; Demba Ba (West Ham U) Free; Yohan Cabaye (Lille) £4,300,000. **Norwich C:** Anthony Pilkington (Huddersfield T) £2,000,000; Elliott Bennett (Brighton & HA) undisclosed; Bradley Johnson (Leeds U) Free; James Vaughan (Everton) £2,500,000; Ritchie De Laet (Manchester U) Loan; Steve Morison (Millwall) £2,800,000. **QPR:** Kieron Dyer (West Ham U) Free; Jay Bothroyd (Cardiff C) Free. **Stoke C:** Jonathan Woodgate (Tottenham H) Free. **Sunderland:** David Vaughan (Blackpool) Free; John O'Shea (Manchester U) £4,000,000; Wes Brown (Manchester U) £1,200,000; Keiren Westwood (Coventry C) Free; Sebastian Larsson (Birmingham C) Free; Craig Gardner (Birmingham C) £5,000,000; Connor Wickham (Ipswich T) £8,100,000; Ahmed Elmohamady (ENPPI Club) £2,000,000. **Swansea C:** Steven Caulker (Tottenham H) Loan; Danny Graham (Watford) £3,500,000; Jose Moreira (Benfica) undisclosed. **Tottenham:** Brad Friedel (Aston Villa) Free. **WBA:** Gareth McAuley (Ipswich T) Free; Billy Jones (Preston NE) Free. **Wigan Ath:** Al Habsi (Bolton W) £4,000,000. **Wolverhampton W:** Dorus De Vries (Swansea C) Free; Jamie O'Hara (Tottenham H) £5,000,000; Roger Johnson (Birmingham C) £7,000,000.

Football League Championship: Barnsley: Scott Wiseman (Rochdale) undisclosed; Jim McNulty (Brighton & HA) undisclosed; Rob Edwards (Blackpool) Free; Miles Addison (Derby Co) Loan. **Birmingham C:** Steven Caldwell (Wigan Ath) Free; Adam Rooney (Inverness CT) Free; Morgaro Gomis (Dundee U) Free. **Blackpool:** Kevin Phillips (Birmingham C) Free. **Brighton & HA:** Craig Mackail-Smith (Peterborough U) undisclosed; Roland Bergkamp (Excelsior) undisclosed; Will Buckley (Watford) £1,000,000; Will Hoskins (Bristol R) undisclosed; Romain Vincelot (Dagenham & R) undisclosed; Kazenga LuaLua (Newcastle U) Loan. **Bristol C:** Ryan Taylor (Rotherham U) undisclosed. **Cardiff C:** Aron Gunnarsson (Coventry C) Free; Robert Earnshaw (Nottingham F) Free; Andrew Taylor (Middlesbrough) Free; Don Cowie (Watford) Free; Joe Mason (Plymouth Arg) undisclosed; Craig Conway (Dundee U) Free. **Coventry C:** Joe Murphy (Scunthorpe U) Free. **Crystal Palace:** Kagisho Dikgacoi (Fulham) undisclosed; Mile Jedinak (Genclerbirligi) Free. **Derby Co:** Adam Legzdins (Burton Alb) undisclosed; Chris Maguire (Aberdeen) undisclosed; Theo Robinson (Millwall) undisclosed; Jason Shackell (Barnsley) undisclosed; Jamie Ward (Sheffield U) undisclosed; Frank Fielding (Blackburn R) undisclosed; Craig Bryson (Kilmarnock) undisclosed. **Doncaster R:** Kyle Bennett (Bury) undisclosed; Richard Naylor (Leeds U) Free. **Hull C:** Paul McKenna (Nottingham F) Free; Dele Adebola (Nottingham F) Free; Joe Dudgeon (Manchester U) undisclosed. **Ipswich T:** Nathan Ellington (Watford) Free; Michael Chopra (Cardiff C) undisclosed; Ivar Ingimarsson (Reading) Free. **Leeds U:** Paul Rachubka (Blackpool) Free; Michael Brown (Portsmouth) Free. **Leicester C:** Matthew Mills (Reading) undisclosed; David Nugent (Portsmouth) Free; Sean St Ledger-Hall (Preston NE) undisclosed; Lee Peltier (Huddersfield T) undisclosed; Kasper Schmeichel (Leeds U) undisclosed. **Middlesbrough:** Curtis Main (Darlington) Free. **Millwall:** Jordan Stewart (Xanthi) Free; Ryan Allsop (WBA) undisclosed; Darius Henderson (Sheffield U) undisclosed. **Nottingham F:** Andy Reid (Blackpool) Free. **Peterborough U:** Craig Alcock (Yeovil T) undisclosed; Paul Jones (Exeter C) Free; Ryan Tunnicliffe (Manchester U) Loan; Nicky Ajose (Manchester U) undisclosed. **Portsmouth:** Stephen Henderson (Bristol C) undisclosed; Luke Varney (Derby Co) undisclosed; Jason Pearce (Bournemouth) undisclosed; David Norris (Ipswich T) Free; Greg Halford (Wolverhampton W) undisclosed. **Reading:** Mikele Leigertwood (QPR) Free. **Southampton:** Jack Cork (Chelsea) undisclosed. **Watford:** David Mirfin (Scunthorpe U) Free; Craig Forsyth (Dundee) undisclosed; Mark Yeates (Sheffield U) undisclosed. **West Ham U:** Kevin Nolan (Newcastle U) undisclosed; Abdoulaye Faye (Stoke C) Free.

Football League 1: Bournemouth: Darryl Flahavan (Portsmouth) Free; Steven Gregory (AFC Wimbledon) undisclosed. **Brentford:** Jonathan Douglas (Swindon T) Free; Niall McGinn (Celtic) Loan; Clayton Donaldson (Crewe Alex) Free. **Bury:** Mark Hughes (North Queensland Fury) Free. **Carlisle U:** Stephen O'Halloran (Coventry C) Free; Andy Welsh (Yeovil T) Free; Jon-Paul McGovern (Swindon T) Free; Liam Noble (Sunderland) Loan. **Charlton Ath:** Bradley Pritchard (Hayes & Yeading U) Free; Danny Hollands (Bournemouth) Free; Matt Taylor (Exeter C) Free; Rhoys Wiggins (Bournemouth) undisclosed. **Chesterfield:** Mark Randall (Arsenal) Free. **Exeter C:** Lenny Pidgeley (Bradford C) undisclosed; Danny Coles (Bristol R) Free; Guillem Bauza (Northampton T) Free. **Hartlepool U:** Colin Nish (Hibernian) Free. **Huddersfield T:** Tommy Miller (Sheffield W) Free; Danny Ward (Bolton W) undisclosed; Liam Cooper (Hull C) Loan; Donal McDermott (Manchester C) undisclosed; Oscar Gobern (Southampton) undisclosed; Calum Woods (Dunfermline Ath) Free.

Leyton Orient: Jamie Cureton (Exeter C) Free; Marc Laird (Millwall) Free; Leon McSweeney (Hartlepool U) Free; Scott Cuthbert (Swindon T) Free. **Milton Keynes D:** Dean Bowditch (Yeovil T) Free; Darren Potter (Sheffield W) Free. **Notts Co:** Jeff Hughes (Bristol R) Free; Charlie Allen (Dagenham & R) Free; Hamza Bencherif (Macclesfield T) Free; Alan Sheehan (Swindon T) Free; Jude Stirling (Milton Keynes D) Free; Julian Kelly (Reading) Free; Ishmel Demontagnac (Blackpool) Free. **Oldham Ath:** Matt Smith (Solihull Moors) undisclosed; Zander Diamond (Aberdeen) Free. **Rochdale:** Andrew Tutte (Manchester C) Free; Ashley Grimes (Millwall) Free; Stephen Darby (Liverpool) Loan. **Scunthorpe U:** Andy Barcham (Gillingham) Free; Jimmy Ryan (Accrington S) undisclosed; Jordan Robertson (St Johnstone) Free. **Sheffield W:** Julian Bennett (Nottingham F) Free; Rob Jones (Scunthorpe U) Free. **Stevenage:** Phil Edwards (Accrington S) Free; Alan Julian (Gillingham) Free. **Walsall:** Ryan Jarvis (Leyton Orient) Free; Kevan Hurst (Carlisle U) Free; Adam Chambers (Leyton Orient) Free. **Wycombe W:** Elliot Benyon (Swindon T) Loan; Scott Donnelly (Swansea C) Loan; James Tunnicliffe (Brighton & HA) Free; John Halls (Aldershot T) Free; Joel Grant (Crewe Alex) Free; Ben Harding (Aldershot T) Free. **Yeovil T:** Gavin Williams (Bristol R) Free.

Football League 2: AFC Wimbledon: Mat Mitchel-King (Crewe Alex) Free; Jack Midson (Oxford U) undisclosed; Max Porter (Rushden & D) undisclosed; Gareth Gwillim (Dagenham & R) Free; Chris Bush (Brentford) undisclosed; Charles Ademeno (Grimsby T) undisclosed. **Accrington S:** Danny Coid (Blackpool) Free. **Aldershot T:** Bradley Bubb (Farnborough T) undisclosed; Ross Worner (Charlton Ath) Free; Jamie Collins (Newport Co) undisclosed; Aaron Brown (Leyton Orient) Free. **Barnet:** Sam Deering (Oxford U) Free. **Bradford C:** Guy Branston (Torquay U) Free; Ross Hannah (Matlock T) Free; Ritchie Jones (Oldham Ath) Free. **Bristol R:** Lance Cronin (Gillingham) Free; Scott McGleish (Leyton Orient) Free; Matt Harrold (Shrewsbury T) undisclosed; Lee Brown (QPR) Free; Adam Virgo (Yeovil T) Free; Craig Stanley (Morecambe) Free; Matthew Gill (Norwich C) Free; Scott Bevan (Torquay U) Free; Cian Bolger (Leicester C) Loan; Kayne McLaggon (Salisbury C) undisclosed. **Burton Alb:** Calvin Zola (Crewe Alex) Free; Chris Palmer (Gillingham) Free. **Cheltenham T:** Sido Jombati (Bath C) nominal; Alan Bennett (Wycombe W) Free; Marlon Pack (Portsmouth) Free; Russell Penn (Burton Alb) Free; Kaid Mohamed (AFC Wimbledon) Free. **Crawley T:** Scott Davies (Reading) undisclosed; Wesley Thomas (Cheltenham T) undisclosed; John Akinde (Bristol C) undisclosed; Jamie Day (Rushden & D) Free; Charlie Wassmer (Hayes & Yeading U) undisclosed; Hope Akpan (Everton) Free; David Hunt (Brentford) Free. **Dagenham & R:** Medy Elito (Colchester U) Free; Robert Edmans (Chelmsford C) undisclosed. **Gillingham:** Lewis Montrose (Wycombe W) Free; Dean Rance (Bishop's Stortford) undisclosed; Adam Birchall (Swindon T) Free; Charlie Lee (Peterborough U) undisclosed; Chris Whelpdale (Peterborough U) undisclosed; Danny Kedwell (AFC Wimbledon) undisclosed; Matt Fish (Dover Ath) Free; Andy Frampton (Millwall) Free; Ross Flitney (Dover Ath) Free. **Hereford U:** Delroy Facey (Lincoln C) undisclosed; Joe Heath (Exeter C) Free. **Macclesfield T:** Scott Kay (Manchester C) Free. **Morecambe:** Lewis Alessandra (Oldham Ath) Free; Izak Reid (Macclesfield T) Free; Kevin Ellison (Rotherham U) Free. **Northampton T:** Adebayor Akinfenwa (Gillingham) Free; Jon-Paul Pittman (Wycombe W) Free; Tony Capaldi (Morecambe) Free; Peter Leven (Milton Keynes D) Free; Andrew Whing (Leyton Orient) Free; Michael Duberry (St Johnstone) Free; Deane Smalley (Oldham Ath) undisclosed. **Rotherham U:** Gareth Evans (Bradford C) Free. **Shrewsbury T:** Reuben Hazell (Oldham Ath) Free; Marvin Morgan (Aldershot T) Free. **Southend U:** Jemal Johnson (Lokomotiv Moscow) Free; Alassane N'Diaye (Crystal Palace) Loan; Neil Harris (Millwall) Free. **Swindon T:** Jonathan Smith (York C) £30,000; Adam Birchall (Dover Ath) undisclosed. **Torquay U:** Chris McPhee (Kidderminster H) undisclosed.

Scottish Premier League: Aberdeen: David Gonzalez (Manchester C) Loan; Isaac Osbourne (Coventry C) Free; Chris Clark (Plymouth Arg) Free; Youl Mawene (Panserraikos) Free. **Celtic:** Victor Wanyama (Beerschot) undisclosed; Adam Matthews (Cardiff C) Free; Kelvin Wilson (Nottingham F) Free. **Dundee U:** Willo Flood (Middlesbrough) Free; Gary Mackay-Steven (Airdrie U) Free; John Rankin (Hibernian) Free. **Dunfermline Ath:** Jason Thomson (Hearts) Loan; Patrick Boyle (Partick Th) Free; John Potter (St Mirren) Free; Paul Gallacher (St Mirren) Free; Andrew Barrowman (Ross Co) Free; Kevin Rutkiewicz (St Johnstone) Free; Paul Burns (Q of S) Free. **Hearts:** Mehdi Taouil (Kilmarnock) Free; Danny Grainger (St Johnstone) Free; John Sutton (Motherwell) Free; Jamie Hamill (Kilmarnock) Free. **Hibernian:** Garry O'Connor (Barnsley) Free. **Kilmarnock:** Paul Heffernan (Sheffield W) Free; Danny Buijs (Den Haag) Free; Danny Racchi (York C) Free; Patrick Ada (Crewe Alex) Free; Gary Harkins (Dundee) undisclosed. **Motherwell:** Nicky Law (Rotherham U) Free; Michael Higdon (St Mirren) Free; Nicky Devlin (Dumbarton) undisclosed. **Rangers:** David Healy (Sunderland) Free. **St Johnstone:** Callum Davidson (Preston NE) Free; David Robertson (Dundee U) Free; Frazer Wright (Kilmarnock) Free. **St Mirren:** Graham Carey (Celtic) undisclosed; Gary Teale (Sheffield W) Free; Graeme Smith (St Johnstone) Free; Paul McGowan (Celtic) Free; Steven Thompson (Burnley) Free.

Leaving the country: Chelsea: Jeffrey Bruma (Hamburg) Loan; Michael Mancienne (Hamburg). **Fulham:** Diomansy Kamara (Eskisehir) Free. **Liverpool:** Dean Bouzanis (Melbourne Victory) Free. **Manchester U:** Bebe (Besiktas) Loan. **WBA:** Gianni Zuiverloon (Mallorca) undisclosed; Scott Carson (Bursa) undisclosed; Abdoulaye Meite (Dijon) Free. **Portsmouth:** Nadir Ciftci (Kayseri) Free. **West Ham U:** Radoslav Kovac (Basle) undisclosed.

Now you can buy any of these other bestselling sports titles from your bookshop or *direct from the publisher*.

FREE P&P AND UK DELIVERY
(Overseas and Ireland £3.50 per book)

Playfair Football Annual 2011–2012	Glenda Rollin and Jack Rollin	£7.99
My Manchester United Years	Sir Bobby Charlton	£8.99
My England Years	Sir Bobby Charlton	£7.99
Gazza: My Story	Paul Gascoigne	£9.99
Being Gazza	Paul Gascoigne	£6.99
The Doc	Tommy Docherty	£8.99
The Autobiography	Alan Mullery	£8.99
Fallen Idle	Peter Marinello	£6.99
Cloughie	Brian Clough	£8.99
Rio: My Story	Rio Ferdinand	£8.99

TO ORDER SIMPLY CALL THIS NUMBER

01235 400 414

or visit our website:
www.headline.co.uk

Prices and availability subject to change without notice.